IRS PRACTICE AND PROCEDURE

REVISED SECOND EDITION

MICHAEL I. SALTZMAN

Partner, White & Case L.L.P.
Member of the New York, California, and
District of Columbia Bars

STUDENT EDITION

WARREN, GORHAM & LAMONT
OF RIA

This publication is designed to provide accurate and authoritative information
in regard to the subject matter covered. It is sold with the understanding that
neither the author(s) nor the publisher is engaged in rendering legal, accounting, or other professional service. If legal advice or other expert assistance is
required, the services of a competent professional should be sought.

In response to IRS Circular 230 requirements, Thomson-RIA advises that any
discussions of federal tax issues in its publications and products, or in third-
party publications and products on its platforms, are not intended to be used
and may not in fact be used to avoid any penalties under the Internal Revenue Code, or to promote, market, or recommend any transaction or subject
addressed therein.

Note to Readers

Because of the profound changes to the workings of the Internal Revenue Service since publication of the Second Edition of *IRS Practice and Procedure*, work on the Third Edition has been an enormous undertaking. This interim edition, the Revised Second Edition, is an effort to bring to the readers a partially revised, partially integrated volume as the author continues his work on a completely revised Third Edition.

Preface to the Revised Second Edition

This new volume of *IRS Practice and Procedure* is a Revised Second Edition. It is not the Third Edition I had expected to complete for publication. My goal of a Third Edition of a treatise that covers the entire range of IRS practice and the law of tax procedure will be met on the more realistic basis of a rolling revision of all eighteen chapters. The new format of the treatise will enable me to accomplish my goal over a relatively short period of time.

Why a Revised Second Edition rather than a Third Edition? The avalanche of information about the reorganization of the Service; the announcements of new procedures and programs; the accretion of changes, significant and minor, in the procedural statutes of the Internal Revenue Code; proposed, temporary, and final regulations; the unprecedented volume of Service positions in the form of Field Service Advice, Chief Counsel Memoranda, Service Center Guidance, and the like, all make the job of my review and judgement about the importance of literally thousands of documents a formidable one.

One illustration may give readers some insight to the task the Service has created. Internal Revenue Manual references are one of the strengths of the treatise for the professional's practice. The Second Edition has about 500 citations to the Manual. Around 1999, the Service changed the numbering system for the Manual and periodically issued Manual provisions with the new numbering system. This change necessitates a review of Manual procedures to find the appropriate section with the new numbering, as well as identifying restatements, reorganization, and changes for the approximately 500 citations to the Manual with the old numbering system. As if this task were not enough, the Service has also revised Manual sections using the new numbering systems. Furthermore, in large part, Manual provisions do not reflect the Service's reorganization.

Change, apparently for change's sake, the volume of change, the frequency of change, the lack of a sense of proportion or thought about the necessity for change—all of this is more than an author with some aspiration to a worthy and rational pursuit can bear.

The Revised Second Edition remains useful for a number of reasons. At least one of them is logistic. The changes and updates described in the previous oversized supplement have been integrated into the text. Another reason is that this revised edition has more than a few chapters that have been completely revised. Finally, the new format will allow revised chapters to be substituted for existing chapters as supplements are issued.

Michael I. Saltzman

August 2002

Preface to the Second Edition

When the first edition of this book was published in 1981, I wrote:

> My decision to write a book on tax procedure was based on two separate circumstances. First, it has been my observation that tax practitioners have generally slighted tax procedure in favor of the substantive provisions of the tax laws. This may be understandable in view of the demands placed on practitioners by the complex, substantive provisions about which they must advise clients. In the process, however, tax procedure has often been relegated to a secondary position. An Eighteenth Century observer's comments about the low standing of punctuation may in our day apply equally to tax procedure: "I know that there are some *Persons* who affect to *despise* it and treat this whole Subject with the utmost *Contempt*, as a Trifle far below *their* Notice, and a Formality unworthy of *their* regard: They do not hold it difficult, but despicable; and neglect it, as being *above* it."* To a degree, this book on tax procedure is an attempt to redress the balance and to accord to this important area of tax practice the standing it necessarily deserves.
>
> The second circumstance that made it important for a book on tax procedure to be written at this time was the publication of the *Internal Revenue Manual*. Previously, the Service's procedures had been set forth in general outlines in various pronouncements such as the Statement of Procedural Rules. These statements provide a broad overview of the Service's procedures; but they are by no means sufficient to indicate how Service personnel actually conduct their day-to-day business. With the publication of the Service's *Manual*, an attempt to describe the Service's procedures and examine their ramifications has become both more possible and more necessary.

Today, it can no longer be said that tax procedure is neglected. Constant legislative change has seen to that. This process started even before publication of the first edition in 1981 with the Tax Reform Act of 1976 and the adoption of changes affecting the summons provisions, the administrative and judicial

---

* Burrow, "A Few Thoughts Upon Pointing..." in Settlement Cases 629, 636 (1768), quoted in D. Mellinkoff, The Language of the Law 165 (1963).

review of jeopardy assessments, and the protection of the confidentiality of tax returns. As the Service, the Treasury, and Congress alike felt that tax shelters and various forms of tax protests threatened the viability of the tax system, procedural amendments of the Internal Revenue Code became less beneficent to taxpayers. Civil penalties were either added to the Code or were increased on a biannual basis with the intention of fostering compliance, but, regrettably, without much reflection on the effect of those penalties, independently or in conjunction with other penalties, on taxpayers or even on the system of tax administration. Not coincidentally, I suggest, the enactment of this profusion of civil penalties and other anti-abuse measures occurred as the Service's traditional administrative capacities lessened when appropriations from Congress proved inadequate to retain and to hire qualified personnel and as burdens caused by rapid changes in the tax laws increased.

It is possible to observe some patterns in the rapidly changing tax procedure landscape. There is a trend of reaction by legislative measure to publicized abuses either on the part of taxpayers or the Service. Rather than addressing an abuse by administrative means and appropriating and dedicating resources to that end, the Service, the Treasury, and Congress have impatiently sought a solution in some specific statutory provisions. For example, tax shelter-related penalties were enacted as the Service slowly marshaled its enforcement resources to deal with a perceived taxpayer abuse. The Taxpayer Bill of Rights was enacted at the same time to protect taxpayers from overzealous examiners and collectors. However, these structural changes came at a price. Dissatisfaction with the civil penalty structure growing out of the same taxpayer sentiment that gave rise to the Taxpayer Bill of Rights resulted in an overhaul of civil penalties in the Improved Penalty Administration and Compliance Tax Act of 1989.

If statutory changes have been eagerly grasped as the solution to abuses in the tax system, organizational and procedural changes have been the apparently desperate response of the Service to its task of administering and enforcing the tax laws with limited and arguably inadequate resources. In the name of better management, functions in the National Office have been reorganized and names changed with such frequency that, at times, the changes have seemed to be devoid of purpose or real meaning.

Never before, therefore, has there been more need for a one-volume description of all the Service's functions and the law of tax procedure. In this environment, tax practitioners cannot denigrate or ignore tax procedure. It supplies the rules according to which increasingly complex substantive provisions of the Code affecting taxpayers' lives and affairs will work themselves out.

Although the circumstances have changed since 1981, my purpose in revisiting the book remains the same: to describe how the Service performs various functions assigned to it under law, with reference to statutes, regulations, and rulings, but with special emphasis on the Service's *Manual*. Where appropriate, case citations also are included; where the procedural provisions of the

Code, such as penalties, are concerned, case citations are quite extensive. It is important to know how the Service operates, not only to enable practitioners to deal effectively with the Service in representing clients, but also to ensure that Service personnel do not overstep the bounds of their authority and fail to act in accordance with Service procedures in dealing with practitioners and their clients. Only if the practitioner knows how the Service operates can he or she adequately represent a client. Techniques practitioners may use in dealing with the Service also are suggested.

Although the text describes how the IRS operates in its various functions, it does not attempt to provide exhaustive citation to cases dealing with various procedural provisions of the Code. Such citation and close analysis of cases would have unduly expanded the size of the book and detracted from its over-all purpose.

The Second Edition covers the complete range of the Service's procedures, from rulings to tax collection, although some areas are dealt with in greater detail than others. Tax collection, for example, is extensively covered in four chapters because so little has been written on the topic and most practitioners' knowledge of tax collection is lacking. Tax returns, on the other hand, are discussed only in the broadest terms that fit in the overall procedural discussion. No attempt has been made to describe each and every tax return that a taxpayer might be called on to file, because such a discussion would be more relevant to a substantive analysis.

In the First Edition, I attempted to provide a description of the Service's functions based on its *Internal Revenue Manual*, a description of the law of tax procedure, as well as practical assistance to tax practitioners in their dealings with the Service. A rigorous attempt to describe those functions and procedures in a straightforward way was and still is appropriate to my purpose and the limitations of a single volume. With a few exceptions, this approach is carried over to the Second Edition. Frequent changes in the Code have required rewriting the chapter on civil penalties, and every chapter has been revised to reflect either statutory or case law developments. This book primarily uses IRS forms to illustrate the Service's functions.

Michael I. Saltzman

New York, New York
September 17, 1990

Acknowledgments

A massive amount of work has gone into publication of this Revised Second Edition. I would be remiss, however, if I did not acknowledge Michelle Wilson, my editor at RIA, who has long suffered my delays and has still managed to prepare invaluable questions and observations to keep me from my grosser infelicities. I also wish to acknowledge Kathy Silva, Director of WG&L Tax Treatises at RIA, for her able assistance, as well as Louise Trinche, Senior Editor at RIA, both of whom cut the "Gordian knot" of constant change and made possible the actual production of this volume. A number of former and current colleagues at White & Case LLP have assisted me over the years. They are Christopher Javens, Sang Ji, Melissa Choi, Amy Robinson, Charles Doumar, Kathleen Pakenham, Todd Simmens, Richard Nessler, and Michael Levin.

My wife, Sandra, has always encouraged me in this effort and without her this volume would not have been possible.

Michael I. Saltzman

Summary of Contents

Table of Contents

1   The IRS as an Administrative Agency

C PRACTICE BEFORE THE IRS

2   Taxpayer Access to Information

A   ACCESS TO INFORMATION FROM THE SERVICE UNDER THE FREEDOM OF INFORMATION ACT

3   Statements of IRS Position and Practice

C   THE PRIVACY OF TAX RETURNS

5   Statutes of Limitations

6   Interest

7A   Criminal Penalties

7B   Civil Penalties

8   The Examination Function

9   The Appeals Function

10   Assessment Procedures

11   Overpayment, Refund, Credit, and Abatement

A   PROCEDURES IN GENERAL

12   The Criminal Investigation Function

13   The Service's Investigatory Powers

A Service and Enforcement

14   The Tax Collection Function: Tax Liens and Levies

15   Avoiding and Minimizing the Effect of Tax Liens and Levies

17   Collection From Nontaxpayers—Transferee Liability

CHAPTER **1**

The IRS as an Administrative Agency

A ORGANIZATION OF THE IRS

A   ORGANIZATION OF THE IRS

¶ 1.01 ORIGINS OF THE IRS

[1] The IRS and Administrative Law

The Internal Revenue Service (the Service) is an administrative agency in the sense that it is "an authority of the Government of the United States," and it is not Congress, the courts, or a military authority.[1] Congress granted to the Secretary of the Treasury those powers of the "Government of the United States" to enforce and administer the tax laws, and the Service does so by delegation from the Secretary.[2] As is true of other administrative agencies, the Service is subject to control by Congress, the President, and the courts. As do other administrative agencies, the Service exercises its power through formal rule or regulation making, investigation, and prosecution, although it acts mostly through such informal procedures as issuing advisory rulings to and negotiating with taxpayers.[3]

The extraordinary volume of tax laws and regulations and the peculiarities of tax practice and procedure can foster the misimpression that the Service is unique and that the general body of administrative law is irrelevant. On the contrary, the ways in which the Service exercises its powers are not unique, and administrative law offers a means to a deeper understanding not only of how and why the Service acts, but also of the standards controlling the validity of IRS actions. There are seven major independent regulatory agencies: the Interstate Commerce Commission, the Federal Trade Commission, the National Labor Relations Board, the Securities and Exchange Commission, the Federal Communications Commission, the Federal Power Commission, and the Civil Aeronautics Board. These agencies are as diverse as the special problems that gave rise to their creation. Each of the seven has developed procedures suited to its own purposes and functions, as have the many other federal agencies. The Service's status as an administrative agency means that administrative law, statutory and decisional, which limits the exercise of power and controls

---

[1] 5 USC § 551(a).

[2] IRC § 7801.

[3] A description of administrative law is not within the scope of this book. Rather, the intention is to indicate another body of law and precedent that may be applicable directly or by analogy to IRS procedure. The discussion here is selective and for purposes of illustration. For treatment of administrative law, see Davis, Administrative Law Treatise (2d ed. 1978); Gellhorn, Byse, Strauss, Rakoff & Schotland, Administrative Law—Cases and Comments (8th ed. 1987); Jaffe & Nathanson, Administrative Law, Cases and Materials (3d ed. 1968); Jaffe, Judicial Control of Administrative Action (1965), E. Gellhorn, A.M. Levin, Administrative Law and Process (4th ed. 1997).

the processes of other administrative agencies, applies to the Service as well. It is also worth noting that judges of federal district courts, the circuit courts of appeals, the Court of Federal Claims, and the Court of Appeals of the Federal Circuit, as well as the justices of the Supreme Court, are familiar with administrative law because they hear cases involving agencies other than the Service. Arguments in these courts sensitive to administrative law concepts can find greater receptivity in these courts if only because they tap a reservoir of familiar applicable precedent.

To accomplish its distinct objective of revenue collection, the Service also operates according to its own body of procedural law, which is either dictated by statute, formulated by regulation, or adopted as guidelines for its employees. Despite their number and diversity, the actions of most if not all administrative agencies present certain fundamental issues, such as the availability of judicial review of agency action. Also, the processes by which agencies arrive at policies and decisions are sufficiently similar to have given rise to a body of general law called administrative law, especially since Congress enacted the Administrative Procedure Act (APA) to regulate formal rule and decision making of all agencies.

Application of administrative law to the Service is important to tax practitioners for at least the following reasons:

First, administrative law dictates the manner in which the Service must perform formal functions such as rule or regulation making. For example, under the APA, the Treasury Department may issue regulations relating to internal revenue laws only after publication of a notice of proposed rule making in the Federal Register and public hearings.[4] Failure to comply with these procedures renders the rule or regulation invalid.[5]

Second, administrative law permits taxpayers to make use of procedures not found in the Internal Revenue Code (the Code) in their dealings with the Service. For example, the APA entitles a person appearing before an agency such as the Service to be represented by counsel and to obtain a transcript of any testimony given.[6] Under a provision of the APA commonly referred to as the Freedom of Information Act (FOIA),[7] a taxpayer may obtain information about the operations of the Service, the treatment of other taxpayers similarly situated, and the degree to which a Service official's actions have conformed to Service policy.[8]

---

[4] 5 USC § 553.

[5] American Standard, Inc. v. United States, 602 F2d 256 (Ct. Cl. 1979) (portion of consolidated return regulations was held invalid because a notice of proposed regulations gave inadequate notice of final regulation in violation of APA).

[6] 5 USC §§ 555(b), 555(a).

[7] 5 USC § 552.

[8] The Freedom of Information Act and the Privacy Act are discussed in Chapter 2.

Third, administrative law enables persons dealing with the Service to assess the validity of Service actions and procedures against the standards of a developed body of law. Under general principles of administrative law, standards of consistency, nondiscrimination, and similar restrictions limit the exercise of discretion of all administrative agencies, including the Service.

Administrative law can be viewed as law defining what administrative agencies cannot do (i.e., the limits on actions and powers of administrative agencies). In this context, an analysis of the Service's procedures must begin with the controls on Service action imposed by Congress and the President, as well as the control that courts exercise by judicial review of administrative action. Administrative law also deals with the manner in which agencies, including the Service, act by formal rule-making power, investigating, prosecuting, or informally advising or negotiating with affected members of the public. These issues are discussed in summary fashion in this chapter. At this point, it is important to understand how the Service is organized and how and why its organization evolved.

[2] A Short History of the Service

Congress established an Office of the Commissioner of Internal Revenue on July 1, 1862, as the head of the Bureau of Internal Revenue. The Bureau of Internal Revenue was formed to meet fiscal needs during the Civil War. The Office of the Commissioner of the Bureau of Internal Revenue was in the Department of the Treasury.[9] This legislation also imposed income and other internal revenue taxes to finance the Union's war efforts in the Civil War. Before 1862, the federal government was supported by revenue from import duties and the proceeds of the sale of public lands. Taxes were collected by "supervisors" of collection districts, who were appointed by the president, subject to confirmation by the Senate. The Revenue Act of 1813 provided for a "collector" and a "principal assessor" for each collection district and for deputy collectors and assistant assessors. After the Civil War, the Bureau's activities declined.

With the ratification of the Sixteenth Amendment in 1913, and Congress's levy of income taxes on individuals and corporations, the modern Internal Revenue Service came into being, although still called the Bureau of Internal Revenue. Again, the financial burdens of war increased the work of the Bureau. In order to meet revenue needs of World War I, the Bureau became an income tax collector, and not a customs duty collector, and during and after the war, the Bureau was faced with the task of enforcing the internal revenue

---

[9] 12 Stat. 432. IRM 1111.2, Organic Act and IRM 1111.32, Background and Evolution of Present Organization (July 7, 1983).

laws on an unprecedented scale.[10] From World War I through 1951, the Bureau was beset by problems of staffing, organization, and coordination, but its basic organization remained unchanged. The Bureau had a Washington headquarters and a field organization with politically appointed district commissioners and collectors of internal revenue. Organization in the field was on a type-of-tax basis, with jurisdictionally separate "units" charged with the administration of different types of taxes. An Income Tax Unit audited income tax returns, while an Alcohol and Tobacco Tax Unit was charged with enforcement of alcohol and tobacco tax. Each unit had different operating jurisdictions; for example, there were thirty-nine Income Tax Unit districts, each under an internal revenue agent in charge, but only fourteen Intelligence Unit districts under special agents in charge. The approximately 200 field offices reported directly to the Washington headquarters, where all decisions were made.[11]

In 1950, as part of a general reorganization of the Executive Branch prescribed by the Reorganization Act of 1949, Congress approved Treasury Department Reorganization Plan No. 26. Under this plan, the functions of all officers and employees of the Bureau of Internal Revenue were transferred to the Secretary of the Treasury, who might authorize the performance of these functions by any other officer or by any agency or employee of the department.[12] To avoid interruption of service, the Secretary of the Treasury promptly redelegated most of its functions back to the Bureau. One set of functions not redelegated to the bureau was left with the Assistant General Counsel of the Treasury serving as the Chief Counsel of the Bureau.

More dramatic changes were made in the bureau under Reorganization Plan No. 1, which became effective on March 15, 1952.[13] Under Plan No. 1, the organization of the Washington office and the field offices changed from one based on the type of tax to one reflecting the Service's functional activities, such as operations (i.e., audit, collection, fraud investigation, appellate), technical advisory, planning, administration, and internal security or inspection services. Three offices, each having the title "Assistant Commissioner of Internal Revenue," were created in the National Office. A system of regional administration was established under regional Commissioners of Internal Revenue. Most field programs were integrated under District Directors of Internal Revenue within each region, who replaced the internal revenue agents and special agents in charge and the collectors of internal revenue. All posi-

---

[10] After the 1913 income tax law, revenue legislation was enacted in nearly every year from 1916 through 1951.

[11] House Comm. on Ways and Means, King Committee Report, HR Doc. No. 327, 82d Cong., 2d Sess. 3 (1952).

[12] Reorg. Plan No. 26 of 1950, § 1(a), 15 Fed. Reg. 4,935, 64 Stat. 1280–1281.

[13] Reorg. Plan No. 1 of 1952, 17 Fed. Reg. 2,243, 66 Stat. 823.

tions below Commissioner were made civil service rather than political appointments. In 1953, the name of the bureau was changed to the Internal Revenue Service.[14]

[3] The Background of the 1998 Reorganization

For the first time in more than forty years, in 1995, Congress began to review the organization, operation, and supervision of the Service. In part, this review grew out of revelations about the lack of success of the Service's systems modernization program, despite Congress's appropriation of billions of dollars and several years of the Service's promises of systems modernization. Taxpayer dissatisfaction with the Service's operations and dealings with the public, which resulted in several Taxpayer Bills of Rights, also led to this review. In 1995, Congress created a National Commission on Restructuring the Internal Revenue Service. This Commission was composed of seventeen members, some of whom were appointed by the President from the Executive branch, as well as from private life; others were appointed by congressional leaders from congressional ranks, with several members also selected from the private sector.[15]

In June 1997, the Commission issued its report, the key recommendations of which were (1) that a new entity for congressional oversight be created to ensure that members of Congress had sufficient information about the Service to make informed decisions about tax administration and policy; (2) that a Board of Directors be created, to be given overall responsibility for Executive branch governance of the Service, but not its law enforcement functions, with members, five of whom should be experienced in running large service organizations; members of this Board should be appointed by the President and confirmed by the Senate (and removable at will by the President) for five-year staggered terms; however, the Department of the Treasury would continue to be responsible for tax policy; (3) that the Commissioner of Internal Revenue, who will be appointed by the Board of Directors for a five-year term, be given greater flexibility in hiring, firing, and salary decisions; (4) that the Service receive stable funding for the next three years so that it can properly plan to re-

---

[14] Treas. Dept. Order 150-29 and TD 6038, 1953-2 CB 443.

[15] Pub. L. No. 104-52, § 637, 109 Stat. 509 (Nov. 19, 1995), amended by Pub. L. No. 104-134, § 2904(a), 110 Stat. 1321 (Apr. 26, 1996), and by Pub. L. No. 104-208, §§ 101(b), 643(a)–643(e), 110 Stat. 3009 (Sept. 30, 1996). In establishing the Commission, Congress found in part that the Service's budget had risen from $2.5 billion in fiscal year 1979 to $7.3 billion in fiscal year 1996, but that returns processing had not become significantly faster, collection rates had not significantly increased, and taxpayer assistance had not significantly improved. Moreover, Tax Systems Modernization, which had already cost $2.5 billion, with an estimated price tag of $8 billion, had been described by GAO as "chaotic" and "ad hoc."

build its foundation; (5) that the Service address training, operations, technology, culture, and taxpayer education if it is to operate efficiently and with taxpayer focus; (6) that the Service update its technology and treat taxpayer information as a strategic asset to improve its customer service and compliance functions; (7) that the Service plan to make paperless filing the most convenient way for taxpayers to file their returns within the next ten years; (8) that further steps be taken to improve taxpayers' ability to recover damages for wrongful actions on the part of the Service, and real efforts be made to protect taxpayers from unnecessary disputes with the Service before they occur; and (9) that the tax laws be simplified to reduce the burden on taxpayers to comply and to facilitate tax administration.[16]

About one month after the Commission's Report was published, two of its congressional members introduced the IRS Restructuring Reform Act of 1997, which attempted to translate the Commission's recommendations into law.[17] Recommendations to improve the efficiency of the Service were not controversial, but the Commission's recommendations about the governance of the Service raised concerns from a number of quarters. Before the Commission had issued its report, Treasury had formed its own governance board, called the Modernization Management Board, made up of high-ranking Treasury and Service officials, to oversee the Service's systems modernization. By contrast, the Commission's recommendation of a board of directors from the private sector seemed to conflict with Treasury's traditional oversight of the Service, and the separation of the Service's law enforcement functions from the Treasury's policy-making functions appeared to interfere with traditional policy-making and tax administration relationships between Treasury and the Service.[18]

---

[16] Report of the National Commission on Restructuring the Internal Revenue Service, "A Vision for a New IRS" (June 25, 1997), published as a Special Supplement by Tax Analysts in 75 Tax Notes (June 30, 1997). The Report is divided into eight parts: Congressional Oversight, Executive Branch Governance, IRS Management, and Budget; Workforce and Culture; Strategic Objectives: Customer Service, Compliance and Efficiency Gains; Modernization; Electronic Filing; Tax Law Simplification; Taxpayer Rights; and Financial Accountability.

[17] HR 2292 and S.1087, introduced July 30, 1997. On October 9, 1997, the House Rules Committee released its report of HR 2676, The IRS Restructuring Act and Reform Act of 1997, which contained the Tax Technical Corrections Act of 1997 (formerly HR 2645), as reported out by the House Ways and Means Committee, and voted on favorably by the House of Representatives on November 5, 1997.

[18] See "Treasury Official Asks ABA Support in IRS Governance Reforms," Tax Analysts, 97 TNT (Aug. 5, 1997) (reporting that Treasury General Counsel appealed to the ABA Tax Section to reject the IRS governance proposals recommended by the Commission).

[4] The IRS Restructuring and Reform Act of 1998

On July, 22, 1998, the President signed into law the IRS Restructuring and Reform Act of 1998 (the 1998 Act), the most significant reorganization of the Service in more than forty-five years. Since 1952, with the adoption of Reorganization Plan No. 1, the Service has been organized under a three-tier geographic structure with a National Office, and regional and district offices in the field. Before the 1998 Act, and its 1995 reorganization, the field organization was divided into four regions (Northeast Region, Southeast Region, Midstates Region, and Western Region), each with a Regional Commissioner, a Regional Counsel, and a Regional Director of Appeals, and thirty-three district offices, in addition to ten service centers and three computing centers. The 1988 Act required the Commissioner to develop and implement a reorganization of the Service, which replaces the three-tier geographic structure with "operating units serving particular groups of taxpayers with similar needs."[19] In other words, the organization of the Service was to be along type-of-taxpayer, not functional/geographic lines. The legislative purpose was to make it easier for taxpayers to deal with the Service, as suggested by the Congressional directive to the Commissioner to revise the mission statement of the Service "to provide greater emphasis on serving the public and meeting taxpayer needs."[20]

¶ 1.02 ORGANIZATION OF THE SERVICE

[1] The IRS Oversight Board and Other Senior Management

[a] The Oversight Board

The 1998 Act established within the Department of Treasury the IRS Oversight Board (Oversight Board).[21] The stated purpose of the Oversight Board is to oversee the Service in its administration, management, conduct, direction, and supervision of the execution and application of the internal revenue laws, related statutes, and tax conventions.[22] As part of its general oversight functions, the Oversight Board is also supposed to ensure that the Service's organization and operation allow it to carry out its mission. However, the Oversight Board has neither the responsibility nor the authority (1) to

---

[19] IRS Restructuring and Reform Act of 1998, HR 2676, 105th Cong., 2d Sess. § 1002 (hereinafter "1998 Act").

[20] 1998 Act § 1002(a).

[21] IRC § 7802(a), as amended by 1998 Act § 1101.

[22] IRC § 7802(c), as amended by 1998 Act § 1101.

develop and formulate tax policy on existing or proposed internal revenue laws, related statutes, and tax conventions; (2) to carry out the Service's specific law enforcement activities, such as its examination, collection, and criminal investigation functions; (3) to carry out the Service's specific procurement activities; or (4) to execute specific personnel actions.

The Oversight Board has specific responsibilities for strategic plans, operational plans, the Service's budget, and taxpayer protection. On strategic plans, the Oversight Board's responsibilities are to review and approve strategic plans, including the establishment of the Service's mission and objectives, and the standards relating to either or both of them, as well as development of the Service's long-range strategic plans. On operations, the Oversight Board is supposed to review the Service's operational functions, including its plans for modernization of its tax system, plans for outsourcing or managed competition, and plans for training and education. On management, the Board will recommend to the President candidates for appointment of the Commissioner of Internal Revenue, as well as recommend to the President the removal of the Commissioner; review the Commissioner's selection, evaluation, and compensation of the Service's senior executives, who have significant functional responsibilities; and review and approve the Commissioner's plans for any major reorganization of the Service. The Board's responsibilities on the Service's budget are to review and approve the Commissioner's budget for the Service; submit the budget to the Secretary of the Treasury; and ensure that the budget supports the Service's annual and long-range strategic plans. The Board has the responsibility of making certain that taxpayers are properly treated by the Service.[23]

There are six members of the Board who are not federal officers or employees and are appointed by the President with the advice and consent of the Senate. In addition, the Secretary of the Treasury (or the Secretary's deputy) serves as a member, as do the Commissioner of Internal Revenue, and a full-time federal employee or a representative of employees, who is appointed by the President with the advice and consent of the Senate.[24] Members of the Board must have qualifications in one or more of the following areas: management of large service organizations; customer service; administration and compliance with the federal tax laws; organizational development; taxpayer needs and concerns; and the needs and concerns of small businesses. The Oversight Board statute also describes the terms of members, ethical considerations, such as financial disclosures and future practice before the Service, and procedures for the Board's operation.

---

[23] IRC § 7805(d), as added by 1998 Act § 1101.
[24] IRC § 7802(b), as added by 1998 Act § 1101.

[b] The Commissioner of Internal Revenue

Unlike prior law, the Commissioner of Internal Revenue is appointed for a five-year term on the nomination of the President with the advice and consent of the Senate, and must have a demonstrated ability in management.[25] This job description suggests that the Commissioner's office will no longer be occupied by tax lawyers, as has been the case for some time. For the first time, the Code spells out the functions of the Commissioner, albeit in broad terms. Subject to delegation by the Secretary (whose decision not to delegate to the Commissioner must be approved by various committees of Congress), the Commissioner has the power to administer, manage, conduct, direct, and supervise the execution and application of the internal revenue laws or related statutes and tax conventions, as well as to recommend to the President the appointment of the Chief Counsel. The Commissioner also consults with the Oversight Board.[26]

Before the 1998 Act, the Internal Revenue Code of 1986 incorporated Treasury Department Reorganization Plans No. 26 of 1950 and No. 1 of 1952.[27] Under Reorganization Plan No. 26, the authority to administer the internal revenue laws was delegated by the Secretary of the Treasury to the Commissioner of Internal Revenue, except for specific functions not delegated to the Commissioner, which remain under the direct authority of the Secretary and the Treasury Department. Under the 1998 Act, however, the Commissioner of Internal Revenue is authorized "to employ such number of persons as the Commissioner deems proper for the administration and enforcement of the internal revenue laws, and the Commissioner shall issue all necessary directions, instructions, orders, and rules applicable to such persons."[28] In other words, the 1998 Act gave the Commissioner greater control of the employment of internal revenue personnel than under prior law, and the Code authorizes the Commissioner to establish procedures and rules governing how those personnel perform their duties. In addition, the Commissioner can decide to designate local offices for Service personnel called "posts of duty" for personnel "engaged in field work or traveling on official business outside the District of Columbia."[29] Also, the Commissioner may order field personnel to duty in the District of Columbia.[30]

---

[25] IRC § 7803, as added by 1998 Act § 1103.

[26] IRC §§ 7803(a)(2), 7803(a)(3).

[27] IRC § 7804(a) before amendment by the 1998 Act.

[28] IRC § 7804(a), after amendment by the 1998 Act.

[29] IRC § 7804(b)(1).

[30] IRC § 7804(b)(2).

[2] The Treasury and the Service

The Service is one of eleven bureaus in the Department of the Treasury. Administration and enforcement of the internal revenue laws are carried out by or under the supervision of the Secretary of the Treasury.[31] The Secretary has delegated most revenue functions and authority to the Commissioner of Internal Revenue by means of Treasury Department orders and Treasury regulations.[32] Certain functions regarding the internal revenue laws have not been delegated to the Commissioner. For example, tax legislation generally originates with the Secretary, whose principal technical adviser is the Assistant Secretary for Tax Policy.[33] The Treasury Department administers those tax laws whose enforcement the Secretary does not delegate to the Service (i.e., alcohol, tobacco, and firearms taxes). With respect to organization, the Secretary retained the authority to determine the number of Internal Revenue Regions (Plan No. 1) and to establish and alter Internal Revenue Districts.[34] In administering or supervising the internal revenue laws, the Secretary of the Treasury is advised by a General Counsel of the Treasury[35] and by an Assistant General Counsel, who is also the Chief Counsel of the Internal Revenue Service and its chief law officer.[36]

The Secretary of the Treasury published an organization chart in 1998 describing the reporting relationships.[37] The Deputy Secretary reports directly to the Secretary of the Treasury, and (among other officers) the Assistant Secretary (Tax Policy) reports through the Deputy Secretary to the Secretary.

---

[31] IRC § 7801(a). The Secretary of the Treasury is appointed by the President with the consent of the Senate.

[32] IRC § 7802(a). The Commissioner is appointed by the president with the consent of the Senate. Treasury Department Order 150-37, dated March 17, 1955, reads in part:

> By virtue of the authority vested in me as Secretary of the Treasury, including the authority of the Internal Revenue Code and Reorganization Plan No. 26 of 1950, it is ordered as follows: 1. Commissioner of Internal Revenue shall be responsible for the administration and enforcement of the Internal Revenue laws.

[33] Under the Assistant Secretary for Tax Policy is the Office of Tax Legislative Counsel, whose staff of lawyers considers technical legal questions of changes in the tax laws and adoptions of regulations, and an Office of Tax Analysis, whose economists provide economic analysis of tax issues and estimates of revenue receipts. The process by which regulations are adopted is described at ¶ 3.02.

[34] IRC § 7601.

[35] IRC § 7801(b)(1).

[36] IRC § 7801(b)(2).

[37] TDO 101-05 (Oct. 29, 1998).

[3] Basic Service Organization

Before the enactment of the 1998 Act on July 22, 1998, the Service had a three-tier geographic structure (the National Office, four regions, and thirty-three districts), which was organized along functional lines (examination, collection, and criminal investigation). There was also a network of ten regional service centers that paralleled the three-tiered structure. Under the Commissioner's reorganization plans, which the Commissioner described in testimony before Congress, and Congress considered developing a Restructuring Act with a type-of-taxpayer organization, having four core operating divisions, each responsible for serving a particular group of taxpayers.[38] After its management consulting firm and a group of its employees worked on a modernized IRS structure for about six months, the National Office produced an IRS Organization Blueprint that "summarizes key decisions and provides a blueprint for the IRS organization of the future."[39] According to the IRS Organization Blueprint:

> The modernized IRS will be built around organizational units with end-to-end responsibility. Four operating divisions [the type-of-taxpayer divisions described above] will be responsible for serving specific groups of taxpayers. Four functional organizations [Counsel, the National Taxpayer Advocate, Criminal Investigation, and Appeals] will be responsible for specific issues and cases. Two support organizations will be responsible for providing common services across the entire agency. Finally, a much smaller National Office will provide high-level strategy and policy setting.[40]

To enable officials who are responsible for making policy decisions and senior managers who are responsible for executing policy decisions to communicate about making policy based on data and experience in the field, the "top management of the agency and of each of the major organizational units will consist of teams, each linked to the next level."[41] For example, at the highest level, the management team that sets policy for the Service will consist of the Commissioner, the Deputy Commissioner, key staff executives, and the heads of each major operating division. At the operational division level, the top management team includes the Commissioner and Deputy Commissioner of

---

[38] Statement of Commissioner Rossotti at Senate Finance Committee, IRS News Release 98-3 (Jan. 28, 1998), 98 TNT 19-12 (Jan. 28, 1998).

[39] IRS Organization Blueprint (Phase IIA) at 7 (May 1999), available on the IRS's Web site at www.irs.gov.

[40] IRS Organization Blueprint (Phase IIA) at 8 (May 1999), available on the IRS's Web site at www.irs.gov.

[41] IRS Organization Blueprint (Phase IIA) at 12 (May 1999), available on the IRS's Web site at www.irs.gov; see Form 1.1.

the operating division, executives within the operating division, and, so that they "understand the needs of the operating division and its taxpayers," representatives from the following functional and support organizations: Counsel, Appeals, Taxpayer Advocate, Criminal Investigation, Information Systems, and Agency-Wide Shared Services.[42]

Initially, the four "taxpayer service units," which would conduct all functional operations, were described as (1) Wage and Investment Income Tax Organization (about 100 million filers); (2) Small Business and Self-Employed Taxpayer Service Organization (about 25 million filers); (3) Large Corporate Taxpayer Service Organization (about 100,000 filers); and (4) Employee Plan/Exempt Organization and State/Local Government Organization (1.8 million filers). These operating units replace the four regions and part of the National Office. When the IRS organization blueprint was announced in May 1999, the units had slightly different names, organized as follows. The Large Taxpayer Service Organization became the Large and Mid-Size Business Operating Division, and the Employee Plan/Exempt Organization and State/Local Government Organization became the Tax Exempt and Government Entity Division.

---

[42] IRS Organization Blueprint (Phase IIA) at 13 (May 1999), available on the IRS's Web site at www.irs.gov. As one observer of the changing IRS organization has noted, the IRS Organization Blueprint, Phase II, represented only the latest of a series of reorganizations, while the Service had yet to deal successfully with the important objective of systems modernization. Structural changes abound in the Blueprint, but business practices cannot be expected to change until the Service modernizes its technological systems, a process which it has been attempting to do for thirty years. Not only has the Service not completed this vital task, but some would say it has not even made significant progress.

FORM 1.1 ———————————————————
IRS ORGANIZATION CHART

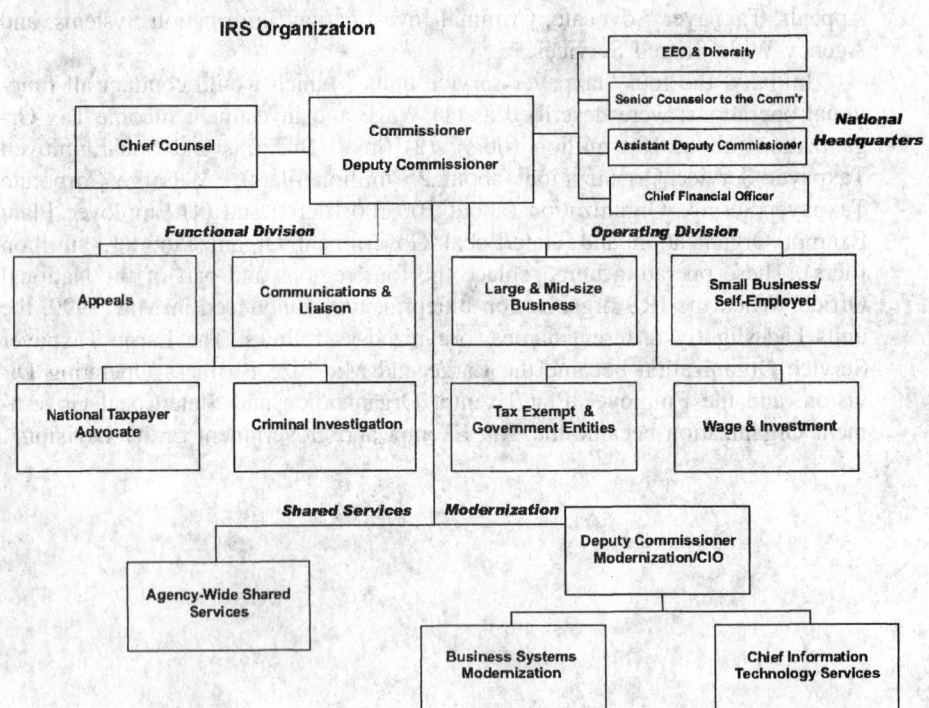

IRS Organization

[4] National Office

The National Office, located in Washington, D.C., makes the major decisions regarding the tax laws for the guidance of Service personnel. The top management in the National Office was restructured under reorganization plans announced in January 1982 and July 1987, and again in 1988, 1989, 1991, 1993, and most recently in 1998.[43] (Form 1.2 shows the organization of the National Office.) As a result of these plans, the National Office is comprised of the Office of the Commissioner of Internal Revenue, assisted by the Deputy Commissioner, who in turn oversees the Chief Headquarters Operations, the Chief Financial Officer, the Chief Information Officer, Chief Management and Administration, Chief Taxpayer Service, the Chief Compliance Officer. In addition, the National Office includes the Chief Counsel, the Appeals Headquarters, and the National Taxpayer Advocate. Also, Commissioners of the four operating divisions have their offices in the National Office.

[a] Chief Counsel

As a result of the IRS Restructuring and Reform Act of 1998, the Chief Counsel no longer has the additional designation as an Assistant General Counsel of the Treasury although the Chief Counsel is in the Department of the Treasury.[44] Duties of the Chief Counsel include the following: (1) to serve as the legal adviser to the Commissioner and Service personnel; (2) to furnish legal opinions for rulings and technical advice, to assist in the preparation of proposed legislation, treaties, regulations, and Executive orders for laws affecting the Service; (3) to represent the Commissioner in tax cases in the U.S. Tax Court and to determine which civil tax actions should be litigated; and (4) to prepare legal recommendations for the Justice Department. The Chief Counsel reports to the Commissioner and the General Counsel of the Treasury on tax advisory matters and interpretations of tax law and litigation. However, where

---

[43] IR 82-8, reprinted in 1982 Stand. Fed. Tax Rep. (CCH) ¶ 6314; see also 14 Tax Notes 213 (1982). The reorganization was put into effect on March 21, 1982; IR 82-39, reprinted in 1982 Stand. Fed. Tax Rep. (CCH) ¶ 6417. The Service's Manual reflects the reorganization. See, e.g., IRM 1111.72 et seq. (1982 Reorganization plan); IRM 1111.74 (1986 Changes); IRM 1111.76 (1988–1989); IRM 1112 (general description of Service organization); IRM 1120 (Office of the Commissioner); IRM 1130 (Office of the Chief Operations Officer); IRM 1170 (Office of Chief Counsel); and IRM 1180 (Office of Regional Commissioner). See also TDO 150-02, 1986-2 CB 746. The 1987 reorganization plan was announced in IR 87-79 (July 2, 1987) and described in 36 Tax Notes 158 (July 13, 1987).

[44] IRC § 7803(b).

tax policy matters are concerned, the Chief Counsel reports to the General Counsel of the Treasury.

Under the IRS Organization Blueprint issued in May 1999, the Chief Counsel's organization went through yet another restructuring.[45] All Counsel attorneys continue to be part of a unified, nationwide Chief Counsel organization; however, to serve each of the Operating Divisions, four new Operating Division Counsel are located with each of the Operating Division Commissioners and will have a staff of attorneys assigned to the legal work of that Operating Division.

Lawyer specialists in the National Office continue to be organized along technical subject specialties, but most of Counsel's field organization are assigned to one of the Operating Division units. Counsel in the field are assigned to one of three Operating Division Counsel areas: Large and Mid-Size Businesses, General Practice, and Tax Exempt. A single contact attorney in each specialty will work with an agent on the same case.

Lawyers in the office of the Associate Chief Counsel (Litigation) perform, as the title denotes, litigation-related activities. The Commissioner generally is represented in the U.S. Tax Court by lawyers assigned to District Counsel offices, under the supervision of a Regional Counsel. The Associate Chief Counsel (Litigation) maintains overall coordination and supervision of Tax Court litigation carried out by lawyers in the Tax Litigation Division. These lawyers also assist the Department of Justice's Tax Division in the defense of refund suits instituted in federal district courts and the Court of Federal Claims, although Tax Division lawyers in the Justice Department lawyers actually represent the Service in these cases.

Lawyers in the General Litigation Division coordinate and supervise lawyers in the field on such matters as the collection of taxes and assist lawyers in the Justice Department's Tax Division actually representing the Service in cases in federal district courts, the Court of Federal Claims, or state courts. The same functions are performed by lawyers in the Disclosure Litigation Division with respect to disclosure of tax information under the Freedom of Information Act, the Privacy Act, and Section 6103.

---

[45] IRS Organization Blueprint (Phase IIA) at 89–94 (May, 1999), available on the Service's Web site at www.irs.gov; see Form 1.3.

FORM 1.2
ORGANIZATION OF THE OFFICE OF THE CHIEF COUNSEL

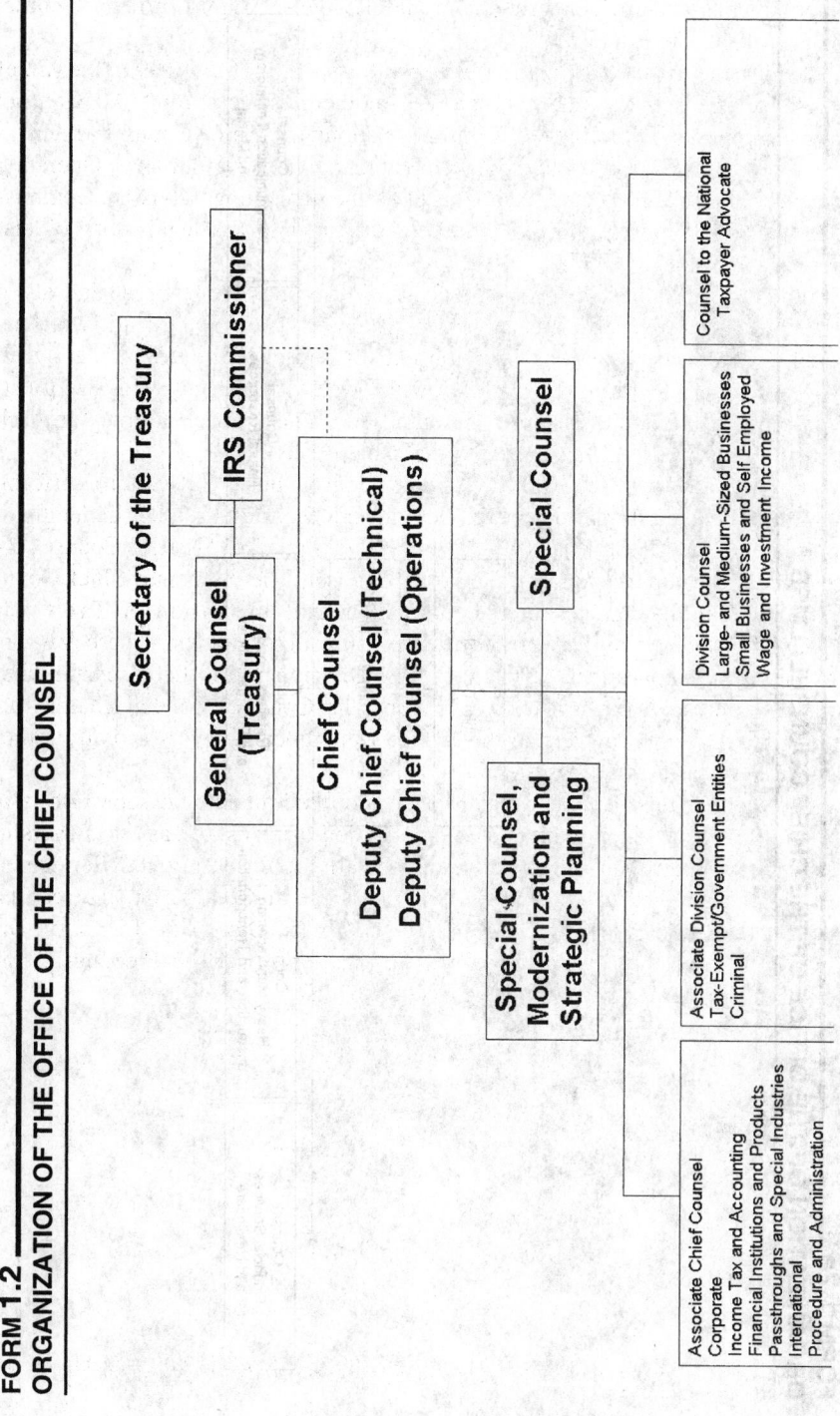

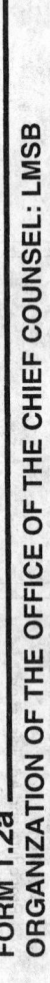

FORM 1.2a
ORGANIZATION OF THE OFFICE OF THE CHIEF COUNSEL: LMSB

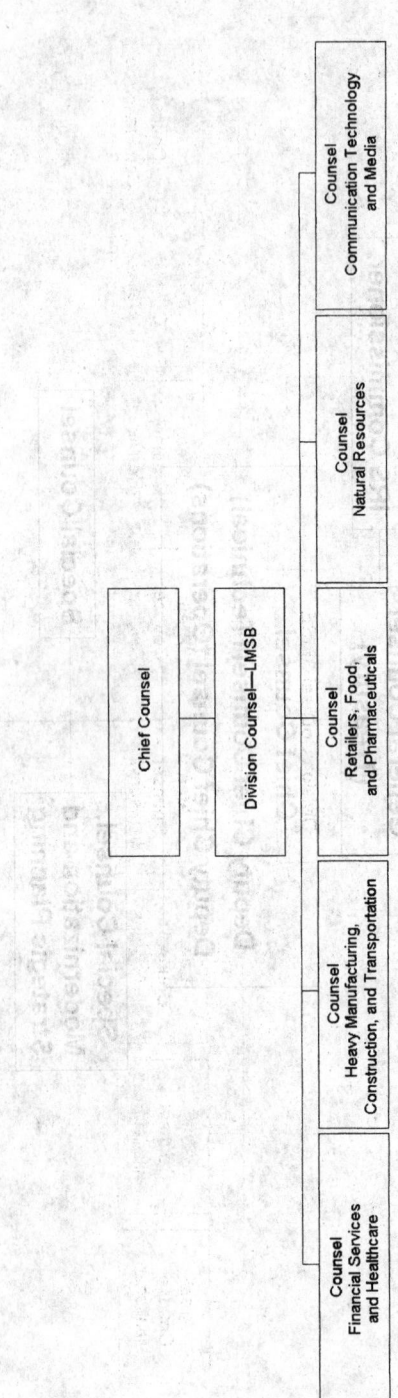

FORM 1.2b
ORGANIZATION OF THE OFFICE OF THE CHIEF COUNSEL: SB/SE

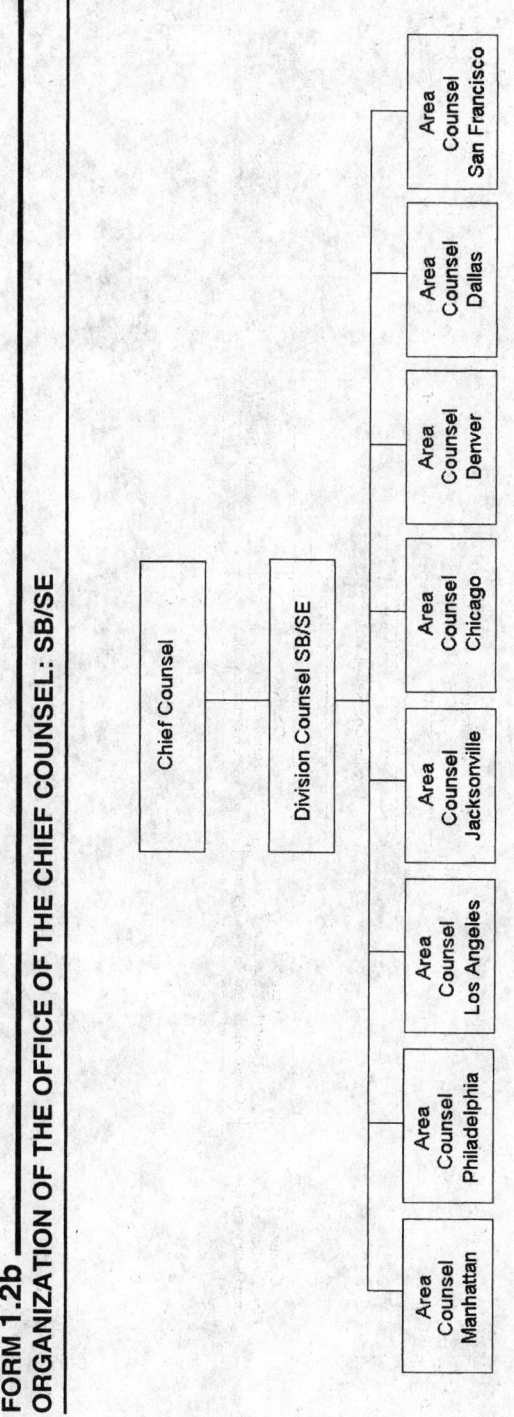

[b] Appeals

Appeals's historical function is to provide taxpayers with review of their cases after an examination has been completed without agreement on one or more issues or collection action has begun. Essentially, Appeals provides the taxpayer with the means for due process review. Appeals is an independent function and gives an impartial review of a dispute between the taxpayer and the local office. Appeals review is the last administrative chance for the taxpayer and the Service to attempt to resolve a dispute before the case goes to court as a deficiency action in the Tax Court or a refund suit in a federal district court or the Court of Federal Claims. The headquarters of Appeals is in the National Office and is headed by the National Director of Appeals.[46] Appeals is identified with the type-of-taxpayer operating divisions, and in the National Office, there is a Director, Appeals, Large and Mid-Size Business (LMSB); a Director, Appeals, for both Small Business and Self-Employed Taxpayers (SB/SE) and Tax Exempt and Government Entities (TE/GE); and a Director, Appeals, Wage and Investment Income (W&I). In the field, Appeals Offices are aligned with the operating divisions with the LMSB Area Headquarters Offices and Area Directors in New York, Houston, Chicago, and Northern California. The SB/SE and TE/GE Headquarters Offices and Area Directors are in New York, Philadelphia, Baltimore, Chicago, Nashville, St. Paul, Dallas, Denver, San Francisco, and Laguna Niguel. The W&I Headquarters is in the National Office, undoubtedly because the service centers handle most of the activities in the field.

[c] National Taxpayer Advocate

The 1998 Act established the Office of the Taxpayer Advocate in the Service, headed by the National Taxpayer Advocate.[47] The National Taxpayer Advocate reports directly to the Commissioner. While the National Taxpayer Advocate replaces the Taxpayer Advocate, who replaced the Taxpayer Ombudsman, as the official in charge of the Problems Resolution function in the field, the 1998 Act gives the National Taxpayer Advocate greater status within the Service's National Office. The National Taxpayer Advocate, in addition to reporting directly to the Commissioner, will receive compensation at the same rate as the highest pay rate of any senior executive in the Service; this is intended to indicate the importance of the Taxpayer Advocate's function. Also, the National Taxpayer Advocate is appointed by the Secretary of

---

[46] Appeals is described in more detail in Chapter 9.

[47] IRC § 7803(c). The Taxpayer Advocate's functions are described in more detail in Chapter 15.

the Treasury after consultation with the Commissioner of Internal Revenue and the Oversight Board.

The Taxpayer Advocate's functions are (1) to assist taxpayers in resolving problems with the Service; (2) to identify taxpayer problems in dealing with the Service; (3) to propose changes in the Service's administrative practices to mitigate taxpayer problems; and (4) to identify appropriate legislation. The Advocate must also monitor the allocation of local office taxpayer advocates, develop guidance for IRS personnel for referral of taxpayer inquiries to local taxpayer advocates, and ensure that telephone numbers of local taxpayer advocates are published. In addition to consulting with the Advocate, the Commissioner is required to establish procedures for formally responding to the Advocate's recommendations within three months after they have been submitted to the Commissioner. At the local office level, the taxpayer advocate has some extraordinary authority. At the initial meeting with a taxpayer, the taxpayer advocate must advise the taxpayer that the taxpayer advocate operates independently of any other Service office and reports directly to Congress through the National Taxpayer Advocate. Also, the taxpayer advocate has the discretion not to contact or disclose information a taxpayer provides to other personnel in the Service, other than the Advocate's office. Taxpayer advocates are required to make reports to the National Taxpayer Advocate's office and to consult with local office supervisory personnel about their daily operations.

A number of changes enhance the visibility and authority of local taxpayer advocates. Internal Revenue Code Section (Section) 6212 is amended to require that each notice of deficiency must include a notice to the taxpayer that the taxpayer has the right to contact a local taxpayer advocate and the location and telephone number of that taxpayer advocate's office. In addition, the taxpayer advocate has the authority to issue a Taxpayer Assistance Order if the advocate determines that the taxpayer "is suffering or about to suffer a significant hardship" as the result of the way in which the tax law is being administered, or the taxpayer meets other requirements that regulations may provide.[48] A "significant hardship" includes the following: (1) an immediate threat of adverse action; (2) a delay of more than thirty days in resolving a taxpayer account problem; (3) significant costs, including professional fees, a taxpayer will incur unless relief is granted; or (4) irreparable injury to, or long-term adverse effect on, the taxpayer unless relief is granted.

Each year, the National Taxpayer Advocate must also report to the tax law writing committees of the Congress (House Ways and Means and Senate Finance) on the activities of the Advocate's office.[49] Specifically, in addition to other information the Advocate chooses to include, the Advocate's report to Congress is supposed to (1) identify the Advocate Office's initiatives for im-

---

[48] IRC § 7811(a)(2).
[49] IRC § 7803(c)(2)(B).

proving taxpayer services and Service responsiveness; (2) describe recommendations the Advocate has received from field personnel with the authority to issue Taxpayer Assistance Orders; (3) contain a summary of at least twenty of the most serious problems encountered by taxpayers; describe the action the Advocate has taken on these initiatives, recommendations, and taxpayer problems; describe the results of those actions, an inventory and estimated completion date of those items that remain to be completed, and the reason for any inaction on an item and the IRS official responsible for the inaction; identify the Taxpayer Assistance Orders; (4) contain recommendations for administrative and legislative action, including action on areas that impose significant compliance burdens on taxpayers; and (5) identify the ten most litigated issues in each taxpayer category.

[d] Criminal Investigation

The Criminal Investigation division is headquartered in the National Office and is headed by a Chief, Criminal Investigation.[50] Special Agents-in-Charge (SACs) report directly to the Headquarters through the Directors of Field Operations. There are thirty-five Special-Agents-in-Charge, and they are responsible for referring cases to the Criminal Tax Section of the Tax Division, Justice Department.

[5] Four Operating Divisions

Four operating divisions are at the core of the Service's reorganization: the Wage and Investment (W&I) Division, the Small Business and Self-Employed (SB/SE) Division, the Large and Mid-Size Business (LMSB) Division, and the Tax Exempt and Government Entity (TE/GE) Division.[51] The Wage and Investment Division is headquartered in Washington, with geographic area headquarters in Buffalo, Greensboro, Indianapolis, New Orleans, Phoenix, St. Louis, and San Francisco.[52] For the Small Business and Self-Employed Division, the headquarters is in New Carrollton, Maryland, and the geographic area headquarters are in Boston, New York, Philadelphia, Baltimore, Jacksonville, Detroit, Chicago, Nashville, St. Paul, Dallas, Denver, Seattle, Oakland, and

---

[50] Information Release (IR)-2000-46 (July 3, 2000). Criminal Investigation is discussed in more detail in Chapter 12.

[51] These divisions are described in more detail in Chapter 8; see also Forms 1.4 and 1.5.

[52] IRS Organization Blueprint (Phase IIA) at 35 (May 1999), available on the IRS's Web site at www.irs.gov, see Form 1.6.

Laguna Niguel.[53] LMSB is divided into industry segments with a headquarters city of Manhattan, for the financial services and health care industry segments; San Francisco, for the communication, technology, and media industries; Houston for the energy and chemical industry; Chicago, for the food and retail industry segments; and central New Jersey, for the manufacturing, construction, and transportation industry segments.[54]

The Tax-Exempt and Government Entities Division is headquartered in Washington, but employee plan and exempt organization issues will be handled in Brooklyn, Philadelphia, Baltimore, Atlanta, Dallas, Chicago, Denver, St. Paul, and Los Angeles.[55]

---

[53] IRS Organization Blueprint (Phase IIA) at 56 (May 1999), available on the IRS's Web site at www.irs.gov.

[54] IRS Organization Blueprint (Phase IIA) at 70–71 (May 1999), available on the IRS's Web site at www.irs.gov; see Form 1.4.

[55] IRS Organization Blueprint (Phase IIA) at 84 (May 1999), available on the IRS's Web site at www.irs.gov; see Form 1.5.

FORM 1.3
ORGANIZATION UNDER THE COMMISSIONER FOR WAGE AND INVESTMENT INCOME

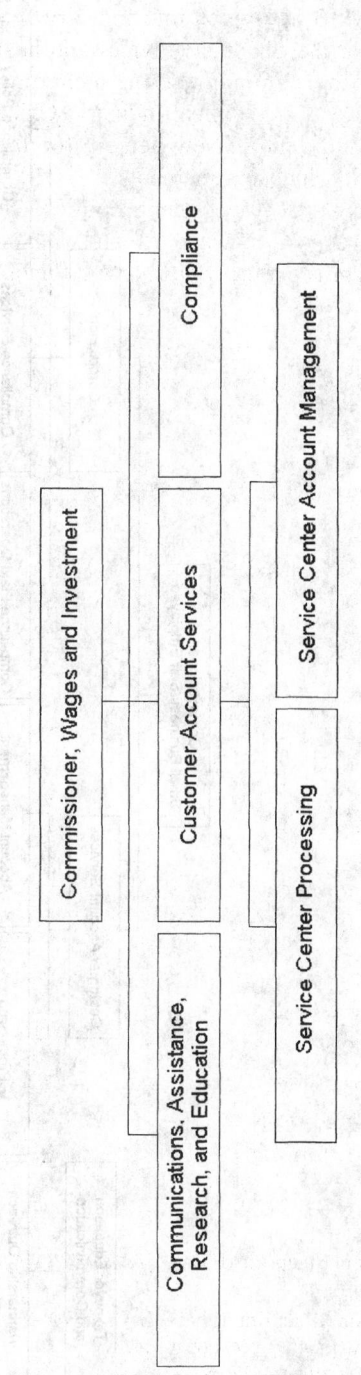

FORM 1.3a
ORGANIZATION UNDER THE COMMISSIONER FOR SMALL BUSINESS/SELF EMPLOYED

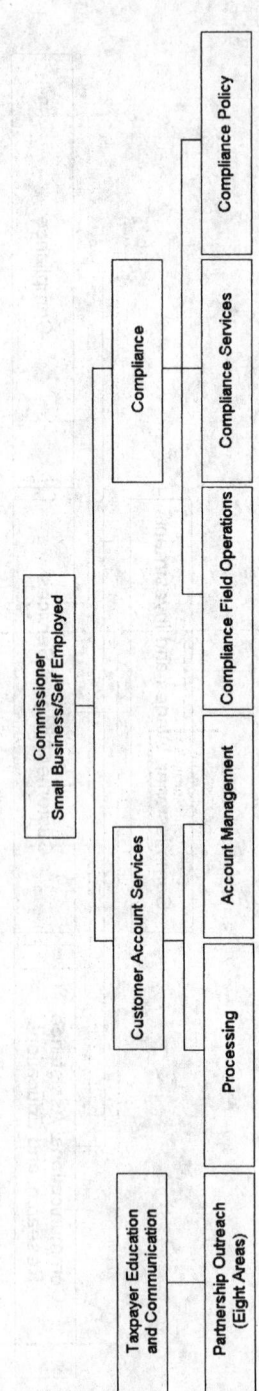

FORM 1.4
LMSB PARTNERSHIPS WITH FUNCTIONAL DIVISIONS

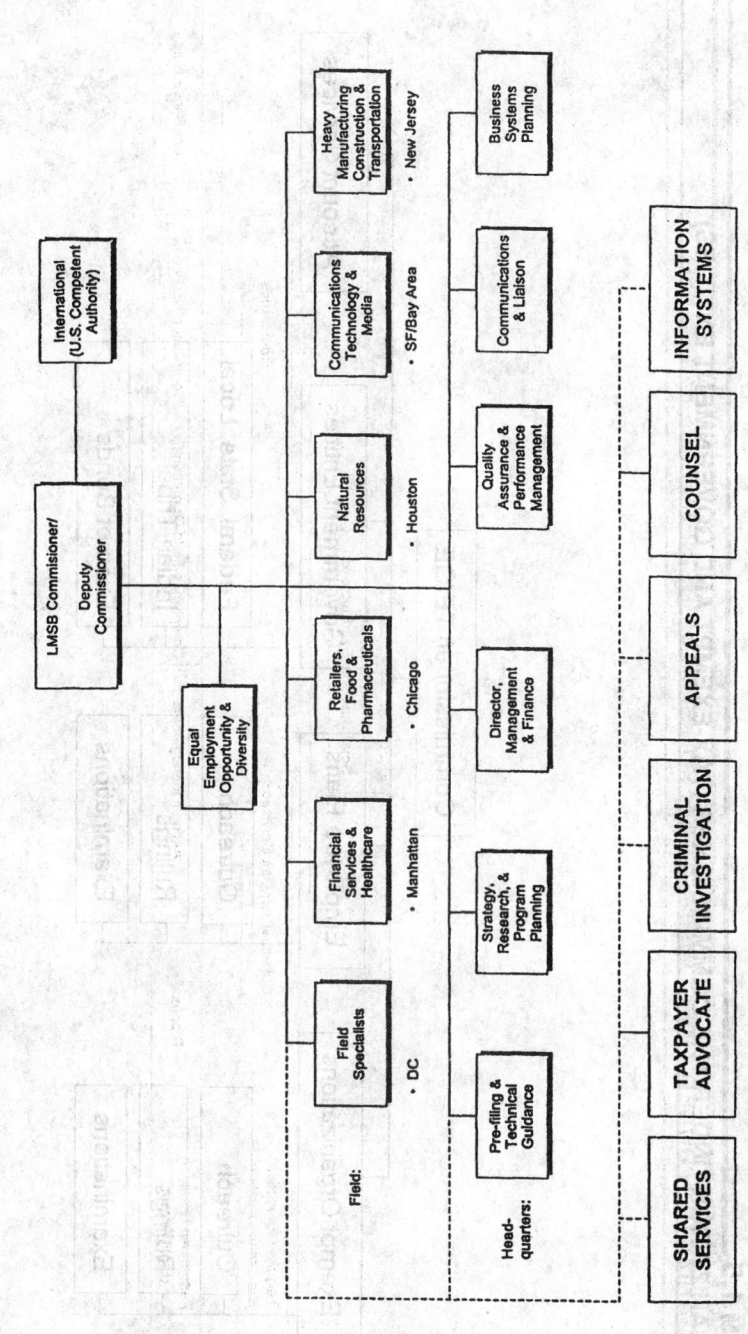

FORM 1.5
ORGANIZATION UNDER THE COMMISSIONER (TAX-EXEMPT AND GOVERNMENT ENTITIES)

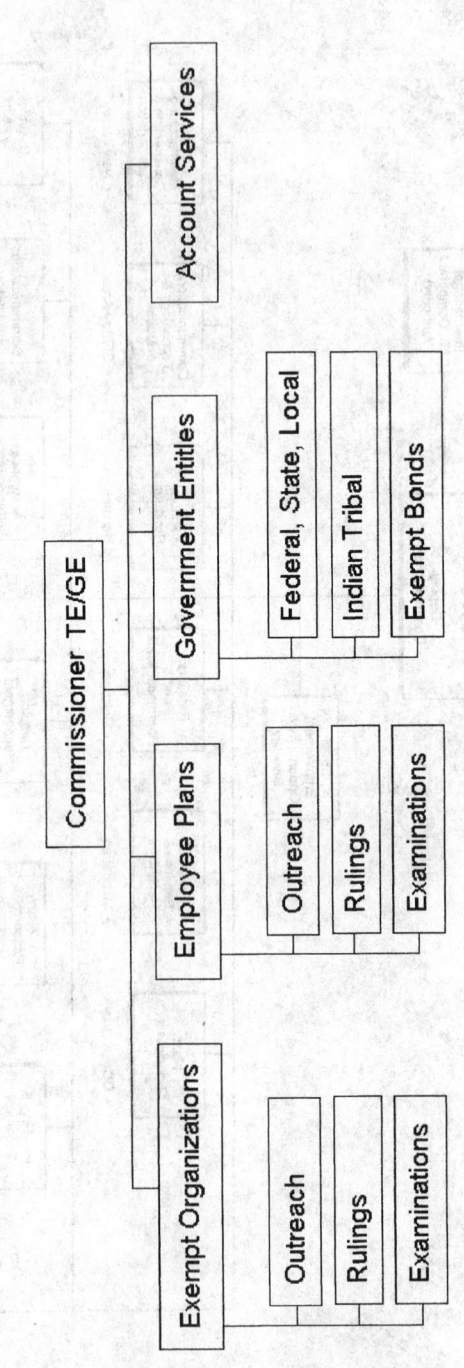

[6] Service Centers

Before the Service's reorganization, ten service centers, each headed by a Director, received and processed tax information returns, conducted audits through correspondence, and took other enforcement action for seven regions. They mass-processed returns and performed mathematical verification of returns and other projects and programs. Important return-processing functions are carried out at the National Computer Center at Martinsburg, West Virginia. Statistical data are also compiled at the IRS Data Center in Detroit, Michigan. Each service center conducted its operations based on the geographic location of the taxpayer without regard to the type of return filed, under the supervision of the Regional Commissioner having jurisdiction over the area.

Under the Service's reorganization plan, activities now performed by ten service centers will be assigned to a service center based on three factors: whether the return is an individual or a business return, the taxpayer's geographic location, and the operating division to which the service center will report.[56] Each service center will now be under the direct authority of either the Wage and Investment Income Division or the Small Business and Self-Employed Division with the expectation that the service center will develop expertise in the respective taxpayer types. Five centers will serve the W&I Division. These five centers are the Andover, Atlanta, Austin, Fresno, and Kansas City service centers. The remaining five centers will serve the SB/SE Division, and will also handle center-based activities for tax-exempt, government entity, and about 200,000 LMSB filers. These service centers are the Cincinnati, Ogden, Memphis, Philadelphia, and Brookhaven service centers. Eight of the centers will handle the receipt and processing of individual returns. These service centers are the five W&I-identified service centers and the Brookhaven, Memphis, and Philadelphia service centers. Cincinnati and Ogden will handle the receipt and processing of business return, including employment tax returns, as well as estate and gift tax returns.

[7] International Tax Functions

International tax matters are administered in a unique way. In addition to the normal National Office functions of an Assistant Commissioner, the office of the Assistant Commissioner (International) performs Area and local office-type functions normally carried out by field offices (i.e., Examinations, Collection, and Criminal Investigations activities).[57] This office administers and enforces the internal revenue laws as to the following:

---

[56] IR 2000-61 (Sept. 9, 2000).

[57] See IRM 4.3.1.11.4, Organization—Assistant Commissioner International Examination Requests (Feb. 26, 1999).

- U.S. citizens traveling or residing abroad[58]
- Income earned by citizens residing or doing business abroad
- Nonresident aliens or foreign corporations who derive income from the United States
- Taxpayers who are required to withhold tax from certain payments to nonresident aliens and foreign corporations

In addition to district-like compliance functions (Examination of Returns, Collection, and Criminal Investigation), the Assistant Commissioner (International) also acts for the Service as the Competent or Taxation Authority in administering and applying tax conventions between the United States and foreign countries and in processing requests for exchange of information and reciprocal tax collection and claims alleging double taxation made under these conventions. (The organization of the office of the Assistant Commissioner (International) is shown in Form 1.6.)

---

[58] The tax returns of resident aliens and foreign subsidiaries of domestic corporations and adjustments arising out of the application of Section 482 are handled by local offices. See Chapter 8.

FORM 1.6
OFFICE OF ASSISTANT COMMISSIONER (INTERNATIONAL)

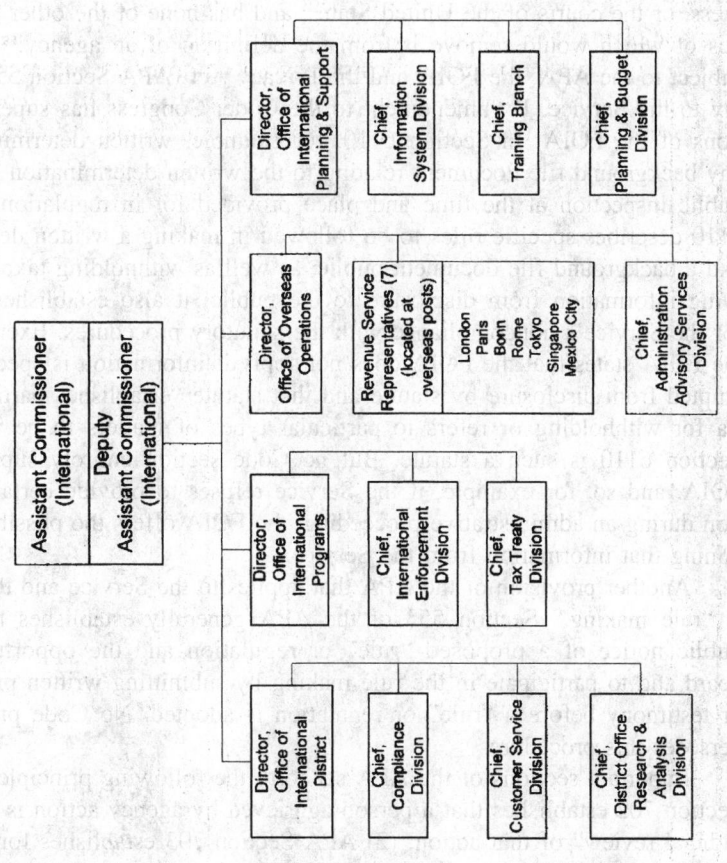

B ADMINISTRATIVE LAW AND THE IRS

¶ 1.03 THE ADMINISTRATIVE PROCEDURE ACT AND THE IRS

For purposes of the APA, the Service is an "agency," which means that it is an "authority of the Government of the United States," and it is not the Congress, or the courts of the United States, and has none of the other characteristics of which would remove it from the definition of an agency.[59] Since it is subject to the APA, the FOIA and the Privacy Act (APA Section 552) also apply to the Service. By amendment to the Code, Congress has superseded portions of the FOIA. In Section 6110, for example, written determinations and any background file document relating to the written determination are open to public inspection at the time and place provided for in regulations.[60] Section 6110 describes specific rules to be followed in making a written determination and a background file document public, as well as withholding taxpayer identifying information from disclosure to the public; it also establishes a remedy for the Service's noncompliance with the statutory procedures. Exemption 3 of the FOIA states that the FOIA does not apply if information is specifically exempted from disclosure by statute and that statute "establishes particular criteria for withholding or refers to particular types of matters to be withheld."[61] Section 6110 is such a statute. But no Code section entirely supersedes the FOIA, and so, for example, if the Service refuses to provide certain information during an administrative proceeding, the FOIA offers the possibility of obtaining that information from the Service.

Another provision of the APA that applies to the Service and the Treasury is "rule making." Section 553 of the APA generally establishes the right to public notice of a proposed "rule" or regulation and the opportunity to be heard and to participate in the rule making by submitting written presentations or testimony before a "rule" or regulation is adopted. No Code provision supersedes this procedure.

Important sections of the APA set forth the following principles: (1) APA Section 702 establishes that a person aggrieved by agency action is "entitled to judicial review" of that action; (2) APA Section 703 establishes forms of judicial review which are proceedings for a declaratory judgment or injunction in a federal district court; (3) APA Section 704 lists the agency action that is judicially reviewable, principally "final agency action." Importantly, the scope of judicial review outlined in Section 706 of the APA gives a framework for judi-

---

[59] 5 USC § 551(a).

[60] IRC § 6110(a).

[61] See 5 USC § 552(b)(3).

cial review of the Service's actions. The reviewing court "shall decide all relevant questions of law, interpret constitutional and statutory provisions, and determine the meaning or applicability of the terms of the agency action."[62] Also, the reviewing court shall "hold unlawful and set aside agency action, findings, and conclusions found to be—(A) arbitrary, capricious, an abuse of discretion, or otherwise not in accordance with law; (B) contrary to constitutional right, power, privilege, or immunity; (C) in excess of statutory jurisdiction, authority, or limitations or short of statutory right; (D) without observance of procedures required by law; . . . (F) unwarranted by the facts to the extent that the facts are subject to trial de novo by the reviewing court."[63]

When Code provisions are compared to these portions of the APA, the results are revealing. On a right to judicial review, APA Section 702 explicitly provides that the person aggrieved by agency action is entitled to judicial review. Code Section 6213 states that after receiving a notice of deficiency, "the taxpayer may file a petition with the Tax Court for a redetermination of the deficiency." Code Section 7422(a) also provides for judicial review, but does not affirmatively give a taxpayer the entitlement to judicial review, but restricts an implied right to review by precluding a suit or proceeding "in any court for the recovery of any internal revenue tax alleged to have been erroneously or illegally assessed or collected. . . . until a claim for refund or credit has been duly filed" with the Service. The APA establishes an explicit right to judicial review, but the Code does not. Might a taxpayer bring an action under APA Section 702 instead of the deficiency and refund actions the Code provides? Both the APA and the Code supply the answer. APA Section 702 states that nothing in the section "affects other limitations on judicial review" or "confers authority to grant relief if any other statute that grants consent to suit [against the agency] expressly or impliedly forbids the relief which is sought." The Code does limit judicial review in the Tax Court to a case where a taxpayer files a timely petition in the Tax Court, and limits judicial review of a suit for refund to a case until a claim for refund has been filed with the Service. Moreover, Code Section 7421, the Anti-Injunction Act, prohibits a "suit for the purpose of restraining the assessment or collection of any tax [from being] maintained in any court by any person." When the Code and the APA are read together, the APA steps aside and does not replace the two types of action the Code permits and limits against the Service or the United States, a deficiency suit or a refund suit, while the Anti-Injunction Act in the words of the APA "impliedly forbids" any other suit against the Service, except as expressly provided in Section 7421(a).

The form of the proceeding under APA Section 703 is described as one "relevant to the subject matter," but frequently the proceeding for judicial re-

---

[62] 5 USC § 706 (flush portion).
[63] 5 USC §§ 706(2)(A)–706(2)(D), and 706(2)(F).

view of an agency's "final action" is by way of a proceeding for an injunction or a declaratory judgement in a federal district court, and in the case of certain agencies that make quasi-judicial decisions by the appropriate court of appeals. In a tax case, the Anti-Injunction Act prohibits a taxpayer from bringing an injunction proceeding to restrain the assessment or collection of any tax, and the Declaratory Judgment Act (28 USC § 2201(a)) excludes taxes from permitted declaratory judgment actions. Judicial review in tax cases differs from judicial review of other agency actions. In tax cases, a taxpayer must use one of the forms of action permitted in the Code, either a deficiency action in the Tax Court or a refund action in a federal district court or the Court of Federal Claims. In tax cases, the action to be reviewed is the administration determination that there is a deficiency in a taxpayer's tax or that a claim for refund is disallowed, but there is no written decision representing the Service's final action. A notice of deficiency appears to be the action the Service takes that is close to a final written determination, but there is disagreement about how much, if any, description of the reasons supporting the Service's action must be included in a notice of deficiency or even whether the notice of deficiency must contain correct information. Similarly, there is no requirement that the Service explain why it has decided to disallow a claim for refund, or even act at all. A taxpayer may file a suit for refund if the Service fails to act for a period of at least six months.[64] In other words, the Service's action is a final action in a specialized way, but not in the way the APA contemplates.

The scope of judicial review described in APA Section 706 materially differs from the scope of review of courts in tax cases. A court review of agency action under APA Section 706 is based on "the whole or those parts of it cited by a party, and due account shall be taken of the rule of prejudicial error." In tax cases, by contrast, the court reviews the case de novo. There is no record to be reviewed, and any prejudice the taxpayer may have suffered during the administrative processing of the case is ignored, unless it reaches constitutional proportions. This is so in the Tax Court as well as courts hearing refund suits. On appeal from an agency's final action, a court of appeals will defer to the agency's expertise, but in tax appeals from final decisions of the Tax Court, the court of appeals conducts appellate review "in the same manner and to the same extent as a decision of the district courts in civil actions tried without a jury."[65] This means that the court of appeals reviews findings of fact made by the Tax Court under a clearly erroneous standard and reviews findings of law de novo.

---

[64] IRC § 6532(a)(1).

[65] IRC § 7482(a)(1).

¶ 1.04 NONJUDICIAL CONTROL OF THE SERVICE

[1] Legislative Control

The most obvious manner in which the legislative branch—Congress—exercises control over an administrative agency is through the provisions of the statute granting the agency the power to act.[66] All administrative authority is conferred directly or by implication from a statute. Congress and the courts combine to prevent the Service from acting outside the scope of its authority (or ultra vires). Under the ultra vires doctrine, administrative actions that are not designed to achieve Congress's expressed intent are held invalid in court as outside the power delegated.

Other legislative action can have even greater impact on an agency. If Congress is dissatisfied with an agency's policy, it can take direct action by changing the agency's authority or overruling its decision. For example, in the Revenue Act of 1978, Congress prohibited the Service from issuing regulations and rulings on the status of workers or employees or independent contractors before January 1, 1980.[67] Congress has also increased the number of situations where taxpayers can obtain judicial review of IRS administrative action by way of declaratory judgment proceedings regarding pension plans, tax-exempt organizations, and industrial development bonds.[68] These proceedings enable taxpayers to avoid the normal statutory procedures for judicial review of IRS action and can be viewed, therefore, as a check on the Service's discretion in these types of cases.

Congress has also adopted procedural safeguards and remedies applicable to all administrative agencies. The APA permits any person to gain access to agency records and information under the FOIA, and it sets standards of administrative procedure in rule or regulation making[69] and in such ancillary matters as right to counsel, access to a transcript of a statement made to the agency, agency subpoenas, and explanations of any request for agency action.[70] Standards are also established for any adjudicative hearing,[71] but since the Service's decisions are subject to de novo judicial review, these provisions do not apply to administrative investigations and appeals. Finally, the APA provides

---

[66] See generally Gellhorn, Byse, Strauss, Rakoff & Schotland, Administrative Law—Cases and Comments 50–146 (8th ed. 1987); Jaffe & Nathanson, Administrative Law, Cases and Material (3d ed. 1968).

[67] Congress extended this prohibition. Revenue Act of 1978, Pub. L. No. 95-600, § 530, 92 Stat. 2885.

[68] IRC §§ 7476, 7428, 7478.

[69] 5 USC § 553.

[70] 5 USC § 555.

[71] 5 USC § 554.

for a general right of judicial review of agency action, although the specific provisions of the Code concerning judicial review take precedence over this general provision.

Congress controls administrative action in other ways. Through appropriations to agencies, Congress can affect the scope of administrative activity and can even refuse to allocate funds for particular activities of the agency in the amount and terms of an appropriations law. In an act to appropriate funds to the Service for its fiscal year ending September 30, 1980, Congress mandated that no funds be used to enforce rulings dealing with the tax-exempt status of segregated schools.[72] Congress also exercises control over the Service through its standing committees, the House Committee on Ways and Means and the Senate Committee on Finance. These standing committees can hold hearings and investigations and propose legislation concerning administrative action, and through congressional subcommittees, the Service may be called on to explain particular actions or positions.

Where the Service's functions are concerned, Congress has established by statute a standing "watchdog" committee, the Joint Committee on Internal Revenue Taxation.[73] This Joint Committee has the duty to investigate the operation and effect of the federal system of internal revenue taxes and the administration of the Service, to investigate and publish proposals concerning the simplification of the tax laws, and to report to the House and Senate standing committees the results of both its procedural and its substantive investigations.[74] The Joint Committee also exercises control over the Service by reviewing determinations made on offers in compromise, involving refunds and credits in excess of $200,000.[75] The Committee may examine tax returns, has subpoena power, may hold hearings in aid of its duties,[76] and has a staff to assist it.[77] The staff of the Joint Committee has been called on to perform a variety of tasks, from analyzing current law on particular subjects and suggesting reforms or changes to auditing the tax returns of a president.

In addition to formal collective action, individual members of Congress can exert influence through private or public intercession in agency affairs. A Congressman can make an inquiry on behalf of a constituent or make known his understanding of the views of Congress concerning legislation that the Service may or may not be interpreting correctly. A private bill is a more formal way of securing special treatment for an individual taxpayer.

---

[72] Pub. L. No. 96-74, §§ 614, 615, 93 Stat. 576 (1979), reprinted in 1979-2 CB 473, 474.

[73] IRC §§ 8001–8005.

[74] IRC § 8002.

[75] IRC § 6015(b). This function is described at ¶ 11.13.

[76] IRC § 8021.

[77] IRC § 8004.

Finally, Congress participates in the appointment process and must approve the appointment of the Commissioner of Internal Revenue and the Assistant Secretary of the Treasury for Tax Policy.

[2] Executive Control

The President controls the Service primarily through appointments, budgets, and reorganization. The President appoints the Commissioner of Internal Revenue and can remove him as well.[78] Because the Chief Executive controls administrative requests to Congress, he may indirectly affect the scope of the Service's action through budgetary restrictions or enabling legislation. Occasional reorganizations of the Service can reflect the judgment of the Chief Executive about the proper direction and operation of the Service. Some power of direction also rests in the hands of the President, and clearly the President may directly participate in an administrative decision. Although few presidents have had particular interest in exercising these powers, the White House has exerted influence and has sometimes placed improper pressures on the Service to institute programs and to investigate individuals and organizations.[79]

[3] Judicial Control

Authority for judicial review of administrative action claimed to be erroneous may be found in (1) a statute that provides a specific method for obtaining judicial review of an agency's orders (specific method of review) or a statute that contains a general provision for judicial review of administrative actions (general method of review) and (2) a grant of general jurisdiction that does not specifically grant a right to review administrative action (nonstatutory re-

---

[78] However, the President's removal power is not free from question. An officer of the Executive branch may be removed (Myers v. United States, 272 US 52 (1926)), but perhaps not a quasilegislative (Humphrey's Ex'r (Rathbun) v. United States, 295 US 602 (1935)) or quasi-judicial officer (Wiener v. United States, 357 US 349 (1958)).

[79] The tax return confidentiality rules of IRC § 6103 were amended in part as a consequence of the misuse of tax return information by the White House under President Nixon. See Staff of Joint Comm. on Taxation, 94th Cong., 2d Sess., General Explanation of the Tax Reform Act of 1976 at 314 (Comm. Print 1976), reprinted in 1976-3 CB (Vol. 2) 326. A recent example of executive control occurred where the White House instructed the Service not to deny tax exemptions to private schools on alleged racial discrimination grounds. The public reaction to this effort to control the activities of the Service may serve as a deterrent to future attempts to control the Service, at least in a public way. See, e.g., "Administration Defends Tax Exempt School Switch," 14 Tax Notes 358 (1982). See also Senate Fin. Comm. Staff Report at 306–328.

view).[80] The most important authority for judicial review of administrative action by the Service is derived from specific statutory provisions. Despite the availability of statutory methods, nonstatutory methods such as injunctions and declaratory judgments also play a limited role in judicial review of IRS actions.[81]

[4] Statutory Review: Refund and Deficiency Procedures

The Code provides two statutory methods of judicial review of administrative action taken by the Service in determining a deficiency in or assessing the correct amount of tax.

1. *Refund methods.* Under the refund method, a taxpayer must pay the full amount of the tax the Service claims to be due and then sue for a refund of the amount the taxpayer claims was erroneously assessed and collected.[82] This suit must be brought either in a federal district court or in the United States Court of Federal Claims, formerly the Court of Claims.[83]

---

[80] See Gellhorn, Byse, Strauss, Rakoff & Schotland, Administrative Law—Cases and Comments 917, 937 (8th ed. 1987); Jaffee & Nathanson, Administrative Law, Case and Materials 191–207 (3d ed. 1968).

[81] The form of proceeding for judicial review of most IRS actions is the specific statutory proceeding specified in the Code. However, Section 702 of the APA appears to grant independent jurisdiction to federal courts to review agency action in providing that "a person suffering legal wrong because of agency action or adversely affected or aggrieved by agency action, within the meaning of a relevant statute, is entitled to judicial review thereof." 5 USC § 702. Moreover, "any applicable form of legal action, including actions for declaratory judgments or writs of prohibitory or mandatory injunction or habeas corpus, in a court of competent jurisdiction" may be used "in the absence or inadequacy" of any statutorily provided-for form of action. 5 USC § 703. Also, final agency action "for which there is no other adequate remedy in a court [is] subject to judicial review." 5 USC § 704. The Judicial Code grant of district court jurisdiction (28 USC § 1331) was amended in 1976, to include, irrespective of the $10,000 limitation, actions "brought against the United States, any agency thereof, or officer or employee thereof in his official capacity." Shortly after this amendment, the Supreme Court held that the APA did not grant jurisdiction to district courts independent of 28 USC § 1331. Califano v. Sanders, 430 US 99, 107 (1977). Therefore, a person bringing an action against the Service or an official must still advance some basis for the district court to exercise its jurisdiction (i.e., to hear the case). One basis may be that the Service or the official has invaded the person's legal rights, committed some legal wrong, committed some tort (see Bivens v. Six Unknown Named Agents of the Fed. Bureau of Narcotics, 403 US 388 (1971)), or violated the person's civil rights (42 USC § 1983).

[82] Flora v. United States, 362 US 145 (1960).

[83] IRC § 7422; 28 USC §§ 1346, 1341. The United States Claims Court was redesignated the United States Court of Federal Claims, effective October 29, 1992, pursu-

2. *Deficiency method.* Under the deficiency method, a taxpayer may, without first paying the tax in issue, file a petition in the U.S. Tax Court for a redetermination of the amount of the deficiency the Service claims is due.[84]

The specific methods of judicial review of IRS actions differ in important respects from judicial review of the actions of other agencies. Judicial review of the actions of agencies other than the Service is typically limited, because courts recognize (or follow explicit statutory directions) that the agency rather than the judiciary is to exercise the power or discretion Congress has delegated.[85] Judicial review of IRS actions is far broader. Both the statutory refund and deficiency methods provide taxpayers de novo judicial review of IRS action in assessing tax or determining the amount of a deficiency.[86] Moreover, in contrast to judicial review of other agency actions, judicial review in tax cases is probably unique in offering taxpayers a choice of court of review (district courts and such specialized courts as the Court of Federal Claims and the Tax Court), each having its own procedures and precedents, which may affect the outcome of a case.

Judicial review of the final orders of most agencies is obtained in a court of appeals by filing a petition for review.[87] The proceeding is to review the agency's action, and the decision is made by the court of appeals on the record of the proceedings conducted before the agency.[88] Both the status of the reviewing court and the nature of the proceeding differ considerably where a taxpayer seeks judicial review under either the refund or the deficiency method.

---

ant to the Federal Court Administration Act of 1992, Pub. L. No. 102-572, 106 Stat. 4506 (1992).

[84] IRC § 6213.

[85] See Gellhorn, Byse, Strauss, Rakoff & Schotland, Administrative Law—Cases and Comments 985, 986 (8th ed. 1987).

[86] See the discussion infra ¶ 1.05[1].

[87] The Federal Rules of Appellate Procedure state that a petition for review includes (1) a petition to enjoin, set aside, suspend, modify, or otherwise review or (2) a notice of appeal. Fed. R. App. P. 15(a). The remedy is usually prescribed by the statute establishing the agency. See, e.g., 29 USC § 160(f) (National Labor Relations Board); 15 USC § 77(i) (Securities and Exchange Commission); 15 USC § 45 (Federal Trade Commission); 16 USC § 825(1) (Federal Power Commission). However, jurisdiction of courts of appeals to review final orders of some agencies, such as the Interstate Commerce Commission and the Federal Communications Commission, is found in the Judicial Code. 28 USC § 2342. Private suits in federal district courts against the agency or officer making the ruling are less frequently provided for in some statutes (e.g., ruling on old age benefits, 42 USC § 405(g)), but these district court actions may be explained in some cases because they typically involve persons of modest means to whom access to a local court is necessary.

[88] See 5 USC § 706; Fed. R. App. P. 16(a).

In view of these differences, statutory review of IRS actions may be productively described in terms of (1) the status of the reviewing court and the nature of the proceeding; (2) the scope of judicial review; and (3) the timing of review.

¶ 1.05 JUDICIAL REVIEW OF SERVICE ACTION: REFUND SUITS IN THE DISTRICT COURTS AND THE COURT OF FEDERAL CLAIMS

[1] The Status of the Reviewing Court

[a] The Federal District Courts

The timing of review. Generally, an affected person contesting a final adverse decision of an administrative agency need not comply with the order before seeking judicial review. Judicial stays of administrative action pending judicial review are authorized by the All-Writs statute, the APA, and at times by specific statutory provision (e.g., the Federal Aviation Act).[89] Under the refund method, however, judicial review of IRS action in tax cases occurs only after the tax has been paid. There are a number of reasons for this practice. Historically, the assessment of a tax had the effect of a court judgment, and so the taxpayer was obliged to satisfy this "decree" immediately.[90] Moreover, as a matter of policy, it is obvious that the public treasury cannot await court review if the government is to operate. The pay-first-litigate-later (refund) method of judicial review reflects this policy, but it obviously has harsh consequences.

The jurisdictional statute for refund suits in the district courts is found in 28 USC § 1346, which provides:[91]

Federal district courts have original jurisdiction over suits for the recovery of internal revenue taxes. Unlike judicial review of final orders of most executive agencies, judicial review of Service action is by the lowest court of general jurisdiction in the federal judicial system.

---

[89] 28 USC § 1651 (All-Units); 5 USC § 705 (APA); 49 USC § 1486(a) (Federal Aviation Act).

[90] Bull v. United States, 295 US 247 (1935).

[91] 28 USC § 1346(a)(1).

[b] The Court of Federal Claims and the Federal Circuit

A taxpayer has the option of instituting a refund suit in the Court of Federal Claims. Under the Federal Courts Improvement Act of 1982, Congress established a new Article I trial court known as the Court of Federal Claims, which inherited the trial jurisdiction of the Court of Claims.[92] A U.S. Court of Appeals for the Federal Circuit was created by a merger of the Court of Federal Claims and the Court of Customs and Patent Appeals into a single appellate court with expanded jurisdiction. This Court of Appeals hears appeals from decisions of the Court of Federal Claims.[93] The Court of Federal Claims is a court of limited jurisdiction created under Article I of the Constitution.[94] Both the Court of Federal Claims and the Tax Court have the same status in that they are both Article I courts or legislative (i.e., legislatively created) courts, while federal district courts are Article III (or constitutional) courts (i.e., provided for in Article III of the Constitution).

The Court of Federal Claims has concurrent jurisdiction with the federal district courts over suits for the recovery of taxes erroneously and illegally assessed by the United States. The Court of Federal Claims also has jurisdiction over such actions under the Tucker Act.[95] In a tax refund suit commenced in a

---

[92] 28 USC § 1491 as amended by the Federal Courts Improvement Act of 1982 § 133, effective October 1, 1982. See also HR Rep. No. 312, 97th Cong., 1st Sess. 16 (1982), reprinted in 1982-24 IRB 52, 53. The Court of Federal Claims was established in the Federal Courts Improvement Act of 1982 to assume the trial jurisdiction of the Court of Claims. The Court of Appeals for the Federal Circuit handles appeals from the Claims Court. Pub. L. No. 97-164 tax-related portions reprinted in 1982-24 IRB 4 et seq. For a case analyzing the jurisdiction of the Court of Federal Claims, see Murray v. United States, 817 F2d 1580 (Fed. Cir. 1987). ("The courts have consistently held . . . that the Claims Court's jurisdiction is limited to such cases where the Constitution or a federal statute requires a payment of money damages compensation for the violation"); Morales v. United States, 90-1 USTC ¶ 50,070 (Cl. Ct. 1990) (Claims Court jurisdiction is based in Tucker Act, but this act creates no substantive rights).

[93] 28 USC § 1295(a). See also HR Rep. No. 312, 97th Cong., 1st Sess. 16 (1982), reprinted in 1982-24 IRB 52, 53.

[94] 28 USC § 171(a). Article III status is reserved for the Court of Appeals for the Federal Circuit. See HR Rep. No. 312, § 18, 97th Cong., 1st Sess. 16 (1982), reprinted in 1982-24 IRB 52. See also Glidden Co. v. Zdanok, 370 US 530 (1962) (the authority of this decision has now become uncertain).

[95] Morales v. United States, 90-1 USTC ¶ 50,070 (Cl. Ct. 1990). The jurisdiction of the U.S. Court of Federal Claims over treaties appears to be settled by Section 7422(f), which provides in part that a suit for refund "may be maintained . . . notwithstanding the provisions of Section 1502 of such title 28 of the United States Code (relating to treaty cases)." Section 1502 states that, except as otherwise stated by Congress, the U.S. Court of Federal Claims does not have any jurisdiction over "any claims against the United States growing out of or dependent upon any treaty entered into with foreign nations." Accordingly, despite Section 1502's prohibition, a taxpayer may institute a refund suit based on an income tax treaty in the U.S. Court of Federal Claims. But see Brown & Wil-

federal district court, either party may request a jury trial,[96] but no right to trial by jury exists in the Court of Federal Claims.[97] Whatever differences there are between the courts, and putting aside certain differences in their procedural rules, a refund suit in the Court of Federal Claims proceeds in the same way as a refund suit in a district court sitting without a jury.

[2] The Nature of the Proceedings

[a] In General

A taxpayer obtains judicial review under the refund method by instituting a suit for refund in a federal district court, having first paid the full amount of the contested tax[98] and filed a claim for refund that the Service has either disallowed or failed to act upon for six months.[99] Initially, the nature of the proceeding is one for debt, based on the common-law count of assumpsit for money had and received.[100] It is now accepted that a suit for refund is a statutory action to recover overpayments of tax that have been illegally and wrongfully collected. To be entitled to judgment, in a refund suit, the taxpayer must (1) prove that the Service's action in assessing and collecting the tax was erroneous and (2) provide an explanation and documentation of the correct tax and the amount owed to him that the Service wrongfully holds.[101] In such proceedings, unlike judicial review of the actions of other agencies, any "record" made in the Service, including the reasons for its assessment, is irrelevant. The action involves a de novo determination of the correct tax and is not a review of the administrative processing of the case.

---

liamson, Ltd. v. United States, 688 F2d 747 (Ct. Cl. 1982) (appearing to say that Section 1502 applies, but failing to mention Section 7422(f)).

[96] 28 USC § 2404.

[97] The absence of jury trials in the Court of Federal Claims derives from the fact that suits against the United States, whether in the Court of Federal Claims or in a district court, require a waiver of sovereign immunity and thus are not "suits at common law" within the meaning of the Seventh Amendment. Glidden Co. v. Zdanok, 370 US 530 (1962) (explaining the jurisdiction and status of the Court of Federal Claims). Congress added to its waiver of sovereign immunity in suits in federal district courts permission for trials by jury, but it did not choose to do so with respect to suits in the Court of Federal Claims and the successor to its trial division, the Court of Federal Claims.

[98] Flora v. United States, 362 US 145 (1960).

[99] IRC §§ 7422(a), 7432(a).

[100] The history of the suit for refund is described by the Supreme Court in Flora v. United States, 362 US 145 (1960).

[101] Helvering v. Taylor, 293 US 507, 514 (1935).

A refund suit in federal district court is commenced by the filing of a complaint and goes through the discovery and trial phases of a case in the same manner as other federal litigation. These procedures are set forth in the Federal Rules of Civil Procedure. Unlike any other court that may hear a tax case, either party may request a trial by jury. In refund suits in federal district courts and the Court of Federal Claims, the United States is represented by lawyers under the jurisdiction of the Assistant Attorney General of the Justice Department's Tax Division.[102]

[b] The Presumption of Correctness and Burden of Proof

In refund suits, the taxpayer has the burden of proving that the Service's assessment and collection was erroneous and the amount of the refund to which the taxpayer is entitled.[103] In other words, a taxpayer has the burden of proving by a preponderance of the evidence that the assessment or determination is incorrect and, in a refund suit, the correct amount, if any, of tax.[104] The presumption of correctness, on the other hand, assigns to the taxpayer the separate burden of coming forward with sufficient evidence from which a trier of fact could find in his favor or of suffering an adverse decision if evidence is not produced.[105] Factual issues are tried de novo in the district court and the Court of Federal Claims under the refund method, as well as in the Tax Court under the deficiency method. No weight is given to findings of fact the Service may have made in its administrative processing of the case. However, in judicial proceedings, the assessment or determination of the Service is presumed to be correct.[106] This presumption may appear to give evidential weight

---

[102] The Authority of the Attorney General is set forth in 5 USC § 291 and in Exec. Order No. 6166, issued by the president on June 10, 1933, pursuant to authority granted by the Act of June 30, 1932, ch. 314, 47 Stat. 383, 413, as amended by the Act of March 3, 1933, ch. 212, 47 Stat. 1489, 1517; see also IRC § 7401.

[103] Helvering v. Taylor, 293 US 507 (1935).

[104] Helvering v. Taylor, 293 US 507 (1935); Rockwell v. Comm'r, 512 F2d 882, 886 (9th Cir.), cert. denied, 423 US 1015 (1975); United States v. Rexach, 482 F2d 10 (1st Cir.), cert. denied, 414 US 1039 (1973).

[105] The Federal Rules of Evidence note the following in regard to presumptions in general in civil actions and proceedings (Rule 301):

> In all civil actions and proceedings not otherwise provided for by Act of Congress or by these rules, a presumption imposes on the party against whom it is directed the burden of going forward with evidence to rebut or meet the presumption, but does not shift to such party the burden of proof in the sense of the risk of nonpersuasion, which remains throughout the trial upon the party on whom it was originally cast.

[106] Welch v. Helvering, 290 US 111, 115 (1933).

to the Service's action, but this is not the case. The presumption of correctness must be distinguished from the taxpayer's burden of proof.[107]

The presumption of correctness is a procedural device for allocating the burden of going forward with evidence. As a matter of policy, it is appropriate to place this burden on taxpayers in part because they may reasonably be said to have control of or access to evidence on the issues.[108] However, the presumption of correctness is not evidence.[109] It drops out of the case once the taxpayer introduces sufficient evidence on which a reasonable trier of fact could reach a conclusion in the taxpayer's favor. Yet, if the taxpayer is to prevail, the evidence adduced must be sufficient to convince the trier of fact that the taxpayer's version of the facts is supported by a preponderance of the evidence; that is, the taxpayer must still satisfy a burden of persuasion, even if the taxpayer has carried the burden of coming forward with evidence.[110]

[3] Appellate Review

To appeal an adverse decision of a district court judge, the taxpayer must file a notice of appeal with the Clerk of the district court. Once the notice of appeal has been filed, the procedural rules for the appeal are governed by the Federal Rules of Appellate Procedure, as well as the Rules of the Circuit Court for appeals from the district court. Appeals from decisions of the Court of Federal Claims are to the Court of Appeals for the Federal Circuit.[111] Appeals from district courts and the Court of Federal Claims will be handled by an attorney in the Appellate Section of the Justice Department's Tax Division.

---

[107] The presumption of correctness must not be confused with the presumption of regularity attaching to official actions by public officers. Official actions are presumed to have been regularly and legally performed because this is the probability and because of the difficulty of proving that the officer conducted himself in a manner that was in all ways regular and legal. IX Wigmore on Evidence (Chadbourne Rev. 1981) § 2534.

[108] Rockwell v. Comm'r, 512 F2d 882 (9th Cir.), cert. denied, 423 US 1015 (1975); Durovic v. Comm'r, 54 TC 1364, 1393 (1970).

[109] Compton v. United States, 334 F2d 212, 216 (4th Cir. 1964); Harbin v. Comm'r, 40 TC 373, 376 (1963).

[110] This distinction between the burden of going forward and the burden of persuasion is discussed in Conforte v. Comm'r, 74 TC 1160, 1178–1179 (1980); Zubone, Jr. v. Comm'r, 883 F2d 1317 (7th Cir. 1989) (good analysis of burden of proof and production in Tax Court cases).

[111] 28 USC § 1295 (Court of Federal Claims); 28 USC § 1291 (district courts).

¶ 1.06 JUDICIAL REVIEW IN THE U.S. TAX COURT: DEFICIENCY ACTIONS IN THE TAX COURT

[1] The Status of the Court

Both the current status of the Tax Court and the nature of proceedings before it are affected by the Tax Court's history.[112] Until 1970, the Tax Court was technically not a court at all, but "an independent agency in the Executive Branch of the Government."[113] Despite the fact that the Tax Court conducted proceedings in a judicial manner, it was considered an administrative agency[114] whose decisions were reviewable by courts of appeals in the same manner as final orders of other agencies.[115] Deficiency proceedings in the Tax Court still reflect a tension between its origins as an administrative agency and its status as a court.

The deficiency method of prepayment Tax Court review was intended to remedy the situation of a taxpayer's being forced to pay the full amount of a proposed deficiency in tax before any review of the Service action could be obtained.[116] Where a Tax Court decision redetermines the amount of a deficiency, the Service must assess and collect the determined tax,[117] and the taxpayer must pay the amount of any deficiency determined by the court unless he files a bond to secure payment of the tax.[118] Also, prepayment review in the Tax Court does not apply to all taxes (e.g., excise and employment taxes) or all taxpayers (e.g., bankrupt taxpayers). Consequently, prepayment judicial review under the deficiency method is still properly seen as an exception to the general rule that a tax must be paid before judicial review may be obtained.

The Tax Court does not have the same status as the federal district courts and the Court of Appeals for the Federal Circuit. Congress established the Tax

---

[112] For a history of the Tax Court, see Dubroff, The United States Tax Court—An Historical Analysis (1979).

[113] This was the language describing the Tax Court, known before 1942 as the Board of Tax Appeals, from the Revenue Act of 1924 (Pub. L. No. 176, § 900, 43 Stat. 336) until the Tax Reform Act of 1969 (Pub. L. No. 91-172, § 951, 83 Stat. 730) amended Section 7441 of the Internal Revenue Code of 1954. See Fairmont Aluminum Co. v. Comm'r, 22 TC 1377, 1384–1385 (1954), aff'd, 222 F2d 622 (4th Cir.), cert. denied, 350 US 838 (1955).

[114] Dobson v. Comm'r, 320 US 489 (1943).

[115] See IRC § 7482(a). The deference paid to Tax Court decisions as a result of this status led to the amendment of Section 7482(a) to provide for appellate review in the same manner and to the same extent as decisions of district courts sitting without a jury. This only confused the status of the Tax Court further.

[116] See IRC § 6213(a).

[117] IRC § 6215(a).

[118] IRC § 7485(a).

Court under one of its legislative powers enumerated in Article I of the Constitution, not pursuant to the authority granted to it in Article III to establish courts of inferior jurisdiction to receive the judicial power described therein. Thus, the Tax Court is a legislative, not a constitutional court, but this difference does not affect the manner in which the court conducts its business.[119] The Tax Court adjudicates cases in the same manner as a federal district court judge sitting without a jury. Unlike federal district courts, the Tax Court performs only those functions Congress has assigned to it, according to the rules and procedures provided in the enabling legislation.[120] Thus, the Tax Court is a "court of record" established under Article I of the Constitution,[121] but its jurisdiction is limited. The Tax Court hears cases involving "deficiencies," a specially defined statutory term, in income, gift, or estate tax and certain excise taxes on private foundations and foundation managers, but not other types of taxes such as employment taxes.[122] Even with respect to taxes over which it has jurisdiction, the Tax Court may not hear the case if an assessment of the tax has been made, unless the assessment is a jeopardy or termination assessment.[123] The Tax Court may determine the amount of an overpayment involving income, gift, or estate taxes, but it may do so only in narrowly drawn circumstances.[124] On the other hand, although declaratory judgments are generally prohibited in tax cases, Congress has given the Tax Court jurisdiction to grant such judgments in certain cases.[125]

---

[119] The main difference between legislative and constitutional courts is that the tenure and compensation of the judges of constitutional courts are protected by Article III of the Constitution. See Northern Pipeline Constr. Co. v. Marathon Pipe Line Co., 458 US 50 (1982); Bator, Mishkin, Shapiro & Wechsler, The Federal Courts and the Federal System 425–428 (3d ed. 1988). C. Wright, Law of Federal Courts (4th ed. 1983) § 11.

While the Tax Court is a court of law, it remains different from federal district courts in a number of ways. For example, Tax Court judges serve fifteen-year terms, while federal district court judges and judges of the courts of appeals hold judicial office during good behavior. One result of this different status is that a Tax Court judge has been held not to be a "judge" for purposes of the recusal statute, 28 USC § 455, because, the circuit court said, there is "no authority in statute or rule for ordering the recusal of a [T]ax [C]ourt judge." Nobles v. Comm'r, 105 F3d 436 (9th Cir. 1997) (motion for mandatory recusal of judge who served as Deputy Chief Counsel and Acting Chief Counsel under 28 USC § 455(b)(3)).

[120] IRC §§ 7441–7448.

[121] IRC § 7441. The Tax Court is a "court of record" and, within a wide definition of the term, it is a "court of law," and its judges exercise judicial power. First W. Gov't Sec., Inc. v. Comm'r, 94 TC 549 (1990).

[122] IRC § 6213(a).

[123] IRC §§ 6861, 6851.

[124] IRC § 6512(b). This jurisdiction applies to the excise taxes on private foundations and foundation managers as well.

[125] IRC §§ 7476 (pension plans), 7428 (exemption organizations), 7478 (the tax-exempt status of certain bonds).

[a] The Equity Jurisdiction of the Tax Court

A persistent issue in Tax Court litigation is whether and to what extent the Tax Court has equity jurisdiction, especially when a claim of equitable estoppel is made. Initially, the Supreme Court's view was that the Tax Court's jurisdiction has been strictly confined by the Supreme Court to the function assigned to it by Congress.[126] Under this view, the Tax Court was held not to have the jurisdiction to do equity—that is, to grant the type of relief, recognized as equitable in nature, that a federal district court may grant as a court of law and equity.[127] The predecessor of the Tax Court had no power to apply the doctrine of equitable recoupment because it "is based upon a determination foreign to the [court's] jurisdiction [and] would be contrary to the expressed will of Congress."[128] The Tax Court itself has said that it cannot expand its jurisdiction by providing relief from statutory requirements, but it can apply equitable principles to decide cases that come within its statutorily prescribed jurisdiction.[129] In *Freytag v. Commissioner*, however, the Supreme Court held that the Tax Court was a "Court of Law."[130] After *Freytag*, one hopes that it is settled that the Tax Court is a court of specialized jurisdiction, but it exercises all of the powers of a court of law within the subject matter jurisdiction.

The nature of the Tax Court's jurisdiction has nevertheless caused some lengthy litigation. In *Estate of Mueller v. Commissioner*, the Tax Court held that its jurisdiction to redetermine estate taxes included jurisdiction to apply the doctrine of equitable recoupment.[131] The Tax Court said that "exercising jurisdiction over petitioner's recoupment defense does not require us to exercise jurisdiction that is beyond the scope of petitioner's main claim for the redetermination of its estate tax deficiency." Thus, the Tax Court now recognizes that it may use equitable principles in deciding cases that come within its jurisdiction and that use of those equitable principles does not constitute an expansion of its jurisdiction. In reaching this conclusion, the Tax Court had Supreme Court support in *Freytag*, holding that the Tax Court is a court of law under the Constitution, exercising within the limits of its statutorily defined jurisdiction full judicial power, as well as the Supreme Court's decision in *Dalm*,[132]

---

[126] Comm'r v. Gooch Milling & Elevator Co., 320 US 418 (1943).

[127] Comm'r v. Gooch Milling & Elevator Co., 320 US 418 (1943).

[128] See Continental Equities, Inc. v. Comm'r, 551 F2d 74 (5th Cir. 1977).

[129] Woods v. Comm'r, 92 TC 776, 784–785 (1989).

[130] Freytag v. Comm'r, 501 US 868 (1991). One circuit court has said that although it is a court of limited jurisdiction, the Tax Court has jurisdiction to hear an equitable estoppel claim "if considering the claim is necessary to the appropriate disposition of the case before it." Bokum v. Comm'r, 992 F2d 1136 (11th Cir. 1993).

[131] Estate of Mueller v. Comm'r, 101 TC 551 (1993) (estate tax deficiency could be redetermined by taking into account recoupment of overpaid income tax).

[132] United States v. Dalm, 494 US 596 (1990).

which at least suggested that the Tax Court has jurisdiction to apply the doctrine of equitable recoupment even though in that case the taxpayer failed to assert the defense or claim in the Tax Court. Despite this Supreme Court authority, the Sixth Circuit, nevertheless, rejected the Tax Court's view of its equitable recoupment jurisdiction.[133] It now appears, however, that the Tax Court recognizes that it has equitable recoupment jurisdiction.[134]

[b] Special Trial Judges

The Tax Court has special trial judges who are appointed by the Chief Judge. The jurisdiction of the special trial judges is limited to (1) any declaratory judgment proceeding; (2) any small case, defined initially in Section 7463 as a case involving a deficiency, where the amount in dispute does not exceed $10,000, but effective July 22, 1998, does not exceed $50,000[135]; (3) any proceeding where neither the amount of deficiency in dispute, as defined under the small case statute, nor the amount of an overpayment, exceeds $10,000 (after July 22, 1998, $50,000); and (4) any other proceeding the Chief Counsel may designate.[136]

In *Freytag*,[137] the Supreme Court settled some of the constitutional issues pertaining to the status and operation of the Tax Court. At issue was the assignment by the chief judge of a complex case for trial by a special trial judge. The taxpayers objected to the assignment, and, because they did so belatedly, one of the issues was whether they had waived the objection. The challenge to the assignment turned on whether the assignment violated the Constitution's Appointments Clause (Article II, Section 2, Clause 3). In substance, the Supreme Court ruled that the chief judge can assign the trial of a case to a special trial judge under a catchall provision in Code Section 7443A(b)(4) because actual decisions in cases assigned to them are made by judges.

In *Gomez v. United States*,[138] the Supreme Court held that the assignment of additional duties to the U.S. magistrates under 28 USC § 636(b)(3) (a provision similar to Section 7443A(b)(4)) did not permit magistrates to supervise juror voir dire in a felony trial over the defendant's objection. According to the Court, the special trial judge in *Freytag* was exercising lesser authority than was the magistrate in *Gomez*. Thus, Section 7443A(b)(4) "permits the chief judge to assign *any* Tax Court proceeding, regardless of complexity or

---

[133] Mueller v. Comm'r, 82 AFTR2d 98-5737 (6th Cir. 1998).

[134] Estate of Branson v. Comm'r, 113 TC 6 (1999), on appeal to the Ninth Circuit.

[135] IRC § 7463, as amended by 1998 Act § 3103.

[136] IRC § 7443A.

[137] Freytag v. Comm'r, 501 US 868 (1991).

[138] Gomez v. United States, 490 US 858 (1989).

amount, to a special trial judge for hearing and the preparation of proposed findings and written opinion."[139]

On the Appointments Clause issue, the Supreme Court concluded in *Freytag* that the special trial judge is an "inferior officer" permissibly appointable by the Tax Court because the Tax Court is a "court of law." With jurisdiction derived from Congress itself, the Tax Court is an Article I court that exercises judicial power to the exclusion of any other function; that is, it is neither an advocate nor a rulemaker as are certain other legislative tribunals, such as the Securities Exchange Commission and the Federal Trade Commission. Also, the Tax Court is independent of the executive and legislative branches.

[c] Collateral Jurisdiction of the Tax Court

The Tax Court's jurisdiction has been expanded so that its judicial business even more closely resembles that of a district court in tax cases. The Tax Court has jurisdiction to carry out the following activities:

1. *Restrain premature assessments of taxes over which the Tax Court has jurisdiction.* The Tax Court has jurisdiction to enjoin collection of an IRS assessment before the ninety-day period within which a taxpayer is permitted to file a Tax Court petition involving an income, gift, or estate tax deficiency. However, the Tax Court has no jurisdiction to enjoin the assessment of an employment tax.[140]

2. *Enforce a decision that a taxpayer petitioner has made an overpayment of tax.* The Tax Court has jurisdiction to order the refund of an overpayment plus interest, if the Service fails to refund the overpayment within 120 days after the Tax Court's decision becomes final.[141]

---

[139] Gomez v. United States, 490 US 858 (1989). Significantly, the Supreme Court did not address the effect of Tax Court Rule 183, which requires the judge to defer to the findings of fact made by the special trial judge. Does that deference effectively mean that the special trial judge both hears and decides issues of fact? See Stone v. Comm'r, 865 F2d 342 (DC Cir. 1989). Since this argument was made late, the Supreme Court said only that a special trial judge has no authority to decide a case. See *Freytag*, 501 US 868 (1991), at n.3. In a case where the specific issue was raised, the Court of Appeals for the Ninth Circuit found that the review by the judge of the special trial judge's recommended findings and opinion was sufficient, although there was no opportunity under Rule 183 of the Tax Court's rules for the opportunity to take exceptions to the special trial judge's report and the procedure for a motion for reconsideration after the judge acted was claimed to be inadequate. Erhard v. Comm'r, 46 F3d 1470 (9th Cir. 1995), cert. denied, 64 USLW 3286 (Oct. 16, 1995).

[140] IRC § 6213(a), added by the Technical and Miscellaneous Revenue Act of 1988 (TAMRA) § 6243(a).

[141] IRC § 6512(b)(2), added by TAMRA § 6244(a) for determined overpayments that have not been refunded by the ninetieth day after enactment.

3. *Review IRS determinations to make jeopardy assessments and levies.*[142] If a jeopardy assessment has been made and the taxpayer has filed a petition in the Tax Court, the Tax Court has jurisdiction to review the IRS determination to sell property it has seized because (a) the expenses of maintenance and conservation will greatly reduce the net proceeds or (b) the property is liable to perish or become greatly reduced in value if kept or cannot be kept without great expense.[143]

4. *Redetermine interest on deficiencies.* The Tax Court can redetermine interest due on a deficiency it has determined to be due from a taxpayer if the taxpayer (a) pays the deficiency; (b) pays the disputed interest; and (c) files a petition in the Tax Court within one year after the decision becomes final.[144]

5. *Modify decision in estate tax cases.* The Tax Court can take such action where the estate is entitled to a deduction for interest paid during an extended payment period on a federal or state estate tax liability.[145]

6. *Declaratory judgment for the determination of employment status.* If the Service determines that one or more of the workers for a taxpayer are employees, or the taxpayer is not entitled to the relief provisions of Section 530 of the Revenue Act of 1978 in the treatment of the worker, the Taxpayer Relief Act of 1997 gives the Tax Court the jurisdiction to redetermine or declare whether the Service's worker status or Section 530 determination is correct.[146] The Tax Court's declaration or redetermination has the force and effect of a decision of the Tax Court and is reviewable as such.

7. *Declaratory judgment relating to the value of certain gifts.* The Taxpayer Relief Act of 1997 also gives the Tax Court jurisdiction to redetermine the value of any gift if (a) there is an actual controversy between the taxpayer and the Service over the value of the gift; (b)

---

[142] IRC § 7429(b)(2)(B), added by TAMRA § 6237(c) for assessments made after June 30, 1989.

[143] IRC § 6863(b)(3).

[144] IRC § 7481(c).

[145] IRC § 7481(d).

[146] IRC § 7436, added by the Taxpayer Relief Act of 1997 § 1454(a), effective on the date of enactment, August 5, 1997. Former Section 7436 was redesignated Section 7437. The person affected by the determination, the putative employer, is the only one who may bring the proceeding, and must do so by filing a pleading in the Tax Court before the ninety-first day after the Service sends a notice of its determination. IRC §§ 7436(b)(1)–7436(b)(2). The putative employer's treatment of the worker during the Tax Court proceeding is not taken into account in the court's consideration of the issue. IRC § 7436(b)(3). The Community Renewal Tax Relief Act of 2000 (CRTRA), Pub. L. No. 106-554, amends Section 7436 to clarify that the Tax Court does have jurisdiction to determine the amount of employment tax, but only to determine employment status. See Ewens & Miller, Inc. v. Comm'r, 117 TC 263 (Dec. 11, 2001).

the gift was shown on a gift tax return, or disclosed on the return or in any statement attached to the return; (c) the donor exhausts all available administrative remedies within the Service; and (d) the donor files a pleading in the Tax Court requesting a determination of value before the ninety-first day after the date the Service mails the donor a notice of determination by certified or registered mail.[147]

8. *Declaratory judgment on the eligibility of an estate to pay estate tax in installments.* Another type of declaratory judgment may be issued by the Tax Court on whether an estate is eligible to make an election under Section 6166 to pay estate tax in installments because the estate consists largely of interest in a closely held business, or whether the extension of time to pay tax provided in Section 6166(a) has ceased to apply with respect to the estate, provided that (a) there is an actual controversy; (b) the executor or a person who has assumed the obligation to pay the estate tax under Section 6166 files a petition requesting the declaration; (c) the petitioner has exhausted all available administrative remedies the Service provides; and (d) the petition is filed before the ninety-first day after the Service sends a notice of its determination by certified or registered mail.[148]

9. *Due process review of lien or levy.* Under the 1998 Act, a taxpayer may obtain due process review of the filing of a lien or serving of a levy by administrative appeal to the Appeals Office within thirty days after notice of the intended action. If the taxpayer or other affected person does not resolve the case in Appeals, the Tax Court is given jurisdiction to provide due process review, as in the similar case of a jeopardy assessment under Section 7429.[149]

10. *Refund jurisdiction.* As described above, the Tax Court has jurisdiction under Section 6213(a) to enjoin the premature assessment and collection of tax; that is, assessment or collection of tax made during the period when assessment and collection is prohibited. If the Service actually collects an amount within this period, the Tax Court has jurisdiction to order the refund of the amount collected.[150] The Tax Court may also order the Service to refund an overpayment if the

---

[147] IRC § 7477, added by the Taxpayer Relief Act of 1997 § 506(c)(1), effective for gifts made after August 5, 1997.

[148] IRC § 7479, added by the Taxpayer Relief Act of 1997 § 505(a), effective for estates of decedents dying after August 5, 1997.

[149] IRC § 6330(d), as amended by the 1998 Act § 3401, effective for collection actions more than 180 days after July 22, 1998. The case may be assigned to a special trial judge for hearing, who has the authority to make the decision of the Court. IRC § 7443(b), as amended by 1998 Act § 3401(c).

[150] IRC § 6213(a), as amended by the 1998 Act § 3464, effective July 22, 1998.

court has found an overpayment to be due to the taxpayer, and the Service does not appeal this portion of the decision.[151]

[2] The Nature of the Proceedings

[a] In General

Judicial review of agency findings of fact is governed by the substantial evidence rule. The APA states that the reviewing court "shall decide all relevant questions of law . . . and . . . shall . . . hold unlawful and set aside agency action, findings, and conclusions found to be . . . (E) unsupported by substantial evidence."[152] Under this standard, courts adopt a middle ground between no review of agency action and a complete substitution of judicial judgment on all questions. The substantial evidence standard requires review of the record as a whole taking into account contradictory evidence or evidence from which conflicting inferences could be drawn.[153] It is similar to the scope of review of a jury verdict. In *NLRB v. Columbian Enameling & Stamping Co.*, the Supreme Court said substantial evidence

> means evidence which [affords] a substantial basis of fact from which the fact in issue can be inferred. . . . [I]t must be enough to justify, if the trial were to a jury, a refusal to direct a verdict when the conclusion sought to be drawn from it is one of fact for the jury.[154]

Unlike review of other agency findings, no substantial evidence rule applies in the judicial review of a tax case. In tax cases, the reviewing court does not inquire whether the IRS assessment or determination is supported by substantial evidence.[155]

A taxpayer starts a deficiency action by filing a petition in the Tax Court within the ninety or 150-day period provided in Section 6213(a). In Tax Court cases, the Commissioner of Internal Revenue is represented by lawyers under

---

[151] IRC §§ 6512(a)(6), 6512(b)(1), as amended by the 1998 Act § 3464.

[152] 5 USC § 706.

[153] In Universal Camera Corp. v. NLRB, 340 US 474 (1951), the Supreme Court said:

> The Board's findings are entitled to respect; but they must be set aside when the record before a Court of Appeals clearly precludes the Board's decision from being justified by a fair estimate of the worth of the testimony of witnesses or its informed judgment on matters within its special competence or both.

Id. at 490.

[154] NLRB v. Colombian Enameling & Stamping Co., 306 US 292, 299–300 (1939).

[155] See supra ¶ 1.05[2][c].

the jurisdiction of the Chief Counsel.[156] The Tax Court has its own rules of practice and procedure, which are similar but not identical to the Federal Rules of Civil Procedure applicable in federal district courts. The Tax Court's Rules of Practice and Procedure will govern the course of the proceedings in the Tax Court. At first reading, the Tax Court's rules may seem much like the Federal Rules of Civil Procedure, but this initial reaction is misleading. The Tax Court permits the appearance before the court of nonlawyers, who cannot practice before a federal district court.[157] The rules do not allow discovery in the same circumstances and to the same degree as the Federal Rules of Civil Procedure.[158] In fact, the Tax Court requires that before a discovery motion, the parties must meet informally, exchange documents, and start the stipulation process. If a party fails or refuses to participate in this informal process, under the rule in *Branerton v. Commissioner*,[159] that party will not be permitted to engage in formal discovery.

The Tax Court's rules provide for written interrogatories (Rule 71), production of documents or things (Rule 72), depositions (Rules 81–84), and requests for admissions (Rule 90). In general, these discovery procedures are derived from the Federal Rules of Civil Procedure. However, these discovery procedures may not be utilized before informal conferences as mandated by the Branerton rule, and they are not a substitute for the stipulation process. The parties must still stipulate the facts of the case, as provided in Rule 91, a procedure having no explicit counterpart in the Federal Rules of Civil Procedure. The Tax Court permits discovery depositions to be taken without the consent of a party in certain cases.[160] The rule itself nevertheless states that the taking of a deposition of a nonparty witness is "an extraordinary method of discovery and may be used only where a nonparty witness can give testimony or possesses documents or things discoverable within the meaning" of certain other rules of the court.[161] Thus, Rule 75 brings the Tax Court's rules of procedure closer to rules applicable in federal district courts, but the Tax Court still does not permit the free-wheeling discovery permitted in federal district courts under the Federal Rules of Civil Procedure.

Even with these differences, the proceeding in the Tax Court is similar to a bench trial in a district court refund suit or one in the Court of Federal Claims. The taxpayer must prove that the Commissioner's deficiency determination is invalid, but unlike a refund suit, the taxpayer need not prove the cor-

---

[156] IRC § 7452.

[157] Tax Ct. R. 200(a)(3).

[158] See Tax Ct. R. 100.

[159] Branerton Corp. v. Comm'r, 64 TC 191.

[160] Tax Ct. R. 75.

[161] Tax Ct. R. 75(b).

rect amount of tax.[162] Any record made in the Service—and thus the reasoning of its agents—is irrelevant to the issues. Once a taxpayer shows that a deficiency is arbitrary and excessive, the Tax Court should take further evidence to establish the correct tax.[163] In the Tax Court, a deficiency is reduced on the basis of approximations derived from available evidence even if the evidence is not conclusive on the issue.[164]

While the Tax Court's deficiency juristidiction is well known, the Tax Court also has overpayment jurisdiction. If the Tax Court finds that there is no deficiency and further finds that a taxpayer has made an overpayment of income tax, for example, or finds that although there is a deficiency the taxpayer has made an overpayment of the tax, the Tax Court has jurisdiction to determine the amount of the overpayment.[165] When the Tax Court's decision becomes final, the amount of the overpayment must be refunded to the taxpayer. In its overpayment jurisdiction, the Tax Court effectively hears and determines a case in the same manner as refund courts. A taxpayer obtains judicial review under the deficiency method by filing a petition for redetermination of the deficiency in the Tax Court. Except in extraordinary circumstances specifically provided for in the Code, where the jurisdiction of the Tax Court is properly invoked, the Service is prohibited from either assessing or collecting the deficiency it has determined until the court's decision becomes final.[166] Because judicial review is obtained in the Tax Court without prior payment of the full amount of the additional tax the Service has determined to be due, the overwhelming number of tax cases, approximately 95 percent, are instituted in the Tax Court rather than in the refund courts.[167]

---

[162] Helvering v. Taylor, 293 US 507, 515–516 (1935).

[163] See, e.g., Gordon v. Comm'r, 63 TC 51, 63 (1974); Nat Harrison Assocs. v. Comm'r, 42 TC 601, 617 (1964).

[164] Apart from Helvering v. Taylor, 293 US 507 (1935), the leading case authorizing approximations is Cohan v. Comm'r, 39 F2d 540 (2d Cir. 1930), involving travel and entertainment expenses that were clearly incurred but whose amounts could not be established with certainty. The Tax Court applies the *Cohan* rule in resolving issues other than travel and entertainment expenses and, at times, without referring to *Cohan*. See, e.g., Nat Harrison Assocs. v. Comm'r, 42 TC 601, 622 (1964).

[165] IRC § 6512(b)(1). See Estate of Baumgardner v. Comm'r, 85 TC 445, 448–449 (1985).

The Tax Court's jurisdiction to determine that an overpayment exists for a year properly before it also includes jurisdiction to determine whether the Service properly credited the overpayment to another year's liability. Belloff v. Comm'r, 996 F2d 607 (2d Cir. 1993).

[166] IRC §§ 6213(a), 6215(a).

[167] See, e.g., Internal Revenue Service, Annual Report 1988, at 38–39.

[b] The Presumption of Correctness

A taxpayer in the Tax Court satisfies its burden of proof if the taxpayer shows by a preponderance of the evidence that the Commissioner's determination is in error. To determine the correct tax, there must be further proceedings. In these further proceedings where the burden of coming forward with evidence has been satisfied and the amount of tax, if any, is the issue, it is unclear whether the taxpayer or the Commissioner has in the first instance the burden of going forward with evidence. The distinction between a deficiency proceeding in the Tax Court and a refund suit may be of slight practical significance. A taxpayer who rests on the record evidence risks a finding that he has not carried his burden of proof (i.e., the burden of persuasion).[168] Although the Tax Court has not specifically addressed this issue,[169] it has stated that while the taxpayer normally has the burdens of proof and production, "a showing by [the taxpayer] that the statutory notice [of deficiency] is arbitrarily excessive or without foundation has the effect of shifting the burden of going forward with the evidence to respondent."[170] Where a taxpayer succeeds in reducing a deficiency against himself by more than 90 percent, the presumption of correctness is not nullified. The presumption continues even if the amount of the deficiency is reduced. A court disregards the presumption where the Commissioner's method of determining the amount of the deficiency in income is arbitrary and invalid.[171] At least where omitted income is involved, the Commissioner has the burden of coming forward with some evidence showing that the taxpayer is connected with the income-generating activity (usually an illegal one).[172] Tax Court Rule 142(a) provides that "in respect of any new matter, increases in deficiency, and affirmative defenses, pleaded in his answer, [the burden of proof] shall be upon [the Commissioner]." The question of what constitutes a new matter seems to depend on whether different evidence would be presented from that related to the notice of deficiency.[173] Where an un-

---

[168] See Tax Ct. R. 142(a).

[169] See Piper & Jerge, "Shifting the Burden of Proof in Tax Court," 31 Tax Law. 303 (1978).

[170] Llorente v. Comm'r, 74 TC 260, 264 (1980), aff'd in part, rev'd and rem'd in part on another issue, 649 F2d 152 (2d Cir. 1981). See also Jackson v. Comm'r, 73 TC 394, 401 (1979).

[171] Turner v. Comm'r, 812 F2d 650 (11th Cir. 1987). See also Cohen v. Comm'r, 266 F2d 5 (9th Cir. 1959). In *Janis*, the Supreme Court said that where "the assessment is shown to be naked and without any foundation," it is not entitled to the presumption of correctness. United States v. Janis, 428 US 433 (1976).

[172] See Weimerskirch v. Comm'r, 596 F2d 358 (9th Cir. 1979).

[173] See Achiro v. Comm'r, 77 TC 881 (1981) (shifting the burden of proof to the Commissioner on a Section 482 claim made five weeks before trial; analyzing cases on the issue). See also McLarney v. Comm'r, TC Memo. 1982-461, 44 TCM 752 (1982); Piper & Jerge, "Shifting the Burden of Proof in Tax Court," 31 Tax Law. 303 (1978).

derpayment is alleged to be due to fraud, the Commissioner has the burden of proof on the issue and must establish fraud with intent to evade tax by clear and convincing evidence.[174]

[3] Appellate Review

With the exception of appeals from the Court of Federal Claims, which are taken to the Court of Appeals of the Federal Circuit, the Courts of Appeals have exclusive jurisdiction to review decisions of the Tax Court "in the same manner and to the same extent as decisions of district courts in civil actions tried without a jury."[175] This means that the Courts of Appeals fully review (that is, de novo) conclusions of law of the Tax Court, but they review findings of fact under a deferential standard, which upholds the findings of the Tax Court unless the reviewing court is left with the firm conviction that the Tax Court has made a mistake.[176] The Court of Appeals for the circuit of the taxpayer's residence or principal place of business reviews the decision of the Tax Court.[177] Circuit court review is obtained by filing a notice of appeal with the Clerk of the Tax Court within ninety days after the Tax Court's decision is entered.[178] The timely filing of a notice of appeal is jurisdictional with the result that if the taxpayer fails to file a notice of appeal within the ninety-day period, the circuit court has no jurisdiction over the appeal.[179] Once the Tax Court enters a decision finding that there is a deficiency in tax, the restrictions on assessment no longer apply to prohibit the Service from assessing and collecting tax, unless the taxpayer files a notice of appeal and also files with the Tax Court a bond in an amount the Tax Court sets, which may not exceed double the amount of the deficiency from which the appeal is taken.[180]

On appeal of a Tax Court decision, the scope of review was at one time influenced by its status as an administrative agency. After the Board of Tax Appeals was established, Court of Appeals review of findings by the Board was limited to questions of law, and, corresponding to review of agency findings, findings of fact were upheld if supported by substantial evidence.[181] The agency status and expertise of the Tax Court also persuaded the Supreme

---

[174] IRC § 7454(a).

[175] IRC § 7482(a)(1).

[176] United States v. U.S. Gypsum Co., 333 US 364, 395 (1948).

[177] IRC § 7483.

[178] IRC § 7483; see also Fed. R. App. P. 13(a).

[179] Davies v. Comm'r, 715 F2d 435, 436 (9th Cir. 1983); Robert Louis Stevenson Apartments, Inc. v. Comm'r, 337 F2d 681 (8th Cir. 1964); Vibro Mfg. Co. v. Comm'r, 312 F2d 253, 254 (2d Cir. 1963).

[180] IRC § 7485(a).

[181] Helvering v. Rankin, 295 US 123 (1935).

Court to accord a special position to Tax Court (as opposed to district court) findings. Narrowing the scope of review even further than the substantial evidence rule, the Supreme Court announced in *Dobson v. Commissioner* that "when the [reviewing] court cannot separate the elements of a decision [between law and fact] so as to identify a clear-cut mistake of law, the decision of the Tax Court must stand."[182] In response to dissatisfaction with the *Dobson* rule, Congress acted in 1948 to remove the Tax Court's favored position. Since then, courts of appeals have had the jurisdiction to review Tax Court decisions "in the same manner and to the same extent as decisions of the district courts . . . tried without a jury."[183]

Whether a taxpayer sues for a refund in a federal district court sitting without a jury or files a petition in the Tax Court, findings of fact in both courts stand on appeal unless they are "clearly erroneous."[184] A finding is clearly erroneous where, although there is evidence to support it, the reviewing court is left with the definite and firm conviction that a mistake has been committed.[185] Some factual findings of a trial court are nevertheless given special weight in tax cases. Under the rule of *Commissioner v. Duberstein*,[186] "primary weight" is given to a trier of fact's conclusion on factual and nontechnical questions of intent and motive. In matters of law, courts of appeal may defer to the expertise of the agency as long as the agency's determination is "rational" or "reasonable."[187] However, in tax cases, reviewing courts regularly substitute their judgment for that of the Service or for a conclusion of law reached by the Tax Court.

[4] Nonstatutory Review: Injunction and Declaratory Judgment

Traditionally, courts have entertained suits for review of administrative action in the form of proceedings for an injunction or a declaratory judgment. The APA provides for judicial review of agency action "except to the extent that—

---

[182] Dobson v. Comm'r, 320 US 489, 502. In *Dobson*, the treatment of a capital loss was considered an accounting problem within the special competence of the Tax Court and, therefore, a nonreviewable question of fact. Post-*Dobson* cases have struggled with the distinction between nonreviewable questions of fact within the Tax Court's special competence and reviewable questions of law.

[183] IRC § 7482(a).

[184] Fed. R. Civ. P. 52(a). Pollei v. Comm'r, 877 F2d 838 (10th Cir. 1989) (application of a law to undisputed facts "is an ultimate question not subject to the clearly erroneous rule"). This standard also applies to the review of findings of fact made by a Tax Court trial judge. Stone v. Comm'r, 865 F2d 342 (DC Cir. 1989).

[185] United States v. United States Gypsum Co., 333 US 364, 394–395 (1948).

[186] Comm'r v. Duberstein, 363 US 278, 289 (1960).

[187] Universal Camera Corp. v. NLRB, 340 US 474 (1951).

(1) statutes preclude judicial review. . . . "[188] In tax cases, Congress has, in the Internal Revenue and Judiciary Codes, expressly removed or excluded jurisdiction of the courts to grant injunctions or declaratory judgments.[189] Properly viewed, this limitation of court jurisdiction to grant nonstatutory review of IRS action represents a legislative attempt to channel tax disputes into the statutory refund or deficiency procedures adopted to provide judicial review. Preclusion of certain types of judicial review is not unique to IRS action, and the issues raised where other agency action is involved will assist in understanding preclusion of injunctions and declaratory judgments in tax cases. These Congressional limitations on judicial review have raised a potential confrontation between equal branches of government. The courts have attempted to avoid this confrontation but have recognized a presumption of judicial review[190] and have permitted some kind of review even in the face of the most explicit statutory language precluding review. In general, statutory preclusion of review has been considered to affect (1) the issues that may be raised on review; (2) the scope of review; and (3) the timing of review.

The jurisdiction of the agency to act in a particular case usually may be raised before a court, even where judicial review of the agency's action is precluded.[191] In a number of situations, Congress has attempted to remove a matter from court review by enacting a provision that agency action is final. However, where vital personal interests are at stake, as in deportation or Selective Service cases, courts have generally responded by reading these statutes not as precluding judicial review but as limiting the scope of review.[192] In Selective Service cases, for example, the order of a local Selective Service board, which was statutorily "final," was held subject to judicial review, but the board's finding needed to be supported only by "some basis in fact."[193] Even where vital personal interests are not at stake because, for example, the benefit is one created by statute, courts have at times given weight to a statutory finality clause,[194] but they have also read them restrictively to find a basis for judi-

---

[188] 5 USC § 701(a).

[189] IRC § 7421; 28 USC § 2201.

[190] Abbott Lab. v. Gardner, 387 US 136 (1967). The APA recognizes a general right of judicial review. 5 USC § 702.

[191] See, e.g., Estes v. United States, 327 US 114 (1946) (Selective Service board decisions "final" by statute; held, board's decision is "final" only if it is within its jurisdiction). See also United States ex rel. Accardi v. Shaughnessy, 347 US 260 (1954) (Attorney General failed to follow his own procedural rules in deportation case).

[192] See, e.g., Shaughnessy v. Pedreiro, 349 US 48 (1955) (deportation decision statutorily "final" held subject to some review).

[193] Oestereich v. Selective Service Bd., 393 US 233 (1968); Estes v. United States, 327 US 114 (1946).

[194] See, e.g., Work v. Rives, 267 US 175 (1925).

cial review.[195] Statutes explicitly precluding judicial review also have been interpreted narrowly to permit some judicial review in order to avoid the constitutional problems of a broad preclusion of review.[196] Sometimes Congress has not attempted to preclude judicial review entirely but to direct challengers of agency action into particular proceedings. In order to avoid due process questions, courts have interpreted a statute apparently precluding review as merely directing aggrieved persons to another court or to another type of proceeding.[197]

[a] Injunctions in Tax Cases

By statute, no suit "for the purpose of restraining the assessment or collection of any tax shall be maintained in any court by any person whether or not such person is the person against whom such tax was assessed."[198] Despite what appears to be an absolute preclusion, jurisdiction to grant an injunction in tax cases exists in a number of situations. Section 7421 itself precludes an injunction "except as provided in section 6212(a) and (c) [requiring the sending of a notice of deficiency and limiting further deficiency letters], 6213(a), [prohibiting assessment and collection during the ninety-day period provided in a notice of deficiency].... 7426(a) and (b)(1) [involving wrongful levies], and 7429(b) [involving jeopardy assessments]." Therefore, courts have jurisdiction to grant an injunction where the Service has failed to follow the requirements imposed by the statutes specifically referred to in Section 7421. District courts also have been held to have jurisdiction to grant injunctions where the IRS has failed to follow other statutory rules.[199]

The Supreme Court in *Enochs v. Williams Packing & Navigation Co.* held that a district court has jurisdiction to grant an injunction restraining assessment or collection of a tax (1) "if it is clear that under no circumstances could the government ultimately prevail ... on the basis of information availa-

---

[195] See, e.g., Gonzels v. Freeman, 334 F2d 570 (DC Cir. 1964).

[196] Johnson v. Rebison, 415 US 361 (1974) (statute precluding judicial review of veterans' benefits held not to preclude class action by conscientious objectors contesting granting of educational benefits to veterans but not class members).

[197] See, e.g., American Ass'n of Councils of Medical Staffs of Private Hosps. v. Califano, 575 F2d 1367 (5th Cir. 1978), cert. denied, 439 US 11, 14 (1979) (preclusion of review held not to preclude action against United States in Court of Claims).

[198] IRC § 7421 (Anti-Injunction Act).

[199] Laing v. United States, 423 US 161 (1976) (failure to send statutory notice of deficiency after termination of taxable year under pre-1976 version of Section 6851); Mrizek v. Long, 187 F. Supp. 830 (ND Ill, 1959) (no demand and levy within ten-day period); United States v. Bonaguro, 294 F. Supp. 750 (EDNY 1968), aff'd sub nom. United States v. Dono, 428 F2d 204 (2d Cir.), cert. denied, 400 US 829 (1970) (failure to take steps required to make termination or jeopardy assessment); Aqua Bar & Lounge, Inc. v. United States, 539 F2d 935 (3d Cir. 1976) (failure to follow sale provisions).

ble to it at the time of the suit . . . [taking] the most liberal view of the law and the facts" and (2) "if equity jurisdiction otherwise exists."[200] Clearly, the *Williams Packing* rule leaves the granting of an injunction to the rare case. However, this result is the same one that would follow if the scope of review of IRS actions were limited to determining whether there was a "basis in fact" to support them. In this sense, the *Williams Packing* rule in tax cases corresponds to judicial interpretation of finality clauses, discussed previously.

The *Williams Packing* exception to the Anti-Injunction Act was drawn from another Supreme Court case decided some thirty years earlier. In *Miller v. Standard Nut Margarine Co.*, the lower court found as a fact that collection of an excise tax from the taxpayer would destroy its business.[201] The same finding was made in *Williams Packing*, and so a basis for equity jurisdiction was present in both cases. Nevertheless, the requested injunction approved in *Standard Nut* was rejected in *Williams Packing*. The rationale for the different results is the "ultimate success" standard articulated in *Williams Packing*. Just what the Supreme Court meant and how it expected the standard to be applied can be seen by comparing the facts of the two cases.

In *Standard Nut*, the manufacturer of "Southern Nut Product" was faced with collection of oleomargarine taxes on its products. Collection was threatened against Standard Nut, but despite the facts, three lower federal courts had held that similar products were nontaxable before the assessment against Standard Nut, and the Service itself had informed Standard Nut by letter that its product was not subject to tax. Under the circumstances, the Supreme Court concluded that "[a] valid oleomargarine tax could by no legal possibility have been assessed against" the taxpayer, and enforcement of the tax could "destroy the business."[202] On the other hand, in *Williams Packing*, a provider of trawlers to fishermen successfully asked a district court to enjoin collection of employment tax on the ground that the fishermen using the trawlers were not its employees. On this nettlesome factual issue, the district court found that the fishermen were not employees, as the company had argued. The district court's finding was made despite contrary evidence that, among other things, the taxpayer and the fishermen had represented that an employer/employee relationship existed for both antitrust and selective service purposes. The evidence that supported the Service's position led the Supreme Court to conclude, despite the district court's finding, that "the record before us clearly reveals that the Government's claim of liability was not without foundation."[203]

In short, under *Williams Packing*, where there is a foundation for the claim or assessment, a court has no jurisdiction to grant an injunction. But, ac-

---

[200] Enochs v. Williams Packing & Navigation Co., 370 US 1, 6 (1962).

[201] Miller v. Standard Nut Margarine Co., 248 US 498 (1932).

[202] Miller v. Standard Nut Margarine Co., 248 US 498, 510 (1932).

[203] Enochs v. Williams Packing & Navigation Co., 370 US 1, 8 (1962).

cording to *Standard Nut*, where there is "no legal possibility" that the tax assessment is valid, an injunction may be granted "if equity jurisdiction otherwise exists." Before a court has jurisdiction to grant an injunction enjoining the Service from assessing or collecting a tax, the aggrieved party must satisfy both conditions of the *Williams Packing* exception: (1) There is no legal possibility that the assessment would be valid (the government could not ultimately prevail) and (2) equitable jurisdiction should be exercised because the aggrieved party will suffer irreparable harm, and no adequate legal remedy is available to the aggrieved party. In later decisions, the Supreme Court examined each of these elements.

[i] **Probability of ultimate success.** Cases where there is no legal possibility that the Service may ultimately prevail are rare. Certainly, taxpayers are not usually supported by a string of favorable lower court decisions or a letter ruling from the Service, as was the case in *Standard Nut*, and cases so finding are legion. So long as there is some basis for the Service's action, the *Williams Packing* exception does not apply. Also, the constitutional nature of the claim of a taxpayer or other aggrieved party as distinct from its probability of success is of no consequence under the Anti-Injunction Act and the *Williams Packing* exception. In *Bob Jones University v. Simon*,[204] an injunction was requested enjoining the Service from revoking the university's tax-exempt status under a policy the Service adopted denying tax-exempt status to private schools with racially discriminatory admissions policies. The university claimed that revocation would violate its rights to free exercise of religion, free association, due process, and equal protection of the laws. Nevertheless, the Supreme Court applied the *Williams Packing* tests. It found that the university's contentions were sufficiently debatable not to foreclose any possibility of government success. In a companion case, *Alexander v. "Americans United," Inc.*,[205] an organization petitioned for a mandatory injunction requiring the Service to reinstate its tax-exempt status under Section 501(c)(3). The Service had ruled that the organization was still tax-exempt under Section 501(c)(4), but its lobbying activities precluded its former Section 501(c)(3) exemption. Despite the organization's claim that the antilobbying provisions of

---

[204] Bob Jones Univ. v. Simon, 416 US 725 (1974). Where parents of black children sought injunctive relief claiming that they had been harmed because the Service had not adopted sufficient standards and procedures to deny tax-exempt status to racially discriminatory private schools, the Supreme Court held that they had no standing to bring the action, and their case was dismissed. Allen v. Wright, 468 US 737 (1984).

[205] Alexander v. "Americans United," Inc., 416 US 752 (1974).

Section 501(c)(3) were unconstitutional, the *Williams Packing* tests were applied, and the legal remedy of the organization was found to be adequate.

[ii] Adequate legal remedy. Access to judicial review is critical to application of the *Williams Packing* exception. The tax system established by Congress gives taxpayers the option of prepayment Tax Court review of a Service-determined tax deficiency or district court/Claims Court review of a postpayment refund suit. Even if this judicial review is delayed, the Supreme Court has found that an adequate legal remedy is present. In *Bob Jones University* and *"Americans United," Inc.*, the Supreme Court recognized that judicial review of the Service's tax-exempt status determination might be delayed, but even delayed access was not inadequate for *Williams Packing* purposes, nor for due process purposes.[206]

Eventual judicial review has long been found an adequate legal remedy in tax cases.[207] In *Phillips v. Comm'r*, the Supreme Court said, "Where only property rights are involved, mere postponement of the judicial enquiry is not a denial of due process, if the opportunity given for the ultimate judicial determination is adequate." This approach appeared to change in 1976. In *Comm'r v. Shapiro*,[208] as the result of a jeopardy assessment, a taxpayer's bank accounts were seized, preventing his posting bail pending a criminal trial and causing him irreparable injury. The government argued that the taxpayer had access to Tax Court review, and so it had no obligation under *Williams Packing* to disclose the basis of its assessments. Without mention of *Bob Jones University*, the Supreme Court held that where irreparable injury may result from a deprivation of property pending final adjudication of the parties' rights, due process requires that the party deprived of property be given an opportunity for some kind of predeprivation or prompt postdeprivation hearing. At this hearing, some showing of the probable validity of the deprivation must be made.[209] The *Williams Packing* exception was held to be consistent with this due process standard in requiring the government to disclose the factual basis for its assessment in order for the court to tell whether it has any chance of ultimately prevailing.[210] No ready test can be drawn from the strict application of

---

[206] Congress attempted to deal with the problem of delayed judicial review by providing a declaratory judgment procedure to review exemption determinations (Section 7428) in the Tax Reform Act of 1976. See ¶ 3.04[3][g].

[207] Phillips v. Comm'r, 283 US 589, 596–597 (1931).

[208] Comm'r v. Shapiro, 424 US 614 (1976).

[209] The Court said, "[I]t is very doubtful that the need to collect revenues is a sufficient reason to justify seizure causing irreparable harm without a prompt post-seizure hearing of any kind into the Commissioner's basis for this claim." Comm'r v. Shapiro, 424 US 614 (1976).

[210] Section 7429, added as part of the Tax Reform Act of 1976, provides a postdeprivation hearing where jeopardy assessments are made. See infra ¶ 10.05[4]. These

the *Williams Packing* exception in *Bob Jones University* and *"Americans United," Inc.*, and the constitutionally sensitive treatment of the same exception in *Shapiro*. It can be said that it is rare to find a case where the no-adequate-legal-remedy standard was satisfied or no remedy at all was found. Aggrieved parties usually cannot avoid the application of the Anti-Injunction Act and the *Williams Packing* standard.

If, as in *Shapiro*, delayed access is not adequate under the *Williams Packing* exception, it is not surprising that the Supreme Court has ruled that the Anti-Injunction Act does not apply at all where there is *no* access to judicial review. In *South Carolina v. Regan*,[211] the state had brought an action for an injunction restraining enforcement of a Code provision dealing with government-issued securities. The Supreme Court held that the Anti-Injunction Act was not intended to apply to actions brought by aggrieved parties for whom it had not provided an alternative remedy.[212]

Where the Service has failed to follow a statutory requirement referred to in Section 7421, an injunction against the Service is permitted by the terms of Section 7421 itself. Nevertheless, an injunction has been denied where the court found the taxpayer did not establish irreparable harm.[213] This result seems misconceived because the statutory omissions that permit the issuance of an injunction are fundamental departures from the tax procedures Congress requires the Service to follow. As a matter of statutory construction, it appears Congress contemplated that a taxpayer could require the Service to comply with the Code by way of obtaining an injunction in the limited cases Congress itself specified. Moreover, even if irreparable harm was required to be shown, a taxpayer should be considered to have established the element. The very omissions referred to in Section 7421 are so fundamental to the tax procedures Congress has established, that the affected taxpayer suffers irreparable harm

---

procedures may mean that taxpayers against whom jeopardy assessments have been made have an adequate remedy at law, which was found missing in *Shapiro*.

[211] South Carolina v. Regan, 465 US 367 (1984).

[212] A declaratory judgment procedure for review of the status and classification of certain governmental obligations is now provided by Section 7478.

[213] See *Cool Fuel, Inc. v. Connett*, 685 F2d 309 (9th Cir. 1982). Accord, *Goodson v. Comm'r*, 82-2 USTC ¶ 9668 (EDNY 1982). Following *Cool Fuel*, the Third Circuit also held that where one of the exceptions listed in Section 7421 is involved, the taxpayer is not required to satisfy the *Williams Packing Co.* rule. However, the taxpayer must still establish the "inadequacy of the legal remedy to prevent irreparable injury." *Flynn v. United States*, 786 F2d 586, 591 (3d Cir. 1986) (taxpayer executed Form 870-AD but claimed he was entitled to and was not sent a notice of deficiency). Compare *Jensen v. IRS*, 835 F2d 196 (9th Cir. 1987) (adhering to *Cool Fuel*, but irreparable harm and no adequate remedy found).

(and a denial of equal protection of the law) precisely because he is denied the same treatment other similarly situated taxpayers receive.[214]

[b] Declaratory Judgment

A taxpayer contesting an IRS determination or assessment can avoid following refund procedures requiring full payment of the assessment if, instead, he seeks a declaratory judgment from a district court. At one time, taxpayers did indeed attempt to bring suits for declaratory judgments in tax cases. However, Congress responded in 1935 by amending the Declaratory Judgment Act to provide:

> In a case of actual controversy within its jurisdiction, except with respect to Federal taxes other than actions brought under section 7428 of the Internal Revenue Code of 1954, or a proceeding under Section 505 or 1146 of title 11, any court of the United States, upon the filing of an appropriate pleading, may declare the rights and other legal relations of any interested party seeking such declaration whether or not relief is or could be sought.[215]

The statute is literally broader in its preclusion of tax-oriented remedies than the Anti-Injunction Act, but the weight of authority holds that the statutory exception is coterminous with that provided by the Anti-Injunction Act.[216] The

---

[214] For further analysis of this issue, see Andrews, "The Use of the Injunction as a Remedy for an Invalid Federal Tax Assessment," 40 Tax L. Rev. 653 (Summer 1985). Where the affected taxpayer has attempted to sue IRS employees for damages arising out of noncompliance with the statute, the attempt has usually proven unsuccessful. See, e.g., the proceedings after the *Laing* decision. Hall v. United States, 773 F2d 703 (6th Cir. 1985). For a case supporting this view, see Philadelphia & Reading Corp. v. United States, 944 F2d 1063 (3d Cir. 1991), in which the Service failed to comply with a condition included in Form 870. As a result, the restrictions on assessment were not waived and the statute of limitations for a timely assessment had expired. The Third Circuit concluded as follows:

> [The Supreme Court] has explained that "[w]here Congress explicitly enumerates certain exceptions to a general prohibition, additional exceptions [such as a failure to show irreparable harm] are not to be implied, in the absence of a contrary legislative intent." . . . The IRS has failed to suggest any contrary legislative intent here. Indeed we think the maxim has special force when the statutory scheme is complex, its parts closely related and, in making important decisions, the persons affected by it depend heavily on the even-handed application of the statute's plain terms.

[215] 28 USC § 2201 (emphasis added).

[216] "Americans United," Inc. v. Walters, 477 F2d 1169, 1176 (DC Cir. 1973), rev'd on other grounds sub nom. Alexander v. "Americans United," Inc., 416 US 752 (1974). The Supreme Court said, with respect to the scope of the "except with respect to Federal taxes" clause of the Declaratory Judgment Act, that "while we take no position on this issue, it is in any event clear that the federal tax exception to the Declaratory Judgment Act

effect of the Supreme Court decisions in *Bob Jones University* and "*Americans United, Inc.*" is to limit the use of the Declaratory Judgment Act by making it more difficult to avoid the Anti-Injunction Act, even though a constitutional issue is involved, and the tax liability of the petitioner is not, at least as a matter of form.

Despite the prohibition of declaratory judgments in tax cases, 28 USC Section 2201(a) itself permits a bankruptcy court to enter a declaratory judgment under Section 505 (a)(1) of the Bankruptcy Code. Consequently, a bankruptcy court is permitted to "determine the amount or legality of any tax. . . ."[217]

Also, Congress itself has increased the number of instances where taxpayers may obtain declaratory judgment relief in cases. Currently, a declaratory judgment may be sought in cases involving certain pension plans,[218] exempt organizations,[219] and the tax-exempt status of certain bonds.[220] Moreover, despite the preclusion of jurisdiction to grant declaratory judgments, courts have granted declaratory judgments in tax cases where ownership of property seized for payment of another's taxes is in issue.[221] Such judgments may still be permitted where a third party seeks to protect a lien claimed to be superior to the Service's lien.[222]

---

is at least as broad as the prohibition of the Anti-Injunction Act." Because the Court held that the Anti-Injunction Act required the action to be dismissed, there was no "occasion" to deal separately with the Declaratory Judgment Act. Spencer v. Brady, 700 F. Supp. 601 (DDC 1988) ("[T]he Declaratory Judgment Act's tax exception, and the anti-Injunction Act, work together to ensure that preemptive taxpayer litigation will not frustrate the efforts of [the IRS] to assess and collect federal taxes"). As is the case with the Anti-Injunction Act, the Declaratory Judgment Act does not preclude a declaration of the rights of the parties by a district court as long as liability for tax is not contested. Just when there is a contest over a liability is not always clear. For example, a taxpayer filed a petition in the Tax Court and also requested competent authority relief. After the Service refused to pursue competent authority negotiations, the taxpayer requested a determination that the denial was arbitrary and capricious. The district court ruled, however, that the "underlying purpose" of the action was to restrain the assessment and collection of tax. Yamaha Motor Corp. v. United States, 779 F. Supp. 610 (DDC 1991).

[217] 11 USC § 505(a)(1). Similar jurisdiction exists in 11 USC § 1146. See Brandt Airflex Corp. DIP v. Long Island Trust Co., 843 F2d 90 (2d Cir. 1988). See also Quattrone Accountants, Inc. v. IRS, 895 F2d 921 (3d Cir. 1990).

[218] IRC § 7476.

[219] IRC § 7428 (in the Tax Court, the district courts, and the Court of Claims).

[220] IRC § 7478.

[221] Bullock v. Latham, 306 F2d 45, 47–48 (2d Cir. 1962). The opportunity of a nontaxpayer to obtain judicial review of a wrongful levy (IRC § 7426) and to secure injunctive relief as well (IRC § 7421(a)) may obviate the necessity of declaratory relief in this type of case.

[222] See Tomlinson v. Smith, 128 F2d 808 (7th Cir. 1942).

¶ 1.07 JUDICIAL CONTROL OF IRS DISCRETION IN FORMULATING POLICY AND LAW

The APA imposes statutory constraints on agency action. Judicial review of factual and legal administrative findings also results in control of agency action, especially in tax cases. Courts also impose other limitations on the power of an agency to make law and policy, as discussed in the following sections.

[1] The Rule of Adherence to Precedent

An agency must either adhere to its precedents or provide a reasoned explanation for its failure to do so. This principle means not that an agency may not change its policies, but rather that if the agency wishes to overrule or distinguish its precedents, it must explain why it acted as it did. The Supreme Court, in *Atchison, Topeka & Santa Fe Railway v. Wichita Board of Trade,* stated that this rule was based on the rationale that a "settled course of behavior embodies the agency's informed judgment that, by pursuing that course, it will carry out the policies committed to it by Congress."[223] These policies are presumed to be carried out best by adherence to the settled rule. Thus, from this presumption comes the agency's duty to explain any departure from "prior norms."

The requirement that the Service adhere to procedures or explain departures from prior behavior is complicated because the Service administers a highly specific statute. Moreover, procedure developed by the Service in the form of written determinations such as a ruling, determination letter, or technical advice memorandum "may not be used or cited as precedent."[224]

Adherence to precedent has been held not to be required where a mistake of law has been made. Even where a taxpayer may have relied to his detriment on a mistaken interpretation of law, the Service may correct the mistake retro-

---

[223] Atchison, T&SF Ry. v. Wichita Bd. of Trade, 412 US 800, 807 (1973) (Interstate Commerce Commission failed to follow precedent without adequately distinguishing prior cases); Secretary of Agric. v. United States, 347 US 645 (1954) (Interstate Commerce Commission order departing from prior decisions held invalid because change not sufficiently explained). As a matter of constitutional law, the equal protection clause does not require that all taxpayers be taxed and treated identically. "It only requires that classification rest on real and not feigned differences, that the distinction have some relevance to the purpose for which the classification was made, and that the different treatments be not so disparate, relative to the difference in classification, as to be wholly arbitrary." Walters v. City of St. Louis, 347 US 231, 237 (1954).

[224] IRC § 6110(k)(3).

actively.[225] In other words, a mistake of law is per se a reasoned explanation for an agency's failure to adhere to precedent.

[2] The Doctrine of Equality of Treatment

Although an agency may make rules and may exercise discretion in that regard, it is bound by some requirement of equality—that is, it must treat similarly situated persons equally. Equality of treatment may be seen as a corollary to the requirement that an agency adhere to precedent because adherence to precedent ensures that agency action will not, in a particular case, be discriminatory (that is, that there will be equality of treatment). If one party is treated differently than another similarly situated party, the agency must state the reasons for the apparent inconsistency.[226]

The leading tax case illustrating this principle is *IBM Corp. v. United States*,[227] where the Service treated competitors in the sale of computer systems differently. Remington-Rand secured a favorable ruling exempting it from excise tax, but when IBM sought the same treatment, the Service waited for more than two years and then denied the ruling request. Subsequently, the Service revoked Remington-Rand's favorable ruling prospectively. This action still left different treatment for roughly two and one-half years. Although the Court of Claims held that the Service abused its discretion under Section 7805(b) in revoking Remington-Rand's ruling prospectively, the rationale was one of equality of treatment. The court said that in exercising discretion, the Commissioner was required to consider "the totality of circumstances," including "the comparative or differential effect on the other taxpayers in the same class,"[228] because the "'Commissioner cannot tax one and not tax another without some rational basis for the difference.' United States v. Kaiser, 363 U.S. 299, 308 (1960) (Frankfurter, J., concurring)."[229] Consequently, the court ruled,

---

[225] Dixon v. United States, 381 US 68, 73 (1965); Automobile Club v. Comm'r, 353 US 180, 183–184 (1957).

[226] Contractors Transp. Corp. v. United States, 537 F2d 1160, 1162 (4th Cir. 1976). For further description of the duty of administrative consistency, see C. Koch, Administrative Law and Practice (1985); Gellhorn, Byse, Strauss, Rakoff & Schotland, Administrative Law—Cases and Comments (8th ed. 1987).

[227] IBM Corp. v. United States, 343 F2d 914 (Ct. Cl. 1965), cert. denied, 382 US 1028 (1966). The problem of discrimination is discussed at ¶ 3.03[6][b].

[228] IBM Corp. v. United States, 343 F2d 914, 920.

[229] IBM Corp. v. United States, 343 F2d 914, 920. In Apache Bend Apartments, Ltd. v. United States, 702 F. Supp. 1285, 1286 (ND Tex. 1988), the equality of treatment doctrine was described this way:

> The equal protection doctrine under the Fifth Amendment requires similarly situated individuals to be treated similarly . . . all people in a class must be treated equally. In addition, a classification of people must bear a rational relationship to a legitimate

IBM was entitled to a refund of manufacturer's excise taxes paid by it during the period Remington-Rand was exempt from tax under the ruling on sales of the machines.

Despite the statements in *IBM* and *Kaiser*, equality of treatment is accepted in a general but not definitive way, and the application of the general principle depends on the circumstances. Where the Service's discretionary action is involved, such as the discretion to apply a ruling prospectively, discriminatory treatment of similarly situated taxpayers, such as those in *IBM*, shows that discretion has been abused absent some explanation.[230] However, where the question is a taxpayer's liability for a tax, the Service's error in failing to collect a tax from a similarly situated taxpayer gives other taxpayers no special rights.[231] Decisions in cases between these two poles are hard to rationalize. Some bedrock belief exists that the Service should not treat similarly situated taxpayers differently, especially where one taxpayer is not taxed, and the other is taxed.[232] At the same time, the Service is permitted to choose among reasonable interpretations of law, but its administrative practice in dealings with other taxpayers (e.g., in letter rulings) can be considered in determining whether the interpretation is reasonable.[233] In other words, although the Service has the discretion to choose alternative interpretations, it must do so consistently. In a situation where a taxpayer claims that because of his reliance on the Service's position, the Service's administrative action is inequitable, the claim is usually considered as one of estoppel. Although consistency, equality of treatment, and estoppel are related doctrines, consistency and equality of treat-

---

governmental purpose. Wheeler v. United States, 768 F2d 1333, 1337 (Fed. Cir. 1985).

[230] IBM Corp. v. United States, 343 F2d 914 (Ct. Cl. 1965), cert. denied, 382 US 1028 (1966). Exchange Parts Co. v. United States, 279 F2d 251, 253–254 (Ct. Cl. 1960).

[231] See Sirbo Holdings Co. v. Comm'r, 509 F2d 1220, 1221 (1975); Davis v. Comm'r, 65 TC 1014, 1022 (1976); Wagner v. United States, 387 F2d 966, 972 (Ct. Cl. 1967).

[232] Sirbo Holdings, Inc. v. Comm'r, 476 F2d 981, 987 (2d Cir. 1973) ("the Commissioner has a duty of consistency toward similarly situated taxpayers; he cannot properly concede capital gains treatment in one case and, without adequate explanation, dispute it in another having seemingly identical facts which is pending at the same time"). IBM Corp. v. United States, 343 F3d 914 (Ct. Cl. 1965), cert. denied, 382 US 1028 (1966). See Oggiony v. Comm'r, 617 F2d 14, 18 (2d Cir.), cert. denied, 449 US 900 (1980) ("consistency over time and uniformity of treatment among taxpayers are proper benchmarks from which to judge IRS actions"). For an extensive analysis of this issue, see Zelanek, "Should Courts Require the Internal Revenue Service to Be Consistent?" 40 Tax L. Rev. 411, 429–430 (1985).

[233] National Muffler Dealers Ass'n v. United States, 440 US 472 (1979) (IRS interpretation not consistently and reasonably applied); Niles v. United States, 710 F2d 1391 (9th Cir. 1983) (IRS letter rulings used to show regular administrative practice in favor of taxpayer's position). The use of rulings is discussed further in Chapter 3.

ment cases involve more than one taxpayer, while estoppel cases tend to involve a single taxpayer and the Service's treatment of that taxpayer.

[3] Compliance With Published Procedural Rules

An agency's action is invalid if the agency fails to comply with its own rules promulgated to benefit a party by entitling it to some procedural safeguard or substantive benefit.[234] In *United States ex rel. Accardi v. Shaughnessy*,[235] regulations of the attorney general delegated certain of his discretionary powers in regard to deportation to the Board of Immigration Appeals and required the board to exercise its own discretion on appeals in deportation cases. The Supreme Court held that so long as the regulations remained in force, the attorney general did not have the authority to exercise the discretion delegated to the board, even though he had the original authority and could reassert it by amending the regulations. This principle was reaffirmed in cases where the discharge of government employees was held an unlawful exercise or noncompliance with departmental regulations establishing procedures and standards for dismissals.[236] The *Accardi* doctrine is a rule of administrative law, but it also rests on due process principles where the rights of individuals are affected by an agency's failure to observe rules promulgated for their protection.[237] In applying the doctrine, the issue is whether the procedural rules the agency has failed to follow in a particular case are such that appropriate judicial intervention is required. An agency's failure to follow some procedural rules will not always require judicial action, but which rules may be disregarded is hard to predict in tax and other cases.

The *Accardi* doctrine has been applied in tax cases. After the IRS issued press releases announcing that its special agents would describe their Criminal Investigation function and give partial Miranda warnings,[238] some courts suppressed evidence obtained by agents who failed to comply with these procedural rules, relying on the *Accardi* doctrine.[239] However, in *United States v.*

---

[234] United States v. Nixon, 418 US 683 (1974) (Justice Department regulation giving Special Prosecutor power to contest claim of executive privilege has force of law); United States ex rel. Accardi v. Shaughnessy, 347 US 260 (1954); Vitarelli v. Seaton, 359 US 535 (1959); Service v. Dulles, 354 US 363 (1957).

[235] United States ex rel. Accardi v. Shaughnessy, 347 US 260 (1954).

[236] Vitarelli v. Seaton, 359 US 535 (1959); Service v. Dulles, 354 US 363 (1957).

[237] Bridges v. Wixon, 326 US 135, 162–163 (1945). See United States v. Caceres, 440 US 741, 757 (1979) (Marshall J., dissenting); Vitarelli v. Seaton, 359 US 535, 547 (1959) (Frankfurter, J., concurring in part and dissenting in part).

[238] The News Release warnings are discussed in Chapter 13.

[239] United States v. Heffner, 420 F2d 809 (4th Cir. 1969); United States v. Sourapas, 515 F2d 295 (9th Cir. 1975). See United States v. Leahey, 434 F2d 7 (1st Cir. 1970). But

Caceres,[240] the Service recorded incriminating statements made by a taxpayer attempting to bribe an agent in violation of its rules requiring advance authorization by the attorney general. The Court did not suppress these statements. The Supreme Court said that a court's duty to enforce an agency regulation is most evident where compliance is mandated by the Constitution or federal law. The Court noted that the IRS was not required to adopt these rules because the Fourth Amendment provided the taxpayer with no protection against the Service recording statements he made to the agent.[241] Similarly, federal law did not grant the taxpayer any protection.[242] No due process violation existed in *Caceres* because the individual had not reasonably relied on IRS rules promulgated for his guidance or benefit, and the Service's breach of the rules had no effect on his conduct (that is, *Caceres* had offered the bribe anyway).

The circumstances of noncompliance and the relief sought (suppression of evidence) were other factors in the Supreme Court's decision in *Caceres*. It refused to adopt "any rigid rule requiring federal courts to exclude any evidence obtained as a result of a violation of [an agency's] rules."[243] Even considering the particular circumstances of the case, there was no reason to suppress evidence obtained in violation of the regulations where the "agency action, while later found to be in violation of the regulations, nonetheless reflected a reasonable, good-faith attempt to comply."[244]

After *Caceres*, then, the type of agency rules, the circumstances of noncompliance, and the nature of the remedy sought all are factors bearing on the court's decision. If the agency rule is not promulgated, and the affected individual could not reasonably have relied on the rule, noncompliance, especially if it is not purposeful and in bad faith, does not warrant judicial intervention to suppress evidence.[245] However, it appears that where the rule is published (e.g., as part of the News Release procedure) and noncompliance cannot have been a mere misinterpretation, suppression may be proper. If *Caceres* is viewed as

---

see United States v. Irvine, 699 F2d 43 (1st Cir. 1983) (*Leahey* is no longer good law in the First Circuit after *Caceres*); United States v. Leonard, 524 F2d 1076, 1089 (2d Cir. 1975).

[240] United States v. Caceres, 440 US 741 (1979).

[241] Lopez v. United States, 373 US 427 (1963); United States v. White, 401 US 745 (1971).

[242] 18 USC § 2511(2)(c).

[243] United States v. Caceres, 440 US 741, 755 (1979).

[244] United States v. Caceres, 440 US 741, 757 (1979). Premonitoring Justice Department authorization had not been obtained because high-ranking IRS officials, who approved the monitoring, believed "exigent circumstances" precluded such authorization in advance of two key meetings between the taxpayer and the agent. The court of appeals concluded that the emergency provisions of the regulation did not apply.

[245] The question of what rules are promulgated and may reasonably be relied on becomes more difficult to determine with the publication of the Internal Revenue Manual.

limiting *Accardi* to rules mandated by the Constitution or federal law, failure to give News Release-Miranda warnings will not result in suppression because no Miranda warnings are required to be given in these circumstances.[246] Still, the courts are likely to continue to hold agencies to compliance with their own rules even if these rules impose a greater burden on the agency than is required by law and the matter involves a vital personal interest.[247] Moreover, the Supreme Court in *Caceres* was troubled by the suppression of clearly relevant evidence of criminal conduct. That case does not preclude the possibility of relief other than suppression where noncompliance with different rules is involved.

Despite the importance of the *Accardi* doctrine, agencies have sometimes been permitted to depart from their own regulations, especially if the regulations were not primarily intended to confer important procedural benefits on persons.[248] For example, an agency may relax or modify its procedural rules in a given case if justice so requires, and the action is not reviewable except on a showing of "substantial prejudice" to the complaining party.[249] Similarly, where taxpayers have been denied administrative hearings provided for by the Service's own regulations, courts generally have held that the Service is not bound by these rules because they are merely "directory," not "mandatory."[250]

---

[246] Beckwith v. United States, 425 US 341 (1976). United States v. Robinson, 811 F. Supp. 1174 (SD Miss. 1993) (*Caceres* said to preclude suppression when IRS agents were claimed to have continued questioning after the taxpayer had requested counsel).

[247] The Supreme Court said that a court's duty to enforce an agency's regulation was "most evident" where it was mandated by law, but it also said that it did not follow "as a matter of either logic or law" that an agency had no duty to obey a regulation not required by law where the rights of individuals were affected. Courts have also exercised their supervisory powers to make and enforce a rule not required by the Constitution or federal law. For example, a prosecutor is not constitutionally required to give target warnings to a target called before a grand jury. United States v. Washington, 431 US 181, 189 (1977). However, some courts have exercised their supervisory powers over United States attorneys and the Department of Justice in requiring target warnings. United States v. Jacobs, 547 F2d 772 (2d Cir. 1976), cert. dismissed, 436 US 31 (1978). See also United States v. Crocker, 568 F2d 1049 (3d Cir. 1977). These supervisory powers may be enforced against the IRS, at least if the taxpayer has standing to raise the claim. United States v. Payner, 444 US 923 (1980).

[248] American Farm Lines v. Black Ball Freight Serv., 397 US 532 (1970) (Interstate Commerce Commission procedural rules held to be for purpose of providing necessary information to the Interstate Commerce Commission).

[249] American Farm Lines v. Black Ball Freight Serv., 397 US 532 (1970).

[250] Rosenberg v. Comm'r, 450 F2d 529 (10th Cir. 1971) (no appellate conference granted despite protest); Cleveland Trust Co. v. United States, 421 F2d 475 (6th Cir.), cert. denied, 400 US 819 (1970); Luhring v. Glotzbach, 304 F2d 556 (4th Cir. 1962) (deficiency notice sent without prior thirty-day letter offering conference); United States v. Goldstein, 342 F. Supp. 661 (EDNY 1972) (denial of conference in criminal case). See also In re Klein, 776 F2d 628 (7th Cir. 1985) (dispute about guidelines promulgated by attorney general; held, guidelines do not affect decision on legality of grand jury subpoena;

These decisions are based on the belief that this administrative hearing is not intended as a procedural safeguard or substantive benefit to the taxpayer but serves the interest of the Service. Therefore, denial of a hearing in a tax case is viewed as not affecting any right of a taxpayer. However, it is unconvincing to say that administrative hearings serve only the interests of the Service. Hearings or conferences enable taxpayers to settle civil cases without going through the expense of a trial and to prevent referral of criminal cases for prosecution without the disgrace of criminal indictment or information. Moreover, denial of a procedural opportunity such as a hearing to one taxpayer where other taxpayers are accorded these hearings raises equal protection and due process questions. These constitutional issues may not be resolved in favor of the Service unless it satisfactorily demonstrates some rational basis for denying one taxpayer some procedural opportunity while others have the benefit of that procedure. Finally, the APA imposes a statutory requirement on an agency hearing to permit a taxpayer to make a presentation on an issue so long as "the orderly conduct" of its business permits.[251]

---

citing *Caceres*). In *Klein*, the court of appeals stated, "[Guidelines] may enable the Department to control those in the field, but once an agent of the Department acts, the legal status of the act depends on other rules of law." Id. at 635. But it is inconsistent for administrative appeal procedures to be minimized when they are now incorporated in Section 7430(b) as "administrative remedies" required to be exhausted before court costs will be reimbursed. See, e.g., Christensen v. United States, 815 F. Supp. 786 (D. Del. 1993) (examining whether the successful taxpayer had exhausted his administrative remedies by requesting an Appeals conference).

In *McKee*, the Sixth Circuit addressed the question of "whether a taxpayer may properly base a challenge to a tax conviction on the IRS's noncompliance with the procedures of its Manual." United States v. McKee, 192 F3d 535 (6th Cir. 1999). Acknowledging that many cases hold that the Service's Manual provides no substantive rights to taxpayers, a majority of the panel held, "However, we believe that the Manual's provisions are, at the very least, relevant in determining whether a taxpayer's constitutional rights have been offended." The circuit court approved of the approach in a number of circuit court decisions that a taxpayer may challenge a conviction by relying on a violation of a provision in the Manual, as long as the alleged Manual violation also violates a constitutional right of the taxpayer. Evidence suggested that the revenue agent had not referred the case to the Criminal Investigation Division after having discovered "firm indications of fraud" in violation of the Service's Manual, but the court "reluctantly" concluded that it could not say the revenue agent had abused her discretion in continuing the investigation. As the court noted, the government's evidence in the criminal prosecution "was practically handed to CID on a silver platter as a result of the civil investigation." Accordingly, the court agreed that the "firm indication of fraud" rule met constitutional requirements, but urged revenue agents "to err on the side of protecting taxpayers' constitutional rights when they conduct investigations."

[251] 5 USC § 555(b).

[4] Estoppel

Generally, the government may not be estopped by the acts of administrative officers or agents, but under appropriate circumstances, courts have held that estoppel is available as a defense against agency action. Agency officials and agents informally give advice to those requesting it. However, if a statute clearly prohibits some conduct or action, no advice from an agency official or agent can supersede the statute. For this reason, a taxpayer may not rely on a mistaken interpretation of law that the Service retroactively corrects.[252] Even where advice was contrary to a regulation, the Supreme Court, in *Federal Crop Insurance Corp. v. Merrill*,[253] narrowly (5-4) held that the agency could not be bound by the erroneous advice. Nevertheless, both agencies and courts have recognized that a no-estoppel rule inflexibly applied to all types of agency conduct would be harsh and unfair. Some statutes make good faith reliance on an interpretation a defense in agency enforcement action.[254] Also, the general rule of no estoppel has been drawn into question by the Supreme Court itself.[255] Some courts have explicitly relied on estoppel principles where "great injustice" would result if the government were not held responsible for the erroneous advice[256] or where there is "affirmative misconduct" in the giving of

---

[252] Automobile Club v. Comm'r, 353 US 180 (1957).

[253] Federal Crop Ins. Corp. v. Merrill, 332 US 380 (1947). The Supreme Court has said that it will not condone any attempts to deviate from the *Merrill* rule, but it has refused to adopt a flat rule prohibiting the defense of estoppel against the government. Office of Personnel Management v. Richmond, 496 US 414, 422 (1990).

[254] For example, the Fair Labor Standards Act allows this defense. 29 USC §§ 258, 260.

[255] United States v. Pennsylvania Indus. Chem. Corp., 411 US 655 (1973) (estoppel terminology not used, but prosecution for failure to obtain a required license held precluded by prior agency action); Moser v. United States, 341 US 41 (1951); Federal Crop Ins. Corp. v. Merrill, 332 US 380, 386 (1947) (Jackson, J., dissenting); see also Heckler v. Community Health Servs., 467 US 51 (1984).

[256] United States v. Lazy FC Ranch, 481 F2d 985, 989 (9th Cir. 1973). Estoppel against the United States has been applied primarily by the Ninth Circuit, but not every circuit agrees with its views. See Goldberg v. Weinberger, 546 F2d 477 (2d Cir. 1976), cert. denied, 431 US 937 (1977). The Eleventh Circuit has developed a three-part test under which the defense of estoppel is available against the government only when (1) the traditional private law elements of estoppel have been pleaded; (2) the government has acted in its private or proprietary capacity as opposed to in its public or sovereign capacity; and (3) the government agent was acting within the scope of the agent's authority. United States v. Vondereau, 837 F2d 1540 (11th Cir. 1988). The Eleventh Circuit has also listed the elements of a traditional equitable estoppel claim to be (1) words, acts, conduct, or acquiescence causing another to believe in the existence of a certain state of things; (2) willfulness or negligence with regard to the acts, conduct, or acquiescence; and (3) detrimental reliance by the other party on the state of things so indicated. Bokum v. Comm'r, 992 F2d 1136, 1141 (11th Cir. 1993).

the erroneous advice.[257] Cases applying estoppel against a government agency do not represent an erosion of the general principle that the government may not be estopped, but rather suggest that the principle is not absolute and that, in appropriate circumstances, an agency may be estopped.[258] In tax cases, es-

---

[257] States v. Wharton, 514 F2d 406, 409–410 (9th Cir. 1975). It has also been said that although the Service may be estopped, the estoppel is limited to cases of affirmative misconduct. In re Lapiana, 909 F2d 221 (7th Cir. 1990) (affirmative misconduct required, but IRS personnel failed to act diligently only in collecting payments from taxpayer; estoppel not applicable).

[258] In Office of Personnel Management v. Richmond, 496 US 414, 423 (1990), the Supreme Court questioned whether equitable estoppel would lie against the government, because it would violate the separation of powers by giving to the executive branch power to overrule the legislative branch. Following *Richmond,* one circuit court has refused to apply estoppel in a tax refund suit. See Kennedy v. United States, 965 F2d 413 (7th Cir. 1992). Other courts interpret the misrepresentation requirement in such a way as to make equitable estoppel practically unavailable against the Service. See Smith S, Inc. v. Comm'r, 837 F. Supp. 130 (EDNC 1993) (failure to file S corporation election; held, neither equitable entitlement nor equitable estoppel prevented IRS from taxing corporation). See also Bray v. United States, 76 AFTR2d ¶ 95-6817 (Bankr. 9th Cir. 1995) (taxpayer argued that taxes were released or dischargeable in bankruptcy because of agreement with a revenue officer and that he had relied on the agreement when he purchased a home and a boat; held, the agreement was not binding, because the revenue officer had no authority to bind the IRS and engaged in no affirmative act of misconduct, while the taxpayer failed to prove serious injustice would result if the agreement were not enforced). The court in *Bray* cited with approval a statement of the Seventh Circuit in Kennedy v. United States, 965 F2d 413, 418–419 (7th Cir. 1992), that "the estoppel doctrine should not be used against the government when the estoppel claimant's detriment is the loss of a windfall that could have never been statutorily effectuated through the process the claimant attempted to use." The Seventh Circuit itself has refused to equitably estop the Service when taxpayers alleged that they had relied on the representations of a revenue agent "because one of the requisite elements to establish equitable estoppel is that the taxpayer reasonably relied on the representations of the IRS agent," and since only a private letter ruling or a closing agreement will bind the Service, the taxpayers were "charged with knowing [the revenue agent's] limited authority so they [could] not demonstrate that their reliance was reasonable." Meyers v. Comm'r, 79 F3d 1150 (7th Cir. 1996).

Absent a closing agreement, even when the Service changes its position on an issue in the course of a Tax Court case, the Court has refused to hold the Service to its original position. See General Dynamics Corp. v. Comm'r, TC Memo. 1996-153, 71 TCM 2586 (1996) (in a report recommending disallowance of claims for refund based on research credits for fixed-price contracts, an engineer had determined the allowable amount, if the Service was wrong on its legal theory; and based on the engineer's report, the Service represented to the court that the parties would be able to agree on the amount of the credits, leaving the legal issue to the court's consideration; however, after the issue was decided by another court adversely to the Service, the Service refused to stipulate to the amount of the research credits in the engineer's report).

Compare the doctrine of judicial estoppel. See Kraft, Inc. v. United States, 30 Fed. Cl. 739 (1994), appeal dismissed, 85 F3d 602 (Fed. Cir. 1996), where the Service was held judicially estopped from denying the veracity of a record it had relied on in an earlier

toppel has not been applied where the Commissioner retroactively corrects a mistake of law.[259] On the other hand, the Service has been estopped where the correction of the error would result, for example, in manifest injustice to an individual taxpayer.[260]

The Supreme Court has not ruled that there are no circumstances in which a taxpayer may use estoppel as a defense against the Service.[261] A majority of the circuits have recognized estoppel as an equitable defense, but as pointed out above, many of these circuit courts impose, in addition to the traditional elements of estoppel, the burden of proving some affirmative misconduct on

---

case involving the same taxpayer. In *Kraft, Inc.*, the court said, "The goal of 'judicial estoppel' is to prevent litigants from playing 'fast and loose' with the courts, to protect judicial integrity . . . and to 'avoid unfair results and unseemliness.'" In the Federal Circuit, judicial estoppel will not be applied when the following seven factors are present: (1) The previously asserted position has not been judicially accepted; (2) there is no risk of inconsistent results; (3) the pleading party's actions have no effect on the integrity of the judicial process; (4) the court has not been misled; (5) there is reliance by the opposing party; (6) the opposing party's case has been prejudiced by the inconsistent position; and (7) the party against whom estoppel has been invoked must have received some benefit from the previously taken position; i.e., won because of it.

[259] Dixon v. United States, 381 US 68 (1965); Automobile Club v. Comm'r, 353 US 180 (1957).

[260] Interstate Fire Ins. Co. v. United States, 215 F. Supp. 586 (ED Tenn. 1963), aff'd per curiam, 339 F2d 603 (6th Cir. 1964) (IRS estopped from denying cost reallocation ordered by revenue agent that produced refund rather than deficiency); Schuster v. Comm'r, 312 F2d 311 (9th Cir. 1962) (IRS estopped from claiming trust includable in estate after agent agreed trust not includable and trust assets distributed); Tonkonogy v. United States, 417 F. Supp. 78 (SDNY 1976) (IRS estopped from claiming default in payment agreement where taxpayer relied on IRS letter extending time for payment); Smale & Robinson, Inc. v. United States, 123 F. Supp. 457 (SD Cal. 1954) (IRS estopped from asserting absence of required statement in a refund claim where agent represented inclusion of the statement was unnecessary). See Miller v. United States, 500 F2d 1007 (2d Cir. 1974) (IRS estopped from claiming statute of limitations where suit brought within erroneous deadline in claim disallowance); Reynolds v. Comm'r, 861 F2d 469 (6th Cir. 1988) (IRS estopped from taking a position in litigation that was inconsistent with one it had successfully asserted in another proceeding).

Compare Bennett v. Comm'r, 935 F2d 1285 (4th Cir. 1991) (no estoppel against IRS, because taxpayer did not reasonably rely on note from Problem Resolution Office about amount of gift tax); L.E.F., Inc. v. United States, 80 AFTR2d 97-5743 (ED Mich. 1997) (motion to amend affirmative defenses to allege that the Service was equitably estopped allowed; taxpayer did not collect diesel fuel excise tax, because the buyer provided certification and a registration number showing that it was registered with the Service as a producer, this information was provided to the Service, and the Service confirmed that it was permissible for the taxpayer to make tax-free sales to the buyer). For further discussion of estoppel in tax cases, see Chapter 3.

[261] See Heckler v. Community Health Servs., 467 US 51, 60 (1984) ("it is well settled that the Government may not be estopped on the same terms as any other litigant"); Office of Personnel Management v. Richmond, 496 US 414 (1990).

the part of government officials.[262] In a case that illustrates the kind of situation where the Service has been estopped, the taxpayer executed and provided to one district office an open-ended waiver, Form 872-A, of the statute of limitations on assessment of income tax for 1977, but then submitted other fixed-date waivers, Forms 872, because another district office insisted that the open-ended waiver had not been received. Although the last fixed-date waiver expired as of June 30, 1984, over eight years later, on July 9, 1992, the Service sent the taxpayer a notice of deficiency. When the taxpayer challenged the timeliness of the notice, the Service produced and relied on the open-ended waiver that Service personnel had insisted did not exist. The circuit court, in reversing the Tax Court, concluded that affirmative misconduct existed because the Service failed to correct its misrepresentation when it learned that the open-ended waiver was on file and decided to rely on that form. The appellate court also concluded that the taxpayer acted reasonably in relying on the Service's misrepresentation that the open-ended waiver was not in its file, and in relying on the subsequent fixed-date waivers both he and the Service executed. Moreover, the misrepresentation was of fact—the nonexistence of the open-ended waiver in the file—not some matter of law. As the result of the misrepresentation, the taxpayer suffered a determent in relying on the Service because the taxpayer could not have earned interest in the market at the rate the Service charged on the 1977 deficiency, especially since after 1984 that rate was at the higher tax-motivated interest rate. Finally, the circuit court found that the public fisc was only minimally affected by its estoppel of the Service, because the result was the same as a finding that the statute of limitations on assessment had expired according to the terms of the last fixed-date waiver.[263]

---

[262] See Fredericks v. Comm'r, 126 F3d 433 (3d Cir. 1997) (gathering cases where the Service and other agencies have been estopped). When the traditional elements of estoppel are combined with the additional element, the elements of an estoppel defense against the Service are (1) a false representation or wrongful or misleading silence; (2) an error in a statement of fact and not in an opinion or statement of law; (3) a person claiming the benefits of estoppel must be ignorant of the true facts; (4) the person claiming estoppel must be adversely affected by the acts or statements of the person against whom estoppel is claimed; and (5) there was some affirmative misconduct on the part of the government officials. Id., quoting from Estate of Emerson v. Comm'r, 67 TC 612, 617–618 (1977); United States v. Asmar, 827 F2d 907, 911 n.4, 912 (3d Cir. 1987).

For an extended review of the case law on estoppel in a situation where taxpayers contended that the Service was estopped from claiming that the claims for refund were untimely under the statute of limitations for filing refund claims, see Chaney v. United States, 84 AFTR2d 99-7137 (Fed. Cl. 1999).

[263] One of the circuit judges, who concurred in part and dissented in part, would have limited the Service to collecting the deficiency that existed in Fall 1984, when the taxpayer would have had the opportunity to file a Form 872-T to terminate the open-ended waiver, and the Service then would have assessed the deficiency.

¶ 1.08 HOW THE IRS EXERCISES ADMINISTRATIVE POWER

Administrative agencies exercise their power by formulating policy in prospective rule making and by way of a final order in adjudicative proceedings. In its rule-making function, the agency engages in quasilegislative activity, while in its adjudicative function, it acts in a quasijudicial fashion. However, the most frequent action agencies take, by far, is informal, where the agency conducts tests, inspections, or examinations; supervises regulated persons; handles applications and claims; negotiates and settles disputes; and gives informal advice. Informal administration is not governed by the APA. Because of its importance, the manner in which the IRS exercises its administrative power by both formal and informal action is discussed.

[1] Rule Making

Regulations (or rules) relating to the internal revenue laws are formulated and promulgated by the Treasury Department, although the IRS plays a role in the regulations process. The APA establishes specific procedures governing agency rule making. The procedures were designed to ensure fairness and mature consideration of agency rules[264] and to give affected members of the public an opportunity to comment.

[2] Adjudications

Determinations of deficiency in tax, as well as other matters, are usually made after a taxpayer has had various opportunities for administrative hearings. For example, in a regional Appeals Office conference, the findings of the district and submissions of the taxpayer are heard by the Appeals Office. The proceeding results in a final decision by the Service about a taxpayer's liability and for this reason appears to constitute an adjudication within the meaning of the APA. However, administrative hearings in the Service constitute a kind of informal adjudication because the APA adjudication rules do not apply if the matter is "subject to subsequent consideration of the law and facts de novo in a court. . . . "[265] Consequently, the APA procedures designed to protect the due process rights of affected individuals where an agency makes a formal adjudication or quasijudicial decision[266] do not apply to informal adjudications that an agency

---

[264] 5 USC § 553. NLRB v. Wyman Gordon Co., 394 US 759, 764 (1969). These procedures are discussed in Chapter 3.

[265] 5 USC § 554(a)(1).

[266] 5 USC § 554. In general, the rules require that a person affected by the adjudication be given notice of the hearing (5 USC § 554(b)) and an opportunity to be heard and

such as the Service may make. Since no attempt has been made in the APA to develop formal procedures to govern the informal adjudications, whatever procedures the Service has adopted are generally the only ones specifically governing its administrative proceedings.

However, the APA does have some impact on IRS informal procedures. A person compelled to appear before the Service is entitled "to be accompanied, represented, and advised by counsel, or, if permitted by the agency, by other qualified representation."[267] A person compelled to submit data or evidence is entitled to a copy of the transcript.[268] Although Treasury regulations are the source of administrative hearing procedures in the Service, the APA appears to give taxpayers the right to such hearings because it allows "an interested person" to appear "before an agency . . . for the presentation, adjustment, or determination of an issue, request, or controversy . . . in connection with an agency function" so long as "the orderly conduct of public business permits. . . . "[269] The APA also requires an agency to give prompt notice of the denial in whole or in part of the written application, petition, or other request of an interested person made in connection with an agency's proceeding.[270] Except in affirming a prior denial or where the denial is self-explanatory, the notice must be accompanied by a brief statement of the ground for denial. Consequently, notice of final action by the Service on the protest of district action to the Appeals Office or on the denial of a claim appears to be required by the APA, irrespective of the Service's own procedural rules.[271]

[3] Informal Action

Informal administrative action is the most frequent manner in which an agency acts to carry out its statutory mandate. As noted previously, informal action can take a number of different forms.

---

present evidence (5 USC § 554(c)) and require the presiding official to make a recommended or initial decision unless he becomes unavailable to the agency.

[267] 5 USC § 555(b); Backer v. United States, 275 F2d 141 (5th Cir. 1960).

[268] 5 USC § 555(c). In investigations, the witness may be limited to inspecting the transcript of the statement where there is "good cause" for the limitation.

[269] 5 USC § 555(b).

[270] 5 USC § 555(c).

[271] But see Cleveland Trust Co. v. United States, 421 F2d 475 (6th Cir.) cert. denied, 400 US 819 (1970) (APA provision does not apply to rejection of an informal conference agreement).

[a] Tests, Inspections, and Examinations

This type of informal procedure is based on the premise that a formal procedure such as an adjudication is time-consuming and does not guarantee any greater accuracy or fairness. The real question, of course, is whether the test or examination is fair and the results reasonably accurate. An agency such as the Service attempts to control the fairness and accuracy of its examinations by having experienced agents set the scope of the examinations to be conducted by district office tax technicians (i.e., issues into which they will inquire and the type of qualifying information that will be acceptable) and by having senior and more experienced officials available to handle any questions from subordinates. The qualifications of the agents assigned to examinations and the standards applied by the review staff in reviewing examinations also work to control fairness and accuracy.[272]

[b] Supervision

The supervisory functions of the Service are especially evident where exempt organizations and pension plans are involved. Exempt organizations, for example, must submit detailed financial and other records to document their compliance with the law and the regulations. IRS supervision is also reflected in the initial application of an organization for exempt status and in the Service's highly developed system of intraagency appeals from district offices.[273]

[c] Applications and Claims

The Service has developed informal procedures for processing claims, rather than holding formal adjudication-type hearings. Methods utilized by the Service in informally processing claims include the use of forms and the informal appeal procedure.[274]

[d] Negotiation and Settlement

Negotiation procedures are incorporated into most agency procedural rules. The APA requires agencies to give respondents in complaint cases an opportunity to settle the case "when time, the nature of the proceeding, and the public interest permit."[275] Therefore, there is some basis for the conclusion that the APA imposes a duty on the agency to consider offers of settlement or

---

[272] The Service's examination activities are discussed in Chapter 8.
[273] The Appeals system is discussed in Chapter 9.
[274] Claims for refund are covered in Chapter 11.
[275] 5 USC § 554(c).

compromise. This duty may well be a ground for reversal of agency action if the agency refuses to permit any settlement negotiations, even where the acceptability of the offer is left entirely up to the agency. The Service has adopted formal appeals procedures that emphasize negotiation and settlement as methods of formally resolving disputes between taxpayers and the Service prior to the institution of legal proceedings in the Tax Court or a refund court. These procedures are successful in the overwhelming number of cases.[276]

[e] Informal Advice

Almost all agencies have developed extensive interpretative services that enable parties to avoid formal proceedings by the agency. The Service has long-standing and highly developed procedures for informally giving advice both to taxpayers and to field personnel. The primary complaint about these procedures has been that there is an opportunity for agency inconsistency, and the agency procedures themselves discourage reliance on the advice given. To some extent, the procedures providing for the publication of letter rulings and technical advice eliminated the existence of a secret body of law available only to a few practitioners. Whether publication has eliminated inconsistency remains to be seen, but it should have a salutary effect in checking the exercise of agency discretion.[277]

C PRACTICE BEFORE THE INTERNAL REVENUE SERVICE

¶ 1.09 PRACTICE BEFORE THE SERVICE

[1] Standards of Practice In General

Standards governing admission to practice as well as duties of those practicing before the Service are designed to protect taxpayers and the quality of representation. The Secretary of the Treasury is authorized to prescribe rules and regulations governing the recognition of persons representing claimants before his department, and he may disbar or suspend any person from practice if that person refuses to comply with those rules.[278] The Treasury Department has adopted rules governing the recognition and conduct of persons representing taxpayers before the Service. These rules have been promulgated in what is

---

[276] Negotiations in the appeals process are discussed in Chapter 9.

[277] IRS ruling procedures are covered in Chapter 3.

[278] 31 USC § 330.

commonly referred to as Treasury Department Circular No. 230.[279] Circular No. 230 is divided into four parts:

1. Rules relating to authority to practice before the Service
2. Duties and restrictions relating to such practice
3. Rules relating to disciplinary proceedings
4. General rules, such as provisions relating to the availability of records

In addition, conference and practice requirements applying to all offices of the Service have been promulgated as Title 26, Part 601 of the Code of Federal Regulations. The Secretary has appointed a Director of Practice in his office to carry out his functions relating to admission to practice and the conduct of disciplinary proceedings.[280]

[2] What Constitutes "Practice" Before the Service

Every person who appears before the Service on behalf of a taxpayer, transferee, or fiduciary must meet the practice requirements of Circular No. 230, unless the person is not engaged in "practice" before the Service.[281] In general, practice occurs where a person makes an advocate's presentation of a client-taxpayer's rights, privileges, or liabilities under IRS-administered laws or regulations.[282] A "presentation" includes the preparation and filing of necessary documents, correspondence with and communications to the Service, and the representation of a client at conferences, hearings, and meetings.[283] But, the preparation and signing of a tax return, claim, or election do not constitute "practice" before the Service.[284] Consequently, a return preparer may represent a taxpayer, answer questions, and supply information to an IRS agent as a witness without having to satisfy the requirements prerequisite to practice and without obtaining a power of attorney.[285] Once a person makes an oral or written presentation that relates to a client's rights, privileges, or liabilities under the internal revenue laws (i.e., advancing the client's position in the manner of an advocate), then that person is considered to be engaged in practice before the Service and is subject to the restrictions and duties of Circular No. 230.

---

[279] 31 CFR pt. 10. Circular No. 230, as amended, was effective, July 26, 2002.

[280] For a description of the duties of the Director of Practice, see Circular No. 230, § 10.1(b).

[281] 26 CFR § 601.502(b).

[282] Circular No. 230, § 10.2(d).

[283] Circular No. 230, § 10.2(d).

[284] See Circular No. 230, § 10.2(d); 26 CFR § 601.501(a).

[285] See Circular No. 230, § 10.7(e)(i)(vii), 10.7(e). Rev. Proc. 68-29, 1968-2 CB 913, outlines the circumstances in which an individual will be considered a witness or a representative.

[3] Who May Practice Before the Service

Three broad classes of persons may practice before the Service: (1) attorneys; (2) certified public accountants; and (3) enrolled agents.[286] Enrolled actuaries and others in specific situations may engage in limited practice before the Service without enrollment.

[a] Attorneys and Certified Public Accountants

Attorneys are permitted by law to represent others before any federal agency and certified public accountants (CPAs) are permitted to represent others before the Service, provided (1) the attorney or CPA submits a written declaration that he is currently qualified to practice and (2) the attorney or CPA is authorized to represent the particular party who is represented.[287] Section 10.3 of Circular No. 230 specifies that an attorney or CPA may practice before the Service provided

- The attorney or CPA is not under suspension or disbarment from practice before the Service[288]; and
- The attorney or CPA submits a written declaration (set forth on the back of the power of attorney forms made available by the Service) that he is currently qualified as an attorney or CPA and is authorized to represent the particular party on whose behalf he wishes to act.

Under proposed amendments to Circular 230, lawyers or accountants who retire from practice and are no longer licensed to practice as such in a state may practice before the Service as enrolled agents if they pass an enrollment examination.[289]

[b] Enrolled Agents

To become an enrolled agent entitled to practice before the Service, a person must demonstrate special competence in tax matters by written examina-

---

[286] Circular No. 230, § 10.4. Government officers and employees or members of Congress may not represent anyone (except a member of the family or an estate of which the person serves as fiduciary) before the Service. State officers and employees who deal with state tax matters also may not practice before the Service if practice would mean disclosure of federal tax information.

[287] Act of Nov. 8, 1965, Pub. L. No. 89-332, 79 Stat. 1282. An attorney is "qualified to practice" only if he is a member of the bar of the highest court in the state. A CPA is qualified if licensed as such by the state.

[288] See Tinkoff v. Campbell, 158 F2d 855 (7th Cir. 1946), cert. denied, 331 US 845 (1947) (disbarred attorney not permitted to practice not denied constitutional rights).

[289] Prop. Reg. § 10.4(d).

tion administered by the Service and must not have engaged in any conduct that would have led to the suspension or disbarment of an attorney or CPA.[290] The person seeking enrollment must file an application, along with a fee, and supply additional information as requested.[291] On becoming entitled to practice, the agent receives an enrollment card entitling him to be considered by Service personnel as duly authorized to practice before the Service.[292] This card is valid for as long as the holder remains enrolled and in good standing before the Service[293] so long as enrollment is renewed as required.[294]

[c] Limited Practice by Nonenrolled Individuals

In limited situations, persons who are not lawyers, CPAs, or enrolled agents may also practice before the Service. Individuals who present satisfactory identification may also appear on their own behalf and engage in limited practice before the Service in certain circumstances.[295] When a nonpractitioner engages in limited practice under Circular No. 230, the nonpractitioner is bound to follow the same standards as a practitioner or is subject to suspension or disbarment.[296] With satisfactory identification and proof of authority, an in-

---

[290] Circular No. 230, § 10.4. Special rules govern the enrollment of former Service employees who apply for enrollment on account of their Service employment.

[291] On receipt of a properly executed application, the applicant may be granted temporary recognition to practice pending a determination whether enrollment should be granted. Circular No. 230, § 10.5(c). If the application for enrollment is denied, the applicant is notified and may, within thirty days, appeal to the Director of Practice in the Department of the Treasury. Circular No. 230, § 10.5(d).

[292] A condition of eligibility for renewal of enrollment is the satisfaction of continuing professional education requirements. Circular No. 230, §§ 10.6(e), 10.6(f). The regulations also contemplate a fee for the renewal of enrollment to defray the costs of administering the program. When the regulations were proposed, the Treasury responded to the comment that its initial proposal was discriminatory by stating that the Agency Practice Act (50 USC § 500) eliminated agency-established admission requirements for licensed attorneys who appear before most federal agencies and for CPAs who appear before the Service. Consequently, under the Agency Practice Act, if the attorney is in good standing or the CPA is duly qualified (and a proper power of attorney, where required, is filed), the Service is required by law to recognize the attorney or CPA. The Treasury believes that it may not impose conditions on eligibility to practice without violating the Agency Practice Act. Also, the Treasury expects that the licensing bodies of each state will have the authority to carry on the continuing education of attorneys and CPAs who are licensed within that jurisdiction. Consequently, the Treasury believes that the continuing education programs in the states would parallel the continuing education requirement imposed on enrolled agents.

[293] Circular No. 230, § 10.6(b).

[294] Enrollment must be renewed every three years. Circular No. 230, § 10.6(d)(2).

[295] Circular No. 230, § 10.7 (1994).

[296] Circular No. 230, §§ 10.7, § 10.7(c)(2)(ii).

dividual who is not a practitioner may represent a taxpayer before the Service even if the taxpayer is not present when (1) the individual is a member of the taxpayer's immediate family; (2) the individual is a full-time employee of the taxpayer; (3) the individual is a general partner or full-time employee of the taxpayer partnership; (4) the individual is a bona fide officer or full-time employee of the taxpayer corporation (or its subsidiary or affiliated corporation), association, or organized group; (5) the individual is a trustee, receiver, guardian, personal representative, administrator, executor, or full-time employee, and the taxpayer is a trust, receivership, guardianship, or estate; (6) the individual is an officer or regular employee acting in the regular course of the individual's business, and the taxpayer is a governmental unit, agency, or authority; (7) the individual is representing a taxpayer before the Service outside the United States; and (8) the individual is the preparer of the tax return under audit, whether the individual signed the return or was not required to sign the return.[297] In addition, an individual may make a special appearance to represent a taxpayer, subject to whatever conditions the district director may set.[298] An individual may also prepare a tax return and appear as a witness before the Service or furnish information to the Service on its request.[299]

- An individual may represent (1) another individual who is his regular full-time employer; (2) the partnership of which he is a partner or for which he works on a regular full-time basis; or (3) a member of his immediate family if he receives no compensation.
- Bona fide officers or full-time employees may represent corporations, including members of multiple corporate groups, trusts, estates, associations, or other organized groups.
- Fiduciaries or their regular full-time employees may represent trusts, receiverships, guardianships, or estates.
- An officer or regular employee in the course of his official duties may represent any governmental unit, agency, or authority.
- Unenrolled individuals may participate in the regulation-making process.
- Enrollment is not required for representation outside the United States, probably because there are few tax practitioners outside the country.
- A return preparer may represent the taxpayer for whom he prepared the return without enrollment as the taxpayer's representative, with or without the taxpayer and before revenue agents and examining officers of the Examination Division in the district offices with respect to the tax liability for the period covered by that return. This limited representation is not an absolute privilege. The standards of conduct and the limi-

---

[297] Circular No. 230, §§ 10.7, § 10.7(c)(1).
[298] Circular No. 230, §§ 10.7, § 10.7(d).
[299] Circular No. 230, §§ 10.7, § 10.7(e).

tations of authority apply, and permission to engage in this limited practice may be denied where the person has engaged in conduct that "would justify" the suspension or disbarment of an attorney or CPA.

In addition to these enumerated cases, the Commissioner, in his discretion, may authorize any person to represent another without enrollment for the purposes of a particular matter.[300]

[4] Representation and Access to Confidential Information

The Service's conference and practice regulations require an individual appearing as an advocate to enter an appearance by filing (1) a power of attorney or tax information authorization permitting the holder to perform certain acts or to receive confidential tax information and (2) a practice declaration, which is a declaration that the person is recognized to practice before the Service.[301] Even where the person is merely to act as a witness, a tax information authorization must be filed if that person is to receive or inspect confidential tax information.

[a] The Power of Attorney or Authorization

A power of attorney or authorization is a prerequisite to representation. In general, a representative cannot receive confidential tax information,[302] and no notice or other written communication (or copy of one) that contains confidential information about a filed tax return will be sent to the representative,[303] unless the representative has on file a power or authorization.[304] A Form 2848 (Power of Attorney) (see Form 1.7) must be filed when the taxpayer's representative is to perform one or more of the following acts on behalf of the taxpayer:[305]

---

[300] Circular No. 230, § 10.7(b).

[301] 26 CFR §§ 601.502(b), 601.502(c).

[302] Under the confidentiality and disclosure rules of Section 6103, a return or return information may be disclosed to a designee of the taxpayer. IRC § 6103(c).

[303] 26 CFR § 601.506(a). If more than one attorney is designated in the power or authorization, the taxpayer should designate the representatives who are to receive notices, or the Service will send notices to the first-named representative. The Service will not send notices to more than two representatives. If the original of a ruling or correspondence relating to a ruling request is to be sent to a representative, the power or authorization should contain a statement to that effect.

[304] Rev. Proc. 68-29, 1968-2 CB 913.

[305] 26 CFR § 601.502(c).

- Receive (but not endorse and collect) a check in payment of any refund of internal revenue taxes, penalties, or interest.[306] The Service does not consider itself bound to deliver any check in payment of a tax refund to a representative, despite the fact that the representative is acting under a power of attorney. Under the Service's general policy, it will mail the check in care of a recognized representative who has filed a power of attorney from the taxpayer specifically authorizing him to receive but not to endorse the check.[307] Where the check is mailed to the representative, it will be made payable to the taxpayer "care of" the representative.[308]
- Execute a waiver of restrictions on assessment or collection of a deficiency in tax, or a waiver of notice of disallowance if a claim for credit or refund.
- Execute a consent to extend the statutory period for assessment or collection of a tax.
- Execute a closing agreement under Section 7121 of the Code.

A Form 8821, Tax Information Authorization, must be used in order for the individual, corporation, firm, organization, or partnership designated by the taxpayer to receive confidential tax information in a matter for the type of tax and the periods designated on the form (see Form 1.7).

The tax information authorization is necessary for the representative to inspect the taxpayer's returns, to receive information at a conference with Service personnel of the Service's position on the taxpayer's liability, to discuss the merits of the taxpayer's request for a ruling or determination letter with the Service, and to receive such notices as a thirty-day letter and examining officer's report. The authorization is not required to receive notices and communications that do not involve the disclosure of confidential information.[309]

---

[306] An income tax return preparer may not endorse or negotiate a refund check issued to a taxpayer without incurring a $500 penalty. IRC § 6695(f). The income tax return preparer rules are discussed in Chapter 4.

[307] A taxpayer may not assign his claim for refund to the representative because such assignment is forbidden by law. 31 USC § 3727 (1983).

[308] 26 CFR § 601.506(b)(1). If the representative requests mailing to an address other than the one on the power of attorney, he must show that the address in the power is no longer his address. If there is more than one representative, the check will be sent to the taxpayer unless all representatives request the check be sent in care of one of them. Also, if the representative has been authorized to receive the check by reason of a substitute power of attorney obtained from a representative designated by the taxpayer, the check will be sent to the taxpayer. Where the claim is in litigation, the check is first sent to the U.S. Attorney in a district court case or to the Assistant Attorney General (Tax Division) in a U.S. Claims Court case for delivery. 26 CFR § 601.506(b)(2).

[309] 26 CFR § 601.502(c)(2).

FORM 1.7
POWER OF ATTORNEY AND DECLARATION OF REPRESENTATIVE

Form **2848** (Rev. February 1993) Department of the Treasury Internal Revenue Service	**Power of Attorney and Declaration of Representative** ▶ For Paperwork Reduction and Privacy Act Notice, see the instructions.	OMB No. 1545-0150 Expires 2-29-96

Part I Power of Attorney (Please type or print.)

1 Taxpayer Information (Taxpayer(s) must sign and date this form on page 2, line 9.)

Taxpayer name(s) and address	Social security number(s)	Employer identification number
ABC CORPORATION 1 WHITNEY STREET NEW YORK, NEW YORK　10000		13 :0000000 Plan number (if applicable)
	Daytime telephone number (212)500-0000	

hereby appoint(s) the following representative(s) as attorney(s)-in-fact:

2 Representative(s) (Representative(s) must sign and date this form on page 2, Part II.)

Name and address	
ALAN MICHAELS, ESQ. 100 PARK PLACE, NEW YORK, NEW YORK　12444	CAF No. .... Telephone No. (212) 637-8900 Fax No. (212)637-8100 Check if new: Address ☐　Telephone No. ☐
Name and address	CAF No. .... Telephone No. (　) .... Fax No. (　) .... Check if new: Address ☐　Telephone No. ☐
Name and address	CAF No. .... Telephone No. (　) .... Fax No. (　) .... Check if new: Address ☐　Telephone No. ☐

to represent the taxpayer(s) before the Internal Revenue Service for the following tax matters:

3 Tax Matters

Type of Tax (Income, Employment, Excise, etc.)	Tax Form Number (1040, 941, 720, etc.)	Year(s) or Period(s)
CORPORATE	1120	1991-1992

4 Specific Use Not Recorded on Centralized Authorization File (CAF).— If the power of attorney is for a specific use not recorded on CAF, please check this box. (See Line 4—Specific Uses Not Recorded on CAF on page 3). . . . . ▶ ☐

5 Acts Authorized.—The representatives are authorized to receive and inspect confidential tax information and to perform any and all acts that I (we) can perform with respect to the tax matters described in line 3, for example, the authority to sign any agreements, consents, or other documents. The authority does not include the power to receive refund checks (see line 6 below) or the power to sign certain returns (see Line 5—Acts Authorized on page 4).
List any specific additions or deletions to the acts otherwise authorized in this power of attorney: ....
....

Note: In general, an unenrolled preparer of tax returns cannot sign any document for a taxpayer. See Revenue Procedure 81-38, printed as Pub. 470, for more information.
Note: The tax matters partner/person of a partnership or S corporation is not permitted to authorize representatives to perform certain acts. See the instructions for more information.

6 Receipt of Refund Checks.—If you want to authorize a representative named in line 2 to receive, **BUT NOT TO ENDORSE OR CASH**, refund checks, initial here _____ and list the name of that representative below.

Name of representative to receive refund check(s) ▶

Cat. No. 11980J	Form **2848** (Rev. 2-93)

Form 2848 (Rev. 2-93)   **Page 2**

7 Notices and Communications.—Notices and other written communications will be sent to the first representative listed in line 2.

a   If you also want the second representative listed to receive such notices and communications, check this box . . . ▶ ☐
b   If you do not want any notices or communications sent to your representative, check this box . . . . ▶ ☐

8 Retention/Revocation of Prior Power(s) of Attorney.—The filing of this power of attorney automatically revokes all earlier power(s) of attorney on file with the Internal Revenue Service for the same tax matters and years or periods covered by this document. If you do not want to revoke a prior power of attorney, check here . . . . ▶ ☐
     YOU MUST ATTACH A COPY OF ANY POWER OF ATTORNEY YOU WANT TO REMAIN IN EFFECT.

9 Signature of Taxpayer(s).—If a tax matter concerns a joint return, **both** husband and wife must sign if joint representation is requested, otherwise, see the instructions. If signed by a corporate officer, partner, guardian, tax matters partner/person, executor, receiver, administrator, or trustee on behalf of the taxpayer, I certify that I have the authority to execute this form on behalf of the taxpayer.

▶ **IF THIS POWER OF ATTORNEY IS NOT SIGNED AND DATED, IT WILL BE RETURNED.**

/s/ JOHN JONES	6-01-93	PRESIDENT
Signature	Date	Title (if applicable)
Print Name		
Signature	Date	Title (if applicable)
Print Name		

Part II   **Declaration of Representative**

Under penalties of perjury, I declare that:

- I am not currently under suspension or disbarment from practice before the Internal Revenue Service;
- I am aware of regulations contained in Treasury Department Circular No. 230 (31 CFR, Part 10), as amended, concerning the practice of attorneys, certified public accountants, enrolled agents, enrolled actuaries, and others;
- I am authorized to represent the taxpayer(s) identified in Part I for the tax matter(s) specified there; and
- I am one of the following:

   a   Attorney—a member in good standing of the bar of the highest court of the jurisdiction shown below.
   b   Certified Public Accountant—duly qualified to practice as a certified public accountant in the jurisdiction shown below.
   c   Enrolled Agent—enrolled as an agent under the requirements of Treasury Department Circular No. 230.
   d   Officer—a bona fide officer of the taxpayer organization.
   e   Full-Time Employee—a full-time employee of the taxpayer.
   f   Family Member—a member of the taxpayer's immediate family (i.e., spouse, parent, child, brother, or sister).
   g   Enrolled Actuary—enrolled as an actuary by the Joint Board for the Enrollment of Actuaries under 29 U.S.C. 1242 (the authority to practice before the Service is limited by section 10.3(d)(1) of Treasury Department Circular No. 230).
   h   Unenrolled Return Preparer—an unenrolled return preparer under section 10.7(a)(7) of Treasury Department Circular No. 230.

▶ **If this declaration of representative is not signed and dated, the power of attorney will be returned.**

Designation —Insert above letter (a–h)	Jurisdiction (state) or Enrollment Card No.	Signature	Date
a	NY (9999)	/s/ ALAN MICHAELS	6-30-93

Form 2848 (Rev. 2-93)   Page **3**

Privacy Act and Paperwork Reduction Act Notice.—We ask for the information on this form to carry out the Internal Revenue laws of the United States. Form 2848 is provided by the IRS for your convenience and its use is voluntary. If you choose to designate a representative to act on your behalf, under section 6109 you must disclose your social security number (SSN) or your employer identification number (EIN). The principal purpose of this disclosure is to secure proper identification of the taxpayer. We also need this information to gain access to your tax information in our files and properly respond to your request. If you do not disclose this information, the IRS may suspend processing the power of attorney and may not be able to fill your request until you provide the number.

The time needed to complete and file this form will vary depending on individual circumstances. The estimated average time is: **Recordkeeping**, 20 min.; **Learning about the law or the form,** 29 min.; **Preparing the form,** 29 min.; **Copying, assembling, and sending the form to the IRS,** 35 min.

If you have comments concerning the accuracy of these time estimates or suggestions for making this form more simple, we would be happy to hear from you. You can write to both the **Internal Revenue Service,** Washington, DC 20224, Attention: IRS Reports Clearance Officer, T:FP; and the **Office of Management and Budget,** Paperwork Reduction Project (1545-0150), Washington, DC 20503. **DO NOT** send this form to either of these offices. Instead, see **Filing the Power of Attorney** below.

General Instructions

Section references are to the Internal Revenue Code unless otherwise noted.

Purpose of Form.—Form 2848 may be used to grant authority to an individual to represent you before the IRS and to receive tax information. You may file this form ONLY if you want to name a person(s) to represent you and that person is a "person recognized to practice before the Service." Persons recognized to practice before the Service are listed in Part II, Declaration of Representative, items a–h. Any person who is not listed in a–h of Part II is not authorized to practice before the IRS under the provisions of Treasury Department Circular No. 230 and therefore cannot act as your representative. However, you can use **Form 8821,** Tax Information Authorization, to authorize any person (or an organization) to receive and inspect confidential tax return information under the provisions of section 6103. For additional information about this or any other matter concerning practice before the IRS, get **Pub. 216,** Conference and Practice Requirements.

Fiduciaries.—A fiduciary (trustee, executor, administrator, receiver, or guardian) stands in the position of a taxpayer and acts as the taxpayer. Therefore, a fiduciary does not act as a representative and should not file a power of attorney. **Form 56,** Notice Concerning Fiduciary Relationship, should be filed to notify the IRS of the existence of a fiduciary relationship. If a fiduciary wishes to authorize an individual to represent or perform certain acts on behalf of the entity, a power of attorney must be filed and signed by the fiduciary acting in the position of the taxpayer.

Authority Granted.—This power of attorney authorizes the individual(s) named to perform any and all acts you can perform, such as signing consents extending the time to assess tax, recording the interview, or executing waivers agreeing to a tax adjustment. Delegating authority or substituting another representative must be specifically stated on line 5. However, the authority granted to an unenrolled preparer may not exceed that allowed under Revenue Procedure 81-38, printed as **Pub. 470,** Limited Practice Without Enrollment.

The power to sign tax returns can only be granted in limited situations. See **Line 5— Acts Authorized** on page 4 for more information.

Filing the Power of Attorney.—File the original, photocopy, or facsimile transmission (fax) of the power of attorney with each IRS office with which you deal. If you choose to file a power of attorney by fax, you must first be sure that the appropriate IRS office is equipped to accept fax transmissions. If the power of attorney is filed for a matter currently pending before an office of the IRS, such as an examination, file the power of attorney with that office. Otherwise, file it with the service center where the related return was, or will be, filed. Refer to the instructions for the related tax return for the service center addresses.

Substitute Form 2848.—If you want to prepare and use a substitute Form 2848, get **Pub. 1167,** Substitute Printed, Computer-Prepared, and Computer-Generated Tax Forms and Schedules. If your substitute Form 2848 is approved, the form approval number must be printed in the lower left margin of each substitute Form 2848 you file with the IRS.

Specific Instructions
Part I—Power of Attorney

Line 1—Taxpayer Information.—

Individuals.—Enter your name, SSN (and/or EIN, if applicable), and street address in the space provided. If a joint return is involved, and you and your spouse are designating the same representative(s), also enter your spouse's name and SSN, and your spouse's address if different from yours.

Corporations, partnerships, or associations.—Enter the name, EIN, and business address. If this form is being prepared for corporations filing a consolidated tax return (Form 1120), do not attach a list of subsidiaries to this form. Only the parent corporation information is required in line 1. Also, line 3 should only list Form 1120 in the Tax Form Number column. A subsidiary must file its own Form 2848 for returns that are required to be filed separately from the consolidated return, such as **Form 720,** Quarterly Federal Excise Tax Return, and **Form 941,** Employer's Quarterly Federal Tax Return.

Employee plan.—Enter the plan name, EIN of the plan sponsor, three-digit plan number, and business address of the sponsor.

Trust.—Enter the name, title, and address of the trustee, and the name and EIN of the trust.

Estate.—Enter the name, title, and address of the decedent's executor/personal representative, and the name and identification number of the estate. The identification number for an estate includes both the EIN, if the estate has one, and the decedent's SSN.

Line 2—Representative(s).—Enter the name of your representative(s). Only individuals may be named as representatives. Please use the identical name on all submissions. If you want to name more than three representatives, indicate so on this line and attach a list of additional representatives to the form.

Enter the nine-digit Centralized Authorization File (CAF) number for each representative. If a CAF number has not been assigned, enter "None," and the IRS will issue one directly to your representative. The CAF number is a unique nine-digit identification number (not the SSN, EIN, or enrollment card number) that the IRS assigns to representatives. The CAF number is not an indication of authority to practice. The representative should use the assigned CAF number on all future powers of attorney. CAF numbers will not be assigned for employee plans and exempt organizations application requests (EP/EO).

Check the appropriate box to indicate if either the address or telephone number is new since a CAF number was assigned. Enter your representative's fax telephone number, if available.

If the representative is a former employee of the Federal Government, he or she must be aware of the post-employment restrictions contained in 18 U.S.C., section 207 and in Treasury Department Circular No. 230, section 10.26. Criminal penalties are provided for violation of the statutory restrictions, and the Director of Practice is authorized to take disciplinary action against the practitioner.

Line 3—Tax Matters.—Enter the type of tax, the tax form number, and the years or period(s). For example, you may list "income tax, Form 1040" for calendar year "1992" and "Excise tax, Form 720" for the "1st, 2nd, 3rd, and 4th quarters of 1992." A general reference to "All years," "All periods," or "All taxes" is not acceptable. Any power of attorney with such general reference will be returned. You may list any tax years or periods that have already ended as of the date you sign the power of attorney. However, the number of future tax periods that can be recorded on the CAF is limited to returns with due dates within 3 years of your signature on Form 2848. If the matter relates to estate tax, enter the date of the taxpayer's death instead of the year or period. If the type of tax, tax form number, or years or periods does not apply to the matter (i.e., representation for a penalty or filing a ruling request or determination), specifically describe on this line the matter to which the power of attorney pertains and enter "Not Applicable" in the appropriate column(s).

Line 4—Specific Uses Not Recorded on CAF.—Generally, the IRS records all powers of attorney on the CAF system. However, a power of attorney will not be recorded on the CAF if it does not relate to a specific tax period or it is for a specific issue. Examples of specific issues include but are not limited to the following: (a) civil penalty issues, (b) trust fund recovery penalty, (c) request for a private letter ruling, (d) application for an EIN, (e) claims filed on **Form 843,** Claim for Refund and Request for Abatement,

(f) corporation dissolutions, (g) a request to change accounting methods, and (h) a request to change accounting periods. Check the specific use box on line 4 if the power of attorney is for a use that will not be listed on the CAF. If the box on line 4 is checked, the representative should bring a copy of the power of attorney to each meeting with the IRS. A specific use power of attorney will not automatically revoke any prior powers of attorney.

Line 5—Acts Authorized.—If you want to modify the acts that your named representative(s) can perform, describe any specific additions or deletions in the space provided. The authority to substitute another representative or delegate authority must be specifically stated on line 5.

If you want to authorize your representative to sign an income tax return, this authorization must be specifically listed and the requirements of Regulations section 1.6012-1(a)(5) must be satisfied. In general, this regulation only permits a representative to sign your return if you are unable to make the return by reason of: (a) disease or injury, (b) continuous absence from the United States (including Puerto Rico), for a period of at least 60 days prior to the date required by law for filing the return, or (c) specific permission is requested of and granted by the district director for other good cause.

If you want to authorize a person other than a representative (an agent) to sign an income tax return, you must

1. Complete the information on lines 1-3.
2. Check the box on line 4, and
3. Write the following on line 5:

"This power of attorney is being filed pursuant to Regulation 1.6012(a)(5), reason (a), (b), or (c), which requires a power of attorney to be attached to a return if a return is signed by an agent. No other acts on behalf of the taxpayer are authorized."

Reasons (a), (b), and (c) are defined above. The agent does not complete Part II, Declaration of Representative.

If any representative you name is an unenrolled return preparer, the acts that person can perform on your behalf are limited by Revenue Procedure 81-38 (Pub. 470). In general, an unenrolled return preparer is permitted to appear as your representative only before revenue agents and examining officers of the Examination Division and the EP/EO Division and is not permitted to represent you before other offices (i.e., Collection Division or Appeals Division) of the IRS. Also, an unenrolled return preparer is not permitted to extend the statutory period, execute waivers, delegate authority, or substitute another representative.

Tax Matters Partner/Person.—The tax matters partner/person (TMP)(as defined in sections 6231(a)(7) and 6244) is authorized to perform various acts on behalf of the partnership or S corporation. The following are examples of acts performed by the TMP that cannot be delegated to the representative: (a) binding nonnotice partners to a settlement agreement under section 6224 and, under certain circumstances, binding all partners or shareholders to a settlement agreement under Tax Court Rule 248; (b) filing a petition for readjustment of

partnership or subchapter S items in the Tax Court, District Court, or Claims Court, under sections 6226 and 6244, based on the issuance of a notice of final partnership administrative adjustment or notice of final S corporation administrative adjustment by the IRS; (c) filing a request for administrative adjustment on behalf of the partnership or S corporation under sections 6227 and 6244; (d) filing a petition for adjustment of partnership items with respect to an administrative request in the Tax Court, District Court, or Claims Court, under sections 6228 and 6244; and (e) extending the statute of limitations on assessment of any tax attributable to partnership or subchapter S items (and affected items) under sections 6229 and 6244.

Line 6—Receipt of Refund Checks.—If you want to authorize your representative to receive, but not endorse, refund checks on your behalf, you must initial and enter the name of that person in the space provided. Section 10.31 of Treasury Department Circular No. 230 prohibits an attorney, CPA, or enrolled agent, any of whom is an income tax return preparer, from endorsing or otherwise negotiating a tax refund check.

Line 7—Notices and Communications.—Notices and other written communications will be sent to the first representative listed. Also, if you want the second representative listed to receive such communications, check box (a) on line 7. The IRS will send notices only to two representatives.

However, if you do not want any notices or communications sent to your representative, you must check box (b) on line 7.

If this form is being filed for a private letter ruling, the taxpayer can request that the original letter ruling be sent to the representative. A statement must be attached to Form 2848 stating this.

Line 8—Retention/Revocation of Prior Power(s) of Attorney.—If there is any existing power(s) of attorney you do not want to revoke, check the box on this line and attach a copy of the power(s) of attorney.

If you want to revoke an existing power of attorney and do not want to name a new representative, send a copy of the previously executed power of attorney to each IRS office where the power of attorney was filed. The copy of the power of attorney must have a current signature of the taxpayer under the signature already on line 9. Write "REVOKE" across the top of the form. If you do not have a copy of the power of attorney you want to revoke, send a statement to each IRS office where you filed the power of attorney. The statement of revocation must indicate that the authority of the power of attorney is revoked and must be signed by the taxpayer. Also, the name and address of each recognized representative whose authority is revoked must be listed.

A representative can withdraw from representation by filing a statement with each office of the IRS where the power of attorney was filed. The statement must be signed by the representative and identify the name and address of the taxpayer(s) and tax matter(s) from which the representative is withdrawing. Include your CAF No. on the statement if one has been assigned to you.

The filing of a Form 2848 will not revoke any Form 8821 that is in effect.

Line 9—Signature of Taxpayer(s).—

*Individuals.—*You must sign and date the power of attorney. If a joint return has been filed and both husband and wife will be represented by the same individual(s), both must sign the power of attorney unless one spouse authorizes the other, in writing, to sign for both. In that case, attach a copy of the authorization. However, if a joint return has been filed and husband and wife will be represented by different individuals, each taxpayer must execute his or her own power of attorney on a separate Form 2848.

*Corporations or associations.—*An officer having authority to bind the taxpayer must sign. However, the tax matters person may sign on behalf of an S corporation.

*Partnerships.—*All partners must sign unless one partner is authorized to act in the name of the partnership. A partner is authorized to act in the name of the partnership if, under state law, the partner has authority to bind the partnership. A copy of such authorization must be attached. For purposes of executing Form 2848, the tax matters partner is authorized to act in the name of the partnership. For dissolved partnerships, see Regulations section 601.503(c)(6).

*Other.—*If the taxpayer is a dissolved corporation, deceased, insolvent, or a person for whom or by whom a fiduciary (a trustee, guarantor, receiver, executor, or administrator) has been appointed, see Regulations section 601.503(d).

Part II—Declaration of Representative

The representative(s) you name must sign and date this declaration and enter the designation (i.e., items a–h) under which he or she is authorized to practice before the IRS. In addition, the representative(s) must list the following in the "Jurisdiction" column:

a   Attorney—Enter the two-letter abbreviation for the state (e.g., "NY" for New York) in which admitted to practice.

b   Certified Public Accountant—Enter the two-letter abbreviation for the state (e.g., "CA" for California) in which licensed to practice.

c   Enrolled Agent—Enter the enrollment card number issued by the Director of Practice.

d   Officer—Enter the title of the officer (i.e., President, Vice President, or Secretary).

e   Full-Time Employee—Enter title or position (e.g., Comptroller or Accountant).

f   Family Member—Enter the relationship to taxpayer (i.e., spouse, parent, child, brother, or sister).

g   Enrolled Actuary—Enter the enrollment card number issued by the Joint Board for the Enrollment of Actuaries.

h   Unenrolled Return Preparer—Enter the two-letter abbreviation for the state (e.g., "KY" for Kentucky) in which the return was prepared.

[The next page is 3137-9.]

FORM 1.8
TAX INFORMATION AUTHORIZATION

Form **8821**
(Rev. February 1993)
Department of the Treasury
Internal Revenue Service

Tax Information Authorization

OMB No. 1545-1165
Expires 2-29-96

1 Taxpayer Information (Taxpayer(s) must sign and date this form on line 7.)

Taxpayer name(s) and address (Please type or print.)	Social security number(s)	Employer identification number
ABC CORPORATION 1 MAIN STREET NEW YORK, NEW YORK 12345		13 : 0000000
	Daytime telephone number (212) 123-4567	Plan number (if applicable)

2 Appointee

Name and address (Please type or print.)
ALAN MICHAELS, ESQ.
100 PARK PLACE
ANYTOWN, NEW YORK   54321

CAF No. ....
Telephone No. (212) 543-2000
Fax No. (212) 543-1000
Check if new: Address ☐   Telephone No. ☐

The appointee is authorized to inspect and/or receive confidential tax information in any office of the IRS for the tax matters listed in line 3.

3 Tax Matters

Type of Tax (Income, Employment, Excise, etc.)	Tax Form Number (1040, 941, 720, etc.)	Year(s) or Period(s)
CORPORATE	1120	1991-1992

4 Specific Use Not Recorded on Centralized Authorization File (CAF).—If the tax information authorization is for a specific use not recorded on CAF, please check this box. (See Line 4—Specific Use Not Recorded on CAF on page 2.) . . . . . ▶ ☐
Do not use lines 5 and 6 if the box on line 4 is checked.

5 Disclosure of Tax Information (you must check one of the following unless box 4 is checked):
   a If you want tax information, notices, and other written communications sent to the appointee on an ongoing basis, check this box. This will cause all computer-generated notices to be sent to the appointee . . . . ▶ ☐
   b If you do not want any notices or communications sent to your appointee, check this box . . . . ▶ ☐

6 Retention/Revocation of Tax Information Authorization.—This tax information authorization automatically revokes all earlier tax information authorizations on file with the Internal Revenue Service for the same tax matters and years or periods covered by this document. If you do not want to revoke a prior tax information authorization, check this box . . . . ▶ ☐
You MUST attach a copy of any tax information authorization you want to remain in effect.

7 Signature of Taxpayer(s).—If a tax matter concerns a joint return, either husband or wife must sign. If signed by a corporate officer, partner, guardian, executor, receiver, administrator, trustee, or party other than the taxpayer, I certify that I have the authority to execute this form with respect to the tax matters/periods covered.

   ▶ **IF THIS TAX INFORMATION AUTHORIZATION IS NOT SIGNED AND DATED, IT WILL BE RETURNED.**

/s/ JOHN JONES	6/01/93	PRESIDENT
Signature	Date	Title (if applicable)
JOHN JONES		
Print Name		
Signature	Date	Title (if applicable)
Print Name		

Privacy Act and Paperwork Reduction Act Notice.—We ask for the information on this form to carry out the Internal Revenue laws of the United States. Form 8821 is provided by the IRS for your convenience and its use is voluntary. If you choose to designate an appointee to inspect and/or receive confidential information, under section 6109, you must disclose your social security number (SSN) or your employer identification number (EIN). The principal purpose of this disclosure is to secure proper identification of the taxpayer. We also need this information to gain access to your tax information in our

files and properly respond to your request. If you do not disclose this information, the IRS may suspend processing the tax information authorization and may not be able to fill your request until you provide the number.

The time needed to complete and file this form will vary depending on individual circumstances. The estimated average time is: Recordkeeping, 7 min.; Learning about the law or the form, 11 min.; Preparing the form, 22 min.; Copying, assembling, and sending the form to the IRS, 20 min.

If you have comments concerning the accuracy of these time estimates or suggestions for making this form more simple, we would be happy to hear from you. You can write to both the **Internal Revenue Service**, Washington, DC 20224, Attention: IRS Reports Clearance Officer, T:FP; and the **Office of Management and Budget,** Paperwork Reduction Project (1545-1165), Washington, DC 20503. **DO NOT** send Form 8821 to either of these offices. Instead, see Filing the Tax Information Authorization on page 2.

Cat. No. 11596P   Form **8821** (Rev. 2-93)

Form 8821 (Rev. 2-93)   Page **2**

General Instructions

Section references are to the Internal Revenue Code unless otherwise noted.

Purpose of the Form.—Form 8821 authorizes any individual, corporation, firm, organization, or partnership you designate to inspect and/or receive confidential information in any office of the IRS for the type of tax and the years or periods you list on this form. You may file a tax information authorization without using Form 8821, but it must reflect all information that is required on Form 8821.

If you want an individual to have the authority to represent you and/or perform other acts on your behalf, such as the execution of waivers, consents, or closing agreements, use **Form 2848**, Power of Attorney and Declaration of Representative, instead of Form 8821.

Fiduciaries.—A fiduciary (trustee, executor, administrator, receiver or guardian) stands in the position of a taxpayer and acts as the taxpayer. Therefore, a fiduciary does not act as an appointee and should not file a tax information authorization. **Form 56**, Notice Concerning Fiduciary Relationship, should be filed to notify the IRS of the existence of a fiduciary relationship. If a fiduciary wishes to authorize an appointee to inspect and/or receive confidential tax information on behalf of the entity, a tax information authorization must be filed and signed by the fiduciary acting in the position of the taxpayer.

Partnership/Subchapter S Items.—Sections 6221-6231 and 6241-6245 authorize a Tax Matters Partner or Tax Matters Person to perform certain acts on behalf of an affected partnership or S corporation. Rules governing the use of Form 8821 do not supersede any provisions of the above referenced sections

Filing the Tax Information Authorization.—File the original, photocopy, or facsimile transmission (fax) of the tax information authorization with each IRS office in which you want your appointee to inspect and/or receive confidential tax information on your behalf. If you choose to file a tax information authorization by fax, you must first be sure that the appropriate IRS office is equipped to accept fax transmissions. If the tax information authorization is filed for a matter currently pending before an office of the IRS, such as an examination, file the tax information authorization with that office. Otherwise, file the tax information authorization with the service center where the related return was, or will be, filed. Refer to the instructions for the related tax return for the service center addresses. Form 8821 must be received by the IRS within 60 days of the date it was signed and dated by the taxpayer.

Line-by-Line Instructions

Line 1—Taxpayer Information.—

Individuals.—Enter your name, SSN (and/or EIN, if applicable), and street address in the space provided. If a joint return is used, enter your spouse's name and social security number also.

Corporations, partnerships, or associations.—Enter the name, EIN, and business address.

Employee plan.—Enter the plan name, EIN of the plan sponsor, three-digit plan number, and business address of the plan sponsor.

Trust.—Enter the name, title, and address of the trustee, and the name and EIN of the trust.

Estate.—Enter the name, title, and address of the decedent's executor/personal representative, and the name and identification number of the estate. The identification number for an estate includes both the EIN, if the estate has one, and the decedent's SSN.

Line 2—Appointee.—Enter the name of your appointee. Please use the identical name on all submissions. If you wish to name more than one appointee, indicate so on this line and attach a list to the form. Enter the nine-digit CAF number for each appointee. If an appointee has been issued a CAF number for any previously filed tax information authorization (Form 8821) or power of attorney (Form 2848), that number should be used. If a CAF number has not been assigned, enter "NONE," and the IRS will issue one directly to your appointee.

The CAF number is a unique nine-digit identification number (not the SSN or EIN) that the IRS assigns to appointees. The CAF number is not an indication of authority to practice. The appointee should use the assigned CAF number on all future tax information authorizations. CAF numbers will not be assigned for employee plans and exempt organization application requests.

Line 3—Tax Matter(s).—Enter the type of tax, the tax form number, and the years or periods. For example, you may list "income tax Form 1040" for calendar year "1990" and "Excise tax Form 720" for the "1st, 2nd, 3rd, and 4th quarters of 1990." A general reference to "All years," "All periods," or "All taxes" is not acceptable. Any tax information authorization with such general reference will be returned. You may list any tax years or periods already ended as of the date you sign the tax information authorization. However, the number of future periods that can be recorded on the CAF is limited to returns with due dates within 3 years of your signature on Form 8821. If the matter relates to estate tax, enter the date of the taxpayer's death instead of the year or period. If either the type of tax, tax form number, or years or periods do not apply to the matter, specifically describe on this line the matter to which the tax information authorization pertains and enter "Not Applicable" in the appropriate column(s).

You may enter on this line any specific information you want the IRS to provide. For example, you may request a transcript of an account, a balance due amount, or whether a return was filed.

Line 4—Specific Use Not Recorded on CAF.—Generally, the IRS records all tax information authorizations on the CAF system. However, a tax information authorization will not be recorded on the CAF if it relates to a specific issue. Examples of specific issues include but are not limited to:
(1) requests to disclose information to loan companies or educational institutions,
(2) requests to disclose information to Federal

or state agency investigators for background checks, (3) civil penalty issues, (4) trust fund recovery penalty, (5) application for employer identification number, and (6) claims filed on Form 843, Claim for Refund and Request for Abatement. Check the specific use box on line 4 if the tax information authorization is for a use that will not be recorded on the CAF. If the box on line 4 is checked, the appointee should bring a copy of the tax information authorization to each meeting with the IRS. A specific use tax information authorization will not automatically revoke any prior tax information authorizations.

Line 6—Retention/Revocation of Prior Tax Information Authorizations.—If there are any existing tax information authorizations you do not want to revoke, check the box on this line and attach a copy of the tax information authorization.

If you want to revoke an existing tax information authorization and do not want to name a new appointee, send a copy of the previously executed tax information authorization to each IRS office where the tax information authorization was filed. The copy of the tax information authorization must have a current signature of the taxpayer under the signature already on line 7. Write "REVOKE" across the top of the form. If you do not have a copy of the tax information authorization you want to revoke, send a statement to each IRS office where you filed the tax information authorizations. The statement of revocation must indicate that the authority of the tax information authorization is revoked and must be signed by the taxpayer. Also, the name and address of each recognized appointee whose authority is revoked must be listed.

The filing of a Form 8821 will not revoke any Form 2848 that is in effect.

Line 7—Signature of Taxpayer(s).—

Individuals.—You must sign and date the authorization. If a joint return is used, either husband or wife must sign. Signatures of both husband and wife are not required.

Corporations.—Generally, Form 8821 can be signed by: (1) an officer having legal authority to bind the corporation, (2) any person designated by the board of directors or other governing body, (3) any officer or employee upon written request signed by any principal officer and attested by the secretary or other officer, and (4) any other person authorized to access information under section 6103(e). (For shareholders in S corporations not excepted and provided for under sections 6241-6245, see **Partnership/Subchapter S Items** above.)

Partnerships.—Generally, Form 8821 can be signed by any person who was a member of the partnership during any part of the tax period covered by Form 8821. For partners in partnerships provided for and defined by sections 6221-6231, see **Partnership/Subchapter S Items** above.)

Other.—If the taxpayer has died, is insolvent, is a dissolved corporation, or if a trustee, guardian, executor, receiver or administrator is acting for the taxpayer, see section 6103(e).

Copyright © August 2003

To identify taxpayers' representatives and the scope of their authority, the Service adopted a Centralized Authorization File (CAF) system.[310] Under this system, if a representative files a power of attorney or tax information authorization and the written practice declaration, information regarding the authorization is reflected on the CAF, which is an automated (i.e., computerized) file. Each representative is or will be assigned an identifying number for inputting and retrieving this information. Forms 2848 and 8821 have been revised to accommodate the use of the representative's identifying number. The stated objective of the CAF system is to enable the Service "to handle matters regarding authorizations and representatives quickly and efficiently" by, for example, identifying representatives and the scope of their authority and automatically directing copies of notices and correspondence to them.[311] Practitioners hope that the system will enable them to communicate with IRS personnel without delays in establishing their authority because their power of attorney is on file with another IRS office.[312] The rules relating to the recognition and au-

---

[310] 26 CFR § 601.502(b)(2).

[311] 26 CFR § 601.502(b)(2)

[312] The Service sent a notice to representatives responding to possible questions about the CAF system. Notice 645 (1-83). Questions and answers included in the notice are as follows:

1. Q: I do not always get copies of notices you send my clients when I have a Power of Attorney from them. Will CAF improve this situation?
   A: Yes. When notices are generated by our computer systems, CAF records will be checked. If a POA is found, a duplicate notice will be generated and sent to the taxpayer's representative.
2. Q: Will CAF mean I need to use a different authorization form?
   A: No. The same forms should be used, such as Forms 2848, 2848-D, 56, and 706.
3. Q: If I detect an error in the way you have my Power of Attorney recorded in your "system," who do I contact and how?
   A: You may contact the Service Center you deal with by mail and explain the problem, and the IRS can correct the file.
4. Q: What if I want to insure that your CAF system includes all the taxpayers I currently represent, can I get a list of those taxpayers I represent from the Service?
   A: No. Our system is not designed to index all the taxpayers represented by a specific individual, but it does automatically generate copies of notices to representatives based on information in each taxpayer's account. Therefore, if you do not receive copies of notices that you are authorized to receive, or, if you should ever receive a copy of a notice that you believe we sent to you in error, please write the Service Center to resolve the problem. For example, if you receive copies of notices for a taxpayer you no longer represent, please let us know and we will delete you as a representative of that taxpayer.
5. Q: Should I use my representative number on future POAs I send to you?
   A: Yes. This number is applicable for current POAs and any new ones you send us. A future revision to Forms 2848 and 2848-D will include an appropriate place to enter your representative number.

thorization requirements, including exceptions to the requirement that a power or authorization be on file, are summarized in Table 1.1.

Representatives initially had to mail or fax power of attorney forms to the service center at which the taxpayer filed the taxpayer's return, but the CAF database was not accessible to Service employees in other areas. To save time, in May 1999, the Service announced that it would permit representatives to fax their signed Forms 2848 and 8821 directly to the Centralized Authorization File Unit located in the service center to which they normally send their tax returns, where the forms will be entered into the CAF database.[313]

[b] The Practice Declaration

To act as an advocate for a taxpayer, a representative must file a practice declaration as well as a power of attorney or tax information authorization. The declaration states that the representative is (1) an attorney who is a member in good standing of the bar of the highest court of the jurisdiction in which he is admitted to practice, a CPA qualified to practice in the jurisdiction in which he practices, or an enrolled agent under Circular No. 230 and (2) not currently under suspension or disbarment from practice before the Service.[314] This declaration is on the reverse side of Form 2848, but the declaration need not be made on these forms.[315] The declaration must be filed when a representative presents himself for the initial meeting in the first office in the Service in which he represents the taxpayer in connection with the matter under consideration.[316] Once evidence of recognition is submitted, it need not be resubmitted in any office of the Service unless a specific request is made.[317]

A power of attorney or tax information authorization must be filed in each office of the Service in which the representative desires to perform one of the enumerated acts or to receive or inspect confidential information. Technically, a power or authorization is required at the district director's office, the Appeals Office, and in the district counsel's office because each is a separate office.[318] Moreover, an additional copy of the power or authorization is required for each taxable period because "each taxable period constitutes a separate matter."[319] However, where a power or authorization is filed in the district office that has the matter under consideration, further filing in the offices that

---

[313] IR-1999-48 (May 24, 1999).

[314] 26 CFR § 601.503(a).

[315] An enrolled agent need show only a "valid" enrollment card.

[316] 26 CFR § 601.503(a).

[317] 26 CFR § 601.503(a).

[318] 26 CFR § 601.501(b)(2).

[319] 26 CFR § 601.501(b)(1). If, in addition to past or present matters, a previously filed power or authorization relates to a taxable period for which a return is not yet due, a

subsequently have the matter under consideration is not required unless a ruling request is made.[320] In that case, a copy of the power or authorization must be submitted with each request if the representative wishes to have a conference or to receive a copy of the ruling.

---

power or authorization must be filed with the return or when the matter is considered by the Service.

[320] 26 CFR § 601.502(c)(2)(ii).

TABLE 1.1

Recognition and Authorization Requirements for Persons Appearing before the Service

Capacity of Person Appearing*	Attorneys and CPAs	Enrolled Agents	Unenrolled Persons Who Are Not Attorneys or CPAs		
			Qualified for Limited Practice under Section 10.7 of Circular No. 230		All Others
			Return Preparers	Others	
As an advocate who is to perform certain acts for taxpayer as prescribed in 26 CFR § 601.502(c)(1) (constitutes "practice" as defined in Circular No. 230)	P/A and D; exception (2) may apply	P/A and E	Ineligible	P/A; exception (2) may apply	Ineligible
As an advocate (constitutes "practice" as defined in Circular No. 230)	TIA and D; exception (1), (2), or (3) may apply	TIA and E; exception (3) may apply	TIA or A; exception (4) applies	TIA; exception (2) or (3) apply	Ineligible
As a witness who may receive or inspect tax information of a confidential nature (does not include "practice" as defined in Circular No. 230)	TIA; exception (1) or (2) may apply	TIA	TIA	TIA; exception (2) may apply	TIA
As a witness for taxpayer to present his books, records, or returns to the examining officer (does not include "practice" as defined in Circular No. 230)	No requirements	No requirements	No requirements	No requirements	No requirements

CODE FOR REQUIREMENTS

P/A — must present or have power of attorney on file.
TIA — must present or have a tax information authorization (or power of attorney) on file if taxpayer is not also present.
D — must present or have a declaration on file. The declaration may be in combination with a TIA or power of attorney.
E — must present evidence of current enrolled status or temporary recognition status.
A — must present or have on file a Form 2848–D authorization for representation by an unenrolled individual tax return preparer, as described in Rev. Proc. 81-38, § 6, 1981-2 CB 592.

EXCEPTIONS

(1) An attorney who prepared the estate tax return and is the attorney of record for the estate will not be required to have a TIA on file, but a declaration must be on file. (26 CFR § 601.502(c)(3)(ii).)

(2) A trustee, a receiver, or an attorney (designated to represent a trustee, receiver, or debtor in possession) may substitute a proper court certificate or a copy of a district court order approving bond in lieu of a P/A or TIA. (26 CFR § 601.502(c)(3)(ii).)

(3) A TIA is not required if the advocacy can be performed without necessitating Service disclosure of tax information of a confidential nature. (26 CFR § 601.502(c)(3)(ii).)

(4) Unenrolled return prepareres are limited to representation of persons during the examination process (ineligible for practice at District or Appellate Conferences). (Circular No. 230 § 10.7(a)(7).)

---

* Each category includes all categories listed below it.

[5] Execution of Powers and Authorizations

[a] Forms

The Service provides that representatives generally will use Form 2848 and Form 8821. Use of these forms is not mandatory, but the instrument purporting to be a power or authorization must clearly express the taxpayer's intention about the scope of the representative's authority and the tax matter to which the authority relates.[321] Generally, a power of attorney must be filed if the representative is to act as attorney-in-fact to perform one or more of the five specific acts listed on the Form 2848. In all other cases involving the receipt of confidential tax information, Form 8821 is used. The Form 8821 authorization has two parts: Part I is a tax information authorization; Part II is a practice declaration. If representation will involve the receipt of confidential tax information, both parts are filled out.

[b] Names and Identifying Numbers

Disclosure of the taxpayer's identifying number is mandatory under Section 6109 to secure proper identification. If the identifying number is not received, the Service may not accept the power or authorization until the information is provided. The following names and identifying numbers must be supplied on the power or authorization:

- If a joint return is involved, the name, social security number, and address (if different) of both husband and wife
- If the taxpayer is a corporation, partnership, or association, the name, employer identification number, and address[322]
- If the taxpayer is a trust, the name, title (e.g., trustee), and address of the fiduciary and the name and employer identification number of the taxpayer-trust
- If the taxpayer is an estate, the name, title (e.g., personal representative), and address of the decedent's personal representative and the taxpayer-estate's identifying number (i.e., the estate's employer identification number and the decedent's social security number)

---

[321] 26 CFR § 601.504(a)(1).

[322] Where the name and Social Security number of each partner have not previously been furnished the Service, the power or authorization for the partnership should include or attach the name and Social Security number of each partner.

[c] Execution

The Service follows certain formalities as to execution of the power or authorization. Some present little problems: An individual (or, in a joint return, both husband and wife)[323] must execute his own power or authorization.[324] A partnership executes the power or authorization by the signatures of all the partners or by the signature of one partner authorized to act for the partnership.[325] In the case of a corporation or an association, an officer certifying his authority to bind the entity may execute a power or authorization.[326] Supplementary evidence of the party or parties executing the power or authorization is usually required in the case of a dissolved partnership, a dissolved corporation, an insolvent taxpayer, a deceased taxpayer or a guardian or other court-appointed fiduciary, or a trustee.[327]

[d] Matters and Tax Periods

The power or authorization must state the type of tax and period(s) to which it relates. Each tax imposed for each period is a separate matter. However, any number of specified periods and types of taxes may be listed in the same power or authorization.[328]

---

[323] One spouse may sign for the other with written authorization.

[324] 26 CFR §§ 601.504(b)(1)(i), 601.504(b)(1)(ii). If a husband and wife are not represented by the same person, the power or authorization may be signed by the spouse represented, but the representative cannot perform any act with respect to the joint return that the represented spouse could not perform alone. 26 CFR § 601.504(b)(1)(ii).

[325] 26 CFR § 601.504(b)(1)(iii). A partner is duly authorized to act in the name of the partnership if he has authority to bind the partnership under state law. See John Arnold Executrak Sys., Inc. v. Comm'r, TC Memo. 1990-6, 58 TCM 1129 (1990) (limited partnership had authority to file a Tax Court petition for a redetermination of a limited partner's taxes under agency principles, the limited partnership agreement, and an executed power of attorney).

[326] 26 CFR §§ 601.504(b)(1)(iv), 601.504(b)(1)(v). It is not necessary that a power of attorney or a tax information authorization granted by a corporation be attested or that the corporate seal be affixed. Spaces provided on power of attorney or tax information authorization forms for affixing the corporate seal are for the convenience of corporations required by charter, or by the law of the jurisdiction in which they are incorporated, to affix their corporate seals in the execution of instruments. 26 CFR § 601.504(c).

[327] 26 CFR § 601.504(b)(2).

[328] If the matter relates to estate tax, the date of the decedent's death, rather than the taxable period, is entered on the power or authorization. A reference to "all years," "all periods," or "all taxes" is not permissible.

[e] Notarization

A power must be acknowledged before a notary public or witnessed by two disinterested individuals unless it is granted to a person recognized to practice before the Service (i.e., an attorney, CPA, or enrolled agent), who completes a declaration evidencing his qualification to practice.[329] However, the signatures on tax information authorizations need not be acknowledged or witnessed.

[f] Modification and Revocation

A new power or authorization must be filed if a power or authorization has already been filed and the taxpayer desires, with respect to the same matter, to take any of the following actions:

- Add to or reduce the number of representatives to perform one or more of such acts or to receive confidential information
- evoke the authority granted to a representative to perform one or more of such acts or to receive such confidential information
- Change the authority granted to a representative[330]

Generally, a new power of attorney or tax information authorization granted by the taxpayer to another representative in the same matter revokes any prior power, whether the acts enumerated in the previous power are the same or different as those in the new power. However, a new power or authorization does not revoke a prior power or authorization if (1) it specifically states that it does not do so and (2) the new power or authorization attaches the prior one or a statement listing the names and addresses of all representatives authorized under the prior power or information authorization. This procedure permits a taxpayer to authorize additional representatives to perform one or more of the specified acts or to receive confidential information.[331]

A taxpayer may revoke a power of attorney or a tax information authorization granted to a representative without authorizing a new representative to act for him. To take such action, the taxpayer must send a signed statement to those offices of the Service where the representative has filed copies of the instrument to be revoked. This statement must list the names and addresses of the representatives whose authority is to be revoked.

---

[329] 26 CFR § 601.504(d). This declaration and the appropriate spaces for notarization and the signatures of witnesses are found on the back of Form 2848.

[330] 26 CFR § 601.505(c)(1).

[331] For rules relating to the practice of the Service in giving notices and other written communications in cases in which a taxpayer has more than one authorized representative, see 26 CFR § 601.506(a).

[6] Effect of Authority Under Power of Attorney

A taxpayer's power of attorney not only permits the taxpayer to be represented by a professional in the taxpayer's dealings with the Service, but also creates an agency relationship between the taxpayer and the representative with the scope of the agency defined by the terms of the Service power of attorney form. As the representative is the agent of the taxpayer, the representative's statements concerning a matter within the scope of the agency established in the power may be used against the taxpayer as the taxpayer's vicarious admissions.[332] Statements of the representative acting pursuant to the power of attorney have been admitted in criminal prosecutions against the taxpayer defendant.[333] Generally, IRS agents must deal with the representative if a power of attorney is filed.[334] However, it appears that even when a taxpayer has executed a power of attorney in favor of an attorney, the taxpayer may be contacted by IRS agents without the knowledge of the representative and any admissions the taxpayer makes may be used against the taxpayer.[335]

¶ 1.10 A BRIEF HISTORY OF DUTIES AND RESTRICTIONS ON PRACTICE

Circular No. 230 imposes twelve duties and restrictions on practice before the Service.

   1. A person authorized to practice before the Service may not interfere with an effort by the Service to obtain information unless the person

---

[332] Fed. R. Evid. 801(d)(2)(D).

[333] United States v. O'Connor, 433 F2d 752, 755–756 (1st Cir. 1970), cert. denied, 401 US 911 (1971); United States v. Dolleris, 408 F2d 918, 921–922 (6th Cir.), cert. denied, 395 US 943 (1969); United States v. Pappas, 806 F. Supp. 1 (DNH 1992) (statements made by defendant's lawyer and accountants to IRS agents not suppressed in criminal prosecution over objection that the statements were not authorized by the power). Cf. United States v. Amelia, 637 F. Supp. 1205 (D. Mass. 1986) (power of attorney form found not to authorize any act other than those specified, which did not include the implied authority to speak for the taxpayer).

[334] See discussion of the conduct of an examination at ¶ 8.06[4] and the issue of conflicting representation at ¶ 13.03[b].

[335] See United States v. Caslan, 795 F. Supp. 196 (SD Ind. 1992) (taxpayer had filed power in a civil examination, and in an interview by special agents made incriminating statements; held, the power was not sufficient to constitute the assertion of the taxpayer's right to counsel).

believes in good faith and on reasonable grounds that the information is privileged or that the effort is of doubtful legality.[336]

2. A person authorized to practice before the Service must, on request, supply the Director of Practice with information about violations of the regulations and must testify in any disbarment or suspension proceeding unless the person believes in good faith and on reasonable grounds that the information is privileged or that the request is of doubtful legality.[337]

3. A person authorized to practice and retained by a client who has not complied with the revenue laws or has made an error in or omission from a return or other document that the client is required by law to execute must advise the client promptly of the noncompliance, error, or omission.[338] It appears that no obligation beyond this advice is necessary, and presumably the final decision to comply or correct the error or omission is the client's. This result is consistent with the American Bar Association's (ABA's) position, which holds that a lawyer has a duty to urge his client to correct the error but states only that the lawyer "may" have to withdraw if the client refuses.[339] The American Institute of Certified Public Accountants (AICPA) takes a similar view and holds that the CPA has the responsibility of advising the taxpayer of the error and the measures to be taken, but if the client does not correct the error, the CPA should only "consider the im-

---

[336] Treas. Dep't Circular No. 230, Regulations Governing the Practice of Attorneys, Certified Public Accountants, Enrolled Agents, Enrolled Actuaries, and Appraisers Before the Internal Revenue Service, 31 CFR, subtit. A, pt. 10, revised as of July 1, 1994. Special Committee on the Lawyer's Role in Tax Practice, Report, "Ethics and The Tax Lawyer," 38 Record 218 (1983). The circumstances described in summaries of disciplinary actions taken by the Director of Practice give some idea how the Director of Practice applies Circular 230. See, e.g., "Summaries of Disciplinary Actions Taken by the Director of Practice," 1991-14 IRB 38 (Apr. 14, 1991).

[337] Circular No. 230, § 10.20(b).

[338] Circular No. 230, § 10.21.

[339] ABA Comm. on Professional Ethics, Opinion No. 314 (1965), 51 ABAJ 671 (1965). A duty to withdraw may become more definite if continued representation requires the lawyer to use false evidence or to make a false statement. ABA Code of Professional Responsibility, Canon 7, DR 7-102(A)(3)–7-102(A)(7). Ethical guidelines in tax practice are also treated in B. Bittker, Professional Responsibility in Federal Tax Practice (1970); Wolfman & Holden, Ethical Problems in Federal Tax Practice (2d ed. 1981); Comm. on Standards of Tax Practice, ABA Tax Section, "Guidelines to Tax Practice," 31 Tax Law. 551 (1978); Saltzman, "Ethical Rules of Conduct for Tax Practitioners: Where Do We Now Stand?" 41 J. Tax. 162 (1974); Sellin, "Professional Responsibility of the Tax Practitioner," 52 Taxes 584 (1974); Comeel, "Ethical Guidelines for Tax Practice," 28 Tax L. Rev. 1 (1972); and Rowen, "When May a Lawyer Advise a Client That He May Take a Position on a Tax Return?" 29 Tax Law. 237 (1976).

plications of this refusal on his future relationship with the client."[340] Also, the ABA's Tax Section has published a statement that a lawyer must disclose a "clear arithmetic error" in the client's favor in a court case.[341] If the case is not in court, with the client's express of implied consent, the lawyer must also disclose "a clear unilateral arithmetic or clerical error." If the client does not consent to the disclosure, the lawyer must withdraw.

4. A person authorized to practice must exercise "due diligence" in preparing and filing returns, documents, and other papers relating to internal revenue matters and in determining the correctness of representations to the Treasury Department and to a client.[342] This duty, it has been said, "suggests a principal concern with making representatives accountable for negligence" and "connotes loyalty and devotion" to the client.[343] Consequently, where a representative deceives his client in a matter before the Service, the representative violates the regulation and may be disbarred or suspended from practice.[344]

What does due diligence oblige a practitioner to do when a tax return is prepared? This seemingly simple question has divided the legal and accounting professions, and the Treasury may have its own view. ABA Opinion 314 stated, with regard to a lawyer's obligation in preparing his client's tax return: "[A] lawyer who is asked to advise his client in the course of the preparation of the client's tax returns may freely urge the statement of positions favorable to the client just as long as there is a *reasonable basis* for the position." (Emphasis added.) In 1984, the ABA's Section of Taxation voted to eliminate the "reasonable basis" standard and asked the ABA's Standing Committee on Ethics and Professional Responsibility to reconsider the "reasonable basis" standard in Opinion 314 with a view to elevating the standard.

On July 7, 1985, the ABA's Ethics Committee issued Formal Opinion 85-352, which stated, "A lawyer may advise reporting a position on a tax return so long as the lawyer believes in good faith that the position is warranted in existing law or can be supported by a good faith argument for an extension, modification or reversal of ex-

---

[340] AICPA, Statements of Responsibilities in Tax Practice, No. 6 (1970).

[341] Standards of Tax Practice, St. 1999-1, 53 Tax L. Rev. 733, 737-8 (Spring 2000).

[342] Circular No. 230, § 10.22.

[343] Harary v. Blumenthal, 555 F2d 1113 (2d Cir. 1977).

[344] In Harary v. Blumenthal, 555 F2d 1113 (2d Cir. 1977), a CPA who was acquitted of bribing an IRS agent had told his client the agent had to be paid $2,000 but paid the agent only $1,250 and pocketed $750 for himself.

isting law and there is some realistic possibility of success if the matter is litigated."[345] In Formal Opinion 85-352, it stated that a lawyer

> may advise reporting a position on a return even where the lawyer believes the position probably will not prevail, there is no substantial authority in support of the position, and there will be no disclosure of the position in the return. However, the position to be asserted must be one which the lawyer in good faith believes is warranted in existing law or can be supported by a good faith argument for an extension, modification or reversal of existing law. This requires that there is some realistic possibility of success if the matter is litigated. In addition, in his role as advisor, the lawyer should refer to potential penalties and other legal consequences should the client take the position advised.[346]

Although the ABA modified the ethical standard from "reasonable basis" to "realistic possibility of success," the AICPA continued to follow the "reasonable basis" standard set forth in its Statement on Responsibilities in Tax Practices No. 10 (1977). In apparent response to the resulting lack of uniformity, amendments to Section 10.34 of Circular 230 were proposed on August 14, 1986, and were published in the Federal Register on August 14, 1986. These proposed amendments provided, in general, that (1) in the exercise of due diligence the statutory requirements of the substantial tax understatement penalty of Section 6661 provided guidance and that accordingly (2) a practitioner was prohibited from recommending or advising that a return should be prepared if the return position may subject the taxpayer penalty attributable to a substantial understatement of tax. Thus, in a non-tax-shelter situation, for example, the proposed requirement would not be met unless there was "substantial authority" for the position or, in its absence, the position had to have been adequately disclosed. Comments on the proposed amendments were solicited. In 1988, the AICPA also adopted the realistic possibility of success standard for return preparation.

Both the AICPA and the Tax Section recommended the adoption of a uniform standard for tax return positions as follows:[347]

---

[345] 39 Tax Law. 631 (1986).

[346] 39 Tax Law. 631, 633–634 (1986). For an analysis of Formal Opinion 85-352, see Falk, "Tax Ethics, Legal Ethics and Real Ethics," 39 Tax Law. 643 (1986).

[347] Both the AICPA and ABA Tax Section submitted comments opposing adoption of the proposed standard (AICPA Letter, dated February 13, 1987, from Herbert Lerner and Leonard Podolin and ABA Tax Section Letter, dated February 12, 1987, from John B. Jones, Jr.). In August 1988, the AICPA Tax Division issued revised Statements on Responsibilities in Tax Practice (SRTPs). SRTP No. 1 (Rev. 1988) is entitled "Tax Return Positions." It contains the standards a CPA should follow in recommending tax return po-

> A practitioner may not advise or recommend to a client that a position be taken with respect to the tax treatment of any item on a return unless the practitioner has a good faith belief that the position has a realistic possibility of being sustained administratively or judicially on its merits if challenged.

Notwithstanding this standard,

> [T]he practitioner may advise or recommend that a position be presented in the context of either: (1) a return on which a position is adequately disclosed, or (2) an amended return that serves as a claim for refund (e.g., a Form 1040X or 1120X), in either case so long as the practitioner concludes that there is a basis for doing so that is not frivolous.

Treasury accepted this recommendation and adopted the realistic-possibility-of-success standard as the standard practitioners must follow when they advise taxpayers on tax matters and when they prepare and sign returns. A practitioner may not sign a return as a preparer (1) if the practitioner determines that there is a position on the return that does not have a realistic possibility of being sustained on its merits, (2) unless the return position is not frivolous, and the practitioner sees to it that this nonfrivolous position is disclosed on the return in accordance with the requirements of the substantial-understatement component of the accuracy-related penalty.[348]

When a practitioner advises a taxpayer on a return position or prepares the portion of the return on which the position is taken, the advising practitioner has the same obligations of complying with the realistic-possibility standard and the disclosure requirement if that standard cannot be met. In addition, the practitioner must describe to the client the penalties "reasonably likely to apply" to the client if the return position is taken, as well as the opportunity of avoiding the penalty if the return position is disclosed.[349]

In making this realistic possibility determination, the practitioner is permitted to rely on information furnished by clients without verifying the information, provided that the reliance is in good faith.[350] This good faith will be lacking if the practitioner ignores the implica-

---

sitions and in preparing or signing tax returns and claims for refund. In December 1990, the AICPA issued SRTP Interpretation No. 1-1, which interpreted the realistic possibility of success standard. The SRTPs and Interpretation No. 1-1 are discussed further in connection with the tax return preparer penalty in Chapter 4.

[348] Circular No. 230, § 10.34(a)(1) (1994).

[349] Circular No. 230, § 10.34(a)(1) (1994), § 10.34(a)(2).

[350] Circular No. 230, § 10.34(a)(1) (1994), § 10.34(a)(3).

tions of information the practitioner receives or knows about, or if the practitioner fails to make reasonable inquiries when the information appears to be incorrect, inconsistent with other known information, or incomplete. Crucial to applying this standard, however, is the meaning of a realistic possibility of success. Circular No. 230 defines the standard in the same terms as the substantial authority standard in the substantial understatement penalty; that is, a position has a realistic possibility of being sustained on its merits "if a reasonable and well-informed analysis by a person knowledgeable in the tax law would lead [that] person to conclude that the position has approximately a one in three, or greater, likelihood of being sustained on its merits."[351] Authorities that are recognized for purposes of the substantial-understatement penalty may be considered for purposes of this realistic possibility analysis. Needless to say, the possibility that the Service will not audit a taxpayer's return is not a realistic-possibility-of-success support for a position, nor is patently improper (i.e., frivolous) support.

It is appropriate that the standard of conduct imposed on practitioners be the same as the standard for preparers of income tax returns enforced through the civil income tax return preparer penalty, and no lower than the standard applied to taxpayers through the substantial-understatement penalty. However, the Circular No. 230 standard is based on the premise that professional groups interpret the realistic-possibility standard the same way as the Service does for purposes of the return-preparer penalty and, because of the stated connection between them, the substantial-understatement penalty as well. The AICPA permits accountants to consider a broader range of material (for example, treatises and articles) in finding support for a position than the Service does in the penalty regulations interpreting substantial authority. The Service does not consider treatises and articles to be authorities for purposes of a substantial authority analysis.[352] Moreover, there is some basis for believing that when the ABA adopted the realistic-possibility-of-success standard that it was imposing a normative standard of conduct, similar to the standard of practice applicable to lawyers in court by Rule 11 of the Federal Rules of Civil Procedure and the duty of care to which tax lawyers would be

---

[351] Circular No. 230, § 10.34(a)(1) (1994), § 10.34(a)(4).
[352] See discussion in Chapter 4.

held in a professional liability case, not a quantitative one-in-three-chance-of-success standard.[353]

Further uncertainty about the standard of conduct is caused by the 1993 change in the disclosure exception to the substantial understatement penalty. Before the change, the penalty could be avoided if the disclosed position was nonfrivolous (not patently improper), but after the amendment, the disclosed position must meet the "significantly higher" reasonable-basis standard.[354] The standard of conduct has therefore come full circle. In 1985, the ABA replaced the reasonable-basis standard with the realistic-possibility-of-success standard because of dissatisfaction with its perceived use by some lawyers to justify frivolous return positions. But by 1993, the reasonable-basis standard returned as a significantly higher standard than a nonfrivolous position. By relating the Circular No. 230 standard to the preparer and substantial-understatement penalties, which now use the same words to connote different or supposedly different meanings, Treasury has made the realistic-possibility standard harder to apply than a standard of conduct should be if it is to affect practitioner conduct in a positive and meaningful way. If practitioners will have some difficulty in understanding the standard of return preparation and advice, they may take some slight comfort in the standard of discipline because it limits the use of suspensions or disbarments from practice to violations of the realistic-possibility standard that are willful, reckless, or the result of gross incompetence.[355]

5. A person authorized to practice must not unreasonably delay the prompt disposition of a matter before the Service.[356]
6. A person authorized to practice may not knowingly and directly or indirectly (a) employ a person disbarred or suspended from practice or accept employment from such a person or (b) accept assistance from a former government employee prohibited by regulations or law from providing assistance.[357]
7. Special rules apply to practice by former government officials[358] or partners of government employees.[359]

---

[353] For a further elaboration of this point, see Saltzman, "The Preparer Penalty's Realistic Possibility of Success Standard: Its Meaning and Application," 43 Fla. L. Rev. 915 (1991).

[354] See Chapter 7B.

[355] Circular No. 230, § 10.34(b) (1994).

[356] Circular No. 230, § 10.23.

[357] Circular No. 230, § 10.24.

[358] Circular No. 230, § 10.26.

[359] Circular No. 230, § 10.25.

8. A person authorized to practice may not notarize papers in a matter in which he is also counsel, attorney, or agent.[360]

9. A person authorized to practice may not charge an unconscionable fee.[361]

10. A person authorized to practice may not represent conflicting interests, except by express consent of all directly interested parties after full disclosure has been made.[362]

11. Advertising and solicitation rules in Circular No. 230 are intended "to liberalize the restrictions currently placed on practitioner advertising." Nevertheless, the regulations prohibit not only a public advertisement that is "a false, fraudulent statement or claim," but also one that is an "*unduly influencing,* coercive or *unfair statement* or claim."[363] Just how this string of redundant and ambiguous terms can serve as meaningful guidance to practitioners is hard to comprehend. The background portion of the notice proposing the regulations[364] sheds some light on Treasury's thinking:

> [C]laims of expertise or attainment without basis would be considered misleading or deceptive. Examples would be references to a professional designation or attainment obtained through "mail order" promotion or where the basis for the designation was not substantive. Such claims as "guaranteed refund" or statements pertaining to win/loss ratios would continue to be considered misleading or deceptive, as will statements intimating that past connections with the Internal Revenue Service allow different results with a tax matter than could be attained by a practitioner without such past connections.

But such terms as "unduly influencing" and "unfair" leave broad discretion in the hands of the field offices and, ultimately, the Director of Practice.

Also, practitioners are not permitted to make uninvited solicitation of employment.[365] A practitioner is nevertheless permitted to seek new business from existing and former clients "in a related matter"

---

[360] Circular No. 230, § 10.27.

[361] Circular No. 230, § 10.28. A practitioner is permitted to charge a contingent fee only if the practitioner preparing a refund claim reasonably anticipated, at the time the claim was filed, that the claim would be denied by the Service and subsequently litigated by the client. Circular No. 230, § 10.28 (1994).

[362] Circular No. 230, § 10.29. Service procedures where a representative appears for multiple parties in an investigation are described at ¶ 13.03[4][b].

[363] Circular No. 230, § 10.30(a)(1) (1994).

[364] 56 Fed. Reg. 77 (Apr. 22, 1991).

[365] Circular No. 230, § 10.30(a)(2).

and solicit by mail (presumably taxpayers other than existing and former clients).[366] Direct mail advertising must carry the legend "Advertisement" at the top of the first page of the mailing and on the envelope and must identify the source of the information used in choosing the recipient.

If costs will be incurred in the representation, fee information must disclose whether the client will be responsible for the costs.[367]

Practitioners may advertise or solicit in professional lists, telephone directories, print media, mailing, and radio and television.[368] But a copy of the direct mailing or an audio recording of a radio or television solicitation must be retained for at least thirty-six months from the date of the transmission or use.

12. Persons admitted to practice may not negotiate a refund check.[369]

¶ 1.11 A BRIEF HISTORY OF DUTIES IN PROVIDING TAX SHELTER OPINIONS

The Treasury has also adopted final rules setting standards for providing opinions used in the promotion of tax shelter offerings.[370] While Congress has used

---

[366] Employees of exempt organizations under Sections 501(c)(3) and 501(c)(4) may make personal solicitations.

[367] Circular No. 230, § 10.30(b) (1994).

[368] Circular No. 230, § 10.30.

[369] Circular No. 230, § 10.31

[370] Reg. § 10.33. The rules are effective for tax shelter opinions provided after May 23, 1984. Final Regulations §§ 10.2, 10.7, 10.51, and 10.52 governing practice before the Service to set standards for opinions used in tax shelter offerings were filed with the Federal Register February 22, 1984. 49 Fed. Reg. 6,719. See Notice 84-4, 1984-1 CB 331.

The Department of the Treasury first published proposed amendments to Circular No. 230, including a revision of Section 10.52, in 1980 to deal with tax shelter opinions. 45 Fed. Reg. 58,594 (1980). Lawyers criticized the proposed amendments as vague and too broad. See, e.g., Sax, "Lawyer Responsibility in Tax Shelter Opinion," 34 Tax Law. 5 (1980); Lewis, "Lawyer's Ethical Responsibilities in Rendering Opinions on Tax Shelter Promotions," 12 Tax Notes 795 (1981). The ABA responded by adopting specific guidelines in the tax shelter area on January 29, 1982. ABA Formal Op. 346 (Revised) (Jan. 29, 1982), 68 ABAJ 471 (1982). As a result of comments and ABA Opinion 346, the Department of the Treasury modified its earlier proposed amendments. 47 Fed. Reg. 56,144 (Dec. 15, 1982), reprinted in 1982 Stand. Fed. Tax Rep. (CCH) ¶ 8947. In general, the revised proposed changes to Circular 230 conformed to the standards expressed in ABA Opinion 346. ABA Tax Section, "Statement on Revisions to Proposed Rule Amending Circular 230 With Respect to Tax Shelter Opinions," 36 Tax Law. 861 (1983) ("The Section of Taxation warmly supports the revised proposal, particularly insofar as it adopted the principles stated in Formal Opinion 346."). The Treasury summarized final regulations

penalties on taxpayers and tax shelter promoters to discourage the use of tax shelters, the Treasury has used the practice rules to impose sanctions on practitioners participating in tax shelters by giving opinions. Punishments for a violation of these tax shelter practice rules include disbarment or suspension from practice before the Service if the violation is (1) willfull or reckless; (2) through gross incompetence (as specially defined in Section 10.51(j)); or (3) part of a pattern of providing tax shelter opinions that fail to comply with the rules.[371] However, these rules are sufficiently broad to include transactions not covered by the substantial understatement penalty arising out of a tax shelter investment. Indeed, the statutory definition of a tax shelter in the substantial understatement penalty was intentionally not used. Therefore, practitioners may not be comfortable with the potential scope of the rules. Moreover, the rules are sufficiently imprecise and onerous to cause practitioners concern even if they conclude the advice they are giving relates to a tax shelter. This result also appears to have been intentional.

Circular 230 broadly defines a tax shelter to include an investment having "as a significant and intended feature" for income or excise tax purposes, either (1) excess deductions that are available to reduce other income in the year or (2) excess credits to offset tax on other income.[372] This definition thus com-

---

and compared them to ABA Opinion 346. See Notice 84-4, 1984-1 CB 331. For practitioner analyses of the final Circular 230 Amendments applying to tax shelter opinions, comparing Circular 230 and ABA Opinion 346, see Goldfein & Cohn, "Final Circular 230 Amendments Prescribe Disciplinary Standards for Shelter Opinions," 60 J. Tax. 330 (June 1984); Schlenger & Watkins, "Exploring the Myths of Circular 230," 62 Taxes 283 (May 1984). Reg. §§ 10.33 and 10.52, in governing standards of practice for attorneys and other practitioners who prepare opinions on tax shelter offerings, do not violate First Amendment guaranties of freedom of speech. Joslin v. United States, 616 F. Supp. 1023 (D. Utah 1985), vacated and remanded on another ground, 832 F2d 7 (10th Cir. 1987) (finding that the standards were legitimate regulation of a profession, not impermissible prohibitions on speech, under authority of Lowe v. SEC, 472 US 181 (1985)).

[371] Reg. § 10.52(b). Reg. § 10.51(j) makes it disreputable conduct for a practitioner to render "a false opinion, knowingly, recklessly, or through gross incompetence, including an opinion that is intentionally or recklessly misleading, or a pattern of providing incompetent opinions on questions arising under the Federal tax laws." Under Reg. § 10.50, this kind of disreputable conduct is ground for disbarment from practice before the Service. Reg. § 10.51(j) is broader than Reg. §§ 10.33 and 10.52(b), since it applies to more than tax shelter opinions. Reg. § 10.51(j) provides definitions of reckless conduct and gross incompetence. Reckless conduct is defined as "highly unreasonable omission or misrepresentation, involving not merely simple or inexcusable negligence, but an extreme departure from the standards of ordinary care that is either known or is so obvious that the competent practitioner must or should be aware of it." Gross incompetence includes "conduct that reflects gross indifference, preparation that is grossly inadequate under the circumstances, and a consistent failure to perform obligations to the client."

[372] Reg. § 10.33(c)(2). A "significant" feature is not defined, but since a determination of whether the feature was intended will depend on the objective facts, evidence of the practitioner's state of mind (or perhaps that of the client) apparently will not be con-

bines an objective and a subjective test. The objective test is whether there are excess deductions or credits. The subjective test is whether these excess deductions or credits are a significant and intended feature of the investment. A tax shelter opinion is advice the practitioner gives concerning the tax aspects of a tax shelter (including the tax risks portion of offering materials) appearing or referred to in the offering materials, used in a sales promotion, and directed to persons who did not engage the practitioner to give the advice.[373] An opinion is broader than advice. Accountants and others who prepare financial forecasts or projections are considered to be rendering a tax shelter opinion if the forecast or projection is based on assumptions about the tax consequences in the transaction reflected in the tax advice.

Circular 230 imposes a requirement of due diligence in tax shelter opinions about factual matters to "[ensure] that any representations as to future activities are clearly identified, reasonable and complete."[374] A practitioner generally need not conduct an independent verification of the facts, unless he has reason to believe that the facts provided by the promoter or another person are untrue.[375] However, appraisal or projection imposes special obligations. The practitioner may not accept an appraisal or financial projection as support for the matters claimed unless it (1) "makes sense on its face"; (2) the practitioner "reasonably believes" that the appraiser or person making the financial projection is competent to do so and is not of "dubious reputation"; and (3) the appraisal is based "on the definition of fair market value prescribed under the relevant Federal tax provisions."[376] If the valuation is based on a stated purchase price, the practitioner must examine the circumstances surrounding the purchase to determine whether the stated purchase price reasonably may be considered the property's fair market value.

In addition to due diligence on factual matters, the practitioner must do the following in a tax shelter opinion:

---

sidered. The term "tax shelter" excludes municipal bonds; annuities; family trusts (but not including schemes or arrangements that are marketed to the public other than in a direct practitioner-client relationship); qualified retirement plans; individual retirement accounts; stock option plans; securities issued in a corporate reorganization; mineral development ventures, if the only tax benefit would be percentage depletion; and real estate, where it is anticipated that in no year is it likely that deductions will exceed gross income from the investment in that year or that tax credits will exceed the tax attributable to gross income from the investment in that year.

[373] Reg. § 10.33(c)(3). Thus, a tax shelter opinion is not given if neither the practitioner's name nor the practitioner's advice is referred to or used in the offering materials or sales promotion.

[374] Reg. § 10.33(a)(1)(i).

[375] Reg. § 10.33(a)(1)(ii).

[376] Reg. § 10.33(a)(1)(iii).

- Relate law to facts and, when addressing issues based on future activities, clearly identify the facts assumed.
- Identify "material issues," as specifically defined, on which there is a "reasonable possibility" of IRS challenge, and fully and fairly address these issues. A "material issue" is an income or excise tax issue whose resolution (1) would make a "significant contribution" toward providing deductions from the tax shelter investment in excess of its income (or excess credits available to offset tax on other income); (2) could have a "significant impact (either beneficial or adverse)" on a tax shelter investor under "any reasonably foreseeable circumstances"[377]; and (3) involves penalties or interest that the Service could reasonably assert with respect to the tax shelter.[378]
- Opine on each material issue that "it is more likely than not that an investor will prevail on the merits." The practitioner must give reasons for being unable to opine as to the likely outcome where a more-likely-than-not opinion cannot be given.
- Give a favorable overall evaluation where possible. The practitioner is supposed to give an evaluation that, in the aggregate, substantially more than half of the material tax benefits will be realized if the Service challenges a typical investor's tax treatment ("a favorable overall evaluation"). If a favorable overall evaluation is not made, the reasons such an evaluation cannot be made must be stated, and those reasons will be given "special scrutiny." Also, if an overall favorable evaluation cannot be made (or the opinion is that overall the material tax benefits will not be realized), this fact must be clearly and prominently disclosed in the offering materials.
- Ensure that the offering materials correctly and fairly represent the nature and extent of the tax opinion.

A practitioner could render an opinion on less than all the material tax issues ("a partial opinion") if (1) some other competent practitioner provides an opinion on the other issues and a favorable overall opinion and (2) the practitioner giving the partial opinion reviews the other opinion and (a) finds no reason to believe it does not comply with the standards for providing a tax shelter opinion and (b) with respect to the favorable overall evaluation fails to find that such an evaluation is incorrect on its face.[379]

In 1985, the Service announced that it planned strict enforcement of the standards of practice where practitioners are connected with abusive tax shelter

---

[377] The examples given are depreciation or investment credit recapture, availability of long-term capital gain treatment, or realization of tax income in excess of cash flow on the sale or other distribution of the tax shelter investment.

[378] Reg. § 10.33(c)(3).

[379] Reg. § 10.33(b).

cases.[380] It has stated that violations of the standards will be referred to the Director of Practice, as a result of which the practitioner may be disbarred or suspended from practice before the Service. Practitioners who will be considered for referral are those who have violated the requirements of Section 10.33 of Circular No. 230; those against whom penalties for promoting abusive tax shelters have been assessed; those who have been enjoined from promoting abusive tax shelters; those who have taken tax shelter losses or credits after having received a prefiling notice from the Service or have clients who have done so on the practitioner's advice; those who have been penalized for giving bad advice that created an understatement of tax; or those who have not complied with the requirements to register a tax shelter.[381] Similarly, the names of CPAs who have signed abusive tax shelter returns will be forwarded to the Director of Practice.[382]

With the condemnation of corporate tax shelters, the ABA's Tax Section proposed amendments add a new Section 10.35 to Circular 230.[383] These amendments articulated minimum standards for the "more likely than not" opinions required to avoid an understatement attributable to investment in a corporate tax shelter. Under the proposal, an opinion to be used to establish that at the time of the particular investment, the tax treatment of a tax shelter item on the taxpayer's return was "more likely than not the proper treatment" must meet each of the following requirements.

1. The practitioner must make a facts and circumstances inquiry to be sure that the practitioner has taken all of the facts and circumstances into account, and has not made any unreasonable factual assumptions. Examples of factual assumptions material to an analysis that a practitioner may not unreasonably make include (a) an assumption that the transaction had a business purpose; (b) an assumption that the transaction was profitable separate and apart from any tax benefits; (c) an assumption of fact an appraiser made in an appraisal;

2. The practitioner may rely on factual representations by persons the practitioner considers to be reliable, but only when it would be reasonable to so, based on the practitioner's prior experience with the client. If the information as represented appears incomplete, incorrect,

---

[380] IR 85-49 (May 17, 1985); see IRM 4297.9, MT 4200-538 (Dec. 22, 1986) (Referrals to the Director of Practice).

[381] The Service also said that referrals may be made to the Director of Practice regardless of whether any penalties have been assessed in connection with an abusive tax shelter case if the situation indicates that the practitioner has failed to follow the rules of practice set forth in Circular No. 230, 26 CFR pt. 10.

[382] IR 85-46 (May 15, 1985).

[383] ABA Section of Taxation, Rec. to Amend 31 CFR pt. 10, Treas. Dep't Circular 230, to Deal With "More Likely Than Not Opinions" Relating to Tax Shelter Items of Corporations (Nov. 1, 1999).

or inconsistent with other information, the practitioner must inquire further;

3. The practitioner's opinion must relate law to facts;

4. The practitioner's opinion must consider both the substance and purpose of the transaction;

5. The practitioner's opinion must identify all material tax issues;

6. The practitioner's opinion must evaluate authorities for their relevance and persuasiveness;

7. The practitioner's opinion must analyze whether the applicable legal authorities support the taxpayer's position in the manner described in the substantial authority portion of the regulations on the substantial understatement penalty.[384] In making this analysis, the practitioner may not assume the favorable resolution of any legal issue material to the analysis;

8. The practitioner's opinion must unambiguously conclude that it is more likely than not that if challenged, the tax treatment of the item would be upheld on its merits; and

9. The practitioner's "more likely than not" opinion may not rely on another person's analysis of the federal tax law, unless the other analysis is limited to a specialized tax issue with which the practitioner is not sufficiently knowledgeable to render an informed opinion, such as the issue about whether interest on a municipal bond is exempt from income tax under Section 103. If the "more likely than not" opinion is intended to provide legal justification for the treatment of the item on a tax return, it must so state, or it will be presumed not to have been intended for that purpose.

A practitioner who meets these requirements satisfies the practitioner's professional obligations, but the fact that the practitioner satisfied these obligations does not control either the substantive issues or the taxpayer's good faith reliance on the practitioner's opinion. A practitioner who recklessly or through gross incompetence violates Section 10.35 may be disbarred or suspended from practice before the Treasury Department, including the Internal Revenue Service.

Lawyers in the ABA's Tax Section commented that the practice of giving "more likely than not" opinions on corporate tax shelters should be addressed in Circular 230 to establish standards of proper practice before the Service.[385] To make the point that this activity is subject to the standards of Circular 230, these practitioners recommended amending the definition of "Practice Before

---

[384] Reg. § 1.6662-4(g)(3).

[385] ABA Tax Section, Special Projects Committee Administrative Recommendation to Amend Circular 230, to Deal With "More Likely Than Not" Opinions Relating to Tax Shelters Items of Corporation (Sept. 2, 1999).

the Internal Revenue Service"[386] to include specific reference to preparation of "more likely than not" opinions so that clients may be able to avoid penalty determinations for corporate tax shelters. At the same time, these lawyers were concerned that confidentiality agreements or restrictions covering the disclosure of opinions could conflict with standards of practice by precluding the use of the opinions as evidence of reasonable cause and good faith. Additionally, tax lawyers have discussed whether the standards of Circular 230, Section 10.33, are adequate to govern one particular feature of corporate tax shelter promotion—the so-called "pre-opinion" opinion, in which a tax practitioner provides a written analysis of the proposed tax shelter to the promoter.

On May 5, 2000, the Service and Treasury requested comments on proposed amendments to Circular 230 regarding the opinion standards of Circular 230, contingent fees, conditions of confidentiality, sanctions, and certain general issues.[387] Comments about tax opinions are requested on (1) whether the standards for opinions used in the marketing of tax shelters[388] should be revised; (2) whether Circular 230 should establish standards for opinions intended to provide legal justification for the treatment of an item under the uniform reasonable good faith and reasonable cause exception of Regulation § 1.6664-4(e); (3) whether a practitioner should be required to state in a "reasonable cause" opinion that it is provided for the purpose described in (3); (4) whether the factual due diligence standard of Section 10.33(a)(1) of Circular 230 should be applied for purposes of opinions other than those used for the marketing of tax shelters; (5) whether the factual due diligence standard should be modified to further limit the circumstances under which a practitioner can rely on factual assertions of other persons; (6) the circumstances under which a practitioner giving an opinion may rely on hypothetical facts, including assumptions about a business purpose for claiming the intended tax benefits of a transaction; (7) whether Circular 230 should be amended to require that a transaction be analyzed under all applicable judicial doctrines, such as the sham transaction doctrine; and (8) whether an opinion should be required to represent that there is a greater than 50 percent likelihood that the taxpayer will prevail on each material tax issue and receive the material tax benefits in the aggregate.[389]

---

[386] Circular 230, § 10.2(e).

[387] TD 9011 (July 25, 2002) (regulations governing practice before the Service).

[388] Circular 230, § 10.33.

[389] Ann. 2000-51, 2000-22 IRB 1142 (May 30, 2000) (Section III(A) concerning requests for comments on opinion standards).

¶ 1.12 FINAL REGULATIONS CIRCULAR 230

On July 25, 2002, the Treasury published final regulations comprising Circular 230, in the Federal Register.[390] This was after three advance notices of proposed rulemaking requesting comments on revisions to Circular 230.[391] The changes cover:

- Who may practice before the Service;
- Procedures about enrollment to practice;
- Information to be furnished;
- Responsibilities of practitioners with knowledge of a client's omission;
- Practitioners' responsibility for diligence as to accuracy;
- The prohibition of assistance from disbarred or suspended persons;
- Practice by partners of government employees;
- Practice by former government employees and their partners and associates;
- Return of client records;
- Conflicts of interest;
- Solicitation;
- Negotiation of taxpayer checks;
- Practitioners' obligations in giving tax shelter opinions used by third parties to market tax shelters;
- "More likely than not" tax shelter opinions;
- Procedures to ensure compliance; and
- Sanctions of persons authorized to practice for violations of standards of practice.

[1] Rules Governing Authority to Practice

The final regulations expand the list of issues on which an enrolled actuary is authorized to represent a taxpayer before the Service. The expanded list of areas of representation includes the following:

- The treatment of funded welfare benefits;
- Qualified asset accounts;
- Transfers of excess pension assets to retiree health accounts;
- Tax on nondeductible contributions to qualified employer plans;
- Taxes with respect to funded welfare benefit plans; and

---

[390] TD 9011 (July 25, 2002) (regulations governing practice before the Service).

[391] See 64 Fed. Reg. 31,994 (June 15, 1999) (requesting comments on legal developments, professional integrity and fairness to practitioners, taxpayer service, and sound tax administration).

• Tax on reversion of qualified plan assets to employers.[392]

Also for enrolled actuaries, the final regulations add a new section providing that the enrollment and renewal of enrollment of actuaries is governed by the regulations of the Joint Board for the Enrollment of Actuaries.[393]

The final regulations also modify the continuing education requirements of Circular 230. The new regulations provide that a course may qualify as a continuing professional education course if the course requires suitable electronic education materials, a written outline, or a textbook.[394]

[2] Duties and Restrictions Relating to Practice Before the Internal Revenue Service

The 2002 version of Circular 230 modifies the rule governing a practitioners' responsibility in responding to information requests made by the Service. Before, there were no exceptions to the requirement that a practitioner must respond to a document or information request. By contrast, the final regulations state that a practitioner must respond to an information request by providing the information "unless the practitioner believes in good faith and on reasonable grounds that the records or information are privileged." However, if the information is not in the possession of either the practitioner or the practitioner's client, the practitioner must notify the Service and "provide any information that either the practitioner or the practitioner's client has regarding the identity of any person who may have possession or control of the requested records or information."[395]

Circular 230 previously required a practitioner to notify a client of any noncompliance, error, or omission under the internal revenue laws. Under the final regulations, however, the practitioner would also be required to advise the client of corrective actions and the possible consequences of not taking corrective action.[396]

The changes to Circular 230 also clarify a practitioner's due diligence requirements. The proposed regulations required a practitioner to exercise due diligence in the preparation or assistance in the preparation of, approving and filing of documents relating to, IRS matters. The final regulations allow a practitioner to meet the due diligence requirements if the practitioner relied on "the work product of another person and the practitioner used reasonable care in engaging supervising, training, and evaluating the person, taking proper ac-

---

[392] Circular 230, § 10.3(d)(2).

[393] Circular 230, § 10.6(o).

[394] Circular 230, § 10.6(f)(2)(i)(C).

[395] Circular 230, § 10.20(a).

[396] Circular 230, § 10.21.

count of the nature of the relationship between the practitioner and the person."[397]

The final regulations also address the rules governing assistance from disbarred or suspended persons. Under the former version of Circular 230, a practitioner may not accept assistance from a person under disbarment or suspension. The final regulations clarify that a practitioner is prohibited from accepting the assistance of such a person if the assistance relates to matters constituting practice before the Service. The final Circular 230 regulations address concerns that practitioners would be required to expel another partner on the basis that the disciplined partners would share in fees derived from practice before the Service.[398]

Following the repeal of 18 USC § 207(c), the final regulations revoked Section 10.25, which precludes partners of former government employees from practice in matters in which the employee personally and substantially participated.[399]

The final regulations modify the rules concerning the use of contingent fees. Section 10.28(b) precludes contingent fees for the preparation of an original tax return. The amendment prohibits practitioners from charging contingent fees for advice rendered in connection with a position taken or to be taken on an original tax return.[400] However, the amendment permits a practitioner to charge a contingent fee for preparation of, and for advice rendered in connection with, an amended return or a claim for refund "if the practitioner reasonably anticipates at the time the fee arrangement is entered into that the amended tax return or refund claim will receive substantive review by the Service."[401] The final regulations would also define a contingent fee to include fees that are based "on whether or not a position taken on a tax return or refund claim is sustained by the Service or in litigation. A contingent fee includes an indemnity agreement, a guarantee, rescission rights, insurance, or "any other arrangement under which the taxpayer or other person would be entitled to be compensated or reimbursed by the practitioner in the event a position taken on a tax return or in a refund claim is not sustained, or any other arrangement that has a similar effect."[402] Section 10.28 requires a practitioner to promptly return all client records at the request of the client, regardless of whether a fee dispute exists between the practitioner and the client. The practitioner may retain a copy of the records.[403]

---

[397] Circular 230, § 10.22(b).

[398] Circular 230, § 10.24(a).

[399] Explanation of Provisions, TD 9011 (July 25, 2002).

[400] Circular 230, § 10.27(b).

[401] Circular 230, § 10.27(b).

[402] Circular 230, § 10.27(b).

[403] Circular 230, § 10.29.

Previously, practitioners were prohibited from representing conflicting interests before the Service unless the practitioner obtained consent from the interested parties. The final regulations clarify the former rules concerning conflicts of interest. In response to written comments, the final regulations provide that any consent must be in writing. The regulations require that the practitioner maintain the written consents for at least thirty-six months and produce the consents if requested by the Service. The final regulations further provide that a practitioner may not represent a party before the Service "if the representation of the party may be materially limited by the practitioner's own interests unless the practitioner reasonably believes the representation will not be adversely affected and the client consents after the practitioner has fully disclosed the potential conflict, including disclosure of the implications of the potential conflict and the risks involved."[404]

Rules concerning solicitation of potential clients are modified. The final regulations expand the current prohibitions on deceptive solicitation to include both private and public solicitations. The regulations also expand the definition of "communication" to include electronic mail, facsimile, and hand-delivered flyers.[405]

Section 10.31 of the final regulations clarifies the rules prohibiting negotiation of taxpayer refund checks to include all checks issued to a client concerning internal revenue matters. Previously, the rule was limited to refund checks for income taxes.[406]

[3] Tax Shelter Opinions

The most noteworthy final changes to Circular 230 are those dealing with tax shelter opinions. The final regulations address two types of tax shelter opinions: (1) opinions used by third parties to market tax shelters and (2) "more likely than not" tax shelter opinions. Treasury and the Service intend to "modify the advice standards in the regulations under section 6662 of the Internal Revenue Code . . . and under section 6664 of the Internal Revenue Code . . . to provide that opinions can satisfy those standards only if such opinions satisfy the standards of Circular 230."[407]

---

[404] Circular 230, § 10.29.
[405] Circular 230, § 10.30.
[406] Circular 230, § 10.31.
[407] Explanation of Provisions, TD 9011 (July 25, 2002).

[a] Opinions Used by Third Parties to Market Tax Shelters

Section 10.33 of the final regulations (1) governs tax shelter opinions that do not conclude that the federal tax treatment of a tax shelter item or items[408] is more likely than not the proper treatment[409]; (2) provides rules for tax shelter opinions prepared for use by third parties, regardless of whether promotional efforts are conducted publicly or privately are also covered[410]; and (3) modifies the definition of a material federal tax issue. A material federal tax issue is defined as "any Federal tax issue the resolution of which could have a significant impact . . . on a taxpayer under any reasonably foreseeable circumstance. A Federal tax issue is also material if it includes the potential applicability of penalties, additions to tax, or interest charges that reasonably could be asserted by the Internal Revenue Service with respect to the tax shelter item."[411]

The practitioner who provides a tax shelter opinion under the final regulations is required to comply with several requirements for each tax shelter item or items. The practitioner is required to

1. Inquire into all relevant facts and not base the opinion on any unreasonable factual assumptions;
2. Clearly identify the facts on which the opinion's conclusions are based and not rely on any unreasonable legal assumptions;
3. Ascertain that all material federal tax issues have been considered and fairly addressed;
4. Clearly provide, where possible, a conclusion as to the likelihood that a typical investor will prevail on the merits with respect to each material federal tax issue;
5. Provide, where possible, an overall conclusion as to the likelihood that the federal tax treatment of the tax shelter item or items is the proper treatment; and
6. Take reasonable steps to assure that any written materials or promotional efforts correctly and fairly represent the nature and extent of the opinion.[412]

These requirements are similar to those in the former regulations, but the former regulations did not contain a provision requiring the practitioner to take

---

[408] A tax shelter item is "an item of income, gain, loss, deduction or credit if the item is directly or indirectly attributable to a tax shelter as defined in section 6662(d)(2)(C)(iii) of the Internal Revenue Code." Circular 230, § 10.33(c)(3).

[409] Circular 230, § 10.33(a).

[410] Explanation of Provisions, TD 9011 (July 25, 2002).

[411] Circular 230, § 10.33(c)(5).

[412] Circular 230, §§ 10.33(a)(1)–10.33(a)(6).

reasonable steps to assure that any written materials or promotional efforts correctly and fairly represent the nature and extent of the opinion.

In addition, the final regulations require that a practitioner "must be knowledgeable in all of the aspects of Federal tax law relevant to the opinion being rendered." The practitioner generally is required to render an opinion that clearly provides a conclusion "as to the likelihood that a typical investor of the type to whom the tax shelter is or will be marketed will prevail on the merits with respect to each material Federal tax issue that involves the reasonable possibility of a challenge" by the Service.[413]

[b] "More Likely Than Not" Tax Shelter Opinions

Under the final regulations a practitioner who provides a written tax shelter opinion that concludes that the federal tax treatment of a tax shelter item or items is more likely than not (or a higher level of confidence) the proper treatment must comply with a series of requirements for each such item. These requirements are similar to those for marketed tax shelter opinions described above. Under the final regulations, the practitioner must

1. Inquire into all relevant facts and not base the opinion on any unreasonable factual assumptions;
2. Clearly identify the facts on which the opinion's conclusions are based and not rely on any unreasonable legal assumptions;
3. Ascertain that all material federal tax issues have been considered and fairly addressed;
4. Clearly provide a conclusion as to the likelihood that a typical investor will prevail on the merits with respect to each material federal tax issue; and
5. Take reasonable steps to assure that any written materials or promotional efforts correctly and fairly represent the nature and extent of the opinion.[414]

Also, a practitioner who renders an opinion must "be knowledgeable in all of the aspects of Federal tax law relevant to the opinion being rendered." "[If] not sufficiently knowledgeable to render an informed opinion with respect to particular material Federal tax issues," the practitioner is permitted to rely on the opinion of another practitioner with respect to such issues.[415] However, if a practitioner relies on the opinion of another practitioner, the practitioner's

---

[413] Circular 230, § 10.33(b)(1)(i).

[414] Circular 230, §§ 10.35(a)(1)–10.35(a)(5).

[415] Circular 230, § 10.35(b).

opinion must identify the other practitioner, state the date the other opinion was rendered, and state the conclusions reached in the other opinion.[416]

[c] Procedures to Assure Compliance by the Practitioner's Firm

The final regulations provide that a practitioner who is a member of, associated with, or employed by a firm "must take reasonable steps, consistent with his or her authority and responsibility for the firm's practice advising clients regarding matters arising under the Federal tax laws, to make certain that the firm has adequate procedures in effect" to comply with the proposed tax shelter opinion regulations.[417]

Disciplinary action may be taken against any practitioner if the practitioner "through willfulness, recklessness, or gross incompetence does not take such reasonable steps and the practitioner and one or more persons who are members of, associated with, or employed by the firm have, in connection with the practice with the firm, engaged in a pattern or practice of failing to comply" with the tax shelter opinion regulations.[418]

The rules also warn that disciplinary action may also be taken against a practitioner even if the practitioner has personally taken reasonable steps, "but [the practitioner] has actual knowledge that (1) one or more persons who are members of, associated with, or employed by the firm have engaged in a pattern or practice of failing to comply [with the tax shelter opinion regulations] and (2) the practitioner, through willfulness, recklessness, or gross incompetence, fails to take prompt action, consistent with the practitioner's authority and responsibility for the firm's practice advising clients regarding matters under the federal tax laws, to correct such pattern or practice."[419]

[4] Sanctions for Violation of the Regulations

Circular 230 formerly authorized the Secretary of the Treasury, after notice and opportunity for proceeding, to suspend or disbar any practitioner from practice before the Service. These actions could be taken if the practitioner (1) was shown to be incompetent or disreputable[420]; (2) refused to comply with

---

[416] Circular 230, § 10.35(b).

[417] Circular 230, § 10.36.

[418] Circular 230, § 10.36.

[419] Circular 230, § 10.36.

[420] The final regulations also modify the definition of "disreputable conduct" to include conviction of any felony "for which the conduct involved renders the practitioner unfit to practice before the Internal Revenue Service." Circular 230, § 10.51(c).

any regulation in [Circular 230]; or (3) with intent to defraud, willfully and knowingly misled or threatened a client or prospective client.[421]

The final regulations permit the Secretary, after notice and opportunity for a proceeding, to censure a practitioner. A censure is a public reprimand for purposes of the regulations. If the practitioner is censured, the practitioner will be permitted to practice before the Service, but future representations "may be subject to conditions prescribed by the Director of Practice designed to promote high standards of conduct."[422]

[5] Rules Applicable to Disciplinary Proceedings

In addition, the final regulations modify the procedures for institution of a suspension or disbarment proceeding including service of the complaint,[423] the answers,[424] a reply to the answers,[425] and motions and requests.[426] The final regulations permit a practitioner to consent to voluntary suspension to prevent the institution of a disbarment proceeding.[427]

Furthermore, while the former regulations prohibited a disbarred practitioner from practicing before the Service until authorized to do so by the Director of Practice, the final regulations permit the Director of Practice to make a practitioner's future representation "subject to conditions prescribed by the Director of Practice designed to promote high standards of conduct."[428]

The final regulations also expand the Director of Practice's ability to suspend a practitioner who has been convicted of a crime. The regulations expand the list of crimes to include any crime under the Code, any crime involving dishonesty or breach of trust, or any felony that involved conduct that renders the practitioner unfit to practice before the Service.[429]

---

[421] Circular 230, § 10.50.
[422] Circular 230, § 10.50.
[423] Circular 230, § 10.63.
[424] Circular 230, § 10.64.
[425] Circular 230, § 10.66.
[426] Circular 230, § 10.68.
[427] Circular 230, § 10.61.
[428] Circular 230, § 10.79.
[429] Circular 230, § 10.82.

¶ 1.13 RESTRICTIONS ON APPRAISERS

Appraisers against whom a penalty for aiding and abetting an understatement of tax has been assessed can be disbarred from practice before the Service or Treasury.[430] Under proposed regulations, the Director of Practice may institute disqualification proceedings.[431] If the appraiser is disqualified (after complaints, hearing, and appeal to the Secretary of the Treasury), appraisals made by the appraiser have no probative value in proceedings before the Service and the Treasury, and the disqualified appraiser is debarred from testifying in an administrative proceeding even if the testimony pertains to a predisqualification appraisal.[432] Although a disqualified appraiser's appraisal has no evidentiary weight in an administrative proceeding to prove value, it can be used to establish the taxpayer's good faith.

¶ 1.14 DISCIPLINARY PROCEEDINGS: DISBARMENT AND SUSPENSION FROM PRACTICE

The Secretary of the Treasury has the power to disbar or suspend any person recognized to practice before the Service who (1) is shown to be incompetent or disreputable; (2) refuses to comply with the rules and regulations in Circular No. 230; or (3) with intent to defraud willfully and knowingly deceives, misleads, or threatens a prospective client by oral or written solicitation.[433] There are ten examples of disreputable conduct for which a representative may be disbarred or suspended:[434]

1. Conviction of any tax crime or a crime involving dishonesty or a breach of trust[435]
2. Knowingly giving false or misleading information to the Service in a matter currently or to be pending before the Service

---

[430] For a description of penalties imposed for valuation over-and understatements, see proposed amendments to 31 CFR pt. 10, filed with the Federal Register February 19, 1985.

[431] See ¶ 7B.02[4].

[432] See infra ¶ 1.14.

[433] The Secretary of the Treasury has the authority, after notice and hearing, to suspend or disbar any practitioner from appearing before the Service. 31 USC § 330(b). Circular 230, § 10.50 (1994), sets forth the grounds for suspension and disbarment.

[434] Circular 230, § 10.51.

[435] See Washburn v. Shapiro, 409 F. Supp. 3 (SD Fla. 1976).

3. Soliciting employment[436]
4. Willful failure to file a tax return, tax evasion, or participating in any way in evading or attempting to evade a tax for the representative or a client
5. Misappropriation of or failure to remit properly and promptly funds received from a client for payment of tax and other federal obligations
6. Bribery of IRS officials[437]
7. Disbarment or suspension from practice as an attorney, CPA, or public accountant by a state
8. Assisting a disbarred or suspended person in practicing before the IRS
9. Contemptuous conduct[438]
10. Giving a false tax opinion, knowingly, recklessly, or through incompetence, an opinion that is intentionally or recklessly misleading, or a pattern of providing incompetent opinions on tax questions[439]

In addition, a person recognized to practice may be disbarred or suspended for willful violation of any of the regulations contained in Circular 230, including, presumably, the standards of and restrictions on practice.[440]

If Service personnel have reason to believe that a person admitted to practice or any other person has information of violation of the rules of Circular 230, a report is made to the Director of Practice in the Treasury Department, on the basis of which the Director may reprimand or commence disbarment or suspension proceedings.[441] Generally, however, a proceeding is not commenced until the person involved is notified of the facts and the conduct that is the

---

[436] See Pollack v. Kurtz, 80-1 USTC ¶ 9117 (DDC 1979) (unenrolled preparer of returns suspended for solicitation).

[437] See Harary v. Blumenthal, 555 F2d 1113 (2d Cir. 1977) (conviction reversed on appeal held to constitute a conviction for disbarment purposes).

[438] Circular 230, § 10.51(i).

[439] Circular 230, § 10.51(j). It is worth noting that for purposes of suspension or disbarment for disreputable conduct, "reckless conduct" means a highly unreasonable omission or misrepresentation that is an extreme departure from the standards of ordinary care a practitioner should follow under the circumstances; a pattern of misconduct will be a factor in the determination.

[440] Circular 230, §10.51(j).

[441] Circular 230, §§ 10.53, 10.54. Once a referral is received, a staff attorney, the field agent, and the Director of Practice review the case to determine if there has been a violation of Circular 230. If the Director decides that there has been such a violation, the Director notifies the practitioner and allows the practitioner to present evidence to refute the allegation. If, after considering the submission, the Director still believes that a violation has occurred, the procedures for formal proceedings, described below, are followed, unless the sanction to be imposed is a reprimand rather than the more serious disciplinary actions of suspension or disbarment.

subject of the complaint.[442] The Director may, but is not required to, offer the person a conference, at which he has the opportunity to convince the Director that no violation has occurred or to consent to a voluntary suspension or resignation, which the Director may, but again is not required to, accept.[443] After the conference (if it is offered), the Director may reprimand the representative, accept the offer of consent to voluntary suspension or resignation, or proceed to file a complaint commencing the disciplinary proceedings.

Formal proceedings are heard by a hearing examiner. After the filing of an answer, motions, trial, and submission of proposed findings, the hearing examiner makes findings of fact and law and an appropriate order for filing with the Director of Practice.[444] Appeal must be filed with the Secretary of the Treasury within thirty days after the decision, but in any event, the Secretary will make the agency's decision.[445]

A disbarred or suspended person may not practice before the Service until reinstated or the period of suspension expires, and notice of disbarment or sus-

---

Periodically, the Director of Practice issues a summary of cases illustrating practitioner actions that violate Circular 230. These actions describe situations where practitioners gave false information to the IRS auditor, acted contemptuously in dealing with an IRS revenue officer, failed to act with due diligence, and failed to advise a client to correct an erroneous return after discovering that the basis for preparing the original return was erroneous.

[442] Circular 230, § 10.54.

[443] Circular 230, § 10.55. This procedure has been held to satisfy the requirements of procedural due process because the practitioner is given notice and an opportunity for a hearing. Ekanem v. IRS, 81 AFTR2d 98-1173 (D. Md. 1998). In *Ekanem*, the practitioner, who was an authorized electronic filer, was suspended for having accepted returns for electronic filing from a paid preparer, rather than directly from the taxpayer, and for having signed a form as the taxpayer's paid preparer, both acts being in violation of Rev. Proc. 96-61, 1996-2 CB 401. He received notice of the suspension and a statement of the grounds for the suspension, and his appeal was denied by the Director of Practice. The practitioner then brought an action claiming that he had been denied due process. The district court noted that the action was not brought as an action for judicial review as provided in Section 706 of the Administrative Procedure Act, but in a constitutional form. Procedural due process required that notice precede a hearing and that a hearing precede administrative action, but the practitioner did not allege, nor did the record show, that he had not been given notice or an opportunity for a hearing. The court held that the analysis is the same whether a due process or a statutory challenge to an agency's action is made. In either case, a court must review "whether the agency decision was procedurally arbitrary and capricious, in the sense of not having been the product of the process required by law and regulation, and/or whether it was substantively arbitrary and capricious, i.e., not based on consideration of relevant factors, or manifesting a clear error of judgment." Although the court believed that suspension for several years was "rather harsh," it observed that arbitrary and capricious review "does not constitute trial de novo or an opportunity for the court to substitute its judgment for that of the administrator."

[444] Circular 230, §§ 10.56–10.70.

[445] Circular 230, §§ 10.71, 10.72.

pension is given not only to Service personnel but also to other federal and state authorities. Notices of disbarment or suspension are published in the Internal Revenue Bulletin.[446] Circular 230 also affects nonpractitioners who are not permitted to practice before the Service, if they prepare returns and engage in limited practice before the Service by representing the taxpayers whose returns they prepared. Any nonpractitioner who is under suspension or disbarment from practice before the Service is prohibited from engaging in limited practice before the Service.[447] Similarly, there are procedures to expedite a practitioner's suspension or disbarment because the practitioner has been convicted of certain crimes in a state or federal court, or because the practitioner's license to practice law or accounting has been suspended for cause, that is, for misconduct, by a state licensing authority.[448] This expedited procedure can be used against any practitioner who, within the previous five years, has been convicted of Title 26 and Title 18 crimes involving dishonesty or breach of trust, or has had his or her license suspended or revoked. Under these accelerated procedures, after a complaint is filed against the practitioner, and after the practitioner files a timely answer requesting a conference, the practitioner will be accorded to a conference with the Director of Practice. After the conference, the Director may suspend or disbar the practitioner. The practitioner still has the right to a formal hearing before an administrative law judge.

---

[446] Circular 230, § 10.74.

[447] Circular 230, § 10.7(c)(2)(i) (1994).

[448] Circular 230, § 10.76.

CHAPTER **2**

Taxpayer Access to Information

¶ 2.01 INTRODUCTION

As an "agency" of the federal government, the Internal Revenue Service is generally required to follow the administrative procedures set forth by the Administrative Procedure Act for all federal agencies.[1] Two of these Administrative Procedure Act provisions are the Freedom of Information Act (FOIA) and the related Privacy Act. Both give taxpayers rights of access to Internal Revenue Service records and documents.[2] Before the FOIA was enacted in 1966, disclosure of information was left to the discretion of administrative agencies themselves and, as a result, disclosures of information to the public were limited, generally based on the requester's need to know the information.[3]

In 1966, Congress enacted the FOIA to implement "a general philosophy of full agency disclosure."[4] To prevent agencies from restricting public access to information by using a "need to know" standard, the FOIA "establishes a presumption that records in the possession of agencies [such as the Service] and departments of the executive branch of the U.S. Government are accessible to the people."[5] The FOIA "seeks to permit access to official information long shielded unnecessarily from public view and attempts to create a judicially enforceable public right to secure such information from unwilling official hands."[6]

While the philosophy underlying the 1966 FOIA changes was to provide full agency disclosure, the FOIA also recognizes the legitimate needs of agencies to restrict disclosure of some information. This recognition is reflected in statutory exemptions from disclosure. The FOIA's exemptions are not intended to detract from the its objective of providing "the fullest possible disclosure of information to the public,"[7] unless information is exempted under clearly delineated statutory language.[8] Accordingly, courts have generally considered the

---

[1] The Service is an "agency" because it is an "authority of the Government of the United States, whether or not it is subject to review by another agency . . . " 5 USC § 551(1). The status of the Service as an agency for purposes of the Administrative Procedure Act was examined in Chapter 1, ¶ 1.03.

[2] 5 USC § 552 (the Freedom of Information Act), and 5 USC § 552a (the Privacy Act).

[3] Committee on Government Reform and Oversight, A Citizens Guide on Using the Freedom of Information Act and the Privacy Act of 1974 to Request Government Records, HR Rep. 105-37, 105th Cong., 1st Sess. (Mar. 20, 1997) at 3 (hereafter "Citizens Guide").

[4] Dep't of Air Force v. Rose, 425 US 352, 360 (1976), quoting S. Rep. No. 813, 89th Cong., 1st Sess. 3 (1965).

[5] Citizens Guide, at 2–3.

[6] EPA v. Mink, 410 US 73, 80 (1973).

[7] Citizens Guide at 3.

[8] Dept. of Air Force v. Rose, 425 US 352, 360 (1976).

FOIA's basic purpose both in developing standards for applying the exemptions and in determining, under the exemptions, those records the agency must disclose and those that the agency may withhold.

The Privacy Act of 1974 is a companion provision that complements the FOIA, and regulates the Service's recordkeeping and disclosure practices. In 1974, Congress "was concerned with curbing the illegal surveillance and investigation of individuals by the federal agencies that had been exposed during the Watergate scandals; [Congress] was also concerned with potential abuses presented by the government's increasing use of computers to store and retrieve personal data by means of a universal identifier—such as an individual's social security number."[9] The Privacy Act establishes "fair information practices" that require, for example, the Service to (1) maintain in its records only such information "about an individual that is relevant and necessary to accomplish a purpose of the agency required by statute;"[10] (2) "collect information to the greatest extent practicable directly from the [taxpayer];"[11] and (3) maintain the records it uses in making a determination about a taxpayer "with such accuracy, relevance, timeliness and completeness as is reasonably necessary to assure fairness to the individual in the determination."[12]

The Privacy Act also restricts both the Service's disclosure of personally identifiable information in the records it maintains and the use of information collected for one purpose from being used for another. An individual taxpayer may request access to the Service's records about the taxpayer and may challenge the accuracy of the information.[13] Civil remedies are provided for individuals whose rights have been violated[14]; however, a taxpayer is prohibited from using the Privacy Act to amend records the Service may maintain about the taxpayer's tax liability or from using the Act to obtain administrative and judicial review of a refusal to correct a record.[15]

---

[9] See also U.S. Dep't of Justice, Freedom of Information Act & Privacy Act Overview (Sept. 1996 ed.) p. 543.

[10] 5 USC § 552a(e)(1).

[11] 5 USC § 552a(e)(2).

[12] 5 USC § 552a(e)(5).

[13] 5 USC § 552a(d).

[14] 5 USC § 552a(g).

[15] Section 7852(e) limits the rights of individual taxpayers to use the Privacy Act by prohibiting the use of the Privacy Act to request amendment of a record determining "the existence, or possible existence of liability (or the amount thereof) . . . for any tax, penalty, interest, fine, forfeiture, or other imposition or offense to which the provisions of the [Code] apply."

[1] Use of the FOIA and Privacy Act in Tax Practice

Both the FOIA and the Privacy Act can be used in tax practice in real and practical ways. However, their use is hedged by provisions in the Code and other federal laws. Since the FOIA reflects "a general philosophy of full agency disclosure unless information is exempted under clearly delineated statutory language,"[16] it permits any person (including a taxpayer who may be, is, or will be the subject of some action by the Service) to obtain a wide range of information from the Service as a matter of right. The taxpayer or other person does not have to demonstrate any need to know; in fact, the Service must justify any claimed need for secrecy to withhold information.[17]

The Privacy Act also permits taxpayers to obtain access to information the Service maintains about them, but the Privacy Act's focus is different from the FOIA's. The Privacy Act is concerned with ways in which a federal agency, such as the Service gathers, maintains, and discloses information it obtains from taxpayers, and imposes fairness standards that limit the way in which the Service gathers and maintains information. As long as the taxpayer does not use the Privacy Act to circumvent the Code's normal dispute resolution procedures for determining the taxpayer's tax liability, the taxpayer may persuade the Service to amend or correct a record in a system of records; it should be noted, however, that the taxpayer may not institute a civil action if the Service refuses to amend or correct the record.[18]

The FOIA has played a dramatic role in opening to public view the Service's operations and the body of working law (or, as it is sometimes called, "secret working law") the Service applies in issuing letter rulings and technical advice. FOIA litigation led to the Service's making available to the public most of the Internal Revenue Manual, which describes the procedures that Service personnel are required to follow in the performance of their duties,[19] as well as private letter rulings and technical advice memoranda.[20] In a number of

---

[16] Dep't of Air Force v. Rose, 425 US 352, 360–361 (1976) (internal quotation marks omitted); see also EPA v. Mink, 410 US 73, 79–80 (1973).

[17] See 5 USC §§ 552(a)(3)(A), 552(a)(4)(B).

[18] IRC § 7852(e) exempts the Service from Privacy Act civil actions to compel amendment of tax records.

[19] See 5 USC § 552(a)(2)(C); Hawkes v. IRS, 467 F2d 787 (6th Cir. 1972) (relying on the requirement of 5 USC § 552(a)(2)(C) that the Manual be made available in reading rooms to hold that the Service must prove the applicability of an exemption before withholding any portion of the Manual); Long v. IRS, 339 F. Supp. 1266 (WD Wash. 1971) (IRS motion to dismiss request to see the Manual denied).

[20] Tax Analysts & Advocates v. IRS, 362 F. Supp. 1298 (DDC 1973), modified in part and remanded, 505 F2d 350 (DC Cir. 1974) (*Tax Analysts & Advocates I*); Tax Analysts & Advocates v. IRS, 405 F. Supp. 1065 (DDC 1975) (*Tax Analysts & Advocates II*); Fruehauf Corp. v. IRS, 369 F. Supp. 108 (ED Mich. 1974), aff'd in part, rev'd in part, 522 F2d 284 (6th Cir. 1975), rev'd and remanded, 429 US 1085 (1977), on remand, 566

instances, FOIA victories have been followed by legislation incorporating case law into statutory procedures. In response to FOIA decisions holding that private rulings should be made public, Congress decided in 1976 to provide comprehensive guidelines for the disclosure of letter rulings and technical advice.[21] As a result, public inspection of rulings, technical advice memoranda, determination letters, and related background files may be obtained only under the rules and procedures of Section 6110, and not under the FOIA. Similarly, courts have ordered the Service to release general counsel memoranda, technical memoranda, and actions on decisions,[22] as well as the legal analysis and conclusions of law contained in field service advice memoranda prepared by the Chief Counsel's office in specific cases.[23] After the circuit court's decision in *Tax Analysts*, rejecting the Service's grounds for withholding access to field service advice, the IRS Restructuring and Reform Act of 1998 seems to foreclose future attempts by the Service to withhold from public view legal advice issues to the field, which Service personnel, including Chief Counsel attorneys, use as a body of "secret working law." Under Section 6110(i), the Service must disclose all Chief Counsel advice (i.e., written advice or instructions under whatever name prepared by the Chief Counsel's office that is issued to the field or service center employees, or regional or district counsel attorneys, and that conveys any legal interpretation of a revenue provision, Service or Chief Counsel position concerning a revenue matter or any legal interpretation of any law relating to the assessment or collection of any liability under a revenue provision).[24] Various deletion procedures are provided to ensure, among other things, that taxpayer return information is not disclosed.

While both the FOIA and the Privacy Act provide access to Service records, several Code provisions sometimes supersede or at least work at cross-purposes with these Acts when the Code provisions restrict the nature or extent of the information the Service is permitted to disclose. To protect the privacy of taxpayers' tax return information, Section 6103 establishes a general rule of confidentiality for returns and return information and also prohibits disclosure of such information for any reason, except in those situations that Sec-

---

F2d 574 (6th Cir. 1977). In *Fruehauf*, the Sixth Circuit held that portions of technical advice memoranda were not within the exemption of Section 6103, and thus were open to inspection and copying to the extent "intended for issuance to taxpayers," but the District of Columbia Circuit held in *Tax Analysts & Advocates I* that technical advice memoranda written in conjunction with income tax returns were exempt from disclosure under FOIA by reason of the return confidentiality rules of the Code (IRC §§ 6103, 7213).

[21] IRC § 6110.

[22] Taxation With Representation Fund v. IRS, 646 F2d 666 (DC Cir. 1981).

[23] Tax Analysts v. IRS, 117 F3d 607 (DC Cir. 1997).

[24] IRC § 6110(i), as amended by the Act § 3509, applicable to Chief Counsel advice issued more than ninety days after July 22, 1998, but the amendment applies to Chief Counsel advice issued after December 31, 1985, at specified intervals.

tion 6103 itself specifically describes. While Section 6103 generally provides for the Service's disclosure to taxpayers of their own tax returns and return information, it also gives the Service the discretion to refuse to disclose return information to a taxpayer if the disclosure would "seriously impair Federal tax administration."[25] The "seriously impair" language itself suggests that discretionary nondisclosure would be limited to the rare or extraordinary case, nevertheless, the Service has contended in FOIA cases involving taxpayers' requests for their own return information that such information is exempt from disclosure because Exemption 3 of the FOIA incorporates Section 6103, including its discretionary nondisclosure provision.[26]

Similarly, while the FOIA establishes a right to full disclosure of information maintained by the Service, Section 6110 provides the exclusive method for obtaining access to the Service's interpretations of law rulings, determination letters, and technical advice memoranda. As a result, Section 5110 supersedes the FOIA in order to avoid disclosing the confidential taxpayer return information that Section 6103 protects. Also, as described above Section 7852(e) prohibits the use of the Privacy Act to correct a Service record reflecting the determination of a taxpayer's tax liability. Other federal law may adversely affect a taxpayer's ability to obtain records under the FOIA and Privacy Act. Both the FOIA and the Privacy Act assume that an agency will have procedures in place that make the information sought under the FOIA readily available for inspection. Where record retention is involved, however, there is an interplay between the FOIA and other federal law regarding an agency's retention of records. The Federal Records Act[27] requires the Service to prepare disposition schedules for its records and to submit these schedules to the National Archives and Records Administration for approval. The Administration reviews the records for their historical value, provides assistance

---

[25] IRC § 6103(c). Section 6103(c) permits the Service to disclose tax return information to the taxpayer or the taxpayer's delegate, but also gives the Service the discretion to withhold information if disclosure would "seriously impair tax administration."

[26] 5 USC § 552(b)(3). For a discussion of this exemption, see infra ¶ 2.03[2]. See, e.g., Chamberlain v. Kurtz, 589 F2d 827 (5th Cir. 1979), cert. denied, 444 US 842 (1979) (taxpayer's request for his tax return information denied); Branch Ministries, Inc. v. Richardson, 970 F. Supp. 11 (DDC 1997) (when a church claimed that the Service improperly revoked its tax-exempt status, the church requested discovery of information about the investigation on the ground that the information was its own tax return information; the court rejected the Service's contention that disclosure of information about the investigation of the church was discretionary on the ground that the Service had not determined that providing the church with its own return information would seriously impair federal tax administration disclosure under Section 6103(c)).

[27] Federal Records Act of 1950, 44 USC chs. 21, 29, 33.

to agencies in their records management programs, and promulgates and administers regulations on federal records.[28]

Despite its limitations, taxpayers and others can use the FOIA in tax practice in several ways, including the following:

- To gain access to facts obtained by agents to support their adjustments and other determinations (e.g., any statement made by a taxpayer and, in limited cases, even the opinions of the agent or other IRS employee)
- To obtain legal memoranda IRS personnel used for an interpretation of law applicable in a particular case (e.g., General Counsel memoranda, actions on decision,[29] and field service advice)[30]
- To obtain information enabling taxpayers to discover how Service personnel are supposed to conduct themselves in order to ensure that their actions are in accordance with Service guidelines set forth in revenue procedures, the Internal Revenue Manual, and other statements the Service uses to control its personnel in performing some administrative act
- To shed more light on the background of legislation or regulations and other agency statements of position (e.g., the meaning of terms and the manner in which Congress or the Treasury meant them to apply)

These are by no means the only uses to which the FOIA may be put in dealing with the IRS. Requests for information are dictated by the particular needs of the taxpayer or requestor. The Service has broad authority to summon information from the taxpayer and third parties that "may be relevant" to its tax determination and collection functions.[31] In this way, the Service is able to gain access to a taxpayer's own records, as well as the records of third parties. With all its limitations, the FOIA is practically the only statutory mechanism available during the administrative processing of a case that allows a taxpayer to obtain pre-trial discovery. Although such mechanism does not equal the Service's summons power, it nevertheless permits taxpayers some access to the information gathered by the Service or the law it applies to the taxpayer's

---

[28] 44 USC chs. 21, 29, 33. In a 1997 report, the GAO found that certain management and policy documents, many of which the Service claimed were subject to the confidentiality restrictions of Section 6103 but also subject to the FOIA and Privacy Act unless the Service proved they were exempt, were not inventoried and scheduled for disposition in violation of the Act's requirements, and that some documents were not stored in satisfactory conditions in the basement of an IRS storage facility. GAO, IRS Records, Inconsistencies Between Statutes Affects Records Appraisal, GAO/GGD-98-4 (Oct. 1997).

[29] These documents have already been ordered released. Taxation With Representation Fund v. IRS, 485 F. Supp. 263 (DDC 1980), aff'd and modified in part, 646 F2d 666 (DC Cir. 1981).

[30] Tax Analysts v. IRS, 117 F3d 607 (DC Cir. 1997) ("Legal analyses contained in FSAs are not 'return information' under section 6103, and the IRS's exemption 3 claim fails").

[31] IRC § 7602(a).

case. To put it another way, the FOIA is a kind of administrative discovery device available to a taxpayer during the course of the examination and appeal of an actual case, as well as a method of obtaining information to evaluate the interpretation and application of Code provisions in advising a taxpayer on a transaction or to inform a practitioner or a taxpayer about to conduct dealings with the Service in future administrative proceedings. Access to information means not only that a taxpayer can be more informed about IRS operations in an abstract sense, but also that taxpayers can make the strongest possible case where Service personnel, in a specific case or situation, (1) have a mistaken view of the facts, (2) have an erroneous understanding of the law, (3) seek to treat one taxpayer differently from another, or (4) fail to follow the Service's own procedures, which may impose on Service personnel a higher standard than does either the law or, perhaps, the Constitution.

[2] The Service's Disclosure Organization

To carry out its responsibilities and process requests under the FOIA and the Privacy Act, the Service has established a disclosure organization (see Form 2.1) and has adopted procedural regulations.[32] Public reading rooms are provided in both the National Office and regional offices under the direction of Disclosure Officers where the FOIA requires that certain information be made available for public inspection and copying.[33] At regional offices, the information available for public inspection and copying includes the following:[34]

- A complete and current Internal Revenue Manual (but not law enforcement manuals)
- The Chief Counsel Directives System, including all manuals issued by the National Office
- Current directives issued by the Regional Counsel
- Current Commissioner, Regional Commissioner, district director, and Service center delegation orders, declassified and unclassified memo-

---

[32] 26 CFR §§ 601.701–601.702. According to the Disclosure of Official Information Handbook, authority to make FOIA determinations about records under their jurisdiction is given to the Director (Office of Disclosure); Assistant Commissioner (International); Chief Inspector; Regional Commissioners; District Directors; Service Center Directors; the Director (Data Center); and their delegates. IRM 1272, 13(20) (Authority), MT 1272-205 (Sept. 18, 1995). For steps taken in processing a request and preparing a response, see IRM 1272, 13(41) (Processing Steps), MT 1272-169 (Sept. 18, 1995).

[33] The addresses of these offices are listed in 26 CFR § 601.702(b)(3)(ii).

[34] IRM 1272, Disclosure of Official Information Handbook § 750 (Contents of the Reading Room), MT 1272-85 (Sept. 4, 1990). The Law Enforcement Manuals are said not to be part of the Internal Revenue Manual and are not placed in the Reading Room).

randa and circulars, along with indexes released under Section 6110 since November 1, 1976

Regional reading rooms are also the place for public inspection of information returns filed by tax-exempt organizations and trusts, approved applications for tax-exempt organizations, accepted offers in compromise, and applications for determination letters for deferred-compensation plans and accounts.

Most individual requests for information that the Service receives are processed by Disclosure Officers in district offices, and any appeal is taken to the National Office.

FORM 2.1
IRS DISCLOSURE ORGANIZATION

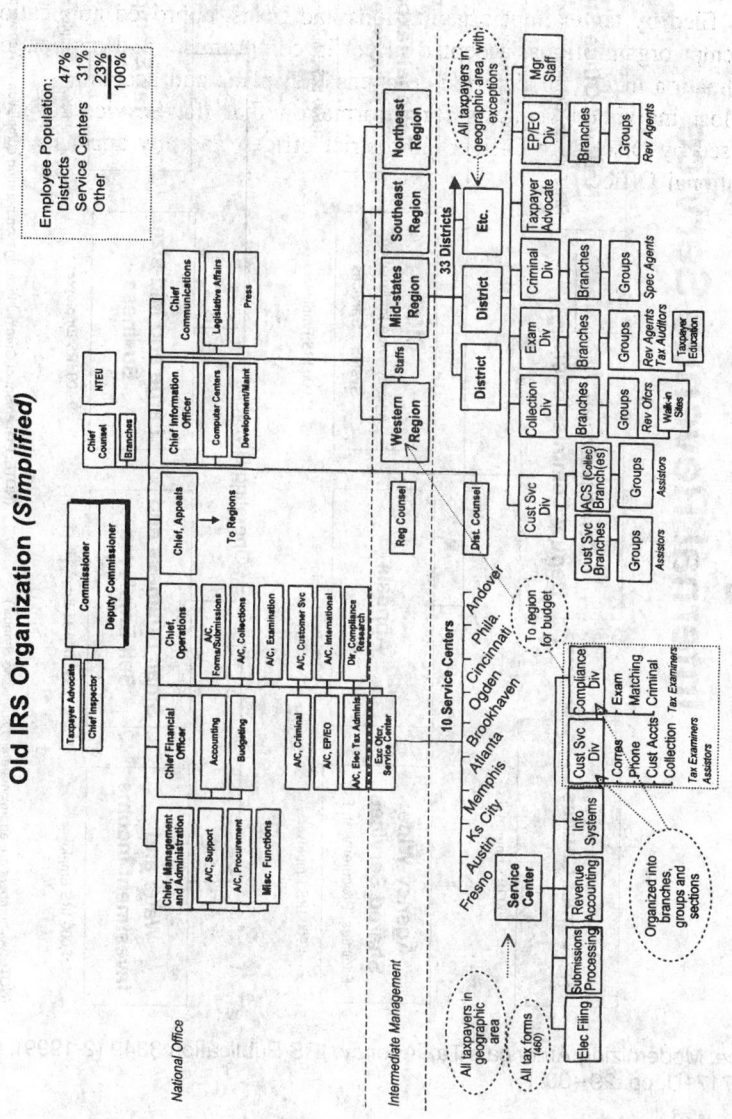

Old IRS Organization *(Simplified)*

Employee Population:
- Districts 47%
- Service Centers 31%
- Other 23%
- 100%

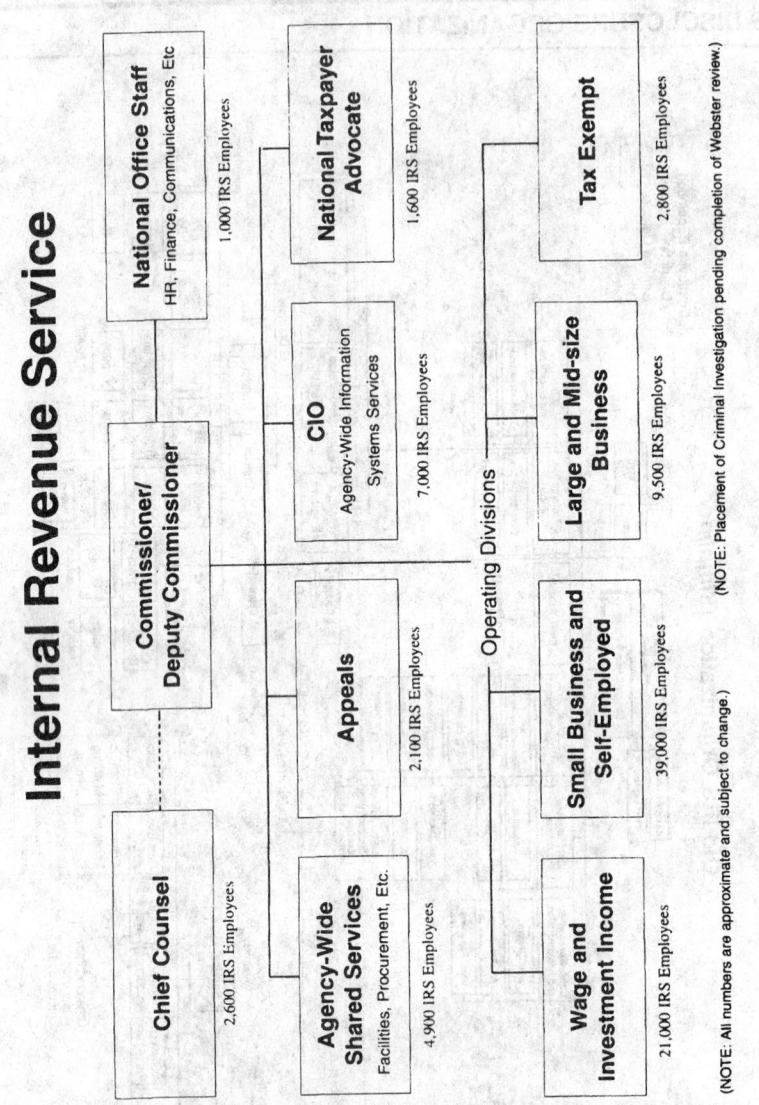

Internal Revenue Service

Commissioner/Deputy Commissioner

Chief Counsel — 2,600 IRS Employees

National Office Staff — HR, Finance, Communications, Etc — 1,000 IRS Employees

Agency-Wide Shared Services — Facilities, Procurement, Etc. — 4,900 IRS Employees

Appeals — 2,100 IRS Employees

CIO — Agency-Wide Information Systems Services — 7,000 IRS Employees

National Taxpayer Advocate — 1,600 IRS Employees

Operating Divisions

Wage and Investment Income — 21,000 IRS Employees

Small Business and Self-Employed — 39,000 IRS Employees

Large and Mid-size Business — 9,500 IRS Employees

Tax Exempt — 2,800 IRS Employees

(NOTE: All numbers are approximate and subject to change.)

(NOTE: Placement of Criminal Investigation pending completion of Webster review.)

Source: Modernizing America's Tax Agency, IRS Publication 3349 (2-1999), Catalog No. 27171U, pp. 29–30.

A. ACCESS TO INFORMATION FROM THE SERVICE UNDER THE FREEDOM OF INFORMATION ACT

¶ 2.02 THE FREEDOM OF INFORMATION ACT IN GENERAL

The FOIA is a single section of the Administrative Procedure Act (APA) in Title 5 of the United States Code. The FOIA was signed into law on July 4, 1966, and went into effect on July 4, 1967. It was amended first in 1974, and later in 1986, 1988, 1989, 1990, and 1996.[35] As the date of its enactment suggests, "[t]he basic purpose of FOIA is to ensure an informed citizenry, vital to the functioning of a democratic society, needed to check against corruption and to hold the governors accountable to the governed."[36] FOIA reflects the legislative policy that "'any person' should have clear access to identifiable agency records without having to state a reason for wanting the information and that the burden of proving withholding to be necessary is placed on the Federal agency."[37]

Under the FOIA, every agency, as defined in the APA,[38] including the Service, must make the information it maintains available to the public in three ways: (1) publishing it in the Federal Register[39]; (2) putting it in reading rooms for public inspection and copying[40]; or (3) making it available in response to the individual request of "any person."[41] This right of access is enforceable in

---

[35] Citizens Guide at 5.

[36] NLRB v. Robbins Tire & Rubber Co., 437 US 214, 242 (1978) (citing Freedom of Information Act Source Book, Subcommittee on Administrative Practice and Procedure, Senate Judiciary Committee, S. Doc. No. 93-82, at 38 (1974)).

[37] House Comm. on Gov't Operations & Senate Comm. on the Judiciary, 94th Cong., 1st Sess., Freedom of Information Act and Amendments of 1974 (Pub. L. No. 93-502) Source Book Legislative History, Texts and Other Documents 9 (Joint Comm. Print 1975) (hereafter Source Book 1975), at 3.

[38] 5 USC § 551(1). The FOIA uses this general definition of "agency," 5 USC § 552(f), and the Privacy Act, 5 USC § 552a(a)(1) uses the definition of the FOIA, thereby including public corporations as well as executive branch agencies.

[39] 5 USC § 552(a)(1).

[40] 5 USC § 552(a)(2).

[41] 5 USC § 552(a)(3). The legislative history of FOIA, along with selected cases decided by 1974, a selected bibliography, and articles, was published in a source book by the Senate Committee on the Judiciary. Senate Comm. on the Judiciary, 93d Cong., 2d Sess., Freedom of Information Act Source Book C Legislative Materials, Cases, Articles (Comm. Print 1974). Legislative materials concerning the FOIA and the Privacy Act are particularly helpful. For example, the Citizens Guide contains not only descriptions of the statutory provisions but also useful form letters and a bibliography as well. The Justice Department's Manual includes a Guide to the FOIA, as well as a case list. The discussion in this treatise is limited to FOIA cases involving the IRS.

court,[42] unless the record fits (1) one or more of nine described categories of exempt information[43] (exemptions) whose release would interfere with specific confidentiality and privacy interests or (2) one of three law enforcement exclusions that permit the record to be treated as excluded from FOIA.[44]

The appropriate disclosure methodology generally depends on the number of persons affected by the nature of the information. Thus, information having the widest interest to, and effect on, the public (e.g., descriptions of agency organization and procedures and rules of general applicability) must be published in the Federal Register. If an agency fails to take this action, no member of the public may be adversely affected by the "unpublished" rule.[45] Other information of general interest (e.g., final opinions, statements, and interpretations not published in the Federal Register, and staff manuals and instructions) must be made available for public inspection and copying in reading rooms, so-called "reading room materials." If the agency fails to make the final order, statement of policy or interpretation, and manual available, the agency may not use them as an authority.[46] Finally, if any person reasonably describes a requested record, and the request is made in accordance with published rules and procedures, the agency must make the record "promptly available."[47]

If information is made available, agencies may charge fees for document search and publication according to a published fee schedule.[48] The agency also must meet certain deadlines in making information available.[49] If the agency denies a FOIA request, the requester may file a complaint in one of the following jurisdictions:

- The federal district court for the district where the requester resides or has its principal place of business
- The federal district court for the district where the agency's records are located
- The district court for the District of Columbia[50]

---

[42] 5 USC § 552(a)(4)(B).

[43] 5 USC §§ 552(b)(1)–552(b)(9).

[44] 5 USC §§ 552(c)(1)–552(c)(3).

[45] 5 USC § 552(a)(1).

[46] 5 USC § 552(a)(2).

[47] 5 USC § 552(a)(3)(B). The agency is required to provide the record in any form or format the requester requests if the record is available in that form or format. The agency is also required to search for the records in electronic form or format, except when the effort would "significantly interfere with the operation of the agency's automated information system." 5 USC § 552(a)(3)(C).

[48] 5 USC § 552(a)(4)(A)(iv).

[49] 5 USC §§ 552(a)(6)(A)–552(a)(6)(C).

[50] 5 USC § 552(a)(4)(B).

The district court has jurisdiction to enjoin the agency from withholding agency records and to order the production of any of the agency records improperly withheld from the complainant requester.[51] If the agency fails to comply with the court's order, the district court may punish the responsible employee for contempt.[52] In this FOIA enforcement proceeding, the agency has the burden of establishing that its withholding of the requested information was proper because, for example, the information is exempt from disclosure.[53] Moreover, in any application of the FOIA, the exemptions from disclosure[54] may be used only to limit the availability of records to the public "as specifically stated" in the exemptions.[55] The exemptions do not, under any circumstance, provide a basis for the withholding of information from Congress.[56] To evaluate agency performance under the FOIA, agencies must also make annual reports to Congress about their operations under the FOIA.[57]

If a taxpayer (or another person) requests information from the IRS under the FOIA and the Service fails to make the information available, in accordance with the FOIA's basic policy in favor of disclosure, the IRS has the burden of proving that the requested material falls within one of the nine statutory exemptions.[58] Unless the IRS successfully carries this burden, records and materials in its possession must be made available to the requester.

---

[51] 5 USC §§ 552(a)(4)(B). See, e.g., U.S. Dep't of Justice v. Tax Analysts, 492 US 136, 142 (1989) (Justice Department ordered to disclose weekly logs of federal court tax opinions and orders that it received in the course of representing the IRS and that were regularly kept in court files to a legal publisher because documents were "agency records" and could only be withheld if they fell within one of the exemptions from disclosure, which they did not).

[52] 5 USC § 552(a)(4)(G).

[53] It would be inconsistent with the broad purpose of the FOIA to require full agency disclosure and to create a judicially enforceable right to requested information for the requester to have the burden of proof. EPA v. Mink, 410 US 73, 79–80 (1973) (FOIA "attempts to create a judicially enforceable public right to secure [official information] from possibly unwilling official hands"); Dep't of the Air Force v. Rose, 425 US 352 (1976); U.S. Dep't of Justice v. Tax Analysts, 492 US 136 (1989) ("The burden is on the agency to demonstrate, not the requester to disprove, that the materials sought are not 'agency records' or have not been 'improperly' withheld").

[54] 5 USC §§ 552(b)(1)–552(b)(9).

[55] 5 USC § 552(d). See also EPA v. Mink, 410 US 73, 79 (1973) ("These exemptions are explicitly made exclusive").

[56] 5 USC § 552(d).

[57] 5 USC § 552(e).

[58] Dep't of Air Force v. Rose, 425 US 352, 361 (1976) (the exemptions "do not obscure the basic policy that disclosure, not secrecy, is the dominant objective of the Act").

¶ 2.03 MATERIALS NOT SUBJECT TO DISCLOSURE

Of the three methods provided by the FOIA for disclosure of information (i.e., publication, public inspection, and individual requests for information), the opportunity to make individual requests for information has the most immediate and practical significance in tax practice. The Federal Register and public inspection and copying methods require the IRS to publish or make available the Federal Register materials (described in 5 USC § 552(a)(1)) and public inspection and copying materials (5 USC § 552(a)(2)). Technically, a taxpayer need not take any action to obtain access to these categories of information, although litigation has been required to obtain access to such public inspection materials as the Internal Revenue Manual and rulings. By contrast, until a member of the general public makes a request for the information, the Service is not required to make available any information available that is neither Federal Register material nor public inspection and copying material. Consequently, the discussion in this chapter focuses on individual requests for information under the FOIA.

To obtain information from the Service in response to a specific request, the taxpayer or other requester must comply with two FOIA requirements: (1) The request must reasonably describe the records sought[59] and (2) the request must be made in accordance with regulations stating the time, place, fees (if any), and the procedures to be followed.[60] It follows that if a record or document is not described with reasonable particularity, the Service is not required to answer questions or interrogatories, conduct legal research, or create documents or opinions in response to specific requests.[61] If the taxpayer or other requester fails to meet the Service's requirements for FOIA requests, the Service is not required to comply with the request.[62] Generally, compliance with these requirements is not difficult, although describing Service internal records may require specialized knowledge obtained only by searching the Internal Revenue Manual. Assuming that the applicable requirements for a specific request for information have been met, a taxpayer's or other requester's access to the information sought depends on whether the information fits within one of the FOIA categories of exempt information. Under FOIA, the following nine categories of information are exempt from disclosure:[63]

---

[59] 5 USC § 552(a)(3)(A).

[60] 5 USC § 552(a)(3)(B); see also 26 CFR § 601.702(c)(4) (1997). Regulations say, "The request for records must describe the records in reasonably sufficient detail to enable [the Service's] employees who are familiar with the subject area of the request to locate the records without placing an unreasonable burden" on the Service.

[61] See National Labor Relations Bd. v. Sears, Roebuck & Co., 421 US 132, 162 (1975).

[62] 5 USC § 552(a)(3); 26 CFR § 601.702(c).

[63] 5 USC § 552(b).

- Classified documents concerning national defense or foreign policy (Exemption 1)
- Internal personnel rules and practices (Exemption 2)
- Information exempt under certain laws other than FOIA and the Privacy Act (Exemption 3)
- Confidential business information (Exemption 4)
- Communications either between or within government agencies (Exemption 5)
- Medical, personnel, and similar files whose disclosure "would constitute a clearly unwarranted invasion of personal privacy" (Exemption 6)
- Certain law enforcement investigatory files (Exemption 7)
- Certain information concerning financial institutions (Exemption 8)
- Geological and geophysical information concerning wells (Exemption 9)

In general, these exemptions are meant to protect public interests in the secrecy of national security information (Exemption 1), effective law enforcement (Exemption 7), the efficient functioning of agencies (Exemption 5), individual interests in personal privacy (Exemption 6), and the confidentiality of business information and trade secrets (Exemptions 8 and 9).

Three general rules apply to all nine exemptions:

Discretionary application. The exemptions are discretionary and were not intended to be mandatory nor to justify an agency's automatic withholding of information. Instead, the exemptions set the outer limits of what an agency such as the IRS may disclose.[64] In other words, an agency is not prohibited from disclosing exempt records.

Segregable information. Access to information may not be denied if exempt information can be segregated from nonexempt information. 5 USC § 552(b) provides: "Any reasonably segregable portion of a record shall be provided to any person requesting such record after deletion of the portions which are exempt under [the nine exemptions of] this subsection."[65]

Balancing interests. Information not exempt from disclosure must be made available to any person, irrespective of interest.[66] However, as the Supreme Court said in *Federal Aviation Administration v. Robertson,* "[n]othing in the Act or its legislative history gives any intimation that all information in all agencies and in all circumstances is to be open to public inspection."[67] The exemptions themselves reflect a balance between the opposing interests of

---

[64] See Chrysler Corp. v. Brown, 441 US 281, 293 (1979) (holding that "congress did not design the FOIA exemptions to be mandatory bars to disclosure"); Senate Comm. on the Judiciary, "Amending the Freedom of Information Act, S. Rep. No. 854, 93d Cong., 2d Sess. (1974), reprinted in Source Book 1975.

[65] 5 USC § 552(b) (flush language).

[66] 5 USC § 552(a)(3).

[67] Federal Aviation Admin. v. Robertson, 422 US 255, 262 (1975).

freedom of information and the protection of rights to the privacy of certain information in government files, as well as accounting for the confidentiality of certain information, such as law enforcement investigatory files necessary for the operation of the government.[68] The FOIA's exemptions are intended to provide a "workable formula" that balance and protect "all interests," and it is in this context that conflicting claims over records and information are considered.[69] A number of exemptions do not contain a "built-in standard,"[70] and therefore require the exercise of discretion or the balancing of the public interest in disclosure against the interest Congress intended to protect.[71] For example, Exemption 3 incorporates the return confidentiality rules of Section 6103. Since Section 6103 permits the Service to exercise discretion in withholding taxpayer return information from the taxpayer (because it would "seriously impair" tax administration), the Service's exercise of its discretion becomes an Exemption 3 issue, and subject to judicial review.[72] Similarly, when the requester seeks trade secrets or commercial or financial information that the Service has obtained from a taxpayer, the Service's decision to disclose the information is subject to judicial review in a reverse FOIA action, although not under the FOIA.[73] Also, the disclosure of information compiled for law enforcement purposes that could "reasonably be expected to constitute an unwarranted invasion of personal privacy" requires the balancing of the public interest in disclosure and the protected individual's personal privacy right.[74]

In making an individual request, the necessary preliminary question is whether the information requested is subject to a disclosure exemption. The following section discusses the exemptions from disclosure in detail. Since the exemptions for classified documents (Exemption 1), personnel, medical, and

---

[68] S. Rep. No. 813, 89th Cong., 1st Sess., 3 (1965).

[69] EPA v. Mink, 410 US 73 (1973).

[70] Federal Aviation Admin. v. Robertson, 422 US 255, 262 (1975).

[71] The Supreme Court has said that balancing the public interest in disclosure and an individual privacy right is required when information, such as addresses, is sought, and Exemption 6 permits the information to be withheld if the disclosure would constitute a "clearly unwarranted invasion of personal privacy." Dep't of Justice v. Reporter's Committee for Freedom of the Press, 489 US 749, 776 (1989); U.S. Dep't of Defense v. Federal Relations Auth., 510 US 487 (1994). See Wine Hobby USA, Inc. v. IRS, 502 F2d 133 (3d Cir. 1974) (court has said that it may balance the interests of the parties seeking disclosure and privacy to determine whether particular information is within a statutory exemption).

[72] Chamberlain v. Kurtz, 589 F2d 827 (5th 1979), cert. denied, 444 US 842 (1979).

[73] Chrysler Corp. v. Brown, 441 US 281 (1979). While the FOIA does not give the affected taxpayer a cause of action in a reverse FOIA case, the Supreme Court suggested that the taxpayer might obtain judicial review under the general right to judicial review provided in the APA, 5 USC § 702.

[74] See U.S. Dep't of Defense v. Federal Labor Relations Auth., 510 US 487, 496, n.6 (1994).

similar files (Exemption 6), information related to reports by or for a bank supervisory agency (Exemption 8), and geological information (Exemption 9) are not usually factors in tax cases, they are not covered here.

[1] Exemption 2: Internal Personnel Rules and Practices

Exemption 2 permits the Service to withhold from disclosure under the FOIA matters "related solely to . . . internal personnel rules and practices."[75] This exemption appears to reflect a judgment that the public does not have a legitimate interest in the disclosure of the Service's "housekeeping" rules, which govern the conduct of agency personnel as employees of the agency rather than their dealings with the public. The purpose of Exemption 2 must be stated tentatively, however, because the Senate and House committees understood the exemption differently when it was adopted.[76] The Senate limited the exemption to trivial matters such as parking space lists and duty hours, while the House referred generally to operating rules and guidelines. After enactment of the FOIA amendments, the Attorney General's memorandum prepared for the use of the various agencies adopted the House explanation.[77] The Supreme Court settled the confusion in *Department of the Air Force v. Rose*,[78] the leading case on the exemption where an individual requested case summaries of Air Force disciplinary proceedings against cadets. In the Court's view, Exemption 2 applied to trivia in which the public could not reasonably be expected to have an interest under the Senate construction. The issue under Exemption 2 was the material's potential for public interest, and not the nature of the rule. Because information about the treatment of cadets in *Rose* had "substantial potential for public interest outside the government," the information was held nonexempt from disclosure.[79] Accordingly, under this construction of Exemption 2, if an internal personnel rule or practice affects interests outside the agency, it is not exempt from disclosure and must be made available to the

---

[75] 5 USC § 552(b)(2).

[76] Compare HR Rep. No. 1497, 89th Cong., 2d Sess. (1966), reprinted in Senate Comm. on the Judiciary, 93d Cong., 2d Sess., Freedom of Information Act Source Book C Legislative, Materials, Cases, Articles 31 (Comm. Print 1974) (hereinafter Source Book 1974), with S. Rep. No. 813, 89th Cong., 1st Sess. (1965), reprinted in Source Book 1974 at 43.

[77] U.S. Attorney General, Memorandum on the Public Information Section of the Administrative Procedure Act, reprinted in Source Book 1974 at 194, 229–230.

[78] Dep't of Air Force v. Rose, 425 US 352 (1976).

[79] Dep't of Air Force v. Rose, 425 US 352, 367 (1976).

public. Internal matters of a relatively trivial nature are sometimes referred to as "low 2" information.[80]

Agency guidelines and techniques, reflected in instructions to agents, have been claimed exempt under internal personnel rules. In *Rose*, the Supreme Court reserved decision on whether the exemption applies "where disclosure may risk circumvention of agency regulations."[81] In cases arising after *Rose*, courts have held the exemption applies to information concerning investigatory techniques the disclosure of which might hamper law enforcement, sometimes called "high 2" risk of circumvention matters (e.g., redacted portions of Bureau of Alcohol, Tobacco, and Firearms pamphlet entitled "Raids and Searches"[82]; the Bureau of Alcohol, Tobacco, and Firearms manual, "Surveillance of Premises, Vehicles, and Persons—New Agent Training"[83]; the Service's Law Enforcement Manual[84]; and an IRS memorandum discussing the features of criminal prosecution of "vow of poverty" cases that make the prosecution attractive or not).[85]

In short, there are two approaches to the exemption. *Rose* clearly supports the view that Exemption 2 applies to "trivial matters." However, since *Rose* did not reject a "risk of circumvention" interpretation, the range of internal rules covered by Exemption 2 also covers many internal rules that, if disclosed, would enable a taxpayer to circumvent agency investigations, such as sensitive portions of criminal law enforcement manuals.[86] Using the *Rose*

---

[80] U.S. Dep't of Justice, Freedom of Information Act Guide & Privacy Act Overview 88, et seq. (1997 ed.).

[81] Dep't of Air Force v. Rose, 425 US 352, 364 (1976).

[82] Caplan v. Bureau of Alcohol, Tobacco & Firearms, 587 F2d 544 (2d Cir. 1978). See also Ginsberg, Feldman & Bress v. Federal Energy Admin., 591 F2d 717 (DC Cir.), aff'd on reh'g en banc, 591 F2d 752 (DC Cir. 1978) (agency manual containing guidelines and instructions to agency employees who audit oil refineries).

[83] Crooker v. Bureau of Alcohol, Tobacco & Firearms, 670 F2d 1051 (DC Cir. 1981) (en banc). In *Jordan v. U.S. Dep't of Justice*, 591 F2d 753 (DC Cir. 1978), the District of Columbia Circuit had said that the words "personnel rules and practices" referred only to minor employment matters, such as pay, pensions, vacations, and hours of work, and granted access to prosecution guidelines. In *Crooker*, the court rejected the limited reading of "personnel rules and practices" of *Jordan*, and said that the words may "cover other rules and practices governing agency personnel, including significant matters like job training for law enforcement personnel."

[84] Tickel v. United States, 86-2 USTC ¶ 9784 (ED Tenn. 1986).

[85] Menard v. United States, 81-2 USTC ¶ 9794 (D. Ariz. 1981); see also Church of Scientology Int'l v. IRS, 845 F. Supp. 714, 723 (CD Cal. 1993) ("information about internal law enforcement techniques, practices, and procedures used by the IRS to coordinate the flow of information regarding Scientology" protected).

[86] See Caplan v. Bureau of Alcohol, Tobacco, & Firearms, 587 F2d 544, 548 (2d Cir. 1978); Hardy v. Bureau of Alcohol, Tobacco, & Firearms, 631 F2d 653, 657 (9th Cir. 1980); Crooker v. Bureau of Alcohol, Tobacco & Firearms, 670 F2d 1051 (DC Cir. 1981).

"trivial matters" rationale, namely that Exemption 2 covers only employer-employee personnel rules and practices, some portions of the Internal Revenue Manual have been ordered to be made available.[87]

No universally accepted standard has been articulated to clarify whether the "trivial matters–low 2" interpretation or the "risk of circumvention–high 2" view applies. In *Crooker v. Bureau of Alcohol, Tobacco & Firearms*, however, the District of Columbia Circuit described a "high 2" test requiring that the requested document be "predominantly internal" and that disclosure of the requested document "significantly risk[s] circumvention of agency regulations or statutes."[88] Although disclosure of any agency procedure or practice might in some general way affect law enforcement simply by making the enforcement process better known, the district court in *Crooker* ruled that such information should not be exempt from disclosure unless disclosure of the technique itself enables a person to evade detection of illegal conduct (e.g., by revealing tolerances below which investigations are not commenced) or endangers the safety of law enforcement officers.[89]

[2] Exemption 3: Materials Exempt by Statute

Under Exemption 3, material need not be disclosed if it is "specifically exempted from disclosure by statute," other than the Privacy Act, provided that the statute "(A) requires that the matters be withheld from the public in such a manner as to leave no discretion on the issue, or (B) establishes particular criteria for withholding or refers to particular types of matters to be withheld."[90] At one time, Exemption 3 applied to all material exempt by statute.[91] Using this exemption, the Service could legally withhold information even though the decision to withhold was entirely a discretionary one made by the agency head under housekeeping statutes granting broad administrative discretion.[92] Existing

---

[87] See Hawkes v. IRS, 467 F2d 787 (6th Cir. 1972) (court noted that 5 USC § 552(a)(2)(C) required all administrative staff manuals to be available in reading rooms, and so only portions of the Manual, disclosure of which would significantly impede the enforcement process, would be exempt); Long v. IRS, 339 F. Supp. 1266 (WD Wash. 1971) (Closing Agreement Handbook and report on sources of returns).

[88] Crooker v. Bureau of Alcohol, Tobacco & Firearms, 670 F2d 1051, 1073–1074 (DC Cir. 1981).

[89] Crooker v. Bureau of Alcohol, Tobacco & Firearms, 670 F2d 1051, 1073–1074 (DC Cir. 1981).

[90] 5 USC § 552(b)(3).

[91] See Source Book 1974 at 12.

[92] Federal Aviation Admin. v. Robertson, 422 US 255 (1975), superseded by statute as stated in Phillippi v. CIA, 546 F2d 1009 (DC Cir. 1976).

regulations recognize the following statutes as specifically exempting or authorizing disclosure:

- Section 4102 (inspection by certain state or local governments of records relating to taxes on petroleum products)
- Section 6103 (confidentiality of tax returns)[93]
- Section 6104 (publicity of information required from certain exempt organizations)[94]
- Section 6108 (publication of statistics of income)[95]
- Section 6110 (public inspection of written determinations)[96]
- Section 7122 (record of compromise of a tax case)[97]
- Section 7213 (penalties for unauthorized disclosure of the Code and unauthorized disclosure of trade secrets and other confidential information)

This list, however, is not exclusive. For example, Rule 6(e) of the Federal Rules of Criminal Procedure has been held to be an exemption statute for Exemption 3 purposes.[98] Accordingly, where a taxpayer, a subject of a grand jury investigation, requested information gathered during the investigation, the Service claimed that such information was grand jury materials exempt from disclosure under Rule 6(e).[99] Nevertheless, absolute discretion is not left to the Service when Rule 6(e) is claimed as the basis for nondisclosure. The Service must also show for each document that the release would reveal a protected aspect of the grand jury's investigation.[100]

The statutory language of Exemption 3 is designed to prevent statutes from granting agencies generalized discretion to withhold information. Exemption 3's function with regard to an exemption statute is illustrated by Section 6103, which requires that returns and return information be kept confidential.

---

[93] 26 CFR §§ 601.702(d)(1), 601.702(d)(2).

[94] 26 CFR §§ 601.702(d)(3), 601.702(d)(4), 601.702(d)(5).

[95] 26 CFR § 601.702(d)(6).

[96] 26 CFR § 601.702(d)(9).

[97] 26 CFR § 601.702(d)(8).

[98] Fund for Constitutional Gov't v. Nat'l Archives & Records Serv., 656 F2d 856, 867 (DDC 1981); see also Linn v. U.S. Dep't of Justice, 80 AFTR2d 97-5242 (DDC 1997) (special agent's report about a grand jury investigation was exempt from disclosure under Exemption 3 in conjunction with the prohibition on disclosure of "matters occurring before [a] grand jury" contained in Fed. R. Crim. P. 6(e)).

[99] Crooker v. IRS, 75 AFTR2d 2375 (DDC 1995).

[100] Crooker v. IRS, 75 AFTR2d 2375 (DDC 1995), rejected a per se rule against disclosure of grand jury information, and required the government to submit affidavits showing "with particularity how disclosure of the grand jury exhibits would disclose a protected aspect of the grand jury's investigation," citing Senate of the Commonwealth of Puerto Rico v. U.S. Dep't of Justice, 823 F2d 574 (DC Cir. 1987).

Tax returns and tax return information have been withheld from disclosure under Exemption 3.[101] Close analysis of Section 6103's confidentiality rules is required to determine when disclosure of the requested information is permitted under that statute and is thus disclosable under the FOIA.

[a] Exemption 3 and Section 6103

The definition of "return information" in Section 6103 is stated in the broadest terms to include not only the tax returns and attached schedules taxpayers file with the Service, but also (1) the Service's administrative action on the return and (2) information the Service gathers in the course of an examination that may come from persons other than the taxpayer.[102] The definition of "return information" specifically excludes "data in a form which cannot be associated with, or otherwise identify, directly or indirectly, a particular taxpayer."[103] Consequently, statistical data derived from individual tax returns, which themselves are confidential, may be disclosed under the FOIA when the Service eliminates identifying information. In fact, the Service may be required to remove or redact information that might identify a taxpayer in order to permit disclosure.[104]

---

[101] Chamberlain v. Kurtz, 589 F2d 827 (5th Cir. 1979), cert. denied, 444 US 842 (1979); Breuhaus v. IRS, 609 F2d 80 (2d Cir. 1979); Fruehauf Corp. v. IRS, 566 F2d 574, 578 (6th Cir. 1977); Belisle v. Comm'r, 462 F. Supp. 460 (WD Okla. 1978); Grenier v. IRS, 449 F. Supp. 834 (D. Md. 1978); Strauss v. IRS, 516 F. Supp. 1218 (DDC 1981); Menard v. United States, 81-2 USTC ¶ 9794 (D. Ariz. 1981); Bernal v. IRS, 80-2 USTC ¶ 9572 (ND Cal. 1980); Otworth v. Comm'r, 82-2 USTC ¶ 9449 (CD Cal. 1982) ("Section 6103 . . . takes precedence over the FOIA when access to tax return information is sought"); Watson v. IRS, 538 F. Supp. 817 (SD Tex. 1982) ("The disclosure of federal tax return information is governed by section 6103").

[102] IRC § 6103(b)(2). Section 6103(b)(2) defines "return information" to mean "[1] a taxpayer's identity, [2] the nature, source, amount of his income, payments, receipts, deductions, exemptions, credits, assets, liabilities, net worth, tax liability, tax withheld, deficiencies, overassessments, or tax payments, [3] whether the taxpayer's return was, is being, or will be examined or subject to other investigation or processing [4] or any other data received by furnished to, or collected by the [Service] with respect to a return or with respect to the existence, or possible existence, of liability (or the amount thereof) of any person under [the Code] for any tax, penalty, interest, fine, forfeiture, or other imposition, or offense. . . . " Privacy of tax returns and return information is described at ¶ 4.06.

[103] IRC § 6103(b)(2). For example, if the information sought contains return information of other taxpayers, such as names, addresses, Social Security numbers, bank information, income amounts, and withholding amounts, the information would be exempt from disclosure under Section 6103, and so exempt from disclosure under Exemption 3. See Barmes v. IRS, 82 AFTR2d 5319 (SD Ind. 1998).

[104] See Long v. IRS, 596 F2d 362 (9th Cir. 1979), cert. denied, 446 US 917 (1980) (data underlying Service's Taxpayer Compliance Measurement Program used to select returns for examinations). See also Long v. Bureau of Economic Analysis, 646 F2d 1310, 1311 (9th Cir. 1981), vacated and remanded, 454 US 934 (1981) (considering effect of

Although it may be possible to remove identifying data,[105] some confidential return information may be incapable of segregation from disclosable tax information.[106] Thus, even if the data cannot be associated with an identifiable taxpayer, the Service is not required to disclose some information, such as the standards it uses for selecting returns for audit or the data to be used for determining these standards, if the Service determines that disclosure will impair tax administration.[107]

Economic Recovery Tax Act of 1981 (ERTA) amendment on IRC § 6103(b)(2)). The position of the Ninth Circuit that return information includes on information that directly or indirectly identifies a particular taxpayer has been followed by the District of Columbia Circuit. Neufeld v. IRS, 646 F2d 661 (DC Cir. 1981). Accord Moody v. IRS, 654 F2d 795 (DC Cir. 1981). In *Moody* and *Neufeld*, the circuit court remanded the case for the district court to decide whether identifying data could be segregated from otherwise disclosable information contained in a document.

Several years after the *Moody* and *Neufeld* cases, the District of Columbia Circuit, sitting en banc, rejected the *Long* interpretation by holding that under Section 6103(b)(2), return information can be nondisclosable even if taxpayers' names and similar identifying data are deleted. To be disclosable, the information must also be reformulated by statistical tabulation or a similar form of combination. Church of Scientology v. IRS, 792 F2d 153 (DC Cir. 1986) (en banc), aff'd, 484 US 9 (1987).

The Eleventh Circuit has also held that once identifying information has been deleted, return information is disclosable under the FOIA. Currie v. IRS, 704 F2d 523, 531 (11th Cir. 1983) (Section 6103(b)(2) "does not require the release of return information if exempt material is readily excisable").

[105] See, e.g., Strauss v. IRS, 516 F. Supp. 1218, 1221 (DDC 1981). Under the Ninth Circuit's decision in *Long*, the government can be required to explain why confidential tax information is not segregable from disclosable matters. Willamette Indus. v. United States, 79-2 USTC ¶ 9520 (D. Or. 1979); Willamette Indus. v. United States, 530 F. Supp. 904, 909 (D. Or. 1981), aff'd, 689 F2d 865 (9th Cir. 1982), cert. denied, 460 US 1052 (1983) (*Long* followed; disclosure of timber sales and valuation data held in individual audit files ordered after redaction of identifying matters). In *Willamette Industries*, the Service argued that the information required to be disclosed in *Long* were "compilations of data" and that *Long* should be limited to this situation. The Ninth Circuit rejected this argument and said that information of the type involved, although contained in the audit file of a particular taxpayer, is a compilation of data relating to timber sales by other taxpayers; 689 F2d at 868.

[106] See also Clarkson v. IRS, 82-2 USTC ¶ 9656 (DSC 1982) (finding that documents pertaining to the Tax Protest Project, various protest groups, and related surveillance activities could not reasonably be segregated into exempt and nonexempt parts, because they were part of an ongoing criminal investigation). Contra Currie v. IRS, 704 F2d 523 (11th Cir. 1983). See also Church of Scientology v. IRS, 792 F2d 146, 151–152 (DC Cir. 1986), aff'd, 484 US 9 (1987) (all information in IRS files is not, as a matter of law, return information, and IRS must make an appropriate showing that "all information [in a 'File of Persons Making Threats of Force or Forcible Assaults'] comes within the statutory definition").

[107] Economic Recovery Tax Act, Pub. L. No. 97-34, § 701, amending IRC § 6103(b)(2). Congress had Long v. IRS, 596 F2d 362 (9th Cir. 1979), cert. denied, 446 US 917 (1980), and Long v. Bureau of Economic Analysis, 646 F2d 1310, 1311 (9th Cir.

It should be noted that Section 6103 permits the Service to make public some tax return information that identifies the taxpayer (e.g., accepted offers in compromise and the amount of outstanding liens). Therefore, if the Service has failed to disclose this information, its release may be demanded under the FOIA.[108] On the other hand, using the provisions of Section 6103, the Service has refused access under the FOIA to certain third-party tax return information. In cases challenging the Service's refusal to disclose this information, the Service's denial has been given deference by the courts.[109]

1981), vacated and remanded, 454 US 934 (1981), in mind when it amended Section 6103(b)(2). HR Rep. No. 201, 97th Cong., 1st Sess. 238–239 (1981). After what might be called the *Long* amendment of Section 6103(b)(2), the Longs lost their attempt to obtain Taxpayer Compliance Measurement Program (TCMP) and DIF formula data under FOIA in the district court. Long v. IRS, 82-2 USTC ¶ 9487 (WD Wash. 1982) (TCMP source data were used for determining standards for the selection of returns for examination within the meaning of Section 6103(b)(2)). The *Long* case was reversed and remanded, Long v. United States, 742 F2d 1173 (9th Cir. 1984). Despite the amendment of Section 6103(b)(2), the Ninth Circuit held that "the Commissioner's determination that disclosure of the specific TCMP data sought . . . would seriously impair assessment, collection or enforcement of the tax laws is subject to de novo review. . . ." 742 F2d at 1182. The Ninth Circuit remanded the case to the district court for a hearing to determine "the correctness of the Commissioner's determination." Id. at 1184. The circuit court said, "[A]lthough we think that the Commissioner's determination is entitled to deference . . . the district court's review is still de novo and . . . the court must satisfy itself, on the basis of detailed and nonconclusory affidavits, that the Commissioner is correct in his belief. . . ." Id. at 1182–1183.

The Service has frequently argued that DIF scores constitute a technique or procedure it uses in selecting returns for examination and that release of the scores would enable taxpayers to analyze tolerance criteria the IRS uses in processing and examining returns, and so falls under Exemption 7(E), discussed infra ¶ 2.03[5]. Courts now say that it is well established that DIF scores are exempt from the FOIA by Exemption 3 in conjunction with Section 6103(b)(2), and FOIA Exemption 7(E). See Buckner v. IRS, 82 AFTR2d 98-5650 (ND Ind. 1998); see also Naranjo v. IRS, 88-2 USTC ¶ 9537 (ED Ky. 1988) (taxpayer's Discriminant Function score held exempt under 5 USC § 552(b)(3) and Exemption (7)(E)).

[108] IRC §§ 6103(k)(1), 6103(k)(2).

[109] See Aronson v. IRS, 973 F2d 962 (1st Cir. 1992) (lawyer specializing in finding taxpayers to whom the IRS owed refunds held not entitled to their names, mailing addresses, refund amounts, and taxpayer identification numbers, because he was not a member of the press or other media, disclosure to whom is provided in Section 6103(m)(1), and the Service's decision not to disclose was not "manifestly contrary to the statute," quoting Chevron USA, Inc. v. Natural Resources Defense Council, Inc., 467 US 837, 844 (1984). See also Fruehauf Corp. v. IRS, 566 F2d 574, 578 (6th Cir. 1977); Belisle v. Comm'r, 462 F. Supp. 460 (WD Okla. 1978); Grenier v. IRS, 449 F. Supp. 834 (D. Md. 1978); Menard v. United States, 81-2 USTC ¶ 9794 (D. Ariz. 1981); Juliano v. IRS, 79-2 USTC ¶ 9521 (ND Ga. 1979); Stephenson v. IRS, 79-2 USTC ¶ 9513 (ND Ga. 1979), aff'd, vacated, and remanded, 629 F2d 1140 (5th Cir. 1980) (third-party tax returns, deposit slips, checks, and transcripts of account held exempt by district court by relying on government affidavit alone); May v. IRS, 82-2 USTC ¶ 9451 (WD Mo. 1982) (request for

Once information initially covered by Section 6103's confidentiality rules is disclosed in accordance with those rules, the Service may not claim that the information is exempt from disclosure under Section 6103 and FOIA.[110]

[b] Review of Nondisclosure Under Section 6103

Suppose a taxpayer wishes to obtain return information pertaining to his own return. Exemption 3 sets out two tests: (1) whether it refers to "particular types of matters to be withheld," and (2) whether the statute establishes "particular criteria."[111] Unquestionably, Section 6103(b) refers to particular types of matters to be withheld (namely, tax returns and return information, both of which are broadly defined), and provides a series of specific situations in which tax returns and return information may be disclosed.[112] Sections 6103(c) and 6103(e)(7) also give the Service discretion to withhold return information from a designee of a taxpayer or a person with a material interest if the Service determines "that such disclosure would seriously impair Federal tax administration." This "serious impairment" standard of both Sections 6103(c) and 6103(e)(7) seems to permit the Service to make a discretionary decision not to disclose information, without using any "particular criteria" in making that decision. Courts nevertheless have held that Section 6103 establishes proper criteria for exercise of agency discretion, and information that may not be disclosed under Section 6103 is, as a consequence, exempt from disclosure under Exemption 3.[113] While Section 6103 does not supersede the FOIA, as a

---

"all information on the Basic Bible Church" held to require disclosure of confidential taxpayer return information); Stine v. IRS, 82-2 USTC ¶ 9645 (WD La. 1982) (disclosure of document pertaining to taxpayer's liability for taxes denied because identity of confidential informant would be revealed).

[110] Cooper v. IRS, 450 F. Supp. 752 (DDC 1977) (documents not confidential under Section 6103, because they had been made part of Tax Court record). See also Hearnes v. IRS, 79-2 USTC ¶ 9526 (ED Mo. 1979) (documents relating to closed criminal case that were not presented to grand jury held not covered by Exemption 3).

[111] IRC § 552(b)(3).

[112] IRC § 6103(e)(7). As one court has said, "[T]he FOIA does not require an agency to disclose information if another statute requires the agency to withhold the information as long as that other statute (1) gives the agency no discretion to disclose, or (2) establishes criteria for withholding, or (3) specifies particular types of information to be withheld." Aronson v. IRS, 973 F2d 962, 964 (1st Cir. 1992).

[113] Chamberlain v. Kurtz, 589 F2d 827 (5th Cir. 1979), cert. denied, 444 US 842 (1979). Courts have almost uniformly followed *Chamberlain*. Some twenty years ago, however, another view was that Section 6103 is a self-contained statutory scheme governing the disclosure of tax information and superseding FOIA. Following IRS action under Section 6103, therefore, the district court was not to review the agency decision de novo, but only determines whether the IRS decision was rational and supported by the record, the same standard of review of an administrative decision pursuant to the APA. See Zale Corp. v. IRS, 481 F. Supp. 486 (DDC 1979).

practical matter, it provides the basis for a claim by the Service that the information is exempt from disclosure under Exemption 3.

When the Service uses Section 6103 as a ground for nondisclosure under Exemption 3, the Service's exemption claim is reviewable by a district court in the same manner as is any other exemption from disclosure claimed by the Service. In the district court FOIA proceeding, the documents or information withheld under the combination of Section 6103 and Exemption 3 are presumed subject to disclosure unless the Service carries its burden of proving that the withheld materials are actually covered by Exemption 3.[114] Most courts have said that the Service's discretionary nondisclosure is subject to de novo review, relying on the language in 5 USC Section 552(a)(4)(B), which states that a court asked to order an agency to produce information under the FOIA "shall determine the matter de novo."[115]

Because the Service's decision under Section 6103 is discretionary, it has also been held that once the district court has decided that the Service has some basis for the exercise of its discretion, the court, in reviewing the Service's claim that the information falls under Exemption 3, must apply ordinary deferential principles of administrative law (i.e., reversal only if the agency's

---

The District of Columbia Circuit itself has rejected the *Zale* approach and has agreed with other circuit courts that "Section 6103 does not supersede FOIA, but rather gives rise to an exemption under Exemption 3, 5 USC § 552(b)(3)." Church of Scientology v. IRS, 792 F2d 146, 150 (DC Cir. 1986). The Eleventh Circuit has refused to follow *Zale* and follows the *Chamberlain v. Kurtz* approach instead. Currie v. IRS, 704 F2d 523 (11th Cir. 1983). After *Currie*, the Fifth Circuit reaffirmed its position in *Chamberlain v. Kurtz* on the applicable law. Linsteadt v. IRS, 729 F2d 998, 1003 (5th Cir. 1984) ("while . . . § 6103 provides the criteria for nondisclosure under Exemption 3 of the Information Act, the agency's denial of disclosure is reviewable under the Information Act, with the government bearing the burden of demonstrating that one of the specific exemptions of the Information Act justifies its non-disclosure").

The Ninth Circuit has also declined to follow *Zale*. See Long v. United States, 742 F2d 1173, 1177 (9th Cir. 1984) ("First, we disagree that Section 6103 is irreconcilable with FOIA. . . . Second, neither Section 6103 nor its legislative history contains any language indicating that Section 6103 should operate independently of FOIA."). See also Willamette Indus. Inc. v. United States, 689 F2d 865 (9th Cir. 1982), cert. denied, 460 US 1052 (1983). The Third Circuit has also refused to follow *Zale*. Grasso v. IRS, 785 F2d 70, 74 (3d Cir. 1986) ("We conclude, as did the Ninth, Fifth and Eleventh Circuits, that section 6103 operates within the confines of FOIA"). See also De Salvo v. IRS, 861 F2d 1217 (10th Cir. 1988) (IRS refusal to disclose documents is subject to de novo review under FOIA; authority of *Zale* questioned).

[114] Aronson v. IRS, 973 F2d 962, 964 (1st Cir. 1992) (Section 6103 "falls squarely within FOIA Exemption 3").

[115] See, e.g., De Salvo v. IRS, 861 F2d 1217 (10th Cir. 1988); Church of Scientology v. IRS, 792 F2d 146 (DC Cir. 1986); Grasso v. IRS, 785 F2d 70 (3d Cir. 1986); Long v. United States, 742 F2d 1173 (9th Cir. 1984); Linsteadt v. IRS, 729 F2d 998 (5th Cir. 1984).

action has been arbitrary and capricious or the agency has abused its discretion), and not the FOIA's de novo review standard.[116]

Using its discretionary nondisclosure authority under Section 6103, the Service has denied a FOIA request for documents referring to or analyzing a taxpayer's own tax liability under Exemption 3 on the ground that disclosure would impair tax administration. The basis for such denial is apparently the same reason that disclosure of an investigatory file is not required; that is, disclosure would give the taxpayer premature access to information and might therefore permit interference with witnesses.[117]

[3] Exemption 4: Trade Secrets and Commercial or Financial Information

The FOIA exempts from disclosure "trade secrets and commercial or financial information."[118] In general, information protected from disclosure under Exemption 4 must be

- Commercial or financial,
- Obtained from a person outside the government, and
- Privileged or confidential.[119]

---

[116] Aronson v. IRS, 973 F2d 962 (1st Cir. 1992). The opinion in *Aronson* was written by Justice Breyer when he was Chief Judge of the First Circuit, which gives this minority view greater weight than it might otherwise have on the issue. According to *Aronson*, "once a court determines that the statute in question is an Exemption 3 statute, and that the information requested at least arguably falls within the statute, FOIA de novo review normally ends." Id. at 967.

[117] Chamberlain v. Kurtz, 589 F2d 827, 841 (5th Cir. 1979), cert. denied, 444 US 842 (1979). See Zale Corp. v. United States, 481 F. Supp. 486 (DDC 1979); Anastas v. United States, 79-2 USTC ¶ 9510 (ND Cal. 1979); Kanter v. IRS, 478 F. Supp. 552 (ND Ill. 1979). See also Strauss v. IRS, 516 F. Supp. 1218, 1221 (DDC 1981) (taxpayer's correspondence with the Service); Watson v. IRS, 538 F. Supp. 817 (SD Tex. 1982) (release of information sought would "impair the ongoing enforcement proceeding against plaintiff by prematurely revealing the scope, direction and limits of the government's investigation. . . .") (quoting government affidavit). See also Otworth v. Comm'r, 82-2 USTC ¶ 9449 (CD Cal. 1982). However, the Third Circuit has held that disclosure of a taxpayer's own statements would not "seriously impair" the administration of the tax laws. Grasso v. IRS, 785 F2d 70 (3d Cir. 1986).

[118] 5 USC § 552(b)(4).

[119] Consumers Union of the United States, Inc. v. Veterans Admin., 301 F. Supp. 796, 802 (SDNY 1969). See also General Services Admin. v. Benson, 415 F2d 878, 881 (9th Cir. 1969) ("this exemption clearly condones withholding information only when it is obtained from a person outside the agency, and that person wishes the information to be kept confidential").

Exemption 4 protects trade secrets from disclosure because trade secrets have traditionally been protected by courts (owing to their confidential nature) and because significant economic losses can be triggered by their disclosure.[120] The exemption also applies to commercial or financial information where (1) the party who submits the information would not ordinarily have revealed it to the public, (2) disclosure would be likely to cause substantial competitive injury (i.e., the same basis for protecting trade secrets), and (3) "nondisclosure is justified by the legislative purpose which underlies the exemption" (i.e., to protect the confidentiality of information that would not ordinarily be disclosed to the public and whose disclosure would impair the government's ability to obtain similar information in the future).[121]

Exemption 4 is unique in that a federal agency has little incentive to claim it; the privacy interest being protected is actually that of the person who submitted the information to the agency and whose business will or may be affected by disclosure. In *Chrysler Corp. v. Brown*, Chrysler Corporation had filed with a Department of Defense agency its written affirmative action programs and annual information reports in connection with its government contracts, which the agency had reviewed for compliance. A third party requested, under the FOIA, that the agency disclose copies of the reports and the agency's compliance reviews.[122] After the agency informed Chrysler of its decision to disclose the information in response to the FOIA request, Chrysler filed a complaint seeking to enjoin the agency from disclosing this information. As the Supreme Court noted, the case belongs to a class of cases that have popularly been denominated "reverse-FOIA" suits. Because the FOIA is "purely a disclosure statute," the Supreme Court held, it gives a person who supplies information to an agency "no private right of action to enjoin agency disclosure."[123] The Court noted that Congress recognized that "much of the information within Government files has been submitted by private entities seeking Government contracts or responding to unconditional reporting obligations imposed by law." Nevertheless, while government agencies had some latitude to afford the confidentiality desired by these submitters, "the FOIA by itself

---

[120] The First Restatement of the Law of Torts defined "trade secret" as follows: "A trade secret may consist of any formula, pattern, device or compilation of information which is used in one's business, and which gives him an opportunity to obtain an advantage over competitors who do not know or use it." § 757, Comment (b) (1939). The second Restatement omitted rules relating to unfair trade practices because they were no longer dependent on principles of tort law. Restatement (Second) of Torts, p.1.

[121] National Parks & Conservation Ass'n v. Morton, 498 F2d 765, 767, 770 (DC Cir. 1974), citing S. Rep. No. 89-813 at 9 (1965).

[122] Chrysler Corp. v. Brown, 441 US 281 (1979). In fact, an agency may even oppose nondisclosure under the exemption. See Charles River Park "A," Inc. v. Department of Hous. & Urban Dev., 360 F. Supp. 212 (DDC 1973), remanded for further proceeding, 519 F2d 935 (DC Cir. 1975).

[123] Chrysler Corp. v. Brown, 441 US 281, 285 (1979).

protects the submitters' interest in confidentiality only to the extent that this interest in endorsed by the agency collecting the information."[124]

Chrysler also argued that the district court had jurisdiction to enjoin the disclosure under the Trade Secrets Act, which makes it a crime for any government employee to disclose trade secrets and financial information furnished to a government agency, "except as authorized by law," and that the Defense Department agency's contemplated disclosure was not "authorized by law." The Supreme Court rejected this argument as well, saying that there is no statutory basis in the Trade Secrets Act, a criminal statute, from which a private right of action may be implied and thereby enforced under the FOIA.[125] However, the Court held that the decision to disclose Chrysler's reports was a reviewable agency action under the APA's general provision affording the right of judicial review of agency action to a person "adversely affected or aggrieved" by that action.[126] Under these provisions, when a person who has submitted trade secret or other proprietary information to a government agency is notified that the agency will disclose the information under the FOIA, the submitter may attempt to enjoin the disclosure, but the jurisdiction of the district court to hear the action is not the FOIA itself, nor the Trade Secrets Act; jurisdiction lies under the general agency judicial review procedure of the APA.

In tax cases, specific provisions of the Code may obligate the Service to withhold the information, and thereby provide the person who submitted the information with administrative and judicial remedies for the review of the Service's decision to disclose that would otherwise be unavailable. For example, if a taxpayer has provided proprietary information to the Service in connection with a request for a letter ruling, determination letter, or technical advice, the provisions of Section 6110 apply. Section 6110(c)(4) exempts from disclosure "trade secrets and commercial or financial information obtained from a person and privileged or confidential. . . ." If the Service decides to disclose a background file document that includes trade secret information, it must notify the taxpayer and permit administrative review of the request to restrain disclosure.[127] The submitter may also file a petition in the Tax Court for judicial review of the proposed disclosure by filing a petition with the Court within sixty days after the date the Service has mailed the notice of intention to disclose to the submitter.[128] These procedures would appear to supersede the

---

[124] Chrysler Corp. v. Brown, 441 US 281, 292–293 (1979).

[125] Chrysler Corp. v. Brown, 441 US 281, 316–317 (1979).

[126] Chrysler Corp. v. Brown, 441 US 281, 317–319 (1979). Section 10(a) of the APA, 5 USC § 702, provides that "[a] person suffering legal wrong because of agency action, or adversely affected or aggrieved by agency action . . . , is entitled to judicial review thereof."

[127] IRC §§ 6110(f)(1), 6110(f)(2).

[128] IRC § 6110(f)(3). Although it is a civil remedy after the disclosure, the submitter also may bring an action for damages if the Service fails to delete trade secret informa-

procedure described in *Chrysler Corp. v. Brown*, at least where the trade secret information was submitted in order to obtain a written determination from the Service.

Moreover, if the trade secret information is reflected in a tax return or constitutes tax return information under the broad definition of Section 6103, the confidentiality of the information is protected under Section 6103, and the Service is required to avoid disclosure of such information under Exemption 3. A failure to claim the exemption in this circumstance might subject Service officials to criminal and civil penalties for disclosure of confidential tax information.[129] Because Section 6103 creates a privacy right in tax return information, and because Congress has provided both civil remedies and criminal penalties for violations of that right, *Chrysler Corp. v. Brown* gives a district court jurisdiction to enjoin disclosure of return information under Section 6103, in addition to the general judicial review procedure of the APA. At any rate, the Service has provided in regulations that business information, defined as "any trade secret or other financial, commercial (including research) information," will not be disclosed pursuant to a FOIA request until the Service provides the submitter of the information with notice of its intent to disclose and an opportunity to object to disclosure.[130] Despite the Supreme Court's decision in *Chrysler Corp. v. Brown*, the Service regulations state that its administrative decision on disclosure is subject to judicial review by way of an action instituted under the FOIA by either the submitter or the requester.[131]

Even if an agency, such as the IRS, has no interest in keeping the information secret, the exemption is applicable if the submitter can show that public disclosure is likely to cause substantial harm to the submitter's competitive position. Concern for a submitter's competitive position and the effect on the agency's access to such information in the future may warrant a court's barring disclosure even when identifying information is deleted.[132] Thus, the willingness of courts in FOIA cases to deny disclosure, even where identifying information has been deleted, may make a submitter's objection under this exemption broader than an objection to disclosure under Section 6103, which permits the disclosure of tax return information where such identifying details have been omitted.

---

tion, or fails to delay disclosure when requested by the submitter (Section 6110(g)). IRC § 6110(i).

[129] IRC § 7213 (criminal action). See 18 USC § 1905 (general criminal liability for disclosure of trade secrets and other confidential information).

[130] 26 CFR §§ 601.702(h)(1)–601.702(h)(6).

[131] 26 CFR § 601.702(h)(7). See 5 USC § 552(a)(4)(B).

[132] See Sterling Drug, Inc. v. FTC, 450 F2d 698 (DC Cir. 1971).

[4] Exemption 5: Inter- and Intra-Agency Memoranda

Exemption 5 authorizes the Service to withhold access to "inter- or intra-agency memorandums or letters which would not be available by law to a party other than an agency in litigation with the agency."[133] Satisfaction of Exemption 5 presents two issues: (1) whether the memorandum reflects deliberative or policymaking processes and (2) whether the memorandum could be discovered in a case in court. Exemption 5 was intended to incorporate "the recognized rule that 'confidential intra-agency advisory opinions . . . are privileged from inspection.'"[134] The purpose of both the exemption and the deliberative process privilege is to encourage and protect a free and candid exchange of ideas during the decision-making process.[135] Exemption 5 is possibly broader and more uncertain than the deliberative process privilege.

In addition to memoranda reflecting the Service's deliberations leading up to an agency's action, Exemption 5 also exempts from disclosure that information a party could not obtain from the agency in a hypothetical court case brought over the agency's refusal to disclose. As the Supreme Court noted in *EPA v. Mink*, however, in litigation between a party and the agency, drawing a line between what may be withheld and what must be disclosed "is not without its difficulties," and so "at best, the discovery rules can only be applied under Exemption 5 by way of rough analogies."[136] The exemption provides no guidance in deciding whether the information would be discoverable, because "we do not know whether the Government is to be treated as though it were a prosecutor, a civil plaintiff, or a defendant," or whether the particularized needs of the individual seeking the information are to be considered, as they are under the discovery rules.[137]

Intra-agency memoranda containing predecisional recommendations on Service policy are also exempt from disclosure under Exemption 5.[138] To be

---

[133] 5 USC § 552(b)(5). Because Exemption 5 is tied to court discovery, if the Federal Rules of Civil Procedure restrict discovery, then access under the FOIA will be similarly restricted. See, for example, Nissei Sangyo Am., Ltd., 81 AFTR2d 98-1053 (DDC 1998) (expert material held not discoverable under FOIA because excepted from discovery, or subject to the restrictions of, Rule 26(b)(4), Fed. R. Crim. P.).

[134] EPA v. Mink, 410 US 73, 86–87 (1973) (quoting Kaiser Aluminum & Chem. Corp. v. United States, 141 Ct. Cl. 38, 49, 157 F. Supp. 939, 946 (1958)).

[135] EPA v. Mink, 410 US 73, 87 (1973); NLRB v. Sears, Roebuck & Co., 421 US 132, 150–151 (1975).

[136] EPA v. Mink, 410 US 73, 86 (1973).

[137] EPA v. Mink, 410 US 73, 86 (1973).

[138] Tabcor Sales Clearing, Inc. v. Department of the Treasury, 471 F. Supp. 436, 438 (ND Ill. 1979) (Treasury Department memoranda commenting on proposals to modify definition of "employer-employee relationship" exempt under both predecisional and deliberative process tests); Dick v. IRS, 78-1 USTC ¶ 9173 (DDC 1978) (memoranda from Chief Counsel to Commissioner containing recommendations on agency investigative poli-

exempt, the memorandum must be both (1) predecisional and (2) deliberative (reflecting the "give and take of the consultative process").[139] Communications prepared before the decision is made are protected because publicity would adversely affect a free and open exchange of ideas. The purpose served by the deliberative process privilege is easy enough to state, but deciding whether the privilege applies in a particular situation to a specific memorandum is another matter. In *Taxation With Representation Fund*, the circuit court considered (1) the function and significance of the document in the decision-making process; (2) the nature of the decision-making authority of the office issuing the disputed document; and (3) whether the document flowed from superiors to subordinates or vice versa.[140] The publicity of factual data does not affect the

---

cies); Common Cause v. IRS, 646 F2d 656 (DC Cir. 1981) (memoranda and correspondence about IRS decision not to disclose contacts with high-ranking federal officials on tax matters of third parties); Cliff v. IRS, 529 F. Supp. 11 (SDNY 1981) (staff opinions, recommendations, comments, and other deliberations concerning proposed IRS Manual Supplements); Rosenthal & Schanfield v. IRS, 80-2 USTC ¶ 9500 (ND Ill. 1980) (IRS Regulations Policy Committee minutes and tentative drafts of regulations not disclosed); Texas Indep. Producers Legal Action Ass'n v. IRS, 605 F. Supp. 538 (DDC 1984) (documents pertaining to development of two proposed Treasury regulations not disclosed).

When the information claimed to be covered by the exemption was alleged to be "opinions, concerns, and questions" that the agent expressed to a district counsel's office in recommending that enforcement action be taken against the taxpayer, the information was held to be exempt because it was predecisional information sought or referred before the district counsel had acted on the summons enforcement, and it was deliberative because it was "employed" by the district counsel in its decision-making process. Brooks v. IRS, 98-1 USTC ¶ 50,161 (ED Cal. 1997); see also Fischer v. IRS, 621 F. Supp. 835 (NDNY 1985) (working papers formulating and expressing opinions about the agency's treatment of tax protestor cases questions held exempt); Barmes v. IRS, 82 AFTR 2d 98-6301 (SD Ind. 1998) ("recommendation" portions of memoranda written by revenue officer to IRS attorney).

[139] See Coastal States Gas Corp. v. Department of Energy, 617 F2d 854, 866 (DC Cir. 1980), quoted in Arthur Andersen & Co. v. IRS, 514 F. Supp. 1173, 1176 (DDC 1981), remanded, 679 F2d 254 (DC Cir. 1982).

The Service recognizes that these are the applicable standards. See Delegation Order 222 (Rev. 2), discussed in IRS Litigation Guidance Memorandum TL-98 (1992), 98 TNT 52-105 ("The delegation order provides that executive privilege may only be claimed for those Internal Revenue Service records and information that are predecisional and deliberative, the disclosure of which would significantly impede or nullify Internal Revenue Service action in carrying out a responsibility or function, or would constitute an unwarranted invasion of personal privacy"). While information only needs to be predecisional and deliberative to be protected, the Service's disclosure policy is not to claim protection unless it meets the self-imposed requirements that the disclosure of the information also significantly impede or nullify IRS action, or invade personal privacy requirement. Purely factual or objective material is acknowledged not to be protected.

[140] Taxation With Representation Fund v. IRS, 646 F2d 666, 678–681 (DC Cir. 1981).

deliberative process and, consequently, this material is nonexempt even if it is compiled before a final decision is reached.[141]

When the government claims the deliberative process privilege, the court can review the documents in camera so that the court can determine whether the government's interest in nondisclosure outweighs "the interests of the litigants and public in disclosure."[142] The factors said to be weighable in this balancing process include (1) the relevance of the evidence; (2) the availability of other evidence; (3) the seriousness of the litigation; (4) the role of the government in the litigation; and (5) the "possibility of future timidity by government employees who will be forced to recognize that their secrets are violable."[143]

Postdecisional memoranda designed to explain the decision do not impair the decision-making process.[144] A postdecisional memorandum, which provides the reasons behind the Service's policy or explains a decision actually adopted (its "working law"), is not protected. For example, the Service distributes the postdecisional document for future use and guidance, as it would with a General Counsel's memorandum (which contains the legal reasons supporting letter rulings, revenue rulings, and technical advice)[145] and with technical memoranda (which contains background information prepared before but is-

---

[141] EPA v. Mink, 410 US 73, 91 (1973) (factual data "inextricably intertwined" with policy making may become protected under the policy-making umbrella). See also Soucie v. David, 448 F2d 1067, 1077 (DC Cir. 1971); Montrose Chem. Corp. v. Train, 491 F2d 63 (DC Cir. 1974).

[142] In re Franklin Nat'l Bank Sec. Litig., 478 F. Supp. 577, 582 (EDNY 1979).

[143] In re Franklin Nat'l Bank Sec. Litig., 478 F. Supp. 577, 583 (EDNY 1979).

[144] NLRB v. Sears, Roebuck & Co., 421 US 132, 151–152 (1975). Exemption 5 protection "ends abruptly the moment a decision is made by the executive," and so '[c]ommunications made after the decision and designed to explain it' are reachable under FOIA." American Soc'y of Pension Actuaries v. IRS, 746 F. Supp. 188, 190 (DDC 1990) (quoting Sears, 421 US at 151). Even if the document is predecisional at the time it is prepared, it can lose that status if it is adopted formally or informally as the agency's position on an issue. American Soc'y of Pension Actuaries v. IRS, supra, at 191 (DDC 1990) (specific budget estimate constitutes adoption of estimates; so calculations and assumptions were held part of IRS's deliberative process but were ordered produced because they became part of the President's budget).

[145] Falcone v. IRS, 479 F. Supp. 985 (ED Mich. 1979) (general counsel memorandum with an attached proposed revenue ruling held not deliberative). Compare Cliff v. IRS, 80-2 USTC ¶ 9596 (SDNY 1980) (nonsubstantive general counsel memorandum not ordered disclosed). See also Taxation With Representation Fund v. IRS, 646 F2d 666 (DC Cir. 1981), aff'd, remanding and modifying 485 F. Supp. 263 (DDC 1980) (extensive discussion of deliberative process privilege, predecisional versus postdecisional documents and working law claims of the Service, and application to general counsel memoranda, technical memoranda, and actions on decision).

sued to explain regulations),[146] as well as actions on decision[147] and field service advice.[148]

Exemption 5 incorporates some of the same privileges and protections that government lawyers raise in tax litigation. If reports, papers, and other documents are not available through discovery in a tax case between the taxpayer and the IRS, this information is exempt from disclosure under Exemption 5. In tax cases, where taxpayers seek to discover IRS memoranda, the government has raised the deliberative process privilege, as well as relevance, work product, and attorney-client privilege objections.[149] Even where docu-

---

[146] See King v. IRS, 684 F2d 517, 521 (7th Cir. 1982) ("Draft Technical Memorandum" apparently never formally adopted or approved discussing a previously promulgated Treasury Regulation held predecisional because it was never "relied on as an accurate statement of agency law. . . ."): Texas Indep. Producers Legal Action Ass'n v. IRS, 605 F. Supp. 538 (DDC 1984) (successive drafts with accompanying comments held not to serve as agency working law; cases analyzed).

[147] Actions on decision, containing the reasons behind the decision to appeal or not to appeal or to acquiesce or not to acquiesce in adverse court decisions, may be nonexempt if they represent final decisions and are distributed to IRS personnel. Arthur Andersen & Co. v. IRS, 514 F. Supp. 1173, 1176 (DDC 1981), remanded, 679 F2d 254 (DC Cir. 1982) (drafts of rulings and background documents found to flow from subordinates to superiors, did not serve as "working law" and were predecisional and deliberative, and thus were held to fall within Exemption 5).

[148] In Tax Analysts, the District of Columbia Circuit held that field service advice memoranda are not covered by the deliberative process exemption (Exemption 5), because they are not "documents produced in the process of formulating policy, [but] are themselves statements of an agency's legal position, and as such, cannot be viewed as predecisional." Tax Analysts v. IRS, 117 F3d 607, 617 (DC Cir. 1997). The circuit court said that field service advice was similar to technical advice because both types of documents reflect "the law the government is actually applying in its dealings with the taxpaying public," even if the field service advice is not formally binding on field offices. Id. at 618. The Service argued that disclosure of field service advice would affect the flow of information within the Service and would subject personnel who request and prepare advice "to pressure from those who disagree with their reasoning. . . ." Id. The circuit court rejected the argument, saying that the Service had shown no damage to the disclosure of technical advice, and so there was no reason to believe disclosure of field service advice would have the adverse consequences the Service described. Id.

[149] LSB Indus. v. Comm'r, 556 F. Supp. 40, 42 (WD Okla. 1982) (IRS conference memoranda and request for grand jury investigation held covered by the attorney-client privilege, work product immunity, and deliberative process privilege; therefore, not disclosable); Green v. IRS, 556 F. Supp. 79 (ND Ind. 1982), aff'd in unpub. op., 734 F2d 18 (7th Cir. 1984) (letter from IRS district counsel to U.S. Attorney's office requesting enforcement of summons held exempt because covered by attorney-client privilege). See also Betke v. IRS, 87-1 USTC ¶ 9262 (D. Neb. 1985) (memoranda between District Counsel and Deputy Regional Counsel and memorandum between District Counsel and District Director pertaining to notice of deficiency and Discriminant Function score held to be exempt).

While inter- and intra-agency letters and memoranda fall within Exemption 5, the District of Columbia Circuit uses a functional, rather than a literal, test in determining

ments reflect deliberations by Service personnel, factual matters generally are held discoverable despite a privilege claim[150] and, in appropriate cases, even opinions may be ordered disclosed.[151] Moreover, the basis for the IRS determi-

---

whether the memoranda are inter- or intra-agency. As a result, information outside the executive branch may fall within the exemption. Durns v. Bureau of Prisons, 804 F2d 701, 704 n.5 (DC Cir. 1986), vacated and remanded, 486 US 1029 (1988); Crooker v. IRS, 75 AFTR2d 95-2375 (DDC 1995) (letter from the IRS to the Assistant Attorney General of the Tax Division dealing with the need for a grand jury protected by the attorney-client privilege and the work product doctrine).

Objection has also been made on the ground that "good cause" for production was absent. See, e.g., Talbott Constr. Co. v. United States, 49 FRD 68 (ED Ky. 1970), 70-1 USTC ¶ 9440; Detroit Screwmatic Co. v. United States, 70-1 USTC ¶ 9175 (SDNY 1970); Conway Import Co. v. United States, 66-1 USTC ¶ 9381 (EDNY 1966); E.W. Bliss Co. v. United States, 203 F. Supp. 175 (ND Ohio 1971). The "good cause" requirement for a motion to produce was removed from the Federal Rules of Civil Procedure as of July 1970, but a showing of particularized need for the production of work product seems to raise a similar requirement, at least for this type of memorandum.

[150] See EPA v. Mink, 410 US 73, 87–88 (1973) ("Memoranda consisting only of compiled factual material or purely factual material contained in a deliberative memoranda and severable from its context would generally be available for discovery by private parties in litigation with the Government"). If the memoranda contain factual and deliberative material, Exemption 5 contemplates that access will be governed by "the same flexible, common sense approach that has long governed private parties' discovery" in litigation with a government agency. Id. at 91–92. See, e.g., ISI Corp. v. United States, 73-1 USTC ¶ 9251 (CD Cal. 1973); Weir Found. v. United States, 72-1 USTC ¶ 9435 (SDNY 1972); Simons-Eastern Co. v. United States, 354 F. Supp. 1003 (ND Ga. 1972); LSB Indus. v. Comm'r, 556 F. Supp. 40 (WD Okla. 1982) (finding factual data inextricably intertwined with recommendation for grand jury investigation). In Mayes v. United States, 86-2 USTC ¶ 9607 (WD Mo. 1986), a "legal analysis" apparently prepared by an appeals officer was held nondiscoverable on the ground that it was irrelevant to the issues in a refund suit and, in any event, was protected by governmental (or deliberative process) privilege.

Exemption 5 and Exemption 3 may overlap. See Casa Inv., Ltd. v. Gibbs, 90-2 USTC ¶ 50,553 (DDC 1990) (Appeal Supporting Statement not released, because portions sought would disclose strategy, investigation, and theory "revealing the Government's case prematurely and effectively thwarting the IRS's duty to enforce the revenue laws"). The law enforcement purpose must be to investigate potential civil or criminal violations of the internal revenue law that the Service is charged with investigating.

[151] Timken Roller Bearing Co. v. United States, 66-1 USTC ¶ 9151 (ND Ohio 1964) (relevance, executive privilege); Branerton Corp., 64 TC 191 (1975) (governmental privilege, attorney-client privilege, relevancy). In both cases, production of opinions and recommendations was necessary to enable the taxpayer to prepare his case with an understanding of the basis for the Service's position.

Opinions of appraisers have been held not to be exempt from disclosure when they were "presumably commissioned in order to assist the IRS in determining what a fair price for the Indian jewelry [the IRS seized] might be at the auction—an action unrelated to taxpayer's return or liability." Kamman v. United States, 56 F3d 46, 49 (9th Cir. 1995). The Service claimed the appraisals were return information within the meaning of Section 6103, but the court found that the affidavits of the Service personnel did not establish that the appraisals were collected for the purpose of determining the existence of or an amount of liability.

nation is relevant for the purposes of discovery in a tax case, even if the information is not legally relevant to a determination of the case.[152] The Service's work product and attorney-client privilege objections to discovery generally fail because IRS reports are not prepared in anticipation of litigation at the direction of or for a lawyer, nor are they communications made for the purpose of obtaining legal advice.[153] Nevertheless, courts have found that the attorney-client privilege and work product immunity protect legal advice given by attorneys for the Service to its agents and revenue officers in connection with a court case against or involving the taxpayer. The courts have determined that these protections apply even when there is no pending legal proceeding, and only administrative action is being considered.[154] Despite this reservation, the

---

With some redactions and exceptions to disclosure, a district counsel's opinion in response to a revenue agent's request for technical assistance was disclosed, over the Service's deliberative process objection. Ginsberg v. IRS, 81 AFTR2d 98-1031 (MD Fla. 1997) (magistrate judge's report). However, the magistrate judge recommended that the request and accompanying exhibits not be disclosed. The legal memorandum was disclosed with redaction to eliminate the possibility of impeding law enforcement although it provided the agents examining the requesters' returns with instructions and legal interpretation of the provisions of the Code, and was predecisional. Reasoning from the circuit court's decision in *Tax Analysts* ordering disclosure of field service advices because they were statements of policy and interpretations, the magistrate judge said that although the memorandum was not from the Chief Counsel's office, "it nonetheless forms the operative body of law found applicable to these taxpayers in this civil examination."

[152] Under Federal Rule of Civil Procedure 26(b)(1), a party is entitled to know the basis of any claim or defense, even if "the information sought will be inadmissible at the trial, if the information sought appears reasonably calculated to lead to the discovery of admissible evidence." In a refund suit, the taxpayer should be permitted to obtain discovery of Service memoranda even if the memoranda will not be admissible at trial (the trial tries the issue de novo) in part because the taxpayer has the burden of proving that he owes no tax at all, or determining the correct tax and overpayment to establish the amount unjustly withheld. Helvering v. Taylor, 293 US 507 (1935).

[153] The Tax Court's analysis of the issues in *Branerton Corp.*, 64 TC 191 (1975), is especially helpful in understanding the privilege and work product issues. For an extensive analysis of a work product claim in a FOIA case, see Moody v. IRS, 682 F2d 266 (DC Cir. 1982). See also Conway Import Co. v. United States, 66-1 USTC ¶ 9381 (EDNY 1966). But see Weir Found. v. United States, 72-1 USTC ¶ 9435 (SDNY 1972), where, contrary to the Tax Court in *Branerton Corp.*, the district court found that an Appeals report was immune from discovery as work product. See also LSB Indus. v. Comm'r, 556 F. Supp. 40 (WD Okla. 1982), holding memoranda of conferences between IRS special agents and attorneys regarding a criminal investigation and a possible grand jury investigation to be covered by the attorney-client privilege and work product immunity because they were in anticipation of "forms of litigation" (i.e., the grand jury).

[154] See Barmes v. United States, 82 AFTR2d 98-5319 (SD Ind. 1998) (The "Law and Analysis" portion of a "pre-decisional memorandum prepared by an IRS attorney in response to a request by a revenue officer to file certain liens . . . apply case law to the facts of the collection case . . . and include recommendations of additional administrative actions that could be taken [and so] were confidential legal advice from an attorney to his client and were prepared in anticipation of litigation (suit to enforce liens)." See also Buckner v.

following specific documents have been held discoverable in tax cases over the
Service's objections:

- Revenue agents' reports[155] and transmittal letters[156]
- Special agents' reports[157]
- Statements of taxpayers[158]
- Witness statements[159]
- Field service advice[160]
- District and appellate conference reports[161]

IRS, 82 AFTR2d 98-5650 (ND Ind. 1998) (memoranda prepared in connection with a
bankruptcy proceeding of the requester).

[155] Abel Inv. Co. v. United States, 72-1 USTC ¶ 9284 (D. Neb. 1971); Peterson v.
United States, 52 FRD 317 (SD Ill. 1971); Roller Bearing Co. v. United States, 66-1
USTC ¶ 9151 (ND Ohio 1964); United States v. Gates, 64-2 USTC ¶ 9832 (D. Colo.
1964); United States v. San Antonio Portland Cement Co., 63-2 USTC ¶ 9784 (WD Tex.
1963); Frazier v. Phinney, 60-1 USTC ¶ 9168 (SD Tex. 1959); Branerton Corp., 64 TC
191 (1975).

When the taxpayer in a tax refund suit moved to compel production of the complete
audit examination report, including the transmittal letter portion of the report, all history
sheets, worksheets, notes, memoranda, and any other material gathered during the examination of the taxpayer's return, the Service produced 1,250 pages, from which it withheld
eleven pages and redacted eight comments. The magistrate judge noted that the withheld
and redacted documents contained opinions regarding tax computations, legal analysis of
the positions of the parties, and recommendations regarding settlement, and so denied the
motion to compel. Armtek Corporation v. United States, 78 AFTR2d 96-5266 (WDNY
1996) (applying Franklin Nat'l Bank Sec. Litig., 478 F. Supp. 577 (EDNY 1979)). However, the district court sustained the government's deliberative process privilege claim in
part, apparently because the government did produce 1,250 pages, from which it withheld
only eleven pages and redacted eight comments. In weighing the government's interest in
nondisclosure against the taxpayer's interest in disclosure, the magistrate judge also called
the argument "compelling" that the mental processes of the agent were not relevant in a
refund suit because the court reviews the Service's action de novo.

[156] Armtek Corp. v. United States, 78 AFTR2d 96-5266 (WDNY 1996).

[157] PT&L Constr. Co. v. Comm'r, 63 TC 404, 411 (1974).

[158] 5 USC § 555(c).

[159] Barger v. Comm'r, 65 TC 925 (1976); Dvorak v. Comm'r, 64 TC 846 (1975);
PT&L Constr. Co. v. Comm'r, 63 TC 404, 411 (1974); Phelps v. Comm'r, 62 TC 513
(1974).

[160] In Tax Analysts, the District of Columbia Circuit held that field service advice
was not protected by the attorney-client privilege, because information communicated by
persons outside the agency, such as taxpayers or their representatives, does not contain
any confidential information concerning the agency that is communicated to the agency's
counsel for the purpose of obtaining legal advice. Tax Analysts v. IRS, 117 F3d 607 (DC
Cir. 1997). Field service advice is subject to work product protection, which means that
not only the mental impressions, conclusions, theories, and the like are protected, but also
"factual materials prepared in anticipation of litigation." Id. ("Any part of an FSA prepared in anticipation of litigation, not just the portions concerning the opinions, legal theories, and the like, is protected by the work product doctrine and falls under exemption 5.")

[161] Abel Inv. Co. v. United States, 72-1 USTC ¶ 9284 (D. Neb. 1971); Peterson v.
United States, 52 FRD 317 (SD Ill. 1971); Timken Roller Bearing Co. v. United States,

[5] Exemption 7: Investigatory Records

Since the FOIA allows any person to seek access to agency information, a taxpayer may request IRS-compiled investigatory records despite an obvious personal, as opposed to public, interest in the records. Taxpayers who have civil tax disputes or who are the subject of criminal investigation frequently make requests for such information. Exemption 7, the law enforcement exemption, permits the Service to deny access to investigatory materials compiled for law enforcement purposes. The 1974 amendments to FOIA substituted "records" for "files"[162] and limited the exemption to cases where one or more of six specified harms are established by the agency. As amended in 1986, Exemption 7 provides that FOIA does not apply to matters that are

> records or information compiled for law enforcement purposes, but only to the extent that the production of such law enforcement records or information (A) could reasonably be expected to interfere with enforcement proceedings, (B) would deprive a person of a right to a fair trial or an impartial adjudication, (C) could reasonably be expected to constitute an unwarranted invasion of personal privacy, (D) could reasonably be expected to disclose the identity of a confidential source, including a State, local, or foreign agency or authority or any private institution which furnished information on a confidential basis, and, in the case of a record or information compiled by a criminal law enforcement authority in the course of a criminal investigation, or by an agency conducting a lawful national security intelligence investigation, information furnished by a confidential source, (E) would disclose techniques and procedures for law enforcement investigations or prosecutions, or would disclose guidelines for law enforcement investigations or prosecutions if such disclosure could reasonably be expected to risk circumvention of the law, or (F) could reasonably be expected to endanger the life or physical safety of any individual.[163]

The 1986 amendment broadened Exemption 7 to cover "records or information compiled for law enforcement purposes," apparently not limiting the records or information to that compiled in investigations. However, the "harm" standard was reduced from "would" to "could reasonably be expected to" in Exemption 7(A) (protecting ongoing proceedings), Exemption 7(C) (protecting personal

---

66-1 USTC ¶ 9151 (ND Ohio 1964); United States v. Gates, 64-2 USTC ¶ 9832 (D. Colo. 1964); United States v. San Antonio Portland Cement Co., 63-2 USTC ¶ 9784 (WD Tex. 1963). But see Casa Inv., Ltd. v. Gibbs, 90-2 USTC ¶ 50,553 (DDC 1990) (Appeals Supporting Statement not disclosed under Exemption 3).

[162] This change was made to prevent an agency from refusing access to otherwise nonexempt information merely by putting it in an investigatory file. Source Book 1975 at 451.

[163] 5 USC § 552(b)(7).

privacy), Exemption 7(D) (protecting informants), and Exemption 7(F) (protecting physical safety).

Another provision of the FOIA, added in 1986, makes it even more unlikely that a person seeking law enforcement records will succeed in gaining access to them. Under this provision, an agency, such as the Service, that conducts criminal investigations can deny the existence of law enforcement records compiled in a criminal investigation where both (1) the subject of the investigation does not know about the investigation and (2) disclosure of the existence of the records "could reasonably be expected to interfere with enforcement proceedings."[164]

Exemption 7 applies where (1) the records or information were "compiled for law enforcement purposes" and (2) one or more of the six enumerated harms will result from production. The substitution of the word "record" for "files" means that, even where an investigation has been made, the courts must "consider the nature of [a] particular document to avoid the possibility of impermissible 'commingling' by an agency's placing in an investigatory file material that did not legitimately have to be kept confidential."[165] For purposes of this exemption, law enforcement appears to include enforcement of civil as well as criminal laws. Consequently, information gathered by the Service during a civil examination, as well as information gathered during a criminal investigation, has been held to be an investigatory record for law enforcement purposes.[166] Litigation in tax cases under Exemption 7 has generally involved interference with enforcement proceedings, invasions of privacy, and confidential informants.

[a] Interference With Enforcement Proceedings

Clause A of Exemption 7 allows an agency to avoid disclosing investigatory records where disclosure "could reasonably be expected to interfere with enforcement proceedings." Although Congress did not specify what type of enforcement proceedings were covered by this clause, it apparently had in mind

---

[164] 5 USC § 552(c).

[165] NLRB v. Robbins Tire & Rubber Co., 437 US 214, 229–230 (1978) (citing Source Book 1975 at 451).

[166] Williams v. IRS, 345 F. Supp. 591 (D. Del. 1972), aff'd, 479 F2d 317 (3d Cir. 1973), cert. denied sub nom. Donlon v. IRS, 414 US 1024 (1973); Luzaich v. United States, 435 F. Supp. 31 (D. Minn.), aff'd without op., 564 F2d 101 (8th Cir. 1977); Chamberlain v. Kurtz, 589 F2d 827 (5th Cir. 1979), cert. denied, 444 US 842 (1979); MacPherson v. IRS, 803 F2d 479 (9th Cir. 1986) (collection of speeches made by tax protester constituted "law enforcement activities" under 5 USC § 552a(e)(7)); Church of Scientology Int'l v. IRS, 995 F2d 916 (9th Cir. 1993) (IRS Exempt Organization Division performs law enforcement function so that documents generated in that division in connection with applications for exempt status may be exempt from disclosure because documents are compiled for law enforcement purposes).

a pending or potential case in court, a proceeding before a regulatory agency, or an investigation leading up to the case or proceeding.[167] However, an agency may properly claim that disclosure of particular types or categories of records will interfere with certain types of enforcement proceedings, and need not establish interference on a document-by-document basis.[168] For example, in *NLRB v. Robbins Tire & Rubber Co.*, the NLRB successfully claimed that because of the danger of witness intimidation, disclosure of witness statements before unfair labor practice proceedings was the kind of interference with enforcement proceedings that clause A was designed to avoid. When FOIA requests are made for information gathered during an ongoing investigation, the Service has successfully contended that production of witness statements before a case comes to court constitutes interference because it would enable a taxpayer to obtain earlier and possibly greater discovery than is provided under court rules.[169] Courts explain that the release of the information would allow

---

[167] Source Book 1975 at 333. The law enforcement purpose must be a response to potential civil or criminal violations of the law. For example, when the Service is participating in a law enforcement investigation of an employee under a nontax statute, it may be acting as an employer, and the investigation will only be for law enforcement purposes if the Service shows that the investigation has focused on acts that could result in civil or criminal sanctions against the employee. Patterson v. IRS, 56 F3d 832 (7th Cir. 1995) (requester was IRS employee against whom disciplinary action had been taken; IRS's affidavit to support claimed exemption held inadequate).

[168] NLRB v. Robbins Tire & Rubber Co., 437 US 214, 236 (1978).

[169] See Bryant v. IRS, 76-2 USTC ¶ 9613 (D. Me. 1976); Barney v. IRS, 618 F2d 1268 (8th Cir. 1980) (all information the Service gathered from January 1, 1977, to present about taxpayers; memoranda by special agent); Levy v. IRS, 531 F. Supp. 485 (SD Fla. 1982) (postinterview notes of witness statement); Lewis v. IRS, 823 F2d 375 (9th Cir. 1987) (700 pages of data collected during a criminal investigation of a taxpayer's failure to file returns; good description of procedure in an Exemption 7 case); Clarkson v. IRS, 811 F2d 1396 (11th Cir. 1987); Stephens v. IRS, 84-2 USTC ¶ 9714 (ND Ill. 1984) (documents revealing investigative procedures and techniques).

In Rosenglick v. IRS, 81 AFTR2d 98-1304 (MD Fla. 1998), there was a request for certain documents gathered in the course of a criminal investigation, and the district court held the information was exempt from disclosure because the declarations of the investigating agents "undisputedly establish" that the information requested was collected for law enforcement purposes and disclosure could reasonably be expected to interfere with enforcement proceedings). As the district court pointed out, to qualify for Exemption 7(A), the records must pass a two-pronged test: first, that the records or information were compiled for law enforcement purposes, and second, that the Service established that disclosure of the documents sought "could reasonably be expected to" interfere with enforcement proceedings. A liberal view of interference made sense, said the court, because if the target could obtain access to information through the FOIA earlier than otherwise, the early discovery could aid the wrongdoer "in secreting or tampering with evidence or witnesses."

Similarly, a Criminal Reference Letter (CRL) prepared on a target taxpayer will not be released to another taxpayer, even if the target provides the other taxpayer with a power of attorney. Casa Inv., Ltd. v. Gibbs, 90-2 USTC ¶ 50,553 (DDC 1990).

the taxpayers to fabricate excuses or evidence to frustrate the government's investigation.[170] Also, "[t]he selectivity in recording would certainly provide clues to the [taxpayers] of the nature and scope of the investigation."[171] However, the segregability rule of the FOIA[172] may apply to permit disclosure of information that would not interfere with an investigation.[173]

FOIA litigation itself may provide information about the contents of investigatory files, even where the Service's exemption claim is upheld. Under *Vaughn v. Rosen*,[174] a court may, on motion of the requester, require the government to file a detailed document index with each claim correlated to the listed document. Taxpayers have been successful in obtaining such indexes in a number of cases.[175] The process of preparing the index can consume the efforts of government investigators and lawyers, and the taxpayer can learn the direction, scope, and nature of the investigation.[176] For this reason, the Service opposes motions for a detailed index and, even if one is prepared, asks that it be reviewed in camera.[177] In response to the Service's objections, some courts

---

[170] For a catalog of possible types of interference, see Kanter v. IRS, 478 F. Supp. 552 at 55 (ND Ill. 1979). Where taxpayers asked for disclosure of a special agent's notes of interviews with them, the Service's claim that the notes were exempt under 5 USC § 552(b)(7)(A) was upheld. See Linsteadt v. IRS, 729 F2d 998, 1005 (5th Cir. 1984); Willard v. IRS, 776 F2d 100 (4th Cir. 1985); Holbrook v. IRS, 914 F. Supp. 314 (SD Iowa 1996) (notes of interview of requester and memorandum of interview were held exempt because the targets of the investigation might tamper with or intimidate potential witnesses, learn about the scope of the investigation, and construct defenses). However, the Third Circuit has refused to follow *Linsteadt* and *Willard* and has found that taxpayer interviews are not covered by Exemption (b)(7)(A). Grasso v. IRS, 785 F2d 70, 76 (8th Cir. 1986) ("The situation posed when the requester seeks disclosure of his or her own statement is far different from that presented when s/he seeks statements of third party witnesses").

[171] Willard v. IRS, 776 F2d 100, 103 (4th Cir. 1985).

[172] 5 USC § 552(b).

[173] See, e.g., Albin v. IRS, 79-2 USTC ¶ 9584 (DDC 1979) (allegation of improper investigative conduct). Compare Kanter v. IRS, 478 F. Supp. 552 at 55 (ND Ill. 1979). For a case finding that Service affidavits were specific enough to permit the court to determine whether or not its decision to disclose was arbitrary and capricious, see Stephens v. IRS, 84-2 USTC ¶ 9714 (ND Il. 1984) (court questioned how 1960–1974 documents ten or more years old could affect a current investigation).

[174] Vaughn v. Rosen, 484 F2d 820 (DC Cir. 1973), cert. denied, 415 US 977 (1974), appeal from remand, 523 F2d 1136 (DC Cir. 1975).

[175] Kanter v. IRS, 433 F. Supp. 812 (ND Ill. 1977). See also Tarnopol v. FBI, 442 F. Supp. 5 (DDC 1977). But see Steinberg v. IRS, 463 F. Supp. 1272 (SD Fla. 1979) (motion for index denied after reconsideration).

[176] See, e.g., Zale Corp. v. United States, 481 F. Supp. 486, 490–491 (DDC 1979).

[177] See Kuzma v. IRS, 775 F2d 66 (2d Cir. 1985); Steinberg v. IRS, 463 F. Supp. 1272 (SD Fla. 1979). The Eighth Circuit has indicated that in camera inspection by the District Court judge and the government's submission of a Vaughn index is not necessary in a case under 5 USC § 552(b)(7)(A) where the government makes an uncontradicted

have permitted the Service to submit affidavits that group documents into generic types and to specify the type of harm alleged to result from production of each category, although the use of affidavits alone has also been criticized.[178]

[b] Unwarranted Invasion of Personal Privacy

Clause C of Exemption 7 provides that law enforcement investigatory records are exempt to the extent that their production "could reasonably be expected to constitute an unwarranted invasion of personal privacy."[179] The language of this clause is the same `` FOIA Exemption 6, except that the phrase "could reasonably be expected to was substituted for "would," and the word "clearly" was deleted. Since the "unwarranted invasion" under clause C need not be clear, the government's burden of proof is somewhat lighter under clause C than under Exemption 6. The privacy invaded must be "personal." What information is private? Disclosure of financial interests, addresses, and personal relationships has been held to invade privacy,[180] as does disclosure of

---

showing that (1) the records were investigatory records compiled for law enforcement purposes and (2) disclosure would interfere with pending enforcement proceedings. Barney v. IRS, 618 F2d 1268, 1272–1273 (8th Cir. 1980). In Lewis v. IRS, 823 F2d 375 (9th Cir. 1987), the Ninth Circuit said that, in regard to each withheld document, the government is not required to make a specific factual showing that disclosure would actually interfere with an enforcement proceeding, citing agreement with *Barney.* Lewis v. IRS, 823 F2d at 380. In *Barney,* the circuit court did not say just how the requester is supposed to contradict the government's affidavits without either of these devices, but left open their use in deciding the applicability of other exemptions. 618 F2d at 1274.

[178] See Stephenson v. IRS, 629 F2d 1140, 1145 (5th Cir. 1980) (disagreeing with the use of affidavits alone); Kuzma v. IRS, 775 F2d 66 (2d Cir. 1985).

[179] 5 USC § 552(b)(7)(C). It has been said that the court must apply a two-pronged analysis to determine the applicability of this exemption. Crooker v. IRS, 75 AFTR2d 95-2375 (9th Cir. 1995). First, the agency must show that the record arose from an investigation related to the enforcement of federal laws, and that the nexus between the investigation and one of the agency's law enforcement duties is based on information sufficient to support at least "a colorable claim" of its rationality, citing Simon v. Department of Justice, 980 F2d 782, 783 (DC Cir. 1992) (which in turn quotes Pratt v. Webster, 673 F2d 408, 420–421 (DC Cir. 1982)). Then, the court must determine whether there has been an invasion of personal privacy, balancing the privacy interest at stake and the public interest in disclosure. See Crooker v. IRS, 75 AFTR2d 95-2375 (9th Cir. 1995) (gathering cases).

In *Crooker,* the requester asked for information about a raid and his arrest, and the IRS withheld the personal information of lower-level IRS and municipal employees. The court held that nondisclosure was proper under Exemption 7(C), and that disclosure would only reveal personal information about the employees, not relevant information about the operations or the conduct of any government agency, and would subject the employees to annoyance and harassment, which are the reasons why the exemption was created.

[180] See Wine Hobby USA, Inc. v. IRS, 502 F2d 133 (3d Cir. 1974) (a sixth-exemption case); May v. IRS, 82-2 USTC ¶ 9451 (WD Mo. 1982) (video training films in

other information that the individual might choose not to personally disclose to the public because of its intimacy or potential adverse effect.[181] In deciding what data would constitute an invasion of privacy if disclosed, a court must balance the individual's privacy interests and the public's interest in access to the material.[182] For this reason, clause C is construed to protect the identity of individuals who provide information to the Service.[183] In other words, disclosure may constitute an unwarranted invasion of an individual's personal privacy if the Service were to disclose not only its investigatory record of that individual, but also personal information about an individual contained in the investigatory file on another individual.

Data compiled during an examination or investigation about a taxpayer constitutes an investigatory file compiled for law enforcement purposes. However, in balancing privacy interest and the public interest in disclosure, such information has been held exempt from disclosure on the ground that privacy interests outweigh the public's interest in disclosure even when information about citizens "reveals little or nothing about the agency's own conduct" (e.g., when a lawyer sought circular letters requesting fee information agents sent to

---

which IRS employees and their families appeared were exempt from disclosure, since disclosure reasonably could be expected to result in harassment of those employees by disgruntled taxpayers).

[181] See Luzaich v. United States, 435 F. Supp. 31 (D. Minn.), aff'd without op., 564 F2d 101 (8th Cir. 1977); U.S. Attorney General, Memorandum on the 1974 Amendments to the Freedom of Information Act, reprinted in Source Book 1975 at 9–10.

[182] Luzaich v. United States, 435 F. Supp. 31 (D. Minn.), aff'd without op., 564 F2d 101 (8th Cir. 1977); Kanter v. IRS, 433 F. Supp. 812 (ND Ill. 1977). See also Wine Hobby USA, Inc. v. IRS, 502 F2d 133 (3d Cir. 1974).

[183] Luzaich v. United States, 435 F. Supp. 31 (D. Minn.), aff'd without op., 564 F2d 101 (8th Cir. 1977) (taxpayer requested a letter in the audit file to learn the identity of an informant; the letter was held exempt from disclosure under Exemption 7(C) because it would constitute an unwarranted invasion of the informant's personal privacy); Lobosco v. IRS, 78-2 USTC ¶ 9578 (EDNY 1978). See also Tarnopol v. FBI, 442 F. Supp. 5 (DDC 1977); Stephenson v. IRS, 629 F2d 1140, 1145 (5th Cir. 1980) (travel arrangements revealing third-party contact). Accordingly, in response to a FOIA request for the information, the Bureau of Prisons claimed that under Exemption 7(C) together with Exemption 7(F) it was entitled to withhold the identities of individuals requiring separation from the requester in prison, cooperating third parties, and witnesses who testified against the requester at trial. The district court upheld the exemption claim for the individuals requiring separation from the requester, as well as cooperating third parties, because their physical safety might be endangered by disclosure of their identities, but this justification did not hold true for witnesses whose identities had already been disclosed at the trial. Linn v. U.S. Department of Justice, 80 AFTR2d 97-5062 (DDC 1997).

the lawyer's clients and the clients' responses,[184] or when a law firm requested records of tax lien filings that had already been made public.[185]

[c] Confidential Sources and Information

Clause D of Exemption 7 has two parts. The first part protects only the identity of a confidential source, but not the information furnished, whether the investigatory record was compiled in a civil or a criminal investigation.[186] However, the agency's determination that disclosure would reveal the identity of the informant must be reasonable. The second part protects the source's identity and the information the informant furnished to the Service, but it applies only to criminal and national security investigations. No express promise of confidentiality need have been given to the source. The protection is implied if an assurance of confidentiality may reasonably be inferred from the circumstances in which the information was provided.[187] Unlike the exemptions

---

[184] Schlabach v. IRS, 82 AFTR2d 98-6221 (ED Wash. 1998) ("The government has shown that the letters to and from the Plaintiff's clients contain information that could reasonably be expected to subject these individuals to harassment or intimidation by the Plaintiff and could affect the continued cooperation of the individuals with the government").

[185] Abraham & Rose, PLC v. United States, 82 AFTR2d 98-7448 (ED Mich. 1998) (although the tax lien information was public, "it is difficult to see how disclosure of this type of information furthers the public interest [and] shed[s] any light on IRS collection procedures"). The district court also agreed that disclosure of the information to a third person had the potential of subjecting the individuals against whom the liens were filed to "'harassment, uninvited solicitations, annoyance, comment, speculation, and stigma.'"

[186] Pope v. United States, 599 F2d 1383, 1386 (5th Cir. 1979) (information concerning possible misconduct that led to consideration of disciplinary proceedings). This exemption applies even if the information furnished the IRS was unsolicited, as it was in *Pope*. Heinsohn v. IRS, 553 F. Supp. 791, 793 (ED Tenn. 1983) (disclosure of documents obtained during criminal investigation not disclosed because nature of data would reveal source); Stine v. IRS, 82-2 USTC ¶ 9645 (WD La. 1982) (entire document held not disclosable because disclosure of any portion would reveal identity of confidential source); Kuzma v. IRS, 775 F2d 66 (2d Cir. 1985).

[187] Kuzma v. IRS, 775 F2d 66 (2d Cir. 1985); Luzaich v. United States, 435 F. Supp. 31 (D. Minn.), aff'd without op., 564 F2d 101 (8th Cir. 1977); Bast v. IRS, 78-1 USTC ¶ 9418 (DDC 1978). See also Sands v. Murphy, 633 F2d 968, 970 (1st Cir. 1980) (*A* gave information to *B*, a state law enforcement agency, which *B* gave to *C*, a federal law enforcement agency; held, indirect informer given implied protection). For a case where an express promise of confidentiality was found, see Gregg v. IRS, 80-1 USTC ¶ 9274 (DDC 1980); Stine v. IRS, 82-2 USTC ¶ 9645 (WD La. 1982) (finding that informant supplied information under circumstances that indicated assurances of confidentiality); Betke v. IRS, 87-1 USTC ¶ 9262 (D. Neb. 1985) (names of third parties who cooperated with IRS during its investigation held to be exempt); Barmes v. IRS, 82 AFTR2d 98-5319 (SD Ind. 1998) (memorandum of an informant's telephone call with revenue officer reporting requesters' violations of the tax laws, including information about the basis for the informant's knowledge, the source, subject, and circumstances of the information, were

for disclosures that would interfere with enforcement proceedings and invade personal privacy, this exemption does not balance the informant's interest in nondisclosure against the requester's purportedly public interest.[188] Clause D is also construed to protect the identity of informants.

In *Department of Justice v. Landano*,[189] the Supreme Court held that "the Government is not entitled to a presumption that a source is confidential within the meaning of Exemption 7(D) whenever the source provides information to [an investigative agency] in the course of a criminal investigation."[190] "Confidential" for purposes of the exemption means that the informant "furnished the information with the understanding that the [agency] would not divulge the communication except to the extent the [agency believes] it necessary for law enforcement purposes."[191] Under Exemption 7(D), "the question is not whether the requested *document* is of the type that the agency usually treats as confidential, but whether the particular *source* spoke with an understanding that the communication would remain confidential."[192] Consequently, no presumption of confidentiality applies. When a FOIA request is made and the government claims the exemption, it must make an individualized showing that the source supplied the information with the understanding that the communication would remain confidential.[193]

---

held confidential based on the revenue officer's affidavit that he prepared the memorandum in the course of an investigation to reflect information about requesters' tax liability, and informant had been given express assurances of confidentiality).

[188] Sands v. Murphy, 633 F2d 968, 971 (1st Cir. 1980). In *Sands*, the circuit court indicated that portions of documents covered by the exemption should nevertheless be disclosed, if segregable. Id.

[189] Department of Justice v. Landano, 508 US 165 (1993).

[190] Department of Justice v. Landano, 508 US 165, 181 (1993).

[191] Department of Justice v. Landano, 508 US 165, 174 (1993).

[192] Department of Justice v. Landano, 508 US 165, 172 (1993). As a result, an agency may withhold confidential information even if the requester or the public knows the source's identity, or if the confidential source testifies in court against the requester. See Crooker v. IRS, 75 AFTR2d 95-2375 (DDC 1995) (IRS deleted information dealing with the names, addresses, telephone numbers, recent activities, and other information tending to reveal the identity of confidential informants, although the requester may already have been aware of their identities; held, Exemption 7(D) was applicable because the informants spoke with express assurances of confidentiality).

[193] See Lodi v. United States, 81 AFTR2d 98-1973 (ED Cal. 1998) (requiring an individualized showing and concluding on review that disclosure of documents redacting names and identifying information of confidential sources satisfied the segregability requirement of the FOIA, and that other documents were exempt because no reasonably segregable portion could be released without disclosing the identity of a confidential source).

[d] Law Enforcement Techniques or Guidelines

Exemption 7(E) makes exempt from disclosure records or information compiled for law enforcement purposes if disclosure "would disclose techniques and procedures for law enforcement investigations or prosecutions, or would disclose guidelines for law enforcement investigations or prosecutions, if [the] disclosure could reasonably be expected to risk circumvention of the law."[194] Since Exemption 2 also permits the Service not to disclose the standards it uses for selecting returns for audit or the data to be used for determining these standards if it determines that disclosure will impair tax administration, there is considerable overlap between Exemption 2 and Exemption 7(E). Read in the context of the other subparts of Exemption 7, it appears that Exemption 7(E) deals with criminal investigations, while the legislative history of Exemption 2 suggests that it applies to the criteria the Service uses to select returns for civil examinations, such as the Taxpayer Compliance Measurement Program and the Discriminant Function System.[195] The Service has nevertheless argued successfully that Exemption 7(E) exempts DIF scores from disclosure.[196]

[6] Exclusions From the Freedom of Information Act

Under certain circumstances, an agency receiving a request for information under the FOIA is permitted to treat records as if they did not exist for purposes of the FOIA. The Freedom of Information Reform Act of 1986 (FOIA Reform Act)[197] added the following three situations where records are excluded from the FOIA:

- Where during a criminal investigation the response to a request could "tip off" the subject of an investigation of its existence[198]

---

[194] 5 USC § 552(b)(7)(E).

[195] See supra ¶ 2.03[2][a].

[196] Small v. IRS, 820 F. Supp. 163, 165–166 (DNJ 1992) (disclosure of IRS's DIF scores would result in circumvention of the tax laws); Inman v. Comm'r, 871 F. Supp. 1275, 1277 (ED Cal. 1994) (same). Accord D'Angelica v. IRS, 76 AFTR2d 95-5719 (ED Cal. 1995). See also Ferguson v. IRS, No. C-89-4048-JPV, unreported op. (ND Cal. Oct. 31, 1990) (1990 US Dist. LEXIS 15293) (portions of IRM held covered by law enforcement exemption, 5 USC § 552(b)(7)(E), because "investigatory techniques not previously known to public, including dollar tolerances and math error codes used to review, process, and examine returns").

[197] Pub. L. No. 99-570, § 1802(b) (1986).

[198] 5 USC § 552(c)(1).

- Where identification of a confidential informant would be threatened by the request[199]
- Where the request involves certain law enforcement records maintained by the FBI pertaining to foreign intelligence or counterintelligence or international terrorism[200]

If the Service makes administrative finding that the requisite circumstances are present, the Service is authorized to treat the records as if they did not exist. In other words, the Service's response will be that there are "no records" meeting the request's description.

Of these exclusions, the "tip off" exclusion has the most significance in tax cases. Where a request is made for records described in Section A of Exemption 7, this exclusion permits an agency, such as the Service, to treat requested records "as not subject to the requirements of" the FOIA. However, the Service may use this exclusion only where (1) there is a pending criminal investigation of "a possible violation of criminal law"; and (2) "there is reason to believe that (i) the subject of the investigation or proceeding is not aware of its pendency, and (ii) disclosure of the existence of the records could reasonably be expected to interfere with enforcement proceedings. . . . "[201] The "tip off" exclusion raises some disturbing issues. The exclusion does not apply to records maintained in a civil enforcement proceeding, but it is available for a mere "possible violation of criminal law," which appears to cover investigatory records maintained or necessary for purposes other than a criminal tax prosecution. Also, the Criminal Investigation Division need only have a "reason to believe" that the subject does not know of the investigation. These standards leave open the possibility of administrative abuse. On the basis of its subjective judgments, the Service might conceal from a requester the existence of an investigatory file, so that the requester will be unable to obtain judicial review of the Service's decision. For example, a taxpayer might not be made aware of a special agent's investigative file, even after the practical likelihood of criminal prosecution has expired, and thus the taxpayer will not be able to obtain review of the Service's decision.

¶ 2.04 INDIVIDUAL REQUESTS FOR INFORMATION

The Service must make those records specifically described and requested by any person promptly available to that person, unless the records are published in the Federal Register or are available at Service offices for inspection and

---

[199] 5 USC § 552(c)(2).
[200] 5 USC § 552(c)(3).
[201] 5 USC § 552(c)(1).

copying. Requests for information must be made in accordance with the Service's published rules with respect to the time, place, fees, and procedures to be followed. If the records are not made available, the requester may sue in a federal district court.

[1] Making a Request

To obtain information from the Service, a written request, reasonably describing the records to which access is sought, must be made to the appropriate district office. The request may be in the form of a letter signed by the requester. (See Form 2.2.) However, such a letter must contain the following information:[202]

- A statement that the request is made pursuant to FOIA. It is also helpful to put "Freedom of Information Act Request" in the lower left-hand corner of the envelope.
- The proper address of the IRS office.[203] In general, the request is sent or hand-delivered to the local district director to the attention of the disclosure officer.
- Identification of the requested records with the greatest possible accuracy. Although it is not required that a document be specified by name or title, the request must "reasonably describe" the information, that is, the description must be sufficient to enable a professional employee of the agency familiar with the subject area of the request to locate the record with a reasonable amount of effort. The regulations state that the reasonable-description requirement is satisfied if the requester gives the name, the subject matter, and (if known) the date and location of the requested record. Although the inclusion of all the data suggested by the regulations may not be required as a matter of law, the more specific and limited the request, the greater the likelihood that it will be processed expeditiously. While the requester is supposed to describe the information sought in sufficient detail to make the search reasonably possible, the Service is required to conduct an adequate search.[204] If the requester's description of the information sought is inadequate, however, it can affect the determination of whether the Service's search was adequate.

---

[202] 26 CFR § 601.702(c)(3).

[203] The addresses of the officials responsible for the control of records are set forth at 26 CFR § 601.702(d).

[204] Patterson v. IRS, 56 F3d 832, 841 (7th Cir. 1995) (finding that the IRS's search was reasonable in light of the requester's request, even though the IRS official submitting the supporting affidavit did not have personal knowledge of the search).

- The facts establishing the requester's identity (e.g., a photocopy of a driver's license or a sworn statement) and right to disclosure, if there is a possible conflict between the FOIA and the privacy or confidentiality rules of either the Privacy Act or Section 6103.
- The address of the person who must be sent notification of any action taken on the request.
- Whether the requester wishes to inspect or desires a copy of the requested record or records.
- An agreement to pay fees for the search and duplication; a statement of the upper limit of the amount of fees the requester is willing to pay; and a statement identifying the requester as either a commercial use requester, media requester, educational institution requester, noncommercial scientific institution requester, or other requester.[205]

---

[205] The Service's fee schedule is set forth at Statement of Procedural Rules, 26 CFR § 601.702(f)(3).

FORM 2.2 _____
FOIA REQUEST LETTER
_____

District Director
Internal Revenue Service
120 Church Street
New York, New York 10008
Attention: Disclosure Officer

Re: Freedom of Information Act Request

Dear Sir:

Under the provisions of the Freedom of Information Act, 5 USC § 552, I request access to the following records: [*Identify records as specifically as possible*].I would like copies made of these records, and I agree to pay any search and duplicating fees. [*Or:* I would like the opportunity to inspect these records first before any copying is made, and I agree to pay any search fees incurred.] I am an "other requester" and agree to pay search and duplicating fees up to [*dollar limit*].Should you determine that any portion of the records or information I request is exempt, please supply me with a copy of the portion considered nonexempt. [*Or:* the records to which I wish to have access are my own tax returns or tax return information relating to me. Accordingly, the records may be disclosed to me under Section 6103. A photocopy of my driver's license is enclosed].

If all or any part of this request is denied, please notify me of the specific exemption(s) you think justifies your refusal to release the information. Any notification regarding this request may be sent to address of noticee.

Sincerely,

[2] Fees and Fee Waivers

The FOIA Reform Act of 1986 established four different categories of users and fees that an agency can assess when an information request is made upon it.[206] It also provided for fee waivers or reductions under certain circumstances. In general, fees must be reduced or waived "if disclosure of the information is in the public interest because it [1] is likely to contribute significantly to public understanding of the operation and activities of the government and [2] is not primarily in the commercial interest of the requester."[207] The Service generally requires that anyone making a request for information attest under penalty of perjury as to the category of user to which they belong,[208] unless it is readily apparent that no fees will be assessed, or the disclosure officer has determined the category of user.[209]

The first type of user is the "commercial" user. A commercial use request is one that "furthers the commercial, trade, or profit interests of the requester or the person on whose behalf the request is made."[210] Among the factors that the Service considers to establish commercial use are (1) the intended use of the information; (2) the identity of the requester in the absence of any explanation to the contrary; (3) the nature of the records requested; or (4) the Service's previous experience with the requester or type of request.[211] Requests made by attorneys, accountants, or other representatives may be commercial use requests when the requests are known to represent principals who would be considered commercial users.[212] With respect to the fees for commercial users, the Manual states that they will be charged for "search, duplication, and review." The Manual also states that commercial users "are not entitled to make requests for the reduction or waiver of fees, and therefore no consideration need be given to such requests."[213] The level of the fee on such requests is limited to "reasonable standard charges."[214]

---

[206] 5 USC § 552(a)(4)(A)(ii).

[207] 5 USC § 552(a)(4)(A). The decision to deny a fee waiver is subject to de novo review, but the court is limited in its review to the record that was before the Service at the time it made its administrative decision. 5 USC § 552(a)(4)(A)(vii).

[208] 26 CFR § 601,702(f)(3)(i). See IRM 1272, Disclosure of Information Handbook, Exhibit 500-1.

[209] IRM 1272, Disclosure of Information Handbook § 521 (FOIA Categories-Categories of Users), MT 1272-301 (Feb. 13, 1995).

[210] 26 CFR § 601.702(f)(3)(i)(A).

[211] IRM 1272, Disclosure of Information Handbook § 521(2)(a).

[212] IRM 1272, Disclosure of Information Handbook § 521(2)(a).

[213] IRM 1272, Disclosure of Information Handbook § 522 (Categories of Services).

[214] 5 USC § 552(a)(4)(A)(ii)(I).

A second type of user is the "educational or noncommercial scientific institution" whose purpose is scholarly or scientific research.[215] An educational institution can be any type of school so long as it has programs for scholarly research.[216] A noncommercial scientific institution is one that is "not operated on a commercial basis," and whose research activities are "not intended to promote any particular product or industry."[217] A third user is the "representative of the news media,"[218] which includes persons associated with news media outlets, such as television or radio stations, wire services, or print media.[219] For both educational or noncommercial scientific institutions and media representatives, the FOIA Reform Act also limits fees to "reasonable standard charges for document duplication."[220] For these second and third categories of users, the Service does not charge a fee for the first hundred pages of duplication, nor require payment for search or review costs."[221] Additionally, the Service considers fee waivers or fee reductions for both these categories of users.[222]

The fourth and most common category of user, and the one into which most taxpayers fall, is simply referred to as "all other requesters."[223] This category includes all users who do not fit into the other three categories. All such requesters are entitled to two hours of free search time and one hundred pages of duplication without charge, and thereafter are only assessed reasonable charges for document search and duplication.[224] Even after the free search time and duplication is given to the requester, no fee is assessed on any subsequent charges "if the costs of routine collection and processing of the fee are likely to equal or exceed the amount of the fee."[225] Table 2.1 lists the fees charged for IRS services.[226]

---

[215] 5 USC § 552(a)(4)(A)(ii)(II).
[216] 26 CFR § 601.702(f)(3)(i)(C).
[217] 26 CFR § 601.702(f)(3)(i)(D).
[218] 5 USC § 552(a)(4)(A)(ii)(II).
[219] 26 CFR § 601.702(f)(3)(i)(B).
[220] 5 USC § 552(a)(4)(A)(ii)(II).
[221] IRM 1272, Disclosure of Information Handbook § 522(4) (Categories of Services).
[222] 26 CFR § 601.702(f)(2)(ii).
[223] 5 USC § 552(a)(4)(A)(ii)(III); 26 CFR § 601.702(f)(3)(i)(E).
[224] 5 USC §§ 552(a)(4)(A)(ii)(III), 552(a)(4)(A)(iv)(II); Reg. § 601.702(f)(3)(ii)(E).
[225] 5 USC § 552(a)(4)(A)(iv)(I).
[226] Reg. §§ 601.702(f)(5)–601.702(g).

TABLE 2.1
Fees for IRS Services

(A) Search services
    (1) Searches other than for computerized records: $17.00 for each hour or fraction thereof spent by any Service personnel in searching for information within the scope of the request
    (2) Searches for computerized records: Actual direct costs, including cost of the computer printout
    (3) Searches requiring travel or transportation (shipping charges for transporting records or cost of transporting an employee): Actual cost of such shipping or transportation
    (4) All other services and materials requested pursuant to the FOIA not covered above: Actual cost
(B) Review services—examination of records in response to a commercial use request that does not fall under a FOIA exemption
    (1) Fees charged for review services: $21.00 for each hour or fraction thereof spent by any Service personnel in reviewing records for disclosure
(C) Duplication other than for returns or related documents
    (1) Photocopy or similar process: $0.15 per copy of page up to 8½" × 14"
    (2) Photographs, film, other materials: Actual cost
    (3) Records released to private contract for copying: Actual cost, so long as it does not exceed the Service's cost
    (4) Records not specifically identified above: Actual cost to the Service
(D) Charges for copies of returns and related documents
    (1) Copy of a return or related document other than an EP/EO return: $4.25 per copy
    (2) EP/EO returns and related documents: $1.00 for the first page and $0.15 for each additional page
(E) Printed materials located at public inspection facilities: Same costs as in (C) above
(F) Search and deletion services with respect to records open to public inspection pursuant to Code Section 6110: Actual cost

---

In cases where the Service expects the fees to exceed $250, it may require advance payment.[227] The Service may also request advance payment where the requester has previously failed to pay fees, has paid them late (more than thirty days), or appears to be incapable of paying (e.g., minor or incompetent).[228] A record request should include a "commitment to pay costs" unless

---

[227] 26 CFR § 601.702(f)(9)(ii). IRM 1272, Disclosure of Information Handbook § 532 (Requests Involving Extensive Efforts). See also Reg. §§ 601.702(f)(4), 601.702(f)(9)(ii).

[228] 26 CFR § 601.702(f)(9)(i). IRM 1272, Disclosure of Information Handbook § 533 (Requests Involving Prior Non-Payment).

fees are not expected to exceed $10. The Service rejects FOIA requests, on the basis of incompleteness, where the request does not include a commitment to pay costs, unless it can be determined that no fees will result.[229]

If a record request, complete and with no errors, is not anticipated to involve fees, contains a commitment to pay costs, or does not require prior payment, the Service will perform all processing necessary to complete the request. However, in cases where payment is required, the Service may defer making copies for release and drafting the final response until payment is received.[230]

Additional authority for the Service's power to assess fees can be found in the Code. Section 6110(j)(l) allows the Secretary to "assess actual costs for duplication of any written determination . . . made available to the public inspection only upon written request" and costs "incurred in searching for and making deletions required under subsection (c) [exemptions] from any written determination . . . available to public inspection only upon written request." Section 6110(j)(l) also provides that the Service may waive or reduce fees where it is furnishing the document primarily to benefit the public interest. Section 6103(p)(2)(A) provides for a reasonable fee to be charged for a "reproduction or certified reproduction of a return" if the person making the request is authorized to receive such material.[231]

The FOIA provides that "[d]ocuments shall be furnished without any charge or at a charge reduced below the fees established under clause (ii) if disclosure of the information is in the public interest because it is likely to contribute significantly to public understanding of the operations or activities of the government and is not primarily in the commercial interest of the requester."[232] To determine whether a requester has met the two-part test for the waiver or reduction of fees for furnishing records and other information, the Service considers such factors as (1) whether the subject of the records concerns the agency's operations or activities; (2) whether the records are likely to contribute to an understanding of the agency's operations or activities; (3) whether the records will contribute to the understanding of the public in general about the Service's operations and activities because of the manner and

---

[229] IRM 1272, Disclosure of Information Handbook § 534 (Commitment to Pay).

[230] IRM 1272, Disclosure of Information Handbook § 535 (Processed Requests).

[231] The Manual also quotes language from what it is the United States Code, which states that "it is the sense of Congress that each service or thing of value provided by an agency to a person is to be self-sustaining to the extent possible. Each charge is to be fair and based upon the costs to the Government, the value of the service or thing to the recipient, the public policy, or interest served and other relevant facts." IRM 1272, Disclosure of Information Handbook § 510 (Background and Authority) (Mar. 1, 1989), citing 31 USC § 9701.

[232] 5 USC § 552(a)(4)(A)(iii). IRM 1272, Disclosure of Information Handbook § 541 (Applicability of Fee Waivers) (Mar. 1, 1989). 26 CFR § 601.702(f)(2)(i).

extent the requester will use to disseminate the information; and (4) whether the information will significantly contribute to the general public's understanding of the agency's operations and activities, or whether the information is already available to the public.[233]

The Service recognizes that various disclosure statutes can overlap so that a request pursuant to either the Privacy Act or the Code may appear to be a FOIA request. Thus, the Service may waive fees regardless of the statute cited in the disclosure request if the services provided are substantially similar to those under FOIA requests.[234] According to a Justice Department memorandum, the statutory fee waiver standard includes two requirements, both of which must be met if there is to be a waiver or reduction in fees.[235] The first requirement is that the disclosure be in the "public interest." The second is that the disclosure not be "primarily in the commercial interest of the requester." If both conditions are met, waiver or reduction of the fee is compelled by statute.[236]

If varying fees are applicable to a particular situation, the Disclosure Officer can exercise discretion and apply the lower fee. Likewise, discretion may also be used to provide copies without charge where it would facilitate administration and examination.[237]

Waiver or reduction requests must be in writing and must include a rationale for the request unless the applicability of such waiver or reduction is self-evident from the material already submitted.[238]

As noted above, where it can be shown that the information sought is in the public interest and will contribute significantly to the public understanding

---

[233] 26 CFR § 601.702(f)(2)(ii). For a case where a requester successfully obtained a fee waiver despite the Service's rejection, see Landmark Legal Found. v. IRS, 82 AFTR2d 98-6544 (DDC 1998) (organization requested information about investigations of Section 501(c)(3) organizations, and the individuals who requested information about these organizations, which it said it would publish on its web site, and communicate through other media; the court held that the requested records would reveal information about the Service's operations and activities in auditing known conservative groups rather than known liberal groups and the manner of dissemination would communicate this information to the general public).

[234] 26 CFR § 601.702(f)(2)(i); IRM 1272, Disclosure of Information Handbook § 541 (Applicability of Fee Waivers).

[235] Dep't of Justice Manual, Dep't of Justice Memorandum: "Guidance on the Fee Waiver Policy" (Apr. 2, 1987). See also 5 USC § 552(a)(4)(A)(iii).

[236] 5 USC § 552(a)(4)(A)(iii).

[237] 26 CFR § 601.702(f)(2)(i); IRM 1272, Disclosure of Information Handbook § 541 (Applicability of Fee Waivers) (Mar. 1, 1989).

[238] IRM 1272, Disclosure of Information Handbook § 542 (Requesting Waivers) (Feb. 13, 1995).

of the IRS, then fees may be waived or reduced.[239] The Service looks at many factors in deciding whether to waive or reduce fees based on the value of the information to the general public, which again revolves around the issue of how the public's understanding of the Service, its history, operations, activities, and mission would be enhanced by the requested information.[240]

Additionally, although mere indigence[241] does not, in and of itself, cause the Service to waive or reduce fees, the showing of a humanitarian purpose may accomplish this goal if it can be shown that the information benefits persons other than the requester.[242]

[3] Requirements for Responses

The Service is required to respond to all requests for information within ten working days after receipt of the request.[243] The ten-day period begins on the date the request is received by the disclosure officer.[244] The Service is entitled to a ten-day unilateral extension for certain "unusual circumstances," such as collecting records from field officers, reviewing a voluminous amount of material, and consulting with another agency in order to fill the request.[245] An automatic exhaustion of administrative remedies is considered to have occurred if the agency misses the statutory time limit, but a court can allow the Service more time for "exceptional circumstances," such as a number of requests far in excess of what Congress anticipated.[246]

---

[239] 26 CFR § 601.702(f)(2)(i); IRM 1272, Disclosure of Information Handbook § 543 (Public Interest) (Mar. 1, 1995).

[240] 26 CFR § 601.702(f)(2)(i); IRM 1272, Disclosure of Information Handbook § 543 (Public Interest) (Mar. 1, 1995).

[241] IRM 1272, Disclosure of Information Handbook § 544 (Indigence) (Mar. 1, 1995).

[242] IRM 1272, Disclosure of Information Handbook § 545 (Humanitarian Requests) (Mar. 1, 1995).

[243] 5 USC § 552(a)(6)(A); 26 CFR § 601.702(c)(7)(i).

[244] If the requester wishes to keep track of the ten-day period, the letter should be sent by certified mail, return receipt requested.

[245] 5 USC § 552(a)(6)(B); 26 CFR 601.702(c)(9). A response to a FOIA request that does not inform the requester of "the right to appeal constitutes a failure to reach a determination within the statutory time limitations" of 5 USC § 552(a)(6)(A). Hudgins v. United States, 85-2 USTC ¶ 9736 (DDC 1985), aff'd in unpub. op., 808 F2d 137 (DC Cir. 1987), cert. denied, 484 US 803 (1987) (as a result of the omission, the requester was considered to have exhausted his administrative remedies and thus was entitled to bring his action).

[246] 5 USC § 552(a)(6)(C). See Open Am. v. Watergate Special Prosecution Force, 547 F2d 605, 610, 615–616 (DC Cir. 1976) ("'exceptional circumstances'" created by a virtual deluge of requests since the effective date of the FOIA amendments. . . ."; agency shown to be exercising due diligence; no "exceptional need or urgency attached to the request justified putting it ahead of all other requests."). But see Schachter v. IRS, 82-2

If the requester has not received a reply by the end of a specified period, allowing for return mailing, a follow-up letter or telephone call should be made to the Service to inquire about the delay. Although the requester has a right to contest the Service's noncompliance in court, it makes obvious sense to permit the Service extra time to comply if it appears to be making a good-faith, diligent effort to obtain the material.

[4] Appeal Procedure

If a request for information is denied, a letter of appeal should be addressed and mailed to the office of the Commissioner of Internal Revenue.[247] (See Form 2.3.) The letter of appeal must be sent within thirty-five days after any notice of denial. The appeal letter should describe the records requested, specify the date of the request, and petition the Commissioner to grant the request for records, as well as setting forth the address where the requester desires to be notified of the determination on appeal. Arguments in support of the appeal should be made in as strong a manner as possible to demonstrate the requester's right to access. It is also important to clarify the request if denial indicates some confusion on the part of the Service as to what is being sought. Although it is not necessary, it may strengthen the appeal if a requester is able to cite court rulings that the agency's use of a particular exemption to withhold information is inappropriate.

All agencies, including the Service, are required to respond within twenty working days after receiving the appeal letter.[248] However, if the Service notifies the requester that it needs additional time and provides a reason, an extension of up to ten working days may be added to the original twenty-day appellate review period.[249] If, after the twenty- or thirty-day period from the time the Service has received the appeal letter, no reply has been received, the case may be taken to court.[250]

USTC ¶ 9636 (DDC 1982), dismissed in unpublished opinion, Nov. 4, 1982 (need for urgency in disclosure shown; Service ordered to make GCM promptly available over Service claim of "exceptional circumstances").

[247] 26 CFR § 601.702(c)(8).

[248] 26 CFR § 601.702(c)(8).

[249] 26 CFR §§ 601.702(c)(8), 601.702(c)(9)(i). The FOIA says that the extension is limited to "unusual circumstances." 5 USC § 552(a)(6)(B).

[250] The Service may also invite the requester "to agree to a voluntary extension of time in which to decide the appeal," which will not constitute a waiver of the requester's right to bring a judicial action. 26 CFR §§ 601.702(c)(8), 601.702(c)(11).

FORM 2.3
FOIA APPEAL LETTER

Commissioner of Internal Revenue
Post Office Box 929
Ben Franklin Station
Washington, D.C. 20044

Re: Freedom of Information Act Appeal

Dear Sir:

This is an appeal of the denial of my request for information made by me pursuant to the Freedom of Information Act, 5 USC § 552.

On [*specify date*], I received a letter from [*specify individual Disclosure Officer's name*] denying my request for access to [*insert description of information sought*]. I am enclosing a copy of this denial along with a copy of my original request.

I believe that the Disclosure Officer's denial of my request was in error for the following reasons: [*Make arguments on each exemption or ground for denial*].

I trust that on examination of this letter the information I seek will be disclosed.

Sincerely,

[*Copy of denial letter*]

[5] Judicial Review

Once a requester has exhausted the prescribed administrative procedures before the Service, and has filed a complaint in federal district court, the district court has jurisdiction to enjoin the Service from withholding agency records and to order production of any Service records improperly withheld from the re-quester-complainant.[251] Jurisdiction in the district court requires a showing that the Service has (1) improperly (2) withheld (3) agency records.[252] Venue is located in the judicial district of (1) the requester's residence; (2) the requester's principal place of business; (3) the location of the records; or (4) the District of Columbia. Accordingly, the complaint filed by the requester must name the agency as defendant and allege the following:

- Jurisdiction is based on the Freedom of Information Act.
- The plaintiff is a person, and the defendant is an agency within the meaning of FOIA and the APA.
- On a specified date, a request for access to certain records was made in accordance with FOIA and the Service regulations.
- There was an initial denial of all or part of the request.
- The plaintiff appealed the denial.
- A final denial of access was made by the Service (or the statutory response time elapsed).
- The agency's denial of access was improper because the records were not exempt in whole or in part.
- The plaintiff is entitled to reasonable attorney fees and other litigation costs pursuant to 5 USC § 552(a)(4)(E).

The statute of limitations on instituting a FOIA review action is six years "after the right of action first accrues."[253] As discussed above, before a complaint may be filed, the complainant must have exhausted administrative remedies the Service makes available. This requirement is less onerous than it seems because, under the FOIA, exhaustion is deemed to have occurred if the agency fails to respond within the applicable time limit.[254] If the Service fails to take any action at all in response to a FOIA request or to the requester's appeal request, the statute of limitations on instituting a judicial review proceeding starts to run on the eleventh or twenty-first working day after the request was initially made. Accordingly, a requester who waits for an agency to act on

---

[251] 5 USC § 552(a)(4)(B).

[252] Gabel v. Comm'r, 75 AFTR2d 95-2223 (9th Cir. 1995).

[253] 28 USC § 2401(a); Spannaus v. Department of Justice, 824 F2d 52, 59 (DC Cir. 1987) (holding that action first accrues on expiration of the ten-day or twenty-day periods in which agency has to respond to initial request or appeal).

[254] 5 USC § 552(a)(6)(C).

an appeal request substantially beyond the required response period, may lose the opportunity for court review.

Essentially, the issue before the court in a FOIA enforcement proceeding is whether the documents covered by the request are exempt.[255] The court must make a de novo determination on this issue.[256] Since the FOIA establishes a presumption of access, the burden of proof in a FOIA case is on the government to justify the nondisclosure of the requested information.[257] If the agency claims that requested information is exempt from disclosure, the court is authorized to examine the contents of the contested documents to determine whether all or any part of them can be withheld so that "reasonably segregable portions"[258] of exempt records may be released.[259] The district court has "broad discretion" to order an in camera review of the documents to determine whether they contain segregable information that must be disclosed.[260] The segregability requirement applies to all documents and all exemptions.[261] For example, even when a document is exempt from disclosure as return information, the district court will still be required to decide whether any portions of the document are segregable. In camera inspection is the exception, and not the rule. As the Supreme Court said, in *NLRB v. Robbins Tire & Rubber Co.*, "The in camera review provision is discretionary by its terms and is designed to be invoked when the issue before the District Court could not be otherwise resolved."[262] Detailed affidavits, a *Vaughn* index (discussed below), and the testimony of government witnesses are said to be the preferred alternative to in camera review because "in camera review is not a substitute for the govern-

---

[255] In order to establish the district court's jurisdiction under FOIA, the requestor must show that the agency has (1) improperly (2) withheld (3) agency records. Gabel v. Comm'r, 75 AFTR2d 95-2223 (9th Cir. 1995).

[256] 5 USC § 552(a)(4)(B).

[257] 5 USC § 552(a)(4)(B).

[258] 5 USC § 552(b).

[259] The District of Columbia Circuit Court has said that an agency must release portions of material not exempted from disclosure unless they are "inextricably intertwined with exempt portions." PHE Inc. v. Department of Justice, 983 F2d 248 (DC Cir. 1993) (quoting Mead Data Cent. v. Department of Air Force, 566 F2d 242, 260 (DC Cir. 1977)). The district court must make explicit findings of segregability of withheld documents, and may not simply permit the Service to withhold an entire document without making a finding on segregability. Church of Scientology v. U.S. Dep't. Of Army, 611 F2d 738, 734 (9th Cir. 1979); see also Weiner v. Federal Bur. of Investigation, 943 F2d 972, 988 (9th Cir. 1991).

[260] Center for Auto Safety v. EPA, 731 F2d 16, 20 (DC Cir. 1984).

[261] Center for Auto Safety v. EPA, 731 F2d 16, 21 (DC Cir. 1984).

[262] NLRB v. Robbins Tire & Rubber Co., 437 US 214, 224 (1978).

ment's burden of proof," imposes a burden on the court, and precludes the adversarial process.[263]

Discovery is permissible in a FOIA case because the FOIA plaintiff faces "peculiar disadvantages" when the government agency has control of the information. For this reason, the requester is permitted to obtain information by way of discovery even if the government moves for summary judgment, absent some national security interest, a sufficient Vaughn index, or responsive answers from the agency.[264]

It is not unusual, however, for issues under the FOIA to be decided by a motion for a summary judgment. The issue to be resolved is "not whether there might exist any other documents possibly responsive to the request, but rather whether the search for those documents was adequate."[265] An agency, such as the Service, must prove that it has conducted a search reasonably calculated to uncover all relevant documents. In attempting to carry its burden of proof, the agency may rely on reasonably detailed, nonconclusory affidavits and declarations submitted in good faith by its personnel. These affidavits or declarations will describe the search that was made for the requested documents. The court will judge the adequacy of the agency's search by applying a standard of reasonableness, and therefore the outcome necessarily depends on the facts of each case.

On the requester's part, the FOIA requires the requester to reasonably describe the records sought. Courts have said that a request is sufficient if it "enables a professional employee of the agency who was familiar with the subject area of the request to locate the record within a reasonable amount of time."[266] It follows that broad or sweeping requests that lack specificity are inadequate, as are requests for information that are not agency records or requests that call for the agency to answer interrogatories.[267]

---

[263] Maricopa Audobon Soc'y v. U.S. Forest Service, 108 F3d 1089, 1093 n.2 (9th Cir. 1997). When the agency had been given two opportunities to submit sufficiently specific affidavits and a Vaughn index, but failed to do so in camera review has been said to be justified because meaningful review of exemptions claims would otherwise not be permitted. Linn v. U.S. Dep't of Justice, 80 AFTR2d 97-5242 (DDC 1997).

[264] See Church of Scientology v. IRS, 991 F2d 560, 562 (9th Cir. 1993), vacated in part, remanded, reh'g denied, 30 F3d 101 (9th Cir. 1994).

[265] Zemansky v. U.S. Environmental Protection Agency, 767 F2d 569, 571 (9th Cir. 1985).

[266] Marks v. United States, 578 F2d 261, 263 (9th Cir. 1978).

[267] See NLRB v. Sears Roebuck & Co., 421 US 132, 162 (1975) ("the act does not compel agencies to write opinions in cases in which they would not otherwise be required to do so. It only requires disclosure of certain documents which the agency requires the agency to prepare or which the agency for its own reasons has decided to create."). See also Terry v. IRS, 80 AFTR2d 97-7605 (D. Ariz. 1997) (request asked for statutory list that form 1040 was a required return; cases gathered).

When the Service claims that the records located are exempt from disclosure under one or more FOIA exemptions, it has also been said that "a threshold predicate to a motion for summary judgment is whether the defendant agency has given the court an adequate factual basis to decide whether or not the withheld documents fit into the prescribed exemptions."[268] Courts agree that there are three ways for the agency to provide a court with an adequate factual basis for a summary judgment on an exemption claim. The agency may submit the following to the court for in camera inspection: (1) sufficiently detailed affidavits, (2) a Vaughn index (discussed infra), and (3) the documents in question.[269] If the Service submits affidavits, the district court will grant summary judgment to the Service only if the affidavits (1) describe the documents the Service withheld and (2) the grounds on which the Service justifies nondisclosure "in sufficient detail and with sufficient specificity to demonstrate that material withheld is logically within the domain of the exemption claimed."[270] This means that the Service's affidavits that do not satisfy these two requirements will not establish an adequate factual basis for the court to order summary judgment for the Service.[271]

[a] The Vaughn Index

Once the case is at issue, the main distinguishing feature of a FOIA case is the particularization of the records with respect to which a claim of exemption is made. The court must make a de novo review of the Service's action. As previously discussed, discovery is permissible in a FOIA case because the FOIA plaintiff faces "peculiar disadvantages" when the government agency has control of the information. For this reason, the requester is permitted to obtain information by way of discovery even if the government moves for summary judgment, absent some national security interest, a sufficient Vaughn index, or responsive answers from the agency.[272]

---

[268] See Becker v. IRS, 34 F3d 398, 402 (7th Cir. 1994), and other cases cited in Buckner v. IRS, 82 AFTR2d 98-5650 (ND Ind. 1998).

[269] See Buckner v. IRS, 82 AFTR2d 98-5650 (ND Ind. 1998).

[270] Patterson v. IRS, 56 F3d 832, 836 (7th Cir. 1995).

[271] See, e.g., Goulding v. IRS, 82 AFTR2d 98-6363 (ND Ill. 1998) ("The Martin declaration is plainly insufficient to support the IRS's assertion of exemption 7(C). First, the declaration does not identify which of the redactions are based on exemption 7(C). Second, as to the documents withheld in full, the court cannot base a finding of segregability solely on Martin's conclusory allegation . . . Third, the Martin declaration never specifies the nature of the 'identity information' such that this court can conclude exemption 7(c) logically applies to each redaction").

[272] In one case, the requesters filed a FOIA request for information about the indices the government had provided in other FOIA cases in order to show that the government's response in their first FOIA case was inadequate. The Second Circuit reversed a summary judgment in favor of the government on the ground that the Tax Division had failed to

To permit the court to determine the propriety of the Service's refusal to disclose requested information, courts have required the Service to submit an index specifying why a particular exemption applies to particular parts of withheld documents.[273] This index, known as a Vaughn index, is suited for use in large document cases,[274] and generally includes the following kinds of information:

- Title of the document
- Date of the document
- Identity of author and recipient
- Adequate factual description of each withheld document or deletion from a released document
- Statement of exemption claimed for each withheld document and the justifications for the exemption claimed

The Vaughn index affords the requester, who generally does not have access to the withheld materials (and therefore is at a disadvantage in challenging the agency's exemption claims), a meaningful opportunity to challenge the agency's position. The index also permits the district court an adequate foundation to review the soundness of the agency's exemption claims.[275]

---

demonstrate the adequacy of its search and the unreasonableness of the search it would have to conduct, and permitted discovery on the issue. Ruotolo v. United States, 53 F3d 4 (2d Cir. 1995).

[273] See Vaughn v. Rosen, 484 F2d 820 (DC Cir. 1973), cert. denied, 415 US 977 (1974), on appeal from remand, 523 F2d 1136 (DC Cir. 1975). Criteria for a Vaughn index have been described in White v. IRS, 707 F2d 897, 899 (6th Cir. 1983) (quoting Founding Church of Scientology v. Bell, 603 F2d 945, 949 (DC Cir. 1979)); Osborn v. IRS, 754 F2d 195, 196 (6th Cir. 1985) ("Examination of a Vaughn Index allows the court to decide whether the government's refusal to divulge information is justified without having the potentially secret nature of the information compromised"); Texas Indep. Producers Legal Action Ass'n v. IRS, 605 F. Supp. 538 (DDC 1984), aff'd in part and rev'd in part, 802 F2d 1483 (DC Cir. 1986) (issues regarding Vaughn index analyzed; i.e., conclusory statements, proof of the nonsegregable nature of the withheld documents, and the adequacy of the search procedure). Similarly, while the Service may limit its search of files to those related to the requester, it cannot carry its burden of justifying its actions by "a generalized assertion that it has examined appropriate subject files. Church of Scientology v. IRS, 792 F2d 146, 151–152 (DC Cir. 1986) (en banc), aff'd, 484 US 9 (1987) (appropriate use of Vaughn index, affidavit, and in camera review discussed).

[274] Ferguson v. IRS, No. C-89-4048-JPV, 1990 US Dist. LEXIS 15293 unreported op. (ND Cal. 1990) ("The Vaughn indexing approach was developed to handle a case where the government had withheld a large number of documents. Where only one document is at issue, . . . [it] would be of no assistance to the court, and would merely represent duplicative busy work for the IRS").

[275] See Brooks v. IRS, 80 AFTR2d 97-5324 (ED Cal. 1997) citing Weiner v. Federal Bur. of Investigation, 943 F2d 972, 977 (9th Cir. 1991) ("The purpose of the [Vaughn index] is to afford the FOIA requester a meaningful opportunity to contest, and the District Court an adequate foundation to review, the soundness of the withholding.").

Different courts have modified the information that must be included in the index, especially since the government has frequently claimed that a document-by-document index is burdensome and, therefore, in many instances, a generic category with its related exemption claim should be adequate.[276] However, the use of affidavits alone has been disapproved.[277] The Service has also attempted to have the index or affidavits submitted to the court in camera where a FOIA action is commenced during an open criminal investigation, but it has not always been successful in this regard.[278] A requester should either

---

In Exemption 7 cases, the Eighth and Ninth Circuits have said that a specific factual showing of actual interference with a particular enforcement proceeding an investigation is not required. Barney v. IRS, 618 F2d 1268, 1273 (8th Cir. 1980); Lewis v. IRS, 823 F2d 375, 380 (9th Cir. 1987) (if the requisite nexus between documents and the law enforcement function is shown, a Vaughn index need not be provided because to do so would defeat the purpose of the exemption).

[276] Courts have said that the affidavit must contain "reasonably detailed descriptions of the documents and allege facts sufficient to establish an exemption," and that whether the government agency has met this burden is a question of law. See Maricopa Audobon Soc'y v. United States, 108 F3d 1089, 1093 (9th Cir. 1997), citing Lewis v. IRS, 823 F2d 375, 378 (9th Cir. 1987); Lead Indus. Ass'n v. OSHA, 610 F2d 70 (2d Cir. 1979) (affidavit and index without in camera inspection). See Tigar & Buffone v. CIA, 81-1 USTC ¶ 9245 (DDC 1981) (index ordered); Britt v. IRS, 547 F. Supp. 808 (DDC 1982) (revised index ordered); Osborn v. IRS, 754 F2d 195, 197 (6th Cir. 1985), citing White v. IRS, 707 F2d 897 (6th Cir. 1983) (requiring Vaughn index and stating it is required "in most FOIA cases" in preference to in camera review). Compare Vaughn v. IRS, 936 F2d 862 (6th Cir. 1991) (category-by-category listing rather than Vaughn index is permissible, but category definitions "must be sufficiently distinct to allow a court to determine, as to each category, whether the specific claimed exemption(s) are properly applied").

[277] See Stephenson v. IRS, 629 F2d 1140, 1145–1146 (5th Cir. 1980) (conclusory government affidavit held inadequate where documents are available; sanitized indexing and in camera inspection of random sample of listed documents ordered). However, despite the absence of a Vaughn index, multiple declarations submitted by Service personnel have been held to satisfy the Vaughn standard because any form of presentation is sufficient so long as it enables the court to make "a reasoned, independent assessment" of the claims of exemption, and the declarations were highly detailed, focused on individual documents, and provided a factual basis for withholding each document in issue. Klunzinger v. IRS, 81 AFTR2d 98-575 (WD Mich. 1998) (requester claimed that determining the basis for the claimed exemption was time-consuming and confusing because the declarations referred to documents and the declarations were interrelated, but court said determining the basis for the claimed exemptions was time-consuming because the requester had made broad requests).

[278] See Kanter v. IRS, 433 F. Supp. 812 (ND Ill. 1977); Steinberg v. IRS, 463 F. Supp. 1272 (SD Fla. 1979) (documents found exempt under Exemption 7(A)); Tarnopol v. FBI, 442 F. Supp. 5 (DDC 1977) (documents exempt under Exemption 7(C)). An in camera examination is appropriate where the identities of agents might be disclosed. Kuzma v. IRS, 775 F2d 66 (2d Cir. 1985). But see Vaughn v. IRS, 936 F2d 862 (6th Cir. 1991) (in camera review is discretionary; adequacy of IRS affidavit made in camera review unnecessary).

make a formal motion for a Vaughn index order or by interrogatory ask for the same information.

[b] Attorney Fees

The award of attorney fees and litigation costs to a requester resulting from a FOIA suit is provided for by statute.[279] The statute gives a court discretion to grant reasonable attorney fees and costs where the requester has "substantially prevailed." To "substantially prevail," the plaintiff must present "convincing evidence" that two threshold conditions have been met: (1) The filing of the FOIA action was necessary to obtain the information sought and (2) the action had a "substantial causative effect" on the ultimate receipt of that information.[280] In deciding whether to award attorney fees to a requester who has substantially prevailed, the court should also consider (1) the public benefit derived from the suit; (2) the commercial benefit to the requester-plaintiff; (3) the nature of the requester's interest in the information sought; and (4) whether the agency had a reasonable basis in law for withholding the information.[281] It should be noted that plaintiff's success in the action is not alone controlling. Courts have denied attorney fees to successful parties, especially

---

[279] 5 USC § 552(a)(4)(E). Where the requester seeks judicial review of an agency action regarding waiver of fees under the FOIA Reform Act, "the court shall determine the matter de novo: *Provided,* That the court's review of the matter shall be limited to the record before the agency." The requester must be both eligible for and entitled to attorney fees and costs. A pro se litigant who is not an attorney is not entitled to attorney fees under the FOIA. Carter v. Veterans Admin., 780 F2d 1479, 1481 (9th Cir. 1986). However, the pro se litigant may still be both eligible for and entitled to costs. See Stigall v. IRS, 81 AFTR2d 98-1209 (ED Cal. 1998) (Service largely ignored requester's request for three months until he filed suit).

[280] Long v. IRS, 932 F2d 1309, 1313 (9th Cir. 1991), citing Church of Scientology v. U.S. Postal Serv., 700 F2d 486, 489 (9th Cir. 1993). See also Cox v. U.S. Dep't of Justice, 601 F2d 1, 5 (DC Cir. 1979) (the plaintiff must "show that prosecution of the action could reasonably be regarded as necessary to obtain the information, [citations omitted] and that a causal nexus exists between that action and the agency's surrender of the information [citations omitted]").

[281] Chamberlain v. Kurtz, 589 F2d 827, 842 (5th Cir. 1979), citing S. Rep. No. 93-1200, reprinted in 1974 USCCAN 6285, 6288; Solomon v. IRS, 79-2 USTC ¶ 9687 (DDC 1979); MCA, Inc. v. IRS, 434 F. Supp. 212 (CD Cal. 1977); Long v. IRS, 932 F2d 1309 (9th Cir. 1991) (criteria for awarding attorney fees reviewed). See Tax Analysts v. IRS, 81 AFTR2d 98-1179 (DDC 1998) (Service objected that requester's fee request of $29,000 in case leading to the release of field service advice should be reduced by five percent; held, fees allowed in full because the requester had prevailed on the Service's basic attorney-client privilege claim and that circuit court had merely narrowed district court's opinion).

where it was found that the documents ordered disclosed had no public interest.[282]

B. ACCESS TO RECORDS FROM THE SERVICE UNDER THE PRIVACY ACT

¶ 2.05 THE PRIVACY ACT IN GENERAL

The Privacy Act of 1974 was enacted after congressional investigations of the Watergate scandal revealed that federal agencies, including the Service, had engaged in illegal surveillance and investigations of individuals.[283] Moreover, due to the increasing use of computers to store and retrieve information about individuals by means of a universal identifier (e.g., a Social Security number), Congress was concerned that government agencies could retrieve and use the information they collect and maintain in ways that harmed individual privacy.[284] As a result of these fears, Congress concluded, in passing the Privacy Act, that "[in] order to protect the privacy of individuals identified in information systems maintained by Federal agencies, it is necessary and proper for the Congress to regulate the collection, maintenance, use and dissemination of information by such agencies."[285]

---

[282] See, e.g., Chamberlain v. Kurtz, 589 F2d 827, 842–843 (5th Cir. 1979), cert. denied, 444 US 842 (1979) (taxpayer obtained fifty-three of ninety-one documents). Court decisions in this area are hard to predict. Compare Moody v. IRS, 654 F2d 795, 801 (DC Cir. 1981) (government attorney possibly breached professional standards by communicating ex parte with judge about particular case and vitiated work product protection so that if requester was found to have substantially prevailed on remand, requester "will then become eligible for an award of attorney's fees") with Cliff v. IRS, 529 F. Supp. 11 (SDNY 1981) (where documents pertaining to a generally applicable Manual Supplement were sought and some disclosed, attorney fees not granted because requester was partner in a major Wall Street law firm who was advising clients in a tax dispute of more than $18 million).

[283] 5 USC § 552a. U.S. Dep't of Justice, Freedom of Information Act Guide & Privacy Act Overview (1996 ed.) at 543 (hereinafter Justice Dep't Guidebook); see also Hitchcock, Overview of the Privacy Act, published in Franklin & Bouchard, Guidebook to the Freedom of Information & Privacy Acts (2d ed. 1991) § 2.02, 2-18.3.

[284] A 1974 study of fifty-four federal agencies found that there were 858 computerized data banks containing 1.25 billion records on individuals. Hitchcock, Overview of the Privacy Act, published in Franklin & Bouchard, Guidebook to the Freedom of Information and Privacy Acts (2d ed. 1991) § 2.02, 2-18.3.

[285] Pub. L. No. 93-579, § 2(a), 88 Stat. 1897 (1974). Section 5 of the Privacy Act established a Privacy Protection Study Commission. Among other things, the Commission was charged with making an assessment of the effectiveness of privacy protection in gov-

The express purpose of the Privacy Act is "to provide certain safeguards against an invasion of personal privacy," and this purpose is served by six provisions.[286] First, an individual is permitted to learn about the records collected, maintained, used or disseminated by government agencies about such individual. Second, an individual can prevent records that an agency obtained for one purpose from being used for another purpose without such individual's prior consent. Third, individuals may gain access to records an agency has about them, and have the information corrected or amended. Fourth, as part of a series of fair information practices, agencies are required to ensure that information about an individual is current and accurate for its intended use and that adequate safeguards were provided to prevent misuse of the information. Fifth, agencies are exempted from the requirements of the Act "only in those cases where there is an important public policy need for such exemption," as specifically provided in the Act. Finally, agencies may be sued for any damages that occur as the result of willful or intentional violations of any person's rights under the Act. It is worth noting the Department of Justice's observation that the Act's four basic policy objectives are (1) to restrict disclosure of personally identifiable records that agencies maintain; (2) to grant individuals increased rights of access to records that agencies maintain about them; (3) to grant individuals the right to seek amendment of records that agencies maintain about them on a showing that the records are not accurate, relevant, timely or complete; and (4) to establish a code of "fair information practices" that requires agencies to comply with specified statutory norms for collecting, maintaining, and disseminating records about individuals.[287]

Congress has amended the Privacy Act several times since its enactment in 1974. In 1984, the relationship between the FOIA and the Privacy Act was finally clarified,[288] and the Computer Matching and Privacy Protection Act of 1988 amended the Privacy Act by adding new provisions to regulate the use of computer matching.[289] Computer matching is the computerized comparison of

---

ernment agencies. In July 1977, it issued a report entitled Personal Privacy in an Information Society, which made a number of recommendations for safeguarding privacy primarily by government. One part of the report (Appendix 2), entitled "The Citizen as Taxpayer," dealt exclusively with tax matters.

[286] Pub. L. No. 93-579, § 2(b), 88 Stat. 1897 (1974); Hitchcock, Overview of the Privacy Act, published in Franklin & Bouchard, Guidebook to the Freedom of Information and Privacy Acts (2d ed. 1991) § 2.02, 2-18.4–2.18.5. The legislative history of the Privacy Act and other useful materials are gathered in Legislative History of the Privacy Act of 1974, S. 3418 (Public Law 93-579), prepared by the Senate Committee on Government Operations and the Subcommittee on Government Information and Individual Rights of the House Committee on Government Operations (Sept. 1996).

[287] Justice Department Guidebook at 543.

[288] Pub. L. No. 98-477, § 2(c), 98 Stat. 2212 (1984). This relationship is discussed at ¶ 2.06, infra.

[289] Pub. L. No. 100-503, 102 Stat. 2507 (1988).

information about individuals for the purpose of determining eligibility for federal programs or continuing compliance with statutory and regulatory requirements under Federal benefit programs, as well as recouping payments and delinquent debts under those programs.[290] Computer matching does not include, however, matches performed to produce aggregate statistical data without any personal identifiers, matches performed to support research or statistical projects that do not affect the rights of specific individuals, matches for criminal or civil law enforcement purposes, and similar purposes.[291] Nor does a computer match subject to regulation by the Privacy Act include matches of tax information by the Service and state tax agencies, including state and local law enforcement agencies enforcing tax laws,[292] provided that it is done for the purposes of tax administration,[293] or for the purposes of intercepting a tax refund under the Social Security Act, or any other tax refund intercept program.[294] In general, matching programs involving federal records, including Service records, must be conducted under a matching agreement between the source agency (e.g., the Service) and the recipient that (1) describes the purpose and procedure of the matching and (2) establishes due process protections for affected individuals to receive notice and to have an opportunity to rebut adverse information at a hearing before having a benefit denied or terminated. Each Federal agency engaged in a matching program must have a Data Protection Board that is empowered to review and approve a matching program agreement, and that is subject to review by the Director of the Office of Management and Budget.[295]

In 1976, shortly after the enactment of the Privacy Act of 1974, Congress revamped Section 6103 (i.e., the tax return privacy provision in the Code) to deal with the particular problems of the privacy and access of tax return information.[296] As a result, the specific provisions of Section 6103 governing the confidentiality and circumstances of disclosure of tax return information neces-

---

[290] 5 USC § 552a(a)(8)(A).

[291] 5 USC §§ 552a(a)(8)(B)(i)–552a(a)(8)(B)(vi).

[292] 5 USC § 552a(8)(B)(iv)(I), incorporating Section 6103(d), dealing with permitted disclosures to state tax officials and state and local law enforcement agencies.

[293] 5 USC § 552a(a)(8)(iv)(II), incorporating the definition of tax administration contained in Section 6103(b)(4).

[294] 5 USC §§ 552a(a)(8)(iv)(III), 552a(a)(8)(iv)(V).

[295] 5 USC §§ 552a(a)(8)(B)(iv), 552a(o) (matching agreements), 552a(p) (verification and opportunity to contest findings), 552a(q) (sanctions for violations of agreements). In 1989, the Office of Management and Budget (OMB) issued guidelines on computer matching. See 54 Fed. Reg. 25,818–25,829 (1989). The Computer Matching and Privacy Protection Amendments of 1990 (Pub. L. No. 101-508) further clarified the due process protections of 5 USC § 552a(q).

[296] Staff of Joint Comm. on Taxation, 94th Cong., 2d Sess., General Explanation of the Tax Reform Act of 1976 at 315 (Joint Comm. Print 1976), reprinted in 1976-3 CB (Vol. 2) 327.

sarily supersede the general "no-disclosure without consent" rules of the Privacy Act for tax return information.[297] Moreover, because Section 6103 specifically regulates the disclosure of tax return information, it has been held that Section 6103, and not the Privacy Act, is the exclusive statutory method for taxpayers to obtain access to their tax returns and return information, although the Privacy Act generally requires agencies to permit an individual access to records pertaining to that individual.[298] Although Section 6103 may override the Privacy Act on the conditions of disclosure and access to tax return information, Section 6103 does not eliminate the relevance of the Privacy Act requirements that the Service publish descriptions of its systems of records, give an accounting of its disclosures, and comply with fair information practices such as making reasonable efforts to ensure that records disclosed outside the Service are accurate, complete, timely, and relevant.

If Section 6103's return confidentiality and disclosure rules supersede the conditions of disclosure and access provisions of the Privacy Act, another Code provision will likely further reduce a taxpayer's effective use of the Privacy Act record amendment provisions. Specifically, the Privacy Act permits an individual to correct his or her records, as well as to grant access to them.[299] An individual taxpayer, however, will not be able to amend records that the Service generates in the course of processing returns and determining tax liability. This is because provisions of the Privacy Act dealing with the right to amend an agency record about an individual do not apply "directly or indirectly, to the determination of the existence or possible existence of [an individual's] liability (or the amount thereof) . . . for any tax, penalty, interest, fine, forfeiture or other imposition or offense to which the provisions of the Code apply."[300] It has been held that, since Section 7852(e) also exempts the Service from the civil remedy provisions of the Privacy Act, subsection (g), it consequently removes from the jurisdiction of a district court the authority to hear an individual's suit for any violation of the Privacy Act that involves, even indirectly, information that the Service obtains to determine such individual's tax liability.[301]

---

[297] 5 USC § 552a(b) ("No agency shall disclose any record . . . to any person, except . . . with the prior written consent of the individual to whom the record pertains").

[298] Lake v. Rubin, 82 AFTR2d 98-7444 (DC Cir. 1998), following Cheek v. IRS, 703 F2d 271 (7th Cir. 1983). The Privacy Act requires an agency to permit an individual to obtain access to records pertaining to the individual (5 USC 552a(d)(1)).

[299] 5 USC § 552a(d)(2).

[300] IRC § 7852(e), excluding tax liability determinations from the operation of 5 USC §§ 552a(d)(2), 552(d)(3)–552a(d)(4).

[301] McMillen v. U.S. Dep't of Treasury, 960 F2d 187 (1st Cir. 1991); England v. Comm'r, 798 F2d 350, 352 (9th Cir. 1986); O'Connor v. United States, 669 F. Supp. 317, 323 (D. Nev. 1987), aff'd, 935 F2d 275 (9th Cir. 1991) (amendment sought of documents identifying taxpayer as a tax protestor); Carter v. IRS, 81 AFTR2d 98-421 (SD Cal.

It should be noted that Section 7852(e) does not mean that the Service is absolutely exempt from all Privacy Act requirements. Instead, Section 7852(e) simply applies to deny a taxpayer the right to seek court assistance in enforcing a Privacy Act–based request for amendment of a record pertaining to that individual.[302] Although the Commissioner has claimed that many of the Service's records are exempt in this regard, and thus has narrowed the obligations it voluntarily assumes under the Privacy Act, a taxpayer may still obtain access to some of the Service's records concerning such taxpayer and, in certain limited circumstances, obtain amendment of those records. It must nevertheless be recognized that most issues about when, what, and to whom tax information may be disclosed are governed by the more specific provisions of the Code's return privacy rules, Section 6103, and not the Privacy Act. As a consequence, the FOIA seems to offer a better opportunity to gain access to taxpayer information maintained by the Service. The FOIA's segregability rules permit disclosure of nonexempt portions of records, and the FOIA's investigatory record exemption (Exemption 3) is narrower than the extremely broad investigatory record exemption of the Privacy Act, which the Service claims for criminal and civil investigatory files. Despite these considerable limitations, the Privacy Act, either in conjunction with a FOIA request or alone, can be used effectively in tax practice.

Despite restrictions on the applicability of the Privacy Act in tax cases, taxpayers may still request access to records the Service maintains about them, and, in conjunction with a request under FOIA and Section 6103, the taxpayer may obtain access to information about why and how the data is being collected. Section 7852(e) exempts the Service from (1) being required to grant an individual's request to amend a tax record, (2) providing an administrative hearing if the individual's request for amendment is denied, and (3) court review of its decision denying the amendment request. Nothing in Section 7852(e), however, prevents the taxpayer from seeking access to a record under Section 6103 and the Privacy Act, having a copy made of all or a portion of the record, presenting information to the Service showing that a tax record is erroneous, and on a case-by-case basis convincing the Service to correct or amend the record. Moreover, the information gathering and maintenance standards of the Privacy Act remain expressions of Congress's sense of fair agency practice. A taxpayer may use these Privacy Act standards to ensure that the records maintained by the Service are as accurate, relevant, timely, and com-

---

1997). The district court in Maxwell v. Rubin, 3 F. Supp. 2d 45 (DDC 1998), also reached this conclusion, but the District of Columbia Circuit said that where court review of denial of access was involved, the district court would have jurisdiction under 31 USC § 1331, even if it did not have jurisdiction under the Privacy Act and the requester could proceed under Section 6103 to obtain his or her tax records. Lake v. Rubin, 82 AFTR2d 98-7444 (DC Cir. 1998).

[302] 5 USC §§ 552a(d)(4), 552a(g)(2).

plete "as is reasonably necessary to assure fairness to the individual in the determination."[303] Individual taxpayers may also be able to use the Privacy Act standards to contend, for example, that the Service should collect information in civil tax matters from the taxpayer rather than from third parties,[304] and that the Service should otherwise comply with the Privacy Act's fairness requirements in compiling and maintaining records.

In an individual case, then, a taxpayer may use the Privacy Act to modify the Service's conduct in investigating the taxpayer and to ensure that the records the Service maintains about the taxpayer are accurate and timely. It can generally be expected that the Service will challenge disclosure and access on the grounds that the investigatory record exemption applies and that the taxpayer is seeking to challenge its determination of the existence or amount of a tax liability, penalty, interest, or fine imposed by the Code.[305] Unless there is a specific reason to do so, however, the Service may not rely on an exemption and provide access and amendment of a record.

In short, the circumstances in which taxpayers may use the Privacy Act are limited, but the Privacy Act remains a procedure to consider as a statutory basis for an appeal to the Service that it treat fairly both the taxpayer and the records it has about the taxpayer.

[1] Overview of the Privacy Act

In general, the Privacy Act is organized along the lines of its objectives with specific sections covering (1) the conditions that restrict an agency's disclosure of information about an individual to certain situations (Section 552a(b)), (2) an individual's right of access to agency-maintained records pertaining to that individual and an individual's right to request amendment of those records (Section 552a(d)), (3) fair information practices that agencies are required to follow in collecting and maintaining records (Section 552a(e)), and (4) remedies that individuals may seek if an agency fails to comply with the provisions of the Act (Section 552a(g)). The Act also provides both general and specific exemptions from these obligations (Sections 552a(j) and 552a(k)).

By its terms, the Privacy Act's protections apply for the benefit of an individual, defined as a U.S. citizen or a resident alien,[306] and they regulate an

---

[303] 5 USC § 552a(e)(5).

[304] 5 USC § 552a(e)(2); IRM 1272, Disclosure of Information Handbook §§ (17)20–(17)24, MT 1271-61 (Feb. 16, 1979, Jan. 27, 1987) (Collecting Information Relating to Individuals From Third Party Sources); see IRM 1272, Disclosure of Information Handbook § 17(22), MT 1272-61 (Jan. 27, 1987) (Inquiries Affected).

[305] IRC § 7852(e).

[306] 5 USC § 552a(a)(2). The definition excludes, of course, corporations, partnerships, and other entities legally distinct from an individual. There is a split in authority about

agency's use of information about an individual that the agency maintains as a record,[307] which is collected and maintained as part of a "system of records." The term "system of records" is fundamental to the Privacy Act, and means a group of any records from which the agency is able to retrieve information by name, Social Security number, or some other identifying symbol assigned to the individual.[308]

The Privacy Act imposes conditions on an agency's disclosure of records contained in a system of records. An agency, such as the Service, is prohibited from disclosing to any person or agency any record contained in a system of records without the individual's written consent, unless the disclosure meets one of twelve conditions.[309] These conditions are met when a disclosure is

- Made to officials and employees of the agency maintaining the records on a "need to know" basis;
- Required by the FOIA;
- For a routine use "compatible with the purpose for which it was collected"[310];
- Made to the Bureau of the Census;
- For statistical research, where the information is transferred in other than in an individually identifiable form;
- Made to the National Archives and Records Administration;
- Made to a federal, state, or local agency for use in an authorized law enforcement activity;
- Made to a person who shows compelling circumstances affecting the health or safety of the individual;
- Made to Congress or to a committee of Congress in a matter under its jurisdiction;
- Made to the Comptroller General;
- Made pursuant to a court order; and
- Made to a consumer reporting agency in accordance with Section 3711(f) of Title 31.

The Service must keep an accurate accounting of certain disclosures it does make, and keep this accounting available to the individual who is the subject of the disclosure.[311] The accounting need not be made available, how-

---

whether a sole proprietorship is an "individual," and the OMB guidelines distinguish between an individual seeking records in his personal or "entrepreneurial capacity." See 40 Fed. Reg. 28,951; Justice Department Guidebook at 547.

[307] 5 USC § 552a(a)(4).

[308] 5 USC § 552a(a)(5).

[309] 5 USC §§ 552a(b)(1)–552a(b)(11).

[310] 5 USC § 552a(a)(7).

[311] 5 USC § 552a(c).

ever, where the disclosure is made to a federal, state, or local civil or criminal law enforcement agency, pursuant to a written request.[312]

The Privacy Act also grants any individual the right to gain access to a record pertaining to that individual, have a copy of such record, and request amendment of the record, so long as the agency has not compiled the information "in reasonable anticipation of a civil action or proceeding."[313] Each agency that maintains a system of records must, on the request of any individual to gain access to his or her records or to any information pertaining to the individual in a system of records, permit the individual (and on the individual's request another person the individual chooses to accompany him or her) to review the record and have a copy of the record made "in a form comprehensible" to the individual.[314] Access to tax return information may be governed by Section 6103, however.[315] Moreover, Section 7852(e) prohibits an individual taxpayer's amendment of a record involving the determination of tax under the Privacy Act.

In general, the Privacy Act requires an agency to permit an individual to request amendment of a record. Not later than ten working days after the date the request is received, the agency must acknowledge receipt of the request in writing, and "promptly" either (1) correct the portion of the record the individual "believes is not accurate, relevant, timely, or complete" or (2) inform the individual of its refusal to amend the record as requested, the reason for the refusal, the procedures established for the individual to intra agency review of that refusal.[316] Even if the Service is not compelled to do so, it is not prohibited from considering a taxpayer's request to correct or amend a record, and may grant the request or include the taxpayer's request and supporting information in the file.

In general, under the Privacy Act's amendment and correction procedures, the agency must also permit the individual, who disagrees with the agency's refusal to amend a record, to request review of that refusal. Not later than thirty working days from the date of the individual's request, the agency must complete the review of the earlier refusal and make a final determination. If the reviewing official concurs with the earlier agency decision not to amend the record as requested, the individual can file a final statement of the reasons for disagreement, and the agency must notify the individual of the provisions

---

[312] 5 USC § 552a(b)(7).

[313] 5 USC §§ 552a(d), 552a(d)(5).

[314] 5 USC § 552a(d)(1).

[315] Lake v. Rubin, 82 AFTR2d 98-7444 (DC Cir. 1998).

[316] 5 USC § 552a(d)(2).

for judicial review of its final determination.[317] These amendment and correction provisions do not apply to records that relate "directly or indirectly to the determination of the existence or possible existence of liability (or the amount thereof) of any person for any tax."[318] If a tax record is not involved, however, the prohibition does not apply and, for this reason, many Privacy Act cases involving the Service deal with Service employee records and records that the Service has maintained on tax protestors.

The Service must also publish a notice of the existence and character of the system of records.[319] All agencies, including the Service, must comply with the Privacy Act's fair information practices requirement in gathering, maintaining, and disseminating records. As an agency, the Service must comply with the following standards:

- Keep only such information about an individual as is relevant to its function[320];
- Inform the individual who is required to supply information as to the purposes and uses to which the information will be put[321];
- Describe the existence and character of systems of records maintained[322];

---

[317] 5 USC § 552a(d)(3). The agency must also note the portion of the record which the individual disputes and provide a copy of the record with the notation to any other agency or person originally provided with the disputed record. 5 USC § 552a(d)(4).

[318] IRC § 7852(e). See also 31 CFR Subtitle A Pt. 1 Subpt. C, App. B § 2 ("The provisions of the Privacy Act of 1974 may not be used by an individual to amend or correct any tax record"). See infra ¶ 2.05[2].

[319] 5 USC §§ 552a(e)(1)–552a(e)(12).

[320] 5 USC § 552a(e)(1).

[321] 5 USC § 552a(e)(3). The IRS supplies taxpayers with a Privacy Act Notification (Pub. L. No. 876), which states in part:

The principal purpose for soliciting tax return information is to administer the Internal Revenue laws of the United States. This includes the determination and collection of the correct amount of tax. In addition, with respect to U.S. Individual Income Tax Returns, IRS is soliciting information concerning place of residence for the Bureau of the Census for revenue sharing and other Census purposes. The completion of all appropriate items requested by the returns forms and related data is mandatory except for the Presidential Election Campaign Fund designation on the U.S. Individual Income Tax Returns, which is voluntary. The routine uses which may be made of tax return information include disclosure to the Department of Justice in connection with actual or potential criminal prosecution or civil litigation; to other Federal Agencies; to States, the District of Columbia, the Commonwealth of Puerto Rico, or possessions of the United States to assist in the administration of their tax laws; to other persons in accordance with and to the extent permitted by law and regulations; and to foreign governments in accordance with treaties.

[322] 5 USC § 552a(e)(4). An IRS employee used this requirement to argue that a computer-based system, the ALERTS system that the IRS created to keep a record of disciplinary actions taken against employees, violated the Privacy Act because the Service had allegedly failed to publish in the Federal Register its policies and practices about the stor-

- Keep records in making a determination about an individual with such accuracy, relevance, timeliness, and completeness as is reasonably necessary to ensure a fair determination[323]; and
- Make a reasonable effort to ensure the records disclosed about an individual are accurate, complete, up-to-date, and relevant before disclosing them.[324]

[2] Section 7852(e): The Code's Limitation on the Use of the Privacy Act

One of the most important remedies granted to aggrieved individuals under the Privacy Act results from its waiver of sovereign immunity in many situations. This waiver permits an individual to obtain an award of damages where an agency fails to follow the Act's requirements. Recall, however, that Section 7852(e) exempts the Service from having to amend and correct an individual's tax records (5 USC § 552a(d)(2)) and provide administrative review of its decision not to correct the record (5 USC § 552a(d)(3)). In addition, Section 7852, prohibits an individual from suing the Service for Privacy Act violations that relate "directly or indirectly to the determination of the existence or possible existence or amount of the individual's tax liability for any tax, penalty, interest, fine, forfeiture, or other imposition or offense to which the provisions of [the Code] apply."[325]

While criminal penalties may be imposed against Service personnel for willful conduct in violation of the Privacy Act, criminal liability cannot arise out of a determination of the existence or amount of the individual's tax liability because such matters are excepted from the operation of the Privacy Act by Section 7852(e).[326]

Finally, while courts have held that Section 7852(e) exempts the Service from suits for any violation of the Privacy Act concerning a refusal to permit an amendment of records and removes jurisdiction of the district courts to hear

---

age, retrievability, access controls, retention, and disposal of the records. Pippinger v. Rubin, 129 F3d 519 (10th Cir. 1997). Because the ALERTS system contained information in paper form which had been disclosed in the Federal Register as a system of records that would be stored on magnetic media, the circuit court rejected the argument, viewing the issue under the standard that what constitutes a "system of records" was narrowly construed. Id. at 527, citing Henke v. U.S. Dep't of Commerce, 83 F3d 1453, 1461 (DC Cir. 1996).

[323] 5 USC § 552a(e)(5).

[324] 5 USC § 552a(e)(6).

[325] IRC § 7852(e). See infra ¶ 2.05[2].

[326] 5 USC § 552a(i).

these suits,[327] there may be a distinction that can be drawn between attempts to seek amendment of a tax record and access to a tax record. Specifically, even if Section 7852(e) exempts the Service from Privacy Act damage suits for failure to amend records, it has been observed that the district court might have jurisdiction under its general federal question jurisdiction (28 USC § 1331) over a claim for injunctive relief resulting from the Service's alleged failure to disclose the records in violation of the Privacy Act's access provision, subsection (d)(1).[328] Where disclosure of records is the basis for the action, Section 7852(e) might not eliminate all district court jurisdiction to hear the case. However, it should be noted that courts have held that the more specific provisions of Section 6103, and not the Privacy Act, are the exclusive method for an individual taxpayer to obtain his or her own tax records.[329] Courts have said that Section 7852(e) protection applies to records generated in the course of processing tax returns and determining liability[330]; records of tax assessments made[331]; records that would explain the Service's determinations adverse to the

---

[327] England v. Comm'r, 798 F2d 350 (9th Cir. 1986) (suit for amendment of records under 5 USC §§ 552a(d)(2) and 552a(d)(3)); McMillen v. U.S. Dep't of Treasury, 960 F2d 187 (1st Cir. 1991) (the waiver of sovereign immunity permitting an individual to obtain damages for an agency's failing to maintain accurate records about him does not apply to the determination of tax liability); O'Connor v. United States, 669 F. Supp. 317, 323 (D. Nev. 1987), aff'd, 935 F2d 275 (9th Cir. 1991); Berridge v. Heiser, 993 F. Supp. 1136, 1145 (SD Ohio 1997); Carter v. IRS, 1997 U.S. Dist. LEXIS 21092 (SD Cal. 1997) ("jurisdiction over records pertaining to tax liability has been expressly removed from district courts by § 7852(e) of the Internal Revenue Code"). See also Maxwell v. Rubin, 3 F. Supp. 2d 45 (DDC 1998), aff'd in part and rev'd in part sub nom. Lake v. Rubin, 82 AFTR2d 98-7444 (DC Cir. 1998).

Similarly, compliance with the Privacy Act has been held not to be a prerequisite to enforcement of a summons. United States v. McAnlis, 721 F2d 334, 337 (11th Cir. 1983), cert. denied, 467 US 1227 (1984); Uhrig v. United States, 592 F. Supp. 349, 353–354 (D. Md. 1984).

[328] Lake v. Rubin, 82 AFTR2d 98-7444 (DC Cir. 1998), reversing on this issue, Maxwell v. Rubin, 3 F. Supp. 2d 45 (DDC 1998). See also Gardner v. United States, 83 AFTR2d 99-1203 (DDC 1999) (following Lake v. Rubin). The Gardner court also discussed another district court case (Sinicki v. U.S. Dep't of the Treasury, 83 AFTR2d 99-2511 (SDNY 1998)), where the court found that Section 6103 does not repeal the Privacy Act as it applies to tax return information, and pointed out that several circuit courts have applied the Privacy Act to taxpayer requests for their own tax records without deciding whether Section 6103 preempts the Privacy Act, citing Taylor v. United States, 106 F3d 833 (8th Cir. 1997); Long v. IRS, 891 F2d 222 (9th Cir. 1989); S.R. Mercantile Corp. v. Maloney, 909 F2d 79, 81 (2d Cir. 1990).

[329] Lake v. Rubin, 82 AFTR2d 98-7444 (DC Cir. 1998); Cheek v. IRS, 703 F2d 271, 271–272 (7th Cir. 1973).

[330] England v. Comm'r, 798 F2d 350 (9th Cir. 1986).

[331] Singer v. IRS, 82 AFTR2d 98-5995 (ED Pa. 1998).

taxpayer[332]; documents identifying a taxpayer as a tax protester[333]; allegedly inaccurate tax records upon which the Service determined a deficiency[334]; as well as "unspecified information that served as the basis for assessments and tax liens against [the plaintiffs] based on the failure to pay income tax."[335] On the other hand, notes and tape recordings of speeches by individuals under surveillance by the Service, because they were believed to be tax protesters, were not protected by the Section 7852(e) exemption.[336]

¶ 2.06 INTERRELATIONSHIP OF THE FREEDOM OF INFORMATION ACT, THE PRIVACY ACT, AND SECTION 6103

The Privacy Act uses different terminology from that used in the FOIA and Section 6103. While the FOIA applies to "information"[337] and Section 6103 applies to "returns" and "return information" as specially defined, the Privacy Act applies to a "record" that is "retrieved" from a "system of records" by reference to the name of an individual "or by some identifying number, symbol, or other identifying particular assigned to the individual."[338] Since "record" is defined as "any item . . . of information about an individual that is maintained by an agency,"[339] the definition literally includes all information associated with an individual. However, the definition of "system of records" limits the information only to that recorded information that the agency in fact retrieves "by the name of the individual or by some identifying number, symbol, or other identifying particular."[340] Any system in which information is not retrieved by name, identifier, or identifying particular is not a system of records subject to the Privacy Act. The apparent rationale of this limitation is that the

---

[332] Maxwell v. Rubin, 3 F. Supp. 2d 45 (DDC 1998).

[333] O'Connor v. United States, 669 F. Supp. 317 (D. Nev. 1987); see also Dydra v. Comm'r, 633 F. Supp. 3 (D. Nev. 1985).

[334] Berridge v. Heiser, 993 F. Supp. 1136 (SD Ohio 1997).

[335] Carter v. IRS, 1997 U.S. Dist. LEXIS 17007 (ED Cal. 1994).

[336] MacPherson v. IRS, 803 F2d 479, 485 n.8 (9th Cir. 1986).

[337] 5 USC § 552(a).

[338] 5 USC § 552a(a)(5).

[339] 5 USC § 552a(a)(4).

[340] 5 USC § 552a(a)(5).

use of recorded information is of concern only if it is readily accessible to decision makers.[341]

An individual's request for information under the FOIA entitles the individual to copies of any information about any person or matter, unless the information is exempt from disclosure. By contrast, the Privacy Act permits only the individual about whom information is maintained in a system of records to gain access to the information and have it corrected or amended. In tax cases, the Privacy Act also permits the individual to obtain certain types of affirmative relief from the Service. However, circuit courts have held that the specific provisions of Section 6103 override the more general provisions of the Privacy Act, and therefore, in many instances, such section "represent[s] the exclusive statutory route for taxpayers to gain access to their return."[342] This means that a taxpayer may not have the same right to his or her return information, as the Privacy Act seems to provide. Moreover, disclosure under Section 6103 permits the Service to exercise its discretion and to withhold the tax return information if disclosure would "seriously impair" tax administration.[343] This discretion serves to further limit a taxpayer's right to access his or her tax information.

At first, the purposes of the FOIA and the Privacy Act seem to conflict. The FOIA's objective is to permit a person access to all information maintained by an agency unless the information is exempt. Even then, the broad objectives of disclosure require segregation of exempt portions of a record from the nonexempt portions. On the other hand, the Privacy Act prohibits disclosures of information an agency maintains about an individual unless certain conditions of disclosure are met. The more specific provisions of Section 6103 also prohibit disclosures except in limited circumstances. This apparent conflict between the FOIA and the Privacy Act is eliminated, however, by the provision of the Privacy Act itself that specifically authorizes disclosures of information without the written consent of the affected individual if disclosure is permitted under the FOIA.[344] Thus, a disclosure permissible under the FOIA is an exception to the Privacy Act restrictions on disclosures.

On the other hand, the Privacy Act is not a statute specifically exempting information from disclosure for purposes of the FOIA, and it does not prevent or restrict access to information under the FOIA.[345] However, Section 6103 is

---

[341] Report of Privacy Protection Study Commission, Personal Privacy in an Information Society, App. 2 ("The Citizen as Taxpayer"), at 4 (1977). This definition is keyed to manual, not computer, searches.

[342] Lake v. Rubin, 82 AFTR2d 98-7444 (DC Cir. 1998), following Cheek v. IRS, 703 F2d 271 (7th Cir. 1983).

[343] IRC § 6103(e)(7).

[344] 5 USC § 552a(b)(2).

[345] 5 USC § 552(b)(3).

considered to be a statute specifically exempting information from disclosure and therefore restricts access to information under the FOIA.[346]

The Privacy Act also provides access to information. In this regard, it overlaps with the FOIA and, in limited circumstances, with Section 6103. The FOIA exemptions do not limit access to information under the Privacy Act. If an individual may have access to the information under the Privacy Act, an agency may not rely on a FOIA exemption to deny access.[347] Consequently, a person seeking information under both the FOIA and the Privacy Act is entitled to access if either statute permits disclosure. As a result, requests are frequently made under both statutes.

Since their purposes are different, it is not surprising that Privacy Act exemptions and FOIA exemptions differ.[348] The first difference is the timing of the exemption determination. Under the FOIA, the Service does not determine whether a record contains exempt information until a requester requests the information. By contrast, before an individual has requested access to a particular record, the Privacy Act requires the Service to decide that a system of records (which may include the particular record) is exempt and must promulgate a regulation stating that there may be exempt records in that system of records. In other words, under the Privacy Act, the Service has exempted systems from disclosure before a request for access is made. Unless it decides that there is a reason to do so, the Service may on a case-by-case basis provide access to a record even if the system of records is exempt, however.

Another difference also derives from the different purposes of the FOIA and the Privacy Act. The FOIA is a disclosure law, and the Service has the burden of proving that it may withhold disclosure because the record is exempt. If it succeeds, the record is not disclosed. Under the Privacy Act, if a system of records is exempt from the disclosure requirements, other Privacy Act requirements still apply. No system of records is exempt from all Privacy Act requirements, such as the requirement that the Service publish a description of the system of records, maintain an accounting of disclosures, maintain information on the exercise of First Amendment rights, and take steps to insure records disclosed outside the Service are accurate, complete, timely, and relevant.

---

[346] See the discussion supra ¶ 2.01[1].

[347] 5 USC § 552a(q). See Bartel v. Federal Aviation Admin., 725 F2d 1403, 1412 (DC Cir. 1983) (even if FOIA requires disclosure of information, Privacy Act does not permit disclosure unless a FOIA request has been made). An agency's denial of disclosure under the Privacy Act has been said to be reviewable under the FOIA. Baronowsky v. Unconstitutionality of the Two Sub-sections of the Privacy Act, 87-1 USTC ¶ 9223 (ED La. 1986).

[348] Citizen's Guide at 27–28.

¶ 2.07 EXEMPTIONS UNDER THE PRIVACY ACT

Two general and seven specific exemptions narrow the scope of the Privacy Act. These exemptions give an agency such as the Service the opportunity to take whole systems of records out from under the more important requirements of the Act.[349] Under the general criminal law enforcement general exemption, an agency or component whose principal function is any criminal law enforcement activity need not disclose systems of records maintained in service of that function (e.g., identification files, investigation records, reports compiled on individuals during the time between arrest and release). Since the Service's Criminal Investigation function investigates criminal violations of the tax law (i.e., tax crimes), under this general exemption, the Service is permitted to maintain systems of records for criminal law enforcement purposes that are not subject to the Privacy Act's requirements on access to or correction of records.[350] The head of an agency is permitted to exempt systems of records within this category, and the Commissioner of Internal Revenue has exempted these records.[351] As a result, the Service's obligations under the Privacy Act with respect to "tax crime"–related records are limited to meeting one of the twelve conditions of disclosure,[352] keeping an accounting of disclosures,[353] and assuring the accuracy and relevance of the records it discloses.[354] The Service need not make this accounting available to the taxpayer, and a taxpayer has no access and correction rights.

This general exemption for a system of records maintained for law enforcement purposes requires further analysis. As noted above, exemption is authorized only if (1) the system is maintained by "an agency or component thereof" that performs "as its principal function any activity pertaining to the enforcement of criminal laws" and (2) if the system of records consists of (a) identifying information, such as "rap" sheets (i.e., prior arrests, convictions,

---

[349] Report of Privacy Protection Study Commission, Personal Privacy in an Information Society, App. 4 ("The Privacy Act of 1974: An Assessment"), at 7–8 (1977). For a case analyzing the application of the Privacy Act's exemptions to a record, see Standley v. Dep't of Justice, 835 F2d 216 (9th Cir. 1987) (list, compiled by a U.S. Attorney, of names of IRS personnel who had received grand jury material did not constitute a court record exempt under the Privacy Act; case remanded to determine whether list constituted a Justice Department record).

[350] 5 USC § 552a(j)(2).

[351] 31 CFR § 1.36, Internal Revenue Service, Notice of Exempt Systems. The Service's Systems of Records and Notice of Exempt Systems have also been published in Document 6372, Privacy Act of 1974, Resource Materials. The information is also listed in IRM 1272, Disclosure of Official Information Handbook, Exhibit (15)00-2, (Mar. 19, 1987).

[352] 5 USC § 552a(b).

[353] 5 USC §§ 552a(c)(1), 552a(c)(2).

[354] 5 USC § 552a(e)(6).

and sentences); (b) "information compiled for the purpose of a criminal investigation, including reports of informants and investigators, and associated with an identifiable individual"; or (c) "reports identifiable to an individual compiled at any stage ... from arrest or indictment through release from supervision."[355] The Service's Criminal Investigation Division does have as its principal function an activity (investigation) "pertaining" to criminal law enforcement. While identifying information (such as that contained on a "rap" sheet and in reports made from arrest to release or probation) are probably not critical for tax crime enforcement, access to investigation reports can obviously be important to a taxpayer, both during and after the investigation.

The general exemption for criminal law enforcement records under the Privacy Act is broader than the FOIA's investigatory record exemption. Consequently, information compiled for investigative purposes and contained in a system of records may be exempt under the Privacy Act, although a person could have access to some of the information under the FOIA because disclosure would not interfere with enforcement proceedings or the information may be segregated from sensitive data. So long as the information may be disclosed under the FOIA, its exemption for Privacy Act purposes does not prevent disclosure.[356] As a result, the Service may be required to release all nonexempt portions of its criminal investigation files under the FOIA, although a taxpayer will not be able to amend these records under the Privacy Act.

In addition to the general Privacy Act exemption for criminal law enforcement records, there are seven specific exemptions under which the head of an agency may exempt any system of records from the requirements of the Privacy Act.[357] The exemptions that the Service might claim are the following:

- Investigatory material compiled for law enforcement purposes;
- Files used solely for statistical purposes;
- Investigatory material used in making decisions concerning federal employment, among other matters; and
- Testing or examination material used solely for employment purposes.

Under the specific exemption for "investigatory material compiled for law enforcement purposes" (Exemption 2), and regulations the Service has promulgated to exempt that system of records from the requirements of the Privacy Act, the Service (1) need not make available an accounting of disclosures to the individual named in the record at his request[358]; (2) need not permit access to the records[359]; (3) need not limit the information gathered only to that which

---

[355] 5 USC § 552a(j)(2).

[356] 5 USC § 552a(b)(2).

[357] 5 USC §§ 552a(k)(1)–552a(k)(7).

[358] 5 USC § 552a(c)(3).

[359] 5 USC § 552a(d).

is "relevant and necessary" to its purpose[360]; and (4) need not publish procedures or agency rules regarding how to obtain notice of whether a record is kept on an individual, how access can be obtained, and the categories of sources of records in the system.[361]

Where a specific exemption is claimed, however, other requirements of the Privacy Act still apply. Even if a system of records is exempt under a specific exemption, the Service is still required to follow the following procedures:[362]

- Individuals asked to supply information must be informed of the uses to which it will be put and whether or not the imparting of it is voluntary or mandatory[363];
- Individuals must be told when the information is disclosed in accordance with compulsory legal process[364];
- Agencies or persons to whom information has previously been disclosed must be told about any corrections or disputes over the accuracy of information[365]; and
- All records must be accurate, relevant, up-to-date, and complete as maintained and disclosed.[366]

The specific exemption that has the most significance in tax practice is the investigatory material exemption. An agency head may claim a specific exemption for investigatory material compiled for law enforcement purposes (Exemption 2), other than the criminal law enforcement records already exempt under the general exemption.[367] In fact, the Commissioner has claimed the exemption for a substantial portion of the Service's "systems of records," including collection, administrative, and appellate case files.[368] The specific

---

[360] 5 USC § 552a(e)(1).

[361] 5 USC §§ 522a(e)(4)(G)–552a(e)(4)(I), 552a(f).

[362] 5 USC § 552a(k).

[363] 5 USC § 552a(e)(3).

[364] 5 USC § 552a(e)(8).

[365] 5 USC § 552a(e)(5).

[366] 5 USC § 552a(e)(6).

[367] 5 USC § 552a(k)(2).

[368] 31 CFR § 1.36 (IRS Notice of Exempt Systems). It is unclear whether this determination is reviewable in the same manner as determinations by the Commissioner under FOIA Exemptions 3 and 7, which some courts have held to be reviewable. See supra ¶¶ 2.03[2], 2.03[5]. This exemption has been upheld. Alt v. Comm'r, 86-1 USTC ¶ 9162 (D. Neb. 1985) (taxpayer asked for records pertaining to him that were maintained by the Service in its Audit Information Management System). See also Lobosco v. IRS, 81-1 USTC ¶ 9366 (EDNY 1981).

investigatory material exemption includes investigatory files the Service has compiled for civil as well as criminal enforcement purposes.[369]

The exemption also applies even if disclosure would not interfere with any enforcement proceedings and sensitive data could be segregated from factual data factors that would result in disclosure of at least some information in investigatory files under the FOIA.[370] It is unclear, however, whether the converse is true. Specifically, where a requester has been denied records under the Privacy Act because of the investigatory material exemption, the circuit courts are divided over the effect of this finding on disclosure under FOIA.[371] In *MacPherson v. IRS*,[372] the circuit court stated that the law enforcement exemptions in the FOIA and the Privacy Act are not analogous, because the purposes of the two acts are different. The court stated:

---

[369] A taxpayer's suit under 5 USC § 552a to amend the Service's records pertaining to him by deleting the words "tax protester" was dismissed under IRC § 7852(e) because the records involved were generated by the Service in the course of determining his tax liability. England v. Comm'r, 799 F2d 350 (9th Cir. 1986) (taxpayer's return had been identified under the Service's Tax Protester Program). See supra ¶ 2.05[2]. See also Rubel v. United States, 89-1 USTC ¶ 9149 (WDNC 1988) (IRS classification of taxpayer as tax protestor reviewed and held reasonable under Section 552(g)(1)(C)).

[370] However, if investigatory materials may be disclosed under FOIA, the Privacy Act does not prevent disclosure. 5 USC §§ 552a(b)(2), 552a(f)(2). On the other hand, if records may be disclosed under the Privacy Act, an agency may not rely on a FOIA exemption to withhold such records from an individual requester. 5 USC § 552a(t)(1). See, e.g., Ely v. FBI, 781 F2d 1487, 1489 n.1 (11th Cir. 1986), citing HR Rep. No. 98-726, reprinted in 1984 USCCAN 3741, 3791. ("Information obtainable under FOIA but not under the Privacy Act must be released if sought under FOIA. Information available under the Privacy Act but not under FOIA must be disclosed if sought under the former").

[371] Compare Greentree v. Customs, 674 F2d 74 (DC Cir. 1982) (holding that the records are per se unavailable under FOIA) with Painter v. FBI, 615 F2d 689 (5th Cir. 1980) and Terkel v. Kelly, 599 F2d 214 (7th Cir. 1979) (holding that the records are automatically exempt under FOIA). See also Baronowsky v. Unconstitutionality of Subsections of Privacy Act, 87-1 USTC ¶ 9223 (ED La. 1986).

[372] MacPherson v. IRS, 803 F2d 479 (9th Cir. 1986). The Ninth Circuit chose to determine whether the exemption granted by Section (e)(7) of the Privacy Act had been violated on a case-by-case basis. Two other circuits have adopted explicit standards. See Clarkson v. IRS, 678 F2d 1368, 1375 (11th Cir. 1982) (Section (e)(7) of the Privacy Act is violated if collection of protected information is "unconnected to any investigation of past, present or anticipated violations of the statutes which [the IRS] is authorized to enforce"); Jabara v. Webster, 691 F2d 272, 279–280 (6th Cir. 1982), cert. denied, 464 US 863 (1983) (no violation if the investigation "is relevant to an authorized criminal investigation or to an authorized intelligence or administrative one"). See Rubel v. United States, 89-1 USTC ¶ 9149 (WDNC 1988) ("[O]nce an IRS agent receives a criminal referral, the agent may investigate the suspect and, in so doing, may observe and record any protestor type writings and attitudes . . . [and] may transmit to the appropriate official an opinion that the suspect is, or may be, an illegal tax protestor").

The FOIA is intended to promote government disclosure of information. The law enforcement exemption to the FOIA is intended to prevent disclosure of sensitive information about innocent individuals and confidential informants and to relieve district courts of potentially onerous in camera inspection of documents. . . . A broad reading of the "law enforcement purposes" exception to the FOIA therefore serves privacy by concealing more information from public view.

Section (e)(7) of the Privacy Act, however, is intended to restrict the information about individuals' First Amendment activities that the government may collect and maintain at all. The "law enforcement activities" exception to the First Amendment protection of section (e)(7) of the Privacy Act is intended merely "to make certain that political and religious activities are not used as a cover for subversive activities." [citation omitted] In the case of section (e)(7), therefore, a narrow reading of "law enforcement activities" better serves the goal of privacy and avoids infringing on the overall First Amendment concerns of (e)(7).[373]

In one situation, the specific investigatory material exemption under the Privacy Act permits access that may be broader than that provided under the FOIA. No investigatory material compiled by the Service may be withheld if it is used to deny a taxpayer a benefit, right, or privilege to which he is entitled by law, unless disclosure would reveal the identity of a confidential source. Consequently, it may be possible for a taxpayer (about whom investigatory material has been gathered) to examine some of the investigatory record on the ground that the taxpayer has been denied a right, privilege, or benefit that he would otherwise be entitled to by federal law but for the maintenance of that record. Statements of individuals who testified before the Service can usually be obtained under this provision, since it is unusual for their statements to have been made "under an express promise that the identity of the source would be held in confidence"[374] or an implied promise made to that effect prior to the effective date of the Privacy Act. This certainly should be the case where investigation has been completed and law enforcement proceedings have been terminated.

However, the meaning of the phrase "any right, privilege, or benefit" is still somewhat uncertain.[375] It would seem difficult for a taxpayer to argue that either freedom from an annual income tax audit a right or that payment of the tax liability for the year in question without the imposition of a penalty is such a right or benefit. Other questions regarding the definition of rights, privileges, or benefits are more difficult to resolve. Suppose a doctor loses some participating status in the Medicare program or a lawyer is disbarred from practice in a federal court or before the Service. Has the doctor or lawyer been denied

---

[373] MacPherson v. IRS, 803 F2d 479, 482 (9th Cir. 1986).

[374] 5 USC § 552a(k)(2).

[375] 5 USC § 552a(k)(2).

"privileges" established under federal law? There is some basis for arguing that the investigatory record should be disclosed in these situations. It is also unclear whether the Service must rely on the specific exemption from disclosure to prevent access to a Criminal Investigation Division file. Those files contain information compiled for the purpose of a "criminal investigation" and are covered by the general exemption provision. On the other hand, the general exemption provision does not appear to cover the Justice Department's Tax Division. Therefore, certain of its records (e.g., a copy of the memorandum declining prosecution) might be available under the Privacy Act. In short, applications of the general and specific exemptions to particular records must await some judicial guidance.

¶ 2.08 PRIVACY ACT REQUEST PROCEDURES

Privacy Act procedures apply only where "an individual desires information or records not in connection with an investigation, audit, or collection activity."[376] Four possible taxpayer requests can be made under the Privacy Act: (1) notification that a system of records has some record pertaining to the taxpayer; (2) access to that record; (3) an accounting of disclosures of that record; and (4) amendment of that record.[377] At the outset, the individual taxpayer must know what systems of records the Service maintains. The various systems of records are published in Document 6372, Privacy Act of 1974, Resource Materials, and also in the Internal Revenue Manual Disclosure of Official Information Handbook, Exhibit (15)00-2. The requirements for the various types of requests are as follows:[378]

---

[376] 31 CFR Subtitle A, Pt. 1, Subpt. C, App. B, P 2. See also IRC § 7852(e). For information or records related to an investigation, audit, or collection activity, "individuals should contact the Internal Revenue Service employee conducting an audit or effecting the collection of tax liabilities to gain access to such records, rather than seeking access under the provisions of the Privacy Act."

[377] However, "[the provisions of the Privacy Act . . . may not be used by an individual to amend or correct any tax record." 31 CFR Subtitle A, Pt. 1, Subpt. C, App. B, ¶ 2. See IRC § 7852(e).

[378] 31 CFR, Subtit. A, Pt. 1, Subpt. C, App. B. When a taxpayer filed a Privacy Act request seeking access to "All records and transmittals concerning" thirty-seven identified document locator numbers, the taxpayer was held not to be entitled access to the records, because they were not retrieved by reference to his name or Social Security number, and because the taxpayer did not name the system of records to which he sought access. Fuller v. IRS, 80 AFTR2d 97-6823 (3d Cir. 1997). Even if the court's opinion displays a rather limited understanding of how the Service uses document locator numbers and their relationship to a taxpayer's taxpayer identification number, the result shows why the requester must track the requirements of the regulations in order to use the protections of the Privacy Act.

- A request for notification, access, or an accounting of disclosures must be labeled as such (e.g., "Request for notification and access"). The request must state that it is made under the Privacy Act and give the name and address of the individual making the request and, if appropriate to secure access, the requester's Social Security number. If the record is a joint return, the names, addresses, and Social Security numbers of both persons are necessary. The request must set forth the name and location of the system of records that is the subject of the request and the title and business address of the custodian. If the request pertains to a period other than a current period, the request should so state, because a request ordinarily is considered to be for current, not past, periods. If the record is the subject of an investigatory material exemption, the request also must establish that the individual has been denied some right, privilege, or benefit he would otherwise be entitled to under federal law as a result of the Service maintaining the record. As with a FOIA request, the individual must state whether he wishes to inspect the record or to have a copy and, if the latter, agree to pay copying charges. The request should be addressed to a person in the access section (the Disclosure Officer) for the particular records. If the request is made by mail, the requester's signature and a copy of another signed form of identification (e.g., a driver's license) should be sufficient to identify the requester for purposes of the Privacy Act. The requester should submit a letter making the request. (See Form 2.4.)
- A request for amendment generally follows the format of a request for notification, access, or an accounting of disclosures. However, it also must state the particular record to be amended and the specific changes, as well as the reason for the changes, that the requester wishes made. (See Form 2.5.)

FORM 2.4
REQUEST FOR NOTIFICATION AND ACCESS

District Director
Internal Revenue Service
[*address of District Office*]
[*city, state, zip*]
Attention: Disclosure Officer

Re: Privacy Act Request for Notification and Access

Dear Sir or Madam:

Under the provisions of the Privacy Act of 1974, 5 USC § 552a, I hereby request that the following systems of records be examined and that I be furnished with a copy of any record pertaining to me. [*Describe as accurately and specifically as possible the record or records you want and provide all the relevant information you have concerning them.*] In order to permit retrieval of this information, I am submitting my Social Security number, which is [*insert number*].

I agree to pay any fees for copying the records I am requesting.

If all or part of this request is denied, please cite the specific exemption(s) you think justifies your refusal to release the information.

In order to expedite consideration of my request, I am enclosing a copy of [*some signed document of identification*].

Thank you for your prompt attention to this matter.

Sincerely,

FORM 2.5 _____
REQUEST FOR AMENDMENT OF A RECORD

District Director
Internal Revenue Service
[*address of District Office*]
[*city, state, zip*]

Re: Privacy Act Request to Amend Records

Dear Sir or Madam:

By letter dated [*date*], I requested access to include [*same description as in request letter*].

In viewing the information forwarded to me, I found that it was [*state basis for amendment, e.g., inaccurate, incomplete, outdated, or not relevant to the purpose of your agency.*] Therefore, pursuant to the Privacy Act of 1974, 5 USC § 552a, I hereby request that you amend my record in the following manner: [*Describe errors, new information, and irrelevance.*] In accordance with the Act, I look forward to an acknowledgment of this request within ten working days of its receipt.

Thank you for your assistance in this matter.

Sincerely,

The Service must respond to a request for notification, access, or an accounting of disclosures in thirty working days, or at least request additional time to complete action on the request within that period. If an individual taxpayer seeks to amend tax records, Section 7852(e) exempts the Service from having to comply with the amendment provisions of the Privacy Act. Nevertheless, the Service may consider a Privacy Act request to amend a record pertaining to an individual. If it does amend the record, under the Privacy Act, the Service has ten working days after the date the request is received to acknowledge receipt of the request and thirty working days (unless extended) to either (1) correct the portion of the record the individual believes is not accurate, relevant, timely, or complete or (2) inform the individual of its refusal to amend the record. If it refuses to amend the record, the Service must inform the individual of the reason for the refusal, the procedures for administrative appeal of the decision, and the name and address of the appeals officer.[379] The individual then has thirty-five days to appeal the adverse determination to the Director (Disclosure Operations Division) in the National Office. (See Form 2.6.) The requester's appeal must be reviewed within thirty working days from the date the individual requests review, although this period may be extended. Again, in the case of tax records, the service is not required to follow these procedures, but if it chooses to do so or the record is not a tax record (and therefore not within the purview of Section 7852(e)), the Privacy Act procedures require that the requester be given the opportunity to state the requester's reasons for disagreement with the Service if the appeal is upheld, and the requester may have this Statement of Disagreement inserted in his file or record. This statement is sent to the same address as the appeal.

---

[379] See 5 USC §§ 552a(d)(2)–552a(d)(4).

FORM 2.6
REQUEST FOR REVIEW OF ADVERSE DETERMINATION

Director, Disclosure Operations Division
Internal Revenue Service
1111 Constitution Avenue
Washington, D.C. 20224

Re: Privacy Act Request for Review of Adverse Determination

Dear Sir:

On [*date*], I received a letter from [*individual's name*] of your agency denying my request for access of [*description of the information sought*]. Enclosed is a copy of this denial along with a copy of my original request. By this letter, I am appealing the denial.

Since Congress intended that information sought under the Privacy Act of 1974, 5 USC § 552(a), be released unless it could be withheld under both this Act and the Freedom of Information Act (FOIA), 5 USC § 552, I hereby request that you also refer to the FOIA in consideration of this appeal.

I am seeking access to these records [*state the reasons for your request if you think it will assist you in obtaining the information and give any arguments you might have to justify its release*].

[*Or*, I am seeking amendment of the following record [*describe*] for the following reasons [*state fully*] and wish to make the following changes therein [*describe changes*]].

Thank you for your prompt attention to this matter.

Sincerely,

Unlike the FOIA, the Privacy Act does not provide for an administrative appeal of a denial of access. However, since Privacy Act requests are frequently joined with requests under the FOIA and Section 6103, the Service's procedures will allow Privacy Act requesters to administratively appeal a denial of access.[380] When access is denied, the Service explains the reason for the denial, naming the system of records, and identifying the exemption that the Service claims is applicable to the system of records. If the taxpayer administratively appeals the denial of access, the basis for the appeal may be that (1) the record is not exempt, (2) the system of records has not been properly exempted, or (3) the record is exempt, but no harm will result if the record is disclosed.

As the form appeal letter shows, the appeal letter should state that the appeal is being made under the Privacy Act of 1974 and, if the request was joined with a FOIA request, state that the appeal is being made under the FOIA as well. The appeal letter should identify the denial that is being appealed and the records that were withheld, and also explain why the action was improper or unnecessary. Finally, the appeal should state the requester's name, address, and phone number. Exhaustion of administrative remedies includes the framing of a proper request, including the payment of costs for locating and duplicating the requested records.[381]

If the determination of a taxpayer's liability for tax is involved, Section 7852(e) exempts the Service from suit for any violation of the Privacy Act, including (1) its determination not to permit amendment of an individual's record in accordance with the individual's request, (2) its refusal to comply with the individual's request for access to a record about the individual, (3) its failure to maintain accurate records about the individual, or (4) its failure to comply with any other provision of the Privacy Act in a way that adversely affects the individual.[382] Since taxpayers may not use the Service's noncompliance with the Privacy Act as a means of disputing tax liability, the failure of the requester to specify which Privacy Act provision was violated has been held to signify a dispute on the merits of a tax liability, and not a taxpayer's status as a tax protester.[383] Consequently, suits against the Service under the Privacy Act will necessarily be few, and will be limited either to situations where tax

---

[380] See Citizen's Guide at 31. The following description of the administrative appeal procedures is derived from this useful publication.

[381] Taylor v. U.S. Treasury Dep't, 127 F3d 470 (5th Cir. 1997).

[382] 5 USC § 552a(g)(2)(A); IRC § 7852(e) (5 USC § 552a(g) does not apply to records that relate to tax liability). Love v. IRS, 80-2 USTC ¶ 9520 (ND Ga. 1980) (IRS failure to amend or expunge references to taxpayer's status as a tax protester). In a civil action under the Privacy Act, a taxpayer's obligation to pay taxes is not excused even if there is a clear violation of the Privacy Act by the Service. Billman v. Comm'r, 83 TC 534 (1984), aff'd, 847 F2d 887 (DC Cir. 1988).

[383] Love v. IRS, 80-2 USTC ¶ 9520 (ND Ga. 1980).

records are not involved or the Service has maintained a record that describes "how any individual exercises rights guaranteed by the first amendment."[384]

Generally, an action to enforce any liability created under the Privacy Act may be brought, within two years from the date on which the cause of action arises, in a federal district court in which the complainant resides or where the agency records are located.[385] The requester must allege which provision of the Privacy Act has been violated by the Service.[386] In an action based on the Service's failure to amend a record other than a tax record, or to permit access to a record other than a tax record, the court determines de novo the reasonableness of the Service's decision.[387] In the case of denial of access, the court may order the Service to produce the improperly withheld agency records and, in deciding whether to do so, may inspect the records in camera.[388] If the action is based on (1) the Service's failure to maintain proper records or (2) a claim that the Service has intentionally or willfully acted contrary to the provisions of the Act in a way that adversely affected the individual, the court may hold the Service liable to the individual for the individual's actual damages or statutory damages of $1,000, as well as costs and reasonable attorney's fees.[389]

---

[384] 5 USC § 552a(e)(7). McPherson v. IRS, 803 F2d 479, 485 n.8. In a proceeding based on the Service's failure to amend a record, the court decides the issue de novo and "may order the [Service] to amend the individual's record in accordance with the [individual's] request or in such other way as the court itself may direct." 5 USC § 552a(g)(2)(A).

[385] 5 USC § 552a(g)(5). But see IRC § 7852(e). 5 USC § 552a(g) does not apply to records that relate to tax liability.

[386] 5 USC §§ 552a(g)(1), 552a(g)(2)–552a(g)(4).

[387] 5 USC §§ 552a(g)(2)(A), 552a(g)(3)(A). If the complainant substantially prevails, reasonable attorney fees and costs may also be awarded. See Anderson v. U.S. Treasury Dep't, 648 F2d 1 (DC Cir. 1981) (IRS employee successfully sued for access to Inspection file on him, but attorney fees were to be limited because requester's attorneys were salaried employees of his union).

[388] 5 USC § 552a(g)(3)(A). But see IRC § 7852(e). If the complainant substantially prevails, the court may award reasonable attorney fees and other litigation costs. 5 USC § 552a(g)(3)(B).

[389] 5 USC § 552a(g)(4). See Johnson v. Dep't of Treasury, 700 F2d 971 (5th Cir. 1983) (actual damages recoverable for violation of the Privacy Act include damages for physical and mental injuries).

CHAPTER **3**

Statements of IRS Position and Practice

¶ 3.01 INTRODUCTION

Taxpayers and others affected by the Internal Revenue Code's legal requirements frequently need guidance to cope with the Code's highly technical and complex provisions. The most authoritative administrative guidance on the Code is provided by the Treasury and the Service in the form of Treasury regulations. The Code itself requires the Secretary of the Treasury to "prescribe all needful rules and regulations for the enforcement" of the provisions of the tax law.[1] When the Treasury promulgates certain regulations, the adoption process for these regulations is subject to the notice and public comment procedures of the Administrative Procedure Act.[2]

In practice, however, tax regulations are sometimes inadequate to answer interpretive questions about the Code. Moreover, on occasion, the regulations themselves are as difficult to understand and apply as the tax law. To meet the need for authoritative interpretations of the Code and the Treasury Regulations, the Service has developed procedures for providing additional information and guidance in the form of informal advisory opinions, private letter rulings (requested by individual taxpayers), and revenue rulings (published by the Service in Internal Revenue Bulletins).[3] In addition to revenue and letter rulings, the Service issues (1) official guidance and advisory opinions in the form of revenue procedures that describe important procedures affecting the rights and duties of taxpayers, Service personnel, and others; (2) technical advice memorandums on specific issues arising during the examination of returns; (3) determination letters that apply the Code's complex rules for pension plans and tax exempt organizations; (4) information letters; (5) publications; and (6) oral advice.

As the result of the Freedom of Information Act,[4] other Service-generated materials and memoranda are also available to the general public, including (1) the Internal Revenue Manual; (2) advice rendered by the Service's National Office to its field personnel (e.g., Field Service Advice); and (3) information regarding the internal procedures that Service personnel must follow in performing their various functions.

Regulations, policy statements, and interpretations take various forms and are issued with different degrees of formality, publicity, and legal effect. Table 3.1 lists the various statements of position and practice as well as the means by which they are issued. These different statements are described separately in the sections that follow.

---

[1] IRC § 7805(a).

[2] 5 USC § 553.

[3] See Rev. Proc. 89-14, 1989-1 CB 814, stating the objectives and standards for the publication of revenue rulings and revenue procedures in the Internal Revenue Bulletin.

[4] Freedom of Information Act, 5 USC § 522.

TABLE 3.1
Statements of IRS Position and Practice

Statement	Issued/ Made by	Formality	Publicity	Reliability
Treasury regulations	Secretary of Treasury under APA	Notice, hearing, and publication	Published in Federal Register	Most reliable statements of position
Revenue rulings	Assistant Commissioners of Internal Revenue (Technical) (EP/EO)	No notice and hearing— informal statement under APA	Published in Internal Revenue Bulletin	Intended to be relied on by IRS personnel and taxpayers
Letter rulings	Assistant Commissioners of Internal Revenue (Technical) (EP/EO)	No notice and hearing— informal statement under APA	Available for inspection under Section 6110; not published by IRS	Binding on IRS only as to party to whom issued
Revenue procedures	Assistant Commissioners of Internal Revenue (Technical) (EP/EO)	No notice and hearing— informal statement under APA	Published in Internal Revenue Bulletin	Intended to be relied on by IRS personnel and taxpayers
Technical advice	Assistant Commissioners of Internal Revenue (Technical) (EP/EO)	No notice and hearing— informal statement under APA	Available for inspection under Section 6110, not published by IRS	Binding on IRS only as to party to whom issued
Determination letters	District offices in most cases	No public notice or hearing	Available for inspection under Section 6110	Binding only as to requesting taxpayer
Internal Revenue Manual	National Office	No public notice or hearing	Available for inspection under the FOIA	Generally not binding on IRS
Information releases	National Office	No public notice or hearing	Published	May be binding on IRS
Information letters	National Office/ District offices	Informal	Issued to requester	Not binding

| IRS publications | National Office | Informal | Published | Not binding |
| Oral communications | Any IRS official | Informal | Not published | Generally not binding on IRS |

¶ 3.02 TREASURY REGULATIONS

Section 7805(a) gives the Secretary of the Treasury general authority to promulgate regulations that "prescribe all needful rules and regulations for enforcement" of the Code. Other, specific grants of authority for the Secretary to promulgate regulations can also be found throughout the Code.[5] Questions about what constitutes a rule or regulation, the process involved in drafting and adoption of regulations, and the legal effect of a regulation require separate treatment and are discussed later in this section.

[1] "Rules," "Regulations," and "Rulings" Defined

In administrative law, a fundamental distinction is drawn between an agency's "rulemaking" (quasi legislative) actions and "adjudication" (quasi judicial) actions.[6] If the action of an agency, such as the Service, is quasi legislative, the APA's rulemaking requirements of preadoption notice and public hearing must be followed before an agency rule is finalized.[7] On the other hand, if the agency's action is quasi judicial, an entirely different set of APA adjudication procedures apply.[8]

There is no clear test for determining whether an agency's action constitutes rulemaking or adjudication. The APA makes a modest attempt to distinguish between the two administrative functions by defining both "rule" and "order" for purposes of the APA. A "rule," under the APA definition, is "an agency statement of general or particular applicability and future effect de-

---

[5] IRC § 7805(a). Section 7805(a) grants the authority to the Secretary, except where "such authority is expressly given by [the Code] to any person other than an officer or employee of the Treasury Department." Also, the Secretary's authority to prescribe "all needful rules and regulations" includes "all rules and regulations as may be necessary by reason of any alteration of law in relation to internal revenue."

[6] The Supreme Court has also said that there is a "recognized distinction in administrative law between proceedings for the purpose of promulgating policy-type rules or standards, on the one hand, and proceedings designed to adjudicate disputed facts in particular cases on the other." United States v. Florida E. Coast Ry., 410 US 224, 245 (1973); Schwartz, Administrative Law, 232 (3d. ed.); Gellhorn et al., Administrative Law 209 et seq. (8th ed.).

[7] 5 USC § 503.

[8] 5 USC § 504.

signed to implement, interpret, or prescribe law or policy or describing the organization, procedure, or practice requirements of an agency."[9] Rulemaking is therefore the "agency process for formulating, amending, or repealing a rule."[10] Consequently, a "rule" in the context of Treasury and Service action has the following three characteristics:

1. A rule is the product of the legislative function of the Treasury and the Service, and resembles a statute in that it applies to a class or category of taxpayers generally. While the definition of "rule" says that it may be directed at a particular situation, this reference is intended to apply to rate-making situations and does not detract from the principle that a rule has general applicability.[11] In the case of federal tax rules directed at a specific, albeit unidentified, person or the particular facts of a transaction or situation, the rule is intended to apply generally to all persons whose facts or transactions are the same as those in the rule.
2. A rule generally has future effect.[12]
3. A rule implements law or policy (legislative or substantive rules), interprets law (interpretive rules), or describes organization or procedure or practice requirements (procedural rules).

By contrast, under the APA, "order" means "the whole or any part of a final disposition, whether affirmative, negative, injunctive, or declaratory in form, of an agency in a matter other than rule making but including licensing."[13] Under this definition, "adjudication" is any agency action that is not rulemaking, and that, at the end of the administrative process, results in a "final disposition" of a matter involving a specific person. That final disposition may be a negative action, an injunction, or declaratory action.

The Code uses the terms "rules" and "regulations" interchangeably and, confusingly, in conjunction (e.g., in the civil penalty for intentional disregard

---

[9] 5 USC § 551(4).

[10] 5 USC § 551(5).

[11] The reference to a rule's "particular applicability" is said to ensure that the definition applies to rulemaking "addressed to named persons." See Administrative Procedure Act, Legislative History 283 n.1, quoted in Schwartz, Administrative Law, p.166 (3d ed. 1991). The reference is also said to be an "historical anomaly" intended to incorporate ratemaking proceedings, such as those public utilities and common carriers file for the approval of tariffs or rate schedules, as rulemaking proceedings rather than adjudications. W. Gelhorn & R. Levin, Administrative Law and Process 300 (West 1997).

[12] See Bowen v. Georgetown Univ. Hosp., 488 US 204, 221 (1988) ("Adjudication deals with what the law was; rulemaking deals with what the law will be"). However, Treasury regulations, under certain circumstances, may be effective retroactively if the Secretary so decides. See IRC § 7805(b). See infra ¶ 3.02[5].

[13] 5 USC § 551(6). "Adjudication" means "agency process for the formulation of an order." 5 USC § 551(7).

of "rules *and* regulations").[14] The Treasury also promulgates certain regulations as Treasury decisions, a term that implies some order or final disposition following an adjudicative process, when, in fact, the Treasury decision refers to a general rule adopted in accordance with its rulemaking function. The Statement of Procedural Rules resolves some of this confusion in terminology when it says that internal revenue "rules" take various forms, the "most important of which are issued as regulations and Treasury decisions prescribed by the Commissioner and approved by the Secretary or his delegate."[15] In other words, a "regulation" is one form of a "rule."

The more difficult question is whether a revenue ruling is a "rule." A revenue ruling differs from a regulation in important respects. First, rulemaking procedures (preadoption notice and public comment) prescribed by the APA govern the process for the Treasury's adoption rules and regulations. No preadoption notice and public comment procedures are required when the Service publishes a revenue ruling. A regulation is therefore the product of the formal process required when the Treasury and the Service states their position on a matter of tax law for future effect, while a revenue ruling is a type of informal statement of the Service's position about the application of the tax law to present or past facts. Because a rule or regulation is the product of a more formal rulemaking process that permits public comment, and presumably further consideration before the regulation is adopted, it is accorded greater weight and legal effect by the courts than a revenue ruling. Furthermore, the Internal Revenue Bulletin, in which revenue rulings are published, states that rulings and procedures reported in the Bulletin "do not have the force and effect of Treasury Department Regulations, but they may be used as precedents [in dealing with the Service]."

There is another fundamental difference between a rule or regulation and a revenue ruling. A regulation may deal with a specific situation or category of taxpayer, but it is intended to have general applicability for future transactions, and therefore the rule it establishes may be applied to facts and circumstances not specifically identified in the rule or regulation. A revenue ruling, by contrast, is the conclusion of the Service on how the law is applied to a specific set of facts. As the Service itself cautions, the conclusion reached in the ruling may not be relied on "unless the facts and circumstances [of the taxpayer] are substantially the same."[16]

---

[14] See IRC § 6662(b)(1).

[15] 26 CFR § 601.601(a)(1).

[16] See Rev. Proc. 2002-1 § 2.05, 2002-1 IRB 1.

[2] The Regulations Process: The Requirement of Notice and Public Comment

Responsibility for drafting regulations rests with the Secretary's delegate, the Assistant Secretary of the Treasury for Tax Policy and the Assistant Secretary's legal advisers in the Office of Tax Legislative Counsel. However, the initial drafting of regulations has been delegated to the Commissioner of Internal Revenue and the Commissioner's legal advisers in the office of an Associate Chief Counsel.[17] When a decision is made to promulgate a new regulation or to amend an existing one, the process from drafting to approval is as follows:

1. An Associate Chief Counsel assigns the project to one of the appropriate branches (functions). An attorney-adviser within the branch prepares a draft with assistance from an attorney from Treasury.
2. Assistance of other necessary personnel in the Service and the Treasury is enlisted.
3. As drafting proceeds, members of the team attempt to reach agreement on a position with the assistance of reviewers. These reviewers can be other attorney-advisers or supervisory personnel, such as the Branch Chief.
4. Depending on the type of project and its significance, the draft also may be reviewed by the Associate Chief Counsel, the Associate Chief Counsel (Litigation), the Associate Chief Counsel (International), and others.
5. The sequence for final review and sign-off on the regulation is to the Associate Chief Counsel, then to the Chief Counsel, thereafter to the Commissioner, and last to Treasury and the Assistant Secretary of the Treasury for Tax Policy.[18] Treasury attorneys may also conduct their own internal review.
6. The regulation as proposed is published in the Federal Register as a notice of proposed rulemaking.
7. Comments are solicited and hearings may be held on the proposed regulation.
8. Final regulations are drafted and adopted or are republished in the Federal Register for further comments.[19]

---

[17] 26 CFR § 601.601(a). See generally Schmid, "The Tax Regulations Making Process—Then and Now," 24 Tax Law. 541 (1971); Rogovin, "The Four R's: Regulations, Rulings, Reliance, and Retroactivity," 43 Taxes 756 (1965); Williams, "Preparation and Promulgation of Treasury Department Regulations," 8 USC Inst. on Fed. Tax'n 736, 741 (1956).

[18] 26 CFR § 601.601(a). This description of the procedure was the one set out in CCDM (39)314.3–(39)314.9, MT (39)-4 (Oct. 7, 1988) (Regulations and Legislation).

[19] See, e.g., Announcement 79-171, 1979-52 IRB 28, announcing public hearings on proposed regulations defining "gross cash rental" for purposes of electing to value certain

When an agency seeks to adopt a "substantive" rule, the APA requires the agency to (1) publish a notice of proposed rulemaking in the Federal Register; (2) give interested persons an opportunity to comment on the proposed rule; and (3) postpone the effective date of the rule until thirty days after publication in the Federal Register.[20] The published notice of the proposed rule must set forth (1) the time, place, and nature of public rulemaking proceedings; (2) the legal authority under which the rule is proposed; and (3) the terms or description of the subjects or issues involved.

Although the APA does not subject interpretive rules to these notice-and-comment procedures, the Treasury Department nevertheless follows them when adopting interpretive rules. Consequently, regulations issued pursuant to statutory authority to implement the statute (legislative regulations) and those advising the public of the agency's construction of a statute (interpretive regulations) are first published in proposed form and go through the notice-and-comment process before they are published in final form.

Temporary regulations must also be issued as proposed regulations. They are permitted to remain in effect for no more than three years after the date of their issuance.[21]

There are two general exceptions to the notice-and-comment procedures. First, the APA does not require the notice-and-comment procedures to be followed when organizational and procedural regulations are adopted. Accordingly, when the rule describes the Service's organization, procedure, or practice, the Treasury may adopt such a rule without providing notice and opportunity for public comment.[22] Second, the Treasury may publish regulations without following the above-discussed "notice-and-public comment" procedures if the regulation states that the Treasury has determined "for good cause" that these procedures are "impracticable, unnecessary, or contrary to the public interest."[23] The Treasury has frequently used this exception to issue temporary regulations for immediate guidance where substantial legislation has been en-

---

farm real property according to its actual use. Proposed regulations were originally published on July 19, 1978, and hearings held on April 3, 1979. On September 19, 1979, a notice was issued withdrawing the portion of the proposed regulations concerning the definition of "gross cash rental."

[20] 5 USC §§ 553(b), 553(c), 553(d).

[21] IRC § 7805(e), added by Technical and Miscellaneous Revenue Act of 1988, § 6232 (Sept. 10, 1988) (effective for regulations issued more than ten days after enactment date).

[22] 5 USC § 553(b)(A).

[23] 5 USC § 553(b)(B).

acted.[24] These temporary regulations are effective until superseded by permanent regulations.

The notice of proposed rulemaking, when required, must be published in the Federal Register at least thirty days before the rule becomes effective.[25] If the final regulation differs materially from the proposed rule (as published), the regulation may be invalid for not having been promulgated in accordance with the APA's notice requirements. In *American Standard, Inc. v. United States*,[26] a notice of proposed rulemaking was published in the Federal Register on September 8, 1966, but the proposed regulation differed substantially from the regulation ultimately adopted on December 30, 1966. The Court of Claims held that the published notice did not give the public fair or adequate notice of the final regulation and that, therefore, the final regulation was invalid because the notice provisions of the APA had been violated.

After a notice of proposed rulemaking is published in the Federal Register, interested persons may submit any data, views, or arguments with respect to the proposed regulations.[27] If a public hearing is announced, they may also make oral comments at the hearing. Persons who wish to be heard at the public hearing must, within the time prescribed in the notice, submit an outline of the topics they want to discuss and the time they will devote to each topic.[28] An agenda is then prepared containing the order of presentation of oral comments and the time (ordinarily ten minutes) allotted to each presentation.[29] Persons making oral comments are requested to avoid the mere restatement of their previously submitted written comments and to be prepared to answer questions not only on the topics listed in the outline of their oral presentation but also on matters related to their written comments.[30]

The APA provides that regulations may not be made effective until at least thirty days after the date the notice of proposed rulemaking is published in the Federal Register. This requirement merely postpones the effective date

---

[24] For a reasoned argument that Treasury should promulgate regulations in proposed form, rather than as temporary regulations, to permit preadoption public comment, see Asimow, "Temporary Regulations," 49 Tax Notes 451 (Oct. 22, 1990).

[25] 5 USC § 553(d).

[26] American Standard, Inc. v. United States, 602 F2d 256 (Ct. Cl. 1979).

[27] 26 CFR § 601.601(b). See, e.g., Announcement 80-25, 1980-8 IRB 27, providing notice of a public hearing on proposed regulations relating to the application of conventions under the Class Life Asset Depreciation Range System. See also Announcement 80-23, 1980-11 IRB 39, announcing public hearings on proposed regulations relating to requirements for depositing Social Security and withheld income taxes.

[28] After a timely request is made, the Treasury may grant additional time to submit the outline.

[29] 26 CFR § 601.601(a)(3)(iii).

[30] 26 CFR § 601.601(a)(3)(ii). A person who wishes copies of written comments of others must make a request for such copies within the time prescribed in the notice of hearing and be prepared to pay copying costs. 26 CFR § 601.601(a)(3)(ii).

of the regulation without stating what that effective date must be once the thirty-day rule is satisfied.[31] In the case of tax rules and regulations, Section 7805(b) also provides that no temporary, proposed, or final regulation may apply to any taxable period ending before the earliest of (1) the date on which the regulation is filed with the Federal Register; (2) in the case of a final regulation, the date on which a related proposed or temporary regulation was filed with the Federal Register; or (3) the date on which a notice substantially describing the expected content of a temporary, proposed, or final regulation was made public.[32] Moreover, where regulations amend existing regulations in a manner adversely affecting taxpayers or restricting treatment previously accorded them, the Treasury delays the effective date of the regulations, usually beyond the statutory thirty-day period.[33] The Service is also required to solicit comments from the Small Business Administration about the impact of proposed and temporary regulations on small business. The Service must take this action after the proposed or temporary regulations are issued (or before the promulgation of final regulations if final regulations are issued directly without the issuance of proposed regulations).[34]

[3] Types of Regulations and Their Legal Effect

Regulations under the 1986 Code have been grouped under Title 26 of the Code of Federal Regulations. Within this title, regulations are divided into parts, and each set of regulations is given a part number. Regulations on income tax sections of the Code are designated Part 1, so that regulations under Section 162 appear in the Treasury Regulations as Section 1.162. As noted previously, there are three types of regulations: (1) legislative or substantive, (2) interpretive, and (3) procedural.

---

[31] The promulgation date of a regulation or Treasury decision is the date the regulation or decision is filed by the Federal Register Division, National Archives and Records Service, for public inspection. Rev. Rul. 56-517, 1956-2 CB 966.

[32] Section 7805(b) applies to regulations relating to legislation enacted on or after July 30, 1996. Retroactive effect may still be given to a regulation if it is adopted to prevent abuse, to correct a procedural defect in a prior regulation, the regulation applies to internal Treasury Department policies, practices, or procedures, Congress has authorized retroactive application, or a taxpayer has elected to apply the regulation retroactively. IRC § 7805(b)(b)(3).

[33] Schmid, "The Tax Regulations Making Process—Then and Now," 24 Tax Law. 541, 542 (1971).

[34] IRC § 7805(f).

[a] Legislative or Substantive Regulations

Legislative or substantive regulations are regulations issued pursuant to a specific authorization from or direction by Congress in particular sections of the Code. These regulations are issued under the particular statute by which Congress makes the delegation to the "Secretary or his delegate." The best known example of this type of regulation is the consolidated return regulations promulgated pursuant to Section 1502, which provides: "The Secretary or his delegate shall prescribe such regulations as he may deem necessary in order that the tax liability of any affiliated group of corporations making a consolidated return and of each corporation in the group . . . may be returned." With this legislative delegation to the Secretary or the Secretary's delegate, Congress enabled the consolidated return regulations, and not the statute, to constitute virtually the entire law dealing with consolidated tax returns. When the Treasury promulgates a legislative regulation, the regulation has the force and effect of law.[35]

In *Rowan Companies*, the Supreme Court described the standard of review applicable to legislative regulations, saying that "[w]here the Commissioner acts under specific authority, our primary inquiry is whether the interpretation or method is within the delegation of authority."[36] A reviewing court has no authority to substitute its judgment about the content of the regulation because Congress has placed maximum discretion in the agency and not in the courts.[37] Legislative regulations do not have the effect of the enabling statute, however, unless they are (1) within the granted power of the agency, (2) issued pursuant to proper procedure, and (3) reasonable.[38]

Since the authority to promulgate legislative regulations derives from the enabling statute, a legislative regulation must be within the granted authority,

---

[35] See Anderson, Clayton & Co. v. United States, 562 F2d 972, 976 n.6 (5th Cir. 1977), cert. denied, 436 US 944 (1978); Union Elec. Co. of Missouri v. United States, 305 F2d 850, 854 (Ct. Cl. 1962).

[36] Rowan Cos. v. United States, 452 US 247, 253 (1981).

[37] Rowan Cos. v. United States, 452 US 247, 253 (1981). Compare City of Tucson v. Comm'r, 820 F2d 1283, 1292 (DC Cir. 1987), where the circuit court stated:

With all due regard for the Treasury Department's pivotal role as administrator of the revenue laws, and as well as its considerable expertise in the field of taxation, we hold that the challenged regulation exceeds the Department's delegated power to implement Section 103(c)(2)(B). The regulation attributes to the statutory word "replace" an unnatural and unreasonably broad interpretation, and thereby enlarges both the section's coverage and the Department's administrative authority beyond the boundaries contemplated by Congress.

[38] See Union Carbide Corp. v. United States, 612 F2d 558, 563 (Ct. Cl. 1979); American Standard, Inc. v. United States, 602 F2d 256, 261, 267 (Ct. Cl. 1979); American Trans-Ocean Navigation Corp. v. Comm'r, 229 F2d 97, 98 (2d Cir. 1956); Comm'r v. General Mach. Corp., 95 F2d 759, 761 (6th Cir. 1938); Corner Broadway-Maiden Lane, Inc. v. Comm'r, 76 F2d 106, 108 (2d Cir. 1935).

or it will be ultra vires. The reasonableness requirement derives from consider-ations of both constitutional due process and the principle of statutory interpre-tation that presumes legislative bodies intend to avoid delegating the power to act unreasonably.[39] Under this doctrine, courts have held legislative regulations invalid when the regulation conflicted with a statute[40] or was unreasonable in attempting to tax income that would otherwise not be taxed.[41] A legislative regulation may also be held invalid if it has not been promulgated according to the requirements of the APA.[42]

[b] Interpretive Regulations

Regulations that explain or construe the meaning of a statutory provision are called interpretive regulations. The explanation or construction offered in such regulations describes the position of the Treasury and the Service, com-mits the Treasury and the Service to an interpretation of law, and is generally binding upon both.[43] Interpretive regulations also give notice to taxpayers of the Service's position on a particular issue or transaction. Unlike legislative regulations, however, there is no specific grant of authority for the promulga-tion of an interpretive regulation. Authority for the promulgation of interpre-tive regulations is derived from the general grant of authority authorizing the Secretary or his delegate "to prescribe all needful rules and regulations for the enforcement of [the tax laws]."[44]

Unlike legislative regulations, an interpretation stated in an interpretive regulation is not controlling on a court. The weight given to an interpretive

---

[39] Davis, Administrative Law Treatise § 5.03 (2d ed. 1978). See, e.g., L&F Sales Corp. v. United States, 912 F2d 377 (9th Cir. 1990) (challenge to DISC regulation re-jected; held, sixty-day rule, rather than two-and-one-half-months rule, not unreasonable).

[40] Union Carbide Corp. v. United States, 612 F2d 558, 563 (Ct. Cl. 1979); American Standard, Inc. v. United States, 602 F2d 256, 261, 267 (Ct. Cl. 1979); Comm'r v. General Mach. Corp., 95 F2d 759, 761 (6th Cir. 1938); Corner Broadway-Maiden Lane, Inc. v. Comm'r, 76 F2d 106, 108 (2d Cir. 1935); Phillips Petroleum Co. & Subsids. v. Comm'r, 97 TC 30 (1991), aff'd, 70 F3d 1282 (10th Cir. 1992). In Tate & Lyle, Inc. v. Comm'r, 103 TC 656 (1994), the Tax Court held that regulations promulgated under Section 267(a)(3), applying the matching principle of Section 267(a)(2) to non-U.S. persons, were invalid because the regulations precluded the accrual and deduction of interest when the payee's noninclusion of income was attributable to an income tax treaty, and not to its ac-counting method as provided in Section 267(a)(2). The Third Circuit, however, reversed and remanded the decision, 87 F3d 99 (3d Cir. 1996).

[41] Joseph Weidenhoff, Inc. v. Comm'r, 32 TC 1222, 1242 (1959).

[42] American Standard, Inc. v. United States, 602 F2d 256 (Ct. Cl. 1979) (notice of regulation's basis and purpose was not published, in violation of the APA).

[43] The binding effect of interpretative regulations is described at ¶¶ 3.02[4][b] and 3.02[5], infra.

[44] IRC § 7805(a).

regulation by a court depends on a totality of circumstances. As the Supreme Court noted in *Skidmore v. Swift & Co.*, in regard to regulations interpreting the Fair Labor Standards Act:

> There is no statutory provision as to what, if any, deference courts should pay to the Administrator's conclusions. . . . This Court has long given considerable and in some cases decisive weight to Treasury Decisions and to interpretative regulations of the Treasury and of other bodies that were not of adversary origin. We consider that the rulings, interpretations and opinions of the Administrator under [the Fair Labor Standards] Act, while not controlling upon the courts by reason of their authority, do constitute a body of experience and informed judgment to which courts and litigants may properly resort for guidance. The weight of such a judgment in a particular case will depend upon the thoroughness evident in its consideration, the validity of its reasoning, its consistency with earlier and later pronouncements, and all those factors which give it power to persuade, if lacking power to control.[45]

In a later statement, the Supreme Court in *National Muffler Dealers Association* described the judicial analysis in the following way:[46]

> In determining whether a particular regulation carries out the congressional mandate in a proper manner, we look to see whether the regulation harmonized with the plain language of the statute, its origin, and purpose. A regulation may have a particular force if it is a substantially contemporaneous construction of the statute by those presumed to have been aware of congressional intent. If the regulation dates from a later period, the manner in which it evolved merits inquiry. Other relevant considerations are the length of time the regulation has been in effect, the reliance placed on it, the consistency of the Commissioner's interpretation, and the degree of scrutiny Congress has devoted to the regulation during the subsequent re-enactments of the statute.

Factors that courts consider to bear on the validity of interpretive regulations include (1) whether the court agrees or disagrees with the regulation; (2) whether the regulation reflects special administrative competence (i.e., the administrator considers the regulation to be reasonable in the context of the statutory scheme); (3) whether the regulation is longstanding; and (4) whether the statute has been reenacted, after promulgation of the regulation, by legislators

---

[45] Skidmore v. Swift & Co., 323 US 134, 139–140 (1944). The Tax Court has not given interpretive regulations as much weight as legislative regulations. See Pacific First Fed. Sav. Bank v. Comm'r, 94 TC 101 (1990) (interpretive regulations are "not entitled to as much deference as that owed to 'legislative regulations'").

[46] National Muffler Dealers Ass'n v. United States, 440 US 472, 477 (1979). See also Comm'r v. Engle, 464 US 206, 224 (1984) (deference accorded to administrative interpretations only sets "framework for judicial analysis; it does not displace it").

who presumably knew the content of the rule. These factors are discussed more fully below.

[i] Reasonableness. Courts generally attach great weight, and thus frequently defer to, the Treasury's construction of a statute. In support of this notion, the Supreme Court stated that a regulation must be upheld "unless unreasonable and plainly inconsistent with the revenue statutes,"[47] and that "the choice among reasonable alternatives is for the Commissioner, not the courts."[48] Nevertheless, despite this principle of deference, a court may find that as a matter of law an interpretive regulation is inconsistent with the statute and therefore is an unauthorized interpretation of it. Once such a finding is made, the interpretive regulation ceases to have any legal effect, and the court's interpretation of the statute will govern resolution of the issue. The rationale for this principle was stated by the Supreme Court in *Manhattan General Equipment Co. v. Commissioner.*

> The power of an administrative officer . . . to administer a federal statute and to prescribe rules and regulations to that end is not the power to make law . . . but the power to adopt regulations to carry into effect the will of Congress as expressed by the statute. A regulation which does not do this, but operates to create a rule out of harmony with the statute, is a mere nullity.[49]

In a decision that has been described as the most important, as well as "notorious," administrative law decision "in recent years," the Supreme Court developed in *Chevron, USA, Inc. v. Natural Resources Defense Council* a two-part process for determining the validity of a regulation:[50]

> First, always, is the question whether Congress has directly spoken to the precise question or issue. If the intent of Congress is clear, that is the end of the matter, for the Court, as well as the agency, must give effect to the unambiguously expressed intent of Congress. If, however, the court determines Congress has not directly addressed the precise question at issue, the court does not simply impose its own construction of the statute, as would be necessary in the absence of an administrative interpretation. Rather, if the statute is silent or ambiguous with respect to the specific issue, the question for the court is whether the agency's answer is based on a permissible construction of the statute.

---

[47] Comm'r v. South Tex. Lumber Co., 333 US 496, 501 (1948).

[48] National Muffler Dealers Ass'n v. United States, 440 US 472, 477, 488 (1979). See also Fulman v. United States, 434 US 528, 533 (1978); Allen Oil Co. v. Comm'r, 614 F2d 336, 340 (2d Cir. 1980); United States v. Correll, 389 US 299, 307 (1967).

[49] Manhattan Gen. Equip. Co. v. Comm'r, 297 US 129, 134 (1936).

[50] Chevron, USA, Inc. v. Natural Resources Defense Council, 467 US 837, 842–843 (1984) (interior footnotes and citations omitted).

The first part of the analysis, concerning whether the regulation is consistent with the statute and its purpose, is in the tradition of the *Manhattan General Equipment* case. The full import of the decision is therefore in the Court's description of the second part of the review process, which courts are to undertake if "Congress has not directly addressed the precise question at issue," and the statute is "silent or ambiguous" on the issue. If Congress did not directly address the issue, *Chevron* says, a court should not independently determine whether the regulation is inappropriate or incorrect. Instead, the court should examine whether the agency was reasonable in determining that its regulation is appropriate in the context of the statutory scheme.[51] If the statute is silent or ambiguous, other statements in *Chevron* make it difficult for a court to take any action other than to defer to the agency's view. Thus, the Court said that the agency's construction of the statute is accorded "considerable weight," and when the agency's choice "represents a reasonable accommodation of conflicting policies that were committed to the agency's care by the statute, [courts] should not disturb it unless it appears from the statute or its legislative history that the accommodation is not one that Congress would have sanctioned."[52] Under the *Chevron* doctrine, an interpretive regulation will not be invalidated by the court's conclusion that the agency interpretation was not the only permissible one or that it would have adopted a different interpretation if the matter had been before it in a judicial proceeding.[53]

Although a long line of Supreme Court cases, including tax cases, adopted a principle of deference to agency legal interpretations,[54] by providing a structure for analysis and application of this principle, *Chevron* has become the most cited case in administrative law in the last fifty years.[55]

After *Chevron*, courts have had to determine (1) whether Congress has "directly addressed" an issue, (2) whether the statute is unambiguous on the issue, and (3) whether the agency's interpretation of the statute is a permissible and reasonable one, even if it is not the correct one in the court's view.

---

[51] Chevron, USA, Inc. v. Natural Resources Defense Council, 467 US 837, 845 (1984).

[52] Chevron, USA, Inc. v. Natural Resources Defense Council, 467 US 837, 844–845 (1984) (quoting United States v. Shimer, 367 US 374, 382, 383 (1961)).

[53] Other administrative law cases have stated the same principle. See, e.g., FEC v. Democratic Senatorial Campaign Comm., 454 US 27, 39 (1981). *Chevron*'s deferential standard is thus similar to the standard of appellate court review of a trial court's decision where the reviewing court must uphold a finding of fact even if the court might have decided the issue differently so long as the finding is not "clearly erroneous."

[54] B. Schwartz, Administrative Law (3d ed. 1991).

[55] J. Reese, Administrative Law, 768 (West, 1995); W. Gellhorn & R. Levin, Administrative Law and Process, 81 (West, 1997) ("*Chevron* is the most widely cited of a long line of cases directing courts to defer to agencies' legal interpretations").

While some degree of deference to an agency's interpretation of a statute is a settled principle even in the case of interpretive regulations, courts (including the Supreme Court) have nevertheless rejected an agency's construction of a statute under certain circumstances. For example, three years after it decided *Chevron*, the Supreme Court carefully reviewed the language and legislative history of two statutory standards in the Immigration and Nationality Act, one for the withholding of deportation and the other for asylum. Upon doing so, the Court rejected the Immigration and Naturalization Service's interpretive rule that the two standards were the same, saying that the question "whether Congress intended the two standards to be identical is a pure question of statutory construction for the courts to decide."[56] The approach of the Court in this case is that courts, not agencies, are the "final authority on issues of statutory construction" (i.e., on the matter of whether Congress has spoken on the issue). As such, the courts are free to reject an administrative construction of a statute that is contrary to Congress's intent.[57] In another case, the Supreme Court applied the *Chevron* principle, and upheld a regulation of the Department of the Interior interpreting the Endangered Species Act. It did so, however, only after it examined the text of the Act, the broad purpose of the Act, and subsequent legislative action, all of which shed light on the meaning of the Act. The Court concluded that Congress did not "unambiguously manifest its intent to adopt" a view different from the agency interpretation, and that the agency's interpretation was a reasonable one.[58]

In tax cases, the Supreme Court has said that it "customarily"[59] defers to a Treasury interpretive regulation as long as it is found to "implement the congressional mandate in some reasonable manner."[60] Deference has sometimes been described in the strongest terms (i.e., foreshadowing *Chevron*), as in *South Texas Lumber Co.*, where the Court said that a regulation could not be held invalid unless the regulation was "plainly inconsistent with the statute."[61] As *Chevron* recognized, deference is given to an agency's construction of a

---

[56] Immigration & Naturalization Serv. v. Cardoza-Fonseca, 480 US 421, 446–448 (1987).

[57] Immigration & Naturalization Serv. v. Cardoza-Fonseca, 480 US 421, 446 (1987). Justice Scalia, concurring, criticized this approach, saying that the Court was erroneously interpreting *Chevron*, "by implying that courts may substitute their interpretation for that of the agency whenever [employing] 'traditional tools of statutory construction,' they are able to reach a conclusion about the proper construction of the statute." Id. at 454. Justice Scalia went on to say that the Court's approach would eviscerate *Chevron* by "authorizing courts to defer [to agencies] only if they would otherwise be unable to construe the enactment at issue." Id.

[58] Babbitt v. Sweet Home Chapter of Comms. for a Great Or., 515 US 687 (1995).

[59] National Muffler Dealers Ass'n, Inc. v. United States, 440 US 472 (1979).

[60] United States v. Correll, 389 US 299, 307 (1939).

[61] Comm'r v. South Tex. Lumber Co., 333 US 496, 501 (1948).

statutory scheme because the agency is entrusted with the administration of the statute and has developed an institutional expertise and familiarity with the statute.[62]

If the agency's familiarity with the statute is fundamental to the *Chevron* doctrine, then the scope of the doctrine, or at least the extent of its applicability, may be questioned when the agency's interpretation is reviewed by a specialized court, such as the Tax Court. Before *Chevron*, the Tax Court stated its approach to the analysis as follows:[63]

> [J]udicial deference is not a substitute for judicial scrutiny and analysis. A regulation which contradicts the unambiguous language of the statute it purports to interpret cannot stand. Moreover, where the statute is unambiguous, and there is no valid reason for adding a requirement to those the statute already provides, the Commissioner may not usurp congressional authority by adding such a requirement by regulation. Finally, although a regulation does not clearly contradict or limit the provisions of the statute it purports to interpret, it is nonetheless invalid if it is inconsistent with the statute's origin and purpose.

This is not *Chevron*-type deference to the Treasury's and the Service's interpretation. However, it should be noted that the Tax Court's specialized juris-

---

[62] Chevron v. Natural Resources Defense Council, 467 US 837, 844 (1984).

[63] CWT Farms, Inc. v. Comm'r, 79 TC 1054, 1062 (1982), aff'd, 755 F2d 790 (11th Cir. 1985). See Edward L. Stephenson Trust v. Comm'r, 81 TC 283, 288 (1983) ("A regulation is not a reasonable statutory interpretation unless it harmonizes with the plain language, origin, and purpose of the statute").

The Tax Court has also said that although an interpretive regulation "is entitled to respect, it is not entitled to the high degree of deference accorded to a legislative regulation." Ann Jackson Family Found. v. Comm'r, 97 TC 534, 538 (1991), aff'd, 15 F3d 917 (9th Cir. 1994) ("Accordingly, the mere fact that the interpretative regulation in the instant appeal was issued by the Secretary of the Treasury some twenty years ago is no argument against either the Tax Court's overturning that regulation or our upholding that ruling if the regulation fails to 'implement the congressional mandate in some reasonable manner'").

For a case illustrating the Tax Court's analysis of the validity of interpretive and legislative regulations, see Sim-Air, USA, Ltd. v. Comm'r, 98 TC 187, 194 (1992) (Reg. § 1.993-3(d)(2)(i)(b) is held to be an interpretive regulation, and its imposition of a one-year limitation with respect to domestic international sales corporation export property is reasonable). Compare St. Jude Medical, Inc. v. Comm'r, 34 F3d 1394, 1402 (8th Cir. 1994) (invalidating for domestic international sales corporation (DISC) reporting purposes one portion of the research and development expenditure regulations, Regulation § 1.861-8(e)(3), because it conflicted with the origin and purpose of the relevant DISC provision, Section 994(b)) with Perkin-Elmer Corp. & Subs. v. Comm'r, 103 TC 464, 481 (1994) (holding that, absent some unequivocal language in the legislative history, another portion of Regulation § 1.861-8(e)(3) describing the sales method of apportioning research and development expenses was not unreasonable, although the taxpayer's method produced better results in certain situations).

diction enables it to determine whether the Service's or Treasury's choice among alternative interpretations is appropriate and reasonable, and the Tax Court may do so with a level of sophistication that courts of general jurisdiction may not be equipped to exhibit.

Still, general propositions do not supply a ready test for predicting the level of deference a court will give an agency's interpretive regulation. Supreme Court decisions, albeit before *Chevron*, illustrate the problem. In *National Muffler Dealers*, the Supreme Court said that, in determining whether a statutory regulation carries out the congressional mandate, it considers whether the regulation "harmonizes" with the "statute, its origin, and its purpose;" the Court then found the regulation in issue to be valid.[64] In *Vogel Fertilizer*, calling upon the same principle, the Court held another regulation invalid.[65]

Courts, including the Supreme Court, have nevertheless struck down regulations because they were unreasonable interpretations of the statute.[66] Cases after *Chevron*, such as *Cardoza-Fonseca*, suggest that, while giving deference to the Treasury's interpretation, courts will not surrender their judicial role of "using the traditional tools of statutory construction" to reach a determination about the proper interpretation of the statute. Courts will determine whether a Treasury regulation is valid by first examining and construing the statute, or, as the Supreme Court said in *National Muffler Dealers*, "the plain language of the statute, its origin, and its purpose." If the statute is unambiguous and the regulation is inconsistent with the statute, that is the end of the matter, and the regulation will be held invalid. If the meaning of the statute is not plain, the court will look to legislative history to determine the origin and purpose of the statute. If Congress has not "directly addressed" the issue, however, *Chevron* requires the court to then uphold the regulation if the Treasury's or Service's interpretation is a permissible or reasonable interpretation of the statute. Despite its principle of deference, both the "directly addressed" and the reasonable interpretation elements of the *Chevron* doctrine give courts the flexibility

---

[64] National Muffler Dealers Ass'n v. United States, 440 US 472 (1979).

[65] Vogel Fertilizer Co. v. United States, 455 US 16 (1982).

[66] For cases in which the Supreme Court found Treasury's interpretation of a statute unreasonable, see United States v. Vogel Fertilizer Co., 455 US 16 (1982) (involving the interpretation of "controlled group of corporations" in IRC § 1563); Rowan Cos., Inc. v. United States, 452 US 247 (1981) (definition of "wages"). Compare Comm'r v. Portland Cement Co., 450 US 156, 170 (1981) (depletion regulations held "reasonable"). Even when the interpretation of the administering agency is given great deference, a regulation may be found unreasonable. See Beneficial Corp. & Subsids. v. United States, 814 F2d 1570, 1574 (Fed. Cir. 1987) (finding nevertheless that the IRS interpretation "pervert[ed] the intent of Congress and [was] unreasonable").

and opportunity to reject the Treasury's or Service's interpretations of Code provisions.

[ii] Timing. Regulations that were promulgated contemporaneously with or shortly after the enactment of a statute are given more weight than regulations enacted later.[67] In the case of Treasury regulations, this practice seems justified where the bill is sponsored by the Administration through the Treasury and the bill survives the legislative process substantially intact. When the Treasury-sponsored bill is enacted, Treasury's regulations interpreting the statute reflect the intention of the writer of the statute (i.e., the Treasury). However, even if a bill does not originate in the Treasury or if a bill originating in the Treasury is substantially changed, the Treasury staff will still be well prepared to formulate regulations that articulate the intentions of Congress (or at least of its committees) because the Treasury staff will have participated in the preparation of the committee reports and the hearings on the bill. In the event that the Treasury staff did not participate in a bill or opposed it, logic (if not experience) indicates that regulations interpreting such statutory provision may not have the same weight.

[iii] Duration. The length of time that a regulation has been in force also is a factor indicating its validity and the level of deference to be accorded to it by the courts. The Supreme Court has even stated that longstanding rules should not be overruled except for weighty reasons,[68] and that "Treasury regulations and interpretations long continued without substantial change, applying to unamended or substantially reenacted statutes, are deemed to have received congressional approval and have the effect of law."[69] Nevertheless, the Supreme Court has declared invalid established regulations with which it has disagreed, longstanding or not.[70]

[iv] Reenactment. The doctrine of legislative reenactment refers to the proposition that Congress implicitly approves all administrative interpretations of a statute it reenacts, thereby giving that administrative interpretation the

---

[67] National Muffler Dealers Ass'n v. United States, 440 US 472, 477 (1979); Comm'r v. South Tex. Lumber Co., 333 US 496, 501 (1948); Fawcus Mach. Co. v. United States, 282 US 375, 378 (1931).

[68] Comm'r v. Estate of Sternberger, 348 US 187, 199 (1955).

[69] Helvering v. Winmill, 305 US 79, 83 (1938); United States v. Correll, 389 US 299, 307 (1939). See Fribourg Navigation Co. v. Comm'r, 383 US 272, 283 (1966); Lykes v. United States, 343 US 118 (1952).

[70] Koshland v. Helvering, 298 US 441 (1936) (regulations had been in force for sixteen years). See also Estate of Kappel v. Comm'r, 615 F2d 91 (3d Cir. 1980) (mitigation regulations in effect since adoption of 1954 Code); Ann Jackson Family Found. v. Comm'r, 15 F3d 917 (9th Cir. 1994) (private foundation excise tax regulation had been in effect for more than twenty years).

force of law. This doctrine has frequently been cited in tax cases.[71] However, at best, the so-called "reenactment doctrine" should have no more status than as "an aid in statutory constructions."[72]

The reasoning of the doctrine assumes that members of the tax committees, or at least their staffs, review all existing regulations prior to reenacting a statute; one could hardly quarrel with judicial approval of a regulation specifically or implicitly approved by Congress. However, with the exponential growth in the number and length of regulations, it is doubtful that members of these committees will have the time or inclination to become sufficiently familiar with all of the Treasury interpretations concerning the reenacted provision to form a judgment as to their position on each individual interpretation. Accordingly, without a clear expression of congressional approval of an existing administrative interpretation, it may not be wise to infer approval from the mere reenactment of a statute after an interpretation thereof has been issued by an agency.

In *Bob Jones University v. United States*, the Supreme Court stated: "Ordinarily, and quite appropriately, courts are slow to attribute significance to the failure of Congress to act on particular legislation," and "[n]onaction by Congress is not often a useful guide."[73] However, the failure of Congress to modify IRS rulings of 1970 and 1971 that denied tax-exempt status to private schools not having a racially nondiscriminatory policy as to students, when it enacted other legislation affecting Section 501, was held to "make out an unusually strong case of legislative acquiescence in and ratification by implication of the 1970 and 1971 rulings."[74] Also, Congress's knowledge of the Service's position was established by "its own studies and by public discourse," as well as the failure of thirteen bills introduced to overturn the IRS interpretation to emerge from any committee. On the other hand, where the record is silent, Congress's failure to act may reflect no more than a willingness to leave details to the special skills of administrators and judges.[75] As Judge Learned Hand put it: "To suppose that Congress must particularly correct each

---

[71] Helvering v. RJ Reynolds Tobacco Co., 306 US 110, 116 (1939). See National Muffler Dealers Ass'n v. United States, 440 US 472, 477 (1979); Comm'r v. South Texas Lumber Co., 333 US 496, 502–503 (1948); Helvering v. Winmill, 305 US 79, 83 (1938). For a case where Treasury's reenactment argument was analyzed and rejected, see Rowan Cos. v. United States, 452 US 247, 260–262 (1981).

[72] Helvering v. Reynolds, 313 US 428, 432 (1941).

[73] Bob Jones Univ. v. United States, 461 US 574, 600 (1983).

[74] Bob Jones Univ. v. United States, 461 US 574, 599 (1983).

[75] Davis, Administrative Law Treatise § 5.07 (2d ed. 1978). The statute in Helvering v. RJ Reynolds Tobacco Co., 306 US 110, 114–116 (1939), was reenacted after regulations were issued, and then reenacted again after the regulations had been changed. Theoretically, Congress can be viewed as having approved both the original and the amended regulations.

mistaken construction under penalty of incorporating it into the fabric of the statute appears to be unwarranted; our fiscal legislation is detailed and specific enough already."[76] Thus, legislative silence may at best mean nothing more than that the matter was not called to the attention of Congress.[77]

[c] Procedural Regulations

The term "procedural regulation" can apply to regulations promulgated in four different circumstances:

1. Otherwise interpretive regulations covering such matters as what information a taxpayer must supply to the IRS on the occurrence of a transaction and when the information must be supplied.[78]
2. Regulations promulgated under the procedural and administrative provisions of the Code.[79]
3. Regulations governing such internal management–type practices as hours, overtime, pensions, and similar matters.
4. Regulations describing, for the benefit of IRS employees and taxpayers alike, how the Service conducts its business.

Unlike legislative and interpretive regulations, the Commissioner of Internal Revenue, not the Treasury, promulgates procedural regulations, such as the Statement of Procedural Rules.[80]

The four distinct types of procedural regulations are issued in different ways and have different legal effect. Regulations setting forth taxpayer obligations to file forms and information, frequently issued as part of interpretive regulations, are promulgated according to the same notice and hearing procedures that accompany interpretive regulations. However, once enacted, they appear to be given the greater weight of legislative regulations. Regulations interpreting the procedural and administrative provisions of the Code are inter-

---

[76] FW Woolworth Co. v. United States, 91 F2d 973, 976 (2d Cir. 1937), cert. denied, 302 US 768 (1938).

[77] United States v. Calamaro, 354 US 351, 359 (1957). See Wendland v. Comm'r, 79 TC 355, 385 (1982) (reenactment doctrine rejected because statute was not considered by Congress during period that regulation and rulings allegedly relied on were adopted). See also McCoy v. United States, 802 F2d 762, 764–766 (4th Cir. 1986) (taxpayer argued that legislative reenactment doctrine applied so that administrative interpretation could only be changed by Congress, but court said the doctrine did not preclude the Service "from later adopting some other reasonable and lawful interpretation of the statute").

[78] See, e.g., Reg. § 1.332-6, regarding the records to be kept and information to be filed with the return filed for the year in which a subsidiary is liquidated.

[79] Reg. §§ 1.6001 et seq.

[80] 26 CFR Part 601.

pretive regulations, and the Treasury treats them as such by using the notice and hearing provisions of the APA.[81]

Internal management rules and descriptions of IRS operations affecting taxpayers are promulgated by the Commissioner of Internal Revenue under the general housekeeping rulemaking authority of the APA at 5 USC § 301. As seen below, these procedural regulations may not be binding on the Service.[82] Moreover, where the Commissioner issues housekeeping-type and procedural regulations, the notice requirements of the APA do not apply.[83]

As a general rule of administrative law, an agency is bound by its procedural regulations, at least where the procedural rule affects some vital personal interest of the taxpayer.[84] For reasons that are not entirely clear, a considerable body of law exists supporting the principle that the Service is not bound by procedural regulations issued by the Commissioner rather than the Treasury.[85] In *Luhring v. Glotzbach*, the Service sent a notice of deficiency to the taxpayer without the prior thirty-day letter required by the Service's procedural regulations. The Court of Appeals for the Fourth Circuit held that compliance with the Statement of Procedural Rules was not essential to the validity of a notice of deficiency, because these rules are promulgated without the approval of the Secretary of the Treasury, and, accordingly, lack the authority of regulations promulgated with the approval of the Secretary. To determine whether the Service is bound by its own procedural rules, the circuit court distinguished between procedural rules "promulgated without the approval of the Secretary . . . laid down by the Commissioner for the regulation of the affairs of his office" under Section 7802 and "formal regulations with the force and effect of law" that are prescribed by the Secretary of the Treasury under Section 7805. Unlike Treasury regulations, the Commissioner's rules were "directory and not mandatory in legal effect," because if they were mandatory, they would oper-

---

[81] See, e.g., Legis. Reg. 160-81, 1982-1 CB 560, containing "proposed regulations relating to the authority of the Service to serve notice of levy by mail," providing for comments and public hearing, but stating, "the Internal Revenue Service has concluded that the proposed regulations herein are interpretative and that the notice and public [hearing] procedure requirements of 5 USC § 553 do not apply."

[82] Luhring v. Glotzbach, 304 F2d 560, 565 (4th Cir. 1962). See also Rosenberg v. Comm'r, 450 F2d 529, 533 (10th Cir. 1971); Cleveland Trust Co. v. United States, 421 F2d 475 (6th Cir. 1970), cert. denied, 400 US 819 (1970).

[83] 5 USC § 553(b)(A).

[84] See the discussion in United States ex rel. Accardi v. Shaughnessy, 347 US 260 (1954), at ¶ 1.06[3].

[85] Luhring v. Glotzbach, 304 F2d 560 (4th Cir. 1962); Rosenberg v. Comm'r, 450 F2d 529 (10th Cir. 1971) (failure to grant appellate conference); Cleveland Trust Co. v. United States, 421 F2d 475 (6th Cir.), cert. denied 400 US 819 (1970); United States v. Goldstein, 342 F. Supp. 661 (EDNY 1972) (taxpayer denied district and regional conferences in criminal case).

ate to curtail the higher authority of the Secretary (in this case, to send a notice of deficiency).

Despite this authority, courts (including the circuit court which decided *Luhring v. Glotzbach*) have nevertheless required, in certain instances, that the Service comply with statements of procedure issued in less formal circumstances than the Statement of Procedural Rules. When special agents investigating criminal violations of the tax law failed to give partial Miranda warnings in accordance with a technical information release, several circuit courts ordered the statements obtained from the taxpayers under investigation suppressed.[86] However, in *United States v. Caceres*,[87] the Supreme Court determined that agents obtained evidence of an attempted bribery in violation of electronic monitoring procedures in the Internal Revenue Manual, but nevertheless held that the agent's failure to comply with the Manual did not warrant suppression of the evidence. The Supreme Court reasoned that the Manual's procedures were not required by either the Constitution or statute, and thus violation of the procedures did not raise constitutional issues. It has apparently escaped courts in later cases, however, that the Supreme Court accepted the principle that the Service, or any other agency for that matter, is bound by the procedural rules it adopts.[88] Specifically, in *Caceres*, the Supreme Court found that the principle did not apply, because (1) the agent's failure to comply with the Manual was the result of a good-faith, although erroneous, interpretation of the Manual's requirements; (2) the electronic monitoring procedures in question were not for taxpayer-defendant's benefit, but for the guidance of Service personnel; and (3) in any event, the defendant did not rely on them to his detriment. Moreover, it was significant to the Court's *Caceres* opinion that the remedy sought was not simply the invalidation of the agency's action under the APA, but the more extreme remedy under a rigid exclusionary rule that, if granted, would result in suppression of all evidence obtained in violation of the procedural rule.[89]

What conclusions regarding the treatment of procedural rules may be drawn from these disparate authorities? First, the Service may be bound by procedural rules it adopts even where these procedures are more stringent than

---

[86] United States v. Sourapas, 515 F2d 295, 298 (9th Cir. 1975); United States v. Leahey, 434 F2d 7, 10–11 (1st Cir. 1970); United States v. Heffner, 420 F2d 809, 812 (4th Cir. 1969); cf. United States v. Leonard, 524 F2d 1076 (2d Cir. 1975). However, after *Caceres*, the First Circuit stated that *Leahey* is no longer good law. United States v. Irvine, 699 F2d 43, 46 (1st Cir. 1983).

[87] United States v. Caceres, 440 US 741 (1979).

[88] The Court also said: "It does not necessarily follow, however, as a matter of either logic or law, that the agency had no duty to obey [regulations more rigorous than either the Constitution or law required]." United States v. Caceres, 440 US 741, 751, n.14 (1979). For further discussion of the effect of administrative rules, see Chapter 1.

[89] United States v. Caceres, 440 US 741, 755 (1979).

the law requires or where important interests of the taxpayer are at stake (the *Heffner* and *Sourapas* cases). Next, strict compliance may not be required where the procedure (e.g., a conference) is less significant. This is because either (1) taxpayers will still have their day in court (the *Luhring v. Glotzbach* line of cases) or (2) the relief requested is drastic (e.g., suppression) and the agency's failure to comply is not intentional (*Caceres*).

[4] The Problem of Retroactivity

Regulations for statutory provisions enacted on or after July 30, 1996, generally may not be given retroactive effect. As amended by the Taxpayer Bill of Rights 2, Section 7805(b) prohibits any temporary, proposed, or final regulation relating to the internal revenue laws to apply to a taxable period ending before the earliest of the following dates: (1) the date on which the regulation is filed with the Federal Register; (2) in the case of a final regulation, the date on which any proposed or temporary regulation that preceded the final regulation was filed with the Federal Register; or (3) the date of any notice "substantially describing" the expected contents of a temporary, proposed, or final regulation is issued to the public.[90]

Elimination of the discretionary authority of Treasury to issue regulations having retroactive effect has certain exceptions. Specifically, the Treasury still has discretionary authority to apply regulations retroactively (1) if they are filed or issued within eighteen months after the date of enactment of the statutory provision to which the regulation relates[91]; (2) if they are given retroactive effect to prevent abuse[92]; (3) if the regulation is given retroactive effect to correct some procedural defect in a previously issued regulation[93]; (4) if the regulations relate to internal Treasury Department policies, practices, or procedures[94]; and (5) if Congress legislatively grants Treasury the authority to prescribe the effective date of the regulation.[95] In addition, Treasury may per-

---

[90] IRC § 7805(b), amended by the Taxpayer Bill of Rights 2, Pub. L. No. 104-168, § 1101(a). According to the Joint Committee explanation of the reason for change in Section 7805(b), "the congress believed that it was generally inappropriate for Treasury to issue retroactive regulations." Staff of Joint Comm. on Tax'n, General Explanation of Tax Legislation Enacted in the 104th Congress, p.44 (Dec. 18, 1996). See also, Cohen & Harrington, "Is the Internal Revenue Service Bound by Its Own Regulations and Rulings?" 51 Tax Law. 675, 714 (1998) ("Taxpayer Bill of Rights 2 should be viewed as having made a significant change in the status of Treasury Regulations which relate to statutory provisions enacted on or after July 30, 1996").

[91] IRC § 7805(b)(2) (1996).
[92] IRC § 7805(b)(3) (1996).
[93] IRC § 7805(b)(4) (1996).
[94] IRC § 7805(b)(5) (1996).
[95] IRC § 7805(b)(6) (1996).

mit any taxpayer to elect retroactive application of any regulation before the date that the regulation is otherwise required to take effect according to Section 7805(b)(1).[96]

With respect to legislation passed before July 30, 1996 (i.e., the effective date of the amended Section 7805(b)), the Treasury and the Service had explicit statutory authority to "prescribe the extent, if any, to which any ruling or regulation, relative to the internal revenue laws, shall be applied without retroactive effect."[97] Treasury had the discretion to apply a regulation prospectively only, but, if Treasury did not exercise this discretion, it appears that a regulation ordinarily had retroactive effect. In its prior form, Section 7805(b) reflected Congress's recognition that when Treasury applied a regulation retroactively, the retroactive application could result in hardship and inequity.[98] The harsh result that may follow a retroactive application of a regulation also led to some judicial restrictions on the Treasury's exercise of its discretion.

These decisions and other case law on retroactive regulations still have relevance today. This is because, as amended, Section 7805(b) gives Treasury the discretion to apply a regulation retroactively when necessary to prevent abuse or when Congress specifically grants the Treasury such authority. Since Section 7805(b) was only amended in 1996, case law under the prior statute offers a background for better understanding the current version and its future development.

Under these pre-amendment cases, a regulation may be retroactively applied where there is (1) no prior administrative practice; (2) conflicting or confused administrative and judicial authority; or (3) under certain circumstances, a change in prior administrative practice or regulation.[99] The issuance of inter-

---

[96] IRC § 7805(b)(7) (1996).

[97] IRC § 7805(b) prior to amendment.

[98] See HR Rep. No. 704, 73d Cong., 2d Sess. 48 (1934). Provisions somewhat similar to Section 7805(b) have been in the tax law since the Revenue Act of 1921. See Helvering v. RJ Reynolds Tobacco Co., 306 US 110, 116 n.11 (1939).

For commentary on how the Treasury should be allowed to exercise its discretion, see Griswold, "A Summary of the Regulations Problem," 54 Harv. L. Rev. 348 (1941) (an analysis critical of retroactivity). See also Nolan & Thuroniyi, "Retroactive Application of Changes in IRS or Treasury Department Position," 61 Taxes 777, 783–785 (1983); Waver, "Retroactive Regulatory Interpretations: An Analysis of Judicial Responses," 61 Notre Dame L. Rev. 167 (1986).

[99] The judicial response to retroactive application of a tax statute provides a context for analyzing the issues raised by the application of a regulation or ruling. In *Welch v. Henry*, the Supreme Court tested whether retroactive application of a tax law was "harsh and oppressive" using three factors: (1) past legislative practice, (2) legislative need, and (3) retroactive periods of relatively short duration. Welch v. Henry, 305 US 134, 148–151 (1938); see also United States v. Darusmont, 449 US 292, 296–297 (1981) (minimum tax enacted October 4, 1976, but made retroactive to January 1, 1976, upheld because there was a "customary congressional practice" to apply tax provisions retroactively" for short and limited periods"). Commentators have noted that the Supreme Court "has exhibited

pretive regulations, after the enactment of a new statute (for which there has been no formal administrative guidance), that are retroactively applicable to the effective date of the statute generally does not constitute an abuse of discretion, even if a taxpayer has in the interim consummated a transaction that adversely affected by the regulation.[100] In *Reynolds*, the Supreme Court said that to hold that a taxpayer "had a vested interest in a hypothetical decision in his favor prior to the advent of the regulations would introduce into the scheme of the Revenue Acts refined notions of statutory construction which would, to say the least, impair an important administrative responsibility in the tax collecting process."[101] Section 7805(b)(2) now incorporates this principle by providing an exception for promptly issued regulations.

Even if no regulation has previously been promulgated, courts have not always permitted the Treasury to apply an interpretive regulation retroactively. The courts first scrutinize the circumstances surrounding the regulation's retroactive application to determine whether retroactivity is proper or fair.[102] In *Chock Full O' Nuts Corp. v. United States*,[103] the taxpayer claimed a deduction

---

extraordinary tolerance to retroactive tax laws, and has applied a deferential standard pursuant to which a retroactive tax statute is not of itself unconstitutional unless it is 'harsh and oppressive,' thus violating due process." Comm. on Federal Legislation, "Retroactive Application of Federal Legislation," The Records of the Ass'n of the Bar of the City of New York, 51:836, 854 (Dec. 1996); see also Bittker, "Constitutional Limits on the Taxing Power of the Federal Government," 41 Tax Law. 3, 11–12 (1987).

[100] Helvering v. Reynolds, 313 US 428, 433 (1941); cf. Chock Full O' Nuts Corp. v. United States, 453 F2d 300, 303 (2d Cir. 1971).

[101] The affected taxpayer could not have reasonably relied on any interpretation in his favor. Helvering v. Reynolds, 313 US 428, 433 (1941).

[102] Compare CWT Farms, Inc. v. Comm'r, 79 TC 1054, 1067–1070 (1982) (retroactive application of regulations upheld, despite change of rules contained in the DISC Handbook, which Treasury said could be relied on until regulations were proposed), aff'd, 755 F2d 790 (11th Cir. 1985), cert. denied, 477 US 903 (1986). Retroactive application of the regulations involved in *CWT Farms, Inc.* was denied, and its reasoning rejected in LeCroy Research Sys. Corp. v. Comm'r, 751 F2d 123, 126 (2d Cir. 1984) (retroactive application an abuse of discretion because Treasury's Handbook for Exporters expressly promised regulations would be applied prospectively). See also Thomas Int'l, Ltd. v. United States, 84-2 USTC ¶ 9857 (Cl. Ct. 1984), rev'd, 773 F2d 300 (Fed. Cir. 1985), cert. denied, 475 US 1045 (1986). For an analysis of the cases and judicial review of Treasury regulations, see Note, "Thomas International Ltd. v. United States," 38 Tax Law. 715 (1985).

When proposed regulations were published in 1983, defining "partnership items" for purposes of the unified partnership proceeding rules, they were intended to apply to tax years beginning after September 3, 1982. The final regulations, promulgated in 1986, were "very similar" to the proposed regulations. For this reason, a court held that the retroactive application of the final regulations was not an abuse of discretion and did not produce an unduly harsh result for the taxpayer. Meserve Drilling Partners v. Comm'r, 82 AFTR2d 98-5818 (9th Cir. 1998).

[103] Chock Full O' Nuts Corp. v. United States, 453 F2d 300, 303 (2d Cir. 1971).

for bond discount, said to have resulted from the sale of convertible debentures at par, equal to the value of the conversion privilege. At the time the debentures had been sold, no Treasury regulation or other authority existed on the subject. Subsequently, a Treasury regulation was promulgated defining "issue price" in such a way as to remove all possibility of discount in the taxpayer's case. The Second Circuit held that, although retroactivity of tax regulations is "presumptively permissible," the courts must determine in each case whether "under all the circumstances retroactive application would be warranted."[104] The court of appeals clearly recognized that taxpayers have no vested right in a hypothetical decision in their favor prior to promulgation of applicable regulations. Nevertheless, the court ruled that the Commissioner (or the Secretary) may not take advantage of the power to promulgate retroactive regulations and thereby, during the course of litigation, provide the Service with an argument based on the presumptive validity of those "just in time" regulations. Although it declined to resolve the issue, the court said: "[I]t is questionable whether [the Treasury regulation] represents a valid exercise of the Commissioner's [sic] power to promulgate retroactive regulations."[105]

A regulation may be retroactively applied where it clarifies confused or otherwise unsettled law. Here, retroactive application usually works no unfairness, since taxpayers cannot have relied on any definitive view or statement of the law in planning and executing the affected transaction. In such instances, the taxpayer acts at its own peril in consummating a transaction using a view of unsettled law that may later be contradicted or challenged in a retroactively applied regulation.[106]

Courts will limit the Treasury's power to apply a regulation retroactively if the new regulation conflicts with a settled administrative practice or regulation that is relied upon by a taxpayer.[107] In this situation, retroactive applica-

---

[104] Chock Full O' Nuts Corp. v. United States, 453 F2d 300, 303 (2d Cir. 1971).

[105] Chock Full O' Nuts Corp. v. United States, 453 F2d 300, 303 (2d Cir. 1971).

[106] Anderson, Clayton & Co. v. United States, 562 F2d 972, 983 (5th Cir. 1977), cert. denied, 436 US 944 (1978).

[107] Compare Wilson v. United States, 588 F2d 1168, 1173 (6th Cir. 1978) (taxpayer could not have relied on settled law because the case relied on by the taxpayer was an aberration, and Service said it would not follow it). See also Wendland v. Comm'r, 79 TC 355, 385 (1982). In *Wendland*, the Service issued a news release on October 29, 1976, stating that it would publish proposed regulations and suspend the application of certain rulings modifying the treatment of advanced royalties under mineral leases as of the news release date. On November 2, 1976, the Treasury published a notice of proposed rulemaking in the Federal Register. The final regulation was promulgated on December 19, 1977, and made retroactive to October 29, 1976. The taxpayer had invested in a coal partnership on December 30, 1976, that purchased a coal lease and other property. The Service challenged the tax treatment of deductions claimed by the partners based on the changed regulations. The Tax Court held that the Service had complied with the APA in promulgating the amended regulation, and had validly and reasonably exercised its authority under Sec-

tion of the regulation has been held to constitute an abuse of discretion, at least where the prior interpretation has been impliedly approved by Congress by its reenactment of the interpreted statute.[108]

If an erroneous interpretation by a taxpayer is not involved, a retroactive change in administrative practice or regulation may constitute an abuse of discretion where it would lead to inequality of treatment between competitor taxpayers or the result in a particular case would be unduly harsh or unfair.[109] By contrast, if the superseding regulation corrects an erroneous interpretation of the statute, it may be applied retroactively despite a taxpayer's detrimental reliance on the superseded but erroneous regulation.[110]

No matter how longstanding the regulation, it cannot alter the statute. As the Supreme Court said in *Manhattan Gen. Equipment Co.*,[111]

---

tion 7805(b) in making the amendment retroactive. The taxpayer had notice of the intent of the Service to apply the proposed change retroactively.

However, in Elkins v. Comm'r, 81 TC 669 (1983), the taxpayer was an investor in a partnership that had been formed, and he had become obligated to pay advanced royalties before October 29, 1976, the effective date of the new regulation. When the final regulations were adopted in 1977, they provided that a partner could not deduct his share of partnership loss resulting from the payment of advanced royalties unless he was a member of the partnership on October 29, 1976. The Treasury's 1976 notice had only stated that the modified regulation would not apply if, prior to October 29, 1976, the payment of advanced royalties was required under a lease "binding . . . upon the party" who pays or accrues the royalties. The Commissioner moved for summary judgment against the taxpayer on the ground that he did not become a partner until after October 29, 1976, and therefore the claimed deductions could be denied under the regulations. The Tax Court denied the motion (and motion for reconsideration of its ruling) on the ground that

it would constitute an abuse of discretion for [the Commissioner] first to state a concise rule through the medium of an official pronouncement and then belatedly to alter that rule to the substantial disadvantage of a taxpayer who had meanwhile acted in reliance on the most reasonable interpretation of it.

Id. at 681. Footnote references omitted.

[108] Helvering v. RJ Reynolds Tobacco Co., 306 US 110, 116 (1939).

[109] See Anderson, Clayton & Co. v. United States, 562 F2d 972, 981 (5th Cir. 1977), cert. denied, 436 US 944 (1978); Chock Full O' Nuts Corp. v. United States, 453 F2d 300, 302–303 (2d Cir. 1971); cf. Wilson v. United States, 588 F2d 1168, 1172–1173 (6th Cir. 1978).

[110] Manhattan Gen. Equip. Co. v. Comm'r, 297 US 129, 134–135 (1936). See Dixon v. United States, 381 US 68, 72–75 (1965); Dickman v. Comm'r, 465 US 330, 343 (1984). For an analysis of the issue of retroactive corrections of erroneous regulations and rulings that concludes that, even though an erroneous regulation or ruling may not be binding on the Service, it may be an abuse of discretion for the Service not to apply the regulation or ruling to a taxpayer who has relied on the Service's published statement of position, see Cohen & Harrington, "Is the Internal Revenue Service Bound by Its Own Regulations," 51 Tax Law. 675 (Summer 1998).

[111] Manhattan Gen. Equip. Co. v. Comm'r, 297 US 129, 135 (1936).

The statute defines the rights of the taxpayer and fixes a standard by which such rights are to be measured. The regulation constitutes only a step in the administrative process. It does not, and could not, alter the statute. It is no more retroactive in its operation than is a judicial determination construing and applying a statute to a case at hand."

¶ 3.03 RULINGS

[1] Types of Rulings

As a matter of policy, the National Office of the Service answers inquiries of individuals and organizations, "whenever appropriate in the interest of sound tax administration," about the tax effects of their acts or transactions or about their status for tax purposes.[112] The Service issues two types of rulings, revenue rulings and private letter rulings, to carry out this policy.

A revenue ruling is the conclusion of the Service on how the tax law applies to a specific set of facts that is published in the Internal Revenue Bulletin.[113] The National Office issues revenue rulings, which are then published in Internal Revenue Bulletin for the purpose of informing and providing guidance on substantive tax issues to taxpayers, IRS personnel, and other interested parties.[114] Because they state the Service's conclusion about the application of substantive tax law, revenue rulings may seem similar to regulations, but (as stated in the introduction to the Internal Revenue Bulletin) revenue rulings "do not have the force and effect of Treasury Department Regulations." This lack of parity between rulings and regulations is specifically recognized by the Service, which cautions taxpayers and others who seek to rely on a revenue ruling "against reaching the same conclusion [as the ruling with regard to their transactions] unless the facts and circumstances are substantially the same" as those in the ruling.[115] Additionally, in contrast to regulations, a revenue ruling is directly responsive to the issues raised by the stated "pivotal" facts recited in the ruling. Thus, the Service's position in the ruling is perforce limited to the issues raised by that particular set of facts. As a consequence, a revenue ruling does not have the general applicability of a regulation.[116]

---

[112] 26 CFR § 601.201(a)(1).

[113] 26 CFR § 601.201(a)(6); Rev. Proc. 2002-1, § 2.05, 2002-1 IRB 1.

[114] 26 CFR § 601.201(a)(6); Rev. Proc. 2002-1, § 2.05, 2002-1 IRB 1 13.

[115] 26 CFR § 601.201(a)(6); Rev. Proc. 2002-1, § 2.05, 2002-1 IRB 1, 8.

[116] See supra ¶ 3.02[1].

   While a revenue ruling does not have the legal effect of a regulation, it still has greater legal weight than a letter ruling for taxpayers other than the one to whom the letter ruling is issued.[117] This is because revenue rulings are intended to be used as "precedents" in the disposition of cases for all taxpayers and, therefore, may be cited and relied on for that purpose. Publication of revenue rulings is intended to promote uniform application of the tax laws by Service employees and to assist taxpayers by informing them, as well as Service personnel, of the National Office interpretations. By publishing its official position in a revenue ruling, the Service expects that the number of letter ruling requests that taxpayers submit to the National Office will ultimately be reduced.

   A letter ruling[118] is a "written statement *issued to a [specific] taxpayer or his authorized representative* by the National Office that interprets and applies the tax laws to a specific set of facts" (emphasis added).[119] Letter rulings on most tax questions are issued by the Chief Counsel's Office by the Associate Chief Counsel (Domestic).[120] A letter ruling's conclusions as to the tax consequences arising from a particular set of facts must be honored by a district office in the determination of tax liability of the taxpayer who requested the ruling, provided that (1) the representations on which the ruling was based reflect an accurate statement of the material facts and (2) the transaction was carried out substantially as represented in the ruling request.[121] Unlike revenue rulings, letter rulings may not be used or cited by any officer or employee of the Service as a precedent in the disposition of other cases[122] and may not be relied upon by taxpayers other than the one to whom it was issued.[123]

   In short, while both revenue rulings and letter rulings address specific sets of facts, a revenue ruling's legal conclusions are intended to be relied on by

---

[117] Rev. Proc. 89-14, 1989-1 CB 814, 815.

[118] Before the Tax Reform Act of 1976, letter rulings were frequently termed private rulings, since they were not made public by the Service. Under Section 6110, added by the Tax Reform Act of 1976, letter rulings are available to the public, and various tax services publish them.

[119] 26 CFR § 601.201(a)(2). See also Rev. Proc. 2002-1, § 2.01, 2002-1 IRB 1, 8.

[120] See Rev. Proc. 2002-1, § 2.01, 2002-1 IRB 1, 9. Letter rulings relating to pension plans and exempt organizations are issued by the Associate Chief Counsel (Employee Benefits and Exempt Organization), as well as under the direction of the Assistant Commissioner (Employee Plans and Exempt Organizations (EP/EO)).

[121] 26 CFR § 601.201(2). See Rev. Proc. 2002-1, § 12.03, 2002-1 IRB 1, 49–50. However, a letter ruling may be revoked or modified if it is "found to be in error or not in accord with the current views of the Service." Id. at § 12.04.

[122] IRC § 6110(k)(3); Rev. Proc. 2002-1, § 12.02, 2002-1 IRB 1, 49. But cf. Rowan Cos. v. United States, 452 US 247, 261 n.17 (1981), where the Supreme Court used a series of letter rulings to show that the Service did not interpret the term "wages" consistently.

[123] Rev. Proc. 2002-1, § 12.02, 2002-1 IRB 1, 49.

taxpayers with the same or very similar factual situations as those described in the revenue ruling, and a letter ruling's legal conclusions are statutorily prohibited from being used as precedent.

[2] Revenue Rulings

A revenue ruling is the Service's official conclusion about how the internal revenue laws, related statutes, tax treaties, and regulations apply to a specific set of facts, and is published by the Service in the Internal Revenue Bulletin.[124] Revenue rulings are prepared from such various sources as letter rulings to taxpayers, technical advice to district offices, studies undertaken by the Associate Chief Counsel (Technical), court decisions, suggestions from tax practitioner groups, and publications. Revenue rulings are issued under the reorganized structure of the Chief Counsel's Office by the Associate Chief Counsel (Domestic), the Associate Chief Counsel (Employee Benefits and Exempt Organizations), the Associate Chief Counsel (Enforcement Litigations), and the Associate Chief Counsel (International). Revenue rulings are Service communications involving substantive tax law; statements of procedure are published as revenue procedures.

[a] Processing of Revenue Rulings

The revenue ruling processing procedure is as follows:[125]

1. A project is assigned to an attorney in the appropriate Division in the office of the Associate Chief Counsel (Technical).

---

[124] In 1953, following an inquiry into the Service's rulings policy and practices by the King Subcommittee of the House Committee on Ways and Means, the Service announced and broadened its policy for published rulings. The publication policy was announced in Rev. Rul. 2, 1953-1 CB 484, and Rev. Rul. 212, 1953-2 CB 449. The current policy is described in Rev. Proc. 89-14, 1989-1 CB 814. Prior to 1953, the Service had published rulings of "general interest," but the number published varied from seventy-eight in 1949 to eighty-six in 1952. After 1952, the numbers published have run from a low of 300 in 1953 to 427 in 1960. The Service published approximately 400 rulings in 1979. Commissioner of Internal Revenue, Annual Report 32 (1979). In 1988, a total of 271 rulings were issued. IRS Annual Report 1988 at 37.

At the same time that the volume of guidance the Service gives to the public has declined, or at least not kept current with legislative changes in the tax law, the National Office has issued various types of internal memoranda, creating a body of secret guidance available only to Service personnel. For an analysis of this problem, see Meadows & Dobrovir, "Who Killed Guidance?" 73 Tax Notes 221 (Oct. 14, 1996).

[125] IRM, Chief Counsel Directive Manual (39)920, Revenue Ruling Handbook, §§ 720–725, MT (39)920-2 (Sept. 28, 1988) (Review).

2. After research, a draft ruling is prepared in the prescribed format, along with a Background Information Note (BIN).
3. The draft is given an in-depth review at the Branch level. This review can be performed by the Branch Chief, the Senior Technical Advisor, or the Assistant to the Branch Chief.
4. The ruling is reviewed by the Associate Chief Counsel (Litigation) to determine whether the position is consistent with the Service's litigating position in pending cases.
5. The ruling is scheduled for Assistant Counsel Review, where it undergoes its strongest scrutiny.
6. The ruling is simultaneously reviewed by the Associate Chief Counsel (Technical) and the Chief Counsel and receives approval.
7. The proposed ruling is simultaneously reviewed by the Commissioner and by the Treasury.
8. The ruling is published in the Internal Revenue Bulletin.

[b] Effect of Revenue Rulings

The Service intends that its employees and taxpayers alike rely on revenue rulings in disposing of cases and in determining the tax treatment of transactions.[126] The invitation to taxpayers is subject to an important qualification, however. The Service states:

> Taxpayers generally may rely upon revenue rulings and revenue procedures published in the Bulletin in determining the tax treatment of their own transactions and need not request specific rulings applying the principles of a published revenue ruling or revenue procedure to the facts of their particular cases. However, taxpayers, Service personnel and others concerned are also cautioned to determine whether a revenue ruling or revenue procedure on which they seek to rely has been revoked, modified, declared obsolete, distinguished, clarified, or otherwise affected by subsequent legislation, treaties, regulations, revenue rulings, revenue procedures or court decisions.[127]

Thus, a revenue ruling's precedential value is qualified by the requirement that taxpayers must determine for themselves whether the facts of their particular transaction are "substantially the same" as those set forth in the revenue ruling.

A revenue ruling is the Service's conclusion about the law applicable to a specific set of facts. Although the Treasury may review revenue rulings, they are issued by the Service. Unlike regulations, revenue rulings are not promul-

---

[126] Rev. Proc. 89-14, §§ 7.01(4), 7.01(5), 1989-1 CB 814.
[127] Rev. Proc. 89-14, § 7.01(5), 1989-1 CB 814. See also Rev. Proc. 2002-1, § 2.05, 2002-1 IRB 1, 8.

gated by the Treasury after the notice and public comment procedures required by the APA.

Before 1953, the Internal Revenue Bulletin said that revenue rulings "do not commit the Department to any interpretation of the law which has not been formally approved and promulgated by the Secretary of the Treasury."[128] Accordingly, it was held that a revenue ruling was of little aid in the interpretation of a statute, since it is not promulgated by or binding on the Treasury.[129] The Internal Revenue Bulletin, however, now states that revenue rulings and revenue procedures "reported in the Bulletin do not have the force and effect of Treasury Department Regulations, but they may be used as precedents."[130]

The Tax Court continues to treat a revenue ruling as simply the Service's position on an issue in litigation, which is not entitled to greater weight than the contention of any other litigant[131] and which cannot therefore bind the courts.[132] In this limited view, a revenue ruling may, at best, be helpful as a guide.[133] Some appellate courts disagree with the Tax Court's view and have accorded revenue rulings almost the same weight as an interpretive regulation, reasoning that the position stated in a revenue ruling is that of the agency charged with administering the statute and is therefore entitled to some measure of deference.[134]

---

[128] 1998-1 CB 1.

[129] See Biddle v. Comm'r, 302 US 573, 582 (1938); Helvering v. New York Trust Co., 292 US 455, 468 (1934). Since the Treasury's review of revenue rulings began after these Supreme Court cases, it might be questioned whether a revenue ruling does not represent an interpretation "binding" on the Treasury. On the other hand, a revenue ruling is not, on account of Treasury review, entitled to any greater weight in the consideration of a court than the contention of a party that may or may not represent a reasonable interpretation of a statute. Indeed, the issuance of revenue rulings that state the Service's litigating positions, for example, in tax shelter cases, only underscores the status of a revenue ruling as the position of one party to a case in court.

[130] 2002-1 IRB 3.

[131] Minnis v. Comm'r, 71 TC 1049, 1057 (1979); Browne v. Comm'r, 73 TC 723, 731 (1980) (concurring opinion).

[132] Stubbs, Overbeck & Assocs. v. United States, 445 F2d 1142, 1146–1147 (5th Cir. 1971) ("[a] ruling is merely the opinion of a lawyer in the agency and must be accepted as such"); Sims v. United States, 252 F2d 434, 438 (4th Cir. 1958), aff'd, 359 US 108 (1959); Burck v. Comm'r, 63 TC 556, 561–562 (1975) ("We emphasize that although there is legislative support for the approach taken in the revenue ruling, we consider it advisory only. . . . It does not carry the force of law, nor bind this Court in the slightest degree. . . . The revenue ruling is but a useful guide. . . ."), aff'd, 533 F2d 768 (2d Cir. 1978).

[133] See Hanover Bank v. Comm'r, 369 US 672, 687 n.21 (1962) (relating to letter rulings).

[134] The Second Circuit has said that a revenue ruling has the force of legal precedent unless it is unreasonable or inconsistent with the statute. Salomon, Inc. v. United States, 976 F2d 837, 841 (2d Cir. 1992); see Galler, "Judicial Review of Revenue Rulings," 72

It should be noted that, in all cases, courts will disregard a revenue ruling when the ruling is not found to be a "reasonable" interpretation of the statute.[135]

Section 7805(b)(8) gives the Commissioner discretionary authority to apply rulings "without retroactive effect." The Service's position is that "[w]hen revenue rulings revoke or modify rulings previously published in the Bulletin, the authority of Section 7805(b) ordinarily is invoked to provide that the new rulings will not be applied retroactively to the extent that the new rulings have adverse tax consequences to taxpayers."[136] This position merely states the applicable law, since retroactive application of a revenue ruling that changes a prior position of the Service as to particular taxpayers who have relied on the earlier ruling to their detriment may constitute an abuse of discretion.[137] However, irrespective of the detrimental reliance of any taxpayer, a revenue ruling may be retroactively revoked or modified to correct a mistake of law.[138] The Commissioner must exercise his discretion under Section 7805(b)(8) by "af-

---

BU L. Rev. 841 (1992) (concluding that court should not give deferential weight to a revenue ruling, because it is merely published position of IRS on particular issue). In Estate of McLendon v. Comm'r, 135 F3d 1017, 1023–1024 (5th Cir. 1998), the Fifth Circuit stated:

> the Tax Court has long been fighting a losing battle with the various courts of appeals over the proper deference to which revenue rulings are due. Whereas virtually every circuit recognizes some form of deference, the Tax Court stands firm in its own position that revenue rulings are nothing more than the legal contentions of a frequent litigant, undeserving of any more or less consideration than the conclusory statements in a party's brief. Although the Supreme Court has not spoken definitively on the subject, its recent jurisprudence tends to support the view that the courts owe revenue rulings a bit more deference than the Tax Court would have us believe. Still, revenue rulings are odd creatures unconducive to precise categorization in the hierarchy of legal authorities. They are clearly less binding on the courts than treasury regulations or Code provisions, but probably (and in this circuit certainly) more so than the mere legal conclusions of the parties. Apart from that, little can be said with any certainty, and in the absence of a definitive statement from on high, the Tax Court continues its crusade to ignore them in toto. [Footnote references omitted.]

[135] See, e.g., Stubbs, Overbeck & Assocs. v. United States, 445 F2d 1142, 1147 (5th Cir. 1971). Accord Estate of Lang v. Comm'r, 613 F2d 770, 776 (9th Cir. 1980).

[136] Rev. Proc. 89-14, § 7.01(3), 1989-1 CB 814. See, however, Rev. Rul. 80-60, 1980-1 CB 97, which requires taxpayers using a method of inventory valuation not in accordance with regulations under Thor Power Tool Co. v. Comm'r, 439 US 522 (1979), to change their method of accounting for their first taxable year ending on or after December 25, 1979.

[137] See, e.g., Barbara (Newburger) Newman, 33 TCM 219 (1974) (government's inclusion of payments under an annulment decree that were previously ruled to be nontaxable held to be abuse of discretion).

[138] Dixon v. United States, 381 US 68, 72–75 (1965); Dickman v. Comm'r, 465 US 330, 343 (1984). The Service may change a position taken in published rulings despite congressional acquiescence in previous revenue rulings advancing that position. Schuster v. Comm'r, 800 F2d 672, 676 (7th Cir. 1986) (*Dickman* followed).

firmative action"—that is, the Commissioner must specifically state that a ruling is nonretroactive; otherwise, the revenue ruling will have retroactive effect.[139]

In the Taxpayer Bill of Rights 2, Congress eliminated the discretion of the Treasury to issue regulations having retroactive effect, except in certain defined situations.[140] For rulings, however, the Service is permitted to "prescribe the extent, if any, to which any ruling (including any judicial decision or any administrative determination other than by regulation) relating to the internal revenue laws shall be applied retroactively."[141]

Despite the limitations noted above, a revenue ruling is useful both in advising taxpayers about proposed transactions and in resolving disputes with the Service. For planning purposes, a revenue ruling is an indication of the Service's position and, as such, marks a safety zone in determining a taxpayer's exposure to challenge on examination. Although a revenue ruling will not bind a court, it nevertheless reflects the Service's administrative practice as well as

---

[139] The requirement that nonretroactivity be specifically stated seems to have been adopted as a result of the decision of the Court of Claims in Crespo v. United States, 399 F2d 191, 193 (Ct. Cl. 1968). In that case, a revenue ruling did not specifically state that it applied retroactively, and the court applied the Service's prior position that rulings "ordinarily are not revoked or modified retroactively" to justify its holding that the ruling only applied prospectively. However, the ruling revoked retroactively in *Crespo* had been in effect for over forty-six years, and the Court of Claims indicated that, under these circumstances, retroactive application of the ruling might be an abuse of the Commissioner's discretion under Section 7805(b).

In Becker v. Comm'r, 751 F2d 146, 150 (3d Cir. 1984), the circuit court said that "in the absence of limitations imposed by statute or the I.R.S., [revenue] rulings generally are entitled to retroactive application." However, where a revenue ruling fails to state that it applies retroactively, courts have not always applied the ruling retroactively. For an illustration of how courts have reached different results on the retroactivity of a ruling, compare Manocchio v. Comm'r, 710 F2d 1400, 1403 (9th Cir. 1983) (applying Rev. Rul. 80-173 retroactively), with Baker v. United States, 748 F2d 1465, 1468–1470 (11th Cir. 1984) (finding that the Commissioner abused his discretion in applying Rev. Rul. 80-173 retroactively because retroactivity resulted in inequality of treatment of taxpayers). See also Becker v. Comm'r, 751 F2d 146, 152 (3d Cir. 1984) (remanding a case so the Tax Court could determine whether the Commissioner abused his discretion in applying Rev. Rul. 80-173 retroactively).

For further discussion of retroactivity of rulings, see infra ¶ 3.03[6][c]. The Service has said in technical advice that "Section 7805(b) does not apply when there is a lack of a pronouncement, but only when there is actually a pronouncement on which the taxpayer could reasonably have relied" in entering into the transaction. Priv. Ltr. Rul. 8604004 (Oct. 21, 1985) (taxpayer failed to demonstrate that it closed concurrent mortgage loan sale/purchase transaction relying on an existing Service practice, so that denial of Section 7805(b) relief would be inequitable).

[140] IRC §§ 7805(b)(1)–7805(b)(7), as amended by the Taxpayer Bill of Rights 2, Pub. L. No. 104-168 § 1101(a), effective for regulations relating to statutory provisions enacted on or after the effective date, July 30, 1996.

[141] IRC § 7805(b)(8) (1996).

its position on the application of the law to a specific set of facts. Moreover, once issued and published, a revenue ruling's stated position is binding on the Service unless the taxpayer's facts and circumstances are not substantially the same as those set forth in the ruling or the ruling has been subsequently revoked or modified by a later revenue ruling. Moreover, if an unrevoked or unmodified revenue ruling supporting the taxpayer's position exists, the ruling represents a litigation hazard to the Service in a contested tax case. This is because, if the Service argues against its own ruling position, such an argument will appear litigation- or outcome-motivated and therefore entitled to less or no deference.[142]

[3] Requesting a Letter Ruling

[a] Availability of Ruling

While a taxpayer decides whether to request a letter ruling from the National Office, the National Office has the discretion to rule or to decline to rule on the issue presented by the ruling. The Service's statement of its policy seems to welcome requests for letter rulings. It says, "it is the policy of the Service to answer inquiries of individuals and organizations regarding their status for tax purposes and the tax effects of their acts or transactions, prior to the filing of returns or reports that are required by the revenue laws."[143] However, this policy statement leaves ample room for the Service to exercise discretion not to rule, since it also says that a ruling will be issued to a taxpayer only "whenever appropriate in the interest of sound tax administration."[144]

Procedures for obtaining letter rulings from the Chief Counsel's Office are published annually in the Internal Revenue Bulletin as the first revenue procedure for the year.[145] Taxpayers may obtain letter rulings on issues within the jurisdiction of the Associate Chief Counsel (Domestic),[146] the Associate

---

[142] See, e.g., the discussion in Chock Full O' Nuts Corp. v. United States, 453 F2d 300, 303 (2d Cir. 1971), regarding regulations promulgated during the course of litigation.

[143] Rev. Proc. 2002-3, § 2.01, 2002-1 IRB 117. The annual revenue procedure governing requests for letter rulings puts the policy more cautiously, saying, "The national office issues letter rulings to answer written inquiries of individuals and organizations about their status for tax purposes and the tax effects of their acts or transactions when appropriate in the interest of sound tax administration." Rev. Proc. 2002-1, § 3, 2002-1 IRB 1, 10.

[144] 26 CFR § 601.201(a).

[145] See, e.g., Rev. Proc. 2002-1, 2002-1 IRB 1.

[146] Rev. Proc. 2002-1, § 3.01, 1999-1 CB 6, 14. Issues under the jurisdiction of the Associate Chief Counsel (Domestic) include issues under the Assistant Chief Counsel (Corporate), and these issues may involve consolidated returns, corporate acquisitions, reorganizations, liquidations, redemptions, spinoffs, transfers to controlled corporations, dis-

Chief Counsel (Employee Plans and Exempt Organizations),[147] the Associate Chief Counsel (Enforcement Litigation),[148] and the Associate Chief Counsel (International).[149] While the Service's general policy is to issue letter rulings, the National Office also announces how it will exercise its discretion by

---

tributions to shareholders, corporate bankruptcies, the effect of certain ownership changes on net operating loss carryovers and other tax attributes, debt versus equity determinations, allocation of income and deduction among taxpayers, acquisitions made to evade or avoid income tax, and certain earnings and profits questions.

Issues under the Assistant Chief Counsel (Financial Institutions and Products) include issues involving income taxes and accounting changes of banks, savings and loan associations, real estate investment trusts (REITs), regulated investment companies (RICs), real estate mortgage investment conduits (REMICs), tax exempt obligations, mortgage credit certificates (MCCs), insurance companies and products, and financial products.

Issues under the Assistant Chief Counsel (Income Tax and Accounting) include issues involving recognition and timing of income and deductions of individuals and corporations, sales and exchanges, capital gains and losses, installment sales, equipment leasing, inventories, the alternative minimum tax, accounting method changes for these and other miscellaneous issues, various administrative provisions, and accounting periods.

Issues under the Assistant Chief Counsel (Passthroughs and Special Industries) include issues involving income taxes of S corporations (except accounting periods and methods) and certain noncorporate taxpayers (including partnerships, common trust funds, and trusts); entity classification; estate, gift, and generation skipping transfers, and certain excise taxes; amortization, depreciation, depletion, and other engineering issues; accounting method changes for depreciation and amortization; cooperative housing corporations; farmers' cooperatives (under Section 521); the low income housing, disabled access, and qualified electric vehicle credits; research and experimental expenditures; shipowners' protection and indemnity associations (under Section 526); and certain homeowners associations (under Section 528).

[147] Rev. Proc. 2002-1, § 3.02, 2002-1 IRB 1, 10. Issues under the jurisdiction of the Associate Chief Counsel (Employee Benefits and Exempt Organizations) include issues involving income tax and other tax aspects of executive compensation and employee benefit programs (other than those within the jurisdiction of the Assistant Commissioner (Employee Plans and Exempt Organizations), employment taxes, and self-employment income.

[148] Rev. Proc. 2002-1, § 3.03, 2002-1 IRB 1, 10. Issues under the jurisdiction of the Associate Chief Counsel (Enforcement Litigation) include issues involving the collection of taxes (which, in turn, are under the jurisdiction of the Assistant Chief Counsel, General Litigation).

[149] Rev. Proc. 2002-1, § 3.04, 2002-1 IRB 1, 11. Issues under the jurisdiction of the Associate Chief Counsel (International) include issues involving the tax treatment of nonresident aliens and foreign corporations; withholding of tax on nonresident aliens and foreign corporations; foreign tax credit; determination of sources of income; income from sources without the United States; domestic international sales corporations (DISCs); foreign sales corporations (FSCs); international boycott determinations; treatment of certain passive foreign investment companies (PFICs); and income affected by treaty.

Special procedures apply to obtaining advance pricing agreements under Section 482, see Rev. Proc. 96-53, 1996-2 CB 375; and Notice 98-10, 1998-6 IRB 9; and competent authority relief, see Rev. Proc. 96-13, 1996-2 CB 616.

describing those situations in which the National Office will issue a ruling letter,[150] as well as those situations when it will not rule or ordinarily not rule.[151]

There are three possible sources for determining whether the National Office will rule on an issue:

1. The annual revenue procedure regarding letter rulings and the current revenue procedure covering the issues on which the Service will or will not rule.[152]

2. A telephone call to the appropriate branch in the National Office will usually result in a response to whether the Service will rule on a particular issue.[153] In this instance, it is not unusual for the branch representative to ask for the taxpayer's name and identifying number, as well as discuss questions relating to procedural matters.[154] If time permits, the branch representative may also discuss substantive tax issues before a ruling request is submitted; this oral discussion, however, is informal and will not bind the Service in general or the Chief Counsel's Office nor form a basis for obtaining retroactive relief under Section 7805(b).[155]

3. Finally, in cases where it will benefit both the Service and the taxpayer, the Service will participate in a pre-request conference with the taxpayer at which it will discuss substantive and procedural issues concerning the tax consequences of the proposed transaction.[156] These conferences are held only when the taxpayer actually intends to make a request, the issue is one on which a letter ruling is ordinarily issued, and there is sufficient time to meet. Generally, before the pre-submission conference, the taxpayer must submit a statement (1) representing that the issue is one on which the National Office ordinarily rules or (2) describing the proposed transaction, issue, and supporting legal analysis. Any statements about the substantive issues made at the conference are advisory, and therefore will not bind the Service or the Chief Counsel's Office, nor form a basis for obtaining retroactive relief under Section 7805(b).

[i] Required rulings. The National Office must issue rulings on prospective or future transactions where the Code or the regulations require it to make

---

[150] See infra ¶¶ 3.03[a][i], 3.03[a][ii].

[151] See infra ¶ 3.03[a][iv].

[152] Rev. Proc. 2002-1, § 5, 2002-1 IRB 1, 12–18; Rev. Proc. 2002-3, 2002-1 IRB 117.

[153] See Rev. Proc. 2002-1, § 2.06(1), 2002-1 IRB 1, 8.

[154] Rev. Proc. 2002-1, § 2.06(1), 2002-1 IRB 1, 8.

[155] 26 CFR § 601.201(k)(l). See Rev. Proc. 2002-1, § 2.06(2), 2002-1 IRB 1, 8.

[156] Rev. Proc. 2002-1, § 11.07, 2002-1 IRB 1, 46.

a determination. Two general areas where rulings are required to be made concern (1) issues relating to alcohol, tobacco, and firearms taxes and (2) employee plan and exempt organization issues.[157] Rulings or consents are also required for changes in accounting methods and accounting periods.[158] As a general rule, where a taxpayer has no discretion about whether to obtain a ruling or consent, the National Office cannot refuse to respond.

　　[ii] Ruling areas—in general. The National Office issues rulings in the following general areas:

- *Income and gift tax matters.* In income and gift tax matters, the National Office issues rulings on (1) prospective transactions or (2) transactions completed before the return for the year of the transaction is filed.[159] The National Office will *not* issue a ruling on only a part of an integrated transaction. Moreover, the National Office will not ordinarily issue a ruling to a taxpayer if, at the time the taxpayer requests a ruling on an issue, the taxpayer's return for a prior period has the identical issue, and the identical issue (1) is being examined by a district office; (2) is being considered by an Appeals Office; (3) is pending in litigation in a case involving the taxpayer or a related taxpayer; or (4) has been examined by a district office or considered by an Appeals office and either (i) the statute of limitations on assessment or refund has not expired or (ii) the district or Appeals has not entered into a closing agreement covering the issue or liability. If a request is pending and the taxpayer has filed a tax return involving the issue posed in the ruling request, the National Office will issue the ruling unless the taxpayer notifies it that an examination of the return has begun. If an examination

---

[157] Rev. Proc. 2002-1, § 4, 2002-1 IRB 1, 12. Procedures for obtaining rulings, determination letters, and the like are described in the general ruling issued under the jurisdiction of the Assistant Commissioner (Employee Plans and Exempt Organizations). See Rev. Proc. 2002-4, 1991-1 IRB 127.

[158] 26 CFR § 601.204.

[159] 26 CFR § 601.201(b)(1); Rev. Proc. 2002-1, § 5.01, 2002-1 IRB 1, 12–13. There are a number of circumstances modifying these general rules dealing with post-return filing ruling requests on specific issues. For example, no letter ruling will be issued on the replacement of involuntarily converted property if the taxpayer has filed his return for the year of conversion. There is an important exception to the rule that the ruling request must be submitted before a return is filed. A § 301.9100 request is considered a request for a letter ruling, and the procedures outlined in Rev. Proc. 2002-1, 2002-1 IRB 1, 15, are to be followed even if a request for an extension of time for filing an election under Reg. § 301.9100 is submitted after the return is filed, or if the return has been examined, or after the issue is being considered by an Appeals office or a federal court. Id. at § 5.02. If district has begun an examination of the year for which the § 301.9100 request has been filed, the taxpayer must notify the National Office, and the National Office will notify the district, appeals officer, or government counsel, as the case may be, and inform the responsible person that the request is pending.

has begun during the pendency of a request, the National Office will ordinarily issue the ruling so long as the district director permits the National Office to rule.

- *Estate tax matters.* In estate tax matters, the National Office issues rulings on transactions affecting the estate tax of a living individual as well as those affecting the estate of decedent before the decedent's estate tax return is filed.[160] The National Office will not issue a letter ruling for a *prospective* estate if the request concerns computations of tax, actuarial factors, or factual matters. If the estate tax return is due to be filed, an extension should, if possible, be obtained during the pendency of the ruling request. If the return is filed before the ruling is issued, the taxpayer must indicate that a request is pending or attach the request to the estate tax return and notify the National Office that the return has been filed.[161]

- *Employment and excise tax matters.* In employment and most excise tax matters, the National Office issues rulings on both prospective transactions and transactions completed either before or after the return is filed.[162] Ordinarily, no ruling is issued if, at the time of the ruling request, (1) the identical issue is being addressed by any district office or Appeals Office as a result of an examination of the same taxpayer for a prior period or (2) the district office or Appeals Office has considered the identical issue with respect to the same taxpayer but the statute of limitations on assessment or refund is open without either office having entered into a closing agreement with the taxpayer.

- *Administrative provisions.* The National Office will rule in administrative provisions matters arising under sections of the Code and regulations relating to (1) the time, place, and manner for filing returns; (2) the procedures for reporting and paying taxes; (3) the assessment and collection of taxes, including interest and penalties; (4) the abatement, credit, or refund of an overassessment or overpayment of tax; and (5) the filing of information returns.[163] However, rulings on these matters

---

[160] Rev. Proc. 2002-1, § 5.05, 2002-1 IRB 1, 14–15. Rulings in generation-skipping transfer tax matters are issued before the return is filed, and either before or after the generation-skipping trust has been established. Id. at § 5.06. The National Office will also issue letter rulings on qualified domestic trusts under Section 2056A, on proposed and completed transactions occurring before the return is filed. Id. at § 5.07. Recapture tax rulings under Section 2032A(c) are issued on prospective transactions and transactions completed before the return is filed. Id. at § 5.08.

[161] Rev. Proc. 2002-1, § 5.05, 2002-1 IRB 1, 14–15. The National Office attempts to rule within three months after the return filing or secures additional time from the district.

[162] 26 CFR § 601.201(b)(3); Rev. Proc. 2002-1, § 5.09, 2002-1 IRB 1, 15–16.

[163] The term "returns" includes "information returns." Rev. Proc. 2002-1, § 5.10, 2002-1 IRB 1, 16.

are not issued if, at the time the request is submitted, either (1) a tax return for a prior period involving the identical issue is under consideration by a district office or a Service center or (2) such a return has been considered by these offices and the statute of limitations on assessment or refund is open without either office having entered into a closing agreement with the taxpayer.[164]

The National Office follows several other self-imposed controls on issuing rulings. Letter rulings will not be issued to business, trade, or industrial associations (or to similar groups) concerning the application of the internal revenue laws to the group's members.[165] Nor will rulings be issued to foreign governments or their political subdivisions concerning either (1) the U.S. tax effects of their laws or (2) on the effect of a treaty on the tax laws of a treaty country for purposes of determining the tax law of the treaty country.[166] Another matter on which the National Office will not issue a letter ruling is the federal tax consequences of any proposed federal, state, local, municipal, or foreign legislation.[167]

On the other hand, the National Office will consider issuing a ruling (that is, it may, but need not, rule) in areas where temporary or final regulations have not been issued or promulgated.[168] In this area, a letter ruling will be issued (1) if the answer seems to be clear from an application of the statute to the facts described, or (2) if the answer seems reasonably certain, but is not entirely free from doubt, and the case involves a business emergency or unusual hardship.[169] No rulings will be issued on these grounds if the letter ruling request presents an issue that cannot be readily resolved before regulation or any other published guideline is issued.[170]

[iii] IRS guidelines in ruling areas. In addition to the general procedures that apply to all ruling requests, the Service issues specific revenue pro-

---

[164] Rules similar to those for income and gift tax rulings apply to ruling requests in administrative matters involving an issue or a return that has been filed or is under examination.

[165] Rev. Proc. 2002-1, § 5.12, 2002-1 IRB 1, 17. But groups may submit suggestions of generic issues that would be appropriate for revenue rulings.

[166] Rev. Proc. 2002-1, § 5.13, 2002-1 IRB 1, 17.

[167] Rev. Proc. 2002-1, § 5.14, 2002-1 IRB 1, 17. The National Office may provide general information in response to an inquiry, however.

[168] 26 CFR § 601.201(b)(5); Rev. Proc. 2002-1, § 5.15, 2002-1 IRB 1, 18.

[169] Rev. Proc. 2002-1, §§ 5.15(1), 5.15(2), 2002-1 IRB 1, 18.

[170] Rev. Proc. 2002-1, § 5.15(3), 2002-1 IRB 1, 18. However, when (1) the Service has closed a regulation project or any other published guidance project that might have answered the issue or (2) it decides not to open such a regulations or guidance project, then the appropriate branch will consider all letter ruling requests unless the issue is covered by the National Office's discretionary authority not to issue letter rulings in certain

cedures and notices describing how it will exercise its discretion in issuing advance rulings on specific issues. These revenue procedure guidelines and checklists establish threshold requirements a taxpayer must meet in order to obtain a favorable ruling. Checklists and guideline revenue procedures are gathered in the annual revenue procedure describing ruling procedures in general.[171] In addition, the National Office issues "safe harbor" revenue procedures to inform taxpayers of those circumstances supporting a favorable ruling.[172] For requests for changes in accounting periods and methods, "automatic change" revenue procedures permit taxpayers that fit an "automatic change" category to file their returns using the new accounting period or method as if the Service's consent to the change had been formally granted.[173]

[iv] "No-ruling" areas and areas where the National Office ordinarily will not rule. Although the Service's usual policy is to issue letter rulings on the tax effects of taxpayers' acts or transactions before they file returns, there are certain areas in which the Service will not rule because of the "inherently factual nature" of the issue involved or other specified reasons.[174] The number of issues on which the National Office will not issue rulings affects the usefulness of the letter rulings program and, over the years, practitioners have noted an increase in the number of these "no-rule" issues.[175] The Service's annual letter ruling revenue procedure generally describes the issues on which the National Office will not rule, but, in addition, the Service issues separate annual revenue procedures that list specific areas in which the Associate Chief Counsel (Domestic), the Associate Chief Counsel (International), and the Associate Chief Counsel (Employee Plans and Exempt Organizations) will not issue advance rulings.[176]

---

areas because of their factual nature or other problems set out in Rev. Proc. 2002-3, 2002-1 IRB 117, and Rev. Proc. 2002-7, 2002-1 IRB 249.

[171] Specific guidelines for rulings under various Code sections are gathered in the annual letter ruling revenue procedure. See Rev. Proc. 2002-1, §§ 9.01, 9.02, 9.03, 2002-1 IRB 1, 40–42, which lists checklists, guideline revenue procedures, safe-harbor revenue procedures, and automatic-change revenue procedures that apply to certain ruling requests.

[172] Rev. Proc. 2002-1, § 9.02, 2002-1 IRB 1, 39–40.

[173] Rev. Proc. 2002-1, § 9.03, 2002-1 IRB 1, 40–42.

[174] Rev. Proc. 2002-1, § 7.01, 2002-1 IRB 1, 20; Rev. Proc. 2002-3, § 2.01, 2002-1 IRB 117.

[175] For example, a committee of the ABA's Tax Section found that the number of no-rule areas increased by 123 percent from 1975 through 1984. ABA, Tax Section, Admin. Practice Comm., Paper, "Internal Revenue Service Private Ruling Program" (July 10, 1985).

[176] Rev. Proc. 2002-3, 2002-1 IRB 117 (Associate, Chief Counsel (Domestic)); Rev. Proc. 2002-7, 2002-1 IRB 249 (Associate Chief Counsel) (International); Rev. Proc. 2002-6, § 3.02, 2002-1 IRB 203, 212–213 (Assistant Commissioner (Employee Plans and Exempt Organizations)). Modifications in the "no-rule" revenue procedure may be made

It should not be assumed, however, that the National Office will rule on issues that are *not* identified on the "no-rule" list. National Office decisions not to rule in individual cases, which do not present "significant pattern issues," are not listed in the "no-rule" revenue procedure.[177] Additionally, apart from issues of an inherently factual nature, the National Office will not rule on only part of an integrated transaction.[178]

Specific areas where the National Office states that it will not rule have exceeded forty in number,[179] but the general areas in which the National Office will not rule are those where[180]

- The request seeks a ruling on the results of transactions that have no bona fide business purpose or have as their principal purpose the reduction of tax.
- The request involves a matter in which the Service is considering whether to accept or contest an adverse court decision.
- The matter involves alternate plans of proposed transactions or "hypothetical situations."[181]
- The request involves the federal tax consequences of any proposed federal, state, local, or municipal legislation.
- The issue is whether reasonable cause, due diligence, good faith, clear and convincing evidence, or a similar standard exists under Subtitle F of the Code (Procedure and Administration).

---

throughout the year, but, in the case of the issues under the jurisdiction of the Associate Chief Counsel (Domestic) and the Associate Chief Counsel (Employee Plans and Exempt Organizations) are incorporated annually in the third revenue procedure of the year.

[177] Rev. Proc. 2002-3, § 2.01, 2002-1 IRB 117.

[178] Rev. Proc. 2002-1, § 7.03, 2002-1 IRB 1, 20. If the National Office will not rule on part of a transaction because it is within a "no-rule" area, it may nevertheless issue a letter ruling on other parts of the transaction. To learn whether the National Office will issue a letter ruling on part of the transaction, the National Office suggests that before preparing the letter ruling request, a taxpayer or taxpayer representative should telephone the branch having jurisdiction over the issue on which the ruling will be sought to discuss the matter. Id.

[179] There were at least fifty-one specific "no-rule" questions and problems in Rev. Proc. 2002-3, § 3.01, 2002-1 IRB 117, 118–121—forty-three specific questions and problems and eight general areas in which rulings and determination letters will not be issued.

[180] The list of issues on which the National Office will not rule is updated annually in the first quarter of each calendar year. Changes are published as they occur during the year. Consequently, it is necessary to check the current Internal Revenue Bulletins and Cumulative Bulletin to find amplifications and modifications of the comprehensive revenue procedure of "no-rule" areas. See Rev. Proc. 2002-3, § 3.02, 2002-1 IRB 117, 121. The areas in which the Associate Chief Counsel (International) will not issue rulings or determination letters are listed in Rev. Proc. 2002-7, § 3.02, 2002-1 IRB 249, 249–250.

[181] Rev. Proc. 2002-1, § 7.02, 2002-1 IRB 1, 20.

- Where the requested ruling is on whether a proposed transaction would subject a taxpayer to a criminal penalty.
- The request does not comply with the procedures set forth in the currently applicable revenue procedure that sets forth the year's guidelines for ruling requests.
- The request is whether under common-law rules for determining the existence of an employer-employee relationship, a professional staffing corporation (loan-out corporation) or subscriber is the employer of individuals, if (1) the loan-out corporation hires employees of the subscriber and assigns the employees back to the subscriber, or (2) the loan-out corporation assigns individuals to subscribers for more than a temporary period (one year or longer).

The National Office also describes those areas in which it will "ordinarily" not issue a letter ruling. If the ruling request would fall within this category, the taxpayer must demonstrate "unique and compelling reasons" to justify the National Office's ruling on the issue. Issues on which the National Office ordinarily will not issue a letter ruling involve the validity of the federal income tax and other taxes provided for in the Code, as well as questions on the Service's authority or jurisdiction to enforce the Code or collect information.[182] In general, the National Office ordinarily will not rule on (1) any matter if the determination requested is primarily one of fact (e.g., market value of property, debt versus equity); (2) situations where the requested ruling deals with only part of an integrated transaction; (3) situations where two or more items or sub-methods of accounting are interrelated, but the requested ruling concerns a change in accounting method involving less than all of the items or sub-methods; (4) the tax effect of any transactions to be consummated at some indefinite future time; (5) any matter dealing with the question of whether property is held primarily for sale to customers in the ordinary course of business; (6) the tax effect of a transaction if any part of a transaction is involved in litigation among the parties affected by the transaction, except transactions involving bankruptcy reorganizations; and (7) situations where the taxpayer or a related party is domiciled or organized in a foreign jurisdiction with which the United States does not have an "effective mechanism" to secure tax information for a civil or criminal investigation.[183]

There are also specific matters as to which the National Office has stated that it will not ordinarily rule, including the issue of who is the true owner of

---

[182] Rev. Proc. 2002-1, § 7.04, 2002-1 IRB 1, 20.

[183] Rev. Proc. 2002-3, § 4.02, 2002-1 IRB 117, 124. If the taxpayer or an "affected person" consents to the disclosure of this foreign-based information, and waives any protection of foreign privacy laws, the taxpayer or affected party will be able to obtain a ruling. Rev. Proc. 2002-3, § 4.02(7), 2002-1 IRB 117, 124.

property that is formally owned by another person.[184] In 1999, there were about fifty specific areas where the National Office said it ordinarily would not rule.

Not only does the National Office identify issues on which it will not or ordinarily will not rule, it also lists areas under extensive study in which rulings or determination letters will not be issued until the Service resolves the issue through publication of a revenue ruling, revenue procedure, regulations, or otherwise.[185] There are also areas covered by automatic approval procedures on which the National Office ordinarily will not issue rulings, the most notable of which are changes in accounting periods and methods of accounting.[186]

[b] Advisability of Ruling

After determining whether the question is in an area where the Service will or may rule if requested, the tax practitioner must consider whether to request a ruling. A number of factors favor requesting a ruling. Clearly, a favorable ruling will provide taxpayers with a measure of certainty as to the tax consequences of a particular transaction, unless, of course, the facts surrounding the transaction turn out to be materially different from those previously stated in the ruling request.[187] This "insurance policy" aspect of a favorable ruling may be a selling point for a transaction or a hedge against promoter or professional liability, and, in other cases, may be a matter of practical necessity such as in the case of the dealings of a public corporation or important transactions. A favorable ruling avoids any controversy with an agent on a subsequent audit concerning the issues resolved in the ruling.

Aside from the benefit of a favorable ruling, the ruling process itself may prove advantageous to a taxpayer. For example, during the course of discussions on the ruling request, the Service may recommend changes in a proposed transaction to assist the taxpayer in reaching the desired tax result.[188] Also, it is reasonable to believe that if the branch representative raises a question about the transaction, other Service personnel may later raise the same question. Accordingly, the ruling process provides a taxpayer with some early warning of danger spots at a time when a transaction is still in proposed form.

---

[184] Rev. Proc. 2002-3, § 4.01(3), 2002-1 IRB 117, 121.

[185] Rev. Proc. 2002-3, § 5, 2002-1 IRB 117, 125.

[186] Rev. Proc. 2002-3, § 6, 2002-1 IRB 117, 125–126.

[187] In Hicks Nurseries, Inc. v. Comm'r, 517 F2d 437, 440 (2d Cir. 1975), the court said that the decision of a tax adviser to go ahead with a Subchapter S election based on an interpretation of a regulation without a ruling, or at least the advice of a tax lawyer, was "unadvisable" under the circumstances.

[188] The branch representative will not recommend substantial changes but may point out minor changes to anticipate questions that the National Office might ask.

On the other hand, there are some definite disadvantages to the filing of a ruling request. Cost is one negative element, since a taxpayer may have to incur substantial fees to professionals that prepare the ruling request and provide assistance in the procedures leading up to and following the filing of the request. The time it takes to get a ruling may be another negative element. Securing a letter ruling takes time and necessarily involves some delay. If time is of the essence in a transaction or if a transaction must be consummated before a certain date, the delay that is part of the ruling process may be unacceptable.[189]

A further risk involved in requesting a ruling is that the ruling received might be unfavorable, such as would occur if the taxpayer will not adjust his plan to meet a condition or change required by the National Office before issuing a favorable ruling. Even if the ruling request is withdrawn in such circumstances, it should be anticipated that the National Office will notify the district office and, as a consequence, there will be a greater likelihood of an audit or examination of the transaction than if no ruling request had been filed. Moreover, there is always the possibility that the National Office attorney or technical personnel may raise collateral issues in the course of the ruling request process that may not be easily answered or dealt with. Finally, the letter ruling may be issued with caveats either because of the particular factual situation or as a matter of form adopted in the particular rulings branch.[190] Such a caveat may be a "red flag" for an agent undertaking a subsequent audit. Consequently, if facts exist that, if known by the Service, may jeopardize a favorable ruling, the risks of an unfavorable letter ruling (as well as a withdrawal of the ruling request) must be weighed against the potential benefits of a favorable ruling before the request is filed.

Another disadvantage of making a ruling request is that any proprietary or confidential business information revealed during the ruling request process may wind up being disclosed to a third party (including a competitor) simply because that information may be in the hands of the National Office and the third party requests that information. Section 6110 is supposed to regulate the disclosure of information provided to the National Office during a request for a letter ruling, but the Service may be less concerned about a disclosure of business information than the taxpayer. The Service may believe, for example, that so long as the taxpayer's identity is not disclosed, the Service has fulfilled its statutory duty. On the other hand, the taxpayer may be justifiably concerned

---

[189] Under certain circumstances, however, the taxpayer may request expedited treatment. 26 CFR § 601.201(e)(12). Rev. Proc. 2002-1, § 8.02(4), 2002-1 IRB 1, 30–31. The taxpayer must submit a separate letter showing need, but, in this showing, usually only the act of third parties (e.g., foreign governments), market conditions, and undue economic hardship will suffice.

[190] For example, in a Section 337 ruling, a caveat as to collapsibility is included as a matter of form.

that a competitor will nevertheless be able to identify the taxpayer from the nature of the limited information disclosed by the Service. Moreover, even under the best of circumstances, the result of disclosure litigation under Section 6110 is uncertain, and a taxpayer may believe that the uncertainty over whether a competitor will obtain proprietary information outweighs the certainty that a favorable ruling will bring.

Accordingly, for the reasons discussed above, a taxpayer may achieve certainty by filing a request for a letter ruling, but the process entails risks as well as benefits. Before, not after, a request for a letter ruling is filed, the risks must be weighed against the benefits of a favorable ruling. Taxpayers and tax practitioners may well decide that, in the close case, the better course of action is to proceed without a ruling and forgo certainty of the Service's position.

[c] Disclosure

Technical personnel use unpublished rulings for reference purposes.[191] Although not explicitly relied upon in the letter ruling to a particular taxpayer, these unpublished rulings have been and are consulted on a regular basis. Before 1976, they had acquired some precedential status. To gain access to this body of precedent, actions were instituted under the Freedom of Information Act (FOIA). As it had done with other FOIA actions to obtain its internal positions, the Service opposed disclosure of letter rulings on the ground that they constituted confidential tax returns or return information (a letter ruling should be attached to a return when filed). Courts of Appeals for both the District of Columbia Circuit[192] and the Sixth Circuit[193] held that letter rulings were subject to disclosure under the FOIA because they were not tax return information required to be kept confidential under Section 6103. These court decisions did not resolve such questions as which parts of rulings should be published, whether letter rulings should be available as "precedent" for other taxpayers, or what procedures should be established to allow taxpayers to claim that protected material should not be disclosed.[194] To incorporate the judicial decisions ordering disclosure and establish procedures for gaining access to letter rulings retained by the Service, as well as to resolve questions not set-

---

[191] At one time, the Manual stated that such rulings "may be used as a guide with other research materials in formulating a district office position on an issue." IRM 424(14).3(3), MT 4200-537 (Nov. 2, 1981) (Application of Private Letter Rulings and Memorandums, Etc.).

[192] Tax Analysts & Advocates v. IRS, 505 F2d 350, 354–355 (DC Cir. 1974).

[193] Fruehauf Corp. v. IRS, 522 F2d 284, 289 (6th Cir. 1975), vacated and remanded for reconsideration in light of Tax Reform Act of 1976, 429 US 1085 (1977).

[194] Staff of Joint Comm. on Taxation, 94th Cong., 2d Sess., General Explanation of the Tax Reform Act of 1976, at 303 (Comm. Print 1976), reprinted in 1976-3 CB (Vol. 2) 315 (hereinafter General Explanation).

tled by the cases, Congress in 1976 added Section 6110 to the Code. The rules of Section 6110 constitute the "exclusive remedy" with respect to the disclosure of rulings and related material.[195] Consequently, the FOIA and other provisions of law are no longer applicable to the disclosure of these written determinations.[196]

Section 6110 requires that the text of any ruling, determination letter, technical advice memorandum, or Chief Counsel advice (a written determination) be open to public inspection[197] after identifying details and other confidential data have been deleted.[198] In addition, any "background file document" relating to such written determination must also be made available for public inspection.[199] However, the disclosable background file information on a written determination is generally meager. It includes (1) the request for the written determination; (2) any supporting written materials that may have been submitted; and (3) any third-party communications received by the IRS before it issued the written determination (other than a communication between the IRS and the Justice Department about a pending civil or criminal case or investigation).[200] Most significantly, the background file does not include internal memoranda or attorney work product leading to the conclusion expressed in the written determination.[201]

Although these written determinations are made public, taxpayers may not rely upon them as precedent.[202] The nonprecedential status of written determi-

---

[195] IRC § 6110(m); General Explanation at 304, reprinted in 1976-3 CB (Vol. 2) at 316.

[196] This does not include discovery rules in a judicial proceeding. IRC § 6110(m). See Grenier v. IRS, 449 F. Supp. 834 (D. Md. 1978); Corelli v. Comm'r, 66 TC 220 (1976); Davis v. Comm'r, 69 TC 697 (1978).

[197] IRC § 6110(a). Special rules apply to Chief Counsel advice, Section 6110(i), discussed below at ¶ 3.04[4]. Procedures for the public place, manner, and copying of written determinations are set forth in Reg. § 301.6110-1(c). Section 6110 originally applied to the disclosure of written determinations made in response to requests filed before November 1, 1976 (the effective date of the statute), and those filed after October 31, 1976. Pre–November 1, 1976, written determinations have also been made public.

[198] IRC § 6110(c).

[199] IRC §§ 6110(b)(2), 6110(e). Procedures for requesting the background file documents relating to a letter ruling or technical advice memorandum issued by the National Office are described in Rev. Proc. 88-11, 1988-1 CB 636.

[200] IRC § 6110(b)(2).

[201] Reg. § 301.6110-2(g)(2). The background file also does not include (1) correspondence pertaining to predisclosure deletions and to postponements of the date on which a written determination is made open or subject to inspection, or (2) a request for a written determination that is withdrawn before it is issued or that the Service declined to answer.

[202] IRC § 6110(k)(3). Nevertheless, the Service uses letter rulings as precedent. At one time, the Service's Manual provided that district offices are permitted to use letter rulings "as a guide along with other research material in formulating a district office position on an issue." IRM 424(14).3(3), MT 4200-537 (Nov. 2, 1981) (Application of Private Let-

nations, however, does not apply to excise tax rulings, which are expressly excluded from the general rule of Section 6110(k)(3). Nevertheless, the written determinations still represent the Service's views on specific transactions, and thus generally indicate the likely result if a ruling request is based on similar facts. Although nonprecedential, written determinations made public under Section 6110 constitute a research resource and a body of authority used by courts, IRS research personnel, and practitioners, even if the authority is not binding on the Service.[203]

If all information contained in a request for a ruling, determination letter, or technical advice were made public, taxpayers might reasonably be reluctant to request a determination. Congress did not intend this result in providing for public disclosures of the Service's written determinations.[204] Accordingly, Section 6110(c) exempts seven categories of information from disclosure, and requires the Service to delete identifying details, as well as other information exempt from public disclosure under the FOIA.[205] Identifying details consist of names, addresses, and any other information the Service believes could identify any person affected by the written determination or background file, except a third-party contact made about the request.[206] A "detail" is considered to identify a person if a reasonable person, generally knowledgeable regarding a community (e.g., a geographical or industrial community) would be able to identify the person, taking into account information available at the time the determination is made public as well as information expected to be made publicly available within a reasonable time thereafter.[207] Trade secrets are exempt from disclosure.[208] Commercial or financial information obtained from a person is exempt from disclosure if such information remains privileged and confiden-

---

ter Rulings and Memorandums, Etc.). The Supreme Court has noted this administrative practice and utilized it in deciding a case. Rowan Cos. v. United States, 452 US 247, 261–262 (1981).

[203] See Hanover Bank v. Comm'r, 369 US 672 (1962); Ogiony v. Comm'r, 617 F2d 14, 17 (2d Cir.) (concurring opinion), cert. denied, 449 US 900 (1980). Disclosure of letter rulings and technical advice troubles the Service because it does not want positions taken in letter rulings, for example, to be considered precedent or to bind the Service in future determinations. In relation to guidance in a new or developing area, the Service feels that unless it can freely change a position taken in a letter ruling or technical advice as dictated by experience and further refection, the viability of the rulings program may be jeopardized. See Portney, "Letter Rulings: An Endangered Species?" 36 Tax Law. 751 (1983). For a reply to this view, see Holden & Novey, "Legitimate Uses of Letter Rulings Issued to Other Taxpayers—A Reply to Gerald Portney," 37 Tax Law. 337 (1984).

[204] General Explanation at 307, reprinted in 1976-3 CB (Vol. 2) 319.

[205] See ¶ 2.03 for a discussion of the FOIA exemptions.

[206] IRC §§ 6110(c)(1), 6110(d)(1).

[207] Reg. § 301.6110-3(a)(1); General Explanation at 305, reprinted in 1976-3 CB (Vol. 2) at 317.

[208] IRC § 6110(c)(4).

tial even after taking into account that the identity of the taxpayer will not be made public (e.g., disclosure will still cause substantial harm to the competitive position of any person).[209] Information also must be deleted if its disclosure would constitute an unwarranted invasion of personal privacy (e.g., a disclosure concerning the details of a pending, but not yet public, divorce, medical treatment, adoption of a child, or gift).[210] Following the FOIA exemptions, Section 6110 also provides for deletion of (1) matters specifically required by executive order to be kept secret in the interest of national defense or foreign policy and (2) geological and geophysical information concerning wells.[211] Information prepared by or for the use of an agency regulating or supervising financial institutions is also to be deleted, since its disclosure could damage the standing of a bank.[212] In addition, information must also be deleted if it is exempt from disclosure under any confidentiality statute applicable to the Service.[213]

Disputes about what information will be disclosed are resolved according to procedures established by Section 6110. These procedures having the following features:

- *Notice of intention to disclose.* Before issuing the written determination, the National Office of district director informs the taxpayer of the information likely to be disclosed.[214] The taxpayer has ten days to respond, but the taxpayer has no right to a conference on any disagreement. On issuing a written determination or receiving a request for a background file document, the National Office must mail (1) a notice of its intention to disclose the written determination and (2) a copy of the written determination as it is to be disclosed to the person requesting the ruling or determination letter or the taxpayer affected by the technical advice.[215]

- *Administrative remedies.* The taxpayer or other affected person has twenty days to request that the Service make additional deletions and to resolve any deletion disagreements with the Service administratively.[216]

- *Action to restrain disclosure.* If the taxpayer or other affected persons are still dissatisfied with the Service's disposition of their deletion re-

---

[209] IRC § 6110(c)(4); Reg. § 301.6110-3(a)(4).

[210] IRC § 6110(c)(5); Reg. § 301.6110-3(a)(5).

[211] IRC §§ 6110(c)(2), 6110(c)(7).

[212] IRC § 6110(c)(6).

[213] IRC § 6110(c)(3).

[214] 26 CFR §§ 601.201(e)(11) (ruling and determination letters), 601.105(b)(5)(iii) (technical advice).

[215] IRC § 6110(f)(1); Reg. § 301.6110-5(a).

[216] 26 CFR § 601.201(e)(16) (rulings and determination letters). Similar administrative procedures apply to technical advice memoranda. 26 CFR § 601.105(b)(5).

quest, after having exhausted all administrative remedies, they may, within sixty days of the mailing of the notice of intention to disclose, file a petition in the Tax Court to restrain disclosure.[217] Notice must be given to any person to whom the ruling or determination pertains so that such person has an opportunity to intervene.[218]

- *Timing of disclosure.* A ruling or other determination must be made available for public inspection no earlier than seventy-five days, and no later than ninety days, after the date the Service mails its notice of intention to disclose.[219] If a court proceeding to restrain disclosure is begun within the sixty-day period after the notice is mailed, the ruling or determination under consideration will not open to inspection until thirty days after the court decision becomes final or later, if the court determines that the Service needs additional time to comply with the court's decision.

- *Postponements of disclosure.* In order to complete a pending transaction, the person who requested the ruling may apply for an extension of the disclosure date for up to fifteen days after the date the National Office determines that the transaction described in the ruling has been completed. However, this additional extension may not result in an extension of more than ninety days in addition to the initial ninety-day period (or a total of 180 days) after the date of the Service's notice of intention to disclose.[220] Nevertheless, if "good cause" can be shown, an additional extension of the disclosure date of no more than 180 days may be obtained.[221]

- *Special timing rules.* Technical advice memoranda and background file documents in a civil fraud case, criminal investigation, or jeopardy or termination assessment need not be disclosed until after the matter is completed.[222] Special timing rules also apply to the disclosure of rulings or determinations relating to the adoption or change of pension plan funding method or plan years, accounting periods or methods, or a partnership's or partner's taxable year.

- *Action for additional disclosure.* A person who wishes to obtain additional disclosure and has exhausted all administrative remedies to obtain disclosure may commence a proceeding in the Tax Court or the District

---

[217] IRC § 6110(f)(3)(A); Reg. § 301.6110-5(b)(2). The Tax Court proceeding, which may be instituted anonymously if appropriate, is for the purpose of obtaining a determination about the portion of the ruling, determination, or background file document the Service intends to disclose.

[218] IRC § 6110(f)(3)(B).

[219] IRC § 6110(g)(1).

[220] IRC § 6110(g)(3).

[221] IRC § 6110(g)(4); Reg. §§ 301.6110-5(c)(2)(ii)(A), 301.6110-5(a)(2)(ii)(D).

[222] IRC § 6110(g)(5).

Court for the District of Columbia seeking an order opening to public inspection any ruling or background file document.[223]

- *Third-party contacts.* If a third party has communicated with the Service about a ruling or other written determination, a notation must be made (on the letter ruling or determination open to public inspection) of the category of the person making the communication and the date.[224] Within thirty-six months after the ruling is open to inspection, a person seeking the identity of the third party may file a petition in the Tax Court or a complaint in the District Court for the District of Columbia for an order requiring disclosure of the third-party contact's identity.[225]
- *Damages.* To ensure compliance with the disclosure rules, an affected person may commence an action for damages in the Court of Federal Claims when the Service fails to make the deletions required by Section 6110(c) or fails to follow the procedures for the timing of disclosure.[226] If the failure to delete or comply is intentional or willful, the person affected may recover actual damages (but not less than $1,000), plus costs with reasonable attorney fees.

[d] User Fees

The Service is required to charge user fees for rulings, opinion letters, determination letters, and similar requests, that (1) vary according to categories and subcategories the Service establishes; (2) are determined after taking into account the average time for complying with the request and the difficulty of the request; and (3) are payable in advance.[227] In accordance with this requirement, the Service publishes a user fee schedule for letter rulings or closing

---

[223] IRC § 6110(f)(4)(A). In this proceeding, the burden of proof is on the person seeking to restrain disclosure, including the Service. However, if, on receipt of notice of the petition or complaint, the Service gives notice of the proceeding to all persons identified by name and address in the ruling or background file, it is not required to defend the action. IRC §§ 6110(f)(4)(A), 6110(f)(4)(B).

[224] IRC § 6110(d)(1). A communication made by the chief of the Joint Committee on Taxation is not a third-party contact. IRC § 6110(d)(2).

[225] IRC § 6110(d)(3). The court is to enter this order if there is evidence in the record from which one could reasonably conclude that an impropriety occurred or that undue influence was exercised in the issuance of the ruling by or on behalf of a third-party contact. The court may also order disclosure of any other deleted material. The person whose identity is sought to be disclosed and the person about whom the third-party contact notation was made must be notified of the action and may intervene anonymously. IRC § 6110(d)(3).

[226] IRC § 6110(g).

[227] Revenue Act of 1987, Pub. L. No. 100-23, § 10511, as amended by the Omnibus Budget Reconciliation Act of 1990, Pub. L. No. 101-508, § 11319, by § 743 of the Uruguay Round Agreements Act of 1994, and by § 2 of the Tax Benefits for Individuals Per-

agreements and determination letters issued by the Associate Chief Counsel (Domestic), Associate Chief Counsel (Employee Plans and Exempt Organizations), Associate Chief Counsel (Enforcement Litigation), and Associate Chief Counsel (International). User fees are set out in fee schedules included with the annual revenue procedures,[228] along with procedures for obtaining a reduced user fee for processing a request for a letter ruling or closing agreement submitted by persons having a gross income of less than $150,000.[229] User fees for determination letters, letter rulings and the like issued by all Assistant Commissioners, except the Assistant Commissioner (Employee Plans and Exempt Organizations), are set out in Form 3.4. A separate fee schedule is also published for letter rulings and determination letters on matters under the jurisdiction of the Assistant Commissioner (Employee Plans and Exempt Organizations), requests for compliance statements under the several compliance programs administered by the Assistant Commissioner (Employee Plans and Exempt Organizations).[230] When a taxpayer submits a request for a letter ruling to the National Office, a check for the amount of the user fee must accompany the request.[231]

---

forming Services in Certain Hazardous Duty Areas of 1996. User fees apply to requests made on February 1, 1988 through October 1, 2003.

[228] Rev. Proc. 2002-1, Appendix A, §§ (1)–(3), Schedule of User Fees, 2002-1 IRB 1, 67–68; Rev. Proc. 2002-8, 2002-1 IRB 252 (Assistant Commissioner (Employee Plans and Exempt Organizations)). The Service periodically revises the fees for processing requests for background file documents relating to a ruling letter or a technical advice memorandum issued by the National Office. Rev. Proc. 95-15, 1995-1 CB 523.

[229] Rev. Proc. 2002-1, Appendix A, § (4), 2002-1 IRB 1, 71. Reduced fees are also charged when there are substantially identical ruling requests or identical accounting method changes. Id. at Appendix A (5).

[230] Rev. Proc. 2002-8, 2002-1 IRB 252. User fees are listed for compliance statements under the Voluntary Compliance Resolution program and the standardized Voluntary Compliance Resolution procedure, as well as correction statements under the Tax Sheltered Annuity Voluntary Program and requests for administrative scrutiny. Id. at § 1 (setting forth the applicable revenue procedures for each of the programs). In addition, user fees are established for such categories as (1) letter ruling requests involving employee plans; (2) requests for certain administrative exemptions; (3) administrative scrutiny determinations on separate lines of business; (4) opinion letters and advisory letters on master and prototype plans; (5) opinion letters on prototype individual retirement accounts/annuities and simplified employee pensions (SEPs), SIMPLE IRAs, SIMPLE IRA Plans, or Roth IRAs; (6) determination letters; and (7) advisory letters on volume submitter plans. Rev. Proc. 2002-8, §§ 6.01–6.07, 2002-1 IRB 252, 255–259. There are also exempt organization user fees for (1) exempt organizations letter rulings; (2) determination letters and requests for group exemption letters; and (3) a summary schedule of Exempt Organization fees, including requests for the processing of applications for exemption. Rev. Proc. 2002-8, §§ 6.08–6.10, 2002-1 IRB 252, 259–261.

[231] Rev. Proc. 2002-1, § 15.08, 2002-1 IRB 1, 57. The method of payment is a check or money order made payable to the Internal Revenue Service in the appropriate amount.

User fees generally apply to requests for (1) letter rulings, determination letters, and advance pricing agreements; (2) closing agreements on certain issues; (3) renewals of advance pricing agreements; and (4) reconsideration of letter rulings and determination letters.[232]

[4] Preparation of Ruling Requests

In its annual revenue procedure describing the process for requesting a letter ruling, the Service provides extensive and detailed instructions for a letter ruling request, as well as a sample format (Form 3.1),[233] a checklist for taxpayers and practitioners to determine whether the ruling request is complete (Form 3.4),[234] and a schedule of user fees.[235] The checklist was developed to advise taxpayers of the information and documents that are necessary to enable the Service to make a quick response to a ruling request. The checklist must be completed, signed by the taxpayer or the taxpayer's representative, and placed on top of the ruling request.

Additionally, from time to time, the Service issues special instructions for ruling requests that involve certain issues or areas. Such requests should be prepared in accordance with these special instructions, checklists, guideline revenue procedures, notices, safe harbor revenue procedures, and automatic change revenue procedures.[236]

Merely because the Service specifies a particular format and content for a ruling request does not mean that the presentation should be a rigid and formal exercise. The primary objective of the request is to persuade the Service to grant the ruling requested.[237] Because the usual purpose of a ruling request is to seek answers for issues that do not have easy solutions, a mere perfunctory statement of the required information, without detailed facts and without persuasive legal or factual analysis, is inadvisable. If a skeleton ruling request is submitted, the Service may not consider itself bound by the ruling if facts that it later believes to be relevant were omitted. A full statement of facts (1) avoids the possibility that the Service will say that the transaction was not completed as described in the ruling, and (2) fosters trust that the taxpayer is not holding back information. On the other hand, the more information that is

---

[232] Rev. Proc. 2002-1, § 15.01, 2002-1 IRB 1, 54–55.

[233] Rev. Proc. 2002-1, Appendix B, 2002-1 IRB 1, 72–74.

[234] Rev. Proc. 2002-1, § 8.01(16), 2002-1 IRB 1, 28.

[235] See 26 CFR § 601.201(e); Rev. Proc. 2002-1, § 8, 2002-1 IRB 1, 21–35. Form 3115 is used for a change in accounting method and Form 1128 and Form 2553 for a change in accounting period.

[236] These revenue procedures are gathered in Rev. Proc. 2002-1, § 9, 2002-1 IRB 1, 35–42.

[237] Rev. Proc. 2002-1, § 8.01(6), 2002-1 IRB 1, 23–24.

disclosed, the greater the opportunity for a revelation of facts that may delay or preclude the issuance of a favorable ruling. Completeness, candor, and reasonableness nevertheless will generally result in successful dealings with the Service.

With this background, a ruling request should include the following information:

- *Address.* Requests for letter rulings should be sent to the Associate Chief Counsel (Domestic), the Associate Chief Counsel (Employee Plans and Exempt Organizations), the Associate Chief Counsel (Enforcement Litigation), or the Associate Chief Counsel (International) at Internal Revenue Service, Attention: CC:Dom:Corp:TSS, P.O. Box 7604, Ben Franklin Station, Washington, D.C. 20044.[238] The package should be marked: RULING REQUEST SUBMISSION.

- *Number of copies.* A request for ruling should be submitted in duplicate if (a) more than one issue is presented in the request or (b) a closing agreement is requested on the issue presented.[239]

- *Statement of facts and supporting data.* The request should include the following information:[240]

  1. The names, addresses, and taxpayer identification numbers of all "interested parties," a term that does not include shareholders in a widely held corporation. The Service does not consider itself bound by a ruling except to the persons for whose benefit the ruling is issued.
  2. The annual accounting period and overall method of accounting of all the interested parties.
  3. The location of the district office that has or will have jurisdiction over the return or report of each interested party.
  4. A description of the taxpayer's business operations.
  5. A statement of the business reasons for the transaction.

---

[238] Rev. Proc. 2002-1, § 8.03(1)(a), 2002-1 IRB 1, 32. If a private delivery service is used, the address is Internal Revenue Service, Attn: CC:Dom:Corp:TSS, Room 6561, 1111 Constitution Avenue, N.W., Washington, D.C. 20224. If the ruling request is hand-delivered, delivery is made to the drop box at the 12th Street entrance of 1111 Constitution Avenue, N.W., Washington D.C. (no receipt is given). Between 8:15 A.M. and 5 P.M. hand-delivery may also be made to the courier's desk at the main entrance of 1111 Constitution Avenue, N.W., Washington, D.C., where a receipt will be given. The package should be addressed to Courier's Desk, Internal Revenue Service, Attn: CC:Dom:Corp:TSS, Room 6561, 1111 Constitution Avenue, N.W., Washington, D.C. 20224.

[239] Rev. Proc. 2002-1, § 8.01(14), 2002-1 IRB 1, 27.

[240] Rev. Proc. 2002-1, § 8.01(1), 2002-1 IRB 1, 21.

6. A detailed description of the transaction that recites the relevant portions of the documents.[241]

- *Documents and foreign law.* True copies of all documents must be submitted with the request, and they should be labeled and attached to the request in alphabetical order.[242] If the transaction is a corporate reorganization or a similar transaction, balance sheets must be attached. If foreign law is relevant to the ruling request, a copy of the statute and a translation must also be submitted with the request.
- *Requested rulings.* A statement of the specific ruling(s) requested should be set forth (e.g., a ruling that a liquidation will qualify under Section 337 of the Code).[243] The taxpayer should draft the language and phrasing of the requested ruling with care because, if the ruling is granted, the Service may use the same words offered by the taxpayer in issuing the ruling. Alternative transactions may not be included in one ruling request. If certain elements are required for a specific type of transaction, all elements must be set forth in the request.
- *Analysis of material facts.* Facts in documents may not merely be incorporated by reference, but must be accompanied by an analysis of their bearing on the issue or issues, specifying the provisions that apply.[244]
- *Same issue in an earlier return.* The request must include a statement about whether the same issue is in an earlier year's return and, if it is, the request must disclose such matters as whether the return is being examined in the district or is being considered by an Appeals office, as well as other relevant information pertaining to the issue on the earlier year's return.[245]
- *Same or similar issue previously submitted or currently pending.* The request must also state whether, to the best of the knowledge of both the taxpayer and the taxpayer's representative, the same or similar issue was previously ruled on or requested, or is currently pending.[246] The statement must say whether the identical issue is in a return of the taxpayer (or of a related taxpayer or a member of an affiliated group within the meaning of Sections 267 and 1504, respectively) and, if so, whether the issue (1) is under examination by any field office or Ap-

---

[241] Rev. Proc. 2002-1, § 8.01, 2002-1 IRB 1, 21–29.

[242] Rev. Proc. 2002-1, § 8.01(2), 2002-1 IRB 1, 22.

[243] Rev. Proc. 2002-1, Appendix B, 2002-1 IRB 1, 72–74. It is curious that with all the detailed instructions in the annual revenue procedure, this important matter is left to the sample format of a letter ruling request attached to the revenue procedure.

[244] Rev. Proc. 2002-1, § 8.01(3), 2002-1 IRB 1, 22.

[245] Rev. Proc. 2002-1, § 8.01(4), 2002-1 IRB 1, 23.

[246] Rev. Proc. 2002-1, § 8.01(5), 2002-1 IRB 1, 23.

peals Office; (2) has been examined and the statute of limitations on assessment or refund has not expired or a closing agreement has not been entered into by a district office; (3) is under consideration by an Appeals Office in connection with a return for a prior period and the statute of limitations on assessment or refund has not expired or a closing agreement has not been entered into by an Appeals Office; or (4) is pending in litigation.[247] If the taxpayer learns that the district office has started an examination of the issue before a ruling is issued, the taxpayer must notify the National Office of the examination. When the taxpayer files a return before receiving a ruling, the taxpayer must attach a copy of the ruling request to the return to alert the district office and avoid premature district action on the issue.

- *Statement of authorities supporting taxpayer's views.* When the taxpayer advocates a particular conclusion, the taxpayer's request must explain the grounds for that conclusion and include the relevant authorities to support it.[248] Even if the taxpayer does not advocate a particular tax treatment of a proposed transaction, the taxpayer's request must still explain the taxpayer's views on the tax results of the proposed transaction as well as describe the authorities that support those views. In addition, the taxpayer's request must state whether the law pertaining to the request is "uncertain," and whether the relevant authorities adequately address the issue. Finally, in presenting the support for the requested ruling, it should be remembered that a branch representative in the Chief Counsel's office will likely give greater weight to regulations, rulings, and other announcements of the Service than to arguments from court decisions.

- *Statement of authorities contrary to the taxpayer's views.* The Service believes that a request that identifies and discusses contrary authorities will enable Branch representatives, having before them the taxpayer's views on the implications of contrary authority, to more quickly understand the issue and the relevant authorities. This more complete form of request is expected to lead to earlier action on the ruling request by making the Service's research easier and avoiding requests for further information. Accordingly, the taxpayer is encouraged, but not required, to inform the National Office about authority the taxpayer believes to be contrary to the requested ruling, and to discuss the implications of this apparently contrary authority. On the other hand, if the taxpayer believes there is no contrary authority, inclusion of a statement to that effect in the ruling "would be helpful."[249] However, in requests involving

---

[247] Rev. Proc. 2002-1, § 8.01(5), 2002-1 IRB 1, 23.
[248] Rev. Proc. 2002-1, § 8.01(6), 2002-1 IRB 1, 23–24.
[249] Rev. Proc. 2002-1, § 8.01(7), 2002-1 IRB 1, 24.

complex or novel issues, if the taxpayer does not present any contrary authority or submit a statement that none exists, the National Office may require the taxpayer to submit a discussion of contrary authorities or a statement that none exists.[250] If the taxpayer then refuses, the National Office may refuse to rule on the request. Since this portion of the request should present the legal justification for the rulings requested in a manner calculated to persuade the branch representative to grant the ruling requested, as a tactical matter, it is better to anticipate adverse or potentially adverse authority and answer it than to wait for the branch representative to discover a problem and ask for additional information. Finally, in presenting authority adverse to the requested ruling, it should be remembered that a branch representative in the Chief Counsel's office will likely give greater weight to regulations, rulings, and other announcements of the Service than to arguments from court decisions.

• *Statement identifying pending legislation.* The taxpayer's request must identify any pending legislative proposal that may affect any ruling on the proposed transaction.[251]

• *Deletion statement required by Section 6110.* To assist in the deletion process for purposes of the disclosure rules of Section 6110, the request for a ruling or determination letter must be accompanied by a separate statement of proposed deletions from disclosure, which is signed and dated by the taxpayer or the taxpayer's representative.[252] This deletions statement must either (1) indicate the deletions proposed (by brackets on a marked copy of the ruling request and accompanying documents) and the statutory basis for each deletion or (2) say that no information other than names, addresses, and taxpayer identification numbers need be deleted. No statement of deletions may appear in the ruling request itself. If the taxpayer's request does not include a copy of the request containing the proposed deletions or otherwise does not meet these requirements, the National Office will notify the taxpayer, and the taxpayer will have thirty days to respond.[253]

• *Procedural matters.* According to the above-discussed general instructions and the sample form for a letter ruling, many statements must be included with the ruling request: the statement about whether the same issue in the letter ruling request is in an earlier return of the taxpayer (or in a return of a related taxpayer)[254]; the statement about whether the

---

[250] Rev. Proc. 2002-1, § 8.01(7), 2002-1 IRB 1, 24.

[251] Rev. Proc. 2002-1, § 8.01(8), 2002-1 IRB 1, 24.

[252] 26 CFR § 601.201(e)(2); Rev. Proc. 2002-1, § 8.01(9), 2002-1 IRB 1, 24–25.

[253] 26 CFR § 601.201(e)(9); Rev. Proc. 2002-1, § 8.01(9), 2002-1 IRB 1, 24–25.

[254] Rev. Proc. 2002-1, § 8.01(4), 2002-1 IRB 1, 23.

Service has ruled on the same or similar issue for the taxpayer[255]; the statement about whether the identical issue has previously been submitted to the Service, but withdrawn by the taxpayer before a ruling was issued[256]; the statement about whether the taxpayer previously submitted a request involving the same or similar issue that is currently pending with the Service[257]; the statement about whether, at the same time that the taxpayer's request is being submitted, the taxpayer is submitting another request involving the same or similar issue to the Service[258]; the statement about whether the law on the ruling request issue is uncertain and whether the issue is adequately addressed by the relevant authorities[259]; the statement that the taxpayer believes that there are no contrary authorities[260]; the statement that the taxpayer wishes to have a conference on the issues involved in the ruling request[261]; the statement that the taxpayer wishes to have the letter ruling sent by facsimile transmission[262]; a statement that the taxpayer is seeking substantially identical letter rulings and wishes to be charged the reduced user fee.[263] The ruling request should also state the following: (1) "The deletions statement and checklist required by [the annual revenue procedure] are enclosed,"[264] (2) "The required user fee of $[the amount of the user fee] is enclosed,"[265] and (3) if the taxpayer is being represented, "A power of attorney in favor of the undersigned [i.e., taxpayer's representative] is enclosed."[266]

- *Signature.* The request must be signed by the taxpayer or the taxpayer's authorized representative.[267] If signed by the representative, the representative's power of attorney must be attached.[268]
- *Penalties of perjury statement.* The request must include an "under penalties of perjury" statement declaration signed by the taxpayer, and not

---

[255] Rev. Proc. 2002-1, § 8.01(5)(a), 2002-1 IRB 1, 24.

[256] Rev. Proc. 2002-1, § 8.01(5)(b), 2002-1 IRB 1, 23.

[257] Rev. Proc. 2002-1, § 8.01(5)(c), 2002-1 IRB 1, 23.

[258] Rev. Proc. 2002-1, § 8.01(5)(d), 2002-1 IRB 1, 23.

[259] Rev. Proc. 2002-1, § 8.01(6), 2002-1 IRB 1, 23–24.

[260] Rev. Proc. 2002-1, § 8.01(7), 2002-1 IRB 1, 24.

[261] Rev. Proc. 2002-1, § 8.02(6), 2002-1 IRB 1, 31–32.

[262] Rev. Proc. 2002-1, § 8.02(5), 2002-1 IRB 1, 31.

[263] Rev. Proc. 2002-1, § 8.02(1), 2002-1 IRB 1, 29–30.

[264] Rev. Proc. 2002-1, § 15.07, 2002-1 IRB 1, 56–57 (statement required for obtaining the user fee provided for in Appendix A(5)(a)).

[265] Rev. Proc. 2002-1, § 15, and Appendix A, 2002-1 IRB 1, 67–71.

[266] Rev. Proc. 2002-1, §§ 8.01(11), 8.01(12), 8.02(2), 2002-1 IRB 1, 29.

[267] Rev. Proc. 2002-1, § 8.01(10), 2002-1 IRB 1, 25.

[268] Rev. Proc. 2002-1, § 8.01(12), 2002-1 IRB 1, 26.

the taxpayer's representative, stating: "Under penalties of perjury, I declare that I have examined this request, including accompanying documents, and to the best of my knowledge and belief, it contains all the relevant facts relating to the request, and such facts are true, correct, and complete."[269] A person signing on behalf of a corporation must be an officer with personal knowledge of the facts. A fiduciary or partner signing on behalf of a trust or partnership also must have personal knowledge of the facts.

---

[269] Rev. Proc. 2002-1, § 8.01(11), 2002-1 IRB 1, 25–26.

FORM 3.1
RULING REQUEST FORMAT

APPENDIX B

SAMPLE FORMAT FOR A LETTER RULING REQUEST

INSTRUCTIONS

To assist you in preparing a letter ruling request, the Service is providing this sample format. You are not required to use this sample format. If your request is not identical or similar to the sample format, the different format will not defer consideration of your request.

(Insert the date of request)

Internal Revenue Service
Associate Chief Counsel *(Insert appropriate*
Associate Chief Counsel)
Attn: CC:PA:T
P.O. Box 7604
Ben Franklin Station
Washington, DC 20044

Dear Sir or Madam:

(Insert the name of the taxpayer) requests a ruling on the proper treatment of *(insert the subject matter of the letter ruling request)* under section *(insert the number)* of the Internal Revenue Code.

[If the taxpayer is requesting expeditious handling, the letter ruling request must contain a statement to that effect. This statement must explain the need for expeditious handling. See section 8.02(4).]

A. STATEMENT OF FACTS

1. Taxpayer Information

[Provide the statements required by sections 8.01(1)(a), (b), and (c) of Rev. Proc. 94-1, 1994-1 I.R.B. 10. Hereafter, all references are to Rev. Proc. 94-1 unless otherwise noted.]

2. Description of Taxpayer's Business Operations

[Provide the statement required by section 8.01(1)(d).]

3. Facts Relating to Transaction

[The ruling request must contain a complete statement of the facts relating to the transaction that is the subject of the letter ruling request. This statement must include a detailed description of the transaction, including material facts in any accompanying documents, and the business reasons for the transaction. See sections 8.01(1)(e), 8.01(1)(f), and 8.01(2).]

B. RULING REQUESTED

[The ruling request should contain a concise statement of the ruling requested by the taxpayer. It is preferred that the language of the requested ruling be exactly the same that the taxpayer wishes to receive.]

C. STATEMENT OF LAW

[The ruling request must contain a statement of the law in support of the taxpayer's views or conclusion and identify any pending legislation that may affect the proposed transaction. The taxpayer also is encouraged to identify and discuss any authorities believed to be contrary to the position advanced in the ruling request. See sections 8.01(6), 8.01(7), and 8.01(8).]

D. ANALYSIS

[The ruling request must contain a discussion of the facts and an analysis of the law. The taxpayer also is encouraged to identify and discuss any authorities believed to be contrary to the position advanced in the ruling request. See sections 8.01(3), 8.01(6), 8.01(7), and 8.01(8).]

E. CONCLUSION

[The ruling request should contain a statement of the taxpayer's conclusion on the ruling requested.]

F. PROCEDURAL MATTERS

1. Revenue Procedure 94–1 Statements

    a. [Provide the statement required by section 8.01(4) regarding whether the same issue in the letter ruling request is in an earlier return of the taxpayer or in a return for any year of a related taxpayer.]

    b. [Provide the statement required by section 8.01(5) regarding whether the Service previously ruled on the same or similar issue for the taxpayer, a related taxpayer, or a predecessor.]

    c. [Provide the statement required by section 8.01(5) regarding whether the taxpayer, a related taxpayer, a predecessor, or any representatives previously submitted the same or similar issue but withdrew it before the letter ruling was issued.]

    d. [Provide the statement required by section 8.01(6) regarding whether the law in connection with the letter ruling request is uncertain and whether the issue is adequately addressed by relevant authorities.]

    e. [If the taxpayer determines that there are no contrary authorities, a statement to that effect would be helpful. See section 8.01(7).]

    f. [If the taxpayer wants to have a conference on the issues involved in the letter ruling request, the ruling request should contain a statement to that effect. See section 8.02(6).]

    g. [If the taxpayer is requesting a copy of the letter ruling to be sent by facsimile (fax) transmission, the ruling request should contain a statement to that effect. This statement must also contain a waiver of any disclosure violations resulting from the fax transmission. See section 8.02(5).]

    h. [If the taxpayer is requesting separate letter rulings on multiple issues, the letter ruling request should contain a statement to that effect. See section 8.02(1).]

2. Administrative

    a. [The ruling request should state: "The deletions statement and checklist required by Rev. Proc. 94–1 are enclosed." See sections 8.01(9) and 8.01(16).]

    b. [The ruling request should state: "The required user fee of $(*Insert the amount of the fee*) is enclosed." See section 14 and Appendix A.]

    c. [If the taxpayer's authorized representative is to sign the letter ruling request or is to appear before the Service in connection with the request, the ruling request should state: "A Power of Attorney is enclosed." See sections 8.01(11), 8.01(12), and 8.02(2).]

Very truly yours,

(*Insert the name of the taxpayer or the taxpayer's authorized representative*)

By:

_____   _____
Signature   Date

_____
Typed or printed name of
person signing request

DECLARATION: [See section 8.01(13).]

Under penalties of perjury, I declare that I have examined this request, including accompanying documents, and to the best of my knowledge and belief, the facts presented in support of the requested letter ruling are true, correct, and complete.

(*Insert the name of the taxpayer*)

By:

_____   _____   _____
Signature   Title   Date

_____
Typed or printed name of
person signing declaration

[If the taxpayer is a corporation that is a member of an affiliated group filing consolidated returns, the above declaration must also be signed and dated by an officer of the common parent of the group. See section 8.01(13).]

FORM 3.2
PENALTY-OF-PERJURY DECLARATION

DECLARATION: (See Rev. Proc. 94-1, § 8.01(13).)

Under penalties of perjury, I declare that I have examined this request, including accompanying documents, and, to the best of my knowledge and belief, the facts presented in support of the requested letter ruling are true, correct, and complete.

[Insert the name of the taxpayer]
By:

....
        (Signature)   (Title)   (Date)

....
    (Typed or printed name of
   person signing declaration)

(If the taxpayer is a corporation that is a member of an affiliated group filing consolidated returns, the above declaration must also be signed and dated by an officer of the common parent of the group. See Rev. Proc. 94-1, § 8.01(13).)

FORM 3.3 _____
STATEMENT OF PROPOSED DELETIONS FROM DISCLOSURE

Statement of Proposed Deletions

Pursuant to the provisions of Section 6110(c) of the Internal Revenue Code of 1986, the following statement of proposed deletions is made.

1. The name, address, and other identifying details of any person, including corporations and shareholders, should be deleted as is required by Section 6110(c)(1).

2. Financial information relating to ABC Corporation should be deleted as is required by Sections 6110(c)(4) and 6110(c)(5) because of its confidential nature and because disclosure would constitute an unwarranted invasion of personal privacy.

3 The corporate charter of ABC Corporation should be deleted as is contemplated by Sections 6110(c)(4) and 6110(c)(5) because disclosure would constitute an unwarranted invasion of personal privacy.

4. The purpose for the proposed transaction should be deleted as is contemplated by Section 6110(c)(5) because disclosure would constitute an unwarranted invasion of personal privacy.

The material requested to be deleted are indicated by brackets on a copy of the ruling request and exhibits that accompany this statement.

....
[Representative]

FORM 3.4 —————————————————
SCHEDULE OF USER FEES
———————————————————————————————

APPENDIX A

SCHEDULE OF USER FEES

(A) *FEE SCHEDULE*

CATEGORY	FEE
(1) User fee for a determination letter request. The user fee for each determination letter request governed by Rev. Proc. 97-1 (this revenue procedure).	$275
(2) User fee for a request for an advance pricing agreement or a renewal of an advance pricing agreement.	See Rev. Proc. 96-53

(3) User fee for a request for a letter ruling or closing agreement. Except for the user fees for advance pricing agreements and renewals, the reduced fees provided in paragraph (A)(4) of this appendix, the user fees provided in paragraph (A)(5) of this appendix, and the exemptions provided in section 15.04 of Rev. Proc. 97-1 (this revenue procedure), the user fee for each request for a letter ruling or closing agreement under the jurisdiction of the Associate Chief Counsel (Domestic), the Associate Chief Counsel (Employee Benefits and Exempt Organizations), the Associate Chief Counsel (Enforcement Litigation), or the Associate Chief Counsel (International) is as follows:

(a) Accounting periods

   (i) Forms 1128 and 2553 .... $250

   (ii) Letter ruling requests for extensions of time to file Form 1128 under § 301.9100–1T $250

(b) Changes in Accounting Methods

   (i) Form 3115 (except as provided in paragraph (A)(4)(a), (b), (c), or (d), or (5)(b) of this appendix) $900

   (ii) Except as provided in paragraph (A)(5)(c) of this appendix, letter ruling requests for extensions of time to file Form 3115 under § 301.9100–1T $250

NOTE: A taxpayer that receives an extension of time under § 301.9100–1T will be charged a separate user fee for the accounting period or accounting method application. No user fee is required if the change in accounting period or accounting method is permitted to be made pursuant to a published automatic change revenue procedure or notice. See section 9.03 of this revenue procedure for the list of automatic change revenue procedures and notices published and in effect as of December 31, 1996.

(c) All other letter ruling requests (which includes accounting period and accounting method requests other than those properly submitted on Form 1128, 2553, or 3115) (except as provided in paragraph (A)(4)(a), (b), (c), or (d), or (5)(a) of this appendix) $3,650

(d) Requests for closing agreements on a proposed transaction or on a completed transaction before a return for the transaction has been filed in which a letter ruling on that transaction is not requested or issued (except as provided in paragraph (A)(4)(a), (b), (c), or (d) of this appendix) $3,650

(4) Reduced user fee for a request for a letter ruling or closing agreement. A reduced user fee is provided in the following situations if the person provides the certification described in paragraph (B)(1) of this appendix:

(a) U.S. citizens and resident alien individuals, domestic trusts, and domestic estates with gross income (as determined under paragraph (B)(2) and (4) of this appendix) of less than $150,000 .... $500

(b) Nonresident alien individuals, foreign trusts, and foreign estates with gross income (as determined under paragraph (B)(3) and (4) of this appendix) of less than $150,000 .... $500

(c) Domestic partnerships and corporations with gross income (as determined under paragraph (B)(5) of this appendix) of less than $150,000 .... $500

(d) Organizations exempt from income tax under "Subchapter F-Exempt Organizations" of the Code with gross receipts (as determined under paragraph (B)(6) of this appendix) of less than $150,000 .... $500

(5) User fee for substantially identical letter ruling requests or identical accounting method changes. If the requirements of section 15.07 of Rev. Proc. 97-1 (this revenue procedure) are satisfied, the user fee for the following situations is as follows:

(a) Substantially identical letter rulings requested $150

Situations in which a taxpayer requests substantially identical letter rulings for multiple entities with a common member or sponsor, or for multiple members of a common entity, for each additional letter ruling request after the $3,650 fee or $500 reduced fee, as applicable, has been paid for the first letter ruling request

(b) Identical accounting method change requested on a single Form 3115 $25

Situations in which a parent corporation requests the identical accounting method change on a single Form 3115 on behalf of more than one member of a consolidated group, for each additional member of the group seeking the identical accounting method change on the same Form 3115 after the $900 fee or $500 reduced fee, as applicable, has been paid for the first member of the group

(c) Extension of time requested to file Form 3115 for an identical accounting method change $25

Situations in which a parent corporation requests an extension of time to file Form 3115 under § 301.9100–1T for the identical accounting method change on behalf of more than one member of a consolidated group, for each additional member of the group seeking the identical accounting method change on the same application after the $250 fee has been paid for the first member of the group

NOTE: A parent corporation and each member of a consolidated group that is entitled to the user fee under paragraph (A)(5)(b) of this appendix, that receives an extension of time to file Form 3115 under § 301.9100–1T will be charged a separate user fee for the accounting method application.

(B) *PROCEDURAL MATTERS*

(1) Required certification. A person seeking a reduced user fee under paragraph (A)(4) of this appendix must provide the following certification in order to obtain the reduced user fee:

(a) If a person is seeking a reduced user fee under paragraph (A)(4)(a), (b), or (c) of this appendix, the person must certify in the request that his, her, or its gross income, as defined under paragraph (B)(2), (3), or (5) of this appendix, as applicable, is less than $150,000 for the last full (12 months) taxable year ending before the date the request is filed.

(b) If an organization exempt from income tax under Subchapter F of the Code is seeking a reduced user fee under paragraph (A)(4)(d) of this appendix, the organization must certify in its request that its gross receipts are less than $150,000 for the last full (12 months) taxable year ending before the date the request is filed.

(2) Gross income of U.S. citizens and resident alien individuals, domestic trusts, and domestic estates. For purposes of the reduced user fee provided in paragraph (A)(4)(a) of this appendix for U.S. citizens and resident alien individuals, domestic trusts, and domestic estates, "gross income" is equal to "total income" as reported on their last federal income tax return (as amended) filed for a full (12 months) taxable year ending before the date the request is filed, plus any interest income not subject to tax under § 103 (interest on state and local bonds) for that period. "Total income" is a line item on federal tax returns. For example, if the 1995 Form 1040, U.S. Individual Income Tax Return, is the most recent 12-month taxable year return filed by a U.S. citizen, "total income" on the Form 1040 is the amount entered on line 22.

In the case of a request for a letter ruling or closing agreement from a domestic estate or trust that, at the time the request is filed, has not filed a federal income tax return for a full taxable year, the reduced user fee in paragraph (A)(4)(a) of this appendix will apply if the decedent's or (in the case of an individual grantor) the grantor's total income as reported on the last federal income tax return filed for a full taxable year ending before the date of death or the date of the transfer, taking into account any additions required to be made to total income described in this paragraph (B)(2), is less than $150,000. In this case, the executor or administrator of the decedent's estate or the grantor must provide the certification required under paragraph (B)(1) of this appendix.

(3) Gross income of nonresident alien individuals, foreign trusts, and foreign estates. For purposes of the reduced user fee provided in paragraph (A)(4)(b) of this appendix for nonresident alien individuals, foreign trusts, and foreign estates, "gross income" is equal to "total effectively connected income" as reported on their last federal income tax return (as amended) filed for a full (12 months) taxable year ending before the date the request is filed, plus any income for the period from United States or foreign sources that is not taxable by the United States, whether by reason of § 103, an income tax treaty, § 871(h) (regarding portfolio interest), or otherwise, plus the total amount of any fixed or determinable annual or periodical income from United States sources, the United States tax liability for which is satisfied by withholding at the source. "Total effectively connected income" is a line item on federal tax returns. For example, if the 1995 Form 1040NR, U.S. Nonresident Alien Income Tax Return, is the most recent 12-month taxable year return filed by a nonresident alien individual, "total effectively connected income" on the Form 1040NR is the amount entered on line 23.

In the case of a request for a letter ruling or closing agreement from a foreign estate or trust that, at the time the request is filed, has not filed a federal income tax return for a full taxable year, the reduced user fee in paragraph (A)(4)(b) of this appendix will apply if the decedent's or (in the case of an individual grantor) the grantor's total income or total effectively connected income, as relevant, as reported on the last federal income tax return filed for a full taxable year ending before the date of death or the date of the transfer, taking into account any additions required to be made to total income or total effectively connected income described respectively in paragraph (B)(2) of this appendix or in this paragraph (B)(3), is less than $150,000. In this case, the executor or administrator of the decedent's estate or the grantor must provide the certification required under paragraph (B)(1) of this appendix.

(4) Special rules for determining gross income of individuals, trusts, and estates. For purposes of paragraph (B)(2) and (3) of this appendix, the following rules apply for determining whether gross income is less than $150,000:

(a) In the case of a request from a married individual, the gross incomes (as defined in paragraph (B)(2) or (3) of this appendix, as applicable) of the applicant and the applicant's spouse must be combined. This rule does not apply to an individual who is legally separated from his or her spouse if the spouses do not file a joint income tax return with each other; and

(b) If there are two or more applicants filing the request, the gross incomes (as defined in paragraph (B)(2) or (3) of this appendix, as applicable) of the applicants must be combined.

(5) Gross income of domestic partnerships and corporations. For purposes of the reduced user fee provided in paragraph (A)(4)(c) of this appendix for domestic partnerships and corporations, "gross income" is equal to "total income" as reported on their last federal income tax return (as amended) filed for a full (12 months) taxable year ending before the date the request is filed, plus "cost of goods sold" as reported on the same federal income tax return, plus any interest income not subject to tax under § 103 (interest on state and local bonds) for that period. If a domestic partnership or corporation is not subject to tax, "total income" and "cost of goods sold" are the amounts that the domestic partnership or corporation would have reported on the federal income tax return if the domestic partnership or corporation were subject to tax.

"Cost of goods sold" and "total income" are line items on federal tax returns. For example, if the 1995 Form 1065, U.S. Partnership Return of Income, is the most recent 12-month taxable year return filed by a domestic partnership, "cost of goods sold" and "total income" on the Form 1065 are the amounts entered on lines 2 and 8, respectively, and if the 1995 Form 1120, U.S. Corporation Income Tax Return, is the most recent 12-month taxable year return filed by a domestic corporation, "cost of goods sold" and "total income" on the Form 1120 are the amounts entered on lines 2 and 11, respectively.

The following rules apply in determining whether gross income is less than $150,000:

(a) In the case of a request for a letter ruling or closing agreement from a domestic corporation, the gross income (as defined in this paragraph (B)(5)) of (i) all members of the applicant's controlled group (as defined in § 1563(a)), and (ii) any related taxpayer that is involved in the transaction on which the letter ruling or closing agreement is requested, must be combined; and

(b) In the case of a request for a letter ruling or closing agreement from a domestic partnership, the gross income (as defined in this paragraph (B)(5)) of (i) the partnership, and (ii) any partner who owns, directly or indirectly, 50 percent or more of the capital interest or profits interest in the partnership, must be combined.

If, at the time the request is filed, a domestic partnership or corporation subject to tax has not filed a federal income tax return for a full taxable year, the reduced user fee in paragraph (A)(4)(c) of this appendix will apply if, in the aggregate, the partners' or the shareholders' gross income (as defined in paragraph (B)(2), (3), or (5) of this appendix, as applicable) is less than $150,000 for the last full taxable year ending before the date the request is filed. In this case, the partners or the shareholders must provide the certification required under paragraph (B)(1) of this appendix.

(6) Gross receipts of an exempt organization. For purposes of the reduced user fee provided in paragraph (A)(4)(d) of this appendix for organizations exempt from income tax under "Subchapter F-Exempt Organizations" of the Code, "gross receipts" is the amount of gross receipts for the last full (12 months) taxable year ending before the date the request for a letter ruling or closing agreement is filed. If there are two or more organizations exempt from income tax under Subchapter F filing the request, the gross receipts of the applicants must be combined in determining whether gross receipts are less than $150,000.

FORM 3.5 ──

CHECKLIST: IS YOUR LETTER RULING REQUEST COMPLETE?

──

APPENDIX C
CHECKLIST—IS YOUR LETTER RULING REQUEST COMPLETE?

INSTRUCTIONS The Service will be able to respond more quickly to your letter ruling request if it is carefully prepared and complete. To ensure that your request is in order, use this checklist. Complete the five items of information requested before the checklist. Answer each question by circling "Yes," "No," or "N/A." When a question contains a place for a page number, insert the page number (or numbers) of the request that gives the information called for by a yes answer to a question. Sign and date the checklist (as taxpayer or authorized representative) and place it on top of your request.

If you are an authorized representative submitting a request for a taxpayer, you must include a completed checklist with the request, or the request will either be returned to you or substantive consideration of it will be deferred until a completed checklist is submitted. If you are a taxpayer preparing your own request without professional assistance, an incomplete checklist will not either cause the return of your request or defer substantive consideration of your request. However, you should still complete as much of the checklist as possible and submit it with your request.

TAXPAYER'S NAME [*Name*]
TAXPAYER'S I.D. NO. [*Number*]
ATTORNEY/P.O.A. [*Name*]
PRIMARY CODE SECTION [*Number*]

CIRCLE ONE	ITEM
Yes No	1. Does your request involve an issue under the jurisdiction of the Associate Chief Counsel (Corporate), the Associate Chief Counsel (Financial Institutions & Products), the Associate Chief Counsel (Income Tax & Accounting), the Associate Chief Counsel (International), the Associate Chief Counsel (Passthroughs & Special Industries), the Associate Chief Counsel (Procedure and Administration), or the Division Counsel/Associate Chief Counsel (Tax Exempt and Government Entities)? See section 3 of Rev. Proc. 2001-1, 2001-1 IRB 1. For issues under the jurisdiction of other offices, see section 4 of Rev. Proc. 2002-1. (Hereafter, all references are to Rev. Proc. 2002-1 unless otherwise noted.)
Yes No	2. Have you read Rev. Proc. 2002-3, 2002-1 IRB 117, and Rev. Proc. 2002-7, 2002-1 IRB 249, to see if part or all of the request involves a matter on which letter rulings are not issued or are ordinarily not issued?

CIRCLE ONE	ITEM
Yes No N/A	3. If your request involves a matter on which letter rulings are not ordinarily issued, have you given compelling reasons to justify the issuance of a letter ruling? Before preparing your request, you may want to call the branch in the Office of Associate Chief Counsel (Corporate), the Office of Associate Chief Counsel (Financial Institutions & Products), the Office of Associate Chief Counsel (Income Tax & Accounting), the Office of Associate Chief Counsel (International), the Office of Associate Chief Counsel (Passthroughs & Special Industries), the Office of Associate Chief Counsel (Procedure and Administration), or the Office of Division Counsel/Associate Chief Counsel (Tax Exempt and Government Entities) responsible for substantive interpretations of the principal Internal Revenue Code section on which you are seeking a letter ruling to discuss the likelihood of an exception. For matters under the jurisdiction of

(a) the Office of Associate Chief Counsel (Corporate), the Office of Associate Chief Counsel (Financial Institutions & Products), the Office of Associate Chief Counsel (Income Tax & Accounting), the Office of Associate Chief Counsel (Passthroughs & Special Industries), or the Office of Division Counsel/Associate Chief Counsel (Tax Exempt and Government Entities), or the Office of the Associate Chief Counsel (Procedure and Administration), the appropriate branch to call may be obtained by calling (202) 622-7560 (not a toll-free call);

(b) the Office of the Associate Chief Counsel (International), the appropriate branch to call may be obtained by calling (202) 622-3800 (not a toll-free call); or

(c) the Office of the Associate Chief Counsel (Procedure and Administration), the appropriate branch to call may be obtained by calling (202) 622-3400 (not a toll-free call).

Yes No N/A Pages	4. If the request deals with a completed transaction, have you filed the return for the year in which the transaction was completed? See sections 5.01, 5.05, 5.06, 5.07, 5.08, and 5.09.
Yes No	5. Are you requesting a letter ruling on a hypothetical situation or question? See section 7.02.
Yes No	6. Are you requesting a letter ruling on alternative plans of a proposed transaction? See section 7.02.
Yes No	7. Are you requesting the letter ruling for only part of an integrated transaction? See sections 7.03 and 8.01(1).
Yes No	8. Are you requesting the letter ruling for a business, trade, industrial association, or similar group concerning the application of tax law to its members? See section 5.12.
Yes No	9. Are you requesting the letter ruling for a foreign government or its political subdivision? See section 5.13.
Yes No Pages	10. Have you included a complete statement of all the facts relevant to the transaction? See section 8.01(1).

CIRCLE ONE	ITEM

Yes No N/A   11. Have you submitted with the request true copies of all wills, deeds, and other documents relevant to the transaction, and labeled and attached them in alphabetical sequence? See section 8.01(2).

Yes No N/A   12. Have you submitted with the request a copy of all applicable foreign laws, and certified English translations of documents that are in a language other than English or of foreign laws in cases where English is not the official language of the foreign country involved? See section 8.01(2).

Yes No
Pages ....   13. Have you included, rather than merely incorporated by reference, all material facts from the documents in the request? Are they accompanied by an analysis of their bearing on the issues that specifies the document provisions that apply? See section 8.01(3).

Yes No
Pages ....   14. Have you included the required statement regarding whether the same issue in the letter ruling request is in an earlier return of the taxpayer or in a return for any year of a related taxpayer? See section 8.01(4).

Yes No
Pages ....   15. Have you included the required statement regarding whether the Service previously ruled on the same or similar issue for the taxpayer, a related taxpayer, or a predecessor? See section 8.01(5)(a).

Yes No
Pages ....   16. Have you included the required statement regarding whether the taxpayer, a related taxpayer, a predecessor, or any representatives previously submitted a request (including an application for change in accounting method) involving the same or similar issue but withdrew the request before the letter ruling or determination letter was issued? See section 8.01(5)(b).

Yes No
Pages ....   17. Have you included the required statement regarding whether the taxpayer, a related taxpayer, or a predecessor previously submitted a request (including an application for change in accounting method) involving the same or similar issue that is currently pending with the Service? See section 8.01(5)(c).

Yes No
Pages ....   18. Have you included the required statement regarding whether, at the same time as this request, the taxpayer or a related taxpayer is presently submitting another request (including an application for change in accounting method) involving the same or similar issue to the Service? See section 8.01(5)(d).

Yes No N/A
Pages ....   19. If your request involves the interpretation of a substantive provision of an income or estate tax treaty, have you included the required statement regarding whether the tax authority of the treaty jurisdiction has issued a ruling on the same or similar issue for the taxpayer, a related taxpayer, or a predecessor; whether the same or similar issue is being examined, or has been settled, by the tax authority of the treaty jurisdiction or is otherwise the subject of a closing agreement in that jurisdiction; and whether the same or similar issue is being considered by the competent authority of the treaty jurisdiction? See section 8.01(6).

CIRCLE ONE	ITEM
Yes No N/A Pages	20. If your request is for recognition of Indian tribal government status or status as a political subdivision of an Indian tribal government, does your request contain a letter from the Bureau of Indian Affairs regarding the tribe's status? See section 8.01(7), which states that taxpayers are encouraged to submit this letter with the request and provides the address for the Bureau of Indian Affairs.
Yes No Pages	21. Have you included the required statement of relevant authorities in support of your views? See section 8.01(8).
Yes No Pages	22. Have you included the required statement regarding whether the law in connection with the request is uncertain and whether the issue is adequately addressed by relevant authorities? See section 8.01(8).
Yes No Pages	23. Does your request discuss the implications of any legislation, tax treaties, court decisions, regulations, notices, revenue rulings, or revenue procedures that you determined to be contrary to the position advanced? See section 8.01(9), which states that taxpayers are encouraged to inform the Service of such authorities.
Yes No N/A Pages	24. If you determined that there are no contrary authorities, have you included a statement to this effect in your request? See section 8.01(9).
Yes No N/A Pages	25. Have you included in your request a statement identifying any pending legislation that may affect the proposed transaction? See section 8.01(10).
Yes No	26. Is the request accompanied by the deletions statement required by IRC § 6110? See section 8.01(11).
Yes No Pages	27. Have you (or your authorized representative) signed and dated the request? See section 8.01(12).
Yes No N/A	28. If the request is signed by your representative or if your representative will appear before the Service in connection with the request, is the request accompanied by a properly prepared and signed power of attorney with the signatory's name typed or printed? See section 8.01(14).
Yes No Pages	29. Have you included, signed, and dated the penalties of perjury statement in the format required by section 8.01(15)?
Yes No N/A	30. Are you submitting your request in duplicate if necessary? See section 8.01(16).
Yes No N/A Pages	31. If you are requesting separate letter rulings on different issues involving one factual situation, have you included a statement to that effect in each request? See section 8.02(1).
Yes No N/A	32. If you want copies of the letter ruling sent to more than one representative, does the power of attorney contain a statement to that effect? See section 8.02(2)(a).
Yes No N/A	33. If you want the original of the letter ruling to be sent to a representative, does the power of attorney contain a statement to that effect? See section 8.02(2)(b).

CIRCLE ONE	ITEM
Yes No N/A	34. If you do not want a copy of the letter ruling to be sent to any representative, does the power of attorney contain a statement to that effect? See section 8.02(2)(e).
Yes No N/A	35. If you are making a two-part letter ruling request have you included a summary statement of the facts you believe to be controlling? See section 8.02(3).
Yes No N/A Pages	36. If you want your letter ruling request to be processed ahead of the regular order or by a specific date, have you requested expedited handling in the manner required by section 8.02(4) and stated a compelling need for such action in the request?
Yes No Pages	37. If you are requesting a copy of any document related to the letter ruling request to be sent by facsimile (fax) transmission, have you included a statement to that effect? See section 8.02(5).
Yes No N/A Pages	38. If you want to have a conference on the issues involved in the request, have you included a request for conference in the letter ruling request? See section 8.02(7).
Yes No	39. Have you included the correct user fee with the request and is your check or money order in U.S. dollars and payable to the Internal Revenue Service? See section 15 and Appendix A to determine the correct amount.
Yes No N/A	40. If your request involves a personal tax issue and you qualify for the reduced user fee when gross income is less than $250,000, have you included the required certification? See paragraphs (A)(4)(a) and (B)(1) of Appendix A.
Yes No N/A Pages	41. If your request involves a business-related tax issue and you qualify for the reduced user fee when gross income is less than $1 million, have you included the required certification? See paragraphs (A)(4)(b) and (B)(1) of Appendix A.
Yes No N/A Pages	42. If you qualify for the user fee for substantially identical letter rulings, have you included the required information? See section 15.07(2) and paragraph (A)(5)(a) of Appendix A.
Yes No N/A Pages	43. If you qualify for the user fee for a Reg. § 301.9100 request to extend the time for filing an identical accounting method change on a single Form 3115, have you included the required information? See section 15.07(3) and paragraph (A)(5)(c) of Appendix A.
Yes No N/A	44. If your request is covered by any of the checklists, guideline revenue procedures, notices, safe harbor revenue procedures, or other special requirements listed in section 9, have you complied with all of the requirements of the applicable revenue procedure or notice?
Rev. Proc.	List other applicable revenue procedures or notices, including checklists, used or relied upon in the preparation of this letter ruling request (Cumulative Bulletin or Internal Revenue Bulletin citation not required).
Yes No N/A Pages	45. If you are requesting relief under IRC § 7805(b) (regarding retroactive effect), have you complied with all of the requirements in section 12.11?

CIRCLE ONE   **ITEM**

Yes No   46. Have you addressed your request to the attention of the
Associate Chief Counsel (Corporate), the Associate Chief
Counsel (Financial Institutions & Products), the Associate
Chief Counsel (Income Tax & Accounting), the Associate
Chief Counsel (International), the Associate Chief Counsel
(Passthroughs & Special Industries), the Associate Chief
Counsel (Procedure and Administration), or the Division
Counsel/Associate Chief Counsel (Tax Exempt and Govern-
ment Entities), as appropriate? The mailing address is:

Internal Revenue Service
Attn: CC:PA:T
PO Box 7604
Ben Franklin Station
Washington, DC   20044

However, if a private delivery service is used, the address is:

Internal Revenue Service
Attn: CC:PA:T, Room 6561
1111 Constitution Avenue, NW
Washington, DC   20224

The package should be marked: RULING REQUEST SUB-
MISSION. Improperly addressed requests may be delayed
(sometimes for over a week) in reaching CC:PA:T for initial
processing.

....
[*Signature*]   [*Title or Authority*]   [*Date*]

....
[*Typed or printed name of person signing checklist*]

[a] The Two-Part Ruling Request

An alternative procedure called the "two-part" ruling request may expedite the processing of a letter ruling request.[270] This procedure permits a taxpayer to submit, in the ruling request, both (1) a complete statement of facts relating to the transaction (together with related documents), and (2) a summary statement of the facts that the taxpayer believes should be control the issue or issues to be resolved by the requested ruling.[271] If the taxpayer's summary statement of controlling facts is accepted, the ruling is based on these facts, and only the summary statement is incorporated in the letter ruling. This alternative procedure can result in an expedited ruling because it simplifies the task of Service personnel. It does not, however, entitle the request to be given priority and thereby reviewed out of turn. Finally, despite the taxpayer's use of this alternative procedure, the Service reserves the right to rule on the basis of a more complete statement of facts it considers controlling and to seek further information developing facts and restating them for ruling purposes.

Use of the two-part ruling request is at the election of the taxpayer, and cannot be required by the Service. However, use of the two-part ruling request may not be elected where it is inconsistent with other procedures applicable to specific situations, such as requests for permission to change accounting methods or periods, applications for exemptions under Section 521, or rulings on employment tax status.

It should be noted that the taxpayer's rights and responsibilities under the two-part ruling request procedure are the same as under the normal ruling request procedure.

[b] Expedited Handling of Ruling Requests

Normally, ruling requests are processed in "regular order," which means in order of receipt. If a taxpayer has a "compelling need" to have a request for processing a ruling ahead of its regular order or by a specified time, the National Office will consider a request for expeditious handling. These requests are not favored because they delay the processing of other rulings. And, in any event, the National Office gives no assurance that the ruling request will be processed by the time requested.

A taxpayer that wishes expedited processing should make the request in a separate letter, with or shortly after filing the ruling request, that clearly de-

---

[270] 26 CFR § 601.201(e)(3); Rev. Proc. 2002-1, § 8.02(3), 1991-1 IRB 1, 30.

[271] Letter rulings made public under Section 6110 may be used as models for the two-part ruling request.

scribes the "compelling need" for such treatment.[272] Circumstances considered compelling are those that are beyond the control of the taxpayer and require the ruling to be issued by a particular time. Compelling circumstances do not include a closing date, or a directors' or shareholders' meeting, or any other occasion scheduled without regard to the time the National Office may need to process a ruling request, nor does it include the possible effect of stock market fluctuations on a transaction.

[5] Processing of Ruling Requests

Requests for letter rulings are processed initially by the Technical Services Staff of the Assistant Chief Counsel (Corporate), hence the address CC:DOM:CORP:TSS. The Technical Services Staff dates the request, examines the request for completeness, processes the user fee, and forwards the file to the appropriate Assistant Chief Counsel or, where the tax ruling request is not under the jurisdiction of the Associate Chief Counsel (Domestic), to the Office of the appropriate Associate Chief Counsel. From these offices, the ruling request is assigned to a branch.[273]

Once the branch receives the ruling request, the review process is as follows:

- Within twenty-one calendar days after the receipt of the request, a branch representative will contact the taxpayer or his representative to discuss informally the procedural and substantive issues involved in the ruling request.[274] Although the Service is not bound by any informal opinion to the representative, the branch representative will say whether (1) the representative will recommend that the Service rule favorably, adversely, or not at all; (2) further information should be submitted; and (3) a tentative conclusion about the ruling cannot be reached because of the nature of the transaction or issue. If something less than a fully favorable ruling is indicated, the branch representative can also indicate whether a modification of the transaction might warrant issuance of a favorable ruling, and, to that end, can offer a conference. This conference constitutes the taxpayer's right to a conference under the conference rules.

- If the letter ruling request involves matters within the jurisdiction of more than one branch or office, the branch representative will notify the

---

[272] Rev. Proc. 2002-1, § 8.02(4), 2002-1 IRB 1, 30–31. If the request for expeditious handling is not sent in a separate letter, the first page of the letter request should be headed "Expeditious Handling Is Requested. See page — of this letter."

[273] Rev. Proc. 2002-1, § 10, 2002-1 IRB 1, 42–46.

[274] Rev. Proc. 2002-1, § 10.02, 2002-1 IRB 1, 42.

taxpayer within the twenty-one-day period that matters within the jurisdiction of the other branch or office have been referred to that branch
or office, and that the other branch or office will contact the taxpayer
within twenty-one calendar days after the referral to discuss informally
procedural and substantive issues.

- Also within twenty-one days, the branch representative will inform the
taxpayer if the representative cannot recommend the ruling that the taxpayer has requested, but will say whether the taxpayer can modify the
transaction to obtain a favorable letter ruling. Although the representative will not recommend or suggest specific changes "that would materially alter the form of the transaction," the representative will say
whether a more favorable ruling will be given if the taxpayer makes
minor changes or follows positions the Service has published.[275] If the
branch representative decides that it would be helpful, the representative
is also permitted to offer a meeting in the National Office to develop or
exchange information with the taxpayer or the taxpayer's representative.[276]

- Informal opinions that the branch representative expresses during this
process are not binding on the Service, nor will they provide any basis
for a taxpayer's obtaining retroactive relief from an unfavorable ruling
under Section 7805(b).

- During the initial contact with the taxpayer, if the ruling request does
not comply with all the National Office's requirements for a ruling request, the branch representative will inform the taxpayer which requirements have not been met.

- If the request omitted "essential information" (including information
needed to satisfy some procedural requirement of the ruling request revenue procedure and substantive changes to the transaction or the documents), the branch representative will advise the taxpayer or the
taxpayer's representative that the missing documentation must be supplied within twenty-one days or the ruling request will be closed.[277]

- When additional information is furnished to the National Office by telephone or telecopier, the information must be confirmed promptly by let-

---

[275] Rev. Proc. 2002-1, § 9.03, 2002-1 IRB 1, 40–42.

[276] Rev. Proc. 2002-1, § 9.03, 2002-1 IRB 1, 40–42. This conference is in addition to
the taxpayer's conference of right in the National Office if the representative says that an
adverse ruling is contemplated.

[277] Rev. Proc. 2002-1, § 10.06, 2002-1 IRB 1, 43–44. This twenty-one-day period
may be extended if the taxpayer justifies the additional time in writing, and the branch
chief of the branch to which the ruling request is assigned approves; certain other senior
staff may approve the extension request as well.

ter to the National Office with an "under penalties of perjury" declaration.[278]

- A conference of right in the National Office is offered to the taxpayer if an adverse ruling is contemplated. Near the completion of the ruling process, after the conference of right is held, but before the National Office issues the ruling, the branch representative will inform the taxpayer or the taxpayer's representative of the branch's conclusion on whether the ruling will still be adverse.[279] If the ruling will be adverse, the taxpayer is given the opportunity to withdraw the ruling.

- When the ruling process is nearly complete, the branch representative may request, in order to accelerate the issuance of the ruling, that the taxpayer submit a proposed draft of the letter ruling based on discussions between the taxpayer and the branch representative.[280]

After the Service has reviewed the facts stated in the ruling request and thoroughly researched the issues raised by those facts, a draft ruling is prepared for review by the branch chief and other personnel within the division. The ruling is then signed by the branch chief, although there may be an additional random review done by the Assistant Chief Counsel. As with any project where the result may be in conflict with another official statement by the Service, such as an Action on Decision or a previous Tax Litigation or field office opinion, there may be referrals to the Assistant Chief Counsel (Litigation). Projects involving subject matters and Code sections exclusively within the jurisdiction of the Assistant Chief Counsel (General Litigation) get

---

[278] Rev. Proc. 2002-1, § 10.07, 2002-1 IRB 1, 44–45. Generally, one copy of the information is sent. The address used to send additional information to the branch representative differs from the ruling request address in including the name, office symbols, and room number of the representative who requested the information. The taxpayer's name and the case control number. When a private delivery service is not used, the additional information is sent to Internal Revenue Service, ADDITIONAL INFORMATION, Attn: [Name, office symbols, and room number of the branch representative who requested the information], P.O. Box 7604, Ben Franklin Station, Washington, D.C. 20044. If a private delivery service is used, the address is Internal Revenue Service, ADDITIONAL INFORMATION, Attn: [Name, office symbols, and room number of the Service representative who requested the information], 1111 Constitution Avenue, N.W., Washington, D.C. 20224.

[279] Rev. Proc. 2002-1, § 10.09, 2002-1 IRB 1, 46.

[280] Rev. Proc. 2002-1, § 10.09, 2002-1 IRB 1, 46. The format, facts, analysis, and letter language for the draft is supposed to be discussed with the branch representative, and, in fact, the representative may provide a sample form of a letter ruling. In addition to a typed draft, the taxpayer is encouraged to submit, on computer disk, an electronic file of the draft. The draft in both formats is sent to the representative, along with an executed "under penalties of perjury" statement, to the same address as any additional information.

mandatory referrals to that Counsel.[281] After signing, the branch chief mails the ruling to the taxpayer and the taxpayer's representative, with a copy to the appropriate district director.[282]

Letter rulings actually issued by the National Office must be in the form desired and requested by the taxpayer. The taxpayer should examine the letter ruling to determine whether any mistakes or omissions have been made. Any mistake or omission should be communicated to the National Office for the purpose of obtaining the appropriate change in the ruling.

[a] Conferences

The National Office grants a conference to taxpayers or their representatives whose request for a ruling is being considered on its merits. If the taxpayer requests a conference in the National Office, the National Office will agree if it considers a conference helpful in deciding the issues. However, the taxpayer is entitled to a conference if the branch has tentatively decided to issue an adverse ruling to any extent.[283]

When the taxpayer requests a conference, the request must be made in writing, with or shortly after the ruling request is filed, and must be accompanied by an explanation of why a conference would be helpful in considering the request.[284] In general, a taxpayer is entitled to only one conference in the National Office as a matter of right.[285] This conference usually is held at the branch level of the appropriate division, and is to be attended by a person who has authority to act for the branch chief.[286] To ensure that there is an informed discussion of the issues, the conference is generally held only after the branch has had an opportunity to study the ruling request. However, at the taxpayer's request, a conference may be held at an earlier stage in the review process. No

---

[281] IRM, Chief Counsel Directive Manual 39(172), MT (39)-4 (Aug. 2, 1996) (Referrals to Litigation).

[282] A letter ruling may also be sent by facsimile if the taxpayer requests it, but the letter ruling is not actually issued until the date that it is mailed. Rev. Proc. 2002-1, § 8.02(5)(a), 2002-1 IRB 1, 31. Rulings are mailed directly to the authorized representative if the power of attorney or authorization specifically provides. If there is no specific provision to this effect, a copy is furnished to the taxpayer. Where two or more representatives are designated, the Service sends copies to the representative first named on the power or authorization that reflects the latest date, but, in any event, no more than two representatives will be sent copies. Rev. Proc. 2002-1, § 8.02(2), 2002-1 IRB 1, 29–30.

[283] 26 CFR § 601.201(f)(1); Rev. Proc. 2002-1, § 11.01, 2002-1 IRB 1, 46–47.

[284] Rev. Proc. 2002-1, § 11.01, 2002-1 IRB 1, 46–47.

[285] 26 CFR § 601.201(f)(2); Rev. Proc. 2002-1, § 11.02, 2002-1 IRB 1, 47. There are certain limited exceptions to the "one-conference" rule.

[286] Rev. Proc. 2002-1, § 11.02, 2002-1 IRB 1, 47.

taxpayer has a right to appeal the action of the branch to an Associate Chief Counsel or any other office in the Service.[287]

Second conferences with the taxpayer or the taxpayer's representative are granted under certain circumstances, for example, where (1) the branch's final answer will reverse a position initially advanced by the branch, and the new position will be less favorable to the taxpayer, or (2) an adverse decision proposed by a branch will become the Service's ruling position, but on either a newer, different issue or grounds substantially different from those on which the branch initially formulated its position. Moreover, provisions limiting the number of conferences to which a taxpayer is entitled do not foreclose an invitation to attend further conferences where, in the opinion of the National Office personnel, a need for such conferences arises.

The conference procedure is relatively simple and informal. If a conference has been requested, the taxpayer is notified of the time and place of the conference. It must be held within twenty-one days after that taxpayer has been contacted concerning the conference; if requested, the Service may grant an extension of this twenty-one-day period.[288] Generally, conferences are conducted in an informal manner for the purpose of discussing the arguments for and against the proposed ruling, and, for this reason, no recording of the conference is permitted.[289] Although a presentation of the relevant facts has already been made in the original ruling request, the conference offers a taxpayer the opportunity to develop or amplify facts not fully presented in the request or to cite new or additional authority not explored in the request. Of course, any new facts discussed and any new authority cited at the conference must be documented for inclusion in the Service's case file so that such new matters may be considered by the branch representative in the preparation of the proposed ruling. It should be noted that, while the Service's representative prepares a conference memorandum, it is the taxpayer's responsibility to furnish (within twenty-one days after the conference) a written record of any new or additional data, lines of reasoning, precedents, and the like presented at the conference, but not previously or adequately presented by the taxpayer in a prior written submission to the Service.

---

[287] The taxpayer may request an additional conference, however. See Rev. Proc. 2002-1, § 11.05, 2002-1 IRB 1, 47–48.

[288] Rev. Proc. 2002-1, § 11.01, 2002-1 IRB 1, 46–47. Normally, the National Office schedules a conference only if it "considers it to be helpful in deciding the case or when an adverse decision is indicated." Id. Normally, the National Office schedules a conference only if it "considers it to be helpful in deciding the case or when an adverse decision is indicated." Id.

[289] Rev. Proc. 2002-1, § 11.03, 2002-1 IRB 1, 47.

[b] Withdrawal of a Ruling Request

The taxpayer's request for a ruling may be withdrawn at any time prior to the signing of the letter of reply.[290] Withdrawing a letter ruling request should be a strategic consideration when the reasons for filing the request have been defeated or frustrated. For example, if the transaction proposed in the request has been completed or canceled, it may be appropriate to withdraw the request because the harm of an adverse ruling may outweigh the benefit of a favorable ruling. For similar reasons, withdrawal is appropriate where the National Office has delayed issuing the ruling. Withdrawal also should be considered if the Service has indicated that an unfavorable ruling would be issued because of (1) the discovery of new or additional facts or (2) changes in law or Service policy. There is no judicial review of an adverse ruling, except in those limited cases where a declaratory judgment procedure has been provided.

If a ruling request is withdrawn, the National Office will notify, and "may" furnish its views to, the district director whose office has or will have audit jurisdiction over the taxpayer's return.[291] The likelihood that the National Office will communicate its views to the district director is greater where the transaction is completed or the district director believes that the taxpayer will complete a proposed transaction. On the other hand, the National Office will not notify the district director if (1) the taxpayer submits, in addition to the withdrawal notice, a written statement to the National Office that the transaction has been or will be abandoned, and (2) the National Office has not formed an adverse opinion to the ruling sought by the taxpayer.[292]

When the National Office communicates with the district director about the withdrawal, it does so by memorandum, and the district can consider this information in any subsequent examination of the taxpayer's return. If this memorandum (1) explains the National Office's reasoning for an adverse position it would have taken on the issues in the request, and (2) acknowledges that the memorandum would constitute Chief Counsel Advice, the taxpayer should be able to obtain a copy of this memorandum under Section 6110(i).

Despite the withdrawal of a request, the National Office will not return the taxpayer's correspondence and exhibits provided to the National Office in the request process,[293] nor will it refund the user fee the taxpayer paid with the request.[294] Furthermore, where appropriate, the subject matter of the ruling request may be published as a revenue ruling or revenue procedure.

---

[290] 26 CFR § 601.201(j); Rev. Proc. 2002-1, § 8.07(1), 2002-1 IRB 1, 34. The ruling request may be withdrawn by a letter stating this fact sent to the same address as the ruling request.

[291] Rev. Proc. 2002-1, § 8.07(2)(b), 2002-1 IRB 1, 34.

[292] Rev. Proc. 2002-1, § 8.07(2)(b), 2002-1 IRB 1, 34.

[293] Rev. Proc. 2002-1, § 8.07(1), 2002-1 IRB 1, 34.

[294] Rev. Proc. 2002-1, § 8.07(3), 2002-1 IRB 1, 34.

[c] Closing Agreements

A closing agreement is the only statutorily authorized agreement between the Service and a taxpayer on a specific issue or liability that is final and binding on the Service, absent a showing of the taxpayer's fraud, malfeasance, or misrepresentation of material fact. A closing agreement may result from the letter ruling request process if either (1) the taxpayer or the National Office desires the tax result to be conclusively resolved or (2) the taxpayer can show that there are good reasons for an agreement and that making the agreement will not prejudice the interests of the Service.[295] Closing agreements are not generally used and, because of their finality, the National Office does not encourage their use. Nevertheless, they do have some utility in the ruling request process. Closing agreements also serve a function in the examination, collection, and appeals processes. Because closing agreements procedures are included in the appeals part of the Internal Revenue Manual, they are discussed more fully in Chapter 9, dealing with the Appeals process.

[6] The Legal Effect of Letter Rulings

A taxpayer who requested a letter ruling from the National Office may rely on the letter ruling the taxpayer received, and a district office must follow the letter ruling in determining the taxpayer's liability.[296] With the publication of redacted letter rulings, the public has access to the text of letter rulings issued to the taxpayers who have requested them, but (for the reasons discussed below) only the taxpayer who received the ruling may rely on it.[297]

However, even in the case of the taxpayer who received the ruling, the district offices do automatically follow the tax treatment prescribed by the National Office in the ruling. Before the taxpayer's adoption and use of the ruling will be approved, the district office will determine whether (1) the taxpayer has properly applied the ruling; (2) the representations made by the taxpayer in obtaining the ruling were accurate and supported by later events; (3) the transaction was carried out substantially as described in the ruling; and (4) there has been any change in the law that applies to the period during which the transaction or a continuing series of transactions was consummated. If the district's determination indicates that the ruling should be modified or revoked, the district's findings and recommendations are sent to the National Office for further action.[298]

---

[295] Rev. Proc. 2002-1, § 2.02, 2002-1 IRB 1, 9.

[296] Rev. Proc. 2002-1, § 12.03, 2002-1 IRB 1, 49–50.

[297] IRC § 6110(k)(3).

[298] Rev. Proc. 2002-1, § 12.02, 2002-1 IRB 1, 49.

Moreover, a letter ruling is the Service's conclusion about the application of the tax law (1) to the particular transaction described in the ruling request and (2) for the purposes of determining the liability of the taxpayer requesting the ruling. Consequently, a ruling issued to a taxpayer is "a holding of the Service on that transaction only,"[299] and one taxpayer may not rely on a letter ruling issued to another taxpayer.[300]

It should be noted that a letter ruling is not binding on the Service. The only statutorily recognized agreement binding on the Service is a closing agreement under Section 7121. As a result, a ruling may be modified or revoked retroactively unless the Commissioner exercises discretion under Section 7805(b) to apply the revocation prospectively. The effect of the "particular transaction" and "specific taxpayer" elements of a ruling and the problem of retroactive revocation are discussed in the following sections.

[a] The "Particular Transaction" Element

Because a letter ruling is a holding on the particular facts set forth, it is binding on a district office only if the district has first determined that (1) the ruling has been properly applied by the taxpayer; (2) the representations made by the taxpayer in obtaining the ruling were accurate and supported by later events; (3) the transaction was carried out substantially as proposed; and (4) there has been no material change in the law that applies to the period during which the transaction or continuing series of transactions was consummated.[301]

The taxpayer who receives the ruling is not permitted to rely on it when (1) there has been a misstatement or omission or material fact in the ruling request[302]; (2) the ruling has been issued on a different tax[303]; or (3) there is failure to comply with a condition of the ruling.[304]

---

[299] Rev. Proc. 2002-1, § 12.01, 2002-1 IRB 1, 49.

[300] Rev. Proc. 2002-1, § 12.02, 2002-1 IRB 1, 49.

[301] 26 CFR § 601.201(e)(2); Rev. Proc. 2002-1, § 12.03, 2002-1 IRB 1, 49–50. If the district believes that a ruling issued to a taxpayer should be modified, the district's findings and recommendations are forwarded to the National Office, and the matter is treated as a request for technical advice.

[302] See Stevens Bros. Found., Inc. v. Comm'r, 39 TC 93, 106 (1962), rev'd and remanded on another issue, 324 F2d 633 (8th Cir. 1963), cert. denied, 376 US 969 (1964); Colombo Club, Inc. v. Comm'r, 54 TC 100, 107 (1970), aff'd, 447 F2d 1406 (9th Cir. 1971).

[303] Mid-Ridge Inv. Co. v. United States, 214 F. Supp. 8, 14 (ED Wis.), aff'd on another issue, 324 F2d 945 (7th Cir. 1963) (ruling on documentary stamp tax inapplicable to income tax).

[304] Gerli & Co. v. Comm'r, 73 TC 1019, 1027 (1980) (failure to comply with condition on Section 367 ruling). The Tax Court's decision in Gerli & Co. was reversed by the Second Circuit, 668 F2d 691 (1982), but on the ground that the condition or toll charge

[b] The "Specific Taxpayer" Element

Only the taxpayer to whom the ruling was issued may rely upon it; this is the "specific taxpayer" element. Other taxpayers may gain some guidance from the Service's analysis of the issues involved, but are not entitled to rely upon a letter ruling issued to another taxpayer.[305] Furthermore, letter rulings, although made public under Section 6110, may not be relied on as precedent.[306] Courts nevertheless have considered them "interpretations put upon the statute by the agency charged with the responsibility of administering the revenue laws."[307] In practice, letter rulings have some status as guides to National Office interpretations, and Service employees consider them in issuing letter rulings to similarly situated taxpayers.[308]

There is a limited exception to the general rule that a taxpayer may not rely on a letter ruling issued to another taxpayer. That exception arises because, as discussed below, the Service generally cannot treat similarly situated taxpayers differently, especially when it results in granting the taxpayer receiving the initial ruling an economic or competitive advantage over the other taxpayer. Accordingly, where the result of denying the tax treatment specified in the ruling to another taxpayer (who requested a similar ruling) would be to apply the internal revenue laws in favor of the taxpayer who received the first ruling to the disadvantage of the other taxpayer, the Service may be required to issue the same ruling to both taxpayers.[309]

As a general principle, the Commissioner is not permitted to tax one taxpayer and not another without some rational basis for the difference.[310] Justice

---

the Service imposed was unreasonable and unlawful. Consequently, failure to comply with the condition did not prevent tax-free treatment.

[305] Minchin v. Comm'r, 335 F2d 30, 33 (2d Cir. 1964); Weller v. Comm'r, 270 F2d 294, 298–299 (3d Cir. 1959), cert. denied, 364 US 908 (1960); Goodstein v. Comm'r, 267 F2d 127, 132 (1st Cir. 1959); 26 CFR § 601.201(e)(6).

[306] IRC § 6110(k)(3).

[307] Hanover Bank v. Comm'r, 369 US 672, 686 (1962).

[308] See Ogiony v. Comm'r, 617 F2d 14, 17 (2d Cir.) (concurring opinion), cert denied, 449 US 900 (1980); Tax Analysts & Advocates v. IRS, 362 F. Supp. 1298, 1306 (DDC 1973), modified in part and remanded in part, 505 F2d 350 (DC Cir. 1974).

[309] For further discussion of the principle of equality applicable to administrative agencies, see Chapter 1.

[310] See United States v. Kaiser, 363 US 299, 308 (1960). See also Ogiony v. Comm'r, 617 F2d 14, 18 (2d Cir.) (concurring opinion), cert. denied, 449 US 900 (1980); Sirbo Holdings, Inc. v. Comm'r, 476 F2d 981, 987 (2d Cir. 1973) ("the Commissioner has a duty of consistency toward similarly situated taxpayers"); Bunce v. United States, 28 Fed. Cl. 500, 508 (1993) ("A duty of administrative consistency certainly exists; the tax laws must be interpreted and applied as uniformly as possible" (footnote reference omitted)).

Frankfurter's statement in his concurring opinion in *Kaiser* is the most frequently cited expression of this principle:[311]

> The Commissioner cannot tax one and not tax another without some rational basis for the difference. And so, assuming the correctness of the principle of "equality," it can be an independent ground of decision that the Commissioner has been inconsistent, without much concern for whether we should hold as an original matter that the position that the Commissioner now seeks to sustain is wrong.

Discriminatory, unequal treatment has been found where the taxpayer who received a ruling was granted an unfair competitive advantage over another taxpayer in the same industry.[312] In *IBM*, Remington-Rand received a letter ruling that certain computers were not subject to excise tax. When IBM learned of this ruling, it applied for a ruling that its computers were not taxable. IBM's ruling request was not acted on for almost two and one-half years, and was finally rejected. Shortly thereafter, Remington-Rand's ruling was revoked prospectively. As a result, from the date Remington-Rand received its ruling until the date that the ruling was withdrawn, IBM was required to collect excise tax, which increased the cost of its equipment, while its competitor Remington-Rand was not required to collect excise tax. The Court of Claims held that the Commissioner had unjustly discriminated against IBM.

On the other hand, it has been held that discrimination does *not* exist where the party claiming to have been discriminated against has failed to make a ruling request seeking the same ruling since that taxpayer is entitled only to the same treatment as similarly situated taxpayers (i.e., those without rulings).[313] In *Bornstein*, a shareholder of six substantially identical corporations

---

[311] United States v. Kaiser, 363 US 299, 308 (1960).

[312] International Business Mach. Corp. v. United States, 343 F2d 914 (Ct. Cl. 1965). See also Oshkosh Truck Corp. v. United States, 123 F3d 1477, 1481 (Fed. Cir. 1997) (under temporary regulations, Service imposed excise tax applying a four percent mark-up on sales of taxpayer's trucks when taxpayer's sales were indistinguishable from sales of trailers, semitrailers, tractors, and similar vehicles which were exempt from the mark-up; held: the Service abused its discretion in treating the taxpayer differently).

[313] Bornstein v. United States, 345 F2d 558 (Ct. Cl. 1965); Goodstein v. Comm'r, 267 F2d 127, 132 (1st Cir. 1959). See also Knetsch v. United States, 348 F2d 932, 940 (Ct. Cl. 1965) ("Insofar as taxpayers' contention is that there is prejudicial discrimination because of a difference in treatment in favor of those who received and relied upon private rulings issued to them as against the instant taxpayers who neither applied for, nor received, a ruling of their own but relied solely on the private ruling issued to other taxpayers, we think there is not merit to such a contention"); Carpenter v. United States, 7 Cl. Ct. 732, 740–741 (1985) (distinguishing IBM, 343 F2d 914 (Ct. Cl. 1965), where there was no request for a private ruling from the taxpayer or any similarly situated taxpayer); Baker v. United States, 748 F2d 1465, 1469 n.9 (11th Cir. 1984) (favorably citing *Knetsch*); Bookwalter v. Brecklein, 357 F2d 78, 84–85 (9th Cir. 1966) ("the Commissioner's decision was based on rational administrative considerations and was not intended

involved in the construction of apartment houses. financed by the Federal Housing Administration, applied for a ruling for one of the six corporations on the basis of advice given by an official assigned to draft the ruling. The ruling granted to the sole applying corporation (i.e., that its distributions would receive capital gain treatment) was not by its terms applicable to the remaining five corporations, which had neither requested nor received any ruling. The Court of Claims refused to find discrimination, and distinguished the *IBM* case on the ground that IBM had made a prompt application to obtain a private ruling to the same effect as Remington-Rand, whereas, in *Bornstein*, the five affected corporations had not asked for rulings.

The specific taxpayer receiving the ruling may rely on the National Office's written advice, and any penalty attributable to tax positions taken in justifiable reliance on this advice must be abated. However, for this reliance to be justified, the taxpayer must have (1) specifically requested the advice in writing; (2) provided adequate or accurate information; and (3) reasonably relied on the advice.[314]

[c] Retroactive Revocation

As a matter of policy and practice, a letter ruling is binding on district offices. However, no statement by any official of the Service other than a closing agreement entered into under Section 7121 legally binds the Service. Except to the extent that it is incorporated in a closing agreement, therefore, the Service may revoke or modify a letter ruling at any time that it finds the ruling to be in error or not consistent with the Service's then current views.[315]

According to its published standards, the National Office may, upon sending a notice to the taxpayer to whom the letter ruling was issued, revoke or modify a letter ruling on the ground that such revocation or modification is required by any one of the following post-ruling events: (1) legislation; (2) ratification of a tax treaty; (3) a Supreme Court decision; (4) promulgation of temporary or final regulations (but not a notice of proposed rulemaking); and (5) publication of a revenue ruling, revenue procedure, notice, or other state-

---

to be nor actually was discriminatory to appellee in regard to others in his situation—i.e., those who had not desired to nor actually did not receive private rulings prior to paying taxes on the assessments").

[314] IRC § 6404(f) (effective for advice requested after December 31, 1988). See Reg. § 301.6404-3.

[315] 26 CFR §§ 601.201(l)(1), 601.201(l)(5); Rev. Proc. 2002-1, § 12.04, 2002-1 IRB 1, 50. For the Service's procedures on the withdrawal of rulings and on the notification of taxpayers, see IRM Chief Counsel Directive Manual (39)633.61 (Nov. 13, 1996) (Nonretroactivity of Rulings General), (39)633.62 (Means of Revoking or Modifying a Previously Issued Ruling), (39)633.63 (General Rule for Nonretroactive Application), (39)633.64 (Application of Nonretroactivity to Particular Transactions).

ment in the Internal Revenue Bulletin. Since the Service is not bound by its own private letter rulings, the above criteria for revocation or modification of a ruling are required to prevent the Service's letter ruling program from being undermined.

If the Service revokes or modifies a ruling, the revocation or modification applies to all years open for assessment purposes, unless the Service, under Section 7805(b), exercises its discretion to apply the revocation or modification prospectively only. Under the Service's current policy, the Service generally exercises this discretion. Accordingly, revocations or modifications are given retroactive application only in "rare and unusual circumstances."[316] Although the Service has not stated what constitutes "rare and unusual circumstances," the Service has indicated that a ruling will be revoked or modified prospectively if

- There was no misstatement or omission of a material fact in the ruling request;
- The facts subsequently developed by the district do not materially differ from the facts submitted in the ruling request;
- There is no change in applicable law;
- The ruling was originally issued for a proposed transaction; and
- The taxpayer acted in good faith in relying on the ruling, and revocation would cause the taxpayer to suffer an unexpected detriment. (Sometimes, the reliance and detriment of a person other than the taxpayer who applied for the ruling may provide the basis for nonretroactivity. For example, a corporation's reorganization ruling will generally not be retroactively revoked or modified where its shareholders justifiably relied on the ruling[317]; on the other hand, the reliance of a member of an industry, who was not directly involved in a ruling issued to another industry member, may not be sufficient to support nonretroactivity for a ruling.)

If these conditions are met, a revocation or modification of the ruling will not be effective before the date the original ruling was modified or revoked, even if the original ruling covered a continuing action or series of actions.[318] These conditions generally are declarative of the law regarding whether retroactive revocation constitutes an abuse of the Commissioner's discretion under Section 7805(b).

A taxpayer may ask the Service to exercise its authority under Section 7805(b) by applying a revocation or modification of a previously issued ruling

---

[316] 26 CFR § 601.201(l)(5); Rev. Proc. 2002-1, § 12.05, 2002-1 IRB 1, 50–51.

[317] Rev. Proc. 2002-1, § 12.05(5), 2002-1 IRB 1, 51. It appears that these examples are intended to reflect the decision of the *Bornstein* case, discussed above.

[318] 26 CFR § 601.201(l)(7); Rev. Proc. 2002-1, § 12.07, 2002-1 IRB 1, 51.

prospectively only—what the Service calls a request to limit the retroactive effect of any revocation or modification of the letter ruling.[319] The request is made to the appropriate Associate Chief Counsel, using a letter in the same form as a request for a letter ruling. In addition to stating that the request is being made under Section 7805(b) and the relief sought, the request must explain the reasons and set forth the arguments for the relief requested, as well as apply the five factors described above to the facts of the particular situation.[320]

Retroactive revocation of a ruling does not amount to an abuse of the Commissioner's discretion where there has been a misrepresentation or omission of material facts on which the issuance of a ruling is based.[321] The issue in such cases in one of fact: namely, was the Service fully and correctly informed, at the time the ruling was issued, as to the material facts of the matter alleged to be the basis for revocation? If the Service was not adequately informed, the ruling may be revoked retroactively. The rationale for permitting revocation has been said to be that "the taxpayer himself is estopped from relying on the ruling in good faith because he has concealed or misrepresented the facts."[322] Retroactive revocation of a ruling usually is justified by the Commissioner on the ground that he is correcting a mistake of law. In this case, it is well established that the Commissioner has the authority to revoke a ruling retroactively.

---

[319] Rev. Proc. 2002-1, § 12.11, 2002-1 IRB 1, 52–53. The request may be made at different times. It may be included in the ruling request itself, made in response to a revenue ruling that has the effect of revoking the letter ruling, or some notice of the Service's change of position, or during an examination (in which case the request is made in the form of a request for technical advice).

[320] Rev. Proc. 2002-1, § 12.11, 2002-1 IRB 1, 52–53. The taxpayer must also include documents bearing on the request.

[321] Colombo Club, Inc. v. Comm'r, 54 TC 100, 107 (1970), aff'd, 447 F2d 1406 (9th Cir. 1971); Birmingham Business College, Inc. v. Comm'r, 276 F2d 476, 482 (5th Cir. 1960); Stevens Bros. Found., Inc. v. Comm'r, 39 TC 93, 106 (1962), rev'd and remanded on another issue, 324 F2d 633 (8th Cir. 1963), cert. denied, 376 US 969 (1964). The Claims Court has adopted the view that the Service's decision not to make a ruling retroactive is reviewed only for an abuse of discretion; no abuse of discretion would exist where retroactivity would work a change in settled law relied on by taxpayers and implicitly approved by Congress, lead to inequality of treatment between similarly situated taxpayers, and create harsh results). Mulholland v. United States, 16 Cl. Ct. 252, 89-1 USTC ¶ 9161 (1989). The Tax Court has held that there is no due process right to a prerevocation hearing when a favorable exempt-organization letter ruling is retroactively revoked. United Cancer Council, Inc. v. Comm'r, 100 TC 162, 167 (1993) [later proceedings].

[322] However, where there has been a good-faith attempt at compliance, the National Office has held that a recapitalization qualified as a reorganization despite the fact that the consummated transaction was not identical to its description as contained in a previously approved letter ruling. See, e.g., Priv. Ltr. Rul. 8308008.

In *Automobile Club of Michigan*,[323] the taxpayer received letter rulings in 1934 and 1938 that stated it was exempt from taxation as a "club," and therefore need not file tax returns. As a result, the taxpayer did not file returns or pay taxes for the years 1933 through 1945. The Commissioner had also issued general statements to the public that similar automobile clubs were exempt from tax. In 1943, the Commissioner changed his position, publicly stating that clubs (such as the taxpayer) were subject to tax. In 1945, the Commissioner revoked the taxpayer's exemption retroactively to 1943, the date of his public change of position. The Supreme Court held that the Commissioner was not estopped from revoking the club's ruling, and implicitly recognized the Commissioner's authority to revoke a ruling retroactively to correct a mistake of law. Later, the Supreme Court, in *Dixon v. United States*,[324] upheld the retroactive revocation of an acquiescence, and articulated a rationale justifying all retroactive corrections of mistakes of law, whether in regulations, rulings, or acquiescences. The rationale is that an erroneous statement of law is a nullity and without legal effect, since only Congress (and not the Commissioner) is charged with prescribing the tax laws. In other words, an agency's erroneous statement or application of law has no legal effect. As such, the revocation or modification of such position is simply official recognition that the prior statement was of no legal effect from the time it was initially issued.[325]

Despite the fact that the Commissioner may without reservation correct a mistake of law, in certain cases, retroactive revocation of a ruling may nevertheless constitute an abuse of his discretion under Section 7805(b). Under these circumstances, an abuse of discretion may occur where (1) the revocation arises only because different inferences have been drawn from the same facts presented in the initial ruling request; (2) the revocation would cause a taxpayer who relied on the ruling unusual hardship; and (3) the revocation results in discrimination in favor of one taxpayer over another.

In *Automobile Club*, the Supreme Court cited, with apparent approval, a number of cases where the Commissioner had attempted an improper correction of a mistaken inference of fact. In one of these cases, *Woodworth v. Kales*,[326] it was held that the Commissioner could not assess additional tax based on a revaluation of stock merely because of a new view of the same evidence that was based on a "matured and better judgment."

---

[323] Automobile Club of Mich. v. Comm'r, 353 US 180 (1957).

[324] Dixon v. United States, 381 US 68, 72–73 (1965). See also Dickman v. Comm'r, 465 US 330, 342–343 (1984) (claimed reliance on administrative practice).

[325] The "mistake of law" basis for revoking a ruling has been criticized where there has been no misrepresentation of fact in the ruling request and no change in the applicable law. Etter Grain Co. v. United States, 462 F2d 259, 265 (5th Cir. 1972) (concurring opinion).

[326] Woodworth v. Kales, 26 F2d 178, 180–181 (6th Cir. 1928).

A retroactive revocation of a ruling may also constitute an abuse of discretion where the taxpayer supplied all of the relevant facts to the Commissioner and there has been no change in the facts since the ruling was requested. In *Automobile Club*, the Supreme Court recognized that the Commissioner's discretionary authority under Section 7805(b) might be abused when the Commissioner retroactively revokes a letter ruling when there has been no change in the relevant facts. The Court stated that "the Commissioner's action may not be disturbed unless, in the circumstances of the case, the Commissioner abused the discretion vested in him by [the predecessor of Section 7805(b)]."[327]

Additionally, abuse of discretion has been found where (1) a taxpayer has undertaken extensive activities in reliance on a ruling, (2) the taxpayer will suffer an economic loss from the retroactive revocation of the ruling, and (3) that loss results as a consequence of the taxpayer's reliance on the ruling.[328] Mere loss of the favorable tax benefits endorsed by the earlier ruling is not alone sufficient, however.

Abuse of discretion also may be found where any of the following results in discrimination in favor of one taxpayer over another: (1) retroactive application of a letter ruling, (2) retroactive revocation of a letter ruling, or (3) in appropriate cases, a failure to retroactively revoke a letter ruling after other similar rulings have been retroactively revoked.[329]

After enactment of the Taxpayer Bill of Rights 2, the Treasury's authority to issue regulations having retroactive effect is limited. Where retroactive effect may be accorded, however, the Service is permitted to prescribe the extent to which a ruling will be applied retroactively.[330]

---

[327] Automobile Club of Mich. v. Comm'r, 353 US 180, 184 (1957) (no abuse of Commissioner's discretion because retroactive revocation applied only to tax years occurring after he published a notice of the change in position and all taxpayers similarly situated had been similarly treated).

[328] See HSD Co. v. Kavanagh, 191 F2d 831 (6th Cir. 1951) (pension plan); Lesavoy Found. v. Comm'r, 238 F2d 589, 592 (3d Cir. 1956) (retroactive revocation of charitable exemption barred when claimed deficiency would have exceeded taxpayer's assets). Compare Manocchio v. Comm'r, 78 TC 989, 1002 (1982) (failure to apply revenue ruling prospectively held not abuse of discretion), aff'd, 710 F2d 1400 (9th Cir. 1983); Boggs v. Comm'r, 784 F2d 1166, 1171 (4th Cir. 1986) (changes in facts held to be immaterial, and therefore revocation was an abuse of discretion). See also Nolan & Thuroniyi, "Retroactive Application of Changes in IRS or Treasury Department Position," 61 Taxes 777 (1983).

[329] Farmers' & Merchants' Bank v. United States, 476 F2d 406, 409 (4th Cir. 1973) (retroactive application of Revenue Ruling 68-630 held abuse of discretion); International Business Machine Corp. v. United States, 343 F2d 914, 923–925 (Ct. Cl. 1965).

[330] IRC § 7805(b)(8) (1996).

¶ 3.04 OTHER STATEMENTS OF IRS POSITION AND PRACTICE

[1] Revenue Procedures

The Service's policy is to publish, in the Internal Revenue Bulletin, statements of procedure that affect the rights and duties of taxpayers or other members of the public.[331] Revenue procedures usually are approved for issuance by the Associate Chief Counsel (Technical), Associate Chief Counsel (International), and Assistant Commissioner (EP/EO), but they are cleared with (and sometimes may even be initiated by) other Assistant Commissioners whose operations are affected.[332]

While revenue procedures usually reflect the contents of the Service's internal management documents, they are also published to announce practices and procedures for the guidance of the public. As a matter of practice, the published procedure includes as much of the Service's internal management document as is necessary for explanatory purposes. Revenue procedures may also concern matters that the Service believes should be public, even though they may not necessarily affect the rights and duties of taxpayers.

Revenue procedures are guidance written for use by the general public. Thus, technical terms that are not generally understood are avoided. The format generally includes sections for "Purpose" (especially if an earlier revenue procedure is superseded), "Background," "Authority," "Effect on Other Documents," and "Effective Date."

The Service's policy is to make revenue procedures effective as of the date of their publication if the procedure adversely affects the rights and duties of taxpayers, such as where taxpayers are obliged to follow procedures that may increase their tax burden. Where appropriate, however, the Service has issued revenue procedures that have retroactive effect.[333]

---

[331] Rev. Proc. 89-14, § 5, 1989-1 CB 814.

[332] Rev. Proc. 89-14, § 8, 1989-1 CB 814. Revenue procedures have been given the same legal effect as revenue rulings. See Snap-On Tools, Inc. v. United States, 26 Cl. Ct. 1045, 92-2 USTC ¶ 50,425 (1992) (revenue procedure "simply announces the IRS position on the issue; it lacks binding precedential value on this court"), aff'd, 26 F3d 137 (Fed. Cir. 1994).

[333] See, e.g., Rev. Proc. 80-5, 1980-1 CB 582, providing a procedure for taxpayers to change their method of accounting for excess inventory pursuant to the Supreme Court's decision in Thor Power Tool Co. v. Comm'r, 439 US 522 (1979). The procedure was released in News Release IR 80-19 on February 8, 1980, and made mandatory to tax years ending on or after December 25, 1979. See also Estate of Shapiro v. Comm'r, 111 F3d 1010, 1017–1019 (2d Cir. 1997) (limits of the Service's obligation to follow revenue procedures discussed).

[2] Technical Advice

[a] Definition and Purpose

Technical advice is guidance that the National Office furnishes by memorandum to a district office or an Appeals Office in response to a request that the National Office interpret and apply the internal revenue laws, tax treaties, regulations, revenue rulings, notices, and other published precedents to a specific set of facts.[334] While a technical advice request is made by the district office or Appeals Office, the request is sometimes initiated by the taxpayer.

Technical advice covers any technical or procedural question that develops during the examination or appeals process, as well as any other review in a field office. Accordingly, technical advice may be requested at various stages of the administrative process (i.e., during the examination of the taxpayer's return); the consideration of a taxpayer's claim for refund or credit; and any other matter involving a specific taxpayer under the Chief, Examination Division or the Chief, Appeals Office level.[335]

Technical advice is useful to a taxpayer because of its effect on the administrative action concerning the disputed issue. Specifically, the district office and the Appeals Office "must process the taxpayer's case on the basis of the conclusion in the technical advice memorandum."[336] If the technical advice is favorable to the taxpayer, field offices have no choice but to resolve a dispute on a legal issue in the taxpayer's favor. Obviously, technical advice adverse to the taxpayer has the opposite effect; that is, it forecloses the possibility that the taxpayer's position will be accepted by the district office.

---

[334] 26 CFR § 601.105(b)(5)(i)(a); Rev. Proc. 2002-2, § 2, 2002-1 IRB 82, 88. Technical advice is also defined as being issued in accordance with the procedures described in the revenue procedure describing technical advice to distinguish it from field service advice or other Chief Counsel advice, which is issued to field offices outside these procedures.

[335] Rev. Proc. 2002-2, § 2, 2002-1 IRB 82, 88. Technical advice may also be requested in any matter under examination or in Appeals pertaining to tax-exempt bonds or mortgage credit certificates. It should be noted that, while technical advice may be requested in a nondocketed case in Appeals, it may not be requested when the issue arises in a docketed case for any taxable year. Nevertheless, if a docketed case involves an estate tax issue, the National Office may issue technical advice memorandum provided that the appropriate Appeals officer and government counsel agree to use the procedure.

[336] Rev. Proc. 2002-2, § 16.01, 2002-1 IRB 82, 105. Technical advice is binding on the district unless (1) the district and the Appeals office believe that the technical advice should be reconsidered, or (2) the case is in the Coordinated Examination Program with an issue in the Industry Specialization Program or International Field Assistance Program and, pursuant to the case manager's settlement authority under Delegation Order No. 247, the case manager decides to settle the issue in accordance with an Appeals settlement guideline or position paper.

Additionally, while adverse technical advice does not have the same preclusive effect in Appeals as it does at the district level,[337] it may significantly decrease the possibility that Appeals will accept the taxpayer's position. Thus, Appeals can rule in favor of the taxpayer, despite the analysis of the issue as set forth in the technical advice, provided that Appeals finds support in existing authority. On the other hand, settlement in Appeals on a basis favorable to the taxpayer is unusual as a practical matter once the National Office has issued technical advice adverse to the taxpayer. Consequently, before a taxpayer initiates a request for technical advice, careful consideration must be given to whether the National Office will issue favorable technical advice on the issue involved.

From the Service's viewpoint, technical advice also serves the purpose of establishing consistent holdings in field offices.[338] Since consistency is one of the objectives of technical advice, the Associate Chief Counsel (Domestic), the Associate Chief Counsel (Employee Plans and Exempt Organizations), the Associate Chief Counsel (Enforcement Litigation), and the Associate Chief Counsel (International) give technical advice to District Directors and Chief of Appeals Offices.[339] Technical advice on issues under the jurisdiction of the Assistant Commissioner (Employee Plans and Exempt Organizations) must be requested from the Assistant Commissioner under procedures separate, but not materially different, from those that apply to other requests for technical advice.[340] Since technical advice is intended to state the Service's position, it is included in the "written determinations" made available to the public under Section 6110, after identifying details have been deleted,[341] but "may not be used or cited as precedent."[342]

Both letter rulings and technical advice state the National Office's conclusions of law as to a particular set of facts. However, there are marked differences between the two types of position statements, as shown in the following table.

---

[337] Rev. Proc. 2002-2, § 17.01(2), 2002-1 IRB 82, 109.

[338] Rev. Proc. 2002-2, § 2, 2002-1 IRB 73, 88.

[339] Rev. Proc. 2002-2, §§ 1, 2, 2002-1 IRB 82, 86–88.

[340] Rev. Proc. 2002-5, 2002-1 IRB 173. Technical advice may be requested from the Assistant Commissioner (Employee Plans and Exempt Organizations) in proceedings involving (1) the examination of a taxpayer's return, (2) consideration of a taxpayer's claim for refund, (3) a request for determination letter, or (4) any other matter involving a specific taxpayer under the jurisdiction of the Chief, EP/EO Division or Chief, Appeals Office, but not issues in docketed Appeals cases. Not all matters are subject to the Assistant Commissioner's procedures; the procedures generally applicable to technical advice must be used to any matter involving tax exempt bonds or mortgage credit certificates. Rev. Proc. 2002-5, § 3, 2002-1 IRB 173, 177.

[341] See the discussion supra ¶ 3.03 [3][c].

[342] IRC § 6110(k)(3).

TABLE 3.2
Characteristics of Letter Rulings and Technical Advice

	Letter Ruling	Technical Advice
Issuer	Associate Chief Counsel	Associate Chief Counsel (Domestic) or Associate Chief Counsel (EP/EO)
Associate Chief Counsel (Domestic) or Associate Chief Counsel (EP/EO)		
Requester	Taxpayer	District or Appeals Office, but taxpayer may initiate
When requested	Pre-return filing transactions	Examination issues after return filed, as well as claims for refund
Effect	Binding on district	Binding on district and Appeals Office if favorable to taxpayer, but not on Appeals Office if unfavorable
Reliability	Revoked or modified retroactively in rare and unusual circumstances	Generally revoked or modifed retroactively
Publicity	Available to public after deletions under Section 6110	Available to public after deletions under Section 6110

[b] Requesting Technical Advice

The taxpayer, the district, and Appeals may initiate a request for technical advice. A taxpayer may request technical advice when (1) existing authorities do not clearly resolve the issue (i.e., there is a lack of uniformity) or (2) the issue is so unusual or complex that it warrants National Office consideration.[343] The National Office suggests that, if an appropriate issue exists, the request for technical advice should be made at the earliest possible stage in the proceeding[344]; however, the district and Appeals should not avoid seeking technical advice because the issue is raised late in the examination or Appeals process.

To expedite the process, a pre-submission conference with the National Office is permitted if the district office or Appeals Office is likely to request technical advice and all parties agree to the request for the conference.[345]

---

[343] 26 CFR § 601.105(b)(5)(i)(e)(iii); Rev. Proc. 2002-2, § 7.01, 2002-1 IRB 82, 91.

[344] Rev. Proc. 2002-2, § 7.03, 2002-1 IRB 82, 91.

[345] Rev. Proc. 2002-2, § 8.01, 2002-1 IRB 82, 91–92. The purpose of the pre-submission conference, which can be held in the National Office or by telephone if district or Appeals personnel cannot attend, is to facilitate (1) the parties' agreement about the scope of the technical advice request; (2) the factual information to be included in the request;

Whether the taxpayer or the Service initiates the request for technical advice, the National Office requires a written request that describes the facts, identifies the issues on which technical advice is requested, discusses the applicable authorities, and makes the arguments in support of the party's position on the issue.[346]

[i] Agreement to request technical advice. If the field office requests technical advice or agrees to request technical advice, the procedure is as follows:[347]

- Whether the taxpayer or the Service initiates the request for technical advice, the district or Appeals (1) notifies the taxpayer that technical advice is being requested, and (2) at or before the request is submitted to the National Office, sends the taxpayer a copy of the arguments supplied to the National Office in support of the field's position.[348] If the district or Appeals initiated the request, the field office will also give the taxpayer a copy of the statement of facts and the issues proposed to be submitted to the National Office for consideration.[349]

- The field office's notice to the taxpayer, advising the taxpayer that a request for technical advice is being sent to the National Office, also informs the taxpayer of the right to a National Office conference if the tentative conclusion is adverse to the taxpayer and asks whether such a conference is requested.[350]

- If the taxpayer disagrees with the field office's statement of facts and the issues as to which technical advice is sought, the taxpayer has ten days (subject to extension for cause) to notify the field office of any disagreement. If any disagreement is not resolved, the field office notifies the taxpayer, and the taxpayer thereafter has ten days (subject to

---

(3) collateral issues that should or should not be included in the request; and (4) any other substantive or procedural matters that will help the National Office provide the parties with technical advice as expeditiously as possible.

[346] Rev. Proc. 2002-2, § 9.01, 2002-1 IRB 82, 92. When a field office initiates the request, the taxpayer is given the opportunity to submit a statement with the same information. Field offices transmit the request for technical advice using a Form 4463 (Request for Technical Advice) (1) in the case of requests from district offices to Internal Revenue Service, Attn: CC:DOM:CORP:TSS, Ben Franklin Station, Washington, D.C. 20044, and (2) in the case of requests from Appeals to Internal Revenue Service, Attn: C:AP:FS, Box 68, 901 D Street, S.W., Washington, D.C. 20024.

[347] Rev. Proc. 2002-2, § 9.01, 2002-1 IRB 82, 92.

[348] Rev. Proc. 2002-2, § 10.01, 2002-1 IRB 82, 93–96.

[349] Rev. Proc. 2002-2, § 10.01, 2002-1 IRB 82, 93–96.

[350] Rev. Proc. 2002-2, § 10.02, 2002-1 IRB 82, 96.

extension for cause) to provide a statement of the taxpayer's version of the facts and issues.[351]

- When a taxpayer initiates the request for technical advice, the taxpayer submits a statement of facts and the issues. The field office notifies the taxpayer of any disagreement it has with such statement of facts and issues, and the taxpayer thereafter has ten calendar (not business) days (subject to extension for cause) to reply to this notice of disagreement.[352]

- The taxpayer is encouraged to submit a statement with the same kind of information included in the request for technical advice (a description of the facts, discussion of the authorities, and argument in support of the taxpayer's position). The taxpayer's statement is forwarded to the National Office with the field office's request for technical advice.

- Since technical advice is subject to disclosure under Section 6110, the taxpayer also must submit a separate statement of proposed deletions, along with supporting reasons, or a statement that no information other than names, addresses, and taxpayer identification numbers need be deleted.[353]

[ii] Denial of request for technical advice. As indicated above, a taxpayer may request referral of an issue, currently under review by a district office or Appeals Office, to the National Office for technical advice. If the examining agent or Appeals Office refuses this request, the taxpayer will be notified, and is given the opportunity to appeal this refusal under the following procedure:[354]

- To appeal the field office's decision not to request technical advice, the taxpayer must submit a statement of the facts and law, as well as argument on the issues and the reasons why the taxpayer believes the matter should be referred to the National Office for advice. This statement must be submitted within ten calendar days (unless an extension is granted) to the examining agent or Appeals Officer.

- The examining agent or Appeals Officer then submits the statement through channels to the Chief (Examination Division) or the Chief (Appeals Office) accompanied by a statement of the agent or Appeals Officer's reasons why the issue should not be referred to the National Office.

---

[351] Rev. Proc. 2002-2, § 10.03, 2002-1 IRB 82, 96–97. The request for an extension must be approved by the Chief (Examination Division) or the Chief (Appeals Division).

[352] Rev. Proc. 2002-2, § 10.04, 2002-1 IRB 82, 97.

[353] Rev. Proc. 2002-2, § 10.05, 2002-1 IRB 82, 97. According to the National Office, a statutory basis for each proposed deletion should be stated.

[354] Rev. Proc. 2002-2, § 11.02, 2002-1 IRB 82, 97.

- If the Chief (Examination Division) proposes to a rejection of the taxpayer's request, he generally must advise the taxpayer in writing of the reasons for the decision. While the decision of the Chief (Examination Division) or the Chief (Appeals Office) is not appealable,[355] a certiorari procedure exists for National Office approval or disapproval of such denial.
- If the taxpayer notifies the Chief within ten calendar days after receipt of the notice that the taxpayer does not agree with the "proposed" denial, the matter is transferred to the National Office for review, and the result of that review is thereafter communicated to the taxpayer.

[iii] Conferences. After review, the National Office attorney or representative to whom the case has been assigned may decide to give advice adverse to the taxpayer. If the taxpayer has requested a conference, the representative arranges a date and time for the conference, which is to be held within twenty-one calendar days after the contact was made.[356] As a matter of right, a taxpayer is entitled to only one National Office conference, and it is normally at the branch level in the Office of the appropriate Associate Chief Counsel.[357]

The National Office conference is supposed to be attended by a person who has authority to act for the branch chief, and possibly also by the examining officer. The purpose of the conference is to clarify the facts of the case.[358] If new and additional data and authorities are proposed by the taxpayer at the conference, they must be submitted within twenty-one calendar days after the conference. Once the branch has reached a decision, a taxpayer has no right of appeal from its decision to any other official in the National Office.

---

[355] "However, if the taxpayer does not agree with the proposed denial, all data on the issue for which the Technical Advice is sought, including taxpayer's written request and statements, will be submitted to the Assistant Commissioner (Examination), or the Assistant Commissioner (International), or the National Director of Appeals, as appropriate." Rev. Proc. 2002-2, § 11.04, 2002-1 IRB 82, 98.

[356] Rev. Proc. 2002-2, §§ 13.01, 13.02, 2002-1 IRB 82, 101. An extension of the period may be granted if the taxpayer so requests in writing before the end of the twenty-one-day period, showing "compelling facts and circumstances," or makes an oral request within the twenty-one-day period followed by the written request after the period.

[357] Rev. Proc. 2002-2, § 14.05, 2002-1 IRB 82, 102–103. After the conference, if an adverse holding is proposed either on a new issue or on the same issue but on a different ground than one discussed at the first conference, the taxpayer is offered an additional conference. The branch may invite the taxpayer to attend further conferences in the National Office when in the opinion of its personnel the need arises. Rev. Proc. 2002-2, § 14.09, 2002-1 IRB 82, 103.

[358] If the advice involves more than one branch, an authorized person from all affected branches must be present. Rev. Proc. 2002-2, § 14.05, 2002-1 IRB 82, 102–103.

[c] Replies to Requests for Technical Advice

When issued, the reply to a request for technical advice is addressed to the district director or Chief, Appeals Office. It is drafted in two parts. Each part identifies the taxpayer by name, address, identification number, and year or years involved.[359] The first part of the reply is a transmittal memorandum. In unusual cases, this memorandum serves as a vehicle for providing the field office with administrative information or "strategic advice" that, under the nondisclosure statutes or for other reasons, may not be discussed with the taxpayer.[360] The second part of the reply is the Technical Advice Memorandum, which (1) states the issues; (2) gives the conclusions of the National Office on the issues; (3) describes the facts the National Office believes bear on the issues; (4) discusses the applicable law, including authorities published in the Internal Revenue Bulletin; and (5) explains the rationale for the conclusions reached by the National Office.

After it has been adopted by the field office, the district director or the Chief of Appeals furnishes a copy of the Technical Advice Memorandum to the taxpayer,[361] along with the disclosure notice and the proposed public version to which the taxpayer may voice objections.[362]

[d] Effect of Technical Advice

In legal effect, technical advice memoranda and a letter rulings are the same. Both are written determinations that "may not be used as precedent."[363] Both have the same procedural effect as a letter ruling with respect to a closed and completed transaction, and the same principles governing legal effect apply to each (i.e., the "particular transaction," the "specific taxpayer," and retroactive revocation rules).[364]

The critical difference between technical advice memoranda and letter rulings is the administrative effect that the Service gives technical advice but does not accord to letter rulings.[365] Both the district office and the Appeals Office must follow technical advice favorable to the taxpayer, and process the taxpayer's case accordingly. Field offices have no discretion to act contrary to

---

[359] Rev. Proc. 2002-2, § 16.14, 2002-1 IRB 82, 108.

[360] Rev. Proc. 2002-2, § 16.14, 2002-1 IRB 82, 108. The transmittal memorandum is a Form M-6000.

[361] Rev. Proc. 2002-2, § 17.03, 2002-1 IRB 82, 109. However, the National Office may instruct a field office not to furnish a copy of the Technical Advice Memorandum to the taxpayer. Id. at § 16.05.

[362] Rev. Proc. 2002-2, § 17.04, 2002-1 IRB 82, 109–110.

[363] IRC § 6110(k)(3).

[364] See the discussion supra ¶ 3.03[6].

[365] Rev. Proc. 2002-2, § 17.01, 2002-1 IRB 82, 108–109.

the National Office's technical advice favorable to a taxpayer, unless the district office and the Appeals Office believe that the conclusions in a technical advice memorandum should be reconsidered. While every effort is made to arrive at a mutually satisfactory conclusion between the National Office and field offices, if the conflict cannot be resolved, the decision of the National Office is final.

Although the district is bound by technical advice unfavorable to the taxpayer, an Appeals Officer is not similarly bound. An Appeals Officer may therefore disregard the technical advice and settle an issue under Appeals general authority in a manner adverse to the taxpayer.[366]

If technical advice is favorable to a taxpayer, the Service will apply it retroactively except in rare or unusual circumstances.[367] Because technical advice is furnished only on closed transactions, a holding adverse to a taxpayer is also applied retroactively, unless the appropriate Associate Chief Counsel exercises discretion under Section 7805(b) to apply the technical advice prospectively only.

Moreover, because technical advice is requested after a transaction is closed, a taxpayer cannot have relied on the technical advice in planning the closed transaction. Accordingly, the self-imposed restraints on the Service's power to retroactively revoke its positions (as in letter rulings) do not ordinarily apply in the case of technical advice. Therefore, except in cases involving an abuse of discretion, there is no limit on the Service's discretionary authority under Section 7805(b) to revoke technical advice retroactively.[368]

As a general rule, technical advice that modifies or revokes prior technical advice is applied retroactively. However, a modification or revocation may be given only prospective effect where the new technical advice (modifying or revoking the prior technical advice) is less favorable to the taxpayer and relates to a continuing transaction. In such a case, because the transaction is ongoing, there is a likelihood that the taxpayer relied on the earlier favorable advice.

Additionally, no retroactive effect will ordinarily be given to technical advice that revokes or modifies an earlier letter ruling or technical advice to the

---

[366] Rev. Proc. 2002-2, § 17.01, 2002-1 IRB 82, 108–109. In a case of a Coordinated Examination Program taxpayer, if the National Office gives adverse technical advice on a coordinated issue in the Industry Specialization Program or International Field Assistance Program and Appeals has a coordinated issue paper containing settlement guidelines or positions for such issue, the Examination case manager may settle the issue contrary to the technical advice; the case manager's settlement authority in such instance is derived from Delegation Order No. 247, 1996-1 CB 356.

[367] Rev. Proc. 2002-2, § 17.02, 2002-1 IRB 82, 96–97.

[368] Rev. Proc. 2002-2, § 18, 2002-1 IRB 82, 98. The discretionary authority under Section 7805(b) is exercised by the appropriate Associate Chief Counsel.

detriment of the taxpayer to whom or about whom such ruling or advice was originally issued if

- There has been no misstatement or omission of material facts;
- The facts subsequently developed are not materially different from the facts on which the ruling or memorandum was based;
- There has been no change in applicable law;
- In the case of a ruling, the ruling was originally issued on a prospective or proposed transaction; and
- The taxpayer directly involved in the ruling or memorandum acted with good faith and in reliance on the ruling or memorandum, and, as a consequence, the retroactive revocation would be to the taxpayer's detriment.[369]

The National Office provides a procedure by which a taxpayer can request, prior to the issuance of the technical advice, that the Service exercise its discretion under Section 7805(b) to apply such technical advice prospectively only.[370] This request must be made in the same form as the request for technical advice, indicate that it is being made under Section 7805(b), set forth the relief sought, and discuss the reasons and arguments in support of the relief sought.[371] The request may be made in an initial request for technical advice or at any time before the National Office issues the technical advice memorandum. The taxpayer has the right to a conference in the National Office to discuss this matter.

---

[369] Rev. Proc. 2002-2, § 18.06(5), 2002-1 IRB 82, 111. The same examples used in Rev. Proc. 2002-1, § 12.05, 2002-1 IRB 1, 50–51, on the retroactive revocation or modification of a letter ruling, are used to describe the circumstances when retroactive revocation of technical advice will or will not be considered to be to the taxpayer's detriment.

[370] Rev. Proc. 2002-2, § 19.02, 2002-1 IRB 82, 112. For example, in Letter Ruling 9131003, the taxpayer requested that revocation of favorable technical advice be applied prospectively. The Service determined there was "good faith reliance," in addition to other factors, for the period starting with the issuance of the favorable technical advice and ending on the date of its revocation. In the ruling, the Service concluded that no reliance on the favorable existed for tax years closed before the favorable technical advice was issued, so that the unfavorable revocation could be applied retroactively to those years.

[371] The request is sent to the district director or Chief, Appeals Office, which will then send the request to the National Office for consideration. Rev. Proc. 2002-2, § 19.03, 2002-1 IRB 82, 112.

[3] Determination Letters

[a] Definition

A determination letter is a written statement (1) issued by a district director (2) in response to a written inquiry by a taxpayer (3) that applies principles and precedents previously announced by the National Office (4) to the specific set of facts.[372] A comparison of a determination letter, a letter ruling, and technical advice is summarized in Table 3.3. All three are official written communications by the Service about the application of the law to the taxpayer's particular facts. The Service considers these written communications to be generally binding, but they may not be used as precedent by the Service or any taxpayer other than the taxpayer whose situation is described in the communication.[373] One feature that distinguishes a determination letter from letter rulings and technical advice is that a determination letter is issued by a district office, not the National Office, as is the case with a letter ruling or technical advice. Also, for the district to issue a determination letter, the law applicable to the issue must be settled; this is unlike the case of technical advice where the applicable law must generally be uncertain.

[b] When Issued

District directors issue determination letters only if the "question presented is specifically answered by a statute, tax treaty, or regulation, or by a conclusion stated in a revenue ruling, opinion, or court decisions published in the Internal Revenue Bulletin."[374] District directors may issue or refuse to issue a determination letter "whenever [the district director considers it] appropriate in the interest of sound tax administration."[375]

Determination letters are usually issued in matters involving pension plans and exempt organizations.[376] However, district directors may issue determination letters on other matters in response to written requests,[377] if they have examination jurisdiction over the returns affected by the requests, including (1) income and gift tax matters where the question presented arises in a completed transaction[378]; (2) estate tax matters where the question affects the return of a

---

[372] 26 CFR § 601.201(a)(3); Rev. Proc. 2002-1, § 2.03, 2002-1 IRB 1, 9.

[373] IRC § 6110(k)(3).

[374] Rev. Proc. 2002-1, § 6, 2002-1 IRB 1, 18–19.

[375] 26 CFR § 601.201(d)(1); Rev. Proc. 2002-1, § 7.01, 2002-1 IRB 1, 20.

[376] See infra ¶¶ 3.03[3][f], 3.03[3][n].

[377] 26 CFR § 601.201(c); Rev. Proc. 2002-1, § 6, 2002-1 IRB 1, 18–19.

[378] While district directors may issue determination letters in a transaction affecting tax returns within their examination jurisdiction, they do not issue determination letters if

deceased taxpayer[379]; and (3) employment tax matters where the question concerns a completed transaction.[380]

A district director may not issue a determination letter in response to an inquiry, even if statutory or Internal Revenue Bulletin precedents cover the matter, where

- It appears that the taxpayer has directed a similar inquiry to the National Office;
- The identical issue involving the same taxpayer is pending in a case before the Appeals Office;
- The determination letter is requested by an industry, trade association, or similar group;
- The request involves an industry-wide problem;
- The request involves an employment tax question that has been or is being considered by the Social Security Administration;
- The request is for a determination of a constructive sales price under Sections 4216(b) and 4216(c) (only the National Office issues these rulings); or
- The request is with regard to a taxpayer or taxpayers who have not filed or are not required to file returns over which the district director's office will have audit jurisdiction.[381]

Moreover, determination letters (like letter rulings) are not issued with regard to questions of an inherently factual nature, alternative plans of proposed transactions, or hypothetical situations.[382] Further, the same circumstances in which a letter ruling will not be issued or will ordinarily not be issued apply as well to the issuance of a determination letter.[383] Finally, even if the subject

---

the same question is presented in an already-filed return. On the other hand, while the district does not issue a determination letter on a proposed transaction, it may issue a determination letter on the consequences of the replacement of involuntarily converted property under Section 1033 if the taxpayer has filed a return for the year in which the property was involuntarily converted but has not yet been replaced. Rev. Proc. 2002-1, § 6.01, 2002-1 IRB 1, 18.

[379] A determination letter will not be issued on tax questions about the application of the estate tax to the potential estate of a living person. Similarly, even though district directors regularly issue determination letters affecting the generation-skipping transfer tax returns over which they have examination jurisdiction, they will not issue determination letters on the application of the generation-skipping transfer tax before the distribution or termination takes place. Rev. Proc. 2002-1, § 6.03, 2002-1 IRB 1, 18.

[380] Requests for a determination of employment status (Form SS-8) must be submitted directly to the appropriate Service office and not to the National Office. Rev. Proc. 2002-1, § 6.04, 2002-1 IRB 1, 19.

[381] 26 CFR § 601.201(c)(4).

[382] 26 CFR § 601.201(e)(2); Rev. Proc. 2002-1, § 7, 2002-1 IRB 1, 20–21.

[383] See Rev. Proc. 2002-3, 2002-1 IRB 117.

of the requested determination letter does not come within any of the areas in which a determination letter will ordinarily not be issued, the district director may refuse to issue a determination letter and refer the request to the National Office.[384] In most cases, these restrictions on a district director's authority to issue determination letters are based on considerations of consistency.

Where the foregoing matters prevent the district director from issuing a determination letter, the request is forwarded to the National Office for reply, and the taxpayer is advised accordingly.[385]

TABLE 3.3

Differences Between Determination Letters, Letter Rulings, and Technical Advice

---

	Determination Letter	Letter Ruling	Technical Advice
Requester	Taxpayer	Taxpayer	District or Appeals Office, but taxpayer may initiate
To whom request made	District Office	National Office	National Office
When issued	Transaction completed	Prospective or pre-return transaction	Post-return transaction
Type of issues	Answer must be clear	Answer may not be clear	Answer may not be clear.

---

[c] Processing of a Request for a Determination Letter

Requests for a determination letter follow the same format as requests for a letter ruling.[386] Unlike letter rulings, however, determination letters issued with respect to income, gift, and certain excise tax matters, or estate and employment tax matters, are not reviewed by the National Office. This is hardly surprising, since a determination letter merely informs a taxpayer of the tax consequences of applying a position previously established in regulations or in

---

[384] 26 CFR § 601.201(g)(1).

[385] 26 CFR § 601.201(g)(1).

[386] 26 CFR § 601.201(d); Rev. Proc. 2002-1, § 8.01(1)–(16), 2002-1 IRB 1, 21–28. See the discussion supra ¶ 3.03[4]. User fees must be paid with the request. See Rev. Proc. 2002-1, Appendix A. The request must be submitted in duplicate if (1) it is for an exemption under Section 501(c) or Section 501(d) of the Code; (2) more than one issue is presented by the request; or (3) a closing agreement is requested with respect to the issue presented. 26 CFR § 601.201(e)(1); Rev. Proc. 2002-1 § 8.01(14), supra.

precedents published in Internal Revenue Bulletins to the taxpayer's particular facts.[387]

If a taxpayer believes that a determination letter is in error, two review procedures are available. The taxpayer may ask the district director to reconsider the matter or he may ask the district director to request technical advice from the National Office. Although the district director may in his discretion refuse to request technical advice, if a request for technical advice is made, the normal procedures for requesting technical advice then apply.[388]

Finally, the same rules that apply to the withdrawal of requests, status of oral advice, and the effect of letter rulings also apply to determination letters.[389]

[d] Legal Effect

A determination letter issued by a district office generally has the same legal effect on the examination of a return as a letter ruling.[390] However, if, on the examination of a return, a district director is of the opinion that "a conclusion contrary to that expressed in the determination letter is indicated," the district director need not refer the matter to the National Office, as must be done where a letter ruling is involved.

Retroactive effect must generally be given to modifications or revocation of determination letters because a district director is not authorized to limit the modification or revocation to prospective effect only. To prevent a modification or revocation from having retroactive effect, the district director must refer the matter to the National Office. There the Associate Chief Counsel (Employee Plans and Exempt Organizations) or the Assistant Commissioner (Employee Plans and Exempt Organizations) may exercise the Commissioner's authority under Section 7805(b) to limit the modification or revocation of the determination letter to prospective effect only.[391]

[e] The Employee Plans and Exempt Organizations Function

Most determination letters are issued on the qualification or status of retirement plans and exempt organizations. The Assistant Commissioner (Em-

---

[387] 26 CFR § 601.201(i)(1).

[388] 26 CFR § 601.201(i)(1). There are special rules for the review of determination letters relating to the qualification of employers' plans under Section 401 (set forth at 26 CFR § 601.201(c)) and to the exemption from federal income tax of certain organizations under Sections 501 and 521 of the Code (set forth at 26 CFR § 601.201(n)).

[389] 26 CFR §§ 601.201(j), 601.210(k), 601.201(l), 601.201(m).

[390] Rev. Proc. 2002-1, § 13.01, 2002-1 IRB 1, 53.

[391] 26 CFR § 601.201(m); Rev. Proc. 2002-1, § 12.11, 2002-1 IRB 1, 52–53.

ployee Plans and Exempt Organizations, or EP/EO) supervises the Service's administration of the tax laws in these areas.[392] The Office of the Assistant Commissioner (EP/EO) has three divisions: the Exempt Organizations Technical Division, the Employee Plans Technical and Actuarial Division, and the Employee Plans and Exempt Organizations Operations Division. Both the Exempt Organizations Technical Division and the Employee Plans Technical and Actuarial Division issue rulings,[393] technical advice, and general technical information in their areas of particular responsibility.[394] These branches also draft revenue rulings, revenue procedures, announcements, releases, manual supplements, and other technical publications.

Four key district offices have audit responsibility for employee plans.[395] These offices have regional responsibility serving states within a set region: the Northeast Key District Office is in Brooklyn; the Southeast Key District Office is in Baltimore; the Midstates Key District Office is in Dallas; and the Western Key District Office is in Los Angeles. The key districts for EP/EO purposes, and the states they serve, are set forth in Table 3.4.[396] Each of these key district offices has an EP/EO Division, to which employee plan and exempt organization specialists are assigned.

[f] Special Rules: Pension Trusts

For employee plan determination letter requests, different procedures apply depending on both the type of request (such as initial qualification, minor plan amendments, termination of plans, and special procedural issues) and the type of plan (such as "specially defined" plans, master and prototype (and regional prototype) plans, volume submitter plans, and multiple employer plans).[397] While additional procedures apply to specific requests, an applicant for a determination letter generally must[398]

---

[392] IRC § 7805(b).

[393] The procedures to be followed are set forth in revenue procedures. Rev. Proc. 2002-4 § 4, 2002-1 IRB 127, 135 (procedures for issuing ruling letters, information letters, and closing agreements).

[394] Rev. Proc. 2002-5, 2002-1 IRB 173 (procedures for the Assistant Commissioner, Employee Plans and Exempt Organizations, to furnish technical advice to key district directors and chiefs of Appeals offices).

[395] Rev. Proc. 2002-5, 2002-1 IRB 173.

[396] Rev. Proc. 2002-6, 2002-1 IRB 203; IRM 11(12)1.51, MT 1100-380 (Jan. 31, 1991) (Chief (EP/EO)).

[397] Rev. Proc. 2002-6, 2002-1 IRB 203.

[398] Rev. Proc. 2002-6, § 6, 2002-1 IRB 203, 215–218.

- File all required information with the district director of the Ohio key district office in order to provide sufficient information to make the requested determination[399];
- Include a complete copy of the plan and trust instrument[400];
- Follow the same format and include the same type of information that must be included in a request for a determination letter[401];
- File Schedule Q, NonDiscrimination Requirements (Form 5300, Application For Employee Benefit Plan) with the determination letter request;
- Submit any prior favorable determination letter[402];
- Pay the required user fee[403]; and
- Before submitting certain requests for a determination letter on the qualified status of certain retirement plans, notify interested parties of the request as required by ERISA and the Code.[404]

A request for a determination letter must include all required information, or it will not be acted upon.[405] Moreover, a determination letter is only as reliable as the accuracy and completeness of the information submitted. Accordingly, if the request fails to disclose a material fact or the request misrepresents a material fact, the applicant will not be able to rely on a favorable determination letter. For this purpose, however, a misrepresentation does not include (1) estimates in demonstrations or required schedules when precise information is unavailable or (2) a prior year's data when the applicant discloses that a prior year's data are being used, the data is for the most recent year available, the data are complete and accurate, there has been no material

---

[399] Requests for determination letters must be addressed to the key district director of the Ohio key district office at the following address: Internal Revenue Service, P.O. Box 192, Covington, Ky. 41011; and if by express mail or delivery service, Internal Revenue Service, 201 West Rivercenter Blvd. Attn. Extracting Stop 312, Covington, Ky. 41011.

[400] A complete copy of the plan and trust instrument need not be included when the application relates to a master and prototype plan filed on Form 5307, Application for Determination for Adopters of Master or Prototype, Regional Prototype, or Volume Submitter Plan, or a minor amendment described in Section 11 of Rev. Proc. 2002-6, 2002-1 IRB 203.

[401] The request must follow the instructions applicable to requests for rulings and determination letters generally. See Rev. Proc. 2002-4 § 9, 2002-1 IRB 127, 142–148.

[402] Schedule Q (Form 5300) Nondiscrimination Requirements need not be filed when the application (1) is filed on Form 6406, Short Form Application for Determination for Minor Amendment of Employee Benefit Plan; (2) relates to state and local government plans or to the qualified status of group trusts; or (3) relates solely to the requirements of IRC § 420.

[403] User fees are listed in regularly issued revenue procedures, see Rev. Proc. 2002-8, 2002-1 IRB 252. Payment should be accompanied by Form 8717, User Fee for Employer Plan Determination Letter Request.

[404] See ERISA § 3001(a); IRC § 7476(b)(2).

[405] Rev. Proc. 2002-6 § 6.15, 2002-1 IRB 203, 217.

change in the facts, and the data are used consistently throughout the application.[406]

In addition to these general requirements for the submission of a request for a determination letter, special procedures must be followed when a determination letter is requested for the following:

- The initial qualification determination for individually designed defined contribution and defined benefit plans (including employee stock ownership plans and collectively bargained plans)[407]
- An employer's adoption of a sponsor's Master and Prototype (M&P) plan (or regional prototype plan) in order to establish that the employer has reliance that the sponsoring organization's or sponsor's plan is qualified under Section 401(a)[408]
- Volume submitter plans (under the Service's program to expedite determination letters in response to applications for approval of individually designed plans when a qualified practitioner has previously submitted a specimen or sample plan that contains provisions that are identical or substantially similar to the provisions in plans that the practitioner's clients have adopted or are expected to adopt, and has obtained an advisory letter approving the specimen plan)[409]
- Multiple employer plans described in Section 413(c)[410]
- Minor amendments of previously approved plans[411]
- The termination or discontinuance of contributions, as well as the required notice of mergers, consolidations, or transfer of assets or liabilities[412]

---

[406] Rev. Proc. 2002-6 § 6.16, 2002-1 IRB 203, 217.

[407] Rev. Proc. 2002-6 § 7, 2002-1 IRB 203, 219–220. These procedures also apply to plan amendments unless (1) the amendment is minor, in which case a short form (Form 6406) and the procedures of Rev. Proc. 2002-6 § 11, 2002-1 IRB 203, 227, are to be used; (2) a restatement of a plan is involved; (3) the amendment arises in the context of a qualification of a plan in the case of partial termination; (4) the amendment involves a change in the scope of a previously received determination letter, e.g., to request the Service to review the plan for certain nondiscrimination requirements that were not within the scope of the original determination letter; or (5) certain other circumstances (excluding plan terminations), such as a change in the demographics of the employer or a change in the method of testing the plan that was used in a demonstration in support of an earlier application.

[408] Rev. Proc. 2002-6, § 8, 2002-1 IRB 203, 220–222.

[409] Rev. Proc. 2002-6, § 9, 2002-1 IRB 203, 223–225.

[410] Rev. Proc. 2002-6, § 10, 2002-1 IRB 203, 226

[411] Rev. Proc. 2002-6, § 11, 2002-1 IRB 203, 227.

[412] Rev. Proc. 2002-6, § 12, 2002-1 IRB 203, 227–229.

- Qualification of a group trust[413]
- Affiliated service group status under Section 414(m) and the effect of leased employees on a plan's qualified status[414]
- Waiver of the minimum funding standard account for a defined contribution plan, and requesting a determination letter on any plan amendment required for the waiver[415]
- Plan language pursuant to Section 420 that permits the transfer of assets in a defined benefit plan to a health benefit account described in Section 401(b)[416]

Other procedures apply to the rights to notice and comment of interested parties.[417]

Applicants have the right to a conference with the key district director concerning the status of the application if it has been pending at least 270 days, and during the conference may only discuss issues relating to the processing of the application, and not any substantive of technical issues.[418] A taxpayer or the taxpayer's representative may seek a pre-submission conference by (1) sending a written request to the key district director, (2) demonstrating that a substantive plan, amendment, or the like has been developed for submission to the Service, and (3) describing the special problems or issues in this case that require a conference.[419] A pre-submission conference will be granted if the key district director decides, based on the taxpayer's request, that a conference will facilitate review and determination when the plan is formally submitted.

Accuracy and completeness in a request for a determination letter are important. First, though issued, a determination letter may not be relied on, and so deductions for contributions and tax exemption may be lost, if (1) the applicant has failed to disclose a material fact or makes a misrepresentation of material fact, (2) the applicant has failed to furnish any of the information or any form called for by an applicable revenue procedure, (3) there has been a

---

[413] Qualified status is determined under criteria described in Rev. Rul. 81-100, 1981-1 CB 326. Rev. Proc. 2002-6, § 13, 2002-1 IRB 203, 229.

[414] Rev. Proc. 2002-6, § 14, 2002-1 IRB 203, 229–231.

[415] Rev. Proc. 2002-6, § 15, 2002-1 IRB 203, 229–230.

[416] Rev. Proc. 2002-6, § 16, 2002-1 IRB 203, 233–234.

[417] Rev. Proc. 2002-6, § 17, 2002-1 IRB 203, 233–235.

[418] Rev. Proc. 2002-6, § 6.19, 2002-1 IRB 203, 218. The request must be in writing and sent to the specialist assigned to review the application or, if the name of the specialist is not known, to the key district director. If the request has been forwarded to the National Office for review together with a request for a waiver of the funding standard, the request should be sent to the actuary assigned to the review of the application or the Chief, Actuarial Branch 1, and the conference will be with the Assistant Commissioner (EP/EO). Rev. Proc. 2002-6, § 6.20, 2002-1 IRB 203, 218.

[419] Rev. Proc. 2002-6, § 19.02, 2002-1 IRB 203, 240.

change in a material fact included in the determination letter request (e.g., a significant change in plan coverage resulting from the operation of the plan), or (4) there has been a change in the law upon which the determination letter was based.[420]

Another reason accuracy and completeness are so important is that the request for the determination letter is part of the administrative record for purposes of Section 7476's declaratory judgment procedures.[421] Since the actual request for a determination letter is an important part of an applicant's declaratory judgment action to review the Service's actions, any incompleteness or inaccuracy in the request will decrease the chance of success in a future declaratory judgment action.

TABLE 3.4
EP/EO Key Districts

The key district that has jurisdiction is:	Entity is in:
Northeast Key District	Brooklyn, Connecticut, Maine, Massachusetts, Michigan, New Hampshire, New Jersey, New York, Ohio, Pennsylvania, Rhode Island, Vermont
Southeast Key District	Baltimore, Alabama, Delaware, District of Columbia, Florida, Georgia, Indiana, Kentucky, Louisiana, Maryland, Mississippi, North Carolina, South Carolina, Tennessee, Virginia, West Virginia, any U. S. possession or foreign country
Midstates Key District	Dallas, Arkansas, Illinois, Iowa, Kansas, Minnesota, Missouri, Nebraska, North Dakota, Oklahoma, South Dakota, Texas, Wisconsin
Western Key District	Los Angeles, Alaska, Arizona, California, Colorado, Hawaii, Idaho, Montana, Nevada, New Mexico, Oregon, Utah, Washington, Wyoming

An applicant may ask the key district office (or Appeals Office) to request technical advice from the National Office if the applicant believes the issue to be appropriate. If the district director refuses, the applicant may appeal

[420] Rev. Proc. 2002-6, § 21.01, 2002-1 IRB 203, 241–242.
[421] Rev. Proc. 2002-6, § 19.03, 2002-1 IRB 203, 240.

the decision not to seek technical advice.[422] If the district director agrees and seeks technical advice as to a plan's status or qualification, the decision of the National Office is final for both the district office and Appeals Office.[423]

[i] **Appeals office review.** If the key district director issues a notice of proposed determination adverse to the applicant, the applicant may appeal the proposed determination to the regional Appeals Office; no intra-agency appeal will be allowed, however, if the district's action was based on previously issued technical advice.[424] If applicants do not appeal an adverse determination within the Service, when such an appeal is permissible, they will not be able to later bring a declaratory judgment action challenging the Service's final determination. This is because the failure to pursue an intra-agency protest of the adverse determination constitutes a failure to exhaust available administrative remedies, which is required before the applicant may bring a declaratory judgment action.[425]

The usual protest procedures apply to appeals of proposed determinations.[426] The protest must be filed within thirty days from the date of the notice, unless an extension is granted. The protest must include the following specific information relating to the application and type of plan:

- Date of the application;
- Name and address of applicant and applicant's representative (if any);
- Key district in which the case is pending;
- Type of plan and type of action (e.g., initial qualification) involved;
- Date of protest and symbols of letter of district's proposed determination;
- Statement of issues and arguments in support of applicant's position; and
- Whether a conference is desired.[427]

If the Appeals Office sought technical advice and the proposed determination is contrary to National Office technical advice concerning qualification, the Appeals Office must refer the case to the Assistant Commissioner (EP/EO)

---

[422] The procedures, described in Rev. Proc. 2002-5, § 9.02, 2002-1 IRB 173, 182, are roughly the same as those for requests in non–EP/EO cases. See supra 3.04[3][c]

[423] Rev. Proc. 2002-5, § 10, 2002-1 IRB 173, 183–186.

[424] 26 CFR § 601.601(o)(6).

[425] IRC § 7476(b)(3); 26 CFR § 601.201(o)(10).

[426] See the discussion of protests in Chapter 9.

[427] 26 CFR § 601.201(o)(6)(ii).

for final decision. After review of the case, the Appeals Office issues a final determination in accordance with the Assistant Commissioner's decision.

[ii] Declaratory judgment procedure. So long as all administrative remedies have been exhausted, Section 7476 permits an employer or plan administrator, depending on who requested the determination letter from the district office, to petition the U.S. Tax Court for a declaratory judgment on the tax-qualified status of an employee benefit plan. This declaratory judgment procedure covers disputes over (1) the initial qualification or the continuing qualification of a retirement plan or (2) the failure of the Service to make a determination with respect to (i) the initial qualification or (ii) continuing qualification if the controversy arises from proposed amendments to the plan or plan termination.[428] A determination about the continuing qualification of a plan includes a revocation or any other change in its qualification.

A petition may be filed only by the employer, the plan administrator, or the employees who are "interested parties" as defined in the regulations.[429] The Pension Benefit Guaranty Corporation also may petition the Tax Court for a declaratory judgment as to a plan's qualification.[430] There are four conditions that must be met before the proceeding may be maintained:

- The Tax Court may find that a petition is premature unless a petitioner establishes compliance with the Service's "notice-to-interested-parties" requirements[431]; the term "interested parties" includes, for example, employees eligible to participate in the plan, subject to age and service requirements and employer contribution requirements.[432]

---

[428] IRC § 7476(a). A notice of deficiency determining that a retirement plan was not exempt does not constitute a determination under Section 7476(a)(1) to which the declaratory judgment procedure applies. Shut Out Dee-Fence, Inc. v. Comm'r, 77 TC 1197 (1981). For a case illustrating the limited jurisdiction of the Tax Court, see Wenzel v. Comm'r, 707 F2d 694 (2d Cir. 1983) (Service's refusal to grant relief did not constitute a determination or failure to determine qualified and tax exempt status of merged pension plans; therefore, Tax Court lacked subject-matter jurisdiction).

[429] Reg. § 1.7476-1(b). For a case where a retired employee was permitted to pursue a declaratory judgment action, see Hawes v. Comm'r, 73 TC 916 (1980). But see Romann v. Comm'r, 111 TC 273 (1998) (retiree is not an interested party for purposes of collectively bargained plans under Section 7476(b)(4) and Reg. § 1.7476-1(b)(4)); Jablonski v. Comm'r, RIA TC Memo. ¶ 98,396 (1998) (a former employee is not an interested party).

[430] IRC § 7476(b)(1).

[431] IRC § 7476(b)(2); Reg. § 1.7476-1(d)(2). The method for giving notice is set forth at Reg. § 1.7476-2(c). It has been held that the giving of notice to interested parties is not an absolute prerequisite to Tax Court review, because such review is discretionary where notice is not given. Federal Land Bank Ass'n v. Comm'r, 573 F2d 179 (4th Cir. 1978).

[432] Reg. § 1.7476-1(b)(1)(i). See also Reg. §§ 1.7476-1(b)(1)(ii) (all other employees at same place of employment), 1.7476-1(b)(6)(ii) (excluded bargaining limit employees).

- Petitioners must have exhausted their administrative remedies before filing.[433] Petitioners are not considered to have exhausted administrative remedies if, after having requested a determination as to initial qualification or continuing qualification of a retirement plan, the petition is filed before expiration of 270 days from the date of the request. Once the 270-day period has expired, declaratory relief is available only if taxpayers are first found to have exhausted their administrative remedies.[434] The steps that must be taken to exhaust administrative remedies are described in the procedural rules.[435]
- The plan or amendment must have been put into effect prior to commencement of the proceeding.[436]
- If the Service has sent a notice of determination, the petition must be filed on or before the ninetieth day after the date of the notice.[437]

The Tax Court has prescribed rules of practice for declaratory judgment proceedings.[438] In general, the case is decided on the basis of the "administrative record," which for retirement plans includes the plan itself, any related trust instrument, any written modification, and all written comments submitted to the Service.[439] The petitioner (i.e., the employer, plan administrator, or employee) generally has the burden of proof as to jurisdictional matters and as to grounds set forth in the notice of determination.[440] As to matters raised by the Service at the time of the Tax Court hearing, the Service has the burden of proof.[441]

---

[433] IRC § 7476(b)(3). See also Efco Tool Co. v. Comm'r, 81 TC 976 (1983) (taxpayer deemed to have exhausted his administrative remedies once final revocation letter had been issued). Compare McManus v. Comm'r, 93 TC 79 (1989) (mutual qualification case; taxpayer failed to exhaust administrative remedies).

[434] Prince Corp. v. Comm'r, 67 TC 318 (1976) (more than 300 days elapsed from date of request).

[435] 26 CFR § 601.201(o)(10).

[436] IRC § 7476(b)(4).

[437] IRC § 7476(b)(5).

[438] Tax Ct. R. Prac. & Proc. 210–218.

[439] Tax Ct. R. Prac. & Proc. 210(b)(11)(i). Thus, the Tax Court will not engage in de novo factual review or consider issues not raised before the Commissioner. TAMKO Asphalt Prod. Inc. of Kan. v. Comm'r, 658 F2d 735, 738–739 (10th Cir. 1981); Jones v. Comm'r, 41 TCM 377 (1980), aff'd, 676 F2d 710 (9th Cir. 1982); McManus v. Comm'r, 93 TC 79 (1989).

[440] Tax Ct. R. Prac. & Proc. 217(c).

[441] Tax Ct. R. Prac. & Proc. 217(c)(1)(ii), 217(c)(2)(ii).

[g] Special Rules: Exempt Organizations

Because the National Office does not generally review determination letters in exempt organization matters before they are issued, procedures restrict the circumstances under which the key district director may issue determination letters. The key district director for the Ohio key district issues determination letters only if the question presented is specifically answered by a statute, tax treaty, or regulation, or by a conclusion stated in a revenue ruling, opinion, or court decision published in the Internal Revenue Bulletin.[442] Both the authority and discretion of the key district director are limited by this "specifically-answered" standard. Generally, the key district director issues determination letters in response to taxpayers' written requests as to completed transactions. However, the key district director does not issue determination letters on the tax consequences of proposed transactions unless it involves (1) the qualification for exempt status of organizations described in Sections 501 and 521 of the Code[443]; (2) the classification of private foundation status[444]; (3) recognition of unusual grants to certain organizations under Sections 170(b)(1)(A)(vi) and 509(a)(2)[445]; (4) requests for relief under Regulations § 301.9100-1 in connection with the recognition of exemption[446]; (5) advance approval under Section 4945 of organizations' grant-making whose determination letter requests or applications disclose (or who have otherwise properly disclosed) a grant program or plans to conduct such a program[447]; (6) whether certain organizations are excepted from filing annual information returns under Section 6303[448]; (7) whether certain organizations qualify as exempt operating

---

[442] Rev. Proc. 2002-4, § 7.01, 2002-1 IRB 127, 139.

[443] Rev. Proc. 2002-4, § 7.04(1), 2002-1 IRB 127, 139. A determination letter concerning qualification for exempt status will be issued only to the extent provided in Rev. Proc. 90-27, 1990-1 CB 514, as modified by the revised schedule for user fees in Rev. Proc. 2002-8, 2002-1 IRB 252. Rev. Proc. 90-27 describes the procedures for organizations seeking recognition of exempt status under Section 501 or Section 521.

[444] Rev. Proc. 2002-4, § 7.04(2), 2002-1 IRB 127, 139. Classification is determined under Rev. Proc. 76-34, 1976-2 CB 656.

[445] Rev. Proc. 2002-4, § 7.04(3), 2002-1 IRB 127, 139.

[446] Rev. Proc. 2002-4, § 7.04(4), 2002-1 IRB 127, 139.

[447] If grant-making procedure questions arise that cannot be resolved on the basis of law, regulations, a clearly applicable revenue ruling, or other published procedure, the key district director will forward such questions to the National Office for technical advice. Rev. Proc. 2002-4, § 7.04(5), 2002-1 IRB 127, 139.

[448] Further procedures are provided in Rev. Procs. 83-23, 1983-1 CB 687; 86-23, 1986-1 CB 564; and 95-48, 1995-2 CB 418. Rev. Proc. 2002-4, § 7.04(6), 2002-1 IRB 127, 139.

foundations described in Section 4904(d)[449]; and (8) advance approval of voter registration activities described in Section 4945(d).[450]

The key district director will not issue a determination letter if it appears that

- The taxpayer has directed a similar inquiry to the National Office;
- The same or a related taxpayer has the same issue pending in a case in litigation or before an Appeals Office;
- An industry or trade association or similar group has requested the determination letter on behalf of individual taxpayers within the group (other than the subordinate organizations covered by a group exemption letter); or
- The request involves an industry-wide problem.[451]

To obtain an exemption letter, the organization must file an application with the key district director for the Ohio key district.[452] Processing of these applications is generally the same as with other determination letters[453]; however, the key district director refers questions that are not specifically covered by published precedent to the National Office.[454] If the organization believes there is no published precedent or there is a lack of uniformity among the districts, the applicant should request that the key district director seek technical advice from the National Office.[455]

The National Office (EP/EO) itself reviews determination letters involving tax-exempt status to ensure uniformity in the application of principles and precedents.[456] It notifies the key district director when it takes exception to a determination letter.[457] If the organization protests the National Office's exception to the determination letter, the file and protest is returned to the National Office and the referral is treated as a request for technical advice.[458]

---

[449] Rev. Proc. 2002-4, § 7.04(7), 2002-1 IRB 127, 139.

[450] Rev. Proc. 2002-4, § 7.04(8), 2002-1 IRB 127, 140.

[451] Rev. Proc. 2002-4, § 7.05, 2002-1 IRB 127, 140.

[452] Rev. Proc. 90-27, 1990-1 CB 514.

[453] Rev. Proc. 2002-4, §§ 9, 10, 11, 2002-1 IRB 127, 142–155.

[454] Rev. Proc. 90-27, § 6.02, 1990-1 CB 514, 516.

[455] Rev. Proc. 90-27, § 6.04, 1990-1 CB 514, 516.

[456] Rev. Proc. 2002-4, § 10.02, 2002-1 IRB 127, 153; Rev. Proc. 90-27, § 8.01, 1990-1 CB 514, 516.

[457] Rev. Proc. 90-27, § 8.02, 1990-1 CB 514, 516. Technical advice procedures are described in Rev. Proc. 2002-5, 2002-1 IRB 173.

[458] In J. David Gladstone Found. v. Comm'r, 77 TC 221 (1981), the Tax Court found that a written protest letter regarding a proposed revocation of nonprivate foundation status was equivalent to a request for a determination.

The effect of a determination letter is generally the same as that of a letter ruling.[459] It is effective as of the date the organization was formed if its activities were consistent with exemption. However, if the organization's activities must be modified in order to qualify, the exemption ruling or determination letter is effective only for the period it specifies. Obviously, an exemption letter may not be relied on if there is a change in the organization's activities.

[i] Appeals. If the key district office issues an initial adverse determination or a letter proposing the revocation or modification of exempt status, the key district must inform the organization of its right to appeal the determination to the Appeals Office.[460] An appeal to the Appeals Office may not be taken, however, if the key district's determination is based on technical advice issued to the district.[461]

To appeal, the organization must file a protest letter (following the usual protest format) within thirty days after the date of the key district's notice (unless the date is extended) (1) requesting Appeals review, (2) stating whether the organization wishes a conference in Appeals, and (3) setting out its statement of the facts, the applicable law, and arguments in support of its position on exempt status.[462] After it receives the protest, the key district may reconsider, but if it adheres to its initial determination, it will send the case to the Chief of the appropriate Appeals Office.

After considering the organization's appeal and any additional information developed at a conference, Appeals will notify the organization of its decision and issue the appropriate determination letter to the organization.[463] If the organization submits additional facts, circumstances, or arguments at Appeals, the Appeals officer may suspend the Appeals procedures and refer the case back to the key district for additional consideration.[464]

It is important for the organization to convince the Appeals office to reverse or modify the key district's decision by making a full presentation of the facts, circumstances, and arguments at the initial consideration by the Appeals Office. To make the case that the key district did not consider all the facts and authorities requires the organization to prepare a full, rather than a skeletal, protest. If proposed action of the Appeals Office is contrary to a prior National Office technical advice or ruling, Appeals must submit the proposed decision through the Office of the Regional Director of Appeals to the Assistant Com-

---

[459] Rev. Proc. 2002-4, § 14.01, 2002-1 IRB 127, 161.

[460] Rev. Proc. 90-27, § 10, 1990-1 CB 514, 516–517.

[461] Rev. Proc. 90-27, § 10.02, 1990-1 CB 514, 517.

[462] Rev. Proc. 90-27, § 10.01, 1990-1 CB 514, 516–517. For the preparation of protests, see ¶ 9.04[3].

[463] Rev. Proc. 90-27, § 11.01, 1990-1 CB 514, 516–517.

[464] Rev. Proc. 90-27, § 11.02, 1990-1 CB 514, 517.

missioner (EP/EO).[465] Once the National Office's decision is made, unless Appeals promptly requests that the National Office reconsider, Appeals must follow the decision of the National Office. Whether reconsideration is requested or not, the Assistant Commissioner makes the final decision.[466]

When either the Appeals Office or the organization believes that an exemption or private foundation status issue is not covered by published precedent or there is a lack of uniformity on the treatment of the issue, the Appeals Office must request technical advice from the National Office,[467] and the organization should ask the Appeals Office to request technical advice.[468] Technical advice issued by the Assistant Commissioner (EP/EO) is final and binding on the Appeals Office.[469]

[ii] **Revocation or modification of exempt status.** Revocation or modification of tax-exempt status can jeopardize the very existence of an organization claiming to be exempt from tax. In two cases decided in 1974, the Supreme Court held that courts were precluded from restraining the Service from withdrawing a favorable determination letter or removing an organization from the list of organizations that may receive gifts qualifying for charitable deductions.[470] According to the Supreme Court's analysis, judicial review of an organization's exempt status could be had only in a Tax Court deficiency proceeding or a suit for refund. However, in 1976, Congress provided a declaratory judgment procedure in Section 7428, which permitted judicial review of the initial or continuing qualification or status of charitable organizations.[471]

A key district director does not have authority under Section 7805(b) to limit the revocation or modification of the determination letter. Therefore, if a key district director proposes to revoke or modify a determination letter, the taxpayer may request limitation of the retroactive effect of the revocation or modification by asking the key district director who issued the determination letter to seek technical advice from the National Office.[472] The Service has es-

---

[465] Rev. Proc. 90-27, § 11.05, 1990-1 CB 514, 517. In a case under Section 521, the proposed disposition is submitted through the Regional Director of Appeals to the Associate Chief Counsel (Employee Plans and Exempt Organizations).

[466] Rev. Proc. 90-27, § 11.05, 1990-1 CB 514, 517.

[467] Rev. Proc. 90-27, § 11.03, 1990-1 CB 514, 517. The Required technical advice procedures are described in Rev. Proc. 2002-5, 2002-1 IRB 173. Technical advice procedures are discussed supra at ¶ 3.04[2].

[468] Rev. Proc. 90-27, § 11.04, 1990-1 CB 514, 517.

[469] This is so unless the Appeals Office believes that the conclusions reached by the National Office should be reconsidered and then requests a reconsideration. Rev. Proc. 90-27, § 11.03, 1999-1 CB 514, 517.

[470] Bob Jones Univ. v. Simon, 416 US 725 (1974); Alexander v. "Americans United," Inc., 416 US 752 (1974).

[471] See infra ¶ 3.04[3][g][iii].

[472] Rev. Proc. 2002-4, § 14.02(3), 2002-1 IRB 127, 161–162.

tablished procedures for organizations seeking intra-agency relief under Section 7805(b) to limit the retroactive effect of the revocation or modification of a determination letter. It should be noted that these procedures constitute an administrative remedy that the organization must exhaust before instituting a declaratory judgment action.[473]

The Service's procedures have the following features:

- *Manner of notice.* Revocation or modification of a ruling or determination letter may be made by (1) a notice to the taxpayer to whom the ruling or determination letter originally was issued; (2) enactment of legislation or ratification of a tax treaty; (3) a Supreme Court decision; (4) issuance of temporary or final regulations; or (5) issuance of a revenue ruling, revenue procedure, or other statement published in the Internal Revenue Bulletin.[474]

- *Prospective or retroactive revocation.* Revocation ordinarily takes effect no later than the time at which the organization received written notice that its exemption ruling or determination letter might be revoked or modified.[475] Revocation may be retroactive if the organization (1) omitted or misstated a material fact; (2) operated in a manner materially different than that originally represented; or (3) engaged in a prohibited transaction that was for the purpose of diverting corpus or income from its exempt purpose and that involved a substantial part of its corpus or income.[476]

- *Request for limitation of retroactive effect.* If a key district director proposes to revoke or modify a determination letter, the organization will only be considered to have exhausted its administrative remedies if it requests the key district director to seek technical advice from the National Office that revocation or modification be applied prospectively under the discretionary authority of Section 7805(b).[477] The organization's request under Section 7805(b) must follow the procedures generally applicable to technical advice in employee plans and exempt organization matters.[478]

- *Appeals Office review.* After the organization is notified of the key district director's decision that the exemption ruling or determination letter should be revoked or modified, the organization may appeal the action by filing a protest with the key district director, requesting Appeals Of-

---

[473] Rev. Proc. 2002-4, § 14.02(3), 2002-1 IRB 127, 161–162.

[474] Rev. Proc. 90-27, §§ 10.01, 14.01, 1990-1 CB 514, 516, 518.

[475] Rev. Proc. 90-27, § 10.01 and § 14.01, 1990-1 CB 514, 516, 518.

[476] Rev. Proc. 90-27, § 14.01, 1990-1 CB 514, 518.

[477] Rev. Proc. 2002-4, § 14.02(3), 2002-1 IRB 127, 161–162; Rev. Proc. 90-27, § 14.01, 1990-1 CB 514, 518.

[478] Rev. Proc. 2002-5, § 18.06, 2002-1 IRB 173, 197–198.

fice review, and stating the facts law, and arguments in support of its position.[479] The organization may ask the district office or Appeals Office to request technical advice in the same manner and circumstances as cases not involving revocation or modification.[480]

[iii] **Declaratory judgment procedure.** Under the provisions of Section 7428, the District Court for the District of Columbia, the Court of Federal Claims, and the Tax Court have concurrent jurisdiction to issue a declaratory judgment in the case of an actual controversy involving a determination of the Service or its failure to make a determination about the initial or continuing qualification or status of an organization as (1) an exempt charitable or other exempt organization under Section 501(c)(3); (2) a qualified charitable contribution donee under Section 170(c)(2); (3) a private foundation under Section 509; or (4) a private operating foundation under Section 4042(j)(3).[481] This remedy applies to situations where a presumably qualified organization has lost its exempt status, but only to an actual determination (or failure to make one) involving initial or continuing tax-exempt qualification or status. It is not available where tax-exempt status has not yet been withdrawn. The Tax Court has interpreted this prerequisite strictly. For example, where the Service has ruled that a proposed transaction will jeopardize an organization's tax-exempt status, no jurisdiction exists to hear the case if the Service has not actually revoked the organization's exemption.[482]

---

[479] Rev. Proc. 90-27, 14.02, 1990-1 CB 518. See ¶ 3.04[3][f][i] for a description of these appeal procedures.

[480] Rev. Proc. 90-27, § 14.02 and §§ 10, 11. The Tax Court has held that there is no due process right to a pre-revocation hearing when a favorable exempt-organization letter ruling is retroactively revoked. United Cancer Council, Inc. v. Comm'r, 100 TC 162 (1993). The court rejected the taxpayer's argument that evolving notions of procedural due process had rendered the Supreme Court's opinion in Bob Jones Univ. v. Simon, 416 US 725 (1974), obsolete.

[481] IRC § 7428(a). The Tax Court has adopted rules for these proceedings. Tax Ct. R. Prac. & Proc. 210–218. Although there is concurrent jurisdiction, where an action is commenced in one court, another action may not be commenced in another court. Basic Bible Church, Inc. v. Regan, 82-2 USTC ¶ 9476 (DDC 1982).

[482] New Community Senior Citizen Hous. Corp., 72 TC 372 (1979). But compare J. David Gladstone Found. v. Comm'r, 77 TC 221 (1981) (Service proposed revocation of nonprivate foundation status, the Foundation protested, and the Service failed to act for more than ninety days; held: the Foundation was entitled to bring an action under Section 7428(a)(2) because the Service had failed to make a determination and the protest was a "request for determination" as to which the Foundation had exhausted its administrative remedies). No final determination had been received in *Gladstone*, but the Tax Court nevertheless found it had jurisdiction to grant declaratory relief under Section 7428. The Tax Court distinguished *New Community*, in part, on the basis of evidence that the Service had already decided to revoke the charitable status of the foundation at the time it filed its petition. Compare Urantia Found. v. Comm'r, 77 TC 507 (1981), aff'd, 684 F2d 521 (7th

The declaratory judgment action is subject to three limitations. First, only the organization whose qualification or status is at issue may bring the action.[483] Second, the action must be instituted no more than ninety days after the date the Service has mailed a notice of determination to the organization.[484] Third, the organization must also have exhausted its administrative remedies before bringing the declaratory judgment action.[485] While the first two requirements pose no unusual problems, satisfaction of the third requirement can be problematic.

Specifically, by statute, an organization is not considered to have exhausted its administrative remedies unless and until 270 days have elapsed since the date on which the Service was properly requested to make a determination and the Service has still not made a determination. Even if this period has expired, it appears that the organization may not bring an action if it has not taken all reasonable steps to secure a determination or the Service has not unreasonably delayed its determination.[486]

Delay in the Service's action can adversely affect an organization whose exempt status is in question, especially an organization seeking initial qualifi-

Cir. 1982) (following *New Community* but recognizing the distinction articulated by *Gladstone*). See also High Adventure Ministries, Inc. v. Comm'r, 80 TC 292 (1983) (the Tax Court found no actual controversy in existence because, at the time of trial, the Service had not yet issued a notice of proposed revocation of exempt status).

[483] IRC § 7428(b)(1). In addition to the prerequisite of standing to bring suit in a declaratory judgment action, the burden of proof is on the taxpayer "where it was determined that the Commissioner followed proper administrative procedures. . . ." Parshall Christian Order v. Comm'r, 45 TCM 488 (1983). Also on standing, see Baptist Hosp., Inc. v. United States, 851 F2d 1397 (Fed. Cir. 1988) (survivor of corporate merger could not obtain declaratory judgment of tax-exempt qualification or status of merged corporation); see also Lee v. IRS, 81 AFTR2d 98-420 (DDC 1997) (founder of organization, whose exempt status was denied, lacked standing to challenge the action under Section 7428, and also lacked standing even if he were bringing the action on behalf of the organization). However, the Service must state on what evidence in the administrative record it relies in revoking exempt status. Otherwise, the court would have to decide what evidence in the record supported the conclusion, thus making the court the initial finder of fact. Airlie Found. Inc. v. United States, 92-2 USTC ¶ 50,462 (DDC 1992).

[484] IRC § 7428(b)(3).

[485] IRC § 7428(b)(2). See discussion at ¶ 3.04[3][f]. The Service has described what it believes are the "steps and remedies required to be exhausted within the Service . . ." for purposes of a proper declaratory judgment proceeding. Rev. Proc. 84-46, § 12, 84-1 CB 541.

[486] See Prince Corp. v. Comm'r, 67 TC 318 (1976) (interpreting the same requirement in Section 7476, involving pension plan declaratory judgments). See also Rev. Proc. 80-25, § 11.02, 1980-1 CB 65; Joint Comm. on Taxation, 94th Cong., 2d Sess., General Explanation of the Tax Reform Act of 1976, at 406 (Comm. Print 1976), reprinted in 1976-3 CB (Vol. 2) 1, at 418.

cation for exempt status.[487] The declaratory judgment provision does not meet this problem, but it does offer assistance to a previously exempt organization faced with the likelihood of exhausting its sources of support during the litigation. If the organization has already qualified for exempt status, it may be entitled to receive contributions as an eligible charitable donee under Section 170(c)(2) during the litigation period, even if the court ultimately determines that the organization has lost its charitable status.[488]

[4] Chief Counsel Advice

Successive amendments to the Freedom of Information Act in 1974 and again in 1976 considerably narrowed the information that the Service could claim was exempt from disclosure. Although the Service fought to keep internally generated procedures and legal positions confidential, as the foregoing description of formerly unavailable letter rulings and technical advice memoranda demonstrates, the Service's efforts in avoiding FOIA disclosure were unavailing.

In response to successful FOIA litigation, Section 6110 was enacted to supersede the FOIA and to establish special procedures for the Service to follow in making "written determinations" (i.e., letter rulings, determination letters, and technical advice) available to the public and at the same time to preserve taxpayer privacy. Chief Counsel attorneys also communicated with field offices in other memoranda, such as field service advice, technical assistance, service center advice, litigation guideline memoranda, tax litigation bulletins, general litigation bulletins, and criminal tax bulletins.

Since 1988, the Chief Counsel has been rendering guidance to field personnel in response to requests for legal guidance on specific taxpayer issues. This advice to the field is called field service advice. The reliance and import to be accorded field service advice is a controversial matter both because the affected taxpayer did not participate in the process, and because such advice appeared to be used by field personnel as a substitute for technical advice.[489]

In *Tax Analysts v. IRS*, the plaintiff sought disclosure of field service advice under the FOIA. The District of Columbia Circuit hearing this case ruled that field service advice memoranda were not confidential return information, and so were subject to disclosure under the FOIA unless portions could not be

---

[487] A refusal to rule is treated as an adverse determination, where the refusal is the result of an organization's inability to describe its purposes and activities completely. 26 CFR § 601.201(n)(7).

[488] IRC § 7428(c).

[489] Staff, Joint Comm. on Taxation, General Explanation of Tax Legislation Enacted in 1998, 105th Cong., 2d Sess., 120 (1998).

made public because of some privilege claim or other FOIA exemption.[490] To provide a statutory procedure for making this information public and also to protect the private information of the affected taxpayers, the IRS Restructuring and Reform Act of 1998 amended Section 6110 to include Chief Counsel advice.[491]

As amended, Section 6110 includes Chief Counsel advice in the definition of "written determination."[492] "Chief Counsel advice" is defined as (1) written advice or instructions under whatever name, prepared by the Chief Counsel's office and issued to the field or service center personnel or to regional or district counsel attorneys (2) that conveys any legal interpretation of a revenue position, or Chief Counsel position concerning a "revenue matter" or any legal interpretation of any law relating to the assessment or collection of any liability under a revenue provision.[493] Accordingly, the Service must now "open to public inspection" Chief Counsel advice and any background file documents relating to the advice.[494]

Generally, there are seven categories of information that the Service must delete before making written determinations public. However, in the case of Chief Counsel advice, the Service need only delete identifying details, such as the names, and addresses of the person to whom the Chief Counsel advice relates and any other person identified in the Chief Counsel advice or any background file document. While Section 6110 does not require deletion of other categories of information from Chief Counsel advice, including those categories covering trade secrets and commercial or financial information, such information may be deleted in the Service's discretion under the FOIA exemptions.[495]

---

[490] Tax Analysts v. IRS, 117 F3d 607 (DC Cir. 1997).

[491] IRC § 6110(i), as amended by Act § 3509, applicable to Chief Counsel advice issued more than ninety days after July 22, 1998; but, the amendment applies to Chief Counsel advice issued after December 31, 1985, at specified intervals. Taxpayer privacy was an important part of Congress's concern in amending Section 6110. The Conference Report says: "[I]t is clear that [field service advice memoranda] are not expressly covered by [S]ection 6110. As a consequence, there exists no mechanism by which taxpayers may participate in the administrative process of redacting their private information from such documents or to resolve disagreements in court." HR Conf. Rep. No. 105-599, at 123.

[492] IRC § 6110(b)(1).

[493] IRC § 6110(i)(1)(A). "Revenue provision" is defined as "any existing or former internal revenue law, regulation, revenue ruling, revenue procedure, other published or unpublished guidance, or tax treaty, either in general or as applied to specific taxpayers or groups of specific taxpayers."

[494] IRC § 6110(a).

[495] IRC §§ 6110(i)(3)(A), 6110(c)(2)–6110(c)(7). Section 6110(i)(3)(B) provides that the Service may make discretionary deletions under the FOIA under the exemptions to disclosure under the FOIA in 5 USC §§ 552(b) and 552(c). See discussion of the FOIA in Chapter 2.

Chief Counsel advice concerning a specific taxpayer or group of specific taxpayers cannot be made public until the Service, within sixty days after the Chief Counsel advice is given, mails a notice of intention to disclose to each affected taxpayer.[496] Of course, if the Chief Counsel advice does not relate to a specific taxpayer, there is no "notice of intention to disclose" requirement.

Within sixty days after the Chief Counsel advice was issued, the advice may be made available to the public with the limited deletions of names and addresses, and, as noted above, other discretionary deletions may be made by the Service for information exempt from disclosure under the FOIA or other federal law.[497]

[5] Acquiescences

The acquiescence program arose out of complaints, made in the 1950s, that official tax policies were known to a select few, but were otherwise unavailable to many tax practitioners having only infrequent contact with the National Office. At this time, complaints were also raised that the Service was refusing to follow selected Tax Court decisions while not appealing them.

Currently, it is the Service's "policy to announce at an early date whether it will follow the holding [of a court] in certain cases."[498] The Service, in its discretion, announces its "acquiescence" or "nonacquiescence" in an Action on Decision "only on unappealed issues decided adverse[ly] to the government." Before 1991, the Service disclosed its acquiescence or nonacquiescence only as to certain regular Tax Court opinions. Thereafter, the Service expanded the program to include the holdings of other courts in civil tax cases where it decides that such guidance is helpful. Accordingly, under the current program, the Service may publish (in the Internal Revenue Bulletin) an acquiescence or nonacquiescence in the holdings of (1) reviewed opinions of the Tax Court; (2) Tax Court memorandum opinions; (3) federal district court opinions; (4) Court of Federal Claims opinions; and (5) Court of Appeals opinions.

The Cumulative Bulletin states: "Actions on Decision shall be relied upon within the Service only as conclusions applying the law in the particular case at the time of the Action on Decision was issued."[499] There is a "same facts" restriction of the use of an Action on Decision, that is, the application of the recommended Action on Decision to a similar case should be extended with "caution" unless (1) the facts and circumstances are "substantially the same,"

---

[496] IRC § 6110(i)(4)(B).

[497] IRC § 6110(i)(4)(A).

[498] 2002-1 IRB 5.

[499] 2002-1 IRB 5.

and (2) the analysis of the issues involved has not been affected by new legislation, regulations, rulings, or subsequent court decisions.

An acquiescence or nonacquiescence may not apply to each issue in a case. Frequently, the announcement relates only to the issue or issues decided adversely to the government. Thus, if a court's holding results in issue 1 being decided adversely for the Service, while issue 2 is decided in favor of the Service, an acquiescence would be necessary only for issue 1.

[a] IRS Policy

The Service policy on acquiescences is as follows:[500]

- The recommendation in every Action on Decision is summarized as an acquiescence, acquiescence in result only, or nonacquiescence.
- Both "acquiescence" and "acquiescence in result only" mean that the Service accepts the holding of the court in the case, and will follow the holding in disposing of cases with the same controlling facts.
- An acquiescence indicates neither approval nor disapproval of the reasons the court gives for its conclusions. Thus, an acquiescence differs from the judicial doctrine of stare decisis, which considers as controlling precedent not only the result but the rationale of the decision. An acquiescence in result only is intended to expressly indicate the Service's disagreement with or concern about some or all of the court's reasons for its decision. Service personnel are thus put on notice that the official policy is against some or all of the reasons for the decision, even though the case may not be appealed. Consequently, field offices are unlikely to follow an acquiescence when it is "in result only."
- Nonacquiescence signifies that, although the Service is not seeking further review, it does not agree with the holding of the court, and generally will not follow the decision in disposing of cases with similar sets of facts involving other taxpayers.
- When the opinion of a circuit court of appeals is involved, a nonacquiescence indicates that, although the Service will recognize the opinion as precedent within the deciding circuit, it will not follow the holding in courts whose decisions are not appealable to that circuit.

Whenever the government loses an issue in tax cases tried in the Tax Court or in a federal district court, an action on decision (AOD) is prepared by a lawyer in the Office of the Associate Chief Counsel (Litigation).[501] The AOD is prepared at the same time that the Chief Counsel lawyer prepares a formal

---

[500] 2002-1 IRB 5.

[501] See Form 1.6, in Chapter 1, for the organization of the Office of the Chief Counsel.

recommendation to the Justice Department regarding appeal of the decision.[502] The AOD presents (1) the issue decided against the government; (2) the pertinent facts; and (3) a discussion of the reasoning supporting the lawyer's recommendation whether or not to appeal. After review in the Tax Litigation Division, the AOD is sent to Technical. If this office is in agreement with the recommendation, the AOD is published for the use of Service personnel.[503]

Where Tax Court decisions are the subject of an AOD, there is frequently a delay in issuing an acquiescence or nonacquiescence.

After an acquiescence or nonacquiescence is published, it may be withdrawn, sometimes after many years.[504] Delays and changes in position are inevitable as the Service develops positions on pending issues and attempts to determine whether the facts of the decided case are the same as those in a current area of interest and the extent to which the legal reasoning of the decided case should be made applicable in other cases.

[b] Effect

In the Service's own words, an Action on Decision, unlike a Treasury regulation or a revenue ruling, "is not an affirmative statement of Service position" and "is not intended to serve as public guidance and may not be cited as precedent." Nevertheless, Service personnel must follow an acquiescence. Therefore, an acquiescence is authoritative in dealing with Service officials on closed transactions, since, as the Cumulative Bulletin states, the acquiescence "shall be relied on" by them. Similarly, in ruling or determination requests, an acquiescence should be useful as authority for the Service's position. In this latter situation, the taxpayer actually relies on the ruling or determination letter received, and not the acquiescence.

On the other hand, if the purpose of the Action on Decision is to correct a mistake in the application of the tax law to particular transactions, an acquiescence may be withdrawn at any time. Such withdrawal can be made with retroactive effect, irrespective of any reliance by taxpayers to their detriment. This principle was announced in *Dixon v. United States*,[505] where the taxpayer, in reliance on the Commissioner's acquiescence in a Tax Court decision on the same issue, reported capital gain on the sale of notes purchased at a dis-

---

[502] This description of the AOD procedure was given by the Service to the district court in Taxation With Representation Fund v. IRS, 485 F. Supp. 263 (DDC 1980).

[503] The IRS has been ordered to make AODs public under FOIA. Taxation With Representation Fund v. IRS, 485 F. Supp. 263 (DDC 1980).

[504] For example, in 1978-1 CB 2, an acquiescence published in VIII-2 CB 27 (1929) was withdrawn and a nonacquiescence substituted.

[505] Dixon v. United States, 381 US 68 (1965).

count.[506] On the same day as its decision in *Dixon*, the Supreme Court decided that the Commissioner's retroactive withdrawal was supported by proper analysis of the law, and held that a sale of notes purchased at a discount was not entitled to capital gain treatment.[507] From the Court's point of view, the initial acquiescence represented a statement of position that was incorrect as a matter of law, while the withdrawal of the acquiescence represented correction of a mistake of law. Based on this reasoning, the Supreme Court held that the Commissioner could correct a mistake of law and that such correction could be made retroactive despite a taxpayer's reliance on the incorrect statement of law adopted by the Service in an acquiescence (or ruling). Having no legal status, the acquiescence could not justifiably be relied upon, and so no notice was required before the acquiescence was withdrawn retroactively.

The Supreme Court's *Dixon* analysis also strictly interpreted the Service's acquiescence to the facts of the case acquiesced in and the basis of the court's opinion in that case. The Court reviewed that Tax Court opinion and found, contrary to the taxpayer's contention, that the Tax Court did not explicitly or "squarely" decide that capital gain treatment was to be accorded to the discount element in the certificate of indebtedness involved. Also, the Court said that the Tax Court decision was limited to retirement of debt instruments and was not extended to a sale of the instrument.

After *Dixon*, it is clear that (1) the Commissioner may not be estopped from retroactively correcting a mistake of law without any prior notice of the action and that (2) both the facts and the actual decision of the adverse Tax Court decision in which the Service has acquiesced limit the extent of the acquiescence. Accordingly, reliance on an acquiescence is hazardous because it may be withdrawn retroactively to correct a "mistake of law" and any authoritative effect it may have is limited to the facts and opinion of the decision that was acquiesced in. As a consequence, an acquiescence can only be given as much weight in tax planning as these limitations allow.

[6] The Internal Revenue Bulletin

The Internal Revenue Bulletin is "the authoritative instrument of the Commissioner of Internal Revenue for announcing official rulings and procedures of the Internal Revenue Service and for publishing Treasury Decisions, Executive Orders, Tax Conventions, legislation, court decisions, and other items of gen-

---

[506] Caulkins v. Comm'r, 1 TC 656 (1943), aff'd, 144 F2d 482 (6th Cir. 1944). The Commissioner initially published a nonacquiescence in Rev. Rul. 11581, 1943-1 CB 28. He published his acquiescence in Rev. Rul. 11907, 1944-1 CB 5, after the court of appeals affirmed the Tax Court decision. The acquiescence was withdrawn in 1955 in 1955-1 CB 7 and Rev. Rul. 55-136, 1955-1 CB 213.

[507] United States v. Midland-Ross Corp., 381 US 54 (1965).

eral interest."[508] The Bulletin is published weekly. These weekly issues are consolidated, usually in semiannual volumes called the Internal Revenue Cumulative Bulletin.[509] The Cumulative Bulletin is prepared in three parts: Part I, 1954 Code, which includes rulings and decisions on provisions of the Code arranged according to Code and regulations sections; Part II, Treaties and Tax Legislation, which includes Subpart A, Tax Conventions (with related Treasury decisions and revenue rulings), and Subpart B, Legislation and Related Committee Reports; and Part III, Administrative, Procedural, and Miscellaneous.

[7] The Internal Revenue Manual

Actions of Service officials are guided almost step by step by the Internal Revenue Manual. The Manual is a compilation of the policies, procedures, instructions, and guidelines governing the Service's organization and operations. It covers in detailed fashion the daily functions of Service personnel. It consists of a basic text with a table of contents, exhibits, and indexes, and is updated by Manual Supplements. In addition, the Manual includes various handbooks for personnel, such as the Handbook for Revenue Officers and the Handbook for Special Agents. Organization of the Manual follows the functional organization of the Service itself.

- Part O, Personnel, Training, and Development
- Part I, Administration
- Part II, Collection Procedure for Office Branches
- Part III, Service Center Procedures
- Part IV, Audit
- Part V, Delinquent Accounts and Returns
- Part VI, Taxpayer Service
- Part VII, Employee Plans and Exempt Organizations
- Part VIII, Appeals
- Part IX, Criminal Investigation
- Part X, Inspection
- Part XXX, Administrative
- Part XXXI, Criminal Tax
- Part XXXIV, General Litigation
- Part XXXV, Tax Litigation
- Part CV, Collection Activity Handbooks

---

[508] 1999-1 CB iii.

[509] Both the weekly bulletins and the semiannual volumes are available from the U.S. Government Printing Office in Washington, D.C. on an individual or subscription basis. There is also an Index-Digest System that is a research and reference service supplementing the Bulletin, available from the Superintendent of Documents.

Each part is then divided into chapters that, in turn, are broken down into sections and subsections. Former Part XI, the Technical portion of the Manual, is located in Part (39) of the Chief Counsel Directive Manual (CCDM).

Manual Supplements contain expanded explanations of material in the Manual. Manual Supplements are issued, in lieu of making Manual revisions, in order to (1) test the practicality and effect of new precedents; (2) provide instructions for immediate release pending later amendment of the Manual; (3) publish temporary instructions; or (4) provide information to specific levels within the Service (i.e., the National Office, a regional office, or regional and district offices and Service centers).[510]

The Service once considered the Manual, with only a limited exception, to be closed to public scrutiny. However, as a result of FOIA litigation, the Manual has been made public, with the exception of those portions exempt under the FOIA, such as those pertaining to tolerances.[511]

The legal effect of the Manual where Service officials fail to act in compliance with its procedures has already been discussed.[512] The effect of a violation of the Manual was squarely before the Supreme Court in *United States v. Caceres*,[513] where conversations with a defendant in a bribery prosecution were monitored without Justice Department approval, as required by the Manual. Holding that the evidence obtained in violation of the Manual was not required to be excluded under the circumstances of the case, the Court also reaffirmed the principle that agencies, such as the Service, are bound by their own procedural rules. For example, the Court said:

> Agency violations of their own regulations, whether or not also in violation of the Constitution, may well be inconsistent with the standards of agency action which the [Administrative Procedure Act] directs the courts to enforce. Indeed, some of our most important decisions holding agencies bound by their regulations have been in cases originally brought under the APA.[514]

The critical point in *Caceres* was that the case was a criminal prosecution, and not an Administrative Procedure Act case. Moreover, the re-

---

[510] CCH Manual, Volume 1, How to Use the Manual at 2. Each Manual Supplement is numbered by a two-digit subject classification code number corresponding to Manual chapter numbers. This number is followed by a code letter corresponding to the level of distribution: G (General distribution), R (Regional-level distribution), RDD (distribution down to Regional Offices, District Directors, and Service Center Directors), or N (distribution in National Office only).

[511] See the discussion of FOIA at ¶ 3.03[3][c]. To the extent that the Manual is public under FOIA, it is available in public reading rooms at district offices and the National Office. Much of the Manual is available on the IRS's website at www.irs.ustreas.gov.

[512] See ¶ 3.02.

[513] United States v. Caceres, 440 US 741 (1979).

[514] United States v. Caceres, 440 US 741, 754 (1979) (footnotes omitted).

quested relief was suppression of incriminating evidence without which there could have been no viable prosecution, and not simply invalidation of agency action.

Determining the legal effect of a violation of the Manual in light of *Caceres* requires the use of a case-by-case approach. There is no rigid rule requiring exclusion for every violation of the Manual. In determining whether exclusion of information, invalidation of action, or some other penalty should be imposed for the Service's violations of the Manual, a court will consider (1) whether the case is civil or criminal; (2) whether the relief sought is invalidation of the Service's action or application of the exclusionary rule; (3) the circumstances of noncompliance with the Manual (i.e., whether or not it was a good-faith failure to comply with the Manual); (4) the nature of the Manual provision (i.e., whether it was a mere housekeeping rule); and (5) whether there are internal sanctions applicable to Service employees for noncompliance.

Given the number of factors to be considered by the courts, generalizations concerning the impact of Manual violations cannot be made. *Caceres* does say that, in criminal cases, the result will turn on whether violation of some constitutional right has resulted from an agent's noncompliance with the Manual and that, absent such a violation, *Caceres* stands as authority for denial of suppression. However, in civil cases, *Caceres* does not support the conclusion that actions in violation of the Manual are immune from challenge based on the denial of administrative due process.

Moreover, the Court's *Caceres* opinion itself recognizes the vitality of the administrative law proposition that an agency is bound by its administrative rules, even if they impose a higher standard than is required by the Constitution or federal law. Other agencies' actions have been invalidated by the courts when a guideline manual or published regulation has not been followed.[515] However, despite these considerations, courts, citing *Caceres* as authority, have indicated that the Manual's provisions are directory and not mandatory, and thus violations of the Manual have no legal ramifications.[516]

---

[515] See Massachusetts Fair Share v. Law Enforcement Assistance Admin., 758 F2d 708 (DC Cir. 1985) ("It has long been settled that a federal agency must adhere firmly to self-adopted rules by which interests of others are to be regulated. This precept is rooted in the concept of fair play and abhorrence of unjust discrimination, and its ambit is not limited to rules attaining the status of formal regulations."); see also Montilla v. INS, 926 F2d 162 (2d Cir. 1991). If (1) the Service violates its Manual, (2) the violation of internal procedures is not a minor one, and (3) the violation affects a substantive right of a taxpayer, there is authority supporting the invalidation of the Service's action. Newman, "The Effectiveness of an Unpublished Rule," 1995 Ann. Survey of Am. Law 1, 16–19.

[516] See Urban v. Comm'r, 964 F2d 888, 890 (9th Cir. 1992); United States v. Horne, 714 F2d 206, 207 (1st Cir. 1983) (*Manual* does not have binding force and effect of law); United States v. Will, 671 F2d 963, 967 (6th Cir. 1982); Continental Ill. Corp. v. United States, 727 F. Supp. 425, 429 (ND Ill. 1989); Notaro v. United States, 93-1 USTC ¶ 50,030 (ND Ill. 1992) (argument that undesignated payment should be applied to trust

[8] Information Letters

An information letter can be issued either by the National Office or by a district office. It is issued to call attention to what the Service believes to be a well-established interpretation or principle of tax law. The general statement, unlike other statements by the Service, is not applied to a specific set of facts.[517] An information letter may be issued where the nature of the request from an individual or an organization suggests that general information is being sought. It may also be issued where the request does not meet all the requirements of a request for a ruling or a determination letter. The primary purpose of the information letter is to provide general information that the Service feels will assist the individual or the organization making the request.

Because the information letter is issued either by the Service's National Office or by district offices, it has the appearance of reliability. However, an information letter is advisory only, and the Service does not consider itself bound by any statements made in an information letter since this type of letter is not a ruling.[518] Consequently, taxpayers should not rely on an information letter in planning or reporting the tax effects of their transactions.[519]

[9] News Releases and Other Publications

The Service also issues news releases (IRs) to the press to bring attention to matters of a general, rather than technical, nature, such as important speeches by Service or Treasury officials and announcements concerning the availability of Service publications.

The Service's statement of policy in an IR has been held to bind it in its dealings with taxpayers. For example, in one instance, prior to the issuance of an IR on the subject, the Service had taken the position that its special agents were not required to give taxpayers suspected of violating the criminal tax laws so-called Miranda warnings. The Service was largely successful in convincing courts of its position. Nevertheless, in 1968, the Service issued a news release stating that, in the future, its special agents were to announce to a tax-

---

fund portion of employment taxes purportedly as described in *Manual*); Dailey v. United States, 78 AFTR2d 96-6610 (SD Fla. 1996) (contention that levy on IRA violated a *Manual* section rejected in injunction proceeding because provision was procedural in nature and did not give taxpayer any substantive right).

[517] 26 CFR § 601.201(a)(5); Rev. Proc. 2002-1, § 2.04, 2002-1 IRB 9; see also Rev. Proc. 2002-4, 2002-1 IRB 127.

[518] 26 CFR § 601.201(a)(5); Rev. Proc. 2002-1, § 2.04, 2002-1 IRB 9; see also Rev. Proc. 2002-4, 2002-1 IRB 127.

[519] Rogovin, "The Four R's: Regulations, Rulings, Reliance, and Retroactivity," 43 Taxes 756, 771 (1965); Taylor, "Tax Rulings: New Rules and Procedures," 21 NYU Inst. on Fed. Tax'n 69, 71–72 (1963).

payer under investigation the nature of their duties and some of the taxpayer's rights as set forth in the *Miranda* case.[520] Since then, when special agents have neglected to follow this procedure, courts followed the *Accardi* doctrine that an agency is bound by its own procedural rules and suppressed evidence obtained in an interview where the Service's procedure was not followed.[521]

As discussed above, in *United States v. Caceres*,[522] however, the Supreme Court concluded that the effect of a failure to comply with Internal Revenue Manual procedure depended upon whether the affected individual could reasonably be expected to rely on it, and the efforts, if any, made by the Service personnel to comply with that procedure. Additionally, after *Caceres*, courts have been less willing to impose sanctions for the failure of Service personnel to comply with Service procedures, and such procedures would certainly include the subject matter of an announcement or press release.[523]

The Service publishes materials both for the public and for the purposes of its own internal management. The publications issued for public use are designed to provide a means of self-help. While these publications perform a useful and laudable function, they may not be relied on by taxpayers in planning future transactions.[524] In *Adler v. Comm'r*, the taxpayer unsuccessfully claimed entitlement to a deduction because he relied on the Service's publication, *Your Federal Income Tax*, in contracting for dance lessons in the belief that the expense qualified as a medical deduction. The Ninth Circuit denied the taxpayer's claim and, in language reflecting the Supreme Court's decision in *Dixon*, said that no "interpretation by taxpayers of the language used in government pamphlets [can] act as an estoppel against the government, nor change the meaning of taxing statutes."[525]

The Service also publishes documents for the information and guidance of various field offices. The Treasury Department issues Department circulars and orders, signed by the Secretary of the Treasury, on matters before the Treasury

---

[520] IR 949 (Nov. 26, 1968).

[521] United States v. Sourapas, 515 F2d 295 (9th Cir. 1975); United States v. Leahey, 434 F2d 7 (1st Cir. 1970); United States v. Heffner, 420 F2d 809 (4th Cir. 1969); cf., United States v. Leonard, 524 F2d 1076 (2d Cir. 1975).

[522] United States v. Caceres, 440 US 741 (1979). See the discussion at ¶ 3.04[7].

[523] After *Caceres*, the First Circuit in United States v. Irvine, 699 F2d 43 (1983), said that its decision in United States v. Leahey, 434 F2d 7 (1970), is no longer good law.

[524] Adler v. Comm'r, 330 F2d 91, 93 (9th Cir. 1964) (concerning Your Federal Income Tax for Individuals); Johnson v. Comm'r, 620 F2d 153, 155 (7th Cir. 1980), aff'g 37 TCM 1763 (1978) (tax information on Individual Retirement Savings Accounts) (concerning Treasury Department's A Handbook for Exporters); Carpenter v. United States, 495 F2d 175, 184 (5th Cir. 1974) (concerning Tax Guide for U.S. Citizens Abroad).

[525] Adler v. Comm'r, 330 F2d 91, 93 (9th Cir. 1964). But see LeCroy Research Sys. Corp. v. Comm'r, 751 F2d 123, 126–128 (2d Cir. 1984) (retroactive application of regulation requirement held improper and abuse of discretion; taxpayer was entitled to rely on Handbook for Exporters' promise to apply change in regulations prospectively).

in general. For example, Circular No. 230 is a Treasury Department circular dealing with practice before the Service.

Additionally, for internal management purposes, the Secretary of the Treasury, Commissioner of Internal Revenue, and Assistant Commissioners delegate authority to other, usually lower-ranking, officials in the Service by means of delegation orders. Thus, the statutory provisions that provide that the "secretary or his delegate" may or shall do some act are executed by means of the formal delegation of statutory or regulatory authority. These orders appear in the Federal Register and the Internal Revenue Bulletin when they affect a taxpayer's rights and duties.

There are other methods of communicating policy. National Office memoranda are used to convey information to other people in the National Office. Regional Commissioners and district directors issue memoranda and circulars distinguished by the letter RC and DIR to indicate the issuing office and also the geographic area affected.

[10] Oral Communications

Taxpayers frequently obtain information relating to tax matters from Service personnel; for example, where a taxpayer consults a Service employee (1) performing the taxpayer assistance function in a district office; (2) during an examination; or (3) in the course of dealings with officials in the National Office. These communications are the least formal and, as such, are the least reliable statements of Service position. Regulations state:

> A taxpayer may, of course, seek oral technical assistance from a district office in the preparation of his return or report, pursuant to other established procedures [e.g., rulings, determination letters, or technical advice]. Such oral advice is advisory only and the Service is not bound to recognize it in the examination of the taxpayer's return.[526]

It has been said that persons dealing with an agent of the government are bound to take notice of the limitations of the agent's authority, with the result that the government is not bound by the unauthorized acts of its agents and is not estopped from asserting lack of authority as a defense.[527] For instance, an agent's oral statement that is incorrect as a matter of law cannot be relied upon

---

[526] 26 CFR § 601.201(k)(2).

[527] The case often cited for this proposition is Federal Crop Ins. Corp. v. Merrill, 332 US 380 (1947), although neither the majority nor the dissenting opinion uses the term "estoppel." In other cases, the Supreme Court has said that, in general, estoppel may not be invoked to bind the United States United States v. San Francisco, 310 US 16, 32 (1940); Utah Power & Light Co. v. United States, 243 US 389, 409 (1917). There is nevertheless a dispute about the principle. Compare United States v. Lazy FC Ranch, 481 F2d 985,

any more than a ruling or acquiescence based on a mistake of law.[528] However, despite this authority, the Service has been equitably estopped from taking a position contrary to the oral representations of one of its employees.[529] Specifically, in tax cases, the Service has been equitably estopped where it has been shown that

- There has been a misrepresentation of fact by government agents acting within the scope of their authority;
- Taxpayers were ignorant of the true facts;
- The circumstances were such that taxpayers could reasonably rely on the government agent's representation;
- Taxpayers did rely on the representation to their detriment; and
- It would be unconscionable not to grant equitable relief.

It should be noted that these elements are not uniformly stated or applied by the courts.[530] Nevertheless, where these elements have been established, the Service has generally been estopped,[531] although several of the estoppel elements may be difficult to establish. For example, it is unclear whether the government agent must have actual or apparent authority. At least one court has

---

988–989 (9th Cir. 1973) (principle not absolute), with Goldberg v. Weinberger, 546 F2d 477, 480–481 (2d Cir. 1976), cert. denied, 431 US 937 (1977).

[528] Automobile Club of Michigan v. Comm'r, 353 US 180 (1957); Dixon v. United States, 381 US 68 (1965); Druker v. Comm'r, 77 TC 867 (1981), aff'd in part and rev'd in part on another issue, 697 F2d 46 (2d Cir. 1982), cert. denied, 461 US 957 (1983); Bornstein v. United States, 345 F2d 558 (Ct. Cl. 1965); Neri v. Comm'r, 54 TC 767, 771–772 (1970).

[529] See also Melnick, "Equitable Remedies Against the Commissioner; Estoppel, Abuse of Discretion and Discrimination," 171-2d BNA TM (1979); Melton & Goldberg, "Equitable Estoppel in Tax Administration," 62 Taxes 77 (Feb. 1984).

[530] These elements are derived from Tonkonogy v. United States, 417 F. Supp. 78, 79 (SDNY 1976), and New York Athletic Supply Co. v. United States, 450 F. Supp. 469, 471 (SDNY 1978). See also Melnick, "Equitable Remedies Against the Commissioner; Estoppel, Abuse of Discretion and Discrimination," 171-2d BNA TM (1979). But compare Morris White Fashions, Inc. v. United States, 176 F. Supp. 760, 764 (SDNY 1959); Underwood v. Comm'r, 63 TC 468, 477–478 (1975), aff'd, 535 F2d 309 (5th Cir. 1976).

[531] Interstate Fire Ins. Co. v. United States, 215 F. Supp. 586 (ED Tenn. 1963), aff'd per curiam, 339 F2d 603 (6th Cir. 1965) (Service estopped from denying cost reallocation, ordered by revenue agent, that produced refund rather than deficiency); Schuster v. Comm'r, 312 F2d 311 (9th Cir. 1962) (Service estopped from claiming trust includable in estate after agent agreed trust not includable and trust assets distributed); Tonkonogy v. United States, 417 F. Supp. 78, 79 (SDNY 1976) (Service estopped from claiming default in payment); Smale & Robinson, Inc. v. United States, 123 F. Supp. 457 (SD Cal. 1954) (Service estopped from asserting absence of required statement in a refund claim when agent represented inclusion of the statement was unnecessary). See Miller v. United States, 500 F2d 1007 (2d Cir. 1974) (Service estopped from claiming statute of limitations when suit brought within erroneous deadline in claim disallowance).

held that the agent must have actual authority.[532] In that case, an IRS Technical representative assigned the ruling request of one corporation was held not to have had the authority to make a representation regarding the necessity of filing ruling requests for five related corporations. However, other courts appear to have found that the Service personnel involved had the apparent authority to make the representation at issue.[533]

Additionally, for there to be an estoppel, the false representation must also be one of fact and not of law.[534] A representation of fact includes a matter of procedure, and here the decisions generally have been favorable to taxpayers. Three examples illustrate this point. In *Schuster v. Commissioner*,[535] estoppel was found where an agent agreed that a trust was not includable in a decedent's estate and, on that basis, the trustee distributed the trust corpus. Later, the Service sought to hold the trustee liable as a transferee after the statute of limitations had run against the estate. The agent's representation was held to be implicitly related to a procedural matter (i.e., transferee liability). Similarly, in *Smale & Robinson, Inc. v. United States*,[536] the Service was estopped from asserting the taxpayer's failure to state a required ground in a refund claim where the ground was omitted in reliance on a revenue agent's representation. The omission of the ground from the refund claim was viewed as a procedural matter. Finally, in *Tonkonogy v. United States*,[537] the Service was estopped from asserting a default under a compromise agreement with the Service where a taxpayer, who was hospitalized at the time a payment was due under the agreement, received a letter apparently extending time for payment. The taxpayer later paid the balance due under the agreement in accordance with the extension. Both the compromise agreement and the alleged extension were procedural matters.[538]

Detrimental reliance is also prerequisite to any estoppel. Where taxpayers have failed to establish this element, the Service has not been estopped.[539]

[532] Bornstein v. United States, 345 F2d 558 (Ct. Cl. 1965).

[533] See, e.g., Tonkonogy v. United States, 417 F. Supp. 78, 79 (SDNY 1976); Interstate Fire Ins. Co. v. United States, 215 F. Supp. 586 (ED Tenn. 1963), aff'd per curiam, 339 F2d 603 (6th Cir. 1965).

[534] See Glassner v. United States, 80-2 USTC ¶ 9498 (SDNY 1980) (agent's erroneous representation of law not binding); Appelgate v. United States, 80-2 USTC ¶ 9567 (WD Va. 1980); Joplin Bros. Mobile Homes v. United States, 524 F. Supp. 800 (WD Mo. 1981) (mutual mistake of law found so there could be no estoppel).

[535] Schuster v. Comm'r, 312 F2d 311 (9th Cir. 1962).

[536] Smale & Robinson, Inc. v. United States, 123 F. Supp. 457 (SD Cal. 1954).

[537] Tonkonogy v. United States, 417 F. Supp. 78, 79 (SDNY 1976).

[538] See also Miller v. United States, 500 F2d 1007 (2d Cir. 1974).

[539] See, e.g., Lemle v. United States, 579 F2d 185 (2d Cir. 1978); New York Athletic Supply Co. v. United States, 450 F. Supp. 469, 471 (SDNY 1978); Underwood v. Comm'r, 63 TC 468, 477–478 (1975), aff'd, 535 F2d 309 (5th Cir. 1976). Compare Ben-

Finally, estoppel must be distinguished from the duty of consistency that taxpayers are said to owe the Service, and that the Service has as well. The elements of estoppel should be compared with those of the so-called "duty of consistency" taxpayers are said to have. This duty applies where (1) a taxpayer has reported an item for tax purposes in one year; (2) the Commissioner has relied on or acquiesced in that fact for that year; and (3) the taxpayer subsequently attempts to change the representation after the statute of limitations on assessment bars adjustments for the prior tax year.[540] This duty of consistency applies to the Service as well, and the elements are similarly stated.[541]

Finally, it should be noted that in appropriate cases a taxpayer might be estopped. Where it is the taxpayer, rather than the Service, who is to be estopped, somewhat different elements are utilized.[542] In a case where taxpayers were estopped,[543] the Tax Court said that the usual elements of equitable estoppel are as follows:

- Conduct amounting to a misrepresentation or concealment of a material fact;
- Actual or imputed knowledge of the misrepresentation by the party to be estopped;
- Absence of knowledge of facts by the party in whose favor estoppel is applied;
- Invention or expectation of the party to be estopped that the representation or concealment will be acted upon by the other party;

---

nett v. Comm'r, 935 F2d 1285 (4th Cir. 1991) (taxpayer did not reasonably rely to her detriment on note from Problems Resolution Office about her gift tax liability, which could not bind Service). Similarly, when a revenue officer and his group manager assured a taxpayer that he would not be assessed a trust fund penalty, and the taxpayer relied on those assurances, estoppel was not found, because the collection personnel did not have the authority to compromise the taxpayer's liability under Section 7122. United States v. Mando, 94-1 USTC ¶ 50,079, 170 BR 104 (ED Ky. 1994); Meyers v. Comm'r, 77 AFTR2d 96-1526 (7th Cir. 1996) (taxpayers were charged with knowing the limited authority of the revenue agent, and so could not demonstrate reliance as a matter of law).

[540] Beltzer v. United States, 495 F2d 211, 212 (8th Cir. 1974); Joplin Bros. Mobile Homes v. United States, 524 F. Supp. 800, 803 (WD Mo. 1981).

[541] See Conway Import Co. v. United States, 311 F. Supp. 5, 14–15 (EDNY 1969); McIntyre v. United States, 88-1 USTC 9142 (D. Colo. 1987) (taxpayer argued that the Service was estopped from assessing additional tax after it entered into an installment agreement with the taxpayer for the payment of withholding and FICA taxes; held: the Service was not estopped, because the taxpayer failed to show the traditional elements of estoppel and affirmative misconduct on the government's part).

[542] See, e.g., cases involving estoppel of taxpayers as the result of the execution of waivers, such as Stair v. United States, 516 F2d 560 (2d Cir. 1975), and Lignos v. United States, 439 F2d 1365 (2d Cir. 1971). See also Clark v. United States, 77-1 USTC ¶ 9397 (D. Kan. 1977).

[543] Sangers Home for Chronic Patients v. Comm'r, 72 TC 105, 115 (1979).

- Reliance by the party seeking the estoppel; and
- Detriment to the party seeking the estoppel resulting from his reliance.

Returns

A. GENERAL RULES RELATING TO RETURNS

A. GENERAL RULES RELATING TO RETURNS

¶ 4.01 INTRODUCTION

The Internal Revenue Code (the Code) makes taxpayers the source of information necessary to compute an internal revenue tax, like the income tax.[1] Taxpayers are required to report information that the Service considers appropriate for the computation of the tax and, based on that information, they enter their computation of the self-assessed tax on tax returns that they then file with the Internal Revenue Service (the Service) at the required time and place, along with a payment of tax (if any is owed). These self-reporting and payment obligations are hardly voluntary. Taxpayers who fail to file returns and pay tax may be penalized by civil penalties and, in egregious cases, criminal penalties.[2]

Requirements for making and filing tax returns are found in Subtitle F of the Code, entitled Procedure and Administration, which begins with Chapter 61, Information and Returns, and is subdivided into the following parts:

- Part I, Records, Statements, and Special Returns, containing Code sections on the general obligation of taxpayers to keep records and make returns as regulations may require;
- Part II, Tax Returns or Statements, containing Code sections setting out the general obligation of taxpayers to make returns (Section 6011), and specifically income tax returns (Sections 6012 through 6017), estate and gift tax returns (Sections 6018 and 6019); and
- Part III, Information Returns, containing Code sections further divided into five subparts dealing with information returns reporting information concerning persons subject to special Code provisions, information con-

---

[1] The alternative to a self-reporting and self-assessment method of taxation is presumptive assessment, which is based on objective criteria obtained from sources other than the taxpayer.

[2] IRC § 6651 (civil delinquency penalties); IRC § 7203 (criminal penalty for failure to file a return or to pay tax).

cerning transactions with other persons, information regarding wages paid employees, information concerning private foundations, registration of and information concerning pension plans, and information concerning income tax return preparers (Sections 6031 through 6060).

In deceptively cryptic terms, the general requirement for filing a tax return states that any person liable for an internal revenue tax "shall make a return" when required by regulations,[3] but provisions for specific taxes require taxpayers to file returns in more emphatic language.[4] For income tax, the Code provides that every individual with gross income in excess of the specified amount, every corporation, every estate, and every trust "must" make an income tax return.[5] For every internal revenue tax, procedural regulations prescribe the forms to be used for the returns or statements that taxpayers must make, as well as the information taxpayers are to include on these forms.[6]

By statute, a taxpayer must sign and verify a return or other document for a tax like the income tax.[7] Taxpayers must also file the returns at the proper time,[8] and in the required place.[9] Finally, taxpayers must pay the tax due on the prescribed dates and in the proper place,[10] although extensions of time for filing returns[11] and paying tax are permitted.[12] These are the general rules, and they correspond to the way in which paper returns must be filed.

By congressional mandate, paper returns are in the process of being phased out. Specifically, in 1998, Congress declared that its policy is that (1) paperless filing should be the preferred method of filing federal tax and information returns; (2) the goal of the Service should be to have at least 80 percent of all tax and information returns filed electronically by the year 2007; and (3) the Service should cooperate with the private sector by encouraging

---

[3] Section 6011(a) merely provides that "[w]hen required by regulations prescribed by [the Treasury] any person made liable for any tax imposed by [Title 26, Internal Revenue] or with the collection thereof, shall make a return."

[4] IRC § 6012 (persons required to make returns of income).

[5] IRC § 6012(a). Other entities must make tax returns as well. Those required to make estate and gift tax returns are described in Sections 6018 (estate tax returns) and 6019 (gift tax returns).

[6] IRC § 6011(a) ("[e]very person required to make a return or statement shall include therein the information required by such form or regulation").

[7] IRC § 6061 (signing of returns and other documents); IRC §§ 6062 (signing of corporation returns), 6063 (signing of partnership returns).

[8] IRC §§ 6071 (time for filing returns or other documents), 6072 (time for filing income tax returns), 6075 (time for filing estate and gift tax returns).

[9] IRC § 6091 (place for filing returns or other documents).

[10] IRC § 6151 (time and place for paying tax shown on returns).

[11] IRC § 6081.

[12] For example, IRC § 6161 (income tax).

competition to increase electronic filing.[13] To achieve this goal, the IRS Restructuring and Reform Act of 1998 (1998 Act) requires that the Treasury (the Secretary of the Treasury, or the Secretary's delegate) adopt a strategic plan to increase electronic filing over the next ten years while maintaining the processing time for paper returns at forty days, and also establishes an Electronic Commerce Advisory Group to assist the Treasury. In furtherance of this purpose, Congress also amended the general return filing requirement authorizing the Service to promote the benefits of electronic filing and even to provide financial incentives for electronic filing.[14] In addition, the Treasury and the Service are directed to develop procedures for a return-free tax system under which "appropriate individuals" will be permitted to comply with the Code without the making of the return required by Section 6012.[15]

As the Service is moving toward an electronic paperless return filing system, special new rules are being developed for this type of filing.[16] Moreover, Congress has also required that the Service develop, no later than December 31, 2006, procedures under which a taxpayer filing returns electronically will be able to review the taxpayer's account electronically, as well as ensure that the privacy of the account information is reasonably safeguarded.[17]

Tax returns the taxpayers are required to file, whether in paper or electronic form, remain the focus of the voluntary compliance system. To ensure that taxpayers disclose accurate information on tax returns for a tax like the income tax, the Code requires that third persons file information returns; namely, returns containing information that the Service uses to audit the accuracy of the taxpayer's own tax return.[18]

This chapter discusses general return filing and tax-payment obligations (Part A), the rules applying to the preparers of income tax returns (Part B), and the important subject of the confidentiality of tax returns and return information (Part C). The tax return is at the core of many other procedural statutes, as well as the Service's administrative procedures. Other procedural statutes and rules are described in later chapters, such as periods of limitations (Chapter 5), interest (Chapter 6), criminal and civil penalties (Chapters 7A and 7B), the examination of returns (Chapter 8), the Service's authority to gather information for the purpose of determining the accuracy return (Chapter 13), and deficiency and assessment procedures (Chapter 10).

---

[13] IRS Restructuring and Reform Act of 1998, HR 2676, 105th Cong., 2d Sess. § 2001 (hereinafter the 1998 Act).

[14] IRC § 6011(f), added by 1998 Act § 2001(c).

[15] 1998 Act § 2004(a).

[16] See infra ¶ 4.02[1].

[17] 1998 Act § 2005(a).

[18] See infra ¶ 4.02[5].

¶ 4.02 TYPES OF RETURNS

[1] Individual Income Tax Returns

Every citizen, whether residing in or outside the United States, and every resident of the United States must file an income tax return if the individual has income that equals or exceeds the exemption amount.[19] The regulations require taxpayers to make this return using a Form 1040.[20] Even a minor is required to file an income tax return in the same way adult individuals do, and the return must be made by the minor him or herself, or by the minor's guardian or person charged with the care of the minor or the minor's property.[21] Neither disease nor injury excuses a taxpayer from the obligation to file a return, and if the taxpayer is unable to make a return, an agent may make the taxpayer's return of income.[22]

Technological developments have affected both the form of a return and the manner in which the return is filed. Taxpayers with a computer and a modem may file their returns electronically.[23] The Service website has links to private sector firms that participate in the Service's e-mail file program. The Service's website (www.irs.ustreas.gov) has links to several company sites, and at these sites, taxpayers may either download software or use an on-line service to complete and e-mail their tax returns.

When on-line filing is used, a taxpayer transmits the completed tax return to an intermediary firm, which electronically converts the file to Service specifications and sends it to the Service. Within forty-eight hours, the Service notifies the taxpayer by e-mail if the return is accepted or, if not, which items the taxpayer must correct. After the Service accepts the return, the taxpayer then mails any Forms W-2 to the Service along with a signed one-page signature document, Form 8453-OL, that the taxpayer has received from the tax preparation or on-line filing company. E-mail filing gives the taxpayer an accelerated refund, if one is due, and the Service will direct deposit the return to the taxpayer's checking or savings account. However, if additional tax is due, the taxpayer must pay the additional tax on or before the date otherwise required for payment for the tax year involved.

---

[19] IRC § 6012(a); Reg. § 1.6012-1(a)(1).

[20] Reg. § 1.6012-1(a)(6).

[21] Reg. § 1.6012-1(a)(4). If a return is not filed, a delinquency penalty may be imposed on the minor, and the applicability of the addition to tax depends on whether there was a lack of good cause and due care on the part of the guardian. Bassett v. Comm'r, 67 F3d 29 (2d Cir. 1995).

[22] Reg. § 1.6012-1(a)(5).

[23] IR 98-10, Feb. 19, 1998. The procedure derives from a limited on-line test that the Service conducted for taxpayers filing Forms 1040, 1040A, or 1040EZ. See Rev. Proc. 96-20, 1996-4 IRB 88 (Jan. 22, 1996).

[a] Returns Prepared by the Service

If a taxpayer fails to make and file a return, the Service itself may prepare a return for the taxpayer, but only in the following situations:

1. If the taxpayer discloses all information necessary for the preparation of the return, the Service will prepare the return for the taxpayer (Section 6020(a)) or
2. If the taxpayer has failed to make and file a return, or has filed a false or fraudulent return, the Service can prepare a return on the basis of the knowledge and information it can obtain through testimony or other means (Section 6020(b)).[24]

In essence, Section 6020(a) is a taxpayer assistance procedure, while Section 6020(b) is a collection device the Service can use to assess and collect unpaid tax. The Service may prepare a return for a taxpayer under Section 6020(a), provided that the taxpayer "consents to disclose all information necessary to the preparation" of the return.[25] When the taxpayer then signs the return the Service has prepared, the Service is permitted to receive the Section 6020(a) return as the "taxpayer's return." When the taxpayer's return is received by the Service, the normal statutory time periods for assessment and collection commence.[26] Once the Section 6020(a) return becomes the taxpayer's return, the taxpayer "for all legal purposes remains responsible for the correctness of the return to the same extent" as if the taxpayer, not the Service, had prepared the return.[27] If the Service thereafter makes an adjustment to the return, the taxpayer is able to make use of deficiency review procedures to challenge the correctness of the Service adjustment.[28]

---

[24] IRC §§ 6020(a), 6020(b); Reg. § 301.6020-1.

[25] Reg. § 301.6020-1(a)(1).

[26] If a taxpayer has not filed a tax return, the Service may ask a taxpayer to sign a Form 870, and when the taxpayer signs it, the Form 870 constitutes the taxpayer's return for purposes of Section 6020(a). Rev. Rul. 74-203, 1974-1 CB 330. The amount shown as tax on the Form 870 is "the amount shown as tax on [the taxpayer's] return," and so the Service takes the position that the taxpayer will become liable for the delinquent payment penalty for having failed to pay the amount reported on the taxpayer's return, and the penalty is retroactive to the due date of the return. Field Service Advice 1998-33 (Apr. 30, 1998). Also, because the tax shown on the Form 870 is treated as the tax reported on the taxpayer's return, the taxpayer will not receive a notice of deficiency because there will be no deficiency in the reported tax. Finally, if the Service fails to assess tax within thirty days after the taxpayer signs the Form 870, the Service's position is that interest is not suspended, as it would be in the ordinary case when a taxpayer signs a Form 870, because in this situation the Form 870 is the taxpayer's return. Id.

[27] Reg. § 301.6020-1(a)(2).

[28] Reg. § 301.6020-1(b)(3).

Section 6020(b) is a collection device because once the Service has prepared the Section 6020(b) return, it is in a position to assess the computed tax and collect the tax assessed.[29] Section 6020(b) contemplates this collection action when it provides that the return, prepared under Section 6020(b), is "prima facie good and sufficient for all legal purposes."[30] Because the Section 6020(b) return is only "prima facie" good and sufficient for all legal purposes, however, the statutory language does not conclusively establish that the Section 6020(b) return is a valid return. The presumption of validity is rebuttable. If a taxpayer produces sufficient evidence to demonstrate that the Service's determination of tax reflected in the Section 6020(b) return is in error, the return is no longer "good and sufficient for all legal purposes"; it is invalid. In the case of income taxes, taxpayers may use deficiency procedures to challenge the validity of a Section 6020(b) return. Despite its presumptive validity for all legal purposes, the return the Service prepares under Section 6020(b) does not permit it to ignore deficiency procedures. In an income tax case, this means that the Service must follow deficiency procedures, and so it must send the taxpayer a notice of deficiency and give the taxpayer an opportunity to file a petition in the Tax Court for a redetermination of the tax determined to be due in the Section 6020(b) return.[31] As the Tax Court has put it, "the historical and traditional purpose of a return prepared and filed by the Commissioner [is] suspended or [does] not take effect until deficiency procedures are complete."[32] The rationale for this suspended validity is that the Service, not the taxpayer, has prepared and executed the return, and the taxpayer has not acknowledged that the amount of tax shown on the return is due.[33]

Despite the apparent finality of the Section 6020(b) return as prepared by the Service, the Section 6020(b) return also does not have the status of the taxpayer's return in a number of procedural settings.

1. In computing the amount of a deficiency, the Section 6020(b) return is not considered to be the return of the taxpayer, with the result that

---

[29] Section 6201(a)(1) requires the Service to assess "all taxes determined by the taxpayer or by the [Service] as to which returns are made" under the Code. Reg. § 1.6201-1(a)(1). The Tax Court observed in *Millsap* that "the return is a consent to assessment of tax in our tax system." Millsap v. Comm'r, 91 TC 926, 932 (1988).

[30] Reg. § 301.6020-1(b)(2).

[31] Taylor v. Comm'r, 36 BTA 427 (1937).

[32] Millsap v. Comm'r, 91 TC 926, 931 (1988).

[33] Accordingly, the Service has ruled that the penalty of Section 6651(a)(2) for failure to pay a reported tax is inapplicable. Rev. Rul. 76-562, 1976-2 CB 430. But the National Office has said that the penalty for failure to pay an assessed tax can apply if the taxpayer fails to pay the amount assessed after the notice and demand was made. Field Service Advice 1998-33 (Apr. 30, 1998).

the amount of the deficiency is the correct tax determined by the Service unreduced by the tax reported on the Section 6020(b) return.[34]

2. Similarly, for purposes of making an election to file a joint return, the Section 6020(b) return is not the taxpayer's return when the taxpayer makes an election on a subsequently filed return.[35] As a result, when the Service prepares a Section 6020(b) return for each of two spouses as married filing separately, and sends them a notice of deficiency, the husband and wife may petition the Tax Court, file a joint return, and challenge the Service's determination of their filing status in the same manner as they contest the amount of the deficiency.

3. For purposes of starting the statute of limitations on assessment and collection, a Section 6020(b) return does not constitute the taxpayer's return.[36]

4. In order to obtain a discharge of tax in bankruptcy, a Section 6020(b) return does not qualify as the return that a taxpayer must have filed to escape the effect of 11 USC § 523(a)(1)(B)(i), which prohibits the discharge of taxes for which a return was not filed.[37]

In determining the failure-to-pay penalty, however, the Section 6020(b) return is considered the taxpayer's return.[38] Because the amount of the deficiency is the amount of tax the Service has determined to be the correct tax, there is necessarily a deficiency, and without payment, the failure-to-pay penalty is attributable to this deficiency.[39] Although the Tax Court did not always believe it had jurisdiction over the failure-to-pay penalty, it is now settled that it does have jurisdiction over that penalty, as long as the court has jurisdiction over the underlying deficiency.[40]

---

[34] IRC § 6211(a).

[35] Millsap v. Comm'r, 91 TC 926 (1988). Section 6013(b) prohibits the later filing of a joint return after the taxpayer files a separate return. In *Millsap*, the Tax Court overruled the Board of Tax Appeals decision in Joe Goldberg, 14 BTA 465 (1928), and refused to follow the decision in Smallridge v. Comm'r, 804 F2d 125, 127–128 (10th Cir. 1986), aff'g TC Memo. 1984-434.

[36] Reg. § 301.6020-1(c)(1), referring to IRC § 6501(b)(3) and Reg. § 301.6501(b)-1(e).

[37] Bergstrom v. United States (In re Bergstrom), 949 F2d 341, 343 (10th Cir. 1991); Rank v. United States (In re Rank), 161 BR 406, 409 (Bankr. ND Ohio 1993) (collecting cases).

[38] IRC § 6651(g)(2).

[39] The failure-to-pay penalty is imposed from the original due date of the return and continues to accrue until the deficiency is paid, according to the National Office, although it also recognizes that the failure-to-pay penalty is subject to deficiency procedures. Chief Counsel Notice N(35)000-169 (Nov. 16, 1999).

[40] IRC §§ 6213(a), 6214(a). Before the amendment of Section 6214(a) in 1986, the Tax Court had held that it did not have jurisdiction over the failure-to-pay penalty, even when it had jurisdiction over the underlying deficiency. Young v. Comm'r, 81 TC 879

Under Service procedures, a revenue officer or revenue agent prepares a Section 6020(b) return from computer-based return information gathered from past filings and information returns or other information from third parties.[41] From these sources, the revenue agent or officer generally is able to obtain the taxpayer's name, address, taxpayer identification number (TIN), filing status, and categories and amounts of taxable income. The initial action is the preparation and filing of a "dummy" return for the taxpayer to open an account on the master file.[42] The dummy return is usually only the first page of a Form 1040 reflecting the taxpayer's name, address, and Social Security number, and is for zero amount. Although the dummy return may have no information from which the amount of tax can be computed and is not signed by Service personnel, a revenue agent may prepare a report from information on the information return master file data base. Simultaneously, the Service employee prepares and mails a thirty-day letter to the taxpayer, along with an explanation of the proposed adjustments and a tax calculation summary report. If the taxpayer responds to the thirty-day letter, the case will be sent to Appeals for a conference with an Appeals officer.[43] If the taxpayer does not respond to the thirty-day letter by filing a protest, the Service sends the taxpayer a notice of deficiency.

To qualify as a return under Section 6020(b), the substitute return the Service prepares must contain (1) taxpayer identifying information (the taxpayer's name, address, and TIN); (2) sufficient data to compute the taxpayer's liability;

(1983). In amending Section 6214(a), Congress reversed this result, and made clear that the Tax Court has jurisdiction over the failure-to-pay penalty where it has jurisdiction over the underlying deficiency. See Nemerov v. Comm'r, TC Memo. 1998-186 (citing the legislative history and acknowledging this jurisdiction).

[41] For individual income tax returns, see Internal Revenue Manual (IRM) 52(10)5.1 (June 12, 1987) (Substitute for Return Procedures—General). For employment, excise, and partnership tax returns, see IRM 5290 (Nov. 15, 1985) (Refusal to File—IRC § 6020(b) Assessment Procedure), IRM 5293.3 (Signing of Tax Returns).

[42] Moreover, since 1986, collection personnel, including the personnel at Service Center Collection Branches, have had the authority to assess individual income tax using Section 6020(b) procedures. Under the Automated Substitute for Return (ASFR) processing applicable to wage earners with less than $100,000, the Service Center Collection Branch prepares substitutes for returns for nonfilers using master file information. IRM 11.8 (May 27, 1999) (Substitute for Returns). In a 1999 Chief Counsel Notice, the Chief Counsel's Office said that at the time, the majority of substitutes for returns were prepared under ASFR procedures. IRS Chief Counsel Notice N(35)000-169 (Nov. 16, 1999). The procedures described in the text are derived from the Internal Revenue Manual and the Chief Counsel Notice; they have also been described in Section 6020(b) cases. See, e.g., Millsap v. Comm'r, 91 TC 926, 928 (1988).

[43] IRM 11.9.3 (May 27, 1999) (Appeals of Unagreed IRC § 6020(b) Cases).

and (3) the signature of an authorized Service employee.[44] If the return includes only taxpayer identifying information (the dummy return described earlier), but not the data from which a tax can be computed, the return is not a valid Section 6020(b) return.[45] Under the Service's procedures, information about the Section 6020(b) return may be found in more than one document. In addition to the dummy return, there may be the revenue agent's report containing an explanation of the taxpayer's income, exemptions, deductions, and filing status; the thirty-day letter; and the notice of deficiency. Courts have found a valid Section 6020(b) return from a combination of Service documents.[46]

[2] Corporation Income Tax Returns

Every corporation subject to income tax must make a return of income, even if it has no taxable or gross income for the year.[47] Corporations have the obligation to file an income tax return as long as they exist for any part of a taxable year. To be relieved of the obligation to file a tax return, a corporation ceases to exist only if it no longer engages in business, dissolves under state law, and retains no assets.[48] A corporation continues to be obligated to file a return even if it is turned over to a receiver or trustee who continues to operate it.[49] A corporation must file its return using the Form 1120. Special forms and schedules must be filed by certain types of corporations:

1. Personal holding companies must file a Schedule PH (Computation of Personal Holding Company Tax) with their Form 1120.
2. Life insurance companies must file their returns on Form 1120L.
3. Mutual insurance companies must file their returns on Form 1120M.
4. Affiliated companies must file their returns on Consolidated Income Tax Returns.

---

[44] See Millsap v. Comm'r, 91 TC 926, 930 (1988). The return must be subscribed by a Service official, but need not be signed under oath. Hartman v. Comm'r, 65 TC 542, 545–546 (1975).

[45] Phillips v. Comm'r, 86 TC 433, 437–438 (1986), aff'd in part and rev'd in part, 851 F2d 1492 (DC Cir. 1988).

[46] Millsap v. Comm'r, 91 TC 926, 928 (1988); see also Conovitz v. Comm'r, TC Memo. 1980-022; Smallridge v. Comm'r, 804 F2d 125, 128 n.3 (10th Cir. 1986).

[47] Reg. § 1.6012-2(a). The definition of a "corporation," Section 7701(a)(3), applies for the purpose of the filing requirement.

[48] Reg. § 1.6012-2(a)(2). Although state law may treat the corporation as continuing to wind up its affairs, such as to sue or be sued, the corporation has ceased to exist for filing purposes. However, if the corporation is suing to collect valuable claims, it is considered to retain property, and therefore to continue to exist, and to be required to file a return. Id.

[49] Reg. § 1.6012-2(a)(2).

5. Charitable organizations and other organizations without unrelated business income must file their returns on Form 990-T.
6. Farmers cooperatives must file their returns on Form 990-C.
7. Foreign corporations must file their returns on Form 1120F.

Members of a group of affiliated corporations may exercise the privilege of filing a consolidated return instead of separate returns, and corporate income tax on the consolidated taxable income of the consolidated group,[50] provided that each corporation in the group files a consent to be governed by the consolidated return regulations under Section 1502.[51] To consent to joining in the making of a consolidated return for a year, a corporation files a Form 1122.[52] However, the Service may determine that the corporation has joined in the making of a consolidated return by taking into account such facts and circumstances as whether the income and deductions of the member were included in the consolidated return, and whether the member filed a separate return for the year.[53] When a group exercises the privilege of filing a consolidated return, the consolidated return must be filed no later than the date the common parent's return must be filed, including extensions.[54] Once a group files a consolidated return, it must continue to file a consolidated return, unless it qualifies for the election to discontinue filing consolidated returns.[55] Also, the common parent becomes the sole agent for each subsidiary in the consolidated group for most purposes and is "duly authorized to act in its own name in all matters relating to the tax liability for the consolidated return year."[56]

[3] Partnership Returns

Although a partnership is not a separate taxable entity,[57] partnerships are required to file returns on Form 1065, reporting items of partnership income and

---

[50] Reg. §§ 1.1502-2(a), 1502-11(a) (describing how consolidated taxable income is determined).

[51] Reg. § 1.1502-75(a)(1).

[52] Reg. § 1.1502-75(a)(b)(1).

[53] Reg. § 1.1502-75(b)(2).

[54] Reg. § 1.1502-75(a)(1).

[55] Reg. § 1.1502-75(a)(2).

[56] Reg. § 1.1502-77(a). The common parent is not the agent of the group for such purposes as the making of the consent to file a consolidated return, required by Reg. § 1.1502-75(a)(1); the making of an election under Section 936 for the Puerto Rico and possession tax credit; the election to be treated as a domestic international sales corporation (DISC) under Reg. § 1.992-2; and a change of annual accounting period pursuant to Reg. § 1.991-1(b)(3)(ii).

[57] A partnership means "partnership" as defined in Section 761(a).

deductions allowed under Subtitle A of the Code.[58] The return must also include the names and addresses of partners, and the amount of each partner's distributive share of partnership income, gain, loss, deduction, or credit, including any items imposed by Section 56 that are allocated to each partner. The return must be made for the taxable year of the partnership, irrespective of the taxable years of the partners. In addition, the partnership must furnish to each person who was a partner during the taxable year, a statement, Form K-1.[59] The statement includes (1) the partner's distributive share of partnership gain, loss, deduction, or credit, which is required to be shown on the partnership return and (2) other information the partnership return form requires.[60] As with other types of returns, partnership returns may be required to be filed on magnetic media,[61] especially if the partnership is a large partnership with over 100 partners.[62]

[4] Information Returns

Categories of information returns, which the Code requires taxpayers and third parties to file, are: (1) information returns to report information about persons subject to special provisions of the Code (Subpart A), such as returns of partnerships and S corporations[63]; (2) information returns concerning transactions

---

[58] Reg. § 1.6031-1(a)(1). The partnership return must contain all the information by the form and accompanying instructions. Reg. § 1.6031-1(a)(2). A partnership that has no income, deductions, or credits for federal income tax purposes for a taxable year is not required to file a partnership return for the year. Reg. § 1.6031-1(a)(3). A foreign partnership is not required to file a partnership return if the partnership has no gross income that is treated as effectively connected with the conduct of a trade or business in the United States, and does not have gross income, including gains, derived from sources within the United States. If the foreign partnership has effectively connected U.S. income or U.S.-source gross income, however, the foreign partnership is required to file a partnership return in the same manner as a domestic partnership. Reg. § 1.6031-1(b)(1). For further return filing and related requirements of foreign partnerships, see Reg. §§ 1.6103-1(b)(2)–1.6103-1(b)(6).

[59] Reg. § 1.6031-1(b)-1T(a)(1).

[60] Reg. § 1.6031(b)-1T(a)(3). The Form K-1 must be provided to the partner on or before the day on which the partnership return is required to be filed, including extensions. Reg. § 1.6031(b)-1T(b).

[61] IRC § 6011(e)(2); see TD 8843, 1999-48 IRB 590, adopting Reg. § 301.6011-3(a) (partnership returns required on magnetic media, applicable for returns for taxable years ending on or after December 31, 2000).

[62] IRC § 775; Reg. § 301.6011-3(a)(1) (magnetic media filing not required for large partnerships with more than 100 partnerships until 2001).

[63] IRC, Subtitle F (Procedure and Administration), Chapter 61 (Information and Returns), Subchapter A (Returns and Records), Part III (Information Returns), Subpart A (Information Concerning Persons Subject to Special Provisions), §§ 6031 (return of

with other persons (Subpart B), such as information returns reporting payments of compensation for services and direct sales[64]; (3) information returns regarding wages paid to employees (Subpart C)[65]; (4) information returns concerning the registration of and information about pension and other deferred compensation plans (Subpart E)[66]; and (5) information returns about return preparers (Subpart F).[67] All told there are over fifty types of information returns or, at least, statutory provisions describing the requirement to file them, eighteen in Subpart A for information about persons subject to special provisions; twenty-seven in Subpart B for information concerning transactions with other persons; three each in Subparts C and E, calling for information returns regarding wages paid to employees, and registration of pension plans; and a single information reporting requirement for tax return preparers in Subpart F. With so many information returns required to be filed, it is not surprising that during its 1996 fiscal year, the Service received more than one billion information returns.[68] The Service uses this information to determine whether taxpayers have reported all their income and otherwise computed the correct tax.[69]

If information returns are filed electronically, the due date for filing the information returns is March 31, rather than February 28, of the year following the calendar year to which the returns relate.[70] Electronically filed information returns to which this later filing date applies are ones likely to report many transactions that are particularly suited to being filed electronically, such as (1) those required to be filed by Sections 6041 to 6050R (Subpart B of Part III, Information Returns), to report the payment of interest and dividends and (2) information required to be filed by Sections 6051 to 6053 (Subpart C) to report information regarding wages paid employees. A study will also be made

---

partnership income) through 6039[G] (information on individuals losing United States citizenship). Section 6031 requires the reporting of partnership income of partners, and Section 6037 is the return of an S corporation.

[64] IRC, Subpart B (Information Concerning Transactions With Other Persons), §§ 6041 (information at source) through 6050R (returns relating to certain purchases of fish).

[65] IRC, Subpart C (Information Regarding Wages Paid Employees), §§ 6051 (receipts of employees) through 6059 (reporting of tips).

[66] IRC, Subpart E (Registration of and Information Concerning Pension, Etc. Plans), §§ 6057 (annual registration, etc.) through 6059 (periodic report of actuary).

[67] IRC, Subpart F (Information Concerning Income Tax Return Preparers), § 6060 (information returns of income tax return preparers).

[68] IRS Data Book (Oct. 1, 2000, to Sept. 30, 2001), Table 25 — Information Reporting Program, at 26.

[69] The Information Reporting Program is described further in connection with the Service's examination of tax returns in Chapter 8.

[70] IRC § 6071(b), as amended by 1998 Act § 2002(b), making former Section 6071(b), a new Section 6071(c), effective for information returns required to be filed after December 31, 1999.

to evaluate whether to extend the date these information returns must be sent to the persons about whose transactions the information is filed, from the present date, January 31 of the year following the reporting year, to some later date.

[5] Estate and Gift Tax Returns

The estate of every citizen or resident must file an estate tax return, Form 706, if the gross estate exceeds $60,000 in value on the date of death.[71] The executor or administrator is required to file the return.[72] The return must contain (1) an itemized inventory by schedule of the property constituting the gross estate and lists of deductions under the proper schedules[73]; (2) a certified copy of the will; and (3) other documents required by Form 706.[74]

Individuals, both citizens and residents,[75] who in any calendar year make any transfer by gift must file a gift tax return on Form 709 for that calendar year, unless the transfer is a gift of no more than $10,000 per donee or an excludable payment of certain educational and medical expenses is not included in the total amount of gifts for that year; or a transfer of an interest that qualifies for the gift tax marital deduction.[76] However, a return is required to be filed even if no tax is due because of a charitable deduction or the unified gift and estate tax credit.[77] If the donor dies before filing a gift tax return, the deceased donor's executor or administrator must file the return, and should the donor become legally incompetent, the donor's guardian or committee must file the return. However, the obligation to file a return may not be delegated. Even if the donor is unable to file a return because of illness, absence, or nonresidence, and an agent makes the return for the donor, the donor must ratify the gift tax return the agent filed within a reasonable time after the donor becomes able to act, or the return will not be considered a qualifying return.[78]

---

[71] Reg. § 20.6018-1(a).

[72] Reg. § 20.6018-2.

[73] Reg. § 20.6018-3(a).

[74] Reg. § 20.6018-4(a).

[75] Reg. § 25.6019-1(f). Returns are required to be filed only by individuals, and not trusts, estates, partnerships, or corporations.

[76] Reg. § 25.6019-1(a). The gift tax exclusions for gifts of $10,000 and certain medical and educational payments must qualify under Sections 2503(b) and 2503(c). The marital deduction under Sections 2503(b) and 2503(c). Property for which a marital deduction is allowed does not include a transfer of qualified terminable interest property for which a return must be filed under Section 2523(f) to make the marital deduction election.

[77] Reg. § 25.6019-1(f). See IRC §§ 2522 (charitable deductions) and 2505 (unified credit).

[78] Reg. § 25.6019-1(h).

¶ 4.03 FORMAL REQUIREMENTS OF A RETURN

[1] Sufficiency of Return

Not every document filed with the Service as a return qualifies as a sufficient return under the Code. Status as a sufficient or qualifying return is important for a number of reasons. Only a sufficient or qualifying return begins the running of the statute of limitations on assessment and avoids the imposition of a delinquency penalty for failure to file a return. As a general rule, a sufficient return must (1) be filed on the proper form; (2) supply enough information to permit the Service to calculate tax; and (3) be properly signed under penalties of perjury. A proper form is required for the filing of a sufficient return to ensure that necessary information is supplied and that the information is furnished in a manner facilitating the administrative processing of a return. In *Commissioner v. Lane Wells Co.*, the Supreme Court explained the sufficiency requirement as follows:

> Congress has given discretion to the Commissioner to prescribe by regulation forms of returns and has made it the duty of the taxpayer to comply. It thus implements the system of self-assessment which is so largely the basis of our American scheme of income taxation. The purpose is not alone to get tax information in some form but also to get it with such uniformity, completeness, and arrangement that the physical task of handling and verifying returns may be readily accomplished.[79]

Similarly, the form must contain "all of the data from which a tax can be computed and assessed" if it is to be a return sufficient to start the statute of limitations on assessment.[80] The third element of a sufficient tax return is statutory. The taxpayer must sign and verify the tax return by a written declaration that it is made under penalties of perjury.[81]

[a] Use of the Proper Form

Regulations prescribe the form a taxpayer must use to report and self-assess tax. Because the regulations are specifically provided for by statute, they

---

[79] Comm'r v. Lane Wells Co., 321 US 219, 223 (1944). For this reason, if an official form is tampered with, the tampered form does not constitute a return. Beard v. Comm'r, 82 TC 766 (1984), aff'd, 793 F2d 139 (6th Cir. 1986) (cases analyzed).

[80] See Chapter 5 for further discussion of returns that are sufficient for limitations purposes. Germantown Trust Co. v. Comm'r, 309 US 304, 308 (1940) (although a corporate return was required, a fiduciary return, which did not report tax, was sufficient because it had information from which tax could be computed).

[81] IRC §§ 6061, 6064.

are given the force of law. In *Lane Wells*, the taxpayer filed a regular corporation income tax return, but did not file a separate personal holding tax return, a Form 1120H, although regulations specifically required a corporation to file a separate return on that form.[82] Lane Wells did not file the return because of its good faith belief that it was not a personal holding company, and claimed that the information called for by the Form 1120H could have been called for by the Form 1120 it did file. The Court responded, "Congress has given discretion to the Commissioner to prescribe by regulation forms of returns and has made it the duty of taxpayers to comply."[83] The regulation requiring two separate returns was a reasonable one and valid in order for the Service to receive the information required with such "uniformity, completeness, and arrangement that the physical task of handling and verifying returns may be readily accomplished."[84] Because Lane Wells had not complied with the regulation by filing a separate personal holding tax return, as matter of law, the statute of limitations on assessment of the personal holding tax did not begin to run. On the other hand, the taxpayer's good faith belief that it was not liable for the tax was a potential reasonable cause defense to the delinquency penalty that raised a question of fact.

Even if the taxpayer does not use the proper form, the taxpayer may still be considered to have filed a return. Before it decided *Lane Wells*, the Supreme Court, in *Germantown Trust Co.*, was faced with a case where a fiduciary filed a fiduciary return, Form 1041, rather than the corporation return the fiduciary was required to file.[85] In this situation, the Court held that the filed fiduciary income tax return was sufficient to start the statute of limitations on assessment because the Form 1041 "contained all of the data from which a tax could be computed and assessed although it did not purport to state any amount due as tax."[86] Not surprisingly, Lane Wells argued that under the decision in *Germantown Trust*, its filed Form 1120 was the equivalent of the separate return called for by the personal holding company regulations. The Supreme Court distinguished *Germantown Trust* on the ground that in *Germantown Trust*, the only tax liability involved was an income tax, "the return

---

[82] The regulation stated: "A separate return is required for the surtax imposed under [the personal holding tax provision]. Such return shall be made on Form 1120H."

[83] Comm'r v. Lane Wells Co., 321 US 219 (1944).

[84] IRC § 6011(a); Reg. § 1.6011-1(a). Copies of the principal forms are available from district directors, but a taxpayer is not excused from filing by the fact that no return has been furnished to him. In the absence of a prescribed form for income tax, a taxpayer may make a statement describing his gross income and deductions. Such a statement is accepted as a tentative return and, if timely filed, avoids delinquency penalties, provided the taxpayer thereafter files a proper form without "unnecessary delay." Reg. § 1.6011-1(b).

[85] Germantown Trust Co. v. Comm'r, 309 US 304, 308 (1940).

[86] Germantown Trust Co. v. Comm'r, 309 US 304, 308 (1940).

was addressed to that liability," and contained "all of the data from which a tax could be computed and assessed," even if the return did not report any tax. The situation in *Lane Wells* was different, said the Court, because the taxpayer was liable for two separate taxes, the taxpayer had disclaimed liability on the filed return for the separate personal holding company tax, and the filed Form 1120 did not show "the facts on which liability [for the personal holding company tax] would be predicated."[87] When *Germantown Trust* and *Lane Wells* are read together it is possible to identify at least three principles:

1. A taxpayer has a duty to file to comply with regulations prescribing the form of return for reporting a specific tax (*Lane Wells*).
2. When liability for only one tax is involved, a return is sufficient, even if it is on the incorrect form, as long as it contains sufficient data to compute the tax (*Germantown Trust*).
3. If, however, the taxpayer is subject to two taxes and files a return for only one of them, the taxpayer will not be considered to have filed a return for the second tax even if the taxpayer believes, in good faith, that the taxpayer is not subject to the second tax.

[b] Complete Information

A return form does not constitute a sufficient return if it makes no reference to income, deductions, and credits.[88] Regulations also require a taxpayer to compute the tax due unless the taxpayer makes a special election under Section 6014 to have the Service compute tax.[89] Failure to make computations can

---

[87] The Supreme Court said that "it seem[ed] admitted that the [Lane Wells] returns did not show the facts on which [personal holding company] liability would be predicated," but the Board of Tax Appeals had found that Lane Wells's returns had shown its income, deductions, and net income, and the circuit court of appeals had found that Form 1120 had shown all the facts necessary to compute the personal holding company tax. In view of the different findings, the Supreme Court's decision can be seen as resting more on Lane Wells's failure to comply with the regulatory requirement of filing the separate personal holding company form for presenting the information, rather than the adequacy of the information on the Form 1120 it did file for computing the personal holding company tax.

[88] Florsheim Bros. Dry Goods v. United States, 280 US 453 (1930) (tentative return for extension not a return); Marko Durovic v. Comm'r, 54 TC 1364, 1387–1388 (1970), aff'd on this issue and rev'd and remanded in part on other issues, 487 F2d 36 (7th Cir. 1973), cert. denied, 417 US 919 (1974) (partnership return did not constitute individual income tax return); Edward A. Cupp v. Comm'r, 65 TC 68, 79 (1975), aff'd in unpublished opinion, 559 F2d 1207 (3d Cir. 1977); Knighten v. Comm'r, 702 F2d 59 (5th Cir. 1983) (return was signed, but blank 1040 does not satisfy the obligation to file income tax returns); John H. Houston, 38 TC 486, 491–492 (1962).

[89] Reg. § 1.6012-1(a)(7)(ii).

result in the imposition of a delinquency penalty, absent reasonable cause.[90] In *Florsheim Bros. Dry Goods*,[91] the Supreme Court held that a tentative return made for the purpose of requesting an extension of the filing date, was not a return. Courts have also held that taxpayers did not file a sufficient or qualifying return when they filed one of the following documents:

- A Form 1040 containing only name, address, and Social Security number
- A Form 1040 containing only identifying information and constitutional or other objections to filing or paying taxes
- A Form 1040 labeled tentative or estimated
- A Form 1040 containing zeroes in all relevant spaces
- A tentative or skeleton Form 1040 containing either identifying information only with tax due or net income with tax due[92]

A return filed on the proper form is sufficient if it contains data from which the tax can be computed, or as the frivolous income tax return penalty if the return form contains information "on which the substantial correctness of the self-assessment may be judged."[93] The fiduciary income tax return the trust company filed in *Germantown Trust* was held sufficient for limitations purposes because the return contained all the data from which the computation could be made and the tax assessed. On the other hand, the corporation income tax return the corporate taxpayer filed in *Lane Wells* did not have sufficient information to compute the personal holding company tax, and the application for extension in *Florsheim Bros.* did not contain sufficient information to make the computation of the corporation's income tax. Complete information suffi-

---

[90] But see McCaskill v. Comm'r, 77 TC 689 (1981), where no late filing penalty was found due from a taxpayer filing a Form 1040 with Schedule C income and no business deductions listed but included income and self-employment tax computation.

[91] Florsheim Bros. Dry Goods v. United States, 280 US 453 (1930).

[92] See McCaskill v. Comm'r, 77 TC 689 (1981), and cases cited therein. In *McCaskill*, a Form 1040 reporting income on Schedule C but listing no business deductions was held to constitute a return. But compare Reiff v. Comm'r, 77 TC 1169 (1981) (thirty-two-page document attached to Form 1040 showing only withheld and estimated tax payments; held, not sufficient return; negligence penalty imposed).

[93] IRC § 6702(a)(1)(A), discussed infra ¶ 4.03[1][b]. Some further understanding of what sufficient information means can also be found in criminal cases involving returns. A taxpayer may be prosecuted under Section 7203 for the misdemeanor of failing to file a tax return, even if the taxpayer files a return form, if the return does not give the Service sufficient financial information to calculate the tax liability. See ¶ 7A.03[1]. Similarly, under Section 7206(1), when the criminal charge is the felony of filing a false return, a return is false if it is false as to a "material matter," and material means material to the Service's function of verifying the accuracy of the return. See the discussion of the elements of the false statement charge, Section 7206(1), ¶ 7A.04[1][b]. Sufficient information for statute of limitations purposes likewise permits it to perform its examination and verification function.

cient to permit assessment of tax is not necessarily enough both for starting the assessment statute and avoiding a penalty.

[i] Frivolous returns. Where a return fails to contain adequate information, a $500 penalty may be imposed in addition to other applicable penalties.[94] This penalty may be imposed on an individual who files a document purporting to be a return but that (1) omits information "on which the substantial correctness of the self-assessment may be judged" or (2) contains information that "on its face indicates that the self-assessment is substantially incorrect. . . ."[95] If the purported return reflects either of these two types of conduct, and the conduct is due to a frivolous position or a desire to impede the administration of the tax laws, the taxpayer is liable for the penalty. In addition, such a taxpayer is not paid interest on a claimed refund if his return is not filed in "processable form."[96] A return is not considered to be in processable form unless it (1) is filed on a permitted form and (2) contains (a) the taxpayer's name, address, and identifying number; (b) the required signature; and (c) "sufficient required information . . . to permit the mathematical verification of tax liability shown on the return."[97] The requirement of computational information probably also means that the return information must comply with the accounting period and method rules.[98] Aside from potential civil penalties, a taxpayer who purposely files insufficient returns for a number of years (e.g., a tax protester) faces the real risk of criminal prosecution for, at the very least, the misdemeanor of willfully failing to file a return in violation of Section 7203.[99]

[ii] Self-incrimination and the return. Taxpayers have the duty to file returns reporting the tax due with sufficient information for the Service to determine the correctness of the self-assessed tax. However, this duty may conflict with an individual taxpayer's privilege against compulsory self-incrimination. If a taxpayer who in the past has failed to include income from a legal or illegal source were to file an honest return, the information on the honest return might be used as evidence in a prosecution of the taxpayer, especially when the taxpayer is already under criminal investigation. If the individ-

---

[94] IRC § 6702. A special procedure for contesting the penalty, similar to the one for the penalties on tax return preparers, is provided. See IRC § 6703.

[95] IRC § 6702(a).

[96] IRC §§ 6611(b)(3), 6611(i).

[97] IRC § 6611(i)(2).

[98] IRC §§ 441 (accounting period), 446 (accounting method).

[99] See ¶ 7A.03[1]. For example, see United States v. Smith, 618 F2d 280 (5th Cir. 1980). Some courts, especially the Ninth Circuit, have a more liberal view of what constitutes sufficient information for a return, at least in criminal cases. United States v. Long, 618 F2d 741 (9th Cir. 1980) (zeroes in Form 1040 constituted information from which taxpayer's income could be computed; Section 7203 conviction reversed).

ual taxpayer files a complete and honest return that supplies information that is or may be incriminating, and might be used against the taxpayer in a tax or other prosecution, the taxpayer will waive the self-incrimination privilege.[100] Clearly there is a conflict between the statutorily mandated tax return filing obligation and the constitutionally protected self-incrimination privilege. Which should be given priority? Long ago, the Supreme Court concluded that a taxpayer's privilege against self-incrimination did not excuse the taxpayer from filing any tax return at all.[101] One individual taxpayer's testimony is not compelled by the general obligation imposed on all taxpayers to file an income tax return. If answers may incriminate the individual taxpayer, the taxpayer must claim the privilege on the return with respect to the particular question believed to be calling for an incriminating answer.[102] These general principles have not answered the vexing issue: What are a taxpayer's obligations when he or she must choose between either filing a return reporting information that may be incriminating, thereby waiving the self-incrimination privilege, or filing a return form that because of the self-incrimination privilege claims does not supply sufficient information to constitute a return?

The general principle that a taxpayer's self-incrimination privilege does not excuse a taxpayer's failing to file any return at all derives from the Supreme Court's 1927 decision in *United States v. Sullivan*,[103] a case where a Prohibition Era bootlegger was subject to criminal prosecution for his illegal bootlegging activities and failed to file any tax returns reporting the income he received from his unlawful business. When he was prosecuted for willfully failing to file his income tax return, Sullivan claimed that he was relieved of the obligation to file any income tax returns by his Fifth Amendment privilege against self-incrimination. The factual situation in *Sullivan* is significant: Even if Sullivan's occupation was illegal, he could have reported the income he received from his illegal business on a return on which he also claimed his Fifth Amendment privilege as to his occupation. It is in Sullivan's particular situation, then, that Justice Holmes cryptically observed that Sullivan's privilege claim to the tax return filing requirement had been pressed too far, because "[i]f the form of return provided called for answers that the defendant was

---

[100] United States v. Garner, 424 US 648 (1976).

[101] United States v. Sullivan, 274 US 259 (1927) (bootlegger subject to prosecution under the National Prohibition Act could not defeat a failure-to-file prosecution by claiming privilege).

[102] United States v. Sullivan, 274 US 259 (1927); United States v. Edelson, 604 F2d 232 (3d Cir. 1979); United States v. Johnson, 577 F2d 1304 (5th Cir. 1978); United States v. Daly, 481 F2d 28 (8th Cir.), cert. denied, 414 US 1064 (1973); United States v. Porth, 426 F2d 519 (10th Cir.), cert. denied, 400 US 824 (1970).

[103] United States v. Sullivan, 274 US 259 (1927).

privileged from making, he could have raised the objection in the return, but could not on that account refuse to make any return at all."[104]

Sullivan stands for the proposition that a taxpayer is required to file a return and claim any Fifth Amendment privilege he or she may have, but may not refuse to file any return at all by the expedient of saying that filing the return would force the taxpayer to waive the self-incrimination privilege. It is also true, however, that if the taxpayer files a return and supplies incriminating information on the return, the taxpayer waives any self-incrimination privilege he may have had, and may not subsequently reclaim the privilege as to the disclosed information.[105] Almost fifty years after *Sullivan*, a gambler named Garner did what Sullivan was convicted of failing to do. He filed a tax return reporting not only his gambling income and losses, but that his occupation was a professional gambler. After Garner filed his returns, he was prosecuted for making use of interstate facilities in his gambling activities, and the prosecution introduced Garner's tax returns on which he admitted he was a professional gambler. Garner claimed that the portion of the return dealing with his occupation was compelled testimony, which could not be used at a later trial because he now claimed his Fifth Amendment privilege as to that information. The Supreme Court rejected Garner's claim that his admission as to his occupation had been compelled, and held that "since Garner made disclosures instead of claiming the privilege on his tax returns, his disclosures were not compelled self-incrimination."[106]

A taxpayer is not immune from all prosecution even if the taxpayer files a return and makes Fifth Amendment privilege claims on the return, as Justice Holmes in *Sullivan* suggests should be done. First of all, a taxpayer may not simply file a return form and make a blanket privilege claim, but must make item-specific privilege claims.[107] To be a valid privilege claim, not only must the taxpayer make specific objections to particular questions on the return, the taxpayer's privilege claim must be based on a real fear that answers to those questions may give rise to prosecution.[108] Moreover, the situation in *Sullivan*

---

[104] United States v. Sullivan, 274 US 259, 263 (1927). Justice Holmes went on, "It would be an extreme if not an extravagant application of the Fifth Amendment to say that it authorized a man to refuse to state the amount of his income because it had been made in crime." Id. at 263–264.

[105] However, again in *Garner*, the Supreme Court was dealing with privilege claim as to occupation, not a privilege claim as to the source of an amount received or of the nature of a deduction. Definitive answers on whether a taxpayer could claim a privilege as to these matters have not yet been given.

[106] Garner v. United States, 424 US 648 (1976) (return reporting income from gambling introduced in nontax prosecution involving gambling activities).

[107] See the cases cited supra note 102.

[108] In United States v. Conforte, 80-1 USTC ¶ 9293 (D. Nev. 1979), the taxpayer, who was engaged in the business of prostitution, filed a "Sullivan"-type tax return, which declared only his net income and tax due based on his own undisclosed computation of

and *Garner* was the relatively easy one. If the only question to which the taxpayer is claiming the privilege is his or her occupation, the taxpayer seems to be able to take comfort in the *Sullivan* and *Garner* cases. Where the taxpayer makes item-specific privilege claims, however, it is unlikely that the taxpayer will have filed a return with sufficient information to permit the Service to compute tax, and thus will not have filed a sufficient or qualifying return, or paid tax. In the absence of information from which the taxpayer's tax may be computed, nothing in *Sullivan* and *Garner* prevents the taxpayer from being prosecuted for the misdemeanor of willfully failing to file a return or supplying information in violation of Section 7203.[109] The more difficult and common situation was before the Supreme Court in another early case. A taxpayer named Murdock had filed returns deducting amounts he paid to others who were apparently government officials, and revenue agents summoned him and asked him to disclose the names of the payees. Murdock refused, saying that if he answered the questions, he would have to give information tending to incriminate him in violation of his privilege against self-incrimination.[110] Murdock was prosecuted under the predecessor of Section 7203 for willful failure to give testimony and supply information. At the trial, Murdock claimed that his privilege claim was made in good faith and based on his actual belief, and so he did not willfully refuse to supply information; however, the trial judge

---

net worth. On Fifth Amendment grounds, no other information was disclosed. The taxpayer was convicted of evasion of withholding taxes. The statement attached to the *Conforte* return is repeated in Conforte v. Comm'r, 74 TC 1160 n.7 (1980).

It has been said that while the source of the income might be protected by the Fifth Amendment, the amount is not. United States v. Booher, 641 F2d 218, 220 (5th Cir. 1981).

[109] In United States v. Grabinski, 727 F2d 681 (8th Cir. 1984), a taxpayer's conviction for failure to file a tax return was upheld when the taxpayer filed a Form 1040 containing objections based on the Fourth and Fifth Amendments and only bottom-line information about the amount of his taxable income. The circuit court applied a "sufficient financial circumstances" test to determine the validity of the tax return for Section 7203 purposes—that is, whether there was sufficient information given from which the IRS could calculate tax liability based on the circumstances of the taxpayer's income years." Id. at 683 (citing cases). See also United States v. Brown, 600 F2d 248, 251–252 (10th Cir.), cert. denied, 444 US 917 (1979) (taxpayer's return form with "unknown" and "Fifth Amendment" entries was not a return).

Criminal penalties are discussed in Chapter 7A, and the failure-to-file offense at ¶ 7A.03. A taxpayer's claim of Fourth and Fifth Amendment protection from including on his tax return any information from which tax liability could be determined was summarily rejected by the Tax Court. Sampson v. Comm'r, 46 TCM 1182 (1983). Similarly, when taxpayers have made what courts consider to be frivolous constitutional claims on a return form, the filing of the return form does not constitute reasonable cause for the failure-to-file or failure-to-pay tax penalties. See, e.g., Kinkead v. Comm'r, 46 TCM 1088 (1983) (taxpayer argued that wages are not taxable income under the Sixteenth Amendment, despite his having filed a return previously).

[110] United States v. Murdock, 290 US 389 (1933) (Murdock II).

refused to let the issue of Murdock's privilege claim go to the jury.[111] In *Murdock II*, the Supreme Court held that the jury was required to decide whether in claiming the privilege, Murdock had acted in good faith and actual belief in making the privilege claim or whether his privilege claim "was so unreasonable and ill founded as to exhibit bad faith and establish willful wrongdoing."[112] It follows that if a taxpayer fails to supply information on self-incrimination grounds either on a tax return or in response to a summons, the taxpayer may be prosecuted for the refusal, but the taxpayer is entitled to have both the reasonableness of the privilege claim and the motive for the claim decided by the jury.[113] The Court's decision in *Murdock II* is not entirely satisfactory guidance on the matters discussed here, but it takes the analysis a further step because (1) the Court accepted the position that a failure-to-file prosecution is an appropriate proceeding in which to test the validity of a taxpayer's self-incrimination privilege claim on a tax return and (2) the Court held that in determining whether the taxpayer has acted willfully, the jury is entitled to consider whether the taxpayer's refusal to answer on privilege grounds was made in good faith and actual belief that his privilege claim was well founded. *Murdock II* also is authority that, if a taxpayer who claims the self-incrimination privilege is prosecuted for failure to file a return or supply information, the taxpayer establishes a good defense by showing that the taxpayer relied in good faith on the advice of counsel.[114]

Suppose the taxpayer claims the Fifth Amendment in error. One circuit court recognized that a good faith but erroneous claim of privilege may negate the "willfulness" element, and said that the defense can be raised if (1) there has been a privilege claim to a specific question, not a blanket privilege claim; (2) the privilege claim is reviewed by a judicial officer to decide whether the information sought would tend to incriminate; and (3) the witness or defendant

---

[111] In *Murdock I*, the Supreme Court remanded the case to the district court because in his appearance before the revenue agents, Murdock had claimed protection of the self-incrimination privilege under state law, not the Fifth Amendment. United States v. Murdock, 284 US 141 (1931). He was thereafter tried and convicted.

[112] United States v. Murdock, 290 US 389, 396 (1933) (Murdock II). The Supreme Court also analyzed the meaning of the term "willfully" and decided that it meant "an act done with evil purpose." About fifty years later, the Supreme Court decided that "willfully" meant a voluntary, intentional violation of a known legal duty. United States v. Pomponio, 429 US 10 (1976). Both formulations of "willfully" still put in issue the taxpayer's intention in refusing to supply information.

[113] Garner v. United States, 424 US 648 (1976); United States v. Murdock, 290 US 389 (1933) (Murdock II); see also United States v. Johnson, 577 F2d 1304, 1311 (5th Cir. 1978).

[114] However, the language in *Garner* raises the possibility that only a valid, as opposed to a good faith invalid, privilege claim is a complete defense in such a prosecution. See Garner v. United States, 424 US 648, 666 (1976) (concurring opinions of Justices Brennan and Marshall).

is not the final arbiter of whether the information sought would tend to incriminate.[115] *Murdock II* does not hold that the taxpayer defendant's privilege claim must be correct, only that it be reasonable and have some basis. Accordingly, a good faith, but erroneous, privilege claim is a valid defense in a failure-to-file or failure-to-supply-information prosecution. The government apparently concedes that a good faith, but invalid, claim of privilege negates the element of willfulness for a Section 7203 prosecution.[116] Even if the taxpayer who claims a self-incrimination privilege on a tax return is not subject to a criminal penalty, however, the taxpayer claiming the privilege may be subject to a civil delinquency penalty for failing to file a return and to timely pay tax.[117]

One exception is recognized to the general requirement that a taxpayer must file even if the taxpayer has a privilege claim. In *Marchetti v. United States* and *Grosso v. United States*, the Supreme Court held that under the particular circumstances, the taxpayers' self-incrimination privilege claims could properly excuse the filing of a return altogether. Both Marchetti and Grosso were engaged in the gambling business and, at the time, gamblers were required to file gambling occupation returns and pay an excise tax. These tax and regulatory requirements were directed solely at gamblers whose activities constituted crimes under most state and some federal laws. As a result, the occupational excise tax return obligation had the direct consequence of requiring incriminating information, rather than the incidental effect a return-filing requirement has when imposed on the taxpaying public as a whole. In 1968, when these cases were heard, there was a real and appreciable hazard of incrimination because the Service was required to make wagering tax information available to state and local prosecuting authorities for nonwagering tax prosecutions. The Supreme Court held that where the return-filing and paying obligations themselves are imposed on a class "inherently suspect of criminal

---

[115] Thompson v. Comm'r, 78 TC 558 (1982) (as a result of blanket privilege claim, filed forms were not returns and taxpayers could not elect joint return status after notices of deficiency were sent; *Johnson* cited). For a case taking this approach, see United States v. Turk, 722 F2d 1439 (9th Cir. 1983), cert. denied, 469 US 818 (1984) ("[e]xamination of Turk's justification for this [blanket] claim of the privilege indicates that he did not validly claim the privilege").

[116] Garner v. United States, 424 US 648, 663 n.18 (1976). But when a taxpayer who had previously filed false withholding forms filed income tax returns claiming the self-incrimination privilege, it was held that the privilege is not a defense to a failure-to-file prosecution because it was used as part of an overall plan to evade the payment of taxes. United States v. Carlson, 617 F2d 518 (9th Cir.), cert. denied, 449 US 1010 (1980).

[117] See Cooper v. United States, 834 F. Supp. 669 (D NJ 1993) (delinquency penalty upheld when a taxpayer under criminal investigation "made no efforts to secure an extension from the IRS, but merely accepted unquestioningly the facially extraordinary advice that they not file any tax documents for an indefinite length of time."); Edward A. Cupp v. Comm'r, 65 TC 68, 79 (1975), aff'd in unpublished opinion, 559 F2d 1207 (3d Cir. 1977) (delinquency penalty imposed where information not supplied because of privilege claims, among others). Delinquency penalties are discussed at ¶ 7B.06.

activities," the taxpayers were excused from filing returns on privilege grounds.[118] After the Supreme Court's decisions, Congress changed the law to restrict the disclosure of this information.[119] Prosecutions under the revised wagering tax laws have been affirmed on the ground that the "real and appreciable" hazards of self-incrimination no longer exist.[120]

Because occupation has played such a pivotal role in decisions of the Supreme Court, it is difficult to derive general principles regarding the filing of a sufficient return to apply to a situation where, for example, a taxpayer already under criminal investigation wishes to claim the privilege for specific information required on an income tax return, such as the specific source and amount of income. *Sullivan* teaches that a taxpayer may not simply refuse to file any return at all, and *Garner* stands as a warning that if the return is fully completed, the privilege will be waived as to the information reported. Moreover, if the privilege is claimed as to the item and amount of the item, it is equally clear that under general principles, the taxpayer will not have filed a sufficient return because of the privilege claim. As *Murdock II* demonstrates, the Service may then prosecute the taxpayer for willfully failing to file a tax return in which the taxpayer's good faith in claiming his privilege will be the focal point.

[c] Signing and Verifying Returns

A tax return is required to be signed by the person making the return[121] and verified by a written declaration that the return is made under penalties of perjury.[122] The phrase "under penalties of perjury" in the return jurat is an his-

---

[118] Marchetti v. United States, 390 US 39 (1968); Grosso v. United States, 390 US 62 (1968).

[119] Permissible disclosures and uses now exist only for tax prosecutions or enforcement. IRC § 4424. The statute does not prohibit the use of wagering tax information that is independently discovered, for example, by the FBI without assistance from the Service. However, such independently discovered evidence has been suppressed in a nontax prosecution as constituting compelled incrimination. United States v. Haydel, 486 F. Supp. 109 (MD La. 1980), aff'd, 649 F2d 1152 (5th Cir. 1981).

[120] United States v. Sahadi, 555 F2d 23 (2d Cir. 1977); United States v. Spica, 483 F. Supp. 1341 (ED Mo. 1980).

[121] IRC § 6061. The signing of returns and other documents is governed by regulations relating to the particular tax involved (Reg. § 301.606-1); income tax (Reg. § 1.6061-1(a)); withholding tax (Reg. § 31.6061-1); returns of foundations (Reg. § 53.6061-1); and real estate investment trusts (REITs) (Reg. § 55.6061-1).

[122] IRC § 6065(a). It has been held, however, that striking out that portion of the return made under penalties of perjury effectively invalidates the return. Bernard Sommer v. Comm'r, 45 TCM 1271 (1983). As a result, the statute of limitations did not bar assessment and collection because no returns had been filed. But see Danol v. United States, 81 AFTR2d 98-1334 (ED Mich. 1998) (taxpayers filed their 1984 return in April 1985, but

torical relic from the time when taxpayers were required to make their returns under oath, and were prosecuted under the perjury statute in the general Criminal Code if they made a false statement on the return.[123] After the statute requiring returns to be sworn was repealed, the jurat was left in return forms and "remains in the present statute as a 'catch phrase' or 'signpost' to indicate what types of documents are covered by [the Code's felony false statement criminal statute, Section 7206(1)]."[124] If the return calls for a signature, it must be signed as follows:

1. An individual return must be signed by the individual taxpayer.[125]

2. A corporate return must be signed by the president, vice president, treasurer, chief accounting officer, or any other officer authorized to act.[126]

3. A partnership or other unincorporated organization return must be signed by a responsible and duly authorized member or officer having knowledge of its affairs.[127]

4. A trust or estate return must be signed by the fiduciary.[128]

A return that is not signed does not constitute a return for tax purposes.[129] As a result, the period of limitations on assessment does not begin to run. Although

---

claimed that wages were not taxable and deleted the attestation portion of the return; after the Service had prepared a return, sent the taxpayers a notice of deficiency, and assessed tax when the taxpayers failed to file a Tax Court petition, the taxpayers argued that the assessment was untimely because their return was invalid, and so the statute of limitations on assessment did not begin to run). Compare McCormick v. Comm'r, 94-1 USTC ¶ 50,026 (EDNY 1993) (taxpayer added "under protest" to jurat of return; held, return filed because taxpayer did not cross out any part of the jurat and exercised his First Amendment rights).

[123] See United States v. Marrinson, 87-2 USTC ¶ 9376 (ND Ill. 1985), aff'd, 832 F2d 1465 (7th Cir. 1987).

[124] Escobar v. United States, 388 F2d 661 (5th Cir. 1967), cert. denied, 390 US 1024 (1965). Without the phrase, "for criminal purposes," a return would be no different than any other document presented to the Service, which when false, may subject the taxpayer to prosecution under the Code's misdemeanor false statement statute, Section 7207.

[125] Reg. § 1.6061-1(a). If the individual is a minor unable to sign, the parent or guardian should sign in the manner set forth in Rev. Rul. 82-206, 1982-2 CB 356.

[126] IRC § 6062.

[127] IRC § 6063; Reg. § 1.6062-1.

[128] Reg. § 1.6061-1(a).

[129] Lucas v. Pilliod Lumber Co., 281 US 245 (1930); Kalb v. United States, 505 F2d 506 (2d Cir. 1974), cert. denied, 421 US 979 (1975); Doll v. Comm'r, 358 F2d 713 (3d Cir. 1966); Peter Vaira, 52 TC 986, 1005 (1969), rev'd on other grounds, 444 F2d 770 (3d Cir. 1971).

no specific penalty is imposed for a failure to sign a return, such a failure may subject the taxpayer to a delinquency penalty.[130]

A person who signs a return fulfills both the signing and the verification requirements and establishes the liability of the signer or his principal for the tax due on the return. Signing and verifying the return also establish the basis for the imposition of sanctions to ensure that honest returns are filed and opens the signer to a criminal penalty for signing and filing a false return[131] if the return is proved to be intentionally false as to a material matter.

[i] **Individuals.** An individual must sign any return or declaration he or she files.[132] The individual's signature on a return is prima facie evidence "for all purposes" that the individual actually signed the return.[133] Absent contrary evidence, an individual's signature alone is sufficient to establish that the person signed the return, although this presumption is not conclusive. A person claiming that he or she did not sign a return must produce evidence to meet the presumption; that is, that the purported signer did not sign the return.[134] The presumption often comes into play in cases where a joint return is allegedly filed, and one of the spouses denies signing the return. Evidence that the signature on the return is not authentic rebuts the presumption.[135] However, where the Service attempts to impose liability on a spouse who has not actually signed a return, the nonsigning spouse's tacit consent is said to be sufficient for finding the filing of a joint return.[136] Moreover, if one spouse fails to

---

[130] See, e.g., Peter Vaira v. Comm'r, 52 TC 986, 1005 (1969), rev'd on other grounds, 444 F2d 770 (3d Cir. 1971), where the penalty was imposed despite the fact that a signed check to pay the reported tax was attached to the return.

[131] IRC § 7206(1).

[132] Reg. § 1.6061-1.

[133] IRC § 6064.

[134] Vincent S. Hennen, 35 TC 747, 748 (1961).

[135] See, e.g., Estate of Hollis R. Temple v. Comm'r, 67 TC 143, 164 (1976); Alma Helfrich, 25 TC 404, 407 (1955).

[136] Myrna S. Howell v. Comm'r, 10 TC 859, 966 (1948), aff'd, 175 F2d 240 (6th Cir. 1949); Heim v. Comm'r, 251 F2d 44, 46 (8th Cir. 1958) ("where a husband files a joint return without the objection of the wife, who fails to file a separate return, it will be presumed that the joint return was filed with the tacit consent of the wife"); Malkin v. United States, 81 AFTR2d 98-2057 (DNJ 1998) (the district court considered four factors to determine whether the wife intended to file a joint return: (1) whether the couple has a history of filing joint returns; (2) whether the wife relied on the husband to handle financial matters; (3) whether the wife's income was reported on the joint return; and (4) whether the wife filed a separate return).

The signing spouse may not rely on the tacit-consent rule, since it derives from the presumption of correctness attaching to the Commissioner's determination that a joint return has been filed. Vincent S. Hennen, 35 TC 747 (1961). For a case finding that the tacit-consent rule was not applicable under the circumstances, see Walsh v. United States, 85-1 USTC ¶ 9411 (D. Minn. 1985).

sign a return, the nonsigning spouse may be considered to have filed a joint return with the signing spouse if the nonsigner intended to file a joint return.[137] The crucial issue in these cases is whether the facts and circumstances establish an intent to file a joint return, not whether the signature appears or is absent. This intent may be inferred from evidence that the nonsigning spouse intended to continue filing a joint return, as that spouse had done in the past[138]; however, evidence that the spouse only acted under duress has been considered to disprove an intent to file a joint return.[139]

---

[137] Estate of Campbell v. Comm'r, 56 TC 1 (1971); Krock v. Comm'r, 46 TCM 1330 (1983); Noonan v. Comm'r, TC Memo. 1997-22 (intention of former wife to file a 1988 return (although she refused to do so) determined, in part, by her signing of indemnification agreement in which she agreed to sign a joint 1988 return).

This rule has been applied in some curious situations, e.g., where a wife refused to sign a return, Irving S. & Sylvia C. Federbush, 34 TC 740 (1960), aff'd per curiam, 325 F2d 1 (2d Cir. 1963); and where neither spouse signed a joint return and the wife, who was using her signature to negotiate with her estranged husband, wrote to the Service that she was not responsible for the taxes her husband reported on the return, Riportella v. Comm'r, 42 TCM 869, 871 (1981).

[138] See Martin v. United States, 411 F2d 1164, 1168 (8th Cir. 1969) (whether a joint return is made "depends on the facts of the case and the taxpayer's intent"); Estate of Upshaw, 416 F2d 737, 742–743 (7th Cir. 1969), cert. denied, 397 US 962 (1970); Tucker v. United States, 85-2 USTC ¶ 9631 (Cl. Ct. 1985). Where a separate return is filed, the lack of the signing spouse's intent to file a joint return may also be determinative. Reather v. Comm'r, 45 TCM 1425 (1983).

It has also been said that both spouses need not file a joint return as long as the couple intended to file jointly. Malkin v. United States, 81 AFTR2d 98-2057 (DNJ 1998) (nonsigning spouse sued for refund of taxes she paid, but complaint dismissed because wife held to have intended to file joint returns). The intent to file a joint return may be inferred from the acquiescence of the nonsigning spouse. Id., citing Crew v. Comm'r, 44 TCM 1145, 1146 (1982). It has also been said that "where a husband files a joint return without the objection of the wife, who fails to file a separate return, it will be presumed that the joint return was filed with the tacit consent of the wife." Heim v. Comm'r, 251 F2d 44, 46 (8th Cir. 1958). Accordingly, the district court in *Malkin* considered four factors when assessing whether the intent to file a joint return exists: (1) whether the couple has a history of filing joint returns; (2) whether the wife relied on the husband to handle financial matters; (3) whether the wife's income was reported on the joint return; and (4) whether the wife filed a separate return.

[139] The surrender of W-2 forms by a nonsigning spouse to the signing spouse, if the surrender is under duress, does not constitute evidence of intent to file a joint return. Stanley v. Comm'r, 81 TC 634 (1983). However, the duress defense has failed where signing spouses have attempted to avoid joint-return liability on the ground that their signature was procured under duress. United States v. Kramer, 83-2 USTC ¶ 9474 (D. Md. 1983), aff'd in unpublished opinion, June 24, 1985 (cases gathered and analyzed; spouse showed that signature was induced by fear of her husband, but failed to show actual duress); Macaux v. Comm'r, 47 TCM 225 (1983) (spouse failed to show that without duress she would not have signed); Anderson v. Comm'r, 47 TCM 1123 (1984) (wife who initially refused to sign return ordered by state court to sign; held, she did not intend to file joint

An agent is permitted to sign a return for a taxpayer in limited circumstances. The agent may sign the return if

- The taxpayer is unable to do so because of disease or injury;
- The taxpayer is continuously absent from the United States for at least sixty days before the date the return is due; or
- The taxpayer requests permission in writing from the district director for the district in which the taxpayer resides or has his or her principal place of business, and the director determines that good cause exists for permitting the agent to make the return.[140]

If an agent does make the return, it must be accompanied by a power of attorney on Form 2848 (Power of Attorney and Declaration of Representative) authorizing the agent to act for the taxpayer in making, executing, and filing the return.[141] Once the return is filed, both the taxpayer and the agent are liable for penalties if it is erroneous, false, or fraudulent.

In the case of joint returns (including declarations of estimated tax), the signatures of both spouses are necessary.[142] Where one spouse is physically unable to sign a joint return because of disease or injury, the other spouse may sign the incapacitated spouse's name to the return with the spouse's oral consent.[143] The signature of the incapacitated spouse must be followed by the words "By Husband [or Wife]" and the signature of the signing spouse in his or her own right. In addition, the signing spouse must attach to the return a dated statement showing all of the following:

- The name of the return being filed
- The taxable year
- The reason for the spouse's inability to sign the return
- That the incapacitated spouse has consented to the signing of the return

These rules are similar to the rules for agents; in fact, the signing spouse is the agent for the incapacitated spouse. In this situation, both the agent spouse and the incapacitated spouse are subject to the penalties provided for filing erroneous, false, or fraudulent returns.

[ii] Corporations. A corporate income tax return must be signed for the corporation by one of the following officers: the president, vice president, treasurer, assistant treasurer, chief accounting officer, or "any other officer duly

---

return because she had no income, believed returns incorrect, and insisted on an indemnity agreement).

[140] Reg. § 1.6012-1(a)(5).

[141] For a discussion of powers of attorney forms, see ¶ 1.08[5].

[142] Reg. § 1.6013-1(a)(2).

[143] Reg. § 1.6012-1(a)(5).

authorized to sign such returns."[144] According to the regulations, an individual's signature on a return, statement, or other document made for the corporation is prima facie evidence that the individual was authorized to sign.[145] A receiver, trustee in dissolution, trustee in bankruptcy, or assignee who has possession or holds title to all or substantially all of a corporation's property or business must make a return for the corporation and sign it.[146]

[iii] Partnerships. A partnership return must be signed by one of the partners.[147] The signing partner's signature on the return is prima facie evidence that the partner was authorized to sign the return on the partnership's behalf.[148]

[iv] Fiduciaries. A "fiduciary" is defined as "a guardian, trustee, executor, administrator, receiver, conservator, or any person acting in a fiduciary capacity for any person."[149] A fiduciary of the estate of a decedent must make an income tax return for the decedent[150] and sign it.[151] A fiduciary acting as the guardian or committee of an insane person, or as the guardian of a minor, must make and sign an income tax return for the insane person or the minor unless the minor makes the return.[152] A receiver who stands in the place of an individual must make and sign that person's income tax return, unless he is receiver of only part of the property, in which case the individual must make his own return.[153] Similarly, a fiduciary in charge of all or substantially all of a corporation's property or business must make a return.[154]

---

[144] Reg. § 1.6062-1(a)(1). A public accountant who prepares a return for a corporation does not become its "chief accounting officer" for signature purposes, although he may sign as preparer. Special Ruling 7-2-52, 525 CCH ¶ 6241.

[145] IRC § 6062; Reg. § 1.6062-1(c).

[146] Reg. § 1.6012-3(b)(4). One exception to the filing rule concerns corporations that are in bankruptcy. If the receiver or trustee shows that the corporation has ceased doing business and has neither assets nor income, the district director can relieve the dissolving corporation of the duty to file a return prior to the granting of a discharge by the bankruptcy court. Rev. Proc. 84-59, 1984-2 CB 504.

[147] IRC § 6063.

[148] IRC § 6063; Reg. § 1.6063-1(b).

[149] IRC § 7701(a)(6). A person must act in a fiduciary capacity to be required to file Form 1041 (Fiduciary Income Tax Return). A bank that serves as an escrowee and merely holds money and pays interest, but performs no administrative duties, is not required to file such a return. Rev. Rul. 82-177, 1982-2 CB 365.

[150] Reg. § 1.6012-3(b)(1).

[151] Reg. § 1.6061-1(a).

[152] Reg. §§ 1.6012-3(b)(3), 1.6061-1(a).

[153] Reg. §§ 1.6012-3(b)(5), 1.6061-1(a).

[154] Reg. §§ 1.6012-3(b)(4), 1.6062-1(a)(2). If the fiduciary is in charge of only a small part of the corporation's property (e.g., in a mortgage foreclosure), the fiduciary need not file a return.

[2] Taxpayer Identification Numbers

TINs enable the Service to identify in its records the type of taxpayer (i.e., a U.S. citizen or resident alien, a nonresident alien individual, or U.S. entity), the type of tax (i.e., individual taxes or business taxes), as well as the taxpayer's account information. A taxpayer must include the TIN on every return, statement, or other document the taxpayer files with the Service. The taxpayer must also furnish the TIN to any other person, such as an information return filer, who is required to include the taxpayer's identifying information on a return, statement, or other document the other person must file with the Service. In general, there are three types of TINs: (1) Social Security numbers; (2) Internal Revenue Service (IRS) individual taxpayer identification numbers; and (3) employer identification numbers (EINs).[155] Both Social Security numbers and IRS individual TINs take the form 000-00-0000, but the IRS individual TIN begins with a number designated by the Service; EINs take the form 00-0000000.

An individual can apply for a Social Security number by filing a Form SS-5, Application for a Social Security Number Card, in accordance with the instructions on the application. An IRS individual TIN is a TIN number the Service issues to an alien individual who is ineligible to obtain a Social Security number but is required to furnish a TIN to comply with filing obligations imposed by the Code.[156] An individual must apply for an IRS individual identification number by filing Form W-7, Application for IRS Individual Identification Number. An EIN must be used by nonindividuals, such as corporations, partnerships, nonprofit associations, trusts, and estates. An EIN is secured by filing a Form SS-4, Application for Employer Identification Number.

When a U.S. person prepares and files a return, statement, or other document, the individual must include his or her TIN, and a U.S. entity its EIN, as required by the forms filed and their accompanying instructions. The U.S. person must also supply the person's TIN to a third party on request if the third party, such as a bank or an employer, files a document that must include the

---

[155] Reg. §§ 301.6109-1(a) et seq. (1996). A fourth type of TIN, an adoption taxpayer identification number (ATIN), is used for children who are in the process of being adopted. Reg. § 301.6109-3. An ATIN is a temporary TIN, and expires two years after the number is assigned to the child. Reg. § 301.6109(3)(a). The Service assigns this temporary TIN on Form W-7A, for use in connection with filing requirements under the Code. When the adoption becomes final, the adoptive parent must apply for a Social Security number for the child.

[156] An "alien individual" is an individual who is neither a citizen nor a national of the United States. Reg. § 301.6109-1(d)(3)(i). Final regulations promulgated for the purpose of describing the procedures for withholding on payments to foreign persons, effective on January 1, 1999, also affect the TIN regulations for foreign persons.

U.S. person's TIN.[157] The same rules apply to (1) a foreign person having income effectively connected with the conduct of a U.S. trade or business; (2) a foreign person having a U.S. office or place of business or a U.S. fiscal or paying agent at any time during the calendar year; (3) a nonresident alien treated as a resident under Section 6013(g) or Section 6013(h); (4) any other foreign person who files a return, amended return, or refund claim, but not information returns, statements, or documents; and (5) a foreign person that makes an election under Regulations Section 301.7701-3(c).[158] Persons, such as information return filers, must supply the Service with the TINs of other U.S. and foreign persons who (1) have income effectively connected with the conduct of a U.S. trade or business during the year; (2) have a U.S. office or place of business; or (3) are nonresident aliens treated as residents.[159] If the payor fails to provide the TIN or other identifying information, the payor is subject to penalties.[160]

---

[157] Reg. § 301.6109-1(b)(1). Financial institutions and certain others may be so-called acceptance agents and may enter into agreements with the Service under which the acceptance agent will be authorized to act on behalf of taxpayers who do not have TINs but are seeking to obtain them from the Service. Reg. § 301.6109-1(d)(3)(iv).

Penalties are imposed for failure to supply taxpayer identifying information; see Sections 6721–6724. Special rules describe the obligations of employees regarding their Social Security numbers; see Employment Tax Regulations, Reg. §§ 31.6011(b)-2(a) and 31.6011(b)-2(b). Employers also have duties in dealing with EINs; see Employment Tax Regulations, Reg. § 31.6011(b)-1.

[158] Reg. § 301.6109-1(b)(2).

[159] Reg. § 301.6109-1(c). The person filing the return must also ask other U.S. or foreign persons for their TINs if the filer does not know their identifying numbers. If, despite asking for the identifying number the return filer still does not know it, the return filer must sign an affidavit on the transmittal document forwarding the returns, statements, or other documents to the Service, so stating.

[160] See ¶ 7B.16-20. The Service established a TIN matching program to permit payors to check the accuracy of a name/TIN combination before filing the information return. See TD 8721, 62 Fed. Reg. 33,008–33,009 (June 18, 1997). Based on the regulations establishing the TIN matching program for employment taxes and collection of income tax at source (Reg. § 31.3406(j)-1), before filing reportable payments, the payor could contact the Service about a TIN the payee has furnished to the payor and the payee has received or is likely to receive a reportable payment, and the Service will inform the payor whether the name/TIN combination furnished matches a name/TIN combination the Service maintains on a data base used for the program. Under the program, the information the Service supplied would not constitute notice of an incorrect name/TIN for purposes of backup withholding or affect a reasonable cause determination for purposes of the penalty.

[3] Amended Returns

For any particular taxpayer, period, and tax, the Code contemplates the filing of only one return. After "the" return has been filed and the date prescribed for filing the return has passed, obvious administrative and legal problems could result from permitting taxpayers to file supplemental information at their option. The Service considers an amended return filed on or before the due date of a return to be the taxpayer's return for the period. However, once a return has been filed and the time prescribed for filing has expired, the Service has the discretion to accept or reject an amended return.[161] Even where an amended return is accepted, the original return is the operative return for purposes of the period of limitations on assessment; the amended return is considered a mere supplement.[162] In *Badaracco v. Commissioner,*[163] the Supreme Court held that the filing of a nonfraudulent amended return after a fraudulent original return had been filed does not start the running of the three-year statute of limitations period on assessment; therefore a tax may be assessed "at any time," despite the fact that more than three years may have elapsed since the filing of the amended return. In reaching this decision, the Court noted that an "amended return is a creature of administrative origin and grace."

In certain cases, the Service requires taxpayers to file an amended return. For example, a taxpayer should claim refund or credit of any tax overpayment on the return when it is originally filed. However, once a return has been filed without such a claim, the Service requires a taxpayer to submit "an amended return" to claim a refund or credit of income tax.[164] Regulations also state that a taxpayer should file an amended return and pay any additional tax due if the taxpayer discovers that an item of income should have been included in gross

---

[161] Rev. Rul. 83-36, 1983-1 CB 358. See Goldstone v. Comm'r, 65 TC 113 (1975), which cited Pacific Nat'l Co. v. Welch, 304 US 191 (1938), as authority for holding a taxpayer to be bound by the treatment of an item reported on his originally filed return. In *Goldstone,* the Tax Court held that the validity of amended returns had been upheld in the following situations: (1) the amended return was filed before the return due date; (2) the taxpayer's treatment of the contested item was not inconsistent with his treatment of that item in his original return; or (3) the taxpayer's treatment of the item in the original return was improper and the taxpayer elected one of several allowable alternatives in the amended return. *Goldstone,* supra at 116. For application of the rule, see Coons v. Comm'r, 47 TCM 767 (1983).

[162] Zellerbach Paper Co. v. Helvering, 293 US 172 (1935); Kaltreider Constr., Inc. v. United States, 303 F2d 366 (3d Cir.), cert. denied, 371 US 877 (1962).

[163] Badarocco v. Comm'r, 464 US 386, (1984). See Espinoza v. Comm'r, 78 TC 412 (1982) (amended return allegedly "filed" with revenue agent, held to raise question of fact).

[164] Individuals must claim income tax refunds or credits on Form 1040X and corporations on Form 1120X. Reg. § 301.6402-3. Other claims for refund or credit are filed on Form 843. Reg. § 301.6402-2(c).

income in a prior taxable year and the period of limitations is open.[165] On this authority, the Service has accepted the filing of an amended return to correct mistakes on a previously filed return. The regulations provide for the filing of amended income tax returns by instructing taxpayers to file such returns with the appropriate Service center.[166]

¶ 4.04 TAX RETURN FILING

[1] Time for Filing

The time for filing a return depends on the type of tax and return involved. Individual income tax returns made on the basis of a calendar year must be filed on or before April 15. Returns made on the basis of a fiscal year must be filed on or before the fifteenth day of the fourth month following the close of the fiscal year.[167] Corporation income tax returns made on the basis of a calendar year must be filed on March 15. Fiscal year corporate returns must be filed on the fifteenth day of the third month following the close of the fiscal year.[168] Other rules apply to different types of taxpayers, as summarized in Table 4.1.

[2] When Returns Are Considered Filed

A tax return is generally considered filed when it is received by the Service (i.e., the date of delivery) on or before the due date of the return.[169] However, there are exceptions to this general rule, as discussed in the following sections.

---

[165] Reg. § 1.451-1(a) (income). See also Reg. § 1.461-1(a)(3) (deductions).

[166] Reg. § 1.6091-2(e).

[167] IRC § 6072(a). The filing date of information returns is governed by Section 6071 and Reg. § 1.6071-1(c).

[168] IRC § 6072(b). In a departure from prior procedure, the Service has instructed its agents that ignorance of the law may be considered reasonable cause for a late-filed return if circumstances support the contention and if the taxpayer demonstrates that he or she has exercised ordinary care and prudence. IRM Penalties Handbook [cite] 4562.2(4), MT 4500-448 (Feb. 25, 1987) (Reasonable Cause and Penalty Consideration).

[169] See United States v. Lombards, 241 US 73 (1916) (document filed "when it is delivered"); Phinney v. Bank of Sw. Nat'l Ass'n, 335 F2d 266, 268 (5th Cir. 1964); Heard v. Comm'r, 269 F2d 911, 913 (3d Cir. 1959).

[a] Timely Mailed, Timely Filed Rule

The postmark date may be considered the date of delivery of a return, claim, or other document, or the date of payment, if the requirements of Section 7502 are met. The postmark date is considered the date of delivery or payment only if all of the following requirements are met:

- The U.S. postmark date is a date within the period for filing or payment or a date that is on or before the date prescribed for filing or payment, including extensions.
- The return, claim, or other document is deposited in the mail in the United States in an envelope or wrapper properly addressed to the appropriate Service office with postage prepaid.
- The return, claim, or other document is delivered to the Service office after the date it was due.[170]

The purpose of this provision is to eliminate the hardships and inequities that might be caused by differences in postal performance and delays in delivery.[171] Before 1996, Section 7502 required the taxpayer to use the U.S. Postal Service, and did not apply to mail delivered by a private delivery service.[172] As of July 30, 1996, for purposes of the timely mailed, timely filed rules of Section 7502, a "designated private delivery service" is treated as the equivalent of the U.S. Postal Service.[173] This means that the date a return or form is recorded or marked as received by a designated delivery service is treated as the date of

---

[170] IRC §§ 7502(a)(1), 7502(a)(2). Obviously, if the document is addressed to the wrong address, Section 7502 does not apply. Zyglis v. Comm'r, 29 F3d 620 (2d Cir. 1994) (unpublished opinion), 74 AFTR2d 94-5512 (notice of appeal from a decision of the Tax Court was required to be filed with the Tax Court within ninety days after the decision, but was erroneously addressed to and received by the court of appeals ninety-three days after the entry of the Tax Court's decision).

[171] For discussion of the purpose and legislative history of this rule, see Sylvan v. Comm'r, 65 TC 548 (1975); Pace Oil Co. v. Comm'r, 73 TC 249 (1979).

[172] For examples of these cases, which are no longer good law, see Pugsley v. Comm'r, 749 F2d 691 (11th Cir. 1985); Petrulis v. Comm'r, 938 F2d 78 (7th Cir. 1991); Correia v. Comm'r, 76 AFTR2d 95-5126 (9th Cir. 1995) ("Section 7502 by its plain and unambiguous language applies to documents delivered by the United States Postal Service . . . [not] to documents delivered by private companies such as Federal Express"); Fanning v. United States, 77 AFTR2d 96-2119 (ND Ga. 1996) (when claimant used UPS, a private parcel delivery service, to deliver a claim for the return of property and the claim was not delivered, a wrongful levy action commenced more than nine months after the levy was dismissed; the limitations period was held not to be extended by delivery to UPS, unlike mail sent through the U.S. Postal Service, which is deemed delivered on the postmark date); Leith v. Comm'r, 47 TCM 255 (1983).

[173] IRC § 7502(f), added by the Taxpayer Bill of Rights 2, § 1210, effective on the date of enactment, July 30, 1996. The Treasury may also provide a rule for designated private delivery services similar to the presumption of delivery in Section 7502(c)(1) when the mailing is by U.S. certified or registered mail.

filing, in the same manner as the U.S. Postal Service postmark. A "designated delivery service" is any business providing a delivery service designated as such by the Treasury that (1) is available to the general public; (2) is at least as timely and reliable as the U.S. mail; (3) records the postmark date electronically on a data base the Service keeps in the regular course of its business or marks the postmark date on the cover in which the item was given to the delivery service for delivery; and (4) meets any other criteria the Treasury prescribes.[174]

---

[174] In Rev. Proc. 97-19, 1997-1 CB 644, the Service provided criteria that the delivery service must satisfy for each type of delivery service it offers. In Notice 97-26, 1997-17 IRB 6 (Apr. 28, 1997), the Service designated specific delivery services to qualify for the timely mailed, timely filed rule; they are Airborne, DHL, FedEx, and UPS. Two sets of rules apply to designated private delivery services, one for services that qualified for designation because their "postmark date" is recorded electronically in their data bases (Airborne, DHL, and UPS), and the other that qualified because the postmark date is marked on the cover of an item (FedEx). For example, the date that an item is delivered to Airborne is electronically recorded in its data base, and that date is considered the postmark date. For items that are received after their due dates, there is a presumption that the postmark date is a date that precedes the delivery date by the normal delivery time of the particular type of delivery service. To rebut this presumption, the taxpayer must provide evidence that shows that the date recorded in the data base is on or before the due date. For FedEx, the postmark date is the date on the label applied by the FedEx employee; however, if the label is applied by the customer, the date on the label will be the postmark date only if the item is received within the normal delivery time.

In Notice 97-50, the Service announced that the list of companies it designated in Notice 97-26 as designated private delivery services satisfying the timely mailed, timely filed rule would remain unchanged, but that the Service would issue a new list of designated private delivery services on or before September 1 of each year. 1997-37 IRB 21.

TABLE 4.1
Date for Filing Returns

Taxpayer	Filing Date	Section
Estates and trusts	Fifteenth day of fourth month following close of year	6072(a); Reg. § 1.6072-1(a)
Decedents (for fractional part of year)	Fifteenth day of fourth month following close of the twelve-month period that began with the first day of the fractional part of year	6072(a); Reg. § 1.6072-1(b)
DISCs	Fifteenth day of ninth month following close of year	6072(e); Reg. § 1.6072-2(e)
Nonresident alien individuals and corporations	Calendar-year taxpayer: June 15; fiscal-year taxpayers: fifteenth day of sixth month following close of year	6072(c)
Cooperative associations (1371(a)(1) and 1381(a)(2))	Calendar-year taxpayers: September 15; fiscal-year taxpayers: fifteenth day of ninth month following close of year	6072(d)
Exempt organizations (other than employee trusts)	Fifteenth day of fifth month following close of year	6072(e)
Estates (estate tax)	Nine months following decedent's death	6075(a)
Donors (gift tax)	April 15 following the close of the donor's calendar year	6075(b)

Because it is an exception to the general rule that a return or other document is filed only when it is delivered to the Service, the three elements of the timely mailed, timely filed rule have been strictly applied.[175] The postmark must be within the prescribed period for filing, and delivery must be made after the prescribed date. If both the postmark and the delivery date are within the prescribed period, Section 7502 does not apply, and the return is filed on the date of actual delivery.[176] For purposes of the timely mailed, timely filed

---

[175] The postmark must be a U.S. postmark; a foreign postmark is not acceptable. Louis Cespedes, 33 TC 214 (1959); see also Blank v. Comm'r, 76 TC 400 (1981). Section 7502 has been held not to apply at all if the document has not been received. Storelli v. Comm'r, 86 TC 443 (1986) (petition not received by Tax Court until 455 days after notice of deficiency). See also Miller v. United States, 784 F2d 728 (6th Cir. 1986); Deutsch v. Comm'r, 599 F2d 44, 46 (2d Cir.), cert. denied, 444 US 1015 (1979); Wiggins v. United States, 87-1 USTC ¶ 9180 (D. Md. 1986) ("When a document or payment is not actually received by the IRS, evidence of date or fact of filing is irrelevant. Without physical delivery, there is no filing."). But see Estate of Wood v. Comm'r, 909 F2d 1155 (8th Cir. 1990).

[176] Pace Oil Co. v. Comm'r, 73 TC 249 (1979). The rationale of *Pace Oil Co.* was followed in First Charter Fin. Corp. v. United States, 669 F2d 1342 (9th Cir. 1982) (Sec-

rule, the prescribed period is the period prescribed for performing the act in question. Thus, the prescribed period is usually the period or date within or by which a tax return (or claim) must be filed. The prescribed period is not necessarily the date for filing the original return, because the date prescribed for performing an act includes any period of extension.[177] Consequently, when the time for filing a return is extended, the timely mailed, timely filed rule applies if the return is mailed before the expiration of the extension period but delivered after the extension period. If the return is both mailed and delivered before the expiration of the extension period, the return is considered filed on the date it is received and the provisions of Section 7502(a) do not apply.[178] Section 7502 can apply in other situations as well. For example, where a spouse who has timely filed a separate return elects to file a joint return, the election may not be made if a notice of deficiency has already been sent; that is, the joint return must be filed before the notice is mailed.[179] The timely mailed, timely filed rule also applies to the filing of an amended return in this situation.[180] For purposes of determining the period of delinquency, however, the timely mailed, timely filed rule does not apply if the return is not posted within the prescribed period. The date of the postmark is crucial because a return mailed after the due date is not considered filed until it is received.[181] Regulations warn that a taxpayer assumes the risk that a document deposited in the mail will be postmarked after the due date, and that in such instances,

---

tion 7502 does not apply to a return mailed and received within extended period for filing; date of delivery controlled expiration of period of limitations on assessment).

[177] Reg. § 301.7502-1.

[178] See, e.g., First Charter Fin. Corp. v. United States, 669 F2d 1342 (9th Cir. 1982). See also Pace Oil Co. v. Comm'r, 73 TC 249 (1979). When an estate received an extension of time to file an estate tax return until Saturday, July 21, 1990, and the return was postmarked and mailed on Friday, July 20, and received on Monday, July 23, 1990, the timely mailed, timely filed rule was held not to apply because the return was received within the extension period. Section 7503 moved the actual due date of the return to Monday, July 23, when the return was actually received. Estate of Mitchell v. Comm'r, 103 TC 520 (1995) (as a result, the notice of deficiency the Service mailed on July 23, 1993, was held timely).

[179] IRC § 6013(b)(2)(C). See Thompson v. Comm'r, 78 TC 558 (1982) (because the forms they filed did not constitute returns, taxpayers were not entitled to elect the filing of joint returns; notices of deficiency sent in the interim).

[180] Charlotte Jacobson v. Comm'r, 73 TC 610 (1979).

[181] The Service said the timely mailed, timely filed rule does not apply to delinquent returns for purposes of computing the delinquency penalty. Rev. Rul. 73-133, 1973-1 CB 605. This interpretation has been approved by the Tax Court. Sanderling, Inc. v. Comm'r, 67 TC 176 (1976), aff'd, 571 F2d 174 (2d Cir. 1978). If a claim for refund is also the return of the taxpayer, Section 7502 does not apply if the mailing is made after the due date of the return, despite its being made within the prescribed period for refund claims. Hartwick v. United States, 83-2 USTC ¶ 9504 (WDNY 1983).

the filing is untimely.[182] Also, if the postmark is illegible or omitted, the taxpayer has the burden of proving when the postmark was made.[183] Furthermore, even if the postmark is timely but the return or document is received after it would ordinarily be received if postmarked on the date indicated, the Service "may require" the taxpayer to prove timely mailing.[184]

Metered mail also presents problems. Section 7502 applies to privately metered mail, but only if (1) the postmark bears a timely date (that is, the metered postmark date must be within the filing period) and (2) delivery occurs within the time that it ordinarily takes for delivery of an envelope bearing a postmark of the U.S. Postal Service, properly mailed on the last day prescribed for filing.[185] If the return or document is received later than the ordinary delivery time, the taxpayer must prove (1) that it was deposited in the mail on time; (2) that the delay was caused in the "transmission of the mail"; and (3) the

---

[182] Reg. § 301.7502-1(c)(iii). In Joseph W. Feldman v. Comm'r, 47 TC 329 (1966), an election required to be made October 31 and deposited in the mail between 7 p.m. and 9 p.m. on October 31 but not postmarked until 3 a.m. on November 1 was held untimely.

[183] Reg. § 301.7502-1(c)(iii). Many of the cases involving Section 7502 arise in the Tax Court because the timely mailed, timely filed rule applies to the Tax Court and the timeliness of petitions that must be filed within ninety days after a notice of deficiency. IRC § 7502(d)(1). Petitions have been found timely filed under Section 7502 where received through the mail on the ninety-first day even where the postmark was illegible (Alexander Molosh, 45 TC 320 (1965)) or the envelope was not postmarked (Sylvan v. Comm'r, 65 TC 548 (1975)).

Absent a legible postmark, a taxpayer may introduce evidence to establish the date of the postmark. See, e.g., Ruegsegger v. Comm'r, 68 TC 463 (1977) (petition arriving in Tax Court on ninety-fourth day after deficiency held timely filed). Booher v. Comm'r, 45 TCM 1246 (1983) (petition deemed timely where it was mailed on the ninetieth day bearing a private meter postmark, despite its receipt on the ninety-fifth day, because it was mailed from Texas during the Christmas card season and a weekend had intervened between mailing and receipt).

[184] Reg. § 301.7502-1(c)(iii).

[185] Reg. § 301.7502-1(c)(iii)(b). For a case applying the regulation, see Raymark Indus., Inc. v. United States, 15 Cl. Ct. 334 (1988) (refund claim stamped by private meter on last date for filing, September 30, not timely filed when received on October 7). See Sable v. Comm'r, TC Memo. 1996-535 (last day prescribed for filing petition was August 22, 1996; privately metered postmark was August 20, 1996; and petition was received by the Tax Court on Monday, August 26, 1996, the third day on which mail could have been delivered; held, petition was timely filed); Guerra v. Comm'r, 45 TCM 510 (1983), holding that a petition enclosed in an envelope bearing a private meter postmark evidencing timely mailing and delivered to the court ninety-four days after a deficiency notice had been mailed to the taxpayer satisfied the timely mailed, timely filed rule. The Tax Court noted in *Guerra* that although the U.S. Postal Service was usually successful in its policy of delivering mail sent from Texas to Washington, D.C., within three days, it was not uncommon for delivery to occur as long as four days from mailing. If an envelope has a postmark made by the U.S. Postal Service and one not made by the Postal Service, the postmark not made by the Postal Service is disregarded. Reg. § 301.7502-1(c)(1)(iii)(b), followed in Malekzad v. Comm'r, 76 TC 963 (1981).

cause of the delay.[186] These regulations have been held valid and can cause taxpayers (and their representatives) almost inextricable difficulty if the return or document is delivered late.[187]

If a taxpayer cannot produce a postmark or a certified or registered mail receipt, can the taxpayer raise a rebuttable presumption of delivery under the common-law mailbox rule by offering other evidence of timely mailing, or does Section 7502 preempt the issue? The Service has contended that compliance with Section 7502 is the exclusive method for establishing filing on mailing rather than on delivery, and some courts agree.[188] However, in *Estate of Wood v. Commissioner*,[189] an estate tax return was mailed by regular mail and was not delivered. The court in *Estate of Wood* noted that a long-standing common-law presumption of delivery exists upon proof of mailing. The Service argued that Section 7502(c), describing the consequences of registered or certified mailing, provides the only circumstances where delivery is presumed. The court concluded, "whether or not the common law presumption continues

---

[186] Id.

[187] In Irving Fishman v. Comm'r, 51 TC 869 (1969), aff'd per curiam, 420 F2d 491 (2d Cir. 1970), a Tax Court petition was mailed from New York City and postmarked September 5, 1961 (the ninetieth day after the notice of deficiency) by private postage meter. When the Tax Court received the petition on September 11 and the parties agreed the normal time for delivery was one day, the taxpayer was unable to establish that the petition was filed on the date of the postmark.

[188] Miller v. United States, 784 F2d 728 (6th Cir. 1986); Surowka v. United States, 909 F2d 148 (6th Cir. 1990); BMC Bankcorp v. United States, 76 AFTR2d 95-5137 (6th Cir. 1995) (unpublished opinion) (district court found that the taxpayer had presented strong proof that the refund claim had been timely mailed because two other claims mailed at the same time had been received, but *Miller* and *Surowka* were followed); see also Deutsch v. Comm'r, 599 F2d 44 (2d Cir. 1979), cert. denied, 444 US 1015 (1980) (taxpayer's testimony and copy of demand letter claimed to have been mailed to the Service were not admissible to prove receipt, because "courts have consistently rejected testimony or other evidence as proof of the actual date of mailing").

In *Carroll*, the Sixth Circuit held that when a taxpayer mails material to the Service by regular mail, it will not be deemed received by the Service on the mailing date under Section 7502 unless the Service acknowledges that the correspondence has been delivered. Carroll v. Comm'r, 71 F3d 1228 (6th Cir. 1995) (taxpayer proved that S corporation election had been mailed with proper postage before filing deadline, but could not prove actual delivery, because the document was lost). In reaching this result, the Sixth Circuit concluded that Section 7502 replaced the common-law doctrine that a properly mailed document is presumed to have been received, the so-called mailbox rule. Consequently, a taxpayer will be entitled to presumption of timely filing only if the statutory provisions of Section 7502 are met; that is, the use of registered or certified mail, or mailing before the due date coupled with actual receipt after that date. This has been the view of the Sixth Circuit for some time. See *Miller v. United States*, supra. In first rejecting the use of the common-law mailbox rule, *Miller* adopted the Second Circuit's view that Section 7502 adopted an "easily applied, objective standard." *Deutsch v. Comm'r*, supra.

[189] Estate of Wood v. Comm'r, 909 F2d 1155 (8th Cir. 1990); see also Anderson v. United States, 966 F2d 487 (9th Cir. 1992).

to exist generally, we simply do not agree that by the enactment of [the timely mailed, timely filed rule of] Section 7502(a), Congress intended to foreclose application of a presumption of delivery within Section 7502(a)(1) in those cases in which the postmark requirements of the section can be conclusively established, as here." The court distinguished other cases (*Miller* and *Deutsch*) on the ground that, in those cases, the only evidence was that of mailing and no postmark was ever established; and, in *Estate of Wood*, a postmark was proved.

Regulations. For the most part, regulations interpret the timely mailed, timely filed rule by repeating the statutory language and the case law. The general rule is that a document or payment will be considered to be filed or paid on the date of the postmark stamped or marked on the envelope in which the document or payment was mailed if (1) the document or payment meets the definition of those terms in the regulations; (2) the envelope containing the document or payment has a postmark that is on or before the last date or day of the period for filing the document or making the payment; and (3) the document or payment is received after the last date or day of the period for filing or payment.[190] Each of the important terms (document, payment, postmark, and delivery) are further defined. A "document" is defined to include a return, claim, or statement that is required to be filed within a prescribed period or by a prescribed date. Excluded from the definition of "document" (and, therefore, from the timely mailed, timely filed rule) are (1) a document required to be delivered by a method other than mailing (e.g., electronic filing); (2) a document filed in any court other than the Tax Court (i.e., the district courts or the Court of Federal Claims, which have their own filing rules), but because the term "document" does include any document filed in the Tax Court, the timely filed, timely mailed rule applies to a Tax Court filing (e.g., a petition); and (3) a document required to be filed with a bank or depository when a deposit of tax is made.[191] "Payment" means any payment that must be made within a prescribed period or before a prescribed date. However, a payment that is required to be delivered by a method other than mailing, such as an electronic funds transfer, is excluded from the definition, as is any payment, whatever the form, unless the Service actually receives and accounts for the amount of the payment (e.g., when a check is honored for payment, when a payment is made to any court other than the Tax Court, and when a deposit is required to be made with a bank or other depository).[192] The statutory timely mailed, timely filed rule does not apply unless the document or payment is properly "mailed," which means that it must be (1) contained in a properly addressed envelope and (2) deposited in the mail in the United States (i.e., with the domestic mail

---

[190] Reg. § 301.7502-1(a). TD 8932, 66 Fed. Reg. 2257–2261 (Jan. 11, 2001).

[191] Reg. § 301.7502-1(b)(1).

[192] Reg. § 301.7502-1(b)(2).

service of the U.S. Postal Service) within the prescribed time and with sufficient postage prepaid.[193] In addition, the envelope must bear a postmark of the U.S. Postal Service with a date that is on or before the last date or period prescribed for the filing or payment.[194] As a result, the sender bears the risk that although the sender deposits the envelope on the last day of the prescribed period, the U.S. Postal Service may not postmark the envelope until the next day, which will be outside the statutory period and too late for the application of the timely mailed, timely filed rule. To avoid this risk, the regulations say that the taxpayer should send the document by registered or certified mail, in which case the postmark date is the date the Postal Service employee postmarks the registration or certification.[195]

The 1998 Act modified the timely mailed, timely filed rule of Section 7502(a) to provide that if any return or other document or a payment is sent by U.S. registered mail, the registration is prima facie evidence that the return or payment has been delivered to the Service office to which it was addressed, and the date of registration is deemed to be the postmark date.[196] Regulations provide the extent to which the date of delivery and the postmark date applicable to registered mail will apply to certified mail and electronic filing.[197]

Acknowledgment of electronic filing. When a document is filed electronically through an authorized electronic return transmitter, the document is treated as being filed on the electronic postmark date given by the electronic return transmitter, which is the record of the date and time (in a particular time zone) that the authorized return transmitter receives the transmission of the taxpayer's electronically filed document on the transmitter's host system.[198]

---

[193] Reg. § 301.7502-1(c).

[194] Reg. § 301.7502-1(c)(1)(iii)(A). The sender also has the burden of proving the actual date of an illegible postmark. If the postmark is not made by the U.S. Postal Service, the postmark must be legible and the document or payment must be received by the Service within the same period as would an envelope mailed with the U.S. Postal Service at the same point of origin. Reg. § 301.7502-1(c)(1)(iii)(B).

[195] Reg. § 301.7502-1(c)(3)(A); see also Reg. § 301.7502-1(c)(2).

[196] IRC § 7502(c)(1), as amended by 1998 Act § 2003(b), effective on the date of enactment, July 22, 1998.

[197] IRC § 7502(c)(2).

[198] Reg. § 301.7502-1(d). The same provisions are included in Prop. Reg. § 301.7502-1(d). An "authorized electronic return transmitter" has the same meaning for purposes of the temporary regulations as it does in Section 3.02(4) of Rev. Proc. 98-50, 1998-8 IRB 8 (Sept. 21, 1998). Rev. Proc. 98-50 describes the procedures to be followed and obligations of participants in the Service Form 1040 e-file Program (formerly known as the Form 1040 Electronic Filing (ELF) Program; Section 3.02(2) of Rev. Proc. 98-51, 1998-38 IRB 20 (Sept. 21, 1998), performs the same functions for the Service's Form 1040 On-Line Filing Program. Section 3.02(4) of Rev. Proc. 98-50 provides that an authorized Service e-file provider includes a transmitter who transmits the electronic portion of a return directly to the Service. Section 3.02(3) of Rev. Proc. 98-51 uses the same definition.

Delivery for purposes of the rule does not occur unless the document or payment is actually delivered to the Service office with which the document is supposed to be filed or the tax paid, and delivery occurs after the due date of the document or payment.[199] Electronic filing presents difficulties for the signing of returns that are electronically filed. Accordingly, the rules relating to the signing of returns have been modified to permit the Service to waive the requirement for a signature, or to provide for alternate methods of signing or subscribing a particular type or class of return, declaration, statement, or other required document.[200] Any alternative method used for signing or subscribing a return is treated for all purposes, civil and criminal, as having been signed under penalties of perjury in the same manner as if it had actually been signed or subscribed.[201]

Moreover, after 1998, all tax forms, instructions, and publications created within the past five years are to be made available on the Internet in a searchable data base at about the same time as those forms, instructions, and publications are made available in paper form.[202] To the extent practicable, the Service is also to make other taxpayer guidance available on the Internet. Procedures are to permit the Service to disclose in electronic form tax returns or return information to persons having a material interest, as provided by Section 6103(e).[203]

Refund claims. The timely mailed, timely filed rule has particular relevance to the timeliness of a refund claim. An example used in the regulations illustrates the point.[204]

EXAMPLE 4-1: Suppose an individual taxpayer, A, files a request for an extension of time to file a 2000 tax return and makes an estimated tax payment. A secures an extension of time to file her 2000 return from April 15, 2001, until August 15, 2001. A files the return on August 14, 2001, making no further payments because the estimated tax payment fully satisfied the tax reported due. On August 14, 2004, A files a claim for refund of a portion of the taxes paid on August 15, 2001, in an envelope postmarked August 14, 2004, but not received by the Service until August 18, 2004. Because A's refund claim was postmarked before the three-year period for filing a claim expired, and the Service received the claim after the date the period for filing a refund claim expired, by applying the timely mailed, timely filed rule, A's refund claim is timely.

---

[199] Prop. Reg. § 301.7502-1(e).

[200] IRC § 6061(b)(1), as amended by 1998 Act § 2003(a), effective on the date of enactment, July 22, 1998.

[201] IRC § 6061(b)(2).

[202] 1998 Act § 2003(d).

[203] 1998 Act § 2003(e).

[204] Reg. § 301.7502-1(e)(3).

In the case of mailed deposits, a special timely mailed, timely filed rule applies. Using the general provisions of the regulations for the timely mailed, timely filed rule, a deposit is treated as having been received on the date it was mailed despite the fact that it is received after the deposit due date, but only if (1) the person making the deposit proves that the date of mailing was on or before the second day preceding the deposit due date; (2) the deposit is mailed to a bank, trust company, or other authorized depositary (but not a Service center); and (3) the amount of the deposit is less than $20,000.[205]

[b] Certified or Registered Mail

Risks assumed with ordinary postage and metered mail can be avoided if the taxpayer sends the return or other document by registered or certified mail. If the return or other document is sent by registered mail, the registration is prima facie evidence that it was delivered to the agency or office to which it was addressed on the registration date, which is considered to be the postmark date. If the return or other document is sent by certified mail, the date the sender's receipt is postmarked is considered to be the postmark (i.e., delivery) date.[206] As with registered mail, proof that a postmarked certified mail sender's receipt was properly issued and that the envelope was properly addressed to the Service office is prima facie evidence of delivery to the Service office.[207]

[c] Saturday, Sunday, or Holiday Filing

In some years, the last day for filing a tax return may fall on a Saturday, Sunday, or legal holiday. Under the provisions of Section 7503, if the last day for filing falls on one of these days, filing is timely if it is made on the next day that is not a Saturday, Sunday, or legal holiday.[208] In most instances, application of this relief provision is clear. For example, if a tax return is due on

---

[205] Reg. § 301.7502-2. Separate rules are provided for deposits by electronic funds transfers. See Section 6302(h) and related regulations.

[206] IRC § 7502(c)(1).

[207] Reg. § 301.7502-1(d)(1). The workings of certified mailings are discussed in Nathaniel A. Denman, 35 TC 1140 (1961).

[208] The term "legal holiday" means a legal holiday in the District of Columbia. These holidays are listed in Reg. § 301.7503-1(b). On the issue of whether the application of Section 7503 is limited to acts required to be performed in connection with the determination, collection, or refund of taxes, the Tax Court and the Service do not agree. The court extends Section 7503 to other acts. In Snyder v. Comm'r, 41 TCM 1416 (1981), the court included the twelve-month period for liquidation distributions under Section 337(a). In E-B Grain Co. v. Comm'r, 81 TC 70 (1983), the court extended Section 7503 to the distribution by an S corporation of previously taxed income under Section 1375(f) (as in effect in 1977). See also Campbell Chain Co., 16 TC 1402 (1951).

April 15 and April 15 falls on a Sunday, a return mailed in accordance with Section 7502 on Monday, April 16, is timely. For purposes of the delinquency penalty, however, regulations provide that once the time for filing has passed, the provisions of Section 7503 do not apply.[209] Under the regulations, if a taxpayer is required to file a return on April 15 and files on May 15, the delinquency period extends to the date of delivery, irrespective of whether delivery could not be made earlier because the preceding day was a Sunday or legal holiday. Courts may not agree with this interpretation.[210] For assessment purposes, the Service has ruled that the period of limitations on assessment begins to run on the actual due date of a return (even if the due date is a Saturday, Sunday, or legal holiday) if the return is filed before the due date.[211] On the other hand, if a taxpayer makes use of Section 7503 because the due date falls on a Saturday, Sunday, or legal holiday, and files a return on the first business day following the actual due date, the period of limitations begins to run on the date the return is filed under Section 7503. Thus, the period of assessment on a return filed on Monday, April 16, 1990, expires April 16, 1993. If April 16, 1993, were to fall on a Saturday, Sunday, or legal holiday, the Service holds that its assessment on the first business day following the Saturday, Sunday, or legal holiday would be timely.

[3] Place of Filing

[a] Filing at Service Centers

Service centers are the designated places for filing most tax returns, information returns, and other documents.[212] The Service center at which an income tax return is to be filed is the one serving the district in which (1) an individ-

---

[209] Reg. § 301.6651-1(b)(3). The Treasury position is based on a literal reading of Section 7503, which grants relief where "the last day prescribed under authority of the internal revenue laws for performing any act falls on Saturday, Sunday or legal holiday. . . . " A return filed late is not filed on the last day prescribed for filing.

[210] This interpretation has been rejected in a case where a taxpayer, to avoid an additional 5 percent penalty, was required to file its return on August 15, a Sunday, but filed on Monday, the next business day. The district court held that the taxpayer avoided the additional penalty where it filed on the next business day. Label-Matic, Inc. v. United States, 74-1 USTC ¶ 9380 (ND Cal. 1974). Cf. Sanderling, Inc. v. Comm'r, 67 TC 176 (1976), aff'd, 571 F2d 174 (2d Cir. 1978).

[211] Rev. Rul. 81-269, 1981-2 CB 243.

[212] IRC § 6091(b). Regulations instruct taxpayers and others to send returns to Service centers. See Reg. §§ 1.6091-2 (income tax returns), 20.6091-1 (estate tax), 25.6091-1 (gift tax), 31.6091-1 (withholding and employment tax returns), 53.6091-1 (private foundations), 55.6091-1 (REITs). The place for filing depends on the particular tax (Reg. § 301.6091-1).

ual, estate, or trust has its legal residence or principal place of business or (2) a corporation has its principal place of business or principal office or agency.[213] Similar rules apply to the filing of estate and gift tax returns.[214] Alternative filing at local district offices is now a relic of the period when the Service was phasing in its automatic data processing at the Service centers, although local filing may still be used if the return is hand-carried.[215] Filing at Service centers does not affect the authority of district directors with whom the return would otherwise have been filed.[216] Centralized filing at Service centers also does not prevent a taxpayer from having a civil or criminal case heard in the judicial district of his or her residence.[217]

[b] Hand-Carrying

A taxpayer may wish to hand-carry a return or other document. By hand-carrying the return a taxpayer can prove that the return has been filed and avoid questions concerning delinquency penalties, which may be significant where there are large tax liabilities. In general, hand-carrying means delivery of the return in person by the taxpayer required to file the return or by an authorized agent to the appropriate local district office.[218] Income tax returns, in-

---

[213] IRC § 6091(b); Reg. §§ 1.6091-2(a), 1.6091-2(b), 1.6091-2(c). Instructions to the returns designate the Service center at which the return must be filed. A person without a legal residence files with the district director in Baltimore, MD, 21202. Individuals living abroad file with the Service center at 11601 Roosevelt Blvd., Philadelphia, PA, 19155. In exceptional circumstances, the place of filing may be changed. Reg. § 1.6091-4.

[214] An estate tax return is filed at the Service center serving the district in which the decedent was domiciled at the time of his death. Reg. § 20.6091-1(a)(1). Gift tax returns are filed with the Service center serving the district of the taxpayer donor's legal residence or principal place of business. Reg. § 25.6091-1(b).

[215] See S. Rep. No. 1625, 89th Cong., 2d Sess. (1966), reprinted in 1966-2 CB 803, 805.

[216] Reg. § 1.6091-4(a)(3).

[217] 28 USC § 1402 requires that an individual taxpayer bring a refund suit against the United States in the judicial district where the taxpayer resides. A corporation must bring a refund suit in the judicial district of its principal place of business, office, or agency, or, if it has none of these, in either the judicial district where the tax return was filed or the District of Columbia. Collection suits may be brought in the judicial district of the taxpayer's residence or place of return filing. 28 USC § 1396. A taxpayer charged with criminal tax offenses under Section 7203 or involving use of the mails (IRC §§ 7201, 7206(1), 7206(2), or 7206(3)) may elect to be tried in the judicial district in which he resided at the time the alleged offense was committed. 18 USC § 3237(b).

[218] Reg. § 301.6091-1(c). Agents include family members; employees; the taxpayer's accountant, lawyer, or tax adviser; or a messenger employed by the taxpayer. The regulations use the phrase "hand delivery" to the district office. A return handed to a revenue agent is not necessarily filed with the district office because it is not part of the revenue agent's duties to transmit the return for filing. See Espinoza v. Comm'r, 78 TC 412

formation returns, statements, and other documents generally required to be filed with the Service center in which the taxpayer's residence or principal place of business is located may be filed with either the local district office (including heads of area, zone, or local offices constituting permanent posts of duty within the district) or the appropriate Service center if they are hand-carried.[219]

[4] Extensions of Time for Filing

Extensions of time for filing returns are permitted under the Code if (1) the extension is requested on or before the due date of the return; (2) the extension request is granted by the Service; and (3) the period of the extension is a reasonable one, not longer than six months.[220] Because the statutory authority is limited to grants before the due date of the return, a request made after the due date of the return is a nullity.[221]

An extension of time to file a return does not extend the time for payment of tax.[222] Even if an extension is granted, interest begins to run from the due date of the return.[223] The grant of the extension allows the taxpayer to avoid

---

(1982) (discussing this point and the decided cases). Therefore, to avoid questions about the date an amended return is filed, the return should be delivered to the district director and copies should be given to the revenue agent.

The taxpayer has the burden of proving delivery if a return or related form is alleged to have been filed by hand delivery, but the Service does not acknowledge actual receipt; and a taxpayer's testimony on the matter is legally insufficient. Deutsch v. Comm'r, 599 F2d 44, 46 (2d Cir. 1979); Prowse v. IRS, 92-2 USTC ¶ 50,508 (EDNY 1992) (taxpayer's testimony that he hand-delivered extension to file return, thereby extending statute of limitations for filing refund claim, was held insufficient to establish filing).

[219] Reg. §§ 1.6091-2(a)(2) (income tax returns), 301.6091-1(b) (information returns).

[220] IRC § 6081; Reg. § 1.6071-1(b). U.S. taxpayers who are outside the United States are excepted from the six-month limitation and are granted an automatic four-month extension. Reg. § 1.6081-2. Regulations under the particular tax govern extensions: Reg. §§ 1.6081-1 (income tax), 20.4081-1 (estate tax), 25.6081-1 (gift tax), 31.6081-1 (employment tax), 53.6081-1 (private foundations), 55.6081-1 (REITs).

[221] But see Eastman Mach. Co. v. United States, 841 F2d 469 (2d Cir. 1988) (discretionary extension filed after due date of return; held, Service had power to grant retroactive extension; letter ruling found to be evidence that Service considered itself to have such power). The Service has privately ruled that a request for an extension filed prior to the date for filing the return, but after the actual filing of a return, does not void the original return and is therefore ineffective to extend the time for making deductible payments to a qualified pension plan. Priv. Ltr. Rul. 8336006 (May 26, 1983).

[222] Reg. § 1.6081-1(a).

[223] IRC § 6601(b)(1).

only the delinquency penalties for late filing[224] and late payment,[225] provided that the tax is paid on or before the extended due date of the return.[226]

Where an extension request is denied, the making of the request for an extension does not alone establish reasonable cause for penalty purposes.[227] Moreover, where an application for an extension of time to file is denied, the return must be filed by the later of the regular due date or ten days from the date of denial.[228] Therefore, it appears that filing within the ten-day grace period is considered filing within the time prescribed by law, presumably for such purposes as delinquency penalties.[229]

There are two types of extensions: discretionary and automatic. In general, a discretionary request for a form other than an individual income tax return (Form 1040) may be made in a letter signed by the taxpayer or his or her authorized agent. This letter must state (1) the form or document and the taxable period for which the extension is requested and (2) the reasons for the request.[230] If an individual income tax return is involved, Form 2688

---

[224] IRC § 6651(a)(1). But see Crocker v. Comm'r, 92 TC 899, 913 (1989) (failure to estimate tax properly voided automatic extension request). If a taxpayer makes false and misleading statements in an application for an extension of time for filing, a granted extension is null and void, and the taxpayer may be subject to the penalty for late filing. Rev. Rul. 83-27, 1983-1 CB 337.

[225] IRC § 6651(a)(2).

[226] The late payment penalty may be imposed unless there is reasonable cause for the delinquency. Regulations state that reasonable cause is presumed if the actual balance due on the tax return of a taxpayer who has filed a request for an automatic extension and paid an estimated tax does not exceed 10 percent of the amount shown as tax on the individual's Form 1040 and the balance is paid with the return. Reg. § 301.6651-1(c)(3).

[227] Taxpayers risk the delinquent filing penalty when they send a request that does not fulfill the regulatory requirements. See, e.g., Custom Component Switches, Inc. v. United States, 396 F2d 514 (9th Cir. 1968) (corporation's extension request rejected because installment not sent); Morrison Indus., Inc., 21 TCM 853 (1962). See also Rev. Rul. 79-113, 1979-1 CB 389–390 (taxpayer who makes false estimate is subject to failure-to-file penalty). See GCM 39014, IRS Positions (CCH) ¶ 1216 (July 25, 1983) (analysis of Service's ability to declare invalid taxpayer's application for extension of time to file a tax return and procedures for enforcing resulting failure-to-file penalty). Prepayment judicial review in the Tax Court is not available to a failure-to-file penalty, except where the penalty is attributable to a tax deficiency. See IRC § 6662(b)(1); Rev. Rul. 78-20, 1978-1 CB 441.

[228] See Rev. Rul. 64-214, 1964-2 CB 472 (elections required to be made within the time prescribed by law held timely made where return was filed within ten-day grace period). However, this ruling applies only to extension requests filed by individuals (Form 2688) and by fiduciaries, partnerships, and small business corporations (Form 2758). It does not apply to regular corporations. However, the Service has warned that this ten-day grace period is not granted automatically, and is not granted if the request is frivolous, IR 1107 (Feb. 16, 1971).

[229] Rev. Rul. 64-214, 1964-2 CB 472 (dealing with effectiveness of elections).

[230] Reg. § 1.6081-1(b)(1).

(Application for Additional Extension of Time to File U.S. Individual Income Tax Return) must be filed. (See Form 4.1.) This form requires the taxpayer to state (1) whether timely returns have been filed in the three preceding years and (2) whether estimated tax payments have been timely made.[231]

Regulations do not specify what reasons are sufficient for extension purposes. The Service has said that "the practitioner's workload in certain circumstances can have a material bearing on the acceptability of an extension request," but the taxpayer must still make a "clear showing" that he has made "timely and reasonable efforts" to file his return on time.[232] In *Estate of Gardner*, the Tax Court held that it has jurisdiction to review the Service's exercise of discretion under Section 6081(a) in denying the request of an executrix for an extension of time to file a decedent's estate tax return.[233] The Service denied a special-use valuation for farmland under Section 2032A on the ground that it was not made on a timely filed estate tax return. In response, the estate argued that because the Service's denial of the extension request was an abuse of discretion, the requested extension should be treated as granted. In deciding this case, the Tax Court found (1) a strong presumption of reviewability in the Administrative Procedure Act and case law; (2) no evidence in the legislative history of Section 6081(a) that nonreviewability was intended; (3) that ascertainable standards for review existed; and (4) that if it reviewed the issue, the Service's functions would not be impaired. Accordingly, the Tax Court held that "the [Service's] denial of an extension of time for filing is not immune from review in this Court . . . [and] that the appropriate standard of review is a narrow one—whether [the Service] has abused [its] statutory discretion."[234] Once the Tax Court's deficiency jurisdiction is invoked, therefore, the Tax Court will review the Service's deficiency determinations, "including [its] exercise of discretion under Section 6081, to the extent that the alleged deficiency and any addition to tax within [the Court's] deficiency jurisdiction (see sec. 6662) turn on [the Service's] discretionary actions."[235]

---

[231] Reg. § 1.6081-1(b)(2).

[232] Announcement 60-90, 1960-45 IRB 31.

[233] Estate of Gardner v. Comm'r, 82 TC 989 (1984).

[234] Estate of Gardner v. Comm'r, 82 TC 989, 1000 (1984). (Citations omitted.)

[235] Estate of Gardner v. Comm'r, 82 TC 989, 999 (1984). (Citations omitted.)

FORM 4.1
APPLICATION FOR ADDITIONAL EXTENSION OF TIME TO FILE U.S. INDIVIDUAL INCOME TAX RETURN

Form **2688**	Application for Additional Extension of Time To File U.S. Individual Income Tax Return	OMB No. 1545-0066
Department of the Treasury Internal Revenue Service	▶ See instructions on back. ▶ You MUST complete all items that apply to you.	**1994** Attachment Sequence No. **59**

Please type or print.	Your first name and initial **John and Mary**	Last name **Doe**	Your social security number **123 : 45 : 6789**
File the original and one copy by the due date for filing your return.	If a joint return, spouse's first name and initial **1776 Main Street**	Last name	Spouse's social security number **987 : 65 : 4321**
	Home address (number, street, and apt. no. or rural route). If you have a P.O. box, see the instructions. **Anytown, NY 00000**		
	City, town or post office, state, and ZIP code		

1 I request an extension of time until ___October 15___, 19 _95_, to file Form 1040EZ, Form 1040A, or Form 1040 for the calendar year 1994, or other tax year ending _____, 19_____.

2 Have you filed Form 4868 to request an extension of time to file for this tax year? . . . . ☒ Yes ☐ No
If you checked "No," we will grant your extension only for undue hardship. Fully explain the hardship on line 3.

3 Explain why you need an extension ▶ ...Taxpayers are limited partners in two limited ......partnerships. The general partner in both entities had advised the limited ......partners that Schedule k-1 will not be available until sometime after August 1, 1995. ......Taxpayer requests a further extension until October 15 to allow for the return ......to be properly prepared.

If you expect to owe gift or generation-skipping transfer (GST) tax, complete line 4.

4 If you or your spouse plan to file a gift tax return (Form 709 or 709-A) for 1994, generally due by April 17, 1995, see the instructions and check here . . . . } Yourself . . ▶ ☐ Spouse . . ▶ ☐

Signature and Verification

Under penalties of perjury, I declare that I have examined this form, including accompanying schedules and statements, and to the best of my knowledge and belief, it is true, correct, and complete; and, if prepared by someone other than the taxpayer, that I am authorized to prepare this form.

Signature of taxpayer ▶ _____ Date ▶ _____

Signature of spouse ▶ _____ Date ▶ _____
(If filing jointly, BOTH must sign even if only one had income)

Signature of preparer
other than taxpayer ▶ _____ Date ▶ _____

File original and one copy. The IRS will show below whether or not your application is approved and will return the copy.

Notice to Applicant—To Be Completed by the IRS

☐ We HAVE approved your application. Please attach this form to your return.

☐ We HAVE NOT approved your application. Please attach this form to your return. However, because of your reasons stated above, we have granted a 10-day grace period from the date shown below or due date of your return, whichever is later. This grace period is considered to be a valid extension of time for elections otherwise required to be made on returns filed on time.

☐ We HAVE NOT approved your application. After considering your reasons stated above, we cannot grant your request for an extension of time to file. We are not granting the 10-day grace period.

☐ We cannot consider your application because it was filed after the due date of your return.

☐ We HAVE NOT approved your application. The maximum extension of time allowed by law is 6 months.

☐ Other ....

Director

_____ By _____
Date

Please type or print	Name
	Number and street (include suite, room, or apt. no.) or P.O. box number if mail is not delivered to street address
	City, town or post office, state, and ZIP code

If you want the copy of this form returned to you at an address other than that shown above or to an agent acting for you, enter the name of the agent and/or the address where the copy should be sent.

For Paperwork Reduction Act Notice, see back of form.   Form **2688** (1994)

Form 2688 (1992)   Page **2**

General Instructions

Paperwork Reduction Act Notice.—We ask for the information on this form to carry out the Internal Revenue laws of the United States. You are required to give us the information. We need it to ensure that you are complying with these laws and to allow us to figure and collect the right amount of tax.

The time needed to complete and file this form will vary depending on individual circumstances. The estimated average time is: **Learning about the law or the form, 7 min.; Preparing the form, 10 min.; and Copying, assembling, and sending the form to the IRS, 20 min.**

If you have comments concerning the accuracy of these time estimates or suggestions for making this form more simple, we would be happy to hear from you. You can write to both the **Internal Revenue Service,** Washington, DC 20224, Attention: IRS Reports Clearance Officer, T:FP; and the **Office of Management and Budget,** Paperwork Reduction Project (1545-0066), Washington, DC 20503. **DO NOT** send this form to either of these offices. Instead, see **Where To File** on this page.

Purpose of Form

Use Form 2688 to ask for more time to file Form 1040A or Form 1040. Use it only if you already asked for more time on Form 4868 and that time was not enough. Form 4868 is the "automatic" extension form.

To get the extra time you **MUST:**

• File Form 2688 on time, **AND**

• Have a good reason why the first 4 months were not enough. Explain the reason on line 3.

Generally, we will not give you more time to file just for the convenience of your tax return preparer. However, if the reasons for being late are beyond his or her control or, despite a good effort, you cannot get professional help in time to file, we will usually give you the extra time.

We usually do not approve Form 2688 unless Form 4868 is filed first. We will make an exception to this rule only for undue hardship. You must clearly explain this reason on line 3.

You cannot have the IRS figure your tax if you file after the regular due date of your return.

An extension of time to file a 1992 calendar year income tax return also extends the time to file a gift tax return for 1992.

Caution: If we give you more time to file and later find that the statements made on this form are false or misleading, the extension is null and void. You will owe the late filing penalty explained on this page.

If You Live Abroad.—U.S. citizens or resident aliens living abroad may qualify for special tax treatment if they meet the required residence or presence tests. If you do not expect to meet either of those tests by the due date of your return, request an extension to a date after you expect to qualify. Ask for it on Form 2350, Application for Extension of Time To File

U.S. Income Tax Return. Get Pub. 54, Tax Guide for U.S. Citizens and Resident Aliens Abroad.

Total Time Allowed

We cannot extend the due date of your return for more than 6 months. This includes the 4 extra months allowed by Form 4868. There may be an exception if you live abroad. See previous discussion.

When To File Form 2688

File Form 2688 by the due date of your return (April 15, 1993, for a calendar year return), or extended due date if you filed Form 4868. For most taxpayers, this is August 16, 1993.

Be sure to file Form 2688 early so that if your request is not approved you can still file your return on time.

Out of the Country.—You may have been allowed 2 extra months to file if you were a U.S. citizen or resident out of the country on the due date of your return. "Out of the country" means either (1) you live outside the United States and Puerto Rico AND your main place of work is outside the United States and Puerto Rico, or (2) you are in military or naval service outside the United States and Puerto Rico.

Where To File

Mail Form 2688 AND a copy to the Internal Revenue Service Center where you send your return.

Filing Your Tax Return

You may file Form 1040A or Form 1040 any time before your extension of time is up. But remember, Form 2688 does not extend the time to pay taxes. If you do not pay the amount due by the regular due date, you will owe interest. You may also be charged penalties.

Interest.—You will owe interest on any tax not paid by the regular due date of your return. The interest runs until you pay the tax. Even if you had a good reason for not paying on time, you will still owe interest.

Late Payment Penalty.—The penalty is usually ½ of 1% of any tax (other than estimated tax) not paid by the regular due date. It is charged for each month or part of a month the tax is unpaid. The maximum penalty is 25%. You might not owe this penalty if you have a good reason for not paying on time. Attach a statement to your return, not Form 2688, explaining the reason.

Late Filing Penalty.—A penalty is usually charged if your return is filed after the due date (including extensions). It is usually 5% of the tax not paid by the regular due date for each month or part of a month your return is late. Generally, the maximum penalty is 25%. If your return is more than 60 days late, the minimum penalty is $100 or the balance of tax due on your return, whichever is smaller. You might not owe the penalty if you have a good reason for filing late. Attach a full explanation to your return, not Form 2688, if you file late.

How To Claim Credit for Payment Made With This Form.—When you file your return, show the amount of any payment

sent with Form 2688. Form 1040A filers should include the payment on line 28d and write "Form 2688" and the amount paid in the space to the left. Form 1040 filers should enter it on line 57.

If you and your spouse each filed a separate Form 2688 but later file a joint return for 1992, enter the total paid with both Forms 2688 on the correct line of your joint return.

If you and your spouse jointly filed Form 2688 but later file separate returns for 1992, you may enter the total amount paid with Form 2688 on either of your separate returns. Or you and your spouse may divide the payment in any agreed amounts. Be sure each separate return has the social security numbers of both spouses.

Specific Instructions

Name, Address, and Social Security Number.—Enter your name, address, and social security number. If you plan to file a joint return, also enter your spouse's name and social security number. If the post office does not bring mail to your street address and you have a P.O. box, enter your box number instead.

Note: If you changed your mailing address after you filed your last return, you should use Form 8822, Change of Address, to notify the IRS of the change. A new address shown on Form 2688 will not update your record. To order Form 8822, call 1-800-TAX-FORM (1-800-829-3676).

Line 3.—Clearly describe the reasons that will delay your return. We cannot accept incomplete reasons, such as "illness" or "practitioner too busy," without adequate explanations. If it is clear that you have no important reason but only want more time, we will deny your request. The 10-day grace period will also be denied.

If because of undue hardship you are filing Form 2688 without filing Form 4868 first, clearly explain why on line 3. Attach any information you have that helps explain the hardship.

Line 4.—If you or your spouse plan to file Form 709 or 709-A for 1992, check whichever box applies. But if your spouse files a separate Form 2688, do not check the box for your spouse.

Your Signature.—This form must be signed. If you plan to file a joint return, both of you should sign. If there is a good reason why one of you cannot, the other spouse may sign for both. Attach a statement explaining why the other spouse cannot sign.

Others Who Can Sign for You.—Anyone with a power of attorney can sign. But the following can sign for you without a power of attorney:

• Attorneys, CPAs, and enrolled agents.

• A person in close personal or business relationship to you who is signing because you cannot. There must be a good reason why you cannot sign, such as illness or absence. Attach an explanation to this form.

An individual taxpayer may obtain an automatic four-month extension by filing Form 4868 (Application for Automatic Extension of Time to File U.S. Individual Income Tax Return) and paying the net amount of the estimated tax due for the year.[236] (See Form 4.2.)

---

[236] This extension is automatic, and a duplicate of the form should be attached to the return when it is filed. Reg. § 1.6081-4(a)(5). The time period for automatic extensions to file for individuals was lengthened to four months from two months, effective for tax years ending on or after December 31, 1982. Reg. § 1.6081-4. The four-month automatic extension runs concurrently with the automatic two-month extension granted taxpayers who are outside the country. Reg. § 1.6081-2.

Procedures for an individual to follow in order to obtain an automatic four-month extension of time to file an individual tax return are simplified under Reg. § 1.6081-4, TD 8703, 61 Fed. Reg. 69,027–69,031 (Dec. 31, 1996), which require only that (1) the application be filed on Form 4868, Application for Automatic Extension of Time to File U.S. Individual Income Tax Return, (2) on or before the prescribed return filing date, (3) with the appropriate Service office designated in the application's instructions, (4) along with the full amount properly estimated as tax for the year. Similar simplified procedures are provided for certain partnerships, corporations, and U.S. citizens and residents, Reg. § 1.6081-5; trust income tax returns, Reg. § 1.6081-6; and real estate mortgage investment conduits (REMICs), Reg. § 1.6081-7.

FORM 4.2 _____

APPLICATION FOR AUTOMATIC EXTENSION OF TIME TO FILE U.S. INDIVIDUAL INCOME TAX RETURN

Form **4868** Department of the Treasury Internal Revenue Service	**Application for Automatic Extension of Time To File U.S. Individual Income Tax Return**	OMB No. 1545-0188 **1999**

General Instructions

A Change To Note

You may be able to use a credit card to get an extension of time to file without sending in Form 4868. See **Extension of Time To File Using a Credit Card** below for more details.

Purpose of Form

Use Form 4868 to apply for 4 more months to file **Form 1040EZ, Form 1040A, Form 1040, Form 1040NR-EZ, or Form 1040NR.**

To get the extra time you **MUST:**

● Properly estimate your 1999 tax liability using the information available to you,

● Enter your tax liability on line 9 of Form 4868, **AND**

● File Form 4868 by the regular due date of your return.

You are not required to make a payment of the tax you estimate as due. But remember, Form 4868 does not extend the time to pay taxes. If you do not pay the amount due by the regular due date, you will owe interest. You may also be charged penalties. For more details, see **Interest** and **Late Payment Penalty** on page 3. Any remittance you make with your application for extension will be treated as a payment of tax.

You do not have to explain why you are asking for the extension. We will contact you only if your request is denied.

Do not file Form 4868 if you want the IRS to figure your tax or you are under a court order to file your return by the regular due date.

If you need an additional extension, see **If You Need Additional Time** on page 3.

Note: Generally, an extension of time to file your 1999 **calendar year** income tax return also extends the time to file a gift or generation-skipping transfer (GST) tax return **(Form 709 or 709-A)** for 1999. Special rules apply if the donor dies during the year in which the gifts were made. See the Instructions for Form 709.

Extension of Time To File Using a Credit Card

You generally can get an extension by phone if you pay part or all of your estimate of income tax due by using a credit card (American Express® Card, MasterCard®, or Discover® Card). To pay by credit card, call **1-888-2PAY-TAX** (1-888-272-9829) toll free by April 17, 2000, and follow the instructions. Your payment must be at least $1 to use this system. Before you call, fill in Form 4868 as a worksheet. You will be asked to enter certain items from the form during the call. A convenience fee will be charged by the credit card processor based on the amount you are paying. You will be told what the fee is when you call and you will have the option to either continue or cancel the call. You can also find out what the fee will be on the Internet at **www.8882paytax.com.**

You will be given a confirmation number at the end of the call. Keep the confirmation number with your records. Once you receive your confirmation number, you have completed the requirements for requesting an extension of time to file. **Do not** send in Form 4868.

Note: Although an extension of time to file your income tax return also extends the time to file Form 709 or 709-A, you cannot make payments of the gift or GST tax with a credit card. To make a payment of the gift or GST tax, send a check or money order to the service center where the donor's income tax return will be filed. Enter "1999 Form 709" and the donor's name and social security number on the payment. **Do not** send in Form 4868.

Out of the Country

If you already had 2 extra months to file because you were a U.S. citizen or resident and were out of the country, use this form to obtain an additional 2 months to file. Write "Taxpayer Abroad" across the top of Form 4868. "Out of the country" means either (**a**) you live outside the United States and Puerto Rico and your main place of work is outside the United States and Puerto Rico, **or** (**b**) you are in military or naval service outside the United States and Puerto Rico.

For Privacy Act and Paperwork Reduction Act Notice, see page 4.   Form **4868** (1999)

▼ DETACH HERE ▼

_____

Form **4868** Department of the Treasury Internal Revenue Service	**Application for Automatic Extension of Time To File U.S. Individual Income Tax Return** For calendar year 1999, or other tax year beginning _____ , 1999, ending _____	OMB No. 1545-0188 **1999**

Identification		Individual Income Tax		
1 Your name(s) (see instructions) Alan & Joanne Smith		4 Total tax liability on your income tax return for 1999	$	14000
Address (see instructions) 2 James Street		5 Total 1999 payments		10430
		6 **Balance.** Subtract 5 from 4		3570
City, town or post office, state, and ZIP code New York, NY 10000		**Gift/GST Tax** — If you are **not** filing a gift or GST tax return, go to Part V now. See the instructions.		
2 Your social security number 123-45-6789	**3** Spouse's social security number 987-65-4321	7 Your gift or GST payment . . . . . . $		
		8 Your spouse's gift/GST tax payment .		
Complete ONLY If Filing Gift/GST Tax Return		Total		
This form also extends the time for filing a gift or generation-skipping transfer (GST) tax return if you file a calendar (not fiscal) year income tax return. Enter your gift or GST tax payment(s) in Part IV and: Check this box ▶ ☐ if you are requesting a GIFT or GST TAX return extension Check this box ▶ ☐ if your spouse is requesting a GIFT or GST TAX return extension Checking box(es) may result in correspondence if Form 709 or 709-A is not filed.		9 **Total liability.** Add lines 6, 7, and 8 . . $		3570
		10 Amount you are paying . . . . ▶		3570
		If line 10 is less than line 9, you may be liable for interest and penalties. See page 3.		

ISA
STF FED5325F.1   Form **4868** (1999)

Form 4868 (1999)   Page **2**

Where To File

If you live in:	And you are making a payment, send Form 4868 with your payment to IRS:	And you are NOT making a payment, send Form 4868 to Internal Revenue Service Center:
Florida, Georgia, South Carolina	P.O. Box 105073 Atlanta, GA 30348-5073	Atlanta, GA 39901
New Jersey, New York (New York City and counties of Nassau, Rockland, Suffolk, and Westchester)	P.O. Box 22423 Newark, NJ 07101-2423	Holtsville, NY 00501
New York (all other counties), Connecticut, Maine, Massachusetts, New Hampshire, Rhode Island, Vermont	P.O. Box 371410 Pittsburgh, PA 15250-7410	Andover, MA 05501
Illinois, Iowa, Minnesota, Missouri, Wisconsin	P.O. Box 970028 St. Louis, MO 63197-0028	Kansas City, MO 64999
Delaware, District of Columbia, Maryland, Pennsylvania, Virginia	P.O. Box 7990 Philadelphia, PA 19162-7990	Philadelphia, PA 19255
Indiana, Kentucky, Michigan, Ohio, West Virginia	P.O. Box 6252 Chicago, IL 60680-6252	Cincinnati, OH 45999
Kansas, New Mexico, Oklahoma, Texas	P.O. Box 970027 St. Louis, MO 63197-0027	Austin, TX 73301
Alaska, Arizona, California (counties of Alpine, Amador, Butte, Calaveras, Colusa, Contra Costa, Del Norte, El Dorado, Glenn, Humboldt, Lake, Lassen, Marin, Mendocino, Modoc, Napa, Nevada, Placer, Plumas, Sacramento, San Joaquin, Shasta, Sierra, Siskiyou, Solano, Sonoma, Sutter, Tehama, Trinity, Yolo, and Yuba), Colorado, Idaho, Montana, Nebraska, Nevada, North Dakota, Oregon, South Dakota, Utah, Washington, Wyoming	P.O. Box 7122 San Francisco, CA 94120-7122	Ogden, UT 84201
California (all other counties), Hawaii	P.O. Box 54916 Los Angeles, CA 90054-0916	Fresno, CA 93888
Alabama, Arkansas, Louisiana, Mississippi, North Carolina, Tennessee	P.O. Box 1236 Charlotte, NC 28201-1236	Memphis, TN 37501
American Samoa or Puerto Rico (or exclude income under section 933); are a nonpermanent resident of Guam or the Virgin Islands; have an APO, FPO, or foreign address; are a dual-status alien; or file Form 2555, 2555-EZ, or 4563	P.O. Box 7990 Philadelphia, PA 19162-7990	Philadelphia, PA 19255
Guam: Permanent residents	Send Form 4868 and payments to:	Department of Revenue and Taxation Government of Guam P.O. Box 23607 GMF, GU 96921
Virgin Islands: Permanent residents	Send Form 4868 and payments to:	V.I. Bureau of Internal Revenue 9601 Estate Thomas Charlotte Amalie St. Thomas, VI 00802

STF FED6325F.2

When To File Form 4868

File Form 4868 by April 17, 2000. Fiscal year taxpayers, file Form 4868 by the regular due date of the return.

If you had 2 extra months to file your return because you were out of the country, file Form 4868 by June 15, 2000, for a 1999 calendar year return.

How To Make Your Payment

● When paying by check or money order with Form 4868, use the addresses in the middle column under **Where To File** on page 2.

● Make your check or money order payable to the "United States Treasury." Do not send cash.

● Write your social security number, daytime phone number, and "1999 Form 4868" on your check or money order.

● Do not staple or attach your payment to the form.

● If you are paying by credit card, see **Extension of Time To File Using a Credit Card** on page 1.

If You Need Additional Time

If the automatic 4-month extension (until August 15, 2000, for most calendar year taxpayers) does not give you enough time, you can ask for additional time later. But you will have to give a good reason, and it must be approved by the IRS. To ask for the additional time, you must **either**:

1. File **Form 2688**, Application for Additional Extension of Time To File U.S. Individual Income Tax Return, or

2. Explain your reason in a letter. Mail it to the address in the right column under **Where To File** on page 2.

File Form 4868 **before** you file Form 2688 or write a letter asking for more time. Only in cases of undue hardship will the IRS approve your request for an additional extension without receiving Form 4868 first. Ask early for this extra time. Then, you can still file your return on time if your request is not approved.

Filing Your Tax Return

You may file your tax return any time before the extension expires.

Do not attach a copy of Form 4868 to your return.

Interest

You will owe interest on any tax not paid by the regular due date of your return. The interest runs until you pay the tax. Even if you had a good reason for not paying on time, you will still owe interest.

Late Payment Penalty

The penalty is usually $1/2$ of 1% of any tax (other than estimated tax) not paid by the regular due date. It is charged for each month or part of a month the tax is unpaid. The maximum penalty is 25%.

The late payment penalty will not be charged if you can show reasonable cause for not paying on time. Attach a statement to your return fully explaining the reason. Do not attach the statement to Form 4868.

You are considered to have "reasonable cause" for the period covered by this automatic extension if at least 90% of your actual 1999 tax liability is paid before the regular due date of your return through withholding, estimated tax payments, or with Form 4868.

Late Filing Penalty

A penalty is usually charged if your return is filed after the due date (including extensions). It is usually 5% of the tax not paid by the regular due date for each month or part of a month your return is late. Generally, the maximum penalty is 25%. If your return is more than 60 days late, the minimum penalty is $100 or the balance of the tax due on your return, whichever is

STF FED5325F.3

smaller. You might not owe the penalty if you have a good reason for filing late. Attach a statement to your return fully explaining the reason. Do not attach the statement to Form 4868.

How To Claim Credit for Payment Made With This Form

When you file your return, include the amount of any payment you made with Form 4868 on the appropriate line of your tax return. If you file Form 1040EZ, the instructions for line 9 of that form will tell you how to report the payment. If you file Form 1040A, see the instructions for line 39. If you file Form 1040, enter the payment on line 61. If you file Form 1040NR-EZ, see the instructions for line 22. If you file Form 1040NR, enter the payment on line 57.

If you and your spouse each filed a separate Form 4868 but later file a joint return for 1999, enter the total paid with both Forms 4868 on the appropriate line of your joint return.

If you and your spouse jointly file Form 4868 but later file separate returns for 1999, you may enter the total amount paid with Form 4868 on either of your separate returns. Or you and your spouse may divide the payment in any agreed amounts. Be sure each separate return has the social security numbers of both spouses.

Specific Instructions

How To Complete Form 4868

Skip Parts II and IV unless you are requesting an extension of time to file a gift or GST tax return.

Part I — Identification

Enter your name(s) and address. If you plan to file a joint return, include both spouses' names in the order in which they will appear on the return.

If you want correspondence regarding this extension to be sent to you at an address other than your own or to an agent acting for you, include the agent's name, if any, and enter that address instead.

If you changed your name after you filed your last return because of marriage, divorce, etc., be sure to report this to your local Social Security Administration office before filing Form 4868. This prevents delays in processing your extension request.

If you changed your mailing address after you filed your last return, you should use Form 8822, Change of Address, to notify the IRS of the change. Showing a new address on Form 4868 will not update your record. You can get IRS forms by calling 1-800-TAX-FORM (1-800-829-3676). You can also download forms from the IRS Internet web site at www.irs.gov.

If you plan to file jointly, enter on line 2 the social security number (SSN) that you will show first on your return. Enter your spouse's SSN on line 3.

If you are filing Form 1040NR-EZ or Form 1040NR, and do not have (and are not eligible to obtain) an SSN, enter your IRS-issued individual taxpayer identification number (ITIN). For information on obtaining an ITIN, get **Form W-7**, Application for IRS Individual Taxpayer Identification Number.

Part III — Individual Income Tax

Line 4 — Total Tax Liability on Your Income Tax Return for 1999

This is the amount you expect to enter on Form 1040EZ, line 10; Form 1040A, line 34; Form 1040, line 56; Form 1040NR-EZ, line 18; or Form 1040NR, line 53. If you expect this amount to be zero, enter zero.

Caution: *You can estimate this amount, but be as accurate as you can with the information you have. If we later find that your estimate was not reasonable, the extension will be null and void.*

Line 5 — Total Payments for 1999

This is the amount you expect to enter on Form 1040EZ, line 9; Form 1040A, line 39; Form 1040, line 64 (excluding line 61); Form 1040NR-EZ, line 22; or Form 1040NR, line 63 (excluding line 57). (For Forms 1040EZ, 1040A, and 1040NR-EZ, do not include in this total payments line the amount you are paying with this Form 4868.)

Line 6 — Balance

Subtract line 5 from line 4. If line 5 is more than line 4, enter zero.

If you find you cannot pay the amount shown on line 6, you can still get the extension. But you should pay as much as you can to limit the amount of interest you will owe. Also, you may be charged the late payment penalty on the unpaid tax from the regular due date of your return. See **Late Payment Penalty** on page 3.

Part IV — Gift/GST Tax

Fill in this part only if you or your spouse plan to file Form 709 or 709-A **and** you are also using Form 4868 to apply for an extension of time to file your 1999 **calendar year** income tax return. **Do not** include income tax on lines 7 and 8.

Enter the amount of gift and GST tax you (or your spouse) are paying on these lines. If your spouse files a **separate** Form 4868, **do not** check the box in Part II for your spouse; enter on your form only the total gift and GST tax you are paying. Pay in full with this form to avoid interest and penalties.

Part V — Total

Enter the total of line 6 (and 7 and 8, if applicable) on line 9. If you are paying your entire estimate of tax liability, lines 9 and 10 should both be the same.

Privacy Act and Paperwork Reduction Act Notice. We ask for the information on this form to carry out the Internal Revenue laws of the United States. We need this information so that our records will reflect your intention to file your individual income tax return within four months after the regular due date. If you choose to apply for an automatic extension of time to file, you are required by Internal Revenue Code section 6081 to provide the information requested on this form. Under section 6109 you must disclose your social security number (SSN) or individual taxpayer identification number (ITIN). Routine uses of this information include giving it to the Department of Justice for civil and criminal litigation, and to cities, states, and the District of Columbia for use in administering their tax laws. If you fail to provide this information in a timely manner, or provide incomplete or false information, you may be liable for penalties and interest.

You are not required to provide the information requested on a form that is subject to the Paperwork Reduction Act unless the form displays a valid OMB control number. Books or records relating to a form or its instructions must be retained as long as their contents may become material in the administration of any Internal Revenue law. Generally, tax returns and return information are confidential, as required by Internal Revenue Code section 6103.

The time needed to complete and file this form will vary depending on individual circumstances. The estimated average time is: **Recordkeeping,** 26 min.; **Learning about the law or the form,** 12 min.; **Preparing the form,** 17 min.; and **Copying, assembling, and sending the form to the IRS,** 10 min.

If you have comments concerning the accuracy of these time estimates or suggestions for making this form simpler, we would be happy to hear from you. You can write to the Tax Forms Committee, Western Area Distribution Center, Rancho Cordova, CA 95743-0001. **DO NOT** send the form to this address. Instead, see **Where To File** on page 2.

STF FED5325F.4

A good faith effort to make the estimate is required.[237] A corporation may obtain an automatic extension of six months for filing a corporation income tax return, provided it files an application on Form 7004 (Application for Automatic Extension of Time to File Corporation Income Tax Return) before the return due date.[238] (See Form 4.3.) This application must set forth the estimated tax due for the year, and the entire amount of the balance due must be remitted. Section 6081(b) denies a corporation requesting an automatic extension the right to remit any unpaid tax liability in installments.[239] Once these conditions have been met, the six-month extension is automatically granted.[240] Similar rules apply for partnerships and trusts.

---

[237] See Crocker v. Comm'r, 92 TC 899 (1989). See Rev. Rul. 79-113, 1979-1 CB 389 (taxpayer who files a Form 4868 showing an estimated income tax liability of zero is not considered to have made a valid filing if ample evidence of tax liability exists). See also Rev. Rul. 83-27, 1983-1 CB 337 ("extension is valid only to extent facts presented in request comport with a reasonable judgment as to the true facts").

[238] Reg. § 1.6081-3(a). For tax years ending before December 31, 1982, corporations were allowed three-month automatic extension.

[239] For taxable years ending in 1983, no further request is necessary to convert a previously granted three-month extension to a six-month extension if full payment of the estimated tax is made at the time of the original request; if, however, the election to pay in installments is made (as it may be for tax years ending before December 1, 1983), the second installment must be remitted within three months of the due date of the first installment in accordance with the procedures set forth in Rev. Proc. 83-37, 1983-1 CB 773. A corporation that expects a net operating loss is granted the automatic extension without making payment as long as the Form 7004 is accompanied by a Form 1138 (Extension of Time for Payment of Taxes by Corporation Expecting a Net Operating Loss Carryback) and the net operating loss will eliminate 50 percent or more of the tentative tax shown on Form 7004. Rev. Rul. 82-47, 1982-1 CB 201.

[240] Reg. § 1.6081-3(a). As in the case of the automatic extension of time provided for individuals by Reg. § 1.6081-4, the district director has discretionary authority to terminate the extension by giving a notice of termination to the taxpayer ten days before its effective date. In the past, if a partnership or trust needed an extension, it had to request a discretionary extension on Form 2758 and include a detailed explanation of the reason for the extension. The Service routinely approved these requests. On March 31, 1988, the Service issued temporary regulations (TD 8190) providing rules for obtaining an automatic extension of time to file partnership and trust income tax returns. Under these rules an automatic three-month extension may be obtained by a partnership or trust by filing Form 2758 with the words "AUTOMATIC EXTENSION UNDER § 6081-2T" typed or legibly printed on line 4 of Form 2758. For taxable years beginning after December 31, 1987, Form 8736 must be used. Form 2758 or Form 8736 must be filed with the proper Service office by the due date for filing the return. In the case of a trust, the return must be accompanied by the full amount of the estimated unpaid tax liability. An automatic extension of time to file a partnership or trust return does not extend the time for filing a partner's or beneficiary's income tax return.

FORM 4.3

APPLICATION FOR AUTOMATIC EXTENSION OF TIME TO FILE CORPORATION INCOME TAX RETURN

Form **7004** (Rev. October 2000) Department of the Treasury Internal Revenue Service	**Application for Automatic Extension of Time To File Corporation Income Tax Return**	OMB No. 1545-0233

Name of corporation	Employer Identification number 01 : 0001000

Number, street, and room or suite no. (If a P.O. box or outside the United States, see instructions.)

City or town, state, and ZIP code

Check type of return to be filed:

☐ Form 990-C	☐ Form 1120-FSC	☐ Form 1120-PC	☐ Form 1120S
☐ Form 1120	☐ Form 1120-H	☐ Form 1120-POL	☐ Form 1120-SF
☐ Form 1120-A	☐ Form 1120-L	☐ Form 1120-REIT	
☐ Form 1120-F	☐ Form 1120-ND	☐ Form 1120-RIC	

● Form 1120-F filers: Check here if the foreign corporation does not maintain an office or place of business in the United States . . . . ▶ ☐

1 Request for Automatic Extension (see instructions)

a Extension date. I request an automatic 6-month (or, for certain corporations, 3-month) extension of time until ...., 20 ...., to file the income tax return of the corporation named above for ▶ ☐ calendar year 20 .... or ▶ ☐ tax year beginning ...., ..., and ending ...., 20 ......

b Short tax year. If this tax year is for less than 12 months, check reason:
☐ Initial return   ☐ Final return   ☐ Change in accounting period   ☐ Consolidated return to be filed

2 Affiliated group members (see instructions). If this application also covers subsidiaries to be included in a consolidated return, provide the following information:

Name and address of each member of the affiliated group	Employer identification number	Tax period

3 Tentative tax (see instructions)		**3**
4 Payments and refundable credits: (see instructions)		
a Overpayment credited from prior year .	**4a**	
b Estimated tax payments for the tax year	**4b**	
c Less refund for the tax year applied for on Form 4466	**4c** ( ) Bal ▶	**4d**
e Credit for tax paid on undistributed capital gains (Form 2439) . .		**4e**
f Credit for Federal tax on fuels (Form 4136)		**4f**
5 Total. Add lines 4d through 4f (see instructions)		**5**
6 Balance due. Subtract line 5 from line 3. **Deposit this amount using the Electronic Federal Tax Payment System (EFTPS) or with a Federal Tax Deposit (FTD) Coupon** (see instructions)		**6**

Signature. Under penalties of perjury, I declare that I have been authorized by the above-named corporation to make this application, and to the best of my knowledge and belief, the statements made are true, correct, and complete.

....
(Signature of officer or agent)   (Title)   (Date)

For Paperwork Reduction Act Notice, see instructions.   Cat. No. 13804A   Form **7004** (Rev. 10-2000)

General Instructions

Section references are to the Internal Revenue Code unless otherwise noted.

A Change To Note

All filers of Form 990-T (and filers of Forms 990 or 990-EZ, 990-BL, and 990-PF) will now use new **Form 8868,** Application for Extension of Time To File an Exempt Organization Return, to request an extension of time to file their exempt organization returns.

Certain filers of Form 1120-ND (section 4951 taxes) will continue to use **Form 2758,** Application for Extension of Time To File Certain Excise, Income, Information, and Other Returns, to request an extension.

Purpose of Form

Use **Form 7004,** Application for Automatic Extension of Time To File Corporation Income Tax Return, to request a 6-month extension of time to file the corporation income tax return.

The extension will be granted if the corporation properly completes this form, files it, and pays any balance due on line 6 by the due date for the return for which the extension applies.

3-month extension of time to file. Foreign corporations that use the automatic 3-month extension of time to file under Regulations section 1.6081-5 (see below) must pay the balance due by the 15th day of the 6th month following the close of the tax year.

Do not file Form 7004 if the corporation is requesting a 3-month extension of time to file and to pay under Regulations section 1.6081-5. Instead, attach a statement to the corporation's tax return stating that the corporation qualifies for the extension to file and to pay under Regulations section 1.6081-5 because it is one of the following:

● A foreign corporation that maintains an office or place of business in the United States;

● A domestic corporation that transacts its business and keeps its books and records of account outside the United States and Puerto Rico; or

● A domestic corporation whose principal income is from sources within the possessions of the United States.

If the corporation is unable to file its return within the 3-month period extended under Regulations section 1.6081-5, file Form 7004 to request an additional 3-month extension. Foreign corporations that maintain an office or place of business in the United States are not considered taxpayers abroad and therefore may not obtain an extension of time to file beyond 6 months from the original due date of the tax return. See Rev. Rul. 93-85, 1993-2 C.B. 297.

When and Where To File

Generally, Form 7004 must be filed by the due date of the return with the Internal Revenue Service Center where the corporation will file its income tax return. See **Where To File** in the Instructions for Forms 1120 and 1120-A, or other comparable instructions. **Do not** attach Form 7004 to the corporation's tax return.

A foreign corporation that does not have an office or place of business in the United States should file Form 7004 by the 15th day of the 6th month following the close of the tax year.

Payment of Tax

Form 7004 does not extend the time for payment of tax.

Domestic corporations must deposit all income tax payments with **Form 8109,** Federal Tax Deposit Coupon, or use the Electronic Federal Tax Payment System (EFTPS), if applicable.

● Foreign corporations that **do** maintain an office or place of business in the United States pay their tax as described above for domestic corporations.

● Foreign corporations that **do not** maintain an office or place of business in the United States may pay the tax by check or money order, payable to the "United States Treasury."

Note: *On all checks or money orders, write the corporation's employer identification number (EIN), the type of tax, and the tax year to which the payment applies.*

Penalty for Late Payment of Tax

A corporation that does not pay the tax when due generally may be penalized ½ of 1% of the unpaid tax for each month or part of a month the tax is not paid, up to a maximum of 25% of the unpaid tax. The penalty will not be imposed if the corporation can show that the failure to pay on time was due to reasonable cause.

If the corporation is granted an extension of time to file, it will not be charged a late payment penalty if **(a)** the tax shown on line 3 (or the amount of tax paid by the regular due date of the return) is at least 90% of the tax shown on line 31 of Form 1120, (or the comparable line on other returns) and **(b)** the balance due shown on the return is paid by the extended due date.

Termination of Extension

The IRS may terminate the automatic extension at any time by mailing a notice of termination to the corporation or to the person who requested the extension. The notice will be mailed at least 10 days before the termination date given in the notice.

Specific Instructions

Address. Include the suite, room, or other unit number after the street address. If the Post Office does not deliver mail to the street address and the corporation has a P.O. box, show the box number instead of the street address.

If the corporation's address is outside the United States or its possessions or territories, enter in the space for "city or town, state, and ZIP code," the information in the following order: city, province or state, and country. Follow the country's practice for entering the postal code. Do not abbreviate the country name.

Line 1a—Extension date. A foreign corporation with an office or place of business in the United States that uses the automatic extension of time to file, as provided in Regulations section 1.6081-5, can use Form 7004 to obtain an additional 3-month extension. See **3-month extension of time to file** above.

Form 7004 (Rev. 10-2000) Page **3**

Note: *For all filers, the date that is entered on line 1a cannot be later than 6 months from the original due date of the return.*

Line 1b—Short tax year. If the box for change in accounting period is checked, the corporation must have applied for approval to change its tax year unless certain conditions have been met.

See **Form 1128,** Application To Adopt, Change, or Retain a Tax Year, and **Pub. 538,** Accounting Periods and Methods, for details.

Line 2—Affiliated group members. Enter the name and address, EIN, and tax period for each member of the affiliated group. Generally, all members of an affiliated group must have the same tax period. However, if a group member is required to file a separate return for a short period and an extension of time to file is being requested, a separate Form 7004 must be filed for that period. See Regulations section 1.1502-76 for details.

Note: *Failure to list members of the affiliated group on line 2 may result in the group's inability to elect to file a consolidated return. See Regulations sections 301.9100-1 through 301.9100-3.*

Line 3—Tentative tax. Enter the tentative amount of total tax for the year, reduced by any nonrefundable credits against the tax. This amount will usually be the tax shown on Form 1120, line 31, or the comparable line of other returns.

Line 4—Payments and refundable credits. Enter the payments and refundable credits described on lines 4a through 4f. On line 4b, include special estimated tax payments for certain life insurance companies and beneficiaries of trusts. On line 4f, include any credit for tax on ozone-depleting chemicals under section 4682(g)(2).

Line 5—Total. Include any backup withholding in the total for line 5. Describe a "write-in" amount on the

dotted line next to the entry space (e.g., for backup withholding, show the amount on the dotted line next to line 5 and write "backup withholding" next to it).

For more information about "write-in" payments and credits, see the Instructions for Forms 1120 and 1120-A, lines 32b through 32h, or the comparable instructions for other applicable forms.

Line 6—Balance due. This is the amount of tax the corporation is required to deposit.

Note: *Except for certain foreign corporations described under Payment of Tax, make all deposits with Form 8109 or use EFTPS, if applicable.* Do not *include the corporation's payment with Form 7004.*

If the corporation expects to have a net operating loss carryback, the corporation may reduce the amount to be deposited to the extent of the overpayment resulting from the carryback, providing all other prior year tax liabilities have been fully paid and **Form 1138,** Extension of Time for Payment of Taxes by a Corporation Expecting a Net Operating Loss Carryback, is filed with Form 7004.

Interest will be charged on any part of the final tax due not shown on line 6. The interest is figured from the original due date of the return to the date of payment.

For certain domestic and foreign corporations that use the automatic extension of time to file under Regulations section 1.6081-5, interest is figured from the 15th day of the 3rd month following the end of the tax year to the date of payment.

Signature. The person authorized by the corporation should sign Form 7004. This person may be:

● An officer of the corporation;

● A duly authorized agent holding a power of attorney;

● A person currently enrolled to practice before the IRS; or

● An attorney or certified public accountant qualified to practice before the IRS.

Paperwork Reduction Act Notice

We ask for the information on this form to carry out the Internal Revenue laws of the United States. You are required to give us the information. We need it to ensure that you are complying with these laws and to allow us to figure and collect the right amount of tax.

You are not required to provide the information requested on a form that is subject to the Paperwork Reduction Act unless the form displays a valid OMB control number. Books or records relating to a form or its instructions must be retained as long as their contents may become material in the administration of any Internal Revenue law. Generally, tax returns and return information are confidential, as required by section 6103.

The time needed to complete and file this form will vary depending on individual circumstances. The estimated average time is:

Recordkeeping . . . 5 hr., 44 min.
Learning about the law or the form . . . 1 hr., 22 min.
Preparing the form . 2 hr., 27 min.
Copying, assembling, and sending the form to the IRS . . . . . . 16 min.

If you have comments concerning the accuracy of these time estimates or suggestions for making this form simpler, we would be happy to hear from you. You can write to the Tax Forms Committee, Western Area Distribution Center, Rancho Cordova, CA 95743-0001. **Do not** send the tax form to this address. Instead, see **When and Where To File** on page 2.

¶ 4.05 PAYMENT OF TAX

[1] Time and Place for Payment

Tax must be paid at the time and place fixed for filing a tax return determined without regard to extensions for filing.[241] Individual taxpayers are required to pay their income tax for a taxable year at the Service center serving the internal revenue district in which their legal residence is located.[242] Alternatively, under the equivalent of hand-carrying, the tax may be paid at the district office for the internal revenue district in which the taxpayer's legal residence is located.[243] The tax that is due and payable is the balance of the tax owed but unpaid; that is, the total income tax less the amount of available credits and withheld or estimated tax previously paid. The full amount of this balance shown to be due on the return must be paid to the internal revenue official with whom the return is filed,[244] without assessment or notice and demand. The date fixed for payment is the last day the return is due whether or not an extension of time to file the return or even to make payment is granted.[245] Because extensions of time for filing or payment do not change the date fixed for payment, interest begins to run on the unpaid tax from the date fixed for payment.[246]

Special rules apply to the use of depositaries for payment of corporate income taxes and estimated income taxes.[247] Corporations must deposit all corporate income tax payments with authorized depositaries, including payment of estimated tax, on or before the date otherwise prescribed for paying the tax.[248]

---

[241] IRC § 6151(a). See the regulations for the time and place for payment of income tax (Reg. § 1.6151-1), estate tax (Reg. § 20.6151-1), and gift tax (Reg. § 25.6151-1). An exception to this general rule for individuals applies where a taxpayer files an individual income tax return and elects under Section 6014 to have the Service compute the tax. In this case, the tax must be paid within thirty days after the date the notice of the amount payable is mailed. Reg. § 1.6151-1(b).

[242] IRC § 6091(b)(1)(A)(ii).

[243] IRC § 6091(b)(1)(A)(i).

[244] IRC § 6151(a).

[245] IRC §§ 6151(a), 6151(c).

[246] Even if the taxpayer obtains an automatic extension by paying the amount of tax he estimates, the delinquent payment penalty may (although probably will not) be asserted. The delinquent payment penalty may be avoided where there is "reasonable cause," but the regulations only say that reasonable cause is presumed on the automatic extension if the balance due is not more than 10 percent of the total tax. Reg. § 301.6651-1(c)(3).

[247] IRC §§ 6151(b)(2), 6302(c); Reg. § 1.6302-1(a).

[248] IRC §§ 6151(b)(2), 6302(c); Reg. § 1.6302-1(a).

These payments must be accompanied by a Federal Tax Deposit Form.[249] The timeliness of the deposit is determined from the date stamped on the deposit form.[250] If the corporation fails to make the deposit within the time fixed for payment, it is subject to a failure-to-deposit penalty under Section 6656.[251] Similar rules are provided for payments by withholding agents from nonresident aliens and foreign corporations,[252] as well as banks or other financial institutions acting as fiduciaries of trusts required to make payments of estimated tax under Section 6654(d).[253] Employers also use the tax deposit system for the payment of withheld income tax and both employer and employee social security taxes.[254]

Payments may be made by check or money order made payable to the Service and collectible in U.S. currency at par.[255] If the check or money order received by the Service is not paid, the taxpayer remains liable for the tax, as well as for interest and penalties, including the delinquent payments penalty under Section 6651(b) and the penalty under Section 6657 for tendering a bad check.[256] If a certified, treasurer's, or cashier's check is not paid, the Service

---

[249] Reg. § 1.6302-1(b). Section 6302(c) provides that the Service may authorize Federal Reserve Banks, and incorporated banks and other financial institutions that are depositories, financial institutions, which are government depositories, or financial agents to receive any tax imposed under the internal revenue laws, and is authorized to describe the procedures for doing so in regulations. A specific method for making payments is statutorily mandated. It requires the Service to establish a paperless electronic funds transfer system to collect federal tax deposits of certain taxpayers. In 1994, the electronic funds transfer system the Service put into place was TAXLINK. See Rev. Proc. 94-48, 1994-2 CB 694. Effective July 15, 1997, all taxpayers making electronic funds transfers must use the Electronic Federal Tax Payment System (EFTPS), a new electronic funds transfer system for making federal tax deposits and payments, and may not use Form 8109, Federal Tax Deposit Coupon to make a federal tax deposit. Rev. Proc. 07-33, 1997-30 IRB 1.

[250] Id. If the deposit is mailed, it is considered received on the date of mailing, provided that the requirements of Section 7502(e) are met.

[251] Reg. § 301.6656-1.

[252] Reg. § 1.6302-2(a).

[253] Reg. § 1.6302-3(a).

[254] Reg. § 31.6302(c)-1(a)(1).

[255] IRC § 6311(a); Reg. § 301.6311-1(a)(1). See Rev. Rul. 76-350, 1976-2 CB 396 (realty is not an acceptable form of payment). Regulations relating to payment by check formerly referred only to checks drawn on a domestic bank or trust company. After amendment, regulations provide that payment may be made by check or draft on any domestic financial institution, which is defined to include not only a bank or trust company, but a building and loan association, a mutual savings bank, a credit union, and a regulated investment company. Reg. §§ 301.6311-1(a)(1)(i) and 301.6311-1(d), TD 8595 (effective Aug. 19, 1994), 59 Fed. Reg. 43,073 (Aug. 22, 1994). The Service also accepts payment of taxes in foreign currency under certain conditions. IRC § 6316; Reg. § 301.6316-1.

[256] IRC § 6311(b)(1).

obtains a lien on all the assets of the financial institution on which the check is drawn.[257]

The Taxpayer Relief Act of 1997 added to permissible tax payment methods "any commercially acceptable means that the Secretary deems appropriate," and provides for in regulations.[258] Accordingly, taxpayers are able to pay their taxes by additional payment methods, such as credit cards, debit cards, and charge cards. In response to Congress's statutory grant of authority for the Service to accept payment of taxes by credit card or debit card, temporary regulations were promulgated that generally permit taxpayers to pay tax by this method, but limit payment by credit or debit cards to certain designated cards, require payments made through certain service providers, and restrict such payments to certain types of taxes.[259] Payment by credit or debit card is deemed made when (1) the card issuer authorizes the transaction; (2) the Service actually receives payment in the ordinary course of business; and (3) the Service is not required to return the payment because of errors in the cardholder's account.[260] In addition, payments of taxes by credit or debit cards are subject to the error resolution procedures of Section 161 of the Truth in Lending Act.[261] While the Service may not charge the taxpayer for the transaction cost, the card issuer may impose such charges.[262]

[2] Extension of Time for Payment of Tax

Extensions of time for paying an income tax either reported on a return, or after the determination that a deficiency is owed, are permitted to be granted to

---

[257] IRC § 6311(b)(2). The Service also has a first priority over any other creditors in payment from the financial institution's assets. If any certified, treasurer's, or cashier's check, other guaranteed draft, or money order is not paid, the United States has a lien for the amount of the check or draft on all assets of the financial institution. Reg. § 301.6311(b)(2).

[258] IRC § 6311, as amended by the Taxpayer Relief Act of 1997, effective nine months after the date of enactment, August 5, 1997.

[259] Reg. § 301.6111-2T(a)(1), added by TD 8793, 1997-7 IRB 15 (Feb. 16, 1999), effective January 1, 1999. A "credit card" means any credit card defined in Section 103(k) of the Truth in Lending Act, 15 USC § 1602(k), and a "debit card" means any accepted card or other means of access as defined in Section 903(1) of the Electronic Funds Transfer Act, 15 USC §§ 1693a(1) and 1693a(3).

[260] Reg. §§ 301.6111-2T(b), 301.6111-2T(c).

[261] 15 USC § 1666, Section 908 of the Electronics Fund Transfer Act, 15 USC § 1693f, or any similar law providing for dispute resolution procedures for resolving credit or debit card disputes.

[262] Reg. § 301.6111-2T(e).

taxpayers by the Service.[263] Such extensions may be obtained for a "reasonable period" not to exceed six months. In the case of a deficiency in tax, the extension may be for eighteen months and, in exceptional cases, for a further period not to exceed twelve months. Where estate tax is involved, extensions of even longer duration are authorized. The time for payment of estate tax or an installment payment of estate tax due under Section 6166 may be extended for a reasonable period not to exceed ten years from the date payment is due or, if later, up to twelve months after the date the last installment is due.[264] Payment of a deficiency in estate tax may be extended for a period of up to four years from the date fixed for payment.[265] Interest continues to run on taxes when their date of payment has been extended,[266] but penalties for delinquent payment are not imposed.

Extensions of time for payment of tax are not freely given. For example, no extension of time for the payment of a tax deficiency is permitted if the deficiency is due to negligence, including intentional disregard of rules and regulations, or fraud.[267] Moreover, to obtain an extension for payment (1) an application must be filed before the due date of the payment[268]; (2) there must be a showing that immediate payment would cause "undue hardship"[269]; and (3) the taxpayer must include supporting financial data (i.e., a balance sheet and income statement for three months).[270]

Although the statute does not require "undue hardship" as a basis for an extension to pay tax shown on a return, the regulations do require a hardship showing. The term "undue hardship" means substantial financial loss, not mere inconvenience to the taxpayer (e.g., loss due to the sale of property at a sacrifice price (rather than the current market price) if property is sold to pay the tax).[271] The taxpayer must also file a financial statement and submit the proposed means by which the government's claim will be secured.

The Service has a number of procedural options when dealing with taxpayers who voluntarily state that they are unable to make a federal tax deposit when required or that they otherwise are not able to pay a tax liability in full on the due date of the return. The Service may ask the taxpayer to

---

[263] IRC §§ 6161(a)(1), 6161(b)(1). A taxpayer who is abroad may be granted an extension of time to pay for more than six months. IRC § 6161(a).

[264] IRC § 6161(a)(2).

[265] IRC § 6161(b)(2).

[266] Reg. § 1.6161-1(d).

[267] IRC § 6161(b)(3).

[268] Reg. § 1.6161-1(c). For applicable estate tax regulations, see Reg. § 20.6161-1. For gift tax regulations, see Reg. § 25.6161-1.

[269] Reg. § 1.6161-1(b).

[270] Reg. § 1.6161-1(c).

[271] Reg. § 1.6161-1(b).

- File a return on time to avoid a failure-to-file penalty;
- File a return with the collection official;
- Submit a financial statement; and
- Agree to pay the tax liability in installments. (This procedure may not be used in all cases.)

B. PENALTIES ON INCOME TAX RETURN PREPARERS

¶ 4.06 PENALTIES ON RETURN PREPARERS

Preparers of income tax returns and claims for refund of income tax, who perform these services for compensation, are subject to statutory standards of return preparation, obligations to make certain disclosures, and civil penalties if they fail to comply with these standards and disclosure obligations. Section 6694(a) requires income tax return preparers to take realistic positions on returns (or claims), and imposes a monetary penalty of $250 for each act of misconduct. If the return preparer willfully understates a taxpayer's tax or recklessly or intentionally disregards a rule or regulation, Section 6694(b) imposes a $1,000 penalty for each violation. Section 6695 requires the return preparer to

- Furnish a copy of the return or claim to the taxpayer;
- Sign the return or claim;
- Include an identifying number on the return or claim;
- Keep copies or a list of the returns;
- Prepare correct information returns;
- Refrain from negotiating refund checks; and
- Exercise due diligence in determining eligibility for the earned income credit, and penalties for failure to comply with these requirements.

Section 6694 imposes standards of preparation, and Section 6695 requires disclosures to enable the Service to identify the returns the preparer prepared.[272] Penalties directed at preparers are in addition to other civil penalties that may be assessed against persons, including preparers, who aid and assist in the preparation of returns (Section 6701), and who promote tax shelters (Section 6700). In addition to these civil penalties, a return preparer who willfully aids and assists in the preparation of a return that is false as to a material matter may be charged with the felony of aiding and assisting in the preparation of a false return (Section 7206(2)). In addition to penalties, preparers of

---

[272] IRC §§ 6694(a), 6694(b).

tax returns and claims for refund are subject to the professional standards of Circular 230, and for violations of these standards are subject to sanction and disbarment from practice before the Service.

Provisions specifically regulating income tax return preparers were first added to the Code in 1976 in response to congressional findings that approximately one half of all taxpayers sought some form of professional assistance in preparing their income tax returns with the result that there had been a tremendous growth in the business of return preparation.[273] Evidence suggested that some return preparers had engaged in improper practices, such as guaranteeing refunds and having taxpayers sign blank returns, and that a significant percentage of returns prepared by return preparers showed fraud potential (although commercial preparers had no significantly greater degree of error than professional return preparers). At the time, however, short of the criminal penalty for aiding and assisting in the preparation of a false return, the Code contained no lesser sanctions applicable to return preparers themselves. To meet this perceived need and to fill the gap in enforcement, Congress, in the Tax Reform Act of 1976 (TRA 1976), added the preparer penalties of Sections 6694(a) and 6694(b) for negligent and willful understatement of income and Section 6695 for various disclosures,[274] along with procedures for preparers to contest penalty assertions (Section 6696), and authorization for the Service to seek prohibitory injunctions against preparers engaging in egregious misconduct (Section 7407). More than a decade later, as part of the 1989 revision of the civil penalty structure, the preparer penalties were amended as follows:[275]

1. The penalty for negligent return preparation was replaced with the "realistic possibility of success" standard (the standard the American Bar Association (ABA) applied to lawyers and the American Institute of Certified Public Accountants (AICPA) imposed on accountants).

2. A disclosure procedure was adopted that permits return preparers to avoid the unrealistic position penalty if the disclosed position is not a frivolous return position.

3. The amount of the penalties for unrealistic positions and willful conduct were increased.

---

[273] Staff of Joint Comm. on Tax'n, 94th Cong., 2d Sess., General Explanation of the Tax Reform Act of 1976 (TRA 1976), at 346–347 (Comm. Print 1976), reprinted in 1976-3 CB (vol. 2) 358–359 (hereinafter General Explanation). The civil penalty for aiding and assisting in the preparation of a false return (Section 6701) was not added to the Code until 1982.

[274] IRC §§ 6107, 6109(a)(4).

[275] HR Rep. No. 101, 1989 Omnibus Budget Reconciliation Act, Pub. L. No. 101-239 (Dec. 19, 1989), 101st Cong., 1st Sess. 294, reprinted in 1989-3 CB 1401 (vol. 3) (hereinafter House Report).

As enacted in 1976 and amended in 1989, return preparer rules are limited in scope, yet they have exceedingly broad application within their statutory limitations. Return preparer penalties apply to preparers of income tax returns and claims for refund of income tax, but they do not apply to preparers of excise, estate, and gift tax returns. The return preparer rules were intended to apply to commercial return preparers and those who prepared large numbers of returns for compensation. However, they also apply to professionals who give advice and do not sign a return, and who would not have considered themselves as engaging in return preparation services. The return preparer penalties were intended to discourage or regulate serious types of misconduct, but even after their increase in 1989, the penalties for each act of misconduct are still relatively light. It is only with multiple acts of misconduct that the cumulative cost of the penalties rises significantly. If a preparer prepares an income tax return understating a taxpayer's income tax due to taking an unrealistic position on a return, the penalty under Section 6694(a) is only $250, but there is no cumulative maximum. When the return preparer takes the same unrealistic position on 100 returns, the aggregate penalty of $25,000 is a heavy one. What gives real force to the return preparer penalties, however, is referral to the Director of Practice, and potential suspension or disbarment from practice before the Service.[276] In egregious cases, where the preparer "continually or repeatedly" engages in acts of misconduct, the preparer risks an injunction prohibiting further practice as an income tax return preparer.[277]

Return preparer provisions may be grouped into the four categories:

1. Standards for tax return preparation, prohibiting preparers from taking unrealistic positions on income tax returns and claims for refund of income tax or willfully understating tax or recklessly or intentionally disregarding rules and regulations in preparing the return or claim[278]
2. Sanctions for violations of these standards[279]
3. Disclosure and reporting rules[280]
4. An injunction remedy that authorizes the Service to prevent by court order a return preparer's improper conduct and deceptive practices[281]

---

[276] IRM 120.1 Penalty Handbook 6.21 (Aug. 20, 1998) (Referral to the Director of Practice) says that referral to the Director of Practice is mandatory where there are violations of the preparer penalties of Sections 6694(a) and 6694(b), and most of the reporting and other penalties of Section 6695.

[277] IRC § 7407.

[278] IRC §§ 6694(a), 6694(b).

[279] IRC §§ 6694(a), 6694(b).

[280] IRC §§ 6695(a)–6695(g). See also IRC § 6107 (return preparer must supply copy of return or claim to the taxpayer and retain a copy or list of the taxpayers and their TINs); IRC § 6109(a)(4) (return or claim must contain the identification number of the return preparer); IRC § 6695 (penalties for failure to comply).

[281] IRC § 7407.

Other provisions define the term "income tax return preparer" (return preparer),[282] and regulations further explain the meaning of return preparer (and adopt a one-preparer-per-firm rule).[283] Regulations also interpret the realistic possibility of success standard,[284] the procedure for avoiding the penalty by disclosing a nonfrivolous return position,[285] reasonable cause,[286] and the willful or reckless disregard penalty.[287] Regulations also explain the obligations preparers have under Section 6695 to (1) furnish copies of the tax returns they prepare to taxpayers; (2) sign the returns; (3) furnish an identifying number; (4) file correct information returns; and (5) transmit refund checks to taxpayers, rather than negotiate them.[288] Section 6696 describes the procedural remedies available to persons against whom penalties have been assessed.[289] These provisions are discussed in the sections that follow.

Return preparers are also subject to other civil and criminal penalties. Section 6701 penalizes any person, including a return preparer who (1) "aids, assists in, procures or advises with respect to, the preparation or presentation of any portion of a *return*, affidavit, *claim*, or other document," (2) knows or has a reason to know that the portion will be used for any material matter under the tax laws, and (3) also knows that if the portion is used, it will result in an understatement of tax for another person.[290] The tax shelter promoter penalty (Section 6700) covers not only the organizer of a tax shelter, but a person "who assists in the organization" of the plan, or "participates (directly or indirectly)" in the sale of the plan, and makes or furnishes a statement about the allowability of any deduction or credit, or other tax benefit to a person participating in the plan that the preparer knows to be false or fraudulent. Therefore, the preparer may be liable for the same penalty as the promoter of an abusive tax shelter.[291] Preparers who willfully aid and assist in the preparation of a false return may be prosecuted for the felony described in Section

[282] IRC § 7701(a)(36).

[283] Reg. § 1.6694-1(b)(1).

[284] Reg. § 1.6694-2(b).

[285] Reg. § 1.6694-2(c).

[286] Reg. § 1.6694-2(d).

[287] Reg. § 1.6694-3.

[288] Reg. §§ 1.6695-1 et seq.

[289] IRC § 6696.

[290] IRC § 6701 (emphasis added). Section 6701 is discussed at ¶ 7B.10. The aiding and abetting provisions of Section 6701 apply without regard to whether the aider actually prepared the taxpayer's return.

[291] IRC § 6700. The Internal Revenue Manual's Penalty Handbook includes the tax shelter promoter penalty in the Return Preparer Penalty Program. IRM 120.1, Penalty Handbook 6.1 (Aug. 20, 1998) (Overview of the Return Preparer Penalty Program).

7206(2).[292] If a return preparer makes an unauthorized disclosure of returns and return information as defined in the tax return privacy rules of Section 6103, the preparer is subject to prosecution under Section 7216 for the unauthorized disclosure.[293]

For assessment of the unrealistic position or willful understatement penalties, the relevant elements to be proved are

1. The preparer is an income tax return preparer;
2. The return prepared has an understatement of income tax;
3. The understatement of income tax is due to an unrealistic position or willful attempt to understate tax;
4. There was no adequate disclosure; and
5. The preparer takes the position without reasonable cause and without acting in good faith.

Each of these elements is described in sections that follow.

[1] Definition of "Return Preparer"

The starting point in applying the return preparer penalties is the definition of the term "income tax return preparer." An "income tax return preparer" (a "return preparer") is defined as (1) any person who prepares (2) for compensation (3) all or a substantial portion of (4) a tax return or a claim for refund under the income tax provisions of the Code.[294] Each element of the definition is discussed separately.

[a] The Preparer

The definition of "income tax return preparer" includes "any person who prepares for compensation, or who employs one or more persons to prepare for compensation," any income tax return or claim for refund of income tax.[295] Under this definition, therefore, the return preparer may be (1) a self-employed return preparer; (2) an employer return preparer; and (3) an employee return preparer. Since a partnership or corporation acts through its employees, there can be more than one preparer: the employer return preparer (the partnership

---

[292] Section 7206(2) is discussed at ¶ 7A.04[2]. In one case, a return preparer who was a financial adviser of church leader was convicted under Section 7602(2) for aiding in the preparation of false returns. United States v. Moon, 718 F2d 1210 (2d Cir. 1983), cert. denied, 466 US 971 (1984).

[293] Penalties for disclosures of return information by return preparer is discussed infra ¶ 4.06[8].

[294] IRC § 7701(a)(36)(A); Reg. § 301.7701-15(a).

[295] IRC § 7701(a)(36).

or corporation) and an employee return preparer (the partner or other employee).[296] To reduce the possibility of having more than one individual associated with a firm treated as the preparer of the same return or claim, regulations adopt a one-preparer-per-firm rule, under which no more than one individual associated with the firm may be the preparer of an income tax return or claim for refund of income tax.[297]

1. *The one-preparer-per-firm rule.* The "one preparer" in a firm is the signing preparer; that is, the individual who signs a return or claim for refund and is associated with the firm. That individual and no other individual in the firm may be the preparer for purposes of Section 6694.[298] Any preparer who is not the signing preparer is a nonsigning preparer.[299] A typical example of a nonsigning preparer is the preparer who provides written or oral advice to a taxpayer or a preparer who is not associated with the same firm as the advising preparer. In a corollary to this one-preparer-per-firm rule, the signing preparer who is subject to the penalty may not rely on the advice of another individual associated with the same firm as the preparer for purposes of the reasonable cause and good faith exception to the penalty.[300] It follows that the signing preparer should be able to rely on the advice of a nonsigning preparer who is not associated with the signing preparer's firm to support a reasonable cause defense.[301]

2. *Nonsigning preparers.* Return preparation includes activities other than physically completing the return. A tax planner or adviser may also be a return preparer. Even when that person does not actually put the information on the return or review it, the person is a return preparer if the person furnishes a taxpayer or other preparer with "sufficient information and advice so that completion of the return or claim for refund is largely a mechanical matter."[302] The Service has held that an individual preparer, *B*, is the return preparer required to sign taxpayer *A*'s return as such (and subject to the failure-to-sign penalty of Section 6695(b) if *B* does not), in the following situations: (1) *B* sends back a statement of all necessary information to *A*, making

---

[296] IRC § 7701(a)(1).

[297] Reg. § 1.6694-1(b)(1).

[298] Reg. § 1.6694-1(b)(1). Suppose two or more individuals associated with the same firm are return preparers, but none is the signing preparer. The regulations say that the one preparer is the preparer with "overall supervisory responsibility" for the advice given by the firm. Id.; Reg. § 1.6694-1(b)(3), Ex.

[299] Reg. § 1.6694-1(b)(2).

[300] Reg. § 1.6694-2(d). However, in certain circumstances, both the individual preparer and the preparer's firm may be subject to the penalty. See Reg. §§ 1.6694-2(a), 1.6694-3(a).

[301] Reg. § 301.6694-2(d)(5).

[302] Reg. § 301.7701-15(a)(1).

it a mere mechanical process for *A* to fill out the return; (2) *B* reviews a draft of the entire return for substantive correctness and "mechanical accuracy," and recommends substantial changes that *A* adopts in filling out the return; and (3) *B* reviews *A*'s signed return in its entirety for both substantive correctness and "mechanical accuracy," questions certain entries, but is satisfied as to the return's correctness and makes no changes.[303]

Preparers of partnership returns may become the preparers of the partners' individual returns. A general partner who prepares a partnership return can be the return preparer of the limited partners' returns in certain situations.[304] The preparer of a partnership return and the Forms K-1 is the preparer of the partners' individual returns, although the individual partner's return has only a single item derived from the partnership.[305] In *Goulding v. United States*, the court reasoned, "Because [Goulding's] analysis of the partnership's financial operations was in essence an analysis of income directly taxable to the partner and losses directly deductible by them, the regulation making him the preparer of their returns reflects the real relationship between Mr. Goulding and the partners."[306]

An adviser on a legal issue is a nonsigning return preparer if the adviser gives advice on completed as opposed to contemplated transactions,[307] or, if the transaction is completed, the adviser gives the advice for other than tax return filing purposes.[308] For example, a lawyer who gives an opinion to an auditor for the purpose of establishing a reserve for taxes in a corporation's financial statement is not a return preparer, but the lawyer becomes a return preparer when the lawyer advises that a loss is classifiable as a business bad debt for return filing purposes. Also, a person who gives advice "directly relevant to the determination of the existence, characterization, or amount of an entry on a return" is regarded as having prepared that entry.[309] Whether the entry represents a substantial portion of the return depends on a comparison of the length and complexity of and tax attributable to that portion of the return to the length and complexity of and tax liability reported on the return as a whole.[310] The one-preparer-per-firm rule applies to nonsigning preparers as well as signing preparers. Thus, the nonsigning preparer may not rely on a

---

[303] Rev. Rul. 84-3, 1984-1 CB 264. For further insight into the reasoning for Rev. Rul. 84-3, see GCM 39322 (Jan. 28, 1985).

[304] Rev. Rul. 81-270, 1981-2 CB 250.

[305] See Goulding v. United States, 957 F2d 1420 (7th Cir. 1992) (preparer of partnership return was held to be preparer of partners' returns by way of the Schedule K-1 he prepared, which was reflected on the partners' returns).

[306] Goulding v. United States, 957 F2d 1420 (7th Cir. 1992).

[307] Reg. § 301.7701-15(a)(2)(i).

[308] Reg. § 301.7701-15(a)(2)(ii).

[309] Reg. § 301.7701-15(b)(1).

[310] Reg. § 301.7701-15(b)(1).

member of his or her firm as a basis for a reasonable cause defense to a penalty.[311]

3. *Persons who are not return preparers.* An income tax return preparer is a return preparer who prepares the return for compensation; therefore, a preparer who prepares a return or claim for refund with no explicit or implicit agreement for compensation is not a return preparer.[312] Four other types of preparers are excepted from the definition of a "return preparer":[313]

    a. A person who types, reproduces, or gives other mechanical assistance in preparing a return

    b. An employee (not an independent contractor) who prepares a return for an employer, an officer of the employer, or for a co-employee, if the preparer-employee is regularly and continuously employed by that employer

    c. A fiduciary who prepares a return

    d. A taxpayer's representative who, in the course of an audit or appeal, prepares a claim for refund

4. *Computerized return preparation packages.* The Service distinguishes between computer programs that perform computational functions and those that perform substantive functions as well. A software developer who designs, develops, and sells a computer program to taxpayers to prepare their own income tax returns is a return preparer if the program provides substantive tax instructions.[314] Similarly, a firm that furnishes a computerized tax return preparation service to tax practitioners is a return preparer if the program goes beyond mere mechanical assistance and makes substantive tax determinations.[315]

5. *Employer preparer and employee preparer liability.* Both the employer return preparer and the employee return preparer may be liable for certain penalties. Generally, only the employee preparer who prepares a return

---

[311] See Reg. § 301.7701-15(a)(1).

[312] Reg. § 301.7701-15(a)(4). The preparer is not compensated even if the preparer receives a gift for preparing the return, a return service, or a favor.

[313] IRC § 7701(a)(36)(B); Reg. §§ 301.7701-15(d)(1)–301.7701-15(d)(4).

[314] Rev. Rul. 85-189, 1985-2 CB 341. In an earlier letter ruling, the National Office had held that when the owner of a microcomputer developed a computer program that he intended to rent to taxpayers, the owner developer was a return preparer because in the Service's view the program explained each entry to be made, unlike computerized tax services that provide computational services to taxpayers who have already made determinations about what income should be included and which deductions are allowable. See Priv. Ltr. Rul. 8111071. See also IR 86-62 (May 5, 1986), announcing the position that companies manufacturing software programs that help taxpayers to prepare their tax returns are return preparers subject to penalties as described in Rev. Rul. 85-189.

[315] Rev. Rul. 85-187, 1985-2 CB 338; Rev. Rul. 85-188, 1985-2 CB 339; Rev. Rul. 85-189, 1985-2 CB 339.

understating the taxpayer's income tax liability owing to an unrealistic position or fraud or reckless disregard of a rule or regulation is subject to the penalty. If the employer or partnership participated in the wrongdoing, failed to establish review procedures, or the employee failed to follow the procedures the firm adopted, the employer or partnership is liable.[316] Only the employer or partnership is the return preparer, however, for purposes of the requirements that a copy of the return be sent to the taxpayer and another copy be kept by the preparer.[317] To determine whether the employer return preparer or the employee return preparer or both are liable for a particular penalty, the regulations relating to that specific penalty or requirement must be consulted.

[b] Compensation

Compensation is a prerequisite to return preparer liability. If an individual prepares a return gratuitously, with no implicit or explicit agreement for compensation, that person is simply not a return preparer.[318] Compensation may be implicit; for example, the preparer of a corporate return who prepares the shareholders' returns apparently for no compensation is considered to have received compensation and is liable as a return preparer.[319] However, a preparer who prepares a return and receives a gift, a service in return, or a favor does not receive compensation.[320]

[c] Substantial Portion

The "substantial portion" language of the definition requires a comparison of the length and complexity of the schedule, entry, or other item on the return with the tax liability or refund involved in the return or claim as a whole.[321]

---

[316] Reg. §§ 1.6694-1(a)(1), 1.6694-1(b)(1).

[317] Reg. § 1.6107(c).

[318] Reg. § 301.7701-15(a)(4).

[319] Papermaster v. United States, 81-1 USTC ¶ 9217 (WD Wis. 1980), aff'd, court order (7th Cir. 1982). Compare Tiddy v. United States, 762 F. Supp. 122 (WDNC 1991) (pre–Rev. Rul. 86-55 case, where returns were prepared without formal charge but preparer received assignments of discounted refund checks; *Papermaster* distinguished). But see Rev. Rul. 86-55, 1986-15 IRB 47 (used-car dealer reviewed return as part of package deal in which refund was applied to price of car; held, dealer was a preparer, although no charge was made for reviewing the return and assignment of refund was invalid).

[320] Reg. § 301.7701-15(a)(4).

[321] Reg. § 301.7701-15(b)(1). The legislative history to the TRA 1976 indicates also that preparation of a single schedule of a return would not be a substantial portion unless the schedule is a dominant part of the return. General Explanation, supra note 273, at 348, reprinted in 1976-3 (vol. 2) 360.

Regulations adopt objective safe harbor rules. Under these rules, if a schedule, entry, or other portion of the return involves amounts that are (1) less than $2,000 or (2) less than $100,000 *and* less than 20 percent of the gross income (or adjusted gross income if the taxpayer is an individual) shown on the return, then the schedule or other portion is not considered a substantial portion.[322] Regulations also address the problem of related or flow-through returns. Generally, the preparer of one return, such as a partnership or S corporation return, is not considered the preparer of another return (the partner's or shareholder's return) merely because an entry on the first return may be affected by an entry on the other return.[323] The crucial matter is whether the entry or entries on the prepared return constitute a substantial portion of the other related return.

[d] Return or Claim for Refund

The term "return" in the definition refers to both an income tax return reporting liability or an entity information return, such as an S corporation, partnership, or domestic international sales corporation (DISC) return. As noted previously, the return preparer provisions do not apply to estate, gift, or excise tax returns or to returns reporting income tax collected at source, declarations of estimated tax, applications for extensions of time to file, and miscellaneous information returns (e.g., Form 1099).[324] The phrase "claim for refund" refers only to claims for the refund of income tax.

[2] Understatement of Income Tax

No return preparer penalty may be imposed on a return preparer under Section 6694 unless there is an understatement of a taxpayer's liability. "Understatement of liability" is defined as any understatement of the net amount payable by the taxpayer or any overstatement of the net amount refundable against the taxpayer's future tax.[325] Understatement of income tax is computed without

---

[322] Reg. § 301.7701-15(b)(2). Goulding v. United States, 957 F2d 1420 (7th Cir. 1992). Based on its decision in *Goulding* upholding Reg. § 301.7701-15(b)(3), the Seventh Circuit also reversed a district court's grant of summary judgment in favor of a preparer of a partnership return and Forms K-1, in a case where the preparer was assessed penalties for each of the partners' individual returns. Adler & Drobney, Ltd. v. United States, 9 F3d 627 (7th Cir. 1993). On remand, the district court was to consider the length, complexity, and tax impact of the partnership loss entry to the return as a whole, and the tax impact of the loss deduction clearly was "significant when compared to the tax liability of the individual investors as a whole, at least in some of the cases." Id. at 630 (footnote omitted).

[323] Reg. § 301.7701-15(b)(3).

[324] Reg. § 301.7701-15(c).

[325] IRC §§ 6694(d), 6694(e).

considering facts in other tax years. When the taxpayer has a net operating loss carried back from another tax year, therefore, the loss carryback does not reduce or eliminate an understatement for return preparer purposes.[326] The result is different if the offsetting adjustment is in the same tax year. When an adjustment that reduces or eliminates the understatement is in the same tax year, the adjustment may be offset against the understatement.[327] On the other hand, if the return preparer creates a net operating loss that is carried forward to the succeeding year because the preparer negligently or fraudulently over-states expenses, the return preparer is liable for the penalty for the succeeding year even if a second return preparer prepares the return for the succeeding year. (The second preparer is not liable for the preparer penalty.)[328]

The understatement for which the preparer is liable may be the result of preparing a related return reflected in the taxpayer's return, such as a Schedule K-1, which is a significant part of the limited partner's return. When a general partner prepares the partnership return and sends Schedules K-1 to the partners, the general partner may be liable for a preparer penalty if an understatement on an individual partner's return is the result of negligence in preparing Schedule K-1 and entries on that schedule.[329] Once an understatement is found, separate proceedings determine the penalty against the return preparer and the taxpayers' actual net amount payable.[330] As a result, a final administrative or judicial determination on the taxpayer's liability is not a necessary condition to the finding that there is an understatement of liability for the preparer penalty. The understatement for the preparer penalty exists if it is shown in fact to exist in the return preparer penalty proceeding. Thus, the taxpayer may not have had a final determination by the time the return preparer's penalty is determined. This does not mean that the preparer may be sanctioned when it is determined that the taxpayer did not understate tax. If there is a final administrative or judicial determination that the taxpayer's liability was not understated, the Service must abate the penalty on the preparer, and refund any amount collected.[331]

---

[326] Rev. Rul. 82-25, 1982-1 CB 214.

[327] Rev. Rul. 82-25, 1982-1 CB 214.

[328] Rev. Rul. 81-171, 1981-1 CB 589.

[329] Rev. Rul. 81-270, 1981-2 CB 250. The result in Rev. Rul. 81-270, and Reg. § 301.7701-15(b)(3) has been upheld. Goulding v. United States, 957 F2d 1420 (7th Cir. 1992) (attorney prepared partnership return and Forms K-1 for partners and prepared substantial portion of partners' returns).

[330] Reg. § 1.6694-1(c).

[331] IRC § 6694(d); Reg. § 1.6694-1(d).

[3] Preparer Misconduct: Unrealistic Positions, Negligence, and Fraud

In its present form, Section 6694 imposes penalties on return preparers, who prepare income tax returns or claims for refund that reflect an "understatement" of a taxpayer's liability by (1) taking an undisclosed position for which there is no "realistic possibility of being sustained on the merits"[332] or (2) making a "willful attempt" to understate in any manner the taxpayer's liability or any reckless or intentional disregard of rules and regulations.[333] This was not always the case. When the return preparer rules were first enacted in 1976, the preparer penalty was imposed for negligence or willful conduct in the preparation of returns. According to the Senate Finance Committee explanation of TRA 1976, the negligence and willful conduct penalties were "primarily aimed at deterring income tax return preparers who prepare a large number of returns from engaging in negligent or fraudulent practices designed to understate a taxpayer's liability."[334] Congress did not adopt the realistic possibility of success standard until 1989, and so for about thirteen years the negligence standard was the penalty standard for return preparation.

In 1989, Section 6694(a) was changed (1) to increase the amount of the penalty from $100 to $250 per return or claim for refund; (2) to modify the standard so that the penalty is imposed if the understatement is due to a position that the preparer knew or reasonably should have known not to have a realistic possibility of success on its merits; (3) to add a disclosure exception for positions that are not frivolous; and (4) to add a reasonable cause and good faith exception. In its present form, Section 6694(a) imposes a preparer penalty if (1) any part of an understatement of liability on a return or claim for refund is "due to a position for which there was not a realistic possibility of being sustained on its merit"; (2) the preparer "reasonably knew or should have known" of the unrealistic position; (3) the unrealistic position was not disclosed in the same manner as a disclosure to avoid a substantial understatement penalty (Section 6662(d)(2)(B)(ii)) or was frivolous; and (4) the preparer failed to show that there is reasonable cause for the understatement and that the preparer acted in good faith. Each of these elements is described later, but because the unrealistic position penalty still uses factors considered in a negligence analysis, the former negligent understatement is also discussed.

The fraud-type preparer penalty of Section 6694(b) was also amended in 1989 to make a heavier penalty to apply to a reckless or intentional disregard of rules or regulations. As amended, Section 6694(b) imposes a penalty of $1,000 on a return statement due (1) to a "willful attempt in any manner" to

---

[332] IRC § 6694(a).

[333] IRC §§ 6694(b)(1), 6694(b)(2).

[334] S. Rep. No. 938, 94th Cong., 2d Sess. 355, reprinted in 1976-3 (vol. 3) CB 393.

understate a tax liability on a return or claim for refund; or (2) to "any reckless or intentional disregard of rules or regulations." This penalty is described later.

[a] Verification of Information

For purposes of both the unrealistic position penalty of Section 6694(a) and the willful understatement penalty of Section 6695(b), return preparers may rely on the information supplied to them by the taxpayers.[335] They need not independently verify a taxpayer's information by auditing, examining, or reviewing the taxpayer's books and records. However, preparers may not ignore the implications of information taxpayers make available to them, and must make reasonable inquiries if the information as furnished appears to be incorrect or incomplete. Certain Code provisions or regulations require that specified facts and circumstances exist; for example, that the taxpayer has maintained certain records before a deduction may be claimed. Consequently, preparers must ask taxpayers whether facts and circumstances exist on which the Code or regulations condition the claiming of a deduction.[336]

[b] The Negligence Standard Before 1989

From 1976 to 1989, Section 6694(a) imposed a penalty on preparers if they understated a taxpayer's liability due to negligence. It is helpful to consider this negligence penalty in understanding the penalty Section 6694(a) imposes on return preparers for taking "unrealistic positions," especially since the legislative history states that the unrealistic position penalty includes negligent conduct as well.[337] The negligence penalty imposed on return preparers was based on the negligence penalty applicable to taxpayers. Negligence in the taxpayer negligence penalty has been defined as "the lack of due care in failing to do what a reasonable and ordinarily prudent person would do under the circumstances."[338] Similarly, the preparer was not considered to have acted negli-

---

[335] Reg. § 1.6694-1(e)(1).

[336] The example in the regulations refers to medical expenses and travel and entertainment expenses, and says that the preparer is not liable for a penalty if he does not ask the taxpayer for documentation of the medical expenses, but does ask about the existence of travel and entertainment records. Reg. § 1.6694-1(e)(2).

[337] See infra note 328.

[338] Marcello v. Comm'r, 380 F2d 499, 506 (5th Cir.), cert. denied, 389 US 1044 (1968); Rev. Rul. 80-28, 1980-1 CB 304. See the discussion of the accuracy-related penalty at ¶ 7B.02[2]. Authority under Section 6653(a) (presumably to excuse imposition of the penalty) was meant to apply to an intentional disregard of rules and regulations in such situations as a taxpayer's good-faith dispute about an interpretation of a statute. See General Explanation, supra note 273, at 351, reprinted in 1976-3 CB (vol. 2) 363.

gently or intentionally disregarded a rule or regulation if the preparer exercised "due diligence" in an effort to apply the rule or regulation to the information the taxpayer had given the preparer for the computation of tax.[339] Negligent return preparation can be divided roughly into two categories: (1) unreasonable conduct or errors in conduct and (2) errors of law. For example, an error-in-conduct-type negligence can be found when the preparer omits or fails to investigate related and relevant records.[340] Error-of-law-type negligence was found where the preparer included contingent debt in depreciable basis with the result that the partnership's depreciation and the partner's loss were overstated.[341]

1. *The Service's interpretation of the standard.* The Service's application of the due diligence standard proved troublesome for the practitioner. Negligence penalties were imposed on a return preparer who (1) failed to compute a minimum tax based on the unsupported belief that it would be offset; (2) omitted computation of the minimum tax through oversight; or (3) was unaware of the minimum tax provision.[342] Liability for a negligent understatement depended on the steps the preparer took to determine the existence or nonexistence of tax. Mere oversight, even if not deliberate, or ignorance of a frequently encountered Code provision, was not sufficient to avoid the penalty. In response to objections to this hard-line approach, the Service issued guidelines for application of the penalty.[343] The Service said that it would take the following factors into consideration in applying the negligent understatement penalty:

For the same reason, the definition of negligence contained in Section 6653(a)(3), as amended by the Tax Reform Act of 1986, applies in determining negligence under the preparer penalty provisions. Section 6653(a)(3) defines negligence as including "any failure to make a reasonable attempt to comply with the provisions of this title, and the term 'disregard' includes any careless, reckless, or intentional disregard." Nevertheless, a general negligence standard has been applied to a return preparer and authority under Section 6653(a) apparently disregarded. Brockhouse v. United States, 749 F2d 1248 (7th Cir. 1984).

[339] Reg. § 1.6694-1(a)(1). Applying the negligence standard, a district court held that due diligence is not present where a preparer's obvious error is caused by physical and mental exhaustion that could have been alleviated by hiring an assistant. 749 F2d 1248 (7th Cir. 1984). Swart v. United States, 568 F. Supp. 763 (CD Cal. 1982), aff'd in unpublished opinion, 714 F2d 154 (9th Cir. 1983).

[340] Brockhouse v. United States, 749 F2d 1248 (7th Cir. 1984), described infra, can be classified as error-in-conduct negligence.

[341] Goulding v. United States, 957 F2d 1420 (7th Cir. 1992).

[342] Rev. Rul. 80-28, 1980-1 CB 304. In other words, a preparer can be penalized for negligence if the preparer fails to apply an obvious requirement through oversight or the preparer does not know an obvious requirement of tax law.

[343] Rev. Proc. 80-40, 1980-2 CB 774.

- The nature of the error causing the understatement (e.g., the magnitude of the error or whether the provision involved was "so complex, uncommon or highly technical that a reasonably competent preparer might be unaware or mistaken as to its applicability");
- The frequency of the error (e.g., whether an understatement is the result of an isolated error or a number of errors); and
- The materiality of the errors (e.g., whether the understatement is material in relation to the correct tax liability, although even an immaterial understatement may result in a penalty if the errors are "sufficiently obvious, flagrant or numerous").

Even if facts suggested that the preparer was negligent, the penalty could be avoided if the preparer (1) has a normal office practice that, when considered together with other facts and circumstances (e.g., the preparer's knowledge) indicates that the error involved would "rarely" occur and (2) has followed this normal practice in preparing the return in question.[344]

A return preparer was not required to exercise due diligence in verifying information supplied by a taxpayer. Generally, the preparer could rely on such information without verification and need not examine or review documents to verify the taxpayer's information.[345] However, the return preparer was required to make reasonable inquiries if the information the taxpayer furnished appeared to be incorrect or incomplete.[346] Also, where provisions of the Code require specific facts and circumstances, including documentation, the return preparer had to make appropriate inquiries to verify that the facts are present or that the taxpayer has adequate documentation to support the deduction.

These guidelines have more than historical significance. They are incorporated in Regulations Section 1.6694-2(d), which describe the reasonable cause and good faith exception to the unrealistic position penalty, as discussed below.

---

[344] In a series of rulings, the Service applied these guidelines to a number of factual situations. Rev. Rul. 80-262, 1980-2 CB 375 (mathematical or clerical error); Rev. Rul. 80-263, 1980-2 CB 376; Rev. Rul. 80-264, 1980-2 CB 377; Rev. Rul. 80-265, 1980-2 CB 377; and Rev. Rul. 80-266, 1980-2 CB 378 (reliance on taxpayer's assurances involving entertainment expenses). See also Priv. Ltr. Rul. 8218005 (return preparer not liable for negligence where the error was the result of technical, mechanical mistakes in the computer program used to prepare the return). However, the adoption of an accepted office practice may work against the preparer; see Brockhouse v. United States, 749 F2d 1248 (7th Cir. 1984) (failure to follow practice itself an act of negligence).

[345] Reg. § 1.6694-1(b)(2)(ii).

[346] These requirements appear to reflect the standard adopted by AICPA Statements on Responsibilities in Tax Practice (SRTP) No. 9, issued in December 1972. This statement, revised in 1988 (and renumbered SRTP No. 3), states, "the CPA may in good faith rely without verification upon information furnished by the client or by third parties," but requires the CPA to make reasonable inquiries if the furnished information is incomplete.

2. *Judicial views of negligent return preparation.* One case illustrates the different judicial attitudes courts could have in reviewing a negligent understatement penalty. In *Brockhouse v. United States,*[347] *B,* a tax return preparer, prepared the 1979 personal income tax returns of a doctor and the corporate return of the doctor's professional corporation. To prepare the corporation's return, *B* used a trial balance the corporation's bookkeeper had prepared. To prepare the doctor's personal return, the preparer used information the doctor's bookkeeper and business manager supplied. The trial balance showed loans to the corporation from a bank and from the doctor, and payments of interest by the corporation (but not the identity of the payees). In preparing the doctor's personal return, *B* omitted this interest income, when in fact, the doctor's corporation had paid over $15,000 in interest to the doctor. A divided circuit court held that *B* was liable for the negligent disregard penalty.[348] Finding that the preparer had negligently disregarded the information supplied to him, rather than that he had negligently disregarded rules and regulations, the majority stated:[349]

> We hold that if the information supplied would lead a reasonable, prudent preparer to seek additional information, it is negligent not to do so. A reasonable, prudent preparer would inquire as to additional information where it is apparent that the information supplied was incorrect or incomplete and it is simple to collect the necessary additional information.

The court further noted:

> A tax preparer negligently disregards a rule or regulation under section 6694(a) if his or her negligent failure to inquire into information provided by the taxpayer results in the filing of a return that violates a rule or regulation.

According to the majority, the standard of negligence applicable to return preparers was a general negligence standard; that is, "a lack of due care or failure to do what a reasonable and ordinarily prudent person would do under the circumstances." Due diligence, it held, means acting "as a reasonable, prudent person with respect to the information supplied to the preparer." The dissent in *Brockhouse* criticized the majority's use of a generalized negligence

---

[347] Brockhouse v. United States, 749 F2d 1248 (7th Cir. 1984).

[348] Brockhouse v. United States, 749 F2d 1248 (7th Cir. 1984). Compare Chandler v. United States, 90-2 USTC ¶ 50,525 (WD Ky. 1990) (taxpayer's agreement to adjustment did not establish negligence and ample evidence of full-time work supported accountant's deduction of amounts paid for spouse's services) with Weidman v. Department of Treasury, 713 F. Supp. 569 (WDNY 1989) (accountant deducted amounts for purported services of "employee" spouse on series of returns despite the fact that the "employee" spouse was employed full-time elsewhere).

[349] Brockhouse v. United States, 749 F2d 1248 (7th Cir. 1984). Compare cases gathered supra note 348.

standard, pointing out that the penalty was imposed for the preparer's negligent "disregard of rules or regulations," unlike the negligence penalty imposed on taxpayers (relied on by the majority), which penalizes taxpayers for tax underpayments attributable to general negligence and intentional disregard of rules or regulations. When applied to return preparation, the general negligence standard gave the Service and courts the jurisdiction to punish preparers for a broader range of tax return preparation conduct than negligently disregarding specific rules and regulations. There was uncertainty, therefore, about just what kind of practice or error could subject the preparer to liability.

[c] The Realistic Possibility of Success Standard

By 1989, the negligence standard was considered inappropriate as a standard to be applied to return preparation and preparers. Taxpayers were able to avoid the negligence penalty on taxpayer understatements if the taxpayer had a "reasonable basis" for the return position. It was believed that lawyers were providing opinions, primarily in tax shelter investments, to provide taxpayers with a reasonable basis for avoiding the negligence penalty. In response to this anecdotal misuse of lawyer opinions, in 1982 Congress adopted the substantial understatement penalty, which required an undisclosed return position to be supported by "substantial authority," which was a new term intended to mean that a return position was supported by more authority than a reasonable basis opinion.[350] This meant, however, that the ABA's professional standard of return preparation, which required that the attorney have a "reasonable basis" for the return position of the client, arguably was lower than the substantial authority standard taxpayers had to meet to avoid the substantial understatement penalty. In 1985, the ABA changed the statement of the professional standard of return preparation from reasonable basis to "a realistic possibility of success if the matter [of the return position] is litigated."[351] In 1988, the AICPA followed suit and also adopted a standard for return preparation that requires lawyers and accountants to have "a realistic possibility of success in court" for reporting a position taken on a tax return.[352] As one of the civil penalty reform measures it adopted in 1989, Congress replaced the negligence standard in the return preparer penalty with the "realistic possibility of success" standard with the express intention of coordinating the professional standards of return preparation and the return preparer penalty standard.[353] In 1994, Treasury replaced

---

[350] See ¶ 7B.02[3].

[351] See ¶ 1.09, ABA Opinion 85-35239 Tax. Law. 631 (1986).

[352] AICPA SRTP No. 1.

[353] House Ways and Means Committee Explanation of the Revenue Reconciliation Act of 1989 (RRA 1989), supra note 275, at 289. The Committee Report states, "the

the Circular 230 standard of "due diligence" in return preparation with the realistic possibility of success standard.[354]

When Congress incorporated the standard of return preparation professional groups applied to lawyers and certified public accountants as the standard of return preparation, it did not eliminate all issues of interpretation. Because it incorporated professional organizations' ethical or practice standard for purposes of the penalty, Congress apparently assumed that the views of those professional organizations about their own standard would also control the Service's interpretation of the standard for penalty purposes. As discussed later, however, regulations interpreting the standard differ in important respects from the AICPA's interpretation of the realistic possibility standard. Congress also believed that the "realistic possibility" standard professional associations had adopted was stricter than the negligence standard in the former version of Section 6694(a) "so that negligent behavior subject to penalty under present law will continue to be subject to penalty under this new standard."[355] This may have been a misreading of the professional realistic possibility standard the professional associations adopted. ABA Opinion 85-352 arguably did not create a higher standard than negligence. In explaining the realistic possibility of success standard, it is noteworthy that ABA Opinion 85-352 states in part, "the position to be asserted must be one which the lawyer in good faith believes is warranted in existing law or can be supported by a good faith argument for the extension of existing law."

As this background shows, return preparers face at least four standards of uncertain meaning, and, as a result, they will have difficulty in deciding whether they are taking penalty-free action in preparing a return. If the realistic possibility standard is stricter than the negligence (reasonable basis) standard, but the negligence standard still applies, it is unclear how the realistic possibility and negligence standards differ, and how each standard applies in practice. The reasonable cause waiver injects still another standard. Add the requirement that a qualifying disclosed position must not be "frivolous," that is, "patently improper," and there is bound to be confusion. One way to retain the original purpose of the preparer penalty in regulating the conduct of return preparers, and to coordinate the standards, is to read Section 6694(a) as requiring the return preparer to (1) make a good faith attempt to determine the proper reporting position; (2) find at least some support for the position (reasonable cause); and (3) after reasonably competent research, find no contrary

Committee has adopted this new standard because it generally reflects the professional conduct standards applicable to lawyers and to certified public accountants."

[354] See supra ¶ 4.06.

[355] House Ways and Means Committee Explanation to RRA 1989, supra note 275, at 289.

authority demonstrating that a court could not practically (i.e., realistically) be expected to sustain the position. Regulations have taken another approach.

1. *The regulations' quantitative view of the standard.* According to regulations, a return preparer is subject to an unrealistic position penalty if any part of an understatement on a return or claim is "due to a position for which there was not a realistic possibility of being sustained on its merits," and the preparer "knew or should have known" of the unrealistic position.[356] A realistic possibility of success exists when "a reasonable and well-informed analysis by a person knowledgeable in the tax law would lead such a person to conclude that the position has approximately a one in three, or greater, likelihood of being sustained on its merits (realistic possibility standard)."[357] It apparently did not occur to the regulation writers that "likelihood" means a probability,[358] and a one-in-three chance of success is obviously less than a probability. Return preparer penalty regulations thus adopt the same type of odds-making standard as regulations interpreting substantial authority for purposes of the substantial misstatement penalty on taxpayers.[359] To what superficially might be viewed as an objective standard (the one-in-three chances of success), regulations also add negligence concepts (the preparer "knew or should have known" element and the "reasonably well-informed professional's" analysis).

For preparer penalty purposes, this quantitative approach converts the ABA and AICPA professional standards into speculative calculation of the chances that the position can be successfully defended. Professionals may be expected to engage in some forecasting of results when they give advice, but the professional standard seems to be normative or qualitative. As interpreted in regulations, the realistic possibility standard clearly focuses on the return position's chances of success on the merits, but it is unclear how the reasonable preparer factor fits into the analysis. As a result, the regulatory standard can mean that the Service employee or a judge will find that the realistic possibility standard is met when the Service employee or the judge agrees with the position, and that the preparer has not met the standard if the employee or judge does not agree with the return position. By contrast, as applied by the professional organizations, the professional standards direct the inquiry to whether the preparer acted in the way a reasonably prudent tax preparer would under the circumstances in saying, in effect, that the return position is defensible in fact and warranted in law.[360] Whether a possibility of success for a return is realistic for signing preparers is determined when the return is signed;

---

[356] Reg. § 1.6694-2(a)(1).

[357] Reg. § 1.6694-2(a)(1).

[358] The American Heritage Dictionary 1042 (3d ed. 1992).

[359] Reg. § 1.6694-2(a)(1).

[360] This language is substantially the same as that of Rule 11, Fed. R. Civ. P., and Rule 33(b), Tax Court R. of Prac. & Proc., which describe the responsibilities of lawyers

for nonsigning preparers, it is determined on the date on which the advice was given.[361]

If a realistic possibility of success analysis works the same way as the substantial authority analysis as interpreted in substantial misstatement penalty regulations, the return preparer will be better able to determine if a realistic possibility of success exists when issues of law, not of fact, are involved, and especially in areas of developed law where it is possible to research court decisions. Its application is confusing in situations where an issue has not been clearly dealt with in either the statute itself or legislative history. The view that the standard is best applied to issues of law is supported by examples in the regulations describing situations when the realistic possibility standard is and is not satisfied. All of the examples involve the weighing of authorities, such as committee reports, proposed regulations, letter rulings, and court decisions.[362]

Ultimately, general statements do not resolve the specific situations facing return preparers. In most cases, there is either clear support for a position or clear authority against it. For those cases in the middle ground, the return preparer must engage in research and analysis to develop a position before the return is filed. However, in this middle ground, the uncertain meaning and application of the realistic possibility standard makes disclosure of the return position the practical option for the preparer. As described below, disclosure is made in the same manner as for purposes of the substantial understatement accuracy-related penalty.

2. *The regulations' limitation of permissible authorities.* Under the realistic position penalty regulations, the only authorities the Service considers proper authority in determining whether a taxpayer's return position has a realistic possibility of success are the same authorities recognized in determining whether the taxpayer's position was supported by "substantial authority" for purposes of the substantial understatement accuracy-related penalty.[363] These regulations differ from the AICPA's interpretation of the realistic possibility standard by restricting the authorities the return preparer may consult to determine the chances of success. According to the AICPA Statements on Responsibilities in Tax Practice, Interpretation No. 1-1, a certified public accountant is entitled to consider well-reasoned treatises, articles in recognized tax publications, and any other reference tools commonly used by tax advisers and return

---

and parties in the filing of pleadings in court. See also ABA Model Rules of Prof. Conduct, Rule 3.1; Wolfram, Modern Legal Ethics, 211, 214 (1986).

[361] Reg. § 1.6694-2(b)(5).

[362] Reg. § 1.6694-2(b)(3), discussed infra note 365.

[363] Reg. § 1.6694-2(b)(2), incorporating by reference Reg. § 1.6662-4(d)(3)(iii).

preparers.[364] Preparer penalty regulations say that while treatises and similar types of secondary sources do not constitute authority, recognized authorities underlying the opinions expressed in secondary sources may give a position favorable to the taxpayer a realistic possibility of being sustained on its merits.[365] This approach still differs from a qualitative standard that would permit the return preparer to consult a wide range of professional material so long as a reasonable professional would rely on the material in practice.

3. *The AICPA's view of the realistic possibility standard and authorities.* In December 1990, the AICPA published an interpretation of the realistic possibility of success standard and, for the first time, gave some guidance to return preparers in arriving at return positions that would avoid, in the view of the AICPA, a violation of the professional standard. Because of the derivation of the preparer penalty standard, however, the AICPA's interpretation is relevant and perhaps determinative of the reasonableness of the Service's application of the preparer penalty. While regulations state that the realistic possibility standard can be expressed in terms of a percentage, the AICPA interpretation states, "the realistic possibility standard cannot be expressed in terms of percentage odds."[366] In contrast to the Service's position on authorities for purpose of the substantial understatement penalty, the AICPA also says, "in determining whether a tax return position meets the CPA's realistic possibility standard, a CPA may rely on authorities in addition to those evaluated in determining whether substantial authority exists."[367] CPAs may rely on well-reasoned treatises, articles in recognized professional tax publications, and any other reference tools of tax analysis "commonly used" by tax advisers and return preparers. The broad range of references are to be used with care, and the weight of each authority is to be considered. In determining the weight of an authority, "the CPA should consider its persuasiveness, relevance, and source."[368] Other important factors the CPA should consider in determining whether the weight of the authority meets the realistic possibility standard are whether the facts stated in the authority are distinguishable from those of the taxpayer client and whether the authority contains an analysis of the issue or merely states a conclusion. After research and a consideration of all of the

---

[364] AICPA SRTP No. 1.07 permits a CPA to consider "well-reasoned articles [and] treatises" that are not treated as "authority" under the substantial understatement penalty, as well as other sources recognized in regulations as authority under this penalty on taxpayers. For a description of what constitutes substantial authority, see Chapter 7B.

[365] Reg. § 1.6694-2(b)(3), Ex. 7 ("[A]s in the case of conclusions reached in treatises and legal periodicals, the authorities underlying the [foreign court's] opinion, if relevant to the taxpayer's situation, may give a position favorable to the taxpayer a realistic possibility of being sustained in its merits. See § 1.6694-2(b)(2) and § 1.6662-4(d)(3)(iii).").

[366] AICPA SRTP, Interpretation No. 1-1 (Dec. 1990).

[367] AICPA SRTP, Interpretation No. 1-1, ¶ 1.07 (Dec. 1990).

[368] AICPA SRTP, Interpretation No. 1-1, ¶ 1.09 (Dec. 1990).

facts and circumstances "known to the CPA," the AICPA acknowledges that more than one position may meet the realistic possibility standard. Preparer regulations incorporate the substantial understatement penalty's limited view of authorities, and unlike the AICPA do not recognize treatises and periodicals, except insofar as the treatises and periodicals cite recognized authorities to give the position a realistic possibility of success.[369]

4. **Application of the realistic possibility standard.** The AICPA applied its general interpretive observations of the realistic possibility standard in fifteen illustrative examples and variations. Because these illustrations spell out the AICPA's interpretation of the realistic possibility standard, they are important enough to be reprinted in Form 4.3. The unrealistic position penalty regulations also have illustrations of the application of the realistic possibility standard. The AICPA's illustrations should be compared with the corresponding examples described in the return preparer regulations (Reg. § 1.6694-2(b)(3)), shown in Form 4.4. Fifteen situations are illustrated in the AICPA Interpretation and nine situations in examples in the regulations, and so they do not cover identical situations. In common situations, however, they generally reach the same conclusions on whether the realistic position standard has been satisfied. Under both AICPA illustrations and preparer regulations, a realistic possibility of success exists when a new statute does not clearly provide favorable tax treatment for a taxpayer's transaction, but (1) prior law supports the taxpayer's position; (2) there are no regulations or other authority; and (3) committee reports say the new statute is not intended to remove the prior favorable tax treatment.[370] Also, under both the AICPA illustrations and the regulations, a position is unrealistic where a new statute adversely affects the tax treatment of a taxpayer's transaction, prior law was favorable to the taxpayer, and the preparer believes that the new statute is inequitable as applied to the taxpayer, as long as the new statutory language is unambiguous, and the committee reports do not deal with the taxpayer's specific situation.[371] On the other hand, if the committee report states that Congress did not intend the new statute to apply to the taxpayer's transaction, a position consistent with either the statute or the committee report satisfies the realistic possibility standard;

---

[369] Reg. § 1.6694-2(b)(3), Ex. 7.

[370] Compare Reg. § 1.6694-2(b)(3), Ex. 1, with AICPA Interpretation No. 1-1, Illustration 2, saying that positions under the statute or the favorable legislative history satisfy the realistic possibility standard.

[371] Compare Reg. § 1.6694-2(b)(3), Ex. 2, with AICPA Interpretation No. 1-1, Illustrations 1 and 3. If the committee reports provide support for the taxpayer's position by saying that no change in the law was intended, under both the regulations and the AICPA Illustrations, there is a realistic position under both the statute and the legislative history, but the position under the legislative history must be disclosed since there is a disregard of rules or regulations. Reg. § 1.6694-2(b)(3), Ex. 3; AICPA Interpretation No. 1-1, Illustrations 3.

but the position consistent with the committee report must be disclosed.[372] The examples in the regulations also make clear that when the Treasury has published interpretations in temporary or final regulations, it is prudent to disclose a return position contrary to an interpretative regulation. Analytically, however, while entitled to great weight, an interpretative regulation is not binding on courts, and it is more than the rare case that a court has held invalid an interpretative regulation, especially when both the Treasury and the Service have incorporated a litigating position into an interpretative statement.

5. *The Circular 230 standard and referral to the Director of Practice.* Circular 230 makes the practitioner's standards of professional conduct that have a realistic possibility of success on the position for giving advice about or preparing a tax return consistent with the preparer penalty. To be considered to have acted with "due diligence" in advising a taxpayer on a return position, practitioners authorized to practice before the Treasury Department and the Service are prohibited by Circular 230 from signing the return "if the practitioner determines that the return contains a position that does not have a realistic possibility of being sustained on its merits (the realistic possibility standard) unless the position is not frivolous and is adequately disclosed to the Service."[373] Following the return preparer and the substantial understatement penalty, Circular 230 interprets that standard as a one-in-three or greater chance of success.[374]

Section 10.53 of Circular 230 requires Service employees to make a written report to the Office of the Director of Practice when there is reason to believe that a practitioner has violated the rules set out in the circular. Under Service procedures, an information referral is mandatory when (1) the penalty asserted is for an unrealistic return position or a willful or reckless understatement under Section 6694(a) or Section 6694(b), respectively; (2) the penalty asserted is for the preparer's endorsement of a taxpayer's refund check under Section 6695(f); or (3) injunction action is taken under Section 7407.[375] Referral is discretionary when a penalty is asserted under Sections 6695(a) through 6695(e)(2). Where there are multiple violations, however, there will be a referral because the number of violations indicate reckless conduct or a lack of

---

[372] Reg. § 1.6694-2(b)(3), Ex. 3.

[373] Circular No. 230, § 10.34(a)(1) (1994).

[374] Circular No. 230, § 10.34(a)(4)(i) (1994), discussed in Chapter 1. Regulations under Section 6664 interpreting the reasonable cause uniform waiver of accuracy-related penalties imposed on taxpayers should be compared. When a taxpayer relies on the advice of a tax professional to avoid an accuracy-related penalty, the tax professional and the taxpayer must have followed very definite steps if the taxpayer is to rely on the tax professional's advice to establish reasonable cause. See Chapter 7B.

[375] IRM 120.1 Penalties Handbook 6.2.1 (Aug. 20, 1998) (Referral to the Director of Practice).

competence. When Congress amended Section 6694, it gave the Service the following instructions about referrals to the Director of Practice:[376]

- If a penalty is imposed, this fact alone should not lead to a referral to the Director of Practice;
- Discretion should be exercised when a case is referred to the Director of Practice; and
- The exercise of discretion in making referrals should not itself lead to an expansion of the Service's investigations of preparer penalty cases.

[376] H. Rep., supra note 275, at 289, 300–301.

FORM 4.4
AICPA INTERPRETATION NO. 1-1—SPECIFIC ILLUSTRATIONS

Specific Illustrations

.12 The following illustrations deal with general fact patterns. Accordingly, the application of the guidance discussed above to variances in such general facts or to particular facts or circumstances may lead to different conclusions. In each illustration there is no authority other than that indicated.

.13 *Illustration 1.* The CPA's client has engaged in a transaction that is adversely affected by a new statutory provision. Prior law supported a position favorable to the client. The client believes, and the CPA concurs, that the new statute is inequitable as applied to the client's situation. The statute is clearly drafted and unambiguous. The committee reports discussing the new statute contain general comments that do not specifically address the client's situation.

.14 The CPA should recommend the return position supported by the new statute. A position contrary to a clear, unambiguous statute would ordinarily be a frivolous position.

.15 *Illustration 2.* The facts are the same as in illustration 1 except that the committee reports discussing the new statute specifically address the client's situation with a position favorable to the client.

.16 In a case where the statute is clear and unambiguous against the taxpayer's position but a contrary position exists based on the committee reports specifically addressing the client's situation, return positions based on either the statutory language or the legislative history satisfy the realistic possibility standard.

.17 *Illustration 3.* The facts are the same as in illustration 1 except that the committee reports can be read to provide some evidence or authority to support the taxpayer's position, but the legislative history does not specifically address the situation.

.18 In a case where the statute is clear and unambiguous, a contrary position based on an interpretation of committee reports which do not explicitly address the client's situation does not meet the realistic possibility standard. However, since the committee reports provide some support or evidence for the taxpayer's position, then such a return position is not frivolous. The CPA may recommend the position to the client if it is adequately disclosed on the tax return.

.19 *Illustration 4.* A client is faced with an issue involving the interpretation of a new statute. Following passage, it was broadly recognized that the statute contained a drafting error and a technical correction proposal has been introduced. The Internal Revenue Service (IRS) issues an announcement indicating how it will administer the provision. The IRS pronouncement interprets the statute in accordance with the proposed technical correction.

.20 Return positions based on either the existing statutory language or the IRS pronouncement satisfy the realistic possibility standard.

.21 *Illustration 5.* The facts are the same as in illustration 4 except that no IRS pronouncement has been issued.

.22 In the absence of an IRS pronouncement interpreting the statute in accordance with the technical correction, only a return position based on the existing statutory language will meet the realistic possibility standard. A return position based on the technical correction proposal may be recommended if it is adequately disclosed, since it is not frivolous.

.23 *Illustration 6.* A client is seeking advice from a CPA regarding a recently amended Code section. The CPA has reviewed the Code section, committee reports that specifically address the issue, and a recently published IRS Notice. The CPA has concluded in good faith that, based upon the Code section and the committee reports, the IRS's position as stated in the Notice does not reflect congressional intent.

.24 The CPA may recommend the position supported by the Code section and the committee reports, since it meets the realistic possibility standard.

.25 *Illustration 7.* The facts are the same as in illustration 6 except that the IRS pronouncement is a temporary regulation.

.26 In determining whether the position meets the realistic possibility standard, the CPA should determine the weight to be given the regulation by analyzing factors such as whether the regulation is "legislative" or "interpretative" or inconsistent with the statute. If the CPA concludes the position does not meet the realistic possibility standard, the position may nevertheless be recommended if it is adequately disclosed, since it is not frivolous.

.27 *Illustration 8.* A tax form published by the IRS is incorrect, but completion of the form as published provides a benefit to the client. The CPA knows that the IRS has published an announcement acknowledging the error.

.28 In these circumstances, a return position in accordance with the published form is a frivolous position.

.29 *Illustration 9.* The client wants to take a position that the CPA has concluded is frivolous. The client maintains that even if the return is examined by the IRS, the issue will not be raised.

.30 The CPA should not consider the likelihood of audit or detection in determining if the realistic possibility standard is met. The CPA should not prepare or sign a return that contains a frivolous position even if it is disclosed.

.31 *Illustration 10.* Congress passes a statute requiring the capitalization of certain expenditures. The client believes, and the CPA concurs, that in order to comply fully, the client will need to acquire new computer hardware and software and implement a number of new accounting procedures. The client and the CPA agree that the costs to comply fully are significantly greater than the resulting increase in tax due under the new provision. Because of cost considerations, the client makes no effort to comply. The client wants the CPA to prepare and sign a return on which the new requirement is simply ignored.

.32 The return position desired by the client is frivolous, and the CPA should neither prepare nor sign the return.

.33 *Illustration 11.* The facts are the same as in illustration 10 except that the client has made a good faith effort to comply with the law by calculating an estimate of expenditures to be capitalized under the new provision.

.34 In this situation, the realistic possibility standard is met. When using estimates in the preparation of a return, the CPA should refer to SRTP (1988 Rev.) No. 4, "Use of Estimates."

.35 *Illustration 12.* On a given issue, the CPA has located and weighed two authorities. The IRS has published its clearly enunciated position in a Revenue Ruling. A court opinion is favorable to the client. The CPA has considered the source of both authorities and has concluded that both authorities are persuasive and relevant.

.36 The realistic possibility standard is met with regard to either position.

.37 *Illustration 13.* A tax statute is silent on the treatment of an item under such statute. However, the committee reports explaining the statute direct the IRS to issue regulations that will require specified treatment of this item. No regulations are issued at the time the CPA must recommend a position on the tax treatment of the item.

.38 The CPA may recommend the position supported by the committee reports, since it meets the realistic possibility standard.

.39 *Illustration 14.* The client wants to take a position that the CPA concludes meets the realistic possibility standard based on an assumption regarding an underlying non-tax, legal issue. The CPA recommends that the client seek advice from its legal counsel, and the client's attorney opines on the non-tax, legal issue.

.40 A legal opinion on a non-tax, legal issue may, in general, be relied upon by the CPA. The CPA must, however, use professional judgement when relying on a legal opinion. If on its face, the opinion of the client's attorney appears to be unreasonable, unsubstantiated, or unwarranted, the CPA should consult his or her attorney before relying on the opinion.

.41 *Illustration 15.* The client has obtained from its attorney an opinion on the tax treatment of an item and requests that the CPA rely on the opinion.

.42 The authorities on which a CPA may rely include well reasoned sources of tax analysis. If the CPA is satisfied as to the source, relevance and persuasiveness of the legal opinion, then the CPA may rely on the opinion when determining whether the realistic possibility standard is met.

FORM 4.5 _____
EXAMPLES IN REGULATIONS § 1.6694-2(B)(3)
_____

Example 1. A new statute is unclear with regard to whether a certain transaction in which a taxpayer has engaged will result in favorable tax treatment. Prior law, however, supported the taxpayer's position. There are no regulations under the new statute, and no authority other than the statutory language and committee reports. The committee reports state that the intent was not to adversely affect transactions similar to the taxpayer's transaction. The taxpayer's position satisfies the realistic possibility standard.

Example 2. A taxpayer has engaged in a transaction that is adversely affected by a new statutory provision. Prior law supported a position favorable to the taxpayer. The preparer believes that the new statute is inequitable as applied to the taxpayer's situation. The statutory language is unambiguous as it applies to the transaction (e.g., it applies to all manufacturers, and the taxpayer is a manufacturer of widgets). The committee reports do not specifically address the taxpayer's situation. A position contrary to the statute does not satisfy the realistic possibility standard.

Example 3. The facts are the same as in Example 2, except that the committee reports indicate that Congress did not intend to apply the new statutory provision to the taxpayer's transaction (e.g., to a manufacturer of widgets). Thus, there is a conflict between the general language of the statute, which adversely affects the taxpayer's transaction, and a specific statement in the committee reports that transactions such as the taxpayer's are not adversely affected. A position consistent with either the statute or the committee reports satisfies the realistic possibility standard. However, a position consistent with the committee reports constitutes a disregard of a rule or regulation and, therefore, must be adequately disclosed in order to avoid the Section 6694(b) penalty.

Example 4. The instructions to an item on a tax form published by the Service are incorrect and are clearly contrary to the regulations. Before the return is prepared, the Service publishes an announcement acknowledging the error and providing the correct instruction. Under these facts, a position taken on a return that is consistent with that of the regulations satisfies the realistic possibility standard. On the other hand, a position taken on a return that is consistent with the incorrect instructions does not satisfy the realistic possibility standard. However, if the preparer relied on the incorrect instructions and was not aware of the announcement or the regulations, the reasonable cause and good faith exception may apply, depending on all facts and circumstances. See Reg. § 1.6694-2(d).

Example 5. A statute is silent with regard to whether a taxpayer may take a certain position on the taxpayer's 1991 federal income tax return. Three private letter rulings issued to other taxpayers in 1987 and 1988 support the taxpayer's position. However, proposed regulations issued in 1990 are clearly contrary to the taxpayer's position. After the issuance of the proposed regulations, the earlier private letter rulings cease to be authorities and are not taken into account in determining whether the taxpayer's position satisfies the realistic possibility standard. See Reg. §§ 1.6694-2(b)(2), 1.6662-4(d)(3)(iii). The taxpayer's position may or may not satisfy the realistic possibility standard, depending on an analysis of all the relevant authorities.

Example 6. In the course of researching whether a particular position has a realistic possibility of being sustained on its merits, a preparer discovers that a taxpayer took the same position on a return several years ago and that the return was audited by the Service. The taxpayer tells the preparer that the revenue agent who conducted the audit was aware of the position and decided that the treatment on the return was correct. The revenue agent's report, however, made no mention of the position. The determination by the revenue agent is not authority for purposes of the realistic possibility standard. However, the preparer's reliance on the revenue agent's determination in the audit may qualify for the reasonable cause and good faith exception, depending on all facts and circumstances. See Reg. § 1.6694-2(d); see also Reg. §§ 1.6694-2(b)(4), 1.6662-4(d)(3)(iv)(A) (affirmative statements in revenue agent's report).

Example 7. In the course of researching whether an interpretation of a phrase incorporated in the Internal Revenue Code has a realistic possibility of being sustained on its merits, a preparer discovers that identical language in the taxing statute of another jurisdiction (e.g., a state or foreign country) has been authoritatively construed by a court of that jurisdiction in a manner that would be favorable to the taxpayer, if the same interpretation were applied to the phrase applicable to the taxpayer's situation. The construction of the statute of the other jurisdiction is not authority for purposes of determining whether the position satisfies the realistic possibility standard. See Reg. §§ 1.6694-2(b)(2), 1.6662-4(d)(3)(iii). However, as in the case of conclusions reached in treatises and legal periodicals, the authorities underlying the court's opinion, if relevant to the taxpayer's situation, may give a position favorable to the taxpayer a realistic possibility of being sustained on its merits. See Reg. §§ 1.6694-2(b)(2), 1.6662-4(d)(3)(iii).

Example 8. In the course of researching whether an interpretation of a statutory phrase has a realistic possibility of being sustained on its merits, a preparer discovers that identical language appearing in another place in the

Internal Revenue Code has consistently been interpreted by the courts and the Service in a manner that would be favorable to the taxpayer if the same interpretation were applied to the phrase applicable to the taxpayer's situation. No authority has interpreted the phrase applicable to the taxpayer's situation. The interpretations of the identical language are relevant in arriving at a well-reasoned construction of the language at issue, but the context in which the language arises also must be taken into account in determining whether the realistic possibility standard is satisfied.

Example 9. A new statutory provision is silent on the tax treatment of an item under the provision. However, the committee reports explaining the provision direct the Treasury to issue regulations interpreting the provision in a specified way. No regulations have been issued at the time the preparer must recommend a position on the tax treatment of the item, and no other authorities exist. The position supported by the committee reports satisfies the realistic possibility standard.

[d] Willful and Reckless Conduct

Section 6694(b) imposes a penalty if any part of an understatement is attributable to the return preparer's "willful attempt in any manner" to understate the tax liability of another person, or to any reckless or intentional disregard of rules or regulations by a return preparer. A return preparer who engages in willful or reckless conduct is subject to a penalty of $1,000 for each return or claim with understated tax. There has been no uncertainty about the willful conduct standard. A "willful attempt in any manner" is the same statutory language used in the criminal evasion statute, which has been interpreted to mean "any conduct the likely effect of which is to mislead or conceal."[377] Misleading conduct constitutes a willful attempt to understate a taxpayer's liability where (1) the preparer disregards information furnished by the taxpayer (e.g., by increasing the number of dependents reported by the taxpayer from two to six) or (2) the preparer makes false legal claims (e.g., by deducting all of a taxpayer's medical expenses, intentionally disregarding the percentage of adjusted gross income limitation).[378]

Reckless or intentional disregard of rules or regulations is more difficult to describe. A willful attempt to understate a taxpayer's liability seems to be a more serious type of misconduct than a reckless or even an intentional disregard of rules or regulations. Even before its amendment in 1989, however, regulations stated that a penalty for willful understatement might be based on an intentional disregard of rules and regulations.[379] Reckless or intentional disregard of rules or regulations was found where as a result of information a bookkeeper supplied, a return preparer was aware that amounts claimed as business deductions on corporation returns were for personal expenses.[380] The preparer acted willfully because he was not permitted "to ignore information which is called to his attention or inferences which are plainly available to him."

Preparer penalty regulations interpreting Section 6694(b) also define a reckless or intentional disregard.[381] These regulations say that a preparer has recklessly or intentionally disregarded a rule or regulation if the preparer takes a position on the return or claim for refund that is contrary to a rule or regula-

---

[377] IRC § 7201; Spies v. United States, 317 US 492, 498–499 (1943).

[378] Reg. § 1.6694-3(b).

[379] These regulations were approved. Judisch v. United States, 755 F2d 823 (11th Cir. 1985) ("[e]very violation of Section 6694(b), based on evidence that the taxpayer [sic] willfully disregarded IRS rules and regulations, is also a violation of [Section 6694(a)]; a violation of section (a) is a violation of section (b) only where the government proves willfullness").

[380] Pickering v. United States, 691 F2d 853 (8th Cir. 1982), aff'g per curiam 82-1 USTC ¶ 9375 (D. Ark. 1980). For other examples of conduct involving willful understatements, see Judisch v. United States, 755 F2d 823 (11th Cir. 1985); United States v. Savoie, 594 F. Supp. 678 (WD La. 1984).

[381] Reg. § 1.6694-3(c)(1).

tion, and (1) "the preparer knows of, or is reckless in not knowing of, the rule or regulation in question" and (2) the preparer is reckless in not knowing of the rule or regulation if the preparer "makes little or no effort to determine whether a rule or regulation exists, under circumstances which demonstrate a substantial deviation from the standard of conduct that a reasonable preparer would observe in the situation." It is instructive to compare these preparer penalty regulations to regulations interpreting the negligent understatement penalty when a taxpayer's disregard of rules or regulations is "reckless" and "intentional."[382] Applying taxpayer penalty regulations to the preparer penalty, a disregard is "reckless" if the preparer "makes little or no effort to determine whether a rule or regulation exists, under circumstances which demonstrate a substantial deviation from the standard of conduct that a reasonable [return preparer] would observe." A disregard is "intentional" when the preparer "knows of the rule or regulation that is disregarded."

Section 6694(b) does not expressly provide for disclosure of a position as a means of avoiding the willful or reckless conduct penalty, but the legislative history reflects an intention that the disclosure rules applicable to avoid the unrealistic position penalty apply to the willful and reckless conduct penalty as well.[383] Preparer penalty regulations permit disclosure to avoid a penalty, stating that a preparer is not considered to have acted recklessly or to have intentionally disregarded a rule or regulation if the position contrary to the rule or regulation is not frivolous, and is adequately disclosed (e.g., on a Form 8275); and when the position is contrary to a regulation, the position represents a good faith challenge to the validity of the regulation, disclosed on Form 8275-R.[384] A reckless or intentional disregard of a contrary revenue ruling or notice (other than a notice of proposed rule making) is not considered to exist when the return position has "a realistic possibility of being sustained on its merits."[385]

Examples in the regulations of willful or reckless conduct give further guidance.[386] If the preparer is supplied with information that identifies both business and personal expenses, and the preparer nevertheless knowingly deducts personal expenses, the preparer's conduct is subject to a willful or reckless understatement penalty.[387] In another example, the preparer disregards a revenue ruling holding that certain expenses must be capitalized, but the Code is silent, and several different courts have held that the expenses may be deducted currently, the regulations say that the preparer is not subject to penalty

---

[382] Reg. § 1.6662-3(b)(2).

[383] House Explanation, supra note 275, at 289.

[384] Reg. § 1.6694-3(c)(2).

[385] Reg. § 1.6694-3(c)(3).

[386] Reg. § 1.6694-3(d).

[387] Reg. § 1.6694-3(d), Ex. 1.

by deducting the expenses on a return, without disclosure, because the position has a realistic possibility of being sustained on its merits.[388] Even if final regulations, rather than a ruling, require the expenses to be capitalized, the return preparer is not subject to a penalty when the Tax Court has expressly invalidated that portion of the regulations, provided that the preparer adequately discloses the position on the return (although the preparer has a realistic possibility of success, he is subject to penalty because he is challenging the regulation, albeit in good faith).[389]

When the penalty under Section 6694(b) is imposed, the Service has the burden of proving that the preparer willfully attempted to understate the taxpayer's liability for income tax.[390] The preparer has the burden of proving that (1) the preparer did not recklessly or intentionally disregard a rule or regulation; (2) the position, although contrary to a regulation, represents a good faith challenge to the validity of the regulation; and (3) disclosure was adequately made.

[e] Imposition of Both Unrealistic Position and Willful Conduct Penalties

Both the willful understatement penalty and unrealistic position penalty may be based on an intentional disregard of rules and regulations. If both a negligence and a willful understatement penalty are imposed, a payment of the unrealistic position penalty reduces the amount of the willful understatement penalty. Thus, a preparer may not be required to pay more than $1,000 for conduct constituting both an unrealistic position and a willful attempt to understate liability.[391]

[f] Employer Liability

Unrealistic position and willful understatement penalties are not imputed to the employer of a return preparer solely because of the preparer's employment. An employer or partnership of a preparer subject to an unrealistic position penalty is liable for the penalty only if one of the following three circumstances is found:

---

[388] Reg. § 1.6694-3(d), Ex. 3.

[389] Reg. § 1.6694-3(d), Ex. 4.

[390] Reg. § 1.6694-3(h).

[391] IRC § 6694(b); Reg. § 1.6694-3(g).

1. If one or more members of the principal management (or principal officers) of the firm or a branch office "participated in or knew of the conduct proscribed" by the unrealistic position penalty.[392]
2. If the employer or partnership "failed to provide reasonable and appropriate procedures for review of the position for which the penalty is imposed."[393]
3. If the employer or partnership had review procedures, and those "procedures were disregarded in the formulation of the advice, or the preparation of the return or claim for refund, that included the position for which the penalty is imposed."[394]

[4] Disclosure

A preparer is not subject to a penalty for a position that in the Service's view, does not have a realistic possibility of being sustained if (1) it is disclosed on a Form 8275, Disclosure Statement (or if the position is contrary to a regulation, on a Form 8275) and (2) the disclosed position is not frivolous. A position is not frivolous if it is not "patently improper."[395] Qualifying disclosure also may be made by complying with the annual revenue procedure issued for purposes of the substantial misstatement component of the accuracy-related penalty.[396] While a preparer's disclosed position must not be frivolous, a taxpayer's disclosed return position must have a "reasonable basis" if the taxpayer is to avoid the substantial understatement penalty. Regulations interpreting the substantial understatement penalty define a "reasonable basis" as "a relatively high standard of tax reporting, that is significantly higher than not frivolous or not patently improper."[397] These different standards for qualifying disclosures can lead to strange, if not unfair results in the usual case where a taxpayer retains a return preparer to prepare the return. With the different standards, it seems possible that the authority for a disclosed position that permits the preparer to avoid a penalty might not be sufficient support for the taxpayer to escape a substantial understatement penalty, although the preparer prepared the taxpayer's return. The taxpayer who relied on the return preparer would have to seek abatement under the reasonable cause waiver, but taxpayers have not

---

[392] Reg. § 1.6694-2(a)(2)(i).
[393] Reg. § 1.6694-2(a)(2)(ii).
[394] Reg. § 1.6694-2(a)(2)(iii).
[395] Reg. § 1.6694-2(c)(2).
[396] Reg. §§ 1.6694-2(c)(1)–1.6694-2(c)(3)(i).
[397] Reg. § 1.6662-3(b)(3).

always been successful in avoiding a substantial understatement penalty based on their reliance on return preparers.[398]

Disclosure for nonsigning return preparers. Nonsigning preparers meet the disclosure requirements if they inform the taxpayer that the position lacks substantial authority, and, therefore, may be subject to penalty unless disclosed.[399] If the advice is given to another preparer, nonsigning preparers meet the disclosure requirements if they inform the other preparer that the position is required to be adequately disclosed on the return or claim for refund.[400]

[5] Reasonable Cause and Good Faith

No penalty is imposed if the preparer can show that "there is reasonable cause for the understatement," and the preparer acted "in good faith."[401] The reasonable cause part of the exception implies a negligence analysis (i.e., whether the preparer was in possession of such facts and legal authority as would have caused a reasonable preparer to take the same return position).[402] This view is consistent with Congress's intention that the negligent behavior subject to penalty under Section 6694 before its revision continues to be subject to penalty under the unrealistic position standard. "Reasonable cause" and "good faith" are also the terms used in the uniform reasonable cause waiver of the accuracy-related penalty (Section 6664(b)) imposed on taxpayers, and similar to the reasonable cause and absence of willful neglect defense to the delinquency penalty (Section 6651). Therefore, reasonable cause interpretations of those terms should also apply to the reasonable cause standard of the preparer penalty. The Service itself instructs its personnel that reasonable cause and good faith for the preparer penalty is a "common sense allowance under the circumstances for omissions or errors."[403]

Return preparer regulations state that there are specific factors to be considered in determining whether a preparer's understatement of income tax is due to reasonable cause and whether the preparer acted in good faith. These

---

[398] See Chapter 7B.

[399] Reg. § 1.6694-2(c)(3)(ii)(A). If the advice is given orally, the disclosure may be given orally, and if the advice is in writing, the disclosure must be made in writing. Obviously, some record should be made of an oral disclosure.

[400] Reg. § 1.6694-2(c)(3)(ii)(B).

[401] The preparer has the burden of proving that the reasonable cause exception applies, or that the position was adequately disclosed on the return. Reg. § 1.6694-2(e).

[402] See Reg. § 1.6662-3(b)(1) ([n]egligence includes "any failure to make a reasonable attempt to comply with the internal revenue laws or to exercise ordinary and reasonable care in the preparation of a tax return").

[403] IRM 120.1, Penalty Handbook 6.1.9(9) (Aug. 20, 1998) (Definitions).

factors include (1) the nature of the error causing the understatement[404]; (2) the frequency of the errors giving rise to the understatement[405]; (3) the materiality of the errors[406]; (4) the preparer's normal office practice[407]; and (5) reliance on the advice of another preparer.[408] While all the facts and circumstances relevant to the understatement are considered, regulations describe these factors as follows:

1. The nature of the error may establish reasonable cause when the understatement "resulted from a provision that was so complex, uncommon, or highly technical that a reasonably competent preparer of returns or claims of the type at issue could have made the error."[409]

2. The frequency of errors is a factor.[410] If the error is an isolated one, such as an inadvertent mathematical or clerical error, rather than one of a "number" of errors, the fact may be considered to establish reasonable cause. An inadvertent error is not considered reasonable cause if it is one of a series of errors, although that error alone might have been eligible for the reasonable cause exception. Even an isolated error will not be considered reasonable cause if the error is "so obvious, flagrant or material that it should have been discovered during a review of the return."

3. An error material to the determination of the taxpayer's correct tax liability does not qualify for the reasonable cause exception, but an error of a relatively immaterial amount does qualify, unless the error is obvious or one of a number of errors.[411]

4. Another factor considered for the reasonable cause exception is whether the preparer has a normal office practice or system "to promote accuracy and consistency" in the preparation of returns or claims.[412] Regulations identify checklists, methods for obtaining necessary information from the taxpayer, a review of the prior year's return, and review procedures as features this system should include. Where the preparer has followed the normal office practice, and such facts as the knowledge of the preparer tend to show that the error would rarely occur under the practice, the preparer may qualify for

---

[404] Reg. § 1.6694-2(d)(1).

[405] Reg. § 1.6694-2(d)(2).

[406] Reg. § 1.6694-2(d)(3).

[407] Reg. § 1.6694-2(d)(4).

[408] Reg. § 1.6694-2(d)(5).

[409] Reg. § 1.6694-2(d)(1).

[410] Reg. § 1.6694-2(d)(2).

[411] Reg. § 1.6694-2(d)(3).

[412] Reg. § 1.6694-2(d)(4).

the exception, unless the error is flagrant, one of a pattern of errors, or repeated on many other returns.

5. Reliance in good faith on the advice of another preparer may qualify for the reasonable cause exception, but only if the other preparer and the other preparer's advice meet certain criteria.[413] The preparer must reasonably believe that the other preparer is competent to give the advice. Good faith reliance is not present, however, if (a) the other preparer's advice is unreasonable on its face; (b) the preparer knew or should have known that the other preparer was not aware of all the facts; or (c) the preparer knew or should have known that the other preparer's advice was no longer reliable as a result of developments in the law since the advice was given.

These factors are the same ones the Service said in a series of revenue rulings that it would consider in determining whether to assess the negligent understatement penalty before the 1989 amendment of Section 6694(a). Guidelines and rulings the Service issued for the negligent understatement penalty apply as well to the reasonable cause and good faith exception to the unrealistic position penalty.[414] Under the prior version of Section 6694, a penalty was imposed if the understatement was caused by the preparer's negligent or intentional disregard of rules and regulations. An increased penalty is now imposed on a reckless or intentional disregard of rules and regulations.[415]

[6] Disclosure and Reporting Requirements

A return preparer is required to perform the following acts or be subject to a penalty under Section 6695:

1. The preparer must furnish a completed copy of a return or refund claim to the taxpayer no later than the original is presented for the taxpayer's signature, as required by Section 6107(a).[416]
2. The preparer must manually sign the return after it is completed and before it is presented to the taxpayer if he is primarily responsible for the accuracy of the return.[417]
3. The preparer must supply his address and EIN or, if the preparer does not have one, his Social Security number. If the return preparer is an

---

[413] Reg. § 1.6694-2(d)(5).

[414] See the discussion supra ¶ 4.06.

[415] IRC § 6694(b)(2).

[416] IRC § 6695(a); Reg. § 1.6695-1(a).

[417] IRC § 6695(b); Reg. § 1.6695-1(b).

employee, the employer must ensure that this information is included on the return.[418]

4. The preparer must retain either a copy of all tax returns and refund claims prepared by the return preparer or a list containing the names and TINs of all taxpayers for whom the return preparer has prepared a claim for three years after the filing of the return, as required by Section 6107(b).[419] This requirement applies only to employer or self-employed return preparers.[420]

5. The preparer must file correct information returns in accordance with Section 6060.[421]

If a return preparer fails to perform any of these required acts, the preparer is subject to a penalty of $50 for each failure, up to a maximum of $25,000 for the calendar year.[422] A penalty of $500 is imposed if the preparer endorses or otherwise negotiates a client's refund check.[423] These penalties may be avoided if the preparer can establish that the failure was due to reasonable cause and not to willful neglect.

   Signing rules. The rules preparers must follow for signing returns are not as straightforward as one would imagine. The general rule is that an individual who is a return preparer of a return must manually sign the return after it is completed and before it is presented to the taxpayer.[424] The individual who

---

[418] IRC § 6695(c); Reg. §§ 1.6109-2(a), 1.6109-2(b). Before the IRS Restructuring and Reform Act amended Section 6109(a), the return preparer's identifying number was the preparer's Social Security number. See IRC § 6109(a). Amended Section 6109 permits the Service to issue regulations providing for alternatives to the preparer's Social Security number, and the Service is developing a system of providing alternative identifying numbers for preparers. See Reg. § 1.6109-2T(a), TD 8835 (Aug. 12, 1999).

[419] IRC § 6695(d); Reg. § 1.6695-1(d).

[420] When the return preparer is a corporation or partnership, and the corporation or partnership dissolves before the end of the three-year period, the retention duty is placed upon those persons responsible under state law for winding up the affairs of the corporation or partnership. Reg. § 1.6107-1(b). Absent a relevant state law, the directors of the corporation or the general partners of the partnership would be required to retain the records for the three-year period.

[421] IRC § 6695(e).

[422] IRC §§ 6695(a)–6695(d).

[423] IRC § 6695(f).

[424] A preparer must write out his signature. Initialing a stamp with the required information is not a signature because the Service needs more positive identification. Priv. Ltr. Rul. 8214006 (Technical Advice). See also Priv. Ltr. Rul. 8214005 (initials held insufficient where they were inserted above stamped reproduction of name, address, and Social Security number or EIN). Gummed labels and facsimile signatures are not allowed. Reg. § 1.6695-1(b)(1). There are only three exceptions to the manual-signature requirement. First, if a master is manually signed, copies may be reproduced if only mathematical changes are made thereafter. Second, if the return is computer-prepared, a manually signed attestation may be attached instead of signing the preparer's jurat. Finally, where

prepares the return must sign it; signature in the firm name does not meet this requirement.[425] If more than one return preparer is involved in the preparation, the individual preparer "who has the primary responsibility as between or among the preparers for the overall substantive accuracy of the preparation" is the return preparer for purposes of the signing requirement.[426] Regulations give the following examples:

1. An employee assigned to prepare a return who gathers information and makes tax-relevant determinations (but is not the employer) is the return preparer primarily responsible and must sign.[427]

2. Similarly, the supervising partner in a national accounting firm whose policies and practice require partner review is the return preparer primarily responsible, even though other employees actually prepare the return.[428]

To identify return preparers and to facilitate a search of returns a preparer has prepared, each preparer required to sign the return must show the preparer's Social Security number or other identifying number, on each return the return preparer prepares.[429] If the individual is an employee or a partner of a firm, the firm's EIN must also be shown.[430] In this context, the $50 penalty for failure to furnish identifying numbers is imposed not on the individual re-

---

the preparer signs a return for a nonresident alien individual, manual signature may also be dispensed with if certain requirements are met. Reg. §§ 1.6695-1(b)(4)(i)–1.6695-1(b)(4)(iii).

[425] Reg. § 1.6695-1(b)(4)(i), TD 8803 (Dec. 31, 1998), permits the return preparer to satisfy the manual signature requirement of Reg. §§ 1.6695-1(b)(1) and 1.6695-1(b)(2) by using a photocopy of a copy of the return or claim for refund that the preparer has manually signed, as long as the preparer has signed a copy of the return or claim and, before it is photocopied, no person other than the preparer has altered any entries, except to correct arithmetical errors discernable from the face of the return. Although the preparer's employer or partnership must retain the manually signed copy of the return or claim, under an alternative procedure, the person required to retain the manually signed copy may choose to retain a photocopy of the manually signed copy or use an electronic storage system to store and produce a copy of the manually signed return or claim.

[426] Reg. § 1.6695-1(b)(2). See also Rev. Rul. 81-246, 1981-2 CB 249 (obligation of licensor of return preparation business).

[427] Reg. § 1.6695-1(b)(3), Ex. 1.

[428] Reg. § 1.6695-1(b)(3), Ex. 2. Examples also illustrate a situation where another preparer may sign the return if the actual preparer is unavailable. Reg. § 1.6695-1(b)(3), Ex. 4; see also IRC § 6109(a)(4).

[429] Reg. § 1.6109-1(b). Alternative identifying numbers may be used by preparers under procedures the Service adopts for the purpose. Reg. § 1.6109-2T(a)(2). For a case where a preparer failed to include his Social Security number and was assessed the penalty under Section 6695(c), see Powell v. Kopman, 511 F. Supp. 700 (SDNY 1981).

[430] Reg. § 1.6109-1(b). Alternative identifying numbers may be used by preparers under procedures the Service adopts for the purpose. Reg. § 1.6109-2T(a)(2). For a case

turn preparer required to furnish the information, but on the employer or partnership.[431]

Other preparer rules. In addition to supplying a taxpayer with a copy of the return or claim, the preparer must either retain a copy of the return or claim for three years, or keep a list of all taxpayers for whom the return preparer has prepared returns or claims, along with their TINs, the taxable years for which the returns or claims were prepared, and the type of return or refund claim prepared.[432] Preparers who fail to meet this requirement are liable for a penalty for each failure, with a maximum penalty of $25,000 applicable to any one return period.[433] Employers of return preparers must retain an annual report on Form 5717 (Annual List of Income Tax Return Preparers)[434] that lists the name, TIN, and place of employment of each return preparer during the year, and make this information available for inspection on request.[435] If the preparer fails or refuses to supply information on request, the preparer risks both a willful or reckless disregard penalty and a mandatory injunction.[436]

A special penalty is imposed on preparers who prepare a return or claim for refund claiming the earned income credit. The preparer of the return or claim claiming the earned income credit will be subject to a $100 penalty unless the preparer meets due diligence requirements imposed by regulations describing how the preparer must determine the taxpayer's eligibility for the earned income tax credit or the amount of any allowable earned income credit.[437]

---

where a preparer failed to include his Social Security number and was assessed the penalty under Section 6695(c), see Powell v. Kopman, 511 F. Supp. 700 (SDNY 1981).

[431] Reg. § 1.6695-1(c)(2). For a discussion of the persons held to be return preparers who are required to sign a return, see supra ¶ 4.06.

[432] IRC § 6107(b).

[433] IRC § 6107(d).

[434] The Service does not require the filing of Form 5717 if the information required to be reported is retained. IR 2137 (June 8, 1979). Presumably, the preparer would still be subject to the penalties of Section 6695(e)(2) if the information is not kept or is incomplete.

[435] IRC § 6060; Reg. § 1.6060-1. A self-employed return preparer or preparer who acts as an independent contractor must file his own annual report.

[436] For a case involving penalties for a preparer's failure to supply either prepared returns or a list of the returns prepared pursuant to Section 6107(b), see United States v. Nordbrock, 941 F2d 947 (9th Cir. 1991) (*Nordbrock I* held that a preparer was entitled to have a jury hear an advice of counsel defense).

When a preparer fails to turn over requested information, the preparer, not the Service, has the burden of proving that the nonproduction was due to reasonable cause and an absence of willful neglect. United States v. Nordbrock, 38 F3d 440 (9th Cir. 1994) (Nordbrock II).

[437] IRC § 6695(g), added by the Taxpayer Relief Act of 1997, § 1085(a)(2). These due diligence requirements are described in Reg. § 1.6695-2T. In general, the preparer is supposed to complete and maintain an Earned Income Eligibility Checklist.

[7] The Service's Preparer Penalty Procedures

Under its Return Preparer Penalty Program, return preparer penalty cases are "the key enforcement vehicle for identifying and penalizing noncompliant preparers."[438] During every field and office examination, examiners are required to consider preparer conduct and apply penalties where evidence of misconduct is found. Penalties on return preparers under Section 6694 are not the only penalties on return preparers in the Service's Return Preparer Penalty Program. Preparers are also subject to the tax shelter promoter penalty (Section 6700) and the aiding and assisting penalty (Section 6701), both of which are not limited solely to return preparers.[439] When examiners determine that return preparer rules have been violated, they must document their penalty determination in workpapers.[440] Although the examiner is cautioned not to propose a preparer penalty in the presence of the taxpayer (because the examination and the preparer violation are separate and distinct proceedings), the examiner does use the examination to develop facts to determine the applicability of the penalty. Generally, no preparer penalty is proposed until the examination is complete at the group level.[441]

The return preparer program includes a Program Action Case procedure, for the examination of returns prepared by a particular preparer where there is evidence of a pattern of noncompliance. Selection and review procedures ensure that a preparer is selected for such examination only if there is strong evidence that she has engaged in a practice of making material errors that demonstrate intentional misconduct or clear incompetence.[442] Preparers in the Electronic Filing Program must meet suitability requirements, and whether the Service has asserted penalties against a preparer is one of the factors in mak-

---

[438] IRM 120.1, Penalty Handbook 6.3.5(1) (Aug. 20, 1998) (Asserting the IRC § 6694 Penalties).

[439] IRM 120.1, Penalty Handbook, 6.1 (Aug. 20, 1998) (Overview of the Return Preparer Penalty Program). The Service has been criticized for both inconsistent enforcement and incomplete data of preparer penalty assessments. In 1983, the General Accounting Office (GAO) found inconsistent enforcement of the penalties and inadequate data to permit the Service to develop guidelines for examiners. The GAO suggested that the Service (1) gather more information about paid return preparers (e.g., information on preparers who commit multiple violations over the course of several years) in order to decide how to manage enforcement and (2) ensure greater consistency in asserting penalties by publishing guidelines defining when the willful misconduct penalty will be imposed. "IRS' Administration of Penalties Imposed on Tax Return Preparers" (Jan. 6, 1983).

In 1990, the GAO found that the Service was understating the number of preparer penalties that were being assessed because multiple penalties were being reflected as single penalties and some preparer penalties were not entered at all. "IRS Preparer Penalty Data Inaccurate and Misleading," GAO/GGD-90-92 (Aug. 1990).

[440] IRM 120.1, Penalty Handbook 6.1.2 (Aug. 20, 1998) (Examination Guidelines).

[441] IRM 120.1, Penalty Handbook 6.1.2 (Aug. 20, 1998) (Examination Guidelines).

[442] IRM 120.1, Penalty Handbook 6.1.6 (Aug. 20, 1998) (Program Action Cases).

ing this determination. As a result, return preparer coordinators notify electronic filing coordinators of all penalties that have been asserted against the preparer.[443] Preparers in the Electronic Filing Program are visited by district personnel to determine whether the preparer has complied with electronic filing procedures, and preparer penalties may be proposed against the preparer.

If injunction is recommended, the agent is instructed (1) to prepare an affidavit or declaration; (2) to obtain affidavits from the taxpayer and others to document the Service's position; and (3) to facilitate the Justice Department's action seeking an injunction.[444] The affidavit is to include the specific positions of the return that are false or fabricated; actions the preparer took when the preparer was informed of the client's examination, such as offering to supply false documents to support false deductions; the experience of the preparer in preparing returns; the preparer's education; where the preparer was working; how the preparer solicits clients; and whether the preparer is continuing to solicit clients. The revenue agent is also asked to include information about how and when the taxpayer met the person under investigation; the information the taxpayer gave the preparer; whether the taxpayer signed the return, was given a copy of the return, and had the return explained to him; the amount and manner of payment for the return preparation; whether the taxpayer paid the preparer before the return was prepared, after it was prepared, or after the refund was received; and whether the taxpayer asked the preparer to put false information in the return.

Before a penalty is asserted, the return preparer is entitled to the same administrative review procedures as are available to other taxpayers.[445] As Section 6696 makes explicit, deficiency procedures do not apply in return preparer penalty cases.[446] However, Service procedures permit preassessment appeal of a penalty.[447] The return preparer receives a thirty-day letter and a copy of the agent's report, and may protest the proposed assessment. If the preparer requests preassessment Appeals consideration, the case will be forwarded to Appeals. If a timely appeal is not received, the penalty will be assessed. The return preparer is notified and asked either to pay the penalty within ten days or to send a written reasonable-cause explanation for consideration in having the penalty abated. If the return preparer fails to pay or respond, the case is sent to the local Collection Division. After full or partial payment has been

---

[443] IRM 120.1, Penalty Handbook 6.1.11 (Aug. 20, 1998) (Electronic Filing Program). See Rev. Proc. 91-69, 1991-2 CB 893, for Electronic Filing Program procedures.

[444] IRM 120.1, Penalty Handbook 6.1.7 (Aug. 20, 1998) (Affidavits).

[445] IRM 120.1, Penalty Handbook 6.1.3 (Aug. 20, 1998) (Appeal Rights). Service procedures also permit a return preparer under investigation to inspect returns to verify his declaration. IRM 1272, Disclosure of Official Information Handbook § 252, MT 1272-180 (Mar. 16, 1982) (Disclosure During the Course of Examination or Investigation).

[446] IRC § 6696(b).

[447] Reg. § 1.6694-4(a)(1).

made, the return preparer must file a claim for refund to challenge the penalty determination. Even when the case is in postassessment status, the Service permits the preparer to obtain Appeals review.

Another program has been adopted to curtail the marketing of abusive tax shelters through the use of prefiling investigative and enforcement procedures.[448] Tax shelter promotions are selected for investigation at the marketing stage and, if judged abusive, trigger the following enforcement mechanisms:

1. The issuance of prefiling notices to investors, warning them of audit if the shelter benefits are claimed;
2. The assessment of penalties against the promoters of the shelter under Section 6700; and
3. The seeking of injunctive relief against the promoters under Section 7408.

Persons subject to the promoter penalties include those who knowingly make a gross valuation overstatement or any false statement with respect to a material tax matter.

---

[448] Rev. Proc. 83-78, 1983-2 CB 595.

FORM 4.6
CLAIM OF INCOME TAX RETURN PREPARERS

Form **6118** (Rev. November 1992) Department of the Treasury Internal Revenue Service	**Claim of Income Tax Return Preparers** ▶ See Instructions on back.	OMB No. 1545-0240 Expires 10-31-95

Please Print or Type

Name of preparer John Preparer	Identifying number (See instructions.) **123-81-1100**
Address to which statement(s) of notice and demand were mailed 1 Main Street	
City or town, state, and ZIP code New York, NY 0000	Address of IRS office that sent statement(s)
Address shown on return(s) for which penalties were assessed (if different from above) Same	

1 Kind of Penalty (Enter letter in column 2(c).)

A Understatements due to unrealistic positions—section 6694(a)

B Willful or reckless conduct (intentional disregard of rules and regulations)—section 6694(b)

C Failure to furnish copy of return or claim for refund to taxpayer—section 6695(a)

D Failure to sign return or claim for refund—section 6695(b)

E Failure to furnish identifying number—section 6695(c)

F Failure to retain copy or list—section 6695(d)

G Failure to file a record of return preparers—section 6695(e)(1)

H Failure to include an item in the required record of return preparers—section 6695(e)(2)

I Negotiation of check—section 6695(f)

2 Identification of Penalties (See *Specific Instructions*.)

	(a) Statement document locator number	(b) Date of statement	(c) Kind of penalty	(d) Amount assessed	(e) Amount paid	(f) Date paid (mo., day, year)
(1)	52653-161-6055-1	5/18/92	C	25	25	5/26/92
(2)	52653-161-6055-2	5/18/92	D	25	25	5/26/92
(3)						
(4)						
(5)						
(6)						
(7)						
(8)						
(9)						
(10)						
(11)						
(12)						
(13)						
(14)						

	(g) Taxpayer's name	(h) Taxpayer's identifying number	(i) Form involved	(j) Tax year
(1)	John Jones	123-45-6789	1040	12/31/90
(2)	John Jones	123-45-6789	1040	12/31/90
(3)				
(4)				
(5)				
(6)				
(7)				
(8)				
(9)				
(10)				
(11)				
(12)				
(13)				
(14)				

3 Amount To Be Refunded (total of column 2(e), lines (1) through (14)) . . . . ▶   50

Under penalties of perjury, I declare that I have examined this claim, including accompanying schedules and statements, and, to the best of my knowledge and belief, it is true, correct, and complete.

Signature ▶ /s/ John Preparer   Date ▶ June 28, 1992

For Paperwork Reduction Act Notice, see back of form.   Cat No. 24415J   Form **6118** (Rev. 11-92)

Paperwork Reduction Act Notice

We ask for the information on this form to carry out the Internal Revenue laws of the United States. You are required to give us the information. We need it to ensure that you are complying with these laws and to allow us to figure and collect the right amount of tax.

The time needed to complete and file this form will vary depending on individual circumstances. The estimated average time is:

Recordkeeping	13 min.
Learning about the law or the form	11 min.
Preparing the form	8 min.
Copying, assembling, and sending the form to the IRS	20 min.

If you have comments concerning the accuracy of these time estimates or suggestions for making this form more simple, we would be happy to hear from you. You can write to both the **Internal Revenue Service**, Washington, DC 20224, Attention: IRS Reports Clearance Officer, T:FP, and the **Office of Management and Budget**, Paperwork Reduction Project (1545-0240), Washington, DC 20503. **DO NOT** send this form to either of these offices. Instead, see **Where and When To File** on this page.

General Instructions

(Section references are to the Internal Revenue Code, unless otherwise noted.)

Purpose of Form.—File Form 6118 if you are a tax return preparer and want to claim a refund of preparer penalties you paid but that you believe were incorrectly charged.

Claims for More than One Penalty.—If you are claiming a refund for more than one of the penalties listed in item 1 on this form, you may or may not be able to claim them on the same form depending on the type of penalty involved.

You may claim a refund for more than one penalty on a single claim for:

1. Penalties G and H, provided you were billed for them on the same statement.

2. Penalties C, D, E, and F, even if you were billed for them on different statements. However, the penalties must all have been imposed by the same IRS office. You may not list penalties imposed by an IRS service center (shown on Form 6335) and penalties imposed by a district office on the same claim. If you file a single claim for penalties billed on different statements, please group the penalties from each statement together.

You must file separate claims for a refund of each penalty A, B, or I, even if you were charged two penalties of the same type.

Where and When To File

File Form 6118 with the IRS service center or IRS district office that sent you the statement(s). Generally, your claim must be filed within 3 years from the date you paid the penalty.

Specific Instructions

Identifying Number.—If you are self-employed or employed by another preparer, enter your social security number. If you are the employer of other preparers, enter your employer identification number.

Items 2 and 3.—Be sure to enter the document locator number (DLN) and the date from each penalty statement you received in columns 2(a) and 2(b) of the form. In column 2(c) show the letter (A through I) from item 1 to indicate the kind of penalty on each line.

Fill in columns 2(d) and 2(g) through 2(j) using the information shown on the statements. Then fill in columns 2(e) and 2(f) and item 3 showing the amount of each penalty, the date you paid it, and the total amount you are claiming as a refund.

Additional Information.—You may want to attach a copy of the penalty statements to your claim.

In addition to completing the form, you must give your reasons for claiming a refund for each penalty you have listed. Identify each penalty by its line number from item 2, and write your explanation next to it. You may use the space below to do this. If you need additional space, attach a separate sheet.

For additional information about refunds of preparer penalties, see Regulations section 1.6696-1.

[8] Judicial Review of Preparer Penalties

Judicial review of a preparer penalty is available only by way of a refund suit, not by prepayment review in the Tax Court.[449] An unrealistic position penalty must be assessed within three years from the date the return is filed, but there is no statute of limitations on the assessment of a preparer penalty where willful conduct is involved.[450] Where disclosure, record-keeping, or refund check negotiation penalties are involved, the Service must assess the penalty within three years after the return is filed.[451] Before the assessment of the penalty, the return preparer is sent a thirty-day letter, which includes the revenue agent's summary report and offers the return preparer an opportunity to appeal to the Appeals Office. If no agreement is reached at the administrative level, the penalty is assessed. After assessment, the return preparer may contest the penalty by paying the full amount of the penalty and filing a refund claim within three years of the date the penalty is paid.[452]

A preparer's claim for refund of a preparer penalty must include:

1. Information identifying the preparer (the preparer's name, identification number, and the address the Service used to send the notice of and demand for payment of the preparer penalty);

2. The Service center or district office that sent the notice and demand to the preparer;

3. Information identifying the penalty to which the claim is directed, such as the form (e.g., Form 1040), the taxpayer's name, and the taxpayer's identification number to which the penalty relates, the amount of the penalty, the type of penalty, any document to which the penalty is related, the amounts paid or collected, and the total amount claimed; and

4. A detailed statement of each ground on which the penalty is claimed to have overpaid, and "facts sufficient to apprise the Internal Revenue Service of the exact basis of each such claim."[453] Grounds for the refund must be set forth in the claim; otherwise, the action may be dismissed.[454]

---

[449] IRC § 6696(b).

[450] IRC § 6696(d)(1).

[451] IRC § 6696(d)(1).

[452] The procedures for filing the claim are set forth in Reg. §§ 1.6696-1(b)–1.6696-1(g). The claim must be filed by the return preparer or his estate. If the preparer is an employee, the employer may prepare the claim but the employee must nevertheless be the filer. Reg. § 1.6696-1(b).

[453] Reg. § 1.6696-1(d).

[454] If the notice to the preparer does not identify the item involved, preparation of the claim still must set forth grounds, at least according to one circuit court. Reiss v. United

Regulations also prescribe the form for filing the preparer's claim, Form 6118, Claim of Income Tax Return Preparers. (See Form 4.6.)[455]

A special exception to the normal full-payment rule is provided where a return preparer seeks judicial review of the assessment of both negligent and willful understatement penalties. If the return preparer pays at least 15 percent of the penalty within thirty days after the date of the notice and demand and files a claim for refund at that time, collection of the balance of the assessment is stayed until after administrative review of the refund claim is completed.[456] The preparer must file a claim for refund, a Form 6118, Claim of Income Tax Return Preparers, to stay collection of the balance of the assessment.[457] If the claim is denied, the return preparer may still avoid collection of the balance of the assessment if suit is instituted within thirty days after denial of the claim.[458] The return preparer can institute a suit for refund in a federal district court.[459]

Refund procedures appear to be the only remedy open to return preparers to challenge return penalty assessments. A preparer's injunction action seeking to restrain collection of a preparer penalty for failure to furnish an identifying number has been held to violate the Anti-Injunction Act (Section 7421).[460] In a refund suit for a divisible portion of the assessment (including the payment of 15 percent of the liability), the government must file a counterclaim for the balance of the assessment.[461] The return preparer has the burden of proving nonliability on all penalties, although the Service appears to have the same burden it has in a civil fraud penalty case, which is to prove by clear and convincing evidence that the preparer's conduct was willful.[462] Trial by jury is permitted.[463] Even if the preparer's challenge to a preparer penalty is unsuc-

---

States, 983 F2d 899 (8th Cir. 1993) (notice gave preparer list of forms, taxpayers, and provisions involved, but preparer's claim did not set forth grounds—a harsh result).

[455] Reg. § 1.6696-1(e).

[456] IRC § 6694(c)(1).

[457] IRC § 6696(a).

[458] IRC § 6694(c)(2). See Mayo v. United States, 82-2 USTC ¶ 9488 (WD La. 1982) (return preparer's refund suit dismissed because he did not institute the refund suit within the thirty-day period).

[459] IRC § 6696(d).

[460] Crouch v. Comm'r, 447 F. Supp. 385 (ND Cal. 1978). If the preparer fails to file a refund claim, the district court does not have jurisdiction over the preparer's complaint about the assessment. Powell v. Kopman, 511 F. Supp. 700 (SDNY 1981).

[461] IRC § 6694(c)(1).

[462] IRC § 7427. Where only civil penalties are being sought from a return preparer, it has been held that the privilege against self-incrimination does not apply. Mertsching v. United States, 704 F2d 505 (10th Cir.), cert. denied, 464 US 829 (1983).

[463] Jury trial has been allowed in a preparer's refund case. Judisch v. United States, 755 F2d 823 (11th Cir. 1985).

cessful, if the final administrative or judicial action of the taxpayer determines that there was no understatement of liability on the return for which the penalty was assessed, the Service must refund to the taxpayer any payment of the penalty.[464]

[9] Injunction Actions

Apart from the sanction of civil penalties, the Service has authority to institute a civil action to secure a district court's injunction against a return preparer to restrain improper conduct or deceptive practices.[465] This procedure is somewhat unusual in tax laws that focus on taxpayers' conduct after the return is due or filed, but is similar to the cease and desist orders other executive regulatory agencies issue or obtain from a court.[466] Section 7407 provides that the Service may commence a civil action to enjoin a return preparer "from further engaging in any conduct described in subsection(b) or from further acting as a return preparer."[467] For an injunction to be granted, the court must also find that "injunctive relief is appropriate under the circumstances." If the court finds that the preparer has "continually or repeatedly" engaged in the proscribed acts of misconduct, and that an injunction would not be sufficient to prevent the preparer's interference with the administration of the tax laws, the court is authorized to enjoin the preparer from acting as an income tax return preparer.[468] Thus, for an injunction to be granted under Section 7407, first, the defendant must be a return preparer; second, the conduct must be one of the four types of improper practices described in Section 7407(b)(1); and third, the court must find that an injunction is "appropriate to prevent a recurrence." An injunction against a return preparer may result if the district court finds that the return preparer:

1. Engaged in any conduct for which the preparer might be penalized under Sections 6694 and 6695, or prosecuted under a criminal statute in the Code[469];

---

[464] IRC § 6694(d).

[465] IRC § 7407(a).

[466] See discussion in United States v. Ernst & Whinney, 735 F2d 1296, (11th Cir. 1984).

[467] See discussion in United States v. Ernst & Whinney, 735 F2d 1296, (11th Cir. 1984).

[468] IRC § 7407(b)(2). Section 7407(b)(2) requires that the prohibited conduct be continual or repeated, but not both. United States v. Nordbrock, 38 F3d 440 (9th Cir. 1994).

[469] IRC § 7407(b)(1)(A).

2. Misrepresented his or her eligibility to practice before the Service, or his or her experience or education as a preparer[470];

3. Guaranteed the payment of a refund or allowance of a credit[471]; or

4. Engaged "in any other fraudulent or deceptive conduct which substantially interferes with the proper administration" of the tax laws.[472]

To establish these four grounds for an injunction under Section 7407(b)(1), the return preparer must have engaged in the proscribed conduct willfully. On the other hand, to defeat a request for an injunction because the preparer is alleged to have engaged in conduct subject to penalty under Section 6694(a), the preparer must prove that there was "reasonable cause for the understatement," and the preparer "acted in good faith."[473] When a preparer refused to turn over a list of the taxpayers for whom he prepared returns in violation of Section 6107(b), with the result that the preparer was subject to a penalty under Section 6695(b), willfulness was held to be an essential element in an action for an injunction.[474] Based on the statutory requirement that the penalty be imposed "unless it is shown that such failure is due to reasonable cause and not due to willful neglect," the circuit court concluded that the preparer had the burden of proving that he or she did not act willfully in refusing to comply with the request.[475] When the Service alleges that the preparer willfully attempted to understate the tax in violation of Section 6694(b) or violated a criminal provision of the Code, it seems that the Service should have the burden of proving this willful element by clear and convincing evidence; that is, the Service must prove that the preparer was aware of the applicable law (and thus the duty to follow the law), and intentionally failed to comply with the law in preparing the income tax return or claim.[476] In view of the nature of the

---

[470] IRC § 7407(b)(1)(B).

[471] IRC § 7407(b)(1)(C).

[472] IRC § 7407(b)(1)(D). The Service has used D-type conduct as grounds for an injunction of an accounting firm's promotional activities in marketing an investment credit service that the Service alleged resulted in false claims. United States v. Ernst & Whinney, 735 F2d 1296 (11th Cir. 1984). For another case applying Section 7407(b)(1)(D), see United States v. Franchi, 91-1 USTC ¶ 50,086 (WD Pa. 1991) (preparer fabricated and inflated taxpayers' car expenses, charitable contributions, and travel expenses).

[473] United States v. Nordbrock, 828 F2d 1401 (9th Cir. 1987) (summary judgment improper because affidavits raised advice of counsel defense).

[474] United States v. Nordbrock, 38 F3d 440 (9th Cir. 1994).

[475] United States v. Nordbrock, 38 F3d 440 (9th Cir. 1994). In *Nordbrock*, the Ninth Circuit said, "We hold that 26 U.S.C. section 6695(d), the statute providing for various tax-return related penalties, on its face places the burden on the tax return preparer to prove that he or she did not act willfully in refusing to comply with an IRS information request."

[476] See United States v. Franchi, 756 F. Supp. 889 (WD Pa. 1991) (Service introduced evidence proving that the preparer engaged in fraudulent conduct, and preparer's response found not to be credible); United States v. Olsen, 80 AFTR2d 97-5708 (D. Colo.

misconduct alleged, the Service also appears to have the burden of presenting evidence that the preparer acted willfully to establish that the preparer engaged in "fraudulent or deceptive conduct which substantially interferes with the proper administration of the Internal Revenue laws."[477]

Even if one or more of the four types of misconduct described in Section 7407(b) are present, the Service also must show that injunctive relief is "appropriate to prevent a recurrence."[478] Factors applied in determining whether an injunction is appropriate are the traditional ones: (1) the significance of the threat of irreparable harm if the injunction is not granted; (2) the balance between the harm and the injury granting the injunction would inflict on the preparer; (3) the probability that the Service will succeed on the merits; and (4) the public interest.[479] Once the courts decide that an injunction is appropriate, they have broad authority to frame any injunctive relief granted to fit the circumstances of the particular case.[480] One possible form of injunction the court may order is an order prohibiting the preparer from preparing returns in the future. The court may enjoin a person "from acting as an income tax return preparer," if (1) the preparer has "continually or repeatedly engaged in any conduct described in subparagraphs (A) through (D)" and (2) the court decides

---

1997) (evidence of knowledge and intent found to support finding that preparer prepared returns for his self-employed taxpayer clients misusing the "spousal wage deduction" in identifying the spouse of the owner of the business as an employee; proof of knowledge and intent was lacking on allegations that preparer advised incorporating businesses and payment of rental to the individuals to evade the payment of FICA and self-employment taxes.

[477] See United States v. Ernst & Whinney, 735 F2d 1296 (11th Cir. 1984).

[478] IRC § 7407(b)(2).

[479] See United States v. Franchi, 91-1 USTC ¶ 50,086 (WD Pa. 1991) (factors applied and injunction granted). See United States v. Ernst & Whinney, 735 F2d 1296 (11th Cir. 1984) ("the decision to issue an injunction under § 7402 is governed by the traditional factors shaping the district court's use of the equitable remedy").

[480] For the form an order may take, see United States v. Owens, 79-2 USTC ¶ 9742 (CD Cal. 1979). The Service has also obtained a mandatory injunction ordering a return preparer to produce a list of the taxpayers for whom he has prepared returns, even though the Service could have obtained the same information by summons. United States v. Nordbrock, 38 F3d 440 (9th Cir. 1994).

To get some sense of the types of orders courts have fashioned, injunction courts have issued under Section 7408 involving tax shelter promoters should also be consulted. See United States v. Landsberger, 534 F. Supp. 142 (D. Minn. 1981), aff'd, 692 F2d 501 (8th Cir. 1982). One tax shelter promoter injunction the Service obtained enjoined the leader of the Wisconsin Society of Educated Citizens from representing that wages are exempt from tax and from assisting in preparation of false Forms W-4, S-4E, 1040X, filing Freedom of Information Act (FOIA) requests, and instituting frivolous court actions. United States v. Kaun, 633 F. Supp. 406 (ED Wis. 1986), aff'd, 827 F2d 1144 (7th Cir. 1987). See also United States v. May, 555 F. Supp. 1008 (ED Mich. 1983).

that an injunction "would not be sufficient to prevent such person's interference with the proper administration" of the tax laws.[481]

The injunction proceeding must be brought in the federal district court for the judicial district in which the return preparer resides or has a principal place of business or in which the taxpayer whose return was prepared resides or has a principal place of business.[482] While Section 7407(a) authorizes the Service to institute a proceeding in the name of the United States, the jurisdiction of the district court to issue an injunction is found in Section 7402(a), the All-Writs Statute.[483] The All-Writs Statute grants district courts, at the request of the Service, "such jurisdiction to make in civil actions, writs and orders of injunction" and other orders "as may be necessary or appropriate for the enforcement of the Internal Revenue laws."[484] Section 7407 contemplates that the Service may join an action to enjoin an income tax return preparer with another action against the preparer. As the preparer injunction statute provides, the district court has jurisdiction over an action to enjoin an income tax return preparer, "separate and apart from any other action brought by the United States against such income tax return preparer or any taxpayer." In *Ernst & Whinney*, the Service brought an action against an accounting firm to enjoin the firm from promoting the use of its investment credit service, which the Service alleged permitted clients to obtain investment tax credit for ineligible property.[485] In its complaint, the Service joined an action under Section 7407 to enjoin the accounting firm for an injunction against the firm based on the firm's alleged misconduct as a return preparer with an action under the All-Writs Statute for an injunction against the accounting firm as a tax adviser. In support of the request for an injunction under the All-Writs Statute, however, the Service did not allege that the accounting firm had breached any specific duty imposed by the Code, and the district court granted the accounting firm's motion to dismiss the injunction action based on the All-Writs Statute. Reversing the district court and rejecting a narrow construction of Section 7402, the circuit court held that in order for an injunction to issue under the All-Writs Statute, the Service is not required to show that the party against whom the injunction is sought violated a particular provision of the Code. Some of the activities the Service alleged the accounting firm engaged in as a "tax adviser" were not those of a return preparer, and, therefore, outside of the preparer misconduct described in Section 7407. As a result, at the Service's request, the

---

[481] IRC § 7407(b).

[482] IRC § 7407(a).

[483] IRC § 7407(a) ("[t]he court may exercise jurisdiction (as provided in section 7402(a)) separate and apart from any other action brought by the United States against such income tax preparer or any taxpayer").

[484] IRC § 7402(a).

[485] See United States v. Ernst & Whinney, 735 F2d 1296 (11th Cir. 1984).

district court had jurisdiction under the All-Writs Statute to enjoin the accounting firm's activities as a tax adviser. In deciding whether to grant an injunction under the All-Writs Statute, the district court's decision is governed by factors courts traditionally consider in requests for an injunctive remedy, rather than the statutory considerations set forth in Section 7407.[486]

C. THE PRIVACY OF TAX RETURNS

¶ 4.07 CONFIDENTIALITY AND DISCLOSURE OF TAX RETURNS

Before 1977, tax returns were "public records," but were only open to inspection under Treasury regulations approved by the president or under presidential order. This apparent contradiction had been part of the revenue laws since 1910.[487] Because Congress was unable to define specific policies to be followed, Section 6103 left decisions regarding disclosures of tax returns by default to the executive branch. By 1974, however, Congress had developed greater sensitivity to the problems created by the use of information gathered from and about citizens by agencies of the federal government. This concern resulted in the Privacy Act of 1974.[488] Soon, however, revelations that the Service had disclosed tax return information to the White House and other federal agencies made it obvious that the Privacy Act would not be adequate to deal with the "unique aspects" of tax returns.[489] Congress noted that the Service had more information about citizens than any other federal agency, and that other agencies sought access to that information. On the other hand, citizens reasonably expected that the tax return information they were required to supply to the Service would be kept private. If the Service abused that reasonable expectation of privacy, the loss of public confidence could seriously impair the tax system.

Accordingly, in 1976, Congress amended Section 6103 to provide that tax returns and tax return information are confidential and are not subject to disclosure, except in limited situations where disclosure is warranted. In situations

---

[486] United States v. Ernst & Whinney, 735 F2d 1296 (11th Cir. 1984).

[487] Report to the Administrative Conference on Administrative Procedures of the Internal Revenue Service, S. Doc. No. 266, 94th Cong., 2d Sess. 835–843 (1976) (hereinafter Report to Administrative Conference). This valuable study traces both the statutory and the administrative history of tax return disclosures prior to the 1976 changes in Section 6103.

[488] See the discussion of the Privacy Act in Chapter 2, Part B.

[489] General Explanation, supra note 273, at 315, reprinted in 1976-3 CB (vol. 2) 327.

of allowable disclosure, Congress attempted "to balance the particular office or agency's need for the information involved with the citizen's right to privacy, as well as the impact of the disclosure upon the continuation of compliance with our country's voluntary tax assessment system."[490] Whether Congress succeeded in this formidable task is open to question.[491] In undertaking direct responsibility for specifying the types and manner of permissible disclosures, Congress adopted a swollen Section 6103, which, in a torrent of statutory language, lists categories and circumstances of permissible disclosures.

However awkward the statute, Congress created a greater sensitivity to return privacy. Even when Section 6103 does not apply, courts have attempted to strike a balance between the privacy of income tax returns and other needs. When the Commodity Futures Trading Commission issued subpoenas directing individuals to produce their retained copies of tax returns said that income tax returns were highly sensitive documents that the Commission could not get directly from the Service and that the "self-reporting and self-assessing character of the income tax system would be compromised were they promiscuously disclosed to agencies enforcing regulatory programs unrelated to tax collecting itself."[492] As a result, the Commission was required to demonstrate some particularized need for the returns, and because it had failed to do so, the circuit court refused to order the copies of the returns produced.

[1] Relationship Between Section 6103 and Freedom of Information Act

While Section 6103 was designed to prevent the Service from indiscriminately disclosing information it obtains from and about taxpayers, the Freedom of Information Act (FOIA) was intended to give citizens the right to have access to government information. In cases in which courts have attempted to resolve this apparent conflict between privacy and public access, the focus has been on Exemption 3 of FOIA, which exempts from disclosing information that another statute withholds from disclosure if the other statute is nondiscretionary or establishes "particular criteria" for withholding the information. The Service has successfully argued that Section 6103 permits the Service to withhold informa-

---

[490] General Explanation, supra note 273, at 315, reprinted in 1976-3 CB (vol. 2) 327.

[491] In 1977, the Privacy Protection Study Commission concluded that, while the amended Section 6103 is a "major step forward," "there are instances in which the statutory authorizations for disclosure . . . are overly broad in describing the types of information that may be disclosed and the purposes for which the information may be used." Report of the Privacy Protection Study Commission, Personal Privacy in an Information Society, App. 2 ("The Citizen as Taxpayer"), at 31 (1977).

[492] Commodities Futures Trading Comm'n v. Collins, 93-2 USTC ¶ 50,410 (7th Cir. 1993).

tion subject to "particular criteria within the meaning of FOIA Exemption 3."[493] Although Section 6103 was intended primarily to control its disclosures to other government agencies, the Service has used Section 6103 as a basis for withholding information from persons, including the taxpayers themselves, who have requested the information under FOIA. It is unlikely that Congress anticipated this affirmative use of Section 6103 by the Service.

The Service has also contended that the Administrative Procedure Act[494] limits judicial review of a decision that specific information need not be disclosed in determining whether the Service's action is arbitrary or an abuse of discretion. This argument has been rejected by most courts.[495] Therefore, in an FOIA proceeding, the returns or return information are presumed to be subject to disclosure unless, after de novo review, the district court decides that the Service has established that the returns or return information are nondiscloseable under Section 6103.

[2] Structure of Section 6103

Section 6103 has a relatively simple structure. The statute starts with the basic proposition that returns and return information "shall be confidential"[496] and sets forth definitions for terms such as "return" and "return information." It then proceeds to articulate in twenty[497] subsections the circumstances under which disclosure is authorized, and establishes the procedures, records, and safeguards relating to disclosure,[498] which are similar to the provisions of the Privacy Act. When revising Section 6103, Congress also increased the criminal penalty for an unauthorized disclosure from a misdemeanor to a felony,[499] and provided a civil remedy for damages in the event of a willful or negligent disclosure.[500] In addition, in 1997, Congress made it a misdemeanor punishable

---

[493] 5 USC § 552(b)(3). This exemption is analyzed in Chapter 2.

[494] 5 USC §§ 701 et seq.

[495] Chamberlain v. Kurtz, 589 F2d 827 (5th Cir.), cert. denied, 444 US 842 (1979); Currie v. IRS, 704 F2d 523 (11th Cir. 1983); Long v. United States, 742 F2d 1173 (9th Cir. 1984); Grasso v. IRS, 785 F2d 70 (3d Cir. 1986) . For further discussion of this issue, see Chapter 2.

[496] IRC § 6103(a).

[497] IRC §§ 6103(c)–6103(o). If disclosures described in more general categories of authorized disclosures are counted, the number balloons to more than thirty-two authorized disclosures.

[498] IRC § 6103(p). The Service has issued a revised delegation order specifying which Service officials are authorized to disclose, and in some instances to withhold, tax information under each of the provisions of Section 6213. CDO No. 156.

[499] IRC § 7213.

[500] IRC § 7431. Congress provided for both actual and punitive damages. However, actual damages must be at least $1,000 for each disclosure. A successful taxpayer is also

by a fine of up to $1,000 or imprisonment for up to one year or both for federal, state, or other employees having access to returns and return information to engage in browsing (that is, willfully inspecting a return without specific authorization in accordance with Section 6103).[501] A return preparer who discloses information furnished to him for return preparation purposes can be held criminally liable.[502]

Within ninety days after the close of each calendar quarter, the Service is supposed to furnish the Joint Committee on Taxation for dissemination to the public, a report, which for each federal agency and certain other entities provides (1) the number of requests for disclosure of returns and return information; (2) the number of completed requests; and (3) the number of taxpayers whose returns or return information were disclosed pursuant to the requests. The Joint Committee Disclosure Report for calendar year 1996 illustrates the flow of information from the Service.[503] This report shows that approximately 2.3 billion disclosures were made, but roughly 1.35 billion of those disclosures were made to states for state tax purposes. At the other end of the use spectrum, only ninety-two disclosures were made to the Department of Justice for purposes of tax administration,[504] but the returns and return information of 2,720 prospective jurors were disclosed in connection with tax cases.[505] On the other hand, 42,307 were disclosed to U.S. Attorneys and 617 to the FBI for purposes of administering laws other than the tax laws. Some of the significant consumers were congressional committees (313 million disclosures) and the General Accounting Office (341 million).

---

entitled to the costs of the action. To assuage the concerns of Service employees, civil liability does not exist if the disclosure results from a "good faith, but erroneous, interpretation."

[501] IRC § 7213A, added by the Privacy Act of 1997 § 2(a), effective for violations occurring on and after August 5, 1997. Civil damages are also available for browsing under Section 7431(c).

[502] IRC § 7216(a). This offense is a misdemeanor. No offense is committed if the disclosure is permitted by regulation. IRC § 7216(b)(3). For permissible disclosures, see Reg. § 301.7216-2(c). See also Rev. Rul. 85-5, 1985-1 CB 385 (accountant may disclose a tax return and related workpapers pursuant to order of a state board of accountancy).

[503] Joint Comm. on Tax'n, Disclosure Report for Public Inspection Pursuant to Internal Revenue Code Section 6103(p)(3)(C) for Calendar Year 1996 (JCX-38-97), July 14, 1997.

[504] IRC § 6103(h)(3)(b). In calendar year 1997, of a total of about 3.2 billion disclosures, about 1.8 billion were made to states, pursuant to Section 6103(d), about 335.6 million were made to congressional committees and their agents, including the GAO, and interestingly the number of disclosures to foreign countries under tax treaties (more than 1 million) far exceeded the number of disclosures to U.S. Attorneys and other federal agencies (about 45,000).

[505] IRC § 6103(h)(5).

[a] Returns and Return Information

For purposes of Section 6103, "return" is defined as any tax return, information return, declaration of estimated tax, or claim for refund under the Code required (or permitted) to be filed on behalf of or relating to any person.[506] A return also includes any amendment, supplemental schedule, or attachment filed with the tax return. The section defines the term "return information" as:[507]

1. The taxpayer's identity;
2. The nature, source, or amount of a taxpayer's income, payments, receipts, deductions, net worth, tax liability, deficiencies, and overassessments;
3. Data received or prepared by the Service regarding a taxpayer's return, including the possible existence of liability under the Code;
4. Information regarding actual or possible investigation of a taxpayer's return[508]; and
5. Any part of a written Service determination or background file document as defined in Section 6110(b) that is not open to public inspection under Section 6110 (providing for public inspection of written determinations, such as rulings and technical advice).

The Fifth Circuit has said that "return information" includes: (1) the taxpayer's identity; (2) the fact that the taxpayer is under investigation or subject to further investigation; and (3) data that the Service has collected about a return.[509] Consistent with the purpose of Section 6103, return information must be information that "at least has passed through the IRS," and the Service must have

---

[506] IRC § 6103(b)(1). Currency Transaction Reports and Reports of Foreign Bank and Financial Accounts are not returns because they are not filed under the provisions of the Code (Title 26, USC), but under Title 31, USC, Money and Finance. See IRM 1272, Exhibit 100-2. Information from a Title 31 report can become return information under Section 6103(b)(2) if the report is used in a civil or criminal tax investigation under the Code. See IRM 1272. Disclosure of Official Information Handbook, Exhibit 100-2, 1272-166.

[507] IRC § 6103(b)(2). See Baskin v. United States, 81 AFTR2d 98-468 (5th Cir. 1998). See also United States v. Bischoff, 75 AFTR2d 95-2071 (5th Cir. 1995) (reversing dismissal of taxpayers' complaint alleging that Service special agents disclosed to current and former employees of taxpayers' businesses that taxpayers had failed to disclose to a pension fund they did not own certain property, disclosed to former and current employees of another pension fund that the taxpayers received a substantial profit on the sale of land to the pension fund, and also disclosed information about their investigation to newspaper reporter).

[508] See Gary L. Ryan v. Bureau of Alcohol, Tobacco & Firearms, 715 F2d 644 (DC Cir. 1983) (divided court) (list of liquor bottle manufacturers registered with the bureau protected against disclosure as return information because the reporting requirement was adopted to protect the revenue).

[509] Huckaby v. United States Dep't of Treasury, 794 F2d 1041, 1046 (5th Cir. 1986).

been the source of the disclosure of the disclosed information.[510] When the Service is not the source of the disclosure, there is no violation of Section 6103; for example, when information is collected by a special agent for a U.S. Attorney's office in the course of a grand jury investigation.[511] As one court said, the language of Section 6103(b)(2)(A) "requires a nexus between the data or information obtained and furtherance of obligations controlled by Title 26."[512] Thus, when the Service disclosed information to a U.S. Attorney regarding a taxpayer's possible Title 18 obstruction of justice violation, the disclosure has been held not to satisfy this nexus requirement.[513]

During tax shelter investigations in the 1980s, the Service sent out prefiling notice letters to investors in named promotions warning them that if deductions or credits are claimed, they will be disallowed and penalties will be imposed. The courts have rejected promoters' claims in this context, that the letters constituted disclosures of tax return information. Some courts have found that these letters did not disclose tax return information because they stated only that the promotions had been reviewed.[514] Alternatively, courts have held that if tax return information has been disclosed, the disclosures relate to the taxpayers' own returns, which is permitted by Sections 6103(e)(1)(A)(i) and 7103(e)(7).[515] Disclosure has also been permitted on the ground that the disclosure of the return information is made in an administra-

---

[510] The Fifth Circuit has said that Section 6103 "requires that the source of the disclosed information must have been the IRS in order for there to be a violation of the general prohibition against the disclosure of return information." Baskin v. United States, 81 AFTR2d 98-918 (5th Cir. 1998) (citing *Huckaby*).

[511] Baskin v. United States, 81 AFTR2d 98-918 (5th Cir. 1998). In *Baskin*, special agents assigned to a grand jury delivered canceled checks obtained by the grand jury to the Houston Police Department Internal Affairs Division, which was also investigating Baskin. Rejecting Baskin's wrongful disclosure claims, the circuit court held that the canceled checks were received by the use of the grand jury subpoena and turned over to special agents in their capacity as agents for the grand jury, and so were not filed with, or disclosed by the Service.

[512] In re Grand Jury Investigation, United States v. Jackson, 688 F2d 1068, reh'g denied, 696 F2d 449 (6th Cir. 1982).

[513] In re Grand Jury Investigation, United States v. Jackson, 688 F2d 1068, reh'g denied, 696 F2d 449 (6th Cir. 1982). In subsequent proceedings, the special agents who made the disclosure were held to have been entitled to rely on the advice of a District Counsel and on the instruction of superiors in determining whether Section 6103(a) had been violated. Jackson v. Romine, 84-1 USTC ¶ 9131 (WD Ky. 1983), opinion and judgment vacated, 84-1 USTC ¶ 9329 (SD Ky. 1984) (dismissal of taxpayer's suit alleging agents' improperly disclosed returns could not be granted on agents' affidavits alone).

[514] Mid-South Music Corp. v. Kolak, 818 F2d 536 (6th Cir. 1984); Balanced Fin. Management, Inc. v. Fay, 87-2 USTC ¶ 9378 (D. Utah 1987); Solargistics Corp. v. United States, 89-2 USTC ¶ 9610 (ND Ill. 1989).

[515] Mid-South Music Corp. v. Kolak, 818 F2d 536 (6th Cir. 1984); Balanced Fin. Management, Inc. v. Fay, 87-2 USTC ¶ 9378 (D. Utah 1987).

tive proceeding and the information directly relates to a transactional relationship between the promoter and the investor/taxpayer.[516]

In general, data that cannot be identified as relating to a particular taxpayer, such as statistical studies, are subject to disclosure.[517] The portion of Section 6103(b)(2) allowing such disclosure, sometimes referred to as the Haskell amendment, makes clear that the provision is not a vehicle for obtaining otherwise protected return information. No duty exists on the part of the Service to redact return information to delete the identifying parts so as to permit disclosure under FOIA.[518] However, there is one exception to the general rule. Although return information data may not identify individual taxpayers, the Service need not disclose the standards it uses for selecting returns for audit or the data for establishing these standards if it determines disclosure will seriously impair tax administration.[519] Under this statutory authority, the Service may refuse to disclose Taxpayer Compliance Measurement Program (TCMP) data it uses for audit selection purposes.[520] Although return information is generally either information supplied by the taxpayer with a tax return or IRS-generated, the term "taxpayer return information" is specifically defined as return information that is filed with or furnished to the Service by the taxpayer or his or her representative.[521]

[b] Disclosure

The term "disclosure" means "the making known to any person in any manner whatever a return or return information."[522] Nothing could be broader than this definition, but its breadth can create analytical problems. Suppose a Service employee discloses a taxpayer's return information to a newspaper or television reporter, and return information is disclosed in the next day's newspaper or on the evening news broadcast. Is the disclosure to the reporter alone or to the purchasers of the newspaper or the television viewers? Faced with

---

[516] First W. Sec., Inc. v. United States, 796 F2d 356 (10th Cir. 1987). See also Solargistics v. United States, 89-2 USTC ¶ 9610 (ND Ill. 1989) (disclosure authorized also under Section 6103(h)(4)(C)).

[517] IRC § 6103(b)(2).

[518] Church of Scientology v. IRS, 484 US 9 (1987) (Section 6103(b)(2) interpreted and legislative history reviewed).

[519] IRC § 6103(b)(2).

[520] This outcome was legislatively intended by the amendment of IRC § 6103(b)(2). The amendment legislatively overrules Long v. IRS, 596 F2d 362 (9th Cir. 1979) permitting access to TCMP data under FOIA. HR Rep. 201, 97th Cong., 1st Sess. 238. For the sequel to the Longs's quest for TCMP data, see Long v. United States, 825 F2d 225 (9th Cir. 1987).

[521] IRC § 6103(b)(3).

[522] IRC § 6103(b)(8).

this question, the Ninth Circuit in *Miller v. United States* said that permitting a taxpayer to recover from those who might read or hear the disclosure was against public policy because in an era of mass communication, "one statement on the worldwide computer network or to a television reporter could result in disseminations that could break our nation's treasury."[523] On the other hand, the Ninth Circuit also said it believed "that the disclosure of information to a person who is likely to publish that information is relevant in determining the degree of negligence or recklessness involved, not the number of disclosures."[524] In other words, in the case of disclosures to the media, the Ninth Circuit would ignore the definition of "disclosure" in Section 6103(b)(8) because statutory damages for those to whom the disclosure was made available would be a "bizarre remedy." Not all courts would agree. The Fourth Circuit's decision in *Mallas* would suggest the statutory amount for each of the readers of the newspaper because a disclosure makes known return information "in manner whatever." Moreover, the extent of the disclosure is a factor that could make punitive damages more likely, and punitive damages would serve to compensate the taxpayer on a more reasonable scale. When the Service conceded that Service agents disclosed return information on a radio talk show, as well as in a letter to the editor, the court ruled that ratings were too speculative to establish the number of disclosures, and used punitive damages of $250,000, as the method for dealing with the letter to the editor.[525]

[c] Permissible Disclosures

Section 6103 covers the following disclosure situations:

1. Disclosures to taxpayer's designees (Section 6103(c))
2. Disclosures to state tax officials (Section 6103(d))
3. Disclosures to persons having a material interest (Section 6103(e))
4. Disclosures to committees of Congress (Section 6103(f))
5. Disclosures to the president and White House (Section 6103(g))
6. Disclosures to federal officers and employees for purposes of tax administration (Section 6103(h))
7. Disclosures to federal officers and employees for purposes of nontax law administration (Section 6103(i))
8. Disclosures for statistical purposes (Section 6103(j))
9. Disclosures for tax administration purposes (Section 6103(k))

---

[523] Miller v. United States, 76 AFTR2d 95-6584 (9th Cir. 1995) ($1,000 damages awarded because Service official said to reporter that the Service had obtained little of value from taxpayer and her former husband).

[524] Miller v. United States, 76 AFTR2d 95-6584 (9th Cir. 1995).

[525] See Ward v. United States, 79 AFTR2d 97-2831 (D. Colo. 1997).

10. Disclosures for purposes other than tax administration (Section 6103(l))[526]
11. Disclosures of taxpayer identity information (Section 6103(m))
12. Disclosures to other persons for storage and similar purposes (Section 6103(n))
13. Disclosures with respect to certain taxes (Section 6103(o))

Confidentiality rules directly related to tax practice are those dealing with (1) the disclosure of returns or return information for tax administration purposes; (2) disclosure in tax cases; and (3) disclosures to federal officers for nontax purposes. Disclosures of returns and return information to designees of taxpayers and those having a material interest, as well as to state tax authorities, are also significant. These topics are discussed more fully in the sections that follow.

[3] Disclosure to Designees of Taxpayers and Persons Having a Material Interest

Section 6103(c) provides that the tax returns and return information of a taxpayer may be disclosed to a person designated by the taxpayer if the taxpayer requests and consents to the disclosure.[527] The request and consent may be in writing or made orally.[528] When a written request is made, the taxpayer must include the taxpayer's mailing address and TIN, the name and address of each person to whom disclosure is to be made, the kinds of returns or return information to be disclosed, and the taxable period(s) covered by the returns or return information, and sign and date any disclosure request and consent.[529] No

---

[526] IRC § 6103(l) specifies the agencies to which disclosure can be made and the conditions of disclosure. For example, Sections 6103(l)(1) and 6103(l)(2) permit disclosure of returns and return information to the Department of Labor and the Pension Benefit Guaranty Corporation for purposes of (but only to the extent necessary in) the administration of Titles I and IV of the Employee Retirement Income Security Act. See amendments to Reg. § 301.6103(1)(2)-3 governing this provision (TD 7911, 1983-2 CB 236).

[527] IRC § 6103(c).
The copying of documents is not free of charge. For example, a request for a copy of the taxpayer's return and related schedules is submitted on Form 4506 and the charge is $23; a return transcript, however, may be obtained free of charge. See Rev. Proc. 97-11, 1997-6 IRB 13.

[528] The Taxpayer Bill of Rights 2 made possible a disclosure to a designee without a written request by amending Section 6103(c) by striking out "*written* request for or consent to such disclosure" (emphasis added), and inserting "request for and consent to such disclosure." IRC § 1207, effective on the enactment date, July 30, 1996.

[529] Reg. § 301.6103(c)-1(a). These regulations have been held to be legislative regulations having the force of law. Therefore, the sixty-day rule strictly applies. Olsen v. Egger, 594 F. Supp. 644 (SDNY 1984) (husband agreed to supply wife with copy of return

disclosure in response to a written request will be made unless the disclosure consent or request is received within sixty days after the date it was signed and dated by the taxpayer.[530]

Under Section 6103(e), disclosure may be made to the following persons:

1. In the case of an individual, the individual, certain trustees, or the individual's spouse where a split gift has been made;
2. Either spouse who filed a joint return[531];
3. The partners of a partnership;
4. In the case of a corporation or its subsidiary, a person designated by the board of directors, an authorized officer or employee, a one percent or more shareholder, certain shareholders if the corporation is a foreign personal holding company, the shareholder of a Subchapter S corporation, or the fiduciary (or person affected) of a dissolved corporation[532];

---

in separation agreement, and wife sued Service apparently without filing request). However, for requests after July 30, 1996, requests need not be in writing.

[530] Taxpayer consent to the release of tax information must be knowing and voluntary. Tierney v. Schwieker, 718 F2d 449 (DC Cir. 1983), rev'g and remanding unreported decision, Trahan v. Regan, 554 F. Supp. 57 (DDC 1982) (notice and consent forms procured by the Social Security Administration from its program beneficiaries declared to be inadequate authorization for Service disclosure of tax return information).

The Service has a fact-of-filing program to respond to requests for fact-of-filing information from firms in the tax-professional community (tax return preparers and advisers) about their employees and associates. Ann. 97-19, 1997-10 IRB 68 (program extended through December 31, 1997). Under the program, in response to requests about the filing of individual income tax returns for 1994 through 1996, the Service will answer either yes or no to the request. The taxpayer about whom the information is requested may request the information himself, but if the taxpayer or the employer asks for the information to be sent to an address that is not the taxpayer's address, the taxpayer must include a Form 8821, Tax Information Authorization, with the request. If the taxpayer has not filed a return, the compliance function in the Service office for the taxpayer's geographic area will be notified.

[531] Unless the statute of limitations bars collection, if the Service has assessed a joint return deficiency, the spouses who filed the return are no longer married or reside in the same household, and one of the spouses requests information about collection of the joint return liability in writing, the Service must disclose in writing to the requesting spouse whether it has attempted to collect a deficiency from the other spouse, the general nature of the collection activities, and the amount collected. IRC § 6103(e)(8), added by the Taxpayer Bill of Rights 2, § 403(a), effective for requests made after the enactment date, July 30, 1996. Before this amendment an ex-spouse might fail to meet the materiality requirements for disclosure despite having filed joint returns for the period in question. Britt v. IRS, 83-2 USTC ¶ 9675 (DDC 1983) (documents sought were compiled by the Service to determine the tax consequences of an alleged "shell game" involving business entities created by former husband).

[532] See Yorkshire v. United States, 26 F3d 942 (9th Cir. 1994) (under Section 6103(e)(1)(D)(iii), more-than-one-percent shareholder member of consolidated group was

5. The administrator, executor, or trustee of an estate (and the heirs of the estate with a material interest that may be affected by the information);

6. The trustee of a trust (and beneficiaries with a material interest);

7. Persons authorized to act on behalf of a dissolved corporation;

8. Receivers or trustees in bankruptcy; or

9. The committee, trustee, or guardian of an incompetent taxpayer.

The Code also permits disclosure (1) where the taxpayer is incompetent[533] or deceased[534]; (2) in certain Bankruptcy Code (Title 11) proceedings and receiverships[535]; or (3) to the taxpayer's authorized attorney in fact.[536] Upon the written request of a person Collection has determined to be liable for the trust fund recovery penalty, the Service may disclose the name of any other person Collection has determined to be liable for the penalty, whether Collection has attempted to collect the penalty from the other person, and the amount collected.[537]

Both Sections 6103(c) and 6103(e) permit the Service to withhold tax information if it determines that disclosure would "seriously impair Federal tax administration." In *Chamberlain v. Kurtz*,[538] a taxpayer contesting civil fraud penalties made an FOIA request for tax return information relating to closed criminal investigations of his own returns. In opposing disclosure, the Service

---

entitled to disclosure of consolidated return, but the shareholder was not entitled to a partnership return of a partnership owned by subsidiaries of one of the other members of the affiliated group because the partnership's return was not necessary for the filing of the partner's return). McAdams v. United States, 77 AFTR2d 96-1902 (WD La. 1996) (during the audit of McAdams, a revenue agent prepared a spreadsheet listing deposits in a McAdams bank account—deposits he believed were diverted from a dissolved corporation, McAdams-Thomason—and disclosed the spreadsheet in a subsequent audit of McAdams-Thomason; held, the disclosure to Thomason was not wrongful, because the information in the spreadsheet was return information not only of McAdams, but also of McAdams-Thomason because it was used to determine the possible existence of additional McAdams-Thomason tax liability; and because under Louisiana law, Thomason had personal liability for claims against the corporation, he had a material interest in McAdams-Thomason).

[533] IRC § 6103(e)(2).

[534] IRC § 6103(e)(3). In determining who is an heir for purposes of this section, state law is applicable. Williams v. Comm'r, 523 F. Supp. 89 (ED Mo. 1981) (under Missouri law an illegitimate child is an heir and thus is entitled to disclosure of decedent's tax return).

[535] IRC §§ 6103(e)(4), 6103(e)(5).

[536] IRC § 6103(e)(6).

[537] IRC § 6103(e)(9), added by the Taxpayer Bill of Rights 2, § 403(a), effective for requests made after the enactment date, July 30, 1996. While the information permitted to be disclosed will be helpful to the requester, the provision does not literally authorize disclosure of statements the other responsible officers may have made about the requester.

[538] Chamberlain v. Kurtz, 589 F2d 827 (5th Cir.), cert. denied, 444 US 842 (1979).

argued that the taxpayer was not entitled to the information because access would impair tax administration. The court of appeals found that while release of the information might benefit the taxpayer in the preparation of his defense, Sections 6103(c) and 6103(e)(7) were designed to avoid the "untimely disclosure" of the Service files the taxpayer wished. Consequently, the Service is able to use Sections 6103(c) and 6103(e)(7) to block a taxpayer's or his designee's access to information under Section 6103 or FOIA by the simple expedient of finding that disclosure would seriously impair tax administration.[539]

There seems to be no rationale on the basis of which one can predict what either the Service or the courts will do in this area. For example, a prefiling notice letter sent to investors in a tax shelter has been held a disclosure of return information of each of the shelter's investors and authorized by Section 6103(e)(7).[540] Also, there is uncertainty about the jurisdiction of district courts to condition enforcement of a summons to keep return information provided to the Service confidential. In *United States v. Zolin*, the Ninth Circuit ruled that when a summons is used, in a summons enforcement action the district court may condition its enforcement order by placing restrictions on the disclosure of the summoned information.[541] Faced with the same issue in *Barrett*, the Court of Appeals for the Fifth Circuit held that a district court may either enforce or refuse to enforce a Service summons, but could not impose conditions on enforcement, such as restrictions on further disclosure of the summoned information.[542] When *Zolin* and *Barrett* came before the Supreme Court, the Court deadlocked on the issue of conditional enforcement, leaving both decisions standing. Reviewing the apparent difference between the views of the Ninth and Fifth Circuits, the Court of Appeals for the Third Circuit observed that the different decisions in *Barrett* and *Zolin* merely created a distinction between limitations on the Service's freedom to disclose information after it has been gathered and limitations on its ability to gather information in the first

---

[539] The curious way in which the confidentiality rules operate is illustrated by how they have been applied in investigations of claimed misconduct by Service personnel. One court has held that the internal investigation file of the Service employee was return information of the employee. Conn v. IRS, 92-1 USTC ¶ 50,123 (ND Cal. 1991) (file in wrongful disclosure investigation); see O'Connor v. United States, 698 F. Supp. 204, 206 (D. Nev. 1988) (reports of assaults and threatened assaults on Service employees by persons other than plaintiff).

Similarly, when appraisals used by the Service for sale of seized property were sought by a bidder, the appraisals were held return information of the delinquent taxpayer, although notice of sale disclosed taxpayer's identity. Kamman v. IRS, 92-1 USTC ¶ 50,208 (D. Ariz. 1992). For further discussion of FOIA exemptions, see Chapter 2.

[540] See Solargistic Corp. v. United States, 921 F2d 729 (7th Cir. 1991).

[541] United States v. Zolin, 109 S. Ct. 2619 (1989), aff'g on this issue, 809 F2d 1411 (9th Cir. 1987).

[542] United States v. Barrett, 837 F2d 1341 (5th Cir. 1988).

place, which is a distinction without a difference.[543] The Third Circuit agreed, however, with the Ninth Circuit that a district court had the jurisdiction to enforce a summons with conditions on future disclosures. Subsequently, the Ninth Circuit abandoned its view in *Zolin*, and agreed with the Fifth Circuit view in *Barrett* that a district court may not condition the enforcement of a summons to prevent further disclosures.[544]

[4] Disclosure for Tax Administration Purposes

Service officers and employees are specifically given permission to disclose returns and return information where the data involve the following:

- Accepted offers in compromise;
- Amounts of outstanding liens;
- Corrections of misstatements of fact (provided the Joint Committee on Taxation approves);
- Information supplied to so-called competent authorities under income tax treaties; and
- Information furnished to state agencies regulating tax return preparers.[545]

Section 6103 also authorizes "investigative disclosures."[546] Under Section 6103(k)(6), a Service employee may, in a civil or criminal tax investigation, "disclose return information to the extent that such disclosure is necessary in obtaining information that is not otherwise reasonably available." The Senate Report states:

> In certain instances, it may be necessary for IRS personnel, in obtaining information with respect to a taxpayer from a third party, to disclose the fact that the request for the information is in connection with an audit or other tax investigation of a taxpayer. In rare and extraordinary cases, it may also be necessary for IRS personnel in obtaining information from a third party to disclose additional return information, such as the manner in which the taxpayer treated on his return a transaction with the third party.

---

[543] United States v. Rockwell Int'l, 897 F2d 1255, 1260–1261 (3d Cir. 1990) ("although the decision in *Zolin* is not binding, we nevertheless think its end result [in affirming the Ninth Circuit's decision] is sound, and we find that IRS summonses may be enforced conditionally").

[544] United States v. Jose, 83 AFTR2d 99-1223 (9th Cir. 1999).

[545] IRC §§ 6103(k)(1)–6103(k)(5). See Harrison v. United States, 90-1 USTC ¶ 50,094 (MDNC 1990) (disclosures by revenue officer held permissible under Sections 6103(k)(2) and 6103(k)(6)).

[546] IRC § 6103(k)(6).

Disclosures under this provision are to be made only in situations and under conditions specified in the regulations.[547]

From this statutory language, it could be inferred that Congress intended that regulations would limit the situations and restrict the conditions where investigative disclosures might be made, but the regulations actually adopted do not do so. Regulations under Section 6103(k)(6) effectively shift to the Service agent or officer the decision of whether and what to disclose to a third party, subject only to the proviso that the disclosure not be made if the information is capable of being obtained in an "accurate and sufficiently probative form, or in a timely manner, and without impairing the proper performance" of the agent's duties.[548] Any apparent restriction on an investigative disclosure is lifted by permission granted the official to disclose information in order to obtain other information (1) that cannot "otherwise reasonably be obtained in accurate and sufficiently probative form," or (2) in a timely manner, and (3) without impairing the proper performance of the official's duties and responsibilities.[549] The regulations also fail to recognize the legislative history, which specifically states that the third-party disclosure exception is to be used only in "rare and extraordinary circumstances."[550] Unquestionably, the Service must be given freedom to investigate the accuracy of returns and return information. Nevertheless, agents who have made inquiries of third persons and casually disclosed information have done substantial damage to the reputations and businesses of taxpayers. Congress apparently intended to restrict these disclosures, but the regulations simply do not reflect that congressional intention.

The Manual gives some illustrations of permissible disclosures:[551]

---

[547] S. Rep. No. 938, 94th Cong., 2d Sess. 342 (1976), reprinted in 1976-3 CB (vol. 3) 380.

[548] Reg. §§ 301.6103(k)(6)-1(a), 301.6103(k)(6)-1(b).

[549] Reg. §§ 301.6103(k)(6)-1(a), 301.6103(k)(6)-1(b). If an agent does not receive information from the taxpayer, a disclosure is authorized. United States v. Arditi, 78-1 USTC ¶ 9435 (SDNY 1978) (agent's third-party disclosures were permissible when taxpayer denied agent access); see also Viti v. United States, 75 AFTR2d 95-1780 (ND Ga. 1995) (citing Reg. § 301.6103(k)(6)-1, and finding that a special agent was authorized to make disclosures of and make inquiries about taxpayer's Schedule C items because agent had unsuccessfully attempted to obtain information from the taxpayer, and the third party had worked in the taxpayer's real estate appraisal business); Stewart v. United States, 75 AFTR2d 95-2248 (SD Ohio 1995) (special agent did not make wrongful disclosure of taxpayer's Social Security number to his bank, because the taxpayer had refused to cooperate by making employment and bank records available).

[550] S. Rep. No. 938, 94th Cong., 2d Sess. 342 (1976), reprinted in 1976-3 CB (vol. 3) 380.

[551] IRM 1.3, Disclosure of Official Information Handbook, 21.1 (Aug. 19, 1998) (Requirements for Investigative Disclosures).

(3) Return information may be disclosed to someone other than the taxpayer or the taxpayer's representative in order to obtain facts needed during an investigation. However, such disclosures will be made only to the extent required to obtain the necessary information.

EXAMPLE 4-2: A revenue agent or special agent contacts a taxpayer's customer regarding the purchases the customer made from the taxpayer during the year under investigation. The agent will usually be able to obtain the needed purchase information only by disclosing the taxpayer's identity and the fact of investigation. However, depending on the facts and circumstances, the agent may also have to inform the customer of the dates of the purchases and the types of merchandise involved.

EXAMPLE 4-3: A tax examiner in a Service Center is processing a return that is missing a schedule. Despite repeated contacts the taxpayer has not responded. The tax examiner can contact the preparer to secure the schedule without the taxpayer's authorization, even if by doing so the employee has to divulge return information such as the taxpayer's address or Social Security Number.

(4) The investigative disclosure must be made to obtain information. Return information may not be divulged solely for the benefit of the recipient.

(5) Disclosures of return information in investigative situations may be made only if the necessary information cannot otherwise be reasonably obtained in accurate and sufficiently probative form, or in a timely manner, and without impairing the proper performance of official duties. Thus, as a general rule, in instances when the taxpayer is aware of the investigation, is cooperating, and is believed to have the needed information, IRS employees should obtain such information directly from the taxpayer or the taxpayer's representative unless to do so might tend to prejudice the investigation.

(6) Situations in which necessary information generally will not be available from the taxpayer or will not be in a usable form include the following:

   1. When corroboration of a taxpayer's statement or records is necessary

   2. When the taxpayer's records are in the possession of a third party and the taxpayer is unwilling or unable to obtain the records

   3. When it is necessary to disclose return information to persons possessing special expertise in areas such as handwriting analysis, photographic development, sound recording enhancement, and voice identification

(7) If the accuracy of the information provided by the taxpayer or the taxpayer's representative needs to be verified, investigative disclo-

sures may be made to third parties to obtain missing or corroborating information.

(8) In determining whether to make an investigative disclosure under Section 6103(k)(6), be certain that the disclosure is consistent with the requirements of that section and the related regulations. In view of the court's decision in Rodgers v. Hyatt, 697 F2d 899 (10th Cir. 1983), the fact that information is already public should not normally be considered in making investigative disclosures.

Caution: In view of conflicting court decisions, caution should be used when considering whether information which is already public should be disclosed in making investigative disclosures. If such a disclosure does not meet 6103(k)(6) standards, and later it is determined that the "public" information was still protected by Section 6103, an unauthorized disclosure may be deemed to have occurred.

---

(9) Questions concerning investigative disclosures should be brought to the attention of one's manager or the Disclosure Officer.

1. *Investigative disclosures and circular letters.* The circular letter is an investigative procedure employed by the Service in criminal investigations to obtain information from third parties. These letters have raised disclosure issues. Where a circular letter states that a taxpayer is under criminal investigation by the Service, the letter has been held to result in a disclosure of return information under Section 6103. In *Calhoun v. Wells*, the district court found that there was no need to state in the circular letter that the taxpayer was under criminal investigation and rejected the Service's argument that an indirect disclosure is required by the Manual because a circular letter must be signed in the name of the Chief, Criminal Investigation Division, saying that such a Manual provision "would require an unnecessary disclosure of return information in violation of [Section] 6103."[552] Moreover, it appears that whether information is "not otherwise reasonably available" within the meaning of Section 6103(k)(6) is a question of fact, the district court must decide whether, in the light of the evidence available, it was necessary to send the letters.[553]

---

[552] Calhoun v. Wells, 80-1 USTC ¶ 9431.

[553] Barrett v. United States, 795 F2d 446 448, 450 (5th Cir. 1986). In Huckaby v. United States, 804 F2d 297 (5th Cir. 1986), the circuit court held that a district court order enforcing a summons in Texas Heart Inst., 755 F2d 469 (5th Cir. 1985), did not collaterally estop a taxpayer from claiming that a violation of Section 6103 had occurred. The circuit court also said that (1) the Service cannot disclose return information to a state agency without some written consent from the taxpayer; (2) the taxpayer's oral consent was insufficient; (3) the issue of the agent's good faith in making the improper disclosure was to be determined under an objective good faith standard; and (4) a disclosure by the special agent to the Texas Alcoholic Beverage Commission violated this standard.

Generally, courts have held that the Manual is not binding on the Service. In determining whether a circular letter was necessary or in the proper form, courts have considered Internal Revenue Manual provisions on criminal investigations regarding circular letters. The Manual acknowledges that there is "some confusion" in the federal courts about what information may be disclosed in a circular letter, and to prevent "any undue problems," the Manual advises as follows: (1) before preparing the circular letter, special agents should review Section 6103(k)(6) and the related regulations; (2) the Chief of the district Criminal Investigation function must approve the circular form letter; (3) inquiries should be made only to third parties who are likely sources of information; (4) the body of the letter must not disclose that the taxpayer is under investigation by Criminal Investigation (the suggested appropriate wording is "The Internal Revenue Service is conducting an investigation of . . . "); (5) neither the signature block nor the heading of the letter should contain the words "Criminal Investigation" (although the letter may use symbols to ensure that the mailed response is returned to the special agent); and (6) the special agent should sign the letter, but the signature block should include only the title "Special Agent" and "Internal Revenue Service."[554] Special agents are also cautioned not to damage the reputation of the target by making the letter either "offensive or suggestive of any wrongdoing" on the part of the taxpayer.

　　　2. *Investigative disclosures and collection.* Confidentiality does not apply to the disclosure concerning the amount of outstanding liens. Revenue officers in the Collection Division may make investigative disclosures in the course of their duties to collect delinquent taxes. Litigation resulted when taxpayers claimed that Service personnel violated their return confidentiality by erroneously filing a notice of lien. In general, courts have held that a disclosure of return information was not wrongful, even when the taxpayer claims the collection action was improper because an improper levy was served[555] or

---

See also Malis v. United States, 87-1 USTC ¶ 9212 (CD Cal. 1986) (disclosures by special agent about taxpayer under investigation were held unauthorized because disclosures were unnecessary to obtain information sought; damages were awarded). Cf. Lambert v. United States, 854 F2d 335 (9th Cir. 1988) ("once return information is lawfully disclosed in a judicial forum, its subsequent disclosure by press release does not violate the Act").

[554] IRM 9.3.1.3.3 (Circular Letters) (Mar. 19, 1998).

[555] Schrambling Accountancy Corp. v. United States, 937 F2d 1484, 1488–1489 (9th Cir. 1991), cert. denied, 112 S. Ct. 956 (1992) (no damages were awarded where information disclosed by improper levy had previously been placed in public domain by properly recorded federal tax lien); Weiner v. IRS, 789 F. Supp. 655 (SDNY 1992), aff'd, 93-1 USTC ¶ 50,124 (2d Cir. 1993) (levy was served after tax was paid through computer error, held, no wrongful disclosure); Maisano v. United States, 89-2 USTC ¶ 9558 (D. Nev. 1989), aff'd, 908 F2d 408 (9th Cir. 1990) (disclosures in notices of tax liens did not violate Section 6103(a)); see also Cuda v. United States, 91-1 USTC ¶ 50,193 (WD Mich. 1991) (revenue officer found only to be attempting to find out whether levied parties had

lien filed.[556] When taxpayers' complaints have been about wrongful collection, courts have also said that the remedy is not a wrongful disclosure action, but a wrongful collection action under Section 7433.[557] There is some authority, however, that an improper notice of levy can disclose tax return information.[558]

3. **Press releases.** The Service's policy is to issue press releases to announce indictments and convictions in criminal tax cases as well as to respond to inquiries about other actions it takes when the matter has become public. Service press releases describing charges against, or the conviction of a taxpayer for a tax crime, have generally been held not to constitute disclosures of return information because the information has already been disclosed in a

---

assets belonging to taxpayer). Even if a levy is wrongful and discloses tax return information, the disclosure does not necessarily constitute a wrongful disclosure. See Haywood v. United States, 642 F. Supp. 188 (D. Kan. 1986) (disclosure of taxpayer's liability was held not to be disclosure of information on return; disclosure to employer was not material, because employer already possessed information).

Once an assessment is properly made, a notice to a financial institution to initiate backup withholding is not an illegal disclosure; Messinger v. United States, 769 F. Supp. 935 (D. Md. 1991); Chandler v. United States, 91-2 USTC ¶ 50,460 (WD Wash. 1991).

[556] Filing a notice of tax lien despite the fact that the liability has been paid has been held not to entitle a taxpayer to damages for wrongful disclosure. Flippo v. United States, 670 F. Supp. 638 (WDNC 1987), aff'd in unpublished opinion, 849 F2d 604 (4th Cir. 1988) (disclosure held authorized under Section 6103(k)(6)).

[557] Where the complaint alleges that collection action has been unlawful, it has been held that the proper remedy is a wrongful collection action under Section 7433, not a wrongful disclosure action. Venen v. United States, 38 F3d 100 (3d Cir. 1994) ("[t]hus, the propriety of the underlying collection action, in this instance the validity of the levy, is irrelevant to whether disclosure is authorized under section 6103 and the basis for liability under section 7431").

[558] In a case where the Service served levies, one of which was to the taxpayer's employer, to collect an erroneous refund, but its collection action was unlawful because it failed to make a timely assessment before serving its levies, the district court agreed that the Service had negligently disclosed the taxpayer's return information. Schipper v. United States, 82 AFTR2d 98-6821 (EDNY 1998) (court awarded damages of $4,800, but refused to award punitive damages).

court proceeding,[559] although in at least one case, where there had been an agreement not to disclose, a wrongful disclosure has been found.[560]

4. **The public records exception.** Although it is not permitted by any statutory exemption, when information has been disclosed in an authorized way and has become a matter of public record (e.g., in the course of a court proceeding or the Service's enforcement activities, such as filing of notice of federal tax lien), some courts have said that the further disclosure of the information does not constitute a violation of Section 6103 for which damages may be awarded under Section 7431. Some courts have adopted a similar public record rationale for disclosures made in press releases.[561] The rationale for this public records exception is that once tax return information is in the public domain, the taxpayer has no reasonable expectation of privacy in the information.[562] However, a nonstatutory public records exception is not universally

---

[559] A Service press release describing the charges against, or criminal conviction of, a taxpayer for a tax crime is generally not held to violate Section 6103, because the information has already been disclosed in a court proceeding. Lampert v. United States, 854 F2d 335 (9th Cir. 1988), cert. denied, 109 S. Ct. 1931 (press release summarizing criminal charges is not disclosure of tax return information); Rice v. United States, 80 AFTR2d 97-5795 (DNM 1997) (public affairs officer prepared one press release from her examination of publicly filed indictment, attendance at the taxpayer-defendant's trial, and research of possible penalties, and prepared second press release by attending the sentencing; held, the press releases did not disclose taxpayer-defendant's return information). See also Thomas v. United States, 671 F. Supp. 15 (ED Wis. 1987); Rubel v. United States, 89-1 USTC ¶ 9149 (WDNC 1988) (damages for disclosures in postconviction press release were denied because government officers acted in good faith and had solid basis in interpretation of Section 6103).

[560] One exception to this general rule is *Johnson v. Sawyer.* Initially, Johnson, who had been a defendant in a criminal case recovered under the Federal Tort Claims Act (FTCA) when a press release was made in violation of plea agreement and contained erroneous information. Johnson v. Sawyer, 980 F2d 1490 (5th Cir. 1992). However, on rehearing, the Fifth Circuit sitting en banc reversed the decision of the panel of the court, and held that under the Texas invasion of privacy tort, none of the facts disclosed was private or under the negligence per se doctrine, and the panel's decision had been based on the return confidentiality law of Section 6103, not Texas law as required for purposes of the FTCA. Johnson v. Sawyer, 47 F3d 716 (5th Cir. 1995). On remand, Johnson recovered compensatory damages of $6 million and punitive damages ranging from $1.5 to $1.6 million. Johnson v. Sawyer, 77 AFTR2d 96-2383 (SD Tex. 1996). The government again appealed, and the decision was reversed and remanded, 120 F3d 1307 (5th Cir. 1997).

[561] See discussion of cases supra note 555.

[562] Lampert v. United States, 854 F2d 335 (9th Cir. 1988) ("[o]nce tax return information is made part of the public domain, the taxpayer may no longer claim a right of privacy in that information"); Schrambling Accountancy Corp. v. United States, 937 F2d 1484, 1488–1489 (9th Cir. 1991). The Sixth Circuit agrees with the Ninth Circuit, "in holding that, once a taxpayer's return information becomes part of the public domain through the filing and recording of a judicial lien it loses its confidentiality and is not protected by [S]ection 6103 if republished by the IRS for tax administration purposes."

accepted, and when the public records exception has been found to apply primarily by the Ninth Circuit, it is often a judicial response to a taxpayer's attempt in a disclosure action to contest the underlying validity of the tax assessment by claiming that the disclosed information was erroneous.[563]

The Fourth Circuit has squarely rejected the view that there is a public records exception to the confidentiality rules of Section 6103. In *Mallas*, even after the circuit court had reversed convictions of tax shelter promoters, the Service continued to send revenue agent reports (RARs) to investors in the tax shelter describing convictions of the promoters and stating that losses claimed through their "financing scheme" were disallowed.[564] The promoters sued for wrongful disclosure and were awarded $73,000 each in damages. On appeal, the government argued that the promoters' return information had not been wrongfully disclosed because the RARs had not been prepared for the promoters' returns. Rejecting this argument, the Fourth Circuit said, "Taxpayer information obtained or prepared by the IRS . . . is 'return information' regardless of the person with respect to whom it was obtained or prepared."[565] Consequently, the promoters' convictions, the reference to "financing scheme" which was gathered from the determination of the promoters' liability, the use of "it was determined" indicating the Service's determinations of how the promoters' fraud was perpetrated—all disclosed tax return information of the promoters. Importantly, the circuit court also rejected the government's argument that the information was not confidential because it was a matter of public record, which the RARs only republished. In the Fourth Circuit's view, there is no "public record" exception to Section 6103, and so it disagreed with the Ninth Circuit's *Lampert* and *Schrambling* decisions finding such an exception. Finally, the circuit court said that all audits are not administrative proceedings with the result that the RARs did not constitute "administrative proceeding" disclosures provided for in Section 6103(h)(4)(C). Disclosures in audits and investigations were intended to be covered, if at all, under the investigative disclosure exception, Section 6103(k)(6).

Rowley v. United States, 77 AFTR2d 96-1071 (6th Cir. 1996) (advertisements of the public sale of seized property contained return information already disclosed in filed notices of federal tax liens and levies).

[563] Weiner v. IRS, 789 F. Supp. 655 (SDNY 1992), aff'd, 93-1 USTC ¶ 50,124 (2d Cir. 1993) (levy was served after tax was paid; held, although error was conceded and taxpayer was entitled to apology from the Service, there was no wrongful disclosure). The rationale stated by some courts in permitting disclosures of erroneous information is that to do otherwise would permit taxpayers to contest the underlying validity of the tax, thereby circumventing the recognized procedures for doing so. Elias v. United States, 91-1 USTC ¶ 50,040 (CD Cal. 1990); Coplin & Assocs., Inc. v. United States, 814 F. Supp. 643 (WD Mich. 1992).

[564] Mallas v. United States, 993 F2d 1111 (4th Cir. 1993).

[565] Mallas v. United States, 993 F2d 1111 (4th Cir. 1993).

In summary, circuit courts have divided over the existence of a nonstatutory public records exception to the general rule of Section 6103 that tax returns and return information are confidential. The Ninth Circuit (*Schrambling Accountancy Corp.*), followed by the Sixth Circuit (*Rawley*) have concluded that a public records exception exists, while the Fourth Circuit (*Mallas*) and the Tenth Circuit (*Rodgers*) have decided that there is no such nonstatutory exception.[566] The Seventh Circuit (*Thomas*) has looked to the source of the information in disclosure, finding that a press release prepared from a Tax Court opinion did not disclose the taxpayer's return information.[567] Finally, the Fifth Circuit (*Johnson*) has sided with the Fourth and Tenth Circuits in rejecting the public records exception to return confidentiality, but modified the rule by adopting the source analysis of the Seventh Circuit.[568] The Service recognizes that no statutory authority supports a public record exception to return information confidentiality, and that there is conflict among the circuits. Therefore, the IRS Manual warns personnel about using the public record exception as a basis for making disclosure of otherwise confidential tax information without advice from the Office of Chief Counsel.[569]

---

[566] Schrambling Accountancy Corp. v. United States, 937 F2d 1484, 1488–1489 (9th Cir. 1991), cert. denied, 112 S. Ct. 956 (1992); Rowley v. United States, 77 AFTR2d 96-1071 (6th Cir. 1996); Mallas v. United States, 993 F2d 1111 (4th Cir. 1993); Rodgers v. Hyatt, 697 F2d 899 (10th Cir. 1983).

[567] Thomas v. United States, 890 F2d 18 (7th Cir. 1989).

[568] Johnson v. Sawyer, 120 F3d 1307 (5th Cir. 1997) (the protection of Section 6103 "does not disappear simply because tax return information has been disclosed in the public record and has therefore lost its confidentiality . . . [and the taxpayer's interest in limiting disclosure] is furthered by a construction of [S]ection 6103 that premises a violation on the *source* of the information claimed to be wrongfully disclosed, not its public or nonconfidential *status*").

[569] IRM 1.3, Disclosure of Official Information Handbook 11.13 (Aug. 19, 1998) (Information Which Has Become Public Record). The manual states that the Service's policy "permits and encourages press releases and responses to media inquiries regarding enforcement activities that have become public record," and that the Service "has consistently argued that tax information that has been placed in the public record in connection with tax administration is no longer confidential and cannot be 'disclosed' within the meaning of section 6103(k)(8) . . . if the Service has already made the information known in public records during tax administration activities." IRM 1.3, Disclosure of Official Information Handbook 11.13(2) and 11.13(3). Service personnel are instructed to exercise "great care" in determining whether information has actually become a matter of public record. The manual warns that "information which is supplemental to that which has become public is subject to the confidentiality provisions." Id.

[5] Disclosure in Tax Cases

Before 1977, the Justice Department's access to tax information maintained by the Service was not seriously restricted.[570] Even in instances where the Service had not referred a tax case to the Justice Department, a lawyer in the Justice Department or in a U.S. Attorney's office investigating a possible violation of the tax laws could obtain tax information upon written request. In addition to obtaining tax information about taxpayers who were subjects of investigations or parties to proceedings, Justice Department lawyers also obtained information from the Service about third persons who were actual or potential witnesses and about jurors.[571] Section 6103(h) now permits the Service, in matters of "tax administration," to disclose to the Justice Department a taxpayer's return or return information as part of a criminal investigation or trial preparation and for use in a proceeding to determine the taxpayer's criminal or civil tax liability.[572] A third person's return or return information may be disclosed to the Justice Department only if it reflects an item or transaction whose disclosure may be related to or affect the resolution of the taxpayer's liability.[573]

Section 6103(h) also codifies the written request procedure. If the Service previously referred a case to the Justice Department, it may make a later disclosure of tax information on its own.[574] Otherwise, a high-ranking Justice De-

---

[570] See General Explanation, supra note 273, at 319–320, reprinted in 1976-3 CB (vol. 2) 331–332.

[571] At one time, the Service provided tax information about prospective jurors in order to detect anti-IRS bias. This practice came to light in the tax prosecution of gambler Frank Costello and, although not approved, was held not to be a prejudicial attempt to find a jury "conditioned" in favor of the Service. United States v. Costello, 255 F2d 876 (2d Cir.), cert. denied, 357 US 937 (1958). On June 27, 1958, the Justice Department's Tax Division directed U.S. Attorneys to cease scanning tax returns of prospective jurors. However, lawyers from the Justice Department and U.S. Attorneys' offices then developed the practice of asking the Service whether it had investigated any prospective juror. If the Service responded in the affirmative, the Service supplied information relating to the investigation. Report to Administrative Conference, supra note 487, at 948–952.

[572] The term "tax administration" is defined in the broadest possible language. IRC § 6103(b)(4). At least one circuit court has given this term even wider scope to include a criminal prosecution of a Service employee primarily on nontax charges where the employee's returns were used, inter alia, as handwriting exemplars. United States v. Mangan, 575 F2d 32 (2d Cir.), cert. denied, 439 US 931 (1978).

[573] IRC §§ 6103(h)(2)(B), 6103(h)(2)(C).

[574] The term "referral" has been interpreted broadly. A referral has been held made where the investigation originated with the Justice Department, which communicated its suspicions to the Service, which then made the request for investigation. United States v. Bachelor, 611 F2d 443 (3d Cir. 1979). See also United States v. Mangan, 575 F2d 32 (2d Cir.), cert. denied, 439 US 931 (1978), where returns were disclosed to the U.S. Attorney apparently before a referral was made. IRM 1.3, Disclosure of Official Information Handbook 22.12.2 (Aug. 19, 1998) (Referred Cases) ("Referral has traditionally included all tax cases where the Secretary has requested the Department of Justice to prosecute, defend, or

partment official must make a written request for the information. This request must come from the attorney general, a deputy attorney general, or an assistant attorney general, and must name the person whose return information is being sought and explain the need for the information.[575] Before 1997, both parties could inquire of the Service whether prospective jurors had been the subject of audit or tax investigation,[576] but the Taxpayer Relief Act of 1997 eliminated this type of disclosure.[577]

Thus, permissible disclosures to the Justice Department under Section 6103(h) fall into two categories: (1) disclosures made for use in and preparation for criminal investigations and proceedings and (2) disclosures for introduction and use in administrative or judicial proceedings.[578]

---

take other actions regarding a criminal matter before a Federal grand jury, or in civil and criminal Federal or State Judicial Proceedings. If The Secretary has analyzed a case, decided that the Justice Department should take action, it is a referred case.").

[575] IRC § 6103(h)(3)(B). The indication is that a request from no other Justice Department official complies with the statute. United States v. Mangan, 575 F2d 32 (2d Cir.), cert. denied, 439 US 931 (1978).

[576] Under former Section 6103(h)(5), the Service would answer yes or no. The request for jury panel information pursuant to Section 6103(h)(5) also had to be timely. When a party was denied access to Section 6103(h)(5) information, most courts held that a presumption of prejudice requiring reversal was created unless negated by the appropriate lines of questioning in voir dire. United States v. Hashimoto, 878 F2d 1126 (9th Cir. 1989); United States v. Nielsen, 1 F3d 855 (9th Cir. 1993) (Service made a substantial search supplying 17 of 100 names, and judge questioned prospective jurors about audit history, with two exceptions; held, Section 6103(h)(5) not violated); United States v. Masat, 896 F2d 88 (5th Cir. 1990) (incomplete audit history supplied, and motion for continuance made and denied; held, denial of motion was in error, but trial judge's questioning elicited same information called for by Section 6103(h)(5)); United States v. Schandl, 947 F2d 462 (11th Cir. 1991) (taxpayer's motion for jury panel information made three months before trial was denied, but judge asked jury panelists whether they had been audited; held, denial of motion for jury panel information effectively denied taxpayer his rights under Section 6103(h)(5)); United States v. Spine, 945 F2d 143 (6th Cir. 1991) (incomplete audit information supplied and motion for continuance denied, but extensive voir dire cured possible noncompliance with Section 6103(h)(5)). See United States v. Axmear, 964 F2d 792, 793 (8th Cir. 1992); United States v. Droge, 961 F2d 1030, 1032–1037 (2d Cir.), cert. denied, 113 S. Ct. 609 (1992). As these decisions suggest, several circuits refused to adopt a per se rule that reversal was required if a defendant was denied Section 6103(h)(5) information regarding a jury panel. But see United States v. Lussier, 929 F2d 25 (1st Cir. 1991) (Section 6103(h)(5) makes no provision for extreme alteration of normal trial arrangements); United States v. Huguenin, 950 F2d 23 (1st Cir. 1991) (error not committed when court cannot accommodate its docket to permit search of jury panel audit records if court obtains answers to voir dire questions).

[577] Former IRC § 6103(h)(5) was deleted by the Taxpayer Relief Act of 1997, § 1283(a), effective for judicial proceedings commenced after August 5, 1997.

[578] These two categories are discussed in more detail infra ¶¶ 4.07[5][a]–4.07[5][b].

[a] Preparation and Investigation Disclosures

Disclosure of a tax return or tax return information may be made to "officers and employees" (not merely attorneys) of the Department of Justice and the U.S. Attorneys' offices who are "personally and directly engaged in" preparing or presenting a case to a grand jury or to any federal or state court.[579] However, there are three limitations on this use. The Service may disclose this information only if

1. The taxpayer is a party to the proceeding;
2. The information is or may be related to the resolution of an issue in the proceeding; or
3. There is or may be a transactional relationship between a party (or potential party) and the taxpayer that affects or may affect an issue in the proceeding or investigation.

The first limitation applies to the taxpayer's return; the other two limitations apply to third-party returns.

The first restriction on access is a party limitation. If a taxpayer's civil or criminal tax liability is at issue, the Service may disclose the taxpayer's return or return information to the Justice Department.[580] Although disclosure is clearly authorized where the taxpayer is a party to the proceeding, the taxpayer need not be a party if the proceeding arises "out of, or in connection with" the determination or collection of the liability.

The second limitation is an item limitation. A third party's return or return information may be disclosed if it reflects the treatment of an item that is or may be relevant to the resolution of an issue in the proceeding or investigation.[581] The legislative history gives several examples.[582] Returns of Subchapter S corporations, partnerships, estates, and trusts can reflect the treatment of certain items that may be relevant to the taxpayer's liability because of some relationship of the taxpayer with the corporation, partnership, estate, or trust (i.e., as shareholder, partner, or beneficiary). Similarly, in cases involving assessment of a penalty for failure to pay over withholding taxes, items on corporate returns, such as wages paid, taxes withheld, and corporate office held by the person, can be relevant to the resolution of the liability issue. Finally, the treatment or absence of treatment of alleged loans and gifts on a return may be relevant to issues raised in criminal fraud cases involving the net worth method.

Under a third limitation or test, there must be a transactional relationship between the third party and the taxpayer whose liability is at issue. As stated

---

[579] IRC § 6103(h)(2).

[580] IRC § 6103(h)(2)(A).

[581] IRC § 6103(h)(2)(B).

[582] General Explanation, supra note 273, at 321, reprinted in 1976-3 CB (vol. 2) 333.

earlier, the Service may disclose a third-party return or return information to the Justice Department where it (1) relates to a transaction between the third party and the taxpayer whose liability is at issue and (2) may affect the resolution of the issue.[583] This transactional limitation appears to have been directed at "whipsaw" cases, where parties to a transaction treat its consequences differently. For example, the treatment on a buyer's return regarding the purchase of a business is relevant to the seller's tax liability resulting from the sale of the business. The buyer may be amortizing what he claims is a covenant not to compete, while the seller may be claiming capital gain treatment on the alleged sale of goodwill. But the transactional relationship test does have its limits. As the TRA 1976 legislative history makes clear, the Justice Department may not use tax returns of third parties to develop evidence such as compensation standards in reasonable compensation cases or prices in Section 482 cases where arm's-length prices for services and products may be at issue.[584] The Service takes the position that it may use third-party return information in its own administrative proceedings, such as a transfer pricing examination where the third-party information is used as comparable price data, and that the "item" and the "transactional relationship" tests only prevent it from disclosing the third-party information to the Justice Department.[585]

[b] Disclosures in Proceedings

Tax returns and return information may be disclosed in judicial and administrative proceedings in four situations.[586] First, the Service may disclose information to the Justice Department if the taxpayer is a party to the proceeding or if the information determines the taxpayer's civil or criminal tax liability or the collection of that liability. The second and third situations for

---

[583] IRC § 6103(h)(2)(C). The Service discloses tax returns or return information about potential witnesses where the intent is to impeach or impugn the witnesses or their testimony, only if the item or transaction tests are satisfied. IRM 1.3, Disclosure of Official Information Handbook, 22.12 (Aug. 19, 1998) (Disclosure to the Department of Justice in Tax Administration Matters), and 22.12.1 (Conditions for Disclosure).

[584] General Explanation, supra note 273, at 321, reprinted in 1976-3 CB (vol. 2) 333.

[585] IRM 1.3, Disclosure of Official Information Handbook 22.20(5) (Aug. 19, 1998) (Use and Disclosure of Third Party Returns and Return Information Relating to Transactions).

[586] IRC § 6103(h)(4). If the testimony of the Service employee is in error, the testimony does not constitute an unauthorized disclosure, at least not when there is no evidence that the misstatements were intentional or knowing. Noske v. United States, 92-2 USTC ¶ 50,429 (D. Minn. 1992) (disclosure of return information of nontaxpayers was authorized because they structured fraudulent conveyance scheme for taxpayers and so had transactional relationship with them); Traxler v. United States, 88-2 USTC ¶ 9627 (ED Cal. 1988) (Section 7431 makes actionable only disclosures that are unauthorized, not those that are simply inaccurate).

disclosure involve third-party returns. Such information may be disclosed in a tax proceeding, subject to the same item and transaction tests applicable in disclosures to the Justice Department, except that the items and transactions must have a "direct relationship" to the resolution of an issue in the proceeding. Thus, the second test for disclosure of a third party's return requires that the treatment of an item reflected on the return be directly related to the resolution of an issue in the proceeding.[587] Under the third test, the return or information must directly relate to a transactional relationship between a party and the taxpayer that directly affects the resolution of an issue in the proceeding.[588] Courts have differed in their approach to this transactional test. One circuit court has interpreted the test liberally and held that the transactional relationship of the third party need only affect "an issue" in the proceeding, not necessarily the taxpayer-party's liability.[589] The district court in *Datamatics* adopted a four-part test that is more restrictive. This test requires that the following conditions be met:

1. The disclosure must occur in the course of a judicial or administrative tax proceeding;
2. A party to the proceeding must have a transactional relationship with the taxpayer whose return information is disclosed;
3. The transactional relationship must directly affect the resolution of an issue in the proceeding; and
4. The disclosure must directly relate to the transactional relationship between the party and the taxpayer.[590]

---

[587] IRC § 6103(h)(4)(B). But see Beresford v. United States, 123 FRD 232 (ED Mich. 1988) (Service required to provide disclosure information on which it based valuation in estate case related to resolution of valuation issue in a judicial proceeding involving beneficiaries).

[588] IRC § 6103(h)(4)(C).

[589] Tavery v. United States, 32 F3d 1423, 1429–1430 (10th Cir. 1994); First W. Gov't Secs., Inc. v. United States, 796 F2d 356, 361 (10th Cir. 1986). See Ryan v. United States, 82 AFTR2d 98-7454 (D. Md. 1998) (a defense witness's tax return information was held to have a transactional relationship with an issue in the defendants' prosecution for evasion of tax on unreported skimming income because the disparity between the income the witness reported on his tax return and his lifestyle suggested that he was involved in the skimming operation with defendants).

[590] Datamatics Servs. Corp. v. United States, 88-1 USTC ¶ 9163 (CD Cal. 1987). See also McDonald v. United States, 75 AFTR2d 95-2366 (ED Cal. 1995) (applying the four-part *Datamatics* test and finding that the government was entitled to summary judgment on allegations that revenue agent's report disclosed plaintiff's name and return information about a loan to the taxpayer when it was sent to the taxpayer's attorney). Beresford v. United States, 123 FRD 122 (WD Mich. 1988) (in estate tax valuation cases, the court compelled the Service to disclose documents relating to third-party taxpayer's treatment of the value of stock and Service treatment of that valuation because information was directly related to issue in suit).

Only that part of the third party's return that reflects the item or transaction in question is subject to disclosure both before and during the tax proceeding. The statutory restrictions on disclosure were designed to prevent the return of a third-party witness from being introduced in a tax proceeding for the purpose of discrediting him as a witness, except on the item and transaction directly related to the proceeding.[591] Section 6103(h)(4)(C) also seems to authorize disclosures to the Department of Justice.[592] The Service was permitted under this section to disclose to investors with a broker/dealer in government securities who had claimed his Fifth Amendment privilege on the ground that the audit was an administrative proceeding, and that the investors to whom the matter was disclosed were themselves parties to the audit.[593]

Finally, disclosure is authorized in criminal cases where required under federal criminal discovery rules. In a criminal case, a district court may order disclosure of a tax return or tax return information under the Jencks Act[594] or under Rule 16 of the Federal Rules of Criminal Procedure, both of which provide for discovery. Before making such a ruling, the court must first give consideration to the congressional policy concerning confidentiality of returns and return information.[595] The Service may refuse to disclose third-party return information for use in a tax proceeding if it determines that the disclosure would identify a confidential informant or seriously impair a pending civil or criminal tax investigation.

[6] Disclosure for Nontax Purposes

Tax returns and tax return information have played a significant role in the discovery and prosecution of violations of nontax federal criminal laws. Before 1977, lawyers in the Justice Department and U.S. Attorneys' offices obtained tax information relating to the defendant and defense witnesses during an investigation, the pretrial period, and at times the trial itself.[596] This tax informa-

---

[591] General Explanation, supra note 273, at 321, reprinted in 1976-3 CB (vol. 2) 333. In Davidson v. Brady, 559 F. Supp. 456 (WD Mich. 1983), the U.S. Attorney attached the financial statement, Form 433, of a third party to a presentence memorandum to show that the defendant had lied to the Probation Office about his debt to that third party. The disclosure was held to be permitted under Section 6103(h)(4)(C).

[592] Cf. Chamberlain v. Kurtz, 589 F2d 827 (5th Cir.), cert. denied, 444 US 842 (1979).

[593] First W. Gov't Secs., Inc. v. United States, 578 F. Supp. 212 (D. Colo. 1984), aff'd, 796 F2d 356 (10th Cir. 1986).

[594] 18 USC § 3500.

[595] IRC § 6103(h)(4)(D).

[596] General Explanation, supra note 273, at 322–323, reprinted in 1976-3 CB (vol. 2) 334–335. In 1975, U.S. Attorneys made 1,350 requests pertaining to 17,678 tax returns of 4,330 taxpayers.

tion was used to cross-examine and impeach the defendant and his witnesses. Government lawyers even obtained tax returns of government witnesses to evaluate their proposed testimony and general credibility. To obtain leads, government lawyers also obtained tax information pertaining to third persons who had some transactional or other relationship with the defendant. The use to which a tax return might be put, even in a nontax criminal prosecution, is illustrated by *United States v. Garner*,[597] a prosecution for various federal crimes arising out of interstate gambling. The government introduced Garner's tax returns for three years; in each of those three years he reported that he was a professional gambler and had derived substantial income from "gambling" or "wagering." The government relied on Garner's familiarity with wagering and gambling, as reflected on his return, "to help rebut his claim that his relationships with other conspirators were innocent ones."[598]

In Section 6103(i), Congress adopted the policy that disclosure of tax returns in nontax criminal cases should be more restricted than in tax prosecutions and that in nontax civil cases tax returns may not be disclosed at all. In nontax criminal cases, with one exception, disclosure may be made by the Service to the Justice Department or another federal agency only on the grant of an ex parte order of a federal district court judge. Furthermore, this order may only be sought on the authorization of the highest-ranking Justice Department or agency official.[599] The rationale for this procedure is the congressional decision that "the information that the American citizen is compelled by our tax laws to disclose to the Internal Revenue Service is entitled to essentially the same degree of privacy as those private papers maintained in his home."[600] Section 6103(i) does not preclude the Service from disclosing to the Justice Department or any other agency information received from sources other than the taxpayer and his representative that would indicate the commission of a nontax federal crime.[601] For similar reasons, the Service is authorized to disclose returns and return information for purposes other than tax administration. Reports of payments in currency in excess of $10,000 (Forms 8300), are filed by third parties with the Service. Upon written request, the Service may disclose these reports of payments in currency, Forms 8300, to any federal

---

[597] United States v. Garner, 424 US 648 (1978).

[598] United States v. Garner, 424 US 648, 650 (1978).

[599] IRC § 6103(i)(1). Authorization must be from the attorney general, deputy attorney general, or assistant attorney general or, if the request is not from the Justice Department, the head of the requesting agency. The Service will adhere strictly to this rule. United States v. Mangan, 575 F2d 32 (2d Cir.), cert. denied, 439 US 931 (1978).

[600] General Explanation, supra note 273, at 328, reprinted in 1976-3 CB (vol. 2) 340.

[601] IRC § 6103(i)(3). The legislative history indicates that before this disclosure may be made the information must be clearly identified as being from sources other than and segregable from taxpayer disclosures. General Explanation, supra note 273, at 325, reprinted in 1976-3 CB (vol. 2) 337.

agency, state or local government, or any agency of a foreign government, as long as the disclosure is not for the purposes of tax administration.[602]

The provisions of Section 6103(i) do not require that the taxpayer be notified of the request, nor do they require that the taxpayer be given an opportunity to oppose the disclosure, as the proceedings are ex parte. However, the district court judge is authorized to issue the ex parte disclosure order only if the government shows sufficient facts to establish the following:

- There is "reasonable cause" to believe, based on information considered to be reliable, that a specific criminal act has been committed.
- There is reason to believe that the return or return information is probative or may be relevant to a matter relating to the commission of a criminal act.
- The return or return information is sought exclusively for use in a federal criminal investigation or proceeding concerning a criminal act, and the information sought to be disclosed cannot reasonably be obtained from any other source.

This showing is made to the district court judge in camera to avoid any unnecessary publicity of the matter.[603] Also, only the parts of the return or return information determined to meet the requirements for disclosure are subject to disclosure.[604]

In 1982, significant changes were made to Section 6103(i).[605] Before amendment, information could be obtained only by way of an ex parte order by a federal district court judge, and return information from sources other than the taxpayer could be obtained only by a written request of high-ranking agency officials to the Service. After amendment, Section 6103(i) permits a magistrate judge as well as a federal district court judge to grant the ex parte order, and permits disclosures to be made to officers and employees of a federal agency who are personally and directly engaged in any federal grand jury proceeding involving enforcement of a federal nontax criminal statute.[606] Offi-

---

[602] IRC § 6103(l)(15), as amended by the Taxpayer Bill of Rights 2, § 1206(a), effective upon the enactment date, July 30, 1996. The disclosure is required to be made on the same basis, and subject to the same conditions, as apply to disclosures of information on currency transaction reports filed under the Bank Secrecy Act, 31 USC § 5313. For a description of (1) how these reports are used in criminal investigations and (2) how the efforts to evade their being filed may serve as an independent basis for prosecution, see Chapter 12.

[603] United States v. Praetorius, 451 F. Supp. 371 (EDNY 1978). See also General Explanation, supra note 273, at 324, reprinted in 1976-3 CB (vol. 2) 336.

[604] General Explanation, supra note 273, at 324, reprinted in 1976-3 CB (vol. 2) 336.

[605] IRC § 6103(i)(1)(A), as amended by the Tax Equity and Fiscal Responsibility Act of 1982, Pub. L. No. 97-248, § 356(a).

[606] IRC §§ 6103(i)(1)(A)(i)–6103(i)(1)(A)(iii).

cials who may authorize application for court-ordered disclosure were also changed. Except for the attorney general, agency heads no longer have authority to ask for such orders, but the number of officials in the Department of Justice who can request the order is increased and now includes any special prosecutor.[607] The standards for issuing the ex parte order have been revised, making the requisite showing by the government less stringent. Before the changes, the information sought had to be probative evidence of a matter in issue related to the commission of a criminal act that could not reasonably be obtained from another source. (Or even if it could be, the return information constituted the most probative evidence of the matter in issue in the criminal investigation.) Now, it need only be shown that the return or return information (1) "is or may be relevant to a matter relating to the commission" of the suspected criminal act and (2) is sought exclusively for use in a federal criminal investigation of the suspected criminal act, and the information sought to be disclosed cannot be obtained, under the circumstances, from another source.[608]

As a result of other modifications of the disclosure rules, persons who may authorize application for court-ordered disclosure may also authorize disclosure of returns and return information for the purpose of locating fugitives.[609] Information not supplied to the Service by the taxpayer may be disclosed to a wider range of government officials.[610] On written request, a taxpayer's Social Security number and name and address may also be disclosed for use in a nontax criminal investigation.[611] In emergency situations (imminent danger of death or physical injury to any individual), the Service may notify federal officials of return information to the extent necessary to apprise them of the imminent flight of a taxpayer-suspect.[612] The use of tax information in nontax administrative or judicial proceedings is expanded to include disclosure in civil forfeiture proceedings, as required by the Jencks Act (18 USC § 3500) or Federal Rules of Criminal Procedure 16.[613]

[a] Ex Parte Application

The restrictions placed on a law enforcement agency that is attempting to secure tax returns or tax information for nontax criminal purposes are not as

---

[607] IRC § 6103(i)(1)(B).

[608] IRC § 6103(i)(1)(B)(ii).

[609] IRC § 6103(i)(5)(A).

[610] IRC § 6103(i)(2)(A).

[611] IRC § 6103(i)(4)(B).

[612] IRC §§ 6103(i)(3)(B)(i), 6103(i)(3)(B)(ii).

[613] IRC § 6103(i)(4)(A).

substantial as they might appear.[614] The first element requires the Justice Department or other agency to establish "reasonable cause," not "probable cause," for the belief a crime has been committed. Probable cause invokes the Fourth Amendment justification for an invasion of a person's privacy by way of a search warrant. Whatever else it may mean for purposes of search and seizure, probable cause requires a magistrate to consider the probabilities and to determine whether a more-than-50-percent probability of those elements necessary for a lawful search exists. Congress intentionally adopted a "reasonable cause" standard to require a lesser showing in disclosure situations.[615] Thus, the first element is satisfied, where it is shown that the probability that a crime has been committed is less than 50 percent, on the basis of information believed to be reliable.[616]

To establish the second element, it need be shown only that the return or return information "is or may be relevant to a matter relating to the commission of the suspected criminal act."[617] This standard is the standard of relevance for purposes of a grand jury subpoena and a Service summons. As a practical and legal matter, it permits the government attorney to seek a return or return information for use in a so-called fishing expedition. The only limitation on relevance would seem to be derived from the third element in the required showing, namely that the information be relevant to an investigation or proceeding concerning the alleged criminal act, because the third element requires that information be sought "exclusively for use in" the criminal investigation or proceeding.

The third element of proof in the ex parte disclosure proceeding also appears to require an attempt to secure the information directly from the taxpayer or his accountant. However, federal law enforcement officers contend that notifying a taxpayer of a pending investigation might seriously impair that investigation. Accordingly, it can be expected that the Justice Department and other

---

[614] The Privacy Protection Study Commission criticized these rules, contending that federal agencies should have no easier access to return information than they would if the information were sought from the taxpayer himself. Accordingly, the commission recommended a hearing or notice to the taxpayer in which the agency had to establish "probable cause" to believe a violation had occurred, that the information was "probative evidence" that the violation had occurred, and that there was no legal impediment (by Fifth Amendment claim) to obtaining the information directly from the taxpayer. Report of the Privacy Protection Study Commission, supra note 491, App. 2, at 41.

[615] General Explanation, supra note 273, at 324, reprinted in 1976-3 CB (vol. 2) 336.

[616] If search warrant cases are any guide, information may be considered reliable where sources are disclosed, such as direct observation, admissions, reasonable conclusions drawn from circumstantial evidence or information from a person in a position to know, or where the source is not disclosed, but sufficient details to support the conclusion have been corroborated. See Spinelli v. United States, 393 US 410 (1969); Draper v. United States, 358 US 307 (1959).

[617] IRC § 6103(i)(1)(B)(ii).

agencies will interpret the provision as not requiring any prior direct approach to the taxpayer.[618] There is no requirement that the information first be sought from the taxpayer or another source, apart from the Service.[619]

[b] Third-Party Source Information

Disclosure of information obtained from third-party sources (e.g., bank records, customer records, or supplier records) may be requested in writing from the Department of Justice or another federal agency.[620] No judicial review is required. The written request need only specify the name of the taxpayer, the kind of tax involved, the taxable period involved, and the reason why inspection is desired. The rationale for the distinction between disclosure of information provided by the taxpayer and disclosure of information about the taxpayer provided by other sources is not entirely clear. Apparently, Congress concluded that the Fifth Amendment and privacy concerns applicable where information is submitted by the taxpayer do not apply where information is supplied to the Service by another source.[621] This decision is curiously inconsistent with the third-party summons rules of Section 7609, which require the Service to give a taxpayer notice and an opportunity to object to a summons served on certain third parties who keep records relating to the taxpayer.[622]

[c] Use in Proceeding or Trial

Once the Justice Department or any federal agency has received returns or return information pursuant to the court order procedure, further disclosure in an administrative hearing or trial relating to the violation of a nontax criminal law is not allowed unless there is a showing to the presiding hearing officer or judge that the return information is "probative of a matter in issue relevant in establishing the commission of a crime or the guilt or liability of a party," or to the extent required by the Jencks Act (18 USC § 3500) or the criminal discovery rule (Fed. R. Crim. P. 16).[623] A return or return information may not be

---

[618] See Report of the Privacy Protection Study Commission, supra note 491, App. 2, at 43.

[619] IRC § 6103(i)(5)(A).

[620] IRC § 6103(i)(2).

[621] General Explanation, supra note 273, at 324–325, reprinted in 1976-3 CB (vol. 2) 336–337. The failure to provide the same protection in the form of court review to third-party-source information was also criticized by the Privacy Protection Study Commission. See Report of the Privacy Protection Study Commission, supra note 491, App. 2, at 44–45.

[622] The third-party summons procedures are discussed at Chapter 13.

[623] IRC § 6103(i)(4)(A). However, the judge may not enter an order unless the request is authorized by the attorney general, deputy attorney general, or assistant attorney

used and be admissible for purposes of collateral impeachment (i.e., discrediting a witness on matters not bearing on the question of guilt of the defendant). Nevertheless, if the return or return information is admitted into evidence without court order or for an authorized purpose, the error is not reversible in any appeal of a judgment or conviction.[624] The Tax Equity and Fiscal Responsibility Act of 1982 amended Section 6103(i)(4) by, among other things, extending disclosure to civil forfeiture proceedings, and permits the use of return information other than taxpayer return information in criminal and civil forfeiture proceedings.[625]

[7] Disclosure to State Tax Officials

Upon the written request of a state official other than the governor, the Service may disclose to the authorized representatives of a state agency or commission named in the request returns any return information for the purpose of administering state tax laws.[626] To satisfy the written request requirement and other provisions of Section 6103(d), the Service has entered into Agreements on Coordination of Tax Administration with each of the fifty states and the District of Columbia. These agreements on coordination have been held to satisfy the written request requirement of Section 6103(d).[627] However, such dis-

---

general, or, if an agency other than the Justice Department is involved, the head of that agency. United States v. Mangan, 575 F2d 32 (2d Cir.), cert. denied, 439 US 931 (1978).

[624] IRC § 6103(i)(4)(E).

[625] IRC § 6103(i)(4)(B).

[626] IRC § 6103(d). See Rev. Proc. 85-33, 1985-2 CB 414 (procedures for federal and state agencies to request data from the Service). It has been held that an investigation by state tax authorities to enforce a personnel regulation prohibiting state revenue employees from moonlighting is "tax administration" within Section 6103(d). Rueckert v. Gore, 587 F. Supp. 1238 (ND Ill. 1984), aff'd, 775 F2d 208 (7th Cir. 1985) (although disclosure of tax return information was made in violation of Section 6103, no liability was imposed because the mistake was made in good faith).

Courts hold that when a state has entered into a coordination agreement with the Service, which contains a blanket request for return information under Section 6103(d), the agreement, while written in general terms, is sufficient to satisfy both the written request requirement (because the coordination agreement is effectively a blanket request) and the written designation requirement (because nothing in Section 6103(d) is said to suggest that the designation cannot be a general one). Smith v. United States, 964 F2d 630 (7th Cir. 1992), cert. denied, 506 US 1067 (1993), followed in McQueen v. United States, 81 AFTR2d 98-646 (SD Tex. 1998) (the tax implementation agreement was held merely to establish ancillary procedures, rather than the specific request found in the coordination agreement).

[627] Long v. United States, 972 F2d 1174 (10th Cir. 1992); Taylor v. United States, 106 F3d 833 (8th Cir. 1997) ("Disclosure of individual taxpayer information by the IRS to a state taxing authority via a standing written agreement that is carefully crafted to satisfy

closure may not be made unless the state adopts a law protecting the confidentiality of federal returns and return information.[628] Also, Section 6103(a)(2) requires that officers or employees of the state treat the tax information furnished by the Service as confidential. The provisions of Section 6103(d) permit the disclosure of income, estate, gift, Social Security (FICA), unemployment (FUTA), self-employment (SECA), withholding, alcohol, tobacco, and highway use tax returns and return information[629] solely for use in the administration of a state's tax laws.[630] Disclosure may also be made to the legal representative of the state tax agency for the purpose of administering state tax laws subject to the statutory relevancy tests that apply to the Department of Justice's access to returns and return information in a federal tax investigation or in tax litigation.

---

concerns for confidentiality implements . . . the will of Congress"); Smith v. United States, 964 F2d 630 (7th Cir. 1992), cert. denied, 506 US 1067 (1993).

A Chief Counsel Notice, entitled Pilot Program for Coordination of FedState matters, describes procedures to be used in the Service's program "to facilitate joint administration projects with state and qualifying local agencies that improve compliance with federal, state, and local tax laws and enable the Service, state and local qualifying agencies to perform their responsibilities more efficiently and cost effectively." Chief Counsel Notice N(35)000-150(b) (Aug. 5, 1998), reprinted in 1999 TNT 48-23. The Service has designated FedState Coordinators in the districts and at each regional office to oversee and coordinate the program; it has also created an Office of FedState Relations in the National Office.

[628] IRC § 6103(p)(4). Apparently, states are not required to enact criminal statutes eqivalent to Section 7213, although the statute (IRC § 7213(a)(2)) applies to state employees.

[629] The procedure of allowing state tax authorities to receive third-party source information the Service has collected, as opposed to written conclusions it has reached on tax issues, seems open to question. But courts have found no disclosure of return information. A district court rejected a taxpayer claim that the disclosure by the Service to Massachusetts tax authorities of the taxpayer's Form 1902-E (Report of Individual Income Tax Audit Changes) violated the confidentiality rules of Section 6103. Davis v. United States, 80-2 USTC ¶ 9794 (D. Mass. 1980), aff'd, 81-1 USTC ¶ 9458 (1st Cir. 1981); Bator v. Department of Treasury, 89-1 USTC ¶ 9138 (D. Nev. 1988), aff'd in unpublished opinion, 899 F2d 1224 (9th Cir. 1990) (disclosure of tax return information by Service to California tax agency pursuant to IRS-California tax convention held permissible under Section 6103(d)).

[630] The Service may also disclose returns and return information relating to alcohol, tobacco, and firearms taxes to federal agencies under Section 6103(o)(1). But disclosure to state authorities of gambling excise tax information appears prohibited by Section 4424, which is incorporated by reference in Section 6103(o)(2).

[8] Penalties for Disclosure

Civil damages for unauthorized disclosure of returns and return information may be obtained by a taxpayer under Section 7431. Not all disclosures are compensable. The disclosure must be made by one of the persons described in Sections 6103(a)(1) through 6103(a)(3)[631]; that is, (1) an "officer or employee of the United States"; (2) an "officer or employee of any State or of any local child support enforcement agency"; or (3) any other person who has access to the information in the capacity of a shareholder, an officer of an educational institution for the purpose of collecting student loans, or a person processing return information for purposes of tax administration.[632] In addition, the disclosing person will not be liable under Section 7431 unless the person acted (1) "knowingly or by reason of negligence" and (2) in violation of Section 6103.[633] Liability is not imposed under Section 7431 for any disclosure that results from "a good faith, but erroneous interpretation of Section 6103."[634]

The crux of the complaint for damages under Section 7431 is a violation of Section 6103.[635] As a result, civil liability exists in one of two possible scenarios: (1) where the person who disclosed the information is described in Sections 6103(a)(1) through 6103(a)(3) or (2) where the person who disclosed the information is not named in Section 6103, but there is no basis for recovery.[636]

---

[631] IRC §§ 7431(a)(1), 7431(a)(2); see Hudson Valley Freedom Theatre, Inc. v. Heimbach, 513 F. Supp. 250 (SDNY), rev'd, 671 F2d 702 (2d Cir. 1981), cert. denied, 459 US 857 (1982) (claim that county official violated Section 6103 was rejected). In Stokwitz v. United States, 831 F2d 893 (9th Cir. 1987), cert. denied, 108 S. Ct. 1592 (1988), Navy employees unlawfully seized copies of the taxpayer's returns and used them in the Navy Department's decision to discharge the taxpayer. The Ninth Circuit dismissed the taxpayer's wrongful disclosure action against the Navy, on the ground that Section 7431 did not apply, because "the statute is concerned solely with the flow of tax data to, from, or through the IRS" (footnote omitted).

[632] IRC §§ 6103(a)(1)–6103(a)(3).

[633] IRC §§ 7431(a)(1), 7431(a)(2).

[634] IRC § 7431(b).

[635] Actual damages of $1,000 were recovered (but punitive damages denied) from a District Chief of the Criminal Investigation Division where he disclosed an allegation that a taxpayer was involved in stolen oil to persons whom he did not believe had any information about the taxpayer. Rodgers v. Hyatt, 697 F2d 899 (10th Cir. 1983), aff'g 81-1 USTC ¶ 9218 (D. Colo. 1981). For other cases brought under Section 7431, see Davidson v. Brady, 559 F. Supp. 456 (WD Mich. 1983), aff'd, 732 F2d 552 (6th Cir. 1984); United States v. President, 591 F. Supp. 1313 (ND Ill. 1984); United States v. Crans, 517 F. Supp. 863 (NDNY 1981). See also Huckaby v. United States, 804 F2d 297 (5th Cir. 1986) (damages of $1,000 awarded for improper disclosure by Service agent to state agency); Malis v. United States, 87-1 USTC ¶ 9212 (CD Cal. 1986) (damages of $6,000 awarded where special agent made disclosures in course of social relationship).

[636] See Hudson Valley Freedom Theatre, Inc. v. Heimbach, 513 F. Supp. 250 (SDNY), rev'd, 671 F2d 702 (2d Cir. 1981), cert. denied, 459 US 857 (1982) (claim that county official violated Section 6103 rejected). In Stokwitz v. United States, 831 F2d 893

When disclosures were made in violation of Section 6103, damages have been awarded.[637] If the disclosure is permitted by Section 6103, however, courts have denied claims for damages. Examples are claims where disclosures have been made for tax administration purposes under Section 6103(k),[638] or where information has already been disclosed under authority of some other provision of Section 6103, such as in a tax case in court (Section 6103(h)).[639] Even when

---

(9th Cir. 1987), cert. denied, 108 S. Ct. 1592 (1988), Navy employees unlawfully seized copies of the taxpayer's returns and used them in the Navy Department's decision to discharge the taxpayer. The Ninth Circuit dismissed the taxpayer's wrongful disclosure action against the Navy on the ground that Section 7431 did not apply because "the statute is concerned solely with the flow of tax data to, from, or through the IRS" (footnote omitted).

[637] Actual damages of $1,000 were recovered (but punitive damages denied) when a District Chief of the Criminal Investigation Division disclosed an allegation that a taxpayer was involved in stolen oil to persons whom he did not believe had any information about the taxpayer. Rodgers v. Hyatt, 697 F2d 899 (10th Cir. 1983), aff'g 81-1 USTC ¶ 9218 (D. Colo. 1981). For other cases brought under Section 7431, see Davidson v. Brady, 559 F. Supp. 456 (WD Mich. 1983), aff'd, 732 F2d 552 (6th Cir. 1984); United States v. President, 591 F. Supp. 1313 (ND Ill. 1984); United States v. Crans, 517 F. Supp. 863 (NDNY 1981); Huckaby v. United States, 804 F2d 297 (5th Cir. 1986) (damages of $1,000 awarded for improper disclosure by Service agent to state agency); Malis v. United States, 87-1 USTC ¶ 9212 (CD Cal. 1986) (damages of $6,000 were awarded where special agent made disclosures in course of social relationship).

A taxpayer may not recover against a Service official for wrongful disclosure in a *Bivens* action, because reputation is not a protected liberty, nor is failure to provide a required notice before collecting a tax a violation of clearly established law. Morales v. Haynes, 890 F2d 708 (5th Cir. 1989) (revenue officer disclosed to local police during seizure of property). However, in Johnson v. Sawyer, 980 F2d 1490 (5th Cir. 1992), a divided panel of the circuit court upheld a $5 million judgment against the Service under the FTCA arising out of Service press release disclosures that resulted in the termination of the taxpayer's employment. The theory of the FTCA complaint was that under Texas tort law, the violation of the standard of behavior set forth in Section 6103 was negligence per se when the person afforded protection of the standard is damaged by its violation. However, on rehearing the Fifth Circuit sitting en banc, reversed the decision of the panel of the court. Johnson v. Sawyer, 47 F3d 716 (5th Cir. 1995). On remand, Johnson recovered compensatory damages of $6 million and punitive damages ranging from $1.5 to $1.6 million. Johnson v. Sawyer, 77 AFTR2d 96-2383 (SD Tex. 1996).

[638] In Mid-South Music Corp. v. Kolak, 756 F2d 23 (6th Cir. 1984), the claim that prefiling notice letter presented colorable claim of violation of Section 6103, but claim under Section 7431(a) is against United States, not individual agents. On remand, the district court in *Mid-South Music Corp.* found that unauthorized disclosures had occurred and that compensatory damages of $174,000, plus punitive damages of $1,000, were owed by the Service. 85-2 USTC ¶ 9782 (D. Tenn. 1985). On appeal, the Sixth Circuit reversed on the ground that no disclosure had occurred. 818 F2d 536 (6th Cir. 1987).

[639] A taxpayer has been denied damages for wrongful disclosure of tax return information where the Service and the U.S. Attorney's Office issued press releases about a government suit for a tax shelter injunction. Lampert v. United States, 87-1 USTC ¶ 9361 (ND Cal. 1987), aff'd, 854 F2d 335 (9th Cir. 1988) (press release assumed, on authority of Johnson v. Sawyer, 640 F. Supp. 1126 (SD Tex. 1986), to be violation of Section

a taxpayer presents evidence that a Service agent has made a wrongful disclosure, courts have regularly found that the taxpayer was not entitled to damages because the agent acted in good faith, but erroneously interpreted Section 6103.[640]

An action for wrongful disclosure is filed in a U.S. district court,[641] and the suit is brought against the United States, if the disclosing person is a government employee of the United States. If the disclosing person is not an employee of the United States, the suit is brought against the person in his or her name.[642] An action for wrongful disclosure must be commenced within two years from the date of discovery of the unauthorized disclosure of return infor-

---

6103, but good faith found because under then-existing tax law press release was not a violation of Section 6103, and Service and Justice Department procedures were followed; good faith standard analyzed). In a related case, an injunction to enjoin disclosure was denied. United Energy Corp. v. United States, 622 F. Supp. 43 (ND Cal. 1985) (promoter who instituted injunction proceeding to stop Service investigation disclosed certain parts of its return information and "lost any entitlement to privacy in that information"). See also Thomas v. United States, 87-2 USTC ¶ 9631 (ED Wis. 1987); Rubel v. United States, 89-1 USTC ¶ 9149 (WDNC 1988) (damages for disclosures in postconviction press release denied because the government officers acted in good faith and had solid basis in interpretation of Section 6103).

[640] See, e.g., Diamond v. United States, 944 F2d 431 (8th Cir. 1991) (erroneous interpretation of regulation applicable to circular letters in criminal investigations was held to have been made in good faith). Even if a circular letter sent by a special agent wrongfully discloses that the taxpayer is under criminal investigation, the disclosure is said to have been made in good faith when the Internal Revenue Manual § 347.2 recommended the disclosure. Schachter v. United States, 866 F. Supp. 1273 (ND Cal. 1994) (citing *Diamond*). However, the standard for applying the "good faith" defense in actions under Section 7431 is an objective standard. Id.; Lebaron v. United States, 794 F. Supp. 947, 955 (CD Cal. 1992) ("[t]he issue is whether the disclosure was contrary to clearly established statutory or constitutional rights of which a reasonable person would have known").

When a disclosure violates Section 6103, the Eighth Circuit has held that "[t]he burden of pleading and proving good faith under [S]ection 7431 rests with the government, not the complaining party." Jones v. United States, 97 F3d 1121 (1996) (the plaintiff in a wrongful disclosure action is not required to prove the government employee's bad faith). In *Jones*, a special agent disclosed the taxpayer's return information to an informant, testified that he had failed to consult IRS Manuals or anyone in the Service before disclosing the information to the informant, and could not cite the specific statute governing disclosure. The agent's disclosure was held to violate Section 6103 and to have been made knowingly or by reason of negligence.

[641] IRC § 7431(a).

[642] IRC § 7431(a)(1).

mation.[643] Statutory damages of $1,000 for each act of disclosure[644] and punitive damages may be recovered, but not both.[645] Even if the taxpayer recovers damages under Section 7431, the Service is permitted to set off the taxpayer's damages against a debt the taxpayer owes the government, such as a tax liability.[646]

The Taxpayer Bill of Rights 2[647] created a civil action for damages that a taxpayer may bring in what presumably is an unusual situation. When a taxpayer's tax adviser provides return information he or she received from the taxpayer to "an officer or employee of the United States" in exchange for a compromise of the adviser's tax liability, the taxpayer may recover damages. Section 7435 provides that a taxpayer may bring a civil action for damages against the United States in a federal district court (1) if any officer of the United States "intentionally compromises the determination or collection of any tax due from an attorney, certified public accountant, or enrolled agent representing a taxpayer," (2) in exchange for information the taxpayer gave to

---

[643] IRC § 7431(d); see, e.g., Mallas v. United States, 92-2 USTC ¶ 50,376 (MDNC 1992), aff'd on other grounds, 993 F2d 1111 (4th Cir. 1993) (complaint timely filed; plaintiffs did not know, and could not be deemed to have known, of alleged wrongful disclosures more than two years prior to filing of complaint); see, e.g., Simpson v. United States, 91-2 USTC ¶ 50,504 (ND Fla. 1991) (notices of lien alleged to have disclosed return information filed in 1985, 1986, and 1987; suit filed in 1990). See also Gandy v. United States, 82 AFTR2d 98-6873 (ED Tex. 1998) (circular letters in 1990, but suit not brought until 1996, and so held untimely).

It has been held that the cause of action for wrongful disclosure survives death because (1) entities as well as individuals can sue and it would be illogical to allow the surviving individual or a corporation to recover, but not the estate of an individual and (2) the statute also is meant to discourage "the tactic of governmental intimidation through disclosure" and to provide a property right in affected taxpayers in the form of damages. Schacter v. United States, 847 F. Supp. 140 (ND Cal. 1993) (one of two partners who instituted a suit for wrongful disclosure died); but see Shapiro v. Smith, 652 F. Supp. 218 (SD Fla. 1986) (finding that the primary thrust of the statute was to protect the individual's privacy right).

[644] For a case deciding what a "disclosure" is for damages purposes, see Mallas v. United States, 92-2 USTC ¶ 50,376 (MDNC 1992), aff'd on other grounds, 993 F2d 1111 (4th Cir. 1993).

[645] Mallas v. United States, 92-2 USTC ¶ 50,376 (MDNC 1992), aff'd on other grounds, 993 F2d 1111 (4th Cir. 1993).

[646] 31 USC § 3728 provides: "(a) The Comptroller General shall withhold paying that part of a judgment against the United States Government presented to the Comptroller General that is equal to the debt the plaintiff owes the Government." For a case where damages were applied to an outstanding tax liability, see Marre v. United States, 80 AFTR2d 97-5126 (5th Cir. 1997). The circuit court also held, however, that the Service could not offset an award of attorney fees because the award of damages and attorney fees under Section 7430 are separate awards, the damages belonging to the taxpayer and the attorney fees to the attorney, and there is no mutuality of debt between the attorney and the government.

[647] Taxpayer Bill of Rights 2, Pub L No. 104-168 (July 30, 1996).

the professional, (3) for the purpose of obtaining advice about the taxpayer's tax liability.[648] The taxpayer may recover damages in an amount equal to the lesser of $500,000, or the sum of the actual economic damages the taxpayer sustains as the proximate result of the information disclosure and costs of the action.

Criminal penalties. Willful unauthorized disclosure of tax returns and return information by a government officer or employee (or a nongovernmental employee performing work for the government) is a felony, punishable by a fine of up to $5,000 and imprisonment for up to five years, as well as loss of office (or employment) upon conviction.[649] Section 7213(a)(3) makes it a felony for any person who has received return information thereafter "to willfully print or publish [the return information] in any manner not provided by law." Section 7213(a)(4) makes it a felony to solicit return information for something of value and to receive the return information. Finally, Section 7216 makes it a misdemeanor for a preparer to disclose or use information furnished to him for the preparation of a return "knowingly or recklessly," except if disclosure is pursuant to some other provision of the Code, is ordered by a court, or is provided for by regulation.[650]

Browsing. When a Service employee in the Taxpayer Services Division, outside the scope of his official duties, knowingly disregarded the Service's rules by accessing one of the Service's computer systems to look for confidential return information of various individuals, he was prosecuted, not for unauthorized disclosure under Section 7213, but for mail fraud and computer fraud under 18 USC §§ 1343, 1346, and 1030(a)(4), crimes whose breadth are attractive to prosecutors. The convictions were reversed because there was insufficient evidence that the employee had done anything more than browsing by accessing taxpayer information, which was not a violation of Service rules.[651]

---

[648] IRC § 7435, added by the Taxpayer Bill of Rights 2, § 601(a), applicable to actions after the date of enactment, July 30, 1996. The cause of action is not permitted if the taxpayer disclosed the information to the professional adviser for the purpose of perpetrating a crime or fraud. Damages also do not include any tax liability for civil penalties, criminal fines, or other losses the taxpayer incurs due to incarceration or other criminal sanctions.

[649] IRC § 7213(a) (federal employees and other persons); IRC § 7213(2) (state and other employees).

[650] Reg. § 301.7216-1.

[651] United States v. Czubinski, 106 F3d 1069 (1st Cir. 1997). The court held that, to sustain a conviction for mail and computer fraud, the government had to prove that the employee had intended to deprive a person of their intangible property interest in their confidential information, and inteded to do so by using interstate wire transmissions. To deprive a person of their intangible property interest in their confidential information, the government had to prove that as a result of the employee's activities, the employee had harmed the holder of the information in some way, or that the employee had intended to have some gainful use of the confidential information by accessing it.

In a direct response to the this case, *United States v. Czubinski*, Congress made browsing (that is, willfully inspecting a return without specific authorization of a provision of Section 6103) by federal and state officers or employees, or other employees having access to tax return information a misdemeanor punishable by a fine of up to $1,000, or imprisonment of up to one year, or both, and discharge from office or employment.[652]

---

[652] IRC § 7213A, added by the Privacy Act of 1997 § 2(a), effective for violations after August 5, 1997. Civil damages for unauthorized inspection may also be recovered from the government equal to $1,000 for each act of unauthorized inspection, or actual damages, and in the case of willful conduct punitive damages, and attorney fees. IRC § 7431, as amended by the Privacy Act of 1997, § 3, effective for inspections and disclosures occurring after August 5, 1997. Congress has made unauthorized inspection of tax returns and tax return information (i.e., browsing of tax return information), by any federal employee, Service contractor, state employee, or other person who acquired tax return information under an exception to Section 6103, both a criminal offense punishable by fine of an amount up to $1,000, or imprisonment, or both (Section 7213A), and a civil cause of action for damages (Section 7431). The taxpayer must also be notified if a person is charged with unauthorized inspection of the taxpayer's return. See the Browsing Protection Act, HR 1226, enacted August 5, 1997.

While Congress has provided both civil and criminal sanctions for Service employee browsing, the GAO concluded that the Service's management systems are inadequate "to describe known browsing incidents precisely or to evaluate their severity consistently," and noted that the percentage of cases resulting in discipline has remained constant during the period 1991 to 1995 despite the Service's "zero tolerance" policy. GAO IRS Systems Security and Funding—Employee Browsing Not Being Addressed Effectively and Budget Requests for New Systems Development Not Justified, GAO/T-AIMD-97-82 (Apr. 15, 1997), at 3.

CHAPTER 5

Statutes of Limitations

¶ 5.01 OVERVIEW

Statutes of limitations, the Supreme Court has said, "are designed to promote justice by preventing surprises through the revival of claims that have been allowed to slumber until evidence has been lost, memories have faded, and witnesses have disappeared. The theory is that even if one has a just claim, it is unjust not to put the adversary on notice to defend within the period of limitation and that the right to be free of stale claims in time comes to prevail over the right to prosecute them."[1] In tax cases, statutes of limitations are "an almost indispensable element of fairness as well as of practical administration of income tax policy."[2] In its 1946 opinion in *Electric Storage Battery Co.*, the Supreme Court described the policy foundation for statutes of limitation in tax cases:

> [Congress has regarded it as] ill-advised to have an income tax system under which there would never come a day of final settlement and which required both the taxpayer and the Government to stand ready forever and a day to produce vouchers, prove events, establish values and recall details of all that goes into an income tax contest.[3]

Statutes of limitations "have come into the law not through the judicial process, but through legislation."[3.1] Internal Revenue Code (the Code) statutes of limitation require the Internal Revenue Service (the Service) to assess and collect tax, and taxpayers to claim refunds or credits of overpayments within stated periods. By definition, these Code statutes of limitations are "arbitrary." Their operation "does not discriminate between the just claim and the unjust claim, or the [avoidable] or unavoidable delay."[4] Taxpayers can use a statute of limitations to avoid paying tax they clearly owe when the Service fails to act within the required assessment period, and at other times the Service can retain an overpaid tax when a taxpayer has failed to file a refund claim within the applicable period.

In operation, statutes of limitations do not distinguish between taxpayers or the Service. But as a matter of statutory construction, when vague or ambiguous, statutes of limitations on assessment and collection are construed strictly in favor of the government, because, as the Supreme Court has said, "the pub-

---

[1] Order of RR Telegraphers v. Railway Express Agency, Inc., 321 US 342, 348–349 (1944), quoted in Rothensies v. Electric Storage Battery Co., 329 US 296, 301 (1946).

[2] Rothensies v. Electric Storage Battery Co., 329 US 296, 300 (1946).

[3] Rothensies v. Electric Storage Battery Co., 329 US 296, 300 (1946).

[3.1] Rothensies v. Electric Storage Battery Co., 329 US 296, 300 (1946).

[4] Chase Sec. Corp. v. Donaldson, 325 US 304, 314 (1945).

lic interest should not be prejudiced by the default or negligence of public officers."[5]

Statutes of limitations are gathered in Chapter 66 of the Code. In turn, Chapter 66 is divided into four subchapters:

1. Limitations on Assessment and Collection (Subchapter A), which includes the general statute of limitations on assessment and collection (Section 6501), the statute of limitations on collection after assessment (Section 6502), and circumstances when the statute of limitations is suspended (Section 6503).
2. Limitations on Credit or Refund (Subchapter B), which contains the statute of limitations on credit or refund (Section 6511), the running of the statute of limitations on assessment and collection when a case is in the Tax Court (Section 6512), the time when a tax return is considered filed and the tax paid for purposes of the running of the statute of limitations on assessment (Section 6513), and the effect of the running of the statute of limitations on the Service's authority to grant a credit or refund (Section 6514).[6]
3. Mitigation of Effect of Period of Limitation Provisions (Subchapter C) relating to the mitigation of the effect of the period of limitations when employment taxes are involved (Section 6521), but the more commonly used mitigation provisions relating to other taxes are contained in Sections 1311 through 1314.
4. Periods of Limitations in Judicial Proceedings (Subchapter D), which includes provisions relating to periods of limitations on criminal prosecutions (Section 6531) and others relating to periods of limitations on suits by taxpayers, the government, and persons other than taxpayers (Section 6532).

The discussion in this chapter focuses on the limitations imposed for the assessment and collection of tax, as well as the mitigation of the effect of these periods of limitations.

---

[5] Bowers v. New York & Albany Lighterage Co., 273 US 346, 350 (1927) (discussing United States v. St. Paul, Minn. & Manitoba Ry., 247 US 310, 314 (1918) (citations omitted).

[6] This subject is discussed in Chapter 11, "Overpayment, Refund, Credit, and Abatement."

¶ 5.02 STATUTE OF LIMITATIONS ON ASSESSMENT

Assessment of any internal revenue tax must generally be made within a three-year period beginning with the date a return is filed.[7] The general rule stated in Section 6501(a) provides, subject to exceptions, "the amount of any tax imposed by this title shall be assessed within 3 years after the return was filed." Even if the return is filed late (i.e., after the due date), the Service still must assess tax within three years after the delinquent return is filed. If the Service fails to assess the tax within three years, it is not only prohibited from collecting the tax administratively by lien and levy, the Service may also not institute a proceeding in court without assessment for the collection of the tax after the three-year period expires.[8] The general period of limitations on assessment applies not only to the principal amount of tax; it also applies to interest and to additions to tax, additional amounts, and penalties that are collected as part of the tax. Whether a tax return is filed or considered filed on the return due date or if the return is filed delinquently after the return due date, the tax must be assessed within the succeeding three-year period, or else it is uncollectible by administrative levy or by a proceeding in court. The critical act that starts the statute of limitations on assessment is the filing of a "return," and the term "return" means "the return required to be filed by the taxpayer (and does not include a return of any person from whom the taxpayer has received an item of income, gain, loss, deduction, or credit)."[9] In other words, the three-year period runs from the date the taxpayer's return is filed, not the date a pass-through entity, such as a partnership or an S corporation files its return.

There are a host of exceptions to the general three-year statute of limitations. These exceptions are listed in Section 6501(c) and summarized subsequently.

1. *False, fraudulent, and no return situations.* No statute of limitations applies if a taxpayer files a false return, engages in a willful attempt to evade tax, or files no return at all.[10]

---

[7] IRC § 6501(a).

[8] Section 6501(a) states that "no proceeding in court without assessment of such tax shall be begun after the expiration of such [three-year] period." Section 6502(a) provides for "collection of levy" only when "the assessment of any tax imposed by this title has been made within the period of limitations properly applicable thereto."

[9] This language was added to Section 6501(a) in 1997 after the Supreme Court had reached this result in Bufferd v. United States, 506 US 523 (1993).

[10] IRC §§ 6501(c)(1), 6501(c)(2), 6501(c)(3). For a fraudulent return or when no return was filed, the deficiency may be assessed at any time. However, the Service will obtain timely consents to extend any unexpired three-year or six-year periods, notwithstanding allegations of fraud. In all cases in which criminal prosecution has been recommended, Regional Counsel must be consulted before obtaining consents.

2. *Extension by agreement.* Rather than the normal three-year period, the Service and the taxpayer may agree to a different statute of limitations on assessment, as long as the agreement is entered into before the three-year statute of limitations expires, and the Service either assesses within the extended agreed-on statute date, or obtains a further extension from the taxpayer.[11] The Service must inform the taxpayer that the taxpayer has a right not to extend the statute.[12]

3. *Tax resulting from changes in certain income tax or estate tax credits.* When a change in a foreign tax credit for income tax purposes results in additional income tax (pursuant to Section 905(c)) or when a change in taxes of a foreign country, state, or other taxing jurisdiction claimed as a credit against estate tax (pursuant to Section 2016) results in additional estate tax, special statutes of limitation apply.[13]

4. *Termination of private foundation status.* When the private foundation status of a foundation is terminated under Section 507, the tax imposed on the termination of the private foundation may be assessed at any time (there is no statute of limitations), or a proceeding in court for the collection of the tax may be instituted at any time.[14]

5. *Special rule for certain amended returns.* When a taxpayer files within the sixty-day period ending with the due date of the return, a written document signed by the taxpayer showing that the taxpayer owes an additional tax for the taxable year, the period for the assessment for the additional tax does not expire until sixty days after the Service received the document reporting the additional tax from the taxpayer.[15]

6. *Failure to notify the Service of certain foreign transfers.* The statute of limitations on assessment will not expire until three years after the taxpayer files the required information with the Service by Section 6038 about certain foreign corporations and partnerships, by Section 6038A about certain foreign-owned corporations, by Section 6038B about certain transfers to foreign persons, by Section 6046 about the organization or reorganization of foreign corporations and about acquisitions of their stock, by Section 6046A about interests in foreign partnerships, or by Section 6048 about certain transactions involving foreign trusts.[16]

---

[11] IRC § 6501(c)(4)(A).

[12] IRC § 6501(c)(4)(B).

[13] IRC § 6501(c)(5).

[14] IRC § 6501(c)(6).

[15] IRC § 6501(c)(7).

[16] IRC § 6501(c)(8).

7. *Gift tax on certain gifts not shown on a gift tax return.* When a donor fails to report a gift, the value of which is required to be reported on a gift tax return (without regard to Section 2503(b)), the Service may assess gift tax at any time, unless the donor has disclosed the item on a return or in a document attached to the return, "in a manner adequate to apprise the [Service] of the nature of such item."[17]

Special statutes of limitation are provided when a taxpayer makes a request for a prompt assessment, a taxpayer files a return with a substantial omission of income, and for carrybacks. When a request for a prompt assessment of a tax other than estate tax is made for which a return is required for a decedent, or by the decedent's estate during the period of administration, or by a corporation, the assessment must be made within eighteen months after the request is received by the Service. Additional income, estate, or gift tax may be assessed within six years from the date the return was filed when the return omits an amount of more than 25 percent of the reported income (Section 6501(e)). In cases involving net operating loss (NOL) carrybacks, the statute of limitations for carryback purposes is that of the loss year. An amended return does not extend the statute of limitations.

Transferee liability may be asserted with respect to a transferor's liability for income, estate, gift, or other taxes; this special statute of limitations is set forth in Section 6901.

Table 5.1 summarizes the expiration date of the statutory period for assessment under Section 6501 for different kinds of tax.[18] The table also lists the Service forms used to file these taxes and extend the periods for assessment.

---

[17] IRC § 6501(c)(9).

[18] IRM 8.1.1, Appeals Return Processing and Control Handbook, Exhibit 8.1.1.2-25.

TABLE 5.1
Expiration Date of Statutory Period for Assessment

Kind of tax[1]	Form No.	Period covered	Due date	Expiration date of statutory period for assessment
1. Income[1]				
(a) Individual	1040	Calendar year	3½ months after close of taxable year (April 15).	3 years after due date (or date return filed if after due date)
		Fiscal year	3½ months after close of fiscal year.	"
(b) Fiduciary	1041	Calendar year	3½ months after close of taxable year (April 15).	
		Fiscal year	3½ months after close of fiscal year.	"
(c) Corporate	1120	Calendar year	2½ months after close of taxable year (March 15).	
		Fiscal year	2½ months after close of fiscal year.	"
2. Estate[1]	706			
(a) Decedents dying before 1/1/71		—	Date of the 15th calendar month after death corresponding to date of death. If no day corresponds to date of death, the last day of 15th month is due date.	3 years after due date (or date return filed if after due date).
(b) Decedents dying after 12/31/70			Date of the 9th calendar month after death corresponding to date of death. If no day corresponds to date of death, the last day of 9th month is due date.	

Kind of tax	Form No.	Period covered	Due date	Expiration date of statutory period for assessment
3. Gift Tax[1]				
(a) Gifts prior to 1/1/71	709	Calendar year	April 15 of following year	3 years from due date of return (or date return filed if after due date).
(b) Gifts after 12/31/70		Calendar quarter	15th day of 2nd month following end of quarter.	"
(c) Gifts after 12/31/81		Calendar year	April 15 of following year.	"
4. Excise	720	Calendar quarter	Last day of 1st month following end of quarter.	3 years from due date or date return is filed, whichever is later.
5. Employment:				
(a) FICA	941	Calendar quarter	Last day of 1st month following end of quarter.	3 years from April 15 of succeeding year or date return was filed, whichever is later.
(b) RRTA	CT-1	Calendar quarter	Last day of 2nd month following end of quarter.	3 years from due date or date return was filed, whichever is later.
(c) FUTA	940	Calendar year	January 31 of next calendar year	3 years from due date or date return was filed, whichever is later.
(d) Withholding	941	Calendar quarter	Last day of 1st month following end of quarter.	3 years from April 15 of succeeding year or date return was filed, whichever is later.
6. Transferee Liability[2]	—	—	—	1 year beyond period for assessment against transferor.
Trust Fund Recovery Penalty assessment IRC 6672 (employees' portion of FICA and withholding).	—	—	—	3 years from April 15 of succeeding year or date return, Form 941, was filed, whichever is later.
7. Information Return	990	Year	15th day of fifth month following close of taxable year.	3 years after due date of taxable return.

Kind of tax	Form No.	Period covered	Due date	Expiration date of statutory period for assessment
8. Information Return	990A	Year	15th day of fifth month following close of taxable year.	3 years after due date of taxable return.
9. Information Return	990-PF	Year	15th day of fifth month following close of taxable year.	3 years after due date of taxable return.
10. Income (Cooperative)	990-C or 1120	Year	15th day of ninth month after taxable year ends.	3 years after due date.
11. Unrelated business income return.	990T	Year	15th day of fifth month following close of taxable year (prior to 1979, 2½ months after close of taxable year).	3 years after due date (or date return filed if after due date).
(a) Domestic or Foreign Trust		Year	3½ months after close of taxable year.	3 years after due date (or date return filed if after due date).
(b) Domestic or Foreign Corporation or Association		Year	2½ months after close of taxable year.	"
(c) Nonresident Organization		Year	5½ months after close of taxable year.	"
12. Highway Use	2290	—	Last day of the next month following the month first used in a given period.	3 years after due date of return or 3 years from date return was actually filed, whichever is later.
13. Initial excise tax on private foundations and disqualified persons	4720	—	Due date for filing Form 990-PF (Form 990, Sch B for 1970 and 1971) and Form 1041-A	Same as expiration date of Form 990, 990-PF, or Form 1041-A.
14. Return of Initial Excise Taxes Related to Pension and Profit-Sharing Plans	5330	Year	On or before the last day of the 7th month after the end of the taxable year of the employer or other person who must file the return.	See IRM 7(10)(14).

Kind of tax	Form No.	Period covered	Due date	Expiration date of statutory period for assessment
15. Annual Return/Reports of Employee Benefit Plans	5500 5500C 5500G 5500K 5500R[3]	Year	On or before the last day of the 7th month following the close of the plan year.	3 years after the due date (or date return filed if after the due date).

General Comments: In the case of a fraudulent return or where no return was filed, the deficiency may be assessed at any time. However, timely consents should be obtained to extend any unexpired three-year or six-year periods, notwithstanding allegations of fraud. In all cases where criminal prosecution has been recommended, Regional Counsel must be consulted before obtaining consents. Where assessment of the tax has been made prior to, or during, Appellate consideration of the case, such as in jeopardy assessment or claim for abatement cases, the six-year period for collection after assessment should be controlled and protected, IRC 6502. In cases involving net operating loss carry backs, the statute of limitations for carrybacks is that of the loss year. An amended return does not extend the statute of limitations. See 630 for determination of expiration date of statutory period for assessment.

[1] Additional income tax, estate tax, or gift tax may be assessed within six years from date return was filed when the return omits an amount of more than 25% of the reported (IRC 6501(c)). (a) Gross income (b) Gross estate (c) Gifts made during the year or quarter.

[2] Transferee liability may be asserted with respect to transferor's liability for income, estate, gift, or other taxes under conditions set forth in IRC 6901. General Comments: In the case of a fraudulent return or where no return was filed, the deficiency may be assessed at any time. However, timely consents should be obtained to extend any unexpired three-year or six-year periods, notwithstanding allegations of fraud. In all cases where criminal prosecution has been recommended. Regional Counsel must be consulted before obtaining consents. Where assessment of the tax has been made prior to, or during, Appellate consideration of the case, such as in jeopardy assessment or claim for abatement cases, the six-year period for collection after assessment should be controlled and protected, IRC 6502. In cases involving net operating loss carry backs, the statute of limitations for carryback purposes is that of the loss year. An amended return does not extend the statute of limitations. See 630 for determination of expiration date of statutory period for assessment.

[3] For additional returns, due dates, and expiration of statutory period for assessments, refer to ADP and IDRS Information, Document 6209.

In accordance with general principles of pleading and proof, taxpayers have the burden of pleading and proving nonliability because of the expiration of the statute of limitations.[19] In a contest over whether the statute of limitations has run, the taxpayer has the burden of proving both that a return has been filed and the date on which it was filed.[20] This means the taxpayer must plead the defense and prove a prima facie case by showing that the notice of deficiency or the assessment was made beyond the normally applicable period. The Service then has the burden of going forward with evidence to show that the bar of the statute is inapplicable because, for example, a valid waiver has been executed.[21]

[1] The Assessment Limitations Start Date: When a Return Is Considered Filed

Assessment of tax must be made within the three-year period following the filing of a return. Several specific rules in Section 6501 govern the time a return is considered filed, and the three-year period of limitations does not begin to run in all instances on the date the return is filed.

[a] Early Returns

An early return (i.e., a return filed before the last date prescribed by law for filing) is not considered filed until the due date.[22] Consequently, if an individual taxpayer files a return before April 15, his or her return is not considered filed until April 15, and the three-year period does not begin to run until the deemed filing date. However, if the individual files his or her return after April 15, the three-year period begins to run from the date the return is actually filed.[23] Early returns of employment and withholding taxes and withhold-

---

[19] Rule 39 of the Tax Court's Rules of Practice and Procedure states, "A party shall set forth in the party's pleading any matter constituting an avoidance or affirmative defense, including . . . the statute of limitations." Federal Rules of Civil Procedure 8(c) similarly provides, "In pleading to a preceding pleading, a party shall set forth affirmatively . . . statute of limitations . . . and any other matter constituting an avoidance or affirmative defense."

[20] See Grosshandler v. Comm'r, 75 TC 1 (1980), in which an attorney failed to convince the Tax Court that he filed returns, despite his testimony, purportedly refreshed by hypnosis. By contrast, Service records were said to be the "most compelling evidence" of nonfiling. Id. at 17.

[21] For a description of the shifting burdens, see Adler v. Comm'r, 85 TC 535, 540 (1985).

[22] IRC § 6501(b)(1).

[23] This result is consistent with the statutory language of Section 6501(a), which states that the amount of any tax must be assessed within three years after the return is

ing tax on nonresident aliens, foreign corporations, or tax-free covenant bonds are not considered filed until the due date. Thus, if these returns are filed before April 15 for any period ending with or within the prior calendar year, they are considered filed on April 15 of the succeeding calendar year.[24]

Under certain circumstances set forth in Section 6020, the Service is permitted to make and execute a return for a taxpayer. However, this so-called Section 6020(b) return is not considered a return for the purposes of the period of limitations on assessment and collection, and an assessment of tax against a taxpayer for whom such a return has been prepared can be made at any time.[25]

A return of excise taxes is considered a return for the purposes of the period of limitations on assessment and collection of all amounts of excise taxes that, if properly paid, would be required to be reported on the return for the period, if the filed return has any entry with respect to the amount of tax or if the entry on the return indicates that no tax liability for the period exists.[26]

Also, the period of limitations begins to run on the day after a return is filed.[27] Thus, if a return is filed on April 15, 2001, the date of filing is excluded and the period of limitations begins to run on April 16, 2001, so that an assessment made on or before April 15, 2004, is timely.

[b] The Timely Mailed, Timely Filed Rule

In proving the date of return filing, the taxpayer may rely on such Code provisions as the timely mailed, timely filed rule of Section 7502,[28] and the rule regarding the timely performance of an act when the last day falls on a Saturday, Sunday, or legal holiday set out in Section 7503.[29] A taxpayer may rely on the timely mailed, timely filed rule, to establish that a return posted in the U.S. mail is considered delivered on the date of the postmark, not the date of actual receipt by the Service, for the purposes of the period of limitations

---

filed "(whether or not such return was filed on or after the date prescribed)." See also United States v. Habig, 390 US 222 (1968) (statute of limitations for criminal prosecution). For a civil case in which this rule was applied, see Prather v. Comm'r, TC Memo 1982-467, 44 TCM 838 (1982).

[24] IRC § 6501(b)(2).

[25] IRC § 6501(b)(3).

[26] IRC § 6501(b)(4).

[27] Burnet v. Willingham Loan & Trust Co., 282 US 437, 439 (1931).

[28] These rules are discussed in more detail at Chapter 4.

[29] See Hotel Equities Corp. v. Comm'r, 546 F2d 725 (7th Cir. 1976). In *Hotel Equities*, a return, which was due July 15, 1970, was mailed on July 14, 1970. The return was delivered on July 17, 1970. A notice of deficiency sent on July 17, 1973, was held to be untimely because the return had been "filed" on July 14, 1970 (i.e., more than three years before the notice of deficiency). Id. at 730.

on assessment and collection.[30] If a return is sent by U.S. registered or certified mail or an authorized private delivery service, the registration or certification or similar evidence of mailing is prima facie evidence of delivery.[31] In instances when a taxpayer has not literally complied with Section 7502, the Service has contended that a return is only filed when it is received.[32]

[c] The Business Day Exception

If the date for performing an act such as filing a return falls on a Saturday, Sunday, or legal holiday, under the provisions of Section 7503, performance on the next succeeding business day is considered timely filing.[33] This remedial procedural rule benefitting taxpayers has a corresponding effect on the running of the statute of limitations on assessment. Section 7503 does not reduce the amount of time statutorily provided for making an assessment. As the Court of Claims observed, "Section 7503 merely considers the performance of [the required] act on the next succeeding business day as being timely and does not operate to negate the effect of the actual date of performance for other purposes, i.e. the actual date of filing for commencing the limitations period on assessment."[34] When a taxpayer files a timely return by operation of Section 7503 because the taxpayer mailed the return on the first business day after a holiday or weekend, then the statutory period for assessment also begins to run on that first business day. If a return is not considered "filed" on the date falling on the Saturday, Sunday, or legal holiday, the statute of limitations on assessment does not begin to run on that day.[35] This principle is confirmed by Section 6501(a), which gives the Service three years after the return is filed to assess a tax "whether or not such return was filed on

---

[30] IRC § 7502(a).

[31] IRC § 7502(c). See ¶ 4.04[2].

[32] The Service has contended that despite Section 7502, delivery, rather than mailing, constitutes "filing" starting the three-year period of assessment. See Hotel Equities Corp. v. Comm'r, 546 F2d 725, 728 (7th Cir. 1976); First Charter Fin. Corp. v. United States, 669 F2d 1342 (9th Cir. 1982) (return mailed and delivered within extension period held filed on date of delivery); Hartwick v. United States, 83-2 USTC ¶ 9504 (WDNY 1983) (return/claim for refund mailed before the due date held filed on date of delivery). See also Emmons v. Comm'r, 92 TC 342 (1989) (untimely return filed for purposes of the three-year assessment on date of receipt, not mailing). For further discussion of the timely mailed, timely filed rule, see ¶ 4.04[2][a].

[33] IRC § 7503.

[34] Rev. Rul. 81-269, 1981-2 CB 243.

[35] See Brown v. United States, 391 F2d 653, 655 (Ct. Cl. 1968). There is language in *Brown* stating that the date of "actual filing" controls; however, it is unclear whether the Court of Claims differs with the Seventh Circuit's decision in *Hotel Equities* that the mailing date can constitute the filing date. For further discussion of this rule, see ¶ 4.03[2][a].

or after the date prescribed." Accordingly, if a taxpayer filed his or her return on Monday, April 16, 2001, the assessment period expires April 16, 2004. The result is different if the taxpayer files an early return. When a taxpayer files an early return, the assessment period begins to run on the actual due date of the return, even if that day falls on a weekend or a holiday.

[2] Returns That Start the Limitations Period

Once a return is filed, the Service has three years to assess the amount of any tax. If a return is not filed, the Service may assess and collect a tax at any time.[36] Consequently, when a taxpayer files a document with the Service, the characterization of the document as a return may control the validity of any subsequent assessment. The form or document need not state any amount due as tax or calculate any tax, provided that it contains all the data from which the tax could be computed and assessed.[37] At a minimum, it must (1) disclose the items of gross income, allowable deductions and credits, and other information prescribed for the purposes of computing the tax in question[38]; (2) be for the proper accounting period and by the proper method of accounting[39]; and (3) be properly executed in accordance with the provisions of the Code.[40]

In other words, a return within the meaning of Section 6501(a) is filed when the return (1) purports to be a return; (2) evinces an honest and reasonable attempt to satisfy the requirements of the tax; (3) contains sufficient information to calculate the taxpayer's tax liability; and (4) is executed by the taxpayer under penalties of perjury.[41] Consequently, whatever the return form or other statement is called, the form or document filed with the Service must disclose this basic data, or it does not start the running of the period of limitations.[42] For example, the return of a partnership does not constitute the individ-

---

[36] IRC § 6501(c)(3).

[37] Germantown Trust Co. v. Comm'r, 309 US 304, 308 (1940).

[38] See also Germantown Trust Co. v. Comm'r, 309 US 304, 307–310 (1940) (taxpayer filed wrong return); cf. Comm'r v. Lane-Wells Co., 321 US 219 (1944) (taxpayer who denied personal holding company status and who did not file a required separate return showing data from which tax could be assessed was held not to have filed a return; period of limitations on assessment did not start to run although a regular return was filed). For further discussion of sufficient returns, see ¶ 4.02[1].

[39] IRC §§ 441 (accounting period), 446 (method of accounting).

[40] Lucas v. Pilliod Lumber Co., 281 US 245 (1930).

[41] Beard v. Comm'r, 82 TC 766, 779 (1984), aff'd per curiam, 793 F2d 139 (6th Cir. 1986).

[42] United States v. Porth, 426 F2d 519, 523 (10th Cir.), cert. denied, 400 US 824 (1970) ("[a] taxpayer's return that does not contain any information relating to a taxpayer's income from which the tax can be computed is not a return within the meaning of the Code or the regulations adopted by the Commissioner"). See Jarvis v. Comm'r, 78 TC

ual tax return of a partner because it does not contain the basic return information of the partner necessary to compute tax.[43] Also, a return with all zeroes,[44] an unsigned return,[45] and a return on which the jurat has been tampered with,[46] is not a return for purposes of Section 6501 and does not start the running of the limitations period on assessment. Applying this test, so-called

---

646, 653–655 (1982) (Form 1040 reporting each item as "less than" a specified de minimis amount held not to be a return, because it did not contain information from which tax could be computed). See also Edwards v. Comm'r, 680 F2d 1268, 1269–1270 (9th Cir. 1982) (protest-type returns were not valid returns starting the statute of limitations).

Similarly, the Service has ruled that an employer who files Form 940, signed or unsigned, has not filed a return if the employer's return does not disclose the amount of remuneration the employer paid during the calendar year, or if the return does not disclose sufficient information to enable the district director to compute the amount of taxable wages. Rev. Rul. 57-554, 1957-2 CB 854; compare Reg. § 40.6011(a)-1(a). Form 720, Quarterly Federal Excise Tax Return, constitutes a return of all taxes listed on the return if the taxpayer enters the word "none" across the return or in the summary portion, provided it "clearly indicates a denial of liability for all taxes."

[43] Durovic v. Comm'r, 54 TC 1364, 1385–1388 (1970), aff'd in part and rev'd in part, 487 F2d 36 (7th Cir. 1973), cert. denied, 417 US 919 (1974). This situation must be compared to one in which partnership and other returns have been considered together with an individual return for the purpose of determining whether there has been a disclosure negativing a more than 25 percent omission of gross income. See IRC § 6501(e)(1)(A)(ii) (extending the limitations period to six years on a substantial omission). This requirement is discussed infra ¶ 5.02[2]. Compare Kelley v. Comm'r, 877 F2d 756 (9th Cir. 1989) (although S corporation not liable for taxes, Service could not make adjustment on return of shareholder of S corporation based on adjustment of return of S corporation after statute of limitations had run on corporation's return). See also ICI Pension Fund v. Comm'r, 112 US 83, 88 (1999) (fiduciary income tax return, Form 1042, is not the return of a pension fund).

[44] Hess v. United States, 785 F. Supp. 137 (ED Wash. 1991) (no entries for dividends, capital gains, business income, or other sources of income from which taxes might have been withheld; held, filing was not sufficient return for limitation period). Nevertheless, a return has been held to constitute a sufficient return if it contains financial data, even untrue financial data, because it permits the computation of tax. United States v. Long, 618 F2d 74, 76 (9th Cir. 1980) (zeroes entered).

[45] See, e.g., Vaira v. Comm'r, 52 TC 986 (1969), rev'd on other grounds, 444 F2d 770 (3d Cir. 1971); Doll v. Comm'r, 358 F2d 713, 714 (3d Cir. 1966); Reaves v. Comm'r, 31 TC 690 (1958), aff'd, 295 F2d 336, 338 (5th Cir. 1961).

[46] Ledbetter v. Comm'r, 837 F2d 708, 710 (5th Cir. 1988) (deletion of verification on return; obliterating words "under penalties of perjury" rendered returns invalid, so that tax could be assessed at any time). See also Beard v. Comm'r, 82 TC 766, 779 (1984) (return that had been tampered with held not to constitute a return).

When the taxpayers crossed out the attestation phrase "[u]nder penalties of perjury," at the bottom of the return form, the taxpayers' refusal to sign the verification portion of the form rendered the return they timely filed invalid so that an assessment could be made at any time pursuant to Section 6503(c). Danol v. United States, 81 AFTR2d 98-1334 (ED Mich. 1998) (gathering cases).

Fifth Amendment returns have not been held to be "returns" because they do not make a reasonable attempt to supply information.[47]

[a] Pass-Through Returns

Does the return of a pass-through entity, such as a partnership or an S corporation, constitute the "return" of the partner or S corporation shareholders for purposes of starting the assessment period of Section 6501(a)? In *Siben*, after the assessment period had expired on the partnership return, an adjustment was made to an individual partner's return based on an adjustment to the partnership's return.[48] The taxpayer argued that because the limitations period had run on the partnership, assessment was barred against the individual partner based on adjustment of the partner's distributive share of the partnership's income. The Second Circuit ruled that

> the "return" that starts the running of the limitations period at issue is that of the taxpayer whose liability is being assessed, and not that of a third person or entity whose return might also report the transaction that gives rise to the liability. On this reading, the return referred to in § 6501(a) would thus be the individual's income tax return for an assessment of individual income tax.[49]

Under the same principle, the assessment of S corporation-derived adjustments against an individual S corporation shareholder is timely even when assessment against the S corporation was barred; the shareholder's return for purposes of Section 6501(a) is the relevant return. The Supreme Court settled this issue in *Bufferd*, holding that the limitations period for assessing the income tax liability of an S corporation shareholder runs from the date on which the shareholder's return is filed.[50] The Court reasoned that as an S corporation, Compo was a pass-through entity with its income, losses, deductions, and credits flowing through and being attributable to the individual shareholders.

---

[47] United States v. Moore, 627 F2d 830 (7th Cir. 1980), cert. denied, 450 US 916 (1981); United States v. Johnson, 577 F2d 1204, 1311 (5th Cir. 1978) (protest return cannot be justified solely on Fifth Amendment grounds); Thompson v. Comm'r, 78 TC 558 (1982) (Fifth Amendment return did not contain essential information from which tax could be computed). Compare Blount v. Comm'r, 86 TC 383, 387–388 (1986) (return with missing W-2 Form held to start three-year assessment period).

[48] Siben v. Comm'r, 930 F2d 1034, 1038 (2d Cir.), cert. denied, 502 US 963 (1991).

[49] Siben v. Comm'r, 930 F2d 1034, 1035 (2d Cir.), cert. denied, 502 US 963 (1991).

[50] Bufferd v. Comm'r, 506 US 523 (1993). After the Supreme Court's decision, the Ninth Circuit held that the statute of limitations on assessment on a partner's liability resulting from a partnership adjustment begins to run on the filing of the individual partner's return. Charlton v. Comm'r, 990 F2d 1161 (9th Cir. 1993) (a pre–TEFRA partnership case; compare IRC § 6229(a)).

Moreover, to determine the tax of the individual shareholder, the shareholder's return had to be examined because the corporation's return did not contain all the relevant information. Finally, the Court did not believe that it was an undue burden for the shareholder to depend on the corporation's records to defend against any deficiency the Service might determine to be due.

The Taxpayer Relief Act of 1997 incorporated the Supreme Court's ruling in *Bufferd* in the statutory language of Section 6501(a) by providing that a "return" for the purposes of the statute of limitations on assessment is "the return required to be filed by the taxpayer and does not include a return of any person from whom the taxpayer has received any item of income, gain, loss, deduction, or credit."[51]

[b] Amended Returns

When a taxpayer files an original return and then an amended return, the period of limitations begins to run from the date of filing of the original return and not from the date the amended return is filed.[52] If a sufficient return is filed at the time required by law, an amended return, even if it modifies or adds to the original return, has no effect for purposes of the period of limitations.[53] No statutory provision exists for filing an amended return, and the Commissioner is not required to accept one. By analogy to criminal cases, the amended return does not cure a defect; rather, it constitutes an admission that the original return was false.

If a taxpayer files a false return and then a correct one, does the period of limitations begin to run from the date the honest return is filed, or is the taint of fraud for limitations purposes unremovable by subsequent conduct? As the first return filed within the statutory period for filing a return, the original fraudulent return is the taxpayer's return, albeit a fraudulent or substantially incorrect one.[54] In *Badaracco*, the Supreme Court held that when a taxpayer files a false or fraudulent return but later files a nonfraudulent amended return, Section 6501(c)(1) applies, and a tax may be assessed "at any time," even if more than three years have expired since the filing of the amended return. The Court reached this result by statutory construction, noting that the absence of any Code provision for a taxpayer's filing, or the Service's accepting, an amended return meant that when "Congress provided for assessment at any time in the

---

[51] IRC § 6501(a), as amended by the Taxpayer Relief Act of 1997 § 1248(a), for tax years beginning after August 5, 1997.

[52] Kaltreider Constr. Co. v. United States, 303 F2d 366 (3d Cir.), cert. denied, 371 US 877 (1962) (original return sufficient to start period for filing claim for refund).

[53] Zellerbach Paper Co. v. Helvering, 293 US 172, 177–178 (1934).

[54] Badaracco v. Comm'r, 464 US 386, 393 (1984). See Goldring v. Comm'r, 20 TC 79 (1953) (original return omitted more than 25 percent of gross income; honest amended return later filed). See also Houston v. Comm'r, 38 TC 486 (1962).

case of a false or fraudulent 'return,' it plainly included by this language a false or fraudulent *original* return."[55] The Court also was not persuaded that good policy required a different result. An unlimited statute of limitations on assessment was good policy because fraud cases were more difficult to investigate than routine tax cases. Moreover, an amended return had no greater guaranty of honesty than the original return. In any event, the Service needs time to prove fraudulent intent for purposes of the penalty; even if the tax is accurately stated on an amended return, the frequent criminal referrals of fraud cases for prosecution impede completion of a civil audit. It has been held that the statute of limitations on prosecution begins to run on the date a fraudulent return is filed (after the normal due date); that is, the offense is completed when the return is filed.[56] From this authority, the Court derived support for the view that, for purposes of the statute of limitations on assessment, the fraud is committed on the filing of the fraudulent return, and no subsequent conduct can purge the fraud.

When an amended return is filed before the due date of the original return, the amended return may be considered part of the original return for purposes of the period of limitations,[57] although there is a distinction between an amended return and a delinquent return. If a taxpayer fails to file a return and then files a delinquent return, the three-year period begins to run from the date of the filing of the delinquent return.[58]

[c] Wrong Return Form

A taxpayer may file the wrong type of return in good faith. Generally, when a taxpayer files the wrong return, the return is not considered sufficient to start the period of limitations, especially if a correct return is required to compute a separate tax.[59] The Code provides certain relief provisions for the more common situations. For example, if a taxpayer determines in good faith

---

[55] Badaracco v. Comm'r, 464 US 386, 393 (1984). In his dissenting opinion, Justice Stevens reviewed the legislative history of Section 6501(c)(1) and concluded that fraudulent returns were treated as no return at all "since neither gives the Commissioner an adequate basis to attempt an assessment." Under this analysis, the amended return becomes the return. Contrary to the majority's conclusion that its reading of Section 6501(c)(1) was supported by good policy, the dissent observed that under the rule adopted, a taxpayer has no incentive to correct past fraud by filing an honest return.

[56] United States v. Habig, 390 US 222 (1968), discussed at Chapter 7A.

[57] Goldring v. Comm'r, 20 TC 79, 82 (1953).

[58] Bennett v. Comm'r, 30 TC 114, 123 (1958), acq. 1958-2 CB 3; Rev. Rul. 79-178, 1979-1 CB 435.

[59] Compare Comm'r v. Lane-Wells Co., 321 US 219 (1944) (correct return was required to compute separate personal holding company tax) with Germantown Trust Co. v. Comm'r, 309 US 304 (1940) (trust erroneously filed a fiduciary return, although it was later found to be taxable as a corporation; only an income tax was involved). See also

that it is a trust or partnership and files a return as such, but it is subsequently held to be a corporation for the taxable year for which the return is filed, the trust or partnership return is considered to be the return of the corporation for purposes of the period of limitations.[60] Also, if a taxpayer determines in good faith that it is an exempt organization and files an information return, but it is subsequently determined to be a taxable organization, the filed return is considered a return of the taxpayer for purposes of starting the period of limitations on assessment and collection.[61] If a corporation determines in good faith that it is a domestic international sales corporation (DISC) and files an appropriate return, this return begins the running of the period of limitations on assessment and collection even if it is later determined that the corporation does not qualify as a DISC.[62] However, when a foreign pension fund believed in good faith that it was exempt from U.S. tax, and failed to file a federal income tax return, the three-year statute of limitations was held not to apply, even though a withholding agent had withheld tax from the fund and paid it over to the Service and filed an Annual Withholding Tax Return for U.S. Source Income of Foreign Persons, Form 1042, and Foreign Person's U.S. Source Income Subject to Withholding, Form 1042S.[63]

Ginter v. United States, 815 F. Supp. 1289 (WD Mo. 1993) (three-year period was not triggered by filing of Forms 1099 when Form 941 was required).

But see Rev. Rul. 82-185, 1982-2 CB 395 (Form 1040 fully reporting income, but not reporting any self-employment tax on Schedule SE or on the applicable line of Form 1040, starts the running of statute of limitations as to the self-employment tax because income and self-employment taxes are so closely connected). Compare Rev. Rul. 79-39, 1979-1 CB 435 (holding an employee has not made a valid return for purposes of Social Security tax on tips when Form 1040 is filed but tip income is not included). Rev. Rul. 82-185 distinguished Rev. Rul. 79-39 on the ground that the Social Security tax was an employment tax and not an integral part of the individual income tax.

[60] IRC § 6501(g)(1). This section codifies the rule of Germantown Trust Co. v. Comm'r, 321 US 219 (1944).

[61] IRC § 6501(g)(2). An organization that files an information return on Form 990, Form 990-A, or Form 990-P may not be considered by the Service to have filed a return sufficient to start the running of the period of limitations for purposes of assessment of unrelated business income tax, because the return for this purpose must be filed on Form 990-T. The Tax Court has held under particular facts that an organization that filed a return on Form 990 filed a return for purposes of the running of the period of limitations on assessment of unrelated business income tax as well. California Thoroughbred Breeders Ass'n, 47 TC 335 (1966), acq. in result only, 1969-2 CB 24 (1969). See also Maynard Hosp., Inc. v. Comm'r, 52 TC 1006 (1969); Colombo Club, Inc. v. Comm'r, 54 TC 100 (1970), aff'd per curiam, 447 F2d 1406 (9th Cir. 1971). However, the Service looks at the Form 990 filed to determine whether it is a sufficient return for purposes of beginning the period of limitations. See Rev. Rul. 69-247, 1969-1 CB 303; see also Rev. Rul. 77-162, 1977-1 CB 400.

[62] IRC § 6501(g)(3).

[63] ICI Pension Fund v. Comm'r, 112 TC 83, 87–88 (1999). The Tax Court concluded that, although regulations (Reg. § 1.6012-1(b)(2)) exempted nonresident alien individuals

¶ 5.03 EXCEPTIONS TO THE GENERAL PERIOD OF LIMITATIONS ON ASSESSMENT

The general rule that an assessment must be made within three years after a return is filed is subject to certain exceptions, which may be grouped as follows:

- Assessments that may be made at any time
- Assessments that may be made within six years
- Assessments that must be made in eighteen months
- Assessment periods extended by agreement
- Assessments effected by carrybacks from an excess loss or credit year to an earlier year

Table 5.2 summarizes the exceptions to the general rule. Each of these categories is discussed more fully in the following sections.

---

who were not engaged in a U.S. trade or business from filing a return if the tax was fully paid, the fund had requested and received a refund of the tax paid. See also Unilever Superannuation Trustees Ltd. v. Comm'r, TC Memo 1999-67, 77 TCM 1494 (1999) (same).

TABLE 5.2 _____
Exceptions to the General Period of Limitations

Exceptions	Statutory Period	Section
1. False or fraudulent returns	No limitation	6501(c)(1), 6501(a)(2)
2. Failure to file a return	No limitation	6501(c)(3)
3. Substantial omission from tax return a. 25 percent of gross income (income tax) b. 25 percent of gross amount of estate (estate tax) c 25 percent of total amount of gifts (gift tax) d. 25 percent of excise taxes	Six years	6501(e)(1)–6501(e)(3)
4. The failure of a personal holding company to report certain items of gross income and all individuals who owned more than 50 percent of the value of outstanding capital stock at any time during the last half of the taxable year	Six years	6501(f)
5. Request for a prompt assesment	Eighteen months after receipt of written request	6501(d)
6. Carrybacks a. Net operating loss b. Investment credit c. Capital loss d. Foreign tax credit	Statute periods for prior years remain open until the expiration of the statute period for the year of loss or credit	6501(h), 6501(j)
7. Extension by agreement period	Statute periods for prior years remain open until one year after expiration of the base year statute period to date agreed upon	
8. Amended returns filed within the sixty-day period ending with the day on which the time prescribed for the assessment of income, gift, or estate tax would otherwise expire	Period for assessment is extended for sixty days after the Service receives the amended return	6501(c)(7)
9. Failure to notify the Service under Section 6038B of any exchange or distribution under Sections 367(a), 367(d), or 367(e)	Period of assessment does not expire before three years after the date on which the Service is notified of the exchange or distribution under Section 6038B	6501(c)(8)

[1] Assessments That May Be Made at Any Time

A tax may be assessed or a proceeding in court to collect the tax without assessment may be begun at any time when a taxpayer

- Files a false or fraudulent return with the intent to evade tax[64];
- Willfully attempts in any manner to defeat or evade an internal revenue tax other than an income, gift, or estate tax[65]; or
- Fails to file a return.[66]

Not only may the tax be assessed at any time if these acts of commission or omission are involved, the Service need not assess the tax at all to collect the tax. Although the tax may not be collected by administrative means (i.e., by levy or distraint), the tax due may be collected without assessment by a proceeding in court to collect the tax. Exceptions to this rule are provided for a tax resulting from changes in certain income or estate tax credits,[67] termination of status as a private foundation,[68] and gift tax on certain gifts not shown on a return.[69]

[a] False or Fraudulent Returns

Tax may be assessed, or a proceeding in court for its collection may be begun at any time, if a taxpayer files a false or fraudulent return "with the intent to evade tax."[70] The language of this exception to the general period of limitations on assessment does not track the civil fraud penalty statute or the tax evasion statute.[71] It is clear, however, that the burden of proof to establish that the taxpayer has filed a false return or has willfully attempted to evade tax is on the Commissioner.[72] The issue is one of fact involving the taxpayer's intent, but evidence of a taxpayer's underpayment in tax due to fraud for purposes of the civil penalty also is evidence that the taxpayer filed a false return or attempted to evade tax.[73] If the return is fraudulent in any respect, "it de-

---

[64] IRC § 6501(c)(1).

[65] IRC § 6501(c)(2).

[66] IRC § 6501(c)(3).

[67] IRC § 6501(c)(5).

[68] IRC § 6501(c)(6).

[69] IRC § 6501(c)(9).

[70] IRC § 6501(c)(1).

[71] Section 6663(b) states that a civil penalty equal to 75 percent of the underpayment is imposed if any part of the underpayment of tax "is due to fraud." Section 7201 makes any person who "wilfully attempts in any manner to evade or defeat any tax" guilty of a felony.

[72] IRC § 7454.

[73] The civil fraud penalty is discussed in Chapter 7B.

prives the taxpayer of the bar of the statute [of limitations] for that year. . . . "[74] When spouses file a joint return but only one spouse has acted fraudulently, Section 6501(c)(1) lifts the bar of the statute of limitations on assessments against both spouses.[75]

To establish the fraud exception to the normal statute of limitations, the Service frequently relies on the preclusive effect of a judgment that a taxpayer criminally violated the tax laws. A taxpayer who has been convicted of willful evasion of tax in violation of Section 7201 is estopped under the doctrine of collateral estoppel from contending that any underpayment of tax for a year of conviction was not due to fraud within the meaning of the civil fraud penalty statute.[76] Estoppel also satisfies the Service's burden on the limitations exception.

Issue preclusion based on a prior conviction does not apply in all situations or to all tax crimes. When a sole stockholder commits fraud with respect to a corporation's returns or when there is more than one stockholder, but all are parties to the fraud, the corporation may be legally chargeable with making a false return with the intent to evade tax.[77] However, when an officer and 50 percent shareholder filed a fraudulent return for a corporation and the other stockholder was completely innocent of any misconduct, the corporation was not chargeable with making a false return with intent to evade tax for purposes of the period of limitations.[78] Moreover, while a judgment of conviction of tax evasion estops the taxpayer from contesting the issue of civil fraud, no such estoppel is found when the conviction is for the crime of filing a false return.[79]

For a case finding evidence that a taxpayer filed a "false or fraudulent return with intent to evade tax," see United States v. Bushlow, 832 F. Supp. 574 (EDNY 1993) (deceased husband's grand jury testimony used to establish fraud).

[74] Lowy v. Comm'r, 288 F2d 517, 520 (2d Cir. 1961), cert. denied, 368 US 984 (1962); accord United States v. Diehl, 586 F2d 1080 (5th Cir. 1978), aff'g per curiam, 76-2 USTC ¶ 9757 (SD Tex. 1976); Bahoric v. Comm'r, 363 F2d 151 (9th Cir. 1966); Worcester v. Comm'r, 370 F2d 713 (1st Cir. 1966).

[75] Ballard v. Comm'r, 740 F2d 659, 663 (8th Cir. 1984); Howell v. Comm'r, 175 F2d 240, 241–242 (6th Cir. 1949); Debrouse v. United States, 91-2 USTC ¶ 50,535 (MD Fla. 1991) (gathering cases); Vannaman v. Comm'r, 54 TC 1011, 1018 (1970) (holding that the wife "is liable for the additions to the tax by virtue of the joint and several liability provision").

[76] Amos v. Comm'r, 43 TC 50 (1964), aff'd, 360 F2d 358 (4th Cir. 1965); Arctic Ice Cream Co. v. Comm'r, 43 TC 68, 75–76 (1964).

[77] Kreps v. Comm'r, 351 F2d 1 (2d Cir. 1965) (president and secretary-treasurer of a corporation, who were also the principal stockholders, caused the corporation to file a fraudulent return).

[78] Asphalt Indus. v. Comm'r, 411 F2d 13 (3d Cir. 1969).

[79] Collateral estoppel on the issue of fraud does not apply when a taxpayer is convicted of filing a false return in violation of Section 7206(1). Wright v. Comm'r, 84 TC 636, 643 (1985). Moreover, a taxpayer, who is convicted of failure to file returns, is not

[b] No Return Filed

If a taxpayer fails to file a return, the tax may be assessed at any time. This exception to the period of limitations does not track the failure-to-file criminal statute, which requires a willful failure to file.[80] A taxpayer who negligently or innocently fails to file a return is still subject to an unlimited period of assessment and collection of tax. The requirements for a return must also be considered when a taxpayer files a document but the document is not considered to be a return.[81]

The rule that the statute of limitations on assessment does not begin to run if the taxpayer fails to file a return applies as well in other situations; for example, the three-year assessment period will not begin to run if a person is required, but fails to report information to the Service about certain foreign corporations and partnerships (Section 6038), information about certain foreign-owned corporations (Section 6038A), notice of certain transfers to foreign corporations (Section 6038B), information about the organization or reorganization of foreign corporations and acquisitions of their stock (Section 6046), returns reporting interests in foreign partnerships (Section 6046A), and information about certain foreign trusts (Section 6048). When a return falling into this category is not filed, the statute of limitations on assessment does not start to run until the information is filed.[82] Also, if a gift of property is required to be reported on a gift tax return, and the gift is not reported on the return, the gift tax may be assessed at any time, or, if the Service institutes a proceeding in court to collect the gift tax without assessment, the proceeding may be begun at any time.[83]

[2] Assessments That May Be Made Within Six Years

When a taxpayer omits more than 25 percent of the taxpayer's gross income, the period for assessment is extended from three to six years. Tax may be assessed or a proceeding in court for the collection of tax may be begun without assessment at any time within six years after the return is filed in the following situations:

---

estopped on the issue of fraud. Woolf v. United States, 578 F2d 1103 (5th Cir. 1978). Issue preclusion and fraud for civil purposes is described in more detail in Chapter 7B.

[80] IRC § 7203. The elements of a criminal failure to file are discussed at Chapter 7A.

[81] See supra ¶ 5.02[1].

[82] IRC § 6501(a)(8), as amended by the Taxpayer Relief Act of 1997, HR Rep. No. 148, 105th Cong., 2d Sess. 429 (June 24, 1997), § 1145(a), effective for information returns due after August 5, 1997.

[83] IRC § 6501(a)(9), added by the Taxpayer Relief Act of 1997 § 1248(a), effective for periods beginning after August 5, 1997.

- A taxpayer files a return that omits more than 25 percent of the taxpayer's gross income.[84]
- A taxpayer omits a constructive dividend from a foreign personal holding company.[85]
- An estate tax return omits more than 25 percent of the gross estate, or a gift tax return omits in excess of 25 percent of the total amount of the gift.[86]
- An excise tax return omits an amount of excise tax properly includable on the return that is in excess of 25 percent of the amount of tax reported in the return.[87]
- A corporation, which is a personal holding company, fails to file with its income tax return a schedule setting forth gross income and shareholder information as required by Sections 543(a) and 544, respectively.[88]

[a] More Than 25 Percent of Gross Income

The extended six-year period of limitations on assessment requires an omission from the return of more than 25 percent of gross income, except when a personal holding company tax return is involved. For the purpose of determining the existence of such an omission from gross income, the term "gross income" generally has the same meaning as for purposes of Section 61, although special rules apply.[89] The Commissioner has the burden of proving the requisite omission. For purposes of a trade or business, "gross income" means the total of the amounts received or accrued from the sale of goods or services before deduction of the cost of such sales and services.[90] In determining the amount of the omission, any amount disclosed in the return or in a

---

[84] IRC § 6501(e)(1)(A).

[85] IRC § 6501(e)(1)(B).

[86] IRC § 6501(e)(2).

[87] IRC § 6501(e)(3).

[88] IRC § 6501(f).

[89] Bardwell v. Comm'r, 38 TC 84 (1962), aff'd, 318 F2d 786 (10th Cir. 1963); Seltzer v. Comm'r, 21 TC 398, 401 (1953). For other cases applying the statutory rule, see Stoller v. Comm'r, TC Memo 1983-319, 46 TCM 345 (1983) (omission of more than 25 percent of gross income not found and six-year statute did not apply); Fritschle v. Comm'r, 79 TC 152 n.3 (1982) (more than 25 percent omission and six-year statute applied); Dapice v. Comm'r, TC Memo 1983-377, 46 TCM 598 (1983) (same); Burbage v. Comm'r, 774 F2d 644 (4th Cir. 1985) (ground lease constituted sale, proceeds of which exceeded 25 percent of reported income so six-year statute applied).

[90] IRC § 6501(e)(1)(A)(i). For a case finding that Section 6501(e)(1)(A)(i) did not apply, apparently because the taxpayer was an investor, not a dealer, see Insulglass Corp. v. Comm'r, 84 TC 203 (1984).

statement attached to the return in a manner "adequate to apprise the Secretary of the nature and amount of [the] item" is not included as part of the omission.[91] Consequently, giving adequate information in a return or on an attached schedule concerning an omitted item helps to avoid a more than 25 percent omission and, thus, to ensure that the shorter three-year period of limitations on assessment applies. This opportunity requires further discussion.

[b] Notice to the Service

A taxpayer who claims entitlement to the notice provision has the burden of proving that the income tax return contains "a statement adequate to apprise the Commissioner of the nature and amount of the item omitted."[92] Because this question is one of fact, a review of the cases generally does not provide helpful guidelines. In the landmark *Colony, Inc.*,[93] case, the Supreme Court established the basic test that the courts have attempted to follow:

> We think that in enacting section 275(c) [now Section 6501(e)], Congress manifested no broader purpose than to give the Commissioner an additional two years [now three years] to investigate tax returns in cases where, because of the taxpayer's omission to report some taxable item, the Commissioner is at a special disadvantage in detecting errors. In such instances, the return on its face provides no clue to the existence of the omitted item. On the other hand, when, as here, the understatement of a tax arises from an error in reporting an item disclosed on the face of the return the Commissioner is at no such disadvantage. And this would seem to be so whether the error be one affecting "gross income" or one, such as overstated deductions, affecting other parts of the return.

As long as the disclosure permits the Service to observe and investigate an error, the Service is at no special disadvantage in detecting the error because a reasonable follow-up will lead to the adjustment. Moreover, the disclosure does not have to be a detailed description of each and every underlying fact. *Colony, Inc.*, was decided under the 1939 Code, and Section 6501(e)(1)(A)(ii) incorporates its holding when it provides, "In determining the amount omitted from gross income, there shall not be taken into account any amount which is

---

[91] IRC § 6501(e)(1)(A)(ii). The courts have interpreted the statute literally. A disclosure made to a revenue agent during an examination does not qualify as a disclosure in the return. Insulglass Corp. v. Comm'r, 84 TC 203 (1984). A disclosure made in an amended return also is not a qualified disclosure. See Goldring v. Comm'r, 20 TC 79, 81–83 (1953); Houston v. Comm'r, 38 TC 486, 492 (1962). Disclosure of one type of income (e.g., wages) from an entity does not constitute a disclosure of other income received from the entity but not reported. *Insulglass Corp. v. Comm'r*, supra.

[92] University Country Club, Inc. v. Comm'r, 64 TC 460, 468 (1975).

[93] Colony, Inc. v. Comm'r, 357 US 28, 36 (1958).

omitted from gross income stated in the return if such amount is disclosed in the return, or in a statement attached to the return." Courts nevertheless use the judicially articulated standard of *Colony, Inc.*, in applying the statutory rule of Section 6501(e)(1)(A)(ii).[94] In *Quick Trust*, the Tax Court observed that "[t]he touchstone in cases of this type is whether [the Service] has been furnished with a 'clue' to the existence of the error" . . . Concededly, this does not mean simply a "clue" which would be sufficient to intrigue Sherlock Holmes. But neither does it mean a detailed revelation of each and every underlying fact." The test is an objective, rather than a subjective one.[95]

A return gives a clue if an adjustment might be apparent from the face of the return to a reasonable man.[96] When a country club reported the dollar value of its Class B stock on the balance sheet of its initial return rather than classifying the proceeds from the sale of the stock as income, the total proceeds received for the stock were held to be shown on the return, although the Commissioner contended that the receipts should have been characterized as income rather than as a contribution to capital.[97] Similarly, an understatement of gross profits on the sale of lots of land as a result of having overstated the basis of the lots by including in their cost certain unallowable items of development expenses was held not to constitute an omission from gross income, since the error was disclosed on the face of the return.[98] In other cases, a partnership or Subchapter S return has been used to supply omitted information to a taxpayer's individual income tax return, thereby furnishing the Commissioner with adequate clues as to the nature and amount of items omitted from the individual return but contained in the other return.[99] The presence or absence of a clue is a factual finding, and so just what a court will find cannot be predicted with certainty. In *Mariani Foods*, the Tax Court stated that it was applying the *Quick Trust* and *University Country Club* standards, yet it found that a taxpayer that filed an income tax return attaching a Form 3646, Income From Controlled Foreign Corporation, disclosing an interest in a foreign corporation

---

[94] Quick Trust v. Comm'r, 54 TC 1336 (1970), aff'd, 444 F2d 90 (8th Cir. 1971) (statute does not require disclosure of exact amount of omitted income, applying Eighth Circuit law, Benderoff v. United States, 398 F2d 132, 136 (8th Cir. 1968)).

[95] Quick Trust v. Comm'r, 54 TC 1336, 1347 (1970), aff'd, 444 F2d 90 (8th Cir. 1971).

[96] University Country Club, Inc. v. Comm'r, 64 TC 460, 471 (1975) ("[t]he proper application of the rule is whether an adjustment might be apparent from the face of the return to the elusive 'reasonable man'").

[97] Quick Trust v. Comm'r, 54 TC 1336 (1970), aff'd, 444 F2d 90 (8th Cir. 1971).

[98] Colony, Inc. v. Comm'r, 357 US 28 (1958).

[99] Davenport v. Comm'r, 48 TC 921, 928 (1967) (discussing Rose v. Comm'r, 24 TC 755, 768–769 (1955) (partnership cases)); Benderoff v. United States, 398 F2d 132 (8th Cir. 1968); Roschuni v. Comm'r, 44 TC 80, 85–86 (1965) (Subchapter S corporation cases).

that had realized foreign personal holding company income (foreign base company income), but no information about the company's gross income did not disclose a clue that the foreign corporation was a foreign personal holding company and that the company had foreign personal holding company income.[100] Disclosure rules corresponding to the income tax rules are provided for estate and gift tax omissions, as well as for omissions from excise tax returns.

[c] Personal Holding Company Tax Returns

When personal holding company tax is involved, Section 6501 provides an exception to the general rule that the statute of limitations does not start when a taxpayer fails to file a return. A company ultimately determined to be a personal holding company may file a regular income tax return, but fail to file the schedules of gross income and the names and addresses of shareholders as required by Sections 543 and 544. In *Lane-Wells Co.*, the taxpayer was subject to personal holding company tax, but failed to file the required schedule, and as a result, was held not to have filed a return, which would have started the running of the period of limitations on assessment.[101] Because the taxpayer had failed to file the personal holding company tax return, the personal holding company tax could be assessed at any time.

The six-year period of limitations for making an assessment of personal holding company tax provided by Section 6501(f) overturns the result of *Lane-Wells*. Rather than the Service's being able to assess the tax at any time when a taxpayer fails to file a personal holding company tax return, the Service must assess the personal holding tax within six years.[102]

---

[100] Mariani Frozen Foods, Inc. v. Comm'r, 81 TC 448, 464–465, 503–505 (1983). See also Insulglass Corp. v. Comm'r, 84 TC 203 (1985); White v. Comm'r, 991 F2d 657 (10th Cir. 1993) (no clue about a distribution to a partner when the partnership return did not disclose a distribution to the partner or real estate assets giving rise to the deemed distribution, and the partner's return did not report any distribution). The Tax Court in *Mariani Foods* questioned whether Section 6501(e)(1)(A)(ii) applied to the six-year assessment period of Section 6501(e)(1)(B) for tax on constructive dividends from foreign personal holding companies that omit foreign personal holding company income. The court indicated that the clue exception did not apply, but declined to decide the issue, because it found no clue had been given the Service. Although it stated that it was not deciding the statutory interpretation issue, the Tax Court viewed the clue factor rather more strictly than it does in cases clearly under Section 6501(e)(1)(A)(ii), such as *Quick Trust* and *Insulglass Corp.*, in which the *Colony, Inc.*, standard was not mentioned and the taxpayer found to have provided no disclosure under Section 6501(e)(1)(A)(ii).

[101] Comm'r v. Lane-Wells Co., 321 US 219 (1944).

[102] Quick Trust v. Comm'r, 54 TC 1336 (1970), aff'd, 444 F2d 90 (8th Cir. 1971).

[d] Withholding Tax Returns

Whether more than 25 percent of gross income has been omitted became an issue for withholding tax purposes. In *Northern Indiana Public Service Co.*, a withholding agent argued that the failure to report on Form 1042 income subject to 30 percent withholding pursuant to Sections 871 and 1441(a) was not an omission of "gross income" but rather an understatement of its generic tax liability.[103] The Tax Court rejected the argument that "the withholding tax liability imposed by [S]ections 1441 and 1461 is a tax on disbursements rather than on the income received by petitioner."[104] Because withholding tax was imposed on the interest paid, and the withholding agent was directly liable for the tax (under Section 1461) the withholding tax *was* a tax; Form 1042 was a return of withholding tax, and the omission of income subject to withholding was an omission from the gross income stated in the return (interest is an item of gross income).[105] The Tax Court also said that Form 1042 was not an information return but a return of withholding tax. Form 1042S is an information return.

[e] Effect of a More Than 25 Percent Omission on Other Items

If there is more than a 25 percent omission of income, the statute of limitations is six years. However, is the statute extended for the assessment of the tax on the omitted income only or for all items? In *Colestock*, the Tax Court held that "if the taxpayer omits the requisite amount of income from his return, the taxpayer's entire tax liability for the particular taxable year is subject to the 6-year limitation period."[106] According to the Tax Court, although the legislative history of Section 6501(e)(1)(A) was not entirely clear, it did suggest that Congress intended to preclude a taxpayer's pleading the bar of the statute of limitations when items of income of such magnitude are omitted. Just what this conclusion can mean is illustrated by *Colestock* itself.

The Colestocks failed to report taxable income arising from certain transactions with a corporation. In the Tax Court proceedings, the Colestocks began to challenge the deficiency, and the Service amended its answer to allege that they were liable for an increased deficiency as the result of the disallowance of a portion of a depreciation deduction they claimed on their return.

---

[103] Northern Ind. Pub. Serv. Co. v. Comm'r, 101 TC 294, 298–300 (1993).
[104] Northern Ind. Pub. Serv. Co. v. Comm'r, 101 TC 294, 298 (1993).
[105] Northern Ind. Pub. Serv. Co. v. Comm'r, 101 TC 294, 298–299 (1993).
[106] Colestock v. Comm'r, 102 TC 380 (1994).

[3] Assessments That Must Be Made in Eighteen Months

The assessment period may be shortened from the normal three-year period to eighteen months by giving the Service a written request for a prompt assessment. Such a request may be made only in two situations:[107]

1. There is any tax other than estate tax for which a return is required and for which a decedent or an estate of a decedent may be liable or

2. There is any tax for which a return is required and for which a corporation that is contemplating dissolution, is in the process of dissolving, or has dissolved may be liable.

The request for prompt assessment shortens the normal period of limitations but does not extend the normal three-year period.[108] For example, if a corporate return for the calendar year 1997 was filed on March 15, 1998, a request for prompt assessment made on March 30, 2000, because the corporation was contemplating dissolution, would not extend the period for assessment beyond March 15, 2001, the normal expiration date of the statute of limitations on assessment.

The procedural prerequisites for filing a request for prompt assessment are quite specific. First, a return must have been filed for the taxable year involved. Second, the appropriate person representing the decedent, his or her estate, or the corporation must file the request for prompt assessment in writing (Form 4810) with the district director for the internal revenue district in which the return was filed. (See Form 5.1.) Third, the request must not be attached to the filed return or any other document. It must be filed separately and must set forth the classes of tax and the taxable periods for which the prompt assessment is requested and clearly indicate that it is a request for prompt assessment. Fourth, if a return is filed after a request is made, another request covering that period must be filed.

For a corporation, the eighteen-month period does not apply unless the request notifies the district director that (1) the corporation contemplates dissolution within the eighteen-month period; (2) the dissolution has begun before the expiration of the eighteen-month period; and (3) the dissolution actually has been completed, whether before or after the expiration of the eighteen-month period.[109] Thus, a corporation contemplating dissolution may not change its plans and still shorten the period of limitations on assessment.

---

[107] IRC § 6501(d).

[108] Reg. § 301.6501(d)-1(b).

[109] Reg. § 301.6501(d)-1(c)(1).

FORM 5.1
REQUEST FOR PROMPT ASSESSMENT UNDER INTERNAL REVENUE CODE SECTION 6501(d)

Form 4810 (Rev. June 1994)	Department of the Treasury — Internal Revenue Service **Request for Prompt Assessment** **Under Internal Revenue Code Section 6501(d)** *(Please see instructions on reverse)*	OMB Clearance Number 1545-0430 Expires: 03-31-97

To Director, Internal Revenue Service	Kind of tax

Tax returns for which prompt assessment of any additional tax is requested

Form Number	Tax Period Ended	Social Security or Employer Identification Number	Name and Address Shown on Return	Internal Revenue Service Office Where Filed	Date Filed
1120	12/31/94		Taxpayer, Inc. 1999 Main Street Anytown, NY 00000	Holtsville, NY	3/15/95

Remarks

If applicable, please provide the following information ▶	Spouse's name *(surviving or deceased)*	Spouse's social security number

If the forms listed above are corporation income tax returns, please check one of the boxes below

☐ Dissolution has been completed.

☐ Dissolution has not begun but is expected by the expiration of the 18-month period of limitation; dissolution will begin before the period expires and will be completed either before or after that period expires.

☒ Dissolution has begun and will be completed either before or after the 18-month period of limitation.

I have attached the following item(s) to help expedite action on my request: ☐ Letters testamentary, or ☐ Letters of administration ☐ Copies of returns listed above *(See "What to File" on the back)* ☐ Other:	Requester's name and address Taxpayer, Inc. 1999 Main Street Anytown, NY 00000

	Requester's signature /s/ John Jones	Date 6/10/95

I request a prompt assessment of any additional tax for the kind of tax and periods shown above, as provided by section 6501(d) of the Internal Revenue Code.

Title
President

Form 4810 (Rev. 6-94)

Information and Instructions

The Internal Revenue Service ordinarily has 3 years after the filing of an income tax return in which to assess any additional tax determined to be due, or in which to begin court action to collect the tax. The fiduciary representing a dissolving corporation or a decedent's estate may, however, request a prompt assessment of tax under section 6501(d) of the Internal Revenue Code. This will limit the time for assessing the tax, or for beginning court action to collect it, to 18 months from the date the request is filed. It will not, however, extend the time beyond 3 years from the date a return was filed.

If the taxpayer or fiduciary did not report substantial amounts of gross income or filed false or fraudulent returns, a request for prompt assessment will not shorten the period provided for assessment or legal action.

When to file. You should not file this form until after you have filed the returns you list on it. Note: The special limitation period will apply only to the returns you list on this form. You must submit a separate request for prompt assessment for any returns filed after the date you file this form.

Where to file. Send your request to the Internal Revenue Service office where you filed the returns.

What to file. This form provides spaces for all information required to process your request. If you prefer to use your own format, the request must be filed separately from any other document and must clearly indicate:

— that it is a request for prompt assessment under section 6501(d) of the Internal Revenue Code

— the kind of tax and tax periods

— the name and social security number or employer identification number shown on the return *(copies of returns may be attached to help identify your return; note at top of return: "Copy - Do not process as original")*

— the date and location of the IRS office where the returns were filed

— verification of your authority to act for the taxpayer, such as letters testamentary, letters of administration, etc.

Paperwork Reduction Act Notice

The Paperwork Reduction Act of 1980 says we must tell you why we are collecting this information, how we will use it, and whether you have to give it to us. We ask for the information to carry out the Internal Revenue laws of the United States. We need it to ensure that taxpayers are complying with these laws and to allow us to figure and collect the right amount of tax. You are required to give us this information.

Form 4810 (Rev. 6-84)

[4] Assessments Affected by Special Rules

In addition to the general exceptions to the standard three-year period of limitations, a number of special rules can affect the length and running of this period.[110] The following sections explain these rules in detail.

[a] Extensions of the Period of Limitations by Agreement

The period of limitations on assessment of any tax, except estate tax, may be extended to a date beyond the normal three-year period on assessment by an agreement in writing between the taxpayer and the Commissioner's delegate made before the expiration of either the normal period of assessment or the date agreed on in a prior agreement between the parties.[111] A taxpayer's representative may execute a consent if so authorized. When a joint return is filed, each taxpayer-spouse has the authority to extend the statute, although if only one does, the statute may expire as to the nonsigning spouse.[112] If the Service asks a represented taxpayer for a consent without notifying the representative, the consent is not necessarily invalid.[113] Similarly, the parent company may execute a consent on behalf of its subsidiaries, even if the subsidiary is less than wholly owned.[114]

The Service's policy regarding consents extending the period of limitations is to (1) request such consents only in unusual circumstances; (2) keep to a minimum the number of consents obtained from taxpayers; and (3) request an extension only for the minimum period required for consideration and processing of the case.[115] Because requests for extensions of the period of limi-

---

[110] Special rules also apply to the period of limitations on assessments for partnership items as defined in Section 6231(a)(3). IRC §§ 6501(o), 6629. See Chapter 8 for a discussion of the procedural rules relating to partnership audits.

[111] IRC § 6501(c)(4). Because a consent may make timely what otherwise appears to be an untimely notice of deficiency, proof of the existence of a waiver can be the subject of dispute. For a case in which the original of a consent was lost or destroyed, but circumstantial evidence was used to establish the existence of a consent, see United States v. Conry, 631 F2d 599 (9th Cir. 1980); Eddins v. United States, 93-1 USTC ¶ 50,027 (SD Miss. 1992), aff'd, 9 F3d 103 (5th Cir. 1993) (Form 895, Notice of Statute Expiration, which was internal control document updated each time consent was obtained, established that the missing consent had been obtained).

[112] Tallal v. Comm'r, 77 TC 1291 (1981), aff'd, 778 F2d 275 (5th Cir. 1985). See Form 872 in Chapter 8.

[113] Neuhoff v. Comm'r, 75 TC 36 (1980), aff'd, 669 F2d 291 (5th Cir. 1982).

[114] Rev. Proc. 72-38, 1972-2 CB 813, as amplified by Rev. Proc. 82-6, 1982-1 CB 409. The National Office has advised that both a subsidiary and its consolidated group parent should sign consents to extend the statue of limitation on assessment. FSA 1999-11198 (Sept. 29, 1993).

[115] See Rev. Proc. 57-6, 1957-1 CB 729; Rev. Proc. 79-22, 1979-1 CB 563, ¶ 2.01.

tations are an integral part of the examination of a return and the appeals process, these matters and the forms are discussed more fully in connection with examinations of tax returns.[116] The focus here is on the legal requirement of a valid extension of the period of limitations.

Individuals who are authorized to sign consents to extend the time for the assessment include the following:

- An executor or an administrator for the estate of a decedent
- Any heirs of an intestate decedent who may be held liable under Section 6901
- Any officer of a corporation who is authorized to take such action, regardless of whether he or she signed the return
- Any authorized officer of a dissolved corporation during the period that corporation continues in existence under state law

When a corporation's existence has been terminated by dissolution, shareholders liable under Section 6901 may sign consents for their own liabilities.[117]

When a TEFRA partnership is involved, Section 6229 permits a partner and the Service to make an agreement extending the period for making assessments attributable to partnership items with respect to that individual partner. However, the tax matters partner (or any partner authorized in writing to take such action) may enter into an agreement with the Service binding on all partners.[118]

[i] IRS forms. The Service uses two basic forms for extensions of the period of limitations by agreement: (1) Form 872 (Consent to Extend the Time to Assess Income Tax) is an extension of the statute of limitations on assessment to a specific agreed-on expiration date (and is called a fixed-date waiver) and (2) Form 872-A (Special Consent Fixing Period of Limitation Upon Assessment of Income Tax) that extends the assessment period indefinitely. Form 872-A is used at the taxpayer's option when a case is to be reviewed by the Appeals Office and an extension is needed to permit additional time for the

---

[116] See infra ¶ 5.02[4][a][ii] for problems regarding the interpretation of waiver agreements.

[117] Rev. Rul. 83-41, 1983-1 CB 349, clarified and amplified, Rev. Rul. 84-165, 1984-2 CB 305, which sets forth factual situations. A consent signed by a duly authorized officer of a corporation's successor-in-interest constitutes a binding agreement to extend the assessment period for the former corporation. San Francisco Wesco Polymers, Inc. v. Comm'r, TC Memo 1999-146, 77 TCM 1945 (1999).

[118] Section 6244 makes these provisions applicable to S corporations. The Manual provides for the use of consents restricted to the items of the partnership or S corporation under consideration. Form 8720, Special Consent to Extend Time to Assess Tax Attributable to Items of Partnership; Form 872-R, Special Consent to Extend the Time to Assess Tax Attributable to Items of an S Corporation. See IRM 8.2.1.1.3.1, Consent Forms (Feb. 17, 1999).

Appeals Office to consider the case.[119] Form 872-A extends the period of limitations to a date ninety days after[120] (1) the Service mails a notice of termination of Service consideration of the case; (2) Form 872-T (Notice of Termination of Special Consent to Extend the Time to Assess Tax) is received from the taxpayer terminating the agreement[121]; or (3) the Service sends a notice of deficiency.[122] If a taxpayer wishes to terminate the Form 872-A extension, the taxpayer must file Form 872-T, as provided for in Form 872-A; no other form of communicating the termination is effective to terminate the unlimited extension of the assessment period provided for in Form 872-A.[123] This

[119] These forms are not the only ones that can be considered an extension agreement. See Caporella v. Comm'r, 86 TC 285 (1986), aff'd, 817 F2d 706 (11th Cir. 1987) (Form 5214 filed under Section 183(d) held to be a general consent to extend assessment period for the year).

[120] Since three specific methods for terminating a Form 872-A are provided, a taxpayer may not object that an assessment was not made within a reasonable period after the Form 872-A was terminated. St. John v. United States, 951 F2d 232, 234–235 (9th Cir. 1991) (distinguishing McManus v. Comm'r, 65 TC 197 (1975), aff'd, 583 F2d 443 (9th Cir. 1978)). A Form 872-A has been held not to have been terminated or superseded even by a later executed closing agreement, because the closing agreement did not specifically refer to the Form 872-A. DeSantis v. United States, 783 F. Supp. 165, 170 (SDNY 1992).

[121] Rev. Proc. 79-22, 1979-1 CB 563. Rev. Proc. 79-22 requires a taxpayer to use a Form 872-T to terminate the unlimited waiver on Form 872-A. Before Rev. Proc. 79-22, other less formal means of terminating the Form 872-A had been approved. See Rault v. Comm'r, TC Memo 1982-283, 43 TCM 1446 (1982) (attorney's letter); Borg-Warner Corp. v. Comm'r, 660 F2d 324 (7th Cir. 1981); Winn v. Comm'r, 67 TC 499 (1976), modified on other grounds, 595 F2d 1060 (5th Cir. 1979); McManus v. Comm'r, 65 TC 197 (1975), aff'd, 583 F2d 443 (9th Cir. 1978); Johnson v. Comm'r, 68 TC 637 (1977).

[122] If the notice of deficiency is not sent to the taxpayer's last known address for purposes of Sections 6212 and 6213, the Tax Court has held that the notice nevertheless constitutes a valid termination of a Form 872-A waiver because the form does not explicitly require receipt by the taxpayer. See Roszkos v. Comm'r, 87 TC 1255 (1986), vacated and remanded, 850 F2d 514 (9th Cir. 1988) . After contrary decisions of the Third, Sixth, and Ninth Circuits, the Tax Court declined to follow Roszkos. Coffey v. Comm'r, 96 TC 161 (1991); see Holof v. Comm'r, 872 F2d 50 (3d Cir. 1989); Hubbard v. Comm'r, 872 F2d 183 (6th Cir. 1989); St. John v. United States, 951 F2d 232 (9th Cir. 1991).

[123] The reason for the rule is that at one time, the waiver was found to have been terminated by any written notice, and the Service suffered a number of losses on the issue. See Tapper v. Comm'r, 766 F2d 401 (9th Cir. 1985) (a taxpayer sent a letter rather than a Form 872-T as required by the revised Form 872-A, the letter was not considered to have terminated the extension—a disturbing result); Aronson v. Comm'r, 989 F2d 105 (2d Cir. 1993) (despite the fact that IRS Publication No. 1035 then indicated that a Form 872-A could be terminated by any written notice, the court held that a Form 872-A can be terminated only by a Form 872-T). The First Circuit held that the time period for making an assessment of tax provided in a closing agreement that does not specifically modify an existing Form 870-A does not supersede the Form 870-A; therefore, termination of the unlimited extension provided in the Form 870-A is governed by the terms of the Form 870-A, not those of the closing agreement. Silverman v. Comm'r, 78 AFTR2d 96-5031 (1st

requirement applies even when a taxpayer has executed a Form 872-A, and only wishes to substitute a fixed-date waiver. The taxpayer may not supersede Form 872-A with a fixed-date waiver, but may only terminate Form 872-A with a T form.[124]

When a taxpayer files a Form 870-T, the form does not constitute a waiver of the restrictions on an assessment. The Service still must send the taxpayer a notice of deficiency in accordance with the provisions of Section 6212; and as is the case with other deficiency procedures, the statute of limitations on assessment is tolled for the period that assessment is prohibited.[125]

Suppose a taxpayer executes a Form 872-A for a year giving rise to a net operating loss carryback, but the open-ended waiver does not include the carryback years. Because it determines that the loss is overstated, the Service sends the taxpayer a notice of deficiency for the carryback years. After the Tax Court decision on the carryback years becomes final, the Service assesses the tax due pursuant to the decision, but the assessment is made more than sixty days after the Tax Court's decision has become final. Is the assessment of tax for the carryback years untimely because the Service is bound by the requirement of Form 870-A executed for the loss year that the assessment must be made within sixty days after the notice of deficiency becomes final? The Federal Circuit held that the assessment for the carryback years was timely because the notice of deficiency was not sent for the year covered by Form 872-A, and so "the clause to terminate the extension was not invoked."[126]

[ii] Agreement as a waiver. A taxpayer has a statutory right to have any assessment of tax made within the normal three-year period of limitations, unless some exception to the general rule applies. But when the taxpayer agrees to extend the normal period of limitations, the taxpayer's agreement constitutes a waiver of this right. The Supreme Court has held that a waiver is not a con-

---

Cir. 1996) (closing agreement provided that the Service would assess within one year after the decision in the controlling case; two years passed and the Service still had not assessed, so taxpayer sent a Form 870-T; DeSantis v. United States, 783 F. Supp. 165 (SDNY 1992), cited with approval).

[124] Grunwald v. Comm'r, 86 TC 85 (1986) (letter from Appeals officer did not terminate Form 872-A; termination is accomplished by filing Form 872-T or statutory notice of deficiency); see also Camara v. Comm'r, 91 TC 957 (1988); Wall v. Comm'r, 875 F2d 812 (10th Cir. 1989). The National Office has concluded that a restricted consent Form 872-A(C) was not effective to modify, terminate, or supersede a previously executed unrestricted consent.

[125] Estate of Camara v. Comm'r, 91 TC 957 (1988) (only way to terminate Form 872-A is Form 872-T or notice of deficiency); Wall v. Comm'r, 875 F2d 812 (10th Cir. 1989) (Service not precluded from sending a notice of deficiency almost six years after Form 872-A was executed; "reasonable time" defense rejected).

[126] Mulder v. United States, 80 AFTR2d 97-7741 (Fed. Cir. 1997) (unpublished opinion). For further discussion of these forms, see infra ¶ 5.03[4][a][ii].

tract but "essentially a voluntary, unilateral waiver of a defense by the tax-payer."[127] At one time, it was felt that the requirement that the Commissioner sign a consent of the extension of the period of limitations was included in the statute merely for administrative purposes. If the taxpayer signed the waiver agreement, but a delegate of the Commissioner did not, the waiver signed was nevertheless valid.[128] This is no longer the case. Until a consent is executed on behalf of the Commissioner, it is not valid.[129] This requirement for validity is now generally recognized.[130]

A consent to the extension of the period of limitations is not considered to be a contract, even though signed by both parties; nevertheless courts have interpreted the consent form as though a contract were involved[131] and have

---

[127] Stange v. United States, 282 US 270, 276 (1931) (discussing Florsheim Bros. Drygoods Co. v. United States, 280 US 453, 466 (1930)); Beer v. Comm'r, TC Memo 1982-735, 45 TCM 401 (1982), aff'd, 733 F2d 435 (6th Cir. 1984).

[128] See Stange v. United States, 282 US 270 (1931); Holbrook v. United States, 284 F2d 747 (9th Cir. 1960); Lesser v. United States, 368 F2d 306 (2d Cir. 1966). The point is well established in the Tax Court. See, e.g., Schulman v. Comm'r, 93 TC 623, 639 (1989).

[129] Reg. § 301.6501(c)-1(d). These regulations did not exist under the 1939 Code. The authority of the Commissioner to sign consents to extension of the assessment and collection periods has been redelegated. The officials to whom the delegation of authority runs are set forth in a Commissioner's Delegation Order (CDO No. 42). The most current revision of this order may be found by checking recent Internal Revenue Bulletins and the Cumulative Bulletin. For a case in which the authority of the officials signing for the Commissioner was questioned, see Cindrich v. Comm'r, TC Memo 1984-294, 48 TCM 252 (1984) (persons who signed were duly authorized delegates under redelegation order). The Service's position is also that unless the waiver is signed on behalf of the Commissioner before the limitations period has expired, the Service will concede that the waiver is not effective. FSA 1998-4 (CC:FS:TL-N4511-92, May 13, 1992), 98 TNT 98-17.

[130] Rohde v. United States, 415 F2d 695 (9th Cir. 1969). Accord United States v. Cook, 494 F2d 573 (5th Cir. 1974). For many years, Form 656, Offer in Compromise, included a waiver and suspension of the statute for assessment and collection during the time the offer was being considered and for one year thereafter. Accordingly, after the taxpayer submitted the signed offer form, and the Service had executed the offer form, the waiver of the statute of limitations and consent had been signed by both parties, despite the fact that the offer had not been accepted (the offer is accepted by a separate notice). See Streck v. Comm'r, TC Memo. 1997-407, 74 TCM 545 (1997).

[131] See, e.g., Aiken v. Burnet, 282 US 277 (1931). See Piarulle v. Comm'r, 80 TC 1035, 1042 (1983) ("[c]ontract principles are significant . . . because section 6501(c)(4) requires that the parties reach a written agreement as to the extension"). Principles of contract construction have been applied. See Constitution Publ'g Co., 22 BTA 426 (1931); United States v. Hodgekins, 28 F3d 610 (7th Cir. 1994); Evinrude v. Comm'r, TC Memo 1980-454, 41 TCM 159, 165, 166 (1980).

Administratively, the Service has applied contract principles. See Priv. Ltr. Rul. 8435014 (May 23, 1984) (technical advice ruling on Forms 872 and 872-A, in which names of two entities omitted through clerical error). For a further critical analysis of the

applied contract principles[132] in such situations as the alteration of a consent,[133] the application of contract defenses, such as incapacity,[134] duress,[135] lack of agreement,[136] and lack of capacity.[137] A consent agreement has also been re-

---

cases, especially cases involving Forms 870-A, see Townsend & Jones, "Interpreting Consents to Extend the Statute of Limitations," 98 TNT 16-108 (Jan. 26, 1998).

[132] See United States v. Hodgekins, 805 F. Supp. 653 (ND Ind. 1992), aff'd, 28 F3d 610 (7th Cir. 1994) (the waiver form reserved the right to reopen in the event Justice Department decided to "*interplead*" potential responsible persons, and acordingly, interpleader was required to reopen even if the form of action the Service meant to use as a condition was *impleader*. Using contract principles, the court said: "We give effect to the words in the [waiver] forms according to their plain meaning, because the plain meaning is the best indication of what the parties intended.").

[133] Amhowitz v. United States, 59 AFTR2d 87-1088 (SDNY 1987) (attachment to consent form prepared by taxpayer was removed by agents and consent was returned to taxpayer signed on behalf of Service; held, consent was ineffective and limitations period on assessment expired); Kronish v. Comm'r, 90 TC 684 (1988) (taxpayer signed form but argued she intended to restrict its terms; held, objective act controlled); Marx v. Comm'r, 13 TC 1099 (1949) (an erroneous date in transmittal returning copy did not affect the agreement evidenced by executed form); compare Ronald H. Scheurman v. Comm'r, TC Memo. 1984-160 (1984) (statements in cover letter may be considered on the issue of assent) with Eckersley v. United States, 90-2 USTC ¶ 50,535 (ND Cal. 1990) (cover letter did not modify generality of Form 872-A waiver). Schwotzer v. Comm'r, 51 TCM 902 (1986) (taxpayer restricted consent, and Service did not intend to execute a restricted consent). See also Southern v. Comm'r, 87 TC 49 (1986) (language permitting an adjustment to taxpayer's distributive share of partnership income in a Form 870-A interpreted to permit an assessment resulting from investment credit recapture).

[134] A waiver can be found void when the taxpayer is incapacitated and the waiver is signed by a representative. In *Halper*, the taxpayer suffered a stroke and was incompetent; the waiver the taxpayer's former representative signed was held invalid because the representative's authority had been invalidated by the taxpayer's incompetency; correspondence between the former representative put the Service on notice that it could no longer rely on the representative's power of attorney. Halper v. Comm'r, TC Memo 1997-58, 73 TCM 1897 (1997).

[135] See, e.g., Robertson v. Comm'r, TC Memo 1973-205, 32 TCM 955 (1973) (taxpayer established that harassment resulted in duress; therefore, waiver was invalid); E. Ray Price v. Comm'r, TC Memo. 1981-693 (1981) (former return preparer who appeared for others before the Service, found not to have signed consent under duress).

[136] When a Form 872 is changed after it has been signed by the taxpayer, the document does not constitute an agreement by both the taxpayer and the Service. Cary v. Comm'r, 48 TC 754, 766 (1967); Piarulle v. Comm'r, 80 TC 1035, 1043–1044 (1983) (Form 872 incorporating three taxable years altered by deleting one year; held, the entire waiver invalid).

[137] For example, the contract principle that unless the rights and obligations created in a contract are personal in nature, they survive death and are binding on executors, with the result that a waiver executed by a deceased taxpayer bound the executors of his estate. Herr v. Comm'r, TC Memo 1992-88, 63 TCM 2056 (1992).

formed to reflect the agreement of the parties.[138] Taxpayers may also be equitably estopped from denying the validity of a waiver.[139] Because the extension statute itself requires that a consent be executed before the expiration of the statute of limitations has expired, a consent is not valid if it is agreed to after the limitations period.[140]

If the taxpayer's agreement to extend the period of limitations is characterized as a waiver of the taxpayer's right to have the assessment made within the applicable period, should the taxpayer be informed of the taxpayer's right to refuse the Service's request for the statute extension? Until 1998, the answer to this question seemed to be no. In search and seizure and other cases involving waiver of constitutional rights and privileges, it has been held that, while a person's knowledge of a right to refuse is a factor to be taken into account in determining "voluntariness," the person's knowledge is not a prerequisite to establishing voluntary consent.[141] Moreover, once the Service produces a waiver valid on its face, the taxpayer has the burden of proving the invalidity of the waivers under Section 6501(c)(4).[142] This was the law until Congress amended the waiver exception of Section 6501(c).[143] Now the Service must no-

---

[138] A waiver form containing the wrong tax year has been reformed to reflect the correct year using contract principles because the change reflected the true agreement of the parties. Buchine v. Comm'r, TC Memo 1992-36, 63 TCM 1838 (1992), aff'd, 20 F3d 173 (5th Cir. 1994) (reformation of agreement form was application of equitable principles, not exercise of general equitable powers to take jurisdiction over matters not provided for by statute); Kelley v. Comm'r, 45 F3d 348 (9th Cir. 1995) ("[t]he Tax Court has a limited equitable power to reform consent-to-extend agreements that are otherwise properly before it as part of the subject matter in dispute").

[139] Benoit v. Comm'r, 25 TC 656 (1955), vacated, 238 F2d 485 (1st Cir. 1956). But see Cary v. Comm'r, 48 TC 754 (1967); Piarulle v. Comm'r, 80 TC 1035 (1983) (estoppel not found because taxpayer had not misled the Service when the document relied on was altered by revenue agent without the taxpayer's consent).

[140] IRC § 6501(c)(4)(A) ("[w]here before the expiration of the time prescribed in this section for the assessment of any tax imposed by this title . . . the Secretary and the taxpayer have consented in writing"). See Tech. Adv. Mem. 8552006 (Sept. 5, 1985) (consent executed more than eighteen months after the filing of a request for a prompt assessment under Section 6501(d), but within three years after return filing; because assessment period had expired, the time for filing a refund claim also had expired). The National Office advised that an assessment extension waiver that was executed after the statute of limitations had expired was valid, relying on Bubinsky v. Becker, 64 F2d 601 (8th Cir. 1933), which interpreted Section 607 of the Revenue Act of 1928. FSA 1999-390 (Nov. 2, 1999).

[141] Schneckloth v. Bustamonte, 412 US 218, 232–233 (1973), on remand, Bustamonte v. Schneckloth, 47 F2d 1047 (9th Cir. 1973).

[142] Crown Williamette Paper Co. v. McLaughlin, 81 F2d 365 (9th Cir.), cert. denied, 298 US 674 (1936). See also Cindrich v. Comm'r, TC Memo 1984-294, 48 TCM 252 (1984) (analyzing cases).

[143] IRC § 6501(c)(4)(B).

tify a taxpayer that the taxpayer has the right to refuse to execute a waiver of the statute of limitations on assessment.

[b] Carrybacks

Taxpayers may apply for refunds of tax based on the carryback of a net operating loss,[144] capital loss,[145] or business tax credit[146] and are permitted to obtain a refund of tax for the carryback year on the basis of a tentative claim arising out of transactions in the loss or credit year.[147] Refunds attributable to loss carrybacks are often made after the normal three-year period of limitations for assessment, the period for assessing deficiencies attributable to these refunds has been extended. Section 6501(h) provides the following rules when net operating losses or capital losses are carried back:

> In the case of a deficiency attributable to the application to the taxpayer of a net operating loss carryback or a capital loss carryback (including deficiencies which may be assessed pursuant to the provisions of Section 6213(b)(3) [dealing with assessments that may arise out of tentative carryback or refund adjustments arising out of excess refunds made under Section 6411]), the deficiency may be assessed at any time before the expiration of the period within which a deficiency for the taxable year of the net operating loss or net capital loss which results in such carryback may be assessed.

The extended assessment period applicable to carrybacks is to ensure adequate time to handle the carryback refund and to take into account the fact that events giving rise to the carryback may not occur until a number of years after the close of the taxable year of overpayment.[148] The period of extension differs according to the nature of the carryback, as follows:

1. *Net operating loss and capital loss.* Three years from date of return for year giving rise to carryback.[149]
2. *Foreign tax credit.* Four years from date of return, for year of excess taxes described in Section 904(d).[150]
3. *Business credit.* Three years from date of return for year of unused credit or, if net operating or capital loss carryback from a later year

---

[144] IRC § 172(b).

[145] IRC § 1212(a)(1).

[146] These credit carrybacks are defined in Section 6511(d)(4)(C). See IRC § 6501(j)(2).

[147] IRC § 6411(a).

[148] Jones v. Comm'r, 71 TC 391, 396 (1978).

[149] IRC § 6501(h)

[150] IRC § 6501(i).

gives rise to investment credit carryback, three years from the date of the return for loss year.[151]

A carryback extends the period of assessment for the carryback year. Assessment of tax attributable to a net operating loss or capital loss carryback may be made at any time before the statute of limitations on assessment for the year of the net operating loss or capital loss giving rise to the carryback.[152] A similar rule applies to a tentative carryback adjustment.[153] Because the period of assessment for both provisions is governed by the general three-year statutory period for the loss year, the assessment period can be extended by agreement, and its running may be suspended for a number of reasons (e.g., by the filing of a Tax Court petition).[154] If the normal assessment period for the loss year is extended by agreement, the extension applies to the carryback years as well.[155] Within the extended period, Section 6501(h) permits the Service to assess a deficiency attributable to items related to the loss carryback, but not one attributable to items unrelated to the loss carryback.[156]

If a deficiency for a carryback year can be assessed as long as the statute of limitations for the loss year is open, what happens if the statute of limitations for the loss year has closed, but the statute for the carryback year is open? Can a deficiency for the carryback year be assessed? In *Calumet Industries, Inc.,*[157] the Tax Court held that as long as, under some provision, the period for assessment of tax for the carryback year is open, the amount of tax due for the carryback year may be redetermined and any deficiency may be as-

---

[151] IRC §§ 6501(j), 6501(p).

[152] IRC § 6501(h).

[153] IRC § 6501(m).

[154] See Midland Mortgage Co. v. United States, 576 F. Supp. 101 (WD Okla. 1983) (taxpayer's filing of Tax Court petition in response to invalid notice of deficiency relating to loss year did not suspend running of limitations period). William F. Smith v. Comm'r, TC Memo. 1989-432 (1989), aff'd; Smith v. Comm'r, 925 F2d 250, 67 AFTR2d 91-509 (8th Cir. 1991) (Form 872-A was signed for carryback year and Tax Court petition was filed, so increased deficiency was not time-barred).

[155] Centennial Sav. Bank FSB v. United States, 670 F. Supp. 195 (ND Tex. 1987).

[156] Leuthesser v. Comm'r, 18 TC 1112 (1952); Bouchey v. Comm'r, 19 TC 1078 (1953). Section 6501(h) has been held not to preclude the Service's basing a deficiency on a carryforward adjustment (to a minimum tax computation), as long as it can be traced directly to a carryback. Note that the statute of limitations on assessment does not bar the recomputation of a loss in a closed year to determine the amount of a deficiency in an open year. First Chicago Corp. v. Comm'r, 742 F2d 1102 (7th Cir. 1984). The circuit court held that a 1972 deficiency could be traced to a carryback from 1974 to 1971. Consequently, the exceptions of Sections 6501(h) and 6501(j) were applicable because the 1972 deficiency was attributable to (i.e., traceable to) the taxpayer's carryback claim. See also Leitgen v. Comm'r, 691 F2d 504 (8th Cir. 1982); ABKCO Indus. v. Comm'r, 56 TC 1083, 1089 (1971), aff'd on other grounds, 482 F2d 150 (3d Cir. 1973).

[157] Calumet Indus., Inc. v. Comm'r, 95 TC 257 (1990).

sessed, even if the assessment period for the loss year has expired. When the carryback year is before the Tax Court, the court reasoned that in redetermining the amount of a deficiency for the open carryback year, Section 6214(b) permits it to consider facts, including the amount of a net operating loss, for a related year. The Tax Court may consider data from another tax year in determining a deficiency in a year before the court, even if the related year is closed and is not in issue before the court. The court also reasoned that because Section 6501(h) was intended to extend the limitations period for assessment of tax for the carryback year, a ruling that shortened the assessment period was inconsistent with legislative intent.

Similarly, when (1) assessment is barred for a year giving rise to a credit or loss carryback but (2) the open carryback year is before the Tax Court, the Tax Court is permitted to redetermine the tax for the barred year; therefore, the amount of the credit or loss available for carryback to the open year is permitted to be redetermined under Section 6214(b).[158]

When a refund is granted under Section 6411 by way of a tentative carryback claim, Section 6501(k) permits the Service to assess a deficiency for the carryback on grounds not attributable to the carryback as long as the deficiency does not exceed the amount of the refund the taxpayer received, reduced by any amount of the deficiency actually attributable to the carryback.[159] The portion of the deficiency attributable to carryback is assessable under Section 6501(h) (if it is a net operating or capital loss carryback), and the balance of the deficiency up to the tentative refund amount is assessable under Section 6501(k).[160] However, owing to the difference between the two provisions, the deficiency may be proved or disproved on any ground to the extent that assessment of the deficiency is attempted under Section 6501(m).[161]

¶ 5.04 JUDICIAL DOCTRINES RELATING TO PERIODS OF LIMITATIONS ON ASSESSMENT

The purpose of periods of limitations is to fix a day beyond which the correctness of a tax need not be subject to contest or justification, in short, to prevent

---

[158] Hill v. Comm'r, 95 TC 437 (1990).

[159] Maxcy v. Comm'r, 59 TC 716 (1973); Pesch v. Comm'r, 78 TC 100 (1982) (quick refund for 1971 obtained by way of carryback of 1974 loss, assessment period for 1974 extended by agreement; held, notice of deficiency as to 1971 sent before extended assessment period for 1974 expired was timely, and 1971 was open even though deficiency not attributable to carryback of the 1974 loss).

[160] Jones v. Comm'r, 71 TC 391 (1978); Reg. § 301.6501(m)-1(a).

[161] Jones v. Comm'r, 71 TC 391, 397 (1978); Maxcy v. Comm'r, 59 TC 716, 730–731 (1973).

the litigation of stale claims.[162] Courts have recognized that it is unfair for either a taxpayer or the government to gain an advantage by waiting until the period of limitations for refund or assessment has expired before taking action that may be construed as inconsistent with the treatment of the same item on a closed year. To remedy this perceived unfairness, courts have developed the doctrines of equitable recoupment, setoff, and estoppel.

At the outset, it must be noted that the statutory mitigation provisions have largely superseded these judicial doctrines; however recoupment, setoff, and estoppel remain relevant for at least two reasons. First, the mitigation provisions were enacted to cure the unpredictable results these judicial doctrines produced, thus the mitigation provisions can be better understood in light of the judicial efforts to deal with some of the same problems.[163] Second, the mitigation provisions do not purport to apply to all cases in which either a taxpayer or the government, by using the statute of limitations, attempts to profit by inconsistency. In situations when the mitigation provisions do not apply, these judicial doctrines still apply.[164] For example, the mitigation provisions apply only to income taxes; recoupment can be applied to cases involving estate tax.[165] Mitigation provisions permit adjustment of tax in a closed year when there is a *single* item of income or deduction with respect to which the taxpayer or the Commissioner has maintained an inconsistent position, and the error and inconsistent position occur in *different* years. Setoff can be applied when the inconsistency is with respect to *different* items in the *same* taxable year.[166]

[1] Recoupment

Recoupment permits a party against whom a claim is asserted to defeat the claim by means of a demand or defense arising from the same transaction. In *Bull v. United States*, there had been the double inclusion of an item of income when, for estate tax purposes, an estate had included in the gross estate

---

[162] Rothensies v. Electric Storage Battery Co., 329 US 296 (1946).

[163] For an analysis of the doctrines of recoupment, setoff, and estoppel documenting the uncertainty of results and their generally pro-government bias, see Maguire & Zimet, "Hobson's Choice and Similar Practices in Federal Taxation," 48 Harv. L. Rev. 1281 (1935); Maguire, Surrey & Traynor, "Section 820 of the Revenue Act of 1938 (Part I)," 48 Yale LJ 509 (1939). See also Willis, "Equitable Recoupment, Tax Mitigation, and Res Judicata," 38 Tax Law. 625 (1985). See also Willis, "Correction of Errors via Mitigation and Equitable Recoupment," 52 Tax Notes 1421 (Sept. 16, 1991).

[164] Benenson v. United States, 385 F2d 26 (2d Cir. 1967); Gooding v. United States, 326 F2d 988 (Ct. Cl.), cert. denied, 379 US 834 (1964); Maguire, Surrey & Traynor, "Section 820 of the Revenue Act of 1938 (Part II)," 48 Yale LJ 719, 773–775 (1939).

[165] Bull v. United States, 295 US 247, 262 (1935).

[166] Lewis v. Reynolds, 284 US 281 (1932).

of a deceased partner an amount the partnership owed the decedent, and also paid income tax on the same amount. After the period of limitations on the refund of the estate tax had expired, the executors filed a claim for refund of either the estate or income tax. The Supreme Court held that the estate was entitled to refund of the estate tax on the theory of recoupment, despite the fact that the claim was untimely.

Using the doctrine of recoupment, the Supreme Court permitted the barred claim describing the doctrine, as "in the nature of a defense arising out of some feature of the transaction upon which the plaintiff's action is grounded" and saying that the defense "is never barred by the statute of limitations so long as the main action itself is timely."[167] A single transaction or item of income was involved (the amount paid by the partnership), and if the Commissioner had sued the estate to collect income tax on this item in the court of claims, the rules of that court would have allowed the estate to recoup the estate tax erroneously paid on the item. Accordingly, the taxpayer's right of recoupment was not lost merely because the taxpayer estate paid the amount of the deficiency and sued for refund rather than the Service's having to sue the taxpayer estate to collect the tax.

Because *Bull* dealt with a single item of income, courts say that equitable recoupment is limited to situations involving a single item or transaction. This "single item" element does not permit a taxpayer to open all returns on which that item or transaction is reported, however. In *Electric Storage Battery Co.*,[168] in 1946, the taxpayer successfully claimed a refund of excise tax paid between 1922 and 1926. When the Service refunded the excise tax, however, it treated the refund as giving rise to additional income tax. To offset this additional income tax, the taxpayer responded by filing a refund claim asserting that it should be permitted to recoup the amount of excise taxes for the years 1919 through 1921 in order to defeat the additional income tax. The Supreme Court said:

> [W]hen this suit was brought in 1943, the claim pleaded as recoupment was for taxes collected over twenty years before and for over sixteen years barred by the statute [of limitations on refund]. That claims dead so long can be resurrected under this doctrine, is enough to show its menace to the statute of limitations—at least as to those taxpayers whose affairs by accident or design take such shape that they can avail themselves of recoupment remedies.[169]

Accordingly, the Court said, a ground for recoupment is not established merely because items are related, especially when the result is that every assessment

---

[167] Bull v. United States, 295 US 247, 262 (1935).

[168] Rothensies v. Electric Storage Battery Co., 329 US 296 (1946).

[169] Rothensies v. Electric Storage Battery Co., 329 US 296 (1946).

of a deficiency and each claim for refund "would invite a search of the tax-payer's entire tax history for items to recoup."[170] *Electric Storage Battery* thus imposes a limitation, albeit an uncertain one, on the single-transaction or taxa-ble-item element of the doctrine of recoupment. Unfortunately, the Supreme Court did not articulate the limits of the doctrine of recoupment with any kind of precision so that the result in other cases might be determined in advance.

[a] Who May Use Equitable Recoupment?

Equitable recoupment may be used by the Service as well as by taxpay-ers, and the doctrine may be used to recover from persons who are related to the taxpayer. When a single transaction or item is involved, the Service may recoup an otherwise barred deficiency from a refund due a related person. In *Stone v. White*,[171] testamentary trustees paid income tax on trust income that the beneficiaries of the trust erroneously excluded from their income. After the Commissioner's claim against the beneficiaries was barred by the period of limitations on assessment, the trustees filed a claim for refund and, when it was disallowed, sued for refund. The Commissioner's denial of the claim was justified as recoupment of tax properly payable by the beneficiaries, although erroneously paid by the trustees. The Supreme Court upheld recoupment, con-cluding that there was no unjust enrichment that entitled the trustees to any re-fund because the error had not increased the tax burden of either the trust or the beneficiaries. Accordingly, the Supreme Court said that the Commissioner had not raised a "counter demand on [the trustees], but [had denied] their equi-table right to undo a payment which, though effected by an erroneous proce-dure, [had] resulted in no unjust enrichment to the Government, and in no injury to [the trustees] or their beneficiary."[172] The Court ruled that the defense of the government inhered in the cause of action and was comparable to "an equitable recoupment or diminution of petitioners' right to recovery."[173]

As these Supreme Court decisions show, when equitable recoupment is used, the result is often unpredictable. During the same term that *Stone v. White* was decided in favor of the Service, the Court also reached a contrary conclusion deciding *McEachern v. Rose*.[174] In *McEachern*, a decedent had made an installment sale of stock in 1924, and, after his death, his administra-tor reported the installments in tax returns for years during which installments were received, including the years 1928 through 1931. However, the 1929 through 1931 returns were erroneous because the value of the unpaid install-

---

[170] Rothensies v. Electric Storage Battery Co., 329 US 296 (1946).

[171] Stone v. White, 301 US 532 (1937).

[172] Stone v. White, 301 US 532, 539 (1937).

[173] Stone v. White, 301 US 532 (1937).

[174] McEachern v. Rose, 302 US 56 (1937).

ments should have been included in the 1928 return as income in respect of a decedent rather than as income received in the subsequent years. Moreover, additional unpaid tax due for 1928 exceeded the overpayments the taxpayer made for the years 1929 through 1931. By the time that the administrator of the taxpayer's estate filed claims for refund of this overpaid tax, the statute of limitations on assessment for 1928 had run.

The Supreme Court held that because the installments were properly excludable for 1929 through 1931, the administrator was entitled to refund of the overpayments for those years. However, it also held that the Commissioner was not entitled to recoup the 1928 deficiency from the 1929 through 1931 overpayments. The Court was not willing to disregard the bar of the statute of limitations altogether, despite the double exclusion of an item of income that was the result of its decision. The Court reasoned that at the time overpayments had been made for 1930 and 1931 the Commissioner was not entitled to credit the overpayment against the 1928 deficiency because assessment of the deficiency was barred. When the 1929 overpayment was made, credit of the overpayment against the 1928 deficiency was not barred, but the amount of the credit was not determined until after the statute of limitations on assessment had run. *McEachern* differed from *Stone* in that assessment and collection of the deficiency were barred at the time the Commissioner sought to credit an overpayment for another year to the deficiency. In *Stone*, assessment and collection of a deficiency against the trustees were not barred.

Deriving meaningful general principles from these Supreme Court decisions is difficult at best. The very uncertainty these decisions created led Congress to adopt the mitigation provisions, and the facts of the cases may be found in some of the circumstances of adjustment and the "related person" features of the mitigation provisions. It can be said, however, that recoupment requires the inconsistent treatment of a single item or transaction, as in *Bull*, in which the same item of partnership income was taxed twice. On the other hand, recoupment does not permit an unlimited review of returns to find a qualitatively identical item of income or deduction if the taxpayer or Commissioner has taken no action for a long period (e.g., the excise taxes erroneously treated by the taxpayer in *Electric Storage Battery* some thirteen years before a refund claim was filed). Both the double inclusion of an item of income (*Bull*) and the double exclusion of an item of income (*Stone*) give rise to a basis for recoupment. Thus, although a deficiency is otherwise barred from assessment against beneficiaries who had excluded an item from their income, the Commissioner may recoup the deficiency from the refund due a trust because the item was excludable from the income of the trust that had erroneously paid tax on it. Less clearly, it seems that recoupment is permitted in a situation when an item of income erroneously excluded in one year is determined to be correctly excluded in another year. Assessment of tax for the year of erroneous exclusion may be made only if assessment can still be made at the time the Service has notice of the erroneous exclusion (*McEachern*). Finally, recoupment is permitted from a refund otherwise due a taxpayer when that taxpayer is related to the taxpayer who has erroneously excluded the item of income (*Stone*).

[b] What Facts Support Equitable Recoupment?

Following *Electric Storage Battery*, courts have applied equitable recoupment to various factual situations with unpredictable results. It is frequently said that the doctrine is "strictly limited" to a single transaction or item of income.[175] On this theory, courts have denied recoupment when the recoupment claim and the refund claim or assessment arise from two transactions or items.[176] One circuit court has held that the doctrine is limited to cases in which a single transaction has been subjected to two taxes on inconsistent legal theories, and ordered a taxpayer to repay taxes erroneously refunded when the taxpayer failed to file a timely refund claim.[177] In other cases, despite what

---

[175] Wilmington Trust Co. v. United States, 610 F2d 703 (Ct. Cl. 1979).

[176] Wilmington Trust Co. v. United States, 610 F2d 703 (Ct. Cl. 1979) (recoupment claim arose from a reduced deduction from gross estate, but refund claim from increased deductions from gross income); Kramer v. United States, 406 F2d 1363 (Ct. Cl. 1969) (government sought recoupment of taxes owed by one beneficiary of a multi-beneficiary estate); Ford v. United States, 276 F2d 17 (Ct. Cl. 1960) (assets valued twice, once for estate tax purposes and once for income tax purposes at the time of subsequent sale, resulting in higher estate tax assessment under first valuation and higher income tax assessment under second valuation); Minskoff v. United States, 490 F2d 1283 (2d Cir. 1974), aff'g 349 F. Supp. 1146 (SDNY 1972) (estate tax paid on estate including cash representing full sale price of recently disposed asset; capital gain tax deficiency for that sale subsequently assessed against the estate); Missouri Pub. Serv. Co. v. United States, 245 F. Supp. 954 (WD Mo. 1965), aff'd, 370 F2d 971 (8th Cir. 1967) (adjustments to correct repeated Service mistreatments of depreciation of assets increased one year's taxes and decreased another's); Kojes v. United States, 241 F. Supp. 762 (EDNY 1965) (essentially the same facts as in *Minskoff*); Provident Nat'l Bank v. United States, 507 F. Supp. 1197 (ED Pa. 1981) (claimed overpayment of capital gain taxes paid by taxpayer-trusts arising out of settlement between settlor's estate and Service held to be two separate taxpayers and recoupment denied); Mann v. United States, 552 F. Supp. 1132 (ND Tex. 1982), aff'd, 731 F2d 267 (5th Cir. 1984) (holding that an estate tax claim and income tax claim did not arise out of a single transaction that had been subjected to two taxes on inconsistent legal theories, because the income tax claim arose out of the taxpayer's right to deduct worthless business debts from ordinary income, whereas the recoupment claim was based on the failure to include the claim for refund on the estate tax return; extensive analysis of the authorities).

[177] United States v. Tomar Hills, Inc., 783 F2d 753 (8th Cir. 1986) ("Taxpayers who do not challenge deficiencies in court should not be granted untimely refunds after the Service's position is held erroneous in another case. Taxpayers should not be encouraged to seek untimely refunds, hoping that they will be erroneously granted, thus providing a chance to apply equitable recoupment."). But see Kolom v. United States, 791 F2d 762 (9th Cir. 1986) (taxpayer liable for tax in 1972 was held entitled to a refund of 1973 tax, although limitations period for filing a formal refund claim had expired and mitigation

appear to be two transactions or items, recoupment has nevertheless been allowed.[178] The Service seems to have taken the view that a single item or transaction is not a prerequisite to equitable recoupment, in ruling that the doctrine of recoupment is not limited to a single transaction or item.[179] In litigation, the Service has claimed, on equitable recoupment grounds, that it was entitled to retain estate taxes of a stepfather's estate, although those taxes had been paid out of a trust that had been established after the mother's death, as the result of a suit her heir brought in which they claimed misappropriation of the mother's separate property.[180] The circuit court held that the claim of equitable

---

provisions did not apply, otherwise the Service would be unjustly enriched; equitable recoupment doctrine applied).

[178] National Biscuit Co. v. United States, 156 F. Supp. 916 (Ct. Cl. 1957) (incorrect excess profits credit led to overpayment of some taxes and underpayment of others); EI du Pont de Nemours & Co. v. United States, 147 F. Supp. 486 (Ct. Cl. 1957) (incorrect treatment of rescission of excess profits tax deferral led to unnecessary payment of interest on one tax deficiency and nonpayment of interest on another); Pond's Extract Co. v. United States, 134 F. Supp. 476 (Ct. Cl. 1955) (incorrect treatment of payment of income tax settlement decreased subsequent excess profits taxes and increased a subsequent income tax); Boyle v. United States, 355 F2d 233 (3d Cir. 1965) (estate tax paid on arrearage of cumulative preferred stock dividends extant at decedent's death; income tax assessed on subsequent payments against the arrearage); United States v. Bowcut, 287 F2d 654 (9th Cir. 1961) (underpayment of income taxes by decedent taxpayer led to overpayment of estate taxes); United States v. Herring, 240 F2d 225 (4th Cir. 1957) (same as Bowcut, but Service did not assert deficiency claim against the estate until after the estate tax limitations period expired).

[179] See Rev. Rul. 71-56, 1971-1 CB 404 (holding that a barred overpayment of estate tax resulting from an income tax deficiency may be applied against the related predeath income tax deficiency owed by the decedent). In Rev. Rul. 71-56, the Service stated that its holding that equitable recoupment could be applied was based on a single item or transaction. But as the later ruling showed, this can be true only by the broadest interpretation of the terms. See Priv. Ltr. Rul. 8333007 (May 15, 1983) (technical advice holding that a barred overpayment of income tax could be applied to an outstanding deficiency in excise tax for the same taxable year under the doctrine of equitable recoupment); Priv. Ltr. Rul. 8342006 (June 30, 1983) (technical advice holding that a foreign mutual insurance company's barred overpayment of income tax erroneously paid on U.S. premium income could be credited against the excise tax actually due on premiums paid by policyholders in the United States under the doctrine of equitable recoupment); Tech. Adv. Mem. 8552005 (Aug. 29, 1985) (after the taxpayer paid assessed additional income tax, applying the equitable recoupment doctrine, the taxpayer was held to be permitted to file a refund claim to recover the income tax to the extent of a barred overpayment of excise tax).

[180] Parker v. United States, 110 F3d 678, 79 AFTR2d 97-1766 (9th Cir. 1997). In rejecting the government's argument, the circuit court noted that there were two or more taxpayers (the stepfather's estate, the mother's estate, and the heirs), two or more transactions (the stepfather's appropriation of the mother's assets, the valuation of the mother's claim against the stepfather, and the establishment of a trust, the income from which was paid to the stepfather, and the corpus of which was payable to the heir on his death), and no inconsistent treatment (the trust corpus had erroneously been included in stepfather's

recoupment was not available because there was no single transaction and no identity of taxpayers. The Service claimed the trust assets were includable in the mother's estate and that the statute of limitations on assessment of her estate tax had expired.

Some sixty-five years after its decision in *Bull*, the Supreme Court had occasion once again to address the nature of equitable recoupment. In *Dalm*, Frances Dalm, the decedent's long time secretary, was named the executrix of his estate and, for her services in this capacity, she received court-approved fees from the estate in both 1976 and 1977.[181] In addition to these fees, the decedent's brother also made payments to her of $180,000 in 1976, and more than $133,000 in 1977. The decedent's brother filed a gift tax return reporting the 1976 payment as a gift; the tax on which Dalm paid to the Service. After an audit, the Service determined that the payments Dalm received from the decedent's brother constituted additional fee income, subject to income tax. Dalm challenged the determination by filing a petition in the Tax Court. During the trial on the gift versus compensation issue, Dalm and the Service settled the case, and later filed a stipulated decision, which stated that Dalm owed additional income tax for both 1976 and 1977. Dalm did not raise any claim for a credit or refund of the amount of 1976 gift tax she had paid. After the settlement of her Tax Court case, in 1984, Dalm filed a claim for refund of the income tax she had paid in 1976, about five years after the three-year statute of limitations on filing a refund claim had expired. Accordingly, when Dalm filed her suit for refund in district court, the Service filed a motion to dismiss on the ground that the court lacked jurisdiction because her refund claim was untimely. Dalm replied that her suit was timely under the doctrine of equitable recoupment. The district court dismissed Dalm's suit, holding that equitable recoupment did not authorize it to exercise jurisdiction over an "independent" suit for refund for a year for which the statute of limitations on refunds had expired. The circuit court reversed, finding that the requirements of equitable recoupment in *Bull* had been satisfied, and saying that Dalm could bring her suit for refund, although it was otherwise barred, because the Service had made a timely claim that she owed a deficiency in income tax, based on a theory inconsistent with her claim in the refund suit that she did not owe gift tax.

The Supreme Court rejected Dalm's equitable recoupment claim because she had not raised the claim defensively in her income tax case, in which the gift versus income tax was in issue. Instead, she had waited to use equitable recoupment offensively in her separate suit for refund of gift tax to justify the court's jurisdiction over her action when that action was barred because a

---

estate, while the Service had erroneously failed to assess the full value of the mother's estate).

[181] United States v. Dalm, 494 US 596, 65 AFTR2d 90-1210 (1990), reh'g denied, United States v. Dalm, 495 US 941 (1990).

timely refund claim had not been filed. Drawing a distinction between *Dalm* and *Bull*,[182] the Court said that when in *Bull*, the executor sought equitable recoupment of estate tax in an action for refund of income tax over which the Court of Claims had jurisdiction, all that was at issue was whether the amount of income tax owed to the Service could be adjusted by the amount of estate tax paid. In *Dalm*, on the other hand, Dalm was challenging her income tax liability that had been determined in the Tax Court, in which she had failed to raise equitable recoupment to adjust the amount of income tax she agreed she owed. In other words, Dalm had voluntarily paid gift tax on the same income that in the Tax Court she had agreed she owed income tax. When Dalm sued for refund of the gift tax she had paid, therefore, she was instituting a second or independent suit to determine her liability for gift tax when she had failed to file a timely refund claim of the gift tax she had agreed she did not owe. Procedurally, therefore, Dalm was not using equitable recoupment as a defense to the collection of two taxes on the same fees but as a basis for the district court's jurisdiction over her otherwise barred case.

What is the lesson of *Dalm*? As the Supreme Court said, "[A] party litigating a tax claim in a timely proceeding may, in that proceeding, seek recoupment of a related, and inconsistent, but now time-barred tax claim relating to the same transaction." Practically speaking, the taxpayer "must" raise the equitable recoupment defense in a timely proceeding because recoupment may not be raised in an *untimely* proceeding. If there is a second action, the taxpayer will not be able to use equitable recoupment as a defense unless that action is timely under the applicable statute of limitations.

[c] Does Tax Court Have Jurisdiction to Apply Equitable Recoupment?

After *Dalm*, there is still uncertainty about the equitable recoupment jurisdiction of the Tax Court. Suppose the same facts as in *Dalm*. The taxpayer has paid a gift tax on an item of income, and, the Service says that an income tax is also owed on that same item of income. After the sending of a notice of deficiency, the taxpayer petitions the Tax Court. But suppose the taxpayer claims that the amount of income tax owed should be adjusted by the amount of gift tax paid, citing the doctrine of equitable recoupment? The majority in *Dalm* said that it was not passing on the question whether Dalm could have raised a recoupment claim in the Tax Court (which has been said not to have equity jurisdiction), and the dissenters roundly criticized the majority for failing to deal with this jurisdictional issue. What seems unclear, therefore, is whether equitable recoupment is a defense the taxpayer might raise in a refund suit or a taxpayer can raise in a tax collection action commenced by the Service to collect

---

[182] Bull v. United States, 295 US 247 (1935).

an unpaid tax assessment. In describing equitable recoupment, the Supreme Court majority referred to inconsistent tax claims related to the same transaction. This suggests that the Tax Court can apply the duty of consistency it recognizes it has the jurisdiction to apply in cases coming before the Tax Court to preclude the Service from collecting tax twice. Moreover, after the Supreme Court's decision in *Freytag*,[183] the Tax Court should be properly viewed as exercising full judicial power within its limited subject matter jurisdiction, thereby having the jurisdiction to permit recoupment of taxes, even if it has historical roots in equity jurisdiction of district courts.

Faced with the opportunity to decide whether it had the jurisdiction to apply the defense of equitable recoupment, the Tax Court held that as part of its statutory jurisdiction to redetermine a deficiency in estate tax, the Tax Court had equity jurisdiction, including the jurisdiction to consider the defense of equitable recoupment.[184] In *Estate of Mueller*, after the Tax Court had increased the value of the shares of the Mueller company stock in the decedent's gross estate, the estate raised the defense of equitable recoupment and claimed that the estate was entitled to recoup against the estate tax deficiency the amount of the income tax the residuary legatee had overpaid because it had used the lower value. Rejecting the Service's argument that the Tax Court, because of its limited statutory jurisdiction, could not hear the defense of equitable recoupment, the Tax Court held that equitable recoupment is part of the entire action to redetermine a deficiency over which it has jurisdiction. When the Tax Court's jurisdiction is invoked to redetermine the amount of a deficiency, the Tax Court said, it had "jurisdiction over the entire tax liability [and] not just the items determined to be erroneous by the Commissioner in the notice of deficiency." Equitable doctrines and principles, such as equitable recoupment, may be applied by the Tax Court in exercising its jurisdiction to redetermine at least an estate tax deficiency, but, it appears, in income and gift tax cases as well.[185]

In *Estate of Mueller II*, the Tax Court based its decision, in part, on the description in Section 6214(b) of the Tax Court's jurisdiction to redetermine the amount of a deficiency. To redetermine the amount of a deficiency in income tax (or gift tax for any calendar year or quarter) for a taxable year over which it has jurisdiction, Section 6214(b) directs the Tax Court to consider facts in taxable years and quarters not before the court, but precludes the court from determining whether the tax for the other year or quarter has been over

---

[183] Freytag v. Comm'r, 501 US 868 (1991).

[184] Estate of Mueller v. Comm'r, 101 TC 551 (1993) (*Estate of Mueller II*).

[185] In Freytag v. Comm'r, 501 US 868 (1991), the Supreme Court held that the Tax Court, although a court of limited jurisdiction, is a "court of law" with all the powers of other courts. As a court of law, *Freytag* suggests that the Tax Court should have jurisdiction over recoupment of income and gift tax deficiencies over which it had acquired jurisdiction, as well as estate tax deficiencies involved in *Estate of Mueller II*.

paid or underpaid. *Mueller II* involved an estate tax deficiency, however, not an income or gift tax deficiency that Section 6214(b) specifically identifies. Although an estate tax deficiency determination is not mentioned in the provision, the Tax Court said that Section 6214(b) did not prevent the court from permitting the estate to offset the barred income tax overpayment from the amount of the estate tax deficiency. Later, the Tax Court was faced with a case that involved income tax deficiencies and facially at least the same restrictions Section 6214(b) imposes on the Tax Court's jurisdiction. In this case the Tax Court permitted the taxpayer to equitably recoup an estate tax overpayment, refund of which was time-barred, from the income tax deficiencies in the years before the court.[186] Despite the Service's argument that Section 6214(b) barred recoupment, the court held that the limitation of its jurisdiction in Section 6214(b) "means, at most, that [S]ection 6214(b) may operate to preclude us from determining the income tax or gift tax for any prior period."[187]

If the Tax Court described an expansive view of the jurisdiction to allow recoupment in *Estate of Mueller II* and *Estate of Bartels*, it limited the application of the equitable recoupment doctrine in *Estate of Mueller III*. The issue in *Estate of Mueller III* was whether the Mueller estate could use equitable recoupment against the Service when, as the result of the Tax Court's redetermination, there was no estate tax deficiency against which the estate needed to defend.[188] According to a majority of the Tax Court, the estate's time-barred income tax overpayment could be used defensively under equitable recoupment only to defend against the Service's deficiency claim in the main action and, once the Tax Court determined the Commissioner's main estate tax deficiency claim to be meritless, the estate could not use recoupment offensively to recover the time-barred overpayment of income tax. As the court concluded, "Where the [Commissioner] claims that the taxpayer owes additional tax and the court finds that there is no additional tax due to the [Commissioner], there

---

[186] Bartels v. Comm'r, 106 TC 430 (1996).

[187] Bartels v. Comm'r, 106 TC 430 (1996). The Tax Court also said that it was confirmed in its conclusion that Section 6214(b) did not apply because historically Section 6214(b) referred only to the limitation on its consideration of facts in other periods for income and gift tax determinations, not estate tax determinations.

[188] Estate of Mueller v. Comm'r, 107 TC 189 (1996) (*Estate of Mueller III*). In *Estate of Mueller I*, the Tax Court had decided that the value of the stock the Commissioner used to arrive at its estate tax deficiency was excessive, and was in fact higher than the estate had used in preparing its estate tax return. Mueller v. Comm'r, TC Memo 1992-284, 63 TCM 3027 (1992) (*Estate of Mueller I*). As a result, the decedent's taxable estate was increased in an amount less than the notice of deficiency and combined with a previously unallowed credit for tax on prior transfers; it was clear that the estate had no deficiency in estate tax and had overpaid income tax for a year on which the refund limitations period had run.

is nothing left to defend against. . . . Any use of equitable recoupment at this point would not be defensive."[189]

As if the Tax Court's equitable jurisdiction were not uncertain enough after the Tax Court's decisions in *Mueller II* and *Mueller III*, the Sixth Circuit compounded the uncertainty by reversing the Tax Court's decision in *Mueller II* and by holding that the Tax Court did not have equitable jurisdiction to apply recoupment.[190] The Sixth Circuit based its opinion on two major grounds: (1) the well-worn proposition that as a court whose jurisdiction was limited to determining the amount of a deficiency, the Tax Court lacked general equitable powers, and (2) a rejection of the Tax Court's reading of Section 6214(b). The Tax Court found jurisdiction to apply equitable recoupment in estate tax cases based on omission of estate taxes from the prohibition in Section 6214(b) from determining whether taxes in other years had been over or underpaid. According to the circuit court, because Section 6214(b) applies to periodic taxes, such as income and gift taxes, not estate tax that is due only once, it made no sense for the statute to include estate tax, and so the "statute's failure to mention estate taxes does not support the theory that the Tax Court's jurisdiction is limited in income and gift tax cases, but unlimited in estate tax cases." Because the Tax Court's jurisdiction is limited, the Tax Court may only determine that an overpayment exists if the overpayment is for the same kind of tax for the same taxable year covered by the notice of deficiency.

[2] Setoff

Under the doctrine of setoff, an underpayment of tax for a year that is barred from collection owing to the expiration of the period of limitations on assessment may be set off against a refund due to a taxpayer for the year of the underpayment. In *Lewis v. Reynolds*,[191] the Supreme Court held that a taxpayer was not entitled to a refund of tax unless there had been an overpayment in tax for the year. In determining whether there has been an overpayment, the Commissioner is permitted to reaudit the return for the year and to take into consideration not only items in which the taxpayer claims tax has been overpaid but also those items on which the Commissioner determines that tax has been underpaid, even if assessment of the unpaid tax is barred. The amount of this underpaid tax is used to set off the amount of the claimed overpaid tax.

---

[189] Estate of Mueller v. Comm'r, 107 TC 189 (1996) (*Estate of Mueller III*).

[190] Mueller v. Comm'r, 153 F3d 302 (6th Cir. 1998).

[191] Lewis v. Reynolds, 284 US 281 (1932). For further discussion of *Lewis v. Reynolds* and setoff, see Chapter 11.

[3] Estoppel

The doctrine of estoppel prevents a person from founding a claim on another's failure to act when the person has induced the omission or nonperformance by his or her own act. Equity imposes a disability on the person who seeks to take advantage of his own inequity or wrong. A classic statement of the doctrine was given in *RH Stearns Co.*,[192] in which the Supreme Court said:

> The applicable principle is fundamental and unquestioned. "He who prevents a thing from being done may not avail himself of the nonperformance which he himself has occasioned for the law says to him in effect "this is your own act, and therefore you are not damnified."[193]

Although the doctrine of estoppel has been applied in tax cases, it has generally been used by the Service and has arisen in cases involving waivers. In *RH Stearns*, the taxpayer was not permitted to contest the validity of an extension of the period of assessment or collection because the taxpayer itself had requested a delay in collection until after returns had been audited so that any overassessment it had for those years might be credited against the amount due for the year of the waiver. On the other hand, in *Botany Worsted Mills*,[194] a case the Supreme Court decided before *RH Stearns*, the taxpayer sued for refund of a tax paid after a settlement with the Service, the terms and form of which did not meet the statutory requirements of a compromise. It appeared that estoppel would have applied to preclude the taxpayer from contesting the validity of the very agreement it voluntarily signed, yet the Supreme Court permitted the action and found no grounds to hold the taxpayers bound by the doctrine of estoppel, at least not when the Code specifically provided a special form to be used for offers in compromise.

Estoppel has frequently been applied in favor of the Service, but has been used far less often on behalf of taxpayers. This one-sided use of estoppel is another reason why the mitigation provisions were adopted. Apart from the uncertain results in particular cases, the continued use of estoppel was objected to as hopelessly lopsided in favor of the government.[195] Nevertheless, the doctrine has continued vitality.[196]

---

[192] RH Stearns Co. v. United States, 291 US 54 (1934).

[193] RH Stearns Co. v. United States, 291 US 54, 61 (1934) (citations omitted).

[194] Botany Worsted Mills v. United States, 278 US 282 (1929).

[195] Maguire, Surrey & Traynor, "Section 820 of the Revenue Act of 1938 (Part 1)," 48 Yale LJ 509, 514 (1939).

[196] See Chapter 1.

¶ 5.05 THE MITIGATION PROVISIONS

The judicial doctrines of recoupment, setoff, and estoppel are used to prevent inequitable results arising from exploitation of the statute of limitations, but they apply to particular situations and produce uncertain results. In 1938, recognizing these limitations, Congress attempted to provide an expanded, more systematic, and objective procedure for dealing with unfair use of the statute of limitations. As the Committee reports note:

> The purpose of the statute of limitations to prevent the litigation of stale claims is fully recognized and approved. But it was never intended to sanction active exploitation by the beneficiary of the statutory bar, of opportunities only open to him if he assumes a position diametrically opposed to that taken prior to the running of the statute. . . . Legislation has long been needed to supplement equitable principles applied by the courts and to check the growing volume of litigation by taking the profit out of inconsistency, whether exhibited by taxpayers or revenue officials and whether fortuitous or the result of design.[197]

Exhibiting unusual longevity for provisions of the internal revenue laws, the mitigation provisions are contained in Sections 1311 through 1314 of the Code in substantially the same form as when they were enacted in 1938. Several principles guide the application of the mitigation provisions:[198]

- To preserve unimpaired the essential function of the statute of limitations, a corrective adjustment should (1) never modify the application of the statute except where the party or parties in whose favor it applies shall have justified such modification by active inconsistency and (2) under no circumstances affect the tax save with respect to the influences of the particular items involved in the adjustment.
- Subject to the foregoing principles, disputes as to the year in which income or deductions belong or as to the person who should have the tax burden of income or the tax benefit of deductions should never result in a double tax or a double reduction of tax or in an inequitable avoidance of tax.
- Disputes about the basis of property should not allow the taxpayer or the Commissioner to obtain an unfair tax advantage by taking one position at the time of the acquisition of property and an inconsistent position at the time of its disposition.

---

[197] S. Rep. No. 1567, 75th Cong., 3d Sess. 48 (1938), reprinted in 1939-1 CB (pt. 2) 779, 865.

[198] S. Rep. No. 1567, 75th Cong., 3d Sess. 48 (1938), reprinted in 1939-1 CB (pt. 2) 779, 865.

- Corrective adjustments should produce the effect of attributing income or deductions to the right year and the right taxpayer and of establishing the proper basis.

As these operating principles make clear, the approach of the mitigation provisions is entirely different from the equitable doctrines of recoupment, set-off, and estoppel. Recoupment and setoff do not correct the error in the earlier year but only take the value of the error in the earlier year to determine the amount of the refund in the later year.[199] In estoppel cases, the earlier error is "frozen," preventing a correct result in a later year because any other course of action permits unfair exploitation of the earlier mistake.[200] The mitigation provisions permit an error to be corrected even though correction of the error in the closed year is prevented by some provision or rule of law.[201] In specifically defined circumstances, the mitigation provisions allow one party to open up a barred year when an error has been made in the inclusion or exclusion of an item of income, in the allowance or disallowance of a deduction, or in the tax treatment of a transaction affecting the basis of property.

The mitigation provisions were developed to achieve an equitable objective—to open up a closed tax year and permit equity to be done by correcting an error in the treatment of an item. Such an objective is justified when one party has exploited a statute of limitations or rule of law by taking a position on an item in an open year inconsistent with the treatment of the item in the closed year. The mitigation provisions include statutory devices calculated to achieve this equitable objective: the determination; the circumstance of adjustment; and the inconsistent position. Together with statutes of limitations and similar rules of law, these devices are factors in the mitigation calculus. The operation of the statutory devices can be stated as a formula, as follows:

$$\text{Adjustment} = \text{determination} + \text{correction in year of error barred} + \text{circumstance of adjustment} + \text{inconsistent position}$$

In other words, for the mitigation provisions to apply, certain conditions must be met.

1. There must be a determination, such as a final Tax Court decision, on an open year about the treatment of an item of income, a deduction or credit, or the basis of property (an item);

---

[199] Maguire, Surrey & Traynor, "Section 820 of the Revenue Act of 1938 (Part I)," 48 Yale LJ 509, 528–529 (1939).

[200] Maguire, Surrey & Traynor, "Section 820 of the Revenue Act of 1938 (Part I)," 48 Yale LJ 509, 522 (1939).

[201] O'Donnell v. Belcher, 414 F2d 833 (5th Cir. 1969).

2. This determination must establish that the same item has been treated erroneously in another year, and created one of the circumstances described in paragraphs (1) through (7) of Section 1312;

3. On the date of the determination, correction of the error in the closed year must be prevented or barred by some provision or rule of law, such as the statute of limitations on filing a refund claim or on assessment; and

4. In the proceeding resulting in the determination, the successful party generally must have taken a position that is inconsistent with the position that it took about the item with respect to the closed year.

Assuming these conditions are met, the error may be corrected by attributing income or deductions to the correct year or taxpayer or by establishing the correct basis of property.[202] If correction of the error results in a refund, the taxpayer may obtain a refund by filing a claim for refund within one year from the date of the determination. Similarly, if the result is a deficiency, the Commissioner has one year to send a notice of deficiency.

[1] When and to What Do the Provisions Apply?

The mitigation provisions apply only to income taxes.[203] They expressly do not apply to employment taxes.[204] In general, the mitigation provisions permit the

---

[202] IRC § 1314.

[203] One court has held erroneously that the mitigation provisions apply to excise taxes. Hall v. United States, 71A AFTR2d 93-4142 (USDC D. Utah 1991), rev'd, Hall v. United States, 975 F2d 722 (10th Cir. 1992) (windfall profits tax not an income tax covered by mitigation provisions); see Willis, "Correction of Errors via Mitigation and Equitable Recoupment," 52 Tax Notes 1421 (Sept. 16, 1991).

[204] IRC § 1314(e); Reg. § 1.1311(a)-2(b). The Court of Appeals for the Tenth Circuit held that mitigation provisions do not apply to the windfall profits tax. Hall v. United States, 975 F2d 722 (10th Cir. 1992) (Reg. § 1.1311(a)-2 approved; Chertkof v. United States, 676 F2d 984 (4th Cir. 1982), was said not to be persuasive).

The mitigation provisions do not apply to estate tax and gift tax determinations. Reg. § 1.1311(a)-2(b); FSA 1999-1044 (undated) (neither mitigation nor equitable recoupment could be asserted against an estate that deducted administrative expenses on both its income and estate tax returns. See Georgia Ketteman Trust v. Comm'r, 86 TC 91 (1986) (mitigation provisions do not apply to gift tax).

When a refund of income taxes is sought as a consequence of a determination (a Tax Court decision) of the value of securities for estate tax purposes, one court held that the mitigation provisions applied. Chertkof v. United States, 676 F2d 984 (4th Cir. 1982). Other courts disagree. See United States v. Provident Nat'l Bank, 507 F. Supp. 1197 (ED Pa. 1981); Evans Nat'l Bank v. United States, 462 F2d 521 (Ct. Cl. 1972) (a Tax Court decision on estate tax liability was held not to constitute a determination bringing into play the mitigation provisions).

correction of errors prevented by any provision of law except Section 7122,[205] relating to compromises, and the mitigation provisions themselves. They also apply if correction is prevented by such Code provisions as the statute of limitations on assessment[206] and credit and refund,[207] as well as to payments, refunds, or credits made after the limitations period,[208] and to restrictions on further deficiency letters[209] or on a taxpayer's suit for refund once a petition in the Tax Court has been filed.[210] Section 1311 may also be applied to correct the effect of an error if, on the date of the determination, correction of the error is prevented by the operation of any rule of law such as res judicata and estoppel.[211]

[2] What Are the Conditions Necessary for Adjustment?

Section 1311(a) authorizes an adjustment in certain cases in which a determination in an open year establishes that an item has been treated erroneously in a closed year, and correction of the error in the closed year is prevented by the expiration of the statute of limitations on assessment or refund or a rule of law, such as res judicata. Mitigation of the effect of statutes of limitation or other rules of law is not available to correct all errors in closed years. Only those errors, or circumstances of adjustment that are specifically described in Section 1312, are permitted to be corrected.

To open a closed year under the mitigation provisions, the facts must fit one of the following seven circumstances of adjustment described in Section 1312:[212]

1. Double inclusion of item of gross income[213]
2. Double allowance of deduction or credit[214]

---

[205] In Hartzog v. United States, 84-2 USTC ¶ 10,006 (Cl. Ct. 1984), a settlement agreement evidenced by a voluntary stipulation of dismissal of a district court case between the taxpayer and the government was held to be a compromise rendering the mitigation rules inapplicable.

[206] IRC §§ 6501, 6901(e).

[207] IRC § 6511.

[208] IRC §§ 6401, 6514.

[209] IRC § 6212(c).

[210] IRC § 6512(a).

[211] Reg. § 1311(a)-2(a).

[212] These seven circumstances of adjustment are discussed infra ¶¶ 5.04[5][a] through 5.04[5][g].

[213] IRC § 1312(1).

[214] IRC § 1312(2).

3. Double exclusion of item of gross income, either with the tax paid[215] or unpaid[216]
4. Double disallowance of deduction or credit[217]
5. Correlative deductions or inclusions for trusts or estates or for legatees, beneficiaries, or heirs[218]
6. Correlative deductions and credits for related corporations[219]
7. Basis of property after erroneous treatment of prior transaction[220]

In addition, one or more of the three conditions set forth in Section 1311(b) must be met. These conditions relate to (1) the maintenance of an inconsistent position; (2) the barring of correction of the error at the time of the erroneous action; and (3) the time a related taxpayer stands in a position of relationship.

[a] Inconsistent Position

In general, the party prevailing in the determination proceeding for an open year must accept the equitable reopening of a closed year if the party prevailed on a position inconsistent with the position it took on the item for the closed year. The regulations state that[221]

[a] position successfully maintained with respect to the taxable year of the determination must be inconsistent with the treatment accorded an item which was the subject of an error in the computation of tax for the closed taxable year.

All but two of the seven circumstances of adjustment described in Section 1312 require that either the taxpayer or the Commissioner has taken an inconsistent position. The two exceptions are (1) adjustments arising from the double exclusion of an item of gross income, when no tax has been paid,[222] and (2) the double disallowance of a deduction or credit.[223] For the remaining circumstances of adjustment (1) either the taxpayer or the Commissioner, as the case may be, must successfully maintain, for the taxable year of the determination, a position concerning the item of income, deduction, or transaction

---

[215] IRC § 1312(3)(A).
[216] IRC § 1312(3)(B).
[217] IRC § 1312(4).
[218] IRC § 1312(5).
[219] IRC § 1312(6).
[220] IRC § 1312(7).
[221] Reg. § 1.1311(b)-1(a).
[222] IRC § 1312(3)(B).
[223] IRC § 1312(4).

affecting basis that is adopted in the determination and (2) such position must be inconsistent with the erroneous treatment of the item in the closed taxable year.[224]

An inconsistent position is required when (1) adjustments result in refunds or credits and (2) adjustments result in additional assessments. For purposes of this requirement, the following questions must be asked:

- Who benefited from the error in the closed year?
- Did this person later take a position inconsistent with the treatment of the item in the closed year?

If the person who benefited from the error took an inconsistent position, the inconsistency requirement has been satisfied.

If correction of the error in the closed year would result in a refund or credit, the Commissioner must be found to have maintained a position (adopted in the determination) that is inconsistent with the treatment of the item in the closed year.

> EXAMPLE 5-1: A taxpayer using the cash method of accounting erroneously includes as income on his 1989 return an item of accrued interest. After the period of limitations for refund has expired, the Service determines that the income is properly includable in 1990, the year it was actually received. A closing agreement constituting a determination under Section 1313(a)(4) is entered into that determines that the item of interest income is includable in 1990 gross income. Thus, the Commissioner has maintained an inconsistent position on the inclusion of the interest item, despite the fact that the taxpayer initially asserted the position, because the Commissioner accepted the return and tax for the year 1989. As a result, correction of the error in 1989 is authorized.[225] The same result would apply if the interest income had been included in 1989 in response to a deficiency assessment. However, if the Commissioner determined a deficiency based on items other than interest, and the taxpayer asserted the interest was includable in 1990 rather than 1989, no adjustment would be authorized for 1989 because the taxpayer and not the Commissioner, would have maintained the inconsistent position on the year of inclusion by including the interest in 1989 and then claiming it was includable in 1990.[226]

If correction of an error in a closed year would result in an additional assessment, then the taxpayer must be found to have maintained a position (adopted in the determination) that is inconsistent with the manner in which the item was treated in the closed year.

---

[224] Reg. § 1.1311(b)-1(a).

[225] Reg. § 1.1311(b)-1(b)(1).

[226] Reg. § 1.1311(b)-1(b)(2).

EXAMPLE 5-2: A taxpayer claims a casualty loss on his 1989 tax return. After filing his 1990 return and after the expiration of the period of limitations on assessment for 1989, the taxpayer discovers that the casualty loss actually had occurred in 1990. The taxpayer then files a claim for refund for 1990 based on the deductibility of the loss in that year, and the Commissioner allows the claim. The taxpayer has maintained a position inconsistent with allowance of the deduction for 1989 by filing a claim for refund for 1990 based on the same deduction. Because the determination of the allowance of the claim for refund adopts the inconsistent position, the Commissioner may open the closed year 1989 to make an additional assessment.[227]

The circumstances of adjustment specified in Section 1312 are themselves examples of inconsistency. Table 5.3 summarizes which party must have adopted the inconsistent position for each circumstance of adjustment.

On the face of the statute, it may be questioned whether the inconsistency requirement adds anything more to the mitigation provisions than the inconsistency inherent in the circumstances of adjustment to which the mitigation provisions apply.

---

[227] Reg. § 1.1311(b)-1(c).

TABLE 5.3

Party Who Must Adopt Inconsistent Position

Section	Circumstances	Party Adopting Inconsistent Position
1312(1)	Double inclusion of item of gross income	Commissioner
1312(2)	Double allowance of deduction or credit	Taxpayer
1312(3)(A)	Double exclusion of item of gross income—tax paid	Taxpayer
1312(3)(B)	Double exclusion of item of gross income—tax unpaid	Not applicable
1312(4)	Double disallowance of deduction or credit	Not applicable
1312(5)	Correlative deductions or inclusions for trusts or estates or for legatees, beneficiaries, or heirs	Trust, estate deduction disallowed, correlative inclusion in beneficiary's income—Commissioner; trust deduction allowed, no correlative inclusion—trustee or fiduciary
1312(6)	Correlative deductions and credits for related corporations	Correlative deduction/credit disallowed—Commissioner: correlative deduction/credit allowed—corporation
1312(7)	Basis of property after erroneous treatment of prior	Erroneous income inclusion/gain recognition/charge to capital—Commissioner; erroneous income omission/gain nonrecognition/deduction—taxpayer

[i] Active versus passive inconsistency. Courts have differed about the meaning of the inconsistent position requirement. These differences derive from the legislative history of the mitigation provisions. The Senate report states that Congress intended to preserve the bar of the statute of limitations "except when the party or parties in whose favor it applies shall have justified such modification by active inconsistency. . . ."[228] This language led some courts, such as the court of claims and the Ninth Circuit, to require that a taxpayer have actively exploited the bar of the period of limitations before any mitigation adjustment is permitted.[229] Other courts, such as the Second Circuit and the Tax Court, believe that the mitigation provisions simply require that the position adopted in the determination be inconsistent with the erroneous treatment in the closed year.[230] This passive-inconsistency view finds support in another portion of the legislative history, which states that the intention of the mitigation provisions is "to take the profit out of inconsistency, whether exhibited by taxpayers or revenue officials, and whether fortuitous or the result of design."[231] This dispute involves only the position taken on the open year. The position on the closed year may be passive; for example, the Commissioner need only have accepted the taxpayer's return reporting the item of income and payment of tax.

The active-inconsistency view does not seem to fit either the statutory language or the purpose of the limitations bar. Active inconsistency focuses on the party who urged the erroneous treatment in the closed year. The mitigation statute requires only that "the position maintained" and accepted in the determination be inconsistent "with the erroneous inclusion, exclusion, omission, allowance, disallowance, recognition, or nonrecognition, as the case may be," in

---

[228] S. Rep. No. 1567, 75th Cong., 3d Sess. 48 (1938), reprinted in 1939-1 CB (pt. 2) 779, 865.

[229] Brigham v. United States, 470 F2d 571 (Ct. Cl. 1972), cert. denied, 414 US 831 (1973); Glatt v. United States, 470 F2d 596 (Ct. Cl. 1972); Heineman v. United States, 391 F2d 648 (Ct. Cl. 1968); Comm'r v. Weinrich, 316 F2d 97 (9th Cir. 1963). Aaron G. Lowery Ins. Agency v. United States, 83-1 USTC ¶ 9296 (EDNC 1982) (taxpayers claimed deductions for covenant not to compete for 1972, 1973, 1974, and 1975 tax years, were successful in refund suit for 1972 and 1973, but did not timely file refund claims for 1974 and 1975; held, taxpayers were not entitled to open the closed years because they, not the Commissioner, actively maintained the position adopted in the refund determination).

[230] Yagoda v. Comm'r, 331 F2d 485 (2d Cir.), cert. denied, 379 US 842 (1964); Chertkof v. Comm'r, 66 TC 496 (1976), aff'd, 649 F2d 264 (4th Cir. 1981); Priest Trust v. Comm'r, 6 TC 221 (1946), acq. sub nom. 1946-1 CB 2 and acq. 1946-1 CB 4. The Fourth Circuit apparently follows the passive-inconsistency view. Chertkof v. Comm'r, 649 F2d 264, 268 (4th Cir. 1981) ("the mitigation provisions can apply regardless of who erroneously excluded the taxable item and who took inconsistent positions").

[231] S. Rep. No. 1567, 75th Cong., 3d Sess. 48 (1938), reprinted in 1939-1 CB (pt. 2) 779, 865.

the closed year.[232] The statute, therefore, focuses on the party who urged the position adopted in the determination. The inconsistent-position requirement is satisfied, therefore, if the position maintained and adopted in the determination is inconsistent with the erroneous treatment in the closed year, and the person in whose favor the determination operates derived the benefit of the erroneous treatment in the closed year (e.g., a double deduction).

The active-inconsistency view also fails to take into account the purpose of the statute, which is to bar litigation of stale claims. Statutorily, the issue is whether the party affected by opening the closed year is disadvantaged by an inability to obtain evidence about the treatment of the item in that year. The person who has successfully maintained a position adopted in a determination as to such an item cannot complain about opening a closed year with respect to the item. Evidence relating to the item is demonstrably available (and not stale) because the party has successfully used the evidence in the determination proceeding. Consequently, the normal justification for the limitation bar is removed. In this context, it is less important that the inconsistent position is actively or passively maintained in the closed year than that the purpose of the mitigation provisions is served by recognizing the inconsistency.[233]

The differing judicial views as to the inconsistency requirement are illustrated by the decisions of the Ninth and Second Circuits in two family partnership cases involving virtually identical facts. With the fact pattern somewhat simplified, the situation was as follows: Taxpayer (T) transferred interests in a partnership to his wife (W) and daughter (D), and each filed a separate individual tax return reporting his or her respective share of partnership income. The Commissioner determined a deficiency in T's income tax on the ground that no bona fide partnership existed, meaning that T was taxable on 100 percent of the income. The Commissioner credited the tax paid by W and D to T's deficiency; T paid the balance of the deficiency and sued for a refund. In the refund suit, T successfully asserted that a partnership existed and that he was taxable only on his partnership share. When the decision of the court became final, the period of limitations on assessment against W and D had expired.

In *Commissioner v. Estate of Weinrich*,[234] the Ninth Circuit held that T had not adopted the actively inconsistent position called for by the legislative history. The fact that this requirement was not met was obviously true when the returns were filed and at the time T filed the claim for refund that resulted in the double exclusion of income, T, W, and D were no longer related parties

---

[232] IRC § 1311(b)(1).

[233] For further reading on this point, see Maguire, Surrey & Traynor, "Section 820 of the Revenue Act of 1938 (Part II)," 48 Yale LJ 719 (1939); Clifford, "Mitigation Provisions: Current Problems and Judicial Inconsistencies," 47 J. Tax'n 68 (1977).

[234] Comm'r v. Estate of Weinrich, 316 F2d 97 (9th Cir. 1963).

(i.e., partners). Consequently, the Ninth Circuit held that the mitigation provisions were not available to the Commissioner. On the other hand, faced with substantially the same facts, the Second Circuit held in *Yagoda v. Commissioner*[235] that the mitigation provisions were available to the Commissioner. The court concluded that all the statute required was that the position adopted in the determination (that a partnership did exist) be inconsistent with the erroneous exclusion of the allocable portions of the partnership income from the gross income of *W* and *D*.[236]

[ii] Use of alternative arguments. The maintenance of an inconsistent position connotes some offensive use of a position inconsistent with the erroneous treatment in the closed year. For example, inconsistency can take the form of an argument that specifies the year of inclusion, such as a taxpayer's contention that (1) an item is taxable and (2) it is taxable not in the year involved in the determination but in the closed year. When a taxpayer makes a single argument and the argument is adopted by a court in making a determination, the taxpayer's position is "inconsistent." However, in some cases, a taxpayer may make alternative arguments. For example, a taxpayer might contend that (1) an item is not taxable at all or (2) if it is taxable, it is taxable in a barred year.

Does the adoption of an alternative argument mean that the taxpayer has taken an inconsistent position? An alternative argument was found to be inconsistent in *Dobson*,[237] in which a taxpayer reported capital gain in 1948 on the sale of stock, although part of the sales proceeds was not received until 1949. The Commissioner asserted a deficiency for 1948 on the ground that the gain should have been treated as dividend income. In the Tax Court, the taxpayer contended that the gain had properly been reported in 1948 or, alternatively, that any proceeds received in 1949 could not be considered dividend income in 1948. The Tax Court sustained the Commissioner on the type of income but sustained the taxpayer's alternative argument on the timing of the income receipt. The Court of Claims concluded that in taking the alternative position adopted by the Tax Court, the taxpayer had maintained a position that was inconsistent with the erroneous omission of the 1949 sales proceeds from the 1949 return.

---

[235] Yagoda v. Comm'r, 331 F2d 485 (2d Cir.), cert. denied, 379 US 842 (1964).

[236] Other courts have held that the Commissioner's allowance of refund claims for open years was the maintenance of a position inconsistent with the disallowance of claims for years barred from refund by the statute of limitations, thereby permitting the opening of the otherwise closed years under the mitigation provisions. Gant v. United States, 441 F2d 1130 (5th Cir. 1971); United States v. Rachal, 312 F2d 376 (5th Cir. 1962). See also Moultrie Cotton Mills v. United States, 151 F. Supp. 482 (Ct. Cl. 1957).

[237] Dobson v. United States, 330 F2d 646 (Ct. Cl. 1964).

However, an alternative position has been found not to be inconsistent if a taxpayer does not change his or her primary argument and alternatively points out that, even assuming the correctness of the Commissioner's argument, the taxpayer's treatment is still correct. For example, in *Commissioner v. Goldstein*,[238] the taxpayers received renewal commissions on liquidation of their corporation. They did not report income in 1950 on the ground that the rights had no ascertainable value, but on the receipt of commissions in 1953 and 1954, they reported the income as capital gain. The Commissioner determined that the corporate dissolution was a closed transaction in 1950 and that the taxpayers realized ordinary income in 1953 and 1954. The taxpayers contended in the Tax Court that their treatment of the transaction and income was correct, but, alternatively, if the renewal commission rights could be valued in 1950, the value was greater than the amounts received in 1953 and 1954, so that the commissions constituted a return of capital, not ordinary income. The Tax Court agreed with the Commissioner's argument on the liquidation, but because it found the value of the rights greater than the amount received, the amounts received in 1953 and 1954 constituted a return of capital. The Second Circuit held that the determination in the Tax Court was inconsistent with the "theory" of the 1950 return but that this determination was based not on an abandonment by the taxpayers of their 1950 theory but on the action of the Tax Court in overruling it.[239]

Similarly, in *Kent Homes, Inc.*, the year income was received was at issue, and the taxpayer argued in the alternative that if the Commissioner were correct that income was realized on execution of an agreement, the agreement itself was not executed until a year after the year at issue. This alternative argument was held to be not inconsistent but "defensive or negative."[240]

[b] Correction Not Barred at Time of Erroneous Action

If there has been (1) a double exclusion of an item from gross income and no tax has been paid[241] or (2) a double deduction or credit,[242] correction of an error is not barred at the time of the erroneous action. In other words, a party is not penalized for having chosen the wrong year when including the

---

[238] Comm'r v. Goldstein, 340 F2d 24 (2d Cir. 1965), aff'g TC Memo 1963-258, 22 TCM 1293 (1963).

[239] Comm'r v. Goldstein, 340 F2d 24, 27 (2d Cir. 1965), aff'g TC Memo 1963-258, 22 TCM 1293 (1963). See also Estate of AW SoRelle v. Comm'r, 31 TC 272 (1958).

[240] Kent Homes, Inc. v. Comm'r, 455 F2d 316, 320 (10th Cir. 1972). The Service has followed the rationale of *Kent Homes* and *Goldstein*. See GCM 39145 (Apr. 14, 1983) (taxpayer who argued item was not income, or if income, it was realized in another year; held, not to have taken an inconsistent position).

[241] IRC § 1312(3)(B).

[242] IRC § 1312(4).

item of income or claiming a deduction provided that correction of the error for the "right" year was permitted at the time the choice was made. In a double-exclusion circumstance, an additional assessment is permitted only if assessment against the taxpayer or a related taxpayer for the taxable year in which the item is includable was not barred by law when the Commissioner first maintained (in a notice of deficiency or before the Tax Court) that the item of income should have been included in gross income for the tax year to which the determination relates.[243] In other words, at the time the Service asserts that income is includable in a later year, the statute of limitations on assessment of tax for the year of proper inclusion must be open.

The rationale for this condition is to prevent the Service from forcing a taxpayer to take an inconsistent position. If a taxpayer erroneously excludes an item of income, the Service could force the taxpayer to maintain an inconsistent position by determining that an item was improperly excluded in any other year. To defend against this position by the Service, the taxpayer might have to contend that the item was properly includable in a closed year at a time when evidence was lacking.

> **EXAMPLE 5-3:** A taxpayer inadvertently fails to include interest income properly includable in his 1984 gross income or in the gross income of any other year. During 1990, the Service sends the taxpayer a notice of deficiency of additional tax for the taxpayer's 1988 year based on the inclusion of the interest income in that year. The taxpayer is successful in the Tax Court. However, the Service may not reopen the 1984 year, because at the time the notice of deficiency was sent the statute of limitations on assessment for the 1984 year had run.

A similar rule applies to correction of the double disallowance of a deduction or credit, described in Section 1312(4). A credit or refund to the taxpayer or a related taxpayer is permitted only if the refund or credit was not barred by law at the time the taxpayer first maintained in writing (e.g., in a tax return, refund claim, or Tax Court petition) that he or she was entitled to the deduction or credit for the taxable year to which the determination relates.[244] The rationale behind this provision is to prevent a taxpayer from forcing the Service to take an inconsistent position. A taxpayer who has incorrectly claimed a deduction in a closed year could force the Service to take an inconsistent position by taking this position in any other year. Thus, the Service would be forced to assert that the taxpayer is not entitled to the deduction in the year of the claim but is so entitled in a closed year. In addition, despite maintaining a successful position on disallowance in the determination year,

---

[243] IRC § 1311(b)(2)(A).
[244] IRC § 1311(b)(2)(B).

the Service might not have evidence justifying lifting the limitations bar because the taxpayer merely failed to prove his or her case.

EXAMPLE 5-4: A taxpayer fails to deduct interest on his 1986 tax return but claims the deduction on his 1987 tax return. The IRS disallows the deduction for 1987, and the Tax Court agrees with this disallowance in 1990. The taxpayer may then open the 1983 year, which is now closed, because when he first claimed entitlement to the deduction, that year was still open.

[c] Time of Existence of Qualifying Relationship

The mitigation rules permit a taxpayer to open a closed year if a determination is made with respect to the tax year of another "related" taxpayer. Section 1313(c) discusses the qualifying relationships and the conditions under which they must exist.[245] An additional condition is imposed by Section 1311(b)(3). With one exception, a deficiency assessment for the closed year of one taxpayer may not be made unless the taxpayer was related to another taxpayer at two points in time. This relationship must exist at (1) some time during the year with respect to which the error was made and (2) the time the related party with respect to whom the determination is made first maintained the inconsistent position. If the inconsistent position is maintained in a return, claim for refund, or Tax Court petition, the taxpayers must be related at the time the document is filed.[246] If the inconsistent position is not made in one of these documents and the determination is made by way of a closing or Section 1313(a)(4) agreement, the relationship must exist on the date of the agreement. The single exception to this relationship condition is the circumstance of a double exclusion from gross income without previous payment of tax,[247] in which no inconsistency is required. In this situation, the relationship need exist only at some time in the tax year in which the error was made.[248]

[3] What Constitutes a Determination?

The determination referred to in Sections 1311 and 1312 is specifically defined in Section 1313(a) to mean four types of actions. Three of these actions are administrative; the other requires action by a court. The following actions qualify as a determination:

---

[245] See infra ¶ 5.04[4].

[246] Reg. § 1.1311(b)-3(b).

[247] IRC § 1312(3)(B).

[248] Reg. § 1.1311(b)-3(a).

1. A decision by the Tax Court or a judgment, decree, or other order by any court of competent jurisdiction that has become final
2. A closing agreement made under Section 7121
3. A final disposition by the Service of a claim for refund
4. An agreement between the taxpayer and the Service authorized by Section 1313(a)(4)

As previously noted, Section 1311 permits the correction of the erroneous treatment of an item or transaction in a tax year otherwise closed by operation of law. In the statutory scheme, the substantive purpose of a determination is to establish whether the mitigation provisions apply. The determination definitively establishes the correct treatment of an item or transaction in the open year and, by so doing, the existence of an error in the treatment of the same item or relevant transaction in another year. Accordingly, the operative determination for the mitigation rules is a determination on the merits of the substantive issue, for example, a final court decision that an item of income is includable in a particular year. Therefore, a determination on a dispositive procedural issue, such as a final court decision that a statute of limitations has expired, does not constitute a determination for mitigation purposes.[249]

In *Fruit of the Loom*, the taxpayer and the Service reflected in a Form 870, their resolution of a dispute about the amount of a loss ($15.2 million versus $19 million) and timing of the loss (1967 versus 1966). The agreement in the Form 870 was subject to a condition, and the Service made an assessment of tax for 1996, as well as 1965 and 1968, in violation of that agreement and collected the net deficiency that had been agreed to. After it sued for refund, the taxpayer succeeded in obtaining a refund of the resulting assessment it paid because the final court decision held that the Service illegally made the assessment in violation of an agreement reflected in the Form 870. The Service then issued a notice of deficiency for 1966, claiming application of the mitigation provisions, because the result of the court decision was that the taxpayer obtained a double deduction of the loss, that is, in both 1966 and 1967. The Tax Court ruled, and the Seventh Circuit agreed, that the Service was not entitled to use the mitigation rules, because the court decisions did not address the issue of whether 1967 was the proper year to deduct the loss, and so there had been no final court decision–type determination on the merits, and the Form 870 was not a determination for the purposes of the mitigation provisions.

As the Seventh Circuit noted, Congress intended that the "determination" for purposes of the circumstances of adjustment described in Section 1312 give "authoritative sanction to the inconsistent position presently maintained

---

[249] See, e.g., Fruit of the Loom, Inc. v. Comm'r, TC Memo. 1994-492 (1994), aff'd, 72 F3d 1338 (7th Cir. 1996).

by the taxpayer . . . and indicated that the previous treatment of the item was erroneous under the applicable provisions of the internal revenue laws."[250]

Consequently, in order for the court determination to have allowed Fruit of the Loom a deduction, the court's decision must have affirmatively approved the deduction in the year before the court (1966), establishing that the deduction in another, closed year was erroneous. Because the prior decisions of the district court and the Third Circuit addressed the validity of the assessments only in view of the agreement reflected on the Form 870, the determination in those cases was not a substantive decision on the merits that established that *Fruit of the Loom* had erroneously been allowed in 1967.[251]

The determination also serves a procedural purpose. The date of the determination (i.e., when it becomes final) is the relevant date for ascertaining whether correction of the error is barred by means outside the mitigation provisions. The date of the determination also triggers the operation of the mechanism for relief under the mitigation provisions. Only after the date of the determination may the taxpayer file a claim for refund (or the Commissioner send a notice of deficiency) under the mitigation provisions seeking correction of the error in the closed year.

Statutorily, the mitigation provisions contemplate two proceedings: The first is to arrive at a determination, and the second is for collection of the adjustment amount.[252] Despite this statutory mechanism, some courts have created a shortcut by holding that taxpayers need not file a second claim for refund if a refund claim they filed before the determination is pending at the time of the determination and the claim apprises the Service of the grounds relied on for adjustment.[253]

---

[250] Fruit of the Loom, Inc. v. Comm'r, TC Memo. 1994-492 (1994), aff'd, 72 F3d 1338, 1345 (7th Cir. 1996) (quoting from HR Conf. Rep. No. 2330, 75th Cong., 3d Sess. 56 (1938), reprinted in 1939-1 CB (pt. II) 817, 835).

[251] See also Fong v. Comm'r, TC Memo 1998-181, 75 TCM 2299 (1998) (stipulated decision only reflected the result of a settlement, not the underlying terms determining the basis of the property; held, the prior decision did not constitute a determination; cases discussed).

[252] Benenson v. United States, 385 F2d 26 (2d Cir. 1967) (taxpayer unsuccessfully attempted to short-circuit the two proceeding requirements by permitting the court's determination to become final and then making the claim for adjustment in the court of appeals). In Rasmussen v. United States, 811 F2d 949 (5th Cir. 1987), a corporation (C) in 1977 adopted a plan of liquidation, sold its assets, and distributed the proceeds after paying tax on the sale. A sole shareholder (R) did not report any gain or loss from the transaction, but after an audit, R agreed to pay additional tax as a consequence of receiving the proceeds of the liquidation. R paid the additional tax in 1981. In 1982, R filed a claim for a refund on behalf of C. The circuit court upheld the government's claim that adjustment of R's tax liability did not constitute a determination in C's tax liability as well.

[253] Moultrie Cotton Mills v. United States, 151 F. Supp. 482 (Ct. Cl. 1957); Esterbrook Pen Co. v. United States, 1960-2 USTC ¶ 9609 (DNJ 1960). But see O'Donnell v.

Not every determination triggers the mitigation provisions. Only a determination that operates to produce one of the seven circumstances described in Section 1312 has this effect. However, it is impossible to tell whether one of the types of inequity the mitigation provisions were designed to avoid actually exists until the specified determination in the open year becomes final. The determination requirement is also closely related to another condition necessary to an adjustment under the mitigation provisions: The condition of inconsistency. In general, the closed year is reopened only when the determination adopts the position of either the taxpayer or the Service and the position is inconsistent with the treatment accorded the item or transaction in the closed year. The determination thus confirms the inconsistency.

One other point must be made about a determination. The question of whether an item or transaction has been treated erroneously in the closed year depends on the authority as it exists at the time of the determination, not the authority in the year of error.[254]

[a] Final Court Decision

The time at which a decision of the Tax Court or any other court of competent jurisdiction becomes final is determined by the rules of the court in question. A court decision generally becomes final when the time for appeal has expired. For example, a Tax Court decision becomes final when (1) the time for filing a notice of appeal expires or (2) if the decision is appealed, when the decision or order of the court of appeals becomes final.[255] The decision of a district court becomes final on the expiration of the time for filing a notice of appeal.[256] The decision of the Court of Appeals for the Federal Circuit or of a circuit court of appeals becomes final at the expiration of the time for filing a petition for certiorari or, if petition for certiorari has been filed, on its denial.[257] A decision of the Supreme Court becomes final when the time

---

Belcher, 414 F2d 833 (5th Cir. 1969) (notice of deficiency sent before a determination was made; held, notice was insufficient; second notice must be sent).

[254] Reg. § 1.1312-8.

[255] IRC §§ 7481(a)(1), 7481(a)(2)(A). Cheng v. Comm'r, 878 F2d 306 (9th Cir. 1989) (when partial summary judgment and the entered order did not conclusively dispose of all claims and terminate litigation, the appellate court lacked jurisdiction owing to the absence of a truly final appealable order). In *Blohm*, the taxpayer reported forgiveness of indebtedness income in 1983. It was later determined by the Tax Court that the taxpayer had unreported income in 1981, arising, in part, from the same transaction that gave rise to the income reported in 1983. Accordingly, the taxpayer filed a refund claim for 1983. The district court held that the mitigation provisions did not apply, because no determination had been made; the taxpayer's appeal from the Tax Court's decision was still pending in the circuit court. Blohm v. United States, 93-1 USTC ¶ 50,106 (SD Ala. 1993).

[256] Fed. R. App. P. 4(a).

[257] IRC § 7481(a)(2)(B).

for filing a motion for reargument expires or on the expiration of thirty days from the date of the issuance of the mandate of the Court.[258]

The finality of a court decision is only the triggering event under the mitigation provisions. Before an adjustment under Section 1314 may be made, the taxpayer or the Commissioner must either file a claim for refund or send a notice of deficiency.

[b] Closing Agreement

A closing agreement is the only method the Code provides to bind the Service. As a consequence, when a closing agreement is entered into, either the taxpayer or the Service may reopen a closed year to correct an error if one of the circumstances of adjustment and the conditions necessary for adjustment are present. A taxpayer may both execute a closing agreement and have a Section 1311 adjustment taken into account for purposes of the payment of tax.[259]

[c] Final Disposition of a Claim for Refund

A determination means a final disposition by the Service of a claim for refund.[260] Finality in the disposition of a claim for refund depends on (1) what action is taken on the item and (2) whether the claim for refund as a whole is allowed or disallowed. A taxpayer's claim can be allowed when it is (1) allowed in full; (2) allowed with respect to some but disallowed as to other items set forth in the claim, but the result is a net refund or credit; or (3) allowed, but the Service raises other items as offsets reducing but not eliminating the net refund or credit.[261] If the taxpayer's claim on the item in question is allowed and the result is a refund or credit, the disposition of the claim becomes final on the date of allowance of the refund or credit.[262] If the taxpayer's claim on the item in question is allowed but the offset of other items result in a disallowance of the claim for refund, the disposition of the claim is final on the date the notice of claim disallowance is mailed.[263]

On the other hand, a claim for refund on an item that is disallowed is finally disposed of two years after the date of the notice of claim disallowance, that is, the expiration of the time within which a taxpayer must bring suit for refund.[264] This rule applies when a claim is (1) unqualifiedly disallowed; (2)

---

[258] IRC § 7481(a)(2)(C).

[259] Reg. §§ 1.1314(c)–1.1314-1(e).

[260] IRC § 1313(a)(3).

[261] Reg. § 1.1313(a)-3(b)(1).

[262] Reg. § 1.1313(a)-3(b)(1).

[263] Reg. § 1.1313(a)-3(b)(2).

[264] Reg. § 1.1313(a)-3(c)(1).

denied on the item in question but allowed as to other items in the claim, so that the result is a net refund or credit; or (3) denied in part and allowed in part on the item in question.[265] Although the taxpayer's claim for refund on the item is disallowed, such a disallowance is not a final determination. However, a taxpayer can shorten the two-year waiting period for filing a suit for refund under the mitigation provisions by using a closing agreement or an informal agreement under Section 1313(a)(4).[266] If a suit for refund is instituted, the final decision of the refund court is the determination.

[d] Agreement With the Service

Section 1313(a)(4) provides for a determination by way of an agreement entered into between the Service and the taxpayer. Form 2259 (Agreement as a Determination Pursuant to Section 1313(a)(4) of the Code) is used for this purpose. (See Form 5.2.) The agreement with the Service must contain the following elements:[267]

1. A statement of the tax liability for the open year, including a reference to any document concurrently executed by which liability is established or altered, such as a waiver or a stipulation in a Tax Court proceeding.
2. A concise statement of the material facts with respect to the item that was erroneously treated in the closed year.
3. A statement of how the item involved was treated in computing the tax liability set forth in the agreement.
4. A statement of the adjustment with respect to the erroneous prior treatment and any related adjustments.
5. A waiver of restrictions on the assessment and collection of any deficiency set forth in the agreement.
6. A heading indicating that the agreement is made pursuant to Section 1313(a)(4).

[4] Who Qualify As Related Taxpayers?

A determination establishing the correct tax treatment of an item or transaction for one taxpayer may serve as the basis for opening a closed year of another taxpayer, if the two taxpayers stand in one of the relationships specified in

---

[265] Reg. § 1.1313(a)-3(c)(1).

[266] Reg. § 1.1313(a)-3(e).

[267] Reg. § 1.1313(a)-4(b).

Section 1313(c). The relationships to which the mitigation provisions extend are the following:

- Husband and wife
- Grantor and fiduciary
- Grantor and beneficiary
- Fiduciary and beneficiary, legatee, or heir
- Decedent and decedent's estate
- Partners
- Members of an affiliated group of corporations as defined in Section 1504 for consolidated return purposes

These relationships are the only ones that qualify for such treatment. Further, they must exist at specific times for adjustment to be permitted under the mitigation provisions.

FORM 5.2
AGREEMENT AS A DETERMINATION

Form **2259** (Rev. May 1980)	Department of the Treasury - Internal Revenue Service **Agreement as a Determination Pursuant to Section 1313(a)(4) of the Internal Revenue Code**

Name of Taxpayers   **Taxable Year Ended**

Taxpayer Rentals Co.   Dec. 31, 1997

Address of Taxpayers

One Main Street, Anytown, NY 00030

We, the above-named taxpayers, and the Commissioner of Internal Revenue agree that the income tax liability for the taxable year shown above is $ 25,200. This liability was established by *(to complete this statement, see Income Tax Regulations section 1.1313(a)-4(b)(1) printed on the back of this form):* Form 870-AD

Executed concurrently herewith

We have attached as a part of this agreement the statement required by Income Tax Regulations sections 1.1313(a)-4(b)(2) and (3) that are printed on the back of this form. This statement consists of   pages.

Upon approval of this agreement for the Commissioner of Internal Revenue, we further agree to the assessment and collection of any deficiency (increase in tax) and accept any overassessment (decrease in tax) shown below, plus interest provided by law. We understand that by signing this agreement we will not be able to contest these years in the United States Tax Court, unless additional deficiencies are determined for these years.

Taxpayers	Taxable Year Ended	Kind of Tax	Increase in Tax	Decrease in Tax
Taxpayer Rentals Co.	Dec. 31, 1997	Income	$25,200	N/A

We further agree that the determination date will be the date on which this agreement is signed for the Commissioner.

Signature of Taxpayers	**Date**
Taxpayer Rentals Co. by /s/ John Jones, President	March 15, 2001
Signature of Related Taxpayers, if any	**Date**
Signature for the Commissioner	**Date**
Title	

Note: Your agreement will not prevent you from filing a claim for refund (after you have paid the tax) if you later believe you are so entitled; nor prevent us from later determining, if necessary, that you owe additional tax; nor extend the time provided by law for either action.

If this agreement is for a year for which a joint return was filed, both husband and wife must sign unless one, acting under a power of attorney, signs as agent for the other.

If the taxpayer is a corporation, this agreement must be signed with the corporate name followed by the signatures and titles of the officers authorized to sign.

This agreement may be signed by an attorney or agent of the taxpayers, provided this action is specifically authorized by a power of attorney which, if not previously filed, must accompany this form.

(See applicable regulations on the back)   Form **2259** (Rev. 5-80)

Form 2259.

Instructions

The original of this agreement will be associated with the return of the taxpayer to whom the determination is made. An additional executed copy will be furnished to each taxpayer involved and one will also be associated with each related tax return.

The statement required by section 1.1313(a)—4(b)(2) and (3) of the regulations must be headed "Statement to be Attached to, and Made a Part of, Form 2259 in the Case of   ", and must be securely attached to this form.

Provisions of the Internal Revenue Code and the Regulations Issued Thereunder Covering the Preparation of an Agreement as a Determination

Code section 1313(a)(4): *Determination.* [For purposes of this part, the term "determination" means. . .] under regulations prescribed by the Secretary, an agreement for purposes of this part, signed by the Secretary and by any person, relating to the liability of such person (or the person for whom he acts) in respect of a tax under this subtitle for any taxable period

Regulations section 1.1313(a)—4: *Agreement pursuant to section 1313(a)(4) as a determination—-(a) In general.* (1) A determination may take the form of an agreement made pursuant to this section. This section is intended to provide an expeditious method for obtaining an adjustment under section 1311 and for offsetting deficiencies and refunds whenever possible. The provisions of part II (section 1311 and following), subchapter Q, Chapter 1 of the Code, must be strictly complied with in any such agreement.

(2) An agreement made pursuant to this section will not, in itself, establish the tax liability for the open taxable year to which it relates, but it will state the amount of the tax, as then determined, for such open year. The tax may be the amount of tax shown on the return as filed by the taxpayer, but if any changes in the amount have been made, or if any are being made by documents executed concurrently with the execution of said agreement, such changes must be taken into account. For example, an agreement pursuant to this section may be executed concurrently with the execution of a waiver of restrictions on assessment and collection of a deficiency or acceptance of an overassessment with respect to the open taxable year, or concurrently with the execution and filing of a stipulation in a proceeding before the Tax Court of the United States, where an item which is to be the subject of an adjustment under section 1311 is disposed of by the stipulation and is not left for determination by the court.

(b) *Contents of agreement.* An agreement made pursuant to this section shall be so designated in the heading of the agreement, and it shall contain the following:

(1) A statement of the amount of the tax determined for the open taxable year to which the agreement relates, and if said liability is established or altered by a document executed concurrently with the execution of the agreement, a reference to said document.

(2) A concise statement of the material facts with respect to the item that was the subject of the error in the closed taxable year or years, and a statement of the manner in which such item was treated in computing the tax liability set forth pursuant to subparagraph (1) of this paragraph.

(3) A statement as to the amount of the adjustment ascertained pursuant to section 1.1314(a)—1 for the taxable year with respect to which the error was made and, where applicable, a statement as to the amount of the adjustment or adjustments ascertained pursuant to section 1.1314(a)—2 with respect to any other taxable year or years; and

(4) A waiver of restrictions on assessment and collection of any deficiencies set forth pursuant to subparagraph (3) of this paragraph.

(c) *Execution and effect of agreement.* An agreement made pursuant to this section shall be signed by the taxpayer with respect to whom the determination is made, or on the taxpayer's behalf by an agent or attorney acting pursuant to a power of attorney on file with the Internal Revenue Service. If an adjustment is to be made in a case of a related taxpayer, the agreement shall be signed also by the related taxpayer, or on the related taxpayer's behalf by an agent or attorney acting pursuant to a power of attorney on file with the Internal Revenue Service. It may be signed on behalf of the Commissioner by the district director, or such other person as is authorized by the Commissioner. When duly executed, such agreement will constitute the authority for an allowance of any refund or credit agreed to therein, and for the immediate assessment of any deficiency agreed to therein for the taxable year with respect to which the error was made, or any closed taxable year or years affected, or treated as affected, by a net operating loss deduction or capital loss carryover determined with reference to the taxable year with respect to which the error was made.

(d) *Finality of determination.* A determination made by an agreement pursuant to this section becomes final when the tax liability for the open taxable year to which the determination relates becomes final. During the period, if any, that a deficiency may be assessed or a refund or credit allowed with respect to such year, either the taxpayer or the Commissioner may properly pursue any of the procedures provided by law to secure a further modification of the tax liability for such year. For example, if the taxpayer subsequently files a claim for refund, or if the Commissioner subsequently issues a notice of deficiency with respect to such year, either may adopt a position with respect to the item that was the subject of the adjustment that is at variance with the manner in which said item was treated in the agreement. Any assessment, refund, or credit that is subsequently made with respect to the tax liability for such open taxable year, to the extent that it is based upon a revision in the treatment of the item that was the subject of the adjustment, shall constitute an alteration of revocation of the determination for the purpose of a redetermination of the adjustment pursuant to paragraph (d) of section 1.1314(b)—1.

Form 2259 (Rev. 5-80)

The relationships specified in Section 1313(c) are ones in which difficulties in allocating income or determining the taxable person are likely to occur. For example, problems may arise in determining whether income is taxable to a fiduciary or to the grantor of a support trust. The same difficulty exists when a grantor and beneficiary are involved. When a fiduciary and beneficiary are involved, it may be difficult to determine whether amounts distributed by the fiduciary are income deductible by the fiduciary and taxable to the beneficiary or whether they represent charges against corpus, taxable not to the beneficiary but to the fiduciary. A similar difficulty exists in allocating many items between a decedent and his or her estate. There may also be improper allocations of partnership income (or loss) between members of a partnership.

State law determines whether the requisite relationship exists. Divorced spouses for purposes of state law do not have the relationship of husband and wife under the mitigation rules. As a result, no relief is afforded in the mitigation provisions to cases involving alimony payments to divorced spouses, although the provisions do grant relief to legally separated spouses when alimonylike payments are made. Also, even though a trust is taxable as a corporation for tax purposes, the grantors and beneficiaries are related under the mitigation provisions if the trust qualifies under state law.[268] In *Ross v. United States*, a father held his son's property in his own name for the benefit of the son, so that under state law there was a resulting trust; the father and son were related as fiduciary and beneficiary for the mitigation rules.[269] If a partner is recognized as such under state law, he or she is considered to be a partner for the mitigation provisions, even if he or she is not otherwise recognized as a partner under the tax law.[270]

Taxpayers who are not related include the following:

- Parent and child[271]
- Donor and donee
- Lessor and lessee
- Principal and agent[272]
- Nephew or niece and aunt or uncle[273]
- Claimants to the ownership of the same property
- Assignor and assignee

---

[268] Lovering v. United States, 49 F. Supp. 1 (D. Mass. 1943).

[269] Ross v. United States, 148 F. Supp. 330 (D. Mass. 1957).

[270] IT 2986, 1949-2 CB 100; cf. Taxeraas v. United States, 269 F2d 283 (8th Cir. 1959) (purported partner failed to prove he was a partner under state law and was held not to be a partner for purposes of the mitigation provisions).

[271] United States v. Rigdon, 323 F2d 446 (9th Cir. 1963).

[272] Taylor v. Comm'r, 27 TC 361 (1956), aff'd, 258 F2d 89 (2d Cir. 1958).

[273] Taylor v. Comm'r, 27 TC 361 (1956), aff'd, 258 F2d 89 (2d Cir. 1958).

- Corporation and stockholder (unless the stockholder is a corporation and both corporations are members of an affiliated group)[274]

If a corporation is ignored for tax purposes as a sham or otherwise, it is treated as an entity unrelated to its shareholder for purposes of Section 1313.[275]

As noted previously, the requisite relationships must also exist at specific times. Section 1313(c) requires that when the taxpayer is seeking relief, the relationship must have been in existence during the taxable year in which the erroneous treatment occurred, although the relationship need not have existed throughout the year. The item with respect to which the error was made does not have to involve a transaction made possible solely because of the existence of the relationship.[276] On the other hand, when the Commissioner is seeking mitigation, the required relationship must exist both at some time during the year in which the erroneous treatment occurred and when the taxpayer's inconsistent position was first maintained.[277]

It is difficult to apply these rules. When a taxpayer erroneously included in income for 1963 a portion of a liquidating distribution, and the taxpayer died the following year, her estate reported a loss attributable to the liquidating distribution on its income tax return.[278] The Service disallowed the loss deduction, and the taxpayer's representatives paid the deficiency and filed for refund claiming that the estate had income tax overpaid for 1963. After the Service disallowed the claim, the estate sued for refund. In response to the estate's contention that the mitigation provisions applied to permit the reopening of the taxpayer's income tax return for 1963, the Service argued that the mitigation rules did not apply because the decedent and her estate were not related in 1963 (the year of the error) because she died the following year. If the Service were correct, relief under the mitigation rules would apply only to situations in which the error (double inclusion of an item of income) is made by an executor. The court of appeals rejected this "narrow construction" on the ground that when the requisite relationship exists, the mitigation provisions should apply, that is, the question of when the relationship exists is less significant than the fact that it does exist. This interpretation does not comport with the literal meaning of the statute, but it is consistent with the remedial purpose of the statute. The Service's contention that the error results only from the relationship seems wrong because, as the regulations recognize, an error correctable under the mitigation rules may be unrelated to the statutory relationship.[279]

---

[274] Rasmussen v. United States, 811 F2d 949 (5th Cir. 1987).
[275] Hindes v. United States, 371 F2d 650 (5th Cir.), cert. denied, 386 US 992 (1967).
[276] Reg. § 1.1313(c)-1.
[277] IRC § 1313(b)(3).
[278] First Nat'l Bank v. United States, 565 F2d 507, 516 (8th Cir. 1977).
[279] Reg. § 1.1313(c)-1.

[5] What Circumstances Warrant Adjustment?

The mitigation provisions allow for the correction of an error under specifically defined circumstances: when an error has been made in the inclusion or exclusion of an item of income, in the allowance or disallowance of a deduction or in the tax treatment of a transaction affecting the basis of property.

[a] Double Inclusion of an Item of Income

Subjecting the same item of income to tax in an open year when the Service has collected tax on the item in a closed year is a circumstance that calls for redress. The first circumstance of adjustment permits the reopening of a closed year when "[t]he determination requires the inclusion in gross income of an item which was erroneously included in the gross income of another taxable year or in the gross income of a related taxpayer."[280] In order for this double-inclusion circumstance to exist, four conditions must be satisfied:

1. An item of income must have been included in a taxpayer's gross income for one year;
2. A determination must be made that the item is includable in the gross income of the taxpayer for another year;
3. The Commissioner's position in the determination proceeding must have been inconsistent with the inclusion of the item in the year of actual inclusion; and
4. At the time of the determination, a claim for refund of tax paid for the year of erroneous inclusion must be barred.

The following example illustrates the occurrence of a double inclusion of an item of income.

EXAMPLE 5-5: A cash method taxpayer erroneously includes an item of accrued rent in his return for 1985. In 1990, when refunds for 1985 are barred, the Commissioner determines that the rent was actually received in 1986 and that there is a deficiency in tax owed for 1986. The Tax Court subsequently upholds this determination. In this instance there has been a determination (the Tax Court decision) establishing the existence of a circumstance of adjustment (the double inclusion of rental income in 1985 and 1986). At the time of the determination, correction of the error is time-barred. Moreover, the Commissioner has taken an inconsistent position by accepting the additional tax for the year of the error (1985) and then successfully contending in the Tax Court that the rent was includable in 1986. Because the taxpayer reported the rental income in both the year of error (1985) and the correct year (1986) and was by determination denied a refund for the error year, he may use the mitigation provisions to

---

[280] IRC § 1312(1).

lift the bar on the closed error year and obtain an adjustment in his favor for the 1985 tax.[281]

The disallowance of a claim for refund can qualify as a determination upon final disposition of a claim, which occurs two years after the notice of claim disallowance. If the taxpayer in the previous example had filed a claim in 1988 for a refund covering 1985, and the claim were disallowed in that year, then on the expiration of the two-year period in 1989, the claim would have been finally disallowed, and the taxpayer could obtain an adjustment under Section 1311.

The matter that has caused the most difficulty in applying the double-inclusion circumstance is the meaning of the term "item" of income. An item of income refers to the type of income received in a qualitative sense—that is, salary and wages, rent, and the other items listed in Section 61.[282] The tax effect of inclusion of the item may be entirely different in the two years, and in that sense, the item need not be quantitatively the same.[283] In *Cocchiara v. United States*, the taxpayer claimed that the mitigation provisions applied because, as a result of the Service's denial of the installment method of reporting gain from the sale of mineral leases, there was double inclusion of an item of income (i.e., the mineral lease sales proceeds). This gain was reported both in 1959 (the year of the sale) and in 1960 through 1965 (the installment years). Moreover, when the Service disallowed the installment sales treatment, taxing the entire gain in 1959, it applied the 1960 through 1965 overpayments to unrelated, but erroneous, assessments. The Service argued that these overpayments lost their character as resulting from mineral lease sale proceeds when

---

[281] Reg. § 1312-1(b), Ex. 1. See Gant v. United States, 441 F2d 1130 (5th Cir. 1971). In *Gant*, the court found that the rejection of refund claims in a closed year while claims for open years were allowed was the maintenance of an inconsistent position. In Bennett v. United States, 89-1 USTC ¶ 9106 (WD Tex. 1988), partners reported income and loss from a partnership in 1977 through 1982 but erroneously included cash distributions from the partnership as additional partnership taxable income. The statute of limitations on a refund claim had run on the years 1977–1979 at the time the partners filed their claims, but the claims for the years 1980–1982 were allowed. The partners claimed that the mitigation provisions applied to lift the bar of the statute on filing the refund claims for the years 1977–1979 because there had been a double inclusion of an item of income, and the cash distribution, for each of those years. The government contended that this circumstance of adjustment applied only to inclusions in different taxable years. The district court held that the statute permits mitigation "when the same item of income is reported in *two different years.*" Moreover, even if the erroneous inclusions of income in 1977–1979 would eventually result, by the adjustment of the partners' capital accounts, in a double inclusion in later years, the years were not sufficiently related within the meaning of the statute, apparently because of the uncertainty of years involved and the absence of a determination covering them.

[282] Cocchiara v. United States, 779 F2d 1108 (5th Cir. 1986).

[283] Maguire, Surrey & Traynor, "Section 820 of the Revenue Act of 1938 (Part II)," 48 Yale LJ 719 (1939).

they were applied to the unrelated assessments. The Fifth Circuit rejected the Service's argument, despite the fact that the earlier decision in the refund suit did not require the inclusion of the proceeds in both 1959 and 1960 through 1965. The Fifth Circuit held that Section 1312(1) refers to the tax due on the items of gross income and not to the items themselves.

When the beneficiary of a trust received trust distributions in 1979 and 1984, and reported the 1979 distribution as income and the 1984 distribution as nontaxable, the Service accepted the tax paid for 1979 and initially asserted a deficiency for 1984, and then appeared to concede the 1984 distribution was nontaxable (although the petition was dismissed without the Service saying so). The taxpayer then filed a claim for refund of the 1979 tax, and claimed that the mitigation provisions permitted the refund after the statute of limitations had run because there had been the double inclusion of an item of income. The district court held that the mitigation provisions did not apply, because the 1979 and 1984 distributions were separate items and not the same item, and the mitigation provisions "only protect against a party taking an inconsistent position on the same item in different tax years, not on similar items in different tax years."[284]

Some courts have further expanded the meaning of the term "item" of income. For example, the Court of Claims has held that inventories constitute an item of gross income and has stated that the term "item of income" should be interpreted "to include any item or amount which affects gross income. . . ."[285] The Service has agreed that inventories are an income item.[286] Applying this broad interpretation of the term, the disallowance of a deduction has been treated as an inclusion in gross income.[287] Other courts have had a less expan-

---

[284] Lichtman v. United States, 75 AFTR2d 95-2699 (ED Pa. 1995) (thereby appearing to apply a quantitative, not a qualitative test, and failing to consider trust distributions as the "item").

[285] Gooch Milling & Elevator Co. v. United States, 78 F. Supp. 94 (Ct. Cl. 1948). See also Central Hanover Bank & Trust Co. v. United States, 163 F2d 60 (2d Cir. 1947).

[286] Rev. Rul. 58-327, 1958-1 CB 16.

[287] First Nat'l Bank v. United States, 565 F2d 507 (8th Cir. 1977). In this case, the decedent erroneously included the amount of a liquidation reserve in income, and her estate later filed an income tax return claiming a loss for the difference between the amount actually received and the amount previously included in income. The Service disallowed the loss and, when the estate sought to reopen the year of erroneous inclusion, claimed that disallowance of the loss did not amount to a double inclusion. The court of appeals implicitly (but not explicitly) treated the loss as an item of income. See also Cocchiara v. United States, 779 F2d 1108 (5th Cir. 1986). But see Schwartz v. United States, 76 AFTR2d 95-6800 (9th Cir. 1995) (deduction for straddle loss claimed to be an item erroneously included in gross income; held, the statutory definition of "gross income," "includes only items that add wealth"). In *Schwartz*, to support its view that a deduction is not an item of income, the Ninth Circuit cited Gardiner v. United States, 536 F2d 903 (10th Cir. 1976), which stated that the meaning of an item of income "does not include everything that results in an increase in tax . . . [i]t does not include negative elements

sive interpretation. The failure to claim a deduction is not considered to be an election to include an item of income.[288] Moreover, the item-as-affecting-income definition has not been adopted by all courts. The Tax Court and the Second Circuit have strictly construed the term "item of income."[289] The Tax Court has held that a determination shifting a taxpayer from the cash to the accrual method, and an adjustment in the closed year arising from this change in accounting method, were not the same items.[290] However, the court of claims held that a change in election of a method of accounting for inventory constitutes an "item,"[291] as does an adjustment involving inventory[292] or deprecia-

---

such as deductions (e.g., depreciation), the omission of which results in increased tax." Although the Ninth Circuit acknowledged that in Gooch Milling & Elevator Co. v. United States, 78 F. Supp. 94 (Ct. Cl. 1948), which involved erroneous inclusions of property in inventory, the court of claims had said that the inventories were used to calculate operating profit and were "vital" in determining the company's profit. The Ninth Circuit distinguished the case by saying that the court of claims did not actually say that a deduction constituted an item of gross income.

[288] M. Fine & Sons Mfg. Co. v. United States, 168 F. Supp. 769 (Ct. Cl. 1958) (gain on sale increased because adjusted basis recomputed to take into account allowable depreciation unclaimed); Skinner v. United States, 202 F. Supp. 598 (SD Tex. 1962) (basis of stock increased when compensation income had been increased on determination of higher fair market value in year of receipt).

[289] See, e.g., American Found. Co. v. Comm'r, 2 TC 502 (1943); Central Hanover Bank & Trust Co. v. United States, 163 F2d 60 (2d Cir. 1947).

[290] MacDonald v. Comm'r, 17 TC 934 (1951); see also Schwartz v. United States, 76 AFTR2d 95-6800 (9th Cir. 1995).

[291] Moultrie Cotton Mills v. United States, 151 F. Supp. 482 (Ct. Cl. 1957); compare United States v. Dubuque Packing Co., 233 F2d 453 (8th Cir. 1956). The Service now follows the view of the court of claims in Moultrie Cotton Mills that such a change results in a circumstance of adjustment that is either a double inclusion of an item of income or a double allowance of a deduction or credit. See Rev. Rul. 72-127, 1972-1 CB 268. See also Schwartz v. United States, 76 AFTR2d 95-6800 (9th Cir. 1995).

[292] Gooch Milling & Elevator Co. v. United States, 78 F. Supp. 94 (Ct. Cl. 1948). See FW Boelter Co. v. United States, 87-1 USTC ¶ 9254 (Cl. Ct. 1987) (taxpayer filed refund claims to correct over valuations of inventory and tax for 1975 through 1981; Service allowed claims for 1977 and 1979 through 1981 but not for 1975, 1976, and 1978; held, allowance of refund claims was not "actively inconsistent" with assertion of statute of limitations; active-inconsistency doctrine justified); compare Hall Paving Co. v. United States, 75 AFTR2d 95-2610 (ND Ga. 1995) (after Service successfully disallowed taxpayer's writedown of soil aggregate in 1978 and 1979 because it constituted an unauthorized change in accounting method for inventory, the taxpayer filed a refund claim for 1975–1977, claiming that it had overpaid tax by including the soil aggregate in inventory for those years; held, the Service's position in the Tax Court was not evidence of inconsistency with its position in the prior years, but a determination that the taxpayer had acted contrary to the rules for changing a method of accounting). In Hall Paving, the court agreed that Boelter did not control the result, but did not believe that the Services's position on taxpayer's noncompliance with the accounting method change rules in 1978 and 1979 adopted any position at all—active or passive—in the earlier years.

tion.[293] The Tax Court also has held that amortization of a bond premium that affects gain or loss on a subsequent sale is not an item.[294] These decisions simply cannot be reconciled. However, it does appear that the liberal interpretations of the court of claims are more consistent with the purposes of the mitigation provisions.

[b] Double Allowance of a Deduction or Credit

A closed year may be opened if "[t]he determination allows a deduction or credit which was erroneously allowed to the taxpayer for another taxable year. . . ."[295] In order for there to be a double allowance of a deduction, the following conditions must exist:

1. The taxpayer must have been allowed a deduction or credit for a taxable year;
2. A determination must allow the deduction or credit in another taxable year;
3. The taxpayer must have maintained in the determination proceeding a position inconsistent with allowance of the deduction or credit in the other year; and
4. At the time of the determination, an assessment in respect to the year of original deduction or credit must be barred.

The following example illustrates the occurrence of a double allowance of a deduction or credit.

EXAMPLE 5-6: A taxpayer claims a casualty loss in his return for 1985. After the return is filed, the taxpayer discovers that the casualty occurred in 1986, not 1985. When the period of limitations for the assessment of a deficiency for 1985 has expired, the taxpayer files a claim for refund for 1986, based on the deduction for the casualty in that year. The Commissioner allows the claim for refund in 1990. An adjustment is authorized for the year 1985[296] because there has been a determination (the allowance of the claim for refund), establishing the existence of a circumstance of adjustment (the double deduction of the casualty loss in 1985 and 1986). At the time of the determination, correction of the error is time-barred. Moreover, the taxpayer has taken an inconsistent position by deducting the casualty loss in 1985 and successfully pursuing the claim for refund for 1986.

---

[293] M. Fine & Sons Mfg. Co. v. United States, 168 F. Supp. 769 (Ct. Cl. 1958).

[294] Brennen v. Comm'r, 20 TC 495 (1953).

[295] IRC § 1312(2).

[296] Reg. § 1.1312-2(b), Ex. 1.

A closed year may be opened when the taxpayer, in whose favor the determination operates by allowing a deduction or credit, is related to the taxpayer who has obtained benefit of the same deduction or credit. The following example illustrates this concept in a beneficiary-trust situation.

EXAMPLE 5-7: In his return for 1986, a beneficiary of a testamentary trust claims and is allowed a deduction for depreciation of the trust property. The Commissioner asserts a deficiency against the beneficiary for 1986 with respect to a different item. In 1989, a final decision of the Tax Court is rendered, so that the Commissioner is prevented by the restriction of Section 6212(c) from sending the beneficiary a further deficiency notice for the year 1986. Thereafter, the trustee files a timely claim for refund, contending that under the terms of the will, the trust and not the beneficiary was entitled to the allowance for depreciation. In 1991, the district court sustains the refund claim. In this situation, an adjustment is authorized for the beneficiary's 1986 year, irrespective of the limitations of Section 6212(c), because the determination has operated in favor of a related party: the trustee.[297]

The Tax Court has adopted a strict view of the term "deduction" for purposes of the double-inclusion circumstance. It considers "deduction" to be a term of art interpreted to mean a specific deduction from gross income granted by Congress in arriving at taxable income. Consequently, an offset employed in the computation of gross income, such as the treatment of basis or cost of goods sold, does not constitute a deduction for the double inclusion circumstance.[298] This narrow interpretation of the term "deduction" must be compared to the more liberal interpretations of an "item" of income. The two interpretations are not easily rationalized, except that the distinction between a deduction and an offset has been established outside the mitigation area[299] and for other circumstances of adjustment as well.[300]

The deduction analysis can become quite refined when adjustments in later years reflect on the accuracy of a deduction on the original return. In

---

[297] Reg. § 1.1312-2(b), Ex. 2.

[298] BC Cook & Sons v. Comm'r, 65 TC 422 (1975), aff'd, 584 F2d 53 (5th Cir. 1978) (embezzlement was allowed for 1965, a portion of which had been included in cost of goods sold; held, cost of goods sold was not a deduction; thus, Section 1312(a) did not apply); Brennen v. Comm'r, 20 TC 495 (1953) (adjustment of basis not a deduction under predecessor of Section 1312(2)).

[299] See, e.g., Dorn v. Comm'r, 54 TC 1651 (1970) (interpretation of deduction in Section 642(g)).

[300] Curtis Gallery & Library, Inc. v. United States, 388 F2d 358 (9th Cir. 1967) (double deduction held not to include overstatement of gross income); Bray v. Comm'r, 46 TC 577 (1966), aff'd, 396 F2d 452 (6th Cir. 1968); Bridges v. Comm'r, 64 TC 968 (1975).

Bolten[301] the taxpayers had claimed net operating losses on their 1975 through 1981 returns. In 1988, they entered into a closing agreement with the Service adjusting the adjusted gross income reported on those returns and established the revised net operating losses for each of the years. As a result of the closing agreement, tax was owed for 1980; but the normal period for assessment of the 1980 liability had expired. At issue was whether the taxpayers had been allowed the 1980 net operating loss in the "determination" (the closing agreement) and also erroneously allowed to the taxpayers on their 1980 return. The taxpayers argued that when the 1980 return had been filed it was not erroneous. The 1980 return was affected by adjustments in related years. The net operating loss on the 1980 return had turned out to be erroneous only some seven years later, when net operating losses for all the preceding years were adjusted in the closing agreement. But for those adjustments, the 1980 return was correct as filed, eliminating one of the elements of the Section 1312(2) circumstance of adjustment. The Tax Court rejected the argument, saying:

> It should be a matter of no consequence why the NOL carryovers that [the taxpayers] used for those years were less than the amounts allowable and in fact allowed in the closing agreement. The point is that for whatever reason, greater amounts of the NOL were allowed to them for 1977–1979 and the remaining amount of that carryover available to reduce taxable income for the period beyond 1979 was thus reduced by precisely the amount of the difference.[302]

The double allowance of a deduction or credit can occur when the Service includes income in the wrong taxable year. In *Hagestad*, the taxpayer took a deduction relating to a computer leasing investment on his 1987 return.[303] On audit, the Service disallowed the deduction but did not find that there was a deficiency for the year because it also determined that an item of income the taxpayer included in his 1987 return was properly includable in his income for 1986, and so eliminated the item of income. Subsequently, the Tax Court agreed with the taxpayer that the income was includable in 1987. Because the statute of limitations on assessment had expired, the effect was that there was no change in the taxpayer's 1987 return, giving him the benefit of a concededly erroneous computer leasing deduction. As a result of the Service's disallowance of the computer leasing deductions and the suspension of those losses, however, the taxpayer was able to claim a portion of the 1987 deduction for 1991 and received a tax refund for that year. The Tax Court concluded that the

---

[301] Bolten v. Comm'r, 95 TC 397 (1990). The *Bolten* case was settled on appeal, but the National Office has stated in Field Service Advice that it believes "quite strongly" that the result is correct. FSA 3916 (Mar. 6, 1992), reprinted in 95 TNT 137-33 (July 13, 1995).

[302] Bolten v. Comm'r, 95 TC 397, 406 (1990).

[303] Hagestad v. Comm'r, TC Memo 1997-273, 73 TCM 3047 (1997).

mitigation provisions applied to permit the Service to reopen the 1987 year to reflect the inclusion of the item of income and the disallowance of the computer leasing deduction. The Court reasoned that there had been an error because of the Service's erroneous treatment of the item of income. When the Service allowed the claim for refund for 1991, the action constituted a determination, as defined in Section 1313(a)(3). This determination, the court found, was with respect to the item giving rise to the error. The Court rejected the taxpayer's argument that the item giving rise to the error was the Service's erroneous position on the item of income, not the computer leasing deduction, on the ground that both deductions and omissions of income affect the determination of taxable income. Finally, the court ruled that the carryforward of the suspended computer leasing deduction was inconsistent with the taxpayer's treatment of the item; that is, the taxpayer had claimed the deduction, and the deduction had in fact been allowed for 1987, irrespective of how the deduction came to be taken into account in determining the taxpayer's tax for the year.

[c] Double Exclusion of an Item of Gross Income

A closed year may be opened under Section 1312(3) if a determination results in the double exclusion of an item of gross income. The object of Section 1312(3) is to permit income to be included in the proper year by permitting an otherwise closed year to be reopened for this purpose. Under Section 1312(3)(A), the determination in an open year must result in the exclusion of an item of gross income that the taxpayer included in gross income in a return the taxpayer filed or on which the taxpayer paid a tax. If the item has not been included in any return, then Section 1312(3)(A) does not apply, although it does cover situations in which the taxpayer has paid tax on the item (which was not included on the return) and has sued for refund. The taxpayer must also have maintained an inconsistent position in the determination proceeding, that is, the taxpayer must have exploited the bar of the statute of limitations by successfully contending that the item excluded was properly includable in a closed year.[304]

Under Section 1312(3)(B), the item of excluded gross income must not have been included on any tax return. In this situation, no inconsistent position is required in the determination proceeding. However, the Commissioner is permitted to reopen a closed year only if, at the time the notice of deficiency was sent, the Commissioner could have made an adjustment for the year in which the item was erroneously excluded because the statute of limitations on assessment was still open. In other words, while an inconsistent position is a condition for use of the Section 1312(3)(A) circumstance, use of Section

---

[304] The inconsistency need not be active. See the discussion of inconsistent positions supra ¶ 5.04[2][a].

1312(3)(B) depends on circumstances existing at the time the notice of deficiency was sent, and if correction of the error was not barred at that time, Section 1311 may be used.

Section 1313(3) describes double exclusions of items of income when tax has been paid on the item and when no tax has been paid on the item. However, the determination of whether there has been a payment or nonpayment is not always clear. In *Kappel v. Commissioner*,[305] the taxpayers failed to include annuity contract proceeds in their 1954 and 1955 returns. In 1962, at a time when the statute of limitations on assessment for the 1954 tax was barred, the Service issued a statutory notice of deficiency for 1955 including a portion of the annuity contract proceeds in that year. The taxpayer paid the deficiency and sued for refund. In 1974, the district court determined that the item of income at issue was received in 1954, not in 1955. Within the one-year period, the Service sent the taxpayer's estate a notice of deficiency for 1954. If the taxpayer had paid tax on the item within the meaning of Section 1312(3)(A), the Commissioner's action was timely, and the year 1954 could be reopened. However, if the tax was not paid within the meaning of Section 1312(3)(B), the deficiency notice was untimely because the limitations period for the 1954 year was not open at the time of the deficiency notice, as required by Section 1311(b)(2)(A).[306] The court of appeals, reversing the Tax Court, held that when a taxpayer has neither included the item on a return for any year nor paid tax, a closed year may be opened only if the notice of deficiency is sent while the limitations period for assessment of tax in the closed year is still open. Because the limitations period in this case was closed when the notice was sent, the mitigation provisions were not available to the Commissioner. The court's rationale for this result was as follows:

> [I]f, when the Commissioner gives a statutory notice, the earlier year is still open, but the taxpayer refrains from acting until the statute of limitations has run, and then asserts that liability belongs in the closed year, the government has been prejudiced by the taxpayer's delay in asserting that position. But where, as here, the earlier year is time-barred at the time the notice of deficiency is sent, the government can in no way be prejudiced with respect to the collection of taxes for the only year still open. That lack of prejudice is no less apparent when the later determination is made in the Tax Court, than when it is made in a suit for a refund.[307]

In short, according to the court, Section 1312(3)(A) protects the Commissioner whenever a taxpayer either includes an item in a return or makes a payment for one year when both years in question are open.

---

[305] Kappel v. Comm'r, 615 F2d 91 (3d Cir. 1980).

[306] See supra ¶ 5.01[2].

[307] Kappel v. Comm'r, 615 F2d 91, 96 (3d Cir. 1980).

A result directly contrary to the result reached by the regulations,[308] was approved by the court of claims in *Birchenough v. United States.*[309] Under the regulations, payment made for a deficiency in one year when the limitations period for assessment of tax due for an earlier year is closed constitutes a payment for purposes of Section 1312(3)(A). In *Birchenough*, the reason for this result was said to be the impossibility of distinguishing between a payment made by a taxpayer who had thought the deficiency was correct and has changed his or her mind and one made by another taxpayer who pays the deficiency solely to start a refund suit. In short, a taxpayer can avoid the effect of Section 1312(3)(A) by not paying the deficiency and taking the case to the Tax Court. Any payment made with respect to an excluded item of income is sufficient for purposes of the statute.

[i] Items included in income. Adjustment is authorized under Section 1311(a) if, as described in Section 1312(3)(A), the determination requires the exclusion from a taxpayer's gross income of an item that was included in a return filed by the taxpayer, or with respect to which a tax was paid, and that was excluded or omitted from the gross income of the same taxpayer for another taxable year or from the gross income of a related taxpayer. This double exclusion circumstance exists when

1. A taxpayer has erroneously excluded an item of income in one year;
2. The taxpayer has included the item of income or paid a tax on the item of income in another year;
3. The determination requires the exclusion of the item for such other year;
4. In the determination proceeding, the taxpayer maintains a position that is inconsistent with the exclusion of the income in the earlier year and that is adopted in the determination proceeding; and
5. At the time of the determination, an assessment of the year of erroneous exclusion is barred.

Section 1312(3)(A) requires that an item has been included in income or a tax paid on it and that the determination establish that it is excluded in another year. As used in this section, the word "included" is a term of art. An item is included only if it has an effect on taxable income. Consequently, an amount was held not to have been included when the taxpayer attached a statement to the return stating erroneously that the item was not taxable.[310] Payment of a deficiency, even if only for the purpose of starting a refund suit, is payment of

---

[308] Reg. § 1.1312-3, Ex. 1.

[309] Birchenough v. United States, 410 F2d 1247 (Ct. Cl. 1969).

[310] Warburton v. Comm'r, 30 TC 34 (1958).

a tax,[311] although there is uncertainty whether payment may be made at a time when the period of limitations for assessment of tax in the error year is still open.[312] A determination that an item is not taxable in a particular year to a single taxpayer or that it is taxable in the closed year to a related taxpayer constitutes an exclusion of the item for the purposes of Section 1312(3)(A).[313]

The following example illustrates the double exclusion circumstance requiring the inclusion of the item.

EXAMPLE 5-8: A taxpayer receives payments for 1990 under a service contract and includes the payments in his 1990 return. After the statute of limitations on assessment for the year 1989 expires, the Commissioner issues a notice of deficiency for 1990 based on other items. The taxpayer files a petition in the Tax Court contesting the notice of deficiency for 1990 and contending, among other things, that he kept his books on the accrual method and that the payments received in 1990 were properly taxable in 1989. The Tax Court then renders a final decision excluding the payments from 1990 income. As a result, the Commissioner is authorized under Section 1311 to make an adjustment in the 1989 tax return whether or not the taxpayer had actually paid tax on the income reported in the 1990 return.[314] The taxpayer has taken an inconsistent position by con-

---

[311] Reg. § 1.1312-3(a)(2), Ex. 1(ii).

[312] Compare Estate of Kappel v. Comm'r, 615 F2d 91 (3d Cir. 1980) with Birchenough v. United States, 410 F2d 1247 (Ct. Cl. 1969).

[313] Cotter v. Comm'r, 40 TC 506 (1963) (nonrecognition of gain under Section 351; held, exclusion of item of income in 1956 occurred because substituted basis of nonrecognition property merely postponed recognition of item to year of taxable transaction). In Mitchell v. United States, 645 F. Supp. 274 (SD Fla. 1986), the deceased husband and surviving wife had deducted losses from a partnership from 1972 through 1976. After an audit, they agreed to the disallowance of the losses and paid additional tax in August 1979. Another partner settled the case with the Service, and was allowed most of the original partnership losses deductions. This settlement was reflected in a stipulated decision entered in April 1982. In February 1983, the Mitchells filed claims for refund for 1973 through 1976 (but apparently not for 1972) based on the settlement the Service had entered into with the other partner. The statute of limitations on filing a claim for refund had expired in 1983, because more than two years had elapsed since the 1979 payment. The Mitchells claimed that Section 1312(3)(A) described the circumstances that entitled them to lift the bar of the statute of limitations. Not surprisingly, the district court held that the Mitchells' case involved deductions, not the exclusion of an item of income. The contention that equitable recoupment applied was also rejected.

[314] Reg. § 1.1312-3(a)(2), Ex. 1. For example, in Chertkof v. Comm'r, 676 F2d 984 (4th Cir. 1982), the taxpayer owed some tax on a stock redemption, either in 1965 or 1966. The taxpayer included the redemption in his 1966 return (but at the capital gains rate). However, the Service determined that the redemption took place in 1965 and was taxable as a dividend. Therefore, it refunded the tax attributable to inclusion of the distribution in 1966. After the taxpayer sued for a refund of the 1965 deficiency tax, the district court ruled in the taxpayer's favor that the redemption took place in 1966. The Service refunded the 1965 tax payment, but issued a notice of deficiency for 1966, al-

tending that the income is excludable in the open year and by having excluded the income from the closed year in which he contends the income
was properly includable. On the other hand, if the taxpayer had not reported the income on any return, no adjustment would be authorized
under this provision.[315]

As shown in the following example, the same result occurs when related parties are involved.

> **EXAMPLE 5-9:** The father in a father-son partnership reports the entire
> partnership income on his 1990 tax return. Shortly before the expiration
> of the period of limitations for making deficiency assessments and refund
> claims for both the father and the son for 1990, the father files a claim
> for refund of that portion of his 1990 tax attributable to the son's half of
> the partnership income. The district court sustains the father's claim in
> 1987. Therefore, an adjustment is authorized for the son's 1990 tax.[316]

[ii] Items not included in income. Section 1312(3)(B) applies if the determination requires the exclusion from gross income of an item that

1. Has not been included in a return filed by the taxpayer, and the taxpayer has not paid tax on it; and
2. Is includable in the gross income of the same taxpayer for another
   taxable year or in the gross income of a related taxpayer for the same
   or another taxable year.

This circumstance is one of the two in which an inconsistent position is not a
requirement for adjustment.[317] However, the Commissioner may open a closed
year for the purpose of including income with respect to which no tax was
paid only as long as correction of the error was not barred when the Commissioner "erroneously" included the income in an open year.[318] In effect, if no
tax has been paid, the Commissioner may proceed for one year and against

---

though the normal period for doing so had elapsed. The court of appeals held that the provisions of Section 1312(3)(A) were fulfilled and rejected the government's contention that
before the double exclusion circumstance could apply, the taxpayer must have erred. The
taxpayer did not err, since he always contended that the redemptions had occurred in
1966.

[315] Reg. § 1.1312-3(a)(2), Ex. 1(ii). However, if the taxpayer had paid the deficiency
for 1971 and sued for refund on the ground that income was properly includable in the
year 1970, an adjustment for 1970 would be authorized. Id. But see the discussion infra
¶ 5.05[5][c][ii].

[316] Reg. § 1.1312-3(a)(2), Ex. 2.

[317] For a discussion of the other circumstance (i.e., double disallowance of a deduction or credit), see IRC § 1312(4), discussed infra ¶ 5.04[5][b].

[318] IRC § 1311(b)(2)(A); Reg. § 1.1312-3(b)(1).

one taxpayer, and the statute of limitations against that taxpayer or a related taxpayer is tolled. The following examples illustrate this provision.

EXAMPLE 5-10: Taxpayer *A* computes his income on the accrual method. He performs services in 1985 for which he receives payment in 1985 and 1986. *A* does not include the payments in either his 1985 or his 1986 return. In 1988, the Commissioner sends a notice of deficiency to *A* for 1985, contending that he should have included all of the payments in 1985. *A* contests the deficiency on the basis that in 1985, he had no accruable right to the payments he received in 1986. In 1991, after the expiration of the statute of limitations on the assessment of any deficiency for 1986, the Tax Court sustains *A*'s position. Thus, the Commissioner may assess a deficiency for 1986, since at the time that the notice of deficiency for 1985 was sent, assessment for 1986 was not barred.[319]

EXAMPLE 5-11: Taxpayers *B* and *C* are partners. *B* reports his one-half share of partnership income, but *C* fails to report his share. The Commissioner sends *C* a notice of deficiency for this tax. *C* successfully contests the inclusion of one-half the partnership income on the basis that there was no partnership. Thus, the Commissioner is authorized to include the entire amount in *B*'s income and assess a tax, provided that the period for assessment had not expired at the time the notice of deficiency was sent to *C*.[320]

[d] Double Disallowance of a Deduction or Credit

The opening of a closed year is authorized if the result of a determination is a double disallowance of a deduction or credit. Such a double disallowance occurs when "[t]he determination disallows a deduction or credit which should have been allowed to, but was not allowed to, the taxpayer for another taxable year, or to a related taxpayer."[321] A double disallowance permits a deduction to be claimed in the correct year and a year otherwise closed to be opened for this purpose. This circumstance of adjustment is one of the two in which the party benefiting from the error (in this case, the Commissioner) need not have maintained an inconsistent position.[322] However, correction of the error by way

---

[319] Reg. § 1.1312-3(b)(2), Ex. 1.

[320] Reg. § 1.1312-3(b)(2), Ex. 2.

[321] IRC § 1312(4). Longiotti v. United States, 819 F2d 65 (4th Cir.), cert. denied, 484 US 985 (1987) (disallowance of net operating loss deduction in 1972, resulting in disallowance of deduction of unused portions of 1973 net operating loss after 1978, and 1974 net operating loss after 1979, held not to constitute a double disallowance because the determination involved only one year; 1973 and 1974 net operating losses could still be carried forward and thus were not disallowed).

[322] IRC § 1311(b)(1).

of claim for refund must not have been barred at the time the taxpayer first maintained in writing before the Service or the Tax Court that he or she was entitled to the deduction or credit in the year at issue in the determination proceeding.[323] The purpose of this requirement is to prevent a taxpayer from going back indefinitely to claim a deduction or credit previously unclaimed. An exceedingly clever taxpayer could do this by claiming a deduction incorrectly in any year and forcing the Service to take an inconsistent position on the correct deduction year, thereby permitting the taxpayer to open the closed year.

To establish an adjustment under this circumstance, the taxpayer must show that the following conditions exist:

1. A deduction or credit was properly allowable for one year but was not allowed in that year;
2. A determination resulted in the disallowance of the deduction or credit in another year;
3. At the time the taxpayer first maintained in writing before the Service or before the Tax Court that he or she was entitled to the deduction or credit in the year at issue in the determination proceeding, the year the deduction or credit was properly allowable was open for the purposes of filing a refund claim; and
4. At the time of the determination, a claim for refund of tax paid for the year of proper deduction or credit was barred.

The following example illustrates this provision.

EXAMPLE 5-12: Taxpayer A, an accrual method taxpayer, deducts for 1986 an item of expense he paid in that year. At the time A files the 1986 return, the statute of limitations on refund or credit for the taxable year 1985 has not expired. Subsequently, the Commissioner determines that a deficiency is due for 1986 because the item of expense should have been accrued in 1985. In 1990, after the period of limitations on filing a claim for refund for 1985 has expired, the Tax Court determines that the Commissioner is correct. Thus, the taxpayer is entitled to an adjustment for the closed taxable year 1985. However, if the Tax Court had determined that the liability should have been deducted in a year that was closed when A deducted the expense item in 1986, the closed year would not be opened.[324]

In *Beaudry Motor Co.*,[325] the taxpayer was able to use the mitigation provisions to file an otherwise barred refund claim for the year in which the investment credit was recaptured (1986) on the ground that the investment credit

---

[323] IRC § 1311(b)(2)(B).

[324] Reg. § 1.1312-3(b), Ex. 1. See also Rev. Rul. 58-12, 1958-1 CB 317; Rev. Rul. 58-24, 1958-1 CB 318.

[325] Beaudry Motor Co. v. United States, 886 F. Supp. 13 (D. Ariz. 1995).

was "disallowed" (for the years 1983 and 1984) when it was made unavailable after the NOL (from 1985) had been carried back, and "because of the determination and the resulting disallowance of those credits in 1983 and 1984, the credits should have been allowed to, but [were] not allowed to, the taxpayer for 1986." The Service argued that unavailability (i.e., disallowance) of investment tax credits and an offset or reduction of the recapture of investment credit were not of the same type of credit, but the district court said that the credits were "based on the same transactions, and in this sense, they are the same."

The Ninth Circuit reversed the district court in an unpublished memorandum decision. Although its decision cannot be cited as authority, the circuit court said that the Service's allowance of Beaudry's NOL carrybacks for 1983 and 1984, which arose in 1985 and were carried back in 1989 to 1983 and 1984, resulting in the unavailability of its investment credits for 1983 and 1984, did not constitute, without more, the disallowance of a deduction or credit. The court also pointed out that Beaudry should have known in 1989, when it carried back the NOLs, that they would not only eliminate the investment credits in 1983 and 1984 but also the investment credit recapture in 1986. Accordingly, the court noted that Beaudry had sufficient time to file the refund claim for 1986, and the situation was not one that the mitigation provisions were intended to remedy.[326]

The double disallowance of a deduction can also occur when a taxpayer claims an ordinary loss that is subsequently determined to be a capital loss, available for carryover to offset capital gain in a later year.[327]

Operation of the provision for related taxpayers is illustrated by the situation in which a husband in a community-property state claims a charitable deduction and the Commissioner successfully disallows one-half the amount deducted on the ground that it properly belongs to the wife. If the deduction was not barred to the wife when her husband claimed it on his return, the closed year can be reopened even though the Commissioner wins his case at a time when the wife could not otherwise claim a refund of tax for the year in which she was entitled to the deduction but did not claim it.[328]

---

[326] Raby & Raby, "Mitigation: No Safety Net for Carelessness," 96 TNT 194-51 (Oct. 3, 1996).

[327] Olin Mathieson Chem. Corp. v. United States, 265 F2d 293 (7th Cir. 1959); Rev. Rul. 68-152, 1968-1 CB 369 (double disallowance occurs when a taxpayer claims a capital loss that is subsequently determined to be an ordinary loss). See also Rev. Rul. 70-43, 1970-1 CB 176 (capital loss subsequently determined to be an ordinary loss may be carried backward and forward).

[328] Reg. § 1.1312-4(b), Ex. 2.

TABLE 5.4 _____
Opening a Closed Year Under Section 1312(5)

Determination	*Error*
1. Allowance of deduction to trust	Omission or exclusion from income of beneficiaries, etc.
2. Inclusion of income of beneficiaries, etc.	Omission or disallowance of deduction to trust, etc.
3. Disallowance of deduction to trust, etc.	Inclusion in income of beneficiaries, etc.
4. Exclusion from income of beneficiaries, etc.	Allowance of deduction to trust, etc.

[e] Correlative Deductions and Inclusions for Trusts or Estates and Legatees, Beneficiaries, and Heirs

Section 1312(5) applies to distributions by a trust or an estate to the beneficiaries, heirs, or legatees and permits an adjustment in two general situations. First, if the determination results in allowance or disallowance of the deduction of a trust or estate under Section 651 or Section 661, an adjustment in the beneficiary's tax is permitted if the beneficiary has erroneously included or excluded the correlative income item. Second, an adjustment is also authorized in the otherwise closed year of the trust or estate if the determination relates to the amount included in the taxable income of the beneficiary required by Sections 652 and 662. This circumstance permits the opening of a closed year by the affected party in four situations, as summarized in Table 5.4.

The first situation in Table 5.4 is when an estate or trust has claimed a deduction for an income distribution, and the beneficiaries, heirs, or legatees have erroneously omitted or excluded the income. The following example illustrates this circumstance of adjustment.

EXAMPLE 5-13: A trustee accumulates and pays a tax on trust income and makes no distribution to the beneficiary. As a result, the beneficiary does not include the trust income in his return for the year 1986.[329] In 1989, a state court holds invalid the clause directing accumulation and determines that the income is required to be distributed currently. It also holds that certain extraordinary dividends that the trustee in good faith allocated to corpus in 1986 were properly allocable to income. In 1990, the trustee, on the basis of the court decision, files a claim for refund for the tax the trust paid for 1986 and thereafter successfully prosecutes the claim in the district court, except as to the tax on the extraordinary dividends. However, the court decision is rendered after the period of limitations on

_____
[329] Reg. § 1.1312-5(b).

assessment of a deficiency in the tax of the beneficiary for the year 1986. Thus, Section 1311(a) permits an adjustment of the beneficiary's 1986 tax to permit the correlative inclusion of the income in the beneficiary's income.[330]

The inclusion-of-income circumstance exists when beneficiaries, heirs, or legatees include in income an amount that has been erroneously disallowed or omitted as a deduction to an estate or trust. This situation is illustrated in the following example.

EXAMPLE 5-14: Assume the same facts as in the previous example, except that, instead of the trustee's filing a claim for refund, the Commissioner, relying on the court decision, successfully asserts a deficiency against the beneficiary in a Tax Court proceeding. The Tax Court decision is rendered in 1991, after the trust's period for filing a refund claim has expired. As a result, an adjustment of the trust's 1986 tax is authorized to permit the correlative deduction.[331]

The deduction-disallowance circumstance applies when an estate or trust deduction has been disallowed, but the beneficiaries, heirs, or legatees have erroneously included the amount in their income.

EXAMPLE 5-15: A trustee claims in the 1990 return for a trust a deduction for the amount of distributable net income. The beneficiary included the amount in his tax return for the year.[332] Subsequently, the Commissioner asserts that capital gains were erroneously included in distributable net income and were taxable to the trust, not the beneficiary. The Commissioner's deficiency determination against the trust is upheld by the Tax Court, after the period for the beneficiary's filing a refund claim for 1990 has expired. Nevertheless, the beneficiary's closed 1990 tax year may be opened to adjust the tax based on the exclusion of the 1990 income previously considered distributed by the trust.

The income-exclusion circumstance occurs when beneficiaries, heirs, or legatees have omitted from income amounts the estate or trust has erroneously deducted. The following example illustrates this situation.

EXAMPLE 5-16: Assume the same facts as in the preceding example with respect to the deduction-disallowance circumstances, except that, instead of the Commissioner's asserting a deficiency, the beneficiary files a refund claim for 1990 on the same ground (i.e., that the trust erroneously included capital gains in distributable net income). Although the district

---

[330] The extraordinary dividends are treated in the manner provided by Subpart D of Subchapter J. See IRC §§ 667, 668.

[331] Reg. § 1.1312-5(c).

[332] Reg. § 1.1312-5(d).

court sustains the refund claim after the period of limitations on the deficiency assessments against the trust for 1990, the Commissioner is nevertheless permitted to adjust the tax of the trust for the otherwise closed year.

[f] Correlative Deductions and Credits for Certain Related Corporations

Section 1312(6) provides that if a determination allows or disallows a deduction (including a credit) to a corporation and if a correlative deduction or credit has been erroneously allowed, omitted, or disallowed for a related corporation, either the corporation or the Commissioner may open a closed year with respect to the item involved. The following example illustrates this provision.

EXAMPLE 5-17: *X* Corporation, a wholly owned subsidiary of *Y* Corporation, pays *Y* $5,000 in 1987 and claims an interest deduction for this amount in its 1987 return. *Y* reports the $5,000 as income on its 1987 tax return. In 1990, the Commissioner disallows *X*'s deduction on the ground that it is a disguised dividend from *X* to *Y*. In June 1990, after the period of limitations on *Y*'s filing of a claim for refund of tax for 1987, the Tax Court sustains the Commissioner's determination, the rationale being that *Y* was entitled to the intercorporate dividends-received deduction with respect to the payment from *X*. Thus, *Y* may open the otherwise closed year to adjust its 1987 tax. On the other hand, if *Y* had filed a claim for refund for the 1987 year based on the dividends-received deduction and its claim had been upheld by a district court at a time when a deficiency assessment could not otherwise be assessed against *X* based on disallowance of the interest deduction claimed on its return for the year, the Commissioner could have opened *X*'s 1987 year and adjusted its tax.[333]

[g] Basis of Property After Erroneous Treatment of a Prior Transaction

Section 1312(7) deals with basis problems. It permits certain taxpayers or the Commissioner to open a closed year if a determination establishes both the basis of property and that one of three specified errors occurred in any transaction on which basis "depends" or in any transaction that was erroneously

---

[333] Reg. § 1.1312-6(b), Ex. 1.

treated as "affecting" basis.[334] The three specified errors that are correctable under Section 1312(7) are:

1. An erroneous inclusion in, or omission from, gross income
2. An erroneous recognition or nonrecognition of gain or loss
3. An erroneous deduction of an item properly chargeable to capital account or an erroneous charge to capital account of an item properly deductible, such as capitalization of current expense or deduction of expense that should have been capitalized

Thus, Section 1312(7) involves situations in which basis depends on the proper treatment of a transaction and either the taxpayer or the Commissioner has asserted a position in the determination proceeding that is inconsistent with an earlier and erroneous treatment of the transaction.

However, in order for a correction to be made under Section 1312(7), the erroneous treatment must have occurred with respect to one of three types of taxpayers:

1. A taxpayer with respect to whom the determination is made;
2. A taxpayer who (a) acquired title in the erroneously treated transaction and (b) transferred the property (mediately or immediately) to another taxpayer with respect to whom the determination is made; or
3. A taxpayer who had title to the property at the time of the erroneously treated transaction and from whom the taxpayer with respect to whom the determination was made derived his or her title (either mediately or immediately) by way of gift so that his or her basis is a carryover basis from the donor taxpayer. Note that an original transferee or a subsequent transferee of the original transference may be the taxpayer with respect to whom the determination was made. No adjustment is authorized for the transferor of the property in a transaction on which the basis of the property depends when the determination is made with respect to the transferor's original transferee or a subsequent transferee.

The operation of Section 1312(7) thus requires that the following questions be answered:

• Was there a transaction (e.g., sale, gift, or redemption) involving the property on which its basis depends?
• Was there a determination that fixes the basis of property?

---

[334] Basis can depend on whether the transaction is a sale or a gift. In Chertkof v. United States, 676 F2d 984 (4th Cir. 1982), the court of appeals held that transfer of stock occurring on the death of a decedent constituted a transaction on which basis depends. This result has been criticized in an extensive analysis, Willis, "Equitable Recoupment, Tax Mitigation, and Res Judicata," 38 Tax Law. 625 (1985).

- Was the taxpayer one of the taxpayers described in Section 1312(7)(B)?
- Did one of the instances of erroneous treatment described in Section 1312(7)(C) occur?

The approach followed by one court in determining whether the statute applies is illustrated by *Chertkof v. United States*,[335] in which gain was erroneously recognized by the executors of an estate when they sold and received liquidating distributions on stocks. This erroneous treatment occurred because in these transactions, they used estate tax return values for the stocks that later were determined in a Tax Court decision involving estate tax to be too low. On appeal, the court found that (1) the Tax Court decision determined the basis of property; (2) there was a transaction on which basis depends (the decedent's death); and (3) the estate was the taxpayer with respect to whom the Tax Court decision (the determination) was made.

For example, when the determination only determines the amount of income or loss a partner must report or may deduct from a leasing transaction, the determination does not necessarily determine the basis of the leased equipment (i.e., the determination may have nothing to do with basis, but merely depend on the ownership).

The operation of Section 1312(7) is illustrated in the following examples, involving (1) a stockholder-corporation exchange; (2) a stockholder-donee transfer; and (3) a dividend or return of capital situation.

EXAMPLE 5-18: In 1984, *A* transfers property that had cost him $5,000 to *X* Corporation in exchange for *X* Corporation stock having a fair market value of $10,000. In his return for 1984, *A* reports no gain. In 1990, a determination upholds the *X* Corporation position that the 1984 exchange was taxable and determines the basis of the property to *X* Corporation as $10,000. Section 1312(7) does not apply to *A* because he is not one of the three types of taxpayers specified in that section. In other words, *A* is not the taxpayer with respect to whom the determination was made, nor did *A* acquire property in the exchange which he transferred to *X*, nor did *X* acquire title to property by gift from *A*. However, if *A* sells the *X* Corporation stock in 1986 and claims a $10,000 basis on the ground that the 1984 exchange was taxable, and *A*'s portion is sustained in a determination that becomes final at a time when an assessment on his year 1984 was barred, a Section 1311 adjustment would be authorized for 1984. Section 1312(7) would apply because *A* is the taxpayer with respect to

---

[335] Chertkof v. United States, 676 F2d 984 (4th Cir. 1982). See American Found. Co. v. Comm'r, 2 TC 502 (1943) (determination determined the amount of gain on the receipt of stock, not the basis of stock); see also undated Chief Counsel FSA 1999-575, reprinted in 1999 TNT 20-89 (applying mitigation provisions to a tax shelter situation and reaching the conclusion that a closing agreement and stipulated decision agreeing on the amount of phantom income for certain years and that income in later years was not subject to tax, was not a determination on a transaction on which basis depended).

whom the determination is made. Also, there would have been an erroneous nonrecognition of gain by *A* in 1984.[336]

EXAMPLE 5-19: *A* receives a dividend of preferred stock on common stock and treats it as nontaxable. He assigns $500 of his common stock basis to the preferred stock. The fair market value of the preferred stock when received is $1,000. *A* makes a gift of the preferred stock to *B*, who later sells the stock. At a time when *A*'s year of the stock dividend is barred to an assessment, a determination sustaining *B* holds that the dividend was taxable to *A* and that *B*'s basis for the preferred stock is $1,000. Thus, Section 1311 adjustment against *A* is authorized. Section 1312(7) applies because (1) the determination fixes the basis of the preferred stock; (2) in the prior transaction (the gift) upon which basis depends, there was an erroneous omission from the gross income of *A*; and (3) *A*, as transferor of the stock received in the erroneously treated transaction, is one of the types of taxpayer specified in Section 1312(7).

Similarly, if the subject of the gift were the common stock and a determination upheld *B* in his contention that his basis for the common stock was *A*'s original basis of the common stock, a Section 1311 adjustment against *A* would be authorized. In this situation, *A* is a covered taxpayer as specified in Section 1312(7).[337]

EXAMPLE 5-20: In 1988, a taxpayer, *A*, who owns no shares of stock in *Y* Corporation, receives $1,000 from *Y*, which she reports as a dividend. In 1990, *Y* is liquidated, and *A* receives a liquidating distribution totaling $8,000. In her 1990 return, *A* reports receipt of the $8,000 and computes her gain or loss on the liquidation by using as a basis the amount she paid for the stock. A determination sustains the Commissioner's position that the basis of the stock distribution in 1988 should be reduced by $1,000, because it was a return of capital. Therefore, Section 1311 permits adjustment in favor of *A* because the basis for gain or loss in 1990 depends on the transaction in 1988, and in the 1988 transaction (upon which the basis of the stock depends), there was an erroneous inclusion in gross income of $1,000 by *A*, the taxpayer with respect to whom the determination was made.[338]

[6] What Is the Amount and Method of the Adjustment?

An adjustment can result in either an overpayment of tax or a deficiency in tax. Both results require action by either the taxpayer or the Service to settle

---

[336] Reg. § 1.1312-7(c), Ex. 1.

[337] Reg. § 1.1312-7(c), Ex. 2.

[338] Reg. § 1.1312-7(c), Ex. 4.

the matter. The amount of the adjustment is limited to correcting only the error in the barred year. The mitigation provisions set out how this amount is to be determined.

[a] Adjustment Procedure

When an adjustment results in an overpayment of tax for the error year, a taxpayer must file a claim for refund within one year of the date of the determination. This period may be extended by agreement. If a refund claim has been filed before and is pending at the time of the determination and the claim adequately apprises the Service of the grounds relied on for adjustment, it has been held that the taxpayer is not required to file a second claim after the determination.[339] If the claim for refund is denied or not acted on by the Commissioner within the period prescribed by law, the taxpayer then may file a refund suit. Ordinarily, in a refund suit, the Commissioner may reduce or eliminate a recovery by offsetting other items. However, in a mitigation situation, the Commissioner does not have this power.

When the adjustment results in a deficiency in tax for the error year, the Commissioner must send a notice of deficiency within one year after the date of the determination. The deficiency notice must be sent after, not before, the determination. A premature notice is not sufficient, as is the case with a taxpayer's refund claim. The one-year period is suspended for the time that the Commissioner is prohibited from making assessment after sending the notice.[340] The taxpayer then may contest the deficiency in the Tax Court or, if the taxpayer chooses, may pay the tax, file a refund claim, and sue for a refund.

For purposes of a Section 1311 adjustment, the statute of limitations on refund or assessment for the taxable year of adjustment is considered to have, on the date of the determination, one year remaining before the expiration of the applicable period.[341] Consequently, the taxpayer has one year after the date of the determination within which to file a claim for refund. If the adjustment is a deficiency, the Commissioner has one year to send a notice of deficiency. When a notice of deficiency is sent, the one-year statute of limitations is suspended.[342] If the taxpayer who receives a notice chooses the refund route, the

---

[339] Moultrie Cotton Mills v. United States, 151 F. Supp. 482 (Ct. Cl. 1957); Esterbrook Pen Co. v. United States, 1960-2 USTC ¶ 9609 (DNJ 1960). But see Benenson v. United States, 385 F2d 26 (2d Cir. 1967) (second refund claim was required because first one failed to involve mitigation provisions).

[340] Bishop v. Reichel, 127 F. Supp. 750 (NDNY 1954), aff'd, 221 F2d 806 (2d Cir.), cert. denied, 350 US 833 (1955).

[341] IRC § 1314(b).

[342] Reg. § 1.1314(b)-1(b).

period for filing a refund claim begins to run on the date of payment in the same manner as in other cases governed by Section 6511.[343]

[b] Amount of Adjustment

The mitigation provisions are predicated on two principles. First, correction of the error in the barred year must be made. Second, the bar of the statute of limitations or rule of law must be made only for the purpose of correcting the error, and for no other purpose. Consequently, the amount of an adjustment may not be reduced by any setoff under the *Lewis v. Reynolds* principle.[344] The amount of an adjustment under the mitigation rules is determined in two steps:

Step 1: The tax previously determined for the taxable year of the error must be ascertained. This tax usually is the amount of tax shown on the taxpayer's return. Any changes in that amount must be taken into account. In these cases, the tax previously determined is the tax shown on the return, increased by any amounts previously assessed as deficiencies and decreased by any amounts previously refunded in respect of the returned tax.

Step 2: With the tax previously determined as the starting point, the increase or decrease in tax resulting from correction of the error is computed. This calculation usually requires a recomputation of the tax shown on the return, as affected by correct treatment of the item involved in the determination. If the amount of tax was previously increased or decreased by reason of deficiencies assessed or amount repaid, the return is in effect reconstructed to reflect these changes. The recomputation is made on the basis of the reconstructed return to ascertain the increase or decrease in tax. The increase or decrease in tax, plus any amounts wrongfully collected from the taxpayer (as additions to tax or interest) as a result of the error, constitutes the amount of the adjustment.

The amount of the adjustment is the difference between the tax for the error year reflected on the return (but subject to any corrections that may have been made by way of refund or deficiency) and the tax as recomputed after the correction of the error.[345] Only the item affected by the mitigation provisions may be corrected.[346] However, if only a portion of a capital gain was included

---

[343] Reg. § 1.1314(b)-1(b).

[344] Lewis v. Reynolds, 284 US 281 (1932); Reg. § 1.1314(c)-1(a).

[345] IRC § 1314(a).

[346] IRC § 1314(c); Reg. § 1.1314(a)-1(c); First Nat'l Bank v. Comm'r, 205 F2d 82 (3d Cir. 1953) (taxpayer, having accrued state taxes in 1942 and having successfully ob-

in income, the total amount of the gain (not just the part actually included) is the item with respect to which the error was made.[347] On the other hand, recomputation of tax for the error year takes into account other Code provisions that depend on the amount of income, such as charitable contributions and medical deductions.[348] Any additions to tax or interest collected because of the error are also taken into account in determining the amount of the adjustment. All recomputations are to be made under the law applicable in the error year.

An adjustment under Section 1311 may have an impact on other closed years. Adjustment is authorized for a taxable year other than the error year when the taxable year or years are affected by an NOL deduction or a capital loss carryover if (1) the NOL deduction or capital loss carryover is determined with reference to the error year and (2) on the date of the determination, an adjustment to the tax paid for the other year is barred (except by a compromise entered into pursuant to Section 7122).[349] The amount of the adjustment for the year affected by an NOL deduction or capital loss carryover is computed in a manner similar to the adjustment for the error year. Then the increase or decrease in tax for the year as affected by the carryover must be recomputed. Again, the only items considered in the recomputation are the NOL deduction and capital loss carryover. This increase or decrease is the amount of the adjustment for the other year.[350]

¶ 5.06 STATUTE OF LIMITATIONS ON REFUNDS AND CREDITS

Taxpayers must also act within statutory limitations periods to obtain a refund or credit of an overpayment of tax. Two statutes of limitations govern the time for filing a claim for refund, either the taxpayer must file (1) a claim within three years after the return is filed or (2) two years from the date a tax is paid. Unless the taxpayer files a refund claim within one of these periods, the Service is not permitted to allow a refund of tax.[351] In the same way that the stat-

---

tained a refund of 1943 taxes based on deducting again the 1942 state taxes, was unable to offset the adjustment to 1942 tax the Commissioner received under Section 1311 by the amount of 1941 state taxes paid in 1942).

[347] Cory v. Comm'r, 261 F2d 702 (2d Cir. 1958), cert. denied, 359 US 966 (1959).

[348] Cory v. Comm'r, 261 F2d 702 (2d Cir. 1958), cert. denied, 359 US 966 (1959).

[349] If the carryover affects an open year, an adjustment for the year is proper with regard to Section 1311.

[350] Reg. § 1.1314(a)-2(b).

[351] IRC § 6511(b)(1) ("[n]o credit or refund shall be allowed or made after the expiration of the period prescribed in subsection (a) for the filing of a claim for credit or re-

ute of limitations on assessment does, the three-year claim period starts with the date the taxpayer filed the applicable tax return and ends three years later. To this extent, the statutes of limitations on assessment and refund are coextensive. During the three-year period that the Service has to conduct an audit of the taxpayer's return, the taxpayer may request a refund of tax the taxpayer has overpaid with the return the taxpayer has filed. If a taxpayer requests a refund during the three-year period, the Service may audit the return, and determine not only whether the taxpayer is entitled to a refund, but whether to assess additional tax. The sequence of the limitations periods is consistent with a taxpayer's having three years after filing a return to claim an overpayment of tax paid or deemed paid on the return due date and paid with the return if filed later than the due date.

The statute of limitations on the filing of a claim for refund or credit of an overpayment in tax is the later of two periods. The second limitations period does not begin with the taxpayer's filing of the taxpayer's return, but with the taxpayer's payment of tax. A taxpayer must file a claim for refund within two years after the taxpayer has paid tax. Requiring the filing of a claim for refund within two years after payment corresponds to the situation in which the Service has audited the taxpayer's return, determined that a deficiency exists, and the taxpayer has paid the deficiency. At least the payment by the taxpayer will have taken place later than the three-year period of limitations.

The nexus between the three-year assessment period and the three-year refund claim filing period is clearly shown by the statutory provision for extending the statute of limitations on assessment. When a taxpayer agrees to extend the statute of limitations on assessment, the statutory period for filing a claim for refund of tax overpaid with a return is also extended for the period of the extension, and for an additional six months.[352]

The statute of limitations on filing a claim for refund is treated in more detail in Chapter 11.

¶ 5.07 THE STATUTE OF LIMITATIONS ON COLLECTION

Once a timely tax assessment has been made, the assessed tax must be collected within ten years after the date of the assessment.[353] In 1990, a simple but far-reaching change was made in the statute of limitations on collection. It

---

fund, unless a claim for credit or refund is filed by the taxpayer within the prescribed period").

[352] IRC § 6511(c)(1).

[353] IRC § 6502(a).

extended the collection period from six years to ten years.[354] This extended collection period applies to taxes assessed after November 5, 1990, as well as to assessed taxes for which the collection period had not already expired on that date. Collection may be made either administratively by levy or judicially by the commencement of a proceeding in court. Unless the amount of the tax is collected by levy within the collection period, the Service is required to commence an action in court to reduce the tax assessment to judgment in order to toll the period of limitations. In 1988 and 1990, Section 6502 was amended to provide as follows:

> If a timely proceeding in court for the collection of a tax is commenced, the period during which such tax may be collected by levy shall be extended and shall not expire until the liability for the tax (or a judgment against the taxpayer arising from such liability) is satisfied or becomes unenforceable.[355]

---

[354] Omnibus Budget Reconciliation Act of 1990, Pub. L. No. 101-508, § 11317(a)(1), amending IRC §§ 6502(a)(1), 6502(a)(2). Section 6323(g), describing the requirement for refiling a notice of tax lien, was similarly amended. When, pursuant to agreement, the six-year period was open on the date Section 6502(a) was amended, the ten-year period was held applicable. Foutz v. United States, 860 F. Supp. 788 (D. Utah 1994), aff'd, 72 F3d 802 (10th Cir. 1995) (taxpayers executed Form 900 extending the six-year period until December 31, 1990; Section 6502(a) was amended in November 1990; held, levy served in December 1991 was timely under ten-year period).

[355] Omnibus Budget Reconciliation Act of 1990, § 11317(a)(1), substituted "10 years" for "6 years" in Section 6502(a)(1). Section 11317(a)(2) of the Act substituted "10 year period" for "6 year period" each time it appeared in Section 6502(a)(2). The Service has issued proposed regulations reflecting the extension of the statute of limitations on collection from six to ten years. See Reg. § 301.6502-1.

Suppose the Service obtains a judgment against the taxpayer in 1984 on a tax assessment made in 1979, but despite the court's order of foreclosure the Service does not issue a levy to seize and sell the property until 1991? A district court ruled that the time during which the Service had to levy expired before the 1988 amendment, and the amendment could not revive the statute of limitations on collection. The Service's levy in 1991 therefore was time-barred. Hillyer v. Comm'r, 73 AFTR2d 94-1950 (MD Pa. 1994), aff'd, 1995 US App. LEXIS 5020, 95-1 USTC ¶ 50,155 (3d Cir.), 75 AFTR2d 95-597 (3d Cir. 1995). At a time when the statute of limitations on collection was six years, the Service served a levy to collect unpaid tax, but did not collect the full amount assessed. However, before the six-year period expired, the Service secured an extension from the taxpayer until December 30, 1990. When the Service served a levy on November 7, 1991, and collected tax, the taxpayer sued for refund claiming that collection was barred by the six-year statute of limitations. The Tenth Circuit held, however, that the levy was not barred, because the taxpayer had agreed in the collection waiver to extend the statutory period, and so the statutory period was open on November 5, 1990, when Congress extended the statutory period to ten years. Foutz v. United States, 72 F3d 802 (10th Cir. 1995).

Thus, the collection agreement was held not to establish a collection period outside and independent of the statutory period, but to have extended the statutory period. Although the circuit court recognized that a waiver is the unilateral waiver of a defense, not a contract, it nevertheless used the language of the waiver form to reach its conclusion.

However, courts have uniformly rejected the argument that the tax collection waiver binds the Service to the extension date, so that the ten-year period does not apply. See

This amendment changed the law. Before the change, if the Service failed to collect the unpaid tax by levy before the expiration of the collection period, but instituted a collection action, collection could be made only by execution on a judgment against the taxpayer. If the Service fails to collect an unpaid tax by levy before the expiration of the collection period, but has instituted a court proceeding within the six-year period, it may not collect a tax by administrative levy after the period has expired. In other words, collection by judicial means is the sole remedy available to the Service after the normal period of collection has run.

As with the period for making an assessment, the taxpayer and the Service may agree to an extension of the normal collection period.

[1] Computation of the Period of Limitations

Several rules are applied in computing the period of limitations on collection. First, the date of assessment is the date the assessment list is signed by the appropriate Service official.[356] Second, the date of the assessment is excluded from the computation.[357] Third, the Service uses a "months-days" method under which a year for purposes of the computation consists of eleven full months and thirty days, but a computation by the number of actual elapsed

---

Foutz, supra (the tax collection waiver is a waiver, not a contract; Kaggen v. Internal Rev. Serv., 57 F3d 163, 165 (2d Cir.) (same), on reh'g 71 F3d 1018 (2d Cir. 1995); Behren v. United States, 82 F3d 1017 (11th Cir. 1996) (accord). In *Behren*, the circuit court pointed out that in Florsheim Bros. Drygoods Co. v. United States, 280 US 453 (1930), the taxpayer also argued that the waiver extending the statutory period was a binding contract so that when the Service instituted a collection action after the period specified in the waiver, but within the statutory collection period, it was time-barred. The Supreme Court rejected the argument and held that "the waivers executed by the parties were not contracts binding on the Commissioner not to make the assessments and collections after the periods specified." *Behren*, supra, at 1019.

Because in Stange v. United States, 282 US 270 (1931), the Supreme Court also said that the waiver is not a contract and that the provision requiring the signature on behalf of the Commissioner "was inserted for purely administrative purposes and not to convert into a contract what is essentially a voluntary, unilateral waiver of a defense by the taxpayer[,]" the precedent against the waiver-as-contract argument is overwhelming. However, these cases also clarify the nature of the statute of limitations on assessment and collection as a defense belonging to the taxpayer. As a personal defense of the taxpayer, the Service cannot properly demand that the taxpayer waive the statute of limitations. See ¶ 15.03[4][a].

Note this principle seems to have been overlooked in the designated summons provision, Section 6503(j), which suspends the running of the statute of limitations when a taxpayer refuses to extend the statute. See ¶ 15.03[4][a].

[356] IRC § 6203; Reg. § 301.6203-1.

[357] Burnet v. Willingham Loan & Trust Co., 282 US 437 (1931).

days (i.e., 5 years and 365 days) also has been approved.[358] Fourth, the date the complaint commencing the collection proceeding in court is filed is included in making the computation.[359] Finally, the date on which a levy on property or rights to property is considered made is the date on which the notice of seizure provided in Section 6335(a) is given.[360]

It is the assessment of tax that starts the running of the statute of limitations on the collection of tax. Accordingly, if the assessment of tax may be made at any time, for example, because a fraudulent return has been filed, it follows that the statute of limitations on the collection of tax will not even begin to run until the Service eventually makes an assessment, and the period for collection will run from that date.

The period of limitations runs in favor only of the taxpayer against whom the tax has been assessed. As a result, usually, one taxpayer may not claim that the Service is barred from collecting from him or her because the period of limitations on collection has run against another taxpayer. For example, the Service may collect from a person against whom a responsible officer penalty assessment has been made within the statutory period following such assessment, although a suit against the corporation that incurred the employment tax liability would not have been timely because it would not have been brought within the statutory period after the assessment against the corporation.[361] In this case, the assessment of the penalty is separate and distinct from the liability for the corporation. However, when the liability is derivative, the collection action must be made within the normal statutory period of limitations that begins to run after assessment against the primary obligor.[362]

---

[358] United States v. Tyrrell, 329 F2d 341, 344 (7th Cir. 1964). The result under the two methods can be different. In *Tyrrell*, under the actual days method, the collection action was untimely, while under the months-days method, the action was timely.

[359] Fed. R. Civ. P. 6(a). United States v. Tyrrell, 329 F2d 341 (7th Cir. 1964); United States v. Harris, 223 F. Supp. 309 (SD Fla. 1963), aff'd per curiam, 337 F2d 856 (5th Cir. 1964); United States v. Besase, 319 F. Supp. 1064 (ND Ohio 1970).

[360] Reg. § 301.6502-1(b).

[361] Bloom v. United States, 272 F2d 215 (9th Cir. 1959), cert. denied, 363 US 803 (1960).

[362] See United States v. Stone, 257 F2d 685 (5th Cir. 1958), aff'g 57-2 USTC ¶ 9864 (ED Tex. 1957) (action instituted against deceased taxpayer rather than taxpayer's estate; amendment to complaint filed after expiration of period of limitations). However, the period of limitations may be tolled until a fiduciary is appointed. United States v. Besase, 319 F. Supp. 1064 (ND Ohio 1970).

[2] Period Extended by Agreement

The period for collection of an assessed tax may be extended by agreement. Form 900 (Tax Collection Waiver) is used for this purpose.[363] An extension or waiver of the normal period for collection is effective if (1) the agreement is in writing; (2) the agreement is entered into before the expiration of the six-year period or prior extension; and (3) the agreement is executed by both the taxpayer and an authorized delegate of the Commissioner.[364] The first two requirements are clearly stated in the statute. The third requirement, although expressed in the statute, is made explicit by regulation.[365] Accordingly, the unilateral act of a taxpayer in signing and submitting a waiver does not effect an extension of the period on collection.[366]

[3] Effect of Offers in Compromise

Although the Service has removed the suspension language from the offer in compromise, it is worth noting that the offer form used to include an extension of the statute of limitations on collection.[367] Any time a taxpayer submits an offer in compromise, the effect on the applicable period of limitations should

---

[363] The matters to be considered before executing such a waiver are discussed infra ¶ 5.07. For example, it appears that extending that collection period permits the Service to collect not only an assessed tax but also an erroneous refund. Sanfellipo v. United States, 90-2 USTC ¶ 50,567 (ND Cal. 1990) (although two-year period on recovery of erroneous refunds had expired, execution of Form 900 permitted the Service to recover erroneous refunds for years covered by waiver).

Because a tax collection waiver can make collection action taken long after a tax assessment legal, the very existence of a waiver can sometimes be an issue. The Service may use circumstantial evidence to prove the existence of a waiver, even when the original is lost or destroyed. See United States v. Conry, 631 F2d 599 (9th Cir. 1980); United States v. McGaughey, 977 F2d 1067, 1071–1074 (7th Cir. 1992) (secondary evidence was received by fact that original form was missing). See Rosenbloom v. United States, 699 F. Supp. 284 (SD Fla. 1988) (erroneous information in collection waiver did not entitle the taxpayer to claim the waiver was invalid.

[364] IRC § 6502(a).

[365] Reg. § 301.6502-1(a)(2)(i).

[366] United States v. Cook, 494 F2d 573 (5th Cir. 1974). Courts holding otherwise may have ignored the change, occurring under the 1954 Code, in Treasury regulations for dealing with offers in compromise, which are a special situation.

[367] Form 656 (Offer in Compromise) used to have a combination waiver and suspension agreement, with the following language:

The taxpayer-proponents waive the benefit of any statute of limitations applicable to the assessment and collection of the liability sought to be compromised, and agree to the suspension of the running of the statutory period of limitations on assessment and collection for the period during which this offer is pending, or the period during which any installment remains unpaid, and for one year thereafter.

be considered even if the offer form does not have an explicit extension of the statute or does not refer to statutes suspending the running of the period. Even without extension language in the form, the Service may require an extension of the statute of limitations on collection to enable it to consider the taxpayer's offer without suffering prejudice, since the period of limitations on collection runs during the time the offer is being considered.[368] An extension of the statutory period can affect the discharge of taxes in bankruptcy because the Service must be able to collect tax after assessment for at least one year before the petition is filed.[369]

When the extension was included in the offer form itself, the terms of extension suspended the running of this period during the pendency of the offer until it was terminated, withdrawn, or formally rejected.[370] Although some suspension period seemed fair, the period of limitations on collection was also extended for one additional year. As a result, when an offer was submitted to compromise an assessed tax, the Service had the full statutory period of collection, plus an additional year, to collect the tax, and so the period of limitations on collection was automatically extended to eleven, not the normal ten, years.[371] This led to considerable litigation and court decisions that have illuminated the nature of the waiver of a statute of limitations as well as the manner in which a waiver should be interpreted. Some courts said that the waiver should be interpreted in the same manner as though the compromise form was a contract. One circuit court held, however, that the waiver's validity is not governed by contract principles. Rather, the waiver is a request on the part of a taxpayer that the Service forgo collection while the taxpayer considers a compromise offer, and as such, "in a non-technical sense [there is] a *quid pro quo*."[372] The mere submission of an offer suspends the limitations period and, in the case, resulted in a finding that the Service's collection action was timely.[373] Even if the waiver is not a contract, the execution of a valid waiver does require execution by both parties—an element of a contract.

---

[368] United States v. Ressler, 576 F2d 650, 652 (5th Cir. 1978), cert. denied, 440 US 929 (1979); United States v. Harris Trust & Sav. Bank, 390 F2d 285 (7th Cir. 1968).

[369] 11 USC § 727(a)(2) (one year); 11 USC § 507(a)(8)(A)(ii) (240 days, plus time offer considered, plus thirty days must be allowed to IRS to collect). See In the Matter of McGoughey, 73 AFTR2d 94-2048 (7th Cir. 1994).

[370] Myrick v. United States, 296 F2d 312 (5th Cir. 1961). The language of the compromise form does not create a fixed-date waiver ending one year after a triggering event, such as rejection. Hussein v. United States, 94-1 USTC ¶ 50,104 (SDNY 1994).

[371] See United States v. Ressler, 576 F2d 650 (5th Cir. 1978), cert. denied, 440 US 929 (1979). See also United States v. Snyder, 82-2 USTC ¶ 9683 (SD W. Va. 1982); United States v. Spurlin, 763 F. Supp. 563.

[372] United States v. McGaughey, 977 F2d 1067 (7th Cir. 1992).

[373] United States v. McGaughey, 977 F2d 1067, 1073 (7th Cir. 1992).

Regulations say that an extension becomes effective only upon an execution of a waiver by both the taxpayer and the director, or on the director's behalf.[374] These rules were illustrated in *United States v. Ressler*[375] in which the taxpayer's offer in compromise was pending from January 6, 1970, until May 3, 1973, a period of three years, three months, and twenty-seven days. The Service rejected the taxpayer's offer on May 3, 1973, and it began collection action against the taxpayer on August 1, 1975. The statute of limitations on collection, which was then six years, would have expired on April 8, 1971, but because the taxpayer had submitted the offer in compromise, the collection statute was extended by the offer for four years, three months, and twenty-seven days, or until August 4, 1975.

After the suspension, the date on which the period of limitations begins to run again usually is easily determined. For example, the date of formal rejection is a matter of record. However, when a fraudulent offer has been submitted, there is some confusion as to whether criminal proceedings instituted against the taxpayer/proponent should be considered an implicit rejection of the offer, thereby restarting the running of the period.[376] The better view is that the civil and criminal proceedings are separate and that a taxpayer who wishes to begin the running of the period of limitations may withdraw his or her offer.

TABLE 5.5

Suspension of Running of the Period of Limitation

Section	*Circumstance*	*Suspension Period*
6503(a)(1)	Notice of deficiency	Period during which assessment or collection is prohibited (i.e., 90 days or 150 days) plus sixty days thereafter
6503(a)(1)	Petition filed	Sixty days after Tax Court decision becomes final

---

[374] Reg. § 301.6502-1(a)(2). Consequently, an agreement to extend the statute of limitations on collection included in an offer in compromise was found not to be binding when there was a dispute about whether the district director had signed the offer. United States v. Simons, 80 AFTR2d 97-8274 (10th Cir. 1997) (as a result, the district court could not rule that the statute of limitations on collection was open when the collection period was extended to ten years).

[375] United States v. Ressler, 576 F2d 650 (5th Cir. 1978), cert. denied, 440 US 929 (1979).

[376] Compare Coy v. United States, 377 F2d 925 (9th Cir. 1967) (date the taxpayer was sentenced on criminal charges arising out of the fraudulent offer was considered the rejection date) with United States v. Ressler, 576 F2d 650 (5th Cir. 1978), cert. denied, 440 US 929 (1979) (actual rejection date was used and the criminal proceedings were said to be entirely separate).

6503(a)(2)	Consolidated return	If notice of deficiency sent to corporation that filed consolidated return, suspension periods for regular notice of deficiency apply to all corporations in consolidated group
6503(b)	Taxpayer's assets in custody of court	Collection period suspended for time of custody or control, plus six months thereafter
6503(c)	Taxpayer outside United States for "continous period of at least six months"	Collection period suspended for period of absence. If taxpayer returns within six months of expiration of collection period, period does not expire for full six months
6503(d)	Extension of time for payment of estate tax (Section 6161(a)(2) or 6161(b)(2) or Sections 6163, 6166, or 6166A)	Collection suspended for period of extension
6503(f)	Wrongful seizure of third party's property	Period of collection against actual taxpayer suspended from date of wrongful seizure to date property returned or, if judgment is obtained under Section 7426, until thirty days after final judgment
6503(i)	Assessment in a Title II case	Assessment—period assessment prohibited, plus sixty days; collection—period collection stayed, plus six months
6872	Bankruptcy and receiverships	Assessment period suspended from date of adjudication or appointment of receiver, plus thirty days after notice of appointment of trustee or receiver is received by district director. Suspension of period may not exceed two years. Collection period suspended when property in custody of court
6694(c)(3)	Tax return preparers	Preparer penalty period of collection is suspended for period during which Service prohibited from collecting by levy or judicial action
6901(f)	Transferees and fiduciaries	Same as for "Notice of deficiency" and "Petition filed"
7609(e)	Third-party summonses	Assessment period suspended for period of proceeding and appeals

| 6503(j) | Designated summons | Assessment period suspended during the period beginning on the day any court proceeding is brought concerning the summons and ending on the date there is a final resolution about the summoned person's response to the summons |

¶ 5.08 SUSPENSION OF RUNNING OF PERIODS OF LIMITATIONS

The running of the three-year assessment period and the ten-year collection period is suspended during certain circumstances, set out primarily in Section 6503 but also provided in other sections of the Code, some of which are summarized in Table 5.5.[377]

[1] Suspension for Deficiency Procedures

On the date the Service mails a notice of deficiency for income, estate, or gift tax, the period of limitations on assessment and collection of the deficiency is suspended for 90 days if the notice of deficiency is addressed to a person within the United States and the District of Columbia, or 150 days if such notice is addressed to a person outside the United States and the District of Columbia,[378] plus an additional 60 days thereafter in either case.[379] If the taxpayer files a petition in the Tax Court contesting the deficiency, the period of limitations is suspended until the decision of the Tax Court becomes final, and for an additional sixty days thereafter.[380] The Tax Court's decision becomes final:

---

[377] Suspension periods also are provided when there has been a recovery of foreign expropriation loss (IRC § 6503(e)); private foundation, qualified plan, and black lung benefits trust violations (IRC § 6503(g)); Bank Holding Company Act divestitures (IRC § 6503(h)); deficiency dividends of real estate investment trusts (IRC § 860(h)); and deficiency dividends of a personal holding company (IRC § 547(f)).

[378] Saturday, Sunday, or legal holidays in the District of Columbia are not counted as the 90th or 150th day.

[379] IRC § 6503(a)(1). The suspension period begins to run on the date of mailing, not the date the notice is received. Whirlpool Corp. v. Comm'r, 61 TC 182 (1973). Elden v. Comm'r, TC Memo 1982-71, 43 TCM 520 (1982) (notice of deficiency mailed two days before the end of three-year statute of limitations was timely, despite the fact that taxpayers did not have notice until more than three years after the date on which the return was deemed filed; held, the date the notice was mailed controlled, not the date of receipt).

[380] IRC § 6503(a)(1). The period of limitations is suspended for the ninety-day appeal period in addition to the sixty-day period even when the taxpayer has waived his right to appeal. See Becker Bros. v. United States, 88-1 USTC ¶ 9262 (CD Ill. 1988).

- On the expiration of the time for filing a notice of appeal if no notice is filed.[381]
- If notice of appeal is filed, on the expiration of the time allowed for the filing of a petition for certiorari in the Supreme Court if no such petition is filed.[382]
- If a petition for certiorari is filed but denied, on the date of the denial.[383]
- If a petition for certiorari is granted, on the expiration of thirty days after the mandate of the Supreme Court if its decision is to affirm the Tax Court or dismiss the appeal.[384]

The same rules apply if a jeopardy assessment is made. Although the assessment triggers the running of the period of limitations on collection, the running of the period is suspended until the Tax Court decision becomes final.[385] If a notice of deficiency is mailed to the taxpayer within the period of limitations and the taxpayer does not appeal to the Tax Court, the notice of deficiency does not suspend the running of the period of limitations on any addi-

---

A waiver of the restrictions on assessment and collection contained in a stipulated decision of the Tax Court does not accelerate the date on which the decision becomes final, which is ninety days after entry. Pesko v. United States, 918 F2d 1581 (Fed. Cir. 1990) (assessment made 148 days after decision was entered was timely because Service had 90 days, plus 60 additional days, to assess after that date). But see Kirch v. United States, 83 AFTR2d 99-2153 (SD Ohio 1999) (assessment was held untimely because the Service mistakenly believed that the taxpayers' Tax Court petition, filed without any prior receipt of a notice of deficiency, suspended the statute of limitations on assessments—petition must be filed in respect of a deficiency in order to suspend the statute of limitations).

[381] IRC § 7401(a)(1). Section 7483 provides that review of a Tax Court decision is obtained by filing a notice of appeal with the clerk of the Tax Court within ninety days after entry of the Tax Court's decision. The ninety-day period must be included in the suspension period even if the decision is a stipulated one that cannot be appealed. Security Indus. Ins. Co. v. United States, 830 F2d 581 (5th Cir. 1987); United States v. Hans, 921 F2d 81 (6th Cir. 1990) (following Security Indus. Ins. Co. and gathering cases from Ninth and Eleventh Circuits).

[382] IRC § 7481(a)(2)(A).

[383] IRC § 7481(a)(2)(B).

[384] IRC § 7481(a)(2)(C); Sherry Frontenac, Inc. v. United States, 868 F2d 420, 424 (11th Cir. 1989) (stipulated Tax Court decisions are "final" ninety days after Tax Court decision is entered); Pesko v. United States, 918 F2d 1581 (Fed. Cir. 1990); United States v. Tranakos, 778 F. Supp. 1220 (ND Ga. 1991) (decision entered on November 19, 1985, became final ninety days later, on February 17, 1986; so February 25, 1986, assessment was timely made within sixty days after Tax Court decision became final).

[385] United States v. Shahadi, 340 F2d 56 (3d Cir.), cert. denied, 381 US 903 (1965); accord United States v. Maxwell, 459 F2d 22 (5th Cir. 1972). See Kahn v. United States, 444 F. Supp. 388 (SDNY 1977), aff'd, 590 F2d 48 (2d Cir. 1978). United States v. Ellis, 86-2 USTC ¶ 9721 (D. Kan. 1986) (calculating the assessment period when a notice of deficiency has been issued).

tional deficiency shown to be due in a subsequent deficiency notice.[386] For purposes of the suspension period, a final decision by the Tax Court restarts the running of the limitations period. Thus, the assessment must be made within a period composed of (1) the days remaining in the normal statutory period for assessment when the notice of deficiency was sent and (2) the sixty-day period after the decision of the Tax Court was final. Because the Tax Court decision becomes final only after the ninety-day period for filing a notice of appeal has expired, the suspension period includes this period as well. Thus, the statute of limitations is tolled for 150 days following the entry of the Tax Court decision—90 days for filing a notice of appeal plus 60 days for assessment.[387]

EXAMPLE 5-21: A taxpayer files a return for the calendar year 1984 on April 15, 1985. The Service mails a notice of deficiency to taxpayer (at an address within the United States), on April 15, 1988, and taxpayer files a petition with the Tax Court on July 14, 1988. The decision of the Tax Court becomes final on November 6, 1989. In this case, the running of the period of limitations for assessment is suspended from April 15, 1988, the date the notice of deficiency was mailed, to January 5, 1990, which is sixty days after the date on which the Tax Court decision became final. If the taxpayer had failed to file a petition in the Tax Court, the running of the period of limitations for assessment would have been suspended from April 15, 1988 (the date of notice), to September 12, 1988, which is sixty days after the expiration of the ninety-day period in which the taxpayer could have filed a petition with the Tax Court.[388]

What happens to the unexpired portion of the limitations period when a petition is filed in the Tax Court? The weight of authority is that the unexpired portion of the limitations period begins to run again sixty days after the final decision.[389] It therefore follows that when a taxpayer has agreed to an extension of the period of limitations and then files a petition in the Tax Court, the

---

[386] If a notice under Section 6212(a) with respect to a deficiency in tax imposed by Subtitle A of the Code for any taxable year is mailed to a corporation, the suspension of the running of the period of limitations provided in Section 6503(a)(1) shall apply to all other corporations with which such corporation made a consolidated income tax return for such taxable year. Under Reg. § 1.1502-77(a), relating to consolidated returns, notices of deficiency are mailed only to the common parent.

[387] In Cole v. United States, 863 F2d 34 (9th Cir. 1988), a Form 872-R extended the assessment date from 1978 to December 31, 1983. A notice of deficiency was sent September 28, 1983, and a Tax Court decision was entered December 28, 1984. The Ninth Circuit held that the statute of limitations was tolled until May 27, 1985, sixty days after decision became final. The court did not tack on the balance of the assessment period (i.e., the time left when the notice of deficiency was sent).

[388] Reg. § 301.6503(a)-1(a).

[389] Olds & Whipple, Inc. v. United States, 22 F. Supp. 809 (Ct. Cl. 1938); Bales v. Comm'r, 22 TC 355 (1954).

unexpired portion of the waiver period is added to the suspension period.[390] However, one court has held that the unexpired term of the waiver is to be disregarded.[391]

[2] Bankruptcy and Other Suspension Periods

There are special circumstances that suspend the running of the limitations period on collection. Section 6503(b) suspends the running of this period while the taxpayer's assets are in the custody or control of a court and for six months thereafter. The rationale behind this rule is that during this period, the taxpayer's assets are not subject to administrative collection action.[392] The bankruptcy court in *Turner* was held to have custody of the taxpayer's assets for purposes of Section 6503(b) from the beginning of the bankruptcy proceeding (i.e., the date the petition is filed) until six months after the first creditors' meeting.[393] Thus, the then six-year limitations period was suspended from the date the bankruptcy petition was filed until one year after the date of the first meeting of creditors.[394] Another court has held that in a bankruptcy case, the suspension period referred to in Section 6503(b) terminates when the taxpayer is discharged as a bankrupt.[395] The Service contended that the suspension period continues until the final order directing the approval of the trustee's account, the trustee's release as trustee, and the closing of the bankrupt's estate.[396] The majority of courts have rejected this view.[397]

To resolve these questions about the suspension period in bankruptcy cases, Congress added a specific suspension provision, Section 6503(h), which suspends the statute of limitations on assessment and collection in a case under the Bankruptcy Code (Title 11 USC) for the period during which the Service

---

[390] Continental Oil Co. v. United States, 14 F. Supp. 533 (Ct. Cl.), cert. denied, 299 US 510 (1936), cert. denied, 301 US 694 (1937); Manz Corp. v. United States, 54 F2d 177 (Ct. Cl. 1931); United States v. Markowitz, 34 F. Supp. 827 (ND Cal. 1940).

The Tax Court has adopted this rule. Aufleger v. Comm'r, 99 TC 109 (1992).

[391] Hoosac Mills Corp. v. Comm'r, 75 F2d 462 (1st Cir. 1935).

[392] S. Rep. No. 1708, 89th Cong., 2d Sess. 24–25 (1966).

[393] United States v. Turner, 625 F2d 328 (9th Cir. 1980).

[394] United States v. Breshears, 698 F2d 394 (9th Cir. 1983).

[395] United States v. Verlinsky, 459 F2d 1085 (5th Cir. 1972); accord United States v. Levasseur, 80-1 USTC ¶ 9349 (D. Vt. 1980).

[396] United States v. Malkin, 317 F. Supp. 612 (EDNY 1970).

[397] McAuley v. United States, 525 F2d 1108 (9th Cir. 1975); United States v. Verlinsky, 459 F2d 1085 (5th Cir. 1972); United States v. Tomasello, 569 F. Supp. 1 (WDNY 1983); United States v. Levasseur, 80-1 USTC ¶ 9349 (D. Vt. 1980); Clark v. Comm'r, 90 TC 6 (1988) (in determining the statute of limitations for taxpayers filing a petition in bankruptcy, the suspension period ends on the date that the discharge is granted, not the date that Service receives notice of the discharge).

is prohibited from assessing and collecting (by the automatic stay provided in the Bankruptcy Code), plus an additional period after the case, which is sixty days for assessment, and six months for collection. Thus, in bankruptcy cases, the collection period can be drastically extended by the period of suspension. This is illustrated by a case in which a partnership entered bankruptcy in 1982, and its plan of reorganization providing for the payment of back taxes was confirmed in 1984, and its reorganization terminated in 1985 when no further tax payments were made.[398] In 1993, about eleven years after the bankruptcy filing, the Service's action against former general partners to collect the unpaid taxes was held timely. Because the collection period was suspended from 1982 through 1985, plus an additional six months, the six-year collection period was still open when the period was increased to ten years. Moreover, collection was suspended against the partnership during the bankruptcy case, and the collection period was also suspended against the partners who were derivatively liable.

When persons are secondarily liable for a tax debt on the basis of the same facts as the primary taxpayer, the tax debt is considered unitary for purposes of the statute of limitations. There is only one period of limitations for both the primary taxpayer and those secondarily or derivatively liable; there are no separate collection periods.[399] Section 6503(c) suspends the running of the collection period for the period of absence if a taxpayer is outside the country for a continuous period of at least six months, and if the taxpayer returns within six months of the expiration of the collection period, the Service is given the full six months to collect.[400]

---

[398] United States v. Wright, 76 AFTR2d 95-7526 (7th Cir. 1995). See also United States v. McCarthy, 81 AFTR2d ¶ 98-7272 (SD Ind. 1998) (collection action timely because responsible person's confirmed plan in prior bankruptcy proceeding only suspended the Service's right to collect as long as the taxpayer was in compliance with the plan, and did not deprive the Service of the additional six months of Section 6502(h) once the responsible person had failed to comply with the plan).

[399] United States v. Wright, 76 AFTR2d 95-7526 (7th Cir. 1995); see also United States v. McCarthy, 81 AFTR2d 98-7272 (SD Ind. 1998). This result is consistent with the principle that if the statute of limitations has expired against the transferor, it has also expired against the transferee. United States v. Updike, 281 US 489 (1930).

[400] Regulations interpret the term "continuous absence" to include a taxpayer who is "generally and substantially absent from the United States, even though he makes casual or temporary visits during that period." Reg. § 301.6503(c)-1(b). This regulation has been held invalid. United States v. Nesline, 590 F. Supp. 884 (D. Md. 1984).

CHAPTER **6**

Interest

¶ 6.01 INTEREST UNDER THE INTERNAL REVENUE CODE

Interest is compensation for the use of money. While Internal Revenue Code provisions authorize the collection of interest on tax underpayments and payment of interest on overpayments, their "underlying objective is to determine in a given situation whose money it is and for how long the other party had use of it."[1] As the Supreme Court analyzed interest in tax matters, interest is put on tax "to compensate the delay in payment of the tax—the detriment of its nonpayment, to be continued during its nonpayment—compensation, not punishment."[2] The distinction the Supreme Court drew between the purpose of interest and penalties is an important one. Interest and penalties serve different purposes: interest compensates either the Internal Revenue Service (the Service) or the taxpayer for the use of money; penalties are financial sanctions the Service imposes on taxpayers and others to insure compliance with the tax laws by punishing taxpayers for their misconduct.[3] Consequently, the Service's delay in assessing and collecting a deficiency due has generally been considered not to result in any injustice to a taxpayer, because the taxpayer has had the use of the money that should have been paid as taxes during the period for which interest was charged.[4] Similarly, a district court does not have equitable power to alter and reduce a statutorily defined period for the accrual of interest.[5]

It must also be noted, however, that the distinction between interest and penalties has been blurred. Before January 1, 1987, interest all taxpayers paid to the Service on deficiencies was deductible from gross income.[6] In 1986, however, the Tax Reform Act of 1986 (TRA 1986) eliminated the deduction for interest on tax deficiencies for noncorporate taxpayers by adding the following to Section 163: "In the case of a taxpayer other than a corporation, no deduction shall be allowed under this chapter for personal interest."[7] After 1986, then, noncorporate taxpayers cannot deduct interest on taxes, but corporate taxpayers may still deduct interest on tax. As a result, payments by noncorporate taxpayers of nondeductible interest on underpayments have the same economic consequences as the payment of a penalty, such as a delinquency penalty. Even if the purpose of interest on tax underpayments is to compensate the government for the use of its money, the pocketbook effect of nondeductible interest is the same as a nondeductible penalty. To make the matter harder

---

[1] Rev. Proc. 60-17, 1960-2 CB 942, modified by Rev. Proc. 84-66, 1984-2 CB 637.

[2] United States v. Childs, 266 US 304 (1924).

[3] United States v. Childs, 266 US 304 (1924). See also Avon Prods., Inc. v. United States, 588 F2d 342, 343 (2d Cir. 1978).

[4] Cibelli v. United States, 585 F. Supp. 799 (D. Conn. 1984); Ingannamorte v. United States, 189 F. Supp. 341, 343 (DNJ 1960). But see Silver v. United States, 202 F. Supp. 1 (NDNY 1962) (Service held not entitled to interest on a proffered partial satisfaction of a jeopardy assessment).

[5] Johnson v. United States, 602 F2d 734, 738–739 (6th Cir. 1979). See also United States v. Means, 621 F2d 236, 238 (6th Cir. 1980).

[6] IRC § 163(a).

[7] This change was phased in beginning in 1987 and was fully effective beginning in 1991.

to swallow for individual taxpayers, when they receive interest on an overpayment, they must include the interest they receive in taxable income.[8]

At one time, the general interest rate charged on underpayments or payable on overpayments often did not correspond to prevailing commercial interest rates. This dislocation encouraged taxpayers to engage in interest arbitrage by borrowing—underpaying tax—from the government in periods of high commercial interest rates. To avoid this situation and to bring interest rates for taxes roughly into line with commercial interest rates, the interest rate on underpayments and overpayments is no longer fixed but is adjusted according to methods described in Section 6621 of the Internal Revenue Code (the Code). Interest payable either by the taxpayer on an underpayment or by the Service on an overpayment is compounded daily;[9] thus, interest is payable on interest.[10] In summary, the Code provides for payment of interest compounded daily[11] on underpayments[12] and overpayments[13] at rates that are adjusted periodically.[14] In general, interest payable by a taxpayer on underpayments (the underpayment rate) is one percent greater than the interest payable by the government on overpayments (the overpayment rate). Where there are overlapping overpayments and underpayments, global interest netting rules apply a net interest rate of zero.[15]

Two basic rules of computation govern interest on underpayments and overpayments. First, interest on underpayments is payable at the applicable rate from the last date the Code prescribes for payment of the tax to the date the taxpayer actually pays the tax. Second, interest on overpayments is payable at the applicable rate from the date the taxpayer makes the overpayment to either the date the overpayment is credited or a date not more than thirty days before the date of the refund check. A similar rule applies to erroneous refunds of an internal revenue tax that are recoverable by suit.[16] Any portion of an erroneously refunded tax (including interest, assessable penalty, additional amount, or addition to tax) bears interest at the applicable rate from the date of the payment of the refund.

---

[8] IRC § 61(a)(4).

[9] IRC § 6622, effective beginning January 1, 1983. Consequently, interest was payable on amounts owed to or by a taxpayer as of this date.

[10] Cohn v. United States, 872 F2d 533 (2d Cir. 1989) (plain meaning of statute and legislative history establish that Section 6622 imposed compounding of interest on taxes and simple interest due at the time that the statute went into effect). See Reg. § 301.6622-1.

[11] IRC § 6622.

[12] IRC § 6601.

[13] IRC § 6611.

[14] IRC § 6621.

[15] IRC § 6621(d).

[16] IRC § 6602.

TABLE 6.1 _____
Summary of Interest Provisions of the Internal Revenue Code

Section 6601(a)	Interest provided on underpayments, nonpayment, or extensions of time for payment
Section 6601(b)	Last date prescribed for payment
Section 6601(e)	Suspension of interest in certain income, estate, gift, and excise taxes
Section 6601(d)	Income tax reduced by carryback of unused deductions
Section 6601(e)	Applicable rules for interest on penalties
Section 6611(a)	Interest on overpayments
Section 6611(b)	Period interest allowed and paid
Section 6611(e)	Advance payment of tax, credit from income tax withholding
Section 6611(e)	Disallowance of interest on certain overpayments
Section 6611(f)	Refunds of income tax caused by carryback of certain unused deductions
Section 6611(g)	No interest until return is in processible form
Section 6621(a)	Determination of overpayment and underpayment rate
Section 6621(b)	Federal short-term rate
Section 6621(c)	Increase in underpayment rate for large corporations
Section 6621(d)	Elimination of interest on overlapping periods of tax overpayments and underpayments
Section 6622	Interest compounded daily

As Table 6-1 shows, the calculation of the amount of interest a taxpayer owes or is owed involves the following four steps:

1. During what period does interest accrue on the taxpayer's underpayment; that is, when was the tax due and when did the taxpayer pay the tax underpayment?[17]
2. During what period does interest accrue on the taxpayer's overpayment; that is, when was the tax overpaid and when did the Service refund the overpayment?
3. What are the applicable rates of interest?[18]
4. How is the interest computed?[19]

Special problems arise in situations where penalties are owed, large corporate underpayments and overpayments are involved, or interest is limited or prohibited under certain provisions of the Code, thereby giving rise to restricted interest.[20]

_____

[17] See ¶¶ 6.02, 6.03.
[18] See ¶ 6.04.
[19] See ¶ 6.05.
[20] See ¶ 6.06.

¶ 6.02 INTEREST ON UNDERPAYMENTS: PROCEDURAL MATTERS

[1] Interest Is Part of the Tax

Interest is assessed, collected, and paid in the same manner as the tax to which it is related.[21] Interest on unpaid taxes is "part and parcel of the tax due under the Internal Revenue Code."[22] This means that for deficiency purposes, interest is not assessed until deficiency procedures have been followed. A notice of deficiency must be sent to the taxpayer, and the taxpayer has the right to challenge the deficiency by filing a deficiency action in the Tax Court. If the taxpayer loses the Tax Court challenge, or the taxpayer permits the deficiency to be assessed, the interest will be assessed at the same time and in the same way as the underlying tax. On assessment, the taxpayer will be sent a notice of the assessment of the tax and accrued interest, and demand for its payment. If the taxpayer fails or refuses to pay the assessment, the Service will take enforced collection action, such as a levy, against the taxpayer to collect tax, including interest. With each notice of levy issued to collect an individual's taxes,[23] the Service is required to include the amount of interest the taxpayer is required to pay, information about the Code Section under which the interest is imposed, and a computation of the interest.

    Liability for interest is a derivative liability; it continues to accrue so long as liability for tax exists. Also, the period of limitations on assessment and collection of interest is the same as the limitations period for assessment and collection of the tax to which the interest relates.[24] Interest continues to run on the unpaid portion of a tax liability until it is satisfied in full. The tax, additions to the tax, additional amounts, and penalties are a part of the tax liability,[25] and a tax liability is not satisfied until all items composing it are satisfied.[26] Liability for interest may not be forgiven if there is an underlying liability for a principal amount of tax. This rule follows from the statute, which provides that in-

---

[21] IRC § 6601(e)(1).

[22] See In re Mark Anthony Constr., Inc., 886 F2d 1101, 1108 (9th Cir. 1989).

[23] IRC § 6331, amended by § 3308(c) of the IRS Restructuring and Reform Act of 1998, HR 2676, 105th Cong., 2d Sess. (hereinafter the 1998 Act) for notices of levy issued after December 31, 2000.

[24] IRC § 6601(g).

[25] IRC § 6659(a).

[26] Blair v. Birkenstock, 271 US 348 (1926). Because only full payment extinguishes an underpayment, a taxpayer owes interest on an assessment even if the taxpayer posts a bond, and even if the assessment has been reduced to judgment but the assessment has not been paid. See SouthTrust Bank of Fla. v. Wilson, 971 F. Supp. 539 (MD Fla. 1997).

terest at the annual rate "shall be paid" for the period of nonpayment.[27] Consequently, the Service may accept less than the full amount of interest only where, for example, a portion of the tax is abated or the entire liability is the subject of a compromise or the Service has abated interest pursuant to Section 6404.

[a] Standard Assessments vs. Interest Assessments

The Service distinguishes between the procedures for making a "standard tax assessment," and the procedures for making an interest assessment, stating:

> Although the term "assessment" is used when interest is posted to a taxpayer's account, a formal summary record of assessment or Form 23-C is not prepared. . . . The interest is simply automatically or manually posted to the account as a computer generated assessment. . . . A separate statute of limitations is provided for the assessment of interest under Section 6601(g).[28]

When the period of limitations on assessment of the tax expires, no interest on that tax may be assessed and collected.

[b] Tax Court's Limited Jurisdiction Over Interest

Deficiency procedures are not applicable to the computation of interest,[29] and only in limited circumstances does the Tax Court have jurisdiction to determine interest as such.[30] If the Tax Court's decision in a deficiency action is decided in favor of the Service, the Service computes the interest due on the deficiency, and includes it in the notice and demand sent to the taxpayer.[31] Overpayments present a different situation. The Tax Court has jurisdiction

---

[27] IRC § 6601(a).

[28] United States v. Toyota of Visalia, Inc., 772 F. Supp. 481 (ED Calif. 1991) (IRS not required to assess interest separately).

[29] Comm'r v. Kilpatrick's Estate, 140 F2d 887 (10th Cir. 1944). The rationale is that, technically, liability for interest does not accrue until after the Tax Court's decision becomes final. When taxpayers and the Service entered into a stipulated Tax Court decision providing, "This agreement constitutes a final civil settlement of taxes due for the years in issue," a district court held that "taxes" included tax and interest. Anthony v. United States, 765 F. Supp. 656, reconsideration denied, 91-2 USTC ¶ 50,393 (D. Colo. 1991).

[30] Estate of Baumgardner v. Comm'r, 85 TC 445, 453 (1985). Similarly, the Tax Court has jurisdiction to determine liability for tax-motivated interest (since repealed), but only as part of a deficiency determination to determine which portion, if any, is attributable to a tax-motivated transaction. Odend'hal v. Comm'r, 95 TC 617 (1990) (taxpayer waived restrictions on assessment for deficiency in tax, but not for tax-motivated interest).

[31] For rules relating to the computation of interest after a Tax Court decision, see Rev. Rul. 56-501, 1956-2 CB 954.

over interest on overpayments. The Tax Court may determine not only whether a taxpayer owes a deficiency in tax, but also whether the taxpayer has overpaid tax for the year.[32] This refund jurisdiction, gives the Tax Court jurisdiction to determine the amount of interest that is *part* of an overpayment, but the Tax Court may not determine the *amount* of interest on the overpayment of tax and interest.

Before 1997, Section 7481(c) permitted the Tax Court to determine the amount of interest the Service claimed to be due on a final decision of the Court. To obtain this Tax Court determination of interest, the (1) Tax Court had to enter a decision in the case and the Service had to assess tax and interest following a Tax Court decision; (2) the taxpayer had to pay the full amount of the deficiency assessment including the interest; and (3) within one year after the date of the Tax Court decision, the taxpayer had to file a petition in a separate post-decision proceeding.[33]

In 1997, Congress decided to permit taxpayers who petitioned for the redetermination of interest to have the interest determination made in a proceeding supplemental to the original deficiency determination. The Taxpayer Relief Act of 1997 amended Section 7481(c) to provide that when (1) the Service has made an assessment of deficiency tax and interest and (2) the taxpayer has paid the entire amount of the deficiency, plus interest, the taxpayer seeking a redetermination of interest may (a) file a motion in the Tax Court, and (b) the Tax Court may then "reopen the case solely to determine whether the taxpayer has made an overpayment of such interest or the Secretary has made an underpayment of such interest and the amount thereof."[34] If the Tax Court finds that the taxpayer has overpaid interest on a deficiency, or that the Service has underpaid interest on an overpayment determined in the deficiency proceeding, the Tax Court treats its interest redetermination under Section 6512(b)(1), as the determination of an overpayment of tax.[35] After the Tax Court enters its interest redetermination, its redetermination is reviewable in the same manner as a decision of the Tax Court.[36]

The Tax Court's jurisdiction to redetermine the amount of Section 7481(c) interest is limited to deciding whether the taxpayer has overpaid "underpayment interest" or the Service has underpaid "overpayment interest" for years involved in a case over which the Tax Court has jurisdiction. The Tax Court's jurisdiction over interest issues does not include claims for "overpay-

---

[32] IRC §§ 6512(a), 6512(b).

[33] This amendment to Section 7481 was made effective for tax deficiencies assessed after November 10, 1988.

[34] IRC §§ 7481(c)(1), 7481(c)(2), as amended by Taxpayer Relief Act of 1997 § 1452, amending IRC § 7481(c), effective on the date of enactment, August 5, 1997.

[35] IRC § 7481(c)(3), as amended by the Taxpayer Relief Act of 1997.

[36] IRC § 7481(b), amended by the Taxpayer Relief Act of 1997.

ment interest" on overpayments refunded or credited outside the Tax Court case, and, therefore, its jurisdiction is limited to the amount of interest involved in the case before it.[37] Suppose that a taxpayer claims it overpaid "underpayment interest" or the Service has underpaid "overpayment interest" in a matter that is outside the Tax Court's jurisdiction. This could occur, for example, where the taxpayer claims that before the taxpayer filed a Tax Court petition involving other adjustments, the Service underpaid the amount of "overpayment interest" on a refund because the Service considered the claim to have been paid during the forty-five-day interest-free period and the taxpayer believes that the Service paid the refund more than forty-five days after the original return claiming a refund was filed. In this situation, the Service would contend that the taxpayer's claim was not within the Tax Court's jurisdiction.[38] It is the Service's view that a taxpayer who claims that the Service has improperly computed "overpayment interest" in a matter outside the scope of the Tax Court case should file a suit for the refund of overpayment interest on amounts that have previously been refunded to the taxpayer, even if the refund suit is filed during pendency of the Tax Court case involving the determination of further deficiencies and overpayments for the same tax period.

Once a taxpayer files a motion under Section 7481(c), the taxpayer may not dismiss the motion to pursue the interest issue in a refund forum. In effect, the motion to redetermine interest invokes the jurisdiction of the Tax Court in the same way that a petition to redetermine a deficiency does. This means that the Tax Court's jurisdiction over the issue is exclusive, with the result either that another proceeding may not be commenced, or that, if already commenced, the proceeding is stayed. The Tax Court may not refuse to exercise its jurisdiction once the jurisdiction of the court has been invoked to decide the motion on the merits. *Hallmark Cards, Inc. v. Comm'r*,[39] illustrates this point. Hallmark and the Service agreed that Hallmark had no income tax deficiency for the year, and when its carryback of a foreign tax credit was taken into account, Hallmark had actually overpaid tax. Hallmark had paid the unreduced amount of the deficiency, but it disagreed with the Service's computation of interest on the portion of the original deficiency that was eliminated by the foreign tax credit carryback. After Hallmark filed a petition in the Tax Court to redetermine the interest computation, the Tax Court ruled against a taxpayer in another Tax Court case on the same interest computation issue Hallmark intended to raise. To avoid the same result in its case, Hallmark filed motion to withdraw its petition. The Tax Court rejected the Hallmark's motion, and decided the interest issue on the same basis as the other case.

---

[37] Bank of Am. Corp. v. Comm'r, 109 TC 1 (1997); Tax Ct. R. 261.

[38] FSA 200012049 (Dec. 13, 1999).

[39] Hallmark Cards, Inc. v. Comm'r, 111 TC 266 (1998).

A taxpayer must make full payment of the deficiency and interest before the Tax Court will have jurisdiction under Section 7481(c). If the taxpayer wishes to appeal the Tax Court's decision, Section 7481(c) gives the taxpayer one year from the date the Tax Court's decision becomes final to pay the tax and interest and file a petition for redetermination of the interest. The Tax Court's decision does not become final until the time for filing a motion for rehearing after a Supreme Court decision has expired.[40] On the other hand, assessment and collection of a deficiency is permitted within ninety days after a Tax Court decision is entered, unless the taxpayer posts an appeal bond to stay collection.[41] Consequently, a taxpayer who does not post an appeal bond will pay the disputed interest substantially before the appellate court decides the appeal. It is uncertain whether a taxpayer who pays assessed interest under protest can petition the Tax Court during the appeal. The availability of prompt judicial review weighs in favor of the Tax Court's hearing the petition, but a literal reading of Section 7481(c) seems to give the taxpayer only the one-year period following the date on which the Tax Court's decision becomes final, which can be after an appeal.

Procedures for computations of interest under Section 7481(c) should not be confused with procedures for review of denials for the abatement of interest under Section 6404(e). Tax Court jurisdiction under Section 7481(c) is limited to recomputations of interest on redetermined deficiencies. When a taxpayer pays the amount of a stipulated decision, and then because of ministerial delay the taxpayer asks the Tax Court to abate interest the Service assessed using Section 7481(c), the Tax Court will not have jurisdiction under Section 7481(c), unless the taxpayer pays both the full amount of the deficiency and the full amount of the interest.[42] Section 7481(c) does not give the Tax Court jurisdiction over taxpayer claims that interest should be abated under Section 6404(e) on account of ministerial delay. In reviewing the Service's administrative decision on abatement, the Tax Court does not exercise full judicial review because, as interpreted, Section 6404(e) gives the Service sole authority to grant a taxpayer discretionary administrative relief.[43]

[c] Exceptions to the Running of Interest on Underpayments

Despite the apparently absolute requirement that interest must be charged on an underpayment, interest is not imposed in two circumstances: (1) when the taxpayer waives the restrictions on assessment and collection and (2) when

---

[40] IRC § 7481(a)(2).

[41] IRC § 7485.

[42] Bax v. Comm'r, 13 F3d 54 (2d Cir. 1993).

[43] This agrees with the Tenth Circuit's decision in Selman v. United States, 941 F2d 1060 (1991).

suspension of interest occurs. Each of these circumstances are described in the following sections.

[i] Waiver of the restrictions on assessment and collection. Interest is not imposed where a taxpayer files a waiver of the restrictions on the assessment of a deficiency, and the following conditions exist:[44]

- A deficiency in income, estate, gift, and certain excise taxes has been determined.[45]
- The taxpayer has filed a waiver of the restrictions on assessment (as provided in Section 6213(d)).
- The Service has failed to send the taxpayer a notice and demand within thirty days after the waiver has been filed.

If these conditions are present, interest on the deficiency stops running on the thirty-first day after the waiver is filed.

Note that the taxpayer's waiver must be "filed." One difficulty associated with this exception is determining when a waiver has been filed. Normally, a waiver of the restrictions on assessment is effective on the date the Service receives the waiver.[46] Waiver forms that local examination offices use are in the Form 870 series, and the forms merely request that a taxpayer "sign and return the form." Because the waiver is filed on the date the Service receives the waiver, interest stops running on the deficiency on the thirty-first day after the Service receives the waiver. The situation is different where a waiver is signed in the Appeals Office. Waiver forms used in the Appeals Office are conditional. Form 870-AD (Offer of Waiver of Restrictions on Assessment and Collection of Deficiency in Tax and Acceptance of Overassessment) specifically states that it is an offer of waiver of the restrictions on assessment "subject to acceptance by the Commissioner" and "shall take effect as a waiver of restrictions on the date it is accepted." Accordingly, this type of waiver has no effect until it is accepted, even if it is delivered to the Service and Service received

---

[44] IRC § 6601(c); Reg. § 301.6601-1(d). After the compounding of interest began on January 1, 1983, the Service failed to suspend the compounding of interest on previously accrued interest on the thirty-first day. Any interest that had accrued up to the execution of the waiver and thirty days thereafter continued to draw interest, even though interest on the underlying deficiency was suspended. TRA 1986 amended Section 6601 to suspend the running of compound interest on accrued interest as well as interest on the deficiency. This change was effective for interest accruing after December 31, 1982, when compound interest itself took effect. IRC § 6601(c). An additional one-year period is allowed for filing a refund claim if the statute of limitations on filing a claim for refund expires within one year after the date of enactment of TRA 1986. TRA 1986 § 1564(b).

[45] The definition of "deficiency" set forth at Section 6211 is incorporated in Section 6601(c).

[46] See IRC § 6213(d).

by the Service before that date.[47] Consequently, when a Form 870-AD is executed, the thirty-day period does not begin to run until the date the waiver is accepted on behalf of the Commissioner.[48] Where a taxpayer executes a conditional waiver or Form 870-AD and also remits the amount of the deficiency listed in the form, the remittance appears to stop the running of interest. A remittance made under these circumstances has been considered payment sufficient to terminate the running of interest against the taxpayer from the date it was received.[49]

A partner in a partnership subject to the uniform partnership proceeding rules may not stop the running of interest by filing a waiver of the restrictions on assessment of the partner's personal tax, because Section 6230, which generally provides that the normal deficiency procedures do not apply to the assessment or collection of any computational adjustment, overrides the general deficiency procedures in a partnership-level audit case.[50]

[ii] Suspension of interest on certain penalties when the Service fails to contact an individual taxpayer. The IRS Restructuring and Reform Act of 1998 (the 1998 Act) added a new circumstance where interest may be abated or suspended. If an individual taxpayer files a timely return, and the Service fails to provide a notice to the taxpayer specifically stating the taxpayer's liability and the basis for the liability before the close of eighteen months in the case of years beginning before 2004 (or the one-year period for years thereafter), the Service must suspend the imposition of any interest, penalty, addition to tax, or additional amount for any failure relating to the return that is computed by reference to the period the failure continues to exist that is properly allocable to the suspension period.[51] The eighteen-month period begins on the later of the date on which the return is filed or the due date of the return without regard to extensions. Curiously, however, the suspension of interest does

---

[47] United States v. Goldstein, 189 F2d 752 (1st Cir. 1951).

[48] Algodon Mfg. Co. v. Gill, 243 F2d 160 (4th Cir. 1957).

[49] State St. Corp. v. United States, 289 F. Supp. 242 (D. Mass. 1968). See United States v. Goldstein, 189 F2d 752 (1st Cir. 1951). The treatment of advance remittances is discussed at ¶ 6.03[1][e].

[50] Monge v. United States, 93-1 USTC ¶ 50,192, 27 Fed. Cl. 720 (1993) (holding that the attempted waiver was a nullity). See also Pilie v. United States, 56 F3d 686 (5th Cir. 1995) (taxpayers were partners in a Tax Equity and Fiscal Responsibility Act of 1982 (TEFRA) partnership and, pursuant to Section 6224(b), executed a settlement agreement agreeing to waive the statute of limitations on assessment of a deficiency arising from the partnership adjustment; they also waived the restrictions on assessment of penalties and interest on their resulting individual partner-level liability; held, normal deficiency procedures, including the suspension of interest under Section 6213(d), do not apply to partnership adjustments, even when as the result of a settlement agreement they become nonpartnership items).

[51] IRC § 6404(g), added by 1998 Act § 3305(a).

not apply to the delinquency penalty imposed by Section 6651. Suspension of interest also is unavailable when the interest and penalty involves a civil fraud case, or certainly a criminal case. The interest suspension period begins after the close of the eighteen-month period and ends on the date which is twenty-one days after the Service sends the explanatory notice.

[iii] Jeopardy assessments. The Service is empowered to assess a tax before a return is due by terminating the taxable year of a taxpayer. Under the termination provision,[52] an assessment is made before the due date of the return. However, for interest purposes, the last date prescribed for payment is determined without regard to any notice and demand for payment issued before the original due date.[53] Consequently, interest does not begin to run until the normal due date of the return for the terminated year. On the other hand, where a jeopardy assessment is made under Section 6861 after the return for the year is due, interest accrues according to the general rule (i.e., from the date the return for the year was due).[54] However, there is a distinction to be made between tax penalties and additions to the tax.

[iv] Stamp and other taxes. In cases where taxes are payable by stamps and in other cases where the date for payment is not prescribed, the last date for payment is considered to be the date the liability for the tax arises, but in no event is later than the date of a notice and demand the Service issued.[55]

¶ 6.03 INTEREST ON UNDERPAYMENTS

As a general rule, all taxpayers who fail to pay the full amount of a tax due under the Code must pay interest at the applicable rate on the unpaid amount from the last date prescribed for payment of the tax until the date the tax is paid.[56] The dates marking the accrual period are (1) "the date prescribed for payment" and (2) the date the tax is "paid."

---

[52] IRC § 6851.

[53] IRC § 6601(b)(3); Reg. § 301.6601-1(c)(3).

[54] IRC § 6601(b)(3).

[55] IRC § 6601(b)(4).

[56] IRC § 6601(a). A portion of estate tax for certain estates not paid pursuant to extension is subject to interest at a rate less than the normal annual rate. IRC § 6601(j)). See ¶ 6.04. No interest is charged on certain adjustments in employment tax. IRC §§ 6601(k), 6205(a).

[1] Interest Runs From the Date Prescribed for Payment

Interest on an underpayment starts to accrue from "the last day prescribed for payment" of the underpaid tax, which generally is the date a taxpayer must file the return reporting the tax due.[57] The day the Code prescribes for an individual taxpayer to pay an income tax is the due date of the return,[58] which for individuals is April 15 of the year following the calendar year for which tax is due, and for corporations is two and one-half months after the close of the year for which tax is due. Interest runs on the correct tax due for the year, which, of course, may not be the tax reported due on the taxpayer's return, but rather the tax the Service has determined to be due after an examination. If it is later determined that the correct income tax is greater than the amount shown on the return, interest runs on the unpaid income tax deficiency from the due date of the return until the date the deficiency is paid. On the face of it, this rule seems reasonable. After all, the taxpayer has had the use of the government's money from the day the tax was due. But consider the situation of a taxpayer whose tax deficiency is the result of a subjective or discretionary adjustment, such as a transfer price adjustment under Section 482, the correctness of which is not determined by final decision until years after the return and payment were due. In the case of a transfer price adjustment, the taxpayer may not have been able to anticipate at the time the tax was due the amount of the Section 482 allocation, but interest will nevertheless start on the due date of payment. In the case of a transfer price adjustment, the taxpayer may not have been able to anticipate at the time the tax was due the amount of the Section 482 allocation, but interest will nevertheless start on the due date of payment. The same can be said of any adjustment that takes years to go through the administrative appeal and litigation stages of review.

The date interest begins to run on a deficiency is critical. When does interest begin to run if the taxpayer has obtained an extension of time to file the return? Although a taxpayer may obtain an extension of time for filing a return or for paying a tax, interest runs on the correct tax from the date the tax return was originally due for payment of the tax. Taxpayers may obtain extensions of time for filing a return for a period not to exceed six months. Corporations are entitled to an automatic six-month extension for filing a corporation income tax return, provided the corporation pays the amount of the properly estimated

---

[57] IRC § 6601(b).

[58] IRC § 6151. See the discussion regarding the due date of returns at ¶ 4.03. Where the due date of a return is a Saturday, Sunday, or legal holiday, the return may be filed on the next business day. However, if payment is not made on that day, interest runs from the actual due date. Rev. Rul. 74-235, 1974-1 CB 347. For example, if a taxpayer timely files his return on Monday, April 16, but does not pay the balance of tax due with his return, interest is computed from Sunday, April 15.

unpaid tax liability.[59] But an extension of time for filing a return is not an extension of the date that payment is due, and the interest provision states that interest begins to run from "the last date prescribed for payment . . . determined without regard to any extension of time for payment."[60] Similarly, where the reported tax is correct, but the full amount is not paid with the return, interest runs on the unpaid amount from the due date of the return without regard to extensions (i.e., the last date prescribed for payment).[61]

[a] The Grace Periods for Payment

A twenty-one-day interest-free period applies to all payments to the Service.[62] No interest is imposed on any amount if taxpayer pays the amount demanded within twenty-one *calendar* days after the date of the notice and demand.[63] If the amount of the notice and demand is $100,000 or more, the interest-free period is ten *business* days. Accordingly, if a taxpayer pays the amount of a .notice and demand within the twenty-one-day (or ten-business-day) period after the date of the notice and demand, no interest is imposed for the period after the notice and demand.

[b] The Date Prescribed for Payment of Interest on Assessable Penalties, Additional Amounts, or Additions to Tax

Interest on penalties, additional amounts, or additions to tax is governed by rules set out in Section 6601(e). Under what is termed the general rule, interest is due on the date of the notice and demand. Penalties to which the general rule applies are the failure to pay penalty and assessable penalties. Rules for the computation of interest have been changed several times[64]— in 1984, 1988, and 1989. These changes removed most penalties from the operation of

---

[59] IRC §§ 6081(a), 6081(b); Reg. § 1.6081-3(a)(3). Extensions of time for filing returns are discussed at ¶ 4.03[4].

[60] IRC § 6601(b)(1).

[61] Section 6601(a) provides that interest runs on "any amount imposed by this title" when it is "not paid on or before the last date prescribed for payment."

[62] IRC § 6601(e)(3).

[63] IRC § 6601(e)(3), as amended by the Taxpayer Bill of Rights 2, § 303(a). For a notice and demand the Service gives a taxpayer before January 1, 1997, the interest-free period was ten calendar days.

[64] Deficit Reduction Act of 1984, Pub. L. No. 369, HR 4170, 98th Cong., 2d Sess., § 158; Technical and Miscellaneous Reconciliation Act of 1988 (TAMRA), § 1015(b)(2)(C); Revenue Reconciliation Act of 1989 (RRA 1989), § 7721(c)(8). The 1984 change was effective for interest accruing after July 18, 1984; the TAMRA change for returns the due date of which was after December 31, 1988; and the OBRA change for returns the due date of which was after December 31, 1989.

the general rule. At the present time, the general rule does not apply to the failure-to-file penalty,[65] the accuracy-related penalties (including the negligence, substantial understatement, and valuation misstatement penalties),[66] the fraud penalty,[67] and the failure to pay stamp tax.[68] For these penalties, interest runs from (1) "the date on which the return of the taxpayer with respect to which such addition to tax is imposed is required to be filed (including any extensions)" until (2) "the date of payment of such addition to tax."[69]

Under the general rule, if the tax is not paid within twenty-one calendar days from the date of the notice and demand (or ten business days if the amount of the notice and demand is $100,000 or more),[70] interest on a penalty, additional amount, or an addition to the tax will be imposed and will accrue for the period from the date of the notice and demand until the date of payment.[71] For example, if a taxpayer receives a notice and demand dated January 10, 2003, reflecting a penalty for failure to pay tax reported on a return filed in 2002, and the taxpayer pays the penalty on January 31, 2003, no interest would be charged on the penalty. If the taxpayer fails to make payment within the twenty-one calendar day or the ten business day period, interest is imposed "for the period from the date of the notice and demand to the date of payment."[72]

For a notice and demand the Service sends after December 31, 1996, the taxpayer must make a payment within the twenty-one-calendar-day or ten-business-day period.[73] For example, suppose a taxpayer timely files a 1989 income tax return on April 15, 1990. Pursuant to a final Tax Court decision in 1993, a notice and demand dated January 10, 1993, is sent to the taxpayer reflecting

---

[65] IRC § 6651(a).

[66] IRC § 6662(a). Accordingly, before the 1984 change, interest starts to run on a penalty on the date of the notice and demand. After July 18, 1984, interest starts to run on a penalty from the date of the notice and demand for payment of the penalty, except for penalties for failure to file, valuation understatement (Section 6659), valuation overstatement (Section 6660), and substantial understatement (Section 6661). If the return due date is after December 31, 1988, interest on a penalty with respect to the return starts to run on the date of the notice and demand for payment of the penalty, except for the failure-to-file penalty, the negligence penalty, the valuation overstatement penalty, the valuation understatement penalty, and the substantial understatement penalty. If the return due date is after December 31, 1989, interest starts to run on a penalty on the date of the notice and demand, except for the penalties for failure to file, pay stamp tax and fraud, as well as the accuracy-related penalty.

[67] IRC § 6663

[68] IRC §§ 6662, 6663.

[69] IRC § 6601(e)(2)(B).

[70] IRC § 6601(e)(2)(A), amended by the Taxpayer Bill of Rights 2, § 303(b)(1).

[71] IRC §§ 6601(e)(2)(A), 6601(e)(3).

[72] IRC § 6601(e)(2)(A).

[73] IRC § 6601(e)(3), amended by the Taxpayer Bill of Rights 2, § 303(a).

the assessment of a deficiency in tax and a negligence-type accuracy-related penalty. If the taxpayer pays the deficiency in tax and the penalty on January 19, 1993, interest is due on the penalty for the period from April 15, 1990, until January 19, 1993.

[i] **Jeopardy assessments.** When a jeopardy assessment is made, the last date prescribed for payment is determined without regard to the date of the notice and demand sent in conjunction with the jeopardy assessment.[74] In other words, Section 6601(e) states that interest starts to run on certain penalties (e.g., the delinquency penalty for failing to pay tax after a notice and demand) unless they are paid within ten days after a notice and demand. However, the notice and demand referred to by Section 6601(e) is not the one issued in the jeopardy assessment process.[75] This rule no longer affects the running of interest on an accuracy-related, fraud, or delinquent-filing penalty that is assessed as part of a jeopardy assessment.

[ii] **Accumulated earnings tax.** Interest is payable on the assessment of an accumulated earnings tax imposed by Section 531 from the due date of the return without regard to any extensions.[76]

[iii] **Transfer price adjustments** Interest on an additional tax due as the result of an allocation under Section 482 also begins to run on the due date of the return, even though a taxpayer might not know the amount of his liability on that date.[77] However, a deficiency resulting from a Section 482 reallocation is not a statutory addition, but rather an adjustment of the tax itself. Thus, it seems unfair to hold a taxpayer liable for interest on such a deficiency when the amount cannot be determined by the taxpayer at the time the return is filed, but the Service must await a largely discretionary action. Because interest on an underpayment compounds daily at a market-sensitive rate, characteri-

---

[74] See IRC § 6601(b)(3).

[75] IRC § 6601(b)(3). For the rule before statutory change, see Decker v. United States, 531 F2d 543 (Ct. Cl. 1976) (interest on fraud penalty assessed by jeopardy assessment runs from post–Tax Court decision notice and demand). Accord Rosenbaum v. Comm'r, No. 5199-72, unreported memorandum sur order (TC Mar. 30, 1987). Interest on a fraud penalty runs from the date of the notice and demand following a final decision of the court and not from the date of the notice and demand following the jeopardy assessments. The Service follows the decisions of the Court of Claims and the Tax Court in *Decker* and *Rosenbaum.* GCM 39755 (revoking GCM 36920).

[76] IRC § 6601(b)(4). Section 6601(b)(4) statutorily overruled such cases as Motor Fuel Carriers v. United States, 420 F2d 702 (Ct. Cl. 1970), which held that interest on the accumulated earnings tax did not run from the due date of the return, because Section 531 contemplated that the tax that might be due under Section 531 would be determined by the Service, not the taxpayer, and would be payable by the taxpayer only on notice and demand for payment.

[77] Morton-Norwich Prods. Inc. v. United States, 602 F2d 270 (Ct. Cl. 1979).

zation of the amount claimed to be due as a penalty subject to the general rule that it is payable on notice and demand is a financially significant one. For example, courts disagree about whether the self-dealing tax of Section 4941 is a penalty or a tax.[78]

[2] The Date Payment Is Received

Interest ceases to accrue on any underpayment in tax on the date the underpayment is paid.[79] For purposes of computing interest, payment ordinarily is made when it is received by the Service, not when it is placed in the mail for delivery.[80] If the timely mailed, timely filed requirements of Section 7502(a) are met, and the payment of tax is actually received and accounted for, the timely mailed, timely filed rule applies to the payment.[81] On the other hand, if the due date falls on a weekend or federal holiday and the first-business-day rule is claimed, the taxpayer's return filed on the first business day will be timely, but interest will start to accrue on the weekend or federal holiday.[82]

[a] Advance Remittances

Interest on tax that is due runs until the date the tax is paid, according to the general rule of Section 6601(a), whether the tax has been underpaid, not paid, or paid late under extension. Payment of the tax not only controls the running of interest, but also affects (1) the Tax Court's jurisdiction; (2) a taxpayer's entitlement to prepayment judicial review in the Tax Court; and (3) the

---

[78] In re Unified Control Sys., Inc., 586 F2d 1036 (5th Cir. 1978) (amount claimed to be due under Section 4941 held to be penalty because it was intended "to curb the described conduct through pecuniary punishment"); Matter of Kline, 403 F. Supp. 974 (D. Md. 1975), aff'd per curiam, 547 F2d 823 (4th Cir. 1977) (considering effect on creditors of classifying tax as penalty); but see Latterman v. United States, 872 F2d 564 (3d Cir. 1989) (amount due under Section 4941 held to be tax because return had to be filed by due date). Cf. MMR Corp. (LA) v. United States, 82 AFTR2d 98-6099 (Bankr. MD La. 1998) (prohibited transactions tax held to be penalty). The courts holding the amount due to be a penalty looked to the bankruptcy law, or at least were influenced by the fact that the case arose in a bankruptcy.

[79] IRC § 6601(a).

[80] Republic Oil Ref. Co. v. Grainger, 98 F. Supp. 921 (WD Pa. 1951), aff'd on other grounds, 198 F2d 161 (3d Cir. 1952).

[81] IRC §§ 7502(a)(1), 7502(a)(2); IRC § 7502(d). The timely mailed, timely filed rule is discussed at ¶ 4.03[2][a].

[82] The first-business-day rule does not apply to payments due on Saturdays, Sundays, and holidays; payment may be made on the following business day, but interest begins to run on the weekend or holiday. See Rev. Rul. 74-235, 1974-1 CB 347.

computation of a tax deficiency over which the Tax Court has jurisdiction.[83] A deficiency is reduced by the amount of tax collected by the Service,[84] and full payment of the tax determined to be due by the Service can eliminate a deficiency. A taxpayer's full payment of the additional tax determined to be due after the Service's examination of a tax return[85] not only stops the running of interest on a deficiency in tax, it eliminates the deficiency in tax. As a result, the Service will not send the taxpayer a notice of deficiency for the taxable period. Without a notice of deficiency, the taxpayer cannot have the examination adjustment reviewed in the Tax Court.[86] Also, interest on an overpayment runs from the date of the overpayment. This interplay of the interest and deficiency/Tax Court provisions of the Code and their possible adverse application or misuse makes it necessary for a taxpayer's remittance to be characterized either as a payment or as something else.

The Service divides remittances made in advance of assessment into four categories:

1. Payments of tax
2. Deposits in the nature of a cash bond
3. Post–statutory notice remittances
4. Undesignated remittances

Administrative procedures permit a taxpayer to make remittances in order to stop the running of interest while at the same time preserving the taxpayer's option of Tax Court review of the deficiency.[87]

---

[83] The characterization of preassessment remittances also controls the computation of interest on overpayments. See infra ¶ 6.03[1][c].

[84] IRC § 6211(a). See ¶ 10.03.

[85] At the end of an examination, the Service encourages voluntary payment of agreed deficiencies or additional taxes plus applicable interest or penalties. Rev. Proc. 63-5, 1963-1 CB 484.

[86] If the Service mails a notice of deficiency and the taxpayer files a petition in the Tax Court, the petition will be dismissed for lack of jurisdiction, even if the notice is sent erroneously. McConkey v. Comm'r, 199 F2d 892 (4th Cir. 1952), cert. denied, 345 US 924 (1953).

[87] Rev. Proc. 84-58, 1984-2 CB 501, effective with respect to remittances made on or after October 1, 1984, superseding Rev. Proc. 82-51, 1982-2 CB 839, which, in turn, superseded Rev. Proc. 64-13, 1964-1 (Pt. 1) CB 674. IRC § 6213(a). The Service has said that Revenue Procedure 84-58 does not apply to post-assessment payments. It has also been held that Revenue Procedure 84-58 does not have the force and effect of law and is not binding on the Service. United States v. Toyota of Visalia, Inc., 772 F. Supp. 481 (ED Cal. 1991) (postassessment payments; questionable decision on binding effect of Rev. Proc. 84-58).

[b] Payments of Tax

A payment of tax is any remittance that (1) is not designated as a deposit; (2) is made in response to a proposed liability (e.g., a revenue agent's report); and (3) fully satisfies the proposed liability.[88] Where a payment is made, (1) the taxpayer is not mailed a notice of deficiency (and therefore no Tax Court review is available); (2) the amount is posted to the taxpayer's account when it is received by the Service, stopping the running of interest on the date received; and (3) any excess is either returned to the taxpayer without interest or applied to other outstanding liabilities.[89] These procedures are followed where the payment equals or exceeds the proposed liability. A remittance of less than the proposed liability (a "partial remittance") is not treated as a payment of tax unless the taxpayer designates which portion of the proposed liability is intended to be satisfied (i.e., the amount of proposed tax intended to be paid).[90]

A partial payment is taken into account in determining the amount of a deficiency included in a notice of deficiency. However, if a partial payment is made, the Service will honor a taxpayer's request to allocate the payment between interest and tax only if (1) the taxpayer consents to assessment and collection of the entire liability by waiving the restrictions on assessment or (2) the taxpayer makes a partial payment of tax as well as interest, and the interest portion is no greater than interest that has accrued on the part of the tax paid (thus, a partial payment alone is not permissible).[91] A remittance not complying with either of these requirements is treated as a deposit in the nature of a cash bond.[92] Payments of tax are treated as any other assessed amount, and in the event that tax has been overpaid, interest is paid on the overpayment.[93]

[c] Post–Statutory Notice Remittances

Normally, the Service is prohibited (or restricted) from assessing and collecting a deficiency in tax until it has sent a notice of deficiency to the taxpayer and waited ninety days for the taxpayer to file a petition in the Tax Court.[94] However, there are exceptions to this general rule. For example, if a taxpayer makes a payment of tax, the Service may (but is not required to) assess the amount of the payment.[95] If the payment equals the amount of the pre-

---

[88] Rev. Proc. 84-58, 1984-2 CB 501, § 4.03(1).
[89] Rev. Proc. 84-58, 1984-2 CB 501, §§ 4.03(2)–4.03(4), § 5.01.
[90] Rev. Proc. 84-58, 1984-2 CB 501, § 4.03(1).
[91] Rev. Proc. 84-58, 1984-2 CB 501, § 6.02.
[92] Rev. Proc. 84-58, 1984-2 CB 501, § 6.03.
[93] Rev. Proc. 84-58, 1984-2 CB 501, § 5.05(1).
[94] IRC § 6213(a).
[95] IRC § 6213(b)(4).

viously determined deficiency, this assessment technically can eliminate the deficiency and the Tax Court review.[96] However, if all or part of the deficiency is paid after a notice of deficiency has been mailed, the Tax Court is not deprived of jurisdiction to review the deficiency despite any assessment.[97] The Service treats any payment in complete or partial satisfaction of the deficiency that is made after a notice of deficiency has been mailed as a payment of tax, and such amounts are posted to the taxpayer's account as soon as possible.[98] If a taxpayer designates a post–statutory notice remittance as "a deposit in the nature of a cash bond," the Service treats it as such.[99] Both the post–statutory notice payment and the deposit stop the running of interest on the date received by the Service,[100] even if the underlying liability is assessed or the remittance is actually applied to the liability at a later time.

[d] Deposits in the Nature of a Cash Bond

A deposit in the nature of a cash bond is a remittance that is (1) made before a notice of deficiency is mailed, and (2) designated by the taxpayer in writing as a deposit in the nature of a cash bond.[101] If a taxpayer makes this kind of remittance (a "deposit"), interest stops running on an assessment on the date the Service receives the deposit, even if the liability is not assessed or the remittance is applied to the taxpayer's account at some later date.[102] A deposit is returned to a taxpayer on request, but without interest, and if the deposit is returned and the liability is subsequently assessed, interest is computed without regard to the period during which the Service had the deposit. In other words, the taxpayer receives no credit for a returned deposit.[103] If the Service determines that the collection of the tax is in jeopardy or "that the amount should be applied against any other liability," it will not return the deposit but rather will apply it against the assessment made on account of jeopardy or against the other liability.[104] A taxpayer who makes a deposit is mailed a no-

---

[96] See IRC § 6211(a).

[97] IRC § 6213(b)(4).

[98] Rev. Proc. 84-58, 1984-2 CB 501, § 4.01.

[99] Rev. Proc. 84-58, 1984-2 CB 501, §§ 4.01 and 5.01. The Service takes the position that this deposit cannot serve as an appeal bond required by Section 7485 to stay assessment and collection. However, the Tax Court determines the adequacy of the bond. It is difficult to understand why a deposit equal to the amount of the deficiency offered by the taxpayer as a bond would not be sufficient.

[100] Rev. Proc. 84-58, 1984-2 CB 501, § 5.01.

[101] Rev. Proc. 84-58, 1984-2 CB 501, § 4.02.

[102] Rev. Proc. 84-58, 1984-2 CB 501, § 5.01.

[103] Rev. Proc. 84-58, 1984-2 CB 501, § 5.01.

[104] The possible application of a deposit to another liability at the Service's option is a negative factor in a taxpayer's consideration of designating a remittance as a deposit.

tice of deficiency as long as he does not execute a waiver of the restrictions on assessment.[105] The deposit is posted as a payment of tax at the expiration of the period for filing a Tax Court petition.[106] Unlike a payment, a deposit may not be allocated between interest and tax until the liability is assessed, when the Service honors an allocation then designated by the taxpayer.[107] Instead of treating the deposit as a payment, the taxpayer may elect to continue the treatment of the deposit as such by making a second request for deposit treatment.[108] Also, the taxpayer may elect to apply an excess deposit to another assessed or unassessed liability.[109] When a taxpayer makes a deposit in the nature of a cash bond, the Service sends a letter of the type illustrated at Form 6.1.

[e] Undesignated Remittances

An undesignated remittance is any remittance made before the Service has proposed additional tax to the taxpayer (e.g., before a revenue agent's or tax examiner's report).[110] Undesignated remittances (1) are treated as deposits; (2) are not subject to claims for refund or credit (i.e., they are not considered overpayments of tax); (3) do not draw interest even to the extent that they exceed the tax ultimately determined to be due; and (4) are returned at the taxpayer's request absent jeopardy or some other outstanding liability.[111] Since they are treated as deposits, undesignated remittances left on deposit until the examination is completed stop the running of interest as of the date of receipt.[112] However, an undesignated remittance that is received and applied after the examination report is applied first to tax, then to penalty, and finally to interest. If more than one period is involved, the remittance is first applied to the earliest period in the same order.[113]

To determine interest, any remittance is automatically treated as a payment as long as a proposed additional tax has been determined. As a result, a taxpayer who intends to seek Tax Court review must either make a partial pay-

---

[105] If the taxpayer waives the restrictions on assessment, he automatically surrenders his right to Tax Court review. Therefore, there is no reason to delay assessment of the amount of the deposit as a payment. See ¶ 8.07.

[106] Although posting of the payment is deferred during the petition-filing period, interest stops running on the date the Service receives the deposit. Rev. Proc. 84-58, 1984-2 CB 501, § 5.01.

[107] Rev. Proc. 84-58, 1984-2 CB 501, § 6.04.

[108] Rev. Proc. 84-58, 1984-2 CB 501, § 4.02(3).

[109] Rev. Proc. 84-58, 1984-2 CB 501, § 4.02(4).

[110] Rev. Proc. 84-58, 1984-2 CB 501, § 4.02(4).

[111] Rev. Proc. 84-58, 1984-2 CB 501, § 5.01.

[112] Rev. Proc. 84-58, 1984-2 CB 501, § 4.04.

[113] Rev. Proc. 84-58, 1984-2 CB 501, § 6.01.

ment of the proposed liability or designate a remittance in writing as a deposit in the nature of a cash bond. Both payments and deposits stop interest from running when received.

[f] Partial Payments

Where a taxpayer voluntarily makes a partial payment, the Service's procedure is to apply the payment in accordance with the specific instructions of the taxpayer.[114] As noted previously, allocations of preassessment payments by a taxpayer are honored by the Service only if the remittance exceeds the full amount of the underlying tax due.[115] The Service does not honor a partial payment remitted before assessment unless the taxpayer waives the restrictions on assessment on the entire liability or the partial payment covers a partial payment of tax as well as interest and the interest portion is not greater than the interest accrued on the underlying tax paid.[116] Where no instructions are given, the Service applies the payment to tax, penalty, and interest in that order for the earliest year and then to each succeeding year in the same order.[117] Absent specific instructions, the payment is not allocated to tax years on a pro rata basis.[118]

---

[114] For post-1982 periods, see Rev. Proc. 84-58, 1984-2 CB 501, § 6.01.

[115] Rev. Proc. 84-58, 1984-2 CB 501, § 6.01.

[116] Rev. Proc. 84-58, 1984-2 CB 501, § 6.02.

[117] Rev. Rul. 73-305, 1973-2 CB 43. Rev. Rul. 79-284, 1979-2 CB 83, states that absent instructions the IRS allocates voluntary partial payments of withheld employment or collected excise taxes "in a manner serving its best interest." This procedure is the same one followed on receipt of involuntary payments (e.g., payments received by way of levy). Id. See also Rev. Proc. 84-58, 1984-2 CB 501.

[118] James F. Keith, 35 TC 1130 (1961).

FORM 6.1
SAMPLE LETTER FROM IRS ACKNOWLEDGING RECEIPT OF PARTIAL PAYMENT AS CASH BOND

Department of the Treasury
Internal Revenue Service

HOLTSVILLE, NY 00501

In reply refer to:
Feb. 19, 1991   LTR 316C
000-00-0000   7912 30 000
                            01976

John and Mary Taxpayer
1 Michael Street
New York, N.Y. 11111

CERTIFIED MAIL

Taxpayer Identification Number: 000-00-0000
              Tax Period(s): Dec. 31, 1979

                Form: 1040

Dear Taxpayer:

Thank you for your payment of   , which we received
            We have applied it as a payment on what you may owe
for 7912 tax for the period(s) shown above.

Although we have not made a final determination of your liability,
we will accept your payment as a cash bond for payment of an amount
that may be assessed later, if you wish us to do so.

Acceptance of your payment as a cash bond means that (1) the deposit
will stop the accrual of interest at the date the payment was received
on that part of any assessment later satisfied by the payment; (2) the
deposit is not subject to a claim for credit or refund as an overpayment of tax, penalties or interest; and (3) interest will not be
paid to you on any of the deposit returned to you should it exceed any
additional tax, penalties or interest later assessed.

If you are not in agreement with the final determination of your
liability, you will be issued a notice of deficiency which allows a
90-day period (150 days if you are outside the United States) to
petition the Tax Court.

Unless you request in writing to continue your remittance as a
deposit in nature of a cash bond before the expiration of the 90- or
150-day period, that part of the deposit that is not greater than the
deficiency proposed, plus any interest that has accrued, will be
posted to your account as a payment.

If these conditions are not satisfactory to you and you would like us
to return your deposit, please sign the statement at the end of this
letter and return it.

Please provide the information requested within 30 days from the date
of this letter If we do not hear from you, your account may reflect
incomplete or incorrect information. We have enclosed an envelope for

Department of the Treasury
Internal Revenue Service

Feb. 19, 1991   LTR 316C
000-00-0000   7912 30 000
                              01977

John and Mary Taxpayer
1 Michael Street
New York, N.Y. 11111

your convenience.

When you write, please include your telephone number, the hours you
can be reached, and a copy of this letter. You may also want to keep
a copy of this letter for your records.
Telephone Number (   )_____ Hours_____

Thank you for your cooperation.

                              Sincerely yours,

                              Bob G. Hughes

                              Bob G. Hughes
                              Director, Service Center

Enclosure(s):
Copy of this letter

[3] Payment and Carrybacks

The Code permits the carryback of a net operating loss,[119] capital loss,[120] and investment credit.[121] The carryback of these losses or credit in one year (the loss or credit year) can result in the reduction or elimination of an underpayment in tax in another year (the carryback year). If an underpayment is satisfied by the application of a carryback, on the underpayment or deficiency does not stop running.[122] In *Manning v. Seeley Tube & Box Co.*, the Supreme Court held that "where a deficiency in interest has been validly assessed under any applicable procedure, a subsequent carryback with an abatement of the deficiency does not abate the interest previously assessed on that deficiency."[123] Section 6601(d)(1) provides that where a net operating loss or capital loss or certain unused credits are carried back, interest runs on the deficiency from the due date for payment of the tax for that year and ends with the filing date for the taxable year in which the loss or credit arises.[124] Interest continues to run beyond the filing date for the loss year, determined without regard to extensions, on any portion of the deficiency that is not eliminated by the carryback.

[4] Carryback of Net Operating Losses

The Service has ruled that when an unassessed deficiency barred by the statute of limitations is offset by the carryback of a net operating loss, interest on the deficiency may not be offset unless the taxpayer is actually due a refund for the carryback year.[125] This ruling covers two situations, as shown in the following examples.

> **EXAMPLE 6-1:** Taxpayer X files its income tax return on a calendar-year basis. X timely files income tax returns for 1998, 1999, 2000, and 2001 and reports no income tax liability for each of these years. In October 2000, the Service examines X's income tax returns for these years. The

---

[119] IRC § 172.

[120] IRC § 1212.

[121] IRC §§ 46 (investment credit), 38 (general business credit), 39 (carryback and carryforward of unused credits).

[122] See Manning v. Seeley Tube & Box Co., 338 US 561, 570 (1950); United States v. Koppers Co., 348 US 254 (1955). But see Pan Am. Van Lines v. United States, 607 F2d 1299 (9th Cir. 1979), where the court incorrectly failed to apply this rule in a case involving the dischargeability of tax in bankruptcy.

[123] Manning v. Seeley Tube & Box Co., 338 US 561, 570 (1950).

[124] IRC §§ 6601(d)(1)–6601(d)(3). See Prop. Reg. § 301.6601(e)(1)(i).

[125] Rev. Rul. 85-64, 1985-1 CB 365.

Service determines that X's taxable incomes for 1998 and 1999 were actually $15x and $8x, respectively. The Service also determines that X had a net operating loss in 2001 that was larger than the combined taxable income of both 1998 and 1999. No changes are made in X's 2000 return. In this situation, the Service ruled that X may carry back to 1999 only the excess of the 2001 net operating loss over $15x, its income for 1998. However, the Service may not further reduce the carryback by the amount of interest on the 1998 deficiency because more than three years have elapsed since the filing of X's 1998 return, and the deficiency is not timely assessed.

EXAMPLE 6-2: Assume the same facts as in Example 6-1, except that X reports taxable income of $6x on its 1998 return and pays tax of $3x. The Service rules that interest owed on the 1998 deficiency may be offset against the refund of tax due to the carryback of a net operating loss to 1998. The Service's rationale is that under *Lewis v. Reynolds*,[126] the taxpayer is not entitled to a refund unless the tax is overpaid, even if the statute of limitations on assessment and collection has expired with respect to the year, as it had for 1998. However, under Section 6601(d)(1), any income tax reduced by reason of a net operating loss does not affect the computation of interest on the tax. Accordingly, the Service found the interest owed on the 1998 deficiency to be capable of offset against the refund of tax due for the year.

The Service also distinguishes situations controlled by Section 6601(d)(1) from the general rule of Section 6601(a).[127] In a situation in which an adjustment in the carryback year is not directly attributable to the carryback itself, the computation of interest under Section 6601(d)(1) does not apply. According to the ruling, Section 6601(d) does not apply to underpayments that could have been determined at the time the payment of tax for the carryback year was due (i.e., a preexisting deficiency) and also situations in which the fact or amount of the underpayment could not be determined until some time after the date payment for the carryback year was due (i.e., a deficiency that "relates back," such as a failure to reinvest in a principal residence under Section 1034). If the adjustment is not attributable to the carryback, and if the year is barred by the statute of limitations, interest accrues and can be collected from a refund due the taxpayer. If the adjustment is directly attributable to the carryback, interest owed on a deficiency barred from assessment or collection by the statute of limitations may not be offset unless the taxpayer is entitled to a refund of tax as the result of the net operating loss carryback.[128]

---

[126] Lewis v. Reynolds, 284 US 281 (1932).
[127] Rev. Rul. 85-65, 1985-1 CB 366.
[128] Rev. Rul. 85-64, 1984-2 CB 501.

[5] Carrybacks of Foreign Tax Credits

The Taxpayer Relief Act of 1997 clarified the computation of interest on an underpayment when the underpayment is reduced or eliminated by the carryback of a foreign tax credit. Section 6601(d)(2) provides that if deficiencies are eliminated by foreign tax credit carrybacks, interest on the deficiency in the carryback year remains payable. There is, however, a two and one-half month difference between the interest accrual periods depending on when the foreign tax credit becomes available. If the credit becomes available in a tax year after August 5, 1997, Section 6601(d)(2) provides that the interest cutoff date is the return due date for that year. Statutory action on the computation of interest where a foreign tax credit carryback is involved became necessary because of litigation on the subject.

In *Fluor Corp.v. United States*, the Court of Federal Claims dealt with foreign taxes actually paid or accrued in taxable years beginning after August 5, 1997, and the court held that if an underpayment for a taxable year is reduced or eliminated by a foreign tax credit carryback from a later tax year in which the foreign taxes were paid or accrued, the carryback does not affect the computation of interest on the underpayment for the period ending with the filing date of the later year's return.[129] In other words, interest continues to accrue on the underpayment in tax until the filing date of the return for the year in which the foreign tax credit carryback arises. Thus, when foreign tax credit carrybacks reduce or eliminate an underpayment, the computation of interest is consistent with the computation of interest in the similar situation where net operating losses or capital losses are carried back. If a net operating loss or net capital loss carryback frees up or increases an excess foreign tax credit, which in turn is carried back to an earlier year, a deficiency in the earlier year is not considered to have been reduced, and an overpayment is not considered to have been created until the filing date of the later year's return in which the loss carryback arose. On appeal, the Court of Appeals for the Federal Circuit reversed the Court of Federal Claims and held that "while the foreign tax credit carryback eliminated the original tax deficiency for the carryback year, it did not release the taxpayer from the obligation to pay interest on that tax deficiency."[130]

Two principles articulated by the Supreme Court, the circuit court said in *Fluor*, supported the conclusion that the elimination of an underpayment by the carryback of a foreign tax credit did not affect the taxpayer's liability for interest. First, although it involved a deficiency that was eliminated by a net operating loss carryback, the same use of the money principle the Supreme Court

---

[129] IRC § 6601(d)(2), added by the Taxpayer Relief Act of 1997 § 1055(a), which also redesignated paragraphs (2) and (3) as paragraphs (3) and (4).

[130] Fluor Corp. v. United States, 122 F3d 1430, opinion whithdrawn and new opinion substituted, 126 F3d 1397 (Fed. Cir. 1997).

articulated in *Seeley Tube & Box Co.*, applied as well to an underpayment eliminated by a foreign tax credit carryback, because "the taxpayer, by its failure to pay the taxes owed, had the use of funds which rightfully should have been in the possession of the United States [, and the] the fact that the statute permits the taxpayer subsequently to avoid the payment of that debt in no way indicates that the taxpayer is to derive the benefit of the funds for the intervening period." Second, because the government is entitled to the use of taxes lawfully due when they become due, a clear legislative expression is required to demonstrate that Congress intended to eliminate the deficiency as of the original due date, thus eliminating the interest charges as well. The circuit court concluded that there was no clear legislative expression that Congress meant to forgive interest on an underpayment merely because the carryback was a foreign tax credit carryback rather than a net operating loss or capital loss or business credit. According to the court, Section 904(c) did not provide a "clear legislative expression" because the phrase "deemed paid or accrued [in the carryback year]" relates to the year in which the credit will be applied; "it does not answer the question of when the reallocation of the foreign tax credit will be deemed to occur."

There is a difference of authority where the credit becomes available in a tax year beginning before August 6, 1997. In *Fluor Corp.*, the Court of Federal Claims held that the cutoff date is the last day of that year, but in *Intel Corp.* the Tax Court disagreed and held that interest runs until the due date of the return. Before the Taxpayer Relief Act of 1997, there was a question whether interest on underpayments of tax for a carryback year eliminated by the carryback of a foreign tax credit should be treated differently from other carrybacks because they were not included in the definition of "credit carryback" under Section 6511(d)(4)(C). Because Section 904(c) provides that excess foreign tax credits "shall be deemed taxes paid or accrued" to foreign countries or possessions of the United States in the carryback year, an argument could be made that no interest should accrue because the tax obligation in the carryback year is changed; it is reduced by the foreign tax that is deemed paid in the carryback year. This argument was recognized by the Court of Federal Claims in *Fluor Corp.*, where an underpayment of tax for 1982 was eliminated by the carryback of an excess foreign tax credit from 1984, and the government claimed that while the carryback eliminated the underpayment, it did not eliminate the interest on the underpayment from the due date of the carryback year return to the due date of the return of the year of the excess foreign tax credit.[131]

---

[131] Fluor Corp. v. United States, 35 Fed. Cl. 520 (1996); see also Intel Corp. v. Comm'r, 111 TC 90 (1998). The circuit court also held, however, that the interest cutoff date was the last day of the year giving rise to the foreign tax credit carryback, rather than, as the amendment to Section 6601(d) made by the Taxpayer Relief Act of 1997 and discussed below provides, the return due date for the year. This is noteworthy because the

The court recognized that Fluor's interpretation would put the taxpayer that timely pays its tax liability for a carryback year and then receives a refund because of the carryback of excess foreign tax credits in a worse position than the taxpayer that does not pay the correct tax when it is due, but whose tax deficiency is subsequently eliminated by a foreign tax credit carryback. However, the court concluded, "[T]here is a clear legislative expression of intent that, notwithstanding the general rule of Section 6601(a), interest is not to be imposed on underpayments of tax that are later satisfied by foreign tax carrybacks."

Frequently, taxpayers credit an overpayment of tax for one year to the estimated tax due for the subsequent tax year. When the Service examines the overpayment return and determines not only that there was no overpayment in tax for the first year, but that there was a deficiency or underpayment, a number of cases show the way through what appears at first to be a difficult interest computation. The common thread in all these cases is the fundamental principle that interest is compensation for the use of money.

[a] The *Avon* Case

In *Avon Products, Inc.*, the taxpayer filed its tax return by September 15, the extended due date, and elected to have the overpayment applied toward an estimated quarterly tax liability due the same day for the following tax year.[132] After the return for the overpayment year was examined, the Service determined that the tax for the first year had not been overpaid and that the taxpayer had underpaid tax for the year, which ended June 15. The circuit court held that interest did not begin to run against the taxpayer on June 15, the end of the fiscal year, as the Service contended, because until September 15, when the taxpayer erroneously applied its refund to the following year's estimated tax liability, there was no amount that was both *due and unpaid*, and so until that date the Service had not been deprived of the taxpayer's money (the use-of-the-money principle).

Federal Circuit decided the case after the changes made by the Taxpayer Relief Act. But see Intel Corp. v. Comm'r, supra (reaching the opposite conclusion); see also Hallmark Cards, Inc. v. Comm'r, 90 TC 26 (1998) (following *Intel Corp.* and holding that interest continued to accrue on deficiency until due date of return for year of excess foreign tax credit carryback). See also Guardian Indus. Corp. v. United States, 84 AFTR2d 99-7492 (ED Mich. 1999) (agreeing with *Intel* and the Tax Court that interest on the deficiency accrued until the due date for the return for the year in which the excess credit arose).

[132] Avon Prods., Inc. v. United States, 588 F2d 342 (2d Cir. 1978).

[b] The *May* Case

Similarly, in *May Department Stores Co.*, the taxpayer reported an overpayment in tax on the return it filed for the first year on October 15, and elected to apply the overpayment to its first installment of estimated tax for the second year.[133] As a result of an audit of the first year's return, the amount of the overpayment was reduced. The Court of Federal Claims held that interest did not begin to run on the excessive overpayment until the date the taxpayer made the election to apply it to the first installment of the second year's estimated tax. Applying the use-of-the-money principle, the court held that the Service had the use of May's money from April 15, the date that May paid the tax it estimated to be due for its first year with its extension request, until October 15, the date May filed its return for the year. The Service assessed interest on the amount May had erroneously applied to the first installment from the date of the installment, May 15. Under the use-of-the-money principle, interest began to run from the date the return for the second year was filed, October 15, when May reported an overpayment and applied it to estimated tax for the third year. After the audit, May had a deficiency for the second year, rather than its reported overpayment. The court held that the Service had the use of May's money from the date May filed its extension request with its estimate of the tax due for the second year until the return for the second year was filed.[134]

The facts in *May* can be stated in a more general fashion. If the taxpayer reports an overpayment in tax on the return it files for Year 1 on October 15 of the year following Year 1, and the taxpayer elects to apply the overpayment to estimated tax for the first installment of estimated tax for Year 2, and then, as the result of an audit, the overpayment is reduced, interest does not begin to run on the excess amount of the overpayment until the date the taxpayer makes the election to apply it to the first installment of Year 2 estimated tax.[135] This is so because under *Avon*'s use-of-the-money principle, the Service had the use of May's money from April 15, the date May paid its estimated Year 1 tax with its extension request, until October 15, the date it filed its return for the year. The Service assessed interest on the amount May had errone-

---

[133] May Dep't Stores Co. v. United States, 36 Fed. Cl. 680 (1996). The Service subsequently announced that it acquiesced in the decision. AOD CC-1997-008 (Aug. 4, 1997). It later issued a revenue ruling applying *May Dep't Stores Co.*; see Rev. Rul. 99-40, 1999-40 IRB 441.

[134] See also Kimberly-Clark Tissue Co. v. United States, 79 AFTR2d 97-1568 (ED Pa. 1997) (taxpayer filed a return for 1983 reporting an overpayment that it applied to the estimated tax for 1984, but it also paid that estimated tax without using the claimed overpayment; the Service determined that a deficiency existed for 1983, but the court held that the taxpayer's 1983 tax was not both due and unpaid from April 15, 1984, until September 15, 1984, and so the Service was not entitled to interest during this period).

[135] See May Dep't Stores Co. v. United States, 36 Fed. Cl. 680 (1996).

ously applied to the first installment from the date of the installment, May 15. Under the same use of the money principle, interest begins to run from the date the return for Year 2 is filed, October 15, when the return reports an overpayment that the taxpayer applies to estimated tax for Year 3; however, after audit, the taxpayer has a deficiency for Year 2 rather than the reported overpayment.[136] The Court of Federal Claims found that the Service had the use of May's money from the date of the payment with the extension request until the date May filed its return for Year 2. In other words, no deficiency existed until the date the return for the year of the erroneous overpayment and credit was filed.

[c] The *Sequa* Case

Sequa filed its return on September 15, reporting an overpayment, applied the overpayment to estimated tax for the second year, but also paid the first quarter estimate for the second year in an amount greater than the amount it ultimately reported due for the second year. In the third year, Sequa discovered an error in its first year's return and amended the return, reducing the amount of the overpayment. The Service claimed that interest was due from April 15 of the second year until the due date of the return for the second year. The district court in *Sequa*[137] applied the use of the money reasoning of *Avon Products* to reject the Service's contention that Sequa was liable for interest from the date of the first installment for the second year interest.

[d] The *Kimberly-Clark* Case

In another situation, *Avon's* use-of-the-money principle was applied once again. Kimberly-Clark filed its 1983 return showing an overpayment of $7,465,035, which it applied to estimated taxes for 1984.[138] Independent of the crediting of its 1983 overpayment to 1984 estimated tax, Kimberly-Clark also paid estimated taxes for 1984 for all four quarters. The Service applied Kimberly-Clark's 1983 overpayment to its first quarter estimate for 1984. Subsequently, the Service determined a deficiency for 1983, and agreed with Kimberly-Clark that the deficiency for the year was $7,148,081. However, the Service contended that interest began to run on the 1983 deficiency on April 16, 1984, when the first quarter estimated tax for 1984 was due. Kimberly-Clark argued that interest properly began to run on September 15, 1984, when it filed the 1983 return applying the overpayment. Based on the reasoning in

---

[136] May Dep't Stores Co. v. United States, 36 Fed. Cl. 680 (1996).

[137] Sequa Corp. v. United States, 80 AFTR2d 97-7824 (SDNY 1996).

[138] Kimberly-Clark Tissue Co. v. United States, 79 AFTR2d 97-1568 (ED Pa. 1997).

May and *Sequa*,[139] the district court ruled that Kimberly-Clark's taxes for 1983 were not both due and unpaid from April 15, 1984, to September 15, 1984, and, accordingly, the Service was not entitled to interest for this period. The Service had the use of the money Kimberly-Clark had paid for 1983, including the amount of the "overpayment" until Kimberly-Clark elected to apply it to its 1984 estimated tax. After suffering several losses, the Service accepted that interest will begin to accrue on an underpayment that results from an individual's application of a purported overpayment to a succeeding year without specifying the estimated tax period to which the overpayment should be credited, when the purported overpayment is applied to the following year's estimated taxes or to the original due date for the following year if the overpayment is not needed to satisfy specific installments of estimated taxes.[140]

In *BankAmerica Corporation*, the taxpayer had deficiencies in its income taxes for Years 1 and 2.[141] In Year 3, the taxpayer had an unused investment credit and carried excess credits back to both Years 1 and 2. In Year 6, the taxpayer had a net operating loss, which it carried back to Year 3. This resulted in the displacement of a Year 3 foreign tax credit, which was then carried back to Years 1 and 2, displacing the investment credit originally carried back and taken in those years. The Service computed the deficiency interest for Years 1 and 2 from the end of Year 3 to the due date of the return for Year 6 on the years 1 and 2 deficiencies, but ignored the effect of the investment credit, which was not displaced until the due date of the Year 6 return and the carryback of the net operating loss to Year 3. Applying the use-of-the-money principle, the Tax Court reasoned that the Service had the use of the investment credit, which is treated as a payment, from the end of Year 3 until the due date of the Year 6 return. Before that date, the Year 6 net operating loss is not considered with the result that the investment credit constituted a payment for Years 1 and 2.

[e] Revenue Ruling 99-40

After *May Department Stores*, *Sequa Corp.*, and *Kimberly-Clark*, the Service changed its position and ruled that when a taxpayer reports an overpayment on its income tax return, which the taxpayer asks to be refunded or applied to the succeeding year's estimated tax, and the Service subsequently determines that there is a deficiency in the original year, the Service will assess interest on the portion of a subsequently determined deficiency for the

---

[139] Sequa Corp. v. United States, 80 AFTR2d 97-7824 (SDNY 1996).

[140] FSA 1999-90010 (Feb. 10, 1999).

[141] BankAmerica Corp. v. Comm'r, 109 TC 1 (1997). The case is also instructive about the Tax Court's jurisdiction under Section 7481(c) to redetermine the amount of interest of a deficiency.

overpayment year that is less than or equal to the overpayment as of (1) the date on which the Service refunded the overpayment to the taxpayer without interest or (2) the date on which the Service applied the overpayment to the succeeding year's estimated taxes.[142] Interest on any remaining portion of the deficiency will be assessed from the original due date of the tax for the overpayment year. In addition, (1) when a taxpayer elects to credit an overpayment for the first year to estimated tax for the succeeding year, the Service will apply the overpayment to unpaid installments for the succeeding year that are due after the date the overpayment arose in the order in which the tax is required to be paid to avoid the penalty for failure to pay estimated tax; (2) the Service will assess interest on a subsequently determined deficiency for the first year from the date the credit is applied to the succeeding year's estimated tax; and (3) pursuant to Section 6513(d), any portion of the overpayment the taxpayer elected to credit against estimated tax for the succeeding year, but which is not needed to satisfy estimated tax for the succeeding year, should be treated as a payment of the succeeding year's income tax as of the due date of the return for the succeeding year, without considering any extensions.[143]

[6] Interest When There Are Both Underpayments and Overpayments

[a] In General

An underpayment may be satisfied by the credit of an overpayment. Before 1958, interest on a credited overpayment was allowed from the date of the overpayment to the date of assessment, while interest on a deficiency ran from the due date of the return to the date of payment. As a result, where a

---

[142] Rev. Rul. 99-40, 1999-40 IRB 441. See also Chief Counsel Notice N(35)000-168 (Nov. 9, 1999) (Change in Litigating Position).

[143] Rev. Rul. 99-40, 1990-40 IRB 441; Chief Counsel Notice N(35)000-168 (Nov. 9, 1999) (Change in Litigating Position); see also FSA 199930031 (Feb. 8, 1999); see also FSA 199930007 (Apr. 6, 1999), and FSA 199932010 (Apr. 26, 1999). See also FSA 199952006 (Aug. 30, 1999) (subsequently determined deficiency, equal to or less than the credit elect, runs interest from the due date of the estimated tax installment payments against which the credit elect is required to be applied; if the credit elect is in excess of the amount needed to pay estimated tax, the excess is deemed a payment for the next succeeding year, and so the corresponding deficiency amount runs interest from the original due date of the succeeding year's income tax return; and, if the deficiency in the first year is greater than the credit elect, the deficiency runs interest from the due date of the return for the first year); FSA 199952008 (Sept. 13, 1999) (if the deficiency for the first year is less than the amount of the unused credit elect for the second year, interest starts running on the entire deficiency amount from the unextended due date of the second year's return).

taxpayer made an overpayment, interest could run on a deficiency until the date the overpayment credit was scheduled to be applied to the deficiency—a date that might be long after the date on which interest on the overpayment was cut off by assessment. Accordingly, in 1958, Congress added Section 6601(f), which provides that interest is not imposed on any portion of a tax for any period during which interest on an overpayment would have been allowed if the overpayment had been refunded.[144] Thus, interest on an underpayment (or deficiency) stops running as of the date of the overpayment when a "mutuality of indebtedness" arises.

In other words, if any portion of a tax is satisfied by credit or an overpayment, interest on the underpayment is traded for interest on the overpayment.[145] As one court said, Section 6601(f) "create[s] a type of legal fiction that payment was made on a certain prior date[,] [and this] is what differentiates a credit from a refund, where the money would then need to be turned over to the Government to satisfy any prior liability and the provisions of [S]ection 6601(f) would apply."[146]

> **EXAMPLE 6-3:** An examination of taxpayer *A*'s returns discloses an underpayment of $800 for 2001 and an overpayment of $500 for 2002. The Service credits the 2002 overpayment against the underpayment. Thus, interest runs on the $800 underpayment from April 15, 2002, the last day prescribed for payment, to April 15, 2003, the date the 2002 overpayment was made. Because interest would have been allowed on the overpayment, if refunded, from April 15, 2003, to a date not more than thirty days before the date of the refund check, no interest is imposed after April 15, 2003, on $500, the portion of the underpayment satisfied by the credit. However, interest continues to run on $300, the portion of the underpayment not satisfied by the credit, to the date of payment.[147]

If an underpayment for one tax year (Year 1) is satisfied by an overpayment caused by excess withholding tax payments that are made for a later tax year (Year 2), interest runs on the Year 1 underpayment until the April 15 fil-

---

[144] See also the discussion of restricted interest infra ¶ 6.06.

[145] IRC § 6601(f). However, if assessment of an underpayment is barred by the statute of limitations, an open overpayment for that year may not be credited against the barred underpayment. IRC § 6514(d).

[146] United States v. LaRosa, 993 F. Supp. 907 (D. Md. 1997) (the court found that the Service erroneously refunded interest because as the result of an agreement between the taxpayers and the Service, overpayments for 1984 and 1985 had effectively been refunded to the taxpayers, not credited to the 1981–1983 tax years, with the result that interest on the 1981–1983 underpayments continued to run). The district court also said that even if there had been a Section 6601(f) credit of the 1984 and 1985 overpayments, interest would have stopped running not only on the 1981–1983 underpayments, but on the 1984–1985 overpayments as well.

[147] See Reg. § 301.6601-1(b)(2), Ex. (1).

ing date of the Year 2 return, even if the Year 2 return is filed early.[148] If the Year 2 return is filed late, the Service has ruled that interest on the Year 1 underpayment continues to run until the date the return is filed because of the operation of Section 6611(b)(3).[149]

> **EXAMPLE 6-4:** Taxpayer A makes an overpayment for 2002 and applies this overpayment to estimated tax due for 2003. Later, the Service determines that there is a deficiency in tax for 2002. The amount of the deficiency is the same as the amount of the overpayment. Interest on the 2002 deficiency runs from the due date of the installment to which the claimed overpayment is applied.[150] Thus, if the 2002 overpayment is not specifically applied to a quarter other than the first quarter, interest on the 2002 deficiency runs from April 15, 2003. If the overpayment is applied to the third quarter, interest on the deficiency runs from September 15, 2003. If A asks that the overpayment be refunded, the interest runs from the date of the refund check.

In Example 6-4, it was assumed that the overpayment was the same amount as the deficiency. If the overpayment is less than the amount of the deficiency, interest on the Year 1 deficiency runs on the portion of the deficiency in excess of the overpayment from the due date of the Year 1 return.

The Service distinguishes between "offsetting," which involves the crediting of overpayments against underpayments for the period when the underpayments and overpayments are *unpaid* and outstanding.[151] Despite Section 6601(f), in a situation called global netting, the Service generally does net interest when a taxpayer has an overpayment in one tax year that overlaps with a deficiency the taxpayer has *paid* for another tax year. The Service also does net interest when a taxpayer has a deficiency in one tax year that overlaps with an overpayment that the Service has already collected for another tax year. The Service's position on global netting is supported by the circuit court's decision in *Northern States Power Co. v. United States*, which held that once a taxpayer's liability was fully paid, there was no "outstanding liability" within the meaning of Section 6402(a) against which the Service had the discretion to apply the taxpayer's subsequent overpayment.[152]

---

[148] Rev. Rul. 88-97, 1988-2 CB 383.

[149] Rev. Rul. 88-97, 1988-2 CB 383, effective for returns filed after October 3, 1982.

[150] Rev. Rul. 89-88, 1988-2 CB 381.

[151] See Notice 96-18, 1996-14 IRB 27 (Apr. 1, 1996).

[152] Northern States Power Co. v. United States, 73 F3d 764 (8th Cir. 1996). In Texas E. Corp. v. United States, 89-2 USTC ¶ 9580 (Cl. Ct. 1989), in 1979 the Service credited overpayments for certain years, 1970 and 1972, against deficiencies for other years, 1970, 1973, and 1974. In 1983, the Service changed its determination that deficiencies were due for 1970 and 1973, and a dispute arose over the amount of statutory interest the Service was required to pay. The Service contended that pursuant to Section 6601(f), it had imposed no deficiency interest on the 1970, 1973, and 1974 deficiencies when it credited the

[b] Elimination of Interest Rate Differential on Overlapping Periods

Pursuant to Congress's directive, in April 1997, Treasury submitted a report to Congress entitled, "Netting of Interest on Tax Overpayments and Underpayments." In addition to describing the issues that arise in global netting when there are different interest rates on overpayments and underpayments, Treasury requested statutory authority to permit global netting. To attempt to solve the interest-netting problem that occurs when taxpayers have both underpayments and overpayments, the 1998 Act provides that there is a zero rate of interest to the extent that underpayments and overpayments were equivalent or overlapped.[153] Section 6601(f), which provides that interest on a tax stops when it is satisfied by the credit of an overpayment, was also amended to provide that Section 6601(f) does not apply to the extent Section 6611(d) applies. This ensures that the zero rate of interest applies as long as there is an overlapping period of underpayment and overpayment, whether or not the overpayment is actually credited to the underpayment, and irrespective of any rate differential. The effective date of this zero rate of interest on overlapping underpayments and overpayments is July 22, 1998, the date of enactment of the 1998 Act, but the zero rate also applies for periods *before* the date of enactment if the taxpayer reasonably identifies and establishes periods of the underpayments and overpayments to which the zero rate applies.[154]

¶ 6.04 ABATEMENT OF UNDERPAYMENT INTEREST

The Service has the authority to abate the interest on a deficiency that is attributable to either a failure by the Service to perform a ministerial act in a timely

---

overpayment. The Court of Federal Claims held that the taxpayer did not pay any deficiency interest when the overpayments were credited against the then determined deficiencies in 1979, even though the Service had the use of the credited amounts until 1983.

[153] IRC § 6621(d), added by 1998 Act § 3301(a). The National Office concluded that it can net overpayment and underpayment interest on different types of taxes (e.g., income, employment, and excise) under Section 6621(d), but that the Service cannot net interest for different taxpayers. FSA 1999-24017 (Mar. 17, 1999). However, the National Office has not decided whether each member of a consolidated group should be treated as the same taxpayer under Section 6621(d). Id. The National Office has also concluded that a taxpayer may apply interest netting as long as the statutory periods for the tax overpayment and underpayment are both open. FSA 1999-18002 (Nov. 4, 1998).

[154] For procedures the Service will follow for interest netting and interest accruing before October 1, 1998, see Rev. Proc. 99-19, 1999-1 CB 842, modified and superseded by Rev. Proc. 99-43, 1999-2 CB 506, discussed infra ¶ 6.04[1]. For procedures applicable to interest accruing on or after October 1, 1998, see Rev. Proc. 2000-26, 2000-1 CB 1257. In general, a net interest rate of zero applies to overlapping tax underpayments and tax overpayments.

manner or an error on the part of the Service in performing a ministerial act.[155] Abatements are subject to the following requirements:

1. There must have been an assessment of interest.
2. The accrual of the interest must be attributable to an error or delay by a Service official in performing a ministerial act.
3. No significant aspect of the delay can have been caused by the taxpayer.
4. The taxpayer must have been contacted by the Service in writing about the deficiency.

Where there has been an erroneous refund, the Service is authorized to abate the assessment of all interest under Section 6602 until the date on which demand for repayment is made unless (1) the erroneous refund exceeds $50,000 or (2) the taxpayer or a related party has caused the delay.[156] It is important to note that this provision is applicable to interest accruing on deficiencies for years after December 31, 1978, and that Congress expects taxpayers to file refund claims for the refund of interest accruing after that year.[157] Abatements of interest apply only to taxes subject to deficiency procedures.[158]

[1] Procedures for Requesting Abatement of Interest

The procedures for requesting abatement of interest are roughly the same as those for seeking the refund of an overpayment of tax, although there is no requirement that the taxpayer must have actually paid the interest.[159] If the Ser-

---

[155] IRC § 6404(e)(1). The Service has issued procedures explaining how taxpayers may apply for a refund, credit, or abatement of interest. Rev. Proc. 87-43, 1987-2 CB 590 (a claim for abatement of an assessment of interest for the period when interest should have been suspended can be filed at any time prior to payment). For IRS procedures, see IRM 45G-342 (May 8, 1988).

[156] IRC § 6404(e)(2).

[157] Magnone v. United States, 89-2 USTC ¶ 9594 (SDNY 1989) (Section 6404(e) applies only to interest accruing on deficiencies for tax years after 1978, and so did not apply to 1974–1976).

[158] IRC § 6404(e)(1). See Woodral v. Comm'r, 112 TC 19 (1999) (because Section 6404(e) refers to the abatement of interest on any payment of any tax described in Section 6212(a) and neither Section 6211 nor Section 6212 refers to employment taxes, "the Commissioner lacks the authority to abate assessments of interest on employment taxes under [Section] 6404(e)").

[159] Rev. Proc. 87-42, 1987-2 CB 589. An abatement request on Form 843 (Claim) should be filed with the Service center where the original return was filed. For further detailed instructions, see Rev. Proc. 87-42, §§ 4.01–4.08. This claim is reviewed by interest abatement coordinators at the Service center and district offices. If the claim is disallowed, the adverse action can be appealed if the taxpayer provides a request for reconsideration in writing describing why the taxpayer believes the adverse action should be

vice denies the taxpayer's request for abatement, judicial review of the action has been denied.[160] It is now settled that the Tax Court, the Court of Federal Claims, and the district courts do not have jurisdiction to review the Service's denial of a taxpayer's request for abatement under Section 6404(e). Courts have given three reasons for not granting judicial review: (1) The statute uses the term "may," not "shall," indicating the Service has discretionary authority; (2) the legislative history implies that abatement was intended to increase the Service's "options for rectifying its errors;" and (3) no standards for judicial review exist.[161]

For interest accruing on deficiencies or payments for tax years beginning after July 30, 1996, if (1) the taxpayer has not caused the error or delay and (2) the Service has contacted the taxpayer in writing, the assessment of interest on a deficiency or payment may be abated to the extent that it is attributable to any "unreasonable" error or delay by Service personnel "in performing a ministerial or managerial act."[162]

---

reconsidered. However, in this type of appeal, the Service does not anticipate that a conference will be necessary, although appeals officers are permitted to hold a conference "when deemed appropriate." Id. at Section 9.

[160] 508 Clinton St. Corp. v. Comm'r, 89 TC 352 (1987). The Court of Federal Claims also stated that it has no jurisdiction to review an IRS refusal to abate interest. Brahms v. United States, 89-2 USTC ¶ 9601 (Cl. Ct. 1989) (IRS refusal to abate interest is not reviewable, because abatement is discretionary, not mandatory, and no standard for judicial review is provided). A district court was also found not to have jurisdiction to review an IRS determination not to abate interest. Horton Homes, Inc. v. United States, 727 F. Supp. 1450 (MD Ga. 1990), aff'd, 936 F2d 548 (11th Cir. 1991) ("short of . . . constitutional contention, judicial review of Service's exercise or nonexercise of discretion under Section 6404(e)(1) is not available"); Selman v. United States, 941 F2d 1060 (10th Cir. 1991) (same).

[161] In *Horton Homes*, the Circuit Court also said,

If the Congress wants the federal courts to review whether the IRS has abused its discretion under section 6404(e)(1) by not granting relief to a taxpayer because of delay by the IRS, then either the Congress must appropriately define what constitutes such a delay, or the Congress must require the Secretary by regulation so to do, or the Secretary, pursuant to his general authority under 26 U.S.C. § 7805, must so do.

The Ninth Circuit in Argabright v. United States, 35 F3d 472 (9th Cir. 1994), followed the decisions in *Selman* and *Horton Homes, Inc.* in concluding that the abatement of interest is a nonreviewable administrative decision. The rationale courts have articulated in judicial review is barred because (1) action is committed to the Service by Section 6404(e)(1); (2) the legislative history provides only an indefinite standard of review; and (3) the Service is authorized to abate interest in its discretion and is not required to abate interest. This rationale is not convincing, because Section 6404(e)(1) itself does not preclude judicial review, and courts review discretionary action by the Service and other administrative agencies under an abuse of discretion standard. There is a possibility that a due process challenge to IRS action may be subject to judicial review. See Argabright v. United States, supra.McDonnell v. Peterson, 93-1 USTC ¶ 50,241 (ND Cal. 1992).

[162] IRC § 6404(e), as amended by the Taxpayer Bill of Rights 2, § 301(a).

[2] Ministerial Acts

Regulations define "ministerial act" as "a procedural or mechanical act that does not involve the exercise of judgment or discretion and that occurs during the processing of a taxpayer's case after all prerequisites to the act, such as conferences and review by supervisors, have taken place."[163] Read literally, this definition restricts interest abatement situations to office delays in issuing notices of deficiencies. Examples of delays caused by ministerial acts, as illustrated in the regulations,[164] include the following:

1. A taxpayer moves before the taxpayer's return is selected for examination, but there is a delay in the transfer of the examination (Ex. 1).
2. There is a delay in the issuance of a notice of deficiency after all conferences and district counsel review have been completed (Ex. 2).
3. In response to a taxpayer's contact of a Service employee and request for the amount owed, the Service employee fails to give the taxpayer current liability information even though the information was available (Ex. 11).

[3] Managerial Acts

Following the legislative history of the change regulations,[165] a managerial act is a loss of records or a personnel management decision, such as the decision to approve a personnel transfer, extended leave, or extended training. Examples of managerial acts included in the proposed regulations are (1) the decision of an agent's supervisor to send an agent to whom the taxpayer's return has been assigned to a training course or another group without reassigning the

---

On January 7, 1998, the Service published proposed regulations. REG-209276-87, proposing to add Prop. Reg. § 301.6404-2. These proposed regulations define "ministerial act," as well as "managerial act," for interest abatement purposes. The term "ministerial act" was used in the Tax Reform Act of 1986 enactment of Section 6404(e)(1) and temporary regulations were issued interpreting the term. See TD 8150, 52 Fed. Reg. 30,162 (Aug. 13, 1987). The proposed regulations were made final by TD 8789, 63 Fed. Reg. 70,012–70,015 (Dec. 18, 1998), effective December 18, 1998, and generally apply to interest accruing for tax years beginning after July 30, 1998. With clarifications regarding estate, gift, and generation-skipping transfer tax, the final regulations do not differ from the proposed regulations.

[163] Reg. § 301.6404-2(b)(2). The National Office has indicated that ministerial acts can include the failure to make a determination on a request for innocent spouse relief for seven years. FSA 1999-24010 (Mar. 15, 1999). The National Office has also ruled that the Service is authorized to abate interest under Section 6404(e) when the tax is the result of a flow-through adjustment of a TEFRA partnership item. FSA 199941010 (July 2, 1999).

[164] Reg. § 301.6404-2(c).

[165] Reg. § 301.6404-2(b)(1).

agent's cases (Exs. 3 and 4) and (2) the misplacing of a file by a clerical employee in a completed examination before a notice of deficiency was prepared and reviewed (Ex. 6).

[4] Net Worth Requirements

For individuals whose net worth does not exceed $2 million or for a business whose net worth does not exceed $7 million, the Tax Court has jurisdiction to determine whether the Service's failure to abate interest under Section 6402 was an abuse of discretion and may order an abatement.[166] The net worth provisions are derived from the provision for the award of attorney fees.[167] It appears that the petitioner in an abatement case must plead and prove that the net worth limitations of Section 7430(c)(4)(A)(ii) and 28 USC § 2412(d)(2)(B) have been satisfied, or the petition will be dismissed.[168]

Because the purpose of Section 6404(g) is to provide increased protection to taxpayers, the Tax Court said that it is inconsistent with that intent to interpret the effective date language "in a manner that would deny judicial review to taxpayers whose requests are continuing, considered, and denied after the date of enactment."[169] However, the Tax Court has held that it does not have jurisdiction over the Service's disallowance of the claim if the claim for abatement was disallowed before the date of abatement.[170] Also, the Tax Court held that the Service did not abuse its discretion in refusing to abate all of the interest that accrued on the taxpayer's deficiency.[171] While a notice of deficiency and a notice of final determination not to abate interest "share similarities in function and purpose," because both are prerequisites to the Tax Court's jurisdiction and start statutorily defined periods for filing a Tax Court petition, without some indication in the notice of deficiency to the contrary, a notice of

---

[166] IRC § 6404(g), added by the Taxpayer Bill of Rights 2, § 302(a).

[167] IRC § 7430(c)(4)(A)(ii).

[168] See Estate of Edward J. Kunze v. Comm'r, TC Memo. 1999-344 (1999) (estate failed to plead and prove that as of the date of death, the net worth of the estate did not exceed $2 million, the net worth limitation for estates under Section 7430(c)(4)(A)(ii) and 28 USC § 2412(d)(2)(B)). Section 6404(g) applies to abatements after the date of enactment, which was July 30, 1996. The Tax Court has ruled that it has jurisdiction over disallowance of claims for abatements that were made before July 31, 1996, if they were disallowed after the date of enactment. Banat v. Comm'r, 109 TC 92 (1997).

[169] Banat v. Comm'r, 109 TC 92, 95 (1997).

[170] White v. Comm'r, 109 TC 96 (1997).

[171] Krugman v. Comm'r, 112 TC 230 (1999).

deficiency does not constitute a notice of final determination not to abate interest.[172]

The taxpayer must file a petition for review in the Tax Court within 180 days after the date of the Service's final determination not to abate the interest.[173] As long as the Tax Court has jurisdiction over a deficiency for a year or years, Section 6512(b) grants the Tax Court jurisdiction to determine the amount of the overpayment either (1) because the Tax Court found that not only is there no deficiency for the year, but that the taxpayer has overpaid the tax due for the year, or (2) that there is a deficiency, but that the taxpayer has made an overpayment. Because an overpayment includes interest, under its overpayment jurisdiction (unlike its deficiency jurisdiction), the Tax Court may review the Service's determination not to abate interest.[174]

When a taxpayer has timely filed a petition for review and has properly invoked the Tax Court's jurisdiction, the court has jurisdiction to review the Commissioner's failure to abate interest under all subsections of Section 6404, not solely denials for claims for abatement the Service has denied under Section 6404(e), as the Service has contended.[175] In *Lee v. Commissioner*, the Tax Court stated that for a taxpayer to prove that the Service abused its discretion in failing to abate interest, the taxpayer must show that the Service "exercised [its] discretion arbitrarily, capriciously, or without sound basis in fact or law."[176] Where a "ministerial act" is alleged to have caused the delay, the Tax

---

[172] Bourekis v. Comm'r, 110 TC 20 (1998). See Gati v. Comm'r, 113 TC 132 (1999) (the Service mailed the final determination letter to the taxpayers on August 13, 1998; the 180-day filing period of Section 6404(g)(1) expired on February 9, 1999, but the taxpayers did not mail their petition to the Tax Court until February 15, 1999, and the Tax Court did not receive the petition until February 17, 1999; held, the petition for review was untimely filed and the Tax Court lacked jurisdiction over the interest abatement petition).

[173] Rules similar to those generally pertaining to the filing of a petition in the Tax Court apply to determine the date of mailing the petition for review. IRC § 6404(g)(2)(A) (1996). Presumably, the timely mailed, timely filed rule applies. In addition, the relief granted in the review proceeding is similar to the overpayment jurisdiction of the Tax Court provided in Section 6512(b). IRC § 6404(g)(2)(B) (1996). The Tax Court's decision is reviewable by the circuit courts of appeal in the same manner as other Tax Court decisions. IRC § 6404(g)(2)(C) (1996).

[174] Winn-Dixie Stores, Inc. v. Comm'r, 110 TC 291 (1998). The Tax Court held that Section 6512(b)(4), which provides that the Tax Court has "no jurisdiction . . . to restrain or review any credit or reduction made by the [Service] under [S]ection 6402" only applies to the Tax Court's review of the Service's use of its discretion under Section 6402 to reduce a refund by way of credit or reduction or the merits of such a reduction of a refund after the Service has made the reduction.

[175] Woodral v. Comm'r, 112 TC 19 (1999). The Service has acquiesced in this decision. AOD 1999-015 (Oct. 18, 1999).

[176] Lee v. Comm'r, 113 TC 145 (1999), citing Woodral v. Comm'r, 112 TC 19, 23 (1999). Note that the delay must be attributable to a post-notice delay of the Service, not a change or clarification of the applicable law. See Sims v. Comm'r, TC Memo. 1999-414

Court, relying on statements in the legislative history of Section 6404(e), limited ministerial acts to nondiscretionary acts where all preliminary administrative and statutory prerequisites to action have taken place. Based on its interpretation that the term "ministerial act" means a nondiscretionary act, the Tax Court held that (1) the eleven years the Service took from the date it sent a notice of deficiency to resolve a Tax Court case with the taxpayer was not the result of a ministerial act but rather the Service's exercise of judgment that as a matter of litigation strategy, a related criminal case should be pursued first; (2) the time to process the taxpayer's innocent spouse claim was necessary to permit the Service to exercise judgment and discretion about whether the taxpayer had met the requirements of the innocent spouse statute; and (3) the taxpayer had not provided Service officials with relevant information, and so any delay was attributable to the taxpayer.[177]

¶ 6.05 INCREASED RATE ON LARGE CORPORATE UNDERPAYMENTS

As described previously, individuals are not permitted to deduct interest on federal taxes after 1990, while corporations are permitted such a deduction. Interest accruing after 1990 on a C corporation's underpayment of any tax that exceeds $100,000 is calculated at a higher rate than the normal underpayment rate.[178] On these large corporate underpayments, instead of the normal underpayment rate equal to the short-term federal rate plus three percentage points, the rate is two percentage points higher—the short-term federal rate plus five percentage points.[179] The events triggering this increased interest rate present some procedural anomalies. In general, however, interest begins to run at the increased rate on the entire amount of an underpayment (i.e., tax, penalty, and interest) thirty days after the date of a thirty-day letter or a notice of deficiency.[180]

The Taxpayer Relief Act of 1997 created an exception to the triggering of the increased interest rate when a letter or notice is received for small amounts. Any letter or notice is disregarded if the amount of the deficiency or proposed deficiency (or the assessment or proposed assessment) set forth in the

---

(1999) (assertion of deficiency was the result of a decision of the Supreme Court on the issue, not Service's delay).

[177] Lee v. Comm'r, 113 TC 145, 150–152 (1999).

[178] IRC § 6621(c), added by Omnibus Budget Reconciliation Act of 1990, § 11341(a).

[179] IRC § 6621(c)(1).

[180] IRC § 6621(c)(2)(A).

letter or notice is not greater than $100,000, excluding penalties, interest, and additions to tax.[181] As the statute stands, "hot interest" begins to run on a large corporate underpayment after the "applicable date," which is the thirtieth day *after* the date on which the first letter of proposed deficiency (the thirty-day letter), a notice of deficiency, or a notice or letter of assessment or proposed assessment is sent to the taxpayer. For periods before January 1, 1998, the amount of the underpayment shown in the letter is irrelevant. However, because of the change made by the Taxpayer Relief Act of 1997, after December 31, 1997, hot interest accrues on an underpayment only to the extent that the underpayment exceeds $100,000, for underpayment periods (not taxable periods) occurring after December 31, 1997.[182]

The statutory reference in Section 6621(c) to the thirty-day letter is unprecedented. Although the Statement of Procedural Rules provides for Appeals conferences and the viability of the judicial system depends on high settlement rates in Appeals, the Code itself is silent about Appeals conferences; and the Service has argued that its procedural rules do not give taxpayers any right to an Appeals conference.[183] Section 6621(c) acknowledges the role of the Appeals system in an explicit way. It provides that interest at the increased rate on large corporate underpayments begins to run thirty days after "the date on which the 1st letter of proposed deficiency which allows the taxpayer an opportunity for administrative review in the Internal Revenue Service Office of Appeals is sent."[184] Thus, one of the events triggering the increased interest rate strips the veil of anonymity away from the Appeals conference, as far as the Code is concerned. It remains to be seen what effect this will have on future Service arguments that taxpayers have no right to an Appeals conference.

---

[181] IRC § 6621(c)(2)(B)(iii), added by the Taxpayer Relief Act of 1997 § 1463(a), is applicable for the purpose of determining interest for periods after December 31, 1997.

[182] If the date of the notice or letter was dated before January 1, 1998, and the amount of the notice is less than $100,000, hot interest runs on the less-than-$100,000 portion of the corporate underpayment from the applicable date and stops on December 31, 1997. Hot interest will still run thirty days after the date of a thirty-day letter, notice of deficiency, or assessment notice if the amount of the letter or notice was in excess of $100,000 on the amount of the underpayment in excess of the $100,000 amount. In other words, if the letter or notice is sent before January 1, 1998, and the amount of the notice is more than $100,000, hot interest will run on the amount in excess of the amount exceeding $100,000 on January 1, 1998; however, if the amount of the letter or notice was less than $100,000, hot interest stops on December 31, 1997. Chief Counsel Significant Service Center Advice 1998-011 (Feb. 2, 1998), reprinted in 98 TNT 104-81.

[183] Jeopardy assessment procedures contemplate an Appeals conference when a request for review is made by a taxpayer. IRC § 7429(a)(2). To recover attorney fees, a taxpayer must have exhausted the administrative remedies the Service provides, including an appeals conference. IRC § 6621(c)(2)(A).

[184] IRC § 6621(c)(2)(A)(i).

If, for some reason (presumably the refusal to extend the statute of limitations or assessment), a notice of deficiency is sent before the thirty-day letter offering the Appeals conference, the increased rate begins to run thirty days after the date of the notice of deficiency.[185] For purposes of this discussion, it is important to note that Section 6213(b)(4) provides, "In any case where such amount [the amount reflected in the statutory notice] is paid after the mailing of a notice of deficiency under section 6212, such payment shall not deprive the Tax Court of jurisdiction over such deficiency determined under section 6211 without regard to such assessment." In other words, the Tax Court can still exercise jurisdiction over a case where a taxpayer makes payment of a deficiency, as long as the payment is made after the date of the notice of deficiency.

The Tax Court does not have jurisdiction over all taxes; therefore, C corporations will not always receive a notice of deficiency. A special rule deals with the increased rate on large corporate underpayments of these nondeficiency taxes, such as many excise taxes and employment and Social Security taxes. Increased interest begins to run on these taxes thirty days after the date of the notice of assessment or proposed assessment.[186]

There is some relief provided to the corporate taxpayer, not in Section 6621(c), but in the Conference Report:[187]

Under present law, the Secretary has the authority to credit the amount of any overpayment against any liability under the Code (sec. 6402). To the extent a portion of tax due is satisfied by a credit of any overpayment, no interest is imposed on that portion of the tax (sec. 6601(f)). The Secretary should implement the most comprehensive crediting procedures under section 6402 that are consistent with sound administrative practice.

Corporations have already experienced difficulties with Service Centers over whether overpayments can be credited and over the date and amounts of credits. Consequently, even assuming that these regulations eventually appear, lively correspondence between corporations and Service Centers can be expected when additional interest payments are at issue.

Regulations interpreting Section 6621(c) have a number of significant features. The most significant feature is the adoption of a concept called the "threshold underpayment of tax," defined as the excess of a tax imposed *excluding* interest, penalties, additional amounts, and additions to tax for the taxable period over the amount of the tax paid on or before the last date

---

[185] IRC § 6621(c)(2)(A)(ii).

[186] IRC § 6621(c)(2)(B)(i).

[187] HR Conf. Rep., 101st Cong., 2d Sess. 102–103 (1990), reprinted in 1990-3 CB (vol. 3) 1100–1101.

prescribed for payment.[188] Thus, the threshold underpayment differs from the normal underpayment in that it includes only the principal amount of tax.

The concept of the threshold underpayment was adopted because, if the general definition of "underpayment of tax" were used to determine whether the Section 6621(c) interest rate were applicable, the amount of an underpayment would depend, at least in part, on how much time passed between the last day prescribed for payment and the assessment date. An underpayment might total less than $100,000 as of the thirty-first day following a thirty-day letter, for example; but as a result of the accumulation of interest, the underpayment might be greater than $100,000 at the time of assessment. The Service felt, therefore, that a taxpayer would not be able to know before the assessment date whether the increased rate applied. The concept of a threshold underpayment is used by the regulations solely for the purpose of determining whether an underpayment is a large corporate underpayment, and it differs from the definition of "underpayment" in that it does not include interest, penalties, and the like.

Several rules affect the calculation of the threshold underpayment. Payments made after the last day prescribed for payment do not reduce the threshold underpayment. For example, if a taxpayer files an amended return, any payment made with that amended return does not affect the threshold underpayment if the payment is made after the last day prescribed for payment. On the other hand, different types of taxes and amounts that relate to different taxable periods are not added together to increase the threshold underpayment. For example, an income tax underpayment and a FICA tax underpayment are not aggregated even if they apply to the same tax year. It is important to note that the temporary regulations adopt a procedural rule that the existence of a threshold underpayment of tax and the amount of a large corporate underpayment are determined only when assessment is made for the taxable period. This means that the amount of a deficiency or proposed deficiency set forth in a letter or notice does not determine whether there is a large corporate underpayment.

The operation of the threshold amount concept is illustrated by several examples in the regulations. The notion that the threshold amount applies to the principal amount of tax rather than the amount of tax and accumulated interest is illustrated by the following example:

EXAMPLE 6-5: *V*, a C corporation, timely files Form 941 on January 31, 1991, for the fourth quarter of 1990. On September 1, 1992, the Service sends *V* a notice and demand reflecting an additional FICA tax liability of $90,000 for the fourth quarter of 1990. On the date of the notice, September 1, 1992, interest computed at the normal underpayment rate totals $15,000. Accordingly, *V*'s underpayment of FICA tax for the fourth quar-

---

[188] Reg. § 301.6621-3T(b)(2)(ii).

ter of 1990 exceeds $100,000. However, the threshold underpayment of FICA tax is $90,000, which is less than $100,000, so that the large corporate underpayment rate does not apply to the underpayment for the fourth quarter of 1990.[189]

Using the above example to continue the illustration, if the amount that was due for the fourth quarter of 1990 was in excess of $100,000 (e.g., $110,000), and on September 1, 1992, the Service sent V a notice and demand, the underpayment would be a large corporate underpayment, and interest at the Section 6621(c) rate would apply to the underpayment if payment were not made by V before October 1, 1992. If V pays the amount of the notice and demand within the thirty-day period beginning after the date of the notice, the notice is disregarded for purposes of determining the existence of a large corporate underpayment.[190]

Significantly, however, the regulations provide that if a taxpayer is sent a notice of deficiency and, within the thirty-day period following the date of the notice, makes a deposit in the nature of a cash bond, the deposit is not considered a payment of the amount shown as due on the ninety-day letter.[191] As a result, if the notice is for an amount greater than $100,000 and this amount is upheld by the Tax Court (or if it is a lesser amount that is greater than $100,000), interest at the higher large corporate underpayment rate would run from the thirty-first day following the date of the notice. However, the deposit reduces the amount of interest that the taxpayer ultimately owes.

There is another aspect of the regulations that can affect interest or a large corporate underpayment. If a taxpayer receives a notice of an adjustment, such as a mathematical error, the notice is considered a situation to which the deficiency procedures do not apply; and it can trigger the large corporate underpayment rate unless it is paid within thirty days after the date of the notice. This can happen if, after the date of the mathematical error notice, the Service examines the tax return of the taxpayer and issues a thirty-day letter. If the taxpayer pays the full amount shown as due on the mathematical error assessment notice within thirty days after the date of the notice, the applicable date for purposes of the Section 6621(c) interest is the thirtieth day after the date on which the thirty-day letter is sent. However, if the taxpayer chooses to contest the mathematical error assessment notice or does not pay it within the thirty-day period, the applicable date is the thirtieth day after the date on which the mathematical error assessment notice is sent.[192]

---

[189] Reg. § 301.6621-3(d), Ex. (1).

[190] Reg. § 301.6621-3(c)(4).

[191] Reg. § 301.6621-3(c)(4)(iii).

[192] Reg. §§ 301.6621-3T(c)(3), 301.6621-3T(d), Exs. (2), (4).

However, the Tax Court has ruled that it lacks jurisdiction to redetermine liability for Section 6621(c) "hot interest" in a deficiency proceeding.[193]

To understand the operation of Section 6621 and why it is anomalous from a procedural point of view, an example may be helpful.

EXAMPLE 6-6: A corporation, having extended the limitations period to allow time for appeals consideration, receives a thirty-day letter and examination report in which the district has determined a $150,000 deficiency in income tax for the year 1989. The thirty-day letter is dated March 1, 1992. The interest rate on the deficiency or underpayment is the normal rate until January 1, 1991. On and after that date, the interest rate is the enhanced rate unless the corporation pays the amount of the deficiency on or before March 31, 1992.

Suppose, however, that the corporation in Example 6-6 wishes to contest adjustments that the district has proposed that are not eliminated or settled in Appeals. If the corporation pays the full amount of the district-proposed deficiency and the accrued normal interest, no notice of deficiency will be sent (and the case cannot be heard by the Tax Court), because there technically is no deficiency. The corporation's payment will have eliminated it. Thus, Section 6621(c) could have the unanticipated result of reducing the flow of cases to the Tax Court. As described, however, if the district sends a notice of deficiency, the corporation can pay the deficiency without the elimination of the deficiency and the Tax Court's jurisdiction.

Assuming that a thirty-day letter is sent, in order to ensure receipt of a notice of deficiency and Tax Court review, the corporation could remit a deposit in the nature of a cash bond, if Service procedures are followed.[194] However, a deposit is not technically a payment; so under a literal interpretation, a deposit would not stop the imposition of Section 6621(c) interest. Whether a deposit or a payment is made, the reality is that district adjustments are significantly reduced at the Appeals level.[195] Although the temporary regulations may mitigate the problem, in the typical case Section 6621(c) appears to require the corporation to pay a greater deficiency and more interest than is likely to be owed, even according to the Service. This can create a windfall for the government because an overpayment is refunded with interest calculated at the lower overpayment rate, and that interest is, of course, taxable. From a financial viewpoint, to make a decision whether to pay after the thirty-day letter or later at a higher rate, corporations figure the cost of borrowing, cash resources, and the after-tax result of payment and refund. Partial payments of district adjustments in order to receive a notice of deficiency require similar calculations

---

[193] Lincir v. Comm'r, 115 TC 293 (2000).

[194] For discussion of these procedures, see ¶ 6.02[3][a][ii].

[195] For Appeals settlement rates, see ¶ 9.01[1].

based, in part, on a forecast of the issues on which Appeals will reverse the district. All of this seems unduly complex from the corporate taxpayer's side, especially when those corporations are operating in difficult economic times.

¶ 6.06 INTEREST ON ERRONEOUS REFUNDS

The Service may make an erroneous refund of an internal revenue tax to a taxpayer. In such instances, the Service may institute a suit for recovery of the erroneous refund.[196] The Service also may recover interest, at the annual rate, from the date of the payment of the refund to the date repayment is received.[197]

¶ 6.07 INTEREST ON OVERPAYMENTS

The government must pay interest at the rate determined under Section 6621 to any taxpayer who has overpaid any internal revenue tax.[198] Overpayment interest is compounded daily.[199] The interest rate on overpayments (the overpayment rate) is the short-term federal rate plus 2 percent.[200] Interest on an overpayment begins to run from the date of overpayment. The 1998 Act changed the overpayment rate for individuals and other noncorporate taxpayers from the federal short-term rate plus 2 percent to the federal short-term rate plus 3 percent.[201] The general overpayment rate for corporations remains at 2 percent. This rate change is effective for the second quarter and succeeding quarters after the date of enactment of the 1998 Act, July 22, 1998.

An overpayment occurs when a taxpayer pays an amount that is greater than the amount required to satisfy his entire correct tax liability.[202] Therefore, a taxpayer cannot make an overpayment in tax until he satisfies the entire tax

---

[196] IRC § 7405.

[197] IRC § 6602.

[198] IRC § 6611(a). Interest is also due on a refund made under a retroactive tax treaty. Brown & Williamson, Ltd. v. United States, 688 F2d 747 (Ct. Cl. 1982). The Service follows this decision and pays interest on refunds from the date tax was paid, not the effective date of the treaty. Rev. Rul. 84-123, 1984-2 CB 244. See also Rev. Proc. 84-60, 1984-2 CB 504.

[199] IRC § 6622. For illustrations of how daily compounding works, see Reg. § 301.6622-1.

[200] IRC § 6621(a)(1), effective for interest after December 31, 1986.

[201] IRC § 6621(a)(1)(B).

[202] See Chapter 11 for a more detailed analysis of overpayments.

liability (including any interest, addition to tax, or additional amount) and then makes a payment that, when added to all others he may have made, is in excess of the tax liability.[203] Of course, the tax liability used in determining whether the payment is an overpayment is the taxpayer's correct tax liability for the year, not the tax liability that may have been reported on the tax return.

To obtain the refund of an overpayment, generally a taxpayer must file a claim for refund within three years after the return was filed, if the overpaid tax is claimed to have been paid with the return, or two years from the date the tax was otherwise paid.[204] Once an overpayment is determined to have been made, interest on the overpayment runs from (1) the date of the overpayment to (2) the date the overpayment is either credited against some other liability or refunded. Interest is not allowed on an overpayment for the period during which a return is delinquent.[205] Also, until a return is filed in processable form (containing such information as the taxpayer's name, address, identifying number, signature, and sufficient information to permit checking a tax computation), the return is not considered filed for purposes of the payment of interest.[206]

The procedure for obtaining interest on overpayments is almost automatic. The Service computes the amount of interest allowable on an overpayment without a separate claim for refund. In other words, a claim for refund of an overpayment implicitly carries with it a claim for refund of interest as provided by law. Careful practitioners nevertheless add language to this effect to a claim for refund.[207] In the event that there is a controversy over the amount of interest, the usual administrative review procedures apply. If both the amount of the overpayment and the interest thereon are in dispute, a taxpayer may seek judicial review under the normal refund procedures by suit in a district court or the Court of Federal Claims.[208] Where a dispute regards only the amount of interest payable, the claim is not simply a claim for refund but a general claim against the United States.[209] Thus, the suit must be brought

---

[203] Reg. § 301.6611-1(b).

[204] IRC § 6511(a).

[205] IRC § 6611(b), applicable to returns filed after October 3, 1982.

[206] IRC § 6611(i).

[207] See ¶ 11.10 for a discussion of claim preparation.

[208] 28 USC § 1346(a)(1).

[209] Rev. Rul. 57-242, 1957-1 CB 452; Rev. Rul. 56-506, 1956-2 CB 959. See also Lyons v. United States, 93-1 USTC ¶ 50,026 (SD Iowa 1992) (taxpayer sought refund of interest on 1979 overpayment that the Service said had been paid by applying amount to contested liability for 1980). The National Office has concluded that a taxpayer who files an application for a tentative refund (Form 1139) has a right to interest on any amounts refunded by the Service after the statutory forty-five-day period. FSA 1999-1058 (July 9, 1993).

within six years after the cause of action first accrues in which the credit or refund is allowed.[210]

[1] The Date of Overpayment

A number of special rules establish the date of overpayment in different situations. However, where there is no special rule, the date the excess payment is received by the district director or Service center controls.[211]

[a] Overpayments Created by Carrybacks

An overpayment can be created by way of the carryback of (1) a net operating or capital loss;[212] (2) a credit;[213] or (3) a foreign tax credit[214] from the year of the excess loss or credit (the loss or credit year) to the tax previously paid in an earlier year (the carryback year). In this situation, there is no actual overpayment in the carryback year. An overpayment resulting from a net operating loss or capital loss carryback, or a credit carryback as defined in Section 6511(d)(4)(C), is treated as having occurred on the due date without regard to extensions of the return for the loss year.[215] The same is true in the case of an

---

[210] Barnes v. United States, 137 F. Supp. 716 (Ct. Cl.), cert. denied, 351 US 933 (1956). The date the overassessment is scheduled would appear to be the date of allowance. IRC § 6407.

[211] See Reg. § 301.6611-1(b); Republic Oil Ref. Co. v. Grainger, 98 F. Supp. 921 (WD Pa. 1951), aff'd on other grounds, 198 F2d 161 (3d Cir. 1952). Where a refund is payable as a result of a retroactive change in law, the date of the overpayment is the date of payment, rather than the effective date of the statute or treaty. Brown & Williamson, Ltd. v. United States, 688 F2d 747 (Ct. Cl. 1982). For returns filed after October 3, 1982, notwithstanding the date the excess payment is received, no interest is allowed before the date that the return is filed, if the return is filed late (determined with regard to extensions). Furthermore, the return is not deemed filed unless it is filed in processable form (as defined). IRC §§ 6611(b)(3), 6611(i).

[212] IRC § 6611(f)(1).

[213] IRC § 6611(f)(3).

[214] IRC § 6611(f)(2), added by the Taxpayer Relief Act of 1997 § 1055(b), effective for foreign tax credit carrybacks arising in taxable years beginning after August 5, 1997.

[215] IRC § 6611(f)(4)(A). The Taxpayer Relief Act of 1997 § 1055(b)(2) redesignated subclause II of Section 6611(f)(4)(B)(ii) as subclause III, and added as a new clause II the provision that the loss year in the case of a foreign tax credit carryback is the taxable year in which the foreign taxes were in fact paid or accrued, or when the carryback was created by the carryback of a net operating loss or capital loss carryback, the taxable year giving rise to the net operating loss or capital loss carryback. For computation of interest on an overpayment caused by an investment credit carryback eliminated by a later net operating loss carryback, see Rev. Rul. 82-172, 1982-2 CB 397. The Treasury has issued proposed regulations providing rules on the period during which interest accrues on under-

overpayment resulting from the carryback of a foreign tax credit.[216] However, the rules for the accrual of interest are different. If an overpayment results from a net operating or capital loss carryback, or credit carryback as defined in Section 6511(d)(4)(C), then (1) the overpayment is treated as an overpayment for the loss year and (2) the return for the loss year is treated as having been filed on the last date prescribed for filing determined without extensions.[217] The effect of this treatment is to deny interest on an overpayment resulting from these types of carrybacks for the period from the date the tax for the carryback year was paid to the filing date of the return for the year in which the net operating loss or credit carryback arose. No interest is payable if the overpayment for the loss year is refunded within forty-five days after the later of the filing of the claim for refund of the overpayment or the filing date of the tax returns for the loss year.[218] If the refund is made after this forty-five day period, then interest accrues from the filing date of the return.

In the case of an overpayment resulting from the carryback of a foreign tax credit, Section 6611(f) does not apply, and the overpayment is treated as an overpayment for the carryback year.[219]

---

payments and overpayments attributable to carrybacks. See LR-280-82, 1984-2 CB 860. See Prop. Reg. § 301.6611-1.

[216] IRC § 6611(f)(2), added by the Taxpayer Relief Act § 1155(b). Section 6611(f)(2) clarifies the principle that if an overpayment of tax for a year results from the carryback of an excess foreign tax credit, the overpayment is not considered to have been made before the filing date of the taxable year giving rise to the excess foreign tax credit. If the foreign tax credit carryback arises from a net operating loss or capital loss carryback from a later year, the overpayment is also considered not to have been made before the filing date for that later taxable year.

[217] IRC § 6611(f)(3)(A).

[218] Reg. § 301.6611(f)(2)(A). Section 6611(f) refers to the return for the loss year. Presumably, an application for tentative carryback adjustment or claim for refund for the carryback year would suffice without the filing of the return for the loss year. Proposed regulations define the due date for purposes of the accrual of interest as "the date fixed for the payment of tax or the several installments thereof." Reg. § 301.6611-1(b)(2)(ii). However, no interest "shall be allowed or paid for any day before the date on which the return is filed (in processable form)." Prop. Reg. § 301.6611-1(b)(4). IRC § 6611(e). The Conference Report (p. 597) indicates that the Service should not have to pay interest if it made a refund within ninety days. For a letter ruling determining the computation of interest both before and after October 4, 1982 (the effective date of the TEFRA amendments to Section 6611), see Ltr. Rul. 8431006 (Apr. 20, 1984).

When a taxpayer submits a tentative carryback claim under Section 6411(a) and the Service refunds the amount claimed within forty-five days pursuant to Sections 6611(f)(3)(B) and 601(e), and the Service later determines that the amount refunded exceeded the amount of the refund actually owed to the taxpayer, the taxpayer is not entitled to interest on the amount that is less than its original claim. Soo Line RR Co. v. United States, 84 AFTR2d 99-6292 (Fed. Cl. 1999).

[219] Section 6611(f) does not apply because Section 6611(f)(2)(B) provides that a credit carryback has the same meaning as given in Section 6511(d)(4)(C), which does not

The taxpayer does need to claim the carryback to start the accrual of interest. At least this was true until the Taxpayer Relief Act of 1997. For foreign tax credit carrybacks arising in taxable years after August 5, 1997, Section 6611(f)(2) provides that when an overpayment results from the carryback of an excess foreign tax credit, the overpayment is considered not to have been made before the filing date for the taxable year in which the foreign tax was in fact paid or accrued; and if the foreign tax credit carryback that produces the overpayment, in turn, became available through the carryback of a later year's net operating loss or capital loss carryback, interest does not begin to run until the due date of the return for the later year.[220] Similarly, the time for filing a claim for refund of the overpayment attributable to the carryback of the foreign tax credit is ten years from the due date of the return for the year in which the foreign taxes were actually paid or accrued.[221] Interest starts to accrue on the actual due date of the tax return for the year in which the foreign taxes were paid or accrued.[222]

[b] Credits of Overpayments

If an overpayment of tax is credited, interest is allowed from the day of the overpayment to the due date of the amount against which the overpayment is credited.[223] Therefore, for interest to be allowable, the overpayment must be made for a year preceding the due date of the tax liability to which it is credited.[224] Otherwise, there is no time during which the government has had use of the taxpayer's money.

---

include carrybacks of foreign tax credits. Consequently, Section 6611(g) governs the date on which an overpayment arises for purposes of Section 6611(b).

[220] IRC § 6611(f)(2) was added by the Taxpayer Relief Act of 1997 § 1155(b), which also redesignated former IRC §§ 6611(f)(2), 6611(f)(3), and 6611(f)(4).

[221] IRC § 6511(d)(3)(A), amended by the Taxpayer Relief Act of 1997 § 1056(a), applicable to foreign taxes paid or accrued in tax years beginning after August 5, 1997. Before amendment, the ten-year period ran from the date with respect to which the claim was made.

[222] IRC § 6611(g). The National Office has issued technical advice to this effect. See Tech. Adv. Mem. 8437011 (May 30, 1984). In Ltr. Rul. 8320004 (Jan. 19, 1983), the Service ruled that it had to pay interest on overpayments that resulted from foreign tax credit carrybacks, even though the carrybacks were eliminated by subsequent refunds of the foreign taxes. It determined that the taxpayer's underlying claims of interest survived until the date that the foreign government refunded the taxes. Thus, under Section 6611(g), prior to amendment by TEFRA, the interest was owing from the day after the close of the taxable year in which the foreign taxes were paid to the day of receipt of the foreign tax refunds.

[223] Reg. § 301.6611-1(h)(1).

[224] See Rev. Proc. 84-58, 1984-2 CB 501, effective for remittances made on or after October 1, 1984.

EXAMPLE 6-7: An overpayment in a taxpayer's income tax is reflected on a timely filed individual 1989 income tax return. This overpayment is credited against a subsequent underpayment in income tax for 1990. Interest is allowed on the overpayment from April 15, 1990, to the due date of the amount against which it is credited, April 15, 1991. However, if an overpayment reflected on the 1989 tax return were credited against an underpayment for a year before the date of overpayment (e.g., 1988), no interest would be allowable because the date of the overpayment (April 15, 1990) is later than the due date of the amount against which it is credited (April 15, 1988).

The due date for payment of a tax generally is the date fixed for payment of tax.[225] Moreover, no interest is allowed on an overpayment shown on a taxpayer's return that he elects to apply to his estimated tax for the following year.[226]

Generally, once an overpayment is credited to satisfy a taxpayer's liability, interest no longer accrues on that liability.[227] The effect of this statutory rule of Section 6601(f) on the compounding of interest on an underpayment is that once an overpayment is credited to satisfy the taxpayer's liability for the interest portion of the underpayment, that credit cuts off any further compounding of interest; that is, interest no longer accrues on the interest portion of the underpayment satisfied by the credit.[228] Also, no interest accrues on the

---

[225] Reg. § 301.6611-1(h)(2). However, the due date when installment payments are made or are due is subject to a number of special rules depending on whether the installment is delinquent or is not yet due. Reg. §§ 301.6611-1(h)(2)(ii)(b), 301.6611-1(h)(2)(iii). If an overpayment is credited against an amount assessed as an additional amount, addition to the tax, or assessable penalty, the due date is the date of assessment. Reg. § 301.6611-1(h)(2)(vi). If an overpayment is credited against a deficiency arising out of an excessive or erroneous refund, the "due date of the amount against which the credit is taken" means the date of the excessive refund check. Tech. Adv. Mem. 9443007 (May 19, 1994).

[226] Reg. § 301.6611-1(h)(2)(vii).

[227] IRC § 6611(f). Marsh & McLennan Co. v. United States, 88 AFTR2d 2001-5381 (Ct. Fed. Cl. 2001) (holding that taxpayer was entitled to interest on overpayment calculated until the due date of the return for the later tax year against which the overpayment was applied).

[228] Reg. § 301.6611-1(h)(2)(v), added by TD 8524, published in the Federal Register dated March 3, 1994, and effective for credits made on or after August 25, 1992. Under "old" Reg. § 301.6611-1(h)(2)(v) interest runs on an overpayment that offsets interest on the deficiency from the due date of the return for the overpayment year until the date the deficiency interest is paid. In 1994, the Treasury amended the regulation to provide that interest is due as it accrues without regard to an assessment, although assessment is to be made as soon as possible. The difference between the two versions of the same regulation was at issue in Pettibone Corp. v. United States, 34 F3d 536 (7th Cir. 1994), because under the old version the taxpayer, which had filed for a reorganization under the Bankruptcy Code, was entitled to greater interest. The circuit court agreed with the taxpayer that the old version applied, holding that the Service had failed to show how the new ver-

taxpayer's overpayment after the overpayment is credited to satisfy the tax-payer's liability for interest.[229] When an overpayment is credited to a penalty, no interest accrues on the overpayment from the due date of the return to which the penalty relates.[230]

[c] Advance Remittances

The classification of a taxpayer's remittance to the Service as an overpay-ment is important for both interest and refund purposes. A taxpayer is entitled to the refund of an overpayment only if he files a claim for refund within two years after the payment date. If a taxpayer files a timely claim, he is also enti-tled to interest on the amount of the overpayment from the date the overpay-ment was made. Accordingly, the interest regulations provide that in the case of an advance payment of a tax, a payment of estimated tax, or a credit of in-come tax withholding, the date an overpayment is made is to be determined under the provisions of the refund statute[231] applicable in determining the date of payment for purposes of the period of limitations on credit or refund.[232]

---

sion had merely "clarified" the old version. The circuit court used the following example to illustrate the differences in the method:

> Suppose that in 1980, the taxpayer had a net underpayment of $1 million and in 1981 had made a $3 million overpayment. Assume further that the interest rate on an un-derpayment is 10 percent. Interest on the $1 million underpayment for one year is $100,000. Under the "new" version of the regulation, the taxpayer would owe $1.1 million at the time that it made the $3 million overpayment. Consequently, the IRS would owe the taxpayer $1.9 million, on which interest runs.

Id. Under the old version, the $100,000 interest would not be deducted from the $2 mil-lion net overpayment, but would be separately stated. Compound interest would continue to run on both the underpayment or deficiency interest of $100,000, and the net overpay-ment of $2 million, until the deficiency interest is assessed.

[229] Reg. § 301.6611-1(h)(2)(v), added by TD 8524, published in the Federal Register dated March 3, 1994, and effective for credits made on or after August 25, 1992. The Na-tional Office has advised that overpayment interest accrues only to the due date of the re-turn for the year in which the overpayment is applied, not to the actual date on which the underpayment arose. FSA 1999-2005 (Mar. 4, 1999). See FSA 200045006 (July 14, 2000) (where a net operating loss carryback from an excess loss year produces an overpayment that is then used to apply to an estimated tax installment due for a future year, the tax-payer is not entitled to interest on the overpayment because it is a "voluntary anticipatory remittance" of the estimated tax installment).

[230] Reg. § 301.6611-1(h)(2)(vi).

[231] IRC § 6513.

[232] Reg. § 301.6611-1(d). For example, when, under Section 1442, a withholding agent withholds tax from a foreign corporation improperly or overwithholds, the taxes withheld at source are deemed paid under Section 6513(b) on the last day prescribed for filing the return required by Section 6012 (i.e., the date when foreign corporations are re-quired to file the Form 1120-F) and, therefore, the tax is deemed overpaid on that date under Section 6611(d). MNOPF Trustees Ltd. v. United States, 33 Fed. Cl. 755 (Cl. Ct.

The classification of a taxpayer's remittance as a mere deposit or as a payment giving rise to an overpayment within the meaning of the refund and interest provisions has been the subject of considerable controversy. This issue arises where a taxpayer remits to the Service an amount of money considered to be sufficient to stop the running of interest or penalties before any tax has been assessed. In *Rosenman v. United States*,[233] the Supreme Court held that the period of limitations on refund claims requiring that a claim be filed within three years "after the payment of tax" begins to run from the date the tax was assessed, rather than from an earlier date when the taxpayer had made a general payment on account of estimated estate taxes. Accordingly, no tax payment was made until there had been an assessment and it had been satisfied in part out of the monies already deposited with the Service. The Supreme Court based its opinion in substantial part on the Service's long-standing position that interest began to run against the government on a taxpayer's payments in excess of the correct tax from the date of assessment. As the Court said, "It will not do to treat the same transaction as payment and not as payment, whichever favors the government."[234]

By the time the Supreme Court decided *Rosenman*, Congress had adopted the current tax payment system, which operates through wage withholding as well as estimated tax payments. Since it was expected that under this system a taxpayer might make excess payments against his tax liability before the return was filed and tax assessed, some flexibility in making a refund or credit of excess current tax payments was considered desirable. Accordingly, Congress enacted the predecessor of Section 6401(c), which, in terms of a double negative, states: "An amount paid as tax shall not be considered not to constitute an overpayment solely (because) there was no tax liability in respect of which (the) amount was paid." Congress intended by this provision that "honest mistakes (in payment) incident to the bona fide orderly compliance with the actual or reasonably apparent duties of the taxpayer" are to be considered overpayments, irrespective of assessment.[235] However, Congress also sought to prevent

---

1995) (U.S. banks improperly withheld tax dividends payable to exempt foreign trust funds, and the Service refunded the tax but computed interest from the date the Service received their refund claims; held, interest was payable from the date the trust funds were required to file their Forms 1120-F). On appeal, the Federal Circuit modified and remanded the Court of Federal Claims decision. MNOPF Trustees Ltd. v. United States, 123 F3d 1460 (1997). The Federal Circuit held that interest accrued in the pension fund trustees' favor from the date prescribed for the custodian banks' filing of the annual returns reporting the withholding tax payments that were made on behalf of the foreign tax-exempt organizations, and these returns were due no later than March 15 following the calendar year for which the taxes were withheld.

[233] Rosenman v. United States, 323 US 658 (1945).

[234] Rosenman v. United States, 323 US 658, 663 (1945).

[235] S. Rep. No. 221, 78th Cong., 1st Sess. (1943) (Current Tax Payment Act of 1943). Reprinted in 1943 CB 1314, 1329–1340.

a taxpayer from rendering the government liable for interest by "merely dumping money as taxes on the Collector, by disorderly remittances to him of amounts not computed in pursuit of the actual or reasonably apparent requirements of the Code, or not transmitted in accordance with the procedures set up by the Code, or by other abuses of tax administration."[236] Therefore, under Section 6401(c), remittance of an amount before assessment may constitute payment. Two apparently contradictory rules thus exist: (1) the statutory rule of Section 6401(c), which recognizes the possibility of a preassessment payment for interest purposes and (2) the judicial rule of *Rosenman* that a preassessment remittance is paid only on assessment. As a result, courts faced with the problem of classifying a remittance as a deposit or a payment have had to accommodate the more flexible provision of the Code reflected in Section 6401(c) to the rather inflexible rule of the Supreme Court in *Rosenman*.[237]

For purposes of computing interest, the Service generally treats a remittance differently depending on whether interest runs in favor of or against the taxpayer. A remittance made before a tax liability has been proposed is not treated as a payment, but rather as a "deposit in the nature of a cash bond."[238] Where a tax has been proposed and a notice of deficiency has been mailed to the taxpayer, the deposit is posted to the taxpayer's account as a payment of tax up to the amount of the deficiency proposed plus accrued interest. If it is later determined that the taxpayer has overpaid the tax, interest runs in the taxpayer's favor only from the date the amount was posted as a tax. No interest is paid on a deposit returned to a taxpayer before or after assessment. This position finds support in Congress's concern that taxpayers might draw interest on haphazard amounts dumped on the Service. It also squares with the *Rosenman* holding that payment does not occur until assessment, even if the amount in question is remitted before assessment. For these reasons, interest does not run in favor of a taxpayer on a remittance made before the date of the assessment.[239] In a case where interest was found to run from the date of a preassessment remittance, the amount was transferred to the Service in response to a notice of deficiency.[240] However, a finding that a post–deficiency notice remit-

---

[236] S. Rep. No. 221, 78th Cong., 1st Sess. (1943) (Current Tax Payment Act of 1943). Reprinted in 1943 CB 1314, 1329–1340.

[237] See the discussion of limitations on claims for refund at ¶ 11.05.

[238] Rev. Proc. 84-58, 1984-2 CB 501, § 4.04(1). See the discussion of Rev. Proc. 84-58 at ¶ 6.02[3][a]. Becker Bros. v. United States, 88-1 USTC ¶ 9262 (CD Ill. 1988) (no interest payable on a deposit on which a timely assessment was not made).

[239] See, e.g., Fortugno v. Comm'r, 353 F2d 429 (3d Cir. 1965) (threat of jeopardy assessment). Rev. Proc. 84-58, 1984-2 CB 501, does not use the term "assessment," but rather the phrase "posting to the taxpayer's account as a payment"; see §§ 4.02(3), 5.05.

[240] Colt's Mfg. Co. v. Comm'r, 306 F2d 929 (2d Cir. 1962) (postdecision remittance in Tax Court case held to draw interest from date of payment); Northern Natural Gas Co. v. United States, 354 F2d 310 (Ct. Cl. 1965) (remittance after notice of deficiency). In at

tance is a payment prevents a claim that the remittance is disorderly because it has no conceivable relationship to liability.

Where interest runs against taxpayers and in favor of the government, the Service, as a matter of practice, considers the remittance a payment if it is made after a notice of deficiency has been sent. The Service assesses the remittance on receipt or as soon as practicable. If the remittance is made before a notice of deficiency is sent, the Service treats the amount as a deposit but terminates the running of interest on the date the remittance is received or any portion of a deficiency is satisfied by application of the remittance.[241]

[2] Date of Credit or Refund

The date when interest ceases to accrue depends on whether the overpayment is credited or refunded. If the overpayment is credited against another tax liability of the taxpayer, interest accrues in favor of the taxpayer from the date of the overpayment to the due date of the amount against which the overpayment is credited.[242] If the overpayment is refunded, interest accrues from the date of the overpayment to a date, as determined by the Service, that precedes the refund check by no more than thirty days.[243]

The thirty-day period described in Section 6611(b)(2) refers to the tender and acceptance of the refund check. Interest can stop thirty days before the date of the check, "whether or not such refund check is accepted by the taxpayer after tender of such check to the taxpayer."[244] However, the thirty-day rule contemplates that a refund check will be tendered by the Service, and, until it is tendered to the taxpayer, interest continues to accrue. The word "tender" has been interpreted as meaning that "a taxpayer has some knowledge of it and an opportunity to accept, or decline to accept, the check."[245] This rule of tender has been held to apply to the forty-five-day rule of Section 6611(e).

---

least one pre-statutory notice situation, the Service has ruled that an advance remittance constitutes a payment. In Revenue Ruling 81-189, 1981-2 CB 240, the Service indicated that this rule also applies to extension payments where income and gift taxes are involved.

[241] Rev. Proc. 64-13, 1964-1 (Pt. 1 CB 674), § 4.01. An exception is made where a waiver of restrictions on assessment has been filed. In such cases, interest terminates thirty days after the waiver is filed. IRC § 6601(c). See Rev. Proc. 84-58, 1984-2 CB 501, for remittances made after October 1, 1984.

[242] IRC § 6611(b)(1). See supra ¶ 6.03[1][b].

[243] IRC § 6611(b)(2). The acceptance of a refund check does not deprive the taxpayer of the right to make a claim for any additional overpayment and interest, provided that the claim is made within the applicable period of limitations. However, if a taxpayer does not accept a refund check, no additional interest on the amount of the overpayment included in the check is allowed. Reg. § 301.6611-1(g).

[244] Doolin v. United States, 918 F2d 15, 18 (2d Cir. 1990).

[245] Doolin v. United States, 918 F2d 15, 18 (2d Cir. 1990).

Tender can be proved by the Service by evidence of actual mailing or proof of procedures followed in the regular course of its operations.[246]

The government is granted a specific period in which it may refund an overpayment without incurring interest. Generally, the interest-free period is forty-five days after the due date of the return or, if a return is filed after the due date, forty-five days after the return was actually filed.[247] The forty-five-day grace period does not start to run until the return is filed in processable form (as defined).[248]

This forty-five-day interest-free period was extended by the Revenue Reconciliation Act of 1993 (RRA 1993) to employment, excise, and estate and gift taxes, as well as to income taxes.[249] In addition to original returns, the interest-free period also applies to refunds of any type of tax arising from amended returns, to claims for refund,[250] and to Service-initiated adjustments.[251] These changes are effective for returns required to be filed (disregarding extensions) on or after January 1, 1994.[252] For amended returns and claims for refund, the changes apply to returns and claims, for whatever period, filed on or after January 1, 1995.[253] The same effective date applies to Service-generated adjustments.[254]

---

[246] Compare Doolin v. United States, 918 F2d 15 (2d Cir. 1990), where such evidence was found to be presented, with Godfrey, Jr. v. United States, 997 F2d 335 (7th Cir. 1993), where evidence of mailing by computer record was found to be adequate.

[247] IRC § 6611(e). A special rule was applied in the case of refunds attributable to taxable years that began in 1974. For these refunds, the regular forty-five-day interest-free period was extended to sixty days if the refund was payable to an individual. The refund period remains at forty-five days for all other taxpayers and all other tax years. Reg. § 301.6611-1(j). Where a delay in the refund of an overpayment is the result of an erroneous past-due child support offset, the Service has ruled that it pays interest on the refund delayed beyond the forty-five-day period of Section 6611(e) unless the error is caused by a state agency. Rev. Rul. 84-171, 1984-2 CB 310.

[248] IRC § 6611(i), effective for returns filed after October 3, 1982.

[249] RRA 1993, § 13271(a), amending IRC § 6611(e) and adding IRC § 6611(e)(1).

[250] RRA 1993, § 13271(a), amending IRC § 6611(e) and adding IRC § 6611(e)(1), adding IRC § 6611(e)(2).

[251] RRA 1993, § 13271(a), amending IRC § 6611(e) and adding IRC § 6611(e)(1), adding IRC § 6611(e)(3).

In Significant Service Center Advice, the National Office has declared that if a return shows a balance due but the Service issues a refund because of errors on the return, interest on a tax refund is computed under Section 6611(e)(3), not under Section 6611(e)(1). SCA 1999-17002 (Oct. 21, 1998).

[252] RRA 1993, § 13271(b)(1).

[253] RRA 1993, § 13271(b)(2).

[254] RRA 1993, § 13271(b)(3).

¶ 6.08 INTEREST RATE ON LARGE CORPORATE OVERPAYMENTS

Not only do corporations face an increased rate of interest on large corporate underpayments,[255] but for taxable periods after December 31, 1994, the interest rate on corporate tax overpayments exceeding $10,000 is lower than the normal overpayment rate.[256] Instead of the normal overpayment rate (the sum of the federal short-term rate, plus 2 percent), the interest rate that will be paid on corporate tax overpayments that exceed $10,000, is the sum of the federal short-term rate, plus 0.5 percent. For example, the interest rate for large corporate overpayments for the first quarter of 1995 was 6.5 percent, while the normal overpayment rate was 8 percent.[257] The interest rates on large corporate overpayments is summarized in Table 6.6.

As the result of the enactment of the reduced corporate overpayment rate, to the extent a corporate overpayment exceeds $10,000, interest on the first $10,000 of the overpayment accrues at the normal overpayment rate (the federal short-term rate, plus two percentage points), but for periods after December 31, 1994, interest accrues on the excess of the overpayment over $10,000 at the reduced GATT rate of the short-term rate, plus one half percentage point. Using the rationale that tax and interest are treated as one, the Service's position is that the GATT reduction in the overpayment rate applies not only to the portion of an overpayment outstanding on January 1, 1995, in excess of $10,000, but also to the accrued interest on the excess portion.[258] For example, if a $12,000 overpayment arises after the effective date of GATT, interest is computed on the $10,000 threshold at the normal overpayment rate, and on the $2,000 excess at the GATT rate. Also, since interest is compounded daily, the GATT rate applies to interest on the $2,000 as well as the $2,000 overpayment itself.[259] Similarly, suppose a corporate taxpayer, on September 15, 1991, overpaid its 1990 income tax by $25,000. The accrued interest as of January 1, 1995, is assumed to be $5,000, and the total amount of $30,000 was refunded to the taxpayer on March 31, 1995. If $2,000 of the accrued interest is accrued on the $10,000 threshold amount, and $3,000 is allocable to the $15,000 ex-

---

[255] See ¶ 6.02[3][e].

[256] Uruguay Round Agreements Act, Pub. L. No. 103-465, amending Section 6621(a)(1) for periods after December 31, 1994.

[257] Rev. Rul. 95-15, 1995-1 CB 212 (Feb. 27, 1995).

[258] Chief Counsel Significant Service Center Advice 1998-015, reprinted in 98 TNT 124-69.

[259] This result is consistent with court decisions on the issue of whether daily compounding applied only to an underpayment outstanding on January 1, 1983, the effective date of the daily compounding statute, Section 6622, or also applied to the simple interest that had accrued on the underpayment before the effective date. See, e.g., RJR Nabisco, Inc. v. United States, 955 F2d 1457 (11th Cir. 1992).

cess portion of the overpayment, the Service's view is that the normal rate of interest applies to the $10,000 threshold amount, as well as to the $2,000 of interest related to the threshold amount, while the GATT rate applies to the $15,000 excess portion and the related $3,000 of interest.[260]

¶ 6.09 INTEREST RATES

The annual rate of interest on tax underpayments and overpayments established under Section 6621 is based on the short-term federal interest rate determined in the same manner as the short-term federal rate in the original issue discount rules.[261] Interest is compounded daily[262] and the rate is adjusted quarterly.[263] The underpayment rate is one percent greater than the overpayment rate. The underpayment rate is the short-term federal rate plus three percentage points,[264] while the overpayment rate is the short-term federal rate plus two percentage points.[265]

The interest rate for underpayments and overpayments has undergone a number of changes over the years. The 1939 and 1954 Codes imposed a 6 percent interest rate that was meant to be higher than the prevailing money market rate to encourage taxpayers to pay their taxes promptly. In 1975, the interest rate was increased to 9 percent because the 6 percent rate was felt to be below the prevailing market rate. Section 6621 tied the interest rate on tax deficiencies to the prime interest rate quoted by commercial banks to their best customers and provided that this rate would be adjusted semiannually. This method of determining the interest rate lasted until January 1, 1987, when, as a result of TRA 1986, the current procedure of basing the rate on the short-term federal rate was adopted. All of these changes were enacted to make the tax interest rate closer to the actual cost of borrowing money to encourage timely refunds and tax payments and "to make certain that 'borrowing' through non-payment of tax (was) no more attractive than other forms of borrowing."[266]

---

[260] Chief Counsel Significant Service Center Advice 1998-015, reprinted in 98 TNT 124-69.

[261] IRC § 1274(d).

[262] IRC § 6622. In Estate of Papson v. Comm'r, 81 TC 105 (1983), the Tax Court held that the change in the interest rate did not violate the due process guaranties in the U.S. Constitution.

[263] IRC § 6621, effective for purposes of determining interest for periods after December 31, 1986.

[264] IRC § 6621(a)(2).

[265] IRC § 6621(a)(1).

[266] Union Pac. RR Co. v. United States, 11 Cl. Ct. 177, 86-2 USTC ¶ 9805 (Cl. Ct. 1986). In In re Connecticut Aerosols, Inc., Debtor, 31 Bankr. 883, 83-2 USTC ¶ 9521

   Table 6.3 shows the underpayment and overpayment rate prior to 1987, when the two rates were the same. In 1983, the Service published daily compounding tables that were reflected in the various revenue rulings the Service published to announce the applicable interest rate. In 1995, however, the Service issued new uniform tables for computing using the daily compounding rules established under Section 6662 for all interest computations made after December 31, 1994.[267] The interest rates for overpayments and underpayments and the applicable rate table are summarized in Tables 6.3 and 6.4.

   The Service publishes uniform tables and procedures for computing interest using the daily compounding rules. Interest accruing after December 31, 1982, must be computed in steps as follows:

   1. Interest on underpayments and overpayments accruing before January 1, 1983, is computed in accordance with Tables 1 through 6 of Revenue Procedure 95-17. As the tables show, the Service used the month-day method of calculating interest before February 1, 1980,[268] and a daily rate from February 1, 1980, through December 31, 1982.

   2. Interest on underpayments and overpayments accruing after December 31, 1982, is computed in accordance with Tables 7 through 54 for non-leap years and Tables 55 through 102 for leap years. Because Section 6621 originally required redetermination of the interest rates semiannually, the effective daily rates for 184 days are included in Revenue Procedure 95-17. Interest on any tax or penalty outstanding as of December 31, 1982, is computed as described above using Tables 1 through 6. All tax, assessed penalty, additions to tax, and interest, whether or not assessed, are totalled to determine the amount to be carried over, and daily interest is charged on the total under the compounding rules.[269]

Compound interest, as opposed to simple interest, imposes a considerably heavier cost on taxpayers who lose disputes with the Service, since such disputes often take years to resolve. Assuming the applicable rate of interest com-

---

(Bankr. D. Conn. 1983), the Bankruptcy Court held that Section 6621 was not applicable to interest payments to be made to the U.S. government pursuant to its allowed tax claim in a bankruptcy case. The court held that the interest rate determined under 28 USC § 1961(a) (rate equal to coupon issue yield equivalent of average accepted auction price of last auction of fifty-two-week U.S. Treasury bills) was a more accurate reflection of the prevailing market rate of interest. However, in In re Stafford, 24 Bankr. 840, 82-2 USTC ¶ 9706 (Bankr. D. Kan. 1982), the bankruptcy court did use Section 6621 to determine the discount factor for a secured claim of the Service for a Chapter 13 bankruptcy petition.

   [267] Rev. Proc. 95-17, 1995-1 CB 556, replacing the interest tables in Rev. Proc. 83-7, 1983-1 CB 583.

   [268] See infra ¶ 6.05.

   [269] Rev. Proc. 95-17, 1995-1 CB 556 (Feb. 27, 1995).

pounded daily continues for ten years (ignoring leap years), the equivalent rate of simple interest for five years would be 24.5 percent, and for ten years, 39.5 percent. The tax and interest on a $1,000 deficiency would be $4,951.29 after ten years with compound interest whereas with 16 percent simple interest, the tax and interest would be $2,600.[270]

¶ 6.10 INTEREST NETTING

When there is both an overpayment of tax for one year and an underpayment in another year, interest runs on the overpayment and underpayment at different rates favoring the Service. If an overpayment exceeding an underpayment and the underpayment are netted, therefore, the Service will lose the benefit of the interest differential on the underpayment. Is the Service required to net the overpayment and the underpayment? Since the abatement authority of Section 6402(a) provides that the Service "may credit the amount of an overpayment . . . against any liability," it has been said that Section 6402 does not apply when a taxpayer has already paid a liability at the time the overpayment is determined, and in any event leaves to the Service the discretion whether to apply overpayments to underpayments or to refund them.[271] As a result, Section 6601(f) does not come into play to stop the running of interest on the portion of the underpayment unless the Service exercises its discretion to apply the overpayment.

The 1998 Act provides a long-awaited statutory solution to the interest-netting problem. It provides that there is a zero rate of interest to the extent that underpayments and overpayments are equivalent or overlap.[272] The effective date of the zero rate of interest on overlapping underpayments and overpayments is July 22, 1998, but the zero rate applies before July 22, 1998, if the taxpayer reasonably identifies and establishes the periods of underpayments

---

[270] 83 Tax Adviser 145 (Mar. 1983).

[271] Northern States Power Co. v. United States, 73 F3d 764 (8th Cir. 1996) (taxpayer wanted overpayments credited against later-accruing underpayments as of the time the underpayments arose so that no underpayment interest would begin to run, a method that would entitle the taxpayer to an additional $460,000). The Service permits crediting of overpayments against underpayments for the period when the underpayments and overpayments are both unpaid and outstanding, even if they are for different tax years or different types of tax (interest netting called "offsetting"), but it has said that it generally does not net interest when a taxpayer has an overpayment in one year that overlaps with a deficiency that a taxpayer has paid in another year (interest netting called "global interest netting"). See, however, IRC § 6621(d). The Service has asked for comments on a number of issues that it believes would exist if it were to implement global interest netting. Notice 96-18, 1996-14 IRB 1. See also the discussion at ¶ 6.02[3][d].

[272] IRC § 6621(d), added by 1998 Act § 3301(a).

and overpayments before July 22, 1998, to which the zero rate applies. Section 6621(d) permits the net zero rate of interest to be applied whether or not the overpayment or underpayment is outstanding, as long as the periods for obtaining a refund and claiming additional interest are still open. It has also been held that Section 6621(d) applies to past periods and permits global interest netting for future periods as long as at least one of the statutes of limitations for claiming a refud of an overpayment or assessing an underpayment is open.[273]

[1] Interest Netting Pre–October 1, 1998

Procedures for claiming the net zero interest rate for interest accruing before October 1, 1998, on overlapping periods of overpayment and underpayment, are described in Revenue Procedure 99-19.[274] Section 6621(d) applies to interest for periods beginning before July 22, 1998 (that is, interest accruing before October 1, 1998). To obtain the benefit of the net zero interest rate under Section 6621(d), a taxpayer must satisfy three conditions: (1) The limitations periods for claims must not have expired; (2) the overlapping periods of underpayment and overpayment must be identified; and (3) the taxpayer must request the zero rate. Accordingly, the net zero rate of interest will not apply to a taxpayer's overpayment and underpayment unless all of the following criteria are met:

1. On July 22, 1998, both the statutory period for the taxpayer's claiming a credit or refund of interest paid on an underpayment and the statutory period for claiming payment of additional interest on an overpayment must be open.
2. The taxpayer must reasonably identify the overlapping periods of tax overpayments and underpayments for which the net interest rate of zero applies.
3. Not later than December 31, 1999, the taxpayer must file a request with the Service to apply the net zero interest rate.[275]

A taxpayer must file a claim for refund of interest paid on an underpayment within three years after the return for the year was filed, or two years

---

[273] See Federal National Mortgage Association v. United States, 91 AFTR2d 2003-1677 (Fed. Cl. 2003)HR Conf. Rep. No. 599, 105th Cong., 2d Sess. 257 (1998). Each overpayment and underpayment may be considered only once.

[274] Rev. Proc. 99-19, 1999-14 IRB 1 (Mar. 16, 1999). Rev. Proc. 99-19 does not apply to interest for periods beginning after July 22, 1999 (i.e., interest accruing on and after October 1, 1998).

[275] Rev. Proc. 99-19, 1999-14 IRB 1 (Mar. 16, 1999).

from the time the interest was paid, whichever period expires later.[276] When the taxpayer claims additional interest is payable on an overpayment under Section 6611, however, the taxpayer must file the claim within the six-year period during which a suit must be commenced under the provisions of Sections 2401 and 2501 of Title 28, United States Code.[277] Both of these periods for claiming a refund or additional interest must be open.

Suppose the Service examined both the 1992 and 1994 tax returns of X, a calendar year corporation, and determined that X has underpaid tax for 1992 in the amount of $40,000, but overpaid tax for 1994 in the amount of $80,000. After the Service sent a notice and demand for payment of the 1992 underpayment dated May 3, 1996, X paid the additional 1992 tax on May 12, 1996, with interest computed from March 15, 1993, to May 3, 1996. If X files a request for the net zero interest on April 27, 1999, for the overlap period from March 15, 1995, the date the 1994 return was filed, to May 3, 1996, the cutoff date of the underpayment interest on the 1992 additional tax, X is not entitled to the net zero interest rate. The six-year period for claiming additional interest for the 1994 year is open, but the two-year period for filing a claim for the refund of interest expired on May 12, 1998.[278] To request the zero rate of interest, the taxpayer must file a Form 843, Claim for Refund and Request for Abatement, with "Request for Net Interest Rate of Zero Under Rev. Proc. 99-19" inserted at the top of the form. In general, the taxpayer must (1) include information "reasonably" identifying the periods of overlapping interest accrual; (2) represent that both periods have not been used before to reduce the taxpayer's liability for underpayment interest; and (3) provide a computation of the amount of interest that should be refunded or abated.[279]

In response to comments, the Service modified and superseded Revenue Procedure 99-19 with Revenue Procedure 99-43.[280] Under the revised procedures, taxpayers had only to file a claim requesting application of the net rate of zero by December 31, 1999, if both applicable periods of limitation would be closed on or before December 31, 1999. In other words, on or before December 31, 1999, (1) the time for filing a claim for the refund of underpayment interest was barred because more than three years had elapsed since the return giving rise to the underpayment determination had been filed, or two

---

[276] IRC § 6511(a).

[277] Rev. Rul. 56-506, 1956-2 CB 959.

[278] Rev. Proc. 99-19, 1999-14 IRB 1 (Mar. 16, 1999), § 5, Ex. (2).

[279] Rev. Proc. 99-19, 1999-14 IRB 1 (Mar. 16, 1999), § 4. No Form 843 is required if the taxpayer's return is currently being audited, or is otherwise being considered by a Service office. In this situation, the taxpayer submits a letter or statement requesting application of the net zero interest rate and other identifying information to the Examination Division office examining the return or the other office considering the taxpayer's return. Id. § 4.06.

[280] Rev. Proc. 99-43, 1999-2 CB 506.

years had passed since the taxpayer paid the underpayment to the Service; and (2) the time for filing a claim for the refund of additional interest on an overpayment is barred because more than six years had passed since the taxpayer could bring an action against the government under 28 USC §§ 2401 and 2501 to collect the overpayment.[281] On the other hand, taxpayers were not required to take action by December 31, 1999, if at least one of the applicable periods of limitation was open after December 31, 1999 (i.e., either the statute of limitations on filing a claim for the refund of overpaid interest on an underpayment, or the six-year period for filing a suit for additional overpayment interest, is still open). If one of the periods was open, the request for a net interest rate of zero must have been made before the expiration of that period for filing a refund.[282] In addition, applications for the net rate of zero are to be sent to the Ogden Service Center, on a Form 843 specifically labeled as "Request for Net Interest Rate of Zero Under Rev. Rul. 99-43," and on the basis of identified overlapping periods of overpayment and underpayment, computing the amount of interest to be credited, refunded, or abated.[283] No Form 843 is required when a computation of interest using a net interest rate of zero is requested by a taxpayer with returns under consideration by any function of the Service (Appeals, Examination, or a case before a federal court, that requires an interest computation).[284] In such a case, the taxpayer must send a letter or statement to the Service.

[2] Interest Netting on or After October 1, 1998

The Service will take "reasonable steps" to identify overlapping periods of tax overpayments and underpayments and apply the net interest rate of zero in Section 6621(d) to interest accruing on or after October 1, 1998.[285] It will also supply the taxpayer with a copy of its computations. The Service itself may fail to identify overlapping periods and to apply the net interest rate of zero; therefore, the Service has cautioned taxpayers to request the net interest rate of zero or, if the taxpayer disagrees with the Service's computation, to ask the Service to recompute the net interest rate of zero. The taxpayer's request for a net interest rate of zero must be "timely."[286] In order for the claim for the

---

[281] Rev. Proc. 99-43, 1999-2 CB 506, § 4.03(1).

[282] Rev. Proc. 99-43, 1999-2 CB 506, § 4.03(2).

[283] Rev. Proc. 99-43, 1999-2 CB 506, §§ 5.01–5.05. The address is Internal Revenue Service, Net Rate Interest Claim, P.O. Box 9987, Mail Stop 6800, Ogden, Utah 84409; or if a private delivery service is used, Internal Revenue Service, Net Rate Interest Netting Claim, 1160 West 1200 South, Mail Stop 6800, Ogden, Utah 84201.

[284] Rev. Proc. 99-43, 1999-2 CB 506, § 5.06.

[285] Rev. Proc. 2000-26, 2000-1 CB 1257, § 4.01.

[286] Rev. Proc. 2000-26, 2000-1 CB 1257, § 4.02.

credit or refund of underpayment interest to be timely filed, it must be filed within the later of three years after the return was filed or two years after interest was paid. For overpayment interest, a claim for additional overpayment must be filed within the six-year period in which a suit must be filed for the recovery of the claim for interest, pursuant to 28 USC §§ 2401 and 2501. It is important to note that the timely filing of the claim will not protect the taxpayer's rights; the taxpayer can protect the claim only by filing suit within the six-year period.

The Service applies the net interest rate of zero for underpayment interest by decreasing the underpayment interest owed by the taxpayer.[287] If the statute of limitations on the refund of underpayment interest is closed at the time the taxpayer's claim is filed, but the period for paying additional overpayment interest is open, the Service will apply the net interest rate of zero by increasing the overpayment interest owed to the taxpayer.[288]

Procedurally, a taxpayer requests the net interest rate of zero by filing a Form 843, Claim for Refund and Request for Abatement.[289] The taxpayer files the Form 843 with the service center where the taxpayer filed its most recent federal income tax return. To identify the nature of the request, the taxpayer is instructed to label the top of the Form 843, "Request for Net Interest Rate of Zero Under Rev. Proc. 2000-26." In the Form 843, the taxpayer must identify the overlapping periods of tax underpayment and overpayment, and provide other information supporting the claim.

When the taxpayer's returns are being considered by the Service, the taxpayer is not required to file a claim form.[290] Instead, the taxpayer needs only to provide a letter or written statement to the contact representative that requests the net interest rate of zero and supplies information about the overlapping periods. Also, if the taxpayer has filed a request under Revenue Procedure 99-43 (or Revenue Procedure 99-19), the taxpayer is not required to file a claim for post–October 1, 1998, interest, and the Service will apply the net interest rate of zero to the entire overlapping period.

¶ 6.11 METHOD OF COMPUTATION

There are three factors to be considered in the computation of interest: (1) the amount of tax, assessed penalties, and additions to tax; (2) the period for which interest is owed; and (3) the interest rate or rates in effect for the inter-

---

[287] Rev. Proc. 2000-26, 2000-1 CB 1257, § 4.03(1).
[288] Rev. Proc. 2000-26, 2000-1 CB 1257, § 4.03(2).
[289] Rev. Proc. 2000-26, 2000-1 CB 1257, § 5.
[290] Rev. Proc. 2000-26, 2000-1 CB 1257, § 5.06.

est period. The Service uses a hybrid combination of the so-called thirty-day method and the 365-day method in computing the period for which interest is owed. The interest period (i.e., the elapsed time) is stated in years and months from the beginning of the interest period to the corresponding date in the last month in the period containing that date, without regard to the number of days in the particular year or month. The remainder of the period is the actual number of days in excess of full years and months. This method produces a result that is slightly different from the result obtained by calculating interest on an actual-day basis for a 365-day period. However, the result has never been contested.

In "borrowing" the number of days, it is the actual number of days in the month preceding the month in which the interest period ends that is borrowed. To illustrate:

If interest period ends in	Transfer to
January	31
February	31
March	28
April	31
May	30
June	31
July	30
August	31
September	31
October	30
November	31
December	30

EXAMPLE 6-8: The due date of a tax is March 15, 1998, and payment is made on January 12, 2000. Under the Service method, the interest period would be computed as follows:

	Year	Months	Days
End of period	1990	1	12
Beginning of period	1988	3	15
Interest period	1	9	28

Because the interest period ends in January, thirty-one days are borrowed from the preceding month, leaving a zero in the months column. Thirty-one days added to twelve days equals forty-three days, and fifteen from forty-three days leaves twenty-eight days. When borrowing months from the year column, the number of months borrowed is always twelve. Thus, twelve months are borrowed here. Because the number of months in the months column is now zero, one year is borrowed from the year column and twelve months are added to the months column. After reduction by three months, nine months are left.

With one year borrowed from 1990, the year column becomes 1989, and the remainder one year.

¶ 6.12 CORRELATING INTEREST ON OVERPAYMENTS AND UNDERPAYMENTS

[1] Restricted Interest

The Code provides that under certain conditions, interest on underpayments and overpayments of tax is prohibited or is limited to specific accrual periods. For example, where an income tax is reduced by a net operating loss carryback, Section 6611(f) restricts interest on any overpayment of tax by providing that the resulting overpayment is not deemed to have been made prior to the filing date for the taxable year in which the net operating loss arises.

Provisions restricting and prohibiting interest are as follows:

TABLE 6.2
Provisions Restricting and Prohibiting Interest

Adjustment Section	Subject	Underpayments	Overpayments
172(b)	Net operating loss carryback		6611(f)
6411(b)	Tentative carryback	6601(d)	6611(f)
901	Foreign tax credit	905(c)	Not restricted
904	Carryback and carryover of foreign tax credit		6611(g)
547(a)	Deficiency dividend deduction—personal holding company		547(b)(1), 547(b)(2)
2011(a)	Credit for state death taxes		2011(c)
2014	Credit for foreign death taxes		2014(c)
2016	Recovery of taxes claimed as a credit		2016

Generally speaking, the special interest-accrual periods are shorter than those that would result if the underpayments and overpayments were subject to the regular interest provisions of Sections 6601 and 6611, respectively. Collectively, these prohibitions and limitations give rise to the term "restricted interest."[291] Some of the provisions of the Code restricting and prohibiting interest are listed in Form 6.4.[292]

An audit determination frequently involves adjustments under more than one section of law, resulting in a deficiency or overassessment attributable to each. The net effect of these deficiencies and overassessments may be (1) no change; (2) a net deficiency to be assessed; or (3) a net overassessment to be allowed. Interest is computed separately on each of the deficiencies (or underpayments) or overassessments resulting from these adjustments and is restricted on some adjustments but not on others.

Correlating interest running separately on underpayments and overpayments is no easy matter. Before 1958, the running of interest on the underpayment and overpayment were not correlated, even though underpayments and overpayments offset each other. Therefore, the Service could collect more interest on the underpayment than it paid on an overpayment, while a taxpayer might collect more interest on an overpayment than he paid on an underpayment. This result occurred because interest on an overpayment of tax credited against an assessed deficiency was allowed from the date of the overpayment to the date of assessment (or, if the amount were refunded, to a date thirty days prior to the issuance of the refund check), but interest on the deficiency ran from the due date of the tax to the date of payment. However, the date a credit might be scheduled as payment of the deficiency might be long after the date on which interest on the overpayment was cut off by assessment of the deficiency. On the other hand, interest on an overpayment might continue to run, while interest on an offsetting deficiency was cut off because a waiver had been filed for thirty days and a notice and demand had not been sent.

In 1958, Congress added what is now Section 6601(f) to correlate the running of interest. Section 6601(f) denies interest to the Service on that portion of an underpayment satisfied by the credit of an overpayment. The period

---

[291] It is not clear whether a Code provision such as Section 6601(j), which provides for a reduction in the interest rate from the annual rate to 4 percent where there is an extension of time for the payment of estate tax for an estate consisting largely of an interest in a closely held business, constitutes a restriction of interest. However, the Service considers Section 2016 (which provides that interest on any additional estate tax due because of the refund of foreign taxes claimed as a credit bears interest to the extent that interest is paid by the foreign country on the refund) to be a provision covered by the term "restricted interest." Revenue Procedure 60-17, 1960-2 CB 942, 943, lays out the procedures to be followed in the computation of restricted interest. It is a tribute to the complexity of restricted interest that Revenue Procedure 60-17 has remained relatively unchanged since it was published. See Rev. Proc. 62-17, 1962-2 CB 496 (modifying § 6.03(2)); Rev. Proc. 65-20, 1965-2 CB 1003 (modifying § 3.02(5)(f)); Rev. Proc. 83-58, 1983-2 CB 575 (modifying § 3.02(4)(b)); Rev. Proc. 84-66, 1984-2 CB 637 (amending § 14.04(2)(a)).

[292] Section 6612(c), entitled "Other Restrictions on Interest," sets forth certain restrictions on interest, but Section 2.02(1) of Rev. Proc. 60-17, 1960-2 CB 942, modified by Rev. Proc. 84-66, 1984-2 CB 637, contains a complete list of provisions of the 1939 and 1954 Codes giving rise to restricted interest situations.

for which interest is denied is the period during which interest would have run on the credited overpayment if the credit had not been made (i.e., if the overpayment had been refunded).[293] At the same time that Section 6601(f) was added to the Code, Section 6611(b)(1) was amended to remove the distinction between refunded and credited overpayments by providing that interest on a credited overpayment runs only from the date of the overpayment to the original due date of the amount against which it is credited.

In computing restricted interest, the basic terms and dates used are the due date of tax and the date of overpayment.[294] The due date of tax is the due date of the return without regard to any extension of time for filing. In a restricted interest case, the due date is the restricted date fixed by law. The due date of interest, penalty, or addition to the tax is the date of assessment. The due date of overpayment is the date of actual receipt of the taxpayer's remittance.[295] In a restricted interest case, the date of overpayment is the date from which interest is allowable on the overpayment.[296] This same date is the terminating date for charging interest on a deficiency satisfied by credit of an overpayment.[297]

[2] Credits of Overpayments

An overpayment in tax may be credited against underpayment. Where such action is taken, it is necessary to determine the amount of interest that has accrued on the underpayment and the interest that has accrued on the overpayment before it was credited. The rules that are to be applied in general are as follows:

1. *Interest on unscheduled overpayments* . Where a net deficiency is to be assessed for a given taxable period, the interest computed on an overpayment for the same taxable period may be less than the interest computed on the deficiencies or underpayments. In such cases, interest due the taxpayer is deducted from interest due the government, and the deficiency, together with only the net amount of interest, is assessed. On the other hand, if the interest on the overpayment is greater than the interest computed on the deficiencies, the entire

---

[293] S. Rep. No. 1983, 85th Cong., 2d Sess. (1958), reprinted in 1958-3 CB 1155–1156.

[294] Rev. Proc. 60-17, 1960-2 CB 942, § 3.02(5), modified by Rev. Proc. 84-66, 1984-2 CB 637.

[295] Taxes withheld at the source or paid as estimated tax are deemed to have been paid on the due date of the return.

[296] See, e.g., IRC §§ 6611(b), 6611(f), 6611(g).

[297] IRC § 6611(f)(1).

amount of deficiency interest is assessed, and the allowable interest is credited to the deficiency and interest assessed.[298]

2. *Interest on overpayments credited against underpayments.* If any portion of a tax is satisfied by credit of an overpayment, no interest is imposed on the portion of the tax satisfied for any period during which a mutuality of indebtedness exists (i.e., when interest would have been allowable on both the underpayment and the overpayment if the overpayment had been refunded).[299]

3. *Interest on underpayments satisfied by credits.* If a tax is satisfied by a credit, interest is allowed on overpayments from the date of overpayment to the due date of the amount against which the credit is taken.[300] For example, if the overpayment is applied as a credit to unpaid tax for a later year, interest is computed and allowed from the date of the overpayment to the due date of the unpaid tax.[301]

These rules are illustrated by the following examples:

EXAMPLE 6-9: An overpayment for 2001 is applied as a credit to unpaid tax (or another type of tax) for an earlier tax year, 2000. No interest is payable on the overpayment because the due date of the amount against which the credit is taken (April 15, 2001) precedes the date of the overpayment (April 15, 2002). However, if the overpayment for 2001 is applied as a credit to an underpayment in a subsequent year, 2002, interest is allowable from the date of the overpayment (April 15, 2002) to the due date of the tax (April 15, 2003).[302]

EXAMPLE 6-10: An overpayment for 2001 is applied as a credit to unpaid interest, a penalty, or an addition to tax due for another year (2002). Interest runs from the date of the overpayment (April 15, 2002) to the date of assessment of the amount to which the credit is applied. If the overpayment is applied as a credit to unpaid interest, a penalty, or an addition to tax due for the same year and the same type of tax, no interest is allowable because these additions are considered part of the tax, and no overpayment exists until all liability is satisfied.[303]

---

[298] Rev. Proc. 60-17, 1960-2 CB 942, § 3.01(2), modified by Rev. Proc. 84-66, 1984-2 CB 637.

[299] IRC § 6601(f); Reg. § 301.6601-1(b)(1); Rev. Proc. 60-17, 1960-2 CB 942, § 3.02(3), modified by Rev. Proc. 84-66, 1984-2 CB 637. See supra ¶ 6.02[3][d].

[300] Reg. § 301.6611-1(h)(1); Rev. Proc. 60-17, 1960-2 CB 942, § 3.02(4), modified by Rev. Proc. 84-66, 1984-2 CB 637.

[301] Rev. Proc. 60-17, 1960-2 CB 942, § 3.02(4)(b), modified by Rev. Proc. 84-66, 1984-2 CB 637.

[302] Rev. Proc. 60-17, 1960-2 CB 942, § 3.03(4), modified by Rev. Proc. 84-66, 1984-2 CB 637.

[303] Reg. §§ 301.6611-1(h)(2)(v), 301.6611-1(h)(2)(vi).

Rules for the computation of interest on an overpayment applied as a credit to unpaid interest for another year are illustrated by *Fruehauf Corp. v. United States*,[304] where an audit of the taxpayer's tax returns revealed a "potential" deficiency of $1.1 million for 1960 and a large net operating loss for 1963. The 1963 net operating loss was carried back to 1960, and the carryback not only extinguished the "potential" deficiency, but also created an overassessment of $500,000 for 1960. Under Section 6601(d)(1), the Service was entitled to interest on the potential deficiency (or underpayment) from 1960 to the end of the loss year, 1963, amounting to $200,000. However, the Service did not assess deficiency interest until February 14, 1969, and after assessing this interest, it applied $200,000 of the $500,000 1960 overassessment in satisfaction of the interest due. The Service allowed interest on the remaining $300,000 overassessment from September 1, 1963, the first day after the end of the applicable loss year, to February 1, 1969, when the interest due the government was assessed.

The taxpayer argued that by applying $200,000 of the $500,000 overassessment, the Service denied it interest on this amount for six years, from the first day after the loss year (1963) to 1969. The government contended that the entire tax liability for 1960 was not satisfied (and thus no overpayment existed) until interest, whether assessed or unassessed, on the deficiency was paid. Thus, it argued that interest on the potential 1960 deficiency was a liability on the first day after the loss year, even though the interest was not assessed until February 14, 1969.

The regulations specifically provide that if an overpayment of tax is credited, interest is allowed on the deficiency from the date of overpayment (the first day after the loss year) to the due date of the amount against which the overpayment is credited, which in the case of assessed interest is the date of assessment of the interest.[305] On the other hand, Section 6601(f) provides that interest on an underpayment satisfied by the credit of an overpayment is stopped during any period of time that these amounts offset each other; that is, when a mutuality of indebtedness arises. In the case of an overpayment that antedates the due date of an underpayment, interest runs on the overpayment only until the due date; that is, a mutuality of indebtedness arises when the liability is due. The Court of Claims concluded that the liability for assessed interest is not due until the date of assessment, even if the related tax is for a period that precedes the date of payment. Thus, because the date of overpayment was September 1, 1963 (the first day after the loss year), which antedated the due date of the deficiency interest (February 14, 1969), the taxpayer

---

[304] Fruehauf Corp. v. United States, 477 F2d 568 (Ct. Cl. 1973).
[305] Reg. § 301.6611-1(h)(v).

was entitled to interest on the overpayment from September 1, 1963, to February 14, 1969.[306]

[3] Carrybacks and the Computation of Interest

As the result of the carryback of net operating or capital loss deductions or the various credits, an underpayment in tax for one year (the carryback year) may be reduced or eliminated by a deduction or credit that arises in a later tax year (the loss or credit year). A carryback may (1) reduce or eliminate an underpayment in the carryback year; (2) create an overpayment in the carryback year; or (3) both eliminate an underpayment and create an overpayment in the carryback year.

Interest is allowable on underpayments or overpayments resulting from the application of a carryback according to the following general rules:[307]

1. Where the carryback loss is the only adjustment involved and is sufficient to cover the unpaid tax, interest on the unpaid original tax is collectible from the due date of the return to the due date of the return for the loss year.
2. If the carryback loss results in an overpayment that is refunded, interest accrues from the first day after the close of the loss year or the date of overpayment, whichever is later, to a date no earlier than thirty days before issuance of the refund check.[308]
3. If the application of the carryback results in an overpayment that is credited to the original or additional tax for a prior year, no interest is allowable.[309]
4. If the loss is credited to an original or additional amount due for a year after the loss year, interest accrues from the first day after the close of the loss year (unless the date of the overpayment is later) to the due date of the return for the subsequent year.[310]
5. If the loss is credited to unpaid interest, a penalty, or an addition to the tax for another year (or tax), interest accrues from the first day after the close of the loss year (or the date of overpayment, if later) to

---

[306] The Service has indicated that it follows the *Fruehauf* decision. Rev. Rul. 83-113, 1983-2 CB 251.

[307] See Rev. Proc. 60-17, 1960-2 CB 942, modified by Rev. Proc. 84-66, 1984-2 CB 637 at § 4.

[308] IRC §§ 6611(f), 6611(b)(2). See Rev. Proc. 60-17, 1960-2 CB 942, § 4.03, modified by Rev. Proc. 84-66, 1984-2 CB 637.

[309] IRC §§ 6611(f), 6611(b)(2). See Rev. Proc. 60-17, 1960-2 CB 942, § 4.03, modified by Rev. Proc. 84-66, 1984-2 CB 637.

[310] IRC §§ 6611(f), 6611(b)(1).

the date of assessment of the interest, penalty, or addition to tax. Because interest is allowed on a tentative carryback allowance, interest is due on an excessive allowance from the same date interest was allowed (the first day after the close of the loss year) to the date of payment.

TABLE 6.3

Table of Interest Rates—Overpayments and Underpayments Before 1987

Period	Rate	Daily Rate Table in 1995-1 CB
Before July 1, 1975	6%	Table 2, p. 557
July 1, 1975–Jan. 31, 1976	9%	Table 4, p. 559
Feb. 1, 1976–Jan. 31, 1978	7%	Table 3, p. 558
Feb. 1, 1978–Jan. 31, 1980	6%	Table 2, p. 557
Feb. 1, 1980–Jan. 31, 1982	12%	Table 5, p. 560
Feb. 1, 1982–Dec. 31, 1982	20%	Table 6, p. 561
Jan. 1, 1983–June 30, 1983	16%	Table 37, p. 591
July 1, 1983–Dec. 31, 1983	11%	Table 27, p. 581
Jan. 1, 1984–June 30, 1984	11%	Table 75, p. 629
July 1, 1984–Dec. 31, 1984	11%	Table 75, p. 629
Jan. 1, 1985–June 30, 1985	13%	Table 31, p. 585
July 1, 1985–Dec. 31, 1985	11%	Table 27, p. 581
Jan. 1, 1986–June 30, 1986	10%	Table 25, p. 579
July 1, 1986–Dec. 31, 1986	9%	Table 23, p. 577

TABLE 6.4

Table of Interest Rates—Overpayments and Underpayments From January 1, 1987–Present

Period	Overpayments			Underpayments		
	Rate	Table	In 1995-1 CB, Page	Rate	Table	In 1995-1 CB, Page
Jan. 1, 1987–Mar. 31, 1987	8%	21	575	9%	2	577
Apr. 1, 1987–June 30, 1987	8%	21	575	9%	23	577
July 1, 1987–Sept. 30, 1987	8%	21	575	9%	23	577
Oct. 1, 1987–Dec. 31, 1987	9%	23	577	10%	25	579
Jan. 1, 1988–Mar. 31, 1988	10%	73	627	11%	75	629
Apr. 1, 1988–June 30, 1988	9%	71	625	10%	73	627
July 1, 1988–Sept. 30, 1988	9%	71	625	10%	73	627
Oct. 1, 1988–Dec. 31, 1988	10%	73	627	11%	75	629
Jan. 1, 1989–Mar. 31, 1989	10%	25	579	11%	27	581
Apr. 1, 1989–June 30, 1989	11%	27	581	12%	29	583
July 1, 1989–Sept. 30, 1989	11%	27	581	12%	29	583
Oct. 1, 1989–Dec. 31, 1989	10%	25	579	11%	27	581
Jan. 1, 1990–Mar. 31, 1990	10%	25	579	11%	27	581
Apr. 1, 1990–June 30, 1990	10%	25	579	11%	27	581
July 1, 1990–Sept. 30, 1990	10%	25	579	11%	27	581
Oct. 1, 1990–Dec. 31, 1990	10%	25	579	11%	27	581

	Overpayments			Underpayments		
Period	Rate	Table	In 1995-1 CB, Page	Rate	Table	In 1995-1 CB, Page
Jan. 1, 1991–Mar. 31, 1991	10%	25	579	11%	27	581
Apr. 1, 1991–June 30, 1991	9%	23	577	10%	25	579
July 1, 1991–Sept. 30, 1991	9%	23	577	10%	25	579
Oct. 1, 1991–Dec. 31, 1991	9%	23	577	10%	25	579
Jan. 1, 1992–Mar. 31, 1992	8%	69	623	9%	71	625
Apr. 1, 1992–June 30, 1992	7%	67	621	8%	69	623
July 1, 1992–Sept. 30, 1992	7%	67	621	8%	69	623
Oct. 1, 1992–Dec. 31, 1992	6%	65	619	7%	67	621
Jan. 1, 1993–Mar. 31, 1993	6%	17	571	7%	19	573
Apr. 1, 1993–June 30, 1993	6%	17	571	7%	19	573
July 1, 1993–Sept. 30, 1993	6%	17	571	7%	19	573
Oct. 1, 1993–Dec. 31, 1993	6%	17	571	7%	19	573
Jan. 1, 1994–Mar. 31, 1994	6%	17	571	7%	19	573
Apr. 1, 1994–June 30, 1994	6%	17	571	7%	19	573
July 1, 1994–Sept. 30, 1994	7%	19	573	8%	21	575
Oct. 1, 1994–Dec. 31, 1994	8%	21	575	9%	23	577
Jan. 1, 1995–Mar. 31, 1995	8%	21	575	9%	23	577
Apr. 1, 1995–June 30, 1995	9%	23	577	10%	25	579
July 1, 1995–Sept. 30, 1995	8%	21	575	9%	23	577
Oct. 1, 1995–Dec. 31, 1995	8%	21	575	9%	23	577
Jan. 1, 1996–Mar. 31, 1996	8%	69	623	9%	71	625
Apr. 1, 1996–June 30, 1996	7%	67	621	8%	69	623
July 1, 1996–Sept. 30, 1996	8%	69	623	9%	71	625
Oct. 1, 1996–Dec. 31, 1996	8%	69	623	9%	71	625
Jan. 1, 1997–Mar. 31, 1997	8%	21	575	9%	23	577
Apr. 1, 1997–June 30, 1997	8%	21	575	9%	23	577
July 1, 1997–Sept. 30, 1997	8%	21	575	9%	23	577
Oct. 1, 1997–Dec. 31, 1997	8%	21	575	9%	23	577
Jan. 1, 1998–Mar. 31, 1998	8%	21	575	9%	23	577
Apr. 1, 1998–June 30, 1998	7%	19	573	8%	21	575
July 1, 1998–Sept. 30, 1998	7%	19	573	8%	21	575
Oct. 1, 1998–Dec. 31, 1998	7%	19	573	8%	21	575
Jan. 1, 1999–Mar. 31, 1999*	7%	19	573	7%	19	573
Jan. 1, 1999–Mar. 31, 1999**	6%	17	571	7%	19	573
Apr. 1, 1999–June 30, 1999*	8%	21	575	8%	21	575
Apr. 1, 1999–June 30, 1999**	7%	19	573	8%	21	575
July 1, 1999–Sept. 30, 1999*	8%	21	575	8%	21	575
July 1, 1999–Sept. 30, 1999**	7%	19	573	8%	21	575
Oct. 1, 1999–Dec. 31, 1999*	8%	21	575	8%	21	575
Oct. 1, 1999–Dec. 31, 1999**	7%	19	573	8%	21	575
Jan. 1, 2000–Mar. 31, 2000*	8%	69	623	8%	69	623
Jan. 1, 2000–Mar. 31, 2000**	7%	67	621	8%	69	623
Apr. 1, 2000–June 30, 2000*	9%	71	625	9%	71	625
Apr. 1, 2000–June 30, 2000**	8%	69	623	9%	71	625
July 1, 2000–Sept. 30, 2000*	9%	71	625	9%	71	625
July 1, 2000–Sept. 30, 2000**	8%	69	623	9%	71	625
Oct. 1, 2000–Dec. 31, 2000*	9%	71	625	9%	71	625
Oct. 1, 2000–Dec. 31, 2000**	8%	69	623	9%	71	625
Jan. 1, 2001–Mar. 31, 2001*	9%	23	577	9%	23	577
Jan. 1, 2001–Mar. 31, 2001**	8%	21	575	9%	23	577
Apr. 1, 2001–June 30, 2001*	8%	21	575	8%	21	575
Apr. 1, 2001–June 30, 2001**	7%	19	573	8%	21	575
July 1, 2001–Sept. 30, 2001*	7%	19	573	7%	19	573

Period	Overpayments			Underpayments		
	Rate	Table	In 1995-1 CB, Page	Rate	Table	In 1995-1 CB, Page
July 1, 2001–Sept. 30, 2001**	6%	17	571	7%	19	573
Oct. 1, 2001–Dec. 31, 2001*	7%	19	573	7%	19	573
Oct. 1, 2001–Dec. 31, 2001**	6%	17	571	7%	19	573
Jan. 1, 2002–Mar. 31, 2002*	6%	17	571	6%	17	571
Jan. 1, 2002–Mar. 31, 2002**	5%	15	569	6%	15	571
Apr. 1, 2002–June 30, 2002*	6%	17	571	6%	17	571
Apr. 1, 2002–June 30, 2002**	5%	15	569	6%	17	571
July 1, 2002–Sept. 30, 2002*	6%	17	571	6%	17	571
July 1, 2002–Sept. 30, 2002**	5%	15	569	6%	17	571
Oct. 1, 2002–Dec. 31, 2002*	6%	17	571	6%	17	571
Oct. 1, 2002–Dec. 31, 2002**	5%	15	569	6%	17	571
Jan. 1, 2003–Mar. 31, 2003*	5%	15	569	5%	15	569
Jan. 1, 2003–Mar. 31, 2003**	4%	13	567	5%	15	569
Apr. 1, 2003–June 30, 2003*	5%	15	569	5%	15	569
Apr. 1, 2003–June 30, 2003**	4%	13	567	5%	15	569

* NONCORPORATE
** CORPORATE

TABLE 6.5

Table of Interest Rates—Large Corporate Underpayments From January 1, 1991–Present

Period	Rate	Table	In 1995-1 CB, Page
Jan. 1, 1991–Mar. 31, 1991	13%	31	585
Apr. 1, 1991–June 30, 1991	12%	29	583
July 1, 1991–Sept. 30, 1991	12%	29	583
Oct. 1, 1991–Dec. 31, 1991	12%	29	583
Jan. 1, 1992–Mar. 31, 1992	11%	75	629
Apr. 1, 1992–June 30, 1992	10%	73	627
July 1, 1992–Sept. 30, 1992	10%	73	627
Oct. 1, 1992–Dec. 31, 1992	9%	71	625
Jan. 1, 1993–Mar. 31, 1993	9%	23	577
Apr. 1, 1993–June 30, 1993	9%	23	577
July 1, 1993–Sept. 30, 1993	9%	23	577
Oct. 1, 1993–Dec. 31, 1993	9%	23	577
Jan. 1, 1994–Mar. 31, 1994	9%	23	577
Apr. 1, 1994–June 30, 1994	9%	23	577
July 1, 1994–Sept. 30, 1994	10%	25	579
Oct. 1, 1994–Dec. 31, 1994	11%	27	581
Jan. 1, 1995–Mar. 31, 1995	11%	27	581
Apr. 1, 1995–June 30, 1995	12%	29	583
July 1, 1995–Sept. 30, 1995	11%	27	581
Oct. 1, 1995–Dec. 31, 1995	11%	27	581
Jan. 1, 1996–Mar. 31, 1996	11%	75	629
Apr. 1, 1996–June 30, 1996	10%	73	627
July 1, 1996–Sept. 30, 1996	11%	75	629
Oct. 1, 1996–Dec. 31, 1996	11%	75	629

Period	Rate	Table	In 1995-1 CB, Page
Jan. 1, 1997–Mar. 31, 1997	11%	27	581
Apr. 1, 1997–June 30, 1997	11%	27	581
July 1, 1997–Sept. 30, 1997	11%	27	581
Oct. 1, 1997–Dec. 31, 1997	11%	27	581
Jan. 1, 1998–Mar. 31, 1998	11%	27	581
Apr. 1, 1998–June 30, 1998	10%	25	579
July 1, 1998–Sept. 30, 1998	10%	25	579
Oct. 1, 1998–Dec. 30, 1998	10%	25	579
Jan. 1, 1999–Mar. 31, 1999	9%	23	577
Apr. 1, 1999–June 30, 1999	10%	25	579
July 1, 1999–Sept. 30, 1999	10%	25	579
Oct. 1, 1999–Dec. 31, 1999	10%	25	579
Jan. 1, 2000–Mar. 31, 2000	10%	73	627
Apr. 1, 2000–June 30, 2000	11%	75	629
July 1, 2000–Sept. 30, 2000	11%	75	629
Oct. 1, 2000–Dec. 31, 2000	11%	75	629
Jan. 1, 2001–Mar. 31, 2001	11%	27	581
Apr. 1, 2001–June 30, 2001	10%	25	579
July 1, 2001–Sept. 30, 2001	9%	23	577
Oct. 1, 2001–Dec. 31, 2001	9%	23	577
Jan. 1, 2002–Mar. 31, 2002	8%	21	575
Apr. 1, 2002–June 30, 2002	8%	21	575
July 1, 2002–Sept. 30, 2002	8%	21	575
Oct. 1, 2002–Dec. 31, 2002	8%	21	575
Jan. 1, 2003–Mar. 31, 2003	7%	19	573
Apr. 1, 2003–June 30, 2003	7%	19	573

TABLE 6.6
Table of Interest Rates—Large Corporate Overpayments From January 1, 1995–Present

Period	Rate	Table	In 1995–1 CB, Page
Jan. 1, 1995–Mar. 31, 1995	6.5%	18	572
Apr. 1, 1995–June 30, 1995	7.5%	20	574
July 1, 1995–Sept. 30, 1995	6.5%	18	572
Oct. 1, 1995–Dec. 31, 1995	6.5%	18	572
Jan. 1, 1996–Mar. 31, 1996	6.5%	66	620
Apr. 1, 1996–June 30, 1996	5.5%	64	618
July 1, 1996–Sept. 30, 1996	6.5%	64	620
Oct. 1, 1996–Dec. 31, 1996	6.5%	64	620
Jan. 1, 1997–Mar. 31, 1997	6.5%	18	572
Apr. 1, 1997–June 30, 1997	6.5%	18	572
July 1, 1997–Sept. 30, 1997	6.5%	18	572
Oct. 1, 1997–Dec. 31, 1997	6.5%	18	572
Jan. 1, 1998–Mar. 31, 1998	6.5%	18	572
Apr. 1, 1998–June 30, 1998	5.5%	16	570
July 1, 1998–Sept. 30, 1998	5.5%	16	570
Oct. 1, 1998–Dec. 30, 1998	5.5%	16	570
Jan. 1, 1999–Mar. 31, 1999	4.5%	14	568
Apr. 1, 1999–June 30, 1999	5.5%	16	570
July 1, 1999–Sept. 30, 1999	5.5%	16	570

Period	Rate	Table	In 1995–1 CB, Page
Oct. 1, 1999–Dec. 31, 1999	5.5%	16	570
Jan. 1, 2000–Mar. 31, 2000	5.5%	64	618
Apr. 1, 2000–June 30, 2000	6.5%	66	620
July 1, 2000–Sept. 30, 2000	6.5%	66	620
Oct. 1, 2000–Dec. 31, 2000	6.5%	66	620
Jan. 1, 2001–Mar. 31, 2001	6.5%	18	572
Apr. 1, 2001–June 30, 2001	5.5%	16	570
July 1, 2001–Sept. 30, 2001	4.5%	14	568
Oct. 1, 2001–Dec. 31, 2001	4.5%	14	566
Jan. 1, 2002–Mar. 31, 2002	3.5%	12	566
Apr. 1, 2002–June 30, 2002	3.5%	12	570
July 1, 2002–Sept. 30, 2002	3.5%	12	566

CHAPTER **7A**

Criminal Penalties

¶ 7A.01 CRIMINAL PENALTIES IN GENERAL

[1] In General

Criminal tax penalties have a long and colorful history. In the 1920s, such notorious criminals as Al Capone were finally convicted for tax crimes rather than for the many other crimes they allegedly committed.[1] More recently, criminal tax penalties have brought down a sitting U.S. vice president and other political figures. Nevertheless, it would be wrong to assume that criminal tax penalties are reserved for career criminals and greedy politicians. These penalties apply to all taxpayers, especially "white collar" criminals with social status and respectability.[2] In 1943, the Supreme Court described the purpose of penalties:

> The United States has relied for the collection of its income tax largely upon the taxpayer's own disclosures. . . . This system can function successfully only if those within and near taxable income keep and render true accounts. In many ways, taxpayers' neglect or deceit may prejudice the orderly and punctual administration of the system as well as the revenues themselves. Congress has imposed a variety of sanctions for the protection of the system and the revenues.[3]

Criminal tax penalties, then, "prohibit and punish fraud occurring in the assessment and collection of taxes."[4] It is believed that the threat of criminal sanctions varying in severity ranging from small fines to heavy prison sentences contributes to maintaining high levels of compliance with the revenue laws.[5]

---

[1] R. Grant & J. Katz, The Great Trials of the Twenties 98 (1998). Although charged with violations of the Volstead Act, Capone was tried only on the charge of tax evasion. The method of proof used was the net worth and expenditures method. Prosecution of organized crime figures did not end in the 1920s. Frank Costello, a gambler and organized crime figure, was charged and convicted of tax evasion for failing to report substantial amounts of income for the years 1947, 1948, and 1949, and the method of proof used was also the net worth method. Costello v. United States, 350 US 359 (1956).

[2] In fact, the Internal Revenue Service's (the Service's) Criminal Investigation Division (CID), which investigates criminal violations of the tax laws, has long had a program of investigating taxpayers in general for criminal tax violations. See Chapter 12 for a description of the CID's programs and investigative techniques.

[3] Spies v. United States, 317 US 492, 495 (1943).

[4] United States v. White, 417 F2d 89, 93 (2d Cir.), cert. denied, 397 US 912 (1969).

[5] This view may have been intuitive at the time the criminal tax laws were enacted, but now support exists in sociological and other data. See T. Tyler, Why People Obey the Law, 42 (Yale Univ. Press 1990) ("research suggests that certainty of apprehension and punishment mostly strongly influences behavior . . ."); Henderson, Jr., Comment, "Criminal Liability Under the Internal Revenue Code: A Proposal to Make the Voluntary Com-

Tax crimes are found in Chapter 75 of the Internal Revenue Code (the Code), "Crimes, Other Offenses, and Forfeitures." Subchapter A describes crimes ranging from the most serious—the felonies of an attempt to evade or defeat a tax "in any manner"[6] and of filing a false return[7] or false document[8]—to the misdemeanor of failing to file a return at all.[9] Another Code provision affecting criminal tax prosecutions is Section 6531, which establishes statutes of limitations on prosecutions.

Both the maximum period of incarceration and the maximum fine are part of the Code's description of tax crimes. Before the Sentencing Reform Act of 1984, within the statutory guidelines, federal district court judges sentenced defendants convicted of tax crimes based on probation reports and their own discretion. Since the first Sentencing Guidelines were published in 1987, the sentencing process is governed by these guidelines, which the U.S. Sentencing Commission adopts and periodically amends. Among other objectives, Sentencing Guidelines are intended to produce greater uniformity in sentencing. For tax crimes, the guidelines also make it likely that the defendant will be sentenced to a period of incarceration (and a longer one at that).[10]

[2] Code Offenses

The most frequently used criminal statutes in the Code are the following:

1. The willful attempt in any manner to evade or defeat tax or the payment of such tax, described in Section 7201 as a felony, punishable by a fine of up to $100,000 in the case of individuals, and up to $500,000 in the case of corporations, or imprisonment for not more than five years, or both, plus the costs of prosecution.
2. The willful failure to pay estimated tax, file a tax return, or supply information, described in Section 7203 as a misdemeanor, punishable by a fine of up to $25,000 ($100,000 in the case of corporations), or imprisoned not more than one year, or both, plus the costs of prosecution.
3. The willful subscribing of a return or other statement containing a written declaration that it is made under penalties of perjury, which

---

pliance System a Little Less Voluntary," 140 U. Pa. L. Rev. 1429 (1992). See also Chapter 12 for a description of the Service's policies in identifying and prosecuting taxpayers who violate the criminal tax laws.

[6] IRC § 7201.

[7] IRC § 7206(1).

[8] IRC § 7207.

[9] IRC § 7203.

[10] USSG § 2T1.1, Tax Evasion—Commentary, at 2.140.

the person signing does not believe to be true and correct as to a material matter, described in Section 7206(1) as a felony punishable by a fine of not more than $100,000 ($500,000 in the case of corporations) or imprisoned not more than three years or both, plus the costs of prosecution.

4. The willful aiding and assisting in the preparation of a false return or other documents that are fraudulent or false as to any material matter, whether or not the person required to file the return or document knows or consents to the falsity, described in Section 7206(2) as a felony punishable in the same manner as the filing of a false return under Section 7206(1).

5. Employment tax offenses described in Section 7204 (fraudulent statement or failure to make statements to employees), Section 7205 (fraudulent withholding exemption certificate or failure to supply information), and Section 7215 (offenses with respect to collected taxes).

6. An attempt to interfere with the administration of the internal revenue laws by any person who "corruptly or by force or threats of force (including any threatening letter or communication) obstructs or impedes or endeavors to obstruct or impede, the due administration of the [tax law]," described in Section 7212(a) as a felony, punishable by a fine of not more than $5,000, or imprisoned not more than 3 years, or both.

As this summary suggests, tax crimes sometimes overlap, so that the taxpayer or other person may be charged under more than one statute. If a taxpayer commits the crime of filing a false income tax return, he may also be committing the crime of tax evasion, if he filed the false return in an attempt to evade the income tax that is due and owing for the year. Evasion may be attempted by the filing of a false return, filing a false document, or failing to file any return at all, coupled with some other act of concealment—all of which are separate tax crimes. In part, this overlapping of possible crimes explains why tax indictments often charge both tax evasion and the filing of a false return.

[3] Title 18 Offenses

Overlapping crimes are not limited to criminal tax offenses in the Code. General federal criminal offenses are described in U.S. Code Title 18. Several of these crimes are used in tax prosecutions: the aiding and abetting statute (18 USC § 2), the conspiracy statute (18 USC § 371), and the false statement statute (18 USC § 1001). Not only do tax crimes described in the Code overlap; they sometimes overlap with these general federal offenses. For example, filing a false return may be prosecuted as tax evasion under Sections 7201 and

7206(1), and it may also be prosecuted under 18 USC § 1001, which makes it a crime for a person to make a false statement to a government official. As a result, two of the continuing issues in the criminal tax law are the extent to which offenses and penalties may be cumulated and whether Code offenses are the exclusive statutes under which a taxpayer may be prosecuted.

[4] Criminal Tax Offenses and the Civil Fraud Penalty

Both criminal and civil penalties are imposed to ensure full and honest disclosure and to discourage fraudulent attempts to evade tax.[11] But criminal and civil tax penalties are separate in theory and sequential in practice. A taxpayer may be liable for a civil penalty if the taxpayer is convicted of a criminal tax offense, or even if the taxpayer is acquitted of the offense. This issue was presented in *Helvering v. Mitchell*,[12] where the chairman of the National City Bank was acquitted of tax evasion for claiming a tax loss on National City Bank stock he had sold to his wife during the 1929 Wall Street crash, and failing to report a fee he received from the National City's management fund. Mitchell then received a notice of deficiency for the tax deficiency based on the stock loss and the omitted income, plus a civil fraud penalty. The Board of Tax Appeals found that Mitchell was not liable for the fraud penalty, because of the preclusive effect of the acquittal in the criminal case; but the Supreme Court disagreed, holding that assessment of the civil fraud penalty was not barred by Mitchell's acquittal on the indictment for the willful attempt to evade and defeat the tax. The Court found that sanctions in the form of money used to enforce compliance had long been held not to be criminal, and "are provided primarily as a safeguard for the protection of the revenue and to reimburse the Government for the heavy expense of investigation and the loss resulting from the taxpayer's fraud."[13] In short, the civil fraud penalty is considered remedial and an indemnity for loss.[14]

Also, in practice, the Internal Revenue Service (the Service) recognizes that the success of a criminal tax prosecution may depend on employees in civil functions of the Service taking no action that compromise the prosecution. To avoid threats to a successful prosecution, the Service generally requires that civil processing be deferred until the criminal aspects of a case are

---

[11] Helvering v. Mitchell, 303 US 391, 399 (1938).

[12] See Helvering v. Mitchell, 303 US 391 (1938) (taxpayer was acquitted of evasion, but found liable for a civil fraud penalty).

[13] Helvering v. Mitchell, 303 US 391, 400, 401 (1938).

[14] See *Halper* and other cases where a civil fraud penalty was argued to be penal in nature, so that its imposition violated the double jeopardy clause of the Constitution. See Chapter 7B.

resolved.[15] As a result, although criminal and civil penalties often punish the same misconduct, they are applied sequentially.

In addition, although both criminal and civil tax penalties are intended to deter noncompliance with tax filing and paying obligations, the procedures used to determine the taxpayer's liability are markedly different. Criminal penalties are imposed only after normal criminal processes, indictment or other charging paper, right to counsel, trial by jury, proof beyond a reasonable doubt, and the same constitutional guaranties and rights other criminal defendants are entitled to. Civil penalties are collected in the same manner as tax (indeed, statutorily, a civil penalty is considered part of the tax), or as the Supreme Court said in *Mitchell*, "a distinctly civil procedure,"[16] and a taxpayer is not liable for a civil penalty until the same procedures are followed that a taxpayer is permitted in disputes over liability for the tax itself.

[5] Tax Money Laundering Offenses

In 1970, Congress adopted the Bank Secrecy Act (BSA),[17] which requires banks and other financial institutions to report currency transactions and to maintain records of those transactions. The act's provisions are intended to assist the Service in developing evidence of violations of the tax law, as well as providing evidence for prosecutors to use in tax prosecutions. In 1984, Section 6050I was added to the Code, and information return reporting provision requires persons engaged in trades or businesses to file information returns, called currency transaction reports, reporting cash receipts of more than $10,000 received in their trade or business. If a person willfully fails to file a report required by Section 6050I, Section 7203 describes the crime as a felony, punishable by fine and imprisonment of up to five years, rather than a misdemeanor punishable by fine and a period of imprisonment of up to one year, as are other failure-to-file crimes.[18] Since this currency reporting provision was added to the Code, the Service was given the responsibility of conducting examinations to ensure compliance with both Section 6050I and the related regulations, and 31 USC § 5312 and the related regulations in 31 CFR Part 103. With two statutes covering substantially the same activities, two sets of regulations and two sets of reporting requirements can apply to the same cash transaction. To avoid duplicative reporting, Section 6050I provides exceptions to its currency reporting rules for (1) currency received in a transaction reported under Title 31 if reporting under Section 6050I would duplicate the reporting

---

[15] IRM 9.5.13.2.1, Criminal and Civil Tax (Dec. 14, 1998). See ¶ 12.01[3].

[16] Helvering v. Mitchell, 303 US 391, 402 (1938).

[17] BSA, 31 USC § 5312.

[18] IRC § 7203.

to the Treasury under Title 31 and (2) cash received by certain financial institutions, as defined in 31 USC § 5312, such as casinos, which are subject to reporting under Title 31.[19]

This chapter focuses on frequently used criminal penalties described in the Code, as well as certain other criminal penalties used in tax prosecutions contained in the Criminal Code, Title 18. Currency crimes contained in Section 6050I and Title 31 are summarized. The Service's Criminal Investigation function, its policies, and procedures, as well as the policies and procedures of the Criminal Tax Section, Tax Division, are described in Chapter 12. Civil penalties, which are also sanctions intended to enforce the filing and paying requirements of the Code, are the subject of Chapter 7B.

¶ 7A.02 THE EVASION STATUTE

[1] Elements of the Statute

[a] In General

Tax evasion is the most serious tax crime, and it is described broadly in Section 7201: "Any person who willfully attempts in any manner to evade or defeat any tax imposed by this title or the payment thereof shall, in addition to other penalties provided by law, be guilty of a felony.... " Three elements of the evasion charge can be identified from the statutory definition: (1) an additional tax due and owing; (2) an attempt to evade or defeat the tax; and (3) willfulness. Each of these elements is discussed in the subsections that follow. At this point, the notable feature of the evasion statute is its scope. By using the term "any person," the potential target of an evasion prosecution is unlimited. Not only may an individual taxpayer be prosecuted for evasion, but so may the taxpayer's attorney, accountant, or bookkeeper,[20] and so may the corporate officer who attempts to evade corporate tax[21] or the administrator of an

---

[19] IRC § 6050I(c).

[20] United States v. Alker, 255 F2d 851 (3d Cir. 1958) (attorney); United States v. Brill, 270 F2d 525 (3d Cir. 1959) (CPA).

[21] Section 7343 defines the term "person" as used in tax offenses set forth in the Code to include "an officer or employee of a corporation, or a member or employee of a partnership, who as such officer, employee, or other member is under a duty to perform the act in respect of which the violation occurs." For a case illustrating the point, see United States v. Berger, 456 F2d 1349 (2d Cir.), cert. denied, 409 US 892 (1972) (president).

estate attempting to evade tax.[22] The "any person" language of the evasion statute also means that the person may be prosecuted as a principal for the crime of tax evasion, or under Section 2 of U.S. Code Title 18 on the ground that the person aided and abetted the taxpayer in the evasion.[23] Since the attempt may be made in "any manner," all sorts of conduct may be charged as the "attempt." Tax evasion is an attempt offense, the attempt being a substantial, if unsuccessful, effort to evade or defeat a tax or its payment. Any type of effort to evade tax is sufficient to support a charge of attempted tax evasion. The tax that is the object of the attempted evasion can be income tax or "any tax" imposed by the internal revenue laws, and so an evasion may be of estate, excise, and employment taxes.[24] Also, the attempted evasion includes not only an attempt to evade liability for tax, but an attempt to defeat its payment.[25] The taxpayer who willfully fails to report income, and the taxpayer who has accurately reported his tax but has attempted to evade or defeat collection of the tax by transferring his assets beyond the reach of the Service, are both guilty of tax evasion.[26]

[b] Evasion of Payment

The evasion statute punishes an attempt to evade or defeat payment of a tax. Some form of transferring assets that would otherwise serve as a source of collection of a tax characterizes an evasion of payment case.[27] Where an at-

---

[22] United States v. Alker, 255 F2d 851 (3d Cir. 1958).

[23] The aiding and abetting statute is discussed infra ¶ 7A.07[1].

[24] See, e.g., United States v. Berger, 456 F2d 1349 (2d Cir.), cert. denied, 409 US 892 (1972) (attempt to evade corporate tax); United States v. Apodaca, 666 F2d 89 (5th Cir.), cert. denied, 459 US 823 (1982) (same); United States v. Alker, 255 F2d 851 (3d Cir. 1958) (estate tax); Kobey v. United States, 208 F2d 583 (9th Cir. 1954) (Social Security and employment tax); United States v. Conforte, 624 F2d 869 (9th Cir.), cert. denied, 449 US 1012 (1980) (evasion of Social Security and employment tax); United States v. Binder, 453 F2d 805 (2d Cir.), cert. denied, 407 US 920 (1972) (excise tax); United States v. Fruehauf, 522 F2d 284 (6th Cir. 1975) (conspiracy to evade excise tax); United States v. Townsend, 31 F3d 262 (5th Cir. 1994) (chief executive officer convicted of evading excise taxes of corporation).

[25] Since Section 7201 charges the single crime of evasion that may be committed by evading either the assessment or payment of taxes, an indictment is not duplicitous if it charges both evasion of the assessment of tax and evasion of payment. United States v. Mal, 942 F2d 682 (9th Cir. 1991).

[26] See, e.g., Lawn v. United States, 355 US 339 (1958) (conversion and diversion of corporate assets; delay of disclosure of income tax liabilities); United States v. Trownsell, 367 F2d 815 (7th Cir. 1966) (transfers to Swiss bank).

[27] See United States v. Trownsell, 367 F2d 815 (7th Cir. 1966) (transfers to Swiss bank account). For other cases involving attempts to defeat payment by removing property from the United States, see United States v. Voorhies, 658 F2d 710 (9th Cir. 1981); United States v. Snyder, 766 F2d 167 (4th Cir. 1985).

tempt to evade is charged, the element of a tax due and owing can be satisfied without a formal tax assessment,[28] but "when the crime charged is one of evading the payment of taxes that have been assessed in civil proceedings, the Government must prove a valid tax assessment."[29] Section 7206(4) also punishes post-assessment misconduct by making it a felony for a person to remove or conceal property subject to levy. While both evasion of payment and removing property subject to levy require proof of a valid assessment, the two crimes have different elements. It must be proved that acts of concealment punishable by Section 7206(4) occurred after the conditions precedent to the use of a levy (i.e., assessment, notice and demand, neglect, and refusal to pay) have occurred.[30]

Separate attempts to evade assessment of several years' taxes are usually charged in separate counts of an indictment because "the fraudulent action of a defendant often directly affects assessment for a particular tax."[31] In a classic evasion of payment case, the defendant was charged with evading payment of several years' taxes in separate counts describing that under a fictitious name, he transferred gold from Canada to a Swiss bank at a time when he had substantial tax liabilities.[32] The circuit court said, "A defendant attempting to evade payment of taxes may, as in this case, engage in transactions designed to conceal assets from the IRS in an attempt to evade payment of the taxes due for a number of years."[33] As a result, in evasion of payment cases, it is logical to charge distinct significant attempts to evade the payments of tax for the same group of tax years in separate counts.

---

[28] United States v. Voorhies, 658 F2d 710, 713 (9th Cir. 1981).

[29] United States v. Dack, 747 F2d 1172 (7th Cir. 1984). See also United States v. McGill, 984 F2d 222, 229 (3d Cir. 1992) (describing the elements of proof in an evasion of payment prosecution); United States v. McLaughlin, 126 F3d 130 (3d Cir. 1997) ("had the government charged the McLaughlins with evasion of payment, it would have had to prove a valid assessment from which the McLaughlins hid assets").

[30] United States v. Hook, 781 F2d 1166 (6th Cir. 1986).

[31] United States v. Pollen, 978 F2d 78, 87 (3d Cir. 1992), cert. denied, 114 S. Ct. 2332. The circuit court held, "As a result in evasion of payment cases, it is logical to charge distinct significant attempts to evade payment of tax for the same group of tax years in separate counts." The defendant argued that the language to evade or defeat "any tax" in Section 7201 meant that while there might be more than one attempt, the allowable unit of prosecution is the tax of a single year, and so the indictment had "impermissibly splintered the crime of tax evasion into potentially innumerable offenses." The circuit court rejected the argument, concluding that the plain language of Section 7201 "evinces the congressional intent to allow distinct, significant, affirmative acts of tax evasion to constitute separate section 7201 offenses."

[32] United States v. Pollen, 978 F2d 78 (3d Cir. 1992), cert. denied, 114 S. Ct. 2332.

[33] United States v. Pollen, 978 F2d 78, 87 (3d Cir. 1992), cert. denied, 113 S. Ct. 2332.

Evasion of payment may take less obvious forms than transferring assets to defeat collection of tax. In *United States v. Huebner*,[34] the defendants devised a scheme to help taxpayers evade tax collection. The defendants advised taxpayers to file petitions in bankruptcy and to backdate promissory notes, with the expectation that payments of the notes could be diverted to the taxpayers while tax collection was stopped by the Bankruptcy Code's automatic stay. A divided court reversed the defendant's conviction for evading and defeating the collection of the taxpayers' income tax, because the automatic stay would not permit the taxpayers to escape tax by making collection impossible. However, the conviction of a conspiracy to defraud was affirmed because the false notes created the deceitful appearance that bankruptcy protection was appropriate.

[2] An Additional Tax Is Due and Owing

To establish the crime of tax evasion, one element the government must prove "beyond a reasonable doubt" is that the taxpayer failed to report his correct tax liability and an additional tax was due and owing.[35] In tax evasion cases, understatements of tax liability usually result from (1) understatements or omissions of income; (2) claims of fictitious or improper deductions[36]; (3) false allocations of income; or (4) improper claims of credit or exemption.[37] Although the government must prove that a taxpayer owed more tax than reported, it need not prove the exact amount of tax evaded nor even the precise amount alleged in the indictment to have been evaded. The evidence need only warrant a finding that the amount of the tax evaded is substantial.[38]

[a] Tax Due and Owing

The correct tax in an evasion prosecution is computed in the same manner as in a civil case, with certain exceptions. For purposes of the evasion statute, a loss realized in a year following the year charged in the indictment may not

---

[34] United States v. Huebner, 16 F3d 348 (9th Cir. 1994).

[35] Sansone v. United States, 380 US 343, 351 (1965).

[36] See, e.g., United States v. Ragen, 314 US 513 (1942) (dividends deducted as "commissions").

[37] See, e.g., Janko v. United States, 281 F2d 156 (8th Cir. 1960), rev'd on other grounds, 366 US 716 (1961) (false dependency exemptions).

[38] United States v. Nunan, 236 F2d 576 (2d Cir. 1956), cert. denied, 353 US 912 (1957); Tinkoff v. United States, 86 F2d 868 (7th Cir.), cert. denied, 301 US 689 (1937); United States v. Schenck, 126 F2d 702 (2d Cir.), cert. denied sub nom. Moskowitz v. United States, 316 US 705 (1942).

be carried back to reduce the additional tax due and owing,[39] because the crime is complete when a false and fraudulent return is filed. But a loss realized before the year for which the false return is filed may be used to reduce the additional tax due and owing, since the loss carryforward is in the nature of an unclaimed deduction.[40] A taxpayer is not permitted to engage in an entire recasting of the return to reduce additional tax—for example, by changing a method of accounting (e.g., from cash to accrual)[41] or by using an accelerated method of depreciation.[42] On the other hand, a certificate of assessment based on a notice of deficiency may be sufficient evidence to establish that there is a tax due and owing, unless the defendant seeks to introduce evidence to rebut the assessment.[43] The assessment itself, not the summary of assessments and payments, must be rebutted. The defendant must be given the opportunity to disprove the assessment amount on the certificate, but not all evidence is sufficient to carry the defendant's burden of coming forward with evidence. In a case where the taxpayer failed to file a return and the Service prepared a substitute return, the taxpayer was unsuccessful in challenging the assessment when he showed that the certificate of assessments assessment was based on the substitute return for which the defendant's gross income was estimated and business expenses were not allowed.[44] Evidence is sufficient to challenge an

---

[39] Willingham v. United States, 289 F2d 283 (5th Cir.), cert. denied, 368 US 828 (1961).

[40] However, in Willingham v. United States, 289 F2d 283 (5th Cir. 1961), the court refused to allow a loss carryforward where the corporate taxpayer had incurred the loss two years before its bankruptcy reorganization and had attempted to carry the loss forward to reduce an understatement in tax for a subsequent year. The issue remains unresolved in cases not involving a corporate reorganization.

[41] United States v. Vardine, 305 F2d 60 (2d Cir. 1962).

[42] In United States v. Helmsley, 941 F2d 71 (2d Cir. 1991), cert. denied, 112 S. Ct. 1162 (1992), despite evidence that personal expenses were deducted, no tax was claimed to be due when depreciation was recalculated under the Accelerated Cost Recovery System, which the defendant had not previously elected to use. The Second Circuit rejected the defense, saying, "Absent the Commissioner's consent, a taxpayer who has used a particular depreciation method may not defend an evasion charge on the ground that, under an alternative method, additional depreciation could have been claimed." Also, according to the Second Circuit, when there are different options, the government's showing of a deficiency "cannot be rebutted by a selection of the most favorable option, where other equally available options result in a deficiency." However, the court noted that when an overpayment is mandatory under applicable law, the deficiency showing may be rebutted by a recalculation. The rather convincing dissent should be read, together with the majority decision, on these points. For another case involving the use of additional depreciation deductions to offset a tax due and owing, see Fowler v. United States, 352 F2d 100, 106 (8th Cir. 1965), cert. denied, 383 US 907 (1966).

[43] United States v. Silkman, 156 F3d 833 (8th Cir. 1998).

[44] On remand, the defendant in Silkman adopted this approach, and was convicted. On appeal, the circuit court rejected the argument, saying that the attack on the certificate

assessment if the defendant produces evidence showing, for example, that no tax was due and owing because the taxpayer's income was offset by business expenses.

[b] Constructive Dividends

Additional tax for purposes of the evasion statute may also be found where a taxpayer has received a constructive dividend. Courts disagree about whether a diversion of funds by a controlling shareholder of a closely held corporation constitutes a taxable constructive dividend if the corporation has no earnings and profits. Several circuits follow the rule in *United States v. Miller.*[45] that in a criminal tax prosecution, funds diverted by a shareholder of a wholly owned corporation constitute taxable income, irrespective of the existence of a sufficient cash surplus to make a distribution as a dividend. The *Miller* court stated that "[t]he difficulty in *automatically* applying the constructive distribution rules to [the false statement case before it] is that it completely ignores one essential element of the crime charged: the willful intent to evade taxes, and concentrates on the nature of the funds diverted."[46] Yet the *Miller* decision fails to answer some serious objections. Without any unpaid tax there can be no evasion, irrespective of an intent to evade. Since under *Miller* certain Code provisions dealing with corporate distributions are not followed, a receipt of funds could be considered taxable for criminal purposes, but not for civil purposes. Also, if these other provisions do not apply, it is unclear how a defendant could establish that no tax was due and owing. Despite the difficulties with *Miller*, no court has required the government to characterize diverted income in a criminal tax case.

---

was not a challenge to the assessment. See United States v. Silkman, 200 F3d 935 (8th Cir. 2000).

[45] United States v. Miller, 545 F2d 1204 (9th Cir. 1976), cert. denied, 430 US 930 (1977). See also Davis v. United States, 226 F2d 331 (6th Cir. 1955); United States v. Williams, 875 F2d 846 (11th Cir. 1989) (following *Miller* and *Davis*, and holding that government need not characterize diverted income in criminal tax cases). See also Bernstein v. United States, 234 F2d 475 (5th Cir. 1976) (disregarding reduction of earnings and profits for penalties). In United States v. Toushin, 899 F2d 617, 622 (7th Cir. 1990), the government argued for a "bright-line test" that money taken by the owner of a wholly owned business is not taxable until the owner uses the money as his own, since otherwise it would be difficult to distinguish skimming from legitimate acts. The circuit court, however, said that the issue was for the jury to evaluate. Where the unreported income is a constructive dividend, it has been said that the government need not prove that the defendant derived a personal benefit from the expenditure and intended to do so, but only that the expenditure was not an expenditure for the corporation's benefit. United States v. Mews, 923 F2d 67 (7th Cir. 1991).

[46] United States v. Miller, 545 F2d 1204, 1214 (9th Cir. 1976).

Other courts, especially the Second Circuit, hold that diverted amounts do not automatically constitute "income," but that the answer depends on the existence of earnings and profits.[47] The Second Circuit first adopted this view in *DiZenzo v. Commissioner*,[48] which involved a civil fraud penalty, but the Second Circuit follows the *DiZenzo* principle in criminal cases. In *United States v. D'Agostino*, the Second Circuit made clear that the *DiZenzo* principle applied in criminal cases, and specifically rejected the *Davis–Williams* cases.[49] The Second Circuit applies a return of capital theory, or "no earnings and profits, no income" rule, under which "diverted corporate finds are treated as a constructive dividend to the shareholder to the extent the corporation had earnings and profits. To the extent that a corporation's distribution to a shareholder is *not* made out of earnings and profits, I.R.C. § 301(c)(2) treats the distribution as a return of capital to the shareholder that is applied against and made in reduction of the adjusted basis of the shareholder's stock; or, if applicable, the distribution is treated as a return of a loan."[50]

The Second Circuit's return-of-capital theory does not depend on the intent of the defendant taxpayer. As long as the defendant proves that there were no earnings and profits, the amounts withdrawn are treated as a return of capital, as they are under the Code for civil tax purposes. At least one court has objected that this bright-line approach goes too far in a prosecution for filing a false corporate return under Section 7206(1). The Seventh Circuit said that in a false statement prosecution, the focus is clearly on the taxpayer's intent, so the court would require the defendant to produce evidence that he intended the amounts diverted from the corporation to be a return of capital. The circuit court found no such evidence of intent had been presented at trial.[51]

---

[47] See United States v. Ruffin, 575 F2d 346, 351 (2d Cir. 1978); Bernstein v. United States, 234 F2d 475 (5th Cir. 1956). However, the defendant bears the burden of production under which the defendant must make an initial showing on each key element of the theory—that is, the defendant must produce credible evidence that the corporation did not enjoy income or profits for the tax year in issue, and that the amount of the taxpayer's capital contribution exceeded the amount of the distribution from the corporation. Absent the defendant's carrying this burden of production, the defendant taxpayer does not establish an adequate basis in the record for the proposed return of capital jury instruction. Id.

[48] DiZenzo v. Comm'r, 348 F2d 122, 125–127 (2d Cir. 1965). See also United States v. Gollapudi, 130 F3d 66 (3d Cir. 1997) (although defendant presented evidence that the withholding amount was correct under a "gross-up" method, false statement about withholding amounts found because, in part, evidence showed that no withholding was actually made).

[49] United States v. D'Agostino, 145 F3d 69, 72–73 (2d Cir. 1998); United States v. Bok, 156 F3d 157 (2d Cir. 1998) (restating the return of capital theory).

[50] United States v. D'Agostino, 145 F3d 69, 72–73 (2d Cir. 1998).

[51] United States v. Peters, 153 F3d 445, 461 (7th Cir. 1998).

[c] Substantial Tax Due and Owing

It is generally accepted that the tax due and owing in an evasion prosecution must be "substantial," but that term has not been defined by the courts with any certainty.[52] A deficiency amount may seem minor or insubstantial in isolation, but significant as a percentage of the tax reported.[53] In *United States v. Nunan*, the court of appeals explained that the requirement of a substantial tax due and owing should be viewed in relation to all the circumstances:

> The showing by the government must warrant the finding that the amount of tax evaded is substantial . . . But this is not measured in terms of gross or net income nor by any particular percentage of the tax shown to be due and payable. All the attendant circumstances must be taken into consideration. . . . But a few thousand dollars of omissions of taxable income may in a given case warrant criminal prosecution, depending upon the circumstances of the particular case. Otherwise the rich and powerful could evade the income tax law with impunity.[54]

If the understatement in tax is insubstantial, a jury may not consider the evidence sufficient to establish a willful attempt to evade unpaid tax,[55] and where the proof shows a significantly smaller tax understatement than alleged in the indictment, a defendant may contend that the indictment unfairly prejudiced the consideration of the jury.

The substantial tax requirement seems to apply whether the proof is direct or circumstantial.[56] In circumstantial proof cases, however, there is a greater

---

[52] Indeed, it has also been said that there is no de minimis exception to the evasion statute. United States v. Marashi, 913 F2d 724 (9th Cir. 1990) (defendant argued that unclaimed deductions would have offset, but concededly would not have eliminated, unreported income).

[53] See, e.g., Janko v. United States, 281 F2d 156 (8th Cir. 1960), rev'd on other grounds, 366 US 716 (1961) (tax evaded was $134 in 1954 and $264 in the next two years, but the percentage of tax evaded equaled 28 percent for 1954 and 38 percent for 1955 and 1956); United States v. Marks, 68-2 USTC ¶ 9535 (D. Or. 1966), aff'd, 391 F2d 210 (9th Cir.), cert. denied, 393 US 839 (1968) (tax evaded was $375); United States v. Beasley, 519 F2d 233 (5th Cir. 1975), vacated and remanded on other grounds, 425 US 956 (1976) (payments of $491 out of a total sum due of $1,707; held, evasion of a substantial tax).

[54] United States v. Nunan, 236 F2d 576, 585 (2d Cir. 1956).

[55] United States v. Celentano, 391 F. Supp. 1252 (SDNY 1975) (understatement in income, not tax, was only $637 for 1965, and the understatement in tax for 1966, 1967, and 1969 was $2,671). But it has also been said that there is no de minimis exception to the evasion statute. United States v. Marashi, 913 F2d 724 (9th Cir. 1990) (argument that unclaimed deductions would have offset, but concededly would not have eliminated, unreported income).

[56] In United States v. Cindrich, 241 F2d 54 (3d Cir. 1957), the court said that a substantial understatement need be proved only in circumstantial or indirect proof (e.g., net

possibility of government error than in specific item method of proof cases. As a practical if not legal matter, therefore, the understatement may have to be larger in circumstantial proof cases than in specific item cases.[57]

[d] Methods of Proof in General

[i] In general. Proof that an additional tax is due and owing may be established either by direct evidence or by indirect or circumstantial evidence. Direct evidence of an additional tax due and owing is evidence of specific transactions affecting taxable income. Under this specific item method of proof, the government attempts to prove that specific transactions in which the taxpayer engaged during the year were not completely or accurately reflected in the income tax return, so that the income tax liability was understated. For example, taxpayers usually maintain books and records in which specific transactions are recorded as they occur. If the books are used to prepare the return, under the specific item method it may be shown that specific transactions (e.g., sales) were not reflected in the books and records. Similarly, if returns were prepared from bank statements for accounts in which business receipts were purportedly deposited, and invoices to customers along with canceled checks in payment of the invoices show that certain receipts were not deposited in the business account, this evidence directly proves an understatement in taxable income. The specific item method may also be used to establish that the taxpayer claimed fictitious deductions, false exemptions, or false tax credits.

The existence of an additional tax due and owing may also be established by circumstantial evidence, which in tax cases is called the circumstantial method of proof. In evasion cases, the circumstantial evidence methods used are almost exclusively the net worth, expenditures, and bank deposits methods. Occasionally, the market of a merchandising business can be sufficiently proved to reconstruct the gross income of a business from its volume of sales.

[ii] The net worth method. The net worth method focuses on what a taxpayer has done with income received rather than on the source of the income. Unexplained funds or acquired property (increases in net worth) in excess of reported income and cash resources is considered the equivalent of unreported income. Here the term "net worth" means the difference between a

---

worth) cases, not direct (specific item) cases. This decision has not been followed, and, in fact, in United States v. Nunan, 236 F2d 576 (2d Cir. 1956), cert. denied, 353 US 912 (1957), the proof was of specific items of omitted income.

[57] For this reason, the Service and the Criminal Section in the Justice Department's Tax Division require a minimum tax deficiency of $10,000 where a circumstantial method of proof is used in a multiyear case. IRM, Chief Counsel Directives Manual (31) 310, MT (31)-28 (Dec. 11, 1989) (Prosecution Standards). 53 J. Tax'n 254 (Oct. 1980) (Justice Department Standards). See also ¶ 12.03[3][a].

person's assets at cost and his liabilities on a given date. If a person's assets at the end of the year are greater than they were at the beginning of the year and his liabilities remain the same, his net worth has obviously increased. As described by the Supreme Court in *Holland v. United States*, the evidence presented under the net worth method is as follows:

> In a typical net worth prosecution, the government, having concluded that the taxpayer's records are inadequate as a basis for determining income tax liability, attempts to establish an "opening net worth" or total net value of the taxpayer's assets at the beginning of a given year. It then proves increases in the taxpayer's net worth for each succeeding year during the period under examination and calculates the difference between the adjusted net values of the taxpayer's assets at the beginning and end of each of the years involved. The taxpayer's nondeductible expenditures, including living expenses, are added to these increases, and if the resulting figure for any year is substantially greater than the taxable income reported by the taxpayer for that year, the government claims the excess represents unreported taxable income. In addition, it asks a jury to infer wilfulness from this understatement, when taken in connection with direct evidence of "conduct the likely effect of which would be to mislead or to conceal." Spies v. United States, 317 U.S. 492, 499 (1943).[58]

To simplify, the net worth method can be restated as follows: (1) an increase in net worth (i.e., assets minus liabilities), plus (2) nondeductible disbursements, minus (3) nontaxable receipts, equals (4) taxable income before exemptions.

Finally, as the Supreme Court made clear in *Holland*, an apparent inadequacy of a taxpayer's records is not a precondition to the use of the net worth method. Even if a taxpayer has records that appear adequate, the government may use the net worth method.

The following sections deal with significant problem areas that arise in net worth prosecutions.

Starting point. The government must establish the taxpayer's net worth at the beginning of the tax year or sequence of tax years with reasonable accuracy. In *Holland*, the Supreme Court said an essential condition in a net worth determination of income is that the prosecution must establish "with reasonable certainty" an opening net worth to serve as a starting point from which to calculate future increases in the taxpayer's net worth.[59] Accuracy in the starting net worth is vital to the proper use of this method, because an inaccurate starting net worth affects the accuracy of the determination of income after the

---

[58] Holland v. United States, 348 US 121, 125 (1954). It is plain error for a court to fail to instruct a jury on the assumptions inherent in the net worth method. United States v. Hall, 650 F2d 994, 999 (9th Cir. 1981).

[59] Holland v. United States, 348 US 121, 122 (1954).

starting point. If a taxpayer's starting net worth is understated, apparent increases in net worth and thus taxable income for the periods in the prosecution will be overstated. In other words, the premise that an increase in net worth plus nondeductible expenditures during the year is equivalent to taxable income is true only if the increase over reported income does not reflect accumulations of wealth from previous taxable years. Not surprisingly, therefore, the most frequent defense in a net worth evasion prosecution is that apparent increases in net worth were the result of a "cash hoard" accumulated in a prior taxable period and spent during the prosecution years.[60]

Evidence of beginning net worth (i.e., the visible assets and liabilities owned and owed by the taxpayer) is usually presented in the form of third-party records, such as

- Bank records;
- County real estate records;
- Brokerage records;
- Bureau of public debt records;
- Federal and state income, inheritance, and gift tax returns and records; and
- Books and records of the taxpayer.[61]

To show that the taxpayer had no cash hoard, the prosecution can present evidence that negates its existence.[62] This evidence may take a number of forms, such as the following:

---

[60] However, the defendant-taxpayer has the burden of proving the existence of a cash hoard. Friedberg v. United States, 348 US 142 (1954); Gay v. United States, 567 F2d 1206 (2d Cir. 1978).

[61] For a description of the government's investigation, see United States v. Costanzo, 581 F2d 28 (2d Cir. 1978), cert. denied, 439 US 1067 (1979); United States v. Mastropieri, 685 F2d 776 (2d Cir. 1982), cert. denied, 459 US 945 (1982) (case with evidence fitting both a net worth and an expenditures analysis).

[62] Compare United States v. Giacolone, 574 F2d 328 (6th Cir.), cert. denied, 439 US 834 (1978), followed in United States v. Smith, 80-2 USTC ¶ 9730 (6th Cir. 1979) (not an error for Service summary to show zero cash on hand in prosecution of gambler, and jury could find a gambler's bankroll stayed about the same during prosecution period and that alleged cash hoard did not exist) and United States v. Scrima, 819 F2d 996 (11th Cir. 1987) (net worth method described; use of cash or cash formula "where cash is unknown but constant factor throughout the prosecution period" following Giacolone; taxpayer's admission on opening net worth was not permitted to be rebutted by his hearsay statement about amount of his available funds) with United States v. Carriger, 592 F2d 312 (6th Cir. 1979) (error for court to exclude evidence of loan of currency to and promissory note given back by taxpayer before opening net worth).

- Written or oral admissions of the taxpayer to the investigating agent concerning his net worth in the form of signed net worth statements, oral statements as to cash on hand, or accountant's work papers[63];
- The taxpayer's prior tax return filing history (e.g., the taxpayer's failure to file returns for years before the indictment period)[64];
- Financial statements given to commercial establishments and other entities[65];
- Evidence of financial deprivation[66]; or
- Low earnings for years prior to prosecution years as shown by records of former employers and the Social Security Administration.[67]

Evidence of a starting point provided by a taxpayer's own admission requires corroboration. In *Smith v. United States*,[68] the defendant gave agents a five-page net worth statement, including a list of his securities, living expenses, and assets for each of the years in the prosecution period. The Supreme Court held that the general rule that an accused may not be convicted on his own uncorroborated confession was applicable to the crime of tax evasion, at least where the statement or admission is made after the fact to an official charged with investigating the possibility of wrongdoing and the statement embraces an element vital to the prosecution's case. The defendant taxpayer's admissions in *Smith* were corroborated by independent evidence in

---

[63] Smith v. United States, 348 US 147 (1954). This is not a requirement that the admission must be made to the special or revenue agent. The taxpayer's admission can be made to any person. See United States v. Scott, 660 F2d 1145 (7th Cir. 1981) (letter from former attorney general of Illinois to his estranged wife). United States v. Mastropieri, 685 F2d 776 (2d Cir. 1982) (statement made to a state probation officer used to corroborate absence of cash on hand at starting point).

[64] Smith v. United States, 348 US 147 (1954). The return or failure to file a return is considered an admission of the amount of taxable income received or the nonreceipt of sufficient taxable income to file a return. The irony and fallacy of accepting a return as an admission is that the same return that is considered accurate for the tax due and owing element is taken to be fraudulent for purposes of the attempt element.

[65] Friedberg v. United States, 348 US 142 (1954).

[66] Holland v. United States, 348 US 121 (1954) (prior indebtedness, compromise of overdue debts, avoidance of bankruptcy); Friedberg v. United States, 348 US 142 (1954) (bankruptcy and mortgage foreclosure).

[67] These examples are not exhaustive. See, e.g., United States v. Terrell, 754 F2d 1139 (5th Cir.), cert. denied, 472 US 1029 (1985) (cash on hand at starting point established by source and application of funds analysis). The results of the government's investigation, the evidence presented in court through testimony, and documentary evidence are summarized in a net worth statement testified to by a special agent.

[68] Smith v. United States, 348 US 147 (1954).

the form of the taxpayer's tax return filing history and expenditures during the prosecution period.[69]

Equation of net worth increase to taxable income. Increases in net worth may be attributable to three possible sources: (1) prior accumulations of income; (2) current income; and (3) nontaxable sources, such as gifts or inheritances. In *Holland*, therefore, the Supreme Court said that "increase in net worth, standing alone, cannot be assumed to be attributable to currently taxable income. But proof of a likely source, from which the jury could reasonably find that the net worth increases sprang, is sufficient. . . . "[70] The assumption that proof of a likely source of taxable income was necessary in every net worth case was later clarified by the Court in *United States v. Massei*,[71] where it said that "should all possible sources of nontaxable income be negatived, there would be no necessity for proof of a likely source."[72] Generally, the source of reported income is the same as the source of unreported income, so that the prosecution has little problem with this element of the net worth case. For example, in *Holland,* the taxpayer's hotel business appeared to increase during the prosecution years while reported profits fell to about one quarter of the amount declared by the previous management in a comparable period. However, even the reported source may have limitations, unless that source is open-ended.[73] Gambling, for example, has been said to have unlimited possibilities.[74] Nontaxable sources of income may be negatived by proving nonre-

---

[69] See also United States v. Calderon, 348 US 160 (1954) (financial history of defendant corroborated his statements about cash on hand); United States v. Mastropieri, 685 F2d 776 (2d Cir. 1982) (special agent's investigation was corroborated by defendant's statements to and questionnaire filed with probation office). It has been held that the corroboration requirement does not necessarily extend to admissions relating to cash on hand, because "the inherent secrecy of the cash hoard makes it impossible for any but the keeper to know even of its existence, let alone the amount." United States v. Normile, 587 F2d 784, 786 (5th Cir. 1979).

[70] Holland v. United States, 348 US 121, 137–138 (1954).

[71] United States v. Massei, 355 US 595 (1958).

[72] United States v. Williams, 837 F2d 1009 (11th Cir. 1988) (government was able to prove that the likely source of taxpayer's unreported income was cash generated in bingo operations; income and expense reports that were not admissible as business records were admissible as the taxpayer's admissions).

[73] The government must introduce some affirmative evidence of the likely source. If the government has not verified that the reported source is the likely source, it has failed to establish an essential element of its case. United States v. Grasso, 629 F2d 805 (2d Cir. 1980). See also United States v. Mastropieri, 685 F2d 776 (2d Cir. 1982) (language in *Grasso* that government must negate "all possible sources of nontaxable source" means government must investigate "reasonably possible sources of income and . . . whatever leads taxpayers or others may proffer"); United States v. Bethea, 537 F2d 1187 (4th Cir. 1976) (increase not shown to be from taxpayer's usual source, carpentry).

[74] Costello v. United States, 350 US 359 (1956), aff'g 221 F2d 668 (2d Cir. 1955). See also United States v. Ford, 237 F2d 57 (2d Cir. 1956) (graft); Ford v. United States,

ceipt of loans, gifts, and inheritances by a taxpayer's own admission. Also, this evidence may be provided by contradicting the taxpayer's assertions of nontaxable sources.[75]

Investigation of leads. In *Holland*, the Supreme Court said that one of the requirements for using the net worth method is that when a taxpayer offers leads or information during the investigation that, if true, would establish his innocence, the prosecution must investigate the leads if they reasonably can be checked. This requirement also extends to a lead or information supplied after the investigation is completed but within a sufficient time before trial to be checked.[76] If the prosecution fails during the trial of the case to show that an investigation into the validity of such information was made, the trial judge may consider the information true and the prosecution's case insufficient to go to the jury.[77] The prosecution's burden is to negate reasonable explanations, not to investigate leads that are not susceptible to reasonable verification.[78] The

---

210 F2d 313 (5th Cir. 1954) (police chief alleged to have received graft); United States v. Scott, 660 F2d 1145 (7th Cir. 1981) (likely source shown to be campaign contributions, not salary); United States v. Vannelli, 595 F2d 402 (8th Cir. 1979) (prior conviction for misappropriation of funds admissible to show likely source); United States v. Klein, 80-1 USTC ¶ 9109 (10th Cir. 1980) (postindictment return used to show law practice likely source). See also United States v. Abodeely, 801 F2d 1020 (8th Cir. 1986) (evidence of income from prostitution and made wagers held admissible in support of both bank deposits and expenditures methods).

[75] In United States v. Adonis, 221 F2d 717 (3d Cir. 1955), the taxpayer claimed in an unrelated case that the $44,000 he used to purchase a house had come from loans and gifts. The government proved that the alleged donor was supported by her family and that the supposed creditors were dummies or of such financial condition as to imply that they had no available assets to lend.

[76] United States v. Vardine, 305 F2d 60 (2d Cir. 1962). A lead first revealed at trial imposes no duty on the government to investigate. United States v. Gay, 567 F2d 1206 (2d Cir. 1978). See United States v. Terrell, 754 F2d 1139 (5th Cir.), cert. denied, 472 US 1029 (1985) (evidence showed that taxpayer concealed information about cattle claimed to have been owned at the starting point). Once the case has begun, the defendant who claims to have a lead or explanation casting doubt on the net worth analysis remains silent at his peril. United States v. Notch, 939 F2d 895 (10th Cir. 1991).

[77] Holland v. United States, 348 US 121 (1954). In United States v. Keller, 523 F2d 1009 (9th Cir. 1975), a conviction for evasion was reversed where the government failed to pursue leads that reasonably could be checked, and the district court erroneously let the case go to the jury. However, an incredible lead need not be followed up by extensive investigation. United States v. Londe, 587 F2d 18 (8th Cir. 1978), cert. denied, 439 US 1130 (1979). See United States v. Blandina, 895 F2d 293 (7th Cir. 1989) (net worth method; where lead checked, IRS agent's testimony about interviews of persons contacted held not hearsay, and government's obligation on another lead discharged where defendant refused to supply records claiming privilege).

[78] Mighell v. United States, 233 F2d 731 (10th Cir.), cert. denied, 352 US 832 (1956) (vague gambling winnings, oral claims to large bills in safes and safe deposit boxes); United States v. Ford, 237 F2d 57 (2d Cir. 1956) (gifts from brother and great-aunt Mary).

leads doctrine nevertheless presents a serious dilemma to taxpayers and their counsel. If a lead is given, the government may be able to prove that the lead is inadequate or insufficient to destroy the prosecution's case. On the other hand, if a lead is not provided, the government is relieved of the obligation to investigate the lead altogether.

Use of charts. In *Holland*, the Supreme Court also contemplated that a summary chart would be used by the prosecution to summarize evidence of net worth increases.[79] Although use of summary charts is generally accepted,[80] the summary chart itself is not evidence, but only an organization of admitted evidence.[81] The court must determine that the summary chart fairly represents and summarizes the evidence on which it is based,[82] and the chart is inadmissible if it contains, for example, an unexplained figure for cash on hand.[83] It is also required that sufficient explanation be provided to allow the jury to see how the numbers in the chart were derived from the underlying evidence.[84]

[iii] The expenditures method. Closely related to the net worth method is the expenditures method of proving income. This method is based on the theory that if a taxpayer's expenditures during a given period exceed his reported income and the sources of those expenditures are established, directly or inferentially, to be taxable, it may be inferred that the expenditures represent unreported income.[85] One circuit court has provided this description of the expenditures method:

> The net worth method involves the ascertaining of a taxpayer's net worth positions at the beginning and end of a tax period, and deriving that part

---

[79] Holland v.United States, 348 US 121 (1954).

[80] United States v. Lawhon, 499 F2d 352, 357 (5th Cir. 1974), cert. denied, 419 US 1121 (1975); United States v. Sorrentino, 726 F2d 876, 877 (1st Cir. 1984) (approving use of government's summary, but also approving exclusion of taxpayer's counter-summary net worth statement). Failure to require production of a special agent's net worth summary under the Jencks Act (18 USC § 3500) has been held to constitute reversible error. *United States v. Sorrentino,* supra.

[81] See United States v. Price, 722 F2d 88 (5th Cir. 1983) (where controverted evidence was involved, line was crossed between laying foundation for use of chart and eliciting testimony bolstering prior testimony and "usurping the jury's rightful place"); United States v. Mann III, 884 F2d 532 (10th Cir. 1989) (use of charts discussed).

[82] United States v. Citron, 783 F2d 307 (2d Cir. 1986) (cases gathered).

[83] United States v. Citron, 783 F2d 307 (2d Cir. 1986) (cases gathered).

[84] United States v. Citron, 783 F2d 307 (2d Cir. 1986) (cases gathered).

[85] United States v. Marshall, 557 F2d 527 (5th Cir. 1977). The government is not required to reestablish the taxpayer's net worth at the beginning of each tax year with evidence independent of the other years. Cash on hand, or its absence, can be established using a source and application of funds analysis, which involves demonstrating that a taxpayer spent more or less than he otherwise had available to him during that time. United States v. Marrinson, 832 F2d 1465 (7th Cir. 1987) (cash hoard disproved).

of any increase not attributable to reported income. This method, while effective against taxpayers who channel their income into investment or durable property, is unavailing against the taxpayer who consumes his self-determined tax free dollars during the year and winds up no wealthier than before. The cash expenditure method is devised to reach such a tax-payer by establishing the amount of his purchases of goods and services which are not attributable to the resources at hand at the beginning of the year or to non-taxable receipts during the year. The beginning and ending net worth positions must be identified with sufficient particularity to rule out or account for the use of a taxpayer's capital to pay for his purchases. If the end-of-year net worth position is equal to that at the beginning of the year, and if there are no non-taxable sources of income during the year, such as gifts or inheritances, the totality of the year's expenditures reflects total taxable income. If ending net worth shows an increase, the increase reflects an added component of income. If ending net worth shows a diminution, the decrease reduces pro tanto the extent to which expenditures reflect income.[86]

In *United States v. Johnson*,[87] the prosecution treated all of the taxpayer's nondeductible disbursements as expenditures without regard to whether they increased his net worth. The expenditures represented investments in realty so that if the realty investments had been treated as reflecting annual net worth increases instead of the continuous outflows of money, the prosecution could have translated the available evidence into annual net worth increases. The Tax Division's Criminal Section prefers to translate expenditures into increases in net worth because the net worth method has been approved by the Supreme Court and is more easily understood, but expenditures cases are still made from time to time.[88]

[iv] The bank deposits method. The bank deposits method is based on the premise that under certain circumstances, proof of deposits is substantial

---

[86] Taglianetti v. United States, 398 F2d 558, 562–563 (1st Cir. 1968) (footnotes omitted), aff'd on another issue, 394 US 316 (1969).

[87] United States v. Johnson, 319 US 503 (1943).

[88] See United States v. King, 563 F2d 559 (2d Cir.), cert. denied, 435 US 918 (1977); United States v. Mastropieri, 685 F2d 776 (2d Cir. 1982) (government apparently chose to prove expenditures case although expenditures used to purchase realty and other invest-ments). In using the expenditures method, as with the net worth method of proof, the gov-ernment proffers summaries of prior testimony in the form of a schedule prepared by and testified to by a special agent. For a case analyzing objections to the use of this type of summary exhibit, see United States v. Radseck, 718 F2d 233 (7th Cir. 1983) (exhibit properly admitted without hearing to determine accuracy of exhibits). But see United States v. Conlin, 551 F2d 534 (2d Cir.), cert. denied, 434 US 831 (1977). Compare United States v. McDonnell, 699 F. Supp. 1348 (ND Ill. 1988) (expenditures method used; exclu-sion of summary charts denied over objections that they contained evidence of other

evidence of taxable receipts. The description of the bank deposits method in *Gleckman v. United States* is the standard one:

> [I]f it be shown that a man has a business or calling of a lucrative nature and is constantly, day by day and month by month, receiving moneys and depositing them to his account and checking against them for his own uses, there is most potent testimony that he has income, and, if the amount exceeds exemptions and deductions, that the income is taxable.[89]

The bank deposits method requires evidence showing that the deposits (1) were regularly or periodically made; (2) have the inherent appearance of business receipts; and (3) have been analyzed to eliminate loans, redeposits, transfers of funds between accounts, and nonincome deposits, from the annual sum of deposits considered to be income.[90] Thus, taxable income is proved through an analysis of all bank deposits and all bank accounts and canceled checks, if available. Since the taxpayer may make cash payments from currency receipts not deposited, cash receipts and cash expenditures must be taken into account in computing additional gross income. The usual formula for determining taxable income by the bank deposits method of a taxpayer whose only source of income is from business operations is as follows:

1. Total deposits
2. Plus: Payments made in cash
3. Subtotal
4. Less: Nonincome deposits and items
5. Equals: Total receipts
6. Less: Business expenses and costs
7. Equals: Net income from business
8. Less: Deductions and exemptions
9. Equals: Taxable income

The bank deposits method does not require proof of a starting point in the same manner as a net worth case. The bank deposits proof itself indicates the receipt of current income reflected in deposits. However, amounts on deposit prior to the tax years in question must be deducted.[91] Also, an accurate cash on

---

crimes contrary to Federal Rules of Evidence 404(b) and that government failed to follow up leads).

[89] Gleckman v. United States, 80 F2d 394, 399 (8th Cir. 1935), cert. denied, 297 US 709 (1936); United States v. Ludwig, 897 F2d 875 (7th Cir. 1990) (jury instructions in bank deposits case, including cash-hoard defense and investigation of leads, reviewed and approved).

[90] United States v. Morse, 491 F2d 149, 152 (1st Cir. 1974); Kirsch v. United States, 174 F2d 595 (8th Cir. 1949). But see United States v. Stone, 770 F2d 842 (9th Cir. 1985) (test check of deposits held sufficient under *Morse* to eliminate nonincome items).

[91] Price v. United States, 335 F2d 671, 677 (5th Cir. 1964).

hand figure for the beginning of the taxable year must be established if deposits from a previously accumulated cash hoard are to be excluded from "income."[92] But the bank deposits method does not require proof of increases in net worth, "because the evidence of bank deposits suffices to raise the inference that the taxpayer's income came from a taxable source."[93]

Essential in the use of the bank deposits method is an analysis of the taxpayer's accounts. The analysis must identify income and nonincome deposits. Deposits from nontaxable sources do not create an inference of unreported taxable income. Where the analysis is inadequate to show what deposits were nonincome deposits, conviction has been reversed.[94] Also, the prosecution must present evidence at trial corroborating the agent's analysis of nonincome deposits.[95] Finally, the "leads" doctrine developed in net worth cases also applies to bank deposits cases.[96] Consequently, the Service's agents are obliged to investigate all reasonable leads as to nonincome deposits.

[3] The Attempted Evasion

Section 7201 states that an evasion attempt "in any manner" is sufficient for the offense. No definition of "attempt" is provided in the evasion statute. Since nonpayment of tax may occur in both evasions and failures to file, the "at-

---

[92] United States v. Slutsky, 487 F2d 832, 842 (2d Cir.), cert. denied, 416 US 937, reh'g denied, 416 US 1000 (1974); United States v. Boulet, 577 F2d 1165 (5th Cir. 1978), cert. denied, 439 US 1114 (1979) ("the government must establish in some fashion the amount of cash the taxpayer had on hand at the start of the period"). However, cash on hand at the end of the year must be added to the sum of deposits to reflect total income for the year.

[93] United States v. Conaway, 11 F3d 40 (5th Cir. 1993) (cash expenditures and bank deposits method used; cash on hand determined from safety deposit box access dates and deposits).

[94] Kirsch v. United States, 174 F2d 595 (8th Cir. 1949). See United States v. Lenamond, 83-1 USTC ¶ 9299 (ND Tex. 1982) (motion of acquittal granted because government failed to conduct full and adequate investigation in a bank deposits case where evidence showed inventory figures "truly anomalous" and defendant had provided leads indicating government's figures were erroneous).

[95] United States v. Morse, 491 F2d 149, 152 (1st Cir. 1974); cf. United States v. Helina, 549 F2d 713 (9th Cir. 1977); United States v. Boulet, 577 F2d 1165 (5th Cir. 1978), cert. denied, 439 US 1114 (1979) (requirement of negating nonincome deposits "may be satisfied by proof that did not disclose nontaxable sources").

[96] United States v. Slutsky, 487 F2d 832, 843 n.14 (2d Cir.), cert. denied, 416 US 937, reh'g denied, 416 US 1000 (1974); United States v. Ramsdell, 450 F2d 130, 133 (10th Cir. 1971); United States v. Stein, 437 F2d 775, 778 (7th Cir.), cert. denied, 403 US 905 (1971); United States v. Boulet, 577 F2d 1165 (5th Cir. 1978), cert. denied, 439 US 1114 (1979) (government checked explanation susceptible to investigation before trial, but another explanation was presented for the first time at trial; held, government "satisfied its obligation to explore leads thoroughly").

tempt" language of the statute distinguishes the evasion statute from a mere failure to file a tax return. In *Spies v. United States*, the Supreme Court said that the evasion statute and the failure-to-file statute covered distinct situations:

> The difference between the two offenses, it seems to us, is found in the affirmative action implied from the term "attempt," as used in the felony subsection. It is not necessary to involve this subject with the complexities of the common law "attempt." The attempt made criminal by this statute does not consist of conduct that would culminate in a more serious crime but for some impossibility of completion or interruption or frustration. This is an independent crime, complete in its most serious form when the attempt is complete and nothing is added to its criminality by success or consummation, as would be the case, say, of attempted murder. Although the attempts succeed in evading tax, there is no criminal offense of that kind, and the prosecution can only be for the attempt.[97]

Accordingly, the term "attempt" contemplates some affirmative conduct. A failure to file a tax return, standing alone, does not make out the crime of evasion, but where the failure to file is coupled with affirmative acts or conduct, there is an attempt within the meaning of the evasion statute.[98]

The attempt may be made "in any manner." In *Spies v. United States*, the Supreme Court listed "by way of illustration" some of the circumstances from which a willful attempt to evade might be inferred:

---

[97] Spies v. United States, 317 US 492, 498–499 (1943). The nature of an attempt for purposes of the evasion statute includes conduct that may serve other purposes, such as concealment of another crime. Id. at 499. For example, steps a lawyer took to conceal his embezzlement from an estate also constituted actions intended to conceal his receipt of the embezzled funds from the Service. United States v. Eaken, 17 F3d 203 (7th Cir. 1994).

[98] United States v. King, 563 F2d 559 (2d Cir.), cert. denied, 435 US 918 (1977) (failure to file a return coupled with concealment of payoffs to policeman); United States v. Copeland, 786 F2d 768 (7th Cir. 1986) ("[w]here a taxpayer has willfully failed to file a tax return in violation of Section 7203, a prior, concomitant or subsequent false statement may elevate the Section 7203 misdemeanor to the level of a Section 7201 felony"); United States v. Frederickson, 846 F2d 517 (8th Cir. 1988) (failure to file coupled with false statements to agents constituted affirmative acts of evasion). See also United States v. Higgins, 2 F3d 1094 (10th Cir. 1993) (twenty years of nonfiling coupled with false statements to special agent and the use of a false Social Security number led to evasion charge); United States v. Klausner, 80 F3d 55 (2d Cir. 1996) (accountant failed to file for four years and then lied to special agent about the number of returns he prepared, his expected tax liability, and his joint adjusted gross income; *Romano*, infra, distinguished on the ground that the defendant in *Romano* corrected his misstatement in the same interview). But see United States v. Romano, 938 F2d 1569 (2d Cir. 1991) (failure to file 1983 return after defendant had attempted to transport currency out of country was held not to be attempt to evade, because of defendant's "overall voluntary attitude" and reliance for nonfiling on advice of counsel).

- Keeping a double set of books[99];
- Making false entries or alterations[100];
- Making false invoices or documents[101];
- Destruction of books or records[102];
- Concealment of assets or covering up sources of income[103];
- Handling one's affairs to avoid the making of records usual in transactions of the kind[104]; and
- "Conduct the likely effect of which would be to mislead or conceal."[105]

In *Spies*, it should be noted, the conduct involved was use of currency and putting property in the names of family members.[106]

As pointed out in *Spies*, the attempt to evade may take many forms. Where a taxpayer has failed to file a return, for example, the taxpayer's filing of a false Form W-4 with his employer constituted an affirmative act for purposes of an evasion charge.[107] In one case, a defendant, King, filed false Forms W-4 on which he claimed to be exempt from withholding in both 1983 and

---

[99] Noro v. United States, 148 F2d 696 (5th Cir. 1945) (classic double set of books—one false set in English, the true set in Japanese).

[100] United States v. Lange, 161 F2d 699 (7th Cir. 1947); United States v. Stoehr, 196 F2d 276 (3d Cir.), cert. denied, 344 US 826 (1952).

[101] United States v. Lange, 161 F2d 699 (7th Cir. 1947); Marienfeld v. United States, 214 F2d 632 (8th Cir.), cert. denied, 348 US 865 (1954); United States v. Walker, 896 F2d 295 (8th Cir. 1990) (personal expenses charged to business with forged invoices, deposits of cash, and failure to report interest). United States v. Townsend, 31 F3d 262 (5th Cir. 1994) ("Townsend prepared a fraudulent Form 637 that contained two forged signatures and a fabricated registration number").

[102] United States v. Ragen, 314 US 513, 585 (1942); Gariepy v. United States, 220 F2d 252 (6th Cir.), cert. denied, 350 US 825 (1955).

[103] Gendelman v. United States, 191 F2d 993 (9th Cir.), cert. denied, 342 US 909 (1952); United States v. Chapman, 168 F2d 997 (7th Cir.), cert. denied, 335 US 853 (1948); United States v. Boone, 951 F2d 1526 (9th Cir. 1991) (failure to file return and channeling money through various trust and corporate accounts and applying to personal use); United States v. Gonzales, 58 F3d 506 (10th Cir. 1995) (defendant attempted to evade payment of employment taxes by directing payment of invoices to a post office box in another town and used the receipts for personal expenditures, and then gave false information to collection officers about the amount of his business's accounts receivable).

[104] Gariepy v. United States, 220 F2d 252 (6th Cir. 1955); Gleckman v. United States, 80 F2d 394 (8th Cir. 1935).

[105] Spies v. United States, 317 US 492, 499 (1943).

[106] See also Smith v. United States, 348 US 147 (1954).

[107] United States v. House, 87-2 USTC ¶ 9561 (WD Mich. 1987) (taxpayer who failed to file tax returns convicted of evasion because he also filed false Forms W-4 claiming exempt status). United States v. Williams, 928 F2d 145 (5th Cir. 1991) (taxpayer failed to file returns for six years, but filing and maintaining false Form W-4 was held affirmative act for purposes of evasion; United States v. Copeland, 786 F2d 768 (7th Cir. 1986), followed); see also United States v. DiPetto, 936 F2d 96 (2d Cir. 1991) ("[t]he fil-

1984, and the Service instructed his employer that the Forms W-4 were incorrect and to withhold.[108] Undeterred, in 1987, King filed another false Form W-4. King was indicted for tax evasion for the years 1989 through 1993, and the prosecution alleged that the false Forms W-4 for 1983, 1984, and 1987 constituted affirmative acts of evasion. King argued that the Forms W-4 could not have constituted acts of evasion, because they expired on February 15 of the years after they were filed. The circuit court rejected King's argument because "[m]aintaining a Form W-4 on file with one's employer effectively represents that one is still entitled to the number of allowances or exempt status claimed . . . [and if] false, the form certainly has the capacity to deceive for as long as it is kept on file."[109] The circuit court reasoned that the employer's failure to request a new Form W-4 from the employee does not change the employee's liability under Section 7201, and to find otherwise would be to allow the employer's negligence "to accrue to the benefit of an employee who has contravened the law in the first place by filing a false and fraudulent Form W-4."[110]

An attempt to evade may also be made after the return is filed. It is generally believed that the attempt to evade or defeat tax is complete on the filing of a return, and, indeed, the usual manner of the attempt alleged in an indictment is the filing of a false and fraudulent return. At least some attempts involve conduct of a continuing nature after the return is filed. A false statement a taxpayer makes to the Service after the taxpayer has filed a return can constitute an attempt to evade the tax if the false statement is for the purpose of concealing income unreported on the return.[111] An attempt to evade collection of a tax, as well as an attempt to evade liability for a tax, is tax evasion, so postfiling conduct may constitute an attempt to defeat payment of the tax, a crime that is not complete until the conduct ends.[112]

---

ing and *maintaining* of false forms W-4 satisfied the affirmative act requirement set forth in *Spies*" (emphasis added)).

[108] King v. United States, 126 F3d 987 (7th Cir. 1997).

[109] King v. United States, 126 F3d 987 (7th Cir. 1997). The Seventh Circuit used the Fifth Circuit's decision in United States v. Williams, 928 F2d 145 (5th Cir. 1991).

[110] King v. United States, 126 F3d 987 (7th Cir. 1997). The Seventh Circuit used the Fifth Circuit's decision in United States v. Williams, 928 F2d 145 (5th Cir. 1991).

[111] United States v. Beacon Brass Co., 344 US 43 (1952).

[112] United States v. Trownsell, 367 F2d 815 (7th Cir. 1966) (attempt to conceal assets by transferring them to Swiss bank); United States v. Mousley, 194 F. Supp. 119 (ED Pa. 1961), aff'd per curiam, 311 F2d 795 (3d Cir.), cert. denied, 372 US 966 (1963) (false statement in offers in compromise); United States v. Sclafani, 126 F. Supp. 654 (EDNY 1954), aff'd on another issue, 265 F2d 408 (2d Cir. 1959) (false statements); United States v. Voorhies, 658 F2d 710 (9th Cir. 1981) (transfer of assets outside the United States).

[4] Willful Conduct

The attempt to evade or defeat tax must be willful, but the meaning of willfulness required several interpretations by the Supreme Court before finally being settled. In *United States v. Murdock*,[113] a misdemeanor prosecution for willful failure to supply certain information about certain deductions under the predecessor to Section 7203, the Supreme Court held that willful conduct meant an act done with a bad or evil purpose. After *Murdock*, some courts approved the use of jury instructions incorporating *Murdock*'s evil-purpose language.[114] Courts also said that the word "willfully" had a different meaning in tax felony statutes than in tax misdemeanor statutes.[115]

In a series of cases, the Supreme Court ultimately rejected the evil-purpose view of willful conduct, as well as belief that "willfully" could have a different meaning for different criminal statutes. The first of these cases involved Cecil Bishop, who was prosecuted for the felony described in Section 7206(1) of filing a false return.[116] At trial's end, Bishop asked the judge for a jury instruction that the jury could find that he was liable for the lesser-included-offense of filing a false document, a misdemeanor described in Section 7207. The trial judge refused, and the issue on appeal was whether "willfully" had the same meaning for both the felony and misdemeanor statutes. Bishop argued that unless the meaning of "willfully" was different in the felony and misdemeanor statutes, they would punish the same misconduct. Demonstrating that the crimes had different elements, but that the term "willfully" was a "simultaneous requirement" in all but two tax offenses, the Court concluded that Congress used the term "willfully" to "describe a constant rather than a variable in the tax formula."[117] That "constant meaning" is "a voluntary, intentional violation of a known legal duty."[118] Interpretative problems arose after *Bishop* because the Court also suggested that willfulness required *Murdock*'s "bad faith or evil intent" language.

Three years after *Bishop*, the Supreme Court removed any doubt that the meaning of the term "willful" might include *Murdock*'s bad faith or evil in-

---

[113] United States v. Murdock, 290 US 389 (1933).

[114] At the time, jury instructions stated, for example: "An act is done (willfully) 'if done purposely with specific intent to disregard the law, or to do that which the law forbids.' The word 'willfully' as used in connection with this offense means with a bad or evil purpose of evading a known tax obligation in order to defraud the government of that tax." LaBuy, "Manual on Jury Instructions in Federal Criminal Cases," pt. 11, § 13.02-2, 36 FRD 457, 555 (1963).

[115] Abdul v. United States, 254 F2d 292 (9th Cir. 1958), cert. denied, 364 US 832 (1960).

[116] United States v. Bishop, 412 US 346 (1973).

[117] United States v. Bishop, 412 US 346, 360 (1973).

[118] United States v. Bishop, 412 US 346, 360 (1973).

tent. In *United States v. Pomponio*,[119] another prosecution for filing a false return, the Supreme Court unequivocally held that "willful" meant "a voluntary, intentional violation of a known legal duty." If *Bishop* and *Pomponio* established the meaning of "willful," then *Cheek v. United States* (a failure-to-file prosecution), described what evidence the prosecution must present to prove that the defendant's conduct was "willful." The prosecution, the Court held, is required "to prove that the law imposed a duty on the defendant, that the defendant knew of this duty, and that he voluntarily and intentionally violated that duty."[120] The defendant's knowledge of a legal duty is to be judged by a subjective, not an objective, standard.[121]

As finally formulated, proof that a defendant's conduct is willful must establish (1) voluntary action; (2) intentional conduct; and (3) knowledge of what the law requires. It follows that an individual's actions are not "willful" if they are done through inadvertence, carelessness, or honest misunderstanding of what the law requires.

[a] Proof of Willful Conduct

Direct proof of a person's intentions is rare, and to say that the defendant's state of mind may be inferred from all the facts and circumstances really does not help one to understand what type of conduct indicates a willful state of mind. In practice, the government presents evidence of *Spies*-type conduct, such as evidence that the taxpayer used currency in his dealings, failed to keep records, or made false statements to agents, thereby proving that not only has the defendant attempted to evade tax, but that the manner of the attempt

---

[119] United States v. Pomponio, 429 US 10, 12 (1976). For a decision holding that "careless and reckless disregard" is inconsistent with the willfulness standard of *Bishop* and *Pomponio*, see United States v. Eilertson, 707 F2d 108 (4th Cir. 1983). Where an indictment for tax evasion alleged that the defendants "well knew" that in the prosecution years their adjusted gross income and tax were in excess of the amounts reported on their income tax returns, the defendants contended that the government was required to meet a higher burden of proof than the *Pomponio* standard of willfulness. The circuit court held that this language was not part of the offense and, as such, was surplusage that the defendants might have had stricken under Rule 7(d) of the Federal Rules of Criminal Procedure. United States v. Hughes, 766 F2d 875 (5th Cir. 1985) (irrelevant facts that are alleged and not challenged are not required to be proven by the government).

[120] Cheek v. United States, 498 US 192, 201 (1991).

[121] Cheek v. United States, 498 US 192 (1991). See discussion infra ¶ 7A.06[1]. In United States v. Alt, 996 F2d 827 (6th Cir. 1993), the jury was charged that it was not necessary for the prosecution to prove that the defendant knew that his act was a violation of law, because it is presumed everyone knows what law forbids. The charge was held to be plain error because, according to *Cheek*, the willful element was intended by Congress to create an exception to the presumed-knowledge rule in view of "the complexity and intricacy of the tax laws."

establishes that the attempt was willful.[122] Also, a pattern of understatement in tax of the kind recognized in *Holland*[123] may also be sufficient to show that the defendant's conduct is "willful."[124] If a tax evasion motive plays any part in the defendant's conduct, an affirmative willful attempt may be inferred from that conduct.[125] In one case, the type of conduct from which a jury could infer willful attempt was the defendant's background as a CPA and businessman, which showed that he was aware of his duty to report his income taxes; false statements to the special agents, from which the jury could infer that the defendant accountant's violation of his duty was voluntary and intentional; and a pattern of understating or failing to report income, which was evidence of willfulness.[126]

To show that their underreporting was not willful, defendants often attempt to show that they relied on a competent tax adviser, they were ignorant of the law, or they made a mistake of law. A mere claim of reliance, ignorance, or mistake are not conclusive. When a defendant claims he relied on his accountant, the issue is not whether the accountant was ordered to falsify the return but whether the defendant knew when he signed the return that it was false.[127] A jury is permitted to infer that the defendant acted willfully where the defendant (1) was aware of the contents of his return and (2) knew that his reportable income significantly exceeded the income reflected on the return. Evidence of a taxpayer's conduct before and after the prosecution years is also admissible on the issue of intent.[128] On the other hand, it has been held that fil-

---

[122] See, e.g., United States v. Marabelles, 724 F2d 1374 (9th Cir. 1984) (cases cited).

[123] In other words, the manner of the attempt may evidence willfulness. See supra ¶ 7A.02[3].

[124] Holland v. United States, 348 US 121 (1954); United States v. Ashfield, 735 F2d 101 (3d Cir.), cert. denied, 469 US 858 (1984) (gathering cases). The circuit court in *Ashfield* stated, "Willfulness may . . . be inferred from circumstantial evidence . . . [and] a jury may find a defendant's tax evasion was willful wholly on the basis of inferential proof." A wide range of evidence is admissible. United States v. Johnson, 893 F2d 451 (1st Cir. 1990) (evidence that a false W-4 was filed for a year after the indictment period held admissible on issue of willfulness).

[125] United States v. Klausner, 80 F3d 55 (2d Cir. 1996).

[126] United States v. Klausner, 80 F3d 55 (2d Cir. 1996).

[127] United States v. Olbres, 61 F3d 967 (1st Cir. 1995), cert. denied, 116 S. Ct. 522 (1995) (even though defendants claimed reliance on their accountant, jury could reasonably find that defendants acted willfully based on circumstantial evidence that defendants signed the return, knew the contents of the return when they signed it, and knew that the return significantly understated their taxable income because they knew that their expenditures substantially exceeded the amount of income they reported, substantial business receipts had not been deposited in the business checking account and were not recorded, not all their rental income had been reported to the accountant, and not all their records were supplied either to the accountant or the Service).

[128] United States v. McKee, 942 F2d 477 (8th Cir. 1992) (gathering Eighth Circuit cases); United States v. Roberts, 22 F3d 744 (7th Cir. 1994) (evidence that the defendant

ing an amended return is not an admission that the defendant knew that the original return was false; as the Second Circuit said, "At most, filing an amended return indicates that the taxpayer now believes he was mistaken at the time he filed the original return; in no way does it shade that minimal assumption toward proof of the requisite fraudulent intent."[129]

[b] Willful Blindness

Willful conduct may also be found where the defendant's conduct amounts to "willful blindness." "Willful blindness" is defined as a "conscious purpose to avoid enlightenment," or deliberately closing one's eyes to what would otherwise have been obvious—all of which amounts to willfulness.[130] The Eighth Circuit has said, "To act 'knowingly' . . . it is not necessary to act only with positive knowledge, but also to act with an awareness of the high probability of the existence of the fact in question. When such awareness is present, 'positive' knowledge is not required."[131]

¶ 7A.03 THE FAILURE TO FILE RETURNS OR PAY TAX STATUTE: SECTION 7203

Section 7203 spells out four possible offenses: (1) willful failure to pay an estimated tax or other tax except for an estimated return declaration; (2) willful

---

owed $2 million in back taxes for years prior to the prosecution period "bears directly on one's motive to evade taxes because the larger the obligation, the greater the incentive to avoid payment"). When the sufficiency of evidence bearing on intent is challenged, the evidence is viewed, not in isolation, but in conjunction with other evidence in the record as a whole. United States v. Rea, 958 F2d 1206 (2d Cir. 1992) (evasion of excise tax on gasoline).

[129] United States v. Dyer, 922 F2d 105 (2d Cir. 1991).

[130] United States v. Callahan, 588 F2d 1078 (5th Cir. 1979). For a discussion of the mistake of law defense, see infra ¶ 7A.06[1]. Cheek v. United States, 498 US 192 (1991) (inadvertence, carelessness, and mistake have been distinguished from "willful blindness").

[131] United States v. Graham, 739 F2d 351, 353 (8th Cir. 1984); see also Mattingly v. United States, 924 F2d 785, 792 (8th Cir. 1991) ("the element of knowledge may be inferred from deliberate acts amounting to willful blindness to the existence of facts or acts constituting conscious purpose to avoid enlightenment"); United States v. Bussey, 942 F2d 1241 (8th Cir. 1991): "Bussey asked no questions, sought no guidance, did no research, all despite his claimed unfamiliarity with partnership taxation. From these actions or each thereof, a jury could reasonably infer that Bussey consciously avoided any opportunity to learn what the tax consequences were, and could then infer this requisite willfulness required by the statute."

failure to file a return; (3) willful failure to keep records; and (4) willful failure to supply information. Section 7203 provides:

> Any person required under this title to pay any estimated tax or tax, or required by this title or by regulations made under authority thereof to make a return (other than a return required under authority of section 6015 [estimated tax returns]), keep any records, or supply any information, who [1] willfully fails to pay such estimated tax or tax, [2] make such return, [3] keep such records, or [4] supply such information, at the time or times required by law or regulations, shall, in addition to other penalties provided by law, be guilty of a misdemeanor. . . .

The Section 7203 penalty for violating one of these offenses, as a misdemeanor, is imprisonment for not more than one year. A taxpayer may also be fined up to $25,000 ($100,000 for a corporation) and required to pay the costs of prosecution.[132] By far, the most frequent prosecution under Section 7203 is for failure to file an income tax return.[133]

[1] Failure to File

To establish a willful failure to file a tax return, the evidence must show (1) the taxpayer was required by law to file a return for the taxable year; (2) the taxpayer failed to file the return at the time required by law; and (3) the failure was willful. Showing that the defendant was required to file a return generally presents few problems for the prosecution: It must merely show that the tax-

---

[132] IRC § 7203, amended by the Tax Equity and Fiscal Responsibility Act of 1982 (TEFRA), Pub. L. No. 97-248, HR 4961, 97th Cong., 2d Sess. § 329(b), for offenses committed after September 3, 1982. United States v. Chavez, 627 F2d 953 (9th Cir. 1980), cert. denied, 450 US 924 (1981); United States v. Wyman, 724 F2d 684 (8th Cir. 1984). In United States v. Palmer, 809 F2d 1504 (11th Cir. 1987), the court decided that a taxpayer's liability for the costs of prosecution upon conviction of willful failure to file does not unconstitutionally burden a defendant's right to a jury trial. The case was remanded for a determination of what portion of the prosecution's costs was reasonable and necessary to the proof of the Section 7203 offense because the taxpayer was not convicted on the Section 7201 charge. For instances where taxpayers have received sentences of fines and imprisonment in failure-to-file cases, see United States v. Sato, 814 F2d 449 (7th Cir. 1976).

[133] The actual sentence is governed by the Sentencing Guidelines. See infra ¶ 7A.09. As a condition of probation or release after a conviction for failure-to-file returns, the taxpayer may be required to file returns. See United States v. Lacy, 658 F2d 396 (5th Cir. 1981); United States v. Wolters, 656 F2d 523 (9th Cir. 1981). A condition requiring the taxpayer to file returns and pay the taxes shown on the returns is proper. United States v. Merritt, 639 F2d 254 (5th Cir. 1981); United States v. Schiff, 876 F2d 272 (2d Cir. 1989) (special conditions of probation that the defendant file all required returns and pay all legally required taxes).

payer received the minimum amount of gross income required by law to file a tax return.[134] There is no requirement in the failure-to-file statute, as there is in a charge of tax evasion, that there be an additional tax due and owing, because the duty to file is imposed by statute, irrespective of any tax that may be owed. Practically speaking, however, failure-to-file cases are not prosecuted where no tax is due because it is difficult to establish that the taxpayer defendant acted willfully where this evidence is lacking.[135]

The nonfiling element is also easily shown.[136] Usually an official with responsibility for maintaining custody of income tax returns testifies that there is no record of any return having been filed by the taxpayer for the particular year in question. A certificate of assessments and payments for the taxpayer is produced to show the taxpayer's return-filing history and that no return has been filed or tax assessed for the year in question. It should be noted that the failure-to-file statute also applies to late filing. A return is due for the purposes of the statute on the last day provided by law or the regulations for filing the return, plus any additional period of time provided in an extension. Consequently, if a taxpayer fails to file a tax return on April 15 or the last day provided in an extension of the filing date, the failure-to-file element of the offense is technically made out.

Even if a taxpayer files what purports to be a return, the taxpayer may be prosecuted for a failure to file the required return. In the view of most courts, a document that does not contain information relating to a taxpayer's income and deductions from which a tax can be computed is not a return for purposes

---

[134] See IRC §§ 6001, 6012(a) (individuals), 6662 (corporations), 6012(b) (fiduciaries), 6031, 6065 (partnerships). For a conviction for failing to file a corporate income tax return, see United States v. Civella, 666 F2d 1122 (8th Cir. 1981); see also United States v. Neal, 93 F3d 219 (6th Cir. 1996) (corporate officer charged with failure to file corporation's quarterly employment tax returns claimed he was under no legal obligation to file for Section 7203 purposes; held, corporation had legal obligation to file under Section 6011(a), and corporate officer was under a duty to file the corporation's returns under Section 7343, which, in part, defines "person" as an officer of a corporation).

[135] See, e.g., United States v. Power, 68-2 USTC ¶ 9443 (D. Wis. 1968). But compare United States v. Parshall, 757 F2d 211 (8th Cir. 1985) (abuse of discretion for district court to exclude defendant's evidence about his lower tax liability and the uncertain state of law, but error was harmless because the "case involved prosecution for willfully failing to file income tax returns, not for failing to report disputed amounts of income"). It has been held that the government may introduce into evidence the defendant's gross income to show that his failure to file a tax return was willful, but the defendant does not have the right to show that because of deductions, exemptions, and the like, his actual tax liability would have been minimal. United States v. Payne, 800 F2d 227 (10th Cir. 1986) (citing cases).

[136] United States v. Hayes, 861 F2d 1225 (10th Cir. 1988) (computer data computations and testimony about Service center procedures permitted under the public records exception to the hearsay rule, Federal Rules of Evidence 803(8), to show that defendant did not file tax returns).

of the criminal statute.[137] Just what constitutes a return is a question for the court.[138] Suppose a taxpayer uses a privilege claim to justify his failure to include information. If the taxpayer has received the minimum amount of gross income, the filed return claiming the self-incrimination privilege is insufficient to constitute a "return" required by the law.[139] Still, the taxpayer may not be guilty of a criminal failure to file. If the taxpayer's self-incrimination privilege claim is made in good faith, the taxpayer's conduct in failing to file a qualifying return appears to negate the willfulness element in a failure-to-file charge, even if the claim is invalid.[140] Even so, to avoid prosecution, the privilege

[137] United States v. Grabinski, 727 F2d 681, 686–687 (8th Cir. 1984) (the test for a "return" is whether it gives sufficient financial information from which the Service can calculate tax liability "based on the circumstances of the taxpayer's income years"); United States v. Edelson, 604 F2d 232 (3d Cir. 1979); United States v. Johnson, 577 F2d 1304 (5th Cir. 1978); United States v. Jordan, 508 F2d 750 (7th Cir.), cert. denied, 423 US 842 (1975); United States v. Daly, 481 F2d 28 (8th Cir.), cert. denied, 414 US 1064 (1973); United States v. Porth, 426 F2d 519 (10th Cir.), cert. denied, 400 US 824 (1970); cf. United States v. Moore, 627 F2d 830 (7th Cir. 1980) (ability of Service to calculate tax not enough; must be "honest and reasonable intent to supply the information required by the tax code").

But compare United States v. Long, 618 F2d 74 (9th Cir. 1980) (zeroes in a return constitute information from which tax can be computed, so failure-to-file conviction reversed; indication that Section 7206(1) charge might have been proper). *Long* has been rejected by a number of circuits. United States v. Moore, 627 F2d 830 (7th Cir. 1980); United States v. Rickman, 638 F2d 182 (10th Cir. 1980); United States v. Mosel, 738 F2d 157, 158 (6th Cir. 1984) ("no reasonable person employing such a symbol in these circumstances could understand that he had submitted the information which is required on a tax return"). The Ninth Circuit adheres to its more liberal view of a qualifying return. United States v. Kimball, 896 F2d 1218 (9th Cir. 1990) (Section 7203 applies only where defendant failed to complete tax form or left it blank; taxpayer "completed" a tax "return" where he filled in asterisks that referred to constitutional objections; conviction under Section 7203 reversed).

[138] A document filed by the taxpayer may be determined, as a matter of law, not to be a return. United States v. Goetz, 746 F2d 705 (11th Cir. 1984) (cases gathered and analyzed). In *Goetz*, the circuit court held that a judge's charge determining that the defendant's returns were not returns erred because it removed the question from the consideration of the jury. However, this view is not followed in all circuits. See United States v. Loniello, 744 F2d 65 (8th Cir. 1984). Similarly, the court decides whether the information sought would tend to incriminate in determining the validity of the self-incrimination privilege claim. Garner v. United States, 424 US 648 (1976). However, the court may not refuse to permit any evidence of good faith to go to the jury, even if the defendant's privilege claim was without legal justification. United States v. Carlson, 617 F2d 518, 523 (9th Cir.), cert. denied, 449 US 1010 (1980).

[139] The requirements of a sufficient return and claims of privilege are discussed at ¶ 4.02[1][a].

[140] See Garner v. United States, 424 US 648, 663 n.18 (1976); United States v. Murdock, 290 US 389 (1933); United States v. Drexler, 74-2 USTC ¶ 9716 (D. Minn. 1973). However, where a taxpayer previously filed false withholding forms and then filed income tax returns claiming the privilege, the claim was found not to be made in good faith. Con-

claim must be made with respect to specific items and questions. A blanket privilege claim has been held to constitute a total failure to file.[141]

[2] Willfulness

As described earlier, the Supreme Court resolved confusion about the meaning of willfulness for purposes of all criminal tax statutes.[142] After *Bishop* and *Pomponio*, "willful" in both tax felony and misdemeanor statutes (such as the failure-to-file statute) has the same meaning: "a voluntary, intentional violation of a known legal duty."[143] After *Pomponio*, most courts held that the standard of willful conduct was a subjective one, so that, for example, the taxpayer's good faith but erroneous belief that he was not required to file a return was a defense to willful nonfiling.[144] Other courts held that defendant's belief had to

---

viction was upheld on the ground that the privilege claim was part of an overall scheme to evade the tax return requirement. United States v. Carlson, 617 F2d 518 (9th Cir. 1980). An erroneous claim of privilege made in good faith is a defense to a Section 7203 charge, but the good faith belief must relate to a fear of criminal prosecution. Saussy III v. United States, 802 F2d 849 (6th Cir. 1986) (fear that information might be disclosed and cause taxpayer harm not sufficient grounds for privilege claim).

   [141] United States v. Daly, 481 F2d 28 (8th Cir.), cert. denied, 414 US 1064 (1973); United States v. Farber, 630 F2d 569 (8th Cir. 1980) (Fifth Amendment claim to income questions is impermissible blanket claim); United States v. Stillhammer, 706 F2d 1072 (10th Cir. 1983) (cases cited).

   [142] Spies v. United States, 317 US 492 (1943); United States v. Murdock, 290 US 389 (1933).

   [143] United States v. Bishop, 412 US 346 (1973); United States v. Pomponio, 429 US 10 (1976).

   [144] United States v. Aitken, 755 F2d 188 (1st Cir. 1985) (analysis of the issue; cases gathered); United States v. Turano, 802 F2d 10 (1st Cir. 1986) (approving a subjective test for determining the taxpayer's good faith belief that he was not required to file a tax return). Apart from United States v. Moore, 627 F2d 830 (7th Cir. 1980), in the Seventh Circuit, the Tenth Circuit stated that the balance of the circuits have either (1) implicitly indicated that only subjective intent to disobey the filing requirement need be proved or (2) explicitly adopted a subjective standard. See United States v. Phillips, 775 F2d 262 (10th Cir. 1985) (cases gathered); United States v. Harting, 879 F2d 765 (10th Cir. 1989) (taxpayer entitled to a jury instruction that a good faith misunderstanding of the duty to file a return can negate willfulness, and the misunderstanding need not have a reasonable basis); United States v. Burton, 737 F2d 439 (5th Cir. 1980); United States v. Jerde, 841 F2d 818 (8th Cir. 1988) (subjective, not objective, standard is applicable in evaluating a good faith defense to a failure-to-file charge; "good faith reason" charge did not convert test from subjective to objective). See also United States v. Payne, 800 F2d 227 (10th Cir. 1986) (jury instruction upheld that "if a person acts without reasonable care, or reasonable grounds in the belief that his conduct was lawful, it is for you to decide whether he acted in good faith, or whether he willfully intended to violate the law"); United States v. Mann III, 884 F2d 532 (10th Cir. 1989) ("a defendant's good faith belief that he is not required

be objectively reasonable.[145] The Supreme Court settled the issue in *Cheek v. United States*.[146] Cheek had claimed that his action in failing to file his income tax returns was not willful because he believed that the tax law was unconstitutional. The Court held that a good faith, but mistaken, belief about what the law required need not be objectively reasonable; otherwise, the element of willfulness would effectively be removed from the consideration of the jury. In such a case, the jury does not decide the issue whether the law is unconstitutional; it decides only whether the defendant's belief was held in good faith. On remand, the Seventh Circuit distinguished claims that the tax law is unconstitutional (which do not serve as a defense, "because they represent a defendant's full knowledge of the provisions of the law") and claims that the taxpayer did not know the tax law or had a mistaken belief or understanding about it (which the jury must be able to consider, no matter how incredible or unreasonable those beliefs might be).[147]

In practice, the difference between a good faith but erroneous belief and an objectively reasonable belief seems slight. If the defendant's claimed belief is bizarre or inconsistent with jurors' everyday experience, they are unlikely to accept the defendant's testimony, however earnest, that his or her belief was held in good faith. At any rate, a good faith disagreement with law is not a defense.[148]

---

to file a return is a valid defense . . . and the beliefs need not be reasonable if actually held in good faith").

[145] One circuit court appears to have accepted this view. United States v. Moore, 627 F2d 830, 833 (7th Cir. 1980), cert. denied, 450 US 916 (1981); United States v. Witvoet, 767 F2d 338 (7th Cir. 1985) ("[n]either this court nor the Supreme Court has overruled *Moore*, and no other circuit has criticized it"). Before *Cheek*, the Second Circuit has said that an objective reasonableness test was not erroneous. United States v. Schiff, 801 F2d 108 (2d Cir. 1986), cert. denied, 480 US 945 (1987).

[146] Cheek v. United States, 498 US 192 (1991).

[147] United States v. Cheek, 931 F2d 1206 (7th Cir. 1991) ("[t]he government remains free to present evidence that [the taxpayer] knew what the law required but simply chose to disregard those duties"); see also United States v. Powell, 936 F2d 1056 (9th Cir. 1991): "The premise of *Cheek* is that a person cannot be convicted of willful failure to file a tax return if he subjectively believes in good faith that the tax laws do not apply to him. The test does not focus on the knowledge of the reasonable person, but rather on the knowledge of the defendant."

In 1992, Cheek was retried. Following a second jury trial before a district judge who gave jury instructions in accordance with the Supreme Court's opinion on the meaning of "willfulness," Cheek was convicted on all counts. On appeal, Cheek claimed the judge had failed to instruct the jury on his advice-of-counsel defense. The claim was rejected because Cheek did not follow the advice of the attorneys with whom he met, and the jury instruction on "willfulness" dealt with Cheek's theory that he acted in good faith reliance on counsel. United States v. Cheek, 3 F3d 1057 (7th Cir. 1993).

[148] However, the failure to file is not willful if the taxpayer honestly relied on the advice that he could legally file a "protest"-type return. United States v. Ellis, 496 F. Supp. 76 (D. Kan. 1980) (one-year prosecution where the taxpayer intended to claim the Fifth

Prosecutions under Section 7203 invariably involve situations where a taxpayer has previously filed tax returns and for one reason or another has failed to file tax returns for a number of years, usually three.[149] The conclusion is almost inescapable that the taxpayer knew he had the obligation to file, but intentionally decided not to file. Moreover, it is not necessary for the government to show some conduct in addition to the intentional nonfiling. This fact is precisely the difference between the failure-to-file statute and the evasion statute.

[3] Failure to Pay

To establish a willful failure to pay tax, it must be shown that (1) the taxpayer was required by law to pay a tax that was due and owing; (2) the taxpayer

---

Amendment in mistaken reliance on Garner v. United States, 424 US 648 (1976), created in part by a protest movement leader, who was himself later convicted. United States v. Tibb, 600 F2d 19 (6th Cir. 1979); United States v. Farber, 630 F2d 569 (8th Cir. 1980), where a taxpayer's reliance on another tax protest leader was rejected, and the instruction approved in United States v. Ware, 608 F2d 400 (10th Cir. 1979) ("neither the defendant's disagreement with the law, nor his own belief that such law is unconstitutional—no matter how earnestly held—constitutes a defense of good faith misunderstanding or mistake"); United States v. Lewis, 671 F2d 1025 (7th Cir. 1982) (failure to instruct more fully on the "knowledge" element of "willfully" where defense theory based on its absence held not an error if foundation in the evidence insufficient). But see United States v. Wyman, 724 F2d 684 (8th Cir. 1984) (defense of good faith misunderstanding, but trial court's refusal to order subpoenas to "experts" on whom taxpayer-defendant relied affirmed).

[149] Failure to file returns both before and after the prosecution years is also evidence of willfulness. See, e.g., United States v. Thompson, 513 F2d 577 (8th Cir. 1975); United States v. Johnson, 386 F2d 630 (3d Cir. 1967) (prior failures); United States v. Luttrell, 612 F2d 396 (8th Cir. 1980); United States v. Farris, 517 F2d 226 (7th Cir.), cert. denied, 423 US 892 (1975) (subsequent failures); United States v. Serlin, 707 F2d 953 (7th Cir. 1983) (subsequent failure); United States v. Kalita, 712 F2d 1122 (7th Cir. 1983) (subsequent failure); United States v. Heise, 709 F2d 449 (6th Cir. 1983) (prior failure); United States v. Rothbart, 723 F2d 752 (10th Cir. 1983) (evidence of conviction of failure to file individual income tax returns properly admitted in prosecution for failure to file employer's quarterly returns, Form 941); United States v. Grumka, 728 F2d 794 (6th Cir. 1984) (prior history of filing).

The willful failure to file can also be inferred from other conduct; for example, the jury can infer the defendant's knowledge of his obligation to file from his regular receipt of Forms W-2 and 1099 and his intentional violation of that duty from his false exculpatory statements to IRS agents about the amount of his income and the payment of tax. See United States v. Hartmann, 86 F3d 1153 (4th Cir. 1996). Evidence of prior bad acts (i.e., prior failures to file returns) can be admitted under Federal Rules of Evidence 404(b) to prove intent. United States v. Fingado, 934 F2d 1163 (10th Cir. 1991) (failure to file for six years before prosecution period; analysis of evidentiary rule). United States v. McCaffrey, 83 AFTR2d 99-967 (7th Cir. 1999) (an accountant who prepared returns for his clients but failed to prepare his own returns for four years).

failed to pay the tax at the time or times required by law or regulations; and (3) the failure to pay was willful. Mere failure to pay a tax is not a crime, since otherwise a taxpayer might be imprisoned for debt. The failure to pay must be willful, which the Supreme Court in *Spies,* said involved a showing that the taxpayer had the ability to pay but intentionally and deliberately refused to do so.[150]

The difficulties in establishing a willful failure to pay tax are demonstrated by the facts of *Palermo v. United States,*[151] where the defendant was charged with willfully failing to pay income tax that he reported on timely filed 1953 and 1954 tax returns on the basis of evidence that he had purchased Cadillacs in 1953 and 1954, and in 1956 had paid almost $7,000 for his daughter's wedding. At trial, however, the defendant presented evidence showing that in 1953, he had also paid approximately $9,500 of his delinquent 1950 and 1951 tax liabilities, and he had unsuccessfully attempted to sell property he owned in order to pay his taxes and other debts. The court of appeals ordered the defendant acquitted on the 1953 failure-to-file count because of payments made on account of delinquent taxes. On the 1954 count, it remanded the case for a determination of whether the history of his payments to the Service and his past record of failure to pay on time established an intentional failure to pay tax on the due date. While a pattern in a taxpayer's behavior may suggest that the taxpayer's conduct was willful, it is not conclusive evidence of a willful failure to pay. Apart from a pattern of behavior, courts have also engaged in a rather refined analysis of the taxpayer's ability to pay.[152] Where a defendant has made lavish expenditures that have rendered him unable to pay his taxes, he has been successfully prosecuted for failure to pay in-

---

[150] In Spies v. United States, 317 US 492, 498 (1943), the Supreme Court said:

> [I]n view of our traditional aversion to imprisonment for debt, we would not without the clearest manifestation of Congressional intent assume that mere knowing and intentional defaults in payments of a tax, where there had been no willful "failure to disclose the liability," is intended to constitute a criminal offense of any degree. We would expect willfulness in such a case to include some element of evil motive and want of justification in view of all the financial circumstances of a taxpayer.

The argument that Section 7203 violates the Fifth Amendment by authorizing imprisonment for debt has been rejected on the basis of this language. See United States v. Shorter, 85-2 USTC ¶ 9673 (DDC 1985), aff'd, 809 F2d 54 (DC Cir.), cert. denied, 108 S. Ct. 71 (1987) (gathering cases).

[151] Palermo v. United States, 259 F2d 872 (3d Cir. 1958).

[152] United States v. Andros, 484 F2d 531 (9th Cir. 1973) (failure to pay successfully said to be willful because taxpayer had won $20,000 betting on a horse race, but dissenting judge believed that other debts of the defendant-taxpayer prevented a finding that the government had proved beyond a reasonable doubt that the taxpayer was on the date at issue financially able to pay the taxes in question). See also United States v. Poll, 521 F2d 329 (9th Cir. 1975), cert. denied, 429 US 977 (1976), reh'g denied, 429 US 1079 (1977) (prosecution under Section 7202 for willful failure to collect and pay over reversed and remanded to consider taxpayer's evidence on ability to pay).

come tax under Section 7203.[153] It is unsettled, however, whether financial inability to pay on the due date is a defense in a failure-to-deposit case.[154]

[4] Failure to Supply Information

A willful failure to supply information at the time or times required by law or regulations may also be prosecuted under Section 7203. The elements of the offense are that (1) the person was under a duty to supply the information; (2) the person failed to supply the information required by law or regulations; and (3) the failure to supply information was willful. The willfulness element in this charge is established if the evidence shows that the person intentionally failed to supply information he knew was required to be supplied. For example, a failure, after repeated requests, to supply a partnership balance sheet as required by regulation to be filed on a separate schedule with the partnership return was held to constitute a willful failure to supply information.[155]

In *United States v. Murdock*,[156] the defendant-taxpayer was convicted of failure to supply information where, based on a claim of privilege, he declined to answer questions regarding deductions. The Supreme Court reversed the conviction because the jury had not been properly charged that an intentional

---

[153] See United States v. Andros, 484 F2d 531 (9th Cir. 1973); United States v. Tucker, 686 F2d 230, 233 (5th Cir.), cert. denied, 459 US 1071 (1982); United States v. Ausmus, 774 F2d 722 (6th Cir. 1985). See United States v. Hatchett, 918 F2d 631 (6th Cir. 1990) (during period of failure to pay, lawyer defendant had substantial fee income, avoided use of bank account, purchased property in other people's names, and spent large sums on personal expenditures).

[154] In United States v. Poll, 521 F2d 329, 333 (9th Cir. 1975), the Ninth Circuit said:

We believe that to establish willfulness the government must establish beyond a reasonable doubt that at the time payment was due the taxpayer possessed sufficient funds to enable him to meet his obligation, or that the lack of sufficient funds on such date was created by (or was the result of) a voluntary and intentional act without justification in view of all the financial circumstances of the taxpayer.

As the Ninth Circuit also said, this evidence on the willfulness issue is also properly presented in a prosecution under Section 7203. However, other circuits disagree. See United States v. Tucker, 686 F2d 230, 233 (5th Cir.), cert. denied, 459 US 1071 (1982) (*Andros* not followed; "mere unavailability of liquid assets on the tax due date does not excuse criminal liability under § 7203"). Moreover, a jury instruction has been approved that includes this language: "As a general rule, financial inability to pay the tax when it becomes due is not a defense to criminal liability for failing to pay income taxes." United States v. Ausmus, 774 F2d 722 (6th Cir. 1985).

[155] Pappas v. United States, 216 F2d 515 (10th Cir. 1954).

[156] United States v. Murdock, 290 US 389 (1933).

and erroneous refusal might nevertheless not be willful if the defendant acted in good faith and on his actual belief that the refusal was justified.[157]

¶ 7A.04 THE PERJURY AND FALSE STATEMENT STATUTE: SECTION 7206

The Code contains its own perjury and false statement statute. This statute makes it a felony, punishable by imprisonment for not more than three years, a fine of up to $100,000 ($500,000 for a corporation), or both, together with the costs of prosecution, for a person to[158]

1. Make a false declaration under penalties of perjury[159];
2. Aid or assist in the preparation or presentation of any return or other document that is false as to a material matter[160];
3. Simulate or fraudulently execute or sign any bond, permit any entry, or other document required by the internal revenue laws, or procure these acts to be done[161];
4. Remove or conceal property with intent to evade or defeat assessment or collection of any tax; or[162]
5. In connection with an offer in compromise and closing agreement, either conceal property or withhold, falsify, or destroy records or make any false statement relating to the financial condition of the taxpayer or other person liable for the tax.[163]

Of these five crimes, the most frequently charged ones are those for filing a false return and for aiding, assisting, or counseling in the preparation of a false return.

---

[157] United States v. Murdock, 290 US 389 (1933), still seems to be good law after the Supreme Court's decision in Garner v. United States, 424 US 648 (1976).

[158] IRC § 7206, amended by TEFRA, Pub. L. No. 97-248, HR 4961, 97th Cong., 2d Sess. § 329(c), for offenses committed after September 3, 1982.

[159] IRC § 7206(1).

[160] IRC § 7206(2).

[161] IRC § 7206(3).

[162] IRC § 7206(4).

[163] IRC § 7206(5).

[1] Declarations Under Penalties of Perjury: Section 7206(1)

Under Section 7206(1), any person who "willfully makes and subscribes any return, statement or other document which contains or is verified by a written declaration that it is made under the penalties of perjury, and which he does not believe true and correct as to every material matter" is guilty of a felony. To prove that a person committed the offense described by Section 7206(1), the person must be shown to have (1) made and subscribed a return or other document under penalties of perjury; (2) known that it was not true and correct as to a material matter; and (3) acted willfully.[164]

The Code's tax offenses overlap considerably, as do general criminal offenses described in Title 18 of the U.S. Code. Both the evasion and false statement statutes punish the filing of a false return, although punishment under the latter felony statute is less severe. However, unlike evasion, no tax due and owning need be proved to establish a false statement on a tax return. For this reason, government prosecutors have frequently "back-stopped" tax evasion charges with false statement counts. In this way, a defendant who defeats the tax-due-and-owing element in the evasion count may nevertheless be convicted on the false statement count. However, to avoid pyramiding sentences, where a defendant is convicted of both evasion and a false statement based on essentially the same conduct, some courts have refused to cumulate penalties beyond the maximum sentence authorized by the evasion statute.[165] Accordingly, a defendant convicted on both evasion and false statement charges for a single year's false return may be fined no more than the maximum fine and sentenced to no more than the maximum period for evasion.

---

[164] The history of Section 7206(1) and its relationship to the general perjury statute in Title 18 of the U.S. Code are discussed in United States v. Marrinson, 87-2 USTC ¶ 9377 (ND Ill. 1985), aff'd, 832 F2d 1465 (7th Cir. 1987) (use of phrase "under penalties of perjury" from language of Section 7206(1) may be outmoded, but it does not impair validity of statute). It has been held that the "person" referred to in Section 7206(1) includes a corporation. United States v. Ingredient Technology Corp., 698 F2d 88 (2d Cir. 1983) (argument that a corporation cannot commit perjury rejected).

[165] United States v. White, 417 F2d 89 (2d Cir.), cert. denied, 397 US 912, reh'g denied, 397 US 1030 (1969); United States v. Lodwick, 410 F2d 1202 (8th Cir.), cert. denied, 396 US 841 (1969); Gaunt v. United States, 184 F2d 284 (1st Cir.), cert. denied, 340 US 917 (1951). Compare United States v. Franks, 723 F2d 1482 (10th Cir. 1983), cert. denied, 469 US 817 (1984) (pyramiding of sentences not found where the evasion conviction was based on understated taxable income and the false statement conviction for misstating foreign bank account information); see also United States v. Helmsley, 941 F2d 71 (2d Cir. 1991) (convictions for false statements on personal income tax returns merged with evasion convictions on same returns, but convictions for false statements on corporate and partnership returns did not merge with personal return evasion convictions), cert. denied, 112 S. Ct. 1162 (1992).

Conduct described by Section 7206 as punishable as a felony are similar to the Code's false statement misdemeanor statute[166] and the Title 18 false statement statute,[167] also punishable as a felony. A false statement punishable under Section 7206(1), however, is one made in a document, usually a tax return, that itself is made under penalties of perjury. The false statement punishable as a misdemeanor under Section 7207 includes a false statement made in *any* document, whether or not it is made under penalties of perjury.[168] Sections 7206 and 7207 cover written false statements. 18 USC § 1001 covers both oral and written false statements and is broad enough to apply to a false statement made under the subsections of Section 7206.[169]

[a] The Statement Element

A false return, document, or statement filed with the Service gives rise to a prosecution under Section 7206(1) if the return, document, or statement contains a jurat or oath. The jurat or oath is precisely the difference between a false document whose filing is punishable as a misdemeanor under Section 7207 and one whose filing is punishable as a felony under Section 7206(1). For purposes of the statute, a return includes not only an actual income tax return, but also accompanying schedules and statements or documents incorporated in the return.[170]

Taxpayers file all sorts of forms with the Service, many of which contain jurats, but it has been held that a false statement may be punishable under the felony statute only if the form on which the false statement is a form authorized by statute or regulation. Clearly, a false answer to a question on a tax return can be the basis for a criminal prosecution.[171] In a less obvious situation,

---

[166] IRC § 7207.

[167] 18 USC § 1001.

[168] At one time, the Department of Justice believed that the misdemeanor false statement statute was confusing and attempted to secure its elimination from the Code.

[169] Although prosecutions for tax-related false statements have been instituted under 18 USC § 1001, there is some question whether the crimes described in the Code were meant to be the exclusive provisions for prosecuting tax-related offenses. The Department of Justice's Tax Division, at any rate, does not encourage prosecutions under provisions outside the Code.

[170] United States v. Henderson, 399 F. Supp. 508 (SDNY 1975) (conviction where backdated document attached to return). See United States v. Franks, 723 F2d 1482 (10th Cir. 1983), cert. denied, 469 US 817 (1984) (Form 4683 regarding foreign bank accounts appended to Form 1040).

[171] United States v. Franks, 723 F2d 1482 (10th Cir. 1983), cert. denied, 469 US 817 (1984). A statement that is literally true cannot constitute perjury or a false statement for purposes of Section 7206(1). For example, when taxpayers filed Forms 1040A that were truthful but omitted other income not called for by Form 1040A that was to be reported on Form 1040, they could not be prosecuted for violating Section 7206(1). United States

the importance of the fact that the form is authorized is illustrated by *United States v. Levy*,[172] where a conviction under Section 7206(1) was reversed, even though statements made on the form were false. Although the false document was a short-form financial statement (Form 433-AB) made under penalties of perjury, the form was neither required nor authorized by statute or regulation.[173] On the other hand, in *United States v. Cohen*,[174] the taxpayer filed Form 656, Offer in Compromise, and Form 433, Statement of Financial Condition, both of which are authorized by regulation, and made a false statement. The conviction was affirmed.

An element in the false statement offense is that the document having the oath must be made and subscribed by the person charged. An individual can "make" a false statement on a return when he supplies incomplete information to his accountant.[175] The taxpayer's signature on the return is not only a statutory requirement, it is at least some evidence that the taxpayer was aware of the return's falsity at the time it was signed.[176] The Code itself provides in this connection that any signature on a return is "prima facie evidence for all purposes that the return, statement or other document was actually signed by him."[177]

---

v. Borman, 992 F2d 124 (7th Cir. 1993); United States v. Reynolds, 919 F2d 435 (7th Cir. 1990), cert. denied, 499 US 942 (1991) (taxpayer filed a Form 1040 EZ that was literally correct, but had received income of a type he had duty to report on a Form 1040).

[172] United States v. Levy, 533 F2d 969 (5th Cir. 1976). Contra Holroyd v. United States, 732 F2d 1122 (2d Cir. 1984) (reversing an order dismissing an indictment for filing a false Form 433-AB and Form 433-A, collection information statements). In *Holroyd*, the Second Circuit said that Section 7206(1) "applies to any verified return, statement or other document submitted to the IRS" and is not limited to documents expressly authorized by statute or regulation.

[173] Since Section 7201 charges the single crime of evasion that may be committed by evading either the assessment or payment of taxes, an indictment is not duplicitous if it charges both evasion of the assessment of tax and evasion of payment. United States v. Mal, 942 F2d 682 (9th Cir. 1991).

[174] United States v. Cohen, 544 F2d 781 (5th Cir.), cert. denied, 431 US 914 (1977).

[175] See United States v. Badwan, 624 F2d 1228 (4th Cir.), cert. denied, 449 US 1124 (1980).

[176] United States v. Drape, 668 F2d 22 (1st Cir. 1982) (signature "sufficient to establish knowledge once it had been shown that the return was false"); United States v. Fontenot, 628 F2d 921 (5th Cir. 1980), cert. denied, 452 US 905 (1981) (corporation's returns signed by taxpayer; evidence showed that he discarded invoices reflecting all the corporation's transactions).

[177] IRC § 6064. United States v. Kim, 884 F2d 189 (5th Cir. 1989) (presumption of Section 6064 held constitutional).

[b] The Material Matter Element

The test of materiality has been variously stated. The generally accepted test is whether, in light of the Service's need for accurate information in order to perform its function, the information is essential to permit the Service to verify the reporting of income.[178] Under this test, a return is not "true and correct" as to a "material matter" if it is not accurate and complete for purposes of examination by the Service.[179] Therefore, even if there is no tax deficiency, the return may not be accurate and complete. Unlike an evasion prosecution, where proof of a "tax due and owing" is a necessary element, a prosecution under Section 7206(1) does not require a tax deficiency to be established if the statement at issue is shown to be false and material.[180]

A material false statement is made not only where the person includes the false statement on a document made and filed under penalties of perjury but also where a material fact is omitted. Material false statements have been found in a taxpayer's failure to attach a Schedule C reporting gross receipts

---

[178] United States v. DiVarco, 484 F2d 670 (7th Cir.), cert. denied, 415 US 916 (1973). Accord United States v. Romanow, 509 F2d 26 (1st Cir. 1975); United States v. Taylor, 574 F2d 232 (5th Cir.), cert. denied, 439 US 893 (1978). See also United States v. Fawaz, 881 F2d 259 (6th Cir. 1989) (understated gasoline purchases were material because they made it more difficult for the Service to verify both the defendant's income tax and excise tax returns).

[179] The government must prove that the defendant did not believe the return to be true and correct as to every material matter. See United States v. Nicolaou, 83 AFTR2d 99-2821 (4th Cir. 1999) (holding that a district court's failure to submit the "willfully and knowing" requirement in Section 7206(1) to the jury constituted error, but that the error was harmless).

[180] In United States v. Rayor, 204 F. Supp. 486 (SD Cal. 1962), appeal dismissed as untimely, 323 F2d 519 (9th Cir.), cert. denied, 375 US 993 (1964), the court said that "material" means material to the contents of the return. Materiality for purposes of Section 7206(1) does not require that there be a substantial tax due. United States v. Citron, 783 F2d 307 (2d Cir. 1986). Thus, a false statement resulting in "minimal under-payments" has been held material. United States v. Greenberg, 735 F2d 29, 31–32 (2d Cir. 1984). One circuit court said in a case involving unreported income, "An accurate reflection of income is critical to determining a taxpayer's liability," and thus was a material matter. United States v. Neder, 81 AFTR2d 98-1367 (11th Cir. 1998). The government may prove that the statement in a return is false by using a circumstantial method of proof, as it would in an evasion case. See United States v. Shetty, 80 AFTR2d 97-5616 (9th Cir. 1997) (net worth method used in proving taxpayer/defendant's false statement about the amount of his income).

and expenses from a business,[181] in the amount of estimated tax paid,[182] in false Subchapter S returns,[183] in false partnership returns,[184] and in other schedules.[185]

The scope of what constitutes a materially false statement is expansive. An item on a return or other document is sufficient to constitute a material false statement.[186] However, statements have been held to be false even where they have not resulted in an underpayment of tax. Where taxpayers did not understate taxable income, but knowingly misstated the source of their income, the knowing misstatement was a material false statement.[187] Similarly, a statement may be false even where tax has been overstated.[188]

---

[181] Siravo v. United States, 377 F2d 469 (1st Cir. 1967). See also United States v. Taylor, 574 F2d 232 (5th Cir.), cert. denied, 439 US 893 (1978), where the defendant failed to report substantial amounts of gross livestock receipts on Schedule F. In United States v. Gurtunca, 638 F. Supp. 296 (ED Wis. 1986), aff'd, 836 F2d 283 (10th Cir. 1987), a defendant charged with falsely stating his gross receipts on Schedule C offered evidence to show that the loan brokerage fees were reportable on the return but not on Schedule C. However, the court found that the amounts were reportable on Schedule C because there was a close relationship between the stated business and the means (albeit fraudulent) by which the amounts were obtained.

[182] United States v. Lopez, 420 F2d 313 (2d Cir. 1969); Edwards v. United States, 375 F2d 862 (9th Cir. 1967). See also United States v. Golapudi, 80 AFTR2d ¶ 97-7861 (3d Cir. 1997) (although defendant presented evidence that the withholding amount was correct under a "gross-up" method, false statement about withholding amounts found because in part evidence showed that no withholding was actually made).

[183] Hickok v. United States, 481 F2d 377 (9th Cir. 1973); DiBenedetto v. United States, 542 F2d 490 (8th Cir. 1976).

[184] Rosenbloom v. United States, 259 F2d 500 (8th Cir.), cert. denied, 358 US 929 (1959).

[185] United States v. Franks, 723 F2d 1482 (10th Cir. 1983), cert. denied, 469 US 817 (1984) (failure to report eight foreign bank accounts on Form 4683). See also United States v. Marchini, 797 F2d 759 (9th Cir. 1986) (false Forms 940 and 941 failed to include cash wages).

[186] United States v. Cohen, 544 F2d 781 (5th Cir.), cert. denied, 431 US 914 (1977) (false statement of assets on financial statement); United States v. Ingredient Technology Corp., 698 F2d 88 (2d Cir. 1983) (overstatement of LIFO (last-in, first-out) inventory); United States v. Krall, 835 F2d 711 (8th Cir. 1987) (optometrist who purportedly assigned his income to foreign trusts was convicted of willfully filing false tax returns under Section 7206(1), even though trust arrangement was not expressly illegal).

[187] United States v. DiVarco, 484 F2d 670 (7th Cir.), cert. denied, 415 US 916 (1973); United States v. Bliss, 735 F2d 294 (8th Cir. 1984) (checks to fictitious payee nominally for purchases claimed to have been cashed to pay for purchases; held, following *DiVarco*, even if the correct amount of income is otherwise fully reported, willful and knowing misstatements about the source of claimed deductions also violate Section 7206(1)). United States v. Jacobson, 547 F2d 21 (2d Cir.), cert. denied, 430 US 946 (1977) (loan shark reported as miscellaneous income usurious interest he received).

[188] In United States v. Greenberg, 735 F2d 29 (2d Cir. 1984), a false statement conviction was upheld despite the fact that although personal expenditures were classified as

Although many circuit courts had a different view,[189] the Supreme Court found in *United States v. Gaudin*[190] that procedurally, whether a false statement is material is a question for the jury to decide along with the other elements of the offense. *Gaudin* was not a tax case but a prosecution under 18 USC § 1001 for statements on Department of Housing and Urban Development loan documents. At the trial, the district court judge charged the jury that the issue of materiality was a matter for the court, not the jury. The Supreme Court reversed, holding that "the Constitution gives a criminal defendant the right to demand that a jury find guilty of all the elements of the crime with which he is charged; one of the elements in [a false statement prosecution] is materiality; the defendant therefore had a right to have the jury decide materiality."[191] Since the Fifth and Sixth Amendments require criminal convictions to rest on a jury determination that the defendant is guilty of every element of the crime, the defendant has the right to have the materiality issue decided by the jury. In a false statement prosecution, the jury's decision whether the statements were material requires it to determine at least two subsidiary questions of purely historical fact—what statement was made and what decision the agency was trying to make—and then to apply the legal standards of materiality, as instructed by the judge, to determine the ultimate question of mixed fact and law: whether the statement was material.

After *Gaudin*, the issue of materiality is to be decided by the jury, and most circuit courts have held that the issue of materiality is for the jury, not

---

business expenses, the business reported more income than it should have for the year in issue, and its net taxable income was stated in the proper taxable amount. United States v. Mastropieri, 685 F2d 776 (2d Cir.), cert. denied, 459 US 945 (1982) (income as process server reported where taxpayer had not received any such income).

[189] United States v. Greenberg, 735 F2d 29 (2d Cir. 1984); United States v. Taylor, 574 F2d 232 (5th Cir.), cert. denied, 439 US 893 (1978); United States v. Romanow, 509 F2d 26 (1st Cir. 1975); United States v. Whyte, 699 F2d 375, 379 (7th Cir. 1983). United States v. Gaines, 690 F2d 849, 858 (11th Cir. 1982); United States v. Strand, 617 F2d 571, 574 (10th Cir.), cert. denied, 449 US 841 (1980). See also United States v. Holecek, 739 F2d 331, 337 (8th Cir. 1984); United States v. Flake, 746 F2d 535 (9th Cir. 1984). But see United States v. Null, 415 F2d 1178, 1181 (4th Cir. 1969) (materiality under Section 7206(1) is a jury issue).

[190] United States v. Gaudin, 515 US 506, 115 S. Ct. 2310 (1995).

[191] United States v. Gaudin, 515 US 506, 115 S. Ct. 2310, 2314.

the court.[192] Also, where issues of fact are related to the false statement, those issues have been left to the jury to decide.[193]

There still remains uncertainty about the application of *Gaudin*. The determination of materiality has been held to involve a pure question of law. In reviewing a conviction for assisting in the filing of false returns, one circuit court said, "While the Supreme Court's determination of materiality [in *Gaudin*] required the resolution by the jury of 'subsidiary questions of purely historical fact,' the determination of materiality in the present case involved purely a question of law and was suitable for resolution by the district court."[194] Using the Seventh Circuit's test of materiality,[195] the Second Circuit held that itemized deductions on tax returns the defendant accountant prepared for his clients constituted material matters sufficient to establish a violation of Section 7206(2). The matters were material because they were essential to the accurate computation of the clients' taxes. The itemized deductions directly affected the calculation of taxable income in the defendant accountant's clients' tax returns, so any false deductions "necessarily" (i.e., as a matter of law) resulted in inaccurate computations of their taxable income. In this situation, the determination of materiality was "purely a legal question," and the jury was not required to make the factual determinations that the jury was required to make in *Gaudin*.

But if the jury does not decide the issue of materiality, is the failure an error, and if so, is the error a plain or harmless error? In *Neder v. United*

---

[192] The First Circuit in *DiRico*; the Fifth Circuit in *McGuire*; the Seventh Circuit in United States v. Domenico, 78 F3d 294, 303 (7th Cir. 1996), cert. denied; the Ninth Circuit in *Uchimura*; the Eleventh Circuit in United States v. Neder, 81 AFTR2d 98-1367 (11th Cir. 1998). A contrary result was reached in a false filing case by the Fifth Circuit, which, without analyzing *Gaudin* as closely as the Second Circuit, simply remanded the case for a new trial with the instruction that whether the false statement was material must be decided by the jury. United States v. McGuire, 79 F3d 1396 (1996). See also United States v. DiRico, 78 F3d 732, 736 (1st Cir. 1996) (applying *Gaudin's* definition of materiality in Section 7206(1), and holding that materiality is a mixed question of law and fact for the jury to decide).

[193] United States v. Uchimura, 107 F3d 1321 (9th Cir. 1997) (*Klausner* not followed; the issue of materiality should have been submitted to the jury because the case involved the fact questions of (1) what statement was made and (2) what information was necessary in the case to make a determination of whether income tax was owed). In a false statement prosecution involving the omission of income, the Tenth Circuit held that the question whether false statement of income was material was for the jury, not the court, to decide. The Tenth Circuit agreed with the Ninth Circuit's opinion in *Uchimura* that after *Gaudin*, the only pertinent question is whether materiality is an essential element of the crime, not whether the element of materiality was an issue of law or fact. United States v. Clifton, 80 AFTR2d 97-7480 (10th Cir. 1997).

[194] United States v. Klausner, 80 F3d 55 (1996) (a divided court).

[195] United States v. Warden, 545 F2d 32, 37 (7th Cir. 1976).

States,[196] the Supreme Court held that although a district court's failure to submit the element of materiality to the jury was error under *Gaudin*, the error was harmless. The defendant did not contest the materiality of the false statement, and materiality had been supported by overwhelming evidence, with the result that absent the error, the jury verdict would have been the same.[197] Also, the Second Circuit has said that when materiality is both an issue for the court and apparent from the evidence, the "better practice" in false return cases is for "the district court to make a determination of materiality, and then inform the jury that the alleged misrepresentation, if found, is material under the statute as a matter of law."[198]

[c] The Willfulness Element

In *United States v. Bishop*,[199] the Supreme Court held that the word "willfully" has precisely the same meaning in both Section 7206(1) (the felony false statement statute) and Section 7207 (the misdemeanor false statement statute). As amplified by *United States v. Pomponio*,[200] "willfulness" means a voluntary, intentional violation of a known legal duty. Proof of willfulness in a false statement prosecution usually involves the same type of evidence outlined in *Spies v. United States*,[201] as probative of willfulness in an evasion prosecution. Thus, for example, use of currency and false names is evidence of willfulness in a false statement case,[202] as is concealment of income from a re-

---

[196] Needer v. United States, 83 AFTR2d 99-2668 (1999).

[197] Needer v. United States, 83 AFTR2d 99-2668 (1999).

[198] United States v. Luiz Ben Zvi, 83 AFTR2d 99-707 (2d Cir. 1999). The court also said that the omission of materiality from a jury charge is "probably not error at all," and, in any event, not plain error.

[199] United States v. Bishop, 412 US 346 (1973).

[200] United States v. Pomponio, 429 US 10 (1976).

[201] Spies v. United States, 317 US 492 (1943).

[202] See, e.g., United States v. Holladay, 566 F2d 1018 (5th Cir.), cert. denied, 439 US 831 (1978); United States v. Doan, 710 F2d 124 (3d Cir. 1983) (among other facts, percentage of unreported income to reported gross income was evidence of willfulness); United States v. Moon, 718 F2d 1210 (2d Cir. 1983), cert. denied, 466 US 971 (1984) (sufficiency of evidence on intent reviewed; "evidence tending to show misconduct through extensive dealings in cash is properly admitted into evidence"). The source of income may be relevant in determining willfulness. In United States v. Tafoya, 757 F2d 1522 (5th Cir. 1985), evidence that the defendant had engaged in assassination efforts was held relevant to show that he "did something to earn the income (the government) alleged he failed to report." The circuit court cited United States v. Carillo, 561 F2d 1125, 1127 (5th Cir. 1977), for the proposition that a prosecution for filing false tax returns by failing to report income would be unintelligible without evidence of source of income; such evidence being "inextricably tied to the basic elements of proof of filing false tax returns." But see United States v. Shorter, 85-2 USTC ¶ 9673 (DDC 1985), aff'd, 809 F2d 54 (DC Cir.), cert. denied, 108 S. Ct. 71 (1987) (evidence of prior years' omissions over twenty-

turn preparer.[203] The taxpayer must have intended, however, to violate a known legal duty. When a taxpayer took deductions for several pension plan contributions he did not in fact make, he was charged under Section 7206(1).[204] The district court dismissed the indictment on the ground that two revenue rulings permitted deductions if the taxpayer intended to make the full contribution by the filing due date. According to the court, "For the indictment to have properly charged a crime under the facts alleged by the government in this case, it should have included additional language to the effect that at the time Defendant subscribed his returns he had no intentions of making the contributions."[205] Similarly, in *United States v. Salerno*,[206] where a former casino manager and his assistant embezzled money through a scheme that made it appear that the missing money had been won by customers, their conviction of attempting to evade the casino's taxes was reversed because the evidence failed to show that the two defendants embezzled the money "not merely for their own benefit but with a specific intent to cause the casino to file false returns." While the filing of the corporate return appeared irrelevant to the embezzlement scheme in *Salerno*, specific intent will be found when the only apparent purpose of the scheme is to obtain some unwarranted favorable tax treatment disguising the receipt of income.[207]

[2] The Preparer Statute: Section 7206(2)

A person who willfully aids or assists in the preparation or filing of a return or other document that is false as to any material matter is guilty of a violation of Section 7206(2). The elements of the crime are (1) that a person has aided or

---

three-year period excluded under the Federal Rules of Evidence 403, because prejudice that would result from proffered evidence outweighed its probative value); United States v. Nielsen, 1 F3d 855 (9th Cir. 1993) (knowing false statement established by evidence that quarterly excise tax returns set forth arbitrary amounts and full-year return carried over same amounts because company was short of cash).

[203] United States v. Greer, 607 F2d 1251 (9th Cir. 1979), cert. denied, 100 S. Ct. 526 (1980); United States v. Drape, 668 F2d 22 (1st Cir. 1982) (taxpayer failed to tell the preparer about the actual date documents were signed, i.e., that they were backdated); Clinkscale v. United States, 729 F2d 940 (8th Cir. 1984) (taxpayer told preparer her husband was unemployed when he was deriving income from prostitution); United States v. Kim, 884 F2d 189 (5th Cir. 1989) ("[g]iving false information to an accountant bears on intent to evade and defeat payment of taxes . . . and the jury was certainly entitled to conclude that Mr. Kim deliberately fabricated the information for the returns").

[204] United States v. Robinson, 811 F. Supp. 1174 (SD Miss. 1993).

[205] United States v. Robinson, 811 F. Supp. 1174, 1176–1177 (SD Miss. 1993).

[206] United States v. Salerno, 902 F2d 1429 (9th Cir. 1990).

[207] See United States v. Dale, 76 AFTR2d 95-5675 (DC Cir. 1995) (proceeds of government contract disguised as a loan and secreted offshore).

assisted in, or has procured, counseled, or advised, the preparation of a return, affidavit, claim, or document; (2) that the document is false as to a material matter arising under the internal revenue laws; and (3) that the conduct was willful.[208] This provision is frequently called the preparer's statute because it is directed at those who aid or assist in the preparation of a return or other document.[209] However, the offense covers a class broader than tax return preparers,

[208] Materiality under Section 7206(2) has been held to be a question of law. United States v. Holecek, 739 F2d 331, 337 (8th Cir. 1984). In *Holecek*, the circuit court also said (739 F2d at 335), "[t]he generally accepted definition of 'false' to be applied in cases such as this is two-pronged: a statement is false if untrue and known to be untrue when made" (footnote omitted). *Holecek*, 739 F2d at 335. But this may no longer be the case. See United States v. Gaudin, 115 S. Ct. 2310 (1995), holding that the failure to permit the jury to decide the issue of materiality in a false statement prosecution under 18 USC § 1001 violated the defendant's Fifth and Sixth Amendment rights. But in reviewing the conviction under Section 7206(2) of an accountant who prepared returns for clients that claimed false itemized deductions, the Second Circuit held that the issue of materiality was an issue of law for the judge to decide, because the falsity of the deductions necessarily prevented the correct computation of the clients' income tax. United States v. Klausner, 80 F3d 55 (1996); but see United States v. Mcguire, 79 F3d 1396 (5th Cir. 1996) (a false statement conviction under Section 7206(1) was reversed and remanded for a new trial in which the issue of materiality would be decided by the jury).

A statement can also be said to be false if it has no basis in fact or in law. See, e.g., United States v. Pacheco, 912 F2d 297 (9th Cir. 1990) (consulting fee based on arbitrary property valuation was clearly excessive and was not actually paid). But to make out a willful violation of Section 7206(2), the government must prove that the defendant acted with specific intent to defraud the Service by filing false tax returns. An employer may file a false tax return when employees embezzle funds from the employer; but this tangential consequence of the embezzlement has been held not to be sufficient to support a Section 7206(2) charge, because the crime requires specific intent. United States v. Solerno, 902 F2d 1429 (9th Cir. 1990) (employees falsified documents to cover up embezzlement); United States v. Foy, 794 F. Supp. 835 (MD Tenn. 1992) (employees falsified invoices to cover up embezzlement).

[209] See United States v. Sassak, 881 F2d 276 (6th Cir. 1989) (defendant need not meet definition of "income tax return preparer to have violated Section 7206(2) so long as there was some affirmative action"). However, it has been held that an element of Section 7206(2) is for the return to have been filed. United States v. Dahlstrom, 713 F2d 1423 (9th Cir. 1983) (a divided court). The taxpayer himself has been prosecuted under Section 7206(2) for supplying false information to the return preparer and thus assisting in the preparation of his own false tax return. See United States v. Greger, 716 F2d 1275 (9th Cir. 1983), cert. denied, 465 US 1007 (1984). Section 7206(2) has been held to be probably not intended for, but applicable to, providing false corporate books and records at a civil audit. United States v. Ecker, 86-2 USTC ¶ 9663 (SDNY 1986) (motion to dismiss Section 7206(2) count dismissed; statute and cases analyzed). In United States v. Isaksson, 744 F2d 574 (7th Cir. 1984), an employer was convicted of aiding and assisting his employees in the preparation of their false income tax returns by paying a portion of their wages to them as independent contractors.

Prior years' returns of a taxpayer whose return an accountant was charged with falsifying might be material in the preparation of an accountant's defense under Federal Rules of Criminal Procedure 16(a)(1)(C). Prior year returns might tend to be materially exculpa-

since it applies to those who procure, counsel, or advise the preparation of a false return or document. Because the statute is directed at conduct that attends the filing of a false return and those whose actions lead to the filing of a false return, a prosecution under Section 7206(2) might be brought under other criminal statutes as well. For example, the "any person" language of Section 7201 indicates that a person who assists in the preparation of a false return may be prosecuted for tax evasion either directly under the statute or as an aider and abettor pursuant to 18 USC § 2.[210] Prosecution could also be based on alleged conspiracy under 18 USC § 371.[211] Although a prosecution under Section 7206(2) may involve some connivance between the taxpayer and the return preparer or tax adviser, it is not necessary for the taxpayer to be charged as well.[212]

The false document involved in a prosecution under Section 7206(2) is usually an income tax return or a partnership information return. Typically, the statute is violated by a return preparer who prepares returns claiming false deductions with the result that his clients obtain refunds.[213] However, unlike Sec-

---

tory by showing that on returns the accountant did not prepare, similar items were treated similarly and information similar to that in the indictment returns was reported, providing impeachment information in questioning a taxpayer-client who testifies he gave the accountant accurate information. United States v. Lloyd, 992 F2d 348 (DC Cir. 1993) (confidentiality of the prior year returns under Section 6103(h)(4)(D) "seems trivial in the circumstances").

Prosecutions for willfully aiding or assisting in the filing of a false return frequently involve the returns of many taxpayers. Analysis of whether there was sufficient evidence to support conviction of violations of aiding and assisting in the preparation of false returns requires a review of the evidence presented in each return and count. This means that the evidence must prove the elements of the crime for each taxpayer's return. When the prosecution has a "global" theory, the requisite evidence on each count may not have been presented. See United States v. Coveney, 995 F2d 578 (5th Cir. 1993) (convictions reversed after count-by-count analysis).

[210] A person who assists another in filing false returns in violation of Section 7206(2) is a principal (not an accessory), and may be indicted only in the district where he acted. An accessory may be prosecuted in the district where he acted or where the principal committed the substantive crime. United States v. Griffin, 814 F2d 806 (1st Cir. 1987) (Section 7206(2) counts dismissed against accountant who rendered services in Massachusetts and was indicted in West Virginia).

[211] See United States v. Kravitz, 281 F2d 581 (3d Cir.), cert. denied, 364 US 941 (1961); United States v. Gleason, 766 F2d 1239 (8th Cir. 1985).

[212] United States v. Brill, 270 F2d 525 (3d Cir. 1959) (accountant was guilty of assisting in preparing false returns for a corporation and some of its shareholders, but neither the corporation nor its shareholders were defendants).

[213] United States v. Herskovitz, 209 F2d 881 (2d Cir. 1954); United States v. Egenberg, 441 F2d 441 (2d Cir.), cert. denied, 404 US 994 (1971) (CPA filed false income tax returns for alien entertainers); United States v. Baum, 435 F2d 1197 (7th Cir. 1970), cert. denied, 402 US 907 (1971) (attorney); United States v. Barnes, 313 F2d 325 (6th Cir. 1963) (lawyer prepared returns claiming fictitious dependents and split refund with tax-

tion 7206(1), the false document need not be a document made and subscribed under penalties of perjury.[214]

In addition, prosecutions are instituted under Section 7206(2) where an individual holding a winning ticket at a horse race asks another person (a so-called 10-percenter) to cash his ticket for him, giving the other person's name and address instead of the winner's on the required information return, Form 1099. The argument that no violation of Section 7206(2) occurs in such an instance because the person to whom the proceeds of the winning ticket were paid gave his correct name and address to the racetrack has been uniformly rejected.[215] The rationale is that an information return is intended to help the government locate and check on recipients of income and amounts they receive, and a scheme that causes the track to record another person as the winner is calculated to defeat the government in this effort.

The statute is broad enough to reach a person who supplied false information and even advice that is used in the preparation of the return.[216] The defendant's action in such a case must be willful. In most cases, this element is

---

payer); United States v. Erickson, 676 F2d 408 (10th Cir. 1982) (husband and wife owners of tax return preparation service that routinely prepared tax returns for taxpayers claiming business expense deductions "regardless of whether the taxpayer was engaged in a business"); United States v. Gleason, 766 F2d 1239 (8th Cir. 1985) (sole proprietorship accounting service assisted taxpayers in using false charitable deductions); United States v. Shortt Accountancy Corp., 785 F2d 1448 (9th Cir. 1986) (accountants advised backdating note). Counseling the filing of a false return is not protected speech where the intent of the speaker and the tendency of his words is to incite an imminent lawless act, tax evasion. United States v. Freeman, 761 F2d 549 (9th Cir. 1985) ("tax protestor" conducted seminars urging the filing of improper returns and giving demonstrations). United States v. Kellogg, 955 F2d 1244 (9th Cir. 1992) (false deductions; special agent posing as taxpayer secretly recorded devastating evidence of meeting).

[214] United States v. Miller, 529 F2d 1125 (9th Cir. 1976) (false return and false documents submitted). See United States v. Damon, 676 F2d 1060 (5th Cir. 1982) (Schedule C held to be integral part of return).

[215] United States v. Haimowitz, 404 F2d 38 (2d Cir. 1968). Accord United States v. LaHaye, 548 F2d 474 (3d Cir. 1977); United States v. Metcalf, 532 F2d 752 (4th Cir. 1976); United States v. Dumaine, 493 F2d 1257 (1st Cir. 1974); United States v. Lincoln, 472 F2d 1183 (5th Cir. 1973).

[216] See, e.g., United States v. Crum, 529 F2d 1380 (9th Cir. 1976) (farmer backdated beaver purchase contracts assisting in false deduction claims); United States v. Wolfson, 573 F2d 216 (5th Cir. 1978) (appraiser who furnished allegedly inflated appraisals used to claim charitable deductions); United States v. Clardy, 612 F2d 1139 (9th Cir. 1980) (preparer advised taxpayers they were entitled to unjustified prepaid interest deductions); United States v. Winograd, 656 F2d 279 (7th Cir. 1981), cert. denied, 455 US 989 (1982) (losses claimed on rigged Mexican peso straddles); United States v. Schulman, 817 F2d 1355 (9th Cir. 1987) (loan transactions were held to be shams as a matter of law so that defendant accountant's "willfulness" in assisting in filing and preparing of taxpayers' false returns was question of fact to be tried by jury); Nealy v. United States, 729 F2d 961 (4th Cir. 1984) (false engineering report about coal reserves).

satisfied by a showing that the return or other document was false and was prepared under circumstances demonstrating that the defendant knew it was falsely prepared. However, the defendants in *United States v. Dahlstrom*[217] were held not to have acted willfully because at the time they advocated a tax shelter program involving the use of foreign trusts, its legality "was completely unsettled by any clearly relevant precedent on the dates alleged in the indictment." A distinction may be drawn between a return that is false as to a matter of fact and a return that is prepared on the basis of a particular legal theory. Where the law is clear, there seems to be no impediment to prosecution under Section 7206(2), but where the law itself is "highly debatable," the requisite intent to violate the law is lacking.[218]

¶ 7A.05 EMPLOYMENT AND WITHHOLDING TAX OFFENSES

A series of criminal offenses deals exclusively with conduct or failure to perform certain acts relating to the withholding of tax from wages. Because the Service has stepped up its employment tax enforcement efforts, the following related criminal statutes and their penalties have become increasingly important:

- An employer or other person who willfully fails to collect or pay over withholding tax is guilty of a felony punishable by imprisonment of up to five years, or a fine of $10,000, or both.[219]

---

[217] United States v. Dahlstrom, 713 F2d 1423 (9th Cir. 1983). However, the "fair warning" limitation does not apply if the transaction would fail under general principles of tax law. See, e.g., United States v. Iles, Sr., 906 F2d 1122 (6th Cir. 1990) (research and development shelters held to be shams).

[218] See James v. United States, 366 US 213 (1961); United States v. Critzer, 498 F2d 1160, 1162 (4th Cir. 1974) (sale of Indian land; "[i]t is settled that when the law is vague or highly debatable, a defendant, actually or impliedly, lacks the requisite intent to violate it"); United States v. Mallas, 762 F2d 361 (4th Cir. 1985) (deduction for minimum advance royalties; "[p]resent authority in support of the [government's] theory is far too tenuous and competing interpretations of the applicable law far too reasonable to justify these convictions. . . . Criminal prosecution for the violation of an unclear duty itself violates the clear constitutional duty of the government to warn citizens whether particular conduct is legal or illegal").

[219] IRC § 7202. It has been held that the statute of limitations on prosecutions under Section 7202 is three, not six, years. United States v. Block, 497 F. Supp. 629 (ND Ga. 1980). See infra ¶ 7A.06[5]. However, the Third Circuit has held that the violation of Section 7202 for willfully failing to collect and truthfully account for and pay over any tax is subject to a six-year statute of limitations because under Section 6513(4), the six-year statute applies to the offense of "willfully failing to pay any tax, or make any re-

- An employer who fails to supply an employee with information regarding his wages and amounts deducted as withheld tax is punishable by imprisonment for not more than one year or a fine up to $1,000, or both.[220]
- An employee who willfully supplies a false exemption certificate is guilty of a misdemeanor punishable by imprisonment for not more than one year or a fine of not more than $1,000 for each false statement or failure to supply information, or both.[221]

---

turn," and the failure to pay any third-party tax; the person who commits the offense described in Section 7202 has willfully failed "to pay any tax" for purposes of Section 6513(4). United States v. Gollapudi, 80 AFTR2d 97-7861 (3d Cir. 1997) (a divided court); see also United States v. Musacchia, 900 F2d 493, 500 (2d Cir. 1990), cert. denied (six-year statute applies to a Section 7202 violation); United States v. Porth, 426 F2d 519, 522 (10th Cir. 1970), cert. denied (same). The Second Circuit reaffirmed its decision in *Musacchia* that a six-year statute applies to a Section 7202 offense. United States v. Evangelista, 122 F3d 112 (2d Cir. 1997). Consequently, despite the fact that two district courts (*Block* and United States v. Brennick, 908 F. Supp. 1004 (D. Mass. 1995)) decided that a three-year statute applies, as did at least one judge on the Third Circuit, the weight of authority is that a six-year statute of limitations applies to a Section 7202 offense.

In a Section 7202 prosecution, the government need not prove that the defendant both willfully failed to truthfully account for and willfully failed to pay over trust fund taxes. *United States v. Evangelista,* supra ("the plain language of the disputed passage in [S]ection 7202 creates a dual obligation—to 'truthfully account for and pay over' trust fund taxes—that is satisfied only by fulfilling *both* separate requirements . . . [the] command of the statute is violated by one 'who willfully fails' *either* 'to account for' or to 'pay over' the necessary funds").

But several circuit courts have held that violations of Section 7202 are subject to a six-year statute under Section 6534(4), because the section is not limited to failures to file and pay described in Section 7203. See *United States v. Musacchia,* supra; *United States v. Evangelista,* supra; *United States v. Gollapudi,* supra; United States v. Porth, 426 F2d 519, 522 (10th Cir.), cert. denied, 400 US 824 (1970).

[220] IRC § 7204. A person who furnishes an employee a Form W-2 containing false information and who files a false statement with the Service on a Form W-3 may be charged with only the misdemeanor described in Section 7204, not with the Section 7206(2) felony of aiding and assisting the employee in filing a false return.

[221] IRC § 7205, amended by the Economic Recovery Tax Act of 1981, Pub. L. No. 97-34 § 721(b). Compare United States v. Kelley, 769 F2d 215 (4th Cir. 1985) (conviction of leader who provided forms and instructions in the preparation of false W-4 forms to members for aiding and assisting in the preparation of false W-4 forms upheld; United States v. Snider, 502 F2d 645 (4th Cir. 1974) where W-4 forms claimed 3 billion dependents held not "deceptive"; distinguished as a "rare case"); United States v. Herzog, 632 F2d 469 (5th Cir. 1980) (employee claimed ninety-nine exemptions because his research led him to conclude wages were not taxable). The Department of Justice has authorized at least one prosecution of taxpayers who filed false withholding exemption certificates under both Sections 7202 and 7212, which deal with obstruction of justice, as well as punishing the use of force against IRS officials. See United States v. Williams, 644 F2d 696 (8th Cir. 1981) (reversing the Section 7212 conviction with a statutory analysis). The Deficit Reduction Act of 1984, Pub. L. No. 98-369, HR 4170, 98th Cong., 2d Sess. § 159,

• A person who fails, after notice from the Service under the provisions of Section 7512, to deposit withheld taxes in a separate trust account payable to the United States is guilty of a misdemeanor, punishable by imprisonment for not more than one year or a fine of $5,000, or both.[222]

Section 7202 literally applies to an employer who is required "to collect, account for, and pay over" withholding taxes for any tax imposed by the Code.[223] Prosecutions under Section 7202 are subject to the defense used in failure-to-pay prosecutions under Section 7203: namely, that the taxpayer did not have sufficient funds to pay the tax. In *United States v. Poll*,[224] the court held that to establish willfulness under Section 7215, the government must establish

> ... beyond a reasonable doubt that at the time payment was due the tax-payer possessed sufficient funds to enable him to meet his obligation or that the lack of sufficient funds on such a date was created by (or was the result of) a voluntary and intentional act without justification in view of all the financial circumstances of the taxpayer.

In a Section 7202 prosecution, therefore, *Poll* requires the government to prove that both the failure to truthfully account for and the failure to pay over were willful. However, it also has been held that the statute punishes a person who fails to complete both the duty of accounting for and the duty of paying over, so that "any intentional failure to complete the required task (to truthfully account for and pay over the tax) constitutes a crime."[225]

The offense described by Section 7215 is noteworthy because it does not require willfulness.[226] Mere failure to make deposits after notification under Section 7512 is sufficient, unless the employer or other person shows that (1)

---

further amended Section 7205 so that its criminal penalty for supplying false or fraudulent withholding information or willfully failing to supply information is in addition to, rather than in lieu of, any other penalty, after the effective date of the legislation. Thus, for example, prosecution for willful evasion (Section 7201) is not barred where prosecution for a false certificate (Section 7205) is also possible. See United States v. Bass, 784 F2d 1282 (5th Cir. 1986) (reversible error in Section 7205 prosecution for court to charge that defendant was an employee; cases and issues analyzed).

[222] IRC § 7215.

[223] Section 7202 also applies to persons who are required to collect, account for, and pay over excise taxes.

[224] United States v. Poll, 521 F2d 329, 333 (9th Cir. 1975).

[225] United States v. Brennick, 908 F. Supp. 1004 (D. Mass. 1995). Thus, the duties constitute an "inseparable dual obligation" and the responsible person may be prosecuted for the failure to complete either one. U.S. Dep't of Justice, Tax Division Manual for Criminal Tax Trials (5th ed. 1973), at 26. For a review of *Brennick* and the related case law, see Lopez & Segal, "Internal Revenue Code Section 7202," 1997 Complex Crimes Journal, ABA Section of Litigation, Criminal Litigation Committee, 41.

[226] United States v. Dreske, 536 F2d 188 (7th Cir. 1976).

there was reasonable doubt that the law required collection or as to who was required by law to collect tax or (2) the failure to comply was due to factors beyond the taxpayer's control. The defendant also has the burden of coming forward with evidence to establish his nonliability by reason of the two statutory exceptions.[227] Once the defendant has satisfied this burden of coming forward, the government must establish that the exception is inapplicable.[228] Although it appears that state of mind does not play a part in such a prosecution, the exception for nonpayment on account of factors beyond the person's control leaves open the possibility of a lack-of-funds defense.

¶ 7A.06 INTERFERENCE WITH SERVICE ADMINISTRATION: SECTION 7212(a)

Section 7212(a) punishes two types of misconduct: (1) attempts corruptly or by force or threats of force to intimidate or impede Service agents or other government officials acting in an official capacity under the Code and (2) attempts "in any other way" corruptly or by force or threats of force to obstruct or impede the due administration of the Code. The first type of misconduct involves interference or use of force or threats of force to interfere with agents. The second type of conduct has been interpreted broadly to reach fraud and misrepresentation, and the means used need not be illegal in themselves.[229] Courts have differed about the breadth of the statute. One court has read the statute broadly, using the same analysis applied to the crime of obstructing justice, to include all types of conduct, even conduct preceding the filing of a re-

---

[227] See, e.g., United States v. Randolph, 588 F2d 931 (5th Cir. 1979) (defendant's preferred defense of impossibility was not proved).

[228] United States v. Paulton, 540 F2d 886 (8th Cir. 1976); United States v. Plotkin, 239 F. Supp. 129 (ED Wis. 1965). See United States v. Gorden, 495 F2d 308 (7th Cir.), cert. denied, 419 US 833 (1974).

[229] United States v. Mitchell, 985 F2d 1275 (4th Cir. 1993) (fraudulent misrepresentation of tax-exempt activities to obtain tax-exempt status); United States v. Popkin, 943 F2d 1535 (11th Cir. 1991), cert. denied, 112 S. Ct. 1760 (1992) (attorney formed corporation to enable client to disguise nature of income); United States v. Williams, 644 F2d 696 (8th Cir.) cert. denied, 454 US 841 (1981) (aiding and abetting filing of false Forms W-4); United States v. Valenti, 121 F3d 327 (7th Cir. 1997) (defendant failed to pay tax, and kept no business records, dealt in currency, maintained no bank accounts, structured banking transactions to avoid the filing of currency transaction reports, did not withhold from employee wages, and, during the Service's investigation, tried to dissuade witnesses from cooperating with the Service; held, the evidence was sufficient to prove that the defendant "corruptly" obstructed the Service from administering the tax laws).

turn.[230] Another court, relying on the principle that a clear warning must be given by a criminal statute, has more strictly construed Section 7202 and held that specific intent to obstruct or impede is impossible to infer unless the defendant has notice or knowledge of a Service proceeding that the defendant's conduct would obstruct or impede.[231] More fundamentally, it has been contended that Congress intended Section 7212(a) "to proscribe only threatening or harassing conduct directed toward IRS agents"—that is, the omnibus clause of Section 7212(a) applies to the same type of conduct as directed toward Service agents, not to all types of conduct that may be interpreted to obstruct or impede the due administration of the tax laws.[232] Despite the argument that such a reading would render the statute unconstitutionally vague, the Second Circuit has pointed out that the omnibus clause renders criminal "any other" action that serves to obstruct or impede the due administration of the tax laws.[233]

An act is "corrupt" within the meaning of Section 7212(a) if it is performed to secure an unlawful benefit for oneself or for another.[234] For exam-

---

[230] United States v. Tolliver, 81 AFTR2d 98-534 (WD Va. 1997) (basketball referee submitted false receipts to the NBA to disguise the receipt of income in the form of unused travel allowances).

[231] United States v. Kassouf, 80 AFTR2d 97-7884 (ND Ohio 1996) (conduct charged, such as the failure to keep records, preceded the filing of the defendant's return).

[232] For a review of the legislative history of Section 7212(a) and the case law, see Fink & Rule, "The Growing Epidemic of Section 7212(a) Prosecutions," J. Tax'n 356 (June 1998).

[233] United States v. Kelley, 82 AFTR2d 98-7322 (2d Cir. 1998) (during an examination of his tax returns, the taxpayer, a lawyer, misrepresented to the revenue agent that he had assigned income to a corporation and that corporation had "picked up" the assigned income; the assignment was found to be a sham and the assignee corporation had not filed a return). Compare United States v. Kassouf, 81 AFTR2d 98-2066 (6th Cir. 1998) (divided on this point) using the requirement of a nexus between the act and the judicial proceeding applied in prosecutions under the obstruction of justice statute, 18 USC § 1503, to limit the imposition of liability under Section 7212(a) to cases where the taxpayer knows that there is an investigation of the return or proceeding of his return, and rejecting use of the statute for conduct which may have occurred long before a Service audit, or even a tax return was filed). For a case rejecting the view that a Service examination or investigation must be pending and that the conduct punished by Section 7212 must fit under defined categories, such as impeding or harassing Service employees, see United States v. Armstrong, 82 AFTR2d 99-5008 (ED Va. 1997) ("In light of other appellate courts' broad construction of the phrase 'in any other way corruptly' in [S]ection 7212(a), this court finds that a pending IRS audit or investigation is not required for [S]ection 7212(a) to apply," following United States v. Mitchell, 985 F2d 1275 (4th Cir. 1993), which said that the omnibus clause of Section 7212(a) was intended to target "creative and multifaceted scheme[s] to evade taxes").

[234] United States v. Reeves, 752 F2d 995, 998–999 (5th Cir.), cert. denied, 474 US 834 (1985); United States v. Yagow, 953 F2d 423, 427 (8th Cir. 1992). For this reason, the corrupt intent element of Section 7212(a) is different from the willfulness element of

ple, when a taxpayer files false Forms 1099 and 1096, falsely reporting substantial payments to others, and files a false income tax return claiming the payments as deductions and claiming a refund of tax, the filing of false information returns constitutes an attempt to obstruct the administration of the Service by "impeding 'the collection of one's taxes, the taxes of another, or the auditing of one's or another's tax records.'"[235] The attempt to obtain the tax refund is performed corruptly because it is to secure an unlawful benefit.

¶ 7A.07 COMMON DEFENSES

Conviction of a substantive tax offense requires each element of the crime to be established beyond a reasonable doubt. Clearly, then, a defense may be constructed with the objective of negating one of the required elements. For example, in an evasion prosecution, a defendant may show that there was no tax due and owing for the year at issue. A defendant may also attempt to prove that unreported income was offset by unclaimed deductions,[236] was reportable by another taxpayer,[237] or constituted a gift or other nontaxable receipt.[238] Further, the method the prosecution uses to establish unreported

---

Section 7206(1). The willfulness element of Section 7206(1) requires proof that the false statement was a voluntary and intentional violation of a known legal duty, while the "corruptly" element of Section 7212(a) involves a false statement made with the intent to gain an improper benefit.

[235] United States v. Kuball, 976 F2d 529 (9th Cir. 1992) (quoting United States v. Reeves, 752 F2d 995 (5th Cir. 1985)); see also United States v. Dykstra, 991 F2d 450 (8th Cir.), cert. denied, 114 S. Ct. 222 (1993).

[236] Koontz v. United States, 277 F2d 53 (5th Cir. 1960) (evasion charged for filing false return claiming deceased wife as an exemption; held, error to exclude evidence of unclaimed ordinary loss offsetting tax deficiency); United States v. Moody, 339 F2d 161 (6th Cir. 1964), cert. denied, 386 US 1003 (1966); Small v. United States, 255 F2d 604 (1st Cir. 1958); Marks v. United States, 391 F2d 210 (9th Cir.), cert. denied, 393 US 839 (1968). But see United States v. Cruz, 698 F2d 1148 (11th Cir.), cert. denied, 464 US 960 (1983) (unsuccessful defense that foreign tax credit reduced U.S. tax liability in evasion prosecution). The burden of coming forward with this evidence shifts to the defendant when it is established that the defendant received more income than he reported. United States v. Bender, 218 F2d 869 (7th Cir.), cert. denied, 349 US 920 (1955).

[237] Poonian v. United States, 294 F2d 74 (9th Cir. 1961).

[238] United States v. Wilkins, 385 F2d 465 (4th Cir.), cert. denied, 390 US 951 (1968) (where defendant successfully argued that income received on construction contracts was reportable in preindictment years, not indictment year); United States v. McCormick, 67 F2d 867 (2d Cir.), cert. denied, 291 US 662 (1933) (deputy city clerk's defense that moneys received from bridegrooms for performing marriage ceremonies constituted gifts rejected on facts). Recharacterization of the receipt may be successfully contended in evasion cases based on constructive dividends from corporations with no earnings and profits. DiZenzo v. Comm'r, 348 F2d 122 (2d Cir. 1965). Contra United States v. Miller,

income may be attacked on the basis of a failure to establish a starting point, follow leads, and the like.[239] Similarly, a prosecution under either Section 7206(1) or 18 USC § 1001 may be defended on the ground that the false statement was not material.[240] Apart from these defenses, there are others relating to the willfulness element common to all tax offenses and affirmative defenses, such as the statute of limitations.

[1] Mistake or Ignorance of Law

The now-standard definition of "willfulness" is an intentional violation of a known legal duty. Only knowing violations are punishable. Since a rule that a violation of law must be knowing would encourage defendants to fabricate ignorance defenses, the well-known maxim that "ignorance of the law is no excuse" is the general rule. But a standard requiring a knowing violation of law becomes more relevant to the issue of a criminal state of mind where the law is a general regulatory statute as complex as the Code. In prosecutions of tax crimes, therefore, ignorance or mistake of law may negate the requisite state of mind (i.e., willfulness), and is a defense,[241] and in support of this defense, the defendant is entitled to produce evidence.[242] Therefore, where the law on the tax treatment of an item of income or deduction is confused, uncertain, or debatable, the defendant lacks the requisite intent as a matter of law.[243]

---

529 F2d 1125 (9th Cir.), cert. denied, 426 US 924 (1976). See also McCormick v. United States, 111 S. Ct. 1807 (1991) (conviction on filing false return was reversed because jury could have convicted state legislator on tax charge, even though it was convinced that payments were nontaxable campaign contributions).

[239] See the discussion supra ¶ 7A.02[2][d][ii].

[240] See the discussion infra ¶ 7A.07[3].

[241] Battjes v. United States, 172 F2d 1, 4 (6th Cir. 1949) ("an actual bona fide misconception of the law, regardless of the presumption that the taxpayer knows the law, will not result in criminal liability"). The Model Penal Code, which has rejected the term "willful," provides in Section 2.04: "Ignorance or mistake as to a matter of fact or law is a defense if—(a) the ignorance or mistake negatives the purpose, knowledge, belief, recklessness or negligence required to establish a material element of the offense."

[242] United States v. Pinner, 561 F2d 1203 (5th Cir. 1977), cert. denied, 439 US 1115 (1979) (failure-to-file conviction vacated and remanded for factual findings on defendant's mistake of law defense); Haigler v. United States, 172 F2d 986 (10th Cir. 1949) (evasion conviction reversed where evidence to support ignorance defense excluded).

[243] See James v. United States, 366 US 213 (1961); United States v. Critzer, 498 F2d 1160, 1162 (4th Cir. 1974) (sale of Indian land; "[i]t is settled that when the law is vague or highly debatable, a defendant, actually or impliedly, lacks the requisite intent to violate it"); United States v. Mallas, 762 F2d 361 (4th Cir. 1985) (deduction for minimum advance royalties; "[p]resent authority in support of the [government's] theory is far too tenuous and competing interpretations of the applicable law far too reasonable to justify these convictions. . . . Criminal prosecution for the violation of an unclear duty itself violates the

Related to the mistake or ignorance of law defense is the defense that a defendant cannot have formed the requisite intent because he has not been given fair warning about his actual legal obligation under the circumstances.[244] In one case, twin sisters were separately prosecuted and convicted for willful evasion and failure to file tax returns. Critical to both cases was the government's contention that moneys their widower admirer gave to them were not gifts, but taxable income.[245] In reversing the convictions in both cases, the Seventh Circuit reasoned:

> We do not remand Harris' case for retrial, however, because Harris had no fair warning that her conduct might subject her to criminal tax liability. Neither the tax code, the Treasury Regulations, or Supreme Court or appellate cases provide a clear answer to whether Harris owed any taxes or not. The closest authority lies in a series of Tax Court decisions—but these cases *favor* Harris' position that the money she received was not income to her. Under this state of the law, Harris could not have formed a "willful" intent to violate the statutes at issue.

This "clear rule of law" requirement has its limits. When the defendant claimed that he believed payments he received from an insurance adjuster were a nontaxable settlement negating the tax due and owing element in an evasion charge, the Seventh Circuit said that, unlike *Harris*, where the tax treatment of the payments was uncertain, the rules governing settlements were clear, and required documentation to benefit from Section 104's personal injury exclusion.[246]

Some rules have been developed in this area:

1. *Disagreement with the law.* Although a bona fide misunderstanding of what the law requires is a defense, a disagreement with the law, no matter how well-intended, is not a defense.[247] For example, when a taxpayer testified to his

---

clear constitutional duty of the government to warn citizens whether particular conduct is legal or illegal"); United States v. Harris, 942 F2d 1125 (7th Cir. 1991) (income versus gift; law held not to supply "clear answer to whether Harris owed any taxes or not").

[244] Cases such as United States v. Garber, 589 F2d 843 (5th Cir. 1979), United States v. Critzer, 498 F2d 1160, 1162 (4th Cir. 1974), and United States v. Mallas, 762 F2d 361 (4th Cir. 1985), can be seen as applying this principle of criminal law.

[245] United States v. Harris, 942 F2d 1125 (7th Cir. 1991).

[246] United States v. Benson, 76 AFTR2d 95-6791 (7th Cir. 1995).

[247] United States v. Schiff, 801 F2d 108 (2d Cir.), cert. denied, 107 S. Ct. 1603 (1986) ("[w]ithout [the distinction between a misunderstanding of the law and disagreement with it], any taxpayer could evade tax obligations simply by stubbornly refusing to admit error despite the receipt of any number of authoritative statements of the law. At some point, such stubbornness becomes unreasonable; the line is crossed between misunderstanding and disagreement and the taxpayer can no longer assert a defense of good faith"); United States v. Ebner, 782 F2d 1120 (2d Cir. 1986) (rejecting good faith belief in tax-exempt status of Life Science Church); United States v. Burton, 737 F2d 439 (5th Cir.

good faith belief that wages were not income, the circuit court observed, "there is a difference between willful defiance of a statute and ignorance of a statute's existence and meaning" and the differences "while arbitrary at their edges distinguish citizens who simply choose not to obey a known duty from those who act out of ignorance or misunderstanding."[248] For this reason, a good faith belief that a law is unconstitutional is not a defense.[249]

2. *Role of the jury.* It is for the jury to decide whether a misunderstanding of the law is bona fide, and the defendant must be allowed to introduce evidence on his claimed misunderstanding regardless of its correctness or credibility.[250] Courts disagree about what type of evidence is admissible on the substantive law claimed to have been misunderstood. It is undisputed that the defendant must be permitted to testify. Expert testimony is another matter. Some courts would refuse to permit expert testimony about uncertainty in the law if the defendant was unaware of it.[251] In an unusual case, a defendant was permitted to introduce expert testimony although there was no claim that the

---

1984); United States v. Karsky, 610 F2d 548 (8th Cir. 1979); United States v. Ware, 608 F2d 400 (10th Cir. 1979); United States v. Kraeger, 711 F2d 6 (2d Cir. 1983) (following *Ware* and *Karsky*).

[248] United States v. Burton, 737 F2d 439, 441–444 (5th Cir. 1984).

[249] United States v. Ware, 608 F2d 400 (10th Cir. 1979).

[250] United States v. Burton, 737 F2d 439 (5th Cir. 1984). However, when a taxpayer claims to have relied on legal authority mistakenly or negligently, but not willfully, elements on which the legal authority is premised must be followed; failure to do so is fatal. United States v. Pacheco, 912 F2d 297 (9th Cir. 1990) (purported reliance on the *Sol Diamond* case did not support partnership's deduction of partnership interest whose value was determined by self-serving valuation). The taxpayer's general educational background is relevant evidence on the issue of mistake. United States v. Fletcher, 928 F2d 495 (2d Cir. 1991) (nonpracticing attorney who had accounting background; held, "the trier of fact may properly consider the general educational background and expertise of the defendant as bearing on the defendant's ability to form the requisite willful intent").

[251] United States v. Ingredient Technology Corp., 698 F2d 88 (2d Cir. 1983), cert. denied, 462 US 1131 (1984) (allowing expert testimony would permit juries "to find that uncertainty in the law negates willfulness whether or not defendants are actually confused about the extent of their tax liability"). In United States v. Fletcher, 928 F2d 495 (2d Cir. 1991), expert testimony was held not erroneously excluded, "especially because explaining the tax law is generally within the purview of the court, not expert witnesses." See also United States v. Daly, 756 F2d 1076 (5th Cir.), cert. denied, 474 US 1022 (1985) (expert opinion is properly excluded absent a showing that the defendant relied on it); United States v. Bryan, 896 F2d 68 (5th Cir. 1990) (expert testimony on legitimate straddles properly excluded when evidence was that trades were fictitious). See also United States v. Curtis, 782 F2d 593 (6th Cir. 1986) (willfulness is personal so evidence of external conflicts is irrelevant and would confuse the jury). If the judge makes the determination of the law, there must be no error. United States v. Pisani, 773 F2d 397 (2d Cir. 1985) (erroneous instruction that political contributions diverted to personal use constitute income as a matter of law resulted in reversal of conviction).

defendant knew of the uncertainty in the law.[252] Other courts have admitted expert testimony on the state of the tax law at least where the defendant claims to have been confused.[253]

3. *Objective versus subjective good faith.* Most courts say that the defendant's mistake need not be objectively reasonable, because to do so would be to remove the case from the consideration of the jury.[254] Other courts do require the defendant's error to be objectively reasonable,[255] or effectively reach that result by approving a "willful blindness" jury instruction permitting the

---

[252] United States v. Garber, 589 F2d 843 (5th Cir. 1979) (case remanded to permit defendant to introduce expert testimony on whether the unreported receipts of defendant-donor's sale of her blood constituted taxable income). But see United States v. Daley, 756 F2d 1676 (5th Cir. 1985) (*Garber* limited to "its bizarre facts—where the level of uncertainty approached legal vagueness").

[253] United States v. Critzer, 498 F2d 1160 (4th Cir. 1974); United States v. Mallas, 762 F2d 361 (4th Cir. 1985); United States v. Clardy, 612 F2d 1139 (8th Cir. 1980) (expert testimony received when there was a good faith dispute as to tax law interpretation); United States v. Dahlstrom, 713 F2d 1423 (9th Cir. 1983); United States v. Schulman, 817 F2d 1355, 1359 (9th Cir. 1987) (trial court must inquire "whether the law clearly prohibited the conduct alleged in the indictment"). The government may also offer expert testimony, at least if the witness is qualified as an expert. See United States v. Benson, 941 F2d 598 (7th Cir. 1991) (revenue agent's testimony that Social Security payments were gross income did not qualify as expert testimony). For a post-*Cheek* case holding that it was error to deny the defendant from presenting expert testimony, see United States v. Lankford, 955 F2d 1545 (11th Cir. 1992) (defendant subjectively believed that $1,500 check he received was gift; divided panel).

[254] United States v. Burton, 737 F2d 439 (5th Cir. 1984) ("[y]et, as far-fetched as it may be, [the defendant's] claim . . . was for the jury because the government is never entitled to a directed verdict in a federal criminal trial"); United States v. Aitken, 755 F2d 188 (1st Cir. 1985); United States v. Turano, 802 F2d 10 (1st Cir. 1986); United States v. Jerde, 841 F2d 818 (8th Cir. 1988); United States v. Phillips, 775 F2d 262 (10th Cir. 1985).

[255] United States v. Moore, 627 F2d 830, 833 (7th Cir. 1980), cert. denied, 450 US 916 (1981); United States v. Cheek, 882 F2d 1263 (7th Cir. 1989) (good faith misunderstanding of law must be objectively reasonable), vacated and remanded, 498 US 192 (1991) (subjective good faith standard adopted). See discussion of *Cheek*, supra ¶ 7A.03[2]. See United States v. Schiff, 801 F2d 108 (2d Cir.), cert. denied, 107 S. Ct. 1603 (1986). In a failure-to-file prosecution after *Cheek*, the following instructions were approved: "The grounds on which the defendant bases his individual claim of good faith in a belief that his conduct was lawful may be considered by the jury in deciding whether he actually acted in good faith." United States v. Barnett, 945 F2d 1296 (5th Cir. 1991) (Supreme Court, "while requiring a subjective standard for such a mistaken belief, clearly anticipated and condoned the jury's consideration of the bases upon which the defendant claims to have held his subjective belief as properly relevant to the ultimate inquiry of whether the defendant *in fact* held such a belief"). In a distinction that will necessarily be difficult for juries to apply and that is hard to reconcile with *Cheek*, it has been held that "although not itself the standard by which to evaluate good faith, the reasonableness of a good-faith defense is a factor which the jury may properly consider in determining whether a defendant's asserted beliefs are genuinely held." United States v. Mann, 884

jury to impute knowledge to the defendant of what should be obvious to him, if the jury finds, beyond a reasonable doubt, a conscious purpose to avoid enlightenment.[256] The Supreme Court resolved the subjective versus objective good faith dispute, holding in *United States v. Cheek*[257] that a good faith misunderstanding of the law or a good faith belief that one is not violating the law need not be "objectively reasonable if it is to be considered as possibly negating the Government's evidence purporting to show a defendant's awareness of the legal duty at issue." In *Cheek,* the defendant contended that he should have been acquitted of willfully failing to file a return and of tax evasion offenses because he believed in good faith that the income tax law is unconstitutional as applied to him, so the Service could not legally impose any duty upon him about which he should have been aware. The district court had charged the jury, however, that a belief that the tax laws are unconstitutional is "not objectively reasonable and cannot serve as the basis for a good-faith misunderstanding of the law defense." The defendant's belief is a question for the fact finder, the Supreme Court said, so characterizing a particular belief as "not objectively reasonable transforms the inquiry into a legal one and would prevent the jury from considering it." Forbidding a jury "to consider evidence that might negate willfulness would raise serious questions under the Sixth Amendment's jury trial provisions." Consequently, it was error for the district court to instruct the jury to disregard evidence of Cheek's understanding that, within the meaning of the tax laws, he was not a person required to file a return or to pay tax on wages, "as incredible as such misunderstandings of and beliefs about the law might be."

4. *The decision in* Cheek: *disagreement with law and mistake of law.* The decision in *Cheek* draws some distinctions about the types of good faith mistake claims that are allowed to constitute a defense to prosecution. Action based on a good faith claim of a Fifth Amendment privilege, an innocent mistake about what the law requires, a frank difference of opinion about the law's requirement, or even an "irrational belief" that the defendant has no duty—all of these claims are inconsistent with the violation of a known legal duty. On the other hand, Cheek's claim that the tax law is unconstitutional revealed that he knew what the law required, but believed, based on research and advice,

---

F2d 532, 537 n.3 (10th Cir. 1989); see also United States v. Collins, 920 F2d 619 (10th Cir. 1990).

[256] In United States v. MacKenzie, 777 F2d 811 (2d Cir. 1985), the convictions of a corporation's president and its general manager under 18 USC § 371 and Sections 7206(1) and 7206(2) were affirmed over the claim that there was uncertainty about the status of workers as independent contractors or employees. The Second Circuit, applying a subjective test, said that there was no evidence that the defendants genuinely thought that what they were doing was lawful and proper or that they were genuinely uncertain about the applicability of the law.

[257] United States v. Cheek, 498 US 192 (1991).

that the tax law was invalid and unenforceable for constitutional reasons. This kind of claim, said the Court, is a submission of a different order because it reveals a disagreement with law.[258] Thus, it appears that the majority would limit its holdings about the irrelevance of the defendant's views to those situations where the defendant claims that the tax statutes are constitutionally invalid, not to situations where the defendant claims there was a good faith mistake of law or a frank difference of opinion with the Service about the meaning of a law.

Where a claim of unconstitutionality is made, "a defendant's views about the validity of the tax statutes are irrelevant to the issue of willfulness, need not be heard by the jury, and if they are, an instruction to disregard them would be proper." This is so because the jury does not decide whether a claim is legally valid; the judge makes that determination. Nevertheless, all asserted misunderstandings are left to the fact finder for decision on whether the prosecution has proved the defendant's knowledge. Consequently, at least where a claim of unconstitutionality of the tax laws is made, the nature of the claim itself does not preclude a finding of willfulness; and the validity of the claim does not go to the jury. Rather, the defendant's asserted beliefs, such as in *Cheek*, that wages are not income and that he was not a taxpayer, must be considered by the jury in deciding whether the actions were willful.[259] After

---

[258] The concurring opinion believed that the majority's rationale would remove any defense that the defendant had a good faith but mistaken belief that a Service pronouncement was invalid. This might follow from the majority's statements about Cheek's knowledge of the law and his own conclusion based, in fact, on advice from others that the law was constitutionally invalid. The majority said Cheek bore the risk of prosecution because he had failed to follow the normal civil routes for judicial review and "when he did was unwilling to accept the outcome." But the majority, and even the dissent, clearly had in mind only the type of claim that Cheek had raised about the constitutional invalidity of the tax law, a claim that had been rejected in other cases involving Cheek and other taxpayers.

[259] In United States v. Powell, 955 F2d 1206 (1992), the Ninth Circuit said:

Although a district court may exclude evidence of what the law *is* or *should* be, . . . it ordinarily cannot exclude evidence relevant to the jury's determination of what a defendant *thought the law was* in § 7203 cases because willfulness is an element of the offense. In § 7203 prosecutions, statutes or case law upon which the defendant claims to have *actually relied* are admissible to disprove that element if the defendant lays a proper foundation which demonstrates such reliance. . . . Legal materials upon which the defendant does not claim to have relied, however, can be excluded as irrelevant and unnecessarily confusing because only the defendant's subjective belief is at issue: the court remains the jury's sole source of the law. (citations omitted)

However, since, after *Cheek*, good faith is an absolute defense to a tax crime such as Section 7206(1), once some evidence to support the defense has been introduced, the district court is required to submit the case to the jury in a manner that enables it to consider the defense fairly. See United States v. Morris, 20 F3d 1111 (11th Cir. 1994) (instruction on good faith mistake and belief defense inadequate in part because jury not instructed that

Cheek, evidence offered on the belief issue is not automatically relevant. One court made a perceptive distinction in a failure-to-file case involving a defendant's alleged belief that he was not required to file a return:

> "Belief" is a mischievous and tricky concept in this context. It is not a single-faceted idea, but is better defined as having both a normative and descriptive side. A normative belief is how Willie *wants* the law to be interpreted and ardently believes it *should* be interpreted. How he believes the law is constitutes a descriptive belief. . . . Thus, (Willie's) belief must be descriptive—he must believe the law *does not* apply to him. A normative belief that the law *should not* apply to him leaves Willie fully aware of his legal obligations and simply amounts to a disagreement with his known legal duty and a "studied conclusion . . . that [the law is] invalid and unenforceable."[260]

5. *Willful blindness after* Cheek. Even after *Cheek*, willful conduct may exist if the defendant taxpayer has acted with willful blindness to obvious or known risks. One circuit court affirmed a jury instruction on willfulness that appeared to distinguish between (1) knowledge of facts that might be inferred from proof that "a defendant deliberately closed his eyes to what would otherwise have been obvious to him" and (2) knowledge of law that might be inferred from the defendant's behavior. According to the Second Circuit, "The conscious avoidance charge is commonly used in this Circuit where a defendant claims lack of some specific aspect of knowledge necessary for conviction but where the evidence may be interpreted as deliberate ignorance."[261]

---

such a finding was a complete defense whether or not the defense is objectively reasonable; conviction reversed and case remanded).

The Seventh Circuit has said that a conviction of tax evasion is improper if the defendants did not know that they owed taxes, and that evidence of a motive unrelated to taxes would bolster a defense that the defendants were not willful, or at least that evidence would be relevant to the issue. United States v. Pittman, 100 F3d 1308 (7th Cir. 1996) (erroneous exclusion of the evidence not plain error because it was far from clear that there was a factual basis for defendants' assertion that they owed no taxes; and "it is extraordinarily unlikely that a jury would have credited this fantastic theory if it had been presented to them").

[260] United States v. Willie, 941 F2d 1384 (10th Cir. 1991).

[261] United States v. Fletcher, 928 F2d 495 (2d Cir. 1991). See also United States v. Sato, 814 F2d 449 (7th Cir. 1987) (charge approved that included "[i]n determining whether Defendant act[ed] knowingly and willfully, you may consider as well whether the Defendant deliberately closed his eyes to what would have been obvious to him"); United States v. Picciandra, 788 F2d 39 (1st Cir. 1986) (authorizing use of charge that willful blindness or ignorance is evidence from which knowledge may be inferred); United States v. Fingaldo, 934 F2d 1163 (10th Cir. 1991) ("[t]he deliberate ignorance instruction may be given when the evidence before the jury supports a finding of intentional avoidance of knowledge"). The Eighth Circuit rejected the argument that a willful blindness charge is improper after *Cheek*. United States v. Bussey, 942 F2d 1241, 1249 (8th Cir. 1991), reh'g denied, 1991 US App. LEXIS 22314, cert. denied, 118 L. Ed. 2d 542, 112 S. Ct. 1936, 60

[2] Advice of Counsel or Other Tax Adviser

Closely related to the mistake of law defense is the defense that the defendant relied on the erroneous advice of counsel or tax adviser. In principle, this defense is not acceptable as a defense to other criminal conduct, because it encourages those bent on unlawful activity to shop for an attorney who gives "good" advice.[262] However, the tax law's complexity has resulted in the acceptance of this defense in tax cases.

A classic formulation of the defense in a jury instruction approved by the Supreme Court stated:

> [I]f a man honestly and in good faith seeks advice of a lawyer as to what he may lawfully do . . . , and fully and honestly lays all the facts before his counsel, and in good faith and honestly follows such advice, relying upon it and believing it to be correct, and only intends that his acts shall be lawful, he could not be convicted of a crime which involves willful and unlawful intent; even if such advice were an inaccurate construction of the law.[263]

The defendant is also entitled to an appropriate instruction to the jury on this issue.[264]

USLW 3780 (US 1992), reh'g denied, 120 L. Ed. 2d 937, 113 S. Ct. 9, 61 USLW 3149 (US 1992) ("*Cheek* did not involve a willful blindness instruction and is therefore irrelevant to Bussey's willful blindness issue on appeal"); United States v. Dykstra, 991 F2d 450 (8th Cir. 1993) (*Bussey* followed).

[262] See Model Penal Code § 2.04(3).

[263] Williamson v. United States, 207 US 425, 453 (1908) (a nontax case). For tax cases, see United States v. Phillips, 217 F2d 435 (7th Cir. 1954); United States v. Raub, 177 F2d 312 (7th Cir. 1949); Benetti v. United States, 97 F2d 263 (9th Cir. 1938); Bursten v. United States, 395 F2d 976 (5th Cir. 1968), cert. denied, 409 US 843 (1972); United States v. Mitchell, 495 F2d 285 (4th Cir. 1974); United States v. Conforte, 624 F2d 869 (9th Cir.), cert. denied, 449 US 1016 (1980). See United States v. Ellis, 496 F. Supp. 76 (D. Kan. 1980) (taxpayer mistakenly relied, not willful). For a case where the court concluded that the tax adviser was not competent and that the taxpayer did not seek tax advice in good faith, see United States v. Farber, 630 F2d 569 (8th Cir. 1980). See also United States v. Rothrock, 806 F2d 318 (1st Cir. 1986) (where reliance on incompetent return preparer was alleged and district court used willful blindness charge, circuit court said, "the purpose of the willful blindness theory is to impose criminal liability on people, who recognizing the likelihood of wrongdoing, nonetheless consciously refuse to take basic investigative steps").

[264] Bursten v. United States, 395 F2d 976 (5th Cir. 1968), cert. denied, 409 US 843 (1972). In United States v. Phillips, 217 F2d 435 (7th Cir. 1954), the Seventh Circuit said that the defendant is entitled to an instruction relating to advice of counsel whether or not the defendant has formally raised the defense. Cf. United States v. Solomon, 825 F2d 1292, 1297 (9th Cir. 1987), cert. denied, 484 US 1046 (1988) (failure to give an instruction on a "good faith" defense is not fatal as long as court clearly instructs jury that spe-

Full disclosure of the material facts to the adviser is an element of the defense. Therefore, reliance on the advice of a tax adviser will fail as a defense if the defendant has withheld material facts from the adviser.[265] A defendant should be entitled to have all evidence considered by the jury—i.e., the assertion of lack of intent based on reliance and the withheld information. It is for the jury to determine whether the information withheld was material and whether, considering all the evidence, the defendant's conduct was willful. A requirement that "all information" be supplied to the adviser seems to defeat the defense before it is considered.[266] Rather, the requirement of providing the adviser with information must be understood in the context of willfulness. It is not the totality of the information given the adviser that is significant but the materiality of the information as evidencing the defendant's explanation that he made an honest effort to seek advice. Thus, withholding information reflects on the defendant's good faith in seeking and relying on the adviser's counsel. However, it must also be remembered that laymen seek advice from tax advisers because of the law's complexity and may reasonably be ignorant of what information is material. Obviously, if the defendant receives proper advice and fails to follow it, the evidence tends to establish that the defendant acted willfully in attempting to do what the law forbids.[267]

---

cific intent is a necessary element of the crime); United States v. Evangelista, 122 F3d 112 (2d Cir. 1997) (citing *Williamson*).

[265] United States v. McCormick, 67 F2d 867 (2d Cir.), cert. denied, 291 US 662 (1933); United States v. Cox, 348 F2d 294 (6th Cir. 1965); United States v. Raub, 177 F2d 312 (7th Cir. 1949). A failure to supply an accountant with all material information to prepare a return similarly defeats a defense of shift of responsibility. United States v. Slutsky, 487 F2d 832 (2d Cir. 1973), cert. denied, 416 US 937 (1974); Black v. United States, 353 F2d 885 (DC Cir. 1965), vacated on other grounds, 385 US 26 (1966); United States v. Scher, 476 F2d 319 (4th Cir. 1973).

[266] The Seventh Circuit has approved an instruction: "Lack of intent may be proven by evidence showing that the defendant did not report the income in question on the advice of counsel, but this is not a defense unless you find that the defendant made a full disclosure of all facts to his attorney." United States v. Baldwin, 307 F2d 577, 579 (7th Cir.), cert. denied, 371 US 947 (1963). United States v. Kelly, 864 F2d 569 (7th Cir. 1989) (promoter of tax shelter convicted of violating Section 7206(1) despite claim that he relied on attorney where evidence showed no engagement for particular purpose and no reliance).

[267] See, e.g., Hill v. United States, 363 F2d 176 (5th Cir. 1964) (accountant who prepared tax returns for corporation and individual owners testified for prosecution that he had been consulted by one of the owners about corporate checks that owners cashed for expenses and that he advised them to file amended returns, which they did not do).

[3] Shift of Responsibility

A defendant may defend against a charge that his conduct was willful by asserting that any deficiencies, omissions, or erroneous entries were the responsibility of the person who prepared the return or kept the books. If established, this defense (like the reliance defense) negates the willfulness element of the crime charged. In *Pechenik v. United States*,[268] the conviction of a corporation's president for evasion was reversed because the evidence showed that a bookkeeper determined how various expenses should be treated and because it did not link the defendant with the corporation's books of account, which erroneously expended capital expenditures. However, where the defendant withholds information from the return preparer or recordkeeper or takes positive action to mislead them, he himself is the cause for the deficiency or error. This evidence tends to show that in fact the defendant knew the return was false,[269] but the entire issue of responsibility goes to the jury.[270] When the defendant claims reliance on, and a shift of responsibility to, an accountant, the prosecution need not show that the defendant ordered the accountant to falsify the return. The prosecution's response can be evidence that the defendant (1) was aware of the contents of the return and (2) knew that the reportable income significantly exceeded the amount reported on the return.[271]

---

[268] Pechenik v. United States, 236 F2d 844 (3d Cir. 1956).

[269] United States v. Slutsky, 487 F2d 832 (2d Cir.), cert. denied, 416 US 937, reh'g denied, 416 US 1000 (1974); United States v. Scher, 476 F2d 319 (4th Cir. 1973); United States v. Stone, 431 F2d 1286 (5th Cir.), cert. denied, 401 US 912 (1971); Black v. United States, 353 F2d 885 (DC Cir. 1965), vacated on other grounds, 385 US 26 (1966). United States v. Drape, 668 F2d 22 (1st Cir. 1982) (in a Section 7206(1) prosecution involving backdated coal tax shelter agreements, taxpayer's alleged reliance on the preparer found not in good faith because the taxpayer did not disclose to the preparer the actual date he executed the papers). With less justification, it has been held that a defendant who should have known his return was false acts willfully. Katz v. United States, 321 F2d 7 (1st Cir.), cert. denied, 375 US 903 (1963).

[270] United States v. Venditti, 533 F2d 217 (5th Cir. 1976) (shift of responsibility defense countered by evidence that defendant controlled information accountant received and knew what income was not taxable, but evidence of accountant's negligence and rebuttal is for jury consideration on issue of willfulness). United States v. Chesson, 933 F2d 298 (5th Cir. 1991) ("the jury was entitled to conclude that the Chessons' reliance upon their accountants to discover the impermissible expenses was not in good faith").

[271] United States v. Olbres, 61 F3d 967 (1st Cir. 1995) (evidence establishing both elements found in the defendants' signing of the return, substantial expenditures in excess of the amount of income reported on the return, failure to deposit receipts into business checking account, knowing underreporting of rental income to accountant, and failure to deliver to accountant bank record of account into which unreported income was deposited).

[4] Mental Disease or Defect

For purposes of a tax offense, an individual may be unable to act willfully owing to some mental disease or defect. The argument that at the time of the alleged criminal conduct or at the time of or after trial the defendant suffered from some mental disease or defect is commonly called the insanity defense. In criminal procedure, this defense serves to determine whether it is appropriate to hold the defendant answerable or responsible under the criminal statutes at trial, sentencing, or commitment, and not to establish that the defendant is or is not "insane."[272]

Varying formulations of the standard applied in evaluating an insanity defense have been articulated. Although these formulations have provoked considerable debate and criticism, they probably have not had different results.[273] The standard formulated by the American Law Institute in its Model Penal Code is adopted in most circuits with or without modification.[274] Under the Model Penal Code, or "substantial capacity," test,

> A person is not responsible for criminal conduct if at the time of such conduct as a result of mental disease or defect he lacks substantial capac-

---

[272] There is a distinction between mental competence at the time of the offense and competence to stand trial. A person who lacks "the capacity to understand the nature of the proceedings against him, to consult with counsel, and to assist in preparing his defense may not be subjected to a trial." Drope v. Missouri, 420 US 162, 171 (1975). Under 18 USC § 4241(a), "the prosecutor, the defendant or the court on its own motion may seek an inquiry into a defendant's competence to stand trial where reasonable cause to believe that he may be presently suffering from a mental disease or defect rendering him incompetent is present." United States v. Auen, 846 F2d 872 (2d Cir. 1988) (sufficient basis in record to warrant competence determination). When the defendant gives notice of reliance on the defense of insanity, the court will order that a psychiatric or psychological examination of the defendant be conducted. 18 USC § 4242(a).

[273] The test most frequently used is the M'Naghten "right-wrong" test, under which an individual is not criminally responsible if, at the time of committing the act, he was laboring under such a defect of reason from disease of the mind, as not to know the nature and quality of the act he was doing, or, if he did know it, that he did not know what he was doing was wrong. A corollary test, called the "irresistible impulse" test, requires acquittal by reason of insanity if it is found that the defendant had a mental disease that prevented his controlling his conduct. An accused is not criminally responsible if his unlawful act was the product of mental disease or defect. Durham v. United States, 214 F2d 862 (DC Cir. 1954). This is called the *Durham* rule.

[274] United States v. Freeman, 357 F2d 606 (2d Cir. 1966); United States v. Currens, 290 F2d 751 (3d Cir. 1961); United States v. Chandler, 393 F2d 920 (4th Cir. 1968); Blake v. United States, 407 F2d 908 (5th Cir. 1969); United States v. Smith, 404 F2d 720 (6th Cir. 1968); United States v. Shapiro, 383 F2d 680 (7th Cir. 1967); Wade v. United States, 426 F2d 64 (9th Cir. 1970); Wion v. United States, 325 F2d 420 (10th Cir. 1963), cert. denied, 377 US 946 (1964). See also Pope v. United States, 372 F2d 710 (8th Cir. 1967) (exact words of formulation not important if charge requires findings as to defendant's cognition, his volition, and his capacity to control his behavior).

ity either to appreciate the criminality (wrongfulness) of his conduct or to conform his conduct to the requirements of law.

[T]he terms "mental disease or defect" do not include an abnormality manifested only by repeated criminal or otherwise anti-social conduct.[275]

For this test, the mental disease or defect need only impair the defendant's "substantial capacity" to appreciate or act; in this sense, diminished capacity rather than total incapacity or impairment is sufficient. Also, the test focuses on the impairment of the defendant's cognition and volitional capacities—i.e., the defendant's knowledge and will.

Decided cases do not provide an accurate picture of the use of the insanity defense in tax cases. It is likely that many cases in which the defense is raised are not brought to trial at all but are disposed of administratively. Also, it is frequently contended that a defendant's conduct was not willful because of some psychological disturbance not amounting to insanity. Courts have treated such an attempt as an unsuccessfully proved insanity defense[276] or have rejected the proffered evidence on the ground that the defendant had not raised the defense of insanity[277] or that it is not relevant to the issue of willfulness.[278] Where the insanity defense is raised in a tax case, expert psychiatric testimony is likely to be conflicting, and, in any event, is not conclusive. The issue is determined from the testimony of all witnesses, lay and expert,[279] and lay testimony can be sufficient to establish responsibility, even if there is expert opinion to the contrary.[280] Since the defendant is likely not to have been incapacitated during the indictment years, evidence that he or she lacked "substantial capacity" to know and to act will be lacking.[281] During an examination, a psychiatrist may ask the taxpayer about the circumstances involved in the prosecution and the taxpayer may disclose incriminating matters, but the de-

---

[275] Model Penal Code § 4.01.

[276] See, e.g., Benus v. Unites States, 196 F. Supp. 601 (ED Pa. 1961), aff'd, 305 F2d 821 (3d Cir. 1962); United States v. Cain, 298 F2d 934 (7th Cir.), cert. denied, 370 US 902 (1961); United States v. Griffin, 432 F2d 558 (8th Cir. 1970).

[277] United States v. Haseltine, 419 F2d 579 (9th Cir. 1969).

[278] Bernabei v. United States, 473 F2d 1385 (6th Cir.), cert. denied, 414 US 825 (1973). See United States v. Felak, 831 F2d 794, 797 (8th Cir. 1987) (psychiatric evidence on defendant's mistaken obsessive belief in nature of voluntary tax payments rejected).

[279] Mims v. United States, 375 F2d 135 (5th Cir. 1967); United States v. Levy, 326 F. Supp. 1285 (D. Conn. 1971), aff'd, 449 F2d 769 (2d Cir. 1971).

[280] Dusky v. United States, 295 F2d 743 (8th Cir.), cert. denied, 368 US 998 (1962); United States v. Lewellyn, 723 F2d 615, 619–620 (8th Cir. 1983) (defendant claiming insanity due to pathological gambling must demonstrate that mental health community generally accepts the principles underpinning his theory).

[281] See, e.g., United States v. Levy, 326 F. Supp. 1285 (D. Conn.), aff'd, 449 F2d 769 (2d Cir. 1971) (lawyer conducted active practice); United States v. Baird, 414 F2d 700 (2d Cir.), cert. denied, 396 US 1005 (1970) (broker employed in brokerage firm).

fendant, having raised the insanity defense, is estopped from claiming his self-incrimination privilege at trial.[282]

Evidence that the defendant did not act willfully because of some mental disturbance nevertheless has been admitted in the trial of a tax case.[283] The rationale for receiving the evidence is not any theory of diminished capacity, but rather that it is admissible to show that the defendant lacked the required state of mind required for conviction.[284] This rationale seems to suggest that the treatment of insanity as an "all or nothing" defense may be waning.

[5] Statute of Limitations

A motion may be made to dismiss one or more counts of an indictment or information on the defense that the statute of limitations bars prosecution. Under Section 6531, the most frequently used tax offenses (i.e., evasion, failure to file, and false statements) are subject to a six-year period of limitations beyond which no person may be "prosecuted, tried or punished." Those tax offenses not described in eight exceptions are subject to a three-year period of limitations for prosecution. The general statute of limitations for Title 18 offenses is five years[285]; however, Section 6531 specifically provides for a six-year period

---

[282] United States v. Baird, 414 F2d 700 (2d Cir.), cert. denied, 396 US 1005 (1970).

[283] See, e.g., United States v. D'Anna, 450 F2d 1201 (2d Cir. 1971) (grief over the drowning of a daughter); United States v. Levy, 326 F. Supp. 1285 (D. Conn.), aff'd, 449 F2d 769 (2d Cir. 1971); United States v. Baird, 414 F2d 700 (2d Cir.), cert. denied, 396 US 1005 (1970). But see United States v. Haseltine, 419 F2d 579 (9th Cir. 1969); Bernabei v. United States, 473 F2d 1385 (6th Cir.), cert. denied, 414 US 825 (1973). A proffer of expert testimony that the defendant could not have acted "willfully" because he was suffering from a compulsive gambling disorder has been rejected on the ground, inter alia, that "there is no general acceptance among the experts in the relevant scientific community that there is a link between the pathological gambling and the failure to pay taxes." United States v. Shorter, 85-2 USTC ¶ 9673 (DDC 1985), aff'd, 809 F2d 54 (DC Cir.), cert. denied, 108 S. Ct. 71 (1987); United States v. Lewellyn, 723 F2d 615 (8th Cir. 1983); see United States v. Sholl, 166 F3d 964 (9th Cir. 1999) (court approved rulings that the testimony of an expert on gambling could be limited to the ten standard criteria in the *Diagnostic Statistical Manual of Mental Disorders*, and that since the expert could not say that all those with a gambling disorder could not file an accurate return, further testimony was excludable on grounds of relevance and possible confusion to the jury). Compare United States v. Barta, 888 F2d 1220 (8th Cir. 1989) (rejection of expert testimony of defendant's detail phobia affirmed because relationship not shown between alleged detail phobia and misstatements of income; cases on psychological defenses gathered).

[284] In United States v. Erickson, 676 F2d 408 (10th Cir. 1982), a doctor testified that the taxpayer was suffering from a delusion about the tax laws with the result that he did not believe he was doing anything wrong in disobeying them. The district court held to have acted properly in instructing the jury that the evidence could be considered only for the limited purpose of determining whether the taxpayer had the requisite specific intent.

[285] 18 USC § 3282.

where the conspiracy is one to attempt to evade or defeat any tax or its payment.[286]

Computation of the statutory period begins with "the commission of the offense." Where a tax offense is committed by the filing of a false return, the normal rules of Section 6513 dealing with the time a return is considered filed apply. Thus, where a return, albeit false, is filed before it is due, the return is considered filed "on the last day prescribed for filing."[287] For example, if an individual taxpayer files his return on January 15, the six-year period begins to run on April 15. A return filed after the due date is considered filed on the actual date of filing, not on the normal due date. In *United States v. Habig*,[288] the defendants contended that the evasion was committed on the normal due date for filing the returns (May 15, 1960), not the dates they were actually filed (August 12 and 15, 1960) pursuant to extensions, because Section 6513(a) literally requires that any extension is to be disregarded for purposes of determining the due date. The Supreme Court rejected this argument on the ground that the statutory period of limitations would then begin to run before the defendants committed the acts on which the crimes were based. Consequently, the rules of Section 6513 apply only where an early return is filed.[289] In computing the limitations period for offenses committed by filing a false tax return, the date of actual receipt controls, rather than the date of mailing, and the day of the offense or act is excluded, while the date on which the indictment is filed is included.[290]

---

[286] IRC § 6531(8). Whether the Code's six-year period or the shorter five-year period applies may be a close question. See, e.g., United States v. Lowder, 492 F2d 953 (4th Cir.), cert. denied, 419 US 1092 (1974). See United States v. Ingredient Technology Corp., 698 F2d 88 (2d Cir. 1983), cert. denied, 462 US 1131 (1984) (six-year statute applies to a conspiracy to defraud). See infra ¶ 7A.07[2][c].

[287] IRC § 6513(a). United States v. Zudick, 523 F2d 848 (3d Cir. 1975).

[288] United States v. Habig, 390 US 222 (1968).

[289] United States v. Zudick, 523 F2d 848 (3d Cir. 1975) (unsuccessful contention that statutory period runs from date of actual filing where filed before due date).

[290] United States v. Mahler, 181 F. Supp. 900 (SDNY 1960); IRC § 7502. It has been held that if the indictment is returned within the six-year period, it may be superseded after the statute has run to add a lesser included offense. United States v. Gerstner, 548 F. Supp. 348 (SDNY 1982) (evasion indictment within statute superseded by indictment charging evasion and filing a false statement under Section 7206(1) after the statute had run). See also United States v. Horowitz, 756 F2d 1400 (9th Cir.), cert. denied, 474 US 822 (1985) (indictment may be refiled within six months after the expiration of the statute of limitations under 18 USC § 3288 (1982) where the earlier accusatory instrument was dismissed for a nonintentional failure to present exculpatory evidence to the grand jury); United States v. Stella, 745 F. Supp. 195 (SDNY 1990): "The indictment in this case on February 21, 1990 was timely because the 1981 return was filed on February 21, 1984, exactly six years before the indictment. In calculating the statute of limitations period, the Court does not count the day of the offense and does not count the last day of the period. Fed. R. Crim. P. 45(a)."

Circuits disagree about whether the statute of limitations defense is jurisdictional or whether it is an affirmative defense that may be waived.[291]

In cases where the attempt to evade is a false statement (as in *United States v. Beacon Brass Co.*),[292] the crime is committed on the date of the false statement. Consequently, an evasion prosecution may be instituted more than six years after a tax return for the year has been filed or was required to be filed. Similarly, the offense of attempting to evade or defeat payment of tax by concealing assets is committed on the last date of the conduct making up the attempt.[293] On this authority, the government has argued that a continuing

---

[291] The majority of circuits have held that the statute of limitations is not a jurisdictional bar to prosecution but a waivable defense. See United States v. Williams, 684 F2d 296 (4th Cir. 1982), cert. denied, 459 US 1110 (1983); United States v. Wild, 551 F2d 418 (DC Cir.), cert. denied, 431 US 916 (1977); United States v. Akmakjian, 647 F2d 12 (9th Cir.), cert. denied, 454 US 964 (1981); United States v. Doyle, 348 F2d 715 (2d Cir.), cert. denied, 382 US 843 (1965); United States v. Waldin, 253 F2d 551, 558 (3d Cir.), cert. denied, 356 US 973 (1958); United States v. Franklin, 188 F2d 182 (7th Cir. 1955); Capone v. Aderhold, 65 F2d 130 (5th Cir. 1933); United States v. Levine, 658 F2d 113 (3d Cir. 1981).

The Sixth and Tenth Circuits have held that the statute of limitations is a jurisdictional bar to prosecution that may be raised at any time by a criminal defendant. Benes v. United States, 276 F2d 99 (6th Cir. 1960); Walters v. United States, 328 F2d 739 (10th Cir. 1964). The Service apparently disagrees with this view. See Legal Memorandum, Assistant Chief Counsel (Criminal Tax), advising that the defendant may waive the criminal statute of limitations. ILM 199923058 (Mar. 3, 1999).

[292] United States v. Beacon Brass Co., 344 US 43 (1952) (false return filed January 5, 1945; false statement made October 24, 1945; indictment March 16, 1951; held, indictment timely); United States v. Mousley, 194 F. Supp. 119 (ED Pa. 1961), aff'd per curiam, 311 F2d 795 (3d Cir. 1963) (tax returns for years 1942 through 1946; false statements in offers in compromise made in 1955, 1956, and 1957; held, crimes committed in 1955, 1956, and 1957); United States v. Sclafani, 126 F. Supp. 654 (EDNY 1954), aff'd on another issue, 265 F2d 408 (2d Cir. 1959) (1947 and 1949 returns, false statements alleged between June 21, 1950, and January 12, 1951; indictment on February 26, 1954, timely).

[293] United States v. Ferris, 807 F2d 269 (1st Cir. 1986) ("it is the date of the latest act of evasion (a false statement to Service agents), not the due date of the taxes, that triggers the statute of limitations"); United States v. Trownsell, 367 F2d 815 (7th Cir. 1966) (offense committed for limitations purposes on date defendant liquidated assets and transferred proceeds to Swiss bank). See also Cohen v. United States, 297 F2d 760 (9th Cir.), cert. denied, 369 US 865 (1962) (Mickey Cohen convicted of evading tax for 1946–1948, indicted and convicted for attempting to defeat payment of tax for 1945–1950 by concealing assets); United States v. Hook, 781 F2d 1166 (6th Cir. 1986) (most damaging evidence against defendant of attempts to evade payment occurred beyond the limitations period, but other evidence occurred within the limitations period and jury instructions did not require jury to consider the acts outside the limitations; dissenting opinion rejected continuing offense theory used by government); United States v. DiPetto, 936 F2d 96 (2d Cir.), cert. denied, 112 S. Ct. 193 (1991) ("The DiPettos violated 26 USC § 7201 by attempting to mislead or to conceal with respect to their tax liability and then willfully failing to file a tax return. . . . In view of *Habig* we conclude that the statute of limitations did

course of conduct existed extending the statute of limitations well beyond the ordinary expiration of the statute of limitations.[294]

Section 7202 makes it a crime to willfully fail to pay over withholding taxes. Section 6531(4) establishes a six-year statute of limitations on prosecutions for "the offense of willfully failing to pay any tax." Does this six-year period apply to a Section 7202 prosecution? It has been held that the term "pay" does not include "pay over," and, as a matter of statutory construction, the language of Section 6531(4) does not apply to a Section 7202 failure-to-pay-over prosecution,[295] but the issue is not entirely free from doubt.[296]

In failure-to-file cases, the offense is complete on the date the return was due. If the taxpayer has requested and received an extension of time for filing, the offense is committed not on the original due date of the return but on the extended due date.[297] Similarly, it has been held that even if a taxpayer's failure to file is not willful on the return due date, the offense is complete on the date the failure to file was willful.[298] Under this view, a prosecution may be instituted more than six years after the return due date if it is commenced within six years after the failure to file became willful.

The running of the statute of limitations may be suspended or tolled—for example, where there is a court proceeding over a third-party summons and where the person committing any of the various offenses under the internal revenue laws "is outside the United States."[299] It is also tolled when the person

---

not begin to run until both of these requirements (filing of false Forms W-4 and passing of filing due date) were met"); United States v. Crocker, 92-1 USTC ¶ 50,008 (D. Del. 1991) (when taxpayer filed false W-4 forms and failed to file tax returns, statute of limitations on charges of evasion and nonfiling was held to run from date tax return was due).

[294] United States v. Shorter, 809 F2d 54 (DC Cir.), cert. denied, 1085 S. Ct. 71 (1987) (twelve counts charging willful attempted evasion of payment of income taxes from 1972 through 1983 held to charge a continuous offense properly chargeable in a single count); United States v. Feldman, 731 F. Supp. 1189 (SDNY 1990) (where there is an ongoing course of allegedly fraudulent conduct, the statute of limitations does not begin to run until the entirety of that conduct is complete; although evasion offense arose out of 1981 returns, conduct continued into 1985, and, so, indictment was timely; *Shorter* discussed and followed).

[295] United States v. Block, 497 F. Supp. 629 (ND Ga. 1980) (well-reasoned opinion).

[296] See United States v. Porth, 426 F2d 519 (10th Cir. 1970) (apparently holding, without explanation, that the six-year statute applies).

[297] Haskell v. United States, 241 F2d 790 (10th Cir.), cert. denied, 354 US 921 (1957); United States v. Twining, 75-2 USTC ¶ 9768 (ND Cal. 1975). If the extension is rejected, the offense is committed ten days after the date of the notice of rejection. United States v. Goldstein, 386 F. Supp. 833 (D. Del. 1975).

[298] United States v. Pelose, 538 F2d 41 (2d Cir. 1976); United States v. Andros, 484 F2d 531 (9th Cir. 1973).

[299] IRC §§ 6531, 7609(e). See, e.g., United States v. Marchant, 774 F2d 888 (8th Cir. 1985) (eleven-day health and pleasure trip to Switzerland during six-year period tolled statute for that time). In United States v. Orlowski, 808 F2d 1283 (8th Cir. 1986), the stat-

committing the offense is a fugitive from justice within the meaning of 18 USC § 3290.[300] Consequently, the statute of limitations stops running when a person committing a tax offense opposes a third-party summons, leaves the country, takes some action to avoid detection by leaving his place of residence, or takes some other action constituting flight from justice. Although flight from the United States may be established without too much difficulty, flight from justice seems to increase the possibility that the statute of limitations will be considered suspended when a defendant moves from the place where he formerly resided and from which he filed tax returns.

The statute of limitations on prosecution is extended if a complaint is filed with a U.S. Magistrate within the period of the statute of limitations.[301] If a complaint is filed, the time for instituting prosecution by an indictment is extended for nine months after the date of the complaint.[302] Normally, the function of a complaint is to serve as the basis for an arrest warrant, and the complaint setting forth "the essential facts constituting the offense charged . . . made upon oath before a magistrate" enables the magistrate to determine whether "probable cause" exists to support the issuance of a warrant.[303] However, in *Jaben v. United States*,[304] the Supreme Court held that the complaint referred to in Section 6531 must also be sufficient to establish probable cause to believe that "an offense has been committed and that the defendant has committed it" within the meaning of Federal Rules of Criminal Procedure 4. In addition, a court must review the complaint to determine whether it supplies an adequate foundation for the magistrate's determination that probable cause existed. In the course of its opinion, the Supreme Court also said that Section

---

ute of limitations on prosecution was held to be suspended under Section 6531 during the sixty-day period when the taxpayer could have appealed (but did not do so) following a district court decision in a summons enforcement proceeding. See also United States v. Meyer, 808 F2d 1304 (8th Cir. 1987).

[300] 18 USC § 3290 provides that "[n]o statute of limitations shall extend to any person fleeing from justice."

[301] IRC § 6531.

[302] However, if the complaint is later dismissed, the nine-month period of extension is vitiated. United States v. Akmakjian, 647 F2d 12 (9th Cir. 1981), quoting Jaben v. United States, 381 US 214 (1965). Consequently, where a taxpayer against whom a complaint has been dismissed was indicted six years, eight months, and twenty-seven days after the alleged violation, the indictment was untimely. Id. However, where a taxpayer enters a plea of guilty, he waives the defense of the statute of limitations (unless the defense is reserved). Therefore, the taxpayer who had entered a guilty plea in *Akmakjian* was held to have waived the defense of the statute of limitations.

[303] Fed. R. Crim. P. 3, 4.

[304] Jaben v. United States, 381 US 214, 217 n.1 (1965). The Court also held that the government must proceed through the further steps of the complaint procedure by affording the defendant a preliminary hearing as required by Federal Rules of Criminal Procedure 5 unless, before the preliminary hearing is held, the grand jury supersedes the complaint procedure by returning an indictment.

6531 "was intended to deal with a situation in which the Government has its case made within the normal limitation period but cannot obtain an indictment because of the grand jury's schedule."[305] The indication in *Jaben* was that there was no grand jury sitting at the time the limitation period expired. However, the complaint procedure has been approved, even where a grand jury was sitting but was not in session at the time of the imminent expiration of the statutory period.[306] In *Jaben*, the Supreme Court also approved a complaint supported by an affidavit of the special agent that he had examined records and interviewed third persons familiar with the defendant's financial condition and had determined that the defendant had attempted to evade tax in a specific amount.[307]

[6] Lesser Included Offenses

A defendant in a felony prosecution may request the judge to charge the jury that it may find the defendant guilty of an offense, usually a misdemeanor, included in the felony with which the defendant has been charged.[308] Although not strictly a defense to the crime charged, a lesser-included-offense instruction has the objective of reducing the grade of the crime of which the defendant is convicted and the punishment for the crime.[309] In *Sansone v. United States*,[310] the defendant conceded that he had understated his income taxes on his return by omitting from income a sale of land, but contended that this understatement was not willful because he believed that future expenses would wipe out profit from the sale. The defendant contended that he was entitled to a lesser-in-

---

[305] Jaben v. United States, 381 US 214, 219–220 (1965).

[306] United States v. Towill, 548 F2d 1363 (9th Cir. 1977); United States v. Miller, 491 F2d 638 (5th Cir.), cert. denied, 419 US 970 (1974). In the denial of certiorari in *Miller*, three justices said that *Jaben* applied to a situation where the grand jury was not in session. United States v. O'Neal, 834 F2d 862 (9th Cir. 1987) (government's use of complaint procedure, rather than securing an indictment, while grand jury was in session was proper because grand jury had no available time to hear case).

[307] See also United States v. Towill, 548 F2d 1363 (9th Cir. 1977), where a special agent filed a *Jaben*-type affidavit but listed only the claimed business deductions and compensation without any allegation of the actual liability of the taxpayer, as was alleged in *Jaben*.

[308] Under Federal Rules of Criminal Procedure 31, "the defendant may be found guilty of an offense necessarily included in the offense charged or an attempt to commit either the offense charged or an offense necessarily included therein if the attempt is an offense."

[309] The lesser-included-offense doctrine also assists the prosecution, since if the jury finds the defendant not guilty of the crime charged, it must also determine guilt or innocence as to a necessarily included lesser offense. United States v. Tsanas, 572 F2d 340 (2d Cir.), cert. denied, 435 US 995 (1978).

[310] Sansone v. United States, 380 US 343 (1965).

cluded-offense instruction to the jury that they might convict him of willfully failing to pay tax or filing a false statement. Rejecting this contention, the Supreme Court held that a lesser-included-offense instruction is proper only where "the charged greater offense requires the jury to find a disputed factual element which is not required for conviction of the lesser-included-offense."[311] Where, on the evidence presented, the factual issues to be resolved by the jury as to both the greater offense and the lesser included offense "cover precisely the same ground," no lesser-included-offense instruction need be given.[312] For example, in an evasion prosecution, the offenses charged in Sections 7203 and 7207 may be lesser included offenses. On the proof offered, the factual elements may be identical, so the defendant will ordinarily be guilty of both crimes or neither—that is, the defendant will be guilty of both evasion and failing to pay or filing a false statement or of neither evasion nor failure to pay or filing a false statement. In the circumstance of identical proof, no lesser-included-offense instruction is proper.[313]

The inquiry, then, is whether a disputed factual element is necessary for conviction of one offense but not the other. A defendant is entitled to a lesser-included-offense instruction based on Section 7203 where, in an evasion prosecution, there is a disputed issue of fact as to the existence of the requisite affirmative act in addition to the Section 7203 omission.[314] Also, if there is evidence of unclaimed deductions that, if believed, would offset specific items

---

[311] Sansone v. United States, 380 US 343, 350 (1965).

[312] Sansone v. United States, 380 US 343, 352 (1965).

[313] However, a lesser included offense should not be submitted to the jury where, considering the evidence presented at the trial, the jury could not rationally acquit the defendant of the greater crime (Section 7201) and convict him of the lesser included one. United States v. Citron, 783 F2d 307 (2d Cir. 1986) (law described). In *Citron*, where the defendant was charged with violations of Sections 7201 and 7206(1), but the false statement was alleged to have resulted in substantial understatements of the tax due, it was held to be an error for the lesser charge to have been submitted to the jury because the proof on the Section 7206(1) charge was identical to proof required by Section 7201. Since the defendant was acquitted of the evasion charge, the jury's conviction of the defendant for violations of Section 7206(1) was reversed. See also United States v. Bender, 606 F2d 897 (9th Cir. 1979).

[314] Even if no lesser-included-offense instruction is proper because, for example, one of the affirmative acts in the evasion charge is the failure to file a tax return, failure to file is a lesser included offense. Where one offense is included in another, it cannot support a separate conviction and sentence. United States v. Buckley, 586 F2d 498, 504–505 (5th Cir. 1978), cert. denied, 440 US 982 (1979); United States v. Snyder, 766 F2d 167 (4th Cir. 1985) (accord; defendant charged under Sections 7201 and 7203). United States v. Doyle, 956 F2d 73 (5th Cir. 1992) ("The jury . . . could have rationally concluded that Doyle did not willfully commit the affirmative act constituting the felony evasion (or attempted evasion) of taxes—filing the inaccurate W-4 forms and at the same time have concluded that Doyle willfully failed to file a tax return in violation of the misdemeanor statute").

of unreported gross receipts, the jury should be instructed that it may acquit under Section 7201 and convict under Section 7207.[315] Sansone conceded that his return did not include the sales income and thus conceded that the return was false for purposes of both the evasion and false statements statutes. On the issue of willfulness, the jury could only find him guilty or not guilty of both the felony evasion and the misdemeanor false statement. Similarly, in *Bishop v. United States*,[316] the defendant contended that he was entitled to a lesser-included-offense instruction on the ground that Section 7207 was an offense not necessarily included in Section 7206(1) because willfulness has a different meaning in the misdemeanor statute[317] than in the felony statute.[318] The Supreme Court rejected this contention, saying that willfulness had the same meaning for both the misdemeanor statute and the felony statute and that consequently the statutes covered precisely the same ground, so that no lesser-included-offense instruction was required.

¶ 7A.08 TITLE 18 OFFENSES

General criminal statutes applicable to federal crimes are gathered in Title 18 of the U.S. Code. In view of the comprehensive statutory scheme applying to tax offenses contained in the Internal Revenue Code, it may be questioned whether there is a congressional purpose to confine tax violations to prosecution under the Code, rather than under Title 18. This view is especially persuasive where the same conduct serves as the basis for the alleged violation of the criminal statutes of both the Code and Title 18—e.g.. attempted evasion by filing a false return and mail fraud for using the mails in the attempt to de-

---

[315] Note, however, that the government may contend that the lesser included offense is the felony false statement statute (IRC § 7206(1)), not the misdemeanor false statement statute, as the Supreme Court assumed in *Sansone*. United States v. Citron, 783 F2d 307 (2d Cir. 1986) (citing cases). See also United States v. Stone, 702 F2d 1333 (11th Cir. 1983) (concluding, without discussion, that Section 7206(1) constitutes a lesser included offense of Section 7201). A defendant has been held not to be entitled to an instruction that Section 7207 is a lesser included offense of Section 7206(1) because the only difference between the two statutes is the requirement of Section 7206 that a false statement be made under penalties of perjury. United States v. Carrodeguas, 747 F2d 1390 (11th Cir. 1984). A failure to pay tax in violation of Section 7201 is an offense in a charge of attempted evasion of payment of a tax in violation of Section 7201. United States v. DeTar, 832 F2d 1110 (9th Cir. 1987) (request for lesser-included-offense charge waives defense of limitations).

[316] Bishop v. United States, 412 US 346 (1973).

[317] IRC § 7207.

[318] IRC § 7206(1).

fraud the United States.[319] Criminal statutes in both the Code and Title 18 overlap, and, if unchecked, sentences for violating these statutes may be inappropriately pyramided. Some courts have avoided cumulative sentences for essentially the same fraudulent conduct by limiting a sentence for conviction on such tax offenses as evasion and filing false statements to the sentence imposed on the greater offense.[320] Implicit in this rule is a policy against fragmenting charges under the Code and Title 18, which permit multiple sentences. This issue is unsettled. However, prosecution under various Title 18 statutes—namely, aiding and abetting, conspiracy, and false statements—have been instituted for so long that it is probable that they qualify as extensions of the Code's system of sanctions. These three Title 18 offenses are discussed in the following sections.

[1] The Aider and Abettor Statute: 18 USC § 2

An individual may be prosecuted as a principal even though he merely aids and abets another in committing an offense described in either the Code or Title 18. An individual who aids or encourages another in attempting to evade the other's tax is subject to prosecution and punishment under 18 USC § 2 as a principal—i.e., as though he committed the attempted evasion himself. The so-called aider and abettor statute, 18 USC § 2, provides:

> Whoever commits an offense against the United States, or aids, abets, counsels, induces, or procures its commission, is a principal.
> Whoever causes an act to be done, which if directly performed by him would be an offense against the United States, is also a principal and punishable as such.

Thus, to establish this offense, there must be proof that (1) a substantive offense has been committed and (2) the defendant aided and abetted the commission of the substantive offense.

Accessory liability is just that—the aider and abettor may be punishable as a principal—but it must be proved that a crime has actually been commit-

---

[319] United States v. Henderson, 386 F. Supp. 1048 (SDNY 1974). *Henderson* was rejected by the Ninth Circuit in United States v. Miller, 545 F2d 1204 (9th Cir.), cert. denied, 430 US 930 (1977). See also United States v. Ready, 574 F2d 1009 (10th Cir. 1978); United States v. Shermetaro, 625 F2d 104 (6th Cir. 1980) (Title 26 does not preempt a conspiracy charge under 18 USC § 371); United States v. Fern, 696 F2d 1269 (9th Cir. 1983) (availability of more specific false statement misdemeanor provisions of Section 7207 did not preclude prosecution under general false statement felony statute, 18 USC § 1001); United States v. Parsons, 967 F2d 452 (10th Cir. 1992) (following *Fern*).

[320] United States v. White, 417 F2d 89 (2d Cir.), cert. denied, 397 US 912, reh'g denied, 397 US 1030 (1969); United States v. Lodwick, 410 F2d 1202 (8th Cir.), cert. denied, 396 US 841 (1969).

ted. However, the government is not required to prove that the principal has been convicted of tax evasion, nor even to establish the identity of the principal,[321] only that someone committed the offense in which the aider and abettor played a part.

Accessory liability requires knowing and purposeful action by the aider and abettor. The aider and abettor must adopt some "purposive attitude" toward the crime and in some way "associate himself with the venture, that he participate in it as something that he wishes to bring about, that he seek by his action to make it succeed."[322] Objective evidence of this purposive attitude may take the form of the aider and abettor's stake in the illegal conduct. For example, the aider and abettor may share in unreported income and facilitate the underreporting of income by not keeping full records of receipts that would ordinarily be kept in the business.

It may appear that it makes little difference whether a person is prosecuted as an aider and abettor or as a co-conspirator under the conspiracy statute, but proof that a person aided and abetted does not establish that he engaged in a conspiracy. Facilitation is not the equivalent of an unlawful agreement. However, under both the aider and abettor and the conspiracy statutes, a defendant may be vicariously liable for the acts of the principal and the acts of co-conspirators, respectively. On the other hand, a prosecution for aiding and abetting an evasion fails if it can be proved that there was no tax due and owing, but a conspiracy still exists even if the substantive offense fails. Also, the aider and abettor statute is broader than Section 7206(2), which makes it a crime for a person to aid in the preparation of a false return or other document. Any person, not merely the preparer or counselor, may be prosecuted as a principal offender if he aids or causes any criminal act described in the Code. Also, the aider and abettor statute and the offense described in Section 7206(2) have been said to be identical with the exception that under Section 2(a), the government must offer proof that the taxpayer committed some offense (i.e., that the taxpayer had knowledge that the return was fraudulent), whereas it need not offer this proof under Section 7206(2).[323]

The operation of the aiding and abetting statute is illustrated by *Imholte v. United States*,[324] where the defendant, a sales manager of an automobile dealership, along with the shareholder-president held back sales income. The two divided this income, so that false corporate returns were filed and tax evaded. The sales manager was indicted in 1954 for evasion of the corpora-

---

[321] United States v. Doughty, 460 F2d 1360 (7th Cir. 1978); Standefer v. United States, 447 US 10 (1980) (history of accomplice liability described).

[322] United States v. Peoni, 100 F2d 401 (2d Cir. 1938); Model Penal Code § 2.06(3)(a).

[323] United States v. Motley, 940 F2d 1079 (7th Cir. 1991) (Section 7206(2) is lesser included offense in aiding and abetting charge under Section 2(a)).

[324] Imholte v. United States, 226 F2d 585 (8th Cir. 1955).

tion's taxes. The president-shareholder, who was also indicted for evasion, entered a plea of not guilty and testified at Imholte's trial. Imholte was convicted of aiding and abetting the filing of a false corporate return for the year 1947, although he did not help prepare or file the return and had not held back any sales income after 1947—i.e., beyond the six-year statutory period for prosecution. The conviction was affirmed on the ground that the filing of the false corporate return on March 15, 1948, by the president constituted the willful attempt to evade, so that Imholte aided and abetted the president's attempted evasion and committed the offense on March 15, 1948, when the return was filed, within the six-year statutory period.

[2] The Conspiracy Statute: 18 USC § 371

The offense of criminal conspiracy has two elements: (1) an agreement between two or more persons either (a) to commit an offense against or (b) to defraud the United States in any manner or for any purpose and (2) an overt act committed by one or more of the conspirators to accomplish the object of the conspiracy.[325] Conspiracy reaches further back into criminal activity than evasion, which is an attempt-type crime requiring affirmative conduct, by punishing mere agreement to commit a crime. In tax cases, the conspiracy charged can be (1) an offense conspiracy, that is, an agreement to commit a substantive tax offense (e.g., evasion), or (2) a fraud conspiracy, that is, a conspiracy to defraud the United States (e.g., by impeding the Service in the determination or collection of tax).[326] All that need be established is that two or more per-

---

[325] The criminal conspiracy statute, 18 USC § 371, provides as follows:

If two or more persons conspire either to commit any offense against the United States, or to defraud the United States, or any agency thereof in any manner or for any purpose, and one or more of such persons do any action to effect the object of the conspiracy, each shall be fined not more than $10,000 or imprisoned not more than five years, or both.

If, however, the offense, the commission of which is the object of the conspiracy, is a misdemeanor only, the punishment for such conspiracy shall not exceed the maximum punishment provided for such misdemeanor.

[326] Thus, the conspiracy statute creates one crime that may be committed in one of two ways. United States v. Minarik, 875 F2d 1186 (6th Cir. 1989) (defraud clause alleged where offense conspiracy proved). Compare Alexander v. Thornburgh, 943 F2d 825 (8th Cir. 1991): "In *Minarik*, the defendants engaged in a narrow course of conduct directed at one object—to sell a house and get the money in an untraceable manner. This obviously is not the circumstance in this case, in which Alexander's conduct is long-spanning, far-reaching, and involves many activities and events." But merely because an indictment charges two conspiracies to defraud in violation of 18 USC § 371 does not mean that a single conspiracy has been divided into multiple violations of the same offense as long as "the totality of the circumstances reveals that the counts address separate agreements." United States v. Noske, 117 F3d 1053 (8th Cir. 1997) (two conspiracies found: (1) a con-

sons[327] have agreed to commit a substantive tax offense or to defraud the United States in some manner.[328] The overt act requirement of the federal conspiracy statute serves to establish the existence of the agreement, and the act need not be particularly significant if it is, in fact, in furtherance of the conspiracy.

Procedurally, the crime of conspiracy differs from other crimes in ways that give prosecutors the following advantages at trial:

1. A conspiracy prosecution may be brought in a judicial district where an overt act took place.[329] This venue rule gives prosecutors an opportunity to elect a place of trial at which conviction is more likely or which may be inconvenient to the defendants.

2. There are rules of evidence peculiar to conspiracy prosecutions. As a general rule, hearsay is not admissible, although this rule is subject to many exceptions.[330] One particular exception is that a statement by a co-conspirator during the course and in furtherance of the conspiracy does not constitute hearsay[331] and is admissible against the defendant. Thus, if conspirator X told witness W that X along with Y and Z planned to hold back business receipts of their corporation, W could testify about the statement, and it would be admissible against both Y and Z as well as against X. The rationale of this rule is the legal fiction that a conspiracy makes the co-conspirators mutual agents. Moreover, although the statement is required to have been made during the course and in furtherance of the conspiracy, any statement relating to the conspiracy is frequently admitted.[332] Also, the defendant's diffi-

---

spiracy to defraud by assisting some clients to evade income tax and (2) a conspiracy to defraud by assisting other clients to evade collection of income tax).

[327] Officers and co-employees of a corporation may conspire to evade or defeat the corporation's tax. United States v. Knox Coal Co., 347 F2d 33 (3d Cir.), cert. denied, 382 US 904 (1965). A corporation may even be one of the co-conspirators in such a conspiracy. See United States v. Cole, 463 F2d 163 (2d Cir.), cert. denied, 409 US 942 (1972). A husband and wife may be co-conspirators. United States v. Dege, 364 US 51 (1960). See also Mitchell v. United States, 213 F2d 951 (9th Cir. 1954), cert. denied, 348 US 912 (1955).

[328] But the co-conspirators must have agreed on the type of fraud they intend to commit. United States v. Rosenblatt, 554 F2d 36 (2d Cir. 1977). The evidence need not show an express or formal agreement; it is sufficient if the evidence shows "a tacit understanding." Iannelli v. United States, 420 US 770, 777 n.10 (1975), cited in United States v. Aubin, 87 F3d 141 (5th Cir. 1996) (participating in concert with others in structuring a transaction intended to impede Service from collecting taxes held sufficient to establish a tacit understanding).

[329] Hyde v. United States, 225 US 347 (1912).

[330] See Fed. R. Evid. 802.

[331] Fed. R. Evid. 802(d)(2)(E).

[332] See LaFave & Scott, Criminal Law 457 (1972).

culties are exacerbated by the willingness of courts to admit these statements before the existence of a conspiracy has actually been established, subject only to an instruction cautioning the jury that evidence is not to be considered unless the conspiracy is proved by independent evidence.[333]

3. Prosecutors enjoy a wide latitude in offering circumstantial evidence to establish a conspiracy. This procedure is justified by the difficulties they would otherwise face in proving the existence of a conspiracy, which by its nature requires secrecy and concealment.[334] Where several defendants have been charged, they may face joint trial, at which evidence damaging to one may be used against all.

4. When more than one group of conspirators has been alleged to be part of a simple overall conspiracy, there is a danger of an "unwarranted imputation of guilt from others' conduct."[335] As a matter of fairness, therefore, the proof must not show multiple conspiracies when the indictment has charged a single conspiracy.[336] Two types of multiple conspiracies may be proved to exist: a wheel conspiracy and a chain conspiracy.[337] In a wheel conspiracy, there is a core group and other individuals (or spokes) who may not have participated in each transaction or may not even have known each other. But they must be aware of each other doing something in furtherance of some single, illegal enterprise; otherwise, the wheel lacks a rim to enclose the spokes. If the conspirators or spokes do not have some dealings with one another on at least one common illegal object, the wheel is incomplete; and two conspiracies exist rather than the one that was

---

[333] See Bourjaily v. United States, 107 S. Ct. 2775 (1987) ("Confrontation Clause does not require a court to embark on an independent inquiry into the reliability of statements that satisfy the requirements of Rule 801(d)(2)(E)"). The admissibility of statements of a conspirator is decided by the court. Before allowing the declarations to be admitted, the judge "must satisfy himself of the defendant's participation in the conspiracy on the basis of the nonhearsay evidence." The declarations may be admitted subject to connection with a cautionary instruction. However, when all the evidence is in, the judge determines whether, in his view, the government has proved participation in the conspiracy by the defendant against whom the hearsay is offered, by a fair preponderance of the evidence independent of the hearsay utterances. United States v. Mastropieri, 685 F2d 776 (2d Cir.), cert. denied, 459 US 945 (1982) (quoting United States v. Gearney, 417 F2d 1116, 1119–1120 (2d Cir. 1969), cert. denied sub nom. Lynch v. United States, 397 US 1028 (1979)). See also United States v. Pack, 85-2 USTC ¶ 9718 (10th Cir. 1985).

[334] See Blumenthal v. United States, 332 US 539, 557 (1947).

[335] Kotteakos v. United States, 328 US 750, 777 (1945).

[336] For this reason, when multiple conspiracies are proved, the judge should give limiting instructions to the jury. Kotteakos v. United States, 328 US 750, 777 (1945).

[337] See Note, "Federal Treatment of Multiple Conspiracies," 57 Colum. L. Rev. 387 (1957).

charged. In a chain conspiracy, each conspirator plays a different but pivotal role in the success of the group as a whole in the same way that different workers on an assembly line or a distribution chain do. Unlike the wheel conspiracy, the conspirators' knowledge of the existence of remote links in the chain may be inferred from the nature of the enterprise. Conspiracies to violate tax laws do not frequently involve the issue, but they do occur.[338]

Procedural advantages prosecutors have in conspiracy cases are offset somewhat by the substantive vagueness and ambiguity of the crime itself. For example, it is not certain what constitutes an agreement for purposes of the conspiracy and what mental state must be shown.[339] This uncertainty and the unfairness it may occasion have prompted the Supreme Court to discourage extensions of the conspiracy offense,[340] and both the Service and the Justice Department's Tax Division to use the charge with restraint.[341]

The rationale of the conspiracy statute is that collective or group activity ought to be punished separate and apart from any substantive crime because it represents a graver threat to society than individual criminal activity. A partnership in crime "both increases the likelihood that the criminal object will be fully attained and decreases the probability that the individuals involved will depart their path of criminality."[342] For this reason, the conspiracy offense is separate and distinct from the crime the conspirators agree to commit, so a conspirator may be punished both for conspiracy and for the contemplated crime. For example, if *A* and *B* agree to raise the deductions of their corporation falsely and, in fact, file false returns for the corporation, they could receive maximum sentences for both evasion and conspiracy.

Punishment under the conspiracy statute has gradations, depending on the offense that the conspirators have agreed to commit. A conspiracy to evade is punishable as a felony in the same manner as the evasion itself. However, if

---

[338] See, e.g., United States v. Rosnow, 977 F2d 399 (8th Cir. 1991) (government alleged defendants shared common goal of harassing enemies through use of false Forms 1099; but evidence showed multiple conspiracies, and inadequate limiting instruction was given).

[339] See, e.g., United States v. Rosenblatt, 554 F2d 36 (2d Cir. 1977) (conspiracy conviction was reversed because a criminal agreement was not proved where the evidence established that two conspirators had agreed to defraud the United States but had not reached agreement on the type of fraud to commit).

[340] Grunewald v. United States, 353 US 391 (1957).

[341] IRM 9781, Special Agent's Handbook § 41(10).3, IRM 9781-1 (Jan. 18, 1980) (Application of Conspiracy Statute). The Handbook says, "[a] practice of self-restraint has been applied with respect to the use of the conspiracy statute. . . . If proof exists to support substantive charges, the addition of conspiracy counts would involve needless duplication."

[342] Callanan v. United States, 364 US 587, 593 (1961).

the conspiracy is to fail to file a tax return, the offense is punished as a misdemeanor with the same punishment as provided by Section 7203.

[a] Conspiracy and Code Offenses

Charges of a substantive tax offense and a conspiracy to commit that offense are separate and distinct.[343] An acquittal or dismissal of a conspiracy count does not bar prosecution for evasion,[344] nor does acquittal in a conspiracy count bar prosecution on a substantive count.[345] However, evidence presented on the two charges is at least parallel. Evidence offered to prove the attempt element of the evasion charge also serves to establish an overt act of the conspiracy. The same evidence used to prove willfulness for the evasion charge can also establish the agreement element of the conspiracy charge. Technically, evidence of a tax due and owing, a required element in an evasion prosecution, is not an element of a conspiracy to defraud, which requires only proof of an overt act.[346]

Where evasion and conspiracy to evade are charged, a finding that no tax is due and owing nevertheless seriously impairs proof of a conspiracy to evade. In *United States v. Klein*,[347] an individual was charged with evasion and conspiring among himself and others to evade individual tax. It was alleged that Cuban and Panamanian corporations were shams and that the income of those corporations derived from the import and delivery of liquor from a Canadian distiller to an American wholesaler was in reality the income of one of the defendants. The court first found that the corporations were not shams, so that individual income taxes could not have been evaded. Once it found individual taxes not due and owing, although it treated the conspiracy count independently of the substantive counts, the court nevertheless dismissed the

---

[343] Pinkerton v. United States, 328 US 640 (1946). See, e.g., United States v. Nealy, 729 F2d 961 (4th Cir. 1984) (indictment charged one count of conspiracy to aid and assist in the preparation of false returns and ten counts of violating Section 7206(2) by aiding and assisting in the preparation of false partnership returns); United States v. DiNiro, 392 F2d 753 (6th Cir.), cert. denied, 393 US 826 (1968) (charging conspiracy to evade estate taxes and estate tax evasion).

[344] United States v. Rosenblum, 182 F2d 956 (7th Cir.), cert. denied, 338 US 893 (1949); United States v. Wenger, 455 F2d 308 (2d Cir.), cert. denied, 407 US 920 (1972).

[345] United States v. Krogstaad, 576 F2d 22 (3d Cir. 1978) (acquittal of conspiracy to defraud did not preclude conviction of aiding and abetting in filing of a false statement, an audit report).

[346] United States v. Baskes, 442 F. Supp. 322, aff'd, 624 F2d 709 (7th Cir.), cert. denied, 450 US 920 (1980) (attorney indicted for conspiracy to defraud although clients not charged with evasion because government admitted no additional tax might be due and owing from clients).

[347] United States v. Klein, 139 F. Supp. 135 (SDNY 1956), aff'd, 247 F2d 908 (2d Cir.), cert. denied, 355 US 944 (1957).

conspiracy charge. Thus, the absence of a tax due and owing can support dismissal of a conspiracy charge as well as a substantive evasion charge.

When a conspiracy to commit a tax offense is charged, the proof must show that the alleged co-conspirators agreed on committing the tax offense. Evidence of a conspiracy and of overt acts in furtherance of that conspiracy does not necessarily show agreement on the commission of a tax offense. Efforts at concealment can reasonably be explainable in terms other than a motivation to evade taxes. If they are, the government must offer independent proof that those who participated in the concealment intended to assist the taxpayer in evading taxes.[348] This rule is derived from the principle that to prove conspiratorial intent, evidence of the defendant's knowledge of the conspiracy and its purposes must be clear and unequivocal.[349]

A finding that a person has engaged in a conspiracy to evade tax may be sufficient to establish his vicarious liability for that substantive offense. In *Pinkerton v. United States*,[350] Pinkerton was indicted both for conspiring with his brother to evade taxes and on substantive counts of tax evasion that his brother committed while Pinkerton was in jail. The trial court instructed the jury that it could convict Pinkerton on the substantive counts if it found that Pinkerton had been engaged in a conspiracy and that the substantive offenses were in furtherance of that conspiracy. The Supreme Court affirmed Pinkerton's conviction, holding that evidence of direct participation in the substantive crimes was unnecessary. Consequently, the vicarious liability of a conspirator for acts of his co-conspirator may be sufficient to establish guilt of substantive crimes if those crimes are in furtherance of the conspiracy.

[b] Conspiracy to Defraud

A conspiracy to defraud combines the vagueness of a conspiracy charge with broad allegations of an attempt to impede or obstruct government func-

---

[348] Ingram v. United States, 360 US 672, 679 (1959) (evidence that participants in illegal gambling business concealed gambling profits was not enough to prove that they intended to evade income taxes); United States v. Pritchett, 908 F2d 816 (11th Cir. 1990) (evidence that defendants participated in concealing drug dealer's assets and income was not sufficient to establish agreement to evade his tax).

[349] See United States v. Pritchett, 908 F2d 816 (11th Cir. 1990); United States v. Rosenblatt, 554 F2d 36 (2d Cir. 1977); United States v. Krasovich, 819 F2d 253 (9th Cir. 1987) (government must prove that defendant who allowed taxpayer to buy assets in defendant's name did so with intent to evade taxes); United States v. Furkin, 119 F3d 1276 (7th Cir. 1997) ("[n]o doubt Lanzotti's conduct was undertaken to hide Allstar's involvement in the illegal gambling market, but it is reasonable to infer that Lanzotti's conduct was also undertaken to hide Allstar's illegal gambling income from the IRS").

[350] Pinkerton v. United States, 328 US 640 (1946).

tions. In *Hammerschmidt v. United States*, the leading case on the defraud clause of 18 USC § 371, the Supreme Court held:[351]

> To conspire to defraud the United States means (1) to cheat the government out of property or money, but it also means (2) to interfere with or obstruct one of its lawful governmental functions by deceit, craft, or trickery, or at least by means that are dishonest.

In *United States v. Klein*, the indictment charged the defendants with a conspiracy to defraud the United States "by impeding, obstructing and defeating the functions of the Department of the Treasury in the collection of the revenue, to wit, income taxes."[352] Intercorporate transactions of considerable complexity were alleged to have concealed the nature and source of the income realized from an immense whiskey-selling business. The Second Circuit said that mere failure to disclose income would not be sufficient to establish the crime of conspiracy to defraud the United States, but that such a charge does include interference or obstruction of lawful government functions by deceit, craft, or trick, or dishonest means. In *Klein*, the acts of concealment were various acts of alteration of books and false statements on tax returns and to Service agents.[353]

In a conspiracy charged under the defraud clause, the prosecution must prove intent to defraud the government, not intent to commit a substantive offense of tax evasion.[354] It has also been held that the government need not

---

[351] Hammerschmidt v. United States, 265 US 182, 188 (1924).

[352] United States v. Klein, 247 F2d 908, 915 (2d Cir. 1957). An indictment for conspiracy to defraud need not contain the *Klein* indictment's language. United States v. Helmsley, 941 F2d 71 (2d Cir. 1991) ("[a]lthough the *Klein* language may have become customary boilerplate in defraud clause indictments, it is not legally required"), cert. denied, 112 S. Ct. 1162 (1992). The indictment need allege only "the essential nature of the alleged fraud." Id. Nevertheless, the conspiracy to defraud charge requires proof of a specific intent to deceive or cheat. United States v. Dale, 76 AFTR2d 95-5675 (DC Cir. 1995) (defendants claimed that imprecision of "conspiracy to defraud" definition left the jury free to convict on the erroneous belief that lawful conduct in the form of the filing of an amended return could demonstrate the requisite disturbance of the governmental process).

[353] Compare United States v. Tarnopol, 561 F2d 466 (3d Cir. 1977), where conviction on a charge to defraud, resting solely on a failure to record certain sales for cash or merchandise on the sales journal and accounts receivable ledger or falsification of records, was dismissed as constituting a mere failure to disclose income. Both *Klein* and *Tarnopol* reflect the view that the conspiracy must obstruct lawful government functions by deceit, craft, or trickery. See Hammerschmidt v. United States, 265 US 182, 188 (1924).

[354] United States v. Zimmerman, 832 F2d 454 (8th Cir. 1988); United States v. Minarik, 875 F2d 1186 (6th Cir. 1989) (conduct amounting to the offense described in Section 7206(4), concealment of sales proceeds subject to levy, could not be charged under the "defraud" clause of 18 USC § 371, but should have been brought under the offense clause). For a conspiracy to defraud case involving failure to file required informa-

have suffered pecuniary loss for the conspiracy to defraud to have existed.[355] Since a conspiracy is an agreement to engage in prohibited conduct, the fact that a false return is not filed does not prevent the finding of a conspiracy to defraud.[356] Thus, in *United States v. Ingredient Technology*, as a result of the

---

tion returns, see United States v. Pack, 85-2 USTC ¶ 9718 (10th Cir. 1985) (credit union fund manager agreed not to report defendant's interest on note payable accounts to Service, nor cash deposits exceeding $10,000).

In United States v. Kraig, 99 F3d 1361 (6th Cir. 1996), the defendant, a lawyer who was charged with conspiracy to defraud by assisting his client to conceal assets to evade collection by the Service, claimed that a different standard applied to lawyers. According to the circuit court, however, evidence showed the lawyer's involvement with his client's affairs was so pervasive that his knowledge of its illegal nature was reasonably certain. On the other hand, the Sixth Circuit has also said that in a prosecution for conspiracy to defraud by impeding the lawful functions of the Service, the intent element of a conspiracy to defraud does not require the prosecution to prove that the conspirators knew that their conduct was illegal or that the conspirators were aware of the criminality of their objective. In a conspiracy to defraud case, the prosecution need only show that the conspirators knew of their liability for federal taxes. United States v. Khalife, 106 F3d 1300 (6th Cir. 1997), reh'g denied, 1997 US App. LEXIS 11378. The Sixth Circuit also said that its dicta in *Minarik* (that the offense and defraud clauses of Section 371 were "mutually exclusive") were confined to the facts of *Minarik*. The court concluded that the defendants' duty not to conceal transactions over $10,000 from the Service, while punishable under the currency reporting statute, need not be charged only under the offense clause of the government need not have suffered pecuniary loss for the conspiracy to defraud to have existed.

[355] See Haas v. Henkel, 216 US 462 (1910); United States v. Freuhauf Corp., 577 F2d 1038, 1071, 1072 (6th Cir.), cert. denied, 439 US 953 (1978); United States v. Buckner, 610 F2d 570 (9th Cir. 1979).

[356] United States v. Ingredient Technology Corp., 698 F2d 88 (2d Cir. 1983), cert. denied, 462 US 1131 (1984). See also United States v. Olgin, 745 F2d 263 (3d Cir. 1984) (argument that Service was not impeded because agents could easily identify seller of scrap metal paid by check-cashing scheme said to be equivalent of saying conspiracy must be successful).

Nevertheless, there must be evidence of an agreement among the conspirators with the intent to "obstruct the government's knowledge and collection of revenue due." United States v. Klein, 139 F. Supp. 135 (SDNY 1956), aff'd, 247 F2d 908, 918 (2d Cir.), cert. denied, 355 US 944 (1957). This evidence may be direct evidence of the agreement, of course, but it is usually circumstantial evidence of the agreement that the prosecution claims establishes the requisite agreement. However, when the government relies on circumstantial evidence to establish a tax conspiracy, the evidence must be sufficient to warrant a jury's finding that the conspirators had some "common design with unity of purpose" to impede the Service. Id. It has been held that evidence of various payments co-defendants received that were not reported to the Service were not sufficient for a jury to infer the requisite agreement to impede the Service, but instead implies a separate purpose to evade taxes, rather than an agreement to do so. United States v. Adkinson, 135 F3d 1363 (11th Cir. 1998) (*Klein* conspiracy to defraud convictions reversed). Even if the evidence were sufficient to establish the requisite agreement, the government failed to show that the object of the conspiracy was to interfere with the lawful functions of the Service in collecting taxes, not a "foreseeable consequence" of some other conspiratorial scheme,

corporation's auditors' inquiry, a sale and resale of inventory agreement for the purpose of evading tax was not given effect in the preparation of a tax return, but a conviction for conspiracy to defraud was upheld.[357]

A *Klein*-type conspiracy (i.e., a conspiracy to defraud by acts of concealment) may be charged against a tax adviser as well as a taxpayer. Just when tax planning becomes concealment is unclear, and determining where the line between legal tax planning and illegal concealment in the context of a criminal conspiracy trial presents difficult and possibly dangerous burdens on the defendant.[358]

---

such as a bank fraud scheme the government alleged was the purpose of the conspiracy in *Adkinson*. Accordingly, the circuit court found that the tax-related activities of the conspiracy were merely part of, not the object of, the conspiracy.

[357] The *Tarnopol* case was distinguished on the ground that the government had failed to prove the defendants had intended to defraud the Service, although they had kept false records, while in *Ingredient Technology* the whole purpose of the agreement was to evade taxes. See also United States v. Montalvo, 820 F2d 686 (5th Cir. 1987) (conviction on conspiracy to obstruct the Service by concealing or disguising the source of currency with the obvious intent and purpose of impeding and obstructing the Service in collecting tax); United States v. Jenkins, 871 F2d 598 (6th Cir. 1989) (money laundering or structuring transactions not illegal at time of alleged conspiracy to defraud held to be the means of the conspiracy need be illegal in themselves). In a conspiracy to defraud, the fraud has to be a purpose or object of the conspiracy and not merely a foreseeable consequence of the conspiratorial scheme. United States v. Goldberg, 105 F3d 770 (1st Cir. 1997). The circuit court said that distinguishing between what is a purpose of the conspiracy and what is merely the foreseeable effect of joint action may be a problem in some cases. In other cases, however, the purpose can be inferred from the facts. In *Goldberg*, the filing of a number of false tax documents misattributing income could interfere so clearly and proximately with Service functions that "we see no sharp distinction under section 371 between a purpose to file such documents and a purpose to interfere."

[358] Nevertheless, this type of prosecution has been used by the Department of Justice with increasing frequency. See, e.g., United States v. Baskes, 442 F. Supp. 322, aff'd, 624 F2d 709 (7th Cir.), cert. denied, 450 US 920 (1980); United States v. Turkish, 623 F2d 769 (2d Cir. 1980) (oil commodity straddles); United States v. Winograd, 656 F2d 279 (7th Cir. 1981) (Mexican pesos, 699 F2d 1017 (9th Cir. 1983), cert. denied, 104 S. Ct. 698 (1984) (cattle-feeding shelter)). On a defense of good faith, see United States v. Heineman, 801 F2d 86 (2d Cir. 1986) (conspiracy to defraud; jury instruction held correct that a defendant may not deliberately close his eyes to what would otherwise be obvious and still be said to have acted in good faith); United States v. Atkins, 661 F. Supp. 491 (SDNY 1987), aff'd, 869 F2d 135 (2d Cir. 1989) ("[e]ven accepting the defendants' contention that losses from tax straddle transactions entered into for the express purpose of realizing a loss are deductible under § 165(c), upon the allegation of the indictment, a jury can find that defendants' commodities straddles were sham transactions devoid of the requisite economic substance" (footnote omitted)); United States v. Schmidt, 935 F2d 1440 (4th Cir. 1991) (trusts were marketed as way of keeping income and assets from Service and other creditors; held, substantive tax law on business purpose and economic substance properly instructed). In *Schmidt*, the defendants were charged with conspiring to defraud the United States "by using sham trust entities known as UBO's to conceal taxable assets from the [Service]."

[c] Statute of Limitations

There is a six-year statute of limitations for conspiracies (1) to defraud or attempt to defraud the United States and (2) to attempt in any manner to evade or defeat any tax or its payment.[359] All other conspiracies are subject to the general five-year statute of limitations applying to crimes described in Title 18.[360] The point at which a conspiracy terminates determines whether the statute of limitations bars a conspiracy prosecution.[361] This determination is especially important in a conspiracy case because each overt act extends the statute of limitations, and, as a consequence, a prosecution for conspiracy is timely if any overt act falls within the statutory period.[362] In other words, the statute of limitations on prosecution begins to run when the conspiracy has terminated or has been abandoned.[363]

In response to the claim that the grand jury and the petit jury were not permitted to consider the factual question of whether the trusts were shams, the circuit court said that in a conspiracy to defraud prosecution the issue is not the question of "sham or no," but whether the trusts "were used to conceal income and assets in a fraudulent manner which made the scheme illegal." See also United States v. Wexler, 31 F3d 117 (3d Cir. 1994) (government's motion for mandamus granted on jury instruction dealing with whether the sham transaction doctrine applied to interest deductions claimed in repo transactions); see also United States v. Noske, 117 F3d 1053 (8th Cir. 1997) (two conspiracies, one of which was to use business trusts and purportedly tax-exempt nonprofit corporations to assist clients to evade income tax; held, lower court instruction that trust arrangements are shams for tax purposes and do not change the way property or income is treated if the trust's grantor retains control over the property or income placed in trust was correct as a matter of law, and the jury should decide whether the trusts were economically viable entities or existed primarily to facilitate the defendants' tax evasion scheme).

[359] IRC §§ 6531(1), 6531(2).

[360] 18 USC § 3282. A claim that the five-year statute of limitations applies to a conspiracy to defraud has been rejected. United States v. Ingredient Technology Corp., 698 F2d 88 (2d Cir. 1983), cert. denied, 462 US 1131 (1984). The problem of determining whether the statute of limitations has run on a conspiracy is complicated where the indictment charges a conspiracy to violate different laws with different statutes of limitations (e.g., a Title 18 offense with a five-year statute and a tax offense with a six-year statute). For an analysis of the law, see United States v. Southland Corp., 760 F2d 1366 (2d Cir.), cert. denied, 474 US 825 (1985).

[361] The termination of the conspiracy also determines whether a statement of a co-conspirator may be used against a conspirator (a statement made after termination would not be admissible) and whether the defendant joined the original conspiracy (in which case all acts and statements might be attributed to him) or a new conspiracy.

[362] Grunewald v. United States, 353 US 391 (1957).

[363] United States v. Kissel, 218 US 601 (1910). The Supreme Court has said that withdrawal from a conspiracy can only be accomplished by affirmative notice to every co-conspirator, disclosure of the illegal enterprise to law enforcement officials, or any affirmative act inconsistent with the object of the conspiracy. United States v. US Gypsum Co., 438 US 422 (1978).

Whether a conspiracy has terminated depends on the scope of the conspirators' agreement.[364] This finding is complicated by acts of concealment that may have been either part of the agreement or those acts ordinarily contemplated by conspirators to avoid detection. If the acts were part of the agreement, they constitute overt acts, but a rule permitting any act of concealment to be by implication part of the agreement would continue the conspiracy indefinitely, effectively resulting in an unlimited statute of limitations for conspiracy cases. In *Krulewitch v. United States*,[365] the Supreme Court rejected the argument that a continuing conspiracy to conceal can be implied even after the central objectives of the actual conspiracy had been accomplished. Consequently, the focus of the inquiry now is whether acts of concealment were part of the central objectives the conspirators agreed upon.

After *Krulewitch*, acts of concealment may not ordinarily be taken as overt acts in furtherance of an implied agreement to conceal. However, in *Grunewald v. United States*,[366] acts of concealment were argued to have been part of the actual agreement of the conspirators. The case involved three defendants indicted for conspiracy to defraud the United States in the exercise of its governmental functions in administering and prosecuting violations of the tax laws. The evidence showed that the defendants used bribes and improper influence to "fix" tax fraud cases by obtaining "no prosecution" rulings in 1948 and 1949. In 1951, the conspirators felt threatened by the King Committee's investigation and took steps to hide their actions. When the indictment was returned on October 25, 1954, the defendants contended that the prosecution was barred by the then three-year (now six-year) statute of limitations. The Supreme Court again rejected the argument that acts of concealment that the prosecution contended occurred after October 25, 1951, within the statutory period, were part of the express original agreement among the conspirators. The Court held that "acts of covering up, even though done in the context of a mutually understood need for secrecy, cannot themselves constitute proof that concealment of the crime after its commission was part of the initial agreement among the conspirators."[367] However, the case was remanded for consideration

---

[364] Grunewald v. United States, 353 US 391 (1957); United States v. Baum, 435 F2d 1197 (7th Cir. 1970), cert. denied, 402 US 907 (1971).

[365] Krulewitch v. United States, 336 US 440 (1949). See also Lutwak v. United States, 344 US 604 (1953).

[366] Grunewald v. United States, 353 US 391 (1957).

[367] Grunewald v. United States, 353 US 391, 402 (1957). Most courts have found that the acts of concealment were necessarily contemplated to accomplish the objective of the main conspiracy. See, e.g., United States v. Gleason, 766 F2d 1239 (8th Cir. 1985) (cases gathered); United States v. Feldman, 731 F. Supp. 1189 (SDNY 1990) (false statements to Service agents were in furtherance of the conspiracy to evade, not a separate conspiracy to conceal; *Grunewald* distinguished). United States v. Fletcher, 928 F2d 495 (2d Cir. 1991) (*Grunewald* applied; division of profits constituted overt act within statute of limitations, but dissolution of partnership did not further conspiracy's main objective). Whether a con-

by a jury of the government's alternative contention that the object of the conspiracy was not merely to obtain "no prosecution" rulings, but a to obtain immunity for the affected taxpayers (which would have occurred within the statutory period).

The problem of applying the continuing conspiracy theory is demonstrated by *Forman v. United States*,[368] involving a conspiracy to evade tax by filing false returns. The defendants had filed tax returns falsely omitting in-

---

spiracy is one scheme or several has been held to be primarily a jury question. Both the expiration of the statute of limitations and a variance between the indictment and the proof (see Kotteakos v. United States, 328 US 750, 773–774 (1946)) depend on the answer. In a case involving a variance claim, the defendant claimed that there was not just one conspiracy for twenty years, pointing out that at the time the alleged conspiracy started, some key members were in high school. Alexander v. Thornburgh, 943 F2d 825 (8th Cir. 1991). The Eighth Circuit held, however, that it was "satisfied that the evidence supported a jury finding of a single *Klein* conspiracy, spanning many years and involving numerous individuals with the common goal of impairing and impeding the IRS in determining the nature and extent of Alexander's businesses." Compare United States v. Jagim, 978 F2d 1032 (8th Cir. 1992) (allegation of single conspiracy, but proof of two separate conspiracies; held, variance was not prejudicial, and severance was not required).

In *Moses*, the indictment alleged a continuing conspiracy to evade taxes and included overt acts of concealment after the taxes for the years 1988 through 1993 were due. United States v. Moses, 82 AFTR2d 98-5253 (3d Cir. 1998). The Third Circuit held that the case was controlled by *Forman*, and upheld the district court's finding that the co-conspirators had to conceal the defendant's failure to pay taxes on kickbacks, which one co-conspirator paid through another co-conspirator and which the defendant used in his corporation, until any action was barred and the evasion was "permanently effected." As a result, when the two co-conspirators falsely testified before the grand jury in 1994, their false statements were held to have been made "during the course of and in furtherance of the conspiracy," and admissible against the defendant under Federal Rules of Evidence 801(d)(2)(E).

[368] Forman v. United States, 361 US 416 (1960). See also United States v. Baum, 435 F2d 1197 (7th Cir. 1970), cert. denied, 402 US 907 (1971) (conspiracy was found not only to file false returns but also to avoid fraud penalty assessments in a later audit).

In *Moses*, the indictment alleged a continuing conspiracy to evade taxes and included overt acts of concealment after the taxes for the years 1988 through 1993 were due. United States v. Moses, 82 AFTR2d 98-5253 (3d Cir. 1998). The Third Circuit held that the case was controlled by *Forman*, and upheld the district court's finding that the co-conspirators had to conceal the defendant's failure to pay taxes on kickbacks, which one co-conspirator paid through another co-conspirator and which the defendant used in his corporation, until any action was barred and the evasion was "permanently effected." As a result, when the two co-conspirators falsely testified before the grand jury in 1994, their false statements were held to have been made "during the court of and in furtherance of the conspiracy," and admissible against the defendant under Federal Rules of Evidence 801(d)(2)(E).

As one court has described the case law after *Grunewald*, "Later cases have recognized that acts of concealment are in furtherance of the conspiracy for limitations purposes where the nature of the conspiracy is such that concealment is part of or in furtherance of the main objectives of the conspiracy." United States v. Mann, 82 AFTR2d 98-7344 (5th Cir. 1998) ("[t]he central aim of the conspiracy extended to concealing the

come beyond the statutory period for prosecution, but had attempted to cover up the omissions by furnishing the Service false records within the statutory period. The Supreme Court affirmed convictions for continuing conspiracy to evade taxes, saying that concealment of the omitted income had to continue if the evasion was to succeed. After *Grunewald* and *Forman*, it can be seen that the line between acts of concealment engaged in after the central object of the conspiracy has been accomplished (*Grunewald*) and acts of concealment in furtherance of the objective of the conspiracy (*Forman*) is hardly a clear one.[369] The issue ostensibly is the scope of the agreement of the conspirators, but it seems that by careful draftsmanship the government may well be able to extend the statute of limitations on a conspiracy prosecution indefinitely.

[3] The False Statement Statute: 18 USC § 1001

[a] In General

The general false statement statute, 18 USC § 1001, punishes by up to five years in prison or a fine of up to $10,000, or both, any person who

> [I]n any matter within the jurisdiction of any department or agency of the United States knowingly and willfully (1) falsifies, conceals or covers up by any trick, scheme, or device a material fact, or (2) makes any false, fictitious or fraudulent statements or representations, or (3) makes or uses any false writing or document knowing the same to contain any false, fictitious or fraudulent statement or entry.

To make out an offense under this statute, the government must prove (1) a statement; (2) its falsity; (3) that the false statement was made knowingly and willfully; and (4) that the false statement was made in a matter within the jurisdiction of any department or agency of the United States. The statute was intended to reach false statements made to governmental agencies and departments that might support fraudulent claims against the government or that might pervert or corrupt the authorized functions of the agencies to which the statements were made.[370] As the Supreme Court has said, the statute was designed "to protect the authorized functions of governmental departments and

---

fraudulent nature of the transaction, in order to evade taxes and maintain control of the [financial] institution in the face of continual regulatory oversight").

[369] For the problems of determining whether a conspiracy has terminated or a conspirator has withdrawn, see United States v. Goodman, 289 F2d 256 (4th Cir.) (Sobeloff, J., dissenting), vacated, 368 US 14 (1961) (conspirator's self-incrimination privilege claim in the course of a Tax Court case was denied on a finding that prosecution for conspiracy was barred by the statute of limitations).

[370] United States v. Bedore, 455 F2d 1109 (9th Cir. 1972).

agencies from the perversion which might result from the deceptive practices described."[371] Except in the Second Circuit,[372] the weight of appellate authority is that the statement must also be "material."[373] No standard adequately explains the results in all of the cases. A perversion of the Service's functions may result where a false statement is made during the course of an investigation.[374]

Both the tax evasion offense and the false statement offense carry a sentence of imprisonment for up to five years. Moreover, a taxpayer who makes a false statement to Service agents during an investigation may be prosecuted alternatively under the evasion statute[375] and under the false statement statute. Although these two statutes can thus serve as overlapping penalties for essentially the same conduct, the false statement statute offers particular advantages in a government prosecution. Under this statute, the government need not prove a willful affirmative attempt to evade a substantial additional tax. It need only prove that a false statement was willfully made to the Service, even if no additional tax is due. Also, the false statement may constitute an offense even if the statement was made with respect to a year barred by the six-year statute of limitations from an evasion prosecution, since it is conduct after the return is filed that is the gist of the offense.

The Service is considered an agency for the purposes of the false statement statute.[376] Although the statute specifies the submission of a false "writing or document," the offense also includes any oral false statement, whether

---

[371] United States v. Gilliland, 312 US 86, 93 (1941).

[372] United States v. McCue, 301 F2d 452 (2d Cir.), cert. denied, 370 US 939 (1962).

[373] Gonzales v. United States, 286 F2d 118 (10th Cir.), cert. denied, 365 US 878 (1960); Robles v. United States, 279 F2d 401 (9th Cir. 1960); United States v. Larocca, 245 F2d 196 (3d Cir. 1957); Freidus v. United States, 223 F2d 598 (DC Cir. 1955); Rolland v. United States, 200 F2d 678 (5th Cir.), cert. denied, 345 US 964 (1953).

[374] United States v. McCue, 301 F2d 452 (2d Cir.), cert. denied, 370 US 939 (1962); Brandow v. United States, 268 F2d 559 (9th Cir. 1959). United States v. Fern, 696 F2d 1269 (9th Cir. 1983) (affirmative, unsolicited false statement, which caused tax auditor initially to conclude that charitable deduction was due taxpayer, violated Section 1001). The test for materiality has also been said to determine "whether the falsification 'has a natural tendency to influence or was capable of influencing, the decision of the tribunal in making a determination required to be made.'" United States v. Parsons, 967 F2d 452 (10th Cir. 1992). In *Gaudin*, the Supreme Court, citing its decision in Kungys v. United States, 485 US 759, 770 (1988), accepted as a definition of "materiality" that the statement must have "a natural tendency to influence, or [be] capable of influencing the decision of the decisionmaking body to which it is addressed."

[375] United States v. Beacon Brass Co., 344 US 43 (1954).

[376] United States v. Beacon Brass Co., 344 US 43 (1954); United States v. McCue, 301 F2d 452 (2d Cir.), cert. denied, 370 US 939 (1962).

under oath or not, where made in an administrative conference.[377] Prosecution under the statute has been instituted where a taxpayer has submitted a false net worth statement,[378] a false tax return,[379] a false document,[380] or a false oral statement.[381]

The false statement statute literally requires a "material fact" be proved only in a prosecution under that portion of the statute dealing with a scheme to defraud. This requirement leaves open the possibility that in a prosecution for any other false statement, whether oral or written, the false statement need not be material. Most courts have held that the word "material" applies to every portion of the statute, although the second clause, dealing with false statements, and the third clause, dealing with writings or documents, do not use this word. One reason for this reading of the statute may be that the false statement statute is graded identically with the more serious offense of perjury, and a broad reading of the statute would tend to obliterate the distinction between false statements and perjury.[382]

Accordingly, a standard of materiality has been used by most courts to limit the circumstances in which a false statement may constitute an offense. In *Gaudin*, a false statement prosecution for false statements made in U.S. Department of Housing and Urban Development loan documents, the Supreme Court held that one of the elements of the false statement crime was materiality and that since the defendant had Fifth and Sixth Amendment rights to demand that the jury find him guilty of every element of the crime with which he was charged, he therefore had the right to have the jury decide material-

---

[377] United States v. McCue, 301 F2d 452 (2d Cir.), cert. denied, 370 US 939 (1962); United States v. Fern, 696 F2d 1269 (9th Cir. 1983) (accountant's statement during conference with tax auditor).

[378] Cohen v. United States, 297 F2d 760 (9th Cir.), cert. denied, 369 US 865 (1962).

[379] Driver v. United States, 199 F2d 860 (5th Cir. 1952).

[380] Neely v. United States, 300 F2d 67 (9th Cir.), cert. denied, 369 US 864 (1962) (lease submitted to agent was false copy omitting option to purchase). United States v. Parsons, 967 F2d 452 (10th Cir. 1992) (false Forms 1099-MISC used to report payments to third persons that were not actually made or received).

[381] United States v. McCue, 301 F2d 452 (2d Cir.), cert. denied, 370 US 939 (1962); Cooper v. United States, 282 F2d 527 (9th Cir. 1960); United States v. Fern, 696 F2d 1269 (9th Cir. 1983).

[382] The general perjury statute, 18 USC § 1621, makes it a felony punishable by imprisonment of up to five years, a fine of up to $2,000, or both, for any person "having taken an oath before a competent tribunal, officer, or person . . . that he will testify . . . or that any written testimony . . . by him subscribed is true, wilfully and contrary to such oath states or subscribes any material matter he does not believe to be true." This point was noted by the Senate Judiciary Committee in its consideration of the proposed Criminal Code. See Senate Comm. on the Judiciary, Report on the Criminal Code Reform Act of 1977, S. Rep. No. 605 (pt. 1), 95th Cong., 1st Sess. 370 (1977).

ity.[383] Rejecting the argument that materiality is a legal question, the Court reasoned that "[d]eciding whether a statement is 'material' requires the determination of at least two subsidiary questions of purely historical fact: (a) 'what statements were made?'; and (b) 'what decision was the agency trying to make?'" The question "whether the statement was material to the decision" requires applying the legal standard of materiality to these historical facts, and this is the kind of mixed question of law and fact typically resolved by juries.

According to *Gaudin*, materiality is a question for the jury to decide, but what happens where the district court fails to instruct the jury on what materiality means? In *Neder v. United States*,[384] a prosecution for mail and wire fraud and bank fraud, the district court had failed to instruct the jury on the element of materiality, but the defendant had not contested the element, nor had he presented any evidence negativing the materiality of the false statements at trial. The Supreme Court held that under these circumstances, the district court's error is reviewed using a harmless error analysis because otherwise the case would have to be remanded for retrial, even on the issues on which the jury had been properly instructed. Under a harmless error analysis, the district court's error was harmless and remand would not effect on the verdict because the overwhelming evidence was that Neder had underreported $5 million on his tax returns, and did not contest the issue that the underreporting was material.

[b] The Exculpatory "No"

Does such a perversion occur where a person merely denies his guilt in the course of an investigation? In *Paternostro v. United States*,[385] the Fifth Circuit held that, even though sworn, the defendant policeman's denials of having received graft or having knowledge of others taking money, which were given to Service agents investigating the payment of graft in the police department, did not constitute "statements" for purposes of Section 1001. The defendant did not initiate the conference or volunteer the false information but gave each answer as a defensive "exculpatory no." The Second Circuit, in *United States v. McCue*,[386] reached precisely the opposite result where false statements were made during the course of a Service investigation.[387] The statements in *Pater-*

---

[383] United States v. Gaudin, 115 S. Ct. 2310, 2314 (1995).

[384] Neder v. United States, 119 S. Ct. 1827 (1999). On remand, the circuit court found that the evidence of a false statement was so overwhelming that a rational jury could not have concluded that they were not material. United States v. Neder, 197 F3d 1122 (11th Cir. 2000).

[385] Paternostro v. United States, 311 F2d 298 (5th Cir. 1962).

[386] United States v. McCue, 301 F2d 452 (2d Cir.), cert. denied, 370 US 939 (1962).

[387] The Ninth Circuit also rejects the "exculpatory no" exception. United States v. Ratner, 464 F2d 101 (9th Cir. 1972). See also Brandow v. United States, 268 F2d 559

nostro were defensive responses made during the course of an investigation that had already focused on the defendant to some extent. This apparent exclusion of false exculpatory denials during investigations has been accepted in a number of decisions.[388]

Finally, in *Brogan v. United States*,[389] the Supreme Court rejected the "exculpatory no" doctrine, holding that a denial of criminal conduct constitutes a false statement punishable under Section 1001. In reaching this conclusion, the Court adopted a plain meaning approach, brushing aside the legislative history of the statute, as well as the Justice Department's instructions about the use of the statute. Since Section 1001 does not have a specific exception for an "exculpatory no" and literally punishes "any false statement," it followed that the statute could not permit a false statement, even one denying guilt, to go unpunished. Similarly, because the statute applied to any false statement made "in any manner within jurisdiction of any department or agency," Congress must have concluded that any false statement made during the course of an agency inquiry was a deceptive practice that might pervert governmental functions, even, as was the situation in *Brogan*, if the agency's function could not have been affected by the false statement, since it already had evidence of the matter the target falsely denied.[390] The Court also had little sympathy for the argument that its interpretation violated the spirit of the Fifth Amendment by forcing targets of an investigation to admit guilt, falsely deny guilt, or remain silent, saying that this "cruel trilemma" was of the target's own making, and in any event, the Fifth Amendment did not exonerate "an otherwise unlawful lie." In response to the argument that its rejection of the exculpatory no doctrine would permit prosecutors to manufacture crimes out of false denials of wrongdoing, and pile on additional charges, the majority's plain meaning approach

---

(9th Cir. 1959) (where false denials were contained in an affidavit); United States v. Protch, 481 F2d 647 (3d Cir. 1973); United States v. Morris, 741 F2d 188 (8th Cir. 1984).

[388] See, e.g., United States v. Philippe, 173 F. Supp. 582 (SDNY 1959); United States v. Stark, 131 F. Supp. 190 (D. Md. 1955). See also United States v. Levin, 133 F. Supp. 88 (D. Colo. 1953) (false statements to FBI agent). The decision in *Philippe* was specifically disapproved by the Second Circuit in United States v. McCue, 301 F2d 452 (2d Cir.), cert. denied, 370 US 939 (1962). The Ninth Circuit rejected *Paternostro* in United States v. Ratner, 464 F2d 101 (9th Cir. 1972). However, the Fifth Circuit reaffirmed its *Paternostro* decision in United States v. Bush, 503 F2d 813 (5th Cir. 1974). The First Circuit, in an en banc opinion, has said, "The judicial engrafting of an 'exculpatory no' exception on a facially all-inclusive statute, if taken literally, would do all the work traditionally expected of perjury statutes free of the latters' burdens and safeguards. We nevertheless acknowledge the arbitrariness of a court-drawn line between affirmative and exculpatory negative responses." United States v. Poutre, 646 F2d 695 (1st Cir. 1980).

[389] Brogan v. United States, 118 S. Ct. 805 (1998).

[390] The dissent of Justice Ginsburg, after reviewing the legislative history, observed, "[I]t [is] doubtful that Congress intended [Section] 1001 to cast so large a net."

led it to say that the grievance was with Congress, not with the hypothetical prosecutors.

A corollary of the "exculpatory no" rationale appears to be that a false statement must be an affirmative or aggressive act, as in the submission of a false claim with the possibility of perverting agency action.[391] The corollary, however, is not uniformly applied. In *Poonian v. United States*,[392] the defendant was convicted for false statements in his tax returns understating "his" income. The evidence showed that the defendant had actually overstated his income, since the omitted income was his mother's, although not reported on her return. The Ninth Circuit reversed the conviction because the statement as to his mother's income, even though intentionally false, was not a material false statement of his income. The return appears to have represented an aggressive statement, not merely an "exculpatory no." The falsity of the statement apparently was not actionable because it was legally impossible for it to have perverted a government function. In *United States v. Hajecate*,[393] on the other hand, the defendants had answered "no" to a return question about their interest in a foreign bank account, and the Fifth Circuit held that the exculpatory no doctrine applied.

It seems, in summary, that a false statement includes neither a false denial of culpability where normally the statement would not be relied upon without further investigation, nor a false statement where perversion of the agency function is legally impossible.

¶ 7A.09 CURRENCY OFFENSES

Currency reporting rules are unabashedly investigative devices for the purpose of notifying the Service that a potential tax crime has been committed, along with evidence that can be used in the prosecution of that crime. In 1970, Con-

---

[391] In United States v. Schmoker, 564 F2d 289 (9th Cir. 1978), for example, the taxpayer submitted false letters to the Service. See also United States v. Bush, 503 F2d 813 (5th Cir. 1974) (submission of a false net worth statement said to constitute a false statement); United States v. Fern, 696 F2d 1269 (9th Cir. 1983) (false oral statement to tax auditor was a material false statement even though it did not actually influence final action by Service); United States v. Morris, 741 F2d 188 (8th Cir. 1984) (false "no" to IRS agent's questions as to whether defendant officer's corporation owned real property). In *Fern*, an accountant falsely stated to a tax auditor that a taxpayer was entitled to a charitable deduction he did not claim. The tax auditor, after consulting her supervisor, asked for further verification. Ultimately, the accountant said the taxpayer did not wish to claim the deduction. The accountant was held to have made a materially false statement that perverted the Service's function. The accountant's alleged recantation came too late.

[392] Poonian v. United States, 294 F2d 74 (9th Cir. 1961).

[393] United States v. Hajecate, 683 F2d 894 (5th Cir. 1982).

gress passed what is now known as the Bank Secrecy Act (BSA) to control the flow of currency of questionable origin into U.S. financial institutions.[394] The Bank Records and Foreign Transactions Act consists of two parts: Title I requires banks and other financial institutions to retain certain financial records for periods of up to five years[395] and Title II, which has become known as the BSA, has the express purpose of requiring "certain reports where they have a high degree of usefulness in criminal, tax or regulatory proceedings."[396] In general, the BSA requires businesses and financial institutions to file currency transaction reports to be filed with the Service, Customs, and the Treasury to be used in "criminal, tax, or regulatory investigations or proceedings."[397] When the California Bankers Association challenged the constitutionality of the domestic currency reporting requirements of Title 31 on Fourth and Fifth Amendment grounds, the Supreme Court held that the record-keeping requirements do not deprive a bank of due process by imposing unreasonable burdens on them and making them agents of the government.[398] No Fifth Amendment claim could be made by banks, since the privilege does not apply to entities. Similarly, in *United States v. Miller*,[399] the Court rejected Fourth and Fifth Amendment challenges a depositor made to the BSA.

Dealings in currency, even in large amounts of currency, are not criminal, but the recipients of cash must report to the Service information assisting it in identifying potential criminal tax cases and in proving the taxpayer guilty of the tax offense. In one criminal tax prosecution, for example, the court observed that the investigation was instigated by the defendants' bank filing a currency transaction report, reporting the purchase of a $100,000 certificate of deposit with $96,000 in currency of small denominations.[400]

---

[394] The Financial Recordkeeping and Reporting of Currency and Foreign Transactions Reporting Act, Pub. L. No. 91-508, much of which is codified in Chapter 53 of Title 31, U.S. Code.

[395] 12 USC §§ 1829(b), 1951–1959; 31 CFR §§ 103.31–103.37.

[396] 31 USC § 5311. As amended, the BSA is technically entitled Records and Reports on Monetary Instruments Transactions, 31 USC §§ 5311–5326. The Audit part of the Manual has an Anti–Money Laundering Handbook. See IRM, Audit, Section 4.3.4, Anti–Money Laundering Handbook. The CID's procedures in cases involving the BSA are set out in the Special Agent's Handbook. IRM 9781, Special Agent's Handbook §§ 560 et seq., Investigation of Title 31 United States Code Violations (Oct. 18, 1995).

[397] 31 USC § 5311.

[398] California Bankers Ass'n v. Shultz, 416 US 21 (1974).

[399] United States v. Miller, 425 US 435 (1976).

[400] See, e.g., United States v. Kaatz, 705 F2d 1237, 1240 (10th Cir. 1983). Currency transaction reports were part of the evidence used against Jerry Lee Lewis, the rock and roll singer, to show that he attempted to evade or defeat taxes, and as a result that tax claims were not discharged in his bankruptcy. Lewis v. United States, 93-1 USTC ¶ 50,218, 151 BR 140 (Bankr. WD Tenn. 1992).

Section 6050I was added to the Code in 1984 to apply to businesses not covered by the BSA and to require them to file information reports of currency transactions over $10,000. The Service was given authority to enforce compliance with the currency reporting requirement. Businesses must file reports of currency transactions under Section 6050I on Forms 8300. One court described how the Service uses the Form 8300 in these terms:

> Whatever other purposes the reporting requirement established by section 6050I may serve, there is indisputably one purpose which is related to legitimate collection concerns. A properly completed Form 8300 gives the IRS the means to verify the source and amounts of discrete items of cash income above a certain figure. A taxpayer who can report cash income without identifying the payor may either hide the source of some of his income by, for example, claiming that income from several sources came from one source, or may underreport his income by understating the amount paid. Unless the IRS can identify the payor, it will simply have to take the taxpayer at his word. Alternative enforcement mechanisms, such as checking the amount shown on a Form 8300 against deposits in the taxpayer's bank accounts, do not provide the same sorts of relevant information as will be available if the payor is named. So, leaving aside any potential for improper use of the reporting requirement, it will generally be the case that the IRS is entitled to have Form 8300 completely and accurately filled out.[401]

Both the BSA and Section 6050I require financial institutions and businesses to report currency transactions. These reporting rules are contained in two statutory regimes, Title 31 and Title 26 of the U.S. Code. As a result, the anti-money laundering and financial crime detection responsibility is split between two administrators, the Treasury and the Service, each administering different statutes and adopting different regulations. The Treasury administers the BSA provisions incorporated in Title 31, U.S. Code; the Service, Section 6050I included in Title 26, U.S. Code. Each administrator has its own sets of rules. For example, the BSA and Section 6050I have different statutes of limitations for instituting cases and different forms of authorization to appear in a case. Different summons procedures apply as well.

Currency offenses may involve a simple failure to report a transaction of more than $10,000 in currency by a bank or some other person engaged in a trade or business to money laundering—i.e., dealings in currency derived from specified unlawful activities. In 1986, the Money Laundering Control Act added the crime of money laundering to Title 18, Sections 1956 and 1957, and increased the penalties for violations of the BSA and added a specific prohibi-

---

[401] In re Hall, 90-2 USTC ¶ 50,442 (ED Ark. 1990) (attorney moved to quash summons served to obtain identity of client referred to in Form 8300).

tion against structuring transactions to evade the reporting requirements of the BSA.

Legislation and regulations of the 1970s and 1980s were directed at the reporting of currency transactions. In the 1990s, the reporting requirements were extended to suspicious transactions and from banks to nonbank financial institutions. In 1992, the Annunzio-Wylie Anti-Money Laundering Act authorized mandatory suspicious transaction reports, and increased the penalties for conspiracies to launder money.[402] Only two years later, the Money Laundering Suppression Act (1) directed the Treasury to reduce the number of filed currency transaction reports by 30 percent; (2) mandated registration of money transmittal businesses, called money service businesses; and (3) clarified the criminal intent required for violation the antistructuring laws, statutorily overruling the Supreme Court's Retzlaf decision, by providing that the government need not prove that the defendant knew that structuring was illegal.[403] Again in 1998, the Money Laundering and Financial Crimes Strategy Act established a new strategy to coordinate federal and state money laundering programs.[404]

The focus here is on tax or tax-related money laundering; that is, offenses arising out of the failure to comply with the cash information reporting rules of the BSA and Section 6050I,[405] rather than the separate crime of money laundering punishable under Title 18, Sections 1956 and 1957, where violations of the tax law are not included in the offenses for which the crime of money laundering may be charged.[406]

[1] The Bank Secrecy Act

[a] In General

Under the BSA, "financial institutions" must report the following transactions: (1) deposits of domestic coins and currency into domestic financial institutions[407]; (2) transactions between or relationships maintained by U.S. persons

---

[402] Pub. L. No. 102-550.

[403] Pub. L. No. 103-325. Ratzlaf v. United States, 510 US 135, 126 L. Ed. 2d 615, 114 S. Ct. 655 (1994).

[404] Pub. L. No. 105-310.

[405] 31 USC §§ 5311–5326.

[406] 18 USC §§ 1956, 1957. However, the specified unlawful activity may be based on a violation arising under the internal revenue laws. 18 USC § 1956(a)(1)(A)(ii). In such a case, Tax Division approval of the prosecution is required. Tax Division Directive No. 99 (Mar. 30, 1993).

[407] 31 USC § 5313.

with a foreign financial agency[408]; (3) foreign currency transactions[409]; and (4) exporting and importing of monetary instruments.[410] If the financial institution fails to file the required report, the person responsible is subject to civil penalties[411] and criminal prosecution.[412] Furthermore, to ensure compliance with the reporting provisions, the Secretary of the Treasury is authorized to obtain search warrants and to seize financial instruments,[413] and also to issue summonses,[414] seek injunctions,[415] and pay rewards to informants.[416] The statute provides a definition of the key term "financial institution."[417] Special rules are provided to deal with structuring transactions to evade reporting requirements.[418] Other rules provide that financial institutions require identification for the purchase of certain monetary instruments,[419] and that the Secretary of the Treasury on his own or on the request of a federal or state law enforcement official may order the financial institutions in a geographic area to keep records of certain coin and currency transactions.[420]

Domestic financial institutions are required by 31 USC § 5313 and the applicable regulations[421] to report currency transactions that involve the payment, receipt, or transfer of U.S. coins or currency[422] of more than $10,000. Multiple cash transactions of under $10,000 occurring in one day at one financial institution and totaling over $10,000 (structuring) must also be reported. Before 1986, courts were divided over whether structuring was illegal.[423] In 1986, however, 31 USC § 5324, was added to expressly prohibit a person for

---

[408] 31 USC § 5314.

[409] 31 USC § 5315.

[410] 31 USC § 5316.

[411] 31 USC § 5321.

[412] 31 USC § 5322.

[413] 31 USC § 5317.

[414] 31 USC § 5318.

[415] 31 USC § 5320.

[416] 31 USC § 5323.

[417] 31 USC § 5312.

[418] 31 USC § 5324.

[419] 31 USC § 5325.

[420] 31 USC § 5326.

[421] 31 CFR § 103.22.

[422] The Secretary of the Treasury may include other monetary instruments.

[423] The First Circuit (Anzalone) and the Ninth Circuit (Varbel) held the conduct not to be criminal absent a clear statement in the statute or regulations prohibiting the conduct. The Fifth Circuit (Thompson) and Eleventh Circuit (Tobon-Builes) held otherwise. See United States v. Thompson, 603 F2d 1200 (5th Cir. 1979). United States v. Anzalone, 783 F2d 10 (1st Cir. 1986); United States v. Tobon-Builes, 706 F2d 1092 (11th Cir. 1983); United States v. Varbel, 780 F2d 758 (9th Cir. 1986); Ratzlaf v. United States, 510 US 135 (1994).

the purpose of evading the reporting requirements, from causing or attempting to cause a domestic financial institution to fail to file a required report of a transaction, or to file a report that contains a material omission or misstatement of fact, and (if there were still any doubt about the matter) from structuring (including an attempt to structure or assisting in structuring) a transaction with one or more domestic financial institutions.

[i] **Financial institutions.** The BSA defines the term "financial institutions" by listing types of financial institutions.[424] Some of these financial institutions are examined by the Service, except brokers or dealers in securities, not currently examined by federal bank supervisory agencies for soundness and safety.[425] There are six types of financial institutions within the definition that the Service examines,[426] and three types the Service generally does not examine.[427] The six types of financial institutions the Service examines are (1) a currency dealer or exchange, including a person engaged as a check casher; (2) an issuer of traveler's checks or money orders; (3) licensed transmitters of funds or another person engaged in the business of transmitting funds; (4) a telegraph company; (5) a casino that is licensed or authorized to do business as such with gross annual revenue from gaming in excess of $1 million; and (6) a card club that is licensed or authorized to do business as such and has gross annual gaming revenue in excess of $1 million. The three types of financial institutions the Service generally does not examine are (1) domestic banks operating within the United States by accepting deposits (as a result, credit unions are considered banks); (2) brokers or dealers in securities (they are examined by the Securities and Exchange Commission); and (3) the U.S. Postal Service, which is a financial institution when it sells money orders. Individual owners, officers, or employees of a financial institution are considered to act for it so that the knowledge, intent, or negligence of the individual may be attributed to the financial institution.[428] The individual is separately liable as individuals for purposes of criminal penalties for willful violations.[429]

[ii] **Reporting.** Reporting requirements depend on the type of entity, the type of transaction, and the amount of the transaction. Many of the rules gov-

---

[424] 31 USC § 5312. Note that 31 CFR § 103.11(3) broadly defines a "financial institution" as "a person who is engaged as a business in dealing in or exchanging currency."

[425] 31 CFR § 103.46.

[426] 31 CFR § 103.11(n).

[427] 31 CFR § 103.11 (definition of "financial institution"), 31 CFR § 103.46 (Service examination authority).

[428] 31 CFR § 103.11.

[429] An individual was held to be a financial institution because he cashed a check and gave a customer $10,000 in cash without filing a currency transaction report and converted $175,000 into cashier's checks without filing currency transaction reports. United States v. Schmidt, 947 F2d 362 (9th Cir. 1991).

erning the reporting obligations of financial institutions under the BSA are found in regulations. In general, these regulations require three reports to be filed:

1. *Currency Transaction Report, Form 4789.* A currency transaction report (also called a CTR) must be filed by domestic banks and other financial institutions with the Service, reporting each large (more than $10,000) currency transaction or other unusual transaction in currency.[430] The financial institution must record the identity of the person involved in the transaction and file the currency transaction report within fifteen days of the transaction.

2. *Report of International Transportation of Currency or Monetary Instruments (CMIR).* This form, Form 4790, must be filed with Customs by each person who transports or causes to be transported in excess of $10,000 in currency and other monetary instruments into or outside the United States.

3. *Report of Foreign Bank and Financial Accounts, Form TDF 90-22.1.* This form must be filed with the Treasury by each person subject to U.S. jurisdiction who has interests in or signature authority over foreign financial accounts, the value of which exceeds $10,000.

4. *Bank Suspicious Activity Report, Form TD F 90-22.47.* Banks must file suspicious activity reports for transactions involving $5,000 value where the transaction has no apparent business reason.

[iii] Exemptions from reporting. The Money Laundering Suppression Act of 1994 reduced the number of currency transaction reports financial institutions must file by, among other things, establishing a two-tier exemption system,[431] consisting of mandatory exemptions from reporting requirements[432] and discretionary exemptions from reporting.[433] The mandatory exemption requires the Secretary of the Treasury to exempt between a depository institution and another depository institution; a federal, state, or local department or agency; any entity established under federal, state, or local law, or under an interstate compact that exercises governmental authority; and any business or category of business whose reports have "little or no value for law enforcement purposes." A discretionary exemption from the reporting requirements may be

---

[430] 31 CFR pts. 103.22, 103.25(a), 103.26. Casinos must file Currency Transaction Reports by Casinos (CTRC), Form 8362, for transactions similar to those for which other financial institutions must file. Nevada Casinos file Currency Transaction Reports of Nevada Casinos (CTRCN), Form 8852.

[431] The act was enacted on September 23, 1994, Pub. L. No. 103-325, 108 Stat. 2243. A depository institution includes a commercial lending company, a corporation chartered under the Federal Reserve Act and any corporation having an agreement with the Board of Governors of the Federal Reserve System under the Federal Reserve Act.

[432] 31 USC § 5313(d).

[433] 31 USC § 5313(e).

granted for transactions between the depository institution and a qualified customer of the institution on the basis of information supplied by the institution, as provided in regulations. If the depository institution is granted an exemption, it is not subject to penalty for failure to file a report for a transaction with a customer, unless the institution knowingly files false or incomplete information with the Treasury about the transaction, or has reason to believe at the time the exemption is granted or the transaction takes place that the transaction does not qualify under the exemption.[434]

[iv] Suspicious transactions. The Secretary of the Treasury is authorized to promulgate regulations requiring financial institutions to report "suspicious transactions" that are subject to the BSA.[435] Since April 1, 1996, banks and other financial institutions are required to file a Suspicious Activity Report (SAR) of suspicious transactions.[436] A suspicious transaction, in general, is a transaction that involves at least $5,000 in funds or other assets, and the bank "knows, suspects, or has reason to suspect" that (1) the transaction involves funds derived from an illegal activity; (2) the transaction is designed to evade the requirements of the BSA; or (3) the transaction has no business or apparent lawful purpose, or is not the sort of transaction in which the customer would normally engage, and the bank knows of no reasonable explanation for the transaction. The report is to be filed with Treasury's Financial Crimes Enforcement Network (FinCEN) no later than thirty calendar days after the date the bank initially detects the facts that constitute the basis for filing the report, although an additional thirty days is permitted to determine the identity of a suspect whose identity cannot be determined on the date the suspicious activity is discovered.[437] When a financial institution reports a suspicious transaction, it may not notify any person involved in the transaction that such a report has been made. In addition, the financial institution is protected from liability "under any law or regulation of the United States or any constitution, law or regulation of any State or political subdivision thereof" for the disclosure or the failure to notify the affected person.

[b] Criminal Penalties for Violations of the BSA

A person who willfully violates 31 USC § 5313 or the regulations promulgated under it commits a felony and is subject to imprisonment for up

---

[434] 31 USC § 5313(f)(1).

[435] 31 USC § 5318(g). 31 CFR § 103.21(a)(2).

[436] 31 CFR § 103.21, 61 Fed. Reg. 4326–4322.

[437] 31 CFR § 103.21(b). Business records relating to a suspicious transaction are required to be kept for five years.

to five years or a fine of up to $250,000, or both.[438] To show that the defendant willfully violated the domestic financial reporting requirements, the government must prove that the defendant actually knew of the currency reporting requirements and voluntarily and intentionally failed to comply with them.[439] The Money Laundering Suppression Act of 1994 amended 31 USC § 5322 to except structuring under Section 5324 from the general crime of "willful" violations of the BSA. The amendment made structuring a separate felony described in Section 5324(c) and eliminated the element that the violation be "willful." According to the legislative history, this change "restores the clear Congressional intent that a defendant need only have the intent to evade the reporting requirement as the sufficient mens rea for the offense."[440] Section 5324(c) only requires proof that the defendant intended to evade the reporting requirement. The government need not prove that the defendant knew that structuring was illegal, although a person who innocently or inadvertently structures or otherwise violates Section 5324 is not supposed to be criminally liable.

[i] Willful conduct and structuring. Before the 1994 Money Laundering and Suppression Act, courts generally held that to be convicted under the antistructuring statute, a defendant must have known of the legal duty to report a currency transaction, but that a defendant need not know that his conduct is illegal to commit an offense under the statute.[441] Other courts, such as the First Circuit, held that a conviction under the anti-structuring statute required proof that the defendant actually knew that structuring was a crime, or at least that the defendant was reckless in his failure to investigate the legality of structuring.[442]

---

[438] 31 USC § 5322(a).

[439] United States v. Warren, 612 F2d 887 (5th Cir.), cert. denied, 446 US 956 (1980). The term "willfully" in Section 5322 requires knowledge of the reporting requirement of Section 5316 for currency imports and exports in excess of $10,000. United States v. Eisenstein, 731 F2d 1540, 1543 (11th Cir. 1984) (defendant who is unaware of the reporting requirement "cannot be expected to recognize the illegality of his otherwise innocent act").

[440] Pub. L. No. 103-325, 1994 U.S. Code Cong. & Admin. News 1881, 2024.

[441] See, e.g., United States v. Scanio, 900 F2d 485, 489–491 (2d Cir. 1990); United States v. Hoyland, 914 F2d 1125, 1128–1129 (9th Cir. 1990); United States v. Brown, 954 F2d 1563 (11th Cir.), cert. denied, 113 S. Ct. 284 (1992). Under Scanio and its progeny, determination of willfulness required only that the defendant (1) know that the bank was legally obligated to report transactions exceeding $10,000 and (2) intends to deprive the government of information to which it is entitled. United States v. Scanio, supra at 491.

[442] United States v. Aversa, 984 F2d 493 (1st Cir. 1993). The court in United States v. Speer, 824 F. Supp. 111 (WD Ky. 1993), went further, holding that mere reckless disregard would not satisfy the willfulness requirement.

Finally, the Supreme Court resolved the uncertainty about what evidence would be sufficient to sustain a conviction for "willfully violating" the antistructuring provision. In *Ratzlaf v. United States*,[443] the Court held that the government did not prove that the defendant willfully violated the antistructuring provision only by proving that the defendant's purpose was to circumvent a bank's reporting obligation by breaking up a single transaction above the reporting threshold into two or more separate transactions below $10,000. To establish that "a defendant 'willfully violat[ed]' the antistructuring law, the Government must prove that the defendant acted with knowledge that his conduct was unlawful." Other provisions of the BSA used the term "willful," the Court observed, and in those instances, courts of appeals had consistently required *both* "knowledge of the reporting requirement" *and* "a specific intent to commit the crime," i.e., "a purpose to disobey the law." Also, contrary to the government's argument, "currency structuring is not inevitably nefarious," because, for example, a business operator might structure deposits to avoid a tax audit.

After *Ratzlaf,* courts concluded that "general consciousness of illegality, the method of structuring, and the status of the defendant can support a reasonable inference of knowledge of illegality."[444] In other words, *Ratzlaf* decided that a defendant's purpose to circumvent a bank's reporting obligation was, without "something more," insufficient to sustain a conviction for "willfully violating" the antistructuring provision. Accordingly, some courts said that evidence of an elaborate scheme to hide the structuring provided the "something more."[445] Other courts said that "evidence that a defendant attempted to conceal the structuring of currency transactions may, with or with-

---

[443] Ratzlaf v. United States, 510 US 135, 126 L. Ed. 2d 615, 114 S. Ct. 655 (1994).

[444] When *Ratzlaf* was the controlling law, the Fourth Circuit reversed a structuring conviction because the evidence did not show that the defendants, who were brothers and Pakistani nationals, acted with the knowledge that their conduct in structuring transactions was unlawful. United States v. Ismail, 97 F3d 50 (4th Cir. 1996). What the evidence showed was that the defendants knew that the bank was required to report cash transactions over $10,000, and that they intended to keep their deposits under that amount to avoid the reports. But this evidence of structuring activity, the court said, did not prove beyond a reasonable doubt that the defendants knew that structuring violated the law and that they willfully violated the antistructuring provision.

[445] One example is the Second Circuit's decision in United States v. Simon, 85 F3d 906 (2d Cir. 1996) (affirming a conviction for structuring transactions to evade currency reporting requirements in violation of 31 USC §§ 5322 and 5324(3) before amendment, and citing cases decided by other circuits). The Second Circuit said "currency structuring is not so 'obviously evil or inherently bad' that the act of structuring itself satisfies the willfulness requirement . . . [h]owever, the method of structuring can provide circumstantial evidence of willfulness." As a result, "when the method of structuring suggests a significant effort not only to avoid the bank reporting requirements but to conceal the currency structuring itself from the authorities, *Ratzlaf's* requirement of 'something more' is satisfied."

out other evidence, support a conclusion that the defendant knew structuring was unlawful."[446] In one such case, a real estate agent received currency in amounts more than the minimum necessary to require filing a currency transaction report, but made deposits of less than $10,000 at different banks.[447]

Post-*Ratzlaf* decisions did not appear to impose a great burden on prosecutors, yet it took Congress very little time to attempt to reverse *Ratzlaf.* In the Money Laundering Suppression Act of 1994, Congress simply sidestepped *Ratzlaf* by making structuring a separate criminal offense for which "willful" conduct was not required.

[ii] **Corporate liability.** Corporate liability can be based on an agency relationship,[448] and a corporation's knowledge can be derived from the collective knowledge of all the corporation's employees.[449] On a corporation's liability for the acts of its agents, the circuit court in *Beusch* approved a district court's jury instruction that read: "A corporation may be responsible for the acts of its agents done or made within the scope of its authority, even though the agent's conduct may be contrary to the corporation's stated policies."[450] Just how a bank may be found to have knowledge was described in an approved jury instruction in *United States v. Bank of New England*: "[T]he bank's knowledge is the totality of what all of the employees know within the scope of their employment. So, if Employee A knows one facet of the currency reporting requirement, B knows another facet of it, and C a third facet of it, the bank knows them all."[451]

[iii] **Failure to comply with record-keeping requirements.** A separate criminal violation of a record-keeping order issued under 31 USC § 5318(a)(2) occurs for each day the violation occurs or continues at any office, branch, or place of business of the financial institution involved.[452] In addition, criminal penalties can be enhanced where the BSA is coupled with other criminal activ-

---

[446] United States v. Beidler, 110 F3d 1064 (4th Cir. 1997).

[447] United States v. Beidler, 110 F3d 1064 (4th Cir. 1997).

[448] United States v. Beusch, 596 F2d 871 (9th Cir. 1980).

[449] United States v. Bank of New Eng., 821 F2d 844 (1st Cir.), cert. denied, 108 S. Ct. 328 (1987).

[450] United States v. Beusch, 596 F2d 871 (9th Cir. 1980).

[451] United States v. Bank of New Eng., 821 F2d 844 (1st Cir.), cert. denied, 108 S. Ct. 328 (1987).

[452] 31 USC § 5322(c). However, under the "one structuring, one violation" rule, a defendant may not be charged with a separate count for each transaction that is a part of an overall structuring. United States v. Davenport, 929 F2d 1169 (7th Cir. 1991) (statute "does not forbid the making of deposits. It forbids the structuring of a transaction"), cert. denied, 112 S. Ct. 871 (1992); United States v. Nall, 949 F2d 301 (10th Cir. 1991) (specifically agreeing with *Davenport* analysis).

ity.[453] A person who willfully violates a provision of or a regulation under the BSA, except the foreign currency transaction reporting requirements of 31 USC § 5315, while violating another law of the United States or as part of a pattern of any illegal activity involving more than $100,000 in a twelve-month period, commits a felony and may be imprisoned for up to ten years or fined up to $500,000, or both.

[iv] Pattern of illegal activity. Enhanced criminal penalties are imposed in part where the violation of 31 USC § 5315 is "part of a pattern" of illegal activity involving transactions of more than $100,000 in a twelve-month period. However, one question that remains to be resolved is whether the pattern of violations must all be of the BSA or whether a violation of the BSA and another illegal act and patterns aggregating the amount of $100,000 will suffice. Most courts have said the violations must be of the BSA.[454] Another issue is whether the pattern of violations of the BSA are violations by the depositor or by the bank. It appears that the depositor and the bank must be considered separately.[455]

[c] Civil Penalties for Violations of the BSA

Civil penalties under the BSA are processed under different procedures than are civil penalties under the Code. Where the facts show that there is no criminal intent, the Service's civil examiners gather evidence to support the assessment civil penalties under the BSA and BSA regulations contained primarily in 31 CFR § 103.47.[456] These examiners may recommend assessment of civil penalties, but do not have the authority to assess them. That authority belongs to the Secretary of the Treasury, and the Secretary has delegated it to FinCEN. The examiner's recommendation of a BSA civil penalty is first sent to the CID. Only after the CID has decided that there is no basis for starting a criminal investigation will the examiner's civil penalty recommendation be sent through the National Office to FinCEN.

---

[453] 18 USC § 5322(b).

[454] United States v. Dickinson, 706 F2d 88 (2d Cir. 1983) (must be violations of the BSA); United States v. Beusch, 596 F2d 871 (9th Cir. 1980); United States v. Valdes-Guerra, 758 F2d 1411 (11th Cir. 1985) (apparently in accord).

[455] United States v. Bank of New Eng., 821 F2d 844 (1st Cir.), cert. denied, 108 S. Ct. 328 (1987) ("[t]he contention that the instruction did not distinguish between a pattern by McDonough and another by the Bank is technically correct, but it ignores the rest of the charge in which the court repeatedly informed the jury that each defendant must be judged separately").

[456] IRM, Audit, 4.3.4, Anti–Money Laundering Handbook Chapter 7, Bank Secrecy Act Penalties (May 21, 1999), especially 7.1, Overview, 7.2, Penalty Authority, and 7.5, Civil Penalties.

Liability for civil penalties depends on the type of the violation, the entity involved, and the violator's intent.[457] Civil penalties are imposed under the BSA when its reporting, record-keeping, or retention requirements are not met. Sanctions for civil violations depend on intent, and the violator's intent may be negligent or willful.

[i] Negligence penalties. Generally, negligent conduct is the failure to exercise due diligence.[458] If the violation is negligent, and the violator is a financial institution, the negligence penalty is $500 per violation, and no penalty is assessed against an individual. A separate and additional penalty of not more than $500 may be imposed on any financial institution that negligently violates a provision of the BSA, and any regulation issued thereunder.[459] As part of the Annunzio-Wylie Anti-Money Laundering Act of 1992, Congress enacted a new penalty for a "pattern of negligent activity." As a result, a financial institution that "engages in a pattern of negligent violations" of the cash transaction reporting requirements may be subject to a fine of not more than $50,000.[460]

[ii] Willful conduct penalties. Willful conduct may include willful blindness to the legal requirements of the BSA or to facts that bring the requirements into play. The Service decides whether the conduct is willful based on the violator's knowledge of the law and the facts. Evidence from which knowledge of the law may be inferred includes the actions of the violator, the education of the principals for whom the violator is acting, the extent of education about the BSA conducted by the business community in which the violator operates, and the extent of the education about the BSA the Service itself has provided.[461] Knowledge of the facts is evidenced by a disregard of facts that should have caused the violator to report or to record, as well as evidence of a personal relationship between the financial institution and the person whose transaction facts were not recorded or reported.[462] A penalty for a willful failure to comply with any BSA requirement may be assessed against both the financial institution and any individual who willfully participated in the violation, such as a partner, director, officer, and employee.

---

[457] Anti-Money Laundering Handbook 7.5(1), Civil Penalties.

[458] Anti-Money Laundering Handbook 7.6.1, Negligence.

[459] 31 USC § 5321(a)(6)(A).

[460] 31 USC § 5321(a)(6)(B).

[461] Anti-Money Laundering Handbook 7.6.2.1, Knowledge of the Law.

[462] Anti-Money Laundering Handbook 7.6.2.3, Knowledge of Facts.

For any willful violation of any record-keeping requirement, a civil penalty may be assessed up to $1,000 per violation.[463] However, if the violation is willful failure to maintain required records by persons having financial interests in a foreign account,[464] a civil penalty may be assessed in an amount equal to the balance in the account at the time of the violation up to a limit of $100,000, or $25,000, whichever is greater.[465] Similarly, if the violation is the willful failure to report a transaction with a foreign financial agency pursuant to a special order of the Secretary of the Treasury,[466] a civil penalty may be assessed equal to the greater of (1) the amount involved in the transaction up to a limit of $100,000, or (2) $25,000.[467] For purposes of computing the penalty for a violating a record-keeping order the Treasury has issued pursuant to 31 USC § 5318(a)(2), a separate violation occurs for each day the violation continues and the violation continues if it occurs or continues at any office, branch, or place of business of the financial institution. An additional or enhanced penalty may be imposed on a person (or that person's agent or bailee) who fails to file the report on exporting and importing monetary instruments, or makes a material omission or misstatement on the report required by 31 USC § 5316, or a regulation thereunder.

Willful violation of any BSA and BSA regulatory requirement is subject to a civil penalty, except for those BSA statutes dealing with the ownership of foreign accounts and the reporting of currency transactions.[468] In addition to the penalty provided by 31 USC § 5321(a)(1), the violator is liable for a civil penalty up to the amount of the monetary instrument for which the report was required, subject to reduction for any amount forfeited under 31 USC § 5317(b).[469] In addition, for violations of the reporting rules of 31 USC §§ 5313(a) and 5324(a), the violator is subject to have property seized and forfeited.[470]

---

[463] 31 CFR § 103.47(c). Violations of record retention requirements are treated as violations of a reporting requirement, and as such are subject to the reporting penalties. Anti-Money Laundering Handbook 7.5.2.3.

[464] 31 CFR § 103.32.

[465] 31 CFR § 103.47(g).

[466] 31 CFR § 103.25.

[467] 31 USC § 5321(a)(1); 31 CFR § 103.47(f).

[468] 31 USC §§ 5314, 5315.

[469] 31 USC § 5321(a)(2).

[470] Civil seizure and forfeiture authority are provided for under the BSA in Section 5317(c) and in 18 USC § 981 for violations of the reporting rules. For the CID's procedures and guidelines for seizures and forfeitures under Title 18, see IRM 9781, Special Agent's Handbook §§ (11)00 et seq., Guidelines for Title 18 Seizures and Forfeitures (Aug. 25, 1995). The subject of seizure and forfeiture under the BSA is beyond the scope of this description of the criminal statutes generally used in tax cases. But see, e.g., Comisky, Feld & Harris, Tax Fraud and Evasion (2d ed. 1999).

Section 5321(a)(4) imposes a civil penalty on any person who willfully engages in acts of structuring described in Section 5324, the penalty amount not to exceed the amount involved in the structured transaction. In 1994, this civil penalty was amended to eliminate the willfulness requirement.[471] After the amendment, any person who structures a transaction with an intent to evade the reporting requirements is liable for a civil penalty without a showing that the person knew that structuring was unlawful.

Failure to file a foreign currency transaction report required by 31 USC § 5315, an accompanying regulation under Section 5315, or a compliance injunction issued at the Treasury's request by a district court pursuant to 31 USC § 5320 is liable for a civil penalty of up to $10,000.[472] Separate penalties are imposed for structuring transactions to avoid the domestic currency transaction reporting requirements of 31 USC § 5313.[473]

[2] Section 6050I

Section 6050I, "Returns Relating to Cash Received in Trade or Business," imposes a currency-reporting requirement on any person[474] (1) who is "engaged in a trade or business"[475] and (2) who, in the course of that trade or business, receives more than $10,000 in cash[476] in one transaction[477] (or two or more related transactions).[478] Each of the terms in Section 6050I is specially defined. The term "trade or business" has the same meaning as in Section 162.[479]

"Cash" includes the coin and currency of the United States or of any other country, "which circulate in and are customarily used and accepted as money in the country in which issued." Cash also includes a cashier's check,

---

[471] The Money Laundering Suppression Act of 1994, Pub. L. No. 103-325, Sept. 23, 1994; 1994 U.S. Code Cong. & Admin. News 1881, 2025.

[472] 31 USC § 5321(c).

[473] 31 USC § 5321(d).

[474] IRC § 6050I(a), added by the Deficit Reduction Act of 1984. The term "person" is defined in Section 7701(a)(1).

[475] Reg. § 1.6050I-1(c)(6). If the cash transaction does not occur during the course of the recipient's trade or business, the recipient is not required to file an information return. Reg. § 1.6050I-1(d)(3).

[476] Cash is specially defined. For amounts received prior to February 3, 1992, "cash" means both U.S. and foreign currency but does not include negotiable or monetary instruments not customarily accepted as money, such as bank checks, traveler's checks, bank drafts, or wire transfers. Reg. § 1.6050I(c)(1)(i).

[477] The term "transaction" means "the underlying event precipitating the payer's transfer of cash to the recipient," such as the sale of goods or services or the making or repayment of a loan. Reg. § 1.6050I-1(c)(7)(i).

[478] Reg. § 1.6050I-1(c)(7)(ii).

[479] Reg. § 1.6050I-1(c)(6).

bank draft, traveler's check, or money order, as long as they have a face amount of not more than $10,000.[480] These monetary instruments are treated as cash if they are received in certain retail sales (a "designated reporting transaction"), or where the recipient "knows that the instrument is being used in an attempt to avoid the reporting of the transaction under Section 6050I."[481] A designated reporting transaction is a retail sale of a consumer durable, a collectible, or travel or entertainment.[482]

Other transactions do not treat monetary instruments as cash for purposes of the reporting requirements is when they are the proceeds of a bank loan. Cashier's checks, bank drafts, traveler's checks, or money orders received in a designated reporting transaction (if the instrument constitutes the proceeds of a bank loan) are not treated as cash payments for purposes of the currency reporting rules.[483] Similarly, cashier's checks and other like instruments are not considered cash if (1) they are received in a designated reporting transaction; (2) they are received in payment on a promissory note or an installment sale; (3) the terms are substantially similar to those used in the ordinary course of the recipient's business; and (4) the payments received on or before sixty days after the date of the sale does not exceed 50 percent of the purchase price of the sale.[484] A similar exception applies for certain down payment plans.[485]

[a] Structuring

The critical issue in currency reporting cases is whether there was structuring to avoid the reporting rules. Structuring can occur when a payer deposits or uses cash in two transactions within a single twenty-four-hour period. To prevent this kind of structuring, the term "related transaction" means "any transaction conducted between a payer (or its agent) and a recipient of cash in a 24-hour period."[486] Transactions during a period of more than twenty-four

---

[480] Reg. § 1.6050I-1(c)(1)(ii).

[481] Reg. §§ 1.6050I-1(c)(1)(ii), 1.6050I-1(c)(1)(iii). This is the definition for amounts received on or after February 3, 1992.

[482] Reg. § 1.6050I-1(c)(1)(ii)(B). Reg. § 1.6050I-1(c)(2) defines a consumer durable as an item of tangible personal property. In technical advice, the National Office, using state law to determine the issue, ruled that a mobile home is personal property for purposes of Section 6050I, despite the fact that it was sold by a manufacturer for use as a family dwelling. At the time of the sale, the mobile home was on wheels and not affixed to land. Accordingly, the manufacturer who received $2,500 in cash and a cashier's check for $9,240 in the retail sale was required to report it. Priv. Ltr. Rul. 9710001 (Nov. 13, 1996).

[483] Reg. § 1.6050I-1(c)(1)(iv).

[484] Reg. § 1.6050I-1(c)(1)(v).

[485] Reg. § 1.6050I-1(c)(1)(vi).

[486] Reg. § 1.6050I-1(c)(7)(ii).

hours can also constitute a related transaction "if the recipient knows or has reason to know that each transaction is one of a series of connected transactions."[487] The payor of the cash is prohibited from structuring transactions to avoid the reporting requirements.[488] Apart from the regulatory definitions, structuring can take other forms. In *United States v. Wilson*,[489] the defendant traded in a 1984 Cadillac toward a co-defendant's purchase of a new 1990 automobile to reduce the purchase price of the co-defendant's automobile below $10,000, and the transaction was held to be structuring.

[b] Reporting

Special rules apply to the time, manner, and form of reporting under Section 6050I. An information return, Form 8300, must be filed[490] by the fifteenth day after the date the cash is received.[491] When completed, this return discloses (1) the name, address, and taxpayer identification number of the person from whom the cash was received; (2) the amount of the cash received; (3) the date and nature of the transaction; and (4) other information required by the form.[492] In addition to filing the information return, the recipient of the cash must furnish a statement to the payor by January 31 of the year following the calendar year in which the cash was received.[493]

Information-reporting requirements cover all cash transactions occurring in the course of a trade or business, but there are certain exceptions, especially for banks and other financial institutions filing currency transaction reports under the BSA[494] and also for "entire transactions occurring outside the United States."[495] Accordingly, the reporting rules of Section 6050I do not apply to (1) cash received by certain financial institutions; (2) cash received by casinos having gross annual gaming revenue in excess of $1 million (these casinos have to file reports with the Treasury under the BSA); (3) casinos that the Ser-

---

[487] Reg. § 1.6050I-1(c)(7)(ii).

[488] IRC § 6050I(f)(1)(C).

[489] United States v. Wilson, 985 F2d 348 (7th Cir. 1993) (witnesses testified the co-defendant's intention was to avoid spending over $10,000).

[490] Reg. § 1.6050I-1(e)(2). Forms 8300 are filed by sending them to Internal Revenue Service, Detroit Computing Center, PO Box 32621, Detroit, MI 48232. A copy of the return must be retained for five years from the date of filing.

[491] Reg. § 1.6050I-1(e)(1).

[492] IRC § 6050I(b)(2); Reg. § 1.6050I-1(e)(2).

[493] IRC § 6050I(e); Reg. §§ 1.6050I-1(f)(1), 1.6050I-1(f)(2). The statements and Form 1099 must include the name and address of the person making the return and the aggregate amount of reportable cash received by the recipient during the year from the payor.

[494] IRC § 6050I(c)(1); Reg. § 1.6050I-1(d)(1).

[495] IRC § 6050I(c)(2); Reg. § 1.6050I-1(d)(4).

vice exempts from Section 6050I because they gross gaming revenue in excess of $1 million and are exempt under the BSA; (4) receipts of cash not in the course of the recipient's business; and (5) receipts of cash in a transaction occurring outside the United States.

[c] Attorney Fees Reporting

One of the most sensitive issues the filing of the Form 8300 has created is whether the attorney-client privilege or the attorney-client relationship permits attorneys not to disclose the names of clients who have paid the attorneys in currency for representation in criminal cases. Courts have generally held that the attorney is obligated to disclose the client's identity.[496] The client's name is not exempt from disclosure under the Sixth Amendment, because that amendment does not state that a defendant is entitled to a lawyer of his choice, nor does it establish the attorney-client privilege. Attorneys are subject to civil and criminal penalties for noncompliance.[497]

[d] Civil and Criminal Penalties

Both civil and criminal penalties are imposed for noncompliance with the requirements of Section 6050I. The civil penalty for a recipient's failure to file an information return is $50 for each failure up to a maximum of $250,000.[498] If the failure is intentional, the penalty rate is $100 or 10 percent of the aggregate amounts required to be reported, without any ceiling on the total amount of the penalty.[499] The criminal penalties for violations of Section 6050I are especially serious. Failure to file a Form 8300 is a felony punishable under Section 7203 by imprisonment for up to five years or a fine of up to $25,000 ($100,000 in the case of corporations), or both.[500]

Filing a false Form 8300 is also a crime, a felony punishable under Section 7206(1), by up to three years imprisonment or a fine of up to $100,000 ($500,000 in the case of a corporation), or both.[501] One element of the crime of filing a false statement is that the statement must be material. Most courts said that the issue of materiality was a legal issue for the court and not the

---

[496] See ¶ 13.11[1][a].

[497] United States v. Goldberger & Dubin, 935 F2d 501 (2d Cir. 1991). For further discussion of this attorney-client privilege issue, see Chapter 13.

[498] IRC § 6721(a). See infra ¶ 7A.08[2][b].

[499] IRC § 6721(e).

[500] Section 7203, which is normally a misdemeanor, states, "In the case of any willful violation of section 6050I, the first sentence shall be applied by substituting '5 years' for '1 year.'"

[501] See supra ¶ 7A.04.

jury to decide; however, in *United States v. Gaudin*,[502] the Supreme Court held in a false statement conviction under 18 USC § 1001 that the failure to submit the issue of materiality to the jury for it to decide violated the defendant's Fifth and Sixth Amendment rights to have the jury decide his guilt of all the elements of the crime with which he was charged.

¶ 7A.10 SENTENCING IN CRIMINAL TAX CASES

The evasion statute, Section 7201, imposes the heaviest penalty of any tax offense described in the Code. A person convicted of tax evasion is subject to imprisonment for up to five years, a fine of up to $100,000 ($500,000 for a corporation), or both,[503] together with the costs of prosecution.[504]The other tax crimes have their own criminal penalties.

Crime	Period of Imprisonment	Fine
Evasion—Section 7201	Up to 5 years	Up to $100,00 ($500,000 for corporations)
Failure to file a return, supply information, pay tax—Section 7203	Up to 1 year	Up to $25,000 ($100,000 in the case of corporations)

---

[502] United States v. Gaudin, 115 S. Ct. 2310 (1995). After *Gaudin*, a conviction for filing a false Form 8300 was reversed and remanded for a new trial in which the jury was to decide the issue of materiality. United States v. McGuire, 79 F3d 1396 (5th Cir. 1996). For further discussion of this issue, see supra ¶ 7A.04.

[503] IRC § 7201, amended by TEFRA, Pub. L. No. 97-248, HR 4961, 97th Cong., 2d Sess. § 329(a), for offenses committed after September 3, 1982. Before TEFRA, the maximum fine was only $10,000 for individuals and corporations. For a case demonstrating the reality of the incarceration portion of the sanction and describing the rights of defendants in the sentencing hearing, see United States v. Walker, 896 F2d 295 (8th Cir. 1990) (sentences of husband to twenty years' and wife to thirty years' imprisonment vacated and remanded for resentencing).

[504] Costs of prosecution include docket fees, witness fees, the stenographer's fees for daily copy of the trial transcript and cost of charts and reproduction of records. United States v. Procario, 361 F2d 683 (2d Cir. 1966). See 28 USC § 1920, which permits a judge or clerk of any federal court to tax special fees, including fees for the court reporter for transcripts, witnesses, and exemplification and copies of papers. See United States v. Dunkel, 900 F2d 105 (7th Cir. 1990) (expenses of transportation and subsistence for witness employed by the government are reimbursable costs). As a condition of probation, the taxpayer may be required to file a return and pay taxes legally owed, but his "ability to fully and fairly question his tax liability" may not be interfered with, and he may legitimately be required to supply financial information only after his tax liability is finally determined, in the same manner as any other judgment debtor. United States v. Stafford, 983 F2d 25 (5th Cir. 1993), reh'g denied, 1993 US App. LEXIS 11030 (5th Cir. Apr. 29, 1993).

Filing a false return or other statement—Section 7206(1); aiding or assisting in the filing of a false return—Section 7206(2)	Up to 3 years	$100,000 ($500,000 in the case of corporations)
Violations of employment tax laws—employer's failure to furnish a withholding statement to employees—Section 7204, or employee's filing a fraudulent statement	Up to 1 year	$1,000
Offenses with respect to collected employment taxes—Section 7215	Up to 1 year	Up to $5,000
Attempted interference with the tax law—Section 7212	Up to 3 years	Up to $5,000

The U.S. Sentencing Commission was created by the Comprehensive Crime Court Act of 1984 to establish sentencing policies and practices for the federal criminal justice system.[505] Tax evaders, the commission found, were sentenced to probation in about half the cases, while in the other half, the defendants received sentences requiring them to serve an average prison term of twelve months.[506] Where sentences in tax prosecutions were concerned, the commission concluded that the number of probationary sentences was too high considering the importance of tax prosecutions in maintaining the integrity of the tax system. As a result, Sentencing Guidelines in tax cases are intended to reduce the number of purely probationary sentences.

Sentencing guidelines were intended to provide honesty in sentencing by eliminating hidden reductions in sentences created by "good time" credits and parole commission action. The guidelines were also intended to impose uniformity in sentencing by narrowing the wide disparity in sentences by different courts for similar criminal conduct by similar offenders. Finally, by imposing appropriately different sentences for criminal conduct of different severity, the guidelines were meant to achieve some proportionality in sentencing. To eliminate hidden reductions in sentences, the act abolished parole and substantially restructured good behavior adjustments (so-called good time) that affected actual time served, with the result that the offender will serve virtually all of any prison sentence imposed. To achieve uniformity in sentences, the Sentencing

---

[505] 28 USC § 994(a).

[506] U.S. Sentencing Comm., Guidelines Manual (hereinafter U.S. Sentencing Guidelines or USSG) § 2T1.1 (Tax Evasion—Commentary), at 2.140.

Commission developed Sentencing Guidelines.[507] The Sentencing Guidelines apply to all crimes committed after November 1, 1987.[508]

Sentencing guidelines were first adopted to apply to crimes committed after November 1, 1987. Where tax offense are involved, significant amendments were added in 1989, 1990, 1991, 1993, and 1998. To avoid uncertainty about which version of the guidelines is to apply to the sentencing as of November 1, 1991, a court uses the guideline manual in effect on the date of the sentencing unless doing so would violate the ex post facto clause of the Constitution (the so-called One Book Rule).[509]

In general, the 1993 guidelines increased the likelihood that a defendant committing a tax crime will receive a sentence including a period of incarceration. Before the 1993 amendments, many defendants convicted of tax crimes were eligible for probation because the defendants had no prior criminal history. Under the then-existing sentencing table, these defendants were in the lowest Criminal History Category (Category 1 of six categories) and fell into Zone A. The 1993 amendments increased the tax tables by two levels, so that the average period of incarceration was increased by six months, and reduced the likelihood that a defendant committing a tax crime will receive an alternative type of incarceration. Before the 1993 amendments, there were separate offense categories for the different tax crimes. The 1993 amendments incorporate convictions for tax evasion, failure to file tax returns, fraudulent or false statements under penalty of perjury, and fraudulent returns under a single consolidated guideline by using a uniform definition of "tax loss," contained in the evasion guideline, for these tax offenses: "the total amount of the loss that was the object of the offense (i.e., the loss that would have resulted had the offense been successfully completed)."[510]

---

[507] USSG 11.2 (Nov. 1989). The guidelines have been held to be constitutional. Mistretta v. United States, 488 US 361 (1989).

[508] The commission was required to send its initial guidelines to Congress by April 13, 1987. They took effect automatically on November 1, 1987. 18 USC § 3551. The commission can submit guideline amendments to Congress each year. These amendments take effect automatically 180 days after submission unless a law is enacted to the contrary. 28 USC § 994(p). When a defendant has committed both preguidelines and postguidelines crimes, the district court has discretion to impose consecutive sentences. United States v. Garcia, 903 F2d 1022 (6th Cir.), cert. denied, 111 S. Ct. 364 (1990) (preguidelines false tax refund followed by postguidelines obstruction of false claim investigation); United States v. Pollen, 978 F2d 78 (3d Cir. 1992), cert. denied, 113 S. Ct. 2332 (same); see also United States v. Dale, 76 AFTR2d 95-7649 (DC Cir. 1993) (gathering circuit court cases).

[509] USSG 7A.09, §§ 1B1.11(a), 1B1.11(b)(1) (Amend. 442).

[510] USSG § 2T1.1(c)(1) (1993).

[1] Determining the Sentence Under the Guidelines—In General

Sentences under the guidelines are determined by the use of a grid, a sentencing table containing guideline ranges in months of imprisonment. (See Table 7A.) The horizontal axis has forty-three offense levels. The vertical axis plots six criminal history categories (I through VI). The intersection of the offense level and the criminal history category on the sentencing table displays the guideline range in months of imprisonment. For example, with an offense level of fifteen and a criminal history category of III, the guideline sentence range is twenty-four to thirty months of imprisonment. If the court sentences within the guideline range, an appellate court reviews the sentence to see if the guideline was correctly applied. If the judge departs from the guideline range, an appellate court may review the reasonableness of the departure.[511]

The guidelines themselves provide step-by-step instructions on how they are to apply to arrive at a sentence:

1. Find the applicable offense guideline section in Chapter Two. For tax offenses, the relevant part of Chapter Two is Part T, Offenses Involving Taxation. An introductory comment describes the philosophy of the Sentencing Commission in devising sentences for criminal tax offenses:

> Because of the limited number of criminal tax prosecutions relative to the relative incidence of such violations, deterring others from violating the tax law is a primary consideration underlying these guidelines. Recognition that the sentence for a criminal tax case will be commensurate with the gravity of the offense should act as a deterrent to would-be violators.[512]

Before 1993, there were separate offense levels for tax evasion,[513] willful failure to file a return or information,[514] filing a false return or statement under penalty of perjury,[515] aiding or assisting in the filing of a false return,[516] and filing a false statement or document.[517] The

---

[511] 18 USC § 3742. Departures from the guidelines are authorized where the offender provides special assistance to authorities. USSG 27A.09, § 5K.1 (Departures), at 5.41.

[512] USSG, pt. T (Offenses Involving Taxation—Introductory Commentary), at 2.151.

[513] USSG § 2T1.1 (Tax Evasion), at 2.151.

[514] USSG § 2T1.2 (Willful Failure to File Return, Supply Information, or Pay Tax), at 2.153.

[515] USSG § 2T1.3 (Fraud or False Statements Under Penalty of Perjury), at 2.155.

[516] USSG § 2T1.4 (Aiding, Assisting, Procuring, Counseling, or Advising Tax Fraud), at 2.156.

[517] USSG § 2T1.5 (Fraudulent Returns, Statements, or Other Documents), at 2.157.

1993 amendments consolidated several tax offenses through a uniform definition in the guideline for tax evasion.[518]

2. Determine the base offense level and any appropriate specific offense characteristics by consulting the particular guideline in Chapter 2 and applying the offense characteristics in the order listed. The base offense level is listed under each tax offense. For example, for tax evasion, specific offense characteristics describe criminal conduct that will increase the base offense level. For tax evasion the base offense level is increased by two levels for "the failure to report or to correctly identify the source of income exceeding $10,000 in any year from criminal activity" and if "sophisticated means were used to impede the discovery of the nature or extent of the offense."[519]

As a result of the 1993 amendments, a uniform definition of "tax loss" applies to all offenses. For individuals, the tax loss is 28 percent of the fraudulent income or deduction items. For corporations, the tax loss is 34 percent of such items. Under the guidelines, the tax loss table is generally two levels higher than previously "to provide increased deterrence" for tax crimes. (The lower end of the tax loss table is less than before.) The effect is to provide more jail time for tax offenses and to virtually guarantee incarceration for the vast majority of tax offenders. For example, a level 10 offense used to apply for a tax loss of between $20,000 and $40,000; under the amended guidelines, a level 10 offense is reached with a tax loss of between only $8,000 and $13,500. In addition, the guidelines provide that the lowest base offense level is 6, which applies to a tax loss of $1,700 or less. Section 2S1.3, dealing with monetary reporting transactions, was newly rewritten. All violations are combined into one guideline with a base offense level of 6 and reference to the fraud table for computation of the loss. § 2T.1, the base offense level is the level from the Tax Table (§ 2T4.1), corresponding to the "tax loss," a specially defined term.[520]

3. Adjust the base offense level to take into account the effect of the offense on a victim, the role of the defendant in the offense, and obstruction of justice. Although tax offenses are not thought of as victim-related offenses, warranting two-level increases in the base offense,[521] tax offenders may well have "willfully obstructed or impeded, or attempted to obstruct or impede, the administration of justice during the investigation, prosecution, or sentencing" of a tax

---

[518] USSG § 2T1.1 (1993).
[519] USSG §§ 2T.1(b)(1), 2T.1(b)(2).
[520] USSG § 2T.1(a).
[521] USSG Ch. 3, pt. A.

offense, so that the base offense level is increased by two levels.[522] "Obstructing" conduct is the type of conduct often associated with tax offenses, such as perjury during the investigation or judicial proceeding, producing false documents during the investigation, or destroying or concealing documents on learning of an investigation.[523] Tax offenses do not often involve organized activity by five or more participants, but if the defendant were involved in a group activity (e.g., a tax protest group) as an organizer or leader, the base offense level is increased by four levels.[524]

4. Repeat steps one through three for each count if there are multiple counts of convictions. Provisions in Chapter 3, Part D, entitled "Multiple Counts," are applied to group or combine all the counts of which the defendant was convicted into a single offense level, and to adjust the offense level according to specific rules. Considerably simplified, in tax offenses, these "combined" offense level rules increase the tax loss by grouping counts of tax evasion, thus increasing the offense level. For example, if the defendant is charged in separate counts for tax evasion in successive years, the tax loss would be the combined amount, and the offense level would be increased accordingly.[525]

5. Adjust the base offense level favorably for the defendant. In general, Chapter Three, Part E—Acceptance of Responsibility, provides that if the defendant "clearly" has demonstrated acceptance of responsibility for the offense, the offense level is decreased by two levels.

6. Determine the defendant's criminal history category, as specified in Part A of Chapter Four, Criminal History and Criminal Livelihood. Under the guidelines, a defendant with a prior criminal record will receive greater punishment than a first offender. In tax offenses, the defendant is typically a first offender, and so does not have increases to the defendant's criminal history category in the sentencing table.[526]

7. Use the sentencing table in Part A of Chapter Five to find the guideline range that corresponds to the intersection of the defendant's of-

---

[522] USSG § 3C1.1.

[523] USSG § 3C1.1, Commentary.

[524] USSG § 3B1.1(a).

[525] USSG Ch. 3, pt. D (Multiple Counts, Introductory Commentary); USSG § 3D1.1. Special rules describe which offenses may be combined as closely related counts (USSG § 3D1.2), the offense level applicable to each group of closely related counts (USSG § 3D1.3), and how to determine the combined offense level (USSG § 3D1.4).

[526] USSG Ch. 4 (Criminal History and Criminal Livelihood, Introductory Commentary). Career offenders and others having a criminal livelihood have the offense levels increased under Part B of Chapter 4.

fense level, as determined above, on the vertical axis and the
defendant's criminal history category on the horizontal axis.

8. For the particular guideline range, identify the sentencing requirements and options, including probation, imprisonment, supervision
conditions, fines, and restitution determined from Part B, Probation;
Part C, Imprisonment; Part D, Supervised Release; Part E, Restitution, Fines, Assessments, and Forfeitures; Part F, Sentencing Options
(such as community confinement, home detention, community service, occupational restrictions); and Part G, Implementing the Total
Sentence of Imprisonment.

9. Finally, review Parts H and K of Chapter Five, entitled "Specific Offender Characteristics and Departures," to find any other policy statements or commentary in the guidelines that might warrant
consideration in imposing sentence.

[2] The First Step: The Base Offense Level and Tax Loss

Tax offenses are found in Part T of Chapter 2 of the guidelines. The first step
in the sentencing determination is to identify the base offense level and then to
apply the appropriate Specific Offense Characteristic described in the guideline. Section 2T1.1 is the guideline for three tax crimes: (1) tax evasion; (2)
willful failure to file a tax return, supply information, or pay tax; and (3)
fraudulent or false tax returns, statements, or other documents. The base offense level is the level indicated by the tax loss table (§ 2T4.1) corresponding
to the "tax loss," or Level 6 if there is no tax loss.[527] Two Specific Offense
Characteristics can increase the base offense level: illegal-source income and
the use of sophisticated means. If the defendant failed to report or correctly
identify illegal-source income exceeding $10,000 in any year, the base offense
level is increased by two levels, and if the offense level before adjustment is
less than a Level 12, the base offense level is increased to Level 12.[528] Similarly if the defendant used sophisticated means to commit the offense, the base
offense level is increased by two levels.[529]

[a] Tax Loss

For tax evasion, as well as other tax offenses, included in the guidelines,
the critical factor in determining the seriousness of the offense is the amount
of "tax loss"; the greater the loss, the higher or more severe the offense level.

---

[527] USSG §§ 2T1.1(a)(1), 2T1.1(a)(2).

[528] USSG § 2T1.1(b)(1).

[529] USSG § 2T1.1(b)(2).

The background of the guidelines states, "Tax offenses, in and of themselves, are serious offenses; however, a greater tax loss is obviously more harmful to the treasury and more serious than a smaller one with otherwise similar characteristics."[530] As the tax loss table shows, a tax loss of $1,700 or less carries an offense level of six, but when the amount of tax loss is more than $8,000 but less than $13,000, the offense level is ten.[531] When the Sentencing Guidelines were made effective in 1987, they defined "tax loss" in the tax evasion guideline. Later amendments changed this definition and consolidated evasion and the crimes of filing a false return and the failure to file a return.

1. Between November 1, 1987, and October 31, 1989, "tax loss" was defined as the greater of "(A) the total amount of tax that the taxpayer evaded or attempted to evade, including interest to the date of the filing of an indictment or information; and (B) the 'tax loss' defined in § 2T1.3 [the guideline for false statement sentences]."[532] "Tax loss" for purposes of the false statement Sentencing Guidelines was defined in terms of applicable tax rates, so that for individuals the tax loss was 28 percent (34 percent for corporations) of the amount by which the greater of gross income and taxable income was understated, plus 100 percent of the amount of false credits claimed.[533]

---

[530] USSG § 2T1.1, Background.

[531] See USSG § 2T4.1, Tax Table (1993), reproduced as Table 7A.2. The tax table was amended, effective November 1, 1993, to read as reflected in Table 7A.2.

[532] USSG § 2T1.1(a) (1987). Tax loss for purposes of USSG § 2T1.1 (1987) includes tax loss in years before the 1987 effective date of the Sentencing Guidelines. United States v. Higgins, 2 F3d 1094 (10th Cir. 1993) (evasion conviction for 1985, 1986, and 1987). The rationale is that the guidelines themselves say that relevant conduct for offenses subject to the guidelines is to be determined without regard to the November 1, 1987, effective date because to do otherwise would be to double the potential sentence with preguideline sentences.

The pre–November 1989 version of § 2T1.1 included interest on unpaid taxes. The Third Circuit held that adding interest properly recognized the time value of money and a rational calculation of the real loss arising from a taxpayer's concealing all of his income from assessment. United States v. McLaughlin, 126 F3d 130 (3d Cir. 1997). Also, in applying the 1987 guidelines, the process of determining the tax loss was said to be a two-step process: (1) the court must calculate the tax due on the amount that should have been included on the return, plus interest, and (2) the court must identify the amount of taxes willfully evaded. United States v. Olbres, 99 F3d 28 (1st Cir. 1996) (court failed to make specific findings on the amount of taxes willfully evaded).

[533] For example, where the defendants were convicted of aiding in the preparation of false returns by marketing sham trusts, the tax loss was held to be equal to 28 percent times non-legitimate deductions plus income distributed to trust owners offshore, not gross income reported by purchasers on their trust tax returns. See United States v. Schmidt, 935 F2d 1440 (4th Cir. 1991). Compare United States v. Bryant, 128 F3d 74 (2d Cir. 1997) (tax loss in an aiding and assisting case may be estimated and extrapolation used

2. In 1989, the Sentencing Commission amended the definition of "tax loss." From November 1, 1989, until October 31, 1993, "tax loss" was defined as "the greater of: (A) the total amount of tax that the taxpayer evaded and (B) the 'tax loss' defined in § 2T1.3."[534]

3. As of November 1, 1993, the definition of "tax loss" was significantly changed from the 1991 definition. For the offenses of tax evasion or a fraudulent or false return, statement or other document, "the tax loss is the total amount of loss that was the object of the offense (i.e., the loss that would have resulted had the offense been successfully completed.)"[535] For failing to file a return, "the tax loss is the amount of tax the taxpayer owed but did not pay." Notes to the guidelines prescribe a calculation of tax loss when the amount of tax loss is otherwise not ascertainable. Some terms (i.e., the percentage rates of tax) were carried over from the pre-1993 guidelines, but the reference to "taxable income" was deleted and the term "gross income" substituted, and an entirely new phrase, "unless a more accurate determination of the tax can be made," was added.[536] As the commentary explains, tax loss does not include interest or penalties, and so tax loss is not the equivalent of a civil deficiency, which would include both penalties and interest. Rather, the amount of the tax loss, also called the "criminal deficiency," is determined by "the same rules that are applicable in determining any of the other sen-

---

where the defendant has been convicted of assisting in the preparation of numerous fraudulent tax returns and there is evidence of many other instances of fraudulent return preparation). See United States v. Fleming, 80 AFTR 2d 97-7314 (6th Cir. 1997) (defendant prosecuted and convicted of filing false refund claims under 18 USC § 287, and, at sentencing, the total amount of the fraudulent tax refund claims defendant filed for others was used to establish "intended loss," without considering whether any of the taxpayers involved might have been entitled to a legitimate refund; held, use of intended loss was not an abuse of discretion).

Under guidelines in effect in 1991, unclaimed deductions were not allowed in computing the amount of tax loss. United States v. Martinez-Rios, Sr., 81 AFTR2d 98-2083 (2d Cir. 1998).

[534] USSG § 2T1.1(a) (1989).

[535] USSG § 2T1.1(c)(1).

[536] USSG App. C, Amendment 491, at 386. The 1993 amendment has been held to be a substantive and not clarifying change, and as a result, under the general One Book Rule of § 1B1.11(b)(2), a defendant was held entitled to choose between being sentenced under the 1991 version of the guidelines in effect at the time the crime was committed, which allowed a lower base offense level, or the 1993 amended version in effect on the date of sentencing, which permitted unclaimed deductions to reduce the tax loss, a step prohibited by the 1991 version. United States v. Minneman, 143 F3d 274 (7th Cir. 1998) (the defendant wanted to use the piecemeal application of the most favorable portions of the 1991 guidelines and a favorable portion of the 1996 guidelines).

tencing factors."[537] Accordingly, indirect methods of proof may be used, but if the amount of tax loss is uncertain, the sentencing court is permitted to make "a reasonable estimate of the amount of tax loss based on the available facts." The tax loss is not reduced by any payment of the tax after the commission of the crime.[538]

As of November 1, 1993, USSG § 2T1.1 describes how tax loss is computed for evasion and filing a false return, as well as failing to file a tax return. When tax loss is not "reasonably ascertainable, special instructions adopt presumptions to determine the amount of tax loss are used," unless the government or defense provide sufficient information to make a more accurate calculation of tax loss. For an offense involving filing a tax return underreporting gross income, the tax loss that was the object is presumed to be equal to 28 percent of the underreported gross income (34 percent if the taxpayer is a corporation) plus 100 percent of any false credits claimed against tax, unless a more accurate determination of the tax loss can be made.[539] If the offense involved the overreporting (or improper claiming) of a deduction or exemption, the tax loss is presumed to be equal to 25 percent of the of the improperly claimed deduction or exemption (34 percent if the taxpayer is a corporation) plus 100 percent of any false credits claimed against tax, unless a more accurate determination of tax loss can be made.[540] Where the offense is failure to file a tax return, "the tax loss is the amount of tax that the taxpayer owed and did not pay."[541] After the tax the taxpayer owed but did not pay is determined, the amount of tax loss is "equal to 20% of the gross income (25% if the taxpayer is a corporation) less any tax withheld or otherwise paid, unless a more accurate determination can be made."[542]

Other issues arise in determining the amount of tax loss for the guidelines. Where the evasion or false statement involve the defendant and his corporation's returns, the tax loss is "the aggregate tax loss from the offenses taken together."[543]

---

[537] USSG § 2T1.1, Commentary (note 2) (1989).

[538] USSG § 2T1.1(c)(5).

[539] USSG § 2T1.1(c)(1), Note (A).

[540] USSG § 2T1.1(c)(1), Note (B). Where the tax offense involves claiming a deduction to provide a basis for tax evasion in the future, the tax loss is computed in the same way as an offense involving an overstated deduction. Id. at Note (C).

[541] USSG § 2T1.1(c)(2).

[542] USSG § 2T1.1(c)(2), Note.

[543] USSG § 2T1.1, Application Note 7. Before the guidelines were amended in 1993 to provide for this treatment, the Seventh Circuit had held, "when a person caused corporate income to be understated, the situation is best viewed in three steps: (1) a corporation failing to pay income taxes on profits; (2) the corporation disbursing those profits as dividends to a shareholder; and (3) the shareholder failing to pay taxes on the dividends." United States v. Wu, 81 F3d 72 (7th Cir. 1996). The tax loss computation follows the

[b] Total Tax Loss: Increase for Related Conduct

In determining the total tax loss attributable to the offense, "all conduct violating the tax laws should be considered as part of the same course of conduct or common scheme or plan unless the evidence demonstrates that the conduct is clearly unrelated."[544] Thus, when more than one year is involved, the tax losses must be added together or aggregated. An application note uses the following examples of the same course of conduct or common scheme or plan:

(a) [t]here is a continuing pattern of violations of the tax laws by the defendant; (b) the defendant uses a consistent method to evade or camouflage income, e.g., backdating documents or using off-shore accounts; the violation involves the same or a related series of transactions; (d) the violation in each instance involves a false or inflated claim of a similar deduction or credit; and (e) the violation in each instance involves a failure to report or an understatement of a specific source of income, e.g., interest from savings accounts or income from particular business activity.

An example of this related conduct principle is the omission of income from a particular source over a three-year period, which means that the tax loss includes the tax evaded on that income for the entire three-year period. In *United States v. Meek*,[545] the district court aggregated the evaded tax for the two years charged, as well as the tax for the two years before the indictment years and the three years after the indictment years. The defendant was previously convicted of failing to file tax returns for the two preindictment years, and had failed to file returns for the three postindictment years. The defendant claimed that it was an error to aggregate tax loss for uncharged failures to file for purposes of an evasion sentence. The failures to file were held to constitute relevant conduct, whether or not charged, because they were part of the same course of conduct within the meaning of USSG § 1B1.3(a)(2). In another case, the defendant was convicted of evasion, but his prior failure to file was held

---

same three-step analysis, with the corporate rate of 34 percent applied to the unreported corporate profit; the imputed dividend reduced by this corporate tax; and the individual rate of 28 percent applied to the reduced corporate dividend.

In reviewing the sentence in another corporate/individual tax evasion case, the Seventh Circuit also approved the determination of tax loss based on the double tax treatment of the unreported corporate taxable income of additional corporate income tax and imputed dividends to the shareholder; but a divided panel went on to approve a two-level enhancement for abuse of trust under USSG § 2T1.1(b)(2), because the taxpayer "had abused the trust of the other shareholders by diverting funds that could have been used to pay dividends or to improve the company's long-term prospects." United States v. Bhagavan, 116 F3d 189 (7th Cir. 1997).

[544] USSG § 2T1.1, Application Notes, Note 2 (1993).

[545] United States v. Meek, 998 F2d 776 (10th Cir. 1993).

not to be relevant conduct, because the failure to file was not shown to be part of a criminal course of conduct.[546]

Calculation of tax loss based on relevant conduct should be distinguished from the grouping rules of the Sentencing Guidelines, which provide that (1) convictions on multiple counts do not result in a sentence enhancement (counts that are grouped together are treated as constituting a single offense for purposes of the guidelines) and (2) when conduct under one count embodies conduct treated as a specific offense characteristic of another count, the counts must be grouped.[547] For example, when a taxpayer was convicted of four counts of the offense of tax evasion, the offenses were grouped.[548] On the other hand, the taxpayer was also convicted of mail fraud, so the district court increased the offense level for tax evasion, because his unreported income was derived from mail fraud, and then increased the tax evasion offense level to increase the offense level for fraud. The circuit court reversed the sentence and remanded the case for resentencing, because the circuit court held that the mail fraud count embodied conduct that was treated as a specific offense characteristic of the tax evasion counts; therefore, the district court had improperly double-counted the mail fraud count.

[c] Increase for Specific Offense Characteristics: Illegal Income and Sophisticated Means

The base offense level can be increased by specific offense characteristics. One offense characteristic is the defendant's failure to report or identify correctly illegal-source income exceeding $10,000 in any year. If the defendant's offense has this characteristic, the base offense level is increased by two levels (and can increase the offense level to twelve). The objective of this offense characteristic is deterrence, and its rationale is that "[c]riminally derived income is generally difficult to establish so that the tax loss in such cases will tend to be understated."[549]

---

[546] United States v. Daniel, 956 F2d 540 (6th Cir. 1992).

[547] USSG § 3D1.2(c).

[548] United States v. Haltom, 113 F3d 43 (5th Cir. 1997) (false invoicing scheme resulted in charges of tax evasion on the proceeds of the scheme and mail fraud on the use of the mails as part of the fraud); cf. United States v. Astorri, 923 F2d 1052 (3d Cir. 1991). After *Astorri*, the Sentencing Commission issued an advisory stating that tax evasion should always be grouped with the offense that generated the illegal income, regardless whether the two-level increase for criminally derived income was actually applied. See Questions Most Frequently Asked About the Sentencing Guidelines, Vol. V, Mar. 1, 1992 (interpreting USSG §§ 3D1.2(c), 2T1.1(b)(1)).

[549] USSG § 2T1.1, Background.

The second offense characteristic is the use of "sophisticated means" to impede discovery of the existence or extent of the crime.[550] If the defendant is found to have used sophisticated means, the offense level is increased by two levels. "Sophisticated means" is defined as "[e]specially complex or especially intricate conduct in which deliberate steps are taken to make the offense, or its extent, difficult to detect."[551] According to the background of the guidelines, "unusually sophisticated efforts to conceal the offense decrease the likelihood of detection and therefore warrant an additional sanction for deterrence purposes." The guidelines provide several examples of sophisticated means, including hiding assets or transactions, or, through the use of fictitious entities, corporate shells, or offshore bank accounts."[552] Sophisticated means have been found when the defendant had falsified and backdated documents[553]; structuring elaborate "land flip" transactions[554]; and used a double set of books or false addresses and other efforts to conceal.[555] On the other hand, merely claiming that withholding tax had been paid when it was not has been held not to involve sophisticated means.[556] But even where sophisticated means is not found to have been used, another enhancement may apply, such as a special skill enhancement. In *United States v. Rice,* where an accountant was held not to have used sophisticated means when he falsely claimed that withholding tax

---

[550] USSG § 2T1.1(b)(2), Application Note 6 (1992). However, the sophisticated means must be tied to the tax offense, not to the concealment of some other crime. See United States v. Stokes, 998 F2d 279 (5th Cir. 1993) ("Any sophisticated means that Stokes employed to hide the money that she took from Tulane occurred in her scheme to embezzle from Tulane. It did not involve the evasion of taxes. . . . ").

[551] USSG § 2T1.1, Application Note 4.

[552] USSG § 2T1.1, Application Note 4.

[553] See United States v. Jagim, 978 F2d 1032 (8th Cir. 1992) (falsification and backdating of documents).

[554] United States v. Charroux, 3 F3d 827 (5th Cir. 1993) (sophisticated means enhancement upheld; "[a]lthough the evidence does not indicate that either James or Charroux were tax experts, it does support the conclusion that they structured elaborate transactions to hide their revenue [from land flips]").

[555] United States v. Salas, 16 F3d 1223 (6th Cir. 1994) (a Section 7206(1) case involving skimming of receipts, keeping a double set of books on a computer, and a secret password to gain access to a computer spreadsheet); United States v. Pierce, 17 F3d 146 (6th Cir. 1993) (use of false documents, multiple addresses, and conduct to avoid detection).

[556] Compare United States v. Rice, 52 F3d 843 (10th Cir. 1995): "Mr. Rice's tax evasion scheme was not sophisticated. He merely claimed to have paid withholding taxes he did not pay." The circuit court said that, in substance, the fraud was the functional equivalent of claiming more in itemized deductions than was actually paid, and if that was a sophisticated scheme, then "every fraudulent tax return will fall within that enhancement's rubric." On the other hand, Rice was given a two-level enhancement for more than minimal planning in connection with a crime involving fraud and deceit (USSG § 2F.1(b)(2)(A)), because he employed "a fairly complicated scheme."

had been paid, the court found that he used his special skill as an accountant to perpetrate his fraud.[557]

[d] Base Offense Levels for Other Tax Offenses

The previous discussion focuses on tax evasion, filing a false return, and failing to file a return. The guidelines are applied in the same way for other tax offenses. First, the base offense level, which can vary, is determined. The base offense level for the offense of aiding and assisting in the filing of a false return is the is the level determined from the tax table corresponding to the tax loss defined in Section 2T1.1, resulting from the "defendant's aid, assistance, procurance, or advice," or if there is no tax loss, Level 6.[558] But an increased offense level is provided "for those in the business of preparing or assisting in the preparation of tax returns and those who make a business of promoting tax fraud because their misconduct poses a greater risk of revenue loss and is more clearly willful."[559] Where the defendant has advised other taxpayers to violate the tax laws by filing false returns, the tax loss misstatements in all returns will be aggregated to determine the tax loss.[560] This aiding and assisting guideline has two Specific Offense Characteristics. The base offense level is increased two levels if "the defendant committed the offense as part of a pattern or scheme from which he derived a substantial portion of his income" or if the defendant was in the business of preparing or assisting in the preparing

---

[557] United States v. Rice, 52 F3d 843 (10th Cir. 1995). Rice's scheme did not simply involve the failure to report income (by overstating the amount of withholding tax his S corporation had paid from his salary). Under the scheme, he failed to report his income on his tax returns for three years. Another two-level enhancement was imposed on the grounds that Rice, an accountant, had used "special skill" in the commission of the crime (USSG § 3B1.3). The use of the special skill enhancement was held not to overlap and to permit impermissible double counting when imposed with either the sophisticated means or the more than minimal planning enhancements. See also United States v. Lewis, 93 F3d 1075 (2d Cir. 1996) (client of accounting firm that used false bank accounts to disguise personal expenses as business expenses and charitable deductions held to have used sophisticated means because scheme was more complex than the routine tax evasion case and similar to the use of shell corporations).

[558] USSG § 2T1.4(b)(1) (1990).

[559] USSG § 2T1.4, Background.

[560] USSG § 2T1.4, Application Note 1.

of tax returns.[561] If the offense involved "sophisticated concealment," the base offense level is also increased by two levels.[562]

The base offense level for a conspiracy to defraud—or as it is entitled in the guidelines, "Conspiracy to Impair, Impede or Defeat Tax," is the greater of (1) the base offense level for tax evasion (USSG § 2T1.1) or aiding or assisting in the filing of a false return (USSG § 2T1.4), depending on the underlying conduct, or (2) a base offense level of ten.[563] Accordingly, if the base offense level under the evasion or false statements guidelines exceeds ten, the base offense level determined under the specific offense guidelines and the tax table applies.[564] Sentencing may also be imposed under other guidelines.[565] A conspiracy to defraud offense also has two offense characteristics that increase the offense level. The base offense level is increased by four levels if the offense involved "the planned or threatened use of violence to impede, obstruct or defeat the ascertainment, computation, assessment, or collection of revenue."[566] An increase of two levels is made if the defendant intended to "encourage persons other than or in addition to co-conspirators to violate the [tax laws]" or defeat the assessment or collection of tax.[567] While an application note to USSG § 2T1.9 lists tax protest groups and fraudulent tax shelters as examples of situations deserving an application of the encouragement enhancement, it has been held that these examples are illustrative, not exclusive.[568]

---

[561] USSG § 2T1.4(b)(1). See also United States v. Welch, 19 F3d 192 (5th Cir. 1994) (professional sports agent submitted phony deduction information to return preparer for his athlete clients; determination that the defendant derived a "substantial portion" of his income made by using the criminal livelihood provisions of USSG § 4B1.3 was proper because USSG § 4B1.3 is intended to supplement specific offenses in the guidelines). Compare United States v. Zapatka, 44 F3d 112 (2d Cir. 1994) (government claimed that defendant derived all her income from her common-law husband; two-level increase on the grounds that her income was derived from prostitution, not from tax-related activity such as the promotion of a fraudulent tax shelter).

[562] USSG § 2T1.4(b)(2) (1998).

[563] USSG § 2T1.9(a). See United States v. Telemaque, 934 F2d 169 (8th Cir. 1991) (conspiracy to defraud; protester's false and obviously exaggerated figures not considered in sentencing under USSG § 2T1.9(a)(2)).

[564] United States v. Kraig, 99 F3d 1361 (6th Cir. 1996).

[565] Where a tax protester submitted false refund claims showing obviously fictitious deductions and no actual loss, as required by USSG § 2T1.3(a)(1), was suffered (USSG § 2T1.3(a)(2)), the "catchall" level-six provision calling for zero-to-six months' incarceration was held applicable. United States v. Krause, 786 F. Supp. 1151 (EDNY 1992).

[566] USSG § 2T1.9(b)(1).

[567] USSG § 2T1.9(b)(2). If both characteristics apply, the greater level increase is used.

[568] United States v. Balagula, 78 AFTR2d 96-6449 (2d Cir. 1996) ("Balagula intended to encourage others to prepare false invoices such that Balagula and his co-conspirators could evade millions of dollars in gasoline excise taxes"). See also United States v. Kraig, 99 F3d 1361 (6th Cir. 1996) (conviction of lawyer for conspiracy to defraud by

[3] Step 2: Adjustments to the Base Offense Level: Aggravating and Mitigating Factors

Once the offense guideline and the specific offense characteristics have been determined, the next step is to apply the appropriate adjustments in Chapter 3 of the Sentencing Guidelines. Chapter 3 describes adjustments to the offense level for a wide variety of offenses, but the ones that seem particularly likely to be present in criminal tax offenses are (1) the role of the defendant in the offense (Part B); (2) whether the defendant willfully obstructed or impeded the proceedings (Part C); (3) the defendant's commission of multiple offenses (part D); and (4) the defendant's acceptance of responsibility (Part E).

[a] Aggravating Factor: Defendant's Role in the Offense

The offense level is increased by four levels if the defendant had an "aggravating role" by being an organizer or leader of a criminal activity that involved five or more participants or was otherwise engaged in extensive criminal activity.[569] On the other hand, if the defendant had a "mitigating role" by being only a minor participant, the offense level is decreased by four levels.[570]

[b] Aggravating Factor: Defendant Willfully Obstructed or Impeded Administration of Justice

If the defendant obstructed or impeded the administration of justice during the investigation, the prosecution, or the sentencing after conviction, the offense level is increased by two levels.[571] The application notes give a nonexhaustive list of the types of misconduct to which the guideline applies: committing perjury; producing a false document; destroying or concealing evidence, such as shredding a ledger after learning that an investigation has or

---

assisting in concealing assets to prevent the collection of taxes; court held, "As to Kraig's role in the conspiracy, the evidence supports the finding that he recruited lawyers and accountants to participate in the scheme").

[569] USSG § 3B.1 (1991) (Aggravating Role). Where the offense level is enhanced because of the defendant's role, the sentencing court may consider only conduct "directly relating" to the specific offense charged in the count of which the defendant was convicted. United States v. Pollen, 978 F2d 78 (3d Cir. 1992), cert. denied, 113 S. Ct. 2332, appeal after remand, 5 F3d 1492 (3d Cir. 1993), cert. denied, 114 S. Ct. 697 (1994) (court considered all "relevant conduct" of the defendant, not the count-specific conduct; held, four-level rather than two-level enhancement not harmless error).

[570] USSG § 3B1.2 (1992) (Mitigating Role).

[571] USSG § 3C1.1 (1992) (Obstructing or Impeding the Administration of Justice).

is about to begin.[572] In a case illustrating this kind of conduct, the taxpayer transferred $280,000 to his wife after he was notified of a civil audit, and then to a Swiss account after he was notified he was under criminal investigation.[573]

[c] Mitigating Factor: Defendant Has Accepted Responsibility

Where the defendant "clearly demonstrates a recognition and affirmative acceptance of personal responsibility for his criminal conduct," the offense level is reduced by two levels.[574] The 1992 guideline states, "If the defendant clearly demonstrates acceptance of responsibility for his offense, decrease the offense level by 2 levels." If the offense level is sixteen or greater, an additional one-level reduction is provided for if the defendant has timely provided complete information to the government about his own involvement in the offense, or gives notice to the authorities that he intends to plead guilty, thereby permitting the government to avoid preparing for trial and permitting the court to allocate its resources efficiently."[575] The commentary says that a defendant "is not required to volunteer or affirmatively admit, relevant conduct beyond the offense of conviction in order to obtain a reduction under subsection (a)." Other examples relevant to tax cases are voluntary payment of restitution prior to adjudication of guilt; postoffense rehabilitative efforts, such as counseling and drug treatment; and the timeliness of the defendant's conduct in manifesting the acceptance of responsibility.[576] But acceptance of responsibility may require more than filing amended returns and paying additional taxes. Although a defendant pleaded guilty and testified for government, a two-level reduction in the offense level was denied because the conviction was based on defendant's perjury and other bad acts.[577] Also, when a lawyer was prosecuted for willful failure to pay taxes, a two-level reduction for acceptance of responsibility was reversed because such a finding could not properly be based on the facts that the defendant supposedly never contested his liability, deterrence had already been served by the adverse publicity about the case, and a longer sentence would damage the defendant's law practice.[578]

---

[572] USSG § 3C1.1, Commentary (note 3) (1992).

[573] United States v. Shetty, 80 AFTR2d 97-5616 (9th Cir. 1997).

[574] USSG § 3E1.1 (1987) (Acceptance of Responsibility).

[575] USSG § 3E1.1(b) (1987) (Acceptance of Responsibility).

[576] USSG § 3E1.1, Commentary (note 1) (1992).

[577] United States v. Jagim, 978 F2d 1032 (8th Cir. 1992).

[578] United States v. Chastain, 84 F3d 321 (9th Cir. 1996).

[d] Other Mitigating Circumstances

A general downward reduction or departure is permitted in USSG § 5K2.0 based on "mitigating circumstance[s] of a kind, or to a degree, not adequately taken into consideration by the Sentencing Commission." Restitution has sometimes been claimed to warrant a downward reduction under USSG § 5K2.0. Most courts have held, however, that restitution is not a basis for a sentencing judge to depart downward from the guideline range under USSG § 5K2.0 because the Sentencing Commission considered that restitution might be a mitigating factor under USSG § 3E1.1, which permits a downward departure when voluntary restitution paid before trial demonstrates an acceptance of responsibility.[579]

[4] Step 3: Prior Criminal Behavior

Although defendants in tax cases do not usually have any prior criminal history, the defendant's criminal history and criminal livelihood also affect the sentence determined under the Sentencing Guidelines. Introductory comments to Chapter Four state, "A defendant with a record of prior criminal behavior is more culpable than a first offender and thus deserving of greater punishment." The criminal history category not only has category ranges from I through VI, but the category depends on the number of criminal history points, from zero or one for Category I, to thirteen or more for Category VI. In other words, the number of points dictate the criminal history category and the number of months of incarceration in the guideline range for an offense level. In general, points are assigned to a defendant depending on the number and length of prior sentences of imprisonment. If a defendant was previously sentenced to imprisonment exceeding one year and one month, he is assigned three criminal history points.[580]

[5] Step Four: Determining the Sentence

A sentence of imprisonment conforms with the guideline range if it is within its minimum and maximum terms. If the minimum term of imprisonment in the guideline range on the sentencing table is zero months, a sentence of im-

---

[579] See United States v. Broderson, 67 F3d 452, 458 (2d Cir. 1995); United States v. Bolden, 889 F2d 1336 (4th Cir. 1989); United States v. Harpst, 949 F2d 860, 863 (6th Cir. 1991); United States v. Seacott, 15 F3d 1380, 1388–1389 (7th Cir. 1994); United States v. Chastain, 84 F3d 321 (9th Cir. 1996) (downward departure to facilitate restitution reversed).

[580] USSG § 4A1.1(a).

prisonment is not required. However, if the minimum term is at least one but not more than six months, the minimum term may be satisfied by (1) a sentence of imprisonment; (2) a sentence of probation that includes a condition or conditions that substitute intermittent confinement, community confinement, or home detention for imprisonment; or (3) a sentence of imprisonment that includes a term of supervised release with a condition that substitutes community confinement or home detention, so long as at least one half the minimum term (but not less than one month) is satisfied by imprisonment.[581] If the minimum term of imprisonment is more than six but not more than ten months, the minimum term may be satisfied by the same options described above, except that no sentence of probation may be imposed.

Apart from imprisonment, probation, or supervised release, the court will impose a fine, unless the defendant is incapable of paying a fine or it would unduly burden the defendant's dependents. The fine table establishes the fine minimum and maximum by reference to the offense level. (See Table 7A.3.)[582]

The sentencing court may also order the defendant to make restitution.[583] However, 18 USC § 3663, which grants the sentencing court the power to order restitution and specifies the crimes for which a court may order restitution, does not include crimes described in Title 26. Accordingly, restitution is not authorized in sentencing for tax crimes. There is an exception under which restitution has been ordered in a tax case. The sentencing court, according to 18 USC § 3662, "may . . . order restitution in any criminal case to the extent agreed to by the parties in a plea agreement." In *Gottesman v. United States*,[584] the Second Circuit said that two consequences flow from this language: first, the court can order restitution only if the parties agreed that the court could do so. Consequently, the circuit court held that when the defendant agreed with the government in his plea agreement that he would pay past taxes due and owing "on such terms and conditions as will be agreed upon by Milton Gottesman and the IRS," he did not agree to court-ordered restitution. But another panel in the Second Circuit limited *Gottesman* to the facts of the case (that is, the terms of the plea agreement precluded restitution). While restitution could not be ordered as part of a sentence, it could be authorized in a tax case as a condition of supervised release, so the circuit court upheld the sentence requiring the defendant to pay a percentage of his monthly income against his personal tax liability.[585]

---

[581] USSG § 5C1.1(c) (1989).

[582] USSG § 5E1.2, at 5.18 (1989).

[583] 18 USC § 3663.

[584] Gottesman v. United States, 122 F3d 150 (2d Cir. 1997).

[585] See United States v. Bok, 82 AFTR2d 98-6383 (2d Cir. 1998).

¶ 7A.11 CONVICTION AND ITS CONSEQUENCES

Sentencing guidelines establish the period of incarceration and the fine, but there are other or collateral consequences of conviction of a tax crime. Apart from the sentence, the taxpayer, as a convicted felon, may suffer such civil disabilities as loss of the right to vote and hold public office, and may find it difficult to obtain many jobs, retain professional licenses, maintain legally enforceable agreements and possibly family relations, and secure insurance and pension benefits.[586] These frequently ignored results of a felony conviction depend on state laws, which are by no means uniform. Under some state laws, a tax offense is a misdemeanor, not a felony. In these states, conviction of evasion may not constitute conviction of a crime of sufficient seriousness ("moral turpitude") to warrant loss of a professional license.[587] The taxpayer is not only liable civilly for the tax evaded but as a result of conviction is collaterally estopped from contesting liability for the civil fraud penalty.[588] However, a defendant may not be required as a special condition of probation to pay a specific sum for unpaid taxes where the amount of the civil liability has not been acknowledged or conclusively established in the criminal proceeding, or finally determined in civil proceedings.[589]

---

[586] In Richardson v. Ramirez, 418 US 24 (1974), a state disenfranchisement law was held constitutional.

[587] See Sellin, "Professional Responsibility of the Tax Practitioner," 52 Taxes 584, 609–614 (1974), for a state-by-state survey of disciplinary rules for tax offenses.

[588] Amos v. Comm'r, 360 F2d 358 (4th Cir. 1965); Tomlinson v. Lefkowitz, 334 F2d 262 (5th Cir.), cert. denied, 379 US 962 (1965). Arctic Ice Cream Co., 43 TC 68 (1964). See the discussion at ¶ 7B.01. The issue of fraud and the amount of tax must be distinguished. Even after conviction of evasion, a taxpayer is entitled to contest the amount of the underpayment in tax.

[589] United States v. Franks, 723 F2d 1482 (10th Cir. 1983), cert. denied, 469 US 817 (1984) (cases gathered). Therefore, it is an error for a court in sentencing to require a taxpayer to pay a charged deficiency as a prerequisite of probation or release. United States v. Touchet, 658 F2d 1074 (5th Cir. 1981). However, a taxpayer who has willfully failed to file returns may be required to file them as part of a sentence. See, e.g., United States v. Lacy, 658 F2d 396 (5th Cir. 1981) (failure to fulfill condition of probation of filing returns). See also United States v. Wolters, 656 F2d 523 (9th Cir. 1981) (such a condition does not violate Fifth Amendment rights of taxpayer). A sentence may not be based on the failure of the defendant's refusal to admit an uncharged crime. United States v. Messer, 785 F2d 832 (9th Cir. 1986) (evasion plea; defendant claimed privilege when asked by probation officer about source and amount of income).

TABLE 7A.1
Sentencing Table (in months of imprisonment)

Offense Level	Criminal History Category (Criminal History Points)					
	I (0 or 1)	II (2 or 3)	III (4, 5, 6)	IV (7, 8, 9)	V (10, 11, 12)	VI (13 or more)
1	0–6	0–6	0–6	0–6	0–6	0–6
2	0–6	0–6	0–6	0–6	0–6	1–7
3	0–6	0–6	0–6	0–6	2–8	3–9
4	0–6	0–6	0–6	2–8	4–10	6–12
5	0–6	0–6	1–7	4–10	6–12	9–15
6	0–6	1–7	2–8	6–12	9–15	12–18
7	1–7	2–8	4–10	8–14	12–18	15–21
8	2–8	4–10	6–12	10–16	15–21	18–24
9	4–10	6–12	8–14	12–18	18–24	21–27
10	6–12	8–14	10–16	15–21	21–27	24–30
11	8–14	10–16	12–18	18–24	24–30	27–33
12	10–16	12–18	15–21	21–27	27–33	30–37
13	12–18	15–21	18–24	24–30	30–37	33–41
14	15–21	18–24	21–27	27–33	33–41	37–46
15	18–24	21–27	24–30	30–37	37–46	41–51
16	21–27	24–30	27–33	33–41	41–51	46–57
17	24–30	27–33	30–37	37–46	46–57	51–63
18	27–33	30–37	33–41	41–51	51–63	57–71
19	30–37	33–41	37–46	46–57	57–71	63–78
20	33–41	37–46	41–51	51–63	63–78	70–87
21	37–46	41–51	46–57	57–71	70–87	77–96
22	41–51	46–57	51–63	63–78	77–96	84–105
23	46–57	51–63	57–71	70–87	84–105	92–115
24	51–63	57–71	63–78	77–96	92–115	100–125
25	57–71	63–78	70–87	84–105	100–125	110–137
26	63–78	70–87	78–97	92–115	110–137	120–150
27	70–87	78–97	87–108	100–125	120–150	130–162
28	78–97	87–108	97–121	110–137	130–162	140–175
29	87–108	97–121	108–135	121–151	140–175	151–188
30	97–121	108–135	121–151	135–168	151–188	168–210
31	108–135	121–151	135–168	151–188	168–210	188–235
32	121–151	135–168	151–188	168–210	188–235	210–262
33	135–168	151–188	168–210	188–265	210–262	235–293
34	151–188	168–210	188–235	210–262	235–293	262–327
35	168–210	188–235	210–262	235–293	262–327	292–365
36	188–235	210–262	235–293	262–327	292–365	324–405
37	210–262	235–293	262–327	292–365	324–405	360–life
38	235–293	262–327	292–365	324–405	360–life	360–life
39	262–327	292–365	324–405	360–life	360–life	360–life
40	292–365	324–405	360–life	360–life	360–life	360–life
41	324–405	360–life	360–life	360–life	360–life	360–life
42	360–life	360–life	360–life	360–life	360–life	360–life
43	life	life	life	life	life	life

TABLE 7A.2 —————————————————————
Tax Loss Table

Tax Loss (Apply the Greatest)	Offense Level
(A) $1,700 or less	6
(B) More than $1,700	7
(C) More than $3,000	8
(D) More than $5,000	9
(E) More than $8,000	10
(F) More than $13,500	11
(G) More than $23,500	12
(H) More than $40,000	13
(I) More than $70,000	14
(J) More than $120,000	15
(K) More than $200,000	16
(L) More than $325,000	17
(M) More than $550,000	18
(N) More than $950,000	19
(O) More than $1,500,000	20
(P) More than $2,500,000	21
(Q) More than $5,000,000	22
(R) More than $10,000,000	23
(S) More than $20,000,000	24
(T) More than $40,000,000	25
(U) More than $80,000,000	26

TABLE 7A.3 —————————————————————
Fine Table

Offense Level	A Minimum	B Maximum
3 and below	$ 100	$ 5,000
4–5	250	5,000
6–7	500	5,000
8–9	1,000	10,000
10–11	2,000	20,000
12–13	3,000	30,000
14–15	4,000	40,000
16–17	5,000	50,000
18–19	6,000	60,000
20–22	7,500	75,000
23–25	10,000	100,000
26–28	12,500	125,000
29–31	15,000	150,000
32–34	17,500	175,000
35–37	20,000	200,000
38 and above	25,000	250,000

Civil Penalties

B.　PENALTIES ON THIRD PARTIES

C.　PENALTIES ON INFORMATION PROVIDERS

¶ 7B.01 OVERVIEW

Civil penalties are gathered in Chapter 68 of the Internal Revenue Code (the Code), which is entitled "Additions to the Tax, and Additional Amounts, and Assessable Penalties." Penalties categorized as additions to the tax and additional amounts include delinquency penalties (Section 6501), failure by individuals to pay estimated income tax (Section 6654), failure by corporations to pay estimated income tax (Section 6655), and failure to make deposit of taxes (Section 6656). Accuracy-related penalties (Section 6662), the fraud penalty, and definitions and special rules are also included as additions to the tax and additional amounts. Assessable penalties are penalties the Service may assess without restrictions applicable in deficiency cases. These penalties are imposed for failure to pay over collected taxes and to file information returns reporting specified information and transactions (Section 6671 through 6716). In addition, there are assessable penalties for failure to comply with certain information reporting requirements, such as failure to file correct information returns (Section 6721), failure to furnish correct payee statements (Section 6722), failure to comply with other information reporting requirements, and a penalty waiver standard, which has its own definitions and special rules (Section 6724).

Many of these civil penalties are discussed in this chapter. In Part I, Taxpayer Penalties, the emphasis is on the fraud and accuracy-related penalties, and then on delinquency penalties on taxpayers. In Part II, penalties on third parties are described. Finally, in Part III, penalties on information providers are examined in general terms.

A. CIVIL PENALTIES ON TAXPAYERS

¶ 7B.02 THE CIVIL FRAUD PENALTY

A civil fraud penalty is imposed by Section 6663(a), as follows: "If any part of any underpayment of tax required to be shown on a return is due to fraud, there shall be added to the tax an amount equal to 75 percent of the underpayment which is attributable to fraud."[1] The fraud element of the penalty has not

---

[1] Omnibus Budget Reconciliation Act of 1989 (OBRA), Pub. L. No. 239, HR 3299, 101st Cong., 1st Sess., Subtitle G, Improved Penalty Administration and Compliance Tax Act (IMPACT) § 7721(a), amending Subchapter A of Chapter 68 (relating to additions to the tax and additional amounts) by striking Section 6662 and adding new Sections 6662 (accuracy-related penalty), 6663 (fraud penalty), and 6664 (definitions and special rules) for returns the due date for which (determined without regard to extensions) is after De-

been changed since the Code of 1954 was enacted. The term "fraud" means "fraud with intent to evade tax," as the statute stated under the 1939 Code.[2]

After the 1954 Code, the amount of the civil fraud penalty remained unchanged for twenty-eight years. Since 1982, the amount of the penalty has changed several times. From the enactment of the 1954 Code until returns required to be filed before September 4, 1982, the penalty was 50 percent of the amount of the underpayment.[3] For returns and taxes due after September 3, 1982, until returns due before January 1, 1986, the penalty was 50 percent of the underpayment, and, in addition, the taxpayer was obliged to pay a "time-sensitive" portion equal to 50 percent of the interest payable on the portion of the underpayment attributable to the fraud to the earlier of the date the tax was assessed or paid.[4] From 1986, until returns due before January 1, 1990, without extensions, the fraud penalty was 75 percent of the amount of the underpayment attributable to fraud.[5] For returns required to be filed after December 31, 1989, the fraud penalty remains 75 percent of the fraud-tainted portion of the underpayment.

Unlike other civil penalties imposed on taxpayers, the Service has the burden of proving a taxpayer's fraud by clear and convincing evidence.[6] However, the burden of proof initially imposed on the Service is coupled with a presumption drawn against the taxpayer when the Service has carried its burden. Once the Service has produced sufficient evidence to establish that any part of an underpayment was due to fraud, "the entire underpayment shall be treated as attributable to fraud, except with respect to any portion of which the taxpayer establishes (by a preponderance of the evidence) is not attributable to fraud."[7]

Several general observations can be derived from this description of the legislative history:

    1. *The penalty amount.* Over time, Congress has decided that the penalty for fraud, the most serious civil infraction of the tax laws, was not substantial enough. The penalty has been increased first by indi-

---

cember 31, 1989. The House Report on IMPACT (hereafter House Report) is contained in the House Report of the Committee on the Budget, HR Rep. No. 247, 101st Cong., 1st Sess. 271–301, reprinted in 1989-3 CB 1381–1406 (vol. 3).

[2] Internal Revenue Code of 1939 293(b).

[3] Internal Revenue Code of 1954 6653(b).

[4] Tax Equity and Fiscal Responsibility Act of 1982 (TEFRA), Pub. L. No. 248, HR 4961, 97th Cong., 2d Sess. § 325(a), amending IRC § 6653(b)(2), for taxes after September 3, 1982.

[5] Tax Reform Act of 1986 (TRA 1986), Pub. L. No. 514, HR 3838, 99th Cong., 2d Sess. § 1503(a), amending IRC § 6653(b), for returns the due date for which is after December 31, 1986.

[6] See IRC § 7454(a).

[7] IRC § 6663(b).

rect means (the "time-sensitive" penalty raiser) and then more directly by increasing the rate.

2. *The penalty base.* The penalty base for fraud has been narrowed. Until 1986, the ad valorem penalty was imposed on the full amount of the underpayment, even if only a portion of the underpayment was attributable to fraud. In many situations, the full underpayment is attributable to the taxpayer's fraud. However, in other situations, where part of an underpayment was innocent, the taxpayer's punishment was still based on the entire underpayment, including the innocently understated amount. Since 1986, the penalty has been limited to the fraud-tainted portion of the underpayment.

3. *Presumptive fraud.* As is fitting with a penalty that is the civil equivalent of tax evasion, the Service has the burden of proof and is required to adduce evidence of the taxpayer's fraud of a high order (clear and convincing evidence). This procedure had never been changed until the penalty base was limited to the fraud-tainted portion of the underpayment. In 1986, the procedure was modified and complicated for taxpayers by the inclusion of a statutory presumption of fraud relating to the entire amount of an underpayment once fraud has been established as to any part of an underpayment. Therefore, at least theoretically, if the Service proves that a taxpayer omitted $100 of interest on a bank account in an assumed name, every other adjustment is treated as due to fraud unless the taxpayer proves otherwise by a preponderance of the evidence.

4. *Coordination.* Penalties for negligence, delinquency, and fraud were coordinated under the 1954 Code. Where the fraud penalty applied, there could not also be a negligence and deliquency penalty.[8] However, until 1989, the fraud penalty was not coordinated with the new generation of penalties, such as the substantial understatement and valuation penalties. Section 6662(b) provides that the five accuracy-related penalties "shall not apply to any portion of an underpayment on which a penalty is imposed under [section] 6663 [for fraud]." Moreover, neither a fraud penalty nor an accuracy-related penalty can be imposed unless a return is filed.[9] This provision was intended to improve coordination between the fraud and accuracy-related penalties and the failure-to-file penalty.[10]

---

[8] IRC § 6653(b)(3) (1986).

[9] IRC § 6664(b).

[10] HR, 101st Cong., 1st Sess. 271, 285. However, this coordination is imperfect. If a return is filed delinquently, it appears that both a delinquency and an accuracy-related or fraud penalty could be imposed.

[1] Procedural Characteristics of the Fraud Penalty

The Supreme Court has said that the fraud penalty is a civil sanction having a remedial character "primarily as a safeguard for the protection of the revenue and to reimburse the Government for the heavy expense of investigation and the loss resulting from the taxpayer's fraud."[11] Both the determination of liability and the procedure for collection of the penalty are distinctly civil in nature. Liability for the penalty is determined in the same manner as the underlying tax deficiency—that is, a notice of deficiency is sent to the taxpayer following an examination offering the taxpayer the opportunity of prepayment review in the Tax Court.[12]

In the Tax Court, the Commissioner has the burden of proof on the issue of whether the taxpayer has been guilty of fraud with intent to evade tax,[13] by

---

[11] Helvering v. Mitchell, 303 US 391, 401 (1938). The fraud penalty has been said not to be "penal" for double jeopardy purposes, because it reimburses the government for the ancillary costs of investigation and prosecution. Forfeiture may constitute punishment for purposes of the Eighth Amendment, and a civil penalty as well as a criminal sanction may also constitute punishment for purposes of the Fifth Amendment. The imposition of tax and penalties on property already forfeited for violations of the Racketeering Influenced and Corrupt Organizations Act (RICO), 18 USC §§ 1962 and 1963, is not prohibited by the Eighth Amendment and does not constitute excessive punishment, nor does collection of fraud penalties constitute double jeopardy in violation of the Fifth Amendment. McNichols v. Comm'r, 13 F3d 432 (1st Cir. 1993) (a marijuana distributor agreed to the forfeiture and admitted receiving the additional income; distinguishing Austin v. United States, 113 S. Ct. 2801 (1993), and United States v. Halper, 490 US 435 (1989)). Circuit courts concluded that the civil fraud penalty was not sufficiently penal in nature to constitute punishment for purposes of the double jeopardy clause, nor so punitive as to violate the excessive fines clause. See, e.g., McNichols v. Comm'r, supra: I & O Publ'g Co., Inc. v. Ward, 80 AFTR2d ¶ 97-5732 (9th Cir. 1997) (relying on United States v. Mitchell, 303 US 391 (1938), as authority that the penalty was remedial and primarily serves as a safeguard for the protection of the revenue and to reimburse the costs of investigation); see also United States v. Alt, 83 F3d 779, 781 (6th Cir. 1996) (also distinguishing Halper and Austin, as well as Department of Revenue v. Kurth Ranch, 511 US 767 (1994)).

The Supreme Court's decision in Hudson v. United States, 118 S. Ct. 488 (1997), should eliminate the contention altogether because the statute itself must be shown to have been enacted to impose a successive criminal, rather than civil, sanction. See Louis v. Comm'r, 83 AFTR2d ¶ 99-549 (9th Cir. 1999) (applying Hudson, and upholding the civil fraud penalty). For further analysis of the cases, see ¶ 7B.01[3][b], infra note 127. The purpose of the civil fraud penalty is said to be to reimburse the Service for the additional costs of a fraud investigation and loss of revenue; therefore, the Tax Court has said that it would frustrate this purpose to permit a taxpayer to reduce the amount of the civil fraud penalty by the amount of the taxpayer's criminal fine imposed as part of the judgment in a criminal prosecution. Schachter v. Comm'r, 113 TC 192 (1999).

[12] IRC §§ 6659(a), 6659(b). The taxpayer may, of course, pay the tax and, after filing a claim for refund, institute a suit for refund in a district court or the Claims Court. Most taxpayers choose to avail themselves of prepayment review in the Tax Court.

[13] IRC § 7454(a).

clear and convincing evidence.[14] On the other hand, the presumption of correctness attaching to the determination of the amount of a deficiency still applies in the Commissioner's favor.[15] The result is a bifurcated proceeding in which the Commissioner must produce evidence to establish fraud and has the burden of proof on this issue, while the taxpayer must produce evidence to disprove the correctness of the Service's deficiency determination and has the burden of proof for the correct amount of tax. The Commissioner's burden of proof on the fraud issue (clear and convincing evidence) is greater than the taxpayer's burden of proof on the deficiency issue (more likely than not). Since the Commissioner must establish fraud by clear and convincing evidence, the government must produce evidence that has a greater probative value than the mere preponderance of the evidence that the taxpayer must produce to justify setting aside the deficiency. Separating these distinct issues and burdens of proof is difficult enough, but the proceeding is complicated still further by the statutory presumption of fraud where the Service establishes that any portion of the underpayment is due to fraud.

The term "underpayment" is specially defined in Section 6664(a). In general, an underpayment is determined in roughly the same manner as a deficiency. In contrast to prior law, where the 50 percent fraud penalty was applied to the entire underpayment, the 75 percent fraud penalty is applied to the fraud-tainted portion of the underpayment.[16] Therefore, if there is a $1 mil-

---

[14] Tax Court Rule 142(b). This rule apparently does not mean the Commissioner must produce affirmative proof of fraud in all cases. Gordon v. Comm'r, 73 TC 736 (1980) (default judgment on fraud issue where taxpayer failed to appear at trial). Where taxpayers have failed to comply with discovery orders of the Tax Court, their petitions are liable to be dismissed with the result that judgment is granted in favor of the respondent. Tax Court Rule 104(c). This situation has been held to result in a default judgment to be granted in favor of the Commissioner on the fraud penalty. Rechtizigel v. Comm'r, 78 TC 132 (1982), aff'd per curiam, 703 F2d 1063 (8th Cir. 1983). The Tax Court also holds that the taxpayer's failure to reply to the Commissioner's answer is deemed an admission of the allegations of fact in the answer, satisfying the Commissioner's burden of proving fraud. Hicks v. Comm'r, 46 TCM 1135 (1983); Breger v. Comm'r, 46 TCM 983 (1983); Hatcher v. Comm'r, 45 TCM 1363 (1983). Compare Douge v. Comm'r, 899 F2d 164 (2d Cir. 1990) (taxpayers actively contested allegations of fraud, but neglected to prepare for trial; held, proper to dismiss petition, but default judgment could not be entered on fraud issue without evidence and findings of fact; Rechtizigel distinguished).

[15] Tax Court Rule 142(a). The presumption of correctness is explained at ¶ 1.05[2][c]. See Zack v. Comm'r, 692 F2d 29 (6th Cir. 1983), cert. denied, 460 US 1084 (1983) (making the distinction between the burdens on the fraud and deficiency issues). The Third Circuit has summarized the issues and applicable law on the presumption of correctness and the distinct burdens of going forward with evidence of proof. See Anastasato v. Comm'r, 794 F2d 884 (3d Cir. 1986).

[16] IRC § 6663(a). For prior law cases, see Biggs v. Comm'r, 440 F2d 1, 6 (6th Cir. 1971); Webb v. Comm'r, 394 F2d 366, 378 (5th Cir. 1968). See O'Connor v. Comm'r, 412 F2d 304, 310 (2d Cir.), cert. denied, 397 US 921 (1969) (same result under 1939 Code). For a discussion of the definition of underpayment, see infra ¶ 7B.05[1].

lion underpayment, but only $100 of the underpayment is due to fraud, the penalty is calculated only on the fraud-tainted portion of the underpayment (i.e., 75 percent of $100).

If any part of an underpayment is due to fraud, no accuracy-related penalty can also be imposed on that portion of the underpayment.[17] It is less certain that a delinquency penalty for failure to file a timely return cannot be imposed if a return has been filed, albeit late, and the penalty for fraud is assessed.[18] However, the penalty for underpayments of estimated tax may be asserted.[19]

There is no lesser-included-offense concept applicable to civil penalties. Courts will not on their own determine that a taxpayer is liable for a negligence penalty where only a fraud penalty is asserted. Therefore, the Commissioner usually alleges, in the alternative, that if the fraud penalty is not due, the taxpayer is subject to a negligence penalty.

The fraud penalty survives death. If the fraudulent return was filed before the taxpayer's death, liability for the penalty survives the taxpayer's death and is collectible from his estate, even if the fraud is discovered after death.[20] A discharge in bankruptcy does not discharge an individual taxpayer from any debt for a fraud penalty.[21] The Service will not claim the penalty in bankruptcy proceedings (although it will claim it in receivership and assignments for benefit of creditors), but will seek payment from the taxpayer-debtor's after-acquired property that is not under the bankruptcy court's jurisdiction.[22] The fraud penalty may also be collected from a corporation where the fraudulent acts of an officer or employee are imputed to the corporation, which can act only through its officers and other agents.[23]

---

[17] IRC § 6662(b).

[18] This result can occur because Section 6653(d) of prior law, which removed the doubt on this issue, was not carried over to Section 6663. It is likely that Congress did not intend both delinquency and fraud penalties to be imposed, since it added an enhanced delinquency penalty (Section 6651(f)) for fraudulent delinquencies.

[19] See, e.g., Roth v. Comm'r, 75 TCM 1624 (1998).

[20] Estate of Reimer v. Comm'r, 12 TC 913 (1949), aff'd per curiam, 180 F2d 159 (6th Cir. 1950); Estate of Rau v. Comm'r, 301 F2d 51 (9th Cir. 1962), cert. denied, 371 US 823 (1962).

[21] 11 USC § 523(a)(1)(C).

[22] Rev. Rul. 68-574, 1968-2 CB 595. The Service will also not set off the fraud penalty against refunds due the bankrupt. Rev. Rul. 71-31, 1971-1, CB 408.

[23] Trans Miss. Corp. v. Comm'r, 494 F2d 770 (5th Cir. 1974); Ruidoso Racing Ass'n v. Comm'r, 476 F2d 502 (10th Cir. 1973); Asphalt Indus., Inc. v. Comm'r, 384 F2d 229 (3d Cir. 1967); Irving S. Federbush, 34 TC 740 (1960), aff'd on other issues per curiam, 325 F2d 1 (2d Cir. 1964); Auerbach Shoe Co. v. Comm'r, 216 F2d 693 (1st Cir. 1954); American Lithofold Corp., 55 TC 904 (1971). When there has been a fraudulent diversion of corporate receipts, earnings and profits of a cash basis taxpayer corporation are not reduced by the amount of accrued but unpaid taxes, penalties, and interest. Mazzocchi Bus

[2] Proof of Underpayment

For the fraud penalty to be imposed, there must be (1) an underpayment of tax required to be shown in a return (2) that is due to fraud. In general, an underpayment for purposes of the fraud and accuracy-related penalty is defined in Section 6664(a) as the amount by which the taxpayer's correct tax is greater than the tax reported on the return.[24] Proof that a taxpayer has underpaid tax serves two purposes. First, a taxpayer's failure to report all of his income or overstated deductions is evidence, albeit not conclusive evidence, from which a taxpayer's fraudulent intent may be inferred.[25] Second, without an underpayment, there is no penalty because there can be no intent to evade tax.[26] Therefore, even if the taxpayer intends to defraud but his return is inadvertently correct, he cannot be liable for the fraud penalty. To put it another way, for purposes of the civil penalty, fraud connotes an attempt to evade a tax as is required by the evasion statute explicitly for purposes of the criminal penalty.[27] Consequently, in establishing a taxpayer's liability for the fraud penalty, the Commissioner has the burden of proving that the taxpayer attempted to evade some tax.[28]

Evidence of an underpayment may be obtained by proof that specific transactions giving rise to gross income were omitted from the return. Apart from direct evidence, the same circumstantial methods of proof used in criminal prosecutions may be utilized by the Commissioner (i.e., net worth, expenditures, bank deposits, and miscellaneous methods). However, in civil penalty cases a wider range of circumstantial methods of proof can be used than are found in criminal cases. For example, in civil penalty cases, the percentage

---

Co. v. Comm'r, 14 F3d 932 (8th Cir. 1994) (Reg. § 1.312-6 applied, which prohibits cash basis taxpayers from using the accrual method in computing earnings and profits). See also FSA 1999-1217 (Nov. 2, 1993) (the National Office has indicated that a corporation can be held liable for the fraud penalty due not only to the actions of its officers, but also to fraud committed by a high-level employee).

[24] IRC § 6664(a). The definition of an underpayment is discussed infra at ¶ 7B.05[1].

[25] Lillian Kilpatrick, 22 TC 446, 457–458 (1954).

[26] Jenkins v. United States, 313 F2d 624, 627 (5th Cir. 1963); Elfmon v. United States, 209 F2d 642, 643 (4th Cir. 1954).

[27] See Derksen v. Comm'r, 50 TCM 1005 (1985) (taxpayer had the subjective intent to defraud the government, but the Service failed to prove that there was unreported income and, therefore, an underpayment). The evasion statute is discussed at ¶ 7A.02.

[28] This point is not always clearly articulated. See Goodwin v. Comm'r, 73 TC 215, 238 (1979) (Featherston, C.J., dissenting) ("[i]t is the attempt to evade tax which is tantamount to fraud"). As a practical matter, in presenting evidence on the fraud issue, the Commissioner will produce prima facie evidence of the amount of the tax allegedly underpaid due to the fraud. The Tax Court later recognized the point. Hebrank v. Comm'r, 81 TC 640, 642 (1983); Wright v. Comm'r, 84 TC 638 (1985) ("the attempt to evade is the gravamen of fraud"). Compare Parks v. Comm'r, 94 TC 654 (1990) (referring to "fraudulent intent," but finding such intent to exist by reasons of attempt-type conduct).

mark-up method has been used,[29] as have projections of income,[30] Department of Labor statistics to establish family income,[31] other statistical analyses,[32] source and application of funds analysis,[33] and even otherwise inadmissible ev-

[29] Hyman B. Stone, 22 TC 893 (1954) (acq.) (profit determined by using same rate of mark-up in 1944 and 1945 as existed in 1943). Monthly gross receipts of a massage parlor have been determined by computing an average gross receipt per towel used. Campise v. Comm'r, 40 TCM 211 (1980). Smith v. Comm'r, TC Memo. 1998-143 (1998) (holding that the Service may use the gross profits method as long as the method is reasonably implemented).

[30] Mitchell v. Comm'r, 416 F2d 101 (7th Cir.), cert. denied, 396 US 1060 (1970); Gerardo v. Comm'r, 34 TCM 1980 (1975), aff'd in part and remanded in part, 552 F2d 549 (3d Cir. 1977); Rowell, Jr. v. Comm'r, 884 F2d 1085 (8th Cir. 1989) (estimated number of returns taxpayer prepared were multiplied by average amount of unreported checks deposited). Bradford v. Comm'r, 796 F2d 303 (9th Cir. 1986) (extrapolation of sales income from sample generated by an FDA surveillance). But compare Weimerskirch v. Comm'r, 596 F2d 358 (9th Cir. 1979), rev'g 67 TC 672 (1977) (projection improper where no evidence linking taxpayer to income-producing activity) and Coleman v. United States, 704 F2d 326 (6th Cir. 1983) (assessments found arbitrary and unenforceable where government did not present any evidence to support its conclusions). Savage v. Comm'r, 63 TCM 2034 (1992) (method used to reconstruct bartender's tip income rejected); Day v. Comm'r, 975 F2d 534 (8th Cir. 1992) ("The Commissioner extrapolated information from 1982 to determine the extent of unreported income (from massage parlor business) for 1983. The approach is not unreasonable."). As *Day* observes, if the taxpayer fails to present any evidence to rebut the Service's income reconstruction method, his objection to the Service's method generally will not be upheld, if only because the taxpayer has failed to prove that the Service's determination was erroneous. Nevertheless, the absence of adequate records does not give the Service "carte blanche for imposing Draconian absolutes." Webb v. Comm'r, 394 F2d 366, 372–373 (5th Cir. 1968).

[31] Giddio v. Comm'r, 54 TC 1530 (1970) (Department of Labor statistics have been used to establish the income a taxpayer must have earned to support a family the size of the taxpayer's in the locality in which he lived); Carroll F. Schroeder, 40 TC 30, 32 (1963).

[32] Davies v. Comm'r, 42 TCM 768 (1981), appeal dismissed, 715 F2d 435 (9th Cir. 1983) (statistical analysis and projections of "tokes" received by blackjack dealers). Formulas based on sales to customers have been used to compute the tip income a waitress or waiter received. Cracchiola v. Comm'r, 643 F2d 1383 (9th Cir. 1981); Mendelson v. Comm'r, 305 F2d 519 (7th Cir.), cert. denied, 371 US 877 (1962).

[33] The cash expenditures (or source and applications of funds) method has been recognized. Petzoldt v. Comm'r, 92 TC 661 (1989); see also Erickson v. Comm'r, 937 F2d 1548, 1553 (10th Cir. 1991); Jones v. Comm'r, 903 F2d 1301, 1303 (10th Cir. 1990). If this method is used, the IRS need not demonstrate a likely taxable source for the money deposited in the taxpayer's account, but it can present evidence that the taxpayer actually had the money by documenting the activity in the taxpayer's account. Erickson v. Comm'r, supra; Williams v. Comm'r, 999 F2d 760 (4th Cir. 1993) (only a "minimal evidentiary showing" is needed to shift burden of proof to taxpayer; link found from narcotics conviction and the criminal trial testimony of an associate); see Tokarski v. Comm'r, 86 TC 74, 76–77 (1986) (in illegal income case, Commissioner must come forward with evidence linking the taxpayer to an income-producing activity when there is no evidence that the taxpayer received anything during the tax period in issue).

idence.[34] Nevertheless, to establish an underpayment in penalty cases, the Service statistically uses the specific items method most frequently and, of the circumstantial methods, the bank deposits method more than the net worth method.[35] Of course, despite its use of different indirect methods of proof, the predominant method of proof it uses is proof of specific items of unreported income or overstated deductions.[36]

[a] Bank Deposits Method

Under the bank deposits method, (1) the taxpayer's bank deposits and cash expenditures are totaled; (2) nonincome deposits, redeposits, or transfers are eliminated; and (3) an excess of deposits as adjusted over reported income is assumed to constitute unreported income. The bank deposits method has been sanctioned in civil tax penalty cases, including those involving the fraud penalty.[37] This method serves to establish additional income and fraud, an issue on which the Commissioner has the burden of proof. Bank deposits standing alone do not prove the receipt of income.[38] Nevertheless, some courts say that bank deposits, where established to be in excess of reported income, are prima facie evidence of income, which shifts the burden of coming forward with evidence to the taxpayer.[39] Use of this method in fraud penalty cases thus creates some confusion over what the Commissioner is required to show in

---

[34] It has been held that the Service is permitted to rely on inadmissible evidence "for the limited purpose of determining whether its reconstruction of gross wagers rested on a reasonable basis." DiMauro v. Comm'r, 706 F2d 882 (8th Cir. 1983) (inadmissible affidavit of person who allegedly placed wagers with taxpayer; citing Avery v. Comm'r, 574 F2d 467 (9th Cir. 1978)).

[35] Hoff, "Tax Withholding at Source Would Reduce Underreporting of Income on False Returns," 15 Tax Notes 443, 446 (1982) (analysis of 359 fraud and negligence penalty cases decided from 1967 through 1977 showed the specific items method was used in 37.6 percent of the cases, the bank deposits method in 25.6 percent, and the net worth method in 13.1 percent of the cases).

[36] There are many cases; but see, e.g., Karcho v. Comm'r, TC Memo. 2000-213 (2000) (where the Service used the taxpayers' records to show unreported cash receipts, and backed up this analysis with an expenditures analysis).

[37] See, e.g., Parks v. Comm'r, 94 TC 654 (1990); Goe v. Comm'r, 198 F2d 851 (3d Cir.) cert. denied, 344 US 897 (1952); Halle v. Comm'r, 175 F2d 500 (2d Cir. 1949), cert. denied, 338 US 949 (1950); Hague's Estate v. Comm'r, 132 F2d 775 (2d Cir. 1943), cert. denied, 338 US 549 (1949); Harper v. Comm'r, 54 TC 1121 (1970); Herman J. Romer, 28 TC 1228 (1957). See also Insolera v. Comm'r, 80-1 USTC ¶ 9164 (2d Cir. 1980).

[38] Goe v. Comm'r, 198 F2d 851 (3d Cir.), cert. denied, 344 US 897 (1952); Henry M. Rodney, 53 TC 287 (1969).

[39] Parks v. Comm'r, 94 TC 654 (1990); Hague's Estate v. Comm'r, 132 F2d 775 (2d Cir. 1943), cert. denied, 338 US 549 (1949). For this reason, it is said that the Commissioner's determination is presumptively correct. Harper v. Comm'r, 54 TC 1121, 1129 (1970).

presenting evidence of additional income and fraud. The confusion may be deepened by the fact that the bank deposits method is used in negligence penalty cases as well.[40] As a result, there has been a tendency to overlook the different burdens of proof in fraud (clear and convincing evidence) and negligence (preponderance of evidence) penalty cases and the party on whom the burden is placed (Commissioner versus taxpayer).[41]

Proper use of the bank deposits method in fraud penalty cases requires the Commissioner to establish the requisite elements of the method as developed in criminal cases. Only in this way can he establish a foundation for the permissible inference of additional income and fraud, as well as the shifting of the burden of coming forward with evidence to the taxpayer.[42] For example, it is properly part of the Commissioner's case to identify and account for nonincome deposits.[43] Without the elimination of nonincome deposits, the Commis-

---

[40] L. Glenn Switzer, 20 TC 759 (1953); Estate of Mason v. Comm'r, 64 TC 651 (1975), aff'd, 566 F2d 2 (6th Cir. 1977).

[41] See, e.g., Harper v. Comm'r, 54 TC 1121 (1970); Estate of Mason, 64 TC 651 (1975), aff'd, 566 F2d 2 (6th Cir. 1977).

[42] In negligence penalty cases, the Commissioner does not have the burden of proof, so presentation of evidence in strict compliance with the bank deposits method may be excused. Nevertheless, the Tax Court has held in a bank deposits case that the Commissioner need not produce evidence linking the taxpayer to an income-producing activity as a precondition to requiring the taxpayer to satisfy his burden of proof. Tokarski v. Comm'r, 87 TC 74 (1986). However, the Third Circuit has stated that "given the obvious difficulties in proving the nonreceipt of income, we believe the Commissioner should have to provide evidence linking the taxpayer to the tax-generating activity in cases involving unreported income, whether legal or illegal." Anastasato v. Comm'r, 794 F2d 884 (3d Cir. 1986). Compare Parks v. Comm'r, 94 TC 654 (1990) ("[r]espondent did not prove a likely source of petitioner's unreported income. Thus, in order to satisfy his burden of proving an underpayment respondent must disprove petitioner's allegation of a cash hoard," i.e., a nontaxable source).

[43] Hoefle v. Comm'r, 114 F2d 713 (6th Cir. 1940); T.O. McCamant, 32 TC 824 (1959); Denny York, 24 TC 742 (1955). See Drinkhouse v. Comm'r, 225 F2d 874 (2d Cir. 1955) (Commissioner has burden of proving unexplained bank deposits derived from currently taxable income); Raymond v. Comm'r, 46 TCM 1556 (1983) (citing Drinkhouse). Redeposits should be eliminated in bank deposits case. See Estate of Mason, 64 TC 651 (1975), aff'd, 566 F2d 2 (6th Cir. 1977) (check kiting found). See also Maddox v. Comm'r, 46 TCM 809 (1983) (deposits analyzed and kiting explanation rejected). There is a difference, albeit one that is not always made, between a claim that the Service has not properly conducted its bank deposits analysis according to the method that has been accepted by courts (a claim going to improper methodology), and the claim that the results of the analysis are incorrect (a claim going to the data used). However, the taxpayer must make some showing in support of either or both claims. See Parks v. Comm'r, 94 TC 654 (1990) ("the burden is on petitioner to prove that respondent's determination of unreported income, computed using the cash deposits and expenditures method of reconstructing income, is incorrect"). On the burden of the Commissioner in a bank deposits case, the Tax Court has also said that when the Commissioner has submitted copies of bank records disclosing all deposits to, and disbursements from, the taxpayer's bank ac-

sioner cannot be said to be using the bank deposits method, but only making the determination that a bank deposit is the equivalent of income. Consequently, it is improper in a fraud case where the bank deposits method is purportedly used for a taxpayer to be required to establish that deposits do not consitute income before the Commissioner takes preliminary steps to identify nonincome deposits. The typical line of defense in bank deposits cases, at any rate, is the identification of nontaxable deposits, such as loans, gifts, inheritances, or deposits of amounts previously accumulated.[44]

---

counts, and submits an analysis of the bank accounts on schedules, which summarize all of the transactions, deposits, and disbursements occurring in the account, the Commissioner has properly calculated the taxpayer's income based on the bank deposits method. DiLeo v. Comm'r, 96 TC 858, 871 (1991), aff'd, 959 F2d 16 (1992). The taxpayer objected that the Commissioner had not submitted proper bank deposits proof (that is, the methodology was not consistent with the method described in criminal tax cases), but this was unpersuasive to the Tax Court because the taxpayer apparently was unable to point to specific errors in the data the Commissioner used. Once the Commissioner has properly used the bank deposits method, the court said, because of the presumption of correctness, the taxpayer bears the burden of proving that the Commissioner's bank deposits determination is incorrect. The distinction is that in civil tax cases, the presumption of correctness, which of course does not apply in criminal tax cases, requires the taxpayer to present evidence to show error in the Commissioner's analysis in order to show that either the methodology or the result or both were flawed. Claims that the Commissioner has failed to follow the precise steps used in a criminal case will not be sufficient. See Day v. Comm'r, 975 F2d 534 (8th Cir. 1992), discussed infra note 63.

[44] See Parks v. Comm'r, 94 TC 654 (1990) ("[r]espondent may disprove [an] alleged specific nontaxable source of [bank deposits and expenditures] through showing that his reconstruction of income is accurate combined with a showing that petitioner's allegation of a cash hoard is inconsistent, implausible, and not supported by objective evidence in the record"). Estate of Sandler v. Comm'r, 38 TCM 915 (1979); Vena v. Comm'r, 29 TCM 195 (1970); Estate of Gladys Horwitz, 24 TCM 1464 (1965); Schlang v. Comm'r, 42 TCM 948 (1981) (a negligence penalty case in which a gift explanation was not accepted); Mahigel v. Comm'r, 46 TCM 1217 (1983) (loan explanation not substantiated). For cases where the taxpayer has presented sufficient evidence to show the existence of a cash hoard, see, e.g., Beard v. Comm'r, TC Memo. 1998-110 (1998) ("In challenging respondent's income reconstruction, petitioners introduced evidence that was intended to corroborate their claim that the deposits were due to nontaxable sources [which] primarily consists of their testimony, bank account statements, credit card statements, and canceled checks."); Kim v. Comm'r, TC Memo. 2000-83 (2000) (loan defense not substantiated because purported lenders did not testify; no evidence was presented about the source of funds for the loans, nor about when, and by what means, the funds were transferred; and the one alleged lender, who did testify, was not credible because her testimony about transferring the amount of an inheritance to the taxpayers was not supported by any documentary evidence).

[b] Net Worth Method

Evidence of unreported income may also be established by the net worth method.[45] An essential condition to the use of the net worth method is the taxpayer's opening net worth, because the taxpayer's opening net worth serves as a starting point from which to calculate future increases in the taxpayer's assets.[46] As part of the use of the method, which equates unexplained increases in net worth to unreported income, the government has the burden of proving the taxpayer's opening net worth with reasonable certainty.[47] Defenses in net worth cases generally are directed at increasing the taxpayer's opening net worth by establishing, for example, the existence of prior accumulated funds[48]

---

[45] Manzoli v. Comm'r, 904 F2d 101 (1st Cir. 1990); Morris Lipsitz, 21 TC 917, 931 (1954), aff'd, 220 F2d 871 (4th Cir.), cert. denied, 350 US 845 (1955) ("when the increase in net worth is greater than that reported on a taxpayer's returns or is inconsistent with such books and records as are maintained by him, the net worth method is cogent evidence that there is unreported income or that the books and records are inadequate, inaccurate or false"). However, the "lead-check" rule of Holland v. United States, 348 US 121 (1954), does not apply in a fraud penalty case if the taxpayer has admitted fraud. Tunnell v. Comm'r, 74 TC 44 (1980), aff'd per curiam, 665 F2d 527 (5th Cir. 1981). Compare Fairchild v. United States, 240 F2d 944 (5th Cir. 1957) ("lead-check" rule applied in a fraud penalty case where the Commissioner had the burden of proving both the underpayment and fraud). Nevertheless, the net worth method must be properly used and proved. See, e.g., Curtix v. Comm'r, 623 F2d 1047 (5th Cir. 1980), aff'd in part and remanding in part, 37 TCM 144 (1976) (no finding of opening net worth). See also Axelrod v. Comm'r, 43 TCM 614 (1982) (failure to produce evidence of all taxpayer's assets and liabilities and likely source of unreported receipts).

The reliability of the net worth method depends on the accuracy of the opening net worth method. The Supreme Court in *Holland* held that "an essential condition in cases of this type is the establishment, with reasonable certainty, of an opening net worth, to serve as a starting point from which to calculate future increases in the taxpayer's assets." *Holland*, supra, at 132.

[46] Holland v. United States, 348 US 121, 132 (1954). See discussion of the net worth method at ¶ 7A.02[1][a].

[47] See, e.g., Yoon v. Comm'r, 81 AFTR2d ¶ 98-471 (5th Cir. 1998) (gathering cases, and holding that the Tax Court erroneously placed the burden of proving the opening net worth on the taxpayers, and that the Tax Court's refusal to reduce the taxpayer's opening net worth by outstanding credit card liabilities "flies in the face of necessary condition of the net worth method that the government establish an opening net worth with reasonable certainty").

[48] Manzoli v. Comm'r, 904 F2d 101 (1st Cir. 1990) (cash hoard defense rejected, in part, because taxpayer borrowed money during period he allegedly had accumulated $200,000 in cash); Meyer J. Safra, 30 TC 1026 (1958); Compton v. Comm'r, 47 TCM 124 (1983) (cash hoard; Commissioner failed to prove living expenses of the amount used in net worth analysis); Gallo v. Comm'r, 46 TCM 548 (1983) (cash hoard; Commissioner's opening net worth erroneous). This defense is the second most frequently advanced defense (after a simple denial). See Hoff, "Tax Withholding at Source Would Reduce Underreporting of Income on False Returns," 15 Tax Notes 443 (1982). More frequently, of course, the cash hoard defenses are unsuccessful. See, e.g., Curtix v. Comm'r,

or reducing the assets included in closing net worth by showing that (1) the asset did not belong to the taxpayer at that date; (2) the asset was overvalued; or (3) the asset never belonged to the taxpayer.[49] A particular problem in civil net worth cases is establishing the net worth increase attributable to each year rather than over a period of years. Where the Commissioner has failed to establish such increases, it cannot be assumed that fraud occurred in each of the years.[50]

[3] Proof of Fraud

Fraud is not defined either in Section 6663(a) or in the regulations. Some clue to the meaning of the term may be found from the version of the penalty contained in the 1939 Code, which imposed the penalty for "fraud with intent to

---

623 F2d 1047 (5th Cir. 1980), aff'g in part and remanding in part, 37 TCM 144 (1976). Barnhill v. Comm'r, 46 TCM 577 (183) (court viewed with jaundiced eye "claim that cash hoard kept in freezer wrapped in meat paper"; other prior accumulation explanations rejected).

Opening net worth can be established when all possible sources of nontaxable income claimed by the taxpayer have been negated. Conti v. Comm'r, 39 F3d 658 (6th Cir. 1994) (cash hoard and loan explanations properly rejected because they were inconsistent with prior statements). Erickson v. Comm'r, 937 F2d 1548 (10th Cir. 1991) (IRS not required to establish opening and closing worth when using expenditures method in civil fraud case).

In *Campfield*, the taxpayers claimed that the Service failed to consider a cash hoard of $143,000, which they kept in a safe deposit box, consisting of $66,000 from an insurance recovery for a 1978 fire loss. Campfield v. Comm'r, 80 AFTR2d ¶ 97-5575 (2d Cir. 1997). The circuit court upheld the Tax Court's rejection of the contention because (1) it was "unlikely that a rational economic actor" would keep a substantial sum in a safe deposit box where it was not earning interest when Campfield maintained an interest-bearing money market account from 1983 through 1986 (during 1983 and 1984, the balances exceeded $40,000); (2) Campfield borrowed money at interest rates of 10 percent and 12 percent during the period the cash hoard allegedly existed; and (3) the modest income Campfield reported in the years before 1984 was insufficient to accumulate about $80,000 in savings, which was part of the cash hoard.

[49] See, e.g., Cleveland v. Comm'r, 46 TCM 257 (1983) (capital loss carryovers available to taxpayer to reduce increases in net worth). The Service does not need to prove both a likely source of taxable income and the absence of nontaxable sources for the income; the test is not conjunctive, and the Service can satisfy its obligation by negating likely sources of nontaxable years. Campfield v. Comm'r, 80 AFTR2d ¶ 97-5575 (2d Cir. 1997) (Service satisfied its burden of proof by showing that Campfield repeatedly denied that at the time he accumulated his cash hoard he had received gifts, insurance proceeds, or inheritances).

[50] W.A. Shaw, 27 TC 561, 570–571 (1956), aff'd, 252 F2d 681 (6th Cir. 1958); cf. Cox v. Comm'r, 54 TC 1735, 1741–1742 (1970).

evade tax."[51] The change in the 1954 Code to the imposition of the penalty for "fraud" from "fraud with intent to evade tax" was made without an apparent legislative purpose to change meaning.[52] Thus, it follows that the fraud referred to in Section 6663(a) is fraud with intent to evade tax. Also, fraud itself signifies an intent to deceive, and this intent to deceive overlaps to some extent the conduct involved in evasion. This overlap is reflected in cases holding that a taxpayer convicted of evasion is collaterally estopped from contesting the issue of fraud in a civil penalty case because the conviction necessarily carries with it the ultimate factual determination that the deficiency was due to fraud.[53] Accordingly, a taxpayer who willfully attempts to evade tax also underpays tax with the requisite fraudulent intent for purposes of the civil penalty statute. The evasion element in fraud makes principles announced in evasion cases— that willful conduct is an intentional violation of a known legal duty (*Pomponio*)[54] and that "conduct, the likely effect of which would be to mislead or conceal," is evidence from which a willful attempt may be inferred (*Spies*)[55]—seem also to apply to the civil fraud penalty. Thus, the longstanding definition of fraud articulated in *Mitchell v. Comm'r*, under the 1939 Code version of the penalty, remains authoritative:

> Negligence, whether slight or great, is not equivalent to the fraud with intent to evade tax named in the statute. The fraud meant is actual, intentional wrongdoing, and the intent required is the specific purpose to evade a tax believed to be owing.[56]

Finally, the deception and misleading conduct characteristic of fraud distinguishes fraud from tax avoidance devices. Both may result in underpayments in tax, but tax avoidance is characterized by disclosure of transactions that are,

---

[51] Section 293(b) of the 1939 Code provided, "[i]f any part of any deficiency is due to fraud with intent to evade tax, then 50 per centum of the total amount of the deficiency (in addition to such deficiency) shall be so assessed, collected, and paid." Section 7454(a), which allocates the burden of proof to the Service in fraud cases states that the burden is on the Service, "[i]n any proceeding involving the issue whether the petitioner has been guilty of fraud with intent to evade tax."

[52] Levinson v. United States, 496 F2d 651 (3d Cir. 1974), cert. denied, 419 US 1040 (1974); Papa v. Comm'r, 464 F2d 150 (2d Cir. 1972); Breman v. Comm'r, 66 TC 61 (1976).

[53] John W. Amos, 43 TC 50 (1964), aff'd, 360 F2d 358 (4th Cir. 1966) (1954 Code case); Arctic Ice Cream Co., 43 TC 68 (1964) (1939 Code case).

[54] United States v. Pomponio, 429 US 10 (1976).

[55] Spies v. United States, 317 US 492 (1943).

[56] Mitchell v. Comm'r, 118 F2d 308, 310 (5th Cir. 1941). Parks v. Comm'r, 94 TC 654 (1990) ("[r]espondent must prove by clear and convincing evidence that petitioner had the requisite fraudulent intent ... the intent to mislead or conceal may be inferred from a pattern of conduct").

in fact, what they appear to be, for example, a sale that is not a sham as a matter of fact, or a sale that takes place on the date stated.[57]

To say that fraud means a willful evasion does not suggest the wide range of conduct that may constitute fraud. This issue is presented in fraud penalty

---

[57] In Helvering v. Mitchell, 303 US 391 (1938), there was a purported sale at a loss by the husband to his wife of stock that she lacked the funds to pay for and that the husband continued to use as collateral for a loan. When a taxpayer has informed the Service of his refusal to file or to pay, the lack of deception or concealment has been found not to be consistent with fraud. Raley v. Comm'r, 676 F2d 980 (3d Cir. 1982); Zell v. Comm'r, 763 F2d 1139 (10th Cir. 1985) (divided court).

Both Raley and Zell were tax protestors, and, in both cases the circuit courts held that the failure to file a return, standing alone, was not clear and convincing evidence of fraud and that there must be some evidence of deception or concealment. In *Raley*, the circuit court acknowledged that the taxpayer had willfully failed to file returns, filed false withholding forms, filed returns falsely designating them as amended returns, and refused to sign the returns under penalty of perjury. In addition, the taxpayer withheld information from which his income tax could be computed. However, the Third Circuit held that the many letters the taxpayer sent notifying the Service that he had terminated withholding and would not file income tax returns "diluted" the Service's evidence of an affirmative indication of an intent to defraud, below the requisite clear and convincing standard. In *Zell*, the Tenth Circuit followed the principle enunciated in *Raley*, but found the evidence of the taxpayer's false Forms W-4s, failure to file a prior notice in two of the years, and failure to cooperate with the Service sufficient to support a fraud finding. At least two other circuits have found that even with prior notification, the failure to file tax returns, coupled with the filing of false Forms W-4 or other affirmatively fraudulent conduct established an intent to evade payment and justified the imposition of a fraud penalty. See Granado v. Comm'r, 792 F2d 91 (7th Cir. 1986); Edelson v. Comm'r, 829 F2d 828 (9th Cir. 1987). It is difficult to reconcile these decisions; however, the Third Circuit in *Raley* clearly weighed the open and declared refusal to comply with the filing obligation along with the other evidence before the Tax Court in determining that the evidence as a whole did not meet the clear and convincing standard, and in that sense held that prior notice was a factor in evaluating the sufficiency of the evidence of fraud. By contrast, the Seventh Circuit in *Granado* seemed to assume that any other evidence of fraud in addition to nonfiling was sufficient to establish fraud by clear and convincing evidence so that the taxpayer's prior notification was irrelevant in the evidence weighing process. In *Edelson*, the taxpayer's conduct went well beyond nonfiling because the evidence established that the taxpayer filed false returns and was intending to evade payment of tax by making fraudulent transfers of property. In the face of this substantial evidence supporting the Tax Court's fraud finding, the Ninth Circuit properly held that the taxpayer's notification was insufficient.

The view of the Third and Tenth Circuits in *Raley* and *Zell* seems to be proper in requiring that, as a matter of law, the finder of fact must consider a taxpayer's prior notice to the Service in weighing the taxpayer's conduct under the clear and convincing standard. However, the Seventh and Ninth Circuits in *Granado* and *Edelson* also seem to be correct in concluding that prior notice alone cannot immunize a taxpayer from a fraud penalty when the evidence supports the conclusion of the finder of fact. The Service, needless to say, believes that the Third and Tenth Circuits were wrong in *Raley* and *Zell*, and that the Seventh and Ninth Circuits correctly rejected them. Litigation Guideline Memorandum TL-23 (Jan. 22, 1998), reproduced in 98 TNT 52-42.

cases where the taxpayer was convicted of a tax crime that was not evasion; namely, a failure to file tax returns. Under the *Spies* standard, there can be no evasion and, thus, no fraud unless, in addition to the omission, there was some affirmative act or conduct to mislead or conceal. This "affirmative act" test is generally applied in civil fraud cases involving failure to file return.[58] However, in some cases, it has been said that an "affirmative indication," rather than an affirmative act, that the taxpayer has willfully attempted to evade tax is sufficient to establish fraud.[59] Decided cases applying the "affirmative indication" test have involved extended periods of nonfiling[60] by taxpayers with considerable business or professional experience,[61] along with other evidence

---

[58] First Trust & Sav. Bank v. United States, 206 F2d 97 (8th Cir. 1953); Jones v. Comm'r, 259 F2d 300 (5th Cir. 1958); Irolla v. United States, 390 F2d 951 (Ct. Cl. 1968); Grosshandler v. Comm'r, 75 TC 1 (1980) (attorney failed to file returns for four years and also made false statements to IRS agents). The fraud penalty has been applied in failure-to-file situations where affirmative acts of fraud have been proved. Habersham-Bey v. Comm'r, 78 TC 304 (1982) (failure to file, coupled with submission of false Forms W-4 to avoid withholding). In *Habersham-Bey*, the Tax Court stated, "[w]hile failure to file tax returns does not itself establish fraud, such failure may properly be considered in connection with other facts in determining whether an underpayment in tax is due to fraud" (citing *Grosshandler*). See also Pollock v. Comm'r, 45 TCM 12 (1982) (failure to file in 1965 and 1968 coupled with false representations to revenue officer and use of nominee accounts); Dudley v. Comm'r, 44 TCM 763 (1982) (seven-year failure to file plus false representations to agents that returns had been filed); Ammen v. Comm'r, 44 TCM 875 (1982) (failure to file sufficient returns plus attempts to hinder IRS investigation). Compare Nelson v. Comm'r, 45 TCM 1397 (1983) (although taxpayer fraudulently evaded taxes in years he filed returns, no evidence of fraud in year return not filed). Vest v. Comm'r, 65 TCM 2830 (1993) (fraudulent intent to underpay tax was established where taxpayer fabricated lease terms for equipment leased to a hospital in order to claim investment credit). The address for filing Form 8264, Application for Registration of a Tax Shelter, is: Internal Revenue Service, Ogden, Utah 84201. Ann. 2001-62, 2001-24 IRB 1337 (June 11, 2001).

[59] The phrase seems to have first been used in Cirillo v. Comm'r, 314 F2d 478, 482 (3d Cir. 1963). See also Stoltzfus v. United States, 398 F2d 1002 (3d Cir. 1968), cert. denied, 393 US 1020 (1969); Powell v. Granquist, 252 F2d 56 (9th Cir. 1958); Anson Beaver v. Comm'r, 55 TC 85 (1970); Gajewski v. Comm'r, 67 TC 181 (1976), aff'd in unpublished opinion (May 5, 1978). Nevertheless, the taxpayer must be shown to have had actual knowledge of the falsity of the return. Stoltzfus v. United States, 398 F2d 1002, 1004 (3d Cir. 1968), cert. denied, 393 US 1020 (1969); Rowlee v. Comm'r, 80 TC 1111 (1983). Compare Katz v. United States, 321 F2d 7, 10 (1st Cir.), cert. denied, 357 US 903 (1963) ("[i]nnocence cannot outdistance ignorance"). See also Porter v. Comm'r, 51 TCM 1062 (1986).

[60] Stoltzfus v. United States, 398 F2d 1002 (3d Cir. 1968), cert. denied, 393 US 1020 (1969) (fifteen years); Beaver v. Comm'r, 55 TC 85 (1970) (six years).

[61] Stoltzfus v. United States, 398 F2d 1002 (3d Cir. 1968), cert. denied, 393 US 1020 (1969) (businessman who negotiated contracts with government agencies); Beaver v. Comm'r, 55 TC 85 (1970) (CPA who prepared tax returns); Grosshandler v. Comm'r, 75 TC 1 (1980) (attorney).

that may well have been construed as the commission of a willful act.[62] Nevertheless, the Tax Court has held that failure to file a tax return standing alone without other independent evidence does not establish fraud, which is "the intentional commission of an act or acts for the specific purpose of evading a tax believed to be owing."[63]

In practice, although an "affirmative act" versus an "affirmative indication" are different formulations, the difference probably does not lead to different results. However, the affirmative indication standard can mask some misconceptions about the fraud penalty. To the extent that the "affirmative indication" test reduces the burden of proof on the Commissioner to establish fraud, it is untenable. The affirmative indication standard appears to reflect confusion between the lesser burden of proof imposed on the Commissioner to establish civil fraud and the element of the intent to evade implicit in the statutory term "fraud." Evidence insufficient to prove beyond a reasonable doubt a willful attempt to evade can be sufficient to establish fraud by clear and convincing evidence. The quantitative difference in the burden of proof has some effect on the qualitative type of evidence adduced on the fraud issue. Although the penalty statute does not literally require an "attempt" to evade but merely an "intent" to evade, purposive conduct to evade and an attempt to evade are hardly distinguishable. It is clear that a failure to file alone does not establish intent to evade, in the same way that the omission to file does not itself constitute an attempt to evade. For example, many taxpayers who fail to file do so because they lack funds and fear the consequences of filing without payment. Nevertheless, the intent-to-evade element opens inquiry in the civil penalty determination to a broader consideration not only of the actions of the taxpayer at the time the returns were due but to his subsequent conduct and his personal characteristics.

With this background, fraud can be described for purposes of the civil penalty as conduct (1) the likely effect of which is to mislead or conceal and (2) in which the taxpayer voluntarily and intentionally engages to evade a tax he knows he has an obligation to pay.

---

[62] Stoltzfus v. United States, 398 F2d 1002 (3d Cir. 1968), cert. denied, 393 US 1020 (1969) (records possibly inadequate; false statement); Anson Beaver v. Comm'r, 55 TC 85 (1970) (income omitted on delinquent returns); Grosshandler v. Comm'r, 75 TC 1 (1980) (false statements, inadequate records, refusal to cooperate).

[63] Kotmair v. Comm'r, 86 TC 1253, 1261 (1986) (Commissioner failed to produce evidence to support the allegation of fraud other than the failure to file; held, fraud penalty not proper).

[a] Evidence of Fraud

Evidence of fraud is generally circumstantial.[64] The trier of fact must infer the taxpayer's state of mind from evidence other than testimony about the taxpayer's state of mind.[65] What circumstantial evidence establishes civil fraud? Because fraud includes a willful attempt to evade, the requisite state of mind for both the civil and criminal penalty may be inferred from the very same conduct. Therefore, the Supreme Court's nonexclusive list in *Spies* is conduct from which fraud may be inferred:

- Keeping a double set of books;
- Making false entries or alterations, false invoices, or false documents.
- Destroying books or records;
- Concealing assets or covering up sources of income; and
- Handling one's affairs to avoid making records usual in transactions of the kind.

One circuit court has said that a nonexclusive list of badges of fraud includes (1) consistent and substantial understatement of income; (2) failure to maintain adequate records; (3) failure to cooperate with the Service's investigation; (4) inconsistent or implausible explanations of behavior; and (5) awareness of the obligations to file returns and pay taxes.[66] According to the Supreme Court,

---

[64] Of course, this general statement is subject to exceptions. For example, estoppel prevents the taxpayer from relitigating in the civil fraud case factual issues finally determined in a criminal evasion case (i.e., the issue of fraud) and perhaps other criminal tax cases as well.

[65] Because a corporation can act only through its officers, the existence of the corporation's fraud depends upon the fraudulent intent of its officers. Irving S. Federbush, 34 TC 740 (1960). See, e.g., Akland v. Comm'r, 46 TCM 51 (1983), aff'd, 767 F2d 618 (9th Cir. 1985) (sales inflating cost of goods sold known to be fictitious by officers). A fraud finding is reviewable and subject to reversal where the finding is clearly erroneous. See IRC § 7482(a). In Henson v. IRS, 835 F2d 850 (11th Cir. 1988), the Tax Court based its decision on the testimony of a witness who it determined was an unbiased party, but the court of appeals found that such a conclusion totally ignored the record, and directed the Tax Court to reevaluate the testimony of the witness in light of his obvious bias. For another case that illustrates this situation, see Roose v. Comm'r, TC Memo. 1995-585 (1995) (drugstore owners had a specialized accounting system for drugstore businesses, but did not reflect in those accounting records certain receipts such as coupon rebates and credit card receipts; while the accountant could have detected the true income from the business's bank statements, he was given only the accounting records, which the taxpayers knew were incomplete to prepare the tax returns). On the other hand, when a corporation's failure to file timely returns and to deposit and pay taxes are due to embezzlement by its officers, the corporation is not automatically vicariously liable for penalties as a result of the officers' acting without apparent authority. In re American Biomaterials Corp., 954 F2d 919 (3d Cir. 1992).

[66] Campfield v. Comm'r, 80 AFTR2d ¶ 97-5575 (2d Cir. 1997).

dealing in currency (*Spies*),[67] a consistent pattern of income understatement (*Holland*)[68] or overstatement of deductions (*Ragen*),[69] and false statements to agents after the return is filed (*Beacon Brass*)[70] also constitute evidence from which a willful attempt to evade and, therefore, fraud may be inferred.

Fraud penalty cases can be considered in the following categories:[71]

1. Understatement of income, especially where there is a pattern of consistent and substantial understatement and no satisfactory explanation for it.[72] In and of itself, an understatement of income is not sufficient to establish fraud,[73] but a pattern of understatement covering a number of years is evidence that the omissions were intentional.

2. Substantial and unjustified overstatements of deductions, usually where clearly personal expenses are deducted as business expenses either by the taxpayer or by a corporation that he controls.[74] The un-

---

[67] Spies v. United States, 317 US 492 (1943).

[68] Holland v. United States, 348 US 121 (1954).

[69] United States v. Ragen, 314 US 513 (1942).

[70] United States v. Beacon Brass Co., 344 US 43 (1954).

[71] Courts have developed other nonexclusive lists of badges of fraud. One list includes (1) understatement of income; (2) inadequate books and records; (3) failure to file tax returns; (4) implausible or inconsistent explanations of behavior; (5) concealment of income or assets; (6) failure to cooperate with tax authorities; (7) filing false returns; (8) failure to make estimated tax payments; (9) dealing in cash; (10) engaging in illegal activity; and (11) attempting to conceal illegal activity. Bradford v. Comm'r, 796 F2d 303, 307 (9th Cir. 1986), aff'g TC Memo. 1984-601 (1984); Recklitis v. Comm'r, 94 TC 316, 334 (1990), cited in McKenna v. Comm'r, TC Memo. 1998-45 (1998).

[72] Adler v. Comm'r, 422 F2d 63 (6th Cir. 1970) (nine-year pattern coupled with weak explanation); Lessmann v. Comm'r, 327 F2d 990 (8th Cir. 1964) (eight-year pattern); Kalil v. Comm'r, 271 F2d 550 (5th Cir. 1959) (three-year pattern and over 100 percent understatements); Lollis v. Comm'r, 595 F2d 1189 (9th Cir. 1979) (four-year pattern); Schwarzkopf v. Comm'r, 246 F2d 731 (3d Cir. 1957) (five-year pattern); Kurnick v. Comm'r, 232 F2d 678 (6th Cir. 1956) (seven-year pattern); Rogers v. Comm'r, 111 F2d 987 (6th Cir. 1940) (three-year pattern); Vannaman v. Comm'r, 54 TC 1011 (1970) (six-year pattern); Ball v. Comm'r, 44 TCM 863 (1982) (five-year pattern and "unbelievable" explanation regarding dealings in gold coins).

[73] See Hyman B. Stone, 22 TC 893 (1954) (acq.) (gross understatement of income not sufficient to establish fraud although strong evidence of fraud). However, it has also been said that purposely engaging in a sham transaction with the intent to disguise ordinary income as capital gain is strong evidence of fraud. Blanton v. Comm'r, TC Memo. 1997-496 (1997) (former governor's attempt to disguise receipt of finder's fees as proceeds of the sale of a partnership interest held to constitute a sham sale and evidence of fraud); see Fazzio v. Comm'r, 959 F2d 630 (6th Cir. 1992), aff'g TC Memo. 1990-608 (1990).

[74] Hicks Co. v. Comm'r, 56 TC 982 (1971), aff'd, 470 F2d 87 (1st Cir. 1973) (officer's salary accrued but not paid, and personal expenses deducted as corporate business expenses); Zeddies v. Comm'r, 264 F2d 120 (7th Cir. 1959), aff'd TC Memo. 1958-14, cert. denied, 360 US 910 (1959) (overstatement of business expenses); Lash v. Comm'r,

derpayment in tax may also occur by other overstatements, such as dependency exemptions.[75]

3. Putting assets in the name of others[76] and similar attempts to conceal assets or cover up sources of income, such as secret bank accounts,[77] use of currency,[78] and the like.[79]

4. Deliberate failure to keep adequate books and records.[80] This evidence becomes particularly probative of fraud where coupled with other evidence showing that the taxpayer knew the records were inad-

---

245 F2d 20 (1st Cir. 1957) (personal expenses deducted as corporate business expenses); Lowy v. Comm'r, 262 F2d 809 (2d Cir. 1959) (same); G. Douglas Strachan, 48 TC 335 (1967) (same); Coast Carton Co. v. Comm'r, 149 F2d 739 (9th Cir. 1945) (compensation deducted without rendition of services); Bennett E. Meyers, 21 TC 331 (1953) (same); Robert Neaderland, 52 TC 532 (1969), aff'd on another issue, 424 F2d 639 (2d Cir.), cert. denied, 400 US 827 (1970) (gross overstatement of business expenses); Joseph H. Imeson, 14 TC 1151 (1950) (pilot's deduction of personal expenses as business expenses).

[75] Zelma Curet Miller, 51 TC 915 (1969); Rowlee v. Comm'r, 80 TC 1111 (1983) (excessive exemptions); Habersahm-Bey v. Comm'r, 78 TC 304 (1982); Hebrank v. Comm'r, 81 TC 640 (1983) (false W-4 form and altered W-2 form). See also Toussaint v. Comm'r, 743 F2d 209 (5th Cir. 1984) (theft loss deduction held to be fraudulently claimed).

[76] Furnish v. Comm'r, 262 F2d 727 (9th Cir. 1958) (concealed ownership of property); Fred N. Acker, 26 TC 107 (1956) (use of nominees); Sam D. Hecht, 16 TC 981 (1951) (same). The Supreme Court in Spies v. United States, 317 US 492 (1943), said that putting assets in the name of family members was evidence from which a willful attempt to evade might be inferred. Coleman v. Comm'r, 46 TCM 1180 (1983) (false statement about number of Forms 1099 received); Estate of Beck, 56 TC 297, 366 (1971).

[77] Friedman v. Comm'r, 421 F2d 658 (6th Cir. 1970).

[78] Robert Leslie Bowlin, 31 TC 188 (1958), aff'd per curiam, 273 F2d 610 (6th Cir. 1960); Parks v. Comm'r, 94 TC 654 (1990) (taxpayer structured purchase of cashier's checks to avoid the filing of Currency Transaction Reports; actions found to be an attempt to conceal possession of large amounts of cash). The Supreme Court in Spies v. United States, 317 US 492 (1943), said that such conduct was evidence from which a willful attempt to evade might be inferred.

[79] Fields v. Comm'r, TC Memo. 1996-425 (1996) (assignment of commissions earned on services rendered outside United States to a Bermuda corporation, payment of personal expenses from the corporation's account, coupled with taxpayer's failure to report all of the commissions received and amounts paid, as well as the interest earned on the corporation's bank accounts); Stotis v. Comm'r, TC Memo. 1996-431 (1996) (Greek immigrant, who rented two apartments in a New York City apartment building but whose wife and children lived in Greece, took checks he received from his landlord to vacate the apartments to Greece, negotiated them there, and gave the proceeds to his family, later failing to inform his return preparer and making a false statement to the agent).

[80] Lollis v. Comm'r, 395 F2d 1189 (9th Cir. 1979); Estate of Mazzoni v. Comm'r, 451 F2d 197 (3d Cir. 1971); Webb v. Comm'r, 394 F2d 366 (5th Cir. 1968); Schwarzkopf v. Comm'r, 246 F2d 731 (3d Cir. 1957); Bryan v. Comm'r, 209 F2d 822 (5th Cir. 1954), cert. denied, 348 US 912 (1955); Tsuneo Otsuki, 53 TC 96 (1969); Herman J. Romer, 28 TC 1228 (1957); Ball v. Comm'r, 44 TCM 863 (1982) (inadequate records did not reflect all payments received from customers and significant dealings in cash).

equate because there were other accurate records,[81] and the records in question were intentionally false.[82]

5. Misleading conduct during the investigation of the case. False statements to an agent during the investigation may constitute an attempt to evade (*Beacon Brass*).[83] They may also establish fraud where the effect is to hide assets or income.[84] Efforts of the taxpayer to hinder the investigation by, for example, failing to supply records can also be considered evidence of fraud.[85] Clearly, then, destruction of records is evidence of fraud.[86] In civil fraud cases there seems to be greater emphasis than in evasion prosecutions on the education and background of the taxpayer for the purpose of assessing his conduct.[87] Where an educated or relatively sophisticated taxpayer fails to cooperate with agents, the failure or refusal is considered evidence of

---

[81] Webb v. Comm'r, 394 F2d 366 (5th Cir. 1968); Stone v. Comm'r, 56 TC 213 (1971).

[82] American Lithofold Corp., 55 TC 904 (1971) (false invoices). In one case, the Tax Court said that the evidence establishing a specific fraudulent intent to evade tax was the failure of the taxpayer to maintain adequate records to substantiate more than $25,000 in deductions, and the apparent presentation of false and fraudulent documents to support the deductions. Fason v. Comm'r, TC Memo. 1999-405 (1999).

[83] United States v. Beacon Brass Co., 344 US 43 (1954).

[84] Upshaw's Estate v. Comm'r, 416 F2d 737 (7th Cir.), cert. denied, 397 US 962 (1969) (false statement about ownership of buildings and costs of remodeling); Goe v. Comm'r, 198 F2d 851 (3d Cir.), cert. denied, 344 US 897 (1952) (false statement about bank accounts); Tsuneo Otsuki, 53 TC 96 (1969) (failure to disclose bank accounts); William H. Parsons, 43 TC 378 (1964) (failure to disclose account); Madeline V. Smith, 32 TC 985 (1959) (false statement about number of bank accounts); Grosshandler v. Comm'r, 75 TC 1 (1980) (false statements about filing returns).

[85] Gajewski v. Comm'r, 67 TC 181 (1976), aff'd in unpublished opinion (May 5, 1978) (no voluntary production of records or cooperation); Robert Neaderland, 52 TC 532 (1969), aff'd on another issue, 424 F2d 639 (2d Cir.), cert. denied, 400 US 827 (1970) (failure to produce records and misleading conduct); Fred N. Acker, 26 TC 107 (1956) (repeated failure to supply records).

[86] Gromacki v. Comm'r, 361 F2d 727 (7th Cir. 1966); Prokop v. Comm'r, 254 F2d 544 (7th Cir. 1958); Estate of Beck v. Comm'r, 56 TC 297 (1971).

[87] See, e.g., Grosshandler v. Comm'r, 75 TC 1, 19 (1980) (taxpayer was aware of his obligation to file returns because he "was an attorney and a well-educated person"); First Trust & Sav. Bank v. United States, 206 F2d 97 (8th Cir. 1953) (taxpayer who never filed returns had no knowledge of bookkeeping or obligation to file); E.S. Iley, 19 TC 631 (1952).

fraud.[88] For example, in *Fred N. Acker*,[89] the taxpayer, a lawyer with a working knowledge of accounting and some familiarity with the tax laws, was held liable for the penalty in part because he repreatedly failed to comply with requests for records, even after his conviction for failure to file returns.

[b] The Effect of Prior Conviction or Acquittal

Liability for the fraud penalty frequently is at issue after the taxpayer has been prosecuted for some tax offense. Where a civil trial follows criminal proceedings based on the same facts, the judicial doctrines of res judicata and collateral estoppel must be considered. Drastically simplified, res judicata means that a judgment in one action has a binding effect in a second action between the same parties involving the same cause of action. However, collateral estoppel provides that where the second action between the same parties is on a different cause of action, the judgment in the first action operates as an estoppel "only as to those matters in the second proceeding which were actually presented and determined" in the first action.[90] The nominal difference in parties in criminal and civil tax cases (the United States and the Commissioner of Internal Revenue) is not relevant,[91] but res judicata and collateral estoppel normally apply only to the party who is actually convicted in the criminal case. Where a civil trial follows a criminal trial involving the same facts, a different cause of action is involved,[92] so that only the doctrine of collateral estoppel must be considered. However, collateral estoppel is confined to "situations where the matter raised in the second suit is identical in all respects with that decided in the first proceeding and where the controlling facts and applicable legal rules remain unchanged."[93]

---

[88] Lord v. Comm'r, 525 F2d 741 (9th Cir. 1975); Grosshandler v. Comm'r, 75 TC 1 (1980); see also Garfinkle v. Comm'r, TC Memo. 1998-131 (1998) (tax attorney, who sold tax shelter investments, substantially underreported taxable income in part from claiming deductions from the shelter, did not timely file a return, failed to maintain accurate books and records, and did not cooperate with Service agents).

[89] Fred N. Acker, 26 TC 107 (1956).

[90] Comm'r v. Sunnen, 333 US 591 (1948). See Restatement (Second) Judgments § 27 ("[w]hen an issue of fact or law is actually litigated and determined by a valid and final judgment, and the determination is essential to the judgment, the determination is conclusive in a subsequent action between the parties, whether on the same or a different claim").

[91] IRC § 7422(c); Tait v. Western, 289 US 620 (1933).

[92] See Helvering v. Mitchell, 303 US 391 (1938).

[93] Comm'r v. Sunnen, 333 US 591, 592 (1948). See Restatement (Second) Judgments § 28 (Exceptions to the General Rule of Issue Preclusion).

These principles apply to civil tax cases that follow criminal prosecutions, with the following results. A taxpayer's prior acquittal of attempted evasion does not bar the Commissioner from proving fraud at a later civil trial.[94] The

---

[94] Helvering v. Mitchell, 303 US 391 (1938) (acquittal on jury verdict); Neaderland v. Comm'r, 52 TC 532 (1969), aff'd on another issue, 424 F2d 639 (2d Cir.), cert. denied, 400 US 827 (1970) (acquittal on motion); Trafficant, Jr. v. Comm'r, 884 F2d 258 (6th Cir. 1989) (imposition of fraud penalty after acquittal in evasion case is not precluded by doctrine of issue preclusion and double jeopardy; *Mitchell* followed). However, the Supreme Court has recognized that a civil sanction may be so disproportionate to any remedial goal that it constitutes "punishment" for purposes of the double jeopardy clause. United States v. Halper, 490 US 435 (1989) (civil penalty under Civil False Claims Act held overwhelmingly disproportionate to damage caused). Applying *Halper* to the imposition of a civil fraud penalty following a conviction for attempted evasion, the Tax Court has held that the 50 percent fraud penalty of former Section 6653(b) was not "grossly disproportionate to the damage caused to the government by the taxpayer's fraud, which includes the loss of the tax itself, plus the costs of investigation, detection, and recovery of the lost money." Barnette v. Comm'r, 95 TC 341 (1990); see also Iannielo v. Comm'r, 98 TC 165 (1992) (also holding that the failure to report income was discrete from the underlying criminal activity).

In 1980, a taxpayer entered into a plea agreement with the Justice Department, under which he agreed to provide the government with evidence, testimony, and cooperation in connection with a drug investigation in Florida, in exchange for the dismissal of charges of possession of a controlled substance. The taxpayer satisfied his obligations and the criminal case brought against him was dismissed. Subsequent to the dismissal, the Service determined federal income tax deficiencies for tax years 1978 through 1989. The taxpayer asserted that the immunity grant prohibited the prosecution for civil tax violations related to income generated before the agreement. The Eleventh Circuit had previously held that the 1980 agreement did not prohibit prosecution for criminal tax violations allegedly committed in the years following the grant of immunity. Similarly, the Tax Court held that the 1980 agreement did not preclude the Service from pursuing taxes for the years 1978, 1979, and the years after 1979. Harvey v. Comm'r, 78 TCM 60 (1999).

After *Halper*, the Supreme Court decided Austin v. United States, 113 S. Ct. 2801 (1993), finding that a civil drug forfeiture of a defendant's property after he had pleaded guilty to possessing cocaine, constituted a successive punishment in violation of the Eighth Amendment's excessive fines clause. Applying *Halper* and *Austin*, the First Circuit held that the imposition of civil fraud penalties on a convicted drug dealer's unreported income did not constitute successive punishment, even if the drug dealer suffered the forfeiture of assets he acquired with his criminal activities, because the civil fraud penalty was remedial in nature (following Helvering v. Mitchell, supra) McNichols v. Comm'r, 13 F3d 432 (1st Cir. 1993).

No sooner had the First Circuit decided *McNichols* than the Supreme Court again decided a case involving the application of the double jeopardy clause to a civil action that was tied to a criminal conviction. Montana Dept. of Revenue v. Kurth Ranch, 114 S. Ct. 1937 (1994). In *Kurth Ranch*, the Supreme Court held that, having punished the defendants criminally for drug possession, Montana's tax on the possession of illegal drugs that was imposed whether or not the defendants had paid tax on income generated from the illegal activity, violated the constitutional prohibition against successive punishments for the same offense. The double jeopardy clause was violated in part because the defendants' $900,000 tax liability to Montana was not rationally related to the damages suffered by Montana. In *Thomas*, the Fourth Circuit followed *McNichols* and held that the civil fraud penalty that the Service imposed on the unreported income of a taxpayer who had been convicted of conspiracy with intent to distribute cocaine and money laundering, fined, and ordered to forfeit substantial property, did not violate the excessive fines and double jeopardy clauses. This was so because the civil fraud penalty was not punitive, and even if the excessive fines clause was implicated, the penalty was based on the tax deficiency, and all taxpayers forced to pay additions to the tax for civil fraud are treated in the same manner. Thomas v. Comm'r, 62 F3d 97 (4th Cir. 1995) ("Although Thomas may feel as if he is continuing to pay a price for crimes for which he has already served time in prison, paid a fine, and forfeited a substantial portion of his net worth, an important distinction exists between the punishment exacted in the criminal arena and the remedial sanction sought in this civil proceeding").

The Sixth Circuit also ruled that civil tax penalties imposed after conviction and punishment for criminal tax offenses are not "punishment" for purposes of the double jeopardy clause. United States v. Alt, 83 F2d 779 (6th Cir. 1996). After reviewing the Supreme Court cases, the Sixth Circuit said that "only civil tax penalties that constitute 'punishment' are those that do not remotely approximate the amount of money that the Government would be entitled to were it simply trying to recoup a loss." In the case of the civil fraud, substantial understatement, and negligence penalties, there was "no convincing discrepancy between the penalty and the actual loss (or anticipated actual loss)."

After this line of cases, finding that a civil sanction was so punitive that it violated the excessive fines clause, the Supreme Court rejected the *Halper* test for determining whether a civil sanction can violate the double jeopardy clause. Hudson v. United States, 118 S. Ct. 488 (1997). The Supreme Court said that starting with the long-held view that the double jeopardy clause protects imposition of multiple *criminal* punishments for the same offense, *Halper* had proved to be unworkable because it failed to focus on whether the legislature intended the particular successive punishment to be "civil" or "criminal" in nature and instead looked at whether the sanction was so grossly disproportionate to the harm caused as to constitute "punishment." The *Halper* test also evaluated the character of the actual sanctions imposed rather than the "statute on its face" to determine whether it provided for what amounted to a criminal sanction. Using this more traditional approach, the Supreme Court held that the double jeopardy clause was not violated when the Comptroller of the Currency imposed monetary penalties and occupational disbarment on three bank officials who were later criminally prosecuted.

About two years after the Supreme Court's decision in *Hudson*, the Ninth Circuit held that when it considered *Hudson*'s "guidepost" factors, the taxpayer, who had been convicted of tax evasion and subsequently determined to owe civil fraud penalties for the same years, had not produced the "clearest proof" that the civil fraud penalties imposed in his case were "so punitive as to overcome clear congressional intent that they be civil rather than criminal in nature." Louis v. Comm'r, 83 AFTR2d 99-1400 (9th Cir. 1999). Civil fraud penalties, the circuit court concluded, "do not amount to an affirmative disability or restraint, nor have they historically [been] regarded as punishment." Id. Rather, the Supreme Court's decision in *Mitchell* was authority for the view that the civil fraud penalty served primarily to reimburse the government for the expense of investigation and loss of revenue. Even if deterrence was an additional purpose of the penalty, that additional purpose did not render the sanction criminal.

In 1980, a taxpayer entered into a plea agreement with the Justice Department, under which he agreed to provide the government with evidence, testimony, and cooperation in connection with a drug investigation in Florida, in exchange for the dismissal of charges of possession of a controlled substance. The taxpayer satisfied his obligations and the criminal case brought against him was dismissed. Subsequent to the dismissal, the Service

difference in the legal rules relating to burden of proof prevents estoppel from applying because the acquittal is merely an adjudication that the proof was not sufficient to overcome all reasonable doubt of the guilt of the defendant taxpayer. The converse of this rule is not true; courts have held that a taxpayer who is convicted of willful attempted evasion, after either trial or guilty plea, is estopped in a later civil trial from contesting the issue of fraud.[95] Under an identical-issue analysis, conviction of a willful attempt to evade by filing a false return necessarily requires the factual determination that (1) the defendant filed a return; (2) the return falsely understated the tax due and owing[96]; and (3) the defendant did so deliberately, knowing that to do so violated his obligation to file a true and correct return. As a matter of ultimate fact, a defendant found to have willfully attempted to evade tax does so with the requisite fraudulent intent for purposes of the civil penalty, despite the difference in statutory language. The difference in the burden of proof does not prevent application of collateral estoppel, since the government has necessarily carried the lesser civil burden in carrying the greater burden of proof in the criminal prosecution.

Thus, collateral estoppel operates (1) to establish fraud for purposes of imposing the fraud penalty; (2) to establish that the normal three-year statute of limitations does not apply because the return was "fraudulent with intent to evade tax"[97]; and (3) to determine specific facts that were actually determined in the criminal proceeding. Only the taxpayer who was a defendant convicted in the prior criminal proceeding is estopped from relitigating the issues. Thus,

---

determined federal income tax deficiencies for tax years 1978 through 1989. The taxpayer asserted that the immunity grant prohibited the prosecution for civil tax violations related to income generated before the agreement. The Eleventh Circuit had previously held that the 1980 agreement did not prohibit prosecution for criminal tax violations allegedly committed in the years following the grant of immunity. Similarly, the Tax Court held that the 1980 agreement did not preclude the Service from pursuing taxes for the years 1978, 1979, and the years after 1979. Harvey v. Comm'r, 78 TCM 60 (1999).

[95] Amos v. Comm'r, 360 F2d 358 (4th Cir. 1965); Moore v. United States, 360 F2d 353 (4th Cir. 1965), cert. denied, 385 US 1001 (1967); Tomlinson v. Lefkowitz, 334 F2d 262 (5th Cir), cert. denied, 379 US 962 (1965); Armstrong v. United States, 354 F2d 274 (Ct. Cl. 1965); Arctic Ice Cream Co., 43 TC 68 (1964). See also Klein v. Comm'r, 880 F2d 260 (10th Cir. 1989) (argument rejected that estoppel should not apply because taxpayer had evidence of mental illness not presented at criminal trial).

[96] It should be noted that the amounts in issue may vary considerably in the civil case that follows a criminal conviction. This point was made by the dissent in John W. Amos, 43 TC 50 (1964), aff'd, 360 F2d 358 (4th Cir. 1966).

[97] IRC § 6501(c)(1). See Manzoli v. Comm'r, 904 F2d 101 (1st Cir. 1990). While the Tax Court has said that a taxpayer's sophistication, education, and intelligence are relevant in determining fraudulent intent, it has also said that the taxpayer's sophistication, education, and intelligence are not in themselves badges of fraud. Compare Niedringhaus v. Comm'r, 99 TC 202, 211 (1992); with Wickersham v. Comm'r, TC Memo. 1999-276 (1999).

a wife whose husband was convicted of evasion is not collaterally estopped on the fraud issues and is not considered in privity with the husband for purposes of estoppel.[98]

Most evasion convictions result from pleas of guilty. Whether conviction is based on a guilty plea or a verdict is not significant for collateral estoppel purposes. Although the Justice Department's Tax Division opposes this policy, a defendant may, with the consent of the court,[99] enter a plea of nolo contendere, which amounts to an admission of guilt only for the purposes of the criminal proceeding in which the plea is entered.[100] Consequently, a conviction based on a nolo plea does not conclusively establish fraud.[101] Apart from the Tax Division's opposition, whether the court accepts or rejects such a plea depends upon the particular judicial circuit, district, or individual judge.

Once there is a criminal conviction on a charge of filing a false return under Section 7206(1), what preclusive effect does the judgment of conviction have on a later civil fraud penalty issue? In *Wright v. Comm'r*, the Tax Court concluded that the fraud penalty issue is not "identical in all respects" to that decided under Section 7206(1) because intent to evade is not an element of the crime covered by Section 7206(1).[102] As the Tax Court stated:[103]

> In a criminal action under section 7206(1), the issue actually litigated and necessarily determined is whether the taxpayer voluntarily and intentionally violated his or her known legal duty not to make a false state-

---

[98] Henry M. Rodney, 53 TC 287 (1969); CBC Super Markets, Inc. v. Comm'r, 54 TC 882 (1970); Stone v. Comm'r, 56 TC 213 (1971).

[99] Fed. R. Crim. P. 11.

[100] Hudson v. United States, 272 US 451 (1926). A taxpayer who pleads guilty to tax evasion under an *Alford* plea (a guilty plea coupled with an assertion of innocence) is estopped from denying fraud in a later civil tax case. Blohm v. Comm'r, 994 F2d 1542 (11th Cir. 1993). An *Alford* plea is not the equivalent of a plea of nolo contendere, which has no preclusive effect in a later civil case.

[101] Bell v. Comm'r, 320 F2d 953 (8th Cir. 1963).

[102] Wright v. Comm'r, 84 TC 636 (1985) ("[t]hus to the extent that they give collateral estoppel effect to a conviction under section 7206(1) on the issue of intent to evade tax under section 6653(b), Considine v. Commissioner . . . and Goodwin v. Commissioner . . . are overruled"). In adopting this rule, the Tax Court overruled an earlier decision finding that a false statement conviction under Section 7206(1) estopped the taxpayer from contesting his fraudulent intent as to the return. Considine v. Comm'r, 68 TC 52 (1977). The Court of Claims reached a contrary conclusion on other years. Considine v. United States, 645 F2d 925 (Ct. Cl. 1981), cert. denied, 459 US 835 (1982). In still another case involving Mr. Considine, a refund suit in a district court, the Ninth Circuit generally agreed with the Court of Claims analysis of the estoppel issue. Considine v. United States, 683 F2d 1285 (9th Cir. 1982).

[103] Wright v. Comm'r, 84 TC 636, 643 (1985). While a false statement conviction is not preclusive in a civil fraud case on the issue of fraud, the Tax Court has said that under *Wright*, the Section 7206(1) conviction is "probative evidence" that the taxpayer intended to evade taxes. See Welker v. Comm'r, TC Memo. 1997-472 (1997).

ment as to any material matter on a return. See United States v. Pomponio, supra at 12; United States v. Bishop, supra at 360. The purpose of section 7206(1) is to facilitate the carrying out of respondent's proper functions by punishing those who intentionally falsify their Federal income tax returns (United States v. Greenberg, 735 F.2d 29, 31 (2d Cir. 1984); United States v. DiVarco, supra at 673), and the penalty for such perjury is imposed irrespective of the tax consequences of the falsification (Gaunt v. United States, 184 F2d 284, 288 (1st Cir. 1950), cert. denied, 340 US 917 (1951); United States v. DiVarco, 342 F. Supp. 101, 103 (N.D. Ill. 1972), aff'd, 484 F.2d 670 (7th Cir. 1973)). As noted above, the intent to evade taxes is not an element of the crime charged under section 7206(1). Thus, the crime is complete with the knowing, material falsification, and a conviction under section 7206(1) does not establish as a matter of law that the taxpayer violated the legal duty with an intent, or in an attempt, to evade taxes.

Even before *Wright*, the Tax Court, applying the doctrine of collateral estoppel, had concluded that the conviction of a shareholder for filing a false corporate return did not preclude the corporation from challenging the issue of fraud as to the corporation's underpayment of tax; that is, estoppel did not run from the shareholder to the corporation.[104]

Conviction on a charge of willfully filing a false return does not constitute fraud with intent to evade tax where the conviction may be for a *DiVarco*-type false statement (e.g., mislabeling an item of income), where there is deception but no underpayment.[105] In this case, the conduct would appear to amount to fraud with intent not to evade tax but to conceal the source of income.[106]

Where the conviction is for willful failure to file a return, the taxpayer is precluded from contesting the determination that the nonfiling was willful. However, this willful conduct does not, without more, amount to fraud with intent to evade tax.[107] In *Kotmair v. Comm'r*, the Tax Court said:

---

[104] American Lithofold Corp. v. Comm'r, 55 TC 904, 923–924 (1971) (sole shareholder convicted of attempted evasion of corporate taxes); Forkston Fireworks Mfg. Co., Inc. v. Comm'r, TC Memo. 1998-188 (1998) (the shareholder was convicted of aiding and assisting in a false corporation return in violation of Section 7602(2), and after reviewing the decisions in other cases, the court held that "controlling case law clearly holds that a corporation is not collaterally estopped by a prior adjudication involving a shareholder in these circumstances.")

[105] In Goodwin v. Comm'r, 73 TC 215 (1979), the taxpayer was convicted of violating Section 7206(1) on his guilty plea, and a majority of the Tax Court judges held that he was estopped.

[106] See Goodwin v. Comm'r, 73 TC 215 (1979) (Featherston, C.J., dissenting); Considine v. United States, 645 F2d 925, 932 n.20 (Ct. Cl. 1981), cert. denied, 459 US 835 (1982); Considine v. United States, 683 F2d 1288, n.5 (9th Cir. 1982).

[107] Kotmair v. Comm'r, 86 TC 1253 (1986).

[F]or purposes of the fraud addition to tax under section 6653(b), the mere failure to file a return, standing alone, is not sufficient. Although such fact may be considered in conjunction with other facts in the case (Beaver v. Commissioner, supra), there must in addition be some other fact proved which would establish fraudulent intent. Such proof, including circumstantial evidence (Rowlee v. Commissioner, supra), can be accomplished in many ways.[108]

Similarly, conviction of mail and wire fraud does not estop a taxpayer on the issue of civil tax fraud, because fraud with intent to evade tax is not an issue in mail and wire fraud prosecution and conviction.[109]

[c] Presumptive Fraud

Section 6663(b) creates a statutory presumption of fraud. Once the Service has "established" that any part of any underpayment is due to fraud, then Section 6663(b) requires that "the entire underpayment shall be treated as attributable to fraud, except with respect to any portion of which the taxpayer establishes (by a preponderance of the evidence) is not attributable to fraud." In terms of evidence law, this statutory presumption means that if the government proves the basic fact (fraud as to any part of an underpayment), the finder of fact must mandatorily find fraud as to the entire underpayment if there is no rebuttal. To rebut the presumption, the taxpayer has the burden of establishing the nonexistence of the presumed fact (fraud as to all portions of an underpayment). This statutory presumption of fraud is unusual in evidence law. A presumption generally "imposes on the party against whom it is directed the burden of going forward with evidence to rebut or meet the presumption."[110] Although the burden of going forward with evidence is allocated to the party against whom the presumption is directed—in this case, the taxpayer—the burden of proof in the sense of the risk of nonpersuasion does not shift.[111] However, in a fraud penalty case, both the burden of going forward with evidence and the burden of proof can shift. At the outset of the trial, the burden of going forward with evidence of fraud and the burden of proof is on the government. Unlike the nonstatutory presumption, both these burdens can shift during the trial to the taxpayer if the government establishes that any part of the underpayment is due to fraud.

Consequently, the effect of the statutory presumption of fraud is to impose on the taxpayer the burden of producing evidence of reasonable cause

---

[108] Kotmair v. Comm'r, 86 TC 1253, 1261 (1986).

[109] In re Carmel, 134 Bankr. 890, 92-1 USTC ¶ 50,042, 134 BR 890 (Bankr. ND Ill. 1991).

[110] Fed. R. Evid. 301.

[111] Fed. R. Evid. 301.

and good faith for all portions of an underpayment. Allocating this burden to the taxpayer is undoubtedly justified on the premise that, the government having established the fraudulent nature of some part of the taxpayer's return, the rest of the underpayment may reasonably be presumed to be fraudulent. The statutory presumption makes for an exceedingly difficult trial for the taxpayer. The allocations of the burdens of going forward and proof can shift during the trial not just as to the item known to be claimed to be fraudulent, but to all items in dispute. The taxpayer will not know for certain that these burdens have shifted without a ruling from the court during trial that the government has or has not "established" fraud as to a part of the underpayment. Although the trial problem can be removed by the government's identifying the items claimed to be fraudulent before trial, nothing in the statute requires such an issue-narrowing gesture.

[4] Common Defenses

Defenses raised in fraud penalty cases to negate the intent elements are the same as in evasion cases.[112]

[a] Personal Attributes of the Taxpayer

Fraud, for purposes of the civil penalty, requires an intent to evade tax. The personal attributes of the taxpayer, such as education, familiarity with bookkeeping, and business experience, are all considered on the issue of intent. As the Tax Court has said, "[i]n determining the presence or absence of fraud, the trier of fact must consider the native equipment and the training and experience of the party charged."[113] Accordingly, a taxpayer's lack of education and knowledge of bookkeeping may negative fraudulent intent.[114] However, these personal attributes are usually also accompanied by other evidence such as co-

---

[112] It is necessary to note that the taxpayer has the burden of coming forward with evidence to establish a claimed defense. The Tax Court has said that a taxpayer may not merely raise a theoretical defense in an attempt to create a reasonable doubt about the Commissioner's evidence. Brooks v. Comm'r, 82 TC 413, 433 (1984), aff'd without pub. op., 772 F2d 910 (9th Cir. 1985).

[113] E.S. Iley, 19 TC 631, 635 (1952).

[114] First Trust & Sav. Bank v. United States, 206 F2d 97 (8th Cir. 1953) (no knowledge of bookkeeping); John Marinzulich, 31 TC 487 (1958) (taxpayer had third-grade education and was ignorant of accounting methods and tax laws); E.S. Iley, 19 TC 631 (1952) (farm boy with high school education who had no experience in bookkeeping).

operation during the examination,[115] reliance on a tax return preparer,[116] or similar evidence inconsistent with intentional concealment or deliberate misrepresentation.[117] For similar reasons, evidence of mental disease or emotional disorders not amounting to insanity may negate fraudulent intent.[118] Also, a person who is not an expert in the tax laws might not be held liable for the fraud penalty where the facts and issues are complicated.[119]

[b] Shift of Responsibility

An underpayment in tax resulting from careless bookkeeping or return preparation may be attributable to the taxpayer in order to establish that the taxpayer intended to evade tax by filing a fraudulent return. It is said that a taxpayer cannot "escape his responsibility for a correct return by committing its preparation to others."[120] Thus, it may be inferred that the filing of a correct return is a nondelegable duty for breach of which, even by an agent, the principal-taxpayer is liable. However, this proposition states the principle too broadly. Taxpayers who have not prepared their return but have been held liable for the penalty have usually known that the records from which the return

---

[115] First Trust & Sav. Bank v. United States, 206 F2d 97 (8th Cir. 1953); Fame v. Comm'r, 46 TCM 794 (1983).

[116] John Marinzulich, 31 TC 487 (1958).

[117] See, e.g., Delfino v. Comm'r, 42 TCM 1656 (1981) (taxpayer filed delinquent returns before being contacted by Service).

[118] Emanuel Hollman, 38 TC 251 (1962) (conflict between psychiatric testimony and taxpayer's astuteness prevented finding of fraud); cf. Anson Beaver, 55 TC 85 (1970) (deteriorating physical condition and mental distress offset by successive advantgeous changes of employement); Jacob D. Farber, 43 TC 407 (1965) (taxpayer suffering from pituitary tumor and personality change did not lack requisite mental capacity); Wilson v. Comm'r, 76 TC 623 (1981) (taxpayer suffered from encephalitis, which seriously impaired mental function as to 1971 but not as to 1972). Compare Chaffin v. Comm'r, 46 TCM 673, 677 (1983) (heavy drinking, or even alcoholism, does not necessarily result in incompetency, which precludes a finding of fraudulent intent).

[119] Danenberg v. Comm'r, 73 TC 370 (1979) (gain realized on foreclosure).

[120] Estate of Louis L. Briden, 11 TC 1095, 1135 (1948), aff'd sub nom. Kirk v. Comm'r, 179 F2d 619 (1st Cir. 1950); American Properties, Inc., 28 TC 1100 (1957), aff'd per curiam, 262 F2d 150 (9th Cir. 1959).

On the other hand, if the taxpayer can show that the reason why income was not reported and tax not paid was that an employee or other person who was responsible for keeping a record of the taxpayer's income has embezzled the taxpayer's funds, the taxpayer may shift responsibility for the fraud—at least for the portions of the unreported income embezzled. See, e.g., Schirle v. Comm'r, TC Memo. 1997-552 (1997) (evidence that lawyer failed to report substantial amounts of fee income countered by evidence that bookkeeper embezzled substantial amounts of that income).

was prepared were incorrect and false.[121] Where, on the other hand, a taxpayer supplies an accountant with books and records conscientiously and honestly intended to be correct and assumes that the accountant is reporting his income and deductions accurately, the facts indicate an absence of fraudulent intent.[122] However, to succeed in shifting responsibility, the taxpayer will probably have to establish that steps were taken to ensure the correctness of the records and that the accountant was not controlled in the preparation of the return.[123] It must also be kept in mind that, in general, return preparation does not require the accountant to audit or verify the taxpayer's records to ensure the accuracy of the return.[124]

[c] Advice of Counsel or Other Tax Adviser

A taxpayer who is ignorant of the tax law may seek expert advice and rely on it without incurring the fraud penalty.[125] Essentially, the defense is one of mistake of law, and such a mistake is not the equivalent of fraud.[126] A taxpayer stands a better chance of using this defense successfully if there is no actual concealment of the incorrectly treated transaction or item on the re-

---

[121] Estate of Louis L. Briden, 11 TC 1095 (1948), aff'd sub nom. Kirk v. Comm'r, 179 F2d 619 (1st Cir. 1950); Estate of William Kahr, 48 TC 929 (1967), aff'd, 414 F2d 621 (2d Cir. 1969); Drieborg v. Comm'r, 225 F2d 216 (6th Cir. 1955); Herbert Eck, 16 TC 511 (1951), aff'd, 202 F2d 750 (2d Cir.), cert. denied, 348 US 822 (1953).

[122] Fred Draper, 32 TC 545, 563–564 (1959); John Marinzulich, 31 TC 487 (1958); Sidney Cohen, 27 TC 221 (1956).

[123] Scallen v. Comm'r, 877 F2d 1364, 1371 (8th Cir. 1989) ("[a] taxpayer may not rely on the errors of his tax return preparer as a defense to a charge of fraud if the taxpayer failed to provide the preparer with the proper documentation correctly to prepare the return"). See also Rivera v. Comm'r, 38 TCM 1338 (1979) (taxpayer's refusal to supply records to preparer that would have revealed income understatement held evidence of fraud); Ortiz v. Comm'r, TC Memo. 1998-141 (1998) (although self-employment income was unreported in both years, and books and records were "not entirely accurate," the court nevertheless found that there was no fraud because "the books and data [the taxpayer] furnished to his accountant and return preparer were apparently sufficient to enable [the accountant] to determine business gross sales, cost of goods sold, and expenses). Groves v. Comm'r, TC Memo. 1999-415 (1999) (court found that a tax attorney with large tax underpayments in two years resulting from sales of stock were attributable to negligence rather than fraud, because although he supplied incorrect information to his accountant, the large understatements of income standing alone did not prove fraud; the information given to the accountant was not intended to mislead him; and his status as a tax attorney, while a factor to consider, did not establish fraudulent intent).

[124] See Estate of Temple v. Comm'r, 67 TC 143, 163 (1976). See also Accardo v. Comm'r, 942 F2d 444 (7th Cir. 1991) (signature of accountant on return was not enough; taxpayer's reliance on preparer's advice must be shown).

[125] Jemison v. Comm'r, 45 F2d (5th Cir. 1930); Durovic v. Comm'r, 54 TC 1364, 1398 (1970), aff'd, 487 F2d 36 (7th Cir.), cert. denied, 417 US 919 (1974).

[126] Welburn Mayock, 32 TC 966, 974 (1959).

turn[127] or in the examination.[128] Merely claiming reliance is not sufficient. The taxpayer must seek advice in good faith, as evidenced by the competence of the adviser, the completeness of the information provided, and the reasonableness of the advice given under the circumstances.[129]

¶ 7B.03 THE ACCURACY-RELATED PENALTY

[1] The Structure of Section 6662

The Improved Penalty Administration and Compliance Tax Act (IMPACT) repealed the 1986 Code penalties for negligent underpayment of tax (Section 6653(a)), valuation overstatements (Section 6659), substantial understatements of income tax (Section 6661), valuation understatements for estate or gift tax purposes (Section 6660), and pension liability overstatement (Section 6661).[130] In place of these five penalties, a single accuracy-related penalty for five different types of misconduct was enacted. Section 6662(a) imposes a 20 percent penalty on the portion of an underpayment attributable to any of the following five types of misconduct:[131]

1. Negligence or disregard of rules or regulations;
2. A substantial understatement of income tax;
3. A substantial valuation overstatement,
4. A substantial overstatement of pension liabilities; or
5. A substantial estate or gift tax valuation understatement.

Before the changes made by IMPACT, penalties were generally uncoordinated. As a result, an individual taxpayer who underpaid tax could be liable for several cumulative penalties. For example, if the taxpayer took a charitable deduction for donated property in excess of the value of the property deter-

---

[127] Welburn Mayock, 32 TC 966, 974 (1959).

[128] Ross Glove Co. v. Comm'r, 60 TC 569 (1973).

[129] See, e.g., Joseph H. Imeson, 14 TC 1151 (1950), where the taxpayer had reason to believe that the advice was dishonest. However, compare the result in *Iemson* with practically identical cases involving the same adviser in which the penalty was not found: Charles C. Rice, 14 TC 503 (1950); Dale R. Fulton, 14 TC 1453 (1950).

[130] IMPACT also repealed the fraud penalty (Section 6653(b)), the special negligence rules applicable to straddles (Section 6653(f)), and the higher interest rate that applied to substantial underpayments attributable to tax motivated transactions (Section 6621(c)). IMPACT, Pub. L. No. 239, HR 3299, 101st Cong., 1st Sess., Subtitle G § 7721(c).

[131] The accuracy-related penalty is applicable for returns due after December 31, 1989, without regard to extensions of time for filing. IMPACT, Pub. L. No. 239, HR 3299, 101st Cong., 1st Sess., Subtitle G, § 7721(a).

mined by the Service, resulting in a $6,000 underpayment in tax, the taxpayer could be liable for (1) a negligence penalty; (2) a substantial understatement or a substantial overvaluation penalty (one of the few instances of penalty coordination); (3) nondeductible interest on the $6,000 deficiency; and (4) interest calculated on deficiencies attributable to tax-motivated transactions.

The accuracy-related penalty eliminates much of the cumulation of penalties by imposing a single 20 percent penalty on the portion of the underpayment that is caused by one or more of the five types of misconduct. As a result, if a $6,000 underpayment in income tax is caused by negligence, constitutes a substantial understatement of income tax, and flows from a valuation overstatement, only one 20 percent penalty is imposed for that $6,000 portion of the underpayment. More than one accuracy-related penalty may be imposed for a single income tax return. Different portions of the total underpayment can be caused by different types of misconduct. For example, a taxpayer might have overvalued property for purposes of a charitable deduction and negligently omitted interest income. Nothing in Section 6662 precludes the imposition of a 20 percent penalty on different portions of the underpayment for a year. Thus, a 20 percent penalty can be imposed on the portion of the underpayment caused by the overvaluation and another 20 percent penalty on the portion of the underpayment caused by the negligently omitted interest.

The accuracy-related penalty is a statutory mechanism for coordinating the five penalties that existed separately under prior law. Few substantive changes have been made to the five penalties other than to incorporate them into a single penalty. Accordingly, the discussion in the following sections of the five components of the accuracy-related penalty incorporates the law as it developed for each of the penalties under prior law.

Under a special provision borrowed from the substantial understatement penalty and expanded to cover all the components of the accuracy-related penalty, no accuracy-related penalty applies if the taxpayer can show that there was reasonable cause for the underpayment and that the taxpayer acted in good faith with respect to the underpayment. This reasonable cause exception applies not only for the accuracy-related penalty but also for the fraud penalty.

[2] Negligence or Disregard of Rules and Regulations

The accuracy-related penalty for negligence or intentional disregard of rules and regulations (Section 6662(c)) is the same as the negligence penalty under prior law with several important exceptions. Since the negligence penalty has undergone several changes from the simple 5 percent penalty that was enacted as Section 6653(a) of the 1954 Code, some review of these legislative changes is necessary to understand the accuracy-related version of the negligence penalty.

From 1954 until 1982, where any part of an underpayment in tax was due to negligence or intentional disregard of rules and regulations, a penalty equal to 5 percent of the entire underpayment was imposed.[132] Thus, so long as some part of the underpayment, which was roughly equivalent to the deficiency, was attributable to negligence, the 5 percent penalty was imposed on the entire underpayment even if it was not caused by the taxpayer's negligence.[133]

From 1982 through 1986, the 5 percent part of the penalty remained, but the effective rate of the negligence penalty was increased by adding to the ad valorem penalty an amount equal to 50 percent of the interest on the negligence-tainted portion of the deficiency from the due date of the return until the earlier of the date the tax was either assessed or paid.[134] For purposes of illustration, if it is assumed that interest on an underpayment accrued at the rate of 10 percent simple interest for each of the years between 1983 and 1986, the negligence penalty would therefore be 5 percent of the entire underpayment, plus an amount equal to 20 percent of the negligence-tainted portion of the underpayment (four years times 10 percent interest divided by 50 percent). Assuming that the entire underpayment were attributable to negligence, the negligence penalty would effectively be 25 percent of the underpayment. In addition, where interest or dividends reported on an information return were omitted, negligence was presumed, and a taxpayer could only rebut this presumptive negligence by presenting clear and convincing evidence of an absence of negligence in the failure to report.[135]

From 1986 through 1988, the negligence penalty continued to have the basic ad valorem penalty of 5 percent and an additional amount based on one half of the accured interest on the negligence-tainted portion of the underpayment. However, three changes were made in 1986. The negligence penalty was made applicable to all taxes, thus permitting, for example, imposition of the penalty for estate taxes. The definition of negligence was also modified to include (1) any failure to make a reasonable attempt to comply with the provisions of the Code and (2) any careless, reckless, or intentional disregard of

---

[132] The amendments to Section 6653(a) made by the Economic Recovery Tax Act of 1981 (ERTA) Pub. L. No. 34, HR 4242, 97th Cong., 1st Sess., applied to taxes the last day for the payment of which, due without regard to extensions, was after December 31, 1981. It has been held that neither estimated tax installments made during 1981 nor withholding during 1981 reduced the amount subject to the time-sensitive portion of the negligence penalty. Jacobs v. Comm'r, TC Memo. 1997-429 (1997) (gathering cases).

[133] Asphalt Prods. Co. v. Comm'r, 482 US 117 (1987).

[134] Interest for purposes of the calculation was the interest rate on an underpayment (Section 6601), which was adjusted periodically. IRC §§ 6653(a)(1), 6653(a)(2), amended by ERTA, Pub. L. No. 34, HR 4242, 97th Cong., 1st Sess., § 722(b), applicable to taxes whose payment due date was after December 31, 1981.

[135] IRC § 6653(g), added by TRA 1986, Pub. L. No. 514, HR 3838, 99th Cong., 2d Sess., § 1503.

rules or regulations.[136] However, behavior considered negligent under prior law remained within the scope of the penalty for negligence, and conduct a court might consider negligent was subject to the penalty even if it was not specifically described in the definition.[137] Finally, the presumptive negligence procedure was expanded to apply to any item reportable on an information return that a taxpayer failed to report. Where a taxpayer omitted information return–type items, he had the obligation of disproving negligence by clear and convincing evidence.[138]

In 1988, the time-sensitive component of both the negligence and fraud penalties was eliminated. However, the 5 percent negligence penalty continued to apply to the full amount of the underpayment. Therefore, the penalty could be imposed on portions of the underpayment that were not due to the taxpayer's negligence.[139] The penalty was effectively increased by changing the method of computing interest on it. Under prior law, interest only began to accrue on the negligence and fraud penalties after assessment. For penalties assessed on tax returns due after 1988, interest began to accrue from the due date of the return, including extensions, and ended on the date of payment.[140]

As part of the accuracy-related penalty, the portion for "negligence or disregard of rules or regulations" has the following features:

1. *Rate.* The rate of the penalty is increased from 5 percent to 20 percent. The amount of the penalty is also increased by the 1988 change in the computation of interest on the penalty that begins to run on the date the return was required to be filed, rather than on the date of assessment.[141]

2. *Penalty base.* Under prior law, the negligence penalty applied to the full amount of the underpayment. The Supreme Court, in *Asphalt Products*, made clear that the penalty applied to the entire underpayment, even if only a small portion of the underpayment was due to negligence and the bulk of the underpayment was untainted by taxpayer fault. The accuracy-related penalty for negligence is imposed

---

[136] IRC § 6653(a)(3), added by TRA 1986, Pub. L. No. 514, HR 3838, 99th Cong., 2d Sess., § 1503(e).

[137] IRC § 6653(a), amended by TRA 1986, Pub. L. No. 514, HR 3838, 99th Cong., 2d Sess., § 1503(a); HR Conf. Rep. No. 841, 99th Cong., 2d Sess., Vol. II-7810.

[138] IRC § 6653(g).

[139] The negligence penalty could not be imposed on the portion of the underpayment that was due to fraud. IRC § 6653(a)(2), added by the Technical Corrections Act of 1988, Pub. L. No. 67, 100th Cong., § 1015(b)(2)(A).

[140] IRC § 6601(e)(2)(B), amended by Technical and Miscellaneous Revenue Act of 1988 (TAMRA), § 1015(b)(2)(C), Pub. L. No. 647, HR 4333, 100th Cong., 2d Sess.

[141] IRC § 6601(e)(2)(B).

only on the portion of the underpayment that is attributable to the negligence.[142]

3. *Presumptions.* Under prior law, the failure to include interest, dividends, and other income information that was supplied to the taxpayer and the IRS by third-party payors was statutorily presumed to be due to negligence unless the taxpayer could prove otherwise by clear and convincing evidence. In the accuracy-related penalty, there is no presumptive negligence. If a taxpayer fails to include income reported on an information return, the taxpayer has the burden of disproving negligence in the sense of having the risk of nonpersuasion if evidence of an adequate explanation is not presented.

4. *Reasonable cause.* Under prior law, there was no statutory procedure for avoiding a negligence penalty. The accuracy-related penalty, on the other hand, does not apply if there was reasonable cause for the understatement and the taxpayer acted in good faith.[143] If the taxpayer can prove these matters, there was no negligence. However, the reasonable cause exception, which permits a taxpayer to avoid an accuracy-related penalty by making a qualifying disclosure, enables taxpayers to disclose and avoid the penalty especially in disregard situations. Changes made in 1993 eliminated the disclosure exception for the negligence penalty and raised the standard for making a qualifying disclosure for disregard of rules or regulations from "not frivolous" to "reasonable basis."[144]

In general, an underpayment is the same as a deficiency (roughly, the difference between the correct tax and the reported tax), with the exceptions that the amount reported on a late return does not reduce the amount of an underpayment, nor does any payment of a deficiency or assessment made after the date the return was due. The same methods of proving a deficiency used in fraud penalty cases (e.g., specific items, bank deposits, net worth) are also used in negligence penalty cases.[145] However, the fact that the taxpayer has the

---

[142] IRC §§ 6662(a), 6662(b)(1).

[143] See Penalty Handbook 120.1.5.7.6 (Aug. 20, 1998).

[144] The Omnibus Reconciliation Act of 1993, Section 13251. Conforming final regulations have been adopted effective September 1, 1995. See TD 8617, adopting final regulations, and amending, inter alia, the negligence and intentional disregard regulations for returns due after December 31, 1993. See Reg. §§ 1.6662-2(d)(2), 1.6662-3(a), 1.6662-3(b)(3)(ii), 1.6662-3(c)(1), 1.6662-3(c)(2).

[145] For a case recognizing the wide latitude the Commissioner has in adopting a method of reconstructing a taxpayer's income, see Catalano v. Comm'r, 81 TC 8 (1983), aff'd without opinion, 735 F2d 1370 (9th Cir. 1984) (cases cited; determination of "toke" income made on the basis of statistical and other data, during surveillance project at Las Vegas casinos, upheld). See Hahn v. Comm'r, 63 TCM 2669 (1992) (surveillance of taxpayer's alleged prostitution operation used projection based on number of days operation

burden of disproving negligence by a preponderance of the evidence has the effect of shifting to the taxpayer the burden of disproving elements the Commissioner would otherwise be required to prove when using circumstantial methods of proof.[146] The Commissioner's determination in a negligence case is presumptively correct.[147]

TABLE 7B.1
Differences Between the Negligence and Fraud Penalties

	Negligence	Fraud
Statute of Limitations	Negligence does not toll running of statute of limitations on assessment	Fraud tolls statute of limitations on assessment indefinitely. IRC §§ 6501(c)(1), 6501(c)(2)
Burden of Proof	Taxpayer has burden of proof; Commissioner's determination is presumptively correct	Commissioner has the burden of proof. IRC § 7454(a)
Standard of Proof	Taxpayer must disprove negligence by preponderance of evidence	Commissioner must prove fraud by clear and convincing evidence.
Presumption	No presumptive negligence	Presumption that entire underpayment is due to fraud if any part proved by IRS to be due to fraud

Both the negligence penalty and the fraud penalty are computed in the same manner, although there are significant procedural differences between the two penalties. Table 7B.1 summarizes these differences.

---

was open multiplied by number of customers serviced per day multiplied by amount received per customer).

[146] Estate of Mason v. Comm'r, 64 TC 651, 657 (1975), aff'd, 566 F2d 2 (6th Cir. 1977) (in bank deposits case, the court said that the taxpayer had the burden of showing duplication of deposits and that the Commissioner did not have to prove the deposits were income); Barry Meneguzzo, 43 TC 824 (1965) (waiter's tips reconstructed; he had the burden of proving the reconstruction was incorrect). Although the taxpayer has the burden of disproving negligence, some facts must support a Tax Court finding of negligence other than the taxpayer's losing substantive issues in a case. See Baxter v. Comm'r, 816 F2d 493 (9th Cir. 1987). Despite taxpayers' burden of proof on the negligence penalty issue, it is surprising to see that, in many cases, no evidence on the issue is offered at all. See, e.g., Lair v. Comm'r, 95 TC 484 (1990) (Taxpayers "have submitted no evidence whatever in this respect. These [negligence] additions must therefore be sustained.").

[147] Vaira v. Comm'r, 444 F2d 770 (3d Cir. 1971); Gibbs v. Tomlinson, 362 F2d 394 (5th Cir. 1966); Lusk v. Comm'r, 250 F2d 591 (7th Cir. 1957), cert. denied, 357 US 932 (1958); Boynton v. Pedrick, 228 F2d 745 (2d Cir. 1955), cert. denied, 351 US 938 (1956).

[a] Definition of Negligence

The term "negligence" is not defined in the Code, except for the statement in Section 6662(c) that "'negligence' includes any failure to make a reasonable attempt to comply with the provisions of this title." It has been said, with respect to the negligence penalty, that "negligence is lack of due care or failure to do what a reasonable and ordinarily prudent person would do under the circumstances."[148] This definition reflects a tort meaning of the term. The *Restatement of the Law of Torts* defines negligence as "conduct which falls below the standard established by law for the protection of others against unreasonable risk of harm to others," and the standard of conduct to which the actor must conform is that "of a reasonable man under like circumstances."[149] Thus, negligence includes acts of omission or commission that a reasonable person would or would not do. This definition accomplishes two things: (1) It imposes an objective and external standard[150] and (2) it covers a broad range of conduct resulting in an underpayment in tax. Finally, although in tort law the term "negligence" is restricted to unintentional conduct, the statute itself joins one type of intentional conduct, "disregard of rules and regulations," with negligence and states that both can result in the imposition of the accuracy-related penalty.[151]

---

[148] Marcello v. Comm'r, 380 F2d 509 (5th Cir. 1967). Negligence has also been defined as the failure to do what a reasonable and ordinarily prudent person would do under the circumstances. Neely v. Comm'r, 85 TC 934, 947 (1985); Emmons v. Comm'r, 92 TC 342 (1989) ("[o]rdinarily, a reasonable and prudent person would comply with a statutorily prescribed deadline applicable to him or her"). The "reasonable person" is not an abstraction, but assumes the general characterstics of a person similarly situated to the taxpayer. See, e.g., Keene v. Comm'r, 44 TCM 1335 (1982) (taxpayer failed to explain why he, a practicing accountant, was not negligent in claiming an unallowable tax credit).

[149] Restatement (Second) of Torts §§ 282, 283. The Internal Revenue Manual similarly adopts the tort meaning of the term, saying that it is "the omission to do something which a reasonable person, guided by those considerations which ordinarily regulate the conduct of human beings, would do, or doing something which a prudent, reasonable person would not do." IRM 4563.11(2), MT 4500-448 (June 30, 1988) (Negligence Penalties—General).

[150] See Restatement (Second) of Torts § 283 comment c. The IRM instructs agents to take into account "the standard of conduct that can reasonably be expected from a taxpayer." IRM 4563.11(2), MT 4500-448 (June 30, 1988) (Negligence Penalties—General).

[151] IRC § 6662(b)(1). Section 6662(c) says that the term "disregard" includes "any careless, reckless, or intentional disregard."

Negligence frequently takes the form of a failure to report income[152] or overstatement of deductions.[153] Understatement of income does not in and of itself establish negligence,[154] but large discrepancies between actual and reported net income are "strong evidence" of negligence, which the taxpayer fails to controvert at his peril.[155] Understatement of income and overstatement of deductions also reflect on the adequacy of a taxpayer's records, which itself is a basis for imposing the penalty. The penalty applies in this situation, in part, because taxpayers are required to keep records sufficient to establish the amount of gross income, deductions, or credits, and other matters required to be shown on a return.[156] Therefore, failure to keep adequate records is evidence not only of negligence, but of intentional disregard of the record-keeping regulations.[157] Nevertheless, it is possible to distinguish between regular books of account that list income and expenses and detailed receipts and a diary to support travel and entertainment expenses. If regular business records have been kept, but not the documentation required under Section 274, it may be possible to avoid the disregard penalty, but entitlement to the amount of travel and entertainment deductions claimed will not be available.[158]

The accuracy-related penalty for negligence has two components, negligence and a separate disregard-type misconduct. The penalty based on disregard comes into play where a taxpayer disregards the Service's "rules and

---

[152] See, e.g., Marcello v. Comm'r, 380 F2d 509 (5th Cir. 1967) (failure to report partnership income); Estate of Mason, 64 TC 651 (1975), aff'd, 566 F2d 2 (6th Cir. 1977) (unreported income of over $51,422 and $84,945, even after eliminations for check kiting); James W. England, Jr., 34 TC 617 (1960) (failure to report income); L. Glenn Switzer, 20 TC 759 (1953) (substantial understatement of partnership income).

[153] Beus v. Comm'r, 261 F2d 176 (9th Cir. 1958) (loss on sale of cattle claimed when no sale in year of deduction); Byron H. Farwell, 35 TC 454 (1960); Howard v. Comm'r, 931 F2d 578 (9th Cir. 1991) (a finding under Section 183 that no reasonably prudent person would have undertaken transactions for profit also established lack of due care).

[154] See, e.g., Charles M. Kilborn, 29 TC 102 (1957), aff'd and rev'd, 58-2 USTC ¶ 9847 (5th Cir. 1958), rev'd, 360 US 715 (1959) (acq.) (omission of less than $1,000 in sales for each of three months found insufficient to establish negligence).

[155] L. Glenn Switzer, 20 TC 759, 766 (1953).

[156] Reg. § 1.6001-1(a).

[157] See, e.g., Marcello v. Comm'r, 380 F2d 509 (5th Cir. 1967) (failure to keep partnership records); Magnon v. Comm'r, 73 TC 980 (1980) (failure to keep adequate records of income and expense); Smith v. Comm'r, 66 TC 622 (1976) (records inadequate to support claimed deductions); Axelrod v. Comm'r, 56 TC 248 (1971) (failure to keep records of claimed entertainment expenses, costs of attending medical meetings, convention expenses, dues to clubs and organizations); Dorothy L. Sutherland, 32 TC 862 (1959) (failure to keep records of tips); Portillo v. Comm'r, 932 F2d 1128 (5th Cir. 1991) (failure to keep adequate sales invoices).

[158] Robinson v. Comm'r, 51 TC 520 (1968), aff'd per curiam, 422 F2d 873 (9th Cir. 1970).

regulations." Disregard misconduct exists where a taxpayer is aware of a rule or regulation and chooses to ignore its requirements.[159] The meaning of the term "rules" in this context is unclear. A statutory rule clearly must be obeyed. However, if the statutory rule is unclear, is a taxpayer subject to a penalty for not following a ruling or other statement by the Service that is not a regulation? Imposition of a penalty for disregarding an IRS ruling is unwarranted,

---

[159] One circuit court has said that the "intentional disregard" penalty was designed to deter taxpayers from abusing prepayment deficiency procedures by intentionally underpaying and then contesting the deficiency. Druker v. Comm'r, 697 F2d 46 (2d Cir. 1982), cert. denied, 103 S. Ct. 2429 (1983). The taxpayers in *Druker* intentionally filed tax returns as married persons filing separately, but used the rate applicable to unmarried individuals, in order to contest the constitutionality of the so-called marriage penalty. The Tax Court had refused to impose the penalty for "intentional disregard of rules and regulations" on the ground that the taxpayers were acting in good faith and did not maintain a position that was frivolous or meritless. 77 TC 867 (1981). The Second Circuit reversed, holding that the penalty is mandatory and permits no "reasonable basis" exception if a taxpayer acts deliberately. According to the circuit court, if a taxpayer wishes to contest a "rule or regulation," his recourse is to pay the tax due and then sue for refund. The result in *Druker* can be changed by a Section 6664(c) disclosure discussed infra ¶ 7B.04[2]. The Tax Court itself has found that a negligence penalty is properly imposed for intentional disregard of rules and regulations where a taxpayer engaged in fictitious straddle transactions. Brown v. Comm'r, 85 TC 968 (1985). See also Cramer v. Comm'r, 64 F3d 1406 (9th Cir. 1995), cert. denied (taxpayers were advised that they could take a position that was contrary to a regulation because it was based on subsequent legislative history; they were nevertheless held liable for both the intentional disregard and substantial understatement penalties). Liability for the accuracy-related penalty can depend on whether the Service takes the position that the understatement was due to an intentional disregard of a regulation or to ordinary negligence. While the Ninth Circuit upheld the Tax Court in finding that the taxpayer in *Cramer* was liable for the intentional disregard penalty, the circuit court reversed the Tax Court on its negligence finding in *Henry*. See Henry v. Comm'r, 83 AFTR2d 99-1394 (9th Cir. 1999). However, the facts in *Henry* were virtually the same as in *Cramer*, and the taxpayer's return was prepared by the same return preparer who made the same determination that the proceeds from the sale of stock options was reportable as capital gain, not as ordinary income. The circuit court makes much of the difference between the cases: The taxpayer in *Cramer* knew of the regulation and the legislative history with which it was inconsistent, while there was insufficient evidence (in the circuit court's view) that the taxpayer in *Henry* knew of the regulation. Since the same accountant participated in the preparation of the returns of both taxpayers and took the same return position, the different results must turn on the fact that the taxpayer in *Cramer* had more knowledge about the return position taken, and so had intentionally disregarded the relevant regulation. This, in turn, leads to the conclusion that a taxpayer who has too much knowledge about his return preparer's position can be punished for having disregarded a regulation, while a taxpayer who does not inquire about the return position will be subject to only a negligence penalty and be able to avoid liability by asserting that he relied on his accountant. In the penalty area, this conclusion gives new meaning to the saying that a little knowledge is a dangerous thing. As a matter of law and policy, a taxpayer who relies on his accountant's good faith but erroneous return position should be able to rely on the accountant's advice to avoid both an *intentional* disregard and a negligence penalty, even if he asks the accountant about the position.

since a ruling is only the Service's position in response to a particular set of facts.[160] Even the disregard of certain interpretative regulations should not be a matter warranting the imposition of a penalty, since interpretations of statutes, even when promulgated by the Treasury, are not "the law." If a statutory requirement has been intentionally disregarded, disregard misconduct has been committed. However, the sense of the statutory phrase "disregard of rules and regulations" can only be kept if it is construed to mean noncompliance with procedural rules and regulations imposed by the Code or the Service that prevents the Service from carrying out its statutorily mandated function of determining and collecting the correct amount of tax—e.g., failing to keep adequate inventory and other records.[161] Where a taxpayer has been convicted of a willful failure to file a return in violation of the criminal statute, Section 7203, the conviction has been held to establish that the taxpayer's failure to file was an intentional disregard of the rules and regulations requiring the filing of returns.[162]

Regulations state that negligence is "strongly indicated" in the following circumstances:

1. A taxpayer omits from an income tax return income that a third party shows on an information return.[163]

2. A taxpayer fails to make "a reasonable attempt to ascertain the correctness of a deduction, credit, or exclusion on a return which would seem to a reasonable and prudent person to be 'too good to be true' under the circumstances."[164]

3. The failure of a partner in a large partnership or TEFRA partnership, or a shareholder in an S corporation, to report items consistently with the partnership and S corporation returns.[165]

A position is also said to be attributable to negligence if it lacks a reasonable basis. Just what "reasonable basis" means in this context is unclear. A substan-

---

[160] See ¶ 3.03.

[161] Carmichael Tile Co., 9 TCM 351 (1950), aff'd, 192 F2d 209 (5th Cir. 1951); Elsie SoRelle, 22 TC 459 (1954).

[162] Kotmair v. Comm'r, 86 TC 1253, 1263–1264 (1986).

[163] Reg. § 1.6662-3(b)(1)(i). This regulatory provision repeats the earlier version of the negligence penalty, which presumed negligence if a taxpayer omitted interest, dividends, and other income shown on an information return unless the taxpayer could prove otherwise by clear and convincing evidence.

[164] Reg. § 1.6662-3(b)(1)(ii). Negligence inferred or presumed for this reason is similar to the failure of an advice of counsel defense to avoid the negligence penalty. See infra cases at note 218.

[165] Reg. §§ 1.6662-1(b)(1)(iii), 1.6662-1(b)(1)(iv). Consistency in reporting is required for partners by Section 6222(a) and for S corporation shareholders by Section 6242, unless the partner or shareholder notifies the IRS. See ¶¶ 8.09[2], 8.09[5].

tial understatement penalty is avoided if there is "substantial authority" for the return position, but substantial authority does not exist if there is "only" a reasonable basis for the return position (i.e., a return position that is arguable, but fairly unlikely to prevail in court).[166] Also, a reasonable basis was considered inappropriate by law in defining the standard applicable to return preparers in preparing tax returns.[167] Consequently, according to the regulations, a position that may not be sufficiently substantial either for the taxpayer to avoid a substantial understatement penalty or for the preparer to avoid a preparer penalty may be sufficient for the taxpayer to avoid a negligence penalty.

A "strong indication" sounds like the evidence law's presumption, which imposes on the party against whom it is directed the burden of going forward with evidence "to rebut or meet the presumption."[168] In many, perhaps most, cases, it is rational to infer negligence from a variance between an income tax return and an information return. But other reasons than negligence may explain why an income tax return did not include precisely what was reported on an information return. Taxpayers should be permitted, and indeed are obligated, to produce evidence that the information return is incorrect, or that there was some nonnegligent reason for the omission.

The "reasonable attempt" inference of negligence seems unnecessarily complicated and ambiguous for the situation apparently intended to be covered. If the taxpayer's conduct did not meet the standard of a reasonably prudent taxpayer attempting to fulfill his tax-reporting obligation, that should be the end of the matter. Adding a "too good to be true" element implies that a taxpayer is in a position to judge the correctness of advice the taxpayer reasonably and prudently seeks from a tax professional, a judgment the Supreme Court in *Boyle* said a taxpayer was not equipped to make. Justification for the use of the term is that it expressed a "typical form of negligent behavior and has been used by a number of courts in describing negligence."[169] As the result of the statutory change made in 1993, a taxpayer may not avoid the negligence penalty by filing a disclosure statement with the taxpayer's return.[170]

The regulations also take the position that "rules or regulations," disregard of which subject a taxpayer to penalty, include revenue rulings and notices published in the Internal Revenue Bulletin. But revenue rulings are not "rules" in the administrative law sense, and they are not given weight in any judicial

---

[166] Reg. § 1.6662-4(d)(2).

[167] See ¶ 1.09.

[168] Fed. R. Evid. 301. Former versions of the negligence penalty also used presumptions, and for the same type of omission.

[169] Comment on this aspect of the proposed regulations was that the standard was too subjective. TD 8381. One case cited was McCrary v. Comm'r, 92 TC 827 (1989).

[170] Reg. § 1.6662-1 (1995).

proceeding.[171] A return position contrary to a revenue ruling nevertheless will be subject to a disregard-type penalty unless the return position has a realistic possibility of being sustained on the merits.[172] As they have done consistently with regard to this standard, the regulations take the position that a realistic possibility of success is said to be a quantitative standard (a one-in-three chance of success), not a qualitative one.[173] In other words, although a revenue ruling is not law, but merely the position of the Service, a taxpayer nevertheless will be considered to have been guilty of intentional disregard if the taxpayer adopts a return position that, in the opinion of the Service, probably would not succeed in court.

Consequently, a taxpayer who takes an undisclosed return position contrary to a revenue ruling or regulation seems likely to face the assertion at the Examination level of a disregard-type penalty. For returns with a due date after December 31, 1993, regulations provide that the penalty for disregard of rules or regulations does not apply if (1) there is a reasonable basis for the position (the reasonable basis standard is significantly higher than the not-frivolous standard applicable to return preparers, as defined in Reg. § 1.6694-2(c)(2)); (2) the position is disclosed on a Form 8275, and if a good faith challenge to the validity of a regulation is made on a Form 8275R, in the same manner as disclosure statements are prepared and filed for purposes of the substantial understatement penalty; and (3) the taxpayer maintains adequate books and records or is able to substantiate items properly.[174] Regulations interpret the term "reasonable basis" as a "relatively high standard of tax reporting," which is significantly higher than "not frivolous or not patently improper," and is "not satisfied by a return position that is merely arguable or that is merely a colorable claim," but it need not satisfy the substantial authority standard as the regulations define that standard (Reg. § 1.6662-4(d)(2)).[175] For purposes of the regulations, a return position will "generally" satisfy the reasonable-basis standard if the return position is "reasonably based on one or more of the authorities set forth in [the list of authorities for substantial authority penalty pur-

---

[171] See ¶ 3.03[2][b]. The error in the regulations is weakly justified by a reference to the legislative history of the return preparer penalty, which explained that the return preparer's disregard of rules and regulations include regulations and "IRS rulings."

[172] Reg. § 1.6662-2(b)(2).

[173] Notice 90-20, 1990-1 CB 328.

[174] Reg. §§ 1.6662-3(a), 1.6662-3(b)(3)(ii), 1.6662-3(c)(1), 1.6662-3(c)(2). For returns due before January 1, 1994 (i.e., returns with a due date after December 31, 1991, but before January 1, 1994), the basis for the disclosed return position had to be at least not frivolous. Reg. § 1.6662-3(c). On November 12, 1996, proposed regulations were issued defining the reasonable basis standard. Prop. Reg. § 1.6662-3(b) and related regulations, IA-42-95, 61 Fed. Reg. 58,020. These proposed regulations were made final by TD 8790, 63 Fed. Reg. 66,433–66,435 (effective December 2, 1998) without substantial change.

[175] Reg. § 1.6662-3(b)(3).

poses in Reg. § 1.6662-4(d)(3)(iii)] (taking into account the relevance and persuasiveness of the authorities, and subsequent developments)."[176] Even if a return position does not satisfy the reasonable-basis standard, the reasonable-cause and good-faith exception of Section 6664 may provide relief from the penalty for negligence or disregard of rules or regulations. Disclosure of a position contrary to a "rule or regulation" seems to be a response to the *Druker* case, where the Second Circuit held that any reporting intentionally contrary to a statute and regulation was an intentional disregard.[177] According to the *Druker* court, the taxpayer who disagrees with the statute is required to pay the tax and notify the IRS by filing a claim for refund. Seen against this background, the regulation appears erroneous. But the expansive definition of "rule," coupled with the specific method in which disclosure is required to be made, broadens the number of situations where intentional disregard penalties can be imposed.

A special rule applies to carrybacks and carryovers when, in a loss or credit year, any part of an underpayment is due to negligence, and the loss or credit is carried back or carried forward. In this situation, the portion of the underpayment caused by the carryback is also subject to the penalty.[178]

[b] Defenses

[i] **Shift of responsibility.** There is a tendency in negligence penalty cases to hold the taxpayer responsible for errors attributable to the mistake of an employee, agent, or return preparer.[179] The taxpayer cannot avoid the duty of filing an accurate return by attempting to shift responsibility to an agent. Therefore, a taxpayer acts negligently, where he fails to (1) ensure that a return is timely filed; (2) supervise a bookkeeper in keeping accurate records[180];

---

[176] Reg. § 1.6662-4(d)(3)(ii) provides rules on relevance, persuasiveness, subsequent developments, and use of a well-reasoned construction of an applicable statutory provision for purposes of the substantial understatement penalty.

[177] See Druker v. Comm'r, 697 F2d 46 (2d Cir. 1982), cert. denied, 103 S. Ct. 2429 (1983).

[178] Reg. § 1.6662-3(d)(i). This is a long-standing IRS position. See infra note 452.

[179] Estate of Louis Briden, 11 TC 1095 (1948), aff'd on another issue, 179 F2d 519 (1st Cir.), cert. denied, 339 US 963 (1950); Inter-Am. Life Ins. Co., 56 TC 497, 512 (1971), aff'd per curiam, 469 F2d 697 (9th Cir. 1973); Pritchett v. Comm'r, 63 TC 149 (1974); James Soares, 50 TC 909 (1968); Leroy Jewelry Co. v. Comm'r, 36 TC 443 (1971); American Properties, Inc., 28 TC 1100 (1957), aff'd, 262 F2d 150 (9th Cir. 1958); Hyman B. Stone, 22 TC 893, 906 (1954); Vern W. Bailey, 21 TC 678 (1954); Elsie So-Relle, 22 TC 459, 489 (1954); Enoch v. Comm'r, 57 TC 781, 802 (1972).

[180] Leroy Jewelry Co., 36 TC 443 (1971); Hyman B. Stone, 22 TC 893 (1954).

and (3) examine a tax return prepared by another to determine whether all income and deductions have been correctly reported.[181]

The line between an unsuccessful attempt to shift responsibility to an agent and reliance on a tax adviser and return preparer is not easily drawn in negligence penalty cases. Although a taxpayer remains vicariously liable for a negligently prepared return, it has also been held that a taxpayer who relies completely on a competent tax adviser and return preparer, supplying the preparer with all relevant records, is not negligent or has not intentionally disregarded rules and regulations.[182] The Supreme Court itself has said,[183] "[W]hen an accountant or attorney advises a taxpayer on a matter of tax law,

---

[181] Pritchett v. Comm'r, 63 TC 149 (1974) (income item of $181,760 omitted by accountant); Vern W. Bailey, 21 TC 678 (1954). See also Henry Schwartz Corp. v. Comm'r, 60 TC 728 (1973) (taxpayer knew omitted item should have been included). The failure to report dividends constituting about 20 percent of the taxpayers' income from a closely held corporation resulted in a negligence penalty although the taxpayers supplied corporate records to the return preparer. Metra Chem Corp. v. Comm'r, 88 TC 654 (1987) (shift of responsibility cases raised questions as to the tax treatment of complex transactions and whether the position taken on the returns with respect to such items had a reasonable basis).

Another type of omission on the part of a taxpayer may be used to defeat a shift of responsibility defense, the failure to comply with a provision of the Code, and the accompanying regulations. In *Asat, Inc.*, the taxpayer argued that it relied on an accounting firm to prepare its tax returns correctly, including the reflection of an arm's length price, but the Tax Court judge rejected the defense on the grounds that the taxpayer (1) failed to keep the records called for by Section 6038A and the regulations interpreting the provision and so prevented the Service from independently determining the correctness of the transfer price used in the intercompany transactions; (2) refused to give the Service an agency authorization during the audit; and (3) apparently ignored the return preparer's warning about the level of the taxpayer's pricing documentation. Asat, Inc. v. Comm'r, 1997 US TC LEXIS 11 (1997). In other words, the taxpayer's failure to comply with regulations, which were record maintenance regulations, and its conduct during the examination, precluded the taxpayer's attempt to shift responsibility to the return preparer.

[182] Betson v. Comm'r, 802 F2d 365 (9th Cir. 1986) (imposition of negligence penalty reversed; "taxpayer relied in good faith on substantive advice of his accountant"); Industrial Valley Bank & Trust Co. v. Comm'r, 66 TC 272 (1976); Athenaise M. Hill, 63 TC 225 (1974), aff'd without published opinion, 551 F2d 313 (9th Cir. 1977); Conlorez Corp. v. Comm'r, 51 TC 467 (1968) (acq.); William A. Brown v. Comm'r, 47 TC 399 (1967) (acq.), aff'd per curiam, 398 F2d 832 (6th Cir.), cert. denied, 393 US 1065 (1968); Leo A. Woodbury, 49 TC 180 (1967) (acq.). See also Heasley v. Comm'r, 902 F2d 380 (5th Cir. 1990) (reliance on a financial adviser coupled with monitoring of investment and honest misunderstanding of the law precluded negligence penalty). It is also said that the taxpayer has the burden of proving that he supplied the correct information to his accountant with respect to the item in question and that the incorrect returns were a result of the accountant's mistake. Enoch v. Comm'r, 57 TC 781, 803 (1972).

See Shane Michael Optical Co. v. Comm'r, TC Memo. 1999-267 (1999) ("Mr. Shane is an elderly man, and both he and Shane Michael relied reasonably on their longtime accounting firm [of 52 years] to prepare their tax returns correctly.").

[183] United States v. Boyle, 469 US 241 (1985).

such as whether a liability exists, it is reasonable for the taxpayer to rely on that advice." Cases in which the taxpayer's reliance has been upheld have generally involved substantive issues or other matters beyond the knowledge of a layman.[184] This view is supported by the observation of one court that failure to consult a tax adviser in order to avoid misinformation is itself evidence of

---

[184] See, e.g., Industrial Valley Bank & Trust Co., 66 TC 272 (1976) (reasonable failure to follow ruling); Athenaise M. Hill, 63 TC 225 (1974), aff'd without published opinion, 551 F2d 313 (9th Cir. 1977) (loss deduction based on depreciation rate and useful lives determined by advisers); Conlorez Corp., 51 TC 467 (1968) (acq.) (gain on involuntary conversion); William A. Brown v. Comm'r, 47 TC 399 (1967) (acq.), aff'd per curiam, 398 F2d 832 (6th Cir.), cert. denied, 393 US 1065 (1968) (taxability of strike benefits); Otis v. Comm'r, 73 TC 671 (1980), aff'd in unpublished opinion (Oct. 22, 1981) (classification of replacement expense as repair or capital expenditure); Sammons v. Comm'r, 838 F2d 330 (9th Cir. 1988) (Tax Court improperly imposed negligence penalty under Section 6653(a) where taxpayers reasonably relied on experts'd valuation of donated property). Sim-Air, USA, Ltd. v. Comm'r, 63 TCM 4738 (1992) ("We are satisfied on the basis of the record as a whole that the instant case falls within the ambit of cases holding a taxpayer not liable for such additions where there has been bona fide reliance on professional advice even though that advice turned out to be erroneous, particularly in light of the complex DISC provisions."). When a professional appraiser's appraisal was attached to the taxpayer's return, the Tax Court found that the taxpayer was nevertheless subject to a negligence penalty because evidence of reasonable reliance had not been produced, other than the attachment of the appraisal. The circuit court reversed in McMurray v. Comm'r, 985 F2d 36 (1st Cir. 1993). The circuit court said: "Reasonable reliance on expert opinion, asserted in good faith, can shield a taxpayer from [negligence and intentional disregard] penalties." The facts that the return attached the appraisal was evidence of reliance and that the different approach to valuation taken at trial had no bearing on the taxpayers' conduct at the time the returns were filed, and evidence that the taxpayers had "some knowledge" of real estate development, fell far short of requiring them to second-guess a licensed appraiser. Finally, the circuit court said that the Tax Court's failure to give any probative weight to the taxpayers' appraiser's opinion does not mandate a finding of bad faith or unreasonable reliance. See also Sammons v. Comm'r, 838 F2d 330, 337 (9th Cir. 1988); Biagiotti v. Comm'r, 52 TCM 588, 595 (1986); Streber v. Comm'r, 81 AFTR2d ¶ 98-610 (5th Cir. 1998) (divided court held that taxpayer daughters reasonably relied on a lawyer's advice that they might treat amounts received in settlement of a dispute over notes their father had given them as a gift; Tax Court's finding of negligence held clearly erroneous).

In Condor Int'l, Inc. v. Comm'r, 78 F3d 1355 (9th Cir. 1996), a case involving both the negligence and the substantial understatement penalties, the circuit court said: "At all relevant times, there was no controlling authority that would have prohibited the creation of a USVI inhabitant corporation to serve as a holding company for stock, or required that corporation to file an income tax return with the IRS in addition to its returns filed with [the Virgin Islands internal revenue]." The court observed that, "Boiled to its essence . . . , the underlying assumption to each of these penalties is that Condor and the Welshes should be punished, not so much for having created an offshore vehicle for deferring taxes that would otherwise have been due and payable upon the transfer of their Arlon stock, but for having failed to anticipate that Congress would eventually amend the Tax Code to eliminate those advantages enjoyed by the inhabitants of the USVI."

negligence.[185] Those cases in which attempts to shift responsibility have generally failed involved the mere failure to record or include income where reliance on the agent was not called for by the complexity of the tax law or the transaction or because the taxpayer was experienced enough to know better.[186]

---

[185] Cooper v. Comm'r, 542 F2d 599 (2d Cir. 1976); Preston v. Comm'r, 47 TCM 417, 418–419 (1983) ("petitioner did not make any reasonable inquiry as to the income tax validity of his actions"); Neely v. Comm'r, 85 TC 934, 947 (1985), cited in Smith v. Comm'r, TC Memo. 1998-91 (taxpayer assumed that by designating business income as trust income, he would not have to report it, but taxpayer did not file a trust return, "nor did . . . [taxpayer] consult an accountant or an attorney to determine whether the $183,585 should be reported. In short, he did not do what a reasonable and ordinarily prudent person would do under the circumstances.").

[186] Reliance on the advice of the adviser must be reasonable under the circumstances. Skeen v. Comm'r, 864 F2d 93 (9th Cir. 1989) (taxpayer relied on accountant in gold tax shelter investment). See also Hansen v. Comm'r, 820 F2d 1464, 1469 (9th Cir. 1987). Compare Hoelzer v. Comm'r, 43 TCM 264 (1982), involving the tax consequences of an assignment of wages to a family trust where the Tax Court, in finding no negligence, said that it might reach a contrary result in future cases because of the numerous decisions adverse to taxpayers on the issue; with a later family trust case, Ferguson v. Comm'r, 43 TCM 1317 (1982), where the negligence penalty was imposed for the taxpayer's use of such "a flagrant tax-avoidance scheme." This approach has been used by at least one court of appeals. Pfluger v. Comm'r, 840 F2d 1379 (7th Cir. 1988) (after taxpayer was put on notice that Service was challenging transaction, his failure to research law to find support for his position constituted an absence of the requisite degree of care; negligence penalty upheld). Where a prospectus notified the taxpayers about high write-offs and risks of audit, the Ninth Circuit has said that the prospectus warned the taxpayers that the deductions were questionable at best, and so they had the obligation to investigate the venture before investing. Sacks v. Comm'r, 82 F3d 918 (9th Cir. 1996). The Ninth Circuit said that "negligence in the claiming of a deduction depends upon both the legitimacy of the underlying investment, and due care in the claiming of the deduction." Id.

The Tax Court itself has said, "Reliance on professional advice, standing alone, is not an absolute defense to negligence, but rather a factor to be considered. First it must be established that the reliance was reasonable." Freytag v. Comm'r, 89 TC 849, 888 (1987), aff'd, 904 F2d 1011 (5th Cir. 1990) (trading in government securities). While this approach is doctrinally sound, it can shift the penalty analysis from the true issue—the conduct of the taxpayer. When this happens, some harsh results follow. See, e.g., Coleman v. Comm'r, 60 TCM 889 (1990) (straddle transactions; negligence penalty imposed when law firm partner relied on his own firm's opinion, but court concluded that standard securities law caveats required second independent opinion); Goldman v. Comm'r, 39 F3d 402 (2d Cir. 1994) (negligence finding upheld because reliance on a sales representative with a conflict of interest and no expertise was not objectively reasonable); see also Spears v. Comm'r, 80 AFTR2d ¶ 97-5694 (2d Cir. 1997) (following *Goldman* on the effect of a conflict of interest by the purported adviser, but also pointing out that the quality of the adviser's advice was inadequate because the adviser's investigation was limited by the terms of the prospectus, he failed to seek an appraisal and other expert information of the property and market involved, and he relied on the biased representations of various interested persons).

The education and occupation of the taxpayer bear heavily in the Tax Court's view of the reliance defense. When the taxpayer is considered "sophisticated," the Tax Court

Some courts have gone further, saying that reliance on the advice of an adviser must be objectively reasonable. These courts read *Boyle* to stand for the proposition that "reliance on an adviser is reasonable where the adviser has expertise in the relevant area."[187] It is unreasonable, these courts say, for a taxpayer to rely on an adviser who lacks those qualifications needed to evaluate the investment.[188] In any event, a reliance defense fails if the taxpayer gives incomplete information,[189] fails to follow advice,[190] or fails to prove that the advice was given at all.[191]

[ii] Mistake. A taxpayer is not liable for a negligence penalty where the underpayment results from a mistake of law or fact made in good faith and on

---

seems to require greater evidence to establish the defense. Cramer v. Comm'r, 64 F3d 1406 (9th Cir. 1995) ("sophisticated" businessmen relied on professionals, but reliance defense rejected because court said copy of option was not provided to the professionals, even though the professionals did not say their advice would have been different); see also Martin v. Comm'r, TC Memo. 1995-448 (1995) (attorney with "impressive resume" claimed that she relied on financial advisor and her return preparers; defense rejected; court said, "There is nothing in the record, however, establishing that any of the persons on whom she allegedly relied was a qualified tax advisor."). See also Heckler v. Comm'r, TC Memo. 1998-49 (1998) ("a reasonable investor would have done more to protect his investment . . . especially one as educated as the [taxpayer, and] the fact that a $3,000 investment yielded a $15,432 loss deduction for that year should have alerted [taxpayers] that their deductions were 'too good to be true.'").

[187] Goldman v. Comm'r, 39 F3d 402, 408 (2d Cir. 1994); Chimblo v. Comm'r, 177 F3d 119, 126 (2d Cir. 1999); Addington v. Comm'r, 205 F3d 54 (2d Cir. 2000) (taxpayer's reliance on tax specialist was objectively unreasonable because tax expert did not advise nor claim the expertise to advise about the business merits of investing in a plastics recycling investment).

[188] See Goldman v. Comm'r, 39 F3d 402, 408 (2d Cir. 1994) (unreasonable to rely on accountant's evaluation of an oil and gas venture); Chimblo v. Comm'r, 177 F3d 119, 126 (2d Cir. 1999) (unreasonable to rely on family accountant for evaluation of investment in publishing venture).

[189] Edison Homes, Inc. v. Comm'r, 90-1 USTC ¶ 50,279 (8th Cir. 1990) (bad debt deduction claimed on transactions where taxpayer was not the seller); McCrary v. Comm'r, 92 TC 827, 849 (1989) (taxpayers found to be aware that the facts on which their deductions depended were not present; cases gathered). Ma-Tran Corp., 70 TC 158 (1978). The defense fails when the taxpayer fails to provide the preparer with complete records. See, e.g., Estate of Weissbart v. Comm'r, 63 TCM 1845 (1992); Welch v. Comm'r, TC Memo. 1998-121 (1998) ("While petitioner used accounting firms to prepare his returns, as far as [one of the accountants] was concerned, petitioner supplied the information in a summary fashion [, and n]one of the other return preparers testified.")

[190] Henry Schwartz Corp. v. Comm'r, 60 TC 728 (1973).

[191] Barnes v. Comm'r, 496 F2d 1197 (6th Cir. 1974). See also Pessin v. Comm'r, 59 TC 473 (1972); Hanson v. Comm'r, 696 F2d 1232 (9th Cir. 1983), aff'd, 42 TCM 1731 (1981) (no lawyer or accountant advised taxpayers that the trust would produce the desired tax advantage). Allen v. Comm'r, 925 F2d 348 (9th Cir. 1991) (no proof of preparer's qualifications or nature of advice, if any, that was given). Sacks v. Comm'r, 82 F3d 918 (9th Cir. 1996) ("The Sacks' argument that they relied upon their accountant

reasonable grounds.[192] In these cases, disclosure of the erroneous or mistaken treatment on the return is a factor in finding for the taxpayer, although nondisclosure may not be held against the taxpayer if there is a reasonable basis for the omission.[193] Nevertheless, the reasonable cause exception provision puts a premium on disclosure, and a failure to establish reasonable cause could appear determinative of disregard.

---

does not preclude a finding of that they were negligent. . . . The Sacks offered virtually no evidence of advice actually given."); see also Chakales v. Comm'r, 79 F3d 726 (8th Cir. 1996) ("The 'advice' that Plastiras gave, on which Chakales now claims to have relied, was little more than a generalized statement that he could lose money on the transaction. Chakales himself was vague about just what 'advice' he had received from Plastiras."). The Ninth Circuit said in *Chakales* that "The underlying premise [of the advice of counsel defense] is that a taxpayer may reasonably rely on advice when that advice involves the application of the attorney's or accountant's relevant expertise." The Service may put taxpayers to their proof when they claim they are not liable for the negligence penalty on the ground that they relied on their tax adviser; and when the tax adviser does not testify, the Service has claimed that an adverse inference may be drawn. See Streber v. Comm'r, 81 AFTR2d ¶ 98-610 (5th Cir. 1998) (while the lawyer who gave the advice did not testify, two other witnesses apart from the taxpayers testified that the advice was given, and the circuit court reversed the Tax Court because it failed to give weight to the two nontaxpayer witnesses).

[192] Scott v. Comm'r, 61 TC 654 (1974) (acq.) (good faith deduction, plus substantial issues of fact and law); Kasey v. Comm'r, 54 TC 1642 (1970) (acq.), aff'd per curiam, 457 F2d 369 (9th Cir. 1972) (same); Lemery v. Comm'r, 54 TC 480 (1970) (acq.) (reliance on confusing and uncertain IRS ruling); Burbank Liquidating Corp., 39 TC 999 (1963), aff'd and rev'd on other issues, 335 F2d 125 (9th Cir. 1964); Wesley Heat Treating Co., 30 TC 10 (1958) (acq.) (profit-sharing plan contribution disallowed). See also Millar v. Comm'r, 577 F2d 212 (3d Cir. 1978), cert. denied, 439 US 1046 (1978) (complexity of issues and confusion resulting from bankruptcy prevented finding of negligence); Belz Inv. Co. v. Comm'r, 72 TC 1209 (1979), aff'd, 661 F2d 76 (6th Cir. 1981) (acq.) (treatment of bankruptcy claim); Freeland v. Comm'r, 51 TCM 253 (1986) (where the law is subject to disagreement, no negligence or intentional disregard of rules and regulations has been found); Lansdown v. Comm'r, 77 AFTR2d ¶ 96-338 (10th Cir. 1996) (taxpayer erroneously believed he was entitled to foreign earned income exclusion, but negligence penalty not imposed because "the tax laws are exceedingly complex and difficult to apply . . . [so that to] find the petitioner negligent for not knowing in advance how these rules ultimately would be applied to his situation is unfair.").

[193] See, e.g., Belz Inv. Co. v. Comm'r, 72 TC 1209 (1979), aff'd, 661 F2d 76 (6th Cir. 1981) (acq.). In Burbank Liquidating Corp., 39 TC 999 (1963), aff'd and rev'd on other issues, 335 F2d 125 (9th Cir. 1964), the petitioner savings and loan company failed to make the disclosure because it was litigating the tax exempt status of the reserves not disclosed.

[3] Substantial Understatement of Income Tax

[a] The Accuracy-Related Penalty and Section 6661

Where an underpayment is attributable to a "substantial understatement of income tax," as specifically described in Section 6662(d), the 20 percent accuracy-related penalty is added to the underpayment. This accuracy-related substantial understatement penalty is virtually identical to the substantial understatement penalty of Section 6661 under prior law. From 1982 through 1989, the substantial understatement penalty was not coordinated with other penalties on taxpayers with the exception of the valuation overstatement penalty. As a result, the substantial understatement penalty was added to such other penalties imposed on the taxpayer as a negligence or fraud penalty. Section 6661 imposed a penalty for substantial understatements in income tax, which was determined, at least in the first instance, without regard to the taxpayer's personal fault. The penalty was originally 10 percent, but in 1986 it was increased to 25 percent.[194] The penalty was imposed where, for whatever reason, (1) there was an understatement in income because a tax due exceeded the returned tax and (2) the understatement was substantial because the tax due exceeded either $5,000 ($10,000 for a corporation) or 10 percent of the tax required to be shown on the return. Except with respect to a tax shelter, the amount of an understatement for penalty purposes could be reduced to the extent that the understatement was attributable to a reported item as to which (1) there was "substantial authority" for the taxpayer's reporting of the item[195] or (2) the "relevant facts" were "adequately disclosed" on or with the return.[196]

Although the Section 6661 substantial understatement penalty has been repealed, a substantial understatement of income tax is still one of the five types of conduct for which an accuracy-related penalty can be imposed. However, Section 6662(b) eliminates any cumulative effect by providing that a single accuracy-related penalty applied "to the portion of any underpayment which is attributable to 1 or more" of the five types of conduct. For returns due after December 31, 1989, the accuracy-related penalty differs from the substantial understatement penalty in the following ways:

---

[194] TRA 1986 provided that the penalty was to be 20 percent effective for returns due after December 31, 1986, but OBRA, enacted one day before TRA, made the penalty 25 percent for penalties assessed after enactment of the Act. In the Technical Corrections Act of 1988, Congress made it clear that the 25 percent penalty applied. Cases involving the retroactive increase in penalty have gone against taxpayers. See, e.g., Karpa v. Comm'r, 909 F2d 784 (1990) (ex post facto argument rejected; Section 6661(a) as amended by OBRA 1986 is civil sanction); Pallotini v. Comm'r, 90 TC 498 (1988).

[195] IRC § 6661(b)(2)(B)(ii).

[196] IRC § 6661(b)(2)(B)(ii). The substantial authority analysis can be made either at the time of return filing or at the time of the tax determination proceeding.

1. *Amount of penalty.* After some confusion over the matter, the substantial understatement penalty of Section 6661 was established to be 25 percent of the understatement. The accuracy-related penalty reduces the rate by a modest 5 percent to 20 percent.

2. *Substantial authority.* No substantial understatement exists attributable to an item if there was "substantial authority" for the taxpayer's return position on the item. Under prior law, the Service excluded from the list of authorities such sources as private letter rulings and the General Explanations of the Staff of the Joint Committee on Taxation (Blue Books). According to the legislative history (but not the statutory language) of Section 6662(d), the list of authorities on which taxpayers may rely for substantial authority has been expanded to include the following:

   • Proposed regulations;
   • Private letter rulings;
   • Technical advice memoranda;
   • Actions on decisions;
   • General counsel memoranda;
   • Information or press releases, notices, and other similar documents published in the Internal Revenue Bulletin; and
   • Blue Books.[197]

3. *The Secretarial list.* By statute, the Service is required to publish a list of positions for which it believes there is no substantial authority.[198]

[b] Substantial Understatement of Income Tax

The accuracy-related penalty is imposed if there is a substantial understatement of income tax. An understatement in income tax is considered to be substantial if it exceeds the greater of 10 percent of the income tax required to be shown on the return or $5,000 ($10,000 for corporations).[199] Potential liabil-

---

[197] HR Rep. No. 247, 101st Cong., 1st Sess. 280–281, reprinted in 1989-3 CB 1389–1390 (vol. 3).

[198] IRC § 6662(d)(2)(D).

[199] IRC §§ 6662(d)(1)(A), 6662(d)(1)(B). The term "income tax" is interpreted to include self-employment tax by Reg. § 1.6661-2(d)(1), and these regulations have been held valid. Cameron v. Comm'r, 98 TC 123 (1992). The IRS, using what it calls a literal reading of the statute, has ruled that the penalty applies to a withholding agent's substantial understatement of tax on Form 1042, Annual Withholding Tax Return for U.S. Source Income of Foreign Persons. GCM 39888 (Apr. 18, 1995). The reasoning is that the tax imposed by Section 1441 is an income tax, and, therefore, comes within the literal language of the substantial understatement penalty. In concluding that the tax imposed by Section

ity for the penalty turns on the amount of the understatement in income tax. An understatement in income tax is defined as the amount by which "the amount required to be shown on the return for the taxable year" is greater than "the amount of tax which is shown on the return, reduced by a rebate."[200] Rebates, in general, are amounts that may have been refunded to the taxpayer because the tax the IRS computed to be due was less than the collected and reported tax, or because of the result of carrybacks of operating losses.[201] Thus, without considering rebates, an understatement is the amount by which the income tax the taxpayer was required to report on the income tax return for the year is greater than the amount of income tax the taxpayer actually reported on the return. However, if the correct tax is greater than the amount that the taxpayer reported on the return, the result is only tentative.[202] Reductions can be made to the amount of this tentative understatement for the following three reasons:

1. If there is or was "substantial authority" for the taxpayer's treatment of the item[203]

2. If the relevant facts affecting the item's tax treatment were "adequately disclosed" in the return or a statement attached to the return[204]

3. If the item is a tax shelter item because tax avoidance or evasion was the principal purpose of the entity, plan, or arrangement giving rise to the item, and, in addition to substantial authority, the taxpayer reasonably believed that the tax treatment of the item was more likely than not the proper treatment,[205] but disclosure will not reduce the understatement[206]

1441 is an income tax, the IRS relied on a Tax Court decision holding that the withholding agent's omission of gross income paid to nonresident aliens constituted the omission of gross income for purposes of the six-year statute of limitations of Section 6501(e)(1). Northern Ind. Pub. Serv. v. Comm'r, 101 TC 294 (1993). The IRS also believed that the application of the penalty to this situation was supportable because the legislative history did not specifically preclude it.

[200] IRC § 6662(d)(2)(A). Note that this definition of "understatement of income tax" is roughly the same as the definition of "deficiency" in Section 6211(a), and this understatement is similarly not reduced by estimated tax and withholding tax credits.

[201] See IRC § 6211(b)(2); Reg. § 301.6211-1(f).

[202] The substantial understatement penalty was routinely asserted at service centers and in district examination divisions. One of the general administrative recommendations Congress made in IMPACT was addressed to this problem and provides: "In the application of penalties, the IRS should make a correct substantive decision in the first instance rather than mechanically assert penalties with the idea that they will be corrected later." HR Rep. No. 247, 101st Cong., 1st Sess. 299. See Reg. § 1.6662-4(b)(3).

[203] IRC § 6662(d)(2)(B)(i). See Reg. § 1.6662-4(b)(6), Ex. (1).

[204] IRC § 6662(d)(2)(B)(ii).

[205] IRC § 6662(d)(2)(C)(i)(II).

[206] IRC § 6662(d)(2)(C)(i)(I).

Since the substantial understatement accuracy-related penalty has its own disclosure provision, there are overlapping disclosure procedures in the accuracy-related penalty and the reasonable cause exception. To assist taxpayers in filing returns, a list of positions affecting a significant number of taxpayers for which the Treasury believes no substantial authority exists is to be published annually.[207] Important elements of the substantial understatement accuracy-related penalty are (1) substantial authority; (2) disclosure; and (3) tax shelter items. These elements are discussed in the following sections.

The amount of the understatement is not determined in the manner in which Section 6662(d) would indicate. Instead, the calculation starts with the correct income tax for the year. However, the amount of tax shown by the taxpayer on the return for the taxable year is determined by recomputing the tax as if individual items of income and deduction that had been incorrectly treated on the return, but covered by one of the three permissible reductions, had received the proper tax treatment.[208] In other words, if a deduction was improperly claimed, but the taxpayer made a qualifying disclosure, the tax shown on the return is computed as if the deduction were properly claimed.

The following example demonstrates the computation that must be made in computing the accuracy-related substantial understatement penalty.

> **EXAMPLE:** In 1990, A, an individual, files a return for 1989, which shows taxable income of $18,200 and a tax liability of $3,914. Subsequent adjustments on audit for 1989 increase the taxable income to $51,500 and tax liability to $17,068. There was a qualifying disclosure (or alternatively, substantial authority) for an item resulting in an adjustment that increases taxable income by $5,300. In computing the amount of the underpayment, the amount of tax shown on A's return is determined as if the item for which there was a disclosure (or substantial authority) had been given the proper tax treatment. The amount of tax that is treated as shown on A's return ($18,200 taxable income actually shown on A's return, plus $5,300, the amount of the adjustment for which there was a disclosure) is $4,837. The amount of the underpayment is $12,231 ($17,068, the amount of tax required to be shown on the return, less $4,837, the amount of tax treated as shown on A's return after adjustment for disclosure). Consequently, the amount of the accuracy-related penalty is $2,426.20 ($12,231 multiplied by 20 percent).

[c] Reduction for Substantial Authority

For purposes of the accuracy-related substantial understatement penalty, the term "understatement" means the excess of the amount of tax required to

---

[207] IRC § 6662(d)(2)(D).
[208] See Reg. § 1.6661-2(d)(3).

be shown on the return for the taxable year over the amount actually shown on the return for the taxable year, reduced by any rebate.[209] The amount of tax shown on the return for the taxable year is determined by computing the tax as if the return (in addition to the items that were properly reported on the return) included items for which there is or was substantial authority for the treatment claimed.[210] In other words, if there is or was substantial authority for the tax treatment of an item (other than a tax shelter item), then the item is treated as if it were shown properly on the return for the taxable year in computing the amount of tax shown on the return.

The actual meaning of "substantial authority" is distressingly vague for a penalty provision. The term is not defined in the statute, and its meaning has been derived from committee reports. "Authority" is a term associated with a court decision, so the term presupposes a legal issue on which authority exists, rather than a factual issue to be resolved by a finder of fact. This suggests an issue on which the facts will not be in dispute, but only the application of some developed law to a set of facts, much in the way a court of appeals would decide an appeal coming before it. Despite the apparent relationship of the standard to the appellate process, the legislative history described the standard in terms applicable in a trial court.[211]

According to the legislative history, the substantial authority standard is less stringent than a "more likely than not" standard (a greater than 50 percent likelihood of being upheld in litigation), but stricter than a reasonable-basis standard (the standard that generally prevented imposition of a negligence penalty under prior law).[212] A taxpayer does not have substantial authority for a position if it is "fairly unlikely to prevail in court upon a complete review of

---

[209] IRC § 6662(d).

[210] See Reg. § 1.6661-3(a)(1).

[211] The Tax Court has said that "substantial authority (in the regulations) refers to legal precedents which would support the taxpayer's application of the law to a given set of facts." The weight of the authorities for the tax treatment of an item is determined by the same analysis that a court would be expected to follow in warranting the treatment of the item. Antonides v. Comm'r, 91 TC 686, 702–703 (1988).

[212] Conf. Rep. No. 760, 97th Cong., 2d Sess. 575 (1982), reprinted in 1982-2 CB 600. For additional critical analysis, see Banoff, "Determining Valid Legal Authority in Advising Clients, Rendering Opinions, Preparing Tax Returns, and Avoiding Penalties: The Impact of IMPACT," 68 Taxes 40 (Jan. 1990); Banoff, "Determining and Weighing Valid Legal Authority to Avoid Penalties: In IRS Notice 90-20, the Empire Strikes Back," 68 Taxes 304 (Apr. 1990). Regulations put the analysis this way: "[a] position with respect to the tax treatment of an item that is arguable but fairly unlikely to prevail in court could satisfy a reasonable-basis standard, but not the substantial-authority standard." Reg. § 1.6661-3(a)(2). This description implies that substantial authority meets a more-likely-than-not chance of success. Regulations state, "The substantial authority standard is less stringent than the more likely than not standard (the standard that is met when there is a greater than 50-percent likelihood of the position being upheld), but more stringent than the reasonable basis standard as defined in [Reg. § 1.6662-3(b)(3)]."

the facts and authorities."[213] In evaluating whether the authorities supporting an item are substantial, the regulations state that the weight of authority supporting the treatment of an item must be substantial "in relation to the weight of authorities supporting contrary positions."[214] Although all authorities are to be taken into account, the taxpayer's belief that the authorities supporting the claimed tax treatment constitute substantial authority does not control the determination. Not all authorities will be considered.

The regulations focus on legal authorities and assume that (1) such authority exists and clearly applies to the return position; (2) the authorities for and against the position are capable of being weighed; and (3) the likelihood of success can be determined with some refinement. Even if the validity of these premises in the committee report and the regulations is granted (and they are not likely to be always valid for every issue on every return) it is fair for a practitioner to be required to make a rough evaluation of the taxpayer's chances of success.[215] It is unfair to expect a lay taxpayer to make this evaluation. Unless the taxpayer was a practitioner or had counsel on the matter, the standard requires a judgment from precisely those persons who are incapable of making it. This problem raises yet another defect with the substantial authority standard. Under certain circumstances, the standard can be applied by practitioners, but the standard is not directed at the conduct of practitioners preparing the taxpayers' returns.[216] Rather, it is included in a penalty imposed

---

[213] Id. When the taxpayer's legal arguments are rejected, it is not surprising that the rejected legal arguments are found not to constitute substantial authority. See, e.g., Lair v. Comm'r, 95 TC 484 (1990). But unless a substantial authority finding involves consideration of whether the taxpayer's conduct was reasonable, a court is likely to find that rejected legal arguments are not substantial authority. Surely, Congress had in mind circumstances other than a taxpayer's being wrong before it believed it was appropriate to penalize a taxpayer. The reasonable cause exception should prompt courts to consider conduct as well as the weight of authority.

[214] Reg. § 1.6661-3(b)(1). The Tax Court seems to have adopted the approach in the regulations. See, e.g., Jamar v. Comm'r, 62 TCM 1390 (1991) ("Substantial authority for a position exists if the weight of authorities supporting the position is substantial when compared to the weight of the authorities contrary to the position. . . . For taxable year 1982, petitioners failed to cite any substantial authority for the positions taken on their tax return.").

[215] Lawyers are required to certify that a pleading, motion, or other paper filed in federal court is "well grounded in fact and warranted by existing law." Fed. R. Civ. P. 11; Tax Court Rule Prac. & Proc. 33(b). But the Tax Court has held taxpayers responsible for essentially faulty legal analysis. See Matlock v. Comm'r, 63 TCM 3108 (1992) (When taxpayers failed to substantiate expenses, the court said, "Even assuming that there were legal authorities that would have supported petitioners' claims (e.g. payments for supplies and bank charges are ordinary and necessary business expenses under section 162), those authorities are 'materially distinguishable.'").

[216] In fact, the standard imposed on return preparers does not require "substantial authority" but a "realistic possibility of being sustained on the merits." IRC § 6694, discussed at ¶ 4.05[3].

on taxpayers, and it is these taxpayers who will pay for the errors or aggressive positions of their preparers. The inherent confusion of the substantial authority standard (that is, it is a standard that confuses the role of the tax adviser and the limited capacity of taxpayers to evaluate a tax position under a concededly complex tax law) brings the tax adviser into the issue of whether the taxpayer had substantial authority for the return position. This is precisely why when taxpayers of limited experience consult tax professionals, the issue of whether the taxpayers acted with reasonable cause merges with the issue whether they had substantial authority for their return positions.[217] Some courts have also been unwilling to narrowly interpret the meaning of substantial authority to exclude the facts of the transaction on which the advice was given. One circuit court has said if substantial authority depends on evidence going both ways, "there is substantial authority from a factual standpoint for the taxpayer's position."[218]

In practice, the substantial authority standard creates a number of anomalous situations. Because it is vague, large corporate and affluent taxpayers with access to sufficient tax expertise to apply the standard utilize the disclosure procedure to avoid any penalty issue. This cautious and practical response indicates an element in the operation of the standard that is unsatisfactory from a policy point of view. Corporations and more affluent taxpayers will be able to retain counsel for both the kind of research and analysis that could develop a substantial authority position or to draft a disclosure statement. On the other hand, individual taxpayers whose returns are prepared by return preparers who are perhaps less sophisticated and certainly more pressured by the number of individual returns being prepared will have to deal with the ambiguity of the

---

[217] Streber v. Comm'r, 81 AFTR2d ¶ 98-610 (5th Cir. 1998) (a divided court), citing Heasley v. Comm'r, 902 F2d 380, 385 (5th Cir. 1990). In both cases, the taxpayers, who were unsophisticated, had consulted tax professionals about issues of tax law, and the circuit court held that they were not liable for a substantial understatement penalty because they acted with reasonable cause.

[218] Osteen v. Comm'r, 62 F3d 356, 359 (11th Cir. 1995) ("only if there was a record upon which the Government could obtain a reversal under the clearly erroneous standard could it be argued that from an evidentiary standpoint, there was not substantial authority . . ."); see also Streber v. Comm'r, 81 AFTR2d ¶ 98-610 (5th Cir. 1998) ("the government makes no effort to assert that the only rational tax treatment of the transaction was as a gift made before 1985"). The Sixth Circuit has agreed with the Tenth Circuit's view in *Osteen* that substantial authority includes factual evidence as well as legal sources, particularly in a case that turns on intent. Estate of Robert G. Kluener v. Comm'r, 82 AFTR2d 98-6151 (6th Cir. 1998). The Sixth Circuit also said that "substantial" authority exists if the taxpayer presents "sufficient facts to support a judgment in the [taxpayer's] favor under the clearly erroneous standard of review, looking at the case as if [the taxpayer] had won on the deficiency." However, the Sixth Circuit disagreed with the analysis in *Osteen* of "substantial," saying that the term "substantial" requires more than a reasonable basis; it requires the taxpayer to present "considerable or ample authority," rather than only "some evidence," as the *Osteen* court said.

standard. Therefore, the operation of the standard in practice is flawed by uncertainties and unfairness inappropriate for a civil penalty.

Based on regulations under prior law[219] and the committee report on the accuracy-related penalty,[220] "authorities," for purposes of the substantial authority analysis, are the following:

- Applicable provisions of the Code and other statutory provisions
- Temporary and final regulations construing such statutes
- Court cases[221]
- Administrative pronouncements (including revenue rulings and revenue procedures)[222]
- Tax treaties and related regulations, and Treasury Department and other official explanations of treaties
- Congressional intent as reflected in committee reports, joint explanatory statements of managers included in conference committee reports, and floor statements made prior to enactment by one of the bill's managers

---

[219] See Reg. § 1.6661-3(b)(2).

[220] After complaints that the list of acceptable authorities was too restrictive, Congress expanded the list of authorities that it said the Treasury should include in regulations. HR Rep. No. 247, 101st Cong., 1st Sess. 280—281. The benefit of increasing the types of "authority" is not without its cost to taxpayers. The greater the number of "authorities," the heavier the research burden to find all those authorities and to weigh them before taking a return position.

[221] Court cases applicable to the taxpayer by reason of the taxpayer's residence in a particular jurisdiction are not taken into account in determining whether there is substantial authority for the tax treatment of an item. However, a controlling precedent of a circuit court of appeals to which the taxpayer has the right of appeal with respect to the item is considered substantial authority. The regulations grudgingly accept this view. Reg. § 1.6662-4(d)(3)(iii). The regulations say that "authority" may lose its status when "it is overruled or modified, implicitly or explicitly, by a body with the power to modify the earlier authority." Reg. § 1.6662-4(d)(3)(iii).

[222] Informal notices and announcements issued by the Service may be relied on for "substantial authority" in the same manner as revenue rulings and revenue procedures. Rev. Rul. 87-138, 1978-2 CB 287. After Congress stated its intention that the list of authorities on which taxpayers may rely that are contained in the substantial understatement penalty regulation should be expanded to include notices the IRS published, the IRS announced that notices published in the Internal Revenue Bulletin constitute "authority." Notice 90-20, 1990-1 CB 328. Notice 90-20 also applied the definition of "authority" in the substantial understatement accuracy-related penalty (Section 6662(d)(2)(B)(i)) retroactively to substantial understatement penalty cases. As a result, Rev. Rul. 87-138 became unnecessary. Rev. Rul. 90-91, 1990-2 CB 262. According to Treasury regulations, actions on decision and general counsel memoranda are considered authority if they were issued after March 12, 1981 or, with regard to general counsel memoranda, if they were published in pre-1955 volumes of the Cumulative Bulletin. Reg. § 1.6662-4(d)(3)(iii).

- A written determination (a letter ruling or a technical advice issued to a taxpayer may constitute substantial authority if it is issued to the taxpayer named and there has been no misstatement of material fact)[223]
- Proposed regulations[224]
- Private letter rulings, technical advice memoranda and actions on decisions, and general counsel memoranda[225]
- Information or press releases, notices and other similar documents published by the Service in the Internal Revenue Bulletin[226]
- Blue Books prepared by the Joint Committee on Taxation[227]

The Service does not consider the following sources to provide authority:[228] conclusions reached in treatises, legal periodicals, legal opinions, or opinions rendered by other tax professionals. However, authorities underlying these expressions of opinion may give rise to substantial authority for an item under the facts of a particular case, and the authorities cited in the opinion may be a basis for waiver of the penalty.

---

[223] Reg. § 1.6662-4(d)(3)(iii).

[224] HR Rep. No. 247, 101st Cong., 1st Sess. 280–281.

[225] HR Rep. No. 247, 101st Cong., 1st Sess. 281. Letter rulings, determination letters, and technical advice are "written determinations" that "may not be used or cited as precedent," according to provisions about the public inspection of written determinations. IRC § 6110(k)(3). Only letter rulings and technical advice memoranda issued after March 12, 1981, are considered to constitute authority in the Treasury regulations. Reg. § 1.6662-4(d)(3)(iii).

[226] HR Rep. No. 247, 101st Cong., 1st Sess. 281. The committee report on IMPACT states that while the intention was to broaden the list of acceptable authorities, the date limitations could be placed on items added to the list. House Report, supra, 281 n.79. For example, consistent with the objective of broadening the list of authorities, a date limitation drawn as narrowly as possible might be used as of which date the item might be considered authority. The committee report uses the example of a regulation that provided letter rulings issued would not be substantial authority before the date they were made public.

[227] HR Rep. No. 247, 101st Cong., 1st Sess. 281. For cases where courts have cited the Blue Book as legal authority, see Holiday Village Shopping Center, Inc. v. United States, 773 F2d 276 (Fed. Cir. 1985); Shenker v. Comm'r, 50 TCM 189 (1985).

[228] See Reg. 1.6662-4(d)(3)(iii). The AICPA differs with this view for purposes of the return preparer penalty. In SRTP Interpretation No. 1-1 (Dec. 1990), the AICPA's Tax Division states as follows (at ¶ .07):

In determining whether a tax return position meets the CPA's realistic possibility standard, a CPA may rely on authorities in addition to those evaluated in determining whether substantial authority exists. Accordingly, CPAs may rely on well-reasoned treatises, articles in recognized tax publications, and other reference tools and sources of tax analyses commonly used by tax advisors and return preparers.

This widening dichotomy between the penalties on preparers and the substantial understatement penalty is simply unjustifiable in logic and principle.

An understatement is reduced by the amount of an item "if there is or was substantial authority" for the return treatment of the item."[229] This statutory language raises the issue of when substantial authority is to be determined—i.e., whether the statutory language "if there is substantial authority" means that the determination is made at the time of the examination or at the time of the return preparation. The plain meaning of these terms is that authority is substantial if it exists either at the time of return preparation or of the tax determination,[230] and the Service has no right to penalize a taxpayer if the taxpayer's position is supportable whenever the support develops.

Supplemental to a list of authorities, the Service is required to publish in the Federal Register, at least annually, a list of positions on issues affecting a significant number of taxpayers for which the Service believes no substantial authority exists.[231] This list is called a Secretarial list and is intended to assist taxpayers and practitioners alike by identifying positions for which the IRS be-

---

[229] IRC § 6662(d)(2)(B)(i). The Tax Court has found "substantial authority" to be lacking and accordingly upheld the imposition of the substantial understatement penalty when the underpayment is due to negligent conduct, rather than frivolous legal positions. See, e.g., Schultheiss v. Comm'r, 63 TCM 2836 (1992) (negligent omission of income also punished by substantial understatement penalty, because no substantial authority for omission); Matlock v. Comm'r, 63 TCM 3108 (1992) (negligent deduction of personal expenses also punished by substantial understatement penalty, because no substantial authority for deduction); Milton Schwartz, Dec'd v. Comm'r, TC Memo 1992-677, 64 TCM 1384 (1992), aff'd per curium, 1994 US App. LEXIS 6984 (11th Cir. 1994) (negligence conceded for failure to report sales income; substantial understatement penalty imposed).

On the other hand, in J.P. Sheahan Assocs., Inc. v. Comm'r, 63 TCM 2842 (1992), while a negligence penalty for the erroneous use of the cash method rather than the accrual method of accounting was not upheld because the taxpayer's returns were prepared by a CPA, a substantial understatement penalty was upheld because case law rejected the use of the cash method under the circumstances. The rationale for this disturbing result was the conclusion that the application of the substantial understatement penalty does not "depend upon the presence or absence of negligence" or reliance on advice of counsel sufficient to relieve the taxpayer of a negligence penalty. 63 TCM at 2848–2849. This view ignores the relevance of the taxpayer's conduct in any penalty analysis. The substantial understatement penalty was intended to punish taxpayers who invested in tax shelters, who used "reasonable basis," i.e., frivolous legal advice, to avoid the negligence penalty. Even when a tax shelter is involved and a taxpayer acts reasonably in retaining a professional adviser, the taxpayer cannot be said to have lacked reasonable cause and good faith. Compare Vorsheck v. Comm'r, 933 F2d 757 (9th Cir. 1991), cert. denied, 112 S. Ct. 591 (1991), with Antonides v. Comm'r, 91 TC 686, 700–704 (1988), aff'd, 893 F2d 656 (4th Cir. 1990). For a case where the taxpayer actually litigated the issue of substantial authority instead of merely relying on the evidence and arguments on the substantive issue, and the district court dealt with the issue in an extended way, see Peerless Indus., Inc. v. United States, 94-1 USTC ¶ 50,043 (ED Pa. 1994).

[230] Nevertheless, under the regulations, substantial authority is determined as of the time the return is filed or on the last day of the taxable year to which the return relates. Reg. § 1.6661-3(b)(4)(iii).

[231] IRC § 6662(d)(2)(D).

lieves there is no substantial authority and that affect a significant number of taxpayers. This Secretarial list is only intended to provide guidance. If a position is not on the list, the Service is not bound by the omission, since there still may be no substantial authority to support the position. Moreover, if a taxpayer takes a position not on the list, but discloses it, a negligence-type accuracy-related penalty could be imposed (e.g., if the position was frivolous).[232]

[d] Reduction by Disclosure

Disclosure of a return position on an item can result in the reduction of an understatement. Where "any item with respect to which the relevant facts affecting the item's tax treatment are adequately disclosed in the return or in a statement attached to the return," the understatement in tax is reduced.[233] In effect, this reduction-by-disclosure treats the disclosed item as if the item were properly reported on the tax return for the taxable year. This procedure was the most notably successful part of the substantial understatement penalty. Undoubtedly, the indefinite nature of the reduction-by-substantial-authority makes the relatively clear-cut reduction-by-disclosure more appealing.

Statutorily, disclosure occurs where (1) the tax treatment of an item is (2) adequately disclosed (a) on the return or (b) in a statement attached to the return. Regulations interpreting the reduction-by-disclosure procedures under prior law[234] were carried over to the substantial understatement part of the accuracy-related penalty.[235] Disclosures for purposes of this penalty are considered adequate if they are made in one of the following ways:

1. *Disclosure in attached statement.* As suggested by the statute, a disclosure can be made by attaching a statement to the return. This disclosure statement can be either an IRS-supplied form or self-prepared. A disclosure statement can be made by a completed Form 8275,[236] or a statement attached to the return that includes (a) a caption identifying the statement as a disclosure under Section 6662; (b) identification of the item (or group of similar items) disclosed; (c) the amount

---

[232] HR Rep. No. 247, 101st Cong., 1st Sess. 281.

[233] IRC § 6662(d)(2)(B)(ii).

[234] Reg. § 6661-4 (1985).

[235] Notice 90-20, 1990-1 CB 328, 330; see Bennett v. Comm'r, 62 TCM 1400 (1991) (disclosure not found, despite attachment of worksheet, deed of gift, and appraisal; absence of loan agreement "made it impossible for respondent to identify the potential controversy"). Merely listing an item, such as income, expenses, and depreciation, on a return is generally not considered by the courts as constituting sufficient disclosure of the potential nature of the controversy concerning the item. See Boreta v. Comm'r, TC Memo. 1997-561 (1997).

[236] Reg. § 1.6661-4(b)(1). When issued, Form 8275 was entitled "Disclosure Statement under Section 6661."

of the item or group of items or similar items; and (d) facts affecting the item that "may reasonably be expected to apprise the [Service] of the nature of the potential controversy concerning the tax treatment of the item."[237]

2. *Disclosure of legal issue.* Instead of setting forth the facts affecting the treatment of an item in the attached disclosure statement, a concise description of the legal issue presented by the facts can be presented in the disclosure statement.[238]

3. *Disclosure on return.* As prescribed in revenue procedures, information provided on a return completed in accordance with the applicable forms and instructions can be considered adequate disclosure.[239] Proving that the return adequately disclosed the item, using the return and attached forms, can be extremely difficult.[240]

---

[237] Reg. § 1.6661-4(b)(1).

[238] Reg. § 1.6661-4(b)(2).

[239] Reg. § 1.6661-4(c). The Service issues annual revenue procedures, identifying the circumstances under which the disclosure on a taxpayer's return of a position with respect to an item is adequate for purposes of reducing the understatement of income tax under Section 6662(d) and for the purpose of the preparer penalty under Section 6694(a). See, e.g., Rev. Proc. 97-56, 1997-52 IRB 18 (applicable to returns filed for 1998); Rev. Proc. 2001-11, 2001-2 IRB 1 (Dec. 7, 2000) (applicable to returns filed in 2000).

[240] For example, although the taxpayer, who purchased, rented, and sold real estate, filed a Form 4797, Gain and Losses from Sales or Exchanges of Assets Used in a Trade or Business and Involuntary Conversions, and carried over the total gain reported to Schedule D of his tax return under the category long-term capital gains, and separately listed each house sale, a divided Ninth Circuit panel held that the disclosures on his returns were inadequate "to disclose the true nature of the sales proceeds as ordinary income, nor did the disclosures supply the critical facts underlying the nature of the Taxpayer's real estate business." Little v. Comm'r, 106 F3d 1445 (9th Cir. 1997). The dissent pointed out that the reporting of 200 real estate sales over a three-year period as capital gains put the Service on notice that Little might have reported capital gains improperly. In other cases, the taxpayer's disclosure argument has failed because the court has concluded that the Service could not have detected the issue from the information provided on the return. See Reinke v. Comm'r, 46 F3d 760 (8th Cir. 1995) (capital gains reported on return would not have indicated the possibility of a controversy because total listed included ordinary income for damage to land and capital gains); Accardo v. Comm'r, 942 F2d 444 (7th Cir. 1991) (nothing on return would have indicated taxpayer's "novel theory" for deducting legal fees and that there was a problem with the deduction); Schirmer v. Comm'r, 89 TC 277 (1987) (no indication on return that a farm was not being used as taxpayers claimed). Compare, Fellouzis v. United States, 896 F. Supp. 1166 (MD Fla. 1995) (couple claimed charitable deductions on their returns for five years and their accountant attached appraisals of artwork contributed to their returns; the Service disallowed the deductions and imposed negligence penalties; held, taxpayers disclosed the relevant facts on which they based their deductions); Pan Am. Life Ins. Co. v. United States, 83 AFTR2d ¶ 99-829 (ED La. 1999) (court held that company adequately disclosed the relevant facts on its returns, thereby properly alerting the Service to the nature of the controversy).

4. *Carryovers and carrybacks and pass-through entities.* Special rules apply to carryovers and carrybacks,[241] but in general the disclosure is made on the return for the year giving rise to the carryover or carryback. Where disclosure is made of a pass-through item, the pass-through entity makes the disclosure on its return. A taxpayer can make a disclosure by attaching a disclosure statement to his return and filing a copy of that disclosure statement with the Service Center where the pass-through entity's return is filed.[242]

However, for returns required to be filed before January 1, 1994, regulations under Section 6662 modify or change these rules in a number of ways:

1. *Limitations on disclosure.* Disclosure will not have an effect if the return position is frivolous or attributable to a tax shelter, or if the taxpayer failed to keep adequate books and records for the item.[243]
2. *Method of disclosure.* The only adequate disclosure is one made on a return or a qualified amended return on a Form 8275 (Disclosure Statement) or, in the case of a position contrary to a regulation, on a Form 8275 (Regulation Disclosure Statement).[244] Disclosure on a return pursuant to the annual revenue procedure remains the same.[245]
3. *Recurring items.* When an item recurs in a number of years and on the returns for those years, the disclosure must be made on each of the returns.[246]
4. *Pass-through entities.* Disclosure on a disclosure statement must be made on the pass-through entity's return, but may also be made on the pass-through participant's return as well.[247]

For tax returns due after December 31, 1993, disclosure will not reduce the amount of an understatement unless (1) the disclosed return position has at least a reasonable basis (i.e., a position that meets a significantly higher standard of support than the not-frivolous standard which permits a return preparer to avoid the return preparer penalty); (2) the item is attributable to a tax shelter; or (3) the item or position is properly substantiated, or the taxpayer failed to keep adequate books and records to support the item or position.[248]

---

[241] Reg. § 1.6661-4(d).

[242] Reg. § 1.6661-4(e) (setting forth information required to be included).

[243] Reg. § 1.6662-4(e)(2).

[244] Reg. § 1.6662-4(f).

[245] Reg. § 1.6662-4(f).

[246] Reg. § 1.6662-4(e)(3).

[247] Reg. § 1.6662-4(e)(4).

[248] Reg. § 1.6662-4(e)(2), effective September 1, 1995. See Prop. Reg. § 1.6662-3(b), 1A-42-95, 61 Fed. Reg. 58,020, for a statement of the Service's view of what "reasonable basis" means.

Although utilized as a basis for exemption from the penalty, as distinguished from a reduction-by-disclosure, an amended return is a kind of disclosure. The penalty can be avoided if an amended return, called a qualified amended return, is filed after the due date of the return but before the earlier of (1) the time the taxpayer is first contacted by the Service concerning an examination of the return or (2) the time a promoter of a tax shelter and others described in Section 6700 is contacted by the Service for an examination of the shelter activity.[249] The Service has ruled that a written statement furnished by a Coordinated Examination Program (CEP) taxpayer to the revenue agent responsible for examining its return will be treated as a qualified amended return.[250]

[e] Tax Shelter Items

Because higher standards for the treatment of an item are applied to a tax shelter, a taxpayer's liability for the substantial underpayment penalty may depend on whether a transaction is a tax shelter. For transactions entered into before August 6, 1997, a tax shelter is defined as a partnership or other entity, any investment plan or arrangement "if the principal purpose of the partnership, entity, plan, or arrangement is the avoidance or evasion of Federal income tax."[251] As a result of the Taxpayer Relief Act of 1997, for transactions entered into after August 5, 1997, the tax avoidance purpose of the entity or arrangement need not be its principal purpose (i.e., tax avoidance purpose exceeds any other purpose), the tax avoidance purpose is only required to be its "significant purpose."[252] The Regulations define a typical tax shelter as a trans-

---

[249] See Reg. § 1.6661-6(c)(2).

[250] Rev. Proc. 85-26, 1985-1 CB 580. To qualify, however, this written statement must be furnished after the return due date and during the nine-day period after the earliest of (1) receipt of a written confirmation of the first formal meeting with the examining agent; (2) the actual day of the meeting; or (3) the day the taxpayer receives a written request for information as part of the examination of the return for the relevant tax year. Revenue Procedure 85-26 applies if the written statement includes the caption "Furnished under Revenue Procedure 85-26," a description of the nature and amount of the items, and a declaration that the statement is made under penalties of perjury. However, recomputation of tax need not be included. Revenue Procedure 85-26 applies to returns whose due date (without regard to extensions for filing) is after December 31, 1982.

[251] IRC § 6662(d)(2)(C)(iii), prior to amendment by the Taxpayer Relief Act of 1997, § 1028(c)(2). See Treas. Reg. § 1.6662-4(g)(2) ("The principal purpose of an entity, plan or arrangement is to avoid or evade Federal income tax if that purpose exceeds any other purpose.").

[252] IRC § 6662(d)(2)(C)(iii), as amended by the Taxpayer Relief Act of 1997, § 1028(c)(2), applicable to transactions after the date of enactment, August 5, 1997. The purpose of this change was to conform the definition of tax shelter to the definition of a tax shelter for purposes of the confidential corporate tax shelter registration requirements. See infra ¶ 7B.16[3].

action structured with "little or no motive for the realization of economic gain, and transactions that use the mismatching of income and deductions over-valued assets or assets with values subject to substantial uncertainty, certain nonrecourse financing, financing techniques that do not conform to standard commercial business practices, or the mischaracterization of the substance of the transaction."[253] On the other hand, the forbidden principal purpose does not exist if the entity, plan, or arrangement has as its purpose the claiming of exclusions from income, accelerated deductions, or other tax benefits "in a manner consistent with the statute and Congressional purpose"; for example, the purchase of tax-exempt securities; claiming accelerated depreciation or depletion allowances; or electing to be taxed as a foreign sales corporation.[254]

For a taxpayer other than a corporation with a substantial understatement attributable to a tax shelter item, the taxpayer may not avoid the understatement by making a qualifying disclosure of the item, and may not rely on the reduction for substantial authority unless "the taxpayer reasonably believed that the tax treatment of the item was more likely than not the correct one."[255] A corporation having a substantial understatement attributable to a tax shelter item may not rely on substantial authority or a qualifying disclosure, and in order to avoid the penalty must show that it reasonably believed that its treatment of the item was more likely than not the correct one.[256] However, a corporation will not be treated as having a reasonable basis for the tax treatment of an item if it is a multiple-party financing transaction, and the treatment does not clearly reflect income.[257]

Attacks on so-called corporate tax shelters began on December 8, 1994, when President Clinton signed legislation to implement the General Agreement on Tariffs and Trade, entitled the Uruguay Round Agreements Act. One of the provisions in the Act, which was intended to finance reduced revenue from tariff reduction, changed the substantial understatement penalty in a way that put even greater pressure than had existed for corporations to document the positions they take on their tax returns. Congress expected that tax revenue

---

[253] Treas. Reg. § 1.6662-4(g)(2)(i).

[254] Treas. Reg. § 1.6662-4(g)(2)(ii). However, a permissible tax benefit may still be a tax shelter item if the permissible tax benefit is related to the principal purpose of avoiding tax. According to an example in the regulations, if a partnership is formed for the principal purpose of avoiding tax by acquiring and overvaluing the basis of the property for the purpose of claiming accelerated depreciation, the depreciation is a tax shelter item. Treas. Reg. § 1.6662-4(g)(3).

[255] IRC § 6662(d)(2)(C)(i)(II); Treas. Reg. § 1.6662-4(g)(3).

[256] IRC § 6662(d)(2)(C)(ii).

[257] IRC § 6662(d)(2)(B), as amended by the Taxpayer Relief Act of 1997, § 1028, effective on the date of enactment, August 5, 1997. See also Reg. § 1.6662-4(e)(3) ("a reasonable corporation will not be treated as having a reasonable basis for its tax treatment of an item attributable to a multi-party financing transaction entered into after August 5, 1997, if the treatment does not clearly reflect the income of the corporation").

will be raised by eliminating the possibility that corporations will be able to avoid the substantial understatement penalty attributable to a tax shelter item, because they are able to show that they had both substantial authority and a reasonable belief that the tax treatment of the item on the return is more likely than not the correct tax treatment. Tax shelter items were defined as a partnership, entity, plan, or arrangement, the principal purpose of which is the avoidance or evasion of income tax (Section 6662(d)(1)(C)), and so all sorts of transactions can be claimed by IRS examiners to be covered by this definition. Accordingly, corporations will be able to avoid the substantial understatement component of the accuracy related penalty after December 8, 1994, only if they can establish reasonable cause under Section 6664(c). This will be even more difficult when tax avoidance need not be the principal purpose, but only a significant purpose.

According to the committee report, the reason for the change in the tax shelter penalty for corporations was that unlike individual taxpayers, the substantial understatement penalty "may" not have been effective enough to deter corporations from entering into aggressive tax shelter transactions.[258] What the change does is to make the 20 percent substantial understatement penalty apply to the tainted portion of a tax understatement, unless the reasonable cause exception applies. But, the report goes on to say, "the intent of the provision is that the standards applicable to corporate shelters be tightened; consequently, in no instance would this modification (of the penalty) result in a penalty not being imposed where a penalty would have been imposed under prior law." To put it another way, the penalty is supposed to be imposed against corporations in more situations than the penalty has been previously applied.

Where noncorporate taxpayers have tax shelter items that have been adjusted, the tax attributable to the adjustment of the items will not be included in the understatement amount where (1) there is substantial authority for the tax treatment of the item and (2) the taxpayer reasonably believed at the time the return was filed that the tax treatment of the item was more likely than not the proper treatment.[259] For corporate taxpayers, all tax shelter items of a corporation are taken into account in computing the amount of the understatement, unless the transaction occurred before December 9, 1994, and the corporation reasonably believed at the time the return was filed that the tax treatment of the item was more likely than not the proper treatment.[260] Reasonable belief is further defined by regulations. If the noncorporate taxpayer does not rely on a professional adviser, the taxpayer will have a reasonable belief only if he analyzes the pertinent facts and authorities, and after the analysis reasonably concludes in good faith that there is a greater-than-50-percent like-

---

[258] HR No. 826, 103d Cong., 2d Sess. 198 (1994).

[259] Reg. § 1.6662-3(g)(1)(i).

[260] Reg. § 1.6662-3(g)(1)(ii).

lihood that the tax treatment of the item will be upheld if challenged by the Service. If the noncorporate taxpayer relies on a professional tax adviser, the taxpayer's belief in the likelihood of the outcome of an IRS challenge will exist only if the adviser's opinion is based on the pertinent facts and authorities, and the adviser unambiguously concludes that there is a greater than 50 percent likelihood that the tax treatment of the item will be upheld if the item is challenged by the IRS.[261] Notice that a disclosure statement will not avoid the penalty whether a noncorporate or corporate tax payer is involved. Moreover, a corporate taxpayer can only avoid the substantial understatement penalty for a tax shelter item if the taxpayer can satisfy the reasonable cause and good faith exception of Section 6664(c).[262]

[4] Substantial Valuation Misstatements

[a] The Accuracy-Related Penalty and Section 6659

Where an underpayment is attributable to a "substantial valuation overstatement under Chapter 1 (normal income taxes and surtaxes)," as specially described in Section 6662(e), the 20 percent accuracy-related penalty is added to the underpayment. This accuracy-related penalty for substantial valuation overstatements is generally the same as the valuation overstatement penalty provided in Section 6659 under prior law.[263] The penalty for valuation overstatements was enacted because it appeared that "taxpayers have been encouraged to overvalue certain types of property and to delay the resolution of valuation issues," because there was tendency to resolve by dividing the differ-

---

[261] Reg. § 1.6662-4(g)(4). In addition, for reliance to be reasonable, the following criteria must be met: (1) the adviser's advice must be based on all pertinent facts and circumstances, all of which the taxpayer must have disclosed to the adviser; (2) the adviser must apply the relevant law to the facts and circumstances; and (3) the adviser must not have made unreasonable assumptions based on the representations, statements, findings, or agreements of the taxpayer or any other person. Reg. § 1.6664-4(c). See infra ¶ 7B.04[1] for a further discussion of the reasonable cause exception.

[262] This exception is discussed infra ¶ 7B.04[1]. Reg. §§ 1.6662-4(g)(1)(ii), 1.6662-4(g)(1)(iv). The term "tax shelter" is defined in a rather detailed way to include plans or arrangements structured with little or no motive for the realization of economic gain, mismatching of income and deductions, overvalued assets, certain nonrecourse financing, nonstandard financing, or mischaracterization of the substance of the transaction. Reg. § 1.6662-4(g)(2). However, the tax shelter definition excludes claimed tax benefits consistent with a statute and Congressional purpose, such as purchasing an obligation having tax-exempt interest, taking accelerated depreciation, or electing domestic international sales corporation or foreign sales corporation status. Id.

[263] IRC § 6659 was added by ERTA, Pub. L. No. 34, HR 4242, 97th Cong., 1st Sess., § 722(a), which redesignated old IRC § 6659 as IRC § 6660.

ences in the values.[264] Recognizing that valuation issues are often difficult, especially where unique property is concerned, Congress adopted a "bright line" test punishing only significant overvaluations by graduated penalty amounts depending on the egregiousness of the significant overvaluation. Since the Section 6659 penalty applied only to individuals, closely held corporations, and personal service corporations, Congress clearly was targetting tax shelter promotions utilizing overvalued property to generate tax deductions when creating the new penalty. However, the penalty can apply in more prosaic transactions, such as charitable contributions of property, purchases of business assets, liquidations, and sale of property received from an estate.[265]

From 1982 through 1989, the substantial valuation overstatement penalty was not coordinated with any other taxpayer penalty, with the exception of the substantial understatement penalty (Section 6661). As a result, this valuation penalty could be imposed in addition to other penalties on taxpayers such as the negligence or fraud penalty. Since Section 6662(b) provides that a single 20 percent penalty applies to the portion of the underpayment attributable to one of five types of conduct, including a substantial valuation overstatement, only a single accuracy-related penalty is imposed where a valuation overstatement is made even if there was also negligence or disregard of rules and regulations with respect to the overvaluation and the tax return position based on it.[266]

For returns due after December 31, 1989, the accuracy-related penalty differs from the substantial overvaluation penalty of Section 6659 in the following ways:

1. *Taxpayers affected.* Section 6659 applied only to individuals, closely held corporations (as described in Section 465(a)(i)(C)), and personal service corporations (as defined in Section 414(m)(3)).[267] The accuracy-related penalty applies to any taxpayer.

2. *Acceptable valuation error.* For purposes of Section 6659, a valuation overstatement existed if the valuation or adjusted basis of property claimed on a return was 150 percent or more of the correct value or adjusted basis.[268] The accuracy-related penalty applies only if the val-

---

[264] HR Rep. No. 201, 97th Cong. 1st Sess. to HR 4242 (ERTA), at 243, reprinted at 1981-2 CB 352, at 398. At the time of the penalty's enactment, the committee report stated that there were 500,000 tax disputes with valuation issues involving $2.5 billion in tax.

[265] Staff of the Joint Comm. on Taxation, General Explanation of the Economic Recovery Tax Act of 1981, 97th Cong., 1st Sess. 333 n.1 (Comm. Print 1981).

[266] If the underpayment involves a valuation overstatement, but is due to fraud, only the fraud penalty is imposed. IRC § 6662(b).

[267] IRC §§ 6659(a), 6659(g) (1986).

[268] IRC § 6659(b) (1986).

uation or adjusted basis of the property is 200 percent or more of the correct value or adjusted basis.[269]

3. *Threshold amount.* Under Section 6659, if the excessive valuation produced an underpayment of $1,000, the penalty could be imposed.[270] For the accuracy-related penalty, the threshold amount is increased fivefold to $5,000 ($10,000 in the case of a corporation other than an S corporation or a personal holding company).[271] Consequently, if an individual taxpayer's excess valuation produces an underpayment of less than $5,000, no accuracy-related penalty for substantial overstatement of value is imposed.

4. *Amount of the penalty.* Under Section 6659, if the excess valuation was between 50 and 200 percent, a 10 percent penalty was imposed.[272] For an excess valuation of from 200 to 400 percent, the accuracy-related penalty was 20 percent.[273]

5. *Maximum penalty rate.* Under prior law, the maximum penalty rate for an excessive valuation (more than 250 percent of the correct value) was 30 percent. For purposes of the accuracy-related penalty, if the excessive valuation is more than 400 percent of the correct value (a gross valuation misstatement), the accuracy-related penalty is 40 percent.[274]

6. *Reasonable cause exception.* Special rules dealing with charitable contributions of property were carried over from pre-IMPACT law. Generally, no accuracy-related penalty is imposed if the taxpayer can show that there was reasonable cause and that he acted in good faith. However, where property has been contributed by the taxpayer to a charity and a deduction has been claimed for income tax purposes, the reasonable cause exception does not apply unless "the claimed value of the property was based on a qualified appraisal made by a qualified appraiser," and the taxpayer made a "good faith investigation of the value of the contributed property."[275]

Minor overvaluations will not be penalized. As the committee report says:[276]

---

[269] IRC § 6662(e)(1).

[270] IRC § 6659(d) (1986).

[271] IRC § 6662(e)(2). A personal holding company for this purpose is defined in Section 542.

[272] IRC § 6659(b) (1986).

[273] IRC § 6662(a).

[274] IRC §§ 6662(h)(1), 6662(h)(2)(A).

[275] IRC §§ 6664(c)(2)(A), 6664(c)(2)(B).

[276] HR Rep. No. 247, 101st Cong., 1st Sess. 282.

> The committee believes that raising both the threshold and the minimum percentage will eliminate from the penalty's scope a number of instances of good-faith valuation disputes that may be subject to penalty under present law.

Nevertheless, excess valuations that do not constitute substantial valuation overstatements may still be subject to the negligence component of the accuracy-related penalty or to a substantial understatement of income tax component of the accuracy-related penalty. Moreover, if the underpayment is due to fraud, the accuracy-related penalty does not apply, but the taxpayer can face the fraud penalty.

[b] Operation of the Overvaluation Component

In operation, the overvaluation component of the accuracy-related penalty requires taxpayers to obtain appraisals of property from qualified appraisers. This is clearly the case if property is donated to a charity, but it is also true in other situations where the valuation of property may be an issue. If there is a dispute about the valuation of property, and the taxpayer and the Service are considerably far apart on the valuation, no reasonable cause exemption can be obtained without an appraisal.[277] Even if a charitable donation is not involved, it is difficult to imagine a set of facts where a taxpayer who had not ever secured an appraisal could establish that there was reasonable cause for the deduction and that the deduction was claimed in good faith. Moreover, since the overvaluation component of the accuracy-related penalty applies to all corporations (not merely closely held and personal service corporations), the penalty puts corporate returns filed after 1989 at risk for the penalty. Transactions involving the valuation of property, such as elections made under Section 338 to treat certain stock purchases as asset acquisitions, can be subject to the overvaluation penalty even though they were entered into before 1990.

The preliminary step in the overvaluation component is to determine that the underpayment was attributable to an overvaluation of property. Not every underpayment in a case involving different valuations of property means that the underpayment was attributable to a valuation overstatement. For example, disallowed deductions can be the result of a finding that no sale of depreciable property to the taxpayer occurred,[278] or that the property had not been placed

---

[277] IRC § 6694(c).

[278] See Zirker v. Comm'r, 87 TC 970, 980–981 (1986) (miscellaneous deductions relating to a cattle investment). See also Soriano v. Comm'r, 90 TC 44, 61 (1988) (disallowance of advance rental deductions not attributable to overvaluation); Ferrel v. Comm'r, 90 TC 1154, 1203–1204 (1988) (disallowed advance minimum royalty deductions too tangentially related to value or bases of leases). But see Gilman v. Comm'r, 933 F2d 143 (2d Cir. 1991) (valuation penalty imposed when transaction was disregarded as sham); see also Zfass v. Comm'r, 118 F3d 184 (4th Cir. 1997) (Tax Court said to have acted cor-

in service during the year.[279] However, where a taxpayer claims a credit or deduction based on an inflated cost, the underpayment is attributable to an overvaluation.[280]

For purposes of the valuation component, "property" includes both tangible and intangible property. Regulations define "tangible property" to include buildings, fixtures, and inventory, while "intangible property" is defined to cover such property as goodwill, covenants not to compete, leaseholds, patents, contracts, contract rights, debts, and choses in action.[281] The breadth of this definition guarantees that in disputes over the valuation of tangible, and especially intangible, property, the valuation misstatement component will be added by examining agents. Where there are multiple valuation misstatements, each valuation misstatement is evaluated separately.[282] On the other hand, the regulations authorize the imposition of an overvaluation component penalty when the correct value or adjusted basis of the property is zero and the valuation misstatement is considered a gross valuation misstatement to which the penalty rate of 40 percent is applicable.[283] The problem with this regulation is that the increased penalty rate is applied regardless of the actual amount of the misvaluation. This approach confuses overvaluation with negligence and possibly with fraud, and it would be better dealt with in the context of those penalties.

Once it is established that all or a portion of the underpayment is attributable to an overvaluation of property, the taxpayer can be penalized only if the overvaluation was substantial—that is, the value of the property (or the adjusted basis of the property) claimed on an income tax return is two or more times the amount determined to be the correct value.[284] If the claimed value is

---

rectly in following the Second Circuit's decision in *Gilman*, as well as decisions in the Sixth and Eighth Circuits when it held "when a transaction lacks economic substance, the correct basis is zero; any amount claimed is a valuation overstatement.").

[279] Todd v. Comm'r, 89 TC 912, 918 (1987), aff'd, 862 F2d 540 (5th Cir. 1988); Gainer v. Comm'r, 893 F2d 225 (9th Cir. 1990) (accord); McCrary v. Comm'r, 92 TC 827, 851 (1989) (*Todd* followed). The Third Circuit refused to follow the Fifth Circuit's decisions in *Todd* and Heasley v. Comm'r, 902 F2d 380 (5th Cir. 1990), and concluded, along with the Second Circuit (*Gilman*) and the Fourth Circuit (*Zfass*) that the disallowance of a claimed benefit does not preclude the imposition of the valuation overstatement penalty when the overvaluation of the property is an essential element component of the tax avoidance scheme. Merino v. Comm'r, 84 AFTR2d 99-6790 (3d Cir. 1999) (unlike the taxpayers in *Heasley*, the taxpayers were sophisticated, and the husband knowledgeable in the plastics business).

[280] Clayden v. Comm'r, 90 TC 656, 677 (1988); Zirker v. Comm'r, 87 TC 970 (1986).

[281] Reg. § 1.6662-5(e)(3).

[282] Reg. § 1.6662-5(f)(1).

[283] Reg. § 1.6662-5(g).

[284] IRC § 6662(e)(1).

more than four times the amount determined to be the correct value, the accu-racy-related penalty amount increases from 20 to 40 percent.[285] The statute uses percentage differences (200 percent or more and 400 percent or more) to describe significant overvaluations. These percentages are easy enough to determine by dividing the taxpayer's claimed value by the correct value. For example, where the claimed value of a carved opal was $292,875 and the correct value was determined to be $27,755, the claimed value was 1,055 percent of the correct value (i.e., $27,755 divided by $292,875).[286]

Not only must there be a substantial valuation overstatement, but the underpayment in income tax attributable to that overstatement must be more than $5,000 ($10,000 in the case of most corporations).[287] In determining the amount of the underpayment attributable to a valuation overstatement, the first step is to calculate the amount of tax liability for the year as if all items had been reported properly (i.e., as if the taxpayer had not claimed any deduction or credit for the property in question). Next, without taking into account any adjustments that are attributable to the valuation overstatement, the amount of tax liability is calculated as if all other items had been reported properly.[288] The difference between the first calculation of the correct tax and the second calculation of the tax liability without regard to the valuation overstatement is the part of the underpayment attributable to the valuation overstatement.

Noncorporate taxpayers who donate property to charities are required to obtain an independent appraisal (a qualified appraisal) and attach a summary of the appraisal to the return, if the value of donated property, other than publicly traded securities, exceeds certain dollar amounts (generally $5,000).[289] Unlike the other accuracy-related penalties, an accuracy-related penalty arising out of a charitable deduction of overvalued property applies unless the taxpayer makes a special reasonable cause showing. For the penalty not to apply the taxpayer must show that the claimed value of the property was (1) based

---

[285] IRC §§ 6662(h)(1), 6662(h)(2)(A). Wyatt v. Comm'r, 62 TCM 1540 (1991) ("We have held that the true value of petitioners's depreciable grove improvements was one-fourth of $700,000, not one-fourth of $2,600,000 that petitioners used in their calculation of the investment tax credit and depreciation deductions. The valuation overstatement exceeds 250 percent.").

[286] Chou v. Comm'r, 58 TCM 1496, 1500 (1990).

[287] IRC § 6662(e)(2). S Corporations and personal holding companies as defined in Section 542 are treated as individual or noncorporate taxpayers.

[288] Todd v. Comm'r, 89 TC 912, 918 (1987), aff'd, 862 F2d 540 (5th Cir. 1988). See also McCrary v. Comm'r, 92 TC 827 (1989), 854–855 (1989).

[289] Reg. § 1.170A-13(c)(2). Taxpayers may also obtain the IRS's valuation of art before filing a return. See Rev. Proc. 96-15, 1996-3 IRB 41, describing procedures for obtaining a Statement of Value for income tax charitable deduction, as well for estate and gift tax purposes.

on a qualified appraisal[290] by a qualified appraiser[291] and that, in addition to obtaining the qualified appraisal, (2) the taxpayer made a good faith investigation of the value of the contributed property.[292]

The overvaluation penalty for contributions of charitable property refers to an entirely new practitioner before the Service—the appraiser permitted to practice before the Service.[293] An appraiser who prepares an appraisal knowing that it will be used in connection with the tax laws and will result in an understatement of tax liability if so used, in violation of Section 6701, may be barred from practice before the Service and Treasury, and the appraisal of such an appraiser may be disregarded for tax purposes.[294]

[c] Transfer Pricing Misstatements: OBRA 1990

The ink had barely dried on the 1989 civil penalty revisions when Congress made a significant change in what had been the substantial valuation overstatement component of the accuracy-related penalty, formerly the valuation overstatement penalty. Responding to perceived abuses by foreign corporations doing business in the United States or with U.S. corporations, Congress

---

[290] A "qualified appraisal" means an appraisal that (1) is made not earlier than sixty days before the contribution of the appraised property; (2) is prepared, signed, and dated by a qualified appraiser (as specially defined); (3) includes all the supporting information required by the regulations (Reg. § 1.170-13(c)(3)(ii)); and (4) is not paid for under a prohibited type of fee arrangement (in general, a fee based on a percentage of the appraised value). Reg. § 1.170A-13(c)(3)(i).

[291] The term "qualified appraiser" excludes any person involved in the transaction or related to the taxpayer or others in the transaction within the meaning of Section 267(b). See also Comm. of Conf. Rep. HR Rep. No. 861, 98th Cong., 2d Sess. 996 (1984), reprinted in 1984-3 CB at 250 (vol. 2). A "qualified appraiser" means an individual who is not the donor, donee, and certain other related persons, and who declares on the appraisal summary that (1) the individual holds himself or herself out to the public as an appraiser; (2) because of the appraiser's qualifications, as described, the appraiser is qualified to make appraisals of the type of property being valued; and (3) the individual understands that a false or fraudulent overstatement of the value of the property described in the appraisal may subject the appraiser to civil penalty for aiding and abetting a tax understatement (Section 6701), with the result that the appraisal may be disregarded under 31 USC § 330(c). Reg. § 1.170-13(c)(5).

[292] See Reg. § 1.170A-13(c)(5)(ii). The donor's actions may disqualify an appraiser. An appraiser is disqualified for "a particular donation" if the donor had knowledge of facts that would cause a reasonable person to expect the appraiser "falsely to overstate the value of the donated property." Id. The regulation gives the example of an appraisal made pursuant to an agreement between the donor and appraiser on the amount at which the property will be appraised, and this agreed-upon appraisal amount exceeds the fair market value of the property.

[293] See discussion of qualified appraisers at ¶ 1.11.

[294] 31 USC § 330(d), added by the Deficit Reduction Act of 1984, § 156, effective for penalties assessed after the date the legislation was enacted.

extended the valuation overstatement component to certain valuation misstatements arising out of reallocations of income or deductions under Section 482.[295] As amended, Section 6662(e) imposes the accuracy-related penalty for substantial overvaluations of property as was provided under the pre-amended version of the component.[296] In addition, however, the accuracy-related penalty can be imposed for Section 482 transfer price and service fee adjustments. Specifically, valuation misstatements are penalized if "the price for any property or services (or for the use of property)" on a related party's return (for purposes of Section 482) is "200 percent or more (or 50 percent or less) of the amount determined under [S]ection 482 to be the correct amount of such price."[297] Alternatively, the penalty may be imposed if "the net [S]ection 482 transfer price adjustment for the taxable year exceeds $10,000,000."[298] Needless to say, the term "net Section 482 transfer price adjustment" is defined as, and the definition says it means that, "the net increase in taxable income for the taxable year (determined without regard to any amount carried to such taxable year from another taxable year) resulting from adjustments under [S]ection 482 in the price for any property or services (or for the use of property)."[299]

This definition is intended to take into account the taxpayer whose regular tax, as defined in Section 55(c), is determined by reference to an amount other than its taxable income.[300] In this case, the other amount is treated as taxable income for purposes of Section 6662(e).[301] Two examples are given in the Conference Report to illustrate the operation of this application of the penalty:

> For example, assume that under section 482 the IRS makes a single adjustment to the net income of a foreign corporation for the taxable year, and that adjustment consists of a $25,000,000 decrease in the foreign corporation's interest expense. Assume also that the foreign corporation is subject to U.S. regular tax only with respect to its gross income which is either derived from sources within the United States or effectively connected with the conduct of a trade or business in the United States (or

---

[295] OBRA 1990, § 11312.

[296] IRC § 6662(e)(1)(A).

[297] IRC § 6662(e)(1)(B)(i).

[298] IRC § 6662(e)(1)(B)(ii).

[299] IRC § 6662(e)(3)(A).

[300] HR Conf. Rep., 101st Cong., 2d Sess. 66 (1990), reprinted in 1990-3 CB (vol. 3) 1074. Section 55(c) provides:

For purposes of this section, the term "regular tax" means the regular tax liability for the taxable year (as defined in section 26(b)) reduced by the foreign tax credit allowable under section 27(a) and the section 936 credit allowable under section 27(b). Such term shall not include any tax imposed by section 402(e) and shall not include any increase in tax under section 47 or subsection (j) or (k) of section 42.

[301] IRC § 6662(e)(3)(C).

both). Further, assume that the section 482 decrease in interest expense increases by less than $10,000,000 the foreign corporation's taxable income effectively connected with the conduct of a trade or business in the United States. Under the conference agreement, the net section 482 transfer price adjustment for the taxable year of the foreign corporation does not exceed $10,000,000.

As another example, assume the same facts as above, except that the foreign corporation is a controlled foreign corporation, and the $25,000,000 interest expense adjustment results in a U.S. shareholder having an additional subpart F inclusion in excess of $10,000,000. Under the provision, the net section 482 transfer price adjustment for the taxable year of the U.S. shareholder may exceed $10,000,000 (assuming neither the reasonable cause exception nor the foreign-to-foreign adjustment exception, as described below, applies).[302]

In determining whether the "net Section 482 transfer price adjustment" exceeds the $10,000,000 benchmark, two possible adjustments must be taken into account. The first adjustment is a special version of the reasonable cause exception already contained in Section 6664(c).[303] A net increase in taxable income arising out of a Section 482 redetermination of a price does not include any portion for which "it is shown that there was a reasonable cause for the taxpayer's determination of [that] price and that the taxpayer acted in good faith with respect to [that] price."[304] The same standards of reasonable cause and good faith in Section 6664(c) apply to this showing to be made by the taxpayer.[305]

Second, in general, the portion of the net increase in taxable income attributable to a transaction solely between foreign corporations is disregarded.[306]

---

[302] HR Conf. Rep., 101st Cong., 2d Sess. 67–68 (1990), reprinted in 1990-3 CB (vol. 3) 1075–1076.

[303] HR Conf. Rep., 101st Cong., 2d Sess. 68 (1990), reprinted in 1990-3 CB (vol. 3) 1076. See infra ¶ 7B.04.

[304] IRC § 6662(e)(3)(B)(i). The $10 million and $20 million adjustments that trigger the penalty may result from a small per-unit intercompany price adjustment on a high-volume intercompany transaction. A number of multinational corporations urged the Service to adopt a de minimis adjustment safe harbor. "Multinationals Urge Reasonable-Cause Exception to Section 482-Related Penalty," DTR (BNA), at G-4 (Feb. 4, 1992). Similarly, the penalty could be triggered by a small percentage of royalty adjustment. The multinational corporations suggested that a reasonable cause exception should apply to taxpayers "whose royalty rates are within a reasonable range of the adjusted royalty rates." The penalty also should not be imposed if the taxpayer can show that it has made a good faith effort to comply with the spirit of the Section 482 regulations by conducting a bona fide transfer pricing study and by establishing a transfer pricing methodology consistent with the fact pattern, the Code, and the regulations.

[305] HR Conf. Rep., 101st Cong., 2d Sess. 68 (1990), reprinted in 1990-3 CB (vol. 3) 1076.

[306] IRC § 6662(e)(3)(B)(ii).

This adjustment is to be made "unless, in the case of [these foreign] corporations, the treatment of [the] transaction affects the determination of income from sources within the United States or taxable income effectively connected with the conduct of a trade or business within the United States."[307] The Conference Report illustrates the operation of this adjustment:[308]

> For example, assume that a net increase in the taxable income of a U.S. shareholder results from an adjustment in the royalty paid by one controlled foreign corporation to another controlled foreign corporation. Assume that neither foreign corporation earns any income from U.S. sources or income effectively connected with the conduct of a trade or business in the United States. Under the conference agreement's foreign-to-foreign adjustment exception, the net increase in the U.S. shareholder's taxable income resulting from the IRS's adjustment of the royalty amount will not be counted in determining whether the net section 482 transfer price adjustment of the U.S. shareholder exceeds $10,000,000 or $20,000,000.
>
> Assume, however, that even without regard to the foreign-to-foreign royalty adjustment the net section 482 transfer price adjustment of the U.S. shareholder exceeds $10,000,000. Under the conference agreement, the penalty does apply to any substantial valuation misstatement resulting from that foreign-to-foreign royalty adjustment (unless an exception, such as reasonable cause, applies).

Gross valuation misstatements, subject to an increased penalty, occur as follows:

1. When property is overvalued by 400 percent or more;
2. When the price of property or a service is overstated by 400 percent or more;
3. When the stated price of property or a service is 25 percent or less than its actual or redetermined Section 482 price; and
4. When the net Section 482 adjustment exceeds $20 million.[309]

[i] Documentation of reasonable effort. Proposed regulations interpreting the transfer price misstatement penalty were issued on January 13, 1993. Although the purpose of the transfer price misstatement penalty was to make the valuation misstatement component of the accuracy-related penalty clearly applicable to transfer price misstatements, the proposed regulations interpreted the statute as though it were a record maintenance and production provision. As the preamble said, "[T]hese regulations are designed to encourage taxpay-

---

[307] IRC § 6662(e)(3)(B)(ii).

[308] HR Conf. Rep., 101st Cong., 2d Sess. 68–69 (1990), reprinted in 1990-3 CB (vol. 3) 1076.

[309] IRC § 6662(h)(2).

ers to document their transfer pricing transactions and to provide the documentation to the Internal Revenue Service on request."

Treasury's focus on document maintenance and production is best seen in its description of reasonable cause and good faith. Reasonable cause is established if the taxpayer shows, through documentation, that it made a reasonable effort to determine its proper tax liability and reasonably believed its efforts produced an arm's-length result.

According to the proposed regulations, adequate documentation is required to establish that a taxpayer has made a reasonable effort to determine its correct tax.[310] But the documentation must exist no later than the date on which the return is filed. The documentation must include "an analysis indicating that the result was an arm's-length result within the meaning of the regulations promulgated under Section 482."[311] If the existence of documentation can establish reasonable cause, but the taxpayer fails to produce documentation within thirty days after the International Examiner or revenue agent requests it, the taxpayer is presumed not to have made a reasonable attempt to determine its tax.[312]

[ii] Reasonable belief. Before the 1993 modification of the penalty,[313] proposed regulations were issued interpreting reasonable belief. Although these regulations were subsequently withdrawn, they still provide some guidance in applying the pre-1993 version of the penalty. A taxpayer's belief that its transfer price methodology produced an arm's-length result must be reasonable. Whether the taxpayer's methodology is one of the acceptable and identified methodologies in the Section 482 regulations—that is, the comparable uncontrolled price method, resale price method, or cost-plus method—is a factor in determining reasonableness.[314]

Reasonable belief required a taxpayer to show that the taxpayer "reasonably believed that the result would be more likely than not sustained on its merits."[315] The more-likely-than-not standard is also the standard for the taxpayer's burden of proof in a case in the Tax Court. Consequently, the proposed regulations required the taxpayer to reasonably believe that it would succeed in court to establish reasonable cause. Nothing in the reasonable cause exception to the accuracy-related penalty requires such a high degree of supportable belief. In fact, only the tax shelter item portion of the substantial understatement penalty requires such a high standard. A transfer price adjustment, suggests the pro-

---

[310] Prop. Reg. § 1.6662-5(ii).

[311] Prop. Reg. § 1.6662-5(ii).

[312] Prop. Reg. § 1.6662-5(ii).

[313] See infra ¶ 7B.03[d].

[314] Prop. Reg. § 1.6662-5(iii).

[315] Prop. Reg. § 1.6662-5(iii)(A).

posed regulations, is essentially the equivalent of a tax shelter item. There is no support for this view. Moreover, the probability of success in court on a tax shelter item is already considered for purposes of a substantial authority reduction. Substantial authority is confusing enough without having it brought into valuation adjustments.

The likelihood of success on the merits is presumed if (1) the taxpayer had a reasonable belief that its methodology would produce an arm's-length result; (2) the taxpayer had a reasonable belief that the underlying critical assumptions of its methodology would not change during the year; and (3) these critical assumptions have not changed by the time the return is filed. If a critical assumption has changed, the taxpayer has an obligation to review its methodology and the result.[316]

Professional advice, including a transfer-pricing study conducted by a professional, is a factor—but only a factor—that is considered in determining a taxpayer's reasonable cause.[317] According to the proposed regulations, however, reliance on the advice must be well-founded. This view echoes some decisions on reliance defenses in negligence penalty cases involving tax shelter items. In a number of tax shelter cases, courts have said that the taxpayer's reliance on the advice of an adviser must have been reasonable under the circumstances.[318] Not all courts accept this approach, however, especially when the taxpayer was relatively unsophisticated.[319] But again, the proposed regulations equate transfer-pricing adjustments and the tax shelter items, and this approach does not seem warranted. When the IRS considers whether the reliance was well-founded, it looks at whether the taxpayers supplied all relevant information about the controlled transaction, the adviser's methodology and the critical assumptions for the advice or study, and the quality and quantity of the data the adviser used relative to the universe of information available in the taxpayer's industry.[320]

It is worth comparing the proposed regulations with the reasonable cause determination used when charitable donations of property have been overvalued. The taxpayer in those circumstances does not have reasonable cause unless (1) the taxpayer also has a qualified appraisal made by a qualified ap-

---

[316] Prop. Reg. § 1.6662-5(iii)(A).

[317] Prop. Reg. § 1.6662-5(iii)(B).

[318] See, e.g., Skeen v. Comm'r, 864 F2d 93 (9th Cir. 1989) (taxpayer relied on accountant in gold tax shelter investment); Ferguson v. Comm'r, 43 TCM 1317 (1982) (penalty imposed because taxpayer used a "flagrant tax-avoidance scheme"); Abernathy v. Comm'r, 63 TCM 2834 (1992) (penalty imposed where tax issue was not difficult or complex).

[319] See, e.g., Eubanks v. Comm'r, 59 TCM 529 (1990) (no penalty imposed on doctors who failed to provide return preparers with copy of lease, because they did not understand tax significance of lease).

[320] Prop. Reg. § 1.6662-5(iii)(B).

praiser and (2) the taxpayer has made a "good faith investigation of the value of the contributed property."[321] The law on the advice of counsel defense differs significantly from these regulations. The Supreme Court, in *Boyle*,[322] stated, "[W]hen an accountant or an attorney advises a taxpayer on a matter of tax law, such as whether a liability exists, it is reasonable for a taxpayer to rely on that advice." In fact, consulting a professional on a tax matter is considered to show ordinary business care and prudence, which is reasonable cause. Cases in which the defense has failed have not been ones where the adviser was wrong; they have involved situations where the taxpayer gave the adviser incomplete information, failed to follow the advice, failed to show that the advice was given at all, or, in some instances, where the taxpayer was experienced enough to know better.[323]

[d] Transfer Pricing Misstatement: The 1993 Penalty Modification

The Revenue Reconciliation Act of 1993 (RRA 1993) modified the accuracy-related penalty for transfer-pricing misstatements by (1) lowering the net Section 482 transfer price adjustment triggering a penalty from $10 million to $5 million[324]; (2) expanding substantial valuation misstatements to include a case where the net Section 482 transfer price adjustment for the taxable year exceeds 10 percent of the taxpayer's gross receipts[325]; and (3) adding two alternative requirements before a net Section 482 transfer price adjustment will be reduced, and the penalty potentially avoided.[326]

To avoid the net adjustment penalty, the first alternative requires the taxpayer to satisfy a three-part requirement.[327] First, the taxpayer must prove ("establish") that the price the taxpayer used was determined in accordance with one of the specific pricing methods described in the Section 482 regulations. Curious to say, the statute also requires the taxpayer to show that use of one of these authorized methods was "reasonable." However, how can the use of an authorized method be "unreasonable"? Second, the taxpayer must prove that it has contemporaneous documentation (documentation in existence at the time of return filing) establishing the price in accordance with the authorized method. Again, and with no apparent logic, the taxpayer's documentation must

---

[321] IRC §§ 6664(c)(2)(A), 6664(c)(2)(B).

[322] United States v. Boyle, 469 US 241, 251 (1985).

[323] Boucher v. Comm'r, 38 TCM 730 (1979) (incomplete information provided); Portemain v. Comm'r, 58 TCM 293 (1989) (failure to follow advice); Abernathy v. Comm'r, 63 TCM 2384 (1992) (taxpayer should have known better).

[324] RRA 1993, § 13236(a), amending IRC § 6662(e)(1)(B)(ii).

[325] RRA 1993, § 13236(a).

[326] RRA 1993, § 13236(b), amending IRC § 6662(e)(3)(B).

[327] RRA 1993, § 13236(c), amending IRC § 6662(e)(3)(B).

also show that the use of the authorized method was reasonable. Finally, the taxpayer must provide this supporting documentation to the IRS within thirty days of a request for such documentation.

Alternatively, the taxpayer may reduce the amount of a new Section 482 adjustment by showing that a method *other than* one of the methods specifically described in the regulations clearly reflects income.[328] The taxpayer must make the three-part showing that (1) none of the methods specifically described in the regulations was likely to result in a price that would clearly reflect income; (2) it used this *other* method; and (3) the *other* method "was likely to result in a price that would clearly reflect income." In other words, while some "other" method is permissible, the taxpayer must prove that the method probably ("likely") clearly reflects income. Of course, if the taxpayer's method probably clearly reflects income, why is a penalty being considered at all? Putting aside this nonsensical aspect of the "other"-method alternative, the taxpayer must also have the contemporaneous documentation and produce the documentation within thirty days to achieve the penalty threshold reduction.

These alternative ways to reduce the transfer-pricing penalty are "coordinated" with the reasonable cause exception of Section 6664(c) in such a way that Section 6664(c) no longer applies to transfer price adjustments.[329] Thus, one of the cornerstones of the 1989 penalty reform—a single reasonable cause standard for all taxpayer penalties—was removed only four years after it was put in place. Where transfer price adjustments are made, the reasonableness of the taxpayer's conduct is not the issue; rather, it is the taxpayer's compliance with the Section 482 regulations and with the Section 6038A regulations dealing with document creation, retention, and production. Dubious policy decisions, formerly reflected only in proposed regulations on pre-1994 years, are enshrined in statute for post-1993 years.[330] Just how taxpayers facing transfer price adjustments for post-1993 years will be treated under the amended penalty cannot be predicted with certainty. However, it can be said that disputes over the penalties, including the transfer price misstatement penalty, will increase with taxpayers having to bear a heavy burden of proof. This will encourage examiners to raise the penalty and to use it as a bargaining chip in the examination and on appeal, a situation that already exists with the substantial understatement penalty.

[i] Regulations interpreting the 1993 penalty clause. Treasury regulations interpret the 1993 addition to the transfer-pricing penalty.[331] These regu-

---

[328] RRA 1993, § 13236(c), amending IRC § 6662(e)(3)(B).

[329] RRA 1993, § 13236(c), amending IRC § 6662(e)(3)(B), adding IRC § 6662(e)(3)(D).

[330] RRA 1993, § 13236(e).

[331] TD 8656 published these regulations, Reg. § 1.6662-6, in final form on February 8, 1996. These regulations were first published in temporary form in TD 8519 on Febru-

lations make clear that in the Treasury's view, the single reasonable cause and good faith exception which was one of the cornerstones of the 1989 civil penalty reform, does not apply to a net Section 482 adjustment in any recognizable or comprehensible way. According to the regulations, if a taxpayer does not satisfy the rules of Treasury Regulations Section 1.6662-6(d) the taxpayer "cannot satisfy the reasonable cause and good faith exception of section 6664(c)."[332] Nevertheless, different reasonable cause determinations must be made in three situations. A transfer-pricing penalty for tax years ending after November 5, 1990, but before January 1, 1994, may be asserted. But the penalty for these years may be avoided by a showing of reasonable cause in accordance with the single reasonable cause exception of Section 6664(c).[333] While the proposed regulations issued on January 21, 1993, are withdrawn, the temporary regulations say that these proposed regulations are considered to be a reasonable interpretation of reasonable cause for purposes of Sections 6662(e) and 6662(h), except that no requirement of contemporaneous documentation will be imposed for transactions before April 21, 1993 (although contemporaneous documentation "may" be helpful in showing reasonable cause). These proposed regulations are discussed above.[334] The second situation involves the transactional penalty that may be imposed when a substantial valuation misstatement is made in a transaction between related parties by the use of a price for property or services that is 200 percent or more (or 50 percent or less) of the correct price. When the transactional penalty is involved, the taxpayer may avoid the penalty by demonstrating reasonable cause under Section 6664(c).[335]

The third situation is the net adjustment penalty that may be imposed when a net Section 482 adjustment exceeds $5 million or 10 percent of the taxpayer's gross receipts, whichever of the two amounts is less. In this case,

---

ary 2, 1994. On July 8, 1994, in TD 8551, new temporary regulations were published to conform these regulations to the final Section 482 regulations.

[332] Temp. Reg. § 1.6664-4T(f) (1996).

[333] TD 8519, Explanation of Effective Date.

[334] See supra ¶¶ 7B.02[4][a][i], 7B.02[4][a][ii]. Rev. Proc. 94-33, 1994-18 IRB 18 (May 2, 1994) states:

[C]ontemporaneous documentation is not mandatory for taxable years beginning prior to April 22, 1993. However, for tax years beginning after April 21, 1993 (the effective date of proposed regulations issued on January 21, 1993), but beginning before January 1, 1994, taxpayers can establish that they acted with reasonable cause and in good faith only if they produce contemporaneous documentation. Regardless of the taxable year, the existence of contemporaneous documentation is a relevant factor in determining whether the taxpayer had reasonable cause and good faith, particularly for transactions after April 21, 1993.

[335] Reg. § 1.6662-6(b)(3) (1996). Final regulations under Reg. § 1.6662-6 say that the transactional penalty will not be imposed on any portion of an underpayment if the requirements of Reg. § 1.6664-4 are met.

reasonable cause and good faith exist only if the taxpayer meets the requirements of Treasury Regulations Section 1.6662-6(d).[336] As the following summary shows, these requirements have more to do with the creation of documents the Service believes are necessary to conduct an audit and with compliance with the Treasury's view of transfer-pricing methods than they do with reasonable taxpayer conduct and reasonable cause as have been interpreted by the courts, especially the courts of appeals. Because these requirements are critical to the Service's penalty determination, they are discussed in summary fashion below.

Exclusion by use of a specified method. A transfer-pricing adjustment will be excluded from the transfer price-triggering amount (the net Section 482 adjustment) if the taxpayer proves that (1) the taxpayer has selected and applied a pricing method described in the Section 482 regulations for the type of transaction and has applied the method in a reasonable manner, and (2) the taxpayer has fulfilled the specified documentation requirements (discussed below).[337] For transfers of tangible property, these methods are the comparable uncontrolled price method, the resale price method, the cost-plus method, and the comparable profits method. For transfers of intangible property, the described methods are the comparable uncontrolled transactions method and the comparable profits method. A qualified cost-sharing arrangement is considered a specified method. A taxpayer's choice of a specified method will be considered reasonable, however, only if the method gives "the most reliable measure of an arm's length result under the principles of the best method rule" described in Treasury Regulations Section 1.482-1(c).[338] Moreover, a taxpayer cannot reasonably conclude that a specified method it selected provides the most reliable result unless the taxpayer has made a reasonable effort to evaluate the potential applicability of the other specified methods under the Section 482 regulations'd best method rule.[339] However, the taxpayer need not conduct an extensive analysis or application of each method. For the taxpayer to establish that it has selected the most reliable method, the taxpayer must make a reasonably thorough search for relevant data and consider which method would prove the most reliable method given that data. The nature of the data located will enable a taxpayer to eliminate a particular method in many cases, the regulations say. Whether the taxpayer's conclusion is reasonable will be determined from specially defined factors. In short, the specified method must be the most reliable method of determining the arm's-length price, taking into account the alternative methods. Why "reasonableness" as specially defined is added to this already high and indeed burdensome standard is hard to fathom.

---

[336] Reg. § 1.6662-6(c)(6); Temp. Reg. § 1.6664-4T(f).

[337] Reg. § 1.6662-6(d)(2).

[338] Reg. § 1.6662-6(d)(2)(ii).

[339] Reg. § 1.6662-6(d)(3)(ii).

Reasonable use of specified method. According to the regulations, the reasonableness of the taxpayer's conclusion that a particular specified method gives the most reliable price will be judged by considering (1) the taxpayer's experience and knowledge, taking into account all members of the taxpayer's controlled group of corporations; (2) the extent to which accurate data available before the end of the taxable year were searched for and used, although the expense of the search will be considered in evaluating the scope of the search; (3) the taxpayer's compliance with the requirements set forth in the Section 482 regulations for the method; (4) the taxpayer's reliance on a pricing study done by an attorney, accountant, or economist, provided that the taxpayer has disclosed all relevant information to the professional about the transaction and, in the Service's view, the study is objective, thorough, and well reasoned[340]; (5) the taxpayer's selection of results derived from uncontrolled comparables[341]; (6) the taxpayer's reliance on a methodology developed in connection with an advance pricing agreement approved by the Service on audit; and (7) the size of the adjustment in relation to the size of the controlled transaction.

The documentation requirement. The taxpayer must maintain sufficient documentation to prove that the most reliable price resulted from the use of a specified method; the taxpayer must supply this documentation to the Service examiner within thirty days after it is requested.[342] Supporting documentation, according to the regulations, must exist no later than when the return is filed.[343] There are two types of supporting documentation: principal documents and background documents. Principal documents[344] are (1) an overview of the taxpayer's business with the economic and legal factors affecting the pricing decision analyzed; (2) a description of the taxpayer's organizational structure and an organization chart covering "all related parties engaged in transactions potentially relevant under Section 482, including foreign affiliates whose transactions directly or indirectly affect the pricing of property or services in the United States"; (3) documentation required by the Section 482 regulations; (4) a written description of the application of the specified method the taxpayer chooses and the reason the method was chosen; (5) a written explanation of

---

[340] Reg. § 1.6662-6(d)(3)(ii).

[341] This factor is considered when a taxpayer uses a range of results to set its price. If a taxpayer uses an extreme point in the range of results to set its price. If a taxpayer uses an extreme point in the range of results, the taxpayer's conclusion will be considered to be arbitrary. Reg. § 1.6662-6(d)(2)(ii)(E). The Section 482 regulations themselves provide that ordinarily the median of the range will be the controlling one. Reg. § 1.482-1(e)(3).

[342] Reg. § 1.6662-6(d)(2)(iii).

[343] Reg. § 1.6662-6(d)(2)(iii)(A). However, the District Director may excuse "a minor inadvertent failure" if the taxpayer has acted in good faith and promptly remedies the failure.

[344] Reg. § 1.6662-6(d)(2)(iii)(B).

the unspecified methods the taxpayer considered and why they were not se-lected; (6) the controlled transactions, including the terms of sale, as well as internal data used to analyze the transactions; (7) the comparable transactions that were used, how they were evaluated as being comparable, and what, if any, adjustments were made; (8) an explanation of the economic analysis and projections the taxpayer relied on in applying the pricing method used[345]; (9) a description of any relevant data the taxpayer obtains after the end of the tax year, before filing a tax return, which would help determine the reasonableness of the taxpayer's selection; and (10) an index (the regulations use the unex-plained term "general index") of the principal and background documents, as well as a description of the taxpayer's system for cataloguing and accessing these documents. Obviously, it is unprecedented for a taxpayer to make and keep an array of records such as these in order to establish that the transfer price method used was reasonable; in fact, these requirements are a substantial departure from the general records taxpayers are required to keep to support their reported income and deductions.[346] After the lengthy list of principal doc-uments, the description of background documents is blissfully brief with, of course, potentially enormous scope—that is, background documents are all documents which support the assumptions, conclusions, and positions in the principal documents. While taxpayers need not turn over background docu-ments on the first request for principal documents, they must deliver back-ground documents within thirty days after the documents are specifically requested.[347]

Exclusion by use of an unspecified method. If a taxpayer uses the pricing methods specified in the Section 482 regulations, but decides that none of the specified methods produces an accurate arm's length price, and then selects an unspecified method that probably results in an accurate transfer price, then a transfer price adjustment will be excluded from the net Section 482 adjust-ment.[348] The same reasonableness factors apply to the Service's analysis of the taxpayer's conclusion. The same exclusion exists if the taxpayer uses an un-specified method because there is no specified method for the particular type of transaction, and if the taxpayer uses a method that the taxpayer reasonably concludes will produce the most accurate transfer price.[349] The taxpayer must

---

[345] If a profit split method is used, in addition to the other principal documents that the taxpayer is required to create and maintain, the taxpayer must provide an explanation of the analysis the taxpayer made to determine how the profits would be split. Reg. § 1.6662-6(d)(2)(ii)(B)(8).

[346] Reg. § 1.6001-1(a).

[347] Reg. § 1.6662-6(d)(2)(iii)(C). The thirty-day rule does not apply to the summary of data acquired after the close of the taxable year or the general index of principal and background documents.

[348] Reg. § 1.6662-6(d)(3)(ii)(B).

[349] Reg. § 1.6662-6(d)(3)(ii)(C).

maintain sufficient documentation to prove that the requirements of the un-specified method regulations have been complied with. Again, this documenta-tion must be turned over to the international examiner within thirty days after a request.[350] The regulations indicate that the same type of documents must be kept—principal and background documents.[351]

Special rules. The regulations provide special rules to deal with situations where there are transactions solely between foreign corporations[352] and in which the tax is determined other than by reference to the regular corporate tax provision,[353] where there are carrybacks and carryovers,[354] and for coordi-nating the transactional and the net adjustment penalties.[355]

Standard of reasonableness. To conform with the final Section 482 regu-lations' modification of the best method rule, the selection and application of a specified method will be considered reasonable only if the taxpayer reasonably concluded that the method selected provided the "most reliable" method of de-termining the arm's-length result (not the "most accurate" measure of the arm's-length result).

[5] Substantial Overstatement of Pension Liabilities

When there is a substantial overvaluation of pension liabilities, the 20 percent accuracy-related penalty can be imposed. A substantial overstatement of pen-sion liabilities occurs "if the actuarial determination of the liabilities taken into account for purposes of computing the deduction (under Section 404(a)(1) or Section 404(a)(2)) is 200 percent or more of the amount determined to be the correct amount of (these) liabilities."[356] If the pension liability is overvalued by 400 percent or more of the actual liability, the accuracy-related penalty is in-creased from 20 to 40 percent.[357] A threshold level of tax underpayments is provided so that no penalty is imposed unless the underpayment in tax caused by the overvalued pension liability exceeds $1,000.

The accuracy-related penalty for substantial overstatements of pension lia-bilities is derived from Section 6659A of pre-IMPACT law.[358] Unlike Section

---

[350] Reg. § 1.6662-6(d)(3)(iii)(A).

[351] Reg. § 1.6662-6(d)(3)(iii)(B).

[352] Reg. § 1.6662-6(d)(4).

[353] Reg. § 1.6662-6(d)(5).

[354] Reg. § 1.6662-6(e).

[355] Reg. § 1.6662-6(f).

[356] IRC § 6662(f).

[357] IRC § 6662(h).

[358] The Service issued guidance as to the operation of Section 6659A in 1989. Notice 89-47, 1989-1 CB 687.

6659A, which penalized excessive claims of 150 percent or more of the amount determined to be correct, the accuracy-related penalty applies only if the actuarial determination of pension liabilities for purposes of computing the deduction under Section 404(a)(1) or Section 404(a)(2) is 200 percent or more of the amount determined to be correct.

[6] Substantial Estate or Gift Tax Valuation Understatements

If property is undervalued by 50 percent or less in calculating estate or gift tax, the portion of the underpayment caused by the undervaluation is subject to the 20 percent accuracy-related penalty.[359] However, no penalty is imposed unless the underpayment exceeds $5,000.[360] Where the undervaluation is grossly misstated—i.e., when the stated value of the property is only 25 percent or

---

[359] IRC § 6662(g)(1). While the undervaluation penalty would appear to apply only to property capable of valuation, the Tax Court has held that the undervaluation penalty, Section 6660, can also be imposed for the underreporting of the amount of an estate's bank account. Estate of Owen, 104 TC No. 25 (1995) (the court reasoned that bank accounts are "property" for estate tax purposes, the value of which is includable in the "value" of the decedent's gross estate). One of the reasons the Tax Court used for reaching this result is that Congress did not explicitly exclude the extension of the penalty to a bank account. This is not convincing statutory interpretation. Surely, Congress was not required to identify possible situations where the penalty was not to be imposed when it described the situation where the penalty was to be imposed—specifically, aggressive undervaluations of property, disputes over which were burdening the Tax Court. The statement of the purpose itself excluded those situations inconsistent with the stated purpose.

In a gift tax case involving the valuation of stock in a closely held family corporation, the taxpayer, based on professional advice, used a 50 percent marketability discount, and the Tax Court found that only a 30 percent marketability discount was proper. Mandelbaum v. Comm'r, TC Memo. 1995-225 (1995). The Service had determined that a valuation understatement penalty under Section 6660 was due in part because the taxpayers should have known that their professionals' valuations were unreasonable based on the results of prior audits. The Tax Court held that the "mere fact that [the IRS] challenged [the taxpayers'] valuation method in prior years does not mean that the method was unreasonable." As for the law of evidence dealing with the effect of a compromise, the court said that the agreements the taxpayers signed in closing the audits of the earlier years "neither bound the parties thereto in future years nor constitutes an acknowledgement that [the IRS] was correct." In view of the taxpayers' reasonable reliance on their professional advisers, the court found that the Service's failure to waive the penalty was an abuse of discretion. Since the Service had determined that the undervaluation component of the accuracy-related penalty applied to gifts in the years 1989 and 1990, the Tax Court also applied the reasonable cause and good faith exception of Section 6664, and found that the taxpayers made a reasonable attempt to assess their proper tax liability, lacked sophistication in valuation and tax matters, reasonably relied on their professionals, and under the facts of the case were not to second guess their advisers' advice.

[360] IRC § 6662(g)(2).

less of its actual value—the accuracy-related penalty is increased to 40 percent from 20 percent.[361]

Although this part of the accuracy-related penalty is derived from Section 6660, it differs in two ways:

1. *Minimum percentage.* Section 6660 applied to claimed values that are 66⅔ percent or less of the amount determined to be correct. The accuracy-related penalty applies only if the value of the property is 50 percent or less of the amount determined to be correct. This increase in the minimum percentage of error is intended to eliminate good faith disputes from the scope of the penalty.

2. *Threshold amount.* Under Section 6660, the penalty was imposed if the undervaluation produced a $1,000 or more reduction in estate or gift tax. This tax differential is increased to $5,000 in the accuracy-related penalty. When the estate or gift tax valuation is grossly misstated because it is 25 percent or less of the actual value of the property, the accuracy-related penalty is increased from 20 to 40 percent.[362]

The following example illustrates the operation of the accuracy-related penalty in this situation.

> **EXAMPLE:** A father dies testate on January 21, 1990, leaving his son stock in a family corporation.[363] For estate tax purposes, the stock is valued at $10,500. After examination of the estate tax return, the IRS determines that the actual value is $80,000. Putting aside the exemption provision, the IRS asserts the accuracy-related penalty for a substantial estate tax valuation understatement. The valuation claimed ($10,500) is only about 17 percent of the IRS-determined value ($80,000). Accordingly, the IRS determines that a penalty of 40 percent of the underpayment attributable to the undervaluation is due. If the Tax Court decides that the correct value of the stock was $30,500, an accuracy-related penalty would be due because the claimed value ($10,500) was less than 50 percent of the correct value ($30,500), but the amount of the penalty would be 20 percent, not 40 percent, because the claimed value was more than 25 percent of the correct value.

As illustrated by the following example, the accuracy-related penalty for underpayment of income tax due to a property valuation overstatement and the penalty for underpayment of estate or gift tax due to a property undervaluation are related.

---

[361] IRC §§ 6662(h)(1), 6662(h)(2)(C).

[362] IRC §§ 6662(h)(1), 6662(h)(2)(C).

[363] See, e.g., the facts in Estate of Newhouse v. Comm'r, 94 TC 193 (1990).

EXAMPLE: A husband (*H*), who dies on December 31, 1989, leaves his wife (*W*) all his property, including a building, with a value of $200,000. For estate tax purposes, the building is valued at $400,500, but because of the marital deduction, no estate tax is paid. *W* later uses the estate tax value for depreciation purposes. On examination, the Service determines that the value is $200,000. Thus, *W*'s return includes a valuation overstatement of 200 percent or more, resulting in *W* underpaying her income tax by more than $5,000. The Service has ruled that in adopting the overstated amount on the estate tax return as her adjusted basis, *W* is subject to a penalty for overvaluation of property.[364]

¶ 7B.04 THE REASONABLE CAUSE EXCEPTION

A reasonable cause exception is provided for the accuracy-related and fraud penalties. Section 6664(c) states, "[n]o penalty shall be imposed under this part (Part II—Accuracy-Related and Fraud Penalties) with regard to any portion of an underpayment if it is shown that there was a reasonable cause for such portion and that the taxpayer acted in good faith with respect to such portion." Therefore, if a taxpayer can show reasonable cause and good faith, these penalties are not properly imposed. Since literally no penalty is permissible if reasonable cause exists, the Service's administrative determination of such a circumstance is reviewable in the same manner and to the same extent as its determination that the penalty was properly imposed. The committee report makes clear that the standardized reasonable cause exception was intended to permit fuller judicial review than existed under prior law,[365] replacing the abuse of discretion review standard applied where the waiver on reasonable cause grounds was within the Service's discretion.[366]

---

[364] Rev. Rul. 85-75, 1985-1 CB 876.

[365] HR Rep. No. 247, 101st Cong., 1st Sess. 285, reprinted in 1989-3 CB 1393–1394 (vol. 3).

[366] Mailman v. Comm'r, 91 TC 1079, 1084 (1988). But see Heasley v. Comm'r, 902 F2d 380 (9th Cir. 1990) (IRS found to have abused its discretion in failing to waive Section 6661 penalty given the taxpayer's inexperience and limited knowledge). Cloud v. Comm'r, 97 TC 613 (1991) ("Had petitioners been presented with respondent's arguments at the time of making the returns in issue, they would have been reasonable in rejecting them."). One circuit court has held, however, that "by failing to offer any reasons for [the Service's] decision [not to waive a substantial understatement penalty], [the Service] failed to demonstrate that [the Service] had exercised [its] discretion and thereby abused that discretion." Fisher v. Comm'r, 45 F3d 396 (10th Cir. 1995) (relying on the administrative law principle that "an administrative agency must provide reasons for its decisions"). The *Fisher* court also said that the Service must provide its reasons during the administrative process, not in court, observing, "The IRS cannot make taxpayers haul it into Tax Court

[1] Meaning of Reasonable Cause and Good Faith

Interpretation of the terms "reasonable cause" and "good faith" is carried over from the interpretation of those terms in the delinquency penalty, and especially under the former stand-alone, substantial understatement penalty.[367] The reasonable cause exception in the delinquency penalty has been interpreted to mean the exercise of ordinary business care and prudence.[368] Generally, a taxpayer that has retained a competent tax adviser, supplied the adviser with relevant information, and relied on the adviser's advice regarding a substantive tax matter, has acted with ordinary business care and prudence, even if the position is in error.[369] For example, the Supreme Court observed in *United States v. Boyle*:[370]

> When an accountant or attorney advises a taxpayer on a matter of tax law, such as whether a liability exists, it is reasonable for the taxpayer to rely on that advice. Most taxpayers are not competent to discern error in the substantive advice of an accountant or attorney. To require the taxpayer to challenge the attorney, to seek a "second opinion," or to try to monitor counsel on the provisions of the Code himself would nullify the very purpose of seeking the advice of a presumed expert in the first place. "Ordinary business care and prudence" do not demand such actions.

Regulations interpreting the reasonable cause waiver in the substantial understatement penalty under prior law impose a heavier burden on taxpayers and seem to require more than ordinary business care and prudence. The focus is on "the extent of the taxpayer's effort to assess the taxpayer's liability under the law."[371] In addition to reliance on the attorney or accountant, the taxpayer is required to show that the reliance was "reasonable and the taxpayer acted in

---

to ascertain that it has ruled on a lawful request or to discover what the rationale for its decision is." The Service will not follow the Tenth Circuit's decision in *Fisher* because it believes that it is not required to provide a written explanation for refusing to wave a Section 6661 penalty, other than a notice of deficiency. AOD re: Fisher v. Comm'r, July 15, 1996, 96 TNT 137-19. Vorsheck v. Comm'r, 933 F2d 757 (9th Cir. 1991) (in overturning the Service's imposition of the negligence penalty, the court reviewed de novo the issue of whether the taxpayers reasonably relied on their tax advisor—abuse of discretion was not discussed).

[367] HR Rep. No. 247, 101st Cong., 1st Sess. 285.

[368] See United States v. Boyle, 469 US 241, 246 (1985); Estate of Paxton v. Comm'r, 86 TC 785, 819 (1986). See also Reg. § 301.6651-1(c)(1).

[369] See the discussion about shift of responsibility and advice of counsel defenses supra ¶¶ 7B.02[4][b]–7B.02[4][c] and 7B.03[2][b].

[370] United States v. Boyle, 469 US 241, 251 (1985) (emphasis in original).

[371] Reg. § 1.6661-6(b).

good faith."[372] Similar limitations on a reliance defense are required where a taxpayer relies on an information return.[373]

What is lost in this approach to reasonable cause and good faith is the reality that it involves evaluations of legal authority on technical issues of tax law. It is in precisely this situation that a taxpayer should be able to seek out and rely on a competent tax professional.[374] If the professional has made a mistake, there is little practical reason to believe that the taxpayer will be able to correct that mistake. It is one thing to require the taxpayer to make a good faith selection of a competent tax professional, but it is quite another to say that the taxpayer should evaluate the advice given by the tax professional. Since the reasonable cause and good faith exception is judicially reviewable and no longer a matter of administrative dispensation, reliance on a competent tax adviser should constitute reasonable cause in the same manner as it does in the case of delinquency, negligence, or fraud penalties.

In 1989, Congress attempted to reform the civil penalty structure by reducing this pyramiding or aggregation of civil penalties that it had added to the Code but had failed to coordinate. Section 6662 achieves coordination by gathering into one accuracy-related penalty, five penalties that might apply to an underpayment, but permitting only one 20 percent penalty to apply to the

---

[372] Reg. § 1.6661-6(b).

[373] A pass-through entity's reasonable cause and good faith or the lack of it was imputed to the taxpayer. Reg. § 1.6661-6(b).

[374] See United States v. Boyle, 469 US 241, 252 (1985). See Gallade v. Comm'r, 106 TC No. 20 (1996) (there was no substantial authority for the position that assignment of pension plan contributions by the owner to his corporation did not constitute a distribution; but no substantial understatement penalty was due because the owner had asked for the advice of his CPA and an actuary, the actuary had contacted the PBGC, a PBGC representative had approved the assignment, and forms disclosing the transaction were filed with the IRS and the PBGC); see also Nestle Holdings, Inc. v. Comm'r, TC Memo. 1995-441 (1995) (holding that it was unreasonable to penalize the taxpayer for relying on the advice of a professional or for not prevailing in the Tax Court).

In *Vorsheck*, the Ninth Circuit accepted the text view in a case where the Tax Court had ruled that the taxpayers had acted prudently in relying on an accountant's advice (and thus they were not negligent), but were found liable for a substantial understatement penalty. Vorsheck v. Comm'r, 933 F2d 757 (9th Cir. 1991), cert. denied, 112 S. Ct. 591 (1991). The Ninth Circuit said:

If the Vorshecks were acting as "an ordinary prudent person in the circumstances," then their reliance upon the investment advice of their accountant was "reasonable" and "in good faith under all the circumstances." See Treas. Reg. § 1-666.6(b) (sic); Heasley [v. Comm'r], 902 F2d [380] at 385 ((5th Cir. 1990)). Thus, the Vorshecks meet the standard for waiver of the penalty under section 6661. Accordingly, we reverse the tax court's decision upholding the Commissioner's assessment of a 10% penalty under section 6661.

Id. at 759. Under the Ninth Circuit's approach, the taxpayer's reasonable cause and good faith for purposes of the negligence penalty also defeats the substantial understatement penalty.

same portion of an underpayment. Another reform was a uniform or standardized reasonable cause exception that was to be used in determining whether the components of the accuracy-related penalty should be waived. This uniform standard provides, "No penalty shall be imposed under this part with respect to any portion of an underpayment if it is shown that there was a reasonable cause for such portion and that the taxpayer acted in good faith with respect to such portion."[375] Reasonable cause for purposes of Section 6664(c) has the meaning that it has in the delinquency penalty as interpreted by courts, including the Supreme Court in *Boyle*, and the reasonable cause exception to the former substantial understatement penalty Congress enacted in 1982. Consequently, Congress could not have expected extensive regulations to be necessary to interpret the exception of Section 6664(c). Fairly extensive and specific regulations have nevertheless been promulgated. These regulations are interpretative regulations, and on that account have a somewhat uncertain legal status. In practice, however, they create a separate body of authority about what constitutes reasonable cause.

Facts and circumstances. Regulations cover some matters that are hardly noteworthy. A reasonable cause determination is to be made on a "case-by-case basis, taking into account all pertinent facts and circumstances."[376] The "most important factor," however, is a carryover from the substantial understatement penalty, discussed above; that is, "the extent of the taxpayer's effort to assess the taxpayer's proper tax liability." Regulations say that an honest misunderstanding of fact or law, which is also reasonable in light of such circumstances as the taxpayer's experience, knowledge, and education, "may" constitute reasonable cause, as may an isolated or transcriptional error. However, the regulations then warn that unless the taxpayer also shows that the reliance was reasonable and the taxpayer acted in good faith, the taxpayer does not necessarily demonstrate reasonable cause by showing that the taxpayer relied on (1) an incorrect information return, (2) the advice of a professional tax adviser, (3) the appraisal of an appraiser, or (4) facts that, unknown to the taxpayer, are incorrect.[377] The regulations engage in circular reasoning here; in effect, they say that a taxpayer's conduct will not necessarily be reasonable unless the taxpayer can demonstrate that the conduct was reasonable. The regulations thus seem both to limit and, as further discussed below, to add unprecedented requirements to the advice of counsel defense. For example, in view of the Supreme Court's statement in *Boyle* that a taxpayer acts with ordinary business care and prudence when the taxpayer consults a tax professional on a matter of tax law, the taxpayer does not seem to have the obligation to make an additional showing of reasonableness.

---

[375] IRC § 6664(c).

[376] Reg. § 1.6664-4(b)(1).

[377] Reg. § 1.6664-4(b)(1).

Examples in the regulations further describe the Service's views about reliance on the advice of counsel, as well as how reliance on erroneous facts, appraisals, and information returns affects a finding of reasonable cause. All of these examples are narrowly drawn and qualify reasonable cause in ways that courts have not done in making a reasonable cause determination. One example describes what seems to be a textbook advice of counsel situation. An individual taxpayer with a question about the deductibility of certain state and local taxes consults a professional tax adviser and gives the tax adviser "full details concerning the taxes." The taxpayer is said to have demonstrated good faith by seeking the advice of the professional tax adviser and to have reasonable cause for any underpayment attributable to the deduction of the taxes. Reasonable cause will not exist even in this simple advice of counsel situation, however, if the taxpayer should have known that the tax professional "lacked knowledge in the relevant aspects of the tax law"; the professional's advice did not meet even the minimum requirements as to form and substance required in the regulations (discussed below); and the taxpayer otherwise acted reasonably and in good faith.[378]

Another example illustrates a qualifying reliance on erroneous facts. In the example, a multi-divisional corporation makes a return error, such as an error in the cost or adjusted basis of property, the date when property was placed in service, or the amount of opening or closing inventory. The error is made because the corporation relied on erroneous information the divisions compiled or financial books and records the divisions prepared. For the corporation to have acted with reasonable cause, however, the corporation must have put into place internal controls and procedures that were designed to detect these types of factual errors.[379] In order for a taxpayer to be able to rely on an appraisal of the value of property, the Service will consider factors such as the appraiser's methodology, the appraiser's assumptions in making the appraisal, the appraised value, the relationship between the purchase price of the property and the appraised value, the circumstances under which the appraisal was obtained, and the appraiser's relationship to the taxpayer or to the activity in which the property is used.[380] A taxpayer may rely on an erroneous information return, such as a Form W-2 or Form 1099, to establish reasonable cause, as long as the taxpayer did not know and had no reason to know that the information was incorrect. However, a taxpayer will be considered to know that

---

[378] Reg. § 1.6664(b)(2), Ex. (1). It is not clear from this requirement whether the taxpayer must consult not merely a tax professional, but also a tax professional having particular expertise in the deductibility of state and local taxes.

[379] Reg. § 1.6664(b)(1).

[380] Reg. § 1.6664(b)(1). But see, e.g., McMurray v. Comm'r, 95 F2d 36 (1st Cir. 1993), where the circuit court found that no negligence or intentional disregard penalty was owed when the taxpayers relied on the appraisal of a professional appraiser, and the Tax Court entirely rejected the taxpayer's appraisal in favor of the Service's appraisal.

the information return is erroneous only if the information on the form conflicts with other information the taxpayer knows, such as the terms of the taxpayer's employment agreement or the rate of interest the taxpayer is entitled to be paid by the obligor.[381]

Reliance on tax advice. For a taxpayer to be considered to have reasonably relied in good faith on advice, including a professional tax adviser's opinion, the regulations say that the advice must meet two "minimum requirements": (1) All facts and circumstances must be considered and (2) no unreasonable assumptions may be made.[382] Even if the advice meets these minimum requirements, the taxpayer still may not be considered to have acted with reasonable cause if the adviser "lacked knowledge in the relevant aspects of the tax law."[383] To meet the all-facts-and-circumstances minimum requirement, the advice (that is, the adviser) must show due diligence in two ways: (1) base the advice on the "pertinent" (that is, relevant) facts and circumstances and relate the applicable law to the facts and (2) in giving the advice, take into account the taxpayer's purposes and the relative weight to be given to those purposes, both for entering into the transaction and for structuring the transaction in a particular manner. Even if the adviser shows due diligence in the ways that the regulations require, the *taxpayer* still may not rely on the advice if the *taxpayer* fails to disclose to the adviser any fact the taxpayer knows or should know to be relevant to the proper tax treatment of the item. Under the second minimum requirement, the adviser must not (1) base the advice on unreasonable factual or legal assumptions, such as an assumption about future events, and (2) unreasonably rely on the representations, statements, findings, or agreements the taxpayer or any other person provides. Moreover, the *taxpayer* cannot rely on advice if it is based on a representation that the *taxpayer* knows or has reason to know is "unlikely to be true," such as the taxpayer's purpose for entering into the transaction or for structuring the transaction in a particular way.

Corporate tax shelter items. For a corporation to use legal justification in its treatment of a tax shelter item as a reasonable cause defense to a penalty for substantial understatement of income tax, the corporation's legal justification must satisfy two minimum requirements: an authority requirement and a belief requirement.[384] The authority requirement is the same substantial author-

---

[381] Reg. § 1.6664(b)(1). An example describes the situation of an hourly worker whose hours were not regular, and so whose paychecks varied in amount. The taxpayer was entitled to rely on an erroneous Form W-2 because it omitted less than 5 percent of the amount that should have been reported. Reg. § 1.6664-4(b)(2), Ex. (3).

[382] Reg. § 1.6664-4(c)(1).

[383] This requirement is difficult to understand, let alone comply with. It seems to say that the taxpayer may not rely on a tax professional who is competent but not experienced in the particular area relevant to the issue.

[384] Reg. § 1.6664-4(e).

ity required to avoid the substantial understatement penalty, as the term "substantial authority" is defined in the substantial understatement penalty regulations, Regulation Section 1.6662-4(d). The corporation will hold the requisite belief only if, at the time its return was filed, it reasonably believed that the tax treatment of the item was more likely than not the proper tax treatment. If the corporation itself determined the tax treatment of the item, its belief will not be reasonable unless the corporation (1) using the method Treasury and the Service have described in the substantial understatement penalty regulations,[385] analyzes the pertinent facts and legal authorities and (2) concludes, on the basis of that analysis, that the corporation's tax treatment of the item will probably be upheld (that is, it has a more than 50 percent chance of success) if the Service challenges it. If the corporation relies on the opinion of a professional tax adviser, then the corporation's adviser must use a substantial understatement penalty analysis and, using this type of analysis, arrive at the conclusion that the tax treatment of the item will probably be upheld if challenged. The adviser's opinion must also satisfy the minimum requirements for general tax advice.

Even if the corporation has arrived at its conclusion about the tax treatment of the item in compliance with these minimum requirements, its conduct in complying with the minimum standards, while an important factor, nevertheless will not control the reasonable cause determination.[386] Although the corporation has satisfied the authority and belief minimum requirements, the corporation will not have acted with reasonable cause if (1) the corporation had no business purpose for the corporation's participation in the transaction; (2) the tax benefits are unreasonable when compared to the corporation's investment; or (3) the corporation and the promoter agreed that the corporation would keep confidential the tax aspects of the shelter's structure. It is possible that factors not described in the regulations, other than the corporation's claimed legal justification, may result in the corporation's being determined not to have reasonable cause for its return position.[387]

[2] Disclosure

As previously noted, a taxpayer can avoid the substantial understatement component of the accuracy-related penalty by making a qualifying disclosure of an item's tax treatment.[388] However, the reasonable cause exception of Section 6664(c) applies to all five components of the accuracy-related penalty, as well

---

[385] Reg. § 1.6662-4(d)(3)(ii).

[386] Reg. § 1.6664-4(e)(3).

[387] Reg. § 1.6664-4(e)(4).

[388] See the discussion supra ¶ 7B.03[3][d].

as the fraud penalty. Disclosure is not explicitly mentioned in Section 6664(c) as a method for establishing reasonable cause and good faith; but, nevertheless, the committee report makes it clear that this result was intended with respect to the negligence component of the accuracy-related penalty. The committee report states:

> The committee believes that the application of standardized exception criteria to the negligence component of the accuracy-related penalty will result in several consequences that are beneficial to taxpayers. First, the complete, item-specific disclosure of a nonfrivolous position on a tax return may generally be considered to permit an exception from the negligence penalty insofar as such disclosure would tend to demonstrate that there was no intentional disregard of rules or regulations. Disclosure must be full and substantive, parallel to the disclosure required under the substantial understatement component of the accuracy-related penalty; completing and filling in a tax form is by itself insufficient disclosure for this purpose. In addition, the disclosure must be clearly identified as being made to avoid the imposition of the accuracy-related penalty. Imposition of the negligence component of the accuracy-related penalty would not be eligible for exception due to disclosure where the taxpayer fails to keep proper books and records or to substantiate items properly.

The reasonable cause exception was intended to be a standardized exception for all components of the accuracy-related penalty and the fraud penalty. Disclosure allows a taxpayer to establish that there was reasonable cause and good faith. However, the method of disclosure itself is not necessarily the same for all components of the accuracy-related penalty. Procedures for making qualifying disclosures for the substantial understatement penalty of prior law were adopted by regulations and apply to the substantial understatement component of the accuracy-related penalty. The committee report shows some definite, and some different, ideas about disclosures for purposes of the negligence component of the accuracy-related penalty. A disclosure made for purposes of the substantial overvaluation component of the accuracy-related penalty must take into account the special rules for a reasonable cause exemption from the overvaluation component of the accuracy-related penalty, even if a charitable donation of property is not involved.

Disclosure of the relevant facts affecting an item's tax treatment in the return or in a statement attached to the return reduces the amount of an understatement for purposes of the accuracy-related penalty for substantial understatement of income tax in the same way it did under the substantial understatement penalty of prior law.[389] Although this disclosure mechanism was borrowed from the substantial understatement penalty of prior law, disclosure

---

[389] Since no change was made in the statutory language, no change was necessary in procedure.

is not unique to the substantial understatement penalty. The question of whether information has been disclosed is also relevant for purposes of the extended statute of limitations on assessment.[390] Therefore, case law interpreting disclosures under this provision is relevant to the issue and should be considered in determining whether a qualifying disclosure has been made for accuracy-related and fraud penalty purposes.[391]

A qualifying disclosure for purposes of the substantial understatement accuracy-related penalty can be made by a disclosure in an attached statement, a disclosure of the legal issue affecting the item, or a disclosure on the return pursuant to the current revenue procedure applicable to this type of disclosure. Following the legislative lead, the Service has described qualifying disclosures for purposes of the negligence and the substantial understatement part of the accuracy-related penalty.[392]

1. The Service will not impose a negligence accuracy-related penalty "if the taxpayer has made a complete, item-specific disclosure of [the] nonfrivolous position."[393] A disclosure is complete and item-specific if it is "full and substantive" and is "clearly identified as being made to avoid imposition of the accuracy-related penalty."[394]

2. Mechanically, the disclosure can be made by attaching a completed Form 8275 (Disclosure Statement Under Section 6661) to the return. If disclosure is not made on a Form 8275, a caption made at the top left-hand corner of the return must state that it is a disclosure under Section 6662 and refer to the page or line number containing the disclosure. For example, a qualifying disclosure about medical expenses would be made at the top left-hand corner of the first page of Form 1040 and read: "Disclosure Made Under Section 6662. See Lines 1–4 of Schedule A."

3. For purposes of a substantial understatement accuracy-related penalty, a qualified disclosure is one qualifying as such under the substantial understatement penalty.[395] For example, a completed Form 8275 also constitutes a disclosure for the substantial understatement accuracy-related penalty.

---

[390] IRC § 6501(e) provides for a six-year statute of limitations on assessment if a taxpayer omits more than 25 percent of gross income from a return, but the amount omitted is reduced if the amount "is disclosed in the return, or in a statement attached to the return, in a manner adequate to apprise the Secretary of the nature and amount of such item."

[391] For a discussion of disclosures under Section 6501(e), see ¶ 5.03[2].

[392] Notice 90-20, 1990-1 CB 328 (Mar. 5, 1990).

[393] Notice 90-20, 1990-1 CB 328 (Mar. 5, 1990).

[394] Notice 90-20, 1990-1 CB 328 (Mar. 5, 1990).

[395] Notice 90-20, 1990-1 CB 328 (Mar. 5, 1990).

There is a difference between the disclosures required to avoid the negligence and the substantial understatement penalty. This difference is indicated in the Service's position that a disclosure might avoid a substantial understatement accuracy-related penalty, but not a negligence accuracy-related penalty, while a disclosure qualifying for the latter penalty will suffice for the substantial understatement accuracy-related penalty.[396] The difference derives from the "full and substantive" requirement. A statement of the legal issue that would qualify as a disclosure for substantial understatement purposes[397] is not necessarily "full and substantive." Consequently, although a notice is adequate disclosure for the substantial understatement accuracy-related penalty, a full presentation and, apparently, a factual and legal presentation, must be made to avoid the negligence accuracy-related penalty.

Disclosure was also intended to avoid imposition of the disregard of rules and regulations component of the accuracy-related penalty. A taxpayer who wishes to make a good faith challenge to the validity of a regulation can avoid the penalty if the taxpayer makes an appropriate disclosure. In addition to the information necessary to make a qualifying disclosure to avoid the negligence component of the accuracy-related penalty, the taxpayer must also state that he is taking a position challenging the specific regulation.[398] Consequently, a disclosure meeting these requirements can avoid the ruling in *Druker v. Comm'r*, where the Second Circuit said that a regulation could only be contested without a disregard of rules and regulations penalty if the taxpayer paid the tax and sued for refund.[399]

Special rules apply where the accuracy-related penalty for a valuation overstatement arises out of a taxpayer's charitable deduction for donated property.[400] The reasonable cause exception does not apply unless (1) the claimed value was based on a qualified appraisal made by a qualified appraiser[401] and (2) in addition to obtaining the appraisal, the taxpayer has made "a good faith investigation of the value of the property."[402] If a taxpayer already acted in

---

[396] Notice 90-20, 1990-1 CB 328 (Mar. 5, 1990). For example, a disclosure made in the return pursuant to a published revenue procedure on the subject might not avoid a negligence penalty.

[397] See Reg. § 1.6661-4(b)(2).

[398] HR Rep. No. 247, 101st Cong., 1st Sess. 285.

[399] Druker v. Comm'r, 697 F2d 46 9 (2d Cir. 1982), cert. denied, 103 S. Ct. 2429 (1983).

[400] IRC § 6664(c)(3). The special rule does not apply to securities for which market quotations are readily available on an established securities market.

[401] The terms qualified appraisal and qualified appraiser have the same meanings as under Section 170(a)(1) and the regulations thereunder.

[402] IRC § 6664(c)(2)(B). See Reg. § 1.6664-4(g), interpreting the reasonable cause exception in a substantial or gross valuation misstatement of charitable deduction property, essentially reciting the provisions of the statute.

sufficient good faith to find and retain a competent appraiser qualified under IRS rules and regulations and to obtain an appraisal meeting the Service's requirements, it is difficult to see what good the second component serves. It is obvious that the intention was to avoid collusive appraisals, but requiring lay taxpayers to make independent investigations of matters outside of their knowledge or experience seems both impractical and out of proportion to the potential problem.

The substantial authority standard was intended to replace the reasonable basis standard, then the standard governing both lawyers and certified public accountants in preparing tax returns. According to critics, reasonable basis was not a supportable enough return position and excused all sorts of positions courts would never accept. Substantial authority is claimed to be a higher standard for undisclosed-return positions than a reasonable basis. One way to avoid uncertainty about the adequacy of the support for a return position is to attach a statement to the return disclosing the position. Regulations attempted to impose a standard for a qualifying disclosure.[403] In order for the disclosure to qualify, the disclosed position still could not be a frivolous one.

The Omnibus Budget Reconciliation Act of 1993 (OBRA 1993) amended the disclosure procedure for the substantial understatement component by requiring a reasonable basis for the disclosed return position.[404] The Conference Report states, "The conferees intend that 'reasonable basis' be a relatively high standard of tax reporting, that is, significantly higher than 'not patently improper.' This standard is not satisfied by a return position that is merely arguable or that is merely a colorable claim."[405] Therefore, for tax returns whose due date, disregarding extensions, is after December 31, 1993, an accuracy-related penalty for substantial understatement of a tax can be avoided by a qualifying disclosure of a return position only if there is a reasonable basis for the disclosed position.[406] In other words, reasonable basis is not good enough support for an undisclosed-return position, but it is required for a disclosed-return position.

In accordance with the 1993 changes to the accuracy-related penalty, regulations state that the penalty for negligence may not be avoided by the disclosure of a return position.[407] Moreover, the penalties for disregarding rules or regulations (Section 6662(b)(1)) and for a substantial understatement of in-

---

[403] Reg. § 1.6662-3(c).

[404] OBRA 1993, § 13251(a), modifying IRC § 6662(d)(2)(B)(ii).

[405] HR Conf. Rep. No. 213, 103d Cong., 1st Sess., on the Revenue Provisions of Title XIII of the Omnibus Budget Reconciliation Act of 1993 (HR 2264), Statement of Conference Managers 205.

[406] OBRA 1993, § 13251(b).

[407] Reg. § 1.6662-7(b). The temporary regulations were adopted in final form on September 1, 1995. TD 8617. These regulations generally apply to returns filed after December 31, 1993, but, in the case of the negligence and intentional disregard portions, the

come tax (Section 6662(b)(2)) will be avoided only by an adequate disclosure if the position has a reasonable basis[408]—that is, support that is "significantly higher" than the not-frivolous standard applicable to preparers under Section 6694 (as defined in Treas. Reg. § 1.6694-2(c)(2)).[409]

[3] Reasonable Cause Under the Consolidated Penalty Handbook

On July 27, 1992, the Service issued a Consolidated Penalty Handbook as part of its Manual.[410] In its current format, the Handbook has the following parts:

1. Introduction and Penalty Relief
2. Failure to File/Failure to Pay Penalties
3. Estimated Taxes
4. Failure to Deposit (Section 6656)
5. Return Related Penalties
6. Preparer, Promoter, Protestor Penalties
7. Information Return Penalties
8. Employee Plans and Exempt Organizations Penalties
9. International Penalties
10. Miscellaneous Penalties

"Consolidated" is the key word in the Handbook's title because the Handbook gathers into a single part civil penalty descriptions and portions formerly scattered and duplicated throughout the Manual. By having one Handbook to look at in applying and abating penalties, IRS personnel (and practitioners) should be able to find and IRS personnel should be able to apply more consistently National Office positions on civil penalties—at least that is the objective. Seen in this light, it is not surprising that the Manual contains little that is new. For example, the description of "reasonable cause" can already be found in the Manual (reasonable cause is discussed later in this chapter). On the other hand, because it is an option overlooked by practitioners and unmentioned by agents, one of the positive features of the Handbook is the prominent description of a taxpayer's appeal rights when a penalty is asserted and not abated.

A useful part of the Penalty Handbook is the Service's description of reasonable cause and related concepts. It is, therefore, appropriate to include the discussion here.

---

temporary regulations do not apply to returns (including qualified amended returns) filed before March 14, 1994.

[408] Reg. § 1.6662-7(c).

[409] Reg. § 1.6662-7(d)(2).

[410] IRM, pt. 20, 120.1.1 et seq. (Aug. 20, 1998). The Penalties Handbook is periodically updated.

1. *Reasonable cause in general.*[411] Reasonable cause is based on all the facts and circumstances in each situation and allows the Service to provide relief from a penalty that would otherwise be assessed. Reasonable cause relief is generally granted when the taxpayer exercises ordinary business care and prudence in determining its tax obligations but is unable to comply with those obligations. In the interest of equitable treatment of the taxpayer and effective tax administration, the nonassertion or abatement of civil penalties based on reasonable cause or other relief provisions provided in the Manual must be made in a consistent manner and should conform with the considerations specified in the Internal Revenue Code, Treasury Regulations, Policy Statements, and Part 120.1, the Penalties Handbook. Although reasonable cause relief is not available for all penalties, other exceptions may apply, depending on the situation.

For those penalties where reasonable cause can be considered, any reason that establishes that the taxpayer exercised ordinary business care and prudence, but was unable to comply with a prescribed duty within the prescribed time, will be considered. If a reasonable cause provision applies only to a specific Code section, that reasonable cause provision will be discussed in the Penalties Handbook chapter relating to that Code section.[412]

An acceptable explanation by a taxpayer is not limited to those given in the reasonable cause part of the Manual. Penalty relief granted because the taxpayer provided an "other acceptable explanation" is identified on either the closing or adjustment document. Also, the terms used to define the reasonable cause exceptions vary. Some penalty sections also require evidence that the taxpayer acted in good faith or that the taxpayer's failure to comply with the law was not due to willful neglect.

2. *Reasonable cause inquiries.* Taxpayers have reasonable cause when their conduct justifies the nonassertion or abatement of a penalty. Each case must be judged individually based on the facts and circumstances. The examiner will make a determination by taking into account the following circumstances, together with specific criteria in the Manual:

- What happened and when did it happen?
- During the period of time the taxpayer was noncompliant, what facts and circumstances prevented the taxpayer from filing a return, paying a tax, or otherwise complying with the law?
- How did the facts and circumstances prevent the taxpayer from complying?
- How did the taxpayer handle the remainder of its affairs during this time?

---

[411] Penalties Handbook 120.1.1.3.1, Reasonable Cause (Aug. 20, 1998).
[412] See Penalties Handbook, Exhibit 120.1.1-2, Penalty Relief-Application Chart.

- Once the facts and circumstances changed, what attempt did the taxpayer make to comply?

Reasonable cause does not exist if, after the facts and circumstances that explain the taxpayer's noncompliant behavior cease to exist, the taxpayer fails to comply with the tax obligation within a reasonable period of time.

3. *Ordinary business care and prudence.*[413] Any reason that establishes that a taxpayer exercised ordinary business care and prudence, but was unable to comply with the tax law, may be considered for penalty relief.[414] In general, ordinary business care and prudence includes making provision for business obligations to be met when reasonably foreseeable events occur. A taxpayer may establish reasonable cause by providing facts and circumstances showing the taxpayer exercised ordinary business care and prudence (taking that degree of care that a reasonably prudent person would exercise), but nevertheless was unable to comply with the law.

In evaluating whether the taxpayer exercised ordinary business care and prudence, the following information must be reviewed in the first instance by the revenue agent or collection official:

a. *Taxpayer's reason.* To show reasonable cause, the taxpayer must present evidence on the particular penalty involved and show that the dates and explanations clearly correspond with events on which the penalties are based. If the dates and explanations do not correspond to the events on which the penalties are based, the examiner must request additional information from the taxpayer that may clarify the explanation.

b. *Compliance history.* The preceding tax years (at least two) will be checked for payment patterns and the taxpayer's overall compliance history. The same penalty, previously assessed or abated, may indicate that the taxpayer is not exercising ordinary business care. If this is the taxpayer's first incident of noncompliant behavior, the examiner must weigh this factor with

---

[413] Penalties Handbook 120.1.1.3.1.2, Ordinary Business Care and Prudence (Aug. 20, 1998).

[414] Penalties Handbook 120.1.1.3.1.1, Standards (Aug. 20, 1998); Accuracy-Related Penalty: 1.6664-4; Failure to Pay Penalty: 301.6651-1(c); Failure to File: 301.6651-1(c); Failure to Deposit Penalty: 301.6656-1(b); 301.6656-2(c); Information Returns Penalty: 301.6723-1A(d); 301.6724-1; Preparer/Promoter Penalties: 1.6694-2(d); 301.6707-1T. The following Internal Revenue Service Policy Statements contain specific criteria that may affect the imposition of penalties:

- P-2-4, Penalties and interest not asserted against federal agencies
- P-2-7, Reasonable cause for late filing of return or failure to deposit or pay tax when due
- P-2-9, Timely mailed returns bearing foreign postmarks
- P-2-11, Certain unsigned returns will be accepted for processing

other reasons the taxpayer gives for reasonable cause, since a first time failure to comply does not by itself establish reasonable cause.

c. *Length of time.* An important consideration is the length of time between the event cited as a reason for the noncompliance and subsequent compliance. The examiner will consider (i) when the act was required by law; (ii) the period of time during which the taxpayer was unable to comply with the law due to circumstances beyond the taxpayer's control; and (3) when the taxpayer complied with the law.

d. *Circumstances beyond the taxpayer's control.* Another factor is whether or not the taxpayer could have anticipated the event that caused the noncompliance. Reasonable cause is said to be generally established when the taxpayer exercises ordinary business care and prudence but, due to circumstances beyond the taxpayer's control, the taxpayer was unable to timely meet the tax obligation. The taxpayer's obligation to meet the tax law requirements is ongoing. Ordinary business care and prudence requires that the taxpayer continue to attempt to meet the requirements, even if the taxpayer is late.

e. *Ignorance of the law.*[415] In some instances taxpayers may not be aware of specific obligations to file and/or pay taxes. The ordinary business care and prudence standard requires taxpayers to make reasonable efforts to determine their tax obligations. Reasonable cause may be established if the taxpayer shows ignorance of the law in conjunction with other facts and circumstances. The examiner will consider:

- The taxpayer's education;
- If the taxpayer has been subject to the tax;
- If the taxpayer has been penalized; or
- If there were recent changes in the tax forms or law that a taxpayer could not reasonably be expected to know.

The level of complexity of a tax or compliance issue is another factor the examiner should consider in evaluating reasonable cause because of ignorance of the law. However, reasonable cause will never be presumed, even in cases where ignorance of the law is claimed. Nevertheless, the taxpayer may have reasonable cause for noncompliance if:

- A reasonable and good faith effort was made to comply with the law, or
- The taxpayer was unaware of a requirement and could not reasonably be expected to know of the requirement.

f. *Mistake was made.*[416] The taxpayer may try to establish reasonable cause by claiming that a mistake was made. Generally, this is not in keeping

---

[415] Penalties Handbook 120.1.1.3.1.2.1, Ignorance of the Law (Aug. 8, 1998).
[416] Penalties Handbook 120.1.1.3.1.2.2, Mistake was Made (Aug. 20, 1998).

with the ordinary business care and prudence standard and does not provide a basis for reasonable cause. However, the reason for the mistake may be a supporting factor if additional facts and circumstances support the determination that the taxpayer exercised ordinary business care and prudence.

g. *Forgetfulness.*[417] The taxpayer may try to establish reasonable cause by claiming that forgetfulness or an oversight by the taxpayer or another party caused the noncompliance. Generally, this is not in keeping with the ordinary business care and prudence standard and does not provide a basis for reasonable cause. Relying on another person to perform a required act is generally not sufficient for establishing reasonable cause. It is the taxpayer's responsibility to file a timely and accurate return and to make timely deposits or payments. This responsibility cannot be delegated. Information to consider when evaluating a request for an abatement or nonassertion of a penalty based on a mistake or a claim of ignorance of the law includes, but is not limited to:

- When and how the taxpayer became aware of the mistake;
- Extent to which the taxpayer corrected the mistake;
- Relationship between the taxpayer and the subordinate;
- Whether the taxpayer took timely steps to correct the failure after it was discovered; and
- Supporting documentation

h. *Death, serious illness, or unavoidable absence.*[418] Death, serious illness, or unavoidable absence of the taxpayer may establish reasonable cause for late filing, payment, or deposit for (i) an individual, if there was a death, serious illness, or unavoidable absence of the taxpayer or a death or serious illness in the taxpayer's immediate family (i.e., spouse, sibling, parents, grandparents, children) and (ii) a corporation, estate, trust, if someone, other than the taxpayer or the person responsible, is authorized to meet the obligation. In evaluating the request for relief of a business, if only one person was authorized, the examiner will evaluate whether this was in keeping with ordinary business care and prudence. When evaluating a request for penalty relief based on reasonable cause due to death, serious illness, or unavoidable absence, the following information will be considered:

- Relationship of the taxpayer to the other parties involved;
- Date of death;
- Dates, duration, and severity of illness;
- Dates and reasons for absence;
- How the event prevented compliance;
- If other business obligations were impaired; and

---

[417] Penalties Handbook 120.1.1.3.1.2.3, Forgetfulness (Aug. 20, 1998).

[418] Penalties Handbook 120.1.1.3.1.2.4, Death, Serious Illness, or Unavoidable Absence (Aug. 20, 1998).

- Whether tax duties were attended to promptly when the illness passed, or within a reasonable period of time after a death or absence.

i. *Unable to obtain records.*[419] The taxpayer's explanations about its inability to obtain necessary records may in some instances constitute reasonable cause. Examiners consider the facts and circumstances relevant to each case and evaluate the request for penalty relief. Reasonable cause may be established if the taxpayer exercised ordinary business care and prudence, but was unable to comply with its tax obligations because of circumstances beyond the taxpayer's control. Information to consider when evaluating such a request includes, but is not limited to, an explanation as to:

- Why the records were needed to comply;
- Why the records were unavailable and what steps were taken to secure the records;
- When and how the taxpayer became aware that it did not have the necessary records;
- Whether other means were explored to secure needed information;
- Why the taxpayer did not estimate the information;
- Whether the taxpayer contacted the Service for instructions on what to do about missing information;
- Whether the taxpayer promptly complied once the missing information was received; and
- Supporting documentation such as copies of letters written and responses received in an effort to get the needed information.

4. *Statutory exceptions and administrative waivers.*[420] These two very separate categories are placed together because in many instances an administrative waiver is an extension of rules that were provided for by statute.

a. *Statutory exceptions.*[421] Some Code sections may provide an exception to a penalty. Specific statutory exceptions can be found in either the penalty-related Code section or the accompanying regulations that are not based on reasonable cause. For example: Section 6654(e)(1), 6654(e)(2), or 6654(e)(3), Estimated Tax Penalties for Individuals[422]; Sections 7502(a) and 7502(e), Timely Mailing Treated as Timely Filing and Paying[423]; Section 6724(a) or 6724(c), Waiver; Definitions and Special Rules, Information Return Penal-

---

[419] Penalties Handbook 120.1.1.3.1.2.5, Unable to Obtain Records (Aug. 20, 1998).

[420] Penalties Handbook 120.1.1.3.2, Statutory Exceptions and Administrative Waivers.

[421] Penalties Handbook 120.1.1.3.2.1, Statutory Exceptions (Aug. 20, 1998).

[422] Penalties Handbook 120.1.3, Estimated Tax Penalties for Individuals.

[423] Penalties Handbook 120.1.2, Timely Mailing Treated as Timely Filing.

ties[424]; Section 6404(f), Abatement of Penalty or Addition to Tax Attributable to Written Advice of the Internal Revenue Service[425]; Section 7508, Time for Performing Certain Acts Postponed by Reason of Service in Combat Zone (this provision applies only in a Presidentially-declared combat zone).

Legislation with retroactive provisions may provide guidance on associated penalties. As a result of that retroactive provision, the Service may issue a News Release or other guidance with instructions for the disposition of the related penalties.

b. *Administrative waiver.*[426] The Service may formally interpret or clarify a provision to provide administrative relief from a penalty that would otherwise be assessed. An administrative waiver may be addressed in either a Policy Statement or News Release, or other formal communication stating that the policy of the Service is to provide relief from a penalty under specific conditions. An administrative waiver may be necessary when there is a delay by the Service in printing or mailing forms, publishing guidance, writing of regulations, or other conditions. An example of an administrative waiver is Notice 93-22.[427] This Notice allowed individuals who requested an automatic four-month extension of time to file an income tax return, an extension of time without remitting the unpaid amount of any tax properly estimated to be due.

5. *Undue hardship.*[428] For undue hardship to support the granting of an extension of time for paying a tax or deficiency, regulations require that the hardship be more than an inconvenience to the taxpayer.[429] The taxpayer must show that it would sustain a substantial financial loss if forced to pay a tax or deficiency on the due date. The extension of time to pay does not provide the taxpayer with an extension of time to file, nor does it relieve the taxpayer of any appropriate penalties. Undue hardship generally does not affect a person's ability to file, and so would not provide a basis for penalty relief in a failure to file situation. However, each request will be considered on a case-by-case basis. For example, undue hardship may establish reasonable cause for failure to file on magnetic media.[430]

Undue hardship may also support relief from the addition to tax for failure to pay tax if the explanation for the noncompliance supports such a determination. A mere inability to pay does not ordinarily provide the basis for

---

[424] Penalties Handbook 120.1.7, Waiver; Definitions and Special Rules, Information Return Penalties.

[425] Penalties Handbook 120.1.1, Abatement of Penalty Attributable to Written Advice of IRS.

[426] Penalties Handbook 120.1.1.3.2.2, Administrative Waiver (Aug. 20, 1998).

[427] Notice 93-22, 1993-1 CB 305.

[428] Penalties Handbook 120.1.1.3.2.3, Undue Hardship (Aug. 20, 1998).

[429] Reg. § 1.6161-1(b).

[430] Reg. § 301.6724-1.

granting penalty relief.[431] The taxpayer must also show that it exercised ordinary business care and prudence in providing for the payment of the tax liability.

The taxpayer may claim that enough funds were on hand but, as a result of unanticipated events, the taxpayer was unable to pay the taxes. An individual taxpayer's inability to pay is a factor when the Service is considering penalty relief if the taxpayer shows that, had the payment been made on the payment due date, undue hardship (as defined in Regulation Section 1.6161-(1)(b)) would have resulted. In the case where a taxpayer files bankruptcy, inability to pay can be a factor if the insolvency occurred before the tax payment date. Employers are required to reserve money withheld from employees' wages in trust until deposited, and not use the money for any other purpose, if a payroll was met, taxes were withheld and should be available for deposit. Undue hardship does not support relief from the IRC Section 6672, Failure to Collect and Pay Over Tax, or attempt to Evade or Defeat Tax (Trust Fund Recovery Program).

When evaluating a request for penalty relief, the examiner should ask the following questions:

- When did the taxpayer know payment could not be made?
- Why was the taxpayer unable to pay?
- Did the taxpayer explore other means to secure the necessary funds?
- What did the taxpayer supply in the way of supporting documentation, such as copies of bank statements?
- Did the taxpayer pay when the funds became available?

6. Advice.[432] There are three basic types of advice that can result in the abatement of a penalty (a) the taxpayer's reliance on the Service's written advice; (b) the taxpayer's reliance on the Service's oral advice; and (c) the taxpayer's reliance on the advice of a tax professional. Information considered when the examiner is evaluating a request for abatement or nonassertion of a penalty due to reliance on advice includes:

- Was the advice in response to a specific request, and was the advice received related to the facts contained in that request?
- Did the taxpayer reasonably rely on the advice?

The following examples address situations where a taxpayer relies on written advice from the Service regarding an item on a filed return.

1. The taxpayer did not reasonably rely on the advice regarding an item included on a return where the advice was received after the date the return was filed.

---

[431] Reg. § 301.6651-1(e).
[432] Penalties Handbook 120.1.1.3.2.4, Advice (Aug. 20, 1998).

2. A taxpayer may be considered to have reasonably relied on advice received after the return was filed if the taxpayer then filed an amended return that conformed with the written advice.

3. A taxpayer may not be considered to have reasonably relied on written advice unrelated to an item included on a return, such as advice on the payment of estimated taxes, if the taxpayer received the advice after the estimated tax payment was due.

Where the taxpayer claims reliance on a tax professional's advice, the critical question is whether the taxpayer provided the tax professional with adequate and accurate information.

To obtain the abatement of a penalty, the taxpayer is advised to submit the necessary supporting information and documentation with Form 843, Claim. However, if the information provided demonstrates that abatement of the penalty is warranted, the penalty should be abated, whether or not a Form 843 is provided.

a. *Written advice from the Service.*[433] The Service is required[434] to abate any portion of any penalty attributable to erroneous written advice furnished by an officer or employee of the Service acting in their official capacity. The taxpayer is entitled to penalty relief for the period during which the taxpayer relied on the advice. The period continues until the taxpayer is placed on notice that the advice is no longer correct or no longer represents the Service's position. The taxpayer is placed on notice as the result of any of the following events that present a contrary position and occurs after the issuance of the written advice:

- Written correspondence from the Service that its advice is no longer correct or no longer represents the Service's position;
- Enactment of legislation or ratification of a tax treaty;
- A Supreme Court decision;
- The issuance of temporary or final regulations; or
- The publication of a revenue ruling, revenue procedure, or other statement in the Internal Revenue Bulletin.

If the taxpayer does not meet the criteria for penalty relief under Section 6404, the taxpayer may qualify for other penalty relief. For example, taxpayers who fail to meet all of the above criteria may still qualify for relief under reasonable cause if the Service determines that the taxpayer exercised ordinary business care and prudence in relying on the Service's written advice.

---

[433] Penalties Handbook 120.1.1.3.2.4.1, Written Advice From the Service (Aug. 20, 1998).

[434] See IRC § 6404(f); Reg. § 301.6404-3.

b. *Oral advice from the Service.*[435] The Service may provide penalty relief based on a taxpayer's reliance on erroneous oral advice from the Service. The Service is required[436] to abate any portion of any penalty attributable to erroneously written advice furnished by an employee acting in his official capacity. Administratively, the Service has extended this relief to include erroneous oral advice when appropriate.

In addition to considering the criteria provided above, the examiner will consider the following:

- Did the taxpayer exercise ordinary business care and prudence in relying on the advice?
- Was there a clear relationship between the taxpayer's situation, the advice provided, and the penalty assessed?
- What is the taxpayer's prior tax history and prior experience with the tax requirements?
- Did the Service provide correct information by other means (such as tax forms and publications)?
- What type of supporting documentation is available?

The types of supporting documentation considered include:

- A notation of the taxpayer's question to the Service;
- Documentation regarding the advice provided by the Service;
- Information regarding the office and method by which the advice was obtained;
- The date the advice was provided; and
- The name of the employee who provided the information.

c. *Advice from tax advisor.*[437] Reliance on the advice of a tax advisor generally relates to the reasonable cause exception in Section 6664(c) for the accuracy-related penalty.[438] However, in "very limited instances," reliance on the advice of a tax advisor may apply to other penalties when the tax advisor provides advice on a substantive tax issue. For example, suppose an employer researched all available Service publications on the subject of contract labor, provided clear and convincing documentation as to the duties of the workers to the tax advisor, and requested an opinion from the tax advisor as to whether the workers were "contract labor" or employees. As a result, the tax advisor

---

[435] Penalties Handbook 120.1.1.3.2.4.2, Oral Advice From the Service (Aug. 20, 1998).

[436] See IRC § 6404(f); Reg. § 301.6404-3.

[437] Penalties Handbook 120.1.1.3.2.4.3, Advice From a Tax Advisor (Aug. 20, 1998).

[438] For a desciption of reasonable cause under the accuracy-related penalty, see Reg. § 1.6664-4(c). See Penalties Handbook 120.1.5, Preparer Promoter Penalty.

advised the employer that the workers were contract labor. The Service later determined that the workers were employees and not contract labor.

Reliance on the advice of a tax advisor is limited to issues generally considered technical or complicated. The taxpayer's responsibility to file, pay, or deposit taxes cannot be excused by reliance on the advice of a tax advisor.

7. *Fire, casualty, natural disaster, or other disturbance.*[439] Relief from a penalty may be requested if the failure to timely comply was due to an impossibility to comply caused by a fire, casualty, natural disaster, or other disturbance. In such a situation, the taxpayer must identify the appropriate basis for reasonable cause. It could be that as a result of a fire the taxpayer was unable to access its records, or as the result of an accident the responsible party was hospitalized and unable to file the return or pay the tax. Fire, casualty, natural disaster, or other disturbance are factors to consider. One of these circumstances by itself does not necessarily provide penalty relief. Penalty relief may be appropriate if the taxpayer exercised ordinary business care and prudence, but due to circumstances beyond the taxpayer's control they were unable to comply with the law. Factors to be considered include:

- Timing;
- Effect on the taxpayer's business;
- Steps taken to attempt to comply; and
- If the taxpayer complied when it became possible.

The determination to grant relief from each penalty must be based on the facts and circumstances surrounding each individual case.

a. *Official disaster area.*[440] When a significant disaster occurs affecting a wide area of taxpayers, the Service often issues special instructions to facilitate evaluating the request for penalty relief. Because there are one-time instructions, they are not incorporated in the Manual. Districts, service centers, and customer service sites will be kept informed of any special instructions affecting their areas.

b. *Service error.*[441] A Service error is any error made by the Service in computing or assessing tax, crediting accounts, and the like. When an analyst, from any area of the Service, identifies a computer programming application that caused a penalty to be assessed in error, that analyst should:

1. Contact Information Services (IS) to resolve the inadequate computer application, and

---

[439] Penalties Handbook 120.1.1.3.2.5, Fire, Casualty, Natural Disaster, or Other Disturbance.

[440] Penalties Handbook 120.1.1.3.2.6, Official Disaster Area (Aug. 20, 1998).

[441] Penalties Handbook 120.1.1.3.3, Service Error (Aug. 20, 1998).

2. Include on the Request for Information Services (RIS) a statement indicating that the computer code must be used to identify any abatement of a penalty resulting from reversal of the computer application.

Other Service errors are manually coded to identify penalties abated as the result of Service errors that occur individually. Some examples are:

1. A math error when manually computing a penalty;
2. An extension of time to file that did not post to the master file; or
3. Any other error, when it can be shown that (a) the taxpayer did in fact comply with the law and (b) the Service did not initially recognize that fact.

8. *Requesting penalty relief.*[442] The initial request for relief may occur either (a) after an examination but before a penalty is actually assessed or (b) with a return that is either filed or paid late. When the request is received, the examiner is to carefully analyze the taxpayer's reasons to determine if penalty relief is warranted. The burden of proof is generally on the taxpayer.

a. Each request must be evaluated on its own merit including:

- The events or parties involved, and
- If the taxpayer exercised ordinary business care and prudence, but due to circumstances or events beyond the taxpayer's control, the taxpayer was unable to meet the tax requirement, or other penalty relief criteria apply.

b. The taxpayer's obligation to meet the requirement is ongoing. Ordinary business care and prudence requires that the taxpayer continue to attempt to meet the requirements, even though late.

c. The examiner is to determine if the taxpayer's explanation addresses the penalty imposed. The dates and explanations should clearly correspond with events on which the penalties are based to show that the taxpayer is entitled to relief from the penalty. The examiner must request additional information from the taxpayer if the dates and explanations do not correspond with the events on which the penalty are based. In addition, the examiner must review available Service information in determining whether or not the taxpayer exercised ordinary business care and prudence (see IRM 1.3.1.2).

d. The examiner is to check the preceding tax years (at least two) for payment patterns and the taxpayer's overall compliance history. The same penalty, previously assessed, may indicate that the taxpayer is not exercising ordinary business care. If this is the taxpayer's first incident of noncompliant behavior, this factor is weighed with other reasons the

---

[442] Penalties Handbook 120.1.1.3.4, Requesting Penalty Relief (Aug. 20, 1998).

taxpayer gives for relief, since a first time failure to comply does not by itself establish reasonable cause.

e. The examiner is to consider the length of time between the event cited as a reason for the noncompliance and the subsequent compliance. The length of time between events may serve to cancel or reduce the event's effect. Penalty relief may not be appropriate if, after considering all facts and circumstances, the taxpayer fails to timely correct noncompliant behavior.

f. The following are examples where penalty relief may *not* be appropriate:

- Taxpayers claimed that they were unable to comply with the filing requirement because of a death in the family. The death occurred several months prior to the due date of the return. The return was filed a year after the due date of the return.
- Taxpayers claimed that they were unable to comply with the filing requirement because the records necessary for filing were in the control of a third party, i.e., a bankruptcy trustee or an accountant. The records were returned to the taxpayer well in advance of the time the return was required to be filed. The return was not filed until several months after the records were returned.

In both of the examples, the timing of the event may prevent the taxpayer from receiving penalty relief unless other factors justify the delay in filing. The examiner must consider whether the taxpayer could have anticipated the event that caused the noncompliance.

¶ 7B.05 DETERMINATION OF THE UNDERPAYMENT FOR THE FRAUD AND ACCURACY-RELATED PENALTIES

[1] Definition of Underpayment

For purposes of computing the negligence and fraud penalties under prior law, the term underpayment was defined as a deficiency (as defined in Section 6211), except that only a timely filed return could be used to reduce the correct tax.[443] Under prior law, therefore, the addition to the tax for fraud was im-

---

[443] Section 6653(c) provided:

For purposes of this section, the term "underpayment" means (1) INCOME, ESTATE, GIFT & CERTAIN EXCISE TAXES.— In the case of a tax to which section 6211 (relating to income, estate, gift, and certain excise taxes) is applicable, a defi-

posed on the difference between the taxpayer's correct tax and the amount of the originally reported tax, irrespective of any tax payments the taxpayer may have made after the original return was filed, but before the penalty assessment.

Under a normal deficiency computation, the correct tax is reduced by any amount previously collected as a deficiency. In an underpayment computation, however, the correct tax is not reduced by the amount of a deficiency a taxpayer may pay on a prior examination before the fraud penalty is asserted or a tax paid with an amended return. In *Papa v. Comm'r*,[444] the taxpayer filed a 1954 tax return and, after a routine audit, paid the amount of the deficiency. Later, IRS agents discovered that the return was fraudulent. Relying on case law under the 1939 Code, the Second Circuit rejected the taxpayer's contention that the deficiency to which the fraud penalty applied was the deficiency in tax existing when the fraud penalty was determined to be due, not the deficiency in tax owed as of the time the return was required to be filed. This view that the provisions of Section 6653(b) work no substantive change in the law developed under Section 293(b) of the 1939 Code is accepted not only by the Second Circuit but by the Third Circuit[445] and Tax Court[446] as well. Consequently, the addition to tax for fraud is imposed on the difference between the taxpayer's correct tax liability and the tax shown on his return, even if, before the assessment of the fraud penalty for the year, additional tax has been paid (1) after an audit of the taxpayer's return by the Service[447]; (2) after an amended return has been filed reporting additional tax[448]; or (3) after a taxpayer files a delinquent return, having fraudulently failed to file a timely return.[449] The rationale of these rules was stated in *Levinson v. United States* as follows:

---

ciency as defined in that section (except that, for this purpose, the tax shown on a return referred to in section 6211(a)(1)(A) shall be taken into account only if such return was filed on or before the last day prescribed for the filing of such return, determined with regard to any extension of time for such filing), . . .

[444] Papa v. Comm'r, 464 F2d 150 (2d Cir. 1972).

[445] Levinson v. United States, 496 F2d 651 (3d Cir.), cert. denied, 419 US 1040 (1974).

[446] Breman v. Comm'r, 66 TC 61 (1976).

[447] Breman v. Comm'r, 66 TC 61 (1976). The same result holds if there have been two audits, after the first of which the deficiency was paid *(Breman)*, or only a single audit, before the end of which a voluntary payment is made. Stewart v. Comm'r, 66 TC 54 (1976).

[448] Maitland A. Wilson, 7 TC 395 (1946); George M. Still, Inc., 19 TC 1072 (1953), aff'd per curiam, 218 F2d 639 (2d Cir. 1955).

[449] Charles F. Bennett, 30 TC 114 (1958); Rev. Rul. 56-54, 1956-1 CB 654. Jenny v. Comm'r, 45 TCM 440 (1983) (return purporting to be amended return after protest return was filed did not reduce fraud penalty).

Had there been only one deficiency assessed coupled with a finding that at least a part of the underpayment was due to fraud, then there would not have been any previously assessed deficiency for which taxpayers could claim a credit under section 6211(a)(1)(B). The fraud penalty quite clearly would have been applied to the total underpayment, i.e., the difference between the correct tax and the tax shown on the original timely filed return. It does not seem likely that Congress would have conditioned the severity of the fraud penalty on such a fortuity as whether or not a routine audit had been conducted prior to the assessment giving rise to the fraud charge.[450]

A loss carried back from another taxable year also does not reduce an underpayment.[451]

The substantial understatement penalty under prior law had no definition of the term underpayment. The Service argued that where no income tax return has been filed, the term "underpayment" meant the entire amount of the tax that should have been shown on the return, irrespective of any withholding or estimated tax credits.[452] Rejecting this approach, the Tax Court held that the substantial understatement penalty was applied only to the unpaid amount, not to the entire understatement in tax.[453] Therefore, for purposes of the substantial understatement penalty, the term underpayment meant the same as the net amount due as used in the delinquency penalty.

---

[450] Levinson v. United States, 496 F2d 651, 654–655 (3d Cir.), cert. denied, 419 US 1040 (1974).

[451] Simon v. Comm'r, 248 F2d 869 (8th Cir. 1957); Auerbach Shoe Co. v. Comm'r, 216 F2d 693 (1st Cir. 1954); Nick v. Dunlap, 185 F2d 674 (5th Cir.), cert. denied, 341 US 926 (1951). In Rev. Rul. 60-215, 1960-1 CB 642, the Service held that the 50 percent fraud penalty was applicable to a deficiency assessed to recover an erroneous tentative carryback. This result has been approved. In *Arc Electrical Constr. Co.*, 1971 tax was underpaid due to fraud, and, as a result, a nonfraudulent new jobs credit was carried back to 1974. The issue was whether a deficiency in 1974 was due to fraud. The Second Circuit held in the affirmative, on the ground that the underpaid tax in 1974 was made possible by the fraud in 1977, the credit carryback being "simply the vehicle for expanding that fraud." Arc Elec. Constr. Co. v. Comm'r, 923 F2d 1005 (2d Cir. 1991); see also Toussaint v. Comm'r, 47 TCM 913, aff'd 743 F2d 309 (5th Cir. 1984) (1974 theft loss carried back to 1971 through 1973; held, because loss was fraudulently claimed in 1974, deficiencies attributable to loss carryback in 1971 through 1973 were fraudulent). Rev. Rul. 84-106, 1984-2 CB 312, expressly holds that underpayment for purposes of the negligence and fraud penalties is computed on the tax originally imposed, unreduced by any later loss carryback. See Elmbrook Home, Inc. v. United States, 559 F. Supp. 787 (DRI 1983) (application of claim of right statute resulted in eliminating underpayment; held, taxpayer nevertheless subject to fraud penalty because returns fraudulent when filed).

[452] Woods v. Comm'r, 91 TC 88, 96 (1988).

[453] Woods v. Comm'r, 91 TC 88, 99 (1988).

Section 6664(a) defines an underpayment as follows:[454]

> For purposes of this part, the term "underpayment means the amount by which any tax imposed by this title exceeds the excess of—
>
> (1) the sum of—
>
> > (A) the amount shown as the tax by the taxpayer on his return, plus
> >
> > (B) amounts not so shown previously assessed (or collected without assessment) over
>
> (2) the amount of rebates made.

No reference is made to the definition of a deficiency, contained in Section 6211, and, in fact, the underpayment definition is expressly for "this part"— i.e., Part II of Chapter 68, "Accuracy and Fraud-Related Penalties." There is also no reference to the rules contained in Section 6211(b) for applying the definition of a deficiency in Section 6211(a). One of these rules is that the tax imposed and correct tax do not take into account withholding and estimated tax payments.[455]

Although there are also differences in the statutory terms, most of these differences simplify and clarify the deficiency definition. However, one change may create some confusion. For purposes of the deficiency definition, the tax imposed is reduced by "the amounts previously assessed (or collected without assessment) as a deficiency."[456] The underpayments definition deletes the words "as a deficiency,"[457] leaving open the possibility that amounts collected from a taxpayer, whether from withholding or estimated tax payments or otherwise, reduce the tax imposed and, therefore, the amount of an underpayment. In short, it is unclear whether an underpayment is a deficiency unreduced by any payments the taxpayer may have made, or whether an underpayment means the net amount of tax due from the taxpayer.

Decisions on the underpayment issue both for the fraud and negligence penalty and the substantial understatement penalty can be coordinated. Pay-

---

[454] According to the House Report, HR Rep. No. 247, 101st Cong., 1st Sess. 286, reprinted in 1989-3 (vol. 3) CB 1381–1406, this provisions states: "This standard definition is intended to simplify and coordinate the definitions in present law; it is not intended to substantively differ from present law." However, Section 6664(b) works a significant change in prior law by imposing the accuracy-related and fraud penalties "only where a return of tax is filed." Where failure to file a return is due to fraud, the misconduct is not punished by the fraud penalty, but by the delinquency penalty (Section 6651(f)), which imposes a maximum penalty equal to 75 percent of the net amount due. See infra ¶ 7B.07.

[455] IRC § 6211(b)(1).

[456] IRC § 6211(a)(1)(B).

[457] IRC § 6664(a)(1)(B).

ments made in the fraud penalty cases previously discussed were made after the original return was filed, while payments made in the substantial understatement penalty case were withholding tax credits. Since a return is required for both the accuracy-related and fraud penalties, it makes sense to take into account withholding and estimated tax credits in determining the amount of the underpayment because the Service has not been impeded by the return from collecting those payments. However, a postreturn payment does not change the fact, for example, that a fraudulent return was filed and that tax was underpaid at the time the return was filed. Regulations take the position that an underpayment is unaffected by withholding tax and estimated tax credits, as well as jeopardy assessment collections.[458]

[2] Computation of the Fraud and Accuracy-Related Penalties

The accuracy-related penalty is 20 percent of the portion of the underpayment to which this section applies.[459] The portion of the underpayment to which Section 6662(a) applies is the portion of the underpayment that is attributable to one or more of the five specified types of misconduct.[460] To arrive at the amount of the underpayment, four factors must be known: (1) the correct tax; (2) the amount of tax shown on the taxpayer's return; (3) the amount of tax previously assessed or collected without assessment; and (4) any rebate. The underpayment is the amount by which the correct tax is greater than the sum of the amount of tax shown on the taxpayer's return, plus the amount of tax previously assessed or collected without assessment, reduced by any rebate. In the same manner as that used in calculating a deficiency, neither the amount of tax imposed nor the amount of tax shown on the return is determined on the return; and they are determined without regard to withholding and estimated tax credits.[461] The amount shown by a taxpayer on a return includes an amount shown as additional tax on a qualified amended return, as long as the items involved were not fraudulent.[462]

A qualified amended return is a kind of voluntary disclosure. It is made on an amended return (or on a request for an administrative adjustment under

---

[458] Reg. §§ 1.6664-2(b), 1.6664-2(c).

[459] IRC § 6662(a).

[460] IRC § 6662(b).

[461] Reg. §§ 1.6664-2(b), 1.6664-2(c). Amounts collected from jeopardy and termination assessments and accumulated earnings tax penalties also do not count. On the other hand, an overstatement of withholding tax or estimated tax credit will reduce the amount of tax shown on the taxpayer's return. Reg. § 1.6664-2(c).

[462] Reg. § 1.6664-2(c)(2). It may also include, however, an amended return that discloses the kind of information disclosed on a disclosure statement for purposes of the substantial understatement penalty and need not report additional tax. Reg. § 1.6664-2(c)(4).

the unified partnership proceedings rules) filed after the due date of the original return and before whichever of the following occurs first:

- Contact by the Service concerning the original return;
- Contact by the Service of a tax shelter promoter under Section 6700 about the claimed tax benefits from the shelter; or
- Where a pass-through entity item is involved, the contact of the pass-through entity by the Service.

In general, rebates arise as the result of a recalculation of the tax the taxpayer has reported on a filed return and the refund of an amount that is in excess of the recalculated tax, or from carrybacks of losses.[463] If situations involving prior assessments and collections as well as rebates are put aside, an underpayment for purposes of the accuracy-related penalty is the amount by which the correct tax exceeds the returned tax. The penalty is imposed on the portion of the excess that is attributable to one or more of the five accuracy-related penalties.

The calculation of the portion of the underpayment attributable to fraud or one or more of the components of the accuracy-related penalty is not described in the statute or legislative history. However, based on case law developed in calculating the overvaluation penalty, the calculation is as follows.[464]

1. Calculate the amount of the tax liability for the year as if all items of income and deduction had been properly reported for the year—i.e., as if there were no item of income or deduction with respect to which a fraud or accuracy-related penalty has been asserted.

2. Without taking into account any adjustment attributable to the item intended to be segregated, calculate the amount of tax liability as if all other items had been reported properly—i.e., calculating the tax as if the deductions had been properly reported, but omitting the penalty tainted item.

3. The difference between the amount of tax calculated under the first and second calculations is attributable to the penalty sought to be segregated.

EXAMPLE: An individual, *T*, files a 1990 return, and, after audit, the IRS makes three adjustments to the return. Interest income received is increased by $2,000. Office-at-home expense of $3,000 is disallowed, as is unreimbursed business expense of $1,000. Suppose an IRS agent asserts

---

[463] See Reg. § 301.6211(f).

[464] See Todd v. Comm'r, 89 TC 912, 918 (1987), aff'd, 862 F2d 540 (5th Cir. 1988). Ordering rules described in the regulations follow this methodology. Reg. § 1.6664-3(b). Unclaimed prepayment credits are applied in the same manner as are the ordering rules, unless the unclaimed credit is allocable to a particular adjustment. Reg. § 1.6664-3(c).

an accuracy-related penalty for negligence with respect to the unreported interest income ($2,000). To calculate the portion of the underpayment attributable to this item, the first step would be to calculate the correct tax by treating all three adjustments as if they had been properly reported. In the second calculation of tax, only the other two disallowed items (the office-at-home expense of $3,000, plus the unreimbursed business expense of $1,000) would be treated as if they had been properly reported on *T*'s return. The amount of the underpayment attributable to the negligence-tainted item would be the difference between the two tax calculations. If the agent were to find that the unreimbursed business expenses also had been claimed negligently, the same calculations would be made, except that only the $3,000 office-at-home expenses would be treated as if they had been properly reported on *T*'s return. An underpayment that is due to the conduct prescribed by the accuracy-related and fraud penalties is not reduced by the carryback of a loss, deduction, or credit to that year.[465]

Computational methodology under the former substantial understatement penalty, Section 6661, may also provide guidance in understanding how the Service computes the substantial understatement component of the accuracy-related penalty. For example, to reduce the understatement for adequately disclosed items, regulations provided that the amount of tax shown on the return is determined by computing the tax as if the items adequately disclosed had been properly reported.[466] In *Craddock*, the Service computed the amount shown on the return for purposes of the substantial understatement penalty by adding the amount of alternative minimum tax (AMT) income actually shown in the taxpayer's return (a negative $5,973,827), the post-audit AMT adjustments of a positive $7,209,720, less the AMT adjustment of $3,378,385 for the adequately disclosed transaction.[467] This resulted in a negative $2,142,492 of AMT income and $0 tax for the amount shown on the taxpayer's return. Consequently, to arrive at the amount of the understatement for penalty purposes, the Service deducted $0 (the amount of tax shown on the return) from $247,299, the correct amount of tax after the Service's audit, to arrive at the understatment of tax of $247,299, and a substantial understatement penalty. The taxpayer argued that all of the understatement of tax related to the disclosed transaction and, therefore, no penalty was due. Under the taxpayer's method, the penalty was computed by taking the corrected amount of AMT income after all audit adjustments relating to the disclosed transaction (the negative $5,973,827 less the positive $7,209,720, leaving a positive $1,235,893), and reversing out the AMT income adjustment attributable to the adequately disclosed transaction, $3,378,385, arriving at a negative AMT income amount of $2,142,492, or $0 tax. From this result, the taxpayer argued that without the

---

[465] Reg. § 1.6664-3(f).

[466] Reg. § 1.6661-2(d).

[467] United States v. Craddock, 81 AFTR2d ¶ 98-656 (10th Cir. 1998).

AMT adjustment from the disclosed transaction, no underpayment would exist, and so he was not liable for the substantial understatement penalty. Although the taxpayer had disclosed the transaction that gave rise to the adjustment, the Tenth Circuit nevertheless upheld the regulation on which the Service relied because the regulation seemed reasonable, and the taxpayer argued that he was being sanctioned although he had disclosed a transaction. The circuit court rejected the taxpayer's argument on the ground that the disclosed transaction accounted for only about half the understated income, which he appeared not to have disclosed.

There is another element in the operation and calculation of the accuracy-related and fraud penalties: interest. Interest on these penalties begins to run on the due date of the tax return,[468] not on the date the penalty is assessed as was the case under prior law. The rationale for this real increase in the amount of the penalty is that the behavior penalized is reflected on the tax return and that the change will dissuade taxpayers from filing improper returns and playing "the audit lottery."[469]

¶ 7B.06 FRIVOLOUS RETURNS: SECTION 6702

In addition to other penalties that may be imposed (e.g., delinquency and negligence penalties), Section 6702 imposes a separate $500 penalty when a taxpayer files a frivolous return.[470] A frivolous return is defined to mean a document that purports to be a return, but that (1) does not contain information "on which the substantial correctness of the self-assessment may be judged;" or (2) contains information that on its face indicates that the self-assessment is substantially incorrect. If the return meets these criteria and the conduct is due to (1) a position that is frivolous or (2) "a desire (which appears on the purported return) to delay or impede the administration of the tax laws," then the taxpayer is subject to the penalty.

The definition of a frivolous return in Section 6702 reflects the applicable law that a return does not qualify as such unless it permits the Service to perform its tax determination and collection function.[471] Consequently, a taxpayer

---

[468] IRC § 6601(e)(2)(B).

[469] HR Rep. No. 247, 101st Cong., 1st Sess. 285.

[470] IRC § 6702, added by TEFRA, Pub. L. No. 248, HR 4961, 97th Cong., 2d Sess. § 326(a).

[471] See the discussion at ¶¶ 4.02[1], 7A.03. If adequate information is provided, the fact that a taxpayer also attaches a protest does not warrant imposition of penalty. Kahn v. United States, 753 F2d 1208 (3d Cir. 1985).

will be penalized if the document purporting to be a tax return is blank[472] or contains frivolous constitutional objections to the tax law.[473]

¶ 7B.07 DELINQUENCY PENALTIES

Delinquency penalties are imposed by Section 6651 for a failure to (1) file a timely return; (2) pay tax; and (3) pay an assessed tax. The Code prescribes specific times for filing income tax and other returns.[474] Where a taxpayer fails to file a return on the due date, including extensions, Section 6651(a) imposes a penalty of 5 percent per month, up to a maximum of five months or 25 percent. The penalty is imposed on the net amount due—i.e., on the difference between (1) the amount required to be shown on the return and (2) the amount paid on or before the due date, plus the amount of any credit against the tax to which the taxpayer is entitled.[475] Section 6651(a)(1) affects any income, gift, or estate tax return, and certain excise tax returns.[476] The "return" referred to in the statute is one conforming to the requirements of the Code and the regulations and, thus, does not include an unsigned return[477] or a return disclosing no information relating to income and deductions.[478] If a taxpayer fails to file one

---

[472] See Fuller v. United States, 786 F2d 1437 (9th Cir. 1986) (taxpayer did not write in numbers, but instead left spaces blank or wrote in "object"; held, self-assessment was zero, and penalty upheld).

[473] Claims that assessment of a penalty for making constitutional objections is itself unconstitutional, have been rejected. Welch v. United States, 750 F2d 1101 (1st Cir. 1985) (First Amendment challenge rejected); Heitman v. United States, 753 F2d 33 (6th Cir. 1984).

[474] See, e.g., IRC §§ 6072 (income tax returns) 6075 (estate and gift tax returns). See also ¶ 4.03 (time for filing returns).

[475] IRC §§ 6651(a), 6651(b)(1). See also Reg. § 301.6651-1 et seq., TD 8703, 61 Fed. Reg. 69027–69031 (Dec. 31, 1996). Because one of the factors in the delinquent filing penalty is the amount required to be shown on the taxpayer's return, the same methods of proving unreported income for regular tax purposes are used in delinquent filing penalty cases. See, e.g., Madigan v. Comm'r, TC Memo. 1997-383 (1997) (bank deposits method used); Driggers v. Comm'r, TC Memo. 1997-354 (1997) (income taxpayer disclosed on two loan applications used to establish income); Frami v. Comm'r, TC Memo. 1997-509 (1997) (IRS used Bureau of Labor Statistics to reconstruct taxpayer's income; Tax Court reduced the IRS's estimates to reflect the taxpayer's particular circumstances).

[476] The penalty applies to alcohol, tobacco, and firearms taxes.

[477] Peter Vaira, 52 TC 986 (1969), aff'd, 444 F2d 770 (3d Cir. 1971). However, the Service's policy is not to assert the penalty if the unsigned return is accompanied by payment and the taxpayer signs the return on request. IRM, Policies of the IRS Handbook P-2-11 (approved Oct. 20, 1970).

[478] Comm'r v. Lane-Wells Co., 321 US 219 (1944); Durovic v. Comm'r, 54 TC 1364, 1387–1388 (1970), aff'd on this issue, 487 F2d 36 (7th Cir. 1973), cert. denied,

of the returns on the date prescribed, including extensions granted by the Service, or fails to file at all, the delinquency penalty must be assessed "unless it is shown that such failure is due to reasonable cause and not to willful neglect."[479]

A delinquency penalty is assessed, collected, and paid in the same manner as taxes; in fact, the reference to "tax" in the Code includes additions to tax such as delinquency penalties.[480] For example, if a taxpayer files a return reporting a tax due, but fails to make payment of the confessed tax, the delinquency penalty may be immediately assessed and collected because the portion of the unpaid principal amount of tax reported on the return may be immediately assessed under Section 6201(a)(1)).[481] Suppose, however, the Service determines that there is a tax deficiency. If the tax deficiency is subject to the deficiency procedures (which, among other things, prohibit immediate assessment of income, gift, estate, and certain excise taxes), the delinquency penalty is likewise subject to the deficiency procedures.[482] Consequently, assessment of the portion of a delinquency penalty attributable to a deficiency in tax may be delayed pending a final decision of the Tax Court. On the other hand, suppose a taxpayer does not contest the deficiency, but wishes to contest the delinquency penalty. If the taxpayer agrees to pay the deficiency in tax before any statutory notice of deficiency is issued, it would appear that any underlying deficiency in tax is eliminated, there is no deficiency to which the penalty is attributable, and, thus, the deficiency procedures (including prepayment Tax Court review) are unavailable.[483] However, in *Estate of DiRezza*, the Tax

---

417 US 919 (1974); Cupp v. Comm'r, 65 TC 68, 79 (1975); John H. Houston, 38 TC 486, 491–492 (1962). This authority raises the question whether a delinquency penalty may be imposed when a taxpayer files a return claiming the privilege. The indication is it may be imposed. United States v. Sullivan, 274 US 259 (1927); Kasey v. Comm'r, 457 F2d 369, 370 (9th Cir.), cert. denied, 409 US 869 (1972). For a discussion of the requirements of a sufficient return, see ¶ 4.02[1].

[479] IRC § 6651(a)(1).

[480] IRC § 6662(a).

[481] The restrictions on assessment do not apply to the collection of a delinquency attributable to the failure to pay the reported tax. Meyer v. Comm'r, 97 TC 555 (1991) (same result applied to failure to pay estimated tax penalty, because both delinquency penalties were based on assessments of taxes computed on basis of tax shown due on taxpayers' returns).

[482] IRC § 6662(b)(1). See Estate of DiRezza v. Comm'r, 78 TC 19 (1982) (discussing the legislative history of Section 6662, which was formerly Section 6659). Section 6662(b) provides first that deficiency procedures do not apply to additions to tax such as delinquency, failure to pay individual estimated tax, and failure to pay corporation estimated tax penalties. It then provides that deficiency procedures do not apply to a deficiency (Section 6662(b)(1)) and to estimated tax penalties for individuals and corporations if no return was filed at all (Section 6662(b)(2)).

[483] Section 6211, which defines the term, reduces a deficiency by the amount of previously assessed tax. The same result might follow from Section 6213(d), which permits

Court held that it had jurisdiction to hear a case where a deficiency in estate tax was agreed to before a statutory notice was issued, but the delinquency penalty attributable to that additional tax was contested.[484]

Beginning in 1987, the amount of the penalty was increased in certain cases from one half of one percent per month to one percent per month. The penalty rate is increased for the month after the month in which the taxpayer is served by the Service with a notice of levy (Section 6331(e)) or a notice of intention to levy on salary or wages (Section 6331(d)).[485] Where this increased failure-to-pay penalty applies, the integration of the failure-to-pay penalty and the failure-to-file penalty is also eliminated so that a taxpayer can pay more than 25 percent of the amount due if there is both a failure to timely file and a failure to pay.[486]

Before 1990, a taxpayer who failed to file a timely return was subject not only to the delinquency penalty, but also to a negligence penalty. The failure to file could also be punished by a fraud penalty (but not a delinquency penalty). For returns due after December 31, 1989, the delinquency penalty and the accuracy-related and fraud penalties are coordinated. Where no return is filed, no accuracy-related or fraud penalty may be imposed. Instead, where the failure to file is fraudulent the delinquency penalty is increased from 5 to 15 percent for each month of delinquency up to a maximum of 75 percent.[487]

Delinquency penalties are also imposed for failure to pay (1) the amount shown on a filed return (Section 6651(a)(2)) and (2) the amount shown on a notice and demand for payment of an assessed tax within ten days after the date of the notice (Section 6651(a)(3)). In both instances, the penalty is 0.5 percent for each month of the delinquency up to a maximum of 25 percent, or fifty months. In the case of failure to pay income tax when due, the penalty is

---

taxpayers to waive the restrictions on assessment of a deficiency. If the deficiency procedures are waived with respect to the deficiency in tax and the amount is assessed, there is no longer a deficiency in tax to which the penalty is attributable.

[484] Estate of DiRezza v. Comm'r, 78 TC 19 (1982) (the court divided on this issue with the majority relying on certain language in the legislative history and the dissenters focusing on the statutory language and operation of Section 6211).

[485] IRC § 6651(d) added by TRA 1986, Pub. L. No. 514, HR 3838, 99th Cong., 2d Sess. § 1502(a), and redesignating former IRC § 6651(d) as IRC § 6651(e). In advice to service centers, the Service's National Office has taken the position that the interest rate of the failure-to-pay penalty of Section 6651(a)(2) is increased under Section 6651(d) when the Service prepares a Section 6020(b) return for a delinquent taxpayer in accordance with its substitute for return procedures. SCA 200004033 (Dec. 1999). After the taxpayer files the delinquent return, the increased interest rate continues to apply where the increased interest rate is already in effect for the same year.

[486] IRC § 6651(e)(1), amended by TRA 1986, Pub. L. No. 514, HR 3838, 99th Cong., 2d Sess. § 1502(b).

[487] IRC § 6651(f), added by IMPACT, Pub. L. No. 239, HR 3299, 101st Cong., 1st Sess., Subtitle 6, § 7741(a).

imposed on the amount shown on the return as due, less amounts that have been withheld, estimated tax payments, partial payments, and other applicable credits. In the case of a notice and demand given after December 31, 1996, the penalty for failure to pay a tax demanded in a notice and demand will not be imposed if the taxpayer pays the tax within twenty-one calendar days from the date of the notice and demand, or within ten business days if the amount of the notice and demand is $100,000 or more.[488] Neither penalty is imposed if it is shown that the failure to pay the tax or the deficiency is due to reasonable cause and not to willful neglect.

These two penalties were enacted in 1969 to prevent taxpayers from delaying payment of taxes at a time when interest charged on delinquencies was less than the prevailing interest rate. Prior to 1969, in the case of a failure to pay an income tax when due, simple interest at an annual rate of 6 percent was required to be paid on the unpaid amount. Since the cost of borrowing money at the time was substantially in excess of the 6 percent interest provided by the Code, taxpayers, by filing a return on the due date and not paying the tax shown as owing on the return, could effectively borrow the amount of the tax at a favorable 6 percent rate for the period the tax remained unpaid. This borrowing could also result from failure to pay deficiencies or to make deposit of taxes. In 1969, to increase the cost of this "borrowing" of tax dollars, Congress added Sections 6651(a)(2) and 6651(a)(3) and amended Section 6656, which deals with deposits of taxes.[489] Congress also provided for a sliding interest rate on unpaid taxes tied to prevailing interest rates, which remains despite the elimination of the reason for its adoption.

A special rule of coordination applies when the Service prepares a substitute return for a taxpayer under Section 6020(b). The return is disregarded for purposes of determining the tax addition for the failure to file penalty, but is treated as the penalty "return" for failure to pay the reported Section 6651(a)(2) tax and failure to pay the tax in a notice and demand under Section 6651(a)(3).[490]

---

[488] IRC § 6651(a)(3), as amended by the Taxpayer Bill of Rights 2, § 303(b)(2).

[489] See S. Rep. No. 552, 91st Cong., 1st Sess. 297–298, reprinted in 1969-3 CB 563. The Tax Reform Act of 1969 amended Section 6656 by increasing a one percent per month penalty to a flat 5 percent penalty.

[490] IRC § 6651(g), added by the Taxpayer Bill of Rights 2, § 130(a), for returns the due date for which is after the date of enactment, July 30, 1996.

[1] Computation of the Penalty

[a] Net Amount Due

Delinquency penalties are imposed upon the "net amount due" as specially defined in Section 6651(b). If there is no net amount due, there can be no delinquency penalty.[491] Unlike a deficiency or underpayment in tax, the net amount due is reduced by payments the taxpayer has made against the tax required to be shown on his delinquent return before the return was due, or the amount shown on the return or notice and demand form.[492] For purposes of the delinquent filing penalty, the amounts of any withholding taxes or estimated taxes paid reduce the net amount due.

EXAMPLE: An individual taxpayer, without reasonable cause, files his 1989 tax return late, on July 15, 1990. The return shows a tax of $800 withheld and estimated tax credits of $300 and $500, respectively. If a deficiency of $200 is subsequently assessed, making the amount required to be shown on the return $1,000, the taxpayer is subject to a delinquency penalty on $200, the net amount due.[493]

The net amount due may also be reduced or eliminated by excess withholding tax,[494] a net operating loss carryover,[495] or offsetting unclaimed deductions,[496] but not by a net operating loss carryback, since a loss in a later year cannot excuse the delinquency.[497]

Similar rules apply to the delinquent payment penalties. The amount of tax shown on the return for failure to pay a reported tax is reduced not only be

---

[491] Since the delinquency penalty is an ad valorem penalty imposed on the net amount due, no penalty, including the $100 minimum penalty, can be imposed if withholding tax credits exceed the amount the taxpayer was required to show on the return. Patronik-Holder v. Comm'r, 100 TC 374 (1993).

[492] See IRC §§ 6211(b), 6653(c). Because there may be a dispute about the amount that should have been reported for delinquency penalty purposes, there are issues about the evidence of the amount, if any, of that unreported income. See, e.g., Osijo v. Comm'r, TC Memo. 1998-38 (1998) (the Service unsuccessfully attempted to use the taxpayer's answer to an interrogatory in his disability claim case as evidence that the taxpayer engaged in the activity he described); Frami v. Comm'r, TC Memo. 1997-509 (1997) (the Service used Bureau of Labor Statistics data to establish the income of a taxpayer who had failed to file a return, but the amounts were reduced after the taxpayer testified).

[493] See Reg. § 301.6651-1(f), Example (1).

[494] Cleveland J. Harris, 51 TC 980, 987 (1969).

[495] Goodwyn Crockery Co., 37 TC 355, 365 (1961), aff'd, 315 F2d 110 (6th Cir. 1963).

[496] Pehlke v. Comm'r, 37 TCM 1088 (1978).

[497] CVL Corp., 17 TC 812, 816 (1951). See Manning v. Seeley Tube & Box Co. of NJ, 338 US 561 (1950).

the amount of any credit claimed on the return but also be any partial payment made on or before the beginning of each month of the delinquency.[498] For example, if a return is filed on April 15 without payment, any payment made before the new month begins on May 16 reduces the net amount due at the beginning of the new month. Also, the amount of tax stated in a notice and demand for purposes of Section 6651(a)(3) is reduced by the amount of any part of the tax paid before the first of the new month.

[b] Month of Delinquency

The late filing penalty runs from the due date of the return to the date the return is actually received, not to the date it was mailed.[499] Consequently, where a late return is filed, the Service's position is that the timely mailed, timely filed rule of Section 7502(a) does not apply. If the date for filing or payment is the last day of a calendar month, the penalty is imposed for each succeeding calendar month or fraction of a month during which the delinquency continues.[500] If the date a return or payment is due is a date other than the last day of a calendar month, a "month" for purposes of delinquency penalties is the period ending on the numerically corresponding date in the following month.[501] Therefore, for a return filed on April 15, a month ends on May 15.[502] According to the regulations, the fact that the due date of filing or payment falls on a Saturday, Sunday, or legal holiday is immaterial for purposes of measuring the number of months of a delinquency.[503] Consequently, although a return would not be late if filed on the first working day after the due date falling on a Sunday,[504] the regulations provide that a month for purposes of the penalty begins on the Sunday due date. However, it has been held that when the last date for filing to avoid penalty for another month falls on a Saturday, Sunday, or legal holiday, the taxpayer can avoid the penalty for the next month if he files on the next working day.[505]

---

[498] IRC § 6651(b)(2).

[499] Rev. Rul. 73-133, 1973-1 CB 605; Sanderling, Inc., 67 TC 176 (1976), aff'd in part and rev'd in part on another issue, 571 F2d 174 (3d Cir. 1978).

[500] Reg. § 301.6651-1(b)(1).

[501] Reg. § 301.6651-1(b)(2).

[502] If there is no corresponding date in the month of February, the period from the corresponding date in January until the last day in February constitutes a "month." Reg. § 301.6651-1(b)(2). Thus, if a return is due on January 30, the first month ends on February 28 (or 29 in a leap year), and the succeeding months end on March 30, April 30, and so on.

[503] Reg. § 301.665-1(b)(3).

[504] IRC § 7503.

[505] Label-Matic, Inc., 74-1 USTC ¶ 9380 (ND Cal. 1974).

[c] Overlapping Penalties

A taxpayer may fail to both file and pay a tax and, thus, incur both delinquency penalties. If the penalties for delinquency in filing and delinquency in payment apply for any month, the delinquent-filing penalty is reduced by the amount of the delinquent payment penalty.

> **EXAMPLE:** An individual taxpayer files his 1988 tax return late and without reasonable cause on July 20, 1989, and the return shows a tax due of $800 and, after withholding credits, a balance due (which is not paid) of $100. A deficiency is later determined in the amount of $200, and the balance due on the return ($100) is paid on August 21, 1989. The failure-to-pay penalty is computed by determining the number of months the delinquency occurred (four full months from April 16 through August 15, plus fractional part of August after August 15, which counts as a whole month). The penalty percentage is 2.5 percent. Since the net amount due is the returned tax ($800) less the paid tax ($700), the penalty is $2.50 ($100 × 2.5 percent). The failure-to-file penalty is computed by multiplying the applicable percentage (20 percent—5 percent for each of the three full months of delinquency, plus the fractional month) by the net amount due ($1,000 − 700), for a penalty of $60. However, since the delinquency penalties overlap for four of the months of delinquency (April 16 through July 20), the delinquent filing penalty is reduced by $2 (0.5 percent × 4 × $100), so that the total penalty due from the taxpayer is $58 for delinquent filing ($60 − $2) and $2.50 for delinquent payment.[506]

The 25 percent ceiling, found in both the failure-to-file and failure-to-pay penalties, applies to each penalty separately, not to the combined penalties.[507] The only exception to this integration is that the failure-to pay and the failure-to-file penalties will not be integrated if the Service has served the taxpayer with a notice of levy or intention to levy on salary or wages.[508] A similar rule applies to overlapping penalties for failure to file and delinquent payment of assessed tax. The delinquent payment penalty is reduced by the failure-to-file penalty attributable to the tax for which assessment and notice and demand have been made.[509]

---

[506] Reg. § 301.6651-1(f), Example (1)(a). For a case following these regulations, see Estate of Rauhoff v. Comm'r, 44 TCM 968 (1982).

[507] Smith v. United States, 571 F. Supp. 664 (SDNY 1983), citing Gerdes v. United States, 498 F. Supp. 485 (ND Cal. 1980).

[508] IRC § 6651(e)(1), amended by TRA 1986, Pub. L. No. 514, HR 3838, 99th Cong., 2d Sess. § 1502(b).

[509] IRC § 6651(c); Reg. § 301.6651-1(f) Example (1)(b)

[d] Minimum Penalty for Failure to File

The nominal delinquency penalty of Section 6651 is imposed on the net amount due. If a taxpayer files a return late, but no amount of tax is due or the taxpayer is owed a refund, there is no net amount due. Thus, there is no amount against which the penalty can be imposed. However, Congress felt that some minimum penalty was appropriate where there was an extended failure to file a return. Accordingly, if an income tax return is not filed within sixty days after the date prescribed for filing the return (determined with regard to extensions of time for filing), the delinquency penalty "shall not be less than the lesser of $100 or 100 percent of the amount required to be shown as tax on such return."[510] The minimum penalty provisions apply where failure to file a required return exceeds sixty days, unless the taxpayer shows that the delinquent filing was due to reasonable cause. The minimum penalty is the lesser of $100 or 100 percent of the amount required to be shown as tax on the return. However, for penalty computation purposes, the amount of tax required to be shown on the return is reduced by the amount of any estimated tax or withholding tax credits or other payments made on or before the date prescribed for payment. The minimum penalty operates in the following manner:

1. If the return is filed within sixty days after the due date, the usual failure-to-file and failure-to-pay penalties apply, not the minimum penalty.
2. If the return is filed more than sixty days past the due date, the failure-to-file penalty, without adjustment for the failure-to-pay penalty, is computed to determine whether it equals or exceeds $100. If the result equals or exceeds $100, the minimum file penalty does not apply.[511]
3. If the failure-to-file penalty computed as described in item (2) is less than $100, the minimum failure-to-file penalty applies. The minimum penalty is based on the amount shown as tax due on the return. If the amount of tax due is less than $100, the applicable minimum penalty is the amount shown as tax due on the return. If the amount of tax due is in excess of $100, the minimum failure-to-file penalty is $100.
4. Where the minimum failure-to-file penalty applies, the Service takes the position that the amount of the failure-to-file penalty is not reduced by the amount of the failure-to-pay penalty, where it is applica-

---

[510] IRC § 6651(a)(1), amended by TEFRA, Pub. L. No. 248, HR 4961, 97th Cong., 2d Sess. § 318(a), for periods after December 31, 1982.

[511] See IRM 5172.212, MT 5100-43 (Nov. 15, 1985) (Minimum Failure to File Penalty).

ble. Instead, both penalties apply concurrently, and the combined total of the penalties is assessed as due.[512]

[2] Fraudulent Failure to File

A failure to file a tax return may be due to fraud—i.e., with the intent to evade tax. In this situation, a penalty for the fraudulent failure to file is imposed. Section 6651(f) increases the monthly penalty rate from 5 to 15 percent for each month of delinquency, up to a maximum penalty of 75 percent of the net amount due.[513] The following procedures apply:

1. *Burden of proof.* In the case of a delinquency penalty, the taxpayer has the burden of proving that the delinquency was due to reasonable cause and that there was an absence of willful neglect. In the case of a fraudulent failure to file, the Service has the burden of proving the fraud element on the increased portion of the penalty by clear and convincing evidence as is provided by Section 7454(a).[514] If the Service fails to sustain its burden of proof, but has alleged, in the alternative, that the taxpayer is liable for the basic delinquency penalty, the court can consider the basic penalty where the burden of proof would be on the taxpayer. If the Service failed to make an alternative determination in the notice of deficiency, but raised the basic delinquency penalty in its answer, the Tax Court can consider the delinquency penalty, but the burden of proof would be on the Service. If the basic penalty is not raised in either the notice of deficiency or in the answer, the Tax Court cannot consider the basic delinquency penalty at all.

2. *Conduct considered.* Under prior law, fraudulent failure to file was punished under the fraud penalty, not the delinquency penalty.[515] Although the fraudulent failure to file is now punished by the increased delinquency penalty, the same evidence of fraudulent conduct considered by courts under the fraud penalty is to be considered under the fraudulent delinquency penalty.[516]

---

[512] See IRM 5172.212, MT 5100-43 (Nov. 15, 1985) (Minimum Failure to File Penalty).

[513] IRC § 6651(f) was added by IMPACT, Pub. L. No. 239, HR 3299, 101st Cong., 1st Sess., Subtitle 6, § 7741(a), for returns due after December 31, 1989.

[514] HR Rep. No. 247, 101st Cong. 1st Sess. 296, reprinted in 1989-3 CB 1402–1403 (vol. 3). See Clayton v. Comm'r, 102 TC 632, 646, 651–653 (1994).

[515] See the discussion supra ¶ 7B.02[3].

[516] HR Rep. No. 247, 101st Cong., 1st Sess. 296–297. Accordingly, a taxpayer's attempts to mislead or conceal, or to prevent or hinder collection of tax may prove a tax-

[3] Defenses

[a] Reasonable Cause

The only statutory basis for escaping a delinquency penalty is if the delinquency is "due to reasonable cause and not to willful neglect."[517] Whether both "reasonable cause" and lack of "willful neglect" exists is a question of fact, and the burden of establishing these facts is on the taxpayer because the penalty is collected as an addition to the tax set forth in the Commissioner's notice of deficiency, which is presumptively correct.[518] Thus, to escape the penalty, a taxpayer must prove both that the failure did not result from "willful neglect" and that it was "due to reasonable cause."

The seemingly self-contradictory "willful neglect" was described by the Supreme Court in *United States v. Boyle* "as meaning a conscious, intentional failure or reckless indifference."[519] Historically, according to the Court, "Congress intended 'willful neglect' to replace 'refusal'—both expressions implying intentional failure—and '(absence of) reasonable cause' to replace 'neglect' to both expressions implying carelessness."[520] Administratively, the regulations state that with certain exceptions, the taxpayer who wishes to avoid the delinquency penalty "must make an affirmative showing of all facts alleged as a reasonable cause" for the delinquency.[521] This requirement clearly places the burden of proof on the taxpayer. The regulations do not explain what a taxpayer must show to carry this burden because they attempt to explain the taxpayer's obligation by substituting another term that itself requires definition.

---

payer's fraudulent intent. See Allen v. Comm'r, TC Memo. 1998-350 (1998) (taxpayer found to have not only failed to file returns for three consecutive years, but to have attempted to conceal his income-producing activities "by encouraging his bank not to comply with respondent's summons, sending respondent a false affidavit, and refusing to provide respondent with relevant information.")

[517] IRC §§ 6651(a)(1), 6651(a)(2). A court lacks jurisdiction to forgive interest and a late payment penalty. Comm'r v. McCoy, 484 US 3 (1987) (after an adverse Tax Court decision, estate failed to post bond, and assessed deficiency was not paid after notice and demand). It has been held that reasonable cause must exist on the date prescribed for payment, regardless of any subsequent changes in a taxpayer's circumstances. Industrial Indem. v. Snyder, 41 BR 882, 84-1 USTC ¶ 9507 (ED Wash 1984).

[518] Lee v. Comm'r, 227 F2d 181, 184 (5th Cir.), cert. denied, 351 US 982 (1956); Sanderling, Inc. v. Comm'r, 66 TC 743, 757 (1976); Tax Court Rule 142(a). However, if the Commissioner raises the issue for the first time in his answer, the burden falls on him. Tax Court Rule 142(a).

[519] See United States v. Boyle, 469 US 241, n.3 (1985).

[520] See United States v. Boyle, 469 US 241 (1985); Southwestern Fin. Co. v. Comm'r, 153 F2d 205 (5th Cir. 1946) ("[r]easonable cause means nothing more than the exercise of ordinary business care and prudence").

[521] Reg. § 301.6651-1(c)(1).

Thus, the regulations state, "[i]f the taxpayer exercised ordinary business care and prudence and was nevertheless unable to file the return within the prescribed time, then the delay is due to reasonable cause."[522]

Of course, the question then becomes, what constitutes "ordinary business care and prudence?" The Service considers the following examples to constitute reasonable cause for the purpose of the delinquent-filing penalty:[523]

---

[522] Reg. § 301.6651-1(c)(1). However, the Supreme Court also said that "disability alone could well be an acceptable excuse for a late filing." United States v. Boyle, 469 US 241, 248, n.6 (1985); see United States v. Isaac, 91-2 USTC ¶ 50,314 (ED Ky. 1991) (taxpayer with paralyzed arms and legs was held unable to prepare 1979 return from 1980 until February 1983 because of illness). The *Boyle* case does not eliminate a shift of responsibility defense altogether. For example, it has been accepted that "systematic deception" by a controller would constitute reasonable cause. Universal Concrete Prods. Corp. v. United States, 90-2 USTC ¶ 50,440 (ED Pa. 1990), aff'd without pub. op., 941 F2d 1204 (3d Cir. 1991). As the lower court noted, the Supreme Court distinguished between reliance on an agent and the effect of a taxpayer's disability and "the essence of the distinction is that a taxpayer should not be penalized for circumstances beyond his or her control." Finding reasonable cause where the delinquency is caused by circumstances beyond the taxpayer's control was said to be supported by Reg. § 301.6651-1(c)(1). The *Manual* provisions (IRM 4562.2, MT 4500-448 (Feb. 25, 1987) (Reasonable Cause and Penalty Consideration)) also support this view. However, in the case, it was found that the corporation did not exercise ordinary business care, because it did not implement an internal system to monitor and control the employee responsible for tax obligations.

[523] IRM 4562.2, MT 4500-448 (Feb. 25, 1987) (Reasonable Cause and Penalty Consideration). The Manual requires answers to the following questions in making a reasonable cause determination:

(a) Do the taxpayer's reasons address the penalty that was assessed?
(b) Does the length of time between the event cited as a reason and the filing or payment date negate the event's effect?
(c) Does the continued operation of a business after the event that caused the taxpayer's noncompliance negate the event's effect?
(d) Should the event that caused the taxpayer's noncompliance or increased liability have reasonably been anticipated?
(e) Was the penalty the result of carelessness or did the taxpayer appear to have made an honest mistake? (Carelessness and forgetfulness are the same as civil willful neglect and are not examples of ordinary business care and prudence.)
(f) Has the taxpayer provided sufficient detail (dates, relationships) to determine whether they exercised ordinary business care and prudence?
(g) Is a nonliable individual being blamed for the taxpayer's noncompliance? What is the nature of the relationship between the taxpayer and this individual? Is the individual an employee of the taxpayer or an independent third party, such as an accountant or lawyer?
(h) Has the taxpayer documented all pertinent facts, i.e., death certificate, doctor's statement, insurance statement for proof of fire, etc?
(i) Does the taxpayer have a history of being assessed the same penalty?
(j) Could the taxpayer have requested an extension or filed an amended return?

Id.

- A return mailed in time but returned for insufficient postage
- A return filed timely but in the wrong district, or directly with the Regional Commissioner or Commissioner of Internal Revenue
- Erroneous information from a Service official
- Death or serious illness of the taxpayer or someone in his immediate family
- Unavoidable absence of the taxpayer
- Destruction of business or business records by fire or other casualty
- A request for proper blanks or returns not timely furnished by the Service
- An effort to obtain assistance or information necessary to complete the return by a personal appearance at an IRS office that was unsuccessful because the taxpayer, through no fault of his own, was unable to see a Service representative

Ignorance of the law is also considered reasonable cause by the Service if other factors support this contention, such as the taxpayer being a first-time filer.[524]

The untimely filing of a return will not be excused under the reasonable cause standard because the taxpayer

- Lacked funds[525];
- Was overworked[526];

---

[524] IRM 4562.2, MT 4500-448 (Feb. 25, 1987) (Reasonable Cause and Penalty Consideration) ("For ignorance of the law to be considered other facts must support the taxpayer's contention, such as first-time filers, or sudden, first-time FTD depository requirements.")

[525] A. Raymond Jones, 25 TC 1100, 1105–1106 (1956), rev'd on other grounds, 259 F2d 300 (5th Cir. 1958); Leo Sanders, 21 TC 1012, aff'd, 225 F2d 629 (10th Cir.), cert. denied, 350 US 967 (1956); Langston v. Comm'r, 36 TCM 1703 (1977).

[526] Crocker v. Comm'r, 92 TC 899, 913 (1989); Odend'hal v. Comm'r, 80 TC 588, 618 (1983), aff'd on this issue and remanded on other grounds, 748 F2d 908 (4th Cir. 1984); Dustin v. Comm'r, 53 TC 491, 507 (1969), aff'd, 467 F2d 47 (9th Cir. 1972); United States v. Craddock, 143 F2d 595 (10th Cir. 1998) ("We recognize Mr. Craddock exercised some care in attempting to keep up with his accounting and tax functions by selectively increasing his accounting staff, having outside accounting firms review tax returns, and replacing his antiquated computer system with one recommended by experts[, but a]lthough the Boyle bright-line test does not apply, since Mr. Craddock did more than just rely on his employees to timely file his tax returns, Mr. Craddock failed to exercise 'ordinary business care and prudence' in ensuring his returns were timely filed and failed to show that he was 'unable' to file his returns on time."). A delinquency penalty has been upheld when the taxpayer filed a return on October 19, 1995, four days late, and attached an extension request, Form 2688, with the return, stating the reason for the request was "tax practitioner's workload." Torres v. Comm'r, TC Memo. 1998-230 (1998) (the phrase "tax practitioner's workload" standing alone on the application does not show reasonable cause for the delay in failing to file the return for the allowed extension to August 15, 1995).

- Allegedly was ignorant of the obligation to file[527];
- Was ill but not incapacitated[528]; or
- Failed to estimate tax properly and so had an automatic extension of time to file voided.[529]

The fact that records are lost, destroyed, or unavailable will not provide reasonable cause for untimely filing if the records did not directly relate to and prevent the filing of the return.[530]

---

[527] See, e.g., Lammerts Estate v. Comm'r, 456 F2d 681 (2d Cir. 1972) (failure to file fiduciary return); Barnes v. Comm'r, 496 F2d 1197 (6th Cir. 1974) (income tax return reporting alimony); I.M. Crawford, 20 TCM 1113 (1961) (employment tax return). But see IRM 4562.2, MT 4500-448 (Feb. 25, 1987) (Reasonable Cause and Penalty Consideration) ("where ignorance of the law is claimed, reasonable cause should not be presumed. Ignorance of the law can be considered for reasonable cause if other facts support this contention, such as first-time filers, sudden first-time FTD depository requirements, etc.").

[528] Hernandez v. Comm'r, 72 TC 1234 (1979) (although hospitalized, accountant could have instructed wife-bookkeeper to prepare return); Alma Williams, 16 TC 893, 906 (1951) (husband allegedly incapacitated, but his wife, in community property state, was familiar with his business affairs). While incapacity on the part of the taxpayer due to mental or physical illness is reasonable cause, see supra note 523, a mental or emotional disorder does not excuse the failure to file a timely return unless it is shown that the disorder rendered the taxpayer incapable of exercising ordinary care and prudence during the period the failure to file continued. See Barber v. Comm'r, TCM 1997-206 (1997) (gathering cases, and finding that although a wife suffered emotional trauma as a result of the arrests of her husband, his criminal trials, and the resulting publicity, she continued to carry on normal activities in her home, failed to present any medical testimony in support of her case, and failed to file a return for 1992 until about nineteen months after her husband's final trial).

[529] Crocker v. Comm'r, 92 TC 899, 913 (1989).

[530] Electric & Neon, Inc. v. Comm'r, 56 TC 1324, 1342–1343 (1971), aff'd without published opinion, 496 F2d 876 (5th Cir. 1974) (net income from rental property was small in relation to total income and could have been estimated with some reasonable accuracy); Crocker v. Comm'r, 92 TC 899 (1989) (failure to replace lost information); Long v. Comm'r, 37 TCM 733 (1978) (deceased mother's records not related to son's return); Estate of Vriniotis v. Comm'r, 79 TC 298, 311 (1982); compare In re Sims, 92-1 USTC ¶ 50,034 (Bankr. ED La. 1991) ("In the present case, the Debtor failed to file his tax returns in timely fashion because the information required to produce and file his return was unavailable.").
Even if the information available is not sufficient to permit preparation of a complete estate tax return by the end of the filing extension period, a return that is as complete as possible must be filed, for example, according to the estate tax. Reg. § 20.6081-1(c). The Reg. § 20.6081-1(c), also permit the filing of supplemental information. Tax Court cases reach the same result. See, e.g., Estate of Vriniotis, supra, at 311; Estate of Maltaman, TC Memo. 1997-110 (1997) (at end of extended filing period of estate tax return, preparer had sufficient information concerning assets included in decedent's estate to file a return, and then could have filed supplemental information; other cases cited). Presumably, the same rationale would apply to the filing of returns for other types of taxes where information necessary to file a complete return was unavailable through no fault of the taxpayer.

IRS Penalty Handbook. The IRS Penalty Handbook provides, in addition to the more common reasons given for reasonable cause determinations, such as those discussed later in this chapter, examples of what the Service considers "sound causes" for delay in paying tax, which, if established, will constitute "other" reasonable cause.[531] These reasons include:

1. When the taxpayer was unable to determine the amount of tax due to reasons beyond the taxpayer's control;
2. When the taxpayer's ability to make payments was materially impaired by civil disturbances (only if the taxpayer's geographic area was declared a disaster area); or
3. The taxpayer's lack of funds, when the taxpayer can demonstrate that the lack of funds occurred despite the exercise of ordinary business care and prudence.[532]

[b] Shift of Responsibility

An attempt is frequently made in delinquency cases to shift responsibility to an employee or return preparer. However, as the Supreme Court held in *Boyle*, "the failure to make a timely filing of a tax return is not excused by the taxpayer's reliance on an agent, and such reliance is not 'reasonable cause' for a late filing under section 6651(a)(1)."[533] *Boyle* involved an executor's reliance on an attorney to prepare and file an estate tax return, but the Supreme Court adopted a "bright-line" rule that is applicable to all returns. Simply put, a taxpayer must determine the deadline for filing a return and file it by the due date, or obtain an extension of time for filing the return. Reliance on an agent who is expected to attend to the matter, even reasonably so, does not relieve the principal of his return filing obligation and is not a defense to a delin-

---

[531] Penalties Handbook 120.1.2.1.3, Penalty Relief (Apr. 27, 2000).

[532] Penalties Handbook 120.1.2.1.3, Penalty Relief (Apr. 27, 2000).

[533] United States v. Boyle, 469 US 241 (1985). *Boyle* resolved a conflict in the circuit courts as to whether reliance on an attorney to file an estate tax return constituted reasonable cause under Section 6651(a)(1). Similarly, a child's nonfiling is not excused by incapacity because of the unique relationship of parent and child. Bassett v. Comm'r, 67 F3d 29 (1993). On appeal, the Second Circuit said, "[W]here the duty to file the return is imposed on the guardian charged with the care of the taxpayer's property, and not in the taxpayer, the inability of the taxpayer is not controlling, and the applicability of additions to tax depends on whether or not there was a lack of good cause and due care on the part of the guardian." Bassett v. Comm'r, 76 AFTR2d ¶ 95-5451 (2d Cir. 1995) (a divided court; the majority said the focus should be on the person with the responsibility to file, i.e., the parents, while the dissent said that "construing an ambiguous tax penalty provision against the interests of an incompetent infant responsible for errors she did not commit . . . [was] so illogical and potentially unfair a result" that it would need to be clearly required by Congress).

quency penalty.[534] When the conduct of corporate officers is the cause of the corporation's delinquency, *Boyle*'s bright-line rule does not always mean the corporation will be liable. There is a distinction between a corporation's unexcused failure to comply with the tax laws as a result of its agents' improper actions and a corporation's excused inability to comply with the tax laws because of those agents' misfeasance or nonfeasance.[535]

When the embezzlement by corporate officers led to the delinquency in filing employment taxes, the Third Circuit held that

> when the officers of a corporation commit criminal acts against the corporation, they do so in the absence of apparent authority. Where their crimes are proved to be the cause of the corporation's failures to fulfill its duties under the tax code, as the district court found, the corporation is not auto-

---

[534] The Supreme Court did not rule on delinquencies due to such circumstances beyond the control of the taxpayer as those set forth in the Manual. See supra note 506. United States v. Boyle, 469 US 241, 242 n.6 (1985). Disability also might be an acceptable excuse. But the illness of the taxpayer's accountant does not establish reasonable cause. Lattman v. United States, 92-2 USTC ¶ 50,423 (NDNY 1992); In re Craddock, 93-1 USTC ¶ 50,084, 149 BR 963 (Bankr. D. Colo. 1993) (delinquency penalty was imposed, despite debtor's reliance on inside and outside accountants, because "circumstances were clearly within Mr. Craddock's ability to control"), aff'd on other grounds sub nom. United States v. Craddock, 143 F2d 595 (10th Cir. 1998). Moreover, delegation to an employee of the duty to pay does not constitute a defense unless the taxpayer has some internal control to review the employee's compliance. See Obstetrical & Gynecological Group, P.A. v. United States, 79-2 USTC ¶ 9511 (DDC 1979); see also Universal Concrete Prods. Corp. v. United States, 90-2 USTC ¶ 50,440 (ED Pa. 1990), aff'd without pub. op., 941 F2d 1204 (3d Cir. 1991); In re American Biomaterials Corp., 954 F2d 919 (3d Cir. 1992) (taxpayer must show evidence of adequate internal corporate controls to establish ordinary business care); Roberts Metal Fabrication, Inc. v. United States, 93-1 USTC ¶ 50,013, 147 BR 965 (Bankr. D. Kan. 1992) (poor health of president and sole shareholder did not constitute reasonable cause, because there were no internal controls); Conklin Bros. of Santa Rosa, Inc. v. United States, 986 F2d 315 (9th Cir. 1993) (reliance on employee not reasonable cause where corporate taxpayer chose to promote controller and withdraw close supervision). Compare McMahon v. Comm'r, 79 AFTR2d ¶ 97-962 (2d Cir. 1997) (taxpayer claimed he relied on his attorney to complete and file a second request for an extension to file his return; held, the nondelegable duty to file a timely return includes the nondelegable duty of filing the return by August 15 unless a second extension is received, and the alleged misrepresentation of his attorney that the extension request had been filed did not relieve the taxpayer of that duty).

Even if a corporate employee's failure to file returns and deposit taxes is assumed to constitute reasonable cause, the employee's misfeasance has been held not to disable the corporation (the equivalent of an individual taxpayer's disability that prevents the individual from filing) because the corporation's president and accountants are to have retained sufficient control to discover the misfeasance. See *Conklin Bros.*, supra; see also Valen Mfg. Co. v. United States, 90 F3d 1190 (6th Cir. 1996) (same); Mason Motors Co. v. United States, 82 AFTR2d 98-6372 (D. Minn. 1998) (following *Conklin Bros.* and *Valen*, and finding no reasonable cause despite corporate employer's failure to file and deposit).

[535] In re American Biomaterials Corp., 954 F2d 919 (3d Cir. 1992).

matically vicariously responsible for the penalties resulting from those failures.[536]

However, even if the corporation as principal is not vicariously liable for the acts of its officers, the corporation still must show reasonable cause and an absence of willful neglect in failing to file timely returns. The corporation can make this showing by evidence that it had "adequate internal corporate controls to establish ordinary business care and reasonable cause" for its failure to ensure the filing of returns.[537]

[c] Advice of Counsel

A distinction is drawn between reliance on the act of an agent and reliance on the advice of a tax adviser. In *Haywood Lumber & Mining Co. v. Comm'r*, the court said: "When a corporate taxpayer selects a competent tax expert, supplies him with all necessary information, and requests him to prepare proper tax returns, we think the taxpayer has done all that ordinary business care and prudence can reasonably demand."[538] This case involved more than mere return preparation. The taxpayer in *Haywood Lumber* had failed to file personal holding company returns, and the expert knew the taxpayer was a personal holding company but failed to advise the client. In this context, erroneous advice or negligence of the adviser is not chargeable to the taxpayer. Consequently, advice sought and received in good faith from a competent adviser constitutes reasonable cause for failure to file a return, at least where the matter is one about which a taxpayer would not normally be aware.[539] Gener-

---

[536] In re American Biomaterials Corp., 954 F2d 919, 927 (3d Cir. 1992).

[537] In re American Biomaterials Corp., 954 F2d 919, 927 (3d Cir. 1992).

[538] Haywood Lumber & Mining Co. v. Comm'r, 178 F2d 769, 771 (2d Cir. 1950). Nevertheless, the *Boyle* rationale has been applied to the delinquent filing of Form 5500-C (Annual Return). Alton OB-Gyn, Ltd. v. United States, 789 F2d 515 (7th Cir. 1986) (in a questionable application of *Boyle*, duty to file information return was held nondelegable, and taxpayer was not entitled to rely on bank).

[539] Haywood Lumber & Mining Co. v. Comm'r, 178 F2d 769 (2d Cir. 1950); Hatfried, Inc. v. Comm'r, 162 F2d 628 (3d Cir. 1947); Orient Inv. & Fin. Co. v. Comm'r, 166 F2d 601 (DC Cir. 1948); Coldwater Seafood Corp., 69 TC 966 (1978); West Coast Ice Co., 49 TC 345 (1968); Reliance Factoring Corp., 15 TC 604 (1950). See Boeving v. United States, 650 F2d 493 (8th Cir. 1981) (penalty imposed even where executor relied on an attorney who was honestly mistaken about the return due date, because the filing date is a matter on which the executor may not rely on others for advice). But see Ballard v. Comm'r, 854 F2d 185, 187 (7th Cir. 1988). ("A taxpayer who does not file any return on the advice of his attorney has shown 'reasonable cause.'") In Dennenburg v. United States, 920 F2d 301 (5th Cir. 1991), the taxpayers claimed that they relied on their accountant's advice that an incorrect return should not be filed, and so the taxpayers did not file their return until a contract had been renegotiated. The Fifth Circuit carefully reviewed advice of counsel cases, but declined to accept advice of counsel as "reasonable

ally, the failure to disclose information or the common knowledge of the matter on which the taxpayer allegedly relies[540] will prevent reliance on an adviser from being a valid defense.[541] This distinction is recognized after *Boyle*. In *Estate of LaMeres*,[542] the executrix of an estate relied on the erroneous advice of an attorney that the estate could obtain a second extension for filing its return.

---

cause." Instead, it found that the adviser had not advised that, as a matter of tax law, the taxpayer's return need not be filed by the due date known to the taxpayer. See also Zabolotny v. Comm'r, 97 TC 385 (1991) ("In this case, petitioners relied on the advice of their tax adviser that no taxable transaction had occurred which would require that [an excise] return be filed."); Condor Int'l, Inc. v. Comm'r, 98 TC 203 (1992) (defense rejected when corporation received conflicting advice about the obligation to file a return, and failed to explain why they proceeded contrary to the correct advice); Inverworld, Inc. v. Comm'r, TC Memo. 1996-301, 71 TCM 3231 (1996) (taxpayer received advice that corporation was not subject to U.S. tax, but advice of counsel defense rejected because the advice did not say that "filing a return was unnecessary"; delinquency and other penalties imposed).

In a case in which a taxpayer who was under criminal investigation relied on an attorney's advice not to file that current year's return, the taxpayer was held subject to a delinquency penalty because the taxpayer did not demonstrate that "erroneous" advice was reasonable. Cooper v. United States, 834 F. Supp. 669 (D. NJ 1993). ("The record indicates that plaintiffs made no efforts to secure an extension from the IRS, but merely accepted unquestioningly the facially extraordinary advice that they need not file any tax documents whatsoever for an indefinite period of time.") Cf. Lilley v. Comm'r, 58 TCM 1517 (1990) ("if a taxpayer reasonably relies upon an attorney's substantive legal advice that he is not required to file a tax return, that reliance constitutes reasonable cause . . . even if that advice is incorrect.") While saying the advice may have been "prudent" considering the taxpayer's potential criminal liability, in *Cooper*, the attorney apparently had not advised the taxpayer to notify the IRS of the reason why a return could not be filed (i.e., the pending investigation and the privilege claim which would have made the return form insufficient to constitute a return), nor to pay the estimated tax due. If both notice and payment had been present, the advice seems to be a reasonable balancing of the taxpayer's return filing and tax payment obligations and the taxpayer's self-incrimination privilege. No court has dealt with a case where the advice of nonfiling has been coupled with notice and payment, nor, in the context of a delinquency penalty, has any court analyzed whether a so-called Fifth Amendment return is a "return."

[540] Estate of Paxton v. Comm'r, 86 TC 785 (1986) (a post-*Boyle* case involving the failure to file an estate tax return on the advice that it was not required); Paula Constr. Co., 58 TC 1055, aff'd, 474 F2d 1345 (5th Cir. 1973) (failure to file corporate returns by Subchapter S corporation); Inter-Am. Life Ins. Co., 469 F2d 697 (9th Cir. 1972); Estate of Rapelje v. Comm'r, 73 TC 82 (1979) (failure to file estate tax return). See also Sanderling, Inc. v. Comm'r, 66 TC 743 (1976) (correct due date of return was uncertain).

[541] See, e.g., Yale Ave. Corp., v. Comm'r, 58 TC 1062 (1972). However, an accountant's advice that no tax is owed does not excuse the nonfiling of the return. Jackson v. Comm'r, 864 F2d 1521 (10th Cir. 1989). See Reed-Merrill, Inc. v. Comm'r, TC Memo. 2000-25 (2000) ("Petitioner, however, did not provide its accountant with sufficient information from which an accurate return could be prepared. Under such circumstances, reliance on accountant's advice is not in good faith and does not establish that the taxpayer acted with reasonable cause."). See Estate of Monroe, 104 TC 352, 366–367 (1995).

[542] Estate of LaMeres, 98 TC 294 (1992).

However, the executrix did not rely on the attorney to file the estate tax return or the extensions. In the Tax Court's view, in seeking the advice of the attorney, the executrix did not rely on the attorney to perform the nondelegable duty of filing a return, as had occurred in *Boyle*. Rather, the executrix had relied on erroneous advice about the due date of the return. The Tax Court concluded, "We hold that reasonable reliance on the erroneous advice of an attorney with respect to the due date of a return can constitute 'reasonable cause' within the meaning of section 6651(a)(1)." The court then went on to determine whether the executrix had acted in good faith. Since the executrix followed the attorney's erroneous advice, the law governing the number of extensions was not entirely clear, and the actions of IRS personnel on the invalid second extension request were initially consistent with accepting the request, the court found that the executrix had acted in good faith.

[d] The Failure-to-Pay Penalty—Ordinary Business Care

The regulations are of some help in determining what is and is not the exercise of ordinary business care and prudence for failure to pay purposes.[543] In

---

[543] Reg. § 301.6651-1(c)(1). Consideration is given to the taxpayer's financial situation and to the nature of the tax the taxpayer failed to pay. Where withholding taxes are not paid over, some courts have said that financial difficulties can never constitute reasonable cause. Brewery, Inc. v. United States, 33 F3d 589 (6th Cir. 1994) (the "circumstances in which a taxpayer could establish reasonable cause for failure to pay withholding taxes are limited to situations in which the taxpayer has made reasonable efforts to protect the trust funds but those efforts have been frustrated by circumstances beyond the taxpayer's control, such as the failure of a financial institution."); see Wolfe v. United States, 612 F. Supp. 605 (D. Mont. 1985), aff'd, 798 F2d 1241 (10th Cir. 1986) ("Almost every non-willful failure to pay taxes is the result of financial difficulties."); see also In the Matter of Upton Printing Co., Debtor, 76 AFTR2d ¶ 95-5072 (Bankr. ED La. 1995) (showing of financial difficulty rejected as reasonable cause); Bostar Foods, Inc. v. United States, 1997 US Dist. LEXIS 1682 (WD Ky. 1997) (failure to pay taxes not excused by company's financial difficulties, nor by the emotional and personal stress experienced by its only active shareholder); East Wind Indus., Inc. v. United States, 83 AFTR2d ¶ 99-707 (DNJ 1999) (as a matter of law, financial difficulties cannot constitute reasonable cause). The Third Circuit reversed the district court in *East Wind Industries, Inc.*, rejecting the bright-line test of *Brewery, Inc.* and adopting the *Fran* approach of the Second Circuit, discussed later in this section. East Wind Indus., Inc. v. United States, 84 AFTR2d 99-6949 (3d Cir. 1999) (the issue is whether under the facts and circumstances, the taxpayers' failure to pay and deposit their employment taxes timely was due to reasonable cause and not willful neglect). Recognizing that operating a business at a minimal level to collect monies owed to the business to pay the taxes and other debts benefits the economy and the Service, the court said that it could not conclude that "choosing to pay those creditors, whose services were essential to maintaining and reworking the inventory, over the trust fund taxes constituted a conscious, intentional failure or reckless indifference," and therefore did not amount to willful neglect. The circuit court said that reasonable cause exists in this case because (1) the taxpayers exercised ordinary business care and prudence and (2) the taxpayers would have suffered undue hardship if they would have paid the trust fund

this context, consideration will be given to all the facts and circumstances of the taxpayer's financial situation, including the amount and nature of the taxpayer's expenditures in light of the income (or other amounts) he could, at the time of the expenditures, reasonably expect to receive prior to the date prescribed for payment of the tax. If a taxpayer incurs lavish or extravagant living expenses in such amounts that the remainder of his assets and anticipated income are insufficient to pay his tax, he has not exercised ordinary business

---

taxes when due because to pay those taxes "no matter what" would have meant closing down the business.

Other courts have taken a more flexible view of the failure to pay. The Second Circuit rejected *Brewery Inc.*'s bright-line rule as "find[ing] no support in either the penalty provisions of the statute or in the longstanding treasury regulations drafted to implement those provisions" and adopted the "facts and circumstances" standard, which permits "consideration of financial difficulties in determining whether reasonable cause has been proven, [and does not] differentiate between trust fund taxes and other taxes which are not kept in trust for the benefit of the IRS." Fran Corp. v. United States, 164 F3d 814 (2d Cir. 1999) (the circuit court found, however, that the substantial loan the taxpayer's shareholder owed the business coupled with the personal expenses the business paid for him was evidence that the taxpayer's financial difficulties did not prevent the payment of taxes). See also Glenwal-Schmidt v. United States, 78-2 USTC ¶ 9610 (DDC 1978) (taxpayer had contract with the Navy Department, but after a dispute the Department began to withhold contract payments, and the taxpayer paid only necessary operating expenses, not withholding taxes; held, since the taxpayer had a right to rely on the Navy and could not foresee the noncompliance by the Navy, its failure to pay its tax liability was with reasonable cause); In re Pool & Varga, Inc., 60 BR 722 (Bankr. ED Mich. 1986) (due to economic recession in the geographic area, the taxpayer decided to pay those expenses necessary to keep the business operating rather than to make timely tax payments; held, the taxpayer "made a sufficient showing that its financial situation was such that its business would have been irreparably injured or terminated had it paid or deposited the taxes in full on the due date; in other words, that it would have imposed an undue hardship").

The Seventh Circuit has said, "In considering whether a taxpayer exercised ordinary business care and prudence, a court should consider all facts and circumstances of the taxpayer's situation, including the amount and nature of expenditures in light of income received prior to the date payment was due." Carlson v. United States, 126 F3d 915 (7th Cir. 1997) ("the Carlsons allowed their tax liabilities to build over 3 years without taking significant steps to reduce or meet those liabilities . . . the Carlsons did not set aside funds out of Mr. Carlson's draw from his firm, make periodic payments when they could, seek financing during those years, or sell their Indiana property, which would have satisfied a large chunk of the IRS' bill [, and while his] son's medical bills totalled $170,000 over the 3 years in question. . . . Mr. Carlson's income as an attorney was just shy of a half a million dollars.") Significantly, the circuit court also said that it believed that "the type of illness or debilitation that might create reasonable cause is one that because of severity or timing makes it virtually impossible for the taxpayer to comply—things like emergency hospitalization or other incapacity occurring around tax time." Although it recognized that the reasonable cause exception could exist in this situation, the court pointed out that the Carlsons had not presented sufficient evidence to establish undue mental and emotional hardship, especially in light of Mr. Carlson's running of his profitable law firm and attending to other business and tax matters.

care and prudence in providing for payment of his tax liability.[544] Similarly, investment in speculative or illiquid investments that may not be sold or pledged as security for a loan also indicate the absence of reasonable business care and prudence. If the taxpayer makes reasonable efforts to conserve sufficient assets in marketable form to satisfy his tax liability and nevertheless is unable to pay all or a portion of the tax when due, the penalty will not be imposed.[545] The nature of the tax involved is also a factor to be considered in determining the imposition of the penalty. Facts and circumstances constituting reasonable cause for nonpayment of an income tax may not be sufficient for nonpayment of withholding taxes.

Before the IRS Restructuring and Reform Act of 1998, the failure of a taxpayer to pay a reported tax was subject to an addition to the tax equal to 0.5 percent of the net amount due (the unpaid tax). This penalty was imposed even if the taxpayer had entered into an installment payment agreement with the Service and was paying the unpaid tax in installments. The 1998 Act mitigates the penalty by reducing the failure-to-pay penalty rate from 0.5 percent to 0.25 percent for each month that an installment payment agreement is in force.[546]

[4] Service Penalty Procedures

No delinquent filing penalty may be assessed if a return is filed pursuant to an extension. The statute specifically provides that the "date prescribed" for filing

---

[544] Jones v. Comm'r, 259 F2d 300 (5th Cir. 1958); Cox v. Comm'r, 54 TC 1735 (1970); Daum Indus., Inc. v. United States, 71-2 USTC ¶ 9609 (D. Idaho 1971); Hopkins v. United States (In re Hopkins), 91-2 USTC ¶ 50,525 (Bankr. D. Colo. 1991). A taxpayer does not exercise ordinary business care and prudence when he fails to use equity in property to pay taxes but rather chooses to use the equity to pay other debts. Duncan v. United States, 84 AFTR2d 99-6260 (D. Or. 1999). The results in these penalty cases, however, depend on the facts. See Broker v. United States, 86 AFTR2d 2000-6784 (ED Pa. 2000) (although the taxpayer used his securities and IRA to pay living expenses and to purchase and refurbish a house, he was not liable for penalty because (1) he relied on his accountant's erroneous advice that he owed no tax and (2) he attempted to borrow to pay the tax he owed).

[545] Gregory v. United States, 80 AFTR2d ¶ 97-5420 (WD Mich. 1997) ("Plaintiff cannot establish reasonable cause for his failure to pay in a timely manner . . . [w]riting of checks out of accounts containing insufficient funds cannot be considered ordinary business care and prudence.")

[546] IRC § 6651(h), added by 1998 Act § 3303(a), effective for purposes of determining the amount of the addition to tax for months after December 31, 1999. For regulations on the reduction of the failure-to-pay penalty when an installment agreement is entered into, see Reg. § 301.6651-1(a)(4), published by TD 8895 (Aug. 17, 2000).

includes extensions.[547] Delinquent payment penalties also are not asserted where an extension to file has been granted, provided that payment is made by the extended due date, but interest is payable from the original due date of the return to the date of payment.[548] If an extension request is denied, the Service will not assert a delinquent filing penalty if the return is filed within ten days of the denial.[549] Obviously, failure to file within the grace or extension period will mean imposition of the penalty,[550] as well as a failure to properly estimate tax, which leads to the voiding of the automatic extension.[551]

Where a late return is filed, an affidavit explaining the reasonable cause for the delinquency should accompany the return.[552] Events occurring before the due date are those relevant in preparing the explanatory statement. As a legal and practical matter, the statement should be carefully prepared. It must be filed under oath, and a perfunctory statement stands a less likely chance of success in persuading the Service official that reasonable cause exists. Initially, the affidavit is reviewed at the service center with which the return is filed. Contact with service center personnel regarding the penalty is with the Taxpayer Service Division. Normally, the deficiency procedures (i.e., notice of deficiency and Tax Court review) do not apply to a delinquency penalty[553]; however, deficiency procedures do apply to the portion of the penalty that is attributable to a deficiency.[554] If the penalty is assessed, the taxpayer has another chance to have the penalty abated when the assessment is sent to the district Collection Division. Should efforts to persuade the revenue officer be

---

[547] IRC § 6651(a)(1). Procedures for filing extension requests should be followed. Although the penalty has not been upheld where individual taxpayers attempt to comply, W.B. Neville v. Comm'r, 26 TCM 452 (1967), corporations are treated more stringently. See, e.g., Custom Component Switches, Inc. v. Comm'r, 396 F2d 514 (9th Cir. 1968); French v. United States, 77 USTC ¶ 9546 (DNM 1976).

[548] Rev. Rul. 75-419, 1975-2 CB 465.

[549] IRM 5172.53(5), MT 5100-38 (Nov. 15, 1985) (Assertion of Failure to File Penalty). The penalty is imposed if the extension requested is frivolous and for the purpose of taking advantage of the grace period.

[550] Marcello v. Comm'r, 23 TCM 1847 (1964), aff'd, 380 F2d 449 (5th Cir.), cert. denied, 389 US 1044 (1967). The Service has ruled that the penalty applies to an income, estate, or gift tax return even where the tax is paid with an extension request, if the return is filed after the extension period. Rev. Rul. 81-237, 1981-2 CB 245.

[551] Crocker v. Comm'r, 92 TC 899, 913–914 (1989).

[552] Reg. § 301.6651-1(c)(1).

[553] IRC § 6659(b).

[554] IRC § 6659(b)(1). See Estate of DiRezza v. Comm'r, 78 TC 19 (1982) (Tax Court has jurisdiction over the unpaid penalty even if the tax deficiency is paid); Judge v. Comm'r, 88 TC 1175 (1987) (so long as it has jurisdiction over the tax on which the penalties are based, the Tax Court has jurisdiction regarding overpayments of delinquency penalties under Sections 6651(a)(1), 6651(a)(2), and 6654, even though deficiency procedures do not apply to these penalties).

unsuccessful, the taxpayer may appeal within fifteen days after notice of denial of the request for abatement to a collection conferee, who must decide the issue within thirty days, during which time collection is suspended.[555] If the appeals officer sustains the penalty, the taxpayer may obtain judicial review in a district court or the Claims Court through the normal refund procedures.

¶ 7B.08 PENALTIES FOR UNDERPAYMENTS IN AND DEPOSITS OF ESTIMATED TAX

[1] Penalty for Underpayment of Estimated Tax by Individuals

An individual who underpays estimated tax is subject to a penalty computed by applying (1) the underpayment rate established under Section 6621; (2) to the amount of the underpayment; (3) for the period of the underpayment.[556] Since the addition to the tax is the underpayment rate established under Section 6621, it is based on the federal short-term rate, plus 3 percent, determined quarterly.[557] Although the penalty is tied to the interest rate provided in the Code,[558] it is clearly not deductible. Apart from the penalty percentage, the other two elements of the penalty are the amount of the underpayment and its duration. The underpayment is the excess of (1) the required installment over (2) the installment, if any, paid on or before the last date prescribed for pay-

---

[555] Rev. Proc. 78-1, 1978-1 CB 550. See ¶ 9.03 for a discussion of appeals in penalty cases.

[556] IRC § 6654(a).

[557] For a description of the operation of Section 6621, see ¶ 6.04. Taxpayers who underpay can choose to permit the Service to compute the penalty or to calculate the penalty themselves using a Form 2210. Taxpayers who compute the penalty can use either a short or regular method. While the interest rate is adjusted quarterly, as of January 1, April 1, July 1, and October 1, the Service updated the Form 2210 annually to account for interest changes. The Taxpayer Advocate's 1996 Report to Congress described the estimated tax penalty rules as extraordinarily complex, and characterized the Form 2210 used for calculating the penalty as one of the most difficult forms taxpayers have to complete. The General Accounting Office criticized the Form 2210 calculation because it requires taxpayers to track each underpayment individually in complicated and numerous calculations to comply with the definition of underpayment. GAO Report "Tax Administration—Ways to Simplify the Estimated Tax Penalty," GAO/GGD-98-96 (May 1998). The GAO suggested allowing taxpayers to track the accumulated underpayment. The GAO also concluded that requiring taxpayers to account for the three or four fifteen-day periods between the interest adjustment date and the penalty calculation date was unnecessarily complex. See also Staff of Joint Comm. on Tax'n, Study of Present-Law Penalty and Interest Provisions As Required by Section 3801 of the IRS Restructuring and Reform Act of 1998 (Including Provisions Related to Corporate Tax Shelters) (JCS 3-99) (July 22, 1999) at 106–122.

[558] IRC § 6621.

ment.[559] Because the penalty is triggered by the untimely payment of a required installment, an overpayment of a later installment or the fact that the taxpayer may be owed a refund at the end of the year does not compensate for the underpayment of an installment. In general, this means that the penalty applies to the difference between payments made by the due date of the installment and the lesser of an installment based on 90 percent of the tax shown on the return for the current year or 100 percent of the tax shown on the prior year's return.[560] Withheld tax is considered payment of estimated tax, and an equal amount of the withholding tax credit is considered paid on each due date for the tax year.[561] Also, if the taxpayer shows the dates the amounts were actually withheld, the withheld tax is considered paid on the dates the amounts were actually withheld.[562] The period of the underpayment runs from the date the installment was required to be paid to the earlier of either (1) the date prescribed for payment (i.e., the fifteenth day of the fourth month following the close of the tax year (April 15 in most cases)) or (2) with respect to any portion of the underpayment, the date on which that portion is paid.

By making "required installments," a taxpayer can avoid an underpayment of estimated tax that would be subject to penalty. A required installment is 25 percent of the lesser of (1) 90 percent of the taxpayer's current income tax[563] or (2) 100 percent ("applicable percentage") of the taxpayer's tax for the preceding year. Under the first alternative, the taxpayer would pay four equal quarterly installments of 90 percent the tax shown in the individual's return for the current tax year. The remaining 10 percent would be paid on the return due date. The second alternative does not call for any projection of the current year's income tax. Simply by paying in each quarter 25 percent of the amount

---

[559] IRC § 6654(b). For farmers and fishermen the percentage is 66 percent. To be considered the return for the year, for penalty purposes, an amended return must be filed by the due date of the original return. Rev. Rul. 83-36, 1983-1 CB 158. In determining underpayments of estimated tax, the Service, for returns filed after December 31, 1983, applies overpayments arising on or before the due date of a return against the first installment payment of the next year's estimated tax, unless the taxpayer notifies the Service that the overpayment should be applied against another installment (and attaches a statement so indicating to the return). Rev. Rul. 84-58, 1984-1 CB 254. The Deficit Reduction Act incorporated this rule by overruling Rev. Rul. 83-111, 1983-2 CB 245, which was revoked by Rev. Rul. 84-58. Thus, a taxpayer may elect to credit an overpayment from a prior year's return to an estimated tax payment arising after the overpayment arose before the election is made (and interest on the estimated tax underpayment will not run).

[560] IRC § 6654(d)(1)(A).

[561] IRC § 6654(g)(1).

[562] IRC § 6654(g)(1).

[563] IRC § 6654(d)(1)(B)(i). The tax shown on the original return, not the tax shown on an amended return filed after the due date of the original return, is the basis for computing the exception to the addition to tax for an estimated tax underpayment. Rev. Rul. 86-58, 1986-16 IRB 7.

shown on the prior year's return, an individual will have paid the required installments for penalty purposes.

If an individual's adjusted gross income shown on the return for the prior taxable year exceeds $150,000, then the applicable percentage is increased from 100 percent to 110 percent.[564] The applicable percentage for such taxpayers, however, has been amended several times.[565] The present estimated tax safe harbor percentages for taxpayers with prior year adjusted gross income over $150,000 is as follows: for prior years beginning in 1998, 105 percent; 1999, 108.6 percent; 2000, 110 percent; 2001, 112 percent; and 2002 and thereafter, 110 percent.[566]

The required installments are the lesser of these two alternatives unless the individual can demonstrate that his "annualized income installment" is lower.[567] The "annualized income installment" requires the computation of the tax for the year based on the annualization of the taxpayer's taxable income, alternative minimum taxable income, and adjusted self-employment taxable income for months in the current year ending before the due date of the installment.[568] This tax is then multiplied by applicable percentages ranging from 22.5 to 90 percent depending on the number of the installment (e.g., the first installment is 22.5 percent of the annualized tax).[569] Finally, the aggregate amount of prior required installments is subtracted. The complexity of this alternative makes its frequent use unlikely, especially with the inclusion of the AMT.

The penalty for underpayment of estimated tax is the only civil penalty imposed with respect to estimated obligations. There is no penalty for failure to file a declaration or for underestimation as such.[570] However, the underpay-

---

[564] OBRA 1993, Pub. L. No. 103-66, § 13214(a) (Aug. 10, 1993).

[565] The Tax Reform Act of 1997, however, established new applicable percentages for taxpayers with prior year adjusted gross income amounts over $150,000. Regarding any installment payment for taxable years before January 1, 2000, 110 percent is replaced by 105 percent if the prior taxable year began in 1998, 1999, 2000, and 112 percent if the prior taxable year began in 2001. These applicable percentages were, again, amended for any installment payment for tax years beginning after December 21, 1999. The Tax and Trade Relief Act of 1998 changed the applicable percentages from 105 to 106 if the prior taxable year began in 1999 or 2000. The Tax Relief Extension Act of 1999 again amended the safe harbor percentage for any installment payment for taxable years beginning after December 31, 1999, by changing the applicable percentage from 106 to 108.6 if the prior taxable year began in 1999, and from 106 to 110 percent if the prior taxable year began in 2000.

[566] IRC § 6654(d)(1)(C)(i).

[567] IRC § 6654(d)(2).

[568] IRC § 6654(d)(2)(B)(i). Annualization of taxable income, alternative taxable income, and self-employment income are governed by regulations. IRC § 6654(d)(2)(C)(i).

[569] IRC § 6654(d)(2)(C)(ii).

[570] IRC § 6651(d).

ment penalty is mandatory. There is no general waiver for reasonable cause and lack of willful neglect, and most extenuating circumstances are therefore irrelevant.[571] No penalty is imposed, however, where (1) the tax shown on the return after deduction for withholding tax credits is less than $1,000[572]; (2) there was no tax liability for the preceding year[573]; or (3) the IRS is authorized to grant a waiver of the penalty.[574] The Service can waive the penalty if the failure to make a payment was due to casualty, disaster, or other unusual circumstances where it would be inequitable to impose the penalty. For example, waiver could be granted where the taxpayer's books and records were destroyed by fire or other casualty, or where payment was not made because of the death or serious illness of the taxpayer. Also, the penalty can be waived where the liability as shown on the return has been substantially overstated by the taxpayer. In addition, the underpayment penalty may be waived for reasonable cause for either of the first two years after the taxpayer retires upon reaching age 62 or becomes disabled.

The penalty for underpayment of estimated tax is collected in the same manner as the tax and must be paid on notice and demand.[575] However, normal deficiency procedures do not apply unless the taxpayer fails to file a return for the year.[576] Failure to file an estimated tax return is not a criminal offense, but failure to pay estimated tax is a misdemeanor if the failure to pay is willful and the individual is subject to the failure-to-pay penalty of Section 6654.[577]

[2] Penalty for Underpayment of Estimated Tax by Corporations

Section 6655 imposes a penalty on corporate taxpayers for any underpayment of estimated corporate tax.[578] As with the underpayment penalty for individuals, the penalty is computed by applying (1) the underpayment rate established

---

[571] Estate of Barney Ruben, 33 TC 1071, 1072 (1960).

[572] IRC § 6654(e)(1).

[573] IRC § 6654(e)(2). For purposes of the preceding year exception, the preceding year must be a period of twelve months, the individual must not have had a tax liability for tax for the preceding year, and the individual must have been a citizen for the entire year.

[574] IRC § 6654(e)(3). See Staff of Joint Comm. on Taxation, General Explanation of the Revenue Provisions of the Deficit Reduction Act of 1984, 708.

[575] IRC § 6659(a)(1).

[576] IRC § 6659(b)(2).

[577] IRC § 7203. The criminal penalty is a fine of not more than $25,000, or imprisonment for not more than one year, or both.

[578] A nonoperating trustee of a bankrupt corporation has been held liable for the payment of estimated corporate income taxes and for penalties under Section 6655 for failure to pay estimated tax. Sapphire SS Lines, Inc. v. Comm'r, 84-2 USTC ¶ 9939 (SDNY 1984), aff'd, 762 F2d 13 (2d Cir. 1985). However, see IRC § 6658.

under Section 6621; (2) to the amount of the underpayment; (3) for the period of the underpayment.[579] The amount of the underpayment is the excess of (1) the required installment and (2) the amount of the installment paid, if any, on or before the due date of the installment.[580] The period of underpayment is the period from the due date of the installment until the earlier of (1) the date the portion of the underpayment is actually paid or (2) the fifteenth day of the third month following the close of the taxable year.[581]

No reasonable cause waiver exists for abatement of estimated tax penalty on corporations, although there is a de minimis exception where the tax on the return for the year is less than $500.[582] A failure to pay 25 percent of the required annual payment will be penalized. In the case of corporations, the penalty can be avoided by utilizing the different alternatives available for calculating the amount of the required annual installment. There are four alternatives available to corporate taxpayers based on the prior year's tax, the current year's tax, annualized income, and adjusted seasonal income. These alternatives are described here in a summary fashion, since they represent methods of penalty avoidance.[583]

The required annual payment is the lesser of (1) 100 percent of the tax shown on the prior year's return or (2) 100 percent of the tax on the current year's return.[584] For large corporations (corporations with taxable income of $1 million or more for any tax year during a testing period),[585] the prior year's return alternative is not available. The large corporation must pay 90 percent of the current year's tax.[586] A large corporation may use last year's tax for determining the amount of the first required installment, but if the first installment

---

[579] IRC § 6655(a).

[580] IRC § 6655(b)(1).

[581] IRC § 6655(b)(1).

[582] IRC § 6655(f).

[583] For completed copies of the IRS forms for calculating additions to the tax, see Saltzman & Saltzman, IRS Practice and Procedure Forms and Analysis, Chapter 2 (Warren, Gorham & Lamont, Inc. 1990).

[584] IRC § 6655(d)(1). If no return was filed for the current year, 100 percent of the tax for the year is used. IRC § 6655(d)(1)(B)(i). However, the prior year tax alternative does not apply if the corporation did not file a return for the year showing a tax liability or if the preceding year was not a taxable year of twelve months. IRC § 6655(d)(1) (flush language).

[585] IRC § 6655(g)(2). In general, the testing period is the three taxable years immediately preceding the tax year involved, IRC § 6655(g)(2)(B)(i). Special rules apply to members of a controlled group (IRC § 6655(g)(2)(B)(ii)) and the effect of carrybacks and carryforwards (IRC § 6655(g)(2)(B)(iii)). The Service's position is that Section 6655(d)(1)(B)(ii) precludes a corporation's avoiding penalties for underpayment of estimated tax if it did not file a return for the preceding taxable year "showing a liability for tax"; that is, a positive corporate income tax liability.

[586] IRC § 6655(d)(2)(A).

under this method is less than the actual amount using the current year method, then the deficiency must be made up in the second installment.[587]

Corporations are permitted to use two other methods of determining the amount of a required installment: the annualized income installment method and the adjusted seasonal installment method.[588] If a corporation can show that any installment calculated according to annualized income method or the adjusted seasonal installment method is less than the amount required under the current year's tax or prior year's tax method, the required installment is the installment determined under either of these alternative methods.[589] The annualized income installment requires the corporate taxpayer to annualize the taxable income, alternative minimum taxable income, and modified alternative taxable income for the first three months of the year in the case of the first installment, the first three or five months of the year in the case of the second installment, the first six or eight months of the year for the third installment, and the first nine or eleven months of the year in the case of the fourth installment.[590] After the annualized tax has been determined, the applicable percentage of the tax due is determined. Since 90 percent of the current year's tax must be paid, the applicable percentages are 22.5 percent for the first installment, 45 percent for the second installment, 67.5 percent for the third installment, and 90 percent with the last installment.[591] The amount of the annualized income installment is the amount of the applicable percentage of the annualized tax less the total of any of the prior installments.[592]

The adjusted seasonal income alternative is intended for corporations that experience a recurring seasonal pattern of income. In general, under this method, the corporation pays its estimated tax in the same seasonal pattern in which its annualized income is earned. If the corporation's income is earned in the second half of the year, this method is particularly advantageous. The test used to determine the seasonal nature of the corporation's income is whether, in the three preceding tax years, taxable income for any six consecutive months averages at least 70 percent of the taxable income for the year.[593] The amount of the adjusted seasonal installment requires calculation of the base-period percentage, which is the average percentage that the taxable income for the base period in each of the three preceding tax years bears to the annual taxable income for each of those years.[594] The adjusted seasonal installment is

---

[587] IRC § 6655(d)(2)(B).

[588] IRC § 6655(e).

[589] IRC § 6655(e)(1).

[590] IRC § 6655(e)(2)(A).

[591] IRC § 6655(e)(2)(B)(ii).

[592] IRC §§ 6655(e)(2)(A)(i), 6655(e)(2)(A)(ii).

[593] IRC §§ 6655(e)(3)(B), 6655(e)(3)(D)(i).

[594] IRC § 6655(e)(3)(D)(i).

90 percent of the annualized taxable income for the months preceding the month when the installment is due, multiplied by the base period percentage for the elapsed months of the taxable year including the month when the installment is due, less the total amount of the prior installments paid for the tax year.[595]

Reaching the safety of one of the alternative calculations is not without its own difficulties, as illustrated by *Evans Cooperage Co. v. United States.*[596] In this case, the taxpayer corporation filed its 1976 return and its 1977 estimated tax computation using the prior year's return method—i.e., the tax shown on the 1976 return. However, through a miscalculation of the quarterly payments, estimated tax was underpaid, and a penalty was assessed and paid. The taxpayer then filed an amended return reflecting a lower tax liability for 1976 and 1977 and claimed a refund. The circuit court in finding against the taxpayer held that "the tax shown on the return" for purposes of the prior year's return method is the tax shown on the original return, not the tax shown on a later filed amended return, as the taxpayer contended. The penalty is also calculated on the basis of the tax reported on the original return, even if that tax is inflated, which it was in this case.[597] The rationale of the court was that Congress intended to provide a predictable escape from any possible penalty liabilities. Such certainty would be defeated if the penalty were based on the liability determined after an audit or even after the filing of an amended return because, in the court's view, an amended return is recognizable by the Service solely as a matter of its discretion.[598] Similarly, the court found no basis for giving "return" a different meaning than the original return the statute unambiguously provided.

¶ 7B.09 ABATEMENT OF PENALTY ATTRIBUTABLE TO ERRONEOUS IRS ADVICE

Section 6404(f) requires the Service to abate "any portion of any penalty or addition to tax attributable to erroneous advice furnished to the taxpayer in writing by an officer or employee [of the Service], acting in [that] officer's or

---

[595] IRC § 6655(e)(3)(A). The calculation is actually computed in a four-step process described in Section 6655(e)(3)(C).

[596] Evans Cooperage Co. v. United States, 712 F2d 199 (5th Cir. 1983).

[597] Applying this interpretation, the taxpayer in *Evans Cooperage* underestimated the minimum amount due by less than $3,000 and, as a result, underpaid estimated taxes by $587,000. Thus, it was found liable for over $24,000 in penalties.

[598] The circuit court expressly followed those cases holding that an amended nonfraudulent return is not a return sufficient to start the normal statute of limitations on assessment, a view now accepted by the Supreme Court. See ¶ 4.03[1].

employee's official capacity."[599] In addition to the limited circumstances requiring abatement of a penalty under this section, the applicability of Section 6404(f) is still further restricted by several statutory limitations[600] and regulations.[601] One statutory limitation requires that (1) the taxpayer must have specifically requested advice in writing; (2) written advice must have been provided; and (3) the taxpayer must have reasonably relied on the advice.[602] The second limitation incorporates a traditional element of the IRS rulings practice, as well as the shift of responsibility or advice of counsel defense— the taxpayer must have provided "adequate or accurate information."[603]

Regulations effectively limit "advice" to a ruling, a determination letter, or technical advice,[604] a conclusion that is supported by both the power of attorney requirement when the written request is made by a taxpayer's representative,[605] and the full disclosure requirement.[606] Moreover, reliance will not be considered reasonable by the Service unless the advice is received before a return is filed[607] or the act or omission occurs.[608] If written advice is provided, there is a reliance period, and certain events occurring after and contrary to the written advice put the taxpayer on notice that the advice no longer represents the Service's position, and terminate the taxpayer's entitlement to rely.[609] These events, as interpreted by the regulations, require the unrepresented taxpayer to become a tax professional keeping up with developments. The taxpayer is put on notice that advice is no longer valid by (1) correspondence from the IRS stating the advice is no longer its position; (2) legislation or a treaty; (3) a Supreme Court decision; (4) issuance of temporary or final regulations; or (5) publication of a revenue ruling, revenue procedure, or other statement in the Internal Revenue Bulletin.[610]

---

[599] IRC § 6404(f)(1). A claim for abatement must be filed within the period the IRS has to collect the penalty. Reg. § 301.6404-3(e). For a discussion of filing procedures for claims for penalty abatement, see Reg. § 301.6404-3(d).

[600] IRC §§ 6404(f)(2)(A); 6404(f)(2)(B).

[601] Reg. § 301.6404-3.

[602] IRC § 6404(f)(2)(A).

[603] IRC § 6404(f)(2)(B).

[604] Reg. § 301.6404-3(c)(1).

[605] Reg. § 301.6404-3(b)(3).

[606] IRC § 6404(f)(2)(B); Reg. § 301.6404-3(b)(4).

[607] Reg. § 301.6404-3(b)(2)(ii).

[608] Reg. § 301.6404-3(b)(2)(iv) (advice not related to a tax return such as an estimated tax issue).

[609] Reg. § 301.6404-3(b)(2)(v).

[610] Reg. § 301.6404-3(b)(2)(v).

¶ 7B.09A ABATEMENT OF PENALTY WHEN THE SERVICE FAILS TO CONTACT TAXPAYER

Section 6404(g) provides that, if the Service fails to contact a taxpayer before the close of the one-year period beginning on the later of (1) the date the return is filed or (2) the due date of the return without regard to extensions, penalties and interest accrual are suspended after such one-year period.[611] Interest and penalties resume after the Service has sent the required notice to the taxpayer.[612] The provision is applied separately with respect to each item or adjustment, and it applies only to taxpayers who have timely filed returns.[613] The suspension period does not apply, however, when a taxpayer has self assessed the tax, the taxpayer is liable for the failure to pay penalty, in cases of fraud, or with respect to criminal penalties.[614]

¶ 7B.10 SPOUSAL LIABILITY FOR PENALTIES

A husband and wife may file a joint return utilizing rates that are lower than those for separate returns. These advantageous rates may be used even if one of the spouses has no gross income or deductions and would not otherwise be required to file a return. For the privilege of filing a joint return and paying a single tax based on the favorable joint-return rate schedule, however, the husband and wife assume joint and several liability for the payment of the single tax, including interest and penalties.[615] Joint and several liability can result in

---

[611] IRC § 6404(g)(1). The one-year period is increased to eighteen months for taxable years beginning prior to January 1, 2004. IRC § 6404(g)(3)(A).

[612] IRC § 6404(g)(3)(B).

[613] IRC § 6404(g)(3)(B).

[614] IRC § 6404(g)(2).

[615] IRC § 6013(d). Joint liablity means that an innocent spouse can be subject to administrative procedures to assess and collect the tax liablity attributable to the other or guilty spouse. Although the IRS may claim that the innocent spouse is liable for tax due on the joint return, the IRS has confounded the efforts of an innocent spouse to respond because it has also claimed that any information it has received from the guilty spouse is confidential return information. Effective March 1, 1996, IRS personnel are supposed to notify one spouse of collection action against the other spouse to collect a joint return liablity. Ann. 96-5, 1996-4 IRB 1.

As part of its administrative initiatives to enhance taxpayer rights, the Service announced in Notice 96-19 that it recognizes that joint and several liablity and community property law present unique issues, especially for divorced or separated taxpayers, and that, accordingly, it was requesting comments on (1) replacing joint and several liablity with a proportionate liability standard, (2) basing spouses' tax obligations and liabilities on the terms of a divorce decree, separation agreement, or other property settlement, (3)

gross inequity where only one of the spouses is responsible for the fraudulent underpayment in tax. One common situation involves a wife who the Service claims is liable for additional tax on a joint return that omitted moneys her husband embezzled from his employer and lost gambling, all without the wife's knowledge. Before 1971, the wife in such a situation was generally held liable for the tax, interest, and fraud penalty although she had no knowledge of her husband's embezzlement and did not benefit from the use of the funds.

On the face of the statute, joint and several liability for the single tax payable on the filing of a joint return is absolute. However, the liability of a spouse for the deficiency, including penalties, is subject to a number of rules. For example, the exception to the normal three-year period of limitations on assessment where a return is "false or fraudulent with intent to evade tax" permits assessment of a deficiency against a spouse filing a joint return even if the fraudulent conduct and intent is that of the other joint-filing spouse.[616] Thus, even if the husband is the one whose conduct was fraudulent in filing the return and making the underpayment, the three-year bar of the statute of limitations is still lifted against the wife, and she is liable for the deficiency by virtue of the joint and several liability provisions of Section 6013(d)(3).

Collateral estoppel applies only to the spouse who was convicted in any prior criminal prosecution.[617] For purposes of estoppel, the unconvicted spouse is not in privity with the convicted spouse and may contest the issue of fraud in a subsequent civil penalty trial.

Under Section 6663(a), even if one spouse is shown to be guilty of fraud in the filing of a joint return by a judgment of conviction for evasion, the other spouse is not liable for the fraud penalty unless the Commissioner also establishes that some part of the underpayment is due to the fraud of that spouse. Thus, Section 6663(c) provides that the penalty does not apply to the tax of a spouse filing a joint return "unless some part of the underpayment is due to the fraud of the spouse." However, even though the spouse acting without fraud is not liable for the fraud penalty, the spouse still remains liable for the deficiency in tax under Section 6013(d)(3), unless the special innocent spouse rule of Section 6015 applies.

A spouse may obtain a limited release from joint liability under Section 6015 for tax (including interest), penalties, and other amounts, as an "innocent spouse,"[618] provided the spouse can prove by a preponderance of the evidence

---

reforming the innocent spouse provisions, and (4) further limiting the effect of *Poe v. Seaborn* in community property jurisdictions. Notice 96-19, 1996-14 IRB 1.

[616] IRC § 6501(C)(1); Vannaman v. Comm'r, 54 TC 1011 (1970).

[617] Henry M. Rodney, 53 TC 287 (1969); CBC Super Markets, Inc., 54 TC 882 (1970).

[618] IRS Restructuring and Reform Act of 1998, Pub. L. No. 105-206, § 3201, applicable to any tax liability arising after July 22, 1998, and any tax liability arising on or before this date but remaining unpaid as of July 22, 1998.

that the prerequisites to relief have been satisfied.[619] Pursuant to Section 6015, in cases where there is an understatement in tax attributable to erroneous items of one individual filing the joint return, the innocent spouse will be relieved of liability provided he or she did not know and had no reason to know that there was an understatement, and it would be inequitable to hold the spouse liable for the deficiency.

[1] Innocent Spouse Relief Under Prior Law

Under former Section 6013(e), relief from joint liability for tax, interest, and penalties was available in limited circumstances. To qualify for relief, an "innocent spouse" was required to show that: (1) the innocent spouse filed a joint return with the guilty spouse; (2) on the joint return, there was a substantial tax understatement (i.e., the amount by which the correct tax exceeds the reported tax is in excess of $500), and this understatement was attributable to "grossly erroneous items" of the other spouse; (3) in signing the return, the spouse did not know and had no reason to know that there was a substantial understatement of tax; and (4) taking into account all "the facts and circumstances," it would have been inequitable to hold the spouse liable for the additional tax attributable to the substantial understatement of the guilty spouse. The appropriate forum for challenging the Service's denial of innocent spouse relief depended on whether an underpayment was asserted or the taxpayer was seeking a refund. The Tax Court did not have jurisdiction to review all denials of innocent spouse relief.[620]

Congress was concerned that the innocent spouse provisions under prior law were inadequate, and that it was too difficult to obtain innocent spouse relief, and, when relief was available, it was provided only if the understatement was large enough and the tax position at issue was "grossly erroneous." The Congress also believed that taxpayers who are no longer living together (because of divorce, separation, or otherwise) should be able to elect to have their tax liabilities separated from that of their spouse (or former spouse).[621] The IRS Restructuring and Reform Act of 1998, therefore, repealed former Section 6013(e) and included a new innocent spouse regime in Section 6015.[622]

---

[619] For further analysis of this subject, see Borison, "Innocent Spouse Relief," 40 Tax Lawyer 819 (1987); Lewis, "Innocent Spouse Cases," 40 Tax Lawyer 865 (1987); Borison, "Getting Equity From the Tax Court in Innocent Spouse Cases," 96 TNT 191-110 (Sept. 30, 1996).

[620] See Staff of Joint Comm. on Tax'n, General Explanation of Tax Legislation Enacted in 1998 (JCS-6-98) (Nov. 24, 1998) at 66–67.

[621] 1998 Blue Book at 67.

[622] IRC § 6015, added by 1998 Act § 3201, applicable to any tax liability arising after July 22, 1998, and any tax liability arising on or before this date but remaining unpaid

[2] The Innocent Spouse Statute: Section 6015

The IRS Restructuring and Reform Act of 1998 replaced the former innocent spouse rules under old Section 6013(e).[623] The new regime under Section 6015 is intended to provide greater protection to innocent spouses who file joint returns and then find themselves liable for their guilty spouse's liability.[624] Section 6015 establishes three procedures for limiting a spouse's liability. First, Section 6105 expands the circumstances under which innocent spouse relief was available under prior law.[625] Second, the rules establish a separate liability election for a taxpayer who is no longer married to, is legally separated from, or has been living apart at all times for at least twelve months from the person with whom the taxpayer originally filed the joint return.[626] Third, the new regime authorizes the Secretary to provide equitable relief in appropriate situations.[627] Section 6015 also grants jurisdiction to the Tax Court over disputes under Section 6015.[628]

[3] Relief From Joint Liability

The 1998 Act expands availability of the circumstances under which a spouse may claim relief from those available under former Section 6013(e). Section 6015(b) releases a spouse who has signed a joint return from liability for tax, interest, penalties, and other amounts if the spouse can establish the following:

1. A joint return has been made for the taxable year[629];
2. On the joint return, there was an understatement of tax attributable to erroneous items of one spouse[630];
3. The innocent spouse establishes that in signing the return, he did not know and had no reason to know, that there was such understatement[631];

---

as of July 22, 1998. See also Cheshire v. Comm'r, 115 TC 183, 189 (2000), aff'd, 2002 WL 200612 (5th Cir. Feb. 8, 2002).

[623] IRC § 6015, added by 1998 Act § 3201, applicable to any tax liability arising after July 22, 1998, and any tax liability arising on or before this date but remaining unpaid as of July 22, 1998.

[624] 1998 Blue Book at 66–67.

[625] IRC § 6015(b).

[626] IRC § 6015(c).

[627] IRC § 6015(f).

[628] IRC § 6015(e).

[629] IRC § 6015(b)(1)(A).

[630] IRC § 6015(b)(1)(B).

[631] IRC § 6015(b)(1)(C).

4. Taking into account all the facts and circumstances, it is inequitable to hold the innocent spouse liable for the deficiency in tax for such taxable year attributable to the deficiency[632]; and

5. The innocent spouse elects the benefits of Section 6015(b) no later than two years after the date on which the Secretary has begun collection activities.[633]

The term "understatement" has the same meaning as it does for purposes of the substantial understatement penalty.[634] In analyzing new Section 6015, the Tax Court will look to cases interpreting former Section 6013(e).[635]

[a] The Joint Return Element

The innocent spouse provisions apply only to situations where a joint return is filed. No relief is accorded a spouse who files a separate return or no return. The separate return exception has harsh results in community property jurisdictions. For example, an innocent wife may be taxable on her community share of income omitted from both her and her husband's separate returns and may be denied relief despite meeting all the other conditions of Section 6015.[636] When both a husband and wife fail to file a return, the innocent spouse may fare somewhat better. An intention to file a joint return will not be inferred and, if, for example, the innocent wife has no income, liability for tax and penalties will not be asserted against the spouse who was not obligated to file a return.[637] If the innocent wife had income requiring the filing of a return, it would seem she also is not liable unless she is in a community property state.

---

[632] IRC § 6015(b)(1)(D).

[633] IRC § 6015(b)(1)(E).

[634] IRC § 6662(d)(2)(A), 6015(b)(3).

[635] Butler v. Comm'r, 114 TC 276, 283 (2000); Rowe v. Comm'r, TC Memo. 2001-325; Bradon v. Comm'r, TC Memo. 2001-69.

[636] Galliher v. Comm'r, 62 TC 760 (1974), aff'd by unpublished opinion (5th Cir. Apr. 24, 1975). If a separate return is filed, this inequity does not occur in a separate property jurisdiction because liability for tax and penalties in the husband's omitted income would be his and his alone. The phrase "on such return" has been interpreted to include erroneous deductions claimed on a Form 1045, Application for Tentative Refund. Friedman v. Comm'r, 97 TC 606 (1991).

[637] Gemma v. Comm'r, 46 TC 821 (1966) (acq.); Rev. Rul. 78-299, 1978-2 CB 304.

[b] Understatement of Tax Attributable to Erroneous Items of Guilty Spouse

Under former Section 6013(e), a spouse was eligible for relief if, among other things, the joint return contained a "substantial understatement of tax attributable to grossly erroneous items of one spouse."[638] Congress, however, believed that it was inappropriate to limit relief only to the most egregious cases where the understatement was large and the tax position was grossly erroneous.[639] New Section 6015 has, in part, lessened the standard in order to expand availability of innocent spouse relief.

The proposed regulations define an "erroneous item" as follows:

An erroneous item is any item resulting in an understatement or deficiency in tax to the extent that such item is omitted from, or improperly reported (including improperly characterized) in an individual income tax return. For example, unreported income from an investment asset resulting in an understatement or deficiency in tax is an erroneous item. Similarly, ordinary income that is improperly reported as capital gain resulting in an understatement or deficiency in tax is also an erroneous item. An erroneous item is also an improperly reported item that affects the liability on other returns (e.g., an improper net operating loss that is carried back to a prior year's return).[640]

[c] Knowledge Element

For elections to limit liability under Section 6015(b)(1), the innocent spouse must establish by a preponderance of the evidence that he or she did not know, and had no reason to know, that there was an understatement of tax.[641] Under the proposed regulations, facts and circumstances that are considered in determining whether a spouse had knowledge or reason to know include: (1) the nature of the item relative to other items; (2) the couple's financial position; (3) the requesting spouse's educational background and business experience; (4) the extent of the requesting spouse's participation in the activity at or before the time the return was signed about items that a reasonable person would question; and (5) whether the erroneous item represented a departure from past years' return positions.[642]

---

[638] Former IRC § 6013(e)(1)(B).

[639] 1998 Blue Book at 67.

[640] Prop. Reg. § 1.6015-1(g)(4).

[641] IRC § 6015(b)(1)(C).

[642] Prop. Reg. § 1.6015-2(c).

Knowledge for purposes of Section 6015(b)(1) need not be actual knowledge of an income omission.[643] However, actual knowledge of the omission before signing the return may be established by a husband's conviction for embezzlement or by an adverse judgment for conversion.[644] The reason-to-know standard appears to incorporate the negligence concept of the "reasonable man." At least one court has held that the test to be applied is whether a reasonably prudent taxpayer would have had reason to know of the omissions.[645] The knowledge referred to is knowledge of the facts relating to the income omission. Thus, ignorance of the legal consequences of a transaction giving rise to the omission are irrelevant.[646] Under the reason-to-know standard, a spouse does not derive knowledge of an income omission merely from ordinary support, nor perhaps even from expenditures beyond current income.[647] Nevertheless, a spouse cannot close his or her eyes to facts such as a special

---

[643] Adams v. Comm'r, 60 TC 300 (1973).

[644] Altman v. Comm'r, 475 F2d 876 (2d Cir. 1973). See Leon v. Comm'r, 42 TCM 1060 (1981) (husband's indictment and conviction on charges arising out of prostitution activities constituted actual notice of his income from prostitution business); Trimmer v. Comm'r, 45 TCM 960 (1983) (husband learned of wife's embezzlement when she was indicted for and convicted of stealing currency). Johnson v. Comm'r, 65 TCM 2760 (1993) (spouse had actual knowledge of unreported embezzlement income where she signed income tax return the day before husband entered guilty plea to forty-one-count embezzlement indictment).

[645] Sanders v. United States, 509 F2d 162 (5th Cir. 1975). The standard applied in determining whether a taxpayer had reason to know of omissions is whether a reasonable person under the taxpayer's circumstances at the time of signing the return could be expected to know of the omissions. Shea v. Comm'r, 780 F2d 561 (6th Cir. 1986) (issue is one of fact, and the Tax Court's finding was not clearly erroneous). See Cox v. Comm'r, 45 TCM 333 (1982) (effect of borderline schizophrenia and reliance on tranquilizers on ability to gain knowledge of wife's embezzlement). In *Day v. Comm'r*, the Tax Court found that the wife had failed to introduce evidence to prove that she did not benefit from the understatement, and therefore was not entitled to innocent spouse status. The Eighth Circuit reversed, 975 F2d 534 (8th Cir. 1992), saying "the tax court required the impossible; that [the wife] explain the distribution of the [undeclared] money of whose existence she claims to be unaware. In doing so, the court incorporated [the husband] into his wife's defense and placed undue burden on [the wife]." The circuit court said, on that remark, that the Tax Court "should determine whether [the wife] substantially benefited from the understatements, and whether a reasonable taxpayer in [the wife's] position would have known, or had reason to know of the understatements." See also McGee v. Comm'r, 979 F2d 66 (5th Cir. 1992) (wife was aware of husband's sole source of income and irresponsible behavior in financial matters, yet failed to question him or accountant or to review documents), reh'g denied, 1993 US App. LEXIS 1281 (5th Cir. 1993). Compare Johnson v. Comm'r, 65 TCM 2760 (1993) (spouse had no reason to know more about embezzled income than interested persons from whom the money was embezzled).

[646] McCoy v. Comm'r, 57 TC 732 (1972) (incorporation of a partnership whose liabilities exceeded the basis of transferred assets); Trimmer v. Comm'r, 45 TCM 960 (1983).

[647] Terzian v. Comm'r, 72 TC 1164 (1979); Mysse v. Comm'r, 57 TC 680 (1972).

account in which unreported payments were deposited,[648] or to unusual or lavish expenditures.[649] Similarly, a spouse can not be expected to ignore the knowledge acquired from actual participation in family finances,[650] or even a spouse's refusal to be forthright about family income.[651]

Where knowledge of a deduction-caused understatement is at issue, some courts have applied the knowledge standard developed in income omission cases. These courts have said, "[t]he knowledge contemplated by [former Section 6013(e)] is not knowledge of the tax consequences of a transaction, but rather knowledge of the transaction itself."[652] In applying new Section 6015, the Tax Court has held that "no knowledge requirement of section 6015(b)(1)(C) is similar to that found in former section 6013(e)(1)(C)."[653] This view, however, is not uniform,[654] and knowledge in income omission cases can be distinguished from knowledge in deduction cases.[655] In *Price v. Commissioner*, the Ninth Circuit said:

> Here, while the [Tax Court] properly concluded that Patricia knew certain facts about the CCM investment, it cannot be said that Patricia was so intimately involved with the investment such that she knew virtually all of the facts of the transaction underlying the deduction, leaving her no option but to rely solely upon ignorance of law as a defense and therefore leaving us no option to conclude that she had reason to know of the understatement.

---

[648] Joss v. Comm'r, 56 TC 378 (1971).

[649] See Mysse v. Comm'r, 57 TC 680 (1972).

[650] Sonnenborn v. Comm'r, 57 TC 373 (1971). See also, e.g., Young v. Comm'r, 42 TCM 1156 (1981) (wife participated in finances and ordered new furniture at about the time her husband submitted false Small Business Administration claim); Ballard v. Comm'r, 44 TCM 829 (1982); Bieber v. United States, 93-1 USTC ¶ 50,028 (Bankr. SD Ga. 1992) (embezzled income paid household bills and mortgage payments, and husband apparently knew of wife's embezzlement, but not that embezzled funds were taxable).

[651] Adams v. Comm'r, 60 TC 300 (1973).

[652] Quinn v. Comm'r, 524 F2d 617, 626 (7th Cir. 1975); Purcell v. Comm'r, 86 TC 228 (1986), aff'd, 826 F2d 470 (6th Cir. 1987), cert. denied, 108 S. Ct. 1290 (1988); Bokum v. Comm'r, 992 F2d 1132 (11th Cir. 1993). In re Freytag, 9302 USTC ¶ 50,531 (Bankr. ND Tex. 1993) (innocent spouse claim rejected, in part because of wife's legal training and occupation, her discussions with her husband, a tax lawyer, and notices received from the Service).

[653] Cheshire v. Comm'r, 115 TC 183, 192 (relief denied when spouse had actual knowledge of the underlying transaction producing omitted income).

[654] Price v. Comm'r, 887 F2d 959 (5th Cir. 1975). As one court observed, courts take into account factors that shed light on whether the putative innocent spouse should have known about the propriety of a deduction because the reading of the return will always give the spouse notice of the underlying transaction. Thus, to find that notice of the transaction is sufficient to preclude innocent spouse protection in deduction cases would entirely gut the exception. IRS v. Meier, 9302 USTC ¶ 50,482 (ED Va. 1993).

[655] Price v. Comm'r, 887 F2d 959 (5th Cir. 1975).

Under the *Price* analysis, knowledge of the transaction itself does not preclude relief. The analysis requires consideration of how much the putative innocent spouse knows about the transaction ("the more a spouse knows about a transaction . . . the more likely it is that she will know or have reason to know that the deduction arising from that transaction may not be valid."). Even if the spouse did not have reason to know that the deduction gave rise to a substantial understatement, the court is also required to determine whether the spouse knew enough facts to put her on inquiry notice (sufficient knowledge that would lead a reasonably prudent taxpayer in her position to question the legitimacy of the deduction).[656] In determining whether the spouse had a reason to

---

[656] Price v. Comm'r, 887 F2d 959, 965. In Erdahl v. Comm'r, 930 F2d 585 (8th Cir. 1991), the Eighth Circuit followed the Ninth Circuit's analysis in *Price v. Comm'r*, 887 F2d (5th Cir. 1975), and Guth v. Comm'r, 897 F2d 441 (1990). Knowledge of the transaction giving rise to the erroneous deduction does not require that the spouse be put on notice that the deduction might result in a substantial understatement, but if the spouse is put on notice, the spouse has a duty to inquire further. Failure to make the inquiry permits a finding that the spouse had constructive knowledge of the transaction. For the duty to exist, the test is a subjective one, that is, whether a reasonably prudent person in the spouse's position would have questioned the legitimacy of the transaction.

The Second Circuit has adopted the test articulated by the Ninth Circuit in *Price*; that is, a taxpayer must establish that "she (or he) did not know and did not have reason to know that the deduction would give rise to a substantial understatement." Hayman v. Comm'r, 992 F2d 1256 (2d Cir. 1993) (knowledge found because wife signed some of the coal shelter documents; she knew of the ventures; she was a vice-president and merchandising director of a retail chain; she was involved in family finances; husband did not hide circumstances; and losses on the returns exceeded income). Compare Epstein v. Comm'r, TC Memo 1996-239 (wife of tax shelter salesman was well educated, but she was found unsophisticated in business matters because she devoted most of her time to her interest in graphic arts and theater and her work experience was selling space for a small local newspaper; her lifestyle was not lavish; her husband and their accountant kept information about the tax shelter deductions from her and systematically refused to explain the returns to her; she was led to believe that tax shelters were "on the up and up" and, like IRAs, a legitimate way to save taxes; and while she and her husband were not divorced, she had used her own money and had sold their house to assist in paying taxes.

In *Friedman*, the Second Circuit said that *Hayman* had listed four factors to consider in deciding whether "a reasonably prudent taxpayer in (the spouse's) position at the time she signed the return" should have known that the return contained a substantial understatement. Friedman v. Comm'r, 53 F3d 523 (2d Cir. 1995). According to the circuit court, "[a] court should look at (1) the level of education; (2) the knowledge and experience in the family's business and financial affairs attained by the spouse claiming to be innocent; (3) whether the family's current standard of living is lavish compared to past levels of income and expenditures; and (4) the conduct of the culpable spouse in concealing the true state of the family's finances from the 'innocent spouse.'" In this case, the circuit court reversed the Tax Court and found the former wife to qualify for innocent spouse status even though she had been the husband's secretary and had learned that the couple's tax liability for 1983 was zero as the result of the tax shelter. (Her reaction, the court said, was a "succinct 'Wow.'") Applying the four factors, however, the court found (1) the former wife had only a high school education and lacked any special training in

know based on knowledge of the facts of the transaction, the *Price* analysis uses factors identified in omission-of-income cases, such as (1) the spouse's level of education; (2) the spouse's involvement in the family's business and financial affairs; (3) the presence or absence of expenditures that appear unusual in comparison with the family's past levels of income, standard of living, and spending patterns; and (4) the culpable spouse's evasiveness or deceit about the couple's finances. It is significant that in *Price*, the Ninth Circuit found that although the spouse had no reason to know that the deduction gave rise to a substantial understatement, she was found to know enough facts to put her on inquiry notice. The court concluded, however, that she had satisfied her duty to inquire by questioning her husband about the deduction and agreed to sign the return only after he had assured her that a reputable professional had prepared it. In *Bokum v. Commissioner*, the Eleventh Circuit rejected the *Price* analysis in favor of the transactional approach applicable in income omission cases.[657]

In *Park v. Commissioner*, the Fifth Circuit upheld a Tax Court decision that found the spouse had a reason to know under both the *Price* and *Bokum* tests.[658] *Bokum*'s transactional test was satisfied because the spouse knew

---

accounting or bookkeeping; (2) she had no active role in the family's financial affairs beyond managing ordinary household expenses; (3) the couple's lifestyle and standard of living remained relatively constant, but their debts increased substantially; and (4) her husband had deceived her about the family's financial affairs by concealing the extent of his gambling addiction and the enormous amounts of money he had lost. Finally, the court concluded that the taxpayer had taken reasonable steps by reviewing the returns she signed as far as she was able to, and "under the circumstances took reasonable steps to enquire about the tax shelter deductions." Because the Tax Court had not made findings about the equities of holding the spouse liable or whether she had derived benefits from the understatement, the case was remanded to the Tax Court.

In still another case, the Second Circuit affirmed, in an unpublished opinion, a Tax Court decision holding that a former wife, who was trained as a stockbroker, had reason to know that the deductions claimed would give rise to a substantial understatement because the deductions offset virtually all of the couple's income, she had the duty of inquiry, and the couple had lived "lavishly." Cockrell v. Comm'r, TC Memo 1995-551, aff'd per curiam in unpublished opinion, 1997 US App. LEXIS 15227 (2d Cir. 1997).

[657] Bokum v. Comm'r, 992 F2d 1132 (11th Cir. 1993). However, as the Second Circuit has said, "(A)pplying the omission of income (or transactional) test to cases involving the disallowance of deductions would eviscerate the innocent spouse defense, since merely looking at the tax return informs the spouse of the transaction—such as a tax shelter—that gave rise to the deduction." Friedman v. Comm'r, 53 F3d 523 (2d Cir 1995).

[658] Park v. Comm'r, 25 F3d 1289 (5th Cir. 1994). In describing both tests, however, the Fifth Circuit showed a distinct preference for the transactional test, and went to considerable lengths to show that the *Price* approach did not mean that a spouse could avoid reason to know on the ground of ignorance of the tax consequences of the deduction, and that the result under both tests often would be the same. However, the Fifth Circuit has expressly rejected the knowledge-of-the-transaction test, holding "the proper test of a spouse's knowledge in an erroneous deduction case is whether the spouse seeking relief

about the transaction and, applying the *Price* approach, even if she was not aware of sufficient facts to give her reason to know that there was a substantial understatement of tax, she did know of sufficient facts to put her on inquiry notice. According to the court, a spouse must at least read a return before signing it, and if there is a large deduction that substantially offsets income from other sources, must take reasonable steps to determine the accuracy of the return. The spouse in *Park* had a duty of inquiry that she could have complied with by making the inquiries as the spouse did in *Price*. In order not to be charged with constructive knowledge of a deduction-caused understatement, therefore, the spouse must at least read the tax return, inquire about any unusually large deductions, and act prudently by confirming that the return was prepared by a competent tax professional.

In *Pietromonaco v. Commissioner*, income apparently derived from the husband's business was omitted from joint returns. Although the wife paid household expenses, and these expenses exceeded reported income, the circuit court, reversing the Tax Court, found that the wife did not have reason to know of the omitted income.[659] The circuit court said that the reasonably-prudent-taxpayer standard adopted in *Price* is an objective standard but that it is not an "abstraction." It is the reasonably prudent taxpayer "in the particular circumstances in which the taxpayer before us was placed." Factors the court said were relevant on the issue were (1) the taxpayer's education; (2) the spouse's involvement in the family's business and financial affairs; (3) the presence of expenditures that appear lavish or unusual when compared with the family's past income and spending patterns; and (4) the culpable spouse's evasiveness and deceit about the couple's finances.

The circuit court rejected the Tax Court's conclusion that the wife was not an innocent spouse because she knew the couple was overspending.[660] According to the circuit court, the spending was not lavish and the couple's

---

knew or had reason to know that the deduction in question would give rise to a substantial understatement of tax on the joint return." Reser v. Comm'r, 112 F3d 1258 (5th Cir. 1997) (although the wife was a practicing lawyer, her education did not extend to complex questions of tax law such as the basis of stock in shares in an S corporation; she invested money in the business, and expected losses during its start-up period, but she played no significant role in the husband's business; and there was no evidence that she and her husband had lavish or unusual expenditures compared with their normal standard of living).

[659] Pietromonaco v. Comm'r, 3 F3d 1342 (9th Cir. 1993); Kistner v. Comm'r, 94-1 USTC ¶ 50,059 (11th Cir. 1994) (while role as homemaker and complete deference to other spouse alone do not establish "no reason to know," wife acted as reasonably prudent taxpayer because she was not involved in family business, was denied access to financial records, and was threatened with violence if she questioned the tax returns).

[660] The wife did not review the return, saying that she relied on the belief that "it was done by a bookkeeper and that should be sufficient." Significantly, the circuit court was not critical of the wife's failure to review the return.

spending not extraordinary. Also, overspending standing alone "does not preclude relief" under the innocent spouse statute when negative cash flow may have its source in borrowing or savings. It would be inequitable to hold the wife liable for the guilty spouse's omissions, because there was no indication that the couple did not live exactly as they had been living. In short, under the *Price* analysis, the spouse's knowledge of the fact of the deduction is not enough; the spouse must also have had a reason to know or knowledge of enough facts about the transaction giving rise to the deduction to put a reasonably prudent taxpayer on notice of the understatement.

[4] Separate Liability Election for Joint Filers No Longer Married or Otherwise Separated

Section 6015(c) provides a special election that applies to the deficiencies of a taxpayer who, at the time of the election, is no longer married to (or widowed from), is legally separated from, or has been living apart at all times for at least twelve months from the person with whom the taxpayer originally filed the return.[661] If an individual has made an election under Section 6015(c), the individual's liability for any deficiency that is assessed with respect to the return will not exceed the portion of the deficiency properly allocable to the individual.[662] The spouse electing separate liability under these rules generally has the burden of proof with respect to establishing the portion of any deficiency allocable to such individual.

[a] Actual Knowledge Required

For a separate liability election for a taxpayer who is no longer married to, is legally separated from, or has been living apart at all times for at least twelve months from the person with whom the taxpayer originally filed the joint return, the knowledge standard is heightened to "actual knowledge."[663] Knowledge for purposes of Section 6015(c) is an "actual and clear awareness (as opposed to reason to know) of the existence of an item which gives rise to the deficiency (or portion thereof)."[664] The Tax Court held that an electing spouse must have an actual and clear awareness of an item of omitted income, not necessarily whether the entry on the return is or is not correct.[665] The proposed regulations provide that "actual knowledge" of the proper tax treatment

---

[661] IRC § 6015(c).

[662] IRC § 6015(c)(1).

[663] IRC § 6015(c)(3)(C).

[664] Cheshire v. Comm'r, 115 TC 183, 195.

[665] Cheshire v. Comm'r, 115 TC 183, 195.

of an erroneous item is not relevant. For example, a requesting spouse's knowledge of how an erroneous item was treated on a tax return is not relevant to the determination of whether the spouse had actual knowledge.[666] Knowledge of the source of an erroneous item (such as the fact of stock ownership but lack of knowledge that a dividend was paid) is not sufficient to establish actual knowledge.[667] Facts and circumstances that may be relied on in showing that a requesting spouse had actual knowledge include whether a requesting spouse made a deliberate effort to avoid learning about an item in order to be shielded from liability. Joint ownership of an asset also may be a factor supporting the finding of actual knowledge.[668]

[b] Allocation of Deficiency

Innocent spouses who do not make the separate liability election but file an election to limit liability under Section 6015(c) are eligible for taxation on an apportioned, not a joint return, basis.[669] In general, under the allocation of liability election, an item giving rise to a deficiency will be allocated in the same manner as it would have been if both spouses had filed separate returns.[670]

[c] Misuse of Innocent Spouse Relief

Special rules are intended to prevent misuse of the separate tax liability election. A former or separated spouse's separate liability election will be ineffective if the Service can prove that as part of a fraudulent scheme, there were transfers of property between the former or separated spouse and the spouse with whom the joint return was filed.[671] Similarly, the separate liability election of a former or separated spouse will not be effective as to the portion of the deficiency not otherwise allocable to the former spouse if, at the time the former spouse signed the joint return, he or she had actual knowledge of any item giving rise to the deficiency.[672] The intended effect of this provision is to treat the affected item as fully allocable to both spouses. Finally, the portion of the deficiency for which the electing spouse is liable is increased by the value of any "disqualified asset" received from the other spouse.[673] A "disqualified asset" is any property or right to property that was transferred to the electing

---

[666] Prop. Reg. § 1.6015-3(c)(2)(i).

[667] Prop. Reg. § 1.6015-3(c)(2)(ii).

[668] Prop. Reg. § 1.6015-3(c)(2)(iii).

[669] IRC § 6015(d).

[670] IRC § 6015(d)(3)(A).

[671] IRC § 6015(c)(3)(A)(ii).

[672] IRC § 6015(c)(3)(C).

[673] IRC § 6015(c)(4)(A).

spouse if the principal purpose of the transfer was to avoid liability for tax or the payment of tax.[674] A statutory reputable presumption presumes that a transfer is made for tax avoidance purposes if the transfer was made less than one year before the date of the proposed deficiency (the thirty-day letter) advising the taxpayer of the right to administrative appeal. The reputable presumption does not apply to transfers made pursuant to a decree of divorce or separate maintenance.[675] The electing spouse also may rebut the tax-avoidance presumption by showing that the principal purpose of the transfer was not the avoidance of tax or the payment of tax.[676]

[5] Equitable Relief From Liability

If the former or separated spouse would file a separate liability election, but is ineligible to make the election because, for example, he or she has not been widowed, divorced, legally separated, or living apart for at least twelve months from the spouse with whom he or she filed a joint return, the innocent spouse may still apply for relief for any deficiency that is attributable to an erroneous item of the guilty spouse. The Service has the discretionary authority to relieve a spouse or former spouse from joint return liability when (1) taking into account all the facts and circumstances, it is inequitable to hold the innocent spouse liable for any unpaid tax or deficiency in tax, and (2) relief is not available to the innocent spouse under the election procedures.[677] Regulations are to provide more detail about the circumstances the Service will consider to be appropriate to use the grant of authority to provide equitable relief, such as when the spouse claiming relief did not know and had no reason to know that the other spouse took funds intended for the payment of tax and used them for personal benefit instead of payment of tax. This authority to treat a taxpayer equitably is intended to permit the Service not only to grant relief for the guilty spouse's understatement of tax but also to grant relief for the nonpayment of a reported tax.

[a] Revenue Procedure 2000-15

In Revenue Procedure 2000-15,[678] the Service provided guidance establishing the threshold conditions that must be met in order to claim equitable

---

[674] IRC § 6015(c)(4)(B).

[675] IRC § 6015(c)(4)(B)(ii)(II).

[676] IRC § 6015(c)(4)(B)(ii)(II).

[677] IRC § 6015(f).

[678] Rev. Proc. 2000-15, 2000-5 IRB 447 (Jan. 18, 2000), superseding and modifying Notice 98-61, 1998 IRB 12 (Dec. 7, 1998).

relief, the conditions under which such relief ordinarily will be granted, and a partial list of factors that will be considered in determining whether it is inequitable to hold a requesting spouse jointly and severally liable for a deficiency.

The threshold conditions that must be met for equitable relief to be considered by the Service include all of the following:

1. The requesting spouse filed a joint return for the taxable year for which relief is sought.
2. Relief is not available to the requesting spouse under Section 6015(b) or Section 6015(c).
3. The requesting spouse applies for relief no later than two years after the date of the Service's first collection activity after July 22, 1998, with respect to the requesting spouse.
4. The liability remains unpaid. A requesting spouse is eligible to be considered for relief in the form of a refund of liabilities for (a) amounts paid on or after July 22, 1998, and on or before April 15, 1999, and (b) installment payments, made after July 22, 1998, pursuant to an installment agreement entered into with the Service and with respect to which an individual is not in default, that are made after the claim for relief is requested.
5. No assets were transferred between the spouses filing the joint return as part of a fraudulent scheme by such spouses.
6. There were no disqualified assets transferred to the requesting spouse by the nonrequesting spouse. If there were disqualified assets transferred to the requesting spouse by the nonrequesting spouse, relief would be available only to the extent that the liability exceeds the value of such disqualified assets.
7. The requesting spouse did not file the return with fraudulent intent.[679]

In cases where the liability reported on a joint return remains unpaid, equitable relief will ordinarily be granted in cases in which the following conditions are satisfied:

1. At the time relief is requested, the requesting spouse is no longer married to, or is legally separated from, the nonrequesting spouse, or has not been a member of the same household as the nonrequesting spouse at any time during the twelve-month period ending on the date relief was requested.
2. At the time the return was signed, the requesting spouse had no knowledge or reason to know that tax would not be paid. The requesting spouse must establish that it was reasonable for the requesting spouse to believe that the nonrequesting spouse would otherwise pay the reported liability. If the requesting spouse would otherwise

---

[679] Rev. Proc. 2000-15, 2000-5 IRB 447, § 4.01.

qualify for relief, except for the fact that the requesting spouse had no knowledge or reason to know of only a portion of the unpaid liability, then the requesting spouse may be granted relief only to the extent the liability is attributable to such portion.

3. The requesting spouse will suffer economic hardship if relief is not granted.

For purposes of this section, the determination of whether a requesting spouse will suffer economic hardship will be made by the Commissioner or the Commissioner's delegate.[680]

In other cases where a spouse who filed joint returns satisfies the threshold conditions but does not qualify for relief under the rules where tax remains unpaid, Revenue Procedure 2000-15 provides a nonexhaustive list of factors to be "weighed appropriately." Factors weighing in favor of relief include: (1) marital status (e.g., whether divorced, separated, or living apart); (2) economic hardship; (3) abuse; (4) no knowledge and no reason to know; (5) nonrequesting spouse's legal obligation pursuant to a divorce decree or agreement to pay outstanding liability. Factors weighing against relief include: (1) unpaid liability or item giving rise to deficiency attributable to the requesting spouse; (2) knowledge or a reason to know of item giving rise to deficiency; (3) significant benefit from unpaid liability; (4) lack of economic hardship; (5) noncompliance with federal income tax laws; and (6) requesting spouse's legal obligation under divorce decree or agreement to pay liability.[681]

[6] Tax Court Jurisdiction

[a] Section 6015

If a spouse or former spouse seeks relief under either the separate liability election (Section 6015(b)) or the limitation of liability election (Section 6015(c)), the Tax Court has jurisdiction to determine the appropriate relief available if the spouse files a petition on the earlier of (1) the date the Service mails a final determination of relief available to the innocent spouse or (2) the date that is six months after the date the innocent spouse files an election with the Service. Under no circumstances may a petition be filed later than ninety

---

[680] Rev. Proc. 2000-15, 2000-5 IRB 447, § 4.02(1). Relief under § 4.02 is subject to the following limitations: (1) if the return is or has been adjusted to reflect an understatement of tax, relief will be available only to the extent of the liability shown on the return prior to such adjustment, and (2) relief will be available only to the extent that the unpaid liability is allocable to the nonrequesting spouse.

[681] Rev. Proc. 2000-15, 2000-5 IRB 447, § 4.03.

days after the date the Service mails its final determination of relief.[682] The Tax Court is required to adopt rules that provide notice to the nonelecting spouse who filed the joint return concerning the electing spouse's proceeding and give the nonelecting spouse an opportunity to become a party in the proceeding.[683]

The same restrictions on the Service's collection of an assessment apply under Section 6213(a); that is, the Service may not begin an enforcement proceeding within the ninety-day period and, if a petition has been filed, it may not begin an enforcement proceeding until the Tax Court's decision has become final. An electing spouse may obtain an injunction against the Service if it violates these restrictions. However, the statute of limitations on collection is suspended during the proceeding.[684]

[b] Tax Court Review of Equitable Relief Determinations

In a series of four cases, the Tax Court filled in some important aspects of the innocent spouse statute's equitable relief procedure. In *Butler v. Commissioner*, the Tax Court ruled that it has jurisdiction to review the Service's discretionary authority to equitably relieve (or not) a spouse or former spouse from joint return liability.[685] In analyzing the Service's argument that the court did not have the jurisdiction to review its decision at the petitioning spouse's request, the court noted that a strong presumption exists in favor of judicial review of agency action and that Section 6015(e) does not expressly preclude the Tax Court's review. The court also noted that the legislative history supported (or at least did not appear to prohibit) Tax Court review of such matters. Finally, the court determined that the Service's discretionary action was not so broad or specialized as to warrant the conclusion that Congress had committed the decision solely to the Service's discretion.

Having concluded that it had jurisdiction to review the Service's denial of equitable relief under Section 6015(f), the Tax Court found that the factors previously considered under the old innocent spouse rule's equitable standard apply as well to equitable relief under Section 6015(f). The court then looked at the existence of evidence in four categories: (1) the level of education of the spouse claiming innocent spouse status; (2) that spouse's involvement in the family's financial affairs; (3) that spouse's awareness of expenses that were lavish or unusual when compared with the family's past income and expenses; and (4) the guilty spouse's evasiveness and deceit (with respect to the purportedly innocent spouse) concerning the couple's finances. When it considered

---

[682] IRC § 6015(e)(1)(A).

[683] IRC § 6015(e)(4).

[684] IRC § 6015(e)(1)(B).

[685] Butler v. Comm'r, 114 TC 276 (2000).

the totality of this evidence, the Tax Court held that the Service's denial of equitable relief was not unreasonable or without basis. In *Culver v. Commissioner*,[686] the Tax Court appeared to impose a heavier burden on the Service. In *Culver*, the court held that in an innocent spouse case, the Service has the burden of showing that the innocent spouse had actual knowledge of the item in question, and rejected the negligence standard the Service used to argue— that the innocent spouse should have known of his wife's embezzlement based on the family's expenditures. When the Service challenged a wife's innocent spouse status on disallowed loss deductions relating to a cattle raising activity, the Tax Court held that the wife was entitled to the innocent spouse relief because the Service did not prove that she had actual knowledge that the deductions were improper.[687] The Tax Court held:

> [I]n determining whether petitioner had actual knowledge of an improperly deducted item on the return, more is required than petitioner's knowledge that the deduction appears on the return or that her former spouse operated an activity at a loss. Whether petitioner had the requisite knowledge is an essential fact respondent was required to establish under section 6015(c)(3)(C).

Only weeks later, the Tax Court again ruled that its jurisdiction under Section 6015 was not limited to issues arising under the Section 6015(b) separate liability election or the Section 6015(c) limitation of liability provision, but extended to the Service's equitable relief decision under Section 6015(f), essentially for the same reasons articulated in *Butler*.[688] Then, in *Charlton v. Commissioner*, the Tax Court held for a third time that it had the jurisdiction to review the Service's administrative decision under Section 6015(f).[689] In *Charlton*, it also ruled that a husband, not entitled to relief under Section 6015(b), was entitled to relief under Section 6015(c), and that it would review the Service's decision as to the wife under Section 6015(f). In a fourth decision, *Corson v. Commissioner*, the Tax Court held that a nonelecting spouse may participate in the administrative proceeding and a Tax Court case of the electing spouse.[690] In *Corson*, the wife had elected relief under Section 6015(c) and the Service agreed, but, when the Service moved for entry of decision, the husband successfully claimed that he could participate in the proceeding to challenge the Service's action, pursuant to Rule 325 of the Tax Court's rules.

---

[686] Culver v. Comm'r, 116 TC 189 (2001).

[687] King v. Comm'r, 116 TC 198 (2001).

[688] Fernandez v. Comm'r, 114 TC 324 (2000).

[689] Charlton v. Comm'r, 114 TC 333 (2000).

[690] Corson v. Comm'r, 114 TC 354 (2000). See also King v. Comm'r, 115 TC 118 (2000) (nonpetitioning spouse permitted to intervene and challenge petitioning spouse's entitlement to innocent spouse relief).

Under Section 6015(e)(1)(A), there is a means by which the spouse or former spouse who was not a petitioner can intervene in a deficiency proceeding that the other spouse (or former spouse) began to establish relief from joint liability. In this so-called stand-alone proceeding,[691] a spouse electing relief under Section 6015(e)(1)(A) petitions the Tax Court for review of the Service's adverse determination and, pursuant to Section 6015(e)(4), the nonelecting spouse is entitled to "adequate notice" and "an opportunity to become a party" to the proceeding. In *Corson*, there was a deficiency proceeding in which both spouses filed a joint petition in the Tax Court following the sending of a notice of deficiency.[692] The Tax Court ruled that in a joint proceeding, rather than a stand-alone proceeding, the nonelecting spouse was entitled to notice and an opportunity to participate in the negotiations between the Service and the electing spouse. However, in *King v. Commissioner*, the nonelecting spouse was not a petitioner, and the Service had assessed a deficiency against him; the Tax Court held that he was nevertheless entitled to intervene and become a party in the deficiency proceeding the electing spouse brought to review her Section 6015 claims for relief from joint liability.[693] As the Tax Court explained in *Corson* and *King*, Sections 6015(e)(4) and 6015(g)(2) "reveal a concern on the part of the lawmakers with fairness to the nonelecting spouse and with providing him or her with an opportunity to be heard on innocent spouse issues."[694]

---

[691] Corson v. Comm'r, 114 TC 354, 363. See also Interim Rules 324 and 325, Tax Ct. Rules of Prac. & Proc.

[692] Corson v. Comm'r, 114 TC 354.

[693] King v. Comm'r, 115 TC 118.

[694] Corson v. Comm'r, 114 TC 354, 365.

FORM 7B.1
REQUEST FOR INNOCENT SPOUSE RELIEF

Form **8857**	**Request for Innocent Spouse Relief**	
(Rev. December 1998)	**(And Separation of Liability and Equitable Relief)**	OMB No. 1545-1596
Department of the Treasury Internal Revenue Service	▶ Do not file with your tax return. ▶ See instructions.	

Your name	Your social security number

Your current address	Apt. no.

City, town or post office, state, and ZIP code. If a foreign address, see instructions.	Daytime phone no. (optional) ( )

Before you begin, you need to understand the following terms. See instructions for descriptions.

- Separation of Liability
- Joint and Several Liability
- Innocent Spouse Relief
- Understatement of Tax
- Equitable Relief
- Underpayment of Tax

TIP The IRS can help you with your request. If you are working with an IRS employee, you can ask that employee, or you can call 1-800-829-1040.

1   Enter the year(s) for which you are requesting relief from liability of tax (see instructions) . ▶ ....

2   Information about your spouse (or former spouse) to whom you were married at the end of the year(s) on line 1.

Name	Social security number

Current home address (number and street). If a P.O. box, see instructions.	Apt. no.

City, town or post office, state, and ZIP code. If a foreign address, see instructions.	Daytime phone no. (if known) ( )

TIP If you only have an **underpayment of tax** (tax shown on your joint return that was not paid), you may only request **equitable relief.** Skip lines 3 and 4 and see line 5 and its instructions.

3   If you have an **understatement of tax,** you may request **Separation of Liability.** You may be relieved of liability for your spouse's (or former spouse's) part of the liability. However, this relief is available only if you and your spouse (or former spouse):
- Are no longer married, or
- Are legally separated, or
- Have lived apart at all times during the 12-month period prior to the date you file this form.

If one of the above conditions apply, attach a statement as explained on page 3 and check here . . . ▶ ☐

4   If you have an **understatement of tax** due to erroneous items of your spouse (or former spouse), you may be allowed **Innocent Spouse Relief.** Attach a statement as explained on page 4 and check here . . . . . ▶ ☐

5   If you have an **underpayment of tax** or you do not qualify for relief under **3** or **4** above, we will automatically consider whether you qualify for **Equitable Relief.** Attach a statement as explained on page 4 and check here . . . . ▶ ☐

Where To File: Generally, send this form to: **Internal Revenue Service Center, Cincinnati, OH 45999-0857.** But if you are meeting with an IRS employee or you received an IRS notice of deficiency, see page 2.

Under penalties of perjury, I declare that I have examined this form and any accompanying schedules and statements, and to the best of my knowledge and belief, they are true, correct, and complete. Declaration of preparer (other than taxpayer) is based on all information of which preparer has any knowledge.

Sign Here Keep a copy of this form for your records.	Your signature ▶			Date
Paid Preparer's Use Only	Preparer's signature ▶	Date	Check if self-employed ☐	Preparer's social security no.
	Firm's name (or yours if self-employed) and address ▶			EIN
				ZIP code

For Privacy Act and Paperwork Reduction Act Notice, see page 4.   Cat. No. 24647V   Form **8857** (Rev. 12-98)

General Instructions

A Change To Note

The Internal Revenue Service (IRS) Restructuring and Reform Act of 1998 made it easier to be relieved from liability of tax related to your spouse (or former spouse). You can now request innocent spouse relief for an understatement of tax no matter how small the amount. If you are divorced, separated, or no longer living with your spouse, you may now request separation of liability between you and your spouse (or former spouse) for an understatement of tax on a joint return. Also, the IRS will consider your request for equitable relief in situations where it would be unfair to hold you liable for tax that should be paid only by your spouse (or former spouse).

The new law applies to any tax liability arising after July 22, 1998, or any tax liability that was unpaid as of that date. For relief of liability for amounts that were paid as of that date, check the box on line 4 and attach the requested statement.

Purpose of Form

Use Form 8857 to request relief from liability for tax, plus related penalties and interest, that you believe should be paid only by your spouse (or former spouse). You generally must have filed a joint return for the year(s) for which you are requesting relief (but see **Community Property Laws** on page 3). The IRS will evaluate your request and tell you if you qualify.

You may be allowed one or more of these three types of relief:

- Separation of liability (see page 3),
- Innocent spouse relief (see page 4), or
- Equitable relief (see page 4).

Attach a statement to Form 8857 explaining why you qualify for relief. Complete the statement using the best information you have available. The IRS will ask you for additional information if needed, or you may provide additional information at any time.

Additional Information

See Pub. 971 for more details.

When and Where To File

When to file. Generally, you should file Form 8857 as soon as you become aware of an unpaid tax liability that you believe should be paid only by your spouse (or former spouse). The following are some of the ways you may become aware of such a liability.

- The IRS has examined your tax return.
- The IRS sends you a notice.

You must file Form 8857 no later than 2 years after the first IRS attempt to collect the tax from you. However, you may file it any time up to 2 years after the first IRS attempt to collect the tax from you that occurs after July 22, 1998. Examples of attempts to collect the tax from you include garnishment of your wages or a notice of intent to levy against your wages or property you own.

Where to file. Do not file Form 8857 with your tax return. Instead, see below.

IF . . .	THEN file Form 8857 with . . .
You are meeting with an IRS employee for an examination, examination appeal, or collection,	That IRS employee.
You received an IRS notice of deficiency, and the 90-day period specified in the notice has not expired.*	The IRS employee named in the notice. Attach a copy of the notice.
None of the situations above apply to you,	**Internal Revenue Service Center Cincinnati, OH 45999-0857**

*Before the end of the 90-day period, you should file a petition with the Tax Court, as explained in the notice. By doing so, you preserve your rights if the IRS is unable to properly consider your request before the end of the 90-day period. Include the information that supports your position, including when and why you filed Form 8857, in your petition to the Tax Court. The time for filing with the Tax Court is not extended while the IRS is considering your request.

Tax Court Review of Request

You may petition (ask) the Tax Court to review your request for innocent spouse relief or separation of liability (but not equitable relief) if:

- The IRS sends you a determination notice denying, in whole or in part, your request for relief, or
- You do not receive a determination notice from the IRS within 6 months from the date you filed Form 8857.

You may petition the Tax Court to review your case no later than the end of the 90-day period that begins on the date the IRS mails you a determination notice. See Pub. 971 for details on petitioning the Tax Court to review your request.

Joint and Several Liability

Generally, joint and several liability applies to all joint returns. This means that both you and your spouse (or former spouse) are liable for any **underpayment of tax** (tax shown on a return but not paid) plus any **understatement of tax** (defined next) that may become due later. This is true even if a divorce decree states that your former spouse will be responsible for any amounts due on previously filed joint returns. Form 8857 allows you to request that joint and several liability not apply to part or all of any unpaid tax.

Understatement of Tax

An understatement of tax, or deficiency, is generally the difference between the total amount of tax that the IRS determines should have been shown on the return, and the amount that actually was shown on the return.

Example. You and your spouse (or former spouse) file a joint return showing $5,000 of tax, which was fully paid. The IRS later audits the return and finds $10,000 of income that your spouse earned but did not report. With the additional income, the total tax becomes $6,500. You and your spouse are both liable for the $1,500 understatement of tax.

Underpayment of Tax

An underpayment is tax that is properly shown on the return, but has not been paid.

Example. You filed a joint return that properly reflects your income and deductions, but showed an unpaid balance due of $5,000. You and your spouse were getting divorced. You gave your spouse $2,500 and your spouse promised to pay the full $5,000, but did not. You and your spouse are both liable for the $5,000 underpayment of tax.

Community Property Laws

You must generally follow community property laws when filing a tax return if you are married and live in a community property state. Community property states are Arizona, California, Idaho, Louisiana, Nevada, New Mexico, Texas, Washington, and Wisconsin. Generally, community property laws require you to allocate community income and expenses equally between both spouses. However, state community property laws are not taken into account in determining whether an item belongs to you or to your spouse (or former spouse) for purposes of requesting any relief from liability.

Note: *If you were married and filed a separate return in a community property state and are now liable for an underpayment or understatement of tax you believe should be paid only by your spouse (or former spouse), you may be allowed equitable relief.*

Specific Instructions

Your Current Home Address

Foreign address. Enter the information in the following order: city, province or state, and country. Follow the country's practice for entering the postal code. Please do not abbreviate the country name.

Line 1

If you want to request relief for more than one tax year, you only need to file one Form 8857. If you are filing Form 8857 for multiple years, clearly indicate in the statement(s) you attach the type(s) of relief you are requesting for each year.

Line 2—Information About Your Spouse (or Former Spouse)

Enter the current name and social security number (SSN) of the person to whom you were married at the end of the year(s) listed on line 1. If the name of your spouse (or former spouse) shown on that year's tax return(s) is different from the current name, enter it in parentheses after the current name. For example: Jane Maple (formerly Jane Oak). Enter the current address and phone number if you know it.

P.O. box. Enter the box number instead of the street address **only** if you do not know the street address.

Foreign address. Enter the information as explained under **Your Current Home Address.**

Note: *The IRS is required to inform your spouse (or former spouse) if you request separation of liability or innocent spouse relief, and to allow your spouse (or former spouse) to participate in the determination of the amount of relief from liability.*

Line 3—Separation of Liability

If you filed a joint return for the year(s) entered on line 1, you may be able to separate liability for any understatement of tax on the return(s) between you and your spouse (or former spouse). Generally, you can request to do so if you and that person:

● Are no longer married, or

● Are legally separated, or

● Have lived apart at all times during the 12-month period prior to the date you file Form 8857.

Note: *A widow or widower is considered no longer married.*

Requesting Separation of Liability

Check the box on line 3 and attach a statement to Form 8857. Show the total amount of the understatement of tax. For each item that resulted in an understatement of tax, explain whether the item is attributable to you, your spouse (or former spouse), or both of you. For example, unreported income earned by your spouse (or former spouse), plus any related self-employment tax, would be allocated to that person. An overstated deduction of home mortgage interest on a home you owned jointly that was paid from a joint checking account would generally be allocated equally between both of you. See Pub. 971 for more details.

Exception. If, at the time you signed the joint return, you knew about any item that would result in part or all of the understatement, then your request will not apply to that part of the understatement.

Line 4—Innocent Spouse Relief

 If you qualify for separation of liability, you may not need to request innocent spouse relief. The amount of relief allowed by requesting separation of liability will usually be equal to or greater than the amount allowed by requesting innocent spouse relief. However, you may still request innocent spouse relief if you wish.

You may be allowed innocent spouse relief if:

● You filed a joint return for the year(s) entered on line 1,

● There is an understatement of tax on the return(s) that is due to erroneous items of your spouse (or former spouse),

● You can show that when you signed the return(s) you did not know and had no reason to know that the understatement of tax existed (or the extent to which the understatement existed), and

● Taking into account all the facts and circumstances, it would be unfair to hold you liable for the understatement of tax.

Erroneous Items

Any income, deduction, or credit is an erroneous item if:

● It is omitted from or incorrectly reported on the joint return,

● It is attributable to your spouse (or former spouse),

● It results in an understatement of tax, **and**

● You either did not know and had no reason to know about the understatement or the extent of it (see **Partial Innocent Spouse Relief** next).

Partial Innocent Spouse Relief

If you knew about any of the erroneous items, but not the full extent of the item(s), you may be allowed relief for part of the understatement. Explain in the statement you attach to Form 8857 how much you knew and why you did not know, and had no reason to know, the full extent of the item(s).

Requesting Innocent Spouse Relief

Check the box on line 4 and attach a statement to Form 8857 explaining why you believe you qualify. The statement will vary depending on your circumstances, but should include the following:

● The amount and a detailed description of each erroneous item, including why you had no reason to know about the item or the extent to which you knew about the item,

● The amount of the understatement of tax for which you are liable and are seeking relief, **and**

● Why you believe it would be unfair to hold you liable for the understatement of tax.

Line 5—Equitable Relief

You may be allowed equitable relief if, taking into account all the facts and circumstances, it would be unfair to hold you liable for any understatement or underpayment of tax that should be paid only by your spouse (or former spouse).

You can only be allowed equitable relief for an underpayment of tax, or part or all of any understatement of liability, that does not qualify for either separation of liability or innocent spouse relief. You should request separation of liability or innocent spouse relief for any understatement of tax, unless you are sure you are not eligible. The IRS will consider equitable relief if it determines that innocent spouse relief and separation of liability do not apply.

Requesting Equitable Relief

Attach an explanation of why you believe it would be unfair to hold **you** liable for the tax instead of your spouse (or former spouse). If you are attaching a statement for separation of liability or innocent spouse relief, include only any additional information you believe supports your request for equitable relief.

Privacy Act and Paperwork Reduction Act Notice. We ask for the information on this form to carry out the Internal Revenue laws of the United States. We need it to determine the amount of liability, if any, of which you may be relieved. Internal Revenue Code section 6015 allows relief of liability. If you request relief of liability, you must give us the information requested on this form. Code section 6109 requires you to provide your social security number. Routine uses of this information include giving it to the Department of Justice for civil and criminal litigation, and to cities, states, and the District of Columbia for use in administering their tax laws. If you do not provide all the information in a timely manner, we may not be able to process your request.

You are not required to provide the information requested on a form that is subject to the Paperwork Reduction Act unless the form displays a valid OMB control number. Books or records relating to a form or its instructions must be retained as long as their contents may become material in the administration of any Internal Revenue law. Generally, tax returns and return information are confidential, as required by Code section 6103.

The time needed to complete and file this form will vary depending on individual circumstances. The estimated average time is: **Learning about the law or the form,** 17 min.; **Preparing the form,** 17 min.; and **Copying, assembling, and sending the form to the IRS,** 20 min.

If you have comments concerning the accuracy of this time estimate or suggestions for making this form simpler, we would be happy to hear from you. You can write to the Tax Forms Committee, Western Area Distribution Center, Rancho Cordova, CA 95743-0001. **DO NOT** send the form to this address. Instead, see **When and Where To File** on page 2.

¶ 7B.11 PROCEDURAL MATTERS

[1] Notice

The IRS Restructuring and Reform Act of 1998 added two procedural requirements when the Service seeks to impose a penalty. Under the first requirement, the Service must include, with each notice of penalty, the name of the penalty and the section of the Code under which the penalty is imposed. Under the second requirement, no penalty may be assessed unless the immediate supervisor of the Service employee making the determination (or higher level official if one is delegated) personally approves the initial determination of the assessment of the penalty in writing.[695] This preassessment approval does not apply to delinquency penalties (Section 6651), failure to pay estimated individual income tax (Section 6654), and failure to pay corporation estimated tax (Section 6655), or any other penalty automatically calculated through electronic means.

[2] Burden of Proof

[a] Shifting the Burden of Proof—In General

In trials of tax cases involving most issues, the taxpayer who is the petitioner in a Tax Court case, or the plaintiff in a refund suit in either a district court or the Court of Federal Claims, must carry two burdens: (1) the burden of going forward with prima facie evidence to support a finding contrary to the Service's determination and (2) the burden of proof or persuasion; that is, the burden of proving that the Service's determination is in error by a preponderance of the evidence.[696] One presumption that allocates the burden of going forward with evidence to the taxpayer is the presumption that the Service's de-

---

[695] IRC § 6751, added by 1998 Act § 3306(a), applicable to notices issued, and penalties assessed after December 31, 2000. CRTRA, Pub. L. No. 106-554, has extended certain deadlines for IRS compliance with penalty, interest, and installment agreement notice requirements. CRTRA Section 302 extends the deadline until June 30, 2001, for the Service to comply with Section 6715, which requires every notice imposing a penalty to include the name of the penalty, the penalty Code section and the computation of the penalty. CRTRA also extends the time for the Service to comply with Section 6631, which requires that every notice that includes interest must include a detailed interest computation and cite the Code section under which interest is being imposed. CRTRA also extends until September 1, 2001, the time for the Service to send every taxpayer that has entered into an installment agreement an annual statement of the starting balance, amounts paid during the year, and the year-end balance.

[696] In a refund suit, the taxpayer also must prove the amount of the overpayment. The legislative history cites Danville Plywood Corp. v. United States, 63 AFTR2d 89-1036 (Ct. Cl. 1989).

ficiency determination or assessment is presumed to be correct. According to the Conference Report on the 1998 Act, the presumption of correctness was judicially recognized, but Congress had never expressly recognized it, although it was assumed to have done so by failing to provide otherwise in legislation.[697] It is well to remember these dual burdens in attempting to understand the significance of the 1998 Act's provision entitled "Burden of Proof."[698]

New Section 7491 provides that in "any court proceeding," if (1) the taxpayer introduces "credible evidence" on any factual issue relevant to ascertaining the taxpayer's liability for any income, estate, or gift tax, the "burden of proof" is shifted to the Service on that issue, provided that on the issue (2) the taxpayer has complied with any requirement to substantiate "any item," (3) the taxpayer has maintained required under the Code and has cooperated with reasonable requests by the Service for witnesses, information, documents, meetings, and interviews, and (4) in the case of a partnership, corporation, or trust, the taxpayer has a net worth of no more than $7 million, the net worth limitation that applies to the awarding of fees under Section 7430 of the Code, which incorporates the Equal Access to Justice Act, 28 USC 2412(d)(1)(b).

To understand each of the four conditions to shifting the burden of proof, the Conference Report is required reading.[699] First, the taxpayer must present "credible evidence," which is defined as "the quality of evidence which, after critical analysis, the court would find sufficient upon which to base a decision if no contrary evidence were submitted (without regard to the judicial presumption of IRS correctness)." Mere implausible factual assertions, frivolous claims, or tax protestor-type arguments are not credible evidence, nor is evidence that the court does not find credible.[700]

If, after hearing all the evidence, the court believes that the evidence is equally balanced, assuming the taxpayer has met all the other conditions of the provision, the court must find that the Service has not sustained its burden of proof. Second, the substantiation requirement means that the taxpayer must comply with all the substantiation requirements of the Code and regulations, whether those substantiation requirements are those imposed for specific deductions, such as those imposed for charitable contributions, or meals, entertainment, and travel expenses. The third requirement is that the taxpayer

---

[697] Conf. Rep. (CCH), at 55.

[698] IRC § 7491, added by 1998 Act § 3001(a), effective for court proceedings arising out of examinations beginning after July 22, 1998, and, in cases where there is no examination, court proceedings occuring after July 22, 1998.

[699] Conf. Rep. (CCH), at 56–59.

[700] See, e.g., Higbee v. Comm'r, 116 TC No. 28 (2001) (taxpayers did not claim uncompensated casualty losses on their original return, and at the Tax Court trial presented only the taxpayer husband's testimony of his estimate of the cost of repairs and uncertified Small Claims pleading in the taxpayers' alleged suit against the insurance company for the cost of repairs; held, the evidence did not constitute credible evidence).

must maintain records the Code and regulations require. Presumably this applies to all recordkeeping requirements, not only ones dealing with substantiation of deductions. Finally, the cooperation requirement means that the taxpayer must provide to the revenue agent, within a reasonable period of time, "access to and inspection of witnesses, information, and documents within the control of the taxpayer, as reasonably requested," including any witnesses, information, and documents located in foreign countries, as well as providing English translations of documents. The taxpayer must establish the applicability of any privilege the taxpayer may claim. Cooperation also means that the taxpayer must exhaust all available administrative remedies, such as protesting adjustments for Appeals review. Cooperation does not mean, however, that the taxpayer must extend the statute of limitations on assessment. No net worth limitation applies in the case of individuals, but partnerships, corporations, and trusts having a net worth in excess of $7 million may shift the burden of proof to the Service.

[b] Burden of Proof on Penalties

In any court proceeding involving a civil penalty on an individual, the Service has the burden of producing evidence that it is appropriate to apply to a particular penalty to the taxpayer before the court may impose the penalty.[701] According to the Conference Report, this provision is not intended to require the Service to introduce evidence to support defenses to the penalty, such as reasonable cause or substantial authority. The taxpayer has the burden of producing evidence to support any defense to a penalty.

[c] Use of Statistical Information on Unrelated Taxpayers

In court proceedings of individual taxpayers, the Service has the burden of proof on any item of income which the Service reconstructed through the use of statistical information of unrelated taxpayers.[702] This provision is directed at the Service's use of such statistical information as Bureau of Labor Statistics data to establish a taxpayer's income in a civil case. Just how frequently the Service has used this kind of information to establish a taxpayer's income is unclear, but court decisions show that the Service has used these statistics to establish living expenses in civil penalty cases when the Service used an indirect method of proving that the taxpayer had unreported income.

---

[701] IRC § 7491(c).
[702] IRC § 7491(b).

B. PENALTIES ON THIRD PARTIES

¶ 7B.12 AIDING AND ABETTING UNDERSTATEMENTS: SECTION 6701

Section 6701(a) imposes a $1,000 penalty ($10,000 for corporate taxpayers) for aiding and abetting in the understatement of tax. This civil penalty is equivalent to the criminal penalty for aiding and assisting in the preparation of a false return.[703] The penalty is imposed on a person who (1) aids or assists, procures, or advises in the preparation or presentation of any portion of a return or other document in a tax matter; (2) knows or has reason to believe that the portion will be used in a material matter arising under the tax laws; and (3) knows that the portion, if used, will result in the understatement of another person's tax liability.[704] The penalty for aiding and assisting understatements applies to any person who "has reason to believe" that a portion of a document will be used in any material matter arising under the internal revenue laws.[705]

---

[703] IRC § 7206(2).

[704] For purposes of the knowledge element, the preparation of a document that is false and the preparer's guilty knowledge about the use of the document need not exist at the same time; i.e., at the time the preparer alters a document he may not know that it will be submitted to the Service and used in a material matter, a later audit. Section 6701 imposes liability either for preparing or presenting a document, and guilty knowledge may be present at the time the document is submitted. See Cheshire v. United States, 80 AFTR2d ¶ 97-5565 (MD Ala. 1997).

IRC § 6701(a), added by TEFRA, Pub. L. No. 248, HR 4961, 97th Cong., 2d Sess. § 324. This provision was effective on September 4, 1982. See Mitchell v. United States, 89-2 USTC ¶ 9494 (Bankr. D. Wash. 1989) (Section 6701 requires that person assessed know or have actual knowledge of understatement of tax liability), aff'd, 90-2 USTC ¶ 50,495 (WD Wash. 1990), aff'd, 977 F2d 1318 (9th Cir. 1992); Mattingly v. United States, 924 F2d 785 (8th Cir. 1991) ("We believe actual knowledge, as opposed to the less stringent willful blindness, is required."), aff'd on this point, 90-2 USTC ¶ 50,495 (WD Wash. 1990) (evidence of direct involvement found lacking); compare Kuchan v. United States, 679 F. Supp. 764 (ND Ill. 1988) (accountant prepared transmittal letters that were to be attached to Schedules C of individual taxpayers liable for penalty). But it has been held that the penalty may be imposed even if the taxpayer has not been shown actually to have understated tax, or even whether the taxpayer ever files a return. Golletz v. United States, 91-1 USTC ¶ 50,233 (ND Ill. 1991) (accountant submitted false documents at Appeals conference); Kuchan v. United States, supra; Bailey v. United States, 77 AFTR2d ¶ 96-734 (D. Ariz. 1996) (preparer claimed that because the claim for refund reported on the amended return was time-barred, no penalty could be imposed; held, statutory language "if so used" indicates that it need not be used; the focus is on the intent of the aider and abetter).

[705] Pub. L. No. 239, HR 3299, 101st Cong., 1st Sess., Subtitle G, IRC § 6701(a)(2), amended by IMPACT, § 7335(a)(1)–7335(a)(3), effective December 31, 1989. The penalty circumstance that a document, or portion of a document, will result in the understatement of another person's tax liability, raises the question about whether some documents

Liability is imposed on a person who acts in violation of the statute through a subordinate (e.g., an officer, director, employee, or agent of the taxpayer) by either ordering or causing the subordinate to act, or knowing of and not attempting to prevent the subordinate from acting.[706] In connection with this penalty, it is not necessary that the person primarily responsible for the document—that is to say, the taxpayer in the case of a return—know of or consent to the understatement.[707]

There is a one penalty per person per period rule. Thus, one penalty is imposed for any false document "relating to" any taxpayer for any tax year.[708] A single document resulting in an understatement by one individual taxpayer for two years or two individual taxpayers for one year can result in a $2,000 penalty assessment. However, two documents resulting in one individual's understatement, even for two different items (for one taxable year),[709] can result only in a single $1,000 penalty.

---

may not be subject to the penalty. For example, it has been held that the penalty does not apply to a Subchapter S corporation's return, in contrast to the related Forms K-1, because the S corporation is not a taxpayer. Mitchell v. United States, 977 F2d 1318 (9th Cir. 1992). On the other hand, a Form 5300 has been held to relate to the corporate tax liability of the sponsor of the pension plan. Berger v. United States, 78 AFTR2d ¶ 96-5040 (2d Cir. 1996). In reversing the district court, which had held that a taxpayer does not rely on a Form 5300 in the same way the taxpayer in an S corporation relies on a Form K-1, the court of appeals in *Berger* said, "The question under [S]ection 6701 . . . is not the nature or extent of another taxpayer's reliance upon the document, but rather whether the preparer knows or has reason to believe that the document 'will be used in connection with any material matter arising under the internal revenue laws,' . . . and further knows that 'if so used,' it 'would result in an understatement of the liability for another person.'"

[706] IRC § 6701(c).

[707] IRC § 6701(d).

[708] IRC § 6701(b). See Kuchan v. United States, 679 F. Supp. 764 (ND Ill. 1998) (penalty imposed based on letters sent to 191 investors). A preparer of an S corporation return and related Form K-1 is liable for the penalty for each Form K-1 filed; but not for the S corporation's return because the S corporation was not a taxpayer. Mitchell v. United States, 977 F2d 1318 (9th Cir. 1992) ("We hold that the amount of the penalty . . . is determined by looking to the type of person whose *tax liability* is understated."). See Berger v. United States, 78 AFTR2d ¶ 96-5040 (2d Cir. 1996), where the circuit court specifically did not rule on whether the penalty for filing false Form 5300s could apply not only to plan sponsors but to beneficiaries as well, but indicating that imposing multiple Section 6701 penalties to the beneficiaries of the plans could lead to "disproportionate liability."

[709] Where carryovers and carrybacks are involved, the issue is whether the carryover or carryback item "relates to" the original tax year. Emanual v. United States, 705 F. Supp. 434 (ND Ill. 1989) (preparer of both tax return and tentative refund claim on Form 1045 is subject to single penalty because both forms relate to same tax year); cf. Mattingly v. United States, 90-1 USTC ¶ 50,012 (ED Mo. 1989) ("documents claiming tax credits for years prior to and subsequent to the original tax return 'relate to' the tax period for which the tax credits are claimed"), rev'd on this issue, 924 F2d 785 (8th Cir. 1991) ("When a § 6701 penalty is imposed with respect to an understatement document in one

The aiding and assisting or preparer penalty is coordinated with other penalties on third parties. The penalty for aiding in understatement of a tax liability and the penalty for promoting a tax shelter (Section 6700) cannot be assessed with respect to the same document.[710] However, both penalties can be imposed for separate documents—e.g., a Section 6700 penalty for the promotional material and a Section 6701 penalty for a later Form K-1 to investors. Also, the return preparer penalties imposed by Section 6694 cannot be assessed as to any document for which a penalty is assessed under Section 6701. However, the person liable for the Section 6701 penalty for aiding in preparing a false return or document may be prosecuted under the criminal provisions of the Code, such as for the felony of aiding and assisting in the preparation of a false return.[711]

If a person engages in conduct subject to penalty under Section 6701 by aiding or assisting a taxpayer in understating tax, the Service may ask a federal district court to enjoin the person from engaging in the proscribed conduct.[712] Such an injunction serves to ensure that promoters will not continue prohibited conduct after the shelter has been organized, such as providing false partnership returns.[713] When one moves from a description of the aiding-and-abetting penalty to its application, confusion sets in. This is so because the statute mixes an element of the willfulness standard ("know") and conduct derived from a negligence standard ("reason to believe"). As a result, the government has contended that the preparer "should have known" that an understatement would result from his tax opinion, although Section 6701 does not use the term.[714] The government has also unsuccessfully argued that the knowledge element permits "willful blindness" to be considered.[715] Thus, the knowledge element means "actual knowledge" and requires evidence from which the finder of fact could find that actual knowledge.[716] The standard of

---

tax period, another penalty may not be imposed on a carryover document of the same taxpayer, based on the same original understatement."); see also Berger v. United States, 79 AFTR2d ¶ 97-879 (D. Conn. 1997) ("Although the Forms 5300 may have resulted in an understatement of tax liability for previous tax years as to each of plaintiff's corporate clients, the conduct allegedly warranting imposition of a section 6701 penalty was the alleged falsification of the forms 5300 . . . [and so] the IRS improperly imposed multiple penalties upon the plaintiff based on each of the 'tax years affected.'").

[710] IRC § 6701(f)(3), added by IMPACT, § 7735(b)(1), effective December 31, 1989.

[711] IRC § 7206(2).

[712] IRC §§ 7408(a), 7408(b), amended by TRA 1984, Pub. L. No. 98-369, § 143.

[713] See Conference Committee Report, HR Rep. No. 861, 98th Cong., 2d Sess. 983–984 (1984), reprinted in 1984-3 CB 237–238; Explanation of Senate Fin. Comm. (CCH) 434 (Apr. 5, 1984).

[714] Gard v. United States, 92-1 USTC ¶ 50,159 (ND Ga. 1992).

[715] Mattingly v. Comm'r, 924 F2d 785 (8th Cir. 1991).

[716] Mattingly v. Comm'r, 924 F2d 785 (8th Cir. 1991) (liability finding upheld because of preparer's knowledge shown by his substantial activities in selling tax shelters).

proof has been said to be a preponderance of the evidence, not the fraud standard of clear and convincing evidence.[717]

¶ 7B.13 PROMOTING ABUSIVE TAX SHELTERS: SECTION 6700

The villain in the tax drama that unfolded from the mid-1970s until at least the passage of TRA 1986 was the tax shelter promoter. Prior to 1986, most of the penalties in the Code applied directly to such individuals, although other penalties dealt with the characteristic elements of tax shelters. For example, the overvaluation penalty applied because property used in tax shelters was frequently overvalued. The substantial understatement penalty dealt with legal positions that were undefensible in the face of existing authority, and the aiding and abetting penalties were aimed at the advisers or appraisers. However, in Section 6700, Congress set its sights on the promoters of tax shelters and those assisting in selling the promotion to taxpayers.

United States v. Bailey, 77 AFTR2d ¶ 96-734 (D. Ariz. 1996) (summary judgment granted; the preparer's knowledge that the taxpayers did not own the amount of stock reported in the year of the amended return was reflected in his own affidavit). Compare Warner v. United States, 726 F. Supp. 1287 (SD Fla. 1989) (the preparer claimed he did not know that the claimed deductions were incorrect and raised a triable issue of fact). In *Warner*, the district court said that "the scienter element of section 6701(a)(3) requires the government to show that the [preparer] was directly involved in aiding or assisting in the preparation or presentation of a false or fraudulent document under the tax laws or directly procured a subordinate to do so"; and that "if the [preparer] knew that portions of the return as prepared and presented would result in the understatement of tax liability, those portions of the returns must necessarily be false and fraudulent." 726 F. Supp., at 1289, 1291. Fraud thus "implies intentional wrongdoing and bad faith," which does not necessarily exist merely because a return is incorrect; the error may be due to negligence. Id.

[717] Id. See also Barr v. United States, 67 F3d 469 (2d Cir. 1995) (adopting the preponderance of evidence standard in aiding and abetting cases).

Section 6700 makes organizers of tax shelters[718] and salesmen of interests in tax shelters subject to penalty under the Code.[719] If, in addition to being an organizer or salesman, an individual who furnishes to another person, either directly or indirectly, (1) a statement about the allowability of any tax benefit arising out of holding an interest in the shelter (the tax opinion) that the organizer or salesman "knows or has reason to know is false or fraudulent as to any material matter"[720] or (2) a gross valuation overstatement about a material matter, is liable for the penalty.[721]

It is a fairly straightforward exercise to determine whether a person has been the organizer of a tax shelter or salesman and has furnished to investors in offering materials a fraudulent tax opinion or a grossly inflated appraisal as part of offering materials. However, it has been more difficult to determine the amount of the penalty. Does the penalty apply to the sale of each limited partnership interest or of each lithograph, book, or the like? Or is the activity the entire promotion? The statute now states that organization activities for "each entity or arrangement shall be treated as (a) separate activity,"[722] and participa-

---

[718] IRC § 6700(a)(1)(A). The organizer is one who "organizes (or assists in the organization of)—(i) a partnership or other entity, (ii) any investment plan or arrangement, or any other plan or arrangement." Id. The statute uses the term "any person" who organizes or sells, and this term has been interpreted to include the partnership as well as the partner promoting the shelter. Bailey Vaught & Robertson v. United States, 828 F. Supp. 442 (ND Tex. 1993). As a result, one court approved the assessments of penalties against both the partners and the partnership, but another court has held to the contrary. Compare Bailey Vaught & Robertson v. United States, supra, with In re Tax Refund Litig., 766 F. Supp. 1248, 1256–1257 (EDNY 1991).

[719] IRC § 6700(a)(1)(B). The seller is one who "participates (directly or indirectly) in the sale of any interest in an entity or plan or arrangement referred to in (Section 6700(a)(1)(A))." Id.

[720] IRC § 6700(a)(2)(A). A promoter was found to have known that his statements about the allowability of interest deductions were false or fraudulent because he knew the "tax shelters were sham transactions in which participants could write off approximately twelve dollars for every dollar of actual out-of-pocket expenses," and this conclusion was supported by evidence that the promoter sent a confidential "comfort letter" to one of his investors indicating that the deductions were not "legitimate" and warning the investor to "[b]e sure this letter does not get into the wrong hands. If IRS would become aware of the offsetting character of your note you would likely lose your interest deduction." Kersting v. United States, 85 AFTR2d 2000-1128 (9th Cir. 2000).

[721] The "know or has reason to know" language suggests that the organizer will not be able to claim an ignorance defense and that "willful blindness" or ignoring obvious facts is sufficient to subject the organizer or salesman to liability. A gross valuation overstatement is any statement of value of property or services "if the value so stated exceeds 200 percent of the amount determined to be the correct valuation . . . " IRC § 6700(b)(1)(A). Not only must the appraisal be twice the actual value, but it must be "directly related to the amount of any deduction or credit allowable . . . to any participant." IRC § 6700(b)(1)(B).

[722] IRC § 6700(a).

tion in each sale of an interest in a tax shelter is treated as a separate activity.[723] Once it is established that a person has engaged in an organizational activity or participated in a sale, the amount of the penalty is $1,000 unless the promoter or salesman establishes that 100 percent of the gross income "derived (or to be derived)" by the person from the activity is less than $1,000.[724] Both the terms "gross income" and "derived (or to be derived)" are vague enough to cause dispute about whether the promoter-organizer, for example, is entitled to deduct the costs of the property that is the subject of the offering. Also, there can be argument about whether the "to be derived" language would require consideration of promissory notes that the IRS would say in the investor cases should not be recognized.[725]

¶ 7B.14 INJUNCTIONS AGAINST PROMOTERS AND AIDERS AND ABETTORS

Apart from penalties for promoting abusive tax shelters (Section 6700) and for aiding and abetting understatements of tax liability (Section 6701), the organizer or salesman or the aider and abettor can be enjoined from engaging in further conduct subject to penalty.[726] Section 7408(a) authorizes a civil action in the name of the United States to be instituted at the request of the IRS in a federal district court for the judicial district in which the person resides, has his principal place of business, or has engaged in the conduct subject to the

---

[723] IRC § 6700(a). The clarification made in Section 6700 by IMPACT should eliminate the difference in judicial interpretation of the penalty base.

[724] IRC § 6700(a). Under prior law, courts of appeals held that the penalty of $1,000 is a minimum penalty, not to be imposed with regard to each sale unless that amount exceeded 10 percent, as Section 6700 then provided, of the gross income derived by the taxpayer against whom it had been made. Spriggs v. United States, 600 F. Supp. 789 (ED Va. 1987), aff'd, 850 F2d 690 (4th Cir. 1988); Gates v. United States, 874 F2d 584 (8th Cir. 1989); Bond v. Comm'r, 872 F2d 898 (9th Cir. 1989).

[725] The Service may look only to unrealized amounts the promoter or other person may reasonably expect to realize. In re Tax Refund Litigation, 989 F2d 1290 (2d Cir. 1993) (unrealized one-time general partner fees included in penalty base). However, in *Tax Refund Litigation*, the circuit court also held that the income of the general partners was includable in the penalty base.

[726] IRC § 7408(a). See, e.g., United States v. Estate Preservation Servs., 38 F. Supp. 2d 846 (ED Cal. 1998), aff'd, 202 F3d 1093 (9th Cir. 2000) (at the Service's request, the court enjoined tax shelter promoters not only from promoting a tax shelter they had already organized, but also—due to prior action—from promoting any abusive tax shelter plan).

penalty.[727] Jurisdiction of federal district courts to hear these actions and to fashion appropriate orders is under the All-Writs Statute "as may be necessary or appropriate for the enforcement of the internal revenue laws."[728] An organizer, salesman, or aider and abettor may be enjoined from engaging in conduct or any other activity subject to penalty under Sections 6700 and 6701, if the court finds (1) that the person has engaged in any conduct subject to the penalties and (2) injunctive relief is appropriate to prevent recurrence of the conduct.[729]

The Service has adopted administrative procedures to be followed in district offices[730] as well as in service centers,[731] and these procedures include the identification of returns claiming benefits from abusive tax shelters, freezing refunds from partnerships determined to be abusive tax shelters,[732] and the sending of "prefiling notice letters" to investors.[733] These letters advise investors in the promotion that "based upon review of the promotion it is believed that the projected tax benefits are not allowable, and also advise the investors of the possible consequences if such tax benefits are claimed on the tax return."[734] Considerable litigation has been generated where the Service has sent these letters, in no small part because they are sent before there has been any judicial determination about the allowability of the deductions. Promoters have usually been unsuccessful in this litigation.[735] Before action is taken to impose a Section 6700 penalty, an application for injunctive relief, or the sending of prefiling notice letters, a meeting is supposed to be arranged between the revenue agent, together with the district counsel attorney, and the promoter.[736] A conference can also be arranged with the Tax Division, Justice Department.[737]

---

[727] Id. Venue is in the District of Columbia if a citizen or resident of the United States does not reside in or have his principal place of business in any judicial district. IRC § 7408(c).

[728] IRC §§ 7204(a); 7408(a).

[729] IRC § 7408(b).

[730] Rev. Proc. 83-78, 1983-2 CB 595.

[731] Rev. Proc. 84-84, 1984-2 CB 782.

[732] Temp. Reg. §§ 301.6231(c)-1T, 301.6231(c)-2T. See also Rev. Proc. 84-84, 1984-2 CB 782, § 2; Rev. Rul. 84-175, 1984-2 CB 296.

[733] Rev. Proc. 83-78, 1983-2 CB 595; Rev. Proc. 84-84, 1984-2 CB 782.

[734] Rev. Proc. 83-78, 1983-2 CB 595, § 6.02.

[735] See, e.g., Corp. v. United States, 818 F2d 536 (6th Cir. 1987) (return confidentiality not violated by prefiling notice letter); cf. Mid-S. Music Corp. v. United States, 579 F. Supp. 481 (MD Tenn. 1983), aff'd in part, 756 F2d 23 (6th Cir. 1984) (promoter's due process rights not violated by letters). See also Western Reserve Oil & Gas Co. v. New, 765 F2d 1928 (9th Cir. 1985), cert. denied, 474 U.S. 1056 (1986) (promoter's damage suit against agents dismissed).

[736] Rev. Proc. 83-78, 1983-2 CB 595.

[737] Dep't of Justice Manual, 6-6.350 (Office of Special Litigation), and 6-6.440 (Opportunity for Conference Regarding Offers).

In the course of these conferences, consent decrees are negotiated, and, where the Service has gone to court, it has been successful,[738] either because a false statement was made[739] or because a gross valuation overstatement was given.[740]

¶ 7B.15 RULES APPLICABLE TO CONTESTING PENALTIES UNDER SECTIONS 6700, 6701, AND 6702

Mitigating the hardship that indiscriminate imposition of the third party and frivolous tax return penalties might cause, Section 6703 establishes burden of proof rules applying to the penalties for promoting abusive tax shelters, preparing documents resulting in understatements, and frivolous returns.[741] Section 6703 also provides a bond procedure to suspend collection of the tax shelter promoter and preparer penalties.[742] Where penalties under Sections 6700 and 6701 against third parties and under Section 6702 against a taxpayer are involved, the Service has the burden of proof on every issue relating to the imposition of the penalty.[743] The normal deficiency procedures do not apply to

---

[738] Compare United States v. Turner, 601 F. Supp. 757, 759 (ED Wis. 1985), aff'd, 787 F2d 595 (7th Cir. 1986) (no injunction ordered because false statement or gross valuation overstatement not personally read or given); and United States v. United Energy Corp., 87-1 USTC ¶ 9216 (WD Cal. 1987) (law of conspiracy applied and all conspirators enjoined).

[739] United States v. Savoie, 594 F. Supp. 678 (WD La. 1984); United States v. Hutchinson, 83-1 USTC ¶ 9322 (SD Cal. 1983).

[740] United States v. Philatelic Leasing Ltd., 794 F2d 781 (2d Cir. 1986); United States v. Campbell, 88-2 USTC ¶ 9525 (ND Tex. 1988).

[741] IRC § 6703, added by TEFRA, Pub. L. No. 248, HR 4961, 97th Cong., 2d Sess. § 322(a).

[742] IRC § 6703 was amended by IMPACT, Pub. L. No. 239, HR 3299, 101st Cong., 1st Sess., Subtitle 6, § 7736(a), deleting this procedure for assessment under Section 6702, for returns filed after December 31, 1989.

[743] IRC § 6703(a). Regarding the quantum of evidence that the government must produce under Section 6700, see Franklet v. United States, 578 F. Supp. 1552, 1559 (ND Cal. 1984), aff'd, 761 F2d 529 (9th Cir. 1985) (preponderance of evidence); United States v. United Energy Corp., 87-1 USTC ¶ 9216 (ND Cal. 1987) (same). Based on "the statutory language, the integrated enactment of §§ 6700-03 and the overall structure of the civil penalty provisions," the Eighth Circuit held that "in actions brought under § 6701, the burden of proof is on the government by a preponderance of the evidence." Mattingly v. United States, 924 F2d 785 (8th Cir. 1991) (Section 6701 was found not to sound in fraud, because, unlike Section 7206(2), willful conduct is not required). But see Warner v. United States, 700 F. Supp. 532 (SD Fla. 1988) (burden of proof is clear and convincing evidence), aff'd, 979 F2d 212 (11th Cir. 1991).

these penalties; therefore, there is no Tax Court jurisdiction.[744] However, judicial review before collection of the full amount of the assessed Section 6700 and 6701 penalties is available if the following conditions are met:[745] (1) Within thirty days after notice and demand of the penalty, at least 15 percent of the penalty must be paid and a claim for refund must be filed[746] and (2)

---

[744] IRC § 6703(b). See Planned Invs., Inc. v. United States, 881 F2d 340 (6th Cir. 1989) ("the form of notice of assessment of a Section 6700 penalty requires only a statement of the amount of the penalty and a demand for payment," but the court considered whether a notice was fair under due process analysis). If the notice omits the years covered by the assessment, it can still provide fair notice. Sage v. United States, 908 F2d 18 (5th Cir. 1990).

[745] IRC § 6703(c). The procedure provided by Section 6703(c) has been held to satisfy due process requirements. Kahn v. United States, 753 F2d 1208 (3d Cir. 1985) (cases gathered and analyzed; "Section 6703(c) allows for eventual full judicial review and the review need not precede deprivation or follow it immediately"); Todd v. United States, 802 F2d 1152 (9th Cir. 1986) (remedies provided to contest Section 6702 penalty were constitutionally adequate). Fifteen percent of the penalty must be paid in order to stop collection of the balance of the assessment. However, since the penalty is a divisible transactional penalty, the taxpayer can pay the penalty on a single transaction and file a refund claim. In this event, the Service is free to collect the balance of the assessment. Courts that hold that the penalty applied to a single activity, not to individual transactions, also say that the penalty is nondivisible. See, e.g., Gates v. United States, 874 F2d 584 (8th Cir. 1989). But see Noske v. United States, 911 F2d 133 (8th Cir. 1990) ("We hold the *Gates* non-divisibility holding should be applied prospectively only, that is, to cases filed after *Gates* was decided."). In further proceedings, the brokers were unsuccessful in their claim that, although they had not paid 15 percent of the assessment, the district court retained jurisdiction over their case. Noske v. United States, 93-1 USTC ¶ 50,087 (D. Minn. 1993). Although a promoter penalty assessment is not a divisible assessment in the Eighth Circuit, both the ground for the assessment and the method of its computation suggest that this issue deserves further consideration.

In *Korobkin*, the Ninth Circuit followed the approach in *Gates* and *Noske*, stating that under the pre-1990 version of Section 6700, penalties were not "assessed on each individual transaction like excise and payroll taxes are—they were assessed based on the aggregate of a person's abusive tax shelter sales during the year." Korobkin v. United States, 988 F2d 975 (9th Cir. 1993).

In district court, a person contesting the imposition of a tax shelter promoter and aider and abettor penalty is entitled to a jury trial. Bailey v. United States, 75 AFTR2d ¶ 95-956 (ND Tex. 1995) (individuals against whom penalties were assessed were debtors in a bankruptcy case, but the penalty claims were held to be actions at law or legal claims, on which debtors were entitled to a jury trial, not equitable claims on which no jury trial is permitted).

[746] The Service has adopted procedures for processing claims for refund on Sections 6700, 6701, and 6702 penalties. See IRM 8(11)61, MT 8-197 (Jan. 23, 1991) (IRC § 6703, Claims for Refund; IRC §§ 6700, 6701, and 6702, Penalties—General). A claim for refund is filed with the district and, if the claim is disallowed, the taxpayer is to be sent a notice advising of the proposed action unless a protest is filed within thirty days requesting Appeals review. Appeals officers are to process claim appeals in the usual manner and may settle cases based on potential hazards of litigation. However, any settlement is subject to approval of the Chief or Associate Chief of Appeals and coordination with

within thirty days after the earlier of the date of denial of the claim for refund
or six months after the filing of the claim, a refund suit must be brought in the
appropriate federal district court (apparently the Claims Court has no jurisdiction over these penalties). If this refund action is commenced, the Service is
prohibited from collecting the penalty until the suit is concluded.[747] If the Service should proceed to collect, the penalized party can get an injunction
against the Service to prohibit collection of the penalty.[748] However, the price
for deferred collection is that the period of limitations on collection is suspended during the period the Service is prohibited from collecting the tax.[749]

In actions under Sections 6700, for the organization and sale of abusive
tax shelters, and Section 6701, the focus is on the merits—i.e., whether the
plaintiff has made or assisted in the making of a false statement about a deduction or credit or about the value of property. However, one defense common to both penalties is not based on the merits; the statute of limitations. No
statute of limitations is specifically provided to deal with the third-party penalties. The IRS contends that the normal statute of limitations that requires an
assessment within three years after return filing in most cases applies to the
third-party penalties because the conduct giving rise to the penalty does not
arise from the obligation to file a tax return.[750] This position has been up-

---

district counsel. IRM 8(11)63, MT 8-197 (June 8, 1990) (IRC § 6703: Appeals Claim Procedures).

[747] In Belloff v. Comm'r, 996 F2d 607 (2d Cir. 1993), the IRS applied a 1986 overpayment to a 1982 Section 6700 penalty assessment, and the taxpayer objected that, having paid 15 percent of the Section 6700 penalty, Section 6703(c)(1) precluded collection
of the balance by setoff of refunds. The Second Circuit held that Section 6703(c)(1)'s collection bar applied only to a levy, not a setoff, following Sage v. United States, 908 F2d
18, 25–27 (5th Cir. 1990), and Hankin v. United States, 891 F2d 480, 482–483 (3rd Cir.
1989). Hankin v. United States, 89-2 USTC ¶ 9562 (ED Pa. 1989) (setoff of refund held
not to violate Section 6703; IRS Policy Statement P-5-16 construed). For a case where the
Service was estopped from contending that a refund suit was not brought within the
thirty-day period, see Producers Brokerage Co. v. United States, 91-2 USTC ¶ 50,358 (D.
Conn. 1991) (Service issued confusing and conflicting communications inconsistent with
its arguments in court); see, e.g., Noske v. United States, 92-2 USTC ¶ 50,429 (D. Minn.
1992) (collection action during gap between rejection of taxpayer's challenge to promoted
penalty and circuit court's sustaining it did not recklessly or intentionally violate stay of
Section 6703(c)).

[748] Id.

[749] Id., adding IRC § 6703(d).

[750] Another statute of limitations might apply even on this theory. There is a general
five-year statute of limitations on government action proceedings for enforcement of any
civil penalty. 28 USC § 2462. Under this statute of limitations, an assessment would be
required to be made within five years after the conduct giving rise to the penalty. However, the IRS could claim that an assessment is not a proceeding for purposes of this statute. Cases have uniformly held that the five-year statute of limitations under 28 USC
§ 2462 does not apply to Section 6700 or Section 6701. See Capozzi v. United States, 980

held.[751] However, Section 6671(a) provides that assessable penalties "shall be assessed and collected in the same manner as taxes," and, if that is so, it follows that the statute of limitations applicable to taxes imposed by Title 26 applies to these assessable penalties on third parties. The return that begins the running of the limitations period is the return affected by the false statement. This procedure is the same one followed where a return preparer penalty is as-

---

F2d 872 (2d Cir. 1992); Lamb v. United States, 977 F2d 1296 (8th Cir. 1992); Mullikin v. United States, 952 F2d 920 (6th Cir. 1991), cert. denied, 113 S. Ct. 85 (1992).

[751] Kuchan v. United States, 679 F. Supp. 764 (ND Ill. 1988); Agbanc, Ltd. v. United States, 707 F. Supp. 423 (D. Ariz. 1988). The theory behind this holding is that the Section 6700 penalty is imposed for prohibited conduct of the promoter. Therefore, the filing of a taxpayer's return does not trigger the three-year statute of Section 6501(a). It is unlikely that this position can be challenged on the basis of the difficulty in determining when a limitation period should start to run. See Kuchan v. United States, supra. Taxpayer-investors file returns containing information identifying the investment as does the vehicle (partnerships, S corporations, trusts). Tax shelter promoters are also supposed to file information returns with the IRS. Apparently recognizing this problem, the government has argued that both Sections 6700 and 6701 are essentially fraud penalties. One circuit court has accepted this argument as a basis for a no-assessment-period finding. Sage v. United States, 908 F2d 18 (5th Cir. 1990) ("Just as with other provisions of the Code enacted to combat fraud no limitations period exists for assessment of a Section 6700 penalty, and consequently no period of limitations is 'properly applicable thereto' (for purposes of Section 6502, the statute of limitations on collection)."). Sage also relied on the rationale of Agbanc, supra, which rejects the argument that Section 6700 assessments depend on the filing of a tax return. But since the accuracy-related penalty punishes a valuation overstatement, even a gross overvaluation, it is not clear why the court in Sage assumed that all conduct covered by Section 6700 is fraudulent. Apparently, the possible applicability of the general five-year statute on government claims (28 USC § 2462) was not argued.

The applicability of 28 USC § 2462 (five-year statute of limitations applicable to government claims) was argued to apply in Mullikin v. United States, 952 F2d 920 (6th Cir. 1991), reh'g denied (6th Cir. 1992) (en banc) (1992 US App. LEXIS 5036). The Sixth Circuit ruled that no statute of limitations is applicable to the aiding and abetting penalty of Section 6701, and so the penalty may be assessed at any time. In substance, the Sixth Circuit reasoned that Section 6701 was an antifraud statute, and no statute of limitations applies in fraud situations under the Code. Mullikin v. United States, supra (adopting fraud analysis and holding "it was the intent of Congress, in enacting Section 6701 that there be no statute of limitations governing the assessment of penalties pursuant to Section 6701; once an assessment is made, however, the statute of limitations on collection of assessed taxes set forth in Section 6502 applies"). Similarly, in Capozzi v. United States, 980 F2d 872 (2d Cir. 1992), the Second Circuit also held that the five-year statute of limitations of 28 USC § 2462 did not apply, because the Section 6700 assessment was not "an action, suit or proceeding" for the enforcement of a penalty. Although an assessment is not a proceeding itself, it is the necessary first step in administrative proceedings to collect the assessment. Just as in Mullikin, the Second Circuit stated that Congress, not the courts, should provide relief "to avoid possibly harsh consequences."

sessed because that penalty must be assessed within three years after the return or claim for refund was filed giving rise to the conduct penalized.[752]

¶ 7B.16 FAILURE TO FURNISH INFORMATION REGARDING TAX SHELTERS

The tax shelter registration and promoter list requirements are similar to requirements that are part of federal and state securities laws. The reasons for their addition to the tax law were stated as follows:[753]

> The committee is concerned that promoters of and investors in syndicated investments and tax shelters are profiting from the inability of the Treasury to effectively examine every return. These promoters know that even if a tax scheme they market is clearly faulty, some investors'd incorrect returns will escape detection and many will enjoy a substantial deferral of tax while the Treasury searches for their returns and coordinates its handling of similar cases.

> The new requirement that promoters keep lists of customers and investments will enable the Treasury to identify quickly all of the participants in related tax-shelter investments. As a result, taxpayers claiming improper treatment will not escape detection and investors in similar schemes will receive more uniform treatment.

The organizer of a tax shelter, as defined, must register the shelter with the Service no later than the day on which the first offering for sale of interests in the tax shelter occurs.[754] Registration is required for any tax shelter when and if any interest is sold to an investor. A tax shelter is registered by the filing of a registration form prescribed by the Service.[755] This form de-

---

[752] IRC § 6696(d).

[753] TRA 1984 Joint Committee Print, Pub. L. No. 369, HR 4170, 98th Cong., JCS 41-84, pt. 13-81.

[754] IRC § 6111, TRA 1984, Pub. L. No. 369, HR 4170, 98th Cong., 2d Sess. § 141, redesignating Section 6111 as Section 6112, and adding new IRC § 6111. The Conference Committee Report is HR Rep. No. 861, 98th Cong., 2d Sess. (1984), and is reprinted in 1984-3 CB (vol. 2). The Conference Committee Report says that terms such as "offering" used in Section 6111 are not necessarily intended to be limited to the meaning the term has under federal or state securities laws. Conference Committee Report, at 980.

[755] IRC § 6111(a). The Service has issued Form 8264 (Application for Registration of a Tax Shelter). This form must be prepared by typing or machine printing of the information required, and no entry may be handwritten except the signature. Form 8264 must be filed with the Internal Revenue Service Center, Kansas City, Missouri 64999. Treas. Reg. § 301.6111-2T. See also Treas. Reg. § 301.6111-1T, A-47. See Announcement 84-85, 1984-35 IRB 8 (Form and instructions).

scribes the investment and the tax benefits represented (or to be represented) to investors and other information the Treasury decides to require by regulation.[756] The person who sells or transfers an interest in a tax shelter must provide the purchaser or transferee with the identification number the Service assigns to the tax shelter.[757] In turn, the purchaser or transferee must include the tax shelter identification number on the return claiming the deduction or credit attributable to the investment.[758] Furthermore, the person who organizes or sells a potentially abusive tax shelter must maintain a list of purchasers, along with identifying information, and make the list available to the Service for up to seven years.[759]

A penalty is imposed on a failure to register (or a false registration) in the amount of $500 or one percent of the aggregate amount invested, whichever is greater, up to a maximum penalty of $10,000 for tax shelters. This penalty applies to tax shelters in which interests were first offered from August 31, 1984, through October 21, 1986. For a failure to register a tax shelter first offered after October 22, 1986, the penalty is either one percent of the aggregate amount invested in the shelter, or $500, whichever is greater.[760] A failure to furnish a tax shelter identification number is subject to a penalty of $100 for each failure.[761] If a taxpayer fails to include a tax shelter identification number on a return, the taxpayer is penalized $50 for each failure, unless the failure was due to reasonable cause. If the failure occurs on a return filed after October 22, 1986, the penalty is $250.[762] If the organizer or seller of an interest in a potentially abusive tax shelter fails to maintain a list of investors, the organizer or seller, absent reasonable cause and willful neglect, will be penalized $50 for each omitted investor, up to a maximum of $50,000 for any calendar year. For

---

[756] Id.

[757] IRC § 6111(b)(1). Mitchell v. United States, 89-2 USTC ¶ 9494 Bankr. D Wash. 1989) (organizer and promoter of shelter held responsible for registration), aff'd, 90-2 USTC ¶ 50,495 (WD Wash. 1990). When a tax shelter organizer accepts a fully paid subscription for a proposed limited partnership, the organizer is not required to furnish investors with the tax shelter registration merely on receipt of the subscription. Rev. Rul. 90-84, 1990-2 CB 253 (Oct. 15, 1990).

[758] IRC § 6111(b)(2). For the prescribed form of the notice, see Temp. Reg. § 301.6111-1T, A-53. The form for reporting a tax shelter's registration number is Form 8271 (Investor Reporting of Tax Shelter Registration Number). Announcement 85-10, 1985-2 IRB 45. For the circumstances when the Form 8271 must be filed, see Announcement 85-33.

[759] IRC §§ 6112, 6122. For the form of the list and the information it must contain, see Temp. Reg. § 301.6112-1T, A-16, A-17. For the rules on who is required to maintain the list, see Temp. Reg. § 301.6112-2T, A-11–A-13.

[760] IRC § 6707(a)(2).

[761] IRC § 6707(b)(1).

[762] IRC § 6707(b)(1), adding IRC § 6707(b)(2); TRA 1986, Pub. L. No. 514, HR 3838, 99th Cong., 2d Sess. §§ 1533(a), 1533(b).

failures occurring after October 22, 1986, the maximum is increased to $100,000.[763]

The penalties for failure to register or falsely registering are summarized in Table 7B.2.

[1] Tax Shelter and Organizer Defined

Definition of the term "tax shelter" triggers the registration requirement. For purposes of registration, the tax shelter definition depends upon the tax benefits to be derived and the number of investors and amount of investment involved. Any investment is a tax shelter if the investor "could reasonably infer" from the representations made or to be made that the "tax shelter ratio" may be greater than 2 to 1 for any of the first five years after the investment.[764] A tax shelter must be registered if (1) the investment offering must be registered under a federal or state securities regulation law (a requirement that usually exists where a number of investors are involved)[765]; (2) the investment is sold under an exemption from a filing requirement with a federal or state securities regulator[766]; or (3) the investment is a substantial investment.[767] The Treasury is given authority to issue regulations exempting other transactions from registration where such registration would not be useful to the Service.[768]

---

[763] IRC § 6708. A separate $100,000 maximum is applied to each transaction for which a list must be maintained. Temp. Reg. § 301.6708-1T (Q&A), Ex. 2.

[764] IRC § 6111(c)(1)(A).

[765] IRC § 6111(c)(1)(B)(i).

[766] IRC § 6111(c)(1)(B)(ii). The inclusion of securities, including those exempt from securities registration, means that private placements, for which notices claiming private placement exemption are required to be filed with a securities regulatory agency, but with a tax shelter ratio greater than 2 to 1, must be registered with the Service.

[767] IRC § 6111(c)(1)(B)(iii).

[768] IRC § 6111(e)(3); Conference Committee Report, HR Rep. No. 861, 98th Cong., 2d Sess. 980 (1984).

TABLE 7B.2
Penalties for Failing to Register or Falsely Registering a Tax Shelter

Conduct	Section	Penalty	Maximum	Minimum	Defenses
1. Failure to register (per § 6111(a))	§ 6707(a)	1% of aggregate amount invested	$10,000 (unlimited if intentional); unlimited for tax shelter interests offered for sale after Oct. 22, 1986	$500	Reasonable cause
2. Failure to furnish tax shelter identification number (per § 6111(b)(1))	§ 6707(b)(1)	$100 per failure; $250 after 1986			
3. Taxpayer's failure to include tax shelter identification number on return (per § 6111(b)(2))	§ 6706(b)(2)	$50 per failure; $250 for failures occurring or continuing after Oct. 22, 1986			Reasonable cause
4. Failure to maintain list of investors (per § 6112)	§ 6708	$50 per omitted person; $100,000 for failures occurring or continuing after Oct. 22, 1986	$50,000 per calendar year		Reasonable cause and no willful neglect

The term "tax shelter ratio" is itself defined as, for any tax year, the ratio which "(A) the aggregate amount of the deductions and 200 percent of the credits which are represented to be potentially allowable to any investor ... for all periods up to (and including) the close of such year, bears to (B) the investment base as of the close of such year."[769] For shelters first offered for sale after December 31, 1986, the tax shelter ratio is changed by increasing the po-

---

[769] IRC § 6111(c)(2). Regulations deal with the computation of the tax shelter ratio, including such matters as the amount of deductions and credits, investment base, and investments subject to securities regulation. Temp. Reg. § 301.6111-1T, A-6, A-9–A10, A11–A-12, A-14, A17–A21. For further interpretation of the computation of the tax shelter ratio, see Rev. Rul. 90-85, 1990-2 CB 255 (Oct. 15, 1990) (effect of tax shelter organizer's representations about passive activity losses); Rev. Rul. 90-86, 1990-2 CB 256 (Oct. 5, 1990) (numerator of ratio calculated for each partner under Section 6111(c)(2) includes each partner's share of partnership's gross deductions).

tentially allowable credit amount to 350 percent.[770] In general, the "investment base" is the amount of cash invested and the adjusted basis of other property contributed by the taxpayer (reduced by any liability to which the property is subject).[771] However, certain borrowed amounts are excluded. These amounts are borrowed from a participant in the organization, sale, or management of the shelter or a person related (within the meaning of Section 168(e)(4)) to a participant in the organization, sale, or management of the shelter.[772] Certain other amounts are excluded from or included in the investment base. No cash or property investment is included in the investment base if it is held in cash equivalent or marketable securities.[773]

The definition of a tax shelter that must be registered also has terms that are further defined. An investment is a substantial investment if "(A) the aggregate amount of which may be offered for sale exceeds $250,000 and (B) there are expected to be five or more investors."[774] The aggregate nominal amount offered for sale includes all cash, all contributions of property, and all loans whether recourse or nonrecourse. In this analysis, the aggregate nominal amount offered for sale is not the same as the investment amount used to compute the tax shelter ratio. The Conference Report to TRA 1984 gives an example of how this definition operates to create substantial investments and thus require registration:[775]

> For purposes of this definition, similar investments organized by the same person are aggregated. For example, suppose a sponsor of tax shelters develops generally similar investment plans or arrangements involving 8 different partnerships, each investing in a different item (such as a separate master recording or film), each with a different general partner, and each with 3 limited partners. If each partner invests $1,000 cash and $10,000 in nonrecourse obligations, there will be 32 investors (1 general partner plus 3 limited partners times 8 partnerships) and an aggregate investment of $352,000 (32 partners times $11,000). Thus, each partnership will constitute part of a substantial investment. If, in this example, representations are made that $1,000 in tax credits and $3,000 in deductions

---

[770] IRC § 6111(c)(2), as amended by TRA 1986, Pub. L. No. 514, HR 3838, 99th Cong., 2d Sess. § 1531.

[771] IRC § 6111(c)(3)(A). See Temp. Reg. § 301.6111-1T, A-13–A-14, A14.

[772] IRC § 6111(c)(3)(B).

[773] IRC § 6111(c)(3)(C)(i). Regulations may exclude from the investment base any amount that is cash or the adjusted basis of property contributed by the investor, and include in the investment base any amount that is not cash or property—if the exclusion or inclusion is necessary to carry out the purposes of the provisions of the statute. IRC § 6111(c)(3)(C)(ii).

[774] IRC § 6111(c)(4).

[775] Conference Committee Report, HR Rep. No. 861, 98th Cong., 2d Sess. 980–981 (1984).

are available to each limited partner in the first year, the sponsor will be required to register all of the partnerships.

A series of persons is obligated to register a tax shelter. The person primarily liable for registration is the tax shelter organizer, who is the person principally responsible for organizing the tax shelter.[776] This person will usually be the promoter, but need not be either the promoter or the general partner. For example, a person who structures or develops a series of related arrangements from which he or a related person will benefit through service contracts or asset purchases is the person who will be treated as the tax shelter organizer, even if each of the arrangements is managed or promoted by different individuals.[777]

If the tax shelter organizer fails to register the shelter, any other person who participates in its organization and sale must register it.[778] Registration must be made before the first offering for sale in order to enable state regulators to prohibit offerings of any unregistered securities.[779] If a person who is primarily or secondarily liable for registering fails to do so, a manager or salesman (i.e., a participant in the management and sale) must register.[780] The Conference Report states that ordinarily a lawyer or accountant who renders professional advice is not considered to be engaged in the organization of a tax shelter.[781] However, if the fee of the lawyer or accountant is based on the number or value of units sold, the Service may reasonably conclude that by virtue of his entrepreneurial risk he is considered an organizer, promoter, or seller of a tax shelter.

[2] Promoter Lists

Before the Deficit Reduction Act of 1984, there was no specific requirement that promoters and sellers of tax shelters maintain lists of investors and make them available for inspection by the Service. When the Service identified a tax shelter it considered abusive, it often had to serve a summons in order to identify investors in the shelter. To enable identification of every purchaser of a

---

[776] IRC §§ 6111(a), 6111(d)(1)(A). Temp. Reg. § 301.6111-1T, A-27, A-29. Temp. Reg. § 301.6111-1T

[777] Conference Committee Report, HR Rep. No. 861, 98th Cong., 2d Sess. 978 (1984). Temp. Reg. § 301.6111-1T, A-30.

[778] IRC § 6111(d)(1)(B).

[779] Conference Committee Report, HR Rep. No. 861, 98th Cong., 2d Sess. 978–979 (1984).

[780] IRC § 6111(d)(1)(C).

[781] Conference Committee Report, HR Rep. No. 861, 98th Cong., 2d Sess. 979 (1984). Temp. Reg. § 301.6111-1T, A-30.

given type of investment, Section 6112 requires that any promoter or seller of a "potentially abusive tax shelter" keep a list of the names of purchasers of the shelter along with such other information to be described in regulations.[782] A "potentially abusive tax shelter" is a shelter that must be registered under Section 6111, and any entity, plan, or arrangement determined by regulations "as having a potential for tax avoidance or evasion."[783] Consequently, regulations may require that organizers and sellers of other tax shelter arrangements that have a tax avoidance potential maintain customer lists, even if the tax shelter need not be registered. Congress contemplated that in those regulations, specific types of investments may be identified, or that the definition of a tax shelter may be modified by requiring, for example, that a plan or arrangement that would be subject to tax shelter registration if the tax shelter ratio were 1 to 1 rather than 2 to 1, must maintain lists of investors.[784]

If a potentially abusive shelter is sold in a series of transactions, a list of customers must be maintained at each level in the series. For example, an organizer who develops several types of tax shelters sold to several promoters, must maintain lists identifying the promoters.[785] When the promoters sell to investors, the promoters must also maintain lists.

[3] Corporate Tax Shelters

[a] Taxpayer Relief Act of 1997

The Taxpayer Relief Act of 1997 expanded the tax shelter registration rules by adding an additional category of tax shelters—confidential corporate tax shelters. As described in the House Report, the purposes served by this type of registration are (1) to give the Service "earlier notification than it generally receive[d] . . . of transactions that may not comport with the tax laws"; (2) to "improve compliance by discouraging taxpayers from entering into questionable transactions"; and (3) to "improve economic efficiency, because investments that are not economically motivated, but that are instead tax-motivated, may reduce the supply of capital available for economically moti-

---

[782] IRC § 6112(a). Temporary regulations have been issued describing the form the list may take and the information it must contain. Temp. Reg. § 301.6111-1T, A-16, A-17. For rules on who is required to maintain the list, see Temp. Reg. § 301.6112-1T, A-11–A-13.

[783] IRC §§ 6112(b)(1), 6112(b)(2).

[784] Conference Committee Report, HR Rep. No. 861, 98th Cong., 2d Sess. 982 (1984). However, in Temp. Reg. § 301.6112-1T, A-4, the investor list requirement has been imposed only on promoters of tax shelters with a tax shelter ratio of 2 to 1.

[785] Conference Committee Report, HR Rep. No. 861, 98th Cong., 2d Sess. 982 (1984).

vated activities, which could cause a loss of economic efficiency."[786] A tax shelter, which must be registered, "includes any entity, plan, arrangement, or transaction" that has three characteristics.[787] First, "a significant purpose" of the structure (not principal purpose) must be the avoidance or evasion of tax for either a direct corporate participant or even an indirect participant which is a corporation. Second, the arrangement is offered to a potential participant "under conditions of confidentiality." Third, the tax shelter promoters may not receive fees for the proposed arrangement in excess of $100,000 in the aggregate. If a tax shelter means an arrangement, which has as merely a significant purpose the avoidance or evasion of tax, many transactions having some intended tax benefit that would not otherwise constitute a tax shelter could be included in the registration provisions. This means that a wide range of transactions must be registered if the confidentiality condition and the promoters' fees elements are met. The offer of the arrangement is confidential alternatively (1) if the potential participant (or someone acting on the participant's behalf) has "an understanding" or enters into an agreement with the promoter (or for the promoter's benefit) to limit disclosure of the tax shelter (or any of its significant features) or (2) the tax shelter promoter claims that the tax shelter (or any of its aspects) is proprietary to the promoter or any person other than the potential participant or that the tax shelter arrangement is otherwise protected from disclosure to or use by others.[788]

If the promoter fails to register the tax shelter as required, and the tax shelter promoter is not a United States person, then each United States person who "discussed participation in [the] shelter" must register the shelter in the same manner as the tax shelter promoter.[789] The unwanted and uncomfortable burden of registering the shelter is on a person who has only discussed possible participation in the tax shelter. This obligation can only be avoided if the person with whom the shelter was discussed notifies the promoter in writing within ninety days after the discussions began that the person will not participate in the shelter, and the person does not in fact participate.[790]

If the tax shelter is not registered, the tax shelter promoter will be subject to a penalty equal to 50 percent of the fees paid to all promoters of the shelter for offerings made before the date the shelter is registered, or $10,000, which-

---

[786] Taxpayer Relief Act of 1997, HR Rep. No. 148, 105th Cong., 2d Sess. 429 (June 24, 1997).

[787] IRC § 6111(d). The Taxpayer Relief Act of 1997, § 1028(a) amended Section 6111 by redesignating subsections (d) and (e) as subsections (c) and (f) respectively. Registration is required for any tax shelter offered to potential participants after the date Treasury issues guidance on the filing requirements.

[788] IRC § 6111(d)(2).

[789] IRC § 6111(d)(3)(A).

[790] IRC § 6111(d)(3)(B).

ever is greater.[791] If the failure to file is intentional, the penalty is increased to 75 percent of the fees. If a person who has discussed participation in the shelter participates in the shelter and does not register the shelter, the person will be required to pay the failure to register penalty, but the amount of the penalty will be based on the fees that the participant has paid and the penalty the participant pays is in addition to the failure to register penalty imposed on any other person.[792] The participant in the shelter also faces a substantial understatement-type accuracy-related penalty, whether or not the shelter is registered, if the shelter is not likely to be upheld. This possibility is increased because the definition of tax shelter for purposes of the substantial understatement penalty also means any arrangement that has as a "significant purpose" the avoidance or evasion of income tax.[793]

[b] Temporary Regulations

On February 28, 2000, the Treasury Department issued temporary and proposed regulations that activated the corporate tax shelter registration rules described above.[794] Treasury also issued temporary and proposed regulations on the maintenance of investor lists and the filing of participant disclosure statements.[795] These temporary and proposed regulations were modified on August 16, 2000, to accomplish the following: (1) to clarify that insurance companies and mutual savings banks conducting life insurance business are subject to the tax shelter disclosure requirements; (2) to revise the record retention requirements by requiring taxpayers to keep a copy of all documents that are material to (a) an understanding of the facts of a reportable transaction, (b) the reportable transaction's expected tax treatment, or (c) the corporation's decision to participate in the reportable transaction; (3) to provide that an exclusivity agreement is a condition of confidentiality; (4) to make clear that the term "tax shelter promoter" has the same meaning as it does under the rules of Section 6111(e)(1) and the accompanying regulations; and (5) to require that list maintenance provisions apply to a tax shelter whether or not the transaction is offered to corporate investors.[796]

---

[791] IRC § 6707(a)(3)(A), as amended by the Taxpayer Relief Act of 1997.

[792] IRC § 6707(a)(3)(B).

[793] IRC § 6662(d)(2)(C)(iii), as amended by the Taxpayer Relief Act of 1997, applicable to items occurring after the effective date of the Act (Aug. 5, 1997).

[794] TD 8876, 65 Fed. Reg. 11215 (Mar. 2, 2000), 65 Fed. Reg. 11272 (Mar. 2, 2000) (proposed). See supra note 779, noting that the corporate tax shelter registration provisions were not self-executing.

[795] TD 8875, 65 Fed. Reg. 11211 (Mar. 2, 2000), 65 Fed. Reg. 11271 (Mar. 2, 2000) (proposed); and TD 8877, 65 Fed. Reg. 11205 (Mar. 2, 2000), 65 Fed. Reg. 11269 (Mar. 2, 2000) (proposed).

[796] TD 8896, 65 Fed. Reg. 49,909–49,913 (Aug. 16, 2000).

On August 7, 2001, the rules were again amended to provide the following: (1) to eliminate the different foreign tax treatment characteristic under the tax shelter disclosure requirements; (2) to clarify the "ordinary course of business" exception under the tax shelter disclosure requirements; (3) to clarify the "no reasonable basis exception" under the tax shelter disclosure requirements; (4) to eliminate the economic substance test from the tax shelter registration rules; (5) to clarify the presumption against confidentiality; and (6) to change the filing location for Form 8264, "Application for Registration of a Tax Shelter."[797]

Corporate tax shelter registration. New registration regulations cover the definition of a corporate tax shelter, and adopt registration requirements and procedures. As described above, registration requirements are triggered if a significant purpose of a transaction is tax avoidance or evasion for a corporate participant, and certain confidentiality requirements and fee thresholds are met.[798] Under the new regulations, there are three categories of transactions that are generally considered to have a significant purpose of tax avoidance or evasion. The first category includes transactions that are the "same as or substantially similar" to a transaction the Service has identified in published guidance as a listed transaction for these purposes.[799] The Service has already issued the first list of these transactions.[800] The second category includes transactions in which the expectation of pre-tax profit is "insignificant" relative to tax savings (on a present value basis), subject to an exception for certain financing transactions.[801] The third category includes transactions that are expected to be presented to more than one potential participant and have as an "important part" the production of tax benefits, but is subject to an ordinary course of business exception.[802] In the case of transactions covered in the second and third categories, there is no significant purpose of tax avoidance or evasion (and thus no registration requirement) if the promoter "reasonably de-

---

[797] TD 8961, 66 Fed. Reg. 41,133 (Aug. 7, 2001).

[798] See text accompanying notes 779–780 supra.

[799] Temp. Reg. § 301.6111-2T(b)(2) (listed transactions).

[800] Notice 2000-15, 2000-12 IRB 826 (Mar. 20, 2000) (including lease strips, lease-in/lease-out transactions (LILOs), and transactions substantially similar to those in ASA Investerings Partnership v. Comm'r, 85 AFTR2d 2000-675 (DC Cir. 2000) and ACM Partnership v. Comm'r, 82 AFTR2d 98-6682 (3d Cir. 1998)). See also Notice 2000-44 adding to the list so-called Son of BOSS (Bond and Option Sales Strategy) transactions; Notice 2001-45, PO-511 (July 26, 2001), disallowing benefits derived from a "basis shifting" tax shelter.

[801] Temp. Reg. § 301.6111-2T(b)(3) (transactions lacking economic substance).

[802] Temp. Reg. § 301.6111-2T(b)(4) (other tax-structured transactions).

termines" that no "reasonable basis" exists under tax law for denial of any "significant portion" of the expected tax benefits.[803]

The new regulations also add to the statutory provisions on the confidentiality and promoter fee requirement. Conditions of confidentiality exist if an offeree's ability to make disclosures about the structure or tax features of the transaction is limited "in any way" by express or implied agreement, regardless of whether such agreement is "legally binding."[804] There is a presumption that confidentiality does not exist where there is a written agreement with every potential participant expressly authorizing disclosure of "every aspect" of the transaction "without limitation of any kind."[805] For purposes of the fee threshold, any consideration is taken into account, including contingent payments, equity, and payments for other transactions as consideration for promotion of the subject shelter.[806]

Potential registrants include the tax shelter's principal organizers, and those who participate in its organization, management, or sale, and any related persons.[807] An exception to inclusion on this list should exist for those involved in organization or management who are not employed by or otherwise related to the tax shelter (or a principal organizer), and who do not receive success-based payments or an interest in the shelter as compensation.[808] Registration is made by filing a modified Form 8264 according to instructions pro-

---

[803] Temp. Reg. § 301.6111-2T(b)(5)(i) (the promoter must not make any unreasonable or unrealistic assumptions of fact, and must consider all relevant aspects of tax law, including legislative history, authoritative administrative guidance, and judicial decisions that establish general principles of tax law (e.g., economic substance)).

[804] Temp. Reg. § 301.6111-2T(c)(3). An implied condition of confidentiality exists where the promoter claims to have a proprietary interest in the tax shelter transaction. Temp. Reg. § 301.6111-2T(c)(1). However, an offer is not considered to be made under conditions of confidentiality if disclosure is restricted in order to comply with federal or state securities laws. Temp. Reg. § 301.6111-2T(c)(2).

[805] Temp. Reg. § 301.6111-2T(c)(2).

[806] Temp. Reg. § 301.6111-2T(d).

[807] Temp. Reg. §§ 301.6111-2T(f) and 301.6111-2T(g)(1) (specifically incorporating previously issued tax shelter temporary regulations, Temp. Reg. § 301.6111-1T (Q&A 26-39), and also expanding the list of potential registrants, for purposes of determining who must register). Note that there is also a special rule for required registrants in the case where all promoters are foreign persons. See Temp. Reg. § 301.6111-2T(g)(2). The definition of "corporate tax shelter promoter" includes the tax shelter organizer and any other person who participates in the organization, management, or sale of the tax shelter, as described in Section 6111(e)(1) and Temp. Reg. § 301.6111-1T (Q&A 26-33), as well as a person related to such a person. Temp. Reg. § 301.6111-2T(f). The promoter required to register the confidential tax shelter is similarly described in Temp. Reg. § 301.6111-1T (Q&A 34-39).

[808] Temp. Reg. § 301.6111-1T (Q&A 30).

vided in the regulations.[809] In the event an attorney or federally authorized tax practitioner is required to register a tax shelter, there are procedures for claiming privilege or protection with respect to omitted information.[810]

The registration rules apply to all corporate tax shelters in which any interests are offered for sale after February 28, 2000.[811] Registration is required no later than the day of the first offering of interests, subject to a transition rule that considers registration timely if made no later than August 29, 2000.[812] In case of uncertainty about the classification of a transaction, the regulations provide a mechanism for seeking a Service ruling or, importantly, filing a protective registration form.[813] A person required to register a shelter who fails to comply with the registration requirements will be subject to the penalties described above.[814]

Maintenance of investor lists. The new regulations describe the circumstances in which organizers (including those who would be potential registrants) of "potentially abusive tax shelters" must maintain a list of investors and other detailed information about the corporate tax shelter; sellers must maintain a list of purchasers with similar detailed information.[815] This information is to be made available for inspection upon request of the Secretary of the Treasury.[816] There are procedures for claiming privilege or protection with respect to information omitted from the list.[817] More transactions are potentially subject to list maintenance requirements than are subject to registration. Potentially abusive tax shelters are those that have a significant purpose of tax avoidance or evasion as defined under the registration regulations.[818] Unlike the registration provisions, there is no condition of confidentiality or promoter fee requirement. The penalty for failure to maintain investor lists is $50 for each person with respect to whom there is a failure, subject to a reasonable

---

[809] Temp. Reg. § 301.6111-2T(e)(2). The address for filing Form 8264, Application for Registration of a Tax Shelter is: Internal Revenue Service, Ogden, Utah 84201. Ann. 2001-62, 2001-24 IRB 1337 (June 11, 2001).

[810] Temp. Reg. § 301.6111-2T(e)(3).

[811] Temp. Reg. § 301.6111-2T(h).

[812] Temp. Reg. § 301.6111-2T(e)(1).

[813] Temp. Reg. § 301.6111-2T(b)(6).

[814] See text accompanying notes 783–785 supra.

[815] These temporary and proposed regulations were issued under Section 6112, which requires the maintenance of investor lists for potentially abusive tax shelters. On August 11, 2000, the Treasury and the Service announced modifications had been made to the tax shelter disclosure regulations to take into account public comments, primarily those concerning documents to be maintained, agreements to retain investor lists, and conditions of confidentiality. News Release, 2000 TNT 156-16 (Aug. 11, 2000).

[816] IRC § 6112(c)(1)(A).

[817] Temp. Reg. § 301.6112-1T (Q&A 17).

[818] Temp. Reg. § 301.6112-1T (Q&A 4).

cause exception and an annual $100,000 cap, which is applied to each transaction for which a list must be maintained.[819] These regulations are effective with respect to all acquisitions of interests in a potentially abusive tax shelter after February 28, 2000. However, the Service will not request to inspect investor lists until August 29, 2000.[820]

Participant disclosure statements. To comply with the new regulations, a corporate taxpayer that has participated in a "reportable transaction" is required to attach a disclosure statement to its return describing the corporate tax shelter.[821] The disclosure statement must be attached to the return for each tax year in which the reportable transaction affects the taxpayer's tax liability.[822] A copy of the disclosure statement must be sent to the Service in Washington, D.C., for the first year of disclosure.[823] In addition, documents related to the transaction must be retained until expiration of the statute of limitations for the return containing the first filed statement.[824] These regulations are effective for returns filed after February 28, 2000.[825]

There are two types of reportable transactions. The first type of reportable transaction is a transaction that (1) is the "same as or substantially similar" to one listed by the Service for these purposes (unless it has affected the taxpayer's tax liability reported on any return filed on or before February 28, 2000), and (2) is expected to reduce the taxpayer's tax liability by more than $1 million in any taxable year (or more than $2 million for any combination of

---

[819] IRC § 6708. Temp. Reg. § 301.6708-1T, Q&A 5, Ex. 2.

[820] Temp. Reg. § 301.6112-IT (Q&A 22).

[821] These temporary and proposed regulations were issued under the specific grant of authority provided the Secretary of the Treasury in Section 6011(a). In general, every taxpayer required to file a return for a taxable year for a corporation's income tax, including savings banks and life insurance companies, which have participated, directly or indirectly, in a reportable transaction, must attach a disclosure statement to its return for each year its federal income tax liability is affected by its participation in the reportable transaction. Temp. Reg. § 1.6011-4T(a).

[822] Temp. Reg. § 1.6011-4T(d).

[823] Temp. Reg. § 1.6011-4T(d).

[824] Temp. Reg. § 1.6011-4T(e). The taxpayer must retain a copy of all documents and other records about a disclosable transaction that (1) are "material to an understanding of the facts of the transaction"; (2) indicate the expected tax treatment of the transaction"; or (3) indicate "the corporation's decision to participate in the transaction." Temp. Reg. § 1.6011-4T(e). The documents to be retained include (1) marketing documents; (2) written analyses used in the decision-making process; (3) correspondence and agreements between the taxpayer and any promoter, advisor, lender, or other party; (4) documents describing the tax benefits of the transaction; and (5) documents concerning the business purpose of the transaction. Id.

[825] Temp. Reg. § 1.6011-4T(g).

taxable years in which the transaction is expected to reduce tax liability).[826] The second type of reportable transaction is a transaction entered into after February 28, 2000 that (1) has at least two out of five listed suspect characteristics, and (2) is expected to reduce the taxpayer's tax liability by more than $5 million in any taxable year (or more than $10 million for any combination of taxable years in which the transaction is expected to reduce tax liability).[827] This second type of reportable transaction is subject to exceptions, including for transactions occurring in the ordinary course of business and for transactions where the taxpayer determines that no basis exists for denial of tax benefits.[828]

A taxpayer's failure to satisfy these disclosure requirements may affect its liability for accuracy-related and fraud penalties on underpayments related to the reportable transaction.[829] The preamble to the regulations warns that reliance on tax advice that a return position is "more likely than not" proper is "not necessarily sufficient" to gain relief under the reasonable cause exception.[830] Improper disclosure (or nondisclosure) of a reportable transaction could indicate a lack of taxpayer "good faith," even if a return position is sufficiently justified for purposes of the reasonable cause exception.[831]

[c] Office of Tax Shelter Analysis

As part of its efforts to combat tax shelters, the Service has created an Office of Tax Shelter Analysis in Washington, D.C.[832] This office is part of the Large and Mid-Size Business Division. The office's activities cover all tax shelter activity. The office's tasks include the review of information about tax shelter transactions and, in coordination with the Office of Chief Counsel and Treasury's Office of Tax Policy, the evaluation of appropriate tax treatment of

---

[826] Temp. Reg. §§ 1.6011-4T(b)(2) and 1.6011-4T(b)(4) (listed transactions). The Service has already issued the first list of listed transactions for purposes of these regulations. See Notice 2000-15, 2000-12 IRB 826 (Mar. 20, 2000).

[827] Temp. Reg. §§ 1.6011-4T(b)(3)(i), 1.6011-4T(b)(4) (other reportable transactions). The six suspect characteristics are confidentiality, contractual protection, presence of contingent promoter fees, book/tax differences, participation of an indifferent taxpayer or person with similar effect, and differing characterization for foreign tax purposes.

[828] Temp. Reg. § 1.6011-4T(b)(3)(ii). The taxpayer determination exception is based on the same standard as that which applies to the promoter determination exception under the registration regulations. See text supra note 794.

[829] See IRC §§ 6662, 6663.

[830] TD 8877, 65 Fed. Reg. 11,205 (Mar. 2, 2000), 65 Fed. Reg. 11,269 (Mar. 2, 2000); see IRC § 6664(c).

[831] TD 8877, 65 Fed. Reg. 11,205 (Mar. 2, 2000), 65 Fed. Reg. 11,269 (Mar. 2, 2000); see IRC § 6664(c).

[832] Ann. 2000-12, 2000-12 IRB 835 (Mar. 20, 2000).

these transactions. The office may also coordinate appropriate Service responses to particular transactions. It is expected that tax shelter information will be gathered through the new disclosure regulations, field personnel activity, and voluntary disclosures by the public.

¶ 7B.17 FAILURE TO MAKE DEPOSITS

To encourage depositors to correct their failures to make deposits, amended Section 6656 creates a four-tier penalty structure in which the amount of the penalty varies with the length of time within which the taxpayer corrects the failure. The penalty is 2 percent if the failure is not more than five days, 5 percent if the failure is for more than five but not more than fifteen days, and 10 percent if the failure is more than fifteen days.[833] Also, if the failure is not corrected on or before ten days after the first delinquency notice to the taxpayer under Section 6303, a depositor is subject to a penalty equal to 15 percent of the amount of the underpayments.[834] In jeopardy cases, under Sections 6861 and 6862 and the jeopardy levy provided in Section 6331(a), the 15 percent rate applies if the taxes are not deposited on or before the date on which notice and demand for immediate payment is given.[835]

Failure-to-deposit penalties have been held not to have matured until the IRS sends the taxpayer notice of the assessed penalty and demands payment.[836] Courts have held that since a notice and demand is required under Sections 6665(a) and 6671(a) before the penalty is payable, the IRS may not pay a failure-to-deposit penalty out of a later deposit before it has sent a notice and demand to the taxpayer. The district court in *Elms* said that until the requisite notice and demand is sent, the penalty is "immature" and not collectible by offsets from other payments.[837] This ruling undoubtedly will frustrate the IRS,

---

[833] IRC § 6656(b)(1)(A).

[834] IRC § 6656(b)(1)(B)(i).

[835] IRC § 6656(b)(1)(B)(ii).

[836] First Nat'l Bank in Palm Beach v. United States, 591 F2d 1143 (5th Cir. 1979); Elms v. IRS, 93-1 USTC ¶ 50,281 (ED Mich. 1993).

[837] In response to the government's motion to alter the initial judgment, the district court in *Elms* said that the issue was not whether the IRS may apply an excess payment to an accrued penalty but whether the IRS may apply an excess "to an *immature* accrued penalty." Elms v. United States, 93-1 USTC ¶ 50,390 (ED Mich. 1993). A delinquency may accrue when the payment is late, but the penalty is not "mature" or "payable" until the IRS provides notice of the penalty to the taxpayer and demands payment. Also, contrary to a government argument, the court said it was not ruling that there was an overpayment in the earlier period but only that Sections 6665(a) and 6671(a) require the IRS to give notice and demand before applying them to outstanding penalties. Finally, the court, rejecting the government's argument, held that Section 6402's setoff authority does

but it serves the salutary effect of permitting a withholding agent to know that what it has actually paid for a period has been applied to that period's liability. An extraordinary amount of time and effort can be expended when a withholding agent faced with penalties attempts to reconcile its accounts with those of the IRS, because the portions of deposits have been applied to assessed but undisclosed penalties.

If a failure-to-deposit penalty is assessed, the taxpayer must make an affirmative showing of reasonable cause, meaning the exercise of ordinary business care and prudence.[838] The Service has described specifically what this showing involves when taxpayers make deposits of tax by electronic funds transfers (EFTs), that is, by telephone or computer by either a debit transaction or a credit transaction. A debit transaction is made by the taxpayer's requesting an authorized financial agent of the Treasury (either Federal Reserve banks or incorporated banks and other financial institutions) to initiate the transfer of funds from the taxpayer's bank account to the Treasury's general account and to transmit the related tax payment data, supplied by the taxpayer, to the Service. A taxpayer makes an EFT deposit by a credit transaction by requesting its financial institution to transfer funds through the Automated Clearing House (ACH) system to the Treasury's general account and to submit the related tax data through the ACH system to a Financial Agent for transmission to the Service. A taxpayer making an EFT deposit through either of these methods may establish reasonable cause for abating the failure to deposit penalty by using the records of the bank instructed to initiate the EFT or by the taxpayer's own books and records, such as a record of the taxpayer's instructions or a saved electronic file of instructions.[839] These records must establish (1) payment instructions; (2) the correct amount of tax to be deposited; (3) the correct type of tax to be deposited; (4) the correct tax period for which the deposit was made; (5) the correct date the funds were to be transferred from the taxpayer's bank account to the Treasury's account; and (6) the number of the taxpayer's bank account with sufficient funds to cover the transfer.

The first-time filer can establish reasonable cause if there is an inadvertent failure to deposit employment taxes and the following criteria are met: (1) The employer's net worth does not exceed $2 million (or if the employer is a business, $7 million) under the attorney's fees recovery rules of Section 7430(c)(4)(A)(ii); (2) the failure occurred during the first quarter the person was required to deposit employment taxes; and (3) the employment tax return

---

not eliminate the IRS's obligation under Sections 6665(a) and 6671(a) to send a notice and demand for penalties.

[838] Reg. § 301.6656-1(b).

[839] Rev. Rul. 94-46, 1994-2 CB 278 (July 18, 1994).

was filed on or before the due date.[840] In 1997, the EFT system provisions under Section 6302(h) were amended to say that no penalty shall be imposed under the Code solely by reason of a failure by a person to use the EFT system if (1) the person is a member of a class of taxpayers first required to use such a system on or after July 1, 1997, and (2) the failure occurs before July 1, 1998. In several notices, the Service extended this first-time filer relief for EFTs.[841]

Designation of periods to which deposits apply. Prior to the 1998 tax changes, the Service would take an amount deposited by a taxpayer (or withholding agent) for one period and apply the amount deposited to a liability for another period, with the result that the failure-to-deposit penalty was generated for the period when the full deposit may have been made. The IRS Restructuring and Reform Act of 1998 amended the failure-to-deposit penalty, Section 6656, by permitting a person who is required to deposit tax reportable on a return for a specified period, to designate the period or periods within which the specified tax period is to be applied.[842] When a designation of the period to which the deposit applies is made, the deposit will be applied to the most recent period or periods within the specified tax period to which the deposit relates, unless the person making the deposit designates a different period or periods to which the deposit applies.[843] The time for making this designation is limited to the ninety-day period beginning on the date the Service sends the taxpayer or withholding agent a notice that a failure-to-deposit penalty has been imposed for a another tax period. Regarding an extension of the waiver of the penalty in a first-time filer situation, the Service is given authority to waive the failure-to-deposit penalty for the first deposit a person making deposits of employment taxes is required to change the frequency of deposits.[844]

---

[840] IRC § 6656(c), added by the Taxpayer Bill of Rights 2, § 304(a), applicable to deposits made after the date of enactment, July 30, 1996. Abatement of the penalty is also permitted if the deposit is inadvertently sent to the Service (for example, an IRS service center) rather than a depository. IRC § 6656(d) (1996).

[841] Notice 97-43, 1997-30 IRB 9, providing relief to first-time filers whose obligation is incurred before December 31, 1997; Notice 98-30, 1998-22 IRB 9, same for obligations incurred on or before December 31, 1998; Notice 99-12, 1999-9 IRB 44, same for obligations incurred on or before June 30, 1999, even if the deposit is made after that date.

[842] IRC § 6656(e)(1), added by 1998 Act § 3304(a). The default ordering rule applies to deposits made after December 31, 2001. Any deposit that is made after December 31, 2001, is to be applied to the most recent period to which the deposit relates, unless the taxpayer explicitly designates otherwise within ninety days immediately after a Service notice imposing a penalty. See Rev. Proc. 2001-58, 2001-50 IRB 579 (Dec. 10, 2001).

[843] IRC § 6656(e)(1).

[844] IRC § 6656(c)(2).

C. PENALTIES ON INFORMATION PROVIDERS

¶ 7B.18 STRUCTURE OF INFORMATION REPORTING AND PENALTIES

Information reporting is a vital part of the Service's return compliance pro-grams. Under its document matching program,[845] the IRS, largely by use of computerized data processing equipment, matches third-party information on items such as wages, interest, dividends, and certain deductions with the amounts reported by taxpayers on their income tax returns.[846] This information is also used to identify those taxpayers who are reported to have received in-come, but did not file returns. During its fiscal year 1988, the IRS received al-most one billion information returns, about 93 percent of which were submitted on magnetic media.[847] When return information does not agree with filed information documents, the IRS asks taxpayers to explain the discrep-ancy.[848] Returns are also solicited from taxpayers who fail to file them.[849] The Service uses information returns to ensure, through the examination, collection, and criminal investigation functions, that taxpayers comply with the tax laws. The focus in this section, however, is on penalties imposed on those who are required to file the information returns.

Provisions calling for the filing of information returns are divided into several categories:

---

[845] This program is also referred to as the Information Returns Program (IRP). See the discussion at ¶ 8.04[3].

[846] IRS Annual Report 1988, at 18.

[847] Included in the total number of returns filed were over 210 million Forms W-2 (Wage and Tax Statement) and W-2P (Statement for Recipients of Annuities, Pensions, Retirement Pay, or IRA Payments), which are received and processed by the Social Secur-ity Administration. Of these documents, some 72 million represented deductions for items such as contributions to individual retirement arrangements and mortgage interest pay-ments. IRS Annual Report 1988, at 18.

[848] In fiscal 1988, the IRS sent about 3.8 million notices reflecting discrepancies to taxpayers. Because discrepancies between information returns filed by payors and taxpay-ers' returns may frequently be resolved, without the IRS's involvement, if taxpayers can contact payors, the IRS now requests that payors voluntarily include their telephone num-bers on taxpayers' copies of the information return. Ann. 96-5, 1996-4 IRB 1. Also, under revised procedures, the IRS is supposed to investigate information reported by payors where a taxpayer challenges the accuracy of the information reported by payors, such as wage income reported to the IRS on Forms W-2 or other income payments reported on Forms 1099. Ann. 96-5, 1996-4 IRB 1, announcing the amendment of IRM 424(16), ef-fective January 31, 1996.

[849] In fiscal 1988, the IRS sent about 3 million of these notices to taxpayers who failed to file returns based on information returns filed.

- Information returns concerning persons such as partnerships, trusts, foreign entities, and persons subject to special provisions (Sections 6031–6039D);
- Information returns concerning transactions with other persons (Sections 6041–6050P).[850]
- Information returns regarding wages paid to employees (Section 6051–6053);
- Registration of and information returns concerning pensions (Sections 6057–6059); and
- Information returns concerning tax return preparers (Section 6060)

Penalties are imposed for failure to file correct information returns (Section 6721), failure to furnish correct payee statements (Section 6722), failure to comply with other information return reporting requirements, and waiver of the penalties and other special rules. For information returns required to be furnished after December 31, 1996, the Taxpayer Bill of Rights 2 amended the information return reporting provisions to require the information provider to include on the information return the name, address, and phone number of the information contact of the information provider.[851] This information is intended to enable the taxpayer affected by the information reported to the Service to correct any incorrect information.

The information reporting penalties differ from prior law in the following ways:

1. *Ceiling on amount.* Under prior law, there was no ceiling on the amount of the late or incorrect filing penalty imposed on payors of dividends and interest. However, there was a $100,000 ceiling on the amount of the same penalty when it was imposed on other filers of information returns. Under Section 6721, interest and dividend returns have the same ceiling as other information returns.

2. *Incentive to file and correct.* Under prior law, there was no distinction made between late filed or late corrected information returns and those that were not filed or corrected. Section 6721 is intended to encourage delinquent information reporters to file or correct information returns by providing reduced penalty rates if the filing or correction is made within thirty days after the required filing date and, if after that date, before August 1.

3. *Special treatment of small businesses.* Under prior law, no relief from the effect of the information return delinquency penalty was given to

---

[850] Under Section 61(a)(12), a taxpayer's gross income includes income from the discharge of indebtedness. Under new Code Section 6050P, lenders are required to file information returns for the discharge of any debt of $600 or more.

[851] See Taxpayer Bill of Rights 2, §§ 1201(a)(1)–1201(a)(12).

small businesses. Under Section 6723, lower maximum penalty levels are provided for small businesses, defined as firms having average annual gross receipts for the most recent three taxable years that do not exceed $5 million.

4. *Waiver standard.* Under prior law, different waiver standards applied for different types of information returns (reasonable cause or, in the case of interest and dividend returns, due diligence). Section 6724 consolidates the waiver provisions under prior law and sets forth a uniform reasonable cause waiver standard.

A procedure existing under prior law has been incorporated into the statute. An exception to the information return delinquency penalty is provided in Section 6721 for minor or insignificant errors in filed information returns that do not impede IRS operations. This exception was provided by regulations under prior law.[852] Final regulations under the new statutory regime have been issued.[853] These regulations are divided into four parts: failure to file correct information returns (Regulations § 301.6721-1), failure to furnish correct payee statements (Regulations § 301.6722-1), failure to comply with specified information reporting requirements (Regulations § 301.6723-1), and the reasonable cause waiver (Regulations § 301.6724-1). Significant features of these regulations are the following:

1. *De Minimis Exception.* The number of returns to which the de minimis exception applies for any calendar year will not exceed ten or 0.5 percent of the total, whichever is greater. If the number of returns on which the filer fails to include correct information exceeds the number of returns to which the de minimis exception applies, the de minimis exception will be applied to those returns that afford the filer the greatest reduction in penalty.[854]

2. *Definition of "Intentional Disregard."* The fact that intentional disregard is decided on the basis of the facts and circumstances is not helpful. But the regulations also specify that the following facts support imposition of the increased penalty: a pattern of repeated failures to file timely or to include correct information, no correction on discovery of the failure, a failure to correct a failure to file or to include correct information within thirty days after receipt of a written request by the Service, and a filer's economic decision to incur the penalty rather than incur the cost of compliance.[855]

---

[852] See Temp. Reg. § 1.6723-1T(a).

[853] TD 8386, 1992-5 IRB 22.

[854] Reg. § 301.6721-1(d)(2).

[855] Reg. § 301.6721-1(f)(3). For a case applying these regulations to determine whether there was intentional disregard in the failure to file information returns, see

3. *Inconsequential Errors.* For purposes of Section 6722, while an inconsequential error or omission will not result in a penalty, certain errors and omissions are never inconsequential: a dollar amount, an address of a payee, a substitute form that is unacceptable to the Service, and the manner of furnishing a statement.[856]

4. *Specified Information.* For purposes of Section 6723, the specified information reporting requirement means: the requirement to provide notice of the transfer of a partnership interest and any requirement under Section 6109 to include a person's taxpayer identification number on a document other than an information return or payee statement or to furnish the number to another person.[857]

5. *Reasonable Cause.* The regulations provide that reasonable cause is present if the filer shows that it acted in a responsible manner both before and after the failure occurred and if the filer establishes further either that there are "significant mitigating factors" or that the failure arose from "events beyond the filer's control." Significant mitigating factors include a first-time filer situation and a history of compliance.[858] Events beyond the filer's control include the unavailability of relevant business records, undue economic hardship for filing on magnetic media, good faith reliance on written IRS advice, reasonable reliance on a filing agent, and payee failure to supply the filer with the correct information.[859] In addition, acting in a responsible manner requires a showing that the filer used reasonable care in obtaining and handling the account information and made efforts to avoid and correct the failure, for example, by requesting extensions, attempting to prevent a failure, removing the cause of failure, or correcting the failure promptly.[860] Special rules are provided for missing or incorrect

---

United States v. Quality Med. Consultants, Inc., 80 AFTR2d ¶ 97-5242 (MD Fla. 1997) (at the time of corporate disputes over management, a corporation's CFO sent Forms 1099-MISC only to individuals, not to corporations, but after new management was installed, information returns were promptly filed after IRS request, and a new CFO was hired; held, the failure to file was not due to intentional disregard but to mistake, and therefore was understandable). See also In re Quality Med. Consultants Inc., Debtor, 81 AFTR2d ¶ 98-469 (Bankr. MD Fla. 1998) (intentional disregard of the filing requirements was found because after the information provider learned of the failure to file a Form 1099, it failed to correct the error).

[856] Reg. § 301.6722-1(b)(2). However, in certain circumstances, an incorrect address may be inconsequential; but the issue will be decided on the facts and circumstances of a particular case.

[857] Reg. § 301.6723-1(a)(4).

[858] Reg. § 301.6724-1(b).

[859] Reg. § 301.6724-1(c).

[860] Reg. § 301.6724-1(d).

taxpayer identification numbers.[861] The due diligence safe harbor applies in the same manner as it did under Section 6676(b) before amendment by IMPACT and the temporary employment tax regulations (Temp. Reg. § 35a.9999-1).[862]

Because the obligation to file an information return may not be clear or may present extraordinary compliance problems for the affected information providers, the Service also develops specific positions on the circumstances under which penalties will (or will not) be imposed.[863]

From time to time, the Service issues notices to clarify the obligations of information providers. These notices establish whether and when a penalty will be imposed for a failure to file information returns in specific situations.[864] When the Service proposes to assess a penalty, it will send the information provider a notice (Notice of Proposed Civil Penalty, Notice 972 CG), which requires a reply within forty-five days.[865] Payers must submit a written reason-

---

[861] Reg. §§ 301.6724-1(e), 301.6724-1(f).

[862] Reg. § 301.6724-1(g).

[863] For example, in Rev. Rul. 93-70, 1993-2 CB 294, the Service ruled that banks and other businesses acting as escrow agents and having oversight functions in the project were required to file information returns reporting reportable payments made on behalf of the owner and general contractor of a construction project. Later, the Service issued Notice 94-37, 1994-1 CB 349 (Apr. 18, 1994), stating that penalties for failure to file would not be asserted for calendar year 1993 and earlier years, unless the bank or other business had been notified of the filing requirement in a letter signed by the district director, in which case the district director had the discretion to assert the penalty.

Similarly, in Notice 94-73, 1994-2 CB 553 (July 18, 1994), the Service announced it would waive penalties for failure to file information returns reporting discharges of indebtedness occurring before the later of January 1, 1995, of the effective date of the final regulations under Section 6050P, in discharges arising under the Bankruptcy Code, resulting from expirations of the statute of limitations on collection on a debt, a discharge of an amount other than principal, or a person other than the primary or first-named debtor on a pre-1995 debt. The waiver does not apply, however, to the reporting requirements for foreclosures and abandonments of secured property.

[864] There are many examples of these notices: In Notice 94-73, 1994-2 CB 553 (July 18, 1994), the Service said that failure to report information about discharges of indebtedness occurring before January 1, 1995, or the effective date of the final Section 6050P regulations would not be punished by penalty if the discharge (1) occurred under the Bankruptcy Code; (2) resulted from the expiration of the statute of limitations on collection of the indebtedness; (3) was for an amount other than principal of a debt in a loan transaction; or (4) involved a person who was not primarily liable for a debt incurred before January 1, 1995.

[865] Ann. 94-93, 1994-29 IRB 40 (July 18, 1994). The notice is used for proposed penalties for missing and incorrect taxpayer identification numbers, late filed returns, and failure to file on magnetic media. The notice is being used by the Service for penalties applying to information returns on Forms 1099-A, B, S, DIV, INT, MISC, OID, PATR, 1098, and W-2G, as well as Forms W-2. Notice 972CG was issued for the calendar year 1994 for 1992 filed information returns.

able cause explanation to show why the penalty should not be assessed.[866] Penalties will be assessed if the payer does not provide a reasonable cause explanation or if the Service does not receive a reply to the notice.

While the Service imposes most civil penalties on the information provider for failing to file timely and correct information to the Service, the information provider is also liable for civil damages to the person affected by the information provider's filing of fraudulent information to the Service.[867] The affected person may recover damages equal to the greater of $5,000 or the sum of actual damages, including the costs of resolving deficiencies the Service claims are due as the result of the fraudulent information, the costs of the action, and, in the court's discretion, reasonable attorney's fees.

¶ 7B.19 FAILURE TO FILE CORRECT INFORMATION RETURNS

If a person required to file an information return fails to file such a return with the IRS on or before the required filing date, or fails to include all the information required to be shown on the return or includes incorrect information, that person is subject to penalty.[868] The basic penalty for late or incorrectly filed information returns is $50 per return, with a maximum penalty of $250,000 per calendar year.[869] However, the basic penalty can be reduced where correction is made within specified periods,[870] and reduced still further where a small business is involved.[871] The penalty can be eliminated altogether if the omitted information is of a minor nature.[872] On the other hand, the penalty amount and ceiling can be increased in the case of an intentional disregard of the filing requirements.

The Code provisions requiring the information returns to which the delinquency penalty of Section 6723 is applicable are listed in Table 7B.3.

---

[866] Payers are also required to compare the taxpayer identification number listings with their records to determine if an annual solicitation must be completed to avoid penalties for taxpayer identification numbers for future years.

[867] IRC § 7434, added by the Taxpayer Bill of Rights 2, § 601(a), applicable to fraudulent returns filed after the date of enactment, July 30, 1996.

[868] IRC §§ 6721(a)(2)(A), 6721(a)(2)(B).

[869] IRC § 6721(a)(1).

[870] IRC § 6721(b).

[871] IRC § 6721(d).

[872] IRC § 6721(c).

TABLE 7B.3
Information Returns Subject to the Delinquency Penalty

Code section	Description of information return
1060(b)	Allocation of the purchase price of a going business among the assets of the business[873]
4093S(c)(4)(A) or 4093(c)(4)(C), or 4093(d)	Information reporting with respect to tax on diesel and nongasoline aviation fuels[a]
6041(a) or 6041(b)	Information at source[a]
6041A(a)	Returns of direct sellers[a]
6041A(b)	Collection and payment of foreign interest or dividends[874]
6042(a)(1)	Payments of dividends[875]
6044(a)(1)	Payments of patronage dividends[c]
6045(a)	Returns of brokers[876]
6045(d)	Returns of brokers[a]
6049(a)	Payments of interest[c]
6050A(a)	Reporting requirements of certain fishing boat operators[a]
6050H(a)	Mortgage interest received in trade or business from individuals[c]
6050I(a)	Cash received in trade or business[877]
6050J(a)	Foreclosures and abandonments of security[c]
6050K(a)	Exchanges of certain partnership interests[d]
6050L(a)	Returns with respect to certain dispositions of donated property[d]
6050N(a)	Payments of royalties[a]
6051(d)	Information returns with respect to income tax withheld[a]
6052(a)	Reporting payment of wages in the form of a group term life insurance[a]
6053(c)(1)	Reporting with respect to certain tips[a]

Section 6721(a)(1) provides that any person who fails to file a correct information return with the Service on or before the prescribed filing date is subject to a penalty, but the amount of the penalty varies based on when, if at all,

---

[873] Where the delinquency is due to intentional disregard, the penalty is increased to the greater of $100 or 10 percent of the aggregate amount required to be reported.

[874] Where the delinquency is due to intentional disregard, the penalty is increased to $100. There is no increased penalty based on the percentage of amount required to be reported on such returns and statements.

[875] The returns required to be filed under these sections are considered to be interest or dividend returns or statements, to which special rules apply.

[876] Where the delinquency is due to intentional disregard, the penalty is the greater of $100 or 5 percent of the aggregate amount required to be reported.

[877] The increased penalty (for failures due to intentional disregard) for each failure to file a return required to be filed under this section is the greater of $100 or either 10 percent of the aggregate amount required to be reported or 10 percent of the taxable income derived from the transaction.

the correct information return is filed. If a person files a correct information return after the prescribed filing date but on or before the date that is thirty days after the prescribed filing date, the amount of the penalty is $15 per return, with a maximum penalty of $75,000 per calendar year.[878] Note that the ceiling helps only those filers who have delinquencies for more than 5,000 returns. If a person files a correct information return more than thirty days after the prescribed filing date but on or before August 1, the amount of the penalty is $30 per return, with a maximum penalty of $150,000 per calendar year.[879] If a correct information return is not filed on or before August 1 of any year, the amount of the penalty is $50 per return, with a maximum penalty of $250,000 per calendar year.[880]

> **EXAMPLE:** Bank B fails to file 15 out of 800 information returns (Forms 1099—INT), relating to interest it paid to depositors in 1989, by the due date, February 1, 1990. B cures the delinquency by filing the 15 returns within thirty days, on March 1. The delinquency penalty for the 15 returns would be $225 ($15 reduced penalty × 15 returns). If B filed the 15 returns before August 1, the penalty would be $450 ($30 reduced penalty rate × 15 returns). However, if B filed after August 1, the penalty would be $750 ($50 full penalty × 15 returns).

The penalty is imposed even if the delinquency is cured within the initial thirty-day period for filing correct information returns, albeit with a lower penalty, because Congress believed that it was vital to the integrity of the self-assessment system that taxpayers receive their payee statements on a timely basis (generally, these must be provided by January 31).[881] The preparation of these payee statements given to taxpayers is integrally connected with the preparation of the parallel information returns given to the Service. This initial thirty-day period was intended to give filers an appropriate amount of time within which to correct failures with respect to documents prepared for the Service without jeopardizing the provision of the payee statements directly to taxpayers on a timely basis. Similarly, the August 1 date was chosen because this date is approximately when the Service begins intensive processing and use of this data.[882] Submission of the data after this date is considered the

---

[878] IRC § 6721(b)(1).

[879] IRC § 6721(b)(2).

[880] IRC § 6721(a)(1).

[881] Report of the Committee on the Budget, HR Rep. No. 247, 101st Cong., 1st Sess. 1383 (1989), reprinted in 1989 USCCAN 1906, 2853. Although the reduced penalty rates available when returns are filed by August 1 give some incentive to information filers, under prior regulations, no penalty at all was imposed if returns were filed by October 1. Temp. Reg. § 301.6723-1T(c)(1).

[882] Report of the Committee on the Budget, HR Rep. No. 247, 101st Cong., 1st Sess. 1383 (1989), reprinted in 1989 USCCAN 1906, 2853. Congress expects that in future

equivalent of failing to provide the data at all. Information return providers who correct errors in payor statements filed with the Service are supposed to make any necessary parallel corrections to payee statements provided to tax-payers.[883]

Information filers can avoid or minimize the delinquency penalty in a number of ways. The IRS permits extensions of time to file most information returns.[884] Moreover, when the delinquency is caused by inaccurate information, the penalty does not apply so long as the inaccuracy is inconsequential.[885] In addition, the penalty can be avoided by a reasonable cause waiver. Even if the penalty is imposed, small business reductions in the amount of the penalty may apply.

[1] De Minimis Error Exception

A special rule is provided where there is a failure to include all the information required to be shown on an information return or incorrect information has been included in the return. Under this de minimis exception, (1) if an information return is originally filed without all of the required information or with incorrect information and (2) the return is corrected on or before August 1, then the original return is treated as having been filed with all the correct required information.[886] The number of information returns that may qualify for this exception for any calendar year is limited to the greater of (1) ten returns or (2) one half of one percent of the total number of information returns that are required to be filed by the person during the calendar year.[887]

The general limitation of this exception to ten returns provides a special small-business exception to this penalty.[888] According to IRS statistics, approximately 84 percent of payors who file information returns with the IRS file ten or fewer forms. As a result, these payors have until August 1 to correct without penalty errors of omission or commission on information returns that were originally timely filed with the IRS. As a practical matter, this limitation

---

years advancements in available technology may permit the Service to utilize these data earlier in the year, and, if this proves to be the case, it expects the Service to request that Congress consider modifying this deadline legislatively.

[883] See IRC § 6722(a).

[884] The form to be used is Form 8809 (Request for Extension of Time to File Information Returns). Forms that can be covered by this request are Forms W-2, W-2P, 1098, 1099, 5498, and W-2G. The request must be filed by the due date of the return.

[885] IRC § 6721(c). See Temp. Reg. § 301.6723-1T(b).

[886] IRC § 6721(c)(1).

[887] IRC § 6721(c)(2).

[888] HR Rep. No. 247, 101st Cong., 1st Sess. 1383–1384 (1989).

means that ten returns will be the maximum excepted under the limitations.[889] If the total number of returns corrected by the taxpayer exceeds the de minimis threshold, only the number of returns exceeding the threshold is subject to penalty. For example, if twenty information returns are corrected by August 1, the delinquency penalty could be imposed for the ten returns not covered by the de minimis exception. The de minimis exception to the delinquency penalty is mechanical—that is, when its requirements are met, no penalty is permitted to be imposed. At the same time, the de minimis exception is limited effectively to ten returns. However, irrespective of the de minimis exception, the information filer can seek and be granted a reasonable cause waiver, and the availability of such a waiver is unaffected by the fact that the de minimis limitation has been exceeded.[890]

[2] Reduced Penalty for Small Businesses

Lower maximum penalty levels are provided for small businesses.[891] Small businesses are defined as firms having average annual gross receipts for the most recent three taxable years that do not exceed $5 million.[892] The maximum penalties for small businesses are $25,000 (instead of $75,000) if the failures are corrected on or before thirty days after the prescribed filing date, $50,000 (instead of $150,000) if the failures are corrected on or before August 1, and $100,000 (instead of $250,000) if the failure is not corrected on or before August 1.[893]

[3] Intentional Disregard

If the failure to file or to provide correct information on one or more information returns is due to "intentional disregard" of the filing requirements (or the correct information reporting requirement), then the remedial provisions of Section 6721 are stripped away. The penalty reduction where a correction is made within the specified period does not apply, nor do the de minimis and the small business exceptions.[894] Moreover, the penalty amount is increased from $50 to $100, or if greater, to certain percentage amounts of the items re-

---

[889] If the information filer has filed more than 2,000 information returns, one half of one percent is greater than 10, and, if filer files less than 2,000 information returns, one half of one percent will be less than 10.

[890] HR Rep. No. 247, 101st Cong., 1st Sess. 1383–1384 (1989).

[891] IRC § 6721(d).

[892] IRC § 6721(d)(2)(A).

[893] IRC §§ 6721(d)(1)(A), 6721(d)(1)(B), 6721(d)(1)(C).

[894] IRC § 6721(e)(1).

quired to be reported correctly.[895] The percentage is 10 percent of the items required to be correctly reported on all information returns except information returns required from brokers,[896] direct sellers,[897] and recipients of mortgage interest received in a trade or business from individuals,[898] as well as information returns related to foreclosures and abandonment of security,[899] exchanges of certain partnership interests,[900] and certain dispositions of donated property.[901] In the case of these specific information returns, the percentage is 5 percent of the aggregate amount of the items required to be reported correctly. In addition, the $250,000 ceiling is eliminated,[902] as well as the lower ceilings provided for returns corrected within specified periods.[903]

Intentional disregard of the filing requirements generally implies some notice or knowledge of the filing requirement and refusal to comply, or notice or knowledge that faulty information has been provided and refusal to correct such erroneous information. Thus, the committee report states that failure to correct information returns within a reasonable period of time after being requested to do so by the Service can be considered intentional disregard.[904] The caps on penalties are removed where there is intentional disregard. This action was intended to discourage payors who are required to file large numbers of returns or payee statements from ignoring the filing requirement and considering the $250,000 cap as a cost of doing business.[905] This rationale for removing the caps also provides the insight that intentional disregard involves knowledge of the filing requirement and refusal to comply.[906]

---

[895] IRC §§ 6721(e)(2)(A), 6721(e)(2)(B).

[896] IRC § 6045(a).

[897] IRC § 6041A(b).

[898] IRC § 6050H.

[899] IRC § 6050J.

[900] IRC § 6050K.

[901] IRC § 6050L.

[902] IRC § 6721(e)(3)(A).

[903] IRC § 6721(e)(3)(B).

[904] HR Rep. No. 247, 101st Cong., 1st Sess. 1384 (1989).

[905] HR Rep. No. 247, 101st Cong., 1st Sess. 1384 (1989).

[906] The rationale also weighs against the Service's position that even if corrected, the penalty may be imposed for information returns that contain certain errors. Temp. Reg. § 301.6723-1T(c)(3) Example (3).

¶ 7B.20 FAILURE TO FURNISH CORRECT PAYEE STATEMENTS

If a person required to file an information return fails to furnish a payee state-ment to the required person by the date required or fails to include all the in-formation required to be included (or includes incorrect information), the person required to furnish the timely and correct payee statement is subject to penalty.[907] The penalty is $50 for each delinquent or incorrect payee statement, up to a maximum penalty of $100,000.[908] However, a failure to supply a timely or correct payee statement due to intentional disregard of this require-ment results in an increase in the per statement penalty and the elimination of the ceiling on the annual penalty amount.[909]

The Code sections requiring payee statements to which the delinquency penalty applies are listed in Table 7B.4.[910]

The term "payee statement" also includes "any form, statement or sched-ule required to be furnished to the recipient of any amount from which tax was required to be deducted and withheld under Chapter 3 (or from which tax would be required to be so deducted and withheld but for an exemption under this title or any treaty obligation of the United States."[911] There has been no change to the deadline by which these payee statements must be furnished. Congress believed that it was vital to the integrity of the self-assessment sys-tem that taxpayers receive their payee statements on a timely basis in order to complete their own tax returns on time. Consequently, unlike Section 6721, there is no time-sensitive element in Section 6722, no de minimis exception, and no small business exception.

Where an intentional disregard exists in the delinquent or incorrect fur-nishing of a payee statement, the per statement penalty increases from $50 to $100.[912] If it is more than $100, the penalty can be 10 percent of the aggregate amount of the items required to be reported correctly on all payee statements other than those (1) required to be furnished by brokers,[913] relating to returns regarding payments of remuneration for services and direct sales[914]; (2) fur-nished in connection with information returns required from direct sellers[915]; (3) relating to mortgage interest received in a trade or business from individu-

---

[907] IRC § 6722(b).
[908] IRC § 6722(a).
[909] IRC § 6722(c).
[910] IRC § 6724(d)(2).
[911] IRC § 6724(d)(2) (flush language).
[912] IRC § 6722(c)(1).
[913] IRC § 6045(b).
[914] IRC § 6041A(e).
[915] IRC § 6041A(b).

als[916]; and information returns relating to (a) foreclosures and abandonments of security[917]; (b) exchanges of partnership interests,[918] and (c) certain dispositions of donated property.[919] Where these specific payee statements are involved, the percentage is reduced to 5 percent of the aggregate amount of the items required to be reported correctly.[920] Where intentional disregard exists, the $100,000 ceiling does not apply for any purpose.[921]

TABLE 7B.4
Payee Statements Subject to the Delinquency Penalty

Code section	Description of payee statement
6031(b) or 6031(c), 6034A, or 6037(b)	Statements furnished by pass-thru entities—Schedules K-1 of Forms 1041, 1065, and 1120
6039(a)	Information required in connection with certain options—Forms 3921 and 3922
6041(d)	Information at source
6041A(e)	Payments of remuneration for services and direct sales
6042(c)	Payments of dividends and corporate earnings and profits
6044(c)	Payments of patronage dividends
6045(b) or 6045(d)	Returns of brokers
6049(c)	Payments of interest—all forms in the 1099 series including Forms 1099-A, 1099-B, 1099-DIV, 1099-G, 1099-INT, 1099-MISC, 1099-OID, 1099-PATR, 1099-R, and 1099-S.
6050A(b)	Reporting requirements of certain fishing boat operations—Form 1099-MISC
6050H(d)	Mortgage interest received in a trade or business from individuals—Form 1098
6050I(e)	Cash received in a trade or business—Form 8300
6050J(e)	Foreclosures and abandonments of security—Form 1099-A
6050K(b)	Exchanges of certain partnership interests—Form 8308
6050L(c)	Certain dispositions of donated property—Form 8282
6050N(b)	Payments of royalties—Form 1099-MIS

[916] IRC § 6050H(d).

[917] IRC § 6050J(e).

[918] IRC § 6050K(b).

[919] IRC § 6050L(c).

[920] IRC § 6722(c)(1)(B).

[921] IRC § 6722(c)(2). A case arising under prior law is instructive on the meaning of intentional disregard for purposes of the reporting requirements. A proprietor of a coin shop who routinely purchased gold bullion and silver coins from his customers and subsequently sold coins at retail was assessed under pre-1989 law the civil penalty for intentional disregard of the obligation of a broker to file an information return as required by Section 6045(a)(3). Robinson v. United States, 75 AFTR2d ¶ 95-750 (MD Fla. 1995). The district court held that there was no intentional disregard because the regulations defining broker were unclear, and, using the Supreme Court's definition of "willful" in Cheek v. United States, 498 US 192 (1991), as a guide to the meaning of intentional disregard, the taxpayer truly believed that the filing was not required. The court also said that case law supported the taxpayer's belief that proposed amendments to the regulation defining "broker" should not control the interpretation of an existing statute.

6051	Receipts for employees—Form W-2
6052(b)	Payment of wages in the form of group term life insurance—Form W-2
6053(b) or 6053(c)	Reports of tips—Form 4070
4093(c)(4)(B)	Purchasers of diesel and aviation fuels—Form 8743

¶ 7B.21 MISCELLANEOUS PENALTIES

[1] Miscellaneous Information Reporting Penalty

Any person who fails to comply with other specified information reporting requirements on or before the prescribed date is subject to a penalty of $50 for each failure, with a maximum penalty of $100,000 per calendar year.[922] Information reporting requirements for this purpose specifically include any requirement to include (1) a correct taxpayer identification number on a return or statement and (2) any requirement to furnish a correct taxpayer identification number to another person.[923] This penalty is coordinated with the penalties for failure to file correct information returns and failure to file correct payee statements, and is inapplicable to failures penalized under Sections 6721 and 6722.[924]

[2] Failure to Meet Magnetic Media Requirements

The ability of the Service to match information returns against taxpayer returns is greatly enhanced when the information is filed on magnetic media compatible with the Service's own computer systems. Information returns filed on paper are less easily and less frequently matched against returns. Accordingly, an effort has been made to require filing on magnetic media and to have that magnetic media of a uniform type compatible with IRS systems.

Uniform magnetic media requirements apply to all information returns filed during any calendar year.[925] This was accomplished by making statutory

---

[922] IRC § 6723.

[923] The penalty also applies to the notice required to be given to a partnership for a transferor's exchange of a partnership interest involving unrealized receivables or inventory. IRC §§ 751(a), 6050K(c)(1).

[924] Under prior law, Section 6723 was used to penalize information filers who failed to file correct returns or to provide correct payee statements. For failures after 1989, these failures are covered by Sections 6721 and 6722.

[925] IRC § 6724(c). See IRC § 6011(e)(2). Magnetic media include all tapes, disks, and diskettes or information in machine-readable form. The requirements specifically apply to the following returns: Form W-2, Form W-2P, Form W2-G, the Form 1099 series, Form 1098, Form 1042S, Form 5498, and Form 8027. IRS Notice 90-15, 1990-1 CB 326.

the requirement formerly contained in IRS regulations that persons filing more than 250 information returns file those returns on magnetic media.[926] Filing on magnetic media is required for all types of information returns, but the penalty for failing to do so when required applies only to the number of returns that exceeds 250.[927] However, the penalty for failure to file correct information returns on a timely basis would apply to the first 250 returns. Payors are supposed to be permitted to file in as many formats as is feasible. Service requirements must keep pace with technological advances.[928]

In granting one-year or multi-year exemptions from this requirement the Service is supposed to take into account the ability of the taxpayer to comply at a reasonable cost with the magnetic-media-filing requirements, and other factors.[929] Other instances of undue hardship, such as temporary equipment breakdowns or destruction of magnetic media equipment, are also considered.

¶ 7B.22 THE UNIFORM WAIVER STANDARD

No penalty for delinquent filing of an information return, failure to furnish correct payee statements, or failure to comply with other information reporting requirements is permissible "if it is shown that such failure is due to reasonable cause and not to willful neglect."[930] The reasonable cause waiver for information return filers and the reasonable cause waiver for taxpayers subject to delinquency penalties are the same. Consequently, the law developed under the taxpayer delinquency penalties is applicable here as well.[931] One distinctive factor in the application of the reasonable cause waiver where information returns are involved is the compliance history of the information provider. If the information provider has an established record of complying with the information reporting requirements, reasonable cause exists.[932] Consideration is also given to other significant mitigating factors. It can be expected that the factors

---

[926] IRC § 6724(c).

[927] IRC § 6724(c). In figuring this exception, each category of return is treated separately so that if, for example, an information provider were filing 200 returns on Form 1099-INT and 350 returns on Form 1099-MISC, only the Forms 1099-MISC would be required to be filed on magnetic media. IRS Notice 90-15, 1990-1 CB 326.

[928] Report of the Committee on the Budget, HR Rep. No. 247, 101st Cong., 1st Sess. 1386 (1989), reprinted in 1989 USCCAN 1906, 2856.

[929] Report of the Committee on the Budget, HR Rep. No. 247, 101st Cong., 1st Sess. 1386 (1989), reprinted in 1989 USCCAN 1906, 2856.

[930] IRC § 6724(a).

[931] See supra ¶ 7B.07.

[932] Report of the Committee on the Budget, HR Rep. No. 247, 101st Cong., 1st Sess. 1385 (1989), reprinted in 1989 USCCAN 1906, 2855. Temp. Reg. § 301.6723-1T(c)(2).

would include whether the omissions or inaccuracies were inconsequential and did not prevent the IRS from processing the returns or correlating the information required to be shown on the return, and whether errors on payee statements could not reasonably be expected to prevent or hinder the payee from timely receiving correct information and reporting it on the payee's tax return.[933]

---

[933] See Temp. Reg. § 301.6723-1T(b).

CHAPTER **8**

The Examination Function

B SPECIAL FEATURES OF EXAMINATIONS BY DIFFERENT OPERATING UNITS

¶ 8.01 OVERVIEW OF EXAMINATIONS OF TAX RETURNS

Examinations of tax returns can be viewed in at least three ways. On one level, examinations of tax returns serve the policy of enforcing compliance with the tax laws. Second, examinations are the day-to-day work of the Internal Revenue Service (the Service), the specific administrative agency charged with the enforcement of the tax laws. Finally, examinations are a product of statute, the Internal Revenue Code (the Code).

Examinations as a compliance mechanism. As the Service describes the policy, examinations of returns are an enforcement measure "to promote the highest degree of voluntary compliance on the part of the taxpayers."[1] The theory is that the greater the number of examinations, the higher the levels of taxpayer compliance with the internal revenue laws.[2] Tax return examinations are not only used to promote higher levels of taxpayer compliance, they are expected to produce additional tax revenue. Limited numbers of examination personnel are available to examine tax returns; the Service therefore uses computer-based techniques and manual review to classify and select returns for examination with the greatest potential for tax change and revenue yield. Despite the Service's belief that audits ensure higher levels of voluntary compliance, the level of taxpayer compliance has been the subject of considerable debate,[3] and audit coverage (i.e., number of examinations divided by the num-

---

[1] IRM 2.1.1.4.10, Policies of the IRS, P-4-21 (approved June 1, 1974) ("[t]he primary objective in selecting returns for examination is to promote the highest degree of voluntary compliance on the part of taxpayers").

[2] Support for this view has long come from legislative, administrative, and academic quarters. Staff of Joint Comm. on Tax'n, "Routes to Better Tax Compliance," __ Tax Notes 1187 (June 27, 1983); Report on Administrative Procedures of the Internal Revenue Service to the Administrative Conference of the United States, S. Doc. No. 266, 94th Cong., 2d Sess. 22 (1976); Dubin, Graetz & Wilde, "Penny-Wise and Pound Foolish: New Estimates of the Impact of Audits on Revenue," __ Tax Notes 789 (May 25, 1987).

[3] Although the matter is subject to much debate, levels of voluntary compliance with the U.S. tax laws are believed to be "one of the highest in the world," with about 83 percent of tax owed on income from legitimate activities voluntarily reported and paid. House Ways & Means Comm., "Overview of the Federal Tax System," HR Rep. No. 28, 101st Cong., 1st Sess. 194. Based on evidence collected by the Service in Taxpayer Compliance Measurement Program (TCMP) examinations (see infra ¶ 8.03[1][b]) and accounting for factors such as inflation, it appears that taxpayer behavior has been relatively stable since at least 1969. S. Long & D. Burnham, "The Numbers Game: Changes in Tax Compliance During the Last 25 Years?" 46 Tax Notes 1177 (Mar. 5, 1990); R. Fratanduono & G. Bucci, Trends in the Voluntary Compliance of Taxpayers Who File Individual Income Tax Returns, 1989 Update, Trend Analysis and Related Statistics, IRC Doc. 6011 (rev. 6-89), at 28–29.

On the other hand, estimates of the difference between the amount of tax that would have been paid if all taxpayers had filed complete and accurate returns (the tax gap) have varied. Id. ($100 billion); IRS, Income Tax Compliance Research, Net Tax Gap and Remittance Gap Estimates (Supp. Pub. 7285) Pub. 1415 (4-90) ($63.5 billion); compare S.

ber of filings), while necessarily small, has declined dramatically over the years.[4] The decline in audit coverage seems irreversible.[5] Audits of corporations produce more revenue than audits of individual returns, so the audit coverage of corporation returns has been better than audit coverage of individual returns over the years; but audits of corporation returns have declined,[6] and even audits conducted under the Coordinated Examination Program (CEP) of the 1,700 largest corporations have been reduced.[7] Low numbers of examinations relative to the number of returns filed may nevertheless produce impressive amounts of revenue, especially when penalties and interest are added to the total amount of recommended additional tax.[8] Audit coverage of high-income individuals with substantial income from a business or profession, is sig-

---

Long & D. Burnham, "Can Bigger IRS Really Dent U.S. Budget Woes," 48 Tax Notes 741, 752 (Aug. 6, 1990) ($23.9 billion).

[4] Audit coverage of individual income tax returns was about 5 percent in the mid-1960s. In fiscal 1999, audit coverage was only 0.43 percent. IRS Data Book 2000, at 15. Although in its fiscal year 1996, the Service's audit coverage for individual returns was 1.67 percent, in fiscal 1998, audit coverage for all classes of individual taxpayers was "the lowest in modern history" at less than 0.5 percent. "IRS Enforcement Drops Sharply," 1999 TNT 69-3 (Apr. 9, 1999).

[5] It has been convincingly contended that with present levels of audit coverage and personnel, examination could produce more revenue by better targeting examinations to those returns with maximum potential for audit change. S. Long & D. Burnham, "The Numbers Game: Changes in Tax Compliance During the Last 25 Years?" 46 Tax Notes 1177 (Mar. 5, 1990).

[6] For corporations, audit coverage increased slightly from 2.36 percent in 1991 to 2.99 percent in 1992, while in 1993, the audit coverage of corporations was 3.05 percent. "IRS Statistics Show Audit Rates Stable for Individuals, Increasing for Others," Daily Tax Rep. No. 108 (June 8, 1993). In fiscal 1993, audit coverage of all corporations dropped to 2.34 percent. IRS Data Book, Oct. 1, 1995, to Sept. 30, 1996, at 12. In 1998, audit coverage for corporations also dropped. "IRS Enforcement Drops Sharply," 1999 TNT 69-3 (Apr. 9, 1999). In 1999, the combined audit coverage of corporation returns was 1.12 percent. IRS Data Book 2000, at 15.

[7] For corporation returns reflecting income of $250 million or more, the audit coverage dropped from 72.86 percent in 1990 to 52.11 percent in 1993. "IRS Audit Rate Falls Below One Percent," 47 Tax Notes 1575 (June 25, 1990). In 1998, the Service audited only 37 percent of the corporations with $250 million or more in assets. "IRS Enforcement Drops Sharply," 1999 TNT 69-3 (Apr. 9, 1999). In 1999, audit coverage of corporation returns of $250 million or more dropped to 31.45 percent. IRS Data Book 2000, at 15.

[8] It is noteworthy that CEP examinations accounted for approximately $15 billion out of the total of $28 billion in recommended additional tax and penalties, and that of the $14.5 billion in adjustments in all CEP corporate audits, CEP audits of corporations with more than $250 million in assets accounted for $13.5 billion in adjustments. IRS Data Book 2000, at 13. In 1999, with a 0.43 percent audit coverage, audits of taxable individual returns still resulted in $3.4 billion of recommended additional tax and penalties. IRS Data Book 2000, at 16.

nificantly higher[9] than the overall coverage rate. Similarly, returns of the largest corporations with substantial assets are audited on an almost continuous basis.[10]

Examinations as a type of test performed by an administrative agency. A second way of looking at examinations is as the work of an administrative agency. The examination of returns is the same type of activity other administrative agencies use when they investigate or test compliance with the statutory jurisdiction of the agencies. Organized into four operating divisions to examine the returns of taxpayers on a type-taxpayer basis, the examination function of each division administers a nationwide program of selecting and examining all types of federal tax returns of the taxpayers included in each division to determine the correct liabilities of taxpayers. Tax auditors conduct examinations through interviews or correspondence, either from service centers or area offices, and revenue agents examine returns in field examinations. To accomplish compliance objectives, the Service uses sophisticated computer technology to classify returns, as well as the accumulated experience of its personnel to classify and select returns for examination. Returns are classified as having audit potential by computer analysis, which numerically scores tax returns according to a mathematically determined probability of error.[11] Returns with the highest scores—i.e., the highest probability of error—are then reviewed manually by experienced agents to confirm audit potential before selection for examination. Other circumstances also lead to the selection of a return for examination. For example, returns with adjusted gross incomes above certain levels and those with respect to which refund or credit claims have been filed are reviewed, and those with audit potential are selected for examination. In the course of an examination, earlier or later returns of the taxpayer

---

[9] Audit coverage of critical categories of returns has declined steadily. For individual returns showing total positive income of $100,000 or more, audit coverage has declined from 5.55 percent in 1990 to 4.03 percent in 1993. On average for the years 1986, 1987, and 1988, with overall coverage rates at about 1.5 percent, approximately 4 percent of the returns of individuals with Schedule C gross receipts of $100,000 or more were examined. S. Long & D. Burnham, "Can Bigger IRS Really Dent U.S. Budget Woes," 48 Tax Notes 741, 752 (Aug. 6, 1990). In 1989, when coverage of all individual income tax returns was 0.92 percent, the coverage of individual returns showing total positive income (TPI) of $100,000 or more was 5.46 percent. IRS Annual Report 1989, Table 7.

[10] IRS Data Book 2000, at 15. In 1985, with 1.34 percent audit coverage for all filed returns, about 87 percent of the returns of corporations with $100 million or more were examined. In 1988, with 1.26 percent audit coverage under the CEP, 1,461 of the largest corporations were examined; these examinations produced $9.58 billion in deficiencies and penalties out of a total of $19.2 billion for the year from all examinations. House Ways & Means Comm., "Overview of the Federal Tax System," HR Rep. No. 28, 101st Cong., 1st Sess. 195. In 1989, when audit coverage was below one percent and the total additional tax and penalties recommended after examinations was about $21.3 billion, the total corporation adjustments were $12.9 billion, IRS Annual Report 1989, Table 9.

[11] See infra ¶ 8.03.

or the returns of related taxpayers, such as the shareholders of a closely held corporation or the partners of a partnership, may be examined.

After selection, returns are examined through correspondence, office interviews, or field examinations by personnel in the operating division's Examination function.[12] Correspondence examinations are conducted by service center personnel,[13] and also by local Examination office technicians.[14] Local office Examination technicians conduct interview examinations as well. Both correspondence examinations and office interview examinations usually involve questionable items on individual taxpayer returns, which may be resolved by the taxpayer's supplying substantiating data. Field examinations, on the other hand, usually involve more complex business returns of individuals or entities, requiring more tax expertise on the part of the examiner than is required of the tax technician.[15]

At the conclusion of the examination, the examiner may accept the return as filed or assert a deficiency. When a deficiency is asserted, the taxpayer has the option of agreeing or disagreeing with the examiner's findings. If the taxpayer agrees with the findings, a form is completed setting forth the adjustments and the taxpayer's agreement to the immediate assessment of the resulting deficiency.[16] After the form is processed, the tax is assessed, and the taxpayer receives a bill for the tax due.

If the taxpayer does not agree with the examiner's adjustments, the examiner prepares a report, which is subject to review by the examiner's supervisor and the area office's Quality Review staff.[17] Following this review, the taxpayer is sent a copy of the examiner's report under cover of a "thirty-day letter," which describes the alternatives available to the taxpayer. The taxpayer may then take one of the following actions:

1. Agree with the adjustments and execute the form enclosed with the thirty-day letter permitting immediate assessment;
2. Disagree with the adjustments, request consideration by a regional Appeals Office, and (if the deficiency exceeds $2,500) file a protest within thirty days (hence the term "thirty-day letter");
3. Do nothing, in which case the taxpayer will receive a notice of deficiency, which permits the taxpayer ninety days to file a petition for redetermination of the local office's deficiency determination in the Tax Court; or

---

[12] See infra ¶ 8.02.
[13] See infra ¶ 8.04.
[14] See infra ¶ 8.05.
[15] See infra ¶ 8.06.
[16] See infra ¶ 8.07.
[17] See infra ¶ 8.08.

4. Wait until the ninety-day period provided for filing a petition in the Tax Court expires, the deficiency is assessed, and a bill is received for the amount assessed. After paying the amount of the assessment, the taxpayer can obtain judicial review of the assessment by filing a refund suit in a federal district court or the claims court. Before instituting a refund suit, the taxpayer must pay the full amount of the assessed tax, file a claim for refund with the Service, and wait at least six months for the Service to act unless the Service disallows the claim before the six months have elapsed.

A statutory view of examinations. A third view of the examination process is a statutory one: a study of the array of tax provisions, which direct and control the examination process. In this view, the examination is the search for and determination of a deficiency. These provisions can be gathered by the purpose they serve in the examination process.

Section 6211(a) defines a "deficiency" as "the amount by which the tax imposed by subtitle A [Income Tax] or B [Estate and Gift Tax], or chapter 41, 42, 43, or 44 [miscellaneous excise taxes] exceeds . . . the amount shown as the tax by the taxpayer upon his return, if a return was made by the taxpayer and an amount of tax was shown by the taxpayer thereon. . . . " In a statutory view, the examination of a tax return is the Service's search for and determination of the difference between "tax imposed" by the income, estate, or gift tax provisions of the Code, and "the amount of shown as the tax by the taxpayer upon his return." In other words, a "deficiency" contemplates that the Service has determined "tax imposed" or the tax due after examining the taxpayer's return.

How does the Code govern the examination process? Section 7602(a) grants the Service authority "for the purpose of ascertaining the correctness of any return, making a return where none has been made, determining of the liability of any person for any internal revenue tax . . . (1) to examine any books, papers, records, or other data which may be relevant or material to such inquiry." The Service's summons authority also authorizes it to summon the person liable for the tax, or the taxpayer's officers and employees or any other person the Service deems proper "to appear before the Service at a time and place named in the summons and o produce such books, papers, records, or other data, and to give such testimony, under oath, as may be relevant to such inquiry" and to take that person's testimony. Although examinations are frequently conducted on an informal basis without a summons, the summons authority is the statutory basis for an examiner's inquiry. In other words, Section 7602(a) gives examination personnel the authority to use a summons to determine the amount of tax due. Section 7603 prohibits unnecessary examinations and second inspections, and in general requires higher level review for approval if a second inspection of a taxpayer's return is to be conducted.

The summons authority under Section 7602(a) is broad enough to permit audit personnel to contact third parties to obtain information about the taxpayer's return. Because of concerns about the privacy of the taxpayer, Section 7602(c) requires the Service to notify the taxpayer of its intent to contact third parties, and Section 7609(a) mandates that the Service give the taxpayer notice that a summons has been served a on a third-party recordkeeper, such as a bank, many financial institutions, an attorney, or an accountant.

Section 7605 establishes the basic standard that the time and place of an examination must be reasonable under the circumstances.

Finally, to resolve disputes about the amount of additional tax due without litigation, Section 7123 requires the Service to establish alternative dispute resolution procedures which taxpayers may use, such as the early referral of issues from examination to the Appeals Office, as well as mediation and arbitration in the Appeals Office. The Service has adopted a number of alternative dispute resolution procedures both before and after this mandate was given.

Another Code provision governing the examination is the statute of limitations on assessment, Section 6501(a). In general, the Service must complete its examination within three years after the taxpayer has filed the return.

A further listing of the relevant statutory provisions would include the refund provisions of the Code, which also presuppose some examination of the taxpayer's claim for refund by requiring the taxpayer to file a claim (Section 6511(a) and Section 7422(a)) and to wait six months to allow the Service to review the claim (Section 6532(a)(1)).

These three perspectives show that the examination function is at the heart of tax compliance efforts. Examination procedures are intended to provide taxpayers with due process rights and ultimately court review to check arbitrary and erroneous action by examiners. At least in important respects, Service examiners are granted powers deemed appropriate to carry out the examination of tax returns, while taxpayers are provided with statutory opportunities to contest the use of summons authority, to resolve disputes with examination personnel without litigation, and if those attempts fail to seek prepayment court review or postpayment suits for refund.

A   ORGANIZATIONAL ASPECTS OF EXAMINATION

¶ 8.02 THE DIVISIONAL ORGANIZATION OF TAXPAYER EXAMINATION

As a result of the IRS Restructuring and Reform Act of 1998 (the 1998 Act) described in Chapter 1, the examination functions of the Service's field organization changed from a geographically and functionally separate organization to an organization based on taxpayer type.[18] Field operations are organized into four operational units or divisions: (1) Wage and Investment Income; (2) Small Business and Self-Employed; (3) Large and Mid-Size Business (LMSB); and (4) Tax Exempt and Government Entities (TE/GE). One of the operations in each of these divisions is compliance, and includes the examination of filed tax returns. Although the organization and name of the examination function has changed, the procedures examiners follow to perform audits of tax returns remain roughly the same as before the reorganization.

---

[18] IRS Restructuring and Reform Act of 1998, HR 2676, 105th Cong., 2d Sess. § 1002.

FORM 8.1
IRS OPERATING DIVISIONS

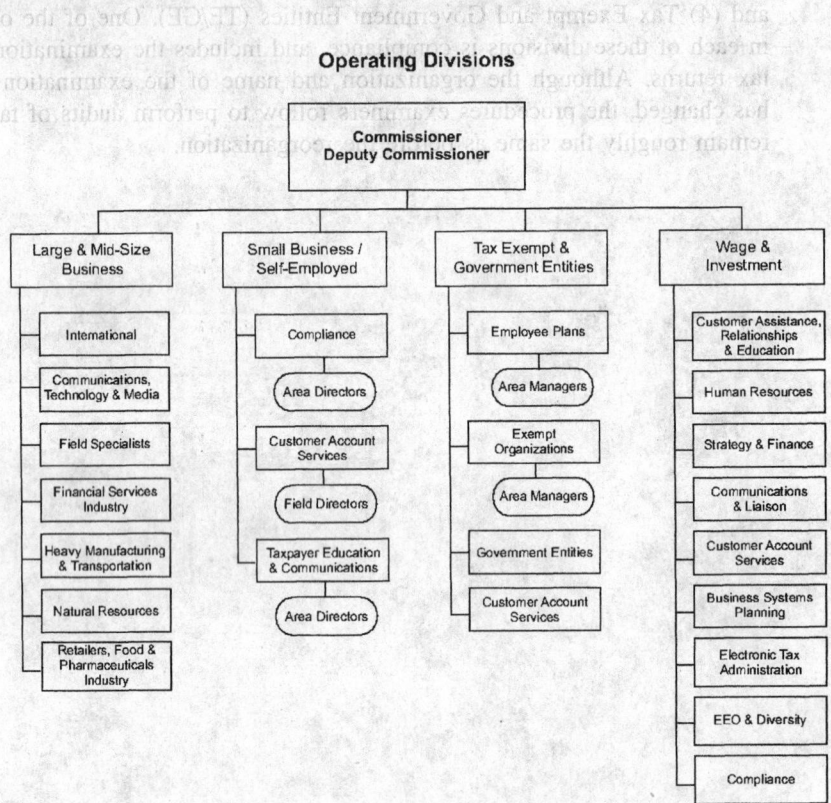

Operating Divisions

Commissioner
Deputy Commissioner

Large & Mid-Size Business	Small Business / Self-Employed	Tax Exempt & Government Entities	Wage & Investment
International	Compliance	Employee Plans	Customer Assistance, Relationships & Education
Communications, Technology & Media	Area Directors	Area Managers	Human Resources
Field Specialists	Customer Account Services	Exempt Organizations	Strategy & Finance
Financial Services Industry	Field Directors	Area Managers	Communications & Liaison
Heavy Manufacturing & Transportation	Taxpayer Education & Communications	Government Entities	Customer Account Services
Natural Resources	Area Directors	Customer Account Services	Business Systems Planning
Retailers, Food & Pharmaceuticals Industry			Electronic Tax Administration
			EEO & Diversity
			Compliance

FORM 8.2
IRS FUNCTIONAL, SHARED-SERVICES, AND MODERNIZATION DIVISIONS

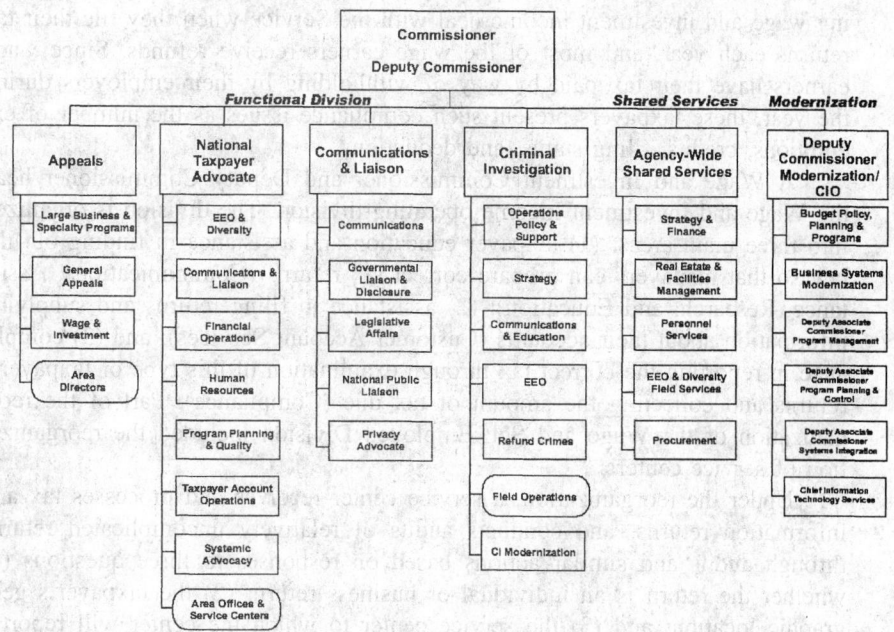

Functional Division, Shared Services, and Modernization

[1] Wage and Investment Income

The Wage and Investment Operating Division has the responsibility for examinations of taxpayers with wage and investment income. The division processes about 88 million filers of tax returns, representing 116 million individual taxpayers, including those who file jointly with wage and investment income only, almost all of which third parties report to the Service. Taxpayers reporting wage and investment income deal with the Service when they file their tax returns each year, and most of the wage earners receive refunds. Since wage earners have their tax paid by way of withholding by their employers during the year, these taxpayers present such compliance issues as the number of exemptions, credits, filing status, and deductions.

A Wage and Investment Commissioner and Deputy Commissioner head the Wage and Investment Income operating division. The division is organized into three main areas: (1) taxpayer education and assistance in finding out the law so that taxpayers can prepare correct tax returns (Communications, Assistance, Research, and Education); (2) assistance in filing returns and supplying information about their accounts (Customer Account Services); and (3) compliance in reporting the correct tax through examination of this type of taxpayer's returns and collecting the amount of tax due (Compliance). Part of the reorganization of the Wage and Self-Employed Division included the reorganization of service centers.

Under the reorganization, a service center receives and processes tax and information returns, and conducts audits of relatively uncomplicated returns through audits and similar actions based on responses to three questions (1) whether the return is an individual or business return; (2) the taxpayer's geographic location; and (3) the service center to which the center will report.[19] Five service centers process Wage and Investment Division returns: Andover, Atlanta, Austin, Fresno, and Kansas City. Eight centers handle the receipt and processing of individual returns. They include the five Wage and Investment centers, and the Brookhaven, Memphis, and Philadelphia centers.

[2] Small Business and Self-Employed

The Small Business and Self-Employed Operating Division includes fully or partially self-employed individuals and small businesses, and has about 45 million filers. Small Business and Self-Employed taxpayers have more complex issues than Wage and Investment taxpayers and have more frequent contacts with the Service. While Wage and Investment taxpayers have from one to four contacts with the Service per filer year, the Service estimates Small Business and Self-Employed taxpayers may have four to sixty contacts with the Service

---

[19] IR-2000-61 (Sept. 1, 2000).

per filer year. Five service centers handle the Small Business and Self-Employed Division, and also handle service center–based activities for TE/GE filers, as well as approximately 210,000 LMSB filers. Cincinnati and Ogden handle the receipt and processing of business returns, which also include employment, estate, and gift tax returns.

[3] Large and Mid-Size Business

The Large and Mid-Size Business Operating Division started to operate in its reorganized form on June 4, 2000, with a Commissioner and Deputy Commissioner, along with International, Field Specialists, and staff functions (the most notable of which is Pre-Filing and Technical Guidance) located in the National Office.[20] In the field, there are five industry organizations, which are organized to provide for the "end-to-end" needs of the following types of taxpayers: (1) Financial Services and Healthcare, headquartered in Manhattan (about 40,000 businesses); (2) Retailers, Food, and Pharmaceuticals, in Chicago (about 25,000 businesses); (3) Natural Resources, in Houston (15,000 businesses); (4) Communications, Technology, and Media, in the San Francisco Bay area (12,000 businesses); and (5) Heavy Manufacturing, Construction, and Transportation, in New Jersey (88,000 businesses).

[4] Tax Exempt and Government Entities

The Tax Exempt and Government Entities Operating Division was established in late 1999 to serve Employee Plans, Exempt Organizations, and Government Entities.[21] The Tax Exempt and Government Entities Division Headquarters is in the National Office, but Employee Plan and Exempt Organization field activities are managed through six area offices. Examination and approval of pension trust plans and exempt organizations and the issuance of determination letters are handled by this division.[22]

Despite reorganization by type of taxpayer, local offices still have Examination organizations, which have five activities: (1) returns classification; (2) review; (3) field examination; (4) office examination; and (5) service. Returns Program Managers develop and administer a program for selecting all types of

---

[20] "IRS's New Large Corporate Division Goes Live," 2000 TNT 108-2 (June 6, 2000); "The New IRS Stands Up," Jan. 13–14, 2000. All four operational units were functioning as of October 2000.

[21] For discussion of the reorganization, see ¶ 1.02[2]. Proceedings, "The New IRS Stands Up," Jan. 13–14, 2000.

[22] For a description of the TE/GE function, see ¶ 3.04[3][e].

returns for examination. They also conduct special studies to identify noncompliance problem areas and recommend audit programs to cope with them.

The compliance function is implemented by Office Branches, which conduct examinations through correspondence or interviews with taxpayers at local offices relating to all types of taxes (except alcohol, tobacco, and firearms), to determine the correct liability of taxpayers for tax and penalties and the validity of claims for refund, credit, or abatement or for redemption of stamps. Office examiners process applications for exemption from collecting admissions tax and compute jeopardy assessments. They also provide technical support to the year-round taxpayer assistance program.

Field Examination Branches are divided into revenue agent groups. These may include regular income tax, training, large case, and specialized groups such as estate and gift, excise, employment, international operations, engineers, valuation, insurance, banking, and brokerage groups. Revenue agents conduct field examinations to determine correct liabilities of taxpayers for tax and penalties, including the examination of claims for refund, credit, or abatement. They also conduct field examinations of offers in compromise, based on either doubt as to liability or inability to pay, and special field examinations, as requested, including joint examinations with special agents of the Criminal Investigation Division (CID) when tax evasion may exist.

To aid its audit function, the branches have specialists in engineering and valuation work. Field Examination Branches also prepare memoranda to accompany closing agreements, recommend jeopardy assessments, and provide technical support to the year-round taxpayer assistance program. International specialists conduct or participate in field examinations of foreign taxpaying entities doing business in the United States.[23]

Quality Review staffs review reports of examinations of all types of tax returns to verify the determination of liability made by the examining officer. The staffs have primary responsibility within the district for maintaining quality standards in examinations and reports and for the technical accuracy of all matters subject to review. When substantial errors are detected in reports of examining agents, the staffs issue correction memoranda. They also direct the issuance of preliminary notices of deficiency to taxpayers, review protests filed in response to notices, and prepare statutory notices of deficiency. The Quality Review staffs prepare closing letters and releases in estate and gift tax cases and review offers in compromise, informants' claims for reward, and the special procedures applicable in cases involving renegotiation.

Service Branches perform clerical services necessary to the processing of returns, reports of examination, case files, and correspondence, including maintaining control of all returns and case files.

---

[23] For a description of the International function, see ¶ 1.02 and infra ¶ 8.10.

¶ 8.03 CLASSIFICATION OF RETURNS FOR EXAMINATION

Some knowledge about how returns are classified and selected for examination is important for at least two practical reasons. First, the way in which the Service classifies and selects returns for examination allows practitioners to anticipate items and issues that are likely to generate examination and to prepare the return using such techniques as disclosure statements and attaching copies of documents and other information to substantiate and explain a return item and possibly avoid examination. Second, the process shows what areas are likely to be important to the Service in an examination.

[1] In General

Classification is "the process of determining whether a return should be selected for examination, what issues should be examined, and how the examination should be conducted."[24] Tax returns are selected for examination by computerized mathematical techniques and by personnel who manually identify them for examination.[25] Mathematical computerized programs, collectively known as the Discriminant Function (DIF) system, analyze the relationship between and among return-line items for tax-change potential. Returns are also manually classified and selected for examination by experienced examiners; for example, where amended returns, information reports, or refund claims are needed. Although a return may be computer classified as having examination potential, it is also manually screened; that is, experienced classifiers identify the issues in need of examination and decide whether to accept as filed returns initially classified by computer.[26] During classification, returns are separated by type of examination (e.g., office examination, field examination, and correspondence examination), and are reviewed for significant items. Selection is made on the basis of characteristics that the return classifiers perceive as requiring special attention.

---

[24] IRM 4.1.5.1, The Examining Process: Overview (May 19, 1999); see also IRM 4.19.1.2.2, What Is Classification (Oct. 1, 2001).

[25] IRM 4.1.5.1, The Examining Process: Overview (May 19, 1999); IRM 4.1.1.2, Identification and Selection of Returns—Methods of Selection (May 19, 1999).

[26] IRM 4.19.1.2.2, What Is Classification (Oct. 1, 2001) ("[c]lassification should be conducted by the technically proficient experienced examiners, who have received appropriate tax law training").

[2] Processing Returns and Classification Operations

As tax returns that taxpayers mail to the Service are delivered to a service center, they are sorted by type (individual, corporation, partnership, and fiduciary).[27] All returns are identified by a document locator number (DLN), which is entered on the check accompanying the return.[28] The return is then examined to see whether the tax due and the amount of the check match. Tax payments are segregated and deposited in banks as quickly as possible. Returns are also examined to see if they are signed and whether taxpayers have given all required information, such as all withholding statements and schedules. If necessary information is lacking and cannot be obtained from other records in the service center, errors or omissions will be communicated to the taxpayer by letter with a request to supply the correct or omitted data.

Service center tax personnel code and edit the return. Also, service center employees edit the return by making illegible items legible and completing incomplete entries, if possible. Numbered codes for such information as the taxpayer's name and address, gross income, withholding credits, refund due, and specific information used in computing the DIF system score are penciled on the return for entry.[29] Coded entries are then put on magnetic tape for computer processing. Computers mathematically check the information and review the return for so-called unallowable items. At the end of each day, two magnetic tapes—a "good" tape and an "error" tape—are produced. Taxpayer return errors are reflected on the error tape, from which is printed an error register. These returns are sent to tax examiners, who review each item on the register (usually by referring back to the tax returns) and track down the cause of the error. If service center examiners discover that an underpayment of tax is the result of a mathematical error and is "not insignificant," a mathematical error assessment is made at the service center, and the service center mails the taxpayer a notice of the correct tax and the amount due.[30] After correction, the data are put on a "good" tape and sent to the Martinsburg Computing Center (MCC).[31]

---

[27] Where an untimely return is filed with a service center, it is stamped with the date of receipt.

[28] The DLN system is a control number given to every return and each subsequent transaction document effecting the return as a means of locating documents processed through the Service's automated data processing system. The DLN system is explained at ¶ 14.03[2].

[29] Coding strip on envelopes supplied to taxpayers for filing returns identify the area in which the taxpayer resides. The DIF system is discussed infra ¶ 8.03[2][a].

[30] The Service's authority to make a summary assessment authority is subject to restrictions imposed by Section 6213(b). See ¶ 10.04[1].

[31] Each year, about 80,000 reels of computer tape are transported to and from Martinsburg by the Service. Minutes, ABA Tax Section, Admin. Practice Comm., Remarks of James Owens, Dep. Comm'r of Internal Revenue 11 (May 3, 1985).

[a] Computerized Classification: The Discriminant Function System

Most returns are classified under the DIF system, which is a computer-based mathematical technique the Service uses to score income tax returns according to their tax-change potential.[32] Under the DIF system, mathematical formulas were developed based on data collected in Taxpayer Compliance Measurement Program (TCMP) examinations, from which computer programs are developed.[33] These programs measure the likelihood of tax change based on the information taken from the return and gives the return a DIF score.[34] Although DIF formulas are confidential, it can be said that the DIF formulas assign weights to certain basic return characteristics, or variables, which are added together to obtain a composite DIF score for each return processed.[35] DIF returns are then ranked according to score from highest to lowest, with the highest scored returns having the greatest audit potential and made available to Examination for manual screening.[36]

Many individual and business returns have sufficiently high DIF scores that they are classified as having tax-change potential (i.e., the DIF score is above the DIF cutoff score). Each year the National Office establishes a national DIF cutoff score, and returns with a DIF score higher than the minimum are added to the DIF inventory and ordered for manual classification.[37] Accordingly, to control the flow of returns into the examination process, these returns are further screened by classifiers.[38] Classifiers consider data that computers cannot recognize, such as return attachments and other explanatory information. Using their experience, classifiers decide whether the return has hidden or obvious issues. If there are issues to be examined, classifiers also make the judgment whether the return will be audited by a tax examiner

---

[32] IRM 4.1.3.1, The Examining Process: Sources of Returns—DIF and Ordering, Overview (May 19, 1999).

[33] The TCMP is discussed infra ¶ 8.03[2][b].

[34] IRM 4.1.5.1.1, Discriminant Function (DIF) System (May 19, 1999).

[35] IRM 4.19.1.2.4.1, How DIF Works (Oct. 1, 2001). DIF formulas for each audit class are more sophisticated than ranges of average deductions and the like. Tax return entries (referred to as variables), such as gross income, filing status, dependents, rents and royalties, dividends and interest, and depreciation, are isolated. There are said to be 200 to 250 variables. The magnitude of tax change recommended in TCMP examinations is correlated to one or more variables on the return. For example, high tax change may correlate with both dividend income of a particular amount and four or more exemptions. Thus, a return with a combination of these two variables (dividend income and four exemptions) may produce a higher average tax change than a return with neither or only one of these variables. Variables or combinations of variables are mathematically weighted according to relative indication of tax change. The DIF score is the sum of these weighted variables.

[36] IRM 4.1.5.1.1, Discriminant Function (DIF) System (May 19, 1999).

[37] IRM 4.1.1.3, Minimum Cutoff Score (May 19, 1999).

[38] IRM 4.1.5.1.1, Discriminant Function (DIF) System (May 19, 1999).

through a correspondence audit, office audit (OA), or revenue agent field audit (FA). Classifiers then sort returns according to whether (1) the return is selected for Field Examination; (2) the return is selected for Office Examination (interview and precontact analysis); (3) the return is selected for Tax Examiners; (4) the return is accepted as filed; and (5) the return is unusual, especially special program returns, such as Tax Shelter and International Issues.[39] The returns that classifiers do not select for examination are accepted as filed.

[b] Taxpayer Compliance Measurement Program Examinations

TCMP examinations provide the information for the development of DIF formulas. The TCMP is a research program for measuring and evaluating taxpayer compliance characteristics through specialized audits. In the past, these audits have included 50,000 to 100,000 individual income tax returns in surveys done from 1965 through 1984.[40] TCMP audits were conducted at approximately three-year intervals or cycles. TCMP cycles have involved random audits of returns from 1965, 1969, 1971, 1973, 1976, 1979, 1982, 1985, and 1989. Until Congress pressured the Service not to conduct the TCMP audits, the Service had planned to conduct a TCMP survey of 1994 returns beginning in October 1995, covering a larger number of returns than prior surveys (153,000 returns versus 54,000 in 1988).[41] After determining the sample size, a statistician, under close supervision, identifies the tax returns to be audited by choosing random ending digits of social security numbers. Without an alternative source of data, variables that the Service uses to score returns for audit potential are based on out-of-date data collected in 1988.[42] Because the Service's present and future compliance programs were based on information expected to be obtained from the TCMP, the General Accounting Office (GAO) recommended that the Service develop a short-term alternative strategy (primarily by reducing the sample size) to minimize the adverse effects of the loss of compliance information.[43]

---

[39] IRM 4.1.5.1.2, Sorting of Classified Returns (May 19, 1999).

[40] For the Service's procedures in assigning TCMP returns, see IRM 4.1.4.35, Taxpayer Compliance Measurement Program (TCMP) (May 19, 1999).

[41] Guttman, "Who Should the IRS Be Auditing," 2000 TNT 49-4 (Mar. 13, 2000). An alternative taxpayer compliance measure called the National Compliance Survey may be a replacement for TCMP audits. This approach still requires some random sampling of taxpayers, but is supposed to effect the least intrusive and burdensome information gathering. Hamilton, "IRS Designs New Taxpayer Compliance Measure," 2000 TNT 70-2 (Apr. 11, 2000).

[42] Guttman, "Who Should the IRS Be Auditing," 2000 TNT 49-4 (Mar. 13, 2000).

[43] GAO, Report to the Commissioner, Internal Revenue Service, Tax Administration—Alternative Strategies to Obtain Compliance Data, GAO/GGD—96–98 (Apr. 1996).

TCMP examinations came to be controversial because they differ from regular examinations in a number of important ways. First, returns selected at random for examination under the TCMP must be examined in a field examination; no correspondence examination is permitted. Second, in the TCMP, the examiner does not have any discretion to accept the return without examination. Also, the TCMP return must be examined in detail, including an examination of all related returns, unless the examiner obtains permission to do otherwise.[44] Fourth, on completion of the audit the examiner must prepare a checksheet with detailed information derived from the examination.

After the TCMP examination is completed, checksheets are forwarded to the Service's Data Center in Detroit for tabulation. Results are analyzed at the National Office to determine significant adjustments that occur more frequently. The DIF formulations are then updated with this information. TCMP tabulations also provide the Service with a model representing the taxpaying public and levels of voluntary compliance. These models are used to focus audit coverage on particular audit classes with low voluntary compliance.[45]

As a substitute for the TCMP, the Service adopted the National Research Program (NRP), which will measure different types of compliance as follows:

1. Filing compliance is measured using sample data from the Census Bureau;
2. Payment compliance is measured using information the Service has available; and
3. Reporting compliance is measured by analyzing a sample of tax returns.[46]

NRP data update the formulas in the DIF system (which are based on data from the late 1980s) that are used to classify returns for examination.

[c] DIF Classification at Martinsburg Computing Center

In Martinsburg, West Virginia, is the heart of the Service's classification and computerized recordkeeping facility. At the MCC, applicable DIF formulas are applied to information received from service center tapes, after which

---

[44] The examining agent may request a deviation from the required procedure of examining all returns related to the TCMP return where the interest of the taxpayer in the related return is minor and would not have a material effect on the results of the TCMP examination.

[45] For example, TCMP studies have shown declining voluntary compliance in individual low-income business returns (adjusted gross income under $10,000) and small corporation returns (asset size below $50,000), thereby suggesting the need for stepped-up audit activity for these taxpayers.

[46] IRS Release No. FS-2002-07, Fact Sheet, National Research Program (Jan. 2002). See IRM 4.22.1 National Research Program (NRP), NRP Overview (Oct. 1, 2002).

each return is assigned a DIF score.[47] For each audit class, a minimum or cut-off DIF score is established. Returns with scores at or above the minimum or cutoff score (i.e., a score indicating a minimum probability of tax change) are listed on a DIF inventory file; returns below the cutoff score (returns with lower-than-minimum scores) are excluded. In addition, the data for each taxpayer are entered on a master tape or file for the type of taxpayer. Individuals have their return information and related transactions reflected in Individual Master Files, and business taxpayers on Business Master Files.

After processing at the MCC, tapes from the DIF inventory files are shipped back to the service centers.[48] These tapes may indicate any number of possible courses of action, including (1) billing; (2) a statement showing whether the taxpayer owes additional tax, is owed a refund, or has paid the correct amount of tax (this is called the Taxpayer Settlement Register); (3) delinquencies; and (4) a directory showing the name, account, and index to the DLN of the taxpayer. From these tapes the service center also produces weekly inventory reports, which show the scores of DIF returns by audit class and posts of duty in each district. These reports provide the district with the information to order the highest scored returns for purposes of examination.

[3] Manual Classification of Returns

Experienced examiners also classify returns, usually those that have not been DIF scored, as having audit potential. Non-DIF returns are manually classified to select returns showing "significant issues likely to result in tax changes or that require examination to achieve voluntary compliance by an identifiable group of taxpayers."[49] As described earlier, DIF and non-DIF returns are classified and screened by classifiers to determine whether they contain "significant" issues likely to result in tax adjustment and the scope of the examination. Regardless of the type of return, classifiers review the entire return (1) to better understand the items of income, deduction, and credit on the return; (2) to evaluate the significance of each of the items; and (3) to exclude as quickly as possible items or areas with low examination potential.[50] Classifiers identify all returns for assignment to a revenue agent, a tax auditor, or a tax examiner based "on the complexity of the issues involved, the degree of tax accounting and auditing skills required to conduct the examination, the de-

---

[47] The Service expects to decentralize the activities of the MCC so that DIF analysis is performed at service centers.

[48] The MCC also ships a tape containing data necessary to issue Treasury checks for any refunds.

[49] IRM 4.1.5.1, Classification—Overview (May 19, 1999).

[50] IRM 4.1.5.1.1, Discriminant Function (DIF) System (May 19, 1999).

gree of law knowledge required, and whether the return can be examined effectively by correspondence."[51]

The key requirement for selection is whether the item or issue to be examined is "significant." To decide whether the item or issue is significant, the classifier compares the size of the item (e.g., a $6,000 questionable expense item in a return reporting total expenses of $30,000 is significant, but the same item would not be significant if the expense were $300,000). Also, the nature of the item may make it significant, such as one the Service is challenging (e.g., airplane expense, even if the amount is not significant). Another factor is evidence of an intent to mislead or conceal, such as a missing or incomplete schedule; this may make an item significant. The way an item is reported may make the item significant if it gives the taxpayer a beneficial result (e.g., an item of expense is reported on a business schedule rather than reported as an itemized deduction). Finally, classifiers consider the relationship of the questionable item to the other items on the return, such as a return that reports business expenses, but no business income.

Returns selected for manual classification are grouped into the following categories:

1. Examinations initiated by the Service and others
2. Claims and requests for refunds
3. Related pickup examinations
4. Multiyear examinations
5. Miscellaneous

Each of these categories is discussed below. In addition to these categories, certain returns are considered automatic returns that must be screened by area classifiers to determine whether the return is worthy of being examined.

[a] Examinations Initiated by the Service and Others

The broadest category of manually selected returns is an examination initiated by the Service and others. Examinations in this category generally are initiated (1) because of information provided by another Service office or a non-Service party (e.g., a tip or referral from the CID); (2) because of a particular compliance project or program adopted by the National Office (e.g., the Returns Preparer Program[52]) to identify areas of noncompliance; or (3) because

---

[51] IRM 4.19.1.2.2, What Is Classification (Oct. 1, 2001).

[52] IRM 4.1.4.28, Return Preparers Program (May 19, 1999). The Examination Return Preparer Coordinator reviews complaints and questions from any source concerning the quality of returns an individual prepares. Leads frequently originate in Office Examinations, and the Return Preparer Coordinator reviews referrals. If a program action case is warranted, the Return Preparer Coordinator obtains returns the preparer has prepared from the Intermediate Data Retrieval System database, and returns on the list are selected, ex-

of the exercise of an examiner's discretion while examining the return of one taxpayer to question the return of another taxpayer (an "independent pickup").

[b] Claims for Refund

When a service center receives a claim or other request for refund or adjustment in tax, the original return may be screened to determine whether an examination is warranted to substantiate and pay the claim.[53]

[c] Related Pickup Examinations

A related pickup examination occurs when the examiner determines that a return of a party related to the taxpayer (e.g., partners, family members, or corporate officers and shareholders) must be examined to determine whether the taxpayer has correctly determined the tax.

[d] Multiyear Examinations

Multiyear examinations occur when an examining officer expands the examination to prior or subsequent years to determine, for example, whether a loss carryback or carryforward is proper, or whether an adjustment made to one year's return should be made to some other year's returns as well.

[e] Miscellaneous

The miscellaneous category is a catchall for examined returns not falling into the other categories, and includes such reasons as TCMP audits,[54] the Information Document Matching Program,[55] and the Unallowable Items Program.[56]

---

amined, and assigned as they are received. Thus, the identity of the return preparer can generate an examination. The Service has compiled information on return preparers so that it can identify, select, and examine all returns filed by taxpayers using a return preparer whose clients have taken positions contrary to Service positions.

[53] IRM 4.1.4.6, Claims (May 15, 1999).

[54] IRM 4.1.4.35, Taxpayer Compliance Measurement Program (TCMP) (May 19, 1999).

[55] IRM 4.1.4.18, Information Returns (May 19, 1999).

[56] The Unallowable Items Program is discussed infra ¶ 8.04[2].

[f] Automatic Returns

Tax returns designated as "automatic" must be screened by classifiers, but merely because a return falls into this category does not mean it will actually be selected for examination and examined.[57] The classifier still must either be selected for examination or accepted as filed. The terms used in the classification of returns as automatic requires some explanation. Total Positive Income (TPI) uses only the positive amounts of certain types of income (in the case of individuals, wages, interest, dividends, and "other" income), while losses are treated as zero.[58] Total Gross Receipts (TGR) are Gross Receipts on Schedule C and from Schedule F, Farm Income.[59] The automatic-return categories are listed below:

Type of Return	Income or Assets
Individual (Form 1040)	Nonbusiness returns with TPI of $50,000 or more
Partnership (Form 1065)	Gross receipts or gross income of $500,000 or more
Fiduciary (Form 1041)	Gross income of $50,000 or more
Corporations (Form 1120)	TGR of more than $25,000—corporate returns with TGR of $100,000 or more constitute a separate category

[4] Area Office Classification and Selection of Returns for Examination

[a] Annual Examination Plan

The Annual Examination Plan is the blueprint for the allocation of staffing.[60] Through an annual planning process, the Service determines how many returns will be audited each year. An annual examination plan is developed in the National Office to allocate available personnel to achieve desired audit coverage.[61] The audit plan is based on the number of returns in each income category and return type that local offices estimate they can examine in the upcoming year. Returns are then selected in different ways to achieve the plan. One part of the planning process is a classification plan, which is used to plan

---

[57] IRM 4.1.4.3, Automatics (May 19, 1999).

[58] IRM 4.1.7.6, Glossary (May 19, 1999), Exhibit 4.1.7-1, Glossary of Terms No. 33.

[59] IRM 4.1.7.6, Glossary (May 19, 1999), Exhibit 4.1.7-1, Glossary of Terms No. 32.

[60] IRM 4.1.7.1, Assignment of Selected Returns (May 19, 1999).

[61] IRM 2.1.2.4.10, Policies of the IRS P-4-21 (approved June 1, 1974); IRM 4.1.1.2, Examination Plan (May 19, 1999).

DIF return orders, schedule agents and auditors for classification details, and establish goals for identification of non-DIF returns.[62]

As described earlier, classifiers screen DIF-scored returns. The classification process in the area office carries out the Annual Examination Plan developed at the regional and national office levels, based in part on estimates of the return examination capacities of the Examination Division. In each area office a Returns Program Manager is responsible for the classification function and the formulation of the area classification plans. The yearly classification plan is developed to ensure a workload of the approximate number of returns in each type (e.g., income, gift, estate, excise, and exempt organizations) and class that can be examined within the work hours allocated to these types and classes in the district's audit programs. To achieve the goals of the Annual Plan, the service center automatically sends returns to the district, and each quarter the Returns Program Manager requisitions returns from the service center. Since the number of returns received in the area office is generally far greater than can be worked by available tax technicians and field revenue agents, further selection processing takes place at the area office.[63]

[b] Classification and Selection of Returns in the Area Office

As described above, classifiers in area offices classify and select returns for examination, and determine the scope of the examination. Individual returns, corporation returns, S corporation returns, and partnership returns are computer-scored under the DIF system. Taxpayer returns are divided into audit classes, each with a different DIF formula. DIF-scored returns are delivered in bulk to area offices under the Examination Plan. Some non-DIF-scored returns are delivered to the area office as "Automatics" for manual screening without the area office's having placed an order with the service or compliance center. Also, certain individual low and medium nonbusiness returns that are appropriate for being conducted by correspondence examinations (CORR) returns are automatically sent to the area office.

All individual returns are computer-scored.[64] While individual returns are generally ordered in bulk, service centers deliver some returns (called Automatics) to local offices, for manual screening according to their Audit Codes. As described earlier, individual nonbusiness returns are divided into classes ac-

---

[62] IRM 4.1.1.2.6, Classification Plan (May 19, 1999).

[63] Classification rates for all classes of returns are closely monitored. For all DIF-ordered returns, selection rates are supposed to be the maximum rates that can possibly be achieved on an examination class, and if the rates fall below the DIF cutoff score for any class, the reason for the low selection rate is reviewed. IRM 4.1.5.3.2, Review of Performance (May 19, 1999).

[64] IRM 4.1.3.1.2, Sources of Returns—DIF and Ordering, Individual Returns (May 19, 1999).

cording to their TPI, which is the sum of all positive income items on the return, and includes such income as wages, dividends, interest, rents, and other income items, with losses and other negative (deduction) items treated as zero.[65] Individual business returns are classified by reference to TGR, which is the sum of all gross receipts on Schedules C and F.[66]

Individual income tax returns sent to a local office can fall into five categories:[67]

1. *DIF regular returns.* These are DIF returns that have received a DIF score above the minimum cutoff score and are not special returns.

2. *CORR returns.* CORR returns are low and medium nonbusiness individual returns that have been computer-identified as possibly having issues susceptible to a correspondence-type examination by tax auditors.

3. *Tax preference returns.* These are returns identified, usually through DIF scores, as possibly having issues that may create minimum tax liability.

4. *Automatic returns.* These are individual returns categorized under undisclosed criteria, which have included individual returns with TPI of $50,000 or more.

5. *Special returns.* These are sent to the area office as part of its workload for classification based on special conditions and, if they are DIF returns, regardless of DIF score. Included in this category are (a) returns with missing schedules, such as Schedule C, D, E, or F, on which the service center contacted the taxpayer without a response; (b) returns referred to Examination on instructions from the CID (e.g., refund mill returns); (c) returns that require prompt audit under Section 6501(d); (d) returns with possible specific unallowable items; (e) returns with international issues; (f) returns manually identified to be included in the Returns Preparers Program; (g) Joint Committee returns with a refund of $2 million or more; (h) prerefund Audit Program returns on Form 1040NR; and (i) self-employment returns for

---

[65] IRM 4.1.7.6, Glossary (May 19, 1999), Exhihit 4.1.7-1, Glossary of Terms No. 33.

[66] IRM 4.1.7.6, Glossary (May 19, 1999), Exhibit 4.1.7-1, Glossary of Terms No 32. In the TPI/TGR class system, certain comparisons are made between TGR and nonbusiness TPI to determine whether a return is classed as a business or nonbusiness return. In general, the intent is to define a return as business or nonbusiness based on the predominant income on the return. Thus, it is possible for certain nonbusiness returns to have Schedule C or Schedule F income.

[67] IRM 4.1.3.1.2, Source of Returns—DIF and Ordering, Individual Returns (May 19, 1999).

service center correspondence audit that reflect income that may be subject to self-employment tax.[68]

Corporation returns that have no balance sheet or that have assets under $10 million are computer-scored under the DIF system.[69] When corporation returns are requested from the service center, the area office uses formula numbers to identify the asset classes of the corporations (e.g., formula numbers from one to five correspond to corporations with no balance sheet, those with assets under $250,000, those with assets of from $250,000 to under $1 million, those with assets from $1 million to under $5 million, and those with assets from $5 million to under $10 million). Corporate returns sent by the service center to area offices fall into three categories:[70]

1. DIF-scored returns

2. High asset returns

3. Miscellaneous categories, which are returns identified as special returns based on specific conditions and delivered to Examination for screening because they show, for example, international transactions, returns claiming miscellaneous refundable credits, and returns with refundable credits in excess of $2 million

S corporation returns are computer-scored under the DIF system if they have assets under $10 million.[71] S corporation returns are categorized into (1) returns having assets under $200,000; (2) returns having assets from $200,000 to under $10 million; and (3) returns having assets over $10 million. Some S corporation returns, identified as Specials, are delivered automatically to area offices for screening. Issues on these returns include partnership issues or a disclosure statement; international issues; a corporation return (Form 1120) that returns processing has converted to a Form 1120S; Form 8283, Non-Cash Charitable Contribution; Form 8586, Low Income Housing Credit; or Form 8609, Low Income Housing Credit Allocation Certificate; and a first year of Subchapter S filing.[72]

Partnership returns are identified by three categories: DIF, non-DIF, and Automatics.[73] Returns with ten partners or less are also scored under the DIF

---

[68] IRM 4.1.5.9, Identifying Issues on Individual Returns (May 19, 1999), Exhibit 4.1.3-1, Individual Returns Audit Codes.

[69] IRM 4.1.3.1.3, Source of Returns—DIF and Ordering, Corporation Returns (May 19, 1999).

[70] IRM 4.1.5.10.1, Corporation Classification—General (May 19, 1999).

[71] IRM 4.1.3.1.4, Source of Returns—DIF and Ordering, S Corporation Returns (May 19, 1999).

[72] IRM 4.1.3.1.4, Source of Returns—DIF and Ordering, S Corporation Returns (May 19, 1999), Exhibit 4.1.3-3, S Corporation Return Audit Codes.

[73] IRM 4.1.5.11, Partnership Issues (May 19, 1999).

system unless they meet automatic criteria, but partnership returns with eleven or more partners are not computer classified. No checksheet is required for DIF scored returns, but classifiers identify significant issues on non-DIF returns on a Partnership Classification Sheet. Screening procedures classifiers follow for partnership returns are the same as for individual and corporation returns. They screen the entire return as well as line items in selecting the returns with the highest examination potential.[74]

Fiduciary returns are manually screened by classifiers, who have enough knowledge and experience to consider the issues peculiar to fiduciary returns.[75]

[c] Preparation of Checksheets

Classifiers also prepare checksheets for each return selected for examination by a tax auditor. These checksheets indicate the particular items to be considered in the examination and whether the examination should be handled by correspondence or interview. They also assist group managers in the assignment of returns by identifying those returns that must be analyzed before the taxpayer is contacted and by identifying the significant items on the return.[76] For correspondence and interview examinations, the checksheet plays an important role because the tax auditor is not permitted to change the scope of the examination unless an issue of significance that is not on the checksheet and that should be examined is found during the examination.[77] For revenue agent returns, classifiers of returns that have not been computer-selected identify the most significant issues on the return (including issues recognized locally to have examination potential) on the checksheet.[78]

---

[74] IRM 4.1.5.11.1, Partnership Features (May 19, 1999).

[75] IRM 4.1.5.12, Fiduciary Returns (May 19, 1999).

[76] IRM 4.1.5.7, Classification Checksheets (May 19, 1999).

[77] IRM 4.1.5.7, Classification Checksheets (May 19, 1999). IRM 4.1.5.7.2, Special Instructions [for the Examination Checksheet] (All Returns) for Forms 6754 (May 19, 1999).

[78] Classifiers of non-DIF returns are supposed to assign one of three codes to the return. The categories illustrate the types of returns that can lead to an examination. Code A returns have one of the following characteristics: (1) potential tax change greater than $50,000; (2) automatic adjustment (i.e., an obvious error such as deduction of an item clearly unallowable); or (3) returns requiring timely examination action (e.g., reorganizations or final year returns). Code B returns have one or more of the following characteristics: (1) a net operating loss; (2) a prime audit issue; or (3) potential issues that may require a significant length of time to audit (e.g., accumulated earnings, Section 482 adjustments, or thin corporations). Code C returns are all other returns. IRM, Part IV, Examination, Chapter 4100, Exhibit 4100-29.

¶ 8.04 SERVICE CENTER EXAMINATIONS

Service center personnel perform various functions under a series of programs that may result in assessment and collection of additional tax.[79] Service center programs involve relatively simple and readily identifiable problems that can be resolved easily by mail. The Service divides service center correspondence programs into two distinct categories: limited-contact and local office-type examinations.

By far, the greater number of contacts is made under programs involving limited contacts by service center tax examiners. The Service does not consider communication under one of its limited-contact programs to constitute an examination of a tax return. Under a limited-contact program, records are not required or requested from the taxpayer to document or substantiate the item being corrected. The Service's position as a limited contact does not preclude examination without the taxpayer's being sent a second inspection letter as required by Section 7605(b) for a second examination of a taxpayer's return.[80] Under a Revenue Protection Strategy, service center examinations are conducted of Earned Income Tax Credit taxpayers. The Earned Income Tax Credit Program is the most important of these examination programs. Other programs are the Mathematical/Clerical Error Abatement Program, the Unallowable Items Program, and the Information Returns Program.

[1] Correcting Mathematical Errors

The term "mathematical error" is defined by statute to include errors other than errors of arithmetic. As defined by Section 6213(f)(2), a "mathematical error" means

> 1. An error in addition, subtraction, multiplication, or division on a return;

---

[79] IRM 4.19.1.5, Examination Programs (Oct. 1, 2001). The programs are (1) Unallowable Items; (2) Multiple Filer Examination; (3) Information Returns; (4) Alimony Compliance Program; (5) DIF CORR; (6) Claims; (7) Federal-State Cooperative Audit; (8) Social Security Form SSA-7000; (9) Married Persons Filing Separately; (10) Math/Clerical Error Abatement; (11) Estate and Gift Tax; (12) IRA; (13) Self-Employment; (14) Refusal to File TDI Cases; (15) Erroneous Refund Program; (16) Alternative Minimum Tax; (17) DATC/ASTA; (18) Qualified Personal Service Corporation; (19) Taxable Gain on Sale of Residence; (20) Zero Bracket Amount; (21) Monitoring Age 65; and (22) Child Support Refund Offset.

[80] Section 7605(b) prohibits unnecessary examinations and second inspections, and, in general, requires higher level review for approval. See ¶ 13.02[4] for further discussion of this provision.

2. An incorrect use of a Service table if the error is apparent from other information on the return;

3. Inconsistent entries on the return;

4. An omission of information required to be supplied on the return to substantiate a return item; and

5. A deduction or credit disallowed by law that is either a specified monetary amount or a percentage, ratio, or fraction—if the items composing the limit appear on the return.

When a mathematical error is identified, the Service is permitted to make a summary assessment (unlike assessment of a tax deficiency assessment, which is prohibited until the taxpayer is given notice and the opportunity to file a petition with the Tax Court). Although it is permitted to make a summary assessment of tax, the Service must also send the taxpayer an explanation of the assessed error. The taxpayer can appeal the assessment by filing, within sixty days from the date of the notice and explanation, a request for abatement of the assessment that states disagreement with the assessed amount. On the receipt of the request for abatement, the Service is required to abate the assessment,[81] and during the sixty-day period it is also prohibited from proceeding to collect the assessment.[82]

Under the Service's Mathematical/Clerical Error Abatement Program, a return with arithmetic and other mathematical errors is identified, and a notice of the assessment, along with an explanation of the correction, is sent by mail to the taxpayer. Requests for abatement or appeals of the assessment are sent to the service center's Taxpayer Service Division. The notice to the taxpayer also solicits an agreement and includes a telephone number and the name of the person to contact so that the taxpayer can call for information.[83] If the taxpayer supplies information substantiating the return, the assessment is abated and the case closed. If the appeal does not justify the figures on the return, the assessment is abated, but the return is identified for examination by the service center's Examination Branch.[84] Before changes to the summary assessment of mathematical errors provision, the Mathematical/Clerical Error Abatement Program affected predominantly low-income taxpayers with adjusted gross income of $10,000 or less. As a result of the expanded definition of the term "mathematical error," this correction program now includes items of deduction that

---

[81] IRC § 6213(b)(2)(A). Assessments of mathematical errors are described at ¶ 10.04[1].

[82] IRC § 6213(b)(2)(B).

[83] IRM 4.19.1.5.6, Math/Clerical Error Program (Oct. 1, 2001).

[84] IRM 4.19.1.1.5.12.1, Unallowables—Response/No Response to Unallowable Notices/Letters (Oct. 1, 2001).

were previously included in the Unallowable Items Program, such as medical expense deductions, and items that exceed statutory limitations.[85]

[2] Questioning Unallowable Items

Under the Unallowable Items Program, the Service questions items on individual income tax returns, identified manually and by computer, that appear to be unallowable by law. Taxpayers who file returns identified as containing unallowable items are contacted by correspondence, and necessary corrections are made.[86] A taxpayer may receive a notice explaining an adjustment in a number of situations, such as where (1) medical expenses reported on the return include personal, living, or family expenses, such as food and lodging; (2) social security and other federal taxes are deducted; or (3) losses that are unallowable, such as termite losses and lost but not stolen items, are claimed.

The Service does not consider a contact it makes under its Unallowable Items Program to be an examination, any more than a contact it makes under the Mathematical/Clerical Error Abatement Program.[87] Consequently, if the Service later contacts the taxpayer for the purpose of examining the return, it does not send the taxpayer a second inspection letter under Section 7605(b). It also treats the adjustment as a mathematical error and follows the procedures provided in Section 6213(b).

Unallowable items are manually identified during the coding and editing process or are computer-identified. The service center receives returns containing potential unallowable items, along with computer-generated initial contact letters to the taxpayer adjusting the tax and explaining the adjustment. These returns are manually reviewed to verify the unallowable items. If the identification is inaccurate, the letter is suppressed. If the identification is accurate and the DIF score of the return is below a set limit, the initial contact letter is sent to the taxpayer. If the DIF score exceeds the set limit, the return is screened for other potentially tax-significant changes. Returns having audit potential are sent to the district for examination.

Letters sent to taxpayers under the Unallowable Items Program ask taxpayers to agree to the proposed adjustment or to give the reasons for disagreement. The agreement or explanation can be written on the letter and returned to the service center. If the taxpayer's explanation is satisfactory, the matter is ended. If the reasons are not satisfactory, the case is retained for a correspondence examination unless the taxpayer requests an interview. An interview is

---

[85] As a result of this change, the number of returns corrected under the Unallowable Items Program decreased from approximately 1.5 million returns to about 354,000 returns. Commissioner of Internal Revenue, Annual Report 24 (1977).

[86] IRM 4.19.1.5.12, Unallowables (Oct. 1, 2001).

[87] Rev. Proc. 85-13, 1985-1 CB 514, § 13.02.

considered necessary if the issues have become too involved, or if the taxpayer cannot express himself in writing. If a taxpayer requests an interview or will be disadvantaged by a correspondence examination, the return is sent to the district for completion of the examination.

The service center retains cases in which no agreement is reached; in such cases, the service center issues a thirty-day letter notifying taxpayers of their appeal rights and, if no request for administrative appeal is received, a notice of deficiency permitting taxpayers to obtain Tax Court review. Not every return meeting the criteria for audit under the service center audit programs is selected for audit by the service center. If, for example, a return meets the audit criteria for the Unallowable Items Program but is found to contain other audit problems indicating a potential for significant tax change, it is referred to the appropriate district office, and no letter to the taxpayer is sent by the service center.

[3] Matching Information Returns

The Service matches the information returns (e.g., Forms W-2 and 1099) of some individual taxpayers with their income tax returns to detect nonfiling or underreporting of income.[88] Under this Information Returns Program, the Service encourages all organizations to file their information returns on computer tape (not all of the information returns filed for individuals on paper can be matched) and matches the information returns on computer tape against the returns of individuals. Where an item of income is discovered, either the return is corrected and the taxpayer billed or (if criminal investigation criteria are met) the file will be referred for criminal investigation.

[4] Examinations by Correspondence

Correspondence examinations are examinations of low and medium nonbusiness individual returns, which have been computer-identified as possibly having issues that are suitable to correspondence-type examinations at service centers. Under the service center correspondence examination program, service center personnel examine single itemized deductions on the highest DIF-scored low- and medium-income nonbusiness returns.[89] These returns will have either a TPI of at least $10,000 but under $25,000 (low nonbusiness returns) or a TPI of between $25,000 and $50,000 (medium nonbusiness returns). Taxpayers are required to produce receipts, canceled checks, and similar items to support an

---

[88] IRM 4.1.5.8, Information Returns Program (May 19, 1999).

[89] IRM 4.19.1.5.16, What Is DIF CORR Source Program (Oct. 1, 2001).

item of income, deduction, or credit on the tax return. After review and selection of the returns to be audited, service center tax examiners request that taxpayers supply substantiating information about such items of deduction as interest and contributions.[90] Correspondence examinations are recognized by the Service to constitute an examination of books and records for the purposes of Section 7602 (and consequently an examination for the purposes of the second-inspection prohibition of Section 7605(b)). Taxpayers who are subject to this type of correspondence examination are entitled to appeal administratively to an Appeals Office and to Tax Court review after a notice of deficiency is sent. Service center personnel forward a case to the appropriate area office if the taxpayer requests an interview examination or if the issues become too involved to be handled effectively by mail or telephone.

Correspondence audit processes have been found to have certain weaknesses.[91] During the fiscal years 1992–1997, the number of correspondence audits varied from about 200,000 to about 1.1 million audits, but the no-change rate in correspondence audits varied from a low of 13 percent to a high of 46 percent, and the amount of additional tax ranged from about $1,300 to $2,800. Also, taxpayers did not respond to notices of the recommended additional tax after Service personnel requested them to do so in 29 to 63 percent of the cases; the Service attributed this percentage of defaults to the number of correspondence audits of returns claiming the earned income credit.

Other weaknesses were found in the correspondence audit process. First, not all traditional correspondence audits closed in 1996 were manually reviewed or classified to identify all issues for audit, and when returns with complex business and investment schedules were classified, the classification was not always done by qualified personnel in local offices. Auditors did not document the support for their recommended audit findings in about one third of the audits. The documentation taxpayers had to submit to justify earned income credit claims varied among the service centers; and service centers did not adequately review closed audits.

---

[90] IRM 4.19.1.5.16, What Is DIF CORR (Source Codes 02 and 06) (Oct. 1, 2001). Correspondence audits at the service centers generally involve one or two audit issues, such as documenting the amount of self-employment income, that are simple and straightforward enough to be audited through correspondence with taxpayers. Area office audits, on the other hand, generally involve multiple, relatively complex audit issues that require face-to-face meetings. More complex issues, such as exemptions, are not covered by this program. For fiscal year 1996, service centers, through their Customer Service Compliance Branches, conducted two thirds of the 1.9 million audits, with the remaining audits done through district Examination Divisions. GAO Report, IRS Audits, Weaknesses in Selecting and Conducting Correspondence Audits, GAO/GGD—99-48 (Mar. 31, 1999).

[91] GAO Report, IRS Audits, Weaknesses in Selecting and Conducting Correspondence Audits, GAO/GGD—99-48 (Mar. 31, 1999).

[5] Tax Shelters

Service center examination operations have included programs to identify tax shelter returns since the 1980s. In 1984, each service center established an Abusive Tax Shelter Detection Team composed of representatives from the Examination, Criminal Investigation, and other affected functions.[92] The team analyzes such returns as Forms 1040, 1041, 1065, and 1120S; amended returns such as Forms 1040X and 1045 (Applications for Tentative Refund); and other forms such as Tax Shelter Registration information. On the basis of this information, the team (1) recommends review of returns and promotions before refunds are issued and (2) identifies tax shelter promotions, promoters, and investors for Compliance and the CID to secure injunctions against persons subject to penalty for promoting abusive tax shelters under Section 6700. On the basis of the team's recommendations, refunds can be suspended or frozen. Cases identified as potential promoter injunction cases are forwarded to the district office for further action.

The Service adopted the Tax Shelter Program "to identify, examine and, in appropriate cases, investigate those tax shelters utilizing improper or extreme interpretations of the law or the facts to secure for investors substantial tax benefits which are clearly disproportionate to the economic reality of the transaction."[93] Under these procedures, the project approach is generally used in the examination of tax shelter promotions because similar packages and promotions are promoted and sold to many investors. Under a project approach, a "key entity" (i.e., a lead or prime tax shelter case or entity) is examined and the results of the examination are consistently applied to all investors in the promotion. The key entity can be a partnership, corporation, S corporation, fiduciary, or other tax return. To achieve uniformity and consistency, responsibility for controlling and monitoring the progress of all related and interrelated cases in the promotion is vested in a key district. The key district generally is

---

[92] Rev. Proc. 84-84, 1984-2 CB 782, § 4.01. For further description of these procedures, see ¶ 7B.11. Functional requirements and procedures for the Abusive Tax Shelter Detection Program have been added to the Manual. IRM 4.1.4.34, Tax Shelters (May 19, 1999). The program uses service center personnel "to identify possible abusive tax shelter promotions from investor returns before processing and before refunds are paid (Front-End Identification)." Under the procedures established, abusive tax shelter returns are identified by computer, and Forms 1040, 1040X, 1041, 1045, 1065, 1120S, 1120X, and 1139 are screened and manually identified as tax shelter returns. Returns in which prefiling notice letters have been issued for the current or prior years are automatically screened. See also Rev. Proc. 84-84, § 3.02. On identified returns where it is determined that the refund is attributable to a potentially abusive tax shelter, refunds claimed are suspended. Cases are to be identified for review for possible criminal investigation, Section 6700 penalties, and Section 7408 injunction action.

[93] IRM 4.1.4.34, Tax Shelters (May 19, 1999).

the district having jurisdiction over the principal promotion, but it may be any other district that expedites the examination process.

Suggested criteria, considered singly or in combination, in identifying a return for inclusion in the Tax Shelter Program are

- A large net loss
- Low gross income
- Large amounts of investment credit
- First-year returns
- Final returns
- A Section 761(a) election
- A nonoperating entity
- A passive investor
- Nonrecourse or not-at-risk questions not answered or answered affirmatively (other than real estate)
- Active engagement in an identified tax shelter area
- Negative capital account if the return is a partnership return and does not involve real estate
- Other factors pertaining to the identification and selection of partnership returns.

Classifiers are also advised to consider information available from Form W-4 requests, Forms 8264 (Application for Registration of a Tax Shelter), Forms 8271 (Investor Reporting of Tax Shelter Registration Number), Forms 8275 (disclosure statement under Section 6661), and other sources, such as state and federal securities filings.

As the returns are identified in the service center, they are categorized and packaged together by promotion or promoter, and are evaluated to determine the impact, scope, and abusiveness of the promotion. Once the case is selected for inclusion in the Tax Shelter Program, all attempts are to be made to identify the promoter and, if applicable, the flow-through entity (e.g., the partnership, S corporation, and fiduciary) to determine whether it is under examination. In general, once the promoter, investor, and flow-through entities have been identified, the key district establishes a project approach to conduct an examination of the key entity and to apply the results consistently to all investors in the promotion.[94]

---

[94] See IRM 8.3.1.3, Appeals—Key Case Approach and Overview (Dec. 18, 2001).

¶ 8.05 AREA OFFICES: OFFICE AND CORRESPONDENCE EXAMINATIONS

[1] Office Examinations

Office examinations are conducted by tax auditors in area offices either through an interview or correspondence or, in limited cases, at the taxpayer's place of business. Returns selected for office examinations include some business returns in addition to the full range of nonbusiness individual income tax returns. In an office interview examination, the most common type of office examination, the taxpayer is asked to go to the local district office for an interview and to bring certain records in support of specific items on the return. An auditor may conduct a field examination with the approval of the Office Audit Supervisor if, for example, it is difficult for the taxpayer to bring requested records to the district office. In an office correspondence examination, the taxpayer is asked to explain items or send supporting evidence by mail. Correspondence examinations are conducted in service centers, but if a complex issue or other circumstance is identified at the service center, the return is sent to an area office.

Individual returns are selected for correspondence examination where information concerning questionable items can be furnished by mail and there are clear indications from review of the tax return that the taxpayer can effectively communicate in writing with the Service.[95] Some examples of items that can be verified by correspondence are itemized deductions for interest, taxes, contributions, and medical expenses; and simple miscellaneous deductions such as union dues and small tools. Although these items can be examined as single issues, the deductions generally are in combination because the Service's experience is that single-issue examinations frequently result in an insignificant or no tax change when other questionable items are not present on the return, particularly if the return was identified by the computer as a CORR return.[96] Items other than itemized deductions, including some dependency exemptions, can, of course, be examined by the correspondence method if they meet these criteria.

[2] Office Interview Returns

Individual returns selected for office interview examinations present issues that require some analysis and judgment in addition to verification of records.[97]

---

[95] IRM 4143.2, Correspondence Examinations (July 24, 1995).

[96] IRM 4143.2, Correspondence Examinations (July 24, 1995).

[97] IRM 4143.3, Tax Auditor Interview Examinations (July 24, 1995).

Business returns are examined by means of an office interview rather than correspondence because of the issues involved. Regardless of the issue, a return is selected for office interview if, in the judgment of the screener, an office interview is needed to give the taxpayer a better opportunity to justify the return. Examples of issues that lend themselves to interview examination are

- Dependency exemptions (unless correspondence criteria are met)
- Income from tips, pensions and annuities, rents and royalties, partnerships, estates and trusts, and occupations where income not subject to tax withholding may have been received
- Determinations of whether the reported income constitutes capital gain or ordinary income
- Deductions for travel and entertainment expenses
- Deductions for bad debts
- Determinations of basis of property
- Complex miscellaneous itemized deductions such as casualty and theft losses where determinations of fair market value are required.

Apart from the issues involved, certain factors may indicate an interview is necessary. For example, a taxpayer's income may be low in relation to his financial responsibilities as suggested by review of the return (e.g., number of dependents or interest expense); or the taxpayer's occupation may be of the type that requires some formal education, yet the appearance of the return (e.g., writing, grammar, neatness) may indicate that the taxpayer is not able to communicate effectively by letter. Some business activities reported on business returns lend themselves to office interview examinations—for example, auto repair shops, barber shops and beauty shops, bowling alleys, restaurants, grocery stores, laundromats, motels, appliance and television service and sales stores, service stations, small building contractors, truckers, farmers, and professional persons.

[3] Controls on Examiners

Whatever the reason for selection of a return for an office examination, the Service's procedures impose substantial controls on the activities of its auditors. These controls are undoubtedly required by the limited education, training, and experience of auditors. The office audit examination is usually initiated by mailing a letter notifying the taxpayer that the return is being examined and requesting the taxpayer to furnish certain information and records by return mail or to bring them to a local office. A questionnaire may also be sent to facilitate a correspondence examination. The auditor has no control over the content, preparation, or issuance of these letters and questionnaires. The taxpayer's return is not assigned to the auditor until after the taxpayer's reply has been received or until the day of or the day before the interview.

The auditor is given little time to prepare for the interview, and the scope of the examination is limited to items on the checklist; however, if the auditor discovers a significant issue not identified and the supervisor agrees, the examination may include a new issue.[98]

[4] Office Examinations: The Taxpayer's View

Appointments for office examinations[99] are handled by a Centralized Scheduling system, which is designed to store returns and schedule initial office examination appointments using computer-generated letters. Taxpayers and their representatives can reduce waiting time in an office audit. To avoid delay, experienced representatives make appointments as early in the office's workday as possible. It also may be possible for a representative who has been notified of two appointments in office examination to call Central Files in Office Examination and have them consolidate the two appointments on one day with one tax technician. Frequently, the cause for delay in an office examination is the failure to bring data to substantiate the type of deduction involved. Both the representative and the taxpayer can save time and expense and go a long way toward ensuring a favorable conclusion to the examination if, before the appearance, every effort is made to secure and organize for presentation such data as (1) the receipts and canceled checks supporting medical expense deductions; (2) a police report, appraisal, insurance claim, or similar documents, to support a theft or casualty loss; and (3) a diary, bills, and canceled checks to substantiate travel and entertainment expense.

Office auditors are supposed to verify records, rather than surmise from casual discourse that a taxpayer is entitled to a claimed deduction.[100] Tax auditors are also instructed to follow pro forma audit aids (i.e., checklists). Pro

---

[98] The Service's expectation that an auditor will close from two to four cases each day also provides some insight into the level of examination by an auditor, although there are exceptions to this description. In identifying a return for examination, the screener may decide that the issue for audit requires planning and analysis before contacting the taxpayer. Examples of returns where this precontact analysis can be performed are (1) returns where verification of gross receipts or cost of goods sold is required; (2) returns showing factors indicating a need to inspect the taxpayer's place of business or residence; and (3) returns where income is low in relation to the taxpayer's obligations and a reconstruction of his income may be required.

[99] A taxpayer can change the place of an office examination to the local office closest to the taxpayer's current residence. Reg. § 301.7605-1(e)(2)(i).

[100] The tax auditor may not be unreasonable in requiring documentation. The Service's policy is that reasonable determinations should be made where deductions are based on a substantial number of small items not susceptible to complete substantiation by documentary evidence if the deduction is legally allowable. IRM 4244, Reasonable Determinations Where Items Cannot Be Fully Documented (Nov. 2, 1981).

forma office aids have also been developed for tax auditors on the following items: miscellaneous expenses, income probe, taxes, interest, contributions, casualty losses, contributions, moving expenses, and rental income and expenses.[101] Failure to keep adequate records for the years examined may result in not only a disallowance of the deduction on the return being examined, but also follow-up audits of intervening years.[102]

[5] Postexamination Procedures

At the conclusion of an interview resulting in a proposed adjustment, the taxpayer is given an opportunity to agree with the findings of the auditor.[103] If the taxpayer agrees with the proposed changes, the auditor asks the taxpayer to execute an agreement form, which permits the immediate assessment of the tax change. The auditor also solicits payment of the amount of the additional tax. If the taxpayer does not agree with the auditor's findings, either the auditor or the taxpayer may request an immediate informal conference with the auditor's supervisor.[104] The purpose of the conference is to resolve differences without the expense and formality of appeal to higher levels within the Service. A high percentage of the cases informally appealed to the supervisor are resolved. If the taxpayer or the representative are inadequately prepared for this immediate appeal, they cannot expect a resolution of the disagreement to be favorable to the taxpayer.

If an immediate conference is not requested, the taxpayer is advised by mail of the auditor's findings and proposed adjustments and is notified of his right to appeal the findings to the Appeals Office. The taxpayer is also given another opportunity to accept the auditor's findings by executing an enclosed agreement form. If the thirty-day letter is ignored, the taxpayer will receive a ninety-day letter (a statutory notice of deficiency), which entitles the taxpayer to petition the Tax Court for a redetermination of the finding.

¶ 8.06 AREA OFFICES: FIELD EXAMINATIONS

Classifiers select returns for field examination because they consider them to have complex issues requiring more advanced accounting skills and knowledge

---

[101] IRM 4231, Tax Audit Guidelines § 228, MT 4231-74 (Jan. 2, 1990) (Pro Forma Audit Aids—Office Examination); see also Pro Forma Aids in IRM Exhibit 200-1.

[102] IRM 4271.2–4271.24, Cases Where Taxpayers Fail to Maintain Proper Records (Nov. 2, 1981).

[103] 26 CFR §§ 601.105(b)(4), 601.105(c)(1)(ii).

[104] Rev. Proc. 74-4, 1974-1 CB 414, § 5.02.

of the internal revenue laws than is required of auditors performing office examinations. In a field examination, a revenue agent examines the taxpayer's books and records, usually on the taxpayer's premises, to make a determination, satisfactory to the agent, of the taxpayer's correct taxable income and correct tax liability. Although no single description can adequately describe the examination of all types of returns (e.g., income, gift, estate, employment, and excise) of all classes of taxpayers (e.g., individual, partnership, corporation, trust, estate, or fiduciary), some general observations can be made.

Factors considered in selecting the return for examination influence the examination itself, such as (1) the type of error apparent from the return; (2) the size of the income (high-income returns usually involve more complex and varied financial or business activities); (3) the type of business (certain businesses require understanding of a complex body of law); and (4) the type of activity (local experience or needs may indicate that the audit should be conducted).

It is reasonable to expect that agents come to an examination believing that the return contains errors in need of correction. Agents are aware that the return has been computer classified as having audit potential and selected by an experienced classifier for examination because it has a greater likelihood than others for tax change. The agents are also likely to take the attitude that they have the duty to assert the Service's position on issues and to "educate" the taxpayer or the taxpayer's representative in the "correct" (i.e., the Service's) interpretation of the law.

To handle an examination effectively, the practitioner must be familiar with all of the following:

1. The techniques used by revenue agents, including the preliminary steps taken before the taxpayer or representative is contacted
2. The scope of the examination
3. The techniques that may be utilized in handling the examination, including settlement with the agent
4. The extension of the assessment period
5. The specialized agents who might be called on during the course of an examination.

These aspects of an examination are discussed in the following sections.

[1] The Audit Cycle

The Service's policy is to complete examinations within a certain time limit after the return is filed, called the audit cycle. Examinations and dispositions of income tax returns must be completed within twenty-six months in the case of individuals, or, in the case of corporation income tax returns, twenty-seven months after the due date of the return or the date the return is actually filed, whichever is later.[105] For examinations for estate tax returns, the audit cycle is eighteen months from the date the return is filed.[106] Under these self-imposed restrictions, the examination of a 1997 corporation income tax return filed on March 15, 1998, and a 1997 individual income tax return filed on April 15, 1998, for example, must have been commenced and completed before June 15, 2000. Certain cases are excepted from the application of the audit cycle—for example, fraud cases, suspense cases, international operations cases, Joint Committee cases, National Office cases (which usually involve taxpayers with assets of $250 million or more), and cases involved in special enforcement programs.

The closer the examination comes to the end of the audit cycle, the more likely the possibility that the agent faced with the obligation to complete the examination will not search further for other adjustments. For this reason, some practitioners believe that delay during the examination can be used to the taxpayer's tactical advantage, since the agent will cut the examination short if there is insufficient time to complete it. If the agent terminates an examination, it is believed that the adjustments proposed will more than likely be limited to the ones that have been developed during the course of the examination before the imminent expiration of the audit cycle. Tactical use of the audit cycle as a means of limiting the scope of an examination can be overestimated. The agent is not precluded from asking the taxpayer to extend the assessment period, and the agent can set up adjustments that have only been partially developed. The agent can also make adjustments bearing heavily against the taxpayer, especially if the agent is suspicious that the representative has attempted to take unfair advantage. Constraints imposed on examining agents by the audit cycle are a fact of life in the examination of tax returns and, when handled with extreme care, may serve the interests of a taxpayer under examination.

[a] Identification of Potential Adjustments

All examinations require a revenue agent to accomplish the following: (1) identify items that indicate adjustment may be proper; (2) verify items on the return by gathering appropriate evidence; and (3) apply the provisions of the Code, as interpreted. Thus, the first phase of an examination is the identification of unusual items requiring further verification.[107] Requirements of the

---

[105] IRM 4.1.1.7.2, Cycle Time Monitoring (May 15, 1999). The examination cycle of claims for refund is twenty-four months and begins when the claim is filed. Delinquent returns are treated as part of the inventory of current year returns. IRM 4.10.2, Excepted Cases (1999).

[106] IRM, Policies of the IRS Handbook, P-4-52 (approved Feb. 20, 1959).

[107] See the discussion of the agent's precontact analysis infra ¶ 8.06[1][a].

Code and the Service's own instructions and guidelines place heavy emphasis on the examination and analysis of substantiating records. Therefore, the second phase of the examination consists of steps the examiner takes to verify the accuracy of amounts reported or required to be reported as taxable income (which in turn is comprised of various items of income and deduction) and the accuracy of any credits claimed against the tax due.[108] After verification of the amounts of the items from which tax liability is computed, the examiner must then analyze transactions or groups of transactions to determine whether the taxpayer has complied with the various provisions of the Code, the regulations, and the other interpretative rulings of the Service.

After reading the prior examination report, the agent is expected to inspect the return for "large, unusual, or questionable" items.[109] The following factors must be considered before the agent identifies an item as large, unusual, or questionable:[110]

1. *Comparative size of the item.* A questionable expense item of $6,000 with total expenses of $30,000 would be significant; however, if total expenses are $300,000, ordinarily the item would not be significant.

2. *Absolute size of the item.* Despite the comparability factor, size by itself may be significant. For example, a $50,000 item may be significant even though it represents a small percentage of taxable income.

3. *Inherent character of the item.* Although the amount of an item may be insignificant, the nature of the item may be significant. For example, airplane expenses claimed on a plumber's Schedule C may be significant.

4. *Evidence of intent to mislead.* This may include missing, misleading, or incomplete schedules or incorrectly showing an item on the return.

5. *Beneficial effect of the manner in which an item is reported.* Expenses claimed on a business schedule rather than claimed as an itemized deduction may be significant.

6. *Relationship to other items on a return.* No deduction for interest expense when real estate taxes are claimed, may be significant. Similarly, the lack of dividends reported when Schedule D shows sales of stock may be significant.

These factors still give only a general idea of what items a revenue agent may decide to pursue in an examination. Thus, the decision of what is "unusual" depends as much on the personal attributes of the agent as on the return itself,

---

[108] See the discussion of the agent's basic audit techniques infra ¶ 8.06[2].

[109] IRM 4.10.2.3.1, Large, Unusual, or Questionable Items (LUQs) Defined (May 14, 1999).

[110] IRM 4.10.2.3.1, Large, Unusual, or Questionable Items (LUQs) Defined (May 14, 1999).

especially since an item may be considered unusual because the agent is unfamiliar with the validity or legality of the item's treatment on the return.

[i] Step 1: Return review to identify large, unusual, and questionable items. The first step in the precontact process is for the examiner to review the return to identify large, unusual, and questionable items (LUQs). Examiners review the return in its entirety. In addition, the return package includes a return charge-out sheet, which has information, such as statute of limitations dates, prior audit results, no-change issues, collectibility indicators, and special messages included in the classification process. Agents are advised to read any examination report and work papers prepared in a prior examination of the taxpayer.[111] The prior examination report may reveal that the taxpayer did not comply with some tax recordkeeping requirement and that some action to correct the deficiency or error should have been made in the examination year or reflected in the return. A prior examination report may also indicate the existence of recurring issues, the presence of which can lead to the audit of years after the assigned year's audit. These multiyear audits usually involve two taxable years (or more) of taxpayers filing business returns. When setting the scope of a field examination, revenue agents are cautioned not to include "timing issues," unless they have long-term, flagrant short-term, indefinite, or permanent deferral features.

Also, classification sheets prepared during the classification process identify specific issues to be considered by office auditors in Office Examination cases, where there has been no precontact analysis, and in Field examinations to identify "unusual or significant reasons" for selecting the return for examination.[112]

Other sources within the Service can provide information as well. Depending on how the return was selected for examination, the case file may contain information from internal sources. For example, DIF selected returns may contain Information Returns Program (IRP) transcripts, reporting the amount of wages, pensions, dividends, interest, gambling winnings, and other items that third-party information reporters reported as paid to the taxpayer and the taxpayer should ostensibly have reported on the return.[113] The Information

---

[111] IRM 4.10.2.6.6, Preliminary Research (May 14, 1999). The assignment sheet may show the results of a prior examination, and if there was no change, the issues involved. During an examination, if the examiner discovers that a prior examination occurred that affects the current examination, he is advised to consider possible recurring issues and recommend that the taxpayer take corrective action. The review of the prior examination record is subject to standards about the scope of the examination. IRM 4.10.2.6.1, Determining the Scope of an Examination (May 14, 1999).

[112] IRM 4.10.2.3.2, In-Depth Pre-Contact Analysis—Step 1: Review to Identify LUQs (May 14, 1999).

[113] IRM 4.10.2.6, Classifying Returns With IRMF Transcripts by Tax Auditors and Revenue Agents (May 14, 1999).

Returns Master File (IRMF) matches information returns and Currency Transaction Reports (CTRs) with any return ordered from the DIF or DIF Correspondence and Self-Employment Tax (SET) inventory files, or delivered as an Automatic/Special return.[114] The IRMF transcript is a listing of the information returns that have been processed for the taxpayer. When the return is classified, the classifier reviews the IRMF transcript to see whether there is unreported income. The revenue agent will review information return transcripts for the prior two years to see whether there have been significant decreases in earnings or deductions.

Other reports and returns can also be checked against the return, such as the prior examination report, CTRs, and informants' communications, as well as a refund claim or carryback claim.[115]

[ii] **Step 2: Examination of income.** There are required precontact analyses for the examination of income for both individual returns and corporations and other business entities.[116]

[iii] **Step 3: Required filing checks.** Minimum requirements apply to the precontact analysis.[117] These minimum requirements are set out in checklists that the examiner must complete. Agents must verify that all returns "within the taxpayer's realm of influence" have been filed.[118] Two internal data bases called Corporate Files on Line (CFOL) and the Midwest Compliance System (MACS) can be used to complete required filing checks for prior and subsequent returns, information returns, employment tax returns, gift tax returns, excise tax returns, and other returns. MACS can be used to obtain a three-year comparative analysis of the return under examination. CFOL is used for on-line research of the taxpayer's tax account and the taxpayer's tax return and related information in the form of the most individual line items on the tax return and accompanying schedules. See Table 14.1 for an illustrative checklist.

---

[114] IRM 4.10.2.3.2, In Depth Pre-Contract Analysis—Step 1: Review to Identify LUQs (May 14, 1999).

[115] A database known as the Midwest Region Automated Compliance System (MACS) provides agents with the capability to do market segmentation, issue identification, and Compliance 2000 Initiatives. The database can be used to retrieve specific taxpayer data, such as a three-year spread of a taxpayer's returns, including a Cash-T analysis. It may also be used to research a market segment to identify samples of returns to determine the level of noncompliance and to decide whether a formal information gathering project should be started.

[116] IRM 4.10.2.3.3, Step 2: Examination of Income (May 14, 1999). See IRM 4.10.4.3.3, Individual Business Returns (May 14, 1999); IRM 4.10.3.4, Corporate and Other Business Returns (May 14, 1999).

[117] IRM 4.10.2.3.4, Step 3: Required Filing Checks (May 14, 1999). See IRM 4.10.5 et seq.

[118] IRM 4.10.5.2.1, Filing Verification (May 14, 1999); IRM 4.10.5.3, Prior and Subsequent Year Returns (May 14, 1999).

If the agent believes additional information is necessary after analyzing the CFOL and MACS information, the return can be requested from the service center or the taxpayer for inspection. This inspection, in the Service's view, is not an examination, but is "essentially the same as classifying a return for examination."[119] Also, since no books and records are requested and no questions are asked of the taxpayer, the inspection does not attempt to determine the taxpayer's tax liability.[120] The distinction between an inspection and an examination is important. Section 7605(b) prohibits unnecessary examinations or unauthorized second inspections, but nothing in the provision prevents the Service from classifying a return and examining the return at a later time if other information indicates examination is appropriate.

[b] Evaluation of Audit Potential

Before a revenue agent decides to conduct an audit, the agent evaluates the audit potential of an examination. Examiners compare the potential benefits of an examination "to the resources required to perform the examination."[121] This comparison, called risk analysis, enables examiners to set priorities so that issues with higher likelihood of tax change are examined over those with lower potential for tax change. Issues having little or no likelihood of tax change are not to be audited. Related to a risk analysis is the question of whether the issue has been subject to repetitive audit. An issue is subject to repetitive audit "when an examination of the same issue in either of the two preceding years resulted in no-change."[122] Also, the examiner should consider the taxpayer's financial status, and while not all taxpayers without the financial resources will be excluded from examination, collectibility is considered when, for example, the taxpayer is deceased or the taxpayer is a defunct corporation and the issue of transferee is not present.[123]

[c] Closed on Survey

After examining the return and its associated documents and researching unfamiliar items, revenue agents can decide that other returns in their inventory show greater audit potential or that audit of the return would result in no material change in tax liability. With the approval of the group manager, the agent may close the case. In Service jargon, the case is closed on "survey after

---

119 IRM 4.10.5.2.2, CFOL and MACS (May 14, 1999).
120 See IRM 4.10.5.2.2, CFOL and MACS, (May 14, 1999).
121 IRM 4.10.2.4.1, Risk Analysis (May 14, 1999).
122 IRM 4.10.2.4.2, Repetitive Audit (May 14, 1999).
123 IRM 4.10.2.4.3, Collectibility (May 14, 1999).

assignment."[124] A case is reported as Closed on Survey After Assignment without contacting the taxpayer. There are some exceptions. For example, when the return is an individual nonbusiness return with no Schedule C or Schedule F, and the taxpayer has been contacted, the case may still be closed on survey after assignment, if the taxpayer responds saying that the same issue in either of the two preceding years resulted in a small or no tax change. Thus, tax returns undergo three levels of inspection before they are selected for actual examination: (1) inspection by the classifier; (2) inspection by the agent's group supervisor; and (3) inspection by the revenue agent. Note also that where a case is closed by the revenue agent on survey after assignment, the taxpayer is not been contacted by the agent and is not notified that the return has been accepted as filed. Nothing in Section 7605(b), which prohibits unnecessary examinations or unauthorized second inspections, prevents the Service from examining the return at a later time if other information indicates examination is appropriate.

¶ 8.07 EXAMINATION OF RETURNS: TECHNIQUES

The examining process starts with the analysis of a return even before the revenue agent contacts the taxpayer. Guidelines for the techniques and procedures used in the examination of returns and specialized examination techniques are described in detail in the Internal Revenue Manual.[125] Audit technique guidelines apply to a revenue agent's examination of the following types of tax returns: (1) individual tax returns—nonbusiness; (2) individual tax returns—business and partnerships; (3) corporation tax returns; and (4) returns of estates and trusts. These techniques are not meant to be exclusive or exhaustive and do not mean that an agent will not take other steps or use other guidelines for the examination of returns of taxpayers in specialized industries. However, they are instructive and indicative of what course the examination should follow.[126] Audit technique guidelines are the ways in which examiners are expected to meet the standard of a quality audit, which is an examination in sufficient depth to develop facts relating to issues of merit and the correct application of law to those developed facts.

---

[124] IRM 4.10.2.5.2, Procedures for Surveying After Assignment (May 14, 1999).

[125] In addition to a section of the examination part of the Manual entitled Examination of Returns (IRM 4.10.1), there are descriptions of programs and many handbooks, including the Industry Specialization Program (IRM 4.4), an Oil and Gas Handbook (IRM 4.4.1), an Insurance Company Handbook (IRM 4.4.2), and a Retail Industry Handbook (IRM 4.4.3).

[126] IRM 4.10.3.1, Examination Techniques—Overview (May 14, 1999).

The audit technique guidelines can be divided roughly into two categories: (1) basic or general standards and procedures and (2) detailed standards
and techniques. Basic standards and procedures apply in all field examinations.
Detailed techniques are to be used at the agent's discretion in the examination
of income, expense, and balance sheet items. In addition, revenue agents use
guidelines for specialized industries in the Industry Specialization Program
(e.g., insurance, oil and gas, banking, public utilities, textiles, timber, mining,
brokerage, railroads, and construction) and types of businesses in the Market
Segment Specialization Program (e.g., auto dealerships).[127] Detailed techniques
are adopted by the Service from time to time to handle specific problems expected to be encountered in special examination programs and areas such as
tax shelters,[128] tax protesters,[129] return preparers,[130] and in-depth fraud examinations.[131]

The 1998 Act[132] limits revenue agent examinations for unreported income.
The Service is prohibited from using financial status or economic reality audit
techniques to determine the existence of unreported income of any taxpayer
unless the Service has a reasonable indication that there is a "likelihood" of
unreported income.[133] Before this statutory change, the Service had used financial status audits as a technique to probe for unreported income. The American
Institute of Certified Public Accountants (AICPA) criticized financial status
audits on a number of specific grounds and has made the following recommendations:[134]

---

[127] IRM 4.10.2.6.7, Referrals for Specialists (May 14, 1999).

[128] IRM (Examination) 42(17)0, Income Tax Examinations (May 14, 1999) (Income
Tax Examinations—Tax Shelter Program).

[129] IRM 4.2.93 (Tax Protesters Program) (Nov. 22, 1989).

[130] IRM 4.2.97 (Return Preparers Program) (Nov. 22, 1989).

[131] IRS Restructuring and Reform Act of 1998, HR 2676, 105th Cong., 2d Sess.
§ 1002.

[132] IRS Restructuring and Reform Act of 1998, HR 2676, 105th Cong., 2d Sess.
§ 1002; IRC § 7206(d).

[133] IRC § 7602(d), added by the 1998 Act § 3412, effective July 22, 1998.

[134] AICPA Tax Division Meeting, "Economic Reality Checks Look Like Fraud
Probes, Accountants Say," 67 Tax Notes 1423 (June 12, 1995). Letter to Commissioner
Richardson, dated April 2, 1996, by Deborah Walker, Chair, Tax Executive Committee,
AICPA, reprinted in 96 TNT 82-22. There were twenty-seven questions revenue agents
asked to uncover possible unreported income, but the Service does not consider this aspect
of the examination to be unusual or part of an in-depth fraud audit. The questions ask taxpayers about their expenditures for home purchases, rental payments, home improvements,
car purchases, other purchases in excess of $10,000, sales of assets, loans to others, repay-
ments of loans, cash advances from credit lines and credit cards, cash on hand, cash transactions, and employee business expenses claimed as deductions. Because the answers to
these questions can potentially establish the taxpayer's tax fraud, the examination technique raised the question whether CPAs and tax lawyers unaccustomed to fraud cases
could continue to represent the taxpayer.

1. To avoid blurring the line between civil audits and criminal investigations, financial status audit techniques should not be used until the end of the audit, and then only if there is a reasonable suspicion or indication of unreported income.
2. Agents should not require taxpayers to complete Form 4822, Statement of Annual Estimated Personal and Family Expenses, or imply that the form is mandatory.
3. The training program, which negatively influenced agents' attitudes and is responsible for an increasingly confrontational atmosphere between agents and representatives, should be withdrawn and revised.
4. Taxpayers should not be required to submit to a face-to-face interview without a representative present because they should be represented in any interview.
5. Financial status audit techniques, requiring small businesses to meet a double entry set of books or strong internal controls standard, should not be used for all small businesses and taxpayers filing Schedule C.

In-depth audits are fraud audits, but special examination techniques used in an examination may be used to probe for unreported income in the same way that an in-depth audit does. Examinations may include specific questions about what the Service terms "economic reality" issues. Detailed techniques followed by revenue agents are of more practical interest than basic standards and procedures, but Audit Standards should not be ignored entirely. It is worthwhile to keep in mind that one of the general standards counsels examiners "to perform this work in a fair and impartial manner, with neither a government nor a taxpayer point of view."[135] Presumably, this instruction means, as the Manual once stated, that issues should be raised only when in the agent's considered opinion they have real merit, and not frivolously, arbitrarily, or for bargaining purposes. When an individual income tax return is assigned to a tax auditor, the scope of the examination has already been set during the classification process.

In other cases, basic standards cover (1) the preliminary planning the examiner is supposed to do to set the scope of the examination, including a review of the prior examination record and documents associated with the return as well as those included in the case file; (2) research of unfamiliar issues; (3)

---

[135] IRM 4233, Tax Audit Guidelines—Partnerships, Estates and Trusts, and Corporations § 120, MT 4233-16 (Apr. 23, 1981) (Statement of Principles of Internal Revenue Tax Administration). The Tax Audit Guidelines require the same standard. IRM 4231 § 120, MT 4231-54 (Apr. 23, 1981) (Statement of Principles of Internal Revenue Tax Administration).

the scope of the examination; (4) the preparation and contents of workpapers; and (5) the interview of the taxpayer.[136]

At least one type of technique used by offices, a compliance check, is not considered by the Service to be an examination, although the Service has specific guidelines for examiners to conduct compliance checks and to conduct examinations if they are considered necessary. The Service does not believe a compliance check is an examination because "it does not seek to make a determination of tax liability," but rather is "an opportunity to educate the taxpayer and encourage compliance."[137] Moreover, examiners and agents are cautioned not to conduct an examination of a taxpayer "under the guise of a compliance check."

Characterization of a compliance check as a taxpayer contact, not as an examination, is important to the Service because Section 7605(b) prohibits the Service from conducting a second inspection of a taxpayer's return without an examiner securing higher level approval.[138] Although the taxpayer's books and records are not supposed to be requested or examined, compliance checks involve requests for information, even if the information requested takes the form of documents that have already been supplied to the Service or should have been supplied to the Service. Compliance checks are used in employment tax cases, especially on worker status issues (whether a worker is an employee or independent contractor), employee withholding allowance certificates (underwithholding is indicated by sampling Forms W-4), information returns and other cash transaction reports, financial institutions' currency transaction reports, and internal procedures to comply with the Bank Secrecy Act.[139]

---

[136] IRM 4.10.2, Prior Examination Record, Scrutiny of Associated Documents, Research of Unfamiliar Items, Scope of the Examination, Workpapers—Definition and Purpose and Initial Interview.

[137] See IRM Administration, Employment Tax Examination Procedure Handbook 12(11) 9.1, § 322, MT 12(11) 9.1-1 (Mar. 1, 1996) (Lead Processing and Assignment of Employment Tax Cases—Compliance Checks). For an analysis of the procedural status of compliance checks, see Stein, "Are IRS Compliance Checks Examinations?" TNT (Mar. 25, 1996).

[138] IRM Administration, Employment Tax Examination Procedure 12(11) 9.1, § 322(5), MT 12(11) 9.1-1 (Mar. 1, 1996) (Guidelines for Compliance Checks).

[139] IRM Administration, Employment Tax Examination Procedure Handbook 12(11) 9.1, § 322, MT 12(11) 9.1-1 (Mar. 1, 1996) (employment tax cases); IRM Administration, Employment Tax Examination Procedure Handbook 12(11) 9.1, § (15)30, MT 12(11) 9.1-1 (Mar. 1, 1996) (Form W-4 Employee's Withholding Allowance Certificate); IRM 4034.5, Examination, MT 4000-256 (July 6, 1994) (Compliance Checks—Information Returns and Other Transaction Reports); IRM Examination, Currency and Bank Reporting Handbook 4234 § 266, MT 4234-4 (Dec. 22, 1986) (Bank Secrecy Act (Title 31)—Compliance Checks).

[1] Initial Contact of the Taxpayer: Time and Place of Examination

Revenue agents usually begin a field examination by telephoning the taxpayer, not the taxpayer's representative, to make an appointment.[140] For corporate returns, contact is made with the treasurer of the corporation or another executive directly connected with the preparation of the return. When a partnership return is to be examined, a partner is contacted. The Service expects that frequently the agent will be referred to the taxpayer's accountant or attorney to set a date for the appointment. After determining that the representative has a valid power of attorney on file, the revenue agent usually telephones the taxpayer's representative for an appointment, but may make an unannounced site visit with the approval of the group manager.[141]

No statutory rule governs the details of the time and place of examination, except that the time and place must be "reasonable under the circumstances."[142] Regulations give some general guidance. Examinations can be scheduled during normal business hours for the Service on a workday during the year without regard to the seasonal fluctuations in a taxpayer's business; nevertheless, examiners will work with taxpayers to minimize any "adverse effects in scheduling."[143] An office examination generally takes place at the local office closest to the taxpayer's residence. A full examination generally occurs "at the location where the taxpayer's books, records and source documents pertinent to the examination are maintained," which is generally either an individual taxpayer's residence or a business taxpayer's place of business.[144] The examiner may make an on-site visit to the taxpayer's residence or place of business "to establish facts that can only be established by direct visit," such as inventory or asset verification "during normal workdays and business hours for the Service."[145]

A field examination of a business return is generally conducted at the taxpayer's place of business because the supporting data should be available, even if the formal books of account of the business are kept at the offices of the accountant. By being on the premises, the agent is able to make observations useful to an examination, has an opportunity to make inquiries of the taxpayer's employees, and avoids unnecessary lack of access to records. However, there is no fixed requirement that the examination must take place at the taxpayer's place of business, and a change in the place of examination can be

---

[140] IRM 4.10.2.7.4, Scheduling the Appointment: Overview (May 14, 1999).

[141] IRM 4.10.2.7.4, Scheduling the Appointment: Overview (May 14, 1999).

[142] IRC § 7605(a).

[143] Reg. § 301.7605-1(b)(1).

[144] Reg. § 301.7605-1(d)(3).

[145] Reg. § 301.7605-1(d)(3)(iii).

requested if, for example, the business is so small that an on-site examination would require the business to close or would unduly disrupt its operations.[146]

The convenience of the taxpayer governs appointments and the place of the examination. Appointments will generally be held at a time and place that will meet the convenience of the taxpayer.[147] Examiners will respect a taxpayer's privacy rights and will enter a taxpayer's private premises only when invited in by the rightful occupant. However, if fraud is a feature or if the interests of the government may be jeopardized, the convenience of the taxpayer need not be regarded as paramount.

If the taxpayer has moved since the return under examination was filed, the taxpayer may also request that the audit be transferred to the district office in which the taxpayer now resides or has its principal place of business.[148] A change in the place of examination can also be requested if the change would allow the Service to conduct the examination more efficiently.[149] Regulations permit the examination to be made at one of the following locations: (1) the location at which the taxpayer's books, records, and source documents are maintained; (2) the location at which the Service can perform the examination most efficiently; or (3) at the Service office requested by the taxpayer if resources are available. The Service considers other factors that indicate that conducting the examination at a particular location "could pose undue inconvenience to the taxpayer." In general, the examination is held at the place where books, records, and source documents are located, even if the examination had been scheduled to be held at some other location.[150]

When making the appointment for the examination, the agent is advised to tell the taxpayer or the representative what books and records should be made available. Such information is especially important when the examination is not held at the taxpayer's place of business. If the agent does not make clear what records should be gathered, the representative should request a clarification, bearing in mind that agents are supposed to avoid permitting the taxpayer or the representative to "preselect" records for the agent.[151] Also, examiners must review certain items during the course of an examination, such as prior

---

[146] Reg. § 301.7605-1T(d)(3)(ii).

[147] Concerning time and place of examination, the appointment must be consistent with IRM 4.10.2.7.6, Place of Examination (May 14, 1999) and IRM 4.10.2.7.7, Time of Examination (May 14, 1999); Reg. § 301.7605-1.

[148] Reg. § 301.7605-1(e)(1).

[149] Reg. § 301.7605-1(e)(1). The convenience of the taxpayer's representative is not one of these factors. Reg. § 301.7605-1(e)(3).

[150] Reg. § 301.7605-1(e)(2)(ii)(B).

[151] The Service's practice is not to permit representatives or taxpayers to select the records to be examined. At any rate, the techniques to be followed in the examination identify the books and records to be examined.

audit results and subsequent and prior year returns.[152] It can be expected that the agent will request certain records, such as the partnership agreement, minutes, books, ledgers and journals, copies of related returns, and subsequent years' returns.

[2] Requesting Information

Revenue agents have sweeping authority to compel production of information that "may be" relevant or material to the examination of a return.[153] In the event that a taxpayer fails or refuses to furnish an agent with the information requested, the agent may serve a summons directing the taxpayer or the keeper of the records to produce the information.[154] Revenue agent requests for records are generally complied with without resort to a summons. A refusal to comply with such a request must take into account the broad scope of the Service's summons authority and the fact that, should the Service decide to pursue it, the matter will end up before a federal district court, which ultimately decides whether or not to order production.

[a] Recordkeeping in General

By statute and regulation, taxpayers are required to maintain and keep books of account or records sufficient to establish the items of income, deduction, and credit and other matters reportable on their returns.[155] No particular form for these books and records is imposed by this requirement. These books and records are to be retained for as long as they "may become material in the administration of any internal revenue law" and kept available for inspection by a revenue agent.[156]

Records fall into two categories for tax examination purposes:

1. Primary (or informal) records are documents, such as invoices, vouchers, bills, receipts, and tapes, on which business transactions are

---

[152] IRM 4263.6, Mandatory Items Requiring Workpaper Comment. A so-called income probe must be made by analyzing bank statements, sales of assets, barter schemes, alimony, pensions, and the like. Revenue agents in some districts have insisted on interviewing taxpayers as part of this income probe. See, e.g., Vol. 12 Manhattan District News & Views No. 2 (Mar. 1986). The Service insists that this request does not bypass the taxpayer's representative.

[153] IRC § 7602.

[154] IRM 4.10.2.9, Requesting Information: Overview (May 14, 1999). The procedures followed on the issuance of a summons and the objections that may be raised to a summons are described in Chapter 13.

[155] IRC § 6001; Reg. § 1.6001-1(a).

[156] Reg. § 1.6001-1(e).

recorded. Inventory lists are primary records of a business in which inventories are an income-determining factor. Canceled checks, duplicate deposit slips, bank statements and notes, and similar records of financial transactions also are primary records.

2. Secondary (or formal) records are the taxpayer's permanent books, work sheets, tallies, and the like, which list or summarize the individual primary records, with necessary adjustments and classifications that permit the taxpayer to determine financial status and profit and loss for any given period.

Audit of an individual nonbusiness taxpayer's return involves selective examination of primary records, while examination of a business return starts at least with an examination of secondary records with spot checks of primary records, which may be necessary to check the accuracy and completeness of the secondary records.

[b] Computer-Based Recordkeeping

Taxpayers are permitted to maintain their books and records by using an electronic storage system that either images their hard copy books and records or transfers their computerized books and records to an electronic storage medium, such as an optical disk; they are also permitted to destroy the hard copy books and records and delete the original computerized records if certain requirements are met.[157]

In general, before the destruction or deletion, the taxpayer must have completed its own test of the electronic storage system's ability to reproduce hard copy or computerized books and records, according to the Service's procedures, and the taxpayer must have instituted procedures that ensure its continued compliance with those procedures. The taxpayer must maintain machine-sensible records for as long as the contents may become "material" under Regulation Section 1.6001-1(e). Materiality continues at least until the statute of limitations on assessment for the year, including extensions, expires.

Because there still may be uncertainty about how long a taxpayer must maintain machine-sensible records, the taxpayer may request a Record Retention Limitation Agreement with the area office. The positive result of this agreement is, or should be, certainty for purposes of a records destruction policy because the taxpayer must identify the records it does not want to retain. However, the area office must agree to a record retention agreement and, before it does, may conduct a "records evaluation" review of the taxpayer's record retention practices—an evaluation some taxpayers may conclude is not worth the certainty of the agreement.

---

[157] Rev. Proc. 97-22, 1997-1 CB 652.

[c] Statistical Sampling

Because records may be so voluminous, revenue agents are permitted to use statistical sampling techniques as long as the estimates of adjustments to tax liabilities resulting from statistical samples are "statistically sound and legally defensible."[158] The Manual says that the Chief Counsel and the Department of Justice have jointly analyzed the legal ramifications of using probability sampling in the examination of large accounts and concluded that substantial authority exists for the determination of deficiencies based on statistical samples.[159] Computer audit specialists usually have responsibility for sampling because of their training. While projections obtained from examination of statistical probability samples of accounting records may be used, sampling is not supposed to be used unless examination of all the records would be prohibitive in terms of time and resources. On the other hand, if it is reasonable to examine 100 percent of the items involved, statistical sampling techniques are not supposed to be used. As a general rule, the proposed adjustment will be determined in such a way that 95 percent of the time, it will not be greater than the actual adjustment obtainable by a 100 percent examination of the population. Statistical sampling of a taxpayer's records should be distinguished from the Service's use of statistical data obtained from third parties to make adjustments, a practice that is prohibited.[160]

[3] Accountants' Workpapers

An accountant may prepare two types of workpapers during an engagement: workpapers made in connection with the preparation of a return (tax workpapers) and audit workpapers. A revenue agent's request for production of tax workpapers usually does not present a problem.[161] For an individual, the workpapers will merely reflect information the taxpayer provided or tallies of bank deposits and classifications of expense items. For a business, the workpapers will reflect extensions of books of account, adjustments of entries, and development of an income statement and balance sheet. Audit workpapers of an independent accountant, on the other hand, are compiled not for the purpose of preparing a tax return but for financial statement purposes. They may

---

[158] IRM 4.47.3, Statistical Sampling Auditing Techniques; IRM 4.47.3, General Instructions (Aug. 31, 2002) ; IRM 4.47.3.3.1, Determination of Proposed Population Adjustment (Aug. 31, 2002. IRM 4.47.3.3.2, Sampling Procedures (Aug. 31, 2002).

[159] See Litigation Guideline Memorandum, "Use of statistical sampling techniques in examination of tax returns," LGM TL-97, 98 TNT 52-104.

[160] IRC § 7491(b).

[161] However, in fraud cases, such a request has led to considerable litigation. See ¶ 13.07[2].

contain information relating to a tax reserve and reflect the opinions and esti-mates of the taxpayer, the tax adviser, and the accountant of questionable items on the return. Production of these workpapers creates the obvious hazard that the amount reserved in the exercise of the auditor's conservative judgment will become a self-fulfilling prophecy by way of the revenue agent's adjust-ment. Clients and their advisers might not communicate openly with auditors if such communication will result in tax adjustments. Understandably, then, audi-tors have resisted a summons or other process for workpapers. In *United States v. Arthur Young & Co.*, the Supreme Court held that tax accrual workpapers prepared by a corporation's independent CPA in the course of regular financial audits were relevant within the meaning of Section 7602, and that the tax ac-crual workpapers were not protected from disclosure.[162]

Revenue agents must follow guidelines in requesting audit workpapers.[163] These guidelines apply to "tax reconciliation workpapers," "audit workpapers," and "tax accrual workpapers." "Audit workpapers" are defined to mean workpapers kept by an independent accountant "of the procedures followed, the tests performed, the information obtained, and the conclusions reached per-tinent to his/her examination."[164] The guidelines do not apply in fraud cases. An agent is instructed to request tax reconciliation workpapers.[165] Access to audit or tax accrual workpapers, on the other hand, is to be requested only in "unusual circumstances."[166]

By use of this standard, the Service has intentionally restricted the use of the summons for audit or tax accrual workpapers. Workpapers are not re-quested because they "may be relevant or material" as the summons statute (Section 7602) provides. The guidelines warn examiners to remember that "the taxpayer's records are the primary source of the factual data to support the tax return." Accountants' workpapers "should normally be used only when such factual data cannot be obtained from the taxpayer's records and then only as a collateral source for factual data, access to which should be requested with dis-

---

[162] United States v. Arthur Young & Co., 465 US 805 (1984). The Supreme Court held that the court of appeals' creation of a work product privilege for the workpapers was misplaced and conflicted with Congress's clear intent. This subject is discussed more fully in Chapter 13 in regard to the Service summons.

[163] IRM 10.2.9.4, Authority to Request Books, Records, and Accountant's Workpapers (May 14, 1999).

[164] IRM 4.10.2.9.4(3), Authority to Request Books, Records, and Accountants Workpapers (May 14, 1999).

[165] IRM 4.10.2.9.4(3), Authority to Request Books, Records, and Accountants Workpapers (May 14, 1999). Unlike audit or tax accrual workpapers, tax reconciliation workpapers "should be requested at the beginning of an examination."

[166] IRM 4.10.2.9.4(3), Authority to Request Books, Records, and Accountants Workpapers (May 14, 1999).

cretion and not as a matter of standard examining procedure."[167] The guidelines give as an example of a permissible request for workpapers an analysis of a taxpayer's bad debt reserve after which the agent decides that audit workpapers "pertaining to the reserve for bad debt are necessary."[168]

An unusual circumstance exists when (1) a specific issue (or issues) has been identified for which the agent needs additional facts; (2) the agent "has sought from the taxpayer all facts known to the taxpayer relating to the identified issue(s)"; and (3) the agent "has sought from the taxpayer's accountant supplementary analysis (not necessarily contained in the workpapers) of facts relating to the identified issue(s)."[169] If an unusual circumstance exists, the agent must nevertheless limit the request to the portion of the workpapers believed to be "material and relevant" to the examination, a concept involving both qualitative and quantitative (i.e., tax significant) judgments. Furthermore, the agent must reconcile the Schedule M-1 before deciding to request access to tax accrual workpapers. Finally, the agent must have the prior written approval of the Chief (Examination Division) and have taken "all reasonable means" to obtain the information from the taxpayer before looking to the auditor. If it is necessary for a summons to be issued, the summons should identify the portion of the workpapers believed to be relevant (unless all are believed relevant), and the background facts of the summons must be reviewed by Counsel.[170]

Tax accrual workpapers reflect a company's tax contingency liability and may include

(a) [a] summary of the transactions recorded in the taxpayer's general ledger pertaining to income tax accounts;

(b) [a] computation of the tax provision for the current year, whether or not the tax is payable in that year; and

(c) [a] memorandum discussing items reflected in the financial statements as income or expense where the ultimate tax treatment is unclear.[171]

---

[167] IRM 4.10.2.9.4(3), Authority to Request Books, Records, and Accountants Workpapers (May 14, 1999).

[168] IRM 4.10.2.9.4(3), Authority to Request Books, Records, and Accountants Workpapers (May 14, 1999).

[169] IRM, CCDM 34.12.3.13.1, Preissuance Review of Summons Issued to Obtain Audit, Tax, or Accrual Workpaper.

[170] IRM 4.10.2.9.4(4)(C), Authority to Request Books, Records, and Accountants Workpaper (May 14, 1999). For a description of summons procedures in such instances, see ¶ 13.11[3].

[171] IRM 4.10.2.9.4(4)(C), Authority to Request Books, Records, and Accountants Workpaper (May 14, 1999).

Under auditing standards of the AICPA, CPAs are required to obtain a written representation letter from their clients "concerning a wide range of subjects, a number of which could have an impact on a taxpayer's liability."[172] Revenue agents are instructed to obtain a copy of this letter to be apprised of the following: (1) records that are not available; (2) transactions that have not been supported by proper documentation; (3) errors in financial statements; and (4) violations of the tax laws that may have a bearing on the taxpayer's tax liability and otherwise to "clarify the correctness of the taxpayer's returns."[173] Auditors also prepare statements regarding detection of errors, irregularities, or illegal acts pursuant to AICPA Statements on Auditing Standards Nos. 16 and 17. These statements may result in a qualified or adverse opinion by the auditor. The agent is responsible for determining both the cause for the issuance of this type of opinion and the tax consequences of the circumstances giving rise to the qualified or adverse opinion.[174]

The Service believes it is entitled to examine tax accrual workpapers. Nevertheless, it has adopted self-imposed restrictions on access to these workpapers, presumably because of the adverse consequences unrestricted access to this information would have on both the openness of the accountant-client relationship and the integrity of financial reporting. The guidelines seem to direct the agent to the taxpayer's records as the primary source of information, leaving access to tax accrual workpapers a possibility only where the information obtained from the records is inadequate.

[4] Third-Party Contacts

Section 7602(c) states that a Service revenue agent or Collection revenue officer[175] may not contact a third party about "the determination or collection of [the taxpayer] without providing reasonable notice in advance to the taxpayer that contacts [with third parties] may be made." In addition to advance notice, the Service is required to provide to the taxpayer periodically a list of all third-party contacts, and the taxpayer may request such a list of contacts.[176] Exceptions to third-party contact notification are (1) contacts the taxpayer authorizes; (2) for good cause the Service's determination that notice to the taxpayer would jeopardize tax collection or might induce a "reprisal" against the person contacted; and (3) criminal investigations.

---

[172] AICPA, Statement on Auditing Standards No. 19 (1977).

[173] IRM 4.10.2.9.4(4)(C), Authority to Request Books, Records, and Accountants Workpaper (May 14, 1999).

[174] IRM 4.10.2.9.4(4)(C), Authority to Request Books, Records, and Accountants Workpaper (May 14, 1999).

[175] Section 7602(c)(1) uses the term "officer or employee."

[176] IRC § 7602(c)(2).

Regulations in proposed form set out the Service's interpretation of the third-party contact procedures of Section 7602(c).[177] These proposed regulations address the issues of (1) what is a third-party contact: (2) who is a person other than the taxpayer; (3) when a contact is "with respect to the determination of a tax"; and (4) when a Service employee discloses the identity of the taxpayer being investigated. These proposed regulations also adopt rules dealing with when the Service employee will give notice to the taxpayer of a third-party contact; when a precontact notice is not required; and when the taxpayer will receive periodic reports; requested reports and the contents of a report of a third-party contact. Exceptions to the notice requirements are also explained; that is, the authorization, jeopardy, and reprisal threat exceptions.

A third-party contact is a communication that is initiated by a Service employee, defined to include all employees of Service, the Chief Counsel, and the Taxpayer Advocate, as well as other persons who are under contract with the Service and subject to the return privacy rules of Section 6103. A contact is initiated by a Service employee "whenever it is the employee who first tries to communicate with a person other than the taxpayer."[178] On the other hand, the Service employee does not initiate a contact when the employee returns an unsolicited telephone call or attempts to speak to the taxpayer must do so by contacting another person. A contact initiated by a Service employee is "with respect to the determination or collection of the tax liability of the taxpayer" when the contact is made "for the purpose of either determining or collecting a particular tax liability."[179] Finally, a Service employee discloses the taxpayer's identity "whenever the employee knows or should know that the person being contacted can readily ascertain the taxpayer's identity from the information given by the employee."[180]

A precontact notice must be made reasonably in advance of the notice and may be made either orally or in writing, whether it is mailed, given to the taxpayer in person, left at the taxpayer's home or usual place of business, or is actually received by the taxpayer.[181] A precontact notice is not required when the taxpayer has received by some other statute, regulation, or procedure, such as a Collection Due Process Notice, which provides reasonable advance notice that contacts with third parties may be made.[182] The Service must give the taxpayer postcontact reports of contacts during the reporting period at least annually, and a taxpayer may request a record of the persons contacted as long as

---

[177] Prop. Reg. § 301.7602-2, added by REG-104906-99, 66 Fed. Regs. 77–84 (Jan. 2, 2001).

[178] Prop. Reg. § 301.7602-2(c)(1).

[179] Prop. Reg. § 301.7602-2(c)(3).

[180] Prop. Reg. § 301.7602-2(c)(4).

[181] Prop. Reg. § 301.7602-2(d)(1).

[182] Prop. Reg. § 301.7602-2(d)(2).

requests are not made with unreasonable frequency.[183] The content of the post-contact report will be sufficient if it discloses without any additional information the name of person contacted.[184]

Exceptions to the precontact notice rules are a contact the taxpayer or the taxpayer's representative authorizes.[185] Neither a general precontact notice nor a postcontact notice will be given to the taxpayer if the Service employee has "good cause" to believe that giving such a notice will lead to (1) hiding or destroying records that "may be relevant" to the examination or collection activity; (2) attempts to prevent the person or persons contacted from communicating with the Service employee by intimidation, bribery, or collusion; or (3) attempts to flee or avoid testifying or producing records that may be relevant to the examination. Good cause to believe that precontact or postcontact notice will result in a taxpayer's harming the person contacted in any way constitutes the reprisal exception to the notice procedures. Precontact and postcontact notices are also not required in pending criminal tax investigations or other criminal investigations, nor to contacts where notice to the taxpayer might lead to revealing the identity of a confidential informant, nor to governmental contacts.

The proposed regulations also state that the precontact and postcontact notice procedures do not apply when the contact is made "during the course of a pending court proceeding."[186] This exception for so-called nonadministrative contacts does not appear in the statutory language; even so, a taxpayer should be entitled to know of such contacts under the discovery rules in district courts or the Court of Federal Claims, as well as under the Tax Court's Rules of Practice and Procedure, even if the contact may not be disclosable under Section 7602(c). In *Seawright v. Commissioner*,[187] the taxpayers alleged that there had been third-party contacts by a Service employee, but they had not been given either a precontact or postcontact notice. Counsel admitted that there had been a third-party contact, but argued that the notice requirement had not been violated. The Tax Court observed that the proposed regulations followed the legislative history, and concluded that "Congress did not intend section 7602(c) to apply to third-party contacts made by the IRS in the course of trial preparation activities, where those contacts are not with respect to examination and collection activities."[188] The Tax Court also noted, however, that although it had not prescribed rules "specifically relating to informal pretrial interviews of potential witnesses," Counsel was "required to identify witnesses in his trial

---

[183] Prop. Reg. §§ 301.7602-2(e)(1), 301.7602-2(e)(2).

[184] Prop. Reg. § 301.7602-2(e)(3).

[185] Prop. Reg. §§ 301.7602-2(f)(1)–301.7602-2(f)(1)(7).

[186] Prop. Reg. § 301.7602-2(f)(7).

[187] Seawright v. Comm'r, 117 TC 294 (2001).

[188] Seawright v. Comm'r, 117 TC 294 (2001).

memorandum, which was required to be submitted to the Court and to the petitioners at least 15 days before the trial session."[189]

[5] Tours of Business Sites

An agent may conduct a tour of the taxpayer's business cite during normal working hours to gather evidence that only be gathered by a "direct visit, such as inventory or asset verification."[190] Tours of business sites are required during the examination. The tour or tours are conducted early in the examination, usually after the initial meeting, to clarify what the agent was told at the initial meeting and to establish a context for a review of information in books of account and other records, such as whether assets identified on the tax return are physically present, and whether assets or inventoriable property not reflected on the return is present or absent. The tour also enables the agent to a sense of the scope and depth of the examination he or she will need to conduct. As the agent tours the business site, the agent will focus on large, unusual, or questionable items the agent has identified during the precontact process.

[6] Related and Pickup Returns

The agent has the discretion to requisition returns related to the return under examination (e.g., returns of a related individual, partnership, corporation, or other entity).[191] In making an examination of an assigned return, an agent is also instructed, as a general rule, to request the taxpayer to produce the retained copy of the subsequent year's return to bring the taxpayer up to date and to avoid repetitive examinations.[192] This inspection is to determine whether examination is necessary, and is equivalent to the classification of the subsequent return for examination. Because books and records are not called for in the classification process, the Service considers this inspection not to constitute an examination. The agent has the discretion to examine a subse-

---

[189] Seawright v. Comm'r, 117 TC 294 n.6 (2001).

[190] Reg. § 301.7605-1(d)(3)(iii). The regulation also permits visits to a taxpayer's residence, but the Service acknowledges that "[d]ue to privacy issues and the intrusiveness of such inspections, their use should be limited."

[191] IRM 4.10.5.4, Related Returns (May 14, 1999). The Manual says: "To the extent practical all individual returns of corporate officers in Examination Division at the time a closely-held corporation return is assigned will also be assigned to the corporation returns examiner." If the corporation's return shows no adjustment affecting the officer's return and the officer has not been contacted, the agent may survey the return. When an officer's return is being examined, the examination is not complete, and the corporation's return is assigned to another agent. The two examinations are supposed to be coordinated.

[192] IRM 4.10.5.3, Prior & Subsequent Year Returns (May 14, 1999).

quent year's return, although the later return may merely be screened to see whether there are any unusual items. If the agent decides not to examine the return, the taxpayer is supposed to be informed of the decision. The agent is also supposed to inform the taxpayer that, as a result of the inspection and Service procedures, the inspected but unexamined return should not be computer-selected for examination. If the examination of the assigned return has produced minor adjustments or no changes, the agent may also accept the subsequent return as filed. Once the agent verifies items on the return, the agent is conducting an examination, and the taxpayer should request a report covering any adjustments. In a report of the examination of the assigned return, the agent will generally state that the return for the subsequent year has been inspected and was not considered worthy of audit.

Pickup returns. In the field examination of an assigned return, revenue agents are also told to inspect the taxpayer's retained copies of returns for the prior year.[193] After inspection, the agent may examine the prior year (a "prior year pickup") at any time before the due date of the return for the year after the return under examination.[194] For example, if a 2000 return were under examination, an agent could pick up a 1999 return any time before April 15, 2002. To pick up a prior year return after that date, the agent must have the group manager's approval. This approval is given only where circumstances warrant exceeding examination cycles[195] for such causes as net operating loss carrybacks, investment credit carrybacks, fraud situations, and significant and material adjustments where failure to examine would result in a serious administrative omission.

¶ 8.08 SPECIAL ISSUES IN EXAMINATIONS

[1] Repetitive Examinations

Repetitive examinations of individuals can be terminated where prior examinations have resulted in small tax change.[196] If the taxpayer (with individual nonbusiness returns having no Schedule C or Schedule F) responds to an initial contact letter or otherwise advises the agent that an examination in either of the two preceding years resulted in no change or a small tax change, the Service will consider whether the examination should continue by reviewing the prior year's case files. The agent's group manager must approve the decision

---

[193] IRM 4.10.5.3, Prior & Subsequent Year Returns (May 14, 1999).

[194] IRM 4.10.5.3, Prior & Subsequent Year Returns (May 14, 1999).

[195] For a description of audit cycles, see supra ¶ 8.06.

[196] IRM 4.10.2.8.5, Repetitive Examinations (May 14, 1999).

to conclude the examination. If the taxpayer's records have been examined, the return will be considered to have been examined without change. Otherwise, the return will be closed on survey after assignment. However, as a matter of law, it is unlikely that a taxpayer's claim that repetitive examination is an abuse of discretion will succeed.[197]

[2] Reopening Closed Examinations

The Service has a well-defined policy against reopening closed cases unless there are strong reasons justifying the action. This policy derives from the provisions of Section 7605(b), which prohibit an "unnecessary examination" and restrict the Service to one inspection of the taxpayer's books for any one taxable period, unless the taxpayer is notified of the need to make the additional examination. The purpose of this curb is not to limit the number of examinations, but to shift the discretion for a reexamination of the taxpayer's books to higher management personnel from the field agent.[198] The Service's policy is not to reopen a closed case to make an adjustment unfavorable to a taxpayer unless one of the following circumstances is present:

1. There is evidence of fraud, malfeasance, collusion, concealment, or misrepresentation of a material fact.
2. The prior closing involved a clearly defined substantial error based on an established Service position existing at the time of the previous examination.
3. Other circumstances exist that indicate that failure to reopen would be a serious administrative omission.[199]

Under Service reopening procedures, when an agreed case is closed for purposes of reopening, the local office must have notified the taxpayer in writing of the final proposal of adjustments of tax liability or acceptance of the return as filed.[200] For purposes of an agreed case, the term "notified in writing" means transmittal to the taxpayer of a Report of Individual Income Tax Audit Changes (Form 1902-E), subject to the conditions on the form. This term also includes a letter transmitting an audit report on excise or employment tax (Let-

---

[197] See, e.g., DuBois v. Comm'r, 81-2 USTC ¶ 9600 (10th Cir. 1981), aff'g TC Memo. 1980-143, 40 TCM 263 (1980); Chapman v. Comm'r, TC Memo. 1982-68, 43 TCM 511 (1982).

[198] United States v. Powell, 379 US 48, 54–55 (1964).

[199] 26 CFR § 601.105(j); Rev. Proc. 85-13, 1985-1 CB 514. Cases may be reopened to make adjustments favorable to the taxpayer without regard to these criteria. IRM, Policies of the IRS Handbook, P-4-3 (approved Dec. 21, 1984).

[200] Rev. Proc. 85-13, 1985-1 CB 514, § 3.01 (definition of "closed cases"). See also IRM 4023.4, MT 4000-239 (June 28, 1989) (Definition of Closed Cases).

ter 898 (DO/IO)) and a letter telling the taxpayer his claim for refund has been disallowed in whole or in part (Letter 569 (SC/DO/IO)). In addition, the term includes a letter to the taxpayer stating that the revenue agent's audit report has been accepted (Letter 987 (DO/IO); and if the taxpayer is a partnership, fiduciary, or small business corporation (Letter 987 (DO)). This result applies in other cases where the revenue agent's examination report is sent to the taxpayer.

Unagreed cases referred to Appeals are not considered closed. An unagreed income, gift, or estate tax case is not considered closed until the time for filing a Tax Court petition has expired without a petition being filed. For unagreed employment and excise tax cases, the term applies where the time for filing a protest has expired without a protest having been filed. Because executors or administrators use closing letters for probate purposes, the Manual also says that estate tax cases previously closed on survey are considered closed and will not be reopened without prior approval. As a matter of law, such a letter is not binding on the Service, nor is the Service estopped from later asserting a deficiency.[201] Unagreed cases referred to Appeals are not to be considered closed. Income, gift, and estate tax cases are considered closed where, after a notice of deficiency has been sent, the ninety-day period has elapsed and the taxpayer has not filed a Tax Court petition.

Reopening because of a "serious administrative omission" covers situations in which a failure to do so could (1) result in serious criticism of the Service's administration of the tax laws; (2) establish a precedent that would seriously hamper subsequent attempts by the Service to take corrective action; and (3) result in inconsistent treatment of similarly situated taxpayers who have relatively free access to information regarding the way the Service treated items on other taxpayers' returns.[202] The type of situation the Service seems to have in mind could arise in the examination of stockholders of a closely held corporation.

> **EXAMPLE 8-1:** *A*, an officer/stockholder of a corporation, was previously examined and a deficiency determined and paid. As a result of a subsequent examination of the corporation, adjustments to income are made on the returns of other individual stockholders (*B* and *C*). In this case, the Service would consider it a serious administrative omission not to open *A*'s return regardless of the amount of the tax deficiency.

Another basis for reopening is the existence of a substantial error. Substantial error cases include three categories: (1) those cases where the reopening will result in a deficiency of $10,000 or more, in which case reopening is

---

[201] See United States v. Bernstein, 39 AFTR2d 77-1115, 77-2 USTC ¶ 9652 (EDNY 1977).

[202] Rev. Proc. 85-13, 1985-1 CB 514.

mandatory; (2) cases where reopening will result in a deficiency between $1,000 and $10,000, in which case approval to reopen depends on the facts and circumstances of the case; and (3) those cases where the reopening will result in a deficiency of less than $1,000, in which case approval to reopen generally is not granted unless fraud is involved or the failure to reopen would constitute a "serious administrative omission."[203] Contacts by the Service with the taxpayer after the tax return has been filed do not always constitute an examination or reopening, and thus do not require a reopening letter.

Under Service procedures, certain contacts do not constitute examination or reopening, such as (1) a contact to correct a mathematical error; (2) a contact to verify a discrepancy between the taxpayer's tax return and an information return; (3) the adjustment of an unallowable item; and (4) reconsideration of a case involving the mitigation provisions, deduction of a carryback, failure to replace involuntarily converted property, and Joint Committee cases (more than $2 million overpayments).[204]

When the examination of a return is to be reopened to make an adjustment unfavorable to the taxpayer, the action must be approved by the Chief (Examination Division) or Chief (Compliance Division) for cases under that Chief's jurisdiction.[205]

[3] Extending Period for Assessment

Extensions of the period of limitations are common in the examination of a return, so it is necessary for the representative to know the Code provisions and the Service's procedures in requesting extensions, as well as the taxpayer's options where a request is made. Section 6501(c)(4) provides that the time within which assessment of any tax other than an estate tax must be made may be extended for any period agreed on in writing by the taxpayer and the Service, as long as the agreement is entered into before expiration of the assessment pe-

---

[203] Rev. Proc. 85-13, 1985-1 CB 514.

[204] Rev. Proc. 85-13, 1985-1 CB 514, § 3.02 (listing contacts and other actions not considered examinations or reopenings). Rev. Proc. 85-13 further elaborates the meaning of verifying a discrepancy under the Service's information document matching program. Verification can include inspection of a taxpayer's books without being considered an inspection under Section 7605(b). However, verification of an item of income not required to be shown as a specific line item on a tax return is such an inspection or examination; therefore, if the Service later seeks to examine the return, a reopening letter would be required. Rev. Proc. 85-13 gives, as an example of an inspection-type verification, a situation where the Service contacts a doctor to verify his inclusion of an insurance company payment reported on a Form 1099-MISC in gross receipts that exceeds the amount reported on the information return.

[205] Rev. Proc. 85-13, 1985-1 CB 514.

riod.[206] No assessment of a tax may be made after the period of limitations on assessment has expired, even if the tax was determined before expiration of the statute. Therefore, to ensure a timely assessment, the Service does not permit a taxpayer to appeal an adjustment in tax from the district to the Appeals Office unless there is sufficient time for both the appeal and assessment. An extension thus serves the interests of both the Service and the taxpayer by avoiding revenue loss and permitting administrative appeal.

[a] The Service's Procedures

The Service monitors the expiration of the assessment period. Minimum procedures have been established by the National Office to avoid the expiration of the period of limitations on assessment. These procedures are generally supplemented by field office procedures. In general, the national procedures place overall responsibility for such monitoring on group supervisors. The group supervisor is required (1) to establish a control file for tax returns having at least 210 days remaining and notify the Service employee responsible for the return that the expiration is approaching and (2) when thirty days remain in the statute period, to take immediate action to "protect the government's interest."[207] Local procedures may start the period at which the supervisor requests the agent to solicit the waiver from six to twelve months before the statute period actually expires.

As the statute of limitations period approaches expiration, the Service has five alternatives. It may

1. Solicit a waiver to extend the limitations period
2. Issue a statutory notice of deficiency to suspend the statute of limitations
3. Make a jeopardy assessment if the circumstances meet the requirements of the jeopardy assessment statute
4. Accelerate the audit and return processing
5. Forgo examination of the return.

Within certain limits, the Service's procedure is to solicit a waiver extending the statutory period for making an assessment. Many taxpayers and some representatives fear that failure to consent to a requested extension of the assess-

---

[206] Reg. § 301.6501(c)-1(d). Authority to enter into consents has been delegated to a district director and regional directors of appeals. Id. These officials may redelegate the authority, but in general, not below the level of group supervisors and Appeals officers. The Commissioner's Delegation Order on this subject is CDO No. 42, which is revised from time to time. To ensure the effectiveness of a consent, the most current revision should be checked in the Internal Revenue Bulletin or one of the commercial tax services.

[207] IRM 25.6.22.1, Special Topics, Statutes of Limitations, Statute Extensions By Agreement, Introduction (Jan. 1, 2000).

ment period will result in a jeopardy assessment. Actually, if execution of a waiver is refused, the next steps the Service follows, in order of priority, are to accelerate the audit and return processing and, failing that, to send a statutory notice of deficiency.[208] Although a waiver is the preferred alternative, the Service recognizes that the granting of a waiver to extend the limitations period is a voluntary action on the part of the taxpayer.[209] Individual taxpayers are supposed to be informed of their options, including the option of not executing the waiver. However, a taxpayer's representative of an employee in a tax department is expected to be familiar with applicable administrative provisions and the taxpayer's options.[210] Publication 1035 (Extending the Tax Assessment Period) is furnished to taxpayers when a written request for consent is made. (See Figure 8.1.) The Service's stated policy is also to request such a consent in the following unusual circumstances:[211]

1. A subsequent year is under examination and there are firm indications that substantial additional tax is due for a prior year and (a) the limitations period for the prior year will expire within 150 days and (b) there is insufficient time to complete the examination and administrative processing of the case.

2. The limitations period for the taxable year under examination will expire within 150 days and there is insufficient time to complete the examination and administrative processing of the case.

3. The limitations period for the taxable year under examination will expire within 180 days, and the taxpayer has requested that the case be transmitted to Appeals.

4. The limitations period for the taxable year under examination will expire within 180 days and the case is included in the CEP or involves a case in which the Form 6658 (Notice of Examination of Flow-Through Entity) procedure is applicable.

5. The limitations period will expire within 210 days and the case is includible in the Tax Shelter Program or involves a case that will be (or has been) placed in suspense.

6. A joint investigation is in progress and there is danger of an early expiration of the statutory period for assessment.

7. A case is open on a consent and closing action may not be completed prior to the expiration of the consent on file.

---

[208] IRM 25.6.22.3, Notification of Taxpayer's Rights (Jan. 1, 2000).

[209] IRM 25.6.22.2.1, Guidelines for Soliciting Extensions-Assessments (Jan. 1, 2000). See ¶ 5.03[4][a].

[210] IRM 25.6.22.2.1, Guidelines for Soliciting Extensions-Assessments (Jan. 1, 2000). Taxpayers are to be given a brief explanation of their rights if the request is made orally. If the waiver is obtained by duress, it is invalid. See ¶ 5.03[4][a].

[211] IRM 25.6.22.2.1, Guidelines for Soliciting Extensions-Assessments (Jan. 1, 2000).

8. A case involves an overassessment not protected by a claim.[212]

A waiver may also be requested where (1) the return is held in suspense status awaiting either a court decision on any similar tax case or the resolution of complex or intricate questions of fact or of doubtful issues of law; (2) there are other conditions beyond the control of the Service, such as the reconstruction of lost or destroyed tax records; and (3) a net operating loss is involved.[213]

Unusual circumstances do not exist if the taxpayer has not been contacted or has filed a refund claim. In cases reopened by the filing of a claim for refund, the taxpayer is not requested to file a waiver unless an examination of the return and case files indicates that a redetermination of tax liability may result in additional tax. The Service's policy also is not to request a waiver in any case in which there has been no previous contact made with the taxpayer, except where "compelling reasons" exist.

FIGURE 8.1

PUBLICATION 1035—EXTENDING THE TAX ASSESSMENT PERIOD

---

[212] IRM 4541.1, Consents Extending Period of Limitations—General (Nov. 2, 1988).

[213] See Rev. Proc. 68-31, 1968-2 CB 917, modified by Rev. Proc. 77-6, 1977-1 CB 539 (Service efforts concerning the language of restricted consents); Rev. Proc. 57-6, 1957-1 CB 729.

Extending the Tax Assessment Period

Department of the Treasury
Internal Revenue Service

www.irs.gov

Publication 1035 (Rev. 12-1999)
Catalog Number 46890Q

Background

We try to examine tax returns as soon as possible after they are filed. To protect you from untimely tax examinations, Congress set deadlines for assessing taxes, making refunds or credit of tax. These deadlines are called statutes of limitations. Without statutes of limitations, a tax return could be examined and tax assessed, refunded, or credited at any time, regardless of when the return was filed.

Statutes of limitations generally limit the time we have to examine returns and make assessments to within 3 years after a return is due or filed, whichever is later. We can't assess additional tax, and we can't make a refund or credit, (unless you filed a claim timely) after the time has expired under any statute of limitations. Even if the tax adjustment was determined before expiration. Also, if you disagree with out findings, we cannot provide you with an appeal within the Service unless sufficient time remains on the statute. Because of these restrictions, we identify tax returns under examination for which the statutory period is about to expire and give you the opportunity to extend the statutes of limitations. This additional time allows you to provide further documentation to support your position, request an appeal if you do not agree with our findings, or to claim a tax refund or credit. It also allows the Service time to finish our examination, make any additional assessment, if necessary, and provide sufficient time for processing.

Congress, recognizing that additional time may sometimes be needed to fairly resolve a tax examination, provided for extending the statutory period by written agreement between you and the Service. These agreements are called "consents" and apply to all kinds of taxes except estate tax.

To provide consistency, we have forms for the written consents and guidelines for any restrictive conditions. There are two basic kinds of consent forms, one sets a specific expiration date for the extension, and the other does not. Either type of consent may be limited by restrictive conditions, explained below.

Length of Extension

Our examiners request an extension period no longer than is necessary to complete the examination, and any action necessary to close the case. We use two kinds of consents to accomplish this, a "fixed date" and an "open-ended" consent.

Fixed date consents expire on the date specified in the consent. Once the date is extended it may be further extended by mutual agreement before the expiration date of the previous extension period. This consent is the one used for most examination and appeal activities. The principal forms used for this purpose are Form 872, *Consent to Extend the Time to Assess Tax*, Form 872-B, *Consent to Extend the Time to Assess Miscellaneous Excise Taxes*, or Form SS-10, *Consent to Extend the Time to Assess Employment Taxes*.

Generally, in an open-ended consent, the extension period remains open until 90 days after either the taxpayer or the Service sends written notice ending the agreement. The procedures for using this consent are given in Revenue Procedure 79-22, 1979-1 C.B. 563. A copy may be obtained by calling the Internal Revenue Service at 1-800-829-1040. This kind of consent may be used by Examination, Employee Plans, or Exempt Organizations for cases placed in suspense and for cases scheduled for regional appeals conferences. It is also used in other situations where it would be advantageous to both you and the Service. Form 872-A, *Special Consent to Extend the Time to Assess Tax* is used for this purpose. However, Form 872-A may not be used for employment and certain miscellaneous excise taxes.

Restricted Consents

In addition to extending the statutory period, consent agreements may also limit further examination or appeal activity to specific tax issues. These agreements are called restricted consents and have a fixed or open-ended date of expiration. As a general rule, we do not accept restricted consents until all of the following conditions exist:

1) The number of unresolved issues that must be covered by the restricted consent do not make it impractical to do so.

2) The scope of the restrictions must be clearly and accurately described for all the unresolved issues.

3) The issues not covered by the restricted consent are agreed and provision is made for assessing any deficiency or, under certain situations, scheduling any over-assessment (refund or credit) for the agreed issues.

4) The use of a restricted consent at the district level is approved by the appropriate Service representative.

Available Options

When asked to sign the consent extending the statutory period, you have three options, with rights and alternatives for each. You have the right to

• **sign an unconditional consent** (the fixed date consent or open-ended consent that does not limit the examination or appeal activities to specific issues). This provides us the same examination authority and you the same appeal opportunities as under the original statutory period.

• **negotiate consent items.** The Internal Revenue Code does not specify the length of the extension period or the extent of examination or appeal activities. This allows you and the Service to negotiate the tax issues contained in a restricted consent and/or the length of the extension period. During any negotiations, factors such as the type and difficulty of issues, whether issues not covered by the restricted consent are agreed, etc., will be considered. Both parties must agree on the terms of the consent before it becomes effective.

• **refuse to sign the consent.** When this occurs, except for employment and certain miscellaneous excise taxes, we will usually take steps to assess any tax we determine due by issuing a notice of deficiency (see Notice of Deficiency below for explanation). This notice neither requires that you make an immediate payment or that you immediately take your case to the Tax Court. The notice gives you 90 days (150 days if the notice was addressed to a person outside the United States) to either agree to the deficiency or file a petition with the United States Tax Court for a redetermination of the proposed deficiency. During this period, you may ask Appeals to reconsider your case. However, any reconsideration of your case will not suspend or extend the 90 or 150-day period you have for filing a petition with the Tax Court. If agreement cannot be reached during the 90 or 150-day period, Appeals will attempt to notify you in sufficient time for you to file a petition with the tax court before the 90 or 150-day period expires. After you have petitioned the court, you will have the opportunity for a pretrial settlement. If agreement cannot be reached, the case will be heard in court. Even if you choose not to sign the consent, you may still be considered to have cooperated with the Internal Revenue Service for purposes of determining who has the burden of proof in any court proceeding.

If you don't agree and don't file a petition during the 90 or 150-day period, the amount shown in the notice of deficiency will be assessed and arrangements for payment must be made. Under no circumstances will a penalty be charged for not signing the consent.

As an alternative, you can pay the disputed amount of tax and file a claim for refund. The claim must be filed within the period of limitations for filing claims; however a timely filed claim can be examined, reviewed, and appealed after the period for filing claims has expired. Of course, if you wish, you can take your case to the United States District Court or the United States Court of Federal Claims within the period specified by Internal Revenue Code Section 6532. That section requires you to wait at least six months after filing your claim before you may file suit, and requires you to file the suit within two years of receiving a notice that your claim has been disallowed.

If you choose not to sign the consent extending the period of limitations for employment taxes or certain miscellaneous excise taxes, we will normally assess the additional tax. Generally, your only recourse is to pay the additional tax when assessed. You may then file a claim for refund within the applicable statutory period of limitations, and upon our disallowance of the claim or six months from the date the claim is filed, file suit in the United States District Court or the United States Court of Federal Claims. We will consider a claim for abatement of the assessment of employment taxes or certain miscellaneous excise taxes if a jeopardy assessment (see jeopardy assessment below) is involved or you establish a meritorious reason for our considering the claim for abatement.

Additional information concerning your appeal rights is contained in Publication 556, *Examination of Returns, Appeal Rights, and Claims for Refund.* Appeal procedures for adverse determinations in Employee Plans and Exempt Organization cases are explained in Notice 402, and Publication 892, respectively. Copies are available free from the Internal Revenue Service by calling 1-800-829-1040.

Notice of Deficiency

If the Commissioner determines there is a deficiency of income, estate, gift, or certain miscellaneous excise taxes, the law authorizes the Commissioner to send notice of such deficiency to the taxpayer by certified or registered mail. District directors and other designated officers are authorized to issue these notices for the Commissioner. The notice is not an assessment of tax. It is a proposed deficiency and gives you 90 days (150 days if the notice is mailed to an address outside the United States) to either agree to the deficiency or file a petition with the United States Tax Court for a redetermination of the deficiency. But once the notice of deficiency is issued, the 90 or 150-day period cannot be suspended or extended.

Jeopardy Assessment

Jeopardy assessments are made when we believe before assessment that collection of a proposed deficiency will be endangered if we follow our regular procedures, see Internal Revenue Code Section 6861. Jeopardy assessments are used sparingly. They are to be reasonable, appropriate, and limited to amounts that can be expected to protect the government's interest. Each jeopardy assessment must receive the approval of the district director, or the Director, International District Operations. In addition written approval from the Chief Counsel (or such delegate) is required.

Jeopardy assessments will be made only if one or more of the following conditions exist.

1) The taxpayer is or appears to be planning to depart the United States quickly or to conceal himself/herself.

2) The taxpayer is or appears to be quickly planning to place their property (including retirement plans) beyond the reach of the Government by removing it from the United States, concealing it, dissipating it, and/or transferring it to other persons: or

3) The taxpayer's financial solvency is or appears to be imperiled. (This does not include investigations where the taxpayer becomes insolvent by the accrual of the proposed assessment of tax, penalty, and interest.)

The Service will promptly consider a taxpayer's written request for administrative review of the decision that collection of the tax was in jeopardy, or that the amount of the assessment was excessive.

Note: Jeopardy assessments are not made because the period of limitations for assessing the tax is about to expire or a taxpayer does not consent to extend the statutory period.

Interest

Generally, interest continues to accrue on any balance due until full payment is made, including the time for appeal within the Service or the courts. A cash bond may be posted to stop the accrual of interest. For information on cash bonds, please contact the person requesting the consent.

Summary

This publication gives general information about the consent process and options available to you if we ask you to extend the statutory period of limitations. Specific questions should be referred to the person requesting the consent.

Examiners are instructed to make every effort to close all cases at the earliest possible date to avoid the necessity for renewal consents.[214]

[b] Fixed-Date and Open-Ended Waivers

Both the Service and the taxpayer must have "consented in writing" to assessment of tax after the normal period of assessment if they do so before the extension becomes effective.[215] A waiver need not be in any particular form nor be limited to any set length of time.[216] The Service has developed specific forms to document the written agreement between itself and the taxpayer, of which two are in general use: Form 872 (Consent to Extend the Time to Assess Tax)[217] and Form 872-A (Special Consent to Extend the Time to Assess Tax).[218] (See Form 8.3.)

---

[214] IRM 25.6.22.2.1, Guidelines for Soliciting Extensions—Assessment (Jan. 1, 2002).

[215] IRC § 6501(c)(4).

[216] However, certain minimum time limits are required for the area review and appeals processing of a case (e.g., in an unagreed case, at least 180 days must remain on the statute for local office review (60 days) and appeals processing (120 days)). IRM 25.6.22.1, Guidelines for Soliciting Consents—Assessment (Jan. 1, 2002).

[217] For problems in interpreting the terms of the waiver form, see ¶ 5.03[4][a].

[218] Other forms are used for special situations or when a tax other than an income tax is involved; for example, Form 872-B (Consent to Extend the Time to Assess Miscellaneous Excise Taxes); Form 872-C, for a private foundation; Form 977 (Consent Fixing Period of Limitation on Assessment of Liability at Law or in Equity for Income, Gift, Estate and Profits Tax Against a Transferee or Fiduciary); and Form SS-10 (Consent to Extend the Time to Assess Employment Taxes). See IRM 25.6.22.4.1, Assessment Consent Forms (Jan. 1, 2002).

FORM 8.3
CONSENT TO EXTEND THE TIME TO ASSESS TAX

Form **872** (Rev. January 2001)	Department of the Treasury-Internal Revenue Service **Consent to Extend the Time to Assess Tax**	In reply refer to: Taxpayer Identification Number

John Jones and Mary Jones

(Name(s))

taxpayer(s) of   **One James Street, New York, NY 100000**

(Number, Street, City or Town, State, ZIP Code)

and the Commissioner of Internal Revenue consent and agree to the following:

(1) The amount of any Federal   **income**   tax due on any return(s) made by or

(Kind of tax)

for the above taxpayer(s) for the period(s) ended   **1997**

may be assessed at any time on or before   **December 31, 2001**   . However, if

(Expiration date)

a notice of deficiency in tax for any such period(s) is sent to the taxpayer(s) on or before that date, then the time for assessing the tax will be further extended by the number of days the assessment was previously prohibited, plus 60 days.

(2) The taxpayer(s) may file a claim for credit or refund and the Service may credit or refund the tax within 6 months after this agreement ends.

MAKING THIS CONSENT WILL NOT DEPRIVE THE TAXPAYER(S) OF ANY APPEAL RIGHTS TO WHICH THEY WOULD OTHERWISE BE ENTITLED.

YOUR SIGNATURE HERE →	/s/ John Jones	1/13/2000
		(Date signed)
SPOUSE'S SIGNATURE →	/s/ Mary Jones	1/13/2000
		(Date signed)
TAXPAYER'S REPRESENTATIVE SIGN HERE →	/s/ Steven Doe	1/13/2000
		(Date signed)
CORPORATE NAME →		
CORPORATE OFFICER(S) SIGN HERE →	(Title)	(Date signed)
→	(Title)	(Date signed)

INTERNAL REVENUE SERVICE SIGNATURE AND TITLE

(Division Executive Name - see instructions)	(Division Executive Title - see instructions)	
BY /s/ District Director		1/13/2000
(Authorized Official Signature and Title - see instructions)		(Date signed)

(Signature instructions are on the back of this form)   www.irs.gov   Catalog Number 20755I   Form **872** (Rev. 1-2001)

Instructions

If this consent is for income tax, self-employment tax, or FICA tax on tips and is made for any year(s) for which a joint return was filed, both husband and wife must sign the original and copy of this form unless one, acting under a power of attorney, signs as agent for the other. The signatures must match the names as they appear on the front of this form.

If this consent is for gift tax and the donor and the donor's spouse elected to have gifts to third persons considered as made one-half by each, both husband and wife must sign the original and copy of this form unless one, acting under a power of attorney, signs as agent for the other. The signatures must match the names as they appear on the front of this form.

If this consent is for Chapter 41, 42, or 43 taxes involving a partnership or is for a partnership return, only one authorized partner need sign.

If this consent is for Chapter 42 taxes, a separate Form 872 should be completed for each potential disqualified person, entity, or foundation manager that may be involved in a taxable transaction during the related tax year. See Revenue Ruling 75-391, 1975-2 C.B. 446.

If you are an attorney or agent of the taxpayer(s), you may sign this consent provided the action is specifically authorized by a power of attorney. If the power of attorney was not previously filed, you must include it with this form.

If you are acting as a fiduciary (such as executor, administrator, trustee, etc.) and you sign this consent, attach Form 56, Notice Concerning Fiduciary Relationship, unless it was previously filed. If the taxpayer is a corporation, sign this consent with the corporate name followed by the signature and title of the officer(s) authorized to sign.

Instructions for Internal Revenue Service Employees

Complete the Division Executive's name and title depending upon your division.

If you are in the Small Business /Self-Employed Division, enter the name and title for the appropriate division executive for your business unit (e.g., Area Director for your area; Director, Compliance Policy; Director, Compliance Services).

If you are in the Wage and Investment Division, enter the name and title for the appropriate division executive for your business unit (e.g., Area Director for your area; Director, Field Compliance Services).

If you are in the Large and Mid-Size Business Division, enter the name and title of the Director, Field Operations for your industry.

If you are in the Tax Exempt and Government Entities Division, enter the name and title for the appropriate division executive for your business unit (e.g., Director, Exempt Organizations; Director, Employee Plans; Director, Federal, State and Local Governments; Director, Indian Tribal Governments; Director, Tax Exempt Bonds).

If you are in Appeals, enter the name and title of the appropriate Director, Appeals Operating Unit.

The signature and title line will be signed and dated by the appropriate authorized official within your division.

Catalog Number 20755I   Form **872** (Rev. 1-2001)

FORM 8.4
SPECIAL CONSENT TO EXTEND THE TIME TO ASSESS TAX

Form 872-A (Rev. October 1987)	Department of the Treasury — Internal Revenue Service **Special Consent to Extend the Time to Assess Tax**	In reply refer to SSN or EIN

John Jones & Mary Jones
_____
(Name(s))

taxpayer(s) of ___1 James Street, New York, N.Y. 00000_____
(Number, Street, City or Town, State, ZIP Code)
and the District Director of Internal Revenue or Regional Director of Appeals consent and agree as follows:

(1) The amount(s) of any Federal_____Income_____tax due on any return(s) made by or
(Kind of tax)
for the above taxpayer(s) for the period(s) ended ___1984____
may be assessed on or before the 90th (ninetieth) day after: (a) the Internal Revenue Service office considering the case receives Form 872-T, Notice of Termination of Special Consent to Extend the Time to Assess Tax, from the taxpayer(s); or (b) the Internal Revenue Service mails Form 872-T to the taxpayer(s); or (c) the Internal Revenue Service mails a notice of deficiency for such period(s); except that if a notice of deficiency is sent to the taxpayer(s), the time for assessing the tax for the period(s) stated in the notice of deficiency will end 60 days after the period during which the making of an assessment is prohibited. A final adverse determination subject to declaratory judgment under sections 7428, 7476, or 7477 of the Internal Revenue Code will not terminate this agreement.

(2) This agreement ends on the earlier of the above expiration date or the assessment date of an increase in the above tax or the overassessment date of a decrease in the above tax that reflects the final determination of tax and the final administrative appeals consideration. An assessment or overassessment for one period covered by this agreement will not end this agreement for any other period it covers. Some assessments do not reflect a final determination and appeals consideration and therefore will not terminate the agreement before the expiration date. Examples are assessments of: (a) tax under a partial agreement; (b) tax in jeopardy; (c) tax to correct mathematical or clerical errors; (d) tax reported on amended returns; and (e) advance payments. In addition, unassessed payments, such as amounts treated by the Service as cash bonds and advance payments not assessed by the Service, will not terminate this agreement before the expiration date determined in (1) above. This agreement ends on the date determined in (1) above regardless of any assessment for any period includible in a report to the Joint Committee on Taxation submitted under section 6405 of the Internal Revenue Code.

(3) This agreement will not reduce the period of time otherwise provided by law for making such assessment.

(4) The taxpayer(s) may file a claim for credit or refund and the Service may credit or refund the tax within 6 (six) months after this agreement ends.

(Signature instructions and space for signature are on the back of this form) Form 872-A (Rev 10-87)

Copyright © May 2003

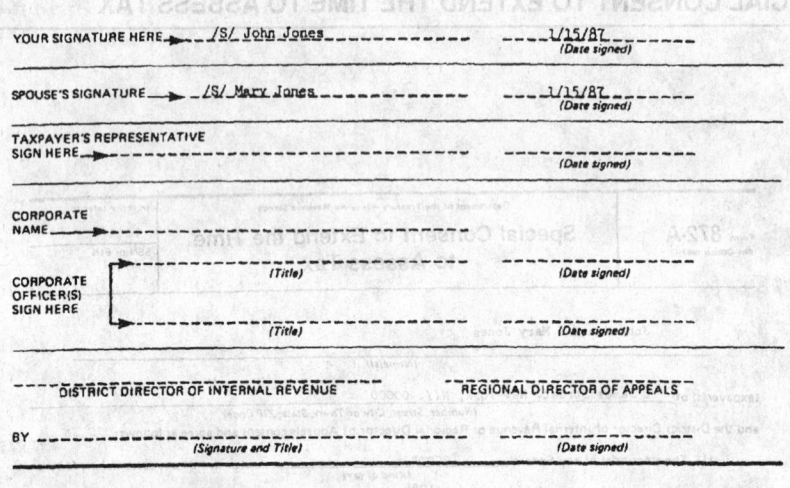

YOUR SIGNATURE HERE ▸ /S/ John Jones   1/15/87
(Date signed)

SPOUSE'S SIGNATURE ▸ /S/ Mary Jones   1/15/87
(Date signed)

TAXPAYER'S REPRESENTATIVE
SIGN HERE ▸
(Date signed)

CORPORATE
NAME

CORPORATE
OFFICER(S)
SIGN HERE   *(Title)*   *(Date signed)*

    (Title)   *(Date signed)*

DISTRICT DIRECTOR OF INTERNAL REVENUE   REGIONAL DIRECTOR OF APPEALS

BY
(Signature and Title)   *(Date signed)*

Instructions

If this consent is for income tax, self-employment tax, or FICA tax on tips and is made for any year(s) for which a joint return was filed, both husband and wife must sign the original and copy of this form unless one, acting under a power of attorney, signs as agent for the other. The signatures must match the names as they appear on the front of this form.

If this consent is for gift tax and the donor and the donor's spouse elected to have gifts to third persons considered as made one-half by each, both husband and wife must sign the original and copy of this form unless one, acting under a power of attorney, signs as agent for the other. The signatures must match the names as they appear on the front of this form.

If this consent is for Chapter 41, 42, or 43 taxes involving a partnership, only one authorized partner need sign.

If you are an attorney or agent of the taxpayer(s), you may sign this consent provided the action is specifically authorized by a power of attorney. If the power of attorney was not previously filed, you must include it with this form.

If you are acting as a fiduciary *(such as executor, administrator, trustee, etc.)* and you sign this consent, attach Form 56, Notice Concerning Fiduciary Relationship, unless it was previously filed.

If the taxpayer is a corporation, sign this consent with the corporate name followed by the signature and title of the officer(s) authorized to sign.

If this consent is for Chapter 42 taxes, a separate Form 872-A should be completed for each potential disqualified person or entity that may have been involved in a taxable transaction during the related tax year. See Revenue Ruling 75-391, 1975-2 C.B. 446.

Form 872-A (Rev 10-87)

The fixed-date waiver on Form 872 sets a specific expiration date for the extension. The extension period requested should be "no longer than is necessary to complete the examination and administrative action incident to the closing of the case."[219] This fixed-date waiver form does not itself set a specific expiration date for the extension period. The extension period is a matter for negotiation between the agent and the taxpayer.[220] There is no limit on the number of agreements the taxpayer and the Service can enter into, as long as before the expiration of the old agreement, the taxpayer and the Service enter into a new agreement in writing, extending the limitations period to a later date.

The special consent form, Form 872-A, is an open-ended consent, rather than a fixed-date form. It is used to extend the period of limitations for an open-ended period required for consideration, plus time for closing action. This period extends to a date ninety days after (1) the Service mails to the taxpayer a written notice of termination of Service consideration; (2) the Service office considering the case receives from the taxpayer a Form 872-T electing to terminate the agreement; or (3) the Service sends a notice of deficiency.[221] Thus, Form 872-A relieves taxpayers and the Service from the inconvenience of obtaining renewal consents. From the taxpayer's standpoint, the limitations period is extended for only as long as is necessary, while incidentally relieving the Service of maintaining the usual controls to ensure against inadvertent expiration of the limitations period on assessment. This open-ended consent is used in both the Examination Division and the Employee Plan/Exempt Organization Division for cases held in suspense pending some judicial or other action that may control the result in the suspended case. It is also used in cases scheduled for Appeals Office review involving complex or intricate facts or unresolved issues of law. However, Form 872-A may not be used for employment and certain miscellaneous excise taxes.

The use of Form 872-T is required because termination of the waiver by correspondence led to situations where the Service failed to send a notice of deficiency within ninety days after the triggering letter.[222] The three ways for termination of a Form 872-A stated in the form are the exclusive means for termination, and alternative methods have not been recognized.[223] A notice of deficiency terminates a Form 872-A, but it must comply with Section 6212 in

---

[219] See IRM 25.6.22.2.1, Guidelines for Soliciting Extensions—Assessments (Jan. 1, 2002).

[220] But see supra note 79.

[221] Rev. Proc. 79-22, 1979-1 CB 563. For further discussion of Form 872-A, see ¶ 5.03[4][a].

[222] See, e.g., Johnson v. Comm'r, 68 TC 637 (1977). Accord Borg Warner Corp. v. Comm'r, 660 F2d 324 (7th Cir. 1981).

[223] Kinsey v. Comm'r, 859 F2d 1361, 1363 (9th Cir. 1988) (failure to respond to thirty-day letter); Kernen v. Comm'r, 902 F2d 17 (9th Cir. 1990) (execution of Form 872).

order to terminate the waiver. Where a taxpayer executes a Form 872-A, and the Service thereafter sends a notice of deficiency that is misaddressed, unde-livered, and unacknowledged, there is no termination of the Form 872-A.[224]

A taxpayer's representative is permitted to sign a waiver for the taxpayer and, if the representative is properly authorized (e.g., by a filed power of attor-ney), the statute of limitations on assessment will be extended in the same manner as if the taxpayer had signed the waiver.[225] Where an agent alters the consent signed by the taxpayer, the consent is ineffective.[226] Extensions may be consented to conditionally, and the conditions can be stated in a letter or writ-ing that accompanies the Form 872.[227] Conditions set forth in a cover letter are binding because they constitute objective manifestations of the taxpayer's con-sent. The Service may not mislead a taxpayer into providing an extension, and if it does, the Service may be equitably estopped from relying on the improp-erly obtained extension.[228] In a case illustrating the point, a taxpayer had exe-cuted Form 872-A, but the revenue agent said that there was no waiver in the file and asked for and received executed fixed-date waivers from the taxpayer; when the Form 872-A was later found, the agent did not notify the taxpayer. The Service was equitably estopped from relying on the fixed-date waivers be-cause of the agent's affirmative misconduct, but the taxpayer was deprived of his opportunity to terminate the Form 872-A, and so penalty interest continued to accrue.

[c] Restricted Consents

Both fixed-date and open-ended agreements have the disadvantage to the taxpayer of permitting new issues to be raised by an examining agent. If an is-sue has been identified by the agent and the assessment period is about to ex-pire, the taxpayer's consent to extend the assessment period can be limited or restricted to the identified issue while the assessment period otherwise expires,

---

[224] Roszkos v. Comm'r, 850 F2d 514 (9th Cir. 1988).

[225] Lefebvre v. Comm'r, TC Memo. 1984-202, 47 TCM 1572 (1984).

[226] Amhowitz v. United States, 59 AFTR2d 87-1088, 87-1 USTC ¶ 9303 (SDNY 1987) (attachment to consent form prepared by taxpayer was removed by agents, and con-sent returned to taxpayer was signed on behalf of the Service; held, consent was ineffec-tive and limitations period on assessment had expired).

[227] Addison H. Gibson Found. v. United States, 91-1 USTC ¶ 50,178 (WD Pa. 1991) (gathering cases). Compare Hubert v. IRS, 78 AFTR2d 96-6535 (CD Cal. 1996) (tax-payer, who signed a Form 870-A that had been sent with a letter from the Service refer-ring to a tax shelter, and who had other correspondence with the Service referring to the same shelter, claimed that the extension was limited to that shelter, so that assessments for two other shelters were barred; held, the extensions were unrestricted because they did not restrict the extension, the correspondence was ambiguous, and no agreement was reached).

[228] Fredericks v. Comm'r, 80 AFTR2d 97-6412 (3d Cir. 1997). The Service has ac-quiesced in this decision. AOD CC-1998-004 (Aug. 28, 1998).

barring any adjustments to the taxpayer's return other than the issues covered by the consent. If an issue has been identified by the agent and the assessment period is about to expire, the taxpayer has the right to request a consent to extend the assessment period restricted to specific issue(s) only, while the statute of limitations is allowed to expire on all other issues.[229] Although the taxpayer has the right to request a restricted waiver, and indeed the Service must notify the taxpayer of the opportunity, the Service has the right to limit the circumstances in which it will agree to enter into a restricted consent.[230] Restricted waivers will only be entered under certain conditions, which are as follows: (1) the number of unresolved issues must not make it impractical for the Service to enter into a restricted waiver; (2) the specific unresolved issues covered in the restricted consent must be clearly described so that there will be no later dispute about what issues are covered in the restricted consent; (3) the issues on which the statute of limitations will be allowed to expire must be agreed, and the assessment of any deficiency or, under certain circumstances, the scheduling of the refund or credit of the amount of an overassessment provided for; (4) the agent's use of a restricted consent is approved by the agent's group manager; and (5) the language of the restricted consent must be approved by the Area Counsel.[231] In addition, until the examination has been completed and the issues have been identified, a restricted will be avoided, if possible. Also, restricted waivers generally will not be accepted if the return involves a Joint Committee Case.

A restricted waiver is permissible under Service practice where "in the light of reasonable tax administration, resolution of such issue or issues requires establishment of a Service position through court decision, regulation, ruling or other National Office action, or where other equally meritorious circumstances exist."[232]

The difficulty with restricted consents and the reason such consents are not frequently used is that the waiver must be carefully written so that both the Service and the taxpayer understand just what changes may be made after the assessment period has otherwise expired. If the scope of the waiver is unclear, a dispute can develop over whether the statutory period was open for assess-

---

[229] IRM 25.6.22.8, Restricted Consents (Jan. 1, 2000).

[230] IRM 25.6.22.8.1, Taxpayer's Rights Concerning Restricted Consents (Jan. 1, 2000).

[231] IRM 25.6.22.8.2, Situations Permitting Taxpayer's Request for Restricted Consent (Jan. 1, 2000). See Rev. Proc. 68-31, 1968-2 CB 917, modified by Rev. Proc. 77-6, 1977-1 CB 539 (Service efforts concerning the language of restricted consents).

[232] IRM 25.6.22.8.2, Situations When the Service May Request Restricted Consents (Jan. 1, 2002).

ment on the adjustment finally proposed.[233] Basic restrictive statement the Service uses in restrictive consent is[234]

> The amount of any deficiency assessment is to be limited to that resulting from any adjustment to (description of the areas of consideration) including any consequential changes to other items based on such adjustment.[235]

The "area of consideration" is the issue that is to remain open, and the "adjustment" is any change within the area of consideration. The "consequential change" is any direct or indirect effect.[236] The effect of a disallowance of an exemption for a dependent in 2000, for example, is a $2,000 increase in taxable income, and this is the adjustment.[237] A possible direct consequence of the adjustment is the disallowance of any medical expenses claimed for the disallowed dependent. If this direct consequence reduces the total itemized deductions to the point that the standard deduction is greater, the disallowance of all itemized deductions and the allowance of the standard deduction would be indirect consequences of the "adjustment."

A restricted consent may be entered into where flow-through issues are present from, for example, partnerships or small-business corporations to individual taxpayers and where the only items determined worthy of examination are those resulting from the flow-through issues.[238]

[d] Taxpayer Options

When asked to waive the period of limitations, a taxpayer has three basic choices, with various rights and alternatives under each:

1. *Taxpayer can refuse to sign the waiver.* When the taxpayer chooses this course, the Service normally issues a statutory notice of deficiency. This notice of deficiency does not prevent the taxpayer from gaining access to the administrative appeal system. Indeed, Service procedures provide for Appeals Office review in the event that a petition is filed in the Tax Court without the taxpayer's having had the opportunity for an appellate conference. The taxpayer can still have an opportunity for review and appeal by paying any dis-

---

[233] IRM 25.6.22.8.2, Situations Permitting Taxpayer's Request for Restricted Consent (Jan. 1, 2000). For a case where an agent used the wrong language suggested in IRM 4541.72 in preparing the restricted consent and thereby failed to identify a flow-through entity, see Goldberg v. Comm'r, 63 TCM 2168 (1992) (taxpayers were not estopped from relying on Form 872-A omitting entity).

[234] IRM 25.6.22.8.12, Basic Restrictive Statement (Jan. 1, 2000).

[235] IRM 25.6.22.8.12, Basic Restrictive Statement (Jan. 1, 2000).

[236] IRM 25.6.22.8.12, Basic Restrictive Statement (Jan. 1, 2000).

[237] IRM 25.6.22.8.12, Basic Restrictive Statement (Jan. 1, 2000).

[238] IRM 25.6.22.8.8, Non-TEFRA Pass-Through Entities (Jan. 1, 2000); IRM 25.6.22.8.8, TEFRA Entity Issues (Jan. 1, 2000).

puted amount and filing a claim for refund. Alternatively, the taxpayer can bypass all administrative opportunities for settlement and seek court review by filing a petition in the Tax Court or, after paying the tax, filing a complaint in a district court or the claims court.

2. *Taxpayer can sign an unconditional waiver extending the period of limitations for a fixed period.* This action permits the Service the same audit authority and the taxpayer the same appeal opportunities as under the original statute of limitations.

3. *Taxpayer can enter into a restricted waiver.* In such a waiver, the specific tax issue with respect to which the period of limitations is waived can be described and an assessment may be made only with respect to those issues.

There are no absolute rules for a taxpayer or representative to follow in deciding which alternative is most appropriate, but some general observations can be made. In most cases, if an agent has not completed the examination, the taxpayer should agree to a waiver, but only for the period necessary to complete the examination. The length of the waiver term is a control over the time the agent can take with the examination. If the examination has already consumed substantial time, a long waiver term should not be necessary for the agent, or unreasonable for the taxpayer to refuse.

A taxpayer probably should also sign a waiver where the agent has completed the examination, even if there are unagreed issues that the taxpayer is ready and able to litigate, if only because it is the least expensive option available to taxpayers and the rate of settlements in Appeals is high. A taxpayer should normally use the Service's administrative dispute-resolution system. His agreement to extend the limitations period is not too high a price to pay for access as long as delays are not inordinate and progress in resolving the disputes is being made or can be foreseen. Bypassing normal administrative review and filing a Tax Court petition to contest adjustments before an Appeals Office hearing is granted is inappropriate in many cases, although it does have tactical advantages.[239] In the usual case, the risk that Appeals will raise a new issue or devise a more technically sound basis for an adjustment is not present. Therefore, bypassing the normal protest-Appeals route leaves the taxpayer with only four months to settle the case. Finally, a restricted waiver, when it can be used, permits the taxpayer to close a portion of the return from further examination and the possibility of adjustment, which is obviously desirable. However, since such a waiver cannot be used in all cases, the restricted consent is an option open to taxpayers only in a limited number of circumstances.

---

[239] See ¶ 9.04.

[4] Fraud Referrals

Referrals from other Service functions are one of the most important sources of fraud cases. Revenue agents and other Service personnel are instructed that a fraud case "begins with the recognition of affirmative indications of fraud by the taxpayer" and that development of these "badges" of fraud assists the employee in establishing "firm indications necessary for a successful fraud case."[240] Revenue agents are told that audit techniques are designed to disclose not only errors in accounting and application of the tax laws but also irregularities indicating the possibilities of fraud. An examining agent who uncovers indications of fraud is required to suspend the examination.[241] This bald requirement does not end the matter for the agent. Other instructions require the agent to exercise extraordinarily delicate judgments about when to discontinue the investigation. On the one hand, the agent must discontinue the investigation "at the earliest opportunity" and do so without disclosing the reason for suspending the audit to the taxpayer. On the other, the agent is told that "earliest opportunity" does not mean "immediately." Agents are cautioned not to discontinue the examination until they have discovered "firm" indications of fraud.[242] When there are indications of fraud, the revenue agent and the agent's superiors and Fraud Coordinator plan to establish that "sufficient affirmative acts exist which confirm fraud."[243] In addition, "[a] refined judgment must be made about when to suspend the audit. If the agent stops too soon all the information necessary to document firm indications of fraud may not be developed sufficiently for the Criminal Investigation (CI) function."[244] At a minimum, the agent will attempt to gather evidence of one or more badges of fraud, noting from whom and when the information was obtained. Also, it is "critical for the [agent] to secure the taxpayer's explanation for any discrepancies."[245]

---

[240] IRM 25.1.2.1, Recognizing and Developing Fraud—Overview (Jan. 1, 2003).

[241] IRM 25.1.3.2, Preparation of Form 2797 (Jan. 1, 2003) . See also Penalty Considerations—Recognizing noncompliance Fraud (May 14, 1999). Fraud is discussed at length in the Fraud Handbook, IRM 25.1, Jan. 1, 2003. Among other things, the procedures state, "The first symptom alerting the examiner to the possibility of fraud will frequently be provided by the taxpayer." See IRM 25.1.3, Investigative Techniques (Jan. 1, 2003). Conduct during the examination (e.g., procrastination and other uncooperativeness) as well as business methods (e.g., failing to keep records or destroying records) are singled out for the agent's attention.

[242] IRM 25.1.3.2, Preparation of Form 2797 (Jan. 1, 2003).

[243] IRM 25.1.2.1, Recognizing and Developing Fraud—Overview (Jan. 1, 2003).

[244] IRM 25.1.2.1, Recognizing and Developing Fraud—Overview (Jan. 1, 2003).

[245] IRM 25.1.2.1, Recognizing and Developing Fraud—Overview (Jan. 1, 2003).

[a] Indicators of Fraud

Indicators of fraud are described at considerable length, and are separated into Indicators of Fraud—Income; Indicators of Fraud—Expenses or Deductions; Indicators—Books and Records; Indicators of Fraud—Allocations of Income; Indicators—Conduct of Taxpayer; and Indicators—Methods of Concealment. These indicators amount to criminal conduct the Supreme Court described in *Spies v. United States* as conduct "the likely effect of which is to mislead or conceal."[246] In the same manner as a taxpayer's criminal misconduct, examples of indicators of fraud in income are

- Omissions of specific items of income, entire sources of income, or substantial amounts of income
- Unexplained increases in net worth
- Unexplained bank deposits.[247]

Indicators of fraud in the conduct of taxpayers include

- False statements about material facts involved in the examination
- Attempts to hinder the examination by failing or refusing to answer questions, canceling appointments, or refusing to supply records
- Employee testimony about irregular business practices
- Destruction of books and records
- Transfers of assets for purposes of concealment.[248]

Even before a criminal referral can be made, the revenue agent may engage in investigation touched off by relatively ambiguous conduct. Agents are told that "[u]nusual, inconsistent or incongruous items should alert examiners to the possibility of fraud and the need for further investigation."[249] Also, "[t]axpayer misconduct should be an early warning sign of possible fraudulent conduct."[250] A lack of internal controls and dealings in cash are said to indicate the filing of improper returns.[251] Another investigative technique emphasizes the importance of the "initial contact" with the taxpayer because it gives the agent "the opportunity to obtain valuable information which may not be readily available later."[252] Because of the importance of the statements the taxpayer may make at this initial interview, the revenue agent will document statements a taxpayer may make in discussions, as well as make note of the

---

[246] Spies v. United States, 317 US 492, 495 (1943).

[247] IRM 25.1.2.2, Indicators of Fraud (Jan. 1, 2003).

[248] IRM 25.1.2.2, Indicators of Fraud (Jan. 1, 2003).

[249] IRM 25.1.2.2, Indicators of Fraud (Jan. 1, 2003).

[250] IRM 25.1.2.3, Investigative Techniques (Jan. 1, 2003).

[251] IRM 25.1.2.3, Investigative Techniques (Jan. 1, 2003).

[252] IRM 25.1.2.3(3), Investigative Techniques (Jan. 1, 2003); IRM 25.1.2.3(4), Investigative Techniques (Jan. 1, 2003) (instruction to prepare memorandum of interview).

taxpayer's failure to respond to questions. Questions are recorded verbatim, and nonresponsive answers are noted. Also, when the revenue agent receives workpapers, the revenue agent notes the tax year summarized, the date of the contact, and who was present during the contact.[253] Importantly, the agent notes information that may provide leads for later inquiry, such as who prepared the information on the tax return, who approves and classifies expense items, who deposits business receipts, and how business receipts on the tax return are determined. During the investigation, the revenue agent must keep a historical record of all contacts and conversations with the taxpayer.[254] The Service believes that this technique is critical in sustaining fraud, so the taxpayer's attorney will want to prepare a "shadow" historical record of what takes place during the examination/investigation in order to keep track of the inquiry and its deficiencies and strong points.

Additional instructions are provided for aiding and abetting;[255] bankruptcy fraud;[256] employment tax fraud;[257] payroll padding;[258] excise tax fraud;[259] willful failure to pay excise tax;[260] and failure to collect and pay over excise tax on diesel fuel, gasoline, and aviation fuel in violation of Section 4103 cases.[261]

[b] Agent Violations in Developing Firm Indications of Fraud

As described earlier, badges of fraud assist agents in recognizing and developing "firm indications" of fraud.[262] A firm indication of fraud is said to be

---

[253] IRM 25.1.2.3(3), Investigative Techniques (Jan. 1, 2003).

[254] IRM 25.1.2.3(3), Investigative Techniques (Jan. 1, 2003).

[255] IRM 25.1.2.3(5), Aiding and Abetting (Jan. 1, 2003) (requiring the agent to determine who, apart from or in addition to the taxpayer, is responsible for the fraudulent acts, such as accountants, attorneys, or appraisers).

[256] IRM 25.1.2.5, Bankruptcy Fraud (Jan. 1, 2003). Among other bankruptcy criminal activity, compliance personnel are warned that an individual may be perpetrating bankruptcy fraud by a so-called bust out where merchandise inventory, cash, or other assets are converted to personal use or personal gain.

[257] IRM 25.1.2.6, Employment Tax (Jan. 1, 2003). Compliance personnel are warned about intentional misclassification of employees and disguised salary payments.

[258] IRM 25.1.2.6.1, Payroll Padding (Jan. 1, 2003). Compliance agents are told that payroll may be padded for a number of reasons and in a number of ways, all of which involve the payment of funds by a business without the recipient paying tax on the income.

[259] IRM 25.1.2.6.1, Excise Tax Fraud (Jan. 1, 2003). Excise tax fraud, examiners are told, has badges of fraud different from other schemes, such as a taxpayer who has paid excise tax previously, but who inexplicably stops doing so; the taxpayer who purchases fuel from a different supplier than the usual one and fails to report the sales; tax passed on to customers, but not reported or paid to the Service.

[260] IRM 25.1.2.7.1, Excise Taxes—Willful Failure to Pay (Jan. 1, 2003).

[261] IRM 25.1.2.7.2, Section 4103 Cases—Referrals to Collection (Jan. 1, 2003).

[262] IRM 25.1.2, Indicators of Fraud (Jan. 1, 2003); IRM 25.1.2.1, Recognizing and Developing Fraud—Overview (Jan. 1, 2003).

distinguishable from a first indication of fraud, "[a] first indication of fraud can be described as a mere suspicion of fraud." The determination of a firm indication of fraud is a factual determination that can be determined only on a case-by-case basis."[263] Another description is, a "firm indication of fraud . . . is something different from a first indication or a mere suspicion that intentional fraud exists."[264] The agent develops firm indications of fraud by examining books and records that may later be unavailable to the Service. Examiners also ask for explanations of discrepancies giving rise to their suspicions, and consult with their group managers and Examination Fraud Coordinator to assist them in deciding whether the indications of fraud are sufficiently developed.

In the process of perfecting indications of fraud, a revenue agent will gather evidence for use in a criminal case without any notice to the taxpayer. This practice poses dangers to taxpayers because, unlike revenue agents, special agents are required to give partial *Miranda* warnings alerting the taxpayer to the agent's function as a criminal investigator and to the possibility that anything the taxpayer says may be used against him in any criminal proceeding.[265] If the compliance employee, such as a revenue agent, follows the investigative techniques in the Manual, the referring agent will obtain incriminating oral statements, extracts, or copies of the taxpayer's records, even before a referral is made and before the special agent has become involved. Although Service guidelines warn about overstepping the bounds of a civil examination, a revenue agent can still cross the line between identifying fraud and gathering evidence for use in a criminal prosecution.

Activities of a revenue agent in violation of these guidelines have sometimes led to suppression of admissions made by the taxpayer;[266] but based on the Supreme Court's decision in *United States v. Caceres,*[267] such evidence may nevertheless be admitted if the violation of the guidelines was not deliber-

---

[263] IRM 25.1.2.1, Recognizing and Developing Fraud—Overview (Jan. 1, 2003); IRM 25.1.2.3, Investigative Techniques (Jan. 1, 2003).

[264] Groder v. United States, 816 F2d 139 (4th Cir. 1987) (revenue agent auditing taxpayer's returns did not violate taxpayer's Fifth Amendment rights where fraud referral was made after taxpayer voluntarily filed amended returns reporting additional income, his attorney supplied agent with explanation of underreporting, and, at agent's request, taxpayer was interviewed).

[265] IRM 9.4.5.11.3, Duty to Advise Individual of Constitutional Rights (May 19, 1999); IRM 9.4.5.5 et seq., Preparation and Planning (May 19, 1999). The special agent will prepare an outline, review available information, organize interview file, and obtain original returns. When there is an interview of a person other than the taxpayer, the format of the interview is prepared for the agent. See Exhibit 9.4.5-1.

[266] Compare United States v. Toussaint, 456 F. Supp. 1069 (SD Tex. 1978) (suppression ordered) with United States v. Lockyer, 448 F2d 417 (10th Cir. 1971) (suppression denied) and United States v. Matis, 476 F. Supp. 1287, 80-1 USTC ¶ 9111 (SDNY 1979) (suppression denied). See ¶ 13.09[6].

[267] United States v. Meier, 607 F2d 215 (8th Cir. 1979), applying United States v. Caceres, 440 US 741 (1979).

ate and the taxpayer, in any event, did not rely on them. In cases where the referring agent engages in active deception in an attempt to gather evidence, the fruits of the deception have been suppressed in subsequent criminal trials.[268] Courts examine whether a revenue agent continued an audit after discovering firm indications of fraud, and will suppress evidence when the revenue agent affirmatively and intentionally misleads the taxpayer of the nature of the investigation in violation of the taxpayer's Fourth and Fifth Amendment rights.[269] Consequently, a taxpayer's representative must be alert to this potential argument of agent misconduct.

The overextension of the examination may jeopardize criminal prosecution by giving the taxpayer a basis for claiming that the criminal case was substantially built by the examiner under the guise of making an audit for civil tax purposes.[270] To avoid a taxpayer's deception argument, the agent is told not to imply that favored treatment will be given if requested information is furnished (e.g., "It will be to your advantage" or "My office will appreciate it").[271] The agent is also instructed not to minimize the nature of the examination by describing it as "routine." A taxpayer's statements to a revenue agent have been suppressed where the agent had indications of fraud and thereafter interviewed the taxpayer on several occasions in violation of the Manual instructions.[272] Courts have used the "firm indication of fraud" standard to determine whether the revenue agent affirmatively misled the taxpayer or the taxpayer's representative and conducted a criminal investigation under the guise of a civil audit. The taxpayer must also show by clear and convincing evidence that the Service affirmatively and intentionally misled the taxpayer, and that the Service's conduct prejudiced the taxpayer's Fourth Amendment and Fifth Amendment due process rights.[273]

Courts have begun to take more seriously Manual instructions to revenue agents to discontinue an examination when they have discovered sufficient evi-

---

[268] United States v. Tweel, 550 F2d 297 (5th Cir. 1977); United States v. Mapp, 561 F2d 685 (7th Cir. 1977).

[269] See United States v. Peters, 153 F3d 445 (7th Cir. 1998), cert. denied; United States v. McKee, 84 AFTR2d 99-6229 (6th Cir. 1999) (applying an abuse of discretion standard when a special agent continued an investigation after having some evidence of fraud, and stating that it had "reservations" about the agent's conduct because she gathered evidence used to convict the taxpayer on a silver platter).

[270] IRM 25.1.2.3, Investigative Techniques (Jan. 1, 2003).

[271] IRM 25.1.2.3, Investigative Techniques (Jan. 1, 2003).

[272] United States v. Toussaint, 456 F. Supp. 1069 (SD Tex. 1978). See also cases gathered in United States v. Peters, 153 F3d 445 (7th Cir. 1998), cert. denied.

[273] United States v. Grunewald, 987 F2d 531 (8th Cir. 1993) ("the mere failure of an IRS agent to inform a defendant that information developed in an audit may result in a criminal investigation does not indicate affirmative and intentional deceit by the IRS"); United States v. Wadena, 82 AFTR2d 98-6049 (8th Cir. 1998) (although revenue agent knew that there was criminal investigation, he did not have a firm indication of fraud when he began his examination).

dence to constitute "firm indications of fraud."[274] In *United States v. Peters,* an inexperienced agent conducted the examination after CI received an information item.[275] Although the agent did not have a firm indication of fraud, the agent made a fraud referral; but because of errors in the referral form and the agent's failure to give the taxpayer an opportunity to explain discrepancies the revenue agent had noted, the revenue agent's group manager rejected the fraud referral. As a result, other revenue agents were assigned, and they requested extension of statute of limitations on assessment and continued to obtain incriminating evidence. The circuit court reluctantly refused to suppress the evidence obtained by the more experienced agents, which was vital in the conviction. In *United States v. McKee,* the Sixth Circuit concluded that the fraud referral part of the Manual is intended to protect taxpayers' constitutional rights, and that "the Manual's provisions are, at the very least, relevant in determining whether a taxpayer's constitutional rights have been offended [by the violation of such a Manual provision]."[276] In the appeal of their criminal convictions, the shareholder taxpayers contended that the revenue agent had violated the Manual when a bookkeeper and another source supplied information to a revenue agent about the taxpayers' charges of personal expenses to their business, and as a result of the revenue agent's interviews and document requests "almost all of the government's evidence against the [taxpayers] was practically handed to CID on a silver platter." The Sixth Circuit held that, although it reached the conclusion "reluctantly," the revenue agent could not be said to have abused her discretion in continuing her investigation and seeking explanations for discrepancies after she had targeted specific items that had been left out of the shareholder loan account.

This result can be justified on the ground that the agent has deceived the taxpayer as to the nature and purpose of the examination and interviews, and the government should be denied the fruits of this deception.[277] Courts have also refused to suppress taxpayer statements made to revenue agents by finding that the agents had not exceeded the bounds of their instructions.[278] Less convincingly, instructions to agents have been said to be for purposes of internal administration, not for the benefit of taxpayers, and thus to give them no legal

---

[274] IRM 25.1.2.3 Ivestigative Techniques (Jan. 1, 2003).

[275] For further discussion of the Fourth Amendment issues and the "consent" issue presented when a revenue agent obtains information during an audit and the information is later used in a criminal prosecution, see ¶ 13.09[4].

[276] United States v. McKee, 84 AFTR2d 99-6229 (6th Cir. 1999).

[277] See, e.g., United States v. Tweel, 550 F2d 297 (5th Cir. 1977) (affirmative acts of deception).

[278] United States v. Lockyer, 448 F2d 417 (10th Cir. 1971). See United States v. Matis, 80-1 USTC ¶ 9111 (SDNY 1979) (agent said unexplained bank deposits would lead to assessment of a "lot of additional tax").

rights.[279] Where the agent intended to deceive the taxpayer, evidence obtained by the agent should be suppressed.[280] The Supreme Court's decision in *United States v. Caceres* lends some support to decisions refusing to suppress evidence obtained after an agent's failure to follow Service rules.[281] Agents in *Caceres* were found to have made a good faith effort to comply with Service rules. Suppression would still seem proper when an agent has deceived the taxpayer and otherwise indicated no effort to comply with directions.

What indicates that a revenue agent or examiner suspects fraud? No bright line has been identified. However, there are warning signals of fraud, such as cases where the agent spends an inordinate length of time with the examination, asks for originals of the taxpayer's records, contacts third persons, asks for amounts of currency the taxpayer had at the beginning of the tax year, or asks the taxpayer and the return preparer for their explanations of the discrepancy. As the foregoing description of Service procedures shows, when the agent or examiner does not contact the taxpayer for a long period without closing the examination with a no-change or proposed adjustments, there is a distinct possibility that a referral to the CID has been made.

[c] Preparation of Fraud Referrals

A Referral Report for Potential Criminal Fraud Cases, Form 2797, is used when an examiner discovers indications of fraud.[282] In general, the agent identifies the fraudulent transaction and makes a narrative outline of the facts to show that (1) there has been a substantial understatement of income and (2) the taxpayer cannot explain the understatement, or the explanation is not plausible. For example, Form 2797 requires the examining agent to document sufficient facts to demonstrate "in a clear and convincing manner that there exists an omission of income or other acts of evasion and that it was a deliberate act on the part of the taxpayer to evade or defraud."[283]

Form 2797 "is a summary of the examiner's evaluation of the indications of fraud . . . [and] provides basic information related to the case, i.e., taxpayer background, amount of additional income, tax due to fraud, etc."[284] This form asks the agent to describe the type of tax evasion and to estimate the tentative additional taxable income due to fraud. It also requires the examiner (1) to de-

---

[279] United States v. Lockyer, 448 F2d 417 (10th Cir. 1971); United States v. Matis, 80-1 USTC ¶ 9111 (SDNY 1979).

[280] In United States v. Matis, 80-1 USTC ¶ 9111 (SDNY 1979), for example, the agent obtained agreement to a civil closing of the case, but his group supervisor refused to approve a civil resolution of the case, and it was referred to CID.

[281] United States v. Caceres, 440 US 741 (1979), discussed at ¶ 1.06[3].

[282] IRM 25.1.3.2, Preparation of Form 2797 (Jan. 1, 2003).

[283] IRM 25.1.3.2, Preparation of Form 2797 (Jan. 1, 2003).

[284] IRM 25.1.3.2, Preparation of Form 2797 (Jan. 1, 2003).

tail all adjustments; (2) to list additional deductions, expenses, or claims; and (3) to list any specific statement made by the taxpayer regarding the amount of cash on hand. The examiner must also describe specific statements or actions taken by the taxpayer that indicate intent to defraud or evade, as well as the taxpayer's and preparer's explanation or defense given in response to the examiner's request for an explanation of the discrepancies that are the basis of the referral.

Referrals from the Examination Division contain the following information:

- A description of the alleged violation (e.g., evasion, failure to file)
- The taxpayer's age, health, marital status, education, and number of exemptions
- The taxpayer's sources of income
- The types of records available and the taxpayer's accounting method
- The estimated unreported income
- The tax due.

Statements made by the taxpayer to the referring agent and a description of the alleged evasion scheme must also be included. In the past, the referring agent omitted information that directly affected the decision to prosecute. For example, a referral can fail to supply information that makes the case unsuitable for prosecution, such as the taxpayer's poor health and limited educational background. In other cases, the referral can contain factually incorrect information, or the unreported income or tax due may be small or involve a single year. Consequently, information supplied on behalf of the taxpayer, even after a special agent has begun an investigation, can establish a defect in the referral that results in the termination of the investigation.

[d] Fraud Coordinator

Procedures in fraud cases were modified in 1996. When the examiner has discovered "the first indications" of fraud, the examiner and the examiner's group manager confer with the "Fraud Coordinator" about the fraud potential of the information obtained.[285] The Fraud Coordinator also participates in the decision of whether the taxpayer knowingly and without reasonable cause failed to file a required return.[286] Once the examiner has discovered "firm indications of fraud," the examiner is supposed to suspend the examination immediately without disclosing to the taxpayer or the representative the reason for the action, and to discuss with the Fraud Coordinator whether or not the facts warrant a criminal fraud referral. Since examiners must know at what point to suspend an investigation, they should seek the advice of the Fraud Coordina-

---

[285] See IRM 25.1.2.1, Overview (Jan. 1, 2003).
[286] IRM 25.1, Fraud Handbook (Jan. 1, 2003).

tor. (If they stop too soon, they may not have obtained all the information CI needs to make a decision, such as information that might account for the understatement, or information that might help to reveal the taxpayer's intent.)

The referring agent's report is forwarded through channels to the Chief (Examination) for the appropriate type of taxpayer local office, who may add comments and transmit the report to the liaison in the office of the Special Agent in Charge. A Collection employee who discovers any indications of fraud utilizes Form 3212 and goes through the same channels as an examiner. A TE/GE specialist who discovers fraud uses Form 2797, which is forwarded to the Special Agent in Charge through the Chief (TE/GE).[287] If the referral is accepted, the case is numbered and assigned to a special agent as the subject of investigation.[288]

[e] Representing a Taxpayer in a Case With Fraud Potential

Representation of a taxpayer in an examination with fraud potential poses extremely difficult issues of judgment.[289] It can be said with some assurance that the potential referral takes the case out of the classification of a civil examination. Although a civil adjustment may result from the examination, so may a criminal investigation. In general, the adverse consequences of a criminal investigation and prosecution are so great that the examination must be handled as though a criminal investigation will be conducted, even if no investigation or prosecution materializes.

Since the Service considers a criminal prosecution to have priority over civil adjustments, so must the practitioner. For this reason, the practice suggestions discussed in Chapter 12 are relevant here and, at a minimum, tax professionals should consider the following:

1. Recognize the difference between the ordinary audit and a fraud investigation. In a fraud investigation, to the extent that it is lawful to do so, information is not produced in an effort to reduce the scope of the investigation. The objective in a civil audit is to present as much evidence as possible to convince the agent or conferee that an adjustment is not appropriate.

2. Inquire of agents what specific questions they have and determine whether a satisfactory explanation to these specific questions can be given.

---

[287] IRM 25.1.3.3, Referral Evaluation (Jan. 1, 2003). See IRM 25.1.3.4, Accepted Criminal Referrals (Jan. 1, 2003).

[288] IRM 25.1.3.4, Accepted Criminal Referrals (Jan. 1, 2003).

[289] In United States v. Matis, 80-1 USTC ¶ 9111 (SDNY 1979), the referral to CI was made after the case had been settled with the revenue agent because the group supervisor would not approve closing the case.

3. Keep a record of conversations with the revenue agent. Under Service procedure, the agent must also keep such a record.[290]
4. Make a full and complete investigation not only of the taxpayer's story but of the evidence available to corroborate or refute the story. Do this before responding to the revenue agent.
5. Silence the taxpayer. No contact between the taxpayer and the agent should be permitted.
6. Do not attempt to bluff or explain an item or transaction. Anything the representative says can be used against the taxpayer. There are no informal conversations with agents. If the explanation is false, it is evidence of fraud.
7. If an explanation is true, the explanation should be provided in the briefest form with supporting evidence and preferably without any direct meeting between the agent and the taxpayer.
8. If there is no explanation, merely say that there is no substantiation or explanation.
9. Cooperation with revenue agents will not carry the day. If there is evidence of criminal conduct and it is sufficient to obtain a conviction, taxpayers will be prosecuted whether or not they have cooperated with the agent. If there is insufficient evidence to prove a crime, taxpayers will not be prosecuted whether or not they have cooperated.
10. If an explanation can be supplied and proved, this form of cooperation can forestall a full-scale investigation.
11. Cooperation can be selective—specific answers to specific questions.

In dealing with the revenue agent, the objective is to (1) limit the scope of inquiry; (2) limit the information provided; and (3) avoid tying the taxpayer to an explanation that cannot be supported. If the case can be closed with a civil adjustment, so much the better for the taxpayer. If there is to be a criminal investigation, the taxpayer is better off if the taxpayer's position is not undermined by an unsuccessful attempt to resolve the case with the revenue agent.

[5] Technical Advice

During the examination of a return, an issue may arise on which the law is unclear and the agent's position is questionable. One way to resolve such a dispute is for the taxpayer to ask the agent to request technical advice on the issue from the National Office. Technical advice is advice or guidance given by the National Office as to the internal revenue laws, related statutes, and regulations with respect to a specific set of facts on the request of a district of-

---

[290] See IRM 25.1.2.3, Investigative Technique (Jan. 1, 2003).

fice in connection with a taxpayer's return or claim for refund or credit.[291] A taxpayer may initiate a request for technical advice where there is inconsistency or a lack of uniformity in the disposition of an issue or where the issue is novel or so complex as to warrant National Office consideration.[292]

A request for technical advice is not without its risks. Technical advice is binding on the district. If the technical advice favors the taxpayer, the agent must follow the advice. However, if it is adverse to the taxpayer, the advice is also binding on the agent and eliminates any possibility of resolving the matter in the taxpayer's favor. Consequently, a request for technical advice must be carefully considered.

Technical advice procedures can be advantageous to the taxpayer; they permit the taxpayer to submit the taxpayer's version of the facts and legal argument, and they provide the taxpayer with the opportunity for a conference in the National Office and the right to receive a copy of the technical advice.

[6] Field Service Advice

Agents may request technical assistance from Field Service personnel in the Chief Counsel's office. Technical assistance or Field Service advice is legal advice provided by lawyers in the office of the Assistant Chief Counsel (Domestic) principally to revenue agents assigned to Examination activities, an Area Counsel (and lawyers in the Area Counsel's office), or Appeals.[293] Technical assistance or Field Service advice may be requested in an examination (i.e., on an issue that agents have not raised with the taxpayer or developed). The Examination Division through the District Counsel (or sometimes directly) requests the Field Service function in the Chief Counsel's office for legal advice on the appropriateness of raising the issue and the factual development necessary to sustain the Service's position. The taxpayer is not notified of the request, is not given the opportunity to review the agent's factual submission and to submit the taxpayer's own version, has no conference right, and does not receive a copy of the response. As a result, the procedures have been criticized for denying taxpayers access to a process that can affect the outcome of the examination.

---

[291] 26 CFR § 601.105(b)(5).

[292] 26 CFR § 601.105(b)(5)(ii)(a). The procedures involved in a request for technical advice are discussed at ¶ 3.04[2][b].

[293] IRC § 6110(j).

¶ 8.09 INDUSTRY AND MARKET SPECIALIZATION PROGRAMS

[1] Industry Specialists

Industry specialization was established to identify accounting and business practices peculiar to certain industries and tax issues within a designated industry, and to provide a procedural system for coordinating the treatment of such issues nationwide.[294] National Industry Coordinators for designated industries, under the direction of the Assistant Commissioner, Examination, provide assistance to Industry Specialists in the field. There are twenty industries in the program, as well as four International issue specialists and two Exempt Organization Industry specialists. Through industry-wide studies and other sources of information, business or economic factors peculiar to the designated industry and tax issues arising in the industry are analyzed and identified, major issues of particular importance to the industry are selected for coordination (Coordinated Issues), and findings and periodic reports are disseminated to Industry Specialists in the field. Industry Specialists are responsible for identifying cases within the industry for regular monitoring (Identified Industry Cases) and advising case managers on industry issues. In addition to specific industries, the Industry Specialization Program also has a team for partnership audits to provide expertise to field examiners on issues raised by the so-called anti-abuse regulations.[295]

When a coordinated issue is identified by a case manager, the Industry Specialist will review the proposed adjustment to ensure uniform treatment, and decide whether technical advice will be requested.[296] In part, coordination is achieved by the use of Coordinated Issue Papers, which are position papers on issues within an industry proposed to the National Office by Industry Specialists and prepared by the National Coordinator, with the assistance of the Chief Counsel lawyers and comment from industry groups. These issue papers describe the Service's current position on an issue, but they are not an official position, such as a revenue ruling or regulation. Nevertheless, because coordinated issues must be raised by examiners and adjusted in accordance with the

---

[294] IRM 4.4, Industry Specialization Program 1.1, Overview (Apr. 30, 1999). The LMSB operating division uses a process called industry issue resolution to resolve an issue common to many taxpayers within an industry by way of both prefiling agreements and dispute resolution techniques.

[295] Ann. 94-87, 1994-27 IRB 124 (July 5, 1994). A determination under the regulations (Reg. § 1.701-2; now in proposed form) must be coordinated with the Issue Specialist and the National Office.

[296] IRM 4.4, Industry Specialization Program 1.2.5, Industry Specialist (Apr. 30, 1999); IRM 4.4, Industry Specialization Program 3.1, Industry Specialist's Duties (Apr. 30, 1999).

position paper, the position paper represents a kind of administrative rule adopted without the procedures followed when formal rules are adopted. One of the results of this informal approach is that position papers are not published by the Service; they are acquired by taxpayers during examinations or obtained by Freedom of Information Act request. This is not a satisfactory procedure when the course of an examination on an issue is controlled by the position adopted in the paper.[297]

[2] Market Segment Specialization Program

The Market Segment Specialization Program is intended to deal with day-to-day issues that affect businesses of all sizes, and to coordinate the activities of Service district functions such as examination and collection.[298] In what appears to be a program parallel to the Industry Specialization Program, the Examination Division has adopted a Market Segment Specialization Program to improve the quality of audits by issuing audit materials for some eighty industries, including those involving attorneys, trucking, mortuaries, cemeteries, taxi drivers, air charters, auto dealerships, commercial fishing, construction, health care, laundromats, and reforestation.[299] The Industry Specialization Program continues to identify mainly technical issues of large businesses. Audit materials issued thus far are similar to the audit handbooks for specialized industries providing examiners with descriptions of the business, the types of records kept, common issues with authorities, and issue checklists and work plans.[300]

¶ 8.10 EXAMINATIONS: USE OF SPECIALIZED AGENTS

Revenue agents examining tax returns can call on the services of a wide range of specialists. There are specialists in excise and employment taxes, estate and gift tax, employee plans and exempt organizations, international operations, engineering, appraisal, computer audits, economics, actuary problems, insurance, banking, and brokerage. Not all offices have these specialists; specialists located in key districts are assigned returns or issues to assist other areas served by the key district.

---

[297] In part because of objection to this procedure, the number of Coordinated Issues has been reduced. See Form 8.3.

[298] IRM 4.28.1, Market Specialization Handbook (May 3, 1999).

[299] See Zeidner, "Service Releases Guidelines for Auditing Attorneys, Various Industries," 60 Tax Notes 1298 (Sept. 6, 1993).

[300] See, e.g., Market Segment Specialization Program, Attorneys, Training 3149-103 (Apr. 1993) Training Publications Distribution System 83 183A.

The Service also conducts a number of programs utilizing the services of specialized agents. In its Computer Assisted Audit Program, computer audit specialists use generalized and custom-designed computer programs to analyze and retrieve data during examinations of taxpayers' computerized accounting systems.[301] The CEP uses a team of experienced revenue agents, economists, computer specialists, engineer agents, international and excise tax examiners, and employee plan specialists to conduct examinations of large business enterprises,[302] especially those susceptible to interdistrict coordination, team audit techniques, and case manager participation.[303] In short, specialized agents whose work must be coordinated must be used to audit the complex returns of diversified and geographically separated corporate enterprises. Similarly, the Service uses specialists in its Industry Specialization Program, under which it engages in concurrent examination of several principal taxpayers in an industry.[304] It performs these audits to ensure nationally uniform and consistent treatment of taxpayers in the particular industry.

There is a difference between the ordinary examination and one in which a specialized agent participates. Because of the specialized agent's expertise, findings of the specialized agent are given greater weight than those of a revenue agent in the administrative review of a return. The specialized agent's expertise may also mean that the taxpayer and the representative require the assistance of an expert. At the very least, it is necessary to understand how and why a specialized agent is assigned to a return and to be aware of any precautions that the assignment indicates.

[1] Engineer Agents

One type of specialist whose services are frequently requested, especially in complex corporation return examinations, is the engineer agent. The issues that may be involved range anywhere from depletion, investment credit, depreciation, and amortization, to demolition or abandonment and obsolescence, fair rental or market value, repairs and maintenance, research and development, ex-

---

[301] IRM 4.3.13, Computer Assisted Audit Program (CAAP) Handbook (May 3, 1999). The Service has ruled that machine-sensible data media used in processing transactions are records within the meaning of Section 6001 and must be retained for examinations. Rev. Rul. 71-20, 1971-1 CB 392. See also United States v. Davey, 543 F2d 996 (2d Cir. 1976) (summons enforcement action to obtain originals of computerized records). Failure to retain these machine-sensible records can lead to imposition of the negligence penalty and possibly criminal prosecution under Section 7203 for failing to keep records. Rev. Rul. 81-205, 1981-2 CB 225.

[302] IRM 4.3.11, Coordinated Examination Program (CEP) Case Manager's Handbook.

[303] IRM 4.3.11, Coordinated Examination Program (CEP) Case Manager's Handbook Definitions. See Exhibit 42(11)0-2, MT 4200-567.

[304] IRM 4.4, Industry Specialization Program (Apr. 30, 1999).

ploration and development, intangible drilling costs, allocation of costs or sale, and similar issues. The importance of the engineer's recommendation is that it is binding on the Service "unless there are clear and compelling reasons for not doing so."[305] A revenue agent must refer certain returns for engineering assistance. Returns requiring referral include the following:

- All corporate returns with assets of $10 million and over that have been selected for examination
- Partnership and joint venture returns with annual gross receipts or deductions of $1 million or more
- Estate and gift tax returns and other returns with fair market valuation issues of $500,000 and more
- Any noncash contributions over $200,000, except publicly traded stocks, bonds, or securities
- Casualty and theft losses in excess of $200,000.[306]

It seems appropriate to take certain steps in cases involving engineering issues. First, valuation issues should be anticipated and prepared for in advance of the examination. Contemporaneous appraisals and valuation data to support allocation of purchase price and valuations of such intangibles as goodwill, franchise patents, and the like will have more credibility and evidentiary weight than after-the-fact appraisals by a Service engineer. At the time of the examination, the following procedures should be considered:

1. Persons who will deal with the engineer agent should have some familiarity with the methods and approaches used in resolving the technical issue.
2. The taxpayer's appraiser or other technical adviser should be qualified by education and experience to be able to testify persuasively in court if necessary.
3. The appraiser's qualifications should enable him to identify and support essential elements of the valuation. If an appraiser is not used, similar substantiating evidence should be gathered and identified.
4. The appraiser or other professional should be equipped to identify omissions or errors in the engineer's and taxpayer's position to remedy, if possible, defects in the taxpayer's case.
5. Before contact with the engineer, an overall position and strategy should be developed.

---

[305] IRM 4.3.16, Engineering Program Handbook (Sept. 8, 1999).

[306] IRM 4.3.1.5, Mandatory Referrals (Sept. 8, 1999). Engineering Program groups are organized into four regions with several key districts in each of the regions. For example, the Midstates Region has groups in Houston; the Northeast Region, in Manhattan; the Southeast Region, in the Delaware-Maryland area office; and the Western Region, in Los Angeles. Engineering groups are located in other area offices as well. See IRM 4.3.1.3, Organization (Sept. 8, 1999).

6. During the course of dealings with the engineer agent, a brief chronological record of the engineer's activities, including conversations, should be kept. The engineer is required to keep this kind of record. The history sheet assists in charting the engineer's direction and recommendation and serves as a check of inaccuracies in the engineer's report and testimony in the event of trial.

7. The representative should be familiar with common errors in valuation and the methods described in the Service's own publications. The IRS Appellate Conferee Training Program entitled "Valuation" is a good description of the valuation methods used by the Service. The Audit Technique Handbook for Estate Tax Examiners (IRM 4350) also has descriptions of various valuation methods used in ascertaining the value of different types of property.

[2] International Examiners

International examiners are revenue agents specially trained to handle international tax issues. Under the Service's International Enforcement Program, these specialized agents are assigned to key districts to participate in district examinations of returns presenting international issues.[307] Issues referred to these agents involve controlled foreign corporations, controlled foreign personal holding companies, Sections 367 and 482, complex foreign tax credit issues, domestic international sales corporations, international boycotts, and Western Hemisphere trade corporations.[308] International examiners may also participate in cases involving complex substantial domestic Section 482 issues.

When a return presents an international issue, a local office revenue agent prepares a referral for participation by an international tax examiner. The referral is reviewed by a local office Program Manager in each local office and ultimately by the local office Program Manager in the key district. If the referral is accepted, the case is assigned to an international examiner in the key district. The international examiner works jointly with the revenue agent, but the examiner, not the revenue agent, has responsibility for the "final development of the international aspects of the case."[309] Therefore, the revenue agent may

---

[307] IRM 4.3.1.2, International Audit Guidelines Handbook. The key districts for the international program are Manhattan, Boston, Hartford, Newark, Philadelphia, Pittsburgh, Richmond, Ft. Lauderdale, Atlanta, Greensboro, New Orleans, Chicago, St. Louis, St. Paul, Cincinnati, Detroit, Cleveland, Oklahoma City, Houston, Dallas, Los Angeles, San Francisco, and Laguna Niguel. IRM 4.3.1.3, Organization (Feb. 26, 1999).

[308] IRM 4.3.1.2, Scope of International Enforcement Program (Feb. 26, 1999). Returns may be surveyed before or after assignment for referral of international issues. IRM 4.3.1.8, Survey of Returns (Feb. 26, 1999). Referral criteria have been established. IRM 4.3.2.2, Referral Criteria (Feb. 26, 1999).

[309] IRM 4.3.5.1, Examination and Processing Procedures (Feb. 26, 1999).

gather information with or without the international examiner, but the international examiner makes the recommendation regarding international adjustments. To obtain information, the international examiner may use a "format document request" calling for books, records, and documents outside the United States, and a taxpayer who fails to "substantially comply" will be precluded from relying on requested information in a later court case.[310]

Activities of international examiners performed under the International Enforcement Program should be distinguished from examinations by agents in the Office of the Assistant Commissioner (International). In general, the Assistant Commissioner (International) is responsible for administration of the tax laws outside the United States, and its agents examine returns of nonresident U.S. citizens, nonresident aliens, and foreign corporations deriving income from the United States.[311] On the other hand, international examiners in key district offices generally examine the returns of resident aliens (including those departing the United States), citizens residing in the United States, and U.S. corporations having transactions involving foreign affiliates or foreign tax.

[3] Tax-Exempt and Government Entity Agents

The Tax Exempt and Government Division has an Examination Branch, composed of employee plans and exempt organizations agent groups.[312] Agents or auditors assigned to these groups examine employee plans, related trusts, and exempt organizations, either on site or in the office by interview or correspondence. The stated objective of this "Employee Plans Enforcement Program" (EP/EO) is to monitor the operations of plans to ensure their compliance with the qualification provisions of the Code,[313] EP/EO carries on independent examinations, but it accepts referral of employee plan issues.[314] Returns with issues involving plans of self-employed individuals or contributions to individual retirement accounts are not referred. Moreover, issues involving the timeliness of contributions are within the jurisdiction of the Examination Division, but EP examiners do provide assistance on such issues as the tax treatment of distributions. If EP/EO accepts a referral, its specialists have "primary responsibility" for developing the EP/EO issues in a case, but they are supposed to coordinate their contacts with the taxpayer with the examiner.

---

[310] IRC § 982. For a discussion of the procedures followed where the Service seeks foreign-based records, see the discussion in Chapter 13.

[311] IRM 4.1.9, International Features (May 19, 1999).

[312] See IRM 4.72, Employee Plans Examination Guidelines (Mar. 1, 2002). There are seven key districts that issue determination letters as well as perform examinations. See ¶ 3.04[3].

[313] IRM 4.72, Employee Plans Examination Guidelines (Mar. 1, 2002).

[314] IRM 4.72, Employee Plans Examination Guidelines (Mar. 1, 2002).

¶ 8.11 CONDUCT OF THE EXAMINATION: THE TAXPAYER'S PERSPECTIVE

[1] Taxpayer Objectives in the Examination

From the taxpayer's point of view, the conduct of a field examination depends on many factors, including the complexity of the return, the availability of substantiating information, and the potential for tax change, as well as the personality of the agent and the experience of the representative. The Service's objective is a "quality" audit, a goal its audit techniques are designed to achieve. The representative's objectives in an examination are (1) to limit the scope of the examination; (2) to keep a record of what the agent has seen (i.e., what the agent knows and does not know); and (3) to move the agent through the examination as quickly as possible.[315]

To accomplish these objectives, the representative should take the following steps:

1. *Assemble files and records of the client in good order.* This task serves several purposes. It helps reduce the time of the examination both for the taxpayer and for the agent. An expeditious examination is convenient for the agent and beneficial for the taxpayer. It conveys to the agent an impression of efficiency and cooperation that can prove to be an intangible benefit to the taxpayer during the course of the examination. Review of the records also gives some indication of what questions the agent is likely to raise.

2. *Remove and separate opinion letters of counsel from files.* In an opinion letter, the taxpayer's tax adviser may have raised possible problems with a transaction. An opinion letter represents only an opinion, not the factual data and underlying records on which taxability rests. Furthermore, the letter may constitute a communication between the attorney and the client that is not subject to disclosure under the attorney-client privilege. The purpose of removing the opinion letter is not to keep its existence secret but to segregate a document as to which the taxpayer may have a privilege or other basis for nondisclosure.[316]

3. *Advise the client and others who may deal with the agent to give the agent what is requested without any explanation unless one is requested.* There is no requirement to volunteer information. Even if the agent asks for an explanation, whether a response should be made and by whom depends on the nature of the request.

4. *Have a preliminary meeting with the agent to present the power of attorney form*[317] *when it is required.* At this meeting, establish the ground rules

---

[315] IRM 4.72, Employee Plans Examination Guidelines (Mar. 1, 2002).

[316] For a discussion of the objections to disclosure, see Chapter 13.

[317] See ¶ 1.08 for a description of the Service's rules of practice.

for the examination. This request is not presumptuous; in a large case examination, the case manager–revenue agent is required to ask for a preexamination conference to do precisely the same thing.[318] It is important, at any rate, for agents to know that they should communicate with the representative rather than with the client.[319] Communication with the representative is necessary to avoid a taxpayer's change in explanation or position.

5. *Ask the agent to make written requests for records.* Records can be produced pursuant to the request with a minimum of delay to the agent and disruption of the client's business. Written requests also facilitate making a record of what the agent has examined.

6. *Ask the agent to hold material questions for the practitioner, preferably at the end of the examination.* This procedure avoids giving the agent misinformation and reduces the possibility of disputes with the agent during the course of the examination. The danger in issue-by-issue meetings with the agent is that a confrontation can cause the agent to (a) dig deeper on a disputed issue to justify their position; (b) look harder to find other issues to "get even"; and (c) deny the representative time to give a considered response. However, if the agent's questions can be answered quickly, the practitioner should do so during the examination.

7. *In small or less complicated examinations, be available to answer questions as they arise.*

8. *In large and more complex examinations, arrange with the client to have some procedure for keeping posted on the progress of the examination.* For example, some current account of the records the agent has requested and is examining should be kept. In this way, the practitioner may have an idea about the direction of the audit and the basis for a proposed adjustment.

9. *Ask the agent to provide a written list of the proposed adjustments.* This will reduce the possibility that the agent will raise additional adjustments. The procedure also gives the practitioner the opportunity to make the kind of issue analysis discussed in the following text before the final meeting with the agent.

Adversaries can represent their respective interests without antagonism or acrimony.[320] Representatives should try to avoid an adversarial climate because

---

[318] IRM 4.3.11, Case Managers Handbook 7.1, Conferences—Overview (May 20, 1999).

[319] This is not to say that the agent will not attempt to bypass the representative. See, e.g., Wegge v. Egger, 84-2 USTC ¶ 9753 (CD Cal. 1984). Revenue agents may also try to interview the taxpayer as an audit technique.

[320] As a result, the Service, in the usual case, will not be estopped from taking a position contrary to settlement with the agent. See the discussion of estoppel at ¶¶ 1.06[4] and 3.04[9]. Taxpayers are charged with knowing the limited authority of revenue agents. See, e.g., Meyers v. Comm'r, TC Memo. 1994-598, 68 TCM 1354 (1994), aff'd in an unpublished opinion, 77 AFTR2d 96-1526 (7th Cir. 1996) (taxpayers claimed that they had

it can cause extensive delay, unnecessary challenges, and excessive costs to the client. To this end, the representative should attempt to establish an atmosphere of credibility and trust with the agent. An agent should be treated with courtesy and consideration. No representation should be made without support, and promises made (e.g., production of records) should not be broken. However, as desirable as a "proper" atmosphere is, in some cases it will not be possible, no matter what the representative's wishes. Failure to provide adequate records to support items on the return, for example, may unavoidably create a credibility gap and either prolong the examination or force the agent to resolve questionable items in the Service's favor, leaning heavily against the taxpayer. Control over all circumstances affecting the result of an examination may not be possible, but representatives will have performed their obligations to clients if they are prepared and deal with the agent in a professional manner.

[2] Preparing for the Final Meeting With the Agent

Effective negotiation requires thorough preparation. Although the amounts involved may put practical limitations on the extent of preparation, the necessity for some preparation nevertheless remains. Before attempting to dispose of a case with an agent, the representative must know the following:

1. *The issues that will be the subject of the discussions.* It is not too much to ask that discussions with the agent be deferred until the agent has determined the proposed adjustments. It can be expected that some issues related to proposed adjustments may arise during the course of discussions, but the representative cannot prepare in a way calculated to be in the client's best interest unless he knows what issues will be discussed.

2. *The facts behind the issues.* This includes those favorable to the Service and those favorable to the taxpayer, including whether evidence to establish those facts is available and how the evidence can be presented. Marshaling the facts at the agent level has two advantages. First, the facts are gathered at a time when they are more likely to be readily available and complete. Second, the effort provides the basis for (a) evaluating the taxpayer's position; (b) determining what the issue is worth (i.e., what an appropriate settlement will cost); and (c) probing for weaknesses in the agent's position. If there is a disagreement on an issue, the agent may dig further for facts. Even if the agent does not obtain additional factual data, someone else in the administrative appeal or litigation process may seek further discovery. If the agent does not have the correct information or does not draw the correct inference from the

---

agreed with a revenue agent regarding the tax treatment of a pension and profit-sharing plan).

facts, the representative's fact investigation will reveal whether the taxpayer can prove the favorable facts.

3. *An updated examination of the law on a particular issue.* If the law has changed in the Service's favor, the representative must know it. Research of Service pronouncements in revenue rulings, acquiescences, and the like will be especially important in resolving an issue or knowing whether the agent has any discretion to dispose of the issue.[321]

4. *A list of points for and against the taxpayer's position.* A fact and law investigation should be used to prepare this list. At the final meeting, the practitioner can mention a factor believed entitled to little weight just to show it was taken into account. It is also useful to prepare short legal memoranda on such issues as travel and entertainment expenses, reasonable compensation, and accumulated earnings. Memoranda not only support the taxpayer's position but enable the revenue agent to justify and more easily accept the taxpayer's position. This preparation should also point to potential issues that may be raised if an agreement is not reached. On appeal, the practitioner may succeed on an issue raised by the agent only to be faced with a more soundly based adjustment raised by an Appeals officer.

5. *Tax computations that show the additional tax that will be payable if an adjustment is agreed to or the effect of a concession on subsequent years' returns.* A concession in the examination year may be offset in a later year or years. In thinking about tax cost, the practitioner must give some consideration to issues that may be used to offset one another. For example, an investment credit may be available if acquisition costs are to be capitalized under the agent's proposed adjustment. Also, there may be an alternative disposition of issues. A proposed disallowance of a deduction may be salvaged, for example, by allowing the taxpayer the amount as a nonbusiness bad debt instead of a business bad debt.

6. *An evaluation of the chances of success at an Appeals Office conference or in court, taking into account the costs of litigation.* This evaluation requires a secure knowledge of the facts and the law pertaining to an issue, the dollar amount involved in the issue, some assessment of the chances of success translated into a percentage, and the estimated costs of litigating the issue. For example, if the proposed deficiency is $50,000, and the taxpayer's chances of success in court are 50 percent and the estimated costs of litigation are $7,500, disposition of the issue by payment of more than $32,500 probably cannot be considered a good result for the taxpayer. A number of similar calculations assuming different success probabilities should be made to get a range of potential settlements.

7. *The potentially adverse effect of discussions with the revenue agent or negotiations with the Appeals officer.* Once made, a concession or proposal is

---

[321] For a discussion of the legal effect of rulings and other Service pronouncements, see ¶¶ 3.03[2] and 3.04.

difficult to recall. The agent may search for further data to support a position on which no agreement is reached. If the issue is not one that the agent can settle, it may be better to put the issue firmly outside discussions and take it up with the Appeals Office.

[3] Settlement With the Agent

Revenue agents have no formal authority to settle cases, but as a practical matter, settlements on issues do occur during the examination. It is to a taxpayer's advantage to dispose of issues or adjustments with the revenue agent after the examination. At the agent level, there is no Service position to justify. There is no administrative record as such, and consequently no need to support any change from the position the agent has taken. However, once the agent takes a position, there is a certain amount of administrative inertia that makes abandonment of the agent's position more difficult. In the administrative review of a case, the taxpayer is perceived by Service officials as having the burden of proving that the agent is wrong and the taxpayer is right in the position taken on the return. Also, the higher up in the appeal process the taxpayer goes, the greater the likelihood that even if the agent is technically in error, a more technically sophisticated or justifiable ground for the agent's position may be discovered and that another adjustment may be found.

If settlement with the agent is desirable, it is by no means assured unless, of course, the taxpayer wishes to concede to all adjustments proposed. An agent has limited authority to dispose of a proposed adjustment developed from an examination of a tax return. The agent is bound by the National Office's position on an issue and cannot settle a prime issue on which the National Office wishes a court decision. The agent must follow not only a regulation or ruling on point but a nonacquiescence to a Tax Court decision adverse to the Service, as well as an internal audit directive. The agent also cannot take into account the hazards of litigation that an Appeals officer may consider in deciding to settle an issue. An agent is more likely to be able to dispose of an issue if it is factual (e.g., valuation or the rate of depreciation) rather than an all-or-nothing legal question. Therefore, no disposition of proposed adjustments should be discussed until an estimate has been made of the stage (e.g., district, Appeals Office, or court) at which the issue can be resolved. If the representative believes the issue is more susceptible to settlement in the Appeals Office, he may be better advised to save the full extent and force of his argument for the Appeals Office conference rather than to give the agent the opportunity to find answering evidence. If the representative feels the best chance is in court, he should consider bypassing administrative review altogether.

Although an agent's settlement authority is limited, in practice, there can still be an agreement with the agent in some circumstances. Where the agent is foreclosed by Service policy from settling a particular issue, usually an issue of law, there may be other issues on which the agent is not so constrained that may be settled, such as a capital versus expense issue. Some agents are willing to settle issues only if they can resolve the entire case as agreed. In this situation, agents refuse to concede or settle issues where there are issues the taxpayer feels will be handled more successfully in an administrative appeal or in court. These agents take an all-or-nothing approach and will let the whole case go to Appeals. This all-or-nothing approach is a questionable tactic, but the only explicit restriction on the agent is the prohibition on setting up an issue for nuisance value or for trading purposes by an Appeals officer at a later time.

[4] Negotiation Process

Negotiation in tax cases involves talking through an issue to reach a mutually acceptable result that reflects the relative strengths and weaknesses of the parties' positions on the facts and the law.[322] A mutually acceptable result is not reached at once, and certainly not by haggling, blind horse-trading, or intimidation. In an examination (and at an Appeals Office hearing), negotiation passes through four stages:

1. *Talking through the issue.* Each side states the facts and the law believed to support its position. In this stage, preparation usually translates into an unspoken recognition of the merits of the other side's position.

2. *Enlarging the areas of agreement and narrowing matters of disagreement.* From the representative's viewpoint, it is important to get the agent to accept the taxpayer's version of the facts, if not to achieve a settlement, to at least ensure that these are the facts included in the agent's report in the event the case goes unagreed on the issue. If a settlement is not reached but the taxpayer's version of the facts is accepted, the taxpayer no longer has the burden of showing what the facts are, and negotiations start from grounds the taxpayer can accept.

3. *Making a specific proposal about how to dispose of the issue.* The representative must consider an offer before the meeting and discuss what he intends to do with the client. Usually the agent does not make the first offer and waits for the representative's proposal. This sequence is not disadvanta-

---

[322] The most helpful discussion of negotiation in tax cases from the Service's point of view was found in the portion of IRM 4350, Audit Technique Handbook for Estate Tax Examiners §§ 21(10) et seq., MT 4350-29 (Mar. 20, 1980). This handbook was revised, and the discussion abbreviated, but some excellent common sense suggestions to examiners remain. See IRM 4350 § 550, MT 4350-31 (Dec. 16, 1987) (How to Handle the First Interview).

geous to the representative or the taxpayer if a proposal has been considered, because negotiations are then based on the taxpayer's offer.

4. *Agreeing or disagreeing on a result.* From the taxpayer's viewpoint, a reasonable result requires calculation of how much the settlement costs him and the exercise of judgment concerning whether to settle the issue, and if so, when.

It is worth mentioning a number of other observations about the negotiation process in a tax examination. Both sides derive advantages from an agreed case. It is to the taxpayer's advantage to dispose of adjustments at the earliest point in the proceedings—that is, with the revenue agent. At the very least, the taxpayer will save professional fees. The agent also wants an agreed case. It takes considerably more time for the agent to write a report in an unagreed case than in an agreed case. To some extent, the agent's ability to get agreed cases affects evaluations of that agent's performance.

Both revenue agents and representatives can use their limited authority in negotiations to gain an advantage. For example, agents may secure a concession on an issue but say that they are unable to concede another issue because, after discussion, the group supervisor will not permit it, or because Service policy prohibits it. A taxpayer's representative can also use limited authority as a negotiation technique. For example, representatives can postpone negotiations until the taxpayer's consent is secured, or they can use the taxpayer as a basis for a refusal to concede an issue. A representative can also counter the agent's use of limited authority by asking to speak to the group supervisor in the event that the agent apparently has no authority to concede or dispose of an issue.

The confidence with which the representative approaches an issue is a direct result of the thoroughness of his preparation on the issue. This is not to say that preparation can cure a totally hopeless position, but many issues are not so clear-cut that preparation will not have some positive effect. This positive effect may mean that the representative rather than the agent controls the negotiations and the result of those negotiations. If the representative is prepared, he may use questions to probe the knowledge of the agent on the factual background of the issue and the law. Where there is a weakness in that knowledge or understanding, the results of the negotiations reflect the representative's training and the weakness of the position of the Service. Questioning agents on the basis for their position also serves to make agents work harder to obtain any concession from the taxpayer and to give the representative a basis upon which to make the judgment that a concession is necessary or appropriate. The representative should also have sufficient information so that the client can be convinced that a concession is desirable.

The representative should not allow a desire to conclude an examination to jeopardize the taxpayer's interests. Only with adequate preparation can representatives determine that there is a point beyond which they need not go in making a concession on an issue. If the taxpayer has a position that warrants either a full concession or a concession the agent feels is appropriate, the representative should let the agent know that no further concession can or will be made. This stance puts the agent on notice that if an agreed case is to be secured, it is the agent who will have to make some concession.

Finally, the representative should be familiar with three more or less mechanical devices that are useful in the negotiation process.

1. *A list of issues serves to focus the negotiations, making it unlikely as a practical matter for the agent to raise other issues.* The Service recognizes that an issue list is a worthwhile negotiating tool and that the order in which issues are listed can be helpful in achieving successful results.[323] If issues on which the taxpayer is prepared to make concessions are put first, the representative will be in a better position to justify a refusal to make concessions on other issues. The Service, it should be noted, tells agents to put strong issues first to show strength and preparation.

2. *Multiple meetings serve a number of purposes.* At the first meeting, neither the agent nor the representative may be willing to express the extent of the adjustments each is willing to accept. Adjournment may be necessary to give the representative an opportunity to gather information on an issue. As a practical matter, it is advantageous to adjourn a meeting when the atmosphere has become strained. After a delay, the parties may be better able to arrive at a settlement.

3. *A concession list memorializes the agreement of the parties and avoids later misunderstanding.* The Service also recognizes this device.[324] It tends to prevent agents from changing their mind and asking for further concessions. It is good practice for the representative to prepare the list and for both parties to initial it.

¶ 8.12 REVENUE AGENT REPORTS

A report is written after each examination, on different report forms depending on whether the case is a regular agreed, unagreed, or excepted agreed case.[325] A regular agreed case is an agreed case in which a copy of the examination report is furnished to the taxpayer before review. This category does not include excepted agreed cases, which are large cases, Joint Committee cases, inade-

---

[323] See IRM 4350, Audit Technique Handbook for Estate Tax Examiners § 550, MT 4350-31 (Dec. 16, 1987) (How to Handle the First Interview).

[324] See IRM 4350, Audit Technique Handbook for Estate Tax Examiners § 550, MT 4350-31 (Dec. 16, 1987) (How to Handle the First Interview).

[325] IRM 4237, Report Writing Guide for Income Tax Examining Officers § 231, MT 4237-24 (Aug. 6, 1992) (Basic Report).

quate records cases, fraud penalty cases, and personal holding company cases where the examination report is not furnished to the taxpayer prior to review. In unagreed and excepted agreed cases, the taxpayer is not furnished a copy of the examination report until after review. The basic form used in preparing a report on an agreed case is a Form 4549 (Income Tax Examination Changes). (See Form 8.5.) This form also includes a waiver of the restrictions on assessment so that when executed, any deficiency in tax may be immediately assessed. Since adjustments are explained at the conclusion of an examination, written explanations are rarely furnished in regular agreed cases. Although the execution of the Form 4549 closes a case, the Service is not prevented from reopening it and making an additional assessment within the period of limitations if it sends a reopening letter pursuant to Section 7605(b).[326]

---

[326] It has been held that a Form 4549 is merely a taxpayer's consent to the assessment of tax, but is not a closing agreement binding on the Service and, in fact, "does not constitute an agreement by the [IRS] to anything, much less a closing agreement." Hudock v. Comm'r, 65 TC 351, 363 (1975); Holland v. Comm'r, 70 TC 1046, 1048–1049 (1978), aff'd, 622 F2d 95 (4th Cir. 1980) (accord). By the same token, the taxpayer should not be prevented from filing a claim for refund within the statutory period and suing on the claim. For a horror story making it painfully clear that there are no informal agreements with revenue agents and no remedy for breach of an informal agreement, see Hearne v. United States, 93-1 USTC ¶ 50,334 (WD Tax. 1993).

FORM 8.5
INCOME TAX EXAMINATION CHANGES

Form 4549 (Rev. 11-93)	Department of the Treasury - Internal Revenue Service		Return Form No 1040
	Income Tax Examination Changes		

Name and Address of Taxpayers	S.S. or E.I. Number	Filing Status
John and Mary Jones 555 East 100th Street New York, NY 10000	123-45-6789	Joint
	Person With Whom Examination Changes Were Discussed	Name and Title Alan Michaels, CPA

		Year: 9812	Year: 9912	Year:
1.	Adjustments to Income			
a	Supplemental Gains and Losses	310,993	843,877	
b	Interest Income - Sch. B	(1562)	(75,940)	
c	Capital Gains and Losses - Sch. D		(935,427)	
d	Interest Expense - Sch. A		281,405	
e	Misc. Deductions		5,250	
f				
g				
2.	Total Adjustments	309,431	119,165	
3.	Adjusted Gross or Taxable Income Shown on Return or as Previously Adjusted	220,475	85,450	
4.	Corrected Adjusted Gross or Taxable Income	529,906	204,615	
5.	Corrected Tax	258,259	98,692	
6. Less Credits	a. Foreign Tax Credit	55	45	
	b. Residential Energy Credit	300	0	
	c.			
7.	Balance (Line 5 less total of lines 6a through 6c)	257,904	98,647	
8. Plus Other Taxes	a.			
	b.			
	c.			
9.	Total Corrected Tax Liability (Line 7 plus total of lines 8a through 8c)	257,904	98,647	
10.	Total Tax Shown on Return or as Previously Adjusted	103,827	36,567	
11.	Adjustments to EIC/Fuels Credits - increase (decrease)			
12.	Deficiency - increase in Tax (Line 9 adjusted by lines 10 and 11)	154,077	65,689	
13.	Overassessment - Decrease in Tax (Line 9 adjusted by lines 10 & 11)			
14.	Adjustments to Prepayment Credits - increase (decrease)			
15.	Balance Due, Excluding Interest and Penalties (Line 12 adjusted by line 14)	154,077	65,689	
16.	Overpayment (Line 13 adjusted by line 14)			

17. Penalties	Code Section
A.	IRC Section 6621(d) penalty on entire deficiency
B.	
C.	
D.	

18. Prepayment on Balance Due   Check #

Examiner's Signature	District Manhattan	Date 3/28/01

Consent to Assessment and Collection - I do not wish to exercise my appeal rights with the Internal Revenue Service or to contest in the United States Tax Court the findings in this report. Therefore, I give my consent to the immediate assessment and collection of any increase in tax and penalties, and accept any decrease in tax and penalties shown above, plus any interest as provided by law. I understand that this report is subject to acceptance by the District Director.

NOTE: If a joint return was filed, both taxpayers must sign.	Signature of Taxpayer	Date	Signature	Date
	Title			Date
By				

Form 4549 (Rev. 11-93)

Form 4549.

The Internal Revenue Service has agreements with State tax agencies under which information about Federal tax, including increases or decreases, is exchanged with the States. If th is change affects the amount of your State income tax, you should file the required State form.

You may be subject to backup withholding if you underreport your interest, dividend, or patronage dividend income and do not pay the required tax. The IRS may order backup withholding at 31 percent after four notices have been issued to you over a 120-day period and the tax has been assessed and remains unpaid.

Form 4549 (Rev. 11-93)

page 744,348P 9/21/94

An explanation of an adjustment may be necessary even in an agreed case. If so, the revenue agent prepares a Form 886-A (Explanation of Items), which is incorporated with the basic report form. The taxpayer or the representative can request the written explanations and the Service will furnish them. An explanation of agreed adjustments can serve a useful purpose for a taxpayer; revenue agents auditing a later return examine the prior report, and although they are not bound by the explanation, they are likely to follow the pattern set by the first agent.

The procedure in an unagreed case is entirely different. In unagreed and excepted agreed cases, a copy of the report is not sent to the taxpayer. When the report has cleared the Quality Review staff, a summary explanation of adjustments is sent to the taxpayer, along with Form 4549-A (Income Tax Audit Changes),[327] which is not the full report prepared by the agent.[328] In addition to the computations and summary explanations, the agent prepares a report transmittal form (Form 4665) in all unagreed cases and as needed in excepted agreed cases. The main purpose of this form is to provide a place to summarize unagreed issues and to present information of a confidential nature—for example, statements and facts involving allegations of fraud; remarks reflecting on the integrity, motives, or ability of the taxpayer; information obtained from informants; and other matters that should not come to the attention of the taxpayer. In addition, the revenue agent prepares an explanation of the items on Form 886-A that describes the various adjustments, along with a statement of facts, law, and argument and the taxpayer's position and the agent's conclusion on the item. The report also includes the revenue agent's audit workpapers, with a form indicating the items that were to be verified at the outset of the examination and the results of the audit. A procedural reminder form is associated with the report. These items (i.e., the transmittal, the full report, and the workpapers) are not produced for the taxpayer. They comprise the case file in the review process. In some cases taxpayers have been able to obtain at least the factual portions of the revenue agent's report under the Freedom of Information Act or by discovery when the case is in court.[329]

---

[327] IRM 4.10.8.5, Report Writing—Partially Agreed Cases (May 4, 1999); IRM 4.10.8.10, Unagreed Case Procedures: Preliminary (30-Day) Letter (May 4, 1999).

[328] Form 4665 (Report Transmittal) is called a T-letter. In Branerton Corp. v. Comm'r, 64 TC 191, 195 (1975), the Tax Court also described the T-letter.

[329] See ¶¶ 2.03[4], 2.03[5].

¶ 8.13 AGREED CASE PROCEDURE

At the conclusion of an office or field examination, the auditor or agent must explain the proposed adjustments to the taxpayer with a view toward obtaining an agreement. If the taxpayer does not agree, the Service follows procedures for unagreed cases and the examining auditor or agent is required to inform the taxpayer of his appeal rights.[330] Whether or not there is an agreement, the examining officer must then prepare a report of his examination. In agreed cases, this report is subject to review by the Quality Review staff in the district. A copy of the report is supposed to be furnished to the taxpayer before submission to the Quality Review staff. The case is not technically closed until the taxpayer receives notice from the district that the case has been accepted by the Quality Review staff. If the taxpayer agrees with the proposed change, the examining agent requests that the taxpayer (1) execute an appropriate agreement form and (2) make an advance payment of the deficiency and accrued interest to eliminate additional interest charges and to save the Service subsequent collection costs.[331] Payment of the deficiency and interest at this point is entirely voluntary, and the agent may merely explain the advantages of making an advance payment.

[1] Agreement Forms

Agreement with the agent in a case involving income, estate, or gift tax is evidenced by execution of a waiver of restrictions on assessment. The forms used are in the Form 870 series, entitled "Waiver of Restriction on Assessment and Collection of Deficiency in Tax and Acceptance of Overassessment."[332] In regular agreed individual and corporate cases, Form 4549 is used. In regular agreed partnership cases, Form 4605, Examination Changes Partnerships, Fiduciaries, Small Business Corporations, and Domestic International Sales Corporations, is used. Where changes in distributions to beneficiaries or to shareholders are involved, the same form is used in fiduciary and small business corporation cases. If the waiver form is executed, the taxpayer must pay the amount of the deficiency before contesting it. The taxpayer will be unable

---

[330] See supra ¶ 8.08.

[331] IRM 4485.2 (June 29, 1992) (Advance Payments Received by Examination Function).

[332] See Form 9.2 at ¶ 9.03[3]. Where a coexecutor signed a Form 890, the other executor was held bound by the act, even if it resulted in the assertion of transferee liability against the nonsigning coexecutor. Ewart v. Comm'r, 814 F2d 321 (6th Cir. 1987). But a waiver may take another form. See United States v. Gilbert, 91-2 USTC ¶ 50,400 (D. Ariz. 1991) (statement made in agreement as part of nolo contendere plea constituted "waiver" of restrictions in assessment).

to contest the deficiency in the Tax Court because the waiver is a consent to the immediate assessment and collection of the deficiency and waiver of the Section 6213 statutory right to a notice of deficiency and the ninety-day period for filing a petition in the Tax Court.[333] The Tax Court is a preassessment, prepayment forum. When a taxpayer executes the waiver of restrictions on assessment, the signed form represents the taxpayer's election not to defer payment of the deficiency and not to contest it in the Tax Court.

A taxpayer who executes a Form 870 does not surrender the right to contest the assessment altogether. Form 870 permits the taxpayer to file a claim for refund and the Service to assert a further deficiency. Consequently, the taxpayer may obtain judicial review in a federal district court or the claims court by way of a refund suit, but the taxpayer must first pay the amount of the assessment, file a claim for refund, and institute the action within the statutory period.[334] If the case is agreed in an office examination, the taxpayer signs a short-form report of the adjustments and computation of the corrected tax liability.[335] The taxpayer is furnished with a copy of the form, and, unless the taxpayer receives notice to the contrary from the district, the case is considered closed thirty days after the signed report is received by the district office. After the taxpayer signs the agreement form and the office auditor prepares a short-form report, the case file is submitted to the group supervisor, who transfers the case to the Quality Review staff, where it is checked for mathematical accuracy. Only a small percentage of office examination cases are actually reviewed by the Quality Review staff.

In a field examination, where the taxpayer agrees with the agent's adjustments, a short-form report of the adjustments to income and computation of the tax liability is submitted to the taxpayer for execution.[336] A copy of this report is furnished to the taxpayer before it is submitted to the Quality Review staff. The case is not considered closed until the taxpayer receives notice from

---

[333] Kalil v. Enochs, 295 F2d 467 (5th Cir. 1961) (taxpayers waived right to petition Tax Court when they executed waiver restrictions on assessments and had no right to require issuance of statutory notice); see also Lampenfield v. IRS, 91-1 USTC ¶ 50,038 (WD Pa. 1991) (taxpayers signed Form 4549).

[334] For a discussion of refund procedures, see Chapter 11. See also the discussion of advance payments at ¶¶ 6.03[1][d] and 11.05[1][b].

[335] The form currently in use for this purpose is Form 1902-E (Report of Individual Income Tax Audit Changes). Other forms sent to the taxpayer reflecting the examiners' adjustments are also not binding when they are not reflected on closing agreement forms, such as a Form 866. See ¶ 9.08[1][b]. Levin v. Comm'r, TC Memo. 1990-226, 59 TCM 526 (1990) (Form 1902-B); Hedrick v. Comm'r, 63 TC 395, 403 n.5 (1974) (Valuation Report); Hagadone v. Comm'r, TC Memo. 1998-352, 76 TCM 592 (1998) (report issued by Problems Resolution Officer was not binding on the Service, because it was not closing agreement and was erroneous).

[336] The Service uses a series of forms for this purpose, but the basic one is Form 4549. See supra ¶ 8.06[8].

the district advising him that the case has been accepted by the Quality Review staff. In large, complex cases, Joint Committee cases, partial agreement cases, and cases involving a fraud penalty, long-form reports are used. In these cases, the taxpayer is asked to sign a Form 870, and, after the agent completes the report, the agent submits the case to the group supervisor for transmission to the Quality Review staff. After approval by the Quality Review staff, the agreed case is sent to the Service staff for administrative action, and a copy of the revenue agent's report is sent to the taxpayer.

[2] Review Process

The Quality Review staff is responsible for reviewing completed examination reports to determine whether there has been a quality audit in the case.[337] Quality Review has shifted its objective from primarily correcting errors in examiners' reports to tracking trends of noncompliance with auditing standards to determine their causes.[338] It is also a mechanism used by the SB/SE Division to measure examination quality.

In general, a statistically valid sample of cases is reviewed because the case is of a type required to be reviewed (mandatory review cases) or because the case was selected on a sample basis from the population of cases completed by examiners.[339] Currently, mandatory review cases are TCMP cases, Joint Committee cases, and Service employee returns.[340]

---

[337] Quality Review processing of income, gift, and estate tax cases after examination is described in IRM Part 4, Examining Process, Chapter 8, Technical Support (Exam).

[338] IRM 4.8.1.4.1, Case Reviews (Sept. 13, 1999). At one time, this section of the Manual stated:

> The reviewer should keep in mind that the role of the Quality Assurance function has been reshaped from a "fix-it" shop to one of quality assessment. In addition, the impact of Reviews Reports on examiners has been modified with the transition of reviews based mostly on statistically valid samples rather than on mandatory reviews, special handling and the former percentage review of field or office cases.

This Manual section goes on to say that "it is the responsibility of the manager to use his or her resources, tools and skills in producing quality examinations by the examiners." Programs have been developed with the objective of applying quality review standards at the revenue group and group manager level, such as the Line Management Quality Assurance System (LMQAS) and the Coordinator Agent/Auditor Program (CATP). See IRS National Advisory Group, "Future of Quality Review July 1989," reprinted in ABA Tax Section, Administrative Practice Comm., Minutes 1990 Midyear Meeting.

[339] IRM 4.8.3, Examination Quality Measurement System (Oct. 21, 2000).

[340] IRM 4.8.2.2.1, Mandatory Review Cases (Sept. 13, 1999). The review of mandatory cases focuses on the quality of the examination as measured by the Auditing Standards. Reviewers apply fifteen Auditing Standards (they previously applied forty-four standards). Review also uses a statistical method to sample mandatory cases, called the EQTRAS. The objective of EQTRAS is to analyze trends in nonconformance with the

In addition to these mandatory cases, an area office has the discretion to designate any type or group of returns for mandatory review when review of the case file is essential.[341] In the past, the types or groups of returns reviewed have included cases involving closing agreements, inadequate records, compromise offers involving doubt as to liability, personal holding companies, cases returned by Appeals, jeopardy and termination assessments, bankruptcy cases, tax protesters, penalty cases involving substantial understatement of liability, return preparer penalties, promoting abusive tax shelters, aiding and abetting tax liability understatement, frivolous returns, valuation overstatements, Special Enforcement Program cases, transferor-transferee returns, fraud cases, suspense cases, Tax Shelter Program cases, international issue cases, windfall profit tax cases, and compliance study cases.

Unagreed cases are also reviewed primarily to determine whether issues have been fully developed in the agent's report. Errors must be corrected either by Quality Review or by the examiner before the case file is forwarded to Appeals.[342] Review of either a mandatory review case or a sample selected case involves (1) the return classification process and (2) the procedural, technical, and managerial aspects of the case.[343] However, if auditing standards have not been complied with, the case is not normally returned to the group for development. Procedural review is essentially a clerical review ensuring that all forms are properly completed and that the case file is complete and properly assembled. The technical review is geared to ensuring that all relevant facts have been developed and that the findings are adequately supported by the law and the facts. This objective is usually accomplished by an independent review of the return to decide which issues should have been investigated and the type of investigation that should have been done. The Quality Review staff official then determines whether the revenue agent's report and workpapers are adequate for this purpose and whether the facts were properly interpreted and the law or the Service's position properly applied.[344]

Auditing Standards to determine their causes. EQTRAS uses a statistically valid sample in a postreview of examined closed cases to accomplish this objective.

[341] IRM 4.8.4, Technical Support (Exam): Mandatory Review (Sept. 13, 1999).

[342] IRM 4.8.3.9, Case Review Procedures (Oct. 1, 2000).

[343] IRM 4.8.3.12, EQMS Reports (Oct. 1, 2000); IRM 4.8.3.14, Feedback to Examiners (Oct. 1, 2000).

[344] More specifically, technical review includes, but is not limited to, the following areas: (1) whether the scope of the examination was limited or expanded as needed (and on corporate returns the balance sheet and Schedule M adjustments were considered); (2) whether sources of unreported income were explored; (3) whether procedures for information returns, package audit requirements, related returns, and prior or subsequent year returns were followed; (4) whether adequate evidence was obtained, including an examination of source documents, an in-depth interview of the taxpayer or representative, and consideration of penalties; (5) whether technical conclusions were correct and were supported by law, regulations, and court cases; (6) whether legible workpapers supported

When a case is returned to the examiner and his group manager, communication is by way of a Reviewer's Report, which identifies errors and inadequacies found in the examining officers' reports. The Reviewer's Report may be used as an inquiry memorandum where it is necessary to return the case for further action by the examiner. After the examiner resubmits the case, the inquiry memorandum may be redesignated by the reviewer as a correction or advisory memorandum, depending on the results of the inquiry. The Reviewer's Report may also be used as an advisory memorandum issued as an initial communication to apprise the group manager of errors of omission or commission in an examining officer's report that have been accepted or corrected with no change in tax liability and without return of the case file to the examiner. The advisory memorandum is intended as a training vehicle for the group manager and is limited to items having an insignificant impact on the tax liability. Finally, the Reviewer's Report may be used as an observation report to give the results of the managerial, procedural, and other aspects of the review. An agreed issue is not reopened, nor is a new issue raised by the reviewer, unless the ground for such action is substantial and the potential effect on the tax liability is material. However, a case is generally reopened, regardless of the significance of the issue, if it is determined to be in favor of the taxpayer.

¶ 8.14 UNAGREED CASE PROCEDURE

In an unagreed case, the district sends the taxpayer a preliminary "thirty-day letter," which states the determination proposed to be made. (See Form 8.6.) Preliminary or thirty-day letters are accompanied by a copy of the examination report (but not the confidential transmittal or T-letter), a waiver of the restrictions on assessment, and Publication 5, a description of the appeals procedures. (See Table 8.3.) The thirty-day letter formally notifies the taxpayer of the examiner's findings, asks him to sign and return an agreement to those findings, and informs him of his appeal rights in the event that he does not accept the findings. If the taxpayer has not presented all the information he wishes to the examiner, he is given fifteen days to mail evidence to the examiner or to set up an appointment to discuss the agent's findings and to present the evidence in person.

If the Service receives no response to this notice within thirty days, the taxpayer is sent a statutory notice of deficiency, which permits the taxpayer to obtain prepayment Tax Court review of the deficiency as long as a petition is

---

conclusions, and audit trails were documented; and (7) whether the examiner's report was accurate, legible, and followed the report writing instructions (IRM 4.10.8, Report Writing (May 14, 1999)).

filed within the ninety-day period. (See Form 8.7.) Thus, the taxpayer who receives a combination fifteen- and thirty-day letter has the following alternatives:

1. The taxpayer can sign and return the enclosed agreement form and consent to assessment and collection. On doing so, the case is closed in Examination. In due course, the taxpayer will receive a bill. If the taxpayer so chooses, after paying the tax, he may file a refund claim with the Service and sue for refund within the statutory period in the appropriate federal district court or the claims court.

2. The taxpayer can, within the fifteen-day period, submit an additional form, requesting a discussion of the examiner's findings.

3. The taxpayer can file a protest within the thirty-day period and request a hearing before the Appeals Office.

4. The taxpayer can bypass administrative appeal, wait for the statutory notice of deficiency, and within the ninety-day period file a petition in the U.S. Tax Court. If the taxpayer chooses this route, he is not required to pay the proposed deficiency unless and until the Tax Court renders an adverse decision that becomes final.

5. The taxpayer can bypass administrative appeal and Tax Court review by not filing either a protest or a Tax Court petition. If the taxpayer pursues this course of action, he will be sent a bill in due course. After payment, the taxpayer can file a claim for refund and obtain judicial review by filing a refund suit in the appropriate federal district court or claims court within the statutory period.

FORM 8.6 ――――――――――――――――――――――――――――――
PRELIMINARY NOTICE OF DEFICIENCY ("THIRTY-DAY LETTER")

Internal Revenue Service
Department of the Treasury
District Director

Date:

Tax Year Ended:

Person to Contact:

Contact Telephone Number:

Contact Address:

Dear

Enclosed are two copies of our report explaining why we believe adjustments should be made in the amount of your tax. Please look this report over and let us know whether you agree with our findings.

If you accept our findings, please sign the consent to assessment and collection portion at the bottom of the report and mail one copy to this office within 30 days from the date of this letter. If additional tax is due, you may want to pay it now and limit the interest charge; otherwise, we will bill you. (See the enclosed Publication 5 for payment details.)

If you do not accept our findings, you have 30 days from the date of this letter to do one of the following:

1. Mail us any additional evidence or information you would like us to consider.
2. Request a discussion of our findings with the examiner who conducted the examination. At that time you may submit any additional evidence or information you would like us to consider. If you plan to come in for a discussion, please phone or write us in advance so that we can arrange a convenient time and place.
3. Discuss your position with the group manager or a senior examiner (designated by the group manager), if an examination has been held and you have been unable to reach an agreement with the examiner.

If you do not accept our findings and do not want to take any of the above actions, you may write us at the address shown above or call us at the telephone number shown above within 30 days from the date of this letter to request a conference with an Appeals Officer. You must provide all pertinent documentation and facts concerning disputed issues to the examiner before your case is forwarded to the Appeals Office. If your examination was conducted entirely by mail, we would appreciate your first discussing our findings with one of our examiners.

The Appeals Office is independent of the District Director. The Appeals Officer, who has not examined your return previously, will take a fresh look at your case. Most disputes considered by Appeals are resolved informally and promptly. By going to Appeals, you may avoid court costs (such as the U.S. Tax Court filing fee of $60), clear up this matter sooner, and prevent interest from mounting. An Appeals Officer will promptly telephone you and, if necessary, arrange an appointment. If you decide to bypass Appeals and petition the Tax Court, your case will normally be assigned for settlement to an Appeals Office before the Tax Court hears the case.

Under Internal Revenue Code Section 6673 the Tax Court is authorized to award damages of up to $5,000 to the United States when a taxpayer unreasonably fails to pursue available administrative remedies. Damages could be awarded under this provision, for example, if the Court concludes that it was unreasonable for a taxpayer to bypass Appeals and then file a petition in the Tax Court. The Tax Court will make that determination based upon the facts and circumstances of each case. Generally, the Service will not ask the Court to award damages under this provision if you make a good faith effort to meet with Appeals and to settle your case before petitioning the Tax Court.

The enclosed Publication 5 explains your appeal rights.

If we do not hear from you within 30 days, we will have to process your case on the basis of the adjustments shown in the examination report. If you write us about your case, please write to the person whose name and address are shown in the heading of this letter and refer to the symbols in the upper right corner of the enclosed report. An envelope is enclosed for your convenience. Please include your telephone number, area code, and the most convenient time for us to call, in case we find it necessary to contact you for further information.

If you prefer, you may call the person at the telephone number shown in the heading of this letter. This person will be able to answer any question you may have. Thank you for your cooperation.

Sincerely yours,

District Director

Enclosures:
Examination Report (2)
Publication 5

FIGURE 8.2

PUBLICATION 5—APPEAL RIGHTS AND PREPARATION OF PROTESTS FOR UNAGREED CASES

Your Appeal Rights and How To Prepare a Protest If You Don' t Agree

IRS
Department of the Treasury
Internal Revenue Service
www.irs.ustreas.gov
Publication 5 (Rev. 01-1999)
Catalog Number 46074I

Introduction

This Publication tells you how to appeal your tax case if you don't agree with the Internal Revenue Service (IRS) findings.

If You Don' t Agree

If you don't agree with any or all of the IRS findings given you, you may request a meeting or a telephone conference with the supervisor of the person who issued the findings. If you still don't agree, you may appeal your case to the Appeals Office of IRS.

If you decide to do nothing and your case involves an examination of your income, estate, gift, and certain excise taxes or penalties, you will receive a formal Notice of Deficiency. The Notice of Deficiency allows you to go to the Tax Court and tells you the procedure to follow. If you do not go to the Tax Court, we will send you a bill for the amount due.

If you decide to do nothing and your case involves a trust fund recovery penalty, or certain employment tax liabilities, the IRS will send you a bill for the penalty. If you do not appeal a denial of an offer in compromise or a denial of a penalty abatement, the IRS will continue collection action.

If you don't agree, we urge you to appeal your case to the Appeals Office of IRS. The Office of Appeals can settle most differences without expensive and time-consuming court trials. [Note: Appeals can not consider your reasons for not agreeing if they don't come within the scope of the tax laws (for example, if you disagree solely on moral, religious, political, constitutional, conscientious, or similar grounds.)]

The following general rules tell you how to appeal your case.

Appeals Within the IRS

Appeals is the administrative appeals office for the IRS. You may appeal most IRS decisions with your local Appeals Office. The Appeals Office is separate from - and independent of - the IRS Office taking the action you disagree with. The Appeals Office is the only level of administrative appeal within the IRS.

Conferences with Appeals Office personnel are held in an informal manner by correspondence, by telephone or at a personal conference. There is no need for you to have representation for an Appeals conference, but if you choose to have a representative, see the requirements under **Representation.**

If you want an Appeals conference, follow the instructions in our letter to you. Your request will be sent to the Appeals Office to arrange a conference at a convenient time and place. You or your representative should prepare to discuss all issues you don't agree with at the conference. Most differences are settled at this level.

In most instances, you may be eligible to take your case to court if you don' t reach an agreement at your Appeals conference, or if you don' t want to appeal your case to the IRS Office of Appeals. See the later section *Appeals To The Courts.*

Protests

When you request an appeals conference, you may also need to file a formal written protest or a small case request with the office named in our letter to you. Also, see the special appeal request procedures in Publication 1660, Collection Appeal Rights, if you disagree with lien, levy, seizure, or denial or termination of an installment agreement.

You need to file a written protest:

■ In all employee plan and exempt organization cases without regard to the dollar amount at issue.

■ In all partnership and S corporation cases without regard to the dollar amount at issue.

■ In all other cases, unless you qualify for the small case request procedure, or other special appeal procedures such as requesting Appeals consideration of liens, levies, seizures, or installment agreements. See Publication 1660.

How to prepare a protest:

When a protest is required, **send it within the time limit specified in the letter you received.** Include in your protest:

1) Your name and address, and a daytime telephone number,

2) A statement that you want to appeal the IRS findings to the Appeals Office,

3) A copy of the letter showing the proposed changes and findings you don't agree with (or the date and symbols from the letter),

4) The tax periods or years involved,

5) A list of the changes that you don't agree with, and why you don't agree.

6) The facts supporting your position on any issue that you don't agree with,

7) The law or authority, if any, on which you are relying.

8) You must sign the written protest, stating that it is true, under the penalties of perjury as follows:

'Under the penalties of perjury, I declare that I examined the facts stated in this protest, including any accompanying documents, and, to the best of my knowledge and belief, they are true, correct, and complete."'

If your representative prepares and signs the protest for you, he or she must substitute a declaration stating:

1) That he or she submitted the protest and accompanying documents and

2) Whether he or she knows personally that the facts stated in the protest and accompanying documents are true and correct.

We urge you to provide as much information as you can, as this will help us speed up your appeal. This will save you both time and money.

Small Case Request:

If the total amount for any tax period is not more than $25,000, you may make a small case request instead of filing a formal written protest. In computing the total amount, include a proposed increase or decrease in tax (including penalties), or claimed refund. For an offer in compromise, in calculating the total amount, include total unpaid tax, penalty and interest due. For a small case request, follow the instructions in our letter to you by: sending a letter requesting Appeals consideration, indicating the changes you don't agree with, and the reasons why you don't agree.

Representation

You may represent yourself at your appeals conference, or you may have an attorney, certified public accountant, or an individual enrolled to practice before the IRS represent you. Your representative must be qualified to practice before the IRS. If you want your representative to appear without you, you must provide a properly completed power of attorney to the IRS before the representative can receive or inspect confidential information. Form 2848, Power of Attorney and Declaration of Representative, or any other properly written power of attorney or authorization may be used for this

Copyright © May 2003

purpose. You can get copies of Form 2848 from an IRS office, or by calling 1-800-TAX-FORM (1-800-829-3676).

You may also bring another person(s) with you to support your position.

Appeals To The Courts

If you and Appeals don't agree on some or all of the issues after your Appeals conference, or if you skipped our appeals system, you may take your case to the United States Tax Court, the United States Court of Federal Claims, or your United States District Court, after satisfying certain procedural and jurisdictional requirements as described below under each court. (However, if you are a nonresident alien, you cannot take your case to a United States District Court.) These courts are independent judicial bodies and have no connection with the IRS.

Tax Court

If your disagreement with the IRS is over whether you owe additional income tax, estate tax, gift tax, certain excise taxes or penalties related to these proposed liabilities, you can go to the United States Tax Court. (Other types of tax controversies, such as those involving some employment tax issues or manufacturers' excise taxes, cannot be heard by the Tax Court.) You can do this after the IRS issues a formal letter, stating the amounts that the IRS believes you owe. This letter is called a notice of deficiency. You have 90 days from the date this notice is mailed to you to file a petition with the Tax Court (or 150 days if the notice is addressed to you outside the United States). The last date to file your petition will be entered on the notice of deficiency issued to you by the IRS. If you don't file the petition within the 90-day period (or 150 days, as the case may be), we will assess the proposed liability and send you a bill. You may also have the right to take your case to the Tax Court in some other situations, for example, following collection action by the IRS in certain cases. See Publication 1660.

If you discuss your case with the IRS during the 90-day period (150-day period), the discussion will not extend the period in which you may file a petition with the Tax Court.

The court will schedule your case for trial at a location convenient to you. You may represent yourself before the Tax Court, or you may be represented by anyone permitted to practice before that court.

Note: If you don't choose to go to the IRS Appeals Office before going to court, normally you will have an opportunity to attempt settlement with Appeals before your trial date.

If you dispute not more than $50,000 for any one tax year, there are simplified procedures. You can get information about these procedures and

other matters from the Clerk of the Tax Court, 400 Second St. NW, Washington, DC 20217.

Frivolous Filing Penalty

Caution: If the Tax Court determines that your case is intended primarily to cause a delay, or that your position is frivolous or groundless, the Tax Court may award a penalty of up to $25,000 to the United States in its decision.

District Court and Court of Federal Claims

If your claim is for a refund of any type of tax, you may take your case to your United States District Court or to the United States Court of Federal Claims. Certain types of cases, such as those involving some employment tax issues or manufacturers' excise taxes, can be heard only by these courts.

Generally, your District Court and the Court of Federal Claims hear tax cases only after you have paid the tax and filed a claim for refund with the IRS. You can get information about procedures for filing suit in either court by contacting the Clerk of your District Court or the Clerk of the Court of Federal Claims.

If you file a formal refund claim with the IRS, and we haven't responded to you on your claim within 6 months from the date you filed it, you may file suit for a refund immediately in your District Court or the Court of Federal Claims. If we send you a letter that proposes disallowing or disallows your claim, you may request Appeals review of the disallowance. If you wish to file a refund suit, you must file your suit no later than 2 years from the date of our notice of claim disallowance letter.

Note: Appeals review of a disallowed claim doesn't extend the 2 year period for filing suit. However, it may be extended by mutual agreement.

Recovering Administrative and Litigation Costs

You may be able to recover your reasonable litigation and administrative costs if you are the prevailing party, and if you meet the other requirements. You must exhaust your administrative remedies within the IRS to receive reasonable litigation costs. You must not unreasonably delay the administrative or court proceedings.

Administrative costs include costs incurred on or after the date you receive the Appeals decision letter, the date of the first letter of proposed deficiency, or the date of the notice of deficiency, whichever is earliest.

Recoverable litigation or administrative costs may include:

- Attorney fees that generally do not exceed $125 per hour. This amount will be indexed for a cost of living adjustment.

- Reasonable amounts for court costs or any administrative fees or similar charges by the IRS.

- Reasonable expenses of expert witnesses.

- Reasonable costs of studies, analyses, tests, or engineering reports that are necessary to prepare your case.

You are the prevailing party if you meet all the following requirements:

- You substantially prevailed on the amount in controversy, or on the most significant tax issue or issues in question.

- You meet the net worth requirement. For individuals or estates, the net worth cannot exceed $2,000,000 on the date from which costs are recoverable. Charities and certain cooperatives must not have more than 500 employees on the date from which costs are recoverable. And taxpayers other than the two categories listed above must not have net worth exceeding $7,000,000 and cannot have more than 500 employees on the date from which costs are recoverable.

You are not the prevailing party if:

- The United States establishes that its position was substantially justified. If the IRS does not follow applicable published guidance, the United States is presumed to not be substantially justified. This presumption is rebuttable. Applicable published guidance means regulations, revenue rulings, revenue procedures, information releases, notices, announcements, and, if they are issued to you, private letter rulings, technical advice memoranda and determination letters. The court will also take into account whether the Government has won or lost in the courts of appeals for other circuits on substantially similar issues, in determining if the United States is substantially justified.

You are also the prevailing party if:

- The final judgment on your case is less than or equal to a "qualified offer" which the IRS rejected, and if you meet the net worth requirements referred to above.

A court will generally decide who is the prevailing party, but the IRS makes a final determination of liability at the administrative level. This means you may receive administrative costs from the IRS without going to court. You must file your claim for administrative costs no later than the 90th day after the final determination of tax, penalty or interest is mailed to you. The Appeals Office makes determinations for the IRS on administrative costs. A denial of administrative costs may be appealed to the Tax Court no later than the 90th day after the denial.

FORM 8.7

STATUTORY NOTICE OF DEFICIENCY ("NINETY-DAY LETTER")

(Use Appropriate Letterhead)

Person to Contact:Contact

Telephone Number:

(Name and Address of Taxpayer)

(Salutation)

    This letter is a NOTICE OF DEFICIENCY. We have determined that your Federal (kind of tax) tax liability for the taxable year(s) .... shows (a) deficiency (deficiencies) of $............... The enclosed statement shows how we computed the deficiency (deficiencies).

    Neither this notice, nor any related action taken by the Internal Revenue Service, affects other sanctions the law provides.

    If you decide not to contest our determination in the United States Tax Court, the law requires us to assess and bill you for the deficiency (deficiencies) after 90 days from the above mailing date of this letter (150 days if this letter is addressed to you outside the United States). However, if you contest this determination by filing a petition within that time with the United States Tax Court, 400 Second Street, N.W., Washington, D.C. 20217, we may not assess any deficiencies and bill you until after the Tax Court has decided your case. You can obtain a copy of the rules for filing a petition by writing to the Clerk of the Tax Court at the Court's Washington, D.C. address stated above. The time within which you may file a petition with the Court (90 or 150 days as the case may be) is fixed by law, and the Court cannot consider your case if your petition is filed late.

    If you have any questions, please contact the person whose name and telephone number are shown above.

                           Sincerely yours,

                           Commissioner
                           By (Signature)
                           (Title)

Enclosure:

Statement

No inflexible rule or set of rules can dictate which option should be chosen in any particular case.[345] At this point, however, experience and practical reality suggest some general observations. Although some taxpayers represent themselves, administrative appeal and certainly litigation usually involve professional representation and cost, and the taxpayer will normally incur this cost no matter what the outcome. Unless the amount in dispute is substantial and significantly more than the projected professional fees, the taxpayer is generally better advised to consent to the assessment and pay the additional tax. Statistically, where the returns of individuals with relatively low or moderate positive incomes are examined, smaller average adjustments are recommended than where the returns of higher income individual taxpayers and business taxpayers are examined. Consequently, fewer lower- or moderate-income cases are appealed. On the other hand, comparing the total adjustments appealed with the total adjustments made, most individual and corporate taxpayers appeal adjustments, and they almost always succeed in reducing the proposed adjustments.[346] Experience with the Service also teaches that once a position is adopted, it is hard to change, despite the involvement of other Service personnel, either in Appeals or Counsel. Accordingly, the least costly option a taxpayer has will be to pursue every possible way of resolving an issue at the district examiner level.

[1] Unagreed Office Examination Cases

At the conclusion of an office examination, the Service makes an immediate attempt to resolve the disagreement. If the taxpayer is present, the tax auditor explains the proposed adjustments to tax liability and solicits an agreement. If the taxpayer disagrees with the adjustment, the taxpayer is given the immediate opportunity to discuss the disputed adjustment with the group manager.[347] The group manager discusses the disputed adjustment with the taxpayer in a further attempt to resolve the issue and obtain the taxpayer's agreement. If there is still no agreement, the taxpayer is advised of his appeal rights. If the

---

[345] The relative merits of these alternatives are discussed at ¶¶ 9.04[1], 9.04[2].

[346] See GAO, Changes to Appeals Process Could Improve Settlements and Increase Taxpayers' Satisfaction 7, 47 (GGD—82-54, 1982); S. Long & D. Burnham, "Solving the Nation's Budget Deficit With a Bigger Tougher IRS: What Are the Realities?" 48 Tax Notes 741, 746–747 (Aug. 6, 1990). Individual taxpayers appeal 60 percent of the additional taxes recommended by examiners. Small corporations with assets of less than $250 million appeal 69 percent of additional taxes, and large corporations appeal 81 percent of the adjustments. The Service estimates that for every $100 of additional taxes an examiner recommends against an individual taxpayer, only $67.20 is ultimately assessed. S. Long & D. Burnham, supra, at 746.

[347] 26 CFR § 601.105(c)(1)(ii). See IRM 4254.1, Concluding the Examination (June 29, 1992); IRM 4255.1, Taxpayer Responses to Proposed Adjustments (May 25, 1988).

taxpayer orally requests an appeal, the request is noted in the file and the case is transferred to Appeals. If the taxpayer does not request an appeal, the taxpayer is sent a thirty-day letter. If an immediate interview or Appeals Office conference is not practical the taxpayer is sent a thirty-day letter from the district office. This letter informs the taxpayer of the proposed adjustments and the alternative courses of action, including appeal, in the event that the taxpayer does not accept the findings.[348] A copy of the auditor's report is transmitted with the letter and explains in summary fashion the basis on which the adjustments are proposed. The taxpayer is also told that (1) if he agrees with the adjustment, he may sign the enclosed agreement form; (2) if he disagrees with the findings, he may request a conference in the Appeals Office; but (3) if a request for a conference is not received within thirty days, the case is processed on the basis of the adjustments shown in the examination report. In an office examination, the taxpayer may obtain an Appeals Office conference without submitting a protest.[349] Consequently, a taxpayer who wishes to appeal an adjustment proposed in an office examination may obtain an Appeals conference by orally notifying the district office (i.e., the examiner) or writing in response to the thirty-day letter that an Appeals conference is requested. If the taxpayer fails to respond to the thirty-day letter, the Service will send the statutory notice of deficiency.[350]

[2] Unagreed Correspondence Examination Cases

If the taxpayer and the auditor fail to agree after a correspondence examination, the taxpayer will receive a thirty-day letter, along with a copy of the auditor's report, an agreement or waiver form, instructions regarding his appeal rights, and a postage-paid envelope. The letter advises the taxpayer that he may choose one of the following courses of action:

1. He may agree to the auditor's determination and sign and return one copy of the enclosed agreement form or "Consent to Assessment and Collection";

2. He may submit additional information or request a discussion of findings; or

3. He may, within thirty days, request a hearing before the Appeals Office.[351]

---

[348] 26 CFR § 601.105(c)(1)(ii). See IRM 4254.1, Concluding the Examination (June 29, 1992); IRM 4255.1, Taxpayer Responses to Proposed Adjustments (May 25, 1988).

[349] 26 CFR § 601.105(c)(1)(i).

[350] IRM 4255.2, No Response to Proposed Adjustments (Aug. 8, 1989).

[351] 26 CFR § 601.105(c)(1)(i); IRM 4255.1, Taxpayer Responses to Proposed Adjustments (May 25, 1988).

If the taxpayer disagrees with the proposed changes, which he may do either by letter or in person at the district office, the auditor will review the case file to consider any additional information submitted that may allow the issue to be resolved at the district level. If additional information indicates that further development is warranted, the examiner is supposed to continue the examination. If the auditor concludes that further correspondence action should not be taken, he may attempt to arrange a personal interview, at which time the disputed items will be discussed with the group manager. If, after the interview with the group manager, the taxpayer does not agree, the same procedures are followed as with an office examination, and the taxpayer can obtain an Appeals conference by orally asking for one or making a written request to the district office.[352] If there is no response to the proposed adjustment letters, the district office may attempt to contact the taxpayer; failing that, if the taxpayer indicates no intention of taking any action or if the taxpayer cannot be contacted, a statutory notice of deficiency is issued.[353]

[3] Unagreed Field Examination Cases

When the taxpayer and a revenue agent cannot agree on proposed adjustments in a field examination, the agent prepares a report explaining the proposed adjustments indicating agreed and unagreed issues. Revenue agent's reports may be given a technical and procedural review by the Quality Review Staff. Once a report is approved, the area office of the operating division sends the taxpayer a summary of the agent's report with a thirty-day letter informing the taxpayer of the options available. A taxpayer has the following alternatives:

1. Accept the findings in the report and sign a waiver of the restrictions on assessment (Form 870);
2. Request a conference in the regional Appeals Office within thirty days of the letter and file a protest within that time if the total amount of the proposed additional tax exceeds $2,500 for any taxable period[354]; or
3. Ignore the thirty-day letter, in which case the taxpayer will be sent a statutory notice of deficiency (ninety-day letter).

If a taxpayer requests a conference in the Appeals Office and files a protest, the district office will forward the taxpayer's protest and case file to the Appeals Office, which then has full control over the case and its disposition.

---

[352] 26 CFR § 601.105(c)(1)(i); IRM 4255.1, Taxpayer Responses to Proposed Adjustments (May 25, 1988).

[353] IRM 4255.2, No Response to Proposed Adjustments (Aug. 8, 1989).

[354] A protest is also required if the proposed overassessment, claimed refund, or tax (plus penalty and interest) sought to be compromised exceeds $2,500.

[4] Settlement at the Area Office Level

There is a single level of administrative appeal within the Service: from the examining agent's findings to an Appeals Office. Although no formal conference procedure exists in the district office, there is an opportunity to discuss the unagreed issues with the agent's group supervisor or manager. There is also an on-the-job visitation program currently in effect in all regions, which can be utilized by a representative to obtain what is essentially an informal conference at the district level.

The on-the-job visitation program requires group managers to make periodic on-the-job visits to the agents in their group. One of the primary purposes of this program is to involve the group manager in the issues in dispute to determine whether a potentially unagreed case can be converted to an agreed case. The representative can request the agent to invite the manager to make a visitation on the next scheduled meeting date when the representative wishes to have an informal conference with the manager. Through this program, the group manager, the agent, and the representative can discuss the issues in dispute at the site of the examination where all the books and records are located and are available for reference, if necessary. The group manager is required to prepare a visitation report after each visit documenting the agent's performance and the extent of the manager's involvement in the case, but need not prepare a conference report as such.

A conference with the group manager will generally be advisable where the issues in dispute were factual, such as valuation, useful life, reasonable compensation, or the like. It should also be appropriate when the examining agent either did not understand the facts or placed a different interpretation on the facts to arrive at the conclusion.

B   SPECIAL FEATURES OF EXAMINATIONS BY DIFFERENT OPERATING UNITS

¶ 8.15 SPECIALIZED PROCEDURES IN LARGE AND MID-SIZE BUSINESS EXAMINATIONS

[1] The Coordinated Industry Care (CIC) Program

Beginning in the late 1960s, the Service has used the Coordinated Explanation Program to examine the returns of approximately 1,700 of the largest and most complex corporate taxpayers.[355] The Service considers the CEP to be its most important audit program because the CEP uses only about 20 percent of the Service's audit resources, yet the CEP revenue agents recommend about two thirds of the total recommended tax from all audits. In a CEP case, a team of revenue agents and specialist revenue agents (such as engineer revenue agents, economists, international examiners, computer audit specialists, excise tax revenue agents, and employment tax revenue agents), under the direction of a case manager, and in accordance with a written plan, conduct multiyear audits ("cycles") of the returns of the taxpayer and its controlled entities.[356] In 2002, LMSB changed the name of the Program to the Coordinated Industry Case (CIC) Program, or the CIC. Industry specialists provide support in the examination of taxpayers in industries in the Industry Specialization Program.[357] Counsel attorneys act as the legal advisers of CEP teams on matters of tax law and policy, such as what information must be developed on issues in order for the issues to be resolved administratively rather than by litigation, although evidence suitable for the administrative dispute resolution process may be usable in court.[358]

For audit purposes, the Service divides large corporations (corporations reporting more than $10 million in gross assets) into two groups. The very largest corporations with assets exceeding $250 million are audited in accordance with the CEP; and the other large corporations are audited under the Ex-

---

[355] IRM 4.3.11, Coordinated Examination Program (CEP) Case Manager's Handbook (May 20, 1999) (hereinafter the CEP Case Manager's Handbook). For a critical review of the CEP, its functions, and effectiveness, see GAO, Compliance Measures and Audits of Large Corporations Need Improvement, GAO/GGD—94-70 (Sept. 1994). The GAO also concluded that although the CEP produces a high rate of return in the form of tax adjustments, when the Service has increased expenditures in large corporate audits, it has not necessarily increased realized additional tax adjustments from those audits. Moreover, the rate of unproductive audits that produce no recommended tax almost doubled over the period of the study. GAO, Tax Administration—Audit Trends and Taxes Assessed on Large Corporations, GAO/GGD—96-6 (Oct. 1995).

[356] See IRM 4.3.11, CEP Case Manager's Handbook 3.14, Definitions (May 20, 1999). See also IRM 4.3.11.8, CEP Case Manager's Handbook 900 (Industry Specialization) and (11)00 (Use of International Enforcement Program Specialists); IRM 42(10)0 (International Enforcement Program); IRM 42(12)0 (Economic Assistance Program); IRM 42(13)0 (Computer Assisted Audit Program (CAAP)); IRM 42(14)0 (Industry Specialization Program); IRM 4.3(16) (Engineering Program).

[357] IRM 4.4, Industry Specialization Program.

[358] Area counsel involvement in Section 482 pricing issues is limited primarily to "potentially significant issues" where the area office has made the preliminary decision to pursue the issue, and (1) the issue is sufficiently complex and technical to require counsel's expertise; (2) the issue has a known sensitivity; or (3) the district is reasonably certain that there will be no agreement on the issue. IRM 4.45.7.3, The Three-Step Process—Step One—Formulate the Examination Scope for General Issues and Have Planning Meetings (Jan. 1, 2002).

amination Division's general program.[359] The CEP was in the process of being reorganized into two categories of companies: middle-market businesses with $5 million to $250 million in assets and large corporations having more than $250 million in assets. With these two new asset categories, CEP examinations may increase from about 1,700 to 170,000 companies. Compliance already has a Market Specialization Program, and the CIC is similarly organized into industry and subindustry groups. The industry groups are Financial Services; Technology and Media; Food and Retail; Energy, Chemical, and Natural Resources; and Manufacturing, Construction, and Real Estate. Generally, Service employees in the corporate division are organized by industry segments as industry specialists, but specialists whose competency is based on technical expertise, not industry knowledge; for example, international examiners and engineers will report to managers in their specialties, not to case managers. Case managers are nevertheless in charge of the examination.[360]

Cases are identified for the CIC based on the following factors:

- The taxpayer's industry (industrial, financial, utilities and insurance companies, mutual funds, and stock brokerages)
- The total gross assets (the starting point is $500 million)
- The number of operating entities (the number of industries in which the taxpayer and its controlled entities operate)
- The number of team members, specialists, support agents, and staff days necessary for the examination.[361]

---

[359] According to a GAO report, the Service identified 46,700 large corporations, of which it selected about 1,700 in the CEP. GAO, "Tax Administration—Factors Affecting Results From Large Corporations," GAO/GGD—97-62 (Apr. 1997), at 1. The GAO found that although the Service was investing more in audits of large corporations than it did in 1988, revenue agents were recommending less additional tax per hour (23 percent less than in 1988) and had doubled their no-change rate. Id. at 3. During the seven-year period from 1988 to 1995, moreover, only 27 percent of additional tax that the revenue agents did recommend was sustained by Appeals. There were several factors GAO identified that adversely affected these audit results and assessment rate: (1) the complexity and vagueness of the Code; (2) the apparently conflicting performance measures used by Examination and Appeals—Examination focused on the amount of additional taxes recommended, and Appeals considered the number of cases settled without litigation and the time taken in the Appeals process; (3) revenue agents working alone without assistance from group managers and district counsel, as well as limited information on the basis of which returns with potential for tax change could be selected, and limited information about previously audited corporations or industry issues, had difficulty in developing support to recommend tax changes; and (4) Appeals did not share with Examination information that could be used to educate revenue agents. Id. at 3–4.

[360] "TEI Asks: Who's Controlling the Audit in the New IRS?" 1999 TNT 57-2 (Mar. 24, 1999).

[361] IRM 4.45.2, Case Selection (Jan. 1, 2002).

Despite the size, complexity, diversity, or geographical dispersion of the principal taxpayer's operations and assets, the objectives of the CIC are

1. To conduct timely, effective examinations that produce "quality results" and minimize the burden to the Service and the taxpayer alike by treating the primary taxpayer and all entities it effectively controls as a single unit;

2. To centralize responsibility for control and management of the entire case in the primary district, avoiding unilaterally initiated examinations by districts other than the primary district;

3. To secure assistance for the primary district from support districts in the planning and examination of CIC cases;

4. To accumulate in the National Office and disseminate to the field offices information about new examination techniques, issues unique to specific industries, avoidance and evasion schemes, and other information useful in planning and executing examinations;

5. To prepare a formal examination plan, a planning file, and a postexamination critique, soliciting the views of the taxpayer;

6. To maintain a National Office system identifying CIC cases (with the taxpayer's effectively controlled entities and divisions), as well as a system for tracking the progress of the cases; and

7. To encourage agents in the program to exchange techniques and procedures to achieve the best and most uniform results.[362]

[2] CIC Examination Plans

Planning is critical in the CIC examination. The Examination Plan is a written document containing agreements with the taxpayer, information for Service personnel, work assignments, audit procedures, time estimates, and special instructions. It is the principal means for the case manager to coordinate the activities of the different specialized agents into an effective team.[363] Case managers develop examination plans in a three-step process. In the first step, before contacting the taxpayer, the case manager studies the taxpayer's returns, prior reports (including specialists' files and planning files), any industry specialist's analysis, financial statements, Securities and Exchange Commission filings, and other information the Service has gathered; meets with specialists and team members; and determines the scope of the examination. In the second step, during preliminary audit work, the team reviews certain of the taxpayer's records and analyzes some accounts to identify procedures necessary to

---

[362] IRM 45.1.1, Introduction (Jan. 1, 2002).

[363] IRM 4.45.7, Constructing the Examination Plan (Jan. 1, 2002).

examine areas of noncompliance and other unusual items or issues. There are discussions with the taxpayer's personnel about the availability of records. In the third step, the team coordinator, team members, and specialists submit suggested procedures to the case manager, who approves or modifies them in accordance with the manager's own views of the scope and depth of the examination.

[a] Parts of the Examination Plan

There are three sections in the Examination Plan:

1. *Taxpayer information section.* This is the first part of the examination plan. It is the overall plan of the examination. It is prepared after the pre-examination conference with the taxpayer, and a copy of it is furnished to the taxpayer. The purpose of this part of the plan is to formalize (and to inform the taxpayer about) the matters to be covered in the examination, and to prevent misunderstandings of commitments made and agreements reached by both the examination team and the taxpayer.

2. *Service management information.* This part of the plan contains the case manager's instructions to team members and information for each team member about the taxpayer, its organization, and structure, including the relationships of its business entities and their business purpose.

3. *Examination procedures.* This part of the plan sets out a summary of the accounts, transactions, examination areas, organizational components, and the team member's examination assignment for carrying out each segment of the examination. This part of the plan also provides administrative information and processing instructions, such as plans for applying computer auditing techniques, special compliance checks to be used (e.g., to determine the existence of nondeductible lobbying expenses and compliance with information reporting regulations for Forms W-4, Forms 1099INT, and Forms 1099NEC), special information reports that will be required, procedures for communicating and requesting information within the Service, confidential case-related information, arrangements with specialists, and industry practices. While only the first part of the plan is routinely provided to taxpayers, at the taxpayer's request, the case manager will provide the second and third parts to the taxpayer, except for specialized audit techniques and law enforcement information intended for internal use.[364]

---

[364] IRM 4.45.7.3, The Three-Step Process (Jan. 1, 2002); IRM 4.45.7.4, Constructing the Examination Plan (Jan. 1, 2002).

[b] Forms Used by Case Managers

Forms case managers most frequently use, described in Form 8.4, indicate the procedures the case manager will follow in the examination. They suggest that the taxpayer should prepare a parallel record during the examination to record, on a daily basis, what the agents and specialists have requested and reviewed, as well as the statements they have made and statements the taxpayer's representatives have made to them. With this information, the taxpayer's representatives can gain some control over the activities of the examiners, and will have a record to use in the event of possible disagreement, such as a disagreement over access to records and the propriety of a summons.

[c] The Planning File

In the planning process, the planning file the case manager prepares and maintains in the planning of the CIC examination is said to be the single most important document. The planning file is intended to prepare the case manager for the next cycle by providing the manager with as much information as possible to develop the examination plan for that cycle.[365] Again, the planning file contents suggest the type of information the taxpayer should keep:

1. Identifying information about the taxpayer and its controlled entities and the taxpayer's history; its organization;
2. Reorganizations, acquisitions, and liquidations; accounting records and procedures; continuing year-to-year analyses;
3. Contracts, documents, and agreements;
4. Examination support;
5. Current data affecting subsequent years;
6. The examination plan and reports;
7. ADP and computer applications;
8. The postexamination critique; and
9. Other information relating to the examination.

FIGURE 8.3

INDEX TO COORDINATED EXAMINATION PROGRAM FORMS

Form Number	Title
4485	Coordinated Examination Support Request
4564	Information Document Request

---

[365] See IRM 4.45.13.4, Examination, CIC, Coordinating and Monitoring Audit Process, Exhibit, Large Case Checklist (Jan. 1, 2002).

4764	Large Case Examination Plan
4764A	CEP Audit Plan (Special Instructions and Summary of Assignment)
4764B	Large Case Examination Plan (Outline of Examination Procedures)
4791	Large Case Proposed Change in Primary District Identity
5696	Large Case Examination Assignment—Short Form
5697	Large Case Examination Assignment—Long Form
5698	Examination History Record
5699	Information Document Request Log
5700	Issue Control Sheet
5701	Notice of Proposed Adjustments
5793	Daily Log—Large Case Examination Activity
6095	Carryover Adjustment Schedule
6352	Industry Specialization Report
6609	CEP Schedule of Working Assignments and Planning Time

[3] Opening Conference

Conferences play an important part in a CIC audit.[366] On the case manager's part, before the opening conference, the case manager has already engaged in planning the examination and, along with the team coordinator, held meetings with selected team members to (1) familiarize themselves with the data that will be needed for the preparation of the plan; (2) establish the scope and depth of the examination; and (3) establish computerized audit procedures.[367] The opening conference is the first meeting the case manager and the team coordinator (and sometimes other team members and specialist supervisors) have with authorized personnel of the corporate taxpayer. Both the internal meetings and the opening conference are "to plan [the examinations] in a cooperative manner with the taxpayer to insure the best use of both parties' resources."[368] In general terms, the purpose of the opening conference is "to summarize agreements on coordination and accommodations and to discuss the scope and depth of the examination."[369]

Opening conferences are intended to cover a number of matters that are important to the case managers and taxpayers alike. Indeed the process of the conference suggests the matters on which the taxpayer must prepare for in defending the audit.

---

[366] IRM 4.45.8, Conferences—Overview (Jan. 1, 2002).

[367] IRM 4.45.8, Conferences—Overview (Jan. 1, 2002)

[368] IRM 4.45.8, Conferences—Overview (Jan. 1, 2002)

[369] IRM 4.45.8, Conferences—Overview (Jan. 1, 2002)

[4] The Audit and Information Gathering

Audit procedures in large case examinations are responses to the scale of large corporate organizations and the complex issues that result from a large corporate enterprise, frequently with international operations conducted in many foreign countries. The procedures used in these audits are a combination of basic audit techniques and specialized audit techniques. Some Team members use procedures that do not differ remarkably from other business examinations. Albeit on a large scale, CIC examinations still include

- Interviews
- Tours of business sites
- Evaluation of the taxpayer's internal controls
- Examining the taxpayer's books and records
- Analyzing Schedules M-1 and M-2
- Bank record reconciliations
- Balance sheet analyses
- Testing gross receipts or sales
- Testing expenses: cost of goods sold
- Testing expenses: operating expenses
- Sampling techniques

At the same time as some Team members are conducting examinations using the basic audit techniques agents follow in other business examinations, the various Specialists on the Team also conduct examinations according to their own specialized audit techniques.

Detail. While both the revenue agents on the CEP Team and the revenue agent conducting the examination of small business will review books of account, balance sheets, and profit and loss statements, Team members follow detailed audit procedures for the analysis of balance sheet accounts, profit and loss statements (income and expenses), and special deductions and credits. These procedures are designed around a chart of account related to different parts of the tax return and keyed to the agent's workpapers with identifying numbers.[370] Although discretionary, this process forces the agent to document his or her actions during the examination, and would seem to assure compliance with the examination techniques.

Specialists. Although Specialists are an integral part of the examination team, they are working separately following specialized industry and type-of-tax audit techniques. Specialists develop issues within their expertise from commencement of the examination, issue information document requests (IDRs), make their own determinations, and their separate examinations can delay the closing of the examination.

---

[370] IRM 4.13.12, Audit Techniques—Standard Audit Index Numbers (SAIN) (Aug. 30, 2000).

Time. A CEP examination requires a company to invest a substantial commitment of time and resources. Without taxpayer planning, the cooperation of the case manager and the taxpayer's personnel, and the taxpayer's use of procedures to expedite the examination, the length of the CIC audit can be measured in years, and not in days.

IDRs. Because of the complexity of the examination, members of the team, including specialists, issue scores of informal minisummonses ("Information Document Requests") far more than in usual business examination. Without a procedure for dealing with these IDRs, taxpayer's personnel will become quickly overwhelmed.

Conferences. The number and type of conferences are a distinctive feature of the CEP examination. They are used to discuss IDRs before they are issued, the language of the IDR will have to be responsive to the taxpayer's business, to determine the status of responses to IDRs, to measure the progress of the examination, and to resolve administrative issues that have developed in the examination. Conferences are also used to resolve issues or to classify issues as unagreed.

Notices of proposed adjustment (NOPAs). As the examination proceeds, adjustments are reflected in NOPAs (Form 5701) to summarize proposed adjustments to the taxpayer. A fuller description of the adjustment and the basis for it is presented in an Explanation of Items (Form 886-A), attached to the Form 5701. The taxpayer and the case manager are expected to agree on how the taxpayer will deal with these NOPAs. Generally, the agreement requires the taxpayer to (1) review the NOPA immediately to identify any erroneous factual statements, and the case manager is responsible for resolving any dispute about factual disputes; (2) respond to proposed adjustments in an agreed manner; i.e., in writing or orally, the team member to whom the response will be provided; and (3) the time within which the taxpayer will respond. The case manager is responsible for maintaining a control list of Forms 5701 that have been issued, and the director of the taxpayer's audit team should likewise maintain a record to avoid any disagreement about when and whether a Form 5701 has been issued and responded to.

Availability of ADR procedures. ADR procedures are not only available, but encouraged in CIC and LMSB examinations. These procedures are not available in the small business examination.

[5] Preparing for and Defending the Audit

As the description of the procedures used in CEP examinations suggests, the taxpayer's audit manager has to have management skills of high order. Initially, the forms the Team Manager uses before and during the examination can be reviewed to give some idea of how the audit process can be controlled. These forms permit the use of a notebook method, computerized or containing written plans and documentation, for preparing for and using the audit process to defend the taxpayer's return reporting position. For example, the Large Case Examination Plan can be used by the audit manger to develop a plan for the audit. The Coordinated Examination Support Request can focus the audit manager on the personnel in the corporation who should be notified of the examination and requested to assist in the examination. The IDR and IDR Log should focus the audit manger on how the IDR process will be handled, and deal with the selection of the single person who will receive the IDRs and deliver responses, and provide a mechanical way to keep track of the IDRs and their status. The Examination History Record should contain the prior audit cycle's audit reports so that the audit manager can review them again and gain some insight into likely or possible audit issues the Team Manager is likely to raise. The IDR Log and the Issue Control Sheet can be used to identify the issues raised in the examination, and what information or law supports the taxpayer's position or treatment. Similarly, the NOPA form the Team Manager uses offers another tracking mechanism for the results of the examination and the development and status of replies. Another important form the Team Manager uses is the Daily Log—Large Case Examination Activity. The audit manager should use a similar file to keep track of what has occurred during the examination on a daily basis, especially record statements made by members of the Team in the event there is an issue about a statement made, an agreement or understanding, and a position taken. The Carryover Adjustment Schedule should be used to record those adjustments which will affect subsequent years returns. The Industry Specialization Report form should identify another section of the audit manager's notebook for comment and reply.

In general, the taxpayer's audit personnel should follow the steps discussed below in preparing for and representing the interests of the large corporation.

Basic Planning. The tax professional who will be in charge of the examination for the taxpayer, called here the director of audits, should be aware of the process the case manager and the CIC team will follow in the examination. This starts with planning. Just as the case manager plans the examination, the director of audits should plan how the taxpayer will respond to the steps in the audit process. At a minimum, the results of the prior audit cycle should be reviewed; e.g., the adjustments made, the revenue agent's reports issued, the agreements reached, and file memoranda of potential issues reviewed. Also, the returns involved in the current cycle should be obtained and reviewed. Personnel who likely will be involved in the examination should be contacted and alerted, and the flow of communications with those personnel established. A person who will serve as the point person for receiving information document requests from the examination team, directing those requests to the appropriate person for response, and, after approval, forwarding those responses to the case manager or specialist. Procedures for preparing responses to IDRs should be put into place. A computer-based tracking program should be established to record the date an IDR is received, the date and person to whom the request is assigned for response, the status of the preparation of the response, and the date of the delivery of the response.

Strategic planning. Obviously, the taxpayer's objective in an examination is for the examination to be concluded in a minimum of time with a minimum of tax adjustment. A strategy to avoid sizable tax adjustments to a filed return will not be fruitful. Developing a plan to minimize the time the examination will take is both realistic and consistent with the stated intention of LMSB. Accordingly, the director of audits should tap the experience of the taxpayer's personnel in handling prior examinations, and consider technology and other relevant factors in reaching some general approach to reducing examination time. Some steps that companies have taken are the use of conferences before an IDR is issued to discuss whether the request is appropriate, and if it is, to make the terms used consistent with the taxpayer's practices. The objectives in the opening conference should be identified and planned for. Also, the audit director should have a general idea of which LMSB ADR procedure will make sense for the taxpayer to utilize to resolve unagreed adjustments.

Document location and review. An examination is about substantiating return positions, which is done by the review of books and records and other documents. The ability or inability to locate records is evidence that a taxpayer has or has not implemented adequate controls, and the effect of the taxpayer's failure to have such controls can be expected to adversely affect the case manager's evaluation of the records that can be produced. As described above, secondary and even primary records may be checked and reviewed during the examination. Even a slight familiarity with the categories of records the team will or is likely to request in the course of the examination provides an early warning to the taxpayer's audit manager that he or she know the location of the corporation's records for the periods under examination beyond those tax workpapers and other records used in the preparation of the tax return and under the direct control of the corporate tax function.

Control of documents becomes more difficult as records are outside the direct control of the tax function of a large case taxpayer. It is not too much to expect that the location of specific categories and vintages of records in a taxpayer's record storage facilities or elsewhere be capable of being determined. In a multinational corporate organization, it may be impossible for the tax director to know the location of every subsidiary, never mind the location of the records of every subsidiary. Yet for financial and tax purposes, it may be possible to establish procedures to identify employees who will or should know the location of records.

It is important not only to be able to produce records, but to review correspondence and other records to identify records potentially privileged from disclosure; e.g., correspondence of lawyers or federally authorized tax practitioners. Corporate counsel should be consulted before a decision is made whether or not to turn over the record. Also, review at some level of detail is necessary in order to know whether and how the record may affect the examination and the making of a potential adjustment.

Making a record during the examination. Case managers will keep a record of what occurs during the examination, and one can be sure that statements made by the taxpayer's audit personnel will be recorded, especially if the statement is adverse to the taxpayer. Differences over what was said and by whom are not only possible, but inevitable. It is obviously good practice, therefore, for the audit director to keep a contemporaneous record of the activities and statements made during the examination, including a written daily history and memoranda of conferences to record what was transpired from the taxpayer's point of view at the conference.

[6] Alternative Dispute Resolution Techniques

One of the distinctive features of the CEP is the authority given to case managers to resolve and settle issues. Case managers are given greater opportunity to resolve and settle issues arising in the course of examination, since the National Office has decontrolled issues in the Industry Specialization Program and the National Office has reduced the number of controlled issues. Three procedures have given case managers the authority to resolve and settle issues during the CEP examination: (1) Delegation Order 236; (2) Accelerated Issue Resolution; and (3) the prefiling determination procedure.

[a] Delegation Order 236

Delegation Order 236 gives case managers discretionary authority to accept settlement offers on rollover and recurring issues, provided the same issues were resolved in Appeals with the same taxpayer in a prior or later period.[371] A rollover issue involves an adjustment arising from the same legal issue in the same transaction or taxable event and affects more than one tax period; for example, the rate of amortization or depreciation of an asset, bad-debt losses, and basis and inventory adjustments. An issue is a recurring issue when the adjustment arises from the legal issue in a separate transaction or a repeated taxable event, and the taxpayer advances the same legal position on

---

[371] Delegation Order 236, effective November 7, 1990, delegates the discretionary authority to compromise cases provided by Section 7121. See IRM 42(11)8, Case Manager's Handbook (14)20 (Case Manager Settlement Authority), MT 42(11)-41 (Feb. 28, 1995). The GAO found that as of November 30, 1996, the limited settlement authority procedure had been used eighty-one times by taxpayers, the highest percentage of which were in the manufacturing industry category (50 percent). See GAO, "Internal Revenue Service—IRS Initiatives to Resolve Disputes Over Tax Liabilities," GAO/GGD—97-71 (May 1997), at 25, 28.

the similar transaction or repeated event as the taxpayer advanced in the prior tax period settled in Appeals; for example, the method of depreciation for similar transactions and the use of the same accounting method for similar transactions. The facts and the legal authority must have remained substantially unchanged, and Appeals must have settled the underlying issue on its merits independent of other issues in the appeal.[372] The case manager's settlement authority extends even to Industry Specialization Program issues, but the case manager must consult with the industry specialist if the case manager is going to exercise the settlement authority. Settlement must also be approved by the case manager's branch chief. Agreements under Delegation Order 236 are reflected in either a closing agreement or a Form 870AD.

Delegation Order 236 was revised in March 1996 because the terms "on the merits" and "rollover and recurring" issues caused confusion, and it did not permit case managers to apply an Appeals settlement to related taxpayers, even when it made sense to do so. As revised, Delegation Order 236 delegates limited settlement authority to case managers under the general settlement authority granted in Section 712 to accept settlement offers on any issue in a CIC case in their jurisdiction.[373] Case managers have this limited authority on an issue irrespective of the following: (1) the amount of the issue; (2) the tax period (i.e., the Appeals settlement on the issue may have been in an earlier, later, or same tax period); (3) whether settlement of the issue in Appeals was a hazards-of-litigation settlement; and (4) whether the Appeals settlement of the issue was with the taxpayer or with another taxpayer who was directly involved in the transaction or taxable event. No settlement may be accepted unless all of the following factors exist:

1. The facts relating to the issue in the examination period are substantially the same as the facts in the settled period.
2. The controlling legal authority has not changed.
3. Appeals must have settled the issue separately from the settlement of other issues (that is, there was no trading of issues).
4. The Appeals settlement of the issue must have been with the same taxpayer (including its consolidated and unconsolidated subsidiaries) or another taxpayer who was directly involved in the transaction or taxable event.

---

[372] This means that an Appeals hazards of litigation settlement can be considered by case managers under Delegation Order 236. IRM 42(11)8, Case Manager's Handbook (14)24 (Settlement Authority Guidelines), MT 42(11)8-41 (Feb. 28, 1995).

[373] Delegation Order 236 (Rev. 2), approved March 15, 1996. Case managers must coordinate settlements of Industry Specialization and International Field Assistance Specialization Program coordinated issues, but the appropriate specialist or coordinator must approve the settlement in accordance with Delegation Order 247, discussed below.

Direct involvement exists when *A* and *B* are directly involved (as parties, for example) in the same transaction or taxable event and would logically be taxed in the same or similar way; if Appeals settles an issue with *A*, and during the examination of *B*, the examination team raises the same issue, the case manager has settlement authority to resolve the settled issue with *B* on a basis that is consistent with the Appeals settlement with *A*. If *A* or *B*, or both of them, are involved in separate, but similar transactions, and during an examination of either *A* or *B* an adjustment of the treatment of the separate transaction raises the same issue as the one settled in Appeals, the case manager may settle the issue consistently with the Appeals settlement of the same issue, although the Appeals settlement was on a different transaction and for a different tax period.

To memorialize the settlement, case managers may use agreements usually used in Appeals, a closing agreement, or a Form 870-AD.

[b] Delegation Order 247

Delegation Order 247 also provides discretionary settlement authority to case managers to accept settlement offers, regardless of the amount of the liability to be compromised, on coordinated issues within both the Industry Specialization Program (ISP) and the International Field Assistance Specialization Program (IFASP), on which Appeals has coordinated settlement guidelines or positions.[374] Before settlement can be finalized, the proposed settlement, together with any related closing agreement or Form 870-AD (Offer of Waiver of Restrictions on Assessment and Collection of Deficiency in Tax) and supporting documentation, shall be reviewed and approved by the appropriate specialists and coordinators for ISP and IFASP within the Examination, International, and Appeals functions. Case managers have the authority to sign closing agreements and Form 870-AD.

[c] Accelerated Issue Resolution

Another settlement option in the CIC permits CIC taxpayers to accelerate the resolution of the same or similar issues arising out of the examination by extending the examination of the issues from the examination periods to more current tax periods ending before the date of the agreement.[375] This process,

---

[374] Delegation Order 247, effective March 15, 1996.

[375] Rev. Proc. 94-67, 1994-2 CB 800 (Oct. 31, 1994); IRM 42(11)8, Case Manager's Handbook (14)30 (Accelerated Issue Resolution), MT 42(11)8-41 (Feb. 28, 1995). GAO found that as of November 30, 1996, the AIR procedure had been used ninety-seven times by CEP taxpayers, most of which were in the manufacturing (53 percent) and finance, insurance, and real estate (21 percent) industry categories. GAO, "Internal Revenue Ser-

called Accelerated Issue Resolution (AIR), does not give the case manager additional settlement authority, but it does have definite advantages in resolving issues affecting other tax years. AIR benefits the Service because it permits the audit team to have access to more current taxpayer records when taxpayer personnel are still likely to be employed by the taxpayer and available for interview, and avoids a taxpayer's having to deal with and reeducate a new audit team.

Because it is voluntary, AIR also focuses both the audit team and the taxpayer on working to resolve not only the AIR issues but the entire examination as well. An AIR agreement is (1) a specific issue−type closing agreement (2) a taxpayer requests of a case manager (3) that involves any issue arising in the course of a CEP examination under the jurisdiction of the district director (4) in a year ending before the agreement and affecting other tax years. Not all issues may be resolved under the AIR procedures.[376]

Two methods can be used in reaching an AIR agreement. Under one method, the case manager will provide the taxpayer with a revenue agent's report, and the taxpayer and the district will enter into a closing agreement, as provided in Revenue Procedure 94-67 (the taxpayer signs a Form 870 waiving the restrictions on the assessment of the tax due under the agreement). Another method uses the same procedures as are used in partial or fully agreed deficiency cases—that is, an agreed case revenue agent's report and a Form 870, waiving the restrictions on assessment of the agreed tax, and an unagreed case report covering those issues not resolved under AIR.[377]

---

vice—IRS Initiatives to Resolve Disputes Over Tax Liabilities," GAO/GGD—97-71 (May 1997), at 25, 28.

[376] Issues that are under the jurisdiction of other Service functions are excluded from AIR, such as issues that are subject to an advance pricing agreement (APA), issues under the jurisdiction of the Assistant Commissioner, Employee Plans and Exempt Organizations (EP/EO), and partnership items governed by the unified partnership audit rules. Other than these jurisdictionally barred issues, any other issue raised in the course of the CEP examination affecting other taxable years can be resolved under the AIR process with the case manager at the district level, unless the issue has already been the subject of a letter ruling, technical advice memorandum, or closing agreement, or has been designated by the Chief Counsel for litigation. Certain issues require the approval of another Service function: for example, issues that are currently coordinated under the Industry Specialization Program, issues under the Appeals Coordinated Issues and Appeals Industry Specialization Programs, issues under Competent Authority consideration for any year, issues under jurisdiction of the Justice Department, and issues involved in multidistrict cases. Rev. Proc. 94-67, 1994-2 CB 800.

[377] There are other methods described in the Manual that can be used to accelerate the resolution of issues. The taxpayer can file an amended return or claim for refund carrying the resolved issues to later tax returns. Although the resolution of an issue under the AIR process may not result in a tax computation or a methodology for computing the adjustment for the later tax periods, the case manager is supposed to bring the AIR issues to

[d] Prefiling Determinations

During the course of the examination, a taxpayer may make a written request for an agreement on the treatment of a completed transaction before the taxpayer has filed a return reporting the transaction. If the examination team agrees, there may be an agreed determination on the treatment of the item.[378] Prefiling determinations must apply principles and precedents previously announced by the National Office to a specific set of facts, and can be issued only when the result is based on clearly established authorities. Not surprisingly, therefore, procedures to be followed are roughly the same as the taxpayer would follow in requesting a ruling, except that the determination is made by a local office, not the National Office.[379] Unlike the issues resolved under Delegation Order 236 and the AIR process, the transaction on which the taxpayer requests a prefiling determination may not involve an issue on a filed return, and the prefiling determination is not reflected on a closing agreement (and so does not have the finality of a closing agreement). A prefiling determination relieves the taxpayer of the burden of an examination of the transaction because the taxpayer is assured as a practical matter that the reported treatment of the transaction will be accepted by the Service.

On February 11, 2000, the Service announced a pilot program for prefiling agreements (PFAs), under which large business taxpayers are permitted to request examination and resolution of specific issues that will be reported on tax returns they expect to file between September and December 2000.[380] It is expected that even before taxpayers file their returns, this program will permit both taxpayers and the Service to resolve the treatment of issues that are otherwise likely to be disputed on audit, thereby reducing the costs and delays of postfiling audits on these issues. In the pilot phase, the program is available to large businesses in the CIC. A PFA is a closing agreement under Section 7121, covering one or more specific issues arising from transactions that the taxpayer has entered into before the date of the agreement that specifies the treatment to be given to that transaction on a tax return the taxpayer will file

---

a conclusion, preferably with a tax computation and accompanying form. IRM 42(11)8, Case Manager's Handbook (14)33 AIR Methods (Feb. 28, 1995).

[378] IRM 42(11)8, Case Manager's Handbook (14)51, Pre-Filing Determinations—Purpose (Feb. 28, 1995).

[379] The request is directed to the local office and contains the penalties of perjury statement required in the revenue procedure describing ruling procedures. The request will then be assigned to the case manager on the taxpayer's examination, although it may also be assigned to another case manager. A prefiling conference on the suitability of the issue for a prefiling determination is permitted. Once the district and the taxpayer agree on the suitability of the issue for a prefiling determination, the taxpayer files a request containing the information required in a ruling request, except that copies of documents need not be supplied. Notice 2000-12, 2000-9 IRB 1 (Feb. 11, 2000).

[380] Notice 2000-12, 2000-9 IRB 1 (Feb. 11, 2000).

after the date of the agreement.[381] Issues or transactions eligible for a PFA are generally factual or involve established or settled legal principles.[382] Examples include (1) the valuation of assets (except for transfer pricing purposes) and the allocation of the purchase or sale price of a business among the assets acquired or sold; (2) the identification and documentation of hedging transactions; (3) the treatment of in-house research expenses under Section 41; (4) the allocation of costs among different categories of deductible and capitalizable items in which there is a published revenue ruling, such as repairs and advertising; and (5) certain valuation issues.

On the other hand, a PFA is not available for issues that (1) can be included in an advance pricing agreement (APA); (2) can be resolved by requesting a change in accounting method; (3) require the resolution of factual matters, such as reasonable cause, due diligence, good faith, and other fact-based standards; (4) concern Tax Equity and Fiscal Responsibility Act of 1982 (TEFRA) partnership items; or (5) are or will be the subject of a ruling request by the taxpayer. Additionally, a PFA is not available where the taxpayer proposes a tax treatment that is either (1) contrary to a letter ruling, technical advice, or closing agreement issued to the taxpayer or about the taxpayer's transaction or (2) contrary to a position adverse to the taxpayer proposed by the Service in response to a ruling request that was withdrawn by the taxpayer. Assuming that a PFA is available, the taxpayer initiates a request by submitting a written application with specified information through the case manager to the LMSB Industry Director.[383] The Service has also announced its position that PFAs are classified as confidential tax return information not obtainable under the Freedom of Information Act.[384]

[e] Early Referral to Appeals

Examinations in CIC can be accelerated under a procedure that is the early referral or transfer of a "developed" unagreed issue to Appeals while the remaining issues in the case continue to be developed by the Examination CIC team.[385] Early referral is optional at the taxpayer's request, but it must be ap-

---

[381] Notice 2000-12, 2000-9 IRB 1, § 2, Description of a Pre-Filing Agreement.

[382] Notice 2000-12, 2000-9 IRB 1, § 3, Subject Matter of an LMSB Pre-Filing Agreement.

[383] Notice 2000-12, 2000-9 IRB 1, § 4, Procedures for Requesting an LMSB Pre-Filing Agreement.

[384] "Corporate Pre-filing Agreements Will Be Secret," 2000 TNT 38-1 (Feb. 25, 2000).

[385] Ann. 94-41, 1994-12 IRB 9 (Mar. 21, 1994). Although GAO considered early referral to be an Appeals program, it found that as of November 30, 1996, the early referral procedure had been used by twenty-three CIC taxpayers, most of which were in the manufacturing (55 percent) and finance, insurance, and real estate (23 percent) industry catego-

proved by both Appeals and the local office, and is initially limited to CIC cases. The obvious purpose of early referral is to resolve cases more quickly. Issues appropriate for early referral, therefore, are those that can be expected to result in a quicker closing of the entire case if they are resolved, where both the taxpayer and Examination agree that the issue should be referred to Appeals, and the issue is not designated for litigation. The taxpayer requests early referral by submitting a written request to the CIC case manager, identifying the period and issues covered by the request, and fully describing the taxpayer's position. If Examination and Appeals agree to the referral, the CIC team prepares a Form 5701, Proposed Adjustment, setting forth Examination's position, to which the taxpayer must respond within thirty days. At this point the file on the issues being referred is sent to Appeals for review in the same manner as unagreed cases, except that the use of a closing agreement may be more likely.

[f] Comprehensive Case Resolution

The corporate division also uses a process called comprehensive case resolution.[386] Under this procedure, a large business can request resolution of all open issues for all open tax years that are under examination by the corporate division, Appeals, and Counsel. Comprehensive case resolution has the objective of reducing delays in resolving open issues in open years, and so it requires the cooperation of the Service and the taxpayer.

[g] Fast Track Mediation and Settlement

A Fast Track Dispute Resolution Program developed by LMSB and Appeals is intended to resolve cases at the examination level, while the taxpayer is still under LMSB jurisdiction.[387] As the procedure's title suggests, the program is intended to provide accelerated issue resolution and cost effectiveness. The Fast Track process is intended to be completed within an average of 90 to 120 days. Fast Track gives taxpayers two alternative techniques to use in resolving a case: Fast Track Mediation and Fast Track Settlement. Either the taxpayer or an LMSB Team Manager may suggest that Fast Track be used.

---

ries. GAO, "Internal Revenue Service—IRS Initiatives to Resolve Disputes Over Tax Liabilities," GAO/GGD—97-71 (May 1997), at 24, 28. Expanded early referral procedures are described in Rev. Proc. 99-28, 1999-2 CB 109 (July 1, 1999). For CIC taxpayers, these procedures generally are the same as those previously available only to CIC taxpayers under the early referral procedures. See Rev. Proc. 96-9, 1996-1 CB 575, superseded by Rev. Proc. 99-28, supra. Early referral procedures are described at ¶ 9.03[1].

[386] Notice 2000-43, IR-2000-55.

[387] Notice 2001-67, 2001-49 IRB 1 (Nov. 14, 2001).

Fast Track is not available for (1) issues the Chief Counsel has designated for litigation; (2) an issue that is the subject of a request for competent authority assistance; (3) an issue for which the taxpayer has requested the simultaneous Appeal/Competent Authority procedure of Revenue Procedure 96-13;[388] (4) issues outside LMSB's jurisdiction; and (5) issues outside Appeals' settlement authority.

Under Fast Track Mediation, an Appeals officer serves as the mediator of a factual dispute between the Team and the taxpayer. As the mediator of the dispute, the Appeals officer assists the parties in arriving at a negotiated settlement. The Appeals officer uses the techniques used by mediators in other mediations. The mediator does not make a decision on the issues, as an arbitrator does. There is no trial, even the type of informal proceeding that takes place in an arbitration. Although there may be variations, the process starts with the parties' selecting the mediator (in Fast Track an Appeals Team Case Leader or an Appeals officer). The parties submit mediation memoranda explaining in summary form what the dispute is about and the party's position on the issues. The mediator communicates the procedures he will follow in the mediation. At the mediation, a decision-maker must be present so that the party may approve any agreement at the mediation itself. At the beginning of the mediation, each party will summarize its position, and the mediator will have an opportunity to ask questions and to restate a party's position. The parties then separate, and the mediator discusses the issues and potential settlements with each party, pointing out weaknesses and exploring possible settlement proposals until it becomes clear that the parties have reached or cannot reach agreement. A party may withdraw from the process at any time. If the parties have reached a basis for settlement, the parties reconvene and prepare a settlement agreement that ultimately will take the form of a closing agreement. Fast Track is protected by the confidentiality and privacy provisions of Section 6103. Note that the end result of mediation is an agreement between the parties. The final result—agreement versus award—is what distinguishes mediation from arbitration, and confirms that the objective of mediation is to assist negotiation and settlement; it is not a trial substitute or a binding decision.

Fast Track Settlement utilizes an Appeals Team Case Leader to facilitate communications between the taxpayer and LMSB to settle both legal as well as factual issues. At the settlement meeting, the parties will have not only the chance to present their positions, but the chance to hear the Appeals' Team Leader present the Leader's views about the respective parties' hazards of litigation if the parties do not settle the case. Fast Track Settlement is not mediation, and it is not arbitration. The procedure is not mediation because the Team Chief presents his views on the issues. Fast Track settlement also is not an arbitration because the Appeals Team Case Leader's views are not binding. If

---

[388] Rev. Proc. 96-13, 1996-1 CB 616, § 8.

the Fast Track Settlement process does not prove successful, the taxpayer still retains its rights to request Appeals consideration on any unagreed issues.

[h] Limited Issue Focused Examinations

A further procedural step in LMSB's use of a cooperative approach in auditing large corporate taxpayer returns is the Limited Issue Focused Examination (LIFE).[389] In this type of examination, one key device is a Memorandum of Understanding, which incorporates the terms and the procedural agreements of the Team Manager and the taxpayer. A prototype of a Memorandum of Understanding is available on the Service's Web site. Another procedure is not strictly speaking a device, but the Team Manager and Team members and the taxpayer meet to discuss the items and issues likely to be involved in the examination and agree upon a limit of materiality below which the Team will not examine, nor will the taxpayer present refund claims.

Under this type of examination, as the Memorandum of Understanding will incorporate, the taxpayer has the obligations to (1) deliver computations for agreed and rollover items; (2) file claims for refund by agreed-upon dates, along with supporting information, in amounts that do not exceed the materiality limit; (3) respond to IDRs by dates the Team and the taxpayer's personnel agree to; and (4) discuss issues as they arise. For its part, the Team must (1) not examine items or issues below the materiality limit; (2) participate in the planning process with the taxpayer's personnel; (3) act on information the taxpayer supplies in response to IDRs; and (4) use appropriate issue resolution techniques throughout the examination as issues arise.

Agreement on the terms and signing the Memorandum of Understanding are not mere formalities. Signatures are a prerequisite to the process. When the taxpayer signs the Memorandum, but fails to comply with one of its terms, the failure will result in the termination of the Memorandum of Understanding, and the LMSB Team may examine items and issues appropriate for examination and without regard to the materiality of the item or issue. If, on the other hand, the Team fails to comply with the Memorandum, although the taxpayer will not be bound by its terms, the taxpayer may enlist the assistance the assistance of the Team Manager to rectify the problem. It makes sense, of course, for both the taxpayer and the Team to give advance notice of an expected failure or inability to comply with a term of the Memorandum of Understanding.

The LIFE examination uses techniques that can be applied in other examinations: the conference between the examiner and the taxpayer, both parties' attempt to identify the items and issues to be examined (where the taxpayer contributes to the item and issue identification process), reducing the agree-

---

[389] Information Release 2002-133 (Dec. 4, 2002).

ment on the examination plan to writing, and, if possible, using dispute resolution procedures during the examination as issues arise.

[7] Qualified Amended Returns

Another procedure peculiar to CIC examinations is available when a CIC taxpayer intends to make a disclosure to avoid either a substantial understatement penalty or the negligence or intentional disregard and substantial understatement components of the accuracy-related penalty.[390] In general, at least if the position is not contrary to a regulation, a qualifying disclosure is made when a disclosure statement (Form 8275) is attached to an original return or a qualified amended return (that is, an amended return filed before the taxpayer is first contacted about an examination). For years ending after December 31, 1993, a qualifying disclosure is made if the CIC taxpayer provides the information that would have been reported on a properly completed Form 8275 or Form 8275-R[egulation] and otherwise satisfies the requirements of the accuracy-related penalty regulations. Special safe harbor rules apply if the taxpayer has been informed that it no longer meets the criteria of the CIC.

¶ 8.16 REOPENING PROCEDURES

Because the objective of the procedures giving settlement and other authority to case managers is to close cases and issues at the local level, reopening a case is restricted. Generally, the Service will not reopen a closed case unless there has been fraud, a prior closing involved a clearly defined substantial error based on an established Service position existing at the time of the previous examination, or some other serious administrative omission.[391] Moreover, if there is a reopening, it must be approved by the local office management, and, under Section 7605(b), a letter must be sent to the taxpayer. In the case of a CIC taxpayer, the inspection of account books for years not under examination is not an "examination" that is subject to the restrictions on reopening, nor will it require a reopening letter if the purpose is to verify the accuracy of adjustments to items (1) in connection with an accelerated issue resolution agreement request or (2) an executed AIR agreement. A prefiling conference in connection with an APA request also is not an examination, nor is the evaluation and processing of an APA request, an annual report, or a renewal request.

---

[390] Rev. Proc. 94-69, 1994-2 CB 804.

[391] Rev. Proc. 94-68, 1994-2 CB 803 (Oct. 31, 1994).

C   TEFRA PARTNERSHIPS AND S CORPORATIONS EXAMINATIONS

¶ 8.17   PARTNERSHIP EXAMINATION PROCEDURES: SECTIONS 6221–6234

Partnerships are tax-reporting, not taxpaying, entities. Individual partners report their distributive shares of income and deductions on their individual returns and pay whatever tax is due after giving effect to the partnership items. During the 1970s, partnerships were used as tax shelter vehicles, and separate proceedings of taxpayers who were also partners in partnerships caused the Service monumental administrative problems in locating individual partners who might reside in different and widely separated parts of the country, and in examining and processing each partner's tax return within the normal three-year statute of limitations on assessment. As a result, a number of partners escaped tax adjustment. For partnerships with large numbers of partners, the Service also had difficulty in coordinating examinations of the individual partners and ensuring that the partners were treated consistently. The Service attempted to act within the statute of limitations on assessment of partnership adjustments by accelerating the sending of notices of deficiency, but this led to the Tax Court's being beset by an avalanche of tax shelter cases instituted by individual partners.

To control these administrative, procedural, and judicial problems, in TEFRA, Congress added a statutory framework for the administrative and judicial review of partnership returns.[392] Sections 6221 through 6232 of the Code, known as the TEFRA partnership rules, were added so that the tax treatment of certain partnership items, such as income, loss deductions, and credits, would be determined in a single, unified partnership-level proceeding, rather than in separate proceedings with each partner.[393]

In substance, the TEFRA rules establish a unified administrative and judicial proceeding to determine the tax treatment of partnership items. The individual partners then apply that determination of partnership items in computing their individual tax liability for the year. Key to the operation of the TEFRA rules is a single general partner, called the tax matters partner (TMP), with

---

[392] TEFRA, Pub. L. No. 97-248, HR 4961, 97th Cong., 2d Sess. (Sept. 3, 1982). These procedures were effective for all partnership taxable years beginning after September 3, 1982, and could be elected by a partnership whose year began before September 3, 1982, but ended after that date. Id. § 402(a). The statutory scheme for the treatment of partnership items in amplified partnership proceedings grew out of studies made by the Treasury and the Service and by the Section of Taxation, ABA, "Section of Taxation Proposal as to Audit of Partnerships," 32 Tax Law. 551 (Spring 1979).

[393] HR Conf. Rep. No. 760, 97th Cong., 2d Sess. 600 (1982). See also Transpac Drilling Venture 1983-63 v. Crestwood Hosps., Inc., 16 F3d 383, 387 (Fed Cir. 1994).

whom the Service will communicate. The TMP is given special procedural rights in the administrative and judicial process in order to facilitate a unified proceeding in which all other partners may participate. These provisions and others permit all partners in the TEFRA partnership to challenge the determinations of the Service in a single proceeding.[394]

Although pre-TEFRA investment partnerships caused administrative and court administration problems, TEFRA's statutory solution creates more than a few problems of its own. General principles distilled from the rules reflected in these Code sections are relatively straightforward and sensible. The following principles are reflected in Sections 6221 through 6233:

1. Partnership items or issues are generally dealt with at the level of the partnership rather than the individual partners for all audit, appeals, and other administrative purposes, as well as in judicial proceedings (Section 6221).

2. In general, in the unified administrative or judicial proceeding, the partnership is represented by a general partner, the TMP (Sections 6223(g) and 6231(a)(7)).

3. Each partner receives a notice of important actions, such as a notice of the Service's intention to commence an examination of the partnership's return (Section 6223).

4. Partners have the right to participate in the administrative examination and appeal, as well as any judicial proceeding (Section 6224).

5. Partners have the right to a settlement consistent with any settlement agreement the Service reaches with another partner (Section 6224(c)).

6. After administrative proceedings are completed, individual partners have the right to judicial review of the partnership adjustment before assessment of tax (Sections 6225 and 6226).

Once particular problems take the practitioner beyond general principles, there seems to be a maze of specific rules, which despite their specificity, leave many questions unaddressed or provide inadequate guidance.

Regulations remedy these uncertainties in many cases, and it is necessary to consult the regulations, rather than to rely solely on the statutes themselves.[395] The role of regulations is provided for in the statutes, and so these

---

[394] Chimbo v. Comm'r, 177 F3d 119, 121 (2d Cir. 1999).

[395] On October 4, 2001, Treasury finalized regulations proposed on December 13, 1984 (49 Fed. Reg. 48,573); April 18, 1986 (51 Fed. Reg. 13,231); and January 26, 1999 (64 Fed. Reg. 3886); and issued as temporary regulations on December 13, 1984 (49 Fed. Reg. 48,536); March 5, 1987 (52 Fed. Reg. 6779); and January 26, 1999 (64 Fed. Reg. 3837). See TD 8695, 66 Fed. Reg. 50,541–50,564. To implement amendments to the TEFRA rules made by the 1997 and 1998 tax acts, those proposed regulations stated that the Service planned on finalizing all of the TEFRA regulations proposed on December 13, 1984, and April 18, 1986. At the same time they issued the proposed regulations, Trea-

regulations have been held to be legislative regulations.[396] As legislative regulations, the TEFRA partnership regulations will be applied unless they are found to be inconsistent with the statute, a result highly unlikely with a complicated statutory scheme, such as the TEFRA rules.

Also, the unified partnership proceeding rules create two proceedings: (1) the proceeding involving the partner's nonpartnership items and (2) the proceeding involving partnership items. If the taxpayer is a partner in more than one TEFRA partnership, a final determination of the taxpayer owes for a year cannot be made until all the TEFRA partnership proceedings have been concluded. As a result, in addition to the examination of the taxpayer's return, the taxpayer can have TEFRA proceedings pending in different levels within the Service with statutes of limitation on assessment expiring at different times as well as judicial proceedings in different courts with still other timetables.

¶ 8.18 CRITICAL TERMS FOR OPERATION OF THE TEFRA RULES

Rules for the treatment of partnership items introduce their own terminology. The more important terms are specially defined.

[1] The TEFRA Partnership and the Small Partnership Exception and Large Partnerships

[a] TEFRA Partnership

A "TEFRA partnership" is any partnership required to file a partnership tax return under the general return filing rules of Section 6031(a). An exception is provided to small partnerships.[397]

Determination that the arrangement is a partnership can control whether the taxpayer may pursue an individual proceeding. If an arrangement is deter-

---

sury and the Service issued temporary regulations containing substantially the same rules, and taxpayers have been operating under these rules. The final TEFRA regulations generally follow the proposed regulations interpreting the TEFRA procedures.

[396] Phillips v. Comm'r, 114 TC 115 (2000).

[397] IRC § 6231(a)(1)(A). TEFRA partnership rules apply to all partnership taxable years beginning after the date of enactment, September 3, 1982. TEFRA § 407(a)(1). Sparks v. Comm'r, 87 TC 1279 (1986); Countess Heart Watch Co. v. Comm'r, TC Memo. 1989-236, 57 TCM 403 (1989) (partnership that obtained minimum funding before TEFRA did not establish pre-TEFRA existence because partners could withdraw; final partnership administrative adjustment (FPAA) held valid).

mined to be a partnership, even if individuals (and putative partners) have received notices of deficiency making disallowances of claimed losses and have filed Tax Court petitions, the Tax Court does not have jurisdiction because the notices of deficiency adjust partnership items that are subject to review in a unified partnership proceeding.[398] The Taxpayer Relief Act of 1997 increases the possibility that a partnership may be subject to the unified partnership proceeding rules. For taxable years ending after August 5, 1997, if the Service reasonably determines on the basis of a partnership return that the unified partnership proceeding rules should apply, those rules apply, even if the Service is wrong.[399] On the other hand, if the Service erroneously decides that the unified partnership proceeding rules should not apply, those rules do not apply.[400] If a corporation return is filed, the partnership rules are applicable. If an entity files a partnership return, and is later determined not to be a partnership, the entity's status is determined under the partnership proceeding rules, and a final determination in the proceeding is binding.[401] For example, a publicly traded partnership is generally treated as a corporation.[402] However, an exception to corporate status is provided for partnerships when 90 percent or more of their gross income is passive income. This determination is made annually.[403] If a publicly traded partnership files a partnership return, it is subject to the partnership audit rules even if it is determined to be a corporation.

[b] Small Partnerships

Since a TEFRA partnership is effectively any partnership, the exception to the TEFRA rules for small partnerships is a notable one. The TEFRA partnership rules do not apply to a small partnership, which is defined as (1) a partnership having ten or fewer partners each of whom is a natural person (but not a nonresident alien) or an estate or (2) a partnership whose partners' shares of each partnership item are the same as their shares of every other item (thus eliminating a partnership with, for example, a special allocation to one partner

---

[398] Bergford v. Comm'r, 12 F3d 166 (9th Cir. 1993).

[399] IRC § 6231(g)(1), added by the Taxpayer Relief Act of 1997, § 1232(a), effective for partnership tax years ending after August 5, 1997.

[400] IRC § 6234(g)(2).

[401] IRC § 6233(a); Reg. § 301.6233-1(c). For example, a determination that the entity filing a partnership return is an association taxable as a corporation will serve as the basis for a computational adjustment reflecting the disallowance of a loss or credit claimed by a purported partner in the entity. Reg. § 301.6233-1(a).

[402] IRC § 7704. "Publicly traded partnership" is defined as any partnership whose interests (1) are traded on an established securities market or (2) are readily tradable on a secondary market. IRC § 7704(b).

[403] IRC § 7704(c). See also IRC § 7704(e) (inadvertent termination).

of a particular deduction).[404] This determination is made annually.[405] The fact that one of the partners in a small partnership is a C corporation, or that there has been a special allocation provision, will not preclude the partnership from meeting the small partnership exception to the unified partnership proceeding rules.[406]

[c] Large Partnerships

The Taxpayer Relief Act of 1997 created a new audit system for electing large partnerships because the TEFRA audit procedures, when applied to large partnerships, were more inefficient and complex than those for other large entities.[407] One reason for the adoption of these procedures was that the Service had to assess a deficiency arising from a partnership audit adjustment against a large number of partners, many of whom could not easily be located or were no longer partners. The procedures were complicated further by partners, acting individually, intervening in the proceedings.

The procedures start with the definition of a large partnership. For any partnership taxable year, the term "electing large partnership" means any partnership that during the preceding partnership taxable year had at least 100 partners and elects to be treated under the special rules for large partnerships.[408] Once made, the election to be treated as a large partnership continues until it is revoked with the consent of the Service or the number of partners

---

[404] IRC § 6231(a)(1)(B). For counting purposes, a husband and wife (and their estates) are treated as one partner. See Reg. § 301.6231(a)(1)-1(a). A partnership that has a nonresident alien partner cannot qualify for the small partnership exception. Id. Despite the provision for a special allocation in a partnership agreement, the determination of whether partners' shares are the same is made from the partnership return and the Form K-1. Harrell v. Comm'r, 91 TC 242 (1988) (no special allocation had been made for the year, and so partners were not entitled to FPAAs). See also Z-Tron Computer Program v. Comm'r, 91 TC 258 (1988).

[405] See Reg. § 301.6231(a)(1)-1(a)(3).

[406] IRC § 6231(a)(1)(B)(i), as amended by the Taxpayer Relief Act of 1997, § 1234(a).

[407] The Taxpayer Relief Act of 1997, § 1222, Subpart D, entitled "Treatment of Electing Large Partnerships." The reasons for the adoption of these procedures are described in the Revenue Reconciliation Act of 1997, HR Rep. No. 148, 105th Cong., 1st Sess. 580. The provisions for large partnerships also deal with substantive partnership issues not covered in this text, such as simplified flow-through rules, and reporting provisions, such as the due date for furnishing information to partners and magnetic media filing requirements. IRC §§ 772 (simplified flow-through), 6031(b), 6724(e) (furnishing information), 6011(e) (magnetic media).

[408] IRC § 775(a), incorporated by reference in IRC § 6255(a)(1), added by the Taxpayer Relief Act of 1997, § 1222(a), effective for partnership taxable years ending on or after December 31, 1997.

falls below 100.[409] Certain large partnerships are excluded from making an election: partnerships, substantially all of whose partners perform personal services, and commodity pools.[410] If, based on the return of the partnership, the Service treats the partnership as a large partnership, the Service's treatment is binding on the partnership and the partners.[411] Special rules apply to partnerships holding oil and gas properties.[412]

[2] Tax Matters Partner

The TMP of any partnership is the general partner designated as such to handle tax matters for the partnership.[413] Regulations permit the TEFRA partnership to designate a TMP for a specific taxable year, but only in a way described in the regulations.[414] A person may be designated as the TMP only if that person (1) was a general partner at some time during the taxable year of designation and (2) is a general partner when the designation is made.[415] The designation of a TMP for a year may be made on the partnership return for that year.[416] Partnership designation of a successor TMP is complete when the current TMP certifies that another partner has been selected as the TMP of the partnership for that taxable year.[417] After a partnership return for a year has been filed, general partners holding a majority interest in the partnership may designate a TMP.[418] Similarly, after the partnership return for the year has been filed, the partners holding a majority interest in the partnership may designate a TMP if all of the general partners are unable to perform the duties of a TMP because they are either deceased (or an entity has been liquidated or dis-

---

[409] IRC §§ 775(a)(1), 775(a)(2); see also IRC § 6255(a)(1).

[410] IRC §§ 775(b)(2), 775(c).

[411] IRC § 775(d).

[412] IRC § 776.

[413] IRC § 6231(a)(7).

[414] Reg. § 301.6231(a)(7)-1(a).

[415] Reg. § 301.6231(a)(7)-1(b)(1). For persons who may not be designated TMPs, see Reg. § 301.6231(a)(7)-1(b)(2). A person who is not a U.S. person may not be designated as a TMP, unless the non-U.S. person meets the general criteria for a person to be a TMP, and secures consent of the Commissioner.

[416] Reg. § 301.6231(a)(7)-1(c).

[417] Reg. § 301.6231(a)(7)-1(d). The certification is a written statement that (1) identifies the partnership and the designated TMP; (2) states the partnership tax year to which the designation relates; (3) declares that it is a designation of a new TMP for the year specified; and (4) is signed by partners who were partners at the close of the taxable year holding more than 50 percent of the aggregate interests in partnership profits held by all partners at the close of the taxable year.

[418] Reg. § 301.6231(a)(7)-1(e). A statement containing identifying information must be filed.

solved), the general partner is adjudicated incapable to handle their own affairs, the general partner's partnership items have been converted into nonpartnership items, or the general partner is no longer a general partner in the partnership.[419]

If the partnership designates a TMP, the document recording that designation may also include the designation of an alternate TMP.[420] The alternate TMP becomes the TMP when the TMP's designation terminates by death or incapacity.[421] The designation of a new TMP supersedes all prior designations.[422] A TMP may resign at any time by filing a statement to that effect with the service center in which the partnership return was filed.[423] Also, the partnership may revoke the TMP's designation at any time after the return for the year has been filed.[424] The partnership may also revoke the TMP's designation by filing a statement with the service center where the partnership return was filed.[425] The designation, resignation, or revocation of TMP status becomes effective when the statements required for those acts is filed with the service center in which the partnership's return is filed.[426] This effective-on-filing rule holds true unless the Service has sent a notice of the beginning of a partnership proceeding. In this circumstance, the Service is not required to accept the designation, resignation, or revocation until thirty days after the requisite statement has been filed.[427]

The TMP's designation can be terminated by such circumstances as death, bankruptcy, or resignation.[428] Apart from death or incapacity, the TMP's designation can terminate if one of the following criteria is met:

1. The entity, which is the TMP, is liquidated or dissolved.
2. The TMP becomes subject to Service enforcement action.
3. The TMP resigns.
4. A newly designated TMP replaces the former TMP.
5. The TMP's designation is revoked.

---

[419] Reg. § 301.6231(a)(7)-1(f)(1). Again, a statement, containing specific information must be filed with the service center where the original partnership return was filed. Reg. § 301.6231(a)(7)-1(f)(2).

[420] Reg. § 301.6231(a)(7)-1(g).

[421] Reg. §§ 301.6231(a)(7)-1(g), 301.6231(a)(7)-1(*l*).

[422] Reg. § 301.6231(a)(7)-1(h).

[423] Reg. § 301.6231(a)(7)-1(i).

[424] Reg. § 301.6231-1(a)(7)(j). A statement with specific information about the partnership and the revocation must be filed with the service center where the return for the year has been filed.

[425] Reg. § 301.6231(a)(7)-1(j).

[426] Reg. § 301.6231(a)(7)-1(k)(1).

[427] Reg. § 301.6231(a)(7)-1(k)(2).

[428] Reg. § 301.6231(a)(7)-1 (*l*)(1).

When a TMP's status is terminated, the validity of any action taken by the partner as TMP before the termination is not affected; e.g., even if the TMP's status is terminated, the TMP's execution of a consent to the extension of the statute of limitations on assessment remains valid.[429] Any subsequent action by the TMP, whose designation has been terminated, takes in his capacity as such is invalid and is not binding on either the partners or the Service.[430]

Despite these clear and obvious rules, termination of the TMP's designation as such can adversely affect the other partners. Suppose a TMP files a petition in the Tax Court, and the limited partners relying on the TMP, do not file separate petitions. If the TMP's status is terminated, the Tax Court has said that the action as commenced by the putative TMP is a nullity,[431] and, presumably, with no qualifying petition having been filed, there would be no restriction on assessment of tax attributable to the computational adjustment.[432] Does a court have jurisdiction to appoint a TMP? The answer is uncertain. When a petition has been filed in the Tax Court, the Tax Court will appoint a TMP, if necessary.[433] In *Computer Programs Lambda, Ltd. v. Commissioner*,[434] the Tax Court took a liberal view of its power to appoint a TMP. The case involved two TMPs, one who had formerly been a general partner and a TMP, who had extended the statute of limitations on assessment, and the other who was the TMP the Service selected who did not extend the statute of limitations on assessment. The Tax Court ruled that even after he was no longer a partner, the general partner who had formerly been the TMP could still be the TMP, as long as he was able to protect the interests of the partnership. Since it found that the former partner was able to protect the interests of the partnership, the Tax Court held that he possessed the power to extend the statute of limitations

---

[429] Reg. § 301.6231(a)(7)-1(*l*)(2).

[430] Barbados #7 Ltd. v. Comm'r, 92 TC 804 (1989) (TMP's status terminated on bankruptcy, and so extension of the assessment period was invalid). See also Computer Programs Lambda, Ltd. v. Comm'r, 89 TC 198 (1989) (TMP's bankruptcy precluded TMP from proceeding as such in partnership proceeding).

[431] See Computer Programs Lambda, Ltd. v. Comm'r, 89 TC 198 (1989) (TMP's bankruptcy precluded TMP from proceeding as such in partnership proceeding); Sierra Design & Research Ltd. Partnership v. Comm'r, 58 TCM 164 (1989). However, even if a TMP has effectively resigned and the partnership is in bankruptcy, a notice partner may institute a partnership proceeding in the Tax Court. 1983 W. Oil & Gas Co. v. Comm'r, 95 TC 51 (1990). The real parties in interest in a partnership proceeding are the partners. As a result, the bankruptcy of the partnership and the automatic stay pending a contrary order of the bankruptcy court do not preclude the Service from sending a valid FPAA to the partners, nor do they preclude the Tax Court from having jurisdiction over a properly commercial proceeding. Chef's Choice Produce, Ltd. v. Comm'r, 95 TC 388 (1990).

[432] NCF Partners v. Comm'r, 89 TC 741, 745–746 (1987).

[433] Tax Ct. R. Prac. & P. 250; Computer Programs Lambda, Ltd. v. Comm'r, 89 TC 198 (1989); Monetary II Ltd. Partnership, 75 AFTR2d 95-777 (9th Cir. 1995).

[434] Computer Programs Lambda, Ltd. v. Comm'r, 89 TC 198 (1989).

on assessment for the partnership.[435] On appeal, however, the circuit court concluded that the Service could select the partner who continued to be a partner during the year in issue to be the TMP for the partnership. On the selection of the successor TMP issue, the circuit court also refused to accept as controlling, the fact that the partner and TMP the Service had selected did not sign the extension of the statute of limitations on assessment on behalf of the partnership. Although the court described the Service's conduct as demonstrating "confusion and perhaps even bad faith," it nevertheless allowed the Service effectively to pick and choose the person it considered to be the TMP, despite the fact that the choice resulted in a situation the partners objected to.

Suppose the partners select a limited partner to be the TMP for the "limited purpose only" of being a TMP to execute an extension of the assessment period or otherwise act for the partnership. Limited partners who try to act as limited purpose TMPs have been held not to be general partners eligible to be TMPs.[436] Moreover, unlike the Tax Court, the Federal Circuit also refused to designate the limited partners as TMPs. The Federal Circuit held that the Court of Federal Claims "does not have the inherent power" to appoint anyone as TMP where the cases are not properly before the court because the petitions were not properly filed. Unless the Service appoints a replacement TMP before the case is filed or a limited partner agrees to become a general partner, it is difficult to see how a partnership without a qualifying TMP can file a petition in the Court of Federal Claims under this approach.

[a] Selection of TMP Where There Is No Designation

The TMP where the partnership has not designated a TMP for the year, or the partnership has designated a TMP, but the TMP's designation has terminated, and the partnership has not designated a new TMP.[437] In this circumstance, the TMP is the general partner with the largest partnership profits interest at the close of the taxable year determined based on the year-end Schedule K-1 for the year (or if there is more than one of these general partners, the one first in alphabetical order).[438]

The Service may select a new TMP (1) if the partnership has not designated a TMP for the year and (2) it is impractical to apply the largest-profits-interest rule.[439] Impracticability occurs when (1) the general partner with the

---

[435] Monetary II Ltd. Partnership, 75 AFTR2d 95-777 (9th Cir. 1995).

[436] Transpac Drilling Venture v. United States, 26 Cl. Ct. 1245, 92-2 USTC ¶ 50,486 (1992), aff'd, 16 F3d 383 (Fed. Cir. 1994) (petition for readjustment filed by limited partners who became general partners for the limited purpose of acting as TMPs).

[437] Reg. § 301.6231(a)(7)-1(m)(1).

[438] Reg. § 301.6231(a)(7)-1(m)(2).

[439] IRC § 6231(a)(7); Reg. § 301.6231(a)(7)-1(n).

largest profits interest is not apparent from the Schedule K-1 or other information; (2) each general partner is deemed to have no profits interest in the partnership because of death, incompetency, liquidation, and conversion of partnership items to nonpartnership items; or (3) the general partner with the largest profits interest is disqualified.[440]

The Service may choose the TMP in three situations. When the Service decides that the statutory largest-profits-interest rule is not apparent under the three conditions of impracticability, the Service may choose any general partner.[441] When each general partner is considered to have no profits interest in the partnership, the Service may choose any partner, general or limited, in accordance with the Service's criteria.[442] When the general partner with the largest profits interest is disqualified, the Service may appoint any other person who was a general partner at any time during the taxable year.[443] If all general partners during the taxable are unable to serve because the designation of the general partner has been terminated on account of the partner's being treated as having no profits interest in the partnership for the taxable year,[444] or the general partner has been disqualified,[445] the Service will select a general or limited partner as the TMP by applying the criteria for selecting a partner as a TMP.[446] The Service's criteria for selecting a partner as a TMP includes such factors as the partner's being a partner in the partnership at the close of the taxable year, as well as more specific criteria indicating the suitability of the partner to be designated as the TMP.[447] If the Service designates a new TMP, the Service will notify both the partner selected and the partnership.[448]

Before the Service selects a TMP, however, the partnership has one last chance to designate a TMP if (1) the partnership acts within thirty days from the date of its notice and (2) the general partners with a majority interest agree.[449] If the partnership does not designate a TMP within the thirty-day period, but does make the designation after the expiration of the period, the designation will become effective, but the service is not required to give effect to the designation until thirty days after the designation statement has been filed.[450]

---

[440] Reg. § 301.6231(a)(7)-1(o).

[441] Reg. § 301.6231(a)(7)-1(p)(1).

[442] Reg. § 301.6231(a)(7)-1(p)(2).

[443] Reg. § 301.6231(a)(7)-1(p)(3)(i).

[444] See Reg. § 301.6231(a)(7)-1(m)(3).

[445] See Reg. § 301.6231(a)(7)-1(o)(3).

[446] Reg. § 301.6231(a)(7)-1(p)(3)(ii).

[447] Reg. § 301.6231(a)(7)-1(q)(2).

[448] Reg. § 301.6231(a)(7)-1(r)(1).

[449] Reg. § 301.6231(a)(7)-1(r)(2)(i)-(ii).

[450] Reg. § 301.6231(a)(7)-1(r)(2)(iii).

The Service is not required to appoint a TMP, at least where there is no prejudice to the other partners because they receive adequate notice.[451] But when no general partner has been appointed, general partners have equal interests; and when one of them files a petition, the petition is not considered as having been filed by the TMP unless the filing general partner precedes the others in the alphabet.[452]

[b] Disqualification of the TMP

A general partner with the largest partnership interest in profits of the partnership may be disqualified from acting as a TMP. The general partner satisfying the largest-profits-interest rule will be disqualified if the general partner (1) has been notified of suspension from practice before the Service; (2) is incarcerated; (3) is residing outside the United States, its possessions, or territories; or (4) cannot be located or cannot perform the functions of a TMP for any reason other than refusal to cooperate with the Service.

When a TMP is disqualified, the effect of acts of the disqualified TMP would seem to be the same as termination of the designation of a TMP; that is, the acts of the TMP before the TMP is disqualified are valid.[453] Accordingly, the TMP's execution of an extension of the statute of limitations on assessment of partnership items before the disqualification would be valid. Limited partners have contended that when the Service notifies their partnership's TMP that the TMP is under criminal investigation, the TMP's status as such terminates,[454] the TMP's partnership items are treated as nonpartnership items,[455] and any extension of the statute of limitations on the assessment of partnership items agreed to by the TMP is ineffective. In *Transpac Drilling Venture 1982-12*, the TMPs were under criminal investigation, but ultimately cooperated with the Service in criminal prosecutions involving the partnerships. The Second Circuit held that the TMPs did not have the authority to bind the partnerships to extensions of the assessment period because of their violation of fiduciary duties to the limited partners and other conflicts of interest.[456] The circuit court also held that the court was not bound by the Service's decision not to remove the TMPs.

On the other hand, the Tax Court has held that the TEFRA partnership regulations are legislative regulations. According to the Tax Court, as legisla-

---

[451] Seneca, Ltd. v. Comm'r, 92 TC 363 (1989).

[452] Amesbury Apartments Ltd. v. Comm'r, 95 TC 227 (1990) (Bowen Equity filed, but Bowen Ballard was TMP).

[453] See Reg. § 301.6231(a)(7)-1(l)(2).

[454] Reg. § 301.6231(a)(7)-1 (*l*)(iv).

[455] Reg. § 301.6231(c)-5.

[456] Transpac Drilling Venture 1982-12 v. Comm'r, 147 F3d 221 (2d Cir. 1998).

tive regulations, the TEFRA regulations are immune from most claims that they are invalid; therefore, the TEFRA regulations dealing with criminal investigations and the conversion of partnership items to nonpartnership items (that require the Service to send written notices of both the investigation and the treatment of partnership items as nonpartnership items) were binding and valid.[457] The result is that if the Service does not send the written notices, the TMP's status remains undisturbed and the extension is valid.

[3] Types of Partners Other Than the TMP: Notice and Pass-Through Partners

Notice partners are those entitled to notice of partnership administrative proceedings. Special rules apply to partners having a less-than-one-percent interest in a partnership of more than 100 partners.[458] These partners are still notice partners for definitional purposes, but under the special rules, notice of administrative proceedings need not be given to them.[459] However, partners with less-than-one-percent profit interests may combine to form a group having in the aggregate 5 percent or more of the profits of the partnership and be entitled to notice as a 5 percent group.[460]

A pass-through partner is a person through whom other persons hold an interest in the partnership, such as a partnership, estate, trust, S corporation, or nominee.[461] The persons who hold interests in the partnership through pass-through partners are called indirect partners.[462]

---

[457] Phillips v. Comm'r, 114 TC 115 (2000).

[458] The proper interests of these partners are generally determined at the end of the partnership's taxable year. If the partner's interest is liquidated or sold, the proper interests are determined immediately before the liquidation or sale. IRC § 6231(d)(1).

[459] IRC § 6323(b)(1).

[460] IRC §§ 6223(b)(2), 6231(a)(11). The request to be treated as a 5 percent group should be filed with the service center with which the partnership return is filed unless it is known that a notice of the beginning of administrative proceeding has been issued, in which case it should be filed with the Service office that mailed the notice. A copy of the request must be provided to the TMP within thirty days of the filing. See Reg. § 301.6223(b)-1.

[461] IRC § 6231(a)(9). The temporary regulations require that a pass-through partner forward a notice or any other information regarding a partnership proceeding from the Service, the TMP, or another pass-through partner to indirect partners within thirty days of receipt. See Reg. § 301.6223(h)-1.

[462] IRC § 6231(a)(10).

[4] Types of Adjustments: Partnership Items, Computational Adjustments, and Affected Items

[a] Partnership Items

A partnership item to which the TEFRA rules apply is any item required to be taken into account for the partnership's taxable year that regulations provide is more appropriately determined at the partnership level than at the partner level.[463] Items that are not classified as "partnership items" are nonpartnership items and are resolved under the general procedures applicable to audits, deficiencies, and refunds, not under the partnership rules.[464]

Partnership items. Regulations list the following items as partnership items, because they are considered to be more appropriately determined at the partnership level:[465]

1. Return items such as the partnership aggregate and each partner's share of each of the following: (a) items of income, gain, loss, deduction, or credit of the partnership; (b) expenditures by the partnership not deductible in computing its taxable income (e.g., charitable contributions); (c) items of the partnership that may be tax preference items under Section 57(a) for any partner; (d) tax-exempt income of the partnership; (e) partnership liabilities; and (f) amounts needed for the computation of investment tax credits, credit recapture, depletion, or the at-risk amounts with partnership activities;

2. Guaranteed payments;[466]

3. Optional adjustments to the basis of partnership property pursuant to an election under Section 754 (including necessary preliminary determinations, such as the determination of a transferee partner's basis in a partnership interest);[467] and

4. Items relating to an amount, the character of an amount, or the percentage interest of a partner in the partnership that are necessary for purposes of the partnership books and records or for purposes of furnishing information to a partner relating to (a) contributions to the partnership; (b) distributions from the partnership; (c) transactions to

---

[463] IRC § 6231(a)(3).

[464] IRC §§ 6231(a)(4), 6231(e). Partnership items must be ignored in deficiency proceedings that relate exclusively to nonpartnership items. Thus, when partnership items are considered by the Service in making proposed adjustments to nonpartnership items, they are ignored in determining whether a deficiency exists that is attributable to nonpartnership items. Maxwell v. Comm'r, 87 TC 783 (1986); Munro v. Comm'r, 92 TC 71 (1989).

[465] Reg. § 301.6231(a)(3)-1.

[466] Reg. § 301.6231(a)(3)-1(a)(2).

[467] Reg. § 301.6231-1(a)(3).

which Section 707(a) applies (including the application of the relating partnership transaction rule of Section 707(b)); and (d) the application of the collapsible partnership rules of Section 751 to a partner who receives a distribution with respect to a transfer of a partnership interest.[468]

Penalties. Because conduct relevant to the determination of whether penalties are due can occur at the partnership level, the definition of a partnership item includes the applicability of any penalty, addition to the tax, or additional amount "which relates to an adjustment to a partnership item."[469] Regulations state that assessment of any penalty must be made based on partnership-level determinations, which include all the legal and factual determinations that underlie the determination of the penalty other than partner-level defenses.[470] Partner-level defenses (i.e., defenses that are personal to the partner and the partner's return) may not be asserted in the partnership-level proceeding.[471] Partner-level defenses (e.g., meeting a required threshold amount of underpayment and the existence of reasonable cause under Section 6664—but not making a qualified disclosure) must be asserted in a separate refund action the partner brings after assessment and payment of the penalty. While a partnership-level determination on a partnership item, including the penalty related to the adjustment, is conclusive if a partner files a claim for refund on the ground that the Service has made an erroneous computational adjustment, the partner may nevertheless raise any partnership-level defenses to the penalty that may apply.[472]

Other items. A partnership item does not include, at least directly, the basis of a partner in his partnership interest because a partnership item is an item required to be taken into account for the partnership's taxable year.[473] A statute of limitations defense concerns a partnership item and must be raised in the partnership proceeding. If they failed to raise the statute of limitations defense in the partnership-level proceeding, therefore, partners contesting computational adjustments flowing from partnership items are barred from raise a stat-

---

[468] Reg. § 301.6231(a)(3)-1(a)(4). Section 707(a) deals with a partner's transaction with his partnership in a capacity other than as a partner.

[469] IRC § 6221, as amended by the Taxpayer Relief Act of 1997, § 1238(a), applicable to partnership taxable years ending after the effective date of the act, August 5, 1997. Conforming amendments were made to other TEFRA provisions.

[470] Reg. § 301.6221-1(c).

[471] Reg. § 301.6221-1(d).

[472] IRC § 6230(c)(4), as amended by the Taxpayer Relief Act of 1997 § 1238(b)(6).

[473] See Dial USA, Inc. v. Comm'r, 95 TC 1, 4 (1995) (an S corporation case reaching this result on the shareholder's basis in his stock). But see University Heights at Hamilton Corp. v. Comm'r, 97 TC 278 (1991) (Subchapter S items affecting the shareholder's basis were reviewed in the S corporation proceeding, although the corporation's income or loss was not affected).

ute of limitations defense in their partner-level proceeding.[474] Tax-motivated interest is not a partnership item because partnership items are limited to items required to be taken into account under any provision of subtitle A of the Code, and Section 6621(c) is in subtitle F.[475] However, the Section 6621(c) determination might be affected by a partnership-level determination, such as whether the partnership entered into a sham transaction, in which case there may be an affected item.[476] Similarly, the Tax Court has held that equitable recoupment is not a partnership item, since any claim of recoupment will be made by a partner after an assessment at the partner level of the computational adjustment that flows from the partnership-level determination on the partnership item.[477]

For a particular partner, a partnership item can become a nonpartnership item under certain circumstances. Special rules apply to determine when a partnership item becomes a nonpartnership item.[478]

Special enforcement areas. In the event of special enforcement situations, such as jeopardy in collection, criminal investigation, indirect methods of proving income, foreign partnerships, and other areas that the Service considers to present enforcement problems, the Service may treat items as nonpartnership items.[479]

Regulations under Section 6231(c) designate claims for refund based on the losses, deductions, and credits attributable to abusive tax shelters as a special enforcement area.[480] Where it is highly likely that false or fraudulent representations were made concerning the tax benefits of the partnership or that there was a gross valuation overstatement, the Service assesses (notwithstanding Section 6225) the tax attributable to the claimed losses or other representations before there is a final partnership-level determination. The Service then mails a notice of the assessment to the partner filing the refund claim. This notice informs the partner of his limited right to elect to treat partnership items as nonpartnership items. A partner may make this election only by filing a statement with the service center that mailed the notice (in the form required) more than one year after the date on which the partnership return giving rise to the loss or other item was filed, and before the date the Service mails the TMP

---

[474] Chimblo v. Comm'r, 177 F3d 119 (2d Cir. 1999).

[475] See Affiliated Equip. Leasing II v. Comm'r, 97 TC 575, 577–578 (1991).

[476] See Smith v. Comm'r, TC Memo. 1990-510, 60 TCM 886 (1990); see also FSA 1999-50008 (Sept. 13, 1999).

[477] Crop Assocs.—1986 v. Comm'r, 113 TC 198 (1999) (applying Reg. § 301.6231(a)(3); the court recognized that to establish equitable recoupment at the partnership level, certain partnership items would have to be determined in the partnership proceeding).

[478] IRC § 6231(b).

[479] IRC § 6231(c). Special rules may be developed in regulations.

[480] Reg. §§ 301.6231(c)-1, 301.6231(c)-2. See also Rev. Rul. 84-2, 1984-1 CB 92.

the notice of final partnership administrative adjustment (FPAA) for the loss year.

Also, regulations have special procedures regarding termination and jeopardy assessments, criminal investigations, indirect methods of proof of income, bankruptcy and receivership, and prompt assessment, all of which are considered problem areas.[481]

[b] Computational Adjustments and Affected Items

Computational adjustments. A computational adjustment is a change in a partner's tax liability properly reflecting the treatment of a partnership item.[482] Regulations say that when a change resulting from a computational adjustment cannot be made without making partner-level determinations, deficiency procedures must be followed in making the changes required at the partner level. However, changes that do not require partner-level determinations are computational adjustments that may be directly assessed.[483] According to the Federal Circuit, the fact "[t]hat the IRS has to ask the taxpayer for a pertinent figure or for the source of a figure does not make the adjustment non-computational."[484] When a computational adjustment of a partnership item is made, it can affect the amount of other items on an individual partner's return.[485]

Affected items. Affected items include items unrelated to items on a partnership return that vary if there is a change in a partner's adjusted gross income as the result of a computational adjustment. For example, the medical expense deduction is an affected item because the deduction varies if there is a change in the partner's adjusted gross income.[486] Similarly, the basis of a partner in the partner's partnership interest is an affected item to the extent that it is not a partnership item.[487] The application of the at-risk limitation of Section 465 to a partner for a partnership loss is an affected item to the extent that it is not a partnership item.[488] The application of the passive loss rules of Section 469 for losses incurred by the partnership is an affected item to the extent that

---

[481] Reg. §§ 301.6231(c)-4 – 301.6231(c)-8.

[482] IRC § 6231(a)(6); Reg. § 301.6231(a)(6)-1.

[483] For a discussion of settlements and computational adjustments, see supra ¶ 8.09[3][c].

[484] Olson v. United States, 172 F3d 1311, 1318 (Fed. Cir. 1999).

[485] IRC § 6231(a)(5). In other words, the term "affected item" for purposes of Section 6231(a)(5) is defined as "any item to the extent that such item is affected by a partnership item." White v. Comm'r, 95 TC 209, 211 (1990).

[486] Reg. § 301.6231(a)(5)-1(a).

[487] Reg. § 301.6231(a)(5)-1(b).

[488] Reg. § 301.6231(a)(5)-1(c).

it is not a partnership item.[489] Also, the term "affected item" includes any penalty, addition to tax, or additional amount ("penalty") provided in subchapter A of Chapter 68 if a penalty which does not contain a floor (or threshold amount of underpayment necessary before the imposition of the penalty) is imposed on a partner as the result of an adjustment of a partnership item.[490] If the penalty has a floor, and the partner would have been subject to the penalty exceeded the floor without the adjustment to a partnership item, the affected item includes only the portion of the penalty computed with reference to the partnership item.[491] If the penalty has a floor, but the floor would not be exceeded before the adjustment to the partnership item, the affected item includes the penalty computed by reference to the entire underpayment or understatement.[492]

The Tax Court has said that there are two types of affected items: (1) those that are affected items only because of a computational adjustment that cannot be made until the partnership level proceeding is completed, such as a medical expense deduction, and (2) those that require factual determinations to be made at the partner level,[493] such as a fault-based negligence penalty. Each of the two types of affected items have different procedural requirements.[494] The affected item resulting from a computational adjustment at the partner level requires no factual determination at the individual partner level. This computational adjustment is required to change the tax liability of a partner to reflect the treatment of a partnership item at the partnership level. Procedurally, when this type of computational adjustment is involved, the Service does not send the taxpayer partners a statutory notice of deficiency; the TEFRA time requirements apply.

The other type of affected item is a substantive computational adjustment and requires factual determinations specific to the individual partner when an adjustment is made at the partner level. On these substantive affected items, the Service is required to follow the non-TEFRA deficiency procedures, and the TEFRA time limitations do not apply.[495] When there is a substantive affected item, therefore, the non-TEFRA refund procedures also apply.[496]

---

[489] Reg. § 301.6231(a)(5)-1(d).

[490] Reg. §§ 301.6231(a)(5)-1(e)(1), 301.6231(a)(5)-1(e)(2).

[491] Reg. § 301.6231(a)(5)-1(e)(3)(i).

[492] Reg. § 301.6231(a)(5)-1(e)(3)(ii).

[493] NCF Energy Partners v. Comm'r, 89 TC 741, 745–746 (1987).

[494] Maxwell v. Comm'r, 87 TC 783 (1986); Woody v. Comm'r, 95 TC 193, 201–202 (1990).

[495] Brookstone Corp. v. United States, 74 AFTR2d 94-6025 (SD Tex. 1994), aff'd per curiam without published opinion, 58 F3d 637 (5th Cir. 1995).

[496] Brookstone Corp. v. United States, 74 AFTR2d 94-6025 (SD Tex. 1994), aff'd per curiam without published opinion, 58 F3d 637 (5th Cir. 1995) (partner's claim for refund was timely filed under non-TEFRA time limits even though it was filed more than six

In summary, partnership item adjustments can be made to an individual partner's return solely through computational adjustments.[497] Affected-item adjustments can be made either through computational adjustments or deficiency proceedings, depending on the nature of the particular affected items.[498] When no partner-level determinations of fact relate to the affected item that must be adjusted, the tax resulting from the adjustment of the affected item must be assessed by a computational adjustment.[499] When fact issues must be decided at the partner level, then the Service makes the adjustment by issuing a notice of deficiency to the partner pursuant to Section 6230(a)(2)(A)(i).[500]

Carrybacks and carryforwards. A partner's carryback or carryforward of a partnership loss or excess credit has been found to be an affected item.[501] When a partnership reported its losses as arising from a trade or business activity, other than rental activity, and the Service did not challenge that characterization in a partnership proceeding, the characterization of the losses as active or passive was held not to be a partnership item, but the Section 469 passive activity loss issue was held to be an affected item requiring a partner-level, not partnership-level, determination. In *Estate of Robert W. Quick v. Commissioner*, the Tax Court ruled that "[d]etermining whether or not petitioners materially participated in such activity for purposes of section 469 has no effect on any item that would affect all of the partners' respective returns, nor does it have any effect on any item on the Partnership's return or on the Partnership's books and records."[502] The Tax Court also concluded that the Service's action in sending a notice of computational adjustment and then an affected-item notice of deficiency was proper because the notice of computational adjustment was for partnership computational adjustments and the notice of deficiency was for affected-item adjustments. The Service sent the taxpayers notices of computational adjustment, rather than notices of deficiency, on the completion of the partnership-level proceeding to reflect the computational adjustments that were reflected on the partnership-level adjustments for those

---

months after the partner received a notice of computational adjustment showing changes resulting from a settlement agreement).

[497] IRC § 6230(a).

[498] Brookes v. Comm'r, 108 TC 1, 5–6 (1997).

[499] IRC §§ 6230(a)(1), 6231(a)(6).

[500] NCF Energy Partners v. Comm'r, 89 TC 741, 745–746 (1987).

[501] See Maxwell v. Comm'r, 87 TC 783, 790 (1986); Woody v. Comm'r, 95 TC 193 (1990). But see Madden v. IRS, 77 AFTR2d 96-1982 (Bankr. DNJ 1996) (net operating loss carryback on the bankrupt taxpayer's 1987 return was held not to be an affected item because no partnership items were reported on the return; as a result, the statute of limitations on assessment barred adjustments to the amount of the net operating loss for partnership adjustments made to years 1984–1986, to which the net operating loss had been carried back).

[502] Estate of Robert W. Quick v. Comm'r, 110 TC 172 (1998).

years. After the taxpayers filed claims for refund based on the partnership-level determination, the Service sent the taxpayers affected-item notices of deficiency raising the passive activity loss issue. In a related decision, the Tax Court held in the partner-level case on the passive loss issue that, under Section 6512(b), it had jurisdiction to find a tax overpayment only as part of a decision on the merits of the Service's affected-item notice of deficiency.[503]

Treatment of spouses. Regulations deal with two situations: where a couple owns a partnership interest as joint property and where a married individual owns an interest in a partnership. In general, spouses holding a joint interest in a partnership are both treated as partners in a partnership.[504] When one spouse owns an interest in a partnership as separate property, and the other spouse signs a joint return with the spouse who is a partner in the partnership, the nonpartner spouse is not treated as a partner once the husband's partnership items convert to nonpartnership items and is not bound by the partnership proceeding.[505] In *Calloway v. Commissioner*, the Second Circuit held that the wife was not bound by the outcome of a unified partnership proceeding where her husband's partnership items converted into nonpartnership items during the proceeding. Since the wife was treated as a partner only because she filed a joint return with her husband, and her tax liability was determined in part by taking into account partnership items, once the husband's partnership items converted to nonpartnership items, there was no longer any reason for her to bound by the partnership proceeding.[506]

Innocent spouse adjustments. When the Service sends a notice of computational adjustment to the spouse of a partner, and the spouse claims he or she is an innocent spouse within the meaning of Section 6015, and so not liable for any tax attributable to the adjustment, the innocent spouse may file with the Service a request for the abatement of the assessment.[507] The request for abatement must be filed within sixty days after the date the Service mailed the notice of computational adjustment to the innocent spouse.[508] Once the Service receives the request for abatement from the innocent spouse, it is required to

---

[503] Esther P. Quick v. Comm'r, 110 TC 440 (1998).

[504] Reg. § 301.6231(a)(12)-1.

[505] Reg. § 301.6231(a)(12)-1.

[506] Calloway v. Comm'r, 231 F3d 106 (2d Cir. 2000). The circuit court distinguished Dubin v. Comm'r, 99 TC 325 (1992), where the Tax Court held that the wife was bound by the outcome of a unified partnership proceeding despite the fact that the husband's partnership items converted into partnership items before the conclusion of the partnership proceeding, in a case where the husband and wife owned the partnership interest jointly.

[507] IRC § 6230(a)(3), added by the Taxpayer Relief Act of 1997, §§ 1237(a) (effective as if included in the 1982 TEFRA amendments), 402 (generally effective for partnership tax years beginning after September 3, 1982).

[508] IRC § 6230(a)(3)(A).

abate the assessment.[509] Any reassessment of the tax abated is subject to normal deficiency procedures.[510] If the request for abatement is made shortly before the expiration of the statute of limitations on assessment, the assessment period is extended so that the Service has sixty days to send a notice of deficiency.[511] If the innocent spouse files a petition in the Tax Court following the request for abatement and notice of deficiency, the Tax Court will have jurisdiction to redetermine only the innocent spouse issue, not the treatment of any partnership item.[512] The innocent spouse may also file a claim for refund on the ground that the Service has failed to relieve the spouse of liability, pursuant to Section 6015, for a tax attributable to a partnership item.[513] The innocent spouse must file this refund claim within six months after the date the Service mailed the spouse the notice of computational adjustment; and, if the Service denies the claim, the spouse may institute a suit for refund to challenge the Service's action on the innocent spouse claim, but not on the treatment of the partnership item.[514]

¶ 8.19 THE ROLE OF THE TMP IN TEFRA PARTNERSHIP ADMINISTRATIVE PROCEEDINGS

[1] Preparing the TEFRA Partnership's Return: The Rule of Consistency

The TMP has the responsibility for the preparation and filing of the partnership return, for the sending of information returns, Forms K-1 to individual partners in the partnership. The positions taken by the TMP on the partnership are important and may be critical to the individual partners because a general rule of consistency applies to partners in the filing of their own returns. Under the rule of consistency, a partner must treat all partnership items on his return in a manner consistent with the treatment of those items on the partnership return as reflected in the Form K-1.[515] If there is consistent treatment of the part-

---

[509] IRC § 6230(a)(3)(A).

[510] IRC § 6230(a)(3)(A).

[511] IRC § 6230(a)(3)(A).

[512] IRC § 6230(a)(3)(B).

[513] IRC § 6230(c)(5)(A), added by the Taxpayer Relief Act of 1997, § 1237(b), effective as if included in the 1982 TEFRA amendments.

[514] IRC §§ 6230(c)(5)(B)–6230(c)(5)(D).

[515] IRC § 6222(a). Section 6031 requires the partnership to furnish every person who was a partner during the year with a copy of the information shown on the partnership return.

nership item on both the partnership's tax returns and the partner's tax returns, no assessment or collection of a deficiency attributable to the partnership item may be made until partnership-level administrative and judicial proceedings are completed.[516] A partner who wishes to report a partnership item in a manner inconsistent with the position taken on the partnership return, however, must notify the Service of the inconsistency.[517] Where it receives a notice of inconsistency, the Service may do nothing, audit the partnership return, or notify the partner that it is treating the item as a nonpartnership item with the result that normal deficiency procedures apply.[518]

When a partner fails to comply with the rule of consistency without giving notice to the Service, the Service is not prohibited from assessing and collecting a deficiency attributable to any partnership item resulting from action taken to make the partner's treatment of the items consistent with treatment of the items on the partnership return.[519] In short, the deficiency may be immediately assessed because the normal deficiency procedures do not apply to the assessment or collection of any computational adjustment.[520] Additionally, the partner may be liable for a negligence penalty for intentional disregard of rules and regulations.[521]

[2] Role of the TMP in Audits and Appeals

The TMP's duties in a partnership proceeding are significant and can determinative of the outcome of the proceeding. The duties of the TMP are as follows:

1. The TMP who receives a notice of the beginning of a partnership proceeding must forward a copy of the notice to partners who are not

---

[516] IRC § 6225(a). If the Service assesses and seeks to collect before the partnership-level proceedings are concluded, it may be enjoined, despite the Anti-Injunction Act. IRC § 6225(b).

[517] IRC § 6222(b)(1). When the partnership has not filed a return, the partner appears to be able to file a return without regard to the consistency requirement, but the statutory language leaves some doubt whether some notice still must be given to the Service (e.g., that the partnership has not yet filed a return for purposes of the consistency rule).

[518] IRC § 6231(b)(2).

[519] IRC § 6222(c).

[520] IRC § 6230(a). However, changes in a partner's tax liability with respect to affected items that require partner-level determinations (e.g., a partner's at-risk amount, which depends on the source from which the partner obtained the funds that the partners contributed to the partnership) are not included in a computations adjustment. See Reg. § 301.6231(a)(6)-1.

[521] IRC § 6222(d), referring to IRC § 6653(a).

entitled to receive the notice from the Service within seventy-five days after the TMP receives the notice.[522]

2. The TMP must, within sixty days after the date of mailing of a notice of final partnership adjustment, forward a copy of the notice to partners who are not notice partners.[523]

3. The TMP must keep each partner informed of a closing conference with the examining agent.[524]

4. The TMP must furnish information to all partners about proposed adjustments, rights of appeal, and requirements for filing a protest;[525]

5. The TMP has authority to bind partners who are not notice partners to a settlement agreement unless such partners file statements with the Service revoking this authority.[526]

6. During the first ninety days following the issuance of an FPAA, the TMP has sole authority to file a petition for readjustment of partnership items in the U.S. Tax Court, a federal district court, or the U.S. Court of Federal Claims. If such an action is filed, all partners are treated as parties to the action and are allowed to participate in the action.[527]

7. The TMP may appeal the court's decision.[528]

8. The TMP may file a request for an administrative adjustment of partnership items serving as a claim for refund of the partnership and, upon disallowance, may file a petition for an adjustment in Tax Court, district court, or the Court of Federal Claims.[529]

9. The TMP is required to provide the Service with information on the identity of partners on request.[530]

---

[522] Reg. § 301.6223(g)-1(a).

[523] IRC § 6223(g); Reg. § 301.6233(g)-1(b). See Computer Programs Lambda, Ltd. v. Comm'r, 89 TC 198 (1987) (TMP's bankruptcy precluded TMP from proceeding as such in partnership proceeding).

[524] Reg. § 301.6223(g)-1.

[525] IRC § 6229(b)(1)(B).

[526] IRC § 6224(c)(3).

[527] IRC § 6226(c); HR Rep. No. 762, 97th Cong. 603 (1982). Other actions for the taxable year are barred.

[528] IRC § 6226(g).

[529] IRC §§ 6227(b), 6229(a).

[530] IRC § 6230(e).

[3] The Role of the TMP in Extensions of the Assessment Period

The period of limitations for making assessments of tax against a partner is three years after the later of (1) the date on which the partnership return for the year in question is filed or (2) the due date of the partnership return (determined without regard to extensions).[531] The statute of limitations provided in Section 6229 seems to be "the" statute of limitations applicable in TEFRA proceedings. It tracks the limitations rules of Section 6501, and is self-contained. But the Tax Court concluded that Section 6229 did not preclude the statute rules in Section 6501 from applying in TEFRA proceedings. In *Rhone-Poulenc Surfactants v. Commissioner*,[532] the Service argued that the six-year statute of limitations of Section 6501(e) applied, and so the Service's determination that a property transfer was not a tax-free partnership contribution, but a taxable transfer, was timely. The determination resulted in an omission in excess of 25 percent of the gross income of the putative partners so that the Service's notice of deficiency was timely. A Tax Court majority held that the three-year statute of limitations of Section 6229(a) was only an alternative and minimum statute, and the general statute of limitations on assessment of Section 6501 controls.[533] As a result, Section 6229 did not preclude a longer period of limitations than the three-year period of Section 6229(a). The Tax Court reasoned that Section 6501(a), which provides limitations periods for the assessment of "tax imposed by this title," provided no exception for deficiencies attributable to partnership items. Applying both Sections 6229 and 6501, the Tax Court also concluded that when the Service issued an FPAA before the expiration of the six-year period applicable to substantial omissions, the limitations period that was suspended was the six-year period of limitations of Section 6501, not the three-year period of Section 6229(a). The decision in *Rhone Poulenc* means that when there is an agreement extending the limitations period, the period is extended not only for the minimum three-year period of Section 6229(a), but for the limitations periods of Section 6501 as well.

A consent to extend the limitations period for the partnership is made on Form 872-P (Consent to Extend the Time to Assess Tax Attributable to Items of a Partnership). (See Form 8.8.) Rules providing special statutes of limitations apply in the case of a false partnership return,[534] a substantial omission of

---

[531] IRC § 6229(a). The Service has taken the position that the limitation period provided by Section 6229 is a *minimum* period for assessing tax attributable to partnership items, and that the general limitation on assessment provided by Section 6501 controls, unless extended by Section 6229. See FSA 1999-22032 (Mar. 2, 1999).

[532] Rhone-Poulenc Surfactants & Specialties, LP v. Comm'r, 114 TC 533 (2000).

[533] Rhone-Poulenc Surfactants & Specialties, LP v. Comm'r, 114 TC 533 (2000).

[534] IRC § 6229(c)(1). There is an unlimited statute for the partners who participated in the preparation of and signed the return, but for other partners the statute of limitations is extended from three to six years.

income,[535] no return,[536] or one prepared by the Service under Section 6020(b).[537]

The TEFRA rules give the TMP the authority to execute the consent to the extension of the statute of limitations on assessment. If the TMP's status has been terminated, the extension is invalid.[538] Regulations provide procedures by which any person, with the approval of all the general partners, may be authorized to extend the period of limitations for making assessments for all the partners.[539] Formal authorization by a partnership for the holder of a power of attorney from one of the general partners is not necessary for the holder of the power to extend the statute of limitations for the partners.[540] A partner may extend the statute for himself or the TMP may extend the statute for all partners by agreement with the Service.[541] If a TMP signs an agreement to extend the statute of limitations on assessment, but the TMP was a debtor in a bankruptcy proceeding at the time the TMP signs the agreement, the TMP's bankruptcy

---

[535] IRC § 6229(c)(2). The statute is six years if more than 25 percent of the partnership's gross income is omitted.

[536] IRC § 6229(c)(3).

[537] IRC § 6229(c)(4).

[538] Barbados #7 v. Comm'r, 92 TC 804 (1989).

[539] Reg. § 301.6229(b)-1.

[540] Amesbury Apartments Ltd. v. Comm'r, 95 TC 227 (1990) (before Temp. Reg. § 301.6229(b)-1T, accountant had power signed by general partner and officer of other general partner; held, partnership failed to prove accountant lacked authority); Transpac Drilling Venture 1983-2 v. United States, 32 Fed. Cl. 810, 75 AFTR2d 95-1202 (Fed. Cir. 1995), aff'd, 83 F3d 1410 (Fed. Cir. 1996) (the partnership had two general partners, Adams and a corporation, Churchill Oil & Gas Corp.; the corporation lost its charter before Adams as president authorized an attorney to sign a Form 872-O, and Adams personally signed two later extensions; held, the extensions were valid because Adams retained the power to extend the assessment period because he was a TMP even when the corporation was disqualified, and he intended to extend the assessment period). In the case, the argument was also made that Adams's cooperation with the government invalidated the extensions applying agency principles. The court refused to apply any agency limitation on Adams's authority to execute the extensions, but held that the six-year fraud statute of limitations applied (Section 6229(c)(1)), and the assessment was therefore timely.

On appeal, the Federal Circuit did not decide the validity of the consent issue. Instead, it concluded that the six-year statute of limitations of Section 6229(c)(1) applied. The partnership returns clearly contained false or fraudulent items. Transpac constituted a partnership, and Adams acted as a partner in signing the false partnership returns. Transpac was a partnership because it represented that it was a partnership, and that Adams was a partner, in various filings. The definitions of "partnership" and "partner" were broad enough to include a partnership organized for illegal purposes and a partner who did not contribute property or services to the partnership. Furthermore, Adams signed the returns in issue with the intent to evade tax.

[541] IRC § 6229(b).

raises questions about the validity of the extension.[542] Uncertainty about this is-sue was removed by the Taxpayer Relief Act of 1997, which added a provi-sion that, if the agreement is signed by a person who would be the TMP, but for the fact that, at the time the agreement is executed, the TMP is a debtor in a bankruptcy proceeding under the Bankruptcy Code, the agreement is binding on all partners in the partnership, unless the Service has received notice of the TMP's bankruptcy proceeding in the manner provided in regulations.[543]

It has been held that a general partner does not have the authority to sign an extension of the assessment period without written authorization from the partnership. Strictly applying the written authorization requirement of Section 6229(b)(1)(B), the Fifth Circuit found that the only written authorization, the partnership agreement, did not contain a broad grant of authority to any indi-vidual general partner that could permit the general partner to execute the ex-tension.[544] In a case appealable to the Ninth Circuit, however, the Tax Court refused to follow the Fifth Circuit's decision in *Medical & Business Facilities*, and held that a partner was estopped to deny the authority of a partner who was neither the TMP nor explicitly authorized by all the other partners to exe-cute a consent binding on the partnership.[545]

Similarly, in *Transpac Drilling Venture 1982-12 v. Commissioner*,[546] part-ners contended that extensions executed by TMPs were invalid so that the stat-ute of limitations had expired when the FPAAs had been issued. The Second Circuit held that TMPs did not have authority to bind partnerships to exten-sions of the statute of limitations when the TMPs were involved in criminal proceedings involving the partnership. The Second Circuit's reasoning was as follows: (1) the TMPs were analogous to the representatives of a class in a

---

[542] Reg. §§ 301.6231(a)(7)-1(*l*), 301.6231(a)(7)-1(*l*)(4), and 301.6231(c)-7(a) provide that on the filing of a petition naming a partner as a debtor in a bankruptcy proceeding, that partner's partnership items are converted into nonpartnership items, and if the debtor was a TMP, that status terminates. The Service believed that these rules were necessary because of the automatic stay provision in the Bankruptcy Code, 11 USC § 362(a)(8).

[543] IRC § 6229(b)(2), added by the Taxpayer Relief Act of 1997 § 1233(c), effective for agreements entered into after the date of enactment, August 5, 1997.

[544] Medical & Bus. Facilities, Ltd. v. Comm'r, 76 AFTR2d 95-5897 (5th Cir. 1995) (refusing to imply authority from Louisiana law or general agency principles because Sec-tion 6229(b)(1)(B) requires the TMP to be authorized in writing to execute the consent); compare cases where the partnership agreement was found to contain a broad grant of au-thority to the general partner, e.g., Cambridge Research v. Comm'r, 97 TC 287 (1991); Georgetown Petroleum—Edith Forrest v. Comm'r, TC Memo. 1994-13, 67 TCM 1952 (1994); Iowa Investors Baker v. Comm'r, TC Memo. 1992-490, 64 TCM 611 (1992).

[545] Cascade Partnership v. Comm'r, TC Memo. 1996-299, 71 TCM 3226 (1996) (manager, who had management authority under the partnership agreement, requested a partner to sign as TMP).

[546] Transpac Drilling Venture 1982-12 v. Comm'r, 82 AFTR2d 98-5078 (2d Cir. 1998).

class action suit and as such had a fiduciary duty to the limited partners, which they breached; (2) the conflict of interest among TMPs prevented them from acting as representatives of the partnership and was not harmless under the circumstances; and (3) the Service's administrative decision not to replace the TMPs under the special enforcement regulations (Temporary Regulation Section 301.6231(c)-5T) was not binding on the court.

Other extensions of the period of limitations on assessment apply to unidentified partners[547] and items converted from partnership to nonpartnership items.[548] Where a partnership item has converted to a nonpartnership item, as, for example, the result of a settlement with the Service, the individual partner, not the TMP, must agree to an extension of the assessment period with respect to the converted partnership item. If a partner enters into a settlement agreement with the Service on some of the partnership items for a taxable year, but other partnership items remain in dispute, the statute of limitations on the assessment of tax on agreed items continues to run as though the partial agreement had not been entered into.[549]

Not only may the statute of limitations on assessment be extended by agreement, the running of the assessment period may also be suspended. The assessment period is suspended during the period when a proceeding for readjustment of an FPAA may be brought, and if such a proceeding is brought, until a decision in that proceeding has become final.[550] The Taxpayer Relief Act of 1997 clarified the period of suspension by striking the original language of Section 6229(d)(1), which provided for suspension for the period during which an action may be brought under Section 6226 "(and, if an action with respect to such administrative adjustment is brought during such period until the decision of the court becomes final)."[551] As amended, the period of suspension is for the period during which an action may be brought under Section 6226 "(and, if a petition is filed under section 6226 with respect to such administrative adjustment, until the decision of the court becomes final)."

In general, the period of assessment and collection of tax against a taxpayer is suspended during bankruptcy under the automatic stay, which the Bankruptcy Code applies to all creditors. The Service is prohibited from as-

---

[547] IRC § 6229(e).

[548] IRC § 6229(f)(1), as amended and renumbered by the Taxpayer Relief Act of 1997, §§ 1235(a)(1)–1235(a)(3), for settlements entered into after the effective date of the act, August 5, 1997.

[549] IRC § 6229(f)(2), added by the Taxpayer Relief Act of 1997 §§ 1235(a)(1)–1235(a)(3), applicable to settlements entered into after the effective date of the act, August 5, 1997.

[550] IRC § 6229(d).

[551] Taxpayer Relief Act of 1997, § 1233(a). The language in Section 6229(a)(1) is applicable to partnership taxable years for which the Service was not barred from assessing tax on or before August 5, 1997, the effective date of the act.

sessing and collecting a tax liability from a debtor during the bankruptcy proceeding, unless the bankruptcy court orders otherwise.[552] Similarly, in a TEFRA partnership proceeding, if a petition is filed naming a partner in a proceeding under the Bankruptcy Code, the period for making an assessment of tax attributable to a partnership item against that partner is suspended for the period during which the Service is prohibited by the automatic stay in the bankruptcy proceeding from assessing tax against the partner, and for sixty days thereafter.[553] Where the partnership is in bankruptcy, however, the automatic stay does not prevent the Service from commencing a partnership-level TEFRA proceeding because "[u]ltimately, . . . it is the tax liability of the individual partners which is affected by the redetermination of the adjustments as to the return of the partnership."[554]

---

[552] See IRC § 6503(h).

[553] IRC § 6229(h), added by the Taxpayer Relief Act of 1997, § 1233(b) for taxable years in which the period for assessing tax has not expired by the effective date of the act, August 5, 1997.

[554] 1983 W. Reserve Oil & Gas Co. v. Comm'r, 95 TC 51, 57 (1990). See also Hoyt & Sons Ranch Properties, Ltd. v. Comm'r, TC Memo. 1998-77, 75 TCM 1850 (1998).

FORM 8.8
CONSENT TO EXTEND THE TIME TO ASSESS TAX ATTRIBUTABLE TO ITEMS OF A PARTNERSHIP

Form **872-P** (Rev November 1992)	Department of the Treasury—Internal Revenue Service **Consent to Extend the Time to Assess Tax Attributable to Items of a Partnership**	In reply refer to:
		Taxpayer Identification Number

ABC Partners _____, a partnership of
(Name)

2 James Street, New York, New York, 00000 _____ and the
(Number, street, city or town, state, and ZIP code)

District Director of Internal Revenue or the Regional Director of Appeals consent and agree as follows:

The amount(s) of any Federal income tax with respect to all partners attributable to any partnership item(s) for the above named partnership for the period(s) ended _____ December 31, 1984 may be assessed at any time on or before December 31, 1988

If a notice of Final Partnership Administrative Adjustment is mailed to the Tax Matters Partner, the time for assessing the tax for the period(s) stated in the notice of Final Partnership Administrative Adjustment shall be suspended for the period during which an action may be brought under section 6226 of the Internal Revenue Code (and, if an action with respect to such administrative adjustment is brought during such period, until the decision of the court in such action becomes final) and for 1 year thereafter.

Signature instructions are on the back of this form.
Making this consent will not deprive the partnership or partners of any appeal rights to which they would otherwise be entitled.

Partnership
Name _____ ABC Partners _____

Under penalties of perjury, I declare that I am not currently in bankruptcy nor have I previously been named as a debtor in a bankruptcy proceeding in which the United States could have filed a claim for income tax due with respect to any partnership taxable year covered by this consent.

Tax Matters Partner Sign Here ____ /s/ John Jones _____	11/15/87
	(Date signed)
Authorized Person Sign Here _____	
(You must also attach written authorization as stated in the instructions on the back of this form.)	*(Date signed)*

District Director of Internal Revenue	; Regional Director of Appeals
By *(Signature and Title)*	Date Signed

Cat. No. 16910J   Form **872-P** (Rev. 11-92)
1/20/93

Instructions for Signing

1. The consent generally applies to partnership returns filed for partnership tax years beginning after September 3, 1982.

2. The consent may be signed for the partnership in the appropriate space by either:

   a. The tax matters partners for the partnership for the year(s) covered by the consent, or

   b. Any other person authorized by the partnership in writing to sign the consent (see item 5 below).

3. If the Tax Matters Partner is not an individual and the consent is signed by a person acting in a representative capacity for the tax matters partner, for example, the trustee of a trust, the declaration above the signature line for the tax matters partner refers to the bankruptcy of the tax matters partner, not the person who actually signed the consent.

4. If the tax matters partner has filed a joint return with his or her spouse for the taxable year(s) covered by the consent and the consent is signed by the tax matters partner, the declaration above the signature line for the tax matter(s) partner refers to the bankruptcy of either spouse, not just to the person who actually signed the consent.

5. If the consent is signed by any person other than the tax matter(s) partner, a copy of the written authorization from the partnership must be attached to the consent. The information that must be included in the authorization is described in Temporary Regulation 301.6229(b)-1 and is listed below. The written authorization must:

   a. Provide that it is an authorization for a person other than the tax matters partner to extend the assessment period with respect to all partners.

   b. Identify the partnership and the person being authorized by name, address, and taxpayer identification number.

   c. Specify the partnership tax year or years for which the authorization is effective, and

   d. Include the signatures of all persons who were general partners at any time during the year or years for which the authorization is effective.

1/20/93

[4] Notice of the Beginning of Administrative Proceedings

The Service must mail to the partnership, each partner entitled to notice, and a 5 percent group a notice of the beginning of an administrative proceeding (NBAP) at the partnership level concerning a partnership item, and an FPAA.[555] The TMP is also responsible for keeping the partners informed about matters arising during the course of the examination,[556] and pass-through partners are required to forward notices.[557] Thus, the TMP has seventy-five days from the date the Service mails the NBAP to forward a copy of this notice to partners who are not entitled to notice from the Service. In most cases, the TMP has the responsibility for providing all the partners with information about the following additional matters arising during the course of the examination:

- A closing conference with the examining agent
- Proposed adjustments, rights of appeal, and requirements for the filing of a protest
- The time and place of any Appeals conference
- Acceptance by the Service of any settlement offer
- Consent to the extension of the period of limitations with respect to all partners
- Filing of a request for administrative adjustment on behalf of the partnership
- Filing by the TMP or any other partner of any petition for judicial review under Section 6226 or Section 6228(a)
- Filing of any appeal with respect to any judicial determination provided for in Section 6226 or Section 6228(a)
- A final judicial redetermination, within thirty days of taking the action or receiving information with respect to that matter.[558]

Under these notice procedures, the Service's primary obligation is to notify the TMP and notice partners. It is the TMP's obligation to notify other

---

[555] IRC § 6223(a). The Service is required to send a notice only if it has received sufficient information from the partnership return, the TMP, or any other person to enable it to determine whether the partner is entitled to notice. IRC §§ 6223(a), 6223(c), 6230(e). Regulations provide procedures for a partner to supply additional information to the Service. Reg. § 301.6223(c)-1. Section 3201(d) requires the Service, "wherever practicable," to send notices relating to a joint return under Section 6013 separately to each spouse. The Service has concluded that this provision "may require the Service to send separate TEFRA Notices to nonpartner spouses where a TEFRA partner files a joint income tax return with his/her spouse," but that the determination of whether it is "practicable" to do so "is a business decision to be made by the Service." SCA 1999-19033 (Mar. 18, 1999).

[556] IRC § 6223(g); Reg. §§ 301.6223(a)-1, 301.6223(g)-1.

[557] IRC § 6223(b).

[558] Reg. § 301.6223(g)-1.

partners whom the Service is not required to notify, such as partners with a less-than-one-percent interest in the partnership. Moreover, pass-through partners are supposed to forward notices to indirect partners. In other words, those partners not entitled to notice are deemed to have constructive notice of the proceeding if the TMP and the pass-through partner receive actual notice. Even if the less-than-one-percent partner or indirect partner with an interest in a pass-through entity does not receive actual notice under the statutory scheme and may receive no notice at all if the TMP or pass-through entity fails to provide notice, courts have held that the procedures satisfy the due process clause.[559] According to these courts, the due process clause does not rigidly require actual notice, and the procedures themselves are reasonably calculated, under the circumstances, to apprise interested direct and indirect partners of the pendency of the proceeding and affords them the opportunity to present their objections.

Apart from the notice rules, other partners are protected by their right to participate in the proceeding,[560] although they may waive that right.[561] Examination of the partnership return and administrative hearings proceed in the normal manner. However, the TMP deals with Service representatives in the administrative proceeding concerning the partnership.

The Service must mail a notice of the beginning of the partnership proceeding at least 120 days before the day on which notice of the FPAA is mailed to the TMP.[562] Although the Service has issued an NBAP, it is not required to issue an FPAA.[563] The Service's right not to issue an FPAA would seem to be noncontroversial, but if the Service does not issue an FPAA after it begins a partnership audit, the partners will be unable to request favorable ad-

---

[559] Kaplan v. United States, 81 AFTR2d 98-389 (7th Cir. 1998) (TMP failed to notify a less-than-one-percent partner); Walthall v. United States, 80 AFTR2d 97-7959 (9th Cir. 1997) (divided panel) (TMP of pass-through entity, a partnership, failed to notify an indirect partner).

[560] IRC § 6224(a). The regulation suggests that special arrangement be made with the TMP to obtain information as to the time and place of any discussion, while Section 6223 and the related regulations do not require a partner's receiving notice of the discussion. Reg. § 301.6224(a)-1.

[561] IRC § 6224(b). The waiver must be made by written statement. Reg. § 301.6224(b)-1. The procedures followed by Appeals are discussed at ¶ 9.05[4].

[562] IRC § 6223(d)(1). However, if an FPAA is mailed less than 120 days after the notice of the commencement of examination and Section 6223(d) is violated by the Service, the FPAA is still valid and suspends the statutory assessment period. Wind Energy Tech. Assocs. III v. Comm'r, 94 TC 787 (1990). Accord White & Case v. United States, 22 Cl. Ct. 734, 91-1 USTC ¶ 50,173 (1991) (election-out option of Section 6223(e) provides exclusive remedy for partners when the Service fails to comply with notice requirements of Section 6223).

[563] See Atlantic Richfield Co. v. Department of Treasury, 79 AFTR2d 97-585 (DDC 1996).

justments unless they have filed a timely administrative adjustment request, called an AAR, requesting a change in the treatment of partnership items.[564]

Since this notice is the functional equivalent of the notice of deficiency, the FPAA also suspends the running of the statutory period of assessment.[565] In the first instance, the Service is required to send partners a notice of the beginning of an examination and an FPAA. If the Service fails to send the partner a timely notice, the partner may elect to have either the FPAA, a court decision, a consistent settlement agreement, or conversion to nonpartnership items apply to the partner's partnership items.[566] The partner's option depends on whether the partnership proceeding is still pending at the time the notice is finally mailed. If the partnership proceeding is pending, the partner becomes a party to the proceeding unless the partner elects to accept the terms of a settlement agreement previously entered into by another partner or to have his partnership items for the taxable year treated as nonpartnership items.[567] On the other hand, if the partnership proceeding is concluded, the partner may elect to have his return changed by one of the following: (1) the adjustment resulting from the administrative proceeding; (2) the decision of judicial proceeding; or (3) a settlement agreement.[568] There is no effect on the proceedings if the TMP, pass-through partner, or member of a notice group fails to notify partners.[569]

---

[564] Reg. § 301.6223(a)-2 states that the Service does not have to issue an FPAA even if it issues and does not withdraw a NBAP.

[565] IRC § 6229(d). The statute is suspended until the decision of the court in the action becomes final and for one year thereafter. See O'Neill v. United States, 44 F3d 803 (9th Cir. 1995) (statute held suspended even when the TMP had filed for bankruptcy before the notice was sent, but filed a timely petition); see also Miller v. Comm'r, 104 TC 378 (1995) (partnership filed petition for readjustment in the district court and dismissed the case without prejudice; the Service then sent an FPAA; held, the period of limitations was suspended for the period during which the action was pending in the district court and for one year thereafter).

[566] Reg. § 301.6223(e)-2(c)(2). The notice must be mailed within forty-five days after the mailing of the FPAA.

[567] IRC § 6223(e)(3). If the partner elects to treat partnership items as nonpartnership items, his return is subject to the normal deficiency procedures, but the statute of limitations on assessment of tax attributable to the item is extended for an additional year. IRC § 6229(f). Under the temporary regulations, the partner must make his election within forty-five days after the date on which the notice regarding the proceeding is mailed by the Service. Reg. § 301.6223(e)-2(c)(2).

[568] IRC § 6223(e). If the partner does not make the election, the partnership items are treated as nonpartnership items. Id. Regulations would treat them as nonpartnership items from the day the Service mails the partner notice of the proceeding. Reg. § 301.6223(e)-2(2).

[569] IRC § 6230(f).

[5] TEFRA Partnership Settlements and Consistent Treatment of Partners

A settlement agreement between the Service and partners concerning a partnership item is binding on the partner-parties to the agreement.[570] Under the unified proceeding rules, when the Service and the partner enter into a settlement agreement about partnership items, the partnership items become nonpartnership items as of the date of the agreement.[571] Partnership items are converted to nonpartnership items by a settlement agreement.[572] Curiously, Section 6224(c)(1) uses the term "settlement agreement," but does not define it, nor does Section 6231(b)(1)(C), which provides that one of the circumstances leading to the conversion of a partnership item to a nonpartnership item is when the Service enters into a settlement agreement with the partner about the partnership item. When a partnership item becomes a nonpartnership item because of the settlement agreement, the Service must make an assessment within one year after the date on which the partnership item becomes a nonpartnership item. Some partners may be bound by settlement agreements they have not entered into themselves. An indirect partner is bound by an agreement entered into by a pass-through partner,[573] and a partner who is not a notice or notice-group member is bound by an agreement entered into by the TMP.[574]

Consistent settlements. Once the Service enters a settlement agreement with one partner, the other partners are entitled to enter into settlement agreements on terms consistent with the first agreement.[575] A partner is entitled to consistent settlement, however, only if (1) the items were partnership items for the partner entering into the original settlement immediately before the original settlement and (2) the items are partnership items for the partner requesting the consistent settlement at the time the partner files the request. Also, settlements must be self-contained. The settlement in regard to the partnership item may not be based on a concession with respect to a nonpartnership item, and settlement must be comprehensive; that is, a settlement may not be limited to se-

---

[570] IRC §§ 6224(c)(1), 6229(f).

[571] IRC § 6231(b)(1)(C).

[572] Brookstone Corp. v. United States, 94-2 USTC ¶ 50,474 (SD Tex. 1994) (cases gathered).

[573] IRC § 6224(c)(1). See also Reg. § 301.6224(c)-1.

[574] IRC § 6224(c)(3)(A). The affected partner may avoid being bound by filing a statement with the Service that the TMP does not have authority to bind him. IRC § 6224(c)(3)(B). The temporary regulations require that this statement be filed with the Service at least thirty days before the day on which the TMP enters into the settlement agreement with the Service. Temp. Reg. § 301.6224(c)-1T.

[575] IRC § 6224(c)(2).

lected items.[576] When there is a partial settlement agreement, the period for assessing any tax attributable to the settled items is determined as if the partial settlement agreement had not been entered into, so that the last partnership item to be resolved for the partnership's taxable year controls.[577] The result is that the one-year period for assessing partnership items applicable to settlement agreements under Section 6231(b)(1)(C) does not apply to partial settlement agreements under Section 6229(f)(2) (although partial agreements have the same binding effect that comprehensive settlement agreements have and convert the settled partnership items to nonpartnership items).[578] A partial agreement has no effect on the partnership items that are not settled; the unsettled partnership items are still subject to the unified partnership audit rules.

This rule of consistent settlement applies only to the terms of settlement agreements entered into before notice of an FPAA has been sent to the TMP, and only if the partner requests the consistent settlement within 150 days after the FPAA has been mailed. Thus, a partner must choose between settlement and litigation because the 150-day period is the one within which the partner must institute a proceeding in court for a readjustment of the partnership item.[579] However, the temporary regulations provide that the request can be made up to (1) the 150th day after the date the FPAA is mailed to the TMP or (2) the 60th day after the date the settlement was entered into, whichever is later.[580]

It is important to note that a partner is entitled to a consistent settlement only if that partner requests a consistent settlement. In *Vulcan Oil Technology Partners v. Commissioner*,[581] some partners attempted to secure consistent treatment under out-of-pocket-cash-settlement offers the Service made that called for acceptance within certain periods. These offers were made before the Service issued FPAAs, and before a favorable decision in a case controlling the treatment of the partners in the shelter. After the decision, however, the Service made no-cash offers to remaining partners, and the complaining partners accepted them. The partners argued that the Service had perpetrated a fraud on the court when it secured their acceptances to the no-cash offers, and that the Service had a duty of consistency to make available to them the most favorable settlement terms that were ever offered to any of the investor partners. The Tax Court found that there was no credible testimony that the TMPs in the partnerships had failed to notify the partners of the offers, and so the

---

[576] Reg. § 301.6224(c)-3(b)(1) (consistent settlement agreements must be identical to the original agreement, whether the original agreement is comprehensive or partial.)

[577] IRC § 6229(f)(2); Reg. § 301.6224(c)-3(b)(2).

[578] IRC § 6229(f)(2); Reg. § 301.6224(c)-3(b)(2).

[579] See IRC § 6226(b).

[580] Temp. Reg. § 301.6224(c)-3T.

[581] Vulcan Oil Tech. Partners v. Comm'r, 110 TC 153 (1998).

limited partners were held to have failed to notify the Service of the acceptance of the offers within their deadlines. Moreover, the partners could not complain that the Service had failed to follow its Manual because, citing *Caceres*,[582] the Manual was not binding on the Service. Finally, the court noted that even if the TMP had failed to give the partners notice of the prior offers, Section 6230(f) provides that the failure of the TMP to give partners notice does not affect the applicability of any proceeding. Also, some of the moving partners attempted to obtain cash settlements that had been offered to partners in other partnerships in the same tax shelter project, but the court held that the partners were not entitled to a settlement with the same terms as one made to the partners in a separate and distinct partnership. On appeal, the Tenth Circuit affirmed the Tax Court decision, saying, "TEFRA states that 'the Secretary shall offer' to any other partner *who so requests* settlement terms for the partnership taxable year which are consistent with those contained in such settlement agreement.'"[583] Partners are presumed to have knowledge of offers because TEFRA requires that the TMP (not the Service) notify partners of a Service offer. The circuit court said that the partners had presented no evidence that the Service had improperly failed to notify them through the TMPs of the terms of the earlier offer.

If a TMP notifies the limited partners of Service adjustments, but the limited partners fail to notify the Service under Section 6224 that the TMP has no authority to bind them, the limited partners will not be able to object to a later assessment based on the settlement.[584]

Settlement agreements. Form 870-P is the settlement agreement used in TEFRA partnership cases. Form 870-P has been treated as if it were a kind of closing agreement, although treating Form 870-P in the same way as Form 870-AD might be more accurate.[585] When a settlement with the Service is conditioned on the execution of Service forms, the agreement with the Service is the primary agreement, not the Service form. The agreement with the Service controls the resolution of whether a "settlement agreement" was actually made.[586]

---

[582] United States v. Caceres, 440 US 741 (1979).

[583] Tucek v. Comm'r, 84 AFTR2d 99-6841 (10th Cir. 1999).

[584] See Clark v. United States, 883 F. Supp. 29 (EDNC 1994) (TMP settled, and the Service notified limited partners but limited partners did not send notice required by Section 6224(c)(3)(B)).

[585] See Thomas v. United States, 75 AFTR2d 95-525 (5th Cir. 1995).

[586] See Estate of Ray v. Comm'r, TC Memo. 1995-561 (1995), aff'd, 112 F3d 194 (5th Cir. 1997); Brookstone Corp. v. United States, 74 AFTR2d 94-6025 (SD Tex. 1994), aff'd per curiam without published opinion, 58 F3d 637 (5th Cir. 1995); see also Cinema '85 v. Comm'r, TC Memo. 1998-213, 75 TCM 2477 (1998) (court concluded that as a factual matter a settlement agreement that contemplated the execution of Service Form 870-P or a closing agreement, but with the partner having failed to sign the form, did not

A closing agreement, Form 906, has been used as a settlement agreement to settle partnership cases. In addition, the Tax Court has held that a Form 870-P qualifies as a settlement agreement under Section 6224(c).[587] In *Crnkovich v. United States*,[588] the partner had signed a closing agreement, Form 906, but the Service argued that the closing agreement did not constitute a settlement agreement because it was a "piggyback" agreement that depended on the result in another case for its implementation; at the time, the other case was undecided. The Court of Federal Claims held that the closing agreement was a settlement agreement, and under the agreement "all that remained was the mechanical exercise of applying that agreement according to its terms"; that is, when the decision in the controlling case became final. Under the terms of the Form 906, the Service had two years from the date of the decision in the controlling case to make assessments, and so the court concluded that the two-year period of the agreement applied, not the one-year period in Section 6229(f).[589]

In one case, the taxpayer and the Service agreed to the treatment of certain partnership items and reflected their agreement in a Form 870-P. However, the TMP had also executed an extension of the statute of limitations on assessment of partnership items. The Service conceded that the extension the TMP executed was invalid because the TMP had filed for bankruptcy protection. In view of the disqualification of the TMP to execute the extension, the question became whether the Form 870-P, which converted the partnership items to individual or nonpartnership items, prevented the taxpayer partner from instituting a refund suit for the amount paid to the Service under the agreement. The circuit court said the taxpayer could recover because the agreement dealt only with the treatment of the items, not with the statute of limitations on assessment.[590] It remains to be said that an agreement is not effective until it is signed on behalf of the Commissioner, and so the one-year statute of

---

constitute a settlement agreement); First Blood Assocs. v. Comm'r, TC Memo. 1998-228, 75 TCM 2565 (1998) (same).

[587] Korff v. Comm'r, TC Memo. 1993-33, 65 TCM 1811 (1993).

[588] Crnkovich v. United States, 81 AFTR2d 98-2399 (Fed. Cl. 1998), aff'd, 202 F3d 1325 (Fed. Cir. 2000).

[589] Crnkovich v. United States, 81 AFTR2d 98-2399 (Fed. Cl. 1998), aff'd, 202 F3d 1325 (Fed. Cir. 2000).

[590] See Thomas v. United States, 75 AFTR2d 95-525 (5th Cir. 1995). See also Toker v. United States, 97 TNT 86-55, 79 AFTR2d 97-2373 (SDNY 1997) (judge sent signed Form-870-P to the Service with letter he claimed said that he understood he would be entitled to a refund, if a court later determined that the original partnership deductions were proper; held, the letter was vague and did not support the claim, and the taxpayer was estopped from claiming that the Form 870-P was invalid on authority using estoppel to bind a taxpayer to the terms of a Form 870-AD).

limitations of Section 6229(f) does not begin to run until the date the Service signs the form, not the date the taxpayer signs it.[591]

Nonpartnership items postsettlement. Once the item becomes a nonpartnership item, the Service can adjust (make a "computational adjustment" of) the tax liability of the partner reflecting the settlement on the partnership item.[592] When the TMP commences a partnership proceeding in the Tax Court, the taxpayer partners participate in the proceeding, and the TMP and the Service enter into a stipulated decision on the partnership items. The Service is not required to send the taxpayer a notice of deficiency for the computational adjustments flowing from the agreement in the partnership proceeding.[593] Once the partnership proceeding is completed, the Service will send a notice of deficiency to the partners about such affected items on their individual returns as additions to tax. However, the requirement of sending a notice of deficiency for the affected items does not mean that the Service is also required to include in the affected-item notice of deficiency the computational adjustments reflecting the very partnership items determined in the completed partnership proceeding. Moreover, because the Tax Court does not have jurisdiction over the partnership items, the partners cannot contest the computational adjustments reflecting the decision in the completed partnership-level proceeding in their partner-level Tax Court case challenging the affected items.[594] The normal deficiency procedures do not apply to the assessment of a computational adjustment, so the partner generally will not receive a notice of deficiency, but rather a tax bill (a notice and demand).[595] There are two exceptions to the general rule that normal deficiency procedures do not apply: (1) a notice of deficiency must be sent if the deficiency is attributable to an item affected by the settlement on the partnership item (an "affected item") or (2) the items giving rise to the deficiency are items that become partnership items for reasons other than a settlement and a judicial proceeding.[596]

Because a settlement agreement, which results in the conversion of partnership items into nonpartnership items, requires computational adjustments to

---

[591] Ray v. Comm'r, 112 F3d 194 (5th Cir. 1997) (settlement reflected in a Form 870-L(AD)).

[592] IRC § 6231(a)(6).

[593] Brookes v. Comm'r, 108 TC 1 (1997).

[594] Brookes v. Comm'r, 108 TC 1 (1997), distinguishing Crowell v. Comm'r, 102 TC 683 (1994), where the partners claimed that they did not receive notice of the partnership-level proceeding and the Tax Court held that the issue of notice could be considered in the partner-level proceeding.

[595] IRC § 6230(a)(1). See Pack v. United States, 992 F2d 955 (9th Cir. 1993) (since deficiency procedures do not apply, interest is not suspended under Section 6601(c) on the resulting deficiency as of the thirty-first day after the settlement agreement/waiver of restrictions on assessment is filed); Harris v. Comm'r, 99 TC 121 (1992).

[596] IRC § 6230(a)(2)(A).

the returns of the individual partners, as well as assessment of the resulting deficiencies, processing a settlement can take considerable time. When a taxpayer waives the restrictions on assessment in the usual deficiency case as part of a settlement agreement with the Service, interest on the deficiency is suspended if the Service does not issue a notice and demand within thirty days after the waiver is filed.[597] The Taxpayer Relief Act of 1997 extended the same treatment for partners who execute settlement agreements.[598] As a result, if a partner executes a settlement agreement and waives the restrictions on assessment of any computational adjustment, but the Service fails to send a notice and demand for the additional tax due within thirty days after the waiver is filed, interest cannot be imposed beginning on the thirty-first day and ending with the date of the notice and demand.

¶ 8.20 JUDICIAL REVIEW IN TEFRA PARTNERSHIP PROCEEDINGS

[1] The Final Partnership Administrative Adjustment and Deficiency-Type Proceedings

If no agreement is reached in the administrative partnership proceeding, the Service sends to the TMP and the other partners a notice of FPAA. Within ninety days after the date on which this notice is mailed to the TMP, the TMP may obtain judicial review of the FPAA by filing a petition for readjustment in one of the following forums: (1) the Tax Court; (2) the federal district court for the district in which the partnership's principal place of business is located; or (3) the Court of Federal Claims.[599] Whichever forum is chosen, it is clear from the statute that the TMP has the first choice of forum.[600] The TMP has

---

[597] IRC § 6601(c).

[598] IRC § 6601(c), as amended by the Taxpayer Relief Act of 1997, § 1242(a), applicable to partnership years beginning after the effective date of the act, August 5, 1997.

[599] IRC § 6226(a). The Tax Court has adopted special rules to govern partnership actions. Tax Ct. R. Prac., tit. XXIV, 240–251. Under the Tax Court rules, the TMP is a party to every partnership proceeding (Rule 247), and there must always be a functioning TMP (Rule 250). Rule 248 describes procedures for settlement of partnership actions. A person who is not a partner is not permitted to file a petition as a TMP; but if a petition purporting to be filed by a TMP was authorized, the Tax Court has permitted the petition to be amended rather than dismissed. Montana Sapphire Assocs. v. Comm'r, 95 TC 477 (1990) (partnership was given time to select TMP and to notify court, and TMP was given time to amend petition).

[600] IRC § 6226(b)(5), as amended by the Taxpayer Relief Act of 1997, § 1240(a), applicable to petitions filed after the effective date of the act, August 5, 1997. The amend-

the exclusive right to file a petition for review of an FPAA during the first ninety days after the notice of FPAA, if any other partner files a petition within that period. At one time it was held that the other partner's petition is subject to dismissal.[601] After the Taxpayer Relief Act of 1997, however, the premature petition of a notice partner or of a 5 percent group is not dismissed, and if no action by another partner is taken within the sixty-day period permitted for doing so by Section 6226(b), the premature petition is treated as having been filed on the last day of the sixty-day period.

The deposit requirement. The FPAA serves the same purpose as a notice of deficiency in normal Tax Court proceedings, but it also operates as a jurisdictional prerequisite in courts where refund suits are normally heard.[602] Partners in a TEFRA partnership have the right to have a final judicial redetermination of the Service's adjustment of partnership items in a partnership-level proceeding before a partner-level proceeding is commenced. The deposit must be made on or before the date the petition is filed. When an action is brought in a district court or the Court of Federal Claims, the filing partner must deposit with the Service "an amount by which the tax liability of the partner would be increased if the partnership return, as adjusted by the notice" of FPAA; i.e., the deposit is equal to the deficiency resulting from the FPAA.[603] The partner is not required to pay other outstanding liabilities to deposit the jurisdictional amount.[604] For example, if the partner, A, files a petition for readjustment in the Court of Federal Claims, and the partner's tax deficiency resulting from the FPAA would increase by $10,000, and A has other unpaid liabilities of $20,000, A only pays a deposit of $10,000, to satisfy the jurisdictional requirement.[605] The amount deposited is treated as a payment of tax for interest computations.[606] By contrast, the deposit for the partnership item–based deficiency is not treated as a payment of tax collection purposes,

---

ment also redesignated former Section 6226(b)(5), dealing with the TMP's right to intervene in another partner's proceeding, as Section 6226(b)(6).

[601] IRC § 6226(a).

[602] In any event, a claim for refund does not have to be filed and acted on administratively; therefore, review of an FPAA in a district court or the Court of Federal Claims is more expeditious than a normal suit for refund. No procedural mechanism requires the Service to send the FPAA, and so the Service can deny the partnership the opportunity for judicial review. As a result, one court has denied a TMP's petition for a mandatory injunction to order the Service to send the TMP an FPAA on the grounds that it violated the Anti-Injunction Act. Atlantic Richfield Co. v. Department of the Treasury, 79 AFTR2d 97-585 (DDC 1997) (partnership had unclaimed tax benefits, and statute of limitations on refunds had expired so that Service's sending of a timely FPAA was argued to be its only remedy).

[603] IRC § 6226(e); Reg. § 301.6226(e)-1(a)(1).

[604] IRC § 6226(e); Reg. § 301.6226(e)-1(a)(1).

[605] Reg. § 301.6226(e)-1(a)(2).

[606] Reg. § 301.6226(e)-1(b).

and the Service may proceed against the depositor for a deficiency based on nonpartnership items without regard to the deposit.[607]

If it is subsequently determined that there is a shortfall in the deposit, the petition will not be dismissed if the partner has made a "good-faith effort to comply" with the requirement and makes up the shortfall in a timely manner.[608] When a partnership's TMP made a timely jurisdictional deposit to permit an FPAA to be challenged in the district court, the Service contended that the amount of the deposit was insufficient, and the partner had not made a good faith effort to comply with the deposit requirement.[609] In support of the bad faith argument, the Service made two basic arguments. First, it claimed that the TMP negligently calculated the jurisdictional deposit because the calculation of the correct amount was straightforward and uncomplicated to a tax professional. Second, the Service argued, before filing the petition for adjustment, the TMP failed to consult with the Service as to what the correct jurisdictional deposit amount should have been, despite being invited by the Service to do so. Rejecting the Service's arguments, the district court held: "Even if [the TMP's] failure to reach a pre-filing agreement as to the correct jurisdictional deposit was largely the result of 'tactical maneuvers' on behalf of [the TMP], it is not indicative of the lack of good faith that would divest the Court of jurisdiction under 26 U.S.C. section 6226(e)." The district court then gave the TMP sixty days to make the additional deposit. If the petition filed in a district court or the Court of Federal Claims is dismissed because of the Tax Court's priority, the deposit will be refunded (without interest), at the partner's request.[610]

Notice. A claim on the part of a partner that the partner was not given notice is treated as a motion to dismiss for lack of jurisdiction on the grounds that the affected-item notices are invalid. Unless the partnership has more than 100 partners, and the partner has a less-than-one-percent interest in the partnership,[611] the Tax Court has held that the Service is required to mail each partner a notice to inform the partner of the beginning of the partnership proceeding and the FPAA.[612] When the Service has failed to give notice to a partner of the proceeding, the Tax Court has effectively considered the validity of an af-

---

[607] Reg. § 301.6226(e)-1(c). If the restrictions on assessment and collection in the TEFRA proceeding lapse, the deposit may be applied to the deficiency that has been assessed. Reg. § 301.6226(e)-1(d).

[608] IRC § 6226(e).

[609] Maarten Investerings Partnership v. United States, 85 AFTR2d 2000-1086 (SDNY 2000).

[610] IRC §§ 6226(e)(2), 6226(e)(3).

[611] See the large partnership rules described below, which specifically apply to partnerships with 100 or more partners.

[612] See supra ¶ 8.09[3][b]. See also Goodman v. Comm'r, TC Memo. 1996-274 (1996) (in an affected-item proceeding, partner claimed that he did not receive a notice of

fected-item notice of deficiency. A different result has been reached, however, when it is the TMP who failed to notify the partners of a partnership settlement the TMP has entered into with the Service, and the Tax Court has entered a decision on the basis of the settlement. Although the partners were entitled to the notice the TMP failed to give, the partners cannot ask the Tax Court to redetermine the tax attributable to partnership items in affected-item proceedings.[613] After the settlement, and the decision based on the settlement, the Tax Court lacks jurisdiction to redetermine to consider partnership items in the affected-item proceeding. Multiple judicial proceedings are not inconsistent with the partnership audit rules.

Suspension of assessment and collection. When the Service sends the partner a notice of adjustment, the statute of limitations on assessment is suspended (1) for the 90-day or 150-day period during which the Service is prohibited from assessing tax, plus another sixty days, and (2) if the partner files a petition in the Tax Court, until the decision of the Tax Court becomes final, plus another sixty days.[614] Just as the Service is subject to restrictions on assessment and collection in the usual deficiency proceeding, the Service is prohibited from making an assessment of a deficiency attributable to any partnership (and taking any action to collect such a deficiency) before the 150-day period after the FPAA was mailed to the TMP. If a petition was filed during the 150-day period, the Service is prohibited from making such an assessment until the date the Tax Court's decision becomes final.[615] If the Service violates the restrictions on assessment and collection of a deficiency attributable to a partnership item, despite the Anti-Injunction Act, the action may be enjoined by the Tax Court or other proper court.[616] The Tax Court does not have jurisdiction to enjoin any prohibited action or proceeding, however, unless a timely petition for a readjustment of the partnership items for the taxable year has been filed, and then only for the adjustments that are the subject of the petition.

If the TMP does not file a petition for readjustment within the ninety-day period following the date of the FPAA, a notice partner or 5 percent group may file a petition for readjustment in the Tax Court, appropriate district court, or Court of Federal Claims within the next sixty days.[617] Each member of a 5

---

a partnership proceeding, and so the affected-item notice of deficiency was invalid; held, partner was not required to be sent a notice because he had less-than-one-percent interest).

[613] Brookes v. Comm'r, 108 TC 1 (1997) (partners were still able to dispute their liability for penalties).

[614] IRC § 6234(e)(2).

[615] IRC § 6225(a).

[616] IRC § 6225(b), as amended by the Taxpayer Relief Act of 1997 § 1239(a), applicable for tax years ending after the effective date of the act, August 5, 1997.

[617] IRC § 6226(b)(1). If a notice partner institutes an action within the ninety-day period, the proceeding will be dismissed. Brookes v. United States, 90-2 USTC ¶ 50,350

percent group must make a deposit. Obviously, this creates the possibility of multiple proceedings in the different courts. Accordingly, there is a rule of priority that provides that the first petition filed in the Tax Court gives that court jurisdiction and that all other petitions will be dismissed.[618] The intended effect is to increase the taxable income that should have been reported on the taxpayer's return. If the final determination in the partnership proceeding reduces the partner's loss or otherwise eliminates the excess shelter from the partnership item, the Service will still have the ability to collect tax on any deficiency attributable to the nonpartnership items. The declaratory judgment on nonpartnership items must be taken into account in determining the amount of any computational adjustment made in connection with any partnership proceeding or deficiency proceedings at the partnership level attributable to items such as affected items that can be determined only at the partnership level.[619]

If the taxpayer does not contest the notice of adjustment within the ninety-day period for filing a petition for declaratory judgment after the taxpayer's partnership items are finally determined in the partnership-level proceeding, the taxpayer has a right to file a refund claim for the tax attributable to the items adjusted in the notice of adjustment. The taxpayer is permitted to file a refund claim on items in a notice of adjustment after the TEFRA proceeding because the notice of adjustment does not require the payment of additional tax. Taxpayers may not challenge the notice when it is issued by paying the tax and instituting a suit for refund.[620]

Apart from extensions and suspensions of the period of limitations on assessment of deficiencies attributable to a partnership item, there are restrictions on the assessment and collection of a deficiency attributable to a partnership item. Section 6225(a) prohibits assessment and collection for 150 days after a

---

(Cl. Ct. 1990). A partner with a less-than-one-percent interest is not entitled to file a petition in the Tax Court as a notice partner, even if the partner actually but erroneously receives an FPAA. Energy Resources Ltd. v. Comm'r, 91 TC 913 (1988). See Buzick v. United States, 15 Cl. Ct. 289 (1988) (150-day period not extended by Claims Court Rule 6, which provides for three additional days for responsive papers when a pleading is served by mail). When a TMP who is also a notice partner does not file within the ninety-day period, but does file within the sixty-day period, the Tax Court has jurisdiction. Barbados #6 Ltd. v. Comm'r, 85 TC 900 (1985). The TMP is the only partner who may file a petition for judicial review in the ninety-day period beginning with the date of the FPAA. For this purpose, if the ninetieth day falls on a Sunday, the TMP may file a timely petition on Monday so that the first day a limited partner may file a petition is Tuesday. Transpac Drilling Venture 1982-22 v. Comm'r, 87 TC 874 (1986).

[618] IRC § 6226(b)(2). If no petition is filed in the Tax Court, the first action brought will go forward with the others dismissed. IRC § 6226(b)(3).

[619] IRC § 6234(g)(1). See IRC § 6230(a)(2) (dealing with deficiency proceedings at the partnership level). See also IRC § 6234(g)(4) for rules describing when the treatment of partnership items has become finally determined.

[620] IRC § 6234(d)(2).

notice of an FPAA is mailed to the TMP and, if a proceeding is begun in the Tax Court, until the court's decision has become final.

Participation in the court case. In a judicial proceeding, all partners are parties, and are entitled to participate,[621] unless the partner does not have an interest in the outcome because (1) the partnership items have become nonpartnership items for his return or (2) the statute of limitations on assessment of any tax attributable to the partnership items has expired as to him.[622] To put it another way, partners whose tax liabilities are affected by the outcome of the partnership proceeding are the real parties in interest in any partnership audit or judicial proceeding. Partnership items of a first-tier partnership must be contested in the first-tier partnership's partnership proceeding, not in the partner's own proceeding, even if the partner is a pass-through partner and a partnership covered by the unified partnership proceeding rules.[623] To be a party to a Tax Court action to review an FPAA, the partner must have an interest in the outcome, unless the partnership items of the partner have become nonpartnership items or the statute of limitations on assessment of any tax attributable to the partnership items against that partner has expired.[624] However, as long as the partner was a partner in the tax year before the court and treated as a party by Section 6226(c), the partner is permitted to participate in the action (or permitted to file a readjustment petition by Section 6226(c)(1)), solely for the purpose of asserting the defense that the statute of limitations has expired on the assessment against the partner of any tax attributable to partnership items, and if the court, including the Tax Court, in which the proceeding is taking place has jurisdiction to hear the partner's statute of limitations defense.[625]

The Tax Court has ruled that if the Service sends a partner in a TEFRA partnership a notice of deficiency for an affected item arising from a partnership adjustment before the completion of the partnership-level proceeding, the notice of deficiency is invalid, and the Tax Court has no jurisdiction over the case. If corporate members of an affiliated group are partners in a TEFRA partnership, and the Service sends the common parent a notice of deficiency for tax due arising from affected items that depended on the resolution of

---

[621] IRC 6226(c). Intervention is accomplished in the Tax Court by way of filing a notice of election with the court. See Tax Ct. R. Prac. & Proc. 244. A petition for judicial review is not a notice of election to participate. Computer Programs Lambda, Ltd. v. Comm'r, 89 TC 198 (1987) (TMP's bankruptcy precluded TMP from proceeding as such in partnership proceeding).

[622] IRC § 6226(d).

[623] Sente Inv. Club Partnership v. Comm'r, 95 TC 243 (1990) (Tax Court had no jurisdiction to hear first partnership items in second-tier partner's partnership proceeding).

[624] IRC § 6226(d).

[625] IRC § 6226(d)(1), as amended by the Taxpayer Relief Act of 1997, § 1239(b), applicable to partnership taxable years ending after the effective date of the act, August 5, 1997.

TEFRA partnership items, the Service's notice of deficiency is invalid because there has been no final resolution and adjustment in the partnership-level proceeding.[626] With the Service's notice of deficiency invalid, the Tax Court lacks jurisdiction over the partner-level proceeding.

The fact that a partner participates in a judicial proceeding for the review of the FPAA does not preclude the possibility that there may be a separate proceeding (possibly in another forum) involving nonpartnership items, or even another judicial proceeding for the review of an FPAA issued to another partnership.[627] Also, when an affected item depends on a factual determination that must be made at the partner level, such as a negligence or substantial understatement penalty, the normal deficiency procedures apply, and, absent agreement, the partner must be sent a notice of deficiency.[628] In this affected-item proceeding, the Tax Court may not adjudicate partnership items or related computational adjustments.[629]

A partner in the partner's own affected-item proceeding can challenge the validity of the affected-item notice of deficiency on the grounds that the Commissioner failed to properly notify the partner of the partnership-level proceeding. For example, if an FPAA includes a negligence penalty, the penalty is an affected item depending on a partnership-level determination and cannot be tried as part of the partner's personal case, until the completion of the partnership-level proceeding.[630] But the Tax Court's jurisdiction in a later proceeding brought by an affected partner must be independently established.[631] In the partnership proceeding, therefore, nonpartnership items may not be heard. This seems to avoid the possibility that the Service can claim res judicata that precludes a partner later suing for refund for the year because the matter might have, but was not, litigated in the Tax Court.[632]

The Tax Court or other court reviewing the FPAA has jurisdiction to determine all partnership items for the taxable year covered by the FPAA and the proper allocation of the items among the partners.[633] If a TMP files a petition in bankruptcy, the designation of the bankrupt partner as TMP terminates as of that date, and the bankrupt partner's partnership items become nonpartnership

---

[626] GAF Corp. v. Comm'r, 114 TC 519 (2000).

[627] Maxwell v. Comm'r, 87 TC 783, 792 (1986).

[628] NCF Energy Partners v. Comm'r, 89 TC 741, 744 (1987).

[629] Saso v. Comm'r, 93 TC 730, 734 (1989).

[630] Crowell v. Comm'r, 102 TC 683, 691 (1994).

[631] See, e.g., White v. Comm'r, 95 TC 209 (1990) (Tax Court had no jurisdiction over partner's liability for tax-motivated interest, because deficiency in issue did not involve alleged tax-motivated transaction).

[632] See Trost v. Comm'r, 95 TC 560 (1990).

[633] IRC § 6226(f); Reg. § 301.6226(f)-1. See Third Dividend v. Comm'r, 88 F3d 821 (9th Cir. 1996) (the bankruptcy court did not have jurisdiction over nondebtors, such as the shareholders, and so the corporation's bankruptcy did not affect them).

items on that date as well. If a TMP files a petition in bankruptcy, the designation of the bankrupt partner as TMP terminates as of that date, and the bankrupt partner's partnership items become nonpartnership items on that date as well.[634]

Review. The decision of the court is reviewable by a court of appeals, but only the TMP, notice partner, or a 5 percent group may seek appellate review.[635] Appeal lies to the circuit court for the circuit in which the partnership's principal place of business is located.[636] The bond for an appeal from the Tax Court is based on an estimate of the aggregate deficiencies of the partners, including penalties and interest.[637]

Partnership items and nonpartnership adjustments. TEFRA rules partnership proceedings and individual partner proceedings are separate. Under prior law, if the Service audited non-TEFRA items in an individual partner's return and determined that the individual partner had a deficiency attributable to nonpartnership items, the Service computed the deficiency attributable to the adjustment of non-TEFRA items by assuming that all items that were subject to the partnership proceeding were correctly reported on the taxpayer's return. Once there was a final decision in the partnership proceeding on partnership items, a separate assessment could be made against the individual taxpayer. In some situations, the partnership loss exceeded the amount of the adjustments that increased the taxpayer's income, and so there was no deficiency for purposes of a non-TEFRA proceeding. If the offsetting partnership loss was subsequently disallowed in a TEFRA partnership proceeding, the Service was unable to assess the resulting deficiency against the individual partner because the period of limitations for making an assessment had expired.

To ensure that the statute of limitations on assessment did not expire in this situation, the Service changed its procedure. The Service sent the individual partner a notice of deficiency covering nonpartnership items by disallowing the TEFRA partnership loss the partner claimed for computational purposes only. The Tax Court ruled that it had jurisdiction to hear the case because there was a deficiency, but disapproved of the method the Service used to compute the partner's deficiency in income tax.[638]

Oversheltered returns. To prevent a situation in which an individual partner would have either an artificially high deficiency assessment to pay, which might later be reduced because some or all of the partnership loss was allowed

---

[634] Computer Programs Lambda, Ltd. v. Comm'r, 89 TC 198 (1987).

[635] IRC § 6226(g).

[636] IRC § 6226(g).

[637] IRC § 7485(b). The Taxpayer Relief Act of 1997, §§ 1241(a)(1)–1241(a)(2), amended Section 7485(b), as of the effective date of TEFRA in 1982, to provide that the Tax Court must estimate the amount of the partners' liabilities, including penalties and interest, in determining the amount of an appeal bond.

[638] Munro v. Comm'r, 92 TC 71 (1989).

in the partnership proceeding, or the Service might not be able to adjust non-partnership items because the assessment period had run, the Taxpayer Relief Act of 1997 reinstated the Service's old procedure by adopting a new declaratory judgment procedure for oversheltered returns. As defined, an "oversheltered return" is a return that shows no taxable income and a net loss from a TEFRA partnership.[639] In this situation, if the Service makes a determination about nonpartnership items, and the resulting adjustments do not give rise to a deficiency, but would produce a deficiency had there been no net loss from a TEFRA partnership, the Service is authorized to send a notice of adjustment reflecting its determination to the taxpayer partner by certified or registered mail.[640]

The taxpayer partner has 90 days (or 150 days if the notice is addressed to a person outside the United States) from the date of the notice to file a petition for the redetermination of the adjustment.[641] The Tax Court is granted jurisdiction to enter a declaratory judgment on any other item to which the notice of adjustment relates, except partnership items and affected items the resolution of which at the partner level must await the determination in the unified partnership proceeding. No tax is due on the entry of the final decision of the Tax Court in this declaratory judgment proceeding, but its decision is treated as a final decision of the court, and is subject to review as such. The final decision in the declaratory judgment proceeding on the treatment of any nonpartnership item has the effect of increasing the taxable income that the taxpayer partner should have reported on the partner's return. During this proceeding, the statute of limitations on assessment is suspended.

[2] The Administrative Adjustment Request and Refund-Type Judicial Review

A request for administrative adjustment (AAR) is a request that partnership items be treated as described in the request, rather than as reported on the partnership return.[642] Either the TMP or any partner may file a request for administrative adjustment.[643] The AAR must be filed within three years after the later

---

[639] IRC § 6234(b), added by the Taxpayer Relief Act of 1997, § 1231(a), applicable to partnership years ending after the effective date of the act, August 5, 1997.

[640] IRC § 6234(a).

[641] IRC § 6234(c).

[642] IRC § 6227(c).

[643] IRC §§ 6227(a)(1), 6227(c) (request by TMP on behalf of partnership), 6227(d) (other requests). The Taxpayer Relief Act of 1997, § 1236(a) amended Section 6227 to add a new subsection (b) to deal with extensions of the period for filing requests, discussed infra, and renumbered former subsections (b) and (c) as subsections (c) and (d), effective as though the changes had been included in the amendment made by TEFRA

of (1) the date the partnership return was filed or (2) the due date of the partnership return (determined without regard to extensions).[644] In the same way that the taxpayer's extension of the period during which the Service may make an assessment extends the period during which the taxpayer may file a claim for refund, the partner's time for filing a request for an administrative adjustment is extended for the period the partner extends the statute of limitations on the assessment of a partnership item, and for six months thereafter.[645] In addition, the AAR must be filed before an FPAA is mailed for the taxable year.

Substituted return requests and refund claims. The AAR takes the form of an amended return that requests either (1) that the treatment of items in the request be substituted for the original partnership return (a substituted return request) or (2) that refunds or credits be allowed, be made to all the partners (a claim for refund), or both.[646] If the TMP files a substituted-return AAR, the Service may treat the changes shown on the AAR as corrections of mathematical or clerical errors appearing on the partnership return.[647] The procedures for immediate assessment of any tax resulting from the mathematical error would be made under Section 6213(b)(1), as an exception to the normal restrictions on assessment. When the TMP files a refund AAR, the Service may allow the refund or credit, conduct a partnership proceeding, or take no action on the request.[648] Where a partner other than a TMP files the AAR, the Service may take the same actions as where the TMP files the request,[649] except that it may give the filing partner notice that all partnership items for the filing partner are

---

§ 402 in 1982 (generally effective for partnership tax years beginning after September 3, 1982).

[644] IRC § 6227(a). The Taxpayer Relief Act of 1997 provides for different limitations periods depending on whether an AAR is based on the deduction by a partnership for a worthless security or a bad debt. Instead of the three-year period, the period for filing an AAR on these grounds is seven years from the due date of the return for the year to which the request relates. IRC § 6227(e), added by the Taxpayer Relief Act of 1997, § 1243(a), effective as though included in the amendments made by TEFRA § 402 in 1982 (generally effective for partnership tax years beginning after September 3, 1982).

[645] IRC § 6227(b), added by the Taxpayer Relief Act of 1997, § 1236(a), effective as though it had been included in TEFRA in 1982 (generally effective for partnership tax years beginning after September 3, 1982).

[646] IRC §§ 6227(c)(1), 6227(c)(2). The AAR must show the effect in distributive shares. IRC § 6227(c)(3).

[647] IRC § 6227(c)(1). Presumably, if the changes on the AAR are not treated as corrections of mathematical errors, the AAR is treated as an amended return. If the AAR is not granted substituted-return treatment, it remains an AAR and the TMP may file suit under Section 6228(a) if the Service fails to take timely action on the request.

[648] IRC § 6227(c)(2).

[649] IRC §§ 6227(d)(1), 6227(d)(2), 6227(d)(4). The language describing the options available to the Service under Section 6227(d) is not identical with that in Section 6227(c), but it is not clear that any different result was intended.

treated as nonpartnership items,[650] thus withdrawing the request from the operation of the special partnership audit rules and leaving the matter to the operation of the normal rules applicable to refund claims.

Judicial review. Procedurally, judicial review of an AAR differs, depending on whether the request was filed by the TMP or another partner. In the TMP's case, the proceeding is one for the adjustment of all partnership items to which the request relates. Another partner's case is treated as a suit for refund, and on the beginning of the action, the partnership items involved are treated as nonpartnership items.[651]

Section 6228(b) applies where the Service has denied, in whole or in part, a request for administrative adjustment; and if the Service has failed to act at all, a taxpayer may not argue that the partnership return is conclusive evidence of his liability and of his right to refund.[652] In *Wall v. United States*,[653] the partner claimed he was entitled to file his refund action under Section 6228 because he was entitled by Section 6230(c) to file a claim for refund on the ground that the Service, in denying his claim, had effectively made an erroneous computational adjustment, established by the conclusive evidence of the partnership return's reporting of the partnership items. The circuit court distinguished the denial of the AAR dealt with in Section 6228 from the erroneous computational adjustment claim described in Section 6230(c)(1)(A). A partner is permitted to file a claim for refund under Section 6230(c)(1)(A) only if the Service has erroneously computed a computational adjustment it considers to be necessary to make the partnership items on the partner's return consistent with their treatment on the partnership's return. In *Wall*, the partner's case was dismissed because there had been no denial of a partner's AAR, nor a computational adjustment.

If the Service fails to allow any part of a TMP's AAR, the TMP may file a petition for adjustment in the Tax Court, the district court in which the principal place of business of the partnership is located, or the Court of Federal Claims.[654] This petition may not be filed until six months after the filing of an AAR or more than two years after the AAR was filed.[655] These periods are analogous to the claim for refund periods provided in Section 6532. As with the claim for refund, the six-month waiting period gives the Service time to re-

---

[650] IRC § 6227(d)(3).

[651] IRC § 6228(b)(2).

[652] Wall v. United States, 133 F3d 1188 (9th Cir. 1998).

[653] Wall v. United States, 133 F3d 1188 (9th Cir. 1998).

[654] IRC § 6228(a)(1).

[655] See U.S. Farm Partners-85 v. United States, 82 AFTR2d 98-6796 (CD Cal. 1998) (petitions for readjustment dismissed because they were filed more than two years after partners had filed AARs with the Service; court rejected argument that period of limitations was suspended because there had been a Tax Court case involving an earlier tax year and the claims were related to the claim in the Tax Court case).

search the claim, and even conduct a partnership proceeding and issue an FPAA. On the other hand, if the Service fails to act on a claim for refund, there is to time limit for filing a complaint. At any rate, no petition for review of an AAR may be filed after the Service has mailed a notice of the beginning of a partnership administrative proceeding or an FPAA.[656] A proceeding for review of a partner's AAR is converted to the Service's FPAA if the FPAA is mailed before a hearing on the partner's petition for adjustment.[657]

In a case the TMP has commenced, the court in the judicial proceeding has jurisdiction to determine only those partnership items in an AAR not allowed by the Service and those adjustments claimed by the Service to be offsets to the adjustments requested by the TMP.[658] Partners other than the TMP are treated as parties and may participate if they have an interest in the outcome.[659] The final decision of the court is reviewable by the appropriate court of appeals, but only the TMP, a notice partner, or a 5 percent group may appeal an adverse decision.[660]

If a partner other than the TMP files an AAR and the Service notifies the partner that all partnership items covered by the request will be treated as nonpartnership items, the AAR is treated as a claim for refund outside the partnership audit rules.[661] Thus, the partner may bring a suit for refund in the district court of his residence or the Court of Federal Claims—but not the Tax Court—within two years after the mailing of the Service's notice regarding the partnership item.[662] If the Service does not allow any part of the AAR of a partner who is not the TMP, the partner may begin a refund suit under Section 7422, but not before six months have elapsed since the filing of the AAR and not more than two years after the AAR was filed.[663] This refund suit is prohibited once the Service mails a notice of the beginning of a partnership proceeding.[664] If the Service mails this notice, but fails to mail an FPAA within the statutory assessment period, an additional six months is added to the two-year period for the partner to bring his refund suit.[665]

---

[656] IRC §§ 6228(a)(2)(B), 6228(a)(3)(A).

[657] IRC § 6228(a)(3)(B). See Tax Ct. R. Prac. & Proc. 247.

[658] IRC § 6228(a)(5).

[659] IRC § 6228(a)(4).

[660] IRC § 6228(a)(6).

[661] IRC § 6228(b)(1).

[662] IRC § 6228(b)(1).

[663] IRC §§ 6228(b)(2)(A), 6228(b)(2)(B). The two-year period may be extended.

[664] IRC § 6228(b)(2)(C).

[665] IRC § 6228(b)(2)(D).

¶ 8.21 AUDITS OF LARGE PARTNERSHIPS

The basic format of the TEFRA audit procedures also apply to the electing-large-partnership procedures. For example, the term "partnership items" is defined in the same manner as under the TEFRA rules, and the tax treatment of partnership items is determined in a partnership-level proceeding, not at the individual partner level;[666] that is, a "partnership adjustment" means "any adjustment in the amount of any partnership item of an electing large partnership."[667] A partnership "takes effect" (1) in the case of an adjustment pursuant to the decision of the court in a proceeding to review the Service's partnership adjustment (an FPAA), when the decision of the court becomes final; (2) in the case of an AAR, when the adjustment is allowed by the Service; or (3) in any other case, when the adjustment is made. The "adjusted year" is "the partnership year to which the item being adjusted relates."[668] One fundamental difference from the TEFRA rules is that partnership adjustments will flow through to current-year partners for the year the adjustment takes effect.[669] Current-year partners' shares of current-year partnership items of income, gains, losses, deductions, and credits are adjusted to reflect partnership adjustments that take effect in that year.[670] Current-year adjustments generally do not affect the returns of partners for prior years, except in the case of changes to a partner's distributive share. In other words, when an audit adjustment is made to the partnership shares of partnership items, the adjustment is made to the distributive shares of partnership items in the year of adjustment, not the adjusted year.

Alternatively, instead of flowing through adjustments for prior years to current-year partners, the large partnership may elect to pay the effect of the adjustment by way of an imputed underpayment, calculated by (1) netting adjustments to the income and loss items of the partnership and multiplying that amount by the highest tax rate, whether that rate is the individual or corporate rate, and (2) adding or subtracting adjustments to tax credits.[671] A partner is not permitted to file a claim for credit or refund when the partnership elects to make this imputed underpayment.[672]

---

[666] IRC § 6242(d)(1).

[667] IRC §§ 6242(d)(2)(A)–6242(d)(2)(C).

[668] IRC §§ 6242(d)(1), 6242(d)(3).

[669] IRC § 6242(a)(1).

[670] IRC § 6242(a)(1).

[671] IRC §§ 6242(a)(2) (election), 6242(b)(4). Regulations govern the manner in which the election is to be made in order to ensure that payment of the imputed underpayment is made by large partnerships, such as foreign partnerships.

[672] IRC § 6240(b)(1).

If an adjustment of a partnership item requires an adjustment in a year after the adjusted year and before the offset adjustment takes effect, the adjustment for the year of adjustment must reflect adjustments to the partnership adjustment in issue for the intervening years.[673] The example used to illustrate this procedure assumes that a partnership deducts a $1,000 item in year one, and the Service determines in an audit in year four that the item should have been capitalized and amortized ratably over ten years.[674] In year four, the adjustment of $700 would reflect the $100 amortization deduction allowable in year one, as well as the $200 allowable in years two and three. Accordingly, the year four partners will be required to include the $700 in income in year four, although the partnership may also amortize the remaining $700, in years four through ten.

The partnership, rather than the individual partners, is liable for interest and penalties that result from the partnership audit.[675] Interest begins to run for the period on the return due date for the adjusted year and ends on the earlier of the partnership's taxable year for the year that the adjustment takes effect or the date the partnership pays the imputed underpayment.[676] Using this same example, the partnership would be liable for interest for four years on a declining balance to take into account the allowable amortization. Similarly, penalties, such as accuracy and fraud penalties, are determined on an annual basis, based on the imputed underpayment.[677] Both liability for a penalty and the application of the uniform waiver standard are determined at the partnership level, treating the partnership as though it were an individual. For purposes of assessment and collection of penalties, the same procedures as those applicable to individuals also apply.[678] The payment of tax, penalties, and interest by the partnership is nondeductible.[679]

If a large partnership elects the large partnership audit rules, the partners must file their separate returns consistently with the partnership's return,[680] or the Service will assess the difference in treatment as a mathematical or clerical error, even if, as under the normal TEFRA rules, the partner notifies the Ser-

---

[673] IRC § 6242(a)(3).

[674] See Revenue Reconciliation Act of 1997, HR Rep. No. 148, 105th Cong., 1st Sess. 580.

[675] IRC § 6242(b).

[676] IRC § 6242(b)(2).

[677] IRC § 6242(b)(3).

[678] IRC § 6242(c).

[679] IRC § 6242(c). If a partnership terminates before a partnership adjustment takes effect, the former partners are required to take the adjustment into account. IRC § 6255(d). The purpose of regulations will be to prevent abuse and to enforce the audit rules in special situations, such as the bankruptcy of the partnership.

[680] IRC § 6241(a).

vice of the inconsistency.[681] In the partnership-level audit, unlike the TEFRA rules, individual partners have no right to participate in settlement conferences or to file a claim for refund.[682] Moreover, the Service is also not required to give notice to individual partners that it has begun a partnership proceeding or that it has made a final adjustment. The Service is only required to give notice to the partnership of a partnership adjustment, sending the notice by certified or registered mail, even if the partnership has terminated.[683] However, the Service must make an adjustment to a partnership for any partnership tax year more than three years after the later of (1) the date on which the partnership return for the year was filed or (2) the due date of the partnership return determined without regard to any extension of time for filing.[684] This three-year adjustment period can be extended in the same manner as the statute of limitations on assessment in Section 6501; that is, by agreement (Section 6248(b)); by the filing of a false or fraudulent partnership return, in which there is no limitations period (Section 6248(c)(1)); by a more-than-25-percent omission of gross income, in which case there is a six-year adjustment period (Section 6248(c)(2)); and by the failure to file any partnership return at all, in which case an adjustment may be made at any time (Section 6248(c)(3)). If the Service prepares a return for the partnership under Section 6020, the return does not qualify as a return for the adjustment period.[685] Once the Service mails a notice of partnership adjustment, the running of the adjustment period is suspended for the period during which an action is pending in court, assuming that the partnership has filed a petition, until the decision of the court has become final, and for one additional year.[686]

If the partnership challenges the final partnership adjustment in court (the Tax Court, the district court where the partnership's principal place of business is located, or the Court of Federal Claims), only the partnership, not the partners individually, is permitted to file a petition for readjustment of the Service's final adjustment.[687] The court having jurisdiction over the partnership's petition for readjustment has the jurisdiction not only to review the partnership's challenge to the Service's adjustment reflected in the notice of final ad-

---

[681] IRC § 6241(b). An electing large partnership must furnish information to its partners by the first March 15 after the close of the partnership year.

[682] See IRC §§ 6240(b)(1), 6245(a).

[683] IRC § 6245(b)(1).

[684] IRC § 6248, added by the Taxpayer Relief Act of 1997.

[685] IRC § 6248(c)(4).

[686] IRC § 6248(d).

[687] IRC § 6247(a). For the jurisdictional requirements that must be met when the action is brought in a district court or the Court of Federal Claims, see IRC § 6247(b).

justment, but also to determine the proper allocation of the adjusted partnership items among the individual partners.[688]

Alternatively, a partnership may file the equivalent of a refund claim, the request for administrative adjustment, requesting the adjustment of any partnership items for a partnership year, as long as the request is filed (1) within three years after the later of (a) the date on which the partnership return for that year was filed or (b) the due date of the partnership return, excluding extensions, and (2) before the mailing to the partnership of a notice of partnership adjustment, the FPAA, for the partnership's tax year.[689] The Service may, of course, allow the request, but if the Service disallows any part of the request, the partnership may file a petition for an adjustment of the disputed partnership items with the Tax Court, the district court in the judicial district in which the partnership has its principal place of business, or the Court of Federal Claims.[690] Following the procedures applicable to the filing of a suit for refund, the partnership must, after filing its request, wait at least six months for the Service to act on it before filing a petition for an adjustment, and the partnership must file its petition for review within two years after the date of its request, apparently whether or not the Service has acted on the request.[691]

Once the petition for adjustment has been filed, the court's jurisdiction to review the Service's action is limited to the items set forth in the request for administrative adjustment in the same manner as a taxpayer may not challenge an item in court that has not been previously raised in a claim for refund. The court's decision in the adjustment proceeding has the same force and effect as a decision of the Tax Court or a final judgment of a district court or the Court of Federal Claims, and is reviewable by an appellate court as such.[692]

---

[688] IRC § 6247(c).

[689] IRC § 6251(a). If the partnership consents to the extension of the adjustment period, the partnership is given an additional six months after the expiration of the extension period to file the request. IRC § 6251(c).

[690] IRC § 6252(a).

[691] IRC § 6252(b). No petition may be filed after the Service has mailed a timely FPAA to the partnership. If the Service mails a timely FPAA to the partnership after the partnership has filed a petition for adjustment but before the hearing on the petition, the petition for adjustment will be treated as a petition for readjustment governed by Section 6247 rather than as a petition for adjustment under Section 6252. IRC §§ 6252(c)(1), 6252(c)(2); see also IRC § 6248.

[692] IRC § 6252(e). The appeal period runs from the date of the decision.

¶ 8.22 S CORPORATION ITEMS

For taxable years beginning after December 31, 1996, the TEFRA audit provisions applicable to S corporations are repealed.[693]

---

[693] Small Business Protection Job Act of 1996, Pub. L. No. 104-88, 104th Cong., 2d. Sess. § 1307(c)(1).

The Appeals Function

¶ 9.01 THE APPEALS PROCESS

Administrative dispute resolution in the Internal Revenue Service (the Service) is by appeal to the Office of Appeals. To minimize expenditures of time and money by the government and taxpayers alike, the Service encourages taxpayers to resolve their disagreements through negotiation and settlement, rather than court litigation. Taxpayers have been entitled to appeal disputes under the Internal Revenue Code (the Code), applicable regulations, and procedures to the Office of Appeals, since 1927.[1] The Office of Appeals is able to resolve disputes because it is "the only administrative function of the Service with the authority to consider settlements of tax controversies, and as such has the primary responsibility to resolve these disputes without litigation to the maximum extent possible."[2] As the Service's Statement of Procedural Rules puts it:[3]

> The Appeals mission is to resolve tax controversies, without litigation, on a basis which is fair and impartial to both the Government and the taxpayer and in a manner that will enhance voluntary compliance and public confidence in the integrity and efficiency of the Service.

The Appeals function is highly successful. In tens of thousands of cases each year, Appeals officers negotiate and in about 85 to 90 percent of the cases settle with taxpayers.[4] If this high rate of settlement were not achieved, the number of unagreed cases soon would overwhelm the courts with hearing tax cases.

Before 1998, the Service's appeals system was barely acknowledged in the Code, and certainly not statutorily mandated.[5] It was a creation of the

---

[1] Administrative appeal has an even longer history in tax matters. The Act of 1789 that established the Treasury Department provided that any person dissatisfied with an audit of his or her account could "within six months appeal to the controller." With the establishment of the income tax laws and the resulting increase in the number of tax controversies, a special advisory committee was established that became known as the technical staff, which was the predecessor of today's Office of Appeals. See Mann, "Administrative Appellate Procedure Before the IRS," 62 ABAJ 377 (1976).

[2] IRM 1.2.1, Policies of the IRS Handbook, 1.8.4, Policy Statement P-8-47(2), Appeals Settlement Authority (approved Apr. 6, 1987).

[3] See IRM 1.2.1, Policies of the IRS Handbook, 1.8.4, Policy Statement P-8-47(1), Consideration to Be Given to Offers of Settlement (approved Apr. 6, 1987); IRM 8.1, Appeals-General, 3.2(2), Appeals Mission (May 19, 1998).

[4] The IRS Annual Report for 1988 states (at p. 36): "Appeals officers, located in major cities, met with taxpayers and their representatives and were usually successful in resolving disputed issues. Appeals closed approximately 93,000 cases, of which 90 percent were agreed."

[5] Section 7429, which provides for administrative review of a jeopardy or termination assessment, appears to require at least district review. Section 7430, which permits taxpayers to recover reasonable litigation costs, also requires the prevailing party to have ex-

Commissioner's Statement of Procedural Rules.[6] In the IRS Restructuring and Reform Act of 1998, however, the Office of Appeals was not only acknowledged, but its independence was required to be protected.[7]

Under the current Service's appeals system, Appeals officers assigned to the different local offices hear taxpayer appeals on matters ranging from tax deficiencies to offers in compromise to collection due process reviews. The following summarized Code sections reflect or acknowledge the existence of the Office of Appeals:

1. Section 7429 provides for administrative due process review of a jeopardy or termination assessment. The administrative review provided for includes Appeals Office review.

2. Section 7430, which permits taxpayers to recover reasonable litigation costs, also requires the prevailing party to have exhausted administrative remedies available to the party within the Service, thereby recognizing the Appeals process. A taxpayer who substantially prevails in an administrative proceeding or an action in court may be awarded a judgment for reasonable costs the taxpayer has incurred in the proceeding. The party moving for costs must also prove that (a) the moving party did not unreasonably protract the proceeding and (b) the moving party was the prevailing party. Appeals has jurisdiction over requests for administrative costs.

3. As a result of the IRS Restructuring and Reform Act of 1998, Appeals has wide jurisdiction in collection cases, including due process review before the filing of a notice of lien (Section 6320); due process review before a levy is made, in which alternatives to levy, such as installment payment agreement will be considered (Section 6320); review of rejected offers in compromise (Section 7122(d)); and the early referral of collection issues (Section 7123).

4. A jeopardy levy is a levy made and served when the Service finds that collection of a tax will be jeopardized by delay, and so the levy calls for the immediate surrender of the taxpayer's property and rights to property without any waiting period.[8] When a jeopardy levy is made, the taxpayer is entitled to the due process review procedures of Section 7429, including administrative review. The Office of Appeals is the forum for final Service review.[9]

---

hausted administrative remedies available to the party within the Service, thereby recognizing the Appeals process.

[6] Statement of Procedural Rules (SPR), 26 CFR pt. 601. Before the Service's 1998 reorganization, SPR, 26 CFR § 601.106(a)(1)(i) stated that "[t]here are provided in each region Appeals offices with office facilities within the region."

[7] IRS Restructuring and Reform Act of 1998, HR 2676, 105th Cong., 2d Sess. § 1001(a)(4) (hereinafter the 1998 Act).

[8] IRC § 6331(a).

[9] IRC § 7429(a)(3).

5. Appeals has jurisdiction to provide independent administrative review of a local office's proposed rejection of an offer in compromise or installment agreement,[10] and also to hear a taxpayer's appeal of the local office's rejection of an offer in compromise or installment agreement.[11]

6. Appeals has jurisdiction under Section 6404(e) over requests for abatement of interest on a deficiency attributable, in whole or in part, to delays of Service managers and employees in performing a managerial or ministerial act, or their error or delay in paying any tax.[12]

7. Section 7123, entitled Appeals Dispute Resolution Procedures, requires the adoption of procedures for taxpayers to request the early referral of unresolved issues to the Office of Appeals, as well as procedures permitting the taxpayer and the Office of Appeals to use the alternative dispute resolution procedures of mediation and arbitration of certain issues.[13]

¶ 9.02 ORGANIZATION OF THE APPEALS FUNCTION

As a result of the IRS Restructuring and Reform Act of 1998, the Service was reorganized by type of taxpayer. As part of the Service's reorganization plan, the Restructuring and Reform Act called for the Commissioner to develop and implement an independent Appeals function.[14] Appeals function's independence was required to be protected in the Commissioner's reorganization plan, in part, by prohibiting "ex parte communications between [A]ppeals officers and other Internal Revenue Service employees to the extent that such communications appear to compromise the independence of [A]ppeals officers."[15]

The Office of Appeals has been reorganized to comprise a headquarters staff in the National Office and three operating units aligned with the larger operating divisions. Accordingly, the three operating divisions are: (1) the Appeals Large and Midsize Operating Unit; (2) the Appeals Small Business and Self-Employed, Tax-Exempt/Government Entities Operating Unit; and (3) the Appeals Wage and Investments Operating Unit.[16] The Office of Appeals has thirty-three offices nationwide. It also has customer service representatives to provide assistance to taxpayers during their administrative appeal. These repre-

---

[10] IRC § 7122(d)(1).

[11] IRC § 7122(d)(2).

[12] IRC § 6404(e)(1).

[13] IRC §§ 7123(a), 7123(b).

[14] The 1998 Act § 1001(a)(4).

[15] The 1998 Act § 1001(a)(4).

[16] IR-2000-57 (Aug. 15, 2000).

sentatives handle taxpayer complaints, ensure that taxpayer rights are not abridged, and participate in National Problem Solving Days.[17]

Table 9.1 provides the locations of all Appeals Offices.[18]

TABLE 9.1 ———————————————————————————————
Location of Appeals Offices

	Appeals Offices	Suboffices
Midstates Region		
Austin, TX (South Texas)	X	
San Antonio, TX		X
Chicago, IL (Illinois)	X	
Morton Grove, IL		X
Peoria, IL		X
Springfield, IL		X
Westmont, IL		X
*Dallas, TX (North Texas)	X	
Houston, TX	X	
Milwaukee, WI (Midwest)	X	
Des Moines, IA		X
Omaha, NE		X
Oklahoma City, OK (Arkansas-Oklahoma)	X	
Little Rock, AR		X
Tulsa, OK		X
St. Louis, MO (Kansas-Missouri)	X	
Kansas City, MO		X
Wichita, KS		X
St. Paul, MN (North Central)	X	
Aberdeen, SD		X
Fargo, ND		X
Northeast Region		
Boston, MA (New England)	X	
Andover Service Center, MA		X
Augusta, ME		X
Burlington, VT		X
Portsmouth, NH		X
S. Portland, ME		X
Springfield, MA		X
Buffalo, NY (Upstate New York)	X	
Albany, NY		X
Newburgh, NY		X
Rochester, NY		X
Syracuse, NY		X
Cincinnati, OH (Ohio)	X	
Cleveland, OH		X

---

[17] Ann. 99-98, 1999-42 IRB 1. The office and telephone numbers for each of the Customer Service Representatives appear at the end of the announcement. Telephone numbers may also be obtained from the Appeals Web site http://www.irs.gov/ind_info/appeals/index.html. Information may also be obtained by phoning the Director, Office of Alternative Dispute Resolution and Customer Service Programs, at (202) 694-1875.

[18] IRM Exhibit 8.1.2-1.

	Appeals Offices	Suboffices
Columbus, OH		X
Dayton, OH		X
Toledo, OH		X
Detroit, MI (Michigan)	X	
Flint, MI		X
Grand Rapids, MI		X
Hartford, CT (Connecticut–Rhode Island)	X	
New Haven, CT		X
Providence, RI		X
Long Island, NY (Brooklyn)	X	
Brookhaven Service Ctr., NY		X
*Manhattan, NY	X	
Newark, NJ	X	
Philadelphia, PA (Pennsylvania)	X	
Pittsburgh, PA		X
Southeast Region		
*Atlanta, GA	X	
Baltimore, MD (Delaware-Maryland)	X	
Washington, DC		X
Wilmington, DE		X
**Fort Lauderdale, FL (South Florida)	X	
Miami, FL		X
Greensboro, NC (North-South Carolina)	X	
Charlotte, NC		X
Columbia, SC		X
Indianapolis, IN (Indiana)	X	
South Bend, IN		X
Jacksonville, FL (North Florida)	X	
Tampa, FL		X
Nashville, TN (Kentucky-Tennessee)	X	
Knoxville, TN		X
Louisville, KY		X
Lexington, KY		X
Memphis, TN		X
New Orleans, LA (Gulf Coast)	X	
Birmingham, AL		X
Jackson, MS		X
Richmond, VA (Virginia–West Virginia)	X	
Baileys Crossroads, VA		X
Charleston, WV		X
Huntington, WV		X
Western Region		
Denver, CO (Rocky Mountain)	X	
Boise, ID		X
Cheyenne, WY		X
Helena, MT		X
Salt Lake City, UT		X
Laguna Niguel, CA (Southern Cal.)	X	
Riverside, CA		X
San Diego, CA		X
Los Angeles	X	
El Monte, CA		X
Glendale, CA		X
Thousand Oaks, CA		X

	Appeals Offices	Suboffices
Phoenix, AZ (Southwest)	X	
Albuquerque, NM		X
Las Vegas, NV		X
Reno, NV		X
*San Francisco, CA (Northern California)	X	
Sacramento, CA		X
Walnut Creek, CA		X
San Jose, CA (Central California)	X	
Fresno, CA		X
Seattle, WA (Pacific-Northwest)	X	
Anchorage, AK		X
Honolulu, HI		X
Portland, OR		X

    * Regional Office
** Cases will continued to be processed in the Miami office.

¶ 9.03 APPEALS OFFICE JURISDICTION

In general terms, the Office of Appeals has the "exclusive and final authority" to determine liability for most taxes in cases originating in a local office located within its area.[19] Appeals authority is exclusive because it is independent of the functions from whose determinations taxpayers appeal.[20] Reaffirming the independence of Appeals representatives, the Statement of Procedural Rules states, "It shall be [the Appeals Officer's] duty to determine the correct amount of the tax, with strict impartiality between the taxpayer and the Government, and without favoritism or discrimination as between taxpayers."[21] Appeals authority is final because there is no appeal from an Appeals Office decision to any other office in the Service. As a result, Appeals Offices serve as tribunals of last resort within the Service, with the objective of "resolv[ing] tax controversies without litigation on a basis which is fair and impartial to both the government and the taxpayer."[22] In carrying out this duty, Appeals officers consider taxpayer appeals, hold conferences, and negotiate settlements.

---

[19] SPR, 26 CFR § 601.106(a)(1).

[20] Before its 1998 reorganization, the Statement of Procedural Rules stated that the Appeals Office represents the Regional Commissioner in "his/her exclusive and final authority" (SPR, 26 CFR § 601.106(a)(1)(ii)) and that under certain conditions the Regional Commissioner may assume direct control over a case in the Appeals Office (26 CFR § 601.106(c)(3)). The exclusive authority of the Appeals Office to make final determinations, including settlements, also appears to result from the fact that this delegation of authority runs directly from the Commissioner of Internal Revenue.

[21] SPR, 26 CFR § 601.106(f)(2) (Rule I).

[22] IRM 8.1.3.2, Appeals Mission (May 19, 1998). See also SPR, 26 CFR § 601.106(f)(2) (Rule II).

[1] Denial of Appeals Conferences

Despite the important role of the Office of Appeals, most courts consider procedural regulations, such as the ones establishing the appeals system, to be directory, not mandatory, statements of procedure for the regulation of the Service itself and not to have the force of law.[23] On this rationale, for example, the Service's failure or refusal to provide an Appeals Office conference to a taxpayer has been found neither to deny the taxpayer due process nor to invalidate a notice of deficiency. Even when a taxpayer has been denied Appeals review, the taxpayer denied Appeals review is sent a notice of deficiency. As a result, the taxpayer is able to obtain prepayment judicial review of a deficiency by filing a petition in the Tax Court. Courts have concluded that due process standards were not violated because due process is said not to require a hearing at any particular point in an administrative proceeding, as long as judicial review is available at some point. Courts have pointed to the Supreme Court's decision in *United States v. Caceres*[24] for authority that the Service is not always held to strict compliance with its rules, at least when the relief requested for noncompliance is drastic. *Caceres* was a bribery prosecution in which the agents had failed to obtain approval for nonconsensual recording in accordance with the Service's Manual. The defendant requested that recorded conversations be suppressed because of the failure; suppression of the conversations would have assured the acquittal of the defendant. A comparable result in a civil case might be the cancellation of the liability determined.[25] However, a less drastic request, such as an order to hold a conference, seems to be acceptable under a *Caceres*-type analysis.[26]

A denial of the Appeals conference procedures also raises the question of whether, in a particular case, the Service's departure from its procedural rules reflects an arbitrariness "inherently characteristic of an agency's violation of

---

[23] Luhring v. Glotzbach, 304 F2d 560 (4th Cir. 1962) (deficiency notices sent without prior thirty-day letter); Rosenberg v. Comm'r, 450 F2d 529 (10th Cir. 1971) (no Appellate Division conference granted, although taxpayer filed a protest); Cleveland Trust Co. v. United States, 421 F2d 475 (6th Cir.), cert. denied, 400 US 819 (1970). See also Einhorn v. DeWitt, 618 F2d 347 (5th Cir. 1980) (rules covering permissible disclosure of information at district criminal investigation division (CID) conference "govern internal affairs" of Service); United States v. Goldstein, 342 F. Supp. 661 (EDNY 1972) (taxpayer denied district and regional conferences in criminal case). Different types of regulations and their legal effect are discussed at ¶¶ 1.06 and 3.02[4][a].

[24] United States v. Caceres, 440 US 741 (1979).

[25] See, e.g., Robert F. Collins v. Comm'r, 61 TC 693 (1974) (failure to comply with Service reopening procedures does not affect validity of notice of deficiency).

[26] One court ordered the Service to grant an Appeals conference when, in response to a thirty-day letter, the taxpayer requested one. Shields v. Sassi, 78-2 USTC 9612 (WD Wash. 1978).

its own procedures."[27] Courts following the authority of *Luhring v. Glotzbach*[28] overlook the long history, frequent use, and mutual benefit of administrative review within the Service. Although one product of this history was creation of the Board of Tax Appeals, now the Tax Court,[29] the availability of judicial review by the Tax Court is not a substitute for administrative review within the Service. Administrative review, as the Service recognizes, is an expeditious and informal procedure that avoids the expense of litigation to the benefit of both the Service and the taxpayer.[30] Moreover, unless the Service can satisfactorily demonstrate some rational basis for denying one taxpayer administrative appeal that it has long been granted to other taxpayers, the denial raises substantial due process and equal protection questions. These issues have not been adequately addressed by the courts, which have refused to hold the Service to its appeals procedures.

[2] Jurisdiction and Functional Authority

More specifically, the jurisdiction of Appeals is as follows:[31]

[a] Preassessment Cases

Appeals has jurisdiction over preassessment cases involving (1) income, estate, gift, and miscellaneous excise tax (whether before or after a notice of deficiency has been issued); (2) employment and certain excise tax liabilities; and (3) additions to the tax and additional amounts (the penalties described in Sections 6651 through 6665), and assessable penalties (described in Sections 6671 through 6724), provided that the taxpayer has requested Appeals Office consideration and, if required, has filed a written protest.[32] Appeals jurisdiction includes cases that are subject to deficiency procedures or involve a tax liability. In most cases, a local office has made a determination of the taxpayer's liability, and sent a preliminary (thirty-day or sixty-day) letter to the taxpayer,

---

[27] See United States v. Heffner, 420 F2d 809, 812 (4th Cir. 1969), applying the doctrine of United States ex rel. Accardi v. Shaughnessy, 347 US 260 (1954).

[28] Luhring v. Glotzbach, 304 F2d 560 (4th Cir. 1962).

[29] See H. Dubroff, The United States Tax Court—An Historical Analysis (1979).

[30] See, e.g., Rev. Proc. 79-34, 1979-1 CB 498. (The work of Appeals Offices is "intended for the benefit of taxpayers and the Government under which the treatment of issues and the disposition of cases generally have been accomplished in a consistent manner.")

[31] SPR, 26 CFR §§ 601.106(a)(1)(ii)–601.106(a)(1)(iv). See IRM 8.1, Functional Authority and Jurisdiction of Appeals, 2.2.2, Jurisdiction of Appeals—General (May 19, 1998).

[32] The protest requirement is discussed infra ¶ 9.05.

and the taxpayer has requested an Appeals conference.[33] In other cases, a local office has determined that an assessable penalty is due. In still another group of cases, the local office has sent the taxpayer a notice of deficiency, and the taxpayer has filed a petition in the Tax Court. It can be said, therefore, that Appeals Offices consider two broad categories of cases: (1) nondocketed cases, in which the taxpayer has filed a protest to the local office's proposed action usually the determination that the taxpayer owes additional income, estate or gift taxes; assessable penalties; the disallowance of a taxpayer's claim for refund of tax; or a rejection of an offer in compromise; and (2) docketed cases, in which the taxpayer has filed a petition for a redetermination in the Tax Court, and the Tax Court has entered the case on its docket.

Generally, cases considered by Appeals involve a disputed tax, but in some cases, there is no immediate tax consequence because no tax liability is in dispute for the period in Appeals. These cases are nevertheless considered by Appeals.[34] For example, suppose adjustments made to a return result in a potential deficiency or overassessment. If a net operating loss carryforward offsets the deficiency or overassessment, Appeals will nevertheless consider the case, as long as a protest is filed.

[b] Postassessment Penalty Cases

Appeals has jurisdiction over an assessment of penalties provided for in Chapter 68 (entitled Additions to the Tax, Additional Amounts, and Assessable Penalties), which are subject to a reasonable cause determination (e.g., delinquent filing or payment).[35] These penalties are an exception to the general rule that Chapter 68 penalties may be appealed only after the penalty has been assessed and paid and a claim for refund has been filed. Postassessment appeal is available if the penalty does not involve a reasonable cause determination (e.g., reasonable cause is not a basis for waiving the penalty for failure to pay estimated tax). Postassessment appeal is not permitted on other penalties subject to deficiency procedures (e.g., negligence, fraud, and trust fund penalties) because the taxpayer has the right to appeal these penalties before assess-

---

[33] IRM 8.1, Functional Authority and Jurisdiction of Appeals, 2.2.2(3), Jurisdiction of Appeals—General (May 19, 1998).

[34] IRM 8.1, Functional Authority and Jurisdiction of Appeals, 2.2.3, "No Immediate Tax Consequence" Cases (May 19, 1998). Other types of "no immediate tax consequences" cases are the carryforward of a net operating loss to a year that has not been examined, Section 6166 estate tax cases, and employee plan determination cases.

[35] Penalty appeal procedures are found in the Statement of Procedural Rules. 26 CFR §§ 601.106(a)(1)(ii)(c), 601.106(a)(1)(iii). See also IRM Penalties Handbook 20.1.4 et seq. (Aug. 20, 1998) (Methods of Appealing Penalties). See Rev. Proc. 86-10, 1986-1 CB 534 (establishing procedure on a trial basis for appeal of reasonable cause penalty assessments).

ment.[36] No postassessment appeal procedure applies to the Section 6700 penalty for promoting an abusive tax shelter because the penalty is subject to the procedural rules of Section 6703, which provide for an extension of the period of collection of the penalty where a person pays not less than 15 percent of the penalty amount.[37] Appeal of a reasonable cause penalty may be made before or after payment, but it must be made before a claim for refund is filed.

Penalty cases reach the Office of Appeals in several different ways. There are at least six methods that a taxpayer can use to protest a proposed or assessed penalty to Appeals:[38]

1. *Deficiency.* When a penalty is based on a liability determined under deficiency procedures, the Appeals Office considers the penalty at the same time as the liability (e.g., the accuracy-related and fraud penalties).

2. *Deficiency-type.* For certain "stand-alone" penalties (i.e., penalties without any relationship to liabilities subject to deficiency procedures), the Service has provided deficiency-type review procedures (e.g., in trust fund recovery penalty cases and tax preparer penalties under Section 6694).

3. *Special claims for refund.* Procedures have been provided by statute to mitigate the potential hardship for taxpayers subject to stand-alone penalties for which deficiency procedures are unavailable. These procedures usually involve the payment of a portion of the assessment and the filing of a claim for refund (e.g., the preparer penalty under Section 6694, the tax shelter promoter penalty of Section 6700, and the aiding and abetting penalty of Section 6701 covered by Section 6703.

4. *Postassessment penalty appeal.* Appeal is available for a penalty subject to abatement on account of reasonable cause or due diligence (e.g., delinquency penalties).

5. *Claims for refund.* All penalties are subject to Appeals Office review if the taxpayer pays the penalty and files a claim for refund.

6. *Offer in compromise.* Taxpayers may file an offer in compromise on either doubt as to liability or doubt as to collectibility of assessed penalties.

[c] Tax-Exempt/Government Entity Cases

The Office of Appeals has jurisdiction over Employee Plan and Exempt Organization cases involving initial or continuing tax exemption or foundation classification, and initial or continuing employee plan qualification, unless the

---

[36] But see Rev. Proc. 84-78, 1984-2 CB 754, § 6 (if there are a number of responsible persons and one has filed suit for refund, the others will be denied an Appeals conference).

[37] SPR, 26 CFR § 601.106(a)(1)(iii)(d).

[38] IRM Penalties Handbook 20.1.4, Methods of Appealing Penalties (Aug. 20, 1998).

case is covered by a National Office ruling or technical advice in which the organization or the plan has either a limited or no right to appeal to the National Office.[39] The Appeals Office also has jurisdiction to review an adverse determination of the tax-exempt status of a bond issue; in fact, the Service is statutorily directed to provide an administrative appeal right to a bond issuer if the Service proposes to the bond issuer that interest on an obligation the bond issuer previously issued is not tax-exempt under Section 103.[40]

[d] Collection Cases

Under the Collection Appeals Program, the Office of Appeals has jurisdiction to review certain actions Collection takes.[41] These appealable actions are seizures, levies, and Notices of Federal Tax Lien. Because the release of a federal tax lien is governed by Section 6325, the appeal of the filing or refusal to release a Notice of Federal Tax Lien is subject to the statutory guidelines. Relief on appeal outside these guidelines normally will be limited to hearing a request that a notice of lien not be filed, that the lien be discharged or subordinated, or that a certificate of nonattachment of lien be issued. Before appeal, the taxpayer must first discuss the collection action with the revenue officer's manager. Appeal of collection action is supposed to be completed within an extremely short period of time. Normally, collection action will be suspended during the appeal, but if delay in collection would be detrimental to ultimate

---

[39] SPR, 26 CFR § 601.106(a)(1)(iv). See IRM 8.16, Employee Plan and Exempt Organization Cases (June 3, 1998).

[40] 1998 Act § 3105. For procedures for issuers to request administrative appeal of a proposed adverse determination on the tax exemption for bond interest, see Rev. Proc. 99-35, 1999-41 IRB 501.

[41] IRM 8.7, Technical and Procedural Guidelines, 1.1.9, Collection Appeals Program (Jan. 1, 1999). There are exceptions to the program for Collection issues, for which separate appeal procedures already apply, such as offers in compromise, trust fund penalties, penalties, and jeopardy levies. If the taxpayer has filed a request for a Taxpayer Assistance Order before the case is sent to the Appeals Office, the request will be sent by the Appeals Office to the Taxpayer Advocate for action. If the request for the Tax Assistance Order is filed after the case is sent to the Appeals Office, the hardship issues will be referred to the Taxpayer Advocate for consideration, while the Appeals Office considers the other issues. The Appeals Office is supposed to complete its action before the Taxpayer Advocate because the Appeals resolution may make action by the Taxpayer Advocate unnecessary. Cases under the jurisdiction of a court and criminal investigations are also excluded.

According to the Director of Appeals, in fiscal year 1997, there were 1,479 Collection appeals filed—376 were related to liens. Through December 31, 1997, of the 287 Collection appeals filed, 109 dealt with lien issues. In fiscal 2001, the number of collection appeals received was 17,522 cases; during the same period, 11,966 collection cases were resolved. Int. Rev. Svc. Data Book 2001, pg. 17. Due process appeals is the reason for the substantial number of appeals in collection cases.

collection of the assessed tax, collection will continue during the appeal process.

As a result of the IRS Restructuring and Reform Act of 1998, the Appeals Office has jurisdiction in collection cases, including due process review before the filing of a notice of lien (Section 6320); due process review before a levy is made, in which alternatives to levy, such as installment payment agreement will be considered (Section 6320); review of rejected offers in compromise (Section 7122(d)); and the early referral of collection issues (Section 7123). Due process appeals are reviewed in Chapter 14, in connection with the discussion of liens and levies.

[e] Jeopardy Levies

A jeopardy levy is a levy made and served when the Service finds that collection of a tax will be jeopardized by delay, and so the levy calls for the immediate surrender of the taxpayer's property and rights to property without any waiting period.[42] When a jeopardy levy is made, the taxpayer is entitled to the due process review procedures of Section 7429, including administrative review. The Office of Appeals is the forum for final Service review.[43]

[f] Claims for Refund and Settlement of Refund Suits

The Office of Appeals has jurisdiction over appeals from rejections of claims for refund proposed by local offices.[44] A request for Appeals Office consideration and a protest are required to secure Appeals review.[45]

[g] Offers in Compromise

The Office of Appeals has jurisdiction to provide independent administrative review of a local office's proposed rejection of an offer in compromise or installment agreement.[46] It also has jurisdiction to hear a taxpayer's appeal of the local office's rejection of an offer in compromise or installment agreement.[47]

---

[42] IRC § 6331(a).

[43] IRC § 7429(a)(3).

[44] SPR, 26 CFR §§ 601.106(a)(1)(ii), 601.106(d)(2)(ii).

[45] 26 CFR § 601.106(a)(1)(ii).

[46] IRC § 7122(d)(1).

[47] IRC § 7122(d)(2).

[h] Administrative Costs and Interest Abatements

Section 7430 provides that a taxpayer who substantially prevails in an administrative or court proceeding may be awarded a judgment for reasonable costs the taxpayer has incurred in the proceeding. The party moving for costs must prove that (1) the moving party did not unreasonably protract the proceeding and (2) the moving party was the prevailing party. The Appeals Office has jurisdiction over requests for administrative costs, as well.

The Office of Appeals has jurisdiction over requests for abatement of interest under Section 6404(e). This interest must be on a deficiency attributable, in whole or in part, to delays by managers and employees of the Service in performing a managerial or ministerial act, or their error or delay in paying any tax.[48]

[3] Limitations on Jurisdiction

As broad as it is, Appeals Office authority is subject to restrictions arising from (1) the subject matter or status of the case and (2) geographic considerations. These limitations are discussed in the following sections.

[a] Subject Matter

The Office of Appeals has exclusive and final jurisdiction over a wide range of cases, but not all. The following types of cases limit the Appeals Office's jurisdiction.

[i] **Docketed cases.** The Office of Appeals generally does not have authority to negotiate or make a settlement in a docketed Tax Court case if the notice of deficiency (a) was issued by the Appeals Office itself; (b) was issued by a Tax-Exempt/Government Entity after an Appeals Office consideration of all petitioned issues; or (c) was issued by a local office and was based on a ruling or technical advice on issues involving qualification of an employee plan, foundation status of an organization, public inspection of a written determination,[49] or a declaratory judgment.[50]

[ii] **Fraud penalty cases.** If criminal prosecution for tax evasion or failure to file a return has been recommended, the Appeals Office must secure the

---

[48] IRC § 6404(e)(1).

[49] IRC § 6110.

[50] IRC § 7478.

agreement of the District Counsel to eliminate the fraud penalty for a year included in a recommendation.[51]

[iii] Criminal cases. The Appeals Office may not act in a case in which criminal prosecution has been recommended, except with the agreement of District Counsel.[52]

[iv] Joint Committee cases. Refunds or credits in excess of $2 million must be reported to Congress's Joint Committee on Taxation. The Joint Committee has no explicit authority to overrule an administrative decision to make the refund or credit, but an Appeals Office settlement is not effective until the Appeals Office has received a notice that the Joint Committee has no objection to the proposed overpayment.[53] In practice, the Service considers the Joint Committee to have authority. The detail required for preparation of a Joint Committee report by the Appeals Office undoubtedly results in a more thorough review of these cases.

[v] Interrelated cases. In so-called whipsaw cases, taxpayers may take inconsistent positions on the same item or transactions. Thus, a settlement reached with one taxpayer may have a direct tax effect on another taxpayer. If an Appeals Office fails to take action to ensure that the taxpayers involved are treated consistently, each taxpayer may receive a tax benefit to the government's detriment. Therefore, procedures have been adopted to deal with these cases. For Appeals purposes, interrelated cases are defined as those in which a determination on an issue in one case has a direct tax effect in another,[54] such as the following: (1) the amount or distribution of net income of a partnership, estate, or trust and (2) gift versus compensation from a corporation to a widow of a deceased employee, or value of goodwill in the sale of a going business.

Usually, all interrelated cases are forwarded together by the District Office to the Appeals Office. In deciding whether to consider cases as interrelated and handle them concurrently, the Appeals Office applies two standards: (1) the best use of the Service's resources and (2) the avoidance of whipsaw

---

[51] SPR, 26 CFR § 601.106(a)(2)(v).

[52] SPR, 26 CFR § 601.106(a)(2)(v). IRM 8.7, Technical and Procedural Guidelines, 1.1.5, Cases Involving Criminal Prosecution and Restrictions on Appeals Jurisdiction in Criminal Cases (Jan. 1, 1999).

[53] IRC § 6405; SPR, 26 CFR § 601.106(g); IRM 8.9, Appeals Joint Committee Cases, 1.1, Introduction to Joint Committee Case Procedures (Apr. 14, 1997), IRM 8.9, Appeals Joint Committee Cases, 1.2, Appeals Responsibility in Joint Committee Cases (Apr. 14, 1997). Joint Committee review is described at ¶ 11.13.

[54] IRM 8.2, Pre-90-Day and Protested Excise and Employment Tax Cases, 1.1.5.1, Definition of Related Cases (Feb. 17, 1999).

situations.[55] To avoid whipsaw situations in interrelated cases, the Appeals Office may take inconsistent positions if all of the taxpayers are unwilling to agree to a settlement acceptable to the Appeals Office, or they are unwilling to have the Appeals Office consider their cases concurrently.[56] The Appeals Office may assume jurisdiction in a related case (interrelated cases are a type of related case) if the taxpayers agree.[57] The fact that interrelated cases are still at the local office level or in different Appeals Offices is not an obstacle to concurrent consideration if the taxpayers agree. The Appeals Office can either request the local office to expedite its action or coordinate action with other Appeals Offices.[58]

[vi] **Bankruptcy cases.** The Office of Appeals jurisdiction in bankruptcy cases is governed by an agreement between the Service and the Justice Department's Tax Division.[59] This agreement is similar to the procedures followed by the Office of Appeals and District Counsel in docketed Tax Court cases. When a bankruptcy petition is filed, the Appeals Office is permitted to continue to work for a period of six months after the filing date on a case already in inventory at the time of the bankruptcy petition or received after the petition, as long as the taxpayer does not file an objection to the Service's proof of claim

---

[55] IRM 8.2, Pre-90-Day and Protested Excise and Employment Tax Cases, 1.1.5.2.1, Appeals Consideration of Interrelated Cases (Feb. 17, 1999).

[56] IRM 8.2, Pre-90-Day and Protested Excise and Employment Tax Cases, 1.1.5.2(6), Scope of Appeals Consideration of Related Cases (Feb. 17, 1999).

[57] See 26 CFR § 601.106(f) (Rule V).

[58] See IRM 8.2, Pre-90-Day and Protested Excise and Employment Tax Cases, 1.1.5.2.1, Appeals Consideration of Interrelated Cases, and 1.1.5.2.2, Appeals Consideration of Principal Cases Without Related Cases (Feb. 17, 1999).

[59] IRM 8.15, Bankruptcy Cases, 1.1.2.1, Department of Justice and the Chief Counsel's Agreement (Nov. 19, 1998).

in the bankruptcy proceeding.[60] If more than six months is needed, the Appeals Office must secure permission from the Justice Department's Tax Division.

[vii] **Regulatory excise tax cases.** Appeals Office authority does not extend to excise tax provisions that are largely regulatory in nature, such as alcohol, tobacco, and firearms excise taxes.[61]

[viii] **Constitutional and religious issues.** Cases embracing arguments based on constitutional, religious, moral, political, or similar grounds are not permitted an administrative appeal.

[b] Geographic Jurisdiction Limitations

The Service has formulated rules to deal with geographic problems that may develop in Appeals Office conferences. An Appeals Office has jurisdiction over cases arising in offices located in its area.

[i] **Transfer of cases.** When a taxpayer has moved to another area, the Service uses a procedure similar to court procedures for transferring a case to a more convenient forum. In a nondocketed case (or in an excise or employment tax case), the Appeals Office for the originating office is authorized to transfer settlement jurisdiction to the region where the taxpayer resides and the taxpayer's books and records are located (or can be made available).[62] Transfer for any other reason requires approval by a Director of Appeals.

In docketed cases, the Appeals Office for the originating local office has similar authority to transfer settlement jurisdiction. Such a transfer depends on the place where the Tax Court hearing will be held. If the Tax Court hearing is to be held in a region where the taxpayer resides and the taxpayer's books and records are located (or can be made available), the jurisdiction of the regional office for the originating district is permitted to transfer the case to the

---

[60] IRM 8.15, Bankruptcy Cases, 1.1.2.3, Time Limitations on Bankruptcy Case Handling (Nov. 19, 1998). On November 6, 1997, the Service began testing, for a six- to twelve-month period, a new administrative process for resolving certain tax-related disputes in some bankruptcy cases. Ann. 97-111, 1997-41 IRB 15. To enter the process, the debtor's bankruptcy case must be open at the time the process is initiated and the debtor must have filed a petition in a bankruptcy court located in Massachusetts, Arizona, the Houston IRS district, or the Indiana IRS district. Disputes are reviewed initially by the Office of Special Procedures within the Collection Division and appeals may be taken to the Office of Appeals. The announcement states that "[t]he processing for disputes should be about 15 days if no appeal is needed, and will generally be 30 days if an appeal is requested."

[61] SPR, 26 CFR § 601.106(a)(3).

[62] SPR, 26 CFR § 601.106(e)(1).

regional office for the place of trial.[63] Counsel may transfer litigation authority to this office as well.

Settlement jurisdiction may be removed from an Appeals Office if it is determined that the government's interests will be better served by the transfer of settlement jurisdiction.[64]

[c] Status Limitations

[i] **Appeals in pre-ninety-day cases.** In a nondocketed case, a statutory notice of deficiency has not been sent to the taxpayer (pre-ninety-day cases) or a statutory notice has been sent to a taxpayer but the ninety-day period for filing the Tax Court petition has not yet expired (ninety-day cases). In a pre-ninety-day or prestatutory notice case, the Appeals Office acquires jurisdiction when (1) the district has not sent a ninety-day letter; (2) the taxpayer requests Appeals Office consideration; and (3) the taxpayer, if required, submits a protest of the district's determination of tax liability.[65] Thus, one of the characteristics of a pre-ninety-day case is the filing of a protest. A taxpayer is sent a thirty-day letter offering the opportunity to protest the finding to the Appeals Office. As a general rule, a thirty-day letter is not sent by a local office unless there is a minimum period of time (at least 120 days) before the expiration of the statutory period on assessment.[66] When a case is received by the Appeals Office and the time remaining on the assessment statute is less than the minimum considered necessary to process the case, the Appeals Office can return the case to the local office.[67]

Once a case is transferred to the Appeals Office, and the taxpayer and the Appeals Office are able to agree on a settlement, the agreement usually is reflected on Form 870-AD (Offer of Waiver of Restrictions on Assessment and Collection of Deficiency in Tax and of Acceptance of Overpayment) (see Form 9.1) or Form 870 (Waiver of Restrictions on Assessment and Collection

---

[63] SPR, 26 CFR § 601.106(e)(2). There is a limited exception if the Tax Court hearing is to be held in Washington, D.C. No transfer can be made to the region in which Washington is located (the Mid-Atlantic Region) unless the taxpayer resides in and has his or her records in Washington.

[64] SPR, 26 CFR § 601.106(e)(3).

[65] SPR, 26 CFR § 601.106(b).

[66] IRM 8.2, Pre-90-Day and Protested Excise and Employment Tax Cases, 1.1.3.1, Period of Limitations on Case Received in Appeals—General (Feb. 17, 1999). In estate tax cases and cases involving the accumulated earnings tax, there must be at least 180 days remaining on the assessment statute.

[67] During the appeals process, the Service can request a consent to extend the assessment period if the statutory period will expire in sixty days. IRM 8.2.1.1.3.3, General Instructions for Consents (Feb. 17, 1999).

of Deficiency in Tax and Acceptance of Overassessment) (see Form 9.2) for income tax cases and on similar forms for cases involving other taxes.[68]

If a settlement cannot be reached, the Appeals Office, rather than the local office, sends the statutory notice of the deficiency to the taxpayer.[69] The amount of the deficiency is not necessarily the same as that determined by the local office. On receiving a statutory notice issued by the Appeals Office, the taxpayer must decide whether to (1) file a petition in the Tax Court within ninety days; (2) permit the ninety-day period to lapse, pay the assessed tax, and file a claim for refund before instituting a refund suit in a district court or the Court of Federal Claims; or (3) permit immediate assessment of the deficiency by waiving the restrictions on assessment by signing a Form 870 or waiting for the ninety-day period to expire after receiving the statutory notice of deficiency.

A case is referred to as a ninety-day case during the period between the date the ninety-day letter is sent until either the date the taxpayer files a petition in the Tax Court or the date on which the ninety-day period expires and the case is processed for assessment. The Office of Appeals sometimes takes settlement jurisdiction during the ninety-day period and attempts to dispose of the case by agreement. The Service Manual states, "Appeals does not consider or reconsider a case during the ninety-day period, unless there are extenuating circumstances, and then only upon specific request by the taxpayer."[70]

Appeals has exclusive jurisdiction to hear and settle ninety-day cases when the statutory notice was issued by a local office and the taxpayer requests Appeals Office consideration.[71] If the taxpayer has had a conference before the Appeals Office during the prestatutory notice status or was given the opportunity for a conference but failed to request one, the Appeals Office will not grant a conference after the mailing of the notice of deficiency, except in "unusual circumstances."[72] A conference might be granted, for example, if the taxpayer may not have had an opportunity for a hearing for reasons beyond the taxpayers's control.

[ii] Appeals in docketed cases. A "docketed case" is a case in which the taxpayer has filed a petition in the Tax Court in response to a statutory notice

---

[68] SPR, 26 CFR § 601.106(d)(2)(i).

[69] SPR, 26 CFR § 601.106(d)(2)(ii).

[70] IRM 8.4, Docketed and 90-Day Cases, 1.5.2, Appeals Consideration of 90-Day Cases (Apr. 16, 1999). Even if the Appeals Office does consider a case, proceedings before the Appeals Office in no way waive or extend the ninety-day period for filing a petition in the Tax Court.

[71] IRM 8.4, Docketed and 90-Day Cases, 1.5.2, Appeals Consideration of 90-Day Cases (Apr. 16, 1999); see also Delegation Order No. 66 (as revised).

[72] IRM 1.2.1, Policies of the IRS Handbook, 1.8.2, P-8-24 (Conferences Not Granted in 90-Day Cases in Absence of Unusual Circumstances) (approved Dec. 23, 1960).

of deficiency sent by a local office. The local office sends a notice of deficiency to a taxpayer if the taxpayer does not file a protest in response to a thirty-day letter, thereby bypassing, either intentionally or not, prepetition appeals procedures. The local office also sends a taxpayer a notice of deficiency when the statute of limitations on assessment is about to expire. Although Appeals Offices do not lose jurisdiction merely because a taxpayer files a petition in the Tax Court, their jurisdiction to negotiate a settlement is limited by the fact that the Chief Counsel represents the Commissioner in proceedings in the Tax Court.

To understand Appeals Office procedures in docketed cases, it is necessary to describe some of the Tax Court's rules of practice. The Tax Court issues the calendar for a trial session no later than ninety days in advance of the opening date of the trial calendar.[73] The Standing Pretrial Order of the Tax Court imposes the following obligations on the parties:

1. At least sixty days before the calendar call, the parties are expected to meet to discuss settlement.

2. At least thirty days before the calendar call, the parties are to submit a Joint Case Status Report.

3. At least twenty days before the calendar call, the parties are required to submit and exchange a trial memorandum.

The deadlines mandated by the Tax Court's Standing Pretrial Order require the Appeals Office to terminate control of a docketed case in sufficient time for the counsel attorney to prepare the case for trial and stand ready to comply with the requirements of settlement discussion, status report, and trial memorandum. The period between the presumptive issuance date of the trial calendar and the opening of the trial session is the presession period. After the opening date of the Tax Court session at which a case is on the calendar for trial, pretrial hearing, or report, the case is referred to as a session case.

Both the timing of Appeals jurisdiction and the procedures the Appeals Office and Counsel must follow in docketed cases is described in revenue procedures that have been modified from time to time.[74] In general, these procedures are designed to (1) use the administrative appeals process in cases for which no Appeals hearing has previously been held and (2) permit counsel further time to prepare docketed cases for trial by discovery, stipulation, and such. The objective of the Appeals Office and Counsel procedures is to have docketed cases settled by the Appeals Office if possible and to have only those

---

[73] Tax Ct. R. Prac. & Proc. 132(a).

[74] Rev. Proc. 87-24, 1987-1 CB 720. See Reg. § 601.106(d)(3)(i) (cases docketed in the Tax Court). See also IRM 8.4.1.1.2, Appeals Authority Over Docketed Cases (Apr. 16, 1999).

cases not susceptible to administrative settlement returned to counsel for trial preparation.

To ensure that the Appeals Office and counsel attorneys perform their respective functions, Appeals and Division Counsel operate under the following procedures:[75]

1. After a case is docketed in the Tax Court, Division Counsel transfers the case to the Appeals Office for settlement consideration, unless Appeals issued the notice of deficiency. Even if the Appeals Office has issued the notice of deficiency, the case may be returned to Appeals unless Division Counsel decides that there is little likelihood that all or part of the case can be settled within a reasonable period of time.[76]

2. When a case involves a tax deficiency of more than $10,000 including tax and penalties, the Appeals Office returns the case to Division Counsel (1) if no progress toward settling all or part of the case is made or (2) the case appears on a trial calendar (unless Division Counsel agrees to extend the period for Appeals consideration).[77]

3. When the case involves a tax deficiency of $10,000 or less (including a case classified as an S case by the Tax Court), counting tax and penalties, the case is referred to Appeals (1) for a period of six months or (2) until one month before the call of the trial calendar if the case was classified by the Tax Court as a regular case or, in an S case, fifteen days before the call of the trial calendar, if earlier. At the end of the applicable period, the case is returned to Division Counsel unless both Appeals and Division Counsel agree that the period of Appeals consideration should be extended.

4. When a case is in the Appeals Office or in Division Counsel's office, that office has sole settlement authority. However, if Division Counsel requests the case file to prepare for trial, or if the case file has been returned, Division Counsel and the Appeals Office can agree that Appeals should continue to attempt to settle the case while trial preparation is taking place.

---

[75] Rev. Proc. 87-24, 1987-1 CB 720.

[76] Rev. Proc. 87-24, 1987-1 CB 720, § 2.01. Division Counsel may return a case to the Appeals Office, even if Appeals has already considered the case, if the transfer "will promote more efficient disposition of the case." Id. at § 2.05.

[77] Rev. Proc. 87-24, 1987-1 CB 720, § 2.02. Counsel may not be ordered by way of a writ of mandamus to enter into a stipulation based on an agreement reached with an Appeals officer. Gilliland v. Brooks, 651 F. Supp. 73 (MD Tenn. 1986) (interpreting 26 CFR § 601.106(d)(3)(iii), which deals with jurisdiction of Appeals Office over docketed Tax Court case). These rules do not apply to a case (or specific issues in a case) in which the notice of deficiency was issued by Appeals, the TE/GE Division or a local office on the basis of a ruling or technical advice on the qualification of an employee plan or tax exemption, or foundation status of an organization. Jurisdiction over the settlement of cases involving disclosure of rulings or technical advice under Section 6110, a declaratory judgment under Section 7428, 7476, 7477, or 7478 is in Division Counsel at the time the case is docketed in the Tax Court. Rev. Proc. 87-24, 1987-1 CB 720, § 3.

5. After an answer has been filed, Division Counsel and the Appeals Office can agree to work on the case jointly, with the Appeals Office having settlement jurisdiction and Division Counsel acting as adviser, which may entail attending conferences. This joint consultation can take place in appropriate cases, such as those involving "significant issues or large deficiencies."

6. At the request of Division Counsel and with the agreement of the Appeals Office, when Division Counsel has jurisdiction over a case, the Appeals Office is permitted to assist in settlement negotiations, trial preparation, or even at the trial of the case.

7. Appeals Office settlement authority over a case or certain issues in a case can be revoked if the Associate Chief Counsel (Litigation) or the Assistant Chief Counsel (International) so decides after consulting with the Director of the Appeals Division and the appropriate Regional Counsel.

8. After a case is received by either Division Counsel or the Appeals Office, the taxpayer, the representative, or both are notified "promptly." This notice states that the office in possession of the case has sole authority to settle the case and, when Division Counsel sends the notice, to try the case as well. If a case is going to be prepared for trial or if Appeals settlement authority has been revoked, the notice will so state.

FORM 9.1 ———————————————————
OFFER TO WAIVE RESTRICTIONS ON ASSESSMENT AND
COLLECTION OF TAX DEFICIENCY AND TO ACCEPT
OVERASSESSMENT

Form 870-AD (Rev. April 1982)	Department of the Treasury—Internal Revenue Service **Offer to Waive Restrictions on Assessment and Collection of Tax Deficiency and to Accept Overassessment**	
Symbols	Name of Taxpayer John Jones & Mary Jones	SSN or EIN 123-45-6789

Under the provisions of section 6213(d) of the Internal Revenue Code of 1986 (the Code), or corresponding provisions of prior internal revenue laws, the undersigned offers to waive the restrictions provided in section 6213(a) of the Code or corresponding provisions of prior internal revenue laws, and to consent to the assessment and collection of the following deficiencies and additions to tax, if any, with interest as provided by law. The undersigned offers also to accept the following overassessments, if any, as correct. Any waiver or acceptance of an overassessment is subject to any terms and conditions stated below and on the reverse side of this form.

Deficiencies (Overassessments) and Additions to Tax					
Year Ended	Kind of Tax	Tax			
1981	Income	$ 45,583	$	$	
1982	Income	$ 38,410	$	$	
1983	Income	$ (21,682)	$	$	
		$	$	$	
		$	$	$	
		$	$	$	

Signature of Taxpayer /S/ John Jones	Date 8/15/87
Signature of Taxpayer /S/ Mary Jones	Date 8/15/87
Signature of Taxpayer's Representative	Date
Corporate Name	Date
By Corporate Officer Title	Date

For Internal Revenue Use Only	Date Accepted for Commissioner	Signature
	Office	Title

Cat. No. 16896Q   (See Reverse Side)   Form **870-AD** (Rev. 4-92)

8/17/93

Form 870-AD.

This offer must be accepted for the Commissioner of Internal Revenue and will take effect on the date it is accepted. Unless and until it is accepted, it will have no force or effect.

If this offer is accepted, the case will not be reopened by the Commissioner unless there was:

- fraud, malfeasance, concealment or misrepresentation of a material fact
- an important mistake in mathematical calculation
- a deficiency or overassessment resulting from adjustments made under Subchapters C and D of Chapter 63 concerning the tax treatment of partnership and subchapter S items determined at the partnership and corporate level
- an excessive tentative allowance of a carryback provided by law

No claim for refund or credit will be filed or prosecuted by the taxpayer for the years stated on this form, other than for amounts attributed to carrybacks provided by law.

The proper filing of this offer, when accepted, will expedite assessment and billing (or overassessment, credit or refund) by adjusting the tax liability. This offer, when executed and timely submitted, will be considered a claim for refund for the above overassessment(s), if any.

This offer may be executed by the taxpayer's attorney, certified public accountant, or agent provided this is specifically authorized by a power of attorney which, if not previously filed, must accompany this form. If this offer is signed by a person acting in a fiduciary capacity (for example an executor, administrator, or a trustee) Form 56, Notice Concerning Fiduciary Relationship, must accompany this form, unless previously filed.

If this offer is executed for a year for which a joint return was filed, it must be signed by both spouses unless one spouse, acting under a power of attorney, signs as agent for the other.

If this offer is executed by a corporation, it must be signed with the corporate name followed by the signature and title of the officer(s) authorized to sign. If the offer is accepted, as a condition of acceptance, any signature by or for a corporate officer will be considered a representation by that person and the corporation, to induce reliance, that such signature is binding under law for the corporation to be assessed the deficiencies or receive credit or refund under this agreement. If the corporation later contests the signature as being unauthorized on its behalf, the person who signed may be subject to criminal penalties for representating that he or she had authority to sign this agreement on behalf of the corporation.

FORM 9.2 ———————————————————————
WAIVER OF RESTRICTIONS ON ASSESSMENT AND COLLECTION OF DEFICIENCY IN TAX AND ACCEPTANCE OF OVERASSESSMENT

Form 870 (Rev. March 1982)	Department of the Treasury — Internal Revenue Service **Waiver of Restrictions on Assessment and Collection of Deficiency in Tax and Acceptance of Overassessment**	Date received by Internal Revenue Service

Names and address of taxpayers (Number, street, city or town, State, ZIP code) John Jones & Mary Jones 1 James Street New York, N.Y. 00000	Social security or employer identification number 123-45-6789

Increase (Decrease) in Tax and Penalties

Tax year ended	Tax	Penalties			
1981	$ 45,583	$	$	$	$
1982	$ 38,410	$	$	$	$
1983	$(21,682)	$	$	$	$
	$	$	$	$	$
	$	$	$	$	$
	$	$	$	$	$
	$	$	$	$	$

(For instructions, see back of form)

Consent to Assessment and Collection

I consent to the immediate assessment and collection of any deficiencies (increase in tax and penalties) and accept any overassessment (decrease in tax and penalties) shown above, plus any interest provided by law. I understand that by signing this waiver, I will not be able to contest these years in the United States Tax Court, unless additional deficiencies are determined for these years.

YOUR SIGNATURE HERE	/s/ John Jones	Date 8/15/87
SPOUSE'S SIGNATURE	/s/ Mary Jones	Date 8/15/87
TAXPAYER'S REPRESENTATIVE HERE		Date
CORPORATE NAME		
CORPORATE OFFICER(S) SIGN HERE		Title	Date
		Title	Data

Catalog Number 16894U   Form 870 (Rev. 3-82)

Form 870.

Instructions

General Information

If you consent to the assessment of the deficiencies shown in this waiver, please sign and return the form in order to limit any interest charge and expedite the adjustment to your account. Your consent will not prevent you from filing a claim for refund *(after you have paid the tax)* if you later believe you are so entitled. It will not prevent us from later determining, if necessary, that you owe additional tax; nor extend the time provided by law for either action.

We have agreements with State tax agencies under which information about Federal tax, including increases or decreases, is exchanged with the States. If this change affects the amount of your State income tax, you should file the required State form.

If you later file a claim and the Service disallows it, you may file suit for refund in a district court or in the United States Claims Court, but you may not file a petition with the United States Tax Court.

We will consider this waiver a valid claim for refund or credit of any overpayment due you resulting from any decrease in tax and penalties shown above, provided you sign and file it within the period established by law for making such a claim.

Who Must Sign

If you filed jointly, both you and your spouse must sign. If this waiver is for a corporation, it should be signed with the corporation name, followed by the signatures and titles of the corporate officers authorized to sign. An attorney or agent may sign this waiver provided such action is specifically authorized by a power of attorney which, if not previously filed, must accompany this form.

If this waiver is signed by a person acting in a fiduciary capacity *(for example, an executor, administrator, or a trustee)* Form 56, Notice Concerning Fiduciary Relationship, should, unless previously filed, accompany this form.

[4] Limitations to Ensure Uniformity

To ensure consistent treatment of specific issues of Service-wide impact or importance, the National Directors of Appeals may identify certain issues as requiring a departure from the normal Appeals practice of resolving cases. Also, taxpayers may seek technical advice from the National Office to ensure uniformity in Appeals Office decisions.

[a] Appeals Coordinated Issues

Issues identified as requiring resolution outside the normal Appeals Office procedures are called Appeals Coordinated Issues (ACIs). Uniform and consistent treatment is accomplished through the coordination of efforts between appeals offices and designated ACI Coordinating Officials.[78] An "ACI issue" is a legal issue in which relevant facts are identical for all taxpayers affected by the issue so that a single settlement position is possible for large groups.[79] An issue that is selected for ACI designation must involve taxpayers in different geographic areas and be common to an entire industry or occupational group; a large number of partners, shareholders, or creditors; or a nationwide tax avoidance scheme or noncompliance transaction. Under ACI procedures, notice is given to a taxpayer that a case involves an ACI and that any settlement of the ACI requires review and approval of the ACI Coordinating Official. Other issues can be settled in the usual way, but the taxpayer has no right to a conference with the ACI Coordinating Official if the taxpayer does not agree with a guideline settlement. Settlement differences are to be resolved by the Appeals Area Director. Appeals Settlement Guidelines are released and updated periodically for Appeals Coordinated Issues and Industry Specialization Program Coordinated Issues. (See Table 9.2.)

[b] Industry Specialization Program Coordinated Issues

An industrywide issue may be designated as an ACI[80] under the Appeals Specialization Coordination Program, located in the National Office. The program has National Industry Coordinators and specialists for each industry lo-

---

[78] Rev. Proc. 79-34, 1979-2 CB 498. IRM 8.7.1.7 (Jan. 1, 1999) (Appeals Coordinated Issues). See also IRM 8.7, Technical and Procedural Guidelines, 1.1.7.12, ACI Descriptions (Jan. 1, 1999).

[79] IRM 8.7, Technical and Procedural Guidelines, 1.1.7.1, Overview of ACI Program (Jan. 1, 1999).

[80] See IRM 8.7, Technical and Procedural Guidelines, 1.1.6.1, Overview of the Industry Specialization Program (ISP) (Jan. 1, 1999).

cated in the field.[81] Based on information and advice from Industry Coordinators and Division Counsel attorneys, the ACI Coordinating Official develops settlement guidelines and forwards an information copy to the National Director of Appeals. Disagreements between Appeals and District Counsel on how to dispose of an industry issue are resolved by the National Director of Appeals and the Assistant Chief Counsel (Tax Litigation).

[c] Settlement Guideline and Position Papers

In the Appeals Office, the Industry Specialization Program (ISP) is intended "to promote consistency in the settlement of [significant industry] issues."[82] Consistency in approach and consistency in results for similarly situated taxpayers are two objectives. If there are differences in the facts of the taxpayers' cases, the results may not be the same; however, the approach to the issue is supposed to be consistent. This distinction is reflected in the Appeals Office's use of settlement guideline papers and settlement position papers.

A settlement guideline paper is used when the case presents factual issues. Settlement guideline papers explain the premise behind the adjustment, describe the positions of the Service and the taxpayers, and identify the key fact elements and law that must be considered to conclude the case. However, settlement guideline papers do not tell Appeals officers what constitutes an acceptance settlement; nor do they give a settlement number or range. Taxpayers and Appeals officers will have to negotiate on the basis of the facts of the case, although the Appeals officer will use the paper as guidance (and, if needed, the ISP coordinator).

Settlement position papers deal with purely legal issues when differences in facts do not exist, because only one form of transaction is involved or because the factual distinctions make no legal difference. These settlement position papers set out specific settlements. Because there are so few purely legal issues, the Office of Appeals issues relatively few settlement position papers and relatively more settlement guideline papers.

---

[81] IRM 8.7, Technical and Procedural Guidelines, 1.1.6.2, Coordinated Issues (Jan. 1, 1999). See Exhibit 8.7.1-1 (Appeals ISP Coordinators, Industries, Specialty Areas, Industrywide Studies, and Coordinated Issues).

ISP Guidelines/Positions are organized by industry: aerospace, banking—commercial banking and savings and loan, construction/real estate, data processing, farmers cooperatives, food, forest products, generic issues, ground transportation—formerly railroads, health, insurance—property/casualty, media/communications, mergers and acquisitions, mining, motor vehicles, petroleum, retail, securities and financial services, shipping, and utilities.

[82] IRM 8.7, Technical and Procedural Guidelines, 1.1.6, Appeals ISP (Jan. 1, 1999).

Before a settlement is reached on an ACI, the Appeals officer is supposed to secure the approval of the ISP coordinator. Differences in views are resolved by the Regional Director of Appeals, and in the final event, by the National Director of Appeals. Although the ISP coordinator plays an important role in settlement, the taxpayer will not be able to negotiate directly with the ISP coordinator. It is possible, however, for the Appeals officer to invite the ISP coordinator to participate in an appeals conference in the case.

[d] Technical Advice

Appeals Offices are permitted to request technical advice from the National Office on any technical or procedural question that develops during the processing or consideration of a case.[83] Technical advice is furnished in a case on the request of Appeals for a case in nondocketed status.[84] This technical advice is intended "as a means of assisting Service personnel in closing cases and establishing and maintaining consistent holdings in the various regions."[85] When technical advice is favorable to a taxpayer, the Appeals Office is bound by the technical advice. If the technical advice is unfavorable to the taxpayer, the Appeals Office may settle the issue, as it would had no technical advice been issued.[86]

Taxpayers are permitted to request that an issue be referred for technical advice on the ground that (1) a lack of uniformity exists as to the disposition of an issue or (2) the issue is so unusual or complex that it warrants National Office consideration.[87]

[5] Maintaining Appeals Independence: Ex Parte Communications

Growing out of the ACI procedures is another development in the Office of Appeals' processing of large cases. Preconference meetings between the Appeals Office, Examination Office, and District Counsel Office take place in

---

[83] SPR, 26 CFR § 601.106(f)(9)(ii)(a). IRM 8.14, Rulings, Technical Advice, Technical Information, and Other Assistance, 1.1.2.1, Request for Technical Advice—General (Aug. 19, 1999).

[84] SPR, 26 CFR § 601.106(f)(9)(i)(a) (Rule IX). There are some situations in which technical advice is not permitted. See 26 CFR §§ 601.106(f)(9)(i)(b)–601.106(f)(9)(i)(d).

[85] SPR, 26 CFR § 601.106(f)(9)(i)(a) (Rule IX). There are some situations in which technical advice is not permitted. See 26 CFR §§ 601.106(f)(9)(i)(b)–601.106(f)(9)(i)(d).

[86] SPR, 26 CFR § 601.106(f)(9)(viii)(c).

[87] SPR, 26 CFR § 601.106(f)(9)(iii)(a). The procedures to be followed when technical advice is issued are discussed at ¶ 3.04[2]. These procedures are also described in 26 CFR §§ 601.106(f)(9)(iii)–601.106(f)(9)(vii).

certain larger cases.[88] These contacts were supposed to be for the benefit of Appeals officers so that they could better understand the issues and request additional information, if necessary. From the perspective of taxpayers and practitioners, the claimed opportunity for faster settlement was offset by doubt about the independence of Appeals officers after these meetings. The ex parte communication rules effectively limit these preconference meetings or at least require notice to the taxpayer to participate.

To comply with the statutory directive to adopt procedures prohibiting ex parte communications, the Service published Revenue Procedure 2000-43.[89] This revenue procedure provides guidance for prohibited and permitted ex parte communications between Appeals officers and the referring or originating function. Under the revenue procedure:

1. *Definition.* An ex parte communication is a communication that takes place between an Appeals officer and another Service function without the participation of the taxpayer or the taxpayer's representative. This definition is not quite complete. An ex parte communication takes place when there is no notice to the other interested party. If there is notice, and no request to participate, there is no ex parte communication. An ex parte communication may be oral or in writing. Communications between or among Appeals officers are not ex parte (they do not compromise Appeals independence), nor does the administrative file contain written ex parte communications.

2. *Preliminary reviews.* During the course of the Appeals officer's preliminary review of a newly assigned case, no ex parte communication takes place when the Appeals officer asks the originating function (a) whether certain information was requested and received from the taxpayer; (b) whether a document referred to in workpapers is available; (c) to clarify illegible documents; (d) questions about case controls; and (e) questions of a mathematical nature about tax calculations.

3. *Prohibited ex parte communications.* Prohibited communications include (a) discussions about the accuracy of the facts the taxpayer has presented and their relative importance to the determination; (b) the relative merits or alternative legal interpretations of the cases and other authorities the taxpayer cited in the protest or the originating function included in its report; and (c) the originating function's view of the credibility of the taxpayer or the taxpayer's representative.

4. *Collection cases.* The ex parte communications rules apply to collection cases, such as collection due process appeals, collection appeals program cases, offers in compromise, and trust fund recovery penalty cases. However,

---

[88] IRM 8.6, Conference and Settlement Practice, 1.2.7, Pre/Post Conference Procedures for Large Cases (Aug. 18, 1999).

[89] Rev. Proc. 2000-43, 2000-43 IRB 404 (Oct. 11, 2000).

Appeals officers may verify in a collection appeal whether the requirements of applicable statutes and administrative regulations have been complied with.

5. *Excluded communications.* The ex parte communications rules do not affect procedures covering premature referrals, raising new issues with the Appeals Office, and acting on new evidence the taxpayer submits. Importantly, during Appeals processing, the Appeals officer may continue to have ongoing communications with the referring function, but the Appeals officer must give the taxpayer or the taxpayer's representative the opportunity to participate.

6. *Communications with counsel.* Chief Counsel attorneys continue to be able to advise Appeals officers on the interpretation of the tax laws and other issues of procedure. However, to avoid ex parte communications issues in cases not docketed in the Tax Court, Appeals officers "should" not communicate with a Chief Counsel field attorney if that attorney has given advice on the same issue to the originating function's employees. In the event of this conflict, the Chief Counsel will reassign the case to another attorney. However, when the Appeals Office request involves an uncertain issue of law, the issue is referred to the National Office and treated as a request for field service advice or technical advice.

7. *Docketed cases and other communications not covered.* The limitations on ex parte communications do not apply to cases docketed in the Tax Court. They also do not apply to processing of a case through the Joint Committee (the rules apply only to intra-Service communications). The ex parte communication prohibition also does not apply to (a) industry specialization issues (existing procedures for review and approval are designed to ensure consistency); (b) communications made during Delegation Order 247 settlement approvals; (c) discussions involving general technical or procedural issues among representatives of the different functions, including Appeals and originating functions, as well as industrywide ISP coordination meetings and similar policy meetings; (d) communications for supervisory purposes between Appeals and high-ranking Service officials; (e) competent authority requests; and (f) communications with the Taxpayer Advocate Service. On the other hand, communications between Appeals and outside consultants or experts are governed by the same rules that apply to communications between Appeals officers and employees of the originating function. Accordingly, Appeals must give the taxpayer or the taxpayer's representative an opportunity to participate in substantive case-specific matters.

8. *Taxpayer's opportunity to participate.* Participation means that the taxpayer or the taxpayer's representative is given a "reasonable opportunity" to attend a meeting or participate in a conference call between the Appeals Office and the originating function when "the strengths and weaknesses of issues or positions in the taxpayer's case" are discussed. The Office of Appeals will give notice of the meeting or telephone conference and an invitation to participate. If the taxpayer or the representative are unable to participate on the date and time scheduled, the date can be rescheduled, assuming the delay is reason-

able under the circumstances. If the requested delay is considered unreasonable, the matter is documented in the Case Activity Record, and the meeting or telephone conference will be held as scheduled. The taxpayer and the representative may also waive the right to participate in one or all of the ex parte communications.

9. *Computational reviews.* When the team conducts a computational review within 120 days after the case has been assigned, and the error involves the interpretation of a legal principle or the application of law to the facts of the case, the taxpayer or the representative should be given the opportunity to participate. If the error is "purely mathematical," the ex parte communication rules do not apply, but before the Appeals Office makes a mathematical correction, both the originating function (the corporate division) and the taxpayer or the representative must be notified.

10. *Preconference and postsettlement conferences.* The prohibition of ex parte communications applies to preconference meetings between the Appeals Office and the corporate division. However, the prohibition does not apply to postsettlement conferences. Discussion of the settlement in the closed cycle is not considered to jeopardize the independence of the Appeals Office. Discussion of open cycles of the taxpayer are supposed to be postponed. On the other hand, ex parte communication procedures do not apply to the processing of refund claims late in the Appeals process. (The claim is referred to the originating function for expedited examination.)

¶ 9.04 ALTERNATIVE DISPUTE RESOLUTION AND OTHER SPECIAL APPEALS PROCEDURES

The IRS Restructuring and Reform Act of 1998 requires the Service to adopt several Appeals dispute resolution procedures by which taxpayers can request the early referral of one or more unresolved issues from the examination or collection functions to the Office of Appeals[90]; mediation[91]; and arbitration.[92] Appeals jurisdiction has expanded to include, sometimes on a test basis, a number of dispute resolution procedures. Some of these procedures have been limited to Coordinated Examination Program (CEP) cases, such as mediation and early referral.

---

[90] IRC § 7123(a).

[91] IRC § 7123(b)(1).

[92] IRC § 7123(b)(2).

[1] Early Referral

Initially, the Service adopted a procedure in CEP cases for the early referral of a developed, but unagreed issue, to the Appeals Office while the Examination Office continues to develop other issues.[93] Early referral of an issue requires the consent of the district CEP team, and so it is as much a CEP procedure as it is part of Appeals jurisdiction. Early referral of an issue for Appeals consideration does not apply to issues designated for litigation or for which the taxpayer has requested competent authority assistance, or intends to request such assistance.

Section 7123, added by the IRS Restructuring and Reform Act of 1998, required the Service to prescribe procedures permitting any taxpayer to request an early referral to Appeals of one or more unresolved issues from a local office examination or collection fuction.[94] Early referral procedures have been used in CEP cases since 1994.[95] By requiring early referral to be made available to "any taxpayer," Section 7123 makes the early referral procedure that only CEP taxpayers could previously use now available to all taxpayers. In CEP examination cases, early referral procedures permitted taxpayers to ask for the early referral to the Appeals activities of one or more developed but unagreed issues arising in an audit, while the audit continued on other issues.[96] As a result, both the Examination and the Appeals activities worked simultaneously on different issues, thereby accelerating the closing of a case. Revenue Procedure 99-28 provides procedures for any taxpayer to request the early referral to the Appeals Office of unagreed issues arising in an audit, a Service-initiated change in a taxpayer's method of accounting, employment tax examinations, collection cases, and employee plans/exempt organizations issues.[97]

Not all developed, unagreed issues arising in an examination division audit are appropriate for early referral, but if an issue falls into an appropriate category, a taxpayer may request early referral of the issue to the Appeals Office. Early referral will not alter the district's authority to audit the return; therefore, the district will continue to audit and develop issues that have not been referred to Appeals.[98] Issues appropriate for early referral are limited to

---

[93] Ann. 94-41, 1994-12 IRB 9. Early referral procedures are described in more detail in Chapter 8.

[94] IRC § 7123(a), added by the IRS Restructuring and Reform Act of 1998 § 3465.

[95] Ann. 94-41, 1994-12 IRB 9, superseded by Rev. Proc. 96-9, 1996-1 CB 575. See ¶ 8.06[6][d][iv].

[96] Ann. 94-41, 1994-12 IRB 9, superseded by Rev. Proc. 96-9, 1996-1 CB 575. See ¶ 8.06[6][d][iv].

[97] Rev. Proc. 99-28, 1999-2 CB 109 (July 19, 1999), superseding Rev. Proc. 96-9, 1996-1 CB 575, superseding Ann. 94-41, 1994-12 IRB 9 (Mar. 21, 1994).

[98] Rev. Proc. 99-28, 1999-2 CB 109, § 2.01 (July 19, 1999), superseding Rev. Proc. 96-9, 1996-1 CB 575, superseding Ann. 94-41, 1994-12 IRB 9 (Mar. 21, 1994). Early re-

those that "(1) if resolved, can reasonably be expected to result in a quicker resolution of the entire case; (2) both the taxpayer and the District agree should be referred to Appeals early; (3) are fully developed; and (4) are part of a case where the remaining issues are not expected to be completed before Appeals could resolve the early referral issue."[99] Not considered appropriate for early referral and thereby excluded from the procedure is an issue: "(1) with respect to which a thirty-day letter has been issued . . . ; (2) that is not fully developed; (3) when the remaining issues in the case are expected to be completed before Appeals could resolve the early referral issue; (4) that is designated for litigation by the Office of Chief Counsel; (5) for which the taxpayer has filed a request for Competent Authority assistance, or . . . for which the taxpayer intends to seek Competent Authority assistance . . . ; or (6) that is part of a whipsaw transaction."[100]

To request the early referral of an issue, the taxpayer must submit a request to the case manager, stating the early referral issues and the taxpayer's positions on the issues, together with a declaration that the matters set forth in the statement are made under penalties of perjury.[101] "When feasible," the case manager is required to notify the taxpayer of the decision to accept or reject the early referral request within fourteen days of receiving the request.[102] If the case manager denies the request, the taxpayer has no formal right to appeal the

ferral also does not affect the authority of the District Office to resolve issues, such as the authority of case managers conducting CEP examinations under Delegation Order 236.

[99] Rev. Proc. 99-28, 1999-2 CB 109, § 2.02 (July 19, 1999), superseding Rev. Proc. 96-9, 1996-1 CB 575, superseding Ann. 94-41, 1994-12 IRB 9 (Mar. 21, 1994). ISP issues can also be early referred to the Appeals Office. For a listing of ISP issues, see IRM, Pt. 8, Exhibit 8.7.1-1.

[100] Rev. Proc. 99-28, 1999-2 CB 109, § 2.03 (July 19, 1999), superseding Rev. Proc. 96-9, 1996-1 CB 575, superseding Ann. 94-41, 1994-12 IRB 9 (Mar. 21, 1994). When a taxpayer requests competent authority assistance, the taxpayer is encouraged to request the simultaneous Appeals/competent authority procedure described in Rev. Proc. 96-13, 1996-1 CB 616, § 8. A whipsaw issue is one in which the Service is faced with conflicting claims of different taxpayers, frequently when the tax consequences to the taxpayers depend on the characterization of a transaction and one taxpayer will be benefited and the other adversely affected by the characterization.

[101] Rev. Proc. 99-28, 1999-2 CB 109, §§ 2.05–2.06 (July 19, 1999), superseding Rev. Proc. 96-9, 1996-1 CB 575, superseding Ann. 94-41, 1994-12 IRB 9 (Mar. 21, 1994). The perjury statement takes the following form: "Under penalties of perjury, I declare that I have examined this request [or submission], including accompanying documents, and to the best of my knowledge and belief, the facts presented are true, correct, and complete." The statement must be signed by any person authorized to sign the taxpayer's income tax return.

[102] Rev. Proc. 99-28, 1999-2 CB 109, § 2.08 (July 19, 1999), superseding Rev. Proc. 96-9, 1996-1 CB 575, superseding Ann. 94-41, 1994-12 IRB 9 (Mar. 21, 1994).

denial, but can request a conference with the case manager's supervisor,[103] and retains the right to appeal the proposed deficiency related to the issue at a later time.[104]

If the local office approves the early referral request, "generally within thirty days from the date the early referral request was accepted," the local office will complete a Form 5701, Notice of Proposed Adjustment, for each early referral issue, describing the issue and explaining the local office's proposed adjustment, and will send the Notification Form to the taxpayer.[105] The Notification Form serves as a revenue agent's report and thirty-day letter, or as the preliminary notice of deficiency. Within thirty days from the date that the Notification Form was sent to the taxpayer, the taxpayer must submit a written response to the case manager (unless extended by the case manager) in a form that corresponds to the original request for early referral.[106] Unless the taxpayer fails to submit a response within the prescribed time, the early referral request is considered withdrawn.[107] After the taxpayer responds to the Notification Form, the district sends the early referral file to the Appeals Office, which then assumes jurisdiction over the early referral issues.[108] On all other issues, the district retains jurisdiction.[109]

The usual conference procedures in the Appeals Office apply to the conference on an early referral issue. If the taxpayer and the Appeals Office reach

---

[103] Rev. Proc. 99-28, 1999-2 CB 109, § 2.09 (July 19, 1999), superseding Rev. Proc. 96-9, 1996-1 CB 575, superseding Ann. 94-41, 1994-12 IRB 9 (Mar. 21, 1994).

[104] Rev. Proc. 99-28, 1999-2 CB 109, § 2.10 (July 19, 1999), superseding Rev. Proc. 96-9, 1996-1 CB 575, superseding Ann. 94-41, 1994-12 IRB 9 (Mar. 21, 1994).

[105] Rev. Proc. 99-28, 1999-2 CB 109, § 2.11 (July 19, 1999), superseding Rev. Proc. 96-9, 1996-1 CB 575, superseding Ann. 94-41, 1994-12 IRB 9 (Mar. 21, 1994). The notice "is not treated as the first letter of proposed deficiency for purposes of computing increased interest under section 6621(c), or for the award of administrative costs under section 7430(c)." Id.

[106] The taxpayer's written response "generally serves the same purpose as an Appeals protest" and, thus, "[e]stablished Appeals procedures, including those governing submissions and taxpayer conferences, apply to early referral issues." Rev. Proc. 99-28, 1999-2 CB 109, § 2.14 (July 19, 1999), superseding Rev. Proc. 96-9, 1996-1 CB 575, superseding Ann. 94-41, 1994-12 IRB 9 (Mar. 21, 1994).

[107] Rev. Proc. 99-28, 1999-2 CB 109, § 2.12 (July 19, 1999), superseding Rev. Proc. 96-9, 1996-1 CB 575, superseding Ann. 94-41, 1994-12 IRB 9 (Mar. 21, 1994).

[108] Rev. Proc. 99-28, 1999-2 CB 109, § 2.13 (July 19, 1999), superseding Rev. Proc. 96-9, 1996-1 CB 575, superseding Ann. 94-41, 1994-12 IRB 9 (Mar. 21, 1994). It is worth noting what the file sent to the Appeals Office contains: (1) applicable portions of tax returns and workpapers; (2) the approved early referral request; (3) the Notification Form; (4) the taxpayer's written response to the Notification Form; (4) the local office's response to the taxpayer's position, if any; and (6) an estimate of the potential tax effect of the proposed adjustment.

[109] Rev. Proc. 99-28, 1999-2 CB 109, § 2.13 (July 19, 1999), superseding Rev. Proc. 96-9, 1996-1 CB 575, superseding Ann. 94-41, 1994-12 IRB 9 (Mar. 21, 1994).

agreement on an early referral issue, the Appeals Office will reflect the agreement in a Form 906, Closing Agreement on Final Determination Covering Specific Matters.[110] The closing agreement is used "to compute the corrected tax as a partial agreement prior to or concurrently with the resolution of any other issues in the case."[111] If agreement is not reached on an early referral issue, the taxpayer may request mediation, provided that the issue meets the Appeals' criteria for mediation. Absent mediation, the early referral file is closed unagreed and returned to the district. If the taxpayer later appeals the entire case by protest, the Appeals Office will not reconsider the early referral issue "unless there has been a substantial change in the circumstances regarding the early referral issue."[112]

If the local office concludes its examination during the pendency of an appeal on early referral issues, the local office will issue a preliminary notice of deficiency (a thirty-day letter), which will include the pending early referral issues. When the only unagreed issues in the case are early referral issues that the Office of Appeals returned to the local office unagreed, the local office will send the taxpayer a statutory notice of deficiency (a ninety-day letter) instead of a thirty-day letter.[113] If the Appeals Office has not resolved the early referral issues, the taxpayer will be sent a thirty-day letter and may protest, because "all issues[,] including all early referral issues that have not yet been settled by Appeals[,] will be considered under established appeals procedures." The Appeals Office will not, however, reconsider an early referral issue that has previously been unagreed by it.[114] If the taxpayer withdraws an issue over which the Appeals Office has taken jurisdiction from the early referral process, the issue is treated in the same manner as an unagreed early referral issue, which means that the Appeals Office will not reconsider the issue on the taxpayer's later protest.[115]

---

[110] Rev. Proc. 99-28, 1999-2 CB 109, §§ 2.14–2.15 (July 19, 1999), superseding Rev. Proc. 96-9, 1996-1 CB 575, superseding Ann. 94-41, 1994-12 IRB 9 (Mar. 21, 1994).

[111] Rev. Proc. 99-28, 1999-2 CB 109, § 2.15 (July 19, 1999), superseding Rev. Proc. 96-9, 1996-1 CB 575, superseding Ann. 94-41, 1994-12 IRB 9 (Mar. 21, 1994).

[112] Rev. Proc. 99-28, 1999-2 CB 109, § 2.16 (July 19, 1999), superseding Rev. Proc. 96-9, 1996-1 CB 575, superseding Ann. 94-41, 1994-12 IRB 9 (Mar. 21, 1994).

[113] Rev. Proc. 99-28, 1999-2 CB 109, § 2.17 (July 19, 1999), superseding Rev. Proc. 96-9, 1996-1 CB 575, superseding Ann. 94-41, 1994-12 IRB 9 (Mar. 21, 1994). The thirty-day letter "generally" will, and the ninety-day letter will, constitute the first letter of proposed deficiency for purposes of Sections 6621(c) and 7403(c). Id.

[114] Rev. Proc. 99-28, 1999-2 CB 109, § 2.18 (July 19, 1999), superseding Rev. Proc. 96-9, 1996-1 CB 575, superseding Ann. 94-41, 1994-12 IRB 9 (Mar. 21, 1994).

[115] Rev. Proc. 99-28, 1999-2 CB 109, § 2.19 (July 19, 1999), superseding Rev. Proc. 96-9, 1996-1 CB 575, superseding Ann. 94-41, 1994-12 IRB 9 (Mar. 21, 1994).

Revenue Procedure 99-28 also addresses the application of the early referral procedures to specific types of issues, such as Service-initiated changes in an accounting method.

[a] Worker Status

The early referral procedure is available for employment tax issues, and allows taxpayers, not just CEP taxpayers, whose returns are being examined, to request the referral of one or more employment tax issues to Appeals.[116] The key issue in this early referral program is the status of a worker as either an independent contractor or employee, and, particularly, whether the taxpayer is entitled to the relief provision of Section 530 of the Revenue Act of 1978. If Section 530 applies, the business that has treated workers as independent contractors will not have an employment tax liability for the workers in issue. Accordingly, the issue is considered appropriate for early referral.

[b] Valuation

The early referral procedure applies to the valuation of art for estate and gift tax purposes, as well as charitable deduction purposes. Unlike the other early referral procedures, the review of the valuation of works of art takes place, indeed must be requested, before the return is filed; moreover, the request for review is sent to the National Office.[117] The request for advanced valuation of art leads to a Statement of Value that can be used to substantiate the value of art for income, and estate and gift tax purposes before filing the return.

[2] Mediation

Mediation and arbitration often are confused. Mediation is an alternative dispute resolution procedure in which a neutral third party attempts to facilitate a settlement between the parties. Mediation is assisted settlement negotiations between the parties. The person who assists or facilitates an agreement is called the mediator. The mediator is neutral, and makes no finding or decision. Mediation is nonbinding in the sense that the parties may terminate the mediation and go to trial. The result of a successful mediation is a settlement agree-

---

[116] Ann. 96-13, 1996-12 IRB 13 (early referral procedures described); Ann. 97-52, 1997-21 IRB 1 (additional one-year test period beginning on May 27, 1997).

[117] Rev. Proc. 96-15, 1996-3 IRB 4 (procedures described). For Appeals Valuation Assistance, Valuation Assistance Procedures, see IRM 8.18.1, Valuation Assistance Procedures (Mar. 30, 2001).

ment. By contrast, in arbitration, the parties present their cases to arbitrators who make a binding decision in favor of one or the other parties. The arbitration decision or award is final. Appeals mediation procedures reflect mediation procedures in general. After negotiations in the Appeals Office have been unsuccessful, and the parties agree to mediation, the taxpayer and the Appeals Office select a neutral third party to assist them in negotiating a settlement.[118]

The mediator is either an Appeals officer from another office and trained in mediation techniques, in which case the Service pays the mediator's costs, or an outside mediator, whose costs are shared by the parties. Mediation is not available for issues designated for litigation, docketed cases, ISP cases, ACI Program cases, or competent authority issues, as well as employment tax issues, collection issues, and employee plans/exempt organizations issues. Mediation is only available (1) for cases that are already in the Appeals administrative process that are not docketed in any court and (2) for issues in the CEP assigned to Appeals Team Chiefs.[119] Factual issues, such as transfer pricing, reasonable compensation, and valuation disputes are considered appropriate for mediation. Mediation is optional. After consulting about using the procedure, a taxpayer or the Appeals Team Chief may request that the Area Director of Appeals—Large Case, approve mediation.

If mediation is approved, the parties will agree on a mediator. Mediation begins with each party's submission to the mediator of a summary of its position. The parties then meet with the mediator and at a joint meeting give opening statements. The parties then separate. and the mediator meets with each party separately, shuttling between them until an agreement is reached or the mediation proves unsuccessful.

As a result of the IRS Restructuring and Reform Act of 1998, mediation in the Office of Appeals will be available for all taxpayers on any issue unresolved at the conclusion of Appeals procedures or unsuccessful attempts to

---

[118] Ann. 95-86, 1995-44 IRB 27 (describing the procedures); see also Ann. 97-1, 1997-1 IRB 62 (extending the test of mediation for a one-year period beginning on January 13, 1997).

[119] Ann. 95-86, 1995-44 IRB 27. Ann. 95-86 has model forms for a mediation agreement, and acknowledgment of disclosure of a return and return information as well as a model mediator's report. The Appeals Office prefers to have an Appeals mediator, and may refuse mediation if the taxpayer will not accept an Appeals mediator, a factor that may weigh against mediation in the Appeals Office. The Chief Counsel has also adopted mediation as an alternative dispute resolution procedure in Tax Court cases. Chief Counsel Notice N (35)000-135 (Oct. 13, 1995). Mediation in docketed Tax Court cases is not limited to CEP issues. Ann. 97-1, 1997-2 IRB 62, extended the test of the mediation procedure described in Ann. 95-86 for an additional one-year period beginning on January 13, 1997. According to the General Accounting Office (GAO), as of November 30, 1996, Appeals had completed two successful mediations, denied five requests for mediation, and two were in process. GAO, "Internal Revenue Service—IRS Initiatives to Resolve Disputes Over Tax Liabilities," GAO/GGD—97-71 (May 1997), at 24.

enter into a closing agreement or offer in compromise.[120] After the passing of the 1998 Act, the Office of Appeals expanded its mediation procedure to cover individual taxpayers' factual issues involving an adjustment of $1 million or more, and, to comply with the 1998 Act, intends to expand the availability of mediation adjustments involving amounts less than $1 million.[121]

[3] Arbitration

As part of its statutory obligation to make arbitration available in the Appeals process, the Service has adopted a program for binding arbitration for factual issues that are already in the Appeals Office, but at the conclusion of normal procedures the issues cannot be resolved, or efforts to enter into a closing agreement or a compromise have proven unsuccessful.[122] Arbitration is an optional alternative dispute resolution procedure; therefore, both the taxpayer and the Appeals Office must agree to resolve the issue by arbitration.[123] Their agreement must be memorialized in a formal Agreement to Arbitrate, which both the taxpayer and the Assistant Regional Director of Appeals must execute. Arbitration may be used only after discussions between the taxpayer and the Appeals Office are unsuccessful, and when, except for the factual issue for which arbitration is to be utilized, all other issues are resolved. Only factual issues, such as valuation and reasonable compensation, are considered suitable

---

[120] IRC § 7123(b), added by the 1998 Act, § 3465(a)(1). Arbitration is also available under Section 7123. FSA 1999-983 (Mar. 26, 1992) (the Administrative Dispute Resolution Act, which authorizes agencies to submit disputes to neutral arbitrators in an effort to reduce litigation, applies to the Service).

[121] Ann. 98-99, 1998-2 CB 650 (Oct. 30, 1998), adopted a two-year test period for more-than-$1-million adjustments, and requesting comments on expansion of the procedure, as required by the 1998 Act. The test of mediation procedures of Announcement 98-99 was extended. Ann. 2001-9, 2001-3 IRB 357.

[122] Ann. 2000-4, 2000-2 IRB 1. The pilot program began on January 18, 2000, and will last for two years. Section 7123(b)(2), added by the 1998 Act, requires the Service to adopt a pilot program under which taxpayers and the Office of Appeals may jointly request binding arbitration on certain issues that cannot otherwise be resolved under normal procedures. Some of the comments made about the arbitration procedures were that: (1) they should be communicated to taxpayers; (2) they should not be limited to factual issues; (3) arbitration should be available even if the taxpayer requests arbitration on only one issue in a multiple issue case, and wishes to resolve the other issues through normal Appeals procedures; and (4) the arbitration agreement should provide the maximum amount of an award, rather than an award within a range agreed to by the parties, as provided in Section 575(2) of the Administrative Dispute Resolution Act of 1999. See 2000 TNT 83-22 (Apr. 28, 2000), Tax Correspondence, "NYSBA Tax Section Suggests Changes to Arbitration Program."

[123] Ann. 2000-4, 2000-2 IRB 1, Overview.

for arbitration.[124] The arbitrator will resolve the unagreed issue by making a finding of fact. The taxpayer and the Appeals Office must be able to agree on the applicable law; that is, the interpretation of law, regulation, ruling, or other legal authority that the arbitrator is to use in his or her deliberations. Because there must be agreement on the applicable law, arbitration is not available for an issue designated for litigation or docketed in any court, an Industry Specialization Issue or an ACI. Other issues that cannot be arbitrated include the substantiation of trade or business expenses or travel and entertainment expenses; and an issue for which the taxpayer has filed, or intends to file, a request for competent authority assistance.

The first step in the arbitration process is an agreement by the taxpayer and the Office of Appeals to arbitrate the issue.[125] The taxpayer must send a written request to the Team Chief or Appeals officer, who sends the request with a recommendation to the Appeals officer's immediate supervisor for approval or disapproval of the request. A final determination is made by the Assistant Regional Director of Appeals after consultation with the Office of Alternative Dispute Resolution in the National Director of Appeals office. If the request is approved, the conference is scheduled to discuss the process with the taxpayer; however, if the request is denied, there is no formal procedure to appeal the denial (although the taxpayer may discuss the denial with the Assistant Regional Director).

The Office of Appeals uses a model arbitration agreement, the significant negotiable points of which are the selection of the arbitrator and the facts to be found.[126] The Appeals Office prefers to use other Appeals personnel as arbitrators, and, because these inside arbitrators have an obvious conflict of interest, the conflict must be waived by the taxpayer.[127] A more practical alternative is an arbitrator outside the Service chosen from a list provided by a national or local arbitration organization that both parties can agree on, who meets criteria such as arbitration experience, substantive tax knowledge, and knowledge of the industry involved.[128] The parties must agree on the factual issues to arbitrate, and may describe their agreement on legal guidance to be considered by the arbitrator. However, both parties will submit a summary of their positions to the arbitrator before the arbitration.[129] Another feature of the arbitration proceeding is the use of an administrator from either the Office of Alternative Dispute Resolution in Appeals or the organization providing the arbitrator. The

---

[124] Ann. 2000-4, 2000-2 IRB 1, Scope of Arbitration.

[125] Ann. 2000-4, 2000-2 IRB 1, Arbitration Process: Arbitration Is Optional.

[126] The Model Agreement is attached to Ann. 2000-4, 2000-2 IRB 1 as Table 1.

[127] Ann. 2000-4, 2000-2 IRB 1, Arbitration Process: Selection of Arbitrators.

[128] Ann. 2000-4, 2000-2 IRB 1, Arbitration Process: Selection of Arbitrators in General, and Criteria for Selection of Arbitrators.

[129] Ann. 2000-4, 2000-2 IRB 1, Arbitration Process: Issues Covered.

administrator communicates with the arbitrator and handles requests for information and submission of documents and other information.[130] The arbitration agreement also controls what evidence the arbitrator will be able to consider, because the parties will agree on the names of persons the arbitrator may interview, and questions the arbitrator may ask in the presence of the parties.[131] The parties will also agree on the documentary evidence the arbitrator may consider. At the conclusion of the arbitration, the arbitrator prepares a report and submits it to the administrator. The arbitrator's report is not a court opinion with findings of fact and an analysis of the law, and it will have no precedential value, unless the parties specifically agree otherwise. The arbitrator's report will set forth only the arbitrator's findings of fact. The arbitrator's report is final; no appeal may be taken from an adverse decision to any court.[132]

[4] Mutually Accelerated Appeals Process

If the Office of Appeals believes that a CEP case has the potential for accelerated resolution, it can ask the CEP taxpayer for its commitment on accelerating the Appeals process.[133] The Appeals Office also will ask the taxpayer whether it is able to resolve the issues at an accelerated rate. The procedure is available for pending and new Appeals cases, although new cases are preferred for this procedure. For pending cases, the Office of Appeals will review open cases to decide whether the resolution of a CEP could be accelerated by the assignment of additional Appeals officers or reassignment of the case.

¶ 9.05 PERFECTING THE APPEAL: THE PROTEST REQUIREMENT

To appeal an unagreed income, estate, or gift tax case or penalty after assessment, taxpayers must request Appeals review and, when required, file with the local office a written protest setting forth specifically the reasons why the district's findings are contested.[134] Procedurally, protests are filed in response to the district's thirty-day letter transmitting a summary of the revenue agent's

---

[130] Ann. 2000-4, 2000-2 IRB 1, Overview.

[131] Ann. 2000-4, 2000-2 IRB 1, Exhibit 1, Model Agreement to Arbitrate, ¶ 5.

[132] Ann. 2000-4, 2000-2 IRB 1, Arbitration Process: Arbitrator's Report.

[133] IR 2000-42 (June 27, 2000).

[134] 26 CFR § 601.106(a)(1)(ii). The same requirements apply to an unagreed employment or excise tax case, an offer in compromise, a termination assessment of income tax, or a jeopardy assessment.

findings within the thirty-day period permitted for this purpose. However, a protest need not be filed in all cases. No protest is required (1) in an office examination case or (2) in a field examination or any other case if the amount of the proposed additional tax, proposed overpayment, or refund is $2,500 or less.[135] An optional procedure is available when the proposed additional tax (including penalties), proposed overassessment, or claimed refund (or, in an offer in compromise, the assessed tax, penalty, and interest sought to be compromised) during any taxable period exceeds $2,500 but does not exceed $10,000. In these instances, a written protest is optional (although a brief written statement of the disputed issues is required) to obtain Appeals Office review in a field examination case.[136]

[1] Decision to File a Protest

A number of factors bear on the decision to file a protest and to request a hearing in an Appeals Office. Although it undoubtedly is good that the Service permits appeals from district determinations, not every case should be immediately appealed to the Appeals Office by filing a protest. Taxpayers can obtain Appeals Office hearings at two different times: (1) when the protest is filed within the thirty-day period described in the thirty-day letter from the District Office (nondocketed cases) or (2) if the thirty-day period is allowed to pass, when the taxpayer, within ninety days after receipt of a statutory notice of deficiency, prepares and files a petition in the Tax Court (docketed cases).

A taxpayer must face the issue of whether to follow the protest procedure or bypass the protest and file a petition in the Tax Court. Under some circumstances, it can be advantageous for the taxpayer to bypass the appeals process altogether and permit the assessment of the deficiency, pay the amount of the assessment, and file a claim for refund before instituting a suit for refund in a district court or the Court of Federal Claims. Before deciding which route to take, the representative must consider the pros and cons of a number of factors.

Some of the factors in favor of filing a protest include:

1. An Appeals Office conference gives the taxpayer and the Service an opportunity to settle a case without the expense of litigation. Unlike a revenue agent, an Appeals officer must weigh the hazards of litigation even when no case is actually pending. Thus, in a sense, this hazards-of-litigation standard gives the taxpayer the benefits of settlement consideration for an action con-

---

[135] 26 CFR §§ 601.105(d)(2), 601.106(a)(1)(ii).

[136] The Statement of Procedural Rules was amended October 16, 1987, to add this procedure. 26 CFR §§ 601.105(c)(2)(iii) (district field examination procedures), 601.105(d)(2)(iv) (thirty-day letter and protest procedures).

testing a deficiency without the taxpayer's having to incur the expense of such an action. Moreover, the chances of settlement are about the same whether the case is in nondocketed or docketed status.[137]

2. The appeals process permits a taxpayer to keep open the option of filing a petition in the Tax Court or instituting a refund suit in a district court or the claims court. If a statutory notice of deficiency is sent to the taxpayer, the taxpayer must choose the forum in which to institute litigation. By keeping his or her forum options open, a taxpayer can see how the authority on a particular issue develops in the different courts and, therefore, determine which court appears to be the most advantageous in the event that a settlement cannot be reached.

3. The protest procedure permits a taxpayer and the Appeals Office to have settlement negotiations over an extended period. In a docketed case, the Appeals Office cannot consider a case after it has appeared on a trial calendar without District Counsel consent.[138] In sizable, complicated cases, this restriction may put the parties under unnecessary time constraints.

4. If a protest is filed, a taxpayer will have more time to defer payment of a tax. Although the interest rate charged on tax deficiencies is adjusted periodically in order to keep it roughly the same as commercial interest rates, a taxpayer may nevertheless be able to earn more on his or her money than the interest that will be charged on any deficiency.

5. A taxpayer who files a protest may obtain further information about the Service's position in the event that a protest is filed. If the Appeals officer can be convinced that the agent or the district was wrong, a court case may be avoided altogether. If the Appeals officer cannot be convinced, there is an informal opportunity for discovery that might not otherwise be available to the taxpayer, especially in the Tax Court in which, despite changes in the rules, there is limited discovery. Furthermore, the taxpayer has more opportunity to prepare the case before any suit is started. Additionally, the taxpayer and his or her representative may realize some benefit by observing the reaction of the Appeals officer to the taxpayer's arguments, thereby allowing the taxpayer to assess which arguments are most effective.

6. When there are related taxpayers or whipsaw issues, the filing of protests by all parties provides for more flexibility in coordinating and resolving these related cases than if only one taxpayer goes to court.

7. A prevailing taxpayer may be able to recover reasonable attorney fees and other costs incurred in connection with administrative proceedings in the Service as well as in court proceedings, provided that the position of the gov-

---

[137] In fiscal year 1988, Appeals Offices settled 34,649 and received 36,942 regular work cases (i.e., non–tax shelter cases) in nondocketed status, while they settled 21,662 and received 21,764 regular work cases in docketed status. IRS Annual Report 1988, Tables 15 & 16, pp. 55–56.

[138] Rev. Proc. 87-24, 1987-1 CB 720, § 2.02.

ernment was not substantially justified.[139] However, to be eligible for recovery of these costs, the prevailing taxpayer "must have exhausted administrative remedies available to (the taxpayer) within the Internal Revenue Service."[140] Although recoverable administrative costs may not include the costs of an Appeals conference,[141] the recovery of costs in litigation are not allowed without such a conference.

Although the foregoing factors weigh in favor of filing a protest, the taxpayer can realize a number of advantages by choosing not to file a protest. The following factors support a bypass of the protest procedure.

1. New issues and grounds are less likely to be raised if a taxpayer, in response to a statutory notice of deficiency issued by a local officer, files a petition in the Tax Court. Appeals officers generally have greater tax experience than revenue agents and can improve on a basis for adjustment assigned by the revenue agent or raise a new issue with a material effect on tax. In pre-ninety-day status cases, the period of limitations on assessment remains open, and the Appeals Office has the opportunity to change or cure a defective basis for adjustment determined by the revenue agent and the District Office. If the statutory notice is sent by the District Office rather than the Appeals Office and a petition has been filed, the risk that a new issue or ground will be raised is reduced by the Tax Court's rules. If a new issue is raised after the District Office has sent a notice of deficiency, under the Tax Court's rules the Commissioner rather than the taxpayer has the burden of proof on any new matter or increase in a deficiency pleaded in the taxpayer's answer.[142] However, if the statutory notice is sent by the Appeals Office, the taxpayer has the burden of proof in a Tax Court suit seeking a redetermination of the deficiency. This change in the normal burden of proof does not eliminate the possibility of the Appeals Office choosing not to raise a new issue or ground, but it does tend to diminish the possibility. Therefore, if there is a significant possibility that a new issue creating a substantial deficiency will be raised, the taxpayer should consider refund rather than deficiency procedures. If a taxpayer pays the assessed tax and files a claim for refund after the period for assessment has expired, the government may raise a new issue in a refund suit only to offset any recovery by the taxpayer.[143] In a refund suit, unlike a defi-

---

[139] IRC § 7430(a).

[140] IRC § 7430(b)(1).

[141] IRC § 7430(c)(2) (costs incurred on or after the date of receipt of an Appeals Office decision or the date of the notice of deficiency). Huffman v. Comm'r, 978 F2d 1139 (9th Cir. 1992) (position of United States starts with earlier of Appeals Office decision or notice of deficiency, but "has room to change toward reasonableness between the administrative or court proceedings").

[142] Tax Ct. R. Prac. & Proc. 142(a).

[143] Refund procedures are described in Chapter 11.

ciency redetermination, the new issue cannot be used affirmatively to collect any additional tax.

2. Appeals officers may not settle fraud penalty cases if a criminal prosecution has been recommended without the concurrence of Division Counsel. If the case is docketed, the presence of a Division Counsel attorney, who has more sensitivity to trial problems, at the conference can help the taxpayer in arriving at a basis for settlement.

3. The taxpayer can gain a psychological advantage in negotiations if the hearing in the Appeals Office concerns a docketed case rather than a nondocketed case. When a petition has been filed, the Appeals officer knows that the taxpayer has sufficient conviction of the rightness of his or her position in order to litigate the matter. However, this factor should not be overestimated: Statistics of settlement of docketed and nondocketed cases are about the same, so that Appeals officers do not appear to be overly influenced by the status of the case. Still, in smaller cases in which an Appeals officer might otherwise believe that a taxpayer is unlikely to pursue the matter in court, the filing of a petition can provide an advantage.

4. The filing of a protest delays the disposition of a case. If a protest is filed, there is generally more delay before a case is resolved than if a petition is filed. In small tax cases, filing a Tax Court petition expedites an Appeals Office hearing. Service procedures appear to contemplate Appeals hearings in docketed cases on a more expedited basis than in nondocketed cases. Consequently, a taxpayer may get a speedier resolution of the case with a docketed rather than a nondocketed status.

5. A settlement in a docketed case has greater finality than a settlement in a nondocketed case. An agreement in a docketed case is reflected in a decision of the Tax Court, which, although entered pursuant to the stipulation, becomes the judgment of the court.[144] On the other hand, a settlement reached in a nondocketed case is generally made on Form 870-AD, which specifically provides that the agreement is not binding if there is any concealment or misrepresentation of a material fact, fraud, or malfeasance. Although Form 870-AD has rarely been avoided by the Service and provides practical insurance against any change of position, there is nevertheless a risk that such a change might occur. This risk is appreciably greater than if a final judgment is entered in the Tax Court.

---

[144] See, e.g., Fluor v. United States, 79-1 USTC 9393 (CD Cal. 1979) (stipulated Tax Court decision for 1967 was res judicata, estopping the Service from assessing additional tax for 1967 arising as result of reduction in a 1970 net operating loss). See Stamm Int'l Corp. v. Comm'r, 90 TC 315 (1988) (unilateral error of government attorney in calculating the dollar cost of the agreement, in absence of misrepresentation by adverse party, was not a sufficient ground to vacate a settlement agreement); Korangy v. Comm'r, 893 F2d 69 (4th Cir. 1990) (taxpayers not relieved from stipulation despite alleged error).

Although the factors controlling the decision in an individual case obviously depend on the circumstances of the case, the professional background of the taxpayer's representative also can play a part in the decision-making process. Accountants and tax lawyers who are not trained to try cases in court and are not authorized to appear in any court, except the Tax Court, are more likely to follow the protest procedure and attempt to settle the case at the least possible cost to the taxpayer. Many accountants do not even consider the possibility that the case can be taken further than an Appeals conference. Lawyers are more likely to consider the possibility of litigation and the advantage in litigation of tying the Service to the position of the District Office. Lawyers may be more sensitive to the risk of having an Appeals officer raise additional issues or sounder grounds for adjustments. This distinction cannot be pressed too far: There are many lawyers who have never seen the inside of a courtroom and who have no intention of pursuing a case in court. Nevertheless, both the taxpayer and his or her representative should discuss all factors before deciding how to proceed.

[2] Choice of Forum

Taxpayers can choose among three different courts in which to litigate the controversy even if they decide to administratively appeal to the Appeals office. As noted previously, taxpayers are permitted to contest a deficiency in the Tax Court or sue for refund in either a district court or the Court of Federal Claims. These courts have different procedures and precedents that can make one court or forum preferable in a particular case. Before deciding on a forum, the taxpayer should consider the factors discussed in the following sections.

[a] Payment of Tax: The *Flora* Rule

The Tax Court is the only prepayment forum for review of a tax deficiency. If a dispute is to be brought before a district court or the Court of Federal Claims, the taxpayer must (1) pay the full amount of the assessed deficiency; (2) file with the Service, after payment, a claim for refund setting forth the grounds for refund; and (3) institute a suit for refund, after disallowance of the claim or the expiration of the statutory six-month waiting period.[145] Under the *Flora* rule, there may be no deviation from the requirement that full payment of the disputed tax be made,[146] but *Flora* does not require the pay-

---

[145] Refund requirements and procedures are discussed in Chapter 11.

[146] Flora v. United States, 362 US 145 (1960). There is no hardship exception to the *Flora* rule. See Curry v. United States, 774 F2d 852 (7th Cir. 1985) (no hardship exception to *Flora*; cases gathered). In *Curry*, because the returns were delinquent, the taxpayers' accountant advised them to file returns that overstated their income and then file

ment of interest.[147] Thus, as a practical matter, the ability of the taxpayer to pay a deficiency dictates whether the deficiency is contested in the Tax Court or in either a district court or the Court of Federal Claims. Not surprisingly, about 95 percent of tax cases are instituted by taxpayers in the Tax Court rather than in the refund courts.

[b] Type of Tax

The type of tax involved also dictates the taxpayer's choice. The Tax Court does not have jurisdiction over certain excise taxes, employment taxes, and certain penalties such as the so-called trust fund recovery percent penalty. A taxpayer who wishes to contest liability for these taxes must follow the refund procedures to obtain judicial review. Fortunately, the burden on these taxpayers is reduced to some extent by the recognition that these taxes are imposed on separate transactions and so are divisible. A taxpayer may pay the tax for a single transaction and bring a refund action based on his or her claimed entitlement to a refund on this transaction in a district court or the Court of Federal Claims. After the complaint has been filed, the government answers and counterclaims for the balance of the assessment, thereby putting the entire assessment in issue. Even if there were no counterclaim as to the issues actually litigated and determined in the case, the judicial determination would collaterally estop their relitigation in a case involving the remaining portion of the assessment.

Although the procedure for obtaining judicial review of a divisible tax assessment appears to compensate taxpayers for being denied access to the Tax Court, problems may nevertheless arise. There is a disturbing lack of recognition by the Collection Division that the assessment-refund procedure used in divisible tax cases is the functional equivalent of Tax Court prepayment review. Unlike other taxpayers, taxpayers against whom divisible tax assessments are made must usually make some security arrangement with the

---

amended returns. When they filed the original returns without full payment and their amended returns were rejected, their refund suit was dismissed on the authority of *Flora*. The circuit court stated, "It is doubtful that there could have been enough flat tires in their area of Indiana in 1975 and 1976 for them to make over $70,000. No citizen should have to pay more taxes than he or she owes, but the Currys have only themselves and their accountant to blame for their predicament." See also Erdman v. United States, 624 F. Supp. 158 (SD Ohio 1985), aff'd in unpublished opinion (government could not be stopped from asserting the jurisdictional defect of taxpayers' failure to pay tax liability before bringing a refund suit).

[147] See Flora v. United States, 362 US 145 (1960). See ¶ 11.06[4].

Collection Division to avoid the filing of tax liens and other enforced collection actions.[148]

[c] Accrual of Interest

Merely because a taxpayer chooses to obtain Tax Court review of a disputed deficiency without paying the tax in advance, interest does not stop running on the deficiency. Should the taxpayer be unsuccessful, he or she must pay not only the deficiency, but the accrued interest as well. In refund cases, the taxpayer has already paid the principal amount of the deficiency assessment and need only pay the interest. The amount of interest can be significant if the Commissioner is successful in the Tax Court. It is not unusual for a tax case to take more than five years to make its way from examination to appellate review to Tax Court decision, and during this period, the interest that has accrued may approximate or even exceed the amount of the original deficiency in tax.[149] A taxpayer can stop the running of interest on a deficiency by remitting the amount of the deficiency to the Service, but unless the taxpayer follows the Service's cash bond procedures, he or she must wait until after the notice of deficiency is received before making payment.[150] If the taxpayer pays the full amount of the deficiency before the notice is sent, a notice of deficiency is not sent, and the Tax Court has no jurisdiction to review the Service's determination because there is no longer any deficiency.

The rate of interest also can influence the route followed by a taxpayer. Despite periodic adjustments in the underpayment rate charged on tax deficiencies,[151] a taxpayer may choose to file a petition in the Tax Court if he or she can earn more on his or her money than the interest that will be charged. When the interest rate on deficiencies is high, taxpayers may be more inclined to pay the tax and follow refund procedures.

[d] Precedent

Tax controversies are probably unique because the Code permits cases to be commenced in three different courts, thus institutionalizing forum shopping. In other federal civil actions, a court might take a dim view of a party's strain-

---

[148] The practical requirement is formalized in Section 6672(b), which provides that no enforced collection is taken if a taxpayer starts a refund suit and files a bond in an amount equal to one and one-half the amount of penalties assessed.

[149] For the calculation of interest on underpayments, see ¶ 6.02.

[150] IRC § 6213(b)(3). The problems in making advance remittances are discussed at ¶ 6.02[3][a]. When the interest rate on deficiencies increased to 20 percent, some taxpayers paid part but not all of the deficiency to stop at least some portion of the interest on the date of deposit. See the discussion of advance remittances at ¶ 6.03[1][c].

[151] IRC § 6621.

ing the rules of jurisdiction and venue to bring suit in the court solely to take advantage of favorable precedent. Of three possible courts available, only the Tax Court hears tax cases exclusively. As a result, it has developed particular expertise in tax questions. This special tax expertise may indicate that a technical issue should be litigated in the Tax Court.

Although the Tax Court has greater technical expertise than district courts, it lacks the equity jurisdiction that the district courts are accustomed to exercising. This difference in jurisdiction may prove to be a handicap in the Tax Court's deciding a case with strong equitable appeal or a case calling for a novel or less technically grounded approach. Such factors indicate that a taxpayer will do better to institute a refund suit in a district court or the Court of Federal Claims. In addition, a local district court judge may more easily appreciate the realities of local business life than a Tax Court judge or Court of Federal Claims judge who only hears a case in the region while traveling on circuit. The Court of Federal Claims traditionally has been receptive to equitable arguments or defenses. The choice between a Tax Court and a district court case has been narrowed on matters of law by the Tax Court's decision in *Golsen v. Commissioner.*[152] As a result of this decision, the Tax Court follows the rule adopted by the court of appeals to which the taxpayer would appeal an adverse decision.

These considerations suggest that a practitioner must (1) thoroughly research the law before advising a client on which route to take; (2) consider what defenses or arguments will be made on the taxpayer's behalf and whether the defenses or arguments because of their equitable nature will be recognized, if at all, only by a district court or the claims court; and (3) determine particularly the law in the appropriate circuit.

[e] Increased Deficiency

Under the rules applicable in Tax Court cases, the Commissioner may claim that an increased deficiency is due, subject only to the requirement that the Commissioner, not the taxpayer, carries the burden of proof on this increased deficiency.[153] The risks of an increased deficiency can be appreciable.

---

[152] Golsen v. Comm'r, 54 TC 742 (1970), aff'd on another issue, 445 F2d 985 (10th Cir.), cert. denied, 404 US 940 (1971).

[153] Tax Ct. R. Prac. & Proc. 142(a). Section 6214(a) gives the Tax Court jurisdiction to determine the correct amount of a deficiency, even if the redetermined amount is higher than that stated in the notice of deficiency. It also allows the Service to decide whether any additional amount or addition to the tax should be assessed, if the Service asserts a claim before the hearing or rehearing. However, an attempt to increase a deficiency has been said to be timely whether it is made during trial or in posttrial briefs, as long as it is made before a decision has been entered and the taxpayer has time to respond. Henningsen v. Comm'r, 243 F2d 954, 959 (4th Cir. 1957). Thus, Tax Court Rule 142(a) permits a

For example, in *Joseph B. Ferguson*,[154] a deficiency of less than $1,200 was increased to more than $300,000. By contrast, in a refund action in a district court or the Court of Federal Claims, brought after the statute of limitations on assessment has run, the government may use an additional tax due only to off-set any recoverable refund. Although the government may use the additional, but time-barred tax, as an offset under the doctrine of equitable recoupment, the taxpayer is not liable for the additional tax exceeding the offset refund.

[f] Discovery Rules

Differences in the discovery rules applicable to cases in the Tax Court, district courts, or the Court of Federal Claims can affect the course of litigation of a tax case in a number of ways. For example, a taxpayer may wish to avoid extensive discovery by the government. Compliance with discovery can be expensive, even more expensive than the trial itself. Frequently, the taxpayer has the advantage of knowing the background of the transaction and what witnesses can be produced to support the taxpayer's position. Discovery enables the government to obtain a degree of equality in such knowledge. On the other hand, in some cases the taxpayer can use discovery to obtain evidence from third persons and from the Service. Freewheeling discovery is most likely to occur in district courts, because the Federal Rules of Civil Procedure encourage discovery in order to facilitate settlement or trial. In many districts, judges do not participate in the discovery stage of the case unless a magistrate is unable to resolve a controversy between the parties. Discovery in the Court of Federal Claims may be limited (but not significantly) by the requirement that a party obtain leave of the court before obtaining discovery by way of depositions, production of documents, or admissions.[155] In the Tax Court, the parties are expected "to attain the objectives of discovery through informal consultation or communication," and discovery is available through depositions only in limited situations.[156] Consequently, a taxpayer who wishes

---

new matter or theory to be raised in response to a new position taken by the taxpayer in pretrial discovery. See Ferrill v. Comm'r, 684 F2d 261 (3d Cir. 1982).

[154] Joseph B. Ferguson v. Comm'r, 47 TC 11 (1966).

[155] Cl. Ct. R. 30 (depositions); Cl. Ct. R. 34 (production of documents); Cl. Ct. R. 36 (admissions). Interrogatories may be served without leave of the court. Cl. Ct. R. 33. With the exception of interrogatories, a showing of good cause is also required for discovery in the claims court. Cl. Ct. R. 26, 33. However, the claims court standard pretrial order requires the parties to submit so much data that their need for discovery is reduced. Cl. Ct. R. 16.

[156] Tax Ct. R. Prac. & Proc. 70(a)(1). This admonition is the source of the difference in pretrial procedure between the Tax Court and the district courts. In the Tax Court, a failure to comply with stipulation procedures can result in sanctions, such as a denial of pretrial discovery. International Air Conditioning Corp. v. Comm'r, 67 TC 89 (1976). The Tax Court Rules permit discovery depositions of a party or nonparty witness if "all the

to limit discovery should consider bringing his or her case in the Tax Court or possibly the claims court, rather than a district court.

[g] Jury Trial

A trial by jury is not available in either the Tax Court or the claims court. The only court having jurisdiction over a tax controversy in which a taxpayer may have issues of fact decided by a jury is a local district court. Frequently, tax cases do not present appealing jury issues because of their complexity. The potential prejudice of jurors who may not be as wealthy as the taxpayer is also a factor. However, certain issues (e.g., casualty losses) may well have jury appeal, especially in areas of the country where members of the jury are likely to identify with the taxpayer.

[3] Preparing the Protest

No Service form is provided for filing a protest. (See Form 9.3 for a sample protest.) When a written protest is required, it must be submitted in duplicate within the thirty-day period granted in the letter transmitting the report of examination, unless extension for filing the protest is granted. The protest should contain the following information:

- The taxpayer's name and address
- The date and symbols from the letter transmitting the proposed adjustments
- The tax periods or years involved
- A statement of the adjustment being protested
- A statement of facts supporting the taxpayer's position on any factual issue
- A statement outlining the law or other authority on which the protest relies

Any statement of facts must be declared true under penalties of perjury, which can be done by executing the following declaration:

---

parties" consent. Tax Ct. R. 74(a). However, the consent requirement obviously limits the use of discovery depositions. Tax Court Rule 75 permits the taking of discovery depositions of nonparty witnesses without leave of the court. Rule 75 provides this "extraordinary method of discovery" to be used only when a nonparty witness can give testimony or possesses documents or things otherwise discoverable within the meaning of Rule 70(b) and when the information sought cannot be obtained through informal consultation (Rule 70(a)(1)) or deposition by consent of the parties (Rule 74). These depositions are properly seen as a method of facilitating the trial of a case, and are, in fact, not permitted until a notice of trial has been issued or the case assigned to a judge or special trial judge of the court.

Under the penalties of perjury, I declare that I have examined the statement of facts presented in this protest and in any accompanying schedules and statements and, to the best of my knowledge and belief, they are true, correct, and complete.[157]

If the protest is submitted by the taxpayer's representative, a substitute declaration may be used stating (1) that the representative had prepared the protest and any accompanying documents and (2) whether the representative personally knows that the statement of facts in the protest and any accompanying documents are true and correct. If the representative has not previously filed a power of attorney, one should be attached to the protest.[158]

The following are a few helpful hints for drafting the protest.

1. *Fact orientation.* The representative moves from strength if he or she makes the protest fact-oriented. The representative also can gain an additional psychological advantage in the Appeals Office conference by attaching documents and affidavits to the protest. Attachments show the Appeals officers that the representative has done the necessary homework and appears ready for trial. Insofar as they support the statements made in the protest, attachments also give the representative a measure of credibility. Both these factors help in negotiations with the Appeals officer.

2. *Demonstrate hazards of litigation.* The presentation of factual and legal arguments in a protest should be directed toward showing that the issue is either inappropriate or hazardous for the Service to litigate. An Appeals officer is more likely to be moved by a demonstration that the Service stands a substantial chance of losing in a court and perhaps of opening an opportunity for other taxpayers to obtain a windfall tax advantage than by an abstract discussion of law with long case analyses. Such a demonstration of the hazards of litigation usually starts by pointing to some fact or authority that the revenue agent has failed to consider or to give appropriate weight. In making a legal argument in a protest, a regulation, revenue ruling, or other Service pronouncement is the most persuasive, if not binding, authority. Finally, the protest should make all possible arguments in favor of the taxpayer's position. Even if the representative does not believe the point is dispositive, the Appeals officer may find that the argument is more substantial or has a cumulative effect in favor of the taxpayer. However, as a tactical matter, an especially telling point may be given more dramatic impact by saving its development for the conference.

3. *Skeletal versus full protest.* As a practical matter, an Appeals officer takes the position that a taxpayer has the burden of proving that the local office made an improper determination. A taxpayer cannot begin to carry this

---

[157] IRS Publication No. 5.

[158] The practice requirements are discussed in Chapter 1, Part C.

burden by filing a skeleton protest and bringing up matters for the first time at a conference. Although it is difficult to generalize, the skeleton protest probably is ineffective in most cases. It puts the whole burden on the representative's presentation at the conference precisely when the Appeals officer may not be completely receptive to the presentation. An Appeals officer who has not been given an opportunity to consider, at least in general outline, a point by seeing it in a protest may feel that he or she is not prepared for a meaningful conference. Further, an Appeals officer made to feel ignorant may become defensive and stubborn in discussing the disposition of the case.

FORM 9.3 ————————————————————

SAMPLE PROTEST
————————————————————

Internal Revenue Service
P.O. Box 0000
Church Street Station
New York, New York 00000
Attention: 30-Day Review Staff

Field Audit Branch Re.—John and Mary Doe

Dear Sirs:

I am in receipt of your letter dated August 3, 1990, and the attached report of the examining agent. On behalf of the taxpayers, John and Mary Doe, protest is hereby made of the adjustments in tax liability set forth therein.

The following information is submitted in support of this protest:

1. *Conference.* A conference relating to this appeal from the findings of the examining revenue agent is requested in the Appeals Office.

2. *Names and address of taxpayers.*

John and Mary Doe
1 Main Street
New York, New York 00000

3. *Date and symbol of letter of transmittal.*

August 3, 1980
Letter 951 (DO) (10-78)

4. *Tax years involved.*

Taxable years 1986 and 1987

5. *Protested adjustments.* The determination appealed from is based on the following errors:

[*Describe in lettered paragraphs the adjustments made by the revenue agent that are believed to be in error.*]

6. *Statement of facts.*

[*Describe the facts related to each of the contested adjustments. Attach copies of documents or affidavits where appropriate.*]

7. *Statement of law.*

[State the law applicable to each of the contested adjustments and apply the applicable law to the facts of the case.]

    I have prepared the foregoing protest for the taxpayers, John and Mary Doe, but I do not know personally that the statements of fact contained in the protest are true and correct.

Very truly yours,

(Representative)

¶ 9.06 APPEALS CONFERENCE PROCEDURE AND PREPARATION

Appeals Office conferences are informal. No stenographer is present to record the discussions of the facts and the law relating to the issue involved. Testimony under oath is not taken. Matters alleged as fact must be submitted in the form of an affidavit or declared to be true under penalties of perjury.[159] A taxpayer is not permitted to withhold evidence from the District Office or present it for the first time at the Appeals Office conference. If new evidence is presented for the first time in the Appeals Office, the Appeals officer has the discretion to return the entire case to the District Office for reconsideration or to transmit the specific evidence to the District Office for verification.[160]

At the conference, the Appeals officer can decide that further factual development is necessary and thus may request that the taxpayer submit additional information. Discussion of a complex case can require additional conferences. In some situations, conferences continue over a long period, while in others a settlement is reached at the first conference. At some point, settlement is discussed. Normally, the Appeals officer asks the taxpayer or the taxpayer's representative to submit an offer of settlement if the officer considers the issue or issues involved to be susceptible to settlement. If this offer is not acceptable, the Appeals officer usually suggests a proposal to the taxpayer's representative.

If the case is settled, the Appeals officer prepares an action/transmittal memorandum and supporting statement, which discusses the issues and evidence, the amount of settlement, and the reasons supporting the settlement. The taxpayer is sent computations and a settlement agreement form. After processing and assessment, the taxpayer is sent a bill for the agreed-on deficiency.

If the case is not settled, the Appeals officer prepares an action/transmittal memorandum and supporting statement, which discusses the settlement offer and the Appeals officer's settlement range.[161] The Appeals Office then requests the issuance of a statutory notice of deficiency. This statutory notice is reviewed by counsel before it is issued.

---

[159] 26 CFR § 601.106(c).

[160] 26 CFR § 601.106(f)(6) (Rule VI).

[161] Taxpayers may be able to obtain a copy of the appeals memorandum by mailing a request under the FOIA. TMM 77-24 (Nov. 21, 1977). See ¶ 2.03[4].

[1] Nondocketed Cases

After a protest is filed, the administrative file containing the protest, returns of the taxpayer, consents, the revenue agent's report, and other documents relating to the taxpayer's liability for the year or years involved is sent to the Appeals Office along with a transmittal memorandum. On receipt, the Appeals Office reviews the file and the protest and any new facts, law, or arguments presented to determine whether further development is required by the local office before the case is ripe for appellate review. However, such cases are rarely returned.

A primary concern of the Appeals Office is the inadvertent expiration of the statute of limitations on assessment. Accordingly, the file is examined to determine whether the statutory period of limitations has expired and, if not, how much of the period of limitations is still available. District Offices are instructed not to transmit a case to the regional Appeals Office unless at least 120 days remain before the expiration of the statutory period for assessment. For certain cases, such as estate tax and accumulated earnings tax cases, at least 180 days must remain. In the event that the time for appellate review is considered inadequate, the taxpayer is requested to extend the statutory period on assessment. In addition to the usual Form 872 (Consent to Extend the Time to Assess Tax), which is used in the District Office to extend the statute for a fixed period, the Appeals Office may use a Form 872-A (Special Consent to Extend the Time to Assess Tax). This form is an open-ended consent that extends the period of assessment until ninety days after either completion of Appeals Office consideration or notice by either party of its desire to terminate the consent.[162]

[2] Docketed Cases

The jurisdiction of the Appeals Office has limited duration.[163] In order to ensure that the period during which the Appeals Office has sole jurisdiction is productively used, the taxpayer should consider taking the following actions:

1. A case should be prepared for an Appeals conference before the Commissioner's answer is filed.

2. When the taxpayer has not adequately developed the facts, he can ask the District Counsel to hold the files rather than send them immediately to the Appeals Office.

---

[162] Form 872-A is described at ¶ 8.06[5][b].

[163] Rev. Proc. 87-24, 1987-1 CB 720, § 2. IRM, Policies of the IRS Handbook, P-8-47 (approved Apr. 6, 1987) (Settlement Practice and Procedure). See also IRM 8412, IRM 8.4.1.1.2 (Apr. 16, 1999) (Appeals Authority Over Docketed Cases).

3. Preparation for the Appeals conference should begin at once.

4. When the taxpayer has prepared for a conference and an answer has been filed, he or she should ask the District Counsel when the file was sent to the Appeals Office, when the file was received, and to whom the case has been assigned.

5. If settlement discussions in the Appeals Office indicate that all issues in the case can be settled, but the period of Appeals jurisdiction is about to expire, the taxpayer can make a request to extend Appeals consideration. The taxpayer should prepare a letter or memorandum demonstrating that (1) there is a substantial likelihood that settlement of the entire case can be reached in a reasonable period and (2) this possibility outweighs the need for commencement of trial preparation.

[3] Preparation for the Conference

The informal nature of the Appeals conference can disarm the taxpayer's representative in appreciating its difficulty. At the conference, unlike a trial, the judge who is to be persuaded is also an adversary, who argues the Service's position. Furthermore, the Appeals officer has a strong psychological edge in tax negotiations; the Appeals officer has no vocal client to satisfy or fee to justify, nor must he or she be as concerned with the time and expense of litigation should no satisfactory basis of settlement be reached. Despite all the difficulties facing the representative, it has been estimated that in approximately 60 percent of all appellate conferences, taxpayers' representatives appear at the initial conference unprepared.[164] Checklist 9.1 is a checklist explaining the steps the representative should take in preparing for the Appeals conference.

[a] The Revenue Agent as Fact Investigator

Although Appeals officers enjoy significant advantages in the conference procedure, the representative can capitalize on an inherent weakness in the position of Appeals officers, as negotiators: Appeals officers do not prepare their own cases. The information given to the Appeals officer, apart from the protest, is derived from the revenue agent's report (RAR). Thus, with adequate preparation, the representative should be more familiar with the facts of the case than the Appeals officer; knowledge is critical in successful negotiations.

The quality of the Appeals officer's information is also affected by the limitations of the revenue agent as a fact investigator. These limitations can be

---

[164] Holloran, "Strategy When Going to Conference and Appellate," in Federal Tax Practice and Procedure 211 (1971).

illustrated by comparing revenue agents and special agents as fact investigators. In a civil tax case, the taxpayers have the burden of proving that the Service determination is erroneous. Therefore, the revenue agent does not have the motivation to dig hard for the facts. On the other hand, because the burden of proof is on the government in a fraud case, the special agent knows that a conviction depends on his or her investigation. The revenue agent is by training more an auditor than a fact investigator and tends to be oriented more toward the rule of law than toward fact. The special agent, on the other hand, is concerned not with complex rules and statutes but, rather, with facts that evidence fraud. Finally, a revenue agent is under considerable pressure to complete an audit, while a special agent may spend more than a year investigating a single case.

The reports of the two types of agents also reflect their differences as fact investigators. The special agent's report organizes and attaches items of evidence (accounting summaries, copies of documents, and affidavits of witnesses) and keys his or her written report to these exhibits for easy reference. The revenue agent's report is rarely prepared in this manner.

[b] Stages of Negotiation at the Conference

A conference with the Appeals officer has the same stages as the conference with the revenue agent.[165] First, the parties talk through the issues, seeking to enlarge the areas of agreement and narrow the matters of disagreement. The Appeals officer then asks the taxpayer's representative to make a specific proposal to dispose of the issues. The parties will either agree or disagree on this settlement proposal. In this process, two major themes emerge: (1) the presentation of the taxpayer's position, including responses to arguments of the revenue agent and the Appeals officer, and (2) settlement discussion. In presenting the taxpayer's position at the conference, the representative should make only his or her strongest arguments. Presenting a weak argument at a conference may only detract from credibility and, possibly, from a stronger argument. The strength of an argument depends on support, and it helps if the representative can point to tangible evidence—something, whether it be a document or an affidavit, other than his representation regarding the matter. Facts in support of the taxpayer's position, including facts that may have been alluded to but not developed in the protest, should be presented. A presentation that makes use of third-party affidavits, expert reports, charts, pictures, or any other physical or demonstrative evidence should be more telling. However, as noted previously, a taxpayer may not refuse to disclose important evidence to the District Office and present it for the first time to the Appeals officer. Although there is no bright line between new evidence and factual development,

---

[165] See ¶ 8.06[4][c].

the Appeals officer can consider the submission to be new evidence and can send it to the district for verification if he or she feels that the tactic is over-reaching.[166] It is also important for the representative to point out some authority or fact that the agent did not or could not consider.

This type of presentation serves several purposes. Negotiation is a delicate art, but experience teaches that it is only after a presentation of the strongest case, factual and legal, for the taxpayer that some spoken or unspoken recognition of the relative merits of the parties' positions will emerge. Then and only then, as a realistic matter, can the merits of the position be translated into a dollar amount and the result be grounded on some matter of fact or appropriate authority, to give the Appeals officer some basis for a settlement to include in his or her report. The representative must bear in mind the requirement that the Appeals officer must justify his action in a written report, for unless he can show the Appeals officer how to overrule the determination of the agent in whole or in part, negotiations will be difficult. The settlement of an issue with an Appeals officer is related to trial advocacy precisely because preparation and readiness for trial allow the representative to deal from strength in negotiations with the Appeals officer. Obviously, an Appeals officer will not be inclined to settle an issue on terms particularly favorable to the taxpayer if the officer feels the taxpayer is not willing to contest the issue.

[c] Factors Bearing on the Presentation

Although the presentation of factual and legal arguments in an Appeals conference and in a case in court is completely different, the dynamics of the Appeals conference has its own complexity. A representative should consider the following:

1. *Rules of evidence.* Appeals officers do not apply the rules of evidence applicable in the Tax Court, a district court, or the claims court. Consequently, all evidence favorable to the taxpayer should be presented, even if the evidence may not be admissible in a court of law. The evidence, even if inadmissible, may persuade the Appeals officer that there is an appreciable hazard of litigation. If the taxpayer has admissible evidence that the District Office has not yet been able to counter, the representative can point out the inadequacy of the District Office's position in a court.

2. *Vicarious admissions.* The representative must remember that factual statements or concessions made in a protest or in an Appeals Office conference constitute an adoptive admission by the taxpayer. In the event that no settlement is reached, the Service can offer the oral or written statement of the taxpayer or taxpayer's authorized representative against the taxpayer as an ad-

---

[166] 26 CFR § 601.106(f)(6) (Rule VI).

mission at a trial.[167] Consequently, the representative should present facts that support the taxpayer but should do so with the understanding that any statement may be used against the taxpayer. However, the fact that the taxpayer has offered to settle the case and the terms of the offer are not admissible in evidence.[168]

3. *Arguments on the law.* Legal authority is difficult to present in a conference unless it is dispositive (which is rare). The representative usually is better able to present the taxpayer's position in writing, either in a protest or in a memorandum, than to carry on extended arguments with the Appeals officer over fine points of tax law.

4. *Authority.* Legal authority is more likely to be dispositive if it is a statement of the Service. The Appeals officer, as a Service official, will be impressed more with statements of position by the Service than with court decisions. Consequently, a point of law will be more successfully made if it is a regulation, ruling, acquiescence, or technical advice.

[d] Factors Bearing on the Offer

Settlement negotiations depend on the success with which the taxpayer's position has been presented. The Appeals officer is unlikely to entertain a settlement offer if the taxpayer has not created some doubt as to the result of presenting the case in court. Also, the Appeals officer will not consider an offer based on the cost to the government in litigating the case (nuisance value). These general observations suggest that the representative consider the following:

1. The initial offer to the Appeals officer must be sufficiently high to indicate a good faith effort to settle the case without necessarily being the taxpayer's best offer.

2. The offer should be framed in terms of the chances of ultimate success in court. The representative should know what the settlement of the case as a whole will look like before the conference, not rely on a running tally as settlement is discussed issue by issue. An Appeals officer understands that a settlement may involve mutual concessions on individual issues based on relative litigating strength or on the percentage or lump-sum portion of the amount of tax each issue involves. Consequently, a taxpayer's proposal should follow these recognized forms.

3. The representative should request that the Appeals officer propose a settlement that the officer would recommend if the initial proposal is not acceptable.

---

[167] Fed. R. Evid. 801(2).
[168] Fed. R. Evid. 408.

CHECKLIST 9.1 _____

PREPARATION FOR APPEALS CONFERENCE CHECKLIST

- ☐ **Interview the Client.** Be a searching cross-examiner. The representative must know "the facts, the exact facts, and all the facts."
- ☐ **Check the Important Facts.** Do not rely solely on what the client says.
- ☐ **Obtain Business Records and Other Documentary Evidence From the Client.**
- ☐ **Formulate the Argument or Arguments After Fact Investigation and Legal Analysis.** After the facts have been investigated and the law analyzed, arrange an outline listing every element the taxpayer must prove, with the documents and witnesses who will support proof of each element. The outline helps to avoid overlooking vital proof and in making an orderly presentation of the case.
- ☐ **Prepare Both Sides of the Case.** Mastery of the facts involves preparing both sides of the issue and anticipating what possible claims the Service might make. Although the taxpayer may not have the best case, preparation of the taxpayer's side of the story in anticipation of opposing arguments permits the representative to deal from the strongest position possible.
- ☐ **Determine What Other Evidence Is Needed.** When appropriate and possible, interview additional witnesses and secure statements from them in the form of affidavits. Such evidence should be obtained from competitors, trade associations, and the like.
- ☐ **Sort and Arrange Exhibits for Ready Use at the Conference.**
- ☐ **Review the Entire File Prior to the Conference.** The objective should be to have the case as fully prepared before the conference as circumstances permit. For this reason, it is generally better to postpone the conference than to make a weak presentation in the expectation that it will be bolstered at a later time.
- ☐ **Formulate a Proposal for Settlement.** In advance of the conference prepare a possible settlement and compute the additional tax, if any, payable under different settlement possibilities.

¶ 9.07 APPEALS SETTLEMENT PRACTICE AND PROCEDURES

The Appeals Office's broad authority to resolve tax controversies without litigation derives from the fact that Appeals officers may settle a case based on an evaluation of the "hazards-of-litigation" if the case were to be litigated in a court of law. As the Service's Statement of Procedural Rules puts it, "Appeals will ordinarily give consideration to an offer to settle a tax controversy on a basis which fairly reflects the relative merits of the opposing views in light of the hazards which would exist if the case were litigated." The stated objective of a conference is a "fair and impartial resolution" of the controversy, which means a disposition of the case that reflects the probable result in the event of litigation. According to the Service, a fair and impartial resolution is one that "reflects on an issue-by-issue basis the probable result in event of litigation, or one which reflects mutual concessions for the purpose of settlement based on the relative strength of the opposing positions where there is a substantial uncertainty of the result in event of litigation."[169]

Not every controversy is disposed of by settlement. Even when the Appeals Office has the authority to settle a case, settlement is not possible unless the taxpayer is able to demonstrate that there is a substantial uncertainty, either in law, fact, or both, as to the correct application of the law to the whole record in the case. Only if this uncertainty exists will the Appeals officer give consideration to an offer that reflects the relative merits of the opposing views, in light of the hazards that would prevail if the case were litigated.[170]

Appeals officers do not have final authority to settle tax cases.[171] No settlement reached with an Appeals officer is binding unless and until it is approved by a reviewing officer in the Appeals Office or is at least submitted to the reviewing officer for approval.[172] Therefore, neither the taxpayer nor his or

---

[169] IRM 8.6, Conference and Settlement Practice, 3.1(2), Settlement Objective (Jan. 22, 1990).

[170] IRM 1.2.1, Policies of the IRS Handbook, 1.8.4, Policy Statement P-8-47(1), Consideration to Be Given to Offers of Settlement (approved Apr. 6, 1987).

[171] Settlement authority is delegated only to "certain officers" of the Appeals Offices. 26 CFR §§ 601.106(a)(1)(i), 601.106(a)(1)(ii). Apart from the Regional Director of Appeals, delegation runs to the Chiefs and Associate Chiefs of Appeals and the Appeals Team Chiefs in large cases handled by a team of Appeals officers. Commissioner Delegation Order (CDO) No. 66 lists the officials empowered to approve settlements. The current revision of CDO No. 66 should be checked by referring to the Internal Revenue Bulletins and Cumulative Bulletins, as well as commercial tax services.

[172] Gardner v. Comm'r, 75 TC 475 (1980) (interpreting the authority of an Appeals officer in a docketed Tax Court case). In *Gardner*, a settlement was reached with the Appeals officer, and settlement documents for filing in the Tax Court were signed by the taxpayers' lawyer. The Appeals officer withdrew the settlement and rejected it. The Tax Court denied the taxpayer's motion for summary judgment based on the withdrawn settlement. See also Boulez v. Comm'r, 76 TC 209 (1981), aff'd, 810 F2d 209 (DC Cir. 1987), cert. denied (the Director of International Operations was held not to have bound the Service because he was not delegated the authority to accept oral offers in compromise). In a case following *Gardner*, a divided panel of the Sixth Circuit refused to hold the Service to a settlement negotiated by an Appeals officer in a docketed Tax Court case despite the fact that the taxpayer was notified by form letter that the settlement had been accepted and the Service negotiated the taxpayer's check, which was sent pursuant to the settlement. Jones Estate v. Comm'r, 795 F2d 566 (6th Cir. 1986) (settlement invalid because it was not executed on behalf of Chief Counsel and filed with the Tax Court). Settlements with the Appeals Office can involve execution of extensions of the limitations period conditioned on a settlement that has been agreed on but not yet formalized. Suppose the Appeals officer reneges on the settlement. Is the extension valid? See Addison H. Gibson Found. v. United States, 91-1 USTC ¶ 50,178 (WD Pa. 1991) (waivers invalid, and as-

her representative should consider a case to be concluded merely because some oral understanding has been reached with the Appeals officer. A settlement can only be considered concluded when it is reflected in a settlement agreement (e.g., Form 870-AD) signed as accepted for the Commissioner.[173]

[1] The Hazards-of-Litigation Standard

Under the "hazards-of-litigation" standard, the Appeals officer reviews the entire file to determine what a court might decide on the basis of (1) the provable facts; (2) the effect of the testimony likely to be presented; and (3) the expected interpretation and application by the court of the Code provisions and applicable regulations in the light of decided cases. The Service's procedural rules state that the Appeals officer has "the duty to determine the correct amount of the tax, with strict impartiality as between the taxpayer and the Government."[174] For this reason, the Appeals officer is sometimes regarded as an impartial judge of the District Office's findings. This view is misleading. There is a difference between the approach the Appeals officer follows in hearing the taxpayer's appeal and in evaluating a case for settlement purposes. At the hearing, the Appeals officer is not a judge, but an employee of the Service who argues the position of the local office. However, to evaluate a case for settlement purposes, the Appeals officer (and the taxpayer's representative) must appraise the facts, law, and litigating prospects as objectively as possible. To the extent that an Appeals officer engages in this objective analysis, he or she is looking at the case in the way he or she believes a court might, rather than attempting to gain the maximum possible result in favor of the government. In this sense, the Appeals officer may be said to adopt a judicial attitude toward settlement.[175]

To evaluate the settlement possibilities of a case properly, the Appeals officer is instructed to consider the following:

- Probative value of the evidence likely to be presented
- Credibility of witnesses (e.g., the taxpayer)

---

sessment of excise tax held untimely; Service held to agreement on income tax prior to expiration of assessment period).

[173] When a settlement is made in a case docketed in the Tax Court, contract principles have been applied, and settlement agreements have been enforced against taxpayers and against the Service when the agreement has been approved by the Office of Appeals during the period of its settlement jurisdiction, and even when the agreement has not been signed on behalf of the Commissioner. See Haiduk v. Comm'r, 60 TCM 864 (1990) (agreement enforced against Service).

[174] SPR, 26 CFR § 601.106(f)(1) (Rule I).

[175] IRM 8.6, Conference and Settlement Practice, 1.1.3.4, Judicial Attitude Towards Settlement (Feb. 18, 1999).

- Availability of witnesses
- Ability of the taxpayer to carry his burden of going forward with evidence
- Likelihood that the evidence the taxpayer can present will carry his burden of proof
- Doubt as to an issue of fact
- Doubt as to a conclusion of law (e.g., the law in the circuit to which the case will be appealed or in which it will be tried)

Consequently, much of the Appeals officer's analysis focuses on the evidence available for presentation in court. However, the Appeals officer does not apply the rules of evidence strictly. Indeed, Appeals officers frequently are not familiar with the use of these rules. Therefore, in evaluating a case, an Appeals officer may choose to consider hearsay or other evidence that is not admissible evidence or that would likely be given little weight if admitted.

Appeals officers must also assess the law applicable to an issue. In this analysis, an Appeals officer does not necessarily give legal authority the same weight as a court might give it. In any legal analysis, a decision of the Supreme Court obviously is controlling, but it would be unusual for a case to reach the Appeals Office if there was a decision directly on point. Although Appeals officers are independent, the Service's position has special importance to them. The Service's position must be considered in the light of the developing law, the importance of the issue, whether the facts of the case present a favorable or unfavorable vehicle to litigate the Service's position, and the effect that an adverse decision will have on that position. An Appeals officer is bound by statute and regulation, but not by revenue rulings in which the Service states its position as to how the tax law applies to particular facts, because revenue rulings do not have the legal effect of a statute or even the weight of a regulation.[176] Consequently, it is possible for an Appeals officer to conclude that a court would decide a case contrary to a revenue ruling on the facts or that an intermediate basis reflects the hazard of litigating the issue and, to that extent, indicates that the Appeals officer should not follow the ruling.

Previously decided Tax Court cases are also important to the Appeals officer's review. Taxpayers who can point to a favorable Tax Court decision should be able to conclude an agreement on the issue. However, even if the Tax Court has decided an issue favorably to a taxpayer, the Appeals officer can refuse to concede the issue if the Commissioner has not acquiesced in the decision and the Service wishes another opportunity to litigate the issue.[177] The

---

[176] For a discussion of the legal effect of a revenue ruling, see ¶ 3.03[2][b].

[177] On a litigated issue, Appeals officers are also advised to check any published Action on Decision (Action) where the court ruled against the Service's position. The Service Manual says, "Actions are valuable guides for evaluating similar issues and should be

law in the circuit to which the taxpayer appeals an adverse decision carries even greater weight than other Tax Court decisions on the same issue because the Tax Court will follow the decisions of this circuit.[178] When the circuit's rule is adverse to the Service, the Appeals officer is instructed to consult with District Counsel to discover the Service's current litigating position.[179] Consequently, it is possible for the Appeals officer to refuse to follow authority adverse to the Service if the Service has made a decision to relitigate the issue. On the other hand, a taxpayer also can rely on authority outside the circuit to which the appeal would lie. Here again, the Appeals officer may not recognize the authority as controlling, such as when an action on decision memorandum reflecting the Service's position on the case states that the Service will not follow the decision and that further litigation is contemplated. Also, if the authority favorable to the taxpayer (and adverse to the Service) is an isolated court of appeals decision or there are conflicting decisions on an issue, the Appeals officer can say that the applicable law is unsettled until the Service abandons a position decided adversely to it or the Supreme Court decides it.

    Thus, the analysis of the law applicable to a disputed issue is a unique amalgam of Service policy and normal recognition of legal authority at the Appeals Office level. Legal authority is not used in the same way as in a court of law; unlike judges, Appeals officers are not bound by precedent if the Service does not consider itself bound by an adverse decision. Although legal reasoning and research are used, the approach is administrative, not judicial, because in the final analysis, the Appeals Office follows the Service's position on an issue.

[2] The Settlement Offer

Appeals officers consider any settlement offer demonstrating a good faith effort to settle the case. Appeals officers are instructed to attempt to reach an agreement with the taxpayer on all issues susceptible of resolution.[180] A settlement offer should cover all issues, and the Appeals officer's approach should

---

applied by Appeals officers in resolving their cases." IRM 8.6, Conference and Settlement Practice, 1.1.3.6(6), Case Evaluation for Settlement Purposes (Feb. 18, 1999).

[178] Jack E. Golsen v. Comm'r, 54 TC 742 (1970), aff'd on another issue, 445 F2d 985 (10th Cir.), cert. denied, 404 US 940 (1971).

[179] IRM 8.6, Conference and Settlement Practice, 1.1.3.6(4), Case for Evaluation for Settlement Purposes (Feb. 18, 1999) ("[i]n cases where the 'Golsen Rule' is applicable, the Appeals officer should consult with Counsel as promptly as possible to determine the amount of litigation activity in other circuits and other relevant information on the Service's posture on the issue(s) involved").

[180] IRM 8.6, Conference and Settlement Practice, 1.1.3.7, Partial Settlements (Feb. 2, 1999).

be to resolve the issues that can be resolved, even if agreement cannot be reached on other issues. However, an offer that is merely an attempt to bargain rather than an actual attempt at settlement of the case based on the hazards-of-litigation, such as a nuisance value offer, is not a good faith offer and is not considered.[181] No clear line divides nuisance value from good faith offers, but a concession of 10 percent or less appears to be the rough guideline frequently used. If an Appeals officer believes that the offer is made in good faith but is unacceptable, the Appeals officer should make a counteroffer or describe a basis for settlement that would be recommended for acceptance.

The Appeals Office takes the same approach in both nondocketed and docketed cases. Thus, an offer unacceptable in a nondocketed case does not become acceptable merely because the case is in docketed status.[182] However, when a case is in docketed status, a Counsel attorney can influence the conference in the appeal and determine whether or not a settlement is reached. For example, the Counsel attorney may be more sensitive than the Appeals officer to problems of proof facing both the Service and the taxpayer, in which case the assessment of the attorney can mean the difference in the settlement discussions. On the other hand, if the Appeals officer would not recommend trying the issue, the officer should concede the issue even if the Service's position might have some merit.[183]

[3] Types of Settlements

There are three types of settlements: (1) mutual concession settlements; (2) split-issue settlements; and (3) nuisance value settlements.

[a] Mutual Concession Settlements

In a mutual concession settlement, both the Service and the taxpayer make concessions for the purpose of settling the case when there is a substantial uncertainty about how a court would interpret and apply the law or about what facts the court would find if the case were litigated. In this type of a set-

---

[181] SPR, 26 CFR § 601.106(f)(2) (Rule II); IRM 1.2.1, Policies of the IRS Handbook 1.8.4, Policy Statement P-8-47. See IRM 8.6, Conference and Settlement Practice, 1.1.3.6(3), Case Evaluation for Settlement Purposes (Feb. 18, 1999) ("[m]inor concessions are not made or accepted on the basis that the outcome of litigation is never absolutely predictable").

[182] IRM 8.6, Conference and Settlement Practice, 1.1.3.6(1), Case Evaluation for Settlement Purposes (Feb. 18, 1999) ("nor does [an unacceptable offer] become more acceptable in a trial calendar period than it was in a prior period").

[183] IRM 8.6, Conference and Settlement Practice, 1.1.3.4, Judicial Attitude Towards Settlement (Feb. 18, 1999).

tlement, both parties recognize the other party's strength so that neither party, with justification, is willing to concede in full the unresolved area of disagreement.[184] A settlement on the valuation or basis of property normally is made by mutual concessions.

[b] Split-Issue Settlements

A split-issue settlement is a form of mutual concession settlement that involves an issue that if litigated would result in a decision completely for the government or for the taxpayer. This type of settlement reflects the relative merits of the opposing views, in a way that a trial of the issue could not, because a trial could not result in a decision at any intermediate point between the positions. A split-issue settlement may be based on an adjustment to taxable income, a percentage of tax in controversy, or a specific amount of tax. This type of settlement is not particularly favored and generally is used when there is no recurring issue and no related case.[185] In situations calling for split-issue settlements, the Appeals officer is instructed to consider whether settlement may have some effect on later years, particularly in carry-over or carry-back situations and in most gift tax cases. In this event, the split-issue settlement should be reflected in terms of an adjustment of taxable income rather than in a percentage or an amount of tax. A settlement involving the issue of whether a debt is a business or nonbusiness bad debt or a fraud penalty will involve a split-issue settlement.

[c] Nuisance Value Settlements

A nuisance value settlement is any concession that is made solely to eliminate the inconvenience or cost of further negotiations or litigation and is unrelated to the merits or the issues. As noted previously, the Service's policy is that no settlement is to be considered if based on nuisance value to either party.[186] Appeals officers are also instructed that if trial of an issue would not be recommended, the issue should be conceded even though it may have some merit.[187]

---

[184] IRM 8.6, Conference and Settlement Practice, 1.1.3.1, Mutual-Concession Settlements (Feb. 18, 1999).

[185] IRM 2.1, Policies of the IRS Handbook 1.8.5, P-8-48, Split-Issue Settlements Considered Under Certain Circumstances (approved Dec. 23, 1960); IRM 8.6, Conference and Settlement Practice, 1.1.3.2, Split-Issue Settlements (Feb. 18, 1999).

[186] IRM 1.2.1, Policies of the IRS Handbook 1.8.4, P-8-47, Consideration Given to Offers of Settlement (Apr. 6, 1987); IRM 8.6, Conference and Settlement Practice, 1.1.3.3, Nuisance Value Settlements (Feb. 18, 1999).

[187] IRM 8.6, Conference and Settlement Practice, 1.1.3.3, Nuisance Value Settlements (Feb. 18, 1999).

[4] New Issues or Reopening Closed Issues

A major concern of the taxpayer in an Appeals Office conference is that the Appeals officer will raise a new issue. The Service's policy is not to reopen an issue on which the taxpayer and the local office are in agreement, nor to raise a new issue, unless the grounds for the action are "substantial" and the potential effect on tax liability is "material."[188] This policy does not apply to new issues raised by taxpayers. When a new issue is raised by a taxpayer, the evidence is to be considered and, if necessary, referred to the local office for verification. In general, a new issue is one that the Commissioner is required to raise in an answer or amended answer in the Tax Court that was not one of the adjustments in the statutory notice of deficiency.[189] Consequently, a new issue generally is anything concerning a taxpayer's return that was not previously raised in the examiner's report or statutory notice of deficiency and that the taxpayer did not cover in a protest or a petition. The term "new issue" is used in its broadest sense and is not limited to a point in debate or a matter in dispute. Anytime the Appeals officer injects a position contrary to the position originally or previously taken by the taxpayer or any government representative this is considered a "new issue."

Appeals officers are instructed not to raise a new issue "casually, indiscriminately or haphazardly" and never to do so, under any circumstances, for bargaining purposes.[190] When a new issue is raised, the taxpayer or the taxpayer's representative should be advised of the new issue, irrespective of the stage of the appellate consideration.

To raise a new issue, the Appeals officer must have a strong reason with real merit.[191] Mere suspicion that something might be wrong with an item is not considered substantial. The Service Manual uses the example of a claimed farm loss that is disallowed by the local office solely on the ground that it was a hobby and that makes no comment about the items composing the loss. The Appeals officer has no substantial grounds for raising as a new issue the amount of the loss, the amount of any item making up the loss, or the nature of any item making up the loss simply because he suspected that the items had not been verified. However, if the examining officer had indicated in the report that the items had not been verified, the Appeals officer might refer the case back to the district for verification. Also, if the local office stated that some of

---

[188] IRM 1.2.1, Policies of the IRS Handbook 1.8.6, P-8-49, New Issues Not to Be Raised Unless Material (approved Dec. 23, 1960); IRM 8.6, Conference and Settlement Practice, 1.1.4, New Issues and Reopening Closed Issues (Feb. 18, 1999).

[189] IRM 8.6, Conference and Settlement Practice, 1.1.4.1, Definitions (Feb. 18, 1999).

[190] IRM 8.6, Conference and Settlement Practice, 1.1.4.2, General Guidelines (Feb. 18, 1999).

[191] IRM 8.6, Conference and Settlement Practice, 1.1.4.2, General Guidelines (Feb. 18, 1999).

the items of claimed expense were personal, the Appeals officer might either raise the new issue or refer the case back to the local office for further investigation. The substantiality test also requires that the Appeals officer be "quite certain" at the time the new issue is raised that the government will prevail if the issue is litigated.

Finally, the issue must have a material effect on tax liability; that is, it must result in an amount of tax that is large in absolute terms even though it may be a small percentage of the taxpayer's tax liability. There is a material effect if failure to correct the error would have an adverse effect on voluntary compliance or would cause the burden of proof before a court to shift to the government.

[5] Settlement of Fraud Cases

Under Service policy, a civil fraud penalty is recommended in every case where evidence of intent to evade tax is found.[192] However, the Appeals Office has the authority in any case under its sole jurisdiction to eliminate or partially concede the fraud penalty to an amount that is less than 75 percent of the underpayment but more than zero.[193] As previously noted, the Appeals Office has sole jurisdiction over nondocketed cases and, in docketed cases, generally until the receipt of the trial status order, unless counsel otherwise agrees.[194] The Office of Appeals does not have sole authority when a fraud penalty is in issue for a year if a recommendation has been made to the Justice Department to prosecute the taxpayer for a criminal tax violation. In such a case, the Appeals officer is required to obtain the consent of counsel before the fraud penalty for that year may be conceded or eliminated, even if the taxpayer has been acquitted in the criminal trial.[195] This limitation on the Appeals officer's authority does not necessarily eliminate the possibility of settlement of a fraud penalty. A counsel attorney can be asked to be present at the Appeals conference. Because the attorney must try the case, he or she will be more sensitive to weaknesses in the government's proof. Thus, the presence of a representative of the

---

[192] See also Rev. Proc. 87-24, 1987-1 CB 720.

[193] IRM 8.11.1.11, Fraud Penalty Cases (Feb. 26, 1999).

[194] Rev. Proc. 87-24, 1987-1 CB 720. IRM 8.11.1.11.1, Appeals, Processing Fraud Penalty Cases (Feb. 26, 1999).

[195] SPR, 26 CFR § 601.106(a)(2)(v). IRM 8.11.1.11.1, Appeals, Processing Fraud Penalty Cases (Feb. 26, 1999) (concurrence of Counsel is required whether or not the recommendation resulted in a conviction and extends "to any other tax year or period of the taxpayer that is related to, or affects, the tax year or period for which criminal prosecution is recommended"). The concurrence of Chief Counsel is also required for the reduction of any criminal fraud income item.

office with concurrent jurisdiction can make settlement easier, if the case can be settled at all.

If, as the result of a settlement, the fraud penalty is conceded to be an amount that is less than 75 percent of the underpayment but greater than zero, the Appeals Office requires the taxpayer to execute a closing agreement.[196] In this closing agreement, the tax liability must not be converted to a fraud penalty solely to reflect the penalty in the settlement, and the fraud penalty must not be converted into tax solely to avoid the appearance of a penalty.

[6] Settlement of Related Cases

An agreement with the Appeals Office on an issue can affect the tax liability of the same taxpayer for other taxable years or the tax liability of a related taxpayer for the same or another taxable year. Both the taxpayer and the Service may wish consistent action to be taken on the issue. For example, if the issue is a continuing one arising in succeeding taxable years, such as the basis of property or the status of the taxpayer as a dealer, it may be to the taxpayer's advantage to have the settlement followed in succeeding years or to limit the effect of settlement to the year or years actually examined and appealed. On the other hand, it may be in the Service's interests to have a particular issue, such as the basis of property, resolved to eliminate unnecessary administrative action. In addition, the Service seeks to avoid "whipsaw" situations, in which it settles one taxpayer's case and another taxpayer files a claim for refund taking a position inconsistent with the settlement after the assessment period for the first taxpayer has expired. If cases are related, the Appeals Office may, and in some instances must, hear them together, thereby ensuring consistency of treatment.

The Service considers cases to be related if they involve (1) a common or similar issue; (2) different years of the same taxpayer and are received at dif-

---

[196] IRM 8.11.1.11.1, Appeals, Processing Fraud Penalty Cases (Feb. 26, 1999). If the three-year period of limitations for assessment (plus any extensions) has not expired, a closing agreement will be secured in nondocketed cases when there is a partial concession of the fraud penalty to an amount representing less than 75 percent of the underpayment but greater than zero. The Service Manual states that it is usually not necessary to obtain a closing agreement in docketed cases because the stipulated decision filed with the court is sufficient. If the period of limitations for assessment has expired except for fraud, the case is nondocketed, and the Appeals officer has concluded that the evidence warrants litigating the penalty, a closing agreement is to be executed when a mutual concession settlement is worked out for a deficiency with no fraud penalty or a fraud penalty representing less than 75 percent of the underpayment but greater than zero. However, the Appeals officer is warned that tax liabilities should not be converted to a fraud penalty solely to reflect the penalty in the settlement nor should the penalty be converted into tax solely to avoid the appearance of a penalty.

ferent times; or (3) the same taxpayer but different kinds of taxes and are received at the same time or at different times.[197] Related cases are, in turn, classified as "interrelated cases" or "other related cases." Interrelated cases are those cases in which a determination in one case has a direct tax effect on another case, such as the amount or distribution of net income of a partnership, estate, or trust; the value of goodwill in the sale of a going business; and the determination of whether a transfer from a corporation to the widow of a deceased employee is a gift or compensation. Perhaps the most common type of interrelated case is the trust fund recovery penalty case in which assessments are made or proposed against a number of responsible persons. In "other related cases," consistency of action on similar issues is desirable, but the determination in one case does not have a direct tax effect in another case, such as taxability of dividends paid on corporate stock and indefinite versus temporary character of employment of a number of taxpayers at a single location.

Suppose a taxpayer wishes to have a settlement include or at least be considered in the examination of later years. The following four options are available:

1. The taxpayer can request that the Appeals Office assume jurisdiction of the later years for which returns have been filed.[198]

2. An overassessment can be applied to a deficiency in a related case. This netting of tax years may be accomplished by adding appropriate language to the agreement form.[199] If the settlement results in an overpayment in later years, the taxpayer may also file a refund claim and request that the cases be associated in the Appeals Office. However, to protect the taxpayer, the representative must be alert to the expiration of the time for filing a refund claim and file a protective claim if necessary.

3. The taxpayer may request a statement reflecting the settlement. The Service does not consider all cases involving a common or similar issue to be related for the purpose of associating them in an Appeals Office conference. Issues such as reasonable compensation, capital gain versus ordinary income on recurring sales of property, and hobby losses are resolved on the basis of

---

[197] IRM 8.2, Pre-90-Day and Protested Excise and Employment Tax Cases, 1.1.5.1, Definition of Related Cases (Jan. 17, 1999); IRM 8.2, Pre-90-Day and Protested Excise and Employment Tax Cases, 1.1.5.2, Scope of Appeals Consideration of Related Cases (Feb. 17, 1999). See also IRM 8.6, Conference and Settlement Practice, 1.1.5, Settlement of Related Cases (Feb. 18, 1999).

[198] IRM 8.6, Conference and Settlement Procedures, 1.1.5.2, Settlement of Nonexamined Years Affected by Appeals Settlements (Feb. 18, 1999); IRM 8.6, Conference and Settlement Procedures, 1.1.3.8, Settlements That Affect Later Taxable Years (Feb. 18, 1999). The District Office must be given an opportunity to complete "any necessary action" on these returns.

[199] IRM 8.8, Agreement Forms 1.2.4, Modification of Agreement-Overpayments Applied Against Deficiencies (Feb. 22, 1997). The Service Manual has suggested language.

the facts and circumstances in each tax year. The Service's position is that a settlement has no effect on later years in these cases.[200] In this type of case, even if the later year is not associated in the Appeals Office, the taxpayer can request that the Appeals officer furnish the taxpayer with a computation of the corrected tax, as agreed on, and a statement and explanation of changes that describe the basis of the settlement. This statement can be shown to a revenue agent, who may examine the returns for the later years, with the usual result that those later years are treated on the same basis as the settlement.

4. If the case involves such issues as basis of property, category of income, or amount of income from installment collections, the taxpayer may request a closing or collateral agreement.[201] When the settlement involves mutual concessions and the subsequent effect on tax is material, a closing agreement should be used. When there is no mutual concession or the tax effect is not material, a closing agreement is not required. However, if the taxpayer requests a closing agreement, one may be executed. In any case, if a closing agreement is not used, a collateral agreement is suggested, because it expresses in writing the understanding of the parties as to the tax effect in later years.

However, a taxpayer may not always wish to achieve final disposition of a continuing issue. To avoid finality, at least if resolution of the issue depends on the facts in each tax year (e.g., reasonable compensation or dealer status), the taxpayer's objective is best accomplished by a split-issue settlement based on a percentage of the tax in dispute. In this way classification is avoided.

From the Service's viewpoint, a closing agreement is ordinarily used in whipsaw cases in order to protect the government's interests if the amount of tax involved is material or there are litigating "uncertainties."[202] In other circumstances, a collateral agreement is used in order to express in writing the understanding of the parties. The objective of the Appeals Office is to avoid duplication of action and whipsaw situations. If taxpayers in interrelated cases refuse to have the cases handled concurrently or cannot work out a mutually acceptable settlement with the Appeals Office, the Service may assert inconsistent positions to protect the government.[203]

---

[200] IRM 8.6, Conference and Settlement Procedures, 1.1.3.8, Settlements That Affect Later Taxable Years (Feb. 18, 1999).

[201] IRM 8.6, Conference and Settlement Procedures, 1.1.3.8, Settlements That Affect Later Taxable Years (Feb. 18, 1999).

[202] IRM 8.6, Conference and Settlement Procedures, 1.15.1, Settlement Procedure in Whipsaw Cases (Feb. 18, 1999).

[203] IRM 8.2.1.1.5.2.1, Appeals Consideration of Interrelated Cases (Feb. 17, 1999). See supra ¶ 9.03[4].

¶ 9.08 SETTLEMENT AGREEMENT FORMS

Appeals uses four types of agreement forms: (1) the usual waiver of restrictions on assessment, Form 870; (2) the special-purpose waiver form used in the Appeals Office, Form 870-AD; (3) a closing agreement; and (4) a collateral agreement. Settlement of a docketed Tax Court case is reflected not on an IRS form but in a stipulated decision, which, when signed and filed by the presiding judge, becomes the judgment of the Tax Court. The stipulated decision generally states that a taxpayer owes a deficiency in a specific amount or that the taxpayer is entitled to an overpayment in some specific amount.

[1] Forms 870 and 870-AD

In nondocketed cases, the settlement of the parties is reflected in agreement forms of the 870[204] and 870-AD[205] series. The Form 870 and Form 870-AD series differ in a number of important respects. The AD agreement contains pledges against reopening, whereas the usual 870 agreement does not.[206] In general, this means that once an AD agreement is executed, the Service may not make an additional assessment, and the taxpayer may not sue for refund. If the normal Form 870 is executed, the Service may make a further assessment, and the taxpayer may sue for refund. Another difference between the two forms is that the 870 agreement becomes effective as a waiver of restrictions on assessment when the Service receives it, but the special AD agreement form becomes effective only on acceptance by or on behalf of the Commissioner.[207] The suspension of interest provided by Section 6601(d) is controlled

---

[204] The Form 870-type agreement series includes Form 4862 (Audit Statement Income Tax Changes), which combines adjustments to income, computation of tax, and a waiver of restrictions on assessment and collection of a deficiency (or acceptance of an overassessment).

[205] The Form 870-AD-type agreement series includes Form 870-AD (income and gift taxes), Form 890-AD (estate tax), Form 2504-AD (excise and employment taxes), and Form 2751-AD (100 percent penalty).

[206] The Service's Manual states that the Form 870-AD, which is called a special form, differs from the Form 870-type of agreement form in that "the AD agreement contains pledges against reopening whereas the usual agreement does not . . . [, and the] usual agreement becomes effective as a waiver of restrictions on assessment when received, whereas the special agreement becomes effective only upon acceptance by or on behalf of the Commissioner." IRM 8.8, Appeals Agreement Forms, 1.1.3, Distinction Between Agreements—Forms 870 and 870-AD (Aug. 22, 1997).

[207] See Estate of Ray v. Comm'r, 112 F3d 194 (5th Cir. 1997) (irrespective of the cover letter's suggestion that the taxpayer's execution of the form represented the acceptance of the Service's settlement offer, the Form 870-L(AD) is effective, according to its explicit terms, when the Service's authorized representative signs the agreement, not when

by the date the special AD agreement becomes effective.[208] The date the form is received is controlling for an 870 agreement.

In general, Form 870 series agreement forms are used when a mutual concession settlement is not involved or when the amount of tax involved in a mutual concession settlement is not material enough to require the finality of the Form 870-AD.[209] The AD form is usually employed in mutual concession types of settlements.

Both the Form 870 and the Form 870-AD may be modified, for example, when agreement can be reached on some but not all issues.[210] If there are mutual concessions, a Form 870-AD is required, but modifications limiting the pledges against reopening are limited to the settled issues, and those issues are identified on the back of the form.[211] The agreement form, Form 870-AD, is used when there is a settlement with reservations, a term that applies to a nondocketed case when settlement is reached but the taxpayer or the Service wishes to reserve one or more issues, and no weight was given to the reserved issue in arriving at the settlement.[212] For example, the back of the Form 870-AD might provide, "The taxpayer reserves the right to timely file a claim for or credit or prosecute a timely claim solely on the grounds," which are then described; however, the Service Manual instructs Appeals officers to add to the reservation the following language, "This offer of restrictions is not to be construed as a claim for refund or credit, formal or informal, concerning the matters for which the right to file a claim is reserved." The Form 870-AD is also modified to reflect carrybacks given effect in the settlement, overpayments used to offset deficiencies in related cases, prepayment credit adjustments, and unverified estate tax credits.[213]

---

the taxpayer signs the agreement). For the legal effect of Forms 870 and 870-AD, see infra ¶ 9.08[2].

[208] Another distinction the Service Manual makes between the Forms 870 and 870-AD is that the suspension of interest under Section 6601(c) is controlled by the date the Form 870-AD becomes effective (i.e., signed on behalf of the Service), while the date the Form 870 is received controls in the case of the usual agreement, the Form 870.

[209] IRM 8.8, Appeals Agreement Forms, 1.1.4, Use of Agreement Forms 870 and 4862 (Aug. 22, 1997).

[210] See IRM 8.8, Appeals Agreement Forms, 1.2.1, Modification of Agreement Form for Partial Settlement (Aug. 22, 1997).

[211] See IRM 8.8, Appeals Agreement Forms, 1.2.1, Modification of Agreement Form for Partial Settlement (Aug. 22, 1997).

[212] See IRM 8.8, Appeals Agreement Forms, 1.2.2, Modification of Agreement for Settlements With Reservations (Aug. 22, 1997). Issues such as corporations with foreign subsidiaries, potential competent authority issues, and taxpayers with distributive shares of partnership income or loss shown on their returns are situations in which taxpayers might request a reservation, the Service Manual says.

[213] IRM 8.8, Appeals Agreement Forms, 1.2.4–8.8.1.2.6 (Aug. 22, 1997). Suggested language for these modifications is included in the Service Manual.

[2] Finality of Forms 870 and 870-AD

As noted previously, the execution of a Form 870 by a taxpayer does not preclude the taxpayer from later filing a claim for refund of the paid deficiency after the statutory period of assessment has run. The Form 870 is merely a waiver of the restrictions on assessment and states: "Your consent will not prevent you from filing a claim for refund (after you have paid the tax) if you later believe you are so entitled." The form does note that by signing the waiver, the taxpayer will not be able to contest the deficiencies in the Tax Court. In addition to leaving open the possibility of a taxpayer's filing a refund claim, the form also states in cautionary terms that execution of the waiver does not prevent the Service "from later determining, if necessary, that (the taxpayer) owe(s) additional tax. . . . " However, Form 870 does not extend the assessment period. Because the language of the form permits reopening of the issues, a taxpayer's request to sign a Form 870 puts the Appeals Office on notice that finality is not contemplated.

The Appeals Office prefers to use Form 870-AD, which states that "no claim for refund or credit shall be filed or prosecuted" for the years involved.[214] For its part, the Service promises in the Form 870-AD that the case will not be reopened by the Commissioner "in the absence of fraud, malfeasance, concealment or misrepresentation of a material fact, an important mistake in mathematical calculation, or excessive tentative allowances of (net operating loss) carrybacks." Even in such instances, the case will not be reopened without high-level approval.[215]

Suppose that a taxpayer and the Service negotiate and settle the disputed deficiency, the taxpayer and the Appeals Office sign a Form 870-AD, and the taxpayer pays the lesser agreed-on amount. After the period for assessment has expired, the taxpayer files a claim for refund. Does the taxpayer's agreement not to file and prosecute a refund claim provided in the Form 870-AD prevent the taxpayer from doing so later? This issue has troubled courts, and there is no unanimity on the answer. It cannot always be assumed that taxpayers who act in violation of the terms of the AD form are seeking to gain unfair advantage. In some cases taxpayers have had legitimate reasons for filing post-agreement refund claims, for example, a retroactive change in the statute[216] or

---

[214] Despite this clear language, one court has said the "language in Form 870-AD is contradictory . . . " because it "purports to prevent taxpayers from reopening a disputed tax case without being a settlement agreement under I.R.C. § 7121." Whitney v. United States, 826 F2d 986, 898 (9th Cir. 1987) (divided court).

[215] IRM 1.2.1, Policies of the IRS Handbook 1.8.7, P-8-50 (approved Apr. 13, 1973).

[216] Guggenheim v. United States, 77 F. Supp. 186 (Ct. Cl. 1948), cert. denied, 335 US 908 (1949).

an intervening court decision favorable to the taxpayer.[217] Although the settlement reflected in a Form 870-AD is neither the closing agreement nor the formal compromise provided for in Sections 7121 and 7122, a less formal method of resolving thousands of tax controversies each year is a matter of administrative necessity.[218]

Generally, by application of equitable estoppel,[219] taxpayers in informal settlements have been prevented from prosecuting their refund claims, even when an agreement with the Service did not constitute a binding closing agreement or compromise. In *Botany Worsted Mills v. United States*, the Supreme Court held that a Form 870-AD agreement was not final and conclusive on the taxpayer and the Service, but specifically left open the question of whether an informal settlement agreement, "though not binding in itself, may when executed become, under some circumstances, binding on the parties by estoppel."[220] The Court did not elaborate on what it meant by "some circumstances," which would estop a taxpayer, because the government conceded that no ground for estoppel was present in the case.

In most other cases, however, the Service has successfully contended that the elements of estoppel were present because the Service had relied on the taxpayer's representation, and so had permitted the period for making an as-

---

[217] Stair v. United States, 516 F2d 560 (2d Cir. 1975); DDI, Inc. v. United States, 467 F2d 497 (Ct. Cl. 1972), cert. denied, 414 US 830 (1973); Whitney v. United States, 826 F2d 896 (9th Cir. 1987).

[218] However, in Hamilton v. United States, 324 F2d 960 (Ct. Cl. 1963), a Form 870-AD was held to constitute a compromise under Section 7122. This decision is questionable, because it makes numerous assumptions in order to find that the statutory requirements of Section 7122(b) have been met. Also, the court ignored the language of Form 870-AD, which states that the execution and filing of the form do not extend the statutory period for refund, assessment, or collection of the tax. The statutory period on assessment and collection is specifically suspended in Form 656 (Offer in Compromise).

[219] Contract principles have been applied to the issue. See, e.g., Flynn v. United States, 786 F2d 586, 591 (3d Cir. 1986) (parol evidence admissible to show absence of agreement). When a case is in court, contract principles, not estoppel, apply in determining whether a settlement has been entered into between the taxpayer and the Service. Robbins Tire & Rubber Co. v. Comm'r, 52 TC 420, 435–436 (1969). Settlement offers made and accepted by letters have been enforced as binding agreements by the Tax Court against taxpayers and the Service. Haiduk v. Comm'r, 60 TCM 864 (1990) (agreement enforced against Service; cases where taxpayers bound cited). For this reason, when a Form 870-AD is signed, but one or more issues are intended to be excluded from the agreement, the agreement must reflect the exclusion; if it does not, the conclusion will be drawn that there was a mutual concession agreement. Kmart v. United States, 94-2 USTC ¶ 50,502 (Fed. Cir. 1994) (parol evidence in the form of the affidavit of Appeals officer saying that issue was not settled rejected in view of the clear language of the Form 870-AD and Supporting Statement); see also Goldman v. Comm'r, 39 F3d 402 (2d Cir. 1994) (application of contract principles used to determine that Form 870-AD did not bind the Service on a later year).

[220] Botany Worsted Mills v. United States, 278 US 282, 289 (1929).

sessment to lapse.[221] Some courts have found that the taxpayer was estopped solely because the statute of limitations on assessment had run.[222] Other courts have applied the elements of estoppel strictly and have found one or more elements lacking, usually either detrimental reliance or a false representation.[223] In either event, when the taxpayer reserves the right to file a claim for refund and sue for refund, the Form 870-AD will preclude the taxpayer's action.[224]

---

[221] The elements of estoppel are, strictly speaking, as follows: (1) There must be a false representation or wrongful misleading silence; (2) the error must originate in a statement of fact, not in opinion or a statement of law; (3) the one claiming the benefits of estoppel must not know the true facts; and (4) that same person must be adversely affected by the acts or statement of the one against whom an estoppel is claimed. Lignos v. United States, 439 F2d 1365, 1368 (2d Cir. 1971).

[222] Stair v. United States, 516 F2d 560 (2d Cir. 1975); Guggenheim v. United States, 77 F. Supp. 186 (Ct. Cl. 1948), cert. denied, 335 US 908 (1949); Daugette v. Patterson, 250 F2d 753 (5th Cir. 1957), cert. denied, 356 US 902 (1958); Cain v. United States, 255 F2d 193 (8th Cir. 1958). In *Cain*, the Eighth Circuit said: "[W]e think it is sufficient to preclude a taxpayer from claiming a refund, in relation to an executed settlement agreement, that the statute of limitations has run against the right of the Commissioner to deal with the situation further." Id. at 199. See also McGraw-Hill, Inc. v. United States, 623 F2d 700, 706 (Ct. Cl. 1980) ("the Court of Claims has consistently adhered to a more 'liberal' view of estoppel . . . [and] has applied the doctrine of equitable estoppel whenever the IRS cannot be placed in the same position as it was when the agreement was executed"); Kretchmar v. United States, 85-2 USTC ¶ 9826 (Cl. Ct. 1985) (first case in Claims Court on the issue applied equitable estoppel to a Form 870-AD; extensive discussion of authorities especially in old court of claims cases).

The Federal Circuit, in considering this liberal approach, has held that equitable estoppel is established if (1) the Form 870-AD was executed as the result of mutual concessions; (2) there was a meeting of the minds that the claims be extinguished; and (3) reopening the case would prejudice the Service because of its reliance on the fact that the parties had agreed that the claims had been extinguished. Union Pac. RR v. United States, 847 F2d 1567, 1571 (Fed. Cir. 1988) (following *Kretchmar*); see also Lowenstein v. United States, 27 Fed. Cl. 38 (1992) (estopping partner from refund based on settlement reached with other partner).

[223] Uinta Livestock Corp. v. United States, 355 F2d 761 (10th Cir. 1966) (Form 870-AD signed with corporation, and statute of limitations ran against shareholders; held, no misleading action or false representation); Joyce v. Gentsch, 141 F2d 891 (6th Cir. 1944) (Form 870 signed, with right to assess a further deficiency reserved; held, Service had all essential information, as well as the right to assess a further deficiency); Whitney v. United States, 826 F2d 896 (9th Cir. 1987) (divided court; majority said Form 870-AD standing alone does not preclude a refund suit and remanded case for further proceedings to determine whether taxpayers made false representations that would justify application of the doctrine of equitable estoppel; dissent said on authority of *Stair* that detrimental reliance by government is sufficient). The *Uinta Livestock* case is still applied in the Tenth Circuit. See Davilman v. United States, 75 AFTR2d ¶95-598 (WD Okla. 1995) ("here, like *Uinta*, the government has shown nothing other than taxpayers' payment of an asserted deficiency the IRS contended was correct, execution of a Form 870-AD, and reliance by the IRS on that admittedly non-binding agreement").

[224] No misrepresentation can occur when a taxpayer reserves the right to contest an issue. For example, in Stroman v. Comm'r, 37 TCM 444 (1978), the taxpayer expressly

When the taxpayer has reneged, many courts view the taxpayer's state-ment in the agreement that no refund claim will be filed to be a misrepresenta-tion of a kind sufficient to ground estoppel.[225] However, in a case involving a single taxpayer, it can be contended with some force that, although the statute has run on assessment, the government has not been prejudiced because it may set off its otherwise barred claim against the refund sought by the taxpayer.[226] Estoppel has nevertheless been applied in a single-taxpayer settlement, despite the taxpayer's no-prejudice argument.[227] A no-prejudice argument loses its force when the informal settlement is arrived at with a taxpayer or taxpayers in addition to the taxpayer seeking the refund. The government cannot set off its claims against these other taxpayers, because they are not parties. Therefore, in multiple-taxpayer cases, estoppel has been applied to defeat the taxpayer's re-fund claim.[228] Consequently, courts denying estoppel are in the distinct minor-ity.

On reflection, the apparent conflict in cases deciding this issue derives not so much from hardline doctrinal differences, but from the courts weighing the

---

stated in a Form 870-AD signed by herself and her ex-husband that she did not waive her right to contest collection from her on the grounds she was an innocent spouse. When the Service assessed the agreed-on deficiency and tried to levy on her property, she brought a successful injunction action (practitioners take note) in which the district court found that no waiver had been intended. As a result, the Service was ordered to issue a notice of de-ficiency. The Service failed to appeal, and the Tax Court refused to reconsider the issue, holding it res judicata. The taxpayer later contended that the notice of deficiency had been untimely sent. She lost this argument as well as her claim that she was an innocent spouse. Stroman v. Comm'r, 77 TC 514 (1981), aff'd, 692 F2d 1 (5th Cir. 1982).

[225] Stair v. United States, 516 F2d 560 (2d Cir. 1975) (cases cited); Elbo Coals, Inc. v. United States, 588 F. Supp. 745 (ED Ky. 1984), aff'd, 763 F2d 818 (6th Cir. 1985) (following *Stair* after analysis of issue and distinguishing *Joyce v. Gentsch*). See also Du-puy v. United States, 598 F. Supp. 520 (WD Va. 1984) (following *Stair* and *Lignos*). But see Whitney v. United States, 826 F2d 896 (9th Cir. 1987). Aronsohn v. United States, 92-2 USTC ¶ 50,542 (MD Pa. 1992) (*Stair* and *Elbo* followed; taxpayer was estopped from seeking refund).

[226] Joyce v. Gentsch, 141 F2d 891 (6th Cir. 1944). The Sixth Circuit distinguished *Joyce* as involving a Form 870, which embodied no promise by the Service not to assess further tax liabilities. See Elbo Coals, Inc. v. United States, 588 F. Supp. 745 (ED Ky. 1984), aff'd, 763 F2d 818 (6th Cir. 1985). See also Whitney v. United States, 826 F2d 896 (9th Cir. 1987). Bennett v. United States, 231 F2d 465 (7th Cir. 1956) (on predeces-sor of Form 870-AD was informal agreement, not formal closing agreement); Combs v. United States, 92-1 USTC ¶ 50,139 (SD Ind. 1992) (Form 2504-AD held not binding, so taxpayer's refund suit not sufficient basis for estoppel); see also McGraw-Hill, Inc. v. United States, 90-1 USTC ¶ 50,053 (SDNY 1990) (Form 870-AD; no estoppel found).

[227] Stair v. United States, 516 F2d 560 (2d Cir. 1975).

[228] Cooper Agency v. United States, 301 F. Supp. 871 (DSC 1969), aff'd per curiam, 422 F2d 1331 (4th Cir.), cert. denied, 400 US 904 (1970); DDI, Inc. v. United States, 467 F2d 497 (Ct. Cl. 1972), cert. denied, 414 US 830 (1973). Accord Cain v. United States, 255 F2d 193 (8th Cir. 1958).

conduct of both the Service and the taxpayer in each case and considering the damage to the respective parties of precluding the taxpayer's refund suit.

[3] Closing and Collateral Agreements

The only statutorily authorized method for entering into an agreement binding on both the Service and a taxpayer is a closing agreement.[229] Because these agreements are final, they require careful consideration by the Service. For this reason, the Service's practice is to discourage the use of a closing agreement in the settlement of an Appeals Office case. The Service Manual instructs Appeals officers to explain the Service's policy on reopening to a taxpayer who requests greater finality and to persuade the taxpayer that a Form 870 or Form 870-AD type of agreement is adequate.[230] However, a closing agreement may be used if the taxpayer still insists on finality and the government will sustain no disadvantage.[231] The Appeals officer may request a closing agreement when there is doubt that a taxpayer or taxpayer's representative will abide by the finality provisions of the Form 870-AD agreement. A closing agreement is also used in (1) certain settlements of fraud cases if the period for assessment of the tax might be barred except for fraud; (2) related cases if there is a risk that the government might be whipsawed to its disadvantage; and (3) continuing-issue cases if the basis of property or similar issues are involved.

The parties may enter into collateral agreements while trying to settle a case. A collateral agreement has the finality of neither a closing agreement nor a compromise. This type of agreement may be used in gift and estate tax cases to express, for example, the agreement of the parties as to the basis of assets received by beneficiaries of an estate or the fair market value of a gift for basis purposes.[232]

¶ 9.09 CLOSING AGREEMENTS

The Code recognizes only two types of binding agreements between taxpayers and the Service to resolve issues of tax liability: (1) a closing agreement (Sec-

---

[229] IRC § 7121. For a detailed description of the closing agreement, see infra ¶ 9.09.

[230] IRM 8.8, Appeals Agreement Forms, 1.1.5, Agreement Used When Taxpayer Requests Greater Finality (Aug. 22, 1997).

[231] The circumstances in which a closing agreement should be requested are discussed infra ¶ 9.09.

[232] IRM 8.8, Appeals Agreement Forms, 1.4 (Aug. 22, 1997) (Collateral Agreements).

tion 7121) and (2) a compromise agreement (Section 7122).[233] The closing agreement procedure has been included in the internal revenue laws since 1921. Early in the Service's history, it was common practice for the National Office to reopen returns examined by field agents whenever an error was suspected or a new administrative position was taken. With respect to the new provision, the Senate Finance Committee report said:[234]

> Under the present method of procedure, a taxpayer never knows when he is through as a tax case may be opened at any time because of a change in ruling by the Treasury Department. It is believed that this provision will tend to promote expedition in the handling of tax cases and certainty in tax adjustments.

The closing agreement was the means chosen to assure taxpayers of finality. A closing agreement is (a) a written agreement that is (b) "final and conclusive" (c) "in respect of any internal revenue tax" (d) for any taxable period ending before or after or after the date of the agreement.[235] Closing agreements may be entered into with "any person" or the person or estate for whom the person acts.[236]

A closing agreement is an agreement provided for by statute. As a statutory agreement, the law of contracts does not govern a closing agreement; for example, legal consideration is not necessary.[237] Closing agreements are "final and conclusive" in the sense that, except on a showing of fraud or malfeasance, or of misrepresentation of a material fact, (1) the agreement may not be reopened as to the matters agreed on nor the agreement modified and (2) in any legal proceeding the agreement, or any administrative action based on the agreement (e.g., assessment, collection, payment, or abatement), the agreement may not be annulled, modified, set aside, or disregarded. Even if, under the agreement, the taxpayer is not liable for any tax for the period to which the agreement relates, the closing agreement may be executed.[238] Although there need be no tax liability as such, there must be a connection between the agreement and either some tax liability past or future or a determination that no liability exists is indicated by the statutory language ("in respect of any internal revenue tax for any taxable period").[239] The use of the term, "in respect of any

---

[233] IRC §§ 7121(a), 7122(a). Compromises, which are most frequently used in collection cases to settle a tax liability for something less than the assessed amount, are discussed elsewhere. See ¶ 15.07.

[234] S. Rep. No. 275, 67th Cong., 1st Sess. (1921), reprinted in 1939-1 (pt. 2) CB 204.

[235] Reg. § 301.7121-1(a).

[236] See H. Dubroff, The United States Tax Court—An Historical Analysis 19 (1979).

[237] Perry v. Page, 67 F2d 635 (1st Cir. 1933), cert. denied, 292 US 632 (1934).

[238] Reg. § 301.7121-1(b)(1).

[239] The Service Manual acknowledges that a closing agreement must be at least arguably consistent with the Code, or a taxpayer might be able to challenge it as not being

internal revenue tax," means that a closing agreement may be entered into despite the fact that under the agreement, the taxpayer is not liable for any tax for the period covered.[240]

A closing agreement for a taxable period ending before the date of the agreement may relate to (1) the total tax liability of the taxpayer or (2) one or more separate items affecting the taxpayer's liability (e.g., gross income, deduction for losses, depreciation, depletion, the year of inclusion of an item of gross income, the year of deduction of an item of loss, or the value of property on a specific date).[241] Such a closing agreement also constitutes a determination for purposes of the mitigation provisions.[242] In contrast, a closing agreement for a taxable period ending after the date of the agreement may only relate to one or more separate items affecting income (e.g., the basis of stock unsold at the date of the agreement).[243] The Service and a taxpayer may enter into more than one closing agreement on the tax liability for a single period.[244]

Any tax or deficiency determined under a closing agreement is assessed and collected, and any overpayment is credited or refunded, in accordance with the provisions of the Code applicable to those administrative actions.[245]

A closing agreement may be entered into for a taxable period at any time before a case involving the period is docketed in the Tax Court.[246] Once a case is in court, a closing agreement may still be executed, but court approval is required (e.g., in bankruptcy).[247]

A closing agreement may be entered into when there appears to be an advantage to having the case closed. However, if a taxpayer wishes a closing agreement, he or she must (1) show good and sufficient reasons for the agreement and (2) satisfy the Service that the government will suffer no disadvan-

---

"in respect of any internal revenue tax." IRM 8.13.1, Appeals Closing Agreement Manual, 1.2.1, General Characteristics of Closing Agreements (May 2, 2001).

[240] Reg. § 301.7121-1(b)(1).

[241] Reg. § 301.7121-1(b)(2).

[242] See ¶ 5.07[2] for a discussion of this requirement for application of the mitigation provisions.

[243] Reg. § 301.7121-1(b)(3).

[244] Reg. § 301.7121-1(b)(1).

[245] Reg. § 301.7121-1(d)(2).

[246] Reg. § 301.7121-1(d)(1). It has been held that a closing agreement may even control a taxpayer's right to receive a notice of deficiency. Hempel, Jr. v. United States, 14 F3d 572 (11th Cir. 1994) (closing agreement contained waiver, but taxpayer claimed waiver was linked to assessment, which had to be made within 365 days after the date of decision in the controlling case, and assessment was made more than two years after the decision; agreement language interpreted).

[247] IRM 8.13.1, Appeals Closing Agreement Manual, 1.2.1(8), General Characteristics of Closing Agreements (May 3, 2001).

tage in entering into the agreement.[248] Although the closing agreement seems to be the answer to the uncertainty of dealings with the Service, as a matter of practice, the Service discourages its use. Section 7121 permits, but does not require, the Service to enter into a closing agreement with a taxpayer. As a result, the Service has the discretion to decide whether and under what conditions a closing agreement is executed. In light of the finality of closing agreements, the Service obviously believes that a large volume of requests for such agreements would be difficult to process. The Service's decision to avoid closing agreements creates a potential conflict between the legislative creation of the remedy and the Service's refusal to make closing agreements as accessible as the statutory language indicates they are. In part, the Service's rulings program, under which a ruling ordinarily is not revoked retroactively, can be viewed as an attempt to give taxpayers a measure of certainty. The same can be said about informal agreement forms, such as Form 870-AD, in which the Service agrees not to reopen a year for which a settlement has been reached.

These agreements may have no conclusive effect on the parties (e.g., Form 4549 (Income Tax Examination Changes) or Form 870), or they may derive some finality as contracts binding, according to their terms, on the taxpayer and the Service alike (e.g., Form 870-AD).[249] However, whatever effect such agreements may have, they remain administrative devices not expressly provided for by statute.[250] Thus, however limited a role it plays in tax practice, the closing agreement is important because it is the only agreement the Code recognizes as binding on the Service.

Reflecting its decision to limit the number of closing agreements, the Service's closing agreement procedures are restrictive and cumbersome. The taxpayer wishing to enter into a closing agreement has a double burden of persuasion to carry: First, that a closing agreement will be to the advantage of the Service, and second, that the taxpayer has good and sufficient reasons for a closing agreement.[251] Although the National Office has delegated authority to execute closing agreements, a request still must pass through layers of admin-

---

[248] Reg. § 301.7121-1(a).

[249] A taxpayer is estopped from suing for refund after executing a Form 870-AD. See supra ¶ 9.08[2]. A Form 4549 is not a closing agreement that prevents the Service from making a further assessment. Shrader v. Tomecek, 81-2 USTC ¶ 9624 (SD Ohio 1980); Person v. Comm'r, 49 TCM 1391 (1985) (same, Installment Payment Agreement, Form 433-D).

[250] Even when the Appeals Office has notified a taxpayer that no assessment will be made against the taxpayer and that no further action is required, the notice does not bind the Service because it is not a closing agreement. Hospitality Servs., Inc. v. United States, 77-1 USTC ¶ 9299 (ED Mich. 1977).

[251] Reg. § 301.7121-1(a). The Service Manual states, "Because of their finality, closing agreements must be entered into with great caution." IRM 8.13.1, Appeals Closing Agreement Manual, 1.2.1, General Characteristics of Closing Agreements (May 3, 2001).

istrative review, and an agreement may be executed only by relatively high-ranking officials.[252]

[1] Use of Closing Agreements

Closing agreements are sometimes requested by the Service before a ruling is issued on certain matters.[253] For example, the Service may ask a taxpayer to enter into a closing agreement as a condition to the issuance of a ruling.[254] Additionally, the taxpayer may request that the Service execute a closing agreement in a ruling situation.[255] At the request of the taxpayer or the Service, a closing agreement may be entered into.

[a] Advantageous to Service

The Service considers the following circumstances to warrant entering into a closing agreement to effect a determination of one or more specific matters or items without disadvantage to the Service:[256]

1. Determining cost, fair market value, or adjusted basis as of a given past date by for example, having both an estate and its legatees, or a donor and donees sign a closing agreement.[257]

2. Dispose of issues involving certain Section 482 allocations.[258]

3. Ensure finality and consistency in disposing of cases involving divisions of community between spouses incident to divorce.

---

[252] Delegations of authority to execute closing agreements are contained in CDO No. 97. The most current version of CDO No. 97 must be checked in the Internal Revenue Bulletin, Cumulative Bulletin, or commercial tax services. Determining that the Service official signing the closing agreement is authorized to do so is not without its complications.

[253] See, e.g., Rev. Proc. 77-11, 1977-1 CB 568 (closing agreement conditioned to issuing ruling to lessors of coal and iron ore receiving bonuses and advance royalties).

[254] Rev. Proc. 89-1, 1989-1 CB 730, 740, § 4.08.

[255] See, e.g., Rev. Proc. 85-44, 1985-2 CB 505 (closing agreement may be requested in connection with ruling on basis adjustment arising from discharge of indebtedness).

[256] IRM 8.13.1, Appeals Closing Agreement Manual, 1.1.2(2), Examples of Use of Closing Agreements (May 3, 2001). A closing agreement may be entered into when the case pending is in the Tax Court. See Estate of Salinitro v. Comm'r, TC Memo. 1992-274, 63 TCM 2994 (1992).

[257] The Service may request that both the estate and its legatees or devisees, or both donors and donees, sign these agreements.

[258] See Rev. Proc. 65-17, 1965-1 CB 833. Rev. Proc. 65-17 was amplified and clarified by Rev. Proc. 70-23, 1970-2 CB 505.

4. Dispose of change of accounting issues in Appeals Office cases involving principles similar to those applied in Revenue Procedure 97-27, 1997-1 CB 680.

5. Determine a fraud penalty reflecting complete or partial concession in cases in which the statute of limitations is otherwise barred.

6. Determine the amount of a net operating loss, tax credit, or capital loss.

7. Provide determinations for the disposition of cases involving the mitigation provisions.[259]

8. Prevent whipsaw situations (e.g., a widow payments case) in which one taxpayer concedes an issue, thereby benefiting another (usually related) taxpayer and then, after the period of assessment against the second taxpayer runs, files a claim for refund.[260]

9. Determine gross income, the amount of income from a transaction, the amounts of deductions for losses, depreciation, depletion, and the like, or the year of includability or deduction.

10. Establish the effect on future years of the disposition of an issue on an intermediate basis when the issue is recurring (but tax treatment in later years will not depend on factual circumstances in those years).

11. Determine the consequences of deferred intercompany transactions of domestic consolidated groups.

12. Close cases involving failure to withhold income tax on payments such as taxable reimbursements of moving expenses.

13. Resolve the settlement of employment tax controversies.

14. Resolve issues involving qualification of employee retirement plans.

15. Reflect competent authority determinations.[261]

16. Resolve an issue in a CEP audit.[262]

17. Finalize an agreement for early referral of an issue under Revenue Procedure 96-9, 1996-1 CB 575.

18. Address a mass error that affects a higher volume of information returns but involves a de minimus amount of understated reported income for select information returns.

---

[259] IRC §§ 1311–1314.

[260] It is unclear whether the Service would consider entering into a closing agreement if a taxpayer might be subject to whipsaw, rather than the Service.

[261] These determinations are those made under Rev. Proc. 96-13, 1996-1 CB 616, as modified by Rev. Proc. 96-53, 1996-2 CB 375.

[262] The issue is one arising under Rev. Proc. 94-67, 1994-2 CB 800.

[b] Good and Sufficient Reasons

A taxpayer must not only make a request for a closing agreement, but show that there is a "good and sufficient reason" for entering into a closing agreement. In nonruling situations, a closing agreement is acceptable when considerations (usually nontax) require certainty of any tax liability. The Service considers the following to be good reasons for entering into a closing agreement without disadvantage:[263]

1. A taxpayer wants to establish its tax liability to facilitate and complete a transaction, such as a sale of stock.

2. A fiduciary of an estate wishes to have a closing agreement so that the fiduciary can be discharged by a probate court.

3. A fiduciary of a trust or a receivership needs to have a final determination before making a distribution.

4. A liquidating corporation wants to have a closing agreement to wind up its affairs.

5. A taxpayer needs a closing agreement to satisfy creditors' demands for authentic evidence of tax liability.

6. The taxpayer wishes to agree to some portion of or all of the assessments, when proposed assessments are contested on the theory that the years are barred.

7. A taxpayer wants certainty that a controversy between the taxpayer and the Service has been disposed of with finality. Although a taxpayer's wish to dispose conclusively of a controversy between the taxpayer and the Service is an acceptable reason for entering into a closing agreement, the Service will inform the taxpayer that other policies may satisfy this concern, e.g., its policy against reopening cases or Appeals special agreement forms, such as the Form 870-AD.

8. A determination of personal holding company tax is required in order to permit deficiency dividends.[264]

9. A closing agreement is requested to reflect and establish with finality a competent authority determination.[265]

---

[263] IRM 8.13.1, Appeals Closing Agreement Manual, 1.1.2(1), Examples of Use of Closing Agreements (May 3, 2001).

[264] IRC § 547.

[265] Rev. Proc. 68-16, 1968-1 CB 770, § 4.01.

[2] Closing Agreement Forms

All closing agreements must be executed on forms provided by the Service.[266] The Service uses two forms, an Agreement as to Final Determination of Tax Liability (Form 866) and a Closing Agreement on Final Determination Covering Specific Matters (Form 906). In addition, the Service uses a combined agreement.

A closing agreement reflected in or adapted from Form 866 determines the tax liability for each period and type of tax covered in the agreement after giving effect to all applicable credits reducing the tax, except those representing payment of the liability. (See Form 9.4.) Final determinations of specific matters are usually reflected on Form 906. (See Form 9.5.) The Service avoids qualified liability determinations in a Form 866. If the parties are unable to agree on an unqualified liability figure, they may resort to a determination of taxable income by use of Form 906, stating the desired reservations and the applicable qualifications.

Neither Form 866 nor Form 906 is specifically designed for closing agreements that determine both tax liability and specific matters. Instead, a typed combined agreement is used that employs a certain format and standard language.[267] The principal reason a combined agreement is necessary is that a determination of liability alone does not determine either the amount of any item of income or deduction or any other related matter that may have been considered in arriving at that liability. This can become important if the amount of one or more of the items affects the computation of taxable income for another year. For example, after entering into a closing agreement, the taxpayer might later be able to prove successfully and make use of a net operating loss for the year for which the tax liability was determined by the agreement, even though the tax liability determination was based on facts that, at the date of the agreement, indicated there was taxable income. Such a result may occur because, although the tax liability for the year has been fixed, the effect of transactions of that year on other years has not. If the parties agree, such a situation can be avoided by determining taxable income for both the year and any applicable carryovers from that year.[268]

Depending on the circumstances, either the taxpayer and his or her representative or the Service drafts the closing agreement. In general, a closing agreement is prepared and executed in duplicate. When more than one party signs, two additional copies of the agreement are required for each additional

---

[266] Reg. § 301.7121-1(d)(1).

[267] The last page of a Form 906 may be used as the last page of the agreement.

[268] It is unclear whether the closing agreement could not in this situation be set aside for misrepresentation of a material fact.

party, one for the additional taxpayer's records and one for attachment to the return.[269]

[3] Contents of Closing Agreements

Closing agreements have five distinct parts: (1) the identification of the parties; (2) the introductory clauses; (3) the agreed determination; (4) the ending clause; and (5) the signatures. Each of these parts of the agreement must be handled with care, but the introductory clauses, agreed determination, and signatures require special consideration.

[a] Introductory Clauses

The introductory clauses lay out the matters on which the closing agreement is based and introduce the subject matter of the agreement.[270] These matters are included in numbered sentences or paragraphs, beginning with the term "Whereas." A closing agreement may not be set aside for a mistake of fact or law, but it is not binding on the Service if there has been a misrepresentation of a material fact. Consequently, these introductory statements should be accurate and should set forth the facts material to the determinations that follow. Because there is the possibility that an inaccuracy or material omission may be characterized later as a misrepresentation of material fact, this part of the agreement should be drafted with care.

[b] The Agreed Determination

For obvious reasons, the agreed determination of tax should be stated with clarity and should be unambiguous as to the taxpayer who realizes the income, the year involved, and the effect on other years.[271] To avoid ambiguity, it is advisable to use statutory terms, for example, if an amount is to be includable in income as long-term capital gain, the agreement should specifically state this fact.[272] When specific matters are being determined, the applicable dollar amounts, dates, and types of taxable income should be set forth.[273] A closing agreement generally relates to past events; the Service does not agree to tax treatment for future years if the correct treatment will depend on post-

---

[269] Rev. Proc. 68-16, 1968-1 CB 770, § 6.09.

[270] Rev. Proc. 68-16, 1968-1 CB 769, § 6.05(a).

[271] Rev. Proc. 68-16, 1968-1 CB 769, §§ 7.04, 7.05.

[272] Rev. Proc. 68-16, 1968-1 CB 769, § 7.04.

[273] Rev. Proc. 68-16, 1968-1 CB 769, § 7.04.

agreement circumstances.[274] Similarly, an agreement that depends on some future act of the taxpayer is discouraged.[275] Normally, a closing agreement does not determine penalties or interest, so that the Service is not precluded from the later assessment of a penalty and interest,[276] unless specifically provided by the closing agreement. The Service's closing agreement forms (Form 866) must be changed if the taxpayer intends to accomplish this result.

[c] Execution

Closing agreements are always signed by or on behalf of taxpayers before being signed for the Service. The Service considers a closing agreement signed only by the taxpayer to be an offer by the taxpayer to enter into a closing agreement. The signature by the appropriate Service official is considered an acceptance and approval.[277]

When the taxpayer does not sign the closing agreement personally, the agreement may not be binding if it was signed by a person unauthorized to bind the taxpayer. Accordingly, specific procedures have been established to ensure the existence of authority.[278] Specific requirements govern execution of a closing agreement by corporations filing consolidated returns, power-of-attorney holders, decedents and estates, trusts, dissolved corporations, partnerships, insolvent taxpayers, and guardians and other court-appointed fiduciaries.[279] In general, fiduciaries, such as executors, administrators, trustees, and receivers, must submit documentary evidence of authority (in the form of attested letters testamentary, court orders, or certified copies of trusts or wills) and execute Form 56 (Notice of Fiduciary Relationship).[280] The hoi_r of a power of attorney may execute a closing agreement, but only if the power expressly provides for such execution.[281]

Similar problems of authority can arise when the agreement is signed on behalf of the Service.[282] A closing agreement is not binding on the Service un-

---

[274] Rev. Proc. 68-16, 1968-1 CB 769, § 7.03.

[275] Rev. Proc. 68-16, 1968-1 CB 769, § 7.06.

[276] Rev. Proc. 68-16, 1968-1 CB 769, §§ 6.15, 6.16.

[277] Rev. Proc. 68-16, 1968-1 CB 769, § 6.071(a).

[278] The evidence of the authority will be attached to the agreement. Rev. Proc. 68-16, 1968-1 CB 769, § 6.07.

[279] Rev. Proc. 68-16, 1968-1 CB 769, §§ 6.072-6.079.

[280] Rev. Proc. 68-16, 1968-1 CB 769, §§ 6.074, 6.079; IRM 8.13.1, Appeals Closing Agreement Manual, 3.4.4.4, Decedents and Their Estates, 3.4.4.5, Trusts (May 2, 2001).

[281] SPR, 26 CFR § 601.502(c)(1)(iv). The Form 2848 power of attorney contains provisions to this effect. See Form 1.1.

[282] Delegations of authority to execute closing agreements are contained in CDO No. 97. The most current version of CDO No. 97 must be checked in the Internal Revenue Bulletin, Cumulative Bulletin, or commercial tax services.

less it is signed by an official who has the delegated authority to so do. For example, when the Associate Chief of Appeals, who normally has delegated authority to execute a closing agreement on behalf of the Commissioner, signed a closing agreement, the agreement was held invalid because the Associate Chief lacks delegated authority when the case is pending in the Tax Court. The Associate Chief signed the agreement at the time the case was docketed in the Tax Court.[283] Not only does the unauthorized execution of the agreement mean that the closing agreement is invalid, it is not binding on either party, and may not be ratified by the Service.[284]

---

[283] See In re Klee, 1997 Bankr. LEXIS 1652 (Bankr. Or. 1997); Webb v. Comm'r, TC Memo. 1994-549 (1994), aff'd without published opinion, 68 F3d 482 (9th Cir. 1995); Stiskin v. Comm'r, TC Memo. 1996-306 (1996) ("[s]ince the case was already docketed in the Tax Court when the closing agreement was signed, the Associate Chief of Appeals here did not have authority to sign the closing agreement on behalf of the Commissioner").

[284] Stiskin v. Comm'r, TC Memo. 1996-306 (1996).

FORM 9.4
AGREEMENT AS TO FINAL DETERMINATION OF TAX LIABILITY

Form 866 (Rev. July 1981)	Department of the Treasury — Internal Revenue Service **Agreement as to Final Determination of Tax Liability**

(Complete three copies of this form)

Under Section 7121 of the Internal Revenue Code, __John Jones & Mary Jones__

(Taxpayer's name, address, and identifying number)

__1 James Street, New York, NY 00000__

TIN: 123-45-6789

and the Commissioner of Internal Revenue agree that the liability of the above taxpayer for the taxable periods and kinds of tax listed in this agreement is as follows: (The applicability or inapplicability of interest or penalties, including additions to tax or additional amounts authorized by Subchapter A of Chapter 68 of the Code, is not determined except as provided in this agreement.)

Taxable Period	Kind of Tax or Penalty	Chapter Number and Subchapter Letter of Internal Revenue Code	Total Tax Liability for Period
1981	Income	1A	$45,583
1982	Income	1A	$38,410
1983	Income	1A	($21,682)

This agreement is final and conclusive except:

(1) the liability it relates to may be reopened in the event of fraud, malfeasance, or misrepresentation of material fact and

(2) it is subject to the Internal Revenue Code sections that expressly provide that effect be given to their provisions notwithstanding any other law or rule of law except Code section 7122.

By signing this agreement, the above parties certify they have read and agreed to its terms.

Your signature __/S/ John Jones__   Date signed __8/25/87__

Spouse's signature (if a joint return was filed) __/S/ Mary Jones__   Date signed __8/25/87__

Signature of taxpayer's representative _____ Date signed _____

Taxpayer (other than individual) _____

By _____ Date signed _____

Title _____

Commissioner of Internal Revenue

By _____ Date signed _____

Title _____

Part 1 — Original   (See back)   Form 866 (Rev. 7-81)

I have examined the return(s) and recommend approval of the proposed agreement.

I have reviewed the return(s) and recommend approval of the proposed agreement.

_____
(Receiving Officer)　　　(Date)

_____
(District/Appeals Reviewing Officer)　　　(Date)

_____
(Title)

_____
(Title)

Form 866　(Rev 7-81)

FORM 9.5
CLOSING AGREEMENT ON FINAL DETERMINATION COVERING SPECIFIC MATTERS

Form **906**
(Rev. August 1994)

Department of the Treasury—Internal Revenue Service

**Closing Agreement On Final Determination
Covering Specific Matters**

Under section 7121 of the Internal Revenue Code _____

_____

(Taxpayer's name, address, and identifying number)

SAMPLE

and the Commissioner of Internal Revenue make the following closing agreement:

SAMPLE

SAMPLE

This agreement is final and conclusive except:

    (1)   the matter it relates to may be reopened in the event of fraud, malfeasance, or misrepresentation of material fact;

    (2)   it is subject to the Internal Revenue Code sections that expressly provide that effect be given to their provisions (including any stated exception for Code section 7122) notwithstanding any other law or rule of law; and

    (3)   if it relates to a tax period ending after the date of this agreement, it is subject to any law, enacted after the agreement date, that applies to that tax period.

By signing, the above parties certify that they have read and agreed to the terms of this document.

Your signature _____   Date Signed _____

Spouse's signature (if a joint return was filed) _____   Date Signed _____

Taxpayer's representative _____   Date Signed _____

Taxpayer (other than individual) _____

           By _____   Date Signed _____

           Title _____

Commissioner of Internal Revenue

           By _____   Date Signed _____

           Title _____

I have examined the specific matters involved and recommend the acceptance of the proposed agreement.

| I have reviewed the specific matters involved and recommend approval of the proposed agreement.

_____
(Receiving Officer)   (Date)

_____
(Reviewing Officer)   (Date)

_____
(Title)

_____
(Title)

SAMPLE

SAMPLE

Form 906 (Rev. 8-94)

SAMPLE

[4] Finality of Closing Agreements

Closing agreements are binding on the parties and may not be modified, annulled, disregarded, or set aside in any suit or proceeding unless one of the statutory bases for setting aside the agreement is established.[285] Although a closing agreement is final, when the Service enters into a specific matters–type agreement, there is no prohibition against the taxpayer and the Service entering into another agreement covering specific matters with the same taxpayer about the same taxable period, but determining other matters not expressly covered in the first closing agreement.[286] Also, differences over the interpretation of one closing agreement can be settled by a second closing agreement stating an agreed-on interpretation of the disputed provision. Absent fraud, malfeasance, or misrepresentation of a material fact, however, the agreement of the parties is final, and even the parties themselves may not rescind or cancel it. For this reason, determinations in the agreement as to taxable periods ending at or before the date of the agreement are not affected by subsequent legislation made retroactively applicable to the years involved in the agreement if the legislation is silent as to its effect on closing agreements.[287]

[a] Retroactive Legislation

The retroactive effect of subsequent legislation will depend on the terms of the closing agreement. In *National Steel Corp.*,[288] the closing agreement essentially provided for the quick refund of income tax for the year 1987, based on the anticipated overpayment for the year arising out of Section 212 of the Tax Reform Act of 1986 (TRA 1986). Section 212 of TRA 1986 permits steel companies to apply certain business credits to income tax due for their first taxable year after 1986, provided that the refund was reinvested in the business. The closing agreement provided for the refund even before National

---

[285] Aetna Life Ins. Co. v. Eaton, 43 F2d 711 (2d Cir.), cert. denied, 282 US 887 (1930); Wolverine Petroleum Corp. v. Comm'r, 75 F2d 593 (8th Cir.), cert. denied, 295 US 743 (1935); In re Marianne Hopkins, Debtor, 1998 US App. LEXIS 12797 (9th Cir. 1998) (closing agreement was a bar to a spouse's later claim, not reserved in the closing agreement, that she was entitled to innocent spouse relief because "closing agreements are meant to determine finally and conclusively a taxpayer's liability for a particular tax year," and citing for the application of the principle to an innocent spouse claim), Katz v. United States, 43 AFTR2d ¶ 79-1125 (D. Mass. 1979) and United States v. Mayfield, 75 AFTR2d ¶ 95-595 (SD Ind. 1994); Bankers Reserve Life Co. v. United States, 42 F2d 313 (Ct. Cl.), cert. denied, 282 US 871 (1930); Cramp Shipbuilding Co., 14 TC 33 (1950).

[286] IRM 8.13.1, Appeals Closing Agreement Handbook, 7.1.1, General Discussion—Finality (May 3, 2001).

[287] Rev. Rul. 56-322, 1956-2 CB 963.

[288] United States v. National Steel Corp., 75 F3d 1146 (7th Cir. 1996).

Steel filed its return for the year 1987. However, National Steel agreed that the time within which the Service could bring a suit to recover any amount of the overpayment determined to be erroneous or excessive would not expire before the expiration of the statute of limitations on assessment, including extensions. No change or modification of applicable statutes could render the agreement "ineffective with respect to the terms herein."

In 1988, Congress amended Section 212 of TRA 1986 retroactively to prohibit the crediting of credits that accrued in 1986. Because the Service already had issued the refund to National Steel, it instituted a suit for erroneous refund for the amount it overpaid based on the retroactive legislation. The Seventh Circuit examined "what exactly the parties agreed to in the closing agreement, for, by virtue of the provision on retroactivity, the 1988 amendment to section 212 of the 1986 Act left intact whatever they agreed to." It concluded that the terms of the agreement were not in conflict with the legislative amendment, because the parties had not agreed to the methodology of determining the amount creditable under Section 212 of TRA 1986, but only the timing of the tentative refund. The court pointed out that the closing agreement permitted the Service to challenge the amount refunded, and this suggested that the method of determining the refund had not been agreed on. The agreement was also "open ended" in that it did not provide the amounts of the credits or specific language on the effect of subsequent legislation on the determination of the allowable credits. Even if the Supreme Court declares a provision unconstitutional or interprets it favorably to the taxpayer after an agreement has been entered into based on the provision, the agreement stands.[289]

[b] Interpretation

A closing agreement is interpreted under ordinary principles of contract law.[290] In *National Steel Corp.*, the Seventh Circuit observed that closing agreements are "contracts in the ordinary legal sense of the term because they contain binding promises."[291] When it is said that closing agreements are not

---

[289] Wolverine Petroleum Corp. v. Comm'r, 75 F2d 593 (8th Cir.), cert. denied, 295 US 743 (1935); Aetna Life Ins. Co. v. Eaton, 43 F2d 711 (2d Cir.), cert. denied, 282 US 887 (1930); Bankers Reserve Life Co. v. United States, 42 F2d 313 (Ct. Cl.), cert. denied, 282 US 871 (1930). See also Appeals Closing Agreement Manual, 7.1.3, Effect of Later Legislation (May 3, 2001).

[290] Smith v. United States, 850 F2d 242, 245 (5th Cir. 1988); Overhauser v. United States, 45 F3d 1085 (7th Cir. 1995) (taxpayer claimed closing agreement was ambiguous and wanted to present parol evidence, but court said that if, "without taking evidence, a court can have reasonable confidence that it knows what the contract means, it ought not to put the litigants (and the trier of fact) to the bother, expense, and uncertainty of a trial or other evidentiary hearing"); see Estate of Magarian v. Comm'r, 97 TC 1 (1991).

[291] United States v. National Steel Corp., 75 F3d 1146 (7th Cir. 1996).

contracts, what is meant is that they are not governed by state contract law but federal common-law contract principles; although the federal common law of contracts is made up of "the core principles of the common law of contracts that are in force in most states."

A closing agreement determines only matters expressly stated therein. For example, a closing agreement determining only tax liability does not determine the amount of gross income or the items of income. It has been held that the fact that a tax liability is determined on a consolidated return basis does not support a later contention by the taxpayer that a consolidated return was validly filed for the year for which the liability was determined.[292]

[c] Specific Provisions and Closing Agreements

Some sections of the Code make their provisions applicable notwithstanding (1) any law or rule of law or (2) any law or rule of law other than a compromise under Section 7122.[293] It may be necessary to give effect in a taxable

---

[292] Export Leaf Tobacco Co. v. Comm'r, 78 F2d 163 (2d Cir.), cert. denied, 296 US 627 (1935). See also BD Phillips v. Comm'r, 8 TC 1286 (1947), aff'd per curiam, 178 F2d 270 (3d Cir. 1949), cert. denied, 339 US 932 (1950) (closing agreement did not determine existence of accumulated earnings); Zaentz v. Comm'r, 90 TC 753 (1988). When closing agreements have settled partnership losses and credits, the Service has been able to assert penalties and interest on the ground that these specific items were not included in the agreement. Smith v. United States, 850 F2d 242, 245 (5th Cir. 1988); Estate of Magarian, 97 TC 1 (1991). However, compare these cases with Cramp Shipbuilding Co., 14 TC 33 (1950), in which the closing agreement specified (1) that the taxpayer could take amortization deductions; (2) the facts giving rise to entitlement to the deductions; and (3) the amounts of the deductions. In re Spendthrift Farms, Inc., 931 F2d 405 (6th Cir. 1991) (Service not barred from collecting interest, because closing agreement did not specifically waive interest); Pack v. United States, 992 F2d 955 (9th Cir. 1993) (suspension of interest as provided in Section 6601(c) not agreed on; "the parties to a closing agreement are bound to the terms agreed upon and not to the premises underlying their agreement"); Quershi v. Comm'r, TC Memo. 1996-169 (1996) (closing agreement provided for tax treatment for the years 1979–1980 and 1982–1983, but not 1984; held, taxpayer was not precluded from challenging the determination for 1984, because the closing agreement had not provided for tax treatment for 1984).

[293] IRM 8.13.1, Appeals Closing Agreement Manual, 6.1.2, Law or Rule of Law Exceptions in Code (May 3, 2001) lists the following Code sections containing language that allows effect to be given to their provisions notwithstanding the execution of a closing agreement: (1) IRC § 183(e)(4) (activities not engaged in for profit); (2) IRC § 453 (installment method); (3) IRC § 481 (adjustments required by changes in methods of accounting) (see IRC § 481(b)(3)); (4) IRC § 1033 (involuntary conversions) (see IRC §§ 1033(a)(2)(C), 1033(a)(2)(D)); (5) IRC § 1034 (sale or exchange of residence) (see IRC § 1034(j)); (6) IRC § 1039 (sales of low-income housing) (see IRC § 1039(e)); (7) IRC § 1311 (mitigation of limitations) (see IRC §§ 1311(a), 1311(b)(2)); (8) IRC § 1481(b) (mitigation-renegotiation of government contracts); (9) IRC §§ 6511(d)(2) (net operating loss and capital loss carrybacks), 6511(d)(4) (investment credit, work incentive program credit, and new employee credit carrybacks), 6511(d)(5) (overpayments of self-

period to provisions in these sections despite the fact that tax liability or a specific matter in the taxable period has been determined by closing agreement. For example, a standard closing agreement determining only income tax liability does not preclude later reduction of the liability (and a refund) by reason of a net operating loss carryback.[294] However, the agreement can prevent a later reopening of the matter by expressly providing the extent to which the particular provision is or will be applicable. Thus, a 1990 agreement can state that the net operating loss carryback from 1989 to 1986 is X or that there is no net operating loss carryback to 1986 from 1987 and 1988.[295]

[d] Fraud, Malfeasance, or Misrepresentation

A closing agreement may be set aside for fraud, malfeasance, or misrepresentation on the part of either the Service or the taxpayer. To determine whether fraud has been perpetrated by a taxpayer, the Service may ask to see the taxpayer's books and records even after a closing agreement has been executed.[296] When the Service believes that there is a ground for setting aside the agreement, the matter is evaluated by the Criminal Investigation Division to determine whether sufficient facts are available to justify setting aside the agreement and for criminal prosecution.[297]

---

employment taxes), 6511(d)(6) (overpayments relating to the reduction of policyholders' surplus account of life insurance companies); and (10) IRC § 6521 (mitigation-related taxes).

[294] See Rev. Rul. 66-270, 1966-2 CB 106.

[295] See IRM 8.13.1, Appeals Closing Agreement Manual, 6.1.2(3) Law or Rule of Law Exceptions in the Code (May 3, 2001) (using later years than those in the text). The Service Manual also warns that no attempt should be made to bar by closing agreement any net operating loss deductions attributable to net operating loss carrybacks resulting from any losses that might arise in years not yet ended at the time the closing agreement is signed for the Commissioner. Id.

[296] Rev. Rul. 72-487, 1972-2 CB 645.

[297] In local office cases, if any examining officer or conferee discovers facts indicating a basis for setting the agreement aside, the matter is referred to the Chief in the local office, whose decision is final. If the facts are found not to warrant setting the agreement aside, the matter is closed. If further investigation is indicated, a request for a second examination of the taxpayer's books is sent to the Regional Commissioner for the issuance of the notice required by Section 7605(b). If criminal prosecution is not indicated, but the agreement should be set aside, a notice is sent to the taxpayer granting thirty days for the filing of a protest of amounts determined to be due. If the closing agreement was not secured while the case was under Appeals Office jurisdiction, there is no appeal to the Appeals Office on the issue of setting aside the agreement with the taxpayer. When the file was recommended by or approved in an appellate-based office, it is transmitted to the National Office through the Appeals Office. The Associate Chief Counsel (Technical) makes the final decision on setting aside or adhering to a closing agreement. IRM 8.13.1, Appeals Closing Agreement Handbook Manual, 6.2.1–6.4. The Service Manual also states,

It follows from principles of contract law that a closing agreement will be set aside if the closing agreement was obtained by the fraud of a party.[298] "Fraud" for this purpose means fraud that goes to matters on which the closing agreement and its determinations are based. Fraudulent conduct may be involved in some other aspect of the transaction, but this conduct will not invalidate the closing agreement unless the fraud goes to the heart of the agreement. For example, a closing agreement between a corporation and the Service was not set aside, when, in entering into the agreement, officers of the corporation perpetrated fraud on the corporation.[299]

The term misrepresentation connotes intentional deceit. For a closing agreement to be set aside for misrepresentation of a material fact, then, there must be more than a misstatement, because it is said that "innocent mistakes should be buried in a closing agreement."[300] A mere mistake of fact or law, whether unilateral or mutual, no matter how material, is not a misrepresentation.[301] In order for an agreement to be set side by reason of misrepresentation under Section 7121(b), "there must be a misrepresentation of a material fact that goes to the essence of the agreement."[302] "A mere mistake of fact or law,

---

"If circumstances indicate reasons for modifying or setting aside a closing agreement entered into by a competent authority, consideration should be given to notifying the National Office by means of a request for technical assistance . . . before taking any action." Id.

[298] Helvering v. Kehoe, 309 US 277 (1940).

[299] Helvering v. Tait, 65 F2d 703 (4th Cir. 1933) (officers reported nonexistent corporate income and entered into closing agreement on deductions); Rev. Rul. 72-486, 1972-2 CB 644.

[300] Comm'r v. Ingram, 87 F2d 915, 916 (3d Cir. 1937) (underreporting of income by taxpayer's accountant). See Robert W. Brinkman v. Comm'r, 57 TCM 331 (1989) (attorney failed to notify taxpayers about possibility of additional deductions under out-of-pocket settlement is not a misrepresentation of the Service); Estate of Magarian v. Comm'r, 97 TC 1 (1991) (settlement of all partnership credits and losses, followed by assertion of penalties related to partnership items, was held not to be misrepresentation); see also Kercheval v. United States, 80 AFTR2d ¶ 97-5685 (D. Md. 1997) (rejecting taxpayer's argument that the Service's erroneous legal position was a "misrepresentation of fact" for which the closing agreement could be set aside).

[301] Comm'r v. Ingram, 87 F2d 915, 916 (3d Cir. 1937) (underreporting of income by taxpayer's accountant). See Robert W. Brinkman v. Comm'r, 57 TCM 331 (1989) (attorney failed to notify taxpayers about possibility of additional deductions under out-of-pocket settlement is not a misrepresentation of the Service); Estate of Magarian v. Comm'r, 97 TC 1 (1991) (settlement of all partnership credits and losses, followed by assertion of penalties related to partnership items, was held not to be misrepresentation); see also Kercheval v. United States, 80 AFTR2d ¶ 97-5685 (D. Md. 1997) (rejecting taxpayer's argument that the Service's erroneous legal position was a "misrepresentation of fact" for which the closing agreement could be set aside). See also Cramp Shipbuilding Co., 14 TC 33 (1950).

[302] Miller v. Internal Rev. Serv., 174 BR 791, 796, 797 (BAP 9th Cir. 1994), aff'd, 81 F3d 169 (9th Cir. 1996).

whether unilateral or mutual, no matter how material is not a misrepresentation."[303] Similarly, in *Aetna Life Insurance Co.*,[304] with respect to the predecessor of Section 7121(b), Aetna argued that the closing agreement had been based on a mistaken interpretation of a tax law, later found to be unconstitutional, and the circuit court held a misrepresentation "excludes mistakes of fact, and a fortiori of law, as grounds for rescission."

¶ 9.10 TEFRA PARTNERSHIP AND S CORPORATION APPEALS AND AGREEMENTS

Under Sections 6221 through 6232, the tax consequences of items of partnership income, loss, deductions, and credits are to be determined at the partnership level through unified administrative and judicial proceedings, although the tax liability that results from the determination is imposed on the separate partners. Sections 6241 through 6245, concerning the tax treatment of S corporation items, provide for the Service to treat S corporations in the same manner as partnership entities for administrative purposes.

[1] Flow of TEFRA Partnership and S Corporation Cases Into Appeals

Upon completion of a unified partnership or S corporation case examination, the revenue agent provides the tax matters partner (TMP) with a summary report.[305] This summary report contains a detailed explanation for each proposed adjustment, including facts, laws, and conclusion. The revenue agent then conducts a closing examination conference, which results in an agreed case, an unagreed case, or a no-change case. After the closing examination conference, the revenue agent prepares an RAR. The RAR and related case file are forwarded to the centralized services function for computation review. Once the quality review staff has reviewed the report and file, it issues a sixty-day letter with a copy of the RAR and Form 870-P (Settlement Agreement for Partnership Adjustments) or Form 870-S (Settlement Agreement for S Corporation Adjustments) to the tax matters partner. (For an illustrative Form 870-P, see

---

[303] Miller v. Internal Rev. Serv., 174 BR 791, 796, 797 (BAP 9th Cir. 1994), aff'd, 81 F3d 169 (9th Cir. 1996).

[304] Aetna Life Ins. Co. v. Eaton, 43 F2d 711, 713–714 (2d Cir. 1930)

[305] IRM 8113, Appeals TEFRA Handbook § 440, Examination Process (Apr. 20, 1990).

Form 9.6.) The sixty-day letter explains the partners' or shareholders' administrative appeal rights with respect to the proposed adjustments.

A copy of the sixty-day letter is sent to the partnership/S corporation district key case service center examination suspense unit, which sends copies to all partners or shareholders along with Form 870-P or Form 870-S. All partners or shareholders are offered an opportunity to enter into an agreement to the adjustments identified on the sixty-day letter by signing Form 870-P or Form 870-S.

If any partner or shareholder submits an acceptable written protest and requests consideration by the Office of Appeals, the case file and written protest are forwarded to the centralized services function for processing and transfer to the Appeals Office serving the partnership or S corporation District Office. For unified partnership or S corporation examinations, only the partnership or S corporation return, not the individual returns of partners or shareholders, are sent to the Office of Appeals.

FORM 9.6
AGREEMENT TO ASSESSMENT AND COLLECTION OF DEFICIENCY IN TAX PARTNERSHIP ADJUSTMENTS

Form **870-P** (Rev. 6-93)	Department of the Treasury — Internal Revenue Service **AGREEMENT TO ASSESSMENT AND COLLECTION OF DEFICIENCY IN TAX FOR PARTNERSHIP ADJUSTMENTS**	IN REPLY REFER TO:
Taxpayer(s) name(s), address and ZIP code	Name of partnership	Tax year(s) ended
	Taxpayer identifying number	
	Name of tax matters partner	
Taxpayers Identifying Number ▶		

OFFER OF AGREEMENT FOR PARTNERSHIP ITEMS

Under the provisions of section 6224(c) of the Internal Revenue Code, the Commissioner of Internal Revenue and the undersigned taxpayer(s) agree to the determination of partnership items of the partnership for the years shown on the attached schedule of adjustments. The undersigned taxpayer(s), in accordance with section 6224(b), also waive(s) the restrictions on assessment and collection of any deficiency attributable to partnership items (with interest as required by law) provided in section 6225(a).

This agreement is conditional, and will not become effective or final until this agreement form is returned to Internal Revenue and is signed for the Commissioner. The one year extension of the period of limitations on assessment under section 6229(f) will not begin to run until the date the Commissioner's representative signs this form for the Commissioner.

If this agreement form is signed for the Commissioner, the treatment of partnership items under this agreement will not be reopened in the absence of fraud, malfeasance, or misrepresentation of fact; and no claim for an adjustment of partnership items or for a refund or credit based on any change in the treatment of partnership items may be filed or prosecuted.

Signature of taxpayer	Date
Signature of taxpayer	Date
By (Signature and title)	Date

(See Instructions For Signing On Next Page)

FOR INTERNAL REVENUE USE ONLY	Date accepted for Commissioner	Signature
	Office	Title

SAMPLE

Department of the Treasury — Internal Revenue Service

AGREEMENT TO ASSESSMENT AND COLLECTION OF
DEFICIENCY IN TAX FOR PARTNERSHIP ADJUSTMENTS

SCHEDULE OF ADJUSTMENTS

NAME OF PARTNERSHIP	TAX YEAR(S) ENDED		
TAXPAYER IDENTIFYING NUMBER			
DETAIL OF ADJUSTMENTS TO ORDINARY INCOME			
SAMPLE			
SAMPLE			
TOTAL ADJUSTMENTS TO ORDINARY INCOME			
OTHER ADJUSTMENTS			
A.			
(1) ADJUSTMENT			
(2) AS REPORTED			
(3) CORRECTED			
B.			
(1) ADJUSTMENT			
(2) AS REPORTED			
(3) CORRECTED			
REMARKS			

SAMPLE

Form **870-P** (Rev. 6-93)

Instructions for signing this agreement:

1. Sign the agreement if you wish to agree to the partnership items as shown on the attached Schedule of Adjustments.

2. If a JOINT RETURN OF A HUSBAND AND WIFE was filed, both spouses must sign, unless one spouse, acting under a power of attorney, signs as agent for the other.

3. If you are a corporation, the officer authorized to sign must sign with the corporate name followed by his/her signature and title.

4. Your attorney or agent may sign for you provided we have received a power of attorney, which if not previously filed, must accompany this form.

Form **870-P** (Rev. 6-93)

[2] Consolidated Appeals Conferences

If any unagreed partner or shareholder requests an Appeals conference, the Appeals Office servicing the area where the partnership or S corporation has its principal place of business holds a consolidated conference[306] that any unagreed partner or shareholder has the right to attend. However, in order to attend the conference, the partner or shareholder must notify the tax matters partner to that effect. Notice must also be given to the tax matters partner in docketed cases in which the tax matters partner or any unagreed notice partner or shareholder filed a petition.

Before the conference, the tax matters partner must furnish the names of the partners or shareholders and representatives who will be attending. The tax matters partner must submit power of attorney forms from the partners or shareholders planning to have representatives attend the conference or inform the Appeals Office if valid power of attorney forms are on file with the Service. The Office of Appeals schedules the consolidated conference with the tax matters partner, who should give notice of the date, time, and place of the conference to all partners or shareholders who have given notice that they plan to attend or plan to have a representative attend. The case file may contain the tax matters partner's summary of the partners' or shareholders' protests, in addition to the individual protests of the partners or shareholders.

[3] Settlement Agreements in Partnership and S Corporation Cases

The Appeals Office uses the following five procedures for settlement agreements in cases involving partnerships and S corporations:[307]

1. The Appeals Office offers all unagreed partners an opportunity to enter into a settlement with the Service by signing a Form 870-P. Shareholders in an S corporation sign Form 870-S. These agreement forms contain the partnership or S corporation adjustments rather than deficiencies.

2. If the Appeals Office changes the original settlement agreement issued by examination, it provides the tax matters partner with a revised Form 870-P or Form 870-S and the name, address, and telephone number of the Appeals officer that partners or shareholders may contact regarding inquiries and/or

---

[306] IRM 8113, Appeals TEFRA Handbook §§ 630–633, Conference Procedures (Apr. 20, 1990).

[307] Settlement procedures have been reorganized and included in IRM 8113, Appeals TEFRA Handbook. See IRM §§ 660–665, Settlement Agreement Without Penalties, MT 8113-1 (Apr. 20, 1990); IRM §§ 670–676, Settlement Agreements With Penalties, MT 8113-1 (Apr. 20, 1990). For a description of the unified partnership provisions pertaining to settlements, see ¶¶ 8.09[3][c] and 8.09[1][d].

submissions of the agreement forms. The tax matters partner must provide a copy of the revised Form 870-P or Form 870-S to all unagreed partners or shareholders. If the tax matters partner is unable to provide the copies, a partner or shareholder may request one from the Appeals Office. The tax matters partner is responsible for advising all unagreed partners or shareholders of any settlement terms. Any partner or shareholder who enters into a settlement agreement with the Service is bound by the settlement.

3. A non-notice partner who is not a member of a notice group is bound by any settlement agreement entered into by the tax matters partner if the tax matters partner states that the agreement binds the non-notice partners. However, such an agreement does not bind any non-notice partner if the partner files a statement prior to the settlement that the tax matters partner does not have authority to bind the partner.

4. The Appeals Office receives and approves all Forms 870-P and Forms 870-S submitted by any previously unagreed partner or shareholder. The original form remains with the partnership/S corporation case file, and one copy is sent to (1) the appropriate partner or shareholder; (2) the tax matters partner; and (3) the partnership/S corporation service center examination suspense unit along with a prepared Form 886-Z(C) (Partners' or S Corporation Shareholders' Shares of Income), Form 886-S (Partners' Shares of Income, Deductions, and Credit), or Form 886-X (Small Business Corporation Shareholders' Shares of Income).

5. The partnership/S corporation service center examination suspense unit forwards the forms to each partner's or shareholder's service center for assessment/overassessment action. The total of each partner's or shareholder's allocated adjustments accounts for the total partnership or S corporation adjustment. The Appeals Office does not compute deficiencies, only individual partner or shareholder adjustments.

If any partner in the partnership does not agree to the settlement, the Appeals Office prepares the notice of final partnership administrative adjustment (FPAA) (Letter 1830 (DO)), if it has not been previously issued.[308] For S corporations, the notice of final S corporation administrative adjustment (FSAA) is prepared (Letter 1828 (DO)). The FPAA/FSAA is similar to a notice of deficiency; however, only partnership or S corporation adjustments are identified. Specific individual partner or shareholder allocations are only shown at this time if allocation of partnership or S corporation items is an issue.

The Appeals Office sends the FPAA/FSAA, Form 870-P or Form 870-S, and a prepared Form 886-Z(C), Form 886-S, or Form 886-X to the partnership/S corporation service center examination suspense unit. The FPAA/FSAA is signed but not dated by the Appeals Office. On the same day, the service

---

[308] IRM 8113, Appeals TEFRA Handbook §§ 680–687, MT 8113-1, Notice of Final Partnership/S Corporation Administrative Adjustment (Apr. 20, 1990).

center mails the FPAA/FSAA package to the tax matters partner and all unagreed notice partners or shareholders. The Service allows a ninety-day period for the tax matters partner to file a petition with the court. At the end of the ninety-day period, if the tax matters partner has not filed a petition, the Service allows an additional sixty-day period for any unagreed shareholder or notice partner (and any 5 percent notice group) to file.

In order for each Appeals Office to have prompt information to determine whether a petition has been filed within the prescribed time limits for an FPAA/FSAA issued by that office, the Office of Chief Counsel has established a procedure to furnish periodic lists of newly docketed U.S. Tax Court, district court, and claims court cases. These lists reflect the following information:

- Docket number
- Name and address of petitioner
- Taxpayer identification number (if known)
- Name of district or Appeals office issuing FPAA/FSAA
- Date FPAA/FSAA was issued

If no petition is filed, the case is defaulted and the partnership or S corporation service center examination suspense unit sends a copy of the FPAA/FSAA and Form 886-Z(C), Form 886-S, or Form 886-X to each partner's/shareholder's service center for tax computation and assessment/overassessment action.

[4] Finality of Settlement Agreements

There have been many cases litigated involving the binding effect of an informal agreement with the Office of Appeals (that is, an agreement which is not a formal closing agreement). The unified partnership proceeding rules and procedures further complicate the issue of whether a partner who signs a Form 870-P or a Form 870-L(AD) will later be precluded from prosecuting a refund claim, especially when the partner's claim is based on the expiration of assessment of the partnership item.[309] One view is that when the partner signs the settlement agreement, the partnership proceeding rules convert the partnership items into nonpartnership items (see Section 6231(b)(1)(C)) so that the prohibition of refund suits attributable to partnership items (see Section 7422(h)) does not apply.[310] In *Alexander v. United States*, a partner learned that in the

---

[309] For a case involving the validity of a settlement agreement, Form 870-P, entered into by limited partners who later filed refund claims, see Fennell v. United States, 830 F. Supp. 1368 (D. Colo. 1993), aff'd without opinion, 43 F3d 1482 (10th Cir. 1994) (rejecting claims that Form 870-P was an invalid contract for lack of consideration, covered nonpartnership items, and procured through Service misrepresentation).

[310] See Alexander v. United States, 44 F3d 328 (5th Cir. 1995).

case of another partner the Service conceded that the statute of limitations had run for assessment of partnership items. Another court has said that this approach "would render any IRS settlement agreement with an individual partner futile, superfluous, and basically, nonsensical, since it would not in fact waive or release any of the claims relating to partnership items, even if these were released or waived under the express terms of the settlement agreement."[311]

The Fifth Circuit in *Alexander* analyzed Form 870-P to determine whether the partner had waived his right to file a refund under the terms of the agreement and concluded that the partner had not waived his right to file a claim based on the expiration of the statute of limitations on assessment. What Form 870-P prohibited was the partner's filing any "claim for refund . . . based on any change in the treatment of partnership items," and the court said that Alexander's refund claim was not in any way based on the change in the treatment of partnership items. However, the Court of Federal Claims in *Slovacek* held that the partner's waiver of the right to file a refund claim based on partnership items in the Form 870-L(AD) effectively waived the right to file a claim for the refund challenging the partnership's extension of limitations on assessment.

An Offer of Settlement of Partnership Items, Form 870-L(AD), permits the Service one year to assess tax and penalties resulting from the settlement. The one-year period runs from the date the agreement is signed on behalf of the Commissioner, not from the date it is signed by the taxpayer.[312]

---

[311] Slovacek v. United States, 36 Fed. Cl. 250 (1996).

[312] Brookstone Corp. v. United States, 94-2 USTC ¶ 50,474 (SD Tex. 1994) (contract principles applied and Form 870-L(AD) found to be an invitation to offer, subject to acceptance by the Commissioner, not an offer by the Service to be accepted by the taxpayer); see also Treaty Pines Inv. Partnership v. Comm'r, 967 F2d 206 (5th Cir. 1992).

CHAPTER **10**

Assessment Procedures

¶ 10.01 IN GENERAL

[1] Definition of "Assessment"

An assessment is the formal recording of a taxpayer's tax liability, fixing the amount payable.[1] This simple statutory description hardly conveys the fundamental importance of an assessment in the administration of the tax laws. The Supreme Court's 1935 decision in *Bull v. United States*, explained why an assessment has such significance:

> A tax is an exaction by the sovereign, and necessarily the sovereign has an enforceable claim against everyone within the taxable class for the amount lawfully due from him. The statute prescribes the rule of taxation. Some machinery must be provided for applying the rule to the facts in each taxpayer's case, in order to ascertain the amount due. The chosen instrumentality for the purpose is an administrative agency whose action is called an assessment. . . . Default in meeting the obligation [of an assessment] calls for some procedure whereby payment can be enforced. The statute might remit the Government to an action at law wherein the taxpayer could offer such defense as he had. A judgment against him might be collected by the levy of an execution. But taxes are the life-blood of government, and their prompt and certain availability an imperious need. Time out of mind, therefore, the sovereign has resorted to more drastic means of collection. The assessment is given the force of a judgment, and if the amount assessed is not paid when due, administrative officials may seize the debtor's property to satisfy the debt.[2]

With this explanation, we can identify several critical ways in which an assessment works in the administration of the tax laws.

First, an assessment enforces a tax statute. Provisions in the Internal Revenue Code (the Code) are not self-enforcing and do not themselves create a collectible liability. An assessment does this by establishing a taxpayer's liability under the tax statute for the amount of tax due and unpaid.

Second, an assessment has "the force of a judgment." The assessment has the same force as the judgment an ordinary creditor obtains after the creditor has successfully prosecuted an action on a debt. There is a difference between assessment-as-judgment and the ordinary creditor's judgment, however. Where assessment of tax is involved, "the usual procedure of debts is reversed . . . [p]ayment precedes defense, and the burden normally on the claimant [the Service] is shifted to the taxpayer. The assessment precedes the pleading, proof

---

[1] IRC § 6203 ("[t]he assessment shall be made by recording the liability of the taxpayer in the office of the Secretary in accordance with the rules and regulations prescribed by the Secretary").

[2] Bull v. United States, 295 US 247, 259 (1935).

and judgment necessary in an action at law [by a creditor], and has the force of such a judgment."[3]

Third, an assessment is the foundation of the Internal Revenue Service's (the Service's) administrative collection procedures. Because the assessment is effectively a judgment, the Service may collect its assessment-as-judgment by using the same types of collection action the ordinary judgment creditor uses to collect a judgment against the debtor. Collection procedures reflect the judgment like character of an assessment. Before the Service may place a charge on a taxpayer's property by lien or seize a taxpayer's property by levy, the Service must give the taxpayer notice of the assessment and demand its payment.[4] The Service records a notice of its assessment lien, in the same manner as the judgment creditor records its judgment. The Service levies on its assessment lien to seize the property of the taxpayer, in the same way as the judgment creditor levies on its judgment to seize property of the judgment debtor.

Perhaps less obvious, but certainly more important, the assessment divides deficiency procedures from refund procedures. It is not too bold to observe that the division of preassessment procedures and postassessment procedures is the most fundamental characteristic in tax procedure. Deficiency procedures grew out of the rigors of assessment procedures. Because a taxpayer was required to make full payment of an assessment before the taxpayer could challenge the assessment, an excessive assessment could prevent the taxpayer who was unable to pay the excessive assessment from securing judicial review of the Service's action. It was precisely this hardship that led Congress to adopt the prepayment judicial review in 1924 in the Board of Tax Appeals, now the U.S. Tax Court.[5] Unlike postpayment refund procedures, prepayment judicial review procedures permit the taxpayer to petition the Tax Court to dispute the Service's administrative determination, where the Service has determined that the taxpayer is liable for a deficiency in income, estate, or gift taxes without the taxpayer's being required to first pay the amount of the deficiency. As Section 6321(a) states,

> Except as provided in Sections 6851, 6852, and 6861, no assessment of a deficiency in respect of any tax imposed by subtitle A or B, Chapter 41, 42, 43, or 44 and no levy or proceeding in court for its collection shall be made, begun, or prosecuted until [a notice of deficiency] has been mailed to the taxpayer, nor until the expiration of such 90-day or 150-day period, as the case may be, nor, if a petition has been filed with the Tax Court, until the decision has become final.

---

[3] Bull v. United States, 295 US 247, 260–261 (1935).

[4] See IRC §§ 6303(a), 6321, 6331; United States v. Coson, 286 F2d 453 (9th Cir. 1961) (no lien where no assessment made).

[5] Flora v. United States, 362 US 145, 158–163 (1960).

Until the Tax Court's decision becomes final, the Service is prohibited from assessing and administratively collecting the deficiency.[6]

Deficiency procedures differ in fundamental ways from assessment procedures. Unlike an assessment, a deficiency does not have the force of a judgment. A deficiency is a provisional determination of the Service, which the Tax Court may modify or reject in whole or in part if the taxpayer timely petitions the court. However, because an assessment has the force and effect of a final judgment, the Service may collect by levy until the taxpayer pays the assessment or judgment in full.[7] When the taxpayer wishes to recover an amount the Service has collected in error, therefore, the taxpayer must pay the full amount of the tax assessed. Refund procedures require the taxpayer to first pay the full amount of the tax, then to file a claim for refund of the tax with the Service, and finally challenge the Service's adverse action on the refund claim within two years, in a refund court, a local federal district court, or the U.S. Court of Federal Claims.[8]

[2] Assessment Procedures

Assessment procedures are found in Chapter 63 of the Code, and include general assessment procedures (Subchapter A), deficiency procedures in the case of income, estate, gift, and certain excise taxes (Subchapter B), and the tax treatment of partnership and Subchapter S items under the unified proceeding rules (Subchapters C and D, respectively).

[a] General Assessment Procedures

General assessment procedures found in Subchapter A include the Service's authority to make all inquiries, determinations, and assessments of taxes imposed by the Code (Section 6201), the Service's authority to adopt regulations governing the mode and time of assessments (Section 6202), the method of assessment (Section 6203), supplemental assessments (Section 6204), and special rules applying to certain employment taxes (Section 6205) and excessive claims for the refund of gasoline excise tax (Section 6206). There are also cross references to the Anti-Injunction Act (Section 7421) and the statute of limitations on assessment (Chapter 66).

---

[6] IRC § 6213(a).

[7] Flora v. United States, 362 US 145 (1960).

[8] IRC § 6231(a).

[b] Summary and Deficiency Assessments

The two most common types of assessments are summary and deficiency assessments. Summary assessments are made for the amounts of tax shown on returns when taxpayers file returns stating their tax liability.[9] The Service has no discretion in making this type of assessment because the statute authorizing the Service to make assessments says that the Service "shall assess all taxes determined by the taxpayer" under the Code,[10] which means that deficiency assessments result from Service examinations of taxpayer returns. No assessment of deficiencies in income, estate, or gift tax, as well as certain excise taxes may, be made until the taxpayer is given the opportunity of seeking prepayment judicial review in the U.S. Tax Court. Under deficiency procedures, the Service is required (1) to give the taxpayer notice of the proposed assessment[11] and (2) to wait the statutorily prescribed waiting period of 90 days (150 days for taxpayers outside the country) before assessing the tax and taking collection action.[12] If the Service attempts to collect a deficiency without sending the required statutory notice or during the ninety-day waiting period, the taxpayer may request that a district court or the Tax Court enjoin the Service from assessing and collecting the assessed tax.[13] If the taxpayer chooses to file a petition in the Tax Court, no collection action may be taken until the Tax Court has reached a final decision. Thus, a deficiency assessment subject to such restrictions may not be assessed until the taxpayer has had an opportunity for Tax Court review before payment of any additional tax. Once the Tax Court has entered its decision that a deficiency exists, the amount of the deficiency may be assessed.[14] At the expiration of the ninety-day period following the sending of a notice of deficiency, a tax determined to be due from a taxpayer may be assessed. Once assessment has been made, the taxpayer is debarred from Tax Court review and must make payment of the assessed tax.

[c] Jeopardy and Bankruptcy Assessments

Two other types of assessments are provided: jeopardy assessments and bankruptcy assessments. There are several types of jeopardy assessments. If the Service determines that collection of an income, estate, or gift tax from a taxpayer will be jeopardized by delay, it may make immediate assessment of the tax either before the return for the year is due by terminating the year (a

---

[9] IRC § 6201(a)(1).
[10] IRC § 6201(a)(1).
[11] IRC § 6212.
[12] IRC § 6213.
[13] IRC § 7421.
[14] IRC § 6215.

termination assessment),[15] or after the return is due by a jeopardy assessment.[16] Unlike normal deficiency procedures, a taxpayer may still obtain Tax Court review when a jeopardy assessment is made. In the case of an excise tax, a jeopardy assessment may also be made.[17] When an individual is found in physical possession of a large amount of cash but does not claim it, or the Service is unable to determine the owner, then the Service is entitled to presume that for jeopardy and termination assessments, the cash constitutes gross income of a single individual in the year the cash is discovered, and that the collection of the tax on the cash will be jeopardized by delay.[18]

[d] Ultimate Collection of Tax

The ultimate collection of a tax is also a consideration when a taxpayer's property comes under the jurisdiction of a receiver as a result of his insolvency. Accordingly, immediate assessment of a tax is made when a taxpayer becomes involved in a receivership proceeding.[19] Only in limited cases may an immediate assessment be made where a taxpayer is in bankruptcy. A bankrupt taxpayer is entitled to receive a notice of deficiency, but either the bankruptcy court or the Tax Court may hear the case. The bankruptcy court makes this forum choice. Deficiencies involving receivership cases are assessed as "quick" assessments. This quick assessment procedure is also used to assess additional taxes and agreed deficiencies where the statutory period for assessment would otherwise expire before these assessments could be made under normal procedures.[20]

Table 10.1 summarizes the features of the various types of assessments. This chapter focuses on the nature of the various types of assessments. The procedures for collection of an assessed tax, as well as the significance of assessment in that process, are discussed in Chapter 14.

---

[15] IRC § 6851.

[16] IRC § 6861.

[17] IRC § 6867.

[18] IRC § 6867.

[19] IRC § 6871.

[20] IRM 4.3.9, Jeopardy/Termination Assessments Handbook, 1.4.1 (Definitions— Jeopardy Assessment), 1.4.2 (Definitions—Termination Assessment) (June 30, 1999).

¶ 10.02 METHOD OF ASSESSMENT

An assessment is the recording of a taxpayer's liability.[21] Whether the assessment is a normal assessment, deficiency assessment, jeopardy assessment, or bankruptcy assessment, the method of recording the taxpayer's liability by an assessment is roughly the same. For purposes of this discussion, procedures followed to make an assessment of tax where a return is filed will be used. For the average taxpayer, the assessment process begins when he files a return stating his tax liability with the appropriate regional Service center. When the return is received in the Service center, it is inspected to determine whether it has been signed and properly executed and the required schedules have been attached. A check for mathematical accuracy is also made. If the return is complete and correct on its face, the tax liability the taxpayer showed on the return is entered on an assessment list with the taxpayer's name, identifying number, the taxable period, and the type of tax.[22] On any date, the total tax liability of all taxpayers for each type of tax to be assessed at the Service center on that day is summarized on Form 23-C (Assessment Certificate). When this summary list is signed by an assessment officer in the Service center, the official act of assessment has occurred for purposes of the Code.[23] The date of an assessment is the date the summary record is signed by the assessment officer.

Because the Assessment Certificate summarizes only the gross amount of the income tax, estate tax, gift tax, and other taxes assessed on a particular day, it is only through supporting records that the taxpayer, type of tax, taxable period, and specific amount of tax can be identified. However, if a taxpayer requests a copy of the assessment, the Service center must furnish a statement that sets forth the name of the taxpayer, the date of the assessment, the type of liability assessed, the applicable period, and the amount assessed.[24] One court has said that the purpose of Section 6203 and the accompanying regulations is "to insure that a proper record is kept in order to avoid slipshod tax accounting practices and to insure that taxpayers may receive a summary of tax records pertaining to their tax liability."[25]

In a court proceeding, if (1) a taxpayer reasonably disputes an item of income reported on an information return a third party has filed with the Service; (2) the Service makes a reasonable request for access to witnesses and information and documents within the taxpayer's control; and (3) the taxpayer

---

[21] IRC § 6201(a).

[22] IRC § 6201(a)(1).

[23] IRC § 6203; Reg. § 301.6203-1. The authority to assess a tax is delegated by the Secretary to the Commissioner to district directors and directors of regional Service centers. IRC § 6201; Reg. § 301.6201-1(a)(1).

[24] Reg. § 301.6203-1. A Service form can be used for this purpose, Form 4506 (Request for Copy of Tax Form).

[25] Gentry v. United States, 962 F2d 555 (6th Cir. 1992).

has fully cooperated with the Service by providing the access and information "within a reasonable time," the Service has "the burden of producing reasonable and probative information concerning [the] deficiency in addition to [the] information return."[26]

Defects in the assessment process may affect subsequent proceedings. Where an assessment list was not signed by an authorized official within the statutory period for collection, a government suit for collection of the assessed tax was barred.[27] Even where the name of the taxpayer on assessment documents was not the name of the taxpayer from whom the tax was collected, however, some courts have nevertheless upheld the validity of the assessment.[28] These decisions are questionable because an assessment made against an erroneously named taxpayer will taint a notice and demand to the correct taxpayer, and so may render collection action defective. A distinction is sometimes drawn between invalidity of the assessment and government action based on the technically defective assessment. Some courts in older cases have been reluctant to strike down collection of an assessed tax based on a technically defective assessment. More recently, courts seem less constrained to prevent government action based on the technically defective assessment even when such action amounts to invalidating the assessment because the statute of limitations on assessment has expired.

[1] Abatement of an Assessment

Once an assessment is made, it may become apparent either that the amount assessed is incomplete or incorrect in a material respect. On its own, the Service may abate the unpaid portion of an assessment that is (1) excessive in

---

[26] IRC § 6201(d), added by the Taxpayer Bill of Rights 2, Pub. L. No. 104-168 § 602(a), effective on the enactment date, July 30, 1996.

[27] See Brafman v. United States, 384 F2d 863, 867 (5th Cir. 1967) (the assessment was not signed by a proper official within the statutory period, and so a collection suit was held barred). It is generally accepted that the government need not produce a copy of Form 23-C to establish that a tax has been properly assessed when a Certificate of Assessments and Payments reflecting the assessment is produced. United States v. Dixon, 672 F. Supp. 503 (MD Ala. 1987) (gathering cases); Long v. United States, 972 F2d 1174 (10th Cir. 1992) (also gathering cases).

[28] Anderson v. United States, 15 F. Supp. 216 (Ct. Cl. 1936), cert. denied, 300 US 675 (1937); 15 F. Supp. 225 (Ct. Cl. 1936), cert. denied, 302 US 695 (1937) rehearing den. 302 US 775 (1937) (assessment in name of decedent, not estate; held, assessment valid); United States v. First Huntington Nat'l Bank, 34 F. Supp. 578 (SD W. Va. 1940), aff'd without opinion, 117 F2d 376 (4th Cir. 1941) (accord); United States v. Munroe, 65 F. Supp. 213 (WD Pa. 1946). See Johnson, "An Inquiry Into the Assessment Process," 35 Tax L. Rev. 285, 288–290 (1980).

amount; (2) assessed after the expiration of the applicable period of assessment; or (3) erroneously or illegally assessed.[29]

[2] Supplemental Assessments

A supplemental assessment is an assessment made within the statute of limitations on assessment "whenever it is ascertained that any assessment is imperfect or incomplete in any material respect."[30] If the initial assessment is less than the amount the taxpayer owed, the Service is also free to make a supplemental assessment as long as (1) it is within the period for making a timely assessment and (2) the taxpayer has been sent a notice of deficiency and has had an opportunity to file a petition in the Tax Court in cases where the deficiency is one of an income, gift, or estate tax.[31]

A supplemental assessment may be made even after an action involving the first assessment has been instituted. Such an action may be the Service's action to reduce the initial assessment to judgment,[32] or a taxpayer's action to quiet title action questioning the procedural validity of the first assessment.[33] The rationale for permitting the Service to make a supplemental assessment during a proceeding involving the first assessment is that during the proceeding on the first assessment, the statute of limitations on assessment may expire. In *Johnson v. United States*,[34] the Service's assessments of the 1980 through 1984 deficiencies were premature because the Tax Court decision on those years had not yet become final. To challenge the propriety of the premature assessment, the taxpayer began a quiet title action. During the pendency of the taxpayer's quiet title action, the Service made a supplemental assessment for 1984 when it determined that the limitations period for that year had not expired. Although the district court found in favor of the taxpayer that the first assessment was premature, the circuit court permitted the Service to make the supplemental assessment during the course of an action involving the first assessment in part on the ground that the Service may "ascertain" that the first assessment is defective without having absolute certainty that the first assessment was defective.[35] As a policy matter, the circuit court said, if the Service must wait until litigation on the first assessment is completed, the statute of

---

[29] IRC § 6404(a). Claims for abatement are also used where employment and excise taxes are assessed. See ¶ 11.04.

[30] IRC § 6204.

[31] IRC § 6204; Reg. § 301.6204-1.

[32] United States v. Vorachek, 563 F2d 884 (8th Cir. 1977) (supplemental assessment approved apparently without the sending of a notice of deficiency).

[33] Johnson v. United States, 80 AFTR2d 97-5869 (2d Cir. 1997) .

[34] Johnson v. United States, 80 AFTR2d 97-5869 (2d Cir. 1997).

[35] Johnson v. United States, 80 AFTR2d 97-5869 (2d Cir. 1997).

limitations on assessment may expire. Since the taxpayer may contest the validity of an assessment in an action to reduce the assessment to judgment, the taxpayer is not prejudiced by the supplemental assessment.

TABLE 10.1
Features of the Various IRS Assessments

Type of Assessment	Deficiency Assessments	Jeopardy Assessments	Termination Assessments	Bankruptcy and Receivership Assessments
2. Section	6211, 6212, 6213	6861, 6862	6851	6871
3. Cause of assessment	Determination of deficiency	Jeopardy in collection	Finding of jeopardy in collection of current year's tax	Notification from bankruptcy or receivership court
4. Restrictions on assessment	Assessment and collection restricted for 90 days and if a petition is filed until the decision of the Tax Court becomes final	No restrictions, assessment is immediate, but notice of deficiency must be sent within 60 days after the assessment	No restrictions, assessment is immediate, but a notice of deficiency must be sent within 60 days after the later of the date the full period return is due or the full period return is filed	No restrictions on assessment, but collection is stayed, and notice of deficiency in bankruptcy cases, but not in receivership cases
5. Restrictions after assessment		Immediate seizure — Section 6331	Immediate seizure — Section 6331	Seizure stayed by the Bankruptcy Code or prohibited by the levy statute — Section 6331
6. Administrative review	Administrative review not required by statute, but can be obtained	Prompt administrative review required by Section 7429	Prompt administrative review required by Section 7429	Administrative review not required by statute, but can be obtained
7. Judicial review	Prepayment judicial review in the Tax Court	Postpayment judicial review in the district court and the Tax Court under Section 7429	Postpayment judicial review in the district court or the Tax Court under Section 7429	Judicial review in the bankruptcy court, the receivership court, or, if the bankruptcy court so orders, the U.S. Tax Court
8. Immediate assessment	No. Assessment is prohibited if the taxpayer files a petition in the Tax Court	Yes. Additional tax may be assessed or abated during the pendency of the case in the Tax Court	Yes. Additional tax may be assessed or abated during the pendency of the case in the Tax Court	Automatic stay prevents collection, but not issuance of notice of deficiency
9. Period of assessment	Full tax years	Full tax years	Partial or full current tax year before the due date of the return	Full tax years
10. Statute of limitations	Any tax years not barred by the statute of limitations on assessment	Any tax years not barred by the statute of limitations on assessment	Assessment is permitted for current or preceding tax year if before due date of return	Assessment not barred by statute of limitations on assessment on date of assessment or due date of return or both
11. Injunction	Injunction may be issued if assessment or collection during the period assessment and collection are restricted	Injunction permitted if Section 7429 not followed	Same as jeopardy assessment	Automatic stay of collection imposed by the Bankruptcy Code

[3] Assessment When a Tax Return Is Filed

When a taxpayer files a return showing that a tax is due, the Service may take one of three possible actions: (1) If no error was made, the tax reported on the return is summarily assessed; (2) if full payment is remitted with the return, the assessment is satisfied, and the result is a zero balance on the Service's records; or (3) if only partial payment is enclosed with the return, the tax reported is assessed and the taxpayer is billed for the balance. The notice sent to a taxpayer after partial payment is a demand for payment, not a notice of deficiency that would entitle the taxpayer to Tax Court review before payment.[36] Where a taxpayer has made a mathematical or clerical error, the return is treated as though it were a partially paid return, and the tax is assessed.[37] The taxpayer is entitled to be informed of the error and to receive an explanation of the adjustment.[38] After the Service sends the taxpayer a notice of the error, the taxpayer has sixty days to request that the Service abate the assessment based on the alleged mathematical or clerical error.[39]

A taxpayer must admit liability for a tax before it may be summarily assessed. If the taxpayer shows a tax on his return, but denies liability for the tax (e.g., by attaching a letter refusing to pay the tax because it is unconstitutional[40] or by a protest that the tax laws are not applicable to him),[41] the amount of tax shown on the return is considered to be zero. Although the taxpayer has shown an amount on the return, he has not admitted that that amount is due and collectible.[42] In short, a tax determined to be due may not be summarily assessed; rather, the normal deficiency procedures apply. When a taxpayer files a return showing a tax due and then files an amended return or claim for refund showing no tax due, the Service summarily assesses the tax shown on the original return (without sending a notice of deficiency) and treats the amended return as a claim for refund.[43]

---

[36] See In re New York Trust Co., 3 BTA 583 (1926) (partial payment; taxpayer filed claims for refund and for abatement, both of which were denied by the Commissioner).

[37] See infra ¶ 10.04[1].

[38] IRC § 6213(b)(1).

[39] IRC § 6213(b)(2).

[40] Penn Mut. Indem. Co. v. Comm'r, 32 TC 653 (1959) (especially concurring opinion of Murdock, J., at 667–668), aff'd, 277 F2d 16 (3d Cir. 1960).

[41] In re Continental Accounting & Audit Co., 2 BTA 761 (1925) (personal holding company).

[42] In re Continental Accounting & Audit Co., 2 BTA 761, 763 (1925).

[43] Kearney v. A'Hearn, 210 F. Supp. 10 (SDNY 1961), aff'd, 309 F2d 487, 489 (2d Cir. 1962); Paccon, Inc. v. Comm'r, 45 TC 392 (1966).

[4] Assessment When No Tax Return Is Filed

If a taxpayer fails to file a tax return or executes a fraudulent return, the Service is authorized to "execute" one for the taxpayer from available information.[44] The return made and executed for the taxpayer is "prima facie good and sufficient for all legal purposes."[45] The Service is not required to prepare and execute a return for a taxpayer who fails to file a return as a condition to making a deficiency assessment. It is not necessary for the taxpayer to consent to disclose all necessary information and to sign the return. Because Section 6020(b) authorizes but does not require the Service to prepare a tax return[46], when a taxpayer fails to file a return, the Service need not make a return under Section 6020(b). Instead, it can determine a deficiency as if a return had been made showing the amount of tax to be zero.[47] If the Service prepares a return for a taxpayer, a deficiency exists to the extent the taxpayer denies liability for the taxes the Service says are owing. For example, where a taxpayer did not file a return, and the Service filed one for him and sent the taxpayer a notice of the amount due,[48] the Board of Tax Appeals held that "to the extent the tax and penalty determined by [the Commissioner] exceed the amount [admitted to be due by the taxpayer], the Commissioner has determined a deficiency. . . ."[49]

¶ 10.03 DEFICIENCY ASSESSMENTS

"Deficiency" is a term of art in the tax law. It not only refers to the additional tax that is due (the deficiency), but also signifies the cornerstone of procedures intended to assure taxpayers that they have a right to prepayment judicial review of the Service's administrative determination that additional tax (the deficiency) is due *before* the Service is permitted to assess and collect the tax. It is this delay in the taxpayer's obligation to pay (if any) that distinguishes defi-

---

[44] IRC § 6020(b)(1). The history of Section 6020(b) is described in United States v. Harrison, 72-2 USTC ¶ 9573 (EDNY 1972), aff'd, 73-1 USTC ¶ 9295 (2d Cir. 1972), cert. denied, 411 US 965 (1973).

[45] IRC § 6020(b)(2); Reg. § 301.6020-1(a)(2).

[46] Hartman v. Comm'r, 65 TC 542 (1975). See United States v. Harrison, 72-2 USTC ¶ 9573 (EDNY 1972), aff'd, 73-1 USTC ¶ 9295 (2d Cir. 1972), cert. denied, 411 US 965 (1973).

[47] Reg. § 301.6211-1(a). This regulation was implicitly approved in Hartman v. Comm'r, 65 TC 542 (1975).

[48] Taylor v. Comm'r, 36 BTA 427 (1938). At first, the taxpayer denied liability altogether, and then admitted liability for about one sixth of the total taxes and penalty the Commissioner said was due.

[49] Taylor v. Comm'r, 36 BTA 427, 429 (1938). For further discussion of Section 6020(b) assessments, see ¶ 5.02[1].

ciency procedures from refund procedures. Prepayment judicial review is not permitted for all taxes. Prepayment judicial review is limited to income, estate and gift, and certain excise taxes on foundations and pension plans. Prepayment judicial review is also limited to the U.S. Tax Court. The U.S. district courts and the U.S. Court of Federal Claims are without jurisdiction to grant taxpayers prepayment judicial review of a proposed deficiency over which the Tax Court has jurisdiction. In short, the U.S. Tax Court is a specialized court Congress established under Article I of the constitution to provide prepayment judicial review of deficiencies.

First of all, the jurisdiction of the Tax Court depends on the type of tax that is the subject of the Service's determination. The term "deficiency" is defined in Section 6211 as an income, estate, or gift tax, as well as certain excise taxes on transactions involving foundations and pension plans. The term "deficiency" is further defined as the excess of the correct tax over the amount shown as due on the return. The amount a taxpayer shows as due on his or her return is not considered a deficiency, and an assessment of the returned amount does not require a notice of deficiency. Before assessment and collection of deficiencies in these taxes may be made, Sections 6212 and 6213 require that the Service must give a taxpayer (1) notice of the deficiency and (2) a 90-day period (150 days for taxpayers outside the United States) for filing a petition in the Tax Court for redetermination.[50] No assessment or collection of the deficiency is permitted to be made (i.e., the Service's authority to do so is restricted) until the expiration of the period for filing a petition in the Tax Court, or, if the taxpayer files a petition, "until the decision of the Tax Court becomes final."[51]

Prepayment Tax Court review of deficiencies in income, estate, or gift tax makes it necessary to know (1) what constitutes a deficiency and (2) what restrictions there are on the making of the assessment.

[1] The Definition and Determination of a Deficiency

In the case of income, estate, and gift tax, as well as certain miscellaneous excise taxes, the "deficiency" is defined in Section 6211(a)(1) to mean the following:

> The amount by which the tax imposed by subtitle A (income tax) or B (estate and gift taxes) or Chapter 41, 42, 43, or 44 (miscellaneous excise taxes) exceeds the excess of

---

[50] Camous v. Comm'r, 67 TC 721 (1977) (married couple who received joint deficiency notice while one spouse was outside the United States was entitled to the 150-day filing period).

[51] IRC § 6213(a).

(1) the sum of

    (a) the amount shown as the tax by the taxpayer upon his return, if a return was made by the taxpayer and an amount was shown as the tax by the person thereon, plus

    (b) the amount previously assessed (or collected without assessment) as a deficiency, over

(2) the amount of rebates . . . made.

A definition is hardly a model of clarity when it uses the very term being defined, and in the case of the term "deficiency," and the use of the term "deficiency" in the definition of a "deficiency" in Section 6211 is no exception.

Two key factors in arriving at the amount of a deficiency are (1) the correct or actual tax the taxpayer owes and (2) the amount the taxpayer has reported on the return. In general, a deficiency is the difference between the two factors; that is, the correct tax and the reported tax. The amount of tax on the return is increased by prior assessments and decreased by rebates. A prior assessment increases the amount reported on the return, and therefore reduces the deficiency in the same way that the tax reported on the return reduces the deficiency. Similarly, a rebate increases a deficiency because the Service has paid or refunded the amount of the rebate to the taxpayer, thereby reducing the amount of tax reported on the return. Both the courts and the Service have accepted a mathematical restatement of this definition:[52]

$$\text{Deficiency} = \text{correct tax} - (\text{tax on return} + \text{prior assessments} - \text{rebates}) \text{ or}$$
$$\text{Deficiency} = \text{correct tax} - \text{tax on return} - \text{prior assessments} + \text{rebates}$$

Prior assessments and rebates are relatively infrequent occurrences. A prior assessment occurs, for example, where the Service has examined a return more than once, and has assessed tax (which the taxpayer has paid) after the first of these examinations.[53] In computing the amount of any new deficiency, credit must be given to the taxpayer for deficiencies previously assessed or collected.[54] Not very instructively, Section 6211(b)(2) defines a "rebate" as "so

---

[52] Morris Kurtzon, 17 TC 1542, 1548 (1952); Rev. Rul. 60-214, 1960-1 CB 700.

[53] In Levinson v. United States, 496 F2d 651 (3d Cir.), cert. denied, 419 US 1040 (1974), the taxpayers filed timely 1974 and 1975 returns paying the reported tax, and examinations were made resulting in the assessment of additional tax. Thereafter, the taxpayers filed amended returns reporting income not included in the original returns, and the Service, after an examination, uncovered additional income.

[54] Levinson v. United States, 496 F2d 651 (3d Cir. 1974). However, *Levinson* holds that this portion of the definition does not apply where a fraud penalty is computed so that a prior deficiency assessment does not reduce the deficiency. Cf. Marie A. Dolan, 44 TC 420 (1965) (deficiency assessed against the taxpayer's husband held not to constitute an

much of an abatement, credit, refund, or other payment, as was made on the ground that the tax imposed (i.e., the correct amount of income, estate or gift and certain excise taxes) was less than the excess of the amount specified in subsection (a)(1) (i.e., the tax the taxpayer reported and previously assessed amounts) over the rebates previously made." In other words, a rebate is the amount refunded to a taxpayer because the taxpayer has reported more tax than the Service computes the taxpayer owed. Regulations give the following example:[55]

> [A]ssume that the amount of income tax shown by the taxpayer upon his return for the taxable year is $600 and the amount claimed as a credit under [S]ection 31 for income tax withheld at the source is $900. If the district director determines that the tax imposed by subtitle A is $600 and makes a refund of $300, no part of such refund constitutes a "rebate" since the refund is not made on the ground that the tax imposed by subtitle A is less than the tax shown on the return. If, however, the district director determines that the tax imposed by subtitle A is $500 and refunds $400, the amount of $100 of such refund would constitute a rebate since it is made on the ground that the tax imposed by subtitle A ($500) is less than the tax shown on the return ($600). The amount of such rebate ($100) would be taken into account in arriving at the amount of any deficiency subsequently determined.

Thus, the elements necessary to compute the amount of a rebate are (1) the correct tax; (2) the returned tax; (3) previously assessed amounts, if any; and (4) previously made rebates, if any.[56] Generally, a rebate occurs when the returned tax is in excess of the correct tax, or in terms of a formula:

$$\text{Rebate} = \text{tax on return} - \text{correct tax}$$

Because a rebate and a prior assessment are relatively infrequent occurrences in the determinations of most deficiencies, a good working definition of a "deficiency" is the difference between (1) the correct tax liability and (2) the amount shown on the taxpayer's return.

[a] The Element of the Correct Tax Due

The correct tax due is the amount the Service "determines" the taxpayer owes under the Code, generally after the Service's examiners have conducted an examination of the taxpayer's return. In administrative law terms, the defi-

---

assessed deficiency for purposes of the definition because to do so would defeat the joint and several liability of spouses filing a joint return).

[55] Reg. § 301.6211-1(f).

[56] For a case where a real life computation of a rebate was made, see Pesch v. Comm'r, 78 TC 100 (1982).

ciency is the Service's administrative finding or determination of the correct tax. In terms of the income tax, a deficiency is the difference between the income tax the Service has determined the taxpayer to owe and the income tax the taxpayer reported on his income tax return. A deficiency should be distinguished from the "net amount of tax due" from the taxpayer. An assessment is made of the net amount of tax due from the taxpayer. But it is the Service's administrative determination of the correct tax that the Tax Court will review. For the purpose of Tax Court prepayment judicial review of the Service's determination, it is unnecessary to know the amount of tax the taxpayer has paid, and it cannot be said what the taxpayer owes until the Tax Court's decision becomes final. As a result, withholding tax and estimated tax are disregarded in determining the correct amount of income tax due, as well as the correctness of the tax shown by the taxpayer on a return.[57]

This distinction between a deficiency and the net amount due is important for the computation of penalties as well as for assessment purposes. Penalties based on the amount of a deficiency are called ad valorem penalties. Ad valorem penalties, such as the accuracy-related and fraud penalties, are generally assessed, collected, and paid in the same manner as any tax imposed by the Code. A taxpayer may obtain prepayment Tax Court review of these ad valorem penalties.[58] On the other hand, penalties based on the net amount due, such as those for delinquency in filing a timely return or for failing to pay estimated tax, are immediately assessed and judicial review may be obtained only by paying the tax and then suing for refund.[59] By contrast, delinquency penalties are subject to the same deficiency procedures as the principal amount of the tax where the penalty for failure to file a timely return is attributable to a deficiency in income, estate, or gift tax, or, if no return is filed, to a penalty for underpayment of estimated tax.[60]

[b] The Element of the Tax on the Return

The other major factor in the deficiency equation is "the amount shown as the tax due by the taxpayer upon his return." The deficiency definition, and indeed the entire voluntary reporting tax system, assumes the filing of a tax return. As discussed earlier,[61] not every document filed with the Service constitutes a tax return. A tax return is considered "sufficient" to be treated as

---

[57] IRC § 6211(b). Special rules apply to credit for withholdings from tax-free covenant bonds held by nonresident aliens and foreign corporations.

[58] IRC § 6659(a).

[59] IRC § 6659(b). The constitutionality of this provision has been upheld. Spencer Press, Inc. v. Alexander, 434 US 914 (1977).

[60] IRC §§ 6659(b)(1), 6659(b)(2).

[61] The requirements of a sufficient return are described in Chapter 4.

such if it sets forth the amount of tax the taxpayer says is due or at least provides enough information to permit the Service to calculate the amount of tax. Nevertheless, a deficiency may be determined where no tax return is filed. If a taxpayer fails to file a return, the returned tax is taken as zero,[62] and the deficiency thus determined may be the subject of a Tax Court proceeding.[63]

A deficiency is computed from the taxpayer's original return. Confusion in computing the amount of a deficiency was created where a taxpayer filed an amended return. In *Badaracco v. Commissioner*,[64] however, the Supreme Court held that because the Code does not provide for the filing or even acceptance of an amended return, the Service's acceptance of an amended return is purely a matter of administrative discretion. As a result, an amended return is not the "return" referred to in the deficiency definition unless the Commissioner chooses in the exercise of his discretion to consider it to be the original return.[65] If the taxpayer files a return showing a tax of $20,000 and then an amended return showing zero tax, and the Service determines the correct tax to be $21,000 (not $20,000), the deficiency is $1,000, not $21,000.[66] If the taxpayer has paid the $20,000 on the original return, the amended return constitutes a valid claim for refund. If the taxpayer files an amended return showing a tax that is greater than the tax on the original return, a different rule applies. In this case, the tax liability shown on the amended return is considered the returned tax for deficiency purposes.[67]

[62] Reg. § 301.6211-1(a).

[63] When no tax return has been filed, the deficiency is the amount of the tax due. Laing v. United States, 423 US 161, 174 (1976); Roat v. Comm'r, 847 F2d 1379 (9th Cir. 1988); Hartman v. Comm'r, 65 TC 542, 546 (1975). When a taxpayer filed a return but the Service erroneously ignored it in determining the amount of a deficiency, the Service nevertheless made a "determination" of a deficiency as required by Section 6212(a). Pearce v. Comm'r, 95 TC 250 (1990) (Scar v. Comm'r, 814 F2d 136 (9th Cir. 1987), distinguished). However, the Tax Court's decision in *Pearce* was reversed. The Fifth Circuit held that the Service did not make a "thoughtful and considered determination" based on the information available to it and that it had not made a valid determination, as a result of which the notices of transferee liability were void ab initio. Pearce v. Comm'r, 946 F2d 1543 (5th Cir. 1991), reh'g denied (5th Cir. Dec. 11, 1991).

[64] Badaracco v. Comm'r, 464 US 386 (1984). See ¶¶ 4.02[3], 5.02[2].

[65] Koch v. Alexander, 561 F2d 1115 (4th Cir. 1977); Kearney v. A'Hearn, 210 F. Supp. 10 (SDNY 1961), aff'd, 309 F2d 489 (2d Cir. 1962).

[66] Koch v. Alexander, 561 F2d 1115 (4th Cir. 1977); Clark v. United States, 81-2 USTC ¶ 9623 (WD Ky. 1981).

[67] Reg. § 301.6211-1(a). For an example of how these regulations caused confusion before they were amended, see DeWelles v. United States, 67-1 USTC ¶ 9314 (CD Cal. 1967), revoking prior opinion and order, 67-1 USTC ¶ 9127 (CD Cal. 1966).

[c] Effect of Rebates

Generally, a rebate is the amount the Service returns to the taxpayer when the Service itself determines that the tax the taxpayer reported on the return is greater than the tax due. There are two types of rebates. The first type of rebate, the Service says, is a rebate refund, which occurs when the Service recalculates the tax the taxpayer reported on a filed tax return and determines that, as a matter of law, the taxpayer's liability under the Code is less than the tax liability the taxpayer reported on the tax return. When the Service determines that this type of rebate exists, it simply refunds the amount of the overpayment. If the Service later recalculates and determines that it misapplied the tax law and regulations, it can collect the erroneous rebate refund by first issuing a notice of deficiency and then making a supplemental assessment, as it did in *Pesch v. Commissioner.*[68]

The second type of refund, a nonrebate refund, is not subject to the normal deficiency procedures. This type of refund is called a nonrebate refund and occurs not because the Service has determined that the taxpayer owed no tax on the refunded amount, but because the Service made a mistake of fact, such as a computer error, or crediting a taxpayer's payment twice. In this type of situation, the Service has argued that it could make a supplemental assessment without following the deficiency procedures, claiming that the amount it assessed did not constitute a deficiency and so deficiency procedures did not apply. The Service has made this argument unsuccessfully to at least three circuits, all of which rejected the rebate refund versus nonrebate refund distinction the Service used to justify summary collection action outside the procedure for summary assessment under Section 6204 or erroneous refund.[69] In another case, the Service made a supplemental assessment under Section 6204 without having first issued a notice of deficiency. The circuit court first noted that the Service did make a supplemental assessment—a practice that other circuit courts have, in the past, criticized the Service for *not* making. The circuit court nonetheless held that, even if the Service's rebate refund versus nonrebate refund distinction were correct, the erroneous refund was an error-of-law rebate refund, and the Service acted improperly under Section 6204 by making a supplemental assessment before sending the taxpayer a notice of deficiency.[70]

The Service may recover an erroneous "quick" refund (i.e., rebate) through use of the deficiency procedures on the grounds that an erroneous re-

---

[68] Pesch v. Comm'r, 78 TC 100 (1982).

[69] Bilzerian v. United States, 86 F3d 1067 (11th Cir. 1996); Clark v. United States, 63 F3d 83 (1st Cir. 1995); O'Bryant v. United States, 49 F3d 340 (7th Cir. 1995).

[70] Singleton v. United States, 128 F3d 833 (4th Cir. 1997) (a divided court) (the time for filing a suit for erroneous refund had expired).

bate gave rise to a deficiency.[71] When the carryback of a loss results in a credit rather than a refund, the amount of the credit is a rebate.[72] To recover an erroneous rebate, the Service may send a notice of deficiency. A deficiency exists even if the refund or credit results from the filing of a claim for quick refund (Form 1045) and the erroneous refund or credit is due solely to the tentative carryback adjustment, but not to any error in the original return as filed.

[2] Restrictions on Assessment and Collection of Deficiencies

Section 6213(a) states that

> no assessment of a deficiency in respect of any tax imposed ... and no levy or proceeding in court for its collection shall be made, begun, or prosecuted until such notice [of deficiency] has been mailed to the taxpayer, nor until the expiration of such 90-day period [for petitioning the Tax Court thereafter] ... nor, if a petition has been filed with the Tax Court, until the decision of the Tax Court has become final.

Prohibitions on or restriction of the Service's authority to assess and collect a deficiency begin when the Service has sent a notice of deficiency to the taxpayer. Assessment and collection are restricted (1) for the 90- or 150-day period the taxpayer is given to file a petition in the Tax Court, and (2) if the taxpayer files a petition, until the Tax Court decision has become final. Restrictions on the Service's authority to assess and collect a deficiency are necessary to protect petitioning taxpayers from the hardship of having to pay the full assessment before the suit for refund is decided. These restrictions are also necessary if the Tax Court's jurisdiction to provide prepayment judicial review of deficiencies is not to be undermined by administrative collection action of the Service. If the Service assesses or seeks to collect tax during the period the restrictions apply, the Tax Court or a federal district court may prohibit the Service from further assessment and any collection action.[73]

    Generally, the so-called Anti-Injunction Act[74] prohibits any suit "for the purpose of restraining the assessment or collection of any tax" to be maintained in any court by any person. However, one of the specific exceptions to this flat prohibition occurs where an assessment is made or a proceeding to collect or levy is begun before a notice of deficiency has been sent to a tax-

---

[71] Pesch v. Comm'r, 78 TC 100 (1982). See infra ¶ 10.04[2].

[72] Baldwin v. Comm'r, 97 TC 704 (1991).

[73] IRC § 6213(a) (Tax Court jurisdiction); IRC § 7421(a) (Anti-Injunction Act exception for violations of the restrictions on assessment and collection in Section 6213(a)).

[74] IRC § 7421(a).

payer and the statutory 90- or 150-day period has run.[75] Thus, Section 6213(a) provides that, notwithstanding the Anti-Injunction Act (Section 7421(a)), an assessment in violation of the restrictions on assessment may be enjoined by a proceeding in a proper court.[76] In *Laing v. United States*,[77] an injunction was upheld when the Service failed to send a notice of deficiency after making a termination assessment.[78] In addition to seeking an injunction of a proposed as-

---

[75] IRC § 7421 states: "Except as provided in Sections . . . 6212(a) and (c), 6213(a) . . . no suit for the purpose of restraining the assessment or collection of any tax shall be maintained." See Dorl v. Comm'r, 507 F2d 406 (2d Cir. 1974). The Tax Court retains jurisdiction to determine the validity of a deficiency once the taxpayer has filed a petition, even when the Service has abated a premature assessment.

[76] Maxwell v. Campbell, 205 F2d 461 (5th Cir. 1953) and Mall v. Kelly, 564 F. Supp. 371 (D. Wyo. 1983) (no notice of deficiency sent; collection enjoined). See also Bromberg v. Ingling, 300 F2d 859 (9th Cir. 1962) (assessment made simultaneously with notice of deficiency); Dierks v. United States, 215 F. Supp. 338 (SDNY 1963) (collection on assessment made during appeal period before Tax Court decision had become final). See Stroman v. McCanless, 391 F. Supp. 1344 (ND Tex. 1975) (reservation of right to contest liability as innocent spouse in waiver held effective so assessment before notice of deficiency invalid). But see Cool Fuel, Inc. v. Connett, 685 F2d 309 (9th Cir. 1982), in which a notice of deficiency was not sent to the taxpayer's "last known address," but an injunction was denied because the taxpayer could not show irreparable injury—a doubtful conclusion in light of the statutory framework creating Tax Court review, and specifically Section 6213(a), which makes premature assessment and collection invalid and subject to injunction.

[77] Laing v. United States, 423 US 161 (1976).

[78] The termination assessment provision (Section 6851) was changed and postassessment procedures on termination and jeopardy assessments (Section 7429) were added to the Code after the *Laing* decision; Laing v. United States, 423 US 161 (1976). However, the principle that Section 7421 does not apply to assessment and collection in violation of the requirement that a notice of deficiency be sent was not questioned by the Supreme Court in *Laing* or by the Service. But see Perlowin v. Sassi, 711 F2d 910 (9th Cir. 1983) (termination assessment invalid when notice of deficiency not sent to taxpayer who failed to file a return, but injunction denied because taxpayer did not prove irreparable harm or inadequacy of legal remedies). In Cool Fuel, Inc. v. Connett, 685 F2d 309 (9th Cir. 1982), the Ninth Circuit also held that despite the Service's failure to comply with the provisions of Section 6213(a), a taxpayer was nevertheless not entitled to an injunction unless he adduced proof of irreparable harm or inadequacy of legal remedies as required by the Supreme Court's decision in *Williams Packing.* For a discussion of injunctions in tax cases, see ¶ 1.05[5][a].

Other courts have followed *Cool Fuel* (inadvisably). See, e.g., August v. Comm'r, 85-1 USTC ¶ 9423 (ED Mich. 1985) (however, deficiency notice had been properly mailed to the taxpayer's last known address). See also Meyer v. Comm'r, 86-2 USTC ¶ 9722 (D. Minn. 1986) (injunction action based on the Service's failure to send a notice of deficiency defeated by evidence that a notice was sent by certified mail). For further discussion, see Andrews, "The Use of the Injunction as a Remedy for an Invalid Tax Assessment," 40 Tax L. Rev. 653 (1985) (concluding that traditional equity prerequisites to a permanent injunction are inapplicable to violations by the Service of Section 6213(a)). Philadelphia & Reading Corp. v. United States, 944 F2d 1063 (3d Cir. 1991) ("[i]n a tax refund action based on an admittedly illegal assessment, the Internal Revenue Code does

sessment and collection of a deficiency where the Service has not complied with the deficiency assessment procedures, the taxpayer can also raise non-compliance as a defense in a suit for collection.[79]

On the simple question of the validity of a premature assessment, courts differ. Some courts hold that a premature assessment can have no legal effect because it is made contrary to the statutes authorizing assessment.[80] In *Philadelphia & Reading Corp.*, the Third Circuit concluded that because Section 6213(b) lists exceptions to the restrictions on assessment, it excludes any other exceptions, such as the absence of equitable considerations making assessment and collection inappropriate. In applying the rule of statutory construction that the inclusion of specific exceptions prohibits others, the Third Circuit continued its reasoning as follows:

> Indeed we think the maxim has special force when the statutory scheme is complex, its parts are closely related and, in making important decisions, the persons affected by it depend heavily on its even-handed application of the statute's plain terms. In this case, the district court should not have considered the equities and, based upon them, ruled in favor of the government.

Consequently, the Third Circuit did not consider the prerequisites for equity jurisdiction if the taxpayer seeks an injunction rather than, as the taxpayer did here, a refund of tax because the assessment period has expired. Other courts, especially the court of claims, have held that a premature assessment is not automatically null and void but merely gives rise to a right to have collection of

---

not permit a Court to balance the equities and determine the amount fairly due from a taxpayer by netting out his liabilities and payments over different taxable years").

[79] See United States v. Williams, 161 F. Supp. 158 (EDNY 1958) (no deficiency notice sent); United States v. Barber, 24 F. Supp. 229 (D. Md. 1938) (assessment void where made prior to board dismissal of a petition filed one day late). Contra United States v. Teti, 75-2 USTC ¶ 9709 (D. Conn. 1975) (premature assessment held valid once taxpayer let period for filing a Tax Court petition expire).

[80] United States v. Yellow Cab Co., 90 F2d 699 (7th Cir. 1937); Ventura Consol. Oil Fields v. Rogan, 86 F2d 149 (9th Cir. 1936), cert. denied, 300 US 672 (1937); Parsons Corp. v. United States, 659 F. Supp. 48 (CD Cal. 1987) (Service violated conditional waiver and then failed to send notice of deficiency; held, assessment was void, not voidable, and collection was invalid; cases analyzed); United States v. Walker, 217 F. Supp. 888 (WDSC 1963). For an analysis of the cases, see Johnson, "An Inquiry Into the Assessment Process," 35 Tax L. Rev. 285 (1980). Philadelphia & Reading Corp. v. United States, 944 F2d 1063 (3d Cir. 1991) (when the Service violated conditional Form 870, its assessment was illegal and, in the interim, the statute of limitations on assessment expired, with result that taxpayer received refund of over $10 million). The Second Circuit has aligned itself with those courts that hold an assessment made contrary to law is void ab initio. Johnson v. United States, 990 F2d 41 (2d Cir. 1993).

the assessed tax enjoined.[81] It is difficult to see why an assessment made without authority in law acquires legality by some failure to act or waiver of a taxpayer.

Assessment and collection are prohibited not only until the Tax Court enters a decision, but until the decision becomes "final." In practical and legal terms, a taxpayer need not be concerned that the Service will assess and collect a disputed tax until the Tax Court has reviewed the Service's determination, and the Tax Court's decision has become final.[82] Once the Tax Court has decided the case, even if the taxpayer appeals, the restrictions on assessment and collection are removed. The Service is free to assess the deficiency in tax that the Tax Court has determined to be due.[83] If a taxpayer wishes to appeal the Tax Court's decision, the taxpayer must post a bond[84] to stay assessment and collection of the redetermined deficiency.

A Tax Court decision becomes final ninety days after it is entered, and this ninety days constitutes the period allowed for filing a notice of appeal.[85] Consequently, an assessment made during the unexpired appeal period is void.[86] In some situations, it is difficult to apply the prohibition of Section 6213(a) of assessment and collection "until a Tax Court decision becomes final." Although under Section 7481(a)(1) a decision becomes final on expiration of the ninety days permitted for filing a notice of appeal, Section 7485 states that appeal of a Tax Court decision will not operate to continue to stay assessment and collection unless a notice of appeal and an adequate bond has been filed with the Tax Court. Consequently, if a taxpayer has filed only a no-

---

[81] Lyddon & Co. v. United States, 158 F. Supp. 951 (Cl. Ct.), cert. denied, 358 US 832 (1958); Lehigh Portland Cement Co. v. United States, 30 F. Supp. 217 (1939); Ryan v. Alexander, 118 F2d 744 (10th Cir.), cert. denied, 314 US 622 (1941); United States v. Teti, 75-2 USTC ¶ 9709 (D. Conn. 1975).

[82] IRC § 6213(a).

[83] IRC § 6215(a).

[84] IRC § 7485(a). For cases determining the amount of a bond to stay assessment, see Poinier v. Comm'r, 96 TC 1 (1991) (Tax Court has jurisdiction to reduce amount of bond).

[85] IRC § 7481(a)(1).

[86] Johnson v. United States, 990 F2d 41 (2d Cir. 1993) (assessment and lien filed fifty-three days after decision). *Johnson I* was a sequel to the *Johnson* case. After the Service made the first assessment and before the circuit court had ruled that the assessment was improper, the Service made a second assessment after the Tax Court's decision had become final. Johnson complained that this assessment was improper as well. Johnson v. United States, 77 AFTR2d 96-749 (D. Conn. 1996). The Service said that the the second assessment was proper under Section 6204(a), which allows the Service to make a supplemental assessment for the purpose of correcting the original assessment. The district court agreed, and because Johnson's reading would unduly restrict the Service's discretion to correct errors, rejected Johnson's argument that Section 6204(a) does not permit a supplemental assessment to be made until the first assessment error has been confirmed. At the time of the second assessment the circuit court had not yet decided *Johnson I.*

tice of appeal, but no adequate bond, the Service may assess—but only after the ninety-day period has expired. Section 7485 would be clearer if it read "the stay of assessment or collection will not continue" unless within the ninety-day period provided for filing a notice of appeal, a notice of appeal is filed, and the taxpayer has also posted an adequate bond with the Tax Court.

[3] Requirement That Notice of Deficiency Be Sent to Taxpayer

If a deficiency is found to exist in income, estate, or gift tax, or a miscellaneous excise tax on pensions and foundations, the Service is required to send a notice of the deficiency by certified or registered mail to the "taxpayer's last known address."[87] A statutory notice of deficiency consists of a letter stating the amount of the deficiency and a summary statement showing how the deficiency was computed.[88]

A notice of deficiency serves three purposes: (1) it serves a jurisdictional purpose because it gives the Tax Court jurisdiction to redetermine the proposed deficiency assessment; (2) it formally gives the taxpayer the opportunity to contest the Commissioner's determination by petitioning the Tax Court, without having to first pay the tax and then sue for a refund[89]; and (3) it gives the taxpayer notice of the Service's claim that additional tax is due and that this tax may be assessed unless the taxpayer takes action.[90] If the taxpayer does not file a petition in the Tax Court within the 90- or 150-day period, the Service may assess the deficiency without giving the taxpayer further notice.[91] Although not immediately apparent, there are marked similarities between the deficiency procedures and the procedures followed in refund suits. The notice of deficiency in a deficiency proceeding, for example, is comparable to a complaint in a refund suit. A notice of deficiency notifies the taxpayer of the Service's claim that there is a deficiency of a certain amount for a particular period. A complaint filed in a refund suit notifies the government of the tax-

---

[87] IRC §§ 6212(a), 6212(b)(1). It has been said that the requirement of certified or registered mailing under Section 6212(a) is "a safe harbor to be relied upon only in those situations in which the taxpayer did not receive actual notice." Balkissoon v. Comm'r, 995 F2d 525 (4th Cir. 1993) (notice not sent certified mail actually received; held valid on timely receipt).

[88] IRM 4.3.19, Statutory Notices of Deficiency Handbook, 1.6, Preparing Notices of Deficiency (July 21, 2000).

[89] Lyddon & Co. v. United States, 158 F. Supp. 951 (Ct. Cl.), cert. denied, 358 US 832 (1958). However, a taxpayer may lose this opportunity if he or she fails to prosecute the case in the Tax Court. See, e.g., Lukovsky v. Comm'r, 692 F2d 527 (8th Cir. 1982), cert. denied, 460 US 1084 (1983) (petition dismissed where taxpayer failed to substantiate deductions by claiming Fifth Amendment).

[90] IRC §§ 6212, 6213. See Tax Ct. R. 13(a).

[91] IRC § 6213(c).

payer's claim that a refund of a certain amount is believed to be due.[92] A complaint in a refund suit must be served on the government by serving the Attorney General and the Office of the United States Attorney for the appropriate judicial district.[93] The government must answer the complaint to challenge the refund claim.[94]

[a] Jurisdictional Nature of Notice

The statutory notice of deficiency is a jurisdictional prerequisite to Tax Court review. It establishes that the Service has determined that a deficiency, as defined in Section 6211(a), exists in a tax over which the Tax Court has jurisdiction. The Tax Court requires a petitioner to attach the notice of deficiency to the petition filed with the court to establish that the court has jurisdiction over the taxpayer's request for redetermination of the Service's deficiency determination.[95] Also, the taxpayer's petition must assign errors in the notice of deficiency and allege facts in support of the petitioner's assignments, and in this way the explanatory paragraphs of the notice become part of the basic pleadings in the Tax Court deficiency action.[96]

The Tax Court has priority in the judicial review of tax cases. Once a notice of deficiency has been sent and the taxpayer files a petition in the Tax Court, the taxpayer may not institute a refund suit for recovery of any part of the tax for the year(s) before the Tax Court.[97] The year before the Tax Court is a single cause of action that the taxpayer is not permitted to split between the Tax Court and a refund court.

---

[92] Fed. R. Civ. P. 4(i).

[93] Fed. R. Civ. P. 4(i).

[94] Fed. R. Civ. P. 7(a).

[95] Tax Ct. R. 34(b)(8).

[96] IRM 4.3.19, Statutory Notices of Deficiency Handbook, 1.6, Preparing Notices of Deficiency (July 21, 2000). This chapter of the handbook contains suggested language for inclusion in a notice of deficiency involving different issues, form letters, and component parts for statutory notices along with detailed instructions on the preparation of the notices.

[97] IRC § 6512(a); see Gustafson v. United States, 27 Fed. Cl. 451 (1993) (taxpayer amended return in year decided by Tax Court and attempted to sue for refund). There are four statutory exceptions, but they are limited and rarely occur. A taxpayer may sue for refund, after the Tax Court has decided the case, (1) to recover overpayments determined by the Tax Court's final decision; (2) to recover collected amounts in excess of the Tax Court's final decision; (3) to recover amounts collected after the expiration of the statute of limitations on collection has expired; and (4) to recover overpayments attributable to partnership items.

[b] Taxpayer Notification

Although no particular form is required for the notice of deficiency, the taxpayer must at least be given notice of the deficiency determination. The material sent to the taxpayer "must inform the taxpayer that a deficiency in tax has been determined and either must state the taxable period in respect to which it has been assessed or at least give enough information that the taxpayer reasonably could not be deceived as to the taxable period."[98] Although one of the purposes of a notice of deficiency is to give the taxpayer the opportunity to petition the Tax Court, a notice of deficiency need not, in order to be valid, "advise the taxpayer of his right to resort to the Tax Court."

Because Section 6212 does not make it clear, two views about what a notice of deficiency must contain have developed. One view is that to comply with the statutory requirement of Section 6212, the contents of the notice are irrelevant; the Service is only required to send the notice to the taxpayer at the taxpayer's last known address.[99] The other view is that the notice must have some content. *Scar v. Commissioner*[100] illustrates this view, which is that the notice must contain sufficiently accurate information to establish that the Service has made a "determination" about the taxpayer's return. Where the notice of deficiency reveals on its face that the Service has failed to make a determination about the return of the named taxpayer, the notice has been held to be a "naked assessment, and thus invalid."[101] In *Scar*, the Service sent a notice of deficiency to Scar disallowing losses he allegedly deducted attributable to a mining tax shelter investment. As it turned out, Scar had not invested in a mining shelter, but in a video production venture. Because the deficiency had no relationship to the taxpayer's return, the circuit court concluded that at least facially, the notice of deficiency did not reflect that the Service had made a

---

[98] Comm'r v. Forest Glen Creamery Co., 98 F2d 968, 971 (7th Cir. 1938), cert. denied, 306 US 639 (1939). The notice is valid even if it is not signed. Tavano v. Comm'r, 93-1 USTC ¶ 50,205 (11th Cir. 1993) (gathering cases). But the notice must show that the Service has followed the statutory requirement of Section 6212 by "determining" that a deficiency exists. See discussion at supra note 96. A prefiling notice letter sent by the Service to investors in tax shelters is not a notice of deficiency entitling taxpayers to petition the Tax Court. See, e.g., Abrams v. Comm'r, 84 TC 1308 (1985), aff'd, 814 F2d 1356 (9th Cir. 1987).

[99] Judge Learned Hand said that, "the notice (of deficiency) is only to advise the person who is to pay the deficiency that the Commissioner means to assess him; anything that does this unequivocally is good enough." Olsen v. Helvering, 88 F2d 650, 651 (2d Cir. 1937).

[100] Scar v. Comm'r, 814 F2d 136 (9th Cir. 1987) (divided court ruled that notice of deficiency in tax based on disallowance of losses in mining shelter, where taxpayer had invested in a videotape activity, was invalid); cf. Campbell v. Comm'r, 90 TC 110 (1988) (notice of deficiency mailed to taxpayer that had computational sheets relating to another taxpayer was valid.)

[101] Janis v. United States, 428 US 433 (1976).

"determination" as it was required to do. Where a facial no-determination is found, the Service is permitted to show that a determination has been made.[102] *Scar* focuses the inquiry on whether a determination has, in fact, been made, however correct or incorrect it may be.

There is also the view that the notice of deficiency must have some evidentiary support as well. When a notice of deficiency was based on a deficiency arising from dealings in narcotics, but the Service failed or refused to produce informants to testify about the taxpayer's illegal income-producing activities, the notice of deficiency was held invalid, the equivalent of a naked assessment.[103]

[c] Timely Notification

The date of mailing rather than the date on the deficiency notice determines the validity of the notice.[104] The Service has the burden of establishing both that a notice of deficiency was prepared and the date the notice was mailed. To accomplish this task, the Service has used the presumption of official regularity and U.S. Post Office (USPS) Form 3877, reflecting mailings of notices of deficiency. Some courts have accepted this evidence.[105] However, it has also been held that habit evidence standing alone does not meet the Service's burden of proof.[106]

Proof in these cases can be quite specific. When the Service mails a notice of deficiency, a USPS Form 3877 is completed, listing the name and address of the taxpayer, the type of mail used (i.e., certified or registered mail), the certified mail number, and the tax years. The notice of deficiency and Form 3877 are delivered to the USPS. A USPS employee compares the certified numbers and the names and addresses on the envelopes with those listed on the Form 3877, initials the form, and dates it with a postmark indicating USPS receipt. The USPS then returns the Form 3877 to the Service as a record of receipt.[107] Once the Service has produced this evidence, the taxpayer has the burden of coming forward with the evidence that the notice was not properly sent. Taxpayers have rarely made this showing, except when there was evidence that the Service did not use due diligence in sending the notice

---

[102] Clapp v. Comm'r, 875 F2d 1396, 1402 (9th Cir. 1989).

[103] Weimerskirsch v. Comm'r, 596 F2d 358 (9th Cir. 1979).

[104] See August v. Comm'r, 54 TC 1535 (1970); Byk v. Comm'r, 46 TCM 1189 (1983).

[105] United States v. Ahrens, 530 F2d 781 (8th Cir. 1976) (presumption of official regularity established mailing); United States v. Zolla, 724 F2d 808 (9th Cir.), cert. denied, 469 US 1067 (1984) (same).

[106] Pietanza v. Comm'r, 92 TC 729 (1989).

[107] IRM (Audit) Vol. II, § 4462.2, MT 4400-269 (Aug. 8, 1981) (Records of Mailing).

to the taxpayer's last known address because, for example, the USPS had returned the notice to the Service undelivered.[108]

[d] "Last Known Address" Requirement

Because no assessment of a deficiency may be made unless a notice of deficiency has been sent to the taxpayer's "last known address," the Service's failure to do so invalidates a wrongly addressed notice and any assessment the Service may have made.[109] The last known address requirement is substantially the same as procedures in the Federal Rules of Civil Procedure for the service of a summons and complaint in a civil action, which call for service to be made on an individual at the individual's "usual place of abode."[110] Nevertheless, the last known address issue has been perhaps one of the most vexatious issues in tax procedure. The "last known address" requirement is intended to assure that a taxpayer is given notice of the Service's impending assessment (unless the taxpayer files a petition in the Tax Court to challenge the Service's deficiency determination) and the rights and duties the taxpayer has under the Code. It follows that the requirement is intended to provide the taxpayer actual or constructive notice of the Service's notice of deficiency. When the Service sends an incorrectly addressed notice of deficiency, but the taxpayer has received it without any prejudicial delay, the notice may still be valid.[111] Just when a delay in receipt of actual notice is prejudicial to the taxpayer's filing of a Tax Court petition is not at all clear.[112] If the notice has been properly

---

[108] See, e.g., McPartlin v. Comm'r, 653 F2d 1185 (7th Cir. 1981); Powell v. Comm'r, 958 F2d 53 (4th Cir. 1992).

[109] IRC § 6213(a). See discussion infra ¶ 10.03[3][d].

[110] Fed. R. Civ. P. 4(e).

[111] Mulvania v. Comm'r, 81 TC 65, 67 (1983), aff'd, 769 F2d 1376 (9th Cir. 1985); Frieling v. Comm'r, 81 TC 42, 57 (1983); followed in Pugsley v. Comm'r, 749 F2d 691 (11th Cir. 1985). Compare Pyo v. Comm'r, 83 TC 626 (1984) (prejudicial delay found where notice of deficiency dated April 13, 1981, received about April 1, 1982); Brown v. United States, 91-2 USTC ¶ 50,537 (D. Md. 1991). See also Bonty v. Comm'r, TC Memo. 1997-372 (1997) (notice sent to wrong address, but taxpayers received the notice dated June 7, on June 28, some twenty-one days later; held, no prejudicial delay).

[112] Prejudicial delay has not been found when the taxpayer had actual notice of the notice when thirty days remained before a petition had to be filed. Loftin v. Comm'r, TC Memo. 1986-322 (1986). On the other hand, prejudicial delay has been found when the notice was received with eight days remaining before a petition had to be filed. Sicker v. Comm'r, 815 F2d 1400, 1401 (11th Cir. 1987), while another court found that receipt of the notice seventeen days before filing was prejudicial. Looper v. Comm'r, 73 TC 690, 699 (1980). For a case where the notice of deficiency was sent to the wrong address, but there was no showing of prejudice, see Bachynsky v. Comm'r, TC Memo. 1997-138 (1997) (undated notice mailed certified mail November 3, 1995, and received by the taxpayer on November 7, 1995, but the Tax Court received the petition on March 14, 1996, 132 days after the date the notice of deficiency was proved to have been sent). The Tax

mailed to the taxpayer's last known address, the taxpayer may not complain even if the taxpayer has not received actual notice.[113]

Generally, a taxpayer's last known address is the address shown on the return for the tax year in question or is the address shown on the taxpayer's most recently filed return. The Tax Court's definition of a "taxpayer's last known address" in *Abeles v. Commissioner*[114] is frequently cited:

> [A] taxpayer's "most recently filed return" is that return which has been properly processed by an IRS service center such that the address appearing on such return was available to [the Commissioner's] agent when that agent prepared to send a notice of deficiency of previously filed return.

Circuit courts have differed about the proper formulation. It is sometimes said that a presumption of reasonable diligence exists when the Service mails the deficiency notice to the address on the taxpayer's most recent return, unless the taxpayer gives the Service clear and concise notice of an address change.[115] It is also said that "the reasonableness of the Commissioner's belief as to what is the taxpayer's last known address is to be assessed as of the time of the IRS mailing . . . [and the] Commissioner has an obligation to exercise reasonable diligence to ascertain the taxpayer's correct address if prior to mailing the deficiency notice she has become aware that the address last known to the agency may be incorrect."[116] The Second Circuit has held that the address shown on

---

Court said, "[I]t is well settled that an improperly addressed notice is nonetheless valid if the taxpayer receives actual notice of the deficiency determination in a timely fashion, i.e., without prejudicial delay." Id., citing McKay v. Comm'r, 89 TC 1063, 1069 n.7 (1987), aff'd, 886 F2d 1237 (9th Cir. 1989); Mulvania v. Comm'r, 81 TC 65, 67 (1983), aff'd, 769 F2d 1376 (9th Cir. 1985).

[113] Hoffenberg v. Comm'r, 905 F2d 665 (2d Cir. 1990).

[114] Abeles v. Comm'r, 91 TC 1019 (1988) ("[a] taxpayer's last known address is that address which appears on the taxpayer's most recently filed return unless [the Service] has been given clear and concise notification of a different address"); King v. Comm'r, 857 F2d 676, 679 (9th Cir. 1988) (accord); Williams v. Comm'r, 947 F2d 1066 (9th Cir. 1991) (same) ("the address from the recently filed return is *available* to the agent issuing a notice of deficiency with respect to a previously filed return, if such address could be obtained by a computer transcript using the taxpayer's TIN [taxpayer identification number] in the case of a separately filed return").

There must be a reasonable amount of time between the filing of the return and the date of deficiency in order to permit processing the information. When a notice of deficiency was sent on June 17, 1987, the taxpayer's return, filed April 15, 1987, had his new address, but the information was not considered to be available to the agent issuing the notice of deficiency. Williams v. Comm'r, 947 F2d 1066 (9th Cir. 1991).

[115] Compare Word v. Comm'r, 907 F2d 517, 521 (5th Cir. 1990); see also Cyclone Drilling, Inc. v. Kelley, 769 F2d 662, 664 (10th Cir. 1985); McPartlin v. Comm'r, 653 F2d 1185 (7th Cir. 1981) (subsequently filed returns are relevant, but not dispositive);

[116] Gaw v. Comm'r, 45 F3d 461, 465 (DC Cir. 1995), followed in Follum v. United States, 128 F3d 118 (2d Cir. 1997).

the taxpayers' most recently filed return was not the taxpayers' last known address where a diligent search on the part of the Service would have revealed a different address.[117] In that case, the Service searched the administrative file and two Service databases, but did not search its Automated Insolvency System (AIS) database, which had received the taxpayers' correct address from the Special Procedures Unit of the Collection Division in connection with one of the taxpayers' personal bankruptcy proceedings. When the Service contended that agents responsible for preparing the taxpayers' notice of deficiency were unaware of the information in the AIS database, the court responded that "[a]n innocent taxpayer should not be penalized because the tax collector neglects to tell his right hand what his left hand is doing."[118]

Other circuit courts, especially the Ninth Circuit, have adopted the Tax Court's formulation, saying "a taxpayer's last known address is that address which appears on the taxpayer's most recently filed return, unless [the Service] has been given clear and concise notification of a different address."[119]

A taxpayer's last known address has also been interpreted to mean the last known permanent address or legal residence of the taxpayer or the last known temporary address of a definite duration to which all communications during the period are to be sent.[120] It is said that the last known address is the address to which, in light of all the circumstances, the Service reasonably believes the taxpayer wishes the notice to be sent.[121] In order for relief to be

---

[117] Sicari v. Comm'r, 98-1 USTC ¶ 50,237 (2d Cir. 1998).

[118] Quoting Crum v. Comm'r, 635 F2d 895 (DC Cir. 1980).

[119] Williams v. Comm'r, 947 F2d 37 (9th Cir. 1991); see also Brignand v. Comm'r, 76 AFTR2d 95-6733 (9th Cir. 1995) (in December 1986, the Service sent duplicate notices of deficiency to two addresses in Reno, Nevada; the taxpayer filed his 1986 return in January 1987; and the Service in April 1987 sent the notice of deficiency to the address in Saudi Arabia shown on the 1986 return; held, the April notice of deficiency was sent to the last known address, and so the Service was not required to send duplicate notices to all three addresses, as taxpayer argued).

[120] Gregory v. United States, 57 F. Supp. 962, 973 (Ct. Cl. 1944), cert. denied, 326 US 747 (1945); Weinroth v. Comm'r, 74 TC 430 (1980); see Marks v. Comm'r, 947 F2d 983 (DC Cir. 1991) (Service had no reason to believe temporary address was permanent or of definite duration). See also order of dismissal in Myerson v. Comm'r, Tax Court Docket No. 026737-96 (Feb. 3, 1998) (prison address that was nothing more than one in a series of numerous and transient places of incarceration was not taxpayer's last known address).

[121] Brown v. Comm'r, 78 TC 215, 219 (1982); Weinroth v. Comm'r, 74 TC 430 (1980). Notice that the focus is on the information available to the Service at the time it mails the notice of deficiency. Eschweiler v. United States, 946 F2d 45 (7th Cir. 1991) (gathering cases). This formulation has been adopted by some circuit courts. Mulder v. Comm'r, 855 F2d 208, 211 (5th Cir. 1988); Powell v. Comm'r, 958 F2d 53 (4th Cir. 1992).

When taxpayer and his wife separated, and taxpayer filed a Form 3198, Special Handling Notice, which a Service agent testified alerted the Service to a change of address for

granted, when the notice of deficiency is not mailed to the taxpayer's last known address, the taxpayer must also be prejudiced by the Service's failure to send the notice to the address required by Section 6212.

In a case where the notice was not mailed to the last known address and the taxpayer was prejudiced because he was unable to file a timely petition, the Tax Court granted a motion to dismiss for lack of jurisdiction, thus preventing collection.[122] However, in a case where the taxpayer received actual notice of the deficiency and had sufficient time to file a petition in the Tax Court, the Tax Court has denied the taxpayer's motion to dismiss.[123] If a notice was, in fact, mailed to the last known address, it is valid even if not actually received by the taxpayer.[124] If the Service sends a notice of deficiency by certified mail to the taxpayer and the taxpayer refuses delivery of the envelope containing the notice, the Ninth Circuit has ruled that the taxpayer has received actual notice, even when the Service may have acted improperly in sending the notice.[125] A taxpayer is also said to have the burden of providing

---

taxpayer, the district court held that the Service had failed to mail the notice of deficiency to taxpayer's last known address; therefore, the assessment and subsequent levy were invalid. Czajkowski v. Tindall & Assocs., PC, 78 AFTR2d 96-5269 (ED Mich. 1996).

[122] Weinroth v. Comm'r, 74 TC 430 (1980). See also Wilson v. Comm'r, TC Memo. 1997-515 (dismissal for lack of jurisdiction because address on deficiency notice inverted the taxpayer's correct address numbers and was not the taxpayer's last known address).

[123] Weinroth v. Comm'r, 74 TC 430 (1980). See also Wilson v. Comm'r, TC Memo. 1997-515 (dismissal for lack of jurisdiction because address on deficiency notice inverted the taxpayer's correct address numbers and was not the taxpayer's last known address). Looper v. Comm'r, 73 TC 690 (1980), acq. 1984-2 CB 1; Gray v. Comm'r, 73 TC 639 (1980); Lifter v. Comm'r, 59 TC 818 (1972); Robinson v. Comm'r, 57 TC 735 (1972). Some support exists for the proposition that the ninety-day period begins to run from the date of actual receipt, at least in cases where the notice has not been sent to the taxpayer's last known address. Sicker v. Comm'r, 815 F2d 1400 (11th Cir. 1987); Powell v. Comm'r, 958 F2d 53 (4th Cir. 1992) (gathering cases).

[124] United States v. Ahrens, 530 F2d 781 (8th Cir. 1976); Delman v. Comm'r, 384 F2d 929 (3d Cir. 1967), cert. denied, 390 US 952 (1968); Luhring v. Glotzbach, 304 F2d 556 (4th Cir. 1962); Boren v. Riddell, 241 F2d 670 (9th Cir. 1957); Lifter v. Comm'r, 59 TC 818 (1973). However, where the evidence is that the notice of deficiency had been returned to the Service, courts have held that the Service did not exercise reasonable diligence to ascertain the taxpayer's last known address. McPartlin v. Comm'r, 653 F2d 1185 (7th Cir. 1981) (failure to receive return receipt should have put the Service on notice); Powell v. Comm'r, 958 F2d 53 (4th Cir. 1992) (accord).

[125] Erhard v. Comm'r, 87 F3d 273 (9th Cir. 1996) (the court adopted a bright-line rule that actual notice occurs when the taxpayer has actual receipt, and the taxpayer may not defeat actual notice by refusing delivery, even if the Service's actions may not have been proper). See also Patmon & Young Professional Corp. v. Comm'r, TC Memo. 1993-143, aff'd, 55 F3d 216 (6th Cir. 1995) ("[o]nce [the Service] places the deficiency notice within the taxpayer's grasp, [it] satisfies the requirement of [S]ection 6212; if the taxpayer turns a blind eye to that information, [the taxpayer] does so at the [taxpayer's] own peril").

the Service with notice of a new address.[126] Absent notice, the Service may rely on the address listed on the taxpayer's return for the year at issue as the taxpayer's last known address.[127] Still, the Service must exercise reasonable diligence in ascertaining the taxpayer's address,[128] and if it knows or has reason to know of a change in address, it must send the notice to that address.[129]

---

[126] Alta Sierra Vista, Inc. v. Comm'r, 62 TC 367 (1974), aff'd, 538 F2d 334 (9th Cir. 1976). See Marvin v. Comm'r, 40 TC 982 (1963). If a formal notice with the information described infra ¶ 10.03[3][d][iii] is not given, it is not clear just who the Service will accept as a "responsible agent" for notification purposes. It need not be the revenue agent assigned to the return in issue if the taxpayer has already given notice of his or her new address to other agents in the same district who were responsible for returns for prior years. Weinroth v. Comm'r, 74 TC 430 (1980) (cases on the subject of notice reviewed); Pyo v. Comm'r, 83 TC 626 (1984). In *Pyo*, after the taxpayers moved from the address listed on the returns in issue, they filed later returns listing their new address, and the same district office auditing the returns in issue corresponded with them on the later years' returns. Nevertheless, the notice of deficiency was sent to the old address and returned to the Service. See Davis v. Comm'r, 661 F. Supp. 733 (MD Ala. 1987) ("[w]here a taxpayer has informed an internal [revenue] agent that she has separated from her husband, [a] notice of deficiency sent to her at her former husband's address is not sent to her 'last known address'").

Compare Marks v. Comm'r, 947 F2d 983 (DC Cir. 1991) (describing as "Chutzpah Doctrine" notion that notice was not sent to taxpayers' last known address when taxpayers failed to notify Service because they were fugitives from criminal prosecution); see also Eschweiler v. United States, 877 F2d 634 (7th Cir. 1989) (agent learned that lease of last known address had expired and that taxpayer was out on bond; but agent had no duty to inquire further, because taxpayer made no attempt to notify Service of new address).

[127] Luhring v. Glotzbach, 304 F2d 556 (4th Cir. 1962); Weinroth v. Comm'r, 74 TC 430 (1980); Tadros v. Comm'r, 763 F2d 89 (2d Cir. 1985) (neither a letter to the Service, nor a return filed after a notice of deficiency was sent, which both indicated the taxpayer's new address, constituted clear and concise notice to the Service of the taxpayer's change of address).

[128] Alta Sierra Vista, Inc. v. Comm'r, 62 TC 367 (1974), aff'd, 538 F2d 334 (9th Cir. 1976); Delman v. Comm'r, 384 F2d 929 (3d Cir. 1967), cert. denied, 390 US 952 (1968); Sorrentino v. Ross, 425 F2d 213 (5th Cir. 1970); Arlington Corp. v. Comm'r, 183 F2d 448 (5th Cir. 1952); United States v. Ahrens, 530 F2d 781 (8th Cir. 1976); United States v. Eschweiler, 877 F2d 634 (7th Cir. 1989); Cyclone Drilling, Inc. v. Kelley, 769 F2d 662 (10th Cir. 1985); McCormick v. Comm'r, 55 TC 138 (1970).

Due diligence on the part of the Service may require it to notify an attorney to file a power of attorney to receive a copy of a deficiency notice when the attorney has informed the Service that he represents the taxpayer, but does not have a power of attorney on file. Gaw v. Comm'r, 45 F3d 461 (DC Cir. 1995).

[129] Expanding Envelope & Folder Corp. v. Shotz, 385 F2d 402 (3d Cir. 1967) (Service failed to send notice to representative who had filed power); DiViaio v. Comm'r, 539 F2d 231 (DC Cir. 1976) (taxpayer's address in Atlanta penitentiary "well-known"); Johnson v. Comm'r, 611 F2d 1015 (5th Cir. 1980) (reasonable diligence not shown where taxpayers submitted power of attorney that superseded previous mailing address and orally notified Service of address change, and Service was conducting criminal investigation at new address); Grafton v. United States, 563 F. Supp. 39 (WD Mo. 1983). Compare Foster v. Comm'r, 43 TCM 731 (1982) (notice of deficiency properly mailed to address on

Accessible computer-based information showing the taxpayer's new address is not attributed to Service employees, but failure to search is a reflection on the "reasonableness" of Service action.[130]

[i] **The address of a representative or other agent.** A taxpayer's last known address may be the address of his or her representative. When a taxpayer's representative files a power of attorney requesting the Service to send all communications to the representative, the representative's address constitutes the taxpayer's last known address.[131] However, if the request simply asks that copies of notices and written communications (rather than all notices and communications) be sent to the representative, a notice sent only to the taxpayer, even if not received, complies with Section 6212.[132] These rules make it

---

power of attorney); Gibson v. United States, 761 F. Supp. 685 (CD Cal. 1991) (subsequent return with new address was filed; Service center had sent refund check to new address; and Service center's knowledge of new address was imputed to Audit Division).

[130] The Tax Court has stated, "Should a brief search of a similar [Service center] computer system disclose that a taxpayer is also the subject of an ongoing investigation of his tax liability for another year at another address . . . the presence of such easily accessible information would necessarily affect any determination whether respondent acts with reasonable diligence when he mails a statutory notice to another address." Pyo v. Comm'r, 83 TC 626 (1984). See also Weinroth v. Comm'r, 74 TC 430 (1980); Crum v. Comm'r, 635 F2d 895, 900 (DC Cir. 1980) (search for most recent address "would take less than a minute today"); Wallin v. Comm'r, 744 F2d 674 (9th Cir. 1984) (given the Service's capacity to perform computer search for Social Security numbers of both spouses listed on return, the Service must perform such a search in cases such as this, where it was aware that the taxpayer had moved).

Many courts have held that a later filed tax return with a new address gives the Service notice. Id. (gathering cases); compare Allen v. LeBaube, 84-2 USTC ¶ 9883 (WD Mo. 1984) ("[s]ubsequently filed returns provide IRS with notice of a change of address"). See also Monge v. Comm'r, 93 TC 22 (1989) (joint notice of deficiency sent to original address of a couple who later separated was invalid as to the wife because she filed a later return for a later year showing her new address, but valid as to the husband whose new address was shown only in a request for filing extension). For an analysis of the many decided cases involving the last known address issue, see Borison, "The Evolving Due Diligence Requirement of the Service in Determining a Taxpayer's Last Known Address," 41 Tax L. Rev. 111 (Fall 1985). See Sicari v. Comm'r, 98-1 USTC ¶ 50,237 (2d Cir. 1998).

[131] Rev. Proc. 61-18, 1961-2 CB 550; Expanding Envelope & Folder Corp. v. Shotz, 385 F2d 402 (3d Cir. 1967); McKay v. Comm'r, 886 F2d 1237 (9th Cir. 1989) (timely receipt of notice of deficiency by attorney for taxpayer held sufficient; taxpayer did not designate attorney to receive communications, but received duplicate of notice). If the notice is sent to the attorney by ordinary rather than certified or registered mail, the notice has been held insufficient. D'Andrea v. Comm'r, 263 F2d 904 (DC Cir. 1959).

[132] Mickens v. United States, 425 F. Supp. 732 (ED Mo. 1977), upholding Rev. Proc. 61-18, 1961-2 CB 550. Thus, the request in the power that copies of correspondence be sent to the taxpayer's attorney is not a direction to make a change in address, and the mailing of copies is a matter of courtesy, not affecting the requirements of Section 6212. Jack D. Houghton, 48 TC 656, 661 (1967). See McDonald v. Comm'r, 76 TC 750 (1981)

advisable for a taxpayer to send a notice of change of address to the Service by certified or registered mail, and include in the notice his name, identifying number, type of tax, and the new and old addresses.[133]

[ii] Notice to consolidated groups. Where a consolidated group of corporations is involved, regulations say that the common parent is the sole agent for each subsidiary in the group, duly authorized to act in its own name in all matters relating to the tax liability for the consolidated return year, and, generally, no subsidiary has authority to act for or to represent itself in any tax matter.[134] The common parent executes all forms, such as waivers of the statute of limitations, closing agreements, and the like, and such a document is considered as having been executed by the subsidiary. On the other hand, the Service may deal directly with the subsidiary as long as the Service notifies the common parent, and if such notice is given, the subsidiary will have full authority to act for itself. Accordingly, when the Service obtained waivers from the common parent, but sent thirty-day letters to both the subsidiary and the parent and sent separate notices of deficiency to the subsidiary and the parent, the Tax Court rejected the subsidiary's argument that the Service's course of separate dealings with the subsidiary precluded the common parent from continuing to act as the subsidiary's agent in executing the waiver, and, therefore, from making the notice of deficiency timely.[135]

[iii] The Service's change of address procedures. Regulations describe procedures the Service will follow in determining a taxpayer's last known address.[136] Adopting the view of the Tax Court in *Abeles*, the general rule is that a taxpayer's last known address is "the address that appears on the taxpayer's most recently filed" tax return.[137] It is not enough for the return to have been filed with the Service; the return must also have been "properly processed" by the Service, so that when Service personnel access the Service's database, the address is available for use in addressing the notice of deficiency. The address on the taxpayer's last return is the taxpayer's "last known" unless the Service is given "clear and concise notification of a different address." Generally, change of address information the taxpayer gives a third party, such as a payer or another government agency, does not serve as notice to the Service of a

---

(failure to send copy to attorney does not invalidate otherwise valid notice of deficiency mailed to taxpayer's last known address).

[133] See Estate of Clark v. Comm'r, 173 F2d 13 (2d Cir. 1949) (notice of change of address for gift tax purposes was not sufficient notice for estate tax purposes).

[134] Reg. § 1.1502-77(a).

[135] Lone Star Ins. Co. v. Comm'r, TC Memo. 1997-465 (1997).

[136] Reg. § 301.6212-2.

[137] Reg. § 301.6212-2(a). See Abeles v. Comm'r, 91 TC 1019 (1988).

taxpayer's change of address.[138] An exception to this rule is that each year, the Service will use the U.S. Postal Service's National Change of Address database to update its own record of the taxpayer's address.[139] The USPS's database retains change of address information for thirty-six months. If the Service's record of a taxpayer's name and address information matches the taxpayer's old address in the U.S. Postal Service's database "within certain tolerances," the new address in the database will be the last known address. The USPS database address is the taxpayer's last known address unless (1) the taxpayer files a tax return with an address different from the Postal Service database, which the Service processes or (2) following the Service's procedures for doing so, the taxpayer gives the Service clear and concise notice of an address different from the USPS database. While the Service will use the USPS's change-of-address database to update its own record, the Service will not consider a change of address the taxpayer gives the USPS to qualify as the taxpayer's last known address unless the taxpayer has notified the USPS "in sufficient time" for the Service to have reflected the change of address on its own database.[140]

The Service has explained how to inform it of a taxpayer's change of address.[141] According to the Service, when taxpayers wish to have their addresses of record changed from the one on the most recently filed return, they can do so by providing the Service center or the Chief (Taxpayer Service Division) with a clear and concise written notification of change of address. This notification should be a signed statement that includes the taxpayer's full name, new address, old address, and Social Security number and/or employee identification number. The Service developed Form 8822 to provide for clear and concise written notification to the Service. After filing a joint return, if either taxpayer changes address, both should send clear and concise written notification to the Service. The Service does not consider a notification to the USPS of change of address to allow forwarding of mail sent to the new address to constitute a clear and concise written notification of a change of address.

These requirements apply to notices that are to be sent to the taxpayer's last known address, including:

[138] Reg. § 301.6212-2(b)(1).

[139] Reg. § 301.6212-2(b)(2).

[140] Reg. § 301.6212-2(b)(3), Exs. 3, 4.

[141] Rev. Proc. 90-18, 1990-1 CB 491. Rev. Proc. 90-18 does not apply to notice requirements under Sections 6221 through 6245 regarding the treatment of partnership and Subchapter S items. Additionally, because of their unique processing requirements, Rev. Proc. 90-18 does not apply to: Form 5330 (Return of Excise Taxes Related to Employee Benefit Plans), Form 5500 (Annual Return/Report of Employee Benefit Plans With 100 or More Participants), Form 5500-C/R (Return/Report of Employee Benefit Plan With Fewer Than 100 Participants), and Form 5500EZ (Annual Return of One-Participant Owners and Their Spouses Pension Benefit Plan).

- A formal document request for the production of foreign-based documentation (Section 982(c)(1))
- A notice of disclosure proceedings (Section 6110(f)(3)(B))
- A notice of deficiency (Section 6212(b))
- A notice and demand for tax (Section 6303(a))
- A notice of revocation of a certificate of release of nonattachment of a lien (Section 6325(f)(2)(A))
- A notice of intention to levy (Section 6331(d)(2)(C))
- A copy of a notice of levy with respect to a life insurance or endowment contract (Section 6332(b)(1))
- Notices of seizure and sale (Sections 6335(a) and 6335(b))
- A notice of liability in transferee cases (Section 6901(g))
- A notice of a third-party summons (Section 7609(a)(2))

It is the taxpayer's duty to inform the Service of any change in address. If any of these notices are sent to the taxpayer's last known address, they are legally effective, even if the taxpayer does not receive them.

A tax return filed with new address information updates the taxpayer's address of record after proper processing, except for gift, estate, and generation-skipping transfer tax returns, which are kept separately and for which separate notice of change of address is required.

[e] Rescission of Notice of Deficiency

If the Service and a taxpayer can agree, a notice of deficiency that has been sent prematurely (e.g., because the taxpayer has extended the limitations period) can be rescinded.[142] If a notice of deficiency is rescinded, it has no effect for purposes of the prohibition against second notices of deficiency,[143] the restrictions on assessment during the period permitted for filing a Tax Court petition,[144] and the running of the limitations period on assessment.[145] A taxpayer has no right to file a Tax Court petition after agreeing to rescission of the notice.[146] A notice of deficiency may be rescinded for any of the following three reasons:

1. The notice was issued as a result of administrative error (e.g., to the wrong taxpayer, for the wrong period, or despite a properly executed consent extending the assessment period).

---

[142] IRC § 6212(d) (applicable for notices issued after December 31, 1986).

[143] IRC § 6212(c).

[144] IRC § 6213(a).

[145] IRC § 6512(a).

[146] The Service has issued rules for the rescission of a notice of deficiency. See Rev. Proc. 88-17, 1988-1 CB 692.

2. The taxpayer submits information establishing that the actual tax due is less than the amount in the notice.
3. The taxpayer requests an Appeals conference, and the Appeals Office consents because settlement is possible.

No rescission is permitted under any of the following four circumstances:

1. Disregarding the notice of deficiency, ninety days or less remain before expiration of the assessment period.
2. The taxpayer has failed to file a Tax Court petition within the time permitted by Section 6213(a).
3. The taxpayer has already filed a Tax Court petition.
4. The Service and the taxpayer have signed a Form 872-A (Special Consent to Extend the Time to Assess Tax).

Even if ninety days or less remain on the assessment period, a rescission is permitted provided that a Form 872 (Consent to Extend Time to Assess Tax) is executed before the assessment period expires (disregarding the notice of deficiency) and, on the date of rescission, the assessment period would have expired but for the statutory notice.[147]

[f] Further Notices

Once the Service has determined a deficiency and sent the taxpayer a notice of deficiency, and the taxpayer has timely filed a petition with the Tax Court for redetermination, the Service may not send any further deficiency notices to the taxpayer.[148] After the taxpayer receives the deficiency notice, and waives his right to file a petition with the Tax Court, the Service is no longer restricted from sending a second or further notice of deficiency.[149] In this situation, the Service is not precluded from sending a second notice of deficiency for the same taxable year,[150] asserting that a deficiency greater than that set forth in the original notice is due. In the Tax Court, the Service can raise the claim that a greater deficiency is due by way of an answer to the taxpayer's

---

[147] Form 8626 (Agreement to Rescind Notice of Deficiency) is used for rescinding a statutory notice. To enter into a rescission agreement, a taxpayer should call the person designated on the notice to find out how to contact the appropriate Appeals Office. Actual preparation and filing of the form is done by the Appeals Office.

[148] IRC § 6212(c)(1). See Zackim v. Comm'r, 887 F2d 455 (3d Cir. 1989) (where fraud is discovered after a decision of the Tax Court has been entered, the Service is not precluded by Section 6212(c) from sending a second notice of deficiency for the year).

[149] See infra ¶ 10.04[6].

[150] Goff v. Comm'r, 18 BTA 283 (1929). The language of this case is even broader than mere waiver by the taxpayer of his right to petition, speaking in terms of failure or declination to appeal the prior notice of deficiency. Id. at 288.

petition, and the Tax Court has jurisdiction to determine the increased deficiency.[151]

The restriction on issuing further notices of deficiency for the same taxable year after the taxpayer has filed a petition in the Tax Court also appears to be limited to deficiencies (1) for the same tax (2) of the same taxpayer (3) based on the same return. In *S-K Liquidating Co.*,[152] the Commissioner issued two notices of deficiency, one for corporate income taxes and another for income taxes required to be withheld by the taxpayer as a withholding agent for amounts paid to nonresident aliens. The second deficiency notice was held not to be a prohibited second notice because the notices were based on two separate returns and two different tax liabilities, albeit both for income tax.[153] Similarly, a notice sent to a taxpayer as a transferee for taxes on the transferor's income does not preclude the sending of a notice on the transferee's own income.[154]

¶ 10.04 EXCEPTIONS TO RESTRICTIONS ON DEFICIENCY ASSESSMENTS: SUMMARY ASSESSMENTS

As described earlier, under normal assessment procedures, the Service is prohibited from assessing and collecting a tax deficiency from a taxpayer until the taxpayer has been sent a notice of the deficiency and has been given a ninety-day period within which to file a petition for redetermination in the Tax Court. If a petition is filed, the Service's authority to assess the deficiency is further suspended until the Tax Court's decision has become final. Four exceptions exist to restrictions on assessment of deficiencies, and these exceptions allow the amount of the deficiency to be summarily assessed. The exceptions are: (1) mathematical errors; (2) tentative carryback adjustments; (3) assessment of the amount paid; and (4) jeopardy assessments. In addition, the restrictions on assessment do not apply where a taxpayer permits the 90-day (or 150-day) period to expire without filing a petition in the Tax Court and where the taxpayer waives the restrictions on assessment.

---

[151] IRC § 6214(a).

[152] S-K Liquidating Co., 64 TC 713 (1975).

[153] See also Rev. Rul. 75-552, 1975-2 CB 476, which looks to the different filing requirements to find income and withholding taxes separate and distinct.

[154] See Michael v. Comm'r, 22 BTA 639 (1931), aff'd per curiam, 75 F2d 966 (2d Cir.), cert. denied, 296 US 579 (1935).

[1] Mathematical Errors

The Service may summarily assess additional tax due as a result of a mathematical error without sending the taxpayer a notice of deficiency and an opportunity to petition the Tax Court.[155] When the Service uses the summary assessment procedure for mathematical or clerical errors, the taxpayer must be given an explanation of the asserted error[156] and a period of sixty days to request that the Service abate its assessment.[157] The Service may not proceed to collect the amount of the assessment until the taxpayer has agreed to it or has allowed the sixty-day period for objecting to expire.[158] If the taxpayer files a request for abatement of the assessment specified in the notice, the Service must abate the assessment.[159] Any reassessment of the abated amount is subject to the ordinary deficiency procedures. This procedure is the only one a taxpayer may use for contesting an assessment arising out of a mathematical or clerical error. The explanation of the error sent to the taxpayer is not a notice of deficiency and does not entitle the taxpayer to file a petition in the Tax Court.[160] Thus, collection of the assessed amount is not prohibited for ninety days after the notice as it would be for a notice of deficiency, but only for the sixty-day period for requesting an abatement.

The term "mathematical or clerical error" is defined to mean[161]

- "[A]n error in addition, subtraction, multiplication or division shown on the return"[162] (e.g., 2 + 2 = 5 and 7 − 0 = 0). However, the Service must be careful that "what appears to be an error in addition or subtraction is not in reality an error in transcribing a number from a work sheet, with the final figure being correct even though an intermediate step appears to be wrong."[163]
- Incorrect use of a Service table if the error is apparent from the existence of other information on the return; for example, where the taxpayer uses a tax rate schedule for single taxpayers but has indicated on the return that he is married filing separately.

---

[155] IRC § 6213(b)(1).

[156] IRC § 6213(b)(1).

[157] IRC § 6213(b)(2)(A).

[158] IRC § 6213(b)(2)(B).

[159] IRC § 6213(g).

[160] IRC §§ 6213(b)(1), 6213(b)(2). See Adler v. Comm'r, 85 TC 535 (1985) (depletion reported in error and mistake in amount of drilling costs made on Form 4625 held not "mathematical errors" because they "were not obvious on their face, and there was nothing else in (taxpayer's) return which would have made it apparent that they were errors").

[161] IRC § 6213(g).

[162] IRC § 6213(g)(2)(A).

[163] Staff of Joint Comm. on Tax'n, 94th Cong., 2d Sess., General Explanation of the Tax Reform Act of 1976, at 372–374, reprinted in 1976-3 CB (vol. 2) 384–386.

- Inconsistent entries on the return; for example, where the taxpayer lists six personal exemptions but multiplies the exemption amount by seven. The Service must be careful when it is uncertain whether the taxpayer has omitted an exemption.[164]
- Omission of information required to be supplied on the return in order to substantiate an item on that return; that is, the Service is permitted to deny beneficial treatment unless the taxpayer supplies the required information.
- An entry of a deduction or credit item in an amount that exceeds a statutory limit that is either (1) a specified monetary amount or (2) a percentage, ratio, or fraction (if the items entering into the application of that limit appear on that return); for example, where a taxpayer who is not married and is filing a joint return claims an excessive dividend exclusion or claims a standard deduction greater than the dollar or percentage limits applicable to that taxpayer.[165]

[2] Tentative Carryback Adjustments

An exception to normal deficiency procedures is provided for assessments arising out of tentative carryback or refund adjustments. After a taxpayer has filed a carryback claim under Section 6411, the Service may decide that the amount it has applied, credited, or refunded to the taxpayer exceeds the overassessment resulting from the carryback. To collect this excess credit or refund, the Service is permitted to assess the excess amount as a deficiency "as if it were due to mathematical error appearing on the return."[166] Where a taxpayer files a

---

[164] Inconsistent entries on a return constitute a clerical or mathematical error only where it is apparent which of the inconsistent entries is correct and which is incorrect. GCM 39,131 (1984). For example, a discrepancy in the tax withheld from a nonresident alien may not be clearly traceable to the incorrect use of a tax table, but rather may be the result of using the wrong income code, country code, or tax table computation. Where this uncertainty exists, summary assessment procedures should not be used. Id.

[165] Derochmont v. Comm'r, 86-2 USTC ¶ 9726 (ED Pa. 1986) (assessment of amount of erroneous refunds the taxpayer had fraudulently obtained by filing a return falsely overstating the amount of tax withheld held to be proper as the assessment of a mathematical error).

[166] IRC § 6213(b)(3); Reg. § 301.6213-1(b)(2). The same procedure applies to an excess refund and the like attributable to a tentative refund claim under a claim of right adjustment. In abusive tax shelter cases, the Service has used the Section 6213(b)(3) assessment procedure when an application for a tentative carryback adjustment under Section 6411 is filed. Reacting to problems it had in recovering tentative refunds improperly claimed on abusive tax shelters, the Service summarily assesses the portion of the tentative refund claim attributable to an abusive shelter and offsets the amount assessed against the scheduled refund. Temp. Reg. § 301.6231(c)-1T(b).

claim for refund based on a tentative carryback of a net operating loss that turns out to have been overstated, and as a result the Service erroneously paid the taxpayer a refund, the Service may assess the amount erroneously refunded without regard to the normal restrictions on assessment. Unlike other mathematical error assessments, it appears that the Service need not send the taxpayer notice of its action, give the taxpayer sixty days to request abatement of the assessment, and refrain from collecting the assessment until the taxpayer agrees to it or fails to file an objection to the assessment within the sixty-day period.[167] The Service can also recover an erroneous refund or credit based on a carryback claim by sending a notice of deficiency[168] or by instituting a suit for erroneous refund under Section 7405.

[3] Payment

As discussed earlier, when a return is filed showing a tax due, the amount must be assessed. If a taxpayer makes payment of the amount of tax the Service has determined to be due before the Service mails a notice of deficiency, the Service is not prohibited by Section 6213 from assessing the amount paid. In this situation, the assessment is discretionary with the local office or Service center director. An amount may be assessed "if such action is deemed to be proper."[169] Any paid but unassessed amount is held in suspense. However, if the amount is assessed, the assessment is taken into account in determining whether there remains a deficiency for which a notice of deficiency must be issued. If assessment is made, there is no deficiency for the Tax Court to review and, consequently, the taxpayer must follow the refund procedures to obtain judicial review in a district court or the claims court. If, after the notice of deficiency is mailed to the taxpayer, payment is made with respect to the deficiency, the amount of the payment may be assessed irrespective of the deficiency assessment restrictions.[170] However, neither payment nor any assessment deprives the Tax Court of jurisdiction to entertain a petition to redetermine the deficiency.[171]

---

[167] Section 6213(b)(3) provides that the assessment is made as if the deficiency were due to a mathematical error "without regard to the provisions of paragraph 2 [of Section 6213(b) dealing with the abatement of mathematical or clerical errors]. . . ."

[168] Reg. § 301.6213-1(b)(2)(ii). For judicial approval of this deficiency notice method, see Pesch v. Comm'r, 78 TC 100 (1982); Baldwin v. Comm'r, 97 TC 704 (1991) (deficiency procedure approved where tentative carryback resulted in credit of tax rather than refund as in Pesch, and there was no error in original return for carryback year as filed).

[169] Reg. § 301.6213-1(b)(3).

[170] IRC § 6213(b)(4); Reg. § 301.6213-1(b)(3).

[171] IRC § 6213(b)(4).

[4] Jeopardy Assessments

If an authorized field office director believes that the assessment or collection of a tax will be jeopardized by delay, the tax may be assessed immediately as a termination assessment under Section 6851 or a jeopardy assessment under Section 6861,[172] although postassessment restrictions may nullify the assessment.[173] Thus, even with immediate assessments, a distinction exists between those where no restrictions apply and those where some form of restriction, albeit postassessment, is imposed.

[5] Failure to File Petition

The Service is required to give a resident taxpayer ninety days from the date of the sending of a notice of deficiency to file a petition in the Tax Court. At the expiration of the applicable period, if the taxpayer has not filed a petition in the Tax Court, the Service may assess the deficiency and demand payment.[174]

[6] Waiver of Restrictions

A taxpayer may at any time waive the restrictions on assessment by signing a notice of waiver form.[175] A waiver may apply to all or any part of a deficiency, thereby allowing a taxpayer to agree to the summary assessment of a portion of a proposed deficiency while the remaining unagreed portion is reserved for Tax Court review. The waiver form must be filed with and accepted on behalf of the district director.[176] A waiver is not effective if it has not been acted upon by the district director, although once it has been acted upon, it may not be withdrawn.[177] A waiver of the restrictions on deficiency assessment

---

[172] IRC § 6213(a).

[173] See infra ¶ 10.05.

[174] IRC § 6213(c).

[175] IRC § 6213(d). The Service uses forms in the 870 series for waivers of the restrictions on assessment.

[176] Statutorily, a waiver of the restrictions on assessment and collection need not be accepted by the Service. IRC § 6213(d). However, waivers are usually incorporated in a revenue agent's report reflecting an agreed case. These reports are reviewed. See Chapter 8. Accordingly, the agreement form containing the waiver states, "It is understood that this report is subject to acceptance by the District Director." See also Reg. § 301.6213(d). In this context, the taxpayer's waiver is subject to acceptance by the Review Staff. However, as a matter of law, interest would be suspended on the amount covered by the waiver on the thirty-first day after the waiver is filed. IRC § 6601(c). See Chapter 8.

[177] Reg. § 301.6213-1(d).

surrenders the taxpayer's right to prepayment Tax Court review.[178] Once the assessment is made, the taxpayer must pay the amount of the assessment; if the taxpayer chooses to contest the matter, he or she must (1) file a claim for refund and (2) after six months (or an earlier denial of the claim), institute a refund suit in a district court or the Court of Federal Claims.

¶ 10.05 JEOPARDY AND TERMINATION ASSESSMENTS

Three types of assessments may be classified as jeopardy assessments: (1) jeopardy assessments of income, estate, or gift tax; (2) termination assessments of income tax; and (3) possessor-of-cash assessments. All three assessments are collection devices the Service is authorized to use to collect tax where the delay of following normal prepayment deficiency procedures might ultimately jeopardize or endanger collection of tax. To protect assessment and collection in these circumstances, the Code authorizes the Service to make immediate assessment of tax without prior notice, and summary enforced collection action before judicial review of the Service's determination. In making jeopardy or termination assessments, the Service's policy is that these assessments "are to be used sparingly and care should be taken to avoid excessive and unreasonable assessments. They should be limited amounts which reasonably can be expected to protect the Government."[179]

Both jeopardy and termination assessments are made for the same reason—jeopardy in collection—but they are made at different times. Jeopardy assessments are made only after the taxpayer has filed a full period return or a deficiency has been (or can be) determined.[180] A jeopardy assessment may be made after the taxpayer's return for the taxpayer's tax year is due and the Service believes collection of an income, estate, or gift tax is in jeopardy. To protect ultimate collection, the Service is authorized to immediately make a jeopardy assessment of the tax.[181] A termination assessment is made in a more extreme situation of jeopardy. A termination assessment may be made even before the taxpayer's return for the current or the preceding year is due and the Service believes that collection of tax is in jeopardy. To protect collection,

---

[178] When a waiver on Form 870-AD was qualified, the right to Tax Court review was found to be retained. See the saga of Mary Frances Stroman. Stroman v. McCanless, 391 F. Supp. 1344 (ND Tex. 1975); Stroman v. Comm'r, 37 TCM 444 (1978); Stroman v. Comm'r, 77 TC 514 (1981), aff'd, 692 F2d 1 (5th Cir. 1982).

[179] IRM 1.2.1, Policies of the IRS Handbook 1.4.27, P-4-88, Jeopardy Assessments, and 1.4.28, P-4-89, Termination Assessments (Jan. 6, 1999).

[180] See Veeder v. Comm'r, 36 F2d 342, 344 (7th Cir. 1929); Ludwig Littauer & Co., 37 BTA 840, 842 (1938).

[181] IRC § 6861(a).

the Service may terminate the taxpayer's taxable year, and immediately make a termination assessment of income tax for the year.[182] In contrast to a jeopardy assessment, therefore, a termination assessment is made before the taxpayer has filed a full period return for the current year or the taxpayer has not filed a return for the preceding tax year because it is not yet due; for example, after income is earned during the course of a taxable year or comes to light under circumstances where collection would be endangered if the taxpayer's normal taxable year were permitted to close and the prepayment deficiency procedures were used.[183]

The possessor-of-cash assessment provides a statutory presumption that assists the Service in making a jeopardy or termination assessment.[184] For purposes of a termination or jeopardy assessment, Section 6867 provides that if an individual found in physical possession of cash or its equivalent in excess of $10,000 does not claim the cash as his or hers or as belonging to another person who can be easily identified and who acknowledges that he or she owns the cash, several presumptions are made: (1) The cash is presumed to be from a single individual; (2) the cash represents gross income for the taxable year in which the possession of the cash is discovered; and (3) the collection of tax is presumed to be jeopardized by delay.

Other types of jeopardy and termination assessments may be made. Section 6862 provides similar authority for the assessment of taxes other than income, estate, or gift taxes, such as employment and excise taxes. Section 6852 provides for a termination assessment against an exempt organization that engages in flagrant political expenditures in violation of its exempt status under Section 501(c)(3).

Other Code provisions provide protection to jeopardy and termination assessment taxpayers. Both jeopardy and termination assessment taxpayers will receive a notice of deficiency, and thus will ultimately have an opportunity for judicial review.[185] The taxpayer may convince the Service to abate a jeopardy assessment on the ground that there is no jeopardy in collection.[186] By posting a bond, a taxpayer will be able to stay collection of termination and jeopardy assessments.[187] Accelerated due process review of termination and jeopardy assessments as well as jeopardy levies is made available by Section 7429, which requires the Service to review the assessment and levy administratively, and requires district courts and the Tax Court to judicially review termination and jeopardy assessments.

---

[182] IRC § 6851(a).

[183] Ludwig Littauer & Co., 37 BTA 840 (1938).

[184] IRC § 6867(a).

[185] IRC § 6861(b) (jeopardy assessment); IRC § 6851(b) (termination assessment).

[186] IRC § 6861(g).

[187] IRC § 6863(a).

[1] The Common Condition of Jeopardy and Termination Assessments: Jeopardy in Collection

Jeopardy and termination assessments each require the Service to determine that assessment or collection of a deficiency will be in jeopardy if the normal assessment and collection procedures are followed. Collection of tax is considered to be in jeopardy when one or more of the following conditions is present:[188] (1) the taxpayer is or appears to be planning ("designing") to leave the United States quickly or to conceal himself[189]; (2) the taxpayer is or appears to be planning to place property, including retirement plan assets, beyond the Service's reach by removing it from the United States, by concealing or dissipating the property, or by transferring the property to another person[190]; (3) the taxpayer's financial solvency (excluding accrued tax liabilities) is or appears to be imperiled[191]; or (4) the taxpayer has in his or her physical possession more than $10,000 in cash, or its equivalent, and denies ownership of the cash, yet refuses to identify the owner of the cash.[192]

Flight, transfer or concealment of assets, and insolvency are evidence of jeopardy, and so the Service instructs examiners to gather evidence proving these conditions before a jeopardy or termination assessment is made. A nonexclusive list of factors that are considered to establish flight, transfer or concealment of assets, and insolvency are set out in Form 10.1.[193] When an individual found to be in physical possession of cash in excess of $10,000, or its equivalent, does not claim the cash as his or hers or as belonging to another person whose identity can be readily ascertained and who acknowledges possession of such cash, a statutory presumption has been created. As a result, when the foundational facts are present, collection of tax is presumed to be in

---

[188] IRM 1.2.1, Policies of the IRS Handbook 1.4.27, P-4-88, Jeopardy Assessments, and 1.4.28, P-4-89, Termination Assessments (Jan. 6, 1999).

[189] See, e.g., Irving v. Gray, 479 F2d 20 (2d Cir. 1973) (the Howard Hughes hoax); Rogan v. Mertens, 153 F2d 937 (9th Cir. 1946) (the design must be of a person in the United States who plans to depart, not a person who has departed).

[190] Perhaps because of the possibility that proceeds of a sporting event may be dissipated or hidden in or outside the United States, termination assessments have been made to ensure collection. See, e.g., United States v. Championship Sports, Inc., 284 F. Supp. 501 (SDNY 1968) (one of the Patterson-Johansson fights). The Service could be expected to take the same action in almost any situation where large sums of money come to light. McGrew v. United States, 85-2 USTC ¶ 9671 (MD Fla. 1985) (jeopardy assessment of Section 6700 penalty where promoter attempted to transfer funds to foreign bank).

[191] IRM 4.3.9, Jeopardy/Termination Assessments Handbook, 2.4.1.1.3, Insolvency (June 30, 1999).

[192] IRC § 6867.

[193] IRM 4.3.9, Jeopardy/Termination Assessments Handbook, 1.6, Conditions (June 30, 1999), and Handbook, 2.4.1.1, Documenting Conditions (June 30, 1999).

jeopardy.[194] Even if there is sufficient evidence of jeopardy to support a jeopardy or termination assessment, the policy of the Service is to require high-level review in "any case which might cause inconvenience to the general public"; for example, when a jeopardy assessment is recommended against a bank, newspaper, insurance company, hospital, or public utility company.[195]

---

[194] IRC § 6867(a) ("it shall be presumed . . . that the collection of tax will be jeopardized by delay").

[195] IRM 1.2.1, Policies of the IRS Handbook 1.4.27, P-4-88(4), Jeopardy Assessments, and 1.4.28, Termination Assessments (approved Jan. 6, 1999); IRM 4.3.9, Jeopardy/Termination Assessments Handbook, 1.4.1, Jeopardy Assessment (June 30, 1999). IRM 4.3.9, Jeopardy/Termination Assessments Handbook, 1.3.1, Prior National Office Notification (June 30, 1999).

CHECKLIST 10.1

FACTORS ESTABLISHING JEOPARDY

1. Factors establishing flight include the following considerations.[196]

   a. Is there evidence which would indicate that if the taxpayer were free on bond, he/she would flee the United States or conceal him/herself?

   b. What is the taxpayer's citizenship status? A resident alien? A nonresident alien temporarily in the United States? An illegal alien? If the taxpayer is an alien legally in the United States, would his/her conviction on a specific offense result in his/her deportation?

   c. Does the taxpayer have a passport? If so, is it in his/her name or in the name of an alias?

   d. Does the taxpayer have any previous convictions for offenses that would indicate that he/she would flee?

   e. Is the taxpayer wanted by the police as a fugitive from another jurisdiction?

   f. Is there any indication that the taxpayer was about to leave the country, such as airline tickets, seized from his/her possession at the time of arrest?

2. Factors establishing concealment/transfer of assets include the following considerations.[197]

   a. Does the taxpayer own any fixed assets, or does he/she deal solely in cash?

   b. If the taxpayer drives a car, is the car registered in his/her name or is he/she using a nominee?

   c. What are the circumstances concerning the taxpayer's residence? If he/she lives in leased premises, are they leased to him/her or to someone acting as a nominee? If the taxpayer was residing in a single-family house, was the title held in his/her name or in the name of a nominee?

   d. If the taxpayer was arrested with a large sum of money on his/her person, what are the circumstances concerning this money? Were there indications that the money belonged to him/her?

   e. Has the taxpayer ever used an alias to conceal his/her identity?

   f. At the time of a taxpayer's arrest, was there an attempt, by the taxpayer, to destroy evidence?

3. Factors establishing insolvency include the following considerations.[198]

   a. Are there any Taxpayer Delinquent Accounts (TDAs) open with respect to the taxpayer under his/her name, or any alias he/she may have used in the past?

---

[196] IRM 4.3.9, Jeopardy/Termination Assessments Handbook, 2.4.1.1.1, Flight (June 30, 1999).

[197] IRM 4.3.9, Jeopardy/Termination Assessments Handbook, 2.4.1.1.2, Transfer/Concealment of Assets (June 30, 1999).

[198] IRM 4.3.9, Jeopardy/Termination Assessments Handbook, 2.4.1.1.3, Insolvency (June 30, 1999).

   b. Did a search of the local court records reveal outstanding judgments
      against the taxpayer?
   c. Has the taxpayer ever been adjudicated a bankrupt?

  4. Financial solvency of the taxpayer must be threatened or there can be no
     jeopardy/termination.

[2] Jeopardy Assessments

The normal restrictions on the assessment of a deficiency in income, estate, or
gift taxes, and in miscellaneous excise taxes on foundations and pension plans
do not apply if the Service "believes" that assessment or collection of the deficiency will be "jeopardized by delay."[199] As Section 6861 states,

> If the Secretary believes that the assessment or collection of a deficiency,
> as defined in section 6211, will be jeopardized by delay, he shall, not-
> withstanding the provisions of section 6213(a) [the prohibition on assess-
> ment or collection during the ninety-day period following the sending of a
> notice of deficiency], immediately assess such deficiency (together with
> all interest, additional amounts, and additions to the tax provided for by
> law), and notice and demand shall be made by the Secretary for the pay-
> ment thereof.

Once the requisite belief is entertained, therefore, Sections 6861 and 6331(a)
authorize the Service to (1) assess the deficiency; (2) deliver a notice and demand for immediate payment of the assessed tax; and (3) levy on the taxpayer's property if the taxpayer fails to pay the assessed tax.

   Although a jeopardy assessment may be made without prior issuance of a
statutory notice of deficiency, restrictions are imposed after the assessment is
made. These restrictions are (1) the prompt sending of a notice of deficiency
and (2) a stay of the sale of seized property.

[a] Sending Notice of Deficiency

   A critical requirement of a jeopardy assessment for taxpayers is that, if
the jeopardy assessment is made before any notice of deficiency for the tax to
which the jeopardy assessment relates has been sent to the taxpayer, the Service must mail a notice of deficiency to the taxpayer according to the rules of
Section 6212 (mailing by certified mail to the taxpayer's last known address)
within sixty days after making the assessment. Before a decision of the Tax
Court, the Service may make a jeopardy assessment of a deficiency greater or
less than the notice of which has been mailed to the taxpayer. The Service is

---

[199] IRC §§ 6213(a), 6861(a).

not bound by the provisions of Section 6212(c) prohibiting the determination of additional deficiencies, and it may make a jeopardy assessment whether or not the taxpayer has theretofore filed a petition with the Tax Court.

Apart from the important fact that an assessment has been made and collection activity has already begun, the judicial remedies available to a jeopardy assessment taxpayer are substantially the same as those available to the normal taxpayer. If a jeopardy assessment is made before the statutory notice of deficiency has been sent to the taxpayer, the Service must send the notice within sixty days after making the assessment.[200] If the notice of deficiency is not sent within the sixty-day period, the assessment is void.[201] Nothing in the statute prohibits the Service from making another jeopardy assessment and then sending the statutory notice of deficiency within the sixty-day period. In practice, the problem usually is what should be done with the money or property seized under the invalid assessment. There is some support for requiring the Service to return the seized money or property.[202] On the other hand, where there were other valid assessments outstanding, some courts have allowed the Service to apply seized funds to the valid assessments.[203] When the Service retains funds, however applied, the taxpayer must file a claim for refund within the period provided in Section 6512(b) to obtain a refund of the seized funds.[204]

On receiving the notice of deficiency, the taxpayer may file a petition in the Tax Court. Alternatively, the taxpayer may pay the amount of the assessment (including any amounts seized), file a claim for refund and, after six months (or sooner if the claim is disallowed), start a refund action in a district court or the claims court. A jeopardy assessment gives the taxpayer an opportunity for Tax Court review on the merits of the assessment. However, unlike the ordinary taxpayer, the jeopardy taxpayer loses the use of whatever property the Service has seized while the Tax Court decides the case. A jeopardy assessment may be made in an amount greater or less than the amount covered by the notice already mailed to the taxpayer, regardless of whether the jeop-

---

[200] IRC § 6861(b).

[201] See Laing v. United States, 423 US 161 (1976); Causey v. United States, 43 AFTR2d 79-636 (D. Minn. 1978) (both involving termination assessments); Perlowin v. Sassi, 711 F2d 910 (9th Cir. 1983); Dorsey v. United States, 54 AFTR2d 84-5803 (D. Cal. 1984). See also Berry v. Westover, 70 F. Supp. 537 (SD Cal. 1947).

[202] Campbell v. United States, 592 F2d 309 (6th Cir. 1979) (funds seized after defective jeopardy assessment did not constitute an overpayment the Service could apply to a second jeopardy assessment); Baylor v. United States, 76-2 USTC ¶ 9654 (EDNY 1976); Dorsey v. United States, 54 AFTR2d 84-5803 (D. Cal. 1984).

[203] Estate of McDonald v. United States, 79-1 USTC ¶ 9182 (ND Cal. 1979); Causey v. United States, 43 AFTR2d 79-636 (D. Minn. 1978); Boyd v. United States, 439 F. Supp. 907 (ED Pa. 1977); Sellers v. Comm'r, 77-1 USTC ¶ 9377 (ND Ga. 1977); United States v. Cooper, 435 F. Supp. 3 (DDC 1976); Harris v. United States, 412 F. Supp. 24 (ED Mich. 1976).

[204] See Hollie v. Comm'r, 73 TC 1198 (1980).

ardy taxpayer has already filed a Tax Court petition. It should be noted that determination of further deficiencies is prohibited against the normal taxpayer.

Before the Tax Court decision is rendered, the Service is permitted to make additional jeopardy assessments or abate all or part of the assessments; however, the Service must notify the Tax Court of any such action. The Tax Court then has jurisdiction to redetermine the entire amount of the deficiency and "of all amounts assessed at the same time in connection therewith."[205] However, if the jeopardy assessment is made after the Tax Court's decision is rendered, the amount of the assessment is limited to the amount of the deficiency the Tax Court determines in its decision.[206] After the Tax Court's decision has become final or after the taxpayer has filed a petition for review of the Tax Court's decision, the Service's power to make a jeopardy assessment expires.[207] Once the Tax Court decision has become final, the amount determined to be due is collected in the usual manner by the issuance of notice and demand. Any amount by which the jeopardy assessment exceeds the Tax Court's determination is abated. Any excessive collection similarly must be credited or refunded, but no claim for refund need be filed.[208]

[b] The Tax Court and Jeopardy Assessments

At any time before the Tax Court enters a decision, the Service may abate the jeopardy assessment, or any unpaid portion of it, to the extent the Service believes the assessment is excessive in amount. The Service must notify the Tax Court of the amount of a jeopardy assessment, or the abatement, if the taxpayer has filed a petition with the Tax Court before the Service has made the assessment, or, if after the jeopardy assessment, the taxpayer has filed a petition with the Tax Court. In turn, the Tax Court has jurisdiction to redetermine at the same time and in the same proceeding the entire amount of the deficiency and all amounts the Service has assessed. After a decision of the Tax Court, the amount of the jeopardy assessment may be only in the amount the Tax Court has determined in its decision.[209] The Service's authority to make a jeopardy assessment expires when the decision of the Tax Court has become final or after the taxpayer has filed a petition for review, that is, an appeal, of the decision of the Tax Court.[210]

---

[205] IRC § 6861(c). Compare this sliding "deficiency" with the amended return regulations.

[206] IRC § 6861(d).

[207] IRC § 6861(e).

[208] IRC §§ 6402, 6861(f).

[209] IRC § 6861(d).

[210] IRC § 6861(e).

[c] Stay of Sale

The right to receive a notice of deficiency within sixty days after a jeopardy assessment is made would be a hollow one if the Service could sell a taxpayer's property while the taxpayer brought a deficiency action in the Tax Court. Of course, the taxpayer could purchase a bond to stay collection.[211] Accordingly, pending a Tax Court decision, Section 6863(b) automatically stays the sale of property the Service has seized to collect the jeopardy assessment until the Service has sent a notice of deficiency, and, if the taxpayer timely files a petition in the Tax Court, until the Tax Court's decision becomes final; that is, during the normal period that assessment would be prohibited if the jeopardy assessment had not been made.[212] The stay of the sale of seized property pending a Tax Court decision does not apply, and the seized property may be sold if (1) the taxpayer consents to the sale; (2) the Service determines that the expenses of conservation and maintenance will greatly reduce the net proceeds; or (3) the property consists of perishable goods that will greatly decrease in value if kept. The stay of sale provision does not apply to bank accounts.[213] Consequently, the relief it accords a taxpayer is limited to seized tangible property, not cash or its equivalent.

[d] Collection of Unpaid Amounts

When the Tax Court has rendered a final decision on the amount the Service should have assessed, the Service is authorized to collect any unpaid portion of the jeopardy assessment, the collection of which has been stayed by bond as provided in Section 6863(b), simply by serving the taxpayer with a notice and demand.[214] Any remaining portion of the jeopardy assessment must be abated. If the Service has already collected an amount in excess of the amount of the Tax Court determined as the amount the Service should have assessed, on its own, the Service must credit or refund the excess collected amount to the taxpayer,[215] without the taxpayer's being required to file a claim for refund. If the amount determined as the amount that should have been assessed is greater than the amount actually assessed, then the Service will assess the difference, and the underpaid amount is collected as part of the tax upon notice and demand from the Service.

---

[211] IRC § 6863(a).

[212] IRC § 6863(b)(3)(A). The stay does not apply to a termination assessment if the taxpayer fails to file a return by the due date, or extended due date.

[213] IRC § 6863(b)(3)(B).

[214] IRC § 6861(f).

[215] The credit or refund is made in accordance with Section 6402(a).

[e] Abatement

The Service may abate the jeopardy assessment if it finds that jeopardy does not exist.[216] During the administrative review of a jeopardy or termination assessment, the Service may be persuaded that the assessment has been improperly made, or is excessive in amount, and accordingly may abate the assessment, in whole or in part.[217] However, the Service loses its authority to abate an assessment on the ground that no jeopardy exists once the Tax Court has rendered a decision in the taxpayer's deficiency action, or, if the taxpayer has not filed a petition with the Tax Court, after the period for filing a Tax Court petition has expired.[218] If the Service abates a jeopardy assessment, the statute of limitations on the Service's making of an assessment and levying on property to collect the assessment or instituting a proceeding in court for collection is determined as if the Service had not abated the jeopardy assessment.[219] An exception to treating the period of limitations as though the jeopardy assessment has not been abated is that the running of the limitations period is suspended from the date of such jeopardy assessment "until the expiration of the 10th day after the day on which such jeopardy assessment is abated."[220]

[f] Employment and Excise Taxes

A jeopardy assessment under Section 6861 may be made only of deficiencies in income, estate, or gift taxes, and in miscellaneous excise taxes on foundations and pensions. Jeopardy assessments of other taxes (i.e., employment and other excise taxes), may be made under Section 6862 if the requisite belief is held that collection will be jeopardized by delay. Once the Service determines that there is jeopardy in collection and the tax is assessed, the Service is authorized to make immediate demand for payment and take immediate collection action by filing a notice of lien or by seizing property by way of levy.[221]

A jeopardy assessment of employment and excise taxes differs from a jeopardy assessment of deficiency taxes under Section 6861 in that the taxes involved are not within the jurisdiction of the Tax Court. Accordingly, the tax-

---

[216] IRC § 6861(g).

[217] Service procedures contemplate the possibility of abatement when the taxpayer requests administrative review of the jeopardy or termination assessment, and it is the policy of the Service, as well as the requirement of the statutory due process review procedures of Section 7429 for there to be such prompt review. See IRM 4.3.9, Jeopardy/Termination Assessments Handbook, 5.2, Abatement Procedures (June 30, 1999).

[218] IRC § 6861(f).

[219] IRC § 6861(f).

[220] IRC § 6861(g).

[221] IRC §§ 6862, 6331(a).

payer against whom a jeopardy assessment of employment or excise tax has been made must file a claim for refund, wait six months (unless the Service earlier denies the claim), and sue for a refund either in a federal district court or the Court of Federal Claims. Two factors lessen the impact of jeopardy assessments of these taxes. First, employment and excise taxes are transactional taxes and divisible by reference to individual transactions. As a result, the taxpayer against whom these taxes are jeopardy assessed is not bound by the normal prerequisite to a refund suit in a federal district court or by the Court of Federal Claims's requirement that the taxpayer make full payment of the amount of the asessment. Thus, the taxpayer may obtain judicial review of the jeopardy assessment of employment or excise tax by (1) paying the tax for one transaction in each taxable period involved; (2) waiting until the earlier of (a) rejection of the claim or (b) the expiration of six months; and (3) filing a complaint in a federal district court or the Court of Federal Claims. Second, in the event that administrative and judicial review of the jeopardy assessment is requested under the due process review procedures of Section 7429, no property seized after the assessment may be sold during the pendency of the review.[222]

[3] Termination Assessments

As described earlier, a termination assessment under Section 6851 is an assessment made to collect income taxes during a tax year and before the return for the year is due. The purpose of an assessment is to secure payment of the tax when it is found that a taxpayer is planning to take some action to defeat its collection. Assessment may be made where there is evidence that the taxpayer plans to evade the tax by a sudden departure from the United States or to remove or conceal his or her property to prevent collection of a tax ultimately determined to be due, as well as in certain cases involving corporate liquidations.[223]

Section 6851 authorizes the Service to take the following actions:

1. Make a determination of tax for the current year or the preceding year if the date for filing the return for the year has not arrived;
2. Assess the amount of tax determined due and payable for the terminated period;
3. Give the taxpayer notice of the assessment and demand immediate payment of the tax assessed; and

---

[222] IRC § 6863(c).

[223] IRC § 6851(a). See GCM 17,195, XV-2 CB 107, 109 (1936), declared obsolete by Rev. Rul. 69-420, 1969-2 CB 264.

4. Take immediate collection action by way of the filing of a notice of lien and service of a levy without regard to the normal ten-day waiting period between demand for payment and seizure.

Thus, the termination statute contemplates four separate acts that are expected to occur within a short period of time: (1) a finding of jeopardy; (2) a determination of tax for the short period; (3) assessment; and (4) collection.

Effectively, a termination assessment reflects the Service's determination that the taxpayer whose year is terminated cannot be trusted, as are other taxpayers, to make a return of his income for the taxable year and to make payment of the tax at the time it is otherwise due. The provision operates in the form of a demand for tax, but the tax demanded is computed under emergency conditions without the benefit of a full audit and is at best an estimated tax. The demanded tax is considered an interim, provisional, or temporary determination made solely for collection purposes.[224] Although a termination assessement imposes liability for an estimated tax before the tax for the year is normally due, it is not penal in nature, rather it is an administrative measure intended to ensure that certain taxpayers pay or provide security for the tax they will ultimately owe for the year. When the taxpayer whose tax year is terminated is compared with the average taxpayer, it can be seen that the termination assessment does not impose disproportionate obligations on the terminated taxpayer. Normally, taxpayers make current payments of tax and, at the time their final returns are due, either pay additional tax or receive a refund of tax. Thus, the termination provision serves much the same purpose in the case of the "untrustworthy taxpayer" as the withholding and estimated tax provisions do in the case of the average taxpayer; that is, to pay tax on a pay-as-you-go basis.

A taxpayer whose taxable year has been terminated need not file a return for the short taxable year, but the Service expects a full-period return to be filed. A termination assessment does not end the taxable year for any purpose other than the computation of the amount of tax to be assessed and collected in the same manner as estimated tax is collected. Although the enforced collection that follows the termination is subject to review under Section 7429, the taxable year continues until its normal end.[225] Within sixty days after the later of the due date of the taxpayer's return for the full taxable year or the date on which the return is filed, the Service must send the taxpayer a notice

---

[224] Ludwig Littauer & Co., 37 BTA 840, 842 (1938); GCM 17,195, XV-2 CB 107, 109 (1936).

[225] See IRC § 6851(b). Staff of Joint Comm. on Tax'n, 94th Cong., 2d Sess., General Explanation of the Tax Reform Act of 1976, at 363, reprinted in 1976-3 CB (vol. 2) 384. Consequently, the Supreme Court's decision in Laing v. United States, 423 US 161 (1976), which held that the tax assessed under Sections 6851 and 6861 constituted a short-period deficiency entitling the taxpayer to a statutory notice, has been legislatively overruled.

of deficiency. No prompt Tax Court review is permitted of the tax demanded after a termination assessment is made, but the termination taxpayer may obtain limited review of the assessment under Section 7429. After the close of the tax year, the taxpayer is expected to file a full period return. The Service is required to send the taxpayer a notice of deficiency for the full tax year "within 60 days after the later of (i) the due date of the taxpayer's return for [the] taxable year (determined with regard to any extension) or (ii) the date [the] taxpayer files [the] return."[226] Consequently, if a taxpayer files an early return, the Service still is not required to send a notice of deficiency until sixty days after the normal due date.

[a] Computation of Tax for Year of Termination

If the Service makes a termination assessment of a current taxable year, the Service is required to compute the tax for the period (or short year) from the first day of the year and ending on the day of the termination assessment. The taxpayer is allowed the standard deduction and credits without proration.[227] The computation of tax is made as though this short period were the taxpayer's taxable year, and must take into account any prior determination affecting the computation of tax for the year.

Examiners are cautioned against making "excessive and unreasonable assessments"; for example, an assessment equal to the amount of money or other property held at the time of arrest would not be considered reasonable unless supported by other facts.[228] After independent investigation and communication with law enforcement officials who may be involved, and with the taxpayer if an interview is permitted, income is generally computed by some accepted method (e.g., specific items, net worth increases, bank deposits, or expenditures).[229] More unusual methods appropriate to illegal activities may also be used, such as estimates of income from narcotics sales (supported by information from a narcotics agent or other expert) and estimates of gambling "taxes" (supported by information from law enforcement officers). The examiner can also estimate the taxpayer's expenses, but it can hardly be expected that an examiner will make estimates in the taxpayer's favor.

---

[226] IRC § 6851(b).

[227] IRC § 6851(a)(2). Any prior determinations of tax are to be taken into account, since more than one termination assessment may be made during a year.

[228] IRM 4.3.9, Jeopardy and Termination Assessments Handbook, Chapter 2, Examination Procedures (June 30, 1999).

[229] For examples of what the Service says are acceptable income computations by different methods, see IRM 4.3.9, Jeopardy and Termination Assessments Handbook, 2.4.1.3.2, Tax Computation (June 30, 1999).

[b] Termination of Current or Preceding Year

A termination assessment terminating a taxable year may be made either for the current taxable year, the preceding taxable year, or both.[230] In the case of a preceding taxable year, however, the Service may not make a termination assessment once the due date of the return for the preceding tax year (determined with regard to extensions) has passed. Instead, the Service may make a jeopardy assessment.[231]

[c] Aliens and Termination Assessments

The Service's termination power extends to three broad classes of taxpayers: (1) the absconding taxpayer; (2) the corporation in liquidation; and (3) the departing alien or citizen.[232] The procedure for all three classes involves a requisite "finding" by the Service. The taxable year of an absconding or alien taxpayer may be terminated only where the Service finds that the taxpayer plans to (1) depart quickly from the United States or remove his property from the country; (2) conceal himself or his property; or (3) take any other act that may prejudice or defeat collection of the income tax for the current or preceding taxable years unless immediate assessment and collection is made.[233]

An alien is prohibited from leaving the United States without first obtaining from the Service a certificate stating that he or she has complied with the tax laws (a so-called sailing permit).[234] If the alien fails to do so, the Service is permitted to make a termination assessment and collect the tax determined to be due. In the case of an alien "about to depart," the Service may waive the use of a termination assessment if it finds that collection will not be jeopardized by the alien's departure. Alien students, industrial trainees, exchange visitors, and their spouses and children, are exempt from the requirement to obtain a certificate of compliance or sailing permit. To qualify for the exemption, aliens must have been admitted to the United States on certain visas (F-1, F-2, H-3, H-4, J-1, or J-2) and must have received U.S.-source income only from (1) allowances for expenses of U.S. study or training, including travel for students or trainees while not physically present in the United States; (2) services or accommodations furnished in connection with the study

---

[230] The language of Section 6851(a)(1) was clarified by the Tax Reform Act of 1976, to avoid further dispute that the Service could terminate a preceding tax year and not the current tax year. See Irving v. Gray, 479 F2d 20 (2d Cir. 1973).

[231] IRC § 6851(a)(4).

[232] IRC §§ 6851(a), 6851(d).

[233] IRC § 6851(a)(1). The statute refers to "proceeding," but historically, a "proceeding" includes levy and distraint as well as a case in court. See Bowers v. New York & Albany Lighterage Co., 273 US 346 (1927).

[234] Reg. § 1.6851-2(a)(2)(ii).

or training; (3) income from federally authorized employment that applies to the alien's visa; and (4) interest on deposits not effectively connected with a U.S. trade or business. Students entering the United States on M-1 or M-2 visas (and their spouses and children) are also eligible for exemption as long as they received no U.S. income other than from the categories of federally authorized employment and interest on deposits not effectively connected with a U.S. trade or business.

[4] Possessor-of-Cash Assessments

A possessor-of-cash assessment is authorized where an individual (1) has more than $10,000 in currency in his physical possession, but (2) does not claim ownership of the currency, or (3) does not claim that the currency belongs to another person whose identity the Service can "readily ascertain and who readily acknowledges ownership of such cash. . . . "[235] If the cash is not claimed, for purposes of termination and jeopardy assessments, it is statutorily presumed that the cash "represents gross income of a single individual for the taxable year in which the possession occurs, and that the collection of tax will be jeopardized by delay."[236] Under statutory rules of assessment, the entire amount of the cash is treated as taxable income for the year in which the individual is discovered in possession of the currency, and is taxable at the highest rate of tax for an individual specified in Section 1 of the Code.[237] Unless the true owner is substituted for the presumed owner, the possessor also is treated as the taxpayer (solely with respect to the cash) for purposes of assessment and collection, as well as the administrative appeal of a jeopardy or a termination.[238]

Regulations describe cash equivalents as including, in general, foreign currency, any bearer instrument, and any medium of exchange that "has been frequently used in illegal activities."[239] Specific cash equivalents include coins, precious metals, jewelry, precious stones, postage stamps, traveler's checks in any form, any kind of negotiable instrument to which title passes on delivery, incomplete instruments with the payee's name omitted, and securities.[240] The

---

[235] IRC § 6867. Cash includes any "cash equivalent" and is specially defined. See IRC § 6867(d). For Service procedures, see IRM 4.3.9, Jeopardy/Termination Assessments Handbook, 5.3, Possessor of Cash (June 30, 1999) (the individual claiming ownership of cash must submit a written request containing specific information, including the person's basis for claiming ownership).

[236] IRC § 6867(a).

[237] IRC §§ 6867(b)(1), 6867(b)(2).

[238] IRC § 6867(b)(3).

[239] Reg. § 301.6867-1(f)(2)(i).

[240] Reg. § 301.6867-1(f)(2)(ii).

possessor of cash is treated as other taxpayers are for assessment purposes, and so is entitled to be sent a notice of deficiency and to file a petition in the Tax Court, solely in his capacity as the possessor of the cash. The possessor is treated as the taxpayer for assessment and collection purposes until the assessment against the possessor is abated, and an assessment against the true owner is substituted.[241] Even if the assessment is abated and the true owner is substituted, the assessment against the true owner is deemed to relate back to the assessment of the possessor of the cash.[242] The true owner of the cash may use the jeopardy and assessment review procedures to contest the assessment, but may not file a petition in the Tax Court until the Service sends a notice of deficiency.[243]

The operation of Section 6867 is illustrated by several Tax Court cases. In *Matut v. Commissioner* (*Matut I*), the Service made a termination assessment against a possessor of cash and, after receiving a notice of deficiency, the possessor, Matut, filed a Tax Court petition in both his individual capacity and as the possessor of cash.[244] Because the statutory presumption of Section 6867 is that the possessor of the cash is deemed to be a taxpayer solely with respect to the cash, Matut's petition in his individual capacity was dismissed, insofar as it asked for review of the deficiency in his individual capacity. On Matut's claim as the possessor of the cash, the Service argued that the Tax Court had no jurisdiction, in reviewing the possessor's claim of nonliability, to determine the true owner of the cash and to permit the person claiming ownership to prove his claim. In *Matut II*, the Tax Court ruled that Section 6867 gave it the jurisdiction to determine the true owner of the cash and to cause that person to be substituted for the possessor.[245] When another person is substituted for the possessor as the true owner, the Tax Court held that the Service

> may, if so advised, abate the assessment previously made pursuant to sections 6867(a) and 6867(b) and replace it with an assessment against the person, firm, or corporation determined by us to be the true owner, as contemplated by section 6867(c). But [the Service] cannot defeat the statutory remedy of the true owner by declining to replace the erroneous assessment and declining to issue a new statutory notice issued pursuant to the presumption of section 6867(a). Our jurisdiction having been properly invoked, we have the power to determine an overassessment in favor of the true owner unless [the Service] chooses to determine a deficiency in

---

[241] IRC § 6867(b)(3); Reg. § 301.6867-1(d).

[242] IRC § 6867(c); Reg. § 301.6867-1(c).

[243] IRC § 6867(c); Reg. § 301.6867-1(e).

[244] Matut v. Comm'r, 84 TC 803 (1985) (Matut I).

[245] Matut v. Comm'r, 86 TC 686 (1986) (Matut II).

the tax liability of the true owner against which the seized cash may be applied.[246]

In *Matut III*, the Eleventh Circuit upheld the Tax Court's jurisdiction to determine the ownership of cash, even if the owner has not been sent a notice of deficiency.[247] Once the true owner of the cash asserts a claim and has been determined to be the owner, the true owner may be substituted for the possessor for all purposes and has the right to have the Tax Court determine his or her tax liability. In *Matut III*, the Eleventh Circuit also said that for purposes of Section 6867, the term "owner" refers to the owner on the seizure date and that this owner must acknowledge his or her ownership on that date in order to be substituted in the proceeding.

What must the possessor do to avoid the presumption of Section 6867(a)? In *Peoples Loan & Trust Co. v. Commissioner*, the Tax Court said: "To avoid the application of the presumptions of section 6867, the statute requires only that the possessor claim that the cash belongs to him or to another identifiable person. A claim requires only that an assertion be made as to the existence of a particular fact."[248] The Tax Court held that the bank had alleged that an identified individual was the owner of the silver in its possession (1) in an application for appointment as the administrator of the owner's estate; (2) in an inventory of the estate's assets filed in court; and (3) in lawsuits. Because only taxpayers are entitled to due process administrative and judicial review procedures under Section 7429, it has been held that these review procedures are unavailable to a possessor of cash because that person is not the taxpayer.[249]

[5] Service Procedures When Jeopardy and Termination Assessments Are Made

High-level review and the predominant role of the examination function mark Service procedures in making jeopardy and termination assessments. These procedures must be viewed in light of the clear requirement that high-ranking examiners must approve a jeopardy or termination assessment before it is

---

[246] Matut v. Comm'r, 86 TC 686, 691 (1986) (Matut II).

[247] Matut v. Comm'r, 858 F2d 683 (11th Cir. 1988), aff'g, vacating, and remanding 88 TC 1250 (1987). Compare Comm'r v. Hendrickson, 873 F2d 1018 (7th Cir. 1989) (procedure under Section 6867 reviewed; bailee who gave notice under Section 6867 should have informed executor so that "equitable owners" of funds could be notified, and the Service could substitute them in assessment proceeding).

[248] Peoples Loan & Trust Co. v. Comm'r, 89 TC 896, 906 (1987). A dissent would have held that the possessor must identify the true owner before being relieved of a deficiency under Section 6867. For later proceedings, see Comm'r v. Hendrickson, 873 F2d 1018 (7th Cir. 1989).

[249] Morgan v. United States, 958 F2d 950 (9th Cir. 1992).

made. The area director must personally approve any jeopardy or termination assessment, as must the counsel for the type-of-taxpayer operating division.[250] If the assessment might cause serious "inconvenience to the general public," such as a jeopardy or termination assessment against a bank, newspaper, insurance company, hospital, or public utility, prior National Office approval is required.

Although jeopardy and termination assessments are collection devices in which the Collection function would appear to have the dominant role, the focal point in the Service's jeopardy and termination assessment procedures is the Jeopardy/Termination Coordinator in the examination function.[251] To ensure coordination with other functions, such as Collection, Appeals, and Criminal Investigation, the Coordinator (1) determines whether the function has the particular taxpayer under active consideration; (2) informs the function that has the taxpayer under consideration that a possible jeopardy or termination assessment is in progress; and (3) alerts Collection of possible action. When recommendations for jeopardy and termination assessments are made, the Coordinator reviews the recommendation for compliance with Service assessment criteria and controls the making of the assessment. After assessment, the Coordinator continues to follow the case.

A jeopardy and termination assessment starts when a Service employee receives information that fits a situation of jeopardy in collection (i.e., flight, concealment or transfer of property, insolvency, or possession of more than $10,00 in cash), and the employee refers the information to the Coordinator.[252] Once the Coordinator approves the case for action, he secures the assignment of an examiner to develop the facts necessary for approval or disapproval as quickly as possible. Specific examination procedures reflect the Service's experience in the few cases where a jeopardy assessment was invalidated either because of the lack of evidence of the taxpayer's being engaged in an income-producing activity or because a projection was unreasonable.[253]

---

[250] Approval of the assessment must be granted by the equivalent of the district director prior to the Service's restructuring. Also, the director of the Foreign Operations District must approve jeopardy and termination assessments for taxpayers under international jurisdiction. As a result of the IRS Restructuring and Reform Act of 1998, the Chief Counsel or the counsel's delegate must approve the assessment in writing. See Delegation Order No. 218, as revised. See also IRM 1.2.1, Policies of the IRS Handbook, 1.4.27, Jeopardy Assessments and 1.4.28, Termination Assessments (Jan. 6, 1999); IRM 4.3.9, Jeopardy/Termination Assessments Handbook, 1.3, Approval (June 30, 1999).

[251] IRM 4.3.9, Jeopardy/Termination Assessments Handbook, 2.2, Jeopardy/Termination Coordinator (June 30, 1999).

[252] IRM 4.3.9, Jeopardy/Termination Assessments Handbook, 2.3 and 2.3.1, Identifying Cases and Reviewing Information (June 30, 1999).

[253] Rinieri v. Scanlon, 254 F. Supp. 469 (SDNY 1966) (the only evidence of an income activity was that a French citizen was found with cash, before the enactment of Section 6867, and was believed to have engaged in narcotics activities); Pizzarello v. United

The examiner is responsible for documenting evidence establishing that one or more of the conditions of jeopardy exists, and that income has been earned, a tax is or will become due, and that the tax will not be collected unless immediate assessment and collection is made.[254] To avoid the claim that the Service failed to present evidence that the taxpayer was engaged in an income-producing activity, the examiner will develop and record specific evidence that the taxpayer received taxable income.[255] To do this, the examiner attempts to interview the taxpayer, an arresting officer, if any, and others with knowledge of the circumstances. In addition to interviews, the examiner documents the facts.[256] In a narcotics, gambling, or other illegal income tax case, the examiner will gather documents relating to the criminal activity from the relevant law enforcement agency, and will obtain the opinion of a law enforcement officer or other expert about the taxpayer's activity. When a projection of income is used, the examiner must gather specific facts to prove that the taxpayer received income over the projection period and that there is "a rational connection between the facts known or ascertained and facts presumed or inferred."[257] The examiner also verifies the tax history of the taxpayer to show that the taxpayer has a history of avoiding payment of tax by failing to file returns for prior years or is delinquent in filing the current year's return.[258] It is important to note that the examiner computes the tax owed using the taxpayer's taxable income determined on the basis of a direct or indirect method of proof and a reasonable estimate of expenses of a business activity, the standard deduction, exemptions, and credits.[259] A narrative explaining the facts, referring to the information and documentary evidence the examiner has gathered, and reason for the examination, completes the examiner's report.

At the end of the examination, the agent prepares a recommendation for a jeopardy or termination assessment and submits the report to the Coordinator, who reviews the recommendation for final action. Counsel also reviews the recommended assessment and determines whether there is a sufficient basis in

---

States, 408 F2d 579 (2d Cir. 1969) (three days of wagers were used to project gambling income over five years).

[254] IRM 4.3.9, Jeopardy/Termination Assessments Handbook, 2.4.1.1, Documenting Conditions, and 2.4.1.2, Developing the Facts (June 30, 1999).

[255] IRM 4.3.9, Jeopardy/Termination Assessments Handbook, 2.4.1.2, Developing the Facts (June 30, 1999).

[256] IRM 4.3.9, Jeopardy/Termination Assessments Handbook, 2.4.1.4, Documenting the Facts (June 30, 1999).

[257] IRM 4.3.9, Jeopardy/Termination Assessments Handbook, 2.4.1.4, Documenting the Facts (June 30, 1999).

[258] IRM 4.3.9, Jeopardy/Termination Assessments Handbook, 2.4.1.2.4(3), Documenting the Facts (June 30, 1999).

[259] IRM 4.3.9, Jeopardy/Termination Assessments Handbook, 2.4.1.3.2, Tax Computations (June 30, 1999).

fact to defend any suit for review of the assessment.[260] After counsel review, the file is sent for personal approval to the local office director and, if approval is given, the assessment is made immediately, usually by faxing the necessary information to the Service center.[261]

After assessment, the taxpayer is served with (1) a Notice of Jeopardy/ Termination Assessment, including a copy of the examiner's computation of the tax; (2) a demand for immediate payment of the assessment; and (3) a form letter informing the taxpayer of appeal rights under Section 7429 (see Pattern Letter P-513).[262] The Service prefers that the notice and demand be served on the taxpayer personally, but delivery by certified mail to the taxpayer's last known address is also allowed. The Service prefers personal service so that immediate collection action by a team of revenue officers may be taken to file a notice of lien and to seize property by service of levies. In the event the taxpayer requests administrative review of the assessment under Section 7429, a conference in Appeals is immediately considered.[263]

Notice of the assessment and demand must be made before collection action is taken. No collection may be made before the notice and demand have at least been served and the taxpayer given the opportunity to make payment. A levy made before notice and demand are served is void.[264] In practice, prompt collection is made by a team of revenue officers. Two revenue officers deliver the notice and demand, while others are stationed near the public office in which notice of the lien will be filed and the bank or other third person on whom a notice of levy will be served. Once the notice and demand has been served, the other revenue officers are informed by telephone of the service and proceed to take collection action, which may mean merely serving a notice of

---

[260] IRM 5.1.4.3.

[261] IRM 4.3.9, Jeopardy/Termination Assessments Handbook, 3.2, Preparing Assessments (June 30, 1999).

[262] See generally IRM 5.1, General Handbook — Jeopardy, Termination, and Prompt Assessments, 4.6, Assessment and Post-Assessment Procedures (Dec. 13, 1999). Although notices of lien are filed in all cases to record the Service lien against the taxpayer's real property, notices of levy to seize personal property are made if it is determined that "the filing of the lien will not provide the degree of protection necessary to ensure that the taxpayer will not dispose of, dissipate or secrete personal property. . . ." Id. Where notices of levy are used, they are used to seize cash or the liquid assets of the taxpayer in the possession of third parties.

[263] IRM 1.2.1, Policies of the IRS Handbook 1.4.27, P-4-88 (approved Jan. 6, 1999).

[264] Section 6331(a) states that, in a jeopardy situation, "notice and demand for immediate payment may be made by the [Service] . . . and, upon failure or refusal to pay such tax, collection thereof by levy shall be lawful." LOC Indus., Inc. v. United States, 423 F. Supp. 265 (MD Tenn. 1976) (notice of prompt assessment not received until some time after 8:30 A.M., and notice of termination delivered at 9:30 A.M., but levy served on first bank at 8:18 A.M.; held, levy invalid and amount seized must be returned). But see Ray v. United States, 78-1 USTC ¶ 9345 (SDNY 1978) (where notice and demand made after an abated assessment was held sufficient; an incorrect result).

lien. However, in cases involving property that can be disposed of, such as automobiles, jewelry, and the contents of safe deposit boxes, levies are served.[265] This sequence of events is important if the Service is to achieve the purpose of the jeopardy and termination assessment in a valid manner. Amounts collected after a termination assessment are credited against the tax finally determined for the taxpayer's taxable year.[266]

Where the taxpayer requests Section 7429 review in writing, the Coordinator will expedite the processing of the request, and it will be considered "immediately."[267] the Service is prohibited from selling seized property during the review unless (1) the property is perishable; (2) the taxpayer consents to the sale; or (3) the Service determines that the expenses of conservation or maintenance would greatly reduce the net proceeds.[268]

[6] Jeopardy Levies

If the Service finds that collection of a tax is in jeopardy, the levy statute, Section 6331(a), authorizes it to make a jeopardy levy. As is required for levies, the Service must give the taxpayer a notice and demand, but in the case of a jeopardy levy, the demand is for immediate payment of the tax, not payment within ten days, as is the case when the usual levy is served. If the taxpayer fails or refuses to make immediate payment, the Service may collect the tax by levy and seize the taxpayer's property without the normal ten-day waiting period. Generally, if collection is in jeopardy, the Service makes a jeopardy assessment, immediately serves a notice and demand on the taxpayer, and then makes a jeopardy levy. However, a jeopardy levy is not automatically authorized when a jeopardy assessment is made. Technically, a separate finding of jeopardy must be made to support a jeopardy levy.[269] But it appears that re-

---

[265] Section 6331(a) states that, in a jeopardy situation, "notice and demand for immediate payment may be made by the [Service] . . . and, upon failure or refusal to pay such tax, collection thereof by levy shall be lawful." LOC Indus., Inc. v. United States, 423 F. Supp. 265 (MD Tenn. 1976) (notice of prompt assessment not received until some time after 8:30 A.M., and notice of termination delivered at 9:30 A.M., but levy served on first bank at 8:18 A.M.; held, levy invalid and amount seized must be returned). But see Ray v. United States, 78-1 USTC ¶ 9345 (SDNY 1978) (where notice and demand made after an abated assessment was held sufficient; an incorrect result).

[266] IRC § 6851(a)(3).

[267] IRM 2.1, Policies of the IRS Handbook, 1.4.27, P-4-88, Jeopardy Assessments (Jan. 6, 1999).

[268] IRC § 6863(b)(3).

[269] It should be noted that the reasonableness of a jeopardy assessment and the reasonableness of a jeopardy levy are two distinct inquiries. Cf. Henderson v. United States, 949 F. Supp. 473 (ND Tex. 1996) (citing Shaw v. United States, 20 F3d 182 (5th Cir. 1994)).

view of a jeopardy levy will take into account at least some of the factors that were considered to establish jeopardy for jeopardy and termination assessment purposes. In a jeopardy levy case reviewed under Section 7429, the district court held that the Service had proven "the jeopardy levy was reasonable by offering evidence that [taxpayer's] liabilities exceeded his assets; he was insolvent or at least in danger of becoming insolvent."[270]

[7] Administrative and Judicial Review of Termination and Jeopardy Assessments: Section 7429

[a] In General

Once a jeopardy or termination assessment is made, the Service immediately files tax liens and serves levies to seize the taxpayer's property with the result that the taxpayer loses access to and is deprived of property. To make matters worse, the amount of the Service's assessment is frequently overstated—sometimes wildly so. Jeopardy or termination assessments are usually computed on the basis of incomplete information, by Service personnel who are not in any way motivated to take positions in favor of taxpayers they believe are attempting to evade tax collection. The jeopardy assessment statute requires that the Service send a notice of deficiency to the taxpayer within sixty days after the date of the jeopardy assessment. But Tax Court review is not so prompt as it might appear. Suppose the Service sends a notice of deficiency to the taxpayer on the last permissible date. Assuming prompt delivery, the taxpayer may be able to file a petition by perhaps the sixty-fifth day after the assessment; nevertheless, the taxpayer still will have waited for more than two months before he could file a deficiency action in the Tax Court, and will wait even longer for the Tax Court to decide the case.

Before 1976, when taxpayers attempted to secure judicial review of Service action in making a jeopardy or termination assessment prior to any Tax Court review, the Service was generally successful in opposing judicial review on the ground that the taxpayer was attempting to restrain assessment and collection of tax in violation of the Anti-Injunction Act.[271] Judicial review in injunction actions had been restricted by the *Williams Packing & Navigation Co.*[272] rule, which required the taxpayer to show that in taking a view of the facts and the law most favorable to the Service, "under no circumstances" could the Service ultimately prevail. In 1976, two Supreme Court cases

---

[270] Crosby v. United States, 86 AFTR2d 2000-5257 (ED Pa. 2000).

[271] In extreme cases, seizures have occasionally been overturned. See, e.g., Rinieri v. Scanlon, 254 F. Supp. 469 (SDNY 1966).

[272] Enochs v. Williams Packing & Navigation Co., 370 US 1 (1962).

changed the treatment of jeopardy and termination taxpayers. The first case, *Laing v. United States*,[273] was a termination assessment case. When it made a termination assessment, the Service did not believe that it was required to send taxpayer Laing a notice of deficiency. However, when the Service terminated Laing's taxable year, he contended that he was entitled to be sent a notice of deficiency in order to obtain Tax Court review of the Service's assessment, and the Supreme Court agreed.[274] The second case was a jeopardy assessment case. In *Commissioner v. Shapiro*,[275] a jeopardy assessment was made against a taxpayer who was charged with criminal acts in both the United States and Israel, and after making a jeopardy assessment, the Service collected amounts that the taxpayer claimed he needed to post bond in Israel, pending his trial there. Absent a bond, he would be incarcerated. Considerations of due process, the Supreme Court held, entitled the taxpayer to a preseizure or at least prompt postseizure hearing. In this hearing, a court would review whether there was a basis in fact for the Service's action. In the course of its opinion, the Court observed that its decision did not preclude another procedure for an expedited inquiry of the basis for the Service's finding and assessment.

At about the same time *Laing* and *Shapiro* were decided, the General Accounting Office (GAO) reported to Congress that jeopardy and termination assessments, while valuable in some instances to prevent tax avoidance, did not produce significant tax revenue.[276] With *Laing* and *Shapiro*'s revealing constitutional defects in termination and jeopardy assessments, and the GAO's report of their practical limitations, Congress adopted a statutory due process remedy that permitted taxpayers to obtain expedited administrative and judicial review of jeopardy or termination assessments. These procedures are contained in Section 7429, which was added to the Code in the Tax Reform Act of 1976. In addition, in 1988, Section 7429 was amended to permit both administrative and judicial review of a jeopardy levy.[277]

[b] Administrative Review

Section 7429 establishes a statutory mechanism for administrative and judicial due process review of the Service's action in making (1) termination assessments of income tax under Section 6851; (2) jeopardy assessments of income, estate, gift, or certain excise taxes under Section 6861; (3) jeopardy

---

[273] Laing v. United States, 423 US 161 (1976).

[274] Laing v. United States, 423 US 161 (1976).

[275] Comm'r v. Shapiro, 424 US 614 (1976).

[276] GAO Report, "Use of Jeopardy and Termination Assessments by the Internal Revenue Service," July 16, 1976.

[277] Technical and Miscellaneous Revenue Act of 1988, Pub. L. No. 100-647 § 6237. See Reg. §§ 301.7429-1–301.7429-3.

assessments of other taxes such as excise and employment taxes under Section 6862; and (4) jeopardy levies. One element of due process is notice; therefore, within five days after the date the Service makes a termination or jeopardy assessment, the Service must give the taxpayer a written statement of the information on which it relied in making the assessment.[278] Within thirty days after the statement is furnished (or required to be furnished), the taxpayer may request the Service to review the propriety of its termination or jeopardy assessment.[279] Due process also requires agency review of its action to determine whether a reasonable basis in fact exists for the action. Section 7429 requires that if the taxpayer makes a request for review, the Service must determine (1) whether the making of the termination or jeopardy assessment is "reasonable" under the circumstances and (2) whether the amount assessed is appropriate under the circumstances.[280] It is also permissible for a taxpayer to request administrative review on "whether or not the levy (served without the thirty-day notice of intent to levy) is reasonable under the circumstances."[281]

Service review of the reasonableness of the assessment takes into account not only information that was available when the Service made the assessment, but also information that became available to the Service after the assessment.[282] If the Service finds that the assessment is inappropriate or excessive in amount, it may abate the assessment in whole or in part. Since the Service

---

[278] IRC § 7429(a)(1). The "last known address" case law under Section 622(b)(1) (discussed supra ¶ 10.03[3][d]) applies in determining whether the taxpayer has been given notice. See Escalera v. Comm'r, 38 TCM 1194 (1979). If the notice is insufficient, the opportunity for administrative and judicial review is not meaningful, and the assessment may be invalidated. See DeLauri v. United States, 492 F. Supp. 442 (WD Tex. 1980); Walker v. United States, 650 F. Supp. 877 (ED Tenn. 1987) (gathering cases on adequacy of Service's Section 6861 notice and finding on facts that notice was inadequate and assessments were unreasonable).

[279] IRC § 7429(a)(2). Rev. Proc. 78-12, 1978-1 CB 590, § 3.01, states that the request must be filed within thirty days after receipt of the Service notice or within thirty-five days after the assessment, whichever is earlier. The thirty-day period begins to run on the date on which the taxpayer receives the notice of termination or jeopardy assessment. Snyder v. United States, 582 F. Supp. 196 (D. Md. 1984); Friko Corp. v. United States, 91-1 USTC ¶ 50,195 (DDC 1991) (accord). But the thirty-day rule is jurisdictional and can be strictly applied. For example, when a request for review by a foreign corporation was received within the thirty-day period, but the taxpayer representative's power of attorney was received outside the thirty-day period, the request for review was held ineffective. Id.

[280] IRC § 7429(a)(3).

[281] IRC §§ 7429(a)(1), 7429(a)(3). Regulations describe procedures for requesting administrative and judicial review. See Reg. §§ 301.7429-2, 301.7429-3.

[282] Reg. § 301.7429-2(b); S. Rep. No. 938, 94th Cong., 2d Sess. 364, reprinted in 1976-3 CB (vol. 3) 397, 402. See Herschhorn v. United States, 685 F. Supp. 68 (SDNY 1988) (the only reasonable ground supporting a termination assessment was rendered unreasonable as a result of information conveyed at the Appeals conference; held, termination assessment abated).

must consider postassessment information, an abatement does not "necessarily" imply that it acted improperly in making the assessment. The Service is also intended to have, and presumably to exercise, discretion to abate an assessment in whole or in part even if the assessment is not found to be inappropriate or excessive "if there is a finding that the taxpayer would suffer unusual hardship."[283] Administrative review of the jeopardy finding is likely to be limited to a determination that one of the three conditions stated in the Manual for the making of a jeopardy or termination assessment exists.[284] Thus a jeopardy or termination assessment will be upheld if there is evidence that the taxpayer was about to leave the country or conceal or dissipate property, or that his or her financial solvency appeared imperiled.

Appeals considers a taxpayer's request for administrative review of a jeopardy or termination assessment.[285] To meet the requirement that due process review be prompt, Appeals is to grant an immediate conference, and within fifteen days after the taxpayer has requested review, Appeals is to determine whether (1) the making of the assessment was reasonable under the circumstances and (2) the amount of the assessment was reasonably correct.[286] After making this determination, Appeals can take one of the following actions: (1) sustain the local office's action in making the assessment in the amount assessed; (2) sustain the local office in part (i.e., redetermine the amount assessed); (3) reverse on the local office finding of jeopardy on the ground that it was not reasonable or warranted; or (4) find that the taxpayer agrees with the action taken on all or part of the amount assessed. If the taxpayer does not agree with the action of Appeals in sustaining the assessment, in whole or in part, the stage is set for judicial review.

In Appeals administrative review, a presentation at a conference should be calculated to challenge (1) the procedural regularity of the assessment (e.g., the assessment was not made in accordance with either statutory or administrative requirements); (2) the propriety of the jeopardy finding (e.g., collection of the tax was not in jeopardy); and (3) the amount of the assessment (e.g., the amount assessed should be redetermined and the excessive amount abated). To do this, the practitioner must (1) investigate the facts relating to jeopardy before, during, and after the assessment; (2) prepare alternative and supportable computations of tax; and (3) identify supporting legal authority. But the

---

[283] S. Rep. No. 938, 94th Cong., 2d Sess. 364 n.5, reprinted in 1976-3 CB (vol. 3) 402.

[284] Congress stated that it believed that the general standards set forth in the Manual relating to the conditions that must exist before a jeopardy or termination assessment may be made are "reasonable." S. Rep. No. 938, 94th Cong., 2d Sess. 364, 367 n.7, reprinted in 1976-3 CB (vol. 3) 405.

[285] IRC § 7429(a)(3).

[286] IRM 4.3.9, Jeopardy/Termination Assessments Handbook, 4.2, Administrative Review (June 30, 1999), and Handbook, 4.3, Judicial Review (June 30, 1999).

nature of the preparation and presentation are more sensitive than an ordinary Appeals conference. Just how the practitioner is to proceed depends on a number of circumstances, some of which are

- Whether the case is likely to be settled
- Whether the case is likely to end up in a judicial proceeding
- Whether there are any pending or potential criminal actions

Any conference can be a source of discovery for the taxpayer, but where the Service has failed to follow the requirements of the Code (e.g., by seizing property before serving notice and demand), presentation of the argument may permit the Service to cure the defect in the assessment or collection without releasing any of the property it seized. A court is more likely to order release of such property if it finds that the Service has not complied with the procedures for assessment and collection.[287] This prospect argues for holding back a procedural-defect argument in the administrative stage, although the taxpayer must offer something in order to negotiate. At the Appeals conference, if the Appeals officer shows some willingness to abate a portion of the assessment, the taxpayer can concede the point of the procedural defect.

The legislative history of Section 7429 approved the Manual's description of the conditions warranting a jeopardy or termination assessment (i.e., flight, transfer or concealment of assets, and insolvency). When the evidence shows that the taxpayer was attempting to leave the country or to conceal, transfer, or dissipate assets, it makes little sense to argue that the finding of jeopardy was erroneous. In such a situation, it is likely to be more productive to challenge the amount of the assessment and discuss terms of payment of tax. Neither the legislative history nor the Manual explain at what point the Service will consider a taxpayer financially solvent and what evidence it will consider, although it does appear that the amount of the assessment is not to be considered a liability. This absence of standards indicates that such a taxpayer's financial solvency may be a matter for discussion, but that presentation of evidence may only give the Service further information about distrainable assets.

The safest challenge at Appeals is the amount of the assessment. The Manual warns against making assessments that are or can be expected to be in excess of the tax due.[288] This warning reflects case law where courts found that the Service had no reasonable basis for the amount of tax demanded.[289]

---

[287] LOC Indus., Inc. v. United States, 423 F. Supp. 265 (MD Tenn. 1976).

[288] IRM 4.3.1, Jeopardy/Termination Assessments Handbook, 2.4.1.3.2, Preparing the Pre-Approved Report—Tax Computations (June 30, 1999).

[289] See United States v. Bonaguro, 294 F. Supp. 750 (EDNY 1968), aff'd sub nom. United States v. Dono, 428 F2d 204 (2d Cir.), cert. denied, 400 US 829 (1970); Pizzarello v. United States, 408 F2d 579 (2d Cir.), cert. denied, 396 US 986 (1969); Lassof v. Gray, 266 F2d 745 (6th Cir. 1959). See also Willits v. Richardson, 497 F2d 240 (5th Cir. 1974);

For example, the number of exemptions may be understated[290]; the taxpayer's cost-of-living figure in a circumstantial method of establishing taxable income may be understated[291]; the amount of income may be based on projections or assumptions that have no factual basis[292]; the tax may not have been properly computed[293]; or the evidence of income may have been tainted by an illegal search by federal agents (rather than state or local police). Another argument that might be made in some cases has been statutorily removed. Section 280E denies a deduction or credit for any amount paid or incurred during the year in carrying on a business consisting of trafficking controlled substances.[294] Case law also limits arguments. In *Janis v. United States*,[295] the Supreme Court held that an illegal search and seizure by state officials does not taint the Service's determination.

Aguilar v. United States, 501 F2d 127 (5th Cir. 1974); Lucia v. United States, 474 F2d 565, 573 (5th Cir. 1973); Rinieri v. Scanlon, 254 F. Supp. 469 (SDNY 1966); Woods v. McKeever, 73-2 USTC ¶ 9727 (D. Ariz. 1973), aff'd in unpublished opinion.

[290] United States v. Bonaguro, 294 F. Supp. 750 (EDNY 1968), aff'd sub nom. United States v. Dono, 428 F2d 204 (2d Cir.), cert. denied, 400 US 829 (1970).

[291] See United States v. Bonaguro, 294 F. Supp. 750 (EDNY 1968), aff'd sub nom. United States v. Dono, 428 F2d 204 (2d Cir.), cert. denied, 400 US 829 (1970); Rinieri v. Scanlon, 254 F. Supp. 469 (SDNY 1966).

[292] Pizzarello v. United States, 408 F2d 579 (2d Cir.), cert. denied, 396 US 986 (1969) (three days' average wages projected over five years); Willits v. Richardson, 497 F2d 240 (5th Cir. 1974) (on the basis of two vials of barbiturates and a scrap of paper, taxpayer said to have earned $60,000 in commissions from sales of $240,000 worth of cocaine). Cf. Hamilton v. United States, 429 F2d 427 (2d Cir. 1970), cert. denied, 401 US 913 (1971) (projections approved). See Breider v. United States, 614 F. Supp. 1200 (ED Wis. 1985) (projections modified).

[293] See, e.g., Giles v. United States, 80-2 USTC ¶ 9546 (MD Fla. 1980) (marijuana dealer entitled to use maximum tax rate of Section 1348).

[294] Presumably, the cost of goods sold can still be used to reduce the gross receipts of a taxpayer. The Senate Finance Committee Report (S. Rep. No. 494, 97th Cong., 2d. Sess. vol. 1 (1982)) provides that adjustment to gross receipts for the cost of goods sold is not affected by the prohibition of Section 280E, denying a deduction or credit for amounts paid or incurred in carrying on a business consisting of trafficking in controlled substances. IRM 4.3.9, Jeopardy/Termination Assessments Handbook, 2.4.1.2.4, Documenting the Facts (June 30, 1999). But see Lopez v. IRS, 614 F. Supp. 1332 (EDNY 1985) (value of contraband to person from whom seized treated as taxable income; held, "[t]hough this method may be a crude estimate, the Court finds nothing obviously inappropriate with its use"). See also Vidiella v. United States, 85-2 USTC ¶ 9677 (SD Fla. 1985) (contraband treated as income; court stated that, "computations made in jeopardy situations are of necessity based on assumptions and, in fact, may be lacking, to some degree, in accuracy").

[295] United States v. Janis, 428 US 433 (1976).

[c] Judicial Review

Section 7429(b) permits a taxpayer to secure expedited judicial review of a jeopardy or termination assessment by instituting a proceeding in either the appropriate federal district court or the Tax Court. The Tax Court has concurrent jurisdiction with federal district courts for challenges to a jeopardy assessment or jeopardy levy if the taxpayer has filed a petition with the Tax Court before the Service has made the assessment or levy with respect to any deficiency covered by the jeopardy assessment or jeopardy levy notice.[296]

A Section 7429 due process review proceeding is specifically excepted from the prohibition of the Anti-Injunction Act.[297] The district court is required to determine whether (1) the making of the jeopardy or termination assessment was "reasonable under the circumstances" and (2) the amount, if assessed, is "appropriate under the circumstances."[298] As part of its review process, the district court also has jurisdiction to review a jeopardy levy to collect the assessment.[299] The requirement of Section 7429(b) that the district court must make such a finding incorporates the rule of *Shapiro*, that a jeopardy taxpayer is entitled to a prompt postseizure review of the propriety of the Service action.[300] *Shapiro* overruled cases that had held a finding of jeopardy to be nonreviewable. These cases no longer apply when Section 7429 review is sought.[301]

---

[296] The Tax Court has jurisdiction if a petition has been filed in the Tax Court before the jeopardy assessment was made and if "1 or more of the taxes and taxable periods before the Tax Court is also included in the jeopardy assessment." Id. See Friko Corp. v. Comm'r, 94-2 USTC ¶¶ 50,306, 50,307 US App. DC (DC Cir. 1994) ("Friko's petition for redetermination of the deficiency was filed after the jeopardy assessment was made, not 'before,' as § 7429(b)(2)(B) requires in order to confer jurisdiction on the Tax Court"). The same result follows when the petition challenges a levy served after the jeopardy assessment. If there is no pending petition for redetermination in the Tax Court, the Tax Court has no jurisdiction over the petition to review the jeopardy levy. Id.

[297] IRC § 7421(a).

[298] IRC § 7429(b)(2).

[299] IRC § 7429(b)(2)(B) effective for assessments made after June 30, 1987. See Melvin Williams et ux. v. Comm'r, 92 TC 920 (1989) (stay granted); Mettenbrink v. United States, 91-1 USTC ¶ 50,212 (D. Neb. 1991) (levy served on same day as notice of jeopardy assessment was held proper, because jeopardy assessment established collection jeopardized by delay and taxpayer had some notice). See also Vonderheide v. United States, 80 AFTR2d 97-8194 (SD Ohio 1997) (levy issued more than thirty days after notice and demand for payment is not a jeopardy levy subject to judicial review under Section 7429).

[300] Comm'r v. Shapiro, 424 US 614 (1976) . For a discussion of the statutory requirement, see supra ¶ 10.05[2]. It has been held that the hearing need not be a full evidentiary hearing. See Chavarria v. United States, 84-1 USTC ¶ 9237 (ND Cal. 1984) (cases gathered).

[301] See, e.g., Melvin Bldg. Co. v. Long, 262 F2d 920 (7th Cir. 1958); Lloyd v. Patterson, 242 F2d 742 (5th Cir. 1957).

[d] Scope of Review

Although Section 7429 is silent on the matter, the legislative history is clear that in making these determinations, the district court is to make an independent, de novo review in which the Service action is to be given no special weight. In this proceeding, the court is to take into account not only the information available to the Service at the time of the assessment but also any other information bearing on the questions at issue.[302] Whatever the result of the proceeding, the determination the court makes under Section 7429 has no effect on the determination of the correct tax in the Tax Court or refund suit.[303]

Judicial review for a determination under Section 7429(b) is both expedited and final. The taxpayer may bring the action in the federal district court for the district in which the taxpayer resides[304] or, under certain circumstances, in the Tax Court,[305] within ninety days after the earlier of (1) the day the Service notifies the taxpayer of its determination on the request for administrative review or (2) sixteen days after the request for administrative review was made.[306] The district court must make its determination within twenty days af-

---

[302] S. Rep. No. 938, 94th Cong., 2d Sess. 364, 365, reprinted in 1976-3 CB (vol. 3) 403; Loretto v. United States, 440 F. Supp. 1168 (ED Pa. 1977). Accord Billig v. United States, 81-2 USTC ¶ 9792 (ND Ga. 1981).

[303] The Senate Report states that the proceeding under Section 7429 is to be a separate proceeding that is unrelated, substantively and procedurally, to any subsequent proceeding to determine the correct tax liability. S. Rep. No. 938, 94th Cong., 2d Sess. 364, 365, reprinted in 1976-3 CB (vol. 3) 403. Accordingly, a district court does not have subject matter jurisdiction in a Section 7429 proceeding to determine the taxpayer's correct tax liability and the amount to be refunded. Estate of Katherine Tinari v. United States, 78 AFTR2d 96-6393 (ED Pa. 1996) (in a proceeding to review a jeopardy assessment made during pendency of Tax Court case, which was settled after the jeopardy assessment, taxpayer asked the court to abate the assessment and amounts seized in excess of the liability refunded).

[304] Venue rules that normally apply in tax actions apply in proceedings under Section 7429. The venue rules of 28 USC §§ 1402(a)(1) and 1402(a)(2) are incorporated by reference. IRC § 7429(e); see also Williams v. United States, 704 F2d 1222 (11th Cir. 1983) (resident alien taxpayer may establish venue under venue rules of 28 USC § 1402(a)(1) for purposes of contesting jeopardy assessment). Venue in a review proceeding is in the judicial district in which the taxpayer resides, rather than in the district where the assessment and levy were made. Alegria v. United States, 945 F2d 1523 (11th Cir. 1991) (resolving apparent conflict between 28 USC §§ 1402(a), 1402(c), 1346(e), and Section 7429(e)). Also, a nonresident alien may institute a review proceeding. Id. (discussing and gathering cases).

[305] IRC § 7429(b)(2)(B).

[306] IRC § 7429(b)(1). The period was extended from thirty to ninety days in 1988 for jeopardy assessments or levies made on or after July 1, 1989. Technical and Miscellaneous Revenue Act of 1988, Pub. L. No. 100-647, § 6237(c), 100th Cong., 2d Sess., 102 Stat. 3342 (Nov. 11, 1988). Saturday, Sunday, or a legal holiday in the District of Columbia are not counted as the last day of any period. IRC § 7429(d). See Fernandez v. United States, 704 F2d 592 (11th Cir.), cert. denied, 464 US 852 (1983); Murphy v. Comm'r, 83-

ter the taxpayer begins the action. This period may be extended for up to forty additional days, but only at the taxpayer's request and on a showing of reasonable grounds.[307] No appeal is permitted from the court's finding.[308]

[e] Hearing Procedures

Neither Section 7429 nor its legislative history make clear what procedures are to be followed in the court review proceeding. Section 7429 does assign the respective burdens of proof to the parties. In the court proceeding, the Service has the burden of proof on the issue of whether the making of the ter-

---

2 USTC ¶ 9576 (ND Miss. 1983); Resnick v. United States, 85-1 USTC ¶ 9405 (D. Minn. 1985) (*Fernandez* followed in strict construction of the time limits under Section 7429(b)). The periods described in Section 7429(b)(1)(B) have been interpreted to mean one forty-six-day period rather than two periods, one ending on the sixteenth day after the taxpayer makes his request to the Service and the second ending thirty days thereafter. Felak v. United States, 87-1 USTC ¶ 9366 (D. Minn. 1987) (forty-six-day method resulted in taxpayer's petition being one day late and the legislatively provided remedial review was therefore denied).

[307] IRC §§ 7429(b)(2), 7429(c). The running of the twenty-day period does not begin before the day on which proper service is made on the United States. IRC § 7429(b)(2), applicable to actions begun after July 18, 1984. In cases instituted before the effective date of amended Section 7429(b)(2), it had been held that under some circumstances at least, the twenty-day rule is not binding. Meadows v. United States, 665 F2d 1009 (11th Cir. 1982) (taxpayer failed to inform the district court of the statutory provision). Although Section 7429(b)(2) requires the district court to act within twenty days, district courts routinely fail to do so. If the petition or complaint is not acted on within twenty days, a taxpayer is not entitled to abatement of a jeopardy assessment if the petition does not require the government to answer within twenty days or if it fails to request review within the twenty-day period. See *Meadows v. United States,* supra, at 1012; United States v. Doyle, 660 F2d 277, 280 (7th Cir. 1981); Boyd v. United States, 724 F. Supp. 1036 (DDC 1989).

[308] IRC § 7429(f). The nonreviewability of the finding of the district court has been reaffirmed where taxpayers have attempted to appeal for various reasons. Meadows v. United States, 665 F2d 1009, 1012 (11th Cir. 1982); Nichols v. United States, 633 F2d 829 (9th Cir. 1980); Vicknair v. United States, 617 F2d 1129 (5th Cir. 1980); Randazzo v. United States, 751 F2d 145 (3d Cir. 1984) (appeal of denial of attorney fees under Section 7430 held nonreviewable because order denying fees incorporated in underlying decision under Section 7429). But see Schuster v. United States, 765 F2d 1047 (11th Cir. 1985) ("where the appeal is based on a procedural error-—i.e., that the district court acted outside its authority, rather than acting erroneously within its authority—this court (of appeals) will review the decision to determine whether such occurred"). Compare Stebco, Inc. v. United States, 916 F2d 556 (9th Cir. 1990), opinion replaced, 939 F2d 686 (9th Cir. 1991) (expansive view of nonreviewability adopted; nonreviewability of district court decision extends to lack of venue issue raised by government); compare Morgan v. United States, 958 F2d 950 (9th Cir. 1992) (when district court's decision is not on merits, appeal is permitted).

mination or jeopardy assessment was reasonable under the circumstances.[309] The taxpayer has the burden of proof on the issue of whether the amount assessed was appropriate, although the Service must provide a written statement that "contains any information with respect to which [its] determination of the amount assessed was based."[310] This division of the burden of proof is similar to the division in civil fraud cases, where the Commissioner has the burden on the issue of fraud and the taxpayer on the amount of the deficiency. The finding of jeopardy need be established only by a preponderance of the evidence, not by the clear and convincing evidence by which the Commissioner must establish fraud for civil penalty purposes.[311] Thus, the Service will succeed on the jeopardy issue if it can establish by a preponderance of the evidence that the taxpayer was about to leave the country, was about to hide or dissipate assets, or was in financial peril. In the absence of other information, an estimate of the taxpayer's liability based on the information available to the Service will be presumed to be reasonable.[312]

In a district court, the action is by its nature a summary proceeding, and local rules control.[313] In the Tax Court, special rules for a summary proceeding have been adopted. Stringent time limitations govern the parties and the reviewing court. In individual cases, procedures may vary, but a reviewing court in a due process review proceeding may consider evidence that would normally be precluded by the Federal Rules of Evidence (e.g., affidavits).[314] Certainly, the Supreme Court in *United States v. Shapiro* expected that the Service would present the basis in fact for its action in the form of affidavits.[315] How-

---

[309] IRC § 7429(g)(1).

[310] IRC § 7429(g)(1). In Penner v. United States, 582 F. Supp. 432, 436 (SD Fla. 1984), the court said that when the taxpayer shows the Service to have been neither diligent nor thorough, the taxpayer has met his burden of proof and has shown that the amount assessed is inappropriate. Hohman v. United States, 535 F. Supp. 1218 (DDC 1982) ("discovery may be permitted in Section 7429 cases but . . . any discovery is circumscribed by the narrow issue before the Court"—i.e., the facts on which the Service relies in supporting the need for a jeopardy assessment).

[311] IRC § 7429(b)(3). See La Rosa v. United States, 841 F2d 544 (4th Cir. 1988).

[312] S. Rep. No. 938, 94th Cong., 2d Sess. 364, 365, reprinted in 1976-3 CB (vol. 3) 403. See Simpson v. IRS, 573 F. Supp. 146 (MD Tenn. 1983).

[313] Haskin v. United States, 444 F. Supp. 299, 304 (CD Cal. 1977); Giles v. United States, 80-2 USTC ¶ 9546 (MD Fla. 1980). See Federal Rules of Civil Procedure 81(a)(3), which applies to civil actions to enforce an internal revenue summons. See Clarke v. United States, 553 F. Supp. 382 (ED Va. 1983) (failure of Service to answer complaint held sufficient evidence of lack of basis for jeopardy assessment). The Service successfully petitioned for a writ of mandamus. For further proceedings on remand in *Clarke*, see Clarke v. United States, 587 F. Supp. 674 (ED Va. 1984).

[314] Billig v. United States, 81-2 USTC ¶ 9792 (ND Ga. 1981); see also Nichols v. United States, 633 F2d 829 (9th Cir. 1980).

[315] United States v. Shapiro, 424 US 614 (1976).

ever, the requirement that the Service provide the taxpayer with a written statement of its basis for the assessment may and probably should lead to one of the following outcomes: (1) an exchange of information; (2) a negotiated settlement of the case; or (3) at the very least, an expedited court proceeding.[316]

As noted previously, the standard of proof in a Section 7429(b) proceeding is the normal "preponderance of the evidence" standard applied in civil cases.[317] Just what the Service must show to establish that its jeopardy finding was "reasonable under the circumstances" is another matter. One often-cited definition of "reasonable under the circumstances" is that the term means something more than "not arbitrary and capricious" and something less than "supported by substantial evidence."[318] According to the legislative history, the relevant circumstances are flight, transfer or concealment or assets, or insolvency, as listed in the Manual.[319] Courts have found other circumstances supporting a determination of jeopardy to be "reasonable."[320] One court has said, "The key consideration must be whether or not the taxpayer appears to be manipulating his property and estate in such a manner as to place them beyond the reach of the government."[321] Also, although the statute speaks of a plan to dissipate property "quickly," this term is a relative one and has been held satisfied where a planned divestiture has emerged from the facts.[322]

The broad and uncertain language of the indexes of jeopardy generally makes it difficult for taxpayers to succeed on the issue of the assessment's rea-

---

[316] S. Rep. No. 938, 94th Cong., 2d Sess. 364, 365–366, reprinted in 1976-3 CB (vol. 3) 403–404. This has not proved to be so in some district courts already overburdened by criminal cases.

[317] S. Rep. No. 938, 94th Cong., 2d Sess. 364, 365, reprinted in 1976-3 CB (vol. 3) 403.

[318] Loretto v. United States, 440 F. Supp. 1168 (ED Pa. 1977). Accord McAvoy v. IRS, 475 F. Supp. 297 (WD Mich. 1979); Giles v. United States, 80-2 USTC ¶ 9546 (MD Fla. 1980); Klotzman v. United States, 618 F. Supp. 112, 113 (D. Md. 1985) (the phrase "reasonable under the circumstances" has been held to mean "something more than arbitrary and capricious and something less than supported by substantial evidence"). Contra Ruth v. Comm'r, 81-1 USTC ¶ 9421 (MD Fla. 1981).

[319] S. Rep. No. 938, 94th Cong., 2d Sess. 364, 365 n.6, reprinted in 1976-3 CB (vol. 3) 403.

[320] See infra ¶ 10.05[7][g]. It should be noted that the reasonableness of a jeopardy assessment and the reasonableness of a jeopardy levy are two distinct inquiries. Cf. Henderson v. United States, 949 F. Supp 473 (ND Tex. 1996) (citing Shaw v. United States, 20 F3d 182 (5th Cir. 1994)).

[321] Revis v. United States, 558 F. Supp. 1071 (DRI 1983).

[322] See Revis v. United States, 558 F. Supp. 1071 (DRI 1983) (two and one-half years); DeLauri v. United States, 492 F. Supp. 442 (WD Tex. 1980) (three years); Harper v. United States, 769 F. Supp. 362 (MD Fla. 1991) (1981 property transfer and 1990 jeopardy assessment against transferee were held proper when transfers constituted fraudulent conveyances under Florida law).

sonableness. For a taxpayer, the difficulty is increased by the view of some courts that both the Service and the reviewing court may rely on information that might be considered inadmissible in a civil or criminal trial.[323] More accurately, the reviewing court in performing its review function may consider a wide range of data that may not be admissible at a trial, but some evidence, whether circumstantial or direct, must support a statement or affidavit of an agent that is not based on personal knowledge.[324]

[f] Evidence of Jeopardy

No standard adequately explains the results in all of the cases. A perversion of the Service's functions may result where a false statement is made during the course of an investigation.[325] The courts have considered a number of factors in deciding whether the Service's finding of jeopardy was reasonable, including the following:[326]

---

[323] Billig v. United States, 81-2 USTC ¶ 9792 (ND Ga. 1981; McAvoy v. IRS, 475 F. Supp. 297 (WD Mich. 1979); Bremson v. United States, 459 F. Supp. 121 (WD Mo. 1978); Miller v. United States, 615 F. Supp. 781 (ND Ohio 1985) (special agent's summary not admissible but apparently considered); Klotzman v. United States, 618 F. Supp. 112 (D. Md. 1985) (revenue officer's affidavit held not rebutted by affidavit with "conclusory allegations").

[324] Northeast Chem., Inc. v. IRS, 81-2 USTC ¶ 9611 (SDNY 1981) (revenue officer's statement not made on personal knowledge and backup records not introduced). See also Satterthwaite v. United States, 81-1 USTC ¶ 9102 (SD Fla. 1980); Dorsey v. United States, 54 AFTR2d 84-5803 (D. Cal. 1984) (taxpayer arrested in 1983 with currency in his possession and under his control; the evidence supported an assessment for 1983 but did not show that taxpayer received unreported income in 1982 from the sale of cocaine; no amount of cocaine sold). Compare Nolan v. United States, 539 F. Supp. 788 (D. Ariz. 1982) (Tucson police testified about results of surveillance, wiretaps, confidential informants, and a known informant). See also Bremson v. United States, 459 F. Supp. 121 (WD Mo. 1978) (Drug Enforcement Agency agent had personal knowledge); Rogers v. United States, 511 F. Supp. 82 (D. Minn. 1980); Danneman v. United States, 84-2 USTC ¶ 9792 (D. Md. 1984) (FBI surveillance for fifteen days in 1979 supported projections of income for 1979 and 1980; stolen goods with $1.25 million value seized at time of arrest).

[325] United States v. McCue, 301 F2d 452 (2d Cir. 1962); Brandow v. United States, 268 F2d 559 (9th Cir. 1959). United States v. Fern, 696 F2d 1269 (11th Cir. 1983) (affirmative, unsolicited false statement, which caused tax auditor initially to conclude that charitable deduction was due taxpayer, violated Section 1001). The test for materiality has also been said to determine "whether the falsification 'has a natural tendency to influence or was capable of influencing, the decision of the tribunal in making a determination required to be made.'" U.S., v. Parsons, 967 F2d 452 (10th Cir. 1992). In *Gaudin*, the Supreme Court, citing its decision in Kungys v. United States, 485 US 759, 770 (1988), accepted as a definition of "materiality" that the statement must have "a natural tendency to influence, or [be] capable of influencing the decision of the decisionmaking body to which it is addressed."

[326] See cases cited supra note 322. The factors enumerated in *Billig* are illustrative, not exclusive. See, e.g., Revis v. United States, 558 F. Supp. 1071 (DRI 1983) (jeopardy

- Possession of or dealings in large amounts of currency[327]
- Possession of narcotics[328]
- Prior tax returns that reported little or no income despite current possession of substantial assets or currency[329]

---

assessment against taxpayer, a resident of Greece and a citizen of the United States, who had over the course of two and one-half years converted various real estate and other interests to cash; held, the taxpayer appeared to be "moving methodically to place his assets beyond the reach of the government"); Pinto v. United States, 599 F. Supp. 432 (D. Kan. 1984) (possible flight to Germany with proceeds of house sale); McGrew v. United States, 85-2 USTC ¶ 9671 (MD Fla. 1985) (transfer of funds to foreign account); Bean v. United States, 618 F. Supp. 652 (ND Ga. 1985) (promoter left United States with large amounts of cash).

[327] Loretto v. United States, 440 F. Supp. 1168 (ED Pa. 1977); McAvoy v. IRS, 475 F. Supp. 297 (WD Mich. 1979; Randahl v. United States, 82-1 USTC ¶ 9356 (D. Minn. 1982); Erath v. United States, 79-1 USTC ¶ 9397 (SD Cal. 1979); Nichols v. United States, 79-1 USTC ¶ 9193 (CD Cal. 1978); Gaston v. United States, 79-1 USTC ¶ 9126 (ND Ga. 1978); Ratzlaff v. United States, 83-2 USTC ¶ 9431 (WD Wis. 1983); Felkel v. United States, 570 F. Supp. 833 (DSC 1983). In Billig v. United States, 81-2 USTC ¶ 9792 (ND Ga. 1981), the taxpayer was arrested at the airport with $106,000 in currency. Currency may be derived from illegal businesses. See, e.g., Hohman v. United States, 535 F. Supp. 1218 (DDC 1982) (prostitution). In Chavarria v. United States, 84-1 USTC ¶ 9237 (ND Cal. 1984), the jeopardy assessment was upheld where the taxpayers were found with $159,410 in currency and had attempted to transfer $119,910 out of the country, despite the absence of direct evidence of participation in illegal drug trafficking. Dorsey v. United States, 54 AFTR2d 84-5803 (D. Cal. 1984) (taxpayer seized with over $106,000 in currency); Howard v. United States, 84-2 USTC ¶ 9550 (SD Miss. 1984) ($82,000 found in windowsill and safe in house); Prather v. United States, 84-2 USTC ¶ 9730 (MD Pa. 1984) (in excess of $400,000 seized).

The fact that the discovered cash is also the subject of a forfeiture action and beyond the reach of the taxpayer has been held not to be inconsistent with a finding that a notice of termination was reasonable. See Gonzalez v. United States, 606 F. Supp. 136 (SD Fla. 1985) ($1,784,700 found in garbage bags in closet subject of state forfeiture action).

[328] Loretto v. United States, 440 F. Supp. 1168 (ED Pa. 1977); McAvoy v. IRS, 475 F. Supp. 297 (WD Mich. 1979; Amyx v. United States, 529 F. Supp. 98 (SD Ohio 1981); Davis v. United States, 511 F. Supp. 193 (D. Kan. 1981); Abercrombie v. United States, 80-2 USTC ¶ 9681 (DSC 1980); Doyle v. United States, 482 F. Supp. 1227 (ED Wis. 1980); Nichols v. United States, 79-1 USTC ¶ 9193 (CD Cal. 1978); Erath v. United States, 79-1 USTC ¶ 9397 (SD Cal. 1979). The possession of narcotics is relevant because narcotics are known to be sold in currency transactions, no record of which is generally kept. Govern v. United States, 82-2 USTC ¶ 9481 (MD Fla. 1982); Bailey v. United States, 82-2 USTC ¶ 9620 (ED Mich. 1982); Noreault v. United States, 85-2 USTC ¶ 9716 (D. Vt. 1985) (indictment for narcotics distribution, dealings in currency, and possession of $34,000 in currency); Miller v. United States, 615 F. Supp. 781 (D. Ohio 1985) (conspiracy to import marijuana; assessment of almost $10 million found appropriate and reasonable under facts).

[329] Nolan v. United States, 539 F. Supp. 788 (D. Ariz. 1982); Billig v. United States, 81-2 USTC ¶ 9792 (ND Ga. 1981); Olah v. United States, 82-1 USTC ¶ 9198 (ED Va. 1981); Erath v. United States, 79-1 USTC ¶ 9397 (SD Cal. 1979); Giles v. United States, 80-2 USTC ¶ 9546 (MD Fla. 1980); Loretto v. United States, 440 F. Supp. 1168 (ED Pa.

- Dissipation of assets through forfeiture, expenditures for attorney fees, appearance bonds, or other expenses[330]
- Taxpayer having no other assets or property from which potential tax liability can be collected[331]
- Use of aliases, which makes it more difficult to locate either the taxpayer or any of his or her assets[332]
- Failure to supply appropriate financial information when requested[333]
- Use of multiple addresses, making it harder for the Service to find the taxpayer[334]

[g] Grounds for Relief

Despite the enormous obstacles a taxpayer faces on the "reasonableness" of the jeopardy determination, some taxpayers have been successful (or rather the Service has been unsuccessful) on this issue.[335] A taxpayer may also be en-

---

1977); Govern v. United States, 82-2 USTC ¶ 9481 (MD Fla. 1982); Bailey v. United States, 82-2 USTC ¶ 9620 (ED Mich. 1982); Petzoldt v. United States, 84-2 USTC ¶ 9991 (D. Ariz. 1984) (evidence that taxpayer intended to leave country and failure to file tax returns for two years); Tucker v. United States, 85-1 USTC ¶ 9394 (Cl. Ct. 1985) (returns not filed for fifteen years; transfers of money out of the United States).

[330] Nolan v. United States, 539 F. Supp. 788 (D. Ariz. 1982); Haskin v. United States, 444 F. Supp. 299, 304 (CD Cal. 1977); Santini v. United States, 80-2 USTC ¶ 9586 (ND Cal. 1979); Hurst v. United States, 80-2 USTC ¶ 9659 (ND Fla. 1980). See Sturman v. United States, 91-1 USTC ¶ 50,202 (CD Cal. 1990) (fine and bail payments by third parties created inference that taxpayer continued "to keep his assets deployed under the nominal title of others").

[331] Loretto v. United States, 440 F. Supp. 1168 (ED Pa. 1977); Erath v. United States, 79-1 USTC ¶ 9397 (SD Cal. 1979); Gaw v. Comm'r, TC Memo. 1995-373 (1995) (taxpayer dissolved partnership, which was his only remaining substantial asset in the United States, and said he would not return to the United States; held, the Service's jeopardy assessment was reasonable under the circumstances despite the taxpayer's successful litigation against the Service).

[332] Billig v. United States, 81-2 USTC ¶ 9792 (ND Ga. 1981); Doyle v. United States, 482 F. Supp. 1227 (ED Wis. 1980); Erath v. United States, 79-1 USTC ¶ 9397 (SD Cal. 1979); Bremson v. United States, 459 F. Supp. 121 (WD Mo. 1978); Berkery v. United States, 544 F. Supp. 1 (ED Pa. 1982); Nesbitt v. United States, 84-2 USTC ¶ 9648 (D. Ala. 1984) (alleged undocumented ownership interest in plumbing business; use of two different Social Security numbers); de la Fuente v. United States, 596 F. Supp. 643 (MD Fla. 1984) (use of nominee to own realty); Munoz v. United States, 87-1 USTC ¶ 9117 (D. Nev. 1986) (purchased business property and automobiles using other names).

[333] Haskin v. United States, 444 F. Supp. 299, 304 (CD Cal. 1977).

[334] Billig v. United States, 81-2 USTC ¶ 9792 (ND Ga. 1981); Gaston v. United States, 79-1 USTC ¶ 9126 (ND Ga. 1978).

[335] See, e.g., Maggio v. United States, 81-2 USTC ¶ 9580 (SD Fla. 1981) (evidence that taxpayer was custodian, not owner of funds); Satterthwaite v. United States, 81-1

titled to relief on grounds other than the unproved reasonableness of the Service jeopardy determination.[336] To carry his or her burden of proof, a taxpayer must prove by a preponderance of the evidence that the amount of the assessment is not an appropriate estimate of the tax he or she may ultimately owe for the full taxable year. Before a taxpayer opposes the appropriateness of the amount assessed, several factors should be considered.

1. A taxpayer who has been arrested and charged with a crime may not be able to contest the assessment without waiving a constitutional privilege or giving evidence that can otherwise be used against him or her.

2. A taxpayer faced with a termination assessment will have a more difficult time than a jeopardy taxpayer, who will at least be able to gather evidence relating to the full year. The statement the Service is required to provide describing the information on which it relied in making the assessment should be carefully analyzed. As indicated earlier, projections of income have met with mixed results in injunc-

---

USTC ¶ 9102 (SD Fla. 1980); Northeast Chem., Inc. v. IRS, 81-2 USTC ¶ 9611 (SDNY 1981). Although the motives behind a taxpayer's transfer of property may be a relevant consideration in making a determination as to reasonableness, they are not dispositive (the issue is ultimate collectibility of the tax). See DeLauri v. United States, 492 F. Supp. 442 (WD Tex. 1980) (and cases cited therein); Burd v. United States, 774 F. Supp. 903 (DNJ 1991) (jeopardy assessment based on uncorroborated testimony of taxpayer's ex-husband was unreasonable; investigation would have shown taxpayer was not attempting to put proceeds beyond reach of government).

[336] See, e.g., DeLauri v. United States, 492 F. Supp. 442 (WD Tex. 1980) (insufficient written statement of basis for assessment); Fidelity Equip. Leasing Corp. v. United States, 462 F. Supp. 845 (ND Ga. 1978). Compare Barry, Jr. v. United States, 534 F. Supp. 304 (ED Tenn. 1982) (acting district director may approve termination assessment; attachments to conclusory notice explained how tax was computed); Penner v. United States, 582 F. Supp. 432 (SD Fla. 1984) (errors in bank deposits analysis); Dorsey v. United States, 54 AFTR2d 84-5803 (D. Cal. 1984) (unsupported projection); Snyder v. United States, 85-1 USTC ¶ 9176 (D. Md. 1984) (taxpayer convicted in December 1981; jeopardy assessment made in June 1984; held, jeopardy not reasonable but used to avoid paying refund to taxpayer); Perillo v. United States, 86-2 USTC ¶ 9638 (EDNY 1986) (jeopardy assessments not reasonably necessary to secure payment of assessment based on seizure of $350,000 in currency where taxpayers owned real property); George F. Harding Museum v. United States, 674 F. Supp. 1323 (ND Ill. 1987) (a jeopardy assessment is not reasonable if its purpose is to gain time to perfect a priority over other claimants). Also, when a jeopardy assessment was made against both a doctor and his professional corporation, and the amount assessed against the corporation was based on full tax on the same income assessed against the doctor personally, the court held that the assessment against the corporation of the same amount was unreasonable. Zamzam v. United States, 97 TNT 74-14 (WD W. Va. 1997) (uncontradicted testimony of accountant was that the net amount received by the corporation would have been paid out to the doctor as compensation, not a dividend).

tion cases,[337] and circumstantial methods of proof (e.g., bank deposits and net worth analyses) must at least meet the criteria of these methods (e.g., by providing for reasonable personal expenses).[338]

3. A taxpayer should document the need for partial abatement due to "unusual hardship," especially if the taxpayer is also the subject of a nontax criminal prosecution.[339] Obviously, the availability of funds for a taxpayer to pay attorney fees is vital to the taxpayer's ability to have legal counsel in nontax and tax controversies. If the amount of tax is appropriate, but the court refuses to abate the assessment, the taxpayer may be put at an unfair disadvantage in defending himself or disputing the amount of the assessment.[340] Courts should balance the interests of the Service and the needs of the taxpayer, and they have done so in cases not involving narcotics, gambling, or similar crimes.[341]

When a taxpayer has been successful in having a jeopardy assessment determined to be improper or excessive, the Service has contended that it is not obligated to refund amounts it has collected. The rationale is that once the jeopardy assessment is abated, amounts collected in excess of the remaining assessment should be considered overpayments to be applied against any other

---

[337] Compare Pizzarello v. United States, 408 F2d 579 (2d Cir.), cert. denied, 396 US 986 (1969) with Hamilton v. United States, 429 F2d 427 (2d Cir. 1970), cert. denied, 401 US 913 (1971). See Breider v. United States, 614 F. Supp. 1200 (ED Wis. 1985) (projection modified in gambling case).

[338] See Nader v. United States, 81-2 USTC ¶ 9554 (ND Ohio 1981) (erroneous inclusion of insurance proceeds as taxable income and opening net worth); Nolan v. IRS, 539 F. Supp. 788 (D. Ariz. 1982); Davis v. United States, 287 F2d 168 (Ct. Cl. 1961). See supra ¶ 10.05[3][a]; Revis v. United States, 558 F. Supp. 1071 (DRI 1983) (source and application of funds or expenditures analysis; funds for personal living expenses not used as offset); Noreault v. United States, 85-2 USTC ¶ 9716 (D. Vt. 1985) (amount of assessment reduced to deduct cost of gun and coin collection found to have been purchased before tax year). For a case where the computation of a penalty was involved in a jeopardy assessment case, see Bean v. United States, 618 F. Supp. 652 (ND Ga. 1985) (Section 6700 penalty applied to each partner's investment, not each partnership).

[339] However, taxpayers have been unsuccessful in obtaining the release of funds to pay attorney fees to contest tax claims. See Fidelity Equip. Leasing Corp. v. United States, 81-1 USTC ¶ 9434 (ND Ga. 1981) (cases collected, but not under Section 7429). This result is questionable in light of the legislative history of Section 7429 and the unfair consequences of jeopardy assessments that completely tie up the taxpayer's resources.

[340] Nevertheless, it has been held that a state forfeiture action has no effect on a Section 7429 determination, and therefore, the taxpayer can be liable for taxes based on cash that has come to light while such funds are seized by a nontax forfeiture. Randahl v. United States, 82-1 USTC ¶ 9356 (D. Minn. 1982).

[341] See, e.g., DeLauri v. United States, 492 F. Supp. 442 (WD Tex. 1980).

outstanding tax assessments, past-due support obligations, and debts owed to other federal agencies.[342]

[h] Authority of the Court

Reviewing courts are expected to rely on information that only becomes available after the assessment and to exercise discretion in abating the assessment, in whole or in part, even if the assessment is found to be inappropriate or excessive, as long as the taxpayer would suffer "unusual hardship." Judicial criteria reviewing courts have considered include (1) improper Service procedure or conduct; (2) excessive assessment; and (3) taxpayer hardship. The reviewing court may order the Service to abate the amount of an improper or excessive assessment or take other action it considers appropriate.[343]

---

[342] While some courts have ordered the seized funds returned to the taxpayer, others have permitted the Service to apply the seized amounts to other unpaid assessments. See Melton v. United States, 1995 WL 804620 (D. Col. 1995) ("Section 7429 proceedings are unrelated substantively and procedurally to any subsequent action for refund brought in a federal district court to determine the correctness of the liability"). If the excess collections are considered overpayments, then the taxpayer must follow the normal procedures for obtaining a refund, such as the filing of a claim within two years after the forced collection of the amount sought to be refunded. When the overpayment to be refunded is for the year of the jeopardy assessment, the taxpayer can seek the refund by raising the issue in a Tax Court petition. But suppose the Service applies the overpayment to another tax year. If the overpayment does not satisfy the full amount of that other tax year's tax liability, the taxpayer will not be able to institute a refund suit, because the taxpayer will not have made full payment, as required under the *Flora* rule, explained infra ¶ 11.06[4].

[343] IRC § 7429(b)(3). In La Rosa v. United States, 841 F2d 544 (4th Cir. 1988), the court noted that "a district court has no jurisdiction to 'fashion an appropriate order' in circumstances where the assessment has been ruled reasonable and appropriate." However, a district court may make such an order if the assessment is unreasonable or excessive. One district court noted that the context and legislative history of Section 7429 permitted the court "to fashion an appropriate remedy even though it has held the Service's determination of jeopardy and amounts of liability to be reasonable." Mrs. Philippines Home for Senior Citizens, Inc. v. United States, 94-1 USTC ¶ 50,065 (D. Md. 1993). The Fourth Circuit reversed, however, saying that once the district court has determined that the amount of an assessment is reasonable and the making of the jeopardy appropriate under the circumstances, the court lacks authority to fashion any remedy. LaRosa v. United States, 841 F2d 544 (4th Cir. 1988). Faced with the circuit court's clear statement, the district court responding creatively, using Rule 62(c) of the Federal Rules of Civil Procedure to enjoin enforced collection by the Service as to property used in the operation of a senior citizens home, pending the appeal to the circuit court. As the district court ruled, there are circumstances when Section 7429 should be read to permit action by either partial abatement or some specifically fashioned order to relieve hardship until there has been a determination of the actual tax liability of the taxpayer.

[8] Minimizing the Effect of Jeopardy or Termination Assessments

Several procedures are available to a taxpayer against whom a termination or jeopardy assessment has been made and collection action taken. The taxpayer may post bond to stay collection if collection has not already been made. Alternatively, the taxpayer may reach an informal arrangement with the local office to secure payment of the assessment. Lastly, the taxpayer may petition the reviewing court to grant an injunction proceeding.[344] Also, as noted previously, a finding may be made of jeopardy abatement in whole or in part after administrative and judicial review of the assessment requested under Section 7429.

[a] Posting Bond

A taxpayer may give the Service security for the collection of the assessed tax by delivering a bond to stay collection of a termination or jeopardy assessment.[345] Because a bonding company usually requires cash or other collateral at least equal to the amount of the bond (and probably more), and charges a fee as well, posting a bond is not a viable alternative except in rare cases where a taxpayer's assets are substantially in excess of the amount of the assessment.[346] Also, the tax lien arising from jeopardy assessments makes a pledge of collateral to the bonding difficult, if not impractical. Finally, few personal sureties are willing to risk having to pay on the bond even if the taxpayer is able to pledge assets to secure the bond. In short, posting a bond is a difficult, if not inaccessible, procedure for a taxpayer.[347]

---

[344] Suits against revenue officers for collecting on jeopardy or termination assessments have generally been unsuccessful because Service officers have qualified immunity when they act in good faith and on reasonable grounds; moreover, Section 7433 provides that a taxpayer may commence an action for wrongful collection. See the discussion at ¶ 15.07. See also Hall v. United States, 704 F2d 246 (6th Cir. 1983) (failure to send notice of deficiency after jeopardy assessment; suit for damages); Epps v. Baer, 696 F2d 989 (4th Cir.), cert. denied, 461 US 929 (1982) (damages incurred following jeopardy assessment); Govern v. Meese, 811 F2d 1405 (11th Cir. 1987) (taxpayer against whom a jeopardy assessment had been made could not obtain a declaratory judgment that property forfeited under the Racketeer Influenced and Corrupt Organizations Act (18 USC § 1963(a)) be applied to assessment because government had not waived sovereign immunity).

[345] IRC § 6863(a). Form 1129 is used for this purpose. It is required, unless the District Counsel approves a substitute or modified version.

[346] The bond procedure has been called a mockery where all the taxpayer's property is tied up. Kimmel v. Tomlinson, 151 F. Supp. 901 (SD Fla. 1957). However, the taxpayer in Millington v. Conley, 74-1 USTC ¶ 9136 (D. Conn. 1974) was able to avoid the threatened sale of his car to collect a termination assessment by posting a $2,000 bond.

[347] See Shelton v. Gill, 202 F2d 503 (4th Cir. 1953); Kimmel v. Tomlinson, 151 F. Supp. 901 (SD Fla. 1957); Macejko v. United States, 174 F. Supp. 87, 89 (ND Ohio 1959).

[b] Informal Arrangements

A taxpayer may be able to arrange to secure the payment of the termination and jeopardy assessment pending court review.[348] Such an arrangement is not as a matter of right under statute or regulation, but is solely in the exercise of the district director's discretion. Under an informal arrangement (1) property might be protected by subordination agreements with other creditors in order to keep a viable business operating; (2) specific property might be discharged from the effect of the lien, sold, and the proceeds used either to maintain other property or to pay the Service in part; or (3) the district director might be given a mortgage on real property. In all likelihood, however, an informal arrangement to secure collection will be difficult to negotiate where assessment has been made based on a finding that collection itself was jeopardized.

[c] Injunctive Relief

The effect of the enactment of Section 7429 on the availability of an injunction against collection is unclear. A person who petitions a court to exercise its equitable jurisdiction to grant an injunction must establish that he or she has no adequate remedy at law. However, the proceeding for review under Section 7429 appears to provide a legal remedy. Congress intended the remedy to be adequate, but there is no indication in either the legislative history or in the Supreme Court's decision in *Shapiro* that an alternative remedy for reviewing a termination or jeopardy assessment would preclude an injunction action.[349]

¶ 10.06 BANKRUPTCY AND RECEIVERSHIP ASSESSMENTS

Special assessment procedures apply where a taxpayer and the taxpayer's property come under the jurisdiction of a bankruptcy court or another court in a receivership proceeding. Section 6871 authorizes the Service, upon the commencement of a bankruptcy case, to make immediate assessments of (1) a tax imposed on the bankruptcy estate (as opposed to the taxpayer/debtor) and (2) a tax imposed on the taxpayer/debtor if liability for the tax has become res judicata against the taxpayer/debtor because of a bankruptcy court determina-

---

[348] The possibilities of minimizing the effect of liens and levies in jeopardy cases are the same as in other collection cases. These options are discussed in Chapter 14.

[349] Comm'r v. Shapiro, 424 US 614 (1976). The Supreme Court said, in fact, that its decision would not "prevent the Government from providing an administrative or other forum outside the Art. III judicial system...."

tion of the tax liability.[350] In all other cases, the normal restrictions on assessment apply when a bankruptcy case is begun. Thus, the taxpayer/debtor is entitled to receive a notice of deficiency and may file a petition in the Tax Court to contest a prebankruptcy tax deficiency. Before the amendment of Section 6781 by the Bankruptcy Tax Act of 1980,[351] the Service was authorized by Section 6871(a) to make immediate assessment of any deficiency in income, estate, or gift tax where (1) a taxpayer filed a petition in bankruptcy; (2) a taxpayer was determined (adjudicated) to be a bankrupt; (3) an involuntary petition in bankruptcy was filed against a taxpayer and the petition was approved; (4) protection of the bankruptcy court in a debtor rehabilitation proceeding was sought by or against the taxpayer, irrespective of any court approval of the petition; or (5) a receiver was appointed for a taxpayer. When a taxpayer's property is placed in receivership, the Service is still authorized to make immediate assessment of tax.[352]

Changes made by the Bankruptcy Tax Act coordinate the internal revenue laws with the provisions of the Bankruptcy Code.[353] On the filing of a bankruptcy petition, all creditors, including the Service, are automatically enjoined or stayed from taking action or continuing action to collect their claims or enforce their liens against property of the debtor.[354] The stay specifically applies to "any act to collect, assess or recover a claim against the debtor that arose before the commencement" of the bankruptcy case.[355] By eliminating immediate assessment of tax against a debtor on the commencement of a bankruptcy case, Section 6871(b) was made consistent with the stay provision that would otherwise prevent such an assessment.

Although the automatic stay prevents the Service from taking administrative action to collect a tax, the bankruptcy stay does not preclude the Service from issuing a statutory notice of deficiency. The automatic stay also enjoins the institution or continuation of proceedings in the Tax Court to challenge an asserted deficiency of the debtor.[356] Because the bankruptcy court has broad jurisdiction to determine the amount of any tax,[357] the effect of the stay and Section 6871 is to give the bankruptcy court the discretion to (1) lift the stay to

---

[350] IRC § 6871(b).

[351] Bankruptcy Tax Act of 1980, Pub. L. No. 95-589.

[352] IRC § 6871(a). See IRM 4.3.10, Bankruptcy Handbook (June 30, 1999).

[353] For a summary of the Bankruptcy Code and its effect on tax collection, see infra ¶ 10.06. For an explanation of the provisions of the Bankruptcy Tax Act of 1980, Pub. L. No. 96-589, see 1980-2 CB 607.

[354] 11 USC § 362(a).

[355] 11 USC § 362(a)(6). The stay provision is applicable to cases under Chapter 7 (liquidation), Chapter 9 (adjustment of debts of a municipality), Chapter 11 (reorganization), and Chapter 13 (adjustment of debts of an individual with regular income).

[356] 11 USC § 362(a)(8).

[357] 11 USC § 505(a)(1).

permit the taxpayer to file a petition in the Tax Court or (2) determine the taxpayer's liability.[358] Section 6213(f) suspends the ninety-day period for filing a Tax Court petition for the period "during which the debtor is prohibited by reason of such case from filing a petition in the Tax Court . . . and for 60 days thereafter." The period of limitations on assessment is extended for the same period.[359] Accordingly, if the bankruptcy court lifts the automatic stay, a taxpayer/debtor may file a petition in the Tax Court to collect a prebankruptcy tax deficiency determination.

Immediate assessment of tax is authorized in the two bankruptcy situations where Congress believed there was no need for the Service to follow normal deficiency procedures, including the sending of a notice of deficiency.[360] When taxes are imposed on the bankruptcy estate of an individual (i.e., where the estate is treated as a separate taxable entity), the bankruptcy court determines the estate's tax liability rather than the Tax Court.[361] In the second situation, where a debtor's personal liability for a nondischargeable tax claim has been heard and determined in the bankruptcy court, the debtor is precluded by the doctrine of res judicata from relitigating the liability in any court. Consequently, no purpose would be served in issuing a notice of deficiency.

The Bankruptcy Tax Act of 1980 also added Sections 1398 and 1399 to the Code. These provisions provide the first comprehensive statutory treatment of issues such as whether the bankruptcy estate constitutes a taxable entity apart from the individual debtor and, if so, how tax attributes are to be allocated between the estate and the debtor. From a procedural viewpoint, Section 1398 is significant because it gives an individual debtor (not a partnership or a corporation) in certain bankruptcy cases (a liquidating bankruptcy under Chapter 7 and a reorganization under Chapter 11, not a wage earners plan under Chapter 13) an election to close his taxable year at the date of bankruptcy.[362] Thus, the debtor rather than the Service may terminate his tax year in this situation. As a result, the taxpayer accelerates examination and deficiency proce-

---

[358] Section 6871(e) permits claims for taxes to be presented to the bankruptcy court even if a case is already pending in the Tax Court.

[359] IRC § 6503(i). The period of collection is suspended for the stay period, plus six months. If the notice of deficiency was issued before the commencement of the bankruptcy case, the unexpired portion of the ninety-day period for filing the Tax Court petition is carried over and added on to the sixty-day period to determine the last day required for filing a timely petition. McClamma v. Comm'r, 76 TC 754 (1981). See also Galanis v. Comm'r, 92 TC 34 (1989) ("the period of limitations on assessment and collection in a title 11 case [may] be suspended during the period in which the automatic stay is in effect").

[360] S. Rep. No. 1035, 96th Cong., 2d Sess. 49 (1980).

[361] 11 USC § 505(b).

[362] IRC § 1398(d)(2)(A).

dures, although no assessment is made. If a debtor makes this election, the debtor's taxable year, which otherwise would include the commencement date of the bankruptcy, is divided into two short taxable years of less than twelve months.[363] The first short year ends on the day before the commencement date[364]; the second begins on the commencement date. By making the election, under the Bankruptcy Code, the debtor's tax liability for the first short taxable year becomes an allowable claim against the bankruptcy estate as a claim arising before bankruptcy.[365] Consequently, any tax liability for the short tax year is collectible from the estate, depending on the availability of estate assets to pay debts of the priority given to federal taxes under the Bankruptcy Code.[366] To the extent that the bankruptcy estate's assets are insufficient to pay the tax for the short tax year, the tax liability of the electing debtor is not dischargeable, and the liability can be collected from the individual debtor after the bankruptcy case.[367] If the debtor does not make an election, no part of the debtor's tax liability for the year of the bankruptcy is collectible from the estate. It is collectible directly from the debtor, presumably out of assets the debtor acquires after the commencement of the bankruptcy case.

Unlike the requirements regarding ordinary taxpayers, if a receiver is appointed for a taxpayer, the Code does not require a notice of deficiency to be sent before an assessment is made. Unlike the jeopardy assessment, a notice of deficiency is not required to be sent within sixty days after the assessment. As a result, the taxpayer in receivership does not have the same rights as other taxpayers to contest a deficiency determination in the Tax Court.[368] However, in further contrast to jeopardy proceedings, the tax assessed under Section 6871 is usually not collected immediately because the taxpayer's property is already under the jurisdiction of the receivership court at the time of the assessment. If the receivership is terminated and a tax claim remains unpaid, the unpaid tax may be immediately collected from the taxpayer's property subject to levy (e.g., after-acquired property) after notice and demand.[369]

---

[363] The election must be made on or before the due date for filing the return for the tax year ending on the day before the bankruptcy case is commenced. Once this election is made, it is irrevocable. IRC § 1398(d)(2)(D).

[364] IRC § 1398(d)(2)(A).

[365] The theory is that it is proper to allow this election because the prebankruptcy income items that gave rise to the liability may have passed to the bankruptcy estate. 1980-2 CB, 607, 632.

[366] For discussion of priority of tax claims, see Chapter 16.

[367] 11 USC § 523(a)(1).

[368] IRC § 6871(c)(2).

[369] IRC § 6873.

[1] Administrative Procedures

Section 6036 and the regulations require that the Service be notified of the pendency of a bankruptcy proceeding.[370] The statute of limitations on assessment is suspended from the date the proceeding is instituted to thirty days after the date the notice is received by the district director, although the period of suspension may not exceed two years.[371] The Service may also receive information of the pendency of proceedings from published notices and reports of revenue officers or revenue agents. In each district office, the Special Procedures Staff of the Collection Division is responsible for determining the commencement of bankruptcy and receivership proceedings.[372]

Stay provisions of the Bankruptcy Code prohibit the assessment and collection of a prebankruptcy tax but do not preclude the sending of a notice of deficiency to a taxpayer/debtor.[373] During the period of the stay, the running of the statute of limitations on assessment and collection is also suspended.[374] When the Special Procedures Staff learns that the taxpayer is involved in a bankruptcy or receivership proceeding with assets available to pay all or part of a tax, it notifies the Examination function of the appropriate taxpayer division.[375] On receiving notice that a bankruptcy "assets" case has commenced, Examination is instructed to determine the taxpayer's liability for income, gift, estate, excise, and employment taxes as expeditiously as possible so that a proof of claim can be filed in the bankruptcy court by the Collection Division.[376] The Examination Division issues a notice of deficiency when prepeti-

---

[370] The trustee or other fiduciary is required to give notice of his qualification within ten days of his appointment. IRC § 6036; Reg. § 301.6036-1(a)(1).

[371] IRC § 6872.

[372] IRM 4.3.10, Bankruptcy Handbook (June 30, 1999). The Assistant Attorney General, Tax Division, Department of Justice, and Chief Counsel have agreed to a bankruptcy referral procedure for efficient processing of tax cases involving taxpayers in bankruptcy proceedings. In general, the Service has six months from the filing date of the bankruptcy petition to resolve the case.

[373] 11 USC §§ 362(a)(6), 362(b)(8).

[374] IRC § 6503(i).

[375] IRM 4583.21, MT 4500-461 (Mar. 2, 1990) (Bankruptcy and Receivership Cases, General Considerations). The Special Procedures Staff determines whether the case is an "asset" or "no asset" case. A "no asset" case is a liquidating bankruptcy case in which (1) a notice of no dividend is included with the notice of the first meeting of creditors or (2) the assets of the debtor are valued at an amount less than the allowable exemptions under federal or state law, plus the estimated costs of administration. Examination is notified of both types of cases.

[376] IRM 4583.221, MT 4500-466 (Mar. 27, 1991) (Processing Forms 2552 Received in "Asset" Cases). In a "no asset" case, the taxpayer's returns are screened, and the returns are accepted as filed, unless examination is considered warranted. A "no asset" bankruptcy case warranting examination is handled in the same manner as an "asset" case.

tion deficiencies of the taxpayer have been determined but not assessed.[377] The notice of deficiency is sent to the taxpayer/debtor, not to the trustee, although the trustee does receive a copy. If a deficiency is determined by the bankruptcy court or the Tax Court, the Service is permitted to and will make assessment of tax, without regard to the automatic stay of assessment, which continues until the case is closed.[378]

In a receivership case, the so-called single assessment is made after the Examination Division determines the existence of any tax liability. With information provided by the Examination Division, the Special Procedures Staff prepares and files a proof of claim.

[2] Judicial Review

The Bankruptcy Code and Section 6871 provide specific rules for the determination of tax liability when a taxpayer is in bankruptcy. The Tax Court and the bankruptcy court have concurrent jurisdiction to determine the taxpayer's liability for tax.[379] However, the bankruptcy court decides which court will actually hear the case. Unless the bankruptcy court lifts the automatic stay of Bankruptcy Code Section 362(a)(8), a taxpayer may not file a petition in the Tax Court or continue a case already pending in that court. Consequently, the bankruptcy court may decide to lift the stay to permit the taxpayer/debtor to file a petition or continue litigation of his or her case, or it may retain jurisdiction and decide the issue itself. If the taxpayer is permitted to and does contest a tax deficiency in the Tax Court, the trustee has the right to intervene.[380] When a debtor's case is pending in the Tax Court but the bankruptcy court assumes jurisdiction over the issue of tax liability, the tax claim may be presented in the bankruptcy court.[381]

IRM 4583.222, MT 4500-458 (Aug. 28, 1985) (Processing Bankruptcy Notices Received in "No Asset" Cases).

[377] IRM 4583.23, MT 4500-466 (June 12, 1986) (Preparation, Review, and Issuance of Bankruptcy Notice of Deficiency). If the case is pending in Appeals at the time the petition is filed, Appeals can retain jurisdiction for six months if the taxpayer files an objection to the Service's proof of claim. IRM 4583.27, MT 4500-466 (May 9, 1984) (Cases Being Considered by Appeals).

[378] IRM 4583.23, MT 4500-466 (June 12, 1986) (Preparation, Review, and Issuance of Bankruptcy Notice of Deficiency). If the case is pending in Appeals at the time the petition is filed, Appeals can retain jurisdiction for six months if the taxpayer files an objection to the Service's proof of claim. IRM 4583.27, MT 4500-466 (May 9, 1984) (Cases Being Considered by Appeals).

[379] 11 USC § 505(a)(1). See IRC §§ 6871(b), 6871(c).

[380] IRC § 7464.

[381] IRC § 6871(c)(1).

There are two exceptions to the concurrent jurisdiction of the bankruptcy court and the Tax Court. If, at the time the bankruptcy case is commenced, the taxpayer has filed a petition in the Tax Court and the matter has been "contested before and adjudicated by" the Tax Court, the bankruptcy court has no jurisdiction to decide the matter.[382] Second, where the tax involved is one over which the Tax Court has no jurisdiction (e.g., employment and most excise taxes), the bankruptcy court has sole jurisdiction to determine the tax liability.

---

[382] 11 USC § 505(a)(2).

FORM 10.1
NOTICE OF JEOPARDY ASSESSMENT

Internal Revenue Service
Department of the Treasury
District Director
Mailing Address: Attn: E:R:30
DP.O. Box 0000
New York, NY 00000

June 1, 1981

Mr. and Mrs. John Doe
1 Main Street
New York, NY 00000

Dear Mr. and Mrs. Doe:

NOTICE OF JEOPARDY ASSESSMENT AND RIGHT OF APPEAL

Under Section 6861 of the Internal Revenue Code, you are notified that I have found you appear to be designing to depart from the United States or to conceal yourself; or appear to be placing your property beyond the reach of the government either by removing it from the United States or concealing it or by transferring it to other persons thereby tending to prejudice or render ineffectual collection of income tax for the period ending December 31, 1978. Accordingly, based on information available at this time, I have approved assessment of tax and additional amounts determined to be due as reflected in the attached computations that do not reflect interest due to the date of payment:

Taxable Period	Tax	Penalty
7812	$125,000.00	$41,500.00

Under Section 7429 of the Internal Revenue Code, you are entitled to request administrative and judicial reviews of this assessment action.

For an administrative review, you may file a written protest with the District Director within 30 days from the date of this letter, requesting redetermination of whether or not:

1. The making of the assessment is reasonable under the circumstances and
2. The amount so assessed or demanded as a result of the action is appropriate under the circumstances.

A conference will be held on an expedited basis to consider your protest. Your protest will be forwarded to the Regional Appeals Office where a conference will be held.

If you submit new information or documentation for the first time at an Appeals conference, the Appeals Office may request comment from the District Director on such evidence or documents.

Enforced collection action may proceed during any administrative appeal process unless arrangements are made regarding collection of the amount assessed. To make such arrangements, please contact:

Revenue Office
Richard Roe
P.O. Box 0000
New York, NY 00000
Tel: (000) 000-0000

Mr. and Mrs. John Doe:

You may request a judicial review of this assessment by bringing a civil suit against the United States in the U.S. District Court in the judicial district in which you reside, or in which your principal office is located. However, in order to have this action reviewed by the District Court, you must request administrative review within 30 days of the date of this letter. Such suit must be filed within 30 days after the earlier of (1) the day the Service notifies you of its decision on your protest, or (2) the 16th day after your protest. The Court will make an early determination of the same points raised in your protest to determine whether the making of the assessment is reasonable under the circumstances, and whether the amount assessed or demanded is appropriate under the circumstances. The Court's determination is final and not reviewable by any other court.

Appeal to the Courts in Case of Income, Estate, Gift, and Certain Excise Taxes

If an agreement is not reached with the Internal Revenue Service, a notice of deficiency is required by law to be issued within 60 days from the date of jeopardy assessment made under Section 6861 of the Internal Revenue Code. You will then have 90 days (150 days if outside the United States) from the date the notice is mailed to file a petition with the U.S. Tax Court.

Very truly yours,

District Director

CHAPTER 11

Overpayment, Refund, Credit, and Abatement

A. PROCEDURES IN GENERAL

¶ 11.01 OVERVIEW OF REFUND PROCEDURES

As described in Chapter 10, an assessment separates deficiency procedures from refund procedures. On making an assessment, the Internal Revenue Service (the Service) has the equivalent of a judgment against the taxpayer.[1] The Service is entitled to collect the amount of its assessment/judgment administratively using roughly the same collection procedures (lien, levy, and seizure) as a judgment creditor uses to collect the judgment from the judgment debtor.[2] For taxpayers, the prospect of the Service's taking enforced collection action after an assessment also brings into play refund procedures. Once the Service makes an assessment against a taxpayer, these refund procedures require a taxpayer to (1) pay the full amount of the assessed tax; (2) file a claim for refund, stating the amount claimed and the grounds for the refund; and (3) if the claim is disallowed, sue for a refund of the amount the taxpayer believes the Service erroneously and illegally collected in a district court, or the U.S. Court of Federal Claims. Because full payment of the amount of the tax is a jurisdictional prerequisite to a suit for refund, refund procedures require the taxpayer to pay first and litigate later.

Refund procedures have long been part of the tax law. Before 1924, if a taxpayer disputed the amount of tax the Bureau of Internal Revenue determined, the taxpayer's only option was to follow the refund procedures. Many taxpayers were unable to make full payment of the amounts of the Bureau assessment. In 1924, Congress responded to the hardships these taxpayers experienced with the requirement of making full payment of the assessed tax before they were entitled to court review.[3] Congress established preassessment procedures, which permitted the taxpayer the opportunity to challenge the correctness of the additional tax the Bureau determined to be owed in a specialized court, the Board of Tax Appeals, now the U.S. Tax Court. During the time the

---

[1] Bull v. United States, 295 US 247 (1935).

[2] See IRC §§ 6303 (notice and demand for payment), 6321 (lien for taxes), 6331 (levy and distraint). The Service's collection procedures are described in Chapter 14.

[3] Flora v. United States, 362 US 145, 154–155 (1960).

taxpayer has to file a petition, and the Tax Court has to decide the case, collection is prohibited. As discussed in Chapter 10, the Internal Revenue Code (the Code) prescribes a statutory framework for deficiency procedures as well as Tax Court jurisdiction. In contrast to refund procedures, the deficiency procedures permit a taxpayer to litigate first and pay later. In addition to deficiency procedures, the Code also describes comprehensive procedures for taxpayers to follow to obtain refunds of overpayments from the Service and, if necessary, a refund court. This chapter analyzes these refund procedures.

As this brief summary of refund procedures shows, the Code establishes two sets of procedures that are fundamentally different in their timing and in the obligations imposed on taxpayers and the government: (1) refund procedures that follow assessment of a tax and culminate in a suit for refund in a district court or the Court of Federal Claims and (2) deficiency procedures that generally precede assessment and result in the filing of a petition for redetermination in the Tax Court. The differences between refund and deficiency procedures are summarized in Form 11.1.

Two factors make a discussion of refund procedures necessary. In a self-reporting tax system, just as some taxpayers will make errors in their favor and underpay tax, others will file returns only to discover that they have erroneously overpaid their tax. Despite procedures to avoid tax disputes, the Code anticipates that at least some taxpayers will be unable to resolve disputes with the Service over the amount of the tax due. After the Service has examined a taxpayer's return and administratively found that the taxpayer has not paid the correct tax, the taxpayer may not agree with the Service's finding. If the taxpayer disagrees with the Service's finding, the taxpayer can challenge it by first paying the tax deficiency the Service found, then filing a claim for refund, and, finally, challenging the correctness of the Service's assessment in a federal district court or the U.S. Court of Federal Claims. As a matter of policy, the refund claim is a prerequisite because it is believed that taxpayers should file a claim for refund with the Service to give the Service a last chance to resolve disputes over the amount of the tax due before the taxpayer takes the dispute to court.

There is a second factor grounded in the history of the tax law. In 1943, Congress adopted the current tax payment system to accelerate the collection of income tax. But the amount of withheld or estimated tax payments intentionally called for collections in excess of the tax actually due for the year. As a result, it was expected that from time to time the Service would collect too much tax from taxpayers or that for a number of reasons excessive amounts will be paid by taxpayers to the Service. Since excess losses or credits for a current tax year may be carried back to prior years, the tax for the prior years, as recalculated, will be less than the original tax paid.

Refund procedures permit taxpayers to recover their overpayments of tax in four alternative ways:

1. By the Service's allowing a claim for refund filed by the taxpayer;

2. By a suit for refund in a federal district court or the U.S. Court of Federal Claims;

3. By the Tax Court's determining that an overpayment exists for a year for which the Service has determined a deficiency; or

4. By voluntary action of the Service without the taxpayer's having filed a claim for refund (e.g., if a mathematical error has been detected in the processing of the return in the Service center).[4]

In more detail, the Code's refund procedures can be summarized as follows:

1. *The existence of an overpayment.* The amount of the overpayment must be determined. Statutorily, any tax paid after the applicable statutes of limitations on assessment and collection have expired constitutes an overpayment, as do excess withholding and estimated tax credits.[5] Generally, any tax payment that exceeds the amount rightfully due for the year is an overpayment.

2. *The required filing of a claim for refund.* Authority is granted to the Service to credit an overpayment against any tax liability the taxpayer may have and to refund the balance.[6] However, even if the Service were to recognize that a taxpayer has overpaid a tax, this refund authority does not exist unless the taxpayer files a claim for refund.[7] After a tax has been assessed and collected, the Service has no authority to refund or credit the overpayment unless the taxpayer files a timely claim for refund. Any refund or credit of an overpayment made after the period for filing a timely claim is considered erroneous and void.[8]

3. *Claims for refund must be timely and satisfy notice and other procedural requirements.* A claim for refund is timely if it is filed within three years from the filing of the return in question or two years from the date the tax was paid.[9] The claim must meet notice requirements by setting forth in detail each ground on which credit or refund of the overpayment is claimed and sufficient facts to inform the Service of the basis for the claim.[10] Finally, the claim must satisfy procedural re-

---

[4] The U.S. Claims Court was redesignated the U.S. Court of Federal Claims effective October 29, 1992, pursuant to the Federal Court Administration Act of 1992, Pub. L. No. 102-572, 106 Stat. 4506.

[5] IRC § 6401.

[6] IRC §§ 6402(a), 6511(b)(1).

[7] IRC §§ 6511(b)(1), 6514.

[8] IRC § 6514(a).

[9] IRC § 6511(a).

[10] Reg. § 301.6402-2(b)(1).

quirements; that is, it must be (1) filed by or on behalf of the "person who made the overpayment"[11]; (2) verified[12]; and (3) filed with the proper Service office.[13]

4. *Limitations on the amount refundable.* Subject to a number of exceptions, the amount of any refund on a timely filed claim is limited to the portion of the tax paid during the three preceding years, plus the period of any extension for filing a return.[14] If a refund claim with respect to the return is filed after a three-year period, the amount of any refund is limited to the portion of the tax paid during the two years immediately preceding the filing of the claim.[15] A taxpayer has no absolute right to the refund of an overpayment. The Commissioner may credit the amount of an overpayment against any internal revenue tax liability of the taxpayer.[16]

5. *The suit for refund.* In the event refund is denied, a taxpayer may commence a civil action for the recovery of an internal revenue tax in a federal district court or the Court of Federal Claims. However, no refund suit may be maintained unless a claim for refund has first been filed with the Service.[17] Also, the refund suit is limited to the ground raised in the filed claim for refund.[18] The Tax Court also has jurisdiction to determine the amount of an overpayment when a deficiency has been determined by the Service to exist for the year.[19]

6. *Refund jurisdiction of the federal district court and Court of Federal Claims.* The suit for refund must be filed within two years from the date the Service mails to the taxpayer the notice of disallowance, as provided in Section 6532(a)(1). If the suit is untimely, a refund court simply lacks jurisdiction to the suit.[20] Jurisdiction for a suit for refund is provided for in 28 USC § 1346, which states:

---

[11] IRC § 6402(a).

[12] Reg. § 301.6402-2(b)(1).

[13] Reg. § 301.6402-2(a).

[14] IRC § 6511(b)(2)(A).

[15] IRC § 6511(b).

[16] IRC § 6402(a).

[17] IRC § 7422(a).

[18] United States v. Felt & Tarrant Mfg. Co., 283 US 269 (1931).

[19] IRC § 6512(a).

[20] Walker v. IRS, 80 AFTR2d 97-7742 (ND Ga. 1997). In addition, the Service cannot confer jurisdiction on a court to hear a refund claim when such jurisdiction does not otherwise exist under applicable law. See Steel v. Comm'r, 81 AFTR2d 98-313 (SDNY 1997) (IRS letter apprising taxpayer of his legal alternatives does not confer jurisdiction on the court to hear a refund claim when the taxpayer failed to pay the disputed tax in full).

(a) The district courts shall have original jurisdiction, concurrent with the United States Court of Federal Claims, of (1) Any civil action against the United States for the recovery of any internal-tax alleged to have been erroneously or illegally assessed or collected without authority or any sum alleged to have been excessive or in any manner wrongfully collected under the internal-revenue laws.

This jurisdictional statute helps to clarify that the suit for refund is based on the allegation that the tax was erroneously or illegally collected. Also, although this statute (28 USC § 1346) establishes the jurisdiction of the district courts and the Court of Federal Claims, the primary jurisdictional statute of the Court of Federal Claims is 28 USC § 1491, which provides in relevant part:

(a)(1) The United States Court of Federal Claims shall have jurisdiction to render judgment upon any claim against the United States founded either upon the Constitution, or any Act of Congress or any regulation of an executive department, or upon any express or implied contract with the United States.

Note that in the Court of Federal Claims jurisdictional statute, the focus is on a claim against the United States arising under the Code, rather than an allegation of wrongful or erroneous collection.

7. *Interest is payable on a refund.* Section 6611(b)(2) provides for the payment of interest in the case of a refund, from the date of the overpayment to a date preceding the refund check by not more than thirty days.

8. *Refunds and credits in excess of $2 million must be reported to the Joint Committee.* No refund or credit of income, estate, or gift tax, and certain other taxes in excess of $2 million is permitted to be made until a report has been made to the Joint Committee on Taxation. The Joint Committee has thirty days to review this report.[21]

9. *The Service may sue for recovery of an erroneous refund.* If the Service makes a refund erroneously, it may commence an action to recover the erroneous refund within two years after making the refund or, if there was fraud, within five years.[22]

---

[21] IRC §§ 6405(a), 6405(b).

[22] IRC §§ 6514(a)(3), 6532(b), 7405.

TABLE 11.1

Deficiency and Refund Procedures for Overpayment of Tax

Deficiency Procedures	Refund Procedures
IRS initiates by sending notice of deficiency.	Taxpayer initiates by filing a claim for refund.
No assessment or collection is permitted until Tax Court decision becomes final, unless there is jeopardy in collection.	Payment and usually assessment have been made.
No formal document required by statute to obtain review of proposed action by Appeals.	Claim for refund required by statute to be submitted to IRS, although IRS requires protest to be filed for Appeals review.
Review in Tax Court before payment of deficiency.	Review by district court or Court of Federal Claims.
Tax Court reviews errors in notice of deficiency assigned in Tax Court petition.	Review limited to grounds in filed claims for refund.
Interest payable to IRS on deficiency.	Interest payable to taxpayer on amount of overpayment or underpayment.

¶ 11.02 "OVERPAYMENT" DEFINED

No refund or credit can be made unless it has first been determined that the taxpayer has made an "overpayment" in tax for the year.[23] Despite the importance of the concept of "overpayment" for refund procedures, the Code contains no explicit definition of this term. Section 6401(a) merely provides that an overpayment "includes" payment of any internal revenue tax that is assessed or collected after the applicable statute of limitations has expired.[24] Since Section 6401 is not instructive, the Supreme Court has had to define the term. In *Jones v. Liberty Glass Co.*, the Court said:

> [W]e read the word "overpayment" in its usual sense, as meaning any payment in excess of that which is properly due. Such an excess payment may be traced to an error in mathematics or in judgment or in interpretation of facts or law. And the error may be committed by the taxpayer or by the revenue agents. Whatever the reason, the payment of more than is rightfully due is what characterizes an overpayment.[25]

In other words, an overpayment is a payment in excess of what properly should have been assessed or collected as tax.

---

[23] IRC § 6401(a).

[24] IRC §§ 6501(a), 6502(a).

[25] Jones v. Liberty Glass Co., 332 US 524, 531 (1947).

Section 6401(a) carries forward the protection to taxpayers from stale demands reflected in the statutes of limitations on assessment and collection.[26] The time-barred assessment and collection of a tax, which Section 6401(a) describes as an overpayment, does not mean that when the Service has made an untimely assessment, the taxpayer has always made an overpayment and is automatically entitled to a refund. Section 6401(a) speaks of the payment of any tax that is assessed and collected after the applicable statute of limitations on assessment or collection has run. Section 6401(a) contemplates a situation such as one where the Service determines that the taxpayer has a deficiency in tax, and it assesses and collects the deficiency (1) after the statute of limitations on assessment has run or (2) even if the assessment was timely, the Service has collected the amount of the assessed tax after the ten-year statute of limitations on collection has expired.[27] In the statutory situation, in short, the payment or collection has occurred after the time-barred administrative action.

But suppose the taxpayer had made payment of tax in the form of withholding tax credits before the statute of limitations on assessment has run, and the Service failed to assess the tax within the statutory period? In this situation, when the taxpayer files a claim for refund claiming that the withheld tax should be refunded, the Tax Court has held that under the principles of *Lewis v. Reynolds*, the Service is permitted to reduce the amount of the taxpayer's refund by the correct tax for the year, even if the Service can no longer assess the amount of any deficiency it may have determined to be due.[28]

Refundable credits that exceed the amount of income tax imposed for the year are "considered" overpayments of tax; thus excessive withholding tax and estimated tax payments are considered overpayments.[29] In addition, Section 6401(c) provides that an amount paid as tax may constitute an "overpayment," even if there is no tax liability for which the tax was paid. This provision is intended to deal with the ambiguous and potentially abusive situation where a taxpayer's remittance may be either a payment of tax on which the government must pay interest if it is in excess of the amount legally due or merely a

---

[26] Based on the statement in Section 6401(a) that an overpayment includes the amount assessed or collected after the expiration of the applicable limitations period, it has also been held that a taxpayer may raise the statute of limitations defense in an action for refund. Walker v. IRS, 333 F2d 768, 771 (9th Cir. 1964); see also Sokolow v. United States, 169 F3d 663, 665; 83 AFTR2d 99-1062 (9th Cir. 1999).

[27] See Bachner v. Comm'r, 81 F3d 1274, 1277 (3d Cir. 1996).

[28] Lewis v. Reynolds, 284 US 281 (1932), discussed infra ¶ 11.02[1]. Bachner v. Comm'r, 109 TC 125 (1997), after remand, 81 F3d 1274 (3d Cir. 1996), aff'd, 82 AFTR2d 98-7321 (3d Cir. 1998) (mem. op.). See also Estate of Michael v. District Dir. of IRS, 81 AFTR2d 98-870 (ED Va. 1998) (Service's offset of a time-barred additional estate tax liability against an agreed-on foreign death tax credit may be permissible under the principles of *Lewis v. Reynolds*, infra).

[29] IRC § 6401(b).

deposit in the nature of a cash bond to stop the running of interest.[30] As the inelegant language of Section 6401(c) suggests, the fact that there has been no actual assessment or reasonably apparent liability for a tax should not of itself negate "payment." Other factors must be present that in conjunction with the absence of a "tax liability" establish that payment has not been made.[31]

With the limited and ambiguous language of Section 6401(c), generally it is more useful to focus on the definition of an "overpayment" in *Liberty Glass*[32] in more detail. An overpayment under the *Liberty Glass* definition has two elements: (1) the correct tax for the year and (2) the amounts paid as tax. Each of these elements is discussed as follows.

[1] Overpayments: The Correct Tax Element

According to *Liberty Glass*, the correct tax is the amount of tax "rightfully due"; that is, the amount of tax finally determined to be legally due by a court, and not necessarily what either the taxpayer or the Service says is due.[33] In this sense, a tax assessed or collected after the expiration of the applicable period of limitations is an overpayment because the tax is not rightfully due.[34] Where the taxpayer pays a tax after the applicable period of limitations on assessment or collection has expired, the taxpayer can recover the overpayment by filing a claim for refund,[35] and, if necessary, instituting a suit for refund.[36] Suppose the taxpayer had remitted amounts to the Service when the Service could have made a timely assessment, but failed to assess until after the statute of limitations on assessment had expired. Finding that the assessment was untimely, some courts have concluded that there is no liability for the assess-

---

[30] Charles Leich & Co. v. United States, 329 F2d 649, 652 (Ct. Cl. 1964). See also Girard Trust Bank v. United States, 643 F2d 725, 727 (Fed. Cir. 1981).

[31] Charles Leich & Co. v. United States, 329 F2d 649, 652 (Ct. Cl. 1964). See also Girard Trust Bank v. United States, 643 F2d 725, 727 (Fed. Cir. 1981). For a discussion of these factors and Section 6401(c), see infra ¶ 11.05[1][b].

[32] Jones v. Liberty Glass Co., 332 US 524 (1947).

[33] Girard Trust Bank v. United States, 643 F2d 725, 727 n.3 (Fed. Cir. 1981).

[34] IRC § 6401(a). See Ewing v. United States, 914 F2d 499 (4th Cir. 1990) ("[s]ince the amounts paid in 1985 were 'collected' by the IRS outside of the period for assessment with no assessment having been made, they come within (the Section 6401) definition of 'overpayment'"); Diamond Gardner Corp., 38 TC 875, 879–881 (1962); Rhodes v. Edwards, 56-2 USTC ¶ 9643 (MD Ga. 1956).

[35] Rev. Rul. 74-580, 1974-2 CB 400. But see Bachner v. Comm'r, 81 F3d 1274, 1277 (3d Cir. 1996).

[36] Bowers v. New York & Albany Co., 273 US 346, 349 (1927) (taxpayers instituted suits for refund of tax collected by distraint after the statutory period for collection had expired). Cohen v. United States, 23 Cl. Ct. 717, 91-2 USTC ¶ 50,384 (1991) (remittance made before untimely assessment and payments made after untimely assessment).

ment-barred year.[37] Other courts have ruled in the context of the taxpayer's suit for refund that the taxpayer's entitlement to a refund turns on whether the government would be unjustly enriched if it retained the payment.[38] The Tax Court, saying it was following *Lewis v. Reynolds*,[39] held that although the Service could no longer assess a deficiency against the taxpayer, the statute bar did not extinguish the right of the government to retain payments already received to the extent that they do not exceed the amount of the taxpayer's actual tax liability.[40]

For purposes of determining whether a taxpayer has made an overpayment, the tax the taxpayer reports on a return is not taken as the correct tax. Any overpayment a taxpayer computes to be owed on his return is tentative and is subject to final audit and adjustment. For example, where a taxpayer files a return showing an overpayment attributable to withholding or estimated tax credits in excess of the returned tax, a refund is made subject to final audit

---

[37] Estate of Goetz v. United States, 286 F. Supp. 128, 131 (WD Mo. 1968) (taxpayer sent check to the Service after she received a notice of deficiency, but the tax was not assessed until after extended assessment period had expired). See Becker Bros. v. United States, 88-1 USTC ¶ 9262 (CD Ill. 1988) (accord); see also Cohen v. United States, 23 Cl. Ct. 717 (1991) (preassessment remittance was deposit that became payment only on making of untimely assessment); see Close v. United States, 79-1 USTC ¶ 9143 (Ct. Cl. 1978) (1976 overpayment could not be credited to 1973 liability because 1973 was time-barred). The Service believes that an overpayment, even if barred from refund, may be applied by a taxpayer to another liability under the doctrine of equitable recoupment. Rev. Rul. 71-56, 1971-1 CB 404 (barred overpayment of estate tax may be applied against outstanding assessment of income tax decedent owed before death). But see ¶ 5.06[1] for a discussion of recoupment.

[38] Crompton & Knowles Loom Works v. White, 65 F2d 132, 133 (1st Cir.), cert. denied, 290 US 669 (1933) (taxpayer paid unassessed interest on a timely assessed deficiency, but interest was not timely assessed; held, interest not refundable because it was legally owed). See also Rev. Rul. 85-67, 1985-1 CB 364 (deficiency and interest paid within assessment period, but assessment made after period expired; held, assessment is untimely, but advance payment does not constitute an overpayment). The unjust enrichment rationale implicit in a suit for refund seems to be the reason why some courts have prohibited the Service from crediting amounts collected under assessments that were illegal rather than untimely. See, e.g., Campbell v. United States, 592 F2d 309 (6th Cir. 1979) (amount collected under illegal assessment was not creditable overpayment); Kabbaby v. Richardson, 520 F2d 334, 335 (5th Cir. 1975) (same). However, courts have not been consistent in their handling of illegal assessments. See the cases cited supra note 20 and ¶ 10.03[2][c].

[39] Lewis v. Reynolds, 284 US 281, 283 (1932).

[40] Bachner v. Comm'r, 109 TC 125 (1997), after remand, 81 F3d 1274, 1277 (3d Cir. 1996). Thus, the Tax Court upheld the Service's position in Rev. Rul. 85-67, 1985-1 CB 364. The Tax Court also held that the Service could reduce the amount of the taxpayer's refund by the amount of negligence and late filing penalties, with the result that the taxpayer's refund claim of $4,396.95 was reduced by $4,301, so that his overpayment for the year was $95.95.

and adjustment.[41] Similarly, a quick refund arising from the carryback of a net operating loss and certain other deductions or credits is made after the Service has run only a preliminary check on the appropriateness of the refund. Thus, the carryback (and any refund) is tentative until full examination is made.[42]

It has long been the rule that when a claim for refund is filed (1) the entire return may be reaudited and not merely the grounds set forth in the refund claim; (2) the tax for the year may be redetermined, irrespective of the result of any previous audit, and the uncollectibility of any deficiency computed; and (3) if the tax as redetermined exceeds the amount of the refund claim, there is no overpayment. In *Lewis v. Reynolds*,[43] the administrator of an estate filed a claim for the refund of additional income tax the estate had paid to the Service after all the estate's deductions except attorney fees had been disallowed in an audit. The Service rejected the claim on the ground that after reaudit, the taxpayer was found to owe tax in addition to the tax paid. Although barred from assessment by the statute of limitations, the additional tax was arrived at by disallowing the attorney fees allowed in the initial audit and by allowing state inheritance taxes that had previously been disallowed. In concluding that the Service's action was proper, the Supreme Court said:

> While the statutes authorizing refunds do not specifically empower the Commissioner to reaudit a return whenever repayment is claimed, authority therefor is necessarily implied. An overpayment must appear before refund is authorized. Although the statute of limitations may have barred the assessment and collection of any additional sum, it does not obliterate the right of the United States to retain payments already received when they do not exceed the amount which might have been properly assessed and demanded.[44]

It follows from *Lewis v. Reynolds* that the Service is not restricted to the specific items or adjustments presented in a refund claim. Where a claim for refund is filed, the ultimate question presented for decision is whether the taxpayer has overpaid tax,[45] which involves the redetermination of the entire tax liability. Also, in a refund suit, the taxpayer has the burden of proving the exact dollar amount of an overpayment.[46] The taxpayer's burden of proof puts in issue every credit or deduction in the return for which the refund is sought as well as a related return.[47] When the redetermination is the result of an adjust-

---

[41] Clark v. Comm'r, 158 F2d 851 (6th Cir. 1946); Rendell Owens v. Comm'r, 50 TC 577 (1968); Henry C. Warren, 13 TC 205 (1949).

[42] IRC § 6411(a).

[43] Lewis v. Reynolds, 284 US 281 (1932).

[44] Lewis v. Reynolds, 284 US 281, 283 (1932).

[45] Lewis v. Reynolds, 284 US 281, 283 (1932).

[46] Helvering v. Taylor, 293 US 507 (1935).

[47] Missouri Pac. RR v. United States, 168 Ct. Cl. 86, 90–91, 338 F2d 668, 671 (1964).

ment from an unrelated return affecting the refund year, however, the burden of proof remains on the government throughout the entire proceeding.[48] The government must establish that "it has some positive evidence, as opposed to a mere theoretical argument, that there is some substance to its claim and is not a mere fishing expedition or a method of discouraging taxpayers from seeking refunds on meritorious claims because of the cost that would result from proving each and every item involved in a return."[49]

After its reaudit, *Lewis v. Reynolds* holds that even if that reaudit deficiency cannot be collected because the period of limitations on assessment or collection has run, the barred deficiency must be considered in determining whether a taxpayer actually overpaid his tax.[50] Interest may also be offset against a refund, even if the interest had not been assessed and the period for assessment of the interest has expired.[51] Similarly, because a penalty is assessed, collected, or paid in the same manner as taxes, when the Service reaudits the taxpayer's return, it may set off penalties from the amount of the refund, even if the Service could not assess the penalties because the statute of limitations on assessment had expired.[52] Where the period of limitations on as-

---

[48] Missouri Pac. RR v. United States, 168 Ct. Cl. 86, 90–91, 338 F2d 668, 671 (1964).

[49] Missouri Pac. RR v. United States, 168 Ct. Cl. 86, 90–91, 338 F2d 668, 671 (1964).

[50] Fisher v. United States, 80 F3d 1576 (Fed. Cir. 1996). The Service has successfully contended that the voluntary payment rule, permitting taxpayers to designate how a voluntary remittance should be applied, does not control the Service's discretion under Section 6402 to credit a tax overpayment against any tax liability of the person who made the overpayment. United States v. Ryan (In re Ryan), 64 F3d 1516 (11th Cir. 1995) (taxpayers overpaid tax for 1990 and requested that the overpayment be applied to 1989; the Service applied the overpayment to another year). The only situation where the Service has voluntarily limited its discretion under Section 6402 is when a taxpayer elects to apply an overpayment for one year to estimated tax for the succeeding year.

[51] Fisher v. United States, 80 F3d 1576 (Fed. Cir. 1996) (government claimed it was entitled to offset against any recovery, the interest that should have been assessed and collected when the deficiency in estate tax was assessed, if it succeeded in establishing that estate tax had been underpaid). The Federal Circuit agreed, saying that under *Lewis v. Reynolds*, "the government may offset against a tax refund claim any additional amounts the taxpayer owes with respect to the tax shown on the return, even though the statute of limitations would bar assessing the additional amount owed." The court refused to treat interest on taxes the taxpayer owed differently from other components of tax liability.

[52] Allen v. United States, 51 F3d 1012 (11th Cir. 1995) (taxpayer convicted of willfully failing to file returns paid civil fraud penalties, but after the Tax Court's decision in Kotmair v. Comm'r, 86 TC 1253 (1986), filed a refund for the fraud penalties paid; held, although the statute of limitations on the assessment of negligence and delinquency penalties had expired, the Service could set off the amount of these penalties from the overpaid fraud penalties); see also Acker v. United States, 519 F. Supp. 178 (ND Ohio 1981) (after statute of limitations on assessment had run, Service set off a fraud penalty against a refund of delinquency and negligence penalties); Brown v. United States, 83 AFTR2d 99-917 (Fed. Cl. 1999) (Federal Circuit's decision in Fisher v. United States, 80 F3d 1576

sessment has not run, the Service may issue a notice of deficiency even if it has previously made a refund to the taxpayer.[53]

Equitable principles inhere in the rules governing refunds of overpayments. *Lewis v. Reynolds* reflects the judgment that when a taxpayer sues for refund, a taxpayer is not entitled to a refund unless the government would be unjustly enriched by permitting it to retain an amount paid as a tax. In *Stone v. White*, which was decided after *Lewis v. Reynolds*, the Supreme Court stated: "The statutes authorizing tax refunds and suits for their recovery are predicated upon the same equitable principles that underlie an action in assumpsit for money had and received . . . "—that is, "to avoid unjust enrichment by the defendant at the expense of the plaintiff. . . . "[54] Thus, the operation of these equitable principles can be seen where a court upholds a taxpayer's claim that he has overpaid a tax because assessment or collection of the tax was invalid for reasons other than the bar of the statute of limitations. One category of such cases involves assessments that are premature or are invalid for some other procedural reason.[55]

Another type of unjust enrichment case involves the collection of tax twice on the same transaction. Obviously, the government is unjustly enriched where the Service makes excessive collections of tax, and the taxpayer can raise the defense of equitable recoupment, as the Supreme Court has said in *Bull v. United States*.[56] However, defenses such as setoff (*Lewis v. Reynolds*) and equitable recoupment (*Bull*) are defenses to excessive collection and do not themselves provide a basis for the jurisdiction of a court to order a refund. Procedural rules regarding the filing of a timely claim still apply so that where the erroneous tax is paid, a claim for refund must be timely filed.[57]

(Fed. Cir. 1996), extended to the set off of penalties and interest on the penalties, assessment of which was barred by the statute of limitations).

[53] Mary R. Milleg, 19 TC 395, 397–398 (1952) (cases discussed). See also Meridian Mut. Ins. Co. v. Comm'r, 44 TC 375 (1965), aff'd, 369 F2d 508 (7th Cir. 1966); Baird v. Comm'r, 42 TCM 1170 (1981) (cases gathered).

[54] Stone v. White, 301 US 532, 534–535 (1937).

[55] Compare Lyddon & Co. (Am.) v. United States, 158 F. Supp. 951 (Ct. Cl.), cert. denied, 358 US 832 (1958) (premature assessment made before the sending of a notice of deficiency was not void and amount collected could not be recovered unless "on the merits" tax was not owed) and Lehigh Portland Cement Co. v. United States, 30 F. Supp. 217, 233 (Ct. Cl. 1939) (premature assessment said to be harmless procedural error that did not go to the validity of tax or right to collect it) with Kabbaby v. Richardson, 520 F2d 334, 335 (5th Cir. 1975) (property seized pursuant to an invalid assessment held refundable and not an overpayment creditable to unsatisfied tax liabilities for other years). See also LaFollette v. United States, 176 F. Supp. 192 (SD Cal. 1959) (collection under threat of distraint barred Service recoupment). See ¶ 10.03[2][c] for further discussion of improper assessments.

[56] Bull v. United States, 295 US 247 (1935).

[57] United States v. Dalm, 495 US 941 (1989). For further discussion of equitable recoupment, see ¶ 5.06[1].

[a] Defensive Use by the Service of an Assessment Item

What actually happens, then, where a claim for refund is filed? Under *Lewis v. Reynolds*, the correct tax for the year of the claimed overpayment must be determined. All adjustments are considered in this calculation—those that decrease tax, including bad debt deductions, and net operating loss and credit carrybacks, as well as those that increase tax. For purposes of computing the correct tax, the statutes of limitations on filing a refund claim or on assessment are disregarded. Any excess of the tax actually paid over the correct tax is an overpayment, although the overpayment amount is not necessarily the amount of the refund. The amount of the overpayment that is credited or refunded to the taxpayer depends on whether (1) the taxpayer has filed a timely claim for refund and (2) the timely claim for refund covers the adjustment decreasing the tax. If the taxpayer has failed to comply with either or both of these requirements, the excess tax paid attributable to this adjustment is not credited or refunded.[58] This procedure is illustrated by the following example.[59]

EXAMPLE 11-1: A corporation files a return reporting taxable income of $800. The following adjustments increase and decrease taxable income:

Taxable income reported on Form 1120 (U.S. Corporation Income Tax Return)		$ 800.00
Adjustments increasing taxable income:		
(1) Decrease in deductions for bad debts		270.00
		$1,070.00
Adjustments decreasing taxable income:		
(2) Additional office expenses	$720.00	
(3) Additional depreciation	100.00	
(4) Additional interest expense	425.00	1,245.00
Corrected taxable income (loss)		$ (175.00)

No deficiency based on adjustment (1) has been assessed or collected and the time for assessing or collecting such a deficiency has expired. Adjustment (2) is covered by a timely claim for credit or refund, but adjustments (3) and (4) are not covered by a claim and the period for filing

---

[58] IRC §§ 6511(b), 6514(a); Rev. Rul. 81-87, 1981-1 CB 580. The authority to credit one year's overpayment to another year's liability is discretionary as an administrative matter, and the Service is not required to offset overpayments for one year against the liabilities of the other year. See Kalb v. United States, 505 F2d 506, 509 (2d Cir. 1974), cert. denied, 421 US 979 (1975); Acker v. United States, 519 F. Supp. 178, 182 (ND Ohio 1981) (following *Kalb*). But see Vishnevsky v. United States, 581 F2d 1249, 1253 (7th Cir. 1978) (mandamus granted requiring the Service to credit taxpayers with an admitted overpayment). Under Lewis v. Reynolds, 284 US 281 (1932), "within-year" credits must be allowed.

[59] This example is taken from Rev. Rul. 81-87, 1981-1 CB 580. For the calculation of an overpayment where there is a net operating loss carryback to a year in which there is a barred adjustment, see infra ¶ 11.05[4].

claims has expired. The amount of the credit or refund is determined as follows:

Taxable income reported on Form 1120	$800.00
Corrected taxable income (loss $175.00)	–0–
Income on which excess tax paid	$800.00
Income covered by a claim	720.00
Income not covered by a claim	80.00

The amount of income on which excess tax was paid, $800, exceeds the amount of income covered by a claim, $720. Consequently, only the tax paid on the $720 may be credited or refunded. Since the tax paid on $800 was not covered by a timely filed claim, it is not credited or refunded.

[b] Defensive Use by a Taxpayer of an Unclaimed Refund Item

An unclaimed item of adjustment or deduction resulting in an overpayment cannot increase the amount of a refund if the period for filing a supplemental claim has run, although a taxpayer can still use the barred overpayment defensively. *Lewis v. Reynolds* permits the government to reduce this amount of a taxpayer's refund by adjustments increasing tax, even if assessment is barred by the period of limitations. But in *Union Pacific Railroad v. United States*, the court of claims held that for the sole purpose of offsetting any set-offs the government might raise, a taxpayer was entitled to raise issues that would have increased the amount of an overpayment even though they were not included in a timely filed refund claim. These offsetting issues can only be used defensively to reduce the government's setoffs to zero, not offensively to increase the amount of any refund.[60] Consequently, under *Lewis v. Reynolds*, a taxpayer can succeed in defeating the government's setoff issues by raising his own offsets, but he may not recover an overpayment attributable to these off-set issues.

[2] Overpayments: The Amount of Tax Payments

Before an overpayment can exist, a taxpayer must have "paid" the amount as tax. Not all remittances are treated as payments of tax when they are received by the Service. For example, remittances of withholding tax and estimated tax made by taxpayers before the due date of the return for the year are not considered "paid" until the due date of payment; that is, the date the return for the

---

[60] Union Pac. RR v. United States, 389 F2d 437, 447 (Ct. Cl. 1968).

year is due without regard to any extension for filing the return.[61] Section 6401(c) indicates that despite the fact that no return is yet due or filed nor an assessment of tax made, a taxpayer may nevertheless be considered to have made an overpayment. Although the Service treats an amount a taxpayer remits before the sending of a notice of deficiency as a deposit in the nature of a cash bond, not as a payment,[62] the issue of whether a remittance is considered a payment or cash bond has provoked much litigation.[63]

¶ 11.03 TENTATIVE OVERPAYMENTS: TENTATIVE CARRYBACK ADJUSTMENTS UNDER SECTION 6411

Under normal procedures, it may take some time for the Service to process and make payment on a claim for refund. Generally, there is a complete audit of the return(s) for the years for which a refund is claimed. However, because a business may have an urgent need for a prompt refund of tax, Congress has provided a special procedure in Section 6411 for net operating losses. This procedure enables a taxpayer to apply for a quick refund based on a tentative carryback adjustment.[64] The right to file an application for a tentative adjustment is not limited to corporations. Any taxpayer who is entitled to carry back a loss or unused credit may apply for a quick refund.[65] An application filed under Section 6411 does not constitute a claim for credit or refund,[66] and the amount carried back results in only the tentative allowance of any refunded overpayment.

The Service must act on a quick refund application (1) within ninety days after the application is filed or (2) within ninety days after the last day of the

---

[61] IRC §§ 6513(a)–6513(c). The "deemed paid" rule of Section 6513(b) has been held to be conclusive, and the taxpayer's intentions to be irrelevant. Ehle v. United States, 720 F2d 1096, 1097 (9th Cir. 1983) (amounts withheld were deemed payments on April 15 following the close of the taxable year, even though the taxpayer intended the amounts to be only a deposit, and he had no tax liability for the years in issue).

[62] Procedures for taxpayers to make remittances in order to stop the running of interest on deficiencies were updated for remittances made on or after October 1, 1984. Rev. Proc. 84-58, 1984-2 CB 501, superseding Rev. Proc. 82-51, 1982-2 CB 839, § 3.02, which, in turn, superseded, for years after 1982, Rev. Proc. 64-13, 1964-1 CB 674. These procedures are described infra ¶ 11.05[1][b].

[63] This subject is discussed infra ¶ 11.05[1][b].

[64] The special procedure has been extended to include tentative carryback adjustments attributable to a net capital loss (IRC § 1212(a)(1)), and a business credit carryback (IRC § 39). FSA 1999-23021 (Mar. 9, 1999) (in considering a request for a quick refund, the Service has discretion to require a taxpayer to provide security for underpayment interest that may be due if the refund must be repaid).

[65] Reg. § 1.6411-1(a).

[66] IRC § 6411(a).

month that the return for the year of loss (or unused credit) is due (including extensions of the return filing date), whichever is later. These time limitations also apply to taxpayers. Corporations must file the application for the tentative carryback adjustment on Form 1139 (Corporation Application for Tentative Refund). (See Form 11.1.) Other taxpayers use Form 1045 (Application for Tentative Refund). (See Form 11.2.) These forms must be filed within twelve months after the end of the year of the net operating loss.[67] The taxpayer's application must set forth the following information:

- The amount of the loss or the unused credit;
- The amount of the tax previously determined for each prior year affected by the loss or unused credit in accordance with Section 1314(a);
- The amount of the decrease in tax in each prior year attributable to the loss or unused credit carryback;
- The amount of unpaid tax in the year affected by the carryback (not including, in the case of a corporation expecting a net operating loss, the tax for the preceding year if it has received an extension of time for payment of the tax under Section 6164); and
- The amount of tax in the year with respect to which the extension under Section 6164 has been granted.[68]

An application for a tentative credit must be filed at the same time as, or after the due date for the filing of, the return of the taxable year, but within the seven- to twelve-month period beginning with the end of the taxable year of the loss or unused credit.[69] If the application is filed before the return, the application is considered filed on the date the return is filed.[70] The application for quick refund must be filed with the same Service center as the return.[71]

When an application for a quick refund is filed, the Service makes a preliminary check on the appropriateness of the refund.[72] An application may be refused if it contains errors of computation or material omissions that the Ser-

---

[67] IRC § 6411(a).

[68] IRC §§ 6411(a)(1)–6411(a)(5).

[69] IRC § 6411(a). See Rev. Rul. 75-327, 1975-2 CB 481 (tentative corporate return does not constitute a return for purposes of Section 6411).

[70] Reg. § 1.6411-1(c). If an unused investment credit in a year results from the carryback of a net operating loss or capital loss from a later year, the unused credit may be carried back three years and a quick refund may be obtained for the taxes affected. However, because this unused investment credit created by the loss carryback affects taxes of a year or years before the three years preceding the loss year, a second Form 1139 must be used for these prior years. This second application must also be filed within twelve months after the end of the year in which the loss arose. Both applications (the first based on the loss carryback and the second based on the investment credit carryback) should be filed together. Id.

[71] Reg. § 1.6411-1(c). But see Reg. § 301.6091-1(b) (relating to hand-carried documents).

[72] IRC § 6411(b); Reg. § 1.6411-3(b).

vice believes cannot be corrected within the ninety-day period.[73] If the Service approves the application, the tax reduction resulting from the carryback is either credited against unpaid taxes or refunded,[74] even if the refund or credit exceeds $1 million. The refund or credit may be made before review by the Joint Committee on Taxation, as is the case with normal refunds of amounts in excess of $2 million.

An application for a tentative carryback adjustment does not constitute a claim for refund or credit.[75] After a tentative quick refund, the Service makes a full examination of the return under its regular auditing procedures. Even if the Service approved the quick refund application, the Service can later determine that the amount refunded or credited on the tentative application was greater than the actual amount of the overassessment for the year, and it can either

1. Send a notice of deficiency within the three-year period during which a deficiency may be assessed for the taxable year of the net operating loss resulting in the carryback[76];
2. Assess the amount of the excessive refund or credit as though it were a mathematical error so that refund procedures are followed[77]; or
3. Commence an action for erroneous refund[78] within the two-year period of Section 6501.

---

[73] If the application is disallowed, the taxpayer's remedy is to file a regular claim for refund. If the Service fails to act within the ninety-day period, no consequences are statutorily provided for, and the Service is permitted to find a deficiency for the year of the alleged loss at a later date. Pearl Zarnow, 48 TC 213 (1967).

[74] Reg. § 1.6411-3(d) (application of decrease in tax).

[75] IRC § 6411(a); Reg. § 1.6411-1(b)(2). Despite the clear statutory language, there has been litigation on the point. See Morse v. United States, 80-2 USTC ¶ 9496 (Ct. Cl. 1980); Badger Materials, Inc., 40 TC 725 (1963), further proceedings, 40 TC 1061 (1963). See also Thrif-Tee, Inc. v. United States, 492 F. Supp. 530 (WDNC 1979), aff'd in unpublished opinion, 628 F2d 1351 (4th Cir. 1980), cert. denied, 449 US 1124 (1981) (taxpayer timely filed tentative carryback claim, but an untimely refund claim; held, refund barred, although Service had not acted on tentative claim).

[76] IRC § 6501(i). As Section 6501(i) makes clear, where a net operating loss is carried back, the three-year period begins to run from the filing date for the loss year's return, not of the year to which the loss is carried back. DuPont v. United States, 483 F. Supp. 588 (D. Del. 1980). The Tax Court also has jurisdiction to determine whether a deficiency should reflect refund checks sent by the Service, but allegedly misappropriated by the taxpayer's lawyer. Naftel v. Comm'r, 85 TC 527 (1985). See also Estate of Baumgardner, 85 TC 445 (1985) (Tax Court has jurisdiction to determine amount of overpayment, including interest).

[77] IRC § 6213(b)(2). See Collegiate Cap & Gown Co. v. Comm'r, 59 TC 449 (1973) (Commissioner need not make assessment under Section 6213(b)(2) relating to mathematical errors).

[78] IRC § 7405. United States v. Lasbury, 83-2 USTC ¶ 9721 (D. Ariz. 1983) (in an action for erroneous refund, the government was entitled to interest for the taxpayers' use of the money even though they voluntarily repaid the refund). See also Tucker v. United States, 89-1 USTC ¶ 9336 (SDNY 1989) (erroneous refund made by Service prior to as-

None of these three methods is exclusive.[79] In many instances, the Service sends a notice of deficiency to recover an erroneous refund.[80]

---

sessment may be recovered by Service not only by means of an erroneous refund suit but also by such other collection procedures as levying on taxpayer's property).

[79] See Collegiate Cap & Gown Co. v. Comm'r, 59 TC 449 (1973) (mathematical error procedure to recover amounts applied, credited, or refunded is not exclusive); Neri v. Comm'r, 54 TC 767 (1970) (suit-for-erroneous-refund procedure not exclusive). Similarly, the Service is not required to reverse the erroneous credit of an overpayment for one year to discharge a liability for another year. It may use deficiency procedures to collect tax for the other year. Fine v. Comm'r, 70 TC 684 (1978). However, the Service may not adjust a taxpayer's account to recover the erroneously refunded amounts. Radinsky v. United States, 622 F. Supp. 412 (D. Colo. 1986), appeal dismissed by stipulation (10th Cir. 1985). See United States v. Young, 79-2 USTC ¶ 9609 (D. Del. 1979). In *Radinsky*, recipients of the refund sued the United States, claiming that the Service adjustments were improper. The district court held that it had jurisdiction over such a suit, although the amounts sought to be recovered technically were not a tax (they were the erroneous refund), and the recipient-plaintiffs were not "taxpayers."

[80] Meridian Mut. Ins. Co. v. Comm'r, 44 TC 375, 378–379 (1965), aff'd, 369 F2d 508 (7th Cir. 1966); Miller v. Comm'r, 23 TC 565 (1954), aff'd, 231 F2d 8 (5th Cir. 1956). For another case upholding the Service's discretion to use deficiency procedures to recover an erroneous refund, see Pesch v. Comm'r, 78 TC 100 (1982) (rejecting the argument that where refund erroneously made because of "mistake of law," the Service must proceed by suit for erroneous refund); Baldwin v. Comm'r, 97 TC 704 (1991) (same result as in *Pesch* where tentative carryback resulted in credit rather than refund). Gordon L. Krieger v. Comm'r, 64 TC 214, 216 (1975) ("the Commissioner may proceed through the deficiency route where there has been an erroneous refund"); Union Equity Coop. Exch., Inc. v. Comm'r, 58 TC 397 (1972), aff'd on another issue, 481 F2d 812 (10th Cir.), cert. denied, 414 US 1028 (1973); United States v. Blansett, 283 F2d 474 (8th Cir. 1960); John S. Neri v. Comm'r, 54 TC 767 (1970).

FORM 11.1
CORPORATION APPLICATION FOR TENTATIVE REFUND

| Form **1139** (Rev. June 1992) Department of the Treasury Internal Revenue Service | **Corporation Application for Tentative Refund** ▶ Read the instructions before completing this form. ▶ Do not attach to the corporation's income tax return—mail in a separate envelope. | OMB No. 1545-0582 Expires 6-30-95 |

Name: **ABC Corporation**
Employer identification number: **12-3456789**

Number, street, and room or suite no. (If a P.O. box, see instructions.): **1 Main Street**
Date of incorporation: **6-24-79**

City or town, state, and ZIP code: **Anytown, NY 00000**
Telephone no. (optional): **(212) 987-0000**

1	This application is filed to carry back:	a Net operating loss (attach computation) ▶	**$11600**	c Unused general business credit (attach computation) ▶	$
		b Net capital loss (attach computation) ▶	$		
2	Return for year of loss, unused credit, or overpayment under section 1341(b)(1) ▶	a Tax year ended **12-31-92**	b Date filed **3-14-93**	c Service center where filed **Holtsville**	

3   If this application is for an unused credit created by another carryback, enter ending date for the tax year of the first carryback. ▶ ....

4a   Was a consolidated return filed for any tax year covered on this application?. . . . . ☐ Yes ☒ No

   b   If "Yes," identify the year and enter the name of the common parent and its EIN, if different from above ▶ ....

5a   If Form 1138 has been filed, was an extension of time granted for filing the return for the tax year of the net operating loss? ☒ Yes ☐ No

   b   If "Yes," give date to which extension was granted ▶ **3-31-93**   c Give date Form 1138 was filed ▶ **3-14-92**

   d   Unpaid tax for which Form 1138 is in effect . . . . ▶ **$33,000**

6   If you changed your accounting period, give date permission to change was granted . . . . . ▶ **N/A**

7   If this is an application of a dissolved corporation, enter date of dissolution . . . . ▶ **N/A**

8   Have you filed a petition in Tax Court for the year or years to which the carryback is to be applied?. . . . . ☐ Yes ☒ No

9   Does this carryback include a loss or credit from a tax shelter required to be registered? If "Yes," attach Form(s) 8271 . ☐ Yes ☒ No

Computation of Decrease in Tax	3rd preceding tax year ended ▶		2nd preceding tax year ended ▶		1st preceding tax year ended ▶	
Note: If no entry in 1a or 1b, skip lines 10–14.	(a) Before carryback	(b) After carryback	(c) Before carryback	(d) After carryback	(e) Before carryback	(f) After carryback
10 Taxable income from tax return	285000	285000				
11 Capital loss carryback (see instructions)						
12 Subtract line 11 from line 10		285000				
13 Net operating loss deduction after carryback		116000				
14 Taxable income (subtract line 13 from line 12)		169000				
15 Income tax	110850	57490				
16 General business credit (see instructions)	18000	18000				
17 Other credits (identify)						
18 Total credits (add lines 16 and 17)	18000	18000				
19 Subtract line 18 from line 15	92850	39490				
20 Personal holding company tax (Sch. PH (Form 1120))						
21 Recapture taxes	1640	1640				
22 Alternative minimum tax and environmental tax						
23 Total tax liability (add lines 19 through 22)	94490	41130				
24 Recomputed tax liability (see instructions)	41130					
25 Decrease in tax (subtract line 24 from line 23)	53360					

26   Overpayment of tax due to a claim of right adjustment under section 1341(b)(1)—attach computation . . . . . ▶

Sign Here   Under penalties of perjury, I declare that I have examined this application and accompanying schedules and statements, and to the best of my knowledge and belief, they are true, correct, and complete.

Keep a copy of this application for your records.

Signature of officer ▶ _____ Date ▶ _____ Title ▶ _____

Preparer Other Than Taxpayer
Name ▶ _____   Date _____
Address ▶ _____

General Instructions

(Section references are to the Internal Revenue Code unless otherwise noted.)

Paperwork Reduction Act Notice.—We ask for the information on this form to carry out the Internal Revenue laws of the United States. You are required to give us the information. We need it to ensure that you are complying with these laws and to allow us to figure and collect the right amount of tax.

The time needed to complete and file this form will vary depending on individual circumstances. The estimated average time is:

Recordkeeping . . . . . 24 hr., 52 min.

Learning about the law or the form . . . . . 3 hr., 16 min.

Preparing the form . . . . . 8 hr., 26 min.

Copying, assembling, and sending the form to the IRS 1 hr., 20 min.

If you have comments concerning the accuracy of these time estimates or

Cat. No. 11170F

Form 1139 (Rev. 6-92)

suggestions for making this form more simple, we would be happy to hear from you. You can write to both the Internal Revenue Service, Washington, DC 20224, Attention: IRS Reports Clearance Officer, T:FP; and the Office of Management and Budget, Paperwork Reduction Project (1545-0582), Washington, DC 20503. DO NOT send the tax form to either of these offices. Instead, see When and Where To File below.

Purpose of Form.—Corporations (other than S corporations) use Form 1139 to apply for:

• A quick refund of taxes from a carryback of a net operating loss (NOL), net capital loss, or unused general business credit.

• A quick refund of taxes from an overpayment of tax due to a claim of right adjustment under section 1341(b)(1).

What To Attach.—Attach copies of the following, if applicable:

• The first two pages of the corporation's income tax return for the loss year.

• Any form or schedule from which the carryback results (e.g., Schedule D (Form 1120), Form 3800, etc.).

• Forms or schedules (e.g., Schedule D (Form 1120), Form 3800, etc.), for items refigured in the carryback years.

• If the loss or unused credit is from a tax shelter, Form 8271, Investor Reporting of Tax Shelter Registration Number, for the year of the loss or unused credit.

• Form 8302, Application for Electronic Funds Transfer (EFT) of Tax Refund of $1 Million or More. If the refund for any carryback year is $1 million or more and the corporation wants the refund wired to a financial institution.

When and Where To File.—File Form 1139 within 1 year from the end of the tax year in which the NOL, net capital loss, unused credit, or claim of right adjustment occurred but not before the corporation files its income tax return for that year. File Form 1139 with the Internal Revenue Service Center where the corporation files its income tax return. Do not mail it with the corporation's income tax return.

If Form 1138, Extension of Time for Payment of Taxes by a Corporation Expecting a Net Operating Loss Carryback, was filed and the corporation wants an additional extension of time to pay, file Form 1139. File it by the last day of the month that includes the due date (with extensions) for filing the return for the tax year of the NOL from which the carryback results.

IRS Actions.—The IRS will act on this application within 90 days from the later of:

1. The date the completed form is filed, or

2. The last day of the month that includes the due date (with extensions) for filing the income tax return for the tax year of the NOL, net capital loss, or unused credit (or the date of the overpayment (under section 1341(b)(1) in the case of a claim of right adjustment).

The IRS may need to contact the corporation or its authorized representative for more information. To designate an attorney or representative, attach Form 2848, Power of Attorney and Declaration of Representative, to Form 1139.

A tentative carryback adjustment is not a claim for credit or refund. It may be disallowed if any required attachments are missing or there are material omissions or math errors that cannot be corrected within the 90-day period. If any part of the tax is disallowed, no suit may be brought in any court for the recovery of that tax.

Any amount applied, credited, or refunded based on this application that the IRS later determines to be excessive may be billed as if it were due to a math or clerical error on the return.

In addition, the accuracy related penalty or the fraud penalty may be assessed. See sections 6662 and 6663. Interest is also charged on amounts erroneously refunded, credited, or applied.

Adjustments to NOL.—In a tax year in which the NOL occurs the following adjustments must be made: (a) the NOL deduction is not allowed; (b) the dividends-received deductions for dividends received from domestic and foreign corporations and for dividends received on certain preferred stock of a public utility are computed without regard to the limitation on the aggregate amount of deductions under section 246(b); and (c) the dividends-paid deduction for dividends paid on certain preferred stock of a public utility is computed without regard to the limitation under section 247(a)(1)(B).

Release of Credits.—When an NOL carryback or a net capital loss carryback eliminates or reduces a credit in an earlier tax year, the released credit may be carried back 3 more years. Use a separate Form 1139 for the earlier year(s). To expedite the processing of Form 1139, file both Forms 1139 at the same time. See section 39 and the instructions for Form 3800, General Business Credit, for additional information on credit carrybacks.

Form 1120X.—Form 1120X may be filed instead of Form 1139 to get a refund. Generally, the corporation must file Form 1120X within 3 years after the later of the due date of the return for the tax year of the NOL, net capital loss, or unused credit or the date the corporation filed its income tax return for that year.

If Form 1120X is filed, attach a computation of the NOL and pages 1 and 2 of Form 1120, for the loss year. Complete a separate Form 1120X for each loss year.

Specific Instructions

Address.—Include the room, suite, or other unit number after the street address. If the Post Office does not deliver mail to the street address and the corporation has a P.O. box, enter the box number instead of the street address.

Line 1a.—A corporation may carry back an NOL to each of the 3 years before the loss year and carry any remaining loss forward to each of the 15 years following the loss year.

A corporation may elect to carry forward an NOL only to each of the 15 years following the year of the loss. To make this election, attach a statement making this election to a timely filed return (including extensions) for the year of the NOL. This election is irrevocable.

Special rules apply for any part of an NOL related to any specified liability loss, including product liability losses. See section 172(b)(1)(C) for details.

Show on a separate attachment all adjustments required to figure an NOL that may be carried back to any year.

Line 1b.—A net capital loss may be carried back 3 years and treated as a short-term capital loss in the carryback year. The net capital loss may be carried back only to the extent it does not increase or produce an NOL in the tax year to which it is carried. For special rules for capital loss carrybacks, see section 1212(a)(3).

Line 1c.—If a tentative refund is claimed based on a carryback of a general business credit, attach a copy of the appropriate credit form for the tax year in which the credit arose. Refigure the credit for each carryback year on Form 3800 and attach it to Form 1139.

Line 4.—If Form 1139 is filed to carry back a loss or unused credit to a year in which the corporation joined in the filing of a consolidated return, the IRS is required to send the refund for that year directly to, and in the name of, the common parent. See Regulations section 1.1502-78(a) and (b).

Lines 10 through 23.—In columns (a), (c), and (e), enter the amount for the applicable carryback year as shown on your original or amended return or per an IRS audit. Use the amounts on the amended return even if the IRS has not acted on it. Also attach a copy of the amended return to Form 1139 and write "Attachment to Form 1139" across the top. If the return was examined, enter the amounts determined as a result of the examination.

When completing lines 15 through 23, take into account any write-in amounts that may have appeared on the original return. For example, if Form 1120, Schedule J, line 10 was increased by interest on tax attributable to a payment received on a timeshare or residential lot, include that amount on line 23.

Line 10.—In columns (b), (d), and (f), enter the amount from columns (a), (c), and (e), respectively.

Line 11.—Enter the capital loss carryback but not more than capital gain net income. Capital gain net income is figured without regard to the capital loss carryback of the loss year or any later year. Attach a copy of Schedule D (Form 1120) for the carryback year. Enter the amount of the capital loss carryback as a positive number on line 11.

Line 15.—In columns (b), (d), and (f), enter the refigured income tax after taking into account the carryback(s). See the instructions for the corporate income tax return for the applicable year for more details on how to figure the tax and attach a detailed computation of the refigured tax. Take into account section 1561 when refiguring the income tax.

Line 16.—In columns (b), (d), and (f), enter the total of the corrected general business credits. Attach all Forms 3800 used to redetermine the amount of general business credit.

Line 22.—For columns (b), (d), and (f), refigure the alternative minimum tax and the environmental tax. Complete and attach Form 4626 for the appropriate year.

Line 24.—In columns (a), (c), and (e), enter the amount from line 23, columns (b), (d), and (f), respectively.

Line 26.—For a tentative refund based on an overpayment of tax under section 1341(b)(1), enter the overpayment on this line and attach a computation showing the information required by Temporary Regulations section 5.6411-1(d).

FORM 11.2
APPLICATION FOR TENTATIVE REFUND

Form **1045**	**Application for Tentative Refund**	OMB No. 1545-0098
Department of the Treasury Internal Revenue Service	▶ Before you fill out this form, read the separate instructions. ▶ Do not attach to your income tax return—mail in a separate envelope. ▶ For use by individuals, estates, or trusts.	**19 93**

Name Mary & John Jones		**Social security or employer identification number** 123-45-6789
Number, street, and apt. or suite no. If you have a P.O. box or a foreign address, see the instructions. One Park Place		**Spouse's social security number** 987 : 65 : 4321
City, town or post office, state, and ZIP code Anytown, NY 00000		**Telephone no. (optional)** (212) 123-0000

1 This application is filed to carry back: **a** Net operating loss (from Schedule A, page 2, line 25) $ 215,949   **b** Unused general business credit $

2a For the calendar year 1993, or other tax year beginning _____, 1993, ending _____, 19 __   **b** Date tax return was filed 4-12-93   **c** Service center where tax return was filed Holtsville

3 If this application is for an unused credit created by another carryback, give year of the first carryback ▶ ....

4 If you filed a joint return (or separate return) for some, but not all of the tax years involved in figuring the carryback, enter the years of the joint or separate returns ▶ ....

5 If social security number for carryback year is different from above, enter a SSN ▶ .... and **b** Year(s) ▶ ....

6 If you changed your accounting period, give date permission to change was granted ▶ ....

7 Have you filed a petition in Tax Court for the year(s) to which the carryback is to be applied? . . . . . ☐ Yes ☒ No

8 Does this carryback include a loss or credit from a tax shelter required to be registered? . . . . ☐ Yes ☒ No

Computation of Decrease in Tax Note: If 1a is blank, skip lines 9 through 15.	3rd preceding tax year ended ▶		2nd preceding tax year ended ▶		1st preceding tax year ended ▶	
	(a) Before carryback	(b) After carryback	(c) Before carryback	(d) After carryback	(e) Before carryback	(f) After carryback
9 Adjusted gross income from tax return or as previously adjusted . . .	11543	11543	206472	206472		
10 Net operating loss deduction after carryback. See instructions . . .				215949		
11 Subtract line 10 from line 9 . . .	11543	11543	206472			
12 Deductions. See instructions . . .	16723	16723	18092			
13 Subtract line 12 from line 11 . . .	(5180)	(5180)	22380			
14 Exemptions	6000	6000	6240			
15 Taxable income. Subtract line 14 from line 13 . . .	(11180)	(11180)	16140			
16 Income tax. See instructions—attach explanation	-0-	-0-	1727			
17 General business credit			1622			
18 Other credits. Identify			105			
19 Total credits. Add lines 17 and 18 .			1727			
20 Subtract line 19 from line 16 . . .			-0-			
21 Recapture taxes						
22 Alternative minimum tax			115722	72277		
23 Self-employment tax	4271	4271	113611	3611		
24 Other taxes						
25 Total tax liability. Add lines 20 through 24	4271	4271	119383	75888		
26 Enter amount from line 25, cols. (b), (d), and (f)	4271		75888			
27 Decrease in tax. Subtract line 26 from line 25	-0-		43495			

28 Overpayment of tax due to a claim of right adjustment under section 1341(b)(1)—attach computation . .

Sign Here Keep a copy of this application for your records.	Under penalties of perjury, I declare that I have examined this application and accompanying schedules and statements, and to the best of my knowledge and belief, they are true, correct, and complete.	
	Your signature	Date
	Spouse's signature (if Form 1045 is filed jointly, BOTH must sign)	Date
Preparer Other than Taxpayer	Name ▶	Date
	Address ▶	

For Paperwork Reduction Act Notice, see separate instructions.   Cat. No. 10670A   Form **1045** (1993)

Form 1045 (1993)   Page **2**

Schedule A—Net Operating Loss (NOL). See instructions.

1	Adjusted gross income from 1993 Form 1040, line 32. Estates and trusts, skip lines 1 and 2 . .		**1**
2	Deductions (individuals only):		
a	Enter amount from your 1993 Form 1040, line 34	**2a**	
b	Enter your deduction for exemptions from 1993 Form 1040, line 36 . .	**2b**	
c	Add lines 2a and 2b		**2c** ( )
3	Combine lines 1 and 2c. Estates and trusts, enter your taxable income		**3**
	Note: If line 3 is zero or more, do not complete rest of schedule. You do not have a net operating loss.		
	Adjustments:		
4	Deduction for exemptions from line 2b above. Estates and trusts, enter exemption amount from your tax return	**4**	
5	Total nonbusiness capital losses before limitation. Enter as a positive number . . .	**5**	
6	Total nonbusiness capital gains	**6**	
7	If line 5 is more than line 6, enter difference; otherwise, enter -0-.	**7**	
8	If line 6 is more than line 5, enter difference; otherwise, enter -0-.	**8**	
9	Nonbusiness deductions. See instructions . .	**9**	
10	Nonbusiness income other than capital gains. See instructions	**10**	
11	Add lines 8 and 10	**11**	
12	If line 9 is more than line 11, enter difference; otherwise, enter -0-		**12**
13	If line 11 is more than line 9, enter difference; otherwise, enter -0-. Do not enter more than line 8	**13**	
14	Total business capital losses before limitation. Enter as a positive number	**14**	
15	Total business capital gains	**15**	
16	Add lines 13 and 15	**16**	
17	If line 14 is more than line 16, enter difference; otherwise, enter -0-.	**17**	
18	Add lines 7 and 17	**18**	
19	Enter the loss, if any, from line 18 of Schedule D (Form 1040). (Estates and trusts, enter the loss, if any, from line 17, column (c), of Schedule D (Form 1041).) Enter as a positive number. If you do not have a loss on that line, skip lines 19 through 21 and enter on line 22 the amount from line 18	**19**	
20	Enter the loss from line 19 of Schedule D (Form 1040). (Estates and trusts, enter the loss from line 18 of Schedule D (Form 1041).) Enter as a positive number	**20**	
21	Subtract line 20 from line 19.	**21**	
22	Subtract line 21 from line 18.		**22**
23	Net operating loss deduction for losses from other years. Enter as a positive number		**23**
24	Add lines 4, 12, 22, and 23		**24**
25	Net operating loss. Combine lines 3 and 24. If the combined amount is less than zero, enter it here and on page 1, line 1a. If the combined amount is zero or more, you do not have a net operating loss		**25**

Form 1045 (1993)   Page **3**

Schedule B—Net Operating Loss Carryover. See instructions.

Complete one column before going to the next column.	(a) 3rd preceding tax year ended ▶	(b) 2nd preceding tax year ended ▶	(c) 1st preceding tax year ended ▶
1 **Net operating loss deduction.** In column (a), enter as a positive number the net operating loss from Schedule A, line 25. In columns (b) and (c), enter amounts from line 8 below, columns (a) and (b), respectively			
2 Taxable income from tax return (or as previously adjusted) before 1993 NOL carryback. (For individuals, if line 37 of Form 1040 is zero, subtract line 36 (Form 1040) from line 35 (Form 1040), and enter the difference as a negative number			
3 Net capital loss deduction from Sch. D (Form 1040) (line 20 of 1992 Sch. D, line 18 of 1991 Sch. D, line 19 of 1990 Sch. D), or from Sch. D (Form 1041), line 18. Enter as a positive number			
4 Adjustments to adjusted gross income. See instructions			
5 Adjustment to itemized deductions. See instructions			
6 Deduction for exemptions from tax return (or as previously adjusted). Estates and trusts, enter your exemption amount			
7 Modified taxable income. Combine lines 2 through 6. If zero or less, enter -0-.			
8 **Net operating loss carryover.** Subtract line 7 from line 1. If zero or less, enter -0-. See instructions . .			
Adjustment to Itemized Deductions (Individuals Only) *Complete lines 9 through 33 ONLY* if, for any of the 3 preceding years, you itemized deductions and line 3 above has an entry other than zero.			
9 Adjusted gross income per return (or as previously adjusted) before 1993 NOL carryback.			
10 Add lines 3 and 4 above			
11 Modified adjusted gross income. Add lines 9 and 10			
12 Medical expenses from Sch. A (Form 1040), line 1.			
13 Multiply line 11 by .075			
14 Subtract line 13 from line 12. If zero or less, enter -0-			
15 Medical expenses from Sch. A (Form 1040), line 4 (or as previously adjusted)			
16 Subtract line 14 from line 15 . . .			

Form 1045 (1993)   Page **4**

Schedule B—Net Operating Loss Carryover *(Continued)*

Complete one column before going to the next column.	(a) 3rd preceding tax year ended ▶		(b) 2nd preceding tax year ended ▶		(c) 1st preceding tax year ended ▶	
17 Modified adjusted gross income from line 11						
18 Enter as a positive number any NOL carryback from a year before 1993 that was deducted in figuring line 9 on page 3						
19 Add lines 17 and 18						
20 Refigure your charitable contributions using line 19 as your adjusted gross income. See instructions						
21 Charitable contributions from Sch. A (Form 1040), line 16 (line 17 of 1990 Sch. A (Form 1040))						
22 Subtract line 20 from line 21 . . .						
23 Casualty and theft losses from Form 4684, line 16						
24 Multiply line 11 by .10						
25 Subtract line 24 from line 23. If zero or less, enter -0-						
26 Casualty and theft losses from Form 4684, line 18 (or as previously adjusted).						
27 Subtract line 25 from line 26 . . .						
28 Miscellaneous itemized deductions from Sch. A (Form 1040), line 21 (line 22 of 1990 Sch. A (Form 1040)) . .						
29 Multiply line 11 by .02						
30 Subtract line 29 from line 28. If zero or less, enter -0-						
31 Miscellaneous itemized deductions from Sch. A (Form 1040), line 24 (line 25 of 1990 Sch. A (Form 1040)) (or as previously adjusted)						
32 Subtract line 30 from line 31 . . .						
33 Combine lines 16, 22, 27, and 32. If the NOL is carried to 1991 or 1992 and line 11 is more than $100,000 for 1991 ($50,000 if married filing separately), or more than $105,250 for 1992 ($52,625 if married filing separately), complete the worksheet on page 4 of the instructions. Otherwise, enter the amount from this line on line 5 (page 3)						

1993

 **Department of the Treasury
Internal Revenue Service**

Instructions for Form 1045
Application for Tentative Refund

Section references are to the Internal Revenue Code unless otherwise noted.

Paperwork Reduction Act Notice

We ask for the information on this form to carry out the Internal Revenue laws of the United States. You are required to give us the information. We need it to ensure that you are complying with these laws and to allow us to figure and collect the right amount of tax.

The time needed to complete and file this form will vary depending on individual circumstances. The estimated average time is:

Recordkeeping	26 min.
Learning about the law or the form	31 min.
Preparing the form . .	5 hr., 39 min.
Copying, assembling, and sending the form to the IRS	56 min.

If you have comments concerning the accuracy of these time estimates or suggestions for making this form more simple, we would be happy to hear from you. You can write to both the Internal Revenue Service, Attention: Reports Clearance Officer, PC:FP, Washington, DC 20224; and the Office of Management and Budget, Paperwork Reduction Project (1545-0098), Washington, DC 20503. DO NOT send Form 1045 to either of these offices. Instead, see Where To File on this page.

General Instructions

Purpose of Form

Form 1045 is used by an individual, estate, or trust, to apply for:

● A quick refund of taxes from the carryback of a net operating loss (NOL) or an unused general business credit.

● A quick refund of taxes from an overpayment of tax due to a claim of right adjustment under section 1341(b)(1).

Note: *An NOL may be carried back 3 years and forward 15 years. However, you may elect to carry forward a 1993 NOL instead of first carrying it back by attaching a statement to that effect to your 1993 tax return filed on or before the due date (including extensions). Once you make the election, it is irrevocable and the carryforward is limited to 15 years.*

When To File

File Form 1045 within 1 year after the end of the year in which the NOL, unused credit, or claim of right adjustment occurred, but only on or after the date you file your 1993 return.

When an NOL carryback eliminates or reduces a credit in an earlier year, you may be able to carry back the released credit 3 more years. See section 39 and the instructions for Form 3800, General Business Credit, for more details on credit carrybacks.

If you carry back the unused credit to tax years before the 3 years preceding the 1993 tax year, use a second Form 1045 for the earlier year(s). File the second application also within 1 year after the 1993 tax year. To expedite processing, file the two Forms 1045 together.

Where To File

File Form 1045 with the Internal Revenue Service Center where you are required to file your 1993 income tax return.

Caution: *Do not mail Form 1045 with your 1993 income tax return.*

What To Attach

Attach copies of the following, if applicable, to Form 1045 for the year of the loss or credit:

● If you are an individual, pages 1 and 2 of your 1993 Form 1040, and Schedules A and D.

● All Schedules K-1 you received from partnerships, S corporations, estates, or trusts that contribute to the loss or credit carryback.

● Any application for extension of time to file your 1993 income tax return.

● All Forms 8271, Investor Reporting of Tax Shelter Registration Number, attached to your 1993 return.

● Any other form or schedule from which the carryback results, such as Schedule C or F (Form 1040), or Form 3468, Form 3800, etc.

● All forms or schedules for items refigured in the carryback years, such as Form 6251 or Form 3468.

Be sure to attach all required forms listed above, and complete all lines on Form 1045 that apply to you.

Otherwise, your application may be disallowed.

Processing the Application

The IRS will process this application within 90 days from the later of:

● The date you file the complete application; or

● The last day of the month that includes the due date (including extensions) for filing your 1993 income tax return (or, for a claim of right adjustment, the date of the overpayment under section 1341(b)(1)).

Before processing certain cases involving abusive tax shelter promotions and before paying refunds, the IRS will reduce refunds of investors when appropriate, and will offset deficiencies assessed under provisions of section 6213(b)(3) against scheduled refunds resulting from tentative carryback adjustments under section 6411(b). See Revenue Procedure 84-84, 1984-2 C.B. 782 and Revenue Ruling 84-175, 1984-2 C.B. 296.

The processing of the Form 1045 and the payment of the refund requested does not mean the IRS has accepted the items carried back to previous years as correct. If it is later determined from an examination of the tax return for the year of the carryback that the claimed deductions or credits are due to an overstatement of the value of property, negligence, or substantial understatement of income tax, you may have to pay penalties. Any additional tax will also generate interest compounded daily.

We may need to contact you or your authorized representative (if you have one) for more information so we can process your application. If you want to designate a representative for us to contact (for example, your accountant or tax return preparer), attach a copy of your authorization to Form 1045. For this purpose, you may use Form 2848, Power of Attorney and Declaration of Representative.

Disallowance of the Application

This application for a tentative carryback adjustment is not a claim for credit or refund. Any application may be disallowed if it has material omissions or math errors that cannot be corrected within the 90-day period. If it is disallowed in whole or in part, no suit may be brought in any court for the recovery of that tax. But you may file a regular claim for credit or refund before the limitation period expires, as explained below under Form 1040X or Other Amended Return.

Excessive Allowances

Any amount applied, credited, or refunded based on this application that the IRS later determines to be excessive may be billed as if it were due to a math or clerical error on the return.

Form 1040X or Other Amended Return

Individuals can get a refund by filing Form 1040X, Amended U.S. Individual Income Tax Return, instead of Form 1045. An estate or trust may file an amended Form 1041, U.S. Fiduciary Income Tax Return. Generally, you must file an amended return no later than 3 years after the due date of the return for the 1993 tax year.

If you use Form 1040X or other amended return, follow the instructions for that return. Attach a computation of your NOL on Schedule A (Form 1045) and, if applicable, your NOL carryover on Schedule B (Form 1045). Complete a separate Form 1040X or other amended return for each year you request an adjustment.

The procedures for Form 1040X differ from those for Form 1045. The IRS is not required to process your Form 1040X within 90 days. However, if we do not process it within 6 months from the date you filed it, you may file suit in court. If we disallow your claim on Form 1040X, you must file suit no later than 2 years after the date we disallow it.

Additional Information

For more details on net operating losses, get Pub. 536, Net Operating Losses.

Specific Instructions

Address

P.O. box.—If your post office does not deliver mail to your home or office and you have a P.O. box, show your box number instead of your home or office address.

Foreign address.—If your address is outside the United States or its possessions or territories, enter the information on the line for "City, town or post office, state, and ZIP code" in the following order: city, province or state, postal code, and the name of the country. Do not abbreviate the country name.

Page 2

Line 1a—Net Operating Loss

Figure your net operating loss (NOL) on Schedule A, page 2.

You must carry the entire NOL back to the 3rd tax year before the loss. Any loss not used in the 3rd year is carried to the 2nd, and then the 1st preceding year. Any loss not applied in the 3 preceding years can be carried forward up to 15 years. Special rules apply to the part of an NOL related to any specified liability loss, including product liability losses. See section 172(b)(1)(C) for details.

If you filed a joint return (or a separate return) for some but not all of the tax years involved in figuring the NOL carryback, special rules apply in computing the NOL deduction. See Pub. 536 for the special rules. Attach a computation showing how you figured the carryback.

Line 1b—Carryback of Unused General Business Credit

If you claim a tentative refund based on the carryback of this credit, attach a detailed computation showing how you figured the credit carryback, and a recomputation of the credit after you apply the carryback. Make the recomputation on Form 3800 for the tax year of the tentative allowance.

If you filed a joint return (or separate return) for some but not all of the tax years involved in figuring the unused credit carryback, special rules apply in computing the carryback. Get the instructions for Form 3800. Attach a computation showing how you figured the carryback.

Line 2a—Tax Year

If the year of the loss, unused credit, or overpayment under section 1341(b)(1) is other than the calendar year 1993, enter the required information.

Lines 9 through 27—Computation of Decrease in Tax

Enter in columns (a), (c), and (e) the amounts for the applicable carryback year as shown on your original or amended return. If the return was examined, enter the amounts determined as a result of the examination.

Computation of deductions, credits, and taxes when the NOL is fully absorbed.—In refiguring your tax for the year to which the NOL is carried and fully absorbed, any income or other deduction based on, or limited to, a percentage of your adjusted gross income must be refigured on the basis of your adjusted gross income

determined after you apply the NOL carryback. This includes items such as medical expenses and miscellaneous itemized deductions subject to the 2% limit. Also, for 1991 and 1992, this includes the overall limitation on itemized deductions and phaseout of the deduction for personal exemptions. Determine the deduction for charitable contributions without regard to any NOL carryback. Any credits based on or limited by the tax must be refigured using the tax liability as determined after you apply the NOL carryback. See Pub. 536 for more information and examples.

Line 10—Net Operating Loss Deduction After Carryback

In column (b), enter as a positive number the NOL from Schedule A, page 2, line 25. If the NOL is not fully absorbed in the 3rd preceding year, first complete Schedule B on page 3. Then, on line 10, column (d), enter the NOL deduction from Schedule B, line 1, column (b). In column (f), enter the NOL deduction from Schedule B, line 1, column (c).

Line 12—Deductions

Individuals.—For columns (a), (c), and (e), enter the amount shown on, or as previously adjusted for, Form 1040, line 34 for 1990, 1991, and 1992. If you used Form 1040A, enter the amount from line 19 for 1990, 1991, and 1992. If you used Form 1040EZ, enter the amount from line 4 if you checked the "Yes" box. If you checked the "No" box for 1990, enter $3,250. If you checked the "No" box for 1991, enter $3,400. If you checked the "No" box for 1992, enter $3,600.

Line 16—Income Tax

For columns (b), (d), and (f), refigure your tax after taking into account the NOL carryback. Include on this line any tax from Forms 4970 and 4972. Attach an explanation of the method used to figure your tax and, if necessary, a detailed computation. For example, write "Tax Rate Schedule—1990" if that is the method used for that year. You do not need to attach a detailed computation of the tax in this case.

Line 17—General Business Credit

In columns (b), (d), and (f), enter the total of the recomputed general business credits. Attach all Forms 3800 used to redetermine the amount of general business credit.

Line 18—Other Credits

See your tax return for the carryback year for any additional credits such as the credit for child and dependent care expenses, credit for the elderly or the disabled, etc., that will apply in that year. If there is an entry on this line, identify the credit(s) claimed.

Line 21—Recapture Taxes

Enter the amount shown on your Form 1040, line 50 for 1990. For 1991 and 1992, enter the amount shown on your Form 1040, line 49.

Line 22—Alternative Minimum Tax

A carryback of an NOL may affect your alternative minimum tax. Use Form 6251 to figure this tax, and attach a copy if there is any change to your alternative minimum tax liability.

Line 23—Self-Employment Tax

Do not adjust the self-employment tax because of any carryback.

Line 24—Other Taxes

See your tax return for the carryback year for any other taxes not mentioned above, such as tax on an IRA, that will apply in that year. If there is an entry on this line, identify the taxes that apply.

Line 28—Overpayment of Tax Under Section 1341(b)(1)

If you apply for a tentative refund based on an overpayment of tax under section 1341(b)(1), enter it on this line. Also attach a computation that shows the information required in Regulations section 5.6411-1(d).

Signature

Individuals.—Sign and date Form 1045. If Form 1045 is filed jointly, both spouses must sign.
Estates.—All executors must sign and date Form 1045.
Trusts.—The fiduciary or an authorized representative must sign and date Form 1045.

Schedule A—Net Operating Loss (NOL)

Complete and file this schedule to determine the amount of your NOL that is available for carryback or carryover.

Line 9—Nonbusiness Deductions

These are deductions that are not connected with a trade or business. They include the following:
● IRA deduction.
● Deduction for payments on behalf of a self-employed individual to a Keogh

retirement plan or a simplified employee pension (SEP) plan.
● Self-employed health insurance deduction.
● Alimony.
● Itemized deductions are usually nonbusiness, except for casualty and theft losses, moving expenses and any employee business expenses.
● Standard deduction if you do not itemize.

Do not enter business deductions on line 9. These are deductions that are connected with a trade or business. They include the following:
● State income tax on business profits.
● Deduction for one-half of self-employment tax.
● Rental losses.
● Loss on the sale or exchange of business real estate or depreciable property.
● Your share of a business loss from a partnership or an S corporation.
● Ordinary loss on the sale or exchange of section 1244 (small business) stock.
● Ordinary loss on the sale or exchange of stock in a small business investment company operating under the Small Business Investment Act of 1958.
● Loss from the sale of accounts receivable if such accounts arose under the accrual method of accounting.
● If you itemized your deductions, casualty and theft losses are business deductions even if they involve nonbusiness property. Moving expenses and employee business expenses such as union dues, uniforms, tools, and educational expenses are also business deductions.

Line 10—Nonbusiness Income Other Than Capital Gains

This is income that is not from a trade or business. Examples are dividends, annuities, and interest on investments.

Do not enter business income on line 10. This is income from a trade or business and includes the following:
● Salaries and wages.
● Rental income.
● Gain on the sale or exchange of business real estate or depreciable property.
● Your share of business income from a partnership or an S corporation.

For more details on business and nonbusiness income and deductions, see Pub. 536.

Schedule B—Net Operating Loss Carryover

Complete and file this schedule to determine the amount of your net operating loss deduction for each carryback year and the amount to be carried forward if not fully absorbed in the carryback years.

If your NOL is more than the taxable income of the earliest year to which it is carried, you must figure the amount of the NOL that is to be carried to the next tax year. The amount of the NOL you may carry to the next year, after applying it to an earlier year(s), is the excess, if any, of the NOL carryback over the modified taxable income of that earlier year. Modified taxable income is the taxable income of the earlier year figured with certain modifications, as explained later.

Note: If you carry two or more NOLs to a tax year, you must deduct them, when figuring modified taxable income, in the order in which they were incurred. First, deduct the NOL from the earliest year, then the NOL from the next earliest year, and so on. After you deduct each NOL, there will be a new, lower total for modified taxable income to compare with any remaining NOL.

Line 2

The NOL carryback from the 1993 tax year or any later tax year is not allowed. However, net operating losses, otherwise allowable as carrybacks or carryforwards, occurring in tax years before 1993, are taken into account in figuring the modified taxable income for the earlier year.

Line 4—Adjustments to Adjusted Gross Income

If you entered an amount on line 3, you must refigure certain income and deductions based on adjusted gross income. These are:
● The special allowance for passive activity losses from rental real estate activities.
● Taxable social security benefits.
● IRA deductions.
● Excludable savings bond interest.

For purposes of figuring the adjustment to each of these items, your adjusted gross income is increased by the amount on line 3. Do not take into account your 1993 NOL carryback. Generally, figure the adjustment to each item of income or deduction in the order listed above and, when figuring the adjustment to each subsequent item, increase adjusted gross income by the total adjustments you figured for the previous items. However, a special rule applies if you received social security

Page 3

benefits AND deducted IRA contributions. Use the worksheets in Pub. 590, Individual Retirement Arrangements (IRAs), to refigure your taxable social security benefits and IRA deductions under the special rule.

Enter on line 4 the total adjustments made to the listed items. Attach a computation showing how the adjustments were figured.

Line 5—Adjustment to Itemized Deductions

Individuals.—Skip this line if, for all 3 preceding years, you did not itemize deductions or line 3 is zero or blank. Otherwise, complete lines 9 through 33 and enter the amount from line 33 or line 12 of the worksheet below, whichever applies, on line 5.

Estates and trusts.—Recompute the miscellaneous itemized deductions you deducted on Form 1041, line 15b, and any casualty or theft losses you claimed on Form 4684, line 18, by substituting modified adjusted gross income (see below) for the adjusted gross income of the estate or trust. Subtract the recomputed deductions and losses from the deductions and losses previously claimed, and enter the difference on line 5, Schedule B of Form 1045.

Modified adjusted gross income. For purposes of figuring miscellaneous

itemized deductions subject to the 2% limit, modified adjusted gross income is figured by adding the following amounts to the adjusted gross income previously used to figure these deductions:

1. The amount from line 3, Schedule B of Form 1045, and

2. The exemption amount from Form 1041, line 20.

For purposes of figuring casualty or theft losses, modified adjusted gross income is figured by adding the amount from line 3, Schedule B of Form 1045, to the adjusted gross income previously used to figure these losses.

Line 8—Net Operating Loss Carryover

Enter the amounts from line 8, columns (a) and (b), on line 1, columns (b) and (c), respectively. Carry forward to 1994 the amount on line 8, column (c).

Line 20

If, for any of the preceding years, you entered an amount other than zero on line 18 and you had any items of income or deductions based on adjusted gross income and listed in the instructions for line 4 of Schedule B, do not use the amount on line 19 as your adjusted

gross income for refiguring charitable contributions. Instead, figure adjusted gross income as follows:

1. Figure the adjustment to each item that affects and is based on adjusted gross income in the same manner as explained on line 4 of Schedule B, except do not take into account any NOL carrybacks when figuring adjusted gross income. Attach a computation showing how the adjustments were figured.

2. Add lines 3, 9, and 18 of Schedule B to the total adjustments you figured in 1 above. Use the result as your adjusted gross income for refiguring charitable contributions.

For net operating loss carryover purposes, you must reduce any contributions carryover to the extent your net operating loss carryover on line 8 is increased by any adjustment made to charitable contributions.

Line 33

If the NOL is carried to 1991 or 1992 and Schedule B (Form 1045), line 11, is more than $100,000 for 1991 ($50,000 if married filing separately), or more than $105,250 for 1992 ($52,625 if married filing separately), complete the worksheet below.

Itemized Deductions Limitation Worksheet—See the Line 33 Instructions (keep for your records)

	1991		1992	
1. Add the amounts from Schedule B (Form 1045), lines 14, 20, 25, and 30, and the amounts from Schedule A (Form 1040), lines 8, 12, 18, and 25				
2. Add Schedule B (Form 1045), lines 14 and 25, Schedule A (Form 1040), line 11, and any gambling losses included on Schedule A (Form 1040), line 25 . . .				
3. Subtract line 2 from line 1. If the result is zero or less, STOP HERE; enter the amount from line 33 of Schedule B (Form 1045) on line 6 of Schedule B (Form 1045) . .				
4. Multiply line 3 by 80% (.80)				
5. Enter the amount from Schedule B (Form 1040), line 11 . . .				
6. Enter $100,000 for 1991 ($50,000 if married filing separately); $105,250 for 1992 ($52,625 if married filing separately) . . .				
7. Subtract line 6 from line 5				
8. Multiply line 7 by 3% (.03)				
9. Enter the smaller of line 4 or line 8				
10. Subtract line 9 from line 1				
11. Total itemized deductions from Schedule A (Form 1040), line 26 (or as previously adjusted)				
12. Subtract line 10 from line 11. Enter difference here and on line 5 of Schedule B (Form 1045)				

¶ 11.04 VOLUNTARY REFUNDS: ABATEMENT

A claim for abatement is a procedure to appeal administratively an assessed tax before paying the assessment.[81] The Service is authorized to abate a tax or liability where (1) the Service determines that the amount of the assessment is excessive; (2) the Service determines that it assessed tax after the period of limitations for making assessments; or (3) the Service determines that it otherwise erroneously or illegally assessed the tax.[82] Abatement of an assessed but unpaid tax is also authorized where it is imprudent to collect a small tax balance or it is inappropriate to collect interest owed by a taxpayer as a result of a mathematical error on a return prepared by the Service.[83] The broad statutory language permitting abatement is deceiving; abatement is simply an administrative device to correct administrative errors. Furthermore, abatement of an assessed income, gift, or estate tax is clearly a matter of administrative discretion because a taxpayer is statutorily precluded from filing a claim for the abatement of those taxes.[84] In practice, claims for abatement are normally used where taxes such as employment and excise taxes are involved.

A claim for abatement of a tax other than an income, gift, or estate tax must be made on IRS Form 843 (Claim).[85] (See Form 11.3.) The completed Form 843 must include identifying information about the taxpayer and about the type and amount of tax assessed and to be abated. The basis for the claim must also be included. Although particular facts of the case are obviously crucial, the specific statutory circumstances in which abatement is authorized must also be considered. For example, a request for abatement of a 100 percent penalty assessed against a putative responsible officer might be grounded on the illegality of the assessment and also might describe facts establishing that no penalty should have been assessed as a substantive matter because, for example, the person had no authority to sign checks, execute returns, or otherwise control priority of payments to creditors.

The completed claim for abatement must be filed with the appropriate regional Service center, unless it is hand-carried to the District Office.[86] If the claim is denied, a taxpayer may not sue for abatement of the assessment, be-

---

[81] The claim for abatement has an interesting administrative history. It was originally an administrative device developed about 1919 when the government made superficial examinations and doubtful assessments to reduce a backlog of unexamined returns. The claim for abatement was the method a taxpayer was to use to defer payment of the assessed tax that the taxpayer believed was erroneous. See H. Dubroff, The United States Tax Court—An Historical Analysis 21–22 (1979).

[82] IRC § 6404(a).

[83] IRC §§ 6404(c), 6404(d).

[84] IRC § 6404(b).

[85] Reg. § 301.6404-1(c).

[86] Reg. § 301.6404-1(c).

cause the suit would be "tantamount to a suit for a declaration of rights as to the correctness of the assessment," and so violate the prohibition of such suits by the Declaratory Judgment Act.[87] The taxpayer's remedy is to pay the tax or—as is usually the case—a divisible portion of the tax and sue for refund in a federal district court or the claims court.

Abatement of an unpaid assessment as excessive appears to cancel the assessment, and collection may follow a new assessment only as long as the assessment period has not expired.[88] However, where an assessment is abated as uncollectible, some courts have apparently viewed the abated assessment as merely suspended, not canceled.[89]

---

[87] 28 USC § 2201. Etheridge v. United States, 300 F2d 906, 909 (DC Cir. 1962).

[88] See Crompton-Richmond Co. v. United States, 311 F. Supp. 1184, 1186 (SDNY 1970).

[89] Carlin v. United States, 100 F. Supp. 451 (Cl. Ct. 1951) (abated $154 assessment used as offset); Crompton-Richmond Co. v. United States, 311 F. Supp. 1184, 1186 (SDNY 1970) (erroneously abated Section 6672 penalty permitted to be reinstated).

FORM 11.3
CLAIM

Form **843**	**Claim for Refund and Request for Abatement**	
(Rev. January 1997)		OMB No. 1545-0024
Department of the Treasury Internal Revenue Service	▶ See separate instructions.	

Use Form 843 only if your claim involves (a) one of the taxes shown on line 3a or (b) a refund or abatement of interest, penalties, or additions to tax on line 4a.

Do not use Form 843 if your claim is for —
- *An overpayment of income taxes;*
- *A refund of fuel taxes;*
- *An overpayment of excise taxes reported on Form 720, 730, or 2290 (see General Instructions).*

Please type or print		
Name of claimant		Your social security number
Address (number, street, and room or suite no.)		Spouse's social security number
City or town, state, and ZIP code		Employer identification number
Name and address shown on return if different from above		Daytime telephone number

1 Period — prepare a separate Form 843 for each tax period
From _____ , 19 ___ , to _____ , 19 ___

2 Amount to be refunded or abated
$

3a Type of tax, penalty, or addition to tax:
☐ Employment ☐ Estate ☐ Gift ☐ Excise (unless reported on Form 720, 730, or 2290 — see instructions.)
☐ Penalty — IRC section ▶ _____

b Type of return filed (see instructions):
☐ 706 ☐ 709 ☐ 940 ☐ 941 ☐ 943 ☐ 945 ☐ 990-PF ☐ 4720 ☐ Other (specify)

4a Request for abatement or refund of:
☐ Interest caused by IRS errors or delays (if applicable — see instructions).
☐ A penalty or addition to tax as a result of erroneous advice from the IRS.

b Dates of payment ▶

5 **Explanation and additional claims.** Explain why you believe this claim should be allowed, and show computation of tax refund or abatement of interest, penalty, or addition to tax.

Signature. If you are filing Form 843 to request a refund or abatement relating to a joint return, both you and your spouse must sign the claim. Claims filed by corporations must be signed by a corporate officer authorized to sign, and the signature must be accompanied by the officer's title.

Under penalties of perjury, I declare that I have examined this claim, including accompanying schedules and statements, and, to the best of my knowledge and belief, it is true, correct, and complete.

Signature (Title, if applicable. Claims by corporations must be signed by an officer.)	Date
Signature	Date

For Paperwork Reduction Act Notice, see separate instructions.   Form **843** (Rev. 1-97)

Department of the Treasury
Internal Revenue Service

Instructions for Form 843

(Revised January 1997)

Claim for Refund and Request for Abatement

Section references are to the Internal Revenue Code.

Paperwork Reduction Act Notice

We ask for the information on this form to carry out the Internal Revenue laws of the United States. Internal Revenue Code sections 6402 and 6404 state the conditions under which you may file a claim for refund and request for abatement of certain taxes, penalties, and interest. Form 843 may be used to file your claim. Section 6109 requires that you disclose your taxpayer identification number (TIN). Routine uses of this information include providing it to the Department of Justice for civil and criminal litigation and to cities, states, and the District of Columbia for use in administering their tax laws.

You are not required to provide the information requested on a form that is subject to the Paperwork Reduction Act unless the form displays a valid OMB control number. Books or records relating to a form or its instructions must be retained as long as their contents may become material in the administration of any Internal Revenue law. Generally, tax returns and return information are confidential, as required by Code section 6103.

The time needed to complete and file this form will vary depending on individual circumstances. The estimated average time is:

Recordkeeping	26 min.
Learning about the law or the form	7 min.
Preparing the form	20 min.
Copying, assembling, and sending the form to the IRS	28 min.

If you have comments concerning the accuracy of these time estimates or suggestions for making this form simpler, we would be happy to hear from you. You can write to the Tax Forms Committee, Western Area Distribution Center, Rancho Cordova, CA 95743-0001. **DO NOT** send Form 843 to this address. Instead, see **Where To File** below.

General Instructions

A Change To Note

New rules apply in certain cases to abatement of interest accrued on deficiencies or payments for tax years beginning after July 30, 1996. See **Line 4** under **Specific Instructions** for more information.

Purpose of Form. — Use Form 843 to file a claim for refund of certain overpaid taxes, interest, penalties, and additions to tax. For example, if on your employment tax return you reported and paid more Federal income tax than you actually withheld from an employee, use this form to claim a refund.

Also use Form 843 to request abatement of an overassessment (or the unpaid portion of an overassessment) if more than the correct amount of tax (except income, estate, and gift tax), interest, additions to tax, or penalties have been assessed.

Do not use Form 843 to claim:

● A refund or to request an abatement of your income tax. Individuals must use **Form 1040X**, Amended U.S. Individual Income Tax Return. Corporations that filed Form 1120 or 1120-A must use **Form 1120X**, Amended U.S. Corporation Income Tax Return. Other income tax filers should file a claim on the appropriate amended tax return.

● A refund of excise taxes reported on Form 720, 730, or 2290. You must use **Form 8849**, Claim for Refund of Excise Taxes. Form 8849 is also used to claim refunds of excise taxes imposed on fuels, chemicals, and other articles used for nontaxable purposes or for which there is a reduced rate of tax.

● A refund of the required payment under section 7519. Instead, file **Form 8752**, Required Payment or

Refund Under Section 7519.

Generally, you must file a separate Form 843 for each tax period and each type of tax. Exceptions are provided for certain claims in the **Specific Instructions** below.

Who May File. — You may file Form 843 or your agent may file it for you. If your agent files, the original or a copy of **Form 2848**, Power of Attorney and Declaration of Representative, must be attached.

If you are filing as a legal representative for a decedent whose return you filed, attach to Form 843 a statement that you filed the return and you are still acting as the representative. If you did not file the decedent's return, attach certified copies of letters of testamentary, letters of administration, or similar evidence to show your authority. File **Form 1310**, Statement of Person Claiming Refund Due a Deceased Taxpayer, with Form 843 if you are the legal representative of a decedent.

Where To File. — File Form 843 with the Internal Revenue Service Center where you filed your return.

Specific Instructions

Social Security Number. — If you are filing Form 843 to request a refund or abatement relating to a joint return, enter social security numbers for both you and your spouse.

Line 3

Line 3a. — Check the appropriate box to show the type of tax, penalty, or addition to tax. If you are filing a claim for refund or request for abatement of an assessed penalty, check the box and enter the applicable Internal Revenue Code (IRC) section. Generally, you can find the IRC section on the Notice of Assessment you receive from the service center.

Line 3b. — Check the appropriate box to show the type of return, if any, that you filed.

Caution: You must attach **Form 941c,** Supporting Statement To Correct Information, or an equivalent statement, if you are claiming a refund of taxes reported on Form 941, 941-M, 941-SS, 943, or 945.

Line 4
Requesting Abatement or Refund of Interest Under Section 6404(e)

Section 6404(e) gives the IRS the authority to abate interest when the additional interest is attributable to IRS errors or delays.

Section 6404(e) applies only if there was an error or delay in performing a ministerial act (defined below) and only relates to taxes for which a notice of deficiency is required by section 6212(a). This includes income, generation-skipping, estate and gift taxes, and certain excise taxes imposed by chapter 41, 42, 43, 44, or 45. Section 6404(e) does not allow abatement of interest for employment taxes or other excise taxes. Get **Pub. 556,** Examination of Returns, Appeal Rights, and Claims of Refund, for more information.

Ministerial Act. — The term "ministerial act" means a procedural or mechanical act that **does not** involve the exercise of judgment or discretion and that occurs during the processing of your case after all prerequisites of the act, such as conferences and review by supervisors, have taken place. See Rev. Proc. 87-42, 1987-2 C.B. 589, for more information.

If you are requesting an abatement of interest, write "Request for Abatement of Interest Under Rev. Proc. 87-42" at the top of Form 843.

On line 1, state the tax period involved. Check the first box on line 4a. On line 4b, show the dates of any payment of interest or tax liability for the tax period involved.

On line 5, state the type of tax involved, when you were first contacted by the IRS in writing about the deficiency or payment, the specific period for which you are requesting abatement of interest, the circumstances of your case, and the reasons why you believe that failure to abate the interest would result in grossly unfair treatment.

Only one Form 843 is required if the interest assessment resulted from the IRS's error or delay in performing a single ministerial act affecting a tax assessment for multiple tax years or types of tax (for example, where 2 or more tax years were under examination).

Tax Years Beginning After July 30, 1996

For interest accruing on payments or deficiencies for tax years beginning after July 30, 1996, section 6404(e) will apply to certain managerial acts as well as ministerial acts, but the errors or delays must be unreasonable. Follow the instructions for line 1 through line 5 above, but do not refer to Rev. Proc. 87-42.

Requesting Abatement or Refund of a Penalty or Addition to Tax as a Result of Erroneous Written Advice

Section 6404(f) gives the IRS the authority to abate any portion of a penalty or addition to tax attributable to erroneous advice furnished to you in writing by an officer or employee of the IRS, acting in his or her official capacity.

The penalty or addition to tax will be abated only if:

1. You reasonably relied on the written advice;

2. The written advice was in response to a specific written request you made for advice; and

3. The penalty or addition to tax did not result from your failure to provide the IRS with adequate or accurate information.

If you are filing a request for abatement or refund of a penalty or addition to tax because of erroneous written advice, write "Request for Abatement of Penalty or Addition to Tax Pursuant to Section 6404(f)" at the top of Form 843. Complete lines 1 through 3. Check the appropriate box on line 4a. On line 4b, show the date of payment if the penalty or addition to tax has been paid.

Send Form 843 to the Internal Revenue Service Center where your return was filed. If the erroneous advice does not relate to an item on a tax return, Form 843 should be sent to the service center where your return was filed for the tax year you relied on the erroneous advice.

You must attach copies of the following information to Form 843:

1. Your written request for advice;

2. The erroneous written advice you relied on that was furnished to you by the IRS; and

3. The report, if any, of tax adjustments identifying the penalty or addition to tax, and the item(s) relating to the erroneous advice.

An abatement of any penalty or addition to tax under this section will be allowed only if you submit the request for abatement within the period allowed for collection of the penalty or addition to tax or, if you paid the penalty or addition to tax, within the period allowed for claiming a credit or refund of such penalty or addition to tax.

Line 5

Explain in detail your reasons for filing this claim and show your computation for the credit, refund, or abatement. Also attach appropriate supporting evidence.

¶ 11.05 RULES APPLICABLE TO CLAIMS FOR CREDIT OR REFUND

Three basic rules apply to claims for refund or credit. The first rule is implicit in Section 6511, found more directly in other Code provisions, and has a basis in long-standing authority: No refund is permitted to be made at all unless a claim for refund is filed. This rule is discussed below. The second and third rules are rules of limitations found in Section 6511. The second rule is a statute of limitations on filing claims for refund. To be timely, a claim for credit or refund "of an overpayment of any tax imposed by this title in respect of which the taxpayer is required to file a return shall be filed by the taxpayer within (1) three years from the date the return was filed or (2) two years from the date the tax was paid, whichever of such periods expires the later, or (3) if no return was filed by the taxpayer, within 2 years from the time the tax was paid."[90] Although it uses much the same language as the statute of limitations on filing a claim, the third basic rule is not a statute of limitations, but rather a set of rules governing the amount of refund allowable. Section 6511(b) states,

> (1) *Filing of claim within prescribed period.* No credit or refund shall be allowed or made after the expiration of the period of limitations prescribed in subsection (a), [the statutes of limitation on filing the claim], unless a claim for credit or refund is filed by the taxpayer within such period.
>
>   (A) *Limit where claim filed within 3-year period.* If the claim was filed by the taxpayer during the 3-year period prescribed in subsection (a), the amount of the credit or refund shall not exceed the portion of the tax paid within the period, immediately preceding the filing of the claim, equal to 3 years plus the period of any extension of time for filing the return. . . .
>   (B) *Limit where claim not filed within 3-year period.* If the claim was filed within such 3-year period, the amount of the credit or refund shall not exceed the portion of the tax paid during the 2 years immediately preceding the filing of the claim.
>   (C) *Limit if no claim filed.* If no claim was filed, the credit or refund shall not exceed the portion of that which would be allowable in subparagraphs (A) or (B), as the case may be, if a claim was filed on the date of the credit or refund is allowed.

Under Section 6511(b), the amount of the refund depends on the time of the filing of the claim, and incorporating the statutes of limitation for filing claims for refund as a guide to the amount of the refund has produced some compli-

---

[90] IRC § 6511(a).

cated issues for the courts to resolve. The third basic rule is actually a set of rules limiting the amount of the credit or refund.[91] Each of the rules is dis-- cussed in the following sections.

[1] Rule That a Claim for Refund Must Be Filed

Section 6511(b)(1) mandates that no credit or refund is permitted to be made to a taxpayer after the expiration of the statute of limitations for filing a claim for credit or refund. However, if only this limitation on the jurisdiction of the Service is considered, a rather cramped understanding of a refund claim is presented. Importantly, the filing of a claim for refund is a jurisdictional pre- requisite for filing a suit for refund. Section 7422(a) requires that a claim for refund be filed by a taxpayer in order for the taxpayer to be able to file a suit for refund. Regulations require that the taxpayer who files a claim must pro- vide a description of the grounds and facts upon which the refund is re- quested.[92] In addition, Section 6532 also prohibits a suit or proceeding under Section 7422(a) for a period of six months.[93] The purpose of this six-month waiting period is obviously to give the Service the opportunity to review the taxpayer's claim. If, within the six-month period, the Service reviews the claim administratively and disallows it, the taxpayer has two years from the date of the disallowance to commence a suit for refund to obtain judicial review. These statutory rules and regulatory requirements are "for the convenience of government officials in passing on claims for refund and in preparing for trial."[94] These requirements are of long standing in the case of erroneous or il- legal collection.[95] At least since 1866, taxpayers had to file appeals or claims for refund with the Commissioner of Internal Revenue, present sufficient infor- mation for administrative reconsideration, and the Commissioner had to be given the opportunity to decide whether to allow the claim; only after this ad- ministrative decision (or a reasonable time to make it) could the taxpayer com- mence an action.

Notice to the Service is at the heart of requirements for claims for refund. The Service requires that claims contain certain information for the purpose of

---

[91] IRC § 6511(b).

[92] Reg. § 301.6402-2(b)(1).

[93] IRC § 6532. If the Service fails to act on the claim, the taxpayer may commence a suit for refund at any time.

[94] Tucker v. Alexander, 275 US 228, 231 (1927).

[95] Flora v. United States, 362 US 145, 154–155 (1960), in part, discusses the history of suits for refund, including the Court's decision in Cheatham v. United States, 92 US 85 (1875), which in turn describes the remedies available to taxpayers under the Act of July 13, 1866, ch. 184, 14 Stat. 152. Section 19 of the act was nearly identical to Section 7422(a).

facilitating their processing, and a document that fails to put the Service on notice impedes the process.[96] For this reason it is said that "[t]he Commissioner should not be left to his own devices in order to discover the precise nature of a taxpayer's claim and thus be placed in a position of having to hazard a guess"[97]; and that the rule is intended to prevent surprise, to give the Service adequate notice of a claim and the facts on which the claim is based, to permit administrative investigation, and to provide the Service with the opportunity to correct errors.[98] Furthermore, while a taxpayer may not raise an entirely new ground in a refund suit, thereby varying the claim against the Service, Section 7422 "goes no further than to require the taxpayer to set forth facts sufficient to enable the Commissioner of Internal Revenue to make an intelligent administrative review of the claim."[99] Seen in this light, imperfect claims do not qualify as claims for refund because they do not serve the purpose of putting the Service on notice and prevent the Service from passing on the claim. Regulations "are calculated to avoid dilatory, careless, and wasteful fiscal administration by barring incomplete or confusing claims."[100]

[2] Rule That a Claim Be Timely Filed

[a] In General

Section 6511 establishes the basic rules for refund or credit of an overpaid tax. Section 6511(a) states, "Claim for credit or refund of an overpayment of any tax imposed by this title in respect of which tax the taxpayer is required to file a return shall be filed by the taxpayer within 3 years from the time the return was filed or 2 years from the time the tax was paid, whichever of such periods shall expire the later. . . . "[101] If the taxpayer does not file a return, the

---

[96] Angelus Milling Co. v. Comm'r, 325 US 293, 300 (1945).

[97] Stoller v. United States, 444 F2d 1391, 1393 (5th Cir. 1971).

[98] First Nat'l Bank v. United States, 727 F2d 741, 744 (8th Cir. 1984).

[99] Scoville Mfg. Co. v. Fitzpatrick, 215 F2d 567, 569 (2d Cir. 1954).

[100] Angelus Milling Co. v. Comm'r, 325 US 293, 297 (1944), citing Tucker v. Alexander, 275 US 228, 231 (1927).

[101] See also IRC § 6514. A taxpayer who seeks a refund for a tax year that was the subject of a Tax Court decision must use the three-year rule for determining the timeliness of the claim. See Mar Monte Corp. v. United States, 503 F2d 254, 257 (9th Cir. 1974); Sachs v. United States, 90-2 USTC ¶ 50,376 (ED Mich. 1990). See also Wadlow v. Comm'r, 112 TC 247 (1999) (a divided court held that a Section 183(e) election extends the assessment period "by operation of law," essentially having the effect of an agreement to extend the statute of limitations on assessments as well as on claiming a refund or credit).

taxpayer must file the claim within two years after the tax was paid.[102] A claim for refund of any tax paid by stamp must be filed within three years of the date of payment.[103]

One interpretation of the three-year period in Section 6511(a) is that the return referred to is a timely return, as suggested by the words "was filed," and by rules limiting the amount of the refund.[104] It does not seem coincidental that there is a three-year statute provided to the Service for auditing the taxpayer's return, and a three-year period for filing a claim for refund. In other words, the statute of limitations on the time for filing a claim for refund (and the limitations on the amount of the credit or refund) seem to be related to the statute of limitations for the Service to assess a deficiency. Normally, a deficiency in tax must be assessed within three years from the date a return is filed. Consequently, where a taxpayer files a claim for refund within three years after filing a return, the Service is not foreclosed from examining the return and assessing a deficiency.

During the assessment period, both the taxpayer and the Service are able to question the entire amount of tax reported on the return. Once the period of limitations on assessment has expired, the Service is not permitted to assess additional tax for the year. If the three-year period for filing and assessment were coextensive, it is reasonable to say that the three-year period for filing a claim for refund presupposes that the taxpayer applies when a taxpayer discovers an overpayment exists in a filed return. Also, in this view, the two-year period would apply to audit adjustments, which the taxpayer pays after the three-year period. Rules limiting the amount refundable on claims a taxpayer files outside the three-year assessment period put the taxpayer in the same position as the Service: Neither can use an error in the return affirmatively—neither the taxpayer by seeking to obtain a refund nor the Service by attempting to collect additional tax.

More certainly, it can be said that by limiting the amount of the credit or refund to the tax paid during the two years immediately preceding the claim, a taxpayer is prevented from extending the time for filing a claim for refund of the tax paid or deemed paid on the due date by the expedient of making a late payment of a small portion of the tax due. Also, since the Service is prohibited from assessing additional tax and can simply defend the government's entitlement to the allegedly overpaid tax, the taxpayer is similarly restricted by being permitted only to contest liability for the tax paid within the prior two years. A

---

[102] See Arnzen v. IRS, 91-1 USTC ¶ 50,020 (WD Wash. 1990); see also Schafer v. United States, 80 AFTR2d 97-8144 (SD Ohio 1997) ("the credit resulting from an overpayment of tax from a previous tax year is not eligible for application to a subsequent year until the tax return for the previous tax year is filed").

[103] IRC § 6511(a).

[104] Weisbart v. United States, 222 F3d 93, 86 AFTR2d 2000-5524 (2d Cir. 2000).

taxpayer who files a claim more than three years after the return was due is generally restricted to recovering an assessed and paid tax deficiency.

Despite the apparent reasonableness of this interpretation, it has not been accepted by the Service, nor by the circuit court in *Weisbart v. United States*.[105] Since the case bears on both the timeliness of a claim for refund and the limitations of the amount of the refund as well, the case is discussed in a later section.

Because the availability of the three-year-from-filing limitations period depends on the filing of a "return," there can be a dispute whether the document filed constitutes a qualifying return.[106] Because the purpose of the statute is to establish periods of limitation for the refund of tax, the return must be one the taxpayer is required to file for tax arising during a year or taxable period. This means that when a return for a year is filed but the event giving rise to the tax liability for the earlier year does not occur until a later year, "the return that starts the running of the statute is the return in which the taxpayer is required to or does report the income."[107]

The statute of limitations on filing a claim is absolute, and tolling of the statute for equitable reasons is not permitted. In *Brockamp v. United States*,[108] the Supreme Court resolved a dispute in the circuit courts over whether the statute of limitations on filing a claim for refund could be equitably tolled because, for example, the taxpayer was ill at the time the refund claim was due. The Supreme Court held that the statute of limitations for filing a claim, Section 6511, which "sets forth its time limits in unusually emphatic form," unlike ordinary statutes using fairly simple language, does not permit the implication of an equitable tolling exception. After the Supreme Court's decision in *Brockamp*, it was clear that the statute of limitations on filing a claim for refund was fixed by statute (Section 6511) and could not be equitably tolled because of a taxpayer's disability. Congress statutorily overruled *Brockamp*, but only for

---

[105] Weisbart v. United States, 222 F3d 93, 86 AFTR2d 2000-5524 (2d Cir. 2000).

[106] See, e.g., Bachner v. Comm'r, 81 F3d 1274 (3d Cir. 1996) (taxpayer unsuccessfully claimed that the Form W-2 his employer filed was a return so that the three-year period permitted refund of withheld tax); see also Zeier v. Comm'r, 80 F3d 1360 (9th Cir. 1996) (the Service successfully argued that Form 706, which did not attach schedules and was said to be based on estimates, was a qualifying return so that the three-year period applied and refund of amounts paid before and with the Form 706 were barred). For further discussion of what constitutes a qualifying tax return, see ¶ 4.02.

[107] Greene v. United States, 84 AFTR2d 99-5619 (Fed. Cir. 1999) (insurance company filed a 1983 return as an insurance company, but failed to qualify as an insurance company in 1984 and 1985, became liable for a phase 3 tax on the surplus in policyholder account for 1983, and filed an amended return reporting additional tax, but later filed a claim for refund of tax; held, the statute of limitations on filing a refund claim for the phase 3 tax began to run with the filing of the amended return, not the original return).

[108] Brockamp v. United States, 519 US 347 (1997).

"financially disabled" taxpayers.[109] Consequently, a late claim, other than one for a "financially disabled taxpayer" cannot serve as a basis for recovery even if late filing might be explained on equitable grounds.[110]

[b] Exception for Financially Disabled Taxpayers

The IRS Restructuring and Reform Act of 1998 (1998 Act)[111] amended Section 6511 to provide that in the case of an individual, the running of the statutory periods for filing a claim (Section 6511(a)) and for determining the amount of the refund (Section 6511(b)), as well as the special rules applicable in the case of the execution of an agreement to extend the statute of limitations on assessment (Section 6511(c)), are suspended during any period that the taxpayer is "financially disabled." An individual is financially disabled if the individual is unable to manage his financial affairs because he has a medically determinable (i.e., verifiable) physical or mental impairment that can be expected to result in death or that has lasted or can be expected to last for a continuous period of not less than twelve months.[112]

---

[109] IRC § 6511(h), added by the IRS Restructuring and Reform Act of 1998 (1998 Act) § 3202(a), effective July 22, 1998.

[110] See, e.g., Spector v. United States, 80-2 USTC ¶ 9658 (DNJ 1980) (Service made error in deficiency assessments resulting from partnership audit; partner who filed claim after discovering error too late barred from recovery); McLeod v. United States, 229 Ct. Cl. 810, 82-1 USTC ¶ 9177 (Ct. Cl. 1982) ("[t]he Service representatives had no authority to waive the time limitation for filing claims for refunds that Congress has imposed"); Ellis v. United States, 229 Ct. Cl. 814, 82-1 USTC ¶ 9214 (Ct. Cl. 1982) (claim not timely filed because of illness); Tallon v. United States, 55 AFTR2d 85-899 (CD Ill. 1984) (taxpayers who had overpaid tax filed return/refund claims for 1976 and 1981 allegedly because Service official said return could be filed at any time if tax was overpaid; held, no estoppel and claim time-barred).

In the absence of an express waiver, the statute of limitations on credit or refund is not extended by later legislation that affects a taxpayer's liability for an earlier tax year. Gebhardt v. United States, 46 AFTR2d 80-5783, 225 Ct. Cl. 612 (Ct. Cl. 1980); Elliott v. United States, 41 AFTR2d 78-1071 (ND Cal. 1991) (legislation affecting investment credit did not waive limitations period on filing refund claims); compare Savoie v. United States, 68 AFTR 2d 91-6080 (WD La. 1991) (oil on which windfall profits tax was paid was classified "de jure" so that former Section 6511(h)(2) extended limitations period).

[111] 1998 Act, HR 2676, 105th Cong., 2d Sess. § 1002.

[112] IRC § 6511(h), adopted in 1998 Act § 3202(a), and redesignating former Section 6511(h) as Section 6511(i). The provision applies to periods of disability before and after July 22, 1998, but does not apply to any claim for refund which without regard to the amendment is barred by the operation of law or rule of law, such as res judicata as of the date of enactment of the 1998 Act, July 22, 1998. This effective date bars the remedy of Section 6511(h) for pre–July 22, 1998, claims. See Johnson v. United States, 84 AFTR2d 99-6787 (SDNY 1999) (deceased taxpayer's claim for refund filed for 1993 was barred for amounts claimed to have been overpaid more than two years before the claim was filed).

Service procedure requires that several statements be submitted with a claim for credit or refund of tax to claim financial disability for purposes of Section 6511(h).[113] A written statement by a qualified physician must include (1) the name and description of the taxpayer's physical or mental impairment; (2) the physician's medical opinion that the physical or mental impairment prevented the taxpayer from managing the taxpayer's financial affairs[114]; (3) the physician's medical opinion that the physical or mental impairment was or can be expected to result in death, or that it has lasted (or can be expected to last) for a continuous period of not less than twelve months; (4) to the best of the physician's knowledge, the specific time period during which the taxpayer was prevented by the physical or mental impairment; and (5) a certification that the physician's statements are true, correct, and complete. In addition, the person signing the claim for refund must certify that no person, including the taxpayer's spouse, was authorized to act on behalf of the taxpayer in financial matters during the period of the taxpayer's physical or mental impairment.[115]

[3] Limitations on Amount of Refund

The amount of the credit or refund is limited in the following situations: (1) where the claim was filed within the three-year period following the filing of the tax return; (2) where the claim was not filed within the three-year period; and (3) where no claim was filed but a credit or refund has been allowed or made. The rules limiting the amount of the refund in these three situations are as follows:

1. *The three-year lookback limitation.* If the taxpayer has filed a tax return and has filed a claim within three years after filing the tax return, the refund amount is measured by and limited to the tax paid within three years before the taxpayer filed the claim, plus any extension of time the taxpayer had for filing the tax return.[116]

---

[113] Rev. Proc. 99-21, 1999-1 CB 960, § 4(1).

[114] "Physician" is defined in the Social Security Act § 1861(r)(1), 42 USC § 1395x(r).

[115] Rev. Proc. 99-21, 1999-1 CB 960, § 4(2). If a person was authorized to act for the taxpayer in financial matters, the dates of that period of authorization must be included.

[116] IRC § 6511(b)(2)(A). The amount of a refund will not be limited under Section 6511(b)(2)(A) when the last day of the limitation period is a Saturday, Sunday, or legal holiday and the claim is filed on the next succeeding day that is not a Saturday, Sunday, or legal holiday. Rev. Rul. 66-118, 1966-1 CB 290, superseding in part Rev. Rul. 57-354, 1957-2 CB 913. See, e.g., Dillard v. Comm'r, 63 TCM 2255 (1992) ("petitioner paid zero tax between October, 1988 and October, 1991 and section 6511(b)(2)(A) limits the amount of credit or refund to zero"). But on the issue of timely filing, the timely mailed, timely filed rules—discussed at ¶¶ 4.03[2][b], 5.02[1], and varying findings by the

2. *The two-year lookback limitation.* If the taxpayer has filed a tax return, but files a claim for refund more than three years after the return was filed (plus any extension of time for filing return), the refund amount is measured by and limited to the tax paid within two years before the taxpayer filed the claim.[117]

3. *No return, but a claim has been filed.* If the taxpayer has not filed a tax return but has filed a claim for refund, the refund amount is measured by and limited to the tax paid within two years before the taxpayer filed the claim.[118]

4. *The Service voluntarily makes a refund.* If the taxpayer has not filed a claim, but the Service allows or makes a refund within three years from the time the return was filed or two years from the time tax was paid, the refund amount is measured by the amount that could be allowed or made if a claim had been filed on the date the credit or refund is allowed.[119]

The limitation rules thus have two elements: the return and the payment. These elements are discussed in detail in the following sections.

[a] Three-Year Lookback Period: Filing of a Return

Section 6511 ties the limitations period to the filing of a return. In some situations, the time a return is deemed filed, and the time the tax is deemed paid is governed by statute.[120] Return filing rules correspond generally to rules

---

courts—come into play. Compare, e.g., Stark v. IRS, 90-2 USTC ¶ 50,552 (ND Ill. 1990) (finding no timely filed claim) with Anderson v. United States, 746 F. Supp. 15 (ED Wash. 1990) (finding claim timely filed).

[117] IRC § 6511(b)(2)(B). The statutory period for filing a claim runs from the filing of a return even if the claim for refund is contingent or uncertain as to amount, or both. Sivietlik v. United States, 779 F2d 1306 (7th Cir. 1985); Pabis v. United States, 92-2 USTC ¶ 50,483 (SD Ind. 1992) (determination of issue of liability and entitlement to refund also did not trigger running of limitations period).

For a case applying the two-years-from-payment rule, see Fogel v. United States, 76 AFTR2d 95-2515 (WD Wis. 1995) (the taxpayer filed 1984 return in 1985, paid an additional assessment between April 15, 1988, and January 23, 1990, and filed his refund claim for $12,976 on December 2, 1991; within the two years preceding the claim, the taxpayer had paid only $1,387; held, the taxpayer's recovery was limited to $1,387).

[118] IRC § 6511(b)(2)(B); see Turco v. Comm'r, TC Memo. 1997-564 (applying two-year rule from the date tax returns were submitted to a Service agent because such returns constituted informal claims for refunds and not filed tax returns).

[119] IRC § 6511(b)(2)(C). See Reg. § 301.6511(b)-1(b)(1). This description of Section 6511(b)(2)(C) is made clear from the legislative history. See HR Rep. No. 2333, 77th Cong., 2d Sess. 118–119 (1942). Section 6514 makes it clear that no credit or refund is permitted to be made after the expiration of the periods for filing a claim for refund.

[120] IRC § 6513.

for assessments. An early return (a return filed before the due date) is considered filed on the due date.[121] An extension of time for filing a return is not given any effect in establishing the date a return is filed for refund purposes[122] because the Supreme Court has held that Section 6513(a) applies only to situations where a return is filed or the tax paid before the statutory due date.[123] If a return is filed after the normal due date but before the extended due date, the date of filing is the date the return is actually received by the Service. Consequently, the period of limitations for filing a claim for refund begins to run from the date the return was actually received and not from the extension date.[124]

Some of the confusion caused by the three-years-from-filing rule is the result of the language in Section 6511, which seems to presuppose a timely return. Section 6511 requires the filing of a claim for credit or refund "within 3 years from the time the return was filed." Also, the interplay between the claim filing rules of Section 6511(a) and the refund limitation rules of Section 6511(b) cause confusion because claim filing periods and the periods limiting the amount of the refund are related (both subsections have a three-year and a two-year rule), but sometimes work independently. For example, how is the taxpayer's refund limited if a taxpayer files a delinquent return? As a result, the rationale for these distinctions in Sections 6511(a) and 6511(b) is not readily apparent; this issue was addressed in *Miller v. United States*.[125]

The following is a summary of the rules dealing with the application of the return filing rules.

1. If a taxpayer does not file a tax return when it is due, but files a delinquent return claiming a refund within the three-year period following the return due date, does the three-years-from-filing period apply or the two-years-from-payment rule apply? In *Miller v. United States*, the Ninth Circuit held that the two-years-from-payment rule applied. When a delinquent return has been filed within three years after the due date of the return, the Service has ruled that although the return is untimely, the claim for refund is timely filed, and the taxpayer is entitled to a refund of withheld and estimated tax credits.[126] One circuit court disagreed with the result in *Miller*.

---

[121] IRC § 6513(a). For the circumstances where a return is considered filed, see ¶ 4.03[2].

[122] Reg. § 301.6513-1(a).

[123] United States v. Habig, 390 US 222 (1968).

[124] Foster v. United States, 221 F. Supp. 291 (SDNY 1963), aff'd on another issue, 329 F2d 717 (2d Cir. 1964) (rule was applied even in the case of an automatic extension granted because the taxpayer was a nonresident alien).

[125] Miller v. United States, 38 F3d 473 (9th Cir. 1994); Richards v. Comm'r, 37 F3d 587 (10th Cir. 1994); see Galuska v. Comm'r, 5 F3d 195 (7th Cir. 1993).

[126] Rev. Rul. 76-511, 1976-2 CB 428; see also Rev. Rul. 57-354, 1957-2 CB 913.

In *Miller*, the Circuit Court reasoned that the point at which one must determine whether a return has or has not been filed, for purposes of the "if no return was filed by the taxpayer" clause must be two years after payment. Otherwise no claim could ever be barred by the two-years-after-payment clause because the taxpayer could at any time file a return and have three more years to assert the claim. To rule otherwise would produce the "anomalous" result that "so long as a taxpayer had paid some taxes within three years of filing a claim, the government would have to process as timely claims relating to overpayments from long ago, regardless of when they were originally made." The *Miller* court observed that Congress wanted to prevent taxpayers from keeping the statute for obtaining refunds open by making small payments to the Service, and the circuit court said its reading of the statute was supported by this legislative history. Another court reached this result on the ground that the tax paid within the relevant period is the tax subject to refund, not any tax paid within the three-year period.[127]

In *Weisbart v. United States*,[128] the Second Circuit held that a timely claim may be filed on a return even if the return itself is untimely. Weisbart obtained an extension to file his 1991 return and did so on August 27, 1995. However, because it had not been filed by the extended due date for filing the 1991 return, it was delinquent. Weisbart's return nevertheless claimed a refund of overpaid withholding tax for 1991. The Service disallowed Weisbart's claim on the ground that refund of withholding tax was barred because the claim had not been filed within the three-years-from-filing period. On appeal, the Service took the unusual step of asking the Second Circuit not to rely on *Miller*, and conceded that Section 6511(a) gave Weisbart three years from the filing of the return to file a refund claim, even when the return itself is untimely, citing Revenue Ruling 76-511. In independently examining *Miller*, the court observed that *Miller* had equated the failure to file a timely return with a taxpayer's filing no return at all (with the result that Weisbart had to file his claim within two years from payment), and his claim had not been filed within two years after the withholding tax had been deemed paid. Also, even before *Miller*, the First Circuit had also noted the anomaly that if a taxpayer were allowed to file a claim for refund on an untimely return, the limitations period of Section 6511(a) would be "illusory" because it would allow "a taxpayer to file a tax return 40 years late and still have 3 additional years in which to file a claim for refund."[129] While conceding that this result is "counter-intuitive," it

---

[127] Lee v. United States, 76 AFTR2d 95-6539 (7th Cir. 1995).

[128] Weisbart v. United States, 86 AFTR2d 2000-5524 (2d Cir. 2000) (taxpayer filed return three years late and claimed refund of taxes paid within the three-year lookback period; held, refund claim was timely).

[129] Oropallo v. United States, 994 F2d 25, 30 (1st Cir. 1993). Case authority was divided on whether a return claiming a refund filed after its due date is a "return" within the meaning of Section 6511(a). See Oropallo v. United States, 994 F2d 25 (1993), cert. de-

observed that "this construction makes sense: a central aim of [S]ection 6511(a) is not to bar stale claims, but to ensure that a taxpayer give the IRS notice of such claims before suing in a federal court." The claim for refund in this view gives the Service the opportunity to "correct claimed errors and, if disagreement persists, to limit the litigation to the issues which have been re-examined by the Service and which it is prepared to defend."[130] Accordingly, if the delinquent return and claim is filed within the three-year period following the return due date, the Second Circuit held that the lookback period is the three-year period provided in Section 6511(b)(2)(A).[131]

2. Suppose a taxpayer fails to file a return, but files a claim for refund. Is the refund amount measured by and limited to the amount of tax paid within the two years preceding the claim?[132] Where claims for refund are made on returns filed more than three years after the payments are deemed made, courts have differed over whether a refund is permitted, using different rules in Section 6511. Some courts apply the three-year limitation and hold that the refund claims were untimely as to those deemed payments.[133] Other courts have held that the claim for refund is timely because it is filed simultaneously with the

---

nied, 114 S. Ct. 705 (1994) (describing cases, and saying, "the government argues that a finding that taxpayers filing late returns have only two years from the time their taxes are paid to file refund claims better reflects the statutory language"). But see the discussion of *Lundy*, infra, as well as new Section 6512(b)(3). The First Circuit declined to resolve the question, finding instead that no amount of a 1982 overpayment deemed made in 1983 could be refunded when the return/claim for refund was filed in 1990 because no part of it had been paid within three years of 1990, following Rainey v. United States, 82-2 USTC ¶ 9442 (ND Ala. 1982) (claim on a delinquent return filed more than three years after the return date was timely; however, taxpayer was not entitled to any refund under Section 6511(b)). When a taxpayer fails to file a return within the three-year period following the due date of a return, the only relevant period for determining the amount of the refund is the two-year period preceding the refund claim. Galuska v. Comm'r, 5 F3d 195 (7th Cir. 1993) (taxpayer had withholding and estimated tax credits for 1986 but failed to file a return until September 19, 1991).

[130] Other courts have said that the refund is limited in this situation to the tax paid within the prior two years for purposes of the refund limitation because the return was not filed within the time required, including "the period of any extension of time for filing the return if that return is to be used in measuring the refund amount." IRC § 6511(b)(2)(A).

[131] Weisbart v. United States, 86 AFTR2d 2000-5524 (2d Cir. 2000). See Curry v. United States, 774 F2d 852 (7th Cir. 1985).

[132] IRC §§ 6511(a), 6511(b)(2)(B). See Arnzen v. IRS, 91-1 USTC ¶ 50,020 (WD Wash. 1990).

[133] Weigand v. United States, 760 F2d 107 (10th Cir. 1985); McLeod v. United States, 229 Cl. Ct. 810, 82-1 USTC ¶ 9177 (1982); Graham v. IRS, 602 F. Supp. 864 (WD Pa. 1984) (following *McLeod*); Chatman v. United States, 82-1 USTC ¶ 9240 (ED Va. 1981); Kreitz v. United States, 82-2 USTC ¶ 9505 (D. Md. 1982); Mills v. United States, 93-1 USTC ¶ 50,019 (ED Tex. 1992) (estimated tax for 1986 was paid on April 15, 1987, and return making claim was not filed until May 3, 1990, within three years after return filed; held, estimated tax was paid more than three years before claim).

return, albeit a delinquent return, but that the refund amount is limited to the tax paid within the three preceding years.[134]

3. Suppose the taxpayer files an original and then an amended return. Which is the return for purposes of Section 6511? Where a taxpayer files an original return and then an amended return, the return referred to in Section 6511 is the original return.[135] An amended return does not affect the running of the limitations period on the filing of a refund claim.

4. What if a taxpayer does not file a return, but files a return only after the Service prepares a return for the taxpayer and sends the taxpayer a notice of deficiency? In this case, the applicable rule is the two-years-from-payment rule.[136]

Under Section 6512(b)(3)(B), the relevant limitation period on the amount of a refund is the one applicable on the date the notice of deficiency was mailed. In *Commissioner v. Lundy*,[137] the Supreme Court dealt with a refund

---

In an unusual case, a trust that had a pending application for tax-exempt status on file nevertheless filed a Form 1041 reporting and paying tax on April 15, 1988. On May 15, 1991, the trust filed a claim for refund. The district court held that the claim was untimely, although the trust became tax-exempt and arguably the taxpayer was not required to file a return as provided in Section 6511(a). Hussey v. IRS, 93-1 USTC ¶ 50,231 (MD Fla. 1993), following Little People's Sch., Inc. v. United States, 842 F2d 570 (1st Cir. 1988) (nonprofit corporation mistakenly filed a return and paid unemployment taxes).

[134] Rainey v. United States, 82-2 USTC ¶ 9442 (ND Ala. 1982) (claim on a delinquent return filed more than three years after the return date was timely; however, taxpayer was not entitled to any refund under Section 6511(b)); McGregor v. United States, 650 F2d 289 (Cl. Ct. 1980); Dixon v. United States, 7 Cl. Ct. 377, 85-1 USTC ¶ 9173 (1985).

[135] Kaltreider Constr., Inc. v. United States, 303 F2d 366 (3d Cir.), cert. denied, 371 US 877 (1962); Rev. Rul. 72-311, 1972-1 CB 398. This must surely be the case after the Supreme Court's decision in Badaracco v. Comm'r, 464 US 386 (1984), in which an amended return was described as having no legal status, but being merely a creature of administrative discretion. See the discussion of this case at ¶ 4.03[2]. See Estate of Zeier v. United States, 80 F3d 1360 (9th Cir. 1996) (on July 16, 1984, an estate filed an estate tax return accompanied by a letter stating that because of difficulties in valuing certain properties, amounts had been estimated and that if necessary an amended return would be filed; and on January 8, 1990, it filed an amended return with complete schedules, requesting a refund; payments had been made before and together with the first return that had been filed; held, the claim for refund was untimely because even if schedules were missing from the original return, it did not prevent the Service from calculating the estate's tax liability; therefore, the return was sufficient for purposes of the running of the refund period).

[136] In Comm'r v. Lundy, 516 US 235 (1996), the Supreme Court resolved this issue, although most circuit courts had also reached this result.

[137] Comm'r v. Lundy, 516 US 235 (1996). In *Lundy*, the Fourth Circuit had ruled that a taxpayer was entitled to a refund of withheld taxes in the Tax Court when, in response to a notice of deficiency, he filed a return more than two but less than three years after the return was due and the taxes deemed paid. Lundy v. Comm'r, 45 F3d 856 (4th Cir. 1995). Virtually every other circuit held to the contrary, holding that for purposes of

claim that was made on a delinquent return filed more than two years and less than three years after the tax return for the year was due and the tax deemed paid. Before the taxpayer filed this delinquent return and claim, the Service had sent the taxpayer a notice of deficiency, and the taxpayer filed a petition in the Tax Court. As a result, the Court considered the lookback period for obtaining a refund of overpaid taxes in the context of the Tax Court's refund jurisdiction. Under Section 6512(b)(2)(B), the Tax Court has jurisdiction to determine that a taxpayer is entitled to a refund only if it first determines that the taxes were paid "within the period which would be applicable under [S]ection 6511(b)(2) . . . if on the date of the mailing of the notice of deficiency a claim had been filed (whether or not filed) stating the grounds upon which the Tax Court finds that there is an overpayment." Consequently, the issue the Supreme Court resolved was "whether the Tax Court can award a refund of taxes paid more than two years prior to the date on which the [Service] mailed the taxpayer a notice of deficiency, when, on the date the notice of deficiency was mailed, the taxpayer had not yet filed a return." In this situation, the Court held that the two-year lookback period applied, and, therefore, that the Tax Court lacked jurisdiction to find the taxpayer entitled to a refund.

Since the Tax Court's refund jurisdiction required application of Section 6511(b)(2), the Supreme Court interpreted the three-year lookback period. The Court said that a taxpayer who fails to file a return before the Service sends a notice of deficiency cannot have filed a deemed claim for refund "within 3 years from the time the return was filed."[138] Absent a filed return, there is no date from which to measure the three-year lookback period. Accordingly, the applicable lookback period is the two-year lookback period. Since Lundy was seeking a refund of the overpaid withholding tax, and that tax was deemed paid on the due date of the return, the notice of deficiency (and hypothetical refund claim) was mailed more than two years after that deemed payment date. Because the claimed tax had been paid more than two years before the notice of deficiency and the hypothetical claim had been mailed, the Tax Court did not have jurisdiction to find that Lundy was entitled to a refund of the withheld tax.

Section 6511(b)(2)(A), if the taxpayer has not filed a tax return at the time that the Service sends a notice of deficiency more than two years after the due date of the return, the applicable lookback period is the two-year period, not the three-year period, so that the Tax Court did not have jurisdiction to find that an individual's remittances for withholding and estimated tax had been overpaid and refundable in whole or in part. See Galuska v. Comm'r, 5 F3d 195 (7th Cir. 1993); Richards v. Comm'r, 37 F3d 587 (10th Cir. 1994); Allen v. Comm'r, 23 F3d 406 (6th Cir. 1994) (unpublished disposition); Davison v. Comm'r, 9 F3d 1538 (2d Cir. 1993) (unpublished disposition). The Supreme Court reversed the Fourth Circuit's decision.

[138] This view would seem to support the conclusion that the three-years-from-filing period cannot apply to a delinquent return/claim.

In *Lundy*, the taxpayer had filed his return late, but within three years from the due date of the return—and had claimed a refund on that return. Why was the claim on the delinquent return not a claim filed within the three-year lookback period, as the Fourth Circuit had held? If a claim for refund is actually filed, the applicable provision governing the Tax Court's jurisdiction to find that the taxpayer has made an overpayment, Section 6512(b)(3)(C), applies only to actual refund claims "filed before the date of the mailing of the notice of deficiency."[139] In the context of the Tax Court's jurisdiction, the Supreme Court refused to permit the actual filing of a refund claim (rather than the date of the mailing of the notice of deficiency) to govern the length of the lookback period. If the actual claim, rather than the hypothetical claim, controlled the determination, the taxpayer who timely filed a return might not obtain a refund if the notice of deficiency was mailed shortly before the expiration of the three-years-from-filing period.

The Supreme Court also refused to accept the argument that the only claim recognized by Section 6512(b)(3)(B) was one filed on a return. If a claim filed on a delinquent return within three years after the return due date was not timely to obtain an overpayment deemed made on the return due date, Lundy argued that different limitations periods applied on a refund case in a district court or the Court of Federal Claims. According to his argument, the claim he filed on his delinquent return would have been timely for purposes of a district court refund suit. However, the Supreme Court rejected this claim of disparate treatment, saying that the rules governing Tax Court litigation "differ in many ways from the rules governing litigation in the district courts and the Court of Federal Claims."[140]

As part of the Taxpayer Relief Act of 1997, Congress statutorily reversed the Supreme Court's decision in *Lundy*, by permitting taxpayers in the Tax Court to recover the overpaid tax deemed paid on the return due date.[141] The amendment of Section 6512(b) accomplishes this by making the three-year period of Section 6511(a) for filing a refund claim and the three-year lookback period for determining the amount of an overpayment apply to a taxpayer who (1) has not filed a return; (2) is sent a notice of deficiency during the third year after the return due date; and (3) files a petition in the Tax Court to obtain a refund of an overpaid tax paid within three years of the date of the notice of deficiency. By making it clear that there is a three-year period for filing

---

[139] Comm'r v. Lundy, 516 US 235, 247 (1996).

[140] Comm'r v. Lundy, 516 US 235, 252 (1996).

[141] IRC § 6512(b)(3), added by the Taxpayer Relief Act of 1997 § 1282, applicable to claims for credit or refund for taxable years ending after the effective date of the Act, August 5, 1997. For an argument that this statutory change still does not create needed certainty, or eliminate confusion in court decisions when a taxpayer files a delinquent return serving as a refund claim, see Lederman, "It's Time to Fix the 'Traps for the Unwary' in the Refund Statutes," 98 TNT 100-94 (May 25, 1998).

a claim and determining the amount of the refund, the Tax Court is permitted under its refund jurisdiction to determine that the taxpayer is entitled to recover any overpayment made within the prior three years.

EXAMPLE 11-2: A taxpayer wishes to obtain a credit or refund of withholding taxes paid for the year 1986 but has failed to file a timely return. To obtain the refund, the taxpayer files a delinquent tax return on April 15, 1990, more than two years after the 1986 return was due, and asks that the reported overpayment be refunded. The Service's position is that the claim is timely and that the refund will be made. But another result can be derived from the statute. Because the taxpayer did not file a timely return, the only refund limitation rule that can apply is the two-year rule. No withholding tax overpayment can be refunded to the taxpayer because withheld tax is deemed paid on the due date of the return without regard to extensions,[142] and this deemed payment was made more than two years before the claim was filed.[143]

EXAMPLE 11-3: A taxpayer files a 1996 return on April 15, 1997, showing a tax liability of $400. On April 1, 1999, he files an amended return showing a tax liability of $600, and he pays the additional $200. In 2000, the taxpayer files a claim for refund of $300, stating that his correct income tax liability for 1996 was $300. The taxpayer is not entitled to a refund of any part of the tax paid with the 1996 return because it was paid more than three years before the claim, but would be entitled to a refund of $200 because it was paid during the two years preceding the claim.[144]

[b] Payment for Refund Claim Purposes

Payment for purposes of the statute of limitations on refund, and the lookback periods used to establish the amount of the refund is an important issue. The starting point for the analysis is Section 6513, which establishes several rules for withholding, estimated tax, and other early payments. If an early remittance is considered a payment that starts the running of the statute of limitations for filing a claim for refund, a claim filed after the statutory period is untimely, and no refund or credit may be made to the taxpayer. Regrettably, there is confusion about the issue of when a remittance constitutes a payment,

---

[142] IRC § 6513(b).

[143] Allen v. United States, 439 F. Supp. 463 (CD Cal. 1977); Harrington v. United States, 83-1 USTC ¶ 9261 (D. Kan. 1983); Poncelet v. Comm'r, 45 TCM 661 (1983); Miller v. United States, 93-1 USTC ¶ 50,018 (WD Wash. 1992) (claim for 1986 was not timely, because delinquent return making claim was filed on April 18, 1990; two-year rule applied); see also Swannack v. IRS, 92-1 USTC ¶ 50,082 (WD Wash. 1992); Musser v. United States, 92-1 USTC ¶ 50,245 (D. Alaska 1992).

[144] Rev. Rul. 72-311, 1972-1 CB 398.

especially when the remittance is made before assessment. Preassessment remittances can be divided into two categories: (1) remittances made before a return is due but deemed paid by statute and (2) other remittances.

The statutory rules of Section 6513 provide the following framework for an analysis:

1. A payment of any tax made before the last date prescribed for payment is considered made on the date payment is due, even if an extension has been granted to the taxpayer to file a return or pay the tax, or the taxpayer has elected to pay the tax in installments.[145]

2. For purposes of Section 6511, withholding income tax deducted from wages or salary during a calendar year is considered to have been paid by the taxpayer on April 15 of the following year.[146]

3. An estimated income tax payment is considered to have been made on the last day for filing the return determined without regard to any extension of time for filing the return.[147]

4. If remuneration or another amount is paid during any period ending with or within a calendar year, any tax paid before April 15 of the next calendar year, is considered paid on April 15 of that succeeding year.[148]

5. Where a taxpayer, reporting an overpayment for a tax year (the first year), elects to credit the overpayment to estimated tax for the next tax year (the second year), the amount credited is considered paid in

---

[145] IRC § 6513(a). This rule also applies for purposes of overpayment determinations made by the Tax Court under Section 6512.

[146] IRC § 6513(b)(1). This rule assumes the taxpayer uses a calendar year. If the taxpayer has a tax year other than a calendar year, the statute states that the payment is deemed made "on the 15th day of the fourth month following the close of his taxable year with respect to which such is allowable as a credit under Section 31." The rules of Section 6511(b) are the same for a Tax Court overpayment determination.

[147] IRC § 6513(b)(2). A similar rule is applied to tax withheld at source on payments to nonresident aliens and foreign corporations. IRC § 6513(b)(3); Reg. § 301.6513-1(b)(3). See Chemical Bank NY Trust Co. v. United States, 275 F. Supp. 26, 29 (SDNY), aff'd, 386 F2d 995 (2d Cir. 1967). It follows that a claim for refund filed more than three years after the return due date is untimely. See also Binder v. United States, 590 F2d 68 (3d Cir. 1978) (remittances alleged to be escrow deposits held to be estimated tax payments).

[148] IRC § 6513(c)(2). This rule applies to withholding and estimated tax, Social Security taxes, and tax withheld at source on payments to nonresident aliens and foreign corporations.

the second year. For refund purposes, the taxpayer can claim that an overpayment has been made in the second year, not the first year.[149]

[i] Tax paid in installments. As with the filing of returns, any extensions of time for paying any tax or an election to pay a tax in installments[150] has no effect on the date payment is made.[151] Consequently, when a tax is paid in installments extending more than three years from the filing date of the return, an estimated tax payment or payment made with the return is not covered by a claim filed after payment of the final installment. Also, Section 6513 does not cover the situation when payment is made after the return is filed.[152] Accordingly, where a tax is paid in installments, it may be necessary to file multiple refund claims to cover both estimated tax and installment payments.[153]

[ii] Credits. A tax can be paid by crediting an overpayment.[154] A tax is considered paid when (1) an overpayment in one type of tax is credited against a deficiency in another type of tax for a single tax year or (2) an overpayment in one year is credited against a deficiency in tax for a different tax year.[155] When an overpayment in one year is applied to a deficiency for another year,

---

[149] IRC § 6513(d).

[150] See, e.g., IRC § 6166.

[151] Reg. § 301.6513-1(a).

[152] See Continental Ill. Nat'l Bank & Trust Co. v. United States, 39 F. Supp. 620 (Ct. Cl. 1941).

[153] For a case where, as a result of failing to file a claim to cover an installment payment, a taxpayer was denied a refund of a tax he admittedly overpaid, see Snyder v. United States, 616 F2d 1187 (10th Cir. 1980).

[154] See IRC §§ 6402(b), 6513(d). However, Section 6402 says that the Service "may" credit the overpayment. Thus, some courts have said the Service is not required to offset overpayments for one year against a liability for another year. See supra ¶ 11.02[1] note 21.

[155] See IRC §§ 6402(b), 6513(d). The Service may not, however, credit the overpayment to a disputed tax liability for a separate tax year. Lyons v. United States, 93-1 USTC ¶ 50,026 (SD Iowa 1992), See Kingston Prods. v. United States, 368 F2d 281 (Ct. Cl. 1966) (refund due on excess profits tax applied to deficiency in income tax for the same year did not constitute payment by credit). Accord Republic Petroleum Corp. v. United States, 613 F2d 518 (5th Cir. 1980) (overpayment is "made" not when Service determines the amount of the overpayment for a single year and applies it to another year, but on the date the return for the year of overpayment is filed). It has been held that crediting an overpayment is entirely within the discretion of the Service; a court does not have jurisdiction to order the Service to apply an overpayment for one year to an underpayment for another year. O'Bryant v. United States, 94-1 USTC ¶ 50,087 (CD Ill. 1994) (taxpayers filed a refund claim that was untimely as to three payments but timely as to one payment and asked the court to apply the overpayment to the balance due to the Service for another year; held, the time-barred overpayments could not be applied). Cf. Vishnevsky v. United States, 581 F2d 1249 (7th Cir. 1978) (overpayment applied because the Service had promised to do so).

the date of payment is the date the Service credits the overpayment against the deficiency, and the two-years-from-payment period begins to run on that date.[156] Once an overpayment has been credited as payment for another year's tax liability, that other year's tax liability has been paid. Accordingly, the taxpayer's remedy for contesting the validity of the tax liability satisfied by the overpayment credit is to file a claim for refund of the tax (paid by means of the credit) within two years from the date on which the overpayment was used to satisfy the outstanding tax liability.[157]

[iii] Example. These rules are illustrated by the following example.

EXAMPLE 11-4: A taxpayer makes quarterly estimated tax payments in the total amount of $8,000, and files his 1997 return early, on March 1, 1998. On April 1, 2000, an income tax deficiency of $6,000 is assessed, which the taxpayer pays in three $2,000 installments on May 1, August 1, and November 1, 2000. A claim filed before April 6, 2001, would be timely as to all payments, including estimated tax payments made in 1997 but deemed made on April 15, 1998, when the tax return for the year was also considered to have been filed. A claim filed on April 20, 2001, would be filed more than three years from the filing period of the return, and no portion of the $8,000 tax paid could be claimed, but the claim would be timely as to all deficiency payments. A claim filed after November 1, 2002, would be untimely as to all deficiency payments, and any claim filed more than two years after each installment would be untimely as to that installment.

---

[156] Republic Petroleum Corp. v. United States, 613 F2d 518 (5th Cir. 1980). See also Rev. Rul. 81-77, 1981-1 CB 582 (merged corporation's deficiency for premerger tax year may not offset an overpayment of second party to merger for premerger tax year to determine whether a refund report must be made to the Joint Committee on Taxation).

[157] Reg. § 301.6402-2; Donahue v. United States, 33 Fed. Cl. 600 (1995). The National Office has advised Service centers that when it satisfies an outstanding liability by crediting an overpayment, payment of the outstanding liability is deemed to occur on the date on which the overassessment is scheduled, which occurs after the return is processed. SCA 1999-17065 (Apr. 30, 1999). This has been the National Office's advice to the field as well. See FSA 200001019 (Oct. 6, 1999).

The applicable statute of limitations for refunds is applied to the tax year that had the deficiency satisfied by the overpayment credit. Thus, the taxpayer may file a refund claim within the two-year period that begins on the date the overpayment was credited against the deficiency or, if a return was filed for that "deficiency year," within the three-year period following the filing of that return. See Republic Petroleum Corp. v. United States, 613 F2d 518 n.19 (5th Cir. 1980); Donahue v. United States, supra; Bazarargani v. United States, 92-1 USTC ¶ 50,312 (ED Pa. 1992); Rev. Rul. 56-506, 1956-2 CB 959.

[c] Deposits Versus Payments

When an amount remitted by a taxpayer before an assessment has been made is not described by one of the statutory payment rules of Section 6513, there is considerable controversy over whether the remittance constitutes a payment for purposes of limitations on refunds set out in Section 6511. The problem arises in the situation where, before any assessment, a taxpayer learns of a possible tax liability and remits to the Service an amount of money considered to be sufficient to stop the running of interest or a delinquency penalty. In this case, is the remittance a payment of tax or merely a deposit to avoid the running of interest and penalties? In *Rosenman v. United States*,[158] the Supreme Court held that the time for filing a claim for refund begins to run from the date the Service makes the assessment, not from the earlier date the taxpayer remitted an amount to the Service.

[i] *Rosenman.* The facts of *Rosenman* require some description. In December 1934, before a return was filed, an estate remitted $120,000 as a payment "on account" of estate tax, but it was said to be made "under protest and duress" and "solely" to stop the running of interest and penalties. After the estate tax return was filed and audited, a deficiency was assessed in April 1938, to which the balance of the remitted amount was applied. The estate paid an additional amount to satisfy the balance of the assessment in April 1938. On May 20, 1940, it filed a claim for refund claiming an amount that included a portion of the remittance made in 1934. The government contended that the claim, except as to the portion paid in 1938, was untimely because "payment" of the tax occurred in December 1934. The Supreme Court, finding for the estate, pointed out that "on December 24, 1934, the taxpayer did not discharge what he deemed a liability nor pay one that was asserted."[159] The tax obligation did not become defined until the date of assessment. The remittance made before this date was the kind of "interim arrangement" the Service recognized and had successfully argued for in other cases where taxpayers claimed interest was owed to them. The Court would not treat "the same transaction as payment and not as payment, whichever favors the Government.... " This holding was especially appropriate where treatment in interest cases carried out the true nature of the arrangement and safeguarded both the Service and the taxpayer.

Although it believed that it did not need to consider them, the Court's decision in *Rosenman* sits rather uncertainly beside a number of Code provisions with which it is not always reconcilable. The reason is largely historical. Before the decision, Congress adopted the current tax payment system that op-

---

[158] Rosenman v. United States, 323 US 658, 662 (1994). See cases cited supra note 20.

[159] Rosenman v. United States, 323 US 658, 662 (1944).

erates through withholding of tax from salary and wages as well as estimated tax payments. These provisions remain in the Code, and reflect certain legislative decisions about how overpayments, refunds, and interest on overpayments would be treated in the current tax payment system Congress adopted in 1943. Under the current tax payment system, amounts were required to be paid against a tax liability, which the Service would not finally determine until after payments were made. Also, before the taxpayer filed a return, the taxpayer could (and depending on withholding rates and estimated tax rules, would) make withholding and estimated tax payments in excess of the tax liability ultimately due. Some flexibility was needed in making a refund or credit of these excess current payments.

This flexibility is provided by Section 6401(c), which using a triple negative states, "an amount paid as a tax shall not be considered not to constitute an overpayment solely because there was no tax liability in respect of which [the] amount was paid."[160] What legislative history there is seems to suggest that "honest mistakes [in payment] incident to the bona fide orderly compliance with the actual or reasonably apparent duties of the taxpayer" are to be considered overpayments, irrespective of assessment. Congress did not want the government to be liable for interest where a taxpayer "merely dumped money as taxes on the collector, by disorderly remittances to him of amounts not computed in pursuit of the actual or reasonably apparent requirements of the Code, or not transmitted in accordance with the procedures set up by the Code, or by other abuses of tax administration."[161]

This background explains why the Code contains the following provisions: (1) a taxpayer may remit an amount to the Service against a tax liability; (2) the Service may, but is not required to, assess the amount as tax[162]; (3) the amount may be considered an overpayment even though no tax assessment for the year has been made[163]; and (4) in the event an amount is remitted as estimated or withheld tax before the time the return for the year is due, it is not considered to have been paid for purposes of determining the time for fixing the amount of a refund claim and the running of interest.[164] These statutory rules leave open the question of how to treat remittances received after the return is due, but before an assessment is made. Courts have come to various

---

[160] Treas. Reg. § 301.6402-4 authorizes district directors and directors of regional Service centers to refund or credit excess current payments without the filing of claims, but cautions taxpayers to file claims for refund as a protective measure.

[161] S. Rep. No. 221, 78th Cong., 1st Sess. (1943), reprinted in 1943 CB 1314, 1939–1940 (Current Tax Payment Act of 1943).

[162] IRC § 6213(b)(4).

[163] IRC § 6401(c).

[164] IRC § 6513.

conclusions in efforts to reconcile the *Rosenman* principle and the various Code provisions.

[ii] Revenue Procedure 84-58. Court decisions on the issue of what constitutes payment for limitations purposes where a preassessment remittance is involved obviously must be considered. However, the Service has promulgated procedures for taxpayers to follow in making remittances in order to stop the running of interest.[165] Since "payment" has the same meaning for both interest and overpayment purposes under *Rosenman*, the Service's administrative procedures on remittances made to stop the running of interest should govern the characterization of a remittance for overpayment purposes as well.

As a matter of practice, the Service instructs its agents to request payment of a deficiency adjustment at the conclusion of an examination. If a taxpayer wants to stop the running of interest and contest the adjustment in the Tax Court, the taxpayer may make a remittance, designating it in writing as a deposit in the nature of a cash bond. If the taxpayer makes such a deposit, the Service does not consider the remittance a payment.[166] The deposit stops the running of interest and, if the taxpayer does not waive the restrictions on assessment, the Service sends the taxpayer a notice of deficiency, thus permitting the taxpayer the option of Tax Court review.[167] On the other hand, the deposit is not considered subject to a claim for refund as an overpayment and does not draw interest as such.[168]

If the taxpayer does not designate the remittance as a deposit, the Service considers the remittance a payment and assesses it.[169] In such a situation, if the remittance equals the amount of the proposed liability (e.g., as reflected in the revenue agent's report), no notice of deficiency is sent to the taxpayer.[170] The Service says a remittance assessed as payment "will be treated as any other assessed amount and interest will be paid on any overpayment under Section

---

[165] Rev. Proc. 84-58, 1984-2 CB 501, superseding Rev. Proc. 81-51, 1982-2 CB 839, for remittance made on or after October 1, 1984. These procedures state when the Service will consider a preassessment remittance as a payment for interest purposes. See ¶ 6.02[3][a].

[166] Rev. Proc. 84-58, 1984-2 CB 501, § 4.02(1). Normally, Section 6213(b)(4) permits assessment of an amount paid as tax on receipt.

[167] Rev. Proc. 84-58, 1984-2 CB 501, §§ 4.02(3), 5.01. If the Service were to assess the remittance as a payment, the amount of the deficiency would be reduced by the amount of the assessment. See IRC § 6211(a). Thus, a full remittance would eliminate a deficiency and Tax Court jurisdiction.

[168] Rev. Proc. 84-58, 1984-2 CB 501, § 4.02(1). A taxpayer may request return of all or part of the deposit at any time before assessment, and, assuming no jeopardy in collection, the deposit will be returned, without interest.

[169] Rev. Proc. 84-58, 1984-2 CB 501, § 4.03(1).

[170] Rev. Proc. 84-58, 1984-2 CB 501, § 4.03(2).

6611 of the Code."[171] It would follow that the remittance assessed as a payment would also be treated as payment of an overpayment for refund purposes.

A remittance made by a taxpayer before a written proposal of a liability (e.g., by way of a revenue agent's report) and not designated by the taxpayer as a deposit will nevertheless be considered a cash bond.[172] Such a deposit is not considered subject to a claim for refund and does not draw interest under Section 6611 as an overpayment.

Administratively, then, a remittance is posted to the taxpayer's account (or assessed) as a payment if the taxpayer does not designate the remittance as a deposit or if he executes a waiver of restrictions on assessment and collection. Although the Service takes this position for purposes of the payment of interest, it also seems to cover refunds of overpayments. Consequently, the date of posting under the Service's interest procedures also begins the running of the period for filing a refund claim.

[iii] Judicial standards. Court decisions seem to have adopted three standards: a bright-line standard, a no-contest standard, and a facts and circumstances standard.

The per se bright-line standard. A remittance made on an agent's request is not considered a payment until assessment.[173] If the amount of the tax cannot be determined, a remittance does not constitute payment for limitations purposes until the date the return is due, but on the return due date such remittances are deemed paid.[174] It also appears that a remittance made after the sending of a notice of deficiency constitutes a payment.[175] In the same general circumstances, other courts have found payment to have occurred where the

---

[171] Rev. Proc. 84-58, 1984-2 CB 501, § 5.05.

[172] Rev. Proc. 84-58, 1984-2 CB 501, § 4.04(1).

[173] See Fortugno v. Comm'r, 353 F2d 429 (3d Cir. 1965), cert. dismissed, 385 US 954 (1966) (interest case where the agent warned of a jeopardy assessment). When a taxpayer claimed that the Service's collection of an assessment against another taxpayer, her daughter, constituted the taxpayer mother's overpayment of tax, lack of assessment was crucial to the Tax Court in its finding that the taxpayer had not made a "payment" of taxes for purposes of the Tax Court's overpayment jurisdiction under Section 6512(b)(1); Terauds v. Comm'r, TC Memo. 1997-64 (1997) (*Fortugno* followed; absent assessment, the court concluded that the Service's assessment and collection from the daughter did not constitute the mother's payment of an asserted liability).

[174] Binder v. United States, 590 F2d 68 (3d Cir. 1978) (estimated tax payments made by or for a person not required to pay; held, made on due date of return); Chemical Bank NY Trust Co. v. United States, 275 F. Supp. 26 (SDNY), aff'd per curiam, 386 F2d 995 (2d Cir. 1967); United States v. Miller, 315 F2d 354 (10th Cir. 1963); Plankinton v. United States, 267 F2d 278 (7th Cir. 1959).

[175] See Colt's Mfg. Co. v. Comm'r, 306 F2d 929 (2d Cir. 1962); Northern Natural Gas Co. v. United States, 354 F2d 310 (Ct. Cl. 1965) (both interest cases). See also Ford v. United States, 618 F2d 357 (5th Cir. 1980) (payment would have been found to have occurred on date of remittance but for earlier authority in circuit).

taxpayer intends the remittance to satisfy the amount of the deficiency.[176] Other decisions hold that payment occurs only on assessment.[177] These decisions cannot be reconciled. Undoubtedly, the requirement that a taxpayer intended to discharge a defined deficiency and to acquiesce in the deficiency can be derived from dicta in *Rosenman*.[178] Finding payment only upon assessment follows the precise holding of the case.

The no-contest standard. Where a remittance is made after a deficiency has been determined, some courts have held that the remittance does not constitute payment if the taxpayer intended to contest the deficiency.[179] Even if intention and a decision not to contest were the appropriate factors, it should be

---

[176] See, e.g., Ameel v. United States, 426 F2d 1270 (6th Cir. 1970). See also Ford v. United States, 618 F2d 357 (5th Cir. 1980). See also Abadi v. United States, 782 F. Supp. 59 (ED Mich. 1992) (preassessment remittance held payment because intended to discharge liability; refund claim filed thirteen days late).

[177] Thomas v. Mercantile Nat'l Bank, 204 F2d 943 (5th Cir. 1953); United States v. Dubuque Packing Co., 233 F2d 453 (8th Cir. 1956). But see Ford v. United States, 618 F2d 357 (5th Cir. 1980) (casting doubt on whether *Mercantile National Bank* should continue to be followed in the Fifth Circuit).

[178] The Supreme Court said the taxpayer "did not discharge what he deemed a liability nor pay one that was asserted." Rosenman v. United States, 323 US 658, 662 (1944).

[179] See Charles Leich & Co. v. United States, 329 F2d 649 (Ct. Cl. 1964); Lewyt Corp. v. Comm'r, 215 F2d 518 (2d Cir. 1954), modified on other issues, 349 US 237 (1955). Contest prevents payments in interest cases. See, e.g., Fortugno v. Comm'r, 353 F2d 429 (3d Cir. 1965), cert. dismissed, 385 US 954 (1966); Northern Natural Gas Co. v. United States, 354 F2d 310 (Ct. Cl. 1965). Ewing v. United States, 914 F2d 499 (4th Cir. 1990) (*Ameel* and *Ford* followed; "in our view, the rule that tax liability is not premised on a per se requirement of previous assessment is the better reasoned one and represents the clear weight of authority"); New York Life Ins. Co. v. United States, 76 AFTR2d 95-7539 (Fed. Cl. 1995) (court concluded that remittance was a deposit despite the fact that the letter accompanying the remittance referred to it as a payment and instructed the Service to apply it as partial payment of taxes, pursuant to Rev. Proc. 84-58, 1984-2 CB 501, § 4.03, dealing with partial payments, because the taxpayer continued to protest its liability, and the Service failed to assess it). The Federal Circuit affirmed the decision of the Court of Federal Claims that the remittance was a deposit, not a payment, on the ground that although it was made after a notice of deficiency, and was referred to as a payment, the remittance was made under protest, and the taxpayer reserved the right to contest to seek recovery of the remittance. New York Life Ins. Co. v. United States, 118 F3d 1553 (Fed. Cir. 1997) (Service argued that remittance was a payment refund, which was barred by limitations period on filing a refund claim, but taxpayer claimed that the Tucker Act, not refund procedures, applied to the recovery of deposits). Factors that courts, such as the Court of Federal Claims, will apply in making this determination include: (1) the taxpayer's intent in remitting the money; (2) how the Service treated the remittance; (3) when, if at all, the Service asserted the liability; and (4) whether the taxpayer contested the liability. Fisher v. United States, 28 Fed. Cl. 88, 91–92 (1993), rev'd on another issue, 80 F3d 1576 (Fed. Cir. 1996).

When a taxpayer failed to file a return, the Service prepared a substitute return, assessed tax, and the taxpayer entered into a partial payment agreement to pay the assessment. The amounts paid pursuant to the partial payment agreement were held to be

recognized that interest cases focus on the "no-contest" element, while the intention factor is applied in limitations cases. One factor justifies the result in interest cases, the other in limitations cases. These contrary results in refund claim and interest cases conflict with the *Rosenman* notion that the same transaction be treated the same way for both purposes.

The facts and circumstances standard. Unless the remittance is labeled a deposit in the nature of a cash bond, a remittance the taxpayer makes after the sending of a notice of deficiency is a payment as of the date of the remittance, and a remittance made before the sending of the notice is not a payment until the date it is assessed. In this approach, neither the intention of the taxpayer nor a later contest is a factor. The relevant dates are objective and have the advantage of consistency with administrative practice for interest and limitations purposes. This result was reached in *Moran v. United States*,[180] where the taxpayer was sent a notice of deficiency, and subsequently made remittances to the Service, in each case stating that the remittance was to be treated as a partial payment of tax and interest, not a deposit in the nature of a cash bond. After the Tax Court decision became final, the Service failed to assess the tax within the limitations period. But rather than refunding the amounts remitted for the now-barred Tax Court years, the Service applied the amounts to open liabilities. The taxpayers then filed a refund claim for the Tax Court–year remittances. The Seventh Circuit ruled that the refund claim was untimely because the remittances were payments, not deposits. Using neither a bright-line assessment nor a no-contest test, the circuit court applied "a more open approach," which it said that the Second, Third, Fourth, Sixth, and Federal Circuits had used, in which the courts held that "a remittance [made] prior to a formal assessment may be a tax payment [and e]xactly when that happens depends on the circumstances of each case, the lack of an assessment being only one consideration among many."[181] In this "open" approach a number of factors play an important role (not only the timing of the assessment); those factors include the taxpayer's intent on making the remittance, how the Service treats the remittance upon receipt, and when the tax liability is defined.

[iv] **Summary.** In view of the uncertainty about the effect of *Rosenman*, a practical solution to the problem is to follow the Service's own procedures.[182] In general, courts after *Rosenman* have concluded that (1) *Rosenman*

"payments," even if the taxpayer does not believe he owes tax. Sy v. United States, 968 F. Supp. 345 (ED Mich. 1997).

[180] Moran v. United States, 63 F3d 663 (7th Cir. 1995).

[181] Moran v. United States, 63 F3d 663 (7th Cir. 1995).

[182] The circuit court found that the remittance constituted a payment because the taxpayers expressly requested that the remittance be treated as a payment, not a deposit; the taxpayers had received a notice of deficiency and remitted the amounts in response to this determination; and the Service's administrative practice recognized that a remittance made

did not establish a rule that no preassessment remittance constitutes a payment until assessment and (2) a remittance made before assessment constitutes a payment if (a) the liability has been defined and (b) the taxpayer intends to discharge that defined liability. A finding of payment works against the taxpayer in limitations cases (the earlier payment date may result in a claim being untimely), but in his favor in interest cases (the overpayment draws interest for a longer period). In *Rosenman*, the Supreme Court said that the same transaction should be treated the same way for both purposes—as a payment or not as a payment. However, the circumstances in which the question arises may nevertheless influence a court's conclusion. A determination that a transaction constitutes a payment for limitations purposes can cut off a taxpayer's entitlement to any refund of an overpaid tax. The same type of determination for interest purposes only means that a taxpayer will receive more or less interest on his or her overpayment.[183]

[v] **Extensions and estimated tax.** Another part of the answer developed in cases where taxpayers attempted to recover overpayments attributable to excess withholding and estimated tax payments made for purposes of obtaining an extension to file a return when refund claims were made on delinquent returns. In an early case,[184] the taxpayer had remitted $25,000 with his applica-

---

after the sending of a notice of deficiency did not require an assessment of the amount the taxpayer remitted to qualify as a payment of tax, citing Rev. Proc. 84-58, 1984-2 CB 501, § 4.01, and Rev. Rul. 89-6, 1989-1 CB 119. Compare New York Life Ins. Co. v. United States, 118 F3d 1553 (Fed. Cl. 1995).

[183] Interest cases are discussed at ¶ 6.02[3][a].

[184] Risman v. Comm'r, 100 TC 191 (1993), rejecting England v. United States, 760 F. Supp. 186 (D. Kan. 1991) and Batton v. United States, 87-2 USTC ¶ 9622 (D. Md. 1987) (holding remittance with Form 4868 to be estimated tax payment as matter of law); Nunziato v. United States, 78 AFTR2d 96-5066 (D. Mass. 1996) (remittance with extension request held payment). See also Blatt v. United States, 830 F. Supp. 882 (WDNC 1993) (in 1987, the executor requested an extension for filing the fiduciary return and transmitted $155,000 toward tax year; in 1988, the return was filed, and the Service, also in 1988, refunded the refund requested on the return; in 1991, however, the executor filed a claim for an additional refund; held, the 1987 remittance was a payment because it satisfied a deemed liability and the 1991 claim was time-barred), aff'd, 34 F3d 252 (4th Cir. 1994).

The wisdom of *Risman* is that it permits the court to look at the circumstances of the remittance to determine its nature as a payment of the estimated tax or a deposit to secure the ultimate payment of an uncertain tax. One court has said that the payment-as-a-matter-of-law view adopted in *Gabelman*, discussed below, "rests on a somewhat precarious foundation" in Tenth Circuit law (because ultimately the Tenth Circuit law, which without analysis, rested on a case where the parties had stipulated that a payment had been made), and favored the use of the facts and circumstances test of *Risman*. Marco v. United States, 81 AFTR2d 98-1540 (D. Conn. 1998) (court said it was not necessary to decide which approach is correct because in the particular facts of the case, a tax liability was known at the time of the remittance, and the taxpayer had treated the remittance as a payment).

tion (Form 4868) for an automatic extension to file his 1981 return, and he filed a claim for refund on a return he filed in 1989. In deciding that the remittance made with the extension was not a payment triggering the statute of limitations on a refund, the Tax Court held that the remittance was merely a deposit, not a payment, because "the [taxpayer's] $25,000 remittance was made by [him] arbitrarily, in an amount which had no good faith relationship to [his] actual joint federal income tax liability for 1981." The court was in the mainstream of authority under the current tax payment system. (The taxpayer had "dumped" money on the government, of the general rule that a deposit is distinguished from a payment by the relationship of the amount remitted to a defined liability and the intention of the taxpayer to satisfy that liability.) Most courts held that a remittance submitted with an extension request on Form 4868 is a payment because the remittance is an amount the taxpayer intends to represent the estimated tax liability, and estimated tax payments are deemed payments on the due date of the return.[185] The rationale that *Gabelman* and the courts that followed *Gabelman* used is that Regulation Section 1.6081-4(a)(4) requires that a taxpayer seeking an extension of time to file a return on Form

---

[185] See Gabelman v. Comm'r, 86 F3d 609 (6th Cir. 1996) ("[w]hile the *Risman* court held that lump sum estimated tax payments should be treated differently than other types of estimated payments, the clear language of the statutes and regulations mandates the opposite conclusion"). See also Estate of Zeir v. United States, 80 F3d 1360 (9th Cir. 1996) (remittances made prior to and at the time of a tentative estate tax return were held to be payments because the return had sufficient information to constitute a return; absent specific designation as a deposit, remittances paid at the time the return was due are payments whether precisely calculated or not). A number of courts followed *Gabelman*'s view that a remittance made with an extension request is a payment as a matter of law. See, e.g., Ott v. United States, 81 AFTR2d 98-1536 (9th Cir. 1998); Ertman v. United States, 972 F. Supp. 706 (D. Conn. 1997) ("[a] remittance in the face of the taxpayer's estimate of a tax liability is logically applied to, and thus a payment of, the tax owed").

In a case appealable to the Sixth Circuit, the Tax Court followed *Gabelman* and held that the remittance made with the extension request was a payment, not a deposit. Austin v. Comm'r, TC Memo. 1996-437 (1996). The Tax Court distinguished *Risman* on the grounds that the remittance in *Risman* was a round amount that bore no good faith relationship to the tax liability and the Service treated the remittance as a deposit, while the remittance in *Austin* was a specific amount, which the Service had treated as a payment. Compare Bachner v. Comm'r, 81 F3d 1274 (3d Cir. 1996) (claim that wage withholding constituted a deposit, not a payment, and so refundable when assessment is late, was found "unpersuasive" in view of Section 6513(b)(1), which treats a taxpayer's withholding as "paid" on the return due date, citing Ehle v. United States, 720 F2d 1096, 1097 (9th Cir. 1983)). On the basis of the *Gabelman* case, the Service announced that it does not acquiesce in the Tax Court's decision in *Risman*. See AOD CC-1997-006, 97 TNT 86-15 (May 2, 1997). The Service's position is that a remittance filed with an extension request is a tax payment. *Gabelman* distinguished the situation where there was no challenge by the Service at the time of the remittance from the situation "where the IRS is challenging determinations and representations made by taxpayers." In the latter situation, the *Gabelman* court said that "a taxpayer may very well submit a remittance merely to stop any penalties from accumulating."

4868 must (1) estimate the tax due for the year and (2) pay the amount of that estimated tax. Because the remittance accompanying the extension request satisfies the estimated tax due, the taxpayer has made a payment, not a deposit. *Gabelman* also derived support for its view in Section 6513(b)(2), which provides that estimated taxes are deemed paid on the date the return for the year is due, without regard to any extensions. It seems that these courts would view the remittance to be a payment when the taxpayer is attempting to satisfy a self-assessed liablity, as distinct from the situation where the Service has determined a liability to be due. One problem with this reasoning is that it ignores the fact that the taxpayer seeking an extension is making only an estimate of the tax that might be owed, and therefore can overestimate the tax due in order to ensure a qualified extension request and avoid any penalties if the return is not filed during the extended period. In other words, the taxpayer may not be admitting any tax liability, but in effect posting a bond to avoid penalties and interest that the Service may determine to be due. This can create a trap for unwary taxpayers.

Finally, in *Baral v. United States*,[186] the Supreme Court affirmed the decision of the court of appeals below and held that wage withholding throughout 1988 and remittance of an estimated payment with Form 1040-ES in January 1989 were both "paid" on April 15, 1989, and so did not fall within the "lookback" period of Section 6511(b)(2)(A) where the return for 1988 was filed in June 1993. The Court relied on straightforward application of Section 6513(b)(1) (withholding) and Section 6513(b)(2) (estimated payments). The Court distinguished *Rosenman*, observing the following:

> But the remittance in *Rosenman*, unlike the ones here, was not governed by a "deemed paid" provision akin to [Section] 6513, and we therefore had no occasion to consider the implications of such a provision for determining when the tax is "paid" under the predecessor to [Section] 6511. Moreover, if the quoted passage had represented our holding, we would have broadly rejected the Government's argument that payment occurred when the remittance of estimated estate tax was made, instead of rejecting the argument, as we did, only because it was not in accord with the "tenor" of the "business transaction."[187]

The Court also stated that it was not addressing other remittances not covered by a provision similar to Section 6513(b), which might include "remittances of any sort of tax by a taxpayer under audit in order to stop the running of interest and penalties."[188]

---

[186] Baral v. United States, 120 S. Ct. 1006 (2000).

[187] Baral v. United States, 120 S. Ct. 1006, 1010 (2000) (internal citations omitted).

[188] Baral v. United States, 120 S. Ct. 1006, 1011 n.2 (2000). The Court noted that the Service has issued guidance on whether such remittances are deposits or payments (Rev. Proc. 84-58, 1984-2 CB 501).

The Court in *Baral* did not explicitly cover the treatment of remittances submitted with a Form 4868, although the taxpayer in *Baral* did file a Form 4868 shortly after the estimated payment remittance. In addition, in framing the issue, the Court cited cases addressing "estimated income tax" and holding that remittances enclosed with Form 4868s constituted payments rather than deposits.[189]

[4] Effect of Extensions of the Assessment Period on Refund Claims

During the course of an audit, a taxpayer may be requested to execute an extension of the normal three-year period of limitations on assessment. The usual form for this agreement is Form 872 (Consent to Extend the Time to Assess Tax). Special rules apply for filing a refund claim where the taxpayer extends the time for making an assessment or agreement. In such cases, the taxpayer is permitted to file a claim for refund or credit of an overpayment at any time within the extended period for assessment provided by the agreement(s) and for an additional six months.[190] An extension agreement becomes effective on the date it is signed both by the taxpayer and on behalf of the Service.[191]

> **EXAMPLE 11-5:** A taxpayer files a 1985 income tax return on April 15, 1986. On April 14, 1988, at the request of the Service, he signs an agreement extending the period of assessment until April 14, 1990. A claim for refund with respect to the 1985 return is timely if it is filed any time on or before October 14, 1990.

The limit on the amount to be credited or refunded also changes where the assessment period is extended by agreement. If a claim is filed within six months after the extended assessment date, the amount of the credit or refund may include not only the portion of the tax paid after the agreement was executed but also the amount of tax that could have been refunded if a claim had been filed on the date the extension agreement was executed.[192] Thus, in the

---

[189] The Court cited both *Dantzler* and *Ertman* as being in "accord" with the court of appeals decision below. Both *Dantzler* and *Ertman* held that estimated tax remitted with extension requests were payments. See Dantzler v. United States, 84 AFTR2d 99-5586 (11th Cir. 1999) and Ertman v. United States, 83 AFTR2d 99-733 (2d Cir. 1999).

[190] IRC § 6511(c). If the period for filing a claim has already expired, the extension does not revive the claim period. Chism's Estate v. Comm'r, 322 F2d 956 (9th Cir. 1963). If no claim is filed, the Commissioner may also allow any refund or credit within the period of extension, plus six months.

[191] Reg. § 301.6511(c)-1(d).

[192] IRC § 6511(c)(2). For cases where this rule was applied, see Berry v. Comm'r, 97 TC 339 (1991) (Form 872-A executed after time for filing refund claim had expired); cf.

preceding example, the taxpayer could request a refund on a claim filed on or before October 14, 1990, not only of the amount of the deficiency assessment paid but also of the tax paid with the return filed on August 15, 1986.

Where a taxpayer files a consent extending the time within which the Service can perform some act, the period for filing a claim is not always extended. An agreement to extend the period of limitations on collection, rather than assessment, does not extend the period for filing a refund claim.[193] The special rules of Section 6511(c) are also limited to the particular periods covered by the extension agreement, and no other. For example, an agreement to extend the assessment period for a loss year does not cover the year to which the loss is carried back.[194] Furthermore, the special rules do not apply to any claims filed either (1) before an extension agreement is entered into or (2) more than six months after the extended assessment date. The first exception applies not only to premature claims filed in anticipation of an extension agreement. When a taxpayer files a claim for refund more than six months after the period of extension, his refund is limited to tax payments made within the prior two years.[195]

[5] Refund Claims and Bad Debts or Worthless Securities

Taxpayers are allowed a deduction for any loss, including losses they sustain during the year as a result of worthless stock or securities that are not compensated for by insurance or otherwise.[196] Taxpayers are also permitted to deduct (1) business bad debts in the year they become partially or wholly worthless and (2) nonbusiness bad debts in the year they become wholly worthless.[197] Actual worthlessness of a stock, security, or bad debt is a condition precedent to deduction. The deduction must be taken in the taxable year of the loss, not a later year. However, whether and when a stock or debt becomes worthless is

---

Estate of Wheeler v. Comm'r, TC Memo. 1979-321, 38 TCM 1236 (1979) (agreements extending assessment period had been timely executed before expiration of limitations period for filing claims for refund). If the period for filing a refund claim is not barred when the assessment period is extended, the Tax Court has jurisdiction to determine the amount of the overpayment. See IRC § 6512(b); *Berry v. Comm'r*, supra; *Estate of Wheeler v. Comm'r*, supra.

[193] Hill v. United States, 57-2 USTC ¶ 9961 (SD Fla. 1957) (1939 Code case).

[194] Brad Foote Gear Works, Inc. v. United States, 288 F2d 894 (Ct. Cl. 1961); Claremont Waste Mfg. Co., 24 TC 1087 (1955), aff'd on other grounds, 238 F2d 741 (1st Cir. 1956).

[195] See Republic Petroleum Corp. v. United States, 613 F2d 518 (5th Cir. 1980) (extension to June 30, 1972, so that time for filing claim expired December 31, 1972, but claim not filed until August 1973).

[196] IRC § 165(g).

[197] IRC § 166.

a question of fact that may not be determinable until after the year in which it appears the loss has occurred. To remedy the problem, an extended time period is provided for filing a claim for refund of an overpayment resulting from a deduction for a worthless security or an entirely worthless bad debt.[198] Rather than the normal three-year period from the return filing date, a claim for refund may be filed within seven years from the date the return was due without regard to any extension for filing the return.[199] This seven-year period for filing the claim may be extended even further. If the deduction for the debt or loss has an effect on a net operating loss carryback, the taxpayer may, in addition to the seven-year period, file a claim within any additional period allowed for the filing of a claim based on loss carrybacks.[200]

[6] Refunds and Loss Carrybacks

Section 6511(d)(2) extends the period for filing a claim for refund where the claimed overpayment results from the carryback of a net operating loss or capital loss. In such cases, the refund claim for the carryback year may be filed within (1) three years after the return due date (including extension) of the loss year or (2) the extended time for filing a claim if the taxpayer has extended the statutory assessment period, whichever is later.[201] Unlike a normal refund or credit, the amount of a loss carryback–generated claim is not limited to the amount of tax paid within the three-year period preceding the filing of the claim,[202] nor is it limited to the tax paid after the taxpayer executed a waiver of the limitations period on assessment and before the date the refund claim was filed.[203] Instead, the amount of the credit or refund can be the entire amount of the overpayment attributable to the loss carryback.[204]

---

[198] Regulations state that the extended period does not apply to a debt that became partially worthless during the taxable year. Reg. § 301.6511(d)-1(d).

[199] IRC § 6511(d)(1). But in *Indiana National Corp. v. United States*, the taxpayer's original 1973 return, filed on September 16, 1974, and claiming both bad debt deductions and a net operating loss generated by the bad debt deduction, was followed first by an amended return sharply reducing the bad debt deduction, but including other increased deductions, and then, on September 15, 1977, by an amended return adjusting the net operating loss. The district court held that the seven-year period did not apply, because Section 6511(d)(1) is applicable only when bad debt deductions are increased or discovered after the filing of the original return. Indiana Nat'l Corp. v. United States, 775 F. Supp. 281 (SD Ind. 1991) (statutory period applicable to net operating loss carrybacks applied); see also Armstrong v. United States, 681 F2d 774, 776 (Ct. Cl. 1982).

[200] IRC § 6511(d)(2).

[201] IRC § 6511(d)(2)(A).

[202] IRC § 6511(b)(2).

[203] IRC § 6511(c)(2).

[204] IRC § 6511(c)(2).

EXAMPLE 11-6: A calendar-year taxpayer, *A, Inc.*, has a net operating loss for 1986 and has timely filed its return for that year on March 15, 1987. It has not executed a Form 872 extending the assessment period for 1986 tax. Thus, *A, Inc.* can file a refund claim for 1986 for the refund of overpaid tax attributable to the carryback of the loss, at any time before March 16, 1990.

The loss year for purposes of the special period for filing a refund claim based on a net operating loss is the year in which the loss arose, rather than the year to which the loss is carried back.[205] The intended result is that the periods for making an assessment and for filing a refund claim are coextensive. Both the assessment period and the date for filing a refund claim expire three years after the return for the loss year is due.[206]

Special rules apply where a taxpayer seeks a refund based on a loss carryback.[207] The limit on the amount of the refund may exceed the portion of the tax paid within the normal three-years-from-filing or two-years-from-payment rules to the extent that the overpayment is attributable to the loss carryback.[208] If the claim is based on a loss carryback *and* other items as well, credit or refund cannot exceed the amount of the overpayment attributable to the loss carryback and the amount that would otherwise be refunded under the general three-year and two-year rules. In cases where a claim involves an overpayment

---

[205] Claremont Waste Mfg. Co., 24 TC 1087 (1955), aff'd on other grounds, 238 F2d 741 (1st Cir. 1956). By now it is settled that the year of the net operating loss is the year the loss is incurred, not the year in which loss is used to reduce a tax liability. Glenwood Coop., Inc. v. United States, 73 F3d 344 (Fed. Cir. 1996) (cooperative's refund claim was untimely because it was not filed within three years after the return for the year in which the net operating loss was incurred; the net operating loss was incurred in the short period from April 1 through September 30, 1983, created by a change of accounting period, with the result that the return was due June 15, 1984; the cooperative argued that the period began to run from the due date of the following year's return because the Service's permission letter provided that the loss be allocated to its patrons in the year after the year of change of period). See, e.g., Malonek v. United States, 77 AFTR2d 96-2098 (D. Wyo. 1996) (1987 loss-year return was amended on August 5, 1990, within three years after the April 15, 1988, filing date. But the amended 1984 return reflecting the carryback was not filed until December 26, 1991, after the three-year period, which closed April 15, 1991).

[206] Because the loss year is the controlling year, where the period for assessment and refund on the carryback year is kept open by agreement (e.g., by Form 872), a claim based on the loss carryback is barred if the period for assessment as to the loss year has expired. Consequently, the limitations periods for both the loss year and the carryback year should be extended. See, e.g., Malonek v. United States, 77 AFTR2d 96-2098 (D. Wyo. 1996) (1987 loss year return was amended on August 5, 1990, within three years after the April 15, 1988, filing date. But the amended 1984 return reflecting the carryback was not filed until December 26, 1991, after the three-year period, which closed April 15, 1991).

[207] Reg. § 301.6511(d)-2. Similar rules apply to overpayments owing to bad debts and worthless securities.

[208] IRC § 6511(d)(2); Reg. § 301.6511(d)-2(a)(2).

based not only on a loss carryback but on another adjustment as well, and the claim with respect to the other items is barred, the mere fact that the claim is based on the carryback of a loss does not permit a barred item to increase the amount of the overpayment.[209] Under the rationale of *Lewis v. Reynolds*,[210] the Service may defeat refund of a claimed overpayment based on a loss carryback by establishing a previously undiscovered deficiency,[211] or by showing that the carryback could have been entirely absorbed by adjustment to income in a carryback year that preceded the year of the claimed overpayment.[212]

By a parity of reasoning, a taxpayer is permitted to use an unclaimed deduction barred from refund by expiration of the period of limitations to reduce the amount of the net operating loss consumed in a carryback year.[213] Consequently, a barred unclaimed deduction increases the amount of the available net operating loss in the next year. The Service does not accept this view and contends that the loss carryback is the first adjustment to taxable income, and any barred adjustment decreasing taxable income is used only to offset barred adjustments increasing taxable income.[214]

If the taxpayer has filed a Tax Court petition, allowance of a claim for refund or credit is prohibited until the court's decision has become final.[215] If the Tax Court has rendered a final decision on the year, the allowance of a refund claim might also be denied under general principles of res judicata.[216] If the refund is based on a loss carryback, a year that is the subject of a Tax Court decision may nevertheless be reopened by the filing of a claim for refund.[217] However, the bar of the decision is not lifted if the tax for the decision year is the result of a compromise under Section 7122.[218] Consequently, to be entitled to this special treatment, a corporate taxpayer must file a refund claim within the three-year period after the due date of the return for the year in which the loss was incurred.[219] The two-years-from-payment period does not apply.[220]

---

[209] Reg. § 301.6511(d)-2(a)(3).

[210] Lewis v. Reynolds, 284 US 281 (1932).

[211] Comm'r v. Van Bergh, 209 F2d 23 (2d Cir. 1954).

[212] Phoenix Coal Co. v. Comm'r, 231 F2d 420 (2d Cir. 1956).

[213] Springfield St. Ry. v. United States, 312 F2d 754 (Ct. Cl. 1963).

[214] Rev. Rul. 81-88, 1981-1 CB 585. See also Rev. Rul. 85-65, 1985-1 CB 366 (if statute of limitations bars assessment of a deficiency, but deficiency is eliminated by a net operating loss carryback, Service will not reduce carryback by amount of deficiency interest unless taxpayer is actually owed a refund).

[215] IRC § 6512(a).

[216] See Fluor v. United States, 79-1 USTC ¶ 9393 (CD Cal. 1979).

[217] IRC § 6511(d)(2)(B).

[218] IRC § 6511(d)(2)(B).

[219] IRC § 6511(d)(2)(A).

[220] Mar Monte Corp. v. United States, 503 F2d 254 (9th Cir. 1974); Longiotti v. United States, 809 F2d 65 (4th Cir.), cert. denied, 484 US 985 (1987) (where taxpayer

[7] Miscellaneous Limitations Periods

The period for filing a claim for refund is also extended for other deductions and credits, such as foreign tax credits, investment credit and work-incentive programs carrybacks, self-employment tax, reduction of policyholders' surplus account of life insurance companies, and income recaptured under qualified plan terminations.[221] Special limitation periods are also provided for certain credits against estate tax, such as for state and foreign death taxes.[222] Where an overpayment of estate tax is attributable to the attorney fees incurred in litigating a claim for refund, any refund allowed to the estate may reflect this increased administration expense, even without a specific claim for refund[223]; for obvious reasons, however, a carefully drafted claim for refund should include provision for attorney fees. The limitations period for refund of excise taxes imposed pursuant to Section 4975 for prohibited transactions by employee benefit plans begins with the filing of the Annual Return/Report of Employee Benefit Plan, Form 5500.[224]

---

seeks to have net operating loss carried back to year closed by a Tax Court decision, a claim for refund must be filed within thirty-nine and one-half months after year of net operating loss; *Mar Monte* followed). Sachs v. United States, 941 F2d 464 (6th Cir. 1991) (following *Longiotti*). In *Akin*, the Tax Court entered a decision holding that the taxpayers owed additional tax for 1983; the taxpayers filed 1984 and 1985 returns claiming net operating losses in October 1985 and October 1986, respectively; and in 1990, they filed a claim for refund of 1983 tax based on the 1984 and 1985 net operating losses. Estate of Akin v. United States, 77 AFTR2d 96-2457 (Fed. Cl. 1996). The Court of Federal Claims, interpreting Section 6511(d)(2)(A), held that the only statute of limitations applicable for the refund of tax for an otherwise closed year based on the carryback of a net operating loss is the period set forth in Section 6511(d)(2)(A); that is, the refund claim is required to be filed within the three-year period after the due date for the filing of the return for the loss year, including extensions. Accordingly, the claim for refund for 1983 based on net operating losses for 1984 and 1985 was required to be filed by October 1988 and October 1989, respectively, and the two-years-from-payment statute was not available.

[221] See IRC §§ 6511(d)(3)–6511(d)(7). See also Section 6511(h) for cross-references to other provisions of the Code. Where a taxpayer filed timely 1964–1967 returns without claiming credit for foreign income tax paid, his claim was held timely under Section 6511(d)(3), not untimely under Section 6511(a). United States v. Woodmansee, 578 F2d 1302 (9th Cir. 1978).

[222] IRC § 2011(c). See also IRC §§ 2014(c), 2015.

[223] Reg. § 20.2053-3(c)(2).

[224] IRC § 6511(f). Section 6511(f) provides that for purposes of any tax imposed by Section 4912, Chapter 42, or Section 4975, the return referred to in Section 6501(a) is "the return specified in [S]ection 6501(l)(1)," and this return is "the return filed by the private foundation, plan, trust, or other organization (as the case may be) for the year in which the act (or failure to act) giving rise to liability for such tax occurred." See Imperial Plan, Inc. v. United States, 95 F3d 25 (9th Cir. 1996) (refund claims filed more than three years after Forms 5500 but less than three years after Forms 5330, Return of Excise Taxes Related to Employee Benefit Plans, were untimely).

The Service has concluded that to challenge a penalty collected under Section 6721 and to obtain its refund, the information provider must file a refund claim within two years after the penalty was collected, or the challenge will be time-barred.[225] The Service concluded that the information provider may not use the alternative three-years-from-return period because the information provider does not file a tax return to report a Section 6721 penalty, and the penalty does not directly relate to a tax reported on a tax return (unlike, for example, the delinquent filing or payment penalties of Section 6511).[226] The Service based its analysis on a regulation that provides, in the case of any tax (other than a tax payable by stamp), if no return is filed, the claim for credit or refund of an overpayment must be filed by the taxpayer within two years from the time the tax was paid.[227]

[8] Summary of Refund Claim Periods

The various periods of limitations for filing refund claims are summarized in Table 11.2.

TABLE 11.2
Limitations Periods for Filing Refund Claims

Item	Section	Period
Limitations on credit or refund	6511(a)	Within three years from the date the return was filed or two years after the date the tax was paid, whichever is later
Limitation on allowance of credits and refunds	6511(b)(1)	(1) No credit or refund allowed if claim is not filed within three years from the time the return was filed or two years from the time the tax was paid, whichever is later
	6511(b)(2)	(2) If a claim was filed within the three-year period, taxpayer may recover taxes paid within the three-year period preceding the claim, plus extension period for filing return
		(3) If claim is not filed within three-year period, refund is limited to the portion of tax paid during the two years immediately preceding the claim
Extensions of time by agreement	6511(c)(1)	Period for filing claim is extended for six months after expiration of the agreement
Bad debts and worthless securities	6511(d)(1)	Seven years from due date of return
Net operating loss and capital loss carrybacks	6511(d)(2)	Three years after the due date of the return for the loss year (including extensions) or six months beyond the expiration of the agreed extension of the assessment period (IRC § 6511(c)), whichever is later
Foreign tax credit	6511(d)(3)	Ten years from the due date of return

---

[225] SCA 200016001 (Aug. 27, 1999) (Significant Service Center Advice).

[226] Reg. § 6511-1(a)(2).

[227] Reg. § 301.6511(a)-1(a)(2).

Business credit carryback	6511(d)(4)	Three years after the due date (including extensions) of the return for the year of the credit or six months beyond the expiration of the agreement extension of the assessment period (IRC § 6511(c)), whichever is later
Self-employment tax	6511(d)(5)	No later than two years after the calendar year in which the state and the Secretary of Health, Education, and Welfare approve the claim agreement made pursuant to Section 218 of the Social Security Act
Income recaptured under qualified plan termination (Employee Retirement Income Security Act of 1974)	6511(d)(6)	Normal three-year period extended one year after the date on which recaptured amount is paid
Partnership items of partnerships covered by unified proceeding rules	6511(g)	Three years from the date the return was filed or the due date of the partnership return, whichever is later, and before the mailing of final partnership administrative adjustment (FPAA) (IRC § 6227); if computational adjustment, six months after date of notice of computational adjustment (IRC § 6230(c)(2)(A)); if failure to make refund after settlement, FPAA, or court decision two years from date of settlement, FPAA, or final decision (IRC § 6230(c)(2)(B))
Credit for state death taxes	2011(c)	Four years after filing the estate tax return (IRC § 6018)
Credit for foreign death taxes	2014(e)	Four years after filing estate tax return (IRC § 6018)
Credit for death taxes on reversionary interests or remainders in property	2015	Before the expiration of the time for payment of the estate tax (IRC §§ 2011 and 2101) or as postponed and extended (IRC § 6163)
Joint returns after filing separately	6013(b)(2)(B)	Before the expiration of three years from the due date of return (determined without regard to any extension granted to either spouse)
Preparer penalties	6696(d)(2)	Refund of understatement penalty (IRC § 6694) or other return preparer penalties (IRC § 6695) within three years from the date the penalty was paid

¶ 11.06 CONSIDERATIONS IN FILING CLAIMS FOR REFUND

[1] Risk of Adjustment

Filing a claim for refund may result in both (1) defensive adjustments by the Service that effectively reduce or eliminate the claimed overpayment by way of setoff or offensive adjustments to create a deficiency in the year covered by the claim or (2) an increase in tax in years other than the year for which the claim is filed. A claim for refund invites the Service to examine the return that is the subject of the refund claim. For this reason, a claim should not be filed without a review of the entire tax return for the period, with the reviewer alert for potential adjustments that might be made if the Service examines or reexamines the return. Unless the risks of adjustment and the relative merits of the issues involved have been carefully considered, it is hardly advisable for a taxpayer to file a claim for refund where the period of limitations on the assessment of a deficiency has not run. Even if the period for the assessment of a deficiency for the year of the claim has run, the Service can still make an adjustment to a carryover or continuing item that affects other returns.

Risk of either an offensive or defensive adjustment is reduced where the taxpayer's return has already been examined. If a deficiency has been asserted, the claim will usually be referred to the revenue agent who made the examination. The agent is unlikely to comb the return for adjustments a second time, although this is a practical likelihood, not a legal prohibition. In *Lewis v. Reynolds*,[228] the Service had conducted an audit, the taxpayer had paid the determined deficiency, and after the taxpayer had filed a refund claim, the Service recomputed the taxpayer's tax on the basis of adjustments that reversed the adjustments in the initial audit. The Supreme Court held that the Commissioner was entitled to make this reaudit for the purpose of determining whether the taxpayer had actually overpaid the tax.[229]

[2] Timing of the Claim

To reduce the risk of an offensive adjustment by the Service, a claim for refund of a deficiency assessment can be filed after the period for assessment has expired. The time within which a claim must be filed and the statute of limitations on assessment frequently expire simultaneously. For example, if an individual's income tax return is timely filed on April 15, 1987, the tax is paid (or considered to have been paid by withholding and estimated tax credits) with the return, and the statute of limitations on assessment is not extended by waiver. Therefore, any additional tax must be assessed on or before April 15, 1990. If the taxpayer wishes to obtain a refund of the tax paid on the due date, the taxpayer must also file a claim for refund on or before April 15, 1990.[230] A taxpayer has a longer period to seek a refund (three years after the return is filed or two years from the date of payment, whichever is later)[231] than it allows the Service to make a tax assessment (three years from the time the return is filed).[232] As a result, when a timely filed return has been examined, a deficiency in tax assessed and paid, and a refund claim filed covering the defi-

---

[228] Lewis v. Reynolds, 284 US 281 (1932).

[229] For an example of this point, see Miller v. United States, 81 AFTR2d 98-2320 (EDNY 1998). In *Miller*, the taxpayers sued for refund, the Service counterclaimed that an erroneous refund had been made, and the taxpayers sought to dismiss the refund case; however, the district court refused to dismiss the Service's erroneous refund claim.

[230] This is not the case where exceptions to the normal assessment period apply, such as the filing of a fraudulent return where the assessment may be made at any time, or a return omitting 25 percent of gross income where the assessment period is six years. IRC §§ 6501(c), 6501(e).

[231] IRC § 6511(a).

[232] IRC § 6501(a).

ciency tax payment, the Service will not be able to assess an additional deficiency relating to the tax return as long as the claim is filed more than three years after the return filing date.

> **EXAMPLE 11-7:** A, an individual taxpayer, files a 1995 return on April 15, 1996. A tax deficiency of $10,000 is assessed on April 26, 1998. On May 1, 1998, A pays this assessment. A could contest his liability for the 1998 payment of $10,000 by filing a claim for refund by May 1, 2000. However, absent an extension agreement, the Service is unable to assess any further deficiency for 1995 tax, after April 15, 1999. Therefore, if A delays filing the claim for refund until after April 15, 1999, and files a claim for refund on September 30, 1999, A can contest the deficiency assessment, but the Service can make no further assessment of tax for 1995. If the claim for refund were filed before April 15, 1999 (e.g., on September 30, 1998) the Service would be able to assess an additional tax for 1995.

In this manner, although a taxpayer's recovery is limited to the amount of the deficiency assessment paid, the bar of the statute of limitations on assessment precludes the government from claiming any further deficiency by way of either assessment or counterclaim. New issues can only be used by the government defensively by way of an offset to the refund.

[3] Estoppel, Settlement Agreements, and Claims for Refund

In most cases, it is statutorily permissible to file a claim for refund of the amount of a paid deficiency assessment after the assessment period has run.[233] Conflicting results have been reached when the Service and the taxpayer have settled the case in the Appeals Office, the taxpayer has paid the amount called for by the settlement, and then filed a refund claim and sued for refund of the payment.[234] In Appeals Office settlements, the Service and the taxpayer usually sign a Form 870-AD, waiving notice of deficiency restrictions on assessments. This form states that "no claim for refund shall be filed or prosecuted" for the years involved. The waiver form also acknowledges that it is not a formal settlement or closing agreement; the only agreements binding on the Service are

---

[233] See Stair v. United States, 516 F2d 560 (2d Cir. 1975). IRS Form 870 specifically states, "Your consent will not prevent you from filing a claim for refund (after you have paid the tax) if you later believe you are so entitled. . . ." Even where the taxpayer agrees to a settlement, a part of which is an agreement not to file a refund claim, the taxpayer is not estopped from filing a refund claim if he specifically provided for the contingency. McGraw-Hill, Inc. v. United States, 623 F2d 700 (Ct. Cl. 1980) (taxpayer reserved the right to file a refund claim if there was a later court decision that tax was not due on moving expense reimbursements).

[234] See the discussion at ¶ 9.08[2].

provided in the Code. Where taxpayers have filed refund claims after the assessment period has run in these informal settlement cases, the settlement agreement, although not binding in itself because it is not a statutorily provided agreement, has generally been held binding on the parties by estoppel, where the claim for refund would have had the effect of undoing settlement agreements involving several taxpayers,[235] or more than one disputed claim made by a single taxpayer, or a single claim made by a single taxpayer.[236] In these cases, the statement that no refund claim would be filed, once the taxpayer has reneged after the assessment period has run, is misrepresentation of a kind sufficient to ground estoppel. In *Joyce v. Gentsch*,[237] the government's equitable estoppel argument was rejected on basically the same facts because the Service possessed all essential information and was not barred from making any further assessment before the assessment period had expired. The results may not be satisfactorily reconciled, but if the *Joyce* rationale were to be followed, the government would at least have the right of setoff.

[4] Requirement of Full Payment: The *Flora* Rule

Jurisdiction of a district court and the Court of Federal Claims over suits for refund is provided in 28 USC § 1346. A federal district court or the U.S. Court of Federal Claims does not have jurisdiction over a suit for refund under the terms of 28 USC § 1346, unless the taxpayer has made full payment of the amount of the assessment. It was not until 1960 in *Flora v. United States*, that the Supreme Court resolved the issue of whether 28 USC § 1346 required full

---

[235] Cooper Agency v. United States, 301 F. Supp. 871 (DSC 1969), aff'd per curiam, 422 F2d 1331 (4th Cir.), cert. denied, 400 US 904 (1970); Cain v. United States, 255 F2d 193 (8th Cir. 1958); DDI, Inc. v. United States, 467 F2d 497 (Ct. Cl. 1972), cert. denied, 414 US 830 (1973); Carland v. United States, 88-1 USTC ¶ 9206 (WD Mo. 1988) (holding a taxpayer was stopped from filing a refund suit after signing a Form 870-AD; cases gathered).

[236] Stair v. United States, 516 F2d 560 (2d Cir. 1975). On facts similar to *Stair*, the court refused to consider the refund suit a misrepresentation for estoppel purposes. Uinta Livestock Corp. v. United States, 355 F2d 761 (10th Cir. 1966). In Whitney v. United States, 826 F2d 896 (9th Cir. 1987), the execution of a Form 870-AD standing alone did not estop the taxpayer from seeking refund. Similarly, when the item giving rise to the claim for refund was an item in a year different from the ones covered by the Form 870-AD, the taxpayer has been held not to be precluded from seeking a refund on that item. McGraw-Hill, Inc. v. United States, 90-1 USTC ¶ 50,053 (SDNY 1990) (*Stair* distinguished). However, most courts follow the result in *Stair*. See, e.g., McGraw-Hill, Inc. v. United States. See also Flynn v. United States, 786 F2d 586, 591 (3d Cir. 1986) (dicta); Elbo Coals, Inc. v. United States, 588 F. Supp. 745 (ED Ky. 1984), aff'd, 763 F2d 818 (6th Cir. 1985); Carland v. United States, 88-1 USTC ¶ 9206 (WD Mo. 1988).

[237] Joyce v. Gentsch, 141 F2d 891 (6th Cir. 1944). See also Girard v. Gill, 261 F2d 695, 699 (4th Cir. 1958).

payment of the tax in issue or only its part payment, and concluded that full payment of the tax in issue was a prerequisite to district court jurisdiction.[238] Since full payment is a jurisdictional prerequisite to a suit for refund, the burden of making that payment is always a factor to be considered in the filing of a refund claim.[239]

In general, if a tax is one over which the Tax Court has jurisdiction (e.g., income, gift, and estate tax), the *Flora* rule applies and the taxpayer must make full payment of assessed tax if the taxpayer wishes to obtain judicial review in a district court (or the Court of Federal Claims) with refund jurisdiction under Section 1346. Transactional taxes, as well as most excise taxes (such as employment tax), do not fall within the Tax Court's jurisdiction, and so the taxpayer has no opportunity for prepayment judicial review. If the tax is one that is imposed on (and may be divided among) individual transactions, such as excise taxes, the taxpayer is considered to make full payment if the taxpayer pays the tax for a single transaction in the applicable period(s).[240] District

---

[238] Flora v. United States, 362 US 145 (1960). The *Flora* rule is applicable to the U.S. Court of Federal Claims as well as to federal district courts. DiNatale v. United States, 12 Cl. Ct. 72, 87-1 USTC ¶ 9243 (Cl. Ct. 1987). The concurrent jurisdiction of federal district courts and the Court of Federal Claims to hear refund. suits is described at ¶ 1.05[2]. Section 7422(d) provides that payment of tax for purposes of a suit for refund is considered to be made by the credit of an overpayment, but the liability considered satisfied by the credit will only be considered to be paid at the time the credit is allowed. When the Service reflects a credit on its records, a payment is considered made even if the credit is subsequently reversed. Simmons v. United States, 94-1 USTC ¶ 50,106, 29 Fed. Cl. 136 (Fed. Cl. 1993). However, since a refund suit is a suit for restitution, it seems contrary to the nature of a refund suit for the matter of payment to depend solely on the bookkeeping of the Service. If a taxpayer has credited an overpayment from another tax period and the Service has failed or refused to honor the taxpayer's allocation or direction to credit the amount, the taxpayer should not be denied the opportunity to sue for refund.

Suppose an overpayment for one year is applied to another year to satisfy a deficiency in that other year. Does the refund court lose jurisdiction over the overpayment year because the payment has been transferred or credited by the Service to the deficiency for the other tax year? One court said no. See Welch, Jr. v. United States, 94-2 USTC ¶ 50,535 (ND Ill. 1994) ("[w]e are not convinced that the 26 USC § 6402 endows the Service with the power to deprive district courts of jurisdiction over refunds for tax years in which there is no deficiency").

[239] The *Flora* rule applies to federal courts, not to the Service. Technically, the rule does not require a taxpayer to pay the full amount of a nondivisible tax assessment when the refund claim is filed, as long as the tax is paid before the suit for refund is commenced.

[240] Flora v. United States, 362 US 145 (1960); Steele v. United States, 280 F2d 89 (8th Cir. 1960); Spivak v. United States, 370 F2d 612 (2d Cir.), cert. denied, 387 US 908 (1967). The Service may contest the taxpayer's allegation that the amount paid represents the full amount of the divisible tax. In *Spivak*, the district court found that the taxpayers failed to sustain their burden of proving "by a fair preponderance of the credible evidence that the sums they paid were in fact the taxes due for one employee for one period. . . ."

courts and the Court of Federal Claims recognize that full payment of an excise tax is made when the tax on an individual transaction for each period in issue is paid before suit is filed. The obligation to pay the tax on only a single transaction before filing a refund claim and a suit for refund where the claim is actually or constructively disallowed eases the burden imposed on a taxpayer by the *Flora* rule.

Flora also ruled that the full-payment rule did not require the payment of interest, unless the taxpayer challenged the amount of interest. *Flora* states: "In some of the cases the only amount remaining unpaid at time of suit was interest. As we have indicated, the statute lends itself to a construction which would permit suit for the tax after full payment thereof without payment of any part of the interest."[241] Of course, where the computation of interest is in issue, under the *Flora* rule, the full amount of the interest must be paid.[242]

If the taxpayer intends to challenge the assessment of a penalty, the amount of the penalty must be paid in full.[243]

[5] The Problem of a Variance Between the Refund Claim and the Refund Complaint

A claim for refund is a notice to the Service that the taxpayer has overpaid a tax and that the overpayment claimed should be refunded or credited. With this notice, the Service will investigate the claim and decide whether to allow or disallow it; in fact, before the taxpayer may commence a suit for refund, the Service must be given six months to review and act on the claim.[244]

Spivak v. United States, 254 F. Supp. 517, 522 (SDNY 1966), aff'd, 370 F2d 612 (2d Cir. 1967), cert. denied; see also 47th St. Setting Corp. v. United States, 84 AFTR2d 99-6691 (SDNY 1999) (refund suit dismissed because taxpayer paid $43.25, and the Service apparently claimed the amount that should have been paid was $415.60, including, erroneously, accrued interest).

[241] Under the *Flora* rule, interest need not be paid. Flora v. United States, 362 US 145 (1960), at n.37(d); Kell-Strom Tool Co. v. United States, 205 F. Supp. 190 (D. Conn. 1962); Leeke v. United States, 737 F. Supp. 1013 (SD Ohio 1990) (accord). In *Shore*, the Court of Appeals for the Federal Circuit settled the question once and for all by holding that the interest portion of an assessment need not be paid under the full-payment rule. Shore v. United States, 9 F3d 1524 (Fed. Cir. 1993). The Federal Circuit said that the full-payment rule referred to the tax only, not to interest and penalties.

[242] Magnone v. United States, 733 F. Supp. 613 (SDNY 1989), aff'd, 902 F2d 192 (2d Cir. 1990) (under the full-payment rule, the taxpayer could not contest liability for interest for years 1974–1976 by paying interest that accrued in 1979 on the deficiencies for those years and suing for refund).

[243] The full-payment rule applies to penalties as well as tax. Professional Eng'rs, Inc. v. United States, 527 F2d 597, 599 (4th Cir. 1975) (delinquency penalty); Francis v. United States, 89-1 USTC ¶ 9229 (D. Nev. 1988) (same).

[244] Section 6523(a)(1) states:

To facilitate the review process, regulations require that the claim provide certain information. In addition to providing forms on which the refund claim should be made, regulations describe the information that should be included in the claim for refund:

> No refund or credit will be allowed after the expiration of the statutory period of limitation applicable to the filing of a claim therefor except upon one or more of the grounds set forth in a claim filed before the expiration of such period. The claim must set forth in detail each ground upon which a credit or refund is claimed and facts sufficient to apprise the Commissioner of the exact basis thereof. The statement of the grounds and facts must be verified by a written declaration that is made under the penalties of perjury. A claim which does not comply with this paragraph will not be considered for any purpose as a claim for refund or credit.[245]

It follows that notice of each ground and supporting facts is necessary to the validity of the claim in the sense that a refund will not be made on any ground not stated in the claim for refund.

Filing a claim for refund with the Service is also a jurisdictional prerequisite to instituting a suit for refund. Unless a claim for refund or credit is filed with the Service, no suit for refund may be maintained under the terms of Section 7422(a). Since Section 7422(a) sets out the terms upon which the government has waived sovereign immunity for suits for refund, a taxpayer's failure to file a qualifying claim for refund also means that the government has not waived sovereign immunity for the refund suit. There is an interplay between the regulatory requirement and the jurisdictional requirement of Section 7422(a). If a complaint sets forth as a ground for refund a ground that has not been included in the claim for refund the taxpayer has filed with the Service, a district court or the Court of Federal Claims will not have jurisdiction over the taxpayer's suit for refund. No "claim for refund" has been previously filed with the Service, as required by Section 7422(a). This failure to have included a ground in the claim for refund upon which the taxpayer relies in the suit for refund is called a variance between the grounds in the claim and the grounds in the suit, and, if true, will result in the dismissal of the suit for refund.

If these statutory and regulatory requirements are taken into account, the claim for refund will be prepared with an eye on a later suit for refund.[246] It is

---

No suit or proceeding under [S]ection 7422(a) for the recovery of any intenal revenue tax, penalty or other sum, shall be begun before the expiration of 6 months from the date of filing the claim required under [Section 7422(a)] unless the Secretary renders a decision thereon within that time, nor after the expiration of 2 years from the date of mailing by certified mail or registered mail by the Secretary to the taxpayer of a notice of the disallowance of the claim to which the suit or proceeding relates.

[245] Reg. § 301.6402-2(b)(1).

[246] IRC § 7422(a).

helpful to view the preparation of a claim for refund as the preparation of the most important allegations in the complaint for the refund suit. As discussed later, the type of pleading in all courts hearing tax cases is notice pleading, and the preparation of a claim for refund is required to provide administrative notice to the Service of the grounds for refund. For jurisdictional purposes, therefore, the refund claim will err on the side of completeness, and include all the grounds on the basis of which the refund can possibly be justified.

[6] The Anti-Assignment Act

Claims against the United States, including claims for the refund of internal revenue tax, are by statute nonassignable.[247] Any assignment in violation of the Anti-Assignment Act[248] is null and void. A refund suit brought by the assignee of the void assignment of a claim for refund is subject to dismissal. However, there are two exceptions to the general prohibition against the assignment of claims: one judicially created and the other provided by the statute itself. The judicially created exception permits the transferee of a claim for refund to prosecute the claim if the transferee becomes the owner by operation of law.[249] Examples of such transferees include the personal representative of a deceased taxpayer,[250] a trustee in bankruptcy,[251] the beneficiaries of an estate on the final distribution of its assets,[252] transferees of claims to shareholders in a corporate liquidation,[253] and transferees of claims in corporate mergers or consolida-

---

[247] 31 USC § 3727 (the Anti-Assignment Act). This statute provides:

An assignment may be made only after a claim is allowed, the amount of the claim is decided, and a warrant for payment of the claim has been issued. The assignment shall specify the warrant must be made freely, and must be attested to by two witnesses. The person making the assignment shall acknowledge it before an official who may acknowledge a deed, and the official shall certify the assignment. The certificate shall state that the official completely explained the assignment when it was acknowledged.

The purpose of the Anti-Assignment Act has been described as follows: "These rather technical requirements are intended, in part, to ensure that the United States is able to avail itself of rights of set-off or cross-claims against original claimants which might not be applicable to an assignee." United States v. Warren Corp., 624 F. Supp. 1163 (D. Mass.), rev'd on another issue, 86-2 USTC ¶ 9804 (1st Cir. 1986).

[248] 31 USC § 3727.

[249] United States v. Aetna Sur. Co., 338 US 366 (1949).

[250] United States v. Aetna Sur. Co., 338 US 366 (1949).

[251] Segal v. Rochelle, 382 US 375 (1966).

[252] Pettengill v. United States, 253 F. Supp. 321 (ND Ill. 1966). Compare Kinney-Lindstrom Found., Inc. v. United States, 186 F. Supp. 133 (ND Iowa 1960) (assignment to beneficiaries before final distribution invalid under Anti-Assignment Act).

[253] Novo Trading Corp. v. Comm'r, 113 F2d 320 (2d Cir. 1940).

tions.[254] The statutory exception applies to the assignment of a claim that satisfies the following requirements:

1. The claim has been allowed;
2. The amount of the claim has been determined;
3. Authorization for payment has been issued;
4. The assignment has been freely made; and
5. The assignment has been executed in the presence of at least two attesting witnesses.

B. MAKING REFUND CLAIMS

¶ 11.07 PROPER PARTIES TO FILE CLAIMS

The Commissioner has authority to credit the amount of an overpayment against any internal revenue tax liability of the "person who made the overpayment" and to "refund any balance to such person."[255] Any claim for refund must be filed within the period of limitations for filing a claim by "the taxpayer,"[256] a term that, for the purposes of the Code, is defined as "any person subject to any internal revenue tax."[257] As a matter of statutory interpretation, the proper party to file a refund claim is (1) the person who was subject to any internal revenue tax who (2) made an overpayment of the tax. Some courts have interpreted the language of Section 6402, which permits a refund to the person who made the overpayment, as authorizing a refund to a person who was not "subject" to the tax. Thus, a payer who assumed liability for the tax has been held the person who made the overpayment.[258] These assumption-of-

---

[254] Seaboard Air Line Ry. v. United States, 256 US 655 (1921); cf. Western Pac. RR v. United States, 268 US 271 (1925).

[255] IRC § 6402(a). For this reason, it is said that "Section 6402(a) is premised upon the claimant having a 'financial interest in the litigation.'" Atlas Hotels, Inc. v. United States, 81 AFTR2d 98-1492 (9th Cir. 1998) (employers lacked standing to sue for refund of employment tax penalties because they had been paid by a payroll service).

[256] IRC § 6511(a).

[257] IRC § 7701(a)(14).

[258] See Scanlon v. United States, 330 F. Supp. 269 (ED Mich. 1971) (employer who paid employee's tax was entitled to refund); Thompson v. United States, 429 F. Supp. 13 (ED Pa. 1977) (bailee who paid taxpayer's tax); United States v. Gilbert, 478 F. Supp. 306, 318 (SDNY 1979) ("it is neither the taxpayer, nor the actual transferor, per se, who is entitled to the refund; rather, we must look to the assumption of liability to determine proper entitlement"). See also Worth v. United States, 633 F2d 1168, 1171 (5th Cir. 1981); cf. Cindy's, Inc. v. United States, 740 F2d 851 (11th Cir. 1984). But the resolution of the issue can depend on who actually pays the tax. Assume the situation where an em-

liability cases do not refer to Section 6511(a), which requires the taxpayer to file a refund claim. The result may be rationalized with the statutory pattern, but not so easily as if the third person were recognized as "the taxpayer" because that person has assumed the obligations of the taxpayer.[259]

The proper party to file a claim for refund is the person subject to the tax, not a person who voluntarily pays the tax of another, even though no tax may be owed. Moreover, in the event a volunteer pays the tax of another, no suit for refund can be brought to recover the tax paid.[260] In response to the obvious hardship this rule presents, some courts have held that, if the payment of a third-party tax was not "voluntary," the person who pays the tax qualifies as

---

ployer pays the tax. As in *Scanlon,* supra, the employer can file a refund claim. See also Hotel Conquistador, Inc. v. United States, 597 F2d 1348 (Ct. Cl. 1979), cert. denied, 444 US 1032 (1980). But when the employer has collected the tax by withholding it from employees, the employer has not been considered the taxpayer or the proper party to file the claim. First Nat'l Bank v. United States, 21 Cl. Ct. 479, 90-2 USTC ¶ 50,519 (1990). The person who actually pays the tax controls the issue.

[259] A similar rationale can be applied to the "involuntary payment" cases discussed infra note 260. However, refunds of overpayments to persons not subject to the tax are not literally provided for by Sections 6402(a) and 6511(a). It should be noted that a taxpayer is not precluded from filing a claim for refund of overpaid tax where the source of the funds is a third party. The problems arise where it is the provider of the funds, rather than the taxpayer, who files the refund claim. See Matrix Dev. Corp. v. United States, 815 F. Supp. 297 (ED Wis. 1993) (tax refund or damage suit is not available to third party claiming wrongful filing of lien).

[260] Stahmann v. Vidal, 305 US 61 (1938); Busse v. United States, 542 F2d 421 (7th Cir. 1976); Spa World Int'l, Inc. v. United States, 82-2 USTC ¶ 9632 (MD Fla. 1982) (nontaxpayer who paid portion of another's tax liability to prevent levy barred from refund suit). See also Cindy's, Inc. v. United States, 740 F2d 851 (11th Cir. 1984) (taxpayer held not to have made overpayment of taxes where a tax deposit was credited to another taxpayer's account because the other taxpayer's tax deposit form was used). Even if a refund action is unavailable, nontaxpayers may sometimes be able to recover from the government on other grounds. In Donaldson, Lufkin & Jenrette Sec. Corp. v. Sirmer, 22 F3d 741 (ND Ill. 1993), the victim of an embezzlement successfully recovered from the government, on Fifth Amendment grounds, the portion of embezzled funds paid over by the embezzler as taxes to the government. The court found the refusal of the government to return the stolen funds to constitute an unlawful taking of private property.

the taxpayer.[261] This result has been based on the finding that the person paying the tax believed himself to be at least potentially liable for the tax.[262]

In *United States v. Williams,*[263] the Supreme Court resolved the issue, at least where a party against whom a tax has not been assessed pays the tax under protest to remove a federal tax lien from her property. The Supreme Court held that under 28 USC § 1346(a)(1), which waives sovereign immunity for and gives federal courts jurisdiction to hear tax refund suits, the person who pays the tax under protest to remove a federal tax lien from property has standing to sue for a refund. This is because Section 1346(a)(1) does not state that only the person assessed may sue, but rather gives the federal courts jurisdiction to hear "*[a]ny* civil action against the United States for the recovery of *any* internal-revenue tax . . . erroneously collected. . . . "[264] In response to the government's claim that allowing a person such as Williams to sue would permit parties to challenge the tax liabilities of others, the Court pointed out that the rule has exceptions, such as the fiduciary's suit to litigate the liability of the taxpayer, and the transferee who may litigate the liability of the transferor.

---

[261] United States v. Halton Tractor Co., 258 F2d 612 (9th Cir. 1958); Parsons v. Anglim, 143 F2d 534 (9th Cir. 1944); David v. United States, 551 F. Supp. 850 (CD Cal. 1982) (corporation officer paid Federal Insurance Contributions Act (FICA) tax on mistaken belief he was personally liable; refund suit allowed under authority of *Parsons*); Noonis v. United States, 576 F. Supp. 853 (WD Tex. 1983) (ex-wife of a taxpayer had standing to bring an action for refund of the tax assessed against her ex-husband but paid by her when a lien was placed on property in which she had interest).

In Schoenherr v. United States, 566 F. Supp. 1365 (ED Wash. 1983), the court allowed a refund suit by taxpayer who, having mistakenly been warned by Service agents that he was personally responsible, involuntarily paid taxes properly assessed against various corporations. The court applied a three-tier test: (1) taxpayer believed he was personally liable for the taxes; (2) his belief was reasonable under the circumstances; and (3) he did not intend by paying the taxes to benefit a third party. When a person who is not liable for a tax pays the tax of another taxpayer, voluntarily but erroneously, it has been held that 28 USC § 1346(a)(1) gives a district jurisdiction over the refund suit because the suit involves a tax alleged to have been "erroneously or illegally assessed or collected." Martin v. United States, 895 F2d 992 (4th Cir. 1990) (divorced wife paid amount of lien arising out of an assessment against her former husband on property that belonged to her after their divorce; held, the plain meaning of 28 USC § 1346(a)(1) allows anyone from whom tax is erroneously or illegally collected to sue for refund of that tax); Williams v. United States, 24 F3d 1143 (9th Cir. 1994) (accord). The Supreme Court reviewed the issue in United States v. Williams, 514 US 527 (1995) (erroneously filed lien was voluntarily paid at closing by nontaxpayer; refund claim filed).

[262] The Court of Federal Claims permitted taxpayers who paid a tax under duress to institute actions against the United States under 28 USC § 1491 on the theory that there is an implied-in-fact contract to repay the money. See Fidelity & Cas. Co. v. United States, 490 F2d 960 (Ct. Cl. 1974). This theory has been rejected by the Second and Third Circuits. Phillips v. United States, 346 F2d 999, 1000 (2d Cir. 1965); First Nat'l Bank v. United States, 265 F2d 297, 300 (3d Cir. 1958).

[263] United States v. Williams, 514 US 527 (1995).

[264] United States v. Williams, 514 US 527 (1995).

Permitting Williams to sue did not violate the privilege completely, because "Williams' main challenge is to the existence of a lien against her property, rather than to the underlying assessment on her husband."[265] Williams's claim was that the government had filed a lien against the wrong property, and so she was "subject to" the tax "in a meaningful and immediate way." Consequently, after *Williams*, when a person pays a tax under protest to challenge the propriety of collection action, a district court or the Court of Federal Claims has jurisdiction to hear the suit for refund.

[1] Husband and Wife

According to regulations, if a joint return was filed for the year for which the claim is filed, both spouses must sign the claim, even if only one spouse had income.[266] Spouses who file a joint return have separate interests in any overpayment. The overpayment is apportionable to each spouse on the basis of the amount he or she contributed to the overpaid tax.[267] The filing of a joint return does not convert the income of one spouse into the income of the other.[268] Ac-

---

[265] United States v. Williams, 514 US 527 (1995).

[266] Reg. § 1.6061-1(a).

[267] Gordon v. United States, 757 F2d 1157 (11th Cir. 1985); Rosen v. United States, 397 F. Supp. 342 (ED Pa. 1975). See Maragon v. United States, 153 F. Supp. 365 (Ct. Cl. 1957); St. John v. Bookwalter, 58-1 USTC ¶ 9216 (WD Mo. 1957); Gens v. United States, 673 F2d 366 (Ct. Cl.), cert. denied, 459 US 906 (1980) ("[t]he overpayment goes to the maker of the overpayment, not the contributor to income"), following Glaubke v. United States, 78-1 USTC ¶ 9206 (ED Va. 1978); Rev. Rul. 74-611, 1974-2 CB 399 (overpayment on joint return filed by husband and wife for tax liability paid by wife not creditable to separate tax liability for husband for prior year).

However, in a community property state, such as California, while the refund may presumptively constitute community property, agreements between the spouses, including prenuptial agreements, may transmute community property into separate property, and, if the agreement provides, the agreement may be used to establish the separate interests of the spouses in the refund. United States v. Elam, 112 F3d 1036 (9th Cir. 1997) (distinguishing Hathaway v. United States, 93-1 USTC ¶ 50,285 (WD Wash. 1993) (applying Washington community property law)). In addition, "to the extent that the income is attributable to one spouse's sole management community property, the refund from the excess tax on that income is the sole management community property of that spouse." Ragan v. Comm'r, 135 F3d 329 (5th Cir. 1998) (entire amount of refund of tax attributable to withholding tax on one spouse's earnings is included in that spouse's bankruptcy estate). The National Office has concluded that if each spouse has a separate interest in a refund, and the Service issues a refund check to only one spouse, the Service is liable to the other spouse for the amount of his or her separate interest in the overpayment. SCA 1999-24056 (Apr. 20, 1999).

[268] Coerver v. Comm'r, 36 TC 252 (1961), aff'd per curiam, 297 F2d 837 (3d Cir. 1962); Marie A. Dolan, 44 TC 420 (1965).

cordingly, each spouse should be able to file a claim for refund of his or her share of the overpayment.[269]

[2] Fiduciaries and Agents

If a return is filed by an individual and, after his death, a refund claim is filed by the decedent's legal representative, the representative must establish his representative status by attaching to the claim certified copies of letters testamentary, letters of administration, and the like.[270] A fiduciary who did not file a return must attach documentary evidence of fiduciary status to the claim. Similarly, a taxpayer's agent may execute and file a claim for refund, but the agent must send a power of attorney with the claim.[271] If the fiduciary (e.g., an executor, administrator, guardian, trustee, or receiver) did file a return, and thereafter files a claim for refund, the fiduciary need not submit documentary evidence to establish his legal authority, provided that he states in the claim that he (1) filed the return and (2) is still acting as fiduciary.[272]

---

[269] See Pettengill v. United States, 253 F. Supp. 321 (ND Ill. 1966). For computation of the amount of a refund, see infra ¶ 11.09[1]. Once one spouse proves that he or she contributed to the tax overpayment, the full amount of an overpayment may not be credited against a tax liability of the other spouse. St. John v. Bookwalter, 58-1 USTC ¶ 9216 (WD Mo. 1957), followed in Glaubke v. United States, 78-1 USTC ¶ 9206 (ED Va. 1978). But see Snodgrass v. United States, 834 F2d 537 (5th Cir. 1987) (wife who sought a refund of federal taxes, penalties, and interest paid by her husband with funds that belonged to her or were community property lacked standing to sue in district court under 28 USC § 1346(a)(1) because she was not the taxpayer). It has been held that where a husband and wife filed separate refund claims, and the Service paid the refund to the wife, the husband's recourse was against his wife, not the Service. Norris Bloomfield, 52 TC 745 (1969) (but separate claims were filed on same day in same handwriting, and couple lived in community property state).

[270] Reg. § 301.6402-2(e).

[271] Reg. § 301.6402-2(e). Oldham's Estate v. Campbell, 217 F. Supp. 819 (ND Tex. 1963) (power of attorney sent after agent filed claim but before claim disallowed; held, requirements of regulations were met).

[272] A claim for refund of an income tax overpayment by a trust or estate discovered after it has been terminated may be made either by a single claim filed by all the beneficiaries or by individual claims filed by each beneficiary in proportion to the tax paid from his or her share. Rev. Rul. 73-366, 1973-2 CB 408.

[3] Corporations

A corporate taxpayer files a claim for refund in the name of the corporation, signed by a duly authorized officer.[273] Where the corporation is a member of an affiliated group of corporations (including a parent-subsidiary group) that elects to file a consolidated return, the common parent is the sole agent for the group and files the claim in its own name. Any refund to the parent discharges any liability of the Service to any member of the affiliated group.[274] If a corporation goes out of existence, the person who would be liable for any unpaid tax of the liquidated corporation as transferee of its assets is the proper person to file a claim for refund. For example, where two or more corporations are combined by way of merger or liquidation of one of them into a surviving or successor corporation, the successor is permitted to file a refund claim on behalf of the liquidated corporation. The name of the taxpayer corporation should be followed by the name of the successor.[275] Evidence establishing the liquidation must be filed with each claim (i.e., certificates of the secretary of state or other public official if the succession is a matter of public record, otherwise certified copies of all pertinent documents).[276]

As a result of a reorganization, the common parent for refund purposes may change. As a general rule, when a refund is claimed as the result of the carryback of a net operating loss or excess credit to a consolidation year, the refund must be made to the common parent.[277] If, as the result of a reorganization, the former common parent becomes unaffiliated with the affiliated group of corporations, and the common parent in the loss or excess credit year is different from the common parent in the carryback year, the common parent at the time of the loss or excess credit year is the agent for refund purposes.[278] The rationale is that, as the result of a reorganization, the common parent became unaffiliated with an affiliated group of corporations, the former common parent's authority terminated, and "it is as though [the former common parent] ceased to exist."[279]

---

[273] Reg. § 1.6062-1(a)(1). See Rainbow Elec. Co. v. United States, 536 F. Supp. 176 (D. Mont. 1982) (unsigned Form 1120X did not constitute valid claim).

[274] Reg. § 1.1502-77(a).

[275] Estate of Bernard H. Stouffer, 48 TC 277, 307 (1967); Rev. Rul. 54-17, 1954-1 CB 160. The same rules apply to corporate consolidations. Rev. Rul. 59-399, 1959-2 CB 488. When an S corporation is involved, the taxpayer is the shareholder, and on this basis, the purchaser of the stock of an S corporation was held to be the taxpayer for purposes of filing a refund claim for a preacquisition period. See Alon Int'l, Inc. v. United States, 910 F. Supp. 233 (WD Pa. 1995); see also FSA 199937003 (May 21, 1999) (concluding that receiver for an S corporation is not the proper party to file a refund claim).

[276] Rev. Rul. 54-17, 1954-1 CB 160.

[277] Reg. § 1.1502-78(b)(1).

[278] Interlake Corp. v. Comm'r, 112 TC 103 (1999).

[279] Interlake Corp. v. Comm'r, 112 TC 103 (1999).

On the other hand, when the common parent remains affiliated with the affiliated group after the reorganization, both the old common parent and the new common parent are agents of the affiliated group for purposes of the issuance of notices of deficiency for years before the reverse acquisition.[280] In both *Union Oil v. Commissioner*[281] and *Interlake Corp. v. Commissioner*,[282] there were reverse reorganizations in which a former subsidiary became the parent of the affiliated group. In *Interlake*, the reverse reorganization was followed by a spinoff of the old parent's stock, and the old parent became an unaffiliated company. In *Union Oil*, the old parent remained part of the affiliated group. In another case, *Southern Pacific v. Commissioner*,[283] there was a reverse acquisition, and the old common parent was merged into the new corporate parent. The Tax Court held that the acquiring corporate parent became the common parent for the years before the reorganization under the reverse acquisition regulations (Reg. § 1.1502-75(d)(3)(i)), because the new corporate parent stepped into the shoes of the old corporate parent.

The lesson to be learned from these cases is that at the time of a restructuring transaction, agreements of the parties should address prior-year consolidated return matters, and although the Service may say that it is not bound by the parties' agreement, regulations require that the Service be notified when a common parent contemplates dissolution and another member of the group is designated to act as the common parent.[284]

[4] Partnerships

A partnership is merely a reporting entity, not a taxpayer. The individual partners are taxpayers with respect to their distributive share of partnership income and, accordingly, are the proper taxpayers to file a claim for refund on their own behalf.[285] If a partner signs a claim for refund for the partnership (and the

---

[280] Union Oil Co. v. Comm'r, 101 TC 130 (1993) (applying Reg. § 1.1502-75(d)(3)(i), which provides that in reverse reorganizations, the acquiring corporation is to be treated as the common parent of the group).

[281] Union Oil Co. v. Comm'r, 101 TC 130 (1993).

[282] Interlake Corp. v. Comm'r, 112 TC 103 (1999).

[283] Southern Pac. Co. v. Comm'r, 84 TC 395 (1985).

[284] Reg. § 1.1502-77(d). See Raby & Raby, "Which Corporate Parent Gets the Refund?" 99 TNT 62-72 (Mar. 31, 1999).

[285] See Reg. § 1.6063-1(a); 26 CFR § 601.504(a)(2). For the rules applicable in unified partnership proceedings, see ¶ 8.09. John Arnold Executrak Sys., Inc. v. Comm'r, 58 TCM 1129 (1990) (general partner of a limited partnership had authority to file a Tax Court petition for a redetermination of a limited partner's taxes under agency principles, the limited partnership agreement, and an executed power of attorney).

partners), it appears that the partner's signature is prima facie evidence that he is authorized to sign the claim.[286]

¶ 11.08 FORMS FOR FILING CLAIMS

[1] Formal Claims

A claim for the refund of an overpayment may be made on the initial return for the year, an amended return, or on a special form provided by the Service. As a general rule, a claim for the credit or refund of an overpayment in income tax must be made on the return filed for the year. A return qualifies as a claim for refund if it sets forth the amount of the overpayment and directions as to its refund or application.[287] If an income tax return has already been filed, the claim for refund must be made on Form 1040X (Amended U.S. Individual Income Tax Return) or Form 1120X (Amended U.S. Corporation Income Tax Return). (See Forms 11.4 and 11.5.) In the case of an income tax return other than an individual or corporation income tax return (e.g., the income tax return of a fiduciary or exempt organization), the claim must be made on the appropriate amended return.[288] Otherwise the regulations require taxpayers to make all claims for the refund of taxes, penalties, and additions to tax on IRS Form 843.[289]

---

[286] Reg. § 1.6063-1(b).

[287] Reg. § 301.6402-3(a)(5).

[288] Reg. § 301.6402-3.

[289] Reg. § 301.6402-2(c). When a taxpayer files a claim for refund on a Form 1040, it has been held that the claim is not a qualifying administrative claim for refund for consideration of the taxpayer's liability of a trust fund recovery penalty, even if the Service has applied the income tax overpayment to the trust fund recovery penalty assessment. Schick v. United States, 80 AFTR2d 97-5999 (DNJ 1997).

FORM 11.4
AMENDED INDIVIDUAL TAX RETURN

Form 1040X (Rev. October 1993)

Department of the Treasury—Internal Revenue Service

Amended U.S. Individual Income Tax Return
▶ See separate instructions.

OMB No. 1545-0091
Expires 10-31-96

This return is for calendar year ▶ 19 ____ , OR fiscal year ended ▶ ____ , 19 ____

Your first name and initial: George	Last name: Franklin	Your social security number: 123 : 45 : 6789

If a joint return, spouse's first name and initial: Linda   Last name: Franklin   Spouse's social security number: 987 : 65 : 4321

Home address (number and street). If you have a P.O. box, see instructions: 617 Palisade Avenue   Apt. no.   Telephone number (optional): ( )

City, town or post office, state, and ZIP code. If you have a foreign address, see instructions: Englewood Cliffs, New Jersey 07632

For Paperwork Reduction Act Notice, see page 1 of separate instructions.

Enter name and address as shown on original return. If same as above, write "Same." If changing from separate to joint return, enter names and addresses from original returns.

Same

A Service center where original return was filed: Holtsville

B Has original return been changed or audited by the IRS? ☐ Yes ☒ No
If "No," have you been notified that it will be? . . . ☐ Yes ☒ No
If "Yes," identify the IRS office ▶

C Are you amending your return to include any item (loss, credit, deduction, other tax benefit, or income) relating to a tax shelter required to be registered? . . . ☐ Yes ☐ No
If "Yes," you must attach Form 8271, Investor Reporting of Tax Shelter Registration Number.

D Filing status claimed. Note: *You cannot change from joint to separate returns after the due date has passed.*
On original return ▶ ☐ Single ☐ Married filing joint return ☐ Married filing separate return ☐ Head of household ☐ Qualifying widow(er)
On this return ▶ ☐ Single ☐ Married filing joint return ☐ Married filing separate return ☐ Head of household ☐ Qualifying widow(er)

Income and Deductions (see instructions)
Caution: Be sure to complete Part II on page 2.

		A. As originally reported or as previously adjusted (see instructions)	B. Net change—Increase or (Decrease)—explain on page 2	C. Correct amount
1	Total income	224500	(6900)	217600
2	Total adjustments (such as IRA deduction, alimony paid, etc.)	7313	--	7313
3	Adjusted gross income. Subtract line 2 from line 1	217187	(6900)	210287
4	Itemized deductions or standard deduction	36200	1800	38000
5	Subtract line 4 from line 3	180987	(8700)	172287
6	Exemptions. If changing, fill in Parts I and II on page 2	8400	--	8400
7	Taxable income. Subtract line 6 from line 5	172587	(8700)	163887
8	Tax (see instructions). Method used in col. C _____	49685	(2697)	46988
9	Credits (see instructions)			
10	Subtract line 9 from line 8. Enter the result but not less than zero	49685	(2697)	46988
11	Other taxes (such as self-employment tax, alternative minimum tax, etc.)			
12	Total tax. Add lines 10 and 11	49685	(2697)	46988
13	Federal income tax withheld and excess social security, Medicare, and RRTA taxes withheld. If changing, see instructions			
14	Estimated tax payments		46500		46500
15	Earned income credit			
16	Credits for Federal tax paid on fuels, regulated investment company, etc.			
17	Amount paid with Form 4868, Form 2688, or Form 2350 (application for extension of time to file)			
18	Amount paid with original return plus additional tax paid after it was filed			3185
19	Total payments. Add lines 13 through 18 in column C			49685

Refund or Amount You Owe

20	Overpayment, if any, as shown on original return or as previously adjusted by the IRS	20	
21	Subtract line 20 from line 19 (see instructions)	21	
22	AMOUNT YOU OWE. If line 12, column C, is more than line 21, enter the difference and see instructions	22	
23	REFUND to be received. If line 12, column C, is less than line 21, enter the difference	23	2697

Sign Here
Keep a copy of this return for your records.

Under penalties of perjury, I declare that I have filed an original return and that I have examined this amended return, including accompanying schedules and statements, and to the best of my knowledge and belief, this amended return is true, correct, and complete. Declaration of preparer (other than taxpayer) is based on all information of which the preparer has any knowledge.

Your signature   Date   ▶ Spouse's signature. If a joint return, BOTH must sign.   Date

Paid Preparer's Use Only

Preparer's signature   Date   Check if self-employed ☐   Preparer's social security no.

Firm's name (or yours if self-employed) and address ▶   E.I. No.   ZIP code

Form **1040X** (Rev. 10-93)

Form 1040X (Rev. 10-93)

Page **2**

Part I Exemptions. See Form 1040 or Form 1040A instructions.

If you are not changing your exemptions, do not complete this part.
If claiming more exemptions, complete lines 24-30 and, if applicable, line 31.
If claiming fewer exemptions, complete lines 24-29.

			A. Number originally reported	B. Net change	C. Correct number
24	Yourself and spouse	24			
	Caution: If your parents (or someone else) can claim you as a dependent (even if they chose not to), you cannot claim an exemption for yourself.				
25	Your dependent children who lived with you	25			
26	Your dependent children who did not live with you due to divorce or separation	26			
27	Other dependents	27			
28	Total number of exemptions. Add lines 24 through 27	28			
29	Multiply the number of exemptions claimed on line 28 by the amount listed below for the tax year you are amending. Enter the result here and on line 6.				

Tax Year	Exemption Amount	But see the Instructions if the amount on line 3 is over:
1993	$2,350	$81,350
1992	2,300	78,950
1991	2,150	75,000
1990	2,050	Not applicable for tax year 1990.

29

30 Dependents (children and other) not claimed on original return:

(a) Dependent's name (first, initial, and last name)	(b) Check if under age 1 (under age 2 if a 1990 return)	(c) If age 1 or older (age 2 or older if a 1990 return), enter dependent's social security number	(d) Dependent's relationship to you	(e) No. of months lived in your home

No. of your children on line 30 who lived with you ▸ ☐

No. of your children on line 30 who didn't live with you due to divorce or separation (see instructions) ▸ ☐

No. of dependents on line 30 not entered above ▸ ☐

31 If your child listed on line 30 didn't live with you but is claimed as your dependent under a pre-1985 agreement, check here ▸ ☐

Part II Explanation of Changes to Income, Deductions, and Credits

Enter the line number from page 1 for each item you are changing and give the reason for each change. Attach all supporting forms and schedules for items changed. If you don't, your Form 1040X may be returned. Be sure to include your name and social security number on any attachments.

If the change pertains to a net operating loss carryback or a general business credit carryback, attach the schedule or form that shows the year in which the loss or credit occurred. See instructions. Also, check here . . . . ▸ ☐

Item 1 - Increase in Subchapter S income $10200.
Section 168 of the Code provides that a full year's depreciation may not be taken in an initial year that is shorter than 12 months - Calculation attached (omitted)

Item 2 - Decrease in Subchapter S income $15200.
Inventory control sheets were incorrectly footed, resulting in a decrease in ending inventory and resultant increase in cost of goods sold. Calculation attached (omitted)

Item 3 - Increase in Schedule A itemized deductions - $1800.
A contribution carryover from 1993 was not utilized. Copy of 1993 Form 1040 attached (omitted)

Item 4 - Mr. Franklin was subject to the alternative minimum tax in 1993 and since no benefit was derived from the state tax deduction the refund is not properly includable as income in 1994.

Part III Presidential Election Campaign Fund. Checking below will not increase your tax or reduce your refund.

If you did not previously want to have $3 (or $1 if a 1992 return) go to the fund but now want to, check here . . . . ▸ ☐ $3 for 1993 ☐ $1 for 1992
If a joint return and your spouse did not previously want to have $3 (or $1 if a 1992 return) go to the fund but now wants to, check here . . . . ▸ ☐ $3 for 1993 ☐ $1 for 1992

Department of the Treasury
Internal Revenue Service

Instructions for Form 1040X
(Revised October 1993)
Amended U.S. Individual Income Tax Return
Section references are to the Internal Revenue Code.

Paperwork Reduction Act Notice

We ask for the information on this form to carry out the Internal Revenue laws of the United States. You are required to give us the information. We need it to ensure that you are complying with these laws and to allow us to figure and collect the right amount of tax.

The time needed to complete and file this form will vary depending on individual circumstances. The estimated average time is: **Recordkeeping,** 1 hr., 12 min.; **Learning about the law or the form,** 20 min.; **Preparing the form,** 1 hr., 11 min.; and **Copying, assembling, and sending the form to the IRS,** 35 min.

If you have comments concerning the accuracy of these time estimates or suggestions for making this form more simple, we would be happy to hear from you. You can write to both the **Internal Revenue Service,** Attention: Reports Clearance Officer, PC:FP, Washington, DC 20224; and the **Office of Management and Budget,** Paperwork Reduction Project (1545-0091), Washington, DC 20503. **DO NOT** send this form to either of these offices. Instead, see **Where To File** on page 2.

General Instructions

Purpose of Form

Use Form 1040X to correct Form 1040, Form 1040A, Form 1040EZ, Form 1040NR, or Form 1040PC. If you used TeleFile to file your original return, you can call 1-800-829-1040 for details on how to complete Form 1040X. You may also use Form 1040X to make certain elections after the prescribed deadline. For details, see Rev. Proc. 92-85, 1992-2 C.B. 490.

File a separate Form 1040X for each year you are amending. If you are changing your Federal return, you may also have to change your state return. Please note that it often takes 2 to 3 months to process Form 1040X.

Filing Form 1045

You may use Form 1045, Application for Tentative Refund, instead of Form 1040X if:

• You are applying for a refund resulting from a net operating loss or general business credit carryback, AND

• Less than 1 year has elapsed since the end of the year in which the loss or credit arose.

For more details, see the separate instructions for Form 1045.

When To File

File Form 1040X only after you have filed your original return. Generally, Form 1040X must be filed within 3 years after the date the original return was filed, or within 2 years after the date the tax was paid, whichever is later. A return filed early is considered filed on the date it was due.

A Form 1040X based on a bad debt or worthless security must generally be filed within 7 years after the due date of the return for the tax year in which the debt or security became worthless. For more details, see section 6511.

A Form 1040X based on a net operating loss carryback or a general business credit carryback generally must be filed within 3 years after the due date of the return for the tax year of the net operating loss or unused credit.

Carryback Claims

You must attach copies of the following to Form 1040X if it is used as a carryback claim.

• Pages 1 and 2 of Form 1040 and Schedules A and D, if applicable, for the year in which the loss or credit originated. At the top of these forms, write "Attachment to Form 1040X—Copy Only—Do Not Process."

• Any Schedules K-1 you received from any partnership, S corporation, estate, or trust for the year of the loss or credit that contribute to the loss or credit carryback.

• Any form or schedule from which the carryback results such as Form 3800 or Schedule C or F.

• The forms or schedules for items refigured in the carryback year such as Form 6251, Form 3468, or Schedule A.

All information described above must be attached to your Form 1040X, if applicable, or your Form 1040X will be returned for the attachments.

Note: *If you filed a joint or separate return for some, but not all, of the years involved in figuring the loss or credit carryback, you may have to allocate your income, deductions, and credits. For details, get the publication that explains the type of carryback you are claiming. For example, get Pub. 536, Net Operating Losses, if you are claiming a net operating loss carryback, or Pub. 514, Foreign Tax Credit for Individuals, for a foreign tax credit carryback.*

Net Operating Loss

Attach a computation of your net operating loss using **Schedule A** (Form 1045) and, if applicable, your net operating loss carryover using **Schedule B** (Form 1045).

A refund based on a net operating loss should not include the refund of any self-employment tax reported on line 11 of Form 1040X. For more details, see Pub. 536.

Other Claims

Injured Spouse Claim.—Do not use Form 1040X to file an injured spouse claim. Instead, file only Form 8379, Injured Spouse Claim and Allocation.

Resident and Nonresident Aliens.—Use Form 1040X to amend Form 1040NR, U.S. Nonresident Alien Income Tax Return. Also, use Form 1040X if you filed Form 1040NR and you should have filed a Form 1040, 1040A, or 1040EZ, or vice versa. For details on resident and nonresident alien filing requirements, get Pub. 519, U.S. Tax Guide for Aliens.

To amend Form 1040NR or to file the correct return, you must do the following:

1. On Form 1040X, fill in your name, address, and identifying or social security number. Also, complete lines A and B, and Part II on page 2. Include in Part II an explanation for the changes or corrections made.

2. Attach the corrected return (Form 1040, Form 1040NR, etc.) to Form

Form 1040X.

1040X. Write "Amended" across the top of the corrected return.

3. If Form 1040X includes a Form 1040NR, file it with the Internal Revenue Service, Philadelphia, PA 19255, U.S.A. Otherwise, file Form 1040X with the service center for the place where you live. For the address, see **Where To File** below

Where To File

Mail your return to the Internal Revenue Service Center for the place where you live. No street address is needed.

If you live in:	Use this address:
Florida, Georgia, South Carolina	Atlanta, GA 39901
New Jersey, New York (New York City and counties of Nassau, Rockland, Suffolk, and Westchester)	Holtsville, NY 00501
New York (all other counties), Connecticut, Maine, Massachusetts, New Hampshire, Rhode Island, Vermont	Andover, MA 05501
Illinois, Iowa, Minnesota, Missouri, Wisconsin	Kansas City, MO 64999
Delaware, District of Columbia, Maryland, Pennsylvania, Virginia	Philadelphia, PA 19255
Indiana, Kentucky, Michigan, Ohio, West Virginia	Cincinnati, OH 45999
Kansas, New Mexico, Oklahoma, Texas	Austin, TX 73301
Alabama, Arkansas, Louisiana, Mississippi, North Carolina, Tennessee	Memphis, TN 37501
Alaska, Arizona, California (counties of Alpine, Amador, Butte, Calaveras, Colusa, Contra Costa, Del Norte, El Dorado, Glenn, Humboldt, Lake, Lassen, Marin, Mendocino, Modoc, Napa, Nevada, Placer, Plumas, Sacramento, San Joaquin, Shasta, Sierra, Siskiyou, Solano, Sonoma, Sutter, Tehama, Trinity, Yolo, and Yuba), Colorado, Idaho, Montana, Nebraska, Nevada, North Dakota, Oregon, South Dakota, Utah, Washington, Wyoming	Ogden, UT 84201
California (all other counties), Hawaii	Fresno, CA 93888
American Samoa	Philadelphia, PA 19255
Guam: Permanent residents	Department of Revenue and Taxation Government of Guam 378 Chalan San Antonio Tamuning, GU 96911

Guam: Nonpermanent residents Puerto Rico (or if excluding income under section 933)	Philadelphia, PA 19255
Virgin Islands: Nonpermanent residents	
Virgin Islands: Permanent residents	V.I. Bureau of Internal Revenue Lockhart Gardens No. 1-A Charlotte Amalie St. Thomas, VI 00802
Foreign country: U.S. citizens and those filing Form 2555, Form 2555-EZ, or Form 4563	Philadelphia, PA 19255
All A.P.O. and F.P.O. addresses	Philadelphia, PA 19255

Information on Income, Deductions, etc.

If you have questions, such as what income is taxable or what expenses are deductible, the instructions for the return you are amending may help you. Be sure to use the Tax Table or Tax Rate Schedules for the right year to figure the corrected tax. The related schedules and forms may also help you. To get prior year forms, schedules, and instructions, call 1-800-TAX-FORM (1-800-829-3676).

Death of Taxpayer

If you are filing a Form 1040X for a deceased taxpayer, write **"DECEASED,"** the taxpayer's name, and the date of death across the top of Form 1040X.

If you are filing Form 1040X as a surviving spouse filing a joint return with the deceased, write "Filing as surviving spouse" in the area where you sign the return. If someone else is the personal representative, he or she must also sign.

Claiming a Refund for a Deceased Taxpayer.—If you are a surviving spouse filing a joint return with the deceased, file only Form 1040X to claim the refund. If you are a court-appointed personal representative or any other person claiming a deceased taxpayer's refund, file Form 1040X and attach Form 1310, Statement of Person Claiming a Refund Due a Deceased Taxpayer, and any other information required by its instructions.

For more details, get Pub. 559, Survivors, Executors, and Administrators.

Paid Preparers

Generally, anyone you pay to prepare your return must sign it. A preparer who is required to sign your return must sign it by hand in the space provided (signature stamps or labels cannot be used) and give you a copy of the return for your records. Someone who prepares your return for you but does not charge you should not sign your return.

Specific Instructions

Above your name, enter the calendar year or fiscal year of the return you are amending.

Name, Address, and Social Security Number

If amending a joint return, list your names and social security numbers in the same order as shown on the original return. If changing from a separate to a joint return and your spouse did not file an original return, enter your name and social security number first.

P.O. Box.—If your post office does not deliver mail to your home and you have a P.O. box, enter the box number instead of your home address.

Foreign Address.—If your address is outside the United States or its possessions or territories, enter the information on the line for "City, town or post office, state, and ZIP code" in the following order: city, province or state, postal code, and the name of the country. Do not abbreviate the country name.

Line D—Filing Status

If you and your spouse are changing from separate returns to a joint return, enter in column A the amounts from your return as originally filed or as previously adjusted (either by you or the IRS). Next, combine the amounts from your spouse's return as originally filed or as previously adjusted with any other changes you or your spouse are making to determine the amounts to enter in column B. If your spouse did not file an original return, include your spouse's income, deductions, credits, other taxes, etc., in determining the amounts to enter in column B. Then, read the instructions for column C on this page to figure the amounts to enter in that column. Both of you must sign Form 1040X. If there is any tax due, it must be paid in full.

Columns A–C

In column A, enter the amounts from your return as originally filed or as you later amended it. If your return was changed or audited by the IRS, enter the adjusted amounts.

In column B, enter the net increase or net decrease for each line you are changing. Show all decreases in parentheses. Explain each change in Part II on page 2 of the form and attach any related schedule or form. For example, if you are amending your return to itemize deductions, attach Schedule A (Form 1040). If you need more space, show the required information on an attached statement.

For column C, add the increase in column B to the amount in column A, or subtract the column B decrease from column A. For any item you do not

Form 1040X.

change, enter the amount from column A in column C.

Example. Anna Arbor had originally reported $11,000 as her total income on her 1992 Form 1040EZ. She received an additional Form W-2 for $500 after she filed her tax return. Ms. Arbor would complete line 1 of Form 1040X as follows:

	Col. A	Col. B	Col. C
Line 1	$11,000	$500	$11,500

Ms. Arbor would also report any additional income tax withheld on line 13 in column B.

Lines 1–31

If you are changing only credits or other taxes, skip lines 1–7 and start with line 8. If changing only payments, skip lines 1–11 and start with line 12.

If you are only providing additional information and there are no changes to the amounts you originally reported, skip lines 1–31 and complete Part II and, if applicable, Part III.

Line 1

Enter income from all sources, such as wages, taxable interest, dividends, and net profit from business. On Form 1040, use line 23.

On Form 1040A, use line 14.

On Form 1040EZ for 1990–1992, use line 3. For 1993, use line 4.

If you are correcting wages or other employee compensation, attach the first copy or Copy B of all additional or corrected Forms W-2 you got after you filed your original return.

Line 2

Enter all adjustments to income, such as an IRA deduction or alimony paid. On Form 1040, use lines 24a–29. Be sure to include any write-in adjustment. For more details, see your Form 1040 instructions.

On Form 1040A, use lines 15a and 15b.

If you are changing the amount of your IRA deduction, write in Part II of Form 1040X "IRA deduction" and the amount of the increase or decrease. If you are changing a deductible IRA contribution to a nondeductible IRA contribution, also complete and attach Form 8606, Nondeductible IRAs.

Line 3

Changes you make to your adjusted gross income (AGI) can cause other amounts to increase or decrease. For example, increasing your AGI may decrease your miscellaneous itemized deductions or your credit for child and dependent care expenses. It may also increase the allowable deduction for charitable contributions or the amount of social security benefits that is taxable.

Also, changes to your AGI may change your total itemized deductions or your deduction for exemptions. You should refigure these items whenever you change your AGI.

Effect on Exemption Deduction.—Use the Deduction for Exemptions Worksheet in the Form 1040 instructions for the year you are amending to figure the amount to enter on Form 1040X, line 6, and if applicable, line 29, if any of the following apply:

• You are amending your 1993 return and your AGI in column A or C is over $162,700 ($108,450 if single; $135,600 if head of household; $81,350 if married filing separately).

• You are amending your 1992 return and your AGI in column A or C is over $157,900 ($105,250 if single; $131,550 if head of household; $78,950 if married filing separately).

• You are amending your 1991 return and your AGI in column A or C is over $150,000 ($100,000 if single; $125,000 if head of household; $75,000 if married filing separately).

Line 4

Itemized Deductions.—If you itemize deductions on Schedule A (Form 1040), enter on line 4 your total itemized deductions. On Schedule A for 1990, use line 27. For 1991–1993, use line 26.

Standard Deduction.—If you do not itemize, enter on line 4 your standard deduction. On Form 1040, use line 34.

On Form 1040A, use line 19.

On Form 1040EZ for 1990–1992, if you checked the "Yes" box on line 4 of that form, enter the amount from line 4 of Form 1040EZ on line 4 of Form 1040X. If you checked the "No" box, enter on line 4 of Form 1040X the amount listed below for the tax year you are amending.

Tax Year	Amount
1992	$3,600
1991	3,400
1990	3,250

On Form 1040EZ for 1993, if you checked the "Yes" box on line 5 of that form, enter on line 4 of Form 1040X the amount from line E of the worksheet on the back of Form 1040EZ. If you checked the "No" box, enter $3,700 ($6,200 if married filing jointly) on line 4 of Form 1040X.

Line 6

If you are changing the number of exemptions claimed, complete the applicable lines in Part I of the form to figure the amounts to enter on line 6. Otherwise, enter in columns A and C of line 6 the amount you claimed for exemptions on your original return. On Form 1040, use line 36. But if changes to your AGI affect your deduction for exemptions (see the line 3 instructions),

enter the net change in column B of line 6 and the correct amount in column C.

On Form 1040A, use line 21.

On Form 1040EZ for 1990–1992, if you checked the "Yes" box on line 4 of that form, enter zero on line 6 of Form 1040X. If you checked the "No" box, enter the amount listed below for the tax year you are amending.

Tax Year	Amount
1992	$2,300
1991	2,150
1990	2,050

On Form 1040EZ for 1993, if you checked the "Yes" box on line 5 of that form, enter on line 6 of Form 1040X the amount from line F of the worksheet on the back of Form 1040EZ. If you checked the "No" box, enter $2,350 ($4,700 if married filing jointly) on line 6 of Form 1040X.

Line 8

Enter your income tax before subtracting any credits. Show on this line the method you use in column C to figure your tax. For example, if you use the Tax Rate Schedules, write "TRS." If you use Schedule D (Form 1040) or, for 1993, the Schedule D Tax Worksheet, write "Sch. D."

Figure the tax on the taxable income you reported on line 7, column C. Attach the appropriate schedule or forms. Include on line 8 any additional taxes from Form 4970, Tax on Accumulation Distribution of Trusts, or Form 4972, Tax on Lump-Sum Distributions.

Line 9

Enter your total credits, such as the credit for the elderly or the disabled, credit for child and dependent care expenses, or credit for prior year minimum tax. On Form 1040 for 1990, use lines 41–45. For 1991–1993, use lines 41–44. Be sure to include any write-in credit.

On Form 1040A, use lines 24a and 24b.

Line 11

Include other taxes, such as alternative minimum tax, self-employment tax, tax on early distributions from qualified retirement plans, or advance earned income credit payments. Also, include any recapture of investment credit, low-income housing credit, or Federal mortgage subsidy. On Form 1040 for 1990, use lines 48–53. For 1991–1993, use lines 47–52. Be sure to include any write-in tax.

On Form 1040A, use line 26.

Lines 13–17

Enter on the applicable lines your payments and credits. On Form 1040 for 1990, use lines 55–61. For 1991–1993, use lines 54–59. If you are amending

Form 1040X.
your 1993 Form 1040 and you filed Form 8841, Deferral of Additional 1993 Taxes, see the instructions for line 14.

On Form 1040A, use lines 28a–28c. Be sure to include any write-in payment.

On Form 1040EZ for 1990–1992, use line 6. For 1993, use line 7.

Line 13.—If you change these amounts, attach to the front of Form 1040X the first copy or Copy B of all additional or corrected Forms W-2 or Forms 1099-R that you got after you filed your original return. Enter in column B any additional Federal income tax withheld shown on Forms W-2 or 1099.

Line 14.—Enter the estimated tax payments you claimed on your original return. If you filed Form 1040-C, U.S. Departing Alien Income Tax Return, include the amount you paid as the balance due with the return.

If you are amending your 1993 Form 1040, include any deferral of additional 1993 taxes from line 58b of that form on line 14 of Form 1040X. Write "Form 8841" in the space to the left of line 14. The amount reported on your original return as deferred additional 1993 taxes cannot be changed even if your taxable income has increased or decreased.

Line 18

Enter the amount you paid from the "Amount You Owe" line on your original return. Also, include any additional tax that may have resulted if your original return was changed or examined. Do not include payments of interest or penalties.

Line 20

Enter the overpayment from your original return. On Form 1040 for 1990, use line 63. For 1991–1993, use line 61. On Form 1040A, use line 29. On Form 1040EZ for 1990–1992, use line 8. For 1993, use line 9. The overpayment amount must be considered in preparing Form 1040X since any refund you have not yet received from your original return will be refunded separately from any additional refund claimed on your Form 1040X.

If your original return was changed or audited by the IRS and as a result there was an additional overpayment of tax, also include that amount on line 20. Do not include any interest you received on any refund.

Lines 21 and 22

If line 21 is a negative amount, treat it as a positive amount and add it to the amount on line 12, column C. Enter the result on line 22. This is the amount you owe.

Attach your check or money order payable to the Internal Revenue Service for the full amount. Write your name, address, social security number, and daytime phone number on your payment. Also, write the year and type of return you are amending. For example, "1992 Form 1040." We will figure the interest due and send you a bill.

If you cannot pay the full amount shown on line 22, you may ask to make monthly installment payments. Get Form 9465, Installment Agreement Request, for more information. But if you and your spouse are changing from separate returns to joint returns, you cannot request an installment agreement.

Line 23

If you are entitled to a larger refund than you claimed on your original return, show only the additional amount due you. This will be refunded separately from the amount claimed on your original return (see the instructions for line 20). We will figure the interest and include it in your refund.

Lines 24–28

In column A, enter the number of exemptions claimed on your original return. In column B, enter any changes to exemptions claimed on your original return. Enter in column C the corrected number of exemptions you are claiming.

Line 29

You may have to use the *Deduction for Exemptions Worksheet* in the Form 1040 instructions to figure the amount to enter on line 29 if the amount in column A or C of line 3 is—

• Over $81,350 if amending your 1993 return,

• Over $78,950 if amending your 1992 return, or

• Over $75,000 if amending your 1991 return.

For details, see Effect on Exemption Deduction on page 3. If you don't have to use the worksheet, multiply the applicable dollar amount on line 29 by the number of exemptions on line 28.

Line 30

If you are amending your return to claim an exemption for a dependent, you may have to enter the dependent's social security number (SSN) in column (c) of line 30. For 1990, you must enter the SSN of any dependent who was age 2 or older on December 31, 1990. For tax years after 1990, you must enter the SSN of any dependent who was age 1 or older on December 31 of the year you are amending. If you do not enter the number or if the number is wrong, you may have to pay a $50 penalty. If your dependent does not have an SSN, see your 1993 Form 1040 or Form 1040A instructions for line 6c.

If you are claiming more than five additional dependents, show the information requested in columns (a) through (e) on an attached statement. When entering the total number of dependents in the boxes to the right of line 30, be sure to include these dependents.

If you are claiming a child who didn't live with you under the special rules for children of divorced or separated parents, you must do one of the following:

• **Check the box on line 31** if your divorce decree or written separation agreement was in effect before 1985 and it states that you can claim the child as your dependent.

• **Attach Form 8332**, Release of Claim to Exemption for Child of Divorced or Separated Parents, or similar statement. If your divorce decree or separation agreement went into effect after 1984 and it unconditionally states that you can claim the child as your dependent, you may attach a copy of the following pages from the decree or agreement instead of Form 8332:

1. Cover page (write the other parent's social security number on this page), and

2. The page that unconditionally states you can claim the child as your dependent, and

3. Signature page showing the date of the agreement.

For more details, see your 1993 Form 1040 or Form 1040A instructions for line 6c.

Part III—Presidential Election Campaign Fund

You may use Form 1040X to have $3 (or $1 if amending a 1992 return) go to the *Presidential Election Campaign Fund* if you (or your spouse on a joint return) did not do so on your original return. This must be done within 20½ months after the original due date for filing the return. For calendar year 1993, this period ends on December 31, 1995. For calendar year 1992, this period ends on December 31, 1994. A "Yes" designation cannot be changed.

FORM 11.5
AMENDED U.S. CORPORATION INCOME TAX RETURN

Form **1120X** (Rev. April 1994) Department of the Treasury Internal Revenue Service		**Amended U.S. Corporation Income Tax Return**		OMB No. 1545-0132 Expires 4-30-97

For tax year ending in ▶ .... (Enter month and year)

	Name		Employer identification number
Please Type or Print	Taxpayer Industries		12-9876543
	Number, street, and room or suite no. (If a P.O. box, see instructions.)		
	1 Main Street		Telephone number (optional)
	City or town, state, and ZIP code		
	Anytown, New York 00000		(212) 249-6666

Enter name and address used on original return (If same as above, write "Same.")

Same

Internal Revenue Service Center where original return was filed ▶ Holtsville

Fill in Applicable Items and Use Part II To Explain Any Changes

Part I Income and Deductions (see instructions)	(a) As originally reported or as previously adjusted	(b) Net change (increase or decrease— explain in Part II)	(c) Correct amount
1 Total income (Form 1120 or 1120-A, line 11)	14,285,00	3,242	14,288,242
2 Total deductions (total of lines 27 and 29c, Form 1120, or lines 23 and 25c, Form 1120-A)	13,615,00	31,414	13,646,414
3 Taxable income. Subtract line 2 from line 1	670,000		641,828
4 Tax (Form 1120, line 31, or Form 1120-A, line 27)	227,800	(9,578)	218,222

Payments and Credits (see instructions)

5a Overpayment in prior year allowed as a credit	210,000	---	210,000
b Estimated tax payments			
c Refund applied for on Form 4466	210,000		210,000
d Subtract line 5c from the sum of lines 5a and 5b . . .			
e Tax deposited with Form 7004			
f Credit from regulated investment companies			
g Credit for Federal tax on fuels			
6 Tax deposited or paid with (or after) the filing of the original return			17,800
7 Add lines 5d through 6, column (c)			227,800
8 Overpayment, if any, as shown on original return or as later adjusted			
9 Subtract line 8 from line 7			227,800

Tax Due or Refund

10 **Tax due.** Subtract line 9 from line 4, column (c). Make check payable to "Internal Revenue Service" (see instructions) . . . . ▶	
11 **Refund.** Subtract line 4, column (c), from line 9 . . . . ▶	9578

Please Sign Here	Under penalties of perjury, I declare that I have filed an original return and that I have examined this amended return, including accompanying schedules and statements, and to the best of my knowledge and belief, this amended return is true, correct, and complete. Declaration of preparer (other than taxpayer) is based on all information of which preparer has any knowledge.		
	/s/ Alan Michaels	5/1/92	President
	Signature of officer	Date	Title

Paid Preparer's Use Only	Preparer's signature ▶		Date	Check if self-employed ▶ ☐	Preparer's social security no.
	Firm's name (or yours if self-employed) and address			E.I. No. ▶	
				ZIP code ▶	

For Paperwork Reduction Act Notice, see instructions on page 3.   Cat. No. 11530Z   Form **1120X** (Rev. 4-94)

Form 1120X (Rev. 4-94) Page **2**

Part II Explanation of Changes to Income, Deductions, Credits, etc. Enter the line number from page 1 for the items you are changing, and give the reason for each change. Show any computation in detail. Attach additional sheets if necessary.

If the change is due to a net operating loss carryback, a capital loss carryback, or a general business credit carryback, see Carryback Claims on page 3, and check here . . . . ▶ ☐

Form 1120X (Rev. 4-94) Page **3**

Paperwork Reduction Act Notice

We ask for the information on this form to carry out the Internal Revenue laws of the United States. We are required to give us the information. We need it to ensure that you are complying with these laws and to allow us to figure and collect the right amount of tax.

The time needed to complete and file this form will vary depending on individual circumstances. The estimated average time is:

Recordkeeping . . . . 12 hr., 12 min.
Learning about the law
or the form . . . . 1 hr., 8 min.
Preparing the form . . . . 3 hr., 14 min.
Copying, assembling, and
sending the form to the IRS . . . . 32 min.

If you have comments concerning the accuracy of these time estimates or suggestions for making this form more simple, we would be happy to hear from you. You can write to both the Internal Revenue Service, Attention: Reports Clearance Officer, PC:FP, Washington, DC 20224; and the Office of Management and Budget, Paperwork Reduction Project (1545-0132), Washington, DC 20503. DO NOT send the tax form to either of these offices. Instead, see Where To File on this page.

General Instructions

Section references are to the Internal Revenue Code.

Purpose of Form

Use Form 1120X to correct Form 1120, U.S. Corporation Income Tax Return, or Form 1120-A, U.S. Corporation Short-Form Income Tax Return, as you originally filed it or as it was later adjusted by an amended return, a claim for refund, or an examination. You may also use Form 1120X to make certain elections after the prescribed deadline. For details, see Rev. Proc. 92-85, 1992-2 C.B. 490.

Do not use Form 1120X to apply for a quick refund of estimated tax, a tentative refund, or to obtain the approval of the IRS for a change in accounting method.

For a quick refund of estimated tax, file Form 4466, Corporation Application for Quick Refund of Overpayment of Estimated Tax. File the form within 2½ months after the end of the tax year, but before the corporation files its income tax return.

For a tentative refund due to the carryback of a net operating loss (NOL), a net capital loss, unused credits, or overpaid tax resulting from a claim-of-right adjustment (section 1341(b)(1)), file Form 1139, Corporation Application for Tentative Refund. Form 1139 can be used only if 1 year or less has passed since the tax year in which the carryback or adjustment occurred. For details on figuring NOL carrybacks, see Pub. 536, Net Operating Losses.

To request the approval of the IRS for a change in accounting method, the corporation generally must file Form 3115, Application for Change in Accounting Method. Form 1120X may not be used to make an accounting method change unless the corporation has received prior approval from the IRS. A change in method of accounting includes a change in practice involving the proper time for including an item in income or taking a deduction. See Rev. Proc. 92-20, 1992-1 C.B. 685, and Pub. 538, Accounting Periods and Methods, for details.

When To File

File Form 1120X only after the corporation has filed its original return. Generally, Form 1120X must be filed within 3 years after the date the original return was due or 3 years after the date the corporation filed it, whichever is later. A Form 1120X based on a net operating loss (NOL) carryback, a capital loss carryback, or a general business credit carryback, generally must be filed within 3 years after the due date of the return for the tax year of the NOL, capital loss, or unused credit. Other claims for refund must be filed within 3 years after the date the original return was due, 3 years after the date the corporation filed it, or 2 years after the date the tax was paid, whichever is later.

Please note that it often takes 3 to 4 months to process Form 1120X.

What To Attach

If the change you are making involves an item of income, deduction, or credit that must be supported with a schedule, statement, or form, attach the appropriate schedule, statement, or form to Form 1120X.

Tax Shelters

If you are amending your return to include any item (loss, credit, deduction, other tax benefit, or income) relating to a tax shelter required to be registered, you must attach Form 8271, Investor Reporting of Tax Shelter Registration Number.

Carryback Claims

If Form 1120X is used as a carryback claim, attach copies of Form 1120 (pages 1 and 3) or Form 1120-A (pages 1 and 2), for both the year the loss or credit originated and for the carryback year. Also attach any other forms, schedules, or statements that are necessary to support the claim. At the top of these attachments, write "Copy Only—Do Not Process."

Information on Income, Deductions, Tax Computation, etc.

See the instructions for Forms 1120 and 1120-A for the tax year you are amending for information about the taxability of certain types of income, the allowability of certain expenses as deductions from income, computation of tax, etc.

Note: Deductions for such items as charitable contributions and the dividends-received deduction may have to be refigured because of changes made to items of income or expense.

Where To File

Mail this form to the Internal Revenue Service Center where the corporation filed its original return.

Specific Instructions

Tax Year

In the space above the employer identification number, enter the ending month and year of the calendar or fiscal year for the tax return you are amending.

P.O. Box

If the post office does not deliver mail to the street address and the corporation has a P.O. box, show the box number instead of the street address.

Form 1120X (Rev. 4-94) Page **4**

Column (a)

Enter the amounts from your return as originally filed or as you later amended it. If your return was changed or audited by the IRS, enter the amounts as adjusted.

Column (b)

Enter the net increase or net decrease for each line you are changing. Use parentheses around all amounts that are decreases. Explain the increase or decrease in Part II.

Column (c)

Lines 1 and 2.—Add the increase in column (b) to the amount in column (a) or subtract the column (b) decrease from column (a). Enter the result in column (c). For an item that did not change, enter the amount from column (a) in column (c).

Line 4.—Figure the new amount of tax using the taxable income on line 3, column (c). Use Schedule J, Form 1120, or Part I, Form 1120-A, of the original return to make the necessary tax computation.

Line 5c.—Enter the amount of tax deposited with Form 7004, Application for Automatic Extension of Time To File Corporation Income Tax Return.

Line 5g.—Include on line 5g any write-in credits or payments, such as the credit for ozone-depleting chemicals or backup withholding.

Line 8.—Enter the amount from the "Overpayment" line of the original return, even if the corporation chose to credit all or part of this amount to the next year's estimated tax. This amount must be considered in preparing Form 1120X

because any refund due from the original return will be refunded separately (or credited to estimated tax) from any additional refund claimed on Form 1120X.

Line 10.—Make the check payable to "Internal Revenue Service" for the amount shown on line 10 and attach it to this form. Do not use the depositary method of payment.

Line 11.—If the corporation is entitled to a refund larger than the amount claimed on the original return, line 11 will show only the additional amount of refund. This additional amount will be refunded separately from the amount claimed on the original return.

Signature

The return must be signed and dated by the president, vice president, treasurer, assistant treasurer, chief accounting officer, or any other corporate officer (such as tax officer) authorized to sign. A receiver, trustee, or assignee must sign and date any return required to be filed on behalf of a corporation.

If a corporate officer completes Form 1120X, the Paid Preparer's space should remain blank. If someone prepares Form 1120X and does not charge the corporation, that person should not sign the return. Certain others who prepare Forms 1120X should not sign. See the instructions for Forms 1120 and 1120-A for more information.

Note: The IRS will figure any interest due or owed and will either include it in the refund or bill the corporation for the interest.

To avoid the Service's rejection of a submitted document on the ground that it does not constitute a valid refund claim, a claim for refund or credit should be made on the requisite forms. A finding that a letter or other document does not constitute a valid claim could lead to disaster if the period for filing a claim has run, because no refund may be made except where a timely claim has been filed.

A return or amended return constitutes a claim for refund or credit only if it contains a statement setting forth the amount determined as an overpayment and informing the Service whether the overpayment is to be refunded to the taxpayer or credited against the taxpayer's estimated tax for the year following the year of the overpayment.[290] That a claim for refund must be filed is required by statute. The information that must be included in the claim for refund is described in regulations; each ground supporting the claim for credit or refund must be set forth in detail on the amended return.[291] The distinction between the statute requiring the filing of a claim for refund (Section 6511) and the regulations regarding the form of the claim was described by the Supreme Court in *United States v. Memphis Cotton Oil Co.*[292]

> The line of division must be kept a sharp one between the function of a statute requiring the presence of a claim within a given period of time, and the function of a regulation making provision as to form. The function of the statute, like that of limitations generally, is to give protection against stale demands. The function of the regulation is to facilitate research.

---

[290] IRC § 6402(b); Reg. § 301.6402-3(a)(5). A taxpayer may not elect to treat an overpayment as a deposit in the nature of a cash bond for payment of deficiencies for taxable years preceding the taxable year of the overpayment. Rev. Rul. 79-430, 1979-2 CB 398. An instruction to credit the overpayment against estimated tax constitutes an irrevocable election. Starr v. Comm'r, 267 F2d 148, 151 (7th Cir. 1959); Rev. Rul. 55-448, 1955-2 CB 595. No interest is allowed on the overpayment credit. Reg. § 301.6402-3(a)(5); Owens-Corning Fiberglass Corp. v. United States, 462 F2d 1139 (Ct. Cl. 1972) (upholding the validity of the regulation). The Service may also credit an overpayment in income tax against any outstanding tax liability; if it does so, only the balance, if any, is applied as the taxpayer has elected. Reg. § 301.6402-3(a)(6). See Martin-Marietta Corp. v. United States, 572 F2d 839 (Ct. Cl. 1978) (taxpayer's election to credit 1968 overpayment to 1969 estimated tax did not prevent the Service from determining which installment payment of 1968 corporate tax (March 1969 or June 1969) was to be applied, and, as a result, interest on the overpayment was reduced).

[291] Reg. § 301.6402-3(a)(5). A taxpayer may use a tax return as the form for filing a claim for refund rather than filing a separate claim for refund. Fearis v. Comm'r, 548 F. Supp. 408, 410 (ND Tex. 1982); McIlvaine v. United States, 23 Cl. Ct. 439, 442, 92-1 USTC ¶ 50,274 (1991); Levitsky v. United States, 27 Fed. Cl. 235 (1992). Having used the proper form, however, does not mean that the taxpayer has set forth specific grounds. Id. (where claim on original return was followed by amended return, and court concluded that both constituted single claim and found that Service knew of underlying facts).

[292] United States v. Memphis Cotton Oil Co., 288 US 62, 71 (1932).

Because of this distinction, the Service may not ignore a taxpayer's failure to file a claim for refund, nor may it accept an untimely claim for refund.[293] The Service does, however, have the administrative discretion to apply or waive the requirements of its regulation. The Service may reject a claim for failure to comply with the regulation's form and particularity requirements, but it need not do so, and so it may also waive the requirements of the regulation and consider a general claim on its merits.[294] On the other hand, a taxpayer may comply with the regulations, and file a claim for refund with specific grounds, but may not allege new and different grounds in a later suit for refund.[295]

[2] Informal Claims

Despite the requirement in regulations that a claim be submitted on one of the IRS forms supplied for that purpose, a document submitted to the Service that fails to satisfy the regulation can be treated as an informal refund claim. Use of an informal claim has long been held valid. In *United States v. Kales*,[296] the Commissioner made a jeopardy assessment against an owner of Ford Motor Company stock who sold the stock in 1919. In March 1925, within the statutory period for filing a refund claim, the taxpayer sent a letter of protest with her payment of the jeopardy assessment. She stated that in the event the Commissioner's 1913 valuation of the Ford stock should be set aside by the courts or administrative action, the tax she paid in 1920 was too high, and accordingly she would "claim a right to a refund of said tax to the extent of such excess."[297] The Supreme Court said that the Commissioner could have been left in no doubt that the taxpayer was setting forth her right to a refund contingent on future events and held that the letter constituted an informal refund claim and had been treated as such by the Service.

The facts and decision in *Kales* established the standards subsequently applied by courts, which are: (1) the issue whether an informal claim has been filed is one of fact; (2) the informal action must be in writing or have a written component[298]; and (3) the matters set forth in the writing must have been

---

[293] IRC § 7422(a).

[294] Tucker v. Alexander, 275 US 228 (1927).

[295] United States v. Felt & Tarrant Mfg. Co., 283 US 269 (1931); United States v. Garbutt Oil Co., 302 US 528 (1937).

[296] United States v. Kales, 314 US 186 (1941).

[297] United States v. Kales, 314 US 186, 195 (1941).

[298] American Radiator & Standard Sanitary Corp. v. United States, 318 F2d 915 (Ct. Cl. 1963); Wrightsman Petroleum Co. v. United States, 35 F. Supp. 86, 96 (Ct. Cl. 1940), cert. denied, 313 US 578 (1941) (taxpayer's oral statements did not constitute informal claim). More recently, the Eleventh Circuit has said, "There are no rigid guidelines except that an informal claim must have a written component and 'should adequately apprise the

sufficient to apprise the Service that a refund is sought and to focus attention on the merits of the dispute so that an examination of the claim may be commenced if the Service wishes.[299] For an informal claim to be valid, it has also been said the claim must (1) have a written component, (2) that is sufficient to apprise the Service that a refund is being claimed, and (3) that specifies the tax and the year or years for which the refund is being sought sufficiently so that the Service can investigate the claim.[300]

A written component is necessary. The written component element is in recognition of the fact that government personnel working on a case may change.[301] The written component need not be in a single document.[302]

Internal Revenue Service that a refund is sought for certain years."' Mills v. United States, 890 F2d 1133, 1135 (11th Cir. 1989), citing Arch Eng'r Co. v. United States, 783 F2d 190, 192 (Fed. Cir. 1986).

The Third Circuit has described the minimum requirements for a written informal claim this way: "If a taxpayer submits to the Internal Revenue Service some sort of written instrument which informs the administrative agency that the taxpayer believes that he has been subjected to an erroneous or illegal tax exaction, and that he desires a refund or credit because of such action, this is sufficient." D'Amelio v. United States, 679 F2d 313, 315 (3d Cir. 1982).

It also is said that the written component "should not be given a crabbed or literal reading, ignoring all the surrounding circumstances which give it body and content. The focus is on the claim as a whole, not merely the written component." Estate of Hale v. United States, 876 F2d 1258, 1276 (6th Cir. 1989) (quoting American Radiator & Standard Sanitary Corp. v. United States, 318 F2d 915, 920 (Ct. Cl. 1963). "In other words, a court must examine the writing, or series of writings, in light of all the existing facts." Estate of Hale v. United States, 876 F2d 1258, 1262, quoted in Estate of Katherine Tinari v. United States, 82 AFTR2d 98-5907 (ED Pa. 1998) (correspondence with the Service and oral statement memorialized in revenue officer's written record held to constitute informal claim).

[299] Angelus Milling Co. v. Comm'r, 325 US 293, 297 (1945); United States v. Commercial Nat'l Bank of Peoria, 874 F2d 1165 (7th Cir. 1989) (cases analyzed; timely letter sent by taxpayer's counsel to the Service satisfied the writing requirement and adequately notified the Service); Crocker v. United States, 83-1 USTC ¶ 9347 (SDNY 1983) (taxpayer's letter to the Service, in conjunction with a subsequently filed refund claim, was treated as an informal claim, since it put the Service on notice as to the factual and legal grounds on which the claim was based). Grovner v. United States, 92-2 USTC ¶ 50,457 (SD Ga. 1992) (protest held to be informal claim); Gray v. United States, 93-2 USTC ¶ 50,557 (ND Tex. 1993) (letter "detailing [administrator's] contentions relating to alleged refunds owed by [Service] to [the administrator] held to constitute an informal claim.)

[300] Mills v. United States, 890 F2d 1133 (11th Cir. 1989).

[301] Disabled American Veterans v. United States, 650 F2d 1178 (Ct. Cl. 1981), aff'd and remanded, 704 F2d 1570 (Fed. Cir. 1983) (oral claim allegedly made to Service agents was not an informal claim, nor was information obtained by Department of Justice attorney from pretrial submission knowledge chargeable to Service).

[302] See Furst v. United States, 678 F2d 147 (Ct. Cl. 1982). A comparison of the *Disabled American Veterans* and *Furst* cases shows how the court of claims dealt with this issue. See also VDO-ARGO Instruments, Inc. v. United States, 3 Cl. Ct. 359, 83-2 USTC ¶ 9605 (1983), aff'd in unpublished opinion, 738 F2d 453 (Fed. Cir. 1984) (alleged infor-

Whether an informal claim has been filed is an issue of fact, and so the mere fact that a writing has been submitted to the Service does not mean that the writing automatically constitutes an informal refund claim.[303] The writing may have been submitted in the course of the audit process to resolve the dispute between the Service and the taxpayer.

Notice to the Service is vital. An informal claim for refund will be recognized only if it alerts the Service to the fact that a refund of taxes is sought for certain years.[304] If a taxpayer can establish that the Service was adequately notified of an intention to claim a refund on a ground omitted from a formal claim for refund, the taxpayer may recover on that omitted ground.[305] However, it is not enough that the Service has in its possession information from which it might find that the taxpayer is entitled to, or might desire, a refund.[306]

---

mal claim followed by untimely formal claim; held, informal claim not valid). See also Wall Indus., Inc. v. United States, 10 Cl. Ct. 82, 86-1 USTC ¶ 9438 (1986) (tax returns and financial statements, coupled with a revenue agent's knowledge that refunds had been claimed, constituted an informal refund claim).

[303] For a case finding that an informal claim was submitted on documents, two of which were created by the Service, and distinguishing other situations where the written submissions were made for dispute resolution purposes, see New Eng. Elec. Sys. v. United States, 32 Fed. Cl. 636 (Fed. Cl. 1995) (taxpayer's objection to adjustment and agent's recording of taxpayer's intention to challenge adjustment held informal claim).

[304] United States v. Kales, 314 US 186, 195 (1941). At one time, the Service Manual recognizing the validity of informal claims emphasized the notice element. An informal claim was described as a "letter or other document which contains all facts necessary to determine that a reduction in tax liability is involved"; IRM § 4121.2 (Sept. 4, 1980). See IRM, Chief Counsel Directive Manual 35.18.12.2, Informal Claims for Refund (Aug. 31, 1982).

[305] Union Pac. RR v. United States, 389 F2d 437 (Ct. Cl. 1968); Carmichael v. United States, 86-2 USTC ¶ 9708 (ED Tenn. 1986) ("it is well settled that all facts and circumstances surrounding the filing of a claim for refund must be taken into account when evaluating whether the Commissioner has been informed and has had an opportunity to address the issue on the merits"). However, it is also possible for the later refund claim omitting the alleged informal claim to serve as evidence that no informal claim was made. Group Life & Health Ins. Co. v. United States, 660 F2d 1042, 1059 (5th Cir. 1981), cert. denied, 457 US 1132 (1982).

[306] Angelus Milling Co. v. Comm'r, 325 US 293, 300 (1945) ("[b]ut it is not enough that somewhere under the Commissioner's roof is the information which might enable him to pass on the claim for refund"); American Radiator & Standard Sanitary Corp. v. United States, 318 F2d 915 (Ct. Cl. 1963). In Barenfeld v. United States, 442 F2d 371, 375 (1971), the court of claims said that, "the Internal Revenue Service is not required to weigh circumstantial evidence in order to determine whether a taxpayer is asking for a tax refund." See D'Amelio v. United States, 679 F2d 313 (3d Cir. 1982) (estate's request for information to determine amount of Service lien may be claim for refund, but not an informal claim). England v. United States, 760 F. Supp. 186 (D. Kan. 1991) (filing of 1983, 1984, and 1985 returns, each showing a net operating loss, along with 1982 return showing tax, did not constitute informal claim). An amended tax return may constitute a claim for refund for the period for which it is filed, but without more specific language, the

Availability of information is not the equivalent of notice. A claim based on the available information must actually be communicated to the Service. For this reason, it has been held that the filing of a claim for another year or different period does not constitute an informal claim.[307]

It must appear from the surrounding facts, including the written element, that the taxpayer is actually requesting a refund. Thus, an attempt to take a deduction that is not allowed on a return does not constitute a refund claim (e.g., a loss erroneously carried back two rather than three years does not constitute an informal claim for the third year).[308] Although the mere filing of an errone-

---

amended return does not constitute an informal claim for future periods. Axtell v. United States, 860 F. Supp. 795 (D. Wy. 1994) (amended estate tax returns did not constitute timely refund claims of estate tax resulting from payment of deferred interest on estate tax in year after the years of the amended returns).

[307] Rosengarten v. United States, 181 F. Supp. 275 (Ct. Cl.), cert. denied, 364 US 822 (1960); Byron Weston Co. v. United States, 87 F. Supp. 955 (Ct. Cl. 1950); cf. Pearl Assurance Co. v. United States, 324 F2d 512 (Ct. Cl. 1963) (net operating loss claims for 1943 and 1944 were sufficient to constitute net operating loss claims for 1942); Pearson v. United States, 443 F. Supp. 878 (EDNY 1978) (communications between the taxpayer and Service established that, in investigating the taxpayer's claim for 1968, the Service had considered his tax liability for 1968 and 1971; held, informal claim for 1971 was made).

However, an application for a tentative refund arising from a loss carryback (Form 1045) has been held not to constitute an informal refund claim. Crismon v. United States, 550 F2d 1205 (9th Cir.), cert. denied, 434 US 807 (1977); Morse v. United States, 47 AFTR2d 80-573 (Ct. Cl. 1980). Reg. § 1.6411-1(b)(2) states that Form 1045 is not a refund claim, as does the form itself. The form serves a purpose other than the one served by a refund claim and involves application of the loss from another period. Similarly, Form 1139 has been held not to constitute an informal refund claim. Thrif-Tee, Inc. v. United States, 492 F. Supp. 530 (WDNC 1979), aff'd in unpublished opinion, 628 F2d 1351 (4th Cir. 1980), cert. denied, 449 US 1124 (1981) (taxpayer timely filed tentative carryback claim but an untimely refund claim; held, refund barred even though Service had not acted on tentative claim).

After a settlement permitting the taxpayer to deduct 70 percent of an item in 1981 and to deduct the balance ratably over the life of a contract, which included 1984, the taxpayer filed claims for 1981, 1982, and other years, but not the year 1984. After the period of limitations for filing a refund claim expired and the taxpayer filed a claim for 1984, the taxpayer claimed that it had filed an informal claim for 1984. The circuit court rejected the argument, in part, on the ground that the taxpayer "had filed nothing except a set of claims, incident to the settlement, that did not mention 1984." BCS Fin. Corp. v. United States, 118 F3d 522 (7th Cir. 1997). The circuit court noted that a "reader of the settlement papers might well infer that [the taxpayer] would be able to claim a refund for [1984] . . . [b]ut to claim a refund for 1981 is not to claim a refund for 1984, even if the logic underlying the 1981 claim would suggest to a person knowledgeable about tax law and the affairs of the taxpayer that the taxpayer would also have a claim for 1984."

[308] Byron Weston Co. v. United States, 87 F. Supp. 955 (Ct. Cl. 1950). See also Kuehn v. United States, 480 F2d 1319 (Ct. Cl. 1973) (instead of carrying back the loss, the taxpayer carried it forward). Compare Malonek v. United States, 923 F. Supp. 1462 (D. Wyo. 1996) (an amended 1987 return reporting a net operating loss carryback was found not to be an informal claim for 1984, because "[a]t most, it contain[ed] information

ous return does not constitute a claim, a qualifying claim was found where there was a written component sufficient to apprise the Service that a refund was requested. Specifically, the taxpayer attached schedules to the return with notations that listed taxes that were refundable based on certain costs, and a revenue agent audited the return.[309]

Under these standards, the following documents have been held to be informal refund claims:

- A notation on the back of a check paying the tax;
- A written protest prior to or accompanying a payment of a tax (even where contingent on the occurrence of a future event)[310];
- A letter attached to a return protesting the constitutionality of an imposed tax[311];

---

from which the IRS might deduce that the taxpayer has a right to and may, in fact, seek a refund. It does not, however, inform the IRS that the taxpayer intends to do so.").

[309] American Radiator & Standard Sanitary Corp. v. United States, 318 F2d 915 (Ct. Cl. 1963). But compare Williams v. District Dir., 82-1 USTC ¶ 9172 (ND Ga. 1981) (amended return claiming refund "based solely on contested income tax issues considered in previously examined returns" held not valid claim). See also Bethlehem Indus., Inc. v. United States, 82-2 USTC ¶ 9686 (ND Ill. 1982) (letter inquiring about status of tentative carryback claim, Form 1139, not an informal claim because Section 6411(a) says such a claim does not constitute a claim for refund).

[310] Newton v. United States, 163 F. Supp. 614 (Ct. Cl. 1958); United States v. Kales, 314 US 186 (1941). A protest can constitute an informal claim for refund if it notifies the Service that an overpayment has been made. Hotel Conquistador, Inc. v. United States, 597 F2d 1348 (Ct. Cl. 1979), cert. denied, 444 US 1032 (1980); Hollie v. Comm'r, 73 TC 1198, 1214 (1980), appeal dismissed (2d Cir. 1981) (excellent analysis of cases).

However, the Court of Federal Claims has held that a protest of a proposed assessment standing alone did not qualify as an informal claim for refund. Skamp Computer Servs., Inc. v. United States, 81 AFTR2d 98-2216 (Fed. Cl. 1998) ("we cannot say — as plaintiff now would have us — that the written protest to the proposed assessment that it filed on September 9, 1993, taken in conjunction with the hearing that followed before the IRS appeals officer — were sufficient to alert the Commissioner to the fact that a refund of the contested tax assessment was intended"). The Court of Federal Claims distinguished *Newton* and other cases on the ground that in those cases the protest served "simply as an add-on notice to refund litigation concerning the same assessed deficiency in tax (although affecting an earlier tax year) that the taxpayer was *then* pursuing in the courts . . . [because] where the protest relates to a tax on which a refund is already being sought through litigation — the Commissioner reasonably can be expected to understand that the protest is meant to preserve the right to a refund if the pending litigation goes in the taxpayer's favor."

[311] Penn Mut. Indem. Co. v. Comm'r, 277 F2d 16 (3d Cir. 1960); Miller v. United States, 82 AFTR2d 98-5414 (CD Ill. 1998) (taxpayer filed a facially frivolous return, deducting the entire amount of his total income, making his adjusted gross income zero, and attached a statement rationalizing his being exempt from tax; held, return constituted a claim for refund).

- A letter attached to a waiver of restrictions on assessment[312]; and
- A letter agreeing to payment of tax in installments.[313]

[3] Protective Claims

A protective claim for refund is filed to protect a right to receive a refund contingent on the occurrence of a future event. A protective claim is a type of claim; it may be filed on a formal claim form or it may be filed as an informal claim. In *United States v. Kales*,[314] not only was the taxpayer's claim for refund in a letter held to be a valid, albeit informal, claim, but in part her letter stated that in the event administrative action or court decision resulted in an increase in the 1913 value of the Ford Motor stock she owned, she "will insist" on the higher valuation and "will claim the right to a refund."[315] The Su-

---

[312] Cumberland Portland Cement Co. v. United States, 104 F. Supp. 1010 (Ct. Cl. 1952); Neilson v. Harrison, 131 F2d 205 (7th Cir. 1942) (conditional waiver). See also Bonwit Teller & Co. v. United States, 283 US 258 (1931) (waiver of the period of limitations executed by taxpayer at the request of the Service to permit refund of determined overassessment; held, filing of informal claim). The Service recognizes this result. Rev. Rul. 68-65, 1968-1 CB 555 (IRS forms of the 870 or 890 series on which a taxpayer agrees to an overassessment of income, estate, or gift tax determined by the Service will be considered a valid claim for refund if timely filed). Form 870 now specifically states that if filed within the period for filing a refund claim, the form is "considered a valid claim for refund . . . ," attributable to the overassessment it sets forth. Consequently, if the Service disallows the claim reflected on the Form 870, the taxpayer must bring an action on the claim within two years. Bauer v. United States, 594 F2d 44 (5th Cir. 1979) (taxpayer's refund suit barred). But see Arch Eng'g Co. v. United States, 783 F2d 190 (Fed. Cir. 1986) (where no actual payment made before they were filed, neither protests nor Forms 870-AD and 870 constituted informal refund claims because they were part of the internal administrative processing of a case before tax was paid, and thus were not actual refund requests). An employer's Form 941-C requesting credit for its share of FICA taxes paid on behalf of an employee was held to constitute an informal refund claim of the employee. Mills v. United States, 890 F2d 1133 (11th Cir. 1989).

[313] Crenshaw v. Hrcka, 237 F2d 372 (4th Cir. 1956), aff'g 140 F. Supp. 350 (ED Va. 1956). But see Tobin v. Tomlinson, 310 F2d 648 (5th Cir. 1962), cert. denied, 375 US 929 (1963).

[314] United States v. Kales, 314 US 186 (1941). Compare D'Amelio v. United States, 679 F2d 313 (3d Cir. 1982). However, in a questionable limitation of the Supreme Court's decision in *Kales*, it has been held that a protective claim applies only to a presently existing right that would be asserted, rather than to a right arising after the filing of a claim, such as subsequently arising administration expenses. Rogan v. Taylor, 136 F2d 598 (9th Cir. 1943). *Taylor* relied in part on Ordway v. United States, 37 F2d 19 (2d Cir. 1930), which itself was decided before *Kales*.

[315] However, a claim for refund that was made contingent on the disallowance of a deduction in a different taxable year was insufficient where the deduction was allowed. National Casket Co. v. United States, 16 AFTR 1001 (SDNY 1934), aff'd per curiam, 79 F2d 1004 (2d Cir. 1935), cert. denied, 298 US 672 (1936).

preme Court held that this part of her claim constituted a valid claim for refund, stating: "The statement that upon the happening of the contingency the claim will be prosecuted is not inconsistent with the present assertion of it."[316] Mrs. Kales's claim for refund was a conditional claim contingent on the happening of certain events, and as such was a proper claim. However, if the condition does not materialize, the claim is not sufficient to constitute a claim for refund, unless the claim states that it will continue to be a claim for refund even if the contingency occurs.[317]

Protective claims are filed when the refund is contingent or uncertain in amount. As one court descibed the procedure, "If a claim for refund is contingent or uncertain in amount or, as here, both, the proper procedure is to file a conditional claim before the statute of limitations runs out, if you fail to do that the statute of limitations will bar the refund."[318] A protective claim may be required to protect potential refunds when a special statutory regime is involved—for example, the tax on insurance companies that fail to qualify as insurance companies for two years after the year they filed returns as insurance companies and become liable for a phase 3 tax for the year they last qualified as insurance companies.[319]

Future contingencies frequently make it difficult to determine the exact amount of administrative expenses for estate tax purposes. Where expenses and liabilities are not ascertainable at the time the return is filed, they become known after the return is filed. If the expenses have been estimated, and disallowed on audit, or if the expenses have not been estimated with the result that the estate has overpaid tax, the taxpayer should file a petition in the Tax Court to contest the deficiency or file a claim for refund to recover the overpayment.[320] If the amount of the liability or expenses is still not ascertainable at

---

[316] United States v. Kales, 314 US 186, 196 (1941).

[317] Sun Chem. Corp. v. United States, 698 F2d 1203 (Fed. Cir.), cert. denied, 464 US 819 (1983) (claim did not state it was made even if condition failed to materialize).

[318] Swietlik v. United States, 779 F2d 1306 (7th Cir. 1985); see also United States v. Commercial Nat'l Bank of Peoria, 874 F2d 1165 (7th Cir. 1989) (counsel's letter about effect of proposed settlement on estate held an informal refund claim contingent on ultimate settlement; Swietlik applied).

[319] However, no protective claim was necessary in John A. Green v. United States, 84 AFTR2d 99-5619 (Fed. Cir. 1999), where the court held that the filing of the later return would start the running of the limitations period for an insurance company that lost qualification and was required to file an amended return and pay tax for the last year it filed as an insurance company.

[320] Reg. § 20.2053-1(b)(3). When the amount cannot be determined, the Tenth Circuit has also said that a protective claim must be filed "to avert the three-year time bar and to suspend the two-year cap on permissible recovery amounts." Amoco Prod. Corp. v. Newton Sheep Co., 85 F3d 1464 (10th Cir. 1996) (although taxpayers' portion of royalties could not be determined until the conclusion of a quiet title action, the taxpayer knew it had a refund claim).

the end of the period for filing a refund claim, a protective claim based on the best available information (and not merely a statement of an intention to file a claim in the future) should be filed to avoid the bar of the statute of limitations.[321] A protective claim may even benefit another taxpayer. For example, an employer's timely filed protective claim for refund of FICA taxes also protects its employees' individual claims filed after the period of limitations has expired.[322]

¶ 11.09 PREPARATION OF CLAIMS

The Service provides forms that may be used in making claims for refund after the original return has been filed: (1) Forms 1040X and 1120X, for refund of income tax and (2) Form 843, for refunds of gift, estate, employment, or excise tax. Forms 1040X and 1120X have the following key parts:

1. The year involved;
2. Information relating to the identity of the taxpayer;
3. The place of filing and status of the original return;
4. Revised amounts of income and deductions and payment credits for the year;
5. Computation of the overpayment to be refunded;
6. An explanation of the changes in computation;
7. Schedules; and
8. The signature of the taxpayer and preparer, if any.

Form 843 calls for the same information, in a somewhat reduced format. Since Form 843 is used for several types of taxes, the type of tax (i.e., employment, estate, excise, gift, or stamp) as well as the kind of return filed must be indicated. The claim form provides space only for the amount to be refunded, not for computations, so the computation of the tax refund must be attached.

One rule applies to all refund claims. In the case of income, gift, and federal unemployment taxes, a separate claim must be prepared and filed for each type of tax for each taxable year or period.[323] For example, a claim for refund of income tax does not constitute a claim for any other class of tax.[324] Taxpay-

---

[321] Kellogg-Citizens Nat'l Bank of Green Bay, Wis. v. United States, 330 F2d 635 (Ct. Cl. 1964).

[322] Rev. Rul. 83-79, 1983-1 CB 346.

[323] Reg. § 301.6402-2(d).

[324] See, e.g., Shanker v. United States, 430 F. Supp. 625 (ED Mo. 1977), aff'd on another issue, 571 F2d 8 (8th Cir. 1978) (claim for refund of overpayments in income tax

ers should not have any difficulty completing those portions of the forms that call for identifying information and computations. However, problems may arise in two areas: (1) computation of the refund amount and (2) the grounds to be set forth in the claim.

[1] Computation of Refund

It is the statement of the grounds for refund, not the computation of the refund, that limits the taxpayer's recovery of an overpayment.[325] At one time, Form 843 contained, after the amount to be refunded, the phrase "or such greater amount as is legally refundable." Where a taxpayer understates the amount of the overpayment, both the courts and the Service agree that the taxpayer is not limited to the lower amount stated in a claim if the grounds for refund are adequately set forth in the claim,[326] whether or not this phrase has

---

that the Service had credited against taxpayer's estate tax liability did not constitute a claim for purposes of the estate tax).

[325] The Service issued rulings for determining each spouse's share in an overpayment made in a year both spouses filed a joint return. Rev. Rul. 80-7, 1980-1 CB 296 (method of computing portion of joint refund creditable against one spouse's preexisting separate liability); Rev. Rul. 80-8, 1980-1 CB 298 (computation of divorced spouse's share of a refund for joint return year); Rev. Rul. 80-6, 1980-1 CB 296 (computation of a divorced spouse's share of a refund resulting from a carryback of a separate net operating loss or investment credit from a postmarriage year to one for which the taxpayer filed a joint return with his or her former spouse). The Service clarified Revenue Ruling 80-7 to describe the conditions under which a joint overpayment can be applied against the separate income tax liability of one of the spouses where the taxpayers live in a community property state. Rev. Rul. 85-70, 1985-1 CB 361. See also Rev. Rul. 86-57, 1986-1 CB 362 (when joint overpayment is credited by carryback of a net operating loss on a former husband's separate return, Service uses a ratio based on hypothetical separate liabilities of spouses as if they had filed separate returns to determine their shares of overpayment); Mitchell v. United States, 403 US 190 (1971) (holding invalid a state law exemption in its community property laws making all community property subject to the premarital or other separate debts of either spouse, but exempting tax claims).

[326] Pink v. United States, 105 F2d 183 (2d Cir. 1939); FW Woolworth Co. v. United States, 15 F. Supp. 679 (SDNY 1936), rev'd on other grounds, 91 F2d 973 (2d Cir. 1937), cert. denied, 302 US 768 (1938). See also Rev. Rul. 81-87, 1981-1 CB 580. When a taxpayer timely filed a claim covering three years, the Service refunded the amount claimed and an agent conducted a field examination. During the examination, it was discovered that the amount of the overpayment had been understated, and the agent's report reflected this error. The taxpayer then filed an informal claim for the additional amount. The district court held that the original claim was sufficient to put the Service on notice of the item regarding which the taxpayer claimed error even if the amount of the claim had been understated, and the refund of the overpayment originally claimed did not extinguish the claim for statute of limitations purposes. Mutual Assurance, Inc. v. United States, 94-1 USTC ¶ 50,082 (ND Ala. 1993), aff'd, 56 F3d 1353 (11th Cir. 1995), nonacq. AOD 1999-014 (Oct. 12, 1999).

been included. Consequently, the rights of a taxpayer are not affected by the presence or absence of the language. Perhaps for this reason, claim for refund forms no longer contain this phrase. It may be advisable to add the language "or such greater amount as is legally refundable" as a precaution. Practitioners who add the phrase should bear in mind that they do not enlarge their tax-payer/client's rights by the effort.

When preparing a claim, it is also appropriate to take the precaution of specifying the amount of any deficiency interest collected along with the principal amount of the tax in the computation of the overpayment. This tactic avoids any possibility that the claim for refund might fail to include this amount as a ground of recovery.[327]

[2] Grounds Set Forth in Claim

The most important part of the claim for refund is the statement of the grounds on which refund is claimed. In a real sense the claim is the administrative equivalent of a pleading in court that may not be amended after the time for filing has expired. A later refund suit must be based on the same grounds stated in a filed claim for refund.[328] An attempt to sue for refund on a ground not included in a claim is subject to attack, the reason being that there would be a "substantial variance" between the suit and the filed claim. The refund claim forms and instructions are cryptic in describing the completion of this vital part of the refund claim, although regulations make its importance clear:

> No refund or credit will be allowed after the expiration of the statutory period of limitation applicable to the filing of a claim therefor except upon one or more of the grounds set forth in a claim filed before the expiration of such period. The claim must set forth in detail each ground upon which a credit or refund is claimed and facts sufficient to apprise the Commissioner of the exact basis thereof. The statement of the grounds and facts must be verified by a written declaration that is made under the penalties of perjury. A claim which does not comply with this paragraph will not be considered for any purpose as a claim for refund or credit.[329]

The rationale behind these requirements has been put this way: The protection of the revenue authorizes the Commissioner to demand information in a particular form, and he is entitled to insist that the form be observed so as to advise him expeditiously and accurately of the true nature of the claim.[330]

---

[327] See Brandt & Brandt Printers, Inc. v. United States, 300 F2d 457 (Ct. Cl. 1962).

[328] IRC § 7422(a); United States v. Felt & Tarrant Mfg. Co., 283 US 269 (1931).

[329] Reg. § 301.6402-2(b)(1).

[330] Angelus Milling Co. v. Comm'r, 325 US 293, 300 (1945); Stoller v. United States, 444 F2d 1391, 1393 (5th Cir. 1971) ("[t]he Commissioner should not be left to his

The claim-as-pleading analogy makes it appropriate to keep in mind the general rules of pleading applied in the Tax Court and the federal district courts. In general, Tax Court Rule 34 requires a petition to set forth (1) an assignment of each error in the Commissioner's notice of deficiency and (2) a statement of facts on which the taxpayer bases each assignment of error. In part, Federal Rules of Civil Procedure 8 requires a pleading to contain "a short and plain statement of the claim showing that the pleader is entitled to relief. . . ." As with pleadings in court, claims for refund may state alternative grounds for refund without regard to whether the claims or grounds are consistent.[331] However, unlike a complaint in a federal district court, a claim for refund may not be based on equitable grounds,[332] although it is advisable to add such grounds to the claim as a protective measure.

[3] Grounds and Facts

Regulations require that both "grounds" and facts be set forth in a claim. It is helpful to remember the Tax Court rules in complying with this requirement. A "ground" for refund should include the item of income, deduction, or credit that gives rise to the overpayment, in whole or in part, and the nature of the change. A statement of a ground for recovery might declare, for example, that $1,000 was erroneously reported as a capital loss under the provisions of Section 166(d) rather than an ordinary loss under the provisions of Section 165(c). However, the statement that the Commissioner failed to "properly compute the taxable income including but not limited to applying Section 281" was held insufficient to constitute a valid claim for refund.[333] The adequacy of the ground

---

own devices in order to discover the precise nature of a taxpayer's claim and thus be placed in a position of having to hazard a guess"); First Nat'l Bank v. United States, 727 F2d 741, 744 (8th Cir. 1984) (reasons for rule are to prevent surprise, to give the Service adequate notice of claim and facts on which claim is based, to permit administrative investigation, and to provide the Service with opportunity to correct errors). While a taxpayer may not raise an entirely new ground in a refund suit, thereby varying the claim against the Service, Section 7422 "goes no further than to require the taxpayer to set forth facts sufficient to enable the Commissioner of Internal Revenue to make an intelligent administrative review of the claim." Scoville Mfg. Co. v. Fitzpatrick, 215 F2d 567, 569 (2d Cir. 1954). This administrative review can occur even when an argument is not raised in the claim for refund but the basic contention is made administratively. See, e.g., Decker v. United States, 93-2 USTC ¶ 50,408 (D. Conn. 1993) (argument based on amended Code section not a variance when section prior to amendment argued to preclude tax).

[331] See United States v. Kales, 314 US 186 (1941).

[332] Reg. § 301.6402-2(b)(2) states, "Neither the district director, nor the director of the regional service center has authority to refund on equitable grounds penalties or other amounts legally collected."

[333] Belt Ry. v. United States, 567 F2d 717 (7th Cir. 1977). The circuit court in *Belt Railway* said that the phrase "including but not limited to" did not give the Service a clue

set out in the claim also determines whether the taxpayer can later pursue a claim in a refund suit. If the claim for refund does not adequately set forth grounds, the claim in the later refund suit will not have been brought to the attention of the Service.[334] Decisions on this issue cannot be rationalized except on the basis that the court felt that the Service was or was not given notice of what error was serving as ground for the claimed refund. Obviously, a claim that omits any factual support is inadequate.[335]

Concise statements of fact in support of the particular ground complete this portion of the claim. The regulations imply that the statement of facts must be detailed. However, since the purpose of the claim is to give the Service sufficient information of the ground to make an investigation of the merits of the claim, it would be more accurate to say that the statement of facts need not be exhaustive, but should include the principal factual elements on which the taxpayer relies.

It does not appear that the claim must make supporting legal argument, although as a matter of practice it may be worthwhile to argue supporting law with the objective of facilitating allowance of the claim without protracted review.

The suggestion might be made that the claim for refund should be as broad as possible consistent with the notice requirement imposed by both the regulations and the courts, although this approach would be dangerous because breadth and generality invite a "variance" attack on a claim in any refund suit that follows rejection.[336] The better approach is to assert grounds that may,

---

to the "nature and details" of the taxpayer's claim, especially where both the alleged error and its amount were also omitted.

[334] See, e.g., Santa Cruz Bldg. Ass'n v. United States, 411 F. Supp. 871 (ED Mo. 1976) (claim merely stated, "Taxpayer qualifies as a tax-exempt organization"; held, claim sufficient because court said the Service knew both the amount and reason why it was at issue). See also Walker v. United States, 143 F. Supp. 566 (ND Tex. 1956), aff'd, 240 F2d 601 (5th Cir.), cert. denied, 354 US 939 (1957) (claim that collection of penalty was unconstitutional held sufficient); Anderson v. United States, 468 F. Supp. 1085 (D. Minn. 1979), aff'd in unpublished order (8th Cir. 1980) (total payment alleged to constitute capital gain understated, but claim held sufficient because Service notified of ground for claim); Nelson, Inc. v. United States, 694 F. Supp. 428 (MD Tenn. 1988) (claim related to substantive issue not negligence penalty, but issues were found to be interrelated; held, there was no variance between them). ITT Corp. v. United States, 770 F. Supp. 863 (SDNY 1991) (while ITT clearly raised issue of proper treatment of forward currency contract gains as either capital gains or ordinary income, it did not raise issue of whether gains were from foreign or domestic source).

[335] Floyd v. United States, 77-1 USTC ¶ 9279 (ND Tex. 1977); Robertson v. United States, 87-1 USTC ¶ 9221 (D. Or. 1987) (taxpayer's claim stating that "[w]e contest all the issues raised by the IRS in the attached notice of deficiency" was held insufficient because it provided "no reason and no factual or legal basis for his claim").

[336] See Edde v. United States, 217 Ct. Cl. 690, 78-2 USTC ¶ 9548 (1978) (claim failed to specify the section under which the loss was claimed and the Service denied the

under the authority of the Supreme Court's decision in *Kales*,[337] be either alternative or inconsistent, but which, in any event, cover any conceivable possibility. If this action is taken and a somewhat broader statement is included to cover an omitted possibility, it can better be argued that the government has been put on notice.

---

claim as a business bad debt; taxpayer's claim on the basis of an ordinary business loss upheld only because the court found the claim to have alleged sufficient facts to put the Service on notice of the alternative theory). Beckwith Realty, Inc. v. United States, 896 F2d 860 (4th Cir. 1990) (Form 1120X stating that taxpayer did not agree with assessment of accumulated earnings tax pursuant to revenue agent report; held, failure to state specific error). Cf. Hall v. United States, 78-1 USTC ¶ 9126 (Ct. Cl. 1977), aff'd, 78-1 USTC ¶ 9,420 (Ct. Cl. 1977) (legal fees claimed to be deductible under Section 212(3) were contended in refund suit to be deductible under Sections 212(1) and 212(2) or 162(e); court refused to permit litigation of new ground for lack of notification to Service); see also Nucorp, Inc. v. United States, 23 Cl. Ct. 234 (1991) (claims failed to identify facts on which they were based, such as identity of oil-producing properties and data to perform net income allocations); Angle v. United States, 996 F2d 252 (10th Cir. 1993) (untimely claim was a new claim, not an amendment of filed claim, and complaint raised new tax-benefit ground not included in a timely claim). A taxpayer was permitted to amend a claim for refund after the statute of limitations on filing a claim had run. In this case, the amended claim corrected a computational error in the timely filed claim and the legal basis for the claim had not changed. Mutual Assurance, Inc. v. United States, 56 F3d 1353 (11th Cir. 1995) (in investigating the original claims the Service discovered that the taxpayer had understated the refund amounts; taxpayer then made an informal amendment to its formal claim).

Following *Edde*, supra, a claim stating that the assessments were made "after the expiration of all applicable statutes of limitations" was held broad enough to include the specific allegation in the refund complaint that the statute of limitations expired on May 3, 1991, and sufficiently specific to put the Service on notice of the claim. Parma v. United States, 84 AFTR2d 99-6534 (Fed. Cl. 1999) (the facts suggest that the taxpayer, taxpayer's counsel, and the Service knew there was an issue about the statute of limitations, but that the Service especially was uncertain about what its position was on the issue because it had raised a new ground in its summary judgment motion).

On the other hand, a later claim was dismissed as "substantially varying," for being based on a different legal theory and factual grounds from the original timely filed claim, when the original claim stated that the taxpayers had no income because the amount they received from their corporation was the repayment of a loan and their later claim took the position that they had no income because the corporation had no earnings or profits. Boyles v. United States, 85 AFTR2d 2000-1042 (MDNC 2000) (situation found different from *Edde* because the taxpayers did not make their claim on the general ground that the distribution of money to the taxpayers could not have been dividends; they specifically claimed that the distribution represented the repayment of loans).

[337] United States v. Kales, 314 US 186 (1941).

[4] The Variance Problem

If the grounds alleged in the suit for refund are different from or vary from the grounds set forth in the claim for refund, then no claim for refund on the grounds raised in the suit has been filed, and the explicit requirement of Section 7422(a) has not been fulfilled. A variance can take the form of a legal theory variance or a factual variance.[338] However, it appears that courts are especially strict where the variance is on the facts as opposed to a legal theory supported by the disclosed facts.[339] Still, it is difficult to predict what will be found to constitute a factual variance or a legal variance,[340] although a legal theory variance may be identified if the factual basis for the ground is entirely different from the one stated in the refund claim.[341]

It is also said that an issue raised in litigation, but not specifically referred to in the refund claim, may meet the requirements of a formal claim, "if the newly raised issue was subsidiary to, or an integral part of, the grounds presented in the refund claim such that the omitted issue must have necessarily been considered by the Service in its review of the refund claim."[342] Lockheed,

---

[338] Hall v. United States, 78-1 USTC ¶ 9126 (Ct. Cl.), aff'd, 78-1 USTC ¶ 9420 (Ct. Cl. 1977) (legal theory variance); Hattaway v. United States, 78-2 USTC ¶ 9581 (Ct. Cl. 1978) (same; failure to raise issue of transferee liability); Sturdivant v. United States, 80-1 USTC ¶ 9422 (DVI 1980) (legal theory variance). Compare Cook v. United States, 599 F2d 400 (Ct. Cl. 1979) (factual variance).

[339] See Burlington N., Inc. v. United States, 82-1 USTC ¶ 9211 (Ct. Cl. Tr. Div. 1982) (discussing cases on this point), rev'd, 684 F2d 866 (Ct. Cl. 1982). See Oregon Metallurgical Corp. v. United States, 12 Cl. Ct. 447, 87-2 USTC ¶ 9388 (1987) (facts were disclosed, but the statutory basis was omitted; variance was not found because no other information than given facts would have been required to make a determination on omitted statutory reference claims).

[340] In Harrison v. United States, 475 F. Supp. 408 (ED Pa. 1979), aff'd in unpublished opinion, 620 F2d 288 (3d Cir. 1980), a refund claim that "the fair market value of the shares received . . . [on] exercise of the qualified stock options had a value substantially lower than the public trading price" was held not to permit the taxpayer to contest the Service valuation on a blockage theory. Compare this result with Dahlgren v. United States, 553 F2d 434 (5th Cir.), reh'g denied per curiam, 557 F2d 456 (5th Cir. 1977), where the taxpayers filed a claim stating that they did not "own more than 80 percent in value of the outstanding stock," and the circuit court held that they were nevertheless permitted to show that a claim against the shares reduced their value to below 80 percent in value. It may be difficult to derive much guidance from a harsh decision such as *Harrison*, but the case illustrates the care required in drafting sufficient claims to cover actual and potential contentions.

[341] See Ottawa Silica Co. v. United States, 82-1 USTC ¶ 9308 (Ct. Cl. Tr. Div. 1982), aff'd per curiam, 699 F2d 1124 (Fed. Cir. 1983) (gross income from mining was distinct from depletion rate claim); Angst v. United States, 87-2 USTC ¶ 9619 (ED Wash. 1987) (deferral of tax because of rollover of gain on sale of residence not raised in refund claim).

[342] Lockheed Martin Corp. v. United States, 80 AFTR2d 97-5917 (Ct. Cl. 1997).

for example, had filed a claim for listed research expenses, but during pretrial discovery discovered other research expenses. The Court of Federal Claims held that the discovered expenses were not factually subsidiary to, or an integral part of, a claim for other research expenditures, despite the revenue agent's report noting that if the taxpayer were successful on other grounds, it would be entitled to a refund on the newly discovered ground, cases analyzed. Under this "theory of recovery" review, if the only element in the formal claim that is changed is the amount of the claim, and the factual and legal grounds remain the same, "the scope of the litigation is not expanded beyond the factual and legal grounds that the IRS was able to review during its administrative review of the refund claim."[343] In the *Lockheed* case, however, the court said that the failure to specifically mention the contract for which the deductions of the expenditures was being sought, denied the Service the opportunity to review the expenditures.

The stringency of the rules requiring a later refund suit to be based on the same grounds as in a filed claim for refund is mitigated by the developed law recognizing informal claims,[344] amendments of filed claims, and the waiver doctrine.[345] The objective, of course, is to avoid having to rely on these authorities by preparing a "ground-sufficient" and "fact-sufficient" claim for refund at the outset.

[5] Amendment and the Waiver Doctrine

A claim is required to "set forth in detail each ground upon which credit or refund is claimed and facts sufficient to apprise the Commissioner of the exact basis thereof."[346] This action facilitates administrative review of a claim, and avoids losing the opportunity to litigate a claim in a subsequent refund suit. Since a claim for refund is a prerequisite to a refund suit, the failure of a claim for refund to set forth a ground raised in a later refund suit constitutes a "substantial variance" between the claim and the suit, thus barring the taxpayer from litigating the matter not previously raised.[347] Some circumstances make it necessary to supplement a filed claim. For example, further information is discovered after the claim has been filed or the original claim was incomplete or deficient in some way because it was prepared and filed by the taxpayer or an-

---

[343] Lockheed Martin Corp. v. United States, 80 AFTR2d 97-5917 (Ct. Cl. 1997).

[344] See supra ¶ 11.08[2].

[345] See infra ¶ 11.11.

[346] Reg. § 301.6402-2(b)(1). Even if the original claim has been allowed, an amendment raising a new ground for refund is untimely if filed after the period of limitations. Stevning v. United States, 79-2 USTC ¶ 9593 (CD Cal. 1979), aff'd per curiam, 654 F2d 604 (9th Cir. 1981).

[347] IRC § 7422(a); United States v. Felt & Tarrant Mfg. Co., 283 US 269 (1931).

other practitioner. Should a filed claim be found inadequate or incomplete, it may be amended at any time before (1) it has been rejected and (2) the period of limitations for filing a claim has expired.[348] Once the claim has been rejected, there is simply no claim pending to amend.[349] If the claim has not been rejected and the period of limitations is open, the claim may be amended, and the amendment and the original claim constitute a single claim.[350] Also, if the period of limitations has not expired, even if the original claim has been rejected, an entirely new claim for refund may be filed.

The waiver doctrine developed out of inconsistent administrative response to the particularity requirements imposed by the regulation. The Service adopted the specificity requirement in a claim for refund to facilitate the administrative review of the claim. It is not required by the statute, which only requires the submission of timely claims to give protection against stale demands.[351] The Service has no authority to ignore the statutory requirement that a timely claim be filed, but it may choose to waive the requirements of its own regulation where it has not been misled by the formal deficiency of a claim to state the ground on which refund was sought.[352] In basic terms, the waiver doctrine recognizes that it is unfair for the Service to use a taxpayer's failure to state the ground on which refund is claimed as the basis for rejecting a claim where it has not been misled by the formal deficiency of the claim and

---

[348] United States v. Memphis Cotton Oil Co., 288 US 62 (1939); Angelus Milling Co. v. Comm'r, 325 US 293 (1945).

[349] See United States v. Memphis Cotton Oil Co., 288 US 62 (1939); Allstate Ins. Co. v. United States, 550 F2d 629 (Ct. Cl. 1977); Kelson v. United States, 503 F2d 1291 (10th Cir. 1974); Stratmore v. United States, 463 F2d 1195 (3d Cir. 1972); Solomon v. United States, 57 F2d 150 (2d Cir. 1932). Compare Pink v. United States, 105 F2d 183 (2d Cir. 1939) (reopening of rejected claim restored its status as an amendable claim).

[350] See United States v. Memphis Cotton Oil Co., 288 US 62 (1939). When a refund claim is filed that repeats portions of the first claim and also alleges other grounds for recovery, the new portion is a separate claim for refund. Allstate Ins. Co. v. United States, 550 F2d 629 (Ct. Cl. 1977); Charlson Realty Co. v. United States, 384 F2d 434 (Ct. Cl. 1967). Although the portion that repeats the first claim is a "single claim," the date of filing is not pushed back to the date of the second claim. Thus, even if the second claim is filed after the three-years-from-filing period, a taxpayer is not limited to the tax paid within the preceding two years. Allstate Ins. Co. v. United States, supra (first claim had been disallowed so that repeated portion was a nullity). On the other hand, a second claim for refund on grounds identical to those in the first does not extend the two-year period for instituting a refund suit, so that a refund suit brought more than two years after disallowance of the first claim is untimely. Einson-Freeman Co. v. Corwin, 112 F2d 683 (2d Cir.), cert. denied, 311 US 693 (1940); Justice v. United States, 616 F. Supp. 829 (WD Va. 1985) (accord).

[351] United States v. Memphis Cotton Oil Co., 288 US 62 (1939).

[352] Tucker v. Alexander, 275 US 228 (1927) (government stipulated that a ground not stated in refund claim was the only one to be decided by the court; held, express waiver as to form and contents of claim).

has considered the claim on its merits. Accordingly, the Service is estopped from rejecting a claim on this basis.

The waiver doctrine has been applied in disputes over the effectiveness of an amendment of a timely claim made after the period for filing a refund claim has run. An untimely amendment of a timely general claim is effective if (1) the original claim has not been rejected at the time the amendment is filed and (2) the amendment merely makes clear specific matters the Commissioner has already considered by investigating the original, formally defective claim.[353] In this situation, the amendment and the original claim constitute a single timely claim because the Commissioner is not asked to make any inquiry other than the one he has already made. Although the Commissioner might have rejected the original claim under the regulation, he has waived the defect if he has heard the claim on its merits. Under the waiver doctrine, it is crucial that the claim has been investigated or heard. The Commissioner does not waive the specificity requirement of the regulation merely by administrative inaction in not rejecting a general claim. The taxpayer must establish that the Commissioner has unmistakenly focused on the matters in dispute and heard them on their merits.[354]

A waiver-by-conduct standard requires a fact-based inquiry, and so it is difficult to predict whether waiver will be found in any particular case. The taxpayer carried the burden in *United States v. Memphis Cotton Oil Co.*[355] because the Commissioner investigated a general claim and, importantly, had notified the taxpayer that an overassessment had been made before rejecting the claim under the regulations. In *Angelus Milling Co. v. Commissioner,*[356] the taxpayer failed to prove that the Service had actually considered its claim rather than the claim of a related taxpayer. Without proof like the correspondence in *Memphis Oil*, the evidence was ambiguous, and so no waiver was found. As a comparison of these cases suggests, waiver is more likely to be found where the taxpayer is able to point to some communication from the

---

[353] United States v. Memphis Cotton Oil Co., 288 US 62 (1939). Compare Nucorp, Inc. v. United States, 23 Cl. Ct. 234 (1991) (original claim did not give adequate notice of specific nature of claim and was amended after notice of disallowance). A taxpayer was permitted to amend a claim for refund after the statute of limitations on filing a claim had run. In this case, the amended claim corrected a computational error in the timely filed claim and the legal basis for the claim had not changed. Mutual Assurance, Inc. v. United States, 76 AFTR2d 95-5732 (11th Cir. 1995) (in investigating the original claims the Service discovered that the taxpayer had understated the refund amounts; taxpayer then made an informal amendment to its formal claim).

[354] Angelus Milling Co. v. United States, 325 US 293 (1945).

[355] United States v. Memphis Cotton Oil Co., 288 US 62 (1939).

[356] Angelus Milling Co. v. Comm'r, 325 US 293 (1945).

Service establishing that the matters in dispute have actually been considered.[357] The Supreme Court stated:

> The showing should be unmistakable that the Commissioner has in fact seen fit to dispense with the formal requirements and to examine the merits of the claim.... The Commissioner's attention should have been focused on the merits of the particular dispute. The evidence should be clear that the Commissioner understood the specific claim that was made even though there was a departure from form in its submission.[358]

A review of the cases shows that courts have found waiver where the Service notified the taxpayer that his claim would be rejected as soon as it was filed. The courts have also found that the Service is right to insist on a procedurally correct claim[359] where the Service's notice to the taxpayer said, "We have reviewed your claim...,"[360] correspondence between taxpayer and the Department of Justice relating to the settlement of a pending tax refund case established that an alternative ground not included in the claim had been considered,[361] evidence showed the Service considered claim on its merits, despite Service argument that claim denied "per audit determination" was not action on merits.[362]

The purported amendment of a specific timely claim and the amendment of a general claim are treated differently. The Service has no authority to waive the statutory period of limitations for filing refund claims, and so a taxpayer's claim limited to a specific item may not be amended out of time to

---

[357] Compare ITT Corp. v. United States, 770 F. Supp. 863 (SDNY 1991) (careful analysis on whether there was government investigation of issue omitted from refund claim; no investigation found). When taxpayer filed an original 1982 return calculating an add-on minimum tax based on intangible drilling costs, then a timely refund claim reducing the amount of the intangible drilling costs and a timely loss carryback to 1982 from 1984, and finally a third claim reducing the intangible drilling costs to zero after the statute, the third claim was held to be an untimely new claim, not an amendment of one of the earlier claims. Angle v. United States, 996 F2d 252 (10th Cir. 1993) (the Service's adjustments based on claims did not constitute examination and waiver of variance between claim and tax-benefit claims in refund suit, especially when agent rejected final claim).

[358] Angelus Milling Co. v. United States, 325 US 293, 297–298 (1945).

[359] Zeeman v. United States, 395 F2d 861 (2d Cir. 1968). But see United States v. Felt & Tarrant Mfg. Co., 283 US 269 (1931) (indicating that the Service may not waive the filing of a claim under any circumstances).

[360] Martinez v. United States, 595 F2d 1147 (9th Cir. 1979) (government's argument that claim was not specific was rejected).

[361] United States v. Henderson Clay Prods., 324 F2d 7 (5th Cir. 1963), cert. denied, 377 US 917 (1964). Henderson is similar to Tucker v. Alexander, 275 US 228 (1927), in that waiver was found in part on the basis of the failure of an attorney for the Commissioner to object to the inadequacy of the claim.

[362] Goulding v. United States, 929 F2d 329 (7th Cir. 1991).

seek refund on account of other, unrelated items.[363] As a result, where the Service investigates an untimely amendment raising entirely new grounds from the timely specific claim, the Service cannot waive the requirement that the new claim be timely filed.[364] Even if a taxpayer files a timely specific claim, which the Service investigates, and the taxpayer later files an untimely amendment that claims a refund on a ground that is entirely different from the original claim, the amendment is simply not an amendment of the timely claim, but rather an untimely new claim.[365] In another early Supreme Court case, *United States v. Andrews*,[366] the taxpayer's original claim was based on a deductible loss owing to worthless securities, and its second claim was based on the ground that proceeds from the sale of stock had been erroneously treated as an item of dividend income. Investigation of the first claim would not have led to a consideration of the ground raised in the purported amendment. Once the document purporting to be an amendment is found instead to be a new claim, the waiver doctrine no longer applies.[367]

Procedurally, the waiver issue usually arises when the government moves to dismiss the plaintiff/taxpayer's complaint in the refund action on the ground that the claim is insufficient. At this point, the taxpayer cannot amend a refund claim, but can argue that the claim is sufficient and that the Commissioner waived any defects. Obviously, in such a motion, the case law demonstrates how critical it is for the taxpayer to produce communications to and from the Service to prove either that the Service considered the ground on which the taxpayer wishes to proceed or that the Service had stated it would reject the claim even if it were submitted. Any administrative refund is void unless a taxpayer submits a timely claim for refund to the Service for processing.[368] Also, a refund court (either a federal district court or the U.S. Court of Federal Claims) does not have jurisdiction over a taxpayer's suit for refund, unless a

---

[363] United States v. Andrews, 302 US 517 (1938); Honeywell, Inc. v. United States, 973 F2d 638 (8th Cir. 1992) (claim of WIN credits for 622 workers constituted new untimely claim, not amendment of timely claim).

[364] United States v. Garbutt Oil Co., 302 US 528 (1938).

[365] United States v. Andrews, 302 US 517 (1938).

[366] United States v. Andrews, 302 US 517 (1938).

[367] When a second claim for refund presents grounds identical to those in a prior claim on which a notice of claim disallowance has been sent, the limitations period begins to run from the notice of claim disallowance on the first claim. Kelson v. United States, 503 F2d 1291, 1293 (10th Cir. 1974); Hiatal v. United States, 675 F2d 239, 242 (9th Cir. 1982). The rationale for the rule is that otherwise a taxpayer could avoid the statute of limitations merely by filing identical refund claims. Jones v. United States, 26 Cl. Ct. 424, 92-2 USTC ¶ 50,468 (Cl. Ct. 1992).

[368] IRC § 6514(a)(1).

claim for refund has been filed and the Service has had at least six months to process the claim.[369]

¶ 11.10 TIME AND PLACE FOR FILING CLAIMS

[1] Timely Filing

For purposes of computing the last day on which a claim for refund can be filed, the day the claim is filed or the tax paid is excluded.[370] If a payment is made on September 30, 2001, the two-years-from-payment period begins to run on October 1, 2001, and does not expire until October 1, 2003. Any claim for refund filed on or before September 30, 2003, would be timely. If the last day for filing a claim for refund falls on a Saturday, Sunday, or "legal holi-day" (as specially defined), a claim filed on the next succeeding day that is not a Saturday, Sunday, or legal holiday is timely.[371] Timely mailing of a claim for refund is considered timely filing, as provided in Section 7502, if the claim (1) is sent in a properly addressed envelope and (2) is postmarked on or before the date for timely filing, or otherwise marked by a private delivery service. If the envelope containing the claim bears a timely postmark, the claim is considered timely filed, even if it is received after the last day of the period prescribed for filing.[372]

---

[369] Section 6523(a)(1) states as follows:

No suit or proceeding under [S]ection 7422(a) for the recovery of any internal reve-nue tax, penalty or other sum, shall be begun before the expiration of 6 months from the date of filing the claim required under [Section 7422(a)] unless the Secretary ren-ders a decision thereon within that time, nor after the expiration of 2 years from the date of mailing by certified mail or registered mail by the Secretary to the taxpayer of a notice of the disallowance of the claim to which the suit or proceeding relates.

[370] IRC § 6501(a).

[371] IRC § 7503. Reg. § 301.7503-1(b) provides that the term "legal holiday" includes all legal holidays in the District of Columbia, as well as all statewide legal holidays. The amount of a refund is not limited under Section 6511(b)(2)(A) where the last day of the limitation period is a Saturday, Sunday, or legal holiday and the claim is filed on the next succeeding day that is not a Saturday, Sunday, or legal holiday. Rev. Rul. 66-118, 1966-1 CB 290.

[372] Reg. § 301.7502-1(a). Note that the timely mailed, timely filed rule of Section 7502 has been held not to apply to a situation where no extension for filing a return has been obtained and a delinquent return claiming a refund of withheld taxes is filed on April 15 of the third year following the due date of the return. King v. United States, 495 F. Supp. 334 (D. Neb. 1980); Lockrey v. United States, 82 AFTR2d 98-6814 (ED Mich. 1998) (return/claim received by the Service on April 19, 1995, two business days after three-year lookback period ended (Apr. 15, 1995), filed too late to recover prepayments of

[2] Place and Manner of Filing

Claims for refund must be filed with the designated Service center.[373] It may become necessary for a taxpayer to prove that a claim for refund was actually filed.[374] A claim for refund may be hand delivered to the office of the appropriate district director rather than a Service center,[375] and proof of hand delivery may be evidenced by an affidavit by the person who made delivery.[376] If a claim is filed by mail, the provisions of the timely mailed, timely filed rules should be followed. These rules are reviewed in Chapter 5. Section 7502 after amendment permits mailing by registered or certified mail, or a recognized private delivery service.[377] The statute considers proper registration or a properly issued certified mail sender's receipt to be prima facie evidence that the claim was delivered to the addressee, provided that the envelope was properly addressed. If a claim is filed by regular mail, the taxpayer has the burden of proving the claim was mailed and posted on or before the date required for

---

tax deemed paid on April 15, 1991, because the mailbox rule of Section 7502(a)(1) did not apply to returns filed after return due date).

[373] Reg. § 301.6402-2(a)(2). If the tax was paid to the Director of International Operations, the claim should be filed with the director. Special rules apply where refunds of alcohol, tobacco, and firearms tax are claimed.

[374] There is division among the courts about whether Section 7502 is the exclusive method of proving delivery of a refund claim. Some courts have said that Section 7502 supersedes the common-law presumption of delivery (only the certified or registered mailing required by Section 7502 suffices). Surowka v. United States, 909 F2d 148 (6th Cir. 1990); Deutsch v. Comm'r, 599 F2d 44 (2d Cir. 1979). But see Wood v. Comm'r, 909 F2d 1155 (8th Cir. 1990) (testimony of postmistress permitted). For other cases showing the division of views, see Sartori v. United States, 88-2 USTC ¶ 9410 (WD Pa. 1988) (taxpayer not permitted to present testimony or other evidence as proof of the actual date of mailing); Buttke v. United States, 87-2 USTC ¶ 9502 (Cl. Ct. 1987); HS&H, Ltd. v. United States, 18 Cl. Ct. 241, 89-2 USTC ¶ 9556 (1989) (absent proof of physical delivery, Section 7502 provides only methods of establishing filing of refund claim). See Hartwick v. United States, 83-2 USTC ¶ 9504 (WDNY 1983) (a claim mailed after the prescribed due date was deemed filed when it was actually received by the Service); King v. United States, 495 F. Supp. 334 (D. Neb. 1980) (the timely mailed, timely filed rule was held not to apply to a refund claim and tax return received by the Service more than three years after the due date); Miller v. United States, 84-2 USTC ¶ 9804 (ND Ohio 1984) (same). In Richard v. United States, 88-1 USTC ¶ 9245 (WD Wash. 1988), refund claims that were deposited in the U.S. mail by the taxpayer's lawyer, which the Service had no record of receiving, were held not to be filed within the statute of limitations. Here, neither of the two exceptions to the physical delivery rule were met: (1) since the refund claim was not received by the Service, the date on the postmark could not be considered the date of delivery, and (2) the claim was not sent by registered mail.

[375] Reg. § 301.6091-1. When a claim is hand-delivered, the Service employee or official receiving the claim should be asked to date-stamp a duplicate of the claim to be retained by the taxpayer.

[376] IRC § 7502(c).

[377] See, e.g., Miller v. United States, 84-2 USTC ¶ 9804 (ND Ohio 1984).

timely filing. Where the timeliness of filing is critical because the expiration of the period for filing is imminent, careful practitioners file duplicate claims.

C. PROCESSING REFUND CLAIMS

¶ 11.11 ADMINISTRATIVE PROCESSING OF CLAIMS

[1] Service Center Review

All requests for refunds and amended returns filed to reduce liabilities previously assessed are filed with regional Service centers, where centralized review and classification of income, excise, and employment claims are conducted.[378] Service center personnel scrutinize all requests for refund (i.e., Forms 1045, 1139, 1040X, and 1120X), informal claims, and amended 1040 or 1120 returns showing decreases in liability, to check for completeness, validity, and timely filing, and to determine whether the claims involve audit matters or should be processed in the Service center.[379] Adjustments in claim cases involving mathematical processing errors, as well as taxpayer contacts to obtain complete schedules (including verification of all needed schedules), are handled at the Service center before the claim is processed and referred for classification. Service center personnel also classify all claims and tentative carryback adjustments after allowance requiring the determination of tax liability or special attention according to audit criteria. Technical personnel in the examination division at the Service centers classify most claims, including amended returns, and make the initial decision to accept a claim if it is determined that the claim issue is allowable in full and that an examination is not warranted.[380] If an examination is believed to be warranted, the claim is referred to the district for examination.

---

[378] Estate and gift tax claims are referred directly to local offices for preliminary examination.

[379] IRM 4511, Centralized Classification of Claims (Nov. 11, 1976); IRM 4512, Preliminary Examination and Disposition of Claims Referred to Examination (Jan. 30, 1987).

[380] Taxpayers who file returns showing overpayments can telephone Service computers to find out the status of their refund checks. See IRS Publication No. 1163 ("Tele-Tax" Guide).

[2] Local Office Review

When a claim is received in the appropriate local office, examination or other audit action must be initiated on the claim promptly. First, the claim is checked to determine whether an examination is permissible or appropriate.[381] For example, a determination is made whether the claim is timely filed, whether the taxpayer waived any refund as part of consideration in a previous settlement, whether the claim relates to a return closed on the basis of a final order of some court, or whether the claim raises issues already allowed. If no such reasons warrant rejection of the claim, it is assigned for examination or survey by a revenue agent. The general procedures for examination of returns, issuance of preliminary letters, district conferences, and reference of cases to field offices of Appeals also apply to cases involving claims for refund of income, estate, and gift taxes.[382] Revenue agents are instructed that examinations initiated in claim cases must be completed as quickly as the taxpayer's cooperation and the complexity of the issues permit.

Examination personnel are instructed to consider both the issues stated in the claim and any offsetting adjustment that may reduce the refundable amount.[383] After the examination, the taxpayer receives a portion of the revenue agent's report, which should disclose the allowance or disallowance of the amount of the claim and the reason therefor. Even where issues stated in a claim are allowed in full, the claim is treated as a partially or wholly disallowed claim if offsetting adjustments are proposed that reduce the refundable amount.[384] Where a claim requests the refund of an amount paid after an audit or examination and assessment, the claim is assigned to the same revenue agent or officer who recommended the assessment. Given the fact that this agent or officer already determined that the taxpayer owed additional tax, it is unlikely that the agent or officer will recommend disallowance of the claim without further investigation (except in unusual circumstances). However, opportunity exists for informal conferences with the agent and the agent's group supervisor. Even if the return has been examined before, it may be appropriate to make use of this conference procedure in certain circumstances, specifically

---

[381] IRM 4512, Preliminary Examination and Disposition of Claims Referred to Examination (Jan. 30, 1987). The full amount of a nondivisible tax need not be paid before a refund claim is considered by the Service, but it must be paid before a refund suit is commenced under the rule of Flora v. United States, 362 US 145 (1960). See IRM 5639.1, Claims for Abatement or Refund, General (Nov. 15, 1985). See also GCM 38932 (Nov. 30, 1982).

[382] IRM 4513, Claims Assigned for Examination (May 2, 1988).

[383] IRM 4513, Claims Assigned for Examination (May 2, 1988).

[384] IRM 4515, Waivers and Acceptances in Claim Disallowance Cases (Jan. 30, 1987). See also Wesley Jung v. United States, 701 F. Supp. 175 (ND Wis. 1988) (district court upheld the government's use of a refund to offset unpaid liability relating to later years).

(1) where no conference was previously held; (2) where there has been a change in the law by way of a favorable court decision or ruling; or (3) where other evidence establishing an error in the treatment of the item has been discovered after the filing of the return or the examination. In short, the taxpayer should employ any available local office conference procedure if the matters presented in the claim have not been previously reviewed within the Service, since otherwise it is unlikely that any previous determination will be reversed.

Disallowance of a claim for refund terminates the administrative processing of the claim. A taxpayer may protest a proposed disallowance or disallowance of a claim for refund and obtain review of local action on the claim by the Appeals Office.[385] However, if the Appeals determination upholds disallowance, or if the Service sends the taxpayer a formal notice of claim disallowance, the taxpayer must file a suit for refund within two years after the date of notice.[386] This statutory period is strictly construed, as are other statutes where the government waives its sovereign immunity.[387] If no notice of claim disallowance is sent, the two-year statute of limitations does not begin to run.

These straightforward rules can trap the unwary when dealing with confusing communications the Service sometimes sends. In *Rosser v. United States*,[388] a taxpayer timely filed a claim for refund, and the Service sent him by certified mail a notice of claim disallowance, which the taxpayer said he did not receive. The taxpayer refiled his refund claim. The Service center sent a form letter stating that the matter was being looked into, but then sent a notice of disallowance stating that the refiled claims were untimely. The first notice of claim disallowance was mailed on January 5, 1988, and the second notice on January 23, 1989. The taxpayer filed his refund suit on January 18, 1991, more than three years after the first notice and five days before the expiration of two years from the date of the second notice. The Eleventh Circuit held that the two-year period of Section 6532(a)(1) for bringing suit "begins to run from the date that the IRS mails, by certified or registered mail, a notice of claim disallowance, regardless of whether the taxpayer actually receives the notice."[389] As described by the circuit court, the legislative history supported Congress's intent to make "the date of disallowance of the claim certain in every case."[390]

---

[385] 26 CFR § 601.106(a)(1)(ii). See ¶ 9.03.

[386] IRC § 6532(a)(1).

[387] United States v. Dalm, 494 US 596 (1990).

[388] Rosser v. United States, 9 F3d 1519 (11th Cir. 1993).

[389] Rosser v. United States, 9 F3d 1519 (11th Cir. 1993). The fact that a notice of claim disallowance is not sent by certified or registered mail is not material when the taxpayer actually receives the notice. See Finkelstein v. United States, 96 TNT 195-10 (DNJ 1996) (letter opinion not for publication).

[390] Rosser v. United States, 9 F3d 1519 (11th Cir. 1993).

In also rejecting the taxpayer's argument that the two-year period had been equitably tolled, the circuit court noted that in cases where equitable tolling had been applied, "the IRS incorrectly informed the taxpayer, in writing, that the taxpayer had two years from the mailing date of a later disallowance in which to file suit."[391] Since the second notice of claim disallowance had no such language or misleading representation, there was no basis for equitable estoppel of the Service.

Determination of whether the suit has been filed within the permissible period is governed by Section 6532 and by the rules of the district courts and the Court of Federal Claims, respectively.[392] Not only must the suit for refund be commenced within two years after the notice of claim disallowance, but the full amount of the disputed tax must be paid.[393] Consequently, a refund court will have no jurisdiction over a suit for refund unless the taxpayer (1) filed a timely claim for refund; (2) commenced the suit within the applicable period; (3) paid the full amount of the disputed tax; and (4) raised the same grounds in the complaint as those that were raised in (i.e., did not vary from) the claim for refund.

If a taxpayer files a claim for refund to satisfy the jurisdictional prerequisite of filing a refund claim before instituting a suit for refund in court, Section 6532(a)(3) permits a taxpayer to accelerate a claim disallowance by filing a written waiver of the requirement that the Service must send the notice of claim disallowance. The waiver, Form 2297 (Waiver of Statutory Notification of Claim Disallowance), accomplishes the same purpose as the sending of a notice of claim disallowance by certified mail. (See Form 11.6.) The effect of this waiver is to start the running of the two-year period for filing suit on the claim from the date the waiver is filed.[394] Although the statute is clear, the Service's handling of this matter can cause confusion, and in some cases the Service has been estopped from asserting that a tax refund suit was barred because it was brought more than two years after the signing of waivers of no-

---

[391] Rosser v. United States, 9 F3d 1519 (11th Cir. 1993).

[392] See, e.g., Rohmann v. United States, 25 Cl. Ct. 274, 92-1 USTC ¶ 50,158 (1992) (claims court did not have jurisdiction because suit commenced two years and one day after the date of notice of claim disallowance).

[393] See supra ¶ 11.06[4].

[394] Reg. § 301.6532-1(c) states that the signing of the waiver does not permit the taxpayer to file suit any earlier than he otherwise could have. See Western Int'l Hotels Co. v. United States, 399 F2d 209 (Ct. Cl. 1968) (effect of filing waiver); Smith v. United States, 539 F. Supp. 137 (D. Neb. 1982) (same). The Fourth Circuit has held that the two-year period begins to run on the date the waiver of notice of claim disallowance is filed, not the date the Service's Appeals officer acknowledged receipt of the waiver. In addition, the court held that the waiver is "filed" as the term is used in Section 6532(a)(3) "when it is delivered to and received by the person or agency, with whom it is to be filed." Hull v. United States, 146 F3d 235 (4th Cir. 1998).

tices of claim disallowances.[395] The Court of Appeals for the Federal Circuit has held that the Court of Federal Claims lacked jurisdiction to hear a refund suit a taxpayer filed more than two years after a waiver of notice of claim disallowance was filed. In the case, the taxpayer filed a waiver of notice of claim disallowance, but the Service nevertheless sent the taxpayer a proposed notice of claim disallowance, and so, the taxpayer requested a conference, and made inquiries regarding the claim. Finally, the Service disallowed the claim.[396]

Although the Supreme Court's ruling in *Brockamp*[397] interpreted Section 6511, the statute of limitations on filing a claim for refund, not Section 6532, the statute of limitations on filing a suit for refund, the Federal Circuit applied *Brockamp*'s reasoning. The circuit court held that regardless of any confusion the Service's actions may have caused the taxpayer, the two-year period provided in Section 6532 does not contain an implied equitable exception, and consideration of equitable principles, such as estoppel, are "inappropriate." In another case of this type, *Marcinkowsky v. United States*,[398] the Service sent the taxpayer notices of claim disallowance, and the taxpayer filed administrative appeals. The Federal Circuit held that the two-year statute started to run with the date of the notice of claim disallowance. The situation in *Marcinkowsky* illustrates how a taxpayer can suffer when the Service fails to follow its own procedures. Under the Service's procedures, the taxpayer should receive a notice of proposed claim disallowance, which the taxpayer can then adminis-

---

[395] Exchange & Sav. Bank of Berlin v. United States, 226 F. Supp. 56 (D. Md. 1964) (waiver was followed by a notice of claim disallowance, and suit was brought within two years after claim disallowance); Miller v. United States, 500 F2d 1007 (2d Cir. 1974) (same). Ohio Nat'l Life Ins. Co. v. United States, 922 F2d 320 (6th Cir. 1990) (action was held timely, but only because lower court found waiver was not proved to have been filed). See also Heath v. United States, 219 Ct. Cl. 582 (1979), and Southeast Bank v. United States, 676 F2d 660 (Ct. Cl. 1982) (notices of disallowance sent); Haber v. United States, 831 F2d 1051 (Fed. Cir. 1987) (taxpayer entitled to rely on Service agent's notice to accountant that prior notice of disallowance had been withdrawn).

Compare Henry v. United States, 88-1 USTC ¶ 9321 (Cl. Ct. 1988), aff'd, 870 F2d 634 (Fed. Cir. 1989) (applying *Tonkonogy* statement of estoppel elements and finding no estoppel where a taxpayer filed waivers of notices of claim disallowance, but continued to receive notices and other communications from the Service). In affirming *Henry v. United States*, the Federal Circuit cited Heckler v. Community Health Servs., 467 US 51 (1984) ("the party claiming the estoppel must have relied on its adversary's conduct . . . and that reliance must have been reasonable in that the party claiming the estoppel did not know nor should it have known that its adversary's conduct was misleading"). Consequently, where a taxpayer files a waiver of claims disallowance, he must take care that suit is brought within the two-year period following the filing of the waiver, sometimes in the face of conflicting signals from the Service. See, e.g., Continental Ill. Corp. v. United States, 727 F. Supp. 425 (ND Ill. 1989) (Form 2297 started running of two-year statute for filing suit; later audit and disallowance did not result in revocation of waiver).

[396] RHI Holdings v. United States, 81 AFTR2d 98-1789 (Fed. Cir. 1998).

[397] Brockamp v. United States, 117 S. Ct. 849 (1997).

[398] Marcinkowsky v. United States, 84 AFTR2d 99-5622 (Fed. Cl. 1999).

tratively appeal. Apparently, the first notice *Marcinkowsky* received was the notice of claim disallowance, warning of the start of the two-year period, but also offering an administrative appeal. Unless the Service informs the taxpayer, in the clearest terms, that the claim is disallowed and that administrative appeal and administrative delay will not affect the running of the period for instituting suit, then the Service is only setting a trap for the taxpayer, not providing administrative due process. A strict interpretation of the statute of limitations can lead to unfair results when the Service sends seemingly conflicting communications; in certain cases courts have found that the Service has orally withdrawn a notice of claim disallowance so that the two-year period did not begin to run until it sent a later notice of claim disallowance.[399]

Normally, the Service solicits a waiver of claim disallowance at the conclusion of the agent's investigation or district conference, if any, where a thirty-day letter with the agent's report is sent to the taxpayer. If the Service determines that a claim should be disallowed in full and no adjustments to the tax liability are necessary, the Service will also solicit a Form 3363 (Acceptance of Proposed Disallowance of Claim for Refund or Credit). (See Form 11.7.) However, if the claim is disallowed in full and adjustments to the tax liability are also proposed, the agreement will be solicited on Form 4549 (Income Tax Audit Changes) in field audit cases, or on similar forms (Form 1902-A or Form 1902-B) in office examinations.[400]

An alternative to the taxpayer's filing a notice of claim disallowance is a request that the Service immediately disallow the claim for refund. The Service says that a notice of claim disallowance will then promptly be sent to the taxpayer.[401] On receipt of the disallowance, the taxpayer has two years to file a refund suit in a district court or the Court of Federal Claims.

---

[399] See Haber v. United States, 831 F2d 1051, modified on reh'g 846 F2d 1379 (Fed. Cir. 1988); see also Cooper v. United States, 84 AFTR2d 99-6222 (WDNC 1999).

[400] IRM 4515, Waivers and Acceptances in Claim Disallowances Cases (Jan. 30, 1987).

[401] IR 1600 (Apr. 26, 1976), 1976 CCH 9 6609.

FORM 11.6
WAIVER OF STATUTORY NOTIFICATION OF CLAIM DISALLOWANCE

Form **2297** (Rev. March 1982)	Department of the Treasury — Internal Revenue Service **Waiver of Statutory Notification of Claim Disallowance**

I, Jane Doe, 123-45-6789 of One Park Place, Anytown, NY 00000

(Name, SSN or EIN)   *(Number, Street, City or Town, State, ZIP Code)*

waive the requirement under Internal Revenue Code section 6532(a)(1) that a notice of claim disallowance be sent to me by certified or registered mail for the claims for credit or refund shown in column (d), below.

    I understand that the filing of this waiver is irrevocable and it will begin the 2-year period for filing suit for refund of the claims disallowed as if the notice of disallowance had been sent by certified or registered mail.

Claims

(a) Taxable Period Ended	(b) Kind of Tax	(c) Amount of Claim	(d) Amount of Claim Disallowed
12/31/2000	Income	$10,000	$5,000

If you file this waiver for a joint return, both you and your spouse must sign the original and duplicate of this form. Sign your name exactly as it appears on the return. If you are acting under power of attorney for your spouse, you may sign as agent for him or her.

For an agent or attorney acting under a power of attorney, a power of attorney must be sent with this form if not previously filed.

For a partnership with excise or employment tax liability, all partners must sign. However, one partner may sign with appropriate evidence of authorization to act for the partnership.

For a person acting in a fiduciary capacity (executor, administrator, trustee), file Form 56, Notice Concerning Fiduciary Relationship, with this form if not previously filed.

For a corporation, enter the name of the corporation followed by the signature and title of the officer(s) authorized to sign.

Your Signature ➤	/s/ Jane Doe _____ (Date signed)
Spouse's Signature If A Joint Return Was Filed ➤	_____ (Date signed)
Taxpayer's Representative Sign Here ➤	/s/ Joe Smith _____ (Date signed)
Partnership/ Corporate Name:	_____
Partners/ Corporate Officers Sign Here	➤ _____ (Title) _____ (Date signed)
	➤ _____ (Title) _____ (Date signed)

NOTE — Filing this waiver within 6 months from the date the claim was filed will not permit filing a suit for refund before the 6-month period has elapsed unless a decision is made by the Service within that time disallowing the claims.

U.S. GOVERNMENT PRINTING OFFICE : 1985 O - 484-015 (20697)

Form 2297 (Rev. 3-82)

FORM 11.7 _____
ACCEPTANCE OF PROPOSED DISALLOWANCE OF CLAIM FOR REFUND OR CREDIT

Form **3363** (Rev. November 1983)	**Acceptance of Proposed Disallowance of Claim for Refund or Credit** Department of the Treasury — Internal Revenue Service

Name(s), SSN or EIN, and address of taxpayer(s) *(Number, Street, City or Town, State, ZIP Code)*

Jane Jones   123–45–6789

One Park Place

Anytown, NY 00000

Year or Period	Date Claim Filed	Kind of Tax	Amount of Claim	Amount of Claim Disallowed	Amount of Claim Allowed
12/31/2000	11/4/2001	Income	$2,000	$1,500	$500

I accept the proposal of the Internal Revenue Service to disallow the claim(s) to the extent described above. This means only that I do not want the Service to consider the claim(s). It does not waive my right to file suit on the disallowance.

If you file this acceptance for a joint return, both you and your spouse must sign the original and duplicate of this form. Sign your name exactly as it appears on the return. If you are acting under power of attorney for your spouse, you may sign as agent for him or her.	**Your Signature** ▶	/s/ Jane Jones .... (Date)
	Spouse's Signature If A Joint Return Was Filed ▶	.... (Date)
For an agent or attorney acting under a power of attorney, a power of attorney must be sent with this form if not previously filed.	**Taxpayer's Representative Sign Here** ▶	/s/ Joe Smith .... (Date)
For a partnership with excise or employment tax liability, all partners must sign. However, one partner may sign with appropriate evidence of authorization to act for the partnership.	**Partnership/ Corporate Name** ▶	....
For a person acting in a fiduciary capacity (executor, administrator, trustee), file Form 56, Notice Concerning Fiduciary Relationship, with this form if not previously filed.	**Partners/ Corporate Officers Sign Here** ▶	.... (Title) (Date)
For a corporation, enter the name of the corporation followed by the signature and title of the officer(s) authorized to sign.		.... (Title) (Date)

☆ U.S. Government Printing Office: 1983—421-041/0431

Form **3363** (Rev. 11-83)

[3] The Refund Check or Payment

Checks in payment of claims allowed are drawn to the order of the taxpayer or fiduciary entitled to payment. These checks are sent directly to the person(s) who made the claim or to the claimant in the case of an attorney or agent who has filed a power of attorney.[402] The Service identifies tax refund checks so that taxpayers can tell exactly what class of tax and period the check covers. The tax class is indicated in symbols in the right-hand corner of the check under the box reflecting the refund amount—for example, "TAX REF" (individual income tax returns), "CORP REF" (corporate income tax refund), "W/ FICA REF" (withholding or Federal Insurance Contributions Act tax refund), and "FUTA REF" (Federal Unemployment Tax Act refund). The period covered is indicated on the left-hand side under the date of the check. The check also shows the regional Service center where it was processed. Where there is a delay in the sending of a refund check and initial inquiries to the Service center have proved unsuccessful, the local taxpayer advocate can be asked to follow up on the inquiry.[403] Tax refunds of $1 million or more are wire-transferred to the financial institution serving the taxpayer if the taxpayer files a written request, Form 8302 (Application for Electronic Funds Transfer (EFT)).[404] However, the wire transfer procedure is a privilege not a right so that where a taxpayer requested a refund by wire transfer and the Service sent a check by mail, the taxpayer is not entitled to additional interest resulting from the delayed receipt.[405]

Interest on overpayments is described in Chapter 6. Briefly, interest is paid on a refund of tax to individual taxpayers at the overpayment rate.[406] Where large corporate overpayments are involved, interest is paid on the refund at a lower rate.[407]

¶ 11.12 JOINT COMMITTEE REVIEW

The Service does not have unfettered authority to refund or credit large overpayments. Among its other investigative functions involving the operation and

---

[402] Reg. § 301.6402-2(f). A refund check need not be mailed to the attorney representing the taxpayer, but can be mailed to the taxpayer, fiduciary, or the like. Carroll v. United States, 50 AFTR2d 82-6111 (ED Wash. 1981).

[403] For a description of the Taxpayer Advocate's Office, see ¶ 15.02.

[404] Ann. 85-14, 1985-4 IRB 43.

[405] Onan Corp. v. United States, 19 Cl. Ct. 678, 90-1 USTC ¶ 50,136 (Cl. Ct. 1990) (option of wire transfer creates no substantive right).

[406] IRC §§ 6611, 6621.

[407] IRC § 6621(c).

effect of the tax laws, the Joint Committee on Taxation reviews cases involving large refunds.[408] The Joint Committee on Taxation has ten members of Congress, five selected from the tax committees of each house (three from the majority party and two from the minority), and employs a full-time staff.[409] No refund or credit of any income, gift, or estate tax[410] (i.e., a Section 6405(a) refund or credit) in excess of $2 million may be made until thirty days after an administrative report of the proposed refund has been submitted to the Joint Committee for review.[411] The report the Service is required to make to the Joint Committee must provide (1) the name of the person to whom the refund or credit is to be made; (2) the amount; and (3) a summary of the facts and the Commissioner's decision.[412] The Code provides only for oversight review for a period of thirty days by the Committee, not for any supervisory role in making a refund or credit of an overpayment.[413] If the Joint Committee staff has any questions or advises the Service that it does not approve a proposed refund for a particular reason, the case is sent back to the Service, further investigation is made, and no refund is actually paid until some agreement with the Joint Committee is reached.

The $2 million rule has a number of limited exceptions. Credits or refunds allowed by reason of tentative carryback adjustments or tentative amorti-

---

[408] Joint Committee review is the only review of a decision to refund or credit an overpayment. At one time, the General Accounting Office disapproved refunds of interest on certain overpayments until Congress prohibited this and other administrative review by adding Section 6406 to the Code. For a critical history of the Joint Committee's review of refunds, recommending that members of Congress be regularly informed of the results of Joint Committee reviews, see Erbsen, "The Joint Committee Refund Review Function: Is It Worth a Damn?" 72 Tax Notes 227 (July 8, 1996).

For Examination's Joint Committee procedures, see IRM Part 4, Joint Committee Handbook 4.3.5; and Appeals' procedures in Joint Committee cases, see IRM 8.9.1, Joint Committee (JC) Case Procedures.

[409] The committee is established pursuant to the provisions of Sections 8001–8023 of the Code.

[410] Certain other taxes are included, namely any tax imposed with respect to public charities, private foundations, operators' trust funds, pension plans, or real estate investment trusts under Chapter 41, 42, 43, or 44 of the Code, as well as war profits and excess profits taxes. IRC § 6405(a).

[411] IRC §§ 6405(a), 6405(b), amended by the Omnibus Budget Reconciliation Act of 1990, § 11834(a), effective as of November 5, 1990, except for credits or refunds on which reports have been written before that date. However, the Joint Committee may conduct a program of postaudit review on selected large cases and issues. See HR Conf. Rep. No. 166, reprinted in 1990-3 CB (vol. 3) 1142–1143. In 2000, the statutory rate was increased to $2 million from $1 million.

[412] IRC § 6405(a).

[413] See American Enka Corp., 30 TC 684, 694 (1958) (acq.), (appeals by Commissioner and taxpayer dismissed; Joint Committee "has a watchdog rather than a supervisory function").

zation are not subject to review by the Joint Committee.[414] Any tentative refund or credit allowed under Section 6411 is made without Joint Committee review until such time as the Service has actually audited the taxpayer's return and determined that the taxpayer is entitled to a refund or credit in excess of $2 million (in which case the refund or credit requires a report and action by the Joint Committee).[415] Similarly, refunds attributable to certain disaster losses may be made before the submission of any report to the Joint Committee.[416]

However, other procedures may push cases into the Joint Committee category. In determining whether the $2 million limit is reached (1) interest is added to the principal amount of the tax refund and (2) the overpayments for more than one year are added together,[417] but (3) an overassessment for one year is not offset by a deficiency of another year.[418] Special rules apply where a tentative credit or refund is involved. Section 6405(b) requires that a tentative credit or refund allowed under Section 6411 not be added to another overpayment. Rather, it is first reduced by any deficiency for the year. For example, if a tentative or refund credit for 2001 were $1.25 million and an examination of the return resulted in the determination of a $270,000 deficiency in the same tax, the case would not be a Joint Committee case, because the tentative allowance reduced by the deficiency is $980,000. On the other hand, if the tentative refund were $1.40 million, and an examination resulted in the determination of an overpayment of $970,000 in the same tax year, the case would not be reportable to the Joint Committee because neither the Section 6405(a) amount of $970,000 nor the Section 6405(b) amount of $940,000 is in excess of $2 million.[419]

---

[414] IRC § 6405(b).

[415] IRC § 6405(b).

[416] IRC § 6405(c).

[417] See Schmitt v. Kavanaugh, 91 F. Supp. 659 (ED Mich. 1950).

[418] The Service has also ruled that "an overpayment and a deficiency relating to two separate taxpayers, which have been reported on two separate returns, cannot be aggregated under Section 6405(a) of the Code, since each liability is dealt with independently." Rev. Rul. 82-77, 1981-1 CB 582 (merged corporation's deficiency for a premerger tax may not be netted against an overpayment of its merger partner for a premerger year to determine whether the Service must make a report to the Joint Committee). IRM 8.9.1, Joint Committee (JC) Case Procedures, 5.4, JC Jurisdiction—Offsetting Deficiency and Overpayment Years (Apr. 14, 1997) ("[i]n determining jurisdiction under both IRC §§ 6405(a) and 6405(b), do not offset a taxpayer's deficiency for one year against an overpayment for another year"). In determining jurisdiction under Section 6405, Appeals may offset a taxpayer's agreed deficiency for one year against an overpayment for another year "in the same Appeals work unit" to determine whether there is a net refund or credit in excess of $1 million (and $2 million) limitation. IRM 8.9.1, Joint Committee (JC) Case Procedures, 5.5, JC Jurisdiction—No Offsetting Deficiencies (Jan. 27, 2000).

[419] IRM 8.9.1, Joint Committee (JC) Case Procedures, 5.3.1 (Jan. 27, 2000).

Authority to make reports to the Joint Committee as required by Section 6405(a) has been delegated.[420] Final action on the report in the Service is taken on behalf of the Commissioner by the Assistant Commissioner (Examination).[421] Cases reportable to the Joint Committee do not require greater documentation or a more intense audit than the Service makes in regular cases under its "quality audit standards."[422] In agreed cases under the jurisdiction of a local office, the case is reviewed by a staff of Joint Committee coordinators located in an office in the same city as the area headquarters. These coordinators prepare the report for the Joint Committee. The Appeals Office prepares reports in unagreed cases and cases under its jurisdiction where an agreement is reached with the taxpayer.[423] After the report has been prepared and acted on by the Chief (Appeals Office),[424] the file is sent to the Joint Committee counsel in the National Office. As a practical matter, a taxpayer has no opportunity to communicate with Service personnel other than the Appeals officer or perhaps the Joint Committee coordinator, and rarely with the staff of the Joint Committee.

Procedures exist for expedited treatment of Joint Committee cases involving Section 6405(a) refunds.[425] The local office or the Appeals Office submits identifying information including a one-sentence summary of the reasons for the refund and a statement that the request is submitted under expedited refund procedures. Related cases (cases where an adjustment in one year may affect the tax in another year) are identified. On receipt, the Joint Committee counsel will date stamp a copy of the request, which is then forwarded to the issuing office. When this acknowledgment is received, a request is forwarded to the Service to process a dummy file to schedule a refund on the thirty-first day after the Joint Committee has date-stamped the request. If no notice is received from the Joint Committee within the thirty-day period, the refund is issued. If

---

[420] To expedite the processing of Joint Committee cases and refunds to taxpayers, the authority to sign Joint Committee reports has been redelegated within the Service. See the current version of the committee's Delegation Order No. 154.

[421] Delegation Order No. 154.

[422] TIR 728 (May 19, 1965), 1965 CCH § 6589; TIR 763 (Sept. 22, 1965), 1965 CCH § 6726.

[423] IRM 8.9.1, Joint Committee (JC) Case Procedures, 6.4, Processing Unagreed JC Case Refunds (Apr. 16, 1999); IRM 8.9.1, Joint Committee (JC) Case Procedures, 6.5, JC Case Involving Unagreed Deficiency (Apr. 16, 1999); IRM 8.9.1, Joint Committee (JC) Case Procedures, 6.6, Agreed Refund, Unagreed Deficiency—Docketed JC Case (Apr. 16, 1999).

[424] IRM 8.9.1, Joint Committee Case (JC) Procedures, 7.4, JC Report Format and Processing (Jan. 27, 2000). For the organization and format of this report, see IRM 8.9.1, Joint Committee Case (JC) Procedures, 7.5.1, Format of JC Report—General (Apr. 16, 1999).

[425] IRM 8.9.1, Joint Committee (JC) Case Procedures, 7.6(4), Format of a JC Report—Overview (Apr. 16, 1999).

the Joint Committee notifies the Service that it has no objection, the refund is also issued. On the other hand, if the Joint Committee objects to the refund, the refund is halted and not released.

¶ 11.13 ERRONEOUS REFUNDS

Erroneous refunds are sometimes issued by the Service, and the Code provides a mechanism for recovery of the erroneous payment. A civil action in the name of the United States is authorized to be brought to recover a refund that was erroneously made because (1) the refund was made by the Service after the time permitted for filing a refund claim or (2) a refund suit was not begun by the taxpayer within the two-year period following the disallowance of a filed claim.[426] Once the taxpayer has paid an assessment, however, the Service must obtain a judgment in an erroneous refund suit before it can file a tax lien.[427] This is so because when the taxpayer pays an assessment in full, the assessment is extinguished, and the Service may not administratively collect the assessment, even if it has made an erroneous refund to the taxpayer. The proper procedure for the Service to collect an erroneous refund is an erroneous refund suit under Section 7405 or a new administrative proceeding beginning with the sending of a notice of deficiency for erroneous refund of income, gift, or estate tax.

If a refund is erroneous for some other reason, a suit may also be instituted.[428] Interest is recoverable on the erroneous refund at the underpayment rate from the date of payment of the refund.[429] The statute of limitations on the suit is relatively short (two years, or the same period a taxpayer has to file a claim for refund after a payment is made and a refund is requested), but the two-year period is extended to five years if any part of the refund was "induced by fraud or misrepresentation of a material fact."[430] This means that a

---

[426] IRC § 7405. See also ¶ 14.08[2][g].

[427] Bilzerian v. United States, 78 AFTR2d 96-5201 (11th Cir. 1996) ("once a tax liability is paid, no erroneous refund—whether rebate or non-rebate—can revive it"). In AOD CC-1998-002, the Service acquiesced in the Bilzerian result only, saying, "We acquiesce to the view of the courts that an erroneous refund of an amount paid by the taxpayer in satisfaction of an assessment does not revive that assessment to the extent of the refund."

[428] Bilzerian v. United States, 78 AFTR2d 96-5201 (11th Cir. 1996).

[429] IRC § 6602.

[430] IRC § 6532(b). The ten-year statute of limitations on collection of an assessment has uniformly been held not to apply to collection of erroneous refund, because the original payment of the assessment extinguished it. See Stanley v. United States, 35 Fed. Cl. 493 (1996), following United States v. Wilkes, 946 F2d 1143 (1st Cir. 1991); O'Bryant v. United States, 49 F3d 340 (7th Cir. 1995); Clark v. United States, 63 F3d 83 (1st Cir.

misrepresentation of law will not support a suit for the erroneous refund of tax.[431]

Apart from a civil action for recovery of the erroneous refund, the proceeds of an erroneously issued refund check represent property for purposes of criminal prosecution for unlawfully converting government property. Under the criminal conversion statute, the government is considered to retain a property interest in the proceeds of the check even after it is received by the taxpayer and the check has been negotiated and paid.[432]

1995). The Service has argued that because a deposit is not the payment of tax, Section 6532 does not apply when the Service seeks to recover interest it erroneously paid to a taxpayer on the return of a deposit in the nature of a cash bond. See United States v. Domino Sugar Corp., 84 AFTR2d 99-6322 (SDNY 1999) (motion to dismiss denied so that Service could establish that the remittance was a deposit and not a payment of tax).

[431] See United States v. Indianapolis Athletic Club (IAC), 785 F. Supp. 1336 (SD Ind. 1991) (representation that amounts remitted were tips rather than wages was not a misrepresentation of material fact); United States v. Northern Trust Co., 85 AFTR2d 2000-1429 (ND Ill. 2000) (suit for refund held time-barred because the alleged misrepresentations that third parties were shareholders was not a misrepresentation of fact; whether third parties were shareholders is a legal question or, at most, a mixed question of law and fact).

[432] United States v. McRee, 94-1 USTC ¶ 50,030 (11th Cir. 1993).

CHAPTER **12**

The Criminal Investigation
Function

¶ 12.01 OVERVIEW OF CRIMINAL INVESTIGATION ACTIVITIES

As described in Chapter 7A, the Internal Revenue Code (the Code) and related criminal statutes establish a comprehensive array of criminal penalties imposing criminal sanctions, fines, and imprisonment to punish various types of intentional misconduct and to deter noncompliance with the tax laws.[1] Administratively, Criminal Investigation (CI) special agents "enforce the criminal statutes relating to tax administration and financial crimes in order to encourage and achieve, directly or indirectly, voluntary compliance with the Internal Revenue laws."[2] To achieve its goals, CI investigates suspected criminal violations and recommends prosecution where evidence is sufficient to establish beyond a reasonable doubt that a criminal statute has been violated and that there is a reasonable likelihood of conviction.[3] There is little argument that control of tax evasion is critical to the voluntary reporting system. No threat of sanction is likely to deter those tempted to violate the law unless suspected violators are successfully prosecuted. In addition, conscientious taxpayers are assured that the Internal Revenue Service (the Service) prosecutes violators when prosecutions are publicized, and, as a result, their confidence in the system is strengthened.[3.1] For CI to achieve this Service policy with limited resources, CI uses selective prosecutions of known instances of violation and provides the public with information about these prosecutions.[4] By selecting only those cases where successful prosecution is probable, the Service achieves a high rate of convictions in criminal tax cases.

---

[1] Social scientists have studied the effect of legal sanctions on tax behavior and have found that although the threat of sanctions can deter people from violations, it appears that they also produce some resistance to compliance. Schwartz & Orleans, "On Legal Sanctions," 34 U. Chi. L. Rev. 283 (1967). Techniques utilizing appeals to conscience and civic responsibility were listed as alternative means of securing compliance.

[2] IRM 9.1.1.2, Criminal Investigation Mission (Apr. 7, 1999).

[3] IRM, Chief Counsel Directive Manual, 31.3.1.1, Prosecution Standards (Mar. 5, 1996).

[3.1] IRM 9.3.2.2, Purpose of Publicity (Mar. 19, 1999) ("[o]ne of the most effective methods to encourage voluntary compliance is through publicity of the legal actions which CI undertakes in the enforcement of the laws within CI's jurisdiction"); see also IRM 9.3.2.5, Information Made Available for the Media (Mar. 19, 1999).

[4] IRM 9.3.2.7.3.1, Sentencing (Mar. 19, 1999) ("A good opportunity to promote voluntary compliance exists at the time of sentencing. The Service may notify the media in advance of the date, time, and place of sentencing.").

[1] The Statutory Framework

The Code contains not only the statutes defining specific tax crimes and related provisions dealing with such matters as statutes of limitations, but it also provides CI special agents with much of their statutory authority for conducting investigations to enforce the tax laws.

CI special agents are authorized to examine books and records, to take testimony under oath, and to use summonses for criminal investigation purposes.[5] CI special agents may continue to use a summons for criminal investigation purposes until such time as CI has sent the case to the Justice Department for criminal prosecution or investigation by use of a grand jury (a "Justice Department referral").[6] It should be noted that a special agent's summons authority gives the agent the right to take handwriting exemplars from a taxpayer.[7] Also, the summons a special agent serves on a third-party summons recordkeeper is excluded from the special procedures for third-party summonses, which in general give the taxpayer notice of the summons and an opportunity to move to quash the summons.[8]

Criminal investigators have the authority to serve and execute search warrants, to make arrests for any offense under the tax laws if the offense takes place in the presence of the investigator, and to make arrests for any tax felony if the investigator has reasonable grounds for believing that the person to be arrested has committed or is committing a tax felony.[9]

CI may make seizures of property subject to forfeiture.[10] CI investigators may also engage in undercover operations within certain limitations.[11]

Other statutes reflect the effect of a criminal investigation on certain procedures, ranging from limiting the confidentiality of communications made to a federally authorized tax practitioner to noncriminal tax matters,[12] to provid-

---

[5] IRC § 7602(b). Since a special agent has the authority to issue a summons, related provisions apply in addition to Section 7602. Some of the provisions related to the use and enforcement of a summons are Section 7603, service of a summons; Section 7604, enforcement of a summons; Section 7605, time and place of examination; Section 7609, special procedures for third-party summonses; Section 7610, fees and costs for witnesses; Section 7622, authority to administer oaths and certify; Section 7402, jurisdiction of district courts; and Section 7210, failure to obey summons.

[6] IRC § 7602(d).

[7] United States v. Euge, 444 US 707 (1980).

[8] IRC § 7609(c)(2)(E).

[9] IRC § 7608(b). Search warrants are also authorized by the Criminal Code, Title 18. See 18 USC Chapter 205, and 18 USC §§ 3105 and 3109, together with Fed. R. Crim. P. 41.

[10] See IRC §§ 7608 and 7321, seizure of property intended for use in violating the tax laws.

[11] IRC § 7608(c).

[12] IRC § 7525(a)(2).

ing that the running of the statute of limitations on a prosecution is suspended during certain civil proceedings.[13]

In other areas, a special agent's authority is limited. The Service has the authority to compromise a tax investigation before its referral to the attorney general, but Chief Counsel makes the decision in cases where criminal proceedings are pending, not the special agent and CI; in fact, CI only investigates offers in response to specific requests of Chief Counsel.[14]

[2] CI Investigations

Every CI investigation is a potential criminal prosecution. The overriding prosecution standard governing criminal tax investigations and prosecution recommendations is that the evidence must be sufficient to establish guilt beyond a reasonable doubt, and that there is a reasonable probability of conviction.[15] That a criminal prosecution, and a successful prosecution at that, is of paramount importance to the Service is also demonstrated by the Service's policy in criminal tax cases. A revenue agent or revenue officer may work with a special agent in a joint civil and criminal investigation, but the criminal investigation has priority because the Service recognizes that attempts to pursue the criminal and civil aspects of a case concurrently can jeopardize successful prosecution of the criminal case.[16] The special agent's primary function is to gather evidence for use in a successful criminal prosecution. As a result, the special agent may gather evidence supporting a civil fraud or other civil penalty, but the CI special agent does not have the responsibility of either determining the taxpayer's correct tax or collecting an assessed tax, except insofar as this determination may be incidental to proving that a tax crime has been committed.

There are three phases in criminal tax cases: (1) the CI special agent's administrative investigation or a grand jury investigation conducted by a U.S. Attorney's office in which the special agent is an agent of the grand jury, assisting an Assistant U.S. Attorney; (2) the review and authorization phase; and (3) the prosecution of the criminal tax case in court. In the investigation and recommendation phase, special agents follow the basic standard and spe-

---

[13] See, e.g., IRC § 7609(c), suspension of statute of limitations on prosecution on a motion to quash a third-party recordkeeper summons.

[14] IRM 9.1.2.5, Authority to Compromise a Tax Investigation (June 30, 1998). After a referral to the attorney general, the Service no longer has the authority to settle a case, and plea negotiations are conducted with the Tax Division or the U.S. Attorney's office. IRM 9.1.2.6, Authority to Settle Criminal Cases (June 30, 1998).

[15] IRM, Chief Counsel Directive Manual 31.3.1.1, Prosecution Standards (Mar. 5, 1996).

[16] IRM 9.5.13.2.1, Criminal and Civil Tax (Dec. 14, 1998).

cific procedures CI has adopted in conducting the investigation. Area Counsel, CI, apply the same standards and policies in reviewing the agent's prosecution recommendation before it makes a final decision to prosecute. In the CI investigation phase, as well as in the review phase, CI's procedures and policies are as important as the rules of evidence and criminal procedure are in the criminal trial.[16.1] Also, CI refers its recommendation to the Justice Department's Tax Division Criminal Section, which makes the final decision on whether or not to prosecute, and in many instances prosecutes the criminal tax case. In proceedings in the Criminal Section, CI has its own policies and procedures.

In its broadest outlines, then, criminal tax investigations and review of prosecution recommendations are guided by these policies and procedures, and so in representing a taxpayer or other person in a criminal tax investigation, the defense lawyer must be familiar with CI's and the Criminal Section's standards and policies. It will be difficult for the defense lawyer to convince CI personnel that no prima facie case of fraud exists or that for one or more reasons no probability of conviction exists, without knowing how and why CI's policies and procedures apply to the consideration of a recommended prosecution.

[3] Priority of Criminal Investigations

As a matter of policy, then, the Service requires that possible criminal prosecution be given precedence over its civil aspects and that any civil enforcement action involving the same tax and periods as an active criminal investigation is suspended or deferred until the criminal aspects of the case are closed.[17] As a result, findings of the CI special agent may serve as the basis for the determination that a taxpayer is liable for certain civil penalties, but these penalties are not asserted until after a criminal prosecution has been concluded or until prosecution of the criminal case is suspended (e.g., owing to insufficient evidence).[18]

[16.1] These procedures and policies are discussed infra ¶ 12.03.

[17] IRM 9.5.13.2.1, Criminal and Civil Tax (Dec. 14, 1998).

[18] IRM 9.5.13.2.1, Investigative Process, Criminal and Civil Tax (Dec. 14, 1998).

¶ 12.02 CRIMINAL INVESTIGATION ORGANIZATION, PROGRAMS, AND PROCEDURES

[1] The CI Organization

Restructuring the Service in 1998 resulted in changes to the organization of CI.[19] CI continues to investigate tax and related crimes. Unlike the type-of-tax-payer basis otherwise adopted in the Service's reorganization, CI has only two levels, headquarters and area/local offices. There are six Area Directors of Field Operations, located in Atlanta, Baltimore, Chicago, Dallas, Philadelphia, and Laguna Niguel, California. The jurisdiction of thirty-five local CI Special Agents in Charge offices corresponds to the judicial districts throughout the country so that U.S. Attorneys' offices will have contact with only one CI office. The majority of CI's field personnel, however, are at the same offices doing the same job as they did before the reorganization. At the ten Service centers, there are ten Fraud Detection Centers, formerly CI branches, that detect fraudulent returns and prevent issuance of related false refunds. While these Fraud Detection Centers report to a Director, Refund Fraud, they also work with CI offices in the field to develop criminal cases. CI Foreign Liaison offices exist in foreign posts of duty located in Canada, Colombia, Germany, Hong Kong, and Mexico, and with INTERPOL in Lyon, France.

CI is a centralized, rather than a geographically decentralized organization supervised by Special Agents in Charge, rather than district directors. CI employees, including more than 2,800 special agents, report directly to the Chief, CI, in the National Office, rather than district directors as had previously been the case. Special agents assigned to the field operations report directly to the National Office through one of the thirty-five Special Agents in Charge, and one of the six Directors of Field Operations. Assistant Chief Counsel (CI) will review recommendations and, where appropriate, refer cases to the Tax Division of the Justice Department or U.S. Attorney's office for prosecution.

By having the jurisdiction of CI's local offices correspond geographically with the jurisdiction of U.S. Attorneys' offices, CI intends to have its investigative activities more integrated with the prosecutorial functions of U.S. Attorneys' offices. Similarly, CI hopes to increase referrals from the operating divisions by maintaining more direct contact with the operating divisions. On the other hand, centralized management in the National Office is expected to ensure consistency in the exercise of the Service's prosecutorial decision making. Also, centralized management is expected to result in the Service selecting

---

[19] IRS News Release, IR-2000-46 (July 3, 2000). See M. Matthews, "Criminal Investigations in the Modernized IRS," in ABA-CLE Publication on Criminal Tax Fraud 2000, at B-4-5.

and referring to the Tax Division and U.S. Attorneys' offices only the best cases for prosecution.

The Chief Counsel's office also particiates in the process. In the National Office, the Division Counsel and the Office of the Division Counsel/Associate Chief Counsel, Criminal Tax, assist CI special agents through Criminal Tax attorneys in the field. In the National Office's Chief Counsel organization, the Deputy Chief Counsel, Operations, supervises the Office of the Division Counsel/Associate Counsel, Criminal Tax. In the field, Criminal Tax attorneys maintain their offices in the same cities as CI Special Agents in Charge. Criminal Tax attorneys are involved in CI cases from the inception of cases to the process for prosecution and declination. During an investigation, counsel attorneys advise the case agent and managerial officials. Attorneys will discuss all types of case-related issues arising out of Title 26 and money laundering investigations with agents. Criminal Tax attorneys advise on (1) substantive crimes CI investigates (tax crimes under Title 26, currency violations, and money laundering); (2) administrative and grand jury issues, including summons enforcement cases, undercover operations, electronic surveillance, search warrants, and forfeitures; (3) the review of completed CI cases; and (4) after evaluating a case, the preparation of a memorandum about the evaluation for the official to whom the case file will be referred (a case evaluation memorandum). Criminal Tax attorneys will also participate in taxpayer conferences at the request of the Special Agent in Charge. Referral and declination authority for CI cases is vested with Special Agents in Charge.

As a direct response to the Webster Report, CI has returned to emphasizing the investigation of tax-related crimes. Although CI also investigates money laundering and financial crimes arising out of narcotics activities, its primary focus is the investigation of the violation of the criminal tax statutes of the Code. Referrals of detected fraud from other Service operating divisions.

[2] CI Programs

CI investigation programs evolved over the years from a balanced enforcement program that investigated both taxpayers in general (under the General Enforcement Program) and career criminals (under the Special Enforcement Program). CI gradually expanded its activities into a wide range of illegal income cases, especially from narcotics trafficking.[20] The Special Enforcement Program (SEP) began to be described as a program that identified taxpayers who

---

[20] CID's Strategic Plan for fiscal years 1989 through 1991 showed a different approach with resources divided among the following areas: white collar tax crimes, including currency crimes and tax compliance information gathering; narcotics crimes; public corruption tax crimes and currency crimes; organized crime; and abusive compliance crimes, such as tax shelter and tax protestor crimes.

derive substantial income from illegal activities, including major racketeers and those taxpayers with income from illegal sources such as narcotics trafficking or corrupt practices.[21] A study showed that by the late 1980s, SEP cases comprised approximately one half of the Service's criminal enforcement activity.[22] In 1988, for example, the ratio of indictments to investigations started by the CID was 64 percent in SEP cases, compared to less than 51 percent in General Enforcement Program (GEP) cases.[23] By contrast, prosecution recommendations in GEP cases declined from 2,898 in 1978, or 84 percent of criminal tax cases, to 1,383 in 1988, or 45 percent of the criminal recommendation cases. In response to this imbalance, eight former Commissioners of Internal Revenue recommended that 75 percent of CI resources be devoted to general enforcement cases.[24] Moreover, far fewer cases originated with the examination function, while the use of grand juries in criminal enforcement increased dramatically.[25] The number of narcotics and grand jury investigations, a large number of which were SEP cases, increased from 4 percent of all criminal tax cases to over 60 percent of the cases.[26]

As a result, there was considerable debate in both the Service and the private bar about CID's role in nontax criminal cases. In 1980, 90 percent of CID's cases involved violations of the criminal tax laws; in 1990, the number

---

[21] From 1989 through 1991, drug traffickers were added to the list of criminals in the SEP. CID special agents assisted U.S. attorneys in grand jury investigations of these individuals. Narcotics crimes programs were scheduled to receive about 25 to 30 percent of special agents' investigative time.

[22] Dubin, Graetz & Wilde, "The Changing Face of Tax Enforcement," 43 Tax Law. 893, 910 (Summer 1990).

[23] Dubin, Graetz & Wilde, "The Changing Face of Tax Enforcement," 43 Tax Law. 893, 910 (Summer 1990).

[24] See "DOJ Tax Division Increasing Number of Tax Fraud Prosecutions, Official Says," Daily Tax Rep. (BNA), at G-5 (May 21, 1991); Letter from Peter L. Faber, Chair, Section of Taxation, ABA, to Commissioner Goldberg (Aug. 19, 1991).

[25] Dubin, Graetz & Wilde, "The Changing Face of Tax Enforcement," 43 Tax Law. 893, 907 (Summer 1990). The percentage of investigations conducted through the use of grand juries increased from 32 percent in 1992 to a projected 50 percent in 1995. Statement, Criminal Section of the Tax Division of the Justice Department at a meeting of the ABA Tax Section Civil and Criminal Penalties Committee (May 20, 1995). In 1995, there were 827 administrative investigation cases referred to the Tax Division's Criminal Section. In 1996, the number rose to 916, an increase of 11 percent. On the other hand, the number of referrals generated by grand jury investigations also increased from 989 referrals in 1995 to 1,010 in 1996. Report of Criminal Section of the Justice Department's Tax Division, Meeting of ABA Tax Section Civil and Criminal Tax Penalties Committee, Minutes, at 2 (May 10, 1997).

[26] Reports of Criminal Tax Policy Subcommittee, ABA Tax Section Civil and Criminal Penalties Committee, at 7.

dropped to only 56 percent.[27] Also, CID's work shifted to currency crimes, the Bank Secrecy Act, and various money laundering statutes. At the same time that referrals from other Service functions dropped from 44 percent to only 16 percent, referrals involving drug-related offenses increased from 2.4 percent in 1980 to 38 percent in 1990. The Commissioner decided to continue CID's focus on illegal income investigations (i.e., financial crimes).[28] However, more resources were supposed to be dedicated to GEP cases. In January 1992, the Commissioner announced the National Office's decision to continue CID's role in investigating illegal-source income cases, usually through grand juries, but also "to revitalize the process of identifying significant legal income cases."[29]

Indiscriminate use of special agents as financial investigators for active U.S. Attorneys' offices did not stop, however, and finally the imbalance in CI's activities resulted in an investigation and report of CI's priorities and suggestions for its return to a balanced enforcement program.

[a] The Webster Report

In April 1999, the CID Task Force (the Webster Commission) published a review of the CID function.[30] The Webster Commission concluded that "CI's focus has drifted from [its] primary mission" of acting as the Service's "criminal investigation component in support of the administration of internal revenue laws."[31] Because it found that "CI now plays a major role in the investigation of offenses that have no obvious direct connection with tax compliance," the Webster Commission recommended that CI should instruct its employees that CI's primary mission is to investigate potential violations of the internal revenue laws.[32] It was clear to the Webster Commission that "the percentage of cases that CI investigates based on referrals from Examination and Collection Divisions has dropped precipitously."[33] To correct problems that it found, the Webster Commission made the following specific recommendations:

---

[27] "Official Says Commissioner Recognizes Too Much Focus Placed on Special Enforcement," DTR (BNA), at G-2 (Mar. 4, 1992).

[28] "IRS Decision to Keep Criminal Investigation Focus on Illegal Sector Raises Questions," DTR (BNA), at G-2 (Jan. 24, 1992).

[29] Memorandum from the Commissioner of Internal Revenue about the Criminal Investigation Study Group Report (Jan. 13, 1972).

[30] Webster Commission, Review of the Internal Revenue Service's Criminal Investigation Division (Apr. 1999) is available on the Service's Web site (http://www.irs.ustreas.gov) (hereinafter Webster Commission Report).

[31] Webster Commission Report, at 1.

[32] Webster Commission Report, at 2.

[33] Webster Commission Report, at 2.

1. CI should remain part of the Service to ensure uniform enforcement of the tax laws, rather than join (in whole or in part) another agency.
2. CI should continue to investigate violations of currency and money laundering statutes in a way that is consistent with an overall compliance strategy.
3. CI should limit narcotics investigations for which it is not reimbursed.
4. CI should "reinvigorate" the fraud referral program with Examination and Collection.
5. Because no evidence was found that increased use of grand jury investigations (as compared with administrative investigations) led to agent misconduct or was "inherently improper," CI should not set a limit on grand jury investigations in which CI will participate.
6. CI special agents should not use search warrants unless they prepare a written report explaining why a search warrant is the least intrusive means necessary to obtain evidence.
7. CI special agents should not participate in high-risk entries during law enforcement operations.
8. CI must address the declining number of special agents.
9. Special agent training should include formal instruction in the tax law.
10. CI should be a separate operating division within the restructured Service, and district directors should be eliminated from the chain of command.
11. There should be CID Counsel in each field division to provide legal advice in investigations, case selection, and prosecution recommendations.
12. CI field offices should have the same jurisdictional boundaries as U.S. judicial districts. CI divisions should be limited in number to fifteen to twenty, with each division headed by a Special Agent in Charge.[34]

[b] Current CI Programs: The Fraud Program and the Narcotics Program

CI conducts only a limited number of investigations each year. To gain maximum impact with limited resources, it works on a program basis. CI has two general programs, its fraud program and its narcotics program. Also, CI has adopted three operational strategies, and these strategies are taken into account in CI's two programs. These strategies are a tax gap strategy, a money

---

[34] Webster Commission Report, at 2–8.

laundering strategy, and an international strategy. The tax gap is the difference between the total true tax and the tax paid voluntarily, and so the tax gap strategy is designed to identify those investigations that will have an impact on the tax gap.[35] Only investigations of legal businesses are included (thus, illegal income investigations, such as narcotics are excluded), but money laundering investigations may fall into the strategy if a tax violation is the primary charge.[36] Under the money laundering strategy, CI investigates and prosecutes the most significant tax, currency, and money laundering offenders, and pursues the assets of those offenders in the United States and internationally.[37] As part of the international strategy, special agents are assigned to strategic posts of duty to gather information in host foreign countries for use in investigations of financial crimes over which CI has jurisdiction.[38] CI's fraud and narcotics programs reflect the use of these strategies. CI's fraud program includes "a broad range of illegal activity, primarily within legal industries (exclusive of those investigations meeting criteria of the narcotics program)," and lists the subprograms as follows:[39]

   A. Bankruptcy—Investigations where bankruptcy fraud is an intrinsic part of a tax evasion scheme.
   B. Excise Tax—Investigations involving violations of the excise tax laws.
   C. Financial Institution Fraud—Investigations wherein income is generated as a result of fraud against or related to a bank, credit union, savings and loan, check cashing business, thrift, stockbroker, or related regulatory agency, possibly even placing the solvency of the institution at risk.[40]
   D. Foreign and Domestic Trusts—Investigations involving fraudulent trusts used to either evade taxes or evade the payment of taxes.[41]
   E. Gaming—Investigations relating to the income generated from the gaming industry (either legal or illegal forms of gaming).[42]

---

[35] IRM 9.1.1.3.1, Tax Gap Strategy (Apr. 7, 1999); IRM 9.1.1.3.1, Tax Gap Defined (Apr. 7, 1999).

[36] IRM 9.1.1.3.1.2, CI Operational Definition—Tax Gap (Apr. 7, 1999).

[37] IRM 9.1.1.3.2, Money Laundering Strategy (Apr. 7, 1999). Money laundering includes the money laundering statutes in the Criminal Code, 18 USC §§ 1956 and 1957; and the conspiracy statutes, 18 USC §§ 371T and 371M; and all Title 31 statutes.

[38] IRM 9.1.1.3.4, International Strategy (Apr. 7, 1999).

[39] IRM 9.1.1.4.1, Criminal Investigation Fraud Programs (Apr. 7, 1999); see also IRM 9.5.3.2, Criminal Investigative Process, Tax Crime Sub-Programs of the Fraud Program (Apr. 7, 1999).

[40] IRM 9.1.3.2.5, Financial Institution Fraud (Apr. 9, 1999).

[41] IRM 9.1.3.2.4, Foreign and Domestic Trusts (Apr. 9, 1999).

[42] IRM 9.1.3.2.5, Gaming (Apr. 9, 1999).

F. General Fraud—Investigations relating to income that does not fall within any of the other subprograms.[43]

G. Health Care Fraud—Investigations relating to income generated from health care fraud. All investigations of insurance fraud involving health care will be included in this program.[44]

H. Insurance Fraud—Investigations involving income generated from or by the insurance industry that is not related to health care insurance.[45]

I. Public Corruption—Investigations of income wherein there is a violation of the public trust of or by a government official or employee.[46]

J. Questionable Refunds—This program includes investigations involving fraudulent tax refund schemes. With electronic filing of tax returns came electronic filing fraud. To control this new type of fraud, CID personnel in CI branches at Service centers that are part of the Service's Electronic Fraud Detection System identify questionable returns after they have been filed electronically. These CID personnel engage in filing fraud detection programs, such as the Questionable Refund Program, which targets questionable refunds generated in electronic refund schemes.[47]

K. Return Preparers—Investigations involving preparers of false and/or fraudulent tax returns.[48]

L. Telemarketing Fraud—Investigations of income wherein telephonic or wire communications are a major element used to promote, solicit, or market products or services.[49]

As described earlier, the fraud program is the modern counterpart of the Taxpayers in General Program, or GEP, under which investigations were conducted of legal-source income subject to all types of taxes and violators in as

---

[43] IRM 9.1.3.2.6, General Fraud (Apr. 9, 1999).

[44] IRM 9.1.3.2.7, Health Care Fraud (Apr. 9, 1999).

[45] IRM 9.1.3.2.8, Insurance Fraud (Apr. 9, 1999).

[46] IRM 9.1.3.2.9, Public Corruption (Apr. 9, 1999).

[47] IRM 9.1.3.2.10, Questionable Refunds (Apr. 9, 1999). See IRM 9.1.4.1 et seq., Refund Fraud (July 30, 1998); see also IRM 9.1.4.1.1.8, The Questionable Refund Program (July 30, 1998). One way CI detects electronic filing fraud is to use up-front filters in the electronic filing system to detect Social Security numbers. Between 1994 and 1995, the number of Social Security number problems identified quadrupled, and refunds were delayed to allow staff to check for possible fraud. General Accounting Office (GAO), IRS Management, Improvement Needed in High-Risk Areas, GAO/T-GGD-97-79 (Apr. 14, 1997).

[48] IRM 9.1.3.2.11, Return Preparers (Apr. 9, 1999). See IRM 9.1.4.1.2, Unscrupulous Return Preparers (July 30, 1998).

[49] IRM 9.1.3.2.12, Telemarketing Fraud (Apr. 9, 1999).

many income brackets, occupations and businesses, and geographic areas as possible to deter other potential violators. Similarly, the narcotics program is roughly the equivalent of the SEP, under which CI special agents conducted investigations of organized crime income and other illegal-source income. Although public attention frequently focused on the SEP, CID historically considered the GEP to be more important because it involved more taxpayers and more money, and its deterrent value had a greater impact. The higher priority was given to the GEP in order to create the "maximum positive impact on the compliance attitude and practices of taxpayers" in general.[50] This strategy was sound from an enforcement viewpoint because the average taxpayer may not identify with a racketeer or narcotics trafficker, but is likely to relate to a friend, neighbor, local businessman, or lawyer caught in the GEP and possibly be deterred from committing or continuing a violation. As the Webster Report suggested, CI will probably give more emphasis to its legal-source fraud program than to its narcotics program.[51]

Under the narcotics program, CI investigates members of high-level drug trafficking organizations and financial activities of individual drug traffickers.[52] Although CID has been criticized for permitting its agents to be coopted for narcotics investigations and participating in investigations of nontax crimes involving illegal-source income, CI nevertheless still plays an important role in multiagency criminal investigations of narcotics trafficking and the laundering of the proceeds of those illegal activities. Within the narcotics program, there are four subprograms: (1) investigations of members of high-level drug trafficking organizations authorized by a multiagency (Organized Crime Drug Enforcement Task Force) committee; (2) investigations of the financial activities of significant individuals or entities who transport, distribute, or finance illegal drugs, or who launder illegal drug proceeds; (3) investigations of organizations or individuals in narcotics trafficking or narcotics money laundering located by a multiagency task force and conducted through the High Intensity Drug Trafficking Area program through the Office of National Drug Policy; and (4) investigations conducted jointly with multiagency committees and programs.[53]

CI also uses special agents in initiatives and emerging issues.[54] For example, CI has initiatives for employment tax, nonfilers, and organized crime; and subprograms have developed from identified emerging issues involving domestic and foreign trusts, health care fraud, insurance fraud, and pension and ex-

---

[50] IRM 9.1.6.1.1, General Enforcement Program (Aug. 16, 1979).

[51] Tax Notes, "CID to Pursue 'Legal Source Tax Crimes,' Officials Say," 1999 TNT 214-4 (Nov. 4, 1999).

[52] IRM 9.1.1.4.2, Narcotics Program (Apr. 9, 1999).

[53] IRM 9.1.1.4.2, Narcotics Program (Apr. 9, 1999). See also IRM 9.1.7.1, Narcotic Investigations (July 30, 1998).

[54] IRM 9.1.3.3, Initiatives and Emerging Issues (Apr. 9, 1999).

empt organization fraud.[55] Special agents have authority to seize property under a variety of federal civil and criminal statutes in the Internal Revenue Code, but more importantly in the Criminal Code, Title 18. These seizures include seizures of evidence of any criminal violation within the jurisdiction of CID, and seizures of forfeiture under the Internal Revenue Code and the seizure and forfeiture authority as a sanction against money laundering violations of the Criminal Code and Bank Secrecy Act.[56]

¶ 12.03 SOURCES OF CID INVESTIGATIONS

The type of investigations CI conducts are criminal investigations, not tax audits. The investigation of tax crimes involves different elements than the usual criminal investigation. A taxpayer (or other person) under investigation cannot be represented adequately unless the representative is familiar with the investigatory process, including how investigations get started, what the special agent does during the investigation, and what policies the CI follows in evaluating whether prosecution should be instituted.[57] These matters are discussed in the sections that follow. CI receives information about potential fraud cases from three general sources:

1. Referrals from other Service functions
2. Information-gathering activities of special agents
3. Information items provided by members of the public, other government agencies, and reports of currency transactions[58]

---

[55] IRM 9.1.3.3, Initiatives and Emerging Issues (Apr. 9, 1999).

[56] IRM 9.1.5.5, Money Laundering Investigations (Oct. 9, 1998). Civil seizure and forfeiture authority for violations of the money laundering statutes (18 USC §§ 1956 and 1957) as well as the currency transaction reporting requirements of the Bank Secrecy Act (31 USC §§ 5313(a) and 5324(a)). The Bank Secrecy Act has a specific civil forfeiture provision, 31 USC § 5317(c). For the CID's procedures in Title 18 seizures and forfeitures see IRM 9.7 et seq., Asset Seizure and Forfeiture.

[57] For reasons that are explained more fully in the following sections, the subject or target of a CID investigation should be represented by a lawyer. It is not advisable for a taxpayer to represent himself or to be represented by an accountant. Although the description of a CID investigation contained herein continues to refer to a "representative," the representative should always be a lawyer.

[58] IRM 9.4.5.5 et seq., Money Laundering (Apr. 4, 1998). Where local Customs officers are maintained, the Chief (CID) may request Customs to relay to them any information regarding importers suspected of substantially undervaluing merchandise. Section 6050I requires cash payments over $10,000 to be reported on Form 8300. Special agents are instructed to use this source of information.

Each of these sources produces information with which the special agent works, and each has[59] different implications for the taxpayer and his representative.

[1] Fraud Referrals From Other Service Functions

Referrals from other Service functions are one of the most important sources of fraud cases. Revenue agents and other Service personnel are instructed that a fraud case "begins with the recognition of affirmative indications of fraud by the taxpayer" and "badges" of fraud will assist the employee in establishing "firm indications necessary for a successful fraud case."[60] When the revenue agent gathers sufficient evidence indicating that the taxpayer has committed fraud, the revenue agent, the agent's superiors, and a Fraud Coordinator develop a plan to show that "sufficient affirmative acts exist which confirm fraud."[61] "A refined judgment must be made about when to suspend the audit. If the agent stops too early in the process, all the information necessary to document firm indications of fraud may not be developed sufficiently for the CI function."[62] At a minimum, the agent will attempt to gather evidence of one or more badges of fraud noting from whom and when the information was obtained. In addition, it is "critical for the [agent] to secure the taxpayer's explanation for any discrepancies."[63]

[a] Badges of Fraud

Badges of fraud are described at considerable length, and are separated into Badges of Fraud—Income; Badges of Fraud—Expenses or Deductions; Badges of Fraud—Books and Records; Badges of Fraud—Allocations of Income; Badges of Fraud—Conduct of Taxpayer; and Badges of Fraud—Methods of Concealment. These badges of fraud amount to criminal conduct the Supreme Court described in *Spies* as conduct "the likely effect of which is to mislead or conceal."[64] In the same manner as a taxpayer's criminal misconduct, examples of badges of fraud in income are omissions of specific items of income, entire sources of income, substantial amounts of income, unexplained increases in net worth, and unexplained bank deposits.[65] Badges of fraud in the

---

[59] IRM 104.2.2.1(2), Recognizing and Developing Fraud—Overview (May 19, 1999).
[60] IRM 104.2.2.1(1), Recognizing and Developing Fraud—Overview (May 19, 1999).
[61] IRM 104.2.2.1(2), Recognizing and Developing Fraud—Overview (May 19, 1999).
[62] IRM 104.2.2.1(3), Recognizing and Developing Fraud—Overview (May 19, 1999).
[63] IRM 104.2.2.1(4), Recognizing and Developing Fraud—Overview (May 19, 1999).
[64] Spies v. United States, 317 US 492 (1943).
[65] IRM 104.2.2.2, Badges of Fraud (May 19, 1999).

conduct of taxpayers include (1) false statements about material facts involved in the examination; (2) attempts to hinder the examination by failing or refusing to answer questions, cancelling appointments, or refusing to supply records; (3) employee testimony about irregular business practices; (4) destruction of books and records; and (5) transfers of assets for purposes of concealment.[66]

Even before a criminal referral can be made, the revenue agent may engage in investigation touched off by relatively ambiguous conduct. Agents are told that "[u]nusual, inconsistent or incongruous items should alert examiners to the possibility of fraud and the need for further investigation."[67] Also, "Taxpayer misconduct should be an early warning sign of possible fraudulent conduct."[68] A lack of internal controls and dealings in cash are said to indicate the filing of improper returns.[69] Another investigative technique emphasizes the importance of the "initial contact" with the taxpayer because it gives the agent "the opportunity to obtain valuable information which may not be readily available later."[70] Because of the importance of the statements the taxpayer may make at this initial interview, the revenue agent will document statements a taxpayer may make in discussions and note the taxpayer's failure to respond to questions. (Questions are recorded verbatim.)

Also, when the revenue agent receives workpapers, the revenue agent notes the tax year summarized, the date of the contact, and who was present during the contact.[71] Importantly, the agent notes information that may provide leads for later inquiry, such as who prepared the information on the tax return, who approves and classifies expense items, who deposits business receipts, and how business receipts on the tax return are determined. During the investigation, the revenue agent must keep a historical record of all contacts and conversations with the taxpayer.[72] The Service believes that this technique is critical in sustaining fraud, and so the taxpayer's attorney will want to prepare a "shadow" historical record of what takes place during the examination/investigation in order to keep track of the inquiry and its deficiencies and strong points.

---

[66] IRM 104.2.2.2, Badges of Fraud—Conduct of Taxpayer (May 19, 1999).

[67] IRM 104.2.2.3(1), Investigative Techniques (May 19, 1999).

[68] IRM 104.2.2.3(2), Investigative Techniques (May 19, 1999).

[69] IRM 104.2.2.3(2), Investigative Techniques (May 19, 1999).

[70] IRM 104.2.2.3(3), Investigative Techniques (May 19, 1999); IRM 104.2.2.3(4), Investigative Techniques (May 19, 1999) (instruction to prepare memorandum of interview).

[71] IRM 104.2.2.3(3), Investigative Techniques (May 19, 1999).

[72] IRM 104.2.2.3(5), Investigative Techniques (May 19, 1999).

Additional instructions are provided for aiding and abetting,[73] bankruptcy fraud,[74] employment tax fraud,[75] payroll padding,[76] excise tax fraud,[77] willful failure to pay excise tax,[78] and failure to collect and pay over excise tax on diesel fuel, gasoline, and aviation fuel in violation of Section 4103 cases.[79]

[b] Agent Violations in Developing Firm Indications of Fraud

As described earlier, badges of fraud assist agents in recognizing and developing "firm indications" of fraud.[80] The agent does this by examining books and records that may later be unavailable to the Service. In the process of perfecting indications of fraud, a revenue agent will gather evidence for use in a criminal case without notifying the taxpayer that what began as an ordinary examination has changed to a potential criminal investigation. This practice is especially dangerous to taxpayers because, unlike revenue agents, special agents are required to give partial *Miranda* warnings alerting the taxpayer to the agent's function as a criminal investigator and to the possibility that anything the taxpayer says may be used against him in any criminal proceeding.[81] If the compliance employee, such as a revenue agent, follows the investigative techniques in the Manual, the referring agent will obtain incriminating oral statements, extracts, or copies of the taxpayer's records, even before a referral

---

[73] IRM 104.2.2.4, Aiding and Abetting (May 19, 1999) (requiring the agent to determine who, apart from or in addition to the taxpayer, is responsible for the fraudulent acts, such as accountants, attorneys, or appraisers).

[74] IRM 104.2.2.5, Bankruptcy Fraud (May 19, 1999). Among other bankruptcy criminal activity, compliance personnel are warned that an individual may be perpetrating bankruptcy fraud by a so-called bust out where merchandise inventory, cash, or other assets are converted to personal use or personal gain.

[75] IRM 104.2.2.6, Employment Tax (May 19, 1999). Compliance personnel are warned about intentional misclassification of employees and disguised salary payments.

[76] IRM 104.2.2.6.1, Payroll Padding (May 19, 1999). Compliance agents are told that payroll may be padded for a number of reasons and in a number of ways, all of which involve the payment of funds by a business without the recipient paying tax on the income.

[77] IRM 104.2.2.7, Excise Tax Fraud (May 19, 1999). Excise tax fraud, examiners are told, has badges of fraud different from other schemes, such as a taxpayer who has paid excise tax previously, but who inexplicably stops doing so; the taxpayer who purchases fuel from a different supplier than the usual one and fails to report the sales; tax passed on to customers, but not reported or paid to the Service.

[78] IRM 104.2.2.7.1, Excise Taxes—Willful Failure to Pay (May 19, 1999).

[79] IRM 104.2.2.7.2, Section 4103 Cases—Referrals to Collection (May 19, 1999).

[80] IRM 104.2.2.1, Recognizing and Developing Fraud—Overview (May 19, 1999).

[81] IRM 9.4.5.11.3, Duty to Advise Individual of Constitutional Rights (May 19, 1999). IRM 9.4.5.5 et seq., Preparation and Planning (May 19, 1999). The special agent will prepare an outline, review available information, organize interview file, and obtain original returns. Where there is an interview of a person other than the taxpayer, the format of the interview is prepared for the agent (see Exhibit 9.4.5.1).

is made and before the special agent has become involved. Although Service guidelines warn about overstepping the bounds of a civil examination, a revenue agent can still cross the line between identifying fraud and gathering evidence for use in a criminal prosecution.

Activities of a revenue agent in violation of these guidelines have sometimes led to suppression of admissions made by the taxpayer[82]; but based on the Supreme Court's decision in *United States v. Caceres*,[83] evidence obtained in violation of the guidelines may nevertheless be admitted if the violation of the guidelines was not deliberate and the taxpayer, in any event, did not rely on them. In cases where the referring agent engages in active deception in an attempt to gather evidence, the fruits of the deception have been suppressed in subsequent criminal trials.[84] Courts examine whether a revenue agent continued an audit after discovering firm indications of fraud, and will suppress evidence when the revenue agent affirmatively and intentionally misleads the taxpayer of the nature of the investigation in violation of the taxpayer's Fourth and Fifth Amendment rights.[85] Consequently, a taxpayer's representative must be alert to this potential argument of agent misconduct.

[c] Preparation of Fraud Referrals

Form 2797 (Referral Report for Potential Fraud Cases) is used when an examiner discovers indications of fraud.[86] This form asks the agent to describe the type of tax evasion and to estimate the tentative additional taxable income due to fraud. It also requires the examiner to (1) detail all adjustments; (2) list additional deductions, expenses, or claims; and (3) list any specific statement made by the taxpayer regarding the amount of cash on hand. The examiner must also describe specific statements or actions taken by the taxpayer that indicate intent to defraud or evade, as well as the taxpayer's and preparer's ex-

---

[82] Compare United States v. Toussaint, 456 F. Supp. 1069 (SD Tex. 1978) (suppression ordered) with United States v. Lockyer, 448 F2d 417 (10th Cir. 1971) (suppression denied) and United States v. Matis, 476 F. Supp. 1287, 80-1 USTC ¶ 9111 (SDNY 1979) (suppression denied). See ¶ 13.09[6].

[83] United States v. Meier, 607 F2d 215 (8th Cir. 1979), applying United States v. Caceres, 440 US 741 (1979).

[84] United States v. Tweel, 550 F2d 297 (5th Cir. 1977); United States v. Mapp, 561 F2d 685 (7th Cir. 1977).

[85] See United States v. Peters, 153 F3d 445 (7th Cir. 1998), cert. denied, 119 S. Ct. 801 (1999); United States v. McKee, 192 F3d 535, 84 AFTR2d 99-6229 (6th Cir. 1999) (applying an abuse of discretion standard when a special agent continued an investigation after having some evidence of fraud, and stating that it had "reservations" about the agent's conduct because she gathered evidence used to convict the taxpayer on a silver platter).

[86] IRM 104.2.3.4, Preparation of Form 2797 (May 19, 1999).

planation or defense given in response to the examiner's request for an explanation of the discrepancies that are the basis of the referral.

Referrals from the Examination Division contain the following information:

- A description of the alleged violation (e.g., evasion, failure to file);
- The taxpayer's age, health, marital status, education, and number of exemptions;
- The taxpayer's sources of income;
- The types of records available and the taxpayer's accounting method;
- The estimated unreported income; and
- The tax due.

Statements made by the taxpayer to the referring agent and a description of the alleged evasion scheme must also be included. This information is important; it can directly affect the decision to prosecute. For example, a referral can fail to supply information that would make the case unsuitable for prosecution, such as the taxpayer's poor health and limited educational background. In other cases, the referral can contain factually incorrect information, or the unreported income or tax due may be small or involve a single year. Consequently, information supplied on behalf of the taxpayer, even after a special agent has begun an investigation, can establish a defect in the referral that results in the termination of the investigation.

The referring agent's report is forwarded through channels to the Chief (Examination) for the appropriate type of taxpayer local office, who may add comments and transmit the report to the liaison in the office of the Special Agent in Charge. A Collection employee who discovers any indications of fraud uses Form 3212 and goes through the same channels as an examiner. A Tax Exempt Plans and Organizations (TE/GE) specialist who discovers fraud uses Form 2797, Referral Report for Potential Fraud Cases, which is forwarded to the Special Agent in Charge through the Chief (TE/GE).[87] If the referral is accepted, the case is numbered and assigned to a special agent as the subject for investigation.[88]

[2] Special Agent Information Gathering

Special agents themselves develop cases by actively seeking out and identifying pockets of noncompliance with the tax laws. With authorization, special agents attempt to determine whether particular individuals, occupations or in-

---

[87] IRM 104.2.3.5, Referral Evaluation (May 19, 1999). See IRM 104.2.3.6, Accepted Criminal Referrals (May 19, 1999).

[88] IRM 104.2.3.6, Accepted Criminal Referrals (May 19, 1999).

dustries, or taxpayers in a geographic area have violated the tax laws. Some projects are nationwide (e.g., narcotics traffickers and preparers of multiple false returns). Other projects focus on narrower targets (e.g., doctors in a particular geographic area). Special agents also use newspaper articles to provide leads to investigations. Because the special agent may gather considerable information before contacting a target, a taxpayer may, in effect, have already made damaging admissions to the special agent himself rather than to revenue agents or revenue officers, who are not trained criminal investigators.

Information gathering is divided into three categories: general investigations, primary investigations, and subject investigations.[89]

[a] General Investigations

A general investigation is a study, survey, or canvassing activity involving a number of individuals or entities within occupations or industries undertaken to identify noncompliance with the tax laws.[90] This type of general investigation has a limited life and is limited to the district for which it has been approved. Other types of general investigations are used to track individuals engaged in a common scheme, a business whose responsible officers are alleged to have violated the tax laws, and federal, state, and local law enforcement investigations (e.g., Financial Investigative Task Forces), as well as other types of investigations that require an authorized imprest fund, such as undercover agent maintenance. General investigations must be approved by the Special Agent in Charge, but general investigations involving sensitive individuals or entities such as clergy, politicians, attorneys, or accountants must be approved by still higher authority in the National Office.

[b] Primary Investigations

A primary investigation is begun in order to investigate alleged violations of the tax laws by individuals where there is believed to be prosecution potential.[91] These individuals may have been identified through a general investigation. If more than one individual is being investigated as part of a common scheme or group, the investigations are linked to the primary investigation of the leader of the scheme or group. Primary investigations are also used to investigate allegations of group and business entity violations of the tax laws where there is prosecution potential, and to evaluate criminal fraud referrals from other Service functions (usually revenue agents in the Examination Divi-

---

[89] IRM 9.3.1.4, General Investigations (Mar. 3, 1999); IRM 9.3.1.5, Primary Investigations (Mar. 3, 1999); IRM 9.3.1.6, Subject Criminal Investigations (Mar. 3, 1999).

[90] IRM 9.3.1.4(1), General Investigations (Mar. 3, 1999).

[91] IRM 9.3.1.5, Primary Investigations (Mar. 3, 1999).

sion), grand jury requests from the U.S. Attorney's office, and information items received in the district or by the Chief (Criminal Investigation) and identified for further development.

[c] Investigative Disclosures

When conducting a general investigation or primary investigation, a special agent is permitted to make investigative disclosures of the type referred to in Section 6103(k)(6) of the tax-return-information confidentiality rules.[92] This type of permissible disclosure allows the special agent to disclose the name of the individual in order to obtain information necessary for the investigation. Permitted contacts mentioned in the Manual are inquiries at federal, state, and local agencies, inquiries at state and local taxing authorities, and contacts with foreign governments (to be coordinated with the International function). These investigative techniques may be used in primary investigations. Also, search warrants are only permitted in primary investigations, while mail covers are permitted only in a subject investigation. In a general or primary investigation involving a Title 31 violation, contacts may be made with financial institutions and participants in the current report to identify the source, disposition, and nature of the currency transaction. Surveillance, consensual monitoring, and undercover activities may be requested in general investigations only if the names of the individuals or entities are unknown.

A special agent making a primary investigation may discuss the referral with the referring officer, verify the taxpayer's filing record with the taxpayer by form letter, and question employers and other filers of information returns. Special agents assigned to the Assistant Commissioner (International) are permitted to contact certain foreign government agencies. For example, in treaties between the United States and their treaty partners, under information exchange provisions, the Service is able to obtain necessary tax records.[93]

[d] Subject Criminal Investigations

A subject criminal investigation is an investigation of an individual or entity that is alleged to have violated the tax laws and that has prosecution potential.[94] The object of this type of investigation is to gather pertinent evidence to prove or disprove a violation of the tax laws. These investigations are only begun after a primary investigation has been completed.

---

[92] IRM 9.3.1.5.6, Authorized Primary Investigation Techniques (Mar. 3, 1999). For further discussion of the confidentiality rules, see ¶ 4.06[4].

[93] IRM 9.13, International Investigations (Mar. 3, 1999).

[94] IRM 9.4.1.6, Subject Criminal Investigations (Mar. 3, 1999).

[3] Information Items Supplied by Members of the Public and Other Sources

Information items represent a significant source of fraud cases. Information items are "tax related communications and information received alleging or indicating a violation" within the Service's investigation jurisdiction.[95] CI frequently receives such information from the general public and other government agencies.[96] Information items include letters, oral communications from informants, tax information from other government agencies, mutilated currency reports, and data about tax violations received by other Service employees. The Service receives more than 200,000 information items each year, which account for approximately 20 percent of all CID cases.

The CI branch at each of the ten Service centers evaluates information items to determine their potential for criminal tax investigations.[97] The criteria used to evaluate information items are, in the final analysis, subjective and depend on the experience of the special agent assigned to the Service center. Information items that have fraud potential are forwarded to the local CI office, and the remaining items are made available to Service center examination or collection representatives for evaluation. Data contained in an information item are entered in a computer system for retrieval by Service center and local personnel. Information items can come from a number of sources.

[a] Informants

CI classifies the categories of individuals who furnish information to the Services as: (1) anonymous informants; (2) confidential sources of information; and (3) confidential informants.[98] All but the anonymous informant may be paid a reward, and only the confidential informant gathers evidence and information at the direction of the Service.[99] Informants can supply information about a taxpayer without which an investigation cannot be successfully com-

---

[95] IRM 9.3.1.2, Authorization to Gather Information (Mar. 3, 1999); IRM 9.3.1.3, Activities Not Requiring Authorized Investigations (Mar. 3, 1999).

[96] For a discussion of the procedures CI uses in processing information items, see infra ¶ 12.04[1].

[97] IRM 9.8.1.2.1, Criminal Investigation Branch Organizational Structure and Responsibilities—Mission Statement (Apr. 14, 1998). The CI branch Mission Statement states that the CI branch detects fraudulent returns and prevents false claims from being acted on, and supports field CI investigations. For a description of this limited type of investigation, see supra ¶ 12.03[2][a].

[98] IRM 9.3.2.5.2, Definition and Classification of an Informant (Apr. 26, 1999).

[99] IRM 9.4.2.5.2.1, Anonymous Informants (Apr. 26, 1999); IRM 9.4.2.5.2.2, Confidential Source of Information (Apr. 26, 1999); IRM 9.4.2.5.2.3, Confidential Informant (Apr. 26, 1999).

pleted.[100] An informant's information can be crucial because the informant may be closely connected to the taxpayer, such as a disgruntled spouse, employee, or relative, and may have devastatingly complete knowledge about the taxpayer's affairs. For example, the informant may be able to take or copy the taxpayer's financial records evidencing the fraud. A brief collection of cases illustrates the point:

- A wife stole or copied records.[101]
- A doctor's employees told agents of separate records showing true income.
- With a search warrant, the Service removed thirty-five cartons of records.[102]
- A warrant to search the defendant's home and office to seize original records after phony one was supplied to the Service, was based on information supplied by his estranged wife.[103]
- A fellow employee seized financial documents from the taxpayer's private desk, copied them, and delivered them to a Service agent the following day.[104]
- An employee supplied company documents to the Service establishing unreported sales.[105]

A spurned spouse makes an excellent witness, especially if the spouse has observed or has been enlisted in the tax evasion scheme. In this context, the marital privilege claim has been rejected because "the greater public interest is to assure a criminal that if he enlists the aid of his spouse, he is creating a potential witness for the government."[106]

Informants are not motivated by altruism. Revenge or self-interest are often motives, and that revenge or self-interest is made even sweeter by the prospect of financial reward the Code provides for information. Form 211 (Application and Public Voucher for Reward for Original Information) is used for this purpose. (See Form 12.1.)[107] Information items are also supplied by federal, state, and local law enforcement agencies that furnish leads to the Service. As of January 1, 1996, Section 7623 permits the Service to pay only

---

[100] IRM 9.4.2.5, Informants (Apr. 26, 1999).

[101] See, e.g., United States v. Jackson, 578 F2d 1162 (5th Cir. 1978).

[102] Hill v. Philpott, 445 F2d 144 (7th Cir.), cert. denied, 404 US 991 (1971).

[103] United States v. Lefkowitz, 618 F2d 1313 (9th Cir. 1980).

[104] United States v. Snowadzki, 723 F2d 1427 (9th Cir. 1984) (the taxpayer's conviction was affirmed because the fellow employee was not acting on his own behalf nor as a government agent).

[105] United States v. Fetter, 831 F2d 734 (7th Cir. 1987).

[106] United States v. Marashi, 913 F2d 724 (9th Cir. 1990).

[107] IRC § 7623. For Service procedures relating to reward claims, see IRM 9.3.2.5.18.3, Payments to an Informant (Apr. 26, 1999).

amounts it "deems necessary for (1) detecting underpayments of tax, and (2) detecting and bringing to trial and punishment persons guilty of violating the internal revenue laws or conniving the same, from the proceeds of amounts (other than interest) collected by reason of the information provided. . . ."[108] Payment of rewards are those squarely within the jurisdiction of the Service.

The regulations interpreting the amended Section 7623 state that (1) rewards may be paid for information that relates to civil as well as criminal violations of the tax laws; (2) rewards must be paid out of the proceeds of amounts, other than interest, collected by reason of the information; and (3) the limit on rewards is increased to 15 percent from the former 10 percent.[109] Also, an individual who acts as a Service informant must wait until additional taxes are collected as a result of his information before he is entitled to a reward.[110] A dispute about a reward may raise a monetary claim against the United States subject to the jurisdiction of the Court of Federal Claims.[111] For example, where an informant was dissatisfied with the interpretation of an agreement made with a district director, the Federal Circuit held that the informant had stated a monetary claim against the United States. On the other hand, where an informant claimed that the Service defrauded him by failing to notify him that it had collected back taxes from the taxpayer he had provided information about, the Court of Federal Claims held that the informant did not make a monetary claim under the Tucker Act, 28 USC § 1491(a). The court also held that it had no jurisdiction under the False Claims Act, 31 USC §§ 3729–3731, to hear his claim for a portion of the recovery the Service had obtained following the false claim filed by the individual he had given information about, because jurisdiction over such qui tam actions was exclusively in the district courts.[112]

The Service has a long-standing practice of prohibiting special agents from compromising the tax liability of an informant in exchange for information about another taxpayer.[113]

---

[108] Taxpayer Bill of Rights 2, § 1209(a).

[109] Treas. Reg. § 301.7623-1.

[110] Petersen v. United States, 80-1 USTC ¶ 9207 (Ct. Cl. 1980).

[111] Merrick v. United States, 846 F2d 725 (Fed. Cir. 1988).

[112] Lloyd v. United States, 80 AFTR2D 97-6520 (Fed. Cl. 1997). See also Krug v. United States, 81 AFTR2d 98-1807 (Fed. Cl. 1998) (information reported to the Service by claimant led to the collection of "millions and millions" of dollars in unpaid taxes, but informant lost argument for reward that IRS Publication No. 733 created an offer to enter into an implied-in-fact contract; court held that Section 7623 vests discretion to pay rewards with the Service).

[113] IRM 9.3.2.5, Informants (Apr. 26, 1999), which includes a specific provision to this effect.

FORM 12.1
APPLICATION FOR REWARD FOR ORIGINAL INFORMATION

Form **211** (Rev. January 1983) Department of the Treasury Internal Revenue Service	**Application for Reward for Original Information**	OMB Clearance No. 1545-0409 Expires 11/30/95 Claim Number

This application is voluntary and the information requested enables us to determine and pay rewards. We use the information to record a claimant's reward as taxable income and to identify any tax outstanding *(including taxes on a joint return filed with a spouse)* against which the reward would first be applied. We need social security numbers and dates of birth on this application in order to process it. Failure to provide the information requested may result in suspension of processing this application. Our authority for asking for the information on this form is 26 USC 6001, 6109, 6011, 7623, 7802, and 5 USC 301.

Name of claimant	Date of Birth			Social Security Number
	Month	Day	Year	
Jane Jones	3	21	39	123-45-6789

Name of spouse	Date of Birth			Social Security Number
	Month	Day	Year	
Jack Jones	8	1	35	987-65-4211

Address, including ZIP code
1 Main Street, Anytown, NY 00000

I am applying for a reward, in accordance with the law and regulations, for original information furnished, which led to the detection of a violation of the Internal Revenue laws of the United States and the collection of taxes, penalties, fines and forfeitures. I was not an employee of the Department of the Treasury at the time I came into possession of the information nor at the time I divulged it.

Name of IRS employee to whom violation was reported Jane Doe	Title Special Agent	Date violation reported *(Month, day, year)* 7-20-92

Name of taxpayer who committed the violation
Jack Jones

Address, including ZIP code
1 Main Street, Anytown, NY 00000

Relative to information I furnished on the above named taxpayer, the Internal Revenue Service made the following payments to me or on my behalf:

Date of Payment	Amount	Name of Person/Entity to Whom Payment Was Made

Under penalties of perjury, I declare that I have examined this application and my accompanying statements, if any, and to the best of my knowledge and belief they are true, correct, and complete. I understand the amount of any award will represent what the District or Service Center Director considers appropriate in this particular case.

/s/ Jane Jones	7-20-92
Signature of claimant	Date

The following is to be completed by the Internal Revenue Service

Allowance of Reward

District	Sum recovered $	Amount of reward

In consideration of the original information that was furnished by the claimant named above, which concerns a violation of the internal revenue laws and which led to the collection of taxes, penalties, fines, and forfeitures in the sum shown above, I approve payment of a reward in the amount stated.

Signature of Service Center Director	Date

FOR PAPERWORK REDUCTION ACT NOTICE, PLEASE SEE THE BACK OF THIS FORM.

Cat. No. 16571S	Form 211 (Rev. 1-83)

PAPERWORK REDUCTION ACT NOTICE. We ask for the information on this form to carry out the Internal Revenue laws of the United States. We need it to insure that taxpayers are complying with these laws and to allow us to figure and collect the right amount of tax. You are required to give us the information if you are applying for a reward.

The time needed to complete this form will vary depending on individual circumstances. The estimated average time is 15 minutes.

If you have comments concerning the accuracy of this time estimate or suggestions for making this form more simple, we would be happy to hear from you. You can write to both the Internal Revenue Service, Washington, DC 20224, Attention: IRS Reports Clearance Officer, T:FP; and the Office of Management and Budget, Paperwork Reduction Project (1545-0409), Washington, DC 20503. DO NOT send this form to either of these offices. Instead, mail or bring it to your local IRS office.

[b] Currency Transaction Reports

One other source of information items merits special attention: currency reports filed by financial institutions.[114] Since 1945, Treasury Department regulations have required every financial institution in the United States to file monthly reports of large and unusual currency transactions. Currency transaction reports (CTRs) were originally developed for the purpose of discovering the large currency transactions of racketeers, but they have proved to be of invaluable assistance to the GEP in breaking income tax evasion cases. In general, whenever a financial institution engages in a currency transaction involving $10,000 or more, it is required by the Bank Secrecy Act of 1971 (BSA) to file a Form 4789 (Currency Transaction Report), showing the identity of the persons involved and the details of the transaction, within fifteen days.[115] (See Form 12.2.) These reports are required because, according to 31 USC § 5311, they have "a high degree of usefulness" in criminal tax cases. Similarly, Form 8300 (Report of Cash Payments Over $10,000 Received in a Trade or Business), which is required by Section 6050I, provides similar information from businesses that are not financial institutions.[116] This information must be filed by any person engaged in a trade or business who, in the course of the trade or business, receives more than $10,000 in cash in one or more related transactions. (See Form 12.2A.)

Although information items are an important source of information for special agents, only a small percentage of the large number of items received ever develop into fraud investigations.[117] Most information items do not provide evidence of tax evasion or are flawed in some manner. For example, an informant's communication may reflect a desire for revenge more than hard information of fraud. Even where the informant is forthright, there still may be deficiencies in the information that preclude successful prosecution. In other words, not every currency transaction is fraudulent; information contained in a currency transaction report may be explicable. Special agents must sift the information items they receive carefully to determine which ones can aid them in their investigations.

---

[114] IRM 9.4.4.2.1.8, Requests for Information—Currency Transaction Reports (Dec. 16, 1998); IRM 9.5.5.5 et seq. describes CI's procedures in money laundering. The Manual states that to show that the subject of the investigation has any CTRs on record, the special agent should search the Currency and Banking Retrieval System (CBRS). The CBRS will contain all of the information from the documents on record. IRM 9.4.4.2.1.8(2).

[115] 31 USC §§ 5311–5326. See 31 CFR §§ 103.11–103.77.

[116] Treas. Reg. § 1.6050-1. For further discussion of the Bank Secrecy Act and Section 6050I, see ¶ 7A.08.

[117] In 1977, for example, only about 7 percent of the information items received were referred by the Service centers to the district CIDs. Comptroller General's Report at 44.

FORM 12.2
REPORTING CASH PAYMENTS OF OVER $10,000

403 7-94   **3539-3**

Form 8300	**Report of Cash Payments Over $10,000 Received in a Trade or Business**	
(Rev. August 1994) Department of the Treasury Internal Revenue Service	▶ See instructions for definition of cash. Please type or print.	OMB No. 1545-0892

1 Check appropriate boxes if: **a** ☐ amends prior report; **b** ☐ suspicious transaction.

Part I   Identity of Individual From Whom the Cash Was Received

2 If more than one individual is involved, see instructions and check here . . . . ▶ ☐

3 Last name Michaels	**4** First name Alan	**5** M.I. P.	**6** Social security number 0 7 0 3 2 1 1 4 2 1
7 Address (number, street, and apt. or suite no.) One Wood Street			**8** Date of birth (see instructions) 0 4 2 9 4 5

9 City Anytown	**10** State KY	**11** ZIP code 10000	**12** Country (if not U.S.)	**13** Occupation, profession, or business Accountant

14 Method used to verify identity: **a** Describe identification ▶ Drivers License **c** Number AB 1234
b Issued by KY

Part II   Person (See Definitions) on Whose Behalf This Transaction Was Conducted

15 If this transaction was conducted on behalf of more than one person, see instructions and check here . . . . . ▶ ☐

16 Individual's last name or Organization's name	**17** First name	**18** M.I.	**19** Social security number
20 Doing business as (DBA) name (see instructions)			Employer identification number

21 Alien identification: **a** Describe identification ▶
b Issued by   **c** Number

22 Address (number, street, and apt. or suite no.)	**23** Occupation, profession, or business

24 City	**25** State	**26** ZIP code	**27** Country (if not U.S.)

Part III   Description of Transaction and Method of Payment

28 Date cash received 0 1 0 1 9 2	**29** Total cash received $ 14,000 .00	**30** If cash was received in more than one payment, check here . . . ▶ ☐	**31** Total price if different from item 29 $ .00

32 Amount of cash received (in U.S. dollar equivalent) (see instructions):

a U.S. currency $ _____ .00 (Amount in $100 bills or higher $ _____ .00)
b Foreign currency _____ .00 (Country ▶ _____)
c Cashier's check(s) _____ .00   Issuer's name(s) and serial number(s) of the monetary instrument(s) ▶ ....
d Money order(s) _____ .00
e Bank draft(s) _____ .00
f Traveler's check(s) _____ .00

33 Type of transaction	**34** Specific description of property or service shown in 33. (Give serial or registration number, address, etc.)
a ☒ personal property purchased **f** ☐ debt obligations paid **b** ☐ real property purchased **g** ☐ exchange of cash **c** ☐ personal services provided **h** ☐ escrow or trust funds **d** ☐ business services provided **i** ☐ other (specify) ▶ **e** ☐ intangible property purchased	▶ 1992 Z Car SBO 000XZ008

Part IV   Business That Received Cash

35 Name of business that received cash Z Motors	**36** Employer identification number
37 Address (number, street, and apt. or suite no.) 1 Route 90	Social security number

38 City Anytown	**39** State KY	**40** ZIP code 10000	**41** Nature of your business Automobile Dealer

42 Under penalties of perjury, I declare that to the best of my knowledge the information I have furnished above is true, correct, and complete.

Sign Here /s/ Donald Jones   Controller   8/6/92   (213) 456-7890
(Authorized signature of business that received cash)   (Title)   (Date signed)   (Telephone number of business)

Form 8300 (Rev. 8-94)

3540

Form 8300 (Rev. 8-94) — Multiple Parties, Page 2

¶ 12.04 TYPES OF SPECIAL AGENT INVESTIGATIONS

Allegations of fraud that CI receives from a referral, an information-gathering activity, or an information item are reviewed by senior special agents to determine whether assignment to a special agent is warranted. Assignments to special agents are of two types: information items and full-scale investigations. Both investigations are aimed at developing a potential criminal case. The investigation of an information item may be limited to gathering additional information necessary to evaluate the information before determining whether a full-scale investigation is warranted. A full-scale investigation, on the other hand, is for the purpose of gathering evidence to prove a criminal tax violation.

The distinction between the types of assignments is important for at least two reasons. First, a special agent assigned an information item may have received an allegation of fraud only as to a specific transaction or item. Thus, a taxpayer may avoid a full-scale investigation if a satisfactory explanation or documentation can be supplied on the specific allegation. Consequently, the taxpayer's attorney must be alert to the possibility that the scope of a special agent's inquiry may be limited. Should the taxpayer be able to provide a satisfactory, nonincriminating explanation, the representative should limit the information supplied to the specific matter raised by the special agent. Second, the limited scope of the preliminary inquiry made by a special agent dramatically demonstrates that by the time a full-scale investigation has begun, the taxpayer has most definitely become the focus of a criminal investigation, and the suspicions of the special agent have become both aroused and informed by some evidence of fraud. By this phase of the investigation, senior agents have screened the information item, the special agent has gathered sufficient information to make the determination that the case warrants further investigation, and supervisors have reviewed and approved the agent's determination.

[1] Information Item Assignments

When an information item is assigned, a special agent makes limited inquiries, including the following:

- Review of the tax returns in question
- Discussion with the referring officer or the informant
- Inquiries of governmental agencies, including taxing authorities
- Contact with the taxpayer

The special agent first examines information readily available in CID files (e.g., CTRs, newspaper clippings, closed files, or other investigations), and then examines information from other sources outside the CID but within the Service. Normally, the special agent's next step is to interview the original sources of the allegation (e.g., the revenue agent who made the referral or the informant). If a revenue agent has made the referral, the special agent's interview covers the following questions:

- What started the audit?
- What records are in the possession of the Service (e.g., returns), and what do the records show?
- What records of the taxpayer exist and are available, and how were they prepared?
- Are supporting data available?
- Has the revenue agent made excerpts from the records?

- What records of third-party witnesses exist?
- What formed the basis of the agent's suspicions, including any offsetting items that might eliminate a deficiency?
- What personal contacts has the agent had with the taxpayer or his representative, including any statement that may have been made and the explanations or defenses indicated?

Similar topics are covered with an informant.

After the special agent has made these inquiries, he is in a position to determine whether the case has prosecution potential. If the agent decides that the case has no criminal potential, the file is closed. However, if the special agent decides that the case has criminal potential, the special agent has already gathered valuable data and gained a definite advantage over the taxpayer's representative. Consequently, the representative must consider the nature of the special agent's inquiry and what it may reveal before responding to the agent's request for information.

[2] Full-Scale Investigations

A full-scale investigation comes after a decision that a case has prosecution potential.[118] The objective of a special agent in a full-scale investigation is to gather sufficient evidence of a criminal tax violation to achieve a successful prosecution of the taxpayer. Once the investigation has started, a special agent does not end it until (1) sufficient evidence to convict has been gathered; (2) the agent determines that there are "insufficient resources" to complete the investigation and that other cases have greater prosecution potential; or (3) circumstances warranting withdrawal are present.

As a general procedure, CI withdraws from an investigation when it determines that prosecution cannot be recommended. More specifically, special agents are instructed to recognize potentially fatal weaknesses in a case as early in the investigation as possible. Fatal weaknesses, which may make the taxpayer immune to prosecution, include such circumstances as the taxpayer's illness (and certainly his death) or the inadmissibility of evidence (e.g., illegal search or seizure). Agents are urged to make every "reasonable effort" to overcome a weakness in a case, but when the weakness cannot be overcome, the agent must withdraw promptly. Thus, the decision to withdraw is not made because of any solicitude for the subject of the investigation or a belief in his innocence, but simply because a successful prosecution cannot be supported and

---

[118] IRM 9.5.1.2.1, Administrative Investigations and General Investigative Procedures—Procedures in Financial Investigations (Dec. 14, 1998).

the agent has other, more promising cases. When CI terminates or discontinues an investigation, it notifies the taxpayer in writing.[119]

CI investigation procedures have important implications for the taxpayer's representative. First, the representative must remember that the special agent is dedicated to finding enough evidence to convict the taxpayer of some criminal tax violation. Second, he should note that the agent can investigate only a limited number of cases. Nationwide, a special agent conducts an average of three investigations per year. Faced with difficulties in obtaining evidence, the agent may decide to withdraw to pursue a more promising case. Therefore, if the representative can avoid providing the special agent with information on the basis of some legitimate ground such as the self-incrimination privilege, he may be able to bring about the agent's withdrawal. The attorney must also be alert to weaknesses in the case and point out such weaknesses to the special agent when such an action can be taken without jeopardizing the taxpayer's chances at a trial. For example, it costs the taxpayer nothing to document his illness. The attorney should remember that the earlier in the investigation some weakness in the case can be pointed out, the more likely that the agent will withdraw. Under CI procedures, an agent cannot withdraw when the investigation has proceeded to the point where all significant inquiries about the case have been made. In this situation, the agent must prepare a report and recommend against prosecution if that is his determination.

In a "joint investigation," a special agent conducts a full-scale investigation jointly with a revenue agent from the Examination Division or a revenue officer from the Collection Division. Cases involving alleged evasion or willful failure to file are usually investigated jointly by a special agent and a revenue agent from the Examination Division, although a special agent may investigate a case involving a willful failure to pay a tax jointly with a revenue officer from the Collection Division.

In any joint investigation, the criminal aspect is predominant. The special agent is responsible for the criminal and civil ad valorem penalty (e.g., fraud, negligence, and delinquency) features of the case, and the cooperating agent is responsible for the audit or collection features. However, the special agent determines the method or plan of the investigation because of the importance of the criminal case. The cooperating agent, who is usually a revenue agent, assists the special agent in interviewing principal witnesses, performing accounting reconstructions (e.g., determining the starting point in a net worth analysis), and verifying records, as well as performing the usual audit functions to determine correct tax. The special agent's use of a revenue agent in an investigation is based on experience and necessity, both of which point to the

---

[119] IRM 9.5.1.3.4.1, Notification to Taxpayers When an Investigation Is Discontinued (Dec. 14, 1998).

advisability of the taxpayer's representative retaining an investigative accountant to serve the same function for the taxpayer's defense.

¶ 12.05 CID'S INVESTIGATIVE TECHNIQUES

[1] Significance of the Particular Offense Investigated

In broad outline, the elements of each criminal tax statute dictate the way in which the special agent will conduct the investigation, especially since the case file must present evidence supporting a prima facie case for criminal prosecution of the particular criminal statute.[120] For example, if the suspected violation is failure to file tax returns, the special agent needs to gather evidence that (1) the taxpayer received the requisite amount of gross income so as to be required to file a return; (2) a return was not filed; and (3) the taxpayer acted willfully, usually because returns were not filed for a three-year period. Although a failure-to-file investigation can be more elaborate than this summary description, it is still relatively simple for the agent. An evasion investigation, on the other hand, requires the special agent to establish that the taxpayer (1) owes tax in addition to the amount paid and (2) made a willful attempt to evade that tax. The tax-due element of this offense can require painstaking work. To gather evidence of omitted income, the agent may have to analyze the taxpayer's net worth over a period of years or examine a substantial number of bank deposits. Although the nature of other tax offenses determines the course of the special agent's investigation, the method used in an evasion investigation is the same one followed in other fraud investigations. Consequently, the investigation in an evasion case requires further discussion. The sections that follow outline the steps that a special agent usually takes in an evasion investigation.

[2] Documentation of Principal's Statements

During an examination, a taxpayer may attempt to avoid detection of his fraud by making a false or misleading statement to the agent. A false or misleading

---

[120] The elements of criminal penalties and methods of proof are discussed in Chapter 7A. The discussion here describes the techniques generally used by special agents. One of the specialized investigative techniques CID uses is the undercover operation. Because this specialized technique to obtain evidence of criminal activity raises constitutional issues, it is discussed at ¶ 13.09[5][b].

statement made after the filing of a return is itself a willful attempt to evade,[121] and certainly is evidence from which willfulness may be inferred. Consequently, any provable false or misleading statements that the taxpayer or suspect may have made to the referring officer or informant are considered determinative by the Service on the issue of intent. A taxpayer's admissions may also be used against him in court. For example, a taxpayer's denial of the existence of a cash hoard may later prevent his attacking a net worth or bank deposit analysis on the ground that increases in net worth or deposits are attributable to previously accumulated funds.

[a] Documenting the Target's Statements

Agents are required to document the taxpayer's statements. Because the Service and the courts consider these statements to be of such importance, the taxpayer's representative should document them as well.

[b] News Release Warnings

At some point during the investigation (usually quite early), the special agent contacts the taxpayer or other suspect. The Service advises special agents that "the confessions or admissions of alleged violations are major factors in resolving tax cases."[122] To avoid any later attack on what the taxpayer said and on whether intimidation was used, the special agent must have at least one other governmental representative present. A special agent is instructed in unequivocal terms to identify himself to the taxpayer and to state that one of his functions is to investigate the possibilities of criminal violations of the tax laws. In addition, under Service-announced procedures, the special agent must advise the taxpayer of his constitutional rights not to speak and to be represented by a lawyer, and must caution him that, if he chooses to speak, anything he says can be used against him.[123] If at any time during the interview, the subject of the interview wishes to exercise his rights to withhold testimony or records or to consult with counsel, the special agent is instructed to terminate the interview.

Also, special agents are instructed to give the same warnings when dealing with a corporate officer or other employee who appears to be implicated in wrongdoing by a corporation under investigation. In addition, the special agent is instructed to say that (1) under the Fifth Amendment, the individual cannot

---

[121] United States v. Beacon Brass Co., 344 US 43 (1952).

[122] IRM 9.4.5.3, Criminal Investigation, Investigative Techniques, Interviews (June 30, 1998).

[123] This warning is the so-called News Release or partial Miranda warnings. The text of the warnings are set out at ¶ 13.10[1].

be compelled to answer any questions or to submit any personal information that might tend to incriminate the individual; (2) any statement the individual makes and any personal documents the individual supplies may be used in a criminal action; but (3) the individual is entitled to the assistance of counsel before responding. If the individual being interviewed is the custodian of corporate records, the special agent will also inform the custodian that he is required to produce the corporation's records, because a corporation has no Fifth Amendment rights.

Despite these warnings, taxpayers often make damaging admissions to special agents.[124] An example of such a situation can be found in a case where a taxpayer convicted of failure to file tax returns attempted to have admissions made to the special agent suppressed:

> On January 10, 1978, Agent Somogyi and Special Agent David Kretchmar met with Meier at Meier's office. Agent Kretchmar identified himself, advised Meier of his rights to remain silent and to consult an attorney, and told him that whatever he said could be used against him in a criminal prosecution. Agent Kretchmar also informed him that the purpose of the investigation was to investigate possible criminal tax violations. Meier responded that he understood his rights and that he wanted to cooperate. At the end of the interview Meier signed a sworn affidavit.

Many suspect taxpayers have neither an understanding of the use to which their testimony may be put nor an appreciation of the significance of what they may say.

[c] The Timing of Interviews

Even where a taxpayer is cautious enough to say little before asking to speak to a lawyer, his belief that he successfully avoided saying anything useful to the agent can be quite erroneous. Taxpayers often underestimate the amount of time spent with the agent and the importance of what they said. In *United States v. Beckwith*,[125] the Supreme Court held that a special agent's interview is noncustodial and so does not require full Miranda warnings. In this case, the special agent came to the taxpayer's house and roused him from his sleep at 8:00 a.m. The special agent engages in considerable advance preparation before interviewing the subject of an investigation.[126] In the unusual case

---

[124] United States v. Meier, 607 F2d 215, 217 (8th Cir. 1979).

[125] United States v. Beckwith, 425 US 341 (1976). Practitioners have complained about these early morning or nighttime visits, but in one Service region, Service representatives, although conceding that these visits are timed to obtain more "candid" replies, said that they are made after prior contacts and are "extremely rare." Minutes, Bar Associations—IRS Liaison Meeting for the North Atlantic Region, at 4 (Nov. 11, 1981).

[126] IRM 9.4.5.5.1, Preparation and Planning for Interviewing (May 19, 1999).

where the taxpayer's representative permits the taxpayer to undergo such an interrogation without claiming the Fifth Amendment privilege, the taxpayer must be exhaustively prepared.

[3] Determination of Types of Available Records

A special agent's access to records is a critical factor in the agent's investigation. Direct evidence of fraud may be established from the taxpayer's records or from records of third parties, such as vendors or customers of the taxpayer. The agent's task is frequently easier where proof is available from the taxpayer's records rather than from third parties. Consequently, the agent must quickly determine (1) what records of the taxpayer are in existence; (2) whether they are available and whether they can be reconciled with returns; (3) what supporting records (e.g., canceled checks, deposit tickets) exist; (4) whether excerpts or copies of records have been made; (5) who kept the records; and (6) how much detailed information is shown by these records.[127] Where the taxpayer is an individual operating as a sole proprietorship, the agent may not be able to compel production of records without protection from waiver of a self-incrimination privilege claim.[128]

If the agent intends to use indirect proof of increases in net worth or a bank deposits analysis, the agent must determine whether all the elements of the method can be established.[129] For example, in a proposed net worth computation, the agent must discover whether it is possible to establish firm starting and cutoff points, and whether income can be allocated to specific years within the period, before he begins to marshal documentary evidence to prove known assets, liabilities, and nondeductible expenditures. Similarly, before documenting the minor facets of a proposed bank deposits computation, the agent must first determine whether the records bear out his basic theory that unreported income was deposited in banks.

These kinds of inquiries allow a special agent to determine what method of proof to use, what immediate action to take, and what witnesses there are to the keeping of records. Conversely, defense preparation must also consider what records are available, what methods of proof are open to the agent, and whether the agent will be able to reconstruct the taxpayer's income from indirect methods if the taxpayer's records are not disclosed to him.

---

[127] IRM 9.3.2.1, Sources of Information—Overview (Apr. 26, 1999).

[128] See the discussion of the Fifth Amendment privilege at ¶ 13.10.

[129] IRM 9.5.9.1, Investigative Process—Method of Proof (July 30, 1998).

[4] Discovery of Third-Party Witness Records

A taxpayer's failure to report income may be proved from third-party records (e.g., banks, brokers, and customers), even if the taxpayer does not permit access to these records under the self-incrimination privilege. Ordinarily, an agent uses third-party records to prove the taxpayer's net worth and nondeductible expenditures and to show periodic deposits in bank deposits cases. The special agent interviews the referring agent or informant to answer such questions as what other records the referring agent found pertinent, to what extent such records are available, what information the previously examined records have disclosed, and whether transcripts or work papers are available and properly identified. Thus, in order to defend the taxpayer properly, the representative must also determine what records were shown and were available to the examining agent and what information was gained from those records.[130]

[5] Use of Records in Possession of the Service

The special agent also gathers records maintained by the Service that may be relevant or may provide investigative leads. These records include tax returns for prior periods, the periods under investigation, and later tax years. The agent should determine who prepared the returns, who signed them, the basis for the returns, and what an analysis of the income, deductions, and credits shows.[131] The taxpayer's signing of a return is considered circumstantial evidence that he had knowledge of the contents of the return.[132] The return or failure to file a return also is considered an admission of the amount of taxable income received or of the nonreceipt of sufficient taxable income, respectively, which can be used by the Service to rebut the existence of a cash hoard accumulated in years before the prosecution period.[133] Consequently, the taxpayer's defense also requires analysis of prior-year and later-year returns.

---

[130] IRM 9.5.2.1, Investigative Process—Sources of Information (Apr. 26, 1999).

[131] IRM 9.4.2.1, Investigative Techniques—Sources of Information (Apr. 26, 1999).

[132] Paschen v. United States, 70 F2d 491 (7th Cir. 1934). See United States v. Drape, 668 F2d 22 (1st Cir. 1982) (taxpayer's signature on his return "was sufficient to establish knowledge once it had been shown that the return was false" (citation omitted)). Section 6064 provides that any signature on a return is "prima facie evidence for all purposes that the return, statement or other document was actually signed by him."

[133] See, e.g., Smith v. United States, 348 US 147 (1954).

[6] Determination of Documentary Sources of Information

Where the taxpayer's records are not available to the special agent, there is no shortage of other information sources to which the agent has recourse. For example, the agent can prove the acquisition of real estate from land records and the acquisition of stocks and bonds from brokerage records. The records of utilities, doctors, and dentists may be used in conjunction with tax records to establish these expenditures. A taxpayer's net worth at the beginning of a period can be proved from any financial statements the taxpayer has filed with his bank. The Manual lists the categories of documentary sources of information that may be used by the agent. The catagories are as follows:[134]

- Confidential sources (e.g., informants)
- Governmental agencies such as the Social Security Administration, Selective Service, Customs Service, and Department of Labor
- Business records of banks, brokers, stock transfer and dividend disbursing agents, title companies, credit agencies, and insurance companies
- Savings and loan records
- Private business records

State and local governmental agencies may also provide information (e.g., state tax returns and the records of the taxpayer obtained in the examination of the state tax returns).

Agents are instructed to use their credentials to obtain records, wherever possible, rather than to request a summons. However, if a summons is requested, the agent will serve one. The third-party summons procedures of Section 7609 apply to limited classes of recordkeepers when the special agent uses a summons.[135] The taxpayer in question receives notices of summonses served by the agent on third-party recordkeepers, showing what sources the agent is using. The taxpayer receives no notice where the third party is not one of the classes of recordkeepers listed in Section 7609 or the agent obtains information without the use of a summons. Consequently, in a criminal tax case, the taxpayer's representative must anticipate what sources the special agent will or can use.

[7] Interviews of Third Parties

In general, the special agent is instructed to interview the taxpayer or other suspect and every witness connected with the case to obtain leads, develop in-

---

[134] IRM 9.4.4.1, Investigative Techniques—Requests for Information (Dec. 16, 1998).

[135] Third-party summons rules are discussed at ¶ 13.04[3].

formation, and document evidence for the purposes of the case.[136] The record of the interview can take the form of a formal question and answer statement made before a stenographer, an affidavit signed by the witness, a memorandum of interview, or a recording of the interview.[137] In addition, the agent makes informal notes or a diary entry of the interview.[138] There are no "off the record" discussions with a special agent. Every statement becomes a part of the agent's case file, in different degrees of formality and accuracy. The question and answer statement and the affidavit are the most formal statements made to the agent. The Service desires formal statements whenever possible, since they are made under oath and the witness is presumably "locked in" to any statement.

The Service permits the person making such a statement to have a copy of an affidavit or a transcript of a question and answer statement.[139] Even if the statement is made with this degree of formality, it may nevertheless be unintentionally inaccurate. For example, a witness may not remember the facts correctly at the time of the statement. Because an affidavit is prepared by the special agent for signature by the witness, the agent's recitation in the affidavit may not accurately reflect the witness's testimony. For these reasons, a witness should be encouraged to obtain a copy of his statement, to make sure that the testimony is accurate, and to have a record of what information he has given the agent.

Memorandums of interview and informal notes are less formal and reliable. These formats present a risk that a witness may deny making statements attributed to him by the agent or may claim that the agent made promises or threats to secure testimony. Consequently, the Service's procedure is to have the special agent accompanied by another Service official (usually the cooperating agent or officer) when an interview is anticipated. (The special agent usually is accompanied at more formal interviews as well.) The witness can ensure that he is not misquoted by notifying the agent in advance of his intention to record the interview.[140]

The accountant who has kept or audited the taxpayer's books and records or has prepared the taxpayer's tax returns in the past is a crucial witness in an agent's investigation. When a return preparer is questioned, a formal statement is usually obtained by having the witness give his testimony under oath and before a stenographer. A taxpayer's failure to include all his income in the

---

[136] IRM 9.4.5.2, Definition (May 19, 1999); IRM 9.4.5.3, Purpose of Interviewing (May 19, 1999).

[137] IRM 9.4.5.7, Record of Interview (May 19, 1999).

[138] IRM 9.4.5.7.5, Informal Notes or Diary Entries of Interview (May 19, 1999).

[139] IRM 9.4.5.8, Right to Record Interview (May 19, 1999); IRM 9.4.5.9, Preserving the Record of Interview (May 19, 1999).

[140] IRM 9.4.5.8, Right to Record Interview (May 19, 1999).

records provided to his return preparer is evidence of willful conduct.[141] Consequently, the purpose of this question and answer statement generally is to establish evidence that the taxpayer has provided incomplete or inaccurate information to the return preparer and that the preparer merely prepared the return based on the information provided to him.[142] The agent should also seek to obtain any work papers or other information compiled or maintained by the taxpayer's return preparer. If appropriate, the agent will question the return preparer regarding such information. For these reasons, the defense investigation must also obtain copies of the work papers and other records in the hands of the return preparer. The taxpayer's representative must also interview the preparer to determine the procedure followed and the statements made by the taxpayer in the course of the preparation.

¶ 12.06 THE SPECIAL AGENT'S REPORT

At the completion of the investigation, the special agent must determine whether there is sufficient evidence to support all elements of the offense and whether all material and implied questions that arose during the investigation have been answered. Where prosecution is recommended, the agent prepares a report. The report is divided into the following seven sections:[143]

1. Introduction, which includes basic information such as the type of violation, tax periods, name and address of the individual, business, and period of limitations, as well as a summary of the cooperating officer's findings regarding income and penalties
2. Personal history of the taxpayer
3. Evidence supporting each element of the alleged offense, including the attachment of exhibits to support the narration of the facts presented

---

[141] United States v. Slutsky, 487 F2d 832 (2d Cir. 1973), cert. denied, 416 US 937 (1974); United States v. Frank, 437 F2d 452 (9th Cir.), cert. denied, 402 US 974 (1971); United States v. Dowell, 446 F2d 145 (10th Cir.), cert. denied, 404 US 984 (1971); United States v. Lindstrom, 222 F2d 761 (3d Cir.), cert. denied, 350 US 841 (1955).

[142] The Manual contains an outline suggested for use by a special agent in questioning a person (other than the taxpayer) who prepared a return under investigation. See IRM Exhibit 9.4.5-1, Suggested Outline for Questioning Person Who Prepared Returns, if Other Than the Taxpayer (June 30, 1998). This outline contains sections entitled "Source of all information on returns," "Instructions and data received from taxpayer and any other person," and "Information as to whether returns were explained to taxpayer, and to what extent."

[143] IRM 9.5.8.4.2, Standard Outline for Final Reports Recommending Prosecution for Violation of Tax Laws (Mar. 19, 1999).

4. Corroborative proof

5. Facts relating to intent

6. Explanation of the principal

7. Evidence relating to sentencing guidelines

8. Conclusions and recommendations

Table 12.1 outlines the standard format of the special agent's report.

Efforts to obtain access to a special agent's report under the Freedom of Information Act[144] for purposes of rebutting conclusions or evidence or of serving as a basis for court action have generally been unsuccessful.[145] Matters considered important in the agent's report do indicate the type of information that the lawyer should gather for defense purposes. In this manner, the types of information available to those reviewing the prosecution recommendation can be anticipated, and areas that the agent may have less interest in developing (e.g., the taxpayer's history and explanation) can be identified for amplification in the review conferences.

The completed report is reviewed by the agent's group supervisor to determine the adequacy of the factual investigation, the sufficiency of the evidence, and the conformance of the report to the legal requirements for prosecution (i.e., whether the elements of the crime have been made out). This review is for quality control purposes; the supervisor normally does not exercise independent judgment to reverse an agent's recommendation. The report is also reviewed at the level of the Special Agent Agent in Charge and the Assistant Commissioner (CI), and if approved, sent to the Tax Division, Justice Department.[146] The information and evidence gathered by a special agent is illustrated in Table 12.2, which is the table of contents of a final report in a specific items case.[147]

---

[144] 5 USC § 552.

[145] For the use of the Freedom of Information Act to obtain investigation reports, see ¶¶ 2.03[4] and 2.03[5]. Anastas v. United States, 79-2 USTC ¶ 9510 (ND Cal. 1979); Steinberg v. IRS, 463 F. Supp. 1272 (SD Fla. 1979); Kanter v. IRS, 478 F. Supp. 552 (ND Ill. 1979); Kanter v. IRS, 433 F. Supp. 812 (ND Ill. 1977). Even where the investigation has been closed without prosecution, access has been refused. Chamberlain v. Kurtz, 589 F2d 827 (5th Cir.), cert. denied, 444 US 842 (1979). The rationale for this result is either that the report is covered by the investigatory record exemption or that its disclosure is prohibited under the privacy rules of Section 6103 and thus is exempt under 5 USC § 552(b)(3). However, where improper conduct by the special agent was alleged, certain information gathered by the Service about the agent's investigation was disclosed with deletions. Albin v. IRS, 79-2 USTC ¶ 9584 (DDC 1979).

[146] See infra ¶¶ 12.05–12.07.

[147] IRM Exhibit 9.5.-2, Specific Items Method Investigation (March 19, 1999).

TABLE 12.1 _____
Format of the Special Agent's Report

1. Introduction
2. History of taxpayer
3. Evidence of income
   a. Theory of the case
   b. Books and records
   c. Preparation and filing of returns
   d. Reconciliation of books and records to tax return (if applicable)
      i.   Reported income
      ii.   Reported expenses
   e. Explanation of appendix items (if applicable)
   f. Evidence for use in criminal proceedings
   g. Additional deductions (if applicable)
   h. Corrected taxable income and tax (if applicable)
4. Corroborative proof (if applicable)
5. Evidence of intent
6. Explanation and defense of taxpayer
7. Evidence relating to sentencing guidelines
8. Conclusions and recommendations

TABLE 12.2 _____
Contents of Special Agents Report

Table of Contents
IM BELL
Chicago, Illinois
36740013A

	Exhibits 600–4
Introduction	Cont. (1–2)
History of Taxpayer	Cont. (2–3)
Evidence of Income	
Theory of the Case	Cont. (4)
Books and Records	Cont. (4)
Preparation and Filing of Returns	Cont. (4)
Reconciliation of Books and Records to Tax Return	Cont. (4)
Reported Income	Cont. (4)
Reported Expenses	Cont. (5)
Explanation of Appendix Items	
Unreported Income	Cont. (5)
Disposition of Proceeds from Unreported Sales	Cont. (6)
Additional Deductions	Cont. (7)
Corrected Taxable Income and Tax	Cont. (7)
Evidence of Intent	Cont. (8)
Explanation and Defense of Taxpayer	Cont. (8)
Conclusions and Recommendations	Cont. (9)
List of Witnesses and Exhibits	Cont. (10–14)
Appendixes A–1–A–4 (Reconciliation of Tax Return to Criminal and Civil Adjustments)	Cont. (15–18)

¶ 12.07 CI STANDARDS AND POLICIES

Evidence gathered by a special agent must meet well-established standards of review before criminal prosecution is recommended. These standards, as well as the policies the Service follows in applying them, are founded on the judgment that maximum deterrence is not achieved by unsuccessful prosecutions. Both the CI and Chief Counsel apply criminal prosecution standards and policies in the investigation and review of a potential criminal case. As a result, a substantial number of the cases investigated by the CI do not result in recommendations of criminal prosecution.[148] Since the standards and policies the Service follows in fraud cases have a definite impact on the course of an investigation and the decision on prosecution, they must be considered during the investigation.

Prosecution is recommended only where (1) there is sufficient evidence to establish guilt beyond a reasonable doubt and (2) a reasonable probability of conviction exists.[149] The first standard requires that a prima facie case must have been made out against the taxpayer; that is, evidence supporting each of the elements of the alleged crime must have been gathered by a special agent before prosecution can be recommended. However, even where sufficient evidence to make out a prima facie case has been gathered, the second standard can nevertheless provide a basis for not recommending prosecution. In general, the special agent is more concerned with the prima facie–case standard, while Criminal Tax Division attorneys are more sensitive to probability-of-conviction factors.

[1] Amount of the Tax

Although a tax evasion case requires proof of a substantial tax deficiency, the amount of tax involved in a case need not be substantial in an absolute dollar amount because the Service seeks out taxpayers from across the tax-paying spectrum as part of a balanced prosecution effort. CI recognizes that a nominal tax deficiency does not make an attractive case for prosecution. As a result,

---

[148] See supra ¶ 12.01[2].

[149] IRM, Chief Counsel Directives Manual (31)310, Prosecution Standards (Dec. 11, 1989).

the amount of tax in question is one of the factors that may be significant in determining whether to recommend criminal prosecution. A small amount may reflect on the "willfulness" of the understatement.[150] Also, where unreported income is to be established by a circumstantial method of proof, the tax evaded must be substantial because the margin for prosecution error increases in the use of these indirect methods of proof. Courts have not defined "substantial" to mean any specific dollar amount of additional tax,[151] but CI has adopted certain criteria to apply to income tax investigations:[152]

1. In evasion cases using the specific item method of proof, prosecution is recommended only if (a) the average yearly additional tax for criminal purposes is $2,500 or more and (b) an uncomplicated fact pattern is involved.

2. In evasion cases using an indirect (e.g., net worth, expenditures, or bank deposits) method of proof or involving complex or sophisticated fact patterns, criminal prosecution is recommended only if the additional tax for criminal purposes totals at least $10,000 for the prosecution period, and the additional tax for any single year is at least $3,000. Thus, for a two-year case, the additional tax must exceed $3,000 in one or both years.

3. In cases involving a failure to file or pay under Section 7203, or filing a false return under Section 7206(1), prosecution is recommended only if the evidence indicates that the average yearly additional tax for criminal purposes is $2,500 or more.

4. In altered document cases under Section 7207, prosecution is recommended only if the additional tax for criminal purposes is $500 or more for any year in question.

5. Investigative preference is given to cases involving three (or more) years rather than those involving only one or two years.

These guidelines do not preclude a recommendation in a case not meeting the dollar criteria. Prosecution may still be sought if "flagrant or repetitious conduct" is involved. Such conduct may include attempts to mislead agents or conceal fraud, the use of a scheme in frequent use by other taxpayers, or conduct so egregious that conviction is probable irrespective of amount.[153] The

---

[150] United States v. Celentano, 391 F. Supp. 1252 (SDNY 1975) (three-year total of tax allegedly evaded was $2,691; held, indictment dismissed).

[151] See the discussion at ¶ 7A.02[1].

[152] IRM, Chief Counsel Directives Manual (31)310, Prosecution Standards (Jan. 17, 1996).

[153] However, the exceptions to the minimum dollar standards are intended to be applied in only a limited number of situations, according to the Chief Counsel's directive. See Litigation Guideline Memorandum: Prosecution Standards. Use of the exceptions is meant to be applied to situations of continued noncompliance or flagrant conduct only

identity of a taxpayer as a racketeer or public official may also result in prosecution regardless of the dollar criteria then in use by the CID.[154]

[2] Evidence of Willfulness

Willfulness is not proved in criminal tax prosecutions by direct evidence. This element of a tax crime must normally be inferred from the taxpayer's conduct. The more flagrant the conduct, the more probable it is that prosecution will be successful. A consistent pattern of substantial tax underpayment or nonfiling is evidence of willful conduct.[155] For this reason, the Service looks for patterns of understatement or nonfiling over a period of years (usually three) as evidence of willfulness. Evidence that destroys or interrupts the pattern reduces the probability of conviction. The pattern may also be affected by the size of the tax deficiency and the number of years involved. Apart from any pattern, the nature of the conduct is also an important consideration. The destruction of records, use of nominees, evidence of keeping phony invoices, or some other badge of fraud is conduct from which willfulness may be inferred. On the other hand, mere understatement alone, even over a three-year period, is not enough to ensure successful prosecution. For example, a situation where a taxpayer fully reflects income from transactions in records but does not report the income because of a mistake of law probably does not make a good prosecution case.[156] In other words, the conduct involved simply may not warrant felony prosecution. The taxpayer's conduct must also be viewed in the context of his education or lack of it, because this fact bears on whether he intended to violate a known legal duty.

---

where there is sufficient basis to warrant the use of criminal sanctions, and are not to be applied so broadly that the exceptions "engulf the rule."

[154] See, e.g., Janko v. United States, 281 F2d 156 (8th Cir. 1960), rev'd and remanded per curiam, 366 US 716 (1961) (involving an employee of a St. Louis racketeer who was convicted of evading tax of $134 and $264, respectively, in two years by falsely claiming his two children, who were living with his former wife, as exemptions).

[155] Holland v. United States, 348 US 121 (1954); United States v. Magnus, 365 F2d 1007 (2d Cir. 1966), cert. denied, 386 US 909 (1967).

[156] See, e.g., United States v. Garber, 607 F2d 92 (5th Cir. 1979) (en banc). In *Garber*, the defendant had failed to report income from the sale of her rare blood, and there was substantial evidence that she acted willfully. Her conviction was at first affirmed (United States v. Garber, 589 F2d 843 (5th Cir. 1979)), but on rehearing en banc, it was reversed and remanded with instructions to permit expert testimony from the defense that there was no taxable gain from such a sale. When the conviction was affirmed by a panel of the Fifth Circuit, the dissenting opinion expressed "serious doubts as to the wisdom of the government's choice to prosecute Mrs. Garber criminally in this case of first impression." Id. at 850.

[3] Voluntary Disclosure

Between 1945 and 1952, the Service had a "voluntary disclosure" policy under which a taxpayer who failed to file a return or declare his full income and pay the tax due could escape criminal prosecution through voluntary disclosure of the deficiency, as long as the voluntary disclosure was made before an investigation was started.[157] Although there was no statutory authority for the policy, once the Service determined that a voluntary disclosure had been made, no recommendation for criminal prosecution would be made to the Department of Justice.[158] This policy caused confusion on such questions as whether a "disclosure" had been made and whether it was "voluntary."[159]

Under the voluntary disclosure policy, no qualifying voluntary disclosure occurred if (1) the taxpayer made the disclosure after an investigation of his tax returns had commenced,[160] whether or not the investigation had begun without the taxpayer's knowledge[161]; (2) the taxpayer failed to make a good faith effort to cooperate with the Service in computing the correct tax[162]; or (3) the taxpayer made only a partial or misleading disclosure.[163] On the other hand, some courts suppressed evidence the Service obtained where an investigation had in fact begun but the taxpayer did not know it at the time the disclosure was made.[164] In an apparent response to this administrative and judicial

---

[157] For quotations from some of the public statements made by Treasury officials encouraging voluntary disclosures, see Wallace, "Penalties and Prosecutions for Evasion of the Federal Income Tax," 1 Tax L. Rev. 329, 341–342 (1946).

[158] The purpose of this policy was to encourage compliance with the tax laws, especially by individuals who had earned income in violation of price control regulations during World War II. The policy achieved remarkable results. Within about four months after it was announced, the Commissioner of Internal Revenue said that 30,000 delinquent or amended returns had been filed voluntarily, accounting for more than $50 million. G. Wallace, "Penalties and Prosecutions for Evasion of the Federal Income Tax," 1 Tax L. Rev. 329, 342 (1946).

[159] The policy was also a source of corruption in the Service. Hearings before the Subcomm. on Administration of the Internal Revenue Laws of the House Comm. on Ways and Means, 82d Cong., 2d Sess. 1071–1077 (1952) (the "King Subcommittee" hearings).

[160] Shotwell Mfg. Co. v. United States, 371 US 341 (1963); United States v. Lustig, 163 F2d 85 (2d Cir.), cert. denied, 332 US 775 (1947).

[161] Lapides v. United States, 215 F2d 253 (2d Cir. 1954).

[162] Centracchio v. Garrity, 198 F2d 382 (1st Cir.), cert. denied, 344 US 866 (1952).

[163] Shotwell Mfg. Co. v. United States, 371 US 341 (1963).

[164] In re Liebster, 91 F. Supp. 814 (ED Pa. 1950). Although the courts could not enforce the voluntary disclosure policy as such, the admission of statements made to the Service in reliance on the policy, it was contended, violated the Fifth Amendment as the product of an unlawful inducement. Compare the discussion with that in Shotwell Mfg. Co. v. United States, 371 US 341 (1963).

confusion, the Service formally withdrew the policy in 1952,[165] and efforts to reinstate it have been unsuccessful.[166]

[a] Voluntary Disclosure for Nonfilers 1993–1995

In September 1992, the Service announced a program to bring nonfilers back into the system.[167] While not described as an amnesty program, the nonfiler program had the important result of amnesty and voluntary disclosure, not prosecution. According to the announcement, the Service will not recommend criminal prosecution of any taxpayer who makes a "true voluntary disclosure" and files an accurate return. In general, the program provides for District Office assistance in obtaining old tax return forms, reconstructing records, and arranging for installment payment of liabilities. Not surprisingly, the program was not available for those taxpayers with illegal sources of income. Moreover, in "egregious cases," criminal prosecution may still be recommended and so high-income nonfilers will have to proceed with professional assistance and caution.

In a related, but somewhat inconsistent program, nonfiling professionals who came forward under the nonfiler program will not "ordinarily" be disbarred or suspended from practice before the Service. There have been some publicized criminal investigations of nonfiling lawyers, however, and the Director of Practice has reminded practitioners that disbarment of one partner may disqualify an entire firm from practice.[168] Accordingly, the Service adopted a one-year test program permitting disclosure of fact-of-filing information.[169]

In 1993, CI's voluntary disclosure practice went through some changes in formulation. The Service's voluntary disclosure practice was changed as part of its nonfiler program. Under the 1993 version of the voluntary disclosure practice, a voluntary disclosure was considered to be made if (1) the taxpayer had legal-source income; (2) the taxpayer had informed the Service of the un-

---

[165] Press Release No. 7-2930 (Jan. 10, 1952).

[166] See, e.g., "Chairman's Letter on Voluntary Disclosure Policy" (letter from William R. Spofford, Chairman, ABA Section of Taxation, to Secretary of the Treasury Dillon and Commissioner of Internal Revenue Caplin), reprinted in 15 Tax Law. 32–40 (1961). See also Lyon & Ritholz, "Voluntary Disclosures," 1980 Rep. to ABA Tax Section Civil and Criminal Penalties Committee; Feld, "Voluntary Disclosures Revisited," ABA Tax Section Newsletter (Winter 1986). One of the major obstacles in formalizing a voluntary disclosure policy is the difficulty in drafting a regulation or statute that would not have the same defects as the original Treasury policy (i.e., defining when a disclosure is voluntary).

[167] IRS News Release, IR-92-94 (Sept. 30, 1992).

[168] See Circular No. 230, §§ 10.24, 10.51(h).

[169] Ann. 93-36, 1993-10 IRB 1.

filed returns before being contacted by the Service by notice, telephone, or personal visit that the taxpayer was under criminal investigation; (3) the taxpayer filed delinquent returns or cooperates in arriving at the tax due; and (4) the taxpayer made full payment of the amounts due or provides for such payment.[170]

[b] Voluntary Disclosure in Cases Other Than Nonfiler Cases

While the guidelines on voluntary disclosures in failure-to-file cases were clear and more liberal than they were in prior statements, the general guidelines on voluntary disclosures merely said that voluntary disclosure occurs when (1) the communication is truthful; (2) the communication is timely; (3) the communication is complete; and (4) the taxpayer shows a willingness to cooperate, and does in fact cooperate with the Service in determining the taxpayer's correct tax liability.[171] No description of when a disclosure would be considered "timely" was given. Coupled with the description of timeliness for nonfiler cases, the cryptic treatment of the timeliness factor suggested some greater flexibility than CI had previously shown with claimed voluntary disclosures. However, long-followed procedures die slowly, and so it is likely that the "triggering event" limitation on a timely disclosure probably continued to be applied in practice.

---

[170] IRM 9781, Special Agents' Handbook § 342.143(3), MT 9781-153 (Apr. 5, 1993). The Service considered the Nonfiler Program a success primarily because it was able to substantially reduce its inventory of nonfilers. The GAO was less certain that the program was successful because data were inadequate to draw any firm conclusions about the impact of the program on compliance. See GAO, "Internal Revenue Service, Results of Nonfiler Strategy and Opportunities to Improve Future Efforts," GAO/GGD-96-72 (May 1996). The Service secured an increasing number of individual returns in fiscal years 1992–1994, from 2,221,751 to 2,360,760; but the number of delinquent business returns dropped during the same period from 1,446,527 to 1,196,615. In terms of collections, the percentage of the net assessment of tax collected with returns of individual taxpayers who took advantage of the program declined over the 1992–1994 period from 6.3 percent to 5.0 percent; and with returns of business taxpayers, from 10.9 percent to 8.5 percent.

At the same time as the Nonfiler Program (including the liberalized voluntary disclosure practice) was encouraging nonfilers to file, the Service said that nonfiling professionals who came forward would not "ordinarily" be disbarred or suspended from practice before the Service. But it also instituted criminal investigations against attorneys who did not act or who did not act quickly enough. Since the Director of Practice reminded practitioners that disbarment of one partner might result in the disqualification of an entire firm from practice before the Service, the Service adopted a fact-of-filing program permitting disclosure of whether an individual had filed a return. Circular No. 230, §§ 10.24, 10.51(h), discussed at ¶ 1.09; see also Ann. 93-36, 1993-10 IRB 1.

[171] IRM 9781, Special Agents' Handbook § 342.142(2), MT 9781-153 (Apr. 5, 1993).

The liberalized voluntary disclosure practice gave rise to a rare case, involving whether a taxpayer had made a qualifying disclosure.[172] The taxpayer, an accountant, attorney, and head of an accounting firm's tax department, had failed to file returns and pay tax for the years 1987 through 1990. After ignoring computer-generated notices from the Service about several years' returns, the taxpayer finally filed his 1986 through 1989 returns in February 1992, but did not file his 1990 return, which was already delinquent, nor did he make any payment. Only after the revenue officer said that she would not consider an installment payment agreement until he did so, did the taxpayer file his delinquent 1990 and 1991 returns. Rather than opting for an installment payment agreement, the taxpayer, through counsel, submitted an offer to compromise the total tax he reported on his returns. The Collection Division rejected this offer. At the time the taxpayer was notified that he was the subject of a criminal investigation of his personal returns, no compromise agreement had been reached with the Collection Division. The Justice Department's Tax Division approved of the failure-to-file prosecution of the taxpayer, and the taxpayer moved to dismiss the information on the ground that he had complied with the Service's voluntary disclosure practice. The Second Circuit found that the taxpayer had not satisfied the voluntary disclosure practice, because he failed to either pay or make bona fide arrangements to pay the taxes he had reported to be due.[173] Agreement between the Service and the taxpayer on a course of payment must exist, according to the court, in order to satisfy the voluntary disclosure practice, and a rejected offer in compromise "clearly is not a bona fide arrangement to pay." While the Service must negotiate with a taxpayer in good faith, the circuit court found that the Service had given the taxpayer a reasonable opportunity to satisfy all of the conditions of the policy, and so it was justified in refusing to treat that taxpayer as a voluntary discloser.[174] Working out some sort of deferred arrangement to pay the delinquent tax with the Collection Division, which is difficult under normal circumstances, becomes crucial, when the delinquent taxpayer is attempting to meet the requirements of the voluntary disclosure practice.

---

[172] United States v. Tenzer, 127 F3d 222 (2d Cir. 1997).

[173] United States v. Tenzer, 127 F3d 222 (2d Cir. 1997). This statement of the case does not include the facts that interest in the taxpayer arose during a grand jury investigation of one of the taxpayer's clients, and that the recommendation for prosecution came from the U.S. Attorney's office conducting the investigation of the client.

[174] The taxpayer had not paid his current taxes. He ignored the revenue officer's demand to sell assets and pay installments to satisfy the assessed liabilities, and he apparently was not going to increase the amount of the offer that had already been rejected.

[c] 1995 Changes

Without publicizing the change, in August 1995, the Service revised its voluntary disclosure practice.[175] In general, the revised voluntary disclosure practice returned to the practice as it existed before the nonfiler program and the initiatives of Compliance 2000. A voluntary disclosure will be considered along with "all other factors" when the CID decides whether to request prosecution. In order for the disclosure to be considered a "true" voluntary disclosure, the communication must be truthful, timely, and complete, and the taxpayer must show a willingness to cooperate with the Service (and actually cooperate) in the determination of the taxpayer's tax liability. The taxpayer's disclosure will not be timely if the taxpayer communicates with the Service only after an event that the Service believes would have eventually led to the discovery of the taxpayer's fraud. If a so-called triggering event has occurred, the disclosure is motivated by fear of detection and is inconsistent with a voluntary act of accepting responsibility for prior misconduct. Accordingly, the Service must receive the disclosure before either the Service has "initiated an inquiry that is likely to lead to the taxpayer, and the taxpayer is reasonably thought to be aware of that investigative activity," or some event has occurred about which the taxpayer knows and that event is likely to cause an audit into the taxpayer's liabilities. This practice should be contrasted with the prior one described above. Note that no distinction is made in the revised practice between voluntary disclosures in nonfiler and amended return cases. There also is a returned emphasis on the triggering event element in a voluntary disclosure; that is, the disclosure must be made before the triggering event occurs if the disclosure is to be timely. Under the 1993 statement of the practice, timeliness was not even defined in an amended return disclosure, and could be made in a nonfiler disclosure even after a contact from Service personnel other than the CID. Moreover, according to the Manual, a disclosure does not qualify as a voluntary disclosure when the identity of the taxpayer is not disclosed (e.g., a letter from an attorney stating that an anonymous client wishes to disclose a tax violation in exchange for immunity).[176]

[d] Current Practice

Under current practice, the Service considers a true "voluntary disclosure" along with other factors in determining whether to recommend prosecution to

---

[175] IRM 31.3.3.1, Criminal Tax Policies and Procedures—Voluntary Disclosure (Jan. 17, 1996).

[176] IRM 31.3.3.1(5), Criminal Tax Policies and Procedures—Voluntary Disclosure (Jan. 17, 1996).

the Department of Justice.[177] The Service's administrative practice recognizes that a taxpayer may still avoid prosecution by voluntarily disclosing a tax violation, provided that there is a qualifying disclosure that is (1) timely and (2) voluntary.[178] A disclosure within the meaning of the practice means a communication that is truthful and complete, and the taxpayer cooperates with Service personnel in determining the correct tax liability. Cooperation also includes making good faith arrangements to pay the unpaid tax and penalties "to the extent of the taxpayer's actual ability to pay."[179] A disclosure is timely if it is received before the Service has begun an inquiry that is (1) "likely to lead to the taxpayer" and (2) the taxpayer is "reasonably thought to be aware" of that inquiry; or the disclosure is received before some triggering or prompting event has occurred (1) that is known by the taxpayer and (2) that triggering event is likely to cause an audit into the taxpayer's liabilities. Examples of triggering events are a newspaper article highlighting commercial bribery in a particular industry, corruption in a government office, or a divorce proceeding. Voluntariness is tested by the following factors: (1) how far the Service has gone in determining the tax investigation potential of the taxpayer; (2) the extent of the taxpayer's knowledge or awareness of the Service's interest; and (3) what part the triggering event played in prompting the disclosure. (Where the disclosure is prompted by fear of a triggering event, it is not truly a voluntary disclosure.)

In its present form, the Service's voluntary disclosure practice reflects the use of criminal prosecutions for deterrent purposes. When a taxpayer makes a true voluntary disclosure before the Service has made any investigation into his returns, the case simply does not have the deterrent impact desired by the Service. Rather than encouraging voluntary compliance with the tax laws, such prosecution might well encourage other taxpayers to continue to conceal whatever omissions they may already have been guilty of in the hope that they will avoid detection. Not only do taxpayers who make voluntary disclosures make poor examples for deterrent purposes, but prosecution of such taxpayers can present significant trial hazards, since a disclosure is evidence from which a finder of fact may determine that the original act or omission was not "willful" in a criminal sense. Nevertheless, the trial hazard to the government presented by a taxpayer's voluntary disclosure should not be overrated by the defense (although it frequently is), because a tax crime is complete on the day the false return was filed.

---

[177] IRM 31.3.1(4), Voluntary Disclosure (Jan. 17, 1996) (the practice "is a matter of internal I.R.S. practice, provided solely for I.R.S. personnel").

[178] IRM 31.3.1, Voluntary Disclosure (Jan. 17, 1996); see "Points to Remember," 32 Tax Law. 181, 184 (1978). For an examination of the voluntary disclosure practice, see Horvitz & Tallichet, "An Examination of the IRS's Voluntary Disclosure Policy," 11 Tax Adviser 545 (1980); Namorato & Timbie, "Voluntary Disclosure Policy," 45 NYU Tax Inst. § 38.01 (1987).

[179] Chief Counsel Directives Manual (31) 330 (4)(d) (Dec. 12, 1991).

No voluntary disclosure can be made by a taxpayer if an investigation by the Service has already begun. Once a taxpayer has been contacted by any Service function (whether it be the Service center, office examiner, revenue agent, or a special agent), the taxpayer cannot make a qualifying voluntary disclosure under Service practice. This no-contact element is crucial for a voluntary disclosure to be a "true" voluntary disclosure, and this was also the case under the practice before the 1993 change for nonfilers and during the 1993 to 1995 period when nonfilers were encouraged to come into the system.

Once the taxpayer is contacted by a Service representative, the taxpayer may no longer rely on the voluntary disclosure practice to avoid prosecution. In a case illustrating this point, the taxpayer was under grand jury investigation after failing to file returns for six years, and a special agent went to the taxpayer's house to take photographs.[180] When the taxpayer spoke to the agent, the agent identified himself as a Service representative, and the taxpayer immediately broke off the contact before learning that the "IRS representative" was a special agent. The taxpayer's attorney thereafter informed the Service that he wanted to participate in the 1993 voluntary disclosure program for nonfilers. The Service responded that the taxpayer was already under criminal investigation for failure to file and tax evasion. At his later prosecution, the taxpayer claimed that his due process rights had been violated by the Service's refusal to recommend that he not be prosecuted under the voluntary disclosure program. The circuit court concluded that the special agent's personal visit to the taxpayer's house "disqualified him from the voluntary disclosure program."[181]

Even if the Service has not actually contacted a taxpayer, it does not necessarily consider a disclosure to have been voluntary if a case file has already been opened. For this reason, one method used to make a voluntary disclosure is for the taxpayer's representative to tell a high-ranking CI official that a named taxpayer wishes to make a voluntary disclosure and to ask whether the taxpayer may make a qualifying voluntary disclosure. If the CI official says that a valid voluntary disclosure can be made, amended or delinquent tax returns can be prepared and filed, and the tax can be paid. At the same time, the taxpayer can send the Service a letter reciting the voluntary disclosure and the fact that the disclosure was timely. Where possible triggering events make it unclear whether CI will accept a disclosure as a voluntary disclosure, a variation of this procedure is sometimes used. This method involves providing a description of the circumstances to the high-ranking CI official, and inquiring whether a disclosure in the described circumstances would be considered voluntary. If the answer is in the affirmative, the returns or amended returns are filed.

---

[180] United States v. Knottnerus, 139 F3d 558 (7th Cir. 1998).

[181] United States v. Knottnerus, 139 F3d 558, 560 (7th Cir. 1998).

If CI's approach is that a voluntary disclosure may not be made, despite the fact that the taxpayer does not know that the Service has selected the return for examination or investigation, the approach may be too restrictive. The same trial problems that face the Service where a true voluntary disclosure is made also exist where the taxpayer makes a voluntary disclosure without knowing of any pending investigation. Consequently, if there is no indication that the Service has started an examination or investigation, some practitioners will send a letter to the Service stating that tax returns of the taxpayer have been found to be incorrect and that amended returns will be filed as soon as they can be accurately and correctly prepared.[182] (See Form 12.3.) This approach has the advantage of putting the taxpayer on record as making a voluntary disclosure at a time when no known investigation is pending. Its disadvantage is that neither the taxpayer nor the lawyer can be completely certain that the voluntary disclosure will prevent the recommendation of criminal prosecution.

Still another approach followed where no examination or investigation of the taxpayer is pending is the preparation and filing of delinquent or amended returns. The advantage of filing delinquent or amended returns without a communication drawing attention to them is that the returns may not even be examined after being received at the Service center. In such an event, the taxpayer not only will have made a voluntary disclosure but will have avoided an examination as well. The obvious disadvantage with this tactic is that during the time the returns are being prepared, the taxpayer may be contacted by the Service and a voluntary disclosure prevented. A taxpayer in this situation is left with the argument—and it is only an argument—that the voluntary disclosure took place when the taxpayer told the lawyer about the delinquency or unreported income and that this date was before the taxpayer was contacted.[183]

[e] Amended Returns

If a taxpayer who cannot make a qualifying voluntary disclosure nevertheless files amended or delinquent tax returns, these returns (1) constitute an admission that the correct income and tax were not reported; (2) if incorrect, may serve as an independent attempt to evade or as a separate false statement; and (3) amount to a waiver of the self-incrimination privilege. As a result, it is critical for the taxpayer's interests that amended returns not be filed without a full appreciation of the risks and uses to which the returns may be put. The hazards of filing amended returns are illustrated by several cases. In *United*

---

[182] This procedure generally is not used when returns have not been filed, but a similar letter could be sent regarding delinquent returns.

[183] To make this argument, the taxpayer's lawyer or accountant must keep an accurate record of the date of the disclosure.

States v. McGrath,[184] the defendant was informed that he was the subject of a Service investigation, and he filed amended tax returns, reporting income from transactions and bank accounts. However, he omitted (although it frequently is) extortion payments. In proving tax evasion, the government used the original and amended returns to show that the defendant had omitted the income reported on the amended returns and had not reported the extortion income at all. In *United States v. Dowell*,[185] amended returns were used as evidence of willfulness because they showed a consistent pattern of underreporting large amounts of income. In *Badaracco v. Commissioner*,[186] the taxpayers filed correct amended returns after federal grand juries subpoenaed their partnership's records, thus admitting that the original filed returns were incorrect. The taxpayers were indicted three months later under Section 7206(1) on fifteen counts of filing false income tax returns and were convicted on their guilty pleas.

---

[184] United States v. McGrath, 558 F2d 1102 (2d Cir.), cert. denied, 434 US 1064 (1977).

[185] United States v. Dowell, 446 F2d 145 (10th Cir.), cert. denied, 404 US 984 (1971).

[186] Badaracco v. Comm'r, 693 F2d 298 (3d Cir. 1982), rev'd on other grounds, 464 US 386 (1984).

FORM 12.3 —————————————————————————
SAMPLE LETTER FROM COUNSEL REGARDING CLIENT'S VOLUNTARY DISCLOSURE

District Director of Internal Revenue
120 Church Street
New York, New York 10008

Re: John Doe

000-00-0000

Dear Sir:

This is to advise you that I am counsel for the above-named taxpayer and that the aforesaid client is making a voluntary disclosure of the fact that his originally filed 1995 and 1996 federal income tax returns contained errors and that he wishes to have these returns corrected as soon as the requisite information can be assembled.

An analysis of the original returns is being conducted to determine their accuracy, and the taxpayer will file amended returns as necessary in due course. The taxpayer has not, prior to the date of this letter, been contacted by the Internal Revenue Service as to these returns. The decision to file amended returns and to disclose errors on the taxpayer's original returns is a completely voluntary one.

If there should be any need to contact the taxpayer in this matter, please do so through counsel at the above address.

So that I may have a record of your receipt of this letter, please date-stamp the enclosed copy of it and return it to me. Thank you for your cooperation.

Sincerely,

[*Representative*]

[*Hand-deliver*]

[f] Risks of Voluntary Disclosure

The Service voluntary disclosure practice has generally worked well as shown by the paucity of cases on the issue. However, this practice can cause problems even for experienced practitioners. For example, in *United States v. Hebel*,[187] the Service apparently believed a qualifying voluntary disclosure had not been made. Taxpayer's counsel had notified the Service that certain returns of two named taxpayers were in error. At a meeting with Service personnel, taxpayers' counsel were told that a revenue agent had already been assigned

---

[187] United States v. Hebel, 668 F2d 995 (8th Cir.), cert. denied, 456 US 946 (1982).

the returns before the disclosure had been received. Despite this warning, the taxpayers filed amended returns and cooperated in the audit. They were later indicted and convicted, one for evasion and the other for filing a false return. The convictions were affirmed, in an opinion in which the court of appeals said, "Taxpayers and their attorneys cannot rely on a long since abandoned policy of nonprosecution when a taxpayer voluntarily discloses a violation of the tax laws."[188] The decision to prosecute in this case obviously gave the Service and the Department of Justice some difficulty, since indictments were handed down five years after the disclosure. Quite possibly, the fact that a revenue agent had already been assigned to the returns was the basis for the decision to consider the disclosure not to have been truly voluntary. Although the taxpayers were prosecuted and convicted, they were not sentenced to prison, so the disclosure appears to have had some beneficial effect.

The foregoing illustrates that making or attempting to make a voluntary disclosure is a matter of judgment, not law. No formula exists, and a taxpayer must endure the uncertainty of the risk that a voluntary disclosure will not be considered truly voluntary by the Service and that an investigation that has already started but has lagged may be pursued more overtly and aggressively as a result of the disclosure. Nevertheless, there appears to be satisfaction with the current practice with all its uncertainties.

[4] Health, Age, and Mental Condition

The Service takes into account the health, age, and mental condition of a taxpayer in deciding whether a recommendation for prosecution will or should be made.[189] Until 1951, the Service would not recommend prosecution of a taxpayer who was seriously ill, either physically or mentally, even if there was a reasonable probability of conviction. Currently, health, age, and mental condition are only factors to be considered in the decision to prosecute. Although a taxpayer's mental condition or the effect of a trial on a taxpayer's health are not matters susceptible to ready determination on an administrative level, a taxpayer whose mental condition raises questions as to his responsibility at the time of the alleged criminal act or a taxpayer who is seriously and pathetically ill is not a satisfactory deterrent example, and his case may entail substantial trial problems for the government. Where there are other arguments against prosecution, the health of the taxpayer may be a decisive consideration.

---

[188] United States v. Hebel, 668 F2d 995, 997.

[189] IRM 31.3.5.1, Health, Age, and Mental Condition (Dec. 11, 1989).

[5] Dual Prosecution

A person may commit more than one criminal offense by the same conduct (e.g., bribery or embezzlement and tax evasion).[190] The Service follows the Justice Department's dual prosecution policy,[191] which precludes federal prosecution following a state or other federal prosecution based on the same act or transaction unless there are compelling reasons to support the prosecution. In criminal tax cases, the Justice Department's Tax Division considers the following factors in determining whether to prosecute:

- The similarity between the sources of unreported income and the activity on which the prior prosecution was based
- The appropriateness of the sentence in the prior prosecution
- The effect of a tax prosecution on rehabilitation efforts following the prior conviction
- The appellate status of the prior conviction
- The additional deterrent value of a tax prosecution
- The appearance of oppressive government action and efficient utilization of manpower[192]

[6] Trial Problems

Counsel reviews a potential case with a view to the actual trial of the case. Counsel attorneys are more sensitive to trial problems than the special agents. A number of trial-related factors may affect the counsel's decision regarding prosecution. For example, if a prosecution requires too many witnesses and documents, the risk that a guilty verdict may not be obtained will work against the prosecution. Of course, some other objective might outweigh these factors (e.g., a foreign bank prosecution). Counsel attorneys also consider substantial accounting problems (e.g., questions about which year an item was reportable)

---

[190] Historically, successive prosecution for the same acts was a consideration in tax prosecution decisions where the prior proceeding was for wartime price control laws and tax had been evaded on black market profits. Lyon, "The Crime of Income Tax Fraud: Its Present Status and Function," 53 Colum. L. Rev. 476, 488 (1953).

[191] IRM 31.3.4.1, Dual and Successive Prosecution (Mar. 5, 1996). Technically, the dual prosecution policy applies to a federal prosecution after a state prosecution. The successive prosecution policy applies to a federal prosecution following a prior federal prosecution based on the same transaction.

[192] The dual prosecution policy is a Department of Justice and Service policy, and neither the Service nor the Department of Justice can be bound by any state official's representation about a later federal tax prosecution. United States v. McIntosh, Jr., 612 F2d 835 (4th Cir. 1979).

and questions of law regarding the substantive treatment of a transaction.[193] Misconduct by investigating agents is regarded as a trial problem because at trial the activities of the agents may deflect the jury's attention from the conduct of the defendant taxpayer, which not only reduces the probability of conviction and increases the chance of jury nullification, but also detracts from the overall deterrence objective of the Service. Other trial problems may also work against a recommendation, such as (1) the conflicting testimony of witnesses or a prior civil settlement and (2) payment of a tax, which might jeopardize a successful prosecution. Even such factors as the taxpayer's advanced age, extreme youth, lack of education, or language ability may present substantial problems for the government in trying a case.

¶ 12.08 SERVICE-INITIATED GRAND JURY INVESTIGATIONS

CI may request the use of a grand jury before an administrative investigation, during an administrative investigation, or after a criminal investigation. The requirements as far as CI is concerned are that (1) using a grand jury is necessary because CI cannot otherwise develop the relevant facts within a reasonable period of time or (2) an administrative investigation has been conducted, but the grand jury process would strengthen the case's prosecution potential.[194] In addition, an Assistant U.S. Attorney may ask for CI's assistance in a grand jury investigation if the available information points to the "the possible commission of crimes under the jurisdiction of the Service."[195] In other words, a grand jury investigation is permitted to be requested where (1) it is apparent that the administrative process cannot develop the relevant facts within a reasonable period of time or (2) (a) the coordination of the tax investigation with an ongoing or proposed grand jury investigation would be more efficient and (b) the case has significant potential.[196] A lack of time for completion of an administrative investigation can include (1) a lack of cooperation by important witnesses; (2) efforts by the taxpayer (or the taxpayer's counsel) to impede an orderly inquiry of witnesses by intimidation or similar tactics; (3) destruction or threat of destruction of records or other evidence; and (4) the

---

[193] For a case illustrating how a technical accounting issue can lead to an acquittal, see United States v. Hestnes, 492 F. Supp. 999 (WD Wis. 1980).

[194] IRM 9.5.2.2, Initiation of Grand Jury Investigations (Sept. 30, 1998).

[195] IRM 9.5.2.2, Initiation of Grand Jury Investigations (Sept. 30, 1998).

[196] IRM 9.5.2.3, Procedures Incident to Grand Jury Requests (Sept. 30, 1998).

imminent expiration of a statute of limitations. In short, the CID requests a tax grand jury when its administrative investigation has been stymied.[197]

Neither CI, nor a government attorney, are authorized to commence a grand jury investigation without approval. Grand jury investigations of suspected tax violations must have the approval of the Criminal Section of the Justice Department's Tax Division.[198] Accordingly, when a grand jury investigation is considered necessary, CI's request is routed to the Special Agent in Charge and the Area Director, with the advice of the Criminal Tax attorney. If approved, the request is then sent to the Tax Division (Justice Department).[199]

Special agents may also become involved in grand jury investigations at the request of local U.S. Attorneys. Such a request may be prompted by information resulting from an ongoing grand jury investigation of nontax criminal violations or simply may be extended to allow the Service to participate in a proposed grand jury looking into possible tax crimes by a subject of a nontax criminal investigation.[200] When a government attorney wishes a special agent from CI to participate in an ongoing grand jury investigation, such participation involves both an informal review of the information gathered by the nontax grand jury investigation for its criminal tax potential and a formal request for CI participation.[201] Where a government attorney furnishes information to CI before any grand jury investigation, a special agent prepares a report for the Special Agent in Charge with information bearing on the recommendation for grand jury investigation.[202] In general, this review and acceptance process also requires the government attorney to secure (1) authorization from the Tax Di-

---

[197] See, e.g., In re Grand Jury Subpoenas, Apr. 1978, 581 F2d 1103, 1107–1108 (4th Cir. 1978); General Motors Corp. v. United States, 573 F2d 936 (6th Cir.), rev'd en banc, 584 F2d 1366 (6th Cir.), cert. denied, 440 US 934 (1978).

[198] 28 CFR §§ 0.70, 71. This authority is derived from Executive Order No. 6166, Aug. 10, 1933, issued pursuant to Pub. L. No. 428, § 16, 47 Stat. 1517, described in Sullivan v. United States, 348 US 170 (1954). See also Dep't of Justice Manual, Tax Div. 6-4.120 (Grand Jury Investigations).

[199] IRM 9.5.2.3, Procedures Incident to Grand Jury Requests (Sept. 30, 1998). See also IRM 9.5.2.3.1.4, Routing of Grand Jury Requests (Sept. 30, 1998); IRM, Chief Counsel Directives Manual (31)550, Referrals for Grand Jury Investigations (Dec. 11, 1989); Dep't of Justice Manual, Tax Div. 6-4.121 (Grand Jury Investigations).

[200] IRM 9.5.2.3.1.2, Government Attorney Initiated Requests (Sept. 30, 1998). The Tax Division has delegated authority to approve requests seeking to expand a nontax grand jury investigation to include inquiry into possible criminal tax violations to U.S. Attorneys and Independent Counsel appointed under 28 USC § 593. A nontax grand jury is expanded into a tax grand jury where there is a "reason to believe, based upon information developed during the course of the nontax grand jury proceedings, that criminal tax violations may have been committed." Dep't of Justice Manual, Tax Div. 6-4.122D (Joint Tax-Nontax Investigations With IRS Participation).

[201] IRM 9.5.2.3.1.2, Government Attorney Initiated Requests (Sept. 30, 1998).

[202] IRM 9.5.2.3.1.2, Government Attorney Initiated Requests (Sept. 30, 1998); IRM 9.5.2.3.1.4, Routing of Grand Jury Requests (Sept. 30, 1998).

vision of the Justice Department and (2) if there is to be access to grand jury information for civil purposes, an order from the district court pursuant to Rule 6(e) of the Federal Rules of Criminal Procedure authorizing disclosure of the grand jury information.[203]

¶ 12.09 DEFENSE TECHNIQUES IN FRAUD INVESTIGATIONS

A taxpayer may need to develop defense tactics and exercise judgment well before a fraud investigation has begun. For example, a taxpayer may elect to disclose his failure to file tax returns for a number of years or his failure to include all taxable income in his returns at a time when no examination or investigation is pending, in an attempt to avoid a fraud investigation altogether.[204] Also, a taxpayer's potential fraud may come to light during the examination of his tax return by a revenue agent. Thus, defense investigations should begin as soon as possible after the taxpayer learns of a Service investigation.

As the discussion of special agent procedures and CI policies in previous sections demonstrates, a taxpayer under CI investigation is a potential defendant in a criminal prosecution. Taxpayers who have had no previous experience with the criminal process in general and criminal tax investigations in particular will want to know the risks of prosecution and conviction. Statistics may provide some solace, but are inadequate and misleading. Even if 60 percent of the investigations do not lead to a recommendation of prosecution, the reality is that in 40 percent of the cases, there is a recommendation, and no attorney can predict at the outset on which side of the statistical division the client will be included. In the dynamics of the first or early meetings with the client, then, the needs of the taxpayer and the attorney are often at odds. The client wants assurances about the result that the attorney cannot honestly give, while the attorney wants information and evidence to formulate a defense situation, which the client finds irrelevant.

Certain practical features mark most tax investigations, however. At a basic level, the taxpayer's representative must be a lawyer rather than an accountant, not because of professional superiority, but because federal law does not recognize an accountant-client privilege.[205] Although the accountant may long have been the taxpayer's adviser, that accountant can be compelled to re-

---

[203] IRM 9.5.2.4.3, Civil or Non–Grand Jury Material (Sept. 30, 1998).

[204] The manner in which a taxpayer should be represented in such circumstances is discussed supra ¶ 12.03[3][c].

[205] Although the text continues to use the term "representative" in reference to the taxpayer's counsel, the representative should always be an attorney. Couch v. United States, 409 US 322 (1973).

veal any statement the taxpayer has made. In fact, CI will interview the accountant at any early stage. Statements the taxpayer makes to a lawyer for the purpose of obtaining legal advice, however, are privileged from disclosure.[206]

A criminal case has three phases: (1) the administrative investigation by a CI special agent or grand jury investigation; (2) the review or authorization phase; and (3) prosecution in court. The special agent follows specific procedures CI has adopted in conducting the investigation. Definite standards and policies are applied in the review of an agent's recommendation before a final decision to prosecute is made.[207] In the first two phases, investigation and review, the Service's procedures, standards, and policies play as important a part as the rules of evidence and criminal procedure do at the criminal trial. When the defense of a criminal tax case is considered in this light, an overall approach to a Service criminal investigation can be formulated. In its broadest outlines, the defense must be geared to establishing that no prima facie case of fraud exists or that for one or more reasons recognized by the Service, no probability of conviction exists.

[1] Preliminary Matters

Defending a taxpayer under criminal tax investigation should take into account CI's and the Tax Division's policies regarding prosecutions, especially since those policies are designed to terminate investigations where successful prosecution is doubtful. As noted previously, the prompt identification of a fatal weakness in a case, a satisfactory explanation of a questioned item, or the presence of circumstances weighing against prosecution under a recognized policy can terminate an information item inquiry or a full-scale investigation. For example, given the Service's attitude toward the health of a target, the taxpayer's representative should immediately supply the agent with any relevant medical information showing that the taxpayer's health weighs against prosecution (e.g., that the taxpayer has heart disease or is under psychiatric care). In fact, a delay in presenting this information may weigh against the seriousness of the illness. Similarly, documentation making out a claimed voluntary disclosure should be furnished early in an investigation. An agent may be more inclined to discontinue a case with a borderline disclosure if he hears of the disclosure before he has expended too much time on the case.

CI also looks for cases involving a pattern of evasion, usually over at least three years, since such a pattern makes it easier to prove willfulness. If the representative can establish that only a single year is involved, the investi-

---

[206] Colton v. United States, 306 F2d 633 (2d Cir. 1962), cert. denied, 371 US 951 (1963). The attorney-client privilege is discussed at ¶ 13.11[1].

[207] These procedures and policies are discussed supra ¶ 12.03.

gation may be terminated. Both CI and the Justice Department also decline prosecutions where the amount of additional tax is too small, because such cases reflect adversely (from the government's standpoint) on the taxpayer's willfulness and on the deterrent effect of prosecution. In addition, since the margin for error in establishing the tax due is increased where a circumstantial method of proof (e.g., net worth) is used by the agent, it may be difficult to establish the tax due in such a case. Disclosures in the course of a circumstantial evidence investigation can be dangerous, but in a case involving specific items of omitted income, the attorney can make arguments to the agent that limit the information the attorney supplies to the agent.

[a] Interview With the Taxpayer

The initial source of information in a tax investigation is the taxpayer, and so the attorney must interview the taxpayer to obtain basic information. A taxpayer under investigation often proves to be a suspect source of information or a source of misinformation, either unintentionally or because he chooses not to tell the representative the whole truth. When the attorney interviews the taxpayer, the understanding should be that the attorney will check the taxpayer's replies and versions of the circumstances. During the interview, the attorney should question the taxpayer about: (1) any prior statements the taxpayer made to a revenue agent, a revenue officer, and the special agent; (2) sources of information in the form of documentary evidence; (3) potential witnesses; (4) any prior examinations of the taxpayer's returns by the Service and any dealings between the taxpayer and the Service; and (5) the taxpayer's personal background in exhaustive detail.

[i] Prior statements. The representative must learn of any prior statements the taxpayer has made to the Service. The Service and the courts consider attempts to mislead agents to be evidence of willfulness. Also, the taxpayer's statements may assist the special agent in using a circumstantial method of proof. For example, a taxpayer's admissions are particularly useful in a net worth analysis. A taxpayer's denial of having any cash at a particular date can be used to establish an opening net worth and the absence of a cash hoard. Also, on the referral of a case from either the Examination Division or Collection Division, the special agent is instructed to inquire about any statements the taxpayer has made. In the interview with the taxpayer, the special agent attempts to document any false statements, admissions, and impossible explanations.

In some cases, agents may obtain admissions in violation of the Service's restrictions on the activities of revenue agents in perfecting indications of

fraud[208] and its requirement that special agents describe their function and give
the taxpayer partial Miranda (or "News Release") warnings.[209] The use of deception or deceit by agents to obtain admissions may violate the taxpayer's
constitutional rights.[210] Consequently, the representative must determine the circumstances of the taxpayer's statements to the Service, as well as their content. If agents have acted improperly, their conduct can be used as a ground
for the Service's declining prosecution.

[ii] Documents. Records and documents of the taxpayer or of third parties may contain traces of criminal activity. The available records dictate not
only whether a criminal case can be made but the type of proof that will be
presented. For example, records of cash receipts may show income greater
than the amount reported on the return. Even where the return is consistent
with books of account, records such as sales invoices may show the receipt of
unreported income. The representative should inquire as to what records the
taxpayer keeps, who maintains the records, and whether the Service has already examined them. The representative should also examine the records of

---

[208] See discussion supra ¶ 12.03[1].

[209] The Service is not required to give Miranda warnings to a taxpayer in a normal
tax investigation because the taxpayer is not in custody. United States v. Beckwith, 425
US 341 (1976). However, the statements of a taxpayer have been suppressed where special agents failed to give the partial Miranda warnings in accordance with Service procedure (the "Heffner-Leahy-Sourapas" rule). United States v. Heffner, 420 F2d 809 (4th Cir.
1969); United States v. Leahey, 434 F2d 7 (1st Cir. 1970); United States v. Sourapas, 515
F2d 295 (9th Cir. 1975). This result is based not on constitutional privilege but on the administrative law (and possibly due process) principle that an administrative agency is
bound by its own administrative rules. The Heffner-Leahey-Sourapas rule was questioned
by at least one other circuit. United States v. Leonard, 524 F2d 1076, 1089 (2d Cir. 1975),
cert. denied, 425 US 958 (1976). The Supreme Court, in United States v. Caceres, 440 US
741 (1979), held that the suppression of evidence was erroneous where agents failed to
follow Service procedures on the use of recording devices. The violation of the procedures
was not deliberate in *Caceres*, and the Court did not consider a "rigid" rule of suppression
appropriate where no statutory or constitutional requirement had been violated. The flexible approach of *Caceres* would seem to leave some vitality to the Heffner-Leahey-
Sourapas rule involving a published procedure about which inadvertent errors of interpretation cannot be expected. But the First Circuit has said in United States v. Irvine, 699
F2d 43 (1st Cir. 1983), that *Leahey* is no longer good law after *Caceres*. For further discussion, see ¶ 13.10[1].

[210] See, e.g., United States v. Tweel, 550 F2d 297 (5th Cir. 1977); United States v.
Mapp, 561 F2d 685 (7th Cir. 1977); United States v. Toussaint, 456 F. Supp. 1069 (SD
Tex. 1978). But see United States v. Lockyer, 448 F2d 417 (10th Cir. 1971); United
States v. Matis, 476 F. Supp. 1287, 80-1 USTC ¶ 9111 (SDNY 1979). See ¶ 13.09[4].

third parties with whom the taxpayer had business transactions (e.g., bank accounts, safe-deposit boxes, and stock brokerage accounts).

[iii] Potential witnesses. Although eyewitness testimony is rare in tax cases, such testimony nevertheless has a dramatic effect on the outcome. Sometimes this effect is attributable to the close relationship between the witness and the taxpayer. It is not unusual for a key prosecution witness to be a former spouse, paramour, relative, or employee. Indeed, this witness may be the person who informed the Service as to the possible violations. The taxpayer's accountant is an obvious potential witness—if only to testify that he prepared the taxpayer's return from information supplied to him by the taxpayer, information that the government establishes is incomplete or false. For purposes of inquiry, potential witnesses may be grouped into return preparers, recordkeepers, income payers (i.e., customers, banks, brokers), and others with knowledge of the circumstances. As part of the interview with the taxpayer, the representative should draw up a list of potential witnesses.

[iv] Prior Service examinations. The probability of conviction is enhanced where a taxpayer repeats a violation after a previous civil examination. If a taxpayer's return has previously been examined and an adjustment made because, for example, an item of income was omitted, the taxpayer will have difficulty in contending that omission of the same item in the investigation year was due to negligence. Furthermore, in a prior examination, the taxpayer may have supplied data, which are still contained in Service files, that provide information useful in the current investigation or that are false. The representative should carefully question the taxpayer in regard to his previous examinations by the Service.

[v] Taxpayer's background. One element of willfulness is knowledge, a state of mind that presumes some minimum level of education and experience with the tax-paying obligation and perhaps with business or financial affairs. The Service believes that a taxpayer's education may show that his conduct was willful rather than attributable to ignorance or negligence. For this reason, the representative should ask the taxpayer about his educational background and other biographical data. Health problems should also be identified.

[b] Importance of Starting Promptly

Prompt defense action is essential at the outset of a CI investigation. The special agent generally has done some preliminary investigation before the taxpayer is contacted or learns of the investigation and by this time is working with some evidence of fraud. Although further investigation by the special agent cannot be stopped, the representative can at least halt an unconsidered flow of information from the taxpayer to the agent. Consequently, the representative should notify the special agent of his involvement, furnish a power of attorney, and request time before replying to any inquiries, as soon as possible.

Key witnesses should be interviewed as early as feasible. Early interviews have the advantage of obtaining information from a witness that he might later forget. Unless the representative makes some early inquiry of witnesses, he will be unable to check the taxpayer's story. Further, the representative should keep ahead of the agent in order to have a better knowledge of the circumstances. Without a prompt defense investigation, the representative will be unable to advise the taxpayer adequately and make judgments during the course of the investigation as to what extent and when to cooperate, and what investigative problems the agent may be encountering.

[c] Use of an Investigative Accountant

[i] In general. As noted previously, in tax evasion prosecutions, government prosecutors use circumstantial or indirect methods of proof to establish that the taxpayer did not report all of his income. These methods build on an analysis of the taxpayer's increases in net worth or of his bank deposits. Even where indirect methods of proof are not involved, records must be analyzed to determine what items of income and deductions will become part of the case. Similarly, the defense investigation should identify unreported or unclaimed deductions to offset unreported income and serve as a basis for a defense argument. The defense may attempt to duplicate any method of proof used by the special agent to check and refute its accuracy. The use of one indirect method to check another can also aid in the administrative review of a case and possibly at trial (e.g., using a net worth analysis to check the use of an expenditures method). An analysis of a taxpayer's bank deposits, increases in net worth, or sources and application of funds also serves as a method of checking the taxpayer's version of the circumstances.

This kind of analysis usually requires the assistance of a competent investigative or forensic accountant. If there is a trial, the investigative accountant may be called upon to testify as an expert or a summary witness. In the administrative stage, the accountant will be able to give the attorney sufficient information in a form the attorney can use to make judgments in dealing with the special agent or in making arguments to the Criminal Tax Counsel or the docket attorney in the Criminal Section of the Justice Department's Tax Division. The accountant also can be present at interviews of witnesses and can testify in the event of any conflict between a statement given at the interview and later testimony. Of course, the taxpayer must consent to the retaining of an investigative accountant, but the fees incurred are usually well spent because the time of the accountant is likely to be less costly than that of the representative for a technical service the representative requires but is usually not equipped to perform himself.

[ii] The Kovel letter. The attorney must take care when engaging the accountant to ensure the confidentiality of the accountant's work product. Analyses prepared by an accountant engaged by a lawyer for the purpose of providing legal counsel to the lawyer's client have been held to be covered by the attorney-client privilege.[211] A letter agreement establishing the relationship of the accountant and the representative is essential. At a minimum, it should include (1) the engagement of the accountant by the representative to assist the representative in rendering legal advice to the client by performing analyses of records; (2) the ownership by the representative of any work papers prepared by the accountant; and (3) provision for payment of the accountant by the representative. (See Form 12.4.) If the accountant who performs the service is the taxpayer's accountant and return preparer, the change in client (from taxpayer to representative) becomes difficult to identify and prove. Also, the accountant, after being retained by the representative, may learn of matters that may incriminate the taxpayer and find it impossible to separate the time when or the capacity in which the information was learned. Consequently, to preserve the integrity of confidential information, the representative usually should retain an accountant other than the taxpayer's accountant to perform necessary analyses. Even if an accountant is engaged by the representative, notes and memorandums prepared by the accountant may become discoverable by the government in some circumstances,[212] especially if the accountant's work papers are for the preparation of tax returns.[213] Accordingly, the accountant should be told to be cautious in making notes. The representative might ask the accountant to report orally first and then to reduce his report to writing with the representative's approval.

[2] CI Delay

Delay is characteristic of tax investigations; both the taxpayer and his representative must realize and accept this basic fact. Investigation and administra-

---

[211] United States v. Kovel, 296 F2d 918 (2d Cir. 1961). For further description of the attorney-client privilege, see ¶ 13.11[1].

[212] Consider the reciprocal discovery provisions of Federal Rules of Criminal Procedure (Fed. R. Crim. P.) 16(c), which allow the prosecution discovery if the defendant taxpayer seeks discovery from the prosecution. See also United States v. Nobles, 422 US 225 (1975), where the prosecution was permitted to discover portions of a pretrial statement given by a defense trial witness, the defense investigator, who testified that prosecution witnesses had made inconsistent statements to him.

[213] See United States v. Brown, 478 F2d 1038 (7th Cir. 1973). See also Colton v. United States, 306 F2d 633 (2d Cir. 1962).

tive review can take several years, and no means of recourse is available to force the Service to take action. Even where a special agent decides to terminate an investigation, such action is not immediate. Because the statute of limitations on the prosecution of tax crimes is six years, the law imposes no requirement on the Service to reach a prompt decision. Unquestionably, taxpayers suffer from the time consumed by investigation and administrative review, but they also benefit from the levels of review when questionable cases are not prosecuted.

[3] Evidence

Evidence, not cooperation, determines the outcome of the investigation. A special agent is an investigator whose primary purpose is to gather sufficient evidence of a criminal violation to secure a conviction. Some harsh realities flow from a criminal investigation. Fraud investigations are contests over evidence. Where sufficient evidence of a tax crime exists to establish a reasonable probability of conviction, and the special agent is able to obtain that evidence, the agent will recommend prosecution whether or not the taxpayer is cooperative during the investigation. If the special agent is unable to obtain sufficient evidence to prove that the taxpayer committed a tax crime, he should terminate the investigation. Realistically then, it is evidence, not the taxpayer's cooperation, that controls the agent's recommendation. As a result, any question about disclosure or nondisclosure of evidence on some legitimate ground, should be resolved in favor of nondisclosure. Attorneys will not advise their taxpayer/clients to provide evidence that conclusively establishes guilt, and they are professionly obligated to consider withholding any evidence with respect to which a privilege can legitimately be claimed. Under developing law, the grounds on which the production of records may be opposed are few and, for the taxpayer, distressingly limited.[214] If no privilege can be claimed or it is decided to turn information over to the agent, at a minimum the attorney must know the significance of the information and be prepared to confront it in a subsequent prosecution.

Because an investigation is a contest for evidence, the attorney must attempt to control not only the data supplied to the agent but also the form of the submission. For example, a taxpayer can supply information in the form of an affidavit without being subject to open-ended questioning. When a witness has supplied an affidavit to the agent, the affidavit may be supplemented, modified, or corrected by another affidavit. When there is a question as to whether the agent has accurately recorded a statement and the witness has favorable testimony, an affidavit can be supplied to make a record. Even where a tax-

---

[214] For the various privileges, constitutional and evidentiary, see Chapter 13.

payer decides to give a statement, the representative and the agent can agree to limit questioning to certain areas.

[4] Dealing With the Special Agent

During an investigation, the taxpayer's attorney interacts with the special agent; therefore, the attorney must adopt an approach in dealings with the agent. First, the attorney must remember that he is the taxpayer's agent once he files his power of attorney with the special agent. Any statement the attorney makes may constitute a vicarious admission and be used against the taxpayer.[215] As a result, the attorney must exercise extreme care in communicating with the special agent because statements he makes in conferences with the agent may be used against the taxpayer as adoptive admissions. Second, the attorney must realize that there are no off-the-record discussions with a special agent. Anything the lawyer says to the agent is likely to be included in the agent's history sheets or chronological notes on the case. For protective reasons alone, therefore, the lawyer should also keep a chronological record of any conversations with the agent. Third, in dealing with the special agent, the lawyer should project the best possible image of himself and the client. The lawyer should show the agent that the lawyer is absolutely sincere and has an unswerving commitment to protect the client's rights under the law and to work as hard on the client's behalf as necessary. Also, the lawyer must project integrity because the lawyer who cannot win some level of trust with the special agent cannot assist the client's cause. Finally, just as the attorney must exercise care in what he says to the agent, he should also use the agent as a source of information. Although the agent wants information from the attorney, the agent can also provide information about the case (e.g., what he thinks the case is about, what violation is involved, and what method of proof is being used).

---

[215] United States v. Dolleris, 408 F2d 918 (6th Cir.), cert. denied, 395 US 943 (1969) (lawyer's statements to agents); Massei v. United States, 241 F2d 895 (1st Cir. 1957), aff'd per curiam on another issue, 355 US 595 (1958) (lawyer's statements); United States v. Pawlak, 352 F. Supp. 794 (SDNY 1972) (accountant's statements); United States v. Parenti, 326 F. Supp. 717 (ED Pa. 1971), aff'd per curiam, 470 F2d 1175 (3d Cir.), cert. denied, 411 US 965 (1973) (accountant's statements). See Feld & Rosenblatt, "Lawyer Beware: The Use of Counsel's Statements as Evidence Against His Client in Tax Fraud Cases," 63 Taxes 618 (Sept. 1985). This line of authority makes all the more notable the Tax Division's policy not to use a lawyer's admissions made in a conference. See supra ¶¶ 12.06, 12.07. However, the Service does not follow the Tax Division's policy. IRM, Chief Counsel Directives Manual (31)420 (July 20, 1990) (Conference Procedures).

[5] Methods of Proof

Tax evasion prosecutions utilize well-defined methods of proof. The taxpayer's own books and the records of third parties, such as vendors or customers, may show that specific items of income were not reported or that deductions were overstated. If a taxpayer's books and records are unavailable or are considered inaccurate or incomplete, the agent may use indirect or circumstantial methods of proof, such as the bank deposits, net worth, or expenditures methods to establish the taxpayer's true income.[216] In a criminal investigation, the attorney must know these methods or theories of proof and determine from either the agent or the manner of his investigation what method the agent is using to make the case. Once the method of proof has been determined, the lawyer should attempt to identify weaknesses or errors in the agent's investigations. Also, the lawyer should duplicate the agent's method to establish, if possible, that no unreported income exists or that the agent has made technical errors in using the method. Errors made by the agent in attempting to determine the taxpayer's income by circumstantial methods of proof can be used in the administrative review of the case to argue that no prima facie case of evasion exists. If the attorney reveals agent errors during review, CI may be able to cure the error and keep the case alive. Consequently, it is a matter of judgment whether and when to reveal agent errors in using a circumstantial method of proof.

[6] Gathering Information to Develop Theory of Defense

Defense investigations in a tax case are similar to other criminal investigations in that ultimately the case turns on a presentation of facts, either at the administrative stage or before a judge or jury. Facts are obtained through an investigation. Since a criminal investigation must have some focus, the attorney must have a theory of defense and develop facts relevant to that theory. Similarly, the representative in a tax investigation must evaluate what theory and method of proof the agent is proceeding under and prepare to rebut that theory and method. Obviously, the representative must reevaluate his theory and his assessment of the agent's theory as the investigation proceeds.

[7] Interviews With Witnesses

Defense interviews of potential witnesses can be obtained only with the witnesses' cooperation, because the representative has no access to processes such as a summons or grand jury subpoena to compel a witness to speak to him. Some witnesses may cooperate because they are well disposed toward the tax-

---

[216] These methods are described in Chapter 7A.

payer on account of business or other relationships. Others may not want to get involved because they suspect further inconvenience. Still others sense that cooperation with the taxpayer may bring some unspecified act of retribution from the Service. These individuals may have tax problems of their own, and agents are not quick to dispel any fears witnesses may have about their own tax returns. Other witnesses may be willing to speak with anyone, but do so without appreciating the importance of the accuracy of their statements. When a potential witness is reluctant to speak, one argument the representative can use is that the witness's testimony does not belong to the Service or to the taxpayer, and that it is proper and may be the duty of the taxpayer's representative as well as the government to interview all persons who may be witnesses.[217] However, the reality is that before a trial, there is little, apart from persuasion, the representative can do to get a witness to say what he knows about the facts of the case.

Even if a witness is willing to discuss the case, the interview must be carefully handled. If the special agent has not yet interviewed the witness, the special agent may interview the witness at a later date. If the attorney has interviewed the witness without taking precautions for the agent's interview, the agent may discovers the attorney's questions, and as a result the areas about which the attorney is concerned. In other words, the attorney's questions may turn out to be leads in the special agent's investigation. Consequently, the attorney must question the witness so as not to indicate areas of concern. Also, the attorney should ask the witness whether the special agent has discussed the case with the witness, and ask what questions the agent asked the witness and what was said in as much detail as possible. If the witness has given a formal statement, the representative should inform the witness that he is entitled to a transcript of testimony or a copy of an affidavit and encourage him to obtain the transcript or copy.[218]

If the witness so requests, a copy of an affidavit or transcript of a question and answer statement "will be furnished [the] witness promptly, except when it is determined by the District Director that release should be delayed until such time as it will not interfere with the development or successful prosecution of a case."[219] A witness is entitled to the question and answer statement whether or not he signs it. The Manual also permits the use of a recording device by a special agent to record an interrogation or conference where no stenographer is readily available. The agent is to advise the witness in advance that the interrogation will be recorded. If the witness objects, the

---

[217] ABA Project on Standards of Criminal Justice, Standards Relating to the Prosecution and the Defense Function § 4.3(c) (1971).

[218] See the discussion supra ¶ 12.03[2][b][vi].

[219] IRM 9.4.5.10.3, Persons Entitled to Copies (June 30, 1999). See also IRM 9.4.5.8, Right to Record Interview (June 30, 1998); IRM 9.4.5.11.1, Right to Advice of Counsel (June 30, 1998).

agent is not supposed to record the statement. If the witness elects to mechanically record the conversation, the Service will make its own recording. Service procedures suggest, then, that a witness should notify the agent that he intends to record the interrogation or conference. If the witness does not notify the agent in advance and the agent does not have a recording device, the agent should adjourn the proceeding until he can obtain a recording device, rather than refuse to allow the witness to record.[220] The possibility of recording an interrogation does not mean that every meeting between a witness and the agent will be recorded. The agent is instructed to determine whether to record on the basis of the particular circumstances, the witness's cooperation, and the judgment of the practitioner. Under current Service procedures, a witness will be furnished a copy only of formal statements, such as an affidavit or a transcript of a question and answer statement, only if the witness requests it. However, the witness is not always told of his entitlement to his formal statement, and does not always get it promptly. Moreover, a witness will not know what an agent includes in a memorandum as information supplied. Recording is at least one solution to these problems.

It is important that another person accompany the representative when a witness is interviewed. The presence of the other person serves two purposes. First, if there is any conflict about what the witness has said, the other person, rather than the representative, can testify. Second, the presence of the other person avoids any charge of intimidation or other questionable conduct in the interview. The representative must remember that obstruction of proceedings before a federal agency by a person who "endeavors to influence, intimidate, or impede any witness" is a felony,[221] and federal prosecutors may not be reluctant to use this charge against the representative.

Witnesses disposed toward the taxpayer may wish to have the taxpayer's representative accompany them to a Service interview. At the same time, the representative may wish to know what happens at the interview. Should the taxpayer's representative also represent the witness? The answer is not as clear as it should be.[222] Multiple representation can entail considerable risks for the representative as well as offer certain tactical advantages.[223] Although it does

---

[220] IRM 9.4.5.8, Right to Record Interview (June 30, 1998).

[221] 18 USC § 1505.

[222] The ethical considerations and the Service's procedures for multiple representation are analyzed at ¶ 13.03[4][b].

[223] The advantages and risks are similar to those present when a lawyer represents a taxpayer under investigation and witnesses before a grand jury. For a discussion of the problems in a grand jury investigation, see Tague, "Multiple Representation of Targets and Witnesses During a Grand Jury Investigation," 17 Am. Crim. L. Rev. 301 (1980). See also Costrilos & Kennelly, "Birds of a Feather," 4 Crim. Justice (ABA) 2 (Winter 1990). The alternative to multiple representation may be joint defense. See Perito, et al., "Joint Defense Agreements," 4 Crim. Justice 6 (Winter 1990).

give the representative the opportunity to discover more information than he might otherwise learn about the direction of the investigation, it can also provoke a disqualification proceeding, which may result in his representing neither the taxpayer nor the witness. Multiple representation may also serve as the basis for criminal-obstruction-of-justice charges. Because of the potential problems of multiple representation, it is appropriate in only the clearest cases where the parties are advised of the potential conflict and choose to pursue this course.

[8] Cooperation and Its Risks

Criminal tax investigations are conducted for the purpose of gathering evidence to use in a prosecution of the taxpayer. Despite the intended use of information provided to a special agent, there is considerable pressure on the representative and the taxpayer to cooperate with the special agent by supplying requested information. Taxpayers under investigation face embarrassment and loss of business when the special agent contacts friends, customers, and business associates. Investigation may extend for a year, and it is not unusual for them to last two or three years. Taxpayers sometimes feel that by supplying information, the ordeal of the investigation can be cut short. The danger of giving in to this natural impulse is that it may shorten not only the time of investigation but the time before the taxpayer begins to serve a period of incarceration. When this danger is explained, the taxpayer usually controls the impulse "to get the matter over with."

FORM 12.4 _____
KOVEL LETTER—RETENTION OF ACCOUNTANT
_____

Mr. Alan Michaels, CPA
[address]

Dear Mr. Michaels:

[Client] has retained me and my firm to represent him in a tax matter and has specifically authorized me to retain an accountant to assist me in rendering legal advice to him. This is to confirm my engagement of you as of [date].

In connection with this engagement, it is understood and agreed that you will do the following:

1. You will assist us in rendering legal advice to the client by, including but not limited to, summarizing and analyzing financial data, and reflecting your work in summaries, analyses, and schedules ("your work product"). Your work product may also be reflected on tax return forms for purposes of our being able to provide advice to the client.

2. You will keep confidential any information you receive that is made available to us as attorneys for the client or which you receive directly from the client. You will not disclose to anyone without written permission the contents or subject matter of any written or oral communications, nor any information obtained from your inspection or review of any record or document submitted to you, nor permit any inspection of those records or documents without our prior written permission.

3. You will open a separate file at your offices marked, "Confidential, Property of Michael I. Saltzman." You will place all documents, records, workpapers, summaries, no matter what the source, in that file. You agree, in this connection, that any workpapers, analyses, summaries, schedules and the like you prepare in the course of this engagement belong to and are the property of Michael I. Saltzman, and that you retain no proprietary interest in this work product.

4. You will report directly to us on matters pertaining to this engagement and will immediately return the file described in Paragraph 3 at our request. By way of illustration and not limitation, you will notify us immediately on the happening of one or more of the following: (a) the use of any of your work product or other records of documents provided to you in a manner not provided for in this agreement; (b) any request by anyone to examine or copy your work product, or records or documents produced to you; and (c) the service or attempted service of any process, such as an administrative summons or court order, to produce the work product, records, or documents.

5. You will bill us directly for the services you render under this engagement, including your regular charges, as well as out-of-pocket disbursements.

If this letter conforms to our understanding, please sign the enclosed copy of this letter and return it to us.

Very truly yours,

Michael I. Saltzman

MIS:rd
Enclosure and cc:[client]

The Service's administrative attitude toward cooperation also weighs against unconsidered cooperation with the agent. The Service is well aware of taxpayers' contentions that cooperation is inconsistent with consciousness of guilt or the commission of an alleged offense and with criminal intent. However, the Service's Handbook for Special Agents states: "This defense is rarely persuasive if the facts and circumstances attending the commission of the alleged offense create an inference of wilfulness. Subsequent cooperation during an investigation may only serve to mitigate the penalty."[224] In short, cooperation only makes the special agent's task easier; it does not change a decision to recommend prosecution.

If the taxpayer fails or refuses to cooperate, the government prosecutor may argue that the taxpayer's silence is an admission of guilt. The taxpayer is privileged from compulsory production of potentially incriminating evidence under the Fifth Amendment, yet some courts have said that a refusal to produce records for reasonable inspection is evidence from which a willful attempt to evade may be inferred.[225] The propriety of an instruction calling attention to a failure to produce records for inspection is doubtful under the Fifth Amendment, but the administrative "no benefit" and the trial "potential risk" of a failure to cooperate make the decision a difficult one for the representative.

With this background, a number of observations about cooperation in a criminal tax investigation can be made. The representative should never voluntarily provide a special agent with information unless there is full appreciation of what is being surrendered and to what use it may be put in the agent's effort to make a case. Cooperation can give the agent an important piece of evidence, and once given to the agent, tax information may not be recalled. Cooperation (as opposed to pointing out some weakness in the case) probably should occur later rather than earlier in an investigation; that is, when the lawyer has a fairly good idea of the case. Also, cooperation need not be an all-or-nothing proposition. Once it can be determined that the data the agent seeks exist and can be obtained from a third party, it makes sense to provide the information to avoid the agent's contacting the third party. A taxpayer may also face a charge of evading substantially greater tax liabilities if the agent uses the net worth, expenditures, or bank deposits method of proving income. Consequently, if the special agent is able to discover the taxpayer's sources of in-

---

[224] See ¶ 7A.02[3].

[225] Even though a blanket instruction has been warned against as creating Fifth Amendment problems, the possibility of an inference is recognized "if an informed defendant allowed a partial examination and then sought to cut it short or to limit investigators." 2 E. Devitt & C. Blackmar, Federal Jury Practice and Instructions § 52.07, at 55 (2d ed. 1970). See also United States v. Gross, 276 F2d 816 (2d Cir.), cert. denied, 363 US 831 (1960); Smith v. United States, 236 F2d 260 (8th Cir. 1956); Beard v. United States, 222 F2d 84 (4th Cir.), cert. denied, 350 US 846 (1955). See ¶ 13.10.

come, investments, and funds for expenditures, it makes sense to provide information about specific items of unreported income. In the final analysis, where there is doubt about the matter, the taxpayer should not cooperate by making a disclosure.

¶ 12.10 CONFERENCES AND EVALUATION IN COMPLETED CRIMINAL INVESTIGATIONS

[1] Overview of the Processing of Criminal Tax Cases

The taxpayer or subject of a criminal prosecution recommendation may have a conference at the local Area Office with the Special Agent-in-Charge's designee.[226] After the Area CI recommends a case for criminal prosecution, CI sends a letter to the taxpayer or other subject of the prosecution recommendation that the case has been forwarded to the Area Counsel's office.[227] Although a conference with Counsel is not a right, Counsel will offer to have a conference unless Counsel concludes that a conference "would serve no purpose,"[228] or the case is one of those cases where no conference will be held.[229] After this conference, Counsel decides whether to recommend prosecution.

If the Counsel recommends prosecution, a criminal reference letter is prepared and the case file is forwarded to the Assistant Chief Counsel, Criminal Tax, in the National Office. If the Assistant Chief Counsel approves the prosecution recommendation, the case file is sent to the Criminal Section of the Department of Justice's Tax Division.[230] The Criminal Section also gives the subject of the Service's recommendation the opportunity to have a conference at the Department of Justice.[231] If the Criminal Section attorney recommends

---

[226] IRM 9.5, The Investigative Process Handbook 12.2, Formal Conference with Principal Upon Completion Of Investigation (Apr. 30, 1999).

[227] IRM, Chief Counsel Directive Manual 31.4.2.4, Conference Opportunity (July 20, 1990).

[228] The authority for holding a conference in cases handled by the Chief Counsel is found in the Statement of Procedural Rules, 26 CFR §§ 601.501–601.509. See IRM, Chief Counsel Directive Manual 31.4.2.2, Conference Procedures- General Authority (July 20, 1990).

[229] IRM, Chief Counsel Directive Manual 31.4.2.5, Cases Where No Conference Will Be Held (July 20, 1990). Where authorized, the case may be referred directly to the local U.S. Attorney for prosecution. IRM, Chief Counsel Directive Manual 31.4.2.5, Cases Where No Conference Will Be Held (July 20, 1990).

[230] IRM, Chief Counsel Directive Manual 31.4.2.1, Conference Procedures—Introduction (July 20, 1990).

[231] See infra ¶ 12.07[4].

prosecution and managers within the Criminal Section authorize prosecution, and the authorization is approved by or on behalf of the Assistant Attorney General of the Tax Division, the case file is forwarded to the office of the U.S. Attorney in the judicial district where venue for prosecution lies for institution of criminal proceedings. If prosecution is declined, the case is returned to the Service, although the Service can protest this decision.

In short, prosecution recommendations in criminal tax cases are subject to successive reviews, ultimately by prosecutors who are criminal tax specialists in the Justice Department's Tax Division.[232]

[2] The CI Office Conference

After the completion of a special agent's investigation, but before the special agent's report (SAR) report is finished, the taxpayer or other person who is the subject of a recommended prosecution may request a conference in the CI office in which the special agent is located, or CI may decide that such a conference is in the best interests of the government.[233] The conference request is usually granted.[234] If the taxpayer fails to request a conference, the taxpayer waives the opportunity for the conference.[235] To make certain that the taxpayer is afforded a conference, therefore, it is good practice for the lawyer to request a conference during the investigation.

A local CI office conference is held with the special agent's group manager or branch chief, and with the special agent.[236] At the conference, the taxpayer's representative is told the "fraudulent features" of the case, such as the criminal offense alleged, the years involved, the nature of the alleged fraud (e.g., unreported dividend or sales income), the method of proof, and the figures in the case (usually the civil, not criminal, figures).[237] Disclosures are left up to the conferees' discretion by provision that they be made "consistent

---

[232] U.S. Attorney's offices grant taxpayer's counsel a conference upon request, but critics of the tiered review process have proposed the elimination of one or more of the criminal case conferences. General Accounting Office, Report to the Joint Comm. on Taxation, Streamlining Legal Review of Criminal Tax Cases Would Strengthen Enforcement of Federal Tax Laws (GGD 81-25, Apr. 29, 1981). For a response to this suggestion, see J. Bray, "A Report and Comment on Proposed Reforms in Criminal Tax Case Conference Procedures," 28 Fed. Bar News 11 (1981).

[233] IRM 9.5.12.2, Formal Conference with Principal Upon Completion of Investigation (Apr. 30, 1999).

[234] 26 CFR § 601.107(b)(2).

[235] Automotive Serv. Inc. v. Kurtz, 45 AFTR2d 80-1465 (MD Fla. 1980).

[236] IRM 9.5.12.2, Formal Conference with Principal Upon Completion of Investigation (Apr. 30, 1999).

[237] See IRM 9.5 12.2, Information to Be Given Principal or His or Her Representative at Formal Conference (Apr. 30, 1999).

with protecting the Government's interests. . . . "[238] If no interest of the government is jeopardized, the lawyer is given "sufficient facts and figures . . . to acquaint [the taxpayer] with the basis, nature, and other essential elements of the criminal charges against him or her."[239] Some, but not all, of this information may be given at the conference, or the information may be conveyed in the most limited and cryptic terms. Efforts to compel the CI to reveal meaningful information at the conference have been unsuccessful.[240]

Theoretically, the representative also has an opportunity to present the taxpayer's defense at the conference, but there is little practical likelihood of overturning the agent's recommendation. As a result, the local office CI conference has proven to have marginal value both to CI and to taxpayers. Lawyers have criticized the conference procedure because there is little opportunity to exchange information. Although the agent and group supervisor listen to explanations and defenses, the conference, apart from the limited information furnished to the representative, is often a one-sided affair.

On balance, a taxpayer probably should accept the offer of a local office CI conference. At the least, the lawyer can discover information useful in preparing for the Counsel conference. The lawyer can also learn what features in the case are the subject of the special agent's recommendation. For example, the investigation may have touched on a number of questionable items or transactions, but the agent may have decided to recommend prosecution on only some of the items investigated. Even the civil figures can indicate the items considered by the special agent, especially in specific-item cases. In some instances, the civil figures can also indicate errors in using an indirect method of proof. Thus, even a limited interchange between the conferees and the representative can be useful in searching out the attitude of district officials to proffered defenses or arguments. Armed with their response, the lawyer can prepare a more telling argument for the Counsel lawyer. Finally, in cases where the propriety of the special agent's conduct has been questioned, the conference should be used to document the taxpayer's objection. In this way, the taxpayer is on record, and even if the conferee does not consider the objec-

---

[238] See IRM 9.5 12.2.2, Information to Be Given Principal or His or Her Representative at Formal Conference (Apr. 30, 1999).

[239] 26 CFR § 601.107(b)(2). See IRM 9.5.12.2.2, Information to Be Given Principal or His or Her Representative at Formal Conference (Apr. 30, 1999).

[240] Short v. Murphy, 368 F. Supp. 591 (ED Mich. 1973), aff'd, 512 F2d 374 (6th Cir. 1975) (extent of disclosure discretionary). Accord Einhorn v. DeWitt, 618 F2d 347 (5th Cir. 1980). Regulations providing for both the conference and disclosures are said not to have the force and effect of law according any rights to taxpayers. Einhorn v. Dewitt, 618 F2d 350 (5th Cir. 1980), citing Luhring v. Glotzbach, 304 F2d 556 (4th Cir. 1962). Pseudonym Taxpayer v. Miller, 497 F. Supp. 78 (DNJ 1980) (petition for injunction to compel disclosure at CID conference and to restrain referral dismissed).

tion to warrant declination, an official acting for the Special Agent-in-Charge may consider the objection meritorious.

When the Special Agent-in-Charge concurs with the special agent's recommendation of prosecution, the subject ordinarily is notified by letter that prosecution has been recommended and that the case is being referred to the Counsel's office.[241]

[3] Division Counsel Review

Recommendations of criminal prosecution made by the CI are reviewed by CI Division Counsel attorney. Counsel's decision on the recommendation is pivotal. If the Counsel attorney approves of the CI recommendation, the case is sent to Division Counsel/Associate Chief Counsel in the National Office, and then to the Criminal Section of the Justice Department's Tax Division. If the Counsel attorney declines prosecution, the case is returned to the referring examination or collection office as a civil tax case.[242] Review at the Counsel level ensures that cases forwarded to the Justice Department's Tax Division meet CI's prosecution standards. Under these standards, (1) there must be sufficient evidence to prove the commission of a crime beyond a reasonable doubt and (2) there must be a reasonable probability of conviction. These standards are applied in accordance with Service policies.[243]

The local CI office ordinarily notifies the taxpayer or the taxpayer's lawyer when it forwards the case to Counsel with a recommendation for prosecution.[244] On receipt of the prosecution recommendation, the special agent's report, and the exhibits to the report, the case is assigned to a docket attorney. Shortly after the file is delivered to the Counsel's office, the administrative file, containing the pertinent tax returns and the revenue agent's report, is received from the CI office that made the recommendation.[245] After the case is assigned to a docket attorney, the attorney prepares a letter to the taxpayer or the taxpayer's lawyer offering a conference and tentatively scheduling the con-

---

[241] 26 CFR § 601.107(a); IRM 9.5.12.5.3, Notification Letter to Principal of the Prosecution Recommendation (Apr. 30, 1999).

[242] Taxpayers are notified in writing when the CI discontinues an investigation. IRM 9.5.12.5, Written Notification to Taxpayer When Criminal Investigation Division Discontinues an Investigation (Apr. 30, 1999).

[243] These policies are discussed at supra ¶ 12.03[3].

[244] 26 CFR 601.107(c). IRM 9.5.12.5.3, Notification to the Principal in the Prosecution Recommendation (Apr. 30, 1999).

[245] IRM, Chief Counsel Directive Manual 31.4.4, Cases Presenting Special Problems or Processing (July 20, 1990).

ference.[246] However, to ensure that the taxpayer does not lose the opportunity of the District Counsel conference, the representative should, immediately after receipt of the CI notice, send a letter to the Area Counsel stating that notice of the referral has been received and that a conference is requested. Although the Service permits the conference to be rescheduled to a mutually convenient date, a conference is normally held within thirty days after the file is received, except in unusual circumstances. Generally, a conference is offered unless the Service concludes that offering a conference would "serve no purpose."[247] Under this standard, a conference is denied where alerting the taxpayer to the pendency of the case in the Counsel's office may result in endangering a witness or flight on the part of the taxpayer.[248]

The docket attorney to whom the case is assigned represents CI at the conference and is accompanied by another Service employee, usually another attorney in Counsel's office. After the conference, the docket attorney prepares a memorandum, which is reviewed by the attorney's reviewer. This memorandum becomes part of the case file.

Based on the special agent's report and the attached exhibits, as well as the other information contained in the file and the submissions that may have been made by the taxpayer or the taxpayer's representative, the docket attorney chooses one of three alternatives:

1. Recommend prosecution to the Justice Department's Tax Division and prepare a "criminal reference letter," which is a type of referral letter.
2. Request that a supplemental investigation be conducted by the special agent to secure certain evidence in order to remedy any deficiency in the proof.
3. Decline prosecution and prepare a "declination memorandum," setting forth the reasons for the declination

If a supplemental investigation is conducted, the results of that investigation are reviewed when received and a determination is made whether or not the deficiencies in proof have been remedied.

Certain types of criminal cases are referred by Special Agents-in-Charge to U.S. Attorneys' offices rather than to the Tax Division Justice Department, and others are referred directly from the Division Counsel's office to U.S. At-

---

[246] IRM, Chief Counsel Directives Manual 31.4.2.6, Prompt Scheduling of Conference (July 20, 1990)

[247] IRM, Chief Counsel Directive Manual 31.4.2.4, Conference Opportunity (July 20, 1990).

[248] IRM, Chief Counsel Directive Manual 31.4.2.4, Conference Opportunity (July 20, 1990).

torneys' offices rather than to the Tax Division Justice Department.[249] Direct referrals to the local U.S. Attorney by the Special Agent-in-Charge are made in cases involving arrests by special agents; violations of the currency transaction reporting provisions of Title 31 and the money laundering crimes of Title 18; and in recommendations of prosecution in OCDETF cases.[250] Also, the CI Division counsel makes direct referrals of tax prosecutions without referring the case to the Justice Department's Criminal Section in the Tax Division in such cases as a failure to file or for filing false Forms 8300 relating to cash received in a trade or business as required by Section 6050I.[250.1] This authority does not cover prosecutions of accountants, physicians, or attorneys (acting in their professional representative capacity) or their employees; local, state, federal, or foreign public officials or political candidates; members of the judiciary; religious leaders; media representatives; labor union officials; and publicly held corporations or their officers.

The Service does not consider a Counsel conference to be a matter of right, and it has been held that the conference is primarily for the Service's, not the taxpayer's, benefit. On this ground, when a taxpayer has been denied a conference, courts have held that the denial did not deprive a taxpayer of administrative due process and that the Service is not bound by its own Manual.[250.2] This view focuses on the wrong issue. A conference serves the interests of both parties: The Service avoids bringing questionable cases, and the taxpayer is able to avoid public indictment on a criminal charge. The real question is whether the exercise of discretion in refusing or denying a taxpayer a conference is rationally made; that is, whether there is some rational basis for treating the taxpayer in question differently from others. Reliance on *United States v. Caceres*[250.3] is also misplaced. The Supreme Court in *Caceres* did not hold that the Service is not bound by its own rules; the Court acknowledged that the Service could adopt rules that were not required by the Constitution or federal statute, and that those rules would be enforced when a personal right was adversely affected.

---

[249] IRM 9.5.12.4, Exceptions to the General Review Process of Prosecution Recommendation Reports (Apr. 30, 1999).

[250] IRM 9.5.12.4.1–9.5.12.4.2.5, Processing Recommendations from the Chief, CI Directly to the U.S. Attorney's Office (Apr. 30, 1999).

[250.1] IRM 9.5.12.4.2, Processing Prosecution Recommendations Directly From District Counsel to the U.S. Attorney's Office (Apr. 30, 1999); IRM 9.5.12.4.2.1, Direct Referral of Form 8300 (Report of Cash Payment Over $10,000 Received in a Trade or Business) Charges to the United States Attorney by District Counsel.

[250.2] United States v. Goldstein, 342 F. Supp. 661 (EDNY 1972), rev'd and remanded on another issue, 479 F2d 1061 (2d Cir. 1973), cert. denied, 414 US 873 (1973); United States v. Matthews, 464 F2d 1268 (5th Cir. 1972); Short v. Murphy, 368 F. Supp. 591 (ED Mich. 1973), aff'd, 512 F2d 374 (6th Cir. 1975); Einhorn v. DeWitt, 618 F2d 347 (5th Cir. 1980).

[250.3] United States v. Caceres, 440 US 741.

[a] CI Policies

Division counsel review the special agent's recommendation in light of CI's policies and practices.[250.4] These policies and practices, such as the voluntary disclosure practice, are described above in connection with the defense lawyer's representation of a taxpayer during an investigation.[250.5] CI Division Counsel applies these policies and practices with more sensitivity and sophistication than special agents in local offices, but it should always be kept in mind that CI's policies and practices do not exist out of any solicitude for the taxpayer who has committed a criminal tax offense. On the contrary, these self-imposed constraints are considered along with facts and circumstances in evaluating whether there is a reasonable probability of conviction.[250.6] Accordingly, in deciding whether to recommend prosecution, Division Counsel attorneys consider whether a voluntary disclosure has been made, whether dual or successive prosecution will result, and whether the age and mental condition of the taxpayer will adversely affect a successful prosecution. Another CI policy is that the active solicitation of a delinquent return is considered detrimental to a prosecution because the defense could claim that the prosecution was commenced solely because of the Service's unsuccessful attempt to dispose of the matter civilly or the prosecution is a substitute for the Service's unsuccessful collection action.[250.7] Obviously, therefore, the taxpayer's lawyer will attempt to fit the taxpayer's case into one of these policies and procedures to discourage a prosecution recommendation. Indeed, any fact or circumstance bearing on the probability of a successful prosecution should be made at the Counsel's conference.

[b] Conference Practice

Review at the Counsel level usually is more objective, and, in any event, should be more detached than at the CI level, and so the conference with the docket attorney may be the best opportunity within the Service to have a recommended criminal prosecution overturned. From the Service's view, the docket attorney conferee welcomes the presentation of exculpatory evidence and defenses for at least two reasons. First, if the defenses are substantial, the government may not be able to successfully prosecute the case, and any acquittal undermines the overriding deterrence policy of the investigation func-

---

[250.4] IRM Chief Counsel Directives Manual 31, Section 3, Criminal Tax Policies and Procedures.

[250.5] See supra ¶ 12.03.

[250.6] IRM, Chief Counsel Directives Manual 31.3.2.1, Exceptions Generally (Dec. 11, 1998).

[250.7] IRM, Chief Counsel Directives Manual 31.3.6.1, Solicitation of Returns (Dec. 11, 1998).

tion. Second, if the defense is not substantial, the attorney may be able to assist in anticipating any defense tactic and thereby improve the prosecution's case. The docket attorney does not disclose information at the conference, except for the criminal statutes involved, the civil tax figures, and the method of proof.[250.8]

The docket attorney usually reads the special agent's report before attending a conference with the taxpayer's representative.[250.9] Any pre-referral advice given by Counsel to the special agent is included with the file. As a result, the docket attorney has some feel for the history of the taxpayer, the nature of the offense, the principal evidence of the omission or understatement, and the principal evidence on the willfulness element. On the other hand, the lawyer who has been engaged during the course of the special agent's investigation will have a good idea of whether the agent has conducted the investigation based on a direct-evidence/specific-item basis or on a circumstantial method of proof, such as a net worth or bank deposits method. In the event that the defense decides to make an all-out effort at the Counsel level, the representative can point out deficiencies in proof. These trial problems may arise from such factors as (1) a prior accumulation of assets or so-called cash hoard, which may wipe out any unexplained increases in net worth; (2) the lack of corroboration of admissions made by the taxpayer; (3) confusion caused by the method of accounting used by the taxpayer; and (4) other problems inherent in the use of the bank deposits method where the taxpayer utilizes an accrual method of accounting.

The taxpayer's lawyer will be able to discuss any defense that the taxpayer may have by reason of reliance on a qualified tax adviser, lack of mental capacity, or unclaimed deductions (particularly in a failure-to-file case) and an analysis of any increases in net worth or bank deposits that disprove unreported income. Since the docket attorney must write a report, a more formal submission in the form of a brief or memorandum summarizing the main points and perhaps documentary evidence should be considered in order to assist the docket attorney as well as to clarify any statements made on behalf of the taxpayer. At any rate, one of the subjects of the docket attorney's conference memorandum is a description of any statement of fact or law made at the conference and the identity of the person making the statement.

If the lawyer is prepared to discuss deficiencies in the proof of the government's case, evidence sufficient to establish a defense, violation of constitutional privileges or other misconduct of the agents, and other factors that the Service considers as bearing on the decision to prosecute, there may be consid-

---

[250.8] IRM, Chief Counsel Directive Manual 31.4.2.15, Conducting the Conference (July 20, 1990).

[250.9] IRM, Chief Counsel Directive Manual 31.4.2.13, Preparation for the Conference (July 20, 1990).

erable give-and-take between the docket attorney and the lawyer at the conference. Although this exchange may be useful for the taxpayer, and sometimes extremely helpful to the taxpayer, the defense counsel must remember that as the taxpayer's representative, any statement made at the conference constitutes a vicarious admission, which can be used against the taxpayer at a trial.[250.10]

¶ 12.11 TAX DIVISION REVIEW

The attorney general is responsible for the prosecution of criminal cases,[251] including criminal tax cases. Under the attorney general's supervision, the U.S. Attorney, an appointee of the president, has the duty, "except as otherwise provided by law," to prosecute all offenses, including tax offenses, against the United States within the judicial district.[252] Actual supervision of tax prosecutions is handled by the assistant attorney general of the Tax Division and the Tax Division's Criminal Section. The Criminal Section consists of staff attorneys, three Section Chiefs, and Assistant Section Chiefs. One of the principal functions of the Criminal Section is to promote uniform enforcement of the tax laws by reviewing cases the Service's CID function has recommended to the Tax Division for prosecution, although these cases may be referred from either the CID as the result of an administrative investigation or a grand jury investigation. The standard of review of criminal tax cases requires that the evidence presented support a prima facie case and a reasonable probability of conviction.[253] The standard applied when the Criminal Section authorizes a grand jury investigation requires "articulable facts supporting a reasonable belief that a tax crime is being or has been committed."[254]

Criminal Section attorneys also prosecute criminal tax cases if requested to do so by a U.S. Attorney. Out of both its review function and its trial functions, the Tax Division has developed definite policies.[255] Although these policies are in many respects the same as those the Service applies in criminal tax cases, differences in emphasis and application arise from the trial orientation of the Tax Division. The fact that review by the Tax Division's Criminal Section is independent and is made from a somewhat different perspective is es-

---

[250.10] IRM, Chief Counsel Directive Manual 31.4.2.15(1)(A)(5), Conducting the Conference (July 20, 1990).

[251] 28 USC § 516. See Sullivan v. United States, 348 US 170 (1954).

[252] 28 USC § 547.

[253] Criminal Tax Manual 6-4.211, Standards of Review (A).

[254] Criminal Tax Manual 6-4.211, Standards of Review (B).

[255] See supra ¶ 12.07[2].

tablished by its declination rate, which varies from year to year but has generally ranged from 10 to 20 percent.[256]

[1] Referral to Tax Division and Direct Referral to U.S. Attorney

On completing an administrative criminal investigation recommending prosecution, the special agent prepares a special agent's report together with supporting exhibits and other supporting information.[257] After review within counsel, a criminal reference letter is prepared and the case is referred to the Criminal Section of the Tax Division for a decision on whether to initiate or decline prosecution. There are two exceptions to this general procedure. First is the so-called direct referral case. In certain criminal cases such as excise tax cases, CI refers cases directly to U.S. Attorneys' offices without prior processing by the Criminal Section, although the Criminal Section receives a copy of the criminal reference letter and monitors the case. Second, while the Tax Division has jurisdiction over offenses involving revenue-producing tax laws, the Criminal Division of the Justice Department has jurisdiction over criminal enforcement of such police or regulatory tax laws as the wagering tax and federal firearms, alcohol, and tobacco tax violations. Moreover, although the Criminal Section has authority to authorize the use of tax grand juries, search warrants in criminal tax cases, and grants of immunity to witnesses in such cases, its authority has been delegated in certain situations to U.S. Attorneys' offices.[258]

---

[256] U.S. Comptroller General, Report, Improved Planning for Developing and Selecting IRS Criminal Tax Cases Can Strengthen Enforcement of Federal Tax Laws 59, GGD-80-0 (Nov. 6, 1979). The serial review process in criminal tax cases with four opportunities for conferences (at the district CID, the District Counsel, Department of Justice's Tax Division, and U.S. Attorney's office) has been criticized as being too time-consuming and expensive. See also Bray, "A Report and Comment on Proposed Reforms in Criminal Tax Case Conference Procedures," 28 Fed. Bar News 11 (Feb. 1981). See also Davis, "Recent Developments in Criminal Tax Matters," 47 NYU Tax Inst. § 46.02[8] (1989).

[257] See discussion and sample table of contents of the special agent's report supra ¶ 12.06.

[258] The Tax Division has delegated some or all of its authority to U.S. Attorneys (1) to permit expansion of nontax grand juries to include the investigation of tax crimes; (2) to approve the execution of search warrants for evidence of tax crimes; and (3) to authorize tax prosecutions for violatons of cash reporting rules of Section 6050I. Dep't of Justice Manual, Tax Div. 6-4.122D (Joint Tax- Nontax Investigations With IRS Participation); 6-4.130 (Search Warrants); 6-8A.206 (Tax Division Directive No. 87-61, Delegation of Authority for Prosecutions Under 26 USC Sec. 6050I). For further discussion of these delegations, see Davis, "Recent Developments in Criminal Tax Matters," 47 NYU Tax Inst. § 46 (1989).

[2] Review in Complex and Noncomplex Cases

On receipt of the criminal reference letter, special agent's report, and exhibits, the case is classified as either complex or noncomplex.[259] Complex cases are generally those involving indirect methods of proof, sensitive issues, or complex questions of law. If a conference request from the taxpayer's representative is on file, a noncomplex case is reclassified as complex, and a conference is granted. If no conference request is on file and the case is classified as noncomplex, it is forwarded to the U.S. Attorney within two weeks. If the U.S. Attorney recommends against prosecution, the Tax Division's Criminal Section will generally follow the recommendation. The U.S. Attorney is also expected to have a greater opportunity to dispose of noncomplex cases, even if there has been a conference in the Criminal Section, Tax Division. The Tax Division estimates that about 25 percent of prosecution referrals can be classified as noncomplex.[260]

[3] Tax Division Conference

The Tax Division's Criminal Section reviews recommendations of criminal prosecution from counsel after the conclusion of the administrative investigation by the CID and counsel review. A conference in the Criminal Section is generally granted, if requested.[261] Counsel notifies the taxpayer's representative and the taxpayer when it refers a case to the Tax Division with a recommendation of prosecution. To ensure that the taxpayer has a Tax Division conference, the representative should send a letter to the Criminal Section immediately after notice of the referral is received from counsel's office. After the case has been classified, it is assigned to a staff attorney in the Criminal Section, who will review the reports prepared and exhibits obtained from the administrative investigation and prepare the action memorandum for the section.

When a conference is requested in the Tax Division, a mutually convenient time is set between the staff attorney and the taxpayer's representative. Usually only one conference with the Criminal Section lawyer is permitted. At the conference, the Criminal Section lawyer advises the taxpayer's representative of the charge recommended by the Service, the years involved, the tentative criminal figures to be included in the indictment, the proposed theory of proof, and only such further information as he believes will be helpful in

---

[259] Dep't of Justice Manual, Tax Div. 6-4.213(B) (Catagories of Matters Reserved).

[260] See United States v. Acceturo, 858 F2d 679 (11th Cir. 1988) (assuming but not deciding that "refusal to grant a tax conference might in some circumstances violate a taxpayer's rights and constitute prejudice . . . "; failure of Justice Department to provide a tax conference did not establish prejudice because there was no exculpatory evidence).

[261] Dep't of Justice Manual, Tax Div. 6-4.214 (Conferences).

reaching the decision on prosecution. After review of the case in the Tax Division, it is either (1) returned to the Service because prosecution is declined; (2) returned to the Service for a supplemental investigation; or (3) referred to the appropriate U.S. Attorney with instructions to institute criminal proceedings.[262] Any recommendation of the staff attorney to decline prosecution must have the approval of an Assistant Section Chief and, in case of disagreement, the Chief of the Criminal Section.

A staff attorney's recommendation of prosecution must be approved by or on behalf of the Chief of the Criminal Section before it is forwarded to the U.S. Attorney. The letter of referral from the Tax Division to the U.S. Attorney sets forth the extent to which prosecution is authorized, cites the statutes involved, calls attention to the earliest statute of limitations deadline, suggests the appropriate indictment or information form to be used as a guide, and discusses any particular problems of law or fact. Once the case is referred to the U.S. Attorney for prosecution, no conference is granted in the Tax Division, although the U.S. Attorney is given the discretion to grant a conference.[263] If the U.S. Attorney disagrees with the decision to prosecute, that difference of opinion is communicated to the Tax Division for reconsideration.[264]

[a] Conference Procedures

After an administrative or a grand jury investigation, conferences in the Criminal Section have at least four features:[265]

[i] Vicarious admissions. Unlike the Counsel conference, the vicarious admissions rule for statements by lawyers attending conferences before the Criminal Section are not used by the Tax Division, except where the lawyer authenticates a written instrument, such as a document, memorandum, or record.

[ii] Administrative investigations. Plea negotiations will be entertained at the conference in non–grand jury matters, consistent with the policies of the appropriate U.S. Attorney's office. The U.S. Attorney's office prepares and en-

---

[262] The Tax Division may authorize a grand jury investigation to be conducted by a Tax Division attorney, or a U.S. Attorney, with the prosecution decision to be made by the Tax Division on completion of the grand jury investigation.

[263] See supra ¶ 12.07[4].

[264] The government has opposed discovery of this letter between the Tax Division and the U.S. Attorney. See Zacher v. United States, 227 F2d 219, 226 (8th Cir. 1955), cert. denied, 350 US 993 (1956) (holding that a preindictment letter to the department from the U.S. Attorney recommending that the case be dropped was a privileged communication).

[265] Dep't of Justice Manual, Tax Div. 6-8A.203 (Tax Division Directive No. 86-58, Conferences).

ters into written plea agreements unless there is a written understanding between the Tax Division and the U.S. Attorney's office to the contrary. Where the prospective defendant indicates a willingness to enter into a plea of guilty to the major count(s) and to satisfy the U.S. Attorney's office policy, the matter is referred to the U.S. Attorney's office for plea disposition.

[iii] Number of conferences. There is no fixed number of conferences that may be granted in any one particular case, but ordinarily, one conference is considered sufficient. In some cases, the Criminal Section acknowledges that more than one conference may be appropriate. The test is not the number of conferences, because the Criminal Section holds that there is no right to a conference, but whether, under the facts and circumstances of the case, sufficient progress is or will be made in either the development of material facts or the clarification of the applicable law, without causing prejudice to the United States. Criminal Section attorneys are warned that delay may prejudice the government and that judgment should be exercised in granting more than one conference in the course of considering a case.

[iv] Witness at conferences. On occasion, the taxpayer or a witness is permitted to attend the conference. In rare situations, the Criminal Section attorneys are told the taxpayer or a witness may attempt to make oral representations or statements at the conference. No restrictions are imposed on the government on the use of these statements. However, the Criminal Section discourages attempts to bring witnesses because it is merely reviewing the result of an investigation and is not conducting either a hearing or an investigation. Under no circumstances will a Criminal Section attorney permit evidence to be presented at the conference in lieu of any person's testifying before a grand jury.

[b] Representing the Taxpayer at the Criminal Section Conference

Before any conference with the taxpayer's representative, the Criminal Section lawyer will have reviewed (1) the special agent's report and attached exhibits; (2) the memorandum of any conference with the counsel lawyer; and (3) the criminal reference letter from counsel, which specifies the violation, the nature of the fraud, and the taxpayer's background and health condition, and provides a summary of the evidence, including the evidence of willfulness, and the taxpayer's defense and any rebuttal. At this point in the administrative review, the Tax Division lawyer has a file with at least formal support for a criminal prosecution. The Criminal Section lawyer looks at the file with the perspective of one who may have to prosecute the case. The Criminal Section lawyer is likely to have tried criminal tax cases, and he may be called upon to provide technical assistance or assume trial responsibility in the case.

This trial orientation of the Criminal Section lawyer has particular impact on the probability-of-conviction standard of review. The Tax Division lawyer may seriously consider factors the Service may have discounted. For example, the extreme age or youth of a potential defendant is a factor that the Tax Division lawyer may consider as affecting the way in which a jury will react. Also, the Service may have concluded that a true voluntary disclosure has not been made, but the Criminal Section lawyer may consider that the circumstances present a significant trial hazard. For example, the taxpayer may have made the disclosure at a time when he did not know that there was a pending investigation (and counsel may have requested the claim), or an accountant or lawyer contacted by the taxpayer may have begun the process of preparing amended returns before the Service contacted the taxpayer to examine the originally filed returns. A Criminal Section lawyer is likely to be more impressed with the size of the tax due than is the Service, and where the tax due and owing is minimal, the lawyer is likely to consider the desirability of prosecution and the hazards of prosecution in light of this evidence. Where a government case depends on the testimony of a witness whose credibility may be seriously undercut, such as an informant, the Criminal Section lawyer is more likely to be sensitive to such trial hazards than the District Counsel lawyer.

As noted previously, the Criminal Section lawyer describes the statutory violation, the method of proof, and the proposed criminal and civil figures at the conference. After providing this information, the Criminal Section lawyer is not likely to be inclined to disclose more of the government's case, but may open the meeting up to a presentation by the representative of matters bearing on the decision to prosecute. It is up to the taxpayer's representative to present arguments to the Criminal Section lawyer as to why prosecution should not be recommended. Obviously, the representative cannot advance his client's interests if his arguments have not been carefully and painstakingly prepared. It bears repeating that the decision to prosecute is a discretionary one and that the purpose of the conference in the Criminal Section, so far as the Tax Division is concerned, is to allow the Criminal Section lawyer to make an informed decision. Consequently, the representative's arguments should be directed at encouraging the lawyer to decline prosecution because of factors that adversely affect the probability of conviction. In the process of making arguments such as these, there normally is some give and take. The Criminal Section lawyer is not going to open up the special agent's files to the defense lawyer for his examination, but in the course of discussing the case, both lawyers will probe the other's statements—the Criminal Section lawyer for the purpose of ascertaining the validity of the representative's argument and the possible inadequacy of the Service's recommendation, the taxpayer's representative for the purpose of ascertaining what evidence the Service has that overcomes the argument being presented.

[4] Grand Jury Cases

Grand juries are used to investigate criminal tax cases. The Criminal Section is involved in the review process in grand jury investigations at two stages. When CI requests a grand jury investigation, the Criminal Section must approve and authorize the use of the grand jury.[266] In general, the Criminal Section must also approve requests from U.S. Attorneys for the initiation of grand jury investigations into possible criminal tax violations.[267] At the conclusion of a grand jury investigation, recommendations for prosecution of a violation of the tax laws resulting from the grand jury investigation must be submitted to the Criminal Section for authorization. At this second stage of the grand jury investigation (but not the first stage), a conference may be held in the Criminal Section, if such a conference has been requested.[268]

U.S. Attorneys' offices are authorized to conduct a tax grand jury investigation in cases referred by the Criminal Section to develop further evidence, and they initiate tax grand jury investigations when the Criminal Section specifically authorizes them. However, U.S. Attorneys and Chiefs of their Criminal Divisions are authorized, without prior authorization, to expand a nontax grand jury investigation to include an inquiry into potential criminal tax violations as long as there is reason to believe a criminal tax violation has been committed, the Service has been requested to provide assistance, and the Service has agreed with the U.S. Attorney's office about the possible criminal tax violation and has agreed to provide assistance. Copies of the U.S. Attorney's request and the Service action are sent to the Criminal Section.

In every grand jury investigation where a conference is requested, the Criminal Section trial attorney contacts the U.S. Attorney's office, discusses the case with the appropriate Assistant U.S. Attorney, and ascertains whether disclosure of any facts of the case is likely to expose any person, including witnesses, to the risk of intimidation or danger. If such a risk exists, the trial attorney then advises the appropriate Assistant Chief of the Criminal Section, who decides the appropriate course of action. The Criminal Section trial attorney advises the Assistant U.S. Attorney that he or she may attend the conference.

---

[266] Dep't of Justice Manual, Tax Div. 6-4.121 (IRS Requests to Initiate Grand Jury Investigations). See supra ¶ 12.03.

[267] Dep't of Justice Manual, Tax Div. 6-4.122 (U.S. Attorney Initiated Grand Jury Investigations). See supra ¶ 12.03[4].

[268] Dep't of Justice Manual, Tax Div. 6-4.214 (Conferences). For this reason, it is advisable to request a conference during the grand jury investigation.

[5] Review in Narcotics Cases

The review process is accelerated in narcotics cases. Under this procedure, the case file need not be sent directly to the Tax Division from the District Counsel's office. The Tax Division attorney can make an "on site" review of the case file as developed by the special agent. After conferring with the District Counsel attorney and the U.S. Attorney's office, the Tax Division attorney can obtain approval from the Criminal Section to present the case to a grand jury.

[6] Simultaneous Referrals

The Tax Division has adopted a program in GEP cases designed to accelerate the processing of cases where a taxpayer wishes to enter a guilty plea.[269] If certain criteria are met, the district CID and District Counsel simultaneously refer the case to the Criminal Section with a recommendation that plea negotiations be commenced with the taxpayer's counsel. The criteria are (1) the taxpayer must be represented by counsel; (2) the sources of income must be legal (e.g., as opposed to income from the sale of narcotics or organized crime); and (3) the representative must indicate that the taxpayer wishes to enter a guilty plea. The special agent needs the approval of both his supervisor and the Chief (CID). The report the CID submits is short, rather than the extensive report normally prepared.

Under this early referral procedure, the Service conducts only a limited investigation to corroborate the elements of the offense and the taxpayer's admissions. Under this procedure the taxpayer avoids a protracted investigation and the taxpayer's representative is allowed to open plea negotiations with the attorney in the Tax Division and in the U.S. Attorney's office to which the case is sent. The early referral procedure does not affect a taxpayer's civil tax liability; nevertheless, taxpayers are expected to cooperate "with the determination and satisfaction of their civil tax liabilities."[270] Should a taxpayer's criminal liability be disposed of under the program, but his civil tax liability remain unresolved, the civil investigation is completed through the Service's Examination Division.

---

[269] Dep't of Justice Manual, Tax Div. 6-4.117 (General Enforcement Plea Program). For Service procedures, see IRM Part IX, Criminal Tax Supp. 9G-154 (Mar. 1, 1986). The Tax Division's position that a plea must be entered to a year covered by the sentencing guidelines, as well as the sentencing guidelines themselves, throw considerable doubt on the viability of the plea program.

[270] Dep't of Justice Manual, Tax Div. 6-4.

¶ 12.12 TAX DIVISION POLICIES

The Tax Division's consideration of a criminal tax prosecution is guided by its standards of review and its policies. First, the standard of review the Tax Division applies to a prosecution recommendation is the same as the dual standard the Service uses: (1) The circumstances and evidence must indicate the commission of a crime beyond a reasonable doubt and (2) there must be a reasonable probability of conviction.[271] Second, the Tax Division has specific policies that affect its handling of recommendations for prosecution. These policies are discussed in the sections that follow.

[1] Compromise of Criminal Liability

Section 7122 permits the attorney general to compromise any civil or criminal tax case after it has been referred to the Justice Department for prosecution or defense. However, since 1958, department policy has been not to consider offers in compromise in criminal tax cases where the offer involves the government forgoing prosecution in exchange for the payment of a fixed sum. The Tax Division considers the criminal case with a view to determining whether a criminal tax offense has occurred. This determination is separate from the matter of civil liability and collection of taxes, penalties, and interest. The criminal aspects of the case are disposed of first. No consideration is given to settlement of the civil liability until after sentence has been imposed in the criminal case.[272] Under a former policy, there was limited provision for such offers, including the requirement that the defendant enter a plea of guilty to at least one major count of the indictment. The Tax Division changed this policy because it sometimes resulted in lengthy delays and because the Tax Division attorneys were required to consider the adequacy of the offer to compromise civil tax liabilities about which they were not sufficiently informed without extended conferences with Service personnel. Also, the Tax Division felt that settlement discussions involved disclosure of the government's case, with the danger that the taxpayer might tamper with evidence or tailor a defense.

[2] Voluntary Disclosure

The Tax Division never had a voluntary disclosure policy, so the Treasury's abandonment of its policy in 1952 did not formally affect the Tax Division's

---

[271] Dep't of Justice Manual, Tax Div. 6-4.213A (Standards for Review).

[272] Dep't of Justice Manual, Tax Div., Part 8A, Criminal Tax Manual 4.06[1] (Offer in Compromise). The Tax Division considers the payment of taxes to represent a trial problem in some cases, but not a defense. Id. at 4.06[2].

handling of prosecution recommendations. The Tax Division's formulation of the voluntary disclosure practice is the same as the Service's practice, although its application of the practice in particular cases may differ from that of the Service. Where a prospective defendant has voluntarily revealed his tax fraud to the Service, the fact that the taxpayer has voluntarily sought to rectify a false return without prodding by investigators or the threat of investigation is given some weight on a case-by-case basis in determining whether to prosecute; however, it is not conclusive on the issue.[273]

[3] Dual Prosecution

The Tax Division follows the Justice Department's *Petite* policy regarding federal prosecutions of a person also prosecuted under state law.[274] The Supreme Court, in *Petite v. United States*,[275] first recognized this principle. Under the Tax Division policy, a person is not prosecuted for alleged criminal behavior if the alleged criminality was an ingredient of a previous state prosecution of the person. An exception is made only if the federal prosecution is specifically authorized in advance by the department itself, on a finding that the prosecution serves "compelling interests of federal law enforcement."[276]

[4] Health Policy

In 1953, the attorney general ordered abandonment of the so-called health policy in criminal tax cases. The question of whether an individual can physically survive the stress and strain of a trial is not controlling in deciding whether a tax case is prosecuted. The Tax Division takes the position that this question should be settled in open court.[277] After the filing of an indictment or information, physical health questions are for the defendant to raise by way of a mo-

---

[273] Dep't of Justice Manual, Tax Div., Part 8A, Criminal Tax Manual 4.01 (Voluntary Disclosure).

[274] Dep't of Justice Manual, Tax Div., Part 8A, Criminal Tax Manual 4.02 (Dual Prosecution and Successor Prosecution). Successive federal prosecutions on charges arising out of the same transaction or occurrence are also covered by the Tax Division's policy.

[275] Petite v. United States, 361 US 529, 531 (1960). This policy was announced after the Supreme Court's decision in Abbate v. United States, 359 US 187 (1959) (federal prosecution and conviction after state conviction for same act held not barred by double jeopardy clause). It is cited in full in United States v. Mechanic, 454 F2d 849, 855 n.5 (8th Cir. 1971), cert. denied, 406 US 929 (1972).

[276] Dep't of Justice Manual, Tax Div., Part 8A, Criminal Tax Manual 4.02.

[277] Dep't of Justice Manual, Tax Div., Part 8A, Criminal Tax Manual 4.04 (Health Policy).

tion for continuance. The court has no power under the Federal Rules of Criminal Procedure or by statute to dismiss indictments on health grounds. If a claim of physical incapacity to stand trial is made on account of a permanent condition, so that trial will be precluded at any time, the U.S. Attorney is instructed to see to it that the health facts and the court's decision are made fully a matter of record. The Tax Division instructs the U.S. Attorney's office to request (1) that the special agent make an investigation to determine the extent of the defendant's daily activities to eliminate the possibility of malingering; (2) that the court appoint a physician (usually a U.S. Public Health Service or Veterans Administration doctor) to conduct an examination; and (3) that a hearing be held in open court to disclose for the record the results of the special agent's investigation and the doctor's report.[278] If the record makes it apparent that the defendant cannot ever stand trial, the U.S. Attorney may request authority to dismiss the indictment, but if the physical condition is only temporary or temporarily disabling, only a temporary continuance is authorized.[279]

[5] Disposition by Plea: The Major Count Policy

The Tax Division's policy is to permit the disposition of tax fraud cases on the basis of a plea of guilty entered to the "major count" if one count is clearly the most important count (i.e., the major count is the count in a multicount indictment or information with the largest tax deficiency).[280] An agreement between the government and the taxpayer/defendant that the taxpayer will enter a plea of guilty to the major count does not mean that the residual counts are excluded from the charging paper. On the contrary, the residual counts are included in an indictment or information if the Tax Division authorizes prosecution. Only after the taxpayer/defendant enters the plea of guilty to the major count, are the residual or remaining counts of the indictment or information dismissed. U.S. Attorneys are instructed not to dismiss the residual counts before the sentencing because of the experience of the Tax Division when residual counts were dismissed simultaneously with the plea. In several cases, where defendants entered a plea to one count and the remaining counts were dismissed simultaneously with the entry of the plea, the defendants, at the sentencing, represented to the court that their pleas were prompted by the desire

---

[278] Dep't of Justice Manual, Tax Div., Part 8A, Criminal Tax Manual 4.04 (Health Policy).

[279] Where competency is involved, the U.S. Attorney is instructed to follow 18 USC §§ 4214, 4241–4247, and, in general, to follow the same steps as with physical health problems. See Dep't of Justice Manual, Tax Div., Part 8A, Criminal Tax Manual 4.05.

[280] Dep't of Justice Manual, Tax Div. 6-4.310 (Major Count(s) Policy/Plea Agreements). See also Part 8A, Criminal Tax Manual 4.08 (Disposition by Plea).

to dispose of the case quickly despite their innocence. The court then permitted the defendant to withdraw the plea or imposed an undeservedly light sentence.

Where the major count is a felony, a plea to a lesser included misdemeanor generally is not accepted. However, in "very unusual circumstances," a plea to a misdemeanor (Section 7207) will be authorized after a case has been sent forward calling for a felony charge. This policy is supported by two considerations. First, the most serious count will most fully support serious punishment in the criminal case; second, conviction on this count will facilitate collection of the civil fraud penalty and the largest amount of tax in the civil tax proceeding following the criminal case.[281] If an Assistant U.S. Attorney violates a plea agreement that has been arrived at with the U.S. Attorney's office, and a timely objection is made by the defendant taxpayer, the judgment and sentence will be set aside.[282] The District Judge is not bound by a plea agreement or a plea to the major count pursuant to an ageement. Sentencing will be governed by the sentencing guidelines.[283]

The Tax Division instructs U.S. Attorneys to oppose accepting a plea of nolo contendere.[284] The government consents to such pleas only in exceptional cases and only with the approval of the Tax Division. The reason for this position is that a plea of nolo contendere is generally held to be inadmissible in subsequent civil tax litigation as evidence to support the existence of civil fraud, and the Tax Division does not believe that the taxpayer should be able to concede willful misconduct in a criminal case and relitigate the issue in a later civil case. However, the court itself has the discretion to accept a nolo contendere plea over any government objection "after due consideration of the views of the parties and the interest of the public in the effective administration of justice."[285]

---

[281] See ¶ 7B.01[3][b].

[282] United States v. Greenwood, 812 F2d 632 (10th Cir. 1987).

[283] See ¶ 7A.09

[284] Dep't of Justice Manual, Tax Div. 6-4.320 (nolo contendere pleas). So-called *Alford* pleas are also opposed. Id. at 6-4.330 (*Alford* pleas). See North Carolina v. Alford, 400 US 25 (1970).

[285] Fed. R. Crim. P. 11(b); Mason v. United States, 250 F2d 704, 706 (10th Cir. 1957).

¶ 12.13 U.S. ATTORNEY ACTIVITIES IN CRIMINAL TAX CASES

[1] U.S. Attorney Communications With Represented Persons

U.S. Attorneys' offices are conducting more investigations of tax crimes than ever before. As a result, investigative policies of the Department of Justice have greater importance. In investigating possible violations of a criminal tax statute, the Assistant U.S. Attorney or Service special agents assigned to the U.S. Attorney's office working with the Assistant U.S. Attorney will contact potential witnesses. The Justice Department has proposed regulations governing the circumstances under which federal attorneys are permitted to communicate with represented persons.[286] Justice Department guidelines accept the principles of the American Bar Association's Code of Professional Responsibility (DR 7-104(A)(1)) and Model Rules of Professional Conduct (Rule 4.2) regarding the obligation of the lawyer generally not to contact represented parties, and acknowledge that federal attorneys are subject to state bar ethical rules except where state rules clearly conflict with lawful federal procedures and practices.[287]

Before a person becomes a party to any proceeding, the proposed regulations permit federal prosecutors and agents to conduct criminal and civil investigations of all individuals as they routinely do whether or not those persons are represented by counsel.[288] Justice Department attorneys are also permitted to make or direct undercover or overt contacts with individuals and organizations represented by counsel for the purpose of developing factual information.[289] This investigative activity must stop, however, at the point that the represented individual is arrested or charged with a crime or named as a defendant in a civil enforcement action. Thus, investigation must be stopped when the represented person becomes a represented party. Also, unless the represented person initiates the contact, federal prosecutors are precluded from making any contacts with represented persons after an arrest, indictment, or the filing of a complaint on the subject matter of the representation.[290] Similarly, federal prosecutors may not attempt to negotiate plea agreements, settlements, or similar arrangements with represented individuals outside the presence of their attorneys or without their attorneys' consent.

---

[286] 28 CFR pt. 77, 59 Fed. Reg. 10,086 et. seq. (Mar. 3, 1994). Additions will be made to the U.S. Attorney's Manual at Title 9, Chapter 13, Section 9-13.200.

[287] 28 CFR §§ 77.1, 77.12.

[288] 28 CFR §§ 77.3, 77.5, 77.7. Rules governing contacts of represented persons apply to investigators acting under the federal attorney's direction. 28 CFR § 77.5.

[289] 28 CFR §§ 77.3, 77.5, 77.7.

[290] 28 CFR § 77.6(c).

Communications with an employee or a member of a represented organization present an issue about whether the communication will be with the represented organization vicariously through the employee or separately with the employee. A communication with a current employee of an organizational party or person will be treated as a communication with the organization subject to the restrictions on contact only if the employee is a controlling individual (i.e., a high-level employee who is known by the prosecutor to participate "as a decision maker in the determination of the organization's legal position in the proceeding or investigation of the subject matter").[291] While a federal attorney may not communicate with a controlling individual of a represented organizational party, the federal attorney may communicate with a controlling individual during the investigative stage of the case even if the organization is represented. Moreover, no restriction applies to communications with lower level employees who are not decision makers (and so not controlling individuals) whether the organization is a represented party in some proceeding or a represented person.[292] If former or current employees are separately represented, or controlling individuals are separately represented, the same protections applicable to represented parties and persons apply.[293]

[2] Conference With Assistant U.S. Attorney

Criminal tax cases are sent to the U.S. Attorney with instructions either to obtain an indictment or information against a taxpayer or to use a grand jury to obtain further information bearing on the decision to prosecute.[294] In both situations, the final decision concerning prosecution is made by the Tax Division of the Department of Justice. However, the U.S. Attorney's office may present its own views, and these views are considered by the Tax Division in making any final decision.

In the usual case, the U.S. Attorney follows the instructions of the Tax Division and, where requested, obtains the appropriate indictment or information. However, many U.S. Attorneys' offices review the files and hold a conference with the taxpayer's representative, if requested. It may be possible to persuade an Assistant U.S. Attorney that the probability of conviction is slight, especially where local factors not considered by the Tax Division in Washing-

---

[291] 28 CFR § 77.10(a).

[292] Similarly, when a controlling individual no longer is an employee and decision maker, the individual is no longer a controlling person, and the restrictions on contact no longer apply even if the organization is represented. 28 CFR § 77.10(b).

[293] 28 CFR §§ 77.10(c), 77.10(d).

[294] The U.S. Attorney also plays an expanded role in the administrative review of noncomplex tax cases, which are referred directly to the U.S. Attorney by the Criminal Section, Tax Division.

ton are well-known to have significance in trials in the particular jurisdiction. It is also possible where the local court has granted a suppression order, thereby eliminating the possibility of introducing important evidence in the government's case. The U.S. Attorney may also interview witnesses in the course of presenting a case to the grand jury and come to the conclusion that statements obtained by the Service are not borne out by the witnesses' testimony or that a critical witness is not credible. In this event, the Assistant U.S. Attorney can attempt to persuade the Justice Department that the case should not be prosecuted. Although such an event rarely occurs, U.S. Attorneys' offices have been exercising more discretion in recent years.[295]

_____

[295] Dep't of Justice Manual, Tax Div. 6-4.245 (Request to Decline Prosecution).

CHAPTER **13**

The Service's Investigatory Powers

B CHALLENGES TO SUMMONS ENFORCEMENT

C OTHER INVESTIGATIVE TECHNIQUES

A　SERVICE AND ENFORCEMENT OF SUMMONSES

¶ 13.01 THE SUMMONS AUTHORITY AND ADMINISTRATIVE PRACTICE

In many examinations and collection investigations, Internal Revenue Service (the Service) revenue agents and collection officers obtain information without the use of any formal compulsory process.[1] Even in criminal investigations, special agents obtain books and records of third parties without the use of a formal summons. Behind the informal requests that these agents and officers make for records to be produced voluntarily is the broad and powerful statutory authority Service field personnel have to order the production of records and testimony by a formal summons.[2] If a taxpayer or third part does not sup-

---

[1] The Service is not required to use a summons, and, when an agent chooses not to use one, the taxpayer will have difficulty in stopping the inquiry. See United States v. Barksdale, 499 F. Supp. 624 (MD Fla. 1980) (circular letters were informal means of inquiry permissible under Section 7602(1); the Service was not required to use a summons under Section 7602(2)). See also Speck v. United States, 76 AFTR2d 95-5226 (9th Cir. 1995) (motion to quash improper because limited to summons; circular letters were informal inquiry, not summons).

[2] IRM 25.5.1.4, Factors to Consider Before Issuing a Summons (Apr. 30, 1999) ("Attempt to obtain information voluntarily from taxpayers and witnesses prior to issuing a

ply information voluntarily, Service revenue agents, collection officers, and criminal investigators are authorized to issue and serve administrative summonses ordering the taxpayer or a third party to appear before them and to produce the records and other information that the agent, collection, and investigator consider to be relevant to the examination or investigation being conducted. The summons may even require a person to produce records outside the United States. A person located in the United States who is subject to the order of a U.S. court located abroad must at least make a reasonable attempt to obtain those records or face the risk of contempt for nonproduction or foreign prosecution for production.[3]

[1] Statutory Provisions Relating to the Use of Summonses

Internal Revenue Code (the Code) sections giving the Service authority to use administrative summonses is contained in Subchapter A ("Examination and Inspection") of Chapter 78 ("Discovery of Liability and Enforcement of Title") of the Code. The broadest authority granted the Service to gather information is contained in Section 7601, which requires the Secretary of the Treasury, "to the extent he deems it practicable, [to] cause officers and employees of the Treasury Department to proceed, from time to time, through each Internal Revenue district and inquire after and concerning all persons . . . who may be liable to pay any internal revenue tax." This statutory provision is rarely cited by the Service since it appears to be directed at excise taxes.[4] The more specific source for the Service's summons authority is Section 7602, which permits use of a summons for the following five authorized purposes:

1. To ascertain the correctness of any return;

---

summons. *Consent may be obtained voluntarily by acquainting the taxpayer or witness with the [summons] provisions of the Internal Revenue Code.*") (emphasis added).

[3] See United States v. Hayes, 722 F2d 723 (11th Cir. 1984) (person ordered must make "all reasonable efforts," and evidence of some efforts is insufficient to rebut prima facie showing of contempt on nonproduction). See also United States v. Bank of Nova Scotia, 691 F2d 1384 (11th Cir. 1982), cert. denied sub nom. Bank of Nova Scotia v. United States, 103 S. Ct. 3086 (1983), further proceedings, 722 F2d 657 (11th Cir. 1983) (remanding case to district court for further proceedings). On remand, the bank was fined $1,825,000, and the contempt order and fine were affirmed. United States v. Bank of Nova Scotia, 740 F2d 817 (11th Cir.), cert. denied, 469 US 1106 (1984) (balancing of interest approach followed; U.S. interest in disclosure of the bank records to uncover the flow of funds in a narcotics investigation outweighed the foreign state's interest in secrecy).

[4] Nevertheless in United States v. Bisceglia, 420 US 141 (1975), the Supreme Court said that the language of Section 7601, coupled with Section 7602, was inconsistent with an interpretation that would limit the issuance of a summons to investigations that have already focused on a particular return, a particular named person, or a particular potential tax liability.

2. To make a return where none has been filed;
3. To determine the liability of any person for any internal revenue tax;
4. To determine the liability at law or in equity of any transferee or fiduciary or any person for any internal revenue tax; and
5. To collect any internal revenue tax liability.[5]

To accomplish these five authorized purposes, Section 7602 permits the Secretary's delegate to (1) examine any books that "may be relevant or material" to the inquiry and (2) summon a taxpayer, custodian of records, or any other person considered proper to appear and to produce records and to give such testimony under oath as may be relevant or material to the inquiry. Section 7602(b) permits these actions to be taken "for the purpose of inquiring into any offense connected with the administration or enforcement of the internal revenue laws." Restrictions are imposed, however, on when such a criminal purpose summons may be issued.[6]

The manner in which a summons is to be served is described in Section 7603, which also requires that where books and papers are to be produced they must be described "with reasonable certainty." The time and place of examination are subject to restrictions set forth in Section 7605, which also prohibits unnecessary examinations and more than one inspection of a taxpayer's records for each taxable year. When a taxpayer is interviewed, Section 7521 gives the taxpayer the right to record the interview and to be represented by and to consult with a lawyer, CPA, or other person authorized to practice before the Service. A witness is entitled to be paid fees and costs for reproducing records sought by any summons under the provisions of Section 7610, provided the witness is not the taxpayer or an officer, employee, or representative of the taxpayer who is acting as such at the time the summons is served.

Special rules in Section 7609 require that when the Service issues a summons to a third-party recordkeeper, a taxpayer (that is, a person affected by the disclosure of information) must be given notice that the summons has been served. These rules also give the taxpayer (the "affected person") the right to restrain compliance with the summons and to contest the propriety of disclosure, as well as the opportunity to move to quash the third-party recordkeeper summons.

In addition to a summons, there are special powers granted to other Treasury officials in Sections 7606 and 7608, such as the execution and service of search and arrest warrants. Where a summons is served but not complied with, Section 7604 grants federal district courts jurisdiction to enforce the summons,

---

[5] When a levy has been served or is about to be made on a taxpayer's property and rights to property, Section 6333 also authorizes the collection officer to order the production of books and records relating to the property or rights to property.

[6] The so-called improper criminal purpose use of a summons is discussed infra ¶ 13.08.

including provision for civil arrest and punishment for contempt. Finally, any person who is duly summoned to appear to testify or produce books and who neglects to take such actions is guilty of a misdemeanor under Section 7610.

TABLE 13.1
Statutory Provisions Relating to Summonses and Their Enforcement

Code Section	Description	Comment
Section 7601	Canvass of districts for taxable persons or objects	Authority related to excise taxes
Section 7602(a)	The general summons authority	Records and testimony which "may be relevant"
Section 7602(b)	Purpose of summons may be to inquire into a criminal offense	Eliminates the improper-criminal-purpose argument
Section 7602(c)	Notice to taxpayer of third-party contacts	Does not apply to criminal cases or jeopardy assessment cases
Section 7602(d)	No summons when case has been referred to Justice Department	Statutory solution to the institutional bad faith challenge to a summons
Section 7602(e)	Limitation on examination of unreported income	Prohibits financial status or economic reality audits without reasonable indication of unreported income
Section 7603(a)	Service of a summons	Personal service or left at the person's last and usual place of abode
Section 7603(b)	Service by mail to third-party recordkeepers	Alternative service by mail when summons is for books and records
Section 7604(a)	Enforcement of summons	Jurisdiction of the district court
Section 7604 (b)	Enforcement of summons	Service may apply to a judge of the district court for enforcement of summons
Section 7605 (a)	Time and place of examination	Time and place must be reasonable under the circumstances
Section 7605(b)	Restrictions on examination of taxpayer	No second examination without high level approval and notice
Section 7606(a)	Entry of premises for examination of taxable objects	See Section 7601. For use in collecting excise tax
Section 7606(b)	Entry at night	
Section 7608(a)	Authority of Internal Revenue Enforcement Officers to carry firearms, execute search warrants, and make arrests	Used to collect excises taxes on liquor, tobacco, and firearms
Section 7608(b)	Authority of criminal investigators to enforce the criminal provisions of the Code	Authorized functions are to execute and serve search warrants, make arrests, or to make seizures of property subject to forfeiture

Code Section	Description	Comment
Section 7608(c)	Rules related to undercover operations	
Section 7609(a)	Special procedures for summonses served on certain third-parties for testimony, records, or the computer software source code	Notice of the summons must be given to the taxpayer within three days after service of the summons and no later than twenty-three days before the return date of the summons
Section 7609(b)	Taxpayer has right to intervene in any proceeding to enforce third-party summons and to institute proceeding to quash a third-party summons	Taxpayer has only twenty days after notice of the third-party summons has been given to institute a proceeding to quash
Section 7609(c)	Exceptions to third-party summons procedures for summonses issued in collection proceedings and criminal investigations	
Section 7609(d)	Examinations of third-party records restricted until the close of the twenty-third day after notice is given or during the course of proceeding to quash	
Section 7609(e)	Statute of limitations on assessment and collection and prosecution is suspended during summons proceeding	Period of suspension is for period the proceeding is pending in the trial court and appeal, and if case is not resolved within six months for the period beginning on the date six months after service of the summons until the final resolution of the response
Section 7609(f)	Additional requirements for a John Doe summons	Ex parte proceeding in which Service must show there is ascertainable group of taxpayers, reasonably believed to comply with the tax laws, and information not otherwise readily available
Section 7609(g)	No notice to taxpayer if, in ex parte proceeding, court finds notice may lead to destruction of records	
Section 7609(h)	Jurisdiction of district court	

Code Section	Description	Comment
Section 7609(i)	Duty of summoned party	Recordkeeper must assemble documents records and be prepared to produce them; Service may give recordkeeper a certificate that no proceeding was begun or taxpayer consents to examination; protection of summoned from liability
Section 7610	Fees and costs for witnesses	No reimbursement for taxpayer's production of records
Section 7611	Restrictions on church tax inquiries and examinations	
Section 7612	Special procedures for summonses for computer software	
Section 6503(j)	Designated summons suspends statute of limitations on assessment if summons issued at least sixty days before the date on which the assessment period would otherwise expire	Summons issued in the course of coordinated program examination

[2] Administrative Practice

The Commissioner of Internal Revenue has delegated authority to issue summonses broadly throughout the Service.[7] Under the summons delegation order, field personnel in territory division offices with responsibility for (1) the examination of tax returns (e.g., revenue agents, tax auditors, estate tax examiners and TE/GE agents, tax law specialists, and tax auditors); (2) the collection of taxes (e.g., revenue officers); or (3) the investigation of any taxpayer's suspected willful failure to comply with the tax laws (e.g., special agents) have the authority to issue a summons. In addition, every Service official with authority to issue a summons may also do the following:

---

[7] The Commissioner's Delegation Order (CDO) regarding authority to issue a summons is CDO No. 4. The current version of this order should be checked in the Internal Revenue Bulletin, Cumulative Bulletin, or a commercial tax service. For a case questioning whether, for lack of publication in the Federal Register, the Secretary of the Treasury has validly delegated authority to the Commissioner to execute the internal revenue laws and hence whether the CDOs are invalid, see Hatcher v. United States, 733 F. Supp. 218 (MD Pa. 1990) (summons not quashed because taxpayer had actual knowledge of delegation and procedural rules). But see United States v. National Commodity & Barter Ass'n, 90-1 USTC ¶ 50,284 (D. Colo. 1990) (delegation of summons authority does not depend on publication in the Federal Register).

- Serve it on the person to whom it is addressed;
- Be the Service official before whom the summoned person must appear in response to a summons;
- Administer the required oath;
- Take the summoned party's testimony under oath;
- Receive whatever data are produced in response to the summons; and
- Apply to a district court to seek enforcement of the summons whenever the person summoned neglects or refuses to obey the summons.[8]

Although the statutory authority to order witnesses to produce records or testimony is extremely broad and widely delegated, Service personnel to whom the summons authority is delegated attempt to obtain information by voluntary means, rather than by summons.[9] This strategy is especially significant where the information is sought from a so-called third-party recordkeeper, such as a bank or credit institution, because without the issuance of a formal third-party recordkeeper summons the notice and other procedural protections of Section 7609 do not come into operation. Before issuing a summons, revenue agents and collection officers consider such factors as (1) the possibility of securing the data by other means and from other sources without the use of a summons; (2) the importance or necessity of the information sought when weighed against the action required to enforce compliance with the summons and the adverse effect on voluntary compliance if enforcement is abandoned; (3) the tax liability involved; (4) the importance of the case when weighed against the importance of the information; and (5) whether a criminal case is pending.[10]

A revenue agent or collection officer will issue a summons when (1) the taxpayer does not make records available to allow for an adequate examination in a reasonable period; (2) the records the revenue agent received are or are suspected to be incomplete, and additional records are presumed to be in the taxpayer's or a broker, bank, or other third party's possession that may disclose material information not reflected in the submitted records; (3) the taxpayer or the taxpayer's representative will not seriously attempt to produce records to substantiate return items or positions, but apparently will make those records available at the Appeals level; and (4) the existence and location of records are in doubt, and a summons for testimony under oath will establish what records exist and where they are located.[11]

---

[8] Reg. §§ 301.7603-1(b) (service of summons), 301-7602-1(b) (hearing officer and oath), 301.7604-1(b) (authority to apply to district court).

[9] IRM 25.5.1.4(2), Factors to Consider Before Issuance of Summons (Apr. 30, 1999).

[10] IRM 25.5.1.4(2), Factors to Consider Before Issuance of Summons (Apr. 30, 1999).

[11] IRM 25.5.1.4(3), Factors to Consider Before Issuance of Summons (Apr. 30, 1999).

Agents and officers are also subject to limitations in using a summons.[12] No summons may be issued in a criminal case for the same taxpayer and the same taxable period either to obtain further information from the taxpayer or a witness or to uncover assets to apply against assessed liabilities, unless the summons is cleared by Criminal Investigation and Area Division Counsel. A summons may not be issued at all when the summons is for the same taxpayer and taxable year if the case is pending in the Criminal Enforcement Section in the Tax Division of the Justice Department. Also, a summons is not to be used to obtain evidence of filing or payment because that information is available in Service records. Employment and excise tax returns can be prepared and processed under the authority of Section 6020(b) to insure that an assessment is made and collection commenced. As a matter of law, when a collection officer serves a summons for the purpose of collecting a tax underpayment, no levy or seizure may be made on the return date of the summons.

¶ 13.02 PREPARATION AND SERVICE OF SUMMONS

[1] Preparation of the Summons

The summons form the Service generally uses is Form 2039, Summons.[13] (Form 13.1 Form 2039, Summons.) The summons form dictates how the summons is to be prepared.[14] After "In the Matter of," the agent or officer inserts the name of the taxpayer whose tax liability is being investigated, collected, or examined, along with the taxpayer's address and other information that might help a third-party comply with the summons. If the liability is that of an individual, the individual's name must appear in the statement of liability, even if the individual's liability results from a corporation.[15] If the liability is that of a corporation, then the name of the corporation must appear in the statement of liability on the summons, but the name of an individual or corporate officer does not appear even if the individual or officer may be the summoned party. When a partnership or a business operating under a trade name, both the busi-

---

[12] See IRM 25.5.1.4.3, Considerations and Limitations on Issuance of a Summons (Apr. 30, 1999).

[13] See Rev. Proc. 84-62, 1984-2 CB 526. There are three additional official summons forms: Form 6637 (Collection Summons, Collection Information Statement), Form 6638 (Collection Summons, Income Tax Return), and Form 6639 (Collection Summons, Financial Records).

[14] IRM Exhibit 25.5.1.2, General Instructions for Preparation of a Summons (Apr. 30, 1999).

[15] If the return is a joint return, both the husband and wife are entered. IRM 25.5.2.2, Preparation and Use [of Summons] (Apr. 30, 1999).

ness and the individual involved must appear. The next part of the summons is the periods involved and the name and address of the summoned party. To the summoned party's name, the title or office of summoned party, such as trustee, custodian, corporate, or public office required to give testimony or produce records is added. The next part states "To Appear Before," which gives the name and title of the agent or officer who will take the testimony or examine the books and records, or before whom the summoned party is to appear before. When the summons requests records and other information, then summoned records and information should be described keeping in mind the nature, ownership, and years involved. In more complex cases, the drafting of the summons is referred to the Area Division Counsel.

[2] Service of the Summons

A summons is served by handing an attested copy of the summons to the person to whom it is directed a witness, or by leaving the summons at the person's "last and usual place of abode."[16] As a matter of practice, the Service encourages agents to make personal service of a summons. Section 7603 does not use the language of Fed. R. Civ. P. 4(e)(2), which authorizes service of a summons and complaint in a civil case by the leaving of papers "at the individual's dwelling house or usual place of abode with some person of suitable age and discretion then residing therein."[17] Where personal service cannot be effected, however, agents are instructed to leave the summons with a person of suitable age and discretion with instructions that the summons be given to the witness.[18] The Service's reading of Section 7603 has been upheld.[19] Where a summons is directed to a specific corporate officer to appear on behalf of the corporation, the person's corporate capacity should be indicated. Service may be made either at the corporation, the person's place of business, "or wherever he/she may be found." A summons directed to a corporation must be served on a corporation officer, director, managing agent, or other person authorized to accept service of process for the corporation.[20]

---

[16] IRC § 7603(a). For a case analyzing whether a place was the summoned party's "last and usual place of abode," see United States v. Hahn, 79-2 USTC ¶ 9595 (ED Wis. 1979). This requirement can be waived if objection is not made. United States v. Myslajek, 568 F2d 55 (8th Cir. 1977), cert. denied, 438 US 905 (1978).

[17] In Section 7603, the words "with some person of suitable age and discretion" are not implicitly included after "the last and usual place of abode." United States v. Bichara, 826 F2d 1037 (11th Cir. 1987) (due process rights of summoned party are protected by formal enforcement proceeding in which show cause order and petition for enforcement must be served in accordance with Rule 4, Fed. R. Civ. P.).

[18] See, e.g., IRM 25.5.3.2, Service of Summons (Apr. 30, 1999).

[19] See United States v. Hahn, 79-2 USTC ¶ 9595 (ED Wis. 1979).

[20] IRM 25.5.3.2, Service of Summons (Apr. 30, 1999).

Section 7603 contemplates that the agent serving the summons will prepare a certificate of service. This certificate, when signed by the person serving the summons, is "evidence of the facts it states" in any later hearing on an application to a district court for enforcement of the summons.[21] The form utilized by the Service as a certificate of service requires the person serving the summons to designate either that the summons was personally handed to the witness or that it was left with a named person at the witness' last usual place of abode.[22] (See Form 13.2.)

---

[21] IRC § 7603. Serving a copy of a summons on the taxpayer that does not contain any certification or affirmation that it is a true and correct copy of the original and does not contain an original signature fails to qualify as an attested summons required by Section 7603. Mimick v. United States, 952 F2d 230 (8th Cir. 1991) (but government acted in good faith, and no substantial rights of taxpayer were lost), on remand, 92-1 USTC ¶ 50,130 (D. Neb. 1992). Where the Service failed to follow the procedures in a delegation order, the summons was enforced. United States v. Gilbert C. Swanson Found., Inc., 772 F2d 440 (8th Cir. 1985) (court should "evaluate the seriousness of the violation under all the circumstances including the government's good faith and the degree of harm imposed by the unlawful conduct"). A certificate of the service of a summons may also be made by mailing the notice to the taxpayers. See Lestrade v. United States, 945 F. Supp. 1557 (SD Fla. 1996) (summonses were served on banks and the certificate was mailed to the Lestrades, who were French citizens, pursuant to the terms of the Hague Convention).

[22] A Certificate of Service form is on the back of the original of the summons. For a description of Service procedures in preparing the Certificate of Notice, see IRM 25.5.3-1, Example of Attestation (Apr. 30, 1999).

FORM 13.1
SUMMONS

Summons

Department of the Treasury
Internal Revenue Service

In the matter of _ABC Manufacturing, Inc._   _114 Easy Street, Anytown, NY 10000_

Internal Revenue District of _Manhattan_   Periods _1995, 1996, and 1997_

The Commissioner of Internal Revenue
Mr. John Oak, President
To _ABC Manufacturing, Inc._

At _114 Easy Street, Anytown, NY 10000_

You are hereby summoned and required to appear before _Ralph M. River_
an officer of the Internal Revenue Service, to give testimony and to bring with you and to produce for examination the following books, records, papers, and other data relating to the tax liability or the collection of the tax liability or for the purpose of inquiring into any offense connected with the administration or enforcement of the internal revenue laws concerning the person identified above for the periods shown.

All records for 1995, 1996, and 1997 of ABC Manufacturing, Inc., including

(1) Retained copies of all financial statements for the years indicated
(2) All books and records related to your federal income tax returns
for 1995, 1996, and 1997
(3) All canceled checks and bank statements for 1995, 1996, and 1997
(4) All correspondence with your customers for 1995, 1996, and 1997

DO NOT WRITE IN THIS SPACE

Business address and telephone number of Internal Revenue Service officer named above:
Room 300, Federal Building, One Broadway, Anytown, NY 10000   (212) 123–4567

Place and time for appearance:

at _Room 300, Federal Building, One Broadway, Anytown, NY_

on the _22nd_ day of _May_ , _2001_ at _10:00_ o'clock _a._ m.

Issued under authority of the Internal Revenue Code this _11th_ day of _May_ , _2001_

/s/ Ralph M. River	Revenue Officer
Signature of Issuing Officer	Title
/s/ Ben Q. Lake	Group Manager
Signature of Approving Officer (if applicable)	Title

Original to be kept by IRS

Form 2039 (Rev. 02-94)
Cat. No. 21405J

[3] Time and Place of Examination

The time and place of an examination made pursuant to the summons authority of Section 7602 must be "reasonable under the circumstances."[23] In the event that the summons calls for a witness to give testimony and to produce books and records, the date fixed for appearance must be at least ten days from the date of the summons[24] unless the witness agrees otherwise and is not a third-party recordkeeper.[25] The ten-day waiting period appears to be for the benefit of the witness, not the taxpayer. Consequently, a taxpayer has no standing to object to a waiver of this period by a witness who is not a third-party recordkeeper.[26] Agents must conduct tax examinations at a reasonable time and place, and criteria for establishing a reasonable time and place are covered by regulations.[27] For this purpose, it is generally unreasonable for the place of examination to be at a Service office other than the one located closest to the taxpayer's home or the taxpayer's place of business if the business premises are so small that the examination would prevent business from being conducted.[28]

As a practical matter, where a witness is considered to be cooperative and only production of records is involved, the summons will be made returnable at a time and place mutually convenient to the witness and the agent. The same practice is followed where an affidavit rather than a formal statement is required. For reasons of control and convenience, if a formal statement made

---

[23] IRC § 7605(a); See IRM 25.5.3.4, Place and Time Set by Summons (Apr. 30, 1999).

[24] IRC § 7605(a); Reg. § 301.7605-1(b)(1). The time for appearance should not be less than eleven full calendar days from the date the summons is served, excluding the date of service but including the date of appearance.

[25] IRC § 7609. See infra ¶ 13.04[3].

[26] Brunwasser v. Pittsburgh Nat'l Bank, 64-2 USTC ¶ 9871 (WD Pa. 1964), aff'd, 351 F2d 951 (3d Cir.), cert. denied, 384 US 986 (1966). The remedy of the taxpayer is to obtain an injunction restraining compliance. Reisman v. Caplin, 375 US 440 (1964).

[27] Conference Report, Technical and Miscellaneous Revenue Act of 1988, 100th Cong., 2d Sess. 212, (hereinafter Conference Report). Reg. § 301.7605-1(d)(3). For a description of the procedures in a tax examination, see ¶ 8.06[1][d].

[28] Reg. § 301.7605-1(d)(3). Examinations can be scheduled during the Service's normal business hours on a workday during the year without regard to seasonal fluctuations in the businesses of taxpayers or their representatives, but the Service will work with taxpayers or their representatives to minimize the adverse effects of scheduling. Reg. § 301.7605-1(b)(1). Even if a field examination is not held at the taxpayer's residence or place of business, Service personnel can make a site visit "to establish facts that can only be established by direct visit, such as inventory or asset verification" during the Service's business hours on a normal workday. Reg. § 301.7605-1(d)(3)(iii). Taxpayer requests to change the place of examination to the location of the taxpayer's current residence or place of business, or the location of the taxpayer's books and records will be considered by the Service on a case-by-case basis. Reg. § 301.7605-1(e).

before a stenographer is required by the agent, the summons will be returnable at the agent's office.

FORM 13.2
SERVICE OF SUMMONS, NOTICE AND RECORDKEEPER CERTIFICATES

Service of Summons, Notice and Recordkeeper Certificates

(Pursuant to section 7603, Internal Revenue Code)

I certify that I served the summons shown
on the front of this form on:

Date 11th day of May, 2001	Time 11:15 A.M.

How Summons Was Served

☒ I handed an attested copy of the summons to the person to whom it was directed.

114 Easy Street
Anytown, NY 10000

☐ I left an attested copy of the summons at the last and usual place of abode of the person to whom it was directed. I left the copy with the following person (if any):

Signature /s/ Ralph M. River	Title Revenue Officer

This certificate is made to show compliance with section 7609, Internal Revenue Code. This certificate applies only to summonses served on third-party recordkeepers and not to summonses served on other third parties or any officer or employee of the person to whose liability the summons relates nor to summonses in aid of collection, to determine the identity of a person having a numbered account or similar arrangement, or to determine whether or not records of the business transactions or affairs of an identified person have been made or kept.

I certify that, within 3 days of serving the summons, I gave notice (Form 2039-D) to the person named below on the date and in the manner indicated.

Date of Giving Notice _____ Time: _____

Name of Noticee: _____

Address of Noticee (if mailed): _____

How Notice Was Given

☐ I gave notice by certified or registered mail to the last known address of the noticee.

☐ In the absence of a last known address of the noticee, I left the notice with the person summoned.

☐ I gave notice by handing it to the noticee.

☐ I left the notice at the last and usual place of abode of the noticee. I left the copy with the following person (if any).

☐ No notice is required.

Signature	Title

I certify that the period prescribed for beginning a proceeding to quash this summons has expired and that no such proceeding was instituted or that the noticee consents to the examination.

Signature	Title

Form 2039 (Rev. 02-94)

If the witness is uncooperative or the agent believes that the witness is attempting to hamper the investigation, Service personnel are advised to have records produced at the agent's office.[29] The authority that exists on this matter is distinctly unfavorable to summoned persons where interference with an examination is alleged.[30]

[4] Notice to the Taxpayer

The IRS Restructuring and Reform Act of 1998[31] amended the summons authority in a significant way. Section 7602(c) prohibits a revenue agent, collection officer, or employee making "contact" with any person other than the taxpayer about the determination or collection of the taxpayer's tax liability unless the agent provides reasonable notice in advance to the taxpayer that "contacts with persons other than the taxpayer may be made."[32] Although the term "contact" is undefined in the statute, a contact includes a summons.[33] In addition, the Service is to maintain and periodically provide to the taxpayer a record of the persons the Service contacted during the period regarding the determination or collection of the taxpayer's liability.[34] This record of contacts is to be provided on the taxpayer's request as well. No notice of contact is required to be given to the taxpayer if

    1. The taxpayer has authorized the contact;

---

[29] IRM 25.5.3.4, Time and Place of Examination Set by Summons (Apr. 30, 1999). However, agents are also told that the authority to require production of records at the agent's office should not be used to penalize the witness.

[30] See, e.g., United States v. United Distillers Prods. Corp., 156 F2d 872 (2d Cir. 1946) (revenue agent's office, twenty-five miles from corporation's place of business, was held to be a proper place for an estimated four-month-long examination of corporation's records where its officers and employees were found to have interfered with the agent's examination).

[31] The IRS Restructuring and Reform Act of 1998, HR 2676, 105th Cong., 2d Sess. § 1002 (hereinafter the 1998 Act).

[32] IRC § 7602(c), as amended by 1998 Act § 3417, applicable to contacts made after the 180th day after July 22, 1998. To provide guidance to Chief Counsel attorneys, the Chief Counsel issued a notice stating that Section 7602(c) does not apply to third-party contacts made during litigation if the contacts relate to a matter being litigated, but is limited to contacts made "in connection with" the determination or collection of a taxpayer's liability. Notice N(35)000-160 (Jan. 22, 1999).

[33] S. Rep. No. 105-74, at 77 (Apr. 22, 1998). Based on failure to comply with Section 7602(c), a district court refused to enforce a summons served in the course of an examination of a corporation on two of the corporation's officers because the Service had failed to give advance notice to the corporation of a contact to a "person other than the taxpayer." United States v. Jillson, 84 AFTR2d 99-7115 (SD Fla. 1999).

[34] IRC § 7602(c)(2).

    2. The Service determines for good cause shown that the notice would jeopardize collection of any tax or the notice might result in a reprisal against the person contacted; or

    3. The contact is made in a criminal investigation.

Regulations on the third-party restriction of the Service's summons authority deal with several important issues left unclear in the statute.[35]

    1. *Third-party contacts.* A third-party contact is a contact by Service employees of "any person other than the taxpayer."[36] Regulations state that a third-party contact does not include the employees of a business taxpayer.[37] In addition, a third-party contact does not include employees of a third-party business entity (e.g., a bank or other business).

    2. *The meaning of "with respect to a determination or collection of tax."* A contact is "with respect to a determination or collection of tax" if it is "directly connected" to the purpose of determining or collecting tax. Interestingly, this interpretation parses the phrase that is frequently found in Code provisions, the phrase "with respect to."[38] According to the explanation, the phrase suggests a "required nexus between the contact" and the two purposes of determining or collecting tax. The words "the" and "such" in Section 7206(c) imply a single affected taxpayer. The proposed regulations interpret "with respect to a determination or collection of tax" to mean a "direct connection between the contact and the purpose of examining or collecting a liability of an identified taxpayer's liability."

    3. *Precontact notice.* A precontact notice may be given orally or in writing in a manner the Service employee reasonably believes will be received by the taxpayer before the contact.[39]

    4. *Postcontact report of persons contacted.* An annual report of third-party contacts is mandated, coupled with a taxpayer's ability to request more frequent reports.[40]

    5. *Record of persons contacted.* Service employees are not required to name all the persons contacted. A Service employee is not required to obtain the name of a person contacted if the employee would not ordinarily do so.[41] If the Service employee obtains the name of the person contacted, the regulations adopt a bright-line rule that the name of an individual satisfies the general standard of reasonable identification. Where a name is not provided, the Ser-

---

    [35] REG-104906-99; Prop. Reg. § 301.7602-2, 66 Fed. Reg. 77–84 (Jan. 2, 2001). These regulations became final on Dec. 17, 2002.

    [36] Reg. § 301.7602-2(a)(6).

    [37] Reg. § 301.7602-2(c)(2).

    [38] Reg. § 301.7602-2(c)(3).

    [39] Reg. §§ 301.7602-2(d)(1), 301.7602-2(d)(2).

    [40] Reg. §§ 301.7602-2(e)(1), 301.7602-2(e)(2).

    [41] Reg. § 301.7602-2(e)(3).

vice employee must provide a reasonable description of the third party, but just what information will be provided will depend on the facts and circumstances.

6. *Reprisal exception.* When either a precontact or a postcontact notice may result in reprisal against a third party, the notice requirements of Section 7206(c) will not apply. Reprisal is interpreted to include not only physical harm but also "emotional or economic harm."[42] Under interim procedures, Service employees have been informing third parties about the requirements of the third-party contact procedures and ask whether the third party has any concern about reprisal if the contact is reported to the taxpayer.

7. *Contacts with other governmental entities.* When Service employees contact other government agencies, the proposed regulations generally provide that contact with government agencies are not reportable.[43]

[5] Unnecessary Examinations and Second Inspections

Section 7605(b) provides: "No taxpayer shall be subjected to unnecessary examination or investigations, and only one inspection of a taxpayer's books of account shall be made for each taxable year (1) unless the taxpayer requests otherwise or (2) unless the Secretary, after investigation, notifies the taxpayer in writing that an additional inspection is necessary." The general prohibition applies to both unnecessary examinations and second inspections. The unnecessary-examination prohibition is absolute—that is, the Service simply may not conduct an unnecessary examination. However, the second-inspection prohibition is conditional—that is, the Service may conduct a second inspection if it so notifies a taxpayer.[44] Examination and inspection do not appear to be synonymous, but at times the terms are interpreted in a manner that gives them no meaning except as descriptions of the same activity. For example, it is said that more than one inspection of a taxpayer's books may take place during a single examination or investigation.[45] Since a second inspection can only take

---

[42] Reg. § 301.7602-2(f)(3).

[43] Reg. § 301.7602-2(f)(5).

[44] For the Service's procedures in reexaminations or reopenings, see ¶ 8.06[3][d].

[45] See, e.g., United States v. Schwartz, 469 F2d 977 (5th Cir. 1972); United States v. Moriarty, 311 F. Supp. 144 (ED Wis. 1969), aff'd, 435 F2d 347 (7th Cir. 1970); United States v. Giordano, 301 F. Supp. 884 (ED Mo. 1969), aff'd, 419 F2d 564 (8th Cir.), cert. denied, 397 US 1037 (1970); United States v. Crespo, 281 F. Supp. 928 (D. Md. 1968). In United States v. Gilpin, 542 F2d 38 (7th Cir. 1976), the Seventh Circuit said no second-inspection notice is required if it is factually established that a revenue agent had not completed his examination when he referred the case to a special agent for further investigation. United States v. Silverstain, 668 F2d 1161 (10th Cir. 1982) (cases gathered). The Service apparently applies this concept. See Tech. Adv. Mem. 8206011 (May 29, 1981) (following the decision in *Crespo*); United States v. Flair Mfg. Corp., 555 F. Supp. 847

place after the examination or investigation ceases, the difference between a prohibited second inspection and an unnecessary examination seems slight as a practical matter.

Challenges that an examination or inspection is unnecessary are infrequent. The issue presented by such a challenge is one of fact: Is the examination or investigation necessary? The answer is not likely to be favorable to the taxpayer because of the broad power granted the Service to determine a taxpayer's tax liability. The prohibition of unnecessary examination does not require courts "to oversee the Commissioner's determinations to investigate."[46] Nevertheless, a taxpayer can contend that if the Service already is in possession of the information being sought, its examination of the taxpayer is presumably unnecessary.[47]

In *United States v. Powell*,[48] the taxpayer refused to give testimony and records because the returns had been examined once and because the three-year statute of limitations barred assessments except in the case of fraud. The Supreme Court held that when read together the statute of limitations provisions and the investigatory power of the Service, do not "impose a probable cause standard . . . from the expiration date of the ordinary limitations period forward."[49] Not only did the legislative history of Section 7605 not impose a probable cause standard, but the Court said:

> This view of the statute is reinforced by the general rejection of probable cause requirements in like circumstances involving other agencies. . . . [T]he Commissioner need not meet any standard of probable cause to obtain enforcement of the summons, either by, before or after the three-year statute of limitations on ordinary tax liabilities has expired.[50]

The enforcing court whose process is invoked need determine only that the inquiry is relevant to a lawful purpose.[51] The purpose of the second-inspection

---

(EDNY 1983) (summons issued after thirty-day letter and protest held not to violate Section 7605(b) because Service made no final determination, agent had not seen documents called for, and canceled checks the agent had seen were part of a continuing investigation); United States v. Morgan, 761 F2d 1009 (4th Cir. 1985) (special agent's examination was continuation of revenue agent's audit, so no second-inspection notice was required).

[46] United States v. Powell, 379 US 48, 56 (1964).

[47] See United States v. Powell, 379 US 48, 56 (1964). Thus, where a special agent attempted to summon records that a revenue agent had already examined, enforcement was denied on the ground that the examination was unnecessary. United States v. Pritchard, 438 F2d 969 5th Cir. 1971). Contra United States v. Silverstain, 668 F2d 1161 (10th Cir. 1982).

[48] United States v. Powell, 379 US 48 (1964).

[49] United States v. Powell, 379 US 48, 56 (1964).

[50] United States v. Powell, 379 US 48, 57 (1964).

[51] The test was announced in Oklahoma Press Publishing Co. v. Walling, 327 US 186 (1964).

prohibition is limited. It is designed to avoid harassment of taxpayers by "low-echelon" revenue agents "by requiring such agents to clear any repetitive examinations with a superior."[52] There need be no "probable cause" for a second inspection as long as the inspection is duly authorized.[53] Moreover, the prohibition applies only to records of a taxpayer. The prohibition does not prevent the Service from seeking information from other sources.[54] Thus, the Service may seek the taxpayer's records in the hands of a third person.[55] Also, the prohibition applies only to an examination of the taxpayer's own liability, and not with respect to information sought concerning another taxpayer.[56]

When a properly authorized reopening letter is sent, the Service may reexamine the taxpayer's books.[57] If the letter is not sent, a taxpayer may refuse to permit the examination and, should the Service seek enforcement of a summons, oppose the application for enforcement.[58] However, if a taxpayer fails to object to a reexamination or second inspection or voluntarily consents to one,

---

[52] United States v. Powell, 379 US 48, 56 (1964).

[53] United States v. Powell, 379 US 48, 56 (1964).

[54] United States v. Howard, 360 F2d 373 (3d Cir. 1966) (records of taxpayer's corporation); Geurkink v. United States, 354 F2d 629 (7th Cir. 1965) (records of taxpayer's wholly owned corporation not subject to Section 7605(b)). But see Moloney v. United States, 521 F2d 491 (6th Cir.), cert. denied, 423 US 1017 (1975) (records of a partnership "merely extension of the person of the taxpayers" and protected by Section 7605(b)). Compare Curtis v. Comm'r, 84 TC 1349 (1985) (inspection of books of limited partnership held not an inspection of the taxpayer-partner's books; *Moloney* distinguished). See also United States v. Lask, 703 F2d 293 (8th Cir. 1983) (summonses issued to third-party recordkeepers for their records of transactions with taxpayers not barred by Section 7605(b)).

[55] Hubner v. Tucker, 245 F2d 35 (9th Cir. 1957) (records in hands of executrix not covered by prohibition).

[56] United States v. Chemical Bank, 593 F2d 451 (2d Cir. 1979); Hubner v. Tucker, 245 F2d 35 (9th Cir. 1957).

[57] There seems to be no statutory requirement that the letter be sent before the examination begins. In re Paramount Jewelry Co., 80 F. Supp. 375 (SDNY 1948). Where a reopening letter is sent, a summons is enforceable even where the Service is trying to use another valuation method more favorable to it. United States v. Clement, 47 AFTR2d 81-1220 (ED Ark. 1981), rev'd, 668 F2d 1010 (8th Cir. 1982).

[58] The Service has long taken this view of a taxpayer's rights under Section 7605(b). See Reineman v. United States, 301 F2d 267 (7th Cir. 1962). On the Service's failure to send a reopening letter, enforcement of a summons has been denied. United States v. Fordin, 30 AFTR2d 72-5249 (EDNY 1972). In what must be considered unusual instances, occurring before the Supreme Court's decision in *Caceres*, failure to send the required notice has resulted in suppression of evidence in criminal cases. In re Leonardo, 208 F. Supp. 124 (ND Cal. 1962); United States v. Avila, 227 F. Supp. 3 (ND Cal. 1963). The Service's position is that even if a second inspection were to take place in violation of one of its procedural rules (see ¶ 8.06[3][d]), the suppression would not be warranted because no constitutional or statutory law was violated. Tech. Adv. Mem. 8206011 (May 29, 1981) (following the decision in United States v. Crespo, 281 F. Supp. 928 (D. Md. 1968).

he waives any rights conferred by Section 7605(b).[59] Consequently, where a taxpayer was aware of the second inspection and did not challenge the unauthorized examination, invalidation of the assessment was considered inappropriate.[60] Courts avoid granting an aggrieved taxpayer relief by finding that Section 7605(b) has been complied with or its protection waived.[61] In *United States v. House*, the Third Circuit said that if the taxpayer was aggrieved by the second inspection, he could have resisted. It concluded: "We can hardly countenance as a ground for suppression an examination to which the taxpayer, having available alternatives, consented."[62]

The lesson seems to be that a taxpayer must challenge a second inspection as soon as he knows one is taking place and refuse access to records sought in the re-inspection. Failure to do so results in a waiver of the protection of Section 7605(b).

Where a taxpayer claims that an illegal second inspection has occurred, the Service often counters by saying that its initial examination was only cursory and therefore insufficient to constitute an "inspection" or "examination." In resolving this question, the time spent by the agent is frequently a significant factor, and courts generally have recognized that a meaningful examination takes time[63] and may involve more than one review of the taxpayer's books.[64]

---

[59] Moloney v. United States, 521 F2d 491 (6th Cir.), cert. denied, 423 US 1017 (1975); United States v. O'Connor, 237 F2d 466 (2d Cir. 1956); Philip Mangone Co. v. United States, 54 F2d 168 (Ct. Cl. 1931).

[60] Moloney v. United States, 521 F2d 491 (6th Cir.), cert. denied, 423 US 1017 (1975) (adjustments were also derived from unprotested examination of corporate records).

[61] United States v. House, 524 F2d 1035 (3d Cir. 1975); Field Enters., Inc. v. United States, 348 F2d 485 (Ct. Cl. 1965), cert. denied, 382 US 1009 (1966). See also Moloney v. United States, 521 F2d 491 (6th Cir.), cert. denied, 423 US 1017 (1975) Collins v. Comm'r, 61 TC 693, 700 n.4 (1974). See Ballantine v. Comm'r, 74 TC 516 (1980) (when second-inspection letter requested, notices of deficiency issued; held, no second inspection and notices valid). However, in *Ballantine*, the Service admitted that "if petitioners show that the notices of deficiency are arbitrary and excessive, the burden of proof will be shifted." Id. at 525.

[62] United States v. House, 524 F2d 1035 (3d Cir. 1975).

[63] United States v. Giordano, 301 F. Supp. 884 (ED Mo. 1969), aff'd, 419 F2d 564, 567 (8th Cir.), cert. denied, 397 US 1037 (1970); In re Magnus, 299 F2d 335 (2d Cir.), cert. denied, 370 US 918 (1962); National Plate & Window Glass Co. v. United States, 254 F2d 92, 93 (2d Cir.), cert. denied, 358 US 822 (1958); United States v. Gambino, 386 F. Supp. 566 (SDNY 1974).

[64] United States v. Crespo, 281 F. Supp. 928 (D. Md. 1968) (if an agent has seen a cash book or other document once, it does not mean he does not need to see it again for another purpose).

[6] Special Procedures for Third-Party Witnesses: Section 7609

Special procedures apply to third-party recordkeepers, such as a summons on a third-party recordkeeper. Both these notice procedures and the method of objecting when a summons is served on a third-party recordkeeper are described later.[65]

[7] Special Procedures for Summonses for Computer Software

Section 7612 limits the Service's authority to issue a summons for any computer source codes unless developed for the internal use of the taxpayer or a related person. In general, except as specifically provided in the provision, the Service may not issue a summons for a tax-related computer software source code, or begin any summons enforcement action for the source code.[66] If the source code is of a protected type, before the Service may issue a summons to obtain the source code, the Service must determine that (1) it is otherwise unable to ascertain the correctness of any item on the return form, the taxpayer's books and records, or the computer software program and associated data; (2) the Service identifies with reasonable specificity the portion of the source code needed to verify the correctness of the item; and (3) the need for the source code outweighs the risk of unauthorized disclosure of trade secrets.[67] The Service will be considered to have satisfied the first two of these requirements if it makes a formal request for the materials to both the taxpayer and the software owner, and the request is not satisfied within 180 days. These limitations do not apply to a summons of computer software source codes the taxpayer acquired or developed primarily for the taxpayer's internal use rather than for commercial distribution.[68] However, the fact that software is developed for internal use is not dispositive of whether the software was intended for internal use for purposes of the tax laws.

The provision establishes a number of specific protections against the disclosure and improper use of trade secrets and confidential information incident to the Service's examination of any computer software program or source code that comes into the Service's possession or control during its examination of the taxpayer. In addition, a court that enforces a summons is authorized to is-

---

[65] See infra ¶ 13.04[3].

[66] IRC § 7612, added by 1998 Act § 3413. The protection of source codes applies to summonses issued after July 22, 1998, and software acquired after that date, and within ninety days after the effective date to source codes the Service acquired before the effective date. For Service procedures, see IRM 25.5.6.10, Software Trade Secret Protection under IRC § 7612 (Apr. 30, 1999).

[67] IRC § 7612(b)(1).

[68] IRC § 7612(b)(2). Investigations of criminal offenses are also excepted from protection.

sue a protective order to prevent the disclosure of confidential information.[69] A willful unauthorized disclosure of a source code the Service obtains is a felony, punishable in the same manner as other unauthorized disclosures.

[8] Designated Summons for Corporate Information

Section 6503(j)(1) suspends the running of any period of limitation on assessment when a designated summons is "issued . . . to a corporation (or to any other person to whom the corporation has transferred records) with respect to any return of tax by such corporation for a taxable year (or other period) for which [the] corporation is being examined under the coordinated examination program (or any successor program). . . ."[70] A "designated summons" is any summons issued for the purpose of determining the amount of any tax imposed by [the Code]" if the summons (1) is issued at least sixty days before the expiration of the statute of limitations on assessment; (2) "clearly states that it is a designated summons" for the purpose of the suspension provision;[71] and (3) no prior summons has been issued that has been treated as a designated summons.[72] The statute of limitations that is suspended is the statute of limitations on assessment. The period during which this limitations period is suspended is called the judicial enforcement period. The judicial enforcement period is the period of a judicial summons enforcement proceeding involving the designated summons or any other summons issued during the thirty-day period starting on the issue date of the designated summons and relates to the same return as the designated summons.[73] The "judicial enforcement period" begins on the day the summons enforcement proceeding is commenced and ends on the day of

---

[69] IRC § 7612(c)(1). Sections 7612(c)(2)(A)–7612(c)(2)(H) set forth the specific safeguards that will be put into place. For Service procedures in designated summons situations, see IRM 25.5.3.3, Designated Summons (Apr. 30, 1999).

[70] The procedures apply to any tax, whether imposed before, on, or after November 5, 1990, if the statute of limitations for assessment of the tax has not run on that date.

[71] IRC § 6503(j)(2)(A). Before amendment of Section 6503(j), Service procedures limited the designated summons to Coordinated Examination Program (CEP) cases, except in unique circumstances; and the Area Division Counsel for the Area in which the examination was taking place had to review the summons before it was issued in order for the period of limitations to be suspended. Ann. 96-5, 1996-4 IRB 1. The administrative procedure was incorporated into Section 6503(j)(1) by the Taxpayer Bill of Rights 2, § 1002(a). IRC § 6503(j)(1), as amended,, is applicable to summonses issued after the effective date, July 30, 1996.

[72] IRC § 6503(j)(2)(B).

[73] IRC § 6503(j)(1)(A). See discussion of suspension of the statute of limitations at ¶ 5.04.

the final "resolution" of the summoned person's response to the designated summons.[74]

Suspension of the statute of limitations can also occur where a designated summons has been issued to the corporate taxpayer and a related summons is issued to another person for information about the corporation's return. For this suspension period to apply, the related summons must be issued within thirty days after the day on which the designated summons is issued.[75] If the related summons is issued within this period, then the running of the assessment period is suspended for the period of a judicial proceeding to enforce the related summons.[76] A further 120 days is added to the suspension period beginning one day after a final decision in the summons enforcement proceeding enforcing the summons.[77] However, even if the court does not enforce the summons, the statute is suspended anyway for the period of the enforcement proceeding and an additional sixty days.[78]

Statutes of limitations on assessment, collection, and prosecution are suspended when there is a proceeding to quash a third-party recordkeeper summons.[79] No suspension operates when a summons is served on the taxpayer or on a person who is not a third-party recordkeeper with the result that a summons enforcement proceeding can still be used as a delaying tactic when such summonses are issued.

Section 6503(j) presupposes a situation where a revenue agent has issued a summons during the course of the examination and has not waited until the imminent expiration of the statute of limitations on assessment. Other suspension periods in Section 6503 are characterized by the inability of the Service to make a timely assessment, either through no fault of the Service (e.g., because of the restrictions on assessment) or through the fault of the taxpayer (e.g., because the taxpayer has fled the country to evade collection). Seen in this statutory context, Section 6503(j) permits the Service to use a designated summons to suspend the statute of limitations on assessment when the Service has been prevented by a taxpayer's failure to provide requested information in a timely manner.

The message of the statute is clear enough. Dilatory summons litigation over a corporation's records should not be used as a tactical device whereby the statute of limitations on assessment prevents the Service from gaining ac-

---

[74] IRC § 6503(j)(3). Section 6503(j)(3)(B) says "ends on the day on which there is a final resolution as to the summoned person's response to such summons." It is assumed that a "final resolution" and a final decision are the same because even settlement is a decision or judgment of the court.

[75] IRC § 6503(j)(1)(A)(ii).

[76] IRC § 6503(j)(1)(A)(ii).

[77] IRC § 6503(j)(1)(B).

[78] IRC § 6503(j)(1) (flush language).

[79] IRC § 7609(e). See infra ¶ 13.04[3][d].

cess to information that may be relevant to examination of the corporation's return. On the other hand, a summons issued sixty days prior to expiration of the assessment period will still qualify as a designated summons. Consequently, can wait until just before statutory period expires to issue a designated summons. This gives agents extraordinary ability to sidestep the statutory period of assessment without regard to any fault they may bear for the delay. It is worth observing, finally, that only the statute of limitations on assessment is suspended, unlike the provision in the third-party recordkeeper statute that suspends the assessment, collection, and prosecution statutes.

There has been one reported designated summons case. In *Derr*, international examiners issued a designated summons although they had previously been obtained successive extensions of the assessment period. Both the district court and the circuit court ordered the designated summons enforced, on the ground that the requirements of *Powell* had been satisfied.[80] The courts in *Derr* refused to read any requirement of taxpayer fault or no agent fault into the designated summons suspension statute. As previously suggested, this ruling leaves agents with the license to obtain data at the end of a lengthy audit, regardless of the corporation's cooperation.[81] Treating the enforcement of a designated summons in the same manner as any other summons enforcement proceeding does give the corporate taxpayer the same objections that it might have raised to any summons, such as that the summons was served to harass the taxpayer and therefore to have violated *Powell*'s requirement that a summons not be served for the purpose of harassing a taxpayer or for some other improper purpose.

[9] Special Procedures for the Examination of Churches

For church tax inquiries and examinations, Section 7611 imposes a special set of restrictions.[82] In general, Section 7611 provides for high-level review within the Service and amplified notice requirements to avoid infringing on the First Amendment rights of any organization claiming to be a church.[83] With the

---

[80] United States v. Derr, 968 F2d 943 (9th Cir. 1992).

[81] In *Derr*, there was evidence that Chevron had been cooperative. It had extended the statute of limitations several times, responded to hundreds of Information Document Requests, and supplied the agents with thousands of documents at considerable expense.

[82] IRC § 7611, added by Section 1033 of the Deficit Reduction Act of 1984. For Service procedures, see IRM 25.8.4, Restrictions on Church Tax Inquiries and Examinations (Apr. 30, 1999).

[83] For the Service's guidelines in church examinations, see IRM 25.5.8.4, Restrictions on Church Tax Inquiries and Examinations (Apr. 30, 1999). Section 7611 procedures do not apply to criminal investigations and violations of the criminal tax laws by an attempt to evade or defeat tax, or the failure to file a return. IRC §§ 7611(i)(1), 7611(i)(4), 7611(i)(5). They also do not apply to the investigation of the tax liability of a person

popularity of mail-order churches, and the attraction of the earthly tax benefits advertised to enhance membership in these organizations, there had been considerable litigation under prior law, but organizations claiming to be churches fought with almost no instance of success in avoiding any tax inquiry at all. Nothing in the statute or the First Amendment prevents an examination to determine whether an organization is engaged in taxable activities,[84] or the service of a summons on a bank where the church maintains an account,[85] although a summons directed at obtaining information about church members is suspect.[86] The Service may not threaten to revoke the tax-exempt status of an organization if it fails to produce records pursuant to a summons.[87] In *Church of World Peace, Inc.*, the Service had actually obtained some records in response to the summons. At a later Tax Court trial, the Service attempted to use copies of the records (the originals having been returned), and the Tax Court refused to suppress or exclude them on the grounds that the summons

---

other than the church, or to a termination or jeopardy assessment. IRC §§ 7611(i)(2), 7611(i)(3).

[84] United States v. Groos Nat'l Bank of San Antonio, 661 F2d 36 (5th Cir. 1981); United States v. Grayson County State Bank, 656 F2d 1070 (5th Cir. 1981), cert. denied sub nom. First Pentecostal Church v. United States, 455 US 920 (1982); United States v. Dykema, 666 F2d 1096 (7th Cir. 1981), cert. denied, 456 US 983 (1982); United States v. City Nat'l Bank & Trust Co., 642 F2d 388 (10th Cir. 1981); United States v. Sommer, 81-1 USTC ¶ 9292 (ND Ill. 1981); United States v. Manufacturers Bank of Southfield, 518 F. Supp. 495 (ED Mich. 1981); Jahns v. United States, 84-1 USTC ¶ 9338 (D. Ariz. 1984) ("the enforcement of a proper IRS summons in order to establish the validity of a church's status or to aid in the collection of taxes due, is only an incidental invasion on the freedom of religion" (citations omitted)). St. German of Alaska, E. Orthodox Catholic Church v. United States, 653 F. Supp. 1342 (SDNY 1987), aff'd, 840 F2d 1087 (2d Cir. 1988) (summons served on church attorneys for real estate records enforced despite Service's criminal investigation of church leader).

[85] Where bank records of an individual are sought, no First Amendment prohibition prevents enforcement even if the individual is active in a church. See United States v. Berg, 636 F2d 203 (8th Cir. 1980); United States v. Manufacturers Bank of Southfield, 518 F. Supp. 495 (ED Mich. 1981). A summons calling for production of bank records of a church has also been held to be outside the scope of Section 7605(c) because the summons calls for the bank's, not the church's, records. United States v. Grayson County State Bank, 656 F2d 1070 (5th Cir. 1981), cert. denied sub nom. First Pentecostal Church v. United States, 455 US 920 (1982) (First Amendment argument also rejected because summons not abusive); McTaggart v. United States, 570 F. Supp. 547, 550–551 (ED Mich. 1983); Troyer v. United States, 84-1 USTC ¶ 9244 (ND Ind. 1984) ("[n]o summons has been issued to a church, convention or association of churches. Thus, a summons to a bank cannot contravene § 7605(c)").

[86] An allegation that for audit purposes, the Service distinguishes between those churches that rely on the mail to further their teachings and others stated a claim for relief. Life Science Church v. IRS, 525 F. Supp. 399 (ND Cal. 1981). See also United States v. Citizens State Bank, 612 F2d 1091 (8th Cir. 1980) (summons for membership records of tax protest group not enforced).

[87] Church of World Peace, Inc. v. IRS, 715 F2d 492 (10th Cir. 1983).

was "arguably valid" at the time it was issued and the agents did not act in bad faith.[88]

Regulations limit the application of Section 7611 by providing that seven types of requests do not constitute a "church tax inquiry" or a "church tax examination."[89] The Service may examine church records only "to the extent necessary to determine" the church's tax liability.[90] Consequently, Section 7611 is interpreted as not applying to an investigation of a member of a church, as opposed to the church itself.[91] When a summons fails to state how or why the data requested are necessary to the investigation of the church, the enforcement of the summons has been denied.[92] As a result the Service has had difficulty in satisfying the statutory requirements of Section 7611. One court has developed a two-part test.[93] First, the Service cannot even begin an investigation by sending an inquiry notice unless it "reasonably believes" the church has the relevant liability. Second, the Service "must show that the material is 'necessary' to the investigation, not necessary to prove liability."[94]. Also, Section 7611 "requires the Service to explain why the particular documents it seeks will significantly help to further the purpose of the investigation."[95]

¶ 13.03 RESPONSES TO THE SUMMONS

[1] Production of Records and Interviews

Section 7602 authorizes the Service to compel production of "such books, papers, records, or other data . . . as may be relevant or material" to its examination or investigation. Generally, the records that the summoned party must

---

[88] Church of World Peace, Inc. v. IRS, 715 F2d 492 (10th Cir. 1983).

[89] Reg. § 301.7611, Q&A 4.

[90] IRC § 7611(b)(1).

[91] Reg. § 301.7611, Q&A 6. Kerr v. United States, 801 F2d 1162 (9th Cir. 1986) (restriction of Section 7611 did not apply where summons served on banks in investigation of individuals and excluded records that "solely concern the Church").

[92] United States v. Church of Scientology of Boston, Inc., 933 F2d 1074 (1st Cir. 1991); United States v. Church of Scientology Western U.S., 973 F2d 715 (9th Cir. 1992) (accord; "meaning of 'necessary' in this context is something more than 'possibly relevant'").

[93] United States v. Church of Scientology of Boston, Inc., 933 F2d 1074 (1st Cir. 1991).

[94] United States v. Church of Scientology of Boston, Inc., 933 F2d 1074, 1078 (1st Cir. 1991).

[95] United States v. Church of Scientology of Boston, Inc., 933 F2d 1074, 1079 (1st Cir. 1991).

produce pursuant to a summons are the type of records a taxpayer is required to keep under the internal revenue laws. Section 6001 of the Code requires: "Every person liable for any tax imposed by this title . . . shall keep such records . . . as the Secretary or his delegate may from time to time prescribe." Regulations state:

> [A]ny person subject to [income] tax . . . or any person required to file a return of information with respect to income, shall keep such permanent books of account or records, including inventories, as are sufficient to establish the amount of gross income, deductions, credits, or other matters required to be shown by such person in any return of such tax or information.[96]

Records include computer-based recordkeeping systems.[97] A taxpayer who has such records must produce the originals and permit their copying. In *United States v. Davey*,[98] production of duplicates of a company's computer-based recordkeeping system was held not to comply with Section 7602 because it speaks of production of the records themselves. As the court said, "Where the accuracy of a taxpayer's return is being checked, the government is entitled to use the original records for purpose of verification rather than be forced to accept purported copies, which present the risk of error or tampering."[99] Authority to compel production includes the right to photocopy.[100] The Service insists on making copies either at the taxpayer's office by using portable equipment or, if the taxpayer refuses, at a territory division office.[101] A taxpayer who voluntarily produces and then demands the return of his personal records on con-

---

[96] Reg. § 1.6001-1(a). Similar regulations exist for specific taxpayers (e.g., farmers) and other types of tax. See, e.g., Reg. §§ 20.6001 et seq. (estate tax); Reg. §§ 25.6001 et seq. (gift tax); Reg. § 41.6001; Reg. § 53.6001 (excise tax); Reg. § 44.6001 (stamp taxes).

[97] Rev. Rul. 71-20, 1971-1 CB 392. Videotapes have been held to constitute "other data" within the meaning of Section 7602(b). United States v. Challman, 520 F. Supp. 64 (SD Ind. 1981); United States v. Schenk 581 F. Supp. 218 (SD Ind. 1984) (master videotape ordered produced).

[98] United States v. Davey, 543 F2d 996 (2d Cir. 1976).

[99] United States v. Davey, 543 F2d 996,1001 (2d Cir. 1976). A taxpayer who wishes to protect himself against the risk of damage or destruction can make duplicates before complying with the summonses.

[100] McGarry v. Riley, 363 F2d 421 (1st Cir.), cert. denied, 385 US 969 (1966); United States v. Ponder, 444 F2d 816 (5th Cir. 1971), cert. denied, 405 US 918 (1972); Boren v. Tucker, 239 F2d 767 (3d Cir. 1956).

[101] IRM 4.10.2.9.4(3), Authority to Request Books, Records and Accountants' Workpapers (May 14, 1999) ("for the sake of convenience, [another suggestion] is that the agent photograph the records").

stitutional grounds is entitled to their return, but the Service may retain copies made before the demand.[102]

Does the summoned party, a taxpayer, have the duty to label or otherwise organize the materials produced pursuant to a summons? In view of the scope of the summons authority, it would seem that the answer is yes, and that the taxpayer is required to demonstrate that the documents were produced just as they appeared in the taxpayer's own records. In one case,[103] however, the Service asked the court to compel a taxpayer to label documents it had already turned over to international examiners conducting a transfer pricing examination in compliance with their designated summons. In the summons enforcement proceeding, the government stated that it based its request that the taxpayer label documents after the examiners concluded that the taxpayer "failed to produce the documents as they are kept in the normal course of business." The court denied the government's motion, noting that "the government, not Chevron, is in a better position to organize the documents according to specific request."

Since taxpayers and others are required to keep certain records by the Code and the regulations for the purpose of verifying or preparing a tax return, records and other data that may be ordered produced must be in existence before the summons is issued. A taxpayer need not prepare or produce records not in existence.[104] However, in *United States v. Euge*,[105] the Supreme Court held that Section 7602 empowered the Service to compel handwriting exemplars relevant to its investigation. This ruling seems to undercut an interpretation of Section 7602 that precludes the Service's authority to order a witness to produce a previously nonexistent document. The Supreme Court declined to express an opinion on the matter, noting that the Service itself disclaims any intention of ordering a witness to create or prepare documents.[106]

---

[102] Mason v. Pulliam, 557 F2d 426 (5th cir. 1977). Accord United States v. Ward, 576 F2d 243 (9th Cir. 1978). See Linn v. Chivatero, 714 F2d 1278 (5th Cir. 1983) (despite the Anti-Injunction Act, a district court had jurisdiction over taxpayer's action for injunction ordering the Service to return his records allegedly retained in violation of his Fourth Amendment rights; on remand, the Service is to be permitted to request enforcement of its summons, and the court is to decide the validity of the taxpayer's constitutional claims). But see Lowrie v. United States, 824 F2d 827 (10th Cir. 1987) (Anti-Injunction Act held to preclude court-ordered return of copies of records to taxpayer because purpose was to prevent collection of additional tax; *Linn* distinguished). Postdemand retention would constitute an unreasonable search.

[103] United States v. Derr, 1993 WL 226100 (ND Cal. 1993).

[104] United States v. Davey, 543 F2d 996 (2d Cir. 1976). See United States v. Brown, 536 F2d 117 (6th Cir. 1976).

[105] United States v. Euge, 444 US 707 (1980).

[106] IRM Exhibit 25.5.1-2, General Instructions for Preparation of a Summons (Apr. 30,1999). These Instructions state: "The summons should not require the witness to do anything other than appear on a given date to give testimony and to bring existing books,

Records whose production may be compelled under Section 7602 include not only the records of U.S. persons but of foreign corporations as well. If records of a foreign corporation are in the United States or may be secured by officers and shareholders who are subject to process of a federal court, they may be ordered produced.[107]

[2] Effect of Summons

A summons is not self-enforcing. To enforce a summons, the Service must commence a proceeding in district court to compel compliance with the summons. Once a summons is served, however, the summoned party is prohibited from making any transfer of the books and papers called for by the summons, and certainly the summoned party's rights will not be expanded nor will the party's obligations be diminished by a postsummons transfer of records. In *Couch v. United States*,[108] an agent served a summons on the accountant for the taxpayer, calling for the accountant to produce the taxpayer's books, and the accountant transferred the books to the taxpayer's attorney. In deciding the case, the Supreme Court ignored the transfer in resolving the taxpayer's claims. The person who transfers such property risks potential criminal liability for obstruction of justice.[109] Since ultimately the court's process is used to enforce the summons, a transferor may be punishable for contempt,[110] and an attorney-transferor may be subject to disciplinary action.[111] Where the transfer takes place during the summons enforcement proceeding, the grounds for imposing sanctions for contempt are even more clearly present.[112] Third-party

---

papers and records. A summons cannot require to prepare or create documents, including returns, that are not currently in existence."

[107] International Commodities Corp. v. IRS, 224 F2d 882 (2d Cir. 1955) (summons directed to resident president of foreign corporation); United States v. Diefenthal, 28 AFTR2d 71-5950 (ED La. 1971) (records of foreign corporation transferred to Panama after summons served), For a discussion of the use of a summons to obtain foreign-based records, see infra ¶ 13.16.

[108] Couch v. United States, 409 US 322, 329 n.9 (1973). See also United States v. Zakutansky, 401 F2d 68 (7th Cir. 1968), cert. denied, 393 US 1021 (1969) (postsummons transfer by accountant to taxpayer).

[109] 18 USC § 1503. See United States v. Curcio, 279 F2d 681 (2d Cir), cert. denied, 364 US 824 (1960).

[110] See, e.g., United States v. Lyons, 442 F2d 1144 (1st Cir. 1971); United States v. Edmond, 355 F. Supp. 435 (WD Okla. 1972) (accountant held in civil contempt and fined $4,040 for turning over his workpapers after summons served).

[111] Any person licensed to practice before the Service may be suspended where the order of a summons is ignored.

[112] See In re DI Operating Co., 240 F. Supp. 672 (D. Nev. 1965) (fine equal to cost of summons enforcement action); United States v. Boudreaux, 328 F. Supp. 154 (Ed La. 1971).

recordkeepers' obligations are statutory. The third-party recordkeeper summons procedures make the obligation of the person served with a summons explicit, at least where that class of third parties is involved. The third party must assemble the records, and be prepared to produce the records on the date called for in the summons.[113]

[3] The Taking of Testimony: Rights of Taxpayers

At an interview of the taxpayer, the taxpayer may be represented by any representative authorized to practice before the Service by Circular 230.[114] The proceeding may be suspended, to permit the taxpayer access to a representative.[115] During the interview, if the taxpayer requests the opportunity to consult with the representative, the agent must suspend the interview for a reasonable period to permit the taxpayer to consult with the representative.[116] Unless a taxpayer is served with a summons, the taxpayer cannot be required to appear for an interview accompanied by a representative, but the agent can request that the taxpayer to attend the interview voluntarily.[117] If the taxpayer abuses the suspension procedure (e.g., by repeated suspensions) the agent may use an administrative summons to require the taxpayer's attendance.

On the return of a summons calling for the testimony of the taxpayer, the taxpayer is permitted to record the proceedings, provided the taxpayer gives prior notice to the agent.[118] The Service is also permitted to record a taxpayer interview, but the agent must give prior notice to the taxpayer, and on the taxpayer's request supply a copy or transcript to the taxpayer when the taxpayer pays the cost of the copy or transcript.[119]

The Service must also explain a taxpayer's rights before a personal interview during an examination and during the collection process.[120] Taxpayers are

---

[113] IRC § 7609(i)(1).

[114] IRC § 7520(c). Although a taxpayer is entitled to be represented, the taxpayer is still required to appear personally on the return date of the summons. United States v. Leach, 71A AFTR2d 93-3665 (D. Kan. 1990).

[115] IRC § 7521(b)(2).

[116] IRC § 7520(c). Although the suspension procedure does not formally apply to an interview pursuant to an administrative summons or criminal investigations, a taxpayer is entitled to be represented at such an interview. Service procedures also require modified *Miranda* warnings to the target of a criminal investigation before the interview takes place.

[117] IRC § 7520(c).

[118] IRC § 7521(a)(1).

[119] IRC § 7521(a)(2).

[120] IRC § 7521(b)(1).

not entitled to notice if their cases have been referred to the Criminal Investigation, but a special agent must give the taxpayer partial *Miranda* warnings.[121]

[4] The Taking of Testimony: Rights of Witnesses

[a] Representation and Assistance

A witness who appears pursuant to a summons is entitled to be represented by counsel and to have that counsel present when questioned in order to give him advice.[122] Moreover, if the subject of the interview is technical in nature, an attorney or accountant may be present to assist the witness in giving testimony.[123] But a taxpayer generally has no right to appear or to have his counsel present at an interview with a witness, even for the limited purpose of making objections to the production of records and testimony called for during the interview.[124] If the witness chooses to have other persons at the interview, they may be able to attend as observers.[125]

[b] A Possible Limitation on Representation: Multiple or "Dual" Representation

At times, representatives of taxpayers have attempted to also represent another summoned third party in an examination or investigation. Multiple repre-

---

[121] IRC § 7520(d).

[122] See IRM 25.5.5.4, Rights and Privileges of Person Summoned (Apr. 30, 1999); IRM 25.5.5.4.2, Right to Be Represented by Counsel (Apr. 30, 1999). The Administrative Procedure Act also provides a right to counsel. 5 USC § 555(b).

[123] IRM 25.5.5.4, Rights and Privileges of Person Summoned (Apr. 30, 1999). Similarly, an interpreter may be present to assist a witness who does not speak English in giving testimony.

[124] United States v. Newman, 441 F2d 165 (5th Cir. 1971). Accord United States v. Nemetz, 450 F2d 924 (3d Cir. 1971), cert. denied, 405 US 988 (1972); United States v. Taylor, 43 AFTR2d 79-790 (ED Va. 1979); United States v. Kershaw, 436 F. Supp. 552 (D. Or. 1977). But see Donaldson v. United States, 400 US 517 (1971) (Douglas, J., concurring). See United States v. Jones, 84 AFTR2d 99-6830 (DSC 1999) (taxpayer's counsel was not permitted to be present at the questioning of the accountant the attorney had engaged to assist him in representing the taxpayer, despite the fact that the accountant was covered by the attorney-client privilege). The district court relied on cases that generally hold that a taxpayer has no right to present when a third-party recordkeeper is questioned, citing United States v. Daffin, 653 F2d 121 (4th Cir. 1981); United States v. Taylor, 43 AFTR2d 79-790 (ED Va. 1979).

[125] United States v. Finch, 434 F. Supp. 1085 (D. Colo. 1977) (witness wished to have other persons present at interview; held, other persons may attend if witness gets waiver of confidentiality rules). Reisman v. Caplin, 375 US 440 (1964), authorizes any interested party to be present to challenge the summons. See the discussion infra ¶ 13.04[1].

sentation usually has occurred in criminal investigations being conducted by a special agent. In multiple or dual representation situations, the lawyer representing the taxpayer under investigation also represents a witness or witnesses, to gain access to information the witness may provide the special agent or to prevent the special agent from totally controlling the course of an interview. Also, lawyers believe that it is appropriate to represent family members or shareholder-officers in a closely held corporation where clients have the same exposure. Primarily because of its concern about the disclosure of information, the Service has objected to this multiple or, as it terms the circumstance, "dual" representation. In egregious cases, the Service has instituted actions to disqualify or exclude counsel.[126]

At odds, in cases where disqualification is involved, are a witness's right to counsel of his choice[127] and the potential impediments to the investigation resulting from multiple representation. The lawyer's ethical considerations are another factor.[128] Where a conflict of interest may be involved, the American Bar Association (ABA) Model Rules of Professional Conduct provide[129]

(a) A lawyer shall not represent a client if the representation of that client will be directly adverse to another client, unless:

(1) the lawyer reasonably believes the representation will not adversely affect the relationship with the other client; and

(2) each client consents after consultation.

(b) A lawyer shall not represent a client if the representation of that client may be materially limited by the lawyer's responsibilities to another client . . . unless:

---

[126] The form of proceeding usually is enforcement of the summons. Backer v. Comm'r, 275 F2d 141 (5th Cir. 1960); In re Johnson, 9 AFTR2d 2071(ED Ill. 1962); In re Richards, 6 AFTR2d 5315 (ND Ill. 1960); Torras v. Stradley, 103 F. Supp. 737 (ND Ga. 1952); United States v. Smith 87 F. Supp. 293 (D. Conn. 1949).

[127] The right is statutory (5 USC § 555(b)) rather than constitutional. See Hannah v. Larche, 363 US 420, 440 n.16 (1960); Kirby v. Illinois, 406 US 682 (1972).

[128] Treasury Department Circular No. 230, § 10.29 ("Conflicting Interests"), 26 CFR § 10.29.

[129] ABA Model Rule 1.7. The ABA's Model Rules of Professional Responsibility were adopted in August 1983. They have been adopted by most states (thirty-seven states and the District of Columbia at last count), as well as the U.S. Tax Court. Before the Model Rules, the ABA's Model Code of Professional Responsibility (see DR 5-105(A)) similarly prohibited simultaneous representation but contained an exception where it was "obvious" the lawyer could represent both clients and they consented after full disclosure (see DR 5-105(C)).

(1) the lawyer reasonably believes the representation will not be adversely affected; and

(2) the client consents after consultation.

Before the Model Rules, Disciplinary Rule 5-105(C) of the ABA's Model Code of Professional Responsibility provided: "In the situations covered by DR 5-105(A) and (B), a lawyer may represent multiple clients if it is obvious that he can adequately represent the interests of each and if each consents to the representation after full disclosure of the possible effect of such representation on the exercise of his independent professional judgment on behalf of each."[130] In short, under the ABA's statements of the applicable professional rules, the lawyer can avoid a potential problem if he discloses the problem and obtains his clients' consent to the multiple representation.

The authorities do not give guidance to a lawyer considering multiple representation, nor do they clearly indicate the circumstances under which a lawyer actually representing a target and witness will be disqualified. It can only be said that (1) multiple representation does not per se constitute a ground for disqualification[131] and (2) disqualification will be ordered only when the lawyer's conduct is egregious.

What are the egregious circumstances warranting disqualification? Multiple representation has not been permitted where a lawyer actively obstructs the interview process by bringing a frivolous action to enjoin an interview and refuses to permit the witness to testify at all.[132] Disqualification also has resulted where a lawyer for the taxpayer also represented a witness who was the taxpayer's employee, presumably because of the lawyer's motive and opportunity to influence the conduct and testimony during the investigation.[133] A lawyer who is himself the target of the investigation may not represent a witness.[134] However, a lawyer was permitted to represent both the taxpayer and his accountant where the lawyer was engaged by the accountant at his expense and

---

[130] All these considerations are also weighed where there is multiple representation of targets and witnesses during a grand jury investigation. For a discussion of the cases and the risks a lawyer who represents a target witness incurs, see Tague, "Multiple Representation of Targets and Witnesses During a Grand Jury Investigation," 17 Am. Crim. L. Rev. 301 (1980).

[131] Backer v. Comm'r, 275 F2d 141 (5th Cir. 1960). See also SEC v. Csapo, 533 F2d 7 (DC Cir. 1976).

[132] See, e.g., Torras v. Stradley, 103 F. Supp. 737 (ND Ga. 1952).

[133] In re Johnson, 9 AFTR2d 2071(ED Ill. 1962); In re Richards, 6 AFTR 5315 (ND Ill. 1960); Torras v. Stradley, 103 F. Supp. 737 (ND Ga. 1952).

[134] See United States v. Clarkson, 567 F2d 270 (4th Cir. 1977) (defense lawyer in grand jury investigation disqualified because he prepared tax returns for his client under investigation by Service).

not at the taxpayer's suggestion and the accountant responded to the questions put to him.[135]

The Service has adopted specific procedures to be followed in dual-representation situations.[136] These procedures have the following features:

1. Dual representation involves a conflict of interest, when the lawyer is obstructing the interview, and whether to suspend the interview. When dual representation exists, the agent will report it to the Group Manager and the Division Area Counsel.

2. Action to disqualify a representative is supposed to be taken only in "extreme circumstances" when the representative actively impedes the process of the interview. The mere existence of dual representation "will not, without some action by the attorney to impede or obstruct the investigation, provide a sufficient basis for seeking a disqualification."[137]

3. The agent may, but is not required to, discuss the potential conflict with the attorney before the interview.

4. If agent is not able to resolve the issue with the attorney, the agent will interview the witness by asking (a) whether the witness wishes the attorney to be present during the questioning; (b) whether the witness hired the attorney for this purpose; (c) whether the witness is paying the attorney fees either alone or in conjunction with someone else and, if the latter, the identity of that person; (d) whether the attorney has told the witness that the attorney is being paid by the taxpayer (or some other person); and (e) whether the witness "realizes that there is a potential conflict of interest."[138]

5. If, after disclosure of the dual or multiple representation has been made, the witness "unequivocally states that he/she wishes the attorney in question to represent him and that he/she is utilizing the services of the attorney in this matter," the interview is to proceed.

6. If the witness does not choose to have the attorney represent him, the interview will be adjourned so that another lawyer can be retained.

7. Despite the witness's choice, the representative will be subject to an action to disqualify him if the representative refuses to permit the witness to answer any question; makes repeated objections; asserts frivolous claims of privilege or defenses on behalf of the witness; or "so disrupts the interview that the interviewing officer, with due diligence and perseverance," is unable to proceed with the interview.[139]

---

[135] Backer v. Comm'r, 275 F2d 141 (5th Cir. 1960).

[136] IRM 25.5.5., Dual Representation (Apr. 30, 1999).

[137] IRM 25.5.5., Dual Representation (Apr. 30, 1999).

[138] IRM 25.5.5.1, Interviewing the Witness (Apr. 30, 1999).

[139] IRM 25.5.5.2, Obstruction of the Interview (Apr. 30, 1999).

8. An attorney will be excluded from an interview (a) if the attorney is the subject of the investigation; (b) if the taxpayer represented by the attorney has inculpated the witness; or (c) if the attorney does not represent the witness.

9. Corporate counsel may be excluded from an interview of an employee-witness if the lawyer does not represent the witness. However, the lawyer's attendance is permitted if (a) the witness refuses to be interviewed unless the corporation's lawyer is present and (b) the corporation's lawyer is authorized to obtain information as a designee of the taxpayer within the meaning of Section 6103(c). The interview also can be suspended in these circumstances if the agent believes that development of the case will be impeded.[140]

The Service's procedures have both positive and negative effects on the complex issue of multiple representation. On the positive side, some guidance is given to revenue and special agents, which should reduce variations in the way these agents respond to this situation. It can be expected that an agent will (1) explore what he sees as a potential conflict with the lawyer before the interview and (2) suspend the interview only when the lawyer "significantly impairs," impedes, or obstructs the interview by active conduct, not mere presence. On the negative side, the procedures leave complex determinations to a layman: the revenue agent or special agent. Without much guidance, the agent must decide for himself that "a potential conflict" exists and that there has been "an obstruction of the orderly inquiry process."[141] The agent must communicate this decision to a witness-client by asking the six questions listed above. Thus, this procedure oversimplifies the problem. It leaves the revenue or special agent generally on his own without the guidance of Area Counsel or other lawyers in the Service and creates an atmosphere that may be conducive to unnecessary interference with the attorney-client relationship.

[5] Transcripts and Recordings

Interviews held pursuant to a summons are conducted with different degrees of formality, and the record of the interview will take one of the following forms, where the agent takes notes, a memorandum of the interview; a statement signed by the witness; the preparation and signing of an affidavit reflecting the interview; or testimony taken in the same manner as a deposition.[142] A transcript must be furnished to any person compelled to appear pursuant to a sum-

---

[140] IRM 25.5.5.3, Suspension of the Interview (April 30, 1999).

[141] IRM 25.5.5.5.2, Obstruction of Interview (Apr. 30, 1999).

[142] See IRM 9.4.5.7, Record of Interview (Mar. 14, 2002). The Criminal Investigation portion of the Manual is more detailed on interviews than is the Summons Handbook.

mons.[143] However, the Service interprets its obligation as requiring it to furnish a transcript only where testimony is given before a reporter or an affidavit is signed.[144] A taxpayer is entitled to record an interview if taxpayer notifies the agent.[145] A witness may record his testimony (indeed, the Service frequently does) and may insist on a competent court reporter, although the taxpayer may retain one.[146] Agents will retain their own contemporaneous notes of interviews used in the preparation of memoranda, affidavits, and the like. Court reporters retain recordings.

[6] Witness Fees and Costs

Witness and mileage fees are paid to a summoned party, without restriction.[147] Use of the term "summoned party" means not only that a third-party witness who is summoned, appears, and requests fees, is entitled to witness and mileage fees, but also apparently a taxpayer who is summoned, although a party is not entitled to witness fees in a case in court.[148]

---

[143] 5 USC § 555(c); 26 CFR § 601.107(d)(1).

[144] See IRM 25.5.5.4.4, Right to Make Audit Recording in the Proceeding (Apr. 30, 1999).

[145] IRC § 7521(a)(1). Although a witness is permitted to have his testimony mechanically recorded, the appearance and testimony apparently may not be videotaped. United States v. Huene, 745 F2d 1216 (9th Cir. 1984), cert. denied, 472 US 1027 (1985); United States v. Black, 804 F2d 1416 (8th Cir. 1986) (audio recording approved, but no showing that denial of videotaping violated taxpayers' due process rights).

[146] Mott v. MacMahon 214 F. Supp. 20 (ND Cal. 1963).

[147] IRC § 7610(a)(1). Attendance fees are the higher of those provided in the regulations or in 28 USC § 1821. Reg. § 301.7610-1(d)(2). The current attendance fee is $30 per day under both the regulations and 28 USC § 1821. Items included in the travel allowance are set forth in Reg. § 301.7610(d)(3) (when private vehicle is used, rate is currently 20 cents per mile). When long-distance travel is required, a subsistence allowance may also be paid. Reg. § 301.7610(d)(4); Roberts v. United States, 397 F2d 968 (5th Cir. 1968) (saying fees are payable to witnesses under Administrative Procedure Act and that no persuasive reason had been presented why fees should not be paid to taxpayers as well); Rev. Rul. 68-645, 1968-2 CB 599 (following *Roberts* regarding witnesses).

In United States v. Coson, 515 F2d 906 (9th Cir.), cert. denied, 423 US 927 (1975), the Ninth Circuit held that the witness and mileage fees set forth at 28 USC § 1821 apply in summons proceedings. The Service agrees. Reg. § 301.7610-1(d). However, the Service is not required to prepay witness fees and travel expenses to persons summoned to appear before it. United States v. Money, 744 F2d 779 (11th Cir. 1984).

[148] The statute is not clear, nor are the regulations. Section 7610(b) specifically excludes payment of reproduction and similar costs to taxpayers and their agents payable under Section 7610(a)(2). Since Section 7610(b) does not mention Section 7610(a)(1), which covers witness fees, it can be inferred that a summoned party entitled to those fees includes a taxpayer. If this is the case, Section 7610 differs from 28 USC § 1821, which authorizes fees only to witnesses, not to parties. One can expect, however, that a taxpayer fee request will result in the Service offsetting the fee against a refund due the taxpayer or

Payments for costs in complying with a summons are provided in Section 7610. Payments may also be made to third parties without the issuance of a summons by Section 7801.[149] Nontaxpayers may also be reimbursed for such costs as are reasonably and directly incurred in searching for, reproducing, or transporting documents or data required by the summons, but statutorily none of these costs may be reimbursed to a taxpayer.[150] The Service offers to perform searches of bank records, but banks themselves have often declined the invitation in order to ensure privacy of customer's bank dealings. If a bank declines assistance, it may not be entitled to reimbursement.[151]

¶ 13.04 SUMMONS ENFORCEMENT PROCEDURES: METHOD OF OBJECTING TO AND CHALLENGING A SUMMONS

[1] Procedure in General

On their face, the provisions of the Code offer a person who is summoned to testify or produce books no alternative to challenge the summons except by risking body arrest, punishment for contempt, and possibly criminal sanctions. Federal district courts have jurisdiction to compel compliance with a summons by "appropriate process" and, if any person "neglects or refuses to obey" a summons, to order "an attachment . . . for the arrest" of the person and to punish him for contempt.[152] Section 7610 makes it a misdemeanor for any person "who, being duly summoned to appear to testify, or to appear and produce books . . . or other papers, as required under . . . [Section] 7602," to neglect "to

---

in its reducing a balance due from the taxpayer by the amount of the fee. Reg. § 301.7610(d)(4).

[149] Procedures and rates of payments are provided in Treas. Dept. Order No. 150-10, dated April 22, 1982; IRS Delegation Order No 178, as revised. See IRM 25.5.9.3, Payments for Costs in Complying With Summons (Apr. 30, 1999).

[150] IRC § 7610(a)(2). Reg. § 301.7610-1(c)(2) establishes payment rates for search costs ($8.50 per person hour), reproduction costs (20 cents per page), appearance fees, and allowances. See also IRM 25.5.9, Fees and Costs for Summoned Witnesses (Apr. 30, 1999).

[151] United States v. Covington Trust & Banking Co., 431 F. Supp. 352 (ED Ky. 1977) A court may not be bound by the rates set in regulations. See United States v. Community Bank & Trust Co., 768 F2d 311 (10th Cir. 1985) (search costs of $10 per hour rather than the Service-set $5-per-hour fee allowed; Section 7610 held not to preclude judicial review of costs); Does v. United States, 866 F2d 1015 (8th Cir. 1989) (district court has jurisdiction to review Service reimbursement rates to avoid a grossly excessive net expense after payment of the Service-established rate).

[152] IRC § 760.

appear or to produce such book . . . or other papers."[153] In the 1964 case *Reisman v. Caplin*,[154] the Supreme Court resolved the apparent dilemma of a person the Service had summoned who objected to the summons.

Reisman was an attorney for taxpayers who were under investigation. Reisman requested an accounting firm to work on the taxpayer's financial records. A special agent had served summonses directing the accountants to produce their audit reports, workpapers, and correspondence. Reisman claimed that these summonses were null and void as an appropriation of his attorney's work product and an unreasonable seizure prohibited by the Fourth Amendment. The accountants had not refused to comply with the summonses, and Reisman alleged that they intended to comply. Accordingly, Reisman petitioned for declaratory and injunctive relief against the Service and the accounting firm. The Supreme Court dismissed Reisman's complaint on the ground that the attorney had an adequate remedy at law so that no equitable relief in the form of an injunction was proper. In reaching its decision adverse to Reisman and his clients in the case, the Court established procedures to be followed in challenging a summons and, in this sense, a "bill of rights" in all future summons proceedings.

Although clarified by later cases, the procedure established in *Reisman* remains authoritative:

1. A summons may be challenged before the Service official presiding at the return date, at which both the parties summoned and "those affected by a summons" may appear and challenge the summons on constitutional or other grounds.

2. At the return of the summons, the agent or officer acting as a hearing official may reject the challenge, but that official is given no power to enforce compliance or to impose sanctions for noncompliance.

3. If the Service wishes to enforce the summons, it must proceed under Section 7402(b), which grants federal district courts jurisdiction to compel compliance with the summons by appropriate process.

4. The summons enforcement action is an adversary hearing that affords judicial review and determination of the challenges of the summons, thereby giving "complete" protection to the witness.

5. Only a refusal to comply with an order of the district judge subjects the witness to contempt proceedings.

6. Any order of the court, whether enforcing the summons or for civil or criminal contempt, is appealable, and a stay pending appeal ensures that a witness will suffer no injury while testing the summons.

---

[153] Penal sanctions for refusal to produce evidence are commonly imposed to aid the jurisdiction of administrative agencies. See, e.g., 15 USC § 50 (failure to produce evidence in obedience of summons of Federal Trade Commission).

[154] Reisman v. Caplin, 375 US 440 (1964).

7. The misdemeanor statute does not apply where the witness appears and interposes good faith challenges to the summons, nor do the bodily arrest and contempt provisions of Section 7604(b). Both the criminal statute and the civil sanction apply to persons who were summoned and who wholly default or contumaciously refuse to comply.

8. Should a witness indicate that he will voluntarily comply with the summons, the taxpayer "or any affected party" may restrain compliance by obtaining a court order until compliance is ordered by a court hearing the summons enforcement proceeding.

The procedure described in *Reisman* is in the mainstream of administrative-law decisions requiring judicial enforcement of an agency's summons. In the same year *Reisman* was decided, the Supreme Court further developed the procedure in a summons enforcement proceeding along the lines previously established in administrative-law cases. In *United States v. Powell*,[155] an agent had already examined Powell's returns once, and Powell refused to comply with a summons issued in a second examination on the ground that the Service was required to establish that there was probable cause to believe that there was fraud because the three-year statute of limitations barred assessments. The Supreme Court held that the statute of limitations provisions of the Code do not, when read together with the investigatory power of the Service, "impose a probable cause standard . . . from the expiration date of the ordinary limitations period forward."[156] This part of the *Powell* opinion is discussed above in connection with second inspections. The Supreme Court went on to describe the nature of the summons enforcement proceeding, and made statements about the process no less significant than those in *Reisman*. The Court observed that it was the process of the court hearing the summons enforcement petition that the Service invoked, and before the court could enforce the summons, the Service had to show that[157]

1. The investigation is to be conducted pursuant to a legitimate purpose;
2. The inquiry is relevant to that purpose;
3. The information sought is not already within the Service's possession; and
4. The Service has followed the administrative steps required by the Code (e.g., the agent has determined the further examination to be necessary and has so notified the taxpayer).

---

[155] United States v. Powell, 379 US 48 (1964).

[156] United States v. Powell, 379 US 48, 56 (1964).

[157] The test was announced in Oklahoma Press Publishing Co. v. Walling, 327 US 186 (1964).

The Commissioner's showing does not make the adversary enforcement hearing meaningless; the taxpayer may challenge the summons on any appropriate ground. In addition, the Court made pointed out that it is the court's process that is invoked to enforce the administrative summons, and a court may not permit its process to be abused. The burden of showing an abuse of the court's process is on the taxpayer. An abuse of process takes place "if the summons has been issued for an improper purpose, such as to harass the taxpayer or to put pressure on him to settle a collateral dispute, or for any other purpose reflecting on the good faith of the particular investigation."[158]

As for the summons enforcement proceeding itself, the *Powell* decision also decided that the Federal Rules of Civil Procedure apply to the enforcement proceeding. These proceedings are instituted by filing a complaint, followed by an answer and hearing. If the taxpayer has contumaciously refused to comply with the administrative summons, and the Service fears he may flee the jurisdiction, application for the sanctions available under Section 7604(b) may be made at the same time the complaint is filed.

In a third case, the Supreme Court added another requirement. In *Donaldson*, a special agent had served a summons on Donaldson's former employer and its accountant to obtain records of Donaldson's employment. After Donaldson had obtained a temporary restraining order and preliminary injunction as to the witnesses, the Service instituted proceedings to enforce the summonses directed at the witnesses. Donaldson attempted to intervene and answer the complaints, but his motion to intervene was denied. Both the denial of the motion to intervene and Donaldson's claim that the summonses were issued for an improper purpose and in bad faith were before the Court.

Donaldson sought to intervene "as of right" under Federal Rule of Civil Procedure 24(a)(2). Under this rule, intervention is allowed where the applicant claims an "interest" relating to the property or the transaction that is the subject of the action and the disposition of the action may impair or impede the applicant's ability to protect that "interest." The Supreme Court held that Donaldson did not have a protectable interest within the meaning of Rule 24(a)(2). The Court said that *Reisman* did not "guarantee" intervention to a taxpayer but required a balancing of "opposing equities."[159] Intervention under Rule 24(a)(2) also required a "significantly protectable interest." Donaldson did not have such an interest in the employer's records because he did not own the records and had no privilege (e.g., attorney-client) with respect to them, and he would not be able to obtain suppression of the records if they were produced by means other than an Service summons (e.g., by voluntary disclosure).

---

[158] United States v. Powell, 379 US 48, 58 (1964).
[159] Donaldson v. United States, 400 US 517, 530 (1971).

However, the Court also indicated that although he might not successfully intervene in the enforcement proceeding, Donaldson could assert a claim of privilege or abuse of process "in due course at its proper place in any subsequent trial."[160] Consequently, a taxpayer may challenge a summons at any subsequent trial if he cannot challenge the summons in an enforcement proceeding."[161]

In summary, after *Donaldson v. United States*, a taxpayer may intervene in a summons enforcement proceeding "as of right" within the meaning of Rule 24(a)(2) of the Federal Rules of Civil Procedure *only* if he has a significantly protectable interest in the matter or documents sought by the summons.[162] Thus, the taxpayer or witness must have a proprietary interest or privilege covering records. A taxpayer's interest in his tax liability is not sufficient to warrant intervention as of right or even at the discretion of the court.[163] But the effect of *Donaldson* has been limited and superseded by later legislation, specifically, the third-party recordkeeper rules. here third-party recordkeepers (such as a bank, attorney, or accountant) are involved.[164] Under

---

[160] Donaldson v. United States, 400 US 517, 531 (1971).

[161] See United States v. Genser, 582 F2d 292 (3d Cir. 1978) (*Genser I*) (postconviction challenge to Service summonses); Garrett v. United States, 511 F2d 1037 (9th Cir. 1975); United States v. Newman, 441 F2d 165 (5th Cir. 1971). For what certainly must be the high-water mark of an improper Service investigation tainting a subsequent criminal case, see United States v. Dahlstrum, 493 F. Supp. 966 (CD Cal. 1980), aff'd, 655 F2d 971 (9th Cir. 1981), cert. denied, 455 US 928 (1982).

[162] Donaldson v. United States, 400 US 517, 530 (1971).

[163] United States v. Income Realty & Mortgage, Inc., 612 F2d 1224 (10th Cir. 1979) (taxpayer had no proprietary interest in employment records); United States v. Exxon Co., 450 F. Supp. 472 (D. Md. 1978) (taxpayers unsuccessfully sought to intervene in proceeding to enforce summons for production of Exxon's records relating to transactions with taxpayers); United States v. Price Waterhouse & Co., 76-1 USTC ¶ 9295 (WD Pa. 1975) (taxpayer, Gulf, sought to intervene in enforcement proceeding against its accountants to require production of audit-related papers).

While a taxpayer may have a proprietary interest in records (which is a "significantly protectable interest"), he may also surrender or abandon that proprietary interest. For example, when a defendant in a state criminal case entered into a plea agreement, which provided in part that the prosecutor would destroy records seized in the execution of a search warrant, and the Service served a summons on the state police for the records, the district court refused to permit the taxpayer (and former defendant) to intervene under Rule 24(a), Federal Rules of Civil Procedure. The court held that "any proprietary interest [the taxpayer] might have had in the records was abandoned when she agreed to have the [police] destroy them." United States v. Preusch, 924 F. Supp. 1021 (D. Nev. 1996) (since the state court had ordered the destruction pursuant to the agreement, the police custodian was faced with conflicting orders; therefore, the Service petitioned to enforce the summons, and the taxpayer moved to intervene). The court also held that "'privacy' or other generalized interests are [not] 'significantly protectable interests' for the purpose of intervention, in a summons proceeding, but merely establish that for those third parties who have intervened, a remedy may exist following actual compliance with a summons."

[164] IRC § 7609, discussed infra ¶ 13.04[3].

these procedures, a taxpayer or related taxpayer has an automatic right to intervene in the summons enforcement proceeding.

[2] Summons Enforcement Proceedings in Practice

A number of courts have adopted local rules that apply in summons enforcement proceedings, subject to the exercise of discretion by the district court.[165] The procedures, suggested by the Third Circuit in *United States v. McCarthy*,[166] describe the procedure generally followed by courts in summons enforcement proceedings:

1. The Secretary or his delegate files a complaint accompanied by an affidavit of the agent who issued the summons, seeking enforcement. The complaint should separately allege compliance with each of the requirements of the *Powell* test of enforceability. The affidavit should support these allegations.

2. Process on the complaint can be in the form of an order to show cause, served on the person summoned, (a) fixing a deadline for filing any responsive pleading, albeit an informal pleading, together with an affidavit and any motions, and (b) directing that person to show cause at a date and time certain why an order should not be entered enforcing the administrative summons. The order should provide that unless the court determines otherwise, any motions and issues raised by the pleadings will be considered at the return date of the order to show cause. In addition, the order should state that only those issues raised in motions or brought into controversy by the responsive pleading and supported by affidavit will be considered at the return of the order and that any uncontested allegation in the complaint will be taken as admitted.

3. At the hearing on the order, the Service should be prepared to prove the allegations of the complaint that the summons complies with the *Powell* requirements, and also be prepared to rebut any proper defenses asserted by the person summoned. The person summoned should be prepared to produce any evidence rebutting the Service's case and also to assume the burden of proof as to affirmative issues raised by him for the purpose of demonstrating that enforcement of the summons would constitute an abuse of the court's process. After completion of the hearing, the district court, in conformity with Fed-

---

[165] United States v. McCarthy, 514 F2d 368 (3d Cir. 1975). See also United States v. Salter, 432 F2d 697 (1st Cir. 1970); United States v. Turner, 480 F2d 272 (7th Cir. 1973); United States v. Kis, 658 F2d 526 (7th Cir. 1981), cert. denied, 455 US 1018 (1982).

[166] United States v. McCarthy, 514 F2d 368 (3d Cir. 1975).

eral Rule of Civil Procedure 52(a), should make the requisite findings of fact and conclusions of law.

4. Although the proceedings are of a summary nature, if the district court concludes that it cannot fairly decide the case on the record before it at the return of the order, it is free to direct further proceedings, including discovery, if requested.

[a] Discovery

Discovery of the government's case can be had either in formal discovery proceedings or in a full-scale evidentiary hearing. To avoid this possibility, government attorneys oppose the taking of discovery and a full evidentiary hearing. This defensive maneuver has met with considerable success, especially where discovery has been sought by taxpayers.[167] The government has argued that discovery should not be permitted before a hearing, at which time, the court can determine its necessity and scope. This argument has generally been accepted.[168] The Second Circuit requires a substantial preliminary showing before discovery is granted.[169] In other words, a limited evidentiary hearing precedes discovery, if it is to be granted at all. Other circuits follow this view.[170] The Fifth Circuit appears to adopt a more lenient approach to discovery by providing full-scale evidentiary hearings as a substitute without requiring the taxpayer to allege a factual background.[171] Moreover, where the government refuses to comply with a court's discovery order, the petition for enforcement has been dismissed.[172]

---

[167] See, e.g., Morgan Guar. Trust Co. v. United States, 572 F2d 36 (2d Cir.), cert. denied sub nom. 439 US 822 (1978); Keech v. United States, 439 US 822 (1978). But compare United States v. Chase Manhattan Bank, 598 F2d 321 (2d Cir. 1979) (limited discovery).

[168] United States v. Salter, 432 F2d 697 (1st Cir. 1970); United States v. Church of Scientology, 520 F2d 818 (9th Cir. 1975). It is generally said that questioning the agent in court is the substantial equivalent of a deposition. See, e.g., United States v. Daffin, 653 F2d 121 (4th Cir. 1981), quoting United States v. Harris, 628 F2d 875, 883 (5th Cir. 1980).

[169] See, e.g., United States v. Chase Manhattan Bank, 598 F2d 321 (2d Cir. 1979).

[170] See United States v. Southern Tanks, Inc., 619 F2d 54 (10th Cir. 1980); United States v. Stuckey, 646 F2d 1369 (9th Cir. 1981), cert. denied, 455 US 942 (1982) (discovery and evidentiary hearing denied; held, denial not "clearly erroneous").

[171] See United States v. Harris, 628 F2d 875, 883 (5th Cir. 1980); United States v. Southeast First Nat'l Bank of Miami Springs, 655 F2d 661 (5th Cir. 1981). See also United States v. Security Bank & Trust Co., 661 F2d 847 (10th Cir. 1981).

[172] United States v. Wright Motor Co., 536 F2d 1090 (5th Cir. 1976).

[b] The Adversary Hearing

According to the *Reisman* and *Powell* cases, the taxpayer or other witness is entitled to an "adversary hearing" before enforcement of a summons is ordered, although it is unclear what constitutes such a hearing. It seems that any hearing on the return of a show cause order obtained by the government constitutes the adversary hearing. The government, in any event, opposes an evidentiary hearing at which testimony is taken on the grounds that its agents should not be exposed to examination during the investigation and that such hearings delay the "summary" nature of the proceeding. Therefore, where a response to the petition to enforce the summons fails to challenge the summons on substantial grounds (e.g., improper purpose, harassment, constitutional privilege, and the like), an evidentiary hearing is not permitted.[173]

[c] The Court's Order

Once the district court finds that the *Powell* requirements have been satisfied and that despite the objection of the summoned party, the summons should be enforced, the court enters an order compelling compliance with the summons at the time and place set forth in the order. Although the Supreme Court in *Powell* made clear that it is the district court's process that the Service invokes to secure enforcement of the summons and that the court may insure that its process will not be abused, it is uncertain whether the district court may impose conditions on the Service in its enforcement order.[174] In *Zolin*, the Ninth Circuit held that the district court could condition enforcement

---

[173] United States v. Newman, 441 F2d 165 (5th Cir. 1971). Cf. United States v. Church of Scientology, 520 F2d 818 (9th Cir. 1975). However, the Fifth Circuit considers an evidentiary hearing to be the "substantial equivalent" of a prehearing deposition and refuses to deny a taxpayer a hearing at which the Service can be questioned. United States v. Southeast First Nat'l Bank of Miami Springs, 655 F2d 661 (5th Cir. 1981). Compare United States v. Stuckey, 646 F2d 1369 (9th Cir. 1981), cert. denied, 455 US 942 (1982), where denial of a hearing was held not to be clearly erroneous. It has been held that the hearing provided for in *Donaldson* need not be a full evidentiary hearing, that an adversary hearing can be sufficient to deal with an objection treated as raised by the taxpayer in a motion for summary judgment, and that a transcript need not be made of such an adversary hearing. United States v. First Nat'l Bank of Mitchell, 691 F2d 386 (8th Cir. 1982). A taxpayer may be denied a hearing where he fails to allege specific facts to support, for example, a claim of privilege. See, e.g., United States v. Kis, 658 F2d 526 (7th Cir. 1981), cert. denied, 455 US 1018 (1982); United States v. First State Bank, 691 F2d 332 (7th Cir. 1982) (hearing properly denied where taxpayer failed to allege specific facts to support attorney-client privilege claim).

[174] United States v. Powell, 379 US 48, 58 (1964) ("It is the court's process which is invoked to enforce the administrative summons and a court may not permit its process to be abused. Such an abuse would take place if the summons has been issued for an improper purpose. . . . The burden of showing an abuse of the court's process is on the taxpayer. . . .").

of a summons,[175] while in *Barrett*, the Fifth Circuit held that once a district court found that the summons should be enforced, it had no jurisdiction to impose any conditions on enforcement.[176]

When the Supreme Court considered *Zolin*, it was equally divided on the issue, and thus it let the Ninth Circuit view go undisturbed. But the affirmance in *Zolin* was not "authority for the determination of other cases, either in [the Supreme Court] or in inferior courts."[177] After *Zolin*, therefore, there was the Ninth Circuit view of conditional enforcement, which was the law in that circuit, and the Fifth Circuit's view that the only options available to the district court were to enforce or not to enforce the summons. However, the Third Circuit took a middle ground that also was consistent with *Powell*'s statement that since the court's process was being invoked in a summons proceeding, the district court could insure that its process was not being abused.[178] In *Rockwell*, the Third Circuit said the difference between the Ninth and Fifth Circuits created a "distinction without a difference," because in cases where "the government's action would be an abuse of process, in whatever context, the court's restrictions are not legal error; rather, they are 'a wise exercise of control.'"[179] In short, the Third Circuit found that "IRS summonses may be enforced conditionally." This did not mean, however, that the appellate court would approve or disapprove a district court's conditional enforcement order, and, in fact, for nonjurisdictional reasons, the Third Circuit remanded the district court's decision.

After *Zolin*, the Ninth Circuit changed its view and adopted the either/or approach of the Fifth Circuit. In *Jose*, a district court in Hawaii conditioned enforcement of an Examination Division summons on the requirement that the Examination Division notify the taxpayer before circulating, transferring, or copying the summoned documents to any other Division, including the Crimi-

---

[175] United States v. Zolin, 809 F2d 1411 (9th Cir. 1987), aff'd in part and vacated in part on other grounds, 491 US 554 (1989) (district court ordered that produced documents "shall not be delivered to any other government agency by the IRS unless criminal tax prosecution is sought or an order of the Court is obtained").

[176] United States v. Barrett, 837 F2d 1341, 1350 (5th Cir. 1988) ("There is no statutory authority, nor Congressional indication that existing statutes supply the authority, nor Supreme Court authority, to allow the district court to make any consideration except whether to enforce or not enforce the summons"). The Fifth Circuit apparently did not believe that the statement in United States v. Powell 379 US 48, 58 (1964) constituted Supreme Court authority for conditional enforcement.

[177] Hertz v. Woodman, 218 US 205, 213–214 (1910).

[178] United States v. Rockwell Int'l, 897 F2d 1255, 1261 (3d Cir. 1990). See also United States v. Norwest Corp., 80 AFTR2d 97-5094 (8th Cir. 1997), where the Service apparently did not object to the district court's conditional enforcement order.

[179] The *Rockwell* court quoted the words of the Ninth Circuit in United States v. Author Servs., 804 F2d 1520 (9th Cir. 1986), modified, 811 F2d 1264 (1987).

nal Investigation.[180] At first, the Ninth Circuit refused to hear the Service's appeal on the ground that it was not ripe for review,[181] but the Supreme Court reversed and remanded the decision, holding that for appellate jurisdiction purposes, the district court's order must be final, not that the issue be ripe for review.[182] After the Supreme Court's remand, the Ninth Circuit, in an *en banc* decision, overruled its decisions in *Zolin* and other cases on conditional enforcement and agreed with the Fifth Circuit's reasoning and holding in *Barrett* that "[t]he sole purpose of the enforcement proceeding is to ensure that the IRS has the summons for a proper purpose and in good faith . . . and hold that the district court is strictly limited to enforcing or denying IRS summonses."[183]

[d] Appeal

Once enforcement has been ordered by a district court, a taxpayer or other affected party may appeal the decision. To ensure that the appeal is not rendered moot, the person directed to comply with the court order must not do so even if he risks contempt.[184] It had been thought that if a summoned party complied with an enforcement order, the party's appeal would be rendered moot because the appellate court could grant no effectual relief. In *Church of Scientology*,[185] however, the Supreme Court held that although summoned

---

[180] United States v. Jose, 93-2 USTC ¶ 50,457 (D. Haw. 1993).

[181] United States v. Jose, 71 F3d 1484 (9th Cir. 1995).

[182] United States v. Jose, 519 US 54, 117 S. Ct. 463 (1996) (per curiam). The Supreme Court also said to gain appellate review, the Service (and presumably any other party aggrieved by the district court's order) was not required to defy the district court's order. Moreover, the Service did not have to comply with the limitation or condition the district court imposed, because the condition was the very portion of the order that the Service challenged on appeal. The Supreme Court was well aware that there was an intercircuit conflict over the authority of the district courts to attach to the order enforcing summonses. Its statement of the issue in conflict is notable. It was not the broad question about whether the district court had the authority to impose any condition on enforcement. Rather, according to the Supreme Court, the issue in conflict was about "judicial limitations on disclosure by the agency seeking summons enforcement to other government agencies." The *Jose* case raised the related but distinct question of the district court's authority to restrict sharing of information within an agency.

[183] United States v. Jose, 131 F3d 1325 (9th Cir. 1997). At any rate, before *Jose*, the Ninth Circuit had refused to permit a district court to impose conditions on the enforcement when it found that the district court had abused its discretion in imposing the conditions. United States v. Abrahams, 905 F2d 1276 (9th Cir. 1990).

[184] See, e.g., United States v. Arthur Andersen & Co., 623 F2d 720 (1st Cir. 1980) (accounting firm complied with court order and its appeal was dismissed as moot). United States v. Kis, 658 F2d 526 (7th Cir. 1981), cert. denied, 455 US 1018 (1982) (collecting cases from different circuits); United States v. Trails End Motel, Inc., 657 F2d 1169 (10th Cir. 1981).

[185] Church of Scientology v. United States, 506 US 9 (1992).

tapes had been delivered to the Service after the compliance order, the Ninth Circuit did have the power to effect a partial remedy by ordering the Service to return or destroy copies of the tapes that it might possess. A stay of the district court's order must be obtained by application to that court or, in the event of denial, from the court of appeals. Absent appeal and a stay, if a person refuses or fails to comply with a court order requiring compliance with the summons, he risks punishment for civil or criminal contempt.[186]

[3] Summonses to Third-Party Witnesses: Section 7609

Summons enforcement proceedings were used by practitioners as a means of delay and an opportunity to obtain information concerning a special agent's investigation. Time taken in a normal summons enforcement proceeding consumed a portion of the period of limitations on prosecution and, for that matter, assessment. In *Reisman*, the Supreme Court had said that the witness, the taxpayer, and any other person "affected" by the summons might intervene at the administrative hearing or later in the enforcement proceeding.[187] This statement encouraged the tactic of time-consuming enforcement proceedings with an eye on the six-year statute of limitations on prosecution. Some seven years after *Reisman*, the Court limited the right of the taxpayer to intervene in these proceedings in *Donaldson v. United States*,[188] apparently out of concern for the ability of a taxpayer to delay the investigative process by forcing protracted enforcement proceedings.

As for the taxpayer, after *Donaldson*, a taxpayer could not intervene in a third-party summons enforcement proceeding absent a significantly protectable

---

[186] United States v. Hankins, 565 F2d 1344 (5th Cir. 1978), clarified, 581 F2d 431 (5th Cir.), cert. denied, 440 US 909 (1978) (civil contempt); United States v. Hankins, 631 F2d 360 (5th Cir. 1980) (civil contempt upheld); Zimmerman v. Speers, 565 F2d 310 (5th Cir. 1977) (civil contempt); United States v. Cotton, 567 F2d 958 (10th Cir. 1978) (civil contempt), cert. denied, 436 US 959 (1978); Steinert v. United States, 571 F2d 1105 (9th Cir. 1978) (criminal contempt). United States v. Rylander, 656 F2d 1313 (9th Cir. 1981) (civil contempt vacated), rev'd, 460 US 752 (1983) reh'g denied); United States v. McAnlis, 721 F2d 334 (11th Cir. 1983) (civil contempt), cert. denied, 467 US 1227 (1984). Compare United States v. Hayes, 722 F2d 723 (11th Cir. 1984) (civil contempt standard is determination that contemnor did not make "all reasonable efforts" to comply and evidence that "some efforts" were made is insufficient to rebut prima facie showing of contempt by noncompliance); United States v. Roberts, 858 F2d 698 (11th Cir. 1988) (civil contempt order fining owner of two corporations $100 per day until documents produced affirmed; proper standard for civil contempt is "all reasonable efforts to comply"). United States v. Young, 532 F. Supp. 334 (ED Mich. 1981) (lawyer-officer of law firm found in civil contempt fined $8,000); United States v. Halsted, 85-2 USTC ¶ 9486 (SDNY 1984) (fine of $100 per day).

[187] Reisman v. Caplin, 375 US 440, 445 (1964).

[188] Donaldson v. United States, 400 US 517, 530 (1971).

interest, but he could nevertheless effectively prevent the enforcement of the summons if the taxpayer could prove to the court's satisfaction that enforcement of the summons would be an abuse of its process. Procedurally, it is not clear just how the claim is heard. In *Donaldson*, the taxpayer had obtained a preliminary injunction preventing compliance and could have had the matter resolved in that proceeding. However, the issue was resolved, albeit against the taxpayer, in the same proceeding. Consequently, it appears that even without intervention, a taxpayer's improper-purpose claim may be heard in the third-party summons enforcement proceeding.

In general, a third person served with a summons was under no legal obligation to inform the taxpayer that a summons has been served and, in most instances, to make any objection to the summons. Should the taxpayer learn of the summons, he might, as *Reisman* indicated, seek an injunction restraining compliance or, having secured the third party's agreement not to comply, attempt to intervene in the enforcement proceeding if he can meet the *Donaldson* standards. Should the third party voluntarily comply with the summons without the knowledge or intervention of the taxpayer, the taxpayer may raise objections to the summons at the time of the trial of any substantive charge or action.[189]

The third-party recordkeeping procedures were strenuously opposed by the Service and the Department of Justice on the grounds that investigation would be delayed and that court calendars would be further clogged with these cases. Three statutory provisions attempt to allay these concerns. Both the summons enforcement proceeding and appeal of any final decision are to take precedence on the docket over all cases and must be assigned for hearing and decided "at the earliest practicable date."[190] In any ex parte proceeding commenced by the government, a court may release the Service from the third-party summons notice rules if on the basis of the facts alleged there is "reasonable cause" to believe that the taxpayer or the witness will engage in acts of spoliation (e.g., concealment, destruction of records, intimidation, or collusion).[191]

Before changes made by the Restructuring and Reform Act of 1998, Section 7609 required the Service to give a taxpayer notice of the service of a summons on a special class of witnesses called "third-party recordkeepers," and to wait at least twenty-four days before it could receive the summoned documents or initiate summons enforcement action.[192] As the statute required

---

[189] Reisman v. Caplin, 375 US 440, 445 (1964); Donaldson v. United States, 400 US 517, 530 (1971); United States v. Genser, 582 F2d 292 (3d Cir. 1978) (*Genser I*).

[190] IRC § 7609(h)(2). See Moutevelis v. United States, 727 F2d 313 (3d Cir. 1984) (evidentiary hearing not mandated in every case where motion to quash filed).

[191] IRC § 7609(g).

[192] The legislative history of Section 7609 is summarized in Staff of Joint Comm. on Taxation, 94th Cong., 2d Sess., General Explanation of the Tax Reform Act of 1976, at

where the Service issued a a summons calling for the production of business records pertaining to an identified person (whether or not the taxpayer) on a "third-party recordkeeper," the Service was required to give notice of the summons to the person affected within three days after the summons is served, but no later than twenty-three days before the return date of the summons.[193] Moreover, this notice had to be personally served.[194] The notice of service of the third-party summons also must contain directions for the taxpayer to stay compliance.[195] On receiving notice, the taxpayer may stay compliance by the third-party recordkeeper. When the Service moved to enforce the summons to the recordkeeper, the taxpayer or other noticee could intervene in the proceeding. To prevent a taxpayer's use of these procedures for the purposes of delay, the statute of limitations on assessment and prosecution is suspended during the pendency of the enforcement proceeding and any appeal.[196] Suspension of the limitations periods applies only where the noticee has mailed a notice to the third-party recordkeeper not to comply with the summons. No suspension occurs where the recordkeeper simply contests the summons, unless the recordkeeper is acting under the taxpayer's direction and control.[197] If the dispute between the third-party recordkeeper and the Service is not resolved within six months after the Service issues a summons, the statutes of limita-

---

364–368 (Comm. Print 1976), reprinted in 1976-3 CB 376–377 (Vol. 2). The statute has been found constitutional. Tucker v. United States, 84-2 USTC ¶ 9919 (ND Ind. 1984).

[193] IRC § 7609(a)(1); Reg. §§ 301.7609-1–301.7609-5. There are three exceptions to the notice requirements: (1) a summons served on the person with respect to whose liability the summons is issued, or any officer or employee of such person; (2) a summons served to determine whether or not records of the business transactions or affairs of an identified person have been made or kept; or (3) a John Doe summons. IRC § 7609(a)(4). Where a summons was served on a holding company and its subsidiary for trading account records of certain individuals, the provisions of Section 7609 were held not to require notice to the account holders because the holding company was a named taxpayer whose tax liability was under investigation. Abraham v. United States, 582 F. Supp. 257 (SDNY), aff'd per curiam, 740 F2d 2 (2d Cir. 1984).

[194] IRC § 7609(a)(2). The notice may be sent to the person's fiduciary if appropriate notice is on file. Section 7603 also requires that when a summons is issued under Section 7602, it "shall be served by the [IRS] by an attested copy" delivered personally to the summoned party or left at his last known address. Most circuits held that the attested copy requirement of Section 7603 was not incorporated in the rules of Section 7609(2) for serving notice on a taxpayer of a third-party summons. See, e.g., Kondik v. United States, 77 AFTR2d 96-1857 (6th Cir. 1996) (citing decisions of the Ninth and Tenth Circuits).

[195] IRC § 7609(a)(1).

[196] IRC § 7609(e). For a case computing the period of suspension, see Edwards v. Comm'r, 42 TCM 1706 (1981).

[197] Comm. Print 1976, at 367, reprinted in 1976-3 CB 379 (vol. 2).

tions on assessment, collection, and prosecution are suspended until the issue is finally resolved.[198]

By contrast when the Service served a summons which was not a third-party recordkeeper summons, the notice and waiting period requirements of Section 7609 did not apply, and the Service only had to wait ten days before it could obtain records from the person served without giving notice to the taxpayer.

The IRS Restructuring and Reform Act of 1998 amended Section 7609 in ways that changed the entire procedure of summons enforcement and challenges. After the 1998 Act, the Service must now follow the notice and waiting period requirements for *all* third-party summonses, except for the five statutory exceptions that Section 7609 previously contained.[199] Specifically, the Service must give notice to the taxpayer and any other person identified in the summons. The date for the return of the summons is no sooner than twenty-four days the date of the notice to be given to the taxpayer and any other person entitled to notice. The summoned party cannot comply with the summons until the twenty-fourth day after the date of the notice, and only then if no person entitled to notice brought a timely proceeding to quash. In the proceeding to quash, the taxpayer or other noticee can challenge the summons on any ground, including any privilege.

[a] Third-Party Recordkeepers for Service by Mail

Section 7603 relating to the service of summonses permits the service of a summons for the production records by a third-party recordkeeper by certified or registered mail to the last known address of the recordkeeper, a manner of service that had not previously been used for notifying third-party

---

[198] HR Conf. Rep. No. 841, 99th Cong., 2d Sess. on HR 3838, Tax Reform Act of 1986 (Sept. 18, 1986), Vol. I, Text of Bill, § 1651 amending IRC § 7609(e). It has been held that the statute of limitations on prosecution is suspended during the sixty-day period for filing an appeal after a district court's summons enforcement order. United States v. Orlowski, 808 F2d 1283 (8th Cir. 1986), cert. denied, 482 US 927 (1987); United States v. Meyer, 808 F2d 1304 (8th Cir. 1987) (same). The statute of limitations is tolled during the summons enforcement proceeding and for an additional sixty days, even if the summoned party complies with the enforcement order during the appeal period. Hefti v. Comm'r, 983 F2d 868 (8th Cir. 1993) (upholding Reg. § 301.7609-5(b)); Maranto v. Comm'r, TC Memo. 1997-122 (1997) (taxpayer argued that the Service's notice of deficiency was untimely because the Service sent its notice seventy-three days after the three-year assessment period had run; Tax Court rejected the argument because taxpayer had filed a petition to quash third-party recordkeeper summonses, and the period from the filing to the date of the order denying the petition and enforcing the summons was eighty-three days).

[199] IRC §§ 7609(c)(2)(B)–7609(c)(2)(F).

recordkeepers.[200] Accordingly, the list of third-party recordkeepers, deleted from the amended Section 7609, is now found in Section 7603, and then solely for the purpose of permitting service by certified or registered mail.[201]

Section 7603(b)(2) defines a "third-party recordkeeper" to mean the following persons:

1. Banks and savings and loan institutions[202]
2. Consumer reporting agencies[203]

---

[200] IRC § 7603(a)(1), as amended by 1998 Act § 3416, applicable to summonses served after July 22, 1998.

[201] IRC § 7603(a)(2).

[202] Literally, Section 7609(a)(3)(A) specifies "a mutual savings bank, cooperative bank, domestic building and loan association and other savings institution chartered and supervised as a savings and loan or similar association under Federal or State law, and any bank (as defined in section 581) or credit union (within the meaning of section 501(c)(14)(A))." Banks are reputed to have lobbied strenuously for the provisions of Sections 7609 and 7610 (permitting payment for search and copying fees), and the elaborate definition and the provisions of Section 7610 offer some evidence of this effort. A mortgage company is not a bank or savings and loan institution and therefore is not a third-party recordkeeper. See Reed v. United States, 55 AFTR2d 85-458 (ND Ind. 1985); Wallen V. United States, 1997 US Dist. LEXIS 3526 (D. Mass. 1997) (magistrate judge's report following Reed); compare Fink v. United States, 578 F. Supp. 617 (ED Miss. 1983) (mortgage company was wholly owned subsidiary of a bank); but see Fink v. United States, 578 F. Supp. 617 (ED Mo. 1983) (corporation that serviced mortgages for mortgage holders held third-party recordkeeper under Section 7609(a)(3)(A)). See United States v. First Bank, 586 F. Supp. 174 (D. Conn. 1983) (co-owner of joint account entitled to notice when summons served on bank; enforcement denied because no notice given), rev'd, 737 F2d 269 (2d Cir. 1984) (notice is only required to be given to person "identified" on summons, even if unidentified joint owner is not given notice). See Vanguard Int'l Mfg., Inc. v. United States, 588 F. Supp. 1229 (SDNY 1984) (First Bank followed where corporate taxpayer had signatory authority over corporate bank account, but was not given notice under Section 7609). Third-party summons rules have been applied even if the taxpayer has a relationship with the financial institution other than as a customer. King v. United States, 684 F. Supp. 1038 (D. Neb. 1987) (taxpayer's petition under Section 7609 to quash a Service summons for the purpose of investigating his financial transactions with a credit union of which he was treasurer was not granted). A mortgage company is not a bank or savings and loan institution and therefore is not a third-party recordkeeper. See Reed v. United States, 55 AFTR2d 85-458 (ND Ind. 1985); Wallen V. United States, 1997 US Dist. LEXIS 3526 (D. Mass. 1997) (magistrate judge's report following Reed); compare Fink v. United States, 578 F. Supp. 617 (ED Miss. 1983) (mortgage company was wholly owned subsidiary of a bank).

[203] The definition incorporates by reference the definition contained in Section 603(d) of the Fair Credit Reporting Act, 15 USC § 1681a(f). Nuttleman v. Vossberg, 585 F. Supp. 133 (D. Neb. 1984) (farmers cooperative held not to be consumer reporting agency because it was only furnishing information of its experience with a consumer), following United States v. Berg, 636 F2d 203, 206 (8th Cir. 1980); Freeman v. Southern Nat'l Bank, 531 F. Supp. 94, 95 (SD Tex. 1983).

3. Persons extending credit through the use of credit cards or similar devices[204]

4. Securities brokers[205]

5. Attorneys[206]

6. Accountants[207]

---

[204] This category has been held to include telephone companies that permit customers to obtain credit cards enabling them to charge the cost of telephone calls. United States v. New York Tel. Co., 644 F2d 953 (2d Cir. 1981), vacating and remanding 80-1 USTC ¶ 9460 (EDNY 1980) (taxpayer had credit card). It also includes telephone companies that extend credit through credit cards and other means, United States v. New York Tel. Co., 682 F2d 313 (2d Cir. 1982) (taxpayer did not have credit card). But see United States v. New Eng. Tel. Co., 81-2 USTC ¶ 9486 (DNH 1981). Cf. Lies v. United States, 91-2 USTC ¶ 50,424 (DNM 1991) (arrears billing system for collecting loans used to finance purchases was held not covered by third-party recordkeeper rules; New York Telephone Co. followed). For a case rejecting the Second Circuit's test for determining whether a telephone company engaged in credit card operations, see Risko v. United States, 85-1 USTC ¶ 9420 (SD Fla. 1985) (finding that there is "no rational distinction between a credit holder and a non-credit card holder"). Issuers of credit cards in other situations have also been found to be included in the term. United States v. Desert Palace, Inc., 79-1 USTC ¶ 9296 (D. Nev. 1979) (gambling casino credit cards); United States v. Exxon Co., 450 F. Supp. 472 (D. Md. 1978) (issuer of credit cards for automobile-related purchases is within category, but summons served on Exxon not in its capacity as an extender of credit). For a case disagreeing with the New York Telephone Co. cases, see United States v. New Eng. Tel. Co., 575 F. Supp. 138 (DRI 1984). An insurance company has been held not to be a third-party recordkeeper because it makes policy loans. Davenport v. Bell, 600 F. Supp. 568 (ND Ill. 1984).

[205] The defintion of a broker contained in Section 3(a)(4) of the Securities Exchange Act of 1934, 15 USC § 78c(2)(4), is incorporated by reference. IRC § 7609(a)(3)(D). A taxpayer can have a difficult time establishing that a company is a "broker" where it denies that status. See United States v. Shivlock, 459 F. Supp. 1383 (D. Colo. 1978), aff'd, 612 F2d 1224 (10th Cir. 1979), cert. denied sub nom. West v. United States, 446 US 952 (1980). See also Winters v. United States, 85-1 USTC ¶ 9131 (ED Cal. 1984) (title company that acted as escrow agent held not to be broker).

[206] It appears that the attorney or the accountant need not have been engaged by the taxpayer, since the statute refers to "any" attorney or accountant. If the summons is served on an attorney other than in his capacity as such, it has been held that the attorney is not a third-party recordkeeper. United States v. Manchel, Lundy & Lessin, 477 F. Supp. 326 (ED Pa. 1979) (attorney was taxpayer's employer). In re Hall, 90-2 USTC ¶ 50,442 (ED Ark. 1990) (statute includes any attorney who is acting as recordkeeper, not that "any attorney is ipso facto a third party record keeper, whether or not the attorney is in possession of another's records of the other's business transactions with third parties").

[207] Regulations (e.g., Reg. § 301.7609-2(a)(1)) defining an accountant as a person "registered, licensed, or certified under State law as an accountant" have been held valid. As a result, a return preparer not registered or licensed by a state board of accountancy has been held not to be an accountant for third-party summons purposes. Wang v. United States, 757 F2d 1000 (9th Cir. 1985). See also Pylar v. United States, 835 F. Supp. 1033 (WD Mich. 1993) (individuals and corporations not claiming to be accountants, but performed services for the taxpayer "in the nature of" accounting services, were not third-party recordkeepers). Where the records of an employer were in the possession of the em-

7. Any barter exchange[208]
8. Any regulated investment company or an agent of a regulated investment company (RIC)[209]
9. Enrolled agents[210]
10. Any owner or developer of a computer software source code.[211]

These categories have been interpreted to exclude records maintained by the recordkeeper of transactions between it and the taxpayer, as opposed to records of the taxpayer's transactions with others,[212] but the distinction between two-party and three-party records has been said to be irrelevant in credit situations as long as the entity served with the summons extends credit.[213]

---

ployer's accountant, an employee was unable to establish that the summons was subject to the third-party summons rules. Tomburello v. Comm'r, 86 TC 540 (1986) (summons was served to examine the employer's business records). Munsell v. United States, 87-1 USTC ¶ 9153 (D. Nev. 1986) (president of one corporation and a partner in a partnership was not permitted to quash the summons directed to these entities because, although he may have served as the entities' accountant, he was also a "person with respect to whose liability the summons was issued").

[208] The additional category for "any barter exchange" is defined in Section 6045(c).

[209] The definition of a RIC is the one contained in Section 851.

[210] IRC § 3(I), added by the Taxpayer Bill of Rights 2, § 1001(a), applicable to summonses issued after the enactment date, July 30, 1996.

[211] Carrying over Section 7612's protection of computer software source codes, the general requirements of notice of a third-party recordkeeper are modified to include a summons for the production of a computer source code. The definition of "source code" referred to is in Section 7612(d)(2).

[212] United States v. Income Realty & Mortgage Co., 612 F2d 1224 (10th Cir. 1979); United States v. Exxon Co., 450 F. Supp. 472 (D. Md. 1978). Accord United States v. Gartland, Inc., 79 FRD 148 (D. Md. 1978); United States v. White Agency, 79-1 USTC ¶ 9300 (WD Mich. 1979); United States v. Manchel, Lundy & Lessin, 477 F. Supp. 326 (ED Pa. 1979). In *Manchel, Lundy & Lessin*, the court said,

When the records are kept for the taxpayer, the business is a third-party recordkeeper and the taxpayer is entitled to intervention in the proceedings. On the other hand, when the records only relate incidentally to the taxpayer, and are really kept for the purposes of the business, no third-party recordkeeper relationship exists and a taxpayer has no rights that would arise from that relationship.

Many courts agree. See United States v. Bass, 784 F2d 1282, 1286 (5th Cir. 1986); Rapp v. Comm'r, 774 F2d 932, 934 (9th Cir. 1985); Doe v. United States, 777 F. Supp. 590 (ED Tenn. 1991) (summonses were not third-party recordkeeper summonses when they "were issued to the law firms to obtain records of their own business transactions to obtain information that they failed to supply on the Forms 8300"). Organtini v. United States, 84-1 USTC ¶ 9281 (ND Ill. 1984) (insurance company held not subject to Section 7609 notice rules). A state employment security agency with which employers filed quarterly reports of employee-taxpayers' wages was held not to be a third-party recordkeeper. United States v. Wheelock, 85-1 USTC ¶ 9136 (WD Wash. 1984) (federal law held to preempt state law requiring prior notice before records released).

[213] See United States v. New York Tel. Co., 644 F2d 953 (2d Cir. 1981), vacating and remanding 80-1 USTC ¶ 9460 (EDNY 1980); United States v. New York Tel. Co.,

[b] Exceptions to the Third-Party Recordkeeper Procedures

Third-party summons procedures do not apply if the summons is issued in one of the following situations:

1. The summons is served on the taxpayer whose liability is involved in the inquiry, or an officer or employee of that person;[214]

2. The summons is issued to determine whether or not records of the business transactions or identified person have been kept;[215]

3. The summons is issued solely to determine the identity of any person that has a numbered account with a bank or other financial institution, defined in Section 7603(b)(2)(A);[216]

4. The summons is "issued in aid of collection" of (a) an assessment made or a judgment rendered against the person about whose liability the summons is issued or (b) the liability at law or equity of any transferee or fiduciary liability of the person whose liability is the subject of the summons;[217]

5. The summons is issued by (a) a special agent in the course of an investigation of a criminal offense involving the administration or en-

---

682 F2d 313 (2d Cir. 1982); United States v. Desert Palace, Inc., 79-1 USTC ¶ 9296 (D. Nev. 1979). Under *New York Telephone Co.*, once an entity is covered by the statute in some of its credit card transactions, then the entity is a third-party recordkeeper of transactions with a customer who has not used his credit card for a particular credit transaction or even a customer who does not have a credit card.

[214] IRC § 7609(c)(2)(A).

[215] IRC § 7609(c)(2)(B).

[216] IRC § 7609(c)(2)(C).

[217] IRC § 7609(c)(2)(D). When a summons served on a bank is broader than merely seeking information about a taxpayer's account balance, the summons is still held to be in aid of collection and excepted from the notice requirements of Section 7609. See Barmes v. United States, 84 AFTR2d 99-7130 (7th Cir. 1999) (form summons served on bank during collection proceeding called for records of a trust account and other specific documents relating to the taxpayers' financial transactions). The exception applies to summonses issued to third-party recordkeepers where the taxpayer, whose tax liability has been assessed, has a recognizable interest in the records summoned. Robertson v. United States, 843 F. Supp. 705 (SD Fla. 1993) (assessment against taxpayers, but summons served on bank for third party's records was not "in aid of collection"). In Ip v. United States, 205 F3d 1168 (9th Cir. 2000,) the Service served a third-party summons on a bank for the records of an individual account holder, and justified the failure to give the account holder notice on the ground that the summons was served for the purpose of collecting of tax from a corporation with which the account holder was supposed to have some connection. The Ninth Circuit struck down the third-party summons, holding that the notice exception for collection applied only to the situation where the assessed taxpayer (the corporation) has a recognizable legal interest in the records summoned, and the Service had not shown that the corporation had any legal interest in the account holder's account. Id.

forcement of the internal revenue laws and (b) served on any person who is not a third-party recordkeeper.[218]

To these five exceptions, another exception could be added for a summons issued after a court permits the use of a John Doe summons,[219] or determines that the summons should be issued without notice to prevent spoliation of evidence.[220]

[c] Taxpayer's Right to Intervene

At an enforcement proceeding, the taxpayer is given statutory standing to raise any objections to the summons he or the recordkeeper may have. Thus, Section 7609 incorporates the injunctive remedy of *Reisman* and statutorily overrules the standing requirements of *Donaldson*, where specific classes of recordkeepers are summoned. However, it does not create any substantive defenses to the enforcement of a summons. In fact, since the Supreme Court has struck down many taxpayer objections to enforcement, Section 7609 may be said to give taxpayers a remedy without the possibility of vindicating any rights.

[4] Taxpayer's Motion to Quash All Third-Party Summonses

[a] General Rules

The IRS Restructuring and Reform Act of 1998 makes significant changes to the third-party summonses rules. Unlike the prior procedure, the Service is required to provide to the taxpayer notice of a "contact" with a third party.[221] The proceeding to quash procedures, which were previously limited to third-party recordkeeper summonses, were expanded to apply to all summonses.[222] Accordingly, the taxpayer whose liability is being investigated will receive a notice of the summons and is entitled to bring a proceeding to quash the summons in a federal district court. During the pendency of this proceeding, the statutes of limitations on assessment, collection, and prosecution are suspended.

---

[218] IRC § 7609(c)(2)(E).

[219] IRC §§ 7609(c)(2)(F), 7609(f).

[220] IRC §§ 7609(c)(2)(F), 7609(g).

[221] IRC § 7602(c); see discussion supra ¶ 13.02[3].

[222] IRC § 7609(c)(1), as amended by 1998 Act § 3415(c), applicable to summonses served after July 22, 1998. Third-party recordkeeper summonses are discussed supra ¶ 13.04[3][a].

To stay compliance of a summons, the person entitled to notice of a third-party summons must institute a proceeding to quash the summons.[223] The proceeding to quash replaces the stay procedure, which placed the burden on the Service to enforce the summons. Under the old procedure, because taxpayers could easily stay compliance with a summons merely by sending a notice, many taxpayers who were under investigation did so without basis in law or fact, nor did they appear at proceedings to compel compliance with the summons. The proper venue for a proceeding to quash a summons directed at a third-party recordkeeper is the venue of the third party's residence rather than the venue of the taxpayer.[224]

The noticee must begin the proceeding to quash within twenty days after the day he is given notice as provided in Section 7609(a)(2).[225] To institute a proceeding to quash:

1. The proceeding must be begun no later than the twentieth day after the notice of the summons was served or mailed to the notified person;

2. The petition to quash is filed in a district court having jurisdiction;

3. The Service is notified by sending a copy of the petition by registered or certified mail to the person designated to receive the copy in the notice of the summons; and

---

[223] IRC § 7609(b)(2).

[224] Masat v. United States, 745 F2d 985 (5th Cir. 1984). See Reg. § 301.7609-3.

[225] The twenty-day period has been strictly construed. The twenty-day period has been so strictly construed that the filing of a petition filed late, even one day late, results in the dismissal of the petition. Stringer v. United States, 776 F2d 274 (1985); Ponsford v. United States, 771 F2d 1305 (9th Cir. 1985); Faber v. United States, 921 F2d 1118 (10th Cir. 1990) (accord); Yocum v. United States, 84-1 USTC ¶ 9322 (ND Ind. 1984); Maikranz v. United States, 612 F. Supp. 590 (SD Ind. 1985). The twenty-day period has been held to run from the date the notice is mailed, not the date the notice is received. Riggs v. United States, 575 F. Supp. 738 (ND Ill. 1983); Brohman v. Mason, 587 F. Supp. 62 (WDNY 1984). See Davis v. United States, 85-1 USTC ¶ 9165 (D. Haw. 1984) (gathering cases); Kaun v. United States, 85-1 USTC ¶ 9305 (ED Wis. 1985) (following *Riggs*). It has also been held that for purposes of the running of the twenty-day period, Saturdays, Sundays, and legal holidays are to be counted. Therefore, when the Service gave notice on Friday, May 26, 1995, the twenty-day period began to run on Saturday, May 27, and the petition had to be filed no later than Thursday, June 15, 1995; thus, the petition filed on Friday, June 16, was untimely. Marlow v. United States, 76 AFTR2d 95-7784 (ND Ga. 1995) (taxpayer contended that under Rule 6(a), Federal Rules of Civil Procedure, Saturdays, Sundays, and legal holidays were to be excluded in counting the twenty-day period, but court held that the rule applies only when the period is less than eleven days). See also Lawson v. IRS, 97 TNT 30-18 (MD Fla. 1997) (following *Marlow*, and dismissing a petition filed one day late); Tarpley v. United States, 1997 US Dist. LEXIS 19627 (SDNY 1997) (petition to quash held untimely because the Service served the third-party summons on the bank account owner by certified mail on June 16, 1997, and she did not file her petition to quash until July 11, 1997, twenty-five days after the Service had mailed its notice to the account owner).

4. The recordkeeper is sent a copy of the petition by registered or certified mail.[226]

Both the Service and the summoned party must be sent the petition to quash.[227] The summoned party may intervene in the proceeding.[228] On receipt of the summons, the summoned third-party recordkeeper must assemble the documents called for and be prepared to produce them on the date specified in the summons.[229] The Service may not examine these records until the twenty-fourth day after notice was given the noticee (taxpayer).[230] When the noticee actually brings on a proceeding to quash, the Service is not permitted to ex-

---

[226] Reg. § 301.7609-3(b)(2). However, there is a presumption that the notice was not timely mailed if the Service does not receive delivery of the petition "within 3 days from the close of the 20-day period allowed to institute" the proceeding to quash. Reg. § 301.7609-2(c). There appears to be no authority for such a presumption, to the extent that its meaning can be fathomed (e.g., does the notice have to be received by the seventeenth day or somtime during days seventeen through twenty?).

[227] IRC § 7609(b)(2)(B). For Service procedures where a proceeding to quash is instituted, see IRM 25.5.6.6, Procedures for Notice, Petition to Quash the Summons, and Compliance or Enforcement (Apr. 30, 1999). It appears that where summonses are served on a number of third-party recordkeepers, the taxpayer must institute separate proceedings to quash and pay separate ($60) filing fees for each of the proceedings as provided in 28 USC § 1914(a). Letter of William M. Nichols, General Counsel to the Administrative Office of the United States Courts, to Melvin A. Coffee, Esq. (Dec. 6, 1982). A party summoned to appear and produce records may not move to quash the summons before the government begins an action in district court to compel compliance with the summons. Caesar Elecs., Inc. v. United States, 86-2 USTC ¶ 9693 (EDNY 1986) (summons served under competent authority provisions of German–U.S. Treaty).
On September 26, 1997, when the taxpayers sent the petition to quash to the clerk, they sent an unstamped copy of the petition to the special agent by certified mail. On October 10, 1997, the taxpayers sent the special agent a copy of the petition they received from the clerk, which was stamped as having been filed on September 30, 1997. The unstamped copy of the petition was held to be a "copy of the petition" for purposes of Section 7609(b)(2)(B). Roebuck v. United States, 81 AFTR2d 98-598 (SD Iowa 1997) (magistrate judge's order).

[228] IRC § 7609(b)(2)(C). The right to intervene applies only to the district court proceeding, not to any appeal from a district court ruling. See Hodges, Grant & Kaufman v. United States, 762 F2d 1299 (5th Cir. 1985).

[229] IRC § 7609(i)(1). The Service may certify to the summoned party that no proceeding to quash has been begun within the twenty-three-day period. If the third-party recordkeeper produces documents pursuant to the certification, the recordkeeper will not be liable for the disclosure. IRC § 7609(i)(3).

[230] IRC § 7609(d)(1). The Service instructs agents to have a summons to a third-party recordkeeper returnable at least twenty-four days from the date of the summons, excluding the date the summons is served and the date of appearance. IRM 25.5.6.6.6, Duty and Rights of Summoned Third-Party (Apr. 30, 1999). However, where a summons was returnable only twenty days after the date of notice, and the taxpayer moved to quash nine days before the return date, the summons was enforced. Vincent v. United States, 85-1 USTC ¶ 9133 (ED Cal. 1984).

amine the records until there is either an appropriate court order or the noticee (taxpayer) consents.[231]

[b] The Enforcement Proceeding

In the enforcement proceeding, the noticee may raise those defenses personal to him. In addition, the noticee may raise "such other issues as could be asserted by the third-party recordkeeper, such as . . . that the summons is ambiguous, vague or otherwise deficient in describing the material requested, or that the material requested is not relevant to a lawful investigation."[232] The legislative intent is that the noticee is to be permitted "to stand in the shoes" of the third-party recordkeeper and assert certain defenses that witnesses are allowed to claim but that may not be available to interveners (under many court decisions) on grounds of standing. However, the noticee is not permitted to raise defenses affecting only the interests of the third-party recordkeeper, such as improper service of the summons (e.g., wrong address) or that it will unduly burden the third party to comply with the summons.[233]

The third-party witness provisions may be mandatory, at least for financial institutions, and at least in courts in the Tenth Circuit. Financial institutions are subject to the Right to Financial Privacy Act (RFPA), which generally prohibits financial institutions from producing their records for the Service, except after notice to the bank customer is made and an opportunity is given to the bank customer to challenge production of the bank records before their release to the Service.[234] One of the exceptions to the requirements of the RFPA permits "the disclosure of financial records in accordance with procedures authorized by title 26."[235] The procedures referred to are the third-party recordkeeper provisions of Section 7609, after which the financial privacy provisions are patterned. Suppose, however, a Service agent seeks to obtain the customer's records by asking a bank to turn the records over *without* a third-party recordkeeper summons. Because of the requirements of the RFPA, it has

---

[231] IRC § 7609(d)(2). On request, the Service certifies the taxpayer's failure to bring on a petition to quash by providing the third-party recordkeeper with a copy of the back of the summons having a certificate to that effect.

[232] Comm. Print 1976, at 367, reprinted in 1976-3 CB (vol. 2), at 379.

[233] See, e.g., Wright v. United States, 1997 US Dist. LEXIS 3450 (MD Fla. 1997) (magistrate judge recommended enforcement of third-party recordkeeper summonses over the taxpayer's objection that the summonses had not been properly served because the objection only affected the rights of the banks the Service had served, not taxpayer).

[234] 12 USC §§ 3401–3422. Congress passed the RFPA in 1978 in response to the Supreme Court's decision in United States v. Miller, 425 US 435 (1976), discussed infra ¶ 13.06 (customer of financial institution has no constitutionally protected privacy interest in bank records of customer's account). See HR Rep. No. 1383, 95th Cong., 2d Sess. 34, reprinted in 1978 USCCAN 9273, 9306.

[235] 12 USC § 3413(c).

been held that a financial institution may not voluntarily provide a customer's records to the Service, thereby avoiding the notice and challenge procedures of Section 7609.[236]

[5] John Doe Summonses

Section 7609(f) authorized the Service to serve a John Doe summons following an ex parte court proceeding in which it establishes to the court's satisfaction that specific factors are present.[237] The Service must show the court that (1) the summons relates to the investigation of a particular person or group;

---

[236] Neece v. IRS, 922 F2d 573 (10th Cir. 1990) (bank president notified the Service and turned over mortgage records to the Service). A customer may obtain damages from the Service and a financial institution for violations of the RFPA. 12 USC § 3417. On remand, the district court in Neece, 93-2 USTC ¶ 50,387 (ND Okla. 1993), used Privacy Act interpretations of "actual damages" and "willful and intentional violations" warranting punitive damages. According to the court, "actual damages" "refers to pecuniary loss, and thus does not extend to generalized mental injuries, loss of reputation, embarrassment, or other nonquantifiable injuries." "Willful and intentional conduct" contemplates action "so patently egregious and unlawful that anyone undertaking the conduct should have known it 'unlawful,'" citing Andrews v. United States, 838 F2d 418, 425 (10th Cir. 1988). The taxpayer was awarded (1) nominal damages of $200; (2) $1,580 in actual damages; (3) no punitive damages, because "the policies and instructions of the [IRS] are not so patently unreasonable as to amount to a willful violation of the RFPA"; and (4) attorney fees of $70,000 and costs of $24,000. Neece v. IRS, 41 F3d 1396 (10th Cir. 1994). The circuit court also held that since the Service relied on the tainted bank information in making a jeopardy assessment, the taxpayers were also entitled under the RFPA to attorney's fees in the jeopardy assessment case, but not in their Tax Court and bankruptcy court cases.

In the Tenth Circuit, because of the *Neece* decision, revenue agents are not supposed to accept information a financial institution offers to provide unless the information comes within the suspected illegal activity exception of the RFPA, § 3403(c). IRM 25.5.1.4.1, Documents From Financial Institutions in the Tenth Circuit (Apr. 30, 1999). The Service does not follow *Neece* in other circuits. The Service has opposed the Tenth Circuit's decision in *Neece* with at least some success. See Peddie v. United States, 80 AFTR2d 97-8234 (4th Cir. 1997) (unpublished and nonprecedential memorandum opinion remanding a district court's finding that the Service violated the RFPA by informally requesting Forms 1099 from three banks to investigate a couple's tax liability; district court's finding remanded because the district court failed to rule on the Service's argument that it was exempt from the notice requirements of the RFPA under RFPA § 3413(b)). See also United States v. US Bancorp, 84 AFTR2d 99-6415 (D. Minn. 1999) (bank unsuccessfully argued that the RFPA exception for Service summonses for financial records issued "in accordance with the procedures authorized by Title 26" applied to Section 7609, which provides for protections similar to the RFPA when a summons is served on a bank, and so the RFPA exception did not apply because the Service issued the summons under authority of Section 7602 rather than Section 7609).

[237] The hearing is ex parte because there is no person to whom notice can be given. However, the hearing is not secret. In re Oil & Gas Producers, 500 F. Supp. 440, 444 (WD Okla. 1980).

(2) there is reasonable basis for believing that this person or group has failed (or may fail in the case of a current transaction) to comply with the internal revenue laws; and (3) the information sought under the summons is not readily available from other sources and information concerning the identity of the person or group involved is also not readily available.[238] Once a court has ruled in the ex parte hearing that the criteria of Section 7609(f) have been met, the summoned party may not challenge enforcement of the summons on the ground that the Service has failed to comply with these criteria.[239]

A summons can be served on a named taxpayer (e.g., a tax shelter promoter) in the course of an investigation of that taxpayer and, with the dual purpose of investigating the tax liabilities of unnamed parties, can seek information about those unknown taxpayers. In *Tiffany Fine Arts*, the Supreme Court recognized that this dual-purpose summons need not comply with the John Doe summons requirement of Section 7609(f) "as long as all the information sought may be relevant to a legitimate investigation of the summoned tax-

---

[238] For decisions applying the provision to particular situations, see United States v. Brigham Young Univ., 679 F2d 1345 (10th Cir. 1982), rev'g 485 F. Supp. 534 (D. Utah 1980) (donors to university had overstated deductions by $16 million; reasonable basis found and summons for names and addresses approved). See also In re Tax Liabilities of John Does, 541 F. Supp. 213 (NDNY 1982), aff'd sub nom. Agricultural Asset Management Co. v. United States, 688 F2d 144 (2d Cir. 1982) (names of investors in dairy cattle program); In re Oil & Gas Producers, 500 F. Supp. 440, 444 (WD Okla. 1980) (summons to Kerr-McGee Corp. denied absent showing of reasonable basis for believing identifiable individuals failed to comply with tax laws). Because of the likelihood income is not reported in barter transactions, John Doe summonses to such groups have been authorized. United States v. Pittsburgh Trade Exch., Inc., 644 F2d 302 (3d Cir. 1981); In re Does, 671 F2d 977 (6th Cir., 1982); United States v. Maxwell, 81-1 USTC ¶ 9378 (D. Nev. 1981); In re Does, 91-1 USTC ¶ 50,248 (D. Nev. 1990) (summons not enforced for "indirectly tipped gaming employees," because it was unclear to which employees summons referred; term was undefined and imprecise). Use of a John Doe summons is not limited to third-party recordkeepers as defined under Section 7609(a)(3). Ungaro v. Desert Palace, Inc., 732 F. Supp. 1522 (D. Nev. 1989) (gathering cases).

[239] Agricultural Asset Management Co. v. United States, 688 F2d 144 (2d Cir. 1982), aff'g 82-1 USTC ¶ 9369 (NDNY 1982); In re Purchasers of Master Recordings From Bowman Recording & Prod. Co., 80-1 USTC ¶ 9448 (ND Ga. 1980); United States v. Hayes, 81-2 USTC ¶ 9627 (ND Ga. 1981); United States v. Coble, 82-2 USTC ¶ 9506 (SD Iowa 1982); First Nat'l Bank of Boston, 84-2 USTC ¶ 9861 (D. Mass. 1984) (following *Agricultural Asset Management Co.*); Does v. United States, 866 F2d 1015 (8th Cir. 1989) (recordkeeper served with John Doe summons could not collaterally challenge district court finding that summons was for good faith investigation of an ascertainable group rather than for research, but could attack it on *Powell* grounds). Contra United States v. Brigham Young Univ., 679 F2d 1345 (10th Cir. 1982) (summoned party not barred from challenging in the enforcement proceeding the prior ex parte determination that there had been compliance with Section 7609(f)). See also United States v. Samuels, Kramer & Co., 712 F2d 1342 (9th Cir. 1983) (divided court) (party resisting a John Doe summons was entitled to a limited evidentiary hearing where it made a sufficient showing from which it might be inferred the Service was not acting in good faith).

payer."[240] In this situation, the self-interest of the summoned taxpayer in opposing arbitrary or irrelevant records production is considered to provide sufficient assurance that the privacy rights of the unnamed parties will be protected.

Tiffany Fine Arts still leaves open the challenge that the Service is not using the summons for a dual purpose, and therefore was required, but failed to use the John Doe summons procedures.[241] For example, in *United States v. Merrill Lynch & Co.*,[242] a summons called for the production of partnership documents reflecting use of the installment sales provisions to determine Merrill Lynch's tax liability. Although it disclosed some information, Merrill Lynch objected to disclosing the names of its clients who were partners in partnerships in which Merrill Lynch served as financial adviser. In the enforcement proceeding, the Service acknowledged that it was interested not only in Merrill Lynch's liability but also in that of the clients; but it argued that this dual purpose was permissible under the *Tiffany Fine Arts* decision. Based on affidavits of the examining agents, the district court concluded that there was sufficient evidence of an examination of Merrill Lynch, as well as compliance with the *Powell* standards, to warrant enforcement of the summons. In another case, however, an agent served a summons on a law firm to obtain information about unnamed clients supplied on Forms 8300, and the district court held that the summons was not a John Doe summons, because the liability involved was the law firm's liability. The district court nevertheless treated the summons to the law firm as a John Doe summons because it found as a matter of fact that the Service was actually interested in clients who made cash payments.

On appeal, the Sixth Circuit affirmed the district court's finding that the Service was actually interested in the law firm's clients, as well as the court's use of the procedures for third-party John Doe summonses, but the circuit court also found that the district court had not followed the John Doe procedures by not holding a hearing before the summons was issued at which the government made the three-part statutory showing.[243] The Sixth Circuit did not require the Service to start the process over because the requisite elements had been determined to exist before the summons was ordered enforced, and said it would "exalt substance over form to make the Service go through the motions of having an ex parte court proceeding, getting the summons issued, serving it, defending a motion to quash, and filing a motion for enforcement, all to bring

---

[240] Tiffany Fine Arts, Inc. v. United States, 469 US 310 (1985). The effect of *Tiffany Fine Arts* may have been limited by Section 6111, at least as to tax shelter investors. Tax shelter promoters must retain and make available lists of investors to the Service, so a summons for the information would ordinarily not be necessary. See ¶ 7B.13[2].

[241] Doe v. United States, 777 F. Supp. 590 (ED Tenn. 1991).

[242] United States v. Merrill Lynch & Co., 93-1 USTC ¶ 50,067 (SDNY 1993).

[243] United States v. Ritchie, 15 F3d 592 (6th Cir.), cert. denied, 115 S. Ct. 188 (1994).

us back to where we are now." The court then reviewed whether the Service had a reasonable basis for believing that the law firm's clients had failed to comply with the internal revenue laws. In response to the law firm's objection that enforcement penalizes clients for exercising their constitutional right to counsel, the court concluded that it was the client's choice to use currency and thus the reporting requirements of Section 6050I, and so "there is no reason to grant law firms a potential monopoly on money laundering simply because their services are personal and confidential; other businesses must divulge the identity of their cash-paying clients in keeping with lawful revenue regulations and law firms should not be an exception to this rule."[244]

As these cases suggest, when the Service directs a summons to a named person as a pretext for investigating other unnamed persons, it is required to use the John Doe summons procedures, and the district court should not enforce the summons, because it has been used for an illegitimate purpose.[245]

B CHALLENGES TO SUMMONS ENFORCEMENT

¶ 13.05 OBJECTIONS TO A SUMMONS

There are a number of objections a taxpayer's representative should consider making when his client is served with a summons or is affected by the service of a summons on a third party because the client is the subject of the investigation. Form 13.2 is a checklist of some of these objections. There are a number of considerations in making a decision to object to a summons. The possibility of raising objection to an agent's request for information under Section 7602 is not confined to criminal investigations. A taxpayer may have good reason to object to the scope of a civil examination where, for example, despite the revenue agent's access to the books and records of the enterprise, the agent also seeks audit workpapers and opinion-type information. In a criminal investigation, the taxpayer's objective is to keep adverse or incriminating evidence out of a special agent's hands by legal means.[246] Where an objection to the production of records or testimony on a particular matter is made, the

---

[244] The Sixth Circuit sided with the Second Circuit's view in Goldberger & Dubin, PC, 935 F2d 501 (2d Cir. 1991).

[245] This pretextual use of a summons has been found when an agent has served a summons on a law firm, but the court determined that the investigation was actually of the law firm's clients, and therefore was illegitimate. United States v. Ritchie, 15 F3d 592 (6th Cir.), cert. denied, 115 S. Ct. 188 (1994); United States v. Gertner, 873 F. Supp. 729 (D. Mass. 1995); compare United States v. Blackman, 72 F3d 1418 (9th Cir. 1995) (district court found that agent was investigating law firm, not its clients).

[246] For defense tactics in a criminal investigation, see ¶ 12.04.

possibility exists that an agent will not pursue the request by seeking enforcement of a summons. If books and other records are available for the agent to make the determination he considers appropriate, the agent may be satisfied with writing a report rather than going through the time-consuming process of a summons enforcement action. An objection made during the course of an interview of a witness by the agent similarly may result in the agent deciding to forgo a particular question or area of inquiry and continuing with the balance of the interview. Again, objection to a summons can result in a narrowing of the summons after discussions with the agent before any enforcement proceeding is begun. During an enforcement proceeding, the taxpayer may be able to learn more about the nature, source of information, direction, and status of the Service's investigation. Although courts rarely grant full-blown discovery in summons enforcement proceedings, the nature of the proceeding does leave open the possibility of discovery in an evidentiary hearing.

Perhaps the most common result of objecting to a summons is a delay in the progress of an examination or a criminal investigation. Objection for the purpose of delay is a tactic strongly condemned by the Service and the Justice Department's Tax Division, with some justification. On the other hand, from the taxpayer's standpoint, delay in a criminal investigation may mean additional time to develop useful evidence or to create the possibility that adverse evidence may become unavailable to the government by reason of lapse of time. In both examinations and criminal investigations, objections also serve the purpose that the law intends—that is, judicial scrutiny of the administrative conduct of the Service and the Justice Department to ensure that information is sought in the manner provided by law and that information that the law permits the taxpayer or a witness to withhold is not produced without the taxpayer's knowing consent.

Although they are often overlooked, there are considerations indicating that objections to enforcement of a summons should be waived. First, objection to a summons will ultimately be heard by a federal district court, with the expense that such a proceeding will entail for the taxpayer. Not all taxpayers have unlimited funds to dispute every potential defect in a summons or to attempt to raise every challenge that conceivably might be raised. In either an examination or an investigation, the taxpayer and his representative must decide where the energies and the expense of professional representation should be focused. In some cases, it is simply more advisable for the taxpayer to prepare to oppose either tax adjustments or a recommendation of prosecution administratively or in court, and, consequently, efforts should be directed to that end. Second, a summons enforcement proceeding may well result in publicity concerning the Service's investigation of the taxpayer. If a special agent has issued the summons, the agent is conducting a criminal investigation, not a tax examination. For the taxpayer's benefit, it may be better to limit the publicity of the investigation, including contacts with third persons, until the matter is resolved administratively or in court. Third, the likelihood that a taxpayer's challenge to a summons will be sustained by a district court or court of appeals is not great. At best, a taxpayer may succeed in narrowing the focus of a summons, achieved by virtue of the taxpayer's concerted effort to convince the district court judge that some participation on the judge's part is appropriate by virtue of the egregiousness of the government's action. By and large, however, the reality is that the vast majority of challenges to summonses are rejected. A taxpayer must consider this likelihood, along with the expense of litigation and the potential of publicity.

Also, although neither the Service nor the Tax Division seems cognizant of the situation, the delays involved in an examination or investigation, whether they be by virtue of opposition to a summons or the time a revenue or special agent takes in processing a case, impose psychological and financial burdens on the taxpayer. It is a fact of life that the Service is far more concerned about the delays that a taxpayer can create by challenging summonses than it is about its own delays in processing a case over several years, during which time the taxpayer sees his personal or business life hang in the balance. Therefore, from the standpoint of opposing a summons, a practitioner must consider the personal effect of delay on the client. Finally, one of the possible results of a wide-ranging strategy of challenging summonses in a criminal investigation is that the special agent will request a grand jury proceeding. An open-ended grand jury does not offer the taxpayer the same range of procedural and substantive advantages as an administrative investigation.[247]

---

[247] See the discussion infra ¶ 13.13.

Table 13.2   IRS PRACTICE AND PROCEDURE   13-68

TABLE 13.2
CHECKLIST OF POSSIBLE OBJECTIONS TO A SUMMONS

1. *Objections pertaining to the procedural validity of the summons.*

- The Service has failed to comply with formal statutory requirements regarding service, time and place of examination, and description of the records to be produced.[248]
- The Service has failed to comply with the time limitations or other requirements of the third-party summons provisions.[249]
- The Service has failed to send a second-inspection letter.[250]
- The summons is being used for research or some other statutorily unauthorized purpose.[251]

2. *Objections pertaining to the scope of the summons*—The summons seeks records or testimony not related (relevant) to the correctness of a tax return.[252]

3. *Objections relating to the use of the court's process to enforce the summons.*

- The summons is being used to gather evidence for a criminal prosecution.[253]
- The Service is using its summons authority in bad faith (e.g., to harass the taxpayer).[254]

4. *Constitutional objections to enforcement.*

- The summons is so overly broad as to constitute an unreasonable search.[255]
- The summons seeks information within the taxpayer's zone of privacy (for example, it seeks information in the possession of the taxpayer's attorney).[256]
- Production of records or testimony would be potentially incriminating.[257]

5. *Evidentiary objections to enforcement*—The summoned person is privileged from producing or testifying as to a matter on the basis of the attorney-client, marital, or doctor-patient privilege, or the matters sought constitute an attorney's work product.[258]

6. *Objections pertaining to the return of the summons* — The witness was not permitted to record his testimony or to have a representative present.[259]

---

[248] See supra ¶ 13.02.

[249] See supra ¶ 13.04[3].

[250] See supra ¶ 13.02[5].

[251] See infra ¶ 13.06.

[252] See infra ¶ 13.07.

[253] See infra ¶ 13.08[2].

[254] See infra ¶ 13.08.

[255] See infra ¶ 13.09[2].

[256] See infra ¶ 13.09[3].

[257] See infra ¶ 13.10.

[258] See infra ¶ 13.11.

[259] See supra ¶ 13.03[3].

¶ 13.06 NONCOMPLIANCE WITH STATUTE

One of the *Powell* elements the Service must establish in order to obtain a district court's order enforcing the summons is that the Service has complied with the applicable provisions of the Code. It follows that if the summons provisions have not been followed, the summons should not be enforced. Although both the purposes of a summons and the scope of a permitted examination are broadly stated, the use of a summons for unauthorized purposes or to compel actions not provided for in the statute is unlawful. A summons is simply not enforceable if the Service has failed to comply with the formal statutory requirements controlling service,[260] the time and place of the examination,[261] description of the records to be produced,[262] unnecessary and second inspections or examinations,[263] and notice when a third-party recordkeeper is served.[264] Judicial recognition of this objection has been spotty at best. A witness waives an objection based on some procedural defect in the service of a summons if the witness fails to object on this ground on the return date of the summons.[265] One judicial approach is that a statutory violation alone will not prevent enforcement of the summons the violation must be evaluated in the context of the surrounding circumstances, the good faith of the agent, and the harm resulting from the violation.[266] For example, failure to serve an attested

---

[260] IRC § 7603. See supra ¶ 13.02[1].

[261] IRC § 7605(a). See supra ¶ 13.02[3].

[262] IRC §§ 7603, 7609(a)(5). Where records are required to be produced, they must be described with "reasonable certainty" (IRC § 7603), and a third-party summons must "provide such other information as will enable the person summoned to locate the records" (IRC § 7609(a)(5)). Although relevance and Fourth Amendment considerations may also be involved, a summons may be so broad and indefinite that courts may refuse to enforce it. See, e.g., Local 174, Int'l Bhd. of Teamsters v. United States, 240 F2d 387 (9th Cir. 1956); United States v. Dauphin Deposit Trust Co., 385 F2d 129 (3d Cir. 1967), cert. denied, 390 US 921 (1968) (limiting request to specified records). But see First Nat'l Bank of Mobile v. United States, 160 F2d 532 (5th Cir. 1947). See also the discussion infra ¶ 13.09[2].

[263] IRC § 7605(b). See supra ¶ 13.02[5].

[264] IRC §§ 7609(a)(1), 7609(b). See supra ¶ 13.04[3].

[265] United States v. Myslajek, 568 F2d 55 (8th Cir.), cert. denied, 438 US 905 (1978), followed in United States v. Payne, 648 F2d 361 (5th Cir.), cert. denied, 454 US 1032 (1981).

[266] United States v. Payne, 648 F2d 361 (5th Cir.), cert. denied, 454 US 1032 (1981). (*Powell* does not preclude enforcement merely because any Code requirement has been violated; the seriousness of the violation had to be evaluated under all the circumstances, including the government's good faith and the degree of harm caused by the unlawful conduct, citing United States v. Bank of Moulton, 614 F2d 1063, 1066 (5th Cir. 1980).) That kind of standard obviously limits the situations in which procedural violations by the Service prevent enforcement of the summons. In both *Myslajek* and *Payne*, the circuit courts noted that the taxpayers who were complaining of defective service in fact appeared on the return date of the summons. One wonders whether the courts would have

copy of the summons on the summoned party pursuant to Section 7603 was held not to preclude enforcement of the summons.[267]

[1] Research Versus Investigation

The purposes enumerated in Section 7602 for which a summons may be used contemplate examination of specific returns of specific taxpayers even if their identity is unknown.[268] A summons served to perform research is unenforceable.[269] Enforcement was denied where a revenue agent "performing research . . . to measure tax compliance" served a summons for production of records of all mineral leases of an oil company, which the company had surrendered to the lessors without production on the leasehold. Although the lessors were required to restore to income the amount of depletion deductions previously taken on the surrender of the lease, the court concluded that a summons in aid of a Section 7601 data-gathering project is not authorized by Section 7602 absent an investigation of specific taxpayers.[270]

There is a distinction between research and an investigation of a specific taxpayer whose identity is unknown. In *United States v. Bisceglia*,[271] the Supreme Court upheld a summons served to obtain production of records that might establish the identity of the depositor of $40,000 in deteriorated $100 bills, since a currency transaction of this magnitude might be evidence of unre-

---

credited the objections if the taxpayers had not appeared at all. Failure to appear seems contumacious if actual notice of the summons has been received. At least this much of the lesson is clear. Where a procedural defect is claimed, objection should be made at the time of appearance in response even to a defective summons.

[267] Mimick v. United States, 91-1 USTC ¶ 50,070 (D. Neb.), rev'd, 952 F2d 230 (8th Cir. 1991), on remand, 92-1 USTC ¶ 50,130 (D. Neb. 1992).

[268] See Lyon, "Government Power and Citizens' Rights in a Tax Investigation," 25 Tax Law. 79, 81 (1971).

[269] United States v. Humble Oil & Ref. Co., 488 F2d 953 (5th Cir. 1974), vacated and remanded, 421 US 943, aff'd on remand, 518 F2d 747 (5th Cir. 1975).

[270] Based on this authority, it has been unsuccessfully contended that a summons served to obtain information for the Service's Taxpayer Compliance Measurement Program (TCMP) rather than for a civil or criminal purpose relating to the specific taxpayer's liability was to be used for research and therefore was not authorized by Section 7602. United States v. First Nat'l Bank in Dallas, 468 F. Supp. 415 (ND Tex. 1979), rev'd, 635 F2d 391 (5th Cir.), cert. denied, 451 US 966 (1981); United States v. Flagg, 80-1 USTC ¶ 9125 (SD Iowa 1979), rev'd and remanded, 634 F2d 1087 (8th Cir. 1980). Similarly, a summons issued in connection with some other Service enforcement program would be enforceable. See, e.g., United States v. Norton, 81-1 USTC ¶ 9398 (ND Cal. 1981) (tax shelter compliance program).

[271] United States v. Bisceglia, 420 US 141 (1975).

ported income.[272] Similarly, a summons to a return preparer to supply names and other information relating to unnamed taxpayers whose returns the preparer prepared is also enforceable where a reasonable basis exists for recommending an investigation.[273] Investigation of specific taxpayers whose identity is unknown is now statutorily permitted in the special John Doe summons procedures.[274]

The authority to examine books and records authorized by Section 7602 refers to books and records that are already in existence, indeed, originals of those books and records.[275] It is generally recognized that Section 7602 does not require production or preparation of records not yet in existence.[276]

Broadly interpreting the Service's authority to compel a taxpayer (and others) "to appear" and then to produce books and records and to give testimony,[277] the Supreme Court held in *United States v. Euge*[278] that the Service has the authority to compel a person to give handwriting exemplars. The rationale of this decision is that witnesses "traditionally" have been compelled in both federal and state courts to give various types of physical evidence without violating constitutional guarantees, such as submitting to fingerprinting, photography, measurements, to write or speak for identification, and the like, and that neither the legislative history nor policy served as a basis for denying the Service the authority to compel enforcement of this type of nontestimonial duty.

---

[272] After its decision in *Bisceglia*, the Supreme Court remanded the *Humble* case to the Fifth Circuit (421 US 943 (1975)). The Fifth Circuit reaffirmed its earlier opinion (518 F2d 747 (1975)).

[273] In these cases, an agent had submitted hypothetical tax information to the return preparer, who prepared returns subsequently determined to be false. United States v. Carter, 489 F2d 413 (5th Cir. 1973); United States v. Berkowitz, 488 F2d 1235 (3d Cir. 1973), cert. denied, 421 US 946 (1975); United States v. Turner, 480 F2d 272 (7th Cir. 1973). Cf. United States v. Theodore, 479 F2d 749 (4th Cir. 1973) (summons not enforced as to work records).

[274] IRC § 7609(f).

[275] United States v. Davey, 543 F2d 996 (2d Cir. 1976). Business records in a computerized world may take the form of tapes provided they are made and kept in the regular course of business. Id. See also Rev. Rul. 71-20, 1971-1 CB 392 (providing retention of computer tapes as records under Section 6001). See the discussion supra ¶ 13.03[1].

[276] See United States v. Davey, 543 F2d 996 (2d Cir. 1976); United States v. Brown, 536 F2d 117 (6th Cir. 1976).

[277] IRC § 7602(a)(2).

[278] United States v. Euge, 444 US 707 (1980).

¶ 13.07 RELEVANCE AND MATERIALITY

The investigative authority of Section 7602 extends to testimony and books that "may be relevant" to the determination of a taxpayer's correct tax liability or its collection from him. The term "relevant" suggests judicial limitations imposed in the litigation of a case in court. Discovery rules in the federal district courts have been broadened considerably, but a party may not go on a "fishing expedition" seeking evidence that is not relevant to the subject matter in the case. However, limitations of relevance applicable in court litigation do not apply to the administrative process as well. In *United States v. Morton Salt Co.*, the Supreme Court said that the administrative investigative power is analogous to that of a grand jury, "which does not depend on a case or controversy for power to get evidence, but can investigate merely on suspicion that the law is being violated, or even just because it wants assurance that it is not."[279] Far from rejecting "fishing expeditions," the Court said: "Even if one were to regard the request for information in this case to be caused by nothing more than official curiosity, nevertheless law-enforcing agencies have a legitimate right to satisfy themselves that corporate behavior is consistent with the law and the public interest."[280] However, there are limitations on the power of an agency to investigate. The Court said:

> Of course a governmental investigation into corporate matters may be of such a sweeping nature and so unrelated to the matter properly under inquiry as to exceed the investigatory power. . . . But it is sufficient (1) if the inquiry is within the authority of the agency, (2) the demand is not too indefinite and (3) the information sought is reasonably relevant.[281]

The standards articulated in *Morton Salt* also apply where the Service seeks access to information under the summons authority of Section 7602. In *United States v. Powell*,[282] the Supreme Court observed that although the Service's summons power derives from a different statute, "analogies to other agency situations" are applicable in determining the scope of its investigative power. Thus, the grand jury subpoena analogy developed in *Morton Salt* applies to a summons.[283] In fact, the standards that the Court formulated in *Powell*, which are required to be met before a summons will be enforced, are drawn from its decision in *Morton Salt*. In *Powell*, the Supreme Court said: "[The Service] must show that the investigation will be conducted pursuant to

---

[279] United States v. Morton Salt Co., 338 US 632, 642–643 (1950).

[280] United States v. Morton Salt Co., 338 US 632, 653 (1950).

[281] United States v. Morton Salt Co., 338 US 632, 652 (1950).

[282] United States v. Powell, 379 US 48 (1964).

[283] United States v. Powell, 379 US 48 (1964). Accord United States v. Euge, 444 US 707 (1980); United States v. Bisceglia, 420 US 141 (1975).

a legitimate (i.e., statutorily authorized) purpose, that the inquiry may be relevant to the purpose, that the information sought is not already within [the Service's] possession, and that the administrative steps required by the Code have been followed."[284]

[1] Relevance and the Summons

When a summons is served, its breadth in the first instance is for the Service's investigators to determine, not the taxpayer, as long as the information sought is "reasonably relevant" to its tax collection functions.[285] Reflecting the grand jury analogy, the test is sometimes also stated to be whether the information sought "might throw light upon" the correctness of a return.[286] In *United States v. Arthur Young & Co.*, the Supreme Court stated:[287]

> As the language of § 7602 clearly indicates, an IRS summons is not to be judged by the relevance standards used in deciding whether to admit evidence in federal court. Cf. Fed. Rule Evid. 401. The language "may be" reflects Congress' express intention to allow the IRS to obtain items of even potential relevance to an ongoing investigation, without reference to its admissibility. The purpose of Congress is obvious: the Service can hardly be expected to know whether such data will in fact be relevant until it is procured and scrutinized. As a tool of discovery, the § 7602 summons is critical to the investigative and enforcement functions of the IRS. See United States v. Powell, 379 U.S. 48, 57 (1964) (the Service therefore should not be required to establish that the documents it seeks are actually relevant in any technical, evidentiary sense).

---

[284] United States v. Powell, 379 US 48, 57 (1964). Because a summons calling for production of records can be considered issued for an improper purpose, objection on this ground is discussed infra ¶ 13.08.

[285] United States v. Acker, 325 F. Supp. 857, 861 (SDNY 1971) (taxpayer, Standard Oil Company of New Jersey, proposed to select which corporate minutes it would produce pursuant to a summons); In re International Corp. Co., 5 F. Supp. 608, 611 (SDNY 1934); United States v. Lewis, 87-2 USTC ¶ 9374 (ED La. 1985) (portion of summons held invalid for failing to describe documents summoned where it called for production of "all information that would be necessary to enable a representative of the Internal Revenue Service to properly determine total income earned or sources of fund received for the period January 1, 1981, through December 31, 1982").

[286] United States v. Harrington, 388 F2d 520, 523–524 (2d Cir. 1968); United States v. Egenberg, 443 F2d 512, 515 (3d Cir. 1971); United States v. Matras, 487 F2d 1271 (8th Cir. 1973).

[287] United States v. Arthur Young & Co., 465 US 805, 814 (1984).

Far from condemning "fishing expeditions," one court has flatly said that the Commissioner is "licensed to fish."[288] This expansive view is applied in a summons directed to a taxpayer's records. Where the summons is directed to a third party's records, however, the standard of relevance may be higher. Thus, in *United States v. Harrington*, the court said that the Service is required to have "a realistic expectation," rather than an "idle hope" that something may be discovered from the third party.[289]

Because relevance has such a broad, almost all-encompassing scope, exercise of the summons authority may interfere with some other legally protected interest. For example, when the Service served a summons calling for production of the copyrighted computer program the taxpayer used to prepare its tax returns, the copyright owner objected to production, and the court had to resolve a potential conflict between the summons authority and the Copyright Act. Unless Congress has clearly stated otherwise, both federal statutes are considered effective. Even if the Service's authority to obtain the information is upheld, the recognizable interest of either the taxpayer or a third party leads to the district court's imposing limitations or protections or providing some other special terms in the order of production.[290] On appeal, the circuit court held that the summons power was broad enough to include the Arthur Ander-

---

[288] United States v. Giordano, 419 F2d 564 (8th Cir. 1969), cert. denied, 397 US 1037 (1969). See also United States v. Acker, 325 F. Supp. 857, 861 (SDNY 1971). Applying this standard, records pertaining to years before the years under examination have been ordered produced. See, e.g., Drum v. United States, 83-2 USTC ¶ 9493 (MD Pa. 1983).

[289] United States v. Harrington, 388 F2d 520, 524 (2d Cir. 1968). The test has been phrased in different ways by other courts. For example, in United States v. Dauphin Deposit Trust Co., 385 F2d 129, 131 (3d Cir. 1967), cert. denied, 390 US 921 (1968), the court said, "The Government is not entitled to go on a fishing expedition through appellant's records." See also Venn v. United States, 400 F2d 207, 209 (5th Cir. 1968); United States v. Luther, 481 F2d 429 (9th Cir. 1973).

[290] United States v. Norwest Corp., 916 F. Supp. 1494 (D. Minn. 1996) (summons for Arthur Anderson's copyrighted software package, Tax Director, enforced). In *Norwest*, the district court's enforcement order required the Service (1) to identify in advance the agents to whom the software would be provided; (2) to notify the court if any other agent was to have access and, if so, to order that other agent to avoid further dissemination; (3) to use the software only in connection with the Norwest audit; and (4) on completion of the Norwest audit, and any collection actions and appeals, to return the software and certify that it has purged its computers and destroyed any documents and notes pertaining to the software. Another type of interest for which a district court might fashion a protective order is a trade secret. See also United States v. CalTex Petroleum Corp., 81 AFTR2d 98-1798 (ND Tex. 1998) (magistrate judge recommended that summons calling for production of source not be enforced because it was issued for an improper purpose, in that the source codes were not needed for the audit, and were "just the first step to gaining unrestricted access to source code[s] for all tax preparation software programs.") In the IRS Restructuring and Reform Act of 1998, use of summonses for computer source codes is sharply restricted. See discussion supra ¶ 13.02[7].

sen proprietary software program, because the program was a "record" or "other data" within the meaning of Section 7602(a) and the Service had established that it met the four Powell factors.[291] The Service claimed that the program was a "critical link" in the audit trail revealing how Norwest's returns were prepared. When Andersen and Norwest argued that the software program was not relevant, the circuit court emphatically rejected the argument, saying that not only did the Service "need not state with certainty how useful, if at all, the summoned material will in fact turn out to be," but that it was for the Service, not the taxpayer "to determine the course and conduct of an audit," and the court would not force the Service to litigate "the reasonableness of its investigative procedures."[292]

[2] Relevance and Accountants' Workpapers

Relevance as opposed to "mere convenience" has also been at issue where the Service has sought access to an accountant's workpapers. There are two kinds of workpapers an accountant may have prepared in the course of an engagement: tax workpapers and audit workpapers. To prepare the taxpayer's return, the accountant may compile workpapers. These tax return workpapers must be produced to the Service whether they are in the hands of the accountant or the taxpayer.[293] The rationale is that there is no accountant-client privilege recognized in federal law[294] and that the workpapers are clearly relevant to a determination of the correctness of a taxpayer's return.

Audit workpapers are not part of a taxpayer's permanent accounting records but are constructed by the accountant for the purpose of preparing formal financial statements and making, adjusting, and closing entries in the journal. Financial statements are used by investors and persons extending credit to a business, as well as for the information of management. In his workpapers, the accountant may accrue a contingent liability for taxes, and his workpapers may indicate the underlying potential adjustment comprising this reserved-for liability. If the Service gains access to this portion of the workpapers, the reve-

---

[291] United States v. Norwest Corp., 116 F3d 1227 (8th Cir. 1997). Two procedural elements about the case are noteworthy. The summons served on Norwest was a designated summons, and the claim that the designated summons for the software program was a pretext to extend the statute of limitations was almost summarily rejected. However, the protections the district court imposed on the use of and access to the program were not seriously challenged on the appeal, and so the circuit court let the order stand without opinion.

[292] United States v. Norwest Corp., citing United States v. Clement, 668 F2d 1010, 1013 (8th Cir. 1982).

[293] Fisher v. United States, 425 US 391 (1976).

[294] See Couch v. United States, 409 US 322 (1973); United States v. Arthur Young & Co., 465 US 805, 814 (1984).

nue agent will have a "road map" of those portions of the return where the taxpayer is considered to have some exposure to adjustment and tax liability. Accountants have recognized that the Service's access to this information is an impediment to the free flow of information from the taxpayer and the taxpayer's advisers to the accountant and, thus, make more difficult the preparation of fairly accurate financial statements.

Audit workpapers also must be produced, even where they were not used in the preparation of a tax return but where compiled by the taxpayer's independent auditors in the course of preparing financial statements for the taxpayer's enterprise. In *Arthur Young & Co.*, the Supreme Court held that audit workpapers were relevant to a Service examination, and, accordingly, an accounting firm was required to produce them in response to a summons.[295] On the relevance of the workpapers, the Court said:

> It is the responsibility of the IRS to determine whether the corporate taxpayer in completing his return has stretched a particular tax concept beyond what is allowed. Records that illuminate any aspect of the return— such as the tax accrual workpapers at issue in this case—are therefore highly relevant to legitimate IRS inquiry.

Even the circuit court had acknowledged the potential relevance of the tax accrual workpapers.[296] The Supreme Court found no basis in law or in the accountant-client relationship for excluding relevant data and creating an immunity from production for accountant's workpapers, even those "highlighting those areas in which the corporate taxpayer has taken a position that may, at some later date, require the payment of additional taxes."

The Court also reaffirmed that no confidential accountant-client privilege exists under federal law, unlike the privilege for attorney-client communications, and that a certified public accountant plays a different role from a lawyer. The public accountant has "a public responsibility transcending any employment relationship with the client." The lawyer, on the other hand, is an advocate whose duty it is to present the client's case in the most favorable light. The Court said, "To insulate from disclosure a certified public accountant's interpretation of its client's financial statements would be to ignore the significance of the accountant's role as a disinterested analyst charged with public obligations." A factor that the Court observed as mitigating the unfairness of disclosing opinions about potential adjustments to the Service was its announced policy of limiting requests for tax accrual workpapers.[297] After the

---

[295] United States v. Arthur Young & Co., 465 US 805, 814 (1984).

[296] However, the district court may not delegate the determination even to an expert. United States v. Rockwell Int'l, 897 F2d 1255 (3d Cir. 1990) (where tax accrual files were summoned, district court erred in delegating the determination of their relevance to an independent outside auditor).

[297] See ¶ 8.06[3][b].

Arthur Young decision, the Service announced it had no plans to change this policy.[298]

In response to the summonses, courts have ordered production of outside audit reports,[299] internal audit reports,[300] and representation and management letters.[301] Courts ordering production have viewed the report or workpapers as throwing light on the correctness of the returns and as being covered by the broad scope of relevance in the summons statute. Neither the availability of a taxpayer's books and records nor the fact that the workpapers were not used in preparing the return was considered by courts ordering production as a limitation on relevance.[302]

[a] Service Procedures

Administrative procedures in civil tax examinations regarding accountant's workpapers, but these procedures are not applicable in fraud cases.[303] In general, the Service instructs agents that they have the authority to request production of audit workpapers but that they should exercise their authority with restraint. Agents are told not to request workpapers "as a matter of standard examining procedure" because the taxpayer's records are the "primary source of information" and the workpapers only a "collateral source." Nevertheless, if an agent believes portions of workpapers, including tax accrual workpapers, to

---

[298] IR 84-45, 10 Stand. Fed. Tax Rep. (CCH) 6454A. For an analysis of the decision from an accountant's point of view, see Buchholz and Moraglio, "IRS Access to Auditors' Work Papers: The Supreme Court Decision," 158 Acct. 91 (Sept. 1984).

[299] United States v. Noall, 587 F2d 123 (2d Cir. 1987), cert. denied, 441 US 923 (1979); United States v. Riley Co., 80-1 USTC ¶ 9157 (ND Ill. 1980) (report by Arthur Andersen on company's internal-accounting system).

[300] First Chicago Corp. v. United States, 79-1 USTC ¶ 9111 (ND Ill. 1978) (write-downs of bond-trading accounts, but not other reports, ordered produced.) United States v. Leaseway Transp. Corp., 523 F. Supp. 1333 (ND Ohio 1981), aff'd in unpublished opinion (2d Cir. 1983), cert. denied, 464 US 960 (1983) (internal audit reports ordered produced; tenuous showing of tax return relevance); United States v. El Paso Co., 682 F2d 530 (SD Tex. 1981), aff'd, 682 F2d 530 (5th Cir. 1982), cert. denied, 466 US 944 (1984) (internal audit reports and tax contingency reserve workpapers ordered produced over attorney-client privilege and work product objections).

[301] United States v. Kroger Co., 566 F. Supp. 1432 (SD Ohio 1983) (representation letters ordered produced; IRM 4024–4024.5, MT 4000-235 (June 8, 1976) (Accountant's Workpapers); United States v. IC Indus., 555 F. Supp. 219 (ND Ill. 1983) (management letters found relevant and ordered produced); United States v. Riley Co., 80-1 USTC ¶ 9157 (ND Ill. 1980). But see First Chicago Corp. v. United States, 79-1 USTC ¶ 9111 (ND Ill. 1978) (request for management report apparently denied).

[302] See especially United States v. Noall, 587 F2d 123 (2d Cir. 1987), cert. denied, 441 US 923 (1979).

[303] IRM 4024–4024.5, MT 4000-235 (June 8, 1976). For a more detailed description of the procedures in civil examination, see ¶ 8.06[3][b].

be "relevant and material" to the examination, the agent may request such portions. He may not request all of the workpapers unless he believes all of them to be relevant. Where a taxpayer's business has been the subject of a certified audit, the examiner may request the written representation letter from management required under auditing standards established by the American Institute of Certified Public Accountants (AICPA).[304] Workpapers reflecting the scope and results of an auditor's examination may also be the subject of an examiner's request.[305]

¶ 13.08 IMPROPER PURPOSE/BAD FAITH USE

The Service is authorized to use a summons for the purposes described in Section 7602, which are generally related to tax determination and collection. When the Service uses its summons power for an unauthorized purpose or for any purpose reflecting on the good faith use of its power, the Supreme Court has said that the summons will not be enforced.[306] Case law and Section 7602(c) make it clear that the Service is not authorized to use this power to assist another agency by, for example, using a summons to investigate a matter already being investigated by a grand jury, or by gathering evidence for the Department of Justice in its prosecution of a criminal case.[307] In general, since it is the court's process that the Service invokes in an enforcement proceeding to obtain compliance with a summons, a court will not use this process by ordering compliance unless it is satisfied that the Service has served the summons in a good faith pursuit of its summons authority.[308]

Before 1982, this authority did not expressly include power to use a summons to investigate a criminal violation of the tax laws. As a result, there was much litigation over the question whether the Service was using a summons for an improper criminal purpose. In 1982, Section 7602 was amended to provide that the statutorily authorized purposes for which a summons may be issued include "the purpose of inquiring into any offense connected with the

---

[304] AICPA, Statement on Auditing Standards No. 19 (June 1977).

[305] The AICPA has established procedures an auditor is to follow. Statement on Auditing Standards Nos. 53 (Apr. 1988), 19 (Jan. 1977).

[306] Reisman v. Caplin, 375 US 440 (1964); United States v. Powell, 379 US 48 (1964).

[307] IRC § 7602(c). United States v. LaSalle Nat'l Bank, 437 US 298 (1978); Donaldson v. United States, 400 US 517 (1971); Reisman v. Caplin, 375 US 440, 445 (1964). It should be noted that the Service may not use a grand jury to gather evidence for a civil case. In re April 1956 Term Grand Jury, 239 F2d 263 (7th Cir. 1956). See United States v. Procter & Gamble Co., 356 US 677 (1958).

[308] United States v. Powell, 379 US 48 (1964).

administration or enforcement of the internal revenue laws."[309] Consequently, the Service is permitted to use a summons to gather evidence of a criminal violation of the tax laws.[310] Section 7602 was also amended to prohibit the use of a summons when a Department of Justice referral for criminal prosecution or grand jury investigation is in effect.[311] To understand these statutory provisions dealing with use of a summons in a criminal investigation, as well as the background of the improper purpose/bad faith objection to enforcement, which covers other uses of a summons, a review of the Supreme Court cases from which the objection developed is in order.

[1] Improper Purpose Before 1982

After its decision in *Reisman*, the Supreme Court recognized the improper-criminal-purpose limitation, but it had considerable difficulty in describing when a summons would be considered to have been issued for an improper criminal purpose. Good faith or the lack of it had had different meanings as the courts responded to different forms of alleged Service abuse of the summons power. Generally, it was said that (1) the Service must have issued the summons before it has referred the taxpayer's case to the Justice Department with a recommendation of criminal prosecution (*Reisman* and *Donaldson*) and (2) even before referral the Service must have issued the summons in good faith pursuit of the statutorily authorized purposes of Section 7602. On the other hand, this good faith use was not present where (1) the summons was issued to harass the taxpayer or put pressure on him to settle a collateral dispute or for some other similar purpose (*Powell*) or (2) at a time when the Service had an institutional commitment to make a referral to the Justice Department and the summons was issued to gather additional evidence for the prosecution rather than to pursue civil tax determination or collection (*LaSalle*).

The improper-purpose limitation was joined in *Powell* with the requirement that the summons be issued in a good faith pursuit of the summons au-

---

[309] IRC § 7602(b).

[310] United States v. Security First Fed. Sav. & Loan, 83-1 USTC ¶ 9325 (MD Fla. 1983) ("Congress has . . . substituted for the 'good faith' standard (of *LaSalle National Bank*) a bright-line test focusing on a Justice Department referral"); Moutevelis v. United States, 561 F. Supp. 1211 (MD Pa. 1983), aff'd, 727 F2d 313 (3d Cir. 1984) (criminal purpose objection of no avail unless there was a referral to the Justice Department before the summons was issued); Godwin v. United States, 564 F. Supp. 1209 (D. Del. 1983) (the Tax Equity and Fiscal Responsibility Act of 1982 (TEFRA) "replaced the vague solely criminal purpose defense with a 'bright line' test under which a summons may be issued so long as there was no 'Department of Justice referral'"); McTaggart v. United States, 570 F. Supp. 547 (ED Mich. 1983) ("'criminal purpose' defense has been rendered irrelevant by the provisions of TEFRA").

[311] IRC § 7602(c).

thority. In *Powell*, the Court said that an abuse of the court's process would take place "if the summons had been issued for an improper purpose, such as to harass the taxpayer, or to put pressure on him to settle a collateral dispute, or for any other purpose reflecting on the good faith of the particular investigation."[312] The conjunction of improper purpose and good faith did not provide clear direction to lower courts, which were faced with a mounting number of challenges to Service summonses.

The Supreme Court attempted to resolve uncertainty over the improper-purpose challenge in a case factually similar to *Boren v. Tucker*, which was cited in *Reisman*. In *Donaldson*, a special agent's summons was challenged on the ground that it was served for an improper purpose because it was in aid of an investigation that could potentially result in a recommendation that criminal prosecution be instituted against the taxpayer. The Supreme Court rejected the challenge, holding that when criminal prosecution is only a potentiality, a summons served by a special agent may not be challenged as seeking material for the improper purpose of obtaining evidence for a criminal prosecution. The Court stated that the improper purpose referred to in *Reisman* exists only where there is a "pending criminal charge (indictment or information) or, at most, . . . an investigation solely for criminal purposes."[313]

The Court made it clear in *Donaldson* that a summons is not served for an improper purpose merely because a special agent who investigated criminal violations of the tax laws has served the summons. Although a criminal prosecution could have developed, the special agent conducted his investigation jointly with a revenue agent from the audit division, and their combined efforts were directed to both civil and criminal infractions. However, other statements in the Court's opinion caused uncertainty. The Court also said that a summons might not be issued for a proper purpose if it were used in "an investigation solely for criminal purposes"[314] and that such a summons would be issued for an improper purpose if it were issued after a recommendation of criminal prosecution had been made or possibly "after the investigation is complete or sufficiently far along so as to support appropriate conclusions (that prosecution be recommended)."[315] Finally, the Court held that "under § 7602 an internal revenue summons may be issued in aid of an investigation if it is issued in good faith and prior to a recommendation for criminal prosecution."[316] The *Donaldson* opinion left lower courts with so many standards that confusion was inevitable. Most courts of appeals focused on the purpose of the special agent in serving the summons. Contrary to this essentially subjective standard, the Sec-

---

[312] United States v. Powell, 379 US 48, 58 (1964).

[313] Donaldson v. United States, 400 US 517, 533 (1971).

[314] Donaldson v. United States, 400 US 517, 533 (1971).

[315] Donaldson v. United States, 400 US 517, 535 (1971).

[316] Donaldson v. United States, 400 US 517, 536 (1971).

ond Circuit said that *Donaldson* had adopted an objective test: A summons was enforceable unless it was issued after a recommendation of criminal prosecution had been made.[317]

As a result of conflict between the circuits about the meaning of *Donaldson* and the improper-purpose standard, the Supreme Court undertook another effort to clarify its position. In *United States v. LaSalle National Bank*,[318] a special agent was conducting an investigation alone. On the basis of the agent's statements and other evidence, the court found the investigation to be solely for criminal purposes. Thus, he was held by the court of appeals to have been using the summons authority in bad faith. Unlike *Donaldson*, where the mere potentiality of criminal prosecution was said by the taxpayer to be an improper purpose, the question in *LaSalle* was whether the special agent's criminal investigation purpose meant that the summons was not issued in good faith pursuit of purposes authorized by Section 7602. The summons the special agent had served on the bank was issued before any recommendation of criminal prosecution had been made by the Service to the Justice Department's Tax Division. Thus, under the objective test this prereferral summons was automatically enforceable. In *LaSalle National Bank*, the Supreme Court affirmed the proposition that the improper-purpose limitation applied to a summons issued before, as well as after, a referral for criminal prosecution. As the Court said, "the Service at all times must use the summons authority in good-faith pursuit of the congressionally authorized purposes of § 7602."[319]

The Court made it clear that resolution of the question of whether an investigation has solely criminal purposes did not depend on the "agent's personal intent." It was "answered only by an examination of the institutional posture of the IRS."[320] The taxpayer opposing enforcement had the burden of proving that the Service did not have "a valid civil tax determination or collection purpose" in serving the summons.[321] The Court recognized that this test imposed a heavy burden on taxpayers: "Because criminal and civil fraud liabilities are coterminous, the Service rarely will be found to have acted in bad faith by pursuing the former."[322] After *LaSalle*, where a taxpayer made an improper-criminal-purpose objection to enforcement of a summons before a referral to the Department of Justice, courts of appeals said that the issue for

---

[317] United States v. Morgan Guar. Trust Co., 572 F2d 36 (2d Cir.), cert. denied sub nom. Keech v. United States, 439 US 822 (1978).

[318] United States v. LaSalle Nat'l Bank, 437 US 298 (1978).

[319] United States v. LaSalle Nat'l Bank, 437 US 298, 318 (1978).

[320] United States v. LaSalle Nat'l Bank, 437 US 298, 316 (1978).

[321] United States v. LaSalle Nat'l Bank, 437 US 298, 316 (1978).

[322] United States v. LaSalle Nat'l Bank, 437 US 298, 316 (1978). The Fifth Circuit later said that the burden of demonstrating that an investigation is for an improper purpose "may, for all practical purposes, be insurmountable." United States v. Price, 655 F2d 56, 58 (5th Cir. 1981) (citations omitted).

determination was whether the Service had institutionally abandoned the civil aspects of the investigation.[323] A great deal of litigation then ensued over the institutional posture of the Service at the time summonses were issued.[324]

[2] Improper Criminal Purpose: Sections 7602(b) and 7602(d)

The *LaSalle National Bank* formulation was statutorily replaced by two amendments to the summons authority in Section 7602(a). Section 7602(b) specifically provides that the purpose of issuing a summons may be to inquire into "any offense connected with the administration or enforcement of the internal revenue laws." Also, Section 7602(d)(1) restricts the Service's authority to issue a summons or begin an enforcement action, "with respect to any person if a Department of Justice referral is in effect with respect to any such person."[325] A Department of Justice referral is in effect if (1) the Service has

---

[323] United States v. Arthur Andersen & Co., 623 F2d 725 (1st Cir. 1980); United States v. Marine Midland Bank of NY, 585 F2d 36 (2nd Cir. 1978); United States v. Genser, 595 F2d 146 (3rd Cir. 1979) (*Genser II*); United States v. McGuirt, 588 F2d 419 (4th Cir. 1978), cert. denied, 444 US 827 (1979); United States v. Holmes, 614 F2d 985 (5th Cir. 1980); United States v. Moll, 602 F2d 134 (7th Cir. 1979); United States v. Kis, 658 F2d 526 (7th Cir. 1981); United States v. Schuttlerle, 586 F2d 1201 (8th Cir. 1978); United States v. Popkin, 623 F2d 108 (9th Cir. 1980); United States v. MacKay, 608 F2d 830 (10th Cir. 1979). The Sixth Circuit did not specifically address the issue.

[324] See, e.g., United States v. Chase Manhattan Bank, 598 F2d 321 (2d Cir. 1979), on remand, 79-2 USTC ¶ 9658 (SDNY 1979) (FBI found to have closed its investigation before Service summons issued). The issue seemed to be whether the Service maintained its independence, despite the contacts. See United States v. Commonwealth Fed. Sav. & Loan, 529 F. Supp. 1246 (ED Pa. 1982) (Service investigation had its genesis in closed grand jury investigation, and special agent had contacts with U.S. Attorney's office during Service investigation about possible new grand jury investigation; summons enforced after findings that agent not used as conduit and that civil purpose not abandoned); United States v. Scholbe, 664 F2d 1163 (10th Cir. 1982) (Service agreement to disclose information to the Department of Environmental Affairs did not taint summons); United States v. Chemical Bank, 593 F2d 451 (2d Cir. 1979) (revenue agent summons; Service held not to be information-gathering agency for Justice Department because Service retained autonomy and no disclosure of tax information authorized); United States v. Serubo, 604 F2d 807 (3d Cir. 1979) (special agent summons and disclosure of tax information authorized; held, "real likelihood" Service used as information-gathering agency). United States v. Cortese, 614 F2d 914 (3d Cir. 1980) (bad faith of informant is not imputable to Service; Service may be shown to have adopted motives of informant); United States v. Richter, 603 F2d 744 (8th Cir. 1979) (agent's "misbehavior" would not establish institutional posture of Service).

[325] IRC § 7602(d), formerly Section 7602(c), was added by TEFRA, § 333(a). The constitutionality of the TEFRA amendement of Section 7602 has been upheld. Frent v. United States, 571 F. Supp. 739 (ED Mich. 1983). Where both the summons and the proceeding to quash the summons preceded the Department of Justice referral, a district court held that Section 7602(d) does not prevent enforcement. Drum v. United States, 85-1 USTC ¶ 9206 (MD Pa. 1985) ("The statute prevents issuance of or commencement of an

recommended to the Justice Department that it conduct a grand jury investigation or criminal prosecution of the person for an internal revenue-connected offense or (2) the Justice Department has requested the disclosure of a return or return information for purposes of tax administration under Section 6103(h)(3)(B).[326] Section 7602(b), authorizing use of a summons to investigate a criminal offense, and Section 7602(d), prohibiting use of a summons after a Department of Justice referral is in effect, leave little, if anything, to the improper-criminal-purpose objection as developed by the Supreme Court.[327] As long as a Department of Justice referral is not in effect, the institutional commitment of the Service to make such a referral seems irrelevant.[328]

A request for disclosure of return information for tax administration purposes does not constitute a referral unless a request is made for a criminal investigation or prosecution.[329] Also, regulations contain five examples illustrating that for purposes of the rule prohibiting issuance or enforcement of a summons when a Department of Justice referral is in effect, each taxable period and each type of tax are treated separately. For example, even if a referral has been made on a tax shelter promoter's income tax liability, a summons may be issued on a potential Section 6700 penalty.[330] A Department of Justice referral terminates when the Justice Department declines prosecution, says it will not authorize a grand jury investigation, or says it will discontinue a grand jury investigation.[331]

[3] Other Improper-Purpose Claims

Persons affected by a summons have made objections that the summons has been issued for improper purposes other than for gathering evidence for use in

---

action to enforce a summons after a Justice Department referral but it does not prevent continued execution of a validly issued and enforced summons").

[326] IRC § 7602(d)(2)(A). A referral to the Area Division Counsel, CI, obviously is not a referral to the Department of Justice for Section 7602(b) purposes. See Frent v. United States, 571 F. Supp. 739 (ED Mich. 1983).

[327] But see Copp v. United States, 968 F2d 1435 (1st Cir. 1992) (analyzing summons under *La Salle*, despite Section 7602(c)).

[328] See, e.g., United States v. Security First Fed. Sav. & Loan, 83-1 USTC ¶ 9325 (MD Fla. 1983); Moutevelis v. United States, 561 F. Supp. 1211 (MD Pa. 1983), aff'd, 727 F2d 313 (3d Cir. 1984); Godwin v. United States, 564 F. Supp. 1209 (D. Del. 1983); McTaggart v. United States, 570 F. Supp. 547 (ED Mich. 1983).

[329] Reg. § 301.7602-1(c)(2)(ii).

[330] Reg. § 301.76021(c)(4)(ii), Ex. (5).

[331] IRC § 7602(c)(2)(B)(i). Termination also occurs where there has been a final disposition of a criminal proceeding relating to the person or the Department of Justice notifies the Service that it will not prosecute a person for whom a return or return information was requested under Section 6103(h)(3)(B). IRC §§ 7602(c)(2)(B)(ii), 7602(c)(2)(B)(iii).

a criminal prosecution. In *LaSalle*, the Supreme Court recognized that a summons might not be enforceable for reasons other than an improper criminal purpose. It said: "Future cases may well reveal the need to prevent other forms of agency abuse of Congressional authority and judicial process."[332] Attempts to expand the scope of the improper-purpose objection do not find a warm judicial reception even where a summons has been served in a civil context.[333] However, it has been held that the TEFRA amendment of Section 7602 did not eliminate the improper-purpose objection. In *Pickel v. United States*,[334] the circuit court said:

> We do not doubt that portions of the *Powell* and *LaSalle* discussions of bad faith retain vitality (after TEFRA) and that where the taxpayer can prove that the summons is issued solely to harass him, or to force him to settle a collateral dispute, *Powell*, . . . or that the IRS is acting solely as an information-gathering agency for other departments, such as the Department of Justice, *LaSalle* . . . or the FBI, the summons will be unenforceable because of the IRS's bad faith.

Where a substantial preliminary showing of abuse of the court's process has been made, a summoned party is entitled to substantiate his allegations by way of an evidentiary hearing.[335]

Other improper uses of a summons include possible retaliation for the taxpayer's role on a Senate committee investigating the Service,[336] harassment,[337] or

---

[332] United States v. LaSalle Nat'l Bank, 437 US 298, 318 n.20 (1978).

[333] See, e.g., United States v. Harper, 662 F2d 335 (5th Cir. 1981) (divided court enforced summons to discover taxpayer's assets to collect tax liability that taxpayer claimed he did not owe; dissent suggested taxpayer should have been able to have hearing on whether any taxes were owed).

[334] Pickel v. United States, 746 F2d 176 (3d Cir. 1984). For a case where a taxpayer established an abuse of process claim, see United States v. Karras, 86-1 USTC ¶ 9166 (DSD 1985) (taxpayer claimed he had discarded his bank records, and the Service apparently refused to serve third-party summons on bank to obtain bank copies).

[335] United States v. Millman, 765 F2d 27 (2d Cir. 1985) (at the hearing, the agents responsible for the investigation and other witnesses may be called). See also United States v. Church of Scientology, 520 F2d 818, 824 (9th Cir. 1975) (limited evidentiary hearing approved); United States v. Author Servs., Inc., 804 F2d 1520 (9th Cir. 1986) (no abuse of discretion in refusing to hold hearing).

[336] United States v. Fensterwald, 553 F2d 231 (DC Cir. 1977) (taxpayer's claims supported by sufficient showing that case was remanded for further proceedings to assess the validity of taxpayer's allegations), on remand, 78-1 USTC ¶ 9245 (DDC 1978) (basis of examination was TCMP audit).

[337] United States v. Church of Scientology, 520 F2d 818 (9th Cir. 1975) (remanded for further proceedings). A summons served in an investigation commenced by the Service primarily to pressure the person to give evidence against another taxpayer has nevertheless been enforced. United States v. Equitable Trust Co., 611 F2d 492 (4th Cir. 1979) (not inappropriate for Service to pressure "minor defendants" to cooperate). The decision (2–1) in *Equitable Trust* is doubtful. See generally 93 Harv. L. Rev. 1574 (1980). The majority ignores the

operation of *Powell* in civil-criminal investigations and uses mainly criminal case authorities to justify the result. It may not be inappropriate for a prosecutor to engage in certain conduct such as plea bargaining, although the propriety of using pressure tactics is not so clear as the court believed. See, e.g., United States v. Dardi, 330 F2d 316, 336 (2d Cir.), cert. denied, 379 US 845 (1964). However, the Service is not supposed to act as prosecutor when using its summons authority.

For other unsuccessful attempts to show Service harassment, see United States v. Mid-west Generator Co., 81-2 USTC ¶ 9818 (ND Ill. 1981) (Service audit scheduled after request to supply information about a Canadian company was not harassment because return was computer selected before request made). See also United States v. Texas Heart Inst., 755 F2d 469 (5th Cir. 1985) (alleged improper disclosures of tax return information in the past held not sufficient evidence of lack of a legitimate purpose, under the facts of the particular case, to warrant nonenforcement); United States v. Balanced Fin. Management, Inc., 769 F2d 1440 (10th Cir. 1985) (harassment alleged because the Service did not centralize a Section 6700 investigation against a promoter in several districts). (*Michaud II*) (case remanded for further findings); Wooden Horse Invs., Inc. v. United States, 92-2 USTC ¶ 50,482 (ED Wash. 1992) (taxpayer's claim that revenue agent issued summons in retaliation for taxpayer's refusal to extend statute of limitations on assessment and in anticipation of litigation in Tax Court was rejected, but protective order limited use of produced documents).

United States v. Administration Co., 94-2 USTC ¶ 50,479 (ND Ill. 1994) presented several harassment claims. There was a three and one-half year delay in the Service's bringing a summons enforcement action, and the Service already was in possession of copies of many summoned documents; nevertheless, the court held that the summons was not stale and ordered originals produced. It was also contended that the summons enforcement proceeding was an attempt by the Service to obtain third-party information it could not obtain under the Tax Court's discovery rules. The court held that "the pendency of a related [T]ax [C]ourt case does not in any way affect the Service's authority to issue, nor the court's authority to enforce an IRS summons." The district court also noted that the summonses were issued before the Tax Court petitions were filed, and that under the Tax Court's opinion in Mary Kay Ash v. Comm'r, 96 TC 459 (1991), the Tax Court's discovery rules would not be abused. The taxpayer claimed, finally, that the Service summons was an attempt to harass the taxpayer and pressure him into a settlement in the Tax Court case. This argument was also rejected. The summons in *Administration Co.* was enforced, but the production before the revenue agent did not satisfy the Service, and it moved for an order of contempt. See United States v. Administration Co., 94-2 USTC ¶ 50,480 (ND Ill. 1994). Enforcement of the summons was affirmed on appeal. United States v. Administrative Enter., Inc., 75 AFTR2d 95-843 (7th Cir. 1995). The circuit court observed that there was no statute of limitations on enforcement of a summons and that the doctrine of laches might apply against the government where there was no statute of limitations, but that the issue did not require resolution, because the defendants could not show "concrete harm" but only the possibility of sanctions for having destroyed summoned records during the three-and-one-half-year hiatus between service of the summons and enforcement. Interestingly, the circuit court said that imposition of sanctions by the district court would be "perverse" and a judgment imposing sanctions would be reversed.

Harassment is difficult to establish once the Service establishes that it has met the four *Powell* factors, including the agent's representation that the summons seeks information that may be relevant to a determination of the taxpayer's correct tax liability. See, e.g., 2121 Arlington Heights Corp. v. IRS, 109 F3d 1221 (7th Cir. 1997) (restaurant unsuccessfully claimed that agent's summons to a phone company for information on years after the years under audit was irrelevant, invaded the privacy rights of its employees, would ruin its business, and was issued in bad faith to force the restaurant to concede its assessed tax liability).

misuse of the Service by some third person or agency.[338] It also appears to be an abuse of the court's process (or a bad faith use of the summons power) to require a taxpayer to produce records already in the Service's possession (e.g., retained copies of tax or information returns),[339] although such a request should

---

In *CalTex Petroleum Corp.*, a magistrate judge found that the Service's summons to obtain the source code for software the taxpayer used to calculate its foreign tax credits was issued for an improper purpose, in part because the Service was issuing the summons as a test case and "a first step to gaining unrestricted access to source code[s] for all tax preparation software programs." United States v. CalTex Petroleum Corp., 81 AFTR2d 98-1798 (ND Tex. 1998). Harpole v. United States, 86 AFTR2d 2000-7101 (D. Alaska 2001) (granting motion to quash third-party summons; in this case, summons was issued by revenue agent without signature of a supervisor because the Service failed to demonstrate compliance with Commissioner's Delegation Order No. 4, and the failure to comply with the Delegation Order raised a material issue of the Service's good faith in issuing the summons).

[338] See Center on Corporate Responsibility, Inc. v. Schultz, 368 F. Supp. 863 (DDC 1973) (evidence of White House use of administrative actions against certain organizations whose views were offensive to the White House). Misuse of the Service by an informant can also occur. See United States v. Cortese, 448 F. Supp. 845 (ED Pa. 1978), remanded, 614 F2d 914 (3d Cir. 1980) (informant's motive does not taint Service's motive, but different result if Service or investigating agent motivated by same animus motivating informant). However, it is not harassment for the Service to reopen a tax return examination if it follows its own procedure. See United States v. Clement, 668 F2d 1010 (8th Cir. 1982) (reexamination of estate tax return after original Service valuation considered too low).

[339] United States v. Powell, 379 US 48 (1964); United States v. Ladd, 471 F. Supp. 1150 (ND Tex. 1979) (tax returns). See United States v. Goldman, 453 F. Supp. 508 (CD Cal. 1978), aff'd, 637 F2d 664 (9th Cir. 1980) (summons for retained copies of tax returns not enforced). But see United States v. Berkowitz, 488 F2d 1235, 1236 (3d Cir. 1973), cert. denied, 421 US 946 (1975) (returns that preparer prepared "would not be readily available to the government since there is no method of retrieval," and to require Service to review all returns "is so obviously burdensome as to make the procedure prohibitive"); United States v. First Nat'l State Bank of NJ, 616 F2d 668 (3d Cir. 1980), modifying and aff'g 469 F. Supp. 612 (DNJ 1979); United States v. First Nat'l Bank of NJ, 616 F2d 668 (3d Cir.), cert. denied sub nom. Levey v. United States, 447 US 905 (1980) (retained copies of Forms 1099 producible despite Service possession of originals where retrieval difficult), followed in United States v. Kis, 658 F2d 526 (7th Cir. 1981), cert. denied, 455 US 1018 (1982); United States v. Security First Fed. Sav. & Loan, 83-1 USTC ¶ 9325 (MD Fla. 1983) (summons for Forms 1099 and Forms 4789 (Currency Transaction Report) already in possession of Service enforced); United States v. Linsteadt, 724 F2d 480 (5th Cir. 1984) ("[t]he 'already possessed' exception . . . to the enforcement of Internal Revenue summonses is narrowly construed"). In *Linsteadt*, the special agent testified that the Forms 1099 sought in the summons were not in retrievable form because they were not computerized for recording or search, nor was any cross-reference made to third-party forms submitted to the payees. See ¶ 8.04[3]. At least one circuit court refused to enforce a summons for retained Forms 1099. United States v. Bank of Cal., 652 F2d 780 (9th Cir. 1980) (summons for bank's retained Forms 1099 not enforced). For a case enforcing a special agent's summons for original records rather than the copies already in his possession, see United States v. Swain, 91-1 USTC ¶ 50,087 (DSC 1991) (gathering cases holding that actual possession or access by Service is not absolute bar to enforcement). For a case where a summons was not enforced, because documents were already in the posses-

be distinguished from a request to inspect records a second time during a single examination. Courts generally have enforced a summons in this situation.[340] The Fifth Circuit has construed the "already possessed" principle enunciated by *Powell* as a gloss on the prohibition of Section 7605(b) against unnecessary examinations, rather than as an absolute prohibition against the enforcement of any summons to the extent it requests production of documents already in the possession of the Service.[341] It has also said that the taxpayer must actually show that the Service possesses the information summoned, and not merely that it has already examined his records.[342]

¶ 13.09 FOURTH AMENDMENT CHALLENGES

The Fourth Amendment to the U.S. Constitution provides, "[t]he right of the people to be secure in their persons, houses, papers, and effects, against unreasonable searches and seizures, shall not be violated, and no warrants shall issue but upon probable cause, supported by oath or affirmation, and particularly describing the place to be searched, and the persons or things to be seized." An internal revenue summons is obviously not a search warrant, nor does a summons present a question of the validity of an actual search and seizure. No revenue official who issues a summons enters on the property of the summoned party against the person's will to search for and seize books, records, or papers without the person's consent. Enforcement of a summons is by way of court order after an opportunity to be heard. Therefore, a challenge to an internal revenue summons based on the Fourth Amendment and its strictures must take into account the reality that no actual search and seizure occurs on the issuance of the administrative order set forth in the summons. However, despite the absence of an actual search and seizure, Fourth Amendment principles do apply when the Service uses its investigative and summons authority. Application of these principles raises the following issues:

---

sion of the Service, see United States v. Moseley, 93-2 USTC ¶ 50,440 (WDNY 1993) (the Service received original records from the taxpayer, copied the records, returned the originals, and then asked for the same original documents)

[340] See, e.g., United States v. Chemical Bank, 593 F2d 451 (2d Cir. 1979); United States v. McGuirt, 588 F2d 419 (4th Cir. 1978), cert. denied, 444 US 827 (1979).

[341] United States v. Texas Heart Inst., 755 F2d 469 (5th Cir. 1985). See also Wright v. United States, 85-2 USTC ¶ 9707 (WD Tex. 1985) (already-possessed principle narrowly construed).

[342] Compare United States v. Pritchard, 438 F2d 969 (5th Cir. 1971) (court found that information sought by the summons was already within the Commissioner's possession; summons was not enforced).

- Whether the taxpayer has standing to raise the Fourth Amendment claim;
- Whether the scope of the summons is so broad, indefinite, or burdensome as to constitute an unreasonable search or invasion of privacy;
- Whether papers sought by the summons are protected as coming within a taxpayer's "zone of privacy";
- Whether the person who claims the protection of the Fourth Amendment has consented to the search; and
- Whether the evidence obtained in violation of the taxpayer's Fourth Amendment claims should be suppressed under the application of the exclusionary rule.

These issues are discussed in the following sections.

[1] The Standing Problem

Only the victim of conduct improper under the Fourth Amendment has standing to challenge such conduct by seeking suppression of the evidence obtained under the exclusionary rule.[343] In short, *A* has no standing to challenge government conduct that may violate the constitutional rights of *B*. The law regarding standing to raise Fourth Amendment challenges has become complex. Analysis is also made difficult because some cases are resolved on the ground that the person or interest in question is or is not entitled to constitutional protection. For purposes of discussion in this section, standing situations can be divided into the following categories: (1) where the person has an interest in the premises searched; (2) where the person owns or has a right to possession of the property seized; and (3) where the person has a reasonable expectation of privacy.

Generally, a person who has an interest in premises searched has standing to challenge an illegal search and seizure.[344] Because of the summons authority, tax investigations usually do not involve entry into premises without a search warrant to search for and seize evidence. Nevertheless, where revenue officers entered the business premises of a corporation and seized records, the corporation had standing to challenge the seizure.[345] However, suppose a taxpayer keeps his records in a bank safe-deposit box. Does he have standing to

---

[343] United States v. Payner, 444 US 923 (1980); United States v. Miller, 425 US 435 (1976); California Bankers Ass'n v. Shultz, 416 US 21 (1974).

[344] Analysis of standing cases and Fourth Amendment cases in general is beyond the scope of this treatise. The focus here is on tax cases and specifically on cases arising in the context of an investigation authorized under Section 7602. For a more general discussion of the Fourth Amendment, see, e.g., McCormick on Evidence (3d ed. 1984); Kamisar, LaFave & Israel, Basic Criminal Procedure (6th Ed. 1974).

[345] GM Leasing Corp. v. United States, 429 US 338 (1977).

raise Fourth Amendment challenges to seizure of those records? Banks usually consider a customer to be a lessee of the box. Despite this status, in *United States v. First National City Bank*,[346] a taxpayer raising Fourth Amendment claims was denied intervention in a proceeding by the Service to enforce levies and to gain access to the box and records. Although the court held that the taxpayer had no right to intervene in the proceeding, it indicated that the taxpayer had some interest in or expectation of privacy with respect to the records for Fourth Amendment purposes.

The assertion of ownership rights in property (e.g., records) seized by the Service gives a taxpayer standing to contest the seizure.[347] A taxpayer who owns records has standing to contest their seizure even if the taxpayer transfers them to a third person for an extended period of time. However, the owner's surrender of possession of property evidences absence of a reasonable expectation of privacy that is fatal to a successful challenge on Fourth Amendment grounds.[348] Similarly, if the taxpayer is the possessor but not the owner of the papers or property sought by the summons, the taxpayer has standing to assert his Fourth Amendment rights, but the challenge will not be upheld.[349] Where the taxpayer is neither the owner nor the possessor of the records sought by the summons, the taxpayer lacks standing to challenge a summons on Fourth Amendment grounds.[350]

A reasonable expectation of privacy in records gives the taxpayer standing to raise Fourth Amendment claims, but standing to raise a challenge does not ensure it will be granted.[351] An expectation of privacy does not exist where

---

[346] United States v. First Nat'l City Bank, 568 F2d 853 (2d Cir. 1977).

[347] See Couch v. United States, 409 US 322 (1973); United States v. First Nat'l City Bank, 568 F2d 853 (2d Cir. 1977). Compare Donaldson v. United States, 400 US 517 (1971) (taxpayer who did not own records of his employer or have a privilege-type interest in them could not move to suppress evidence from them if they were turned over voluntarily to Service).

[348] Couch v. United States, 409 US 322 (1973).

[349] Fisher v. United States, 425 US 391 (1976) (taxpayer constructively possessed workpapers owned by accountants). See Dixon v. Comm'r, 90 TC 237 (1988) (taxpayers, who did not contend that their Fourth Amendment rights were violated, did not have standing to suppress otherwise admissible evidence on the ground that it was unlawfully seized from a third party not before the court).

[350] United States v. Miller, 425 US 435 (1976); California Bankers Ass'n v. Shultz, 416 US 21 (1974); Donaldson v. United States, 400 US 517, 530 (1971) (taxpayer neither owned nor possessed bank records of employer). The reasoning in *Miller* applies to the records of other third persons doing business with the taxpayer. See, e.g., Mauroni v. United States, 84-2 USTC ¶ 9705 (ND Cal. 1984) (title companies).

[351] Fisher v. United States, 425 US 391 (1976) (taxpayer had standing but claim rejected); United States v. First Nat'l City Bank, 568 F2d 853 (2d Cir. 1977).

the records are of commercial transactions betwee the third person and the tax-payer that the third person is likely to keep.[352]

[2] Reasonableness and Breadth

An investigation that the Service conducts under Section 7602 must meet standards of reasonableness deriving from the Fourth Amendment. Although it is not a search warrant, an administrative summons must contain a "specification of the documents to be produced adequate, but not excessive, for the purpose of the relevant inquiry."[353] Any administrative summons that is indefinite or broad may be so onerous as to constitute an unreasonable search.[354] This reasoning also applies to an internal revenue summons,[355] but the burden of the request is considered more of a factor where the summons is directed at a third party rather than at the taxpayer.[356] Fourth Amendment principles of specificity and reasonableness merge into the determination that data sought by a sum-

---

[352] United States v. Miller, 425 US 435 (1976) (bank records). A taxpayer has been held not to have standing to object to a third party's production of records of transactions between it and the taxpayer even where the identity of the third party was allegedly obtained by deceit. United States v. Manufacturers Hanover Trust Co., 485 F. Supp. 653 (SDNY 1979).

[353] Oklahoma Press Publishing Co. v. Walling, 327 US 186, 209 (1946).

[354] Oklahoma Press Publishing Co. v. Walling, 327 US 186, 209 (1946); McMann v. SEC, 87 F2d 377, 379 (2d Cir. 1937), cert. denied, 301 US 684 (1937).

[355] Hubner v. Tucker, 245 F2d 35, 38 (9th Cir. 1957). For a summons struck down as unreasonably broad, see Local 174, Int'l Bhd. of Teamsters v. United States, 240 F2d 387 (9th Cir. 1956). However, it is said that although a summons may be broad, it need not be overbroad, and the mere fact that a summons requests extensive records and documents does not render it overbroad. United States v. Giordano, 301 F. Supp. 884 (ED Mo.), aff'd, 419 F2d 564 (8th Cir. 1969), cert. denied, 397 US 1037 (1970). See also United States v. Michaud, 897 F2d 264 (7th Cir. 1990) (Michaud I) (summons directing taxpayers to be fingerprinted at a local police station could not be quashed because it was "heavy-handed"), reh'g en banc United States v. Michaud, 907 F2d 750 (7th Cir. 1990) (Michaud II) (case remanded for further findings).

[356] Compare United States v. Harrington, 388 F2d 520, 524 (2d Cir. 1968) (requiring a "realistic expectation" rather than an idle hope that something may be discovered when a third-party summons is served); United States v. First Nat'l Bank of Mobile, 160 F2d 532 (5th Cir. 1968); Local 174, Int'l Bhd. of Teamsters v. United States, 240 F2d 387 (9th Cir. 1956); Venn v. United States, 400 F2d 207 (5th Cir. 1968); United States v. Luther, 481 F2d 429 (9th Cir. 1973); with United States v. Acker, 325 F. Supp. 857 (SDNY 1971) (no Fourth Amendment violation found although summons called for production of corporate minutes to determine relevancy). United States v. Moseley, 93-2 USTC ¶ 50,440 (WDNY 1993) ("The mere fact that the IRS summons requests general correspondence and administrative files does not make it vague and overbroad so long as the request is limited to the tax liability of Moseley").

mons are not "relevant," and the line between the constitutional and administrative law concepts is not distinguished with ease.[357]

[3] Protected Persons and Interests

Fourth Amendment guarantees apply to artificial as well as natural persons, unlike Fifth Amendment protections.[358] A warrantless search may not constitutionally be made on private premises, even business premises, whether they belong to corporations or individuals, to enforce tax laws applicable to taxpayers in general.[359] Consequently, a warrantless entry by revenue officers into the business premises of a corporation was in violation of the corporation's Fourth Amendment rights.[360] However, if a business voluntarily engages in a highly regulated activity, such as the sale of firearms or liquor, warrantless searches are permissible.[361] This principle has been used in tax-related cases. For example, the Bank Secrecy Act of 1970 imposed domestic reporting requirements upon financial institutions to report currency transactions in excess of $10,000 voluntarily entered into between banks and their customers. These requirements were held not to constitute either an unreasonable search or a seizure of bank records.[362]

It is established that protection under the Fourth Amendment has more to do with reasonable and legitimate expectations of privacy than with property concepts.[363] In summons cases, a taxpayer has no legitimate expectation of pri-

---

[357] However, it is significant that the *Harrington* line of cases, which reflect judicial sensitivity to the burden imposed on third parties when a summons is served, was relied upon in the *Coopers & Lybrand* decision, holding that accountants' tax accrual files and audit programs were not sufficiently relevant to warrant production in an audit of the client-taxpayer's return. The Service's use of a summons to examine accounting workpapers is discussed supra ¶ 13.07[2]. See United States v. Wyatt, 637 F2d 293 (5th Cir. 1981) (distinguishing between concepts of overbreadth and relevance in enforcing a summons calling for answers to the eleven questions). But see United States v. Richards, 613 F2d 341 (4th Cir. 1980) (indicating summons exceeding "relevant scope of the summons power" would not be enforced). See supra ¶ 13.07[1].

[358] GM Leasing Corp. v. United States, 429 US 338 (1977); Oklahoma Press Publishing Co. v. Walling, 327 US 186, 205–206 (1946); Go-Bart Importing Co. v. United States, 282 US 344 (1931). See United States v. City of Seattle, 387 US 541 (1967).

[359] GM Leasing Corp. v. United States, 429 US 338 (1977).

[360] GM Leasing Corp. v. United States, 429 US 338 (1977).

[361] United States v. Biswell, 406 US 311 (1972) (enforcement of Gun Control Act); Colonnade Catering Corp. v. United States, 397 US 72 (1970) (liquor regulation).

[362] California Bankers Ass'n v. Shultz, 416 US 21 (1974); United States v. First Nat'l City Bank, 568 F2d 853 (2d Cir. 1977) (court in dicta distinguished a seizure of bank and personal records stored in a bank safe-deposit box).

[363] Katz v. United States, 389 US 347 (1967).

vacy in records that he neither owns nor possesses.[364] The Fourth Amendment also does not protect a taxpayer's own books and records delivered to the keeping of an accountant where the accountant is expected to make the contents of the records known to the Service by way of the filing and audit of a tax return.[365] In Fourth Amendment terms, there is no expectation of privacy where books and records, even those owned by the taxpayer, are delivered to an accountant to prepare the taxpayer's return. Return preparation, by its nature, contemplates the making of a disclosure, and there is no accountant-client privilege recognized in federal law upon which a taxpayer may rely in expecting confidentiality. Moreover, a taxpayer does not have a legitimate expectation of privacy in communications to an accountant reflected in the accountant's replies to the taxpayer's letters or in workpapers.[366]

On the other hand, where a taxpayer transfers his own books and records to a lawyer for the purpose of obtaining legal assistance, the attorney-client privilege recognized in federal law creates an expectation of privacy. Therefore, a summons served on the lawyer may be challenged under a combination of the Fourth Amendment and the attorney-client privilege.[367] The success of this Fourth Amendment/attorney-client privilege claim in a summons enforcement proceeding depends on the applicability of the attorney-client privilege to the records, writings, or other communications sought to be protected. A taxpayer does not increase protection of records by transferring them to a lawyer. If the client would not be protected from producing the record, writing, or other communication, the attorney-client privilege does not apply and neither, therefore, does any Fourth Amendment privilege. Thus, the Fourth Amendment's protection and attorney-client privilege are coextensive. Where the privilege does not apply, the Fourth Amendment protection is unavailable.

This analysis was applied by the Supreme Court in *Fisher v. United States*, and, presumably, this analysis is to be followed where evidentiary privileges other than the attorney-client privilege are involved. In *Fisher*, the Supreme Court concluded that an accountant's workpapers were preexisting documents that could have been obtained by court process from the client and, thus, from his lawyer as well.[368] Some records (e.g., a diary) may be inherently private for Fourth Amendment purposes. In *Fisher*, the Supreme Court left this

---

[364] United States v. Miller, 425 US 435 (1976) (bank's records); California Bankers Ass'n v. Shultz, 416 US 21 (1974) (bank's records); Donaldson v. United States, 400 US 517 (1971) (employer's records).

[365] Couch v. United States, 409 US 322 (1973).

[366] United States v. Beattie, 522 F2d 267 (2d Cir. 1975), vacated and remanded, 425 US 967 (1975); Fisher v. United States, 425 US 391 (1976).

[367] Fisher v. United States, 425 US 391 (1976).

[368] The privilege only protects disclosures that might not have been made absent the privilege. This principle places preexisting documents outside the scope of the privilege.

question open, but there appears to be no record so personal that it may not be seized by a valid search warrant.[369]

The limitations of the Fourth Amendment have been dramatically revealed where a taxpayer has attempted to secure the return of books and records stolen from him by an employee or other person and turned over to the Service, and to have the evidence suppressed. As long as the Service has not been involved in the theft by its knowledge or complicity, it has been permitted to use the records because the taxpayer is constitutionally protected only from government searches and seizures.[370]

[4] The "Consent" Problem

A warrantless search of a person's premises and papers may constitutionally be made if there is a valid consent to the search. In Fourth Amendment cases, a "voluntary" consent to a search and the "seizure" of evidence in the course of that search may constitute a waiver of the person's constitutional rights under the amendment.[371] Thus, the determination of what is a "voluntary" and, therefore, valid consent to a search is a question of fact to be determined from all the circumstances. In tax investigations, the "consent" problem can arise where a revenue agent purportedly conducting a civil audit actually obtains evidence for use in a criminal tax prosecution[372] and the taxpayer contends that no "consent" was given to the search for and seizure of the evidence the revenue agent

---

[369] United States v. Bennett, 409 F2d 888 (2d Cir. 1969), cert. denied, 415 US 1113 (1969) (diary). See also Andresen v. Maryland, 427 US 463 (1976) (business records of individual).

[370] Meister v. Comm'r, 504 F2d 505 (3d Cir. 1974), cert. denied, 421 US 964 (1975); Resmondo v. United States, 536 F. Supp. 19 (SD Fla. 1981). Where an employee repeatedly copied records of an employer and gave them to a special agent, a later summons for records was nevertheless enforced. See United States v. Feffer, 85-2 USTC ¶ 9644 (WD Wis. 1984).

[371] Schneckcloth v. Bustamonte, 412 US 218 (1973).

[372] The consent problem can also arise where the Service engages in an undercover operation. In Jones v. Berry, 524 F. Supp. 645 (D. Ariz. 1981), under the Service's Business Opportunities Project (BOP), a special agent posed as a prospective purchaser of a business to learn if skimming was taking place, and obtained information for the purpose of obtaining a search warrant. The district court held that the operation constituted an illegal search that was warrantless as well as deceptive. Thus, the information gathered could not be used to support a search warrant. The court also ordered all seized records returned and the evidence gathered suppressed. The Ninth Circuit reversed, finding no Fourth Amendment violation. Jones v. Berry, 722 F2d 443 (1983), cert. denied, 466 US 971 (1984). See also United States v. Security Bank of Nev., 82-2 USTC ¶ 9588 (D. Nev. 1982) (BOP project summonses directed to bank and accountant's records rather than those of taxpayers enforced over Fourth Amendment objection). For other BOP cases following Jones v. Berry, see United States v. Centennial Builders, Inc., 747 F2d 678 (11th Cir. 1984); Hiller & Dawen, Inc. v. United States, 600 F. Supp. 14 (ND Ga. 1984).

obtained. A distinction is drawn between a discovery of wrongdoing in the course of a routine investigation and a failure on the part of an agent (usually a revenue agent) to disclose the purpose of his investigation at its inception where suspicion of wrongdoing exists.

A consent search is unreasonable under the Fourth Amendment if the consent was induced by deceit, treachery, or misrepresentation of an internal revenue agent.[373] However, to establish the existence of fraud, the taxpayer must present evidence showing some affirmative misrepresentation.[374] Silence is only equated with fraud where there is a duty to speak or where silence would be intentionally misleading.[375] Where a revenue agent initiates an investigation for the purpose of obtaining evidence to use against a taxpayer already suspected of criminal acts, or works on the instructions of a special agent who is behind the scene, the fraud and deceit perpetrated on the taxpayer vitiates a valid consent.[376]

Similarly, where the revenue agent represents that the information will be used for civil, not criminal, purposes, the taxpayer's consent to an examination or search has been held invalid and any evidence obtained has been suppressed.[377] As the circuit court in *Grunewald* ruled, the Service "may not de-

---

[373] United States v. Tweel, 550 F2d 297 (5th Cir. 1977); United States v. Prudden, 424 F2d 1021 (5th Cir.), cert. denied, 400 US 831 (1970); United States v. Sclafani, 265 F2d 408 (2d Cir.), cert. denied, 360 US 918 (1959).

[374] United States v. Prudden, 424 F2d 1021 (5th Cir.), cert. denied, 400 US 831 (1970); United States v. Sclafani, 265 F2d 408 (2d Cir.), cert. denied, 360 US 918 (1959). See also United States v. Matis, 476 F. Supp. 1287 (SDNY 1979) (revenue agent obtained agreement to additional income tax but group manager refused to approve it and referred the case for criminal investigation; held, revenue agent did not deceive).

[375] United States v. Prudden, 424 F2d 1021 (5th Cir.), cert. denied, 400 US 831 (1970). See also United States v. Tonahill, 430 F2d 1042 (5th Cir.), cert. denied, 400 US 943 (1970). It has been contended that the Manual provisions on fraud referrals create some obligation on the part of the revenue agent, but courts have generally said that the Manual is not for the protection of taxpayers. See, e.g., United States v. Lockyer, 448 F2d 417 (10th Cir. 1971); United States v. Mapp, 561 F2d 685 (7th Cir. 1977); United States v. Matis, 476 F. Supp. 1287 (SDNY 1979). But see United States v. Toussaint, 456 F. Supp. 1069 (SD Tex. 1978).

[376] United States v. Wheeler, 149 F. Supp. 445 (WD Pa. 1957), vacated and remanded on other grounds, 256 F2d 745 (3d Cir.), cert. denied, 358 US 873 (1958). In re Bodkin, 165 F. Supp. 25 (EDNY 1958), appeal vacated as moot, 266 F2d 55 (2d Cir. 1959). But see United States v. Esser, 520 F2d 213 (7th Cir. 1975), cert. denied, 426 US 947 (1976) (revenue agent asked list of questions supplied by the special agent concerning discrepancy between bank deposits and return; held, no Fourth or Fifth Amendment violation because no unreasonable delay in referral and no collusion).

[377] United States v. Tweel, 550 F2d 297 (5th Cir. 1977) (revenue agent assigned to Organized Crime Drive); United States v. Guerrina, 112 F. Supp. 126 (ED Pa. 1953), modified, 126 F. Supp. 609 (ED Pa. 1955). But compare United States v. Cleveland Trust Co., 474 F2d 1234 (6th Cir. 1973), cert. denied sub nom. Miceli v. United States, 414 US 866 (1973) (enforcing a revenue agent summons although agent assigned to Organized

velop a criminal investigation under the auspices of a civil audit."[378] Under the Manual, the revenue agent who detects a "firm indication" fraud is required to suspend the audit and refer the case for evaluation to CID.[379] To determine whether the Service has acted deceptively, and that evidence the revenue agent obtained should be suppressed in a later prosecution, the *Grunewald* court adopted a three-part test, which requires the taxpayer defendant to prove that (1) the Service had "firm indications" of the taxpayer's fraud; (2) there is clear, convincing evidence that the Service affirmatively and intentionally misled the taxpayer defendant; and (3) the Service's conduct resulted in prejudice to the taxpayer defendant's constitutional rights.[380] However, it is also said that

---

Crime Drive "Strike Force"); United States v. Chemical Bank, 593 F2d 451 (2d Cir. 1979). For other cases where Strike Force-related summonses were enforced, see United States v. Nuth, 605 F2d 229 (6th Cir. 1979); United States v. Ryan, 485 F. Supp. 1285 (SDNY 1980).

[378] United States v. Grunewald, 987 F2d 531, 534 (8th Cir. 1993).

[379] See the description of the Service's procedures when a revenue agent suspects fraud during the course of a civil examination at ¶ 8.06[7].

[380] See United States v. Grunewald, 987 F2d 531 (8th Cir. 1993); see United States v. Wadena, 82 AFTR2d 98-6049 (8th Cir. 1998), applying the *Grunewald* test, and finding that the defendants had failed to prove the factors by clear and convincing evidence. See also United States v. Peters, 82 AFTR2d 98-5719 (7th Cir. 1998). In determining whether a consensual search is unreasonable under the Fourth Amendment and the Fifth Amendment's due process clause because it was induced by fraud, deceit, trickery, or misrepresentation, the Seventh Circuit uses a standard similar to the *Grunewald* standard. To prevail, the taxpayer defendant must produce clear and convincing evidence that the agents affirmatively misled him as to the true nature of their investigation, and that the misinformation was material to his decision. United States v. Serlin, 707 F2d 953, 956 (7th Cir. 1983).

However, the Seventh Circuit approved the approach of the district court and other courts, including the Eighth Circuit, that in evaluating whether affirmative misleading took place, if there was clear and convincing evidence that a revenue agent continued to audit the taxpayer defendant after the revenue agent had "a firm indication of fraud," the revenue agent would be found to have engaged in a "covert criminal investigation." *United States v. Peters*, supra. The circuit said that the "firm indication of fraud" standard was difficult to apply because "it is inherently vague and depends in large part on the good faith and professional judgment of agents conducting the investigation." Despite the difficulty in applying the standard, the "firm indication of fraud" standard is a "tool for courts to utilize in determining whether revenue agents made an affirmative misrepresentation to a defendant or her representative concerning the nature of their investigation." Id. In applying the standard, the circuit court pointed to other cases where courts had found impermissible deception, for example, if the agent is conducting an audit at the behest of the criminal enforcement agency conducting a criminal investigation; CID personnel have an active involvement in the civil audit before the criminal referral has been completed; continuation of the audit after the revenue agent begins preparation of the fraud referral; the agent has determined that the agent has found that the taxpayer "engaged in a consistent pattern of substantial underreporting and/or overstatement of deductions such that an intent to evade taxes can be inferred"; the revenue agent having discovered a potential violation of the tax laws, the revenue agent has interviewed the taxpayer, and the taxpayer's

when a routine tax audit has begun, the revenue agent may obtain evidence of misreporting without warning the taxpayer of the changing direction of the examination.[381] In this view, the statement that the purpose of an investigation is a routine audit is "not the equivalent of a promise that only civil liability will be considered regardless of what the examination reveals."[382] According to the court in *United States v. Sclafani*, the Fourth Amendment requires only that "when his consent is sought the taxpayer be apprised of the government's concern with the accuracy of his reports, and therefore of such hazards as may be

---

explanation is incredible in view of the taxpayer's knowledge of the tax law and business practices. On the other hand, a first indication of fraud is not a firm indication of fraud.

In Kontny v. United States, 238 F3d 815 (7th Cir. 2001), the Service began a civil examination of the taxpayers after receiving a tip from an employee. The agent assigned to the matter interviewed the taxpayers. The revenue agent explained to the taxpayers that he was investigating allegations that they had failed to withhold payroll taxes. One of the taxpayers asked whether she needed to have a lawyer present, to which the agent replied that it was "a civil exam," but that if he discovered fraud he would refer the matter for a criminal investigation. The taxpayers made inculpatory statements to the agent, and the agent referred the matter for a criminal investigation. The taxpayers were later indicted and convicted of fraudulent nonpayment of federal payroll taxes. On appeal, the circuit court held that the district court did not err in denying motion to suppress the statements the taxpayers/defendants had made to the agent. The circuit court found that *Miranda* was not implicated because the statements were voluntary. According to the court, the agent "was unarmed, un-uniformed, unaccompanied. The [defendants] were at no disadvantage in dealing with him. They were under no pressure to answer his questions." Furthermore, "even if [the agent] was pretending to be conducting a civil investigation but was really . . . conducting a criminal one, this would not, under the rules that govern the admissibility of incriminating statements (written and oral) made to government officers even by a suspect who is in custody, make the statements inadmissible." Id.

[381] United States v. Sclafani, 265 F2d 408 (2d Cir.), cert. denied, 360 US 918 (1959). But see United States v. Toussaint, 456 F. Supp. 1069 (SD Tex. 1978) (statement taxpayer made to revenue agent after the agent had firm indications of fraud suppressed). In United States v. Powell, 835 F2d 1095 (5th Cir. 1988), the taxpayer, who was convicted of willfully attempting to evade income taxes under Section 7201, sought to suppress the evidence on the ground that it was obtained through the fraud, trickery, and deceit of Service agents, and in violation of the Manual. The court found that a revenue agent did not mislead the taxpayer and had no duty to inform him that her investigation might result in criminal charges. In addition, the Service agent did not violate the provisions of the Manual by failing to file a fraud referral report with the Criminal Investigation Division when she first considered referring the case. There was sufficient evidence in the record that the agent and her manager did not believe that enough evidence of fraud existed to refer the case until the time when the fraud report was actually filed. "The mere failure of an IRS agent to inform the defendant that information developed in an audit may result in a further criminal investigation does not indicate affirmative and intentional deceit by the IRS." United States v. Grunewald, 987 F2d 531, 534 (8th Cir. 1993).

[382] United States v. Sclafani, 265 F2d 408 (2d Cir.), cert. denied, 360 US 918 (1959). United States v. Prudden, 424 F2d 1021 (5th Cir.), cert. denied, 400 US 831 (1970); United States v. Wolrich, 119 F. Supp. 538, 540 (SDNY 1954).

incident to a voluntary disclosure."[383] Nevertheless, agents may not obscure the warning inherent in the request to search, through an examination of the returns, by assuring the taxpayer that no proceeding against him will occur.[384]

In summary, a taxpayer validly consents to a search of his papers for Fourth Amendment purposes when he voluntarily permits the agent to examine his returns, provided the agent has not begun or continued the investigation for the purpose of gathering evidence of criminal wrongdoing already suspected, or has not misrepresented the use to which any findings may be put.

Although a taxpayer may consent to a search and seizure of his personal papers, the consent may be limited or withdrawn. If a search exceeds the scope of the actual consent given, the portion of the search not covered by the consent is considered unreasonable.[385] Where the basis for the search is a consent, the taxpayer may withdraw his consent and obtain the records being held, but he may not obtain copies of the records made prior to the demand for the records.[386]

[5] Obtaining Information Without the Use of a Summons

The Service typically uses its broad summons authority to obtain information from and about taxpayers. However, the summons is not the only method it uses; it also employs search warrants, grand juries, wiretaps, and mail covers. From time to time, the Service tries new information-gathering devices that sometimes present Fourth Amendment problems.

---

[383] United States v. Sclafani, 265 F2d 408, 415 (2d Cir.), cert. denied, 360 US 918 (1959).

[384] United States v. Sclafani, 265 F2d 408, 415 (2d Cir.), cert. denied, 360 US 918 (1959); United States v. Guerrina, 112 F. Supp. 126 (ED Pa. 1953), modified, 126 F. Supp. 609 (ED Pa. 1955).

[385] United States v. Dichiarinte, 445 F2d 126 (7th Cir. 1971) (consent to search for narcotics but search extended to papers; held, any item in papers inadmissible). See United States v. Miller, 491 F2d 638, 650 (5th Cir.), cert. denied, 419 US 970 (1974).

[386] Mason v. Pulliam, 557 F2d 426 (5th Cir. 1977) (agent asked taxpayer whether he could remove and copy records; taxpayer withdrew consent one week later). Accord United States v. Ward, 576 F2d 243 (9th Cir. 1978). Laviage v. Lyons, 93-1 USTC ¶ 50,292 (SD Tex. 1993) (consent withdrawn; special agent ordered to return original books and copies). Once the taxpayer withdraws his consent, the Service has no right to examine or photocopy his documents, and if the Service wants to examine or use the documents further, it must file a summons enforcement proceeding.In these cases, the withdrawal of consent was grounded in a claim for protection of constitutional rights. Where the demand for return is not made on constitutional grounds, retention does not make continued examination an unreasonable search. United States v. Ponder, 444 F2d 816 (5th Cir. 1971), cert. denied, 405 US 918 (1972) (demand for business reasons).

[a] Court Intervention

In *United States v. Mobil Corp.*, the Service sought a permanent mandatory injunction requiring Mobil to make certain records available to it.[387] The records the Service wanted were magnetic tapes containing data (e.g., income, sick pay, exemptions claimed) regarding employees whose payroll records were processed by computer. The Service contended that Mobil was required to keep these records by the general recordkeeping statute, Section 6001. The district court found that Mobil would be required to generate new records to supply this information and held that it was not obligated by Section 6001 to do so.[388] Initially, the district court indicated that the Service might obtain its mandatory injunction if only records falling within Section 6001 existed. However, in a later case, the district court was faced squarely with a Service demand for documents kept under Section 6001. It reached the conclusion on "the more basic question" that the summons procedures of Sections 7602 through 7610 constituted "the exclusive enforcing mechanism for IRS inspection of documents required to be kept by Section 6001." Apart from an interpretation of the statutory provisions and their legislative history, the Service contention, according to the court, raised "serious" constitutional issues under the Fourth Amendment.[389]

[b] Undercover Operations

An undercover operation is a technique used by the Service in such investigations as those of return preparers and tax shelter promoters.[390] In an undercover operation, a Service employee assumes another identity to secure information or evidence for an ongoing criminal tax investigation.[391] Statutory authority for criminal investigation undercover operations is found in Section

---

[387] United States v. Mobil Corp., 499 F. Supp. 479 (ND Tex. 1980); United States v. Mobil Corp., 543 F. Supp. 1420 (ND Tex. 1981) (injunction denied).

[388] The district court also questioned whether Mobil could be required to produce records about the tax liability of its employees rather than of Mobil itself under Section 6001.

[389] In arriving at this interpretation of Section 6001, the district court expressly rejected United States v. Ohio Bell Tel. Co., 475 F. Supp. 697 (ND Ohio 1978), the only case authorizing Service discovery under Section 6001.

[390] IRC § 7608(c)(4)(B), as amended by the Taxpayer Bill of Rights 2, § 1205(c), effective on the enactment date of the Act, July 30, 1996.

[391] IRM 9.4.8.1, Undercover Operations—Overview (April 2, 2002). The Manual says that undercover techniques can be used in the investigation of unscrupulous return preparers and tax shelter promoters, and in the BOP, and describes undercover operations as a "lawful and essential technique in the detection of tax frauds, political corruption, organized crime, money laundering, narcotics trafficking, questionable preparers, and other priority areas related to crimes." Id. Recognizing that undercover operations can be "controversial and potentially dangerous undertakings," the Manual says that they will be used

7608(c), which permits Service appropriations to be used in commercial activities engaged in by criminal investigators as part of undercover operations, but requires high-level certification (the Commissioner, Deputy Commissioner, or Assistant Commissioner) of the operation. In addition, the Service must submit an annual report of undercover operations to Congress reporting the number of operations, the number of programs using undercover operations, the number of operations closed, and for each operation, the date of the operation and required high-level certification, the expenditures for and proceeds from the operation, how the proceeds were used, a detailed description of the potential violation investigated, whether the operation was or is being conducted under grand jury auspices, and the results of the operation and any related criminal proceedings. Section 7608(c) uses the term "undercover investigative operation" as opposed to undercover operation, but the term means generally and undercover investigative operation of the Service. National Office approval for undercover operations of substantial duration or having sensitive characteristics, such as an investigation of a public official, a political candidate, the activities of a foreign government, the activities of a religious or political organization, or the activities of the news media.[392] Other less-sensitive operations require approval at the regional commissioner level.[393]

---

only after "judicious decision-making." IRM 9.4.8.2, General Information (April 25, 2002).

    To ensure that undercover operations are fully authorized, CID distinguishes between surveillance, for which experienced special agents do not require even group manager authorization, and undercover operations, for which high-level approval is required. IRM 9383.11, MT 9-378 (Aug. 17, 1992). See IRM 9.4.6, Surveillance and Non-Consensual Monitoring (July 16, 2002), and IRM 9.4.8.1, Undercover Operations—Overview (April 25, 2002). Surveillance has the purpose of observing ongoing activities and individuals, where interaction with the subject and third party is not initiated. When interaction does occur, it is limited to three telephone communications for the purpose of verifying the allegations of illegal activities, and approval by the Special Agent in Charge is required. Conversations with the subject are incidental and not recorded. The special agent has limited cover, is usually from the local office, and is not specially trained. In an undercover operation, the purpose is to initiate or participate in activities and to have interaction with identified targets. The undercover agent will initiate and direct conversations to further the objectives of the operation, which may be recorded; and the undercover agent will normally have a documented cover, be trained in undercover operations, and will not usually be from the local district office.

    [392] IRM 9.4.8.3, Classification of Undercover Operations (April 25, 2002); IRM 9.4.8.3, Group 1 Undercover Operations (April 25, 2002). The Assistant Commissioner (Criminal Investigation) must approve all Group 1 undercover operations. Other sensitive factors that require National Office approval show why this investigative technique is so controversial. These factors include damaging falsehoods about an innocent third person; attending meetings covered by the attorney-client privilege; and posing as an attorney, physician, clergyman, or member of the news media. Id.

    [393] IRM 9.4.8.3.2, Group II Undercover Operations (April 25, 2002). Approval is required from the Director of Field Operations.

An early case involving an undercover operation illustrates the issues presented by this tactic, as well as the judicial response. To uncover evidence of skimming receipts not reported on returns, the Service developed an undercover operation where a special agent posed as a prospective purchaser. The objective was to secure information to support a search warrant. Initially, this device was held to violate the Fourth Amendment. However, on appeal, the agent's action in posing as a prospective purchaser was held not to have violated the taxpayer's Fourth Amendment rights, even though the taxpayer was induced to reveal incriminating information by the agent's disguise.[394] The circuit court applied the so-called misplaced confidence doctrine, holding that the Fourth Amendment affords no protection to a wrongdoer's misplaced belief that a person to whom he voluntarily confides his wrongdoing will not reveal it.

[6] Remedies for Fourth Amendment Violations

[a] Suppression Under the Exclusionary Rule

The exclusionary rule is a remedy for enforcing rights and privileges guaranteed by the Constitution. Under this rule, evidence is inadmissible in a criminal trial if obtained in violation of constitutional rights and privileges. This rule has traditionally been applied to violations of the Fifth Amendment privilege against self-incrimination, since that provision specifically prohibits the use of "compelled" testimony in a criminal case.[395] However, the exclusionary rule also applies to searches and seizures that violate the Fourth Amendment, whether the evidence to be used in a criminal prosecution was

---

[394] Jones v. Berry, 524 F. Supp. 645 (D. Ariz. 1981), rev'd, 722 F2d 443 (9th Cir. 1983). In *Jones*, the circuit court said that its "conclusion that there had been no fourth amendment violation should not be misconstrued as approval of the tactics employed by the IRS agents." The Service agents had failed to obtain National Office approval until after the investigation began. Also, the circuit court was concerned about the effect of undercover operations, saying, "[d]emocratic governments are based on a relationship of trust between government and the governed." 722 F2d at 448. See also United States v. Security Bank of Nev., 82-2 USTC ¶ 9588 (D. Nev. 1982) (BOP summons to taxpayer's bank and accountant enforced over Fourth Amendment claim). For a post-*Jones* approval of undercover operations, see United States v. Little, 753 F2d 1420 (9th Cir. 1984) (undercover operations do not exceed Service authority; agent's denial that he was with the Service not misconduct because undercover agent is under no duty to respond truthfully). See also United States v. Centennial Builders, Inc., 747 F2d 678 (11th Cir. 1984); Hiller & Dawen, Inc. v. United States, 600 F. Supp. 14 (ND Ga. 1984). United States v. Kellogg, 955 F2d 1244 (9th Cir. 1992) (special agent posed as client seeking return preparation services).

[395] Boyd v. United States, 116 US 616 (1886); Miranda v. Arizona, 384 US 436 (1966).

obtained by federal officers for use in a federal court, by federal officers for use in a state court, by state officers for use in a federal court, or by state officers for use in a state court.[396] Furthermore, the exclusionary rule may not be avoided by the indirect use of illegally obtained evidence. Any evidence obtained as a direct result of a lead from an illegal search, wiretap, or other improper governmental activity is excluded under the "fruit of the poisonous tree" doctrine.[397] Similarly, where evidence is obtained in violation of certain federal statutes, such as those dealing with wiretapping, the evidence illegally obtained has been excluded.[398] On the other hand, evidence obtained by foreign police officers in violation of Fourth Amendment standards is admissible in U.S. courts unless the method of obtaining such evidence shocks the conscience of the court.[399]

These general exclusionary rule principles apply in tax prosecutions. Where incriminating, compelled testimony is obtained in violation of a taxpayer's Fifth Amendment privilege, the evidence is inadmissible in a criminal tax prosecution.[400] Evidence obtained by internal revenue agents in violation of a taxpayer's Fourth Amendment rights is also not admissible in a criminal

---

[396] Weeks v. United States, 232 US 383 (1914) (federal officers, federal court); Reg v. United States, 350 US 214 (1956) (federal officers, state court); Elkins v. United States, 364 US 206 (1960) (state officers, federal court); Mapp v. Ohio, 367 US 643 (1961) (state officers, state court).

[397] Silverthorne Lumber Co. v. United States, 251 US 385 (1920); Wong Sun v. United States, 371 US 471 (1963); Brown v. Illinois, 422 US 590 (1975).

[398] Federal Communications Act of 1934, 47 USC § 605, 18 USC § 2510; Nardone v. United States, 302 US 379 (1937) (state officer federal court); Lee v. Florida, 392 US 378 (1968) (federal officers, federal court); Benanti v. United States, 355 US 96 (1957) (state officer, federal court) Lee v. Florida, 392 US 378 (1968) (state officers, state court).

[399] United States v. Wolfish, 525 F2d 457 (2d Cir.), cert. denied, 423 US 1059 (1975).

[400] Mathis v. United States, 391 US 1 (1968) (in-custody statement obtained by revenue agents without Miranda warning held inadmissible although taxpayer in custody of state for nontax crimes). See also Marchetti v. United States, 390 US 39 (1968) (gambler's Fifth Amendment privilege prevented prosecution for failure to comply with gamblers' excise tax and reporting requirements); cf. Beckwith v. United States, 425 US 341 (1976) (incriminating statement made by taxpayer who was focus of criminal investigation but not in custodial or coercive circumstances). District courts also have jurisdiction to suppress evidence even before any civil or criminal proceeding under their so-called anomalous jurisdiction deriving from the inherent authority of the courts over their officers. This jurisdiction has been invoked and analyzed, especially in the Fifth Circuit. See United States v. Chapman, 559 F2d 402 (5th Cir. 1977); Mason v. Pulliam, 557 F2d 426 (5th Cir. 1977); Richey v. Smith, 515 F2d 1239 (5th Cir. 1975).

prosecution.[401] Similarly, where evidence has been obtained by an illegal wire-tap, the tainted evidence is inadmissible in a criminal tax prosecution.[402]

Principles have been developed in nontax cases to serve as guidelines in the application of the exclusionary rule in criminal tax prosecutions, but, un-like other criminal prosecutions, collection of a tax due and owing invariably follows (and sometimes proceeds along with) a criminal tax prosecution. As a result, there have been fewer guidelines available to courts and taxpayers in the application of the exclusionary rule in civil tax proceedings, and, not sur-prisingly, there has been greater uncertainty in the results in these cases. The intramural Supreme Court debate on the desirability of the exclusionary rule has also promoted uncertainty.[403]

The exclusionary rule applies to evidence illegally obtained by state offi-cials and made available on a "silver platter" to federal officials.[404] There is no distinction between intersovereign or intrasovereign violations of constitutional rights in criminal cases. The tainted evidence simply may not be admitted in criminal prosecutions. However, at least where an illegal search and seizure is involved, the rule is different in civil tax proceedings. Where internal revenue officials obtain evidence by way of an illegal search and seizure, the evidence has been held inadmissible for the purpose of supporting an assessment or a

---

[401] United States v. Tweel, 550 F2d 297 (5th Cir. 1977) (microfilm copies of records obtained by revenue agent assigned to audit taxpayer's returns at request of Justice Department's Organized Crime Drive; held, "sneaky deliberate deception" secured invalid consent to search and seizure); United States v. LeClair, 315 F. Supp. 853 (ED Wis. 1970); Goodman v. United States, 285 F. Supp. 245 (CD Cal. 1968); United States v. Young, 215 F. Supp. 202 (ED Mich. 1963); United States v. Lipshitz, 132 F. Supp. 519 (EDNY 1955). See also Riland v. Comm'r, 79 TC 185 (1982) (hearing ordered on allega-tion that Service used return preparer to gather information in violation of taxpayer's rights). Where the Service has acquired information through a Fourth Amendment viola-tion, a later summons has been denied enforcement. United States v. Deak-Perera, Inc., 566 F. Supp. 1398 (DDC 1983) ("[a]ssuming arguendo that a single IRS special agent possesses all the attributes of a grand jury . . . when he issues a subpoena [sic], and that it is, indeed, the spirit of the exclusionary rule which inhabits this Court's finding of an abuse of process in the agent's use of the subpoena here . . . to decline to enforce it will have the salutary effect of deterring calls for regulatory inspections to gain entre to an in-spectee's premises on less benign errands . . . "). But see Jones v. Comm'r, 97 TC 7 (1991) (revenue agent engaged in "inappropriate" and "reprehensible" conduct to mislead taxpayers; but evidence nevertheless was received by Tax Court, because there was no af-firmative deceit).

[402] Black v. United States, 385 US 26 (1966); United States v. Schipani, 44 FRD 461, (EDNY 1968), aff'd, 414 F2d 1262 (2d Cir. 1969), cert. denied, 397 US 922 (1970).

[403] See, e.g., the majority and dissenting opinions in Stone v. Powell, 428 US 465 (1976).

[404] Elkins v. United States, 364 US 206 (1960).

civil actio to collect a tax.[405] In *United States v. Janis*,[406] local police officers seized gambling paraphernalia under a search warrant that was invalid under developing constitutional principles relating to the specificity of allegations required to obtain a warrant. The evidence was suppressed at the state prosecution of the taxpayer but was communicated to the Service, which began a proceeding to collect additional tax from the taxpayer. The Supreme Court refused to exclude the evidence in the civil tax proceeding on the ground that the application of the exclusionary rule to the use of tainted evidence obtained by local police officers in federal civil tax proceedings would not deter future violations by the police. The Court drew the distinction between intersovereign violations and intrasovereign violations and limited the exclusionary rule in civil tax cases to intrasovereign violations (where internal revenue or other federal officials committed the constitutional violations).

In summary, in civil proceedings after *Janis*, the exclusionary rule only applies to intrasovereign violations, so that where state officials who engage in unconstitutional conduct make tainted evidence available to Service officials, the evidence may be used in a federal tax proceeding.[407] Finally, evidence ille-

---

[405] GM Leasing Corp. v. United States, 429 US 338 (1977); Pizzarello v. United States, 408 F2d 579 (2d Cir. 1969), cert. denied, 396 US 986 (1969). See Singleton v. Comm'r, 65 TC 1123 (1976) (airport search found to constitute a valid search). For a case where federal officers participated in a search by state officers having a state warrant, see Tirado v. Comm'r, 74 TC 14 (1980), aff'd, 689 F2d 307 (2d Cir. 1982) (evidence seized was within scope of the warrant). See also United States v. Stelten, 867 F2d 446 (9th Cir. 1989) (state search warrant held not to violate Fourth Amendment, although it authorized seizure of evidence of defendants' conspiracy to defraud).

[406] United States v. Janis, 428 US 433 (1976).

[407] The Tax Court has applied *Janis*, refusing to suppress evidence obtained by state police officers in violation of the taxpayer's Fourth Amendment rights. Guzzetta v. Comm'r, 78 TC 173 (1982). See also Black Forge, Inc. v. Comm'r, 78 TC 1004 (1982) (claim that Service participated in state search rejected; therefore, no intrasovereign violation). Even where a statutory violation has been considered to occur in the use of a summons, the evidence obtained can still be used for a civil case. Weiss v. Comm'r, 919 F2d 115 (9th Cir. 1990) (criminal case had been dismissed, thereby punishing illegal governmental action); Houser v. Comm'r, 96 TC 184 (1991) (no "federal participation" in state search, although Service agents counted currency, inventoried precious stones, and identified records later used in determining deficiencies).

The exclusionary rule is applied "where the deterrent effects are likely to outweigh the increased costs to the societal interest in law enforcement" and this determination in civil cases is made "by reference primarily to the nature of the proceedings." A second step in the analysis considers other factors, such as whether the proposed use of the unconstitutionally seized material is intersovereign or intrasovereign, whether the search and the secondary proceeding were initiated by the same agency, whether there was an explicit understanding between the two agencies or some statutory mandate for sharing resources, and the relationship between "the law enforcement responsibilities and expertise of the seizing officials and the type of proceeding at which the seized material is being offered." Wolf v. Comm'r, 13 F3d 189 (6th Cir. 1993) (evidence obtained from an allegedly illegal search by FBI agents held admissible in Tax Court proceedings because the "tax defi-

gally obtained by foreign government officials without the request of the United States has been held admissible at least in a civil tax proceeding, presumably because the method used (i.e., raid and seizure of documents and wiretapping) did not shock the conscience of the court.[408]

[b] Suppression Under the Supervisory Power and Related Doctrines

The supervisory power of a federal court over federal prosecution operates very much in the same way as the exclusionary rule. Evidence that is obtained by illegal conduct or by a bad faith hostility to a constitutional right is excluded. Like the exclusionary rule, exercise of the court's supervisory power serves to deter illegality and to protect the court's integrity.[409] Previously, it was thought that the supervisory power was exercisable where the taxpayer did not have standing for Fourth Amendment purposes to vindicate violation of the right because the victim of the unconstitutional conduct was a third person. However, in *United States v. Payner*, the Supreme Court ruled that "the supervisory power does not authorize a federal court to suppress otherwise admissible evidence on the ground that it was seized from a third party not before the Court."[410] In *Payner*, Service employees had engaged in illegal conduct to photocopy bank records in the possession of a Bahamian bank official while he was in the United States. Under the *Payner* ruling, the evidence obtained by the illegal conduct of Service personnel could be used in the prosecution of the

---

ciency proceedings are too remote from the 'zone of primary interest' of the narcotics agent who made the seizure to deter future violations"); see also Tirado v. Comm'r, 689 F2d 307 (2d Cir. 1982), cert. denied, 460 US 1014 (1983) (evidence seized by narcotics agent also permitted to be used in Tax Court case). See also Grimes v. Comm'r, 82 F3d 286 (9th Cir. 1996) (FBI illegally seized material from taxpayer's home, and when the Service served requests for admissions from the taxpayer in the Tax Court case that followed, he refused to answer on the ground that they were the product of the illegal search and asked the Tax Court to exclude evidence having no source independent of the search). In *Grimes*, the circuit court held that the intrasovereign use of illegally seized evidence in a civil tax proceeding, even one involving a civil fraud penalty, does not tilt the balance of the deterrent effect of exclusion versus the the loss of admissible and probative evidence in favor of exclusion. For another example of the Tax Court's reluctance to suppress evidence seized by state and local police during a search, see Marquart v. Comm'r, TC Memo. 1998-335 (1998) (marijuana dealer claimed police acted in bad faith when they searched his house and seized documents from which the Service determined his liability; court refused to assume bad faith from circumstances that were subject to conflicting interpretations and rejected the argument "to portray a straightforward police operation as a conspiracy to subvert his privacy rights").

[408] United States v. Stonehill, 405 F2d 738 (9th Cir. 1968), reh'g denied, cert. denied, 395 US 960, reh'g denied; United States v. Stonehill, 420 F. Supp. 46 (CD Cal. 1976) (renewed motion to suppress).

[409] United States v. Payner, 447 US 727 (1980).

[410] United States v. Payner, 447 US 727 (1980).

taxpayer-depositor because a third party's rights, not the taxpayer's, were violated. Standing for purposes of the exclusionary rule and exercise of the supervisory powers are thus coextensive.

Evidence has also been excluded from criminal tax investigations where it has been obtained in violation of neither a constitutional nor a statutory provision. Where agents have failed to follow the Service's own procedures requiring partial Miranda warnings, the evidence obtained has been excluded under the *Accardi* doctrine.[411] However, the Supreme Court, in *United States v. Caceres*,[412] denied suppression of evidence obtained by Service personnel in violation of certain Service procedures where there was a reasonable good faith attempt to comply.[413] Both the type of agency procedure violated and the circumstances of noncompliance must be analyzed before a court will suppress evidence obtained in violation of agency procedures. In addition, a procedure affecting some fundamental interest must be involved and the circumstances of noncompliance egregious. *Caceres* does not eliminate suppression under *Accardi* as a remedy, but merely recognizes that the remedy is an extreme one appropriately used in limited circumstances.

There are a number of exceptions to the exclusionary rule, one of which is the inevitable-discovery exception. Under the inevitable-discovery exception, unlawfully obtained evidence is admitted at trial when the government demonstrates that discovery of that evidence by legitimate means was inevitable.[414] Admission of what is conceded to be illegally seized evidence is intended "to block setting aside convictions that would have been obtained without police misconduct."[415] In *United States v. Eng*, a Service special agent assigned to the Drug Enforcement Agency's Southeast Asian Task Force began a tax investigation after identifying the taxpayer as the purchaser of a building. Using the expenditure method of proof, Eng was indicted on nontax charges and arrested. At the time of his arrest, property was seized and searched; various documents contained in a safe at one of the properties were unlawfully seized. About six months later, Eng was charged in a superseding indictment with tax evasion. Because there was an active and ongoing tax investigation of Eng's tax violations at the time of the unlawful search, the records contained in the safe were found to be admissible under the inevitable-discovery exception. However, the

---

[411] United States ex rel. Accardi v. Shaughnessy, 347 US 260 (1954). See United States v. Leahey, 434 F2d 7 (1st Cir. 1970); United States v. Heiner, 420 F2d 809 (4th Cir. 1969); United States v. Sourapas, 515 F2d 295 (9th Cir. 1975). But see United States v. Leonard, 524 F2d 1076 (2d Cir. 1975). Moreover, after the decision of the Supreme Court in *Caceres*, the First Circuit has said that "Leahey and its successors is no longer good law." United States v. Irvine, 699 F2d 43 (1st Cir. 1983).

[412] United States v. Caceres, 440 US 741 (1979).

[413] The *Accardi* and *Caceres* cases are also discussed at ¶ 1.03[2][c].

[414] Nix v. Williams, 467 US 431, 444 (1984).

[415] Nix v. Williams, 467 US 431, 443 n.4 (1984).

district court was required to identify "demonstrated historical facts capable of ready verification or impeachment" supporting the finding that a preexisting and ongoing tax investigation was in progress, as well as particularized findings of inevitable discovery of each of the items seized from the safe, e.g., bank account records and credit card records.[416]

¶ 13.10 FIFTH AMENDMENT CHALLENGES

The Fifth Amendment to the U.S. Constitution provides that "no person . . . shall be compelled in any criminal case to be a witness against himself." Although literally applicable only to criminal cases, the Fifth Amendment has been held to grant individuals the option or privilege of refusing to answer potentially incriminating questions when compelled to appear before an administrative agency.[417] If the individual is forced to answer over his privilege claim, nothing he discloses may thereafter be used against him.[418] In general, the Fifth Amendment may not be claimed in civil tax cases, even where a civil fraud penalty is involved, as long as there is no threat of criminal prosecution.[419]

---

[416] United States v. Eng, 971 F2d 854, 856 (2d Cir. 1992) (*Eng I*), on remand, United States v. Eng, 819 F. Supp. 1198 (EDNY 1993), aff'd, 997 F2d 987 (2d Cir. 1993) (*Eng II*).

[417] Smith v. United States, 337 US 137 (1949). Although, generally, there is no doubt that a taxpayer under an administrative criminal investigation by special agents has the Fifth Amendment privilege, at least one district court in the Ninth Circuit enforced a summons despite the taxpayer's privilege claim because it was persuaded that there was a "Tax Crime Exception" to the privilege. On appeal, the Justice Department's Tax Division confessed error, stating to the circuit court that "the self-incrimination clause of the Fifth Amendment applies in all instances where a taxpayer has reasonable cause to apprehend criminal prosecution, whether tax related or not." United States v. Troescher, 99 F3d 933 (9th Cir. 1996). See also United States v. Grable, 98 F3d 251 (6th Cir. 1996) ("[W]hen Grable appeared at the [summons enforcement] contempt proceeding, the district court should have conducted an inquiry to determine the validity of his claim of privilege rather than mistakenly advising Grable that no Fifth Amendment privilege against compulsory self-incrimination existed . . . [i]t was clear error and an abuse of discretion for the district court to advise Grable that a taxpayer has no Fifth Amendment privilege when required by the IRS to produce documents that may be incriminating").

[418] Garrity v. New Jersey, 385 US 493 (1967); Murphy v. Waterfront Comm'n, 378 US 52 (1964).

[419] However, if the taxpayer's apprehension of criminal prosecution is objectively reasonable, the Fifth Amendment's protection against self-incrimination applies in any type of proceeding, whether civil, criminal, administrative, investigatory, or adjudicatory. Maness v. Meyers, 419 US 449, 464 (1975). What if the taxpayer fears prosecution in a foreign country? Does the fear serve as the basis for a Fifth Amendment claim? In 1998, the Supreme Court refused to extend the application of the Fifth Amendment privilege to individuals who feared prosecution in a foreign country, although it was conceded that Bal-

Although the privilege protects against incriminating testimony, what may incriminate is not always easily determined, especially in tax cases. In addition to the admission of a crime itself, testimony carrying the risk of incrimination is also able to be protected by a privilege claim. The Supreme Court has described the scope of the privilege this way:

> The privilege afforded not only extends to answers that would in themselves support a conviction . . . but likewise embraces those which would furnish a link in the chain of evidence needed to prosecute the claimant. . . . To sustain the privilege, it need only be evident from the implications of the question, in the setting in which it is asked, that a responsive answer to the question or an explanation of why it cannot be answered might be dangerous because injurious disclosure could result.[420]

---

sys, the taxpayer in question, had a "real and substantial fear" that his answers could subject him to prosecution in Lithuania. United States v. Balsys, 524 US 666 (1998). This case has obvious relevance where a summons is served under a treaty to obtain information for a foreign prosecution. In *Balsys*, the majority opinion in dicta said that the fear of prosecution should not be characterized as truly "foreign" in this case because (1) there was sufficient cooperation between the foreign country and the government prosecutors to justify a finding that the government prosecutors were "agents" of foreign law enforcement; (2) the crime was common to both countries; and (3) it could be shown that the United States was granting immunity from U.S. prosecution for the purpose of obtaining evidence to be delivered to the foreign country. However, the Third Circuit rejected this very argument in a case involving price fixing and anticompetitive activities where employees who had been granted immunity nevertheless refused to answer questions about activities that took place outside the United States or related to foreign markets. In re Impounded, 178 F3d 150, 155 (3d Cir. 1999). Estate of Ryan v. Comm'r, 568 F2d 531 (7th Cir. 1977), cert. denied, 439 US 820 (1978) (claim of privilege rejected because grant of use immunity removed danger of self-incrimination); Nickell v. United States, 79-1 USTC ¶ 9206 (D. W.Va. 1979); Harper v. Comm'r, 54 TC 1121 (1971). The principle that a civil penalty generally is not sufficiently "criminal" in nature to trigger the Fifth Amendment now seems settled. United States v. Ward, 448 US 242 (1980). The civil fraud penalty in tax cases has been held not to be criminal or quasi-criminal in nature. Helvering v. Mitchell, 303 US 391 (1938). But it has also been said that the privilege against self-incrimination "may apply in the context of an IRS investigation into civil tax liability, given the recognized potential that such investigations have for leading to criminal prosecutions." United States v. Sharp, 920 F2d 1167, 1170 (4th Cir. 1990); accord United States v. Argomaniz, 925 F2d 1349 (11th Cir. 1991).

[420] Hoffman v. United States, 341 US 479, 486–487 (1951). Applying the *Hoffman* description of the privilege's scope, it has been held that a summons seeking financial information from a taxpayer in order to collect her civil tax liability was not enforceable over her privilege claim because the answers might provide a link in the chain of evidence needed to prosecute. United States v. Haworth, 386 F. Supp. 1099 (SDNY 1975); United States v. Jones, 703 F2d 473 (10th Cir. 1983) (the Service had obtained judgment against taxpayers and sought financial information from them; privilege claim upheld because answers might be link in chain of evidence for attempt to evade payment prosecution under Section 7201). United States v. Sharp, 920 F2d 1167 (4th Cir. 1990) (compulsion order in revenue officer summons enforcement proceeding, reversed on finding that incriminating nature of information sought was facially evident). The appropriate device for obtaining

Conversely, where an individual gives incriminating testimony without claiming the privilege, the privilege cannot be invoked as to all questions on the same subject matter.[421] Courts have generally been inclined to find against waiver;[422] nevertheless, a taxpayer who makes disclosures risks waiver of the privilege.[423]

In general, when a taxpayer claims the protection of the Fifth Amendment privilege in a summons enforcement proceeding, the district court conducts an inquiry to determine the validity of the claim.[424] The court can require the taxpayer to identify the basis for the Fifth Amendment claim by asking the taxpayer to assert the privilege as to each question or on a document-by-

---

answers to incriminating questions, according to *Sharp*, is to grant use immunity under 18 USC §§ 6002 and 6003. But the result depends on the court's own finding on whether the taxpayer's fear of incrimination is realistic. These findings vary depending on the facts of the case. See, e.g., United States v. Moss, 90-2 USTC ¶ 50,531 (D. Md. 1990) (taxpayer filed return, but claimed privilege when asked to complete financial statement); United States v. Cates, 686 F. Supp. 1185 (D. Md. 1975) (taxpayer failed to file returns and claimed privilege when asked to produce records to determine his tax liability); compare United States v. Sanchez, 90-2 USTC ¶ 50,439 (SD Fla. 1990) (revenue officer attempted to obtain financial data to collect delinquent tax from taxpayer previously convicted on nontax charge; held, no realistic fear of incrimination, but privilege could be claimed regarding source of income, not amount); see also United Liquor Co. v. Gard, 81-2 USTC ¶ 9613 (D. Ariz. 1981) (civil action under IRC § 7217 for disclosure of tax information; reporter refused to disclose source of information on self-incrimination grounds; held, disclosure might have been link in chain of evidence needed to prosecute under IRC § 7213); United States v. Blumberg, 787 F. Supp. 67 (SDNY 1992) (collection summons enforced over privilege claim because statute of limitations on prosecution had expired). There are two corollary principles derived from *Hoffman*. "The central standard for the privilege's application has been whether the claimant is confronted by substantial and 'real,' and not merely trifling or imaginary, hazards of incrimination." Marchetti v. United States, 390 US 39, 53 (1968). The second principle is "when the danger is not readily apparent from the implications of the question asked or the circumstances surrounding the inquiry, the burden of establishing its existence rests on the person claiming the privilege." Estate of Fisher v. Comm'r, 905 F2d 645, 649 (2d Cir. 1990).

[421] Rogers v. United States, 340 US 367 (1951).

[422] See, e.g., United States v. O'Henry's Film Works, Inc., 598 F2d 313 (2d Cir. 1979).

[423] See, e.g., Hankins v. Civiletti, 614 F2d 953 (5th Cir. 1980) (taxpayer who testified on direct about lack of possession of books waived privilege as to cross-examination).

[424] This description of privilege claim procedure is taken from United States v. Grable, 98 F3d 251 (6th Cir. 1996). Because the privilege must be claimed question by question, the district court then conducts a particularized inquiry into the merits of the privilege claims. This required inquiry is made in an in camera proceeding, where the claimant is given the opportunity to substantiate his claim and the district court is given "the opportunity to consider the questions asked and the documents requested by the summons." United States v. Argomaniz, 925 F2d 1349, 1355 (11th Cir. 1991). If the court fails to make this particularized inquiry, its order of contempt will be reversed and the case remanded for the hearing on the validity of the privilege claim on a question-by-question basis. See United States v. Drollinger, 77 AFTR2d 96-1636 (9th Cir. 1996).

document basis. If the taxpayer's claim is that the act of production of a document is privileged,[425] the court will order the party to produce the documents, not to the official in the Service who summoned the records, but to the court for in camera inspection. If the taxpayer refuses to produce the documents to the court, the taxpayer will be considered to have waived the privilege. If the taxpayer produces the documents to the district court for an in camera proceeding, the court must give the party the opportunity to assert the privilege claim as to each document, and must rule on the validity of each claim. After the district court's ruling, if the taxpayer fails to turn over to the Service any document for which the court has ruled there is no privilege, the failure to comply will support a finding of contempt. If the court has ruled that the taxpayer has a valid claim of privilege for the act of production, the taxpayer will be required to produce the documents, but only if the taxpayer is granted use immunity.

For there to be a valid claim of privilege under the Fifth Amendment, three elements are required.

1. There must be some sort of compulsion.
2. The compulsion must ordinarily be directed against the individual whom the compelled disclosure will incriminate, not against another party.
3. The compulsion must be directed toward extracting a kind of incriminating evidence constituting "communications" or "testimony," rather than corporeal or physical objects or demonstrations.

These three elements are discussed in the following sections.

[1] The Element of Compulsion

[a] Statements: The Factor of Custody

A person is privileged from being compelled to be a witness against himself under the Fifth Amendment. However, an incriminating statement voluntarily made by submitting to an agent's interrogation, completing a return, or supplying other written information to the Service is not barred by the Fifth Amendment and may be admitted against the person who made the statement.[426] Does an incriminating statement made by a taxpayer at a local office

---

[425] See infra ¶ 13.10[3][a].

[426] Beckwith v. United States, 425 US 341 (1976) (interrogation); Garner v. United States, 424 US 648 (1976) (return); United States v. Smith, 348 US 147 (1954) (net worth statement). See Groder v. United States, 816 F2d 139 (4th Cir. 1987) (revenue agent auditing taxpayer's returns did not violate taxpayer's Fifth Amendment rights where fraud referral was made after taxpayer voluntarily filed amended returns reporting additional in-

differ from an incriminating statement made at a police station? When, in short, is an incriminating statement made in a tax investigation "voluntary" rather than "compelled" in the Fifth Amendment sense? Since 1966, the Supreme Court has answered these questions through the application of the Miranda rule, which is objective and automatic: Any incriminating statement made in the course of a custodial interrogation is inadmissible, unless the procedural safeguards enunciated have been followed.[427]

Just when is an interrogation "custodial" for purposes of the Miranda rule? In the usual tax case, a taxpayer suspected of fraud is not in custody in the same manner as a suspect taken to a police station. However, where a taxpayer was in custody for a nontax crime, he was held to be entitled to Miranda warnings when he was questioned by revenue agents.[428] A taxpayer interrogated by special agents may not be physically in custody, but he has certainly become the focus of a criminal investigation and is subject to certain pressures that may be described as coercive. In *Beckwith v. United States*,[429] the Supreme Court held that *Miranda* warnings were not required to be given to a taxpayer who made incriminating statements to agents who questioned him at his home. Although Beckwith had concededly become the focus of a criminal investigation, he had not been placed under arrest when he was questioned, nor was the interrogation found to be coercive, despite Beckwith's contention that he was under psychological restraints that were the functional equivalent of custody.

The Supreme Court in *Beckwith* adopted an objective rather than the officer's intention. For purposes of the *Miranda* rule, a taxpayer is not the focus of an investigation until after he has been taken into custody, and, consequently, any incriminating statement made during the noncustodial interrogation is "voluntary." However, in *Beckwith*,[430] the Supreme Court did recognize the possibility that even a noncustodial confession might be suppressed where the actions of agents are such as to overbear the taxpayer's "will to resist" and produce statements "not freely self-determined" (i.e., involuntary). Therefore,

---

come, his attorney supplied agent with explanation of underreporting, and, at agent's request, taxpayer was interviewed). In *Groder*, the court stated that a "firm indication of fraud . . . is something different from a 'first' indication or a mere suspicion that intentional fraud exists." An agent's interview of the taxpayer did not automatically establish bad faith or a violation of the Service's own procedures as stated in the Manual.

[427] In Miranda v. Arizona, 384 US 436, 479 (1966), the Court said:

(The individual) must be warned prior to any questioning that he has the right to remain silent, that anything he says can be used against him in a court of law, that he has the right to the presence of an attorney, and that if he cannot afford an attorney one will be appointed for him prior to any questioning if he so desires. Opportunity to exercise these rights must be afforded to him throughout the interrogation.

[428] Mathis v. United States, 391 US 1 (1968).

[429] Beckwith v. United States, 425 US 341 (1976).

[430] Beckwith v. United States, 425 US 341 (1976).

Miranda warnings are not required to be given to a taxpayer who has not been taken into custody and is interrogated by special agents of the Service,[431] and any statements made during the interrogation are not barred by the Fifth Amendment unless there is other evidence reflecting on the voluntariness of the statements.[432]

In 1967 and 1968, the Service announced in two news releases that a special agent would be required to identify himself, to describe his function as a criminal investigator, and to give partial Miranda warnings.[433] The administratively required "News Release" warnings are

> As a Special Agent, one of my functions is to investigate the possibility of criminal violations of the Internal Revenue Laws, and related offenses. I would like to ask you some questions. However, first I advise you that under the Fifth Amendment to the Constitution of the United States I cannot compel you to answer any questions or submit any information if such answers or information might tend to incriminate you in any way. I also advise you that anything you say may be used against you in criminal proceedings which may be undertaken. I further advise you, if you wish, seek the assistance of an attorney before responding.

These warnings differ from *Miranda* warnings in that the taxpayer is not told that he has a right to remain silent, that an attorney can be present at any interview, and that if the taxpayer cannot afford one, an attorney will be appointed at his request.

This administrative procedure adopted preceded the decision in *Beckwith*,[434] but how the Supreme Court would rule if an agent failed to give such warnings after *Beckwith* is uncertain, especially since news release warnings had been given in that case. However, some courts have suppressed statements given by taxpayers when the administratively required warnings were not given, not on *Miranda* grounds but because the agents had failed to follow the

---

[431] See also United States v. Fitzgerald, 545 F2d 578 (7th Cir. 1976) (some partial Miranda warnings as in *Beckwith* were given); United States v. Venditti, 533 F2d 217 (5th Cir. 1976) (statements made to tax technician without any Miranda warnings were made in noncustodial and noncoercive setting and held admissible). In the absence of the a custodial interrogation of coercive circumstances, a taxpayer's statements (admissions) may be used in a civil tax case, even if the agent failed to give Miranda-type warnings. Nickell v. United States, 79-1 USTC ¶ 9206 (D. W.Va. 1979); Singleton v. Comm'r, 65 TC 1123 (1976) (taxpayer in noncoercive but custodial setting, no Miranda but news release warnings given).

[432] Romanelli v. Comm'r, 466 F2d 872 (7th Cir. 1972), rev'g 54 TC 1448 (1970) (no Miranda warnings but coercive circumstances; evidence held inadmissible). See also United States v. Crans, 517 F. Supp. 863 (NDNY 1981) (taxpayer's will was not overborne because he was questioned in a noncustodial setting although he was sick with the flu).

[433] IRS News Releases 987 (Oct. 3, 1967), 949 (Nov. 26, 1968).

[434] However, the agents in *Beckwith* followed the Service procedure.

Service's own procedures.[435] The rationale of the decision to suppress a taxpayer's statements where no news release warnings were given is the so-called *Accardi* doctrine applied in administrative law cases. This doctrine holds that once an agency adopts procedural rules affecting substantial rights of a person, these rules must be followed by administrative officials. All was well until 1979 when the Supreme Court decided *United States v. Caceres*[436] held that under the circumstances of that case evidence obtained from a defendant in the course of negotiating a bribe of a revenue agent in violation of Manual procedures for approval of nonconsensual monitoring was not sufficient to warrant suppression of the evidence. After *Caceres*, many courts have assumed that *Caceres* held that that agents are not bound by the Service's Manual. This is not what Caceres held, but the *Caceres* is repeatedly cited for this proposition, and so *Caceres* casts doubt on the *Heffner* line of cases. There are sharp differences between *Caceres* and the *Heffner* line of cases. One difference is that unlike the formalities of the consensual-monitoring procedures in *Caceres*, the warning procedure was publicly announced.

[b] Required Records

Records required to be kept by the law are not protected by a privilege claim that they constitute compelled testimony. The "required records" doctrine was enunciated in *Shapiro v. United States*,[437] where a fruit wholesaler charged with violations of the Emergency Price Control Act was served with a subpoena to produce business records at a Price Administration hearing. The Supreme Court recognized that there were limits the government could not exceed in requiring the keeping of records for inspection by an administrative agency and for use, over a privilege claim, in prosecuting statutory violations of the recordkeeper. However, these constitutional limits are not overstepped where "there is a sufficient relation between the activity sought to be regulated and the public concern so that the government can constitutionally regulate or forbid and basic activity concerned."[438] The "required records" doctrine, if pressed to its logical conclusion in tax cases, would sound the death knell of

---

[435] United States v. Heffner, 420 F2d 809 (4th Cir. 1969). See also United States v. Sourapas, 515 F2d 295 (9th Cir. 1975). Contra United States v. Leonard, 524 F2d 1076 (2d Cir. 1975). The First Circuit initially followed *Heffner*, but has since stated that the Service is not bound by the news release procedure. United States v. Leahey, 434 F2d 7 (1st Cir. 1970). But see United States v. Irvine, 699 F2d 43 (1st Cir. 1983) (*Leahey* no longer good law in First Circuit after *Caceres*).

[436] United States v. Caceres, 440 US 741 (1979). The effect of *Caceres* on Service violations of its own procedural rules is discussed at ¶ 1.03[2][c].

[437] Shapiro v. United States, 335 US 1 (1948).

[438] Shapiro v. United States, 335 US 1, 32 (1948).

the privilege as to a taxpayer's own records because of the recordkeeping requirements of the Code.[439]

However, the required records doctrine does not apply to tax records, except in limited situations. Before *Shapiro*, the Supreme Court had held that the privilege did not excuse the failure to file a tax return as required by law.[440] After *Shapiro*, in cases involving violations of the gambling tax provisions of the Code, the Supreme Court refused to apply the doctrine in "an area permeated by criminal statutes" to a group "inherently suspect of criminal activities."[441] The Supreme Court observed that the gambling tax provisions differed from the Office of Price Administration regulations in *Shapiro* in three ways: First, the records in Shapiro were of the same kind that the businessman customarily kept. Second, the records in *Shapiro* had a public aspect, which did not depend solely on the interest of the government. Finally, the purpose of the government was essentially regulatory. These three characteristics were simply not present in the gambling tax provisions. However, they may be present where the general class of taxpayers, rather than a limited group inherently suspect of criminal activities, is "required" to keep records if the records have a "public aspect." In fact, the required records doctrine has been applied in certain regulatory aspects of the internal revenue laws.[442]

Personal financial records are "required records" for privilege purposes, with the qualification that no definitive judicial statement on the issue has been given. Before *Marchetti v. United States* and *United States v. Grosso*, decisions of two circuits applied the required records doctrine. In *Falsone v. United States*, a summons directed to an accountant was enforced, consistent with the result of the later-decided *Couch v. United States*.[443] Nevertheless, the Fifth Circuit in dicta observed that the records could have been ordered produced from the taxpayer as required records. In *Beard v. United States*, the defendant in a tax evasion prosecution claimed that a jury instruction, that the jury might consider the defendant's refusal to permit inspection of his records

---

[439] Section 6001 requires "every" person liable for "any" tax to keep such records as the regulations require. The regulations require any person required to file a return to keep "such permanent books of account or records, including inventories, as are sufficient to establish" information shown on the return. Reg. § 1.6001-1(a).

[440] United States v. Sullivan, 274 US 259 (1927).

[441] United States v. Marchetti, 390 US 39 (1968); Grosso v. United States, 390 US 62 (1968).

[442] United States v. Turner, 480 F2d 272, 278 (7th Cir. 1973) (records of tax return preparer required under Reg. § 1.6065-1(b)). See also United States v. Silverman, 449 F2d 1341, 1345 (2d Cir. 1971), cert. denied, 405 US 918 (1972) (records of real estate closing required to be filed by attorneys with state court were held admissible in evasion prosecution).

[443] Falsone v. United States, 205 F2d 734 (5th Cir.), cert. denied, 346 US 864 (1953); Beard v. United States, 222 F2d 84 (4th Cir.), cert. denied, 350 US 846 (1955). Couch v. United States, 409 US 322 (1973).

as bearing on willfulness, violated his Fifth Amendment privilege not to permit disclosure. There was no evidence that the defendant had relied on his privilege, but the Fourth Circuit said the privilege was inapplicable because of the required records doctrine. Certiorari was denied in both *Falsone* and *Beard*, but in opposing review in *Beard*, the Solicitor General represented that the government was not contending that a taxpayer could not claim the privilege as to his personal records. After *Marchetti* and *Grosso*, the government adopted a policy of not arguing that the doctrine applies to personal tax records, although it has used the requirement to keep such records as evidence that the taxpayer had no expectation of privacy.[444] Apart from the government's restraint, it may be contended after *Marchetti* and *Grosso* that financial records are not required records for purposes of the privilege because they have no "public aspect" for regulatory purposes merely because they must be kept and produced, for example, to substantiate deductions the taxpayer may claim and that the Service may deny in the absence of such substantiation.

[c] Individual Records

Is a writing voluntarily prepared before any compulsion in the form of a summons or other process covered by the privilege? The answer seems to be no, but the production of the document may be protected. In two Supreme Court cases, *Fisher v. United States* and *Andresen v. Maryland*,[445] the papers in question (accountant's workpapers in *Fisher* and an attorney's records in *Andresen*) had been prepared before any compulsion in the form of the summons

---

[444] See, e.g., United States v. Helina, 549 F2d 713 (9th Cir. 1977); Mahon, "Privileged Communications and Self-Incrimination," 32 NYU Inst. on Fed. Tax'n 1251, 1269–1270 (1974), quoting the government's brief in Stuart v. United States, 416 F2d 459, 460 n.2 (5th Cir. 1969), and in Couch v. United States, 409 US 322 (1973). In its Supreme Court brief in *Couch*, the Solicitor General said:

> Moreover, while we do not contend that the required records doctrine of Shapiro v. United States, 335 U.S. 1, should, or need, be applied here for Fifth Amendment purposes, it is significant that taxpayers are required by statute to keep records sufficient to disclose their taxable income, deductions, and such other matters (under section 6001 of the 1954 Code). Since the records here involved are in that category, petitioner for this reason as well could not reasonably expect her accountant to withhold them from a tax investigation.

In dicta, one circuit court noted that the Code does not require a taxpayer to retain a copy of a tax return so that the retained copy is not a required record. However, the court went on to say, " *Garner* and *Doe* . . . make the required-records exception to the Fifth Amendment privilege largely, perhaps entirely, superfluous, because records that are not required are by the same token not privileged." Commodity Futures Trading Comm'n v. Collins, 997 F2d 1230 (7th Cir. 1993). See note, "Tax Return Confidentiality Under the Fifth Amendment and the 'Required Records' Doctrine," 48 Tax L. 923 (1995).

[445] Fisher v. United States, 425 US 391 (1976); Andresen v. Maryland, 427 US 463 (1976).

and warrant, respectively, and the Supreme Court rejected any privilege claim. The rule that documents prepared before the service of compulsory process are not privileged was made explicit in *United States v. Doe*, where the Supreme Court held that the contents of an individual proprietor's business records are not privileged.[446] As the Court stated, "where the preparation of business records is voluntary, no compulsion is present."[447] A subpoena that demands production of business records (there was a grand jury subpoena in *Doe*, but the same would hold true for a summons) does not compel oral testimony nor does it force the proprietor to restate, repeat, or affirm the truth of their contents. Consequently, the contents of voluntarily prepared busines records of a proprietor are not privileged.

[i] The implicit authentication doctrine. If *Fisher* established that the privilege does not protect writings voluntarily made before the service of compulsory process, it nevertheless recognized that the act of producing documents may compel the taxpayer to make a testimonial communication. On producing the documents called for by a summons or subpoena, the taxpayer tacitly or implicity concedes the existence of the documents, the taxpayer's possession and control of the documents, and the taxpayer's belief that the documents are those described in the summons or subpoena.[448] However, unless the tacit averments of the taxpayer are both "testimonial" and "incriminating," compulsion may be present, but, for example, the compulsion present when a summons directs a taxpayer to produce his records is not proscribed by the Fifth Amendment.

[ii] Individual records. When the tacit averments are both testimonial and incriminating, the act of production is privileged, at least where an individual's documents are the subject of the summons or subpoena. In *Doe*, the Supreme Court upheld the sole proprietor's privilege claim where there was an explicit finding by the lower court that the act of producing the documents

---

[446] United States v. Doe, 465 US 605 (1984).

[447] United States v. Doe, 465 US 605, 610 (1984). United States v. Doe, 1 F3d 87 (2d Cir. 1993), a split panel of the Second Circuit enforced a grand jury subpoena issued in the course of a parallel Securities and Exchange Commission (SEC)–U.S. Attorney's Office investigation. At issue was a calendar appointment book, copies of which had been produced to the SEC, but that the U.S. Attorney's Office believed had been altered. The majority held that the Fifth Amendment does not protect the contents of private papers that are not business documents. Relying on the Supreme Court's decisions in *Fisher* and *Doe*, the majority concluded that the calendar was a voluntarily prepared writing made before the grand jury subpoena had been served, and, thus, the calendar itself was entitled to no testimonial protection under the Fifth Amendment. No act of production privilege was involved, said the majority, because all that the individual was required to do was to surrender the original, there being no issue about the existence of the document.

[448] Fisher v. United States, 425 US 391, 410 (1976). See discussion infra ¶ 13.10[3].

would involve testimonial self-incrimination.[449] In short, even if an individual's preexisting documents are not privileged, the individual's act of producing those documents (i.e., production by a sole proprietor) can be privileged.[450]

[iii] **Corporate records.** However, where the records do not relate to the individual who is the custodian, the act of production has been held not to involve self-incrimination. A sharply divided Supreme Court ruled 5 to 4 in *Braswell v. United States* that the custodian of corporate records may not resist a subpoena for corporate records on the ground that the act of production will incriminate him in violation of the Fifth Amendment because the custodian acts as a representative of the corporation.[451] The *Braswell* majority said that different constitutional considerations apply to the records of a collective entity, such as a corporation, than apply to the business records of a sole proprietorship, as in *Doe*. In *Fisher*, and later in *Doe*, the Court had changed the privilege analysis from the nature of the documents to whether the act of producing the documents had testimonial aspects and incriminating effect.

This change in the analysis had led some courts to say that neither the nature of an entity that owns the documents, nor the contents of the documents were significant factors for the privilege against self-incrimination, and the only issue was the communicative or noncommunicative nature of the compelled production.[452] *Braswell* shifted the analysis back to the nature of the documents. The Supreme Court reaffirmed that the nature of the entity that owned the documents (there, the records of closely held corporations) continued to be a factor in the privilege analysis.[453] Under the collective entity rule, records of a corporation or other entity are not private papers, but rather the corporation's records, which the custodian holds in a representative, not a personal capacity. As the corporation's representative, the custodian's act of production is the act of the corporation. Since the corporation possesses no privilege, the custodian of corporate records "may not interpose a Fifth

---

[449] United States v. Doe, 465 US 605, 613–614 (1984). This finding distinguished *Doe* from *Fisher*, where the act of production was determined to have only minimal testimonial value and, thus, would not operate to incriminate the taxpayer.

[450] See infra ¶ 13.10[3]. In *Doe*, the district court based its finding on the inference that since the five subpoenas called for production of myriad documents, the government was not able to prove that the documents existed or that the individual was connected with the business entities under investigation and, therefore, was using him to supply that information. See also United States v. Schmidt, 816 F2d 1477 (10th Cir. 1987) (revenue agent's summons to sole proprietor enforced over "act of production" Fifth Amendment claim because fear of criminal prosecution was generalized).

[451] Braswell v. United States, 487 US 99 (1988).

[452] See In re Grand Jury Matter (Brown), 768 F2d 525, 528 (3d Cir. 1985) (en banc), quoted in Braswell v. United States, 487 US 99, 109 (1988).

[453] Braswell v. United States, 487 US 99, 109–110 (1988), citing Fisher v. United States, 425 US 391 (1976).

Amendment objection to the compelled production of corporate records, even though the act of production may prove personally incriminating."[454]

In short, records of even a wholly owned corporation are not personal records, and the custodian has no privilege objection to the production of such records whether the custodian's production of corporate records is deemed not to constitute testimonial self-incrimination, or whether the custodian has waived the right to exercise the privilege by choosing to do business in the form of an artificial or collective entity. However, although the custodian of corporate records may not refuse to produce such records on privilege grounds, the government may make no evidentiary use of the custodian's act of production in any criminal prosecution of the custodian.[455]

[2] The Element of Personal Compulsion

The Fifth Amendment privilege is personal in the sense that the compulsion it protects against must be directed at the same individual who may be incriminated by the testimonial act sought to be compelled. Thus, an individual, *A*, compelled to testify may not refuse to do so under the Fifth Amendment on the ground that the testimony will incriminate another person, *B*.[456] Nor can *A* claim protection of the privilege where testimony that may incriminate *A* is sought to be compelled from *B*.[457] The person subject to the compulsion and the person who may be incriminated by the testimony sought to be compelled must be the same. This rule has undergone considerable refinement (one might say overtechnical refinement) in tax cases, and two corollary rules have developed. First, the privilege is applicable only to natural persons, not to entities (e.g., a corporation) having an identity independent of their individual owners or members. As a result, production of the entity's records may be compelled whether those records incriminate the entity (which has no privilege) or an owner or custodian (with respect to whom the records are third-party records). Second, the privilege does not protect from compelled disclosure records that are not in the personal possession of the person whom they may incriminate.

---

[454] Braswell v. United States, 487 US 99 (1988).

[455] Braswell v. United States, 487 US 99, 118 (1988). This limited evidentiary use of the custodian's act of production is discussed infra ¶ 13.10[2][b].

[456] Rogers v. United States, 340 US 367, 371 (1951).

[457] United States v. Miller, 425 US 435 (1976) (bank records incriminating customer); Fisher v. United States, 425 US 391 (1976) (accountant's workpapers incriminating client); California Bankers Ass'n v. Shultz, 416 US 21 (1974) (bank records). See also Donaldson v. United States, 400 US 517 (1971) (employer's records), where, in an extension of the *Miller* and *Fisher* cases, a taxpayer was ordered to consent to the disclosure of any bank records concerning accounts the taxpayer had at Bahamian branches of a Canadian bank. See the discussion infra ¶ 13.10[3][d].

[a] Individuals Versus Entities

The Fifth Amendment privilege is available only to natural persons because it is the extraction of testimonial or communicative acts that the privilege protects. Since an artificial "person" is itself incapable of being questioned, it cannot be entitled to protection of the privilege. Thus, a corporation has no Fifth Amendment privilege, and compulsory process requiring production of a corporation's records may not be opposed on Fifth Amendment grounds,[458] even where the corporation is dissolved and the records are in the hands of the individual who had been the corporation's sole shareholder.[459] It also does not apply even if a corporation is owned by a single individual who operates it as an alter ego[460] or is a Subchapter S corporation whose separate identity is disregarded for tax purposes.[461] In *Braswell*, the collective entity rule was held to preclude a Fifth Amendment objection by the sole shareholder and custodian of a corporation to the compelled production of corporate records, although the act of production may prove personally incriminating.[462] The decisions denying protection of the privilege to corporations were also based on characteristics peculiar to the corporate form: its status as an artificial person having limited powers granted to it by the state in its charter, and the "visitorial powers" the state retained to investigate its activities.[463]

From the time the policy decision was made not to extend the privilege to corporations, there has been a steady process of denying the privilege to entities that, while not corporations as such, have been considered to have an identity independent of the constituent individual members. Thus, in *United States v. White*,[464] the Supreme Court denied a claim of privilege to the custodian of the records of an unincorporated association, specifically, a labor union. The test, said the Court, was

> [W]hether one can fairly say under all the circumstances that a particular type of organization has a character so impersonal in the scope of its membership and activities that it cannot be said to embody or represent

---

[458] Hale v. Henkel, 201 US 43 (1906); Wilson v. United States, 221 US 361 (1911).

[459] Grant v. United States, 227 US 74 (1913).

[460] United States v. Rosenstein, 474 F2d 705 (2d Cir. 1973). The Supreme Court's decision in United States v. Doe, 465 US 605 (1984), which involved corporations with a sole stockholder, does not change this principle. See In re Grand Jury Subpoena Dated January 28, 1985, 775 F2d 43 (2d Cir. 1985). Once a taxpayer has incorporated, the courts will not look through the form of the business to find, in substance, a sole proprietorship whose business records might be privileged. United States v. Sancetta, 788 F2d 67 (2d Cir. 1986) (one-man medical corporation).

[461] United States v. Mid-Western Bus. Forms, Inc., 474 F2d 722 (8th Cir. 1973).

[462] Braswell v. United States, 487 US 99 (1988).

[463] See Wilson v. United States, 221 US 361, 382–385 (1911).

[464] United States v. White, 322 US 694 (1944).

the purely private or personal interests of its constituents, but rather to embody their common or group interests only.

If the organization represents only group interests, the privilege cannot be invoked by the organization or its representatives in their official, as contrasted with their personal, capacity.[465]

Although an association may become large enough to have an identity independent of its members, members of small associations or partnerships join together primarily as a means of convenience for accomplishing objectives that are essentially personal.[466] Nevertheless, in exploring the "outer limits" of the *White* test, a three-man law partnership in *United States v. Bellis* was held to have acquired "an institutional identity independent of its individual partners."[46.'] Despite the absence of a formal partnership agreement, the continuation of the partnership for fifteen years (the partnership had dissolved some four years before the subpoena was served) and its operation as an entity hiring employees, dividing profits, and owning property according to state partnership law gave the partnership its organizational character so that its records were held by Bellis in a representative, not personal, capacity.[468]

It was observed in *Bellis* that there might be a different result if a small, family partnership were involved,[469] but no basis was articulated for distin-

---

[465] United States v. White, 322 US 694, 701 (1944).

[466] E. Cleary, McCormick on Evidence § 128, at 311 (3d ed. 1984).

[467] United States v. Bellis, 417 US 85, 95 (1974). The Court also believed that the partner was holding the records in a representative, not personal, capacity, as a co-owner and fiduciary with respect to the other partners. The partnership in *Bellis* was dissolved, but this fact did not affect the nature of the records for privilege purposes. If there is a dispute about whether records are those of an entity or of a proprietorship, a taxpayer needs to present only a "minimal" amount of evidence at the hearing to show cause to be entitled to an evidentiary hearing to determine whether an entity is separate from its creator and whether records are held in a representative capacity.

[468] Following the rationale of *Bellis*, the privilege has been held not to apply to documents of a trust held by an individual in a purely representative capacity. United States v. Harrison, 653 F2d 359 (8th Cir. 1981). Accord Watson v. Comm'r, 690 F2d 429 (5th Cir. 1982) (summary calendar). See also cases involving abusive trusts. United States v. Crum, 87 AFTR2d 2001-2301 (ND Ind. 2001), adopted United States v. Crum, 88 AFTR2d 2001-5335 (ND Ind. 2001) (magistrate judge and recommendation) (summoned parties were in possession of trust documents as comanagers, and so were holding the documents in a representative, not personal, capacity; held, summoned parties could not claim protection of the Fifth Amendment); United States v. Wooten, 86 AFTR2d 2000-5125 (ND Ohio 2000) (summonses were served on person in her representative capacity as trustee, and so she could not claim the Fifth Amendment). After *Bellis*, the point is well settled. See United States v. Harrison, 653 F2d 359 (8th Cir. 1981); Watson v. Comm'r, 690 F2d 429 (5th Cir. 1982); In re Grand Jury Subpoena, 973 F2d 45, 47–49 (1st Cir. 1992) (trusts are collective entities, and so the Fifth Amendment cannot be claimed to avoid producing trust documents).

[469] See United States v. Slutsky, 352 F. Supp. 1105 (SDNY 1972) (where brothers owned and operated a large hotel).

guishing the institutional identity of a partnership of unrelated partners from a partnership of related partners. Therefore, not surprisingly, the privilege has been held not to apply to a family partnership.[470]

The *White* and *Bellis* tests raise the question whether a business conducted by a sole proprietor can acquire an established identity independent of its owner. In *Bellis*, the Court stated that the "privilege applies to the business of a sole proprietor or sole practitioner, as well as to personal documents containing more information about the individual's private life."[471] However, two 1976 decisions of the Court cast doubt on this statement. In *Fisher*,[472] accountant's workpapers that reflected an individual taxpayer's own records were held not to be protected by the privilege, even though the workpapers were deemed to be in the hands of the taxpayer. In *Andresen v. Maryland*,[473] a lawyer's records were seized pursuant to a valid search warrant and introduced at trial, despite his privilege claim. In both cases, the Supreme Court seemed to consider that the papers in question were not intended to be "private," despite its attempt to separate Fourth Amendment privacy concepts from Fifth Amendment compelled testimony situations. Finally, in *Doe*, despite the statements in *Bellis* about the privilege's applying to the business of a sole proprietor, the records of a sole proprietor were held not to be privileged because they had been prepared before any service of compulsory process.[474]

If articulation of an underlying rationale is put aside, it is possible to derive some general principles from these cases. Under the collective entity rule, the records of a corporation are not privileged, even if the corporation is owned by a single shareholder (*Braswell*). Just what constitutes a collective entity subject to the rule will be interpreted broadly but the class of business forms stops short of a sole proprietorship (the *White-Bellis* line of cases). Although a collective entity does not include the business of a sole proprietorship, records of a proprietorship having been voluntarily prepared before service of process for that reason are not privileged (*Doe*). To put the matter bluntly, business records are not covered by the Fifth Amendment either because they belong to a collective entity, which has no privilege, or because they were voluntarily prepared.

---

[470] United States v. Hankins, 565 F2d 1344 (5th Cir. 1978), cert. denied, 440 US 909 (1979). See also United States v. Alderson, 646 F2d 421 (9th Cir. 1981) (partners were brothers).

[471] United States v. Bellis, 417 US 85, 87–88 (1974).

[472] Fisher v. United States, 425 US 391 (1976).

[473] Andresen v. Maryland, 427 US 463 (1976).

[474] United States v. Doe, 465 US 605 (1984).

[b] Custodians

Under the *White-Bellis* rule, neither the organization nor the custodian are shielded from compelled production of the organization's records on self-incrimination grounds because the organization's records are not the personal papers of the custodian, and the custodian's possession is not in a personal capacity but in an official or representative capacity. Despite any Fifth Amendment privilege the custodian may have, the custodian must produce the organization's records in response to compulsory process. This rationale was stated in *Bellis*:

> In view of the inescapable fact that an artificial entity can only act to produce its records through its individual officers or agents, recognition of the individual's claim of privilege with respect to the financial records of the organization would substantially undermine the unchallenged rule that the organization itself is not entitled to claim any Fifth Amendement privilege, and largely frustrate legitimate governmental regulations of such organizations.[475]

If merely personal possession does not cloak third-party or impersonal records with the privilege, does the custodian lose his own privilege by the fact of possession of those records? The custodian must produce records in response to compulsory process, although by that act alone he implicitly testifies that the records produced are the ones called for by the summons.[476] In *Braswell*, the Supreme Court held that the custodian of corporate records acts as a representative of the corporation and so may not refuse to produce records on personal self-incrimination grounds.[477] The Court reasoned:[478]

> Artificial entities such as corporations may act only through their agents, *Bellis*, . . . and a custodian's assumption of his representative capacity leads to certain obligations, including the duty to produce corporate records on proper demand of the government. Under those circumstances, the custodian's act of production is not deemed a personal act, but rather an act of the corporation. Any claim of Fifth Amendment privilege asserted by the agent would be tantamount to a claim of privilege by the corporation—which of course possesses no such privilege.

In *Braswell*, the Supreme Court left open the question "whether the agency rationale supports compelling a custodian to produce corporate records when the custodian is able to establish, by showing . . . that he is the sole employee and officer of the corporation, that the jury would inevitably conclude that he pro-

---

[475] United States v. Bellis, 417 US 85, 90 (1974).
[476] Fisher v. United States, 425 US 391 (1976).
[477] Braswell v. United States, 487 US 99, 110 (1988).
[478] Braswell v. United States, 487 US 99, 110 (1988).

duced the records."[479] However, where the person served with a grand jury subpoena duces tecum for corporate records was the president and sole shareholder of the target corporation, the president/shareholder's privilege claim has been rejected on the ground that, as the corporation's custodian, he had no privilege.[480]

[i] **Procedural implications of *Braswell***. Because it believed recognizing a Fifth Amendment privilege for custodians of collective entities would have "a detrimental impact on the Government's efforts to prosecute "white-collar crime,'" the Court, in *Braswell*, also made two rulings regarding the procedure to be followed.[481] First, by addressing the subpoena to the corporation, the corporation must find some means of complying with it, which most commonly means choosing an agent or alternate custodian to produce the records who can do so without incriminating himself.[482] Second, in contrast to the proprietor who produces proprietorship records, as in *Doe*, the government need not grant statutory immunity for the testimonial acts of production. Nevertheless, the government is precluded from the evidentiary use of the custodian's act of production in any prosecution of the custodian.[483]

---

[479] Braswell v. United States, 487 US 99, 118 n.11 (1988).

[480] See In re Grand Jury Subpoenas Dated October 22, 1991, and November 1, 1991, 959 F2d 1158 (2d Cir. 1992); United States v. Moseley, 832 F. Supp. 56 (WDNY 1993).

[481] Braswell v. United States, 487 US 99, 118 (1988).

[482] United States v. Barth, 745 F2d 184 (2d Cir. 1984), cert. denied, 105 S. Ct. 1356 (1985); In re Grand Jury Subpoena Issued to Thirteen Corps., 775 F2d 43 (2d Cir. 1985). Where a summons or subpoena is issued to the corporation, if the shareholder-custodian claims his privilege, the corporation must produce the records through a designated employee or agent. United States v. Sancetta, 788 F2d 67 (2d Cir. 1986) ("[A]n individual stockholder, as any other representative of a collective entity, may assert that the act of production incriminates him. If his personal claim is successful, the records must be produced by another").

[483] Braswell v. United States, 487 US 99 (1988). Suppose, in addition to producing the records, the custodian is asked to provide oral testimony that will bring the records within the business records exception to the hearsay rule, Rule 803(6), Federal Rules of Evidence, and so assure their eventual admission at a trial. In the case of In re Custodian of Records of Variety Distrib., Inc., 927 F2d 244 (6th Cir. 1991), the Sixth Circuit ordered the testimony to be given, saying that the testimony was implicit in the act of production and that statements that the custodian is familiar with the company's recordkeeping practices and knows that it regularly keeps the records in the course of a regularly conducted business activity were not of themselves sufficiently incriminating. However, a district court refused to order the business records testimony from a custodian, saying that less is required to authenticate records under *Braswell* than is to qualify the records as business records under Rule 803(6), "specifically testimony regarding the conduct of the corporation at the time the subpoenaed records were created." In effect, the *Variety Distributing* decision impermissibly expands *Curcio* and *Braswell*. In re Grand Jury Empanelled on April 6, 1993, 869 F. Supp. 298, 304 (DNJ 1994).

Because the custodian acts as a representative, the act is deemed one of the corporation and not the individual. Therefore, the Government concedes, as it must, that it may make no evidentiary use of the "individual act" against the individual. For example, in a criminal prosecution against the custodian, the Government may not introduce into evidence before the jury the fact that the subpoena was served upon and the corporation's documents were delivered by one particular individual, the custodian. The Government has the right, however, to use the corporation's act of production against the custodian. The Government may offer testimony—for example, from the process server who delivered the subpoena and from the individual who received the records—establishing that the corporation produced the records subpoenaed. The jury may draw from the corporation's act of production the conclusion that the records in question are authentic corporate records, which the corporation possessed, and which it produced in response to the subpoena. And if the defendant held a prominent position within the corporation that produced the records, the jury may, just as it would had someone else produced the document, reasonably infer that he had possession of the documents or knowledge of their contents. Because the jury is not told that the defendant produced the records, any nexus between the defendant and the documents results solely from the corporation's act of production and other evidence in the case.[484]

Disagreeing with the majority opinion, the dissenters would "require the Government to use the only mechanism yet sanctioned for compelling testimony that is privileged: a request for immunity as provided by [18 USC §§ 6002–6003]."[485]

[ii] Compelled testimony of the custodian. The custodian may be compelled over a privilege claim to produce summoned records but may not be compelled to testify about the records. Although it has been held that a custodian may be compelled to identify produced records at a trial, the act of production in response to a summons is identification for the purpose of the proceeding.[486] In the event that records are not produced because they are no

---

[484] Braswell v. United States, 487 US 99 (1988).

[485] Braswell v. United States, 487 US 99 (1988).

[486] United States v. Austin-Bagley Corp., 31 F2d 229, 233 (2d Cir.) cert. denied, 279 US 863 (1929) (defendant who was secretary-treasurer of corporation required to identify corporate books and records); United States v. Daisart Sportswear, Inc., 169 F2d 856, 861 (2d Cir. 1948) (corporate secretary required to identify corporate records in Office of Price Administration prosecution). Cf. Curcio v. United States, 354 US 118, 125 (1957) (*Austin-Bagley* line of authority where union official required to testify as to whereabouts of unproduced records). The rule is that once a defendant voluntarily produces documents pursuant to process and implicitly represents them to be the subpoenaed corporate records, he cannot be heard to contend that the records did not originate from the company. United States v. Lawrence, 934 F2d 868 (7th Cir. 1991) (subpoenaed documents were delivered by defendants' attorney and were identified by government witnesses), cert. denied, 112 S.

longer in the possession of the summoned party, the individual may not be compelled to respond to questions to locate the corporate or association records.[487] The custodian must say that he does not possess the demanded records,[488] and one court was found that if he does so, he does not waive the privilege.[489]

[iii] Contempt and the custodian. A custodian may not respond to an order to show cause why a summons calling for books and records should not be enforced may be held in contempt for failing to comply with the court's summons enforcement order. In *United States v. Rylander*,[490] the president of two corporations, Rylander, was served with a summons for the production of records. He did not appear at the summons enforcement hearing and was ordered to produce the records. After failing to produce the records in response to the district court's order, a contempt proceeding was instituted. At the contempt hearing, Rylander claimed lack of possession or control of the records for the first time. The Supreme Court said that in a contempt proceeding a person ordered by the court to produce the records has the burden of coming forward with evidence in support of any raised defenses, including the defense that he is then unable to comply with the court order because he lacks possesion or control of the records.

Under the facts in *Rylander*, the court order enforcing the summons implied that no defense of lack of possession or control had been raised or sustained in the summons enforcement proceeding. At the contempt hearing, Rylander had merely submitted an ex parte affidavit and refused to be cross-examined, claiming the Fifth Amendment privilege. Accordingly, the Court held that Rylander's privilege claim did not satisfy his burden of production on a defense that he lacked present ability to comply with the enforcement order

---

Ct. 372 (1991). In *Medlin*, the summons called for production by the target "in his capacity as custodian of records, representative, registered agent, officer, director or stockholder of twenty named corporations." United States v. Medlin, 986 F2d 463 (11th Cir. 1993). It was conceded by the Service that Medlin was entitled to "*Braswell* protections," but could not refuse to comply with the summons "on grounds that his act of selecting the documents to produce and producing those documents in his capacity as custodian for the corporations may be used to personally incriminate him." According to the court, "*Braswell* prohibits the revelation of his 'individual act' of selecting and producing the records being used against him." Braswell v. United States, 88-2 USTC ¶ 9546, 487 US 99, 114–115 (1988).

[487] Curcio v. United States, 354 US 118 (1957).

[488] McPhaul v. United States, 364 US 372 (1960).

[489] United States v. O'Henry's Film Works, Inc., 598 F2d 313 (2d Cir. 1979). However, it has also been held that where a custodian has been held in contempt for failing to comply with an order enforcing a summons, direct testimony denying possession constitutes waiver of the privilege as to cross-examination on "matters relevant to his direct examination." Hankins v. Civiletti, 614 F2d 953 (5th Cir. 1980).

[490] United States v. Rylander, 460 US 752 (1983).

because he lacked possession or control. The Court distinguished *Curcio*, saying that in *Curcio*, the conviction rested solely on the individual's failure to testify about the location of records. This case differed from *Curcio* because Rylander was not ordered to testify about the whereabouts of the records. In the contempt proceeding, the district court upheld Rylander's privilege claim when he refused to answer questions about the location of the records. However, Rylander was properly held in contempt because he failed to produce evidence to show he lacked possession or control of the records. His claim of privilege, according to the Supreme Court, did not excuse his failure to produce evidence of nonpossession.

Thus, the law after *Rylander* is this: A custodian may still claim his Fifth Amendment privilege in response to questions about the whereabouts of records, even in a contempt proceeding following an order to produce those records. However, if he failed to raise the defense of lack of possession or control of records at the summons enforcement proceeding and has been ordered to produce the records, he must be prepared to prove in the contempt proceeding that he is then unable to comply with the enforcement order.[491] He cannot carry this burden by merely denying he has possession of the records and claiming his privilege as to their whereabouts. The lesson of *Rylander* is that the custodian must testify about conditions or events that might corroborate his lack of possession, and produce other evidence on the issue of present ability or inability to comply with the court order.[492]

---

[491] A custodian is entitled to the assistance of counsel in the contempt proceeding, and, if he is indigent, counsel should be appointed for him. United States v. Bobart Travel Agency, 699 F2d 618 (2d Cir. 1983). For a post-*Rylander* decision where no contempt was found, see United States v. Beckman, 545 F. Supp. 1284 (MD Fla. 1983) (taxpayer's own testimony that he could not produce the summoned records because they were not in his possession or control held sufficient to establish his inability to comply with the order, thereby providing him with justification for his lack of compliance).

[492] There may be a distinction between a defense of nonpossession and a privilege claim. A privilege claim has been held not barred even if it is raised for the first time in the contempt hearing, because the privilege claim cannot be properly litigated in the enforcement hearing. United States v. Rendahl, 746 F2d 553 (9th Cir. 1984) (privilege claim upheld on offer of proof that production of records could subject summoned party to criminal liability); United States v. Grable, 98 F3d 251 (6th Cir. 1996) (following *Rendahl*, but stating that in determining whether taxpayer waived the privilege in the prior enforcement action, an "important factor" is whether taxpayer was unrepresented by counsel). See also United States v. Edgerton, 734 F2d 913 (2d Cir. 1984); United States v. Sorrells, 877 F2d 346 (5th Cir. 1989) (once court orders production, only defense in contempt proceeding is lack of present possession or control; defendant held in contempt not because he claimed privilege but because he failed to produce credible evidence of inability to comply with court's order).

[c] The Factor of Possession

It is a fundamental precept that the privilege protects a person against his compelled testimonial acts. Consequently, if a taxpayer's financial records are called for by a summons directed to a person other than the taxpayer who is in possession of those records, the privilege is inapplicable because the taxpayer-owner of the records is not being compelled to testify by complying with the summons. The result is similar to that where the privilege has been held inapplicable to the records of a third person in the hands of a custodian, even though the custodian may have made the entries in those records himself.[493] In short, there is no personal compulsion for Fifth Amendment purposes if the summons or other process is directed at a third person in possession of records that may incriminate a taxpayer, even if the taxpayer is the owner of such records.

This rule of possession has been rather strictly applied by the Supreme Court in two tax cases: *Couch v. United States* and *Fisher v. United States.*[494] In *Couch*, the taxpayer was the sole proprietress of a restaurant who delivered the records of her business to her accountant to prepare her tax returns and customarily left the records with him after the returns were completed. A special agent served a summons on the accountant calling for production of five years' worth of business records, which were in the accountant's possession.[495] The Supreme Court rejected the taxpayer's claim that her Fifth Amendment privilege barred production. Since the summons and court order were directed against the accountant, he was the only one compelled to do anything, and he did not claim the privilege. Thus, for Fifth Amendment purposes, "[i]nquisitorial pressure or coercion against a potentially accused person, compelling her, against her will, to utter self-condemning words or produce incriminating documents [was] absent."[496]

There are circumstances where no waiver of the privilege is implied despite the rule of possession. For example, the privilege has been held to apply to personal records held in a safe on a corporation's premises to which others

---

[493] Wilson v. United States, 221 US 361 (1911).

[494] Couch v. United States, 409 US 322 (1973); Fisher v. United States, 425 US 391 (1976).

[495] The accountant returned the records after the summons was served, but the delivery was ignored for purposes of the summons. The taxpayer who retrieves his records used to prepare his tax returns from his accountant after the accountant has been served with a summons may not claim his self-incrimination privilege with respect to the retrieved records. United States v. Daffin, 653 F2d 121 (4th Cir. 1981). However, when the taxpayer's books and records have been transferred to the taxpayer's accountant for the convenience of the Service, the transfer is held not to prevent the taxpayer from claiming the Fifth Amendment privilege at a later date. See Stuart v. United States, 416 F2d 459 (5th Cir. 1969); Streett v. United States, 83 AFTR2d 99-2922 (WD Va. 1999) (accord).

[496] Couch v. United States, 409 US 322, 329 (1973).

had no access.[497] Also, since records not physically in an individual's possession may be considered to be in his constructive possession, then the individual's temporary surrender of records to another for tax advice would seem to be another form of constructive possession. In *Couch*, the professional relationship between the accountant and the taxpayer seemed to form a basis for a constructive possession finding. The Supreme Court acknowledged that "situations may well arise where constructive possession is so clear or the relinquishment of possession so temporary and insignificant as to leave the personal compulsions on the accused substantially intact."[498] Nevertheless, in *Couch*, neither situation was found to exist because of the absence of any federally recognized accountant-client privilege. Also, the surrender of the records was for the purpose of making mandatory disclosures on returns not confidential, and the long period of surrender was inconsistent with any expectation of confidentiality.[499]

The relationship between an attorney and a client is distinguishable from the one between an accountant and his client. Federal law recognizes both the constitutional importance of a lawyer's assistance and the confidentiality of communications between a taxpayer-client and his attorney.[500] Consequently, where a taxpayer-client transfers records to his lawyer, the client would seem to retain constructive possession of the records for Fifth Amendment purposes. Despite the policy reasons supporting constructive possession in this situation, the Supreme Court in *Fisher* held that where a taxpayer surrenders possession of his records by delivering them to his lawyer, the taxpayer loses the opportunity of claiming the privilege directly. In the *Fisher* case, a taxpayer had obtained possession of the accountant's workpapers and turned them over to his lawyer, Fisher. A special agent, having failed to obtain the workpapers from the accountant, served a summons on the lawyer. The Supreme Court again applied a strict rule of possession and held that a taxpayer could not on Fifth Amendment grounds object to enforcement of a summons directed at his attor-

---

[497] United States v. Guterma, 272 F2d 344 (2d Cir. 1959).

[498] Couch v. United States, 409 US 322, 333 (1973). Constructive possession has been limited to situations where the party claiming the privilege has personal control and the other person is a mere custodian. See United States v. Silverstain, 668 F2d 1161 (10th Cir. 1982) (records in possession of accountant who was supposed to represent the taxpayer in an audit of returns he did not prepare); United States v. Jones & Horton, 630 F2d 1073 (5th Cir. 1980) (constructive possession not found where records in possession of accountants for six months and accountants were not regular accountants).

[499] It was significant in *Couch* that the accountant was an independent contractor who did very little work for the taxpayer. The government noted in oral argument that had the accountant been a full-time employee of the taxpayer, she would have retained dominion over the records and the option of claiming the privilege. Couch v. United States, 409 US 322, 334 n.18 (1973). See also United States v. Slutsky, 352 F. Supp. 1105, 1109 n.2 (SDNY 1972).

[500] Fisher v. United States, 425 US 391 (1976).

ney and calling for production of workpapers because production by the attorney did not compel the taxpayer to do anything. However, the Court recognized that a taxpayer has a legitimate expectation of privacy in seeking legal assistance and, therefore, could oppose production under a combination of the Fourth Amendment and the attorney-client privilege.

Therefore, where a client delivers possession of potentially incriminating records to his lawyer, the issue is whether and to what extent the taxpayer-client had an expectation of confidentiality in the surrendered records, recognizing that a client cannot enlarge his privilege merely by delivering papers to an attorney. In *Fisher*, the Supreme Court said that the taxpayer-client had an expectation of confidentiality only if the client could not have been compelled to produce the workpapers had he himself retained them, and he had served with the summons. In this hypothetical situation, the Court held that the taxpayer could be compelled to produce the workpapers because they were the property of a third party (the accountant). Production of this third person's records did not compel the taxpayer's implicit authentication (testimony) vouching for the accuracy or genuineness of the workpapers and, thus, would not violate the taxpayer's Fifth Amendment privilege.[501]

The *Couch* and *Fisher* cases left open the possibility that a sole proprietor would not be able to claim the privilege if records of his sole proprietorship are in the custody of an employee. If a summons is served on the employee, does the proprietor have constructive possession of the records? The answer would seem to be yes, if the taxpayer takes action to ensure confidentiality of the records by, for example, preparing them himself or restricting access to them. However, just where the Supreme Court's strict rule of possession leads is disturbingly unclear if the employee is considered to have possession of records for privilege purposes. Under a strict rule of possession, a summons served on the employee rather than on the proprietor may defeat the proprietor's privilege claim.[502] After the Supreme Court's pronouncement in *Doe* that

---

[501] However, it has also been held that *Fisher* would require production of the accountant's workpapers even if the taxpayer could show that he owned the workpapers he obtained from the accountant as well as had them in his possession. In re Witte, 544 F2d 1026 (9th Cir. 1976); United States v. Coratti, 81-1 USTC ¶ 9277 (NDNY 1981); United States v. Sneeky Theef Records, Inc., 526 F. Supp. 434 (NDNY 1981) (a not very happily named enterprise under the circumstances). Where an accountant's records and personal financial records of the taxpayer were delivered to the taxpayer's attorney, who in turn delivered them to a second accountant retained by the attorney, a summons served on the attorney was enforced over the claim that production would constitute self-authentication violating the taxpayer's privilege. United States v. Clark, 847 F2d 1467 (10th Cir. 1988) (finding that the case was closer to *Fisher* than to *Doe*, apparently because the personal financial records had been in the accountant's hands and, thus, could be produced without a privilege violation).

[502] See, e.g., In re Grand Jury Empanelled, 597 F2d 851 (3d Cir. 1979) (grand jury subpoena served on employee for sole proprietor's records held enforceable in part because proprietor had delegated exclusive responsibility for preparation and custody of

no privilege applies to a sole proprietor's records, lack of possession served only as an alternative ground for rejecting any privilege claim. On the other hand, if the proprietor has possession of the records, the privilege claim will be upheld only if the act of production will be both testimonial and potentially incriminating.

It can be said that a taxpayer's privilege claim with respect to financial records and writings cannot be made at all unless the documents are in the taxpayer's possession (*Couch* and *Fisher*) and possibly unless the taxpayer owns the documents (*Fisher*). If the taxpayer lacks personal possession, the privilege may not be claimed where the actual possessor is an accountant (*Couch*) or even the taxpayer's attorney (*Fisher*). However, if records are in the hands of an attorney, there is a recognized expectation of privacy that requires analysis under the attorney-client privilege to determine whether the client could have been required to produce the records (*Fisher*). Thus, after *Fisher*, personal possession is a prerequisite to having a privilege claim, although that claim will not necessarily be upheld. If personal possession is lacking, the claim will not stand at all. Even if the taxpayer has possession of potentially incriminating evidence, the Fifth Amendment protects the taxpayer from production of the evidence only if the taxpayer will be compelled to make a testimonial communication that is incriminating (*Fisher* and *Doe*).

[3] The Element of Compelled Testimony

The compulsion that the Fifth Amendment protects must be directed at extorting from the individual testimony or some communicative response. The Fifth Amendment itself derives from the common-law injunction that no man shall be compelled to be a witness against himself. The privilege clearly applies to compelled oral testimony, and it has long been held that the compelled production of a private document is also a constitutionally prohibited form of compelled testimony. In *Boyd v. United States*, the Supreme Court considered the Fourth and Fifth Amendments as running "almost into each other" on the facts before it, and it said that the doctrines of those amendments

> [A]pply to all invasions on the part of the government and its employees of the sanctity of a man's home and the privacies of life. It is not the breaking of his doors, and the rummaging of his drawers, that constitutes the essence of the offense; but it is the invasion of his indefeasible right of personal security, personal liberty and private property.... Breaking into a house and opening boxes and drawers are circumstances of aggra-

---

records to her). But compare United States v. Slutsky, 352 F. Supp. 1105, 1109 n.2 (SDNY 1972) (pre-*Fisher* case indicating that records prepared by employee-accountant would be protected by privilege). See also United States v. Guterma, 272 F2d 344 (2d Cir. 1959) (records in safe held privileged).

vation; but any forcible and compulsory extortion of a man's own testimony or of his private papers to be used as evidence to convict him of crime or to forfeit his goods, is within the condemnation [of those amendments].[503]

Although *Boyd* emphasized privacy as the criterion for the privilege's protection of writings, later decisions have looked to the act of producing writings as the test of whether incriminating testimony was being compelled.

[a] The Implicit Authentication Doctrine

The prevailing rationale for application of the privilege to compelled production of documentary evidence is that compliance with the subpoena tacitly concedes the existence of the papers and their possession or control by the individual, as well as indicating the individual's belief that the papers are those described in the subpoena.[504] When this "implicit authentication" doctrine was applied in a tax investigation in *Fisher*, the Supreme Court narrowed it in this way:

> The elements of compulsion are clearly present (when an individual complies with a summons), but the more difficult issues are whether the tacit averments of the taxpayer are both "testimonial" and "incriminating" for purposes of applying the Fifth Amendment. These questions perhaps do not lend themselves to categorical answers; their resolution may instead depend on the facts and circumstances of particular cases or classes thereof.[505]

The Court went on to analogize the production of an accountant's workpapers to the production of third-party records held by a custodian, despite the fact

---

[503] Boyd v. United States, 116 US 616, 630 (1886).

[504] Schmerber v. California, 384 US 757, 763–764 (1966) ("[t]he privilege reaches . . . the compulsion of responses which are also communications, for example, compliance with a subpoena to produce one's papers"). Boyd v. United States, 116 U.S. 616"); Couch v. United States, 409 US 322, 335, 346–348 (1973) (Marshall. J., dissenting) (the person complying with the subpoena "implicitly testifies that the evidence he brings forth is in fact the evidence demanded"); United States v. Beattie, 522 F2d 267, 270 (2d Cir. 1975), vacated and remanded, 425 US 967 (1975) ("a subpoena demanding that an accused produce his own records is . . . the equivalent of requiring him to take the stand and admit their genuineness"); 8 Wigmore, Evidence § 2264 at 380 (McNaughton, Ed.; rev. ed. 1961) (the testimonial component involved in compliance with an order for production of documents or chattels is "the witness's assurance (compelled as an incident of the process) that the articles produced are the ones demanded"); E. Cleary, McCormick on Evidence § 126, at 307 (3d ed. 1984) ("[complying with a subpoena] communicates at least the following information: (a) the items produced exist; (b) the items were within the possession or control of the respondent; and (c) the respondent believes or has some reason to believe the items produced are those described in the subpoena").

[505] Fisher v. United States, 425 US 391, 410 (1976).

that producing the documents tacitly admits their existence and their location in the hands of their possessor. Although the act of producing the accountant's papers had some minimal testimonial significance, it posed no realistic threat of incrimination to the taxpayer. It was "doubtful," said the Court, that implicitly admitting the existence and possession of the papers posed, in *Fisher*, "any realistic threat of incrimination of the taxpayer."[506] Production expressed nothing more than the taxpayer's belief that the papers were those described in the summons, an act that did not authenticate or vouch for the accuracy of the accountant's workpapers.

According to *Fisher*, compliance with a summons directing a taxpayer to produce his accountant's workpapers summarizing the taxpayer's records involves no incriminating testimony within the Fifth Amendment. Does compliance with a summons directed at the taxpayer and calling for the taxpayer to produce his own records call for potentially incriminating testimony? The Supreme Court left this question open in *Fisher*. However, in *United States v. Doe*, it removed any doubt, holding that the contents of business records, even of a sole proprietor, are not privileged. Nevertheless, the act of producing a proprietorship's records may be privileged. In *Doe*, it was found as a fact by the lower court, and accepted by the Supreme Court, that the act of production in the case would have involved testimonial self-incrimination. In part, this finding was based on the individual's refusal to concede the existence of the records. The argument on behalf of *Doe* was that producing the records would tacitly admit their existence and possession and relieve the government of the need for authentication. The Supreme Court thought that under the circumstances, the risk of incrimination was "substantial and real," and not "imaginary and trifling," as the government contended. However, it pointed out, that the government is not foreclosed from rebutting an individual's claim of privilege "by producing evidence that possession, existence and authentication was a 'foregone conclusion.' " In *Doe*, the government failed to make such a showing. In other cases, such a showing might be made with the result that no privilege claim could be made.

---

[506] Fisher v. United States, 425 US 391, 418 (1976). For cases where the fact of existence of possession of records did pose such a threat, see United States v. Karp, 80-1 USTC ¶ 9423 (SDNY 1980); In re Grand Jury Subpoena Duces Tecum, 466 F. Supp. 325 (SDNY 1979). The act of production may be privileged in a civil tax investigation because the taxpayer can legitimately fear criminal prosecution before a Service investigation in the civil stage is transferred to CID. United States v. Argomaniz, 925 F2d 1349 (11th Cir. 1991) (revenue officer summons, and taxpayer invoked privilege to avoid act of producing records; held, taxpayer could legitimately fear prosecution for failure to file return). But a generalized privilege claim is not sufficient. In an in camera proceeding, the district court must make a particularized inquiry, question by question, about "first, whether the taxpayer has the records sought and second, whether under the existing circumstances, they are incriminating." Id.

The principle seems to be that if the government establishes that specific records or papers exist, that they are in the possession of the person served with process, and that they are authentic, then requiring the individual to produce the records or papers involves no self-authentication of them and, thus, does not violate the Fifth Amendment. In short, the act of production requires no testimony because possession, existence, and authentication are a foregone conclusion.

The court weighs evidence of possession, existence, and authentication in deciding whether the basis for an act-of-production privilege claim exists.[507] The limited circumstances in which the privilege will be recognized by a custodian require the individual claiming the privilege to prove that (1) he would be incriminated by producing the documents and (2) the act of producing the documents would be communicative. Under *Doe*, the individual claiming the privilege must show that the risks of incrimination are "substantial and real," not merely "trifling or imaginary." The government may then rebut the taxpayer's evidence by showing that possession, existence, and authentication are a "foregone conclusion."[508] This process is illustrated by the approach of the

---

[507] See, e.g., United States v. Fox, 721 F2d 32 (2d Cir. 1983), rev'g 549 F Supp 1362 (SDNY 1983). In *Fox*, the district court said that the doctor's tax returns and the revenue agent's affidavit describing them "demonstrate that the existence and taxpayer's possession of the three categories of summoned documents (business records, bank account records, and tax records) are established by other evidence to the point that admitting their existence and possession does not rise to the level of testimony under the Fifth amendment." (Citations omitted.) The Second Circuit reversed the district court's decision, saying that the Service did not have such detailed information about the taxpayer's records that his production of the records would not result in compelled testimony from him. Compare United States v. Schlansky, 709 F2d 1079 (6th Cir. 1983), cert. denied, 465 US 1099 (1984) (production of ring binder containing taxpayer's records specifically described in summons held not to compel taxpayer's testimony because it would not confirm the existence or location of materials otherwise unknown to the government, nor supply assurance of their authenticity). See also In re Grand Jury Subpoenas (Heuwetter), 584 F. Supp. 119 (SDNY 1984) (the mere existence of a proprietorship is not enough to affirm the existence of any documents so that summonses to two law firms calling for "any and all records" of the proprietorship, without specifying who has what, demonstrated uncertainty about the existence of the documents); United States v. Edgerton, 734 F2d 913 (2d Cir. 1984) (privilege claim upheld in part because existence of records was an open question); United States v. Lang, 792 F2d 1235 (4th Cir. 1986) (production of corporation's orders, bank statements, and loan agreements would not amount to compelled authentication because existence of records was undisputed and known to special agent). Compare United States v. Berry, 807 F. Supp. 439 (WD Tenn. 1992) (act of production privilege claim sustained because agent did not have "specific knowledge of either the existence or contents of the [summoned] records").

[508] In this procedure, conclusory assertions that production would be self-incriminating are insufficient. See United States v. Darwin Constr. Co., 873 F2d 750 (4th Cir. 1989), aff'g an unreported district court decision. See also United States v. Schmidt, 816 F2d 1477 (10th Cir. 1987) ("Thus, in order to invoke the Constitutional protection under the Fifth Amendment that bars compelled self-incrimination, [the sole proprietors] must

Second Circuit where the subpoenaed records are required records. In *In re Two Grand Jury Subpoenas Duces Tecum Dated Aug. 21, 1985*, retainer agreements and closing statements were subpoenaed from lawyers who were required to file them with a state court. The circuit court stated, "[B]ecause the records must be kept by law, the record-holder, 'admits' little in the way of control or authentication by producing them . . . [and] this is especially true where, as here, the record-keeper is required not merely to maintain certain records, but to file them with a public body."[509]

Under the circumstances of the case, the Supreme Court in *Doe* held that the act of production would involve testimonial self-incrimination, although the records covered by the subpoena were not described as having been prepared by the proprietor, Doe. In some cases before *Doe*, courts had applied the implicit authentication rationale only to records that had been personally prepared by the individual to whom the summons or subpoena was issued.[510] Nevertheless, the Supreme Court's decision in *Doe* seems to make the distinction between taxpayer-prepared and third-party-prepared records irrelevant. The issue is whether, in producing the records called for, the proprietor would be compelled to testify because the possession, existence, and authentication of the records is not a foregone conclusion. If the existence of the records or the taxpayer's possession of them is unclear, ordered production would violate the proprietor's privilege even if he is not the author of the records.

Even where the custodian of a collective entity is compelled to produce the entity's records, the act of production doctrine applies. In *Braswell*, the Supreme Court held that "[a] custodian may not resist a subpoena for corporate records on Fifth Amendment grounds," but it limited the evidentiary use of the custodian's act of production. Since the custodian's production is a representative act, not a personal act, no evidentiary use of the individual custodian's act may be made against the individual. Thus, the fact that the records produced are authentic corporate records may be used in a prosecution of the custodian,

---

demonstrate that they have a 'reasonable cause to apprehend danger' upon giving a responsive answer that 'would support a link in the chain of evidence needed to prosecute' them for a violation of the criminal statutes.").

[509] In re Two Grand Jury Subpoenas Duces Tecum Dated Aug. 21, 1985, 793 F2d 69 (2d Cir. 1986). United States v. Doe, 465 US 605 (1984).

[510] See, e.g., United States v. Beattie, 541 F2d 329 (2d Cir. 1976) (Service summons calling for taxpayer's letter to his accountant held privileged, but not letter from accountant to taxpayer); In re Grand Jury Proceedings (Martinez), 626 F2d 1051 (1st Cir. 1980) (grand jury subpoena in nontax investigation directing doctor to produce patient logs he kept); United States v. Plesons, 560 F2d 890 (8th Cir. 1977), cert. denied, 434 US 966 (1977) (patient medical files subpoenaed from doctor in nontax case); In re Bernstein, 425 F. Supp. 37 (SD Fla. 1977) (tape recordings of own conversations with third persons). See also United States v. Klir, 81-1 USTC ¶ 9422 (ED Tex. 1979) (canceled checks and deeds in which taxpayers were grantors were privileged, but bank statements and deeds in which they were grantees were not privileged).

but not the fact that the custodian produced the records. In short, the act of production has consequences even if the corporate custodian is not entitled to resist a summons or subpoena on the ground that the custodian's production will be personally incriminating.

[b] Use Immunity for the Act of Production

In *Doe*, the Supreme Court sanctioned a procedure for the government to obtain records even if an individual's production of described records pursuant to a summons or subpoena would require the individual to implicitly authenticate such records or documents. A grand jury subpoena was involved in *Doe*. Under 18 USC Sections 6002 and 6003, whenever a witness refuses on the basis of his privilege against self-incrimination to testify or produce records in a proceeding before a grand jury, on the request of the U.S. Attorney, the district court may order the witness to comply with the grand jury subpoena. Where a request is made and an order issued under 18 USC Sections 6002 and 6003, "no testimony or other information compelled under the order (or any information directly or indirectly derived from such testimony or other information) may be used against the witness in any criminal case, except a prosecution for perjury, giving a false statement, or otherwise failing to comply with the order."[511]

In *Doe*, the government had not made a statutory request to the district court to grant use immunity. It was argued that a doctrine of constructive use immunity should be adopted precluding the government's use of the incriminatory acts of production against the individual claiming the privilege without recourse to the statutory procedures of 18 USC Sections 6002 and 6003. The Supreme Court rejected this procedure, saying

> We decline to extend the jurisdiction of courts to include prospective grants of use immunity in the absence of the formal request that the statute requires. (note omitted) . . . The decision to seek use immunity necessarily involves a balancing of the Government's interest in obtaining information against the risk that immunity will frustrate the Government's attempts to prosecute the subject of the investigation. See United States v. Mandujano, 425 U.S. 564, 676 (plurality op.). Congress expressly left this decision exclusively to the Justice Department.[512]

---

[511] 18 USC § 6002. Section 6002 defines the scope of the immunity protection as follows:

[N]o testimony or other information compelled under the order (or any information directly or indirectly derived from such testimony or other information) may be used against the witness in any criminal case, except a prosecution for perjury, giving a false statement, or otherwise failing to comply with the order.

The immunity protection described in Section 6002 is use and derivative use immunity.

[512] United States v. Doe, 465 US 605 (1984).

Therefore, even if an individual's production of records called for by a summons or subpoena would require the individual to implicitly authenticate the records, the individual may be compelled to produce the records as long as the government makes a statutory request to the district court under 18 USC Sections 6002 and 6003.[513] If use immunity is granted under the statutory procedure, the Supreme Court made it clear that the grant will not cover the contents of the documents produced. Since the privilege extends only to the act of production, "any grant of use immunity need only protect [the individual] from the self-incrimination that might accompany the act of producing his business records."[514]

The Service has authority to grant use immunity under 18 USC § 6004 and has procedures to use this provision and to compel testimony for investigations conducted by the Criminal Investigation Division.[515] There seems to be no reason under *Doe* why the Service could not grant administrative immunity to compel the custodian or possessor to produce records.

---

[513] Section 6002 defines the scope of immunity, and Section 6003 provides for compulsion orders to witnesses in court and grand jury proceedings. Sections 6004 and 6005 apply to witnesses in proceedings before United States agencies and Congress, respectively. For a case where use immunity pursuant to 11 USC §§ 6002 and 6003 was requested at the time of the enforcement proceeding, see United States v. McPhaul, 617 F. Supp. 58 (WDNC 1985). In United States v. Municipal Bond & Collection Servs., 810 F2d 46 (3d Cir. 1987), the Service gave a corporation president, and target, use immunity with respect to the testimony he presented to substantiate his custodial duties. The district court in *Municipal Bond* ordered after the hearing that the records be produced and that the testimony of the president to attempt to establish his custodial responsibilities not be used against him in a criminal case. It also ordered that the act of production by the president not be used as evidence against him in any later proceeding. Although the corporation appealed the decision, the president failed to appeal and was held to have waived his Fifth Amendment rights.

[514] United States v. Doe, 465 US 605 (1984), at n.17.

[515] Although the procedure has been available for some time, the National Office of the Service only began granting requests for administrative immunity in 1984 and 1985. The district court may issue an order only on application by the United States Attorney. 18 USC § 6003(a). The U.S. Attorney makes the immunity application with the approval of the Attorney General, when a determination is made that (1) the witness's testimony is "necessary to the public interest" and (2) the witness will invoke the privilege against self-incrimination. 18 USC §§ 6003(b)(1), 6003(b)(2). Chief Counsel has requested that the Department of Justice apply for orders compelling an individual to testify, or to provide other information, in significant Tax Court cases. See Litigation Guideline Memorandum re: Immunity Request in Tax Court Cases, TL-36 (Jan. 10, 1990) (describing the status of the Fifth Amendment law and policy considerations as well as procedures to be used in seeking compulsion orders in Tax Court cases).

[c] Nontestimonial Compelled Acts

The Supreme Court has adhered to the principle that the Fifth Amendment does not independently prohibit the compelled production of every sort of incriminating evidence but applies only where the accused is compelled to make a testimonial communication that is incriminating. Thus, the focus has been on communications in the sense of disclosures or speech rather than on the act of compulsion itself. Accordingly, the privilege does not extend to situations where individuals are compelled to give blood samples,[516] handwriting exemplars,[517] or voice exemplars,[518] or are compelled to wear a shirt worn by the perpetrator.[519] These cases have themselves been criticized as unwarranted extensions of a distinction between "communications" and "real or physical evidence" articulated by Wigmore and taken up by the Court.[520] Therefore, in view of the developed principles in nontax cases, a summons that requires a taxpayer to prepare handwriting exemplars has been upheld over Fifth Amendment privilege claims.[521]

Compelled testimony has also been held not to include a court order to a grand jury investigation target to sign an authorization permitting "any bank" at which the target may have a bank account to disclose the records of the account.[522] The situation was held analogous to cases where a suspect is compelled to furnish blood samples or to provide a handwriting or voice exemplar. To be testimonial, according to the Supreme Court's decision in *Doe II*, "[a]n accused's communication must itself, explicitly or implicitly, relate a factual assertion or disclose information."[523] Since the consent directive involved in the case was considered hypothetical and did not make reference to a specific account, the Court concluded that neither the form nor its execution communi-

---

[516] Schmerber v. California, 384 US 757, 763–764 (1966).

[517] Gilbert v. California, 388 US 263 265–267 (1967).

[518] United States v. Wade, 388 US 218 (1967).

[519] Holt v. United States, 218 US 245 (1910).

[520] Schmerber v. California, 384 US 757, 764 (1966).

[521] United States v. Euge, 444 US 707 (1980); see United States v. Mordini, 76 AFTR2d 95-5043 (EDNY 1995) (summons directing taxpayer to provide handwriting exemplars and to be photographed enforced after the Service made in camera proffer to judge, despite the fact that the Service already possessed a document concededly signed by the taxpayer). See also United States v. Tanoue, 94 F3d 1342 (9th Cir. 1996) (summons enforced for handwriting exemplars of employee of taxpayer under investigation in order to determine whose handwriting appeared on the tax returns and bookkeeping records).

[522] John Doe v. United States, 108 S. Ct. 2341 (1988). Although *Doe II* arose in the context of a compelled consent directive to obtain access to records in foreign banks, it has also been used to compel defendants in a state criminal case to request access to tax returns from the Service, albeit over their Fifth Amendment objections. Commonwealth v. Burgess, 426 Mass 206; 688 NE 439 (Mass. Sup. Jud. Ct. 1997).

[523] John Doe v. United States, 108 S. Ct. 2341 (1988).

cated any factual assertions, implicit or explicit, or conveyed any information to the Government."[524] Thus, the form did not acknowledge the existence of an account at a foreign financial institution or, assuming that such an account existed, whether any documents were available, and did not identify any bank or financial institution.[525]

¶ 13.11 EVIDENTIARY PRIVILEGES

A person summoned pursuant to Section 7602 may refuse to answer questions or produce a writing and, where appropriate, may prevent another from being a witness or producing a writing on the ground that the answer or writing is privileged from disclosure. The privileges referred to are those recognized at common law "as they may be interpreted by the courts of the United States in the light of reason and experience."[526] A federal common law of evidentiary privileges applies in summons proceedings, and state privileges are inapplicable.[527] Privileges are strictly construed because they are said to contravene the fundamental principle that "the public . . . has a right to everyman's evi-

---

[524] John Doe v. United States, 108 S. Ct. 2341 (1988).

[525] Since the form thus received judicial approval and will, for that reason, likely be used in other cases, it is set forth here. John Doe v. United States, 108 S. Ct. 2341, 2344 (1988).

> I . . . , of the State of Texas in the United States of America, do hereby direct any bank or trust company at which I may have a bank account of any kind or at which a corporation has a bank account of any kind upon which I am authorized to draw, and its officers, employees and agents, to disclose all information and deliver copies of all documents of every nature in your possession or control which relate to said bank account to Grand Jury 84-2, empaneled May 7, 1984 and sitting in the Southern District of Texas, or to any attorney of the District of Texas, or to any attorney of the United States Department of Justice assisting said Grand Jury, and to give evidence relevant thereto, in the investigation conducted by Grand Jury 84-2 in the Southern District of Texas, and this shall be irrevocable authority for so doing. This direction has been executed pursuant to that certain order of the United States District Court for the Southern District of Texas issued on connection with the aforesaid investigation, dated . . . . This direction is intended to apply to the Confidential Relationships (Preservation) Law of the Cayman Islands, and to any implied contract of confidentiality between Bermuda banks and their customers which may be imposed by Bermuda common law, and shall be construed as consent with respect thereto as the same shall apply to any of the bank accounts for which I may be a relevant principal.

[526] Fed. R. Evid. 501. It is not entirely clear that the Federal Rules of Evidence apply at the return of a summons before an agent or officer. See Fisher v. United States, 425 US 391 (1976). However, the rules would be applicable in a summons enforcement proceeding in a federal district court because it is not a type of proceeding excluded from application of the rules. See Fed. R. Evid. 1101.

[527] Fed. R. Evid. 501; Couch v. United States, 409 US 332, 335 (1973) ("no state-created privilege has been recognized in federal cases").

dence."[528] Constitutional protections, such as Fourth and Fifth Amendment privileges, are generally classified as privileges in the law of evidence. Exclusion of evidence of compromise, offer to compromise, and statements made in compromise negotiations may be said to have the character of a privilege,[529] but the most frequently encountered evidentiary privileges in tax cases are the attorney-client, marital, and physician-patient privileges. Courts have recognized these privileges, in general, to encourage full disclosure in the course of certain relationships considered to be of such societal importance that sacrifice of these sources of relevant evidence is justified.

The examination of evidentiary privileges in tax summons cases is a study of the tension between the Service's demand for relevant evidence and a taxpayer's right to privacy, as the brief description of the law in the following sections demonstrates.

[1] The Attorney-Client Privilege

Where legal advice of any kind is sought (1) from a professional legal adviser in his capacity as such; (2) the communications relevant to that purpose; (3) made in confidence by the client; (4) are at his instance protected permanently from disclosure either by himself or his legal adviser; (5) except where the protection is waived.[530] There is no universally accepted statement of the scope of the attorney-client privilege, but for the purposes of this dicussion, the formulation in Wigmore's *Evidence* will be sufficient.[531] However stated, certain issues have arisen in the context of summons cases. These issues fall into the following categories: (1) the "client"; (2) the "attorney"; (3) the subject matter of the privilege; and (4) the meaning of confidential communication. As the following discussion will show, the statement that communications between a client and his lawyer are confidential requires more than a few qualifications.

---

[528] Trammel v. United States, 445 US 40, 50 (1980), quoting United States v. Bryan, 339 US 323, 331 (1950).

[529] Fed. R. Evid. 408. See E. Cleary, McCormick on Evidence §§ 72.1, at 274 (3d ed. 1984).

[530] Wigmore, Evidence § 2292 (McNaughton, ed.; rev. ed. 1961).

[531] The attorney-client or lawyer-client has been variously formulated. The Supreme Court adopted a lawyer-client privilege in Rule 503 of the proposed Federal Rules of Evidence, but it was deleted by Congress. See 2 Weinstein & Berger, Weinstein's Evidence ¶ 503 (1989). There are other statements of the privilege. See, e.g., United States v. United Shoe Mach. Corp., 89 F. Supp. 357, 358–359 (D. Mass. 1950); Uniform R. of Evid. 26.

[a] The Privileged Relationship: The "Client"

The attorney-client privilege belongs to the "client," not to the attorney or third persons.[532] However, where the client is a corporation, the question is, Who represents the corporation, since it cannot itself make communications to its lawyer? In summons cases, the issue is important because the Service has with greater frequency sought information compiled internally in corporate investigations or in audits (e.g., investigations of foreign bribery or other illegal payments). At least two standards have been developed under which a greater or lesser number of officers and employees are included as representatives of the client whose communications are privileged. The standards are the "control group" and the "subject matter" tests. Under the more restrictive control group test, only communications made by officers or employees who are in a decision-making or control capacity are covered by the privilege.[533] Even if the officer or employee is not in the control group, the privilege protects an employee's communications under the subject matter test.

[I]f (1) the communication was made for the purpose of securing legal advice; (2) the employee making the communication did so at the direction of his corporate superior; (3) the superior made the request so that the corporation could secure legal advice; (4) the subject matter of the communication is within the scope of the employee's corporate duties; and (5) the communication is not disseminated beyond those persons who, because of the corporate structure, need to know the contents.[534]

The Supreme Court, in *Upjohn Co. v. United States*, rejected the control group test.[535] The Court observed:

Middle-level and indeed lower-level employees can, by actions within the scope of their employment, embroil the corporation in serious legal difficulties, and it is only natural that these employees would have the relevant information needed by corporate counsel if he is adequately to advise the client with respect to such actual or potential difficulties.[536]

---

[532] However, a trustee in bankruptcy may waive the privilege of a bankrupt corporation. Commodity Futures Trading Corp. v. Weintraub, 471 US 343 (1985).

[533] The test was first articulated in City of Philadelphia v. Westinghouse Elec. Corp., 210 F. Supp. 483, 485 (ED Pa.), mandamus and prohibition denied sum nom. General Elec. Co. v. Kirkpatrick, 312 F2d 742 (3d Cir. 1962), cert. denied, 372 US 943 (1963).

[534] Diversified Indus., Inc. v. Meredith, 572 F2d 596, 609 (8th Cir. 1978) (en banc). A somewhat different statement of this test had been adopted in the Seventh Circuit. Harper & Row Publishers, Inc. v. Decker, 423 F2d 487, 491–492 (1970), aff'd mem. by an equally divided court, 400 US 348, reh'g denied, 401 US 950 (1971).

[535] Upjohn Co. v. United States, 449 US 383 (1981).

[536] Upjohn Co. v. United States, 449 US 383 (1981).

The communications in *Upjohn Co.* were responses made by employees to questionnaires sent by corporate counsel about the nature and extent of questionable foreign payments. The factual investigation was conducted for the purpose of putting the counsel in a position to give legal advice to the company. Thus, the Court concluded, "[t]he communications concerned matters within the scope of the employees' corporate duties, and the employees themselves were sufficiently aware that they were being questioned in order that the corporation could obtain legal advice."[537] Based on these facts, while refusing to adopt a standard applicable in all cases, the Court decided that the communications were covered by the privilege.

Thus, without a uniform rule, communications of lower-echelon employees may be privileged, depending on the facts of the particular case. Maintaining the privilege in a corporate setting is nevertheless difficult. The interview process itself may destroy the privilege if persons not falling within the client group are present. There is also the problem of maintaining confidentiality where a large number of persons are considered to have a need to know.[538] A destruction of confidentiality can also occur in planning and audit situations where third persons are involved.[539]

In *Mobil Corp.*, a summons was issued to the manager of tax administration for Mobil Administrative Services Company to obtain information in an examination of Mobil's intercompany pricing of Saudi crude oil.[540] The summons sought documents relating to a German tax audit of Mobil's pricing and resulted in a settlement between the German tax authorities and Mobil's German subsidiary. One of the documents claimed to be privileged was a communication between attorneys for different related entities. The district court applied a Ninth Circuit test stating that communication between employees of a subsidiary and counsel for parent is privileged "if the employee possesses information critical to the representation of the parent company and the communication concerns matters within the scope of employment."[541]

---

[537] Upjohn Co. v. United States, 449 US 383, 385 (1981).

[538] United States v. Bonnell, 483 F. Supp. 1070 (D. Minn. 1979), aff'd without opinion (8th Cir. 1982) (notes of conference stolen when sent to special counsel).

[539] See In re Sealed Case, 676 F2d 793 (DC Cir. 1982); In re John Doe Corp., 675 F2d 482 (2d Cir. 1982); United States v. Brown, 536 F2d 117 (6th Cir. 1976) (accountant was present at meeting with lawyer at taxpayer's request, and lawyer's memorandum was held in accountant's files).

[540] United States v. Mobil Corp., 149 FRD 533 (ND Tex. 1993).

[541] Admiral Ins. v. United States Dist. Court for Dist. of Ariz., 881 F2d 1486, 1493 n.6 (9th Cir. 1990). The Ninth Circuit said that the situation of communications between former employees and corporate counsel "would be privileged if the employee possesses information critical to the representation of the parent company and the communication concerns matters within the scope of the employment."

The Tax Court has held that in a docketed Tax Court case, Service attorneys may engage in ex parte communications with taxpayers' former employees without violating the

Also, the court observed that protection would serve the purpose of the privilege because the communication related to "tax consequences for certain actions involving the activity between parents and subsidiaries." Documents specifically related to the German audit, including documents describing German law, strategy, proposed settlement and negotiations, and the final settlement, were also found privileged. On the other hand, a letter from Mobil's supervisory tax counselors to three other counselors in Mobil's tax department relating to the legal consequences of selling Saudi crude above or below the official selling price was protected by attorney-client privilege even though it was not generated in anticipation of litigation.[542] While documents may have been classified as privileged, some were found not to be covered by work product protection because they did not discuss the German audit and, therefore, did not appear prepared in anticipation of litigation.

[b] The Privileged Relationship: The "Attorney"

The privilege only applies to professional legal advisers acting in that capacity. If the attorney is consulted for legal advice, the communication is protected. However, if the attorney is not consulted in his capacity as such but as a friend, business adviser, or accountant, the inquiry may not be privileged.[543] Determining whether the attorney is acting in a privileged legal capacity and in

---

ethical rules of Model Rule 4.2 of the ABA's Model Rules of Professional Conduct, which generally prohibits a lawyer from communicating ex parte with a party known to be represented by counsel. However, the Tax Court also said, "[W]e recognize that circumstances may arise where certain precautions (including a narrowly drawn protective order) may be warranted to ensure that such ex parte contacts are not simply a forum for counsel to seek information protected by the attorney-client privilege." Fu Inv. Co. v. Comm'r, 104 TC 408 (1995).

[542] Similarly, a review of the tax laws of certain countries and the obligations of Mobil and its subsidiaries under various contracts sent by General Counsel of one of Mobil's subsidiaries to its finance director was held privileged but not protected as work product.

[543] Olender v. United States, 210 F2d 795 (9th Cir. 1954) (attorney consulted in his capacity as accountant to prepare net worth statements); Pollock v. United States, 202 F2d 281 (5th Cir. 1953) (deposit of funds not communication to an attorney in his professional capacity); McFee v. United States, 206 F2d 872 (9th Cir. 1953) (purchases of cashier's checks); Colton v. United States, 306 F2d 633, 639 (2d Cir. 1962), cert. denied, 371 US 951 (1963) ("[a]ttorneys frequently give their clients business or other advice which, at least insofar as it can be separated from their essentially professional legal services, gives rise to no privilege whatever").

An attorney who acts as his client's agent for the receipt from and disbursement to third parties of money or property is not acting in a legal capacity and records of the transactions are not privileged. United States v. Wells, 929 F. Supp. 423 (SD Ga. 1996) (during investigation of an attorney for failing to file tax returns, the agent summoned records of the lawyer's trust account about a $64,000 cash bank deposit, and the attorney challenged the summons in part on the ground that it reflected only a client's real estate transaction).

some nonprivileged capacity is a matter of proof on the person claiming the privilege. Cases seem to fall into categories involving corporate counsel and professionals who are both lawyers and accountants. Another question that arises in tax cases is the persons who are included in the privilege group covered by the term "attorney."

[i] Corporate counsel. Proof that a corporate counsel is acting as a legal adviser is difficult in a corporate setting because an in-house legal counsel can provide both business and legal advice. Consequently, some courts have said that the corporation that raises the privilege claim to protect a communication to in-house counsel must prove the communication was made primarily for the purpose of seeking legal advice.[544]

In *Upjohn Co.*, protected communications from employees to in-house counsel were made pursuant to a directive from the chairman of the company, which stated that the information was necessary for the purpose of securing legal advice from the counsel.[545] The matter is one of proof, and the corporation must prove that the in-house counsel's advice was given in a professional legal capacity.[546] Since the corporation must prove that the purpose of making the communication was to secure the advice of counsel as such, the corporation cannot shield internal documents from discovery merely by having copies sent to counsel. When a document is prepared for simultaneous review of a document by legal and nonlegal personnel, the corporation will find it difficult to show that the document was prepared primarily for the purpose of obtaining legal advice.[547]

[ii] The attorney-accountant. A similar problem exists when the attorney is also an accountant and return preparer. In *Frederick*, documents were submitted to the attorney/accountant both for the preparation of the taxpayers' returns and possible litigation ("dual-purpose documents"), while other documents were submitted that were prepared in connection with the audit of the taxpayers' returns.[548] Dual-purpose documents were held not privileged because otherwise taxpayers "would be able to invoke, in effect, an accountant's privilege, provided that they used their lawyer to fill out their tax returns." Even if a document is also to be used in preparing for litigation, the document is not privileged because of its nonprivileged use in return preparation. In other words, the nonprivileged use waives protection for a potential privileged

---

[544] United States v. Chevron Corp., 77 AFTR2d 96-1548 (ND Cal. 1996) (gathering cases).

[545] Upjohn Co. v. United States, 449 US 383 (1981).

[546] In re Sealed Case, 737 F2d 94, 99 (DC Cir. 1984) (clear showing required).

[547] See United States v. Chevron Corp., 77 AFTR2d 96-1548 (ND Cal. 1996); see also United States v. IBM Corp., 66 FRD 206 (SDNY 1974).

[548] United States v. Frederick, 182 F3d 496 (7th Cir. 1999).

use. Similarly, when a document is prepared for use in an audit, it is not privileged if the document is to be used to substantiate an item on the return. If the document is prepared for the lawyer's use in addressing issues of statutory interpretation or case law, however, the lawyer is doing "lawyer's work," and the attorney-client privilege may attach. Again, the nonprivileged use precludes attorney-client privilege protection. *Frederick* makes certain judgments about the nature of the attorney's work: the preparation of tax returns and the submission of data to the Service substantiating such returns are not lawyer's work, but the analysis of law, even if it is done for the purpose of assisting the client at an audit, is lawyer's work.[549]

[iii] The "attorney": The Kovel case. It is recognized that attorneys must have agents, so that a consultation in the attorney's office is privileged even where the subject matter becomes known to associates, stenographers, and the like, but the privilege is not confined to "menial or ministerial" employees. The privilege also applies to communications made by the client in the presence of an accountant employed by the attorney to assist him in rendering legal advice to the client.[550] Analogizing accounting to a "foreign language" for many lawyers, the court in *United States v. Kovel* stated: "The attorney, ignorant of the foreign language, sends the client to a non-lawyer proficient in it, with instructions to interview the client on the attorney's behalf and then render his own summary of the situation, perhaps drawing on his own knowledge in the process, so that the attorney can give the client proper legal advice."[551] When the attorney hires the accountant, the *Kovel* court went on:

> Hence the presence of an accountant, whether hired by the lawyer or by the client, while the client is relating a complicated tax story to the lawyer, ought not destroy the privilege any more than would that of the linguist . . . ; the presence of the accountant is necessary, or at least highly useful, for the effective consultation between the client and the lawyer which the privilege is designed to permit.[552]

---

[549] The Seventh Circuit held that the documents in issue would also not be protected by the federally-authorized practitioner provisions of Section 7525 because "these non-lawyer practitioners are [not] entitled to privilege when they are doing other than lawyer's work."

[550] United States v. Kovel, 296 F2d 918, 922 (2d Cir. 1961).

[551] United States v. Kovel, 296 F2d 918, 922 (2d Cir. 1961).

[552] United States v. Kovel, 296 F2d 918, 922 (2d Cir. 1961). When an accountant prepared workpapers for an attorney and accountant, the Fourth Circuit said that the issue to be determined was whether the accounting services were performed primarily to allow the attorney to give advice as attorney or to prepare a tax return as accountant. United States v. Bornstein, 977 F2d 112 (4th Cir. 1992). On remand, the district court in *Bornstein* held that the accountant's workpapers were protected by the attorney-client privilege because they were prepared so that the accountant-lawyer could render legal advice to his

Under this approach, it makes no difference if the lawyer instructs the client to tell his story in the first instance to the accountant, who then interprets it for the lawyer so that the lawyer may better give legal advice. But a rather arbitrary line has been drawn. A communication made by the client to an accountant before the client consults the lawyer is not privileged,[553] but if the client consults a lawyer who retains an accountant, the communications are protected.[554] However, for the *Kovel* protection to apply, the person claiming the privilege must prove that, in fact, the lawyer retained the accountant for the purpose of assisting the lawyer in rendering legal advice to the client, as the following cases illustrate.

In *Adlman*, a corporation's tax counsel claimed that memoranda prepared by the corporation's outside accountants were confidential under authority of *Kovel* because the counsel had requested the accountants to prepare the memoranda so that he could advise the corporation's management about a proposed transaction. But the memoranda were held not to be protected by the attorney-client privilege when no contemporaneous documentation showed that the accountants had prepared and supplied the memoranda to the counsel pursuant to an arrangement with him that was different from the tax advisory services the accountants regularly provided to the corporation in the course of their general engagement.[555] The Second Circuit noted that in *Kovel*, it had recognized that

---

client in anticipation of litigation with the government. United States v. Bornstein, 93-1 USTC ¶ 50,130 (D. Md. 1992).

[553] Gariepy v. United States, 189 F2d 459, 463 (6th Cir. 1951). See United States v. Kovel, 296 F2d 918, 922 (2d Cir. 1961).

[554] The communication may be protected if the client consults the lawyer with his own accountant present. United States v. Kovel, 296 F2d 918, 922 (2d Cir. 1961). See also United States v. Schwimmer, 892 F2d 237 (2d Cir. 1989). ("Schwimmer has carried the burden of establishing that the information he furnished to Glickman, the accountant hired by Renda's attorney to serve the joint interests of Renda and himself, was protected by the attorney-client privilege.") In *Schwimmer*, the contention was that information derived from the schedules and work papers of the *Kovel* accountant was indirectly used by the government in the prosecution. Compare the result when there is no formal engagement of the accountant by the attorney, and it appears that the accountant is providing services independently to the taxpayer. Bernardo v. Comm'r, 104 TC 677 (1995) (absent evidence of the accountant's engagement by the lawyer, communications from the attorney to the accountant and from the accountant to the attorney during the examination were held not privileged, because made during accountant's services in handling the audit). See also United States v. Adlman, 68 F3d 1495 (2d Cir. 1995) (the court said that no formal engagement letter was required, but the evidence had to establish that the corporation's counsel in fact retained the accountant as a *Kovel* accountant).

[555] United States v. Adlman, 68 F3d 1495 (2d Cir. 1995). For a case where the dispute was about whether documents accountants had prepared were retained by the defendant's attorney as such, but there were insufficient findings on the issue of their protection, if any, under the attorney-client privilege, see In the Matter of the Grand Jury Proceedings, 86 AFTR2d 2000-5318 (7th Cir. 2000) (remanding the case for further findings).

"the privilege would extend to communications by an attorney's client to an accountant hired by the attorney to assist the attorney in understanding the client's financial information." But the evidence in the case showed that while the accounting firm had prepared a draft and final version of a tax memorandum describing the tax consequences of a proposed transaction for the counsel, it had also provided a summary of the advice to another corporate officer, and did not distinguish in its billing between the services for the counsel and the rest of the services regarding the transaction. The transaction ultimately occurred in accordance with the advice given by the accounting firm. The circuit court did not require that there be a separate retainer agreement or individualized billing, but the absence of documentary proof supporting the corporation's interpretation of the facts and the presence of contemporaneous documentation supporting the Service's interpretation, strongly supported the district court's interpretation that no *Kovel* relationship existed.

As *Adlman* suggests, there is judicial reluctance to expand the protection of *Kovel* beyond the facts of the case. In *Ackert*, for example, a corporation's counsel discussed the details of a proposed transaction with a representative of an investment banker who had presented the transaction to the corporation, but the circuit court that decided both *Kovel* and *Adlman* held that the communications were not covered by *Kovel*.[556] Although the corporate counsel was gathering the information for the purpose of rendering legal advice to the corporation, the principle of *Kovel* did not make the corporate counsel's/investment banker's communications privileged, because the investment banker's "role was not as a translator or interpreter of client communications." Moreover, the importance of the communications to the legal advice rendered by the counsel to the corporation did not make the communications privileged. It was assumed that the communications significantly assisted the counsel in rendering legal advice to the corporation, but the communication with the investment banker was nevertheless a communication with a third party and, therefore, not an attorney/client communication.

In another case, taxpayers' in-house counsel consulted with an accountant and sent certain documents to him.[557] Taxpayers claimed that the documents were privileged because the accountant was a *Kovel* accountant assisting the in-house counsel in rendering legal advice to the corporation. According to the court, a *Kovel* accountant is one who functions as a translator or facilitator of communications to assist the attorney in rendering legal advice to the client. After considering the evidence, however, the court concluded that, in fact, the accountant acted as a consultant on tax accounting implications of complex transactions, but as a tax adviser who did not interact with the client was not protected the attorney-client privilege.

---

[556] United States v. Ackert, 169 F3d 136 (2d Cir. 1999).

[557] United States v. ChevronTexaco Corp., 241 F. Supp. 2d 1065 (ND Cal. 2002).

[c] The Subject Matter of the Privilege

The attorney-client privilege has been interpreted to protect only those disclosures necessary to obtain informed legal advice that might not have been made absent the privilege.[558] It is obvious that the attorney must be fully informed on a matter by the client and that clients would withhold information if the law could compel the attorney to repeat it in court.[559] However, it is precisely the process of obtaining and rendering informed legal assistance that itself sets the limits of the privilege. Not all communications the lawyer receives in the course of rendering legal assistance are made in confidence by the client for the purpose of securing that assistance. As a result, no blanket claim of the attorney-client privilege can prevent a court from inquiring into the general nature of the services performed and the communications made.[560] The privilege must be established on a document-by-document basis. The statement of one court on the subject is typical.[561]

> We hold that when, as here, a party asserting the attorney-client privilege against a tax summons sets out specific facts establishing the elements of the privilege and detailing the general nature of the withheld documents, there is no plain error if the district court fails to make a *sua sponte*, document-by-document finding of the privilege's applicability.

An attorney may also be required to respond to questions by the Service to determine the existence of the attorney-client relationship and its duration and to further the search for unprivileged information.[562] Thus, the attorney may be required to disclose the general date and nature of the services he performed on the taxpayer's behalf and whether the attorney received any remuneration for his services and the amount thereof. The attorney also may be required to respond to questions in aid of the Service's attempt to discover the nature of

---

[558] Fisher v. United States, 425 US 391 (1976).

[559] See Wigmore, Evidence § 2290 (McNaughton, ed.; rev. ed. 1961).

[560] Colton v. United States, 306 F2d 633 (2d Cir. 1962), cert. denied, 371 US 951 (1963); United States v. Hodgson, 492 F2d 1175, 1177 (10th Cir. 1974); United States v. Finley, 434 F2d 596 (5th Cir. 1970); United States v. Alario, 78-1 USTC ¶ 9304 (EDNY 1978); United States v. Davis, 636 F2d 1028, 1029 n.20 (5th Cir. 1981); United States v. El Paso Co., 81-2 USTC ¶ 9819 (SD Tex. 1981), aff'd, 682 F2d 530 (5th Cir. 1982), cert. denied, 104 S. Ct. 1927 (1984) ("[b]lanket assertions of privilege are not acceptable"). In attempting to establish protection of the privilege, the party claiming the privilege has the burden of proof. Id. United States v. Rockwell Int'l, 897 F2d 1255 (3d Cir. 1990) (although tax-accrual workpapers may be subject to privilege, claimant must establish on document-by-document basis that they constituted legal advice and that there was no waiver by communication to independent auditors).

[561] United States v. Bornstein, 977 F2d 112 (4th Cir. 1992).

[562] Colton v. United States, 306 F2d 633 (2d Cir. 1962), cert. denied, 371 US 951 (1963).

the papers in the attorney's possession in order to determine which are privileged and which are not.

The privilege is claimed by way of a privilege log, which identifies each document withheld on privilege grounds and the particular privilege being asserted (e.g., attorney client privilege or work product). A Local Rule of the District Court for the Southern District of New York illustrates the information to be included in a privilege log:[563] (1) the type of document; (2) the general subject matter; (3) the date; and (4) such other information sufficient to identify it for a subpoena duces tecum, including where appropriate the author, the addressee, and, where not apparent, the relationship of the author and addressee to each other. It is not unusual for there to be a dispute about privilege logs, such as the burden of preparing the privilege log for large number of documents (courts have discretion to ease the requirements of the privilege log) and whether the privilege log is adequate. When the privilege log is found to be inadequate, the court may find that the privilege claim has not been established. If the inadequacy is not cured, the court may order that the party seeking the documents may make an offer of proof as to what the documents in question would establish if they were available as exhibits in the case and may draw adverse inferences from the privilege claimant party's failure to produce the documents.[564]

[i] The identity of the client. In general, neither the name of a client nor the fee and related matters are subject to the attorney-client privilege. Without more, a client's name is not a communication made for the purpose of obtaining legal advice and, thus, generally falls outside the privilege.[565] This general principle has become known more for a notable limited exception. The privilege will protect a client's identity where, because of information already

---

[563] See Local Rule 46, Local Rules of the U.S. District Court for the Southern District of New York.

[564] See Cabot v. United States, 77 AFTR2d 96-2068 (Fed. Cl. 1996) (taxpayer made generalized attorney-client privilege and work product claims and failed to comply with an order to cure). For a case involving a privilege log prepared using categories of information, which was unsatisfactory, see United States v. KPMG, 237 F. Supp. 2d 35 (DDC 2002).

[565] See Cabot v. United States, 77 AFTR2d 96-2068 (Fed. Cl. 1996) For a nontax case holding that the name of a client is not privileged, see In re Grand Jury Proceedings (Pavlick), 680 F2d 1026 (5th Cir. 1982) (en banc). Case Comment, 21 Am. Crim. L. Rev. 81 (1983). Compare United States v. Liebman, 742 F2d 807 (3d Cir. 1984) (list of clients who paid fees over three-year period for purchases of tax shelters held privileged because subject matter of communications involved not just client names); Tornay v. United States, 840 F2d 1424 (9th Cir. 1988) (summons issued to taxpayers' attorney for the amount, date, and form of legal fees did not violate the attorney-client privilege). United States v. Goldberger & Dubin, 935 F2d 501 (2d Cir. 1991) (client names were not exempt from disclosure under attorney-client privilege for Form 8300); United States v. Garland, 92-1 USTC ¶ 50,218 (ND Ga. 1992) (accord).

possessed by or disclosed to another, disclosure of the client's name will also disclose other matters ordinarily falling within the privilege.[566] Where special circumstances exist, the name of the client may be a communication. One type of case in which the limited exception has been applied is so-called conscience payment cases. In *Baird v. Koerner*,[567] attorney *A* was consulted by attorney *B*, whose unnamed client has understated his tax and wanted to remedy the situation without precipitating a fraud investigation. Attorney *B* paid the client's funds to Attorney *A*, who remitted a check to the Service in the amount of the delinquent tax on behalf of an unnamed taxpayer. It has generally been accepted that the client's name under these circumstances is privileged.[568] Another case of this type involved an identified taxpayer who also understated his liability on a previously filed return, and retained an attorney to deliver a cashier's check to the Service without, of course, disclosing the taxpayer's identity.[569] The Service served a summons ordering the attorney to disclose the name of his client. The Ninth Circuit's rationale in *Baird* was that the client's identity was a communication that must remain confidential in order to prevent complete disclosure of the taxpayer's fraud or at least unpaid tax liability. In *Baird*, by paying the client's tax the attorney had informed the Service that the unnamed client owed tax, and disclosure of the client's name would reveal not only his identity but that he owed tax. In *Tillotson*, the Seventh Circuit also concluded that the substance of the attorney-client communication had already been communicated to the Service at the time the attorney remitted the cashier's check. If the attorney were compelled to reveal the identity of the client, the entire communication both the taxpayer client and the communication he made to the attorney would be revealed.[570]

The exception these rare cases illustrate must be determined to apply on a case-by-case basis. It should be noted that even if the exception applies, the Service is not precluded by the attorney-client privilege from requesting the bank records of the attorney, and those records may disclose the name of the client-taxpayer.[571] Also, a lawyer who is asked to be a conduit for funds is not normally rendering legal services.[572] In another case, therefore, a court might

---

[566] Baird v. Koerner, 279 F2d 623 (9th Cir. 1960); Tillotson v. Boughner, 350 F2d 663 (7th Cir. 1964).

[567] Baird v. Koerner, 279 F2d 623 (9th Cir. 1960).

[568] Baird v. Koerner, 279 F2d 623 (9th Cir. 1960); Tillotson v. Boughner, 350 F2d 663 (7th Cir. 1964).

[569] Tillotson v. Boughner, 350 F2d 663 (7th Cir. 1964).

[570] Tillotson v. Boughner, 350 F2d 663, 666 (7th Cir. 1964).

[571] Gannet v. First Nat'l State Bank of NJ, 546 F2d 1072 (3d Cir. 1976); Shulze v. Rayunec, 350 F2d 666 (7th Cir. 1965).

[572] See Gannet v. First Nat'l State Bank of NJ, 546 F2d 1072 (3d Cir. 1976); Pollock v. United States, 202 F2d 281 (5th Cir. 1953) (deposit of funds not confidential communication).

well reach a different conclusion than the circuit courts did in *Baird* and *Tillot-son* reached. More than a decade after its decision in *Baird*, the Ninth Circuit said that it would only apply the *Baird* rule where a "strong probability" exists that the information sought would implicate the client "in the very criminal activity for which the legal advice was sought."[573] In a later case, this rule was modified, and the true principle, as restated, was that the privilege applies where in the circumstances of the case disclosure of the identity of the client is in substance "a disclosure of the confidential communication in the professional relationship between the client and the attorney."[574] Yet another more recent restatement of *Baird* holds that the correct test "is whether the fee-payer's identity and the fee arrangements are so intertwined with confidential communications that revealing either . . . would be tantamount to revealing a privileged communication."[575]

[ii] The Section 6050I cases. Under Section 6050I, lawyers and others receiving currency of $10,000 or more are required to report the transactions, including the identity of the payer, on Form 8300. When lawyers refused to report the identity of clients who paid them in currency on the ground of attorney-client privilege, following authority generally requiring disclosure of a client's identity and fee information, courts have enforced summonses for the missing information,[576] holding that client-identifying information is not ex-

---

[573] United States v. Hodge & Zweig, 548 F2d 1347 (9th Cir. 1977).

[574] In re Grand Jury Subpoena (Osterhoudt), 722 F2d 591 (9th Cir. 1983).

[575] Ralls v. United States, 52 F3d 223, 226 (9th Cir. 1995); see also United States v. Blackman, 77 AFTR2d 96-313 (9th Cir. 1995) (citing other Ninth Circuit decisions) (*Baird v. Koerner* limited to the principle that "the attorney client privilege does not apply where disclosure would convey information tantamount to a confidential communication").

[576] United States v. Goldberger & Dubin, PC, 935 F2d 501 (2d Cir. 1991) (client names are not exempt from disclosure on Forms 8300 under the attorney-client privilege and Sixth Amendment); United States v. Leventhal, 961 F2d 936 (11th Cir. 1992) (accord); United States v. Ritchie, 19 F3d 13 (6th Cir. 1994) (accord); United States v. Sindel, 94-2 USTC (CCH) ¶ 50,300 (ED Mo. 1994) (summons enforced over claims of attorney-client privilege and Sixth Amendment violation), aff'd in part and rev'd in part, 53 F3d 874 (8th Cir. 1995), United States v. Blackman, 72 F3d 1418 (9th Cir. 1995) (privilege claim rejected). On appeal, in *Sindel*, the circuit court reversed the district court on the attorney-client privilege claim for Jane Doe's Form 8300 because based on an in camera review of the special circumstances, the lawyer "could not release the information about the payments on behalf of Jane Doe without revealing the substance of a confidential communication." However, the court affirmed on the rejection of the privilege claim for John Doe, following the Second Circuit's analysis in *Goldberger & Dubin*. The Eighth Circuit acknowledged that there were serious Sixth Amendment implications in Sindel's claim that an attorney becomes a de facto agent for the government when compelled to offer an opinion about whether a particular cash payment was a "suspicious transaction," a question added to the January 1990 version of Form 8300. Sindel had used this version of the Form 8300 when he filed for Jane Doe, and the court had upheld the attorney-client privilege. It refused to decide the constitutional claim on the John Doe form because the

empt from disclosure on Forms 8300 under the attorney-client privilege and the Sixth Amendment. covered. Not only were attorneys unsuccessful in their privilege claims to completing the Forms 8300, the privilege claim does not constitute reasonable cause for the attorney's refusal to file the form. In fact, the failure has been said to be willful, with the result that the attorney is liable for the civil penalty for failure to file the Form 8300 imposed by Section 6721.[577]

[iii] The tax shelter summons cases. In tax shelter investigations, the Service has targeted promoters, accounting firms, and law firms. In sum-

---

possibility that the reporting requirements of Section 6050I would permit prosecutors to subpoena and force the disqualification of the attorney was too speculative.

The ethical implications of requiring lawyers to disclose the identity of clients who pay them in currency are discussed and analyzed by a committee of lawyers in United States v. Monnat, 853 F. Supp. 1304 (D. Kan. 1994) (*Monnat II*); see also United States v. Monnat, 853 F. Supp. 1301 (D. Kan. 1994) (*Monnat I*). In summary, the committee on conduct of attorneys for the District of Arkansas said that since concealment of a client's identify is generally not included in the attorney-client privilege, the attorney has a duty to advise the client about the limitations of confidentiality. A lawyer may advise a client about the law in order to assist the client to make an informed decision, but the lawyer may not advise the client for purposes of evading the statue. Finally, a lawyer does not act unethically by complying with Section 6050I or an order of the court directing compliance; because the lawyer is permitted to do so when the lawyer reasonably believes that disclosure is required by law or court order. Whatever accommodation is made with state-created ethical obligations, however, the lawyer cannot justify refusal to comply with a summons on the basis of a state-imposed duty on the lawyer to avoid disclosures of a client's confidences and secrets. United States v. Blackman, 72 F3d 1418 (9th Cir. 1995); see also United States v. Sindel, supra.

[577] Lefcourt v. United States, 78 AFTR2d 96-5051 (SDNY 1996) (attorney received clear notice in the *Goldberger* case that civil and criminal penalties might be imposed). The Second Circuit affirmed the district court's decision. Gerald B. Lefcourt, PC v. United States, 125 F3d 79 (2d Cir. 1997). In affirming the district court, the Second Circuit held that Lefcourt was liable for the $25,000 penalty for intentionally disregarding the requirement of filing a complete Form 8300, and Lefcourt acted intentionally in omitting the payor's name since "only a civil penalty" was involved; and for purposes of a civil penalty, not a criminal penalty, the intentional disregard in Section 6721 means conduct that is willful, but in the context of a civil penalty, this "requires only that a party act voluntarily in withholding the requested information, rather than accidently or unconsciously." Lefcourt did not act with reasonable cause for purposes of the uniform waiver standard of Section 6724, because his reason for omitting the payor's name was not "objectively reasonable under the circumstances." In evaluating the reasonableness of Lefcourt's actions, the circuit court said it was proper to consider his particular "business"; that is, "whether the law firm's decision to withhold client-identifying information was consistent with the standard of care that a reasonably prudent attorney would use under the circumstances in the course of his or her business." Lefcourt did not meet that standard of care, because he had argued that the attorney-client privilege protected him from disclosing client-identifying information in certain "special circumstances," which applied to the completion of the Form 8300. The Second Circuit rejected this reasonable cause explanation on the ground that Lefcourt should have known that the Second Circuit did not

monses issued to accounting firms, the summons has called for the identity of the firm's clients who entered into tax shelter transactions that fit within transactions which the Service has identified in notices as being potentially abusive tax shelter transactions. Clients whose identities might be disclosed have intervened in the summons enforcement actions or instituted their own proceedings to quash the summons in the name of John Doe. In these proceedings, the unnamed clients have contended that by virtue of the federally authorized tax practitioner privilege (which is roughly coextensive with the attorney-client privilege), their identities were privileged confidential communications. The authority cited for this identity confidentiality are the *Baird* and *Tillotson* cases. After considerable litigation on the issue, in *BDO Seidman v. United States, Appeals of John Doe and Jane Doe*,[578] the Seventh Circuit concluded that no disclosure of a confidential communication would be made if documents the accounting firm produced in response to a summons revealed the identity of the Does. Documents responsive to the summonses also did not contain any tax advice, and in fact the accounting firm's specifically did not include "any legal and/or tax opinions regarding any strategies that may be implemented." Other documents had been generated for the purpose of preparing tax returns, and this accountant's work was not covered by Section 7525. Also, a group of unidentified clients who attempted to intervene had produced no agreements on the basis of which confidentiality could be inferred. The court found that the taxpayers could not have had any expectation that their identities would be confidential because the tax shelter reporting rules required the accounting firm to make and retain a list of investors in potentially abusive tax shelters. As the court held, "[t]his list-keeping provision precludes the Does from establishing an expectation of confidentiality in their communications with [the accounting firm], an essential element of the attorney-client privilege and by extension the § 7525 privilege."[579] Consequently, the Does "should have known that the [accounting firm] was obligated to disclose the identities of clients engaging in such financial transactions."[580] The court recognized that the case was unlike *Tillotson* (where the communication revealed the substance of the confidential communication) in that the Service did not know what if any relationship the Does had with the twenty notice transactions listed in the summons to the accounting firm. But the accounting firm's "affirmative

---

recognize any "special circumstance" that "possible or even likely client incrimination constitutes a special circumstance justifying nondisclosure."

[578] BDO Seidman v. United States, Appeals of John Doe and Jane Doe, 337 F3d 802 (7th Cir. 2003).

[579] BDO Seidman v. United States, Appeals of John Doe and Jane Doe, 337 F3d 802 (7th Cir. 2003) at slip op. 15.

[580] BDO Seidman v. United States, Appeals of John Doe and Jane Doe, 337 F3d 802 (7th Cir. 2003) at slip op. 15.

duty" to disclose the clients' participation in a potentially abusive tax shelters made the Does' situation distinguishable from the conscience payment cases.[581]

[iv] Fees. It is clear that a fee is not a protected communication under the attorney-client privilege, nor are records such as bills and notations concerning tax liabilities and arrangements for paying fees.[582] Where an attorney representing the target of a grand jury investigation has been served with a subpoena calling for the attorney's testimony and production of his fee records pertaining to the target, more than the attorney-client privilege is at stake. Although fees are not themselves privileged attorney-client communications, by calling an attorney as a witness against his client, the government is creating the potential for the attorney's disqualification. Thus, the subpoena affects the client's right to have counsel of his own choosing in the event an indictment is returned against him. In this situation, the Second Circuit held that the government is not required to make a preliminary showing of need before a grand jury subpoena is enforced against an attorney for fee information.[583] The court

---

[581] The Seventh Circuit's decision in the *BDO* case resulted in the district court hearing *United States v. Arthur Andersen, John and Jane Doe*, which had previously found an identity privilege, to amend its prior order and to hold that Andersen must reveal the identities to the Service; denied the Does' request for a determination of the responsiveness of the transaction to summonses; and denied the request to intervene of clients because they did not timely raise an identity privilege. The district court followed the Seventh Circuit's *BDO* opinion with some misgivings because it believed that the Seventh Circuit ruled as it did based on the particular facts of *BDO*, while the facts in Andersen arguably supported an identity privilege: Andersen provided tax advice and tax opinions to the clients, none of which was used to prepare tax returns; Andersen provided tailored tax strategies to provide specific results to a specific situation; and the clients relied on opinions Andersen gave to them that their transactions were not subject to the tax shelter reporting rules, although the district court suggested that *BDO* did not call for the circuit court's establishing such a broad rule.

[582] Colton v. United States, 306 F2d 633 (2d Cir. 1962), cert. denied, 371 US 951 (1963); United States v. Hodge & Zweig, 548 F2d 1347 (9th Cir. 1977); In re Michaelson, 511 F2d 882, 887–888 (9th Cir. 1975); United States v. Haddad, 527 F2d 537 (6th Cir. 1975); In re Wasserman & Carliner, 198 F. Supp. 564 (DDC 1961). United States v. Davis, 636 F2d 1028 (5th Cir. 1981). But see In re Grand Jury Subpoenas (Salas and Waxman), 695 F2d 359 (9th Cir. 1982) (demands for "attorney time records, describing the services performed by the attorneys, retainer agreements, contracts, letters of agreement, and related correspondence . . . [are] an unjustified intrusion into the attorney-client privilege").

[583] To balance the need of the grand jury for all available information and the integrity of the attorney-client relationship, a panel of the Second Circuit initially adopted a rule requiring the government to make a preliminary showing of relevance and need where (1) a subpoena is issued to an attorney to testify before a grand jury investigating his client, whom he had previously represented, and (2) the attorney will be disqualified if he testifies. In re Grand Jury Subpoena Served Upon John Doe, Esq., 759 F2d 968 (2d Cir. 1985) (enforcement denied). See also In re Shargel, 742 F2d 61 (2d Cir. 1984) (similar facts, subpoena quashed). However, the circuit court sitting en banc vacated this panel decision.

pointed out that since the client had not been indicted, the client's Sixth Amendment right to counsel had not yet attached. Thus, the Second Circuit holds that client awards and fee arrangements are not protected by the attorney-client privilege.[584] Also, client identity information is not privileged in the absence of special circumstances.[585] Other circuits have also refused to adopt such a limiting rule.[586] The Seventh Circuit has stated that the lawyer and prosecutor may differ and necessity may become a factor if, for example, the work product doctrine is involved. However, "[c]oncern about the possible effects of disclosure on legal representation at trial is not a reason—apart from the extent to which it is reflected in the privilege—to resist disclosure." The district court must resolve all claims, and appeal will only be heard thereafter.[587]

[v] The crime/fraud exception. The subject matter of the privilege does not include advice that assists the client in the commission of a crime or fraud. This crime/fraud exception to the attorney-client privilege is well-recognized.[588] A two-pronged test is applied to decide whether this exception exists: (1) Is there prima facie evidence showing that the client was engaged in criminal or fraudulent conduct when be sought the advice, that he was planning such conduct when he sought the advice, or that he committed a crime or fraud after receiving the benefit of counsel's advice and (2) is there evidence that the attorney's assistance was obtained in furtherance of the criminal or fraudulent conduct or that it was closely related to it?[589] Under this exception, no privilege applies where the desired advice refers not only to prior wrongdoing, but to future wrongdoing—i.e., to further either the crime charged in an indict-

---

[584] In re Grand Jury Subpoena Ducas Tecum (Shargel), 742 F2d 61 (2d Cir. 1984); In re Two Grand Jury Subpoenas Duces Tecum Dated Aug. 21, 1985, 793 F2d 69 (2d Cir. 1986).

[585] In re Grand Jury Subpoena Served on John Doe, Esq., 781 F2d 238 (2d Cir.) (en banc), cert. denied, 106 S. Ct. 1515 (1986).

[586] In re Klein, 776 F2d 628 (7th Cir. 1985) ("the grand jury may call a lawyer as a witness without making any preliminary showing of need. The lawyer may assert any privileges the client possesses, and he must do so, as Walsh, 623 F2d 489 (7th Cir. 1980), cert. denied, 449 US 994 (1980), holds, one document at a time").

[587] See also In re Grand Jury Investigation (Harvey), 769 F2d 1485 (11th Cir. 1985).

[588] See generally 8 Wigmore, Evidence § 2298 (McNaughton, ed., rev. ed. 1961) (and cases cited.)

[589] In re Schroeder, Jr., 842 F2d 1223 (11th Cir. 1987) (cases gathered; any legal assistance provided by the counsel to the taxpayer in generating income or in disposing of income was related to the taxpayer's failure to report income). The analysis in *Schroeder* would exclude any protection to sources of income even if the sources disclosed prior criminal conduct rather than the tax evasion being investigated. However, the court also found that the source communications were made in connection with legal assistance related to ongoing criminal activity, namely, the lawyer had assisted the taxpayer in establishing several offshore companies.

ment or future illegality.[590] In opposing an attorney-client privilege claim on grounds of the crime/fraud exception, the Service may request that the district court conduct an in camera review of allegedly confidential communications to determine whether these communications fall within the crime/fraud exception.[591] the Supreme Court in *United States v. Zolin* stated that before the request can be granted, the party seeking in camera review "must present evidence sufficient to support a reasonable belief that in camera review may yield evidence that establishes the exception's applicability."[592]

The purpose of the privilege "is to encourage clients to make full disclosure to their attorneys."[593] The privilege protects communications by the client to the lawyer in both oral and written form—that is, the client may make the communication orally or in writing to the lawyer.[594] But the client may not make preexisting records confidential communications simply by delivering them to an attorney. If a client has turned records over to a lawyer, the status of the records in the lawyer's hands depends on their status in the taxpayer-client's hands.[595] This was the analysis the Supreme Court used in *Fisher v. United States*, where the Court distinguished between a document that already had independent existence, the information in which is communicated to a lawyer, and physical possession of a preexisting document. The preexisting document is not covered by the privilege unless it is otherwise confidential in the hands of the taxpayer-client. For this reason, a taxpayer's attorney may be compelled to produce an accountant's workpapers because such workpapers would not have been privileged from production in the hands of the taxpayer-client.

[d] Confidentiality and Tax Services

Communications protected by the attorney-client privilege are communications made in order to obtain or render legal assistance. Whether a particular

---

[590] See, e.g., United States v. Friedman, 445 F2d 1076, 1085–1086 (9th Cir. 1971). Thus, under the crime/fraud exception, attorneys were required in response to a Service summons to produce documents that evidenced payment of fees by one member of a drug conspiracy for the defense of himself and for the defense of third parties both named and unnamed. Payment of the fees was found to be in furtherance of the conspiracy and ordered disclosed. United States v. Hodge & Zweig, 548 F2d 1347 (9th Cir. 1977).

[591] United States v. Zolin, 109 S. Ct. 2619 (1989).

[592] United States v. Zolin, 109 S. Ct. 2619, 2642 (1989) (showing must be based on any relevant evidence, lawfully obtained, that has not been adjudicated to be privileged).

[593] Fisher v. United States, 425 US 391 (1976).

[594] McCormick, ¶ 89, at 214. See United States v. Hankins, 631 F2d 360 (5th Cir. 1980) (citing the *McCormick* reference and holding that the privilege covers what records and documents a client shows the attorney).

[595] Fisher v. United States, 425 US 391 (1976). For a case following the *Fisher* analysis with painstaking care, see United States v. Davis, 636 F2d 1028 (5th Cir. 1981).

communication was made in confidence depends on the circumstances of the case. In resolving the issue, it seems that the objective (rather than subjective) intention of the client is considered—i.e., whether the client can reasonably have expected the communication to be held confidential.

Where a client makes communications to a lawyer in connection with the preparation of a tax return, the privilege may apply to some but not all of the matters disclosed. Giving of tax advice and the preparation of tax returns certainly involves the rendering of legal assistance,[596] but not all tax-related communications are intended by the client to be confidential. Where an estate tax examiner who was examining an estate tax return served a summons on partners of a law firm for documents relating to the formation, operation, and valuation of a limited liability company included in the estate, and the partners refused to produce the documents, a district court granted the lawyers' motion to quash.[597] The court rejected the Service's argument that the withheld documents were business, not legal, advice on the ground that factually the documents were prepared in the course of estate planning services the decedent and her son had previously requested. Also, as the documents demonstrated, third parties present at meetings were to assist the taxpayer in obtaining confidential legal advice or were assistants of the attorneys in rendering that advice in confidence. Finally, valuation and financial information were so intertwined with privileged communications that the financial information was privileged.

Communications made for the purpose of including them in tax returns are not considered privileged because the communications were not intended to be kept confidential.[598] Under this rationale, workpapers compiled in the process of amending income tax returns were held not to be privileged, even though the accountant was employed by the taxpayer's attorney to prepare the amended returns.[599] This result is clearly indicated where the information ob-

---

[596] Colton v. United States, 306 F2d 633, 637 (2d Cir. 1962), cert. denied, 371 US 951 (1963) (there are "matters sufficiently within the professional competence of an attorney to make them prima facie subject to the attorney-client privilege").

[597] Segerstrom v. United States, 87 AFTR2d 2001-1702 (ND Cal. 2001).

[598] Colton v. United States, 306 F2d 633, 638 (2d Cir. 1962), cert. denied, 371 US 951 (1963); United States v. Cote, 456 F2d 142 (8th Cir. 1972), aff'g 326 F. Supp. 444 (D. Minn. 1971); Olender v. United States, 210 F2d 795 (9th Cir. 1954). The Court in *Colton* said that "particularly in the case of an attorney preparing a tax return" much of the information communicated to him by the client-taxpayer "is not intended to be confidential, but rather is given for transmittal by the attorney to others—for example, for inclusion in the tax return." *Colton v. United States*, supra, at 638. For this reason, tax return workpapers and the records on which they are based may not be privileged. United States v. Davis, 636 F2d 1028, 1043 (5th Cir. 1981); see also United States v. Swain, 91-1 USTC ¶ 50,087 (DSC 1991) (accountant, not client, gave workpapers to attorney).

[599] United States v. Cote, 456 F2d 142 (8th Cir. 1972), aff'g 326 F. Supp. 444 (D. Minn. 1971). See also United States v. Brown, 349 F. Supp. 420 (ND Ill.), aff'd, 478 F2d 1038 (7th Cir. 1972) (accountant retained before attorney consulted). Where a client employs an attorney to research the possibility of filing a public document, such as a ruling

tained is actually set forth on the completed return or has been received from persons other than the client or his agent.[600] However, information supplied to an attorney for the purpose of preparing a return is generally supplied with the understanding that the attorney will make a determination as to what should be included and how the information should be treated for return-filing purposes.[601] This process seems to be the essence of legal advice rendered by an attorney in the preparation of a tax return.[602]

For this reason, oral communications and written summaries made or otherwise communicated to the attorney in connection with the preparation of a tax return should not automatically be considered communications that the client does not expect to be held confidential by the attorney in his capacity as such.[603] However, some courts seem to have accepted the notion that the prep-

---

request, the client's communications have been held confidential. In re Grand Jury 83-2, 748 F2d 871 (4th Cir. 1984) (analyzing cases; distinguishing *Cote*; ruling request not privileged because there was no evidence the client had instructed the attorney not to file it; other documents pertaining to dissolution on which client decided not to go forward held confidential).

[600] United States v. Threlkeld, 241 F. Supp. 324 (WD Tenn. 1965).

[601] United States v. Judson, 322 F2d 460 (9th Cir. 1963); In re Schroeder, Jr., 842 F2d 1223 (11th Cir. 1987) ("the preparation of a tax return should not be viewed as legal advice"). United States v. Schlegel, 313 F. Supp. 177 (D. Neb. 1970). In *Schlegel* the court said, "a more realistic rule would be that the client intends that only so much of the information will be conveyed to the government as the attorney concludes should be, and ultimately is, sent to the government. In short, whatever is finally sent to the government is what matches the client's intent." Id. at 179.

[602] Colton v. United States, 306 F2d 633 (2d Cir. 1962), cert. denied, 371 US 951 (1963). But see United States v. Davis, 636 F2d 1028 (5th Cir. 1981) (lawyer who prepares tax returns is merely performing same function as accountant as to whom no privilege applies, so that no basis exists for finding privilege applies at all to return preparers).

[603] United States v. Abrahams, 905 F2d 1276 (9th Cir. 1990) ("[a]lthough communications made *solely* for tax return preparation are not privileged, communications made to acquire legal advice about what to claim on tax returns may be privileged"). See also United States v. Schlegel, 313 F. Supp. 177 (D. Neb. 1970); United States v. Baucus, 74-2 USTC ¶ 9594 (D. Mont. 1971); United States v. Jeremiah, 76-1 USTC ¶ 9441 (D. Or. 1975); United States v. Threlkeld, 241 F. Supp. 324 (WD Tenn. 1965). Because returns are prepared primarily by accountants, return preparation appears to some courts to be an accounting service, not a legal service covered by the privilege. But the tax law is still law, and advice about the law is legal advice if it is given by an attorney, even if an accountant may also give advice about the tax law. When the return preparer is both an accountant and an attorney, deciding whether the service rendered was an accounting or legal service is difficult. See, e.g., United States v. Bornstein, 977 F2d 112 (4th Cir. 1992) (attorney and accountant prepared client's tax return making Fifth Amendment privilege claim).

In United States v. Bell, 95-1 USTC ¶ 50,006 (ND Cal. 1994), a transfer pricing study prepared by an accounting firm retained by the corporation's counsel was held subject to the attorney-client privilege and covered by work product protection. However, because it was unclear whether the accounting firm had assisted in the preparation of the tax

aration of tax returns is automatically outside the scope of the attorney-client privilege.[604]

[i] Waiver. Voluntary disclosure of the subject matter of the communication by the client may constitute a waiver of the privilege and strip the communication of its confidentiality.[605] Once public disclosure is made, the privilege has been held to be permanently waived.[606] For example, where ledgers were given to an agent by the taxpayers' accountant for a civil tax examination in 1976 and later were returned to the taxpayers' lawyer, the attorney-client privilege could not protect the ledgers when they were later subpoenaed for criminal tax prosecution of the taxpayers.[607]

Waiver may also be implied. Where some disclosure is made, fairness may prevent the client from withholding the remainder.[608] Thus, the client's voluntary disclosure of certain transactions to a government agency may constitute a waiver of the privilege as to communications underlying the disclosure.[609] Similarly, a corporation waived privilege where questionable payments

---

return, an activity the judge assumed could not be legal services, the judge reviewed the study in camera, and decided it was privileged.

[604] United States v. Cote, 456 F2d 142 (8th Cir. 1972), aff'g 326 F. Supp. 444 (D. Minn. 1971); United States v. Brown, 478 F2d 1038 (7th Cir. 1973); United States v. Blackburn, 74-2 USTC ¶ 9696 (MD Fla. 1974); United States v. Young, 76-1 USTC ¶ 9448 (ED Mich. 1976). In United States v. Merrell, 303 F. Supp. 490 (NDNY 1969), because it concluded that the privilege did not apply to materials included in a tax return, the court ordered the production of income and expense summaries prepared by the client and the attorney's workpapers made in preparing the return. United States v. Davis, 636 F2d 1028 (5th Cir. 1981).

[605] Wigmore, Evidence § 2327, at 634 (McNaughton, ed.; rev. ed. 1961).

[606] McCormick, ¶ 4, § 93, at 227. There is an exception when the disclosed information falls under the "common interest rule," which "serves to protect the confidentiality of communications passing from one party to the attorney for another party where a joint defense effort or strategy has been decided upon and undertaken by the parties and their respective counsel." United States v. Schwimmer, 892 F2d 237, 243 (2d Cir. 1989). The common interest rule was found applicable when the Service served a summons to obtain documents prepared by the counsel and tax counsel of members of a consortium, which had been formed to compete with General Electric, regarding among other things the tax structure of the entity. See United States v. United Techs. Corp., 80 AFTR2d 97-6614 (D. Conn. 1997).

[607] United States v. Miller, 660 F2d 563 (5th Cir. 1981) (a divided court).

[608] Wigmore, Evidence § 2292 (McNaughton, ed.; rev. ed. 1961).

[609] In re Sealed Case, 676 F2d 793 (DC Cir. 1982). See also United States v. Massachusetts Inst. of Tech., 957 F. Supp. 301 (D. Mass. 1997) (minutes and billing statements were not subject to the attorney-client privilege when the Service summoned them, because the privilege had been waived when they had previously been turned over to the Defense Contract Audit Agency), aff'd in part and vacated and remanded on the Service's appeal as to certain documents, 129 F3d 681 (1st Cir. 1997) (several documents district court held were privileged, were held by the circuit court to be reports on legal matters, not legal advice). In re Pioneer Hi-Bred Int'l, Inc., 238 F3d 1370 (Fed. Cir. 2001) (an in-

report was shown to an auditor and an underwriter in connection with a proposed securities offering.[610]

Also, waiver is implied when a client makes affirmative use of an attorney-client communication, but refuses to disclose it. Accordingly, when a taxpayer uses the advice of an attorney or federally authorized practitioner to support a reasonable cause defense to a civil penalty, there is a risk that this type of implied waiver will be found to have occurred. In *G-I Holdings*,[611] taxpayers were found to have waived the attorney-client privilege as to certain transactions because in response to a government interrogatory regarding an accuracy-related penalty, they had raised the reasonable cause defense which was the equivalent of an "advice of counsel" defense. The court also held that the taxpayers had permanently waived the privilege, and that their waiver extended to the subject matter about which they responded (the specific transactions). Consequently, the waiver allowed the government access to relevant communications about the tax and penalty issues in the case. Thus, when a reasonable cause or reliance defense has been raised, a waiver will occur and the scope of that waiver is the subject matter of the with respect to which the affirmative defense was raised.[612]

Waiver, albeit an inadvertent one, can take place during discovery in a large document case. Courts have different views on the effect of a disclosure of otherwise attorney-privileged documents in the course of discovery, but the precautions that at least some courts require to support a finding that the privilege has not been waived are instructive about the level of care that must be taken to avoid a waiver of the privilege. For example, in a tax refund suit, the Court of Federal Claims reviewed the following different approaches courts have taken when an attorney inadvertently discloses privileged communications during discovery: (1) the traditional per se rule that disclosure results in waiver of the privilege, irrespective of the precautions taken to avoid it; (2) the

---

house counsel was required to testify about and produce documents relating to the effect of a merger on certain licenses on the ground that a waiver occurred when the corporation relied on or disclosed privileged opinions and communications concerning tax implications of the merger in the proxy statement filed with the SEC; however, the attorney-client privilege was not waived with respect to tax advice on other issues). For a case involving both disclosure and reliance on an opinion, see Long-Term Capital Holdings v. United States, 91 AFTR2d 2003-2606 (D. Conn. 2003).

[610] See In re John Doe Corp., 675 F2d 482 (2d Cir. 1982); In re Sealed Case, 676 F2d 793 (DC Cir. 1982). These cases also involved an exception to the privilege holding that advice in a criminal or fraudulent transaction is not protected. In both *In re Sealed Case* and *John Doe Corp.*, the circuit courts would not permit the privilege to prevent disclosure of the full record in an in-house investigation when to do so might result in a coverup of some crime or fraud.

[611] See In re G-I Holdings, 92 AFTR2d 2003-6070, (DNJ 2003).

[612] See In re G-I Holding, 92 AFTR2d 2003-6070, (DNJ 2003). The increase in tax shelter litigation is likely to supply additional responses to this issue soon enough.

contrary view that no waiver occurs when the attorney inadvertently discloses an attorney-client communication, because the privilege belongs to the client; and (3) the view of some courts that to determine whether the waiver was truly inadvertent, the circumstances of the disclosure must be considered.[613] In the case, the court applied the third approach and reviewed the precautions the attorneys had taken to avoid the disclosure of confidential communications. When it found that the attorneys used conclusory representations to describe their precautions rather than the specific procedures used and instructions given which had been unavailing, the court ruled that the taxpayer had not proved that it had taken sufficient steps to prevent the disclosure of privileged documents. One learns from the case, therefore, that the client's intention to maintain confidentiality (and to avoid waiver) must be proved, and, to carry this burden of proof, the client should establish specific procedures that are required to be followed.

The requirement that the communication be made in confidence excludes communications made in the presence of strangers, although if the lawyer is to be able to render legal services, it is recognized that some disclosure beyond the lawyer himself may be made without destroying confidentiality. At the least, these persons include the lawyer's staff and associates. In tax matters, a communication made to an accountant retained by the lawyer to assist him in rendering legal advice is considered made to the lawyer.[614]

Even where the client intends that communications not be disclosed, the privilege has traditionally not prevented an eavesdropper from revealing the communication.[615] The rationale behind this position is that the risk is on the client to see to it that the circumstances in which the communications are made are adequate to ensure secrecy, although the availability of modern eavesdropping devices has resulted in some movement toward abandoning the traditional view and preventing anyone from testifying to a confidential communication.[616] However, the traditional view still may be used. Where notes that a taxpayer's lawyer made were copied by a messenger who gave the copy to the Service, the notes were not ordered returned.[617] Although the notes were found not to be covered by the attorney-client privilege (they were the lawyer's work product), the distinction had no apparent impact on the result.

---

[613] International Bus. Mach. Corp. v. United States, 37 Fed. Cl. 599 (Fed. Cl. 1997).

[614] United States v. Kovel, 296 F2d 918 (2d Cir. 1961).

[615] Wigmore, Evidence § 2326 (McNaughton, ed.; rev. ed. 1961).

[616] See 2 Weinstein & Berger, Weinstein's Evidence ¶ 503(b)(02) (1989).

[617] United States v. Bonnell, 483 F. Supp. 1070 (D. Minn. 1979), aff'd without opinion (8th Cir. 1982).

[2] Discovery Protection for Work Product

Although it is not an evidentiary privilege, a lawyer's work product is conditionally protected from compulsory disclosure in civil and criminal litigation.[618] The elements of the work product doctrine are now restated in Rule 26(b)(3) of the Federal Rules of Civil Procedure as follows:[619]

> A party may obtain discovery of documents and tangible things otherwise discoverable . . . and prepared in anticipation of litigation or for trial by or for another party or by or for that other party's representative (including the other party's attorney, consultant, . . .) Only upon a showing that the party seeking discovery has substantial need of the materials in the preparation of the party's case and that the party is unable without undue hardship to obtain the substantial equivalent of hte materials by other means. In ordering discovery of such materials when the required showing has been made, the court shall protect against disclosure the mental impressions, conclusions, opinions, or legal theories of an attorney or other representative of the concerning the litigation.

In short, an attorney's fact work product is discoverable only on a showing of substantial need, but an attorney's opinion work product in the form of mental impressions, and the like are not discoverable. Compare the rule with the facts of *Hickman v. Taylor*, the case in which the Supreme Court first recognized a protection for a lawyer's work product.[620]

Even in language of the rule, the doctrine still reflects the facts of the case. In *Hickman v. Taylor*, tugboat owners retained a law firm to represent them after one of their tugboats sank and several crew members drowned, because they anticipated that claims would be made by the estates of the drowned crew members. There was an official hearing about the accident, and the testimony of the witnesses who testified was available to interested parties. The tugboat owners' lawyer interviewed witnesses who testified at the hearing and others, securing signed statements from some and taking notes of the other interviews. All of the estates of the drowned crew members made claims, as the tugboat owners anticipated, and all the claims were settled except one. In

---

[618] In civil cases, see Fed. R. Civ. P. 26(b)(3). In criminal cases, see United States v. Nobles, 422 US 225 (1975); In re Grand Jury Investigation (Sun Co.), 599 F2d 1224 (3d Cir. 1979); In re John Doe, Inc., 675 F2d 482 n.46 (2d Cir. 1982); In re Murphy, 560 F2d 326 (8th Cir. 1977); In re Grand Jury Proceedings (Duffy), 473 F2d 840 (8th Cir. 1973).

[619] Fed. R. Civ. P. 26(b)(3) provides for discovery only where there is a showing "that the party seeking discovery has substantial need of the materials in the preparation of his case and that he is unable without undue hardship to obtain the substantial equivalent of the materials by other means."

[620] Hickman v. Taylor, 329 US 495 (1947). In *Hickman*, the statements the lawyer obtained and the notes he made were held not to be protected by the attorney-client privilege.

the course of the discovery in the case brought by the remaining estate, the tugboat owners answered all interrogatories and production requests, except the one calling for the statements and notes the lawyer had made in interviewing the witnesses. Since the witnesses' identities and testimony were a matter of public record as available to the estate as they had been to the tugboat owners' lawyer, the estate could not show that it was unable to obtain the same information it was seeking in discovery.

Accordingly, in holding that the interview statements and lawyer's notes were confidential, the Supreme Court made the protection available (1) to documents a lawyer obtains and notes the lawyer prepares; (2) in anticipation of litigation; and (3) when the party seeking the information in discovery is unable to show that production of the lawyer's work product is needed to prepare the party's case, or that denial of discovery would cause undue hardship or injustice. While a showing of need (that is, the information is not otherwise available) may result in the loss of confidentiality of witness statements and the like (what is called fact work product), the Court said that the lawyer's mental impressions (opinion work product) are not discoverable.

Where a summons has been directed to an attorney, the challenge has sometimes been made that disclosure of the summons data is shielded by the work product doctrine. It is now established that the work product doctrine applies in a summons enforcement proceeding.[621] Work product protection is available only when the work product is prepared in anticipation of litigation. In tax situations it has been said that litigation might be anticipated and work product protection apply to a tax analysis of a proposed transaction prepared before the transaction occurs,[622] before the return has been filed,[623] after the return has been filed, but before the return has been examined,[624] and after the Commisioner's Art Advisory Panel has acted, but before a notice of deficiency has been sent to the taxpayer.[625]

In *Adlman* II, the Second Circuit adopted an interpretation recognized by a number of other circuits and well-known commentators that a document is prepared "in anticipation of litigation," if "'in light of the nature of the document and the factual situation in the particular case, the document can be fairly said to have been prepared or obtained because of the prospect of litigation.'"[626] According to the court, when a document is created because of the

---

[621] Upjohn Co. v. United States, 449 US 383, 396 (1981) ("[t]he Government concedes, wisely, that the Court of Appeals erred and that the work-product doctrine does apply to IRS summonses").

[622] See United States v. Adlman, 68 F3d 1495 (2d Cir. 1995).

[623] United States v. Bell, 95-1 USTC ¶ 50,006 (ND Cal. 1994).

[624] Upjohn Co. v. United States, 449 US 383, 385 (1981).

[625] Bernardo v. Comm'r, 104 TC 677 (1995).

[626] United States v. Adlman, 134 F3d 1194 (2d Cir. 1998) (*Adlman II*) (quoting 8 Wright, Miller, & Marcus, Federal Practice & Procedure § 2024:343 (1994)).

prospect of litigation and analyzes "the likely outcome of that litigation, it does not lose protection under this formulation [of the work product doctrine] merely because it is created in order to assist with a business decision."[627] This approach does not protect documents prepared in the ordinary course of business or that have been created in essentially the same form, whether or not there was a prospect of litigation. Thus, if a court finds that a taxpayer, such as the corporation in *Adlman II*, would have prepared the document as part of the ordinary course of its restructuring, then it will conclude that the document is not entitled to protection. Moreover, even if the document qualifies as work product, it is not protected if the party seeking the document establishes substantial need for the document and satisfies the other requirements of Rule 26(b)(3).[628]

In *Upjohn Co.*, the Supreme Court was faced with the responses of employees to questionnaires sent by corporate counsel and notes and memoranda of interviews. The Court did not establish a definitive rule, but it did hold that to the extent that the notes and memoranda reveal the attorney's mental processes in evaluating communications, they constitute work product which, under Federal Rule of Civil Procedure 26(b)(3), "cannot be disclosed simply on a showing of substantial need and inability to obtain the equivalent without undue hardship."[629] The Court indicated that a substantial showing of necessity and unavailability is required to compel disclosure.[630]

[a] Waiver

As with the attorney-client privilege, work product protection can be waived by voluntary disclosure. Also, waiver by implication has been found under circumstances where work product protection would permit the claimant to deceive. In one case where an implied waiver of the work product immunity was found, a public corporation had apparently made improper payments the

---

[627] The court also said that if "the company declines to make a [candid analysis of litigation risks] or scrimps on candor and completeness to avoid prejudicing its litigation prospects, it subjects itself and its co-venturers to ill-informed decision making." United States v. Adlman, 134 F3d 1194 (2d Cir. 1998).

[628] The circuit court remanded the case once again for the district court to make findings applying the "because of" standard and other findings consistent with its opinion.

[629] Upjohn Co. v. United States, 449 US 383, 401 (1981); United States v. Rockwell Int'l, 897 F2d 1255 (3d Cir. 1990) (tax-accrual workpapers subject to work product protection only if created by attorneys because of the prospect of litigation).

[630] This view throws into doubt earlier circuit court decisions in which the public interest in enforcement of the tax laws was considered relevant in determining the showing of necessity the Service needed to make to compel disclosure. See, e.g., United States v. Amerada Hess Corp., 619 F2d 980 (3d Cir. 1980); United States v. Brown, 478 F2d 1038 (7th Cir. 1973); United States v. Bonnell, 483 F. Supp. 1070 (D. Minn. 1979), aff'd without opinion (8th Cir. 1982).

circumstances of which it purportedly disclosed to the Securities and Exchange Commission (SEC), under the Commission's voluntary disclosure program.[631] When a grand jury began an investigation for possible conspiracy to defraud the government and obstruction of justice, it subpoenaed certain documents that clearly constituted work product. The documents also shed light on the accuracy of the report supplied to the SEC and statements that officers of the company had given the Service. The circuit court concluded that work product protection was impliedly waived when the corporation made the disclosure to the SEC because a purportedly unconditional disclosure may carry with it, if the circumstances warrant, an implied waiver of "any material necessary for a fair evaluation of [the] disclosure." The circuit court also applied to the work product immunity the crime/fraud exception applicable to the attorney-client privilege. It established a two-part test: (1) There must be a prima facie showing of a violation sufficiently serious to defeat work product immunity and (2) the court must find some valid relationship between the work product under subpoena and the prima facie violation.

After *Sealed Case*, federal courts have applied the doctrine of implied waiver in civil cases.[632] Where there has been a disclosure of an internal investigation to a government agency, it has been said that "litigants must not manipulate the work product doctrine for their own benefit by attempting to selectively disclose their attorney's work product."[633] In *Subpoena Duces Tecum*, the circuit court said that considerations of fairness and consistency prohibit litigants from gaining "the substantial advantages accruing to voluntary disclosure of work product to one adversary . . . while being able to maintain another advantage inherent in protecting that same work product from other adversaries."[634] In *Harding*, the fact of the internal investigation was used in a state agency's inquiry and as a defense to a sex discrimination case, and an implied waiver to work product protection for the internal investigation was found. The same kind of situation could arise in a corporation's use of an internal investigation in a civil tax penalty case (for example, a transfer pricing penalty or a reasonable cause defense to a negligence penalty, and later nontax litigation in which the corporation attempts to keep the investigation confidential; or in a corporation's use of an internal investigation for SEC purposes, and a claim that the investigation is confidential for Service purposes). In this context, an observation by the *Harding* court is worth noting, "Corporate litigants hoping to counter charges of respondeat superior liability may easily avoid this result in the future either by separating the role of the investigator

---

[631] In re Sealed Case, 676 F2d 793 (DC Cir. 1982).

[632] See In re Subpoena Duces Tecum, 738 F2d 1367, 1371 (DC Cir. 1984); Harding v. Dana Transp., Inc., 914 F. Supp. 1084, 1098 (DNJ 1996); see also Westinghouse v. Republic of the Phillipines, 951 F2d 1414, 1428–1430 (3d Cir. 1990).

[633] Harding v. Dana Transp., Inc., 914 F. Supp. 1084, 1098 (DNJ 1996)

[634] In re Subpoena Duces Tecum, 738 F2d 1367, 1371–1372 (DC Cir. 1984).

from that of litigator, or by refraining from defending themselves on the basis of reasonable investigation."[635]

[3] The Self-Critical Analysis Privilege

Similar to the work product doctrine is the self-critical analysis privilege. This privilege, which is recognized by some courts, protects internal investigations.[636] Under the self-critical analysis privilege, absent evidence of extraordinary circumstances, the public interest may be a reason for not permitting inquiry by discovery into particular matters, such as an internal report, or where confidentiality is essential to the free flow of information to promote recognized public interests. One court made these observations about this emerging privilege:

> First, materials protected have generally been those prepared for mandatory governmental reports. Second, only subjective, evaluative materials have been protected; objective data contained in those same reports in no case have been protected. Finally, courts have been sensitive to the need of the plaintiffs for such materials, and have denied discovery only where the policy favoring exclusion of the materials clearly outweighed plaintiff's need.[637]

In addition, protection has been provided for generalized reports, such as the corporation's overall compliance with a legal requirement, rather than an individual situation or complaint.[638]

[635] Harding v. Dana Transp., Inc., 914 F. Supp. 1084, 1099 (DNJ 1996).

[636] Bredice v. Doctor's Hosp., Inc., 50 FRD 249, 251 (DDC 1970), aff'd, 479 F2d 920 (DC Cir. 1973); Banks v. Lockheed-Georgia Co., 53 FRD 283 (ND Ga. 1971); United States v. Dexter Corp., 132 FRD 8, 9 (D. Conn. 1990); Todd v. South Jersey Hosp. Sys., 152 FRD 676 (DNJ 1993); Harding v. Dana Transp., Inc., 914 F. Supp. 1084, 1099 (DNJ 1996). See also Note, "The Privilege of Self-Critical Analysis," 96 Harv. L. Rev. 1083 (1983).

[637] Webb v. Westinghouse Elec. Corp., 81 FRD 431, 434 (ED Pa. 1078).

[638] Compare Banks v. Lockheed-Georgia Co., 53 FRD 283 (ND Ga. 1971) (general study of corporation's affirmative action compliance), with Harding v. Dana Transp., Inc., 914 F. Supp. 1084, 1099 (DNJ 1996) (applying a balancing test and permitting discovery of investigation of specific sex discrimination complaint).

[4] Accountant-Client Privilege

Although many states recognize an accountant-client privilege, there is no such privilege recognized in federal law.[639] It is now established that an accountant's workpapers prepared from the taxpayer's records are not protected from production pursuant to an internal revenue summons, even where the accountant has voluntarily surrendered the workpapers to his taxpayer client.[640] However, where the accountant is an employee of the taxpayer,[641] or where the accountant is retained by an attorney for the purpose of rendering legal advice,[642] the accountant's workpapers may be protected from disclosure under either the Fifth Amendment privilege or the attorney-client privilege, but not under the accountant-client privilege.

Federally Authorized Tax Practitioners. The IRS Restructuring and Reform Act of 1998 creates a new confidentiality privilege for taxpayer communications with federally authorized practitioners. Procedurally, the new Section 7425 establishes equal or coextensive confidentiality for taxpayer communications for the purpose of obtaining tax advice. Such communications may be between the taxpayer and a lawyer or between the taxpayer and a federally authorized tax practitioner (certified public accountants, enrolled agents, and, for limited subjects, an enrolled actuary).[643] There are several limitations that are important. One limitation is not reflected in the statute, but in the case law of the attorney-client privilege. Since the new privilege is coextensive with the attorney-client privilege, the same limitations that apply to the attorney-client privilege apply to the accountant/enrolled agent privilege. In general, the attorney-client privilege is not as broad as many attorneys believe. Accountants and enrolled agents will also find that the new attorney-like protection is hedged by many limitations and waiver circumstances that narrow the scope of the attorney-client privilege.

[a] Practice Before the Service

One limitation the statute provides is that the communication must be for the purpose of obtaining tax advice on a matter within the accountant/enrolled

---

[639] Couch v. United States, 409 US 322, 342 (1973) ("no confidential accountant-client privilege exists under federal law, and no state-created privilege has been recognized in federal cases"). United States v. Arthur Young & Co., 104 S. Ct. 1495 (1984) (explaining rationale for not recognizing an accountant-client privilege).

[640] Fisher v. United States, 425 US 391 (1976).

[641] United States v. Slutsky, 352 F. Supp. 1105, 1109 (SDNY 1972) ("the work product of an accountant hired full time for the purpose of keeping his employer's records belongs to the employer").

[642] United States v. Kovel, 296 F2d 918 (2d Cir. 1961).

[643] IRC § 7525, added by 1998 Act § 3411, applicable for communications made on or after July 22, 1998, the effective date of the Act.

agent's authority to practice before the Service.[644] This limitation may seem benign, but it also reflects the limitation on the attorney-client privilege that the privilege only applies to legal, not business, advice, and raises issues about the confidentiality of communications between the practitioner and the taxpayer about the preparation of a tax return when the communications themselves are not reflected on the return.

[b] Corporate Tax Shelters

Even tax advice will not be confidential if it is "[1] a written communication between [the accountant/enrolled agent] and a director, shareholder, officer, or employee, agent, or representative of a corporation [2] in connection with the promotion of the direct or indirect participation of [that] corporation in any tax shelter, [3] as that term is defined in [the substantial understatement component of the accuracy-related penalty]."[645] Since the substantial understatement accuracy-related penalty defines a tax shelter as any plan or arrangement, "a significant purpose" of which is the avoidance or evasion of income tax, the broad scope of the definition may sharply limit confidentiality for advice that accountants may give to their corporate clients.

[c] Criminal Matters

Another statutory limitation on the protection is that the accountant/enrolled agent privilege may only be asserted in any noncriminal matter before the Service.[646] It follows that confidentiality does not apply in any "criminal matter" before the Service. But what is a "criminal matter"? If the same standard that applies in summons cases is used, a criminal matter might not be said to exist even when Service special agents are investigating the taxpayer for potential criminal violations of the tax laws. This is because the taxpayer's case has not been referred for criminal prosecution, and, therefore, the Service has not institutionally committed itself to a criminal prosecution until then. Putting aside this "criminal matter" limitation, however, the new confidentiality applies in civil tax proceedings in any federal court brought by or against the United States.[647]

---

[644] IRC § 7525(a)(3)(B).

[645] IRC § 7525(b).

[646] IRC § 7525(2)(A).

[647] IRC § 7525(2)(B).

[5] Husband-Wife Privilege

Communications of a confidential nature between a husband and a wife occurring within a marriage cannot be used in court if the privilege is claimed and not waived. There are two distinct privileges arising out of the marital relationship: the first prevents one spouse from testifying adversely to the other; the second bars the testimony of one spouse as to confidential communications with the other. The testimonial privilege in federal courts rests in the witness spouse alone, and this spouse may neither be compelled to testify nor be prohibited from testifying.[648] This rule applies only to criminal cases. A spouse may be compelled to testify in a civil tax case, at least where the husband and wife have been granted immunity for criminal prosecution purposes.[649]

The marital communication privilege is limited to expressions intended by one spouse to convey a meaning to the other, usually in the form of words (oral or written) rather than acts that are not intended to be communications.[650] This principle applies in tax cases.[651] Under these general principles, it is questionable whether such matters as a husband's hiding records of a foreign bank account or similar conduct is protected under the marital communication privilege, especially where it is generally held that communications in furtherance of a crime or fraud are not privileged.[652]

[6] Physician-Patient or Psychotherapist-Patient Privilege

A communication made or information acquired in confidence, expressed or implied, to or by a person in his professional capacity as a physician and necessary for enabling him to give treatment is privileged from disclosure.[653] This privilege protecting the confidentiality of communications between a physician and patient occasionally arises in summons enforcement cases.[654] The privilege

---

[648] Trammel v. United States, 445 US 40 (1980) (wife granted immunity not foreclosed from testifying).

[649] Ryan v. Comm'r, 568 F2d 531 (7th Cir. 1977).

[650] Pereira v. United States, 347 US 1, 6 (1954); United States v. Lewis, 433 F2d 1146, 1151 (DDC 1970).

[651] United States v. Ashby, 245 F2d 684 (5th Cir. 1957).

[652] United States v. Kahn, 471 F2d 191, 195 (7th Cir. 1972), cert. denied, 411 US 986 (1973). Bassett v. United States, 80-1 USTC ¶ 9116 (DNH 1979) (testimony of wife in wrongful levy action about ownership of money allegedly derived from drug trafficking admitted over marital privilege claim).

[653] Wigmore, Evidence § 2380 (McNaughton, ed.; rev. ed. 1961).

[654] In re Albert Lindley Lee Memorial Hosp., 209 F2d 122 (2d Cir. 1953); United States v. Williams, 337 F. Supp. 1114 (SDNY 1971), appeal dismissed (psychotherapist-patient privilege). It has been held that since no physician-patient privilege is recognized as a matter of federal common law, it therefore is not available in a summons enforce-

is only as broad as the purpose it serves, which is weighed against the Service's need to know the information. The names of patients of a doctor under investigation were ordered disclosed after the court determined that the patients could not be injured by a disclosure of the fact.[655] However, the names of patients of a psychotherapist-taxpayer listed on message slips of a telephone-answering service were not ordered disclosed where the court perceived that the harm that might result from the contact of the patients outweighed the advantage the disclosure might have in the tax investigation.[656]

In *Jaffee v. Redmond*, the Supreme Court resolved the issue about whether a psychotherapist-patient privilege is a recognized new testimonial privilege for purposes of the Federal Rules of Evidence, and held that communications between a psychotherapist and his or her patient are confidential.[657]

---

ment proceeding. United States v. Providence Hosp., 507 F. Supp. 519 (ED Mich. 1981), followed in United States v. Schneider, 513 F. Supp. 286 (ND Ind. 1981) (patient-accounting records ordered produced provided that names of patients not copied, citing Gretsky v. Basso, 136 F. Supp. 640 (D. Mass. 1955)); United States v. Wettstein, 733 F. Supp. 1212 (CD Ill. 1990) (Illinois Mental Health Act claimed to protect psychologist's appointment books; held, not recognized in federal court and so "state-created privacy right must yield in the face of the expansive, congressionally-bestowed summons power of the IRS"). However, the proposition that no privilege exists seems overstated when some courts (*Schneider* and *Basso*) make efforts to avoid disclosure of patients' names, treatment, and diagnoses. In *Providence Hospital*, the summons seemed limited to the number of operations performed, but the district court, following authority in the Sixth Circuit, did hold that no such privilege exists in federal common law. Whatever the status of the privilege, courts allow sensitivity to the privacy rights of patients and the adverse effect on such rights of a disclosure of medical as opposed to financial information are given weight in a summons case. Id. See also United States v. Humedco Enters., Inc., 512 F. Supp. 1302 (ED Pa. 1981); United States v. Texas Heart Inst., 755 F2d 469 (5th Cir. 1985) (summons served on hospital to obtain names of doctors' patients; on remand, district court to determine whether concern for patient privacy bars enforcement).

[655] In re Albert Lindley Lee Memorial Hosp., 209 F2d 122 (2d Cir. 1953). See also United States v. Humedco Enters., Inc., 512 F. Supp. 1302 (ED Pa. 1981).

[656] United States v. Williams, 337 F. Supp. 1114 (SDNY 1971).

[657] Jaffee v. Redmond; 518 US 1 (1996). The privilege also applies to the social worker and client. The Second Circuit has declined to recognize a psychotherapist-patient privilege as part of federal common law. In re Doe, 711 F2d 1187 (2d Cir. 1983) (facts weighed against existence of any relationship of trust because Doe, who allegedly used medical clinic as a front for the illegal sale of quaaludes, conducted brief interviews with up to seven people a day). See also United States v. Lindstrom, 698 F2d 1154 (11th Cir. 1982) (indicating privilege does not exist); United States v. Meagher, 531 F2d 752 (5th Cir.), cert. denied, 429 US 853 (1976) (rejecting the privilege). In re Zuniga, 714 F2d 632 (6th Cir.), cert. denied, 464 US 983 (1983); United States John Doe v. Diamond, 964 F2d 1325, 1328 (2d Cir. 1992). But see United States v. Moore, 970 F2d 48 (5th Cir. 1992) (refusing to adopt doctor (psychotherapist)-patient privilege, but finding that such privilege, if recognized, would not cover accounts receivable records). The Second Circuit modified its decision in *Diamond* and recognized the privilege, but said that "the privilege amounts only to a requirement that a court give consideration to a witness's privacy inter-

C OTHER INVESTIGATIVE TECHNIQUES

¶ 13.12 SEARCH WARRANTS

The Service is authorized to use a search warrant to search for and seize books and records of a taxpayer.[658] The Code itself authorizes warrants to seize property used in violating the internal revenue laws[659] and authorizes a criminal investigator to execute search warrants.[660] Under Service guidelines, applications for warrants are only to be used in significant tax cases based on such factors as the amount of tax due, the nature of the fraud, and the impact of the case on voluntary compliance.[661] The Service does not use search warrants without the approval of the Tax Division, Justice Department. The Justice Department has delegated authority to approve a search warrant in tax cases under Title 26 or Title 18 of the U.S. Code to U.S. Attorneys or to Assistant U.S. Attorneys in charge of criminal functions.[662] Search warrants covered by this delegation may be directed at "offices, structures, premises, etc. owned, controlled or under the dominion of the subject or target of a criminal investigation," except for the following subjects or targets:[663]

- Accountants
- Lawyers
- Physicians
- Domestic or foreign public officials or political candidates
- Members of the clergy
- News media representatives
- Labor union officials
- Officials of tax-exempt organizations

The use of search warrants by the Service dates from the Supreme Court's decision in *Warden v. Hayden*,[664] holding that a search warrant could properly be used to seize "mere evidence" of a crime, as well as instrumentali-

---

ests as an important factor to be weighed in the balance in considering the admissibility of psychiatric histories or diagnoses."

[658] See 18 USC § 3103; Fed. R. Crim. P. Rule 41(b).

[659] IRC § 7302.

[660] IRC § 7608(b). See IRM 9.4.9.3, Authority for Searches & Seizures with Warrants (June 30, 1998). See also IRM 9.4.9.5, Affidavit for Search Warrant (June 30, 1998).

[661] IRM 9.4.9.6.1, Approval for Search Warrant—Title 26 Investigations and Tax-Related Title 18 Investigations (June 30, 1998).

[662] Department of Justice Manual, Tax Division, 6-4.130 (Search Warrants).

[663] Department of Justice Manual, Tax Division, 6-4.130 (Search Warrants). IRM 9.4.9.6.2, Search of Attorney Premises (June 30, 1998).

[664] Warden v. Hayden, 387 US 294 (1967).

ties, fruits of a crime, or contraband. After *Warden v. Hayden*, the Service has from time to time used search warrants to seize records for use in tax prosecutions.[665] The Federal Rules of Criminal Procedure provide for the issuance of a warrant to search for and seize, inter alia, "property that constitutes evidence of the commission of a criminal offense."[666] The Supreme Court's decision in *Andresen v. Maryland*[667] further encouraged the Service to use search warrants. In *Andresen*, it was held that seizure of records, even personal records, pursuant to a search warrant violates neither the Fourth nor Fifth Amendment. If an adequate showing of probable cause can be made to a magistrate and the things to be seized are described with some particularity, the Fourth Amendment is not violated. And since seizure incident to execution of the warrant requires no testimonial communication from the taxpayer, the Fifth Amendment is not violated.[668]

Under the current state of the law, a taxpayer has few grounds on which to contest seizure of his records by search warrant. Why then are warrants not used more frequently? First, apart from the delays it complains of where a summons is opposed, the Service is by and large successful in its use of summonses. Second, a search warrant, unlike a summons, may not be issued by a special agent. The Service must go before a magistrate and make the necessary showing before the warrant will issue. Third, in a tax investigation, it is not always possible to describe with particularity the records to be seized and to make a showing of probable cause that the things sought are connected with criminal activity. However, a search warrant has the obvious advantage of permitting a seizure of records before they can be altered, concealed, or de-

---

[665] Truitt v. Lanahan, 529 F2d 230 (6th Cir. 1976), cert. denied, 427 US 912 (1976); Shaffer v. Wilson, 523 F2d 175 (10th Cir. 1975); VonderAhe v. Howland, 508 F2d 364 (9th Cir. 1974); Hill v. Philpott, 445 F2d 144 (7th Cir. 1971), cert. denied, 404 US 991 (1971); United States v. Erickson, 676 F2d 408 (10th Cir. 1982) (based on incriminating information given by three former employees and one current one); United States v. Rosenberger, 872 F2d 240 (8th Cir. 1989) (search warrant of chiropractor's offices on allegations of conspiracy, evasion, and violations of currency reporting law; 31 USC § 5322); Hearn v. Internal Revenue Agents, 597 F. Supp. 966 (ND Tex. 1984) (search warrant used to seize client files in tax shelter planning consultant's offices). Compare In re Impounded Case (Law Firm), 840 F2d 196 (3d Cir. 1988) (search warrant based on information given by accountant, and confidential informant was used to seize certain documents and to search offices of law firm suspected of various crimes including tax evasion and filing false or fraudulent returns; attorney-client privilege was protected by requirement that government obtain leave of court before examining any seized items).

[666] Fed. R. Crim. P. 41(b).

[667] Andresen v. Maryland, 427 US 463 (1976).

[668] Andresen v. Maryland, 427 US 463 (1976). To the extent that Hill v. Philpott, 445 F2d 144 (7th Cir. 1971), cert. denied, 404 US 991 (1971), and VonderAhe v. Howland, 508 F2d 364 (9th Cir. 1974), hold that seizure of an individual's business records violates the Fifth Amendment, they have been overruled by Fisher v. United States, 425 US 391 (1976), and Andresen v. Maryland, 427 US 463 (1976).

stroyed. Litigation about the warrant follows seizure, unlike disputes over a summons where the taxpayer frequently has possession of the records during the litigation.

A search warrant can be challenged on grounds that probable cause was lacking and that the warrant was overbroad. For probable cause, the Service must present substantial evidence establishing the probability that (1) the items sought are connected with criminal activity and (2) the items will be found in the place to be searched. However, the Supreme Court has recognized that the nature of the offense charged affects the supporting information that must be included in a supporting affidavit. Tax evasion is not a crime that is "subject to establishment by blunt and concise factual allegations," such as "A saw B file a false tax return", and "often require[s] reconstruction of the taxpayer's income from many individually unrevealing sources."[669] Still, the person supplying the information must show that it is more probable than not that the records sought are connected with criminal activity. A finding of probable cause may be based on hearsay evidence.[670] In reported tax cases where search warrants have been used, the Service has generally relied on information supplied by former employees, sometimes coupled with a preliminary investigation indicating substantial omissions of income.[671] Even if this showing is made, since records may have been moved from a location, an affidavit in support of a search warrant must also contain a statement as to the time when the facts relied upon occurred.

The Fourth Amendment requires a particular description of things to be seized. However, the Supreme Court's decision in *Andresen* indicates that taxpayers will have difficulty challenging search warrants on specificity grounds. In the case, search warrants were issued by a Maryland state court judge on the application of a fraud unit that had been investigating certain real estate settlement transactions of Andresen, an attorney. One warrant authorized the search of Andresen's law office and the other the search of the office of the development corporation of which he was the sole shareholder. The allegation was of fraud by Andresen in connection with the sale and conveyance of Lot 13T, and the warrant authorized search and seizure of specified documents pertaining to the sale of that lot "together with other fruits, instrumentalities and evidence of crime at this time unknown." The investigators seized various

---

[669] See Jaben v. United States, 381 US 214 (1965) (not a search warrant case, but one discussing probable cause in the context of a tax case).

[670] Fed. R. Crim. P. 41(b).

[671] Truitt v. Lanahan, 529 F2d 230 (6th Cir. 1976), cert. denied, 427 US 912 (1976); (tip from former employee plus revenue agents' determination); Shaffer v. Wilson, 523 F2d 175 (10th Cir. 1975) (affidavit of former employees about log and separate "cheat" book); VonderAhe v. Howland, 508 F2d 364 (9th Cir. 1974) (affidavit from former and current employees about records not disclosed to revenue agent); Hill v. Philpott, 445 F2d 144 (7th Cir. 1971), cert. denied, 404 US 991 (1971) (employee affidavit that doctor told employees to destroy red letter folders if tax man visited office).

business records, including those relating to a real estate sale that was not described in the search warrant. Andresen was charged with the crimes of false pretenses and fraudulent misappropriation by a fiduciary, and moved to suppress the seized documents. The Supreme Court upheld the search warrant against the claim that it was unreasonably broad. It reaffirmed the principle of *Warden v. Hayden*, that mere evidence may be seized pursuant to a duly authorized search warrant as long as there is probable cause to believe that it will aid in a particular apprehension or conviction. Despite the general language of the warrant and the quantity of documents returned or suppressed, the Court also said that a description of categories of documents, rather than specified papers, is adequate to sustain the warrant.

¶ 13.13 GRAND JURY INVESTIGATIONS

[1] In General

The Service need not utilize its summons authority to conduct an investigation. Instead, it may request the authorization of the Assistant Attorney General for the Tax Division for a grand jury to investigate suspected violations of the internal revenue laws. Specific authorization from the Tax Division is required for tax cases to be presented to a grand jury.[672] Apart from Service requests, prosecutorial emphasis on investigating white-collar and racketeer cases has resulted in the Tax Division's receiving an increasing number of requests for tax grand jury authorizations from U.S. Attorneys and requests to expand a nontax grand jury investigation to include inquiry into possible criminal tax violations.[673] On its own, the Tax Division may also authorize use of a grand jury where, after the Service has referred a case for criminal prosecution, the determination is made that the case has prosecution potential and further investigation is needed.[674] However, the focus in this section is on requests from the Service before a referral for prosecution. A discussion of the so-called open-

---

[672] Department of Justice Manual, Tax Division, 6-4.120 (Grand Jury Investigations). See Exec. Order No. 6166. (Aug. 10, 1933) (issued pursuant to Act of Mar. 3, 1933, Pub. L. No. 428, § 16, 47 Stat. 1517, described in Sullivan v. United States, 348 US 170 (1954)); 28 CFR § 71. See also IRM 9.5.2.3.1.4, Routing of Grand Jury Requests (July 29, 2002) ("All tax grand jury requests must be approved by the Supervisory Special Agent (SSA), SAC, and Director of Field Operations."). The request then goes to the Area Counsel, and then to the Tax Division Justice Department.

[673] Department of Justice Manual, Tax Division, 6-4.122 (U.S. Attorney Initiated Grand Jury Investigations).

[674] Department of Justice Manual, Tax Division, 6-4.126 (U.S. Attorney Initiated Grand Jury Investigations) (Tax Division Requests). At this point, the Tax Division cannot simply send the case back to the Service to let it use a summons to investigate because of

ended grand jury investigation in a tax case may be divided into (1) the circumstances when the Service will request a grand jury investigation; (2) the features of a grand jury as opposed to a Service investigation; and (3) objections that may be made to the grand jury process.

A grand jury investigation is considered "necessary and appropriate" where[675]

- It is apparent that the administrative process cannot develop the relevant facts within a reasonable period of time or
- Coordination of the tax investigation with an ongoing grand jury investigation would be more efficient and
- The case has significant deterrent potential.

Circumstances indicating that the administrative process cannot develop the relevant facts in a reasonable time include (1) lack of cooperation by important witnesses; (2) efforts by the taxpayer to impede orderly investigation by intimidation of witnesses; (3) destruction or threat of destruction of records or evidence; and (4) severe time constraints imposed by the statute of limitations. Essentially, the Service requests an open-ended grand jury where its investigation has become stymied.[676]

A special agent may initiate a request for a grand jury investigation. In this case, the agent's recommendation and report go through channels from the Supervisory Special Agent (SSA) to the Special Agent in Charge (SAC) to the Director of Field Operations, and finally to the Area Counsel. If the Area Counsel agrees, the request goes to the Justice Department's Tax Division for final approval.[677] In practice, a request for an open-ended grand jury is reviewed in the Tax Division's Criminal Section, although final approval is given by the Assistant Attorney General (Tax Division).[678]

The Service may also become involved in a grand jury investigation where evidence of tax violations is found during the course of an investigation of nontax crimes initiated by the Justice Department or a local U.S. Attorney. If the government attorney desires to investigate possible tax crimes by grand jury, the attorney must secure (1) approval from the district Chief (CID),

---

the restrictions of United States v. LaSalle Nat'l Bank, 437 US 298 (1978), against a post-treferral summons.

[675] IRM 9.5.2.3.1, Grand Jury Requests Involving Potential Tax Violations (July 29, 2002).

[676] See, e.g., In re Grand Jury Subpoenas, April 1978, 581 F2d 1103, 1107–1108 (4th Cir. 1978); General Motors Corp. v. United States, 573 F2d 936 (6th Cir.), rev'd en banc, 584 F2d 1366 (5th Cir.), cert. denied, 439 US 876 (1978).

[677] IRM 9.5.2.3.1.1, Service-Initiated Requests (July 28, 2002). Differences within the Service between District Counsel and the district may be resolved in the National Office by the Director (CID).

[678] Department of Justice Manual, Tax Division, 6-4.121 (IRS Requests to Initiate Grand Jury Investigation).

before Service assistance is provided and (2) a Rule 6(e) order releasing the information from the grand jury secrecy provisions.[679] The Tax Division has delegated to the U.S. Attorneys its authority to approve requests seeking to expand nontax grand jury investigations into possible criminal tax violations.[680]

A grand jury investigation radically changes the procedural setting of a tax investigation. A grand jury performs the constitutionally mandated function in federal felony cases of formally charging a person with a criminal violation on finding probable cause that the crime has been committed and that the accused has committed the crime.[681] To perform this function, the grand jury has broad investigatory powers.[682] Procedurally, the district court impanels the grand jury but retains no direct role in the grand jury's proceedings except for such matters as immunity grants and contempts.[683] The Justice Department initiates and prepares cases coming before the grand jury.[684] Grand jury subpoenas issued in the name of the court over the signature of the clerk[685] are obtained by Assistant U.S. Attorneys in blank without any exercise of prior control by the court. This uncontrolled use of the court's process is one of the reasons the grand jury is said to be an instrument of the prosecutor. The Assistant U.S. Attorney fills in the subpoena to testify (ad testificandum) or to produce records (duces tecum), and, in tax cases, the subpoena is usually served by a special agent. A witness who has an objection to a grand jury subpoena may respond by a motion to quash the subpoena or, after appearing before the grand jury and refusing to comply with the subpoena, wait for an application

---

[679] See IRM 9.5.2.3.1.2, Government Attorney Initiated Requests (July 29, 2002). See also IRM 9.5.2.3.1.3, Special Agent in Charge's Review of Government Attorney Initiated Requests (July 29, 2002). The government attorney's request for assistance must also be approved by the chain of command. The Service has modified the procedures for access to grand jury information. Internal Audit personnel will review (1) material obtained before the grand jury referral and (2) matters considered not occurring before the grand jury. See IRM 9.5.2.4.1, Grand Jury Access List (July 29, 2002); CID is supposed to inform Internal Audit when full disclosure of all items in the file cannot be made, owing to some items being covered by Rule 6(e); but CID may disclose the type of item not being released (e.g., a transcript of an individual's testimony).

[680] Department of Justice Manual, Tax Division, 6-4.123 (Joint Tax-Nontax Investigations with IRS Participation).

[681] Branzberg v. Hayes, 408 US 665, 686 (1972) (grand jury is convened to determine "if there is probable cause to believe that a crime has been committed"). The Fifth Amendment prohibits any person from being federally prosecuted for a felony without having been indicted by a grand jury.

[682] United States v. Calandra, 414 US 338, 343 (1974) ("[t]raditionally the grand jury has been accorded wide latitude to inquire into violations of law").

[683] See Fed. R. Crim. P. 7 (a); 18 USC § 6003 (immunity); 28 USC § 1826 (contempt).

[684] For a discussion of the powers and functions of the Attorney General and U.S. Attorney, see In re Persico, 522 F2d 41 (2d Cir. 1975).

[685] Fed. R. Crim. P. 67(a).

for contempt.[686] In either event, the proceeding is a civil proceeding before the district court, at which time all appropriate defenses may be raised.[687] In this regard, a motion to quash or for contempt is analogous to a summons enforcement proceeding.[688]

With this background, the following points can be made about the powers of a grand jury. This discussion also helps to point out the differences between the grand jury's investigation and the Service's administrative investigation.

1. *The grand jury's investigative powers are not defined by statute.* However broad the Service's investigative power may be, it is limited to the statutory authority conferred and the manner of exercise described in the statute.

2. *The grand jury investigation looks toward the filing of a criminal charge.* The grand jury may not be used for the sole purpose of gathering evidence for a civil case.[689] No such restriction applies to the use of a summons, which is recognized to have a dual criminal-civil purpose.[690]

3. *A grand jury can investigate without having a specific target or particular crime in mind.*[691] The tax return of a specific taxpayer must be under investigation, even if his identity is unknown, for a summons to be valid.

4. *The target of a grand jury investigation has no right to be informed of his status as a target but must be given Miranda warnings.*[692] Although some courts require target warnings under exercise of their supervisory powers,[693] the Service requires that all special agents give Miranda-type warnings to targets in administrative investigations.

---

[686] Fed. R. Crim. P. 17(g).

[687] 28 USC § 1826(a).

[688] In re Grand Jury Proceedings (Schofield), 486 F2d 85, 90 (3d Cir. 1973) (*Schofield I*) ("[t]he enforcement mechanism of 28 U.S.C. § 1826(a) is the same as that for the typical administrative subpoena"). The Third Circuit in *Schofield I* said procedures governing administrative summons enforcement proceedings apply in grand jury subpoena proceedings. Thus, for example, the government attorney must "make some preliminary showing by affidavit that each item is at least relevant to an investigation being conducted by the grand jury and properly within its jurisdiction, and is not sought primarily for another purpose." Id. at 93. The Third Circuit's procedures are not applied in every circuit. See, e.g., In re New York Law School, 448 F. Supp. 822 (SDNY 1978) (no evidentiary hearing unless witness's failure to make showing documents had no conceivable relevance to subject matter of inquiry).

[689] United States v. Procter & Gamble Co., 356 US 677, 683–684 (1958).

[690] IRC §§ 7602(a)(2), 7602(b). See also United States v. LaSalle Nat'l Bank, 437 US 298 (1978).

[691] See Hale v. Henkel, 201 US 43 (1906).

[692] United States v. Washington, 431 US 181 (1977); United States v. Mandujano, 425 US 564 (1976).

[693] See, e.g., United States v. Jacobs, 547 F2d 772 (2d Cir. 1976), cert. dismissed, 436 US 31 (1977).

5. *In a tax grand jury investigation, the only process that may be used is a grand jury subpoena.* A summons served after a Service request for a grand jury would violate the Supreme Court's decision in *United States v. LaSalle National Bank.*

6. *A witness has no right to be accompanied by counsel in the grand jury room, although the witness has a right to be excused from the grand jury room to confer with counsel.*[694] The Service recognizes that a witness has a right to be accompanied by counsel.

7. *A grand jury has an almost unlimited scope of inquiry.* A person seeking to quash a grand jury subpoena must show that a particular category of documents can have no conceivable relevance to any legitimate object of investigation.[695] Although it is analogous to a grand jury subpoena, the Service's summons can require production of records that may only "throw light upon" the taxpayer's return.

[2] Challenges to the Grand Jury Process

Grounds for challenging grand jury process fall roughly into the same categories as those for objecting to a Service summons: (1) procedural objections (e.g., composition of the grand jury, some defect in the subpoena); (2) objections relating to the use of the grand jury's process; (3) constitutional challenges; and (4) evidentiary objections and testimonial privileges.[696] Prospective defendants in tax cases probably have fewer possibilities of challenging a grand jury's process than in objecting to a summons.

A witness may object to a grand jury subpoena on the Fourth Amendment ground that a subpoena duces tecum is "too sweeping in its terms 'to be regarded as reasonable.'" Hale v. Henkel, 201 U.S. 43, 76."[697] Restrictions on an overbroad subpoena duces tecum have been said to be based not on the Fourth Amendment but on the less-stringent requirements of the due process clause.[698] However, whatever the source of the restriction, the standard applied is whether the records sought are potentially relevant to the subject matter of the investigation or can have no conceivable relevance to any legitimate object of

---

[694] See United States v. Mandujano, 425 US 564 (1976).

[695] In re Horowitz, 482 F2d 72 (2d Cir. 1973).

[696] For a more detailed treatment of the grand jury and objections to its process, see National Lawyers Guild, Grand Jury Defense Office, Representation of Witnesses Before Federal Grand Juries—A Manual for Attorneys (1979); A. Amsterdam, Trial Manual 5 of the Defense of Criminal Cases (1989).

[697] United States v. Dionisio, 410 US 1, 11–12 (1973), citing Hale v. Henkel, 201 US 43 (1906).

[698] In re Horowitz, 482 F2d 72 (2d Cir. 1973); In re Morgan, 377 F. Supp. 281 (SDNY 1974).

the investigation.[699] On application of such a standard, a challenge to a subpoena stands little chance of being sustained. A witness may also object to a grand jury subpoena on the Fifth Amendment ground that it compels him to incriminate himself either by producing records or by giving testimony.[700] This Fifth Amendment objection is likely to be resolved in the same manner as summons cases.[701] Also, evidentiary privileges claimed in response to a subpoena are reviewed by reference to the same authorities used in summons cases. However, unlike summons cases, the work product doctrine is clearly recognized in grand jury proceedings.[702]

Abuse of process objections to a grand jury subpoena are of particular interest in tax cases. The objection is similar to the claim that a summons has been issued for an improper purpose or in bad faith. The following types of objections can be made.

[a] Improper Civil Purpose

A grand jury must pursue a bona fide inquiry looking to indictment. It may not pursue some other purpose, such as gathering evidence for a civil case.[703] Thus, for example, the Service may not issue a summons, fail to seek

---

[699] In re Morgan, 377 F. Supp. 281 (SDNY 1974). In *Morgan*, the court said, "Relevancy, in the context of a Grand Jury proceeding is not a probative relevancy, for it cannot be known in advance whether the document produced will actually advance the investigation." Id. at 285.

[700] A witness must usually appear and assert a privilege claim. However, in some districts, as a matter of practice, where a witness is subpoenaed and will claim the Fifth Amendment privilege, a grand jury appearance may be avoided if a letter is sent to the prosecutor stating that the privilege will be claimed to each question propounded in the grand jury room except the witness's name and address. If the government lawyer consents, the letter is made part of the record, and the appearance is excused.

[701] See the discussion supra ¶ 13.10.

[702] See, e.g., In re Grand Jury Proceedings (Duffy), 473 F2d 840 (8th Cir. 1973). Accord In re General Counsel, John Doe, Inc., 599 F2d 504 (2d Cir. 1979). See In re Terkeltoub, 256 F. Supp. 683 (SDNY 1966). Fed. R. Crim. P. 16(b)(2) provides no postindictment discovery of a defense lawyer's work product regardless of substantial need.

[703] See United States v. Procter & Gamble Co., 356 US 677 (1958); In re Grand Jury Subpoenas, April 1978, 581 F2d 1103 (4th Cir. 1978) (special agents assisted in grand jury investigation, but use of grand jury found to be in good faith in criminal investigation); Robert Hawthorne, Inc. v. Director of Internal Revenue, 406 F. Supp. 1098 (ED Pa. 1975) (special agent summonses issued during grand jury investigation later withdrawn; agents assisted government attorney; held, not bad faith abuse of grand jury process); In re Morgan, 377 F. Supp. 281 (SDNY 1974) (special agent had served summonses, and, after refusal to comply, grand jury subpoena served).

enforcement, and resort to the grand jury to get the information if the matter is in no way criminal but purely civil.[704]

[b] Harassment and Other Prosecutorial Misconduct

The court's process may be abused if the grand jury is being used as a means of harassment rather than for a legitimate investigation.[705] However, conduct that a subpoenaed witness claims is harassment is often justified as the exercise of the broad powers of the grand jury to investigate, as is the case when a summons is challenged. A grand jury may at least investigate potential criminal violations on the basis of a tip or information supplied by an informer no matter what the informer's motive may be.[706] A prosecutor's misconduct may be the basis for a claim of harassment.[707] Also, a government attorney may not use a grand jury subpoena as a means of interviewing the witness in the attorney's office outside the presence of a grand jury.[708]

[c] Conflict of Interest

A potential conflict of interest by a government attorney may compromise the secrecy of the grand jury. In a grand jury investigation of General Motors Corporation, the Regional Counsel attorney who had recommended use of the grand jury was designated a special attorney for the United States to assist in the investigation but remained on the payroll of the Service. A panel of the Sixth Circuit found that these circumstances presented an appearance of professional impropriety and that potential misuse of the grand jury warranted termination of the grand jury and a protective order.[709]

[i] Lack of Authority A grand jury investigation conducting an open-ended tax investigation must have Tax Division authorization, and, failing this,

---

[704] In re April 1956 Term Grand Jury, 239 F2d 263 (7th Cir. 1956).

[705] United States v. Dionisio, 410 US 1 (1973).

[706] See Costello v. United States, 350 US 359 (1956) (tax indictment returned on the basis of hearsay evidence is sufficient).

[707] See In re Doe, 546 F2d 498, 502 (2d Cir. 1976) (subpoena to investigator assisting defense attorney withdrawn; motion to enjoin grand jury investigation denied; prosecutor admonished, "[a] grand jury is not a prosecutor's plaything and the awesome power of the Government should be used deliberately, not in haste, and without unwarranted or idle threats, direct or implied"). See also United States v. Terkeltoub, 256 F. Supp. 683 (SDNY 1966) (attorney for indicted but untried defendant subpoenaed to testify about attorney's trial preparation).

[708] Durbin v. United States, 221 F2d 520, 522 (DC Cir. 1954).

[709] General Motors Corp. v. United States, 573 F2d 936 (6th Cir.), rev'd en banc, 584 F2d 1366 (5th Cir.), cert. denied, 439 US 876 (1978). This type of case may be avoided in the future by amendment of Federal Rule of Criminal Procedure 6(e), which provides

the investigation by the U.S. Attorney should be enjoined. However, one court has held that it is not an abuse of process for a grand jury to investigate non-tax crimes and potential tax violations without Tax Division approval.[710] Also, once an indictment has been returned by the grand jury, the indictment is not invalid if the case was presented without prior authorization from the Justice Department.[711]

[ii] Violation of Grand Jury Secrecy Grand jury secrecy serves such purposes as protecting witnesses against reprisals, limiting obstruction of justice and perjury before the grand jury, prevention of flight, and protection of those the grand jury ultimately finds innocent of wrongdoing.[712]

[3] Grand Jury Secrecy

Disclosures of "matters occurring before the grand jury" may only be made pursuant to Rule 6(e) of the Federal Rules of Criminal Procedure. Before 1977, Rule 6(e) limited such disclosures to "attorneys for the government for use in the performance of their duties."[713] Therefore, where there was evidence of participation by Service personnel in the grand jury investigation, motions were made to quash grand jury process or dismiss an indictment because of disclosures to unauthorized persons (i.e., Service personnel).[714] However, attorneys for the government were generally permitted to disclose grand jury material, without a court order, to Service personnel assisting the grand jury,

---

that disclosures of matters occurring in the grand jury may be made to those government personnel the Justice Department attorney deems necessary to assist him. However, the principle that the prosecutor must avoid the appearance of impropriety remains.

[710] In re Berkovitz, 74-2 USTC ¶ 9507 (ED Pa. 1973). The Supreme Court has held that absence of Justice Department approval did not invalidate an indictment. Sullivan v. United States, 348 US 170 (1954). Similarly, action taken by a grand jury is not invalid because the defendant was not granted administrative conferences in the Service as he would have in a normal tax case. United States v. Stofsky, 527 F2d 237, 249 (2d Cir. 1975) (power of grand jury to indict "not conditioned upon taxpayers being given an opportunity to explain their conduct to a government official any more than to the grand jury itself"); United States v. Goldstein, 342 F. Supp. 661 (EDNY 1972).

[711] Sullivan v. United States, 348 US 170 (1954).

[712] See United States v. Procter & Gamble Co., 356 US 677 (1958).

[713] Federal Rule of Criminal Procedure 54(c) defines attorneys for the government to mean "the Attorney General, an authorized assistant to the Attorney General, a United States Attorney, and an authorized assistant of the United States Attorney."

[714] See, e.g., General Motors Corp. v. United States, 573 F2d 936 (6th Cir.), rev'd en banc, 584 F2d 1366 (5th Cir.), cert. denied, 439 US 876 (1978); In re Grand Jury Subpoenas, April 1978, 581 F2d 1103 (4th Cir. 1978); In re Morgan, 377 F. Supp. 281 (SDNY 1974). See also Robert Hawthorne, Inc. v. Director of Internal Revenue, 406 F. Supp. 1098 (ED Pa. 1975) (mandamus for return of records).

provided the agents and the material remained under the control of the government attorney and the disclosure was made for criminal purposes.[715]

In 1977, Rule 6(e) was amended to make it clear that government attorneys may utilize the services of other government employees to assist in evaluating evidence. The rule now provides that a government attorney may make disclosures "to such government personnel as are deemed necessary . . . to assist [him] in the performance of [his] duty to enforce federal criminal law."[716] The only restrictions on disclosures are that (1) they may be made only for criminal, not civil, purposes and (2) the names of the agents to whom disclosures are made must be furnished to the district court.[717] Consequently, motions to quash based on secrecy violations are not available during the course of a criminal investigation. However, these issues still arise where grand jury evidence is sought to be used in civil tax proceedings.

The Service may obtain access to grand jury evidence for use in a civil case. Under Rule 6(e)(3)(C)(i), the government makes an ex parte application for an order of disclosure "preliminarily to or in connection with a judicial proceeding." The government must (1) generally describe the materials sought, to allow the court to decide whether they are rationally related to a civil proceeding, and (2) satisfy the court that the grand jury proceeding has not been used as a subterfuge for obtaining records for a civil investigation or proceeding.[718] To obtain disclosure for use in a civil proceeding, the government must also make a showing of "particularized" need for the disclosure of the transcript and exhibits requested.[719] This showing is considered necessary to ensure that the grand jury's criminal process is not used to elicit evidence in a civil case. Despite this apparent restriction on Service access to grand jury evidence,

---

[715] See, e.g., Robert Hawthorne, Inc. v. Director of Internal Revenue, 406 F. Supp. 1098 (ED Pa. 1975); In re Grand Jury Investigation (William H. Pflaumer & Sons), 53 FRD 464 (ED Pa. 1971). See also Coson v. United States, 533 F2d 1119 (9th Cir. 1976).

[716] Fed. R. Crim. P. 6(e)(2)(A)(ii). As a result, the special agent's report is a "matter occurring before the grand jury" when the report is based on documents subpoenaed before the grand jury and grand jury witness testimony. United States v. Randell, 924 F. Supp. 557 (SDNY 1996). A taxpayer may wish to see the special agent's report to prepare his defense in a civil fraud penalty case. While the report is grand jury material, if the taxpayer makes an application under Rule 6(e) showing particularized need, the application may result in the disclosure of at least portions of the report. See id. (although the taxpayer was unsuccessful in making the requisite showing, portions of the report pertaining to the taxpayer and made public at trial were disclosed).

[717] Fed. R. Crim. P. 6(e)(3)(B). A 1985 amendment to Fed. R. Crim. P. 6(e)(3)(B) states that the government attorney must certify to the district court persons to whom disclosure was made under Rule 6(e)(3)(A)(i).

[718] In re Grand Jury Subpoenas, April 1978, 581 F2d 1103 (4th Cir. 1978). But see United States v. Sells Eng'g, Inc., 463 US 418 (1983).

[719] See United States v. Procter & Gamble Co., 356 US 677 (1958). See United States v. Sells Eng'g, Inc., 463 US 418 (1983).

disclosure was generally granted under Rule 6(e),[720] although some courts exercised discretion against disclosure.[721] This procedure changed after the decisions in *United States v. Sells Engineering, Inc.* and *United States v. Baggot.*[722]

In *Sells Engineering*, the government attempted to justify access to grand jury materials without obtaining a court order. A corporation and two of its officers were indicted after a grand jury investigation on charges of conspiracy and filing false tax returns. After their guilty pleas to one count of conspiracy, the government moved the district court for an order disclosing all grand jury materials to attorneys in the Department of Justice's Civil Division for use in preparing a civil False Claims Act suit. The government contended that all Department of Justice attorneys qualified for automatic disclosure of the grand jury materials under Rule 6(e)(3)(A)(i), because the disclosure was being made to "an attorney for the government for use in the performance of such attorney's duty." The Supreme Court, rejecting this argument, held that Rule 6(e)(3)(A)(i) disclosure was limited to disclosure to government attorneys for criminal use.[723] Thus, to obtain disclosure for civil purposes, the government was required to seek a court order under Rule 6(e)(3)(C)(i) by showing particularized need for the grand jury materials.

According to *Sells Engineering*, the particularized need standard to be applied in the access hearing is a flexible one. The party seeking disclosure under Rule 6(e), including the government, must show that the materials sought are needed "to avoid a possible injustice in another judicial proceeding, that the need for disclosure is greater than the need for continued secrecy, and that [the] request is structured to cover material only so needed."[724] In considering disclosure, the district court's duty is to weigh the competing interests carefully in the light of "the relevant circumstances," including "any relevant considerations, peculiar to government movants, that weigh for or against dis-

---

[720] See, e.g., In re July 1973 Grand Jury, 374 F. Supp. 1334, 1335 (ND Ill. 1973); In re Grand Jury Investigation (William H. Pflaumer & Sons), 53 FRD 464 (ED Pa. 1971); Robert Hawthorne, Inc. v. Director of Internal Revenue, 406 F. Supp. 1098 (ED Pa. 1975).

[721] United States v. Doe, 341 F. Supp. 1350 (SDNY 1972) (Rule 6(e) request that Service agent be granted access to books and records subpoenaed by pending grand jury to determine civil tax liabilities as well as to assist prosecutor denied because no justification "for allowing the intentional use of a strictly criminal weapon . . . for the combined purposes"). See also Coson v. United States, 533 F2d 1119 (9th Cir. 1976).

[722] United States v. Sells Eng'g, Inc., 463 US 418 (1983); United States v. Baggott, 463 US 476 (1983).

[723] This holding paralleled the Court's decision earlier in 1983, refusing to interpret the Clayton Act as granting state attorneys general an exemption from making a particularized showing. Illinois v. Abbott & Assocs., 460 US 557 (1983).

[724] United States v. Sells Eng'g, Inc., 463 US 418, 443 (1983), quoting Douglas Oil Co. v. Petrol Stops NW, 441 US 211, 222–223 (1979).

closure in a given case."[725] By way of example, the Supreme Court said that a court could consider (1) the fact that disclosure to the Justice Department poses less risk of improper use than disclosure to private parties; (2) the public interest, if any, served by disclosure to a government body; and (3) the availability of alternative disclosure tools available under law to the agency seeking disclosure.[726]

The Supreme Court in *Baggot* dealt with a request made under Rule 6(e)(3)(C)(i) for disclosure of grand jury information to the Service for civil purposes, and specifically whether a Service audit is "'preliminar[y] to' a redetermination proceeding [in the Tax Court] or a refund suit within the meaning of Rule 6(e)(3)(C)(i)." The Court concluded that "disclosure [of grand jury materials] is not appropriate for use in an IRS audit of civil tax liability, because the purpose of the audit is not to prepare for or conduct litigation, but to assess the amount of tax liability through administrative channels." According to the Court, the Service's audit determination did not require resort to litigation to accomplish its goal of tax assessment,[727] and, under this circumstance, the audit would not be preliminary to a judicial proceeding for purposes of Rule 6(e)(3)(C)(i).[728] On the other hand, it is not necessary for a Tax Court case actually to be pending for disclosure to be preliminary to litigation. The Court said that the Service could seek disclosure of grand jury materials after it had concluded its audit and mailed a notice of deficiency, where the taxpayer had clearly expressed its intention to seek Tax Court review, even if no petition had yet been filed.[729]

The decisions in *Baggot* and *Sells Engineering* limit the Service's access to matters occurring before the grand jury, for use in civil tax proceedings. Materials developed in terminated grand jury investigations may not simply be turned over by Department of Justice attorneys to Service district counsel attorneys, nor from Department of Justice attorneys in and outside of the Tax

---

[725] United States v. Sells Eng'g, Inc., 463 US 418, 443 (1983).

[726] Once the district court rules, the taxpayer has the daunting task of showing that the district court has abused its discretion. See, e.g., In re Grand Jury Subpoena Duces Tecum, 904 F2d 466 (8th Cir. 1990) (district court sealed government submission and denied taxpayer's access to materials the Service reviewed).

[727] This analysis may be questioned. After all, as a matter of law (Section 6213(a)), no assessment may take place until a notice of deficiency is mailed that is itself a condition precedent to a Tax Court proceeding. See Lyon, "Disclosure of Grand Jury Materials: Why the Supreme Court Was Wrong in Baggot," 39 Tax L. Rev. 215 (1984). On the other hand, the Court rejected *Baggot's* argument that litigation was a remote contingency (because he could settle) on the ground that as a factual matter the chances of litigation were not so low as to not be considered a realistic possibility. Id. at n.7.

[728] It has been held that *Baggot* governs the validity of disclosure orders previously issued by district courts. In re Grand Jury Investigation of Peter A. Sells, 719 F2d 985 (9th Cir. 1983).

[729] In re Grand Jury Proceedings (Miller Brewing Co.), 687 F2d 1079 (7th Cir. 1982).

Division to attorneys handling civil tax cases *(Sells Engineering)*. The attorneys involved in the civil case must seek a disclosure order showing particularized need *(Sells Engineering)*. They will not be able to show such need if the Service proceeding is still in the audit stage *(Baggot)*. Thus, access is postponed until some as yet undefined point in the administrative process. Once events have crystallized or progressed to a point preliminary to a judicial proceeding and the Service requests access, the issue shifts to the "particularized-need" showing to be made and ruled upon by the district court.[730]

District courts are called on to make judgments weighing the interests of the parties concerned, including witnesses before the grand jury. These judgments are not always easy ones to make.[731] It is not clear how government attorneys can make particularized-need showings without knowing what has occurred before the grand jury (matters that are supposed to be secret). However, since the government request is made ex parte, taxpayers are not able to participate, and, even if they could, they would have great difficulty in showing why disclosure should not be made without knowing what occurred before the grand jury.

Apart from the procedural issues, after the *Baggot* and *Sells Engineering* cases, in a later civil tax case, it is in the interest of taxpayers for testimony of

---

[730] The decision to grant a Rule 6(e) order remains in the hands of the district court, at least in the first instance. It remains to be seen whether district courts will view the *Baggot* and *Sells* decisions as a signal to restrict access. The Supreme Court in *Baggot*, 463 US 476 (1983), at n.6, refused to decide how firm the Service's decision to litigate must be before its investigation can be characterized as preliminary to a judicial proceeding, or even whether the decision can ever be regarded as preliminary to a judicial proceeding before the termination of the administrative investigation. This holding leaves open the possibility of access during the appeals process.

[731] See In re Doe, 537 F. Supp. 1038 (DRI 1982) (analyzing the different approaches of the courts). The Tax Court will not review the Rule 6(e) of a federal district court ordering the disclosure of grand jury materials. Arc Elec. Constr. Co. v. Comm'r, 91 TC 947 (1988). The Second Circuit has developed a rather broad standard for deciding on the applicability of Rule 6(e). United States v. Interstate Dress Carriers, Inc., 280 F2d 52 (2d Cir. 1960). Under *Interstate Dress*,

> when testimony or data is sought for its own sake—for its intrinsic value in the furtherance of a lawful investigation—rather than to learn what took place before the grand jury, it is not valid defense to disclosure that the same information was revealed to a grand jury or that the same documents had been, or were presently being, examined by a grand jury.

280 F2d at 54. In Di Leo v. Comm'r, 959 F2d 16 (2d Cir. 1992), no Rule 6(e) order was obtained for bank records subpoenaed by a grand jury that investigated and charged the taxpayers. The records were subsequently subpoenaed by the Service for a Tax Court trial involving the taxpayers, and the banks gave permission to the Service, which still had the records, to produce them. Applying *Interstate Dress*, the Second Circuit held that since the bank records were sought for their own sake and not to learn what took place before the grand jury, the records were not "matters occurring before the grand jury" within the meaning of Rule 6(e). However, the court criticized the Service for simply disclosing the records without a court order, thereby risking contempt and sanctions.

witnesses and documents to constitute matters before the grand jury because witnesses testify in the grand jury (rather than giving statements to prosecutors) and documents are produced pursuant to grand jury subpoena (rather than summons). By the same token, the interest of the Service is to have evidence obtained outside the grand jury (e.g., by greater use of its summons power before referring a case for grand jury investigation). The thrust of the *Baggot* and *Sells* decisions also makes it necessary for the Service to resort more frequently to the summons in auditing returns for civil purposes after closed grand jury proceedings and criminal cases.[732]

One of the initial problems of the *Baggot* and *Sells* decisions was whether and how they would affect those tax cases with outstanding Rule 6(e) orders. In *Kluger v. Comm'r*, the Tax Court concluded that *Baggot* and *Sells* would not be applied retroactively in a case where a Rule 6(e) order did not satisfy the standards announced in those cases.[733] Retroactively was not warranted because the *Baggot* and *Sells* decisions were cases of first impression, their holdings were not necessary consequences of prior case law, and it would not beneficially affect the accuracy of the trial (the grand jury materials were presumably accurate), nor would retroactive application restore grand jury secrecy.[734]

---

[732] For other practical implications of the *Baggot* and *Sells* cases, see Garbis, Schwait & Saltzman, What the Tax Practitioner Should Know About the Supreme Court's Baggot and Sells Decisions (1983).

[733] Kluger v. Comm'r, 83 TC 309 (1984). The decision in *Kluger* has been generally approved. Syufy v. IRS, 85-1 USTC ¶ 9195 (ND Cal. 1984), aff'd, 818 F2d 1457 (9th Cir. 1987); Caprio v. Comm'r, 787 F2d 109 (3d Cir. 1985) (*Baggot* not applied retroactively; suppression not warranted where Service agents who used grand jury information acted in good faith reliance on facially valid Rule 6(e) order issued by district court); In re Grand Jury 78-3, 783 F2d 450 (4th Cir. 1986) (*Baggot* and *Sells* do not apply retroactively). Although *Baggot* and *Sells* have not been applied retroactively, a curative order has been considered proper to bar further disclosure. In re Grand Jury Proceedings (Henry Kluger, Deceased), 86-2 USTC ¶ 9490 (EDNY 1986), aff'd, 827 F2d 868 (2d Cir. 1988) (although Gluck v. United States, 771 F2d 750, 775 (3d Cir. 1985), denied relief, "the better approach is to prohibit further disclosure of the grand jury material in pending civil proceedings unless the government shows a particularized need for the materials"). One court of appeals has said that a Rule 6(e) order entered before the *Baggot* and *Sells* decisions is a final order that can be set aside only on a showing of exceptional circumstances. In re Disclosure of Grand Jury Material, Basic Earth Science Sys., Inc., 821 F2d 1290 (7th Cir. 1987). See also In the Matter of Dec. 3, 1979 Houston Div. Fed. Grand Jury, 889 F2d 1466 (5th Cir. 1989), cert. denied, 58 USLW 3835 (1990) (accord).

[734] The Tax Court applied the criteria described by the Supreme Court in Chevron Oil Co. v. Huson, 404 US 97, 106–107 (1971) in deciding the retroactivity issue. In Hajecate v. Comm'r, 90 TC 280 (1988), notices of deficiency based on information obtained from grand jury materials disclosed as a result of pre-*Baggot* and *Sells* Rule 6(e) orders were valid. However, the court said, "[r]eexamination of the materials by respondent, after a five-year lapse in which he lost custody and no longer remembers the contents of the materials, is, in the ordinary sense of the words, a new use or disclosure." To obtain disclosure of the materials, the court held that the Service was required to obtain a new Rule

If *Baggot* and *Sells* standards are applied and a notice of deficiency has been prepared with improperly used grand jury materials, the Service is not precluded from asserting a deficiency from the taxpayer. In *Graham v. Comm'r*, the Tax Court assumed, for the purposes of decision, that *Baggot* and *Sells* applied retroactively, and that the Service's use of the grand jury material under the outstanding Rule 6(e) orders involved was improper.[735] It nevertheless held that the statutory notices of deficiency issued by the Service were not invalid. A majority followed the general rule that the Tax Court will not look behind a notice of deficiency to examine the evidence used or the propriety of the Service's motives or conduct in determining the deficiency. It concluded: "Thus, even assuming the illegality of [the Service's] use of the grand jury materials in this case, such use does not render the statutory notices null and void, requiring invalidation of the statutory notices." (Footnote omitted.) What the Tax Court refused to do was invalidate the statutory basis of its own jurisdiction—i.e., the notice of deficiency.[736]

To prevent doubt about the origin of information for civil use, agents are instructed to prepare a record and index of information in the Service's possession before any receipt of grand jury information.[737] Only non–grand jury information may be used in a civil tax case in the absence of a Rule 6(e)

6(e) order that could be granted only upon a showing of particularized need. For further proceedings in *Hajecate*, see In re Dec. 3, 1979 Houston Div. Fed. Grand Jury, n.61 (new production order issued and affirmed).

[735] Graham v. Comm'r, 82 TC 299 (1984). The decision in *Graham* was affirmed, 770 F2d 381 (3d Cir. 1985). Information obtained in violation of a Rule 6(e) order may also be used for purposes of issuing a summons to obtain additional information and to support a notice of deficiency, irrespective of *Baggot* and *Sells*. Gluck v. United States, 771 F2d 750 (3d Cir. 1985). In *Gluck*, the Third Circuit stated that the agents had acted in good faith on a facially valid Rule 6(e) order, so the remedy the taxpayer had asked for (suppression of evidence obtained by the Service) was inappropriate. In *Graham*, the taxpayer wanted his notice of deficiency canceled, but he did not contest the amount of the deficiency. The Second Circuit, contrary to *Gluck*, would issue a protective order restricting further disclosure in future civil proceedings. See In re Grand Jury Proceedings (Henry Kluger, Deceased), 86-2 USTC ¶ 9490 (EDNY 1986), aff'd, 827 F2d 868 (2d Cir. 1988). Use of grand jury materials pursuant to a Rule 6(e) order naming one spouse does not authorize use of those materials against the other spouse. Altman v. United States, 90-2 USTC ¶ 50,357 (EDNY 1990).

[736] However, it appears that in *Graham*, a motion to suppress the tainted evidence obtained in violation of Rule 6(e) or one to shift the burden of going forward or of proof might have been successful. See especially the concurring opinions of Judges Nims and Cohen.

[737] After the *Baggot* and *Sells* decisions, the Service also adopted guidelines to identify personnel who assist the attorney for the government in a grand jury investigation. IRM 9.5.2.5, Investigative Techniques Peculiar to Grand Jury Investigations (Sept. 30, 1998), and IRM 9.5.2.5.1, Subpoenas (July 29, 2002).

order,[738] unless the protection of Rule 6(e) does not apply. Rule 6(e) protects only materials that reveal "some secret aspect of the inner workings of the grand jury."[739]

---

[738] When Service agents obtained grand jury materials without a Rule 6(e) order, the evidence obtained was suppressed in a Tax Court case and the Service was required to bear the burden of going forward with evidence obtained independent of the grand jury investigation. Cohen v. Comm'r, 42 TCM 312 (1981). Where the government disclosed grand jury material during allocution on his guilty plea, the defendant moved to seal the court record to prevent the circumventing of Rule 6(e) and *Baggot* and *Sells*. The court of appeals held that the prosecutor did not show bad faith and intentional "use of grand jury materials designed to circumvent the prohibitions announced in Sells and Baggot." United States v. Manglitz, 773 F2d 1463 (4th Cir. 1985) (fact that the defendant did not object to the introduction of the materials played a part in the decision). *Baggot* and *Sells* do not prevent evidence that is presented at a criminal trial from being used in a later civil tax proceeding. Siskin v. Comm'r, 790 F2d 480 (6th Cir. 1986) (court also stated that even if the evidence is presented to a grand jury after an administrative investigation, it may be used for civil purposes); Anaya v. United States, 815 F2d 1373 (10th Cir. 1987) ("[t]he IRS was in pursuit of a legitimate investigation, and revelation of information learned by other governmental agencies in a parallel investigation without disclosure of what had been submitted to the grand jury was not improper" because "it is not the information itself, but the fact that the grand jury was considering the information which is protected by Rule 6(e)"). In Hajecate v. Comm'r, 90 TC 280 (1988), notices of deficiency based on information obtained from grand jury materials disclosed as a result of Rule 6(e) orders in effect before *Baggot* and *Sells* were valid. However, the court said, "[r]eexamination of the materials by respondent, after a five-year lapse in which he lost custody and no longer remembers the contents of the materials, is, in the ordinary sense of the words, a new use or disclosure." The court held that in order to obtain disclosure of the materials the Service must obtain a new Rule 6(e) order, which can be granted only upon a showing of particularized need.

[739] Davies v. Comm'r, 61 F3d 910 (9th Cir. 1995) (quoting United States v. Dynavac, Inc., 6 F3d 1407, 1413 (9th Cir. 1993)). Merely because business books and records are presented to a grand jury does not mean that they become matters occurring before the grand jury for purposes of Rule 6(e). When a taxpayer contended that disclosure of his corporation's business records that had been presented in a grand jury investigation of the taxpayer would reveal the grand jury's deliberations, the Tax Court rejected the contention. Levitt v. Comm'r, TC Memo. 1995-464 (1995). The court said that while a general request of all the grand jury records relating to the taxpayer and his corporation would, in effect, be a disclosure of the grand jury proceedings, a specific request for the corporation's books and records, prepared independent of the grand jury proceeding, would not reveal secret grand jury deliberations.

Similarly, when a witness provides information to the Service independent of the grand jury proceeding, Rule 6(e) does not apply, because a witness's "knowledge and information" is not covered by the rule. *Davies v. Comm'r*, supra.

¶ 13.14 WIRETAPS AND SIMILAR DEVICES

Nonconsensual monitoring of telephone and nontelephone conversations is expressly prohibited by the Service.[740] Nonconsensual monitoring may only be authorized by court order under Title III of the Omnibus Crime Control and Safe Streets Act[741] in order to investigate criminal offenses specified in 18 USC Section 2516. Tax offenses in the Code are not among the criminal offenses specified in that Section. Thus, the Service is prohibited from doing its own wiretapping as opposed to consensual monitoring. The Service is permitted to receive wiretap information from another federal or state agency that lawfully conducted a wiretap if the Service's special agent or revenue agent is "another investigative or law enforcement officer," at least to the extent that the disclosure "is appropriate to the proper performance of the official duties of the officer making or receiving the disclosure."[742] The Service believes its agents are investigative or law enforcement officers for these disclosure purposes, and there is some support for this position.[743] However, it is anomalous for the Service to be excluded from directly conducting wiretaps to discover evidence of tax violations and still be permitted to receive information from other federal agencies to use in a tax prosecution or proceeding. The likelihood is that law enforcement officers to whom disclosures could be made are those who enforce statutes covered by the direct-wiretapping provision.[744]

Consensual monitoring (i.e., monitoring a conversation with the consent of at least one of the parties) is permitted, but special authorization is required.[745] Such monitoring of telephone conversations requires National Office authorization. Consensual monitoring of nontelephone conversations occurs most frequently in bribery investigations where one of the parties is wired with a recording device. Consensual monitoring of nontelephone conversations requires the advance written authorization of the Director, Field Operations, or Deputy Assistant Commissioner (Criminal Investigation), except for emergency

---

[740] IRM 9.4.6, Surveillance and Non-Consensual Monitoring (July 16, 2002).

[741] 18 USC § 2510.

[742] 18 USC § 2517(1).

[743] United States v. Iannelli, 477 F2d 999, 1001 (3d Cir. 1973), aff'd on other grounds, 420 US 770 (1975).

[744] James v. McKeever, 73-2 USTC ¶ 16,119 (D. Ariz. 1973).

[745] IRM 9.4.7.3, Consensual Monitoring of Telephone Conversations (June 30, 1998). Monitoring of telephone conversations with the consent of one participant can be authorized by the Special Agent in Charge (SAC) for the areas. However, where a recording device is to be installed, the Chief or Deputy Chief, Criminal Investigation (CI) must authorize the monitoring. See also IRM 9.4.7.4.1, Consensual Monitoring of Non-Telephone Conversations (June 18, 2003).

situations, when designated officials in the Department of Justice may grant prior approval.[746]

These administrative requirements were examined by the Supreme Court in *United States v. Caceres*[747] where, in the consensual monitoring of a nontelephone conversation, the Service failed to obtain the prior written authorization of the specified Justice Department officials and justified the failure under the emergency exception. With National Office approval, a revenue agent recorded conversations in which Caceres made bribe offers to the agent. Both the district court and the court of appeals suppressed tapes of the conversations because they concluded no emergency existed and the agents had failed to comply with the Service's own regulations. The Supreme Court reversed, saying that the "emergency" finding by the Service officials, even if erroneous, "was not obviously so." Where a regulation is violated, errors of interpretation of the applicable regulation do not raise constitutional questions or warrant a "rigid rule of exclusion." Thus, the type of regulation and the circumstances of noncompliance determine whether evidence obtained in violation of regulations will be suppressed. The decision in *Caceres* raises questions about taxpayers' recourse where Service procedures are violated.[748]

¶ 13.15 MAIL COVERS

The Service uses so-called mail covers in the investigation of tax felonies, such as tax evasion. Under this procedure, the Service makes a request for a mail cover pursuant to which request the Postal Service makes a record of all data appearing on the outside of all mail and checks the contents of second-, third-, or fourth-class mail.[749] The Postal Service then furnishes the Service with such information as the name of the addressee, the postmark, the name and address of the sender (if it appears), and the class of mail, and delivers the mail itself to the addressee.

Use of mail covers presents issues of Fourth Amendment violations and compliance with both the Service's and the Postal Service's regulations. Thus far, taxpayers have been unsuccessful on these issues. Mail covers have been held to violate no Fourth Amendment privacy right in the sender because the information is voluntarily conveyed to the Postal Service and its employees

---

[746] IRM 9.4.7.4(2), Emergency Authorization of Non-Telephone Conversations (June 18, 2003).

[747] United States v. Caceres, 440 US 741 (1979).

[748] These questions are discussed at ¶ 1.03[2][c].

[749] IRM 9.4.10.2, Mail Covers (March 26, 2002).

and there is no reasonable expectation of privacy.[750] Although the Supreme Court has not ruled on the issue, a mail cover seems indistinguishable from bank-reporting requirements and bank records in Fourth Amendment terms.[751] Moreover, an attempt to challenge the failure to comply fully with administrative procedures in mail cover requests must distinguish the Supreme Court's decision in *United States v. Caceres*,[752] refusing to suppress evidence obtained after noncompliance.[753] A challenge must at least find that the noncompliance was in bad faith and violated some fundamental interest of the taxpayer.[754]

D INTERNATIONAL USES OF SUMMONSES AND OTHER METHODS OF ACCESS TO FOREIGN-BASED INFORMATION

¶ 13.16 TERRITORIAL LIMITS OF THE SUMMONS AUTHORITY

[1] Summons to Determine U.S. Tax Liability

The Service's summons authority is used to gather information to determine or collect liability for not only an internal revenue tax of the United States, but also a tax imposed by a foreign country having a treaty with the United States. A person located in the United States who is subject to the order of a U.S. court enforcing a summons for records located abroad faces the risk of contempt for nonproduction or foreign prosecution for production.[755] Use of a

---

[750] United States v. Choate, 576 F2d 165 (9th Cir. 1978), cert. denied, 99 S. Ct. 350 (1978) (extended discussion of mail covers); United States v. Leonard, 524 F2d 1076 (2d Cir. 1978) (outside of envelopes were photocopied); United States v. Balistrieri, 403 F2d 472 (7th Cir. 1968), cert. denied, 394 US 985 (1969). See United States v. Bianco, 534 F2d 501 (2d Cir. 1976).

[751] See United States v. Choate, 576 F2d 165 (9th Cir. 1978), cert. denied, 99 S. Ct. 350 (1978).

[752] See, e.g., United States v. Choate, 619 F2d 21 (9th Cir. 1980), cert. denied, 449 US 951 (1980).

[753] United States v. Caceres, 440 US 741 (1979).

[754] The Supreme Court's decision in *Caceres* is discussed at ¶ 1.03[2][c].

[755] See United States v. Hayes, 722 F2d 723 (11th Cir. 1984) (person ordered must make "all reasonable efforts," and evidence of some efforts is insufficient to rebut prima facie showing of contempt on nonproduction). See also United States v. Bank of Nova Scotia, 691 F2d 1384 (11th Cir. 1982), cert. denied sub nom. Bank of Nova Scotia v. United States, 103 S. Ct. 3086 (1983), further proceedings, 722 F2d 657 (11th Cir. 1983) (remanding case to district court for further proceedings). On remand, the bank was fined $1,825,000 and the contempt order and fine were affirmed. United States v. Bank of Nova

summons to obtain records in a foreign country having a treaty with the United States rather than the "competent authority" provisions of that treaty has been approved.[756] In general, the courts have balanced the relative interests of the United States and the foreign country. This balancing is provided in a five-part test laid down in the *Restatement (Second) of Foreign Relations Law* and adopted by many courts.[757] On the basis of this balancing test, a summons to the Hong Kong branch of a U.S. bank for banking records of a Hong Kong corporation was ordered enforced.[758]

It has also been held that nothing in Section 7602 precludes issuance of a summons to a foreign parent that has information relevant to the tax liability of its domestic subsidiary, and, indeed, Code provisions such as Section 482 appear to contemplate such an inquiry.[759] The district court enforced a sum-

---

Scotia, 740 F2d 817 (11th Cir.), cert. denied, 469 US 1106 (1984) (balancing of interest approach followed; U.S. interest in disclosure of the bank records to uncover the flow of funds in a narcotics investigation outweighed the foreign state's interest in secrecy).

[756] United States v. Vetco, Inc. 644 F2d 1324 (9th Cir.), cert. denied, 454 US 1008 (1981) (potential criminal liability in Switzerland did not excuse failure to produce records under the particular circumstances). See also Marc Rich & Co., AG v. United States, 707 F2d 663 (2d Cir.) cert. denied, 103 S. Ct. 3555 (1983) (sanctions for failure to comply with grand jury subpoena upheld although subpoena served on Swiss parent to produce records that were prohibited from production by Swiss law). Compare United States v. First Nat'l Bank of Chicago, 699 F2d 341 (7th Cir. 1983) (district court's order to U.S. bank to produce records of a branch in Greece reversed because Greek law would be violated by enforcement; an order requiring the bank to seek permission from the Greek government to obtain the summoned information was to be considered).

If the person whose bank account is in the foreign country is himself in the United States and subject to the order of a U.S. court, the person may be ordered to produce the records of the foreign bank account, as long as the Service establishes that the prerequisites in *United States v. Powell* have been met (see discussion supra ¶ 13.04[1]). See, e.g., United States v. Monahan, 80 AFTR2d 97-6694 (WD Wash. 1997) (couple ordered to produce records of offshore accounts after the Service showed that the husband had transferred large amounts of money to and from the offshore accounts).

[757] Restatment (Second) of Foreign Relations Law § 40 (1965). Marc Rich & Co., AG v. United States, 707 F2d 663 (2d Cir.) cert. denied, 103 S. Ct. 3555 (1983); United States v. First Nat'l Bank of Chicago, 699 F2d 341 (7th Cir. 1983).

[758] United States v. Chase Manhattan Bank, NA, 584 F. Supp. 1080 (SDNY 1984). see also Garpeg, Ltd. v. United States, 583 F. Supp. 799 (SDNY 1984); Garpeg, Ltd. v. United States, 588 F. Supp. 1237, 1239 (SDNY 1984). See Vanguard Int'l Mfg., Inc. v. United States, 588 F. Supp. 1229 (SDNY 1984) (balancing test applied and enforcement ordered although Hong Kong court had entered an order of preliminary injunction prohibiting the bank involved in *Garpeg* and *Chase Manhattan* from complying with the summons, and the matter had been referred to the grand jury). See IRM 42.2.1.1, Issuance of Summons Under IRC Section 7602 (June 15, 1988).

[759] United States v. Toyota Motor Corp., 561 F. Supp. 354 (CD Cal. 1983). For further proceedings in the case, see United States v. Toyota Motor Corp., 569 F. Supp. 1158 (CD Cal. 1983) (service of summons on officer of managing agent held proper; pricing data originating in Japan and claimed by Japan not to be subject to compelled production under international law held required to be produced).

mons issued to a foreign parent in connection with an audit of its domestic subsidiary because the foreign parent could be "found" in the judicial district in which the proceeding was filed within the meaning of Section 7604(a), which gives districts courts jurisdiction to compel a summoned person who resides or is "found" in the district to comply with a summons. The statutory term "found" in Section 7604(a) was read expansively "to extend at least as far as the administrative summons power accorded the IRS by Section 7602." The district court also concluded that due process considerations limited its jurisdiction to claims arising out of or resulting from the parent's foreign-related activities.

Summonses crossing territorial boundaries have been enforced in the following situations:

1. *U.S. bank with foreign branch.* A U.S. court can enforce a Service summons calling for non-U.S.-based records from the foreign branch of a U.S. company. In the *First National City Bank of New York*, a U.S. bank was found to have control over its Panamanian branch's records.[760] In the case, Panamanian law was held not to be violated. The court said that if production had violated Panamanian law, production would not have been ordered. However, in *United States v. First National Bank of Chicago*, the summons to obtain records of the Athens branch of a U.S. bank was not enforced.[761] Under the Greek bank secrecy law, criminal penalties were imposed on disclosures of depositors' information. The circuit court considered factors set forth in the *Restatement (Second) of Foreign Relations Law* to decide the case. The factors considered were the vital national interest of each country, the extent and nature of the hardship that inconsistent actions would cause, the nationality of the person affected, and the likelihood that enforcement action would achieve compliance with a rule prescribed by the country seeking enforcement. The threat of criminal prosecution was considered by the court to represent a case of potential hardship, but the court remanded the case for consideration by the lower court of an order requiring the U.S. bank to make a good faith effort to get the Greek authorities to permit the disclosure. The so-called "Gucci summons litigation" cases involved accounts at Chase Manhattan Bank's branch in Hong Kong, which was subject to Hong Kong's bank secrecy laws.[762] In addition, a Hong Kong court order was obtained enjoining Chase from complying with the Service summons. Despite the order, the courts in New York ordered the summonses enforced. The courts found that Hong Kong law did not clearly

---

[760] First Nat'l City Bank of NY v. IRS, 271 F2d 626 (2d Cir.), cert. denied, 361 US 948 (1959).

[761] United States v. First Nat'l Bank of Chicago, 699 F2d 341 (7th Cir. 1983).

[762] See United States v. Chase Manhattan Bank, NA, 584 F. Supp. 1080 (SDNY 1984); Garpeg, Ltd. v. United States, 583 F. Supp. 799 (SDNY 1984); Garpeg, Ltd. v. United States, 588 F. Supp. 1237, 1239 (SDNY 1984); Vanguard Int'l Mfg., Inc. v. United States, 588 F. Supp. 1229 (SDNY 1984.

prohibit disclosure and that there were only civil, not criminal, penalties for disclosure. The courts also said that if there were contempt citations sought in Hong Kong, Chase could always use the U.S. court order as a defense.

2. *Non-U.S. bank with U.S. branch.* A U.S. court can order a non-U.S. corporation with a U.S. branch to produce records based abroad. In *United States v. Bank of Nova Scotia*, a grand jury in Miami was conducting a narcotics and tax investigation. A grand jury subpoena was served on the Miami branch of the Bank of Nova Scotia for records of the Bank of Nova Scotia branch in the Bahamas, which was subject to the Bahamian bank secrecy laws.[763] In general, the courts found that the interests of the United States in tax collection are more vital than the Bahamas' interests in bank secrecy. The substantial fines that were imposed on the Bank of Nova Scotia were imposed because of the finding that it had not made a good faith effort to comply with the subpoena. Ultimately, the fine against the bank was $1.8 million. In a variation of this situation, in *United States v. Bache–Halsey Stuart, Inc.*, a summons was enforced against Bache–Halsey Stuart in New York to obtain information maintained in Switzerland.[764]

3. *U.S. parent with foreign subsidiary.* A summons can be served on a U.S. parent to obtain records of its foreign subsidiary. In *United States v. Vetco, Inc.*, the Service served a summons in a criminal investigation to obtain records of a Swiss subsidiary of a California corporation.[765] Despite Swiss secrecy laws, the summons was ordered to be enforced. The court held that the treaty between the United States and Switzerland was not the exclusive means for the Service to obtain information. Also, the threat of criminal prosecution under Swiss law was found not to exist. Balancing the competing interests, even hardship, the court found the interests of the United States paramount.

4. *Non-U.S. parent with U.S. subsidiary.* A summons can also be used to obtain information concerning a non-U.S. parent from a U.S. subsidiary. In *United States v. Toyota Motor Corp.*, a summons was served for records of Toyota (Japan), as well as its U.S. subsidiary (Toyota, US).[766] The court said that while mere ownership of the U.S. subsidiary is not enough to conclude jurisdiction, where the parent uses the subsidiary as a marketing conduit, it acquires a presence in the United States and, thus, can be "found" here for purposes of the summons authority. The same result was reached in the grand jury subpoenas involved in *Marc Rich & Co., AG v. United States*.[767] In both

---

[763] United States v. Bank of Nova Scotia, 740 F2d 817 (11th Cir.), cert. denied, 469 US 1106 (1984).

[764] United States v. Bache–Halsey Stuart, Inc., 563 F. Supp. 898 (SDNY 1982).

[765] United States v. Vetco, Inc., 644 F2d 1324 (9th Cir.), cert. denied, 454 US 1008 (1981).

[766] United States v. Toyota Motor Corp., 569 F. Supp. 1158 (CD Cal. 1983).

[767] Mark Rich & Co., AG v. United States, 707 F2d 663 (2d Cir.) cert. denied, 103 S. Ct. 3555 (1983).

Toyota Motor Corp. and *Marc Rich*, it was significant to the courts considering enforcing the processes of the U.S. courts that there were interlocking directorates, with the same individuals sitting on the board of directors of both the non-U.S. corporation and the U.S. subsidiary.

5. *Foreign parent present in the U.S.* A non-U.S. national of a country with bank secrecy laws who is present in the United States, can be compelled to give testimony in violation of those laws. In *United States v. Field*, a Cayman Islands bank official was served with a grand jury subpoena at the Miami airport as he was about to depart from the United States.[768] He was nevertheless compelled to testify despite the bank secrecy laws of the Cayman Islands, again because the interest of the United States in enforcing its tax laws was believed to outweigh the interest of the Cayman Islands in its secrecy laws.

6. *U.S. person present in the U.S. with foreign bank account.* A person present in the United States can be compelled to consent to the disclosure of information that is based abroad and is subject to non-U.S. secrecy laws. In *Doe v. United States*, the U.S. Supreme Court held that a court order compelling the target of a grand jury investigation to execute an authorization permitting "any bank" at which the petitioner "may have a bank account" to disclose the records relating to such account did not violate his Fifth Amendment right against self-incrimination, since the consent directive in question did not acknowledge the existence of any such account.[769] Similarly, an individual may be compelled to consent and not to resist U.S. foreign evidence-gathering efforts in foreign courts.[770] Under the same line of authority, a U.S. person may be compelled to repatriate funds,[771] or a U.S. bank with a foreign branch may be ordered to freeze funds in a taxpayer's account.[772]

[2] Other Code Provisions Providing Access to Foreign-Based Information

[a] Foreign-Owned Domestic Corporations—Section 6038A

Section 6038A takes a direct and heavy-handed approach to difficulties the Service may have had in the past in gaining access to information about transactions between U.S. taxpayers and the foreign corporations that control them. Section 6038A addresses the allocation, pursuant to Section 482, of in-

---

[768] United States v. Field, 532 F2d 404 (5th Cir.), cert. denied, 429 US 940 (1976). See also In re Sealed Case, 825 F2d 494 (DC Cir. 1987).

[769] Doe v. United States, 487 US 201 (1988). See the discussion supra ¶ 13.10.

[770] United States v. Davis, 767 F2d 1025 (2d Cir. 1985).

[771] United States v. McNulty, 446 F. Supp. 90 (ND Cal. 1978).

[772] United States v. First Nat'l City Bank, 379 US 378 (1965).

come, deductions, and credits between related taxpayers to clearly reflect their income—in this case, domestic corporations and the foreign corporations or individuals that control them. The statute presupposes a domestic corporation (or a U.S. branch operation of a foreign corporation) that (1) is 25 percent foreign-owned[773] and (2) engages in a transaction with the foreign shareholder or foreign persons related to either the foreign shareholder or the domestic corporation or branch operation.[774] Three separate requirements are imposed on the domestic corporation or branch operation:

1. *Reporting requirements.* The domestic corporation or branch operation (called the reporting corporation) must report "transactions between it and each foreign person which is a related party to the reporting corporation," as well as certain identifying information for the foreign persons with which the transaction took place.[775]

2. *Maintaining records.* The reporting corporation is itself required to maintain, "in the location, in the manner and to the extent prescribed in regulations," or cause another person to maintain, information to determine the correct tax treatment of the related party transaction.[776] This requirement is even more far-reaching than the language suggests. According to the Committee report:

   a. Regulations will control the type and form of the records that must be maintained.

   b. The reporting corporation must obtain and compile records not in the reporting corporation's possession or ensure that another person obtains, compiles, and maintains the records.

   c. Duplicates as well as original documents may satisfy the record maintenance requirement.

   d. The Service has the authority "to adjust the level of record maintenance in the United States on a case-by-case basis."

   e. Because a foreign corporation may not wish to disclose some information to the reporting corporation, the reporting corporation must

---

[773] A corporation is 25 percent foreign-owned if at least 25 percent of the total voting power of all classes of voting stock or at least 25 percent of the value of all classes of the corporation's stock are owned by one foreign person. IRC § 6038A(c)(1).

[774] IRC § 6038A(a). Section 6038A was amended in 1989 by the Revenue Reconciliation Act of 1989, Pub. L. No. 239, 101st Cong., 1st Sess., § 7403, for tax years beginning after July 10, 1989. For a discussion of the legislative purpose of the amendments, see HR Rep. No. 166-168, reprinted in 1989-3 CB 1296–1299 (vol. 3) (hereinafter House Report). A related party means (1) any 25 percent shareholder; (2) any person who is related to the reporting corporation or to a 25 percent shareholder within the meaning of Section 267(b) or Section 707(b)(1); or (3) any other person who is related to the reporting corporation within the meaning of Section 482. IRC § 6038A(c)(2).

[775] IRC §§ 6038A(b)(3), 6038A(b)(1), 6038A(b)(2).

[776] IRC § 6038A(a).

obtain the required information but need not keep this information under its control.

3. *Authorized agent for service.* The foreign shareholders or any other related party must authorize the reporting corporation to act as agent for purposes of a Service request "to examine records or produce testimony related to [the related-party] transaction or . . . any summons by the [IRS] for such records."[777] As the Committee report observes, "this requirement will ensure IRS examination requests and summonses with respect to related-party transactions involving U.S. taxpayers can be served on related foreign persons that do not directly engage in trades or businesses in the United States."[778]

If the reporting corporation fails to furnish the required information or to maintain required records, it can be penalized $10,000.[779] If the reporting corporation fails to cure its delinquency for more than ninety days after it is notified of the delinquency, this penalty can be increased by an additional $10,000 for each month or portion thereof for which the noncompliance continues.[780] A delinquency in filing or maintaining records can be avoided if the reporting corporation can establish "reasonable cause."[781] Some consideration is to be given to small corporations that promptly comply with Service requests for records, but reasonable cause does not exist where a foreign country would impose a civil or criminal penalty for disclosing records the Service requires.[782]

If the foreign corporation or other related party refuses to authorize the reporting corporation to receive process, an unusual penalty is imposed. The Service, in its "sole discretion" from the information available to it, is permitted to determine the amount of any deduction for any payment or amount due to the foreign corporation or other related party, and the cost to the reporting corporation for property it acquires from the foreign corporation or other related party.[783] Once the Service determines the amount of the reporting corpo-

---

[777] IRC § 6038A(e)(1).

[778] House Report, at 167. Congress was aware that requiring the reporting corporation to serve as agent for service of a Service summons might subject foreign corporations and individuals to nontax legal actions in the United States. Accordingly, the reporting corporation's status is described as an agency limited to Service inquiries and summonses. Section 6038A(e)(1) also states, "[T]he appearance of persons or production of records by reason of the reporting corporation [sic] being such an agent shall not subject such person or records to legal process for any purpose other than determining the correct treatment under this title of any transaction between the reporting corporation and such related party."

[779] IRC § 6038A(d)(1).

[780] IRC § 6038A(d)(2).

[781] IRC § 6038A(d)(3).

[782] House Report, at 170.

[783] IRC § 6038A(e)(3).

ration's deductions or costs, the sole discretion standard ensures that in a judicial review proceeding, the reporting corporation will usually be unable to overturn the determination.[784] Because the Service is permitted to exercise its sole discretion, the reporting corporation bears the burden of proving by clear and convincing evidence that the Service abused its discretion. Consequently, the Service's determination will be overturned only if the reporting proves that it was made with improper motive or was clearly erroneous after accepting as true all reasonably credible interpretations, assumptions of facts, and inferences that may have supported the Service's determination.

Section 6038A in itself does not authorize the Service to serve a summons. That authority is found in the general summons authority of Section 7602(a). Consequently, when the Service seeks documents and information described in Section 6038A and its regulations, and the reporting corporation wishes to challenge the validity of the summons, the procedures followed and the principles developed in summons cases are used.[785] When the Service serves a summons on any person, the reporting corporation has the right to institute a proceeding in a federal district court to quash the summons, provided that the proceeding is begun not later than ninety days after the date the summons was issued.[786] If the Service serves a summons and the reporting corporation provides records in response to the summons, but the Service determines that the reporting corporation has not "substantially complied in a timely manner" with the summons, the reporting corporation can seek judicial review of the determination.[787] This review proceeding must be begun within ninety days after the date on which the Service mails its notice of determination.[788] If a review proceeding is not instituted, the Service's determination of the correct tax treatment of the related-party transaction (the one made in its sole discretion under Section 6038A(e)(3)) "shall be binding and shall not be reviewed by any court."[789]

Some description of the procedure applicable in these proceedings is in order. Only federal district courts have jurisdiction over these review proceed-

---

[784] ASAT, Inc. v. Comm'r, 108 TC 147 (1997) (quoting House Conference Report on the standard to be applied; holding that agent's determination was not an abuse of discretion because it was based on her experience with a similar taxpayer, advice given by a Service economist, and published industry data; and rejecting reporting corporation's Section 482 analysis).

[785] Nissei Sangyo Am., Ltd. v. United States, 31 F3d 435 (ND Ill. 1995) ("However Section 6038A standing alone does not grant the power to issue an investigatory summons. The summons power of the IRS emanates from Section 7602 . . . "). See the description of summons procedures supra ¶ 13.04[3].

[786] IRC § 6038A(e)(4)(A). The Service can also ask the court to order compliance in this proceeding.

[787] IRC § 6038A(e)(4)(B).

[788] IRC § 6038A(e)(4)(B).

[789] IRC § 6038A(e)(4)(B).

ings, and the appropriate district court to institute the proceeding is the district court in which the summoned party "resides or is found."[790] The Federal Rules of Civil Procedure apply in the proceeding,[791] and the district court's decision is an appealable final order.[792] If the reporting corporation institutes a review proceeding, statutes of limitations on assessment, collection, and criminal prosecution are suspended during the pendency of the review proceeding and any appeal, and for ninety days after a final decision in the case.[793]

Amendments to Section 6038A made in 1989 expanded and modified the reporting and related requirements of Section 6038A, which were applicable only to taxable years beginning after July 10, 1989. The Omnibus Budget Reconciliation Act of 1990 extended the application of the 1989 Act so that the reporting and related requirements apply to future acts and failures to act in connection with taxable years beginning before July 11, 1989.[794] Similarly, a limited agent who must be appointed to receive a summons after November 5, 1990, must be authorized to receive a summons calling for information relating to tax years beginning before July 10, 1989. Obviously, then, a summons issued pursuant to Section 6038A after November 5, 1990, may call for information relating to tax years beginning before July 10, 1989. For a tax year beginning before July 10, 1989, if the reporting corporation fails to comply with the amended Section 6038A before November 5, 1990, and the noncompliance after that date, the penalty provision of Section 6038A(a)(2) applies for purposes of determining the amount of the penalty for each thirty-day period of delinquency.[795]

In 1991, the Service issued final regulations interpreting Section 6038A. The regulations are organized into seven sections: general requirements and definitions (Regulation Section 1.6038A-1); requirement of return (Regulation Section 1.6038A-2); maintenance of records (Regulation Section 1.6038A-3); application of the monetary penalty for the failure either to furnish information or to maintain records (Regulation Section 1.6038A-4); authorization of an agent for purposes of Sections 7602, 7603, and 7604 (Regulation Section 1.6038A-5); failure to furnish information requested by a summons (Regula-

---

[790] IRC § 6038A(e)(4)(C).

[791] See Fed. R. Civ. P. 81(a)(3).

[792] IRC § 6038A(e)(4)(C).

[793] IRC § 6038A(e)(4)(D).

[794] Omnibus Budget Reconciliation Act of 1990, §§ 11314(a)(1)–11314(a)(4). If the time for furnishing information under the amended Section 6038A(a) is after November 5, 1990, the 1989 amendments therefore apply, whenever the taxable year began that the information covers. The same holds true for records required under Section 6038A(a) to be maintained that were in existence on or after March 20, 1990. Even if the records pertain to tax years beginning before July 10, 1989, the record maintenance rules of Section 6038A apply.

[795] Omnibus Budget Reconciliation Act of 1990, § 11314(b).

tion Section 1.6038A-6); and application of the noncompliance penalty for failure by the related party to authorize an agent or for the reporting corporation to substantially comply with a summons (Regulation Section 1.6038A-7). It is something of an understatement to say that the regulations have been controversial.[796] Since it is beyond the scope of this description of the Service's summons authority and access to information to analyze substantive aspects of the regulations, the discussion here focuses on several procedural aspects of the regulations.

1. *Required records.* According to the regulations, a reporting corporation must keep "permanent books of account or records as required by Section 6001 that are sufficient to establish the correctness of the federal income tax return of the (reporting) corporation, . . . to the extent they may be relevant to determine the correct treatment of transactions with related parties."[797] However, neither Section 6001 nor the regulations promulgated under it with respect to income tax say anything about the keeping of records that "may be relevant" to determine the correct treatment of transactions.[798] The regulations speak in terms of keeping permanent books of account or records "as are sufficient to establish the amount of gross income, deductions, credits, or other matters required to be shown by such person in any return of such tax or information."[799] The "may be relevant" standard is the scope of inquiry described in the summons authority of the Service at Section 7602(a). But the books and records required to be maintained to establish the amount of income, deductions, and credits to be reported on a return, and the information that may throw light on the correctness of items of gross income, deductions, credits, and so on that are reported on a filed return, are not necessarily the same. By using the summons standard, the regulations apply the broad standard for document discovery to define the records that are required to be maintained by a reporting corporation. This confusion of the standard of discovery with the standard of record maintenance hardly provides guidance on what records must be maintained. The situation is exacerbated by the requirement that these records must be maintained for related corporations as well. Records must be maintained in the United States, except where the reporting corporation agrees to produce foreign-based records under an alternative procedure;[800] and records of transactions between a reporting corporation and the related parties, includ-

---

[796] More than fifty comments on the proposed regulations were received, some of which were longer than the regulations. "IFA Conferees Hear Gideon's Views on Info Reporting," 50 Tax Notes 1056 (Mar. 11, 1991). For an argument that Section 6038A itself is unconstitutional and violative of international law, see Palmieri, "Section 6038A Violates the Constitution and International Law," 54 Tax Notes 1017–1021 (Feb. 24, 1992).

[797] Reg. § 1.6038A-3(a)(1).

[798] Reg. § 1.6001-1(a).

[799] Reg. § 1.6001-1(a).

[800] Reg. § 1.6038A-3(b)(1).

ing directly or indirectly related transactions, must be maintained in the United States.[801] In addition, the records must not only be maintained in the United States but also be translated into English within thirty days after a request for translation is made.[802]

The alternative procedure requires an annual election whereby the reporting corporation agrees to the production of records by either (1) delivering duplicates of them to the Service within sixty days after a request (followed by translations of the documents within thirty days after a translation request) or (2) moving duplicates of the original documents to the United States within sixty days after a request; providing an index, the name and address of the custodian, and the location of the records; and maintaining the records in the United States so that they may be subject to a summons.[803] Finally, the records required to be maintained must be maintained "as long as they may be relevant to determining the correct treatment of any transaction between the reporting corporation and a related party."[804]

The Service's power to require translations is not unlimited. Because the Service must use its general summons power to secure the translations, the *Powell* standards and other principles developed in summons enforcement cases are applicable to limit the Service's demands. Under the general summons power, the Service may call for a reporting corporation to produce documents and other information that "may be relevant," and this broad power would permit the Service to require that documents be translated. Thus, the Service can require that basic financial records be kept in English in order to permit it to conduct an audit. But when the Service seeks translations of other documents under the Section 6038A regulations, it can demand that the reporting corporation produce translations of the documents only after the reporting corporation has produced the documents, the Service has reviewed the documents, and the Service has identified the specific documents that need to be translated.[805] Accordingly, when the Service seeks translated documents under the Section 6038A regulations, the sequence is (1) the Service requests documents; (2) the reporting corporation has sixty days to produce the documents; (3) before requesting translations, the Service must review the produced docu-

---

[801] Indirectly related records include, for example, records possessed by a foreign subsidiary of a foreign-related party that document the raw material or component costs of the product that is manufactured or assembled by the subsidiary and sold as a finished product by the foreign-related party to the reporting corporation. Reg. § 1.6038A-3(b)(2).

[802] Reg. § 1.6038A-3(b)(4).

[803] Reg. § 1.6038A-3(f)(1).

[804] Reg. § 1.6038A-3(g).

[805] Nissei Sangyo Am., Ltd. v. United States, 31 F3d 435 (7th Cir. 1994) (summons called for translations of all summoned documents without any review of documents, translated documents, translations of random samples of documents, and translations of titles of 1,441 pages of correspondence that had been produced).

ments; and (4) after reviewing the documents, the Service may request translations of specific documents, giving the reporting corporation thirty days to provide translations of those specific documents. When the Service serves a summons on a reporting corporation for translations of documents, and the reporting corporation believes the request burdensome, the reporting corporation must, by interview, written summaries, or some other method, provide the Service with a level of translation sufficient to show that the documents need not be produced under the *Powell* standards (e.g., because the documents are already in the Service's possession or are unrelated to the Service's audit). When a summons is served on the reporting corporation as agent of a third party calling for the production and translation of documents, the request must be reasonable, and the summons may be quashed if it is unduly burdensome.[806]

2. *Creation of records.* While a taxpayer is required to keep permanent books of account or records sufficient to establish the gross income, deductions, credit, or other matters required to be shown on a tax return,[807] a taxpayer is not required to prepare records not yet in existence.[808] Nevertheless, in order to meet a safe harbor exception to the record maintenance provisions, the regulations require the creation of a record, a "material profit and loss statement" for a product line or service for all members of a related group.[809] Whether a profit and loss statement is material is also covered by a set of complicated rules.[810] It is one thing to require a taxpayer to produce existing profit and loss statements, but it is quite another to require taxpayers to create profit and loss statements for each manufactured product line and then to maintain records from which the profit and loss statement is compiled or suffer penalties for failure to do so.

3. *Authorization of agent for service of summons.* A foreign-related party must authorize the reporting corporation to be its agent for the purposes of Sections 7602, 7603, and 7604 and for the service of process pursuant to Rule 4(d)(3) of the Federal Rules of Civil Procedure.[811] As the regulations make clear, the appointment of the reporting corporation as an agent effectively means the end of cases involving the reach of judicial process of U.S.

---

[806] Nissei Sangyo Am., Ltd. v. United States, 31 F3d 435 (7th Cir. 1994). The district court said that "in reality" a summons issued to the parent of the reporting corporation was issued to a third party, so that a reasonable request requirement applied in considering enforcement of a summons. The foreign parent could object to a summons calling for the foreign parent to produce documents in translated form on the ground that "the burden of translating is disproportionate to the ends sought."

[807] Reg. § 1.6001-1(a).

[808] See supra ¶ 13.06[1].

[809] Reg. § 1.6038A-3(c).

[810] Reg. §§ 1.6038A-3(c)(3)–1.6038A-3(c)(6).

[811] Reg. §§ 1.6038A-5(a), 1.6038A-5(b).

courts.[812] Thus, there should no longer be a case such as *Toyota Motor Corp.*,[813] where the issue is the reach of a summons or court order to produce records of a foreign parent corporation selling its products through a U.S. corporation. As long as a domestic corporation is a reporting corporation during the tax year in issue, the Tax Court held in *ASAT, Inc.* that the domestic corporation continues to be required to obtain the agency authorization from the foreign corporation, which was the 25 percent foreign shareholder during the year, even if at the time the Service requests the agency authorization, the domestic corporation is no longer 25 percent or more owned by the foreign corporation.[814]

4. *Sanctions for noncompliance.* There are, of course, monetary penalties for noncompliance with the information return filing, record maintenance, and record production provisions of Section 6038A.[815] But what is remarkable about Section 6038A is the carte blanche that it gives the Service to revise the return of the reporting corporation and determine the amount of tax. The regulations impose this sanction when the reporting corporation unsuccessfully moves to quash a Service summons.[816] Thus, there is a penalty for losing an effort to quash a Service summons, and the penalty is an extraordinary one indeed. No effort is made to determine whether the objection to the summons was made in good faith. This seems to be such an extreme position that it may result in applications to the court hearing the summons case to order the Service not to take such drastic action. One should be entitled to expect that if there is a good faith, nonfrivolous objection to a summons, compliance with the court order should not entail further sanctions in the form of Service recomputation of the reporting corporation's tax. In fact, if the Service is successful in a summons enforcement proceeding, its use of its power to determine tax as though the records have not been produced seems to be an

---

[812] See cases cited supra ¶ 13.09[5][a].

[813] United States v. Toyota Motor Corp., 561 F. Supp. 354 (CD Cal. 1983); United States v. Toyota Motor Corp., 569 F. Supp. 1158 (CD Cal. 1983).

[814] ASAT, Inc. v. Comm'r, 108 TC 147 (1997). To interpret Section 6038A otherwise, the court said, "would have us read into [S]ection 6038A(e) the additional requirement that the petitioner be a reporting corporation at the time the request for authorization of agent is made upon it by the IRS . . . [, but if] the statute could be rendered inapplicable by subsequent ownership changes in a reporting corporation, then it might lose a substantial part of its efficacy for its stated purpose." The court also noted that the legislative history did not anticipate that the reporting corporation would be permitted to avoid liability because, as the result of a change in ownership, it could no longer obtain the agency authorization from the foreign owner.

[815] Reg. § 1.6038A-4(a).

[816] Reg. § 1.6038A-6(a)(1). Moreover, if the summons is quashed because the reporting corporation has not maintained the required records, the District Director may also unilaterally determine the amount of the deduction or cost to the reporting corporation. Reg. § 1.6038A-6(a)(2).

unjustifiable abuse of the court's process to secure enforcement of the summons itself.

[b] Notice of Certain Transfers to Foreign Corporations

When a U.S. person transfers property to a foreign corporation in an exchange described in Sections 332, 351, 354, 355, 356, or 361, or makes a distribution described in Section 336 to a person who is not a U.S. person, the U.S. person must report the exchange to the Service.[817] The legislative purpose of this notice is that "[w]ithout a mechanism of apprising the IRS of outbound transfers, the IRS generally would have to depend on audits to detect outbound transfers of property subject to section 367 and any instances of failure to pay tax on such transfers . . . [and] the audit process is not a reliable means of isolating exchanges subject to section 367."[818] According to regulations, the information about the transfer must be filed on a Form 926, Return by Transferor of Property to a Foreign Corporation, Foreign Estate or Trust, or Foreign Partnership.[819] If the required information is not filed, a failure to file penalty is imposed equal to 25 percent of the gain realized on the exchange, unless the United States person is able to show that the failure was due to reasonable cause and not willful neglect.[820]

The Taxpayer Relief Act of 1997 made several important changes to Section 6038B. The amount of the penalty was changed from 25 percent of the gain realized on the transfer to 10 percent of the fair market value of the property transferred, and a ceiling of $100,000 limits the penalty unless the United States person has acted with intentional disregard of the reporting requirements.[821] In addition, for the purpose of making the reporting rules applicable to foreign partnerships conform to those applicable to foreign corporations, the reporting obligations of Section 6038B extend to foreign partnerships, and apply to transfers to a foreign partnership in a contribution described in Section 721, or as other contributions regulations dictate. Exceptions are provided when a United States person transfers property to a foreign partnership, but after the transfer, the United States person owns at least a 10 percent interest in the partnership, or the value of the property transferred exceeds $100,000.[822] In

---

[817] IRC § 6038B(a).

[818] S. Rep. No. 98-169, vol. 1 at 363–364 (1984).

[819] Reg. § 1.6038B-1T sets forth the filing requirements.

[820] IRC § 6038B(b).

[821] The Taxpayer Relief Act of 1997 § 1144(c), effective for transfers made after the enactment date, August 5, 1997.

[822] IRC § 6038B(b)(1). Former Section 6038B(b) was redesignated 6038B(c) by the Taxpayer Relief Act of 1997 § 1144(b).

addition, Section 482 adjustments are treated as having taken place no earlier than the date specified in the regulations.[823]

[c] Foreign Corporation Related-Party Transactions

Section 6038A is applicable only where the foreign corporation is 25 percent foreign owned. Section 6038C, added by the Omnibus Budget Reconciliation Act of 1990, imposes the same information-reporting, record maintenance, and summons service requirements as Section 6038A does; but these rules apply to all foreign corporations that carry on trades or businesses in the United States. Unlike Section 6038A, Section 6038C is applicable to related-party transactions in the case of any foreign corporation with the U.S. trade or business, regardless of whether the foreign corporation is foreign owned. Section 6038C goes even further than Section 6038A. It applies the reporting, record maintenance, and summons service rules to other information that may be required by regulations about items not directly connected with a related-party transaction.[824]

Section 6038C states that if a foreign corporation is engaged in a U.S. trade or business, it becomes a reporting corporation and, as such, must report transactions between it and each foreign person to which it is related.[825] Apart from reporting these related-party transactions, the reporting corporation must maintain records considered appropriate by the Service to determine the reporting corporation's tax liability.[826] Failure to furnish information or to maintain required records is punished in the same manner as under Section 6038A(d),[827] unless the related party authorizes the reporting corporation to act as the related party's limited agent for the sole purpose of receiving a summons for information that may be relevant to the determination of any U.S. tax liability.[828] As under Section 6038A, if the foreign corporation or the authorized agent fails to comply with a summons and the summons is not quashed, the Service, in its "sole discretion," is permitted to determine the treatment of the related-party transaction or the amount and treatment of an item of income or deduc-

---

[823] IRC § 6038(b)(2).

[824] IRC § 6038C(b)(2).

[825] IRC § 6038C(a), added by Omnibus Budget Reconciliation Act of 1990, § 11315, if the time for furnishing the information is after November 5, 1990. The terms "related party," "foreign person," and "records" have the same meanings as they do under Section 6038A.

[826] IRC § 6038C(a)(2), applicable to records in existence on March 20, 1990. The reporting corporation can satisfy the record maintenance provision by causing another corporation to maintain the records.

[827] See supra ¶ 13.16[2][a].

[828] IRC § 6038C(d)(1).

tion from the transaction from the information available to it.[829] The procedures for judicial review of a Section 6038C summons are the same as for a summons under Section 6038A.[830]

[d] Partnership Audits

To assist the Service in obtaining records from foreign countries, special rules apply in both partnership audits and summons proceedings. Special rules also relate to the use of records kept in foreign countries in tax litigation in the United States. The partnership return-filing requirements of Section 6031 are applicable to any partnership that has U.S. partners (direct or indirect). Under the partnership audit rules, in the case of a partnership where the tax matters partner resides outside the United States or where the books are maintained outside the United States, no loss or credit is allowable if the partnership fails to file a partnership return or to make its books and records available for inspection on request.[831] Jurisdiction for summons enforcement actions involving U.S. citizens or residents living abroad is established in the federal district court for the District of Columbia, by treating those persons as residents of the District of Columbia for summons enforcement purposes.[832]

[e] Foreign Document Requests

Section 982 establishes rules governing the admissibility of foreign-based documents. If a taxpayer has failed to "substantially comply" with a "formal document request" (FDR) arising out of an examination within ninety days after the date of the request, a court hearing a civil tax case involving the tax treatment of an item must, on the Service's motion, rule that evidence in the form of "foreign based documentation" is inadmissible.[833] An FDR is any request made in the course of an audit after normal request procedures have failed for the production of foreign-based documentation.[834] The FDR must be mailed by certified or registered mail to the taxpayer at his last known address and must set forth (1) the time and place for production; (2) a statement as to

---

[829] IRC §§ 6038C(d)(2), 6038C(d)(3).

[830] IRC §§ 6038C(d)(4). See supra ¶ 13.16[2][a].

[831] IRC § 6231(f).

[832] See IRC § 6230(j).

[833] IRC § 982(a). The foreign document request procedure and sanction does not preclude the Service from seeking and the Tax Court from ordering discovery. The Hong Kong & Shanghai Banking Corp. v. Comm'r, 85 TC 701 (1985).

[834] IRC § 982(c)(1). Foreign-based documentation is any documentation that may be relevant to the tax treatment of the examined item and kept out of the United States by a foreign entity whether or not controlled by the taxpayer. IRC § 982(d).

why any previously produced documentation is insufficient; (3) a description of the documents sought; and (4) the consequences of a failure to produce.[835]

When an FDR is sent, the taxpayer is permitted to contest the Service's action by instituting a proceeding to quash the request.[836] In this proceeding, the standards for enforcement of an FDR are the same as those applied in a summons case, that is, the standard adopted by the Supreme Court in the *Powell* case.[837] In *Yujuico*, for example, the taxpayers' claim that the Service agents had failed to follow administrative steps required by the Code was rejected, because the taxpayer had failed to produce much of the information requested in many Information Document Requests (IDRs). The taxpayers argued that they had reasonable cause for failing to produce the records. One of the taxpayers was found to have practical control over the records, however, in part because he transferred stock in foreign corporations after the first FDR and guaranteed loans to those corporations after the stock was transferred. This proceeding must be instituted within ninety days after the date the request was mailed[838] in the federal district court for the district in which the person served resides or is "found."[839] The decision of the district court is a formal order appealable as such.[840] Statutes of limitation on assessment, collection, and criminal prosecution are suspended during the pendency of the proceeding.[841]

Evidence preclusion is not required if the taxpayer proves that the failure to provide documentation is due to reasonable cause.[842] Reasonable cause has been found where the foreign document request was addressed to the taxpayers' corporation in the Philippines and not to the taxpayers, whose liability was

---

[835] IRC § 982(c)(1).

[836] IRC § 982(c)(1).

[837] International Mktg. Ltd. v. United States, 90-2 USTC ¶ 50,476 (ND Cal. 1990); Yujuico v. United States, 818 F. Supp. 285 (ND Cal. 1993). See supra ¶ 13.08[1] for discussion of *Powell*. However, the Service believes that the FDR is not so attractive an alternative to a summons, where the records are needed to determine liability; therefore, in this situation, it will use a summons rather than a foreign document request. IRM (42)220, cited in ILM 199938002 (July 28, 1999).

[838] International Mktg. Ltd. v. United States, 90-2 USTC ¶ 50,476 (ND Cal. 1990).

[839] IRC § 982(c)(2).

[840] IRC § 982(c)(2).

[841] IRC § 982(e).

[842] Whether a taxpayer has substantially complied with an FDR depends on all the facts and circumstances, such as the overall compliance of the taxpayer and making the determination on an issue-by-issue basis. Staff of Joint Comm. on Taxation, General Explanation of Tax Equity and Fiscal Responsibility Act of 1982, HR 4961, 97th Cong., 2d Sess. 246–247. For a case prohibiting introduction of documents after noncompliance with an FDR, see Flying Tigers Oil Co., Inc. v. Comm'r, 92 TC 1261 (1989) (Service complied with preliminary requirements of Section 982; taxpayer's failure to respond "deemed to concede that the request was for material and relevant documents and that no reasonable cause existed for its failure to produce the requested documents").

in issue in the Tax Court.[843] However, reasonable cause does not exist by reason of the fact that a foreign jurisdiction would impose a civil or criminal penalty on the taxpayer (or any other person) for disclosing the requested documentation.[844] One court has said that the evidence-preclusion sanction is so harsh that it should only be employed upon a finding of culpability on the part of the noncomplying party amounting to willfulness or bad faith.[845]

¶ 13.17 SUMMONS TO DETERMINE FOREIGN TAX LIABILITY

A summons served to obtain information concerning liability for a foreign country's tax has been enforced, at least where there is a tax treaty with the foreign country that requests the information under a "competent authority" provision in the treaty.[846] At one time, it was unclear whether a summons should be enforced where it would not be enforceable if issued to obtain information regarding U.S. tax or where the foreign country's laws do not provide for compulsory process to obtain tax-related information. The Model Treaty used by the Treasury provides that a requesting party may not take advantage of an information system of another party if it is wider than the information system of the requesting party. However, in *United States v. Stuart*, the Supreme Court settled the issue.[847] Canada's Department of National Revenue had asked the Service for assistance under the United States–Canada Tax Convention in obtaining records of bank accounts maintained in the U.S. by Canadian citizens and residents. The Service used its summons authority to obtain

---

[843] Santa Maria v. Comm'r, TC Memo. 1994-622 (1994) (the taxpayers claimed that they were not required to report the interest on certain bank accounts; the Service argued that they were precluded by the foreign document request from offering evidence on the true ownership of the bank accounts).

[844] IRC § 982(b)(2). See Chris-Marine USA, Inc. v. United States, 892 F. Supp. 1437 (MD Fla. 1995) (taxpayer claimed the FDRs requested information between unrelated corporations in aid of a criminal investigation by both the Service and Swedish authorities; motion to quash denied because the FDRs sought information that might be relevant to the determination of whether a parent-subsidiary relationship existed and the Service had not made a formal criminal referral or abandoned in an institutional sense its civil examination).

[845] Aruba Bonaire Curacao Trust Co. v. Comm'r, 777 F2d 38 (DC Cir. 1985).

[846] United States v. Burbank Co., 525 F2d 9 (2d Cir.), cert. denied, 426 US 934 (1975). In an FSA, the office of the Assistant Chief Counsel, International, concluded that the Service did not have authority to use a Postal Service "mail cover" at the request of a treaty partner, because a mail cover was permitted only to detect acts punishable under U.S. law. FSA 1998-100, dated August 19, 1992, published June 6, 1998, in 98 TNT 132-29.

[847] United States v. Stuart, 109 S. Ct. 1183 (1989).

information for the Canadian Department of National Revenue. The Supreme Court held that the Service was entitled to enforcement of its summons, whether or not the Canadian investigation was directed toward criminal prosecution under Canadian law. The Court found that Section 7602(c), restricting the use of a summons after the referral of the case to the Justice Department, does not apply to a treaty-related summons because it speaks only to possible violations of U.S. revenue laws. On the other hand, the investigation of the foreign country must meet the *Powell* standards applicable to Service summonses for its own investigations. Therefore, the foreign country's investigation must have been instituted for a lawful purpose, the inquiry must be relevant to that purpose, the information must not already be in the possession of the foreign taxing authority, and the proper administrative steps required by law (e.g., the provisions of the treaty providing for mutual assistance) must have been followed.[848]

A summary of some of the cases involving the Service's use of its summons authority to assist a foreign country's tax inquiry is instructive on this point. In *Fernandez-Marinelli v. United States*,[849] pursuant to two agreements between the United States and Mexico, the Convention for the Avoidance of Double Taxation and the Prevention of Fiscal Evasion with Respect to Taxes, and the Exchange of Information with Respect to Taxes, the Service served a summons on a Mexican citizen's New York broker to obtain information for the Mexican government's investigation of his 1989 tax liability. In enforcing the summons, the district court noted that before it issued the summons, the Service had determined that an ongoing Mexican investigation existed and that the Mexican authorities had notified the taxpayer that he was being audited based on his 1989 tax liability. The court considered the taxpayer's arguments attacking the legitimacy of the Mexican investigation and observed that while he might have shown that the investigation had an illegitimate purpose if the applicable Mexican statute of limitations had run, the summons was served before the expiration of that period. Similarly, in another case,[850] the taxpayer claimed that the summons served under the Canadian treaty violated Canadian law; however, the district court held that Canadian law was irrelevant to the issue whether the summons should be enforced.

In *Barquero v. United States*,[851] the taxpayer moved to quash the Service summons requesting bank documents pursuant to a Tax Information Exchange Agreement (TIEA) between the United States and Mexico for the exchange of information with respect to taxes. The competent authority from Mexico made a request for information pursuant to the TIEA to determine the plaintiff's

---

[848] For a discussion of the *Powell* standards, see supra ¶ 13.08[1].

[849] Fernandez-Marinelli v. United States, 76 AFTR2d 95-8102 (SDNY 1995).

[850] Azouz v. United States, 85 AFTR2d 2000-1217 (SDNY 1999).

[851] Barquero v. United States, 1993 WL 328030 (SD Tex. 1993).

Mexican tax liability. The taxpayer argued, among other things, that (1) the Service cannot use an administrative summons to obtain documents and other information pursuant to a request by Mexico under the TIEA; (2) the summons was not issued pursuant to a proper or legitimate purpose; and (3) the TIEA failed to comply with the Federal Right to Financial Privacy Act of 1978. The court held that the Service's broadly worded summons authority under Section 7602 enabled the Service to retrieve documents "as if the I.R.S. was requesting the documents for its own investigation." It also held that the requirements of *Powell* were met. Finally, the court held that the summons issued pursuant to the TIEA complied with the Right to Financial Privacy Act of 1978.

Also, when the Service served third-party summonses on two U.S. banks to obtain information for the French fiscal authorities under the United States–France Income Tax Convention, the summonses and certificates of service of the summonses were held to have been properly made by mailing them to the French taxpayers, applying the Hague Convention.[852]

The principle that the Service must meet the *Powell* requirements when it serves a summons for a treaty partner may result in the Service's refusing to issue a summons for the information, limiting the summons, or requesting further information from the treaty partner to support the issuance of a summons. For example, when the competent authority of a treaty partner requested the Service to serve a summons on two banks believed to be owned by two corporate clients of the person the treaty partner was investigating, calling for the production of all bank statements and canceled checks of the corporate clients for a two-year period, the office of the Assistant Commissioner, International, concluded that the treaty partner had not supplied sufficient information or explanation to establish a "clear nexus" between some of the requested information and the person being investigated to support the issuance of a summons.[853]

---

[852] Lestrade v. United States, 78 AFTR2d 96-6470 (SD Fla. 1996) (Article 10(a) of the Hague Convention, which says the Convention does not interfere with the "freedom to send judicial documents, by postal channels, directly to persons abroad" and thus permits service by mail).

[853] FSA 1998-108, dated in 1993, published June 6, 1998, in 98 TNT 137-40. Lidas, Inc. v. United States, 87 AFTR2d 2001-801 (2001) (the Service was authorized to issue summons to obtain documents for French fiscal authorities because documents under the France–United States tax treaty related to a foreign tax liability; to succeed on motion to enforce summons at the request of a tax treaty partner, the Service must establish that it has complied with *Powell* and applicable statutes). Yeong Yae Yun v. United States, 87 AFTR2d 2001-1408 (CD Cal. 2000) (enforcing summons where the Service served summonses on behalf of Korean taxing authorities and holding that the Service may serve summons pursuant to a tax treaty, even where no U.S. tax audit is pending).

[1] Exchanges of Information

Exchange of information articles are part of U.S. tax treaties and, as discussed below TIEAs. For purposes of the exchange of information, TIEAs, although not tax treaties are treated the same as treaties. Exchange of Information articles usually have three provisions: (1) A general obligation for competent authorities to exchange information for purposes of carrying out the treaty or the the domestic tax laws relating to the taxes covered by the treaty; (2) restrictions on the use and disclosure of information received to those permitted access under the treaty; and (3) and language which relieves the competent authority of any obligation to provide information which (a) is not obtainable either by the requesting competent authority under the treaty partner's laws or by the receiving competent authority; (b) would require the receiving competent authority to carry out administrative procedures contrary to its own laws or those of the requesting treaty partner; or (c) would disclose trade secrets or other information contrary to public policy.[854]

Generally, tax treaties also provide for the competent authority of the United States and a treaty partner to resolve double taxation and other treaty problems by mutual agreement procedures (MAP).[855] Tax information is exchanged to the extent necessary to resolve particular tax disputes involving double taxation. The designated U.S. competent authority under the tax treaties is the Director, International (LMSB). The taxpayer requesting the assistance of the U.S. competent authority is informed of the information provided to, and the positions taken with, the treaty partner.

Sections 927(e) and 274(h)(6)(C) permit the Secretary of the Treasury to enter into an agreement for the exchange of information with any foreign country.[856] Under this authority, TIEAs have been entered into not only with "beneficiary countries" as defined in Section 212(a)(1)(A) of the Caribbean Basin Economic Recovery Agreement but with other foreign countries as well.[857] Under a TIEA, when information is requested by a contracting country, through its competent authority, the United States must obtain the requested information as though the tax was that of the United States and the information was requested for a Service investigation.[858] For this reason, a summons

---

[854] IRM 4.60.1.1, Exchange of Information Overview (Jan.1, 2002).

[855] IRM 4.60.1.2.1, Exchangeable Information [Under Tax Treaties and TIEAs] (Jan.1,2002): IRM 4.60.2, Mutual Agreement Procedures and Report Guidelines (Jan. 1, 2002).

[856] See Barquero v. United States, 18 F3d 1311 (1994).

[857] The United States has entered into TIEAs with Mexico, Bermuda, and other countries.

[858] For example, the U.S.–Mexico TIEA provides:

[I]f information is requested by a Contracting State [Mexico] . . . the requested State [United States] shall obtain the information requested in the same manner, and pro-

issued by the Service for information requested by another country under a TIEA is tested under the *Powell* standards (discussed above).[859] Since information is to be obtained "in the same manner" as if the Service were seeking information for its own investigation, the RFPA applies. Under the RFPA, therefore, the Service is required to give the taxpayer notice of a summons issued to a bank or other financial institution, and the bank must obtain a certificate to that effect.[860]

The Service has five general procedures for *exchanging* information under tax treaties:[861]

1. Specific requests other than under the Simultaneous Examination Programs;
2. Specific requests under the Simultaneous Examination Programs;
3. Industrywide exchanges;
4. Exchanges of "know-how" with both treaty and nontreaty countries; and
5. Spontaneous exchanges of information uncovered during an audit or other investigation of a specific taxpayer.

In addition, the Service conducts investigations outside the United States through collateral investigations and other information-gathering activities of the Office of the Assistant Commissioner (International) (which has fourteen posts located throughout the world, each having a revenue service representative, and on-site examinations by district agents). The types of information exchangeable under these programs are (1) information about tax law changes; (2) information concerning double taxation; (3) information exchanged on a routine basis; and (4) information exchanged on a specific request about a particular case.[862]

[a] Specific Request Information

Two types of specific requests may be mase under treaties: specific requests about particular cases, and specific requests made during examinations under the Simultaneous Examination Programs conducted by the Service and the fiscal agency of the treaty partner.[863] Suppose a revenue agent examining a

---

vide it in the same form, as if the tax of the applicant State were the tax of the requested State and were being imposed by the requested State.

Art. 4, para. 5.

[859] See infra ¶¶ 13.04[1], 13.08[1], for a discussion of the four-part *Powell* standard.

[860] See Barquero v. United States, 18 F3d 1311 (1994).

[861] IRM 4.60.1.1, Exchange of Information Overview (Jan. 1, 2002).

[862] IRM 4.60.1.1, Exchange of Information Overview (Jan. 1, 2002).

[863] IRM 4.60.1.2, Specific Exchange Program (Jan. 1, 2002).

taxpayer in New York wants information from outside the United States. The agent must prepare a request for the Area Director, who forwards the request to the Director, International (LMSB). This request must contain specific identifying information. The request is sent to the Director (Office of International Programs) who decides whether to secure the information through the revenue service representative or to request the information through a treaty-partner competent authority.

Suppose a treaty partner wishes to obtain information within the United States. The Service handles specific requests for information from a treaty partner on a case-by-case basis. The Director (Office of International Programs) forwards specific requests to the appropriate Territory Manager for the appropriate Division, with an information copy to the Area Director. The Territory Manager forwards the requested information to the Director (Office of International Programs) with a written recommendation of whether the information should be disclosed. A copy of this recommendation is sent to the Area Director. The Assistant Commissioner (International) then forwards the information to the foreign competent authority who requested the information, or explain why the information is not available or cannot be disclosed. Although the Territory Manager's recommendation will be considered, the ultimate decision is made by the Assistant Commissioner (International).[864] The request must specifically identify the taxpayer and the information requested.[865] It also must show that it concerns a person or entity subject to the treaty partner's tax laws and is required in good faith for material necessary to determine a tax liability covered by the treaty.

Once the Service decides to supply information to a treaty partner, it uses its own summons power to obtain the information. Where a person in the United States has refused to supply information for transmission to the treaty partner, the Service's use of its summons power on behalf of the treaty partner has been approved by the Supreme Court. In *Stuart v. United States*, Canada's Department of National Revenue asked the Service for assistance under the United States–Canada Tax Convention in obtaining records of bank accounts maintained in the United States by Canadian citizens and residents. The Supreme Court held that the Service was entitled to enforcement of its summons, whether or not the Canadian investigation was for the purpose of a criminal

---

[864] IRM 4.60.1.2, Specific Request Program (Jan.1, 2002). This request must contain general information identifying the taxpayer, a description of the tax issues and why the information is needed, as well as any efforts to secure the information, data supplied by the taxpayer and the foreign government's interest, if any, and identifying information about an affiliate or witness if the affiliates or witness of the affiliates are to be examined or the witness is to be interviewed.

[865] IRM 4.60.1.1(6), Exchange of Information Overview (Jan. 1, 2002).

prosecution under Canadian law.[866] Not surprisingly, in light of this authority, a summons has been enforced in the United States to obtain information to be supplied to Canada for civil purposes.[867] An even more far-reaching extension of the Service's summons power for the benefit of a treaty partner was involved in *United States v. Bache–Halsey Stuart, Inc.*, where, under the United States–Netherlands Treaty, a U.S. firm's branch was required to disclose Swiss-based information about a Dutch resident for communication to the Dutch authorities.[868]

Is information exchanged under treaties confidential? The Service is permitted by the confidentiality provisions of the Code to disclose information under treaties.[869] Trade secrets and proprietary information are generally protected by the treaties themselves.[870] Once the Service discloses the information, it may remain confidential, because many treaties provide that exchanged information may not be disclosed except to persons involved in tax administration of the tax covered by the treaty.[871] In-bound information is not disclosed by the Service to the affected party if the Service decides that disclosure would "seriously impair" tax administration.[872] At any rate, the Service is supposed to consult its treaty partner if a disclosure is to be made and to keep a record of the disclosures.[873]

---

[866] Stuart v. United States, 109 S. Ct. 1183 (1989). However, the summons must be for an authorized governmental purpose and issued in a good faith pursuit of that purpose rather than to harass a taxpayer.

[867] United States v. AL Burbank Co., Ltd., 525 F2d 9 (2d Cir. 1975).

[868] United States v. Bache–Halsey Stuart, Inc., 563 F. Supp. 898 (SD NY 1982).

[869] IRC § 6103(k)(4).

[870] See 1981 Draft United States Model Income Tax Treaty, Article 26(2)(c).

[871] To prevent unauthorized disclosures, the Office of Assistant Commissioner (International) will note the following on all information disclosed under the tax treaty: "This information was secured under provisions of income (estate or gift) tax treaty. Its use and disclosure must be governed by the provisions of such treaty." IRM 4.60.1.2.2, Confidentiality, Disclosure and Treaty Secrecy (Jan. 1, 2002).

[872] IRC § 6103(e)(7).

[873] IRM 4.60.1.2.2, Confidentiality, Disclosure and Treaty Secrecy (Jan.1, 2002). The Chief Counsel, International, concluded in an FSA that the information obtained under the competent authority provision of a treaty with one treaty partner is confidential return information subject to the confidentiality rules of Section 6103(k)(4), and the extent to which the Service may disclose the information is determined under Section 6103. There is an exception, however. If the exchange-of-information portion of the treaty is more restrictive than Section 6103, the treaty will control. Accordingly, the information obtained from the first treaty partner should not be disclosed to the second treaty partner without the consent of the first treaty partner. FSA 1998-109 (Aug. 4, 1993), published in 98 TNT 149-23. On the other hand, if the information requested by the treaty partner was developed during the course of the Service's own examination of a U.S. taxpayer, the information could be exchanged with the treaty partner for use in developing a comparable price in transfer pricing examination because the return information so gathered could be disclosed under Section 6103(k)(4).

[b] Specific Requests Under the Simultaneous Examination Programs

Simultaneous examinations are examinations conducted under the information exchange provisions of income tax treaties and Tax Information Exchange Agreements conducted through the Competent Authority, who is the Commissioner, LMSB, and certain treaty partners under income tax treaties.[874] The compliance benefits the Service sees as resulting from this program are the assessment of tax based on a more complete factual development of the circumstances pertaining to tax liability; information exchange on apparent tax avoidance techniques or patterns; information exchange on tax haven transactions; information exchange on cost sharing arrangements; and information exchange on profit allocation arrangements, including those involving global trading and new financial instruments.[875] Each country separately and simultaneously examines the related taxpayers under its jurisdiction. During the examination, information is exchanged under the provisions of the treaty. The Service conducts simultaneous examination programs with Australia, Canada, France, Germany, Italy, Norway, Sweden, the Philippines, Japan, Korea, and the United Kingdom.

The type of taxpayers the Service believes are candidates for these types of examinations includes not only large, multinational corporations, but smaller corporations, as well as individuals, partnerships, and trusts with multinational contacts. In addition, the Service also has a limited number of multilateral simultaneous examination programs, in which each treaty partner independently identifies specific taxpayers for simultaneous examination. Each partner notifies the other that it wishes to participate in the examination of the identified taxpayer, and then each treaty partner separately and simultaneously examines the same tax years. In the course of these examinations, specific exchanges of information take place between the Service and the treaty partner. However, the Service does not exchange information it receives from another treaty partner.

[c] Industrywide Exchanges of Information

The purpose of industrywide exchanges of information between the Service and fiscal authorities of foreign countries is to secure comprehensive data on worldwide industry practices and operating patterns.[876] The Service uses personnel with the necessary expertise. There are industrywide information exchange programs with Australia, Canada, Denmark, Germany, France, Italy, Japan, and the United Kingdom. Under these programs, information about

---

[874] IRM 460.1.3, Simultaneous Examination Program (Jan. 1, 2002).

[875] IRM 460.1.3.1, Purpose, Objectives and Benefits (Jan. 1, 2002).

[876] IRM 4.60.1.4, Industrywide Exchanges of Information (Jan.1, 2002).

pricing and operations is exchanged in such industries as banking, commodities, forest products, grain, and petroleum.

[d] Routine Exchanges of Information

The program of routine exchanges of information is a spontaneous exchange of information program. It is perhaps the oldest and most active program of the Service. Each year, the Service sends between 500,000 and 600,000 information documents to treaty partners and receives approximately 800,000 to 850,000 information documents in return.[877] The information exchanged under this program is Form 1099-type information about interest and dividend income received by U.S. taxpayers. For example, the Service provides foreign treaty partners with information supplied by U.S. payors of passive income to persons claiming foreign status. The information that treaty partners supply to the Service is converted to Forms 1099 and is used in the Service's Information Returns Program under which information return data are matched against filed income tax returns. The Service will disclose to a treaty partner information it discovers during an examination without specific request.[878] Such information is sent through the chain of authority to the Commissioner (LMSB), who then sends it to the competent authority for exchange. The Service monitors information exchanges under this program to ensure that treaty partners also supply such information.

---

[877] Olsen, "Written Remarks," UCLA Second Annual Tax Disputes Inst., at 8 (1985).
[878] IRM 4.60.1.1(6), Exchange of Information Overview (Jan. 1, 2002); IRM 4.60.1.5, Spontaneous Exchanges of Information (Jan. 1, 2002).

CHAPTER **14**

The Tax Collection Function: Tax Liens and Levies

¶ 14.01 OVERVIEW: DEBTOR-CREDITOR RELATIONS AND THE TAX CLAIM

Debtor-creditor relations divides the types of creditors into general, government, and lien creditors. The Internal Revenue Service (the Service) is a government creditor, and its claim that a taxpayer owes taxes is a type of debt. Once the Service makes an assessment of tax, the Service may, without judicial intervention, summarily collect the assessment by seizing the taxpayer's property. This extraordinary authority to collect an assessed tax by administrative means is restricted by statutory provisions,[1] but the Service's tax collection power remains an awesome one. Assessment creates quite a different kind of debt from the one a debtor owes to the general creditor, because the Service's tax assessment is the equivalent of judgment obtained by a general creditor. To collect a debt, a general creditor must commence a proceeding in court, carry the burden of proof that the debt is owed and the general creditor is entitled to payment, obtain a judgment, and collect on the judgment against the judgment debtor. When the assessment is made, however, the usual procedure the general creditor follows to recover a debt (pleading proof, judicial proceeding, judgment, and execution on the judgment) is "reversed in the field of taxation."[2] When the Service makes an assessment of the tax claim, "pay-

---

[1] See, e.g., the collection due process rights taxpayers have where the Service has filed a notice of lien (Section 6320) or intends to serve a levy (Section 6330).

[2] Bull v. United States, 295 US 247, 260 (1934).

ment precedes defense, and the burden of proof, normally on the claimant, is shifted to the taxpayer."[3] The assessment "supersedes the pleading, proof and judgment necessary in an action at law, and has the force of such a judgment."[4] The Supreme Court stated the rationale for this distinction between the debt owed a general contractor and one owing to the government in *Bull*:

> [T]axes are the lifeblood of government, and their prompt and certain availability an imperious need. Time out of mind, therefore, the sovereign has resorted to more drastic means of collection (than an action at law for the amount due). The assessment is given the force of a judgment, and if the amount assessed is not paid when due, administrative officials may seize the debtor's property to satisfy the debt.[5]

Once assessment is made, the only way a taxpayer can challenge the amount assessed is to follow the refund procedures by paying the amount of the tax assessed, filing a claim for refund, and if the claim is denied, filing a suit for refund in a district court or the Court of Federal Claims. It is precisely because the effect of assessment can be so drastic (e.g., suppose the taxpayer does not have the funds to pay the full amount of the assessment) that the Service and the Internal Revenue Code (the Code) provide for administrative reviews and even prepayment judicial review in the U.S. Tax Court before the Service makes an assessment. At these stages the Service's determination that a taxpayer owes an additional income tax, for example, is not a tax debt, but a claim for tax, and it might be said that the tax claim is an inchoate debt.

This section compares the collection process a general creditor might use and the procedure available to the government in the collection of a tax debt. A comparison of an ordinary creditor and the Service's demands for payment of a tax debt is helpful because it not only reveals the special characteristics of the tax claim and the extraordinary powers of the government-as-creditor; it provides a basis for a better understanding of the tax collection process. If the tax debt differs from the debt owed to a general creditor, the process by which the Service-as-creditor collects its tax debt and the process by which a general collector collects a debt are quite similar.

[1] Collection of a Debt by a General Creditor

The general creditor who is unable to collect a debt from his debtor may start the collection process by using such extrajudicial means as a "dunning letter." If this pressure is unsuccessful, the general creditor is usually forced to resort

---

[3] Bull v. United States, 295 US 247, 260 (1934).

[4] Bull v. United States, 295 US 247, 259–260 (1934).

[5] Bull v. United States, 295 US 247, 259–260 (1934).

to court action.[6] An unsecured creditor has no right against other claimants or creditors of the debtor until he has established his rights by a judgment and, under most state laws, by taking some further action such as docketing the judgment or delivering the judgment to the sheriff. Before obtaining a final judgment, such procedures as prejudgment attachment, garnishment, arrest, receivership, preliminary injunction, and lis pendens are available as part of the collection process to prevent the debtor from rendering the final judgment ineffectual. These remedies are called prejudgment or provisional remedies as opposed to postjudgment or final remedies. Prejudgment remedies are used at an early stage in the proceedings to ensure that the creditor receives actual relief in the form of payment or recovery of property from a final judgment in his favor,[7] and because they depend for their effect on the results of the action the creditor is required to bring on the underlying debt.

For the purposes of this discussion, the provisional remedies of prejudgment attachment and garnishment are of particular interest because they permit the seizure of property before a final judgment in a manner similar to a tax levy. Attachment is the act of seizing property from the debtor. Garnishment effects a kind of seizure of the debtor's property in the hands of some third party by way of a warning or notice to the third party (the garnishee) that the creditor (garnishor) claims the right to have the debtor's property applied in satisfaction of his claim and that the garnishee should hold the property until the creditor's suit has been tried and any judgment satisfied. Under both procedures, a general creditor obtains a specific lien on the property seized as of the time of the levy or the service of process on the garnishee, which establishes the rights of the creditor as against other creditors in the specific property seized. A final judgment is needed to perfect the attachment or garnishment lien, but when the final judgment is rendered, the rights of the creditor relate back to the date the levy or service of process was made under the attachment or garnishment process.

Attachment and garnishment were at one time available to a creditor by summary ex parte procedures often involving nonjudicial officers, such as the court clerk. Four Supreme Court decisions dealing with these provisional or prejudgment remedies establish the rule that procedural due process requires a preseizure notice and hearing unless procedural safeguards are afforded the debtor, such as the requirement that the creditor make a specific showing to a judicial officer and provision for a prompt postseizure hearing.[8] The Court has

---

[6] Where a secured creditor is involved, the Uniform Commercial Code (UCC) and other state laws give the creditor certain powers of self-help repossession. UCC § 9-503.

[7] The provisional remedies of attachment or garnishment may also serve the purpose of creating a proper basis for jurisdiction of a court.

[8] Sniadach v. Family Fin. Corp., 395 US 337 (1969) (prejudgment wage garnishment); Fuentes v. Shavin, 407 US 67 (1972) (prejudgment replevin of chattels); Mitchell v. WT Grant Co., 416 US 600 (1974) (prejudgment sequestration statute provided prompt

ruled that only "extraordinary situations" necessary to secure an important governmental or general public interest, such as the collection of taxes, justify postponing notice and opportunity for a hearing.[9]

Even where a creditor may use a provisional remedy that satisfies the requirements of procedural due process, the creditor still has not secured satisfaction of the debt owed by the debtor. A debt owed to a general creditor is only a chose in action—that is, it creates in the creditor a right to recover the amount or property by a suit at law. What the creditor obtains by a prejudgment attachment or garnishment is security for the ultimate payment of a court judgment. The creditor's right to the property, which is security, depends upon the creditor obtaining a favorable judgment from the court and taking the appropriate steps to enforce the judgment.

Assume that the creditor has obtained a final judgment against the debtor. A judgment in favor of a creditor is not in itself the equivalent of satisfaction; it only creates in the judgment creditor a right to levy on the judgment debtor's property to the exclusion of intervening creditors. To obtain satisfaction of a judgment, the judgment creditor must secure a writ of execution to have the judgment debtor's property seized and sold. The clerk of the court issues a writ to a sheriff and orders him to levy on certain property and, usually after appraisal and notice, to sell the property at a public sale. To prevent execution sales for unfair prices, most states provide for appraisal of the property before sale and require that an execution sale must bring not less than a certain percentage of the appraised value or that a stated percentage of the appraised value must be credited on the debt. Another device aimed at avoiding unfair sales prices is the execution debtor's redemption or repurchase of the real property within a stated time and at a stated price.

---

postsequestration hearing); North Ga. Finishing, Inc. v. DiChem, Inc., 419 US 601 (1975) (prejudgment garnishment of bank account without provision for early hearing).

[9] At one time, the Supreme Court distinguished between property and personal rights for due process purposes with the result that collection could take place and a postseizure hearing delayed in a tax case without a violation of the taxpayer's due process rights. Phillips v. Comm'r, 283 US 589, 596–597 (1931) ("Where only property rights are involved, mere postponement of the judicial enquiry is not a denial of due process, if the opportunity given for the ultimate judicial determination of the liability is adequate"). *Sniadach* and the other prejudgement attachment cases signaled an end to this view. Compare Sniadach v. Family Fin. Corp., 395 US 337 (1969) (prejudgment wage garnishment) with Mitchell v. WT Grant Co., 416 US 600 (1974) (prejudgment sequestration statute provided prompt postsequestration hearing). The change in tax cases came in Comm'r v. Shapiro, 424 US 614 (1976) where the Court held that due process required that a taxpayer faced with collection of a jeopardy assessment to be accorded a preseizure hearing or a prompt postdeprivation hearing.

[2] Internal Revenue Code Procedures

Once it is recognized that the assessment of tax is the equivalent of a final judgment, Code provisions dealing with the collection of a tax are more comprehensible and may even seem less draconian. The general lien which exists on the assessment of a tax, on "all property and rights to property" of the taxpayer is similar to the judgment lien the general creditor has after a judgment for the debt is entered on the docket of the court and other state procedures are followed, such as delivering the judgment to the sheriff.[10] The Code authorizes the Service to use its investigatory power to discover property or rights to property of the taxpayer to effect collection.[11] A general creditor, on the other hand, may discover such information only after obtaining a judgment by instituting so-called supplementary proceedings. The Code provides that an assessment may be collected by levy upon all property and rights to property of the taxpayer in the taxpayer's or a third party's hands.[12] A general creditor does not have the right to levy upon property of the debtor until he secures a final judgment.

Seizure, sale, and redemption all occur after a creditor obtains a favorable final judgment. However, property seized by levy to collect an assessed tax may be sold after notice, within certain limits.[13] At the sale of seized property, the buyer is given a certificate of sale with respect to personal property and a deed with respect to realty,[14] which generally provide prima facie evidence that the sale was valid and conveys all the taxpayer's rights in the property sold.[15] The taxpayer whose property has been levied upon may redeem it at any time prior to the sale by paying the amount of tax due plus costs of the proceeding. After the sale, personal property may not be redeemed, and real estate may be redeemed only within 180 days of the sale.[16] Finally, the provisions of the Anti-Injunction Act[17] that prohibit a person from restraining the assessment and collection of a tax in court are explicable in part if the assessment is viewed as a final judgment.

The assessment-as-final-judgment interpretation does not explain all provisions dealing with collection. The requirements of Section 6323 with respect to the filing of a notice of lien are the kind of filing requirements imposed on both a secured creditor without a judgment and a judgment creditor. However, the rule that the interest of a claimant or creditor competing with a tax lien be

---

[10] IRC § 6321.

[11] IRC §§ 6333, 7602.

[12] IRC § 6331.

[13] IRC §§ 6335, 6336.

[14] IRC § 6338.

[15] IRC § 6339.

[16] IRC § 6337.

[17] IRC § 7421.

"perfected" becomes more comprehensible (and defensible) if the tax lien is considered as having the force of a judgment—that is, the competing lien is not entitled to priority unless it has achieved the same status as a later tax assessment.

Finally, for some purposes, an assessment has been treated in the same manner as a provisional remedy and has been held subject to the same restrictions. A jeopardy or termination assessment is made in situations similar to those where provisional remedies are used—for example, where a debtor is about to conceal or remove himself or his property and thus jeopardize ultimate collection of a debt. At one time, there seemed to be no constitutional infirmity in enforced collection of these assessments, since the Supreme Court, in *Sniadach* and *Fuentes*, had accepted the notion that a preseizure notice and hearing were not constitutionally required in such extraordinary situations as the collection of taxes.[18] In *Commissioner v. Shapiro*,[19] the Court recognized that, although the government's interest in collecting taxes was sufficiently important to justify seizure of a taxpayer's property without a preseizure notice and hearing, "it is very doubtful that the need to collect revenues is a sufficient reason to justify seizure causing irreparable injury without a prompt postseizure hearing of any kind into the Commissioner's basis for this claim."[20]

In the Tax Reform Act of 1976, Congress incorporated the *Shapiro* requirement of a prompt postseizure hearing. Under the Code, despite provisions of the Anti-Injunction Act prohibiting taxpayer suits to restrain collection of taxes, a taxpayer is permitted to bring a civil action against the United States in a district court or the Tax Court to determine whether or not the making of a jeopardy or termination assessment is reasonable under the circumstances and whether or not the amount assessed is appropriate under the circumstances.[21]

In 1998, *Shapiro*'s due process protection was extended to the collection process. Taxpayers are entitled to collection due process hearings before or after a notice of federal tax lien is filed and before a levy is served, and the op-

---

[18] Sniadach v. Family Fin. Corp., 395 US 337–339 (1969); Fuentes v. Shavin, 407 US 67, 91–92 (1972).

[19] Comm'r v. Shapiro, 424 US 614 (1976).

[20] The decision in *Shapiro* modified the ruling of the Supreme Court in Phillips v. Comm'r, 283 US 589, 596–597 (1931) ("[w]here only property rights are involved, mere postponement of the judicial enquiry is not a denial of due process, if the opportunity given for the ultimate judicial determination of the liability is adequate") that preseizure hearing was not required if a provision was ultimately made for a judicial hearing. Although the case was not cited, the requirement of a prompt postseizure hearing, which helped validate the Louisiana sequestration statute in Mitchell v. WT Grant Co., 416 US 600 (1974) was found necessary to validate the jeopardy assessment and collection procedures utilized under the provisions of the Code.

[21] IRC § 7429.

portunity to appeal the action of the local collection office, as well as limited judicial review of the Service's review.[22]

In short, there are substantial similarities in collection procedures where both general creditors and the Service attempt to collect a judgment or a judgment equivalent (the Service's assessment), but there are also differences in the procedures general creditors must follow and those available to the Service. Where general creditors attempt to use prejudgment attachment or garnishment, their debtors must be accorded a preseizure hearing or a prompt postseizure hearing. After the assessment of a tax, a lien attaches to the taxpayer's property and rights to property, but the taxpayer is entitled to a due process hearing. If the Service intends to use a levy to seize property, the taxpayer is also entitled to a due process hearing. These lien and levy due process hearings do not determine the correct tax. To obtain such judicial review, the taxpayer has the burden of paying the full amount of the tax, filing a claim for refund, and commencing a suit for refund in which the taxpayer bears the burden of proof, and obtain a judgment. in the taxpayer's favor. Refund procedures can be seen as providing the taxpayer something like a prompt postseizure hearing. Some of these similarities and differences between general creditor and Service collection are summarized in Form 14.1.

---

[22] IRC §§ 6320 (liens), 6330 (levies).

TABLE 14.1 ———
Debt Collection Procedures

Debtor-Creditor Procedure	IRS Collection Procedure
Dunning letters	Same
Attachment or garnishment after preseizure hearing or prompt postseizure hearing	Assessment and notice and demand, but taxpayer is entitled to collection due process hearing on lien filing and service of levy
Attachment lien is specific, and encumbers only property attached: judgment needs to be obtained and docketed before lien is general	Assessment lien is a general lien encumbering "all property" and "rights to property"
Final judgment needed to perfect attachment lien	No final judgment needed to perfect lien; filing of notice of lien perfects against competing creditors, purchasers, holders of security interests, mechanic's lienors, and judgment creditors
Sale of property after final judgment in court and docketed and writ of execution issued by clerk of court	Sale of property without judgment after Service gives notice
Appraisal of property sold at sheriff's sale is usually required by law	Service must determine "minimum price" but it is not necessarily value of property
Redemption or repurchase within time provided by law	Same

A   ORGANIZATION AND OPERATION OF THE COLLECTION FUNCTION

¶ 14.02 ORGANIZATION OF THE COLLECTION FUNCTION

[1] Service Center Operations

Before the Service's reorganization, its ten service centers received and processed tax and information returns, managed taxpayer accounts, and conducted simple audits through correspondence and other procedures. These activities were assigned to a specific center based on the taxpayer's geographic location, irrespective of the type of return. After the reorganization, the former service center activities are assigned to a center or campus based on three factors: whether the return is an individual or business return; the taxpayer's geographic area; and the operating division to which the center or campus will report.[23] Consequently, each center is under the direct authority of either the Wage or Investment Division or the Small Business/Self-Employed (SB/SE) Division with the objective of having center personnel develop expertise in their taxpayer segments. Five centers are under the authority of the W&I Division: Andover, Atlanta, Austin, Fresno, and Kansas City. Similarly, five centers are under the SB/SE Division. SB/SE also handles service center activities for tax exempt/government entity returns, and some large and midsize business returns. Eight centers handle the receipt and processing of individual returns: the five W&I centers and the Brookhaven, Memphis, and Philadelphia centers. Cincinnati and Ogden handle the receipt and processing of business returns, including employment and estate and gift tax returns.

Service centers perform data processing work for the Operating Divisions field organization organized into regions and territories. In collection activities, this means processing returns, information documents, and payments, and entering the data on computer tapes that are sent by service centers to the National Computing Center (NCC) in Martinsburg, West Virginia, where master account files are kept in a data base. When new tapes are received from the NCC (after the master files have been updated), notices are sent out and files (tapes) of the data base shared by the service center and the local offices are updated. In addition, service center Collection branches conduct the initial attempts to collect delinquent accounts through notices and correspondence with taxpayers and handle delinquency penalty assessments and abatements of such penalties. Accounts that are not resolved in the service center collection branch are assigned to the Automated Collection System (ACS) for collection primarily by the Compliance/Collection enforcement organization in area and territory offices in the SB/SE Division.

[2] Area/Territory Collection Operations

The SB/SE Division has the field collection function in local area/territory offices, organized into an Automated Collection Branch, a field branch (consisting of a number of revenue officer groups), and a Special Procedures Staff.[24]

[a] Automated Collection System

The ACS is a series of computer databases on which most delinquent accounts and delinquency investigations are maintained that the office branch of the local Collection function formerly handled in paper form. ACS call sites are located in each service center, and there are Automated Collection

---

[23] Info. Rel. 2000-61 (Sept. 1, 2000).

[24] IRM 5.3.1.2.5 New Collection Group Realignments (Nov. 30, 2001).

Branches in many territory offices. Delinquent accounts and delinquency investigations appear on the ACS at the same point when delinquency accounts and investigations are sent to the local office collection function—that is, in routine cases, after two to four notices have been sent to the taxpayer by the service center.

To handle delinquent accounts and delinquency investigations, ACS personnel are provided with data that the Service has about the taxpayer from tax returns, information returns, and the tax records maintained at the NCC. ACS personnel use this information to perform four functions:

1. Contact taxpayers by telephone to demand full payment of a delinquent tax;

2. Search for taxpayers and their assets by telephoning third parties, among other means;

3. Handle incoming calls, respond to taxpayer correspondence, and make adjustments of accounts; and

4. Support the Automated Collection Branch in a district by researching suspense files, inputting account actions in the computer database accessible by the district (the Integrated Data Retrieval System (IDRS)), and responding to correspondence, liens, and levies generated by the ACS.

FORM 14.1
COLLECTION ORGANIZATION

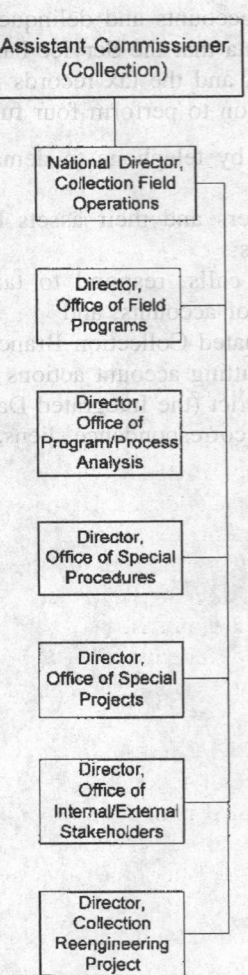

[b] Area Collection Groups of Revenue Officers

Areas have a number of revenue officer groups, each of which is under the supervision of a group manager and has an assigned territory within the particular area. Within his assigned area and territory, the revenue officer has the duty to collect delinquent accounts and secure delinquent returns.[25] The revenue officer is also armed with the considerable collection powers of the Service to collect delinquent taxes by filing notices of lien, serving levies, and seizing and selling real and personal property. Revenue officers recommend, subject to managerial review, jeopardy assessments and suits to enforce collection of taxes or for failure to honor a levy. Investigations of applications to discharge or subordinate tax liens, or in connection with most offers in compromise, are made by revenue officers. Area groups receive some delinquent accounts directly from the service center because they require considerable field work or some expertise in handling—for example, penalty assessments against responsible officers with respect to delinquent employment taxes.[26]

[c] The Special Procedures Staff

The Special Procedures Staff furnishes advisory assistance on technical matters to the other branches in the Collection Division and performs litigation-related functions for the Collection Division. It also (1) recommends civil suits to enforce collection or to protect the government's interests; (2) processes suits against the United States or the district director; and (3) provides liaison for the district director with the Department of Justice, including the U.S. Attorneys, the Chief Counsel, and Division Counsel, on all collection matters. In insolvency and decedents' estates proceedings, the Special Procedures Staff ascertains tax liability and files proof of claims. The Staff also examines, reviews, and processes (1) seizure and sale reports; (2) applications for discharge of property from the effect of federal tax liens; (3) applications for certificates of nonattachment of federal tax liens, certificates of subordination of the federal tax lien, and filed notices of federal tax liens; and (4) certificates of release (executed collection waivers). Where offers in compromise are involved, the staff analyzes and determines the sufficiency of various forms of collateral offered as security for release of a lien or postponement of a collection action and furnishes technical advice, assistance, and recommendations for or against entry into suitable escrow agreements for the collection of delinquent accounts. The Special Procedures Staff also reviews recommendations for 100 percent penalty and transferee assessments.

---

[25] IRM 5.3.1.2.5 Area Collection Group Realignments (Nov. 30, 2001); IRM 5.3.1.3.2 Revenue Officer Responsibilities (July 31, 2001).

[26] IRM 5.3.1.3.2 Revenue Officer Responsibilities (July 31, 2001).

¶ 14.03 THE PROCESSING OF COLLECTION CASES

[1] The Integrated Data Retrieval System

After returns are filed with the appropriate service centers in the country, data on the returns are edited and coded for computer processing and entered into computers. Magnetic computer tapes containing this data are sent to the NCC at Martinsburg, West Virginia, where master accounts for taxpayers are kept. These master accounts are reflected on computer tapes (called "master files") for various classes of taxpayers.[27] Computerized master files contain such information as (1) the debits and credits to the account, including penalties and interest; (2) the nature of the tax; and (3) a history of the account. Computer system data bases, called the IDRS, are maintained at the service centers and updated with information from the master files at the NCC. The IDRS permits data input and retrieval concerning taxpayer tax returns and other current account information. Revenue officer groups have access to this information via computer terminals.

[2] Document Locator Numbers

The Service also uses a system for to identify and locate documents, called the document locator number (DLN) system.[28] The DLN is a control number given to every return and each subsequent transaction affecting the return input through the Service's automated data processing system. A thirteen-digit number is assigned to every return and document input through the automatic data processing (ADP) system that affects a taxpayer account.[29] A fourteenth digit, the year of processing, is assigned by the submission site processing computer. The DLN should not be confused with the taxpayer identification number (TIN), which is either an individual's nine-digit social security number or a business's employer identification number. The DLN is a document tracking system, not a number used to identify a taxpayer. For example, the DLN stamped on a taxpayer's canceled check indicates to what specific liability the amount was applied. Separate documents may have different DLN numbers, but all DLN numbers are tied together by a TIN within the computer files

---

[27] For example, for individual income taxpayers there is an Individual Master File (IMF); for all taxpayers having Employer Identification numbers (EINs), a Business Master File (BMF); and a Non-Master File (NMF) and Residual Master File (RMF) for listings of taxpayers who do not appear in the other master files.

[28] IRM 3.0.273 Administrative Reference Guide Exhibit 3.0.273-2, Glossary (Jan. 1, 2004).

[29] IRM 3.0.273 Administrative Reference Guide Exhibit 3.0.273-2, Glossary (Jan. 1, 2004).

maintained at the service center and on the master files. Any DLN reference may be keyed into the appropriate files and records necessary for resolving a question. Using the IDRS computer terminals, which are updated on a weekly basis from master files of taxpayers' accounts, a Service employee is able to answer questions about a taxpayer's account. The DLN and information on any outstanding items pending may be obtained from a combination of the tax-payer's name and his social security number or employer identification number, which are cross-referenced to the IDRS files.

A fourteen-digit DLN is used on computer-generated documents, although DLNs may have different numbers of digits. The format for a DLN is as follows:

1	2		3		4	5		6	7	8		9	10	11		12	13		14
2	8		2		1	0		1	0	5		6	0	0		2	5		4

Reading from left to right, the first two digits are the filing location code (e.g., service center or district office). The third digit is the tax class each transaction involves (e.g., 1 is withholding and FICA tax; 2, individual income tax, fiduciary income tax, partnership returns; and 3, corporate income tax). The fourth and fifth digits are the document codes (e.g., 17 is the code for a subsequent payment input by a service center; 18, the code for a subsequent payment input by district office; and 47, the code for an examination adjustment). The sixth, seventh, and eighth digits are the numeric days of the year that the return or document was numbered for processing (e.g., the deposit date of remittance received with a return or payment documents may be the 105th day of the year). The ninth, tenth, and eleventh digits are the processing block numbers. The twelfth and thirteenth numbers are the control serial numbers; the maximum number within a block is 100, and they are serially numbered 00 through 99. The fourteenth digit is the last digit of the processing year.

A similar system is used for processing remittances with returns, subsequent payments, estimated payments, and extensions. An examination trail is printed at the bottom edge of the back of the remittance. This trail includes the full DLN, transaction code, TIN, tax period, and payment date.

[3] Notices

When an assessment is made and a balance is due on the account, the service center computers are programmed to send a series of notices to taxpayers who are individual or business taxpayers. Individual taxpayers receive notices as follows:[30]

1. A first notice is generated when a balance due is entered on the taxpayer's account or master file. This notice represents the notice of the assessment and demand for payment of the amount assessed within ten days, required by Section 6303.

2. Five weeks later, a first follow-up balance due notice is mailed. This "Reminder of Unpaid Tax" includes a late payment penalty and requests payment within ten days to avoid additional interest and penalty charges. (See Form 14.2.)

3. A second follow-up letter is mailed after five weeks. This follow-up notice states "Overdue Tax," and again requests payment within ten days so as to avoid interest and penalty charges. (See Form 14.3.)

4. A third follow-up balance due notice is mailed after another five weeks. This notice is headed "Urgent—Payment Required." (See Form 14.4.)

5. A final follow-up notice is mailed in another five weeks. This notice warns that it is a final notice before enforcement action is taken. (See Form 14.5.)

6. If the taxpayer still does not pay the balance due within five weeks after the mailing of the Form 8126, a taxpayer delinquent account (TDA) is automatically generated by the computer for processing by the local office.[31]

7. The Taxpayer Bill of Rights 2 added a new notice the Service is required to send to taxpayers with assessed but unpaid liabilities. At least annually, the Service is required to send a written notice to a taxpayer who has a delinquent account, setting out the amount of the tax delinquency as of the date of the notice.[32]

As a matter of law, the Service is required to send to the taxpayer a notice stating the amount and demanding payment (called the notice and demand).[33] The content of the notice and demand is not left solely in the discretion of the Service. Section 7521(a) requires tax due notices to "describe

---

[30] The first notice is postdated by the computer to permit screening and verification for errors. If the taxpayer claims to have made payment, this information may be written on a duplicate of the notice and inserted in a window envelope that has the address of the service center.

[31] A business taxpayer is first sent an initial notice. Five weeks later, a Form 8125 is sent, and four weeks after that a Form 8126. If payment has still not been made, a TDA is generated by the computer for processing by the local office.

[32] IRC § 7524, added by the Taxpayer Bill of Rights 2, § 1204(a), applicable to years after 1996.

[33] IRC § 6303.

the basis for, and identify the amounts (if any) of, the tax due, interest, additional amounts, additions to the tax, and assessable penalties included in (the) notice." Although an inadequate description does not invalidate the notice, the intention of the provision is to ensure that the notice is sufficiently clear to enable the taxpayer to understand the adjustments or penalties applied to the tax return.[34]

---

[34] HR Conf. Rep. No. 1104, Technical and Miscellaneous Revenue Act of 1988, 100th Cong., 2d Sess. 219, reprinted in 1988-3 CB 219.

FORM 14.2 _____
REQUEST FOR PAYMENT OF BALANCE DUE

CP501—Reminder of Unpaid Tax

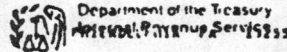

Department of the Treasury
Internal Revenue Service 19255

DATE OF NOTICE   06-24-91   9138   CP501
TAXPAYER IDENTIFYING NUMBER
FORM 1040   TAX PERIOD 12-31-88

FOR ASSISTANCE YOU MAY CALL US AT

574-9900 LOCAL PHIL.
1-800-829-1040 OTHER PA

OR YOU MAY WRITE TO US AT THE
ADDRESS SHOWN AT THE LEFT. IF
YOU WRITE, BE SURE TO ATTACH
THE BOTTOM PART OF THIS NOTICE

REMINDER OF UNPAID TAX

ACCORDING TO OUR RECORDS, YOU HAVE NOT PAID THE FEDERAL TAX YOU OWE FOR THE TAX PERIOD SHOWN ABOVE. PLEASE PAY IT TODAY.

THE AMOUNT OUR RECORDS SHOW YOU OWE IS $4,230.56.
WE FIGURED THIS AMOUNT BY ADDING:

AMOUNT UNPAID FROM PRIOR NOTICES	$3,922.82
LATE PAYMENT PENALTY	$74.61
INTEREST	$229.13

THE AMOUNT UNPAID FROM PRIOR NOTICES MAY INCLUDE TAX, PENALTIES, AND INTEREST YOU STILL OWE IRS. IT ALSO SHOULD REFLECT ANY CREDITS AND PAYMENTS WE RECEIVED FROM YOU SINCE THE LAST NOTICE WE SENT.

WE COMPUTED PENALTY AND INTEREST TO THE DATE OF THIS NOTICE. TO AVOID ADDITIONAL PENALTIES AND INTEREST, SEND YOUR PAYMENT FOR THE AMOUNT YOU OWE BY 07-04-91. OTHERWISE, WE MAY HAVE TO CHARGE YOU ADDITIONAL PENALTIES AND INTEREST.

MAKE YOUR CHECK OR MONEY ORDER FOR THE AMOUNT YOU OWE PAYABLE TO THE INTERNAL REVENUE SERVICE. WRITE YOUR TAXPAYER IDENTIFICATION NUMBER ON YOUR PAYMENT AND SEND IT WITH THE BOTTOM PART OF THIS NOTICE IN THE ENCLOSED ENVELOPE.

IF YOU THINK THIS BILL IS INCORRECT, SEND THE AMOUNT YOU BELIEVE YOU OWE AND A STATEMENT EXPLAINING THE DIFFERENCE. BE SURE TO INCLUDE THE BOTTOM PART OF THIS NOTICE WITH YOUR REPLY.

TO MAKE SURE IRS EMPLOYEES GIVE COURTEOUS RESPONSES AND CORRECT INFORMATION TO TAXPAYERS, A SECOND EMPLOYEE SOMETIMES LISTENS IN ON TELEPHONE CALLS. KEEP THIS PART FOR YOUR RECORDS

RETURN THIS PART WITH YOUR PAYMENT OR INQUIRY

9133

DATE OF NOTICE 06-24-91   9138   CP501
TAXPAYER IDENTIFYING NUMBER
FORM 1040   39   TAX PERIOD 12-31-88

828 2381

WH   30 0 8812 670 00000423056

INTERNAL REVENUE SERVICE
PHILADELPHIA PA 19255

AMOUNT YOU OWE . . . . .
SUBTRACT PAYMENTS WE
HAVEN'T INCLUDED . . . . .
PAY ADJUSTED AMOUNT $

$4,230.5

FORM 14.3 _____
PAYMENT OVERDUE

Department of the Treasury
Internal Revenue Service

Philadelphia, PA 19253

If you have any questions, refer to this information
Date of This Notice
Taxpayer Identifying Number:
   Form   Tax Year Ended
      1120   12/31/96

Call   574-9900 (Local Phil.)
       1-800-424-1040 (Elsewhere in Pa.)
or

Write: Chief, Taxpayer Assistance Section
       Internal Revenue Service Center

Allentown, PA 12208

If you write, be sure to include the bottom part of this notice

Overdue Tax

We have previously written to you about the federal tax shown below.
Additional interest and penalties are included. Please pay it now.

Send full payment by check or money order payable to the Internal
Revenue Service. Write your taxpayer identification number on your
payment. Include the bottom part of this notice with your payment so
we can quickly identify and credit your account.

If you think this bill is incorrect, send the amount you believe is
due and explain the difference. You may use the flap on the return
envelope to help us locate payments not applied to your account.

We have calculated penalty and interest to the date of this notice.
If your payment is not received within ten days from the date of this
notice, additional penalties and interest may be charged.

                      Tax Form: 1120
                    Tax Period: 12/31/96

Balance of Prior Assessments	$ 9,182.22
Late Payment Penalty	$ 999.91
Interest	$ 1,315.78

Total Amount Due	$11,097.91

If you have any questions, you may call or write—see information in the upper right corner of this notice. To make sure IRS
employees give courteous responses and correct information to taxpayers, a second employee sometimes listens in on telephone calls.
See back of this notice for more information.
Keep this part for your records.   ↓ DETACH HERE ↓   Form 13131 (Rev. 4-86)
Send this part with your payment or inquiry. Please
correct any errors in your name, address, or taxpayer
identifying number.

Date of This Notice:
Taxpayer Identifying Number:
   Form   Tax Year Ended

Internal Revenue Service

Amount You Owe . . . .   _____
Subtract Payments We Haven't
   Included . . . .
Pay Adjusted Amount . . . . . . $ _____

FORM 14.4 _____
FOLLOW-UP FORM LETTER

Department of the Treasury
Internal Revenue Service
Austin, TX 73501

If you have any questions, refer to this information

Date of This Notice: 08/15/99   503   8836
Taxpayer Identifying Number: BV
Form   Tax Year Ended   Document Locator
                                        Number
1040EZ   12/11/96   18274-502-55360-8

Call   965-0440 (Local Houston)

or   1-800-474-1040 (Elsewhere in TX)

Write: Chief, Taxpayer Assistance Section
         Internal Revenue Service Center
         Austin, TX 73501

Orange, TX 77640-9012

If you write, be sure to include the bottom part of this notice

Urgent—Payment Required

Your full payment of the federal tax shown below has still not
been received. We have previously billed you for the overdue tax and
must now consider filing a notice of federal tax lien and seizing your
property, wages, or other Assets to satisfy your unpaid tax. The amount
due includes additional interest and penalties which will continue to
increase until the balance is paid in full. We have calculated the
interest and penalty amounts to ten days from the date of this notice.

Send full payment today by check or money order payable to the
Internal Revenue Service. Write your taxpayer identification number
on your payment. Include the bottom part of this notice with your
payment so we can quickly identify and credit your account.

If you think this bill is incorrect, send the amount you believe
is due and explain the difference. If payments have not been credited
to your account, follow the instructions on the back of this notice.

If you are unable to pay in full, contact us immediately
to explain your financial condition. We will review your circumstances
to help you determine how to pay the amount due. Installment payments
or payroll deduction may be considered.

Your prompt response is necessary.

Balance of Prior Assessment:	$1,001.50
Late Payment Penalty:	$ 17.10
Interest:	$ 31.99
Total Amount Due:	$1,050.59

Enclosures: Envelope

If you have any questions, you may call or write—see information in the upper right corner of this notice. To make sure IRS
employees give courteous responses and correct information to taxpayers, a second employee sometimes listens in on telephone calls.

See back of this notice for more information.
Keep this part for your records.   ▼ DETACH HERE ▼   --------------

Send this part with your payment or inquiry. Please
correct any errors in your name, address, or taxpayer
identifying number.

Date of This Notice:
Taxpayer Identifying Number:
   Form   Tax Year Ended   Document Locator
                                        Number

Internal Revenue Service

Amount You Owe . . . .
Subtract Payments We Haven't
   Included . . . .
Pay Adjusted Amount . . . $ _____

FORM 14.5
FINAL NOTICE BEFORE SEIZURE

Department of the Treasury
Internal Revenue Service

Past Due
Final Notice (Notice of Intention to Levy)
Read Carefully

Muskogee, OK 74403-6121

If you have any questions, refer to this information
Date of This Notice 07/04/99 504 8830
Taxpayer Identifying Number: QA
Form   Tax Year Ended   Document Locator
                                          Number

1040   12/31/93   49254-614-65698-5

Call   1-800-424-1040

or

Write: Chief, Taxpayer Assistance Section
        Internal Revenue Service Center
        Austin, TX 73301

If you write, be sure to include the bottom part of this notice

This is your final notice. Your full payment of the federal
tax shown below has still not been received. If full payment is not
received within ten days from the date of this notice, we will begin
enforcement proceedings.

A notice of federal tax lien may be filed, which is a public
notice that there is a tax lien against your property. As provided
by section 6331 of the Internal Revenue Code, your property or rights
to property may be seized. This includes salary or wages, bank
accounts, commissions, or other income. Real estate and personal
property such as automobiles may also be seized and sold to pay
your tax.

To prevent this action, send full payment today by check
or money order payable to the Internal Revenue Service. Write
your taxpayer identification number on your payment. Include the
bottom part of this notice with your payment so we can quickly
identify and credit your account.

We have calculated penalty and interest amounts to ten
days from the date of this notice. If payment is not received
by then, additional interest and penalties will be charged.
The failure-to-pay penalty increases from one-half percent
per month to one percent per month after this notice.

If you recently paid the amount due or if you cannot pay
this amount in full, contact the office shown above today.

Reply within 10 days
to avoid enforcement actions
and additional penalties.

If you have any questions, you may call or write—see information in the upper right corner of this notice. To make sure IRS
employees give courteous responses and correct information to taxpayers, a second employee sometimes listens in on telephone calls.

See back of this notice for more information.
Keep this part for your records.   ↓ DETACH HERE ↓

Send this part with your payment or inquiry. Please
correct any errors in your name, address, or taxpayer
identifying number.

Date of This Notice:
Taxpayer Identifying Number:
Form   Tax Year Ended   Document Locator
                                         Number

Internal Revenue Service

Amount You Owe ....
Subtract Payments We Haven't
  Included ....
Pay Adjusted Amount .... $

[4] Taxpayer Contacts

Initial taxpayer contacts either by telephone or field visit are supposed to be made by revenue officers handling a delinquent account or delinquency investigation.[35] In these contacts by officers, the taxpayer has certain rights. The taxpayer is entitled to an explanation of the collection process and the taxpayer's rights in that process.[36] Also, the time and place of the interview must be reasonable under the circumstances.[37] At the interview, the taxpayer may record what occurs as long as prior notice is given,[38] and the taxpayer is entitled to consult with a professional representative and to retain one.[39] During the initial contact, the revenue officer will attempt to (1) verify compliance with all filing and payment requirements when the taxpayer claims that the tax was paid, the return filed, or both; (2) demand full or partial payment of all delinquent accounts; (3) demand filing of all delinquent returns; and (4) determine and document the taxpayer's compliance with current filing and paying requirements.[40] If the taxpayer cannot pay the full amount due, the revenue officer will attempt to obtain the maximum amount that can be paid immediately and the balance in the shortest period possible. Significantly for the taxpayer, the revenue officer will try to learn enough about the taxpayer's assets so that enforcement action can be taken without further contact, for example, if the taxpayer fails to keep a commitment to make a payment by a certain date.

Before a notice of federal tax lien is filed, a number of factors are considered.[41] The Service's practice is not to file a notice of lien until the taxpayer has been contacted and the amount of tax due and the value of the taxpayer's property and rights to property considered.[42] Some limitations on filing and certainly levy are a matter of law. No levy may be made on any property if the amount of the expenses of levy and sale which the revenue officer estimates at the time of the levy will exceed the fair market value of the prop-

---

[35] The time frames have varied, but can range from sixty calendar days for return compliance efforts to fifteen calendar days for a federal tax deposit delinquency. IRM 5.1.10.3.1 Initial Contact Time Frames (Apr. 1, 2003).

[36] IRC § 7521(b)(1)(B). The Service sends Publication 1, Your Rights as a Taxpayer, with follow-up notices, and Publications 586A and 594, The Collection Process Income Tax Accounts and Employment Tax Accounts), with the Final Notice (Notice of Intention to Levy). IRM 5181.33, MT 5100-60 (July 18, 1989) (Notification of Taxpayer Rights).

[37] IRC § 7605(a). Procedures regarding the time and place and conduct of an interview are discussed in Chapter 15.

[38] IRC § 7521(a).

[39] IRC §§ 7521(b)(2), 7521(c).

[40] IRM 5.1.10.3.2 Effective Initial Contact (Apr. 1, 2003).

[41] IRM 5.12.1.3.1 Review Process (Feb. 22, 2000).

[42] IRM 5.12.1.3.1 Review Process (Feb. 22, 2000).

erty.[43] Once the decision has been made to file a lien, the Service uses Form 668(Y) (Notice of Federal Tax Lien Under Internal Revenue Laws). (See Form 14.6.)

---

[43] IRC § 6331(f). See also IRM 5.12.1.3.1 Review Process (Feb. 22, 2000). The possible responses to this first contact available to taxpayers are described in Chapter 15.

EXHIBIT 14.1
CRITERIA FOR FILING NOTICE OF FEDERAL TAX LIEN[a]

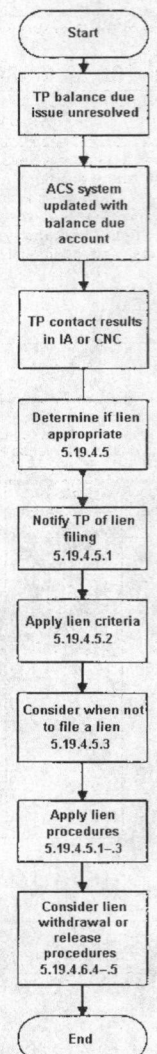

```
        ┌──────────────┐
        │    Start     │
        └──────────────┘
                │
    ┌───────────────────────┐
    │ TP balance due        │
    │ issue unresolved      │
    └───────────────────────┘
                │
    ┌───────────────────────┐
    │ ACS system            │
    │ updated with          │
    │ balance due           │
    │ account               │
    └───────────────────────┘
                │
    ┌───────────────────────┐
    │ TP contact results    │
    │ in IA or CNC          │
    └───────────────────────┘
                │
    ┌───────────────────────┐
    │ Determine if lien     │
    │ appropriate           │
    │ 5.19.4.5              │
    └───────────────────────┘
                │
    ┌───────────────────────┐
    │ Notify TP of lien     │
    │ filing                │
    │ 5.19.4.5.1            │
    └───────────────────────┘
                │
    ┌───────────────────────┐
    │ Apply lien criteria   │
    │ 5.19.4.5.2            │
    └───────────────────────┘
                │
    ┌───────────────────────┐
    │ Consider when not     │
    │ to file a lien        │
    │ 5.19.4.5.3            │
    └───────────────────────┘
                │
    ┌───────────────────────┐
    │ Apply lien            │
    │ procedures            │
    │ 5.19.4.5.1–.3         │
    └───────────────────────┘
                │
    ┌───────────────────────┐
    │ Consider lien         │
    │ withdrawal or         │
    │ release               │
    │ procedures            │
    │ 5.19.4.6.4–.5         │
    └───────────────────────┘
                │
        ┌──────────────┐
        │     End      │
        └──────────────┘
```

---

[a] References are to sections of the Manual.

FORM 14.6
NOTICE OF FEDERAL TAX LIEN UNDER INTERNAL REVENUE LAWS

Form **668 (Y)**	Department of the Treasury - Internal Revenue Service	For Optional Use by Recording Office
(Rev. January 1991)	**Notice of Federal Tax Lien Under Internal Revenue Laws**	

District		Serial Number		For Optional Use by Recording Office
	Manhattan		987654321	

As provided by sections 6321, 6322, and 6323 of the Internal Revenue Code, notice is given that taxes (including interest and penalties) have been assessed against the following-named taxpayer. Demand for payment of this liability has been made, but it remains unpaid. Therefore, there is a lien in favor of the United States on all property and rights to property belonging to this taxpayer for the amount of these taxes, and additional penalties, interest, and costs that may accrue.

Name of Taxpayer   Jane Jones

Residence   One Main Street
Anytown, NY 10000

IMPORTANT RELEASE INFORMATION: With respect to each assessment listed below, unless notice of lien is refiled by the date given in column (e), this notice shall, on the day following such date, operate as a certificate of release as defined in IRC 6325(a).

Kind of Tax (a)	Tax Period Ended (b)	Identifying Number (c)	Date of Assessment (d)	Last Day for Refiling (e)	Unpaid Balance of Assessment (f)
1040	12/31/97	123–45–6789	2/18/00	3/20/06	312,655
1040	12/31/98	123–45–6789	2/18/00	3/20/06	177,677
1040	12/31/99	123–45–6789	2/18/00	3/20/06	138,172

Place of Filing	Clerk's Office Anytown County Anytown, NY 10000	Total $	628,504

This notice was prepared and signed at _____ 000 Park Place, New York, NY 10000 _____ , on this,

the __2nd__ day of __February__, 19 __99__ .

Signature		Title	
	/s/ John Doe		Revenue Officer

(NOTE: Certificate of officer authorized by law to take acknowledgments is not essential to the validity of Notice of Federal Tax lien Rev. Rul. 71-466, 1971 - 2 C.B. 409)

Form **668 (Y)** (Rev. 1-91)

Part 2 - To Be Receipted and Returned to Internal Revenue Service TDA Copy

No. _____

United States

vs.

Notice of Tax Lien

Filed this ____ day of ____, 19 ____ at ____ m.

_____
Clerk (or Registrar).

Form 668 (Y) (Rev. 1-81)

Account Satisfied (Date)	BY: (Cash, M.O., Cert. Check, Personal Check (Not Cert.), Abatement, etc.)	☐ Bond Accepted
Revenue Officer (Signature)		Date

Form 668(Y).

Administrative Appeal of the Erroneous filing of Notice of Federal Tax Lien/CAP

Under Internal Revenue Code section 6326, you have the right to file an administrative appeal if you believe the filing of this notice of lien was erroneous. The intent of the appeal process is to correct any erroneous filing of notices of lien and is not to be used for the purpose of challenging the calculation of the tax, penalty or interest which includes 100 percent penalty assessments.

Filing of a notice of lien is erroneous if:

* all tax, penalty and interest was paid prior to filing the notice of lien;

* tax was assessed after the date on the petition for bankruptcy in violation of the automatic stay (Title 11);

* tax was assessed in violation of your rights under IRC 6213 (notice of deficiency was mailed to the wrong address or a petition was timely filed with the Tax Court);

* the statute of limitations for collection expired prior to the filing of the notice of lien.

All request must be in writing and contain the following:

* the person's name, current address and SSN/EIN;

* provide a copy of the notice of lien as filed, if available;

* the specific reason why you think we were in error;

* provide the canceled check or other evidence of payment;

* information identifying the bankruptcy court, docket number and petition date.

All requests should be addressed to the District Director, attention of the Chief, Special Procedures function in the district where the notice of lien is filed.

Excerpts From Internal Revenue Code

Sec. 6321. Lien For Taxes

If any person liable to pay any tax neglects or refuses to pay the same after demand, the amount (including any interest, additional amount, addition to tax, or assessable penalty, together with any costs that may accrue in addition thereto) shall be a lien in favor of the United States upon all property and rights to property, whether real or personal, belonging to such person.

Sec. 6322. Period Of Lien.

Unless another date is specifically fixed by law, the lien imposed by section 6321 shall arise at the time the assessment is made and shall continue until the liability for the amount so assessed (or a judgment against the taxpayer arising out of such liability) is satisfied or becomes unenforceable by reason of lapse of time.

Sec. 6323. Validity and Priority Against Certain Persons.

(a) Purchaser's, Holders Of Security Interests, Mechanic's Lienors, And Judgment Lien Creditors. — The lien imposed by section 6321 shall not be valid as against any purchaser, holder of a security interest, mechanic's lienor, or judgment lien creditor until notice thereof which meets the requirements of subsection (f) has been filed by the Secretary.

(f) Place For Filing Notice; Form. —

(1) Place For Filing - The notice referred to in subsection (a) shall be filed-

(A) Under State Laws

(i) Real Property - In the case of real property, in one office within the State (or the county, or other governmental subdivision), as designated by the laws of such State, in which the property subject to the lien is situated; and

(ii) Personal Property - In the case of personal property, whether tangible or intangible, in one office within the State (or the county, or other governmental subdivision), as designated by the laws of such State, in which the property subject to the lien is situated; except that State law merely conforming to or reenacting Federal law establishing a national filing system does not constitute a second office for filing as designated by the laws of such State; or

(B) With Clerk Of District Court - In the office of the clerk of the United States district court for the judicial district in which the property subject to lien is situated, whenever the State has not by law designated one office which meets the requirements of subparagraph (A), or

(C) With Recorder Of Deeds Of The District Of Columbia - In the office of the Recorder of Deeds of the District of Columbia, if the property subject to the lien is situated in the District of Columbia.

(2) Situs Of Property Subject To Lien - For purposes of paragraphs (1) and (4), property shall be deemed to be situated-

(A) Real Property - In the case of real property, at its physical location; or

(B) Personal Property - In the case of personal property, whether tangible or intangible, at the residence of the taxpayer at the time the notice of lien is filed.

For purposes of paragraph (2) (B), the residence of a corporation or partnership shall be deemed to be that of a taxpayer at which the principal executive office of the business is located, and the residence of a taxpayer whose residence is without the United States shall be deemed to be in the District of Columbia.

(3) Form - The form and content of the notice referred to in subsection (a) shall be prescribed by the Secretary. Such notice shall be valid notwithstanding any other provision of law regarding the form or content of a notice of lien.

Note: See section 6323(b) for protection for certain interests even though notice of lien imposed by section 6321 is filed with respect to:

1. Securities
2. Motor vehicles
3. Personal property purchased at retail
4. Personal property purchased in casual sale
5. Personal property subjected to possessory lien
6. Real property tax and special assessment liens
7. Residential property subject to a mechanic's lien for certain repairs and improvements
8. Attorney's liens
9. Certain insurance contracts
10. Passbook loans

(g) Refiling Of Notice. — For purposes of this section-

(1) **General Rule.** — Unless notice of lien is refiled in the manner prescribed in paragraph (2) during the required refiling period, such notice of lien shall be treated as filed on the date on which it is filed (in accordance with subsection (f)) after the expiration of such refiling period.

(2) **Place For Filing.** — A notice of lien refiled during the required refiling period shall be effective only-

(A) If-

(i) such notice of lien is refiled in the office in which the prior notice of lien was filed, and

(ii) in the case of real property, and the fact of refiling is entered and recorded in an index to the extent required by subsection (f) (4); and

(B) in any case in which, 90 days or more prior to the date of a refiling of notice of lien under subparagraph (A), the

Secretary received written information (in the manner prescribed in regulations issued by the Secretary) concerning a change in the taxpayer's residence, if a notice of such lien is also filed in accordance with subsection (f) in the State in which such residence is located.

(3) **Required Refiling Period.** — In the case of any notice of lien, the term "required refiling period" means-

(A) the one-year period ending 30 days after the expiration of 10 years after the date of the assessment of the tax, and

(B) the one-year period ending with the expiration of 10 years after the close of the preceding required refiling period for such notice of lien.

Sec. 6325. Release Of Lien Or Discharge Of Property.

(a) Release Of Lien. — Subject to such regulations as the Secretary may prescribe, the Secretary shall issue a certificate of release of any lien imposed with respect to any internal revenue tax not later than 30 days after the day on which —

(1) Liability Satisfied or Unenforceable - The Secretary finds that the liability for the amount assessed, together with all interest in respect thereof, has been fully satisfied or has become legally unenforceable; or

(2) Bond Accepted - There is furnished to the Secretary and accepted by him a bond that is conditioned upon the payment of the amount assessed, together with all interest in respect thereof, within the time prescribed by law (including any extension of such time), and that is in accordance with such requirements relating to terms, conditions, and form of the bond and sureties thereon, as may be specified by such regulations.

Sec. 6103. Confidentiality and Disclosure of Returns and Return Information.

(k) Disclosure of Certain Returns and Return information For Tax Administration Purposes. —

(2) Disclosure of amount of outstanding lien. - If a notice of lien has been filed pursuant to section 6323(f), the amount of the outstanding obligation secured by such lien may be disclosed to any person who furnishes satisfactory written evidence that he has a right in the property subject to such lien or intends to obtain a right in such property.

[5] Approval Process for Liens, Levies, and Seizures

The IRS Restructuring and Reform Act of 1998 directs the Service to develop and implement procedures under which a Service employee's decision to file a notice of lien, serve a notice of levy, or seize property is required to secure the review of a supervisor before the action is taken.[44] This review is to be provided "where appropriate."[45] Under the procedures, if review procedures are not followed, the employee or the supervisor or both are to be disciplined. The review process may include a certification that the supervisor reviewed the taxpayer's information, verified that a balance is due, and affirmed that the proposed action is appropriate given the taxpayer's circumstances, considering the amount due and the value of property involved.

B   THE GENERAL TAX LIEN

¶ 14.04 EFFECT OF THE GENERAL TAX LIEN

A lien is a claim or charge on property for the payment of a debt. By itself, the creditor's lien does not transfer the debtor's property to the creditor. A transfer of the debtor's property can be effected only by a levy or seizure. The tax lien is the government's claim or charge on a taxpayer's property for the payment of a tax debt; similarly, the tax lien itself does not seize or deprive a delinquent taxpayer of property. The government obtains possession or custody of property when the Service actually seizes the property, or at least serves a notice of levy.[46] Not only does the tax lien not seize the taxpayer's property, the Service may choose not to record the tax lien immediately so that the government's claim is not a matter of public record.[47] This forbearance is based on

---

[44] The IRS Restructuring and Reform Act of 1998, HR 2676, 105th Cong. 2d Sess. § 3421 (hereinafter the 1998 Act). The review procedure applies to general collection action on the effective date of the 1998 Act, July 22, 1998, but the procedure did not apply to the ACS until after December 31, 2000.

[45] See IRM 5.12.1.3.1 Review Process (Feb. 2, 2000).

[46] Because of the difference between the tax lien and the tax levy, release of a levy does not release the underlying notice of lien. United States v. Norse, Inc., 77 AFTR2d 96-2135 (D. Guam 1996) (Service released levy and then bank made loan, but Service lien had priority in surety bond proceeds). The notice of levy transfers constructive possession of the taxpayer's property to the Service although the taxpayer's title is not divested until the property is sold. United States v. Whiting Pools, Inc., 462 US 198 (1983); Phelps v. United States, 421 US 330 (1975).

[47] The Service's stated policy is not to file a notice of lien (except in jeopardy cases) until "reasonable efforts" have been made to contact the taxpayer and to afford the tax-

the belief that filing of liens adversely affects the taxpayer's ability to pay and so hampers the collection process.[48]

How does the filing of notices of lien affect those dealing with the delinquent taxpayer? In general (except for "superpriority" interests), once notices of the lien are filed, persons deal with the taxpayer at their peril. If they acquire property from the taxpayer, it is acquired subject to the tax lien and any claim the person has will be paid out of the taxpayer's property in a position subordinate to the tax lien. Careful prospective creditors or transferees will check whether a tax lien is on file in the appropriate office and will not deal with the taxpayer if a lien is on file. As a result, a taxpayer can be deprived of the opportunity to acquire the means to pay a delinquent tax.

However, without actual deprivation of property and even public notice of its existence, the delinquent taxpayer can be deluded about the precariousness of his financial situation once the assessment or general lien exists.

Other than collection due process review, few limitations prevent the Service from seizing a taxpayer's property after a general lien attaches to the property. Once the lien exists, the Service need only wait thirty days after giving the taxpayer notice of its intention to levy before it may, without judicial intervention, levy upon, seize, and sell "all property and rights to property" of the taxpayer.[49] The government need not proceed administratively by levy. Once the tax lien exists, it may institute any proceeding in court[50] that it considers appropriate under the circumstances.

A taxpayer cannot avoid payment of the liability secured by a lien by making gratuitous transfers of property so as to nullify potential enforced collection action because the transferred property will be encumbered by the general tax lien,[51] and the transfers may be set aside as fraudulent.[52] The taxpayer who seeks to render himself "judgment-proof" risks criminal liability as well.[53]

---

payer an opportunity to make payment. IRM, Policies of the IRS Handbook, P-5-47 (approved Mar. 17, 1992).

[48] IRM, Policies of the IRS Handbook, P-5-47 (approved Mar. 17, 1992).

[49] IRC § 6331(d). But see IRC § 6330.

[50] See the discussion infra ¶ 14.09.

[51] See, e.g., United States v. Bess, 357 US 51 (1958).

[52] See, e.g., United States v. Livingstone, 381 F. Supp. 607 (D. Mass. 1975).

[53] United States v. Trownsell, 367 F2d 815 (7th Cir. 1966) (conviction of willful attempted evasion under Section 7201 where taxpayer liquidated his assets and deposited them in a Swiss bank). See also United States v. Schwartz, 390 F2d 1 (3d Cir. 1968) (prosecution under Section 7206(4) where attorney made false entries in corporate books to conceal assets subject to levy); United States v. Bregman, 306 F2d 653 (3d Cir. 1962), cert. denied, 372 US 906 (1963) (conviction of mailing false statement under Section 7206(4) where taxpayer attempted to conceal trailers subject to levy by making entries that they had been repossessed). But see United States v. Palermo, 259 F2d 872 (3d Cir. 1958) (unsuccessful prosecution for willful failure to pay tax under Section 7203). For further discussion of criminal penalties for attempts to evade payment or willful failure to

Suppose a taxpayer wishes to deal with others despite the existence of a lien. If a notice of lien has not been filed, some persons having dealings with the taxpayer (e.g., purchasers, holders of security interests, judgment creditors, and mechanic's lienors) are protected from the effect of the tax lien.[54] If the purchaser of real property has recorded the deed or otherwise complied with state recording law before the Service has recorded its tax lien, the purchaser is protected under Section 6323(a) from the later-filed tax lien, even if the purchaser has actual notice of the existence of the unfiled tax lien.[55] However, persons who are not protected by the statute because they are not in a protected class or have failed to take sufficient steps to perfect their interests must face the fact that once the lien exists the government is not merely a general creditor of the taxpayer before the claims of a general creditor, but a creditor with security (i.e., the lien) entitled to payment. If the taxpayer has transferred property to an unprotected person, the transferred property is still subject to the government's lien.[56]

Even if notice of a tax lien is not filed, persons having actual knowledge of the lien must exercise care in their dealings with the taxpayer or the taxpayer's property. Persons who make purchases from or loans to the taxpayer having "actual notice or knowledge" of the existence of a tax lien lose their protected status even where they would have otherwise been entitled to "superpriority" over a filed lien.[57] Furthermore, since the lien makes "all property and rights to property" of the taxpayer security or collateral for the payment of the tax claim, a bailee holding the taxpayer's property, or a person indebted to the taxpayer with actual knowledge of the tax lien, may be liable for conversion if the person dissipates the government's "security"[58] or may be liable for the amount of the money paid in derogation of the lien.[59] The serious implications of such action against debtors of a delinquent taxpayer have led the Service to

---

pay tax, see ¶¶ 7A.02, 7A.03[2]. The attempt constitutes an attempted evasion of payment of the tax punishable as the most serious in the Code by felony, under Section 7201. In addition, Section 7206(4) makes it a felony to remove or conceal property subject to levy with intent to evade or defeat collection.

[54] IRC § 6323(a).

[55] United States v. McCombs, 30 F3d 310 (2d Cir. 1994). The purchaser must qualify as a purchaser under Section 6323(h)(6); see ¶ 16.03[1].

[56] United States v. Bess, 357 US 51, 57 (1958) ("transfer of property subsequent to the attachment of the lien does not affect the lien, for 'it is in the very nature and essence of a lien that no matter into whose hands the property goes, it passes cum onere.'")

[57] See IRC §§ 6323(b)(1) (purchasers of securities), 6323(b)(2) (purchasers of automobiles), 6323(b)(3) (purchasers of personal property at retail), 6323(b)(4) (casual sales), 6323(b)(9) (insurance policy loans), 6323(b)(10) (passbook loans), 6323(c)(1) (commercial lenders).

[58] Nomellini Constr. Co. v. United States, 328 F. Supp. 1281 (ED Cal. 1971).

[59] United States v. Allen, 207 F. Supp. 545 (D. Wash. 1962) (escrow agent with notice of lien liable for making payment).

state that it will not assert any tort liability against insurance companies, banks, or domestic building and loan associations acting in the regular course of business, even if they possess actual notice or knowledge of the tax lien (e.g., by way of a previous unsatisfied levy) with respect to payment made to an insured or a depositor (or his order).[60] However, the very existence of this announced position raises questions of potential liability for persons who do not fall within its specific provisions.

¶ 14.05 WHEN AND HOW THE GENERAL TAX LIEN ARISES

The general rule is that "if any person liable to pay any tax neglects or refuses to pay the same after demand, the amount (including any interest, additional amount, addition to tax, or assessable penalty, together with costs that may accrue in addition thereto) shall be a lien in favor of the United States upon all property and rights to property, whether real or personal, belonging to the taxpayer."[61] Several terms used in the statute need further description. What does the statute mean when it states that the lien applies to "a person liable to pay any tax"? A taxpayer's liability for a tax is established by an assessment of the tax. Consequently, the person liable for the tax is a taxpayer against whom the Service has assessed a type of tax for a particular period or year. The demand referred to is the demand the Service is required to make of the taxpayer "as soon as practicable" and in no event later than sixty days after an assessment.[62] The notice and demand used by the Service accords the taxpayer ten days to make payment, drawing on the levy provision that prohibits collection within ten days after the notice and demand.[63] If the taxpayer fails to pay the assessed tax after a notice and demand, the amount for the tax and any additions "shall be a lien" on all the taxpayer's property. It follows that a general tax lien (the lien attaches to all property and rights to property) arises by operation of law where (1) the Service has made an assessment of a tax assessment; (2) the Service has sent the taxpayer a notice of the assessment stating the amount and demanding its payment; but (3) the taxpayer has failed to pay the amount assessed within ten days after the notice and demand.

Only when these three events have occurred does a tax lien arise that is enforceable against "all property and rights to property, whether real or per-

---

[60] Rev. Rul. 67-162, 1967-1 CB 356.

[61] IRC § 6321. The amount of the tax lien includes the amount of tax, penalties, and interest accruing until the date of the payment of the tax. IRC §§ 6321, 6601(a), 6665(a); Paul Revere Life Ins. Co. v. Brock, 28 F3d 551 (6th Cir. 1994).

[62] IRC § 6303(a).

[63] IRC § 6331(a).

sonal, belonging to the (taxpayer)" as of the date the assessment was made.[64] Because the lien arises after assessment and attaches generally to all property and rights to property, it is called the assessment lien or general tax lien. These interchangeable terms distinguish the assessment or general lien from the special gift and estate tax lien that arises without any assessment and attaches to a limited class of property.[65]

The assessment lien comes into existence automatically. Nothing more needs to be done to establish the government's interest in the taxpayer's property as against other creditors of the taxpayer and persons having dealings with or claims against the taxpayer. There is a limited class of creditors and a transferee of the taxpayer against whom the assessment lien does not have priority. In the lien priority statute, Section 6323, the assessment lien is not valid against purchasers, holders of security interests, judgment lien creditors, and mechanic's lienors unless notice of the federal tax lien has been filed before these creditors have perfected their interests under local law. Even if a notice of federal tax lien is filed, it is not valid against a class of "superpriority" interests.[66] Because the assessment lien so significantly affects the taxpayer's property and those having dealings with the taxpayer—the lien is literally the basis for collection of a tax administratively and judicially—the three prerequisites for the lien are examined separately in this section.

[1] Prerequisites to the Assessment Lien: Assessment

An assessment is the official act of recording the liability of a taxpayer on a summary list.[67] More precisely, the official act of assessment occurs when a responsible officer in the Service signs the assessment certificate (Form 23-C). The Service uses computers to record a taxpayer's liability in processing returns and payments. Consequently, a distinction is drawn between assessment and the mechanical recording of the taxpayer's liability. Assessment does not occur where the taxpayer's liability is recorded through computer operations; it requires the signing of the assessment certificate by the assessment officer.[68]

---

[64] IRC §§ 6321, 6322.

[65] IRC § 6324. The special estate and gift tax lien is discussed in Part D of this chapter.

[66] IRC § 6323. The priority of federal tax liens is discussed in Chapter 16.

[67] IRC § 6203; Reg. § 301.6203-1.

[68] Reg. § 301.6203-1. Brafman v. United States, 384 F2d 863, 867 (5th Cir. 1967) (assessment certificate not signed by the proper official within the statutory period for assessment; therefore, suit for collection barred). A Form 23-C that had an incorrect assessment amount and listed "tax period ending September 30, 1985," rather than each of the tax periods for which assessment was made, was held valid. Curley v. United States, 791 F. Supp. 52 (EDNY 1992) (no showing that assessment was arbitrary, without foundation, or so technically flawed as to amount to violation of due process; Brafman said to be sig-

Two assessment records exist: a summary record of assessment, which is a Form 23-C, and a supporting record or supporting records, which together with the Form 23-C identify (1) the taxpayer; (2) the character of the liability assessed; (3) the taxable period, if applicable; and (4) the amount of the assessment. The date the Form 23-C is signed is the date of the assessment. The supporting record varies with the type of tax. For example, when a trust fund recovery penalty assessment is made, a Form 2749, Request for Trust Fund Recovery Penalty Assessment, is a supporting record.[69]

Much litigation has taken place over the government's use of Form 4340, Certificate of Assessment and Payment, to establish that as an assessment against the taxpayer. Form 4340 is neither a summary record of assessment nor a supporting record; it is a certification of what Service records show about the assessment against, and payments made by, a taxpayer of a particular tax. As an official record, the Certificate of Assessment and Payment is not hearsay,[70] and it is self-authenticating.[71] In a suit to reduce an assessment to judgment, it is generally held that the government need not produce the Form 23-C, and can satisfy its burden of proof that an assessment been made by producing a certificate of assessments and payments.[72] When original records are used by the Service to prepare the summary record, however, those records have been said not to be required on the debatable authority of the regulations themselves.[73] Many courts have also said that for purposes of a summary judgment, the certificate of assessments and payments (Form 4340) is sufficient evidence that an assessment was made in the manner prescribed by Section 6203 and Reg. § 301.6203-1.[74] On the other hand, it is also held that the Form 4340 is not conclusive evidence of the matters stated. Rather, the certificate creates a presumption of regularity or correctness that shifts the burden of coming forward with evidence and proof to the taxpayer to show that the information in the certificate is incorrect (Fed. R. Evid. 301). Many cases so hold.[75]

---

nificant violation of regulation). Cf. Jones v. United States, 93-2 USTC ¶ 50,446 (D. Nev. 1993) (*Brafman* applied to Form 23-C, not Form 4340, Certificate of Assessments and Payments).

[69] See Moore v. United States, 72 AFTR2d 93-6571 (ED Cal. 1993) (erroneous social security number did not invalidate assessment).

[70] Fed. R. Evid. 803(8).

[71] Fed. R. Evid. 901(b)(7).

[72] United States v. Dixon, 672 F. Supp. 503 (MD Ala. 1987) (gathering cases); United States v. Hesse, 90-1 USTC ¶ 50,049 (SDNY 1990) (certificate of assessments and payments is admissible secondary evidence of assessment date, but assessment shown to have been made on an earlier date).

[73] Gentry v. United States, 962 F2d 555 (6th Cir. 1992).

[74] Long v. United States, 972 F2d 1174 (10th Cir. 1992) (gathering cases).

[75] See, e.g., Psaty v. United States, 442 F2d 1154, 1158–1160 (3d Cir. 1971); Long v. United States, 972 F2d 1174 (10th Cir. 1992); Fidelity Bank v. United States, 616 F2d

Assessment of tax is the first step in the collection process, but the timing of the assessment may be more important to the taxpayer than the fact that an assessment has been made. Assessments may be made at widely varying times. Where a taxpayer files a return acknowledging a tax liability, the acknowledged or confessed tax is assessed almost immediately.[76] The timing of an assessment may be accelerated where collection of the tax might be jeopardized by delay[77] or where there is a receivership or bankruptcy.[78] In these situations, the restrictions on assessment, such as the ninety-day waiting period, do not apply, and assessment may or must be made immediately.[79] On the other hand, before a deficiency is assessed, the return must be audited at the local level, and the taxpayer may choose to protest unagreed items and take the disagreement to the Appeals Office. Even after this administrative review, before an assessment may be made in the normal case, a notice of deficiency must be sent to the taxpayer permitting him ninety days to file a petition for redetermination of the proposed assessment in the Tax Court. Finally, if a petition is filed and the matter passes through the pleading, stipulation, trial, and briefing stages to judgment, an assessment made on the basis of a judgment unfavorable to the taxpayer may by stayed pending appeal to a court of appeal by the filing of a bond in the amount of the assessment plus accrued interest. Where this route is taken, an assessment sometimes will not be made for more than three years.

The timing of an assessment is significant in determining whether the assessment is valid. For an assessment of tax to be valid, it obviously must be made within the three-year period of limitations or any agreed extension of that period.[80] An untimely assessment taints later action to collect tax.[81] Also, assessment of tax is prohibited at certain times, for example, during the ninety-day period after the date of a notice of deficiency and during the pendency of a Tax Court proceeding.[82] An assessment made during prohibited periods is void.[83]

1181 (10th Cir. 1980); United States v. Chila, 871 F2d 1015 (11th Cir. 1989), cert. denied, 493 US 975 (1989).

[76] IRC § 6201(a)(1).

[77] IRC §§ 6851, 6861.

[78] IRC § 6871.

[79] IRC § 6213(a).

[80] IRC § 6501(a). The statute of limitations on collection is discussed at ¶ 5.04.

[81] See, e.g., Brafman v. United States, 384 F2d 863, 867 (5th Cir. 1967).

[82] IRC § 6213(a).

[83] See, e.g., Dierks v. United States, 215 F. Supp. 338 (SDNY 1963) (assessment made before Tax Court decision had become final). For a discussion of the assessment process, see ¶ 10.02. See also Johnson v. United States, 990 F2d 41 (2d Cir. 1993) (assessment made and lien filed during ninety-day appeal period following Tax Court's decision that it was held invalid).

[2] Prerequisites to the Assessment: Demand

Once the formal act of assessment takes place, the Service must, "as soon as practicable, and within 60 days, after the making of an assessment of a tax, give notice to each person liable for unpaid tax, stating the amount and demanding payment thereof, . . . " by leaving the notice and demand "at the dwelling or usual place of business of such person" or by mailing it to his "last known address."[84] Although there is an explicit statutory requirement that a taxpayer receive notice of the assessment and demand for payment of the amount assessed, a demand need not be formal—that is, by way of official government form.[85] However, the Service does usually use Form 3446 to give notice of the assessment and make demand for the payment of the assessed amount.

Under the collection mechanism established by the Code, once tax has been assessed, a taxpayer is subject to the summary nonjudicial procedures (lien and levy) available to the Service to collect the assessed tax. Because a notice and demand is required to be sent by Section 6303, the taxpayer is warned that the taxpayer must take some action to resolve the delinquent account if these summary collection procedures are to be avoided. Preseizure notice thus serves an important practical, and possibly a due process, purpose in

---

[84] IRC § 6303(a). For a discussion of what constitutes a taxpayer's last known address, see ¶ 10.03[2][a][i]. The person receiving the notice and demand must pay "at the place and time stated in such notice the amount of any tax (including any interest, additional amounts, additions to tax, and assessable penalties) stated in such notice and demand." IRC § 6155(a).

It has been held that, when taxpayers complain that they did not receive a notice and demand, the determinative issue is not whether the taxpayer actually received the notice and demand, but rather whether it has been mailed to the person's last known address. See United States v. Zolla, 724 F2d 808, 810 (9th Cir. 1984); Pursifull v. United States, 849 F. Supp. 597, 601 (SD Ohio 1993); Koss v. United States, 81 AFTR2d 98-2049 (ED Pa. 1998) (parties agreed that the issue was whether the Service had sent a notice and demand, but after the Service was requested to produce backup documents for Certificate of Assessments and Payments and admitted it had no record of a notice's having been sent, the court found the Service failed to present hard evidence that a notice was actually mailed, despite the Service's claim that a notice had been manually sent).

[85] Guaranty Trust Co. v. McKenrick, 5 F2d 553 (4th Cir. 1925) (verbal demand); Laing v. United States, 364 F. Supp. 469, 472 n.6 (D. Vt. 1973), aff'd on other grounds, 496 F2d 853 (2d Cir. 1974), rev'd on other grounds, 423 US 161 (1975) (same). A proof of claim has been held to constitute a valid demand. In re Fidelity Tube Corp., 278 F2d 776 (2d Cir. 1960). The fact that a notice and demand was made on a taxpayer may be established from the Service's records. United States v. Lorson Elec. Co., 72-2 USTC ¶ 9614 (SDNY 1972), aff'd per curiam, 480 F2d 554 (2d Cir. 1973); In re Resyn Corp., 945 F2d 1279 (3d Cir. 1991) (proof of claim in bankruptcy proceeding "did not satisfy the notice requirements of section 6303(a) because it was not left at Resyn's usual place of business or mailed to Resyn at its last known address").

the statutory scheme.[86] A taxpayer's liability is recorded by the official act of assessment, but where no Section 6303 notice is given, or an invalid notice is given, a statutory prerequisite is missing and, absent compliance with the Code, any collection action that follows is invalid. No lien can arise, nor can a levy be effective, absent a notice and demand.[87] The principle that the failure to give notice under Section 6303(a) bars administrative collection action (but not a judicial action to collect tax) has been accepted by several circuit courts.[88] Where the government elects to collect tax by a civil suit, the complaint gives the taxpayer notice, and collection cannot be taken without court approval. A Section 6303 notice does not appear to be required where liability is asserted in a judicial proceeding.[89]

---

[86] See Shapiro v. Secretary of State, 499 F2d 527, 531 n.12 (DC Cir. 1974), aff'd on other grounds, 424 US 614 (1976) ("In the present case there are allegations that the Commissioner failed to provide the taxpayer the required notice prior to serving 'Notices of Levy' on the taxpayer's New York banks. If so, the Commissioner may well have violated Shapiro's right to due process").

[87] Jenkins v. Smith, 99 F2d 827 (2d Cir. 1938) (failure to give notice of assessment barred levy under predecessor of Section 6303); United States v. Coson, 286 F2d 453 (9th Cir. 1961); Bauer v. Foley, 404 F2d 1215 (2d Cir. 1968), on reh'g, 408 F2d 1331 (2d Cir. 1969) (effect on lien of no or faulty notice); LOC Indus., Inc. v. United States, 423 F. Supp. 265 (MD Tenn. 1976) (no notice and demand prior to levy; held, seized funds must be returned); Mrizek v. Long, 187 F. Supp. 830 (ND Ill. 1959) (levy served five days before notice and demand; held, invalid). This principle is acknowledged also in United States v. Jersey Shore State Bank, 781 F2d 974, 975–976 (3d Cir. 1986) aff'd, 479 US 442 (1987); United States v. Berman, 825 F2d 1053 (6th Cir. 1987).

[88] United States v. Berman, 825 F2d 1053 (6th Cir. 1987); United States v. McCallum, 970 F2d 66 (5th Cir. 1992); United States v. Kohnke, 923 F2d 864 (9th Cir. 1991) (unpublished); United States v. Chila, 871 F2d 1015, 1019 (11th Cir.), cert. denied, 493 US 975 (1989). This result was stated in *Berman*, and the text was adopted in Blackston v. United States, 778 F. Supp. 244 (D. Md. 1991) ("[n]evertheless, this Court concludes, consistent with the Sixth Circuit view in *Berman*, . . . that the appropriate 'sanction' against the IRS for its failure to comply with § 6303(a) and give timely notice and demand is to take away its awesome non-judicial collection powers"). In *Blackston*, defective notice and demand were held no bar to government action to reduce assessment to judgment. See also Stevens v. United States, 49 F3d 331, 336-37 (7th Cir. 1983) (failure to give notice and demand does not prevent the Service from pursuing an action for collection against the taxpayer). See also Marvel v. United States, 719 F2d 1507 (10th Cir. 1983) (defective notice and demand did not defeat government claim for employment taxes raised by counterclaim in refund suit.)

For an analysis distinguishing the different factual situations in the cases, and concluding that an injunction could be issued to enjoin collection if a notice and demand was not sent, see Gordon, "Failure to Give Notice and Demand: Enjoining the IRS from Administrative Collection Action," 98 TNT 100-100.

[89] This distinction between administrative collection and judicial collection was recognized in the litigation over whether a lender claimed by the government to be liable under Section 3505 for withholding taxes was entitled to receive a notice and demand, as was the common law employer against whom the unpaid tax was assessed. United States v. Jersey Shore State Bank, 781 F2d 974, 975–976 (3d Cir. 1986) aff'd, 479 US 442

The right to receive a notice and demand within the sixty-day period is a defense personal to the taxpayer and may not be raised by a taxpayer's creditor.[90] The statute also requires that a notice and demand be sent to "each taxpayer" at his last known address. The "each taxpayer" requirement has proved to be somewhat troublesome (e.g., where a joint return was filed and there has been a separation or divorce).[91] However, generally speaking, where an agency relationship between or among taxpayers exists, a single notice to one is notice to all.

The requirement that a notice and demand be left at the taxpayer's principal place of business or usual place of abode or mailed to the taxpayer's last known address is similar to the language of Section 6212(b) dealing with the mailing of a notice of deficiency. Consequently, cases arising under that section should apply as well to the mailing of a notice and demand.[92]

[3] Prerequisites to the Assessment Lien: Nonpayment

Since the Service uses a series of notices, the ten-day grace period for making payment provided in the initial notice and demand may, as a practical matter, be much longer than ten days. Practical delay aside, on the expiration of the ten days without payment (the statute literally requires "neglect or refusal to

---

(1987); United States v. Berman, 825 F2d 1053 (6th Cir. 1987) ("[N]otice of assessment and demand for payment only would be necessary if the government wanted to proceed administratively to collect the tax"). The Ninth Circuit has said that the failure to send a notice and demand does not invalidate an assessment so that the Service is permitted to use the statutory period on collection to institute a collection action. See Purcell v. United States, 1 F3d 932 (9th Cir. 1993). See also Jones v. United States, 93-2 USTC ¶ 50,446 (D. Nev. 1993) (suggesting that a failure to send a notice and demand would not prevent the Service from instituting a collection action).

[90] United States v. Lorson Elec. Co., 72-2 USTC ¶ 9614 (SDNY 1972), aff'd per curiam, 480 F2d 554 (2d Cir. 1973); Macatee, Inc. v. United States, 214 F2d 717 (2d Cir. 1954); cf. Georgia-Pac. Corp. v. Lazy Two T Ranch, Inc., 76-2 USTC ¶ 9666 (CD Cal. 1976) (notice not mailed to taxpayer's last known address; held, assessment invalid despite government's argument that debtor (Lazy Two T Ranch) lacked standing to raise claim).

[91] See, e.g., Bauer v. Foley, 404 F2d 1215 (2d Cir. 1968), on reh'g, 408 F2d 1331 (2d Cir. 1969) (notice and demand sent to husband ineffective as to estranged wife).

[92] See ¶ 10.03[2][a]. However, in Bauer v. Foley, 404 F2d 1215 (2d Cir. 1968), on reh'g, 408 F2d 1331 (2d Cir. 1969), in which a notice and demand was involved, a mailing to the husband was held ineffective, although it appears that the mailing of a notice of deficiency would have been effective under Section 6212(b)(2) had it been mailed to the husband, unless the Service were notified that either spouse had established a separate residence.

pay") the general assessment lien attaches to all the taxpayer's property as of the date the assessment was made.[93]

¶ 14.06 DURATION OF THE GENERAL TAX LIEN

The lien for taxes imposed by Section 6321 "shall arise at the time the assessment is made and shall continue until the liability for the amount so assessed (or a judgment arising out of such liability) is satisfied or becomes unenforceable by lapse of time." The period of the lien is thus tied to the statute of limitations for collection after assessment. The period for collection after assessment is ten years after the date of assessment.[94] Generally, a levy or collection proceeding in court against a taxpayer will not be valid unless collection action is taken within ten years.[95] Accordingly, the general tax lien has the same duration as the statutory period of collection. Unless the Service has collected the tax by levy or the government has begun a court proceeding to collect the tax before the expiration of the statutory collection period, the lien will expire and be unenforceable at the end of the statutory period on collection.[96]

---

[93] IRC § 6322; United States v. Wintner, 200 F. Supp. 157 (ND Ohio 1961), aff'd per curiam, 312 F2d 749 (6th Cir. 1963), rev'd on other grounds, 375 US 393 (1964) (partial payment constitutes "neglect or refusal"). See also United States v. Bess, 357 US 51, 55 (1958). There is authority that the taxpayer must be given the opportunity to refuse. LOC Indus., Inc. v. United States, 423 F. Supp. 265 (MD Tenn. 1976).

[94] See IRC § 6502(a). Section 6502(a) was amended by the Omnibus Budget Reconciliation Act of 1990, § 11317, amending Section 6502(a) for taxes assessed after November 5, 1990, the date of enactment. Before 1990, the statutory period on collection was six years; but for taxes assessed after November 5, 1990, the ten-year period applies. For a discussion of the statute of limitations on collection and its extension, see ¶ 5.04.

[95] IRC § 6502(a). When a taxpayer agreed to extend the then six-year period of limitations so that the period was open when Congress extended the period to ten years, it was held that the ten-year period applied. Foutz v. United States, 860 F. Supp. 788 (D. Utah 1994) (Form 900 extended collection period until December 31, 1990, and Section 6502(a) amended on November 5, 1990: held, levy made on November 7, 1991, was valid).

[96] See Bowers v. New York & Albany Lighterage Co., 273 US 346 (1927) (interpreting the predecessor of Section 6502(a) and saying, "it was the intention of Congress . . . to protect taxpayers against any proceeding whatsoever for the collection of tax claims not made and pressed within [the applicable statutory period of] years"). However, the statute of limitations will not prevent collection after the limitations period when the Service institutes a court proceeding on a cause of action separate and distinct from its underlying action to collect taxes from the taxpayer (e.g., when the taxpayer delivered a bond to the Service to suspend collection of outstanding taxes, and the Service sues on the bond after the collection period has expired). United States v. John Barth Co., 279 US 370 (1929) (bond to suspend collection); Gulf States Steel Co. v. United States, 287 US 32 (1932) (taxpayer issued bonds to prevent immediate collection shortly before the collection period

The statutory period for assessment after collection is modified in a number of instances. The ten-year statute of limitations on collection is not subject to extension by agreement after December 31, 1999,[97] but the ten-year period after assessment applies absolutely with the exception of two situations:

1. If before the ten-year period has expired, the taxpayer and the Service have entered into an installment payment agreement that provides for an agreed-upon period of collection, the Service may collect during the ninety days after that agreed-upon period expires or

2. If the taxpayer and the Service have agreed upon a release of levy after the ten-year collection period has expired, the Service may collect within any period the taxpayer and the Service have agreed upon.[98]

Also, if a proceeding in court for the collection of the tax is commenced within the ten-year period, the period during which tax may be collected by levy is extended and does not expire until the liability for the tax (or a judgment against the taxpayer arising from the liability is satisfied or becomes unenforceable.[99]

Suspension of the running of the period of limitation on collection. Because the statute of limitations on collection begins to run on the date tax is assessed, suspension of the statute of limitations on assessment affects the running of the statute of limitations on collection. The same rules that apply to the statute of limitations on collection apply to the duration of the tax lien. Thus, if the period for collection is extended by agreement or by one of the circumstances of suspension described in Section 6503, the period of the lien is extended as well.[100]

---

expired, achieved delay in collection until the period expired, and then argued that the Service could not enforce the obligation because the collection period had expired; held, strict construction of the statute of limitations on collection would be "manifestly unjust, if not absurd"); Julicher v. IRS, 76 AFTR2d 95-5793 (ED Pa. 1995) (although Section 6502 prohibits collection of taxes after the statute of limitations has expired, "the precedents . . . John Barth Company and Gulf States clearly demonstrate that the letter of credit which [the taxpayer] executed afforded the Service a cause of action separate and distinct from an action to collect taxes").

[97] IRC § 6502(a), as amended by the 1998 Act § 3461(a), effective for requests after December 31, 1999. Requests obtained before the effective date will still expire at the latter of the ten-year period or December 31, 2002. An extension agreed upon as part of an installment agreement expires on the ninetieth day after the expiration of the agreed-upon period.

[98] IRC § 6502(a)(2)(B).

[99] IRC § 6502(a) (flush language).

[100] The problem of a tax lien's continuing validity beyond the normal six-year period, thereby misleading a creditor of a taxpayer who assumed the lien was no longer enforceable, was the reason Congress imposed a refiling requirement on tax liens as part of the Federal Tax Lien Act of 1966 (FTLA). S. Rep. No. 1708, 89th Cong., 2d Sess. (1966), reprinted in 1966-2 CB 876, 884. Under Section 6323(g), the Service must refile a notice of

The running of the statutory period on collection is suspended during certain periods set forth in Section 6503. When the running of the statute of limitations on collection is suspended, the period of the lien is extended. In the following circumstances, when the running of the period of limitations is suspended, the duration of the tax lien is extended:

1. A notice of deficiency has been issued;[101]
2. Assets of the taxpayer are in the control or custody of a court;[102]
3. The taxpayer is outside the United States;[103]
4. A third party's property has been wrongfully seized to satisfy the taxpayer's tax;[104] or
5. Bankruptcy proceedings have begun.[105]

The period of limitations on assessment and collection is suspended for the 90-day (or 150-day) period after the sending of a statutory notice of deficiency in income, gift, or estate tax. If a petition for redetermination is filed in the Tax Court, the period is suspended until the court's decision becomes final, and for sixty days thereafter.[106]

Assets of a taxpayer are not subject to administrative collection procedures while they are in the custody of a court. Therefore, the statute of limitations on collection is suspended for the period the assets of the taxpayer, including the estate of a deceased or incompetent taxpayer, are in the control or custody of the court during any proceeding, and for six months thereafter.[107]

The running of the statutory period of limitations on collection after assessment is also suspended for the period during which the taxpayer is outside the United States if the absence is for a continuous period of at least six

---

lien within the one-year period ending thirty days after the expiration of the six-year period.

[101] IRC § 6503(a)(1).

[102] IRC § 6503(b).

[103] IRC § 6503(c).

[104] IRC § 6503(f).

[105] IRC § 6503(i). Section 6503(i) has been renumbered as Section 6503(h).

[106] IRC § 6503(a)(1). The Tax Court decision becomes final on the expiration of the three-month period for filing an appeal or, if appeal is made, on expiration of further judicial procedures for review available to a taxpayer. IRC § 7481. A levy made during the three-month period is invalid. Dierks v. United States, 215 F. Supp. 338 (SDNY 1963). However, if the taxpayer fails to file an appeal bond along with his notice of appeal, assessment and collection may be made. IRC § 7485. Consequently, the period of limitations on assessment and collection would start to run again sixty-one days after the three-month appeal period if no appeal were filed.

[107] IRC § 6503(b). United States v. Shahadi, 340 F2d 56 (3d Cir. 1965) (collection statute suspended where Tax Court petition filed). See United States v. Davenport, 61-1 USTC ¶ 9270 (WDSC 1960), aff'd on another issue, 297 F2d 284 (4th Cir. 1962).

months.[108] To make certain that the government has an opportunity to collect the tax after the taxpayer's return, the collection period does not expire (where the taxpayer has been out of the country for six months or more) until six months after the taxpayer's return to the country.

A taxpayer might wait until the period of limitations has run and then help a third party recapture property the Service erroneously believes is the taxpayer's because the government had no recourse with respect to the taxpayer. In this situation, the running of the period of limitations on collection is suspended during the period the Service holds a third person's property (including money) wrongfully seized or received. The suspension continues to the date the property is administratively returned pursuant to Section 6343(b), or the date on which a judgment secured pursuant to Section 7426 with respect to such property becomes final, and for thirty days thereafter.[109] Where the period of limitations is suspended under this provision, it is suspended only as to that part of an assessment equal to the amount of money or value of specific property that initially has been wrongfully taken from a third party and subsequently is returned to him.[110]

The running of the collection period is also suspended during the period when a taxpayer's case under the Bankruptcy Code (11 USC) is pending, and for six months after the termination of that case.[111]

If a proceeding in court is begun before the expiration of the statutory period and a judgment against the taxpayer for the amount of the tax assessment is obtained, whether before or after that period, the general assessment lien continues independent of any judgment until the underlying tax liability is satisfied or becomes unenforceable by reason of lapse of time. What happens if the Service levies within the statutory collection period? Is the levy, even if the full tax is uncollected, sufficient to extend the collection period and lien as well? If a levy served within the statutory period could extend the period of

---

[108] IRC § 6503(c).

[109] IRC § 6503(f).

[110] This amount or value is to be determined as of the date of return.

[111] IRC § 6503(i). Section 6503(i) has been renumbered as Section 6503(h). When the statute of limitations on collection was suspended because of the bankruptcy of the partnership, the statute of limitations on collection was also held suspended on collection from the partners. United States v. Wright, 57 F3d 561 (7th Cir. 1995) (when a suit against the taxpayer would be timely, then suit is also timely against persons derivatively liable). The Seventh Circuit reached its conclusion in *Wright* on the basis of two cases in which statute of limitations was treated as governing the debt as a whole, rather than applying it separately to each obligor's circumstances: United States v. Updike, 281 US 489 (1930), which held that because the period of limitations had run against the corporate taxpayer, it had also run against the transferees of the corporation, and United States v. Associates Commercial Corp., 721 F2d 1094, 1096–1098 (7th Cir. 1983), which involved the suspension of the period of limitations when funds are in the custody of a court (Section 6503(b)), and concluded that suits against persons derivatively liable for taxes are timely, or not, according to rules for timeliness against taxpayers.

the lien, there simply would be no limitations period on collection from a tax-payer.[112] The statutory scheme contemplates the use of summary administrative collection procedures to collect a tax for the collection period. Once the collection period has expired, assuming a suit has been instituted before the expiration date, the government must use the process of the court to collect the judgment against the taxpayer rather than an administrative levy. However, with the amendment of Section 6502 if a proceeding in court to collect a tax is begun within the ten-year period, the Service is permitted to continue collection action by levy until the judgment becomes unenforceable.

Once a judgment against the taxpayer is obtained, the assessment lien does not merge with the judgment. Section 6322 provides that the assessment lien continues until the liability "or a judgment against the taxpayer arising out of such liability" is satisfied or becomes unenforceable by reason of lapse of time. There are two reasons for this rule. If the assessment lien did not continue when it was reduced to judgment, the government might lose its priority under the lien as against competing creditors and take a new priority only as of the later date of the judgment. Also, if the lien did not continue after the judgment, the government could not enforce the lien but would have to pursue the more cumbersome process of foreclosing its judgment. Congress thought neither of these situations desirable. Since the same liability gives rise to the lien and to the judgment, the purpose of Section 6322 is to ensure the government's continued priority as against other creditors. Similarly, since the judgment merely confirms the validity of the lien, the intention is that the government's power to foreclose the lien is not curtailed. The effect of Section 6322 is seen when the life of the tax lien is extended by the court proceeding. In this situation, the lien continues to have priority over competing creditors who might have acquired liens on the taxpayer's property between the date of the assessment and the date of the judgment.[113]

State statutes of limitations do not affect the assessment lien.[114] However, a judgment lien arising from an action to reduce the tax assessment to judgment is subject to state statutes as to duration.[115] Where the Service reduces a tax assessment to a judgment, the judgment rendered by the district court is a

---

[112] Nevertheless, in dicta, one district court has said (incorrectly) that a levy is sufficient to extend the statutory period of collection. Valley Bank v. City of Henderson, 528 F. Supp. 907 (D. Nev. 1981). It has been held that there is no statute of limitations on enforcement of a levy served on a third person and that the provisions of Section 6502 apply only to actions against taxpayers. United States v. Weintraub, 613 F2d 612 (6th Cir. 1979). If an unlimited period of limitations can be found in one action, the possibility of an unlimited lien exists.

[113] Moyer v. Mathas, 71-2 USTC ¶ 9533 (MD Fla. 1971), aff'd, 458 F2d 431 (5th Cir. 1972); Moyer v. O'Donnell, 71-1 USTC ¶ 9411 (MD Fla. 1971). See also United States v. Mandel, 377 F. Supp. 1274 (SD Fla. 1975).

[114] United States v. Summerlin, 310 US 414 (1939).

[115] 28 USC § 1962 states:

lien on property located within the state in which the district court sits in the same manner, to the same extent, and under the same conditions as a judgment of a court of general jurisdiction in that state and ceases to be a lien in the same manner and time.[116]

However, postjudgment remedies in the Federal Debt Procedure Act provide that a judgment in a civil action creates a lien on all real property of the judgment debtor upon the filing of a certified abstract of the judgment in the same manner as a notice of lien would be filed under Code Section 6323(f).[117] This judgment lien is for the amount necessary to satisfy the judgment, including costs and interest, and unless satisfied, has a duration of twenty years.[118] The lien may be renewed for one additional period of twenty years upon the filing of a notice of renewal if (1) the notice of renewal is filed before the twenty-year period expires and (2) the court approves the renewal. Release of the judgment lien occurs on the filing of a satisfaction of judgment or release of lien filed in the same manner as the judgment lien. Moreover, once a judgment is obtained, the assessment lien may not be enforced by administrative action after the period of limitations on collection would have run but for the government's action in court.[119] This provision recognizes that there comes a time when it is inappropriate for the government to collect by administrative levy action without court supervision. Where the judgment arising out of the underlying assessment becomes unenforceable by reason of lapse of time under state law, the extended assessment lien also expires, the purpose for the extension (preserving the government's priority as against other creditors) having been served.[120]

Every judgment rendered by a district court within a State shall be a lien on the property located in such State in the same manner, to the same extent and under the same conditions as a judgment of a court of general jurisdiction in such State, and shall cease to be a lien in the same manner and time.

[116] 28 USC § 1962.

[117] 28 USC § 3201(a) (1996). The judgment has priority over any other lien or encumbrance which is perfected after the date of filing. On application to the court, the court may order the United States to the real property subject the lien, following the procedures set forth in 28 USC §§ 2001 and 2002. Filing of notices of tax lien is discussed at ¶ 16.03[5].

[118] 28 USC § 3201(c) (1996).

[119] Moyer v. Mathas, 71-2 USTC ¶ 9533 (MD Fla. 1971), aff'd, 458 F2d 431 (5th Cir. 1972). This matter was set to rest, at least so far as Congress was concerned, in the legislative history of the FTLA. S. Rep. No. 1708.

[120] If the assessment lien did not expire when the judgment lien expired, the assessment lien would continue indefinitely, and the government could seek to foreclose it at any time by another civil suit. This situation would result in relitigating the taxpayer's liability after it had been determined in the time-barred prior judgment, which is precisely the result the doctrine of res judicata and statutes of limitations were meant to avoid. In United States v. Palmer, 86-2 USTC ¶ 9719 (ND Ill. 1986), the government reduced tax assessments to judgment in November 1964. In 1983, the government instituted an action

First, if the taxpayer and the Service have entered into an installment payment agreement, the tax may continue to be collected until "the date which is 90 days after the expiration of any period for collection agreed upon in writing by the Service and the taxpayer at the time of the installment payment agreement was entered into."[121]

Changes in the statute of limitations on collections, Section 6502(a), have created uncertainty about the timeliness of collection action. In one case, income tax for the years 1970 through 1976 were assessed on June 14, 1979, at a time when the collection statute was six years.[122] On September 16, 1983, the government obtained a judgement for the assessed tax, and the judgment was entered on July 3, 1984. On November 7, 1991, more than twelve years after the assessment and eight years after the judgment was obtained, the Service levied on the taxpayer's property and seized his real property. To halt the sale of his residence and other real estate, the taxpayer asked for an injunction. Granting an injunction to the sale of the residence, the district court rejected the government's contention that the 1988 amendment of Section 6502 operated to make the period that the Service could levy coextensive with the period during which a judgment could be enforced. The court concluded that the Service's authority to levy on the 1979 assessment expired in 1985, six years after the date of the assessment, and the 1988 amendment could not "breathe new life into a right that no longer existed."[123] As a result, the 1991 levy was invalid.

The normal statute of limitations on collection may be extended by waiver. Collection is timely if it is made before the expiration of any period for collection agreed upon in writing by the Service and the taxpayer as long as the agreement (or waiver of the normal statute) is entered into before the period expires.[124] The taxpayer may also agree to extend or waive the statute

---

to set aside a fraudulent conveyance of real estate by the judgment debtor-taxpayer. The district court held that the action was not time barred because the assessment lien had been extended by the government's collection action, even if the judgment lien it obtained had expired under Illinois law. This conclusion is incorrect. The assessment lien does not merge into the judgment. It exists only for so long as the judgment lien exists.

[121] IRC § 6502(a)(2)(B).

[122] Hillyer v. Comm'r, 817 F. Supp. 532 (MD Pa. 1993). When a tax was assessed and, during the six-year collection period then in existence, the Service only filed a notice of tax lien, the tax lien was not a secured tax lien and the failure to levy or begin a proceeding in court meant that the statute of limitations on collection expired and the lien was unenforceable. In re Abich, 94-1 USTC ¶ 50,046, 164 BR 581 (Bankr. ND Ohio 1993).

[123] Hillyer v. Comm'r, 817 F. Supp. 532, 536 (MD Pa. 1993).

[124] IRC § 6502(a)(2). This period may in turn be extended by subsequent agreements in writing made before the expiration of the previously agreed-upon period. IRC § 6502(a). However, a waiver may not be valid if it is not executed by "the taxpayer," a circumstance that could arise where the taxpayer is not an individual. Where the taxpayer presents prima facie evidence that collection is barred by the statute of limitations, the

of limitations on collection by submitting an offer in compromise, which contains an extension of the period of collection during which the offer is pending and for one year thereafter.[125] An exception to this rule permits an agreement to be entered into after the statutory period if the consideration given by the government is the release of a levy (under Section 6343) before the expiration of the statutory period.[126]

¶ 14.07 SCOPE OF THE GENERAL TAX LIEN

[1] General Principles

After assessment, demand, and failure to pay, the general tax lien attaches automatically to "all property and rights to property, whether real or personal, belonging to the [taxpayer]."[127] The types of property subject to the general lien are unlimited, but there are certain principles that apply to the general tax lien irrespective of the type of property involved.

[a] The Government's Interest Is Derivative

Although the tax lien attaches to all a taxpayer's property and rights to property, the security of the lien is derivative—that is, it is only as good as the taxpayer's interest in the property. Thus, it is said that the government as lienor "stands in the taxpayer's shoes," which means that while the tax lien attaches to and encumbers the taxpayer's property, it is subject to the same restrictions, conditions, and disabilities as the taxpayer has with respect to the property. For example, the tax lien may attach to a taxpayer-lessee's leasehold interest, but the lien is terminated when the lessee's interest is terminated by a state court judgment.[128] Similarly, the tax lien may be defeated if a taxpayer

---

Service must present proof that a valid waiver exists. See Schenk v. Comm'r, 35 TCM 1652 (1976) (citing cases). Where a waiver procured by a Service revenue officer incorrectly stated the period for which taxes were assessed, the waiver was ineffective to extend the period for collection of the taxes in issue and collection was barred. United States v. Grabscheid, 82-1 USTC ¶ 9382 (ND Ill. 1982).

[125] United States v. Hackl, 82 AFTR2d 98-5284 (WD Wis. 1998) (collection statute would have expired but for the submission of an offer in compromise, which ultimately was rejected 200 days after it was initially submitted).

[126] IRC § 6502(a)(2). However, the Service requires the taxpayer to execute a waiver prior to release. Reg. § 301.6502-1(a)(2)(ii).

[127] IRC § 6321.

[128] Carolina Apartment Investors "A" v. United States, 77-1 USTC ¶ 9262 (CD Cal. 1977); Hedlund v. Brellenthin, 520 F. Supp. 81 (WD Wash. 1981) (forfeiture of real es-

holds an option that expires unexercised,[129] the taxpayer has failed to record an interest in order to perfect it against an intervening third party,[130] or the taxpayer's life interest in property terminates.[131] On the other hand, there are certain restrictions that might operate to limit the right of a taxpayer but that do not limit the general tax lien—for example, a state statute of limitations that runs against the taxpayer does not run against the government,[132] and an insurance clause requiring the insured-taxpayer to surrender the policy in order to receive its surrender value does not affect the operation of the lien.[133]

---

tate contract after taxpayer default left no property interest that was subject to lien); United States v. Maniscalco, 523 F. Supp. 1338 (ED La. 1981) (under Louisiana law, tax lien did not attach to the property conveyed under defaulted sales contract, but did attach to portion of purchase price paid); Kansas City, Mo. v. Tri-City Constr. Co., 666 F. Supp. 170 (WD Mo. 1987) (after taxpayer defaulted on contract, it had no rights in future payments to which tax lien could attach; the rights belonged to the surety). See also Chicago Mercantile Exch. v. United States, 840 F2d 1352 (7th Cir. 1988) (proceeds of the sale of a taxpayer's seat on a commodities exchange were not subject to levy because the taxpayer had no interest in the proceeds to which the tax lien could attach until claims required to be paid under the commodities exchange rules were satisfied). Compare United States v. 110–118 Riverside Tenants Corp., 886 F2d 514 (2d Cir. 1989), cert. denied, 110 S. Ct. 2560 (1990) (distinguishing Chicago Mercantile and holding shares of stock in a cooperative corporation entitled shareholder to full property interest of the shares, despite default and consent requirement of lease). Note that even if another party claims an interest in the property, that interest or lien must be choate at the time the lien is filed. See ¶ 16.02[2]. See, e.g., In re Terwilliger's Catering Plus, Inc., 911 F2d 1168 (6th Cir. 1990).

Because the Service stands in the shoes of the taxpayer, the Service's tax lien can be defeated by infirmities in the taxpayer's property interest under state law. Under Kansas law, a divorced spouse has an interest in marital property as of the date the divorce petition was filed, but the extent of that interest is undetermined before the divorce decree is entered. Accordingly, when the wife filed for divorce and the Service later assessed tax against her husband, the Service's assessment lien against the husband's property did not attach to property awarded to the wife under a later divorce decree. Gardner v. United States, 34 F3d 985 (10th Cir. 1994).

[129] Rev. Rul. 54-154, 1954-1 CB 277.

[130] Avco Delta Corp. v. United States, 321 F. Supp. 241 (SD Ill. 1971); Reiter v. Kille, 143 F. Supp. 590 (ED Pa. 1956); United States v. Dickerson, 101 F. Supp. 262, 272–273 (ED Mo. 1951).

[131] United States v. William, 160 F. Supp. 761 (DNJ 1958).

[132] United States v. Summerlin, 310 US 414, 416 (1940); United States v. Polan Indus., Inc., 196 F. Supp. 333 (SD W. Va. 1961); United States v. Fernon, 640 F2d 609 (5th Cir. 1981).

[133] Equitable Life Assurance Soc'y v. United States, 331 F2d 29 (1st Cir. 1964); United States v. Fried, 309 F2d 851 (2d Cir. 1962); United States v. Metropolitan Life Ins. Co., 256 F2d 17 (4th Cir. 1958); Knox v. Great W. Life Assurance Co., 212 F2d 784 (6th Cir. 1954).

[b] The Lien Encumbers After-Acquired Property

The general tax lien that attaches to "all property and rights to property" of the taxpayer as of the assessment date continues until the liability is satisfied or becomes unenforceable by lapse of time.[134] Accordingly, the tax lien attaches not only to property belonging to the taxpayer on the assessment date, but also to "after-acquired property" (property acquired after the date the lien attaches) until the tax is paid or collection becomes barred by the statute of limitations.[135]

[c] The Lien Does Not Attach to Property Transferred Before the Assessment Date

The general tax lien does not attach to property the taxpayer has completely transferred before the assessment date because the transferred property does not "belong" to him as of that date.[136] Such a transfer must be bona

---

[134] IRC § 6322.

[135] Glass City Bank v. United States, 326 US 265 (1945); Bigheart Pipeline Corp. v. United States, 835 F2d 766 (10th Cir. 1987) (lien on undeveloped oil and gas lease attached to proceeds from sale of oil from well drilled after lease was transferred; held, "[b]ecause the proceeds of the sale of oil is a 'right to property' to which a lien can attach under Oklahoma law, the district court correctly concluded that a federal tax lien attached to such property under 26 USC § 6321"); United States v. Safeco Ins. Co., 870 F2d 338 (6th Cir. 1989) (fees earned by standing Chapter 13 bankruptcy trustee held to constitute rights to property subject to tax lien).

[136] The Eighth Circuit has said that the plain meaning of the words "belonging to" in Section 6321 "suggests that the [tax] lien attaches to property interests owned by the taxpayer, not property interests vulnerable to the taxpayer's judgment creditors . . . [which] is a potentially larger universe." Thomson v. United States, 66 F3d 160 (1995). In reviewing the case law, the Eighth Circuit said that the First Circuit's opinion in United States v. V&E Eng'g & Constr. Co., 635 F. Supp. 153 (DPR 1986), aff'd, 819 F2d 331 (1st Cir. 1987), finding that the Service had no interest in property after the taxpayer had transferred it, was more consistent with the Supreme Court's decision in *First National Bank of Commerce* than were the Fifth Circuit's decisions in the Prewitt v. United States, 792 F2d 1353 (5th Cir. 1986) and *Creamer* cases. Those cases said that the Service was a creditor, entitled to protection as such under the state recording statute. Minnesota's recording statute made an unrecorded conveyance void as against subsequent bona fide purchasers and judgment creditors. Even if the transfer was not recorded under the Minnesota statute, the taxpayer-transferor retained no property right to which the tax lien could attach. But the taxpayer subsequently transferred his unrecorded equitable interest in property to his wife pursuant to a divorce decree, and later received a warranty deed purporting to give him a joint tenant's interest. These conveyances raised questions to be answered on remand about whether, in light of the divorce decree, the warranty deed gave the taxpayer/husband a property interest subject to lien, and even if it did, whether the nature and extent of the wife's interest nevertheless rendered the levy wrongful.

See Continental Oil Co. v. United States, 326 F. Supp. 266 (SDNY 1971); United States v. Lester, 235 F. Supp. 115 (SDNY 1964); United States v. General Motors Corp.,

fide.[137] A mere formal transfer will be ineffective to defeat the attachment of the lien (e.g., where a taxpayer transfers title but retains proceeds from the transferred property). Similarly, the tax lien attaches to property of a taxpayer even if it is held by an alter ego.[138] Liens and levies have been held to attach

---

929 F2d 249 (6th Cir. 1991) (an assignment of accounts receivable before the assessment was held under Michigan law to have resulted in a transfer of the accounts before the lien arose); Commonweal, Inc. v. IRS, 94-2 USTC ¶ 50,477, 171 BR 405 (Bankr. MD Fla. 1994) (stock of real estate corporation was purchased by taxpayer and given by taxpayer and his wife to their children, but while corporate formalities were followed, the corporation was a "mere instrumentality" of the taxpayer and was his nominee or alter ego).

In United States v. General Motors Corp., 929 F2d 249 (6th Cir. 1991), an assignment of accounts receivable before the assessment was held under Michigan law to have resulted in a transfer of the accounts before the lien arose. Compare Hamilton v. United States, 806 F. Supp. 326 (D. Conn. 1992) (real property was transferred before tax lien was filed, but quitclaim deed was not recorded; held, transferee was entitled to property, although deed was unrecorded because taxpayer could not legally sell property second time); United States v. Dalessandro, 94-1 USTC ¶ 50,023 (MD Pa. 1993) (deed to real property was delivered to transferee before tax was assessed and, although the deed was not recorded, Service had notice of the conveyance; held, under Pennsylvania law the conveyance was made before the assessment, and Section 6323 therefore did not apply).

[137] State law can determine the transfer issue. For a case where a lien on a husband's property was ineffective because he transferred the property to his wife for valuable consideration before the tax lien arose, see United States v. Mentelos, 81-1 USTC ¶ 9257 (SD Fla. 1980). See also Midland Ins. Co. v. Friedgood, 577 F. Supp. 1407 (SDNY 1984) (money deposited by a third party as collateral for an insurance company bail bond did not "belong" to the taxpayer under New York law; therefore, lien did not attach to the money on exoneration of the bail). SEC v. Levine, 881 F2d 1165 (2d Cir. 1989) (tax lien did not attach to disgorged assets turned over to receiver before assessment). Under Puerto Rico law, a deed transferring real property from the taxpayer to a purchaser left the taxpayer with no "property subject to a tax lien although the purchaser did not qualify under Section 6323 as a purchaser entitled to notice." United States v. V&E Eng'g & Constr. Co., 635 F. Supp. 153 (DPR 1986), aff'd, 819 F2d 331 (1st Cir. 1987).

Compare Prewitt v. United States, 792 F2d 1353 (5th Cir. 1986) (although taxpayer transferred real property pursuant to a divorce decree before a tax lien was filed, tax lien had priority over purchaser's interest in property because deed was not recorded and Service was creditor without notice entitled to protection under Texas recording statute; Creamer Indus. followed); United States v. Wood, 877 F2d 453 (6th Cir. 1989) (federal tax lien for unpaid tax liabilities recorded against property of taxpayer's spouse was enforceable because taxpayer agreed to pay the taxes when she received the property in a property settlement pursuant to a divorce).

[138] GM Leasing Corp. v. United States, 429 US 338 (1977); Wolfe v. United States, 798 F2d 1241 (9th Cir. 1986), cert. denied, 482 US 927 (1987) (applying the alter ego doctrine, a sole shareholder was held to be his corporation's alter ego; therefore, the corporation's taxes could be collected from the shareholder's assets). See, e.g., Pacific Dev., Inc. v. United States, 79-1 USTC ¶ 9138 (DDC 1979), aff'd, Valley Fin., Inc. v. United States, 629 F2d 162 (DC Cir. 1980) (corporation found to be alter ego of taxpayer); Manhattan Constr. Co. v. K & E Constr. Co., Inc., 89-1 USTC ¶ 9119 (ND Ga. 1988) (100 percent assessment collected from responsible officer's corporation because it was his alter ego; cases and factors on alter ego doctrine gathered and discussed); Pennbright Indus., Inc. v. District Dir., 90-1 USTC ¶ 50,091 (SD Tex. 1990) (corporate taxpayer transferred

to property nominally held by the taxpayer's corporate alter ego under state creditor's rights law permitting creditors to collect a debt of the corporation from its shareholder (the alter ego doctrine), and piercing the corporate form to reach corporate assets to collect a debt owed by the shareholder (reverse piercing).[139] State law may determine whether an individual is the taxpayer's nominee, allowing the taxpayer to avoid his or her financial obligations, and state law may identify certain badges of fraud in deciding the issue, such as (1) lack of consideration; (2) transfers of the taxpayer's entire estate; (3) taxpayer's relationship to the alleged nominee; (4) pendency or threat of litigation; (5) secrecy or hurriedness of the transfer; (6) departure from usual method of business; (7) taxpayer's retention of possession of the transferred property; and (8) reservation of benefit to the taxpayer.[140]

Typical factors considered in determining the alter ego issue are (1) whether the individual is in a position of control or authority over the entity;

---

property to shareholder who transferred property to second corporation; held, levy served on transferee corporation was valid because it was not an entity separate from taxpayer and transfer was a fraudulent conveyance under Texas law).

Cf. United States v. Bruce, 82-1 USTC ¶ 9280 (SD Tex. 1982) (Service failed to prove that taxpayer's corporation was his alter ego; therefore, real property in name of corporation was not subject to the lien against the taxpayer's property). Grant Inv. Fund v. IRS, 91-2 USTC ¶ 50,406 (D. Mont. 1991). For a list of factors considered by some courts to establish alter ego status, see Century Hotels v. United States, 952 F2d 107, 110 n.5 (5th Cir. 1992); United States v. Good Samaritan Church, 93-1 USTC ¶ 50,052 (D. Alaska 1992); see also United States v. JEB Properties, Inc., 80 AFTR2d 97-5256 (ED La. 1997) (holding that the factors in *Century Hotels* were applicable to determine whether one partnership was the alter ego of another partnership).

One unique aspect of this creditor's equitable remedy is the corollary stated by some courts that where a tax debt is involved, the Service need not show fraud in order to disregard the corporate entity. See Towe Antique Ford Found. v. IRS, 999 F2d 1387 (9th Cir. 1993); Valley Fin., Inc. v. United States, 629 F2d 162, 172 (DC Cir. 1980).

[139] See Towe Antique Ford Found. v. IRS, 999 F2d 1387 (9th Cir. 1993) (piercing permitted when findings established corporation was alter ego, but no actual fraud shown; split panel); Century Hotels v. United States, 952 F2d 107, 110 (5th Cir. 1992) (corporation alter ego of taxpayer, even though taxpayer had no ownership interest); Shades Ridge Holding Co., Inc. v. United States, 888 F2d 725, 728 (11th Cir. 1989), cert. denied, 494 US 1027 (1990) (same); Loving Saviour Church v. United States, 728 F2d 1085, 1086 (8th Cir. 1984) (unincorporated association alter ego); Valley Fin., Inc. v. United States, 629 F2d 162, 172 (DC Cir. 1980) (corporation liable for shareholder's tax debt). But see Floyd v. IRS, 82 AFTR2d 98-5574 (10th Cir. 1998) (attempt to collect tax assessment against shareholder from corporation (which is called outside reverse-piercing) not allowed because Kansas law did not allow creditors such a right). For a case involving an application of Minnesota alter ego law to taxpayers' transfers of property to trusts, finding that the entities were shams created on behalf of and used by the taxpayers to evade payment of their tax liabilities, so that the trusts were equally liable for the taxpayers' taxes under reverse piercing, see United States v. Scherping, 187 F3d 796 (8th Cir. 1999).

[140] Scoville v. United States, 85 AFTR2d 2000-502 (WD Mo. 1999) (Missouri law applied to defeat "sometime" wife's claim to her tax protestor husband's transferred property).

(2) whether the individual controls the entity's actions without need to consult others; (3) whether the individual uses the entity to shield himself from personal liability; (4) whether the individual uses the business entity for personal financial benefit; (5) whether the individual mingles his own personal affairs in the affairs of the business entity; and (6) whether the individual uses the business entity to assume his own debts, or the debts of another, or whether the individual uses his own funds to pay the business entity's debts.[141] Another list of factors establishing nominee status is (1) the taxpayer exercises dominion and control over the property while the property is in the nominee's name; (2) the nominee paid little or no consideration for the property; (3) the taxpayer placed property in the nominee's name in anticipation of a liability or lawsuit; (4) a close relationship exists between the taxpayer and the nominee; and (5) the taxpayer continues to enjoy the benefits of the property while the property is in the nominee's name.[142] Many of the alter ego cases have used a "reverse piercing" theory, that is, piercing the corporation to reach assets to pay the tax debt owed by the shareholder, rather than attempting to reach the assets of the shareholder to pay the debt of the corporation.

Also, a taxpayer generally may not defeat a tax lien by abandoning an interest in property.[143] Abandonment of an interest can take a form other than a renunciation of an interest in an estate.[144] A situation that illustrates this princi-

---

[141] See, e.g., Towe Antique Ford Found. v. IRS, 999 F2d 1387 (9th Cir. 1993); see also Porta-John of Am., Inc. v. United States, 4 F. Supp. 2d 688 (ED Mich. 1997) (applying Bodenhamer Bldg. Corp. v. Architectural Research Corp., 873 F2d 109, 111 (6th Cir. 1989), which said, "'The general principle in Michigan is that separate corporate identities will be respected, and thus corporate veils will be pierced only to prevent fraud or injustice . . . [and that a] court may find identity between business entities and pierce the corporate veil upon proof of three elements: first, the corporate entity must be a mere instrumentality of another entity or individual; second, the corporate entity must be used to commit some fraud or wrong; third, there must have been an unjust loss or injury to the plaintiff'"). For a review of the cases and the Service's position as of 1989, see Litigation Guideline Memorandum, In re: Administrative Action Against Nominee Alter Ego, or Transferee of a Taxpayer, LGM GL-21 (Oct. 31, 1989).

[142] See United States v. Reed, 88 AFTR2d 2001-5502 (D. Utah 2001) (gathering cases and holding that the taxpayer's mother was the nominee of son and daughter-in-law's residence as security for mother's alleged loan); see also Scoville v. United States, 87 AFTR2d 2001-2347 (8th Cir. 2001) (another list of factors establishing nominee status, and finding that a wife was the title owner of a farm and insurance policy, but that the taxpayer/husband was the beneficial owner of the insurance proceeds, and so they were subject to levy).

[143] See Scottsdale Ins. Co. v. English Furniture Indus., Inc., 83 AFTR2d 99-1714 (SD Ind. 1999) (taxpayer and taxpayer's transferee had allowed judgments to be entered against them).

[144] See, e.g., United States v. Mitchell, 403 US 190, 204–206 (1971) (holding renunciation under state law is ineffective to defeat a federal tax lien that attached to property rights that vested before the renunciation); United States v. Comparato, 22 F3d 455, 457–458 (2d Cir. 1994) (retroactive renunciations of interest in property pursuant to New York

ple is when a taxpayer with preexisting liens against his property inherits property, and then renounces the inheritance or disclaims any interest in the decedent's estate. In *Drye*, the Supreme Court settled the issue about the effect of a renunciation and held that the disclaimer cannot defeat the tax lien.[145]

[d] There Are No Exemptions From the Effect of the Lien

The general tax lien attaches to literally all property belonging to the taxpayer as of the assessment date or acquired by him during the time the lien is in effect. The Code provides for no exemptions with respect to the general tax lien, although certain types and amounts of property are exempt from levy.[146] A tax lien technically could be foreclosed even against exempt property, al-

---

law are ineffective against a federal tax lien); Drye Family 1995 Trust v. United States, 152 F3d 892 (8th Cir. 1998), aff'd sub nom. Drye v. United States, 120 S. Ct. 474 (S. Ct. 1999). Compare the decisions of the Ninth and the Fifth Circuits interpreting Arizona and Texas law, respectively. Mapes v. United States, 15 F3d 138 (9th Cir. 1994) (renunciation under Arizona law was effective to defeat a preexisting federal tax lien from attaching to an interest in an estate); Leggett v. United States, 120 F3d 592 (5th Cir. 1997) (renunciation under Texas law prevented a preexisting tax lien from attaching to interest in an estate). One view of the cases is that the conflicting results do not arise from different interpretations of federal lien law, but only as a result of different interpretations of the applicable state disclaimer laws. See Lawrence, Note, Drye Family 1995 Trust v. United States, 52 Tax Law. 627, 633–634 (1999).

[145] Drye v. United States, 528 US 49 (1999).

[146] Compare IRC § 6321 with IRC § 6334 (discussed infra ¶ 14.14[1]). United States v. Barbier, 896 F2d 377, 379 (9th Cir. 1990) (household effects exempt from levy held subject to lien in a Chapte 13 proceeding; "The plain words of section 6321 allow a tax lien to be attached to all of the taxpayer's property including property exempt from IRS levy"); Matter of Voelker, 42 F3d 1050 (7th Cir. 1994) (accord; gathering cases); American Trust v. American Community Mut. Ins. Co., 142 F3d 920 (6th Cir. 1998) (accord; Service successfully claimed lien attached in an interpleader action).

Despite the common law doctrine of custodia legis that prohibits any attachment of property and prevents the court from allocating the property in accordance with the purpose for which it was deposited, the tax lien has been held to attach to property in the custody of a court. See United States v. Van Cauwenberghe, 934 F2d 1048, 1063, n.12 (9th Cir. 1991) ("tax liens may attach to property held in custodia legis"), followed in In the Matter of the Application for Return to Brose & Poswistilo, Assignee of Albert R. Boettger, 75 AFTR2d 95-2640 (ED Pa. 1995) (cash seized from taxpayer was held in the custody of the state court when the Service made a jeopardy assessment, filed a notice of lien, and attempted to levy on the funds over the objection of the law firm assignee; held, the Service's lien attached to the funds, and was superior to the other claimants). On the same basis, an appeal bond a taxpayer paid into court to protect the Service was held subject to a Service lien and levy after the appeal was heard. See Plachter v. United States, 80 AFTR2d 97-6197 (SD Fla. 1997).

Note, however, that Section 6331 provides that property is not subject to levy if it has already been subject to attachment or garnishment under judicial process, or if it is in the custody of the court in which a bankruptcy of receivership proceeding is pending. IRC § 6332(a); Reg. § 301.6323-3, discussed infra ¶ 14.14[2].

though such property could not be administratively seized by levy. The pervasiveness of the tax lien is evidence that Congress intended to occupy the field as far as tax liens are concerned. Accordingly, any state statute purporting to exempt specified property from the claims of creditors is not effective against the general tax lien. Any exemption from the effect of the lien (to the extent that one exists at all) must be found in federal, not state, law, even where a state exemption law is incorporated into a nontax federal statute.[147]

[e] State Law Determines What Rights a Taxpayer Has in Property, and Federal Law Governs Whether Those Rights Constitute "Property" Subject to the Lien

Section 6321 creates the general tax lien that attaches to "all property" and "rights to property" of the taxpayer, but it does not create the rights, powers, and privileges, or interests, the sum of which is called "property." State law controls just how cognizable property interests are created. State law governs whether the legal interests the taxpayer has constitute "property" which can be reached by the general tax lien.[148] Federal law attaches the consequences to the determination. Section 6321 itself "creates no property rights but merely attaches consequences, federally defined, to rights created under state law."[149] The formulation approaches the metaphysical, but whether and to what extent the taxpayer has a property interest is a matter of state law, while whether the state-created property interest constitutes "property or rights to property," as well as the consequences of that determination (e.g., lien priority or sale), is a matter of federal law.[150] Several Supreme Court decisions illus-

---

[147] State exemption laws are incorporated by reference into the Bankruptcy Code (and the prior Bankruptcy Act). 11 USC § 522. Sears v. United States, 474 F. Supp. 988 (SD Tex. 1979); United States v. Heffron, 158 F2d 657 (9th Cir.), cert. denied, 331 US 831 (1947). However, it is clear that a tax lien nevertheless attaches to this property.

[148] Aquilino v. United States, 363 US 509 (1960); Morgan v. Comm'r, 309 US 78, 82 (1940).

[149] United States v. Bess, 357 US 51, 55 (1958); cf. Meyer v. United States, 375 US 233, 236 (1963) (citing Bess but saying, "[O]ur recent cases . . . [held] that state law controls the determination of what is included within . . . 'property or rights to property'").

[150] See Fidelity & Deposit Co. v. New York City Hous. Auth., 241 F2d 142, 144 (2d Cir. 1957) ("the statute [IRC § 6321] was fashioned to require the courts to determine for federal purposes whether those state-created interests are 'property' or 'rights to property'"); Randall v. H. Nakashima & Co., 542 F2d 270 (5th Cir. 1976) ("a federal court looks to state law to determine whether an interest exists, and then determines under a federal standard whether such an interest amounts to a 'property' interest"). Compare this rule to the developed bankruptcy rule that "property" is a question of federal law and whether a particular item of property is transferable or leviable is a matter of state law. See Segal v. Rochelle, 382 US 375 (1966) loss-carryback tax refunds constituted "property" for purposes of the old Bankruptcy Act despite contrary state law).

trate the operation of these principles. In *United States v. Bess*,[151] New Jersey law (1) gave the insured a right to change beneficiaries; (2) prohibited the insured the right to receive the proceeds of a policy while the insured lived; (3) gave the insured a chose in action to collect the cash surrender value of the policy; and (4) exempted the insured's chose in action from the lien of a private creditor, which otherwise could have attached to the insured's chose in action. New Jersey law, the Supreme Court held, should be followed to the extent that it gave the insured a chose in action to collect the cash surrender value of the policy, but New Jersey law could not exempt the chose in action from tax collection. New Jersey law governed the recognition of a property right, the chose in action, but New Jersey law could not be followed on the exemption of the chose in action from collection because exemption from a tax lien was a matter of federal law. In another case, *Aquilino v. United States*,[152] New York's Lien Law created a trust for monies owed to a contractor in which subcontractors had a right in the trust to monies. New York law applied to determine whether the taxpayer-contractor held monies in trust for the subcontractors, and if the contractor did hold the monies in trust, then the contractor did not have a right to property subject to the tax lien. Similarly, in *Durham Lumber Co.*,[153] under North Carolina law, the general contractor had a property interest in the face amount of the general construction contract only to the extent that the amount exceeded the aggregate of the claims of the subcontractors. Applying North Carolina law, the interest of the contractor which was subject to lien, could only be the residue left after the claims of the subcontractors.

Later cases describing the role of state law have greater emphasis on the point at which federal takes over the determination of whether the taxpayer's interest constitutes property and rights to property. Where the Service levied on a joint bank account to collect tax one of the joint owners owed to the Service, and state law prohibited creditors of one of the joint account owners from depleting the account, the Supreme Court in *National Bank of Commerce*, stated that state law determines what rights the taxpayer has in the property, [t]he question whether state law rights constitute 'property' or 'rights to property' is a matter for federal law."[154] *National Bank of Commerce* was decided in 1985, but by 1999, when it decided *Drye*, the Court self-critically observed that its earlier decisions might not have stated "meticulously" the division between state and federal law in deciding issues of whether property was subject to lien and levy. The Court concluded that it was satisfied that "the Code and interpretative case law place under federal, not state, control the

---

[151] United States v. Bess, 357 US 51, 55 (1958).

[152] Aquilino v. United States, 363 US 509 (1960).

[153] Durham Lumber Co. v. United States, 363 US 522 (1958).

[154] United States v. National Bank of Commerce, 472 US 713, 727 (1985).

ultimate issue whether a taxpayer has a beneficial interest in any property subject to levy for unpaid taxes."[155]

The Court in *Drye* also stated, "[W]e look initially to state law to determine what rights the taxpayer has in the property the Government seeks to reach, then to federal law to determine whether the taxpayer's state-delineated rights qualify as 'property' and 'rights to property' within the compass of the federal tax lien legislation." In resolving the issue in the case, the Court looked to Arkansas law, which, the Court concluded, gave the taxpayer at his mother's death a valuable, transferrable, and legally protected right to his share of property in his mother's estate. On the other hand, the taxpayer's right under state law to disclaim his inheritance was a personal right, not a valuable right that he could transfer to a third party. Under state law, therefore, the taxpayer's right to channel the inheritance by disclaiming or not disclaiming the inheritance ("a control rein") "rendered the inheritance 'property' or 'rights to property' belonging to the taxpayer within the meaning of section 6321, and hence subject to the federal tax lien." In other words, state law controlled a determination of the taxpayer's interest in his mother's estate (a valuable and transferrable right under Arkansas law), but federal law controlled the effect of the disclaimer (the right to channel the estate, which, if exercised, could defeat the federal tax lien).

Several years later, the Supreme Court returned to this question in a case involving the effect of a lien against one of the spouses holding real property as tenants by the entirety.[156] The Court evaluated the effect of the tax lien against one of the spouses under Michigan law noting that "despite the fiction [that neither tenant has a separate interest in entireties property], each tenant possesses individual rights in the estate sufficient to constitute 'property' or 'rights to property' for the purposes of the lien." Under Michigan law, the husband could not alienate the property himself (he needed the wife's consent), but he had the right to use the property, the right to income from the property, and the right to exclude others from the property. These state-created rights, the Supreme Court held, were sufficient under federal law to constitute "property" and "rights to property" belonging to the husband under federal law so that his interest in the entireties property was subject to the lien.

Some general observations can be drawn from these Supreme Court cases. State law defines the rights a taxpayer has in and to property. State law is also consulted to identify limitations on the rights of the taxpayer in the property. Where the rights of a creditor to the taxpayer's interests in the property are limited under state law, those limitations will be disregarded as an improper interference with the sovereign right of the United States to create exemptions from levy.

---

[155] Drye v. United States, 528 US 49, 58 (1999).
[156] United States v. Craft, 535 US 274, 276, 282–283 (2002).

[2] Real Property

Because of the broad scope of the general tax lien ("all property and rights to property"), any interest a taxpayer may have in land is likely to be subject to the lien. A focal point for analyzing an interest or "estate" in land is the right to possession—that is, where a person's right to possession begins and its duration. For purposes of the tax lien, the issue is whether the lien will attach to an interest or estate in land whose duration is or may be limited and whether the lien will attach to a right to possession in the future.

[a] Terminable Interests in Land

The greatest bundle of rights (the "estate") a person may own in land is a fee simple absolute, and there is no question that the tax lien will attach to such an estate. A life estate created by deed or will terminates at the death of the life tenant or other measuring life. A tax lien attaches to the interest of the delinquent taxpayer/life tenant, however, provided that the lien arises before the death of the life tenant or other measuring life.[157]

Dower and curtesy. The life estates of dower and curtesy arose out of the marital relationship and have been created by operation of law.[158] In general, the tax lien attaches to the delinquent spouse's property, irrespective of dower or curtesy rights.[159] Suppose property is bequeathed to a taxpayer, but the tax-

---

[157] See United States v. Schofield, 179 F. Supp. 332 (ED Pa. 1959) (assessment and demand made after death of life tenant). The same rule would apply to an estate in land that will be or is subject to be defeated or divested on the occurrence of a specific event (so-called qualified or defeasible fees). The property of the owner-delinquent taxpayer would be subject to the lien as long as the lien arises before the estate has expired or has been terminated or divested. United States v. United Banks of Denver, 542 F2d 819 (10th Cir. 1976). In United States v. Baran, 996 F2d 25 (2d Cir. 1993), the taxpayers requested the opportunity to satisfy the government's lien against a life estate before sale of the property. The court held that the Service could properly value the life estate through use of an actuarial table.

[158] Dower is the name given a wife's right in the husband's property; curtesy, the right of a husband in the wife's property. These legal life estates have been abolished in a majority of the states and do not exist in community-property states.

[159] If the delinquent taxpayer is the husband, the tax lien attaches to the property irrespective of the wife's right of dower. However, it appears that the Service will respect the priority of the dower or curtesy right if the marriage took place prior to the time the federal tax lien arose, unless the interest could be defeated by creditors of the spouse or by conveyance by him alone. Rev. Rul. 79-399, 1979-2 CB 398. Compare Washington v. United States, 402 F2d 3 (4th Cir. 1966), cert. denied, 402 US 978 (1971) (United States entitled to sell taxpayer's real estate free of his wife's contingent or inchoate dower interest), with United States v. Gearries, 82-2 USTC ¶ 9705 (ED Ky. 1981) (husband's right of curtesy to his wife's property was inchoate and did not become an interest in property to which a federal lien could attach until her death, and lost postnuptial agreement effectively released any rights he had in the property after her death).

payer disclaims any interest in the gift, does the tax lien against the taxpayer have any property right to which to attach under the applicable state law?[160]

The homestead exemption. The legal life estates of dower and curtesy should be distinguished from the homestead exemption provided in many states to exempt the homestead or residence of a debtor from execution or forced sale by creditors. Since these statutes do not create property rights as such but only restrict the right of a creditor to execute on the property of a debtor, they neither prevent the attachment of the tax lien nor exempt the property from levy since federal law governs in these matters.[161]

The homestead exemption does not defeat a tax lien or levy against the interest of a taxpayer-spouse, and it does not even protect the nondelinquent spouse from a sale of the homestead. In *United States v. Rodgers*, the Supreme Court held that a homestead exemption does not protect property held as a homestead by a nondelinquent spouse from sale under Section 7403, which generally permits a court to sell property subject to a lien.[162] Consequently, the Texas homestead exemption claimed by the widowed Mrs. Rodgers did not prevent a federal district court from enforcing tax liens against her deceased husband's interest in the homestead by selling the house in which she and her children still lived. If the Court recognized the state-created exemption, the forced sale authorized by Section 7403 would be nullified, a result that would violate the Constitution's supremacy clause. Accordingly, the Supreme Court held that Section 7403 grants power to a federal court to order the sale of the home itself, not just the delinquent taxpayer's interest in the property.

Where the home is sold, the nondelinquent spouse is entitled, as part of the distribution of proceeds required under Section 7403, to so much of the

---

[160] See Leggett v. United States, 120 F3d 592 (5th Cir. 1997):

> Under Texas law, [the taxpayer] had the right to accept Leggett's intended gift by taking possession of it, by exercising control and dominion over it, or by taking no action within the set time. She also had the right to reject Leggett's intended gift by filing a valid disclaimer within nine months. This right of decision was not, itself, a property right under Texas law. Because the [taxpayer] rejected the intended gift, she never had a property right. Therefore, the federal tax lien had nothing to which to attach.

See also Mapes v. United States, 15 F3d 138 (9th Cir. 1994) (tax lien did not attach because taxpayer made a timely disclaimer under Arizona law). Cf. United States v. Comparato, 22 F3d 455 (2d Cir. 1994) (holding that a disclaimer under New York law was rendered ineffective by a federal tax lien).

[161] Carter v. United States, 399 F2d 340 (5th Cir. 1968) (Louisiana homestead exemption held ineffective against tax lien); United States v. Heasley, 283 F2d 422 (8th Cir. 1960) (North Dakota homestead statute); United States v. Heffron, 158 F2d 657 (9th Cir.), cert. denied, 331 US 831 (1947) (California homestead exemption); United States v. St. Clair, 80-1 USTC 9364 (ND Tex. 1980) (Texas homestead exemption). Proceeds from the sale of homestead property are subject to a tax lien when both spouses are liable for tax. San Antonio Sav. Ass'n v. United States, 86-2 USTC 9665 (WD Tex. 1986).

[162] United States v. Rodgers, 461 US 677 (1983).

proceeds as represents complete compensation for the loss of the nondelinquent spouse's separate homestead interest. Sale of the homestead is not required to be authorized under all circumstances. Section 7403 gives a court limited discretion not to order a sale after engaging in an "individualized equitable balancing" of the interest of the government and the nondelinquent spouse. The Supreme Court has provided a nonexhaustive list of factors to be used in making this determination, but warned that it is not to be used as a mechanical checklist "to the exclusion of common sense and special circumstances." The Court suggested that the district court should consider such factors as the following:

- The extent to which the government's financial interests would be prejudiced if the forced sale of the partial interests actually liable for the delinquent taxes was ordered;
- Whether the nondelinquent spouse had a legally recognized expectation that the separate property would not be subject to forced sale by the delinquent taxpayer or his or her creditors;
- The likely prejudice to the nondelinquent spouse both in personal dislocation costs and in practical undercompensation; and
- The relative character and value of the nonliable and liable interests held in the property (e.g., whether the interest is possessory and the worth of the nonliable spouse's interest).

These factors indicate that a district court may refuse to order the sale of property for reasons at least similar to ones that support the recognition of the homestead exemption. In *Rodgers*, no individualized balancing of these factors had yet been attempted and the case was remanded.[163]

---

[163] United States v. Rodgers, 461 US 677, 710–712 (1983). For a circuit court's response to a *Rodgers*-type problem after the Supreme Court's decision in that case, see United States v. Pilla, 711 F2d 94 (8th Cir. 1983) (remand for the district court to determine "whether this is an appropriate case for the exercise of equitable discretion, and, if not, the extent to which (the spouse) should be compensated for the loss of her homestead interest, if at all").

For district court cases, see United States v. Bachman, 584 F. Supp. 1002 (SD Iowa 1984) (sale ordered); United States v. Molina, 584 F. Supp. 1011 (SD Tex. 1984) (sale ordered; percentage of proceeds to be paid to spouse not determined, but to be based on present discounted value of life estate using statutory or commercial actuarial tables). See also Indiana Nat'l Bank v. Gamble, 612 F. Supp. 1272 (ND Ill. 1984) ("although a forced sale would, of course, cause personal dislocation to Mrs. Gamble, the only way to avoid that dislocation would be to allow Dr. Gamble to continue in possession of his house without paying off his creditors first"); United States v. Thomassen, 610 F. Supp. 386 (D. Neb. 1985) (sale of taxpayer's one-half interest would not prejudice the Service where innocent co-tenant would suffer some financial hardship if entire property sold); Harris v. United States, 764 F2d 1126 (5th Cir. 1985) (use of Treasury single-life actuarial tables to determine value of the wife's homestead interest).

The interest of a lessee is an estate for a term of years, which terminates at the expiration of the lease term. A tax lien attaches to the lessee-taxpayer's leasehold, even if the lease contains a restrictive covenant requiring approval of the lessor before a transfer of the leasehold interest may be made.[164] If the lessor has terminated the lease for a breach of any covenant or condition prior to the time the lien arises, the lessee has "no property" to which the lien could attach.[165]

A delinquent taxpayer's right to possession of land may begin in the future after the expiration of a life estate or a term of years or on the occurrence or nonoccurrence of an event in the creating instrument (e.g., a possibility of reverter or a right of reentry). As a general matter, these so-called future interests are transferable and subject to the claims of creditors and, accordingly, are subject to the tax lien. For example, the reversionary interest of the grantor of a ten-year trust is subject to the federal tax lien.[166] However, if the interest is contingent, so that ultimate possession is uncertain because some condition precedent must be fulfilled, the interest of the remaindermen may be so contingent as not to constitute "property or a right to property"—for example, where an interest is subject to the condition that the remainderman survive the life tenant.[167]

[b] Concurrent Ownership

In the modern law of real property, there are five principal forms of co-ownership: a tenancy in common, joint tenancy, tenancy by the entirety, community property, and tenancy in partnership.

Tenancy in common and joint tenancy. In a tenancy in common, each of the co-tenants has a distinct and separate interest in the property, but the right

---

Cf. United States v. Bierbrauer, 936 F2d 373, 376 (8th Cir. 1991) (sale of residence, despite spouse's homestead interest, was approved; no real prospect that taxpayer spouse's interest could be sold separately).

It has been said that the *Rodgers* factors "serve to limit the district court's equitable discretion *not* to sell, and to provide a framework under which it must justify its refusal to order a sale under [S]ection 7403 . . . so that [c]onsideration of these undue hardship factors is thus a matter of judicial grace, not entitlement." United States v. Davenport, 106 F3d 1333 (7th Cir. 1997).

[164] Stagecrafters Club v. District of Columbia Div. of Am. Legion, 211 F2d 811 (DC Cir. 1954), aff'g 110 F. Supp. 481 (DDC 1953).

[165] Carolina Apartment Investors "A" v. United States, 77-1 USTC ¶ 9262 (CD Cal. 1977).

[166] In re Lackey, 72-2 USTC 9578 (MDNC 1972).

[167] But see United States v. United Banks of Denver, 542 F2d 819 (10th Cir. 1976) (Colorado Supreme Court certified that interest of remainderman was vested interest subject to complete defeasance, not future interest subject to condition precedent and, therefore, contingent).

of possession is common to all co-tenants. The separate and distinct interest of a tenant is subject to the claims of creditors and, accordingly, to the general tax lien.[168] What distinguishes a joint tenancy from other types of ownership is that joint tenants have one and the same interest, accruing by one and the same conveyance, commencing at one and the same time, and held by one and the same possession.[169] For some purposes joint tenants are viewed as a unity (a single person), but for other purposes they are recognized as having individual rights with respect to the property. One of the characteristics of joint tenancy is the right of survivorship. On the death of one of the joint tenants, his interest does not pass to his heirs or under his will. The entire ownership remains in the surviving joint tenants; in effect, the interest of the deceased joint tenant disappears. This unity of ownership and the disappearing interest characteristic of joint tenancy raise the question of whether the interest of a joint tenant/taxpayer is "property" to which the lien attaches. Most courts have brushed aside the "property" question and have held that the delinquent taxpayer/joint tenant has an "interest" in the property that is subject to the tax lien[170] and that, in an event, may be foreclosed pursuant to Section 7403 (authorizing a district court to decree the sale of property in which a delinquent taxpayer has "any right, title or interest" to satisfy the tax lien) against the entire property to satisfy the liability of the delinquent joint tenant.[171]

Tenancy by the entirety. A tenancy by the entirety is a kind of co-ownership peculiar to husband and wife in which the unity of ownership is even more pronounced than in a joint tenancy. Although the right of survivorship exists as it does in a joint tenancy, in the majority of states a husband and wife have equal rights to possession, use, and revenues from the property. Also, under many state laws, neither spouse can individually transfer his or her interest during marriage or his or her right of survivorship. Should state law control in determining whether the delinquent taxpayer/spouse had an interest in entireties property to which the tax lien could attach? Faced with the issue, some courts concluded that the debtor or delinquent spouse had no interest in

---

[168] See Rev. Rul. 79-55, 1979-1 CB 400 (lien attaches to a delinquent taxpayer's interest in a time-sharing condominium unit and related areas but not to the interests of any other owners in the condominium unit or the condominium itself).

[169] Cunningham, Stoebuck, & Whitman, The Law of Property § 5.3, 202–203 (1984).

[170] Shaw v. United States, 331 F2d 493 (9th Cir. 1964).

[171] United States v. Kocher, 468 F2d 503 (2d Cir. 1972), cert. denied, 411 US 931 (1973); Washington v. United States, 402 F2d 3 (4th Cir. 1966), cert. denied, 402 US 978 (1971); United States v. Trilling, 328 F2d 699 (7th Cir. 1964); United States v. Overman, 424 F2d 1142 (9th Cir. 1970) (community property). Contra Folsom v. United States, 306 F2d 361 (5th Cir. 1962); United States v. Gurley, 415 F2d 144 (5th Cir. 1969) (delinquent taxpayer himself had "no property" in the jointly owned property). Compare Medaris v. United States, 884 F2d 832 (5th Cir. 1989) (Texas community property law permits levy on delinquent husband's entire earnings to satisfy lien against him; *Overman* distinguished).

the property that was subject to tax lien.[172] In *United States v. Craft*, the Supreme Court resolved uncertainty about the attachment of the federal tax lien to the interest of a spouse in entireties property.[173] A couple in Michigan held real property as tenant by the entireties. The Service assessed income tax owed by the husband and claimed that its tax lien attached to the husband's interest in the property. The Court held that "despite the fiction [that neither tenant has separate interest in entireties property], each tenant possesses individual rights in the estate sufficient to constitute 'property' or 'rights to property' for the purposes of the lien." Evaluating the husband's interests under Michigan law, the court found that although the husband could not alienate the property himself, he could do so with the consent of his wife; he also had the right to use the property, the right to income from the property; and the right to exclude others from the property. These state-created rights, the Supreme Court held, were sufficient under federal law to constitute "property" and "rights to property belong to" the husband, and so his interest in entireties property was subject to the tax lien.

Where both spouses owe the tax, the lien attaches to the entire property.[174] But the where there is an innocent spouse and a tax-delinquent one, courts reached different results.[175] Some states permit creditors to reach the debtor-

---

[172] American Nat'l Bank of Jacksonville v. United States, 255 F2d 504 (5th Cir. 1958) (under Florida law, liens for taxes owed by a husband do not attach to Florida real property held by husband and wife as tenants by the entirety); Benson v. United States, 442 F2d 1221 (DC Cir. 1971) (applying District of Columbia law); United States v. Hutcherson, 188 F2d 326 (8th Cir. 1951) (applying Missouri law). Geiselman v. United States, 961 F2d 1 (1st Cir. 1992) ("Massachusetts law governing tenancies by the entirety . . . gives the husband a significant personal interest in the estate that is both distinguishable and separable from that of his wife. . . . The husband's creditors can attach his interest; the wife's creditors can attach nothing"); Talbot v. United States, 850 F. Supp. 969 (D. Wyo. 1994) (under Wyoming law, tax lien against husband did not attach to property owned with wife as tenancy by the entirety).

[173] United States v. Craft, 535 US 274, 276, 282–283 (2002). See Notice 2003-60, 2003-39 IRB 643 (Sept. 11, 2003), providing guidance on collection of property held in a tenancy by the entirety where only the spouse owes taxes after *Craft*. In general, the Service recognizes the potential hardship to the nonliable spouse and will decide whether to seize and sell the property on a case-by-case basis, and will consider the taxpayer's interest in the property to be limited to one-half of its value.

[174] Where both spouses are liable for the tax, a tenancy by the entirety does not prevent collection of the tax. Tony Thornton Auction Serv., Inc. v. United States, 791 F2d 635 (8th Cir. 1986). Angello v. United States, 93-2 USTC ¶ 50,391 (MD Pa. 1993) (applying Pennsylvania law and finding entireties property was subject to tax lien because there was a joint and several liability of the husband and wife). Cf. United States v. Scharf, 91-1 USTC ¶ 50,205 (ED Mo. 1991) (finding that tenancy by entireties had not been created under Missouri law).

[175] Consider the effect of different state laws on the results in In re Rudie William Pletz, 80 AFTR2d 97-8355 (Bank. D. Or. 1997) (tax lien attached to taxpayer-debtor's interest in entireties property owned with his nondebtor spouse under Oregon law, and so

spouse's interest, subject to the other spouse's right of survivorship, with the result that the lien can attach to a one-half possessory or income interest for the joint lives of the tenants, and the entire fee if the debtor-spouse survives.[176]

the Service could sell the property to satisfy its tax lien) and In re the Marriage of Foust, 82 AFTR2d 98-5210 (SD Ind. 1998) (divorced spouse had priority over the tax lien in the proceeds of the sale of entireties property and one half of the interest on the proceeds, applying Indiana law).

[176] See Hiles v. Fisher, 144 NY 306, 39 NE 337, 338 (1895) (creditor becomes a tenant in common with the nonliable spouse, subject to the nonliable spouse's right of survivorship); King v. Greene, 330 NJ 395, 153 A2d 49 (1959). While the right of survivorship survives transfers if the nondebtor-spouse retains an interest in the property, it does not survive a sale by the nondebtor-spouse.

When the taxpayer-husband transferred his interest in entireties property to his wife, she took his interest subject to the tax lien, but the tax lien, in turn, was subject to the wife's right of survivorship. After they were divorced, the wife sold the property. Applying New Jersey law, the wife's right of survivorship was held to be terminated, and the sale vested the buyers with a fee simple interest subject to the Service's lien. United States v. Diemer, 859 F. Supp. 126 (DNJ 1995). The tax lien attached to a one-half interest in the property, the court held, so that the Service was not entitled to one half of the current value of the property; it was entitled only to one half the value of the property, subject to any other liens having priority over the tax lien, on the date the taxpayer-husband transferred the property to his nondebtor-wife.

Diemer was reversed on appeal. United States v. Avila, 88 F3d 229 (3d Cir. 1996). The circuit court reversed the district court's holding that the value of the lien on the debtor-spouse's interest was limited to the value of his share of the property on the transfer date, pointing out that the debtor-spouse's transfer of his interest in the property to his wife did not affect the tax lien that had already attached, and which under Section 6322 continued until the assessed liability was collected or became unenforceable because of lapse of time. The circuit court also applied New Jersey law to find that in the divorce settlement, when the wife received the debtor-spouse's interest in the property held by the entireties, the tax lien that attached to the debtor-spouse's one-half interest he conveyed continued to attach to his interest, subject to the nondebtor-wife's right of survivorship.

Accordingly, if the debtor-spouse predeceased the nondebtor-wife, the tax lien would be extinguished. However, if the nondebtor-wife predeceased the debtor-spouse, the tax lien would attach to the entire property. The circuit court also concluded that when the nondebtor-wife transferred the property to the Avilas, she transferred the debtor-spouse's right of survivorship subject to the tax lien. Under the circumstances, the transfer did not terminate the right of survivorship. Because there was no evidence about whether either the debtor-spouse or the nondebtor-wife were alive, the case was remanded. The Diemers, who had purchased the property from the Avilas, were held to succeed to the Avilas' right of subrogation against the amount of the tax lien.

In another case involving the value of a tax lien on jointly owned property, the lien attached before the taxpayer spouse's death and the Service foreclosed on its lien two years after the taxpayer spouse's death. The innocent spouse argued that the Service could recover only one half the value of the property on the date of the taxpayer's death ($76,250), but the Service contended successfully that it was entitled to one half of the proceeds on the date of the foreclosure sale ($86,550). United States v. Librizzi, 108 F3d 136 (7th Cir. 1997). A circuit court majority interpreted Wisconsin law and concluded that when the taxpayer's one-half interest passed to the innocent spouse by operation of law, it came encumbered by the tax lien so that when the Service later foreclosed its lien, the

On the death of the delinquent spouse, the Service has also contended that the survivor spouse is liable as a transferee for the spouse's delinquent income taxes. Courts have generally rejected this contention and found no transfer to have taken place, because the survivor of a joint tenancy or tenancy by the entirety takes the full estate by virtue of the original grant of tenancy, not by a transfer from the deceased co-tenant.[177]

The timing of the creation of the tenancy by the entirety is important. If the tax lien has attached to the property before, not after the debtor spouse has transferred the property into a tenancy by the entirety, the innocent or nondebtor spouse takes the property subject to the tax lien.[178] Similarly, where property held by the entireties was sold after the couple filed for bankruptcy protection, the sale terminated the tenancy by the entireties.[179] However, when the nondebtor spouse died during the bankruptcy proceeding, the proceeds became the sole property of the debtor husband's bankruptcy estate, and available to the Service, one of his sole creditors, rather than to only joint creditors of the husband and deceased wife.

[3] Personal Property

Personal property includes all objects and rights capable of ownership, except estates and interests in land, and generally means money, goods, chattels (i.e., tangible movable property), and intangible property, such as choses in action, literary property and copyrights, patents, and trademarks. The owner of a chose in action must do something to obtain the money or tangible property to which he has a right. In other words, a chose in action is a "thing" (money or tangible property) that a person does not yet have possession of but has a right

---

Service was entitled to the value of the lien at that time. The majority also pointed to Wisconsin law, under which liens other than judgment liens remain in force against the surviving joint tenant. Thus, the majority refused to accept that the lien was extinguished on the date of death, or that the lien's value was "frozen" on the date of death.

[177] Tooley v. Comm'r, 121 F2d 350, 354, 356 (9th Cir. 1941). Accord Parker v. Comm'r, 122 F2d 230, 231 (9th Cir. 1941); Irvine v. Helvering, 99 F2d 265 (8th Cir. 1938); Fecarrota v. United States, 154 F. Supp. 592, 597–598 (D. Ariz. 1956). This result would not appear to apply if the joint tenancy arises by gift, rather than on the original grant (Arlington F. Brown, 24 TC 256, 266–267), nor to gift and estate taxes (IRC § 6324). See generally Comment, "Section 6901: Transferee Liability," 30 Tax Law. 433, 446 (1977). For a further description of transferee liability, see Chapter 17.

[178] United States v. Davenport, 106 F3d 1333 (7th Cir. 1997) (joint tenancy existing at the time the tax lien attached was converted into tenancy by the entirety under Illinois law).

[179] Ballard v. United States (In re Ballard), 65 F3d 367 (4th Cir. 1995) (a divided court; because the sale took place in the course of a bankruptcy proceeding for the purpose of paying creditors, the dissent would have divided the proceeds of the sale between the bankruptcy estates for distribution to their respective creditors).

to or a right to demand in an action at law. Therefore, chose in action includes, money due on a bond, note, or contract; damages due for breach of contract; open or unliquidated accounts; or a claim for damages arising out of tortious conduct and a policy of insurance. For example, a debt owed to a taxpayer is subject to lien and can be seized by levy on the debtor. The predecessor of Section 6331 provided for levies, inter alia, "evidences of debt."[180] The general tax lien attaches to all personal property, but the variety of types of personal property makes further discussion necessary.

[a] Accounts and Executory Contracts

An executory contract (i.e., a contract not yet performed) has been held not to constitute "property or rights to property" at least where the performance involved was one for personal services.[181] The theory is that, although earned salary and wages are subject to a lien for unpaid taxes, future earnings contingent on the performance of services by the taxpayer represent a contingent rather than an existing right that may be subject to the lien. Where personal services are not involved, the result is less clear, but the weight of authority favors the proposition that the lien attaches to the contract right, especially since the UCC is in force in all states except Louisiana. Under the UCC, an "account"[182] may be the subject of a security interest. Consequently, under the UCC, a contract right or account constitutes "property" to which a tax lien may attach even if payment has not been earned by performance.[183]

---

[180] United States v. Long Island Drug Co., 115 F2d 983, 985–986 (2d Cir. 1940); United States v. Williams, 959 F. Supp. 210 (SDNY 1997) (shareholder owned the stock of a parent corporation, and had borrowed from both the parent and one of its subsidiaries; the parent and the subsidiaries filed a consolidated return and had a tax liability; the Service served levies on the shareholder to seize the shareholder's debt to the parent and the debt to the subsidiary, and the levies were upheld because all the debts to the consolidated group were subject to lien and levy).

[181] United States v. Long Island Drug Co., 115 F2d 983 (2d Cir. 1940).

[182] The UCC defines "account" as "any right to payment for goods sold or leased or for services rendered which is not evidenced by an instrument or chattel paper, whether or not it has been earned by performance." UCC § 9-106. Prior to 1972, the UCC used the term "contract right," which was defined as "any right to payment under a contract not yet earned by performance and not evidenced by an instrument or chattel paper." J. White and R. Summers, Uniform Commercial Code, Vol. 2, Ch. 23 (1988).

[183] Randall v. H. Nakashima & Co., 542 F2d 270 (5th Cir. 1976) (contract was partially performed); Pine Builders, Inc. v. United States, 413 F. Supp. 77 (ED Va. 1976) (account held to constitute a bilateral contract). In a pre-UCC case following United States v. Long Island Drug Co., 115 F2d 983 (2d Cir. 1940), the Third Circuit held that an executory contract between the taxpayer and A to sell incomplete jackets from cutout materials did not constitute property to which the tax lien could attach where, after tax lien filing, the taxpayer assigned to C amounts to become due from A under the executory contract. On notice of the assignment, A agreed to pay C directly all monies to become due under

[b] Alimony

The Service has long maintained that alimony payments are subject to the federal tax lien,[184] and this position has received judicial support.[185] The problem is that alimony and support payments are subject to modification. Consequently, although it is clear that the tax lien attaches to the property in the alimony or support payments, there are obvious, and as yet unresolved, problems in enforcing the lien.[186]

[c] Bank Accounts

Under most state laws, a person who places money on general deposit in a bank is entitled to the money and becomes a creditor of the bank. Thus, a tax lien would attach to the "chose in action" owned by the delinquent taxpayer.[187] The issue that frequently arises is whether an indebtedness the depositor owes to the bank, which creates a right of setoff in the bank, reduces to that extent the "property" of the taxpayer in the bank deposit subject to the lien. The weight of authority is that in order for the property of the taxpayer to be reduced, the bank must have taken some affirmative action to exercise its right of setoff.[188] A joint bank account is subject to lien and levy and although

---

the contract with the taxpayer. The Third Circuit held that the result was a purchase-money mortgage because C, the assignee, financed the property producing the transaction. In re Halprin, 280 F2d 407 (3d Cir. 1960); Harter v. District Dir., 68-2 USTC 9458 (D. Wash. 1968). This result was criticized in *Randall v. H. Nakashima & Co.* In United States v. General Motors Corp., 929 F2d 249 (6th Cir. 1991), before the tax was assessed and the lien arose, the taxpayer assigned accounts receivable, one of which was due from General Motors, to a bank as security for a loan. Under Michigan law, the assignment was held to have transferred the taxpayer's "property" in the account to the bank, so that General Motors held no "property" of the taxpayer for the Service to seize by levy.

[184] Rev. Rul. 53-89, 1953-1 CB 474.

[185] United States v. Russell, 74-2 USTC 9540 (D. Conn. 1974); United States v. Rye, 550 F2d 682 (1st Cir. 1977) (support payments).

[186] See United States v. Rye, 550 F2d 682 (1st Cir. 1977).

[187] United States v. Citizens & So. Nat'l Bank, 538 F2d 1101 (5th Cir. 1976), cert. denied, 430 US 945 (1977).

[188] United States v. Citizens & So. Nat'l Bank, 538 F2d 1101 (5th Cir. 1976), cert. denied, 430 US 945 (1977); United States v. Sterling Nat'l Bank & Trust Co., 494 F2d 919, 921–922 (2d Cir. 1974); United States v. First Nat'l Bank, 348 F. Supp. 388, 389 (D. Ariz. 1970), aff'd per curiam, 458 F2d 513 (9th Cir. 1972); United States v. Central Bank of Denver, 843 F2d 1300 (10th Cir. 1988) (bank's "right of setoff was not exercised in a timely and certain manner so as to defeat the IRS administrative levy"; bank made the setoff after it received the notice of levy); Cache Valley Bank v. United States, 866 F2d 1242 (10th Cir. 1989) (where lien attaches before bank right of setoff, the bank takes the deposits subject to the lien on exercising its setoff right). A bank's setoff claim also is an issue where a levy is served. See infra ¶ 14.14[4]. But see IRC § 6323(b)(10) with respect to relative priority where a passbook loan is made. Cf. United States v. Intermoun-

the lien technically applies only to the taxpayer's interest in the account, the account may be seized by levy even if only one of the co-owners is liable for the tax.[189] However, the nature and extent of the interest of the taxpayer and the co-owner depend on the facts and state law.[190]

[d] Suits Against Third Parties

A right to property (chose in action) is subject to a general tax lien. The right is not exempt from the lien merely because it would take a lawsuit to collect, whether the claim is definite in amount or unliquidated and whether it arises out of contract or tort.[191]

[e] Insurance

During his life, the insured-taxpayer has the right to change the beneficiary, borrow on the policy, and take its cash surrender value. If the taxpayer assigns the insurance policy to the beneficiary or an employer owns the policy on the life of the insured employee, only a tax lien arising out of a tax assessment against the policy owner, not the insured, would attach to the policy's

---

tain Region Concrete Co., 636 F. Supp. 280 (D. Utah 1986) (a tax lien could not be foreclosed on a taxpayer's bank account because title to the deposit of money in a bank was held to have passed to the bank and was subject to the bank's right to apply the obligation of the taxpayer-customer). This case is discussed further at ¶ 16.03[2]. See also United States v. Intermountain Region Concrete Co., 636 F. Supp. 280 (D. Utah 1986) (where bank offset debtor-taxpayer's bank balances pursuant to a right of offset, bank's right was superior to tax lien because Service's right was no greater than that of taxpayer).

[189] United States v. National Bank of Commerce, 472 US 713 (1985). See discussion infra ¶ 14.14[4]. United States v. Ragsdale, 206 F. Supp. 613 (WD Tenn. 1962).

[190] Rev. Rul. 55-187, 1955-1 CB 197; United States v. Bershad, 58-2 USTC ¶ 9528 (D. Ariz. 1958); Cole v. Bookwalter, 170 F. Supp. 527 (WD Mo. 1959). If the account is held by husband and wife as tenants by the entirety, under most state laws the account would not be subject to a lien against one spouse. See the cases cited supra at notes 175–180, regarding entireties.

[191] United States v. Hubbell, 323 F2d 197 (5th Cir. 1963) (contractor's right to recovery for extra work performed); Bottom v. Grace, 79-2 USTC 9504 (SD Ohio 1979) aff'd per curiam sub nom. Bottom v. United States, 636 F2d 1216 (6th Cir. 1980) (personal injury claim settlement); Greenup v. United States, 239 F. Supp. 330 (D. Mont. 1965) (cause of action for unjust enrichment). For a case illustrating the reach of the federal tax lien, see United States v. Camparato, 850 F. Supp. 153 (EDNY 1993) (taxpayers' interests in settlement proceeds of malpractice actions for their son's pain and suffering before his death and for his wrongful death, determined under New York law); United States v. Stonehill, 83 F3d 1156 (9th Cir. 1996) (under California law, the taxpayers' interests in lawsuits against a municipality were property subject to lien, and so subject to sale under the procedures provided in 28 USC § 2001).

cash value.[192] The insured-taxpayer's rights terminate at his death. What is the effect of a tax lien that attaches to all property and rights to property of the taxpayer before his death, on the proceeds of the policy the insurance company pays to a beneficiary? The Supreme Court answered this question in *United States v. Bess*,[193] saying that the full proceeds of the policy paid to the beneficiary were not subject to the tax lien because the insured himself could not have obtained these funds. However, the premiums paid in and accumulated were, in effect, a fund held by the insurer for the insured, and this "fund" was subject to the lien even where paid over by the insured to the beneficiary.[194]

What if a tax assessment is not made until after the death of the taxpayer? At death, the taxpayer's rights in the policy have terminated. Consequently, there is no "property" to which the lien can attach. Because life insurance proceeds are transferred to the beneficiary at the death of the taxpayer, the Service has asserted that the beneficiary is liable as transferee for the deceased taxpayer's tax to the extent of the insurance proceeds.[195] In *Commissioner v. Stern*, the Supreme Court held that the transferee liability provision of the Code is a procedural statute only; thus, the liability of the transferee-beneficiary depends upon applicable state law.[196] The tax lien also attaches to property insurance proceeds.[197]

---

[192] United States v. Burgo, 175 F2d 196 (3d Cir. 1949). However, in this situation the question then becomes: who is the policy owner? If the insured retains the right to change the beneficiary and to withdraw the cash value, the fact that the beneficiary pays the premiums may not, without more, make the beneficiary the owner. United States v. Fried, 309 F2d 851 (2d Cir. 1962) (applying New York law).

[193] United States v. Bess, 357 US 51 (1958). Procedural problems with respect to a levy served on an insurer to seize the "property or rights to property" of the insurer were resolved in FTLA by amending Section 6332(b).

[194] However, if, at the insured's death, the policy is pledged for a debt senior to the tax lien, only the net amount of the policy's cash value may be reached in the beneficiary's hands to satisfy the tax lien. Meyer v. United States, 375 US 233, 236 (1963) (Supreme Court refused to apply the doctrine of marshaling of assets so that the senior debt, a policy loan, would be satisfied out of the excess of the proceeds over the cash value, leaving the cash value to satisfy the tax lien). See also Section 6323(b)(9) with respect to the relative priority of a policy loan and tax lien. If the insured died intestate, under Missouri law, it has been held that the decedent did not own property after his death, and so a tax lien did not attach to the property in the estate. Igoe v. United States, 717 SW2d 524 (Mo. 1986).

[195] IRC § 6901.

[196] Comm'r v. Stern, 357 US 39 (1958) (transferee held not liable because Kentucky law provided that beneficiary of life insurance policy not liable to insured's creditors absent fraud).

[197] See PPG Indus., Inc. v. Hartford Fire Ins. Co., 384 F. Supp. 91 (SDNY 1974), aff'd, 531 F2d 58 (2d Cir. 1976). However, in cases where a person had a security interest in collateral and "proceeds," most courts have concluded that the insurance proceeds were proceeds of the collateral subject to the security interest. Id.; Aetna Ins. Co. v. Texas Thermal Indus., Inc., 436 F. Supp. 371 (ED Tex. 1977). As a result, if the security interest

[f] Licenses and Franchises

In general, a license or franchise reflects the permission or authority granted by a sovereign or public authority to a person or corporation to engage in a particular activity or enterprise affecting the public. The determination of whether a license or franchise is "property" depends on state law, but the weight of authority is that a license such as a liquor license or franchise is a kind of personal property subject to the lien[198] and that the taxpayer's property

---

had priority over the tax claim, the secured party, not the Service, would take the proceeds. See also United States v. Paladin, 539 F. Supp. 100 (WDNY 1982).

[198] United States v. McFadden Express, 67-2 USTC 9635 (D. Conn. 1967). See Barr v. United States, 337 F2d 693 (6th Cir. 1964); United States v. California, 281 F2d 726 (9th Cir. 1960) (liquor license). In re American Way Food Serv. Corp. v. IRS, 48 BR 79, 85-1 USTC 9296 (Bankr. WD Mich. 1985) (following *Barr*, Michigan liquor license held subject of tax lien); JFWIRS, Ltd. v. United States, 607 F. Supp. 566 (MD Pa. 1985) (Pennsylvania liquor license). See also 21 W. Lancaster Corp. v. Main Line Rest., Inc., 790 F2d 354 (3d Cir. 1986) (Pennsylvania liquor license constitutes "property" for purposes of a tax lien, but creditor of taxpayer could not obtain security interest in license because license was not property for purposes of a security interest under Pennsylvania law); In re Bay Ridge Inn, 94 F2d 555 (2d Cir. 1938) (liquor license held to be a privilege). See Chicago Mercantile Exch. v. United States, 650 F. Supp. 141 (ND Ill. 1986), aff'd, 840 F2d 1352 (7th Cir. 1988) (commodities exchange membership seat was not "property" subject to a tax lien until all claims were satisfied in accordance with Chicago Mercantile Exchange rules).

Some courts have said that "property" means anything of pecuniary value so that state law does not control. Paramount Fin. Co. v. United States, 379 F2d 543 (6th Cir. 1967). Accord Commonwealth of Ky. Dep't of Alcoholic Beverage Control v. United States, 77-1 USTC 9340 (WD Ky. 1977) (liquor license not property under Kentucky law, but found to constitute property anyway because it had pecuniary value). This approach seems in error because it ignores the role of state law in defining "property" for purposes of the tax lien.

As cases cited above show, a liquor license has generally been considered to constitute "property" or "rights to property" subject to levy and sale, because the state has created valuable rights in the license that could be transferred or sold. See also In re Terwilliger's Catering Plus, Inc., 911 F2d 1168 (6th Cir. 1990) (applying Ohio law, citing *Paramount Fin. Co.*, supra, and *21 W. Lancaster Corp.*, supra). See also United States v. Comptroller of the Treasury, 80 AFTR2d 97-6149 (D. Md. 1997) (finding that although a liquor license was not regarded as property with Maryland, the Service's tax lien attached to the taxpayer's rights in the liquor license, and following *Terwilliger*, held that the Service tax liens had priority in the proceeds in the sale of the license, because at the time the Service's tax liens were filed, Maryland's restriction on the transfer of the license when state taxes were unpaid was contingent and inchoate). See also In re Main St. Beverage Corp., Debtor, 83 AFTR2d 99-457 (D. NJ 1999) (liquor license under New Jersey law constituted "property" for purposes of a tax lien, but was not property in which a taxpayer could grant a security interest, even in the proceeds of the sale of the license, following the Third Circuit's decision in *21 West Lancaster Corp.*, supra, which involved a Pennsylvania-issued liquor license, and noting that after *21 West Lancaster Corp.*, Pennsylvania changed its law to permit a creditor to have a security interest in a liquor license).

interest may be defeated by the licensing authority's refusal to honor the transfer.[199] On the other hand, an Interstate Commerce Commission certificate is held to be a privilege and not "property" subject to the lien.[200] Accordingly, the Service attempts to secure approval of the transfer from the licensing authority before foreclosing its lien and selling a license.[201] If sale is approved, the tax lien clearly attaches to the proceeds of the sale.[202]

[g] Trusts

If the grantor-taxpayer may revoke a trust, the tax lien attaches to the corpus of the trust.[203] In a sense, the trust in this circumstance is an alter ego of the taxpayer. Also, where a grantor establishes a trust for himself for life and reserves a general power of appointment, both the income and the settlor's beneficial life interest are subject to a tax lien.[204] Similarly, a tax lien attaching to the property of a beneficiary should attach to his interest in a trust if, for example, he has the power to invade the corpus. On the other hand, where the

---

The Ninth Circuit has held that the license is subject to the right of the state to refuse to transfer the license when the owner is delinquent in the payment of taxes. *United States v. California*, supra; In re Farmers Mkts., Inc., 792 F2d 1400 (9th Cir. 1986). But the Sixth Circuit has held that such a state or lien must be choate in order to take priority over a federal tax lien. *In re Terwilliger's Catering Plus, Inc.*, supra (Ohio's lien inchoate because not enforceable at time assessment was made). For a description of the choate lien doctrine, see ¶ 16.02[2].

[199] United States v. California, 281 F2d 726 (9th Cir. 1960) (state imposed restriction of transferability—i.e., payment of delinquent sales taxes). But cf. Business Title Corp. v. Division of Labor Law Enforcement, 76-2 USTC 9644 (Cal. 1976) (where transfer is approved, state priority rules as to proceeds of sales cannot defeat tax lien priority).

[200] Fidler v. United States, 72-2 USTC 9506 (NDNY 1972) (ICC and Public Service Commission certificates); In re Tri-State Transp., Inc., 81-1 USTC 9395 (SD Ga. 1981) (Georgia Public Service Commission certificates held property subject to lien following *Fidler* and refusing to follow Sandri v. United States, 266 F. Supp. 139 (D. Mass. 1967); United States v. Berkshire St. Ry. Co., 219 F. Supp. 861 (D. Mass. 1963) (street railway license held a privilege, not a property right subject to lien). Proceeds from the sale of an FCC license constitute property within the meaning of Section 6321, although the FCC has ruled that FCC licenses may not be subjected to private liens. In re Atlantic Bus. & Community Dev. Corp., 994 F2d 1069 (3d Cir. 1993) (finding no interference with regulatory scheme when Service is creditor and that liquor license cases are analogous).

[201] When a common-carrier certificate was sold under levy and the state then withheld consent to the transfer, the purchaser was permitted to recover the price. Sandri v. United States, 266 F. Supp. 139 (D. Mass. 1967).

[202] United States v. Blackett, 220 F2d 21 (9th Cir. 1955).

[203] United States v. Pulle, 159 F. Supp. 45 (EDNY 1958).

[204] United States v. Ritter, 558 F2d 1165 (4th Cir. 1978) (general power of appointment). But see United States v. Baldwin, 77-1 USTC 9341 (D. Md. 1976), aff'd, 586 F2d 324 (4th Cir. 1978) (settlor's reserved right to income for life held subject to lien, but not the corpus of the trust).

taxpayer-beneficiary has only a remainder interest, the interest may be so contingent as not to constitute a property right (e.g., if the remainderman must survive another to be entitled to receive trust property).[205]

Discretionary trusts. Also, where a trustee has the discretion to apply the income for the benefit of the beneficiary or his wife, children, or next of kin, the trust is a discretionary trust. The beneficiary himself cannot compel the trustee to pay over any part of the trust fund, and so his assignees or creditors, including the government, are in no better position. If the trustee has the discretion whether or not to pay, a beneficiary has been held not to have any right to income that a creditor might attach.[206] If the trustee must pay the trust income, even if it is to be paid to a group of beneficiaries, including the taxpayer, the right to income is subject to a tax lien.[207] But such a discretionary-forfeiture trust provision has been held subject to the tax lien because there

---

[205] See United States v. United Banks of Denver, 542 F2d 819 (10th Cir. 1976) (remainder interest found under Colorado law to be a vested remainder subject to complete defeasance rather than a contingent remainder subject to condition precedent, and therefore probably "property" for purposes of lien). United States v. Solheim, 91-1 USTC ¶ 50,108 (D. Neb. 1991) (interest in trust contingent upon survival was not subject to lien, but Service had right to income and principal payments as they came due under terms of trust). If there is a tax lien at the time a taxpayer renounces his interest in a trust, the tax lien attaches to the taxpayer's interest and prevents a renunciation effective to defeat the lien. United States v. Solheim, 953 F2d 379 (8th Cir. 1992) ("Taxpayer's acceptance of some of the benefits of the trust and his failure to renounce within a reasonable time preclude renunciation").

[206] Hamilton v. Drogo, 241 NY 401, 150 NE 496 (1926). Applying National Bank of Commerce, 472 US 713 (1985), which held that the interest of a joint owner of a bank account was property even though either owner could withdraw funds from the account, the First Circuit held that where trustees had the power to terminate a beneficiary's interest in a trust's income and corpus, the beneficiary/taxpayer had a sufficient interest in the income and corpus at the time the tax lien was filed, and that the interest therefore constituted "property" for purposes of the tax lien statute. United States v. Murray, 86 AFTR2d 2000-5077 (1st Cir. 2000).

[207] Magavern v. United States, 550 F2d 797 (2d Cir. 1977). A spendthrift trust had a forfeiture provision providing that taxpayer's beneficial interest terminated and would vest in another person, if a creditor attached the taxpayer beneficiary's interest. When the Service served a levy to seize the interest, it was held that the levy did not retroactively defeat the tax lien that had attached to taxpayer's beneficial income interest before the levy. Bank One Ohio Tr. Co. NA v. United States, 80 F3d 173 (6th Cir. 1996). The Sixth Circuit said that the lien attached to all of the taxpayer's property, including his interest in the trust, when he failed to make payment after demand, because "state-law restraints on the alienation of property rights created under the state law do not affect the status of such rights as 'property' or 'rights to property' within the meaning of those terms as used in [S]ection 6321." The income interest in the trust was a matter of Ohio law: But alienability and restraints on alienability, are "to borrow a term used in *Bess*, a 'consequence' as to which federal tax law is controlling." Accordingly, while the levy may have been sufficient under the forfeiture provision to terminate the taxpayer's previously nondiscretionary interest in the trust, under federal law, "any such termination came too late to defeat the government's right to the money."

was no absolute forfeiture.[208] Once the trustee decides to make a distribution, the amount distributed is clearly subject to the tax lien.[209]

Spendthrift trusts. Where the interest of the beneficiary cannot be assigned by him or reached by his creditors, the trust is called a spendthrift trust. Not all states recognize spendthrift trusts. Many states have statutes that permit a creditor to enforce his claim against trust income, except for a sum necessary for the education and support of the beneficiary.[210] Viewing the prohibition of private creditors from enforcing their claims against trust property as the equivalent of a state-created exemption, it is not surprising that exemption cannot bar the Service from reaching the interest of a beneficiary of a spendthrift trust to enforce its claim for unpaid taxes.[211]

Pension trusts. Assets of a qualified pension trust are subject to lien and levy.[212]

---

[208] United States v. Taylor, 254 F. Supp. 752 (ND Cal. 1966).

[209] See, e.g., Hamilton v. Drogo, 241 NY 401, 150 NE 496 (1926).

[210] Scott's Abridgment of the Law of Trusts, § 152.1, at 286, 287 (1960).
A distinction is sometimes drawn between a support or spendthrift trust and a discretionary trust. The Service may collect the beneficiary's tax from a support trust. (See below.) However, the Service's ability to collect from a discretionary trust depends on state law. Applying New York law, the Second Circuit permitted collection from a discretionary trust in *Magavern*, but, applying Maryland law, a district court held that a taxpayer (and, thus, the Service) had an interest in the income, but not the corpus, of a discretionary trust, First of Am. Trust Co. v. United States, 93-2 USTC ¶ 50,507 (CD Ill. 1993).

[211] Leuschner v. First W. Bank & Trust Co., 261 F2d 705 (9th Cir. 1958) (California law held inapplicable because construed to create an exemption); In re Rosenberg's Will, 269 NY 247, 199 NE 206 (1935), cert. denied, 298 US 669 (1936). Accord Howard v. United States, 78-1 USTC 9396 (Tenn. 1978). A beneficiary's interest in a spendthrift trust constitutes "property or a right to property" subject to a federal tax lien and levy. LaSalle Nat'l Bank v. United States, 636 F. Supp. 874 (ND Ill. 1986) (applying Illinois law); United States v. Riggs Nat'l Bank, 636 F. Supp. 172 (DDC 1986) (under Maryland law trustee vested with discretion to distribute income among beneficiaries, including taxpayer-beneficiary, held not to preclude levy).

[212] Reg. § 1.401(a)-13(b). See In re Taylor, 91-2 USTC ¶ 50,354 (Bankr. D. Md. 1991). On the authority of *Leuschner*, a pension and 401(k) plan were held rights to property subject to lien despite restrictions on immediate withdrawal. Raihl v. United States, 93-1 USTC ¶ 50,290, 152 BR 615 (Bankr. 9th Cir. 1993). It has been held that the tax lien attaches to retirement plans. See, e.g., Jacobs v. United States, 93-1 USTC ¶ 50,118 (Bankr. WD Pa. 1992) (federal tax lien attaches to debtor's interest in pension plan, notwithstanding nonalienation provisions in ERISA); see also Raihl v. United States, 93-1 USTC ¶ 50,290, 152 BR 615 (Bankr. 9th Cir. 1993) ("Federal tax lien can attach to debtor's fully vested interest in pension and § 401(k) plans, which were property interests under Alaska law"); Hyde v. United States, 93-2 USTC ¶ 50,432 (D. Ariz. 1993) (taxpayer's community property interest in a retirement plan resulted in a levy on one half the fund). Similarly, the tax lien attaches to property purchased for maintenance and support with workers' compensation proceeds, although workmen's compensation amounts are exempt from levy under Section 6334(a)(7). See Sills v. United States, 82 F3d 111 (5th Cir. 1996).

Constructive trusts. State law also plays a part in determining title to currency, a problem frequently encountered in connection with criminal activities.[213] Applying state law, it has been held that title to embezzled funds remained in the victim, so that no lien against property of the taxpayer-embezzler attached to the funds.[214] The Service has agreed that a tax lien does not attach to properties subject to a constructive trust, because even though the taxpayer may have legal title, the constructive trust gives its "beneficiary" equitable title.[215] However, if, for example, a constructive trust is found to exist because of the taxpayer's breach of fiduciary duties or fraud, property subject to the trust must be traced.[216] Tracing can create difficult problems of proof.[217]

Other state-recognized property rights have been held subject to tax liens.[218]

---

[213] See, e.g., Katsaris v. United States, 499 F. Supp. 282 (ND Fla. 1980) (when arrested, taxpayer said $220,000 belonged to others; held, property "abandoned" under Florida law before assessments); Metropolitan Dade County v. United States, 635 F2d 312 (5th Cir. 1981) (currency seized incident to arrest held contraband that escheated to state; therefore, taxpayer had no property rights in funds). See also the discussion of Section 6867 in ¶ 10.05. See also United States v. Badger, 930 F2d 754 (9th Cir. 1991) (cash bond in criminal case is subject to levy).

[214] Atlas, Inc. v. United States, 459 F. Supp. 1000 (DND 1979) (wrongdoer obtains no more than naked title to property and holds it as trustee for party who should have it; applying North Dakota law); First Nat'l Bank v. United States, 412 F. Supp. 422 (ND Ga. 1976) (applying Georgia law); SEC v. Paige, 85-2 USTC ¶ 9588 (DDC 1985), aff'd, 810 F2d 307 (DDC 1987) (unpublished disposition) (taxpayer obtained no title or rights to converted funds, but held funds as constructive trustee for defrauded corporation; consequently, even where transferred into escrow account pursuant to court order, funds were not subject to lien and levy). See also Mervis Indus., Inc. v. Sams, 866 F. Supp. 1143 (SD Ind. 1994) (embezzler transferred funds to third party who was constructive trustee under Indiana law, and Service lien did not have priority because beneficiary of constructive trust had prior judgment; however, beneficiary's summary judgment denied because tracing not clearly established).

[215] TMG II v. United States, 778 F. Supp. 37 (DDC 1991); see also United States v. Fontana, 528 F. Supp. 137 (SDNY 1981).

[216] TMG II v. United States, 778 F. Supp. 37 (DDC 1991).

[217] See TMG II v. United States, 93-2 USTC ¶ 50,503 (DC Cir. 1993) (partnership failed to avoid tracing requirement).

[218] See United States v. Paladin, 539 F. Supp. 100 (WDNY 1982) (after tax lien arose, insurance proceeds purportedly assigned by taxpayer were held converted under New York law; therefore, assignee held liable for amount of lien at time of conversion); Bigheart Pipeline Corp. v. United States, 600 F. Supp. 50 (ND Okla. 1984) aff'd, 835 F2d 766 (10th Cir. 1987) (oil and gas lessee has, under Oklahoma law, a right to prospect, but not title to oil or gas until it is reduced to possession by extraction; held, tax lien attaches to this state-defined interest); Commonwealth Ky. v. Laurel County, 805 F2d 628 (6th Cir. 1986) (state law controls whether the taxpayer had a property interest in money owed by county agencies to the taxpayer). United States v. Wood, 877 F2d 453 (6th Cir. 1989) (government was a third-party beneficiary to a property settlement that required wife to

State law is applied in many situations to determine whether the taxpayer has "property" or a "right to property." Interests under state versions of the Uniform Commercial Code (UCC). Under state law only the taxpayer's equity in property in his possession under a conditional sales contract, a purchase-money mortgage, or a UCC purchase-money security interest constitutes property belonging to the taxpayer for the purposes of the lien.[219]

¶ 14.08 COLLECTION DUE PROCESS: NOTICE TO A TAXPAYER AND OPPORTUNITY FOR A HEARING WHEN A LIEN IS FILED

One of the due process rights that the IRS Restructuring and Reform Act of 1998 gives taxpayers is a notice and opportunity for a hearing when a notice of lien is filed.[220] Section 6320 requires that the taxpayer be given notice of the filing of a lien and provides for the right to a fair hearing. The Service is required to notify in writing the person whose property and rights to property will be encumbered by the public notice of the Service's lien.[221] This written

---

apply sale proceeds of marital residence to a federal tax lien against the husband; thus, government was entitled to judgment against taxpayer for breaching her promise).

[219] Rev. Rul. 68-57, 1968-1 CB 553; HR Rep. No. 19884, 89th Cong., 2d Sess. (1966), reprinted in 1966-2 CB 815, 817. See also Slodov v. United States, 436 US 238 (1978); U.S. v. Stamps, 93-1 USTC ¶ 50,280 (SD Ill. 1993) (taxpayer's interest in Illinois land trust was subject to tax lien).

[220] IRC § 6320(a), added by 1998 Act § 3401(a).

[221] Approximately one year after the 1998 Act, the GAO issued a report on the collection process and the new due process procedures. GAO, "IRS Seizures, Needed for Compliance, But Processes for Protecting Taxpayer Rights Have Some Weaknesses," (GAO/GGD-00-4) (Nov. 29, 1999). GAO found that during the period after the 1998 Act, the Service's use of its seizure authority was "in transition," and the number of seizures had declined by about 98 percent, at least in part because there was a lack of guidance given to revenue officers on when to make seizures in light of the act. GAO found that in the Service's fiscal year 1997, 42 percent of the seizures resulted in full resolution because the taxpayers made full payment in order to have their property returned; in 22 percent of the seizures, little revenue was produced and little contribution was made to resolving taxpayers' delinquencies. Statistically, the greater the amount of unpaid tax, the greater the likelihood of seizure, although likelihood of seizure varied significantly from district to district. After the 1998 changes in taxpayer rights, GAO reported weaknesses in the Service's seizure processes, such as the failure to send notices to taxpayers, inadequate postseizure processes to ensure public sales were attended by more than one bidder, proper documentation that taxpayer protections were considered, and reliance on manual reviews of revenue officer case files as a means of controlling the use of seizure authority.

The GAO Report prompted further comment on due process procedures for collection activities. Senator Roth of the Senate Finance Committee stated, "While the GAO report confirms many of the weaknesses documented during Congressional hearings and demon-

notice of the lien must be given in person, left at the dwelling or usual place of abode, or sent by certified or registered mail to the person's last known address not more than five business days after the date the lien is filed.[222] In the notice, the Service must describe in simple and nontechnical terms such information as the following:[223]

1. The amount of the unpaid tax;
2. The right of the person to hearing during the thirty-day period beginning on the day after the five-day period following the filing of the notice of lien;
3. The administrative appeal available for review of the lien filing and the procedure for taking this administrative appeal; and
4. A description of the procedures for obtaining a release of lien.

The person affected by the filed lien is entitled to a fair hearing, as long as that person requests the hearing within the thirty-day period after the five-day period following the filing of the notice of lien.[224] The hearing will be conducted by an Appeals officer who has had no prior involvement with the unpaid tax that gave rise to the filing of the lien.[225] Only one hearing before this impartial official is permitted.[226]

Regulations fill in the procedures the Service will follow in complying with these statutory rules.[227] When a notice of federal tax lien is filed after January 19, 1999, the office responsible for filing the lien (the Area-Territory office, service center, or the office of the Assistant Commissioner, International) will serve the taxpayer personally or by mail with a notice of the lien

---

strates how some persist despite new law, I remain optimistic that positive change is taking hold within the agency." "Roth Statement on GAO Report on Seizures," 2000 TNT 6-66 (Jan. 3, 2000).

[222] IRC § 6320(a)(2).

[223] IRC § 6320(a)(3). The listed information is inclusive, not exclusive.

[224] IRC § 6320(b)(1).

[225] IRC § 6320(b)(3). See Mesa Oil, Inc. v. United States, 86 AFTR2d 2000-7312 (D. Colo. 2000) (the taxpayer requested a hearing and attached a letter describing the company's financial condition and requesting an installment payment agreement; the Appeals Officer replied with a letter stating that the filing of the notice of tax lien was not premature and denying an installment payment agreement; held, the letter from the Appeals Officer established that the Appeals Officer had prejudged the issue and had not been impartial, as required by Sections 6320(b)(1) and 6330; accordingly, the case was remanded for a due process hearing before another Appeals Officer).

[226] IRC § 6320(b)(2). To the extent practicable the due process hearing in Appeals for the lien is to be coordinated with the due process hearing on the serving of the levy under Section 6330. IRC § 6320(b)(4).

[227] See Reg. §§ 301.6230-1 et seq. The Service also published "Collection Appeal Rights," Publication 1660, describing the collection actions of lien filing and levy, the actions the taxpayer may appeal, and the taxpayer's collection appeal rights.

filing.[228] Along with the notice of lien filing, the Service will include information about the tax secured by the lien, a Collection Due Process Hearing Notice, and a Request for a Due Process Hearing, Form 12153.

There are very specific and short periods that govern the collection due process hearing procedure. Care must be taken about the time for filing a request for a due process hearing. First, the Service has five business days after the notice of lien filing to notify the taxpayer of the lien filing and due process hearing right. Second, the taxpayer has thirty calendar days after the five business-day period to file a request for a due process hearing.[229] If the taxpayer does not file a request for a due process hearing within the thirty-day period, the taxpayer will lose the opportunity for full collection due process review. But even if the taxpayer does not request collection due process review in a timely fashion, the Service will permit the taxpayer an Appeals hearing, in this instance called an equivalent hearing, if the taxpayer so requests, but the taxpayer will not be entitled to judicial review of the Appeals determination.[230] In the case of an equivalent hearing, Appeals will issue a Decision Letter, not a Notice of Determination.

The taxpayer's request for a hearing must be in writing, preferably on the Service's Request for Due Process Hearing form, and this has several reasons: to prove that the taxpayer requested a hearing and permit the reviewing court to determine that it has jurisdiction over a subsequent appeal of the Appeals determination; to establish the date for the beginning of the period of suspension on the statute of limitations on administrative collection, prosecution, and collection suits.[231]

Appeals has the authority to determine whether the Area/Territory office's notice of the right to a due process hearing is valid, contains sufficient information, and is timely. Before making a final decision on the taxpayer's appeal, Appeals is required to verify that the Service office collecting the tax or filing

---

[228] Reg. §§ 301.6320-1(a)(1), 301.6320-1(a)(2), at A-A9. If a notice of filing is sent to the taxpayer's last known address by certified or registered mail, or left at the taxpayer's dwelling or usual place of abode, the thirty-day period begins to run even if the taxpayer does not actually receive the notice.

When the liabilities are those of a deceased taxpayer, the same procedures are followed as those for sending a notice of deficiency. First, inquiry is made to determine whether a fiduciary has been appointed, and if a Form 56, Notice Concerning Fiduciary Relationship, has been filed, the Collection Due Process notice is sent to John Doe (Decd.), Richard Doe, Executor, at Richard Doe's address.

The mailing address for a CDP notice for partnership delinquent accounts is governed by the information on the Notice of Federal Tax Lien; therefore, if the notice is in the name of the partnership only, the CDP notice is addressed to the partnership, and if the tax lien reflects the names of the partners, CDP notices will be sent to the partnership and each of the named partners. Reg. § 301.6320-1(a)(2), at A-A1.

[229] Reg. §§ 301.6320-1(a)(2), 301.6320-1(b)(1), at A-A2.

[230] Reg. § 301.6320-1(i).

[231] Reg. § 301.6320-1(c)(2), at A-C2.

the lien has followed the requirements of applicable law and administrative procedures.[232] At the Appeals hearing, the taxpayer may raise a number of arguments: an innocent spouse defense, challenge the appropriateness of the lien filing, or propose an offer in compromise or other collection alternative. However, the taxpayer may only dispute the existence or amount of the tax liability identified in the notice of lien if the taxpayer did not receive a notice of deficiency for the tax liability or did not otherwise have an opportunity to dispute the Service's determination that the taxpayer was liable for the tax assessed. In addition, Appeals will consider whether continuing to have the tax lien on file balances the need for efficient collection with "the legitimate concern of the taxpayer that any collection be no more intrusive than necessary."[233]

If the taxpayer and Appeals are unable to resolve the taxpayer's appeal, Appeals will issue a Notice of Determination.[234] To obtain judicial review of action, the taxpayer must file a petition in the Tax Court (or district court in cases where the Tax Court does not have jurisdiction over the tax involved, such as employment and excise taxes) within thirty days after the date of the notice.[235] The court will consider only those issues which the taxpayer raised at the hearing in Appeals. Once the taxpayer requests due process review, the statutes of limitation on collection, prosecution, and collection suits are suspended from the date the Service receives the request until ninety days after the date of the determination of Appeals or the reviewing court becomes final because the time for seeking review or reconsideration has expired.[236]

After an unsuccessful hearing in Appeals about the filing of a notice of federal tax lien and the Service's collection action, the taxpayer may file a petition in the U.S. Tax Court. The Tax Court has jurisdiction to review the Appeals determination to proceed with lien.[237]

---

[232] Reg. §§ 301.6320-1(d)(1), 301.6320-1(d)(2), at A-E1.

[233] Reg. § 301.6320-1(d)(2), at A-E1. Even after the appeal, Appeals retains jurisdiction, and may consider a change in the taxpayer's circumstances. Reg. § 301.6320-1(h).

[234] Reg. § 301.6320-1(f)(1).

[235] Reg. § 301.6320-1(f)(1). If the taxpayer seeks review of an Appeals determination on innocent spouse status under Sections 6015(b) and 6015(c) only (that is, the issue is one of liability, not the propriety of the Service's collection action), the period for filing the petition for review is governed by Section 6015, and is ninety days. Id., at A-F2.

Unless the jurisdiction of the court to which an appeal lies is recognized, the taxpayer's appeal will be delayed. See Moore v. Comm'r, 114 TC 171 (2000) (taxpayer appealed a trust fund recovery penalty assessment to the Tax Court, which did not have jurisdiction over the underlying trust fund liability); McCune v. United States, 85 AFTR2d 2000-1240 (ND Tex. 2000) (district court has jurisdiction over review action only if Tax Court did not; district court dismissed review action because the underlying tax was an income tax and the taxpayer had failed to pay the full amount of the tax under *Flora* rule.) See McCune v. Comm'r, 115 TC 114 (2000) (petition must be filed within thirty days after mailing of the determination letter in order for the Tax Court to have jurisdiction).

[236] Reg. § 301.6320-1(e)(1).

[237] IRC § 6330(d)(1).

¶ 14.09 GOVERNMENT SUITS INVOLVING LIENS

[1] Request and Authorization Procedure

A civil action for collection of taxes must be authorized by the Chief Counsel (the delegate of the Secretary of the Treasury) and instituted at the direction of the Assistant Attorney General of the Tax Division (the delegate of the Attorney General).[238] Absent this specific request and authorization, a collection action should be dismissed. Although the Chief Counsel's authorization is required as a matter of law, the process by which the request is made begins in most cases with the revenue officer. When the revenue officer's recommendation is approved at the local office level, it is forwarded to the office of the Area Counsel for review. If the Area Counsel believes a suit is warranted, the Counsel attorney prepares a letter addressed to the Assistant Attorney General, Tax Division, Department of Justice, requesting the institution of a suit. Signed by or on behalf of the Chief Counsel, this suit letter contains the Chief Counsel's specific request for the Attorney General to institute proceedings, a discussion of the necessary facts, supporting documents, tax information, and the applicable statutes and pertinent judicial decisions that may be involved in the case.[239] The suit letter and file are forwarded to the Office of the Deputy Chief Counsel's General Litigation Division, where they are reviewed. If the Chief Counsel's office concurs, the letter is forwarded to the Assistant Attorney General of the Tax Division.

As Sections 7401 and 7403 state, the Justice Department's Tax Division has jurisdiction over civil tax litigation in federal and state courts.[240] When the suit request is received in the Tax Division, it is routed to the appropriate Civil Trial Section, where the final determination regarding institution of suit is made. If the action requested is considered appropriate, as it usually is, the authorization to institute suit along with a draft complaint is sent to the U.S. Attorney in the appropriate judicial district. A trial attorney in the Tax Division in Washington usually has primary responsibility for the preparation and trial of the case, although there are exceptions to this rule depending on the type

---

[238] IRC §§ 7401, 7403. See also 28 CFR § 0.70 (describing the matters assigned to the Assistant Attorney General in charge of the Tax Division).

[239] See Dep't of Justice Manual, Tax Div. 6-5.110 (Suits to Collect Tax and Foreclose Tax Liens). To determine whether the statutory request has been made, the government should be requested to produce this letter by a motion to produce.

[240] Civil litigation within the jurisdiction of the Tax Division is handled, supervised, or coordinated by four Civil Trial Sections, a Court of Federal Claims Section, which handles litigation in that Court, and an Office of Special Litigation, which handles tax shelter-related litigation. 4 Dep't of Justice Manual 6-5.000 (Civil Tax Case Procedures). U.S. Attorneys' offices in the Southern District of New York and the districts of California have their own tax units.

and importance of the case and the judicial district.[241] After a case is referred to the Justice Department, the Tax Division must approve a settlement agreement with the taxpayer,[242] although the recommendation of the Chief Counsel's office (which in turn will request the views of the Division Counsel) on the proposed terms of the settlement usually will be solicited.

[2] Types of Civil Actions

There appear to be no limitations on the kinds of actions the Service may bring to effect collection of a tax or on the jurisdiction of district courts to hear such actions. District courts are granted jurisdiction "to make and issue in civil actions, writs and orders of injunction, and of ne exeat republica, orders appointing receivers, and such other orders as may be necessary and appropriate for the enforcement of the internal revenue laws."[243] Not only is this "all writs" jurisdiction very broad indeed, but jurisdiction of the district courts is "in addition to and not exclusive of any and all other remedies of the United States in such courts or otherwise to enforce such [internal revenue] laws." Thus, the remedies available to the government seem to be limited only by constitutional restrictions on the district courts (e.g., the requirement that there be a case or controversy) or by some constitutional guarantee (e.g., a Fourth or Fifth Amendment right or privilege) that the requested relief would violate. The following sections summarize some of the more common collection actions brought by the government.

[a] Suit to Reduce Tax Assessment to Judgment

A suit to reduce a tax assessment to judgment is generally instituted to prevent the statute of limitations on collection from running where collection

---

[241] Even if the U.S. Attorney's office is given primary responsibility for trial of the case, the Tax Division retains general responsibility for control purposes.

[242] IRC § 7122(a). For Tax Division procedures, see Dep't of Justice Manual 6-6.000 (Compromises and Concessions). In general, Chiefs of the Civil Trial Sections, the Court of Federal Claims Section, and the Office of Special Litigation have authority to settle cases where the government's concession, exclusive of interest, does not exceed $200,000, and to approve administrative settlement not to exceed $100,000. Cases involving greater amounts are acted on either by the Chief of the Office of Review, or by Deputy Assistant Attorneys General and Special Counsel to the Assistant Attorney General. U.S. Attorneys are authorized to reject offers to compromise judgments in favor of the government regardless of amount and accept offers to compromise judgments for amounts not exceeding $200,000. Dept. of Justice Manual 6-6.1300 (Redelegation of Authority to Compromise, Settle, and Close Claims—Tax Div. Directive No. 54).

[243] IRC § 7402(a). See United States v. First Nat'l City Bank, 568 F2d 853 (2d Cir. 1977).

cannot be accomplished by administrative methods (levy and sale) within the normal six-year collection period.[244] To reduce a tax assessment to judgment or collection action, the government has the burden of proving that a timely assessment has been made against the taxpayer and that the collection suit is timely.[245] The government usually proves the assessment, its timeliness, and amount by submitting a certificate of assessments and payments to the court.[246] The government establishes a prima facie case when it shows a timely assessment was made. Once this evidence has been produced, the burden shifts to the taxpayer to prove by a preponderance of the evidence that the assessment was erroneous. In so doing, the taxpayer may contest the merits of the tax assessment.[247] If a judgment in favor of the government is obtained, the Justice Department has primary responsibility for its collection, but local U.S. Attorneys usually supply the initiative to collect judgment.[248] Under Rule 69(a) of the Federal Rules of Civil Procedure, the district court in executing judgments must follow the law of the state in which the district court is located.[249] This was true as to judgments obtained before May 29, 1981. The Federal Debt Collection Act, which became effective May 29, 1991, creates a uniform framework for enforcing debts owed to the government. The statute of limitations for the government to collect on a judgment lien in a civil action under this act is twenty years.[250]

---

[244] Authority for this type of action is found in Section 7403(a). For Tax Division procedures, see Dep't of Justice Manual 6-3111.

[245] United States v. Lease, 346 F2d 696 (2d Cir. 1965); United States v. Besase, 623 F2d 463 (6th Cir. 1980); Higgenbotham v. United States, 556 F2d 1173 (4th Cir. 1973).

[246] See cases cited supra ¶ 14.05[1]. See also United States v. Janis, 428 US 433, 440 (1976); United States v. Strebler, 313 F2d 402, 403 (8th Cir. 1964); Holland v. United States, 209 F2d 516, 520 (10th Cir. 1954); United States v. Chila, 871 F2d 1015 (11th Cir.), cert. denied, 493 US 975 (1989). Production of the Certificate of Assessment and Payments, Form 4340, by a witness who had no personal knowledge of its contents has been held admissible under 28 USC § 1733(a), which makes admissible "books or records of accounts or minutes of proceedings of any department or agency of the United States." Holland v. United States, 209 F2d 516, 520 (10th Cir. 1954).

[247] United States v. O'Connor, 291 F2d 520 (2d Cir. 1961).

[248] Section 7406 provides that all judgments and moneys recovered or received for taxes, costs, forfeitures, and penalties shall be paid to the Secretary or his delegate as collection of internal revenue taxes. When a compromise agreement is entered in a district court proceeding, the settled amount of "taxes" includes interest. Anthony v. United States, 765 F. Supp. 656 (D. Colo. 1991).

[249] See also 28 USC § 1962. See United States v. Little, 52 F3d 495 (4th Cir. 1995) (applying Maryland law, which has a twelve-year statute of limitations on judgments to a judgment obtained more than ten years before the effective date of the Federal Debt Collection Act).

[250] 28 USC § 3201(c) (1992). The act does not apply to judgments entered more than ten years before the statute's effective date. United States v. Little, 52 F3d 495 (4th Cir. 1995).

[b] Foreclosure of Tax Liens

The government can either levy administratively on the taxpayer's property only or it can proceed by judicial action against property of which the taxpayer owns a part. Where there has been a refusal or neglect to pay any tax, and it is not feasible to seize and sell the delinquent taxpayer's real or personal property administratively to satisfy the tax liability, an action may be commenced in a federal district court to foreclose the tax lien against specific property.[251] A suit to enforce or foreclose a tax lien is generally initiated where title to property claimed to be subject to the lien is in dispute, conflicting claims to a fund being levied upon exist, or the taxpayer employs many people and the Service desires to sell the business as a going concern to preserve the jobs of the employees. There may be other reasons why levy would result in substantially less recovery for the government or why the levy would otherwise be inappropriate. For example, although a levy procedure is available as a collection tool with respect to life insurance or endowment contracts, the government may elect to bring an action to foreclose a lien or enforce a levy so as to reach any equity the taxpayer may have in term and extended term insurance; consequently, it must commence lien foreclosure action. A lien foreclosure suit also is instituted where the property involved is in possession and control of a third person who either claims an interest or claims that someone else has an interest in the property that is superior to the tax claim. This situation occurs where a third person unknowingly purchases property subject to a tax lien; where he is in possession, although he has no legal claim to the property; or where he has received notice of other claims and is fearful to take it upon himself to determine what claim is entitled to priority.

All persons having liens upon or claiming any interest in the property involved must be made parties to this action.[252] The form of action is a proceeding in rem, so that venue is determined by the location of the property, and a jury trial is not available.[253] After the parties have been "duly notified of the action," the court proceeds to adjudicate all matters involved and finally determines the merits of all claims to and liens on the property.

Once the claim or interest of the government is established, Section 7403 authorizes the district court to order that the property be sold and the proceeds of the sale be distributed according to the court's findings.[254] In *United States*

---

[251] IRC §§ 7402(a), 7403(a).

[252] IRC § 7403(b).

[253] Equitable Life Assurance Soc'y v. United States, 331 F2d 29 (1st Cir. 1964) (in rem action nonjury); United States v. Polk, 59-1 USTC 9246 (D. Nev. 1959) (venue). If a personal judgment for taxes owed is sought, then personal jurisdiction over the taxpayer must be obtained.

[254] IRC § 7403(c). Although the suit to reduce a tax assessment to judgment is used to extend the statutory period of collection rather than to foreclose the tax lien, the proce-

v. Rodgers, the Supreme Court interpreted Section 7403 "to contemplate, not merely the sale of the delinquent taxpayer's own interest, but the sale of the entire property (as long as the United States has any 'claim or interest' in it), and the recognition of third-party interests through the mechanism of judicial valuation."[255] Consequently, a state-created exemption cannot prevent a federal district court from ordering the sale of property under Section 7403.

The district court is not required to order a forced sale in all instances. The district court's power "is limited to some degree by equitable discretion."[256] If the property in which a non-delinquent third person has an interest (*Rodgers* involved a homestead interest) is sold, the nondelinquent person is entitled, as part of the distribution of proceeds required under Section 7403, to so much of the proceeds as represents complete compensation for the loss of the interest.[257]

In a lien foreclosure suit, the court may order either a public or a private sale.[258] A purchaser at a judicial sale is generally willing to pay more for property that at a sale following administrative seizure. The price at an administrative sale is often lower because only the taxpayer's interest is sold, and the taxpayer's interest or title may not be readily determined without threat of future litigation. At a judicial sale, the purchaser can expect a good marketable title without the necessity of further litigation. The practical difference in the results of an administrative seizure and sale versus a lien foreclosure suit presents the government with an option that is generally resolved in favor of

---

dural aspects of both actions are very much the same, and, in most lien foreclosure suits, the complaint includes a request for judgment in the amount of the tax assessment.

[255] United States v. Rodgers, 461 US 677 (1983) (legislative history and meaning of Section 7403 reviewed).

[256] United States v. Rodgers, 461 US 677 (1983). For a description of the "individualized equitable balancing" of the interests of the government and a nondelinquent third party having an interest in the property the government wants sold. The Supreme Court also said in *Rodgers* that it would almost never be an impermissible exercise of discretion to order the sale of property where the interest sought to be protected was not that of the delinquent taxpayer. However, even in such a situation, equitable considerations might require postponement of a sale or the setting of an upset price. For a case in which the calculation of the innocent spouse's interest was determined, see Harris v. United States, 764 F2d 1126 (5th Cir. 1985) (Treasury actuarial table used).

[257] Harris v. United States, 764 F2d 1126 (5th Cir. 1985). However, the Supreme Court, in United States v. Rodgers, 461 US 677 (1983), recognized that "in practical terms financial compensation may not always be a completely adequate substitute for a roof over one's head." It also noted other problems in valuing a homestead interest.

[258] If the court orders a public sale, the provisions of 28 USC §§ 2001(c) and 2002 govern the sale of real property, and 28 USC § 2004 governs the sale of personal property. If the court orders a private sale, the provisions of 28 USC § 2001(b) govern the terms of the sale.

judicial sale, thus cutting off the statutory right of redemption accorded the taxpayer and others when administrative collection action is taken.[259]

[c] Appointment of a Receiver

At the request of the government, the court may (1) appoint a receiver to enforce the tax lien or (2) during the pendency of the proceeding, upon certification of the Commissioner that it is in the public interest, appoint a receiver with all the powers of a receiver in equity.[260] The first situation usually occurs after the priorities of various encumbrances have been determined with respect to the property or assets involved. The government can request that a receiver be appointed to negotiate the sale of the property, in which instance the receiver is paid from the sale proceeds and his actions are approved by the court. This type of receivership might occur where the property consists of a number of securities that, by appointment of a receiver, may be sold through negotiation rather than by auction. A receiver may also be requested on certification by the Commissioner that a receiver is in the public interest.[261] The Commissioner certifies to the court that it is in the public interest that a receiver be appointed with all the powers of a receiver in equity, which includes the power to conduct the business of the taxpayer, safeguard his assets, and liquidate the business to pay creditors.[262] The effect of the appointment of this type of receiver is that the taxpayer is no longer allowed to conduct his affairs or business with respect to the property subject to the tax lien. The receiver has complete control over the assets, subject, of course, to the court's supervision.

[d] Intervention

If the United States is not a party to a civil action or suit, it may intervene in the action or suit to assert any tax lien on the property that is the sub-

---

[259] Where the taxpayer's property is encumbered by other liens, unless a tax liability is so small that it can reasonably be anticipated that a distraint sale will satisfy the taxpayer's liability, serious consideration is given to a suit under Section 7403.

[260] IRC § 7403(d).

[261] It is sufficient if the government makes a prima facie showing that a substantial tax liability probably exists and that collection of the tax may be jeopardized if a receiver is not appointed. United States v. O'Connor, 291 F2d 520 (2d Cir. 1961). See United States v. Ross, 302 F2d 831 (2d Cir. 1962) ("probable existence of a substantial tax liability" is sufficient).

[262] Goldfine v. United States, 300 F2d 260 (1st Cir. 1962) (receiver for corporation); United States v. Ross, 302 F2d 831 (2d Cir. 1962) (receiver to hold stock of foreign corporations).

ject of the action or suit.[263] The statutory authorization for intervention does not require the court to grant the government's motion to intervene, but makes it clear that if the motion is granted, the court will be able to settle the entire controversy in one suit. If the original action has been instituted in a state court, the government's intervention usually removes the action from a state court to a federal district court.[264] If the government's motion to intervene is denied, the proceedings have no effect on the tax lien. The government can enforce the lien against property by foreclosure.

[e] Action to Open Safe-Deposit Box

If a taxpayer refuses to cooperate and voluntarily consent to the opening of his safe-deposit box, the government can make an application in a district court for a court order directing the keeper of the box to open it for inspection or seizure of the contents by the government.[265] This action is commenced ex parte, and the taxpayer has no right to intervene in it.[266] At one time the action was considered to be one to enforce a levy, but in *United States v. First Nat'l City Bank*,[267] the Second Circuit found jurisdiction instead under the All-Writs statute (IRC § 7402).

[f] Order of Entry to Effect Levy

In the same manner as it proceeds to open a safe-deposit box, the Service can make ex parte applications to a federal district court for authorization to enter a taxpayer's premises to seize property for tax collection purposes.[268] This procedure was adopted following the Supreme Court's decision in *GM Leasing Corp. v. United States*, where revenue officers' warrantless entry into

---

[263] IRC § 7424. For Tax Division procedures, see Dep't of Justice Manual 6-5.120 (Intervention by United States in Court Actions).

[264] 28 USC § 1444.

[265] IRC § 7402.

[266] United States v. First Nat'l Bank, 348 F. Supp. 388, 389 (D. Ariz. 1970), aff'd per curiam, 458 F2d 513 (9th Cir. 1972). See also United States v. New Eng. Merchants Nat'l Bank, 465 F. Supp. 83 (D. Mass. 1974). But see United States v. Mellon Bank, NA, 521 F2d 708 (3d Cir. 1975) (district court permitted taxpayer to intervene under Federal Rule of Civil Procedure 24(b)); United States v. Bowery Sav. Bank, 76-2 USTC 9796 (SDNY 1976) (postjudgment petition for order authorizing entry and seizure of contents of safe-deposit boxes.)

[267] United States v. First Nat'l Bank, 348 F. Supp. 388, 389 (D. Ariz. 1970), aff'd per curiam, 458 F2d 513 (9th Cir. 1972).

[268] Jurisdiction of a district court is found in 26 USC § 7402(a) and 28 USC § 1345. In re Carlson, 580 F2d 1365 (10th Cir. 1978). This order is also called a writ of entry or an order to enter. Denial of authorization constitutes an appealable order. Id.; United States v. Shriver, 645 F2d 221 (4th Cir. 1981).

a taxpayer's premises was held to violate the Fourth Amendment's prohibition of unreasonable searches and seizures.[269] The Fourth Amendment violation in *GM Leasing* involved revenue officers' entry into the home office of the taxpayer, the rummaging through desk drawers, and the seizure of certain books and records, but the Court held that the seizure of cars parked on the street and open places outside the home office was not a Fourth Amendment violation. Courts have found that the Service is entitled to seize property such as an automobile from semiprivate areas such as driveways or front lawns.[270] In its decision, the Supreme Court indicated that, had the revenue officers obtained a warrant, their search and seizure would have been valid. The Service has responded by making an ex parte application supported by a revenue officer's affidavit for an order permitting entry into a taxpayer's premises and seizure of property.[271] The Service must make a showing of "probable cause," although what constitutes an adequate probable cause showing has been differently interpreted.[272] In general, the revenue officer's affidavit recites that (1) a tax assessment has been made against the taxpayer; (2) notice and demand has properly been made; (3) the taxpayer has neglected or refused to pay the assessment within the ten-day grace period; and (4) property subject to seizure presently exists at the premises to be searched that either belongs to the taxpayer or is subject to lien. The Tenth Circuit has stated that the probable cause standard in administrative entry cases is different from the one applied in criminal cases.[273] In *United States v. Shriver*,[274] the Fourth Circuit said judges are simply "to determine whether the application and supporting affidavit showed probable cause to enter, search for, and levy upon personal property in aid of summary collection of assessed and unpaid taxes (citing *Carlson*)." The court also held that the Service must establish by affidavit that (1) it has a right to levy and seize assets of a taxpayer and (2) "there is probable cause to believe that there are assets which may be seized on the premises to be entered").[275] The Ninth Circuit has held that the application must have sufficient specificity to enable the judge to make an independent determination of whether probable

---

[269] GM Leasing Corp. v. United States, 429 US 338 (1977).

[270] United States v. Riccio, 981 F2d 587, 561 (1st Cir. 1992); Maisano v. Welcher, 940 F2d 499, 501 (9th Cir. 1991) (revenue officers seized vehicles from taxpayer's driveway; Service granted a summary judgment on taxpayer's Fourth Amendment claim).

[271] In re Carlson, 580 F2d 1365 (10th Cir. 1978); In re Gerwig, 461 F. Supp. 449 (CD Cal. 1978); In re Brickner, 453 F. Supp. 91 (ED Wis. 1978). The Service has adopted detailed procedures for preparing a request for a writ of entry. See IRM 56(12)4.5, MT 5600-34 (June 3, 1991) (Writ Procedures). For Tax Division procedures, see Dept. of Justice Manual 6-5.130 (Order for Entry to Effect Levy).

[272] In re Carlson, 580 F2d 1365 (10th Cir. 1978).

[273] See In re Tax Indebtedness of L. Shyrl Brown, 84-2 USTC ¶ 10,002 (D. Utah 1984).

[274] See United States v. Shriver, 645 F2d 221 (4th Cir. 1981).

[275] See United States v. Shriver, 645 F2d 221 (4th Cir. 1981).

cause exists and to prevent the Service revenue officers from having uncontrolled discretion to rummage everywhere in search of seizable items once lawfully within the premises.[276] A writ of entry is not identical to a search warrant, because the purpose of the writ of entry is to permit the collection by the sale of seized property, whereas the search warrant seeks only the seizure of certain property. In search warrant cases, the probable cause standard is stated in these words, "The task of the issuing magistrate is simply to make a practical, common sense decision whether, given all the circumstances set forth in the affidavit . . . , there is a fair probability that contraband or evidence of a crime will be found in a particular place."[277]

Assuming that a district court has jurisdiction to issue a warrant or writ of entry, it clearly has jurisdiction to require specificity as to the items sought and to narrow any order it may choose to issue,[278] especially where the government is seeking to enter the premises of someone other than the taxpayer.[279] Attempts to prevent the execution of a writ of entry have been held to constitute civil contempt.[280]

In 1993, however, the Supreme Court decided *United States v. James Daniel Good Real Property*,[281] a civil forfeiture case, in which the question was whether, in the absence of exigent circumstances, the Due Process Clause of the Fifth Amendment prohibits the government from seizing real property without first affording the owner notice and an opportunity to be heard. The Court held that ex parte preseizure hearings violate the Due Process Clause in certain cases. The Court observed:

> The *ex parte* preseizure proceeding affords little or no protection to the innocent owner. In issuing a warrant of seizure, the magistrate judge need determine only that there is probable cause to believe that the real property was "used, or intended to be used, in any manner or part, to commit, or to facilitate the commission of" a felony narcotics offense. . . . The Government is not required to offer any evidence on the question of innocent ownership or other potential defenses a claimant might have . . . nor would that inquiry, in the *ex parte* stage, suffice to protect the innocent owner's interests.[282]

---

[276] United States v. Condo, 782 F2d 1502 (9th Cir. 1986).

[277] See Illinois v. Gates, 462 US 213, 235 (1983).

[278] In re Gerwig, 461 F. Supp. 449 (CD Cal. 1978); see also United States v. Condo, 782 F2d 1502 (9th Cir. 1986).

[279] In re Brickner, 453 F. Supp. 91 (ED Wis. 1978).

[280] United States v. Campbell, 761 F2d 1181 (6th Cir. 1985) (husband thwarted efforts of Service to effect a levy on automobiles to satisfy wife's taxes; held, husband in civil contempt of writ of entry authorizing entry onto his premises).

[281] United States v. James Daniel Good Real Property, 510 US 43 (1993).

[282] United States v. James Daniel Good Real Property, 510 US 43 (1993).

The Supreme Court held that due process required prior notice and an opportunity to be heard. Importantly, the Court said that the issue was not determinable solely on Fourth Amendment grounds, so that the mere intervention of a judicial officer, a magistrate, satisfied all relevant constitutional requirements. More than a search and seizure incident to a criminal prosecution is involved in a forfeiture. Since the government sought "to assert ownership and control over the property itself, . . . government action of this consequence must comply with the Due Process Clause of the Fifth and Fourteenth Amendments."[283]

Good Real Property distinguishes tax cases where the taxpayer had a preassessment deficiency action to determine the amount of tax owed. But since the Tax Court has jurisdiction over income, estate, and gift taxes, the Supreme Court's decision suggests that, at least in the case of employment and excise taxes, orders to permit revenue officers to enter on property to make seizures require prior notice and hearing. If this interpretation is correct, the service may not use the ex parte procedure it has followed after *GM Leasing*.

Absence of prior notice and hearing is permitted in some cases where the property could be concealed or moved if advance warning were given, as when a yacht was involved. However, real property can neither be moved nor concealed. In deciding whether due process requires preseizure notice and hearing, the Court applied a three-part test: "(1) the private interest affected by the official action; (2) the risk of an erroneous deprivation of that interest through the procedures used, as well as the probable value of additional safeguards; and (3) the Government's interest, including the administrative burden that additional procedural requirements would impose."[284]

On the second part of the test, the Supreme Court said that an adversary hearing had the purpose of ensuring "the requisite neutrality that must inform all government decisionmaking." That protection was of particular importance where the government has a "direct pecuniary interest in the outcome of the proceeding."[285]

The third part of the analysis dealt with whether ex parte seizure was justified by a pressing need for prompt action. The Court concluded that no pressing need existed, primarily because, unlike a yacht, which might have disappeared had advance warning been given, real property cannot abscond. Moreover, the government could have secured its legitimate interests without seizing the property, by, for example, obtaining an ex parte restraining order or other appropriate relief on a proper showing in district court.

Because prepayment judicial review is available in income, gift, and estate tax cases, the Court said its ruling did not apply to the collection of those taxes. However, employment taxes may be assessed and collected without pro-

---

[283] United States v. James Daniel Good Real Property, 510 US 43 (1993).
[284] United States v. James Daniel Good Real Property, 510 US 43 (1993).
[285] United States v. James Daniel Good Real Property, 510 US 43 (1993).

viding a taxpayer prepayment judicial review. As a result, the Service's use of a writ of entry to collect unpaid employment or excise taxes presents the same Due Process problems that are present in a civil forfeiture. There is a basis, therefore, for *Good Real Property* to apply to orders or warrants of entry to collect employment or excise taxes. The implications of *Good Real Property* for ex parte motions for orders or warrants of entry are fairly clear. Due process requires that the Service give notice and that there be a hearing before revenue officers may enter on property to make seizures. In the event a risk exists that the property may be moved or destroyed, the Service may be able to apply ex parte, but usually for injunctive relief. An ex parte order to permit entry on and seizure of property will be limited to property that might be easily moved or concealed or facilitate flight, like a motor boat, but even in this situation, the Service would seem to have the burden of showing why means short of seizure are not adequate to protect its interests without first affording notice and an adversary hearing.

[g] Miscellaneous Actions

To collect a tax, the United States may bring any suit available to creditors in general. The government may obtain a court order restraining the taxpayer from leaving the country (a writ ne exeat republica).[286] Some of the factors that courts have found relevant in determining whether to issue a writ ne exeat republica are (1) the amount of the tax liability; (2) whether the taxpayer has transferred his assets outside the United States or is in the process of doing so; (3) whether the taxpayer has established a permanent residence outside the United States or is likely to do so; (4) whether it is likely that the Service will prevail on the merits of the underlying liability determination; and (5) whether the taxpayer's assets are subject to collection absent the writ.[287]

Where a third party holds a taxpayer's "property or rights to property" subject to a tax lien, the government can sue the third party, even if no levy

---

[286] IRC § 7402(a); 28 USC § 1651; United States v. Shaheen, 445 F2d 6 (7th Cir. 1971).

[287] See United States v. Shaheen, 445 F2d 6 (7th Cir. 1971); United States v. Lipper, 47 AFTR2d 81-1289 (ND Cal. 1981) (taxpayer had not filed returns for many years and was in the process of liquidating assets, and there was evidence he was intending to establish a residence in France); United States v. Robbins, 235 F. Supp. 353 (ED Ark. 1965); see also Chief Counsel Litigation Memorandum re: Writs of Ne Exeat Republica, INTL-2, GL-7 (Apr. 17, 1990).

The Chief Counsel has said in field advice that a writ ne exeat republica cannot be used to detain a person in the United States for the purpose of compelling to disclose information, and that the Tax Division of the Justice Department requires the Service to be able to prove that the taxpayer has transferred assets out of the country in order to avoid the payment of taxes. FSA 1999-578, reprinted in 99 TNT 20-100.

has been served, for tortious conversion of the government's "collateral."[288] State fraudulent conveyance statutes can be used to set aside transfers of property by a taxpayer that are fraudulent or that are without adequate consideration at a time when the transferor is insolvent or rendered insolvent by the transfer.[289] Forfeiture of property is provided for by Section 7302, which makes it unlawful for a person "to have or possess any property intended for use in violating the provisions of the internal revenue laws . . . and no property rights shall exist in any such property." To work a forfeiture under Section 7302, all that needs to be shown is that "the property in question had been intentionally used as an 'active aid' in the violation of the internal revenue laws."[290] Proceeding under Section 7302, the Service has instituted forfeiture proceedings against a Rolls Royce that was used in a backdating tax shelter scheme.[291]

Any portion of any internal revenue tax that has been erroneously refunded to a taxpayer may be recovered by administrative action or a suit in court.[292] Although assessment and collection may be used to collect the tax due and erroneously refunded to a taxpayer, a suit generally is used because the statute of limitations on assessment has run.[293] However, the suit for erroneous refund must be brought within a relatively short period—within two years from the making of the refund or within five years if any part of the refund

---

[288] Nomellini Constr. Co. v. United States, 328 F. Supp. 1281 (ED Cal. 1971). See also United States v. Allen, 207 F. Supp. 545 (ED Wash. 1964).

[289] See, e.g., United States v. Livingstone, 381 F. Supp. 607 (D. Mass. 1974).

[290] United States v. One 1968 Ford LTD, 425 F2d 1084, 1085 (5th Cir. 1970).

[291] United States v. One 1954 Rolls Royce Silver Dawn, 777 F2d 1358 (9th Cir. 1985).

[292] IRC § 7405.

[293] However, if the Service makes a timely assessment, it may collect the assessment by administrative means as long as the collection takes place during the applicable period of collection. Ideal Realty Co. v. United States, 561 F2d 1123 (4th Cir. 1977) (erroneously refunded interest on assessed principal collected by levy within six years of assessment). The Service is not required to institute a civil action. It may also reassess the tax if the statute of limitations on assessment is open. Brookhurst, Inc. v. United States, 931 F2d 554 (9th Cir. 1991). One court has said in regard to the erroneous refund of withheld tax that the statutory period of Section 6501(a) did not apply to the erroneous refund assessment, because Section 6501(a) applies to assessments of tax; and, in this situation, the assessment was of an "amount" for an "overstatement of the credit for income tax withheld at the source" under Section 6201(a)(3). deRochemont v. United States, 23 Cl. Ct. 80, 91-1 USTC ¶ 50,237, 23 Cl. Ct. 80 (1991). However, when a taxpayer has made a payment against a tax assessment, the assessment is extinguished in the amount paid, and the assessment is not revived by the Service's paying an unsolicited erroneous refund. When the Service makes a nonrebate erroneous refund in the circumstance where the assessment has been extinguished, it cannot collect the erroneous refund by administrative means. O'Bryant v. United States, 49 F3d 340 (7th Cir. 1995); United States v. Wilkes, 946 F2d 1143 (5th Cir. 1991).

was induced by fraud or misrepresentation of material fact.[294] The two-year period begins to run from the date of delivery of the refund check.[295] The Service has two options: The first option is to file a civil suit within two years after the erroneous refund; the second option is to reassess a taxpayer's liability, taking into account the erroneous refund, within three years after the filing of the taxpayer's return, subject to any period of suspension during the pendency of the case in the Tax Court and for sixty days thereafter. When the Service fails to institute a civil action to recover the erroneous refund within the refund period, it is barred from recovering the refund, even if it results in a windfall to the taxpayer.[296]

Erroneous refunds sometimes tempt taxpayers to cash the checks and use the proceeds. Not only is the taxpayer personally liable for the amount of the refund under Section 7405, but the taxpayer may even face criminal prosecution for converting money of the United States.[297] In one case, a taxpayer who was sent a refund check—despite an outstanding tax assessment—had disbursed the funds in a series of transactions, and was prosecuted for converting government property.[298] A divided circuit court reversed the conviction, saying that "when the named payee receives and uses an erroneously issued tax refund check that the recipient in no way induced, the check is not government

---

[294] IRC § 6532(b).

[295] United States v. Wurts, 303 US 414 (1938). See United States v. CPC Int'l, 875 F. Supp. 264 (DNJ 1995) (Service issued refund check on or about October 30, 1990, and government instituted suit for erroneous refund on July 8, 1994, more than two years later; held, government's suit was time-barred).

It has also been held that an erroneous refund is "made" when it is "received," and a refund is "received" when the refund check clears the Federal Reserve Bank and the Treasury authorizes payment, not the date the taxpayer receives the refund check. United States v. Commonwealth Energy Sys., 994 F. Supp. 80 (D. Mass. 1998) (taxpayers received the refund check on July 27, 1995, and deposited the check in their account; however, the check cleared the Federal Reserve Bank and Treasury authorized payment on August 2, 1995, and erroneous refund filed July 30, 1997, held timely, rejecting the date of mailing argument, and citing O'Gilvie v. United States, 117 S. Ct. 452, 458 (1996)).

[296] Stanley v. United States, 81 AFTR2d 98-1307 (Fed. Cir. 1998) (Service also failed to reassess within the assessment period, even after taking into account the suspension of the assessment statute during the Tax Court case, and original assessment was not sufficient because it did not take into account the erroneous refund).

[297] 18 USC § 641 imposes a find of $10,000 or imprisonment for up to ten years, or both when property belonging to the government is fraudulently used by the defendant for his own purpose or the purposes of another, and the defendant did so knowingly with the intent to deprive the government of the property. United States v. McRee, 984 F2d 1144 (11th Cir. 1993), decision vacated, and reh'g en banc ordered, 93-1 USTC ¶ 50,254 (11th Cir. 1993).

[298] United States v. McRee, 984 F2d 1144 (11th Cir. 1993), decision vacated, and reh'g en banc ordered, 93-1 USTC ¶ 50,254 (11th Cir. 1993); see also United States v. Spear, 734 F2d 1 (8th Cir. 1984) (social security checks erroneously sent to deceased mother were cashed by sons).

property under Section 641."[299] But the majority said that prosecution might have been proper under another criminal statute for attempting to hide the proceeds of the erroneously issued check.[300]

[3] Foreign Enforcement of Tax Liens

The general tax lien attaches to property of the taxpayer wherever it is located and thus encumbers property outside the United States. Although the lien may attach to property outside the United States, enforcement of the lien is quite another matter. Generally, foreign jurisdictions have not enforced tax claims.[301] A foreign government's cooperation may not be necessary if a court in the United States has jurisdiction over the taxpayer. The court may order the person to repatriate the property located in the foreign country as long as no foreign law would be violated.[302] Moreover, the court may order a person within its jurisdiction not to act with respect to property of the taxpayer outside the United States.[303] However, state law can be applied in rather curious ways. In *United States v. First National City Bank* (the "Omar" case), the Supreme Court followed state law to find "long-arm jurisdiction" for a federal district court to issue an injunction directed to a New York bank with a Montevideo, Uruguay, branch restraining the transfer of funds on deposit in Montevideo to the taxpayer. On the other hand, the Court ignored New York law that treated the branch as a separate entity and gave the depositor no "right" (subject to a tax lien) against the New York bank until there had been a demand and wrongful refusal at the foreign branch.

---

[299] United States v. McRee, 984 F2d 1144 (11th Cir. 1993), decision vacated, and reh'g en banc ordered, 93-1 USTC ¶ 50,254, at 87,656 (11th Cir. 1993).

[300] 18 USC § 2322.

[301] United States v. Harden, 63-2 USTC ¶ 9768 (Can. 1963). Her Majesty the Queen ex rel. British Columbia v. Gilbertson, 433 F. Supp. 410 (D. Or. 1977) aff'd, 597 F2d 1161 (9th Cir. 1979). See also Johnson et al., "Reciprocal Enforcement of Tax Claims Through Tax Treaties," 33 Tax Law. 469 (1980). Although treaties have provided for exchanges of information by competent authorities for tax enforcement purposes, broad mutual collection provisions have not been considered desirable. Under the most frequently used provision (see U.S. Model Treaty, Article 26), obligations are assumed by signatories for the purpose of ensuring that treaty benefits are obtained only by those entitled to them. More general enforcement provisions are found in the five income tax treaties with Denmark, France, the Netherlands, the Netherlands Antilles, and Sweden.

[302] United States v. Ross, 302 F2d 831 (2d Cir. 1962), aff'g 196 F. Supp. 243 (SDNY 1961); United States v. McNulty, 446 F. Supp. 90 (ND Cal. 1978) (taxpayer who won Irish sweepstakes ordered to repatriate from the Island of Jersey assets sufficient to satisfy taxes owed).

[303] United States v. First Nat'l City Bank, 379 US 378 (1965) (injunction restraining New York bank with branch in Uruguay from transferring taxpayer's funds deposited with that branch upheld).

¶ 14.10 RESPONSES TO COLLECTION ACTIONS—DEFECTS IN THE GENERAL TAX LIEN

As described previously, the general tax lien is a statutory lien, arising by operation of law when specific statutory conditions exist. These statutory conditions exist only where the Service complies with statutory procedures for assessment, giving notice to the taxpayer of the assessment and permitting the taxpayer to make a voluntary payment. Where the Service has not complied with these statutory procedures, the prerequisites to the lien do not exist. A taxpayer may defend against collection of tax by the Service administratively or in court on the ground that the procedures in the Code have not been followed. It should be noted that any procedural defense might be dismissed as a "technical defense." However, as one court has noted:[304]

> Any procedural defense is in a sense "technical." The procedures set forth in the Internal Revenue Code were prescribed for the protection of both Government and taxpayer. Neglect to comply with those procedures may entail consequences which the neglecting party must be prepared to face, whether such party be the taxpayer or the Government.

Based on the previous discussion, the following procedural defenses can be used against the general tax lien:

- The assessment was made at the time prohibited by law.
- The Service failed to send the taxpayer a notice of the assessment and demand for its payment.
- A notice and demand was received, but the Service did not give the taxpayer the opportunity to make payment within the ten-day period.
- A notice and demand was given, but the Service did not send it to the taxpayer's last known address.
- Collection of the assessed tax by foreclosure of the tax lien is prohibited by the statute of limitations on collection.
- The interest of the taxpayer that the Service asserts is subject to the tax lien does not constitute "property or rights to property" of the taxpayer.

---

[304] United States v. Lehigh, 201 F. Supp. 224, 234 (WD Ark. 1961), quoted with approval in Brafman v. United States, 384 F2d 863, 868 (5th Cir. 1967).

C   ENFORCED COLLECTION PROCEDURES

¶ 14.11   OVERVIEW OF LEVY AND SALE PROVISIONS

The Service may collect the amount of an assessment by levy against all property and rights to property (except certain property exempt from levy under Section 6334) in the hands of the taxpayer or subject to the tax lien may be seized after the Service has sent the taxpayer a notice and demand and the taxpayer has failed to pay the amount assessed.[305] The person in possession of (or obligated with respect to) property or rights to property subject to levy on which levy has been made must surrender the property on demand.[306] Failure to honor the levy renders the person served personally liable and subject to penalty,[307] but if the person does honor the levy, he is discharged from any liability to the taxpayer arising from surrender or payment.[308] The Service may also demand that books or records containing information with respect to property subject to levy be opened to it.[309]

Seized property must be sold quickly after notice within the time limits, at the place, in the manner, and under the conditions set forth in Section 6335. Special rules are provided for perishable goods.[310] The buyer at the execution sale must be given a certificate of sale with respect to personal property and a deed with respect to realty,[311] which documents generally are prima facie evidence that the sale was valid and conveys all the taxpayer's right in the property sold.[312] Although the person whose property has been levied upon may redeem the property at any time prior to sale by paying the amount due plus costs of the proceeding, personal property may not be redeemed after the sale, and real estate may only be redeemed within 180 days of the sale.[313] The Service need keep records only of sales of realty,[314] but it must determine expenses of levy and sale[315] and apply the proceeds first against these expenses and then against any specific tax liability on the seized property. Only after

---

[305] IRC § 6331.

[306] IRC § 6332.

[307] IRC § 6332(c).

[308] IRC § 6332(d).

[309] IRC § 6333.

[310] IRC § 6336.

[311] IRC § 6338.

[312] IRC § 6339.

[313] IRC § 6337.

[314] IRC § 6340.

[315] IRC § 6341.

these other liabilities have been satisfied are the proceeds applied against the delinquent tax liability.[316]

The Service has the authority to release a levy to facilitate collection of a tax against the taxpayer or, where a third person is involved, if the levy is wrongful.[317] Generally, however, a taxpayer may not maintain an action to enjoin or restrain the collection of a tax,[318] although this prohibition does not apply to a third person who claims the levy was wrongful.[319]

The discussion in this part describes (1) the levy authority and its limits; (2) the property subject to levy; (3) the obligations of persons served with the levy; and (4) levy and sale procedures.

¶ 14.12 ISSUES RELATING TO THE VALIDITY OF LEVY AND SALE

Levy and sale are authorized only if the Service has followed the provisions of the Code and the constitutional rights of the taxpayer have been respected. Although all of the potential issues that may arise where enforced collection action is taken cannot be anticipated, the following list identifies some of them.

1. A levy may be made only after there has been an assessment, notice and demand and, in nonjeopardy situations, a notice of intention to levy given at least thirty days before the levy.[320]
2. The manner of the levy must be effective to seize the property in question.[321]
3. The levy must be served on the proper person.[322]
4. The property purportedly seized must have been in the hands of the person served with the levy on the date of the levy.[323]
5. The levy must have been served within the statutory period of collection.[324]
6. The seizure must not have violated the constitutional rights of the levied party.[325]

---

[316] IRC § 6342.

[317] IRC § 6343.

[318] IRC § 7421.

[319] IRC §§ 7421, 7426.

[320] See infra ¶ 14.12.

[321] See infra ¶¶ 14.12, 14.15.

[322] See infra ¶ 14.14[2].

[323] See infra ¶ 14.14[5].

[324] See infra ¶ 14.15[4][b].

[325] See infra ¶ 14.15[4][a].

7. The property purportedly seized must have been subject to levy.[326]
8. The levy must have been made by an authorized revenue officer.[327]
9. Seizure and sale must have met the requirements of the Code as to notice and date of sale.[328]

¶ 14.13 WHEN AND HOW LEVY IS MADE

[1] In General

The property of a delinquent taxpayer may be seized and sold, without judicial intervention, where (1) tax has been assessed; (2) the taxpayer has been given notice of the assessment and a demand for its payment; (3) the taxpayer has neglected or refused to pay the assessed tax within ten days after the notice and demand; and (4) the Service has notified the taxpayer of its intention to levy more than thirty days before the levy. If these conditions exist, Section 6331(a) allows the Service to satisfy a tax liability "by levy upon all property and rights to property belonging to the taxpayer or on which there is a lien." As the Supreme Court has stated, a levy is a "summary, non-judicial process, a method of self-help authorized by statute which provides the Commissioner with a prompt and convenient method for satisfying delinquent tax claims."[329] Once the Service has levied on a taxpayer's property or a third party's property to pay the taxpayer's tax liability, the taxpayer is no longer entitled to instruct the Service on how to allocate payments.[330]

There are, however, limitations on the peremptory use of the levy. The Service is required to send three notices to a taxpayer before it may seize by levy property belonging to the taxpayer: the Section 6303 notice and demand, the Section 6330 collection due process notice, and the Section 6331(d) notice before levy. Both the collection due process notice and the notice before levy must either be given personally to the taxpayer, left at the taxpayer's residence or usual place of business, or sent to the taxpayer's last known address by cer-

---

[326] See infra ¶ 14.15.

[327] See infra ¶ 14.15.

[328] See infra ¶ 14.18.

[329] United States v. National Bank of Commerce, 472 US 713 (1985), quoting United States v. Sullivan, 333 F2d 100, 116 (3d Cir. 1964).

[330] See Theodore A. Pride & Assocs. v. United States, 87 AFTR2d 2001-881 (ED Pa. 2001) (holding that taxpayers may not designate the application of tax payments to the Service that are involuntarily made, and that payments the Service received as result of levy were involuntarily made).

tified or registered mail.[331] Both notices must be given no less than thirty days before the day of the levy and must include with the notice "a brief statement" describing the following information:[332]

1. The Code provisions and procedures dealing with levy and sale of property;
2. Administrative appeal rights and procedures about a levy and sale;
3. The alternatives available to a taxpayer that could avoid a levy, including an installment payment agreement; and
4. The Code provisions and procedures relating to redemptions of property and release of liens on property.

A levy made before assessment or before the sending of a notice and demand is outside the statutory authority and void.[333] In addition, unless there has been a finding that collection of the tax is in jeopardy, a taxpayer is given a ten-day grace period after a notice and demand before "it shall be lawful for the (Service) to collect such tax. . . . "[334] A levy made within the grace period is void.[335] In addition to the ten-day grace period following the Section 6303

---

[331] IRC §§ 6330(a)(2), 6331(d)(2).

[332] IRC §§ 6330(a)(3), 6331(d)(4). The waiting period under Section 6331 before the Service can levy increased from ten to thirty days for levies issued after June 30, 1989. Conference R. 1104, Technical and Miscellaneous Revenue Act of 1988, 100th Cong., 2d Sess. 220–222, reprinted in 1988-3 CB 710–712.

[333] Dierks v. United States, 215 F. Supp. 338 (SDNY 1963) (levy made before Tax Court decision had become final under Section 7481 and thus when assessment was prohibited); LOC Indus., Inc. v. United States, 423 F. Supp. 265 (MD Tenn. 1976) (no notice and demand prior to levy); Mrizek v. Long, 187 F. Supp. 830 (ND Ill. 1959) (levy made prior to notice and demand). See Shapiro v. Secretary of State, 499 F2d 527, 531 n.12 (DC Cir. 1974), aff'd, 424 US 614 (1976). However, the Service's position is that failure to give notice of the tax liability within the sixty-day period does not invalidate the assessment (Reg. § 301.6303-1(a)), so that a levy made ten days after an untimely notice and demand is valid. As explained at supra ¶ 14.05, this position is not supported by the statute nor by the cases, which have generally held the Service to strict compliance with statutorily required procedures. See, e.g., Laing v. United States, 423 US 161 (1976).

However, the use of a signature stamp to sign a levy instead of an original signature does not invalidate a levy, nor does it violate the taxpayer's due process rights. Biegelsen v. Albert, 82 AFTR2d 98-6382 (2d Cir. 1998).

[334] IRC § 6331(a).

[335] Martinez v. United States, 669 F2d 568 (9th Cir. 1982) (Service mailed notice and demand to taxpayer on same day it levied on cash and car; held, seizure improper and property ordered returned); Mrizek v. Long, 187 F. Supp. 830 (ND Ill. 1959). Compare Callahan v. Haxton, 84-2 USTC 9734 (MD Fla. 1984) (levy mailed nine days after Service demand for payment; held, prematurely sending a notice of levy does not render underlying levy illegal where levied party did not "react" until over twenty days after notice). See also McBride v. United States, 87-1 USTC 9244 (DNJ 1987), aff'd in unpublished opinion (3d Cir. July 23, 1987) (Service may rely on presumption of validity of government actions, but not where issue was whether it had sent notice of intention to levy; notice found to have been sent).

notice and demand, a levy is not permitted until a notice before levy has been given to the taxpayer no less than thirty days before the day of the levy.[336] Absent a finding of jeopardy in collection,[337] a levy made without a prelevy notice or within the thirty-day period is unauthorized and void.

Section 6331(a) allows the Service to satisfy a tax liability by levy, but it does not prescribe how a levy should be made. The levy statute only says (Section 6331(b)) that levy "includes the power of distraint and seizure by any means" and that in any case in which the Service may levy on property, it may seize and sell property. Curiously, at common law, distraint was a summary extrajudicial remedy that consisted of the seizure and holding (but not selling) of tangible personal property for the purpose of compelling payment of a debt.[338] No further guidance about how a levy or seizure is to be made is given except for two specific rules: (1) wages and salary of a government employee may be seized by a notice of levy served on his employer[339] and (2) the taxpayer must be given a notice before levy is made upon salary and wages and other property of any person to collect an unpaid tax.[340] Although the statute grants the Service the power of distraint and seizure "by any means," the usual method is by the service of a notice of levy.[341] Levy can also be effected by physical seizure of the property.[342] Where seizure is not feasible, property can be posted or tagged. A levy on intangible property is effected by serving

---

[336] IRC § 6331(d). The notice of intention to levy must be sent to the taxpayer's last known address. Chandler v. Department of Treasury, 91-1 USTC ¶ 50,209 (ND Ohio 1991) (notice of intention to levy sent to last known address because address was address on most recently filed return).

[337] IRC § 6331(g)(2).

[338] Raffaele v. Granger, 196 F2d 620 (3d Cir. 1952). Although a person aggrieved by distraint could at common law bring an action of replevin against the distrainor, no such act is permitted against the United States. 28 USC § 2463.

[339] IRC § 6331(a).

[340] IRC § 6331(d).

[341] Phelps v. United States, 421 US 330, 337 (1975) ("[h]istorically, service of notice has been sufficient to seize a debt and notice of levy and demand are equivalent to seizure"). See also Reg. § 301.6331-1(a)(1) ("levy may be made by serving a notice of levy on any person in possession of or obligated with respect to property" belonging to the taxpayer). Levy on property or rights to property of a taxpayer in the hands of a third party can be effected by service of a notice of levy. Schiff v. Simon & Schuster, Inc., 780 F2d 210 (2d Cir. 1985); United States v. Donahue Indus., Inc., 90-2 USTC ¶ 50,343 (9th Cir. 1990). Simon v. Playboy Elsinore Assocs., 91-1 USTC ¶ 50,231 (ED Pa. 1991) ("A Notice of Levy and a Demand to Comply therewith have been held to be equivalent to seizure").

[342] Revenue officers may not enter a taxpayer's house or business premises to seize property without violating the taxpayer's Fourth Amendment rights, but they may constitutionally seize a taxpayer's car parked on a street. GM Leasing Corp. v. United States, 429 US 338, 350 (1977); Reg. § 301.6331-1(a)(1).

the notice of levy. It has even been said that a revenue officer's oral instructions concerning property already seized are binding.[343]

A levy may be made either by actually seizing property or by serving a notice of levy that transfers constructive possession of the property to the government.[344] Levy on property in the hands of the taxpayer is made by the seizure and public sale of the property.[345] Seizure procedures are often used to take a taxpayer's car, house, or business property.[346] Levy on property in the hands of a third party is made by serving a notice of levy on the third party, especially when the taxpayer's property can be turned over by writing a check.[347] When a notice of levy is served on a third party, the contact is considered a third-party contact, and the taxpayer is entitled to reasonable notice of the Service's intention to make such a contact.[348] Also, before property can be levied, the taxpayer is entitled to receive a notice and demand, a notice of intention to levy, and notice of a right to a Collection Due Process hearing.

[2] Notice of and Opportunity for Hearing Before Levy

The Service may not levy on any property or right to property of any person unless the Service has notified the person in writing of the right to a hearing before the levy is made.[349] The notice is required only once. Service of the notice is made in the same way as the notice of the filing of the lien, provided in Section 6320, but the notice must be served not less than thirty days before the day of the first levy to collect the amount of the unpaid tax. The notice must include the following:

1. The amount of the unpaid tax;
2. The right to request a hearing during the thirty-day period before the Service serves the levy; and

---

[343] St. Louis Union Trust Co. v. United States, 617 F2d 1293 (8th Cir. 1980).

[344] United States v. Whiting Pools, Inc., 462 US 198 (1983).

[345] IRM 5.11.1.1.2 Notice of Levy vs. Seizure (Jan. 19, 1999). Before a third party can be held liable for failure to honor a levy, a final demand is contemplated by Section 6332(a). A separate Form 668-C (Final Demand) is used for this purpose. (See Form 14.11.)

[346] Authority to levy on certain property has been delegated to local managers. See Delegation Order No. 191 (Rev. 3).

[347] See Reg. § 301.6331-1(a)(1). A notice of levy can be served by mail. Reg. § 301.6331-1(c). Where a levy is mailed, the date and time of the levy is the date and time the notice of levy is delivered to the person served, which is presumed to be when an authorized person signs and dates the return receipt.

[348] IRC § 7602(c). The Service uses Notification of Potential Third Party Contact, Letter 3164 and Notice 1219, to give this notice.

[349] IRC § 6330(a).

3. The proposed action by the Service and the rights of the person when such action is taken, including

   a. A brief statement describing the levy and sale provisions of the Code;
   b. The procedures the Service follows in making the levy and sale of property;
   c. The administrative appeals available when a levy and sale are contemplated;
   d. The procedures to be followed for an appeal; and
   e. The alternatives available by which the taxpayer could prevent levy on property, including installment agreements under Section 6159, and the Code provisions dealing with redemption of property after levy and the release of a tax lien on property.

If the person affected by the contemplated levy requests it, the Appeals office will hear the issue of the proposed levy.[350] The Appeals officer must obtain verification from the district that the requirements of applicable law and procedures have been met, and will consider at the hearing such matters as appropriate spousal defenses, challenges to the appropriateness of the collection action, and offers of collection alternatives, such as the posting of a bond, substitution of assets, an installment payment agreement, or an offer in compromise. At the appeal, a taxpayer may also challenge the underlying liability, but only if the taxpayer has not received a notice of deficiency for the tax or did not otherwise have an opportunity to dispute the tax liability.

In making a decision, the Appeals officer may consider whether the procedures of the Code for the levy have been followed, the defenses and challenges the taxpayer raises, and whether any proposed collection action "balances the need for the efficient collection of taxes with the legitimate concern of the [taxpayer] that any collection action may be more intrusive than necessary."[351] Certain issues may not be raised at this prelevy Appeals confer-

---

[350] IRC § 6330(b). A hearing at the Appeals Office complies with Section 6330(b) when the hearing is offered to the taxpayer at the Appeals Office located nearest to the taxpayer's residence, or the taxpayer is offered a hearing with the Appeals officer by telephone conference. Katz v. Comm'r, 115 TC No. 26 (2000) (the taxpayer claimed that the office nearest his residence would place an undue burden on his witnesses, and the Appeals officer granted the taxpayer a hearing by telephone conference). A qualifying hearing does not take place if the Appeals officer sends determination letters and then schedules a hearing. Meyer v. Comm'r, 115 TC No. 31 (2000).

[351] IRC § 6330(c). Section 6330(c)(2)(B) provides that the person may also raise the issue of the underlying tax liability "if the person did not receive any statutory notice of deficiency for such tax liability or did not otherwise have an opportunity to dispute such tax liability." Unless the petitioner in a Tax Court collection due process hearing alleges these matters, the issue of the underlying liability will be deemed not to have been raised, and as a result that issue will not go before the Tax Court. See Goza v. Comm'r, 114 TC

ence, such as an issue that was raised and considered at a prior hearing under Section 6320 or any other prior administrative or judicial proceeding, and the person attempting to raise the issue materially participated in such a hearing or proceeding.

There is an opportunity for a due process in the Tax Court involving collection of income, gift, and estate taxes, if the Appeals determination on the lien or levy review is adverse to the taxpayer or other person.[352] Since review in the Tax Court, and by the Appeals office, is a due process review, the scope of review is limited.[353] The normal standard of due process review is whether

---

176 (2000). Where the underlying liability is not in issue, the court only reviews the Service's administrative determination for abuse of discretion. Sego v. Comm'r, 114 TC 604 (2000); Goza v. Comm'r, supra, at 181–182. In an Appeals collection due process hearing, the Tax Court has also held that the taxpayer is not entitled to subpoena witnesses and documents, reasoning that the informality of an Appeals conference, about which Congress knew at the time the prelevy hearing was adopted, was inconsistent with the formalities of the taking of testimony under oath, or the compulsory attendance of witnesses. Davis v. Comm'r, 115 TC 35 (2000).

On August 12, 1999, the Service issued to Mesa Oil, Inc., a Notice of Intent to Levy and Notice of Your Right to a Hearing. After a due process hearing was held, the Appeals officer issued a determination finding that the Notice of Federal Tax Lien was appropriate. Mesa appealed the Appeals decision to the district court. Citing Sections 6320 and 6330, the court held that the taxpayer was entitled to a new due process hearing with a new Appeals officer. The court found that (1) the Appeals officer gave no statement of facts, no legal analysis, and no explanation of how or why the proposed levy balanced the needs for collection with Mesa's interests; (2) the Appeals officer was not a "neutral officer"; and (3) the Service failed to make a record of the hearing, thus damaging the taxpayer's statutory right to judicial review. Mesa Oil, Inc. v. United States, 86 AFTR2d 2000-7312 (D. Colo. 2000).

[352] IRC § 6330(d). The petition for review must be both timely and filed in the appropriate court; that is, the taxes proposed to be collected are taxes over which the court normally has jurisdiction. A petition for review must be filed in the Tax Court or in the district court within thirty days of the date of mailing of the determination letter. See Offiler v. Comm'r, 114 TC 492 (2000) (taxpayer did not request a due process hearing within thirty days after the final of intent to levy, and so Appeals did not make a determination from which the taxpayer could appeal to the Tax Court, with the result that the Tax Court lacked jurisdiction over the taxpayer's petition); McCune v. Comm'r, 115 TC 114 (2000). A petition for review of the proposed collection of taxes over which the Tax Court does not have jurisdiction will be dismissed. See Van Es v. Comm'r, 115 TC 324 (2000) (dismissing a petition for review of a collection action to collect a frivolous return penalty); Moore v. Comm'r, 114 TC 171 (2000) (dismissing a petition for review of a collection action to collect trust fund taxes). In Landry v. Comm'r, 116 TC 60 (2001), the Tax Court held that it has jurisdiction under Section 6330(d)(1) even though the record was unclear as to whether the Service determined a deficiency against the taxpayer because "the underlying tax liability relates to Federal income taxes, over which [the Tax Court has] jurisdiction."

[353] Shapiro v. United States, 424 US 614 (1976). The standard of review has been described as an abuse of discretion standard, not a de novo standard. AJP Mgmt. v. United States, 87 AFTR2d 2001-347 (CD Cal. 2000), citing Goza v. Comm'r, 114 TC 176, 179–180 (2000); and Sego v. Comm'r, 114 TC 604 (2000).

there is probable cause for the Service's proposed action (or that it has a basis in fact). An existing Code provision providing for limited due process review is the jeopardy assessment review procedure of Section 7429. There is no requirement in a due process hearing for formality, and according to the Supreme Court's decision in *Shapiro*, affidavits may be used. The case may be assigned to a special trial judge of the Tax Court, and the special trial judge has the authority to make the decision of the Tax Court.[354] In the meanwhile, collection of the tax is suspended, but the statutes of limitations on collection, criminal prosecution, and other suits are also suspended.[355] During the review process, the Appeals office retains jurisdiction on the collection actions taken or proposed to be taken on the lien or levy, and after all administrative remedies have been exhausted, any change in the circumstances of the taxpayer.[356]

Regulations describe the procedures the Service will follow in more detail.[357] Section 6330 required the Service to alter its notice procedures. After an assessment, the Service will continue to send a notice and demand for payment. Absent a determination that collection is in jeopardy, a taxpayer may be sent an Urgent Notice to inform the taxpayer that the Service may levy on the taxpayer's state tax refund after thirty days from the date of the notice. The date of the Urgent Notice will also begin the increase in the failure to pay penalty if the taxpayer fails to pay the assessed tax within ten days. After January 19, 1999, if a Service office (a local office, service center, or the office of the Assistant Commissioner) intends to levy on property, the office must first notify the taxpayer of the intention to levy and of the taxpayer's right to the opportunity for a prelevy Collection Due-Process hearing with the Appeals office.[358] The Service must personally serve the taxpayer with the notice, leave the notice at the taxpayer's dwelling or usual place of abode, or mail the notice by certified or registered mail to the taxpayer's last known address.

Both in the case of (1) levy to be served to seize a state tax refund to which the taxpayer might be entitled and (2) a jeopardy levy, the Service does not notify the taxpayer of its intent to levy and or the taxpayer's right to a due process hearing; instead, the Service will give the taxpayer a notice of the taxpayer's right to a due process hearing within a reasonable time after the levy is served (a postlevy due process notice).[359] The notice of the Service's intent to levy will include a notice of the taxpayer's right to a due process hearing, the statutory provisions and administrative procedures applicable to the seizure and sale of property, the procedures for administrative appeal, and the statutory and

---

[354] IRC § 7443(b), as amended by 1998 Act § 3401(c).

[355] IRC § 6330(e).

[356] IRC § 6330(d)(2).

[357] Reg. § 301.6330-1.

[358] Reg. § 301.6330-1(a)(1).

[359] Reg. § 301.6330-1(a)(2).

administrative procedures for the redemption and release of liens on property.[360] Along with this information, the Service will include a Request for a Due Process Hearing, Form 12153. The taxpayer must file a request for a due process hearing on the Service's form or otherwise in writing within thirty days beginning on the day after the date of the notice.[361] In general, the procedures the Service will follow when the taxpayer requests a due process hearing are the same as those the Service will follow in due process appeals of filed liens;[362] indeed, the Service will hold the due process hearings together.

¶ 14.14 GENERAL PRINCIPLES APPLICABLE TO LEVIES

Certain principles apply to levies in general, and a review of these principles will answer questions about the scope of the levy authority and its limitations.

[1] A Levy May Be Made by "Any Means"

The means the Services uses to seize property depends upon the nature of the property. Tangible personal property capable of delivery, such as an automobile, is physically seized. Where intangible property is levied upon, a notice of levy is usually sufficient. If the property is in the hands of a third party, a notice of levy is used. Because of its size, bulk, or quantity (e.g., a going business), other personal property may not be removable, as may also be the case with real property. Therefore, other than a notice of levy, some additional steps must be taken to evidence the transfer of possession to the government, such as notice and padlocking.[363] Where a piece of paper represents a right to property (e.g., a promissory note or a stock certificate), an actual seizure of the document must be made; otherwise, the payor on a negotiable promissory note might remain liable to pay any holder who presents it after the notice of levy.[364]

---

[360] Reg. § 301.6330-1(a)(3), at A-A6.

[361] Reg. § 301.6330-1(a)(3), at A-A8.

[362] See the description of the due process hearing procedures following the filing of a notice of lien at supra ¶ 14.07.

[363] GM Leasing Corp. v. United States, 429 US 338 (1977) (upholding seizure of car parked on street). See, e.g., Freeman v. Mayer, 253 F2d 295 (3d Cir. 1958) (operating business padlocked and notices posted).

[364] United States v. Bowery Sav. Bank, 297 F2d 380 (2d Cir. 1961) (negotiable note); Rev. Rul. 75-355, 1975-2 CB 478 (negotiable certificate of deposit); UCC § 8-317 (attachment or levy on security or share of stock); cf. In re Frank, 55-2 USTC 9772 (SD Cal. 1955) (stock certificates). It is necessary to seize the stock certificate itself because a stock certificate is a certified security and a negotiable instrument that is freely transfera-

[2] Notice Must Be Given to the Proper Person

To be effective to seize property, a notice of levy must be directed to the proper person.[365] For example, a levy on accounts receivable is not effected by padlocking the business location where the account creditor's books are located; notices of levy must be served on the individual account debtors.[366] Similarly, to levy on the contents of a safe-deposit box, the notice of levy must be served on the bailee bank.[367]

[3] The Levy Seizes Only the Taxpayer's Interest in Property

The effect of a levy is to seize and transfer to the Service the taxpayer's right, title, and interest in the seized property. That a levy seizes only the taxpayer's interest in property follows from the scope of the tax lien. The tax lien encumbers only the taxpayer's interest in property, and a levy seizes only property "belonging" to the taxpayer or property in the hands of a third person who is subject to the lien.[368] Moreover, where the Service sells the seized property af-

---

ble without notice to the issuing corporation; without seizure of the stock certificate, the corporation could be subjected to double liability. See UCC §§ 8-102(1)(a), 8-105(1), 8-313(1)(a), 8-313(1)(c), 8-313(1)(d), 8-317(1). The National Office's position on the matter is that actual seizure of stock certificates is required if the Service wishes to sell the stock certificates. ILM 1999-18010, GL-808855-98 (Dec. 22, 1998). The owner of an interest in a mutual fund is technically a part owner of the fund. When the Service seizes a taxpayer's interest in a mutual fund, however, the levy permits the Service to ask for the certificates that represent the taxpayer's interest in the fund. The National Office says that Collection can direct the broker/manager to obtain the actual stock certificates and certificates representing the taxpayer's mutual fund shares, although it notes that, in most cases, managers pay over the cash value of the shares instead of surrendering certificates. Id.

[365] Reg. § 301.6331-1(a) ("Levy may be made by serving a notice of levy on any person in possession of or obligated with respect to property or rights to property subject to levy . . . "). The proper person in the case of the tax liability of a consolidated group of corporations includes a debtor on a debt owed to a subsidiary in the consolidated group because "the common parent corporation and each subsidiary which was a member of the group during any part of the consolidated return year shall be severally liable for any tax for such year." Reg. § 1.1502-6(a). United States v. Williams, 959 F. Supp. 210 (SDNY 1997) (shareholder of parent corporation of a consolidated group had promissory notes outstanding to both the parent and one of the subsidiaries, and so it was proper for the Service to levy against any money owed to the parent and subsidiary to collect taxes of the consolidated group).

[366] Freeman v. Mayer, 253 F2d 295 (3d Cir. 1958).

[367] Salsbury v. United States, 356 F2d 822 (DC Cir. 1966).

[368] IRC § 6331(a). See United States v. Rodgers, 461 US 677 (1983). Property belonging to a taxpayer extends to obligations. An obligation exists when the liability of the obligor is "fixed and determinable," although the right to receive payment may be deferred until a later date. Reg. § 301.6331-1(a)(1). An allowed administrative expense against a bankruptcy estate is "property" under Washington law subject to levy, and since

ter it has levied, the certificate of sale only transfers "to the purchaser all right, title, and interest of the party delinquent in and to the property sold."[369] Thus, the sale provisions indicate that a levy seizes only the taxpayer's interest in the property and that the taxpayer's interest, whatever it may be, is transferred to the Service for later sale.

[4] A Levy on Property Transfers Custody of the Property to the Service

A levy on property (real and tangible personal property) constructively transfers custody of the property to the Service, not title to the property. Although they generally do not mention the sale provisions, the cases support this view. In *Phelps v. United States*,[370] a notice of levy was served on an assignee for the benefit of creditors of the delinquent taxpayer. When the taxpayer was later adjudicated bankrupt, the bankruptcy court, exercising the summary jurisdiction it had under the old Bankruptcy Act, ordered the assignee who had not complied with the levy to turn the proceeds over for administration as part of the bankrupt estate. The question was whether the levy removed the property from the bankrupt's estate. The Supreme Court held that the bankruptcy court lacked summary jurisdiction over the proceeds because after the levy the assignee had possession of the proceeds not for the bankrupt, but on behalf of the Service. The levy created a "custodial relationship between the assignee and the United States and thereby reduced (the proceeds) to the United States'

---

the allowed administrative expense was a "fixed and determinable" liability at the time the notice of levy was served on him, the trustee held an obligation of the taxpayer. United States v. Hemmen, 51 F3d 883 (9th Cir. 1995) (a divided panel). Consequently, if a trustee is served with a levy seizing property of a taxpayer, and the trustee has allowed the taxpayer's claim as an administration expense, the trustee must pay the funds to the Service rather than to the delinquent taxpayer once the estate is liquidated and the proposed distribution is approved. The decision of the majority believed that the automatic stay in bankruptcy did not apply, and never addressed the possible exception in Section 6332(a) for property in the custody of the court. Nevertheless, once notice of the Service's claim to property has been given, there is a risk of personal liability of the trustee if payment in derogation of the Service's interest is made.

Similarly, in a bankruptcy case where a taxpayer acted as a business broker and was entitled to a commission if the sale he arranged was approved by the bankruptcy court, the taxpayer's commission was fixed and determinable for levy purposes when the bankruptcy court approved the sale even if the commission was not payable until the bankruptcy court approved the payment. United States v. Ruff, 99 F3d 1559 (11th Cir. 1996) (when the trustee paid the commission to taxpayer rather than the Service, the trustee was liable for a penalty for willful failure to honor the levy served before the sale was approved).

[369] IRC § 6329(a)(2) (personal property). See IRC § 6339(b)(2) (real property).

[370] Phelps v. United States, 421 US 330 (1975).

constructive possession."[371] *Phelps* arose under the Bankruptcy Act, which has since been replaced by a revamped version of bankruptcy laws, called the Bankruptcy Code. However, when the Supreme Court considered the effect of a prepetition levy under the Bankruptcy Code, it reached a somewhat different result than it had in *Phelps*. In *United States v. Whiting Pools, Inc.*, the Service served a notice of levy to seize the taxpayer-debtor's tangible personal property. On the next day, the taxpayer-debtor filed a petition for a reorganization under the Bankruptcy Code.[372] The Supreme Court held that the reorganization estate included the property seized by the Service and that the Bankruptcy Court was authorized to order the Service to turn over the property it seized.[373] Just as any other secured creditor, the Service was bound by the Bankruptcy Code's turnover provision in 11 USC § 542(a), which requires an entity holding property of the debtor that the trustee can use in the reorganization to turn the property over to the trustee. The Supreme Court said that levy is a procedural device to satisfy a lien but does not transfer ownership of seized property to the Service.

> The Service's interest in seized property is its lien on that property. The Internal Revenue Code's levy and seizure provisions . . . §§ 6331 and 6332, are special procedural devices available to the IRS to protect and satisfy its liens, United States v. Sullivan, 333 F. 2d 100, 116 (CA 3, 1964), and are analogous to the remedies available to private secured creditors. . . . They are provisional remedies that do not determine the Service's rights to the seized property, but merely bring the property into the Service's legal custody. . . .[374]

However, in *Phelps*, the Court had said that a notice of levy not only transferred constructive possession to the Service, it gave the Service "full legal right" to the seized property.[375] Faced with this contradictory language, the Court explained its earlier statement in *Phelps*, as "merely a restatement of the proposition that the levy gave the Service a sufficient possessory interest to avoid the bankruptcy court's supremacy jurisdiction (a proposition now irrelevant because of the expanded jurisdiction of bankruptcy courts under the Bankruptcy Code)."[376]

---

[371] Phelps v. United States, 421 US 330, 337 (1975).

[372] United States v. Whiting Pools, Inc., 462 US 198 (1983).

[373] See ¶ 16.11 for the effect of the Bankruptcy Code on tax liens.

[374] United States v. Whiting Pools, Inc., 462 US 198 (1983). On the basis of this analysis, the Sixth Circuit has said that the levy "gives the IRS the right to all property levied upon, and creates a custodial relationship between the person holding the property and the IRS so that the property comes into constructive possession of the Government." State Bank of Fraser v. United States, 861 F2d 954, 958 (6th Cir. 1988).

[375] Phelps v. United States, 421 US 330, 337 (1975).

[376] United States v. Whiting Pools, Inc., 462 US 198 (1983).

It appears, that the statements of some courts that a levy effectively transfers a substantial interest in property amounting to ownership are no longer correct.[377] The levy, according to *Whiting Pools*, does not transfer ownership of property, such as tangible personal property, to the Service. The levy brings the property into the "legal custody" of the Service subject to a sale that divests the taxpayer of the title to the property, which leaves open the effect of a levy on a bank account that need not be sold to satisfy the taxpayer's lien.[378]

---

[377] In re Pittsburgh Penguins Partners, 598 F2d 1299 (3d Cir. 1979) ("*Phelps*' further indication that service of a levy effectively transfers "full legal right" to the property levied upon is . . . sufficient to give the government a 'substantial adverse claim' of ownership as well"); United States v. Pittman, 449 F2d 623 (7th Cir. 1971) ("A valid and effective levy . . . is 'an absolute appropriation in law' and a seizure of the property levied upon, tantamount to a transfer of ownership"); Phelps v. United States, 421 US 330, 337 n.8 (1975) ("the pre-bankruptcy levy displaced any title of [the debtor]"). In United States v. Whiting Pools, Inc., 674 F2d 144 (2d Cir. 1982), the circuit court said that a taxpayer-debtor loses not title but possession of tangible personal property where it is seized by levy. According to the court, "ownership is extinguished not by the levy but only by a subsequent sale." Faced with the language of *Phelps* cited in the text, the court said it was limited to the particular circumstances "where the tax claim vastly exceeded the amount of the levy and the seizure was of cash which did not need to be sold" (citation omitted). In substantial part, the position of the Second Circuit was adopted by the Supreme Court.

[378] Phelps v. United States, 421 US 330, 337 (1975) (bankruptcy); In re Pittsburgh Penguins Partners, 598 F2d 1299 (3d Cir. 1979) (Chapter 11); In re Bush Gardens, Inc., 10 Bankr. 506 (DNJ 1979) (same result under Bankruptcy Code). The Second Circuit left this question open in United States v. Whiting Pools, Inc., 674 F2d 144 (2d Cir. 1982); Altman v. Comm'r, 88-1 USTC 9166 (D. Haw. 1987) (levy on trust funds gave Service full legal rights to funds; *Phelps* followed, and *Whiting Pools* distinguished); Brewer v. United States, 91-2 USTC ¶ 50,453 (SDNY 1991) (title to funds in union annuity and vacation fund passed to Service at time of levy).

In *Challenge Air International, Inc.*, the Eleventh Circuit rejected the Service's argument that a prebankruptcy levy on cash equivalent accomplished a seizure, unlike the levy on tangible property involved in *Whiting Pools*. Challenge Air Int'l, Inc. v. United States, 952 F2d 384 (11th Cir. 1992). According to the Eleventh Circuit, ownership of property is not determined by a levy, and the court refused to find even that constructive possession had been transferred to the Service before the taxpayer filed its Chapter 11 petition. This view of the effect of a levy is inconsistent with the analysis of the Second Circuit and the Supreme Court in *Whiting Pools*, which pointed to Code provisions dealing with the sale of personal and real property as showing that title to those classes of property was transferred only on sale. The Third Circuit also believes that constructive possession of a bank account passes to the Service on the service of a levy. See Resolution Trust Corp. v. Gill, 960 F2d 336 (3d Cir. 1992) ("Assuming the levy preceded the issuance of the checks, the levy seized the funds in Gill's IRA accounts and transferred constructive possession of the funds to the IRS").

There is more uncertainty about a receivable, with one circuit (pre–*Whiting Pools*) holding that the Service need not turnover an account seized by levy to satisfy an amount greater than the account because the taxpayer's right of redemption is valueless. See Cross Elec. Co. v. United States, 664 F2d 1218 (4th Cir. 1981); In re Eisenbarger, 93-2 USTC ¶ 50,538, 160 BR 542 (Bankr. ED Va. 1993) (the Service entitled to retain cash it had levied on before bankruptcy, and did not need to turn the cash over to bankruptcy court).

Even if a levy only transfers "legal custody" of property to the Service, the control the Service has over the property prevents the Service from penalizing a taxpayer for any postlevy diminution in the value of the property attributable to the Service's conduct.[379]

[5] The Levy Does Not Seize After-Acquired Property

A levy does not seize after-acquired property. A notice of levy does not operate to seize property acquired by the taxpayer or a third person holding prop-

---

An account receivable is not the equivalent of money. Consequently, applying the rationale of *Whiting Pools*, a levy served on an account debtor to seize receivables owed to a creditor-taxpayer does not transfer ownership of the receivables to the Service. In re Federation of Puerto Rican Orgs. of Brownsville, Inc., 93-2 USTC ¶ 50,454, 155 BR 44 (EDNY 1993) (Service also not a secured creditor, because it did not perfect its lien by filing a notice of federal tax lien). When the Service serves a levy to seize an account receivable, it obtains constructive possession or custody of the receivable. The taxpayer retains the right to a notice of sale, the right to redeem the property prior to sale by paying the tax obligation, and the right to any surplus realized on the sale of the property. The taxpayer has been held to have a sufficient property interest in the receivables for them to become part of a Chapter 11 estate. Id. In a bankruptcy proceeding, bankruptcy courts have differed over whether a prelevy bankruptcy is subject to turnover order, with some courts believing that even when the levy is on cash or cash equivalents, the taxpayer debtor retains sufficient residual rights in the cash to support a turnover order. Hancock Bank of La. v. District Dir. (In the Matter of Jerry Creel), 79 AFTR2d 97-2621 (Bankr. ED La. 1997) (gathering bankruptcy cases).

Other courts agree that the Service's levy on a bank account does not transfer ownership of the account to the Service, and they may conclude that constructive possession passes to the Service, but they still find that the account proceeds are included in the bankruptcy estate and subject to the jurisdiction of the bankruptcy court. See Gouveia v. Internal Revenue Service, In re Quality Health Care, 80 AFTR2d 97-5879 (ND Ind. 1997):

> The Court is persuaded by the reasoning of the majority of the courts . . . and concludes that the fact that the IRS served its Notice of Levy on the Bank Prepetition did not, standing alone, transfer ownership of the Bank account to the IRS, and thus, the monies remitted by the Bank to the IRS Postpetition remain property of the Debtor's Estate pursuant to section 541(a) [of the Bankruptcy Code]. However, the Court also concludes that at the time of the Notice of Levy was served on the Bank the Notice effectively put a freeze on the account, and placed the account in the constructive possession of the IRS as of the date the Notice was served on the Bank, or prior to the Petition date.

[379] United States v. Pittman, 449 F2d 623 (7th Cir. 1971) (Service served notice of levy to seize real property and exercised rights of owner to rent; held, taxpayer entitled to credit for value of property on date it should have been sold). Accord Barlows, Inc. v. United States, 84-1 USTC 9233 (Bankr. Ct., ED Va. 1984), aff'd in unpublished opinion (4th Cir. July 22, 1985) (post–*Whiting Pools* case saying *Pittman* still "viable as precedent" and holding that taxpayer entitled to credit for full value of account receivable, even though Service failed to collect full amount from account debtor).

erty of the taxpayer after the date of the levy.[380] Thus, a notice of levy served on a bank at which a taxpayer has an account does not operate to seize a deposit made to the taxpayer's account after the date of the notice.[381] There are exceptions to this rule. A levy on salary and wages payable to or received by a taxpayer is continuous from the date the levy is first made until the levy is released under Section 6343.[382] Since a levy has no prospective effect, except where wages and salary are involved, the statute contemplates that successive seizures will be made until the amount due from the taxpayer is fully paid.[383]

There is another exception to the general rule that a levy seizes only property or rights to property belonging to the taxpayer on the date of the levy.[384] A continuous levy of up to 15 percent of the amount of the payment is provided for specified payments to or received by a taxpayer from the date of the levy until the date the levy is released.[385] A specified payment, subject to the 15 percent continuous "levy," means "any Federal payment *other than* a payment for which eligibility is based on the income or assets (or both) of a payee."[386] This means that a continuous levy applies to non-means-tested recurring Federal payments, such as social security payments, which were not subject to levy under prior law. In addition, a continuous levy attaches to 15 percent of unemployment benefits; worker's compensation benefits; the nonexempt amount of wages, salary, and other income;[387] as well as certain public assistance payments.[388]

---

[380] Section 6331(b) states: "A levy shall extend only to property possessed and obligations existing at the time thereof."

[381] Reg. § 301.6331-1(a)(1).

[382] IRC § 6331(e).

[383] IRC § 6331(c).

[384] IRC § 6331(h), added by the Taxpayer Relief Act of 1997 § 1024(a)(1)–1024(a)(2) applicable to levies issued after the effective date of the act, August 5, 1997. The act redesignated Section 6331(h) as Section 6334(i). On December 14, 1998, the Service announced that as of that date it had no procedures for serving levies under Section 6331(h), and that no levies under authority of Section 6331(h) had been or would be issued until continuous levy procedures are issued. Notice 98-62, 1998-51 IRB 1. When such procedures are released, they will require that a continuous levy must be clearly identified on the face of the levy as a levy made pursuant to Section 6331(h) to distinguish it from an ordinary levy.

[385] IRC § 6331(h)(1).

[386] IRC § 6331(h)(2)(A).

[387] IRC § 6331(h)(2)(B). See also IRC § 6334(a)(9).

[388] IRC § 6331(h)(2)(C). In June 2000, the Service announced that it had adopted the Federal Payment Levy Program, which collects overdue taxes by a continuous levy on certain federal payments. IRS News Release (IR) 2000-45 (June 29, 2000). Initially, continuous levies will apply to federal retirement benefits paid to individuals through the Office of Personal Management and federal payments to vendors doing business with the government. The program will be expanded to federal employment salaries, some social security benefits, and other federal payments. However, the program does not apply to

[6] A Summons May Be Used to Discover Property Subject to Levy

Information may be ordered produced to identify property subject to levy. To effect a levy that has already been made or one that is about to be made, the Service may require "any person having custody or control of any books or records, containing evidence of statements relating to the property" of the taxpayer to supply information.[389] This power to seek information adds little, if anything, to the already broad powers the Service has to examine books by virtue of Section 7602 for the purpose of "collecting any [internal revenue] liability."[390] However, the Service typically uses the demand of Section 6333 for the purpose of obtaining information from a bank concerning the balances and accounts of a taxpayer Form 2270 (Notice to Exhibit Books and Records) is used for this purpose. (See Form 14.7.) This demand is not subject to the restrictions otherwise imposed upon the use of a third-party summons directed to a bank. The third-party summons rules[391] do not refer to a demand under Section 6333 and, in any event, exclude a summons "in aid of the collection of" an assessed tax.[392] Nevertheless, this does not mean that a demand under Section 6333 could not be subject to some of the same objections that may be raised where a summons is served under Section 7602.[393]

---

payments to a delinquent taxpayer when the taxpayer is in bankruptcy, in a hardship situation, or had applied for relief as an innocent or injured spouse. Similarly, the program does not apply to such federal insurance payments as those for black lung disease.

[389] IRC § 6333.

[390] But see United States v. Agin, 81 AFTR2d 98-451 (3d Cir. 1997). In *Agin*, when the Service summoned the taxpayer/corporation's president to appear and give testimony and produce books and records about the taxpayer's finances, and apparently to prepare financial statements for Collection Information Statement for Business (Form 433B) and Collection Statement for Individual (Form 433A), the district court held that the Service "may not require [the president] to prepare those forms," struck the language so requiring the creation of new documents, and otherwise enforced the summons. The circuit court affirmed the order. The corporation's president also claimed a Fifth Amendment privilege as grounds for not honoring the summons and the district court's order, but the circuit court said that he was required to claim the privilege on a question-by-question and document-by-document basis.

[391] IRC § 7609.

[392] IRC § 7609(c)(2)(B).

[393] For objections to a summons, see Chapter 13.

FORM 14.7
NOTICE TO EXHIBIT BOOKS AND RECORDS

Form **2270** (Rev. October 1992)	Department of the Treasury — Internal Revenue Service **Demand to Exhibit Books and Records**	
To *(Name and address of person holding books or records)* Alan Michaels, CPA One Main Street Anytown, NY 10000		
Taxpayer *(Name and address)* John and Mary Doe One Main Street Anytown, NY 10000		**Taxpayer Identifying Number**

Please have ready for our examination any books or records in your possession or control containing information on property or rights to property belonging to the taxpayer identified above. We must inspect these records, because a levy is about to be made (or was made) on property or rights to property belonging to this taxpayer.

This authority is authorized by section 6333 of the Internal Revenue Code and corresponding regulation, quoted below.

Revenue Officer *(Signature)* /s/ Revenue Officer	Office address and telephone number One Broadway Anytown, NY 00000 (212) 123–4567	Date 7/17/01

Excerpt From Internal Revenue Code

Section 6333. Production of Books

If a levy has been made or is about to be made on any property, or right to property, any person having custody or control of any books or records, containing evidence or statements relating to the property or right to property subject to levy, shall, upon demand of the Secretary, exhibit such books or records to the Secretary.

Regulation Issued Under Section 6333

Section 301.6333-1. Production of Books

If a levy has been made or is about to be made on any property or rights to property, any person, having custody or control of any books or records containing evidence or statements relating to the property or rights to property subject to levy, shall, upon demand of the internal revenue officer who has made or is about to make the levy, exhibit such books or records to such officer.

Right to Financial Privacy Act of 1978
(Public Law 95-630)

The Right to Financial Privacy Act of 1978 contains provisions governing the disclosure of information contained in the financial records of customers to certain government authorities. Under Section 1113(c) of the Act, nothing prohibits the disclosure of financial records in accordance with procedures authorized by the Internal Revenue Code.

* U.S Government Printing Office1992-343-049/71909   Form **2270** (Rev. 10-92)

¶ 14.15 PROPERTY SUBJECT TO LEVY

There are two broad categories of property subject to levy. A levy may be made on "all property and rights to property (except such property as is exempt under Section 6334) [1] belonging to . . . (the taxpayer) or [2] on which there is a lien provided in this chapter for the payment of such tax (the assessed tax set forth in the notice and demand)."[394] It is understandable that property belonging to a taxpayer—that is, in which he has "property or rights to property"—may be seized by levy where that property is in the taxpayer's possession.[395] A levy may also be made of property belonging to the taxpayer even if it is not formally in his possession. Seizure by levy may be made of property in the hands of an alter ego of the taxpayer.[396] The situations in which an alter ego levy has been used are many and varied. The contents in a safe at a parent's house were held to belong to the son and subject to levy;[397] the "owner" of a safe-deposit box failed to prove a valid gift of the box and its contents by the taxpayer who retained coaccess to the box;[398] a property transfer by taxpayers to a church was a sham—the church was the alter ego of the taxpayers and property held by the church was in fact property of the taxpayers;[399] and Missouri law applied to defeat a "sometime" wife's claim to her tax protestor husband's transferred property.[400]

---

[394] IRC § 6331(a). The term "property" for the purposes of levy is further amplified in Section 6331(b), which provides that, "in any case in which the Secretary or his delegate may levy upon property or rights to property, he may seize and sell such property or rights to property (whether real or personal, tangible or intangible)."

[395] By the same token, property that does not belong to the taxpayer is not subject to levy. See, e.g., Zimler v. United States, 79-1 USTC ¶ 9395 (EDNY 1979) (certificates of deposit held not subject to levy to satisfy assessment against divorced husband because the wife had legal title to them); Belton v. Comm'r, 562 F. Supp. 30 (DDC 1982), reconsideration denied, 562 F. Supp. 30 (DDC 1982) (wrongful levy of wife's bank account to pay husband's tax liability). When the taxpayer had assigned accounts receivable before the lien arose and before levy was made on the account debtor, the account debtor, under Michigan law, held no property belonging to the taxpayer subject to levy. United States v. General Motors Corp., 929 F2d 249 (6th Cir. 1991).

[396] GM Leasing Corp. v. United States, 429 US 338 (1977); United States v. Plastic Electro-Finishing Corp., 313 F. Supp. 330 (EDNY 1970), aff'd, 443 F2d 501 (2d Cir. 1971) Tri-State Equip. v. United States, 79 AFTR2d 97-2502 (ED Cal. 1997) (trust, which owned equipment and purportedly leased it to the taxpayer, was held alter ego of taxpayer using California alter ego law); United States v. Landsberger, 80 AFTR2d 97-7296 (D. Ariz. 1997) ("The 'nominee/alter' ego theory is clearly viable in this instance even though the assets are held by a trust, and not a corporation").

[397] See, e.g., Bassett v. United States, 80-1 USTC ¶ 9116 (DNH 1979).

[398] Vicknair v. United States, 80-2 USTC ¶ 9746 (SD Fla. 1980).

[399] Loving Saviour Church v. United States, 556 F. Supp. 688 (DSD 1983).

[400] Scoville v. United States, 85 AFTR2d 2000-502 (WD Mo. 1999).

The alter ego doctrine is generally applicable to corporations, but it can also be applied to other business entities, including trusts. For example, the Service has successfully used the doctrine when new company "purchased" assets and assumed liabilities of the taxpayer-corporation, except taxes; when corporate funds were used to pay personal expenses;[401] where a church was found to be alter ego of taxpayers;[402] where the taxpayer treated church property as his own and levy on church's bank account upheld);[403] and where the property of a family trust belonged to taxpayer.[404] Also, there is a difference between the issue of whether a corporation is a separate taxable entity for income tax purposes and whether it is an alter ego for tax collection purposes,[405] and the same is true for trusts formed to defeat collection.[406] In determining whether property belongs to the taxpayer or to the third person, the Service also uses an approach similar to one the courts have adopted in choosing the proper taxable person where the assignment-of-income, sham-transaction-or-business-purpose, and substance-over-form doctrines are applied.

State law may determine whether an individual is the taxpayer's nominee, allowing the taxpayer to avoid his or her financial obligations, and state law may identify certain badges of fraud in deciding the issue, such as (1) lack of consideration; (2) transfers of the taxpayer's entire estate; (3) taxpayer's relationship to the alleged nominee; (4) pendency or threat of litigation; (5) secrecy or hurriedness of the transfer; (6) departure from usual method of business; (7) taxpayer's retention of possession of the transferred property; and (8) reservation of benefit to the taxpayer.[407]

The second category of property subject to levy is property a delinquent taxpayer has transferred. Since the Service may levy only after making an assessment of tax against the taxpayer, providing the taxpayer with a notice and demand, and the taxpayer's failure or refusal to pay, property the taxpayer transfers after the assessment date is encumbered by the general assessment lien. Consequently, property that belonged to the taxpayer on the assessment date but that is in the hands of a transferee or subsequent transferee on the date of levy may be seized from the transferee.[408] The seizure of property from postassessment transferees of delinquent taxpayers has been recognized by a

---

[401] Pacific Dev., Inc. v. United States, 79-1 USTC ¶ 9138 (DDC 1979), aff'd, Valley Fin., Inc. v. United States, 629 F2d 162 (DC Cir. 1980).

[402] Loving Saviour Church v. United States, 728 F2d 1085 (8th Cir. 1984).

[403] All One Faith in One God State Universal Life Church, Inc. v. United States, 76-1 USTC 9409 (SD Cal. 1976).

[404] Itz v. United States, 85-1 USTC ¶ 9345 (WD Tex. 1985).

[405] See Wolfe v. United States, 798 F2d 1241 (9th Cir. 1986).

[406] See United States v. Geissler, 94-1 USTC ¶ 50,060 (D. Idaho 1993).

[407] Scoville v. United States, 85 AFTR2d 2000-502 (WD Mo. 1999).

[408] Reg. § 301.6331-1(a)(1).

number of courts.[409] Not all transferees are exposed to levy. If the transferee is entitled to "superpriority" or is a person otherwise protected under Section 6323 from the effect of the tax lien, then the transferee is also protected from levy.[410]

[1] Specific Property Subject to Levy

[a] Salary and Wages

Notice of an intention to levy is required when any property of a taxpayer is to be seized. The Service uses Form 668-W (Notice of Levy on Wages, Salary, and Other Income) to provide such notice. (See Form 14.8.) At one time salary and wages were the only type of property where a special notice of intention to levy had to be given. A taxpayer has thirty days after the date of the prelevy notice to work out his tax debt. Unlike a levy served to seize other property, a levy served on salary or wages is continuous.[411] As previously noted, the levy is effective from the date the levy is first made until the date the levy is released for one of the reasons set out in Section 6343: (1) the liability is satisfied or becomes time barred; (2) release will facilitate collection; (3) an installment payment agreement has been entered into; and (4) the levy is determined to be creating an economic hardship due to the financial condition of the taxpayer.[412] In providing this exception to the levy rules, Section 6331(e) overruled *United States v. Long Island Drug Co.*[413] and similar cases

---

[409] Busse v. United States, 542 F2d 421 (7th Cir. 1976) (family home transferred by husband to wife under divorce decree was encumbered by tax liens at the time filed against the husband and so subject to lien and levy in hands of former wife); Falsone v. Foley, 66-2 USTC ¶ 9478 (WDNY 1966). Cf. Hill v. United States, 94-1 USTC ¶ 50,037 (WDNC 1993) (daughter established that she did not own house as nominee for taxpayer father so that levy was wrongful; cases discussed).

[410] Reg. § 301.6331-1(a)(1). Issue involving the priority of the tax lien and other liens are discussed in Chapter 16.

[411] The term "wages or salary payable to or received by a taxpayer" in Section 6331(e) has been held to include commissions paid to an independent contractor. United States v. Jefferson-Pilot Life Ins. Co., 49 F3d 1020 (4th Cir. 1995) ("[t]he underlying purpose of the provision is to provide a means of levying upon remuneration payable to a taxpayer on a recurring basis for personal services performed by the payor").

[412] IRC §§ 6331(e), 6343(a)(1) When a levy is served on wages, the Service levy begins on the first payroll period after the employer receives the levy. United States v. Metro Interior, Inc., 93-2 USTC ¶ 50,389 (WD Mo. 1993). If the taxpayer leaves a job after a notice of levy has been served, and the employer pays severance pay, the severance pay is subject to levy, with exemptions based on the terms of the payment (e.g., if the taxpayer receives biweekly paychecks, two weeks' exempt amount i subtracted from each of the checks).

[413] United States v. Long Island Drug Co., 115 F2d 983 (2d Cir. 1940).

that, in effect, required successive levies to seize wages or salary earned by the performance of services after an initial levy. The Taxpayer Relief Act of 1997 significantly changed the amount that the Service can seize from a taxpayer's salary and wages by limiting the amount subject to the continuous levy to 15 percent of the non-exempt amount the employer pays (the exempt amount of salary, wages, and other income is calculated under Section 6334(d)).[414] Section 6343 was also amended in 1998 to provide that in the case of a levy on wages and salary payable to the taxpayer, the Service may release the levy on agreement with the taxpayer that the tax is not collectible.[415] Deferred compensation payable under a pension plan is subject to levy.[416]

[b] Insurance Policies

Life insurance and endowment policies of living taxpayers may be levied upon, but since 1966 a special procedure has been provided in Section 6332(b). The taxpayer has ninety days after the service of a levy on an insurer to find the funds to pay the delinquent tax or work out some other arrangement with the Service.[417] After the ninety-day period, the insurer is required to honor the levy by paying over the amount the taxpayer could have had advanced to him on the ninetieth day (i.e., the cash loan value of the policy), plus any amounts the insurer improperly advanced the taxpayer-insured after the insurer had actual notice or knowledge of the tax lien.[418] As a result, the policy continues to protect the taxpayer's family, but the amount the taxpayer could have borrowed on the policy from the insurer is paid to satisfy the tax liability. After honoring the levy, the insurer may deal with the taxpayer-insured as it wishes, at least until it receives a new notice of lien.[419] The government has contended that the loan value should be determined as of the date of

---

[414] See IRC §§ 6331(h)(2)(B) and 6334(a)(9). See IRC § 6334(d)(4) for the calculation of the exempt amount of wages, salary, and other income. For Service procedures, see IRM 5.11.5.4 Exempt Amount (May 5, 1998). See Notice 97-71, 1997-49 IRB 9, providing tables for 1998, which show the amount of an individual's income that is exempt from a notice of levy used to collect delinquent tax in 1998, on Forms 668-W, 668-W(c), and 668-W(c)(DO).

[415] IRC § 6343(e), as amended by 1998 Act § 3433(a), applicable to levies effected after December 31, 1999.

[416] Reg. § 1.401(a)-13(b).

[417] The taxpayer may transfer the insurance policy to the beneficiaries during the ninety-day period, and they may obtain a discharge of the tax lien on the policy by paying over the cash loan value to the Service. S. Rep. No. 1708, 89th Cong., 2d Sess. (1966), reprinted in 1966-2 CB 876, 888–889. An annuity contract is not a life insurance or endowment policy covered by Section 6332(b). United States v. Metropolitan Life Ins. Co., 874 F2d 1497 (11th Cir. 1989).

[418] IRC § 6332(b)(2).

[419] IRC § 6323(b)(9)(C).

the levy. This contention has been rejected in favor of determining the amount of the loan value as of the ninetieth day after service of the levy.[420] If the taxpayer defaults in paying premiums during the ninety-day period and the policy is automatically converted to paid-up term insurance, the levy may reach nothing.[421] However, the government may foreclose the tax lien against whatever equity the taxpayer has in the term insurance, but it cannot exercise the insured's option to surrender the policy for its net cash value within three months from the date of default.[422]

[c] Bank Accounts

A deposit by one party of money in a bank is generally considered to create a debtor-creditor relationship between the bank and the depositor, the amount of the debt being the amount on deposit. Normally, the levy is made by serving a notice of levy on the debtor-bank with whom the taxpayer's funds are on deposit.[423] Irrespective of state banking laws or bylaws of the banking institution that may provide that the amount on deposit may not be paid except on presentation of the passbook, the bank must honor a notice of levy served on it notwithstanding a failure on the part of the government to present the passbook or to guarantee to indemnify the bank if necessary.[424] On the other hand, where the bank account is evidenced by a certificate of deposit, the government must actually seize the certificate and present that certificate in order to obtain payment.[425]

A special rule applies to the surrender of deposits by a bank.[426] Under Section 6332(c) a bank need only surrender deposits after the expiration of

---

[420] United States v. Prudential Ins. Co., 461 F2d 208 (5th Cir. 1972). Accord United States v. Equitable Life Assurance Co., 442 F. Supp. 500 (SDNY), aff'd, 78-2 USTC ¶ 9749 (2d Cir. 1978).

[421] United States v. Prudential Ins. Co., 461 F2d 208 (5th Cir. 1972); United States v. Equitable Life Assurance Co., 442 F. Supp. 500 (SDNY), aff'd, 78-2 USTC ¶ 9749 (2d Cir. 1978). But see Reg. § 301.6332-2(c)(2), Ex. (3).

[422] United States v. Prudential Ins. Co., 461 F2d 208 (5th Cir. 1972).

[423] See Resolution Trust Corp. v. Gill, 960 F2d 336 (3d Cir. 1992) ("[The bank] continued to owe an obligation [to the taxpayer-depositor] to pay a sum of money equal to the amount that existed in the IRA accounts . . . the IRS levy attached to the bank's obligation").

[424] United States v. Bowery Sav. Bank, 297 F2d 380 (2d Cir. 1961) (negotiable note).

[425] Rev. Rul. 75-355, 1975-2 CB 478.

[426] Regulations set forth guidance for banks in complying with the twenty-one-day holding period. A levy on a bank account applies to those funds on deposit at the time the levy is made, up to the amount of the levy. No withdrawals may be made against the funds reached by the levy during the twenty-one-day holding period. At the end of the twenty-one-day period, the bank must also surrender any interest that accrues on the deposits, unless it would exceed the amount of the levy. See Reg. § 301.6332-3.

twenty-one days following service of the levy. Where a bank account is the property levied upon, a taxpayer has thirty days after the notice of intention to levy, and another twenty-one days after the levy is served on the bank to resolve the delinquent account with the Service.

A joint checking or savings account may be seized by levy even if only one of the co-owners is liable for the tax. The Supreme Court, in *United States v. National Bank of Commerce*, held that the Service had the right to levy on joint accounts where only one of the co-owners was liable, at least where the taxpayer–co-owner had the unqualified right to withdraw the full amounts without notice to his co-owner.[427] What the levy seizes in this situation is the taxpayer–co-owner's property or right to property consisting of his unrestricted right to withdraw. The levy seizes this right although other claims to the funds may exist and ownership of the account may be unresolved at the time the levy is served. Conflicting claims are not affected by the levy, according to the Court, because the levy is provisional and is subject to the later claim by a codepositor that the money in fact belongs to him. In other words, Section 6331 "is a provisional remedy, which does not determine the rights of third parties until after the levy is made, in postseizure administrative or judicial hearings (under Sections 6343(b) and 7246)" (note omitted).[428]

A savings account may be in the name of the taxpayer in trust for another party, a type of account referred to as a "Totten trust." Whether a levy will reach a Totten trust depends on who the taxpayer is (the depositor or the beneficiary) and whether or not an irrevocable trust was established. If the taxpayer-beneficiary predeceases the party establishing the trust, a levy is ineffective because the tentative trust is terminated by the taxpayer's failure to

---

[427] United States v. National Bank of Commerce, 472 US 713 (1985). Cf. Raffaele v. Granger, 196 F2d 620 (3d Cir. 1952) (tenancy by the entirety in a bank account recognized under Pennsylvania law not subject to levies); United States v. Third Nat'l Bank & Trust Co., 111 F. Supp. 152 (MD Pa. 1953) (account in joint tenancy subject to levy with the result that tenancy in common created). See also United States v. Equitable Trust Co., 524 F. Supp. 1133 (D. Md. 1982) (evidence established that depositors opened joint checking account that was labeled a trust account solely due to bank practice); Rev. Rul. 55-187, 1955-1 CB 197 (joint checking account subject to levy only to the extent of taxpayer's interest). The effect of *National Bank of Commerce* on these authorities is unclear. The Supreme Court indicated that it was not deciding substantive ownership issues, but only the procedure to be followed — that is, under its rule, the levy transfers the account provisionally to the Service, and the innocent account owner must apply to the Service for return of funds belonging to that owner. At that time, the innocent owner will raise state law and ownership claims.

[428] United States v. National Bank of Commerce, 472 US 713, 731 (1985). On remand, the circuit court stated that the Supreme Court had not resolved the constitutional issues in the case — that is, whether Section 6331 would be unconstitutional under the due process clause, as applied to joint bank accounts, unless it was interpreted to require the Service to notify all codepositors and give them a reasonable amount of time to claim an ownership interest in the bank account. 772 F2d 438 (8th Cir. 1985).

survive the depositor.[429] On the other hand, if the taxpayer-settlor has delivered the passbook to the beneficiary or the settlor has died without having revoked the trust, an irrevocable trust has been established that is not subject to levy.[430] A levy may be made upon checks drawn in favor of the taxpayer and, when properly endorsed by the district director, may be presented to the drawee bank in payment when demanded. Where the taxpayer has drawn checks on an account prior to levy, but the checks are not presented to the debtor bank until after the notice of levy is served, or the checks are honored before the service of levy but the amounts paid have not been charged on the bank's books to the depositor's account, the levy is ineffective because the bank is not in possession of any property or rights to property of the taxpayer-depositor.[431]

Generally, a branch bank is considered an agent of the main bank and not a separate and distinct institution. The Service takes the position that a notice of levy served on the main bank reaches an account in a branch bank.[432] However, in *United States v. First National City Bank*,[433] it was held that where moneys were deposited in a foreign branch of a U.S. bank and the foreign branch had contracted to pay the depositor at the foreign branch only, the depositor did not under New York law have any property in New York at the main office of the bank subject to levy. However, since the district court had jurisdiction over the main bank, it ordered the bank to freeze property under its control, wherever that property was situated, pending acquisition by the United States of jurisdiction over the taxpayer and adjudication of the case on its merits.

[d] Setoff

The problem of setoff is often encountered where a notice of levy is served upon a third-party debtor of the taxpayer, such as a bank or employer. The third party claims a right to set off against the debt that he owes the taxpayer a portion of or an amount equal to the indebtedness of the taxpayer to the third party. Where taxes were assessed and the taxpayer subsequently bor-

---

[429] United States v. Williams, 160 F. Supp. 761 (DNJ 1958).

[430] United States v. Emigrant Indus. Sav. Bank, 122 F. Supp. 547 (SDNY 1954); United States v. Williams, 160 F. Supp. 761 (DNJ 1958).

[431] United States v. Guaranty Bank & Trust Co., 56 F. Supp. 470 (EDNC 1944). On the other hand, the Service has ruled that where, by custom or agreement, a bank customer is entitled to draw on uncollected funds, the bank must treat uncollected funds in the customer's account as being subject to levy whether or not the uncollected items later reach final settlement. Rev. Rul. 79-38, 1979-1 CB 406.

[432] Reg. § 301.6332-1(a)(2). The levy reaches branch banks only if it specifically so states.

[433] United States v. First Nat'l City Bank, 321 F2d 14 (2d Cir. 1963) and 325 F2d 1020 (2d Cir. 1964), rev'd on another issue, 379 US 378 (1965).

rowed money from a bank and executed a promissory note payable on demand, the notice of levy served upon the bank has been held to reach all the funds of the taxpayer-depositor.[434] Where the bank's loan to the taxpayer is made prior to the date the tax lien arose, setoff cannot be made until there exists the right to do so (e.g., upon default in payment of a note). Therefore, a levy served before the default would be entitled to priority.[435] Even a levy served after default is entitled to priority unless the bank takes some positive act (such as making transfer entries) before the levy is served.[436] In *Congress Talcott Corp.*, the debtor corporation officers had entered into cash collateral

---

[434] Bank of Nev. v. United States, 251 F2d 820 (9th Cir.), cert. denied, 356 US 938 (1958) (no demand had been made for payment of the note, notwithstanding a general lien or right of offset in favor of the bank created by state law and by contract with the debtor-depositor); Peoples Nat'l Bank of Wash. v. United States, 608 F. Supp. 672 (WD Wash. 1984) (unexercised right of setoff does not defeat a tax levy; *Bank of Nevada* followed; cases cited); United States v. Illinois State Bank of E. Alton, 86-2 USTC ¶ 9738 (SD Ill. 1986) (a bank that failed to exercise its setoff rights against a taxpayer's bank account had no defense to a levy served to seize the amount); State Bank of Fraser v. United States, 861 F2d 954 (6th Cir. 1988) (since great weight of authority under state law was against priority of bank's unexecuted right to setoff, bank did not have reasonable cause; penalty imposed).

[435] See cases cited supra at note 434. United States v. Graham, 96 F. Supp. 318 (SD Cal. 1951), aff'd sub nom. California v. United States, 195 F2d 530 (9th Cir.), cert. denied, 344 US 831 (1952) California was denied the right to set off against its debt to the taxpayer taxes that the taxpayer owed to the state where federal taxes were assessed well in advance of any right to setoff in the state); Beeghly v. Wilson, 152 F. Supp. 726 (ND Iowa 1957) (insurer denied right to set off from renewal commissions due former employee, expenses, and attorney's fees incurred in garnishment proceeding brought by judgment-creditor of the taxpayer, where notice of levy served after garnishment proceedings but federal taxes assessed before the proceeding). See Rev. Rul. 73-365, 1973-2 CB 407 (earned commissions credited against advance commissions previously paid held not subject to levy). Compare United States v. Guittard Chocolate Co., 81-2 USTC ¶ 9805 (ND Cal. 1981) (potential defense to a claim by taxpayer was not a judgment that could be set off against amount owed to taxpayer).

[436] United States v. Citizens & So. Nat'l Bank, 538 F2d 1101 (5th Cir.), cert. denied, 430 US 945 (1976); Citizens and Peoples Nat'l Bank of Pensacola v. United States, 570 F2d 1279 (5th Cir. 1978) (levy served after depositor-taxpayer delivered checks to bank but before bank made decision to pay checks drawn on account; held, levy had priority). Compare United States v. Philadelphia Nat'l Bank, 81-2 USTC ¶ 9493 (ED Pa. 1981) (the levy did not prejudice bank's rights because, under Pennsylvania law, when depositor gave bank security interest in deposits, depositor had no rights in the bank account and bank could make setoff at any time). See also Pittsburgh Nat'l Bank v. United States, 657 F2d 36 (3d Cir. 1981) (under Pennsylvania law, a bank's automatic right of setoff extinguishes the taxpayer's property rights in the bank account when the obligation to the bank matures). United States v. First National Bank & Trust Co., 695 F. Supp. 194, 195 (WD Pa. 1988) (demand obligation is due at time levy is served); United States v. Third Nat'l Bank, 589 F. Supp. 155 (MD Tenn. 1984) (gathering cases and analyzing Tennessee law); Trust Co. of Columbus v. United States, 735 F2d 447 (11th Cir. 1984) (distinguishing *Citizens & Southern Nat'l Bank* and Georgia law).

agreements to provide additional collateral to an asset-based lender.[437] Under the cash collateral agreement (which incorporated the factoring agreement), the lender could apply any part of the cash collateral to satisfy claims owed to the lender by the corporate debtor. After assessments against both officers for employment tax from another of their businesses, the Service served levies on the lender to seize the cash collateral accounts. The circuit court majority held that the officers had property rights in the collateral accounts because, as pledgors of the funds, they retained beneficial interests in the accounts subject to levy.[438] The lender had not offset any amounts from the collateral accounts until after the levies had been served, and this fact (coupled with the absence of substantial evidence of the borrower's default) precluded the lender from claiming that the lender's right of setoff had reduced the officers' property in the accounts when the levy was served.

However, if a right of setoff against future wages is claimed by virtue of an indebtedness owing from the taxpayer-employee to the employer and an agreement exists whereby the employee has the right to satisfy the indebtedness from future wages, a notice of levy would only reach any accrued wages due the taxpayer in excess of the amount to be set off at the time of service of levy.[439] Thus, it appears that if the tax lien arises before the right of setoff in a third party, or a loan is made before the tax lien arises but levy is made before the right of setoff accrues or the right to set off is perfected by some affirmative act, a notice of levy reaches all the taxpayer's property or right to property in the hands of the third party undiminished by any offsets,[440] except perhaps where contingent rights to compensation for personal services dependent upon future performance are assigned prior to the vesting of such rights.[441]

---

[437] Congress Talcott Corp. v. Gruber, 993 F2d 315 (3d Cir. 1993).

[438] The levy could attach to this contingent interest, according to the circuit court. See also United States v. Marine Midland Bank, 675 F. Supp. 775, 780 (WDNY 1987) (relied on by the circuit court).

[439] United States v. Long Island Drug Co., 115 F2d 983 (2d Cir. 1940). Accord United States v. Wagner, 573 F2d 447 (7th Cir. 1978).

[440] However, state law governs what interests the taxpayer actually had at the time of the levy.

[441] United States v. Long Island Drug Co., 115 F2d 983 (2d Cir. 1940); United States v. Wagner, 573 F2d 447 (7th Cir. 1978). But cf. Randall v. H. Nakashima & Co., 542 F2d 270 (5th Cir. 1976) (taxpayer's rights in a partially executed contract to purchase personal property were held to constitute "property" subject to a federal tax lien (and therefore subject to levy)).

[2] Property Not Subject to Levy

[a] Property in the Custody of a Court

Apart from property exempt from levy under Section 6334, and regardless of the priority of the tax lien, property is also not subject to levy if it has already been subjected to attachment or execution under judicial process.[442] Similarly, taxes cannot be collected by levy upon assets in the custody of a court in which a bankruptcy or receivership proceeding is pending.[443] When funds are in the custody of a court, but not in connection with a bankruptcy or receivership proceeding, the funds are subject to both lien and levy. This is because the common law doctrine of custodia legis that prohibits attachment of property in the custody of a court has been held not to preclude the attachment of the Service's lien and levy to the taxpayer's property when it is seized in the course of an arrest or forfeiture and deposited with the court.[444] Other courts have reached the same conclusion because the lien attaches to the taxpayer's interest in funds in the custody of the court.[445]

---

[442] IRC § 6332(a); Reg. § 301.6332-1(a); Walker v. Paramount Eng'g Co., 353 F2d 445, 448 (6th Cir. 1965); United States v. Board of County Comm'rs, 80-2 USTC 9526 (ND Ohio 1978) (proceeds of foreclosure sale held by sheriff following an order of distribution held under Ohio law not to be under judicial process and so subject to levy); SEC v. Paige, 85-2 USTC 9588 (DDC 1985) (escrowed assets in custody of court in connection with securities case); Federal Home Life Ins. Co. v. Ross, 84-1 USTC 9331 (ND Ga. 1984) (funds deposited by insurance company in an interpleader action in registry of court held subject to levy); United States v. Swink, 41 F. Supp. 98 (ED Pa. 1941) (state action to collect taxes brought delinquent taxpayer's property into the custody of the court and levy was ineffective). See also United States v. McPherson, 631 F. Supp. 269 (MDNC 1986) (where a state court-appointed receiver held assets of a dissolved law firm, the assets were in the custody of the court, and the receiver was not liable for failing to honor a levy to collect taxes owed by one of the partners; Swink followed). Parties may agree to an arrangement to secure payment of a judgment in a pending action in lieu of using the court's process to attach property. This consensual agreement in lieu of attachment has been held not to bring the property into the custody of the court. St. Louis Union Trust Co. v. United States, 617 F2d 1293 (8th Cir. 1980).

[443] Reg. § 301.6332-3. This rule holds true whether the court's custody is incident to a bankruptcy or receivership proceeding. Courts do not take lightly interference with their jurisdiction. Where the Service levied upon property in the bankruptcy court, one court ordered return of the funds seized and enjoined the Service from further collection. In re Thomas, Inc., 79-1 USTC 9204 (WD Va. 1979). See also United States v. McPherson, 631 F. Supp. 269 (MDNC 1986) (state court receivership).

[444] See United States v. Van Cauwenberghe, 934 F2d 1048, 1063, n.12 (9th Cir. 1991); In the Matter of the Application for Return to Brose & Poswistilo, Assignee of Albert R. Boettger, 75 AFTR2d 95-2640 (ED Pa. 1995) (cash seized from the taxpayer and held by the court was subject to Service lien and levy).

[445] See United States v. Francis, 646 F2d 251 (6th Cir.), cert. denied, 454 US 1082 (1981) (taxpayer claimed funds had been improperly seized); Field v. United States, 263 F2d 758 (5th Cir.), cert. denied, 360 US 918 (1959) (same); Welsh v. United States, 220

[b] After-Acquired Property

Once a general tax lien exists, it makes no difference when the taxpayer's property or right to property comes into existence because the lien attaches to after-acquired property.[446] Consequently, a levy collects property or rights to property that come into existence after the date the tax is assessed, but a levy extends "only to property possessed and obligations existing at the time thereof."[447] Service of a notice of levy results in the seizure of property or rights to property at the time of service of levy. If property comes into the possession of the taxpayer or third party after service of the levy, another levy must be made to seize the property, although the tax lien itself automatically attaches to the after-acquired property.[448] The regulations use the example of a levy served on a bank to seize the balance in an account of a delinquent taxpayer. The levy has no effect on deposits made in the bank by the taxpayer after the levy. The subsequent deposits may be reached only by a second (or successive) levy on the bank.[449] In fact, the making of successive levies is specifically contemplated.[450] As noted above, there are exceptions to the rule that successive notices of levy must be served in order to seize property acquired after the initial levy. A levy on salary and wages is continuous from the date of the levy until the liability out of which the levy arose is satisfied or becomes unenforceable by lapse of time.

Although a levy generally reaches obligations in existence at the time the levy is made, an obligation may be in existence when the liability of the obligor is fixed and determinable even though the right to receive payment is deferred to a later date—for example, a right to receive future payments under a trust or contract, provided the right to receive such payments is not contingent upon future services.[451] In other words, where the right to future income is a fixed or present right to property, it is appropriated by levy notwithstanding the fact that the taxpayer's enjoyment of the property is postponed to some fu-

---

F2d 200 (DC Cir. 1955) ("Congress has not specifically exempted from the [tax] lien . . . money in custodia legis, and we think that we may not write such an exception into [Section 6321 or Section 6323] in the situation here").

[446] Glass City Bank v. United States, 326 US 265 (1945).

[447] IRC § 6331(b). The Service took this position before the statutory language was added to the Code. Rev. Rul. 66-210, 1966-2 CB 238.

[448] United States v. Long Island Drug Co., 115 F2d 983 (2d Cir. 1940); Reg. § 301.6331-1(a)(1); Rev. Rul. 66-210, 1966-2 CB 238.

[449] Reg. § 301.6331-1(a)(1).

[450] Section 6331(c) provides that if property is not sufficient to satisfy the tax claim, the Service "may, thereafter, and as often as may be necessary, proceed to levy in like manner upon any other property liable to levy of the person against whom such claim exists, until the amount due from him, together with all expenses is fully paid."

[451] St. Louis Union Trust Co. v. United States, 617 F2d 1293 (8th Cir. 1980) (taxpayer had right to income from escrowed securities).

ture date.[452] Service of notice of federal tax lien is of no consequence in terms of the right to levy upon and sell the taxpayer's property.[453]

[3] Property Exempt From Levy

No property or right to property is free from the general assessment lien, although certain property of limited types and amounts is exempt from levy.[454] Section 6334 enumerates thirteen categories of property exempt from levy:

1. Items of wearing apparel and such school books necessary for the taxpayer or for members of his family.
2. If the taxpayer is the head of a family, so much of the fuel, provisions, furniture, and personal effects in his household, and of the arms for personal use, livestock, and poultry of the taxpayer, as does not exceed $1,650 ($1,500 in the case of levies issued during 1989) in value. In 1998, the exemption amount for a levy on fuel, provisions, furniture, and personal effects was raised from $2,500 to $6,250.[455]
3. Books and tools necessary for the trade, business, or profession of the taxpayer that do not exceed in the aggregate $1,100 ($1,050 in the case of levies issued during 1989) in value. In 1998, the exemption

---

[452] Dallas Nat'l Bank v. United States, 167 F2d 468 (5th Cir. 1948) (spendthrift trust).

[453] United States v. Dean, 82-2 USTC 9684 (MD Ga. 1982) (taxpayer-lessor's rights to receive rent subject to levy, and lessees had to pay rent for periods after date of levy to Service). See also United States v. Antonio, 91-2 USTC ¶ 50,482 (D. Haw. 1991) ("When the United States served the second levy on the defendant, the effect of the levy was to transfer or 'assign' to the United States by operation of law [the McLeans'] right to be compensated for the sandblasting services the taxpayer performed on the Barber's Point & Pearl Harbor contracts").

[454] In re Voelker, 42 F3d 1050 (7th Cir. 1994) ("the federal tax lien attaches to all of a debtor's property, without exception. ... Thus, if a debtor later sells the exempt property, the Service could move to collect the proceeds from the sale"); United States v. Barbier, 896 F2d 377 (9th Cir. 1990).

[455] IRC § 6334(a)(2), as amended by 1998 Act § 3431(c), applicable to levies issued after July 22, 1998. The value of the fuel, provisions, furniture, and personal effects exempt from levy under Section 6334(a)(2) was increased from $1,650 to $2,500 by the Taxpayer Bill of Rights 2, effective for levies issued after December 31, 1996. In addition, the exemption amount will be adjusted for inflation for each year beginning after 1997. The inflation adjustment will be an amount equal to the amended dollar amount multiplied by the cost-of-living adjustment determined under Code Section 1(f)(3) for the calendar year, except that the calendar year 1996 will be substituted for the calendar year 1992. IRC § 6334(f), added by the Taxpayer Bill of Rights 2, § 502(c), effective for levies issued after December 31, 1996.

amount for books and tools of a trade or business was raised from $1,250 to $3,125.[456]

4. Any amount payable to an individual with respect to his unemployment (including any portion payable with respect to dependents) under an unemployment compensation law of the United States, any state, the District of Columbia, or the Commonwealth of Puerto Rico.

5. Mail addressed to any person that has not been delivered to the addressee.

6. Annuity or pension payments under the Railroad Retirement Act, benefits under the Railroad Unemployment Insurance Act, special pension payments received by a person whose name has been entered on the Army, Navy, Air Force, and Coast Guard Medal of Honor roll, and annuities based on retired or retainer pay.[457]

7. Any amount payable to an individual as workmen's compensation (including any portion thereof payable with respect to dependents) under a workmen's compensation law of the United States, any state, the District of Columbia, or the Commonwealth of Puerto Rico.[458]

8. If the taxpayer is required by judgment of a court of competent jurisdiction, entered prior to the date of levy, to contribute to the support of his minor children, so much of his salary, wages, or other income as is necessary to comply with this judgment.[459]

---

[456] IRC § 6334(a)(3), as amended by 1998 Act § 3431(c), applicable to levies issued after July 22, 1998. The value of books and tools of a trade, business, or profession exempt from levy by Section 6334(a)(3) was increased from $1,100 to $1,250 by the Taxpayer Bill of Rights 2, effective for levies issued after December 31, 1996. The exemption amount will be adjusted for inflation, as described in Form 7.2.

[457] 38 USC § 562 (Medal of Honor roll); 10 USC Chapter 73 (retired or retainer pay). However, assets of qualified pension trusts are subject to levy. See Reg. § 1.401(a)-13(b). Before amendment of the exemption, military retirement benefits were subject to levy. See Melechinsky v. Secretary of the Air Force, 83-1 USTC ¶ 9373 (D. Conn. 1983).

[458] Note that it has been held that the exemption does not apply to worker's compensation benefits once they have been paid on the ground that the exemption applies only to amounts that are payable. Fredyma v. United States, 98-1 USTC ¶ 50,166 (DNH 1998); Cathey v. United States, 82 AFTR2d 98-6951 (SD Tex. 1998) (accord).

[459] IRC § 6334(a)(8); Reg. § 301.6334-1(a). The statute and regulations have been literally interpreted to prevent the wife of a taxpayer and support judgment debtor rather than the taxpayer and judgment debtor himself (he failed to appear) from claiming the exemption on her husband's behalf. Fidelity Equip. Leasing Corp. v. United States, 462 F. Supp. 845 (ND Ga. 1981). But see Woods v. Simpson, 93-2 USTC ¶ 50,377 (WD Ky. 1993) (bequest to child claimed by child's ex-spouse for past-due child support; held, bequest constituted "other income" and exempt from Service lien and levy). When child support is sheltered by the exemption from levy, it has been held, the lien also cannot attach, thus preventing the Service from arguing that its lien has priority over the support judgment creditor. Don King Prods., Inc. v. Thomas, 749 F. Supp. 79 (SDNY 1990), aff'd in part and rev'd in part on other grounds, 945 F2d 529 (2d Cir. 1991).

9. Any amounts payable to or received by an individual as wages or salary for personal services, or as income derived from other sources, during any period, to the extent that the total of such amounts payable to or received by him during the period does not exceed the applicable "exempt amount."[460]

10. Amounts payable to an individual as a service-connected disability benefit.[461]

11. Amounts payable to an individual as a recipient of public assistance for aid to families with dependent children or supplemental security income for the aged, blind, and disabled. State or local government public assistance or public welfare programs for which eligibility is determined by a needs or income test.

12. Amounts payable to a participant under the Job Training Partnership Act[462] from funds appropriated pursuant to such act.

13. The principal residence of the taxpayer (within the meaning of Section 1034) unless there has been approval by the area or territory manager or unless there has been a finding that collection of the tax is in jeopardy. If the amount of the levy is $5,000 or less, the IRS Restructuring and Reform Act of 1998 exempts from levy the taxpayer's residence or the taxpayer's property that is used as a residence by another individual.[463] A principal residence is exempt whatever the amount of the levy, unless a judge or magistrate of a district court approves the levy in writing. The same exemption applies to the tangible personal and real property of an individual taxpayer used in a trade or business, unless the area or territory manager approves the levy in writing, or the collection of the tax is believed to be in jeopardy. Approval may not be given unless the official making the determination decides that the taxpayer's other assets subject to

---

[460] The exempt amount is defined in Section 6334(d).

[461] IRC § 6334(a)(10). The Service has successfully argued that Exemption 10 applies only to benefits before they have been paid, and that once they have been paid, the benefits are subject to levy. Hughes v. IRS, 83 AFTR2d 99-2516 (EDNY 1999). The definition of service-connected disability is in 38 USC § 101(16) and applies to benefits under 38 USC subchapter II, III, IV, V, or VI of Chapter 11, or Chapter 13, 21, 23, 31, 32, 34, 35, 37, or 39.

[462] 29 USC § 1501.

[463] IRC § 6334(a)(13), added by 1998 Act § 3445(a), effective July 22, 1998. The Service's procedures require Chief Counsel attorneys to prepare a suit letter requesting and authorizing the Tax Division of the Justice Department to seek court approval of the seizure of a residence. The letter must include information about (1) the taxpayer's tax liability; (2) ownership interest in the residence; (3) the record of administrative review proceedings; and (4) a thorough consideration of alternative collection methods. Chief Counsel Notice N(34)700-2 (Feb. 5, 1999). Under these procedures, the Service will also use a suit to reduce a tax assessment to judgment and to foreclose its lien against a residence if a third person has or claims to have an interest in the residence.

collection are insufficient to pay the amount due, together with expenses of the seizure and sale.

The exempt amount, in the case of an individual who is paid wages, salary, and other income on a weekly basis is defined by Section 6334(d) to be the standard deduction and the aggregate amount of deductions for personal exemptions under Section 151, divided by fifty-two. Individuals who are paid on other than a weekly basis are entitled to have, under Treasury regulations, as nearly as possible, an equivalent amount exempt from levy.[464]

If it is approved by a delegated Service official, specified payments of (1) unemployment benefits (exemption 4); (2) workmen's compensation benefits (exemption 7); (3) certain means-tested public assistance payments (exemption 11); and (4) annuity or pension payments under the Railroad Retirement Act or benefits under the Railroad Unemployment Insurance Act (exemption 6) are not exempt from levy under Section 6331(h).[465] A continuous levy may also be served on wages, salary, and other income notwithstanding the minimum exemption of the exempt amount determined under Section 6334(d). As a result, a continuous levy attaches to up to 15 percent of these previously exempt amounts from the date of the levy until the levy is released. However, by limiting the amount that the Service may seize under a continuous levy to 15 percent of taxpayers' wages and salary, taxpayers will be able to retain a greater portion of their wages and salary than under the previous exempt amount computation, which left delinquent taxpayers with little income that was exempt from levy.

The exemptions provided in Section 6334 occupy the field where exemption from a levy for a federal tax is concerned. State law determines the existence, nature, and extent of a taxpayer's property for the purposes of the lien statute. However, state law and even federal law exemption statutes (apart from the Bankruptcy Code, which has its own set of exemption rules) are ineffective to prevent the seizure of state-created property or rights to property by levy to collect a delinquent tax.[466]

---

[464] See Reg. § 301.6334-3.

[465] IRC § 6334(f), added by the Taxpayer Relief Act of 1997 § 1025(a), effective for levies issued after the date of enactment, August 5, 1997, and redesignating Section 6334(f) as Section 6334(g).

[466] IRC § 6334(c); United States v. Offshore Logistics Int'l, Inc., 483 F. Supp. 1055 (WD La. 1979) (seaman's wages exempt from attachment under 46 USC § 601 subject to levy). Before the enactment of Section 6334(c), state exemption statutes were held not to affect the validity of a levy. United States v. Bess, 357 US 51 (1958); Fried v. New York Life Ins. Co., 241 F2d 504 (2d Cir.), cert. denied, 354 US 922 (1957) (disability benefits from life insurance policies); United States v. Ocean Accident & Guar. Corp., 76 F. Supp. 277 (SDNY 1948) (workmen's compensation). Section 6334(c) itself states that social security benefits are not exempt from levy, when it provides, "Notwithstanding any other law of the United States (*including section 207 of the Social Security Act*), no property or

Pension benefits of a beneficiary in a qualified pension plan under ERISA are subject to levy.[467] The rationale is that Section 6334, which lists property exempt from levy, does not exempt pension plan benefits from collection. Moreover, Section 7334(c) makes Section 6334(a) the exclusive source of exemptions from levy "notwithstanding any other law of the United States (including section 207 of the Social Security Act). . . . " ERISA itself states that it is not intended to supersede any other law or regulation.[468] To ensure that an absurd result does not occur as the result of a levy on a taxpayer's pension plan or IRA, the early withdrawal tax is eliminated when an amount is withdrawn as the result of a levy.[469] A levy on a taxpayer debtor's IRA and Keogh accounts is not covered by ERISA's bar against assignment or alienation of an individual's interest in a qualified retirement plan.[470]

Similarly, 401(k) plan accounts are subject to lien because they constitute "property" or "rights to property," and are not made specifically exempt by Section 6334.[471] Also, a Thrift Savings Plan account that 5 USC § 8437(e)(2) makes not assignable or transferrable is subject to a tax lien, and not exempt from levy.[472] In addition, an annuity is subject to lien and levy, and no part of the annuity is exempt under the minimum exemptions from levy of wages, salary, and other income of Section 6334(a)(9) if the taxpayer has other income that equals or exceeds the amount exempt from levy.[473]

The Service believes that it not only has the authority to levy on the rights of the taxpayer to receive pension plan benefits on retirement, but when the plan gives participants the right to elect early retirement, the levy reaches that right as well, and permits the Service to elect early retirement on the tax-

---

rights to property shall be exempt from levy other than the property specifically made exempt by subsection (a)." (Emphasis added).

[467] Shanbaum v. United States, 32 F3d 180 (5th Cir. 1994) (plan administered by the Pension Benefit Guaranty Corporation (PBGC) after the plan was terminated, and levy was served on PBGC's paying agent to collect taxpayer's monthly pension benefits as they became due).

[468] 29 USC § 1144(d).

[469] IRC § 72(t)(2)(A), as amended by 1998 Act § 3436(a). As the result of the change in the law, the Service withdrew its litigating position that the taxpayer was subject to a withdrawal penalty when it seized funds from a pension plan, and will no longer assess a Section 72(t) on distributions from a qualified retirement plan made on account of a levy.

[470] Ameritrust Co. v. Derakhshan, 830 F. Supp. 406 (ND Ohio 1993) (Treas. Reg. § 1.401(a)-13(b) found valid despite anti-alienation provision of Section 206(d) of ERISA).

[471] Schaffer v. United States (In re Schaffer), 80 AFTR2d 97-5012 (Bankr. D. Idaho 1997).

[472] Melton v. Teachers Ins. & Annuity, 114 F3d 557 (5th Cir. 1997).

[473] Internal Revenue Serv. (In re Cheryl Jones), 206 Bankr. 614 (Bankr. DDC 1997).

payer participant's behalf—even if it means that, on exercise, the taxpayer participant will receive substantially reduced early retirement benefits.[474]

---

[474] ILM 199936041 (June 8, 1999) (the Chief Counsel memorandum says, however, that

> Careful consideration must be given where the Service seeks collection from a retirement plan that, absent waiver, requires benefits to be paid in the form of a joint and survivor annuity. In these cases, the Service may only levy upon that joint and survivor annuity, and may not elect another form of benefit for collection purposes without the consent of a spouse.

FORM 14.8
NOTICE OF LEVY ON WAGES, SALARY, AND OTHER INCOME

Form 668-W(c) (Rev. July 1992)	Department of the Treasury - Internal Revenue Service **Notice of Levy on Wages, Salary, and Other Income**

Date Reply:	District:	Telephone Number of IRS Office

NAME AND ADDRESS OF TAXPAYER

TO: [Employer]
       1 Park Place
       Anytown, NY 00000

John Jones
1 Main Street
Anytown, NY 00000

IDENTIFYING NUMBER(S)

Kind of Tax	Tax Period Ended	Unpaid Balance of Assessment	Statutory Additions	Total
Income	12-31-90	$15,000.00	$875.50	$15,875.50
Income	12-31-91	$ 8,400.00	$690.00	$ 9,090.00
			Total amount due ▶	$24,965.50

Interest and late payment penalty have been figured to _____

This is not a bill for taxes you owe. This is a notice of levy used to collect money owed by the person named in the upper right of this form.

The Internal Revenue Code provides that there is a lien for the amount that is owed. Although notice and demand that are required by the Code have been made, the amount owed has not been paid. This levy requires you to turn over to us: (1) this taxpayer's wages and salary that have been earned but not paid yet, as well as wages and salary earned in the future until this levy is released, and (2) this taxpayer's other income that you have now or for which you are obligated.

These are levied to the extent they are not exempt, as shown on the instructions. Do not offset money this person owes you without contacting us at the telephone number shown above for instructions.

If no money is owed to this person, please complete the back of part 3. Attach it as a cover to the rest of this form and return all of the parts in the enclosed envelope.

If money is owed to this person, please see the back of this page for instructions.

Signature of Service Representative /s/ John Doe	Title Special Agent

Part 1 - For Employer or other Addressee

Form 668-W(c) (Rev. 7-92) 16748F

IF FUNDS ARE DUE THIS TAXPAYER

Give the taxpayer Parts 2, 3, 4, and 5, as soon as you receive this levy. Part of the taxpayer's wages, salary, or other income is exempt from levy. To claim exemptions, the taxpayer must complete and sign the Statement of Exemptions and Filing Status on Parts 3, 4, and 5 and return Parts 3 and 4 to you within 3 work days after you receive this levy. The taxpayer's instructions for completing the Statement of Exemptions and Filing Status are on the back of Part 5.

Send us the taxpayer's take home pay minus the exempt amount which is described below. Payments are to be made to us on the same dates that payments are made, or are due, to the taxpayer. Unless we tell you that a deduction should not be allowed, allow the taxpayer's payroll deductions which were in effect when you received this levy in determining the take home pay. Do not allow the taxpayer to take new payroll deductions while this levy is in effect.

When you send us your check, **complete the back of Part 3 of this form, attach it to the check, and mail them to us in the enclosed envelope. Make your check payable to the Internal Revenue Service. Please write on the check (not on a detachable stub) the taxpayer's name, identifying number(s), kind of tax, and tax periods shown on Part 1, and the words "LEVY PROCEEDS".**

This levy remains in effect for all wages and salary for personal services until you are issued a release of levy. Wages and salary include fees, commissions, and bonuses. If more than one payment is necessary to satisfy the levy, send additional payments to the Internal Revenue Service address shown on your copy of this levy, and make out your check as described above.

For income **other** than wages and salary, this levy is effective only for currently obligated funds. We may issue another levy if necessary. However, this levy attaches to *all* obligations you owe the taxpayer at the time the levy is received, even though the payment is deferred to a later date.

INSTRUCTIONS FOR FIGURING THE AMOUNT EXEMPT FROM THIS LEVY

There are three steps in figuring the amount exempt from this levy.

1. When you receive the completed Parts 3 and 4 from the taxpayer, use item 1 of the enclosed Table (Publication 1494) to figure how much wages, salary, or other income is exempt from this levy. Find the correct block on the Table using the taxpayer's filing status, number of personal exemptions claimed, and pay period. Be sure you allow one exemption for the taxpayer, in addition to one for each person listed on Parts 3 and 4, unless, "I cannot claim myself as an exemption," is written next to the taxpayer's signature. If you do not receive the completed Parts 3 and 4, then the exempt amount is what would be exempt if the taxpayer had returned them indicating married filing separate and only the taxpayer is claimed as a personal exemption. Do not use the information on the taxpayer's Form W-4, Employee's Withholding Allowance Certificate, to determine the amount that is exempt from this levy. That information can be different from what is filed on the employee's Individual Income Tax Return.

2. If the taxpayer, or the taxpayer's spouse, is at least 65 years old and/or blind, an additional amount is exempt from this levy. To claim this, the taxpayer counts one for each of the following: (a) the taxpayer is 65 or older, (b) the taxpayer is blind, (c) the taxpayer's spouse is 65 or older, and (d) the taxpayer's spouse is blind. Then, this total (up to 4) is entered next to "ADDITIONAL STANDARD DEDUCTION" on the Statement of Exemptions and Filing Status. If the taxpayer has entered a number in this space, use item 2 of the enclosed Table to figure the additional amount exempt from this levy.

3. The amount the taxpayer needs to pay court ordered support for minor children is also exempt from levy, but the court order must have been made before the date of this levy. These children cannot be claimed as personal exemptions on Parts 3, 4, and 5.

If the taxpayer's exemptions, filing status, or eligibility for additional standard deduction change while this levy is in effect, a new Statement can be given to you to change the amount that is exempt. You can get more forms from an IRS office. If you are sending payments for this levy next year, the amount that is exempt does not change merely because the amount that all taxpayers can deduct for exemptions, filing status, and additional standard deduction on Individual Income Tax Returns changes for the new year. However, if the taxpayer asks you to recompute the exempt amount in the new year by submitting a new Statement of Exemptions and Filing Status, even though there may be no change from the prior Statement, you may use the new year's exemption Table. This change applies to levies you already have as well as this one. If you are asked to recompute the exempt amount and you do not have the new year's exemption Table, you may order one by calling 1-800-829-3676. Ask for publication 1494. The taxpayer submits the information under penalties of perjury, and it is subject to verification by the Internal Revenue Service.

Form 668-W(c) (Rev. 7-92) 16748F

[4] Other Limitations on the Levy Authority

Other limitations on the service's levy authority are constitutional, statutory, and administrative limitations.[474.1]

[a] Constitutional Limitations

A revenue officer is not permitted to use force in the seizure of property,[475] nor is a revenue officer to attempt to enter a personal residence unless the taxpayer or another adult gives him specific permission (nonconsensual entry is unconstitutional under *GM Leasing Corp. v. United States*).[476] A revenue officer may seize personal property on public property (e.g., vehicles parked on streets) or open space without requiring a taxpayer's permission or invading his privacy.[477] If personal property is located outside the residence but on private premises, the revenue officer may enter on the premises and seize the property as long as there is no obstruction or enclosure that would indicate entry would constitute invasion of the taxpayer's privacy.[478] To avoid constitutional issues, consent of the taxpayer or a writ of entry is sought to seize property in a taxpayer's personal residence. However, where the residence itself is seized, neither consent nor a writ of entry is required because no entry is made into the residence.[479] Similarly, where improved realty used as business property is seized, no consent or writ is requested; warning notices are posted on the outside of the building. A safe-deposit box is seized by placing a Seal for Securing Safety Deposit Boxes on the box.[480]

[i] The statute of limitations on collection.

As a general rule, any tax may be collected by levy only if it is made within ten years after the assess-

---

[474.1] Administrative limitations are described at ¶ 14.16.

[475] IRC §§ 7433, 6304.

[476] GM Leasing Corp. v. United States, 429 US 338 (1977).

[477] GM Leasing Corp. v. United States, 429 US 338 (1977) ("[t]he seizures of the automobiles in this case took place on public streets, parking lots, or other open space, and did not involve any invasion of privacy").

[478] GM Leasing Corp. v. United States, 429 US 338 (1977). If at any point force or violence is threatened, the revenue officer is to withdraw and report the matter to his group manager, who may request the assistance of the Criminal Investigation Division or Inspection Division. Revenue officers are permitted to use sufficient but not excessive force to defend themselves.

[479] IRC §§ 6334(e); 6334(a)(13). However, unimproved real property may be seized, without obtaining the taxpayer's consent or a writ. IRM 5.10.2.14 Securing Managerial Approval of Seizure Actions (Jan. 1, 2003).

[480] IRM 5.10.3.12 Safe Deposit Boxes (Jan. 1, 2003). If the taxpayer refuses to open the box, a writ of entry is requested.

ment of the tax.[481] A levy is considered made not on the date the notice of
levy is served, but on the date the notice of seizure provided for in Section
6335(a) is given.[482] Consequently, the six-year period of limitations on collection may still run if there is delay in giving the notice of seizure. The collection period is not extended (or shortened) because the government has obtained
a judgment against the taxpayer. Once the period for collection by summary
administrative action has expired, a personal judgment against the taxpayer for
the assessed tax liability does not extend the period. For example, a tax liability assessed on April 20, 1984 and reduced to judgment on April 20, 1988
may be collected by levy during the remaining two years of the six-year statutory period. However, after April 20, 1990, the government may not collect by
administrative levy but only by foreclosing its judgment lien.

As a general rule, any tax may be collected by levy only if it is made
within ten years after the assessment of the tax.[483] A levy is considered made
not on the date the notice of levy is served, but on the date the notice of
seizure provided for in Section 6335(a) is given.[484] Consequently, the six-year
period of limitations on collection may still run if there is delay in giving the
notice of seizure. The collection period is not extended (or shortened) because
the government has obtained a judgment against the taxpayer. Once the period
for collection by summary administrative action has expired, a personal judgment against the taxpayer for the assessed tax liability does not extend the period. For example, a tax liability assessed on April 20, 1984 and reduced to
judgment on April 20, 1988 may be collected by levy during the remaining
two years of the six-year statutory period. However, after April 20, 1990, the
government may not collect by administrative levy but only by foreclosing its
judgment lien.

[ii] Application of fair debt collection procedures. The IRS Restructuring and Reform Act of 1998 added a new Section 6304, which imposes fair
tax collection practices on the Service.[485] Without the prior consent of the taxpayer given to the Service or a court of competent jurisdiction, the Service
may not communicate with a taxpayer about the collection of an unpaid tax (1)
at any unusual time or place or a time or place known to be inconvenient to a

---

[481] IRC § 6502(a)(1). If the levy is served within the statutory collection period, a
suit to enforce the levy may be instituted after the collection period has expired. See
United States v. Weintraub, 613 F2d 612 (6th Cir. 1980), cert. denied, 447 US 905;
United States v. Atlantic Richfield Co., 73-1 USTC 9437 (ED Pa. 1973).

[482] IRC § 6502(b).

[483] IRC § 6502(a)(1). If the levy is served within the statutory collection period, a
suit to enforce the levy may be instituted after the collection period has expired. See
United States v. Weintraub, 613 F2d 612 (6th Cir. 1980), cert. denied, 447 US 905;
United States v. Atlantic Richfield Co., 73-1 USTC 9437 (ED Pa. 1973).

[484] IRC § 6502(b).

[485] IRC § 6304, added by 1998 Act § 3466(a).

taxpayer; (2) if the Service knows that the taxpayer is represented; or (3) at the taxpayer's place of employment. The generally authorized hours of contact are between 8 AM and 9 PM. The Service also is not permitted to engage in conduct the natural consequence of which is to harass, oppress, or abuse any person in connection with the collection of an unpaid tax. If these restrictions are violated the taxpayer may institute an action for wrongful collection under Section 7433.

¶ 14.16 LEVY PROCEDURE

[1] Prelevy Procedures

Levy procedures are designed to give taxpayers a reasonable chance to settle their tax liabilities voluntarily before administrative action is taken to collect delinquent taxes. Before a levy is permitted, three notices must be given to the taxpayer—the Section 6303 notice and demand, notice of taxpayer due process rights (Section 6330), and the notice before levy (Section 6331(d)). Both the collection due notice and the notice before levy must be given at least thirty days before the day of the levy.[486] The notice before levy must state each tax period to be reflected on the notice of levy.[487] This notice must also be accompanied by a statement that sets out the following:

- The levy and sale provisions of the Code;
- The procedures applicable to the levy and sale of property;
- The administrative appeals available to a taxpayer;
- Alternatives, such as an installment payment agreement, that might prevent a levy on property;
- The redemption of property and release of lien provisions of the Code; and
- The procedures applicable to redemption and release.[488]

---

[486] IRC § 6331(d)(1). The Service uses Forms 4840 (Notice of Intent to Levy) and 668-A (Notice of Levy) for this purpose. (See Forms 14.9 and 14.10.) Except in unusual circumstances such as jeopardy, the revenue officer is required to see that the taxpayer has received a notice of intent to levy within the last 180 days before taking seizure action. If the taxpayer has not received a notice within this 180-day period, the Service will issue a new notice, unless the Service has given the taxpayer notice by having taken current collection action (e.g., within the last sixty days). IRM 5.10.1.5.1 Timeliness of Pre-Seizure Taxpayer Notification (Jan. 1, 2003).

[487] Manual provisions describe the required procedures before issuing a levy. IRM 5.11.1 (Background, Pre-Levy Actions and Restrictions on Levy) (July 26, 2002). IRM 5.11.2.1.1 Serving Notices of Levy—General (May 5, 1998).

[488] IRC § 6331(d)(4).

The notice of intention to levy and the accompanying information must be (1) given in person; (2) left at the dwelling or usual place of business; or (3) sent by certified or registered mail to the taxpayer's last known address.[489] Just as the ten-day grace period normally provided to a taxpayer who receives a Section 6303 notice and demand is eliminated on a finding that collection of tax is in jeopardy, no notice of intention to levy need to be given where collection of tax is found to be in jeopardy.[490] After the notice of intention to levy has been given, the Service may levy on a taxpayer's property and rights to property.

[2] Administrative Review Before a Levy Is Served

The Service's sensitivity to the use of a levy involving third parties is reflected in the explicit instruction to collection personnel that a notice of levy "should be used only when there is evidence or reasonable expectation that the third party has property or rights to property of the taxpayer."[491] Also, the seizure and sale of a going business is a sensitive matter. Before a decision is reached to seize a going business, the possible adverse effect on innocent employees who will be put out of work if the business is seized are to be considered, and the determination made that every reasonable effort has been made to collect the delinquent taxes on a voluntary basis.[492] However, apart from advising the revenue officer to see his group manager in these situations, little guidance is given to help a revenue officer determine whether and when to use the levy power; that matter is largely left to the discretion of individual revenue officers.

The IRS Restructuring and Reform Act of 1998 amended Section 6331 by adding the requirement that no levy may be made on property that is to be sold under Section 6335 until a thorough investigation has been made of the status of the property. This investigation must include the following:[493]

---

[489] IRC § 6331(d)(2).

[490] IRC § 6331(d)(3).

[491] See Delegation Order 191 (Rev. 3).

[492] IRM, Policies of the IRS, Policy Statement P-5-34 (collection is to be enforced through seizure and sale of assets of a taxpayer only after thorough consideration of all factors and alternative collections methods). According to the Manual, while Policy Statement P-5-34 requires that "thorough consideration be given to the facts and circumstances of a particular case before a decision is reached to seize a going business . . . failure to turn over trust fund taxes is a high priority tax delinquency . . . [and so b]usinesses will not be allowed to continue pyramiding these taxes." The revenue officer and the manager will decide whether a reasonable attempt has been made to collect the delinquent taxes without seizing the business. An important consideration in this process is the taxpayer's record of paying current trust fund taxes while paying delinquent taxes as agreed.

[493] IRC § 6331(j), added by 1998 Act § 3444(a), applicable on July 22, 1998. The Community Renewal Tax Relief Act of 2000 (CRTRA), Pub. L. No. 106-554, states that

1. Verification of the taxpayer's liability;
2. The complete analysis provided in Section 6331(f);
3. The determination that the equity in the property is sufficient to yield net proceeds from the sale of the property to apply the liability; and
4. A thorough consideration of alternative collection methods.

Statutory rules must be followed. No levy is permitted if the levy would be uneconomical because the expenses of levy and sale exceed the fair market value of the property at the time of the levy.[494] Also, a levy may not be served on the day a taxpayer is required to appear in response to a summons.[495] If the property to be seized is the principal residence of the taxpayer, a district director or assistant district director must personally approve the levy in writing.[496] After much criticism of Collection Division's seizure procedures, the Service expanded the role of higher level district Collection management in approving seizures, and requires that the chief of the district Collection Division must approve all seizures, with the district director continuing to be required to approve the seizures involving a taxpayer's residence, the contents, and perishable goods.[497]

Administrative actions required to be taken after the decision has been made to seize property and property has actually been seized can be divided into the following categories: actions prior to seizure, seizure actions, actions prior to sale, sale procedures, and report of sale.[498] The revenue officer is directed to take "exclusive dominion and control" over the seized property and to attach warning notices. Once these actions have been taken, the revenue officer takes an inventory at which the taxpayer or his representative are invited

---

the Tax Court and the district courts have authority to enjoin collection activity during the resolution of a collection due process dispute.

[494] IRC § 6331(f). Regulations require that an estimate of the fair market value be made for this purpose is to be made on an aggregate basis rather than with respect to each individual item of property potentially subject to seizure. Reg. § 301.6331-2(b). The estimate, which may be formal or informal, is to be made at the time of the seizure or within a reasonable period of time prior to a seizure. Before the revenue officer seizes property, the Manual requires the revenue officer to determine whether the taxpayer has sufficient equity in the property to be seized to yield net proceeds from the sale to apply to the unpaid liabilities. This entails searching public records for senior and other lienholders. IRM 5.10.1.3.3 Equity Determination (Jan. 1, 2003). Once the revenue officer has decided to seize property, the revenue officer submits the case file and the Form 688-B to the officer's group manager for review. IRM 5.10.1.3.3. The group manager will review the case to ensure that a seizure is warranted, considering such factors as the ability of the taxpayer to pay based on an analysis of the taxpayer's income and expenses, equity in assets, and the taxpayer's efforts to pay or provide for payment of the tax liability.

[495] IRC § 6331(g).

[496] IRC §§ 6334(a), 6334(e).

[497] Info. Rel. 97-46 (Dec. 8, 1997).

[498] Exhibit 5600-24, MT 5600-33; IRM 56(12)1.1.

to be present. This inventory is not ordinarily delayed, even if redemption is planned by the taxpayer, because the Service is responsible for the seized property. "As soon as practicable," a copy of Form 2433 (Notice of Seizure) is given to the owner (or, in the case of personal property, the possessor) or mailed to his last known address by the revenue officer.[499] The notice must specify the sum demanded. Until this notice is sent, the levy is not considered as having occurred. Thereafter, the revenue officer must make some arrangement for storage and protection of the property pending redemption or disposition of the property. For example, the officer may arrange to have the assets moved commercially and stored in government or private facilities or may hire custodians to guard the property and request the district director to authorize hiring an auctioneer. Finally, the property is appraised for purposes of establishing an inventory value.[500]

---

[499] IRC § 6335(a).

[500] IRM 5.10.3.9 Notice of Seizure—Preparation (Jan. 1, 2003), IRM 5.10.3.18 Notice of Seizure—Delivery. (Jan. 1, 2003). An appraisal is made to comply with monetary accounting control requirements imposed upon federal agencies. The value referred to is, in general, the property's fair market value, using, if possible, the comparable sales (market data) method. IRM 5.10.1.3.3(2) Equity Determination (Jan. 1, 2003).

FORM 14.9 ————————————————————————
NOTICE OF INTENT TO LEVY

Department of the Treasury
Internal Revenue Service

		Date of This Letter
		7/15/01
	If you inquire about	▶ Taxpayer Identification Number
John and Mary Doe	your account, please	123-45-6789
One Main Street	refer to these numbers	Document Locator Number
Anytown, NY 12345	or attach this letter	
	▶	

Intent to Levy

Our records show that we have previously sent you notices but we have not received full payment of the Federal tax liability shown below. This is your final notice.

A Notice of Federal Tax Lien, which is a public notice that there is a tax lien against your property, may be filed at any time to protect the interest of the government. If you do not take the requested action within 30 days from the date of this notice, we may, without further notice to you, levy upon and seize your property and rights to property. Section 6331 of the Internal Revenue Code allows us to seize wages, bank accounts, commissions, and other income. Real estate and personal property such as business assets and automobiles may also be seized. The enclosed publication contains an explanation of the actions we may take.

To prevent action from being taken, send full payment today by check or money order payable to the Internal Revenue Service. Write your social security number or employer identification number on your payment. Include the bottom part of this notice with your payment so we can quickly credit your account.

We have calculated penalty and interest amounts to the date of this notice. If full payment is not received within 10 days from the date of this notice, additional interest and penalties will be charged and will continue until the account is fully paid. The failure-to-pay penalty increases from one-half to one percent.

If you recently sent the amount due or if you cannot pay this amount in full, contact the office shown above today.

Enclosures:
Envelope
Copy of this letter

Reply within 30 days
To avoid enforcement action

Tax Form Number	1040
Tax Period Ended	9912
Balance of Prior Assessment	$ 234,175
Late Payment Penalty	75,000
Interest	70,215
Total Amount Due	$ 379,390

Reply to:

Form 4840 (Rev. 1-81)

FORM 14.10 _____
NOTICE OF LEVY

| Form 668-A | Department of the Treasury-Internal Revenue Service |
| (Rev August 1990) | **Notice of Levy** |

DATE 0/21/01   DISTRICT Manhattan   TELEPHONE NUMBER
                                         OF IRS OFFICE 1-800-123-4567

REPLY TO IRS
          PO Box 000
          Holtsville, NY 00000

NAME AND ADDRESS OF TAXPAYER

TO   Acme National Bank   Jane Jones
     One Main Street   One Park Place
     Anytown, NY 12345   Anytown, NY 10000

IDENTIFYING NUMBER(S) 123-45-6789

THIS ISN'T A BILL FOR TAXES YOU OWE. THIS IS A NOTICE OF LEVY WE ARE USING TO COLLECT MONEY OWED BY THE TAXPAYER NAMED ABOVE.

Kind of Tax	Tax Period Ended	Unpaid Balance of Assessment	Statutory Additions	Total
1040	12/31/99	$ 9832.70	$ 437.26	$ 10,269.96

	Total Amount Due	$ 10,269.96

THIS LEVY WON'T ATTACH FUNDS IN AN IRA, SELF-EMPLOYED INDIVIDUALS RETIREMENT PLAN, OR ANY OTHER RETIREMENT PLAN IN YOUR POSSESSION OR CONTROL, UNLESS IT IS SIGNED IN THE BLOCK TO THE RIGHT.

We figure the interest and late payment to   9/19/01

   The Internal Revenue Code provides that there is a lien for the amount that is owed. Although we have given the notice and demand required by the Code, the amount owed hasn't been paid. This levy requires you to turn over to us this person's property and rights to property (such as money, credits and bank deposits) that you have or which you are obligated to pay this person. However, don't send us more than the "Total Amount Due."
   Money in banks, credit unions, savings and loans, and similar institutions described in section 401(n) of the Internal Revenue Code must be held for 21 days from the day you receive this levy before you send the money. Turn over any other money, property, credits, etc. that you have or are already obligated to pay the taxpayer, when you would have paid it when this person asked for payment.
   Make a reasonable effort to identify all property and rights to property belonging to this person. At a minimum search your records using the taxpayer's name, address, and identifying number shown on this form. Don't offset money this person owes you without contacting us at the telephone number shown above for instructions. Ddo not subtract a processing fee from the amount you send us.
   To respond to this levy
   1   Make your check or money order payable to the Internal Revenue Service
   2   Write the taxpayer's name, identifying number(s), kind of tax, and tax period shown on this form, and write "PROCEEDS" on your check or money order (not on the detachable stub)
   3   Complete the back of Part 2 of this form and mail it to us with your own payment in the enclosed envelope
   4   Keep Part 1 of this form for your records and give the taxpayer Part 3 within two days
   If you do not owe any money to the taxpayer, please complete the back of Part 2, and mail this form back to us in the enclosed envelope.

Signature of Service Representative   /s/ John Doe   Title   Special Agent

Part 3 ADDRESSEE'S COPY   Catalog No. 35X   Form 668-A (Rev. 8-90)

FORM 14.11
FINAL DEMAND

Form **668-C** (Rev. July 1989)	Department of the Treasury — Internal Revenue Service **Final Demand**	
To Acme National Bank One Main Street Anytown, NY 12345	Date Sept. 14, 2001	
	District Anytown, NY	

On _____ August 21 _____, 2001, a notice of levy was served on

Mr. Head Teller _____ at Acme National Bank, One Main Street. The notice

of levy attached property, rights to property, money, credits, and bank deposits then in your possession, to the credit of, belonging

to, or owned by _____ Jane Jones _____

of One Park Place, Anytown, NY . Identifying Number(s) 123-45-6789 .

At the time the notice was served, that person owed and still owes the United States unpaid internal revenue taxes, with additions

provided by law, in the amount of $ 10,269.96 . Demand was made on you for the amount shown in the notice

of levy, or for any smaller sum you may have owed the taxpayer. That demand has not been met.

Please see the provisions of section 6332 of the Internal Revenue Code on the back of this form.

Demand is again made for the amount of $ 10,269.96 , shown in the notice of levy,

or for any smaller sum you may have owed the taxpayer at the time the notice of levy was served. Remit payment in accordance

with the instructions received in the levy. If you comply with this final demand within 5 days from its service, no action will be

taken to enforce the provisions of Code section 6332. However, if you do not comply within the 5-day period, we will consider it

your final refusal and may then start proceedings under Code section 6332.

Other claims asserted against this property—see reverse of this form.

Signature /s/ John Doe	Address *(City and State)*
Title Revenue Officer	Telephone Number 123-4567	IRS One Broadway Anytown, NY 12345

Part 2 — Third Party   *(over)*   Form **668-C** (Rev. 7-89)

¶ 14.17 SURRENDER OF PROPERTY THAT HAS BEEN SEIZED BY LEVY

Because a taxpayer and others may not acquiesce in the forcible collection of taxes, the Code has provisions designed to facilitate collection and to protect revenue officials engaged in collection. Criminal penalties are imposed on a person who corruptly or forcibly interferes with collection or forcibly rescues seized property.[501] This crime can be committed where a taxpayer removes notices of seizure and removes padlocks.[502] It is a felony for a person to remove, deposit, or conceal any property subject to levy with intent to defeat collection of a tax.[503] Civil penalties are also imposed if an individual does not comply with a levy. A person in possession of property or rights to property subject to levy must, on demand, surrender the property, or suffer personal liability for failing to honor the levy.

After demand, if the person served fails or refuses to honor a levy, he is personally liable for an amount equal to the value of the property or the tax liability for which the levy was made, whichever is less.[504] Costs and interest at the same rate as that running on the tax liability from the date of the levy are also added to this personal liability.[505] If the person subsequently satisfies the levy, the amount paid, as well as any interest owed, is credited to the account of the delinquent taxpayer. Since this liability is a collection device similar to the trust fund penalty of Section 6672, satisfaction of the levy terminates the personal liability of the levied-upon party, unless the failure or refusal to honor the levy was without reasonable cause. A penalty equal to 50 percent of the

---

[501] IRC §§ 7212(a), 7212(b); see also 18 USC §§ 111, 114. For a case involving the conviction of a lawyer for "corruptly" interfering with the collection process, see United States v. Popkin, 943 F2d 1535 (11th Cir. 1991) (lawyer formed corporation to assist his client in laundering profits).

[502] United States v. Johnson, 424 F. Supp. 631 (D. Or. 1976). See also United States v. Harris, 521 F2d 1089 (7th Cir. 1975) (removal of warning stickers on seized car). United States v. Hardaway, 731 F2d 1138 (5th Cir. 1984) (taxpayer removed vehicles with notices of seizure affixed from lot to which Service had towed them).

[503] IRC § 7206(4).

[504] IRC § 6332(c)(1). It is unclear what statute of limitations applies to a suit for failure to honor a levy, especially where the statute of limitations on collection has expired against the taxpayer. But see United States v. Antonio, 91-2 USTC ¶ 50,482 (D. Haw. 1991) (apparently holding that statute is six years from date of levy). Cf. United States v. Peloquin, 91-2 USTC ¶ 50,538 (D. Ariz. 1991) (apparently holding that action is timely if tax lien on taxpayer's property is still in effect).

[505] IRC § 6332(c)(2). When a levy was served two weeks before the taxpayer filed a bankruptcy petition, interest did not accrue because the automatic stay prevented the levied party from releasing the funds. United States v. Giffels Assocs., 78 AFTR2d 96-6228 (ED Mich. 1996).

amount recoverable is imposed where the failure to surrender was without reasonable cause.[506] This amount is not credited against the taxpayer's liability.

The statute permits the person upon whom levy and demand has been made only two defenses for noncompliance: (1) that the person is not in possession of property of the taxpayer subject to levy and (2) that the property is subject to prior judicial attachment or execution.[507] With respect to the first defense, it has been held that a party upon whom a levy describing particular property has been served is not required to determine the true owner of the property, nor whether the property is subject to levy,[508] although persons who surrender property not subject to levy may be liable to a third party.[509] Where there is a dispute about the ownership of property, at least where the property is a joint bank account or similar property, the person on whom the levy is

---

[506] IRC § 6332(c)(2). This penalty may even be imposed where the taxpayer has paid the delinquent tax, although it is unclear from the statute that the 50 percent penalty may be imposed where the 100 percent penalty also has been assessed. See United States v. Sterling Nat'l Bank & Trust Co., 360 F. Supp. 917 (SDNY 1973), rev'd on another issue, 494 F2d 919 (2d Cir. 1974); United States v. Kamin, 77 AFTR2d 96-677 (ED Mich. 1995) (levy served on taxpayers' debtors under promissory note, but they nevertheless paid the taxpayers after the levy was served; held, the debtors were liable for the full amount of the debt owed to the taxpayers on the date of the levy, plus a penalty equal to 50 percent of that amount).

[507] IRC § 6332(a); United States v. Manufacturers Hanover Trust Co., 198 F2d 366 (2d Cir. 1952); United States v. Sterling Nat'l Bank & Trust Co., 494 F2d 919, 921–922 (2d Cir. 1974); United States v. Weintraub, 613 F2d 612 (6th Cir. 1979). However, there are special rules for levies served on insurers under life insurance and endowment contracts (IRC § 6332(b); Reg. § 301.6332-1(a)(1)) and banks (IRC § 6332(c)).

[508] Determan v. Jenkins, 111 F. Supp. 604 (ND Ga. 1953) (police official acted properly where he turned currency over pursuant to levy although he knew title to the currency was in dispute). Of course, persons on whom a levy has been served may claim that they are not in possession of property subject to levy. See, e.g., United States v. Equitable Life Assurance Co., 442 F. Supp. 500 (SDNY 1977), aff'd, 78-2 USTC ¶ 9749 (2d Cir. 1978) (suit for failure to honor a levy holding taxpayer-insured's policy was valueless ninety days after levy so insurer not holding property subject to levy); United States v. Donahue Indus., Inc., 905 F2d 1325 (9th Cir. 1990) (taxpayer-debtor's transfer of accounts receivable was already subject to lien so that bank was required to surrender property even after taxpayer's interest was extinguished); United States v. New Eng. Merchants Nat'l Bank, 465 F. Supp. 83 (D. Mass. 1979) (suit to enforce levy finding bank in possession of safe-deposit box for levy purposes). Some courts have held that the burden rests on the party opposing the levy to show that the taxpayer does not have an interest in the property in issue. See, e.g., Flores v. United States, 551 F2d 1169 (9th Cir. 1977); United States v. Capital Sav. Ass'n, 576 F. Supp. 790 (ND Ind. 1983). There is authority to the contrary. See United States v. Stock Yards Bank of Louisville, 231 F2d 628 (6th Cir. 1956) (burden on government to prove taxpayer's interest); United States v. Bailey, 707 F2d 19 (1st Cir. 1983) (government has the burden of proving the value of property in the hands of the levied party). However, this authority antedated the wrongful-levy statute (Section 7426) and was distinguished on this ground in United States v. National Bank of Commerce, 472 US 713 n.11 (1985).

[509] Reg. § 301-6332-1(c).

served must turn the property over to the Service, "leaving ownership disputes to be resolved in a post-seizure administrative or judicial proceeding,"[510] such as the filing of a wrongful-levy claim and wrongful-levy action under Section 7426.[511] It has been said that where money has been levied upon by the Service, but the holder claims an interest in the funds, the proper procedure is for the third party claimant to surrender the funds and then sue for their return under Section 7426 because the prior lien is not a defense to a tax levy.[512] After it had instituted a foreclosure proceeding and received a levy, a bank sold the taxpayer's mortgaged property and interpleaded the surplus proceeds. Despite the bank's interpleader, the failure of the bank to pay over the surplus to the Service pursuant to the levy rendered the bank liable.[513] Although the interpleader court transferred the surplus to the taxpayer based on his false statement, the court did not consider whether the circumstances constituted "reasonable cause." When a trustee in bankruptcy had allowed an administrative claim of a delinquent taxpayer and the Service served the trustee with a levy, the trustee held an obligation belonging to the taxpayer, and, accordingly, the trustee failed to honor the levy when the trustee paid the taxpayer, not the Service.[514]

The second defense points up a difference between a tax levy and lien. A levy is not effective to seize property already subject to an attachment lien, but for lien priority purposes the tax lien would have priority over a lien arising from the attachment.[515] In other words, the statutory rule merely removes the

---

[510] United States v. National Bank of Commerce. 472 US 713, 730 (1985).

[511] United States v. National Bank of Commerce. 472 US 713, 730 (1985).

[512] Trust Co. of Columbus v. United States, 735 F2d 447, 449 (11th Cir. 1984). This means, for example, that a bank may not decide for itself that it has priority over the tax lien and simply refuse to turn over account proceeds to the Service pursuant to the levy. If the bank ignores the levy, it may be held liable not only for the account proceeds on the date of the levy, but also for the 50 percent penalty. To assert that it has priority over the tax lien and levy, therefore, the bank must pay over the account and file a wrongful-levy claim under Section 7426.

[513] United States v. Rockland Trust Co., 860 F. Supp. 895 (D. Mass. 1994).

[514] See United States v. Bank of W., 83 AFTR2d 99-933 (ND Cal. 1999) (unpublished order; bank claimed that its refusal to honor the levy was reasonable because it believed that its lien on the account had priority over the tax lien, and it attempted to have the taxpayer pay the tax assessed). United States v. Hemmen, 51 F3d 883 (9th Cir. 1995) (a divided court); see also United States v. Ruff, 99 F3d 1559 (11th Cir. 1996) (taxpayer's commission for the sale of property in a bankruptcy estate became fixed and determinable when the sale was approved, not when the payment was approved, so that the trustee's payment to taxpayer despite the levy was a willful violation of the levy, and rendered the trustee liable for the 50 percent penalty).

[515] Property subject to a prior judicial attachment is in the custody of a court and cannot be collected by administrative levy. United States v. McPherson, 631 F. Supp. 269 (MDNC 1986) (receiver had valid defense in failure to honor levy action because the

possibility that administrative action will collide with the judicial process, but it does not affect any right the government may have by way of its tax lien.

Note that these are the only two defenses provided for failing to honor a levy. The person served may not raise defenses the taxpayer might raise, such as the amount and validity of the assessment, statute of limitations, absence of notice and demand, and collection within the ten-day grace period.[516]

The person served with a levy is subject to a 50 percent penalty for failure to honor the levy, if the failure was without "reasonable cause." What constitutes reasonable cause? The regulations reflecting the legislative history of the statute provide little information,[517] saying only that the penalty is inapplicable where a "bona fide dispute" exists concerning the amount to be surrendered or the legal effectiveness of the levy.[518] If a court sustains the levy in an enforcement suit and the levied party refuses a later levy made under similar circumstances, reasonable cause "usually" does not exist.[519]

If the penalty provisions are the "stick" where a levy is concerned, the provision of the statute discharging the person who honors the levy from liability to the taxpayer is intended to be the "carrot." Where the person served honors a levy and surrenders property, the person is discharged by operation of

---

property levied upon was subject to prior judicial attachment by virtue of being the subject of receivership under state court supervision). See also supra ¶ 14.14[2].

[516] United States v. Penn Mut. Life Ins. Co., 130 F2d 495 (2d Cir. 1942); Commonwealth Bank v. United States, 155 F2d 327 (6th Cir. 1940). But see Georgia-Pac. Corp. v. Lazy Two T Ranch, Inc., 76-2 USTC ¶ 9666 (CD Cal. 1976).

[517] Reg. § 301.6332-1(b)(2); S. Rep. No. 1708, 89th Cong., 2d Sess. (1966), reprinted in 1966-2 CB 876, 889.

[518] A dispute between the taxpayer and the Service about whether the taxpayer is liable for the tax is not reasonable cause. United States v. First Nat'l Bank of Bellaire, 83-2 USTC ¶ 9648 (SD Tex. 1983). United States v. Marine Midland Bank, 675 F. Supp. 775 (WDNY 1987) (contingent debt was attachable; bank was not subject to penalty, because it had reasonable cause for withholding payment of tax). State Bank of Fraser v. United States, 861 F2d 954 (6th Cir. 1988) (penalty because no unsettled area of law provided reasonable ground for refusal to honor levy); United States v. Metropolitan Life Ins. Co., 874 F2d 1497 (11th Cir. 1989) (claim that annuity contract not subject to levy rejected as having "no justification in logic or in the case law"; penalty imposed); United States v. Donahue Indus., Inc., 905 F2d 1325 (9th Cir. 1990) (bank's dispute held not bona fide); United States v. Metro Interior, Inc., 93-1 USTC ¶ 50,073 (WD Mo. 1992) (no bona fide legal dispute that levy on employer seized accrued wages).

[519] See United States v. Sterling Nat'l Bank & Trust Co., 360 F. Supp. 917 (SDNY 1973), rev'd on another issue, 494 F2d 919 (2d Cir. 1974), in which a bank, after a levy, exercised a believed right of setoff. Applying the standard of the regulations, the district court upheld the 50 percent penalty against the bank on the basis of two Ninth Circuit decisions on the setoff issue. However, the circuit court (with one dissent) reversed only by straining to find contrary authority of doubtful weight. See also United States v. First Nat'l Bank of Commerce, 73-2 USTC ¶ 9751 (ED La. 1973), aff'd, 493 F2d 1228 (5th Cir. 1974).

law from any liability to the taxpayer.[520] This provision does not discharge liability to a third person who actually owns the property surrendered, although the third person may seek the return of the surrendered property from the Service under Section 6343(b) or institute a civil action for wrongful levy under Section 7426.[521]

¶ 14.18 SEIZURE AND SALE

To satisfy a tax debt due, Section 6335 authorizes the Service to sell seized personal and real property. The Service must follow definite procedures in the sale of seized property prior to, during, and after the sale. These procedures are discussed in the following sections.

[1] Preseizure Requirements

In general, Section 6335 requires that (1) a notice of seizure be delivered to the owner of the property seized; (2) a notice of sale be delivered to the owner and be publicly made; and (3) the sale take place not less than ten nor more than forty days from the date of the notice of sale. These notice and timing requirements are conditions precedent to the sale, and the Service's failure to follow them makes the sale voidable.[522]

---

[520] IRC § 6632(e). See, e.g., United States v. Bonneville, 85 AFTR2d 2000-2036 (10th Cir. 2000) (taxpayer transferred a joint venture interest in Green River to another controlled corporation, Bonneville, but when the Green River joint venture dissolved, it paid Bonneville's share to the Service; held, Green River was discharged of any liability to Bonneville). The levied party must actually surrender property to the Service that is subject to levy. In *Farr*, the taxpayer's employer, United Airlines, turned over workmen's compensation benefits to the Service, even though those benefits were exempt from levy under Section 6334(a)(7), and the notice of levy specifically excluded exempt property. Farr v. United States, 990 F2d 451 (9th Cir. 1993). As a result, United was not discharged from liability to the taxpayer.

[521] Reg. § 301.6331-1(c).

[522] See IRC §§ 6335(a), 6335(b), and 6335(d). Margiotta v. District Dir., 214 F2d 518 (2d Cir. 1954) (failure to post notice at two public places held fatal to validity of sale); Reese v. Scoggins, 506 F2d 967 (5th Cir. 1975); Aqua Bar & Lounge, Inc. v. United States, 438 F. Supp. 655 (DNJ 1977); United States v. Conry, 74-1 USTC ¶ 9187 (ND Cal. 1974) (sale held invalid due to failure to notify property owner of sale's adjournment). But see United States v. City of New York, 233 F2d 307 (2d Cir. 1956) (substantial compliance with notice requirement of predecessor of Section 6335 held sufficient where notice posted at General Post Office rather than branch nearer property sold); Silver Bell Indus., Inc. v. United States, 76-1 USTC ¶ 9432 (10th Cir.), cert. denied, 429 US 822 (1976) (claimed failure to comply with sale provisions rejected). The failure to comply with sale requirements may be raised in an action to quiet title under 28 USC

[a] Notice of Seizure

After seizure of property, a written notice of seizure must be given "as soon as practicable" to the owner of the property or, in the case of personal property, to its possessor.[523] The Service uses Form 2433 (Notice of Seizure) for this purpose. (See Form 14.12.) The notice of seizure must be (1) delivered to the owner or possessor personally; (2) left at his usual place of abode or at his place of business if it happens to be located in the district in which the seizure took place; or (3) if the person cannot be readily located or has no place of abode or business in the district, mailed to his last known address. The notice must specify the sum demanded and, in the case of realty, must describe the seized property sufficiently to identify it and, in the case of personalty, must provide a list sufficient to identify the property seized.

---

§ 2410(a)(1). Where the nontax lien is a specific rather than a general lien, the notice requirement may be interpreted more strictly. Verba v. Ohio Cas. Ins. Co., 851 F2d 811 (6th Cir. 1988) (notice of sale to specific property lienor held constitutionally inadequate despite publication in general circulation newspapers and posting). Even if the Service has not complied with the statutory requirements, where a taxpayer-owner had actual notice before the sale and failed to act, or ratified the sale by subsequently accepting the excess proceeds, courts have refused to void the sale. Johnson v. Gartlan, 470 F2d 1104, 1106 (4th Cir.), cert. denied, 414 US 865 (1973) (subsequent ratification); Lawrence v. Beaman, 90-2 USTC ¶ 50,514 (D. Mass. 1990) (actual prior notice and subsequent ratification); Howard v. Adle, 538 F. Supp. 504, 508–509 (ED Mich. 1982) (actual prior notice); McCoy v. United States, 92-2 USTC ¶ 50,530 (D. Colo. 1992) (taxpayer had actual prior notice, and because she was represented, she was deemed to have made knowing waiver of sale defects).

[523] IRC § 6335(a); Reg. § 301.6335-1(a) (1996). See also IRM 5.10.1 Pre-Seizure Considerations (Jan. 1, 2003); IRM 5.10.3 Conducting the Seizure (Jan. 1, 2003). It is unclear whether the failure to provide this notice renders the levy ineffective. At least some courts have considered whether the property was cash or tangible property and whether the value of the property exceeded the amount of the levy. Altman v. Comm'r, 88-1 USTC ¶ 9166 (D. Haw. 1988). Cf. Dunne Trucking Co. v. IRS, 32 Bankr. 182 (Bankr. ND Iowa 1983) (notice of seizure held to be required before levy effective so that where taxpayer filed for bankruptcy on the day after notice of levy, a bank account held subject to bankruptcy court turnover order). A divided panel of the Second Circuit has held that notice of seizure need not be a formal notice, and that in "the normal course of events all of us know that depositors are sent monthly bank statements by banks. . . ." so that it was only reasonable to conclude that the taxpayer received actual notice of the Service's levies through his monthly bank statements. Kaggen v. IRS, 75 AFTR2d 95-2715 (2d Cir. 1995), reaff'd on reh'g, 71 F3d 1018 (2d Cir. 1995) (the panel remained divided over the applicability of judicial notice). The Service contended that the notice of seizure requirement applied only to tangible property, not intangible property, but the majority declined to resolve the issue.

[b] Notice of Sale

In the same manner as a notice of seizure, and as soon as practicable after the seizure of property, notice of sale must be given to the owner.[524] A notice specifying the property to be sold and the time, place, manner, and conditions of sale must also be published.[525] The Service uses Form 2434 (Notice of Public Auction Sale) for this purpose. (See Form 14.13.) This notice must be printed in a newspaper published in the county where the seizure is made or a newspaper generally circulated in that county. If no newspaper is published or generally circulated in the county, notice of the sale must be posted at the post office nearest the place of seizure and in at least two other public places.[526]

---

[524] IRC § 6335(b); Reg. § 301.6335-1(b)(1). See also IRM 5.10.4 Returns Prior to Sale (Jan. 1, 2003). In addition to giving notice of sale in newspapers, other methods of giving notice if the nature of the property to be sold is believed to warrant a wider or more specialized advertising coverage will enhance the possibility of obtaining a higher price for the property. Reg. § 301.6335-1(b)(2). If a jeopardy levy is served, the Service is prohibited from giving a public notice of sale of the property seized within the ten-day period provided in Section 6331(a), unless the procedures of Section 6336, dealing with the seizure of perishable goods, apply.

[525] A description of real property in a notice of sale is sufficient if the land can be identified, provided the portion of the description that is left out would add nothing to the certainty of such description. Keely v. Sanders, 99 US 441 (1879). In describing personal property to be sold, it is not necessary that each item be listed and completely detailed. Sacks v. Machiz, 58-2 USTC ¶ 9918 (D. Md. 1958) (suit to enjoin a sale based in part on alleged inadequate description of personal property was dismissed although it is not clear whether the petitioner had failed to prove his case or had run afoul of the Anti-Injunction Act).

For collection procedures, see IRM 5.10 Seizure and Sale.

[526] IRC § 6335(b). The delinquent taxpayer's premises do not constitute a public place even if the sale takes place there. Margiotta v. District Dir., 214 F2d 518 (2d Cir. 1954). See United States v. City of New York, 233 F2d 307 (2d Cir. 1956) (posting at the General Post Office, although there was a branch nearer the place of seizure, was held substantially to comply with the posting requirements).

FORM 14.12
NOTICE OF SEIZURE

Department of the Treasury
Internal Revenue Service
Form 2433 (Rev. March, 1988)

Notice of Seizure

Name and Address

John Jones
One Main Street
New York, NY 00000

Under the authority in section 6331 of the Internal Revenue Code, and by virtue of a levy from the District Director of Internal Revenue of the district shown below, I have seized the property below for nonpayment of past due internal revenue taxes.

Due from	Amount	Internal Revenue District *(City and State)*
John Jones One Main Street New York, NY 00000	$ 675,000	Manhattan, NY

Description of property

All of that certain plot, place, or parcel of land with the buildings and improvements thereon erected, situate, lying and being in the City of Anytown and the State of New York, bounded and described as follows:

Beginning at a point on the westerly side of Main Street, distant 260 feet from the northerly corner formed by the intersection of the westerly side of Main Street with the westerly side of Park Place, measured along the westerly side of Main Street, running westerly on a line which is the extension of a radius of a circle of which the westerly side of Main Street is the circumference 100 feet; thence northerly 65 feet to a point which is 115 feet westerly from the westerly side of Main Street on a line which is the radius of the said circle and passes through the westerly side of Main Street, which is the circumference of the said circle at a point 55 feet northerly from the point of beginning.

The said premises being known as One Main Street.

Signature of Revenue Officer making seizure /s/ John Doe	Address One Broad Street Anytown, NY 12345	Date 7/20/01
Signature of accompanying employee /s/ Michael Alans	Address One First Street Anytown, NY 54321	Date 7/20/01

Part 1 — Taxpayer Copy   Form **2433** (Rev. 3-88)

FORM 14.13
NOTICE OF PUBLIC AUCTION SALE

Notice of

Department of the Treasury / Internal Revenue Service

Public Auction Sale

Under the authority in Internal Revenue Code section 6331, the property described below has been seized for nonpayment of internal revenue taxes due from

John Jones

The property will be sold at public auction as provided by Internal Revenue Code section 6335 and related regulations.

Date of Sale: March 16   , 2001

Time of Sale: 10:00   (am) pm

Place of Sale: 100 Main Street, Anytown, NY 10000

Title Offered: Only the right, title, and interest of _____ John Jones _____
in and to the property will be offered for sale. If requested, the Internal Revenue Service will furnish information about possible encumbrances, which may be useful in determining the value of the interest being sold (see the back of the form for further details).

Description of Property:
Three-Family House
909 Park Place
Anytown, NY 12345

Property May Be Inspected at: _____

Payment Terms:
☐ Full payment required on acceptance of highest bid
☒ Deferred payment as follows:

Form of Payment: All payments must be by cash, certified check, cashier's or treasurer's check or by a United States postal, bank, express, or telegraph money order. Make check or money order payable to the Internal Revenue Service.

Signature /s/ Jane Doe	Name and Title (Typed) Jane Doe—Revenue Officer	Date 2/10/01
Address for Information about the Sale 100 Main Street, Anytown, NY 10000		Phone (212) 765-4321

Form **2434** (Rev. 2-84)

Nature of Title The right, title, and interest of the taxpayer (named on the front of this form) in and to the property is offered for sale subject to any prior valid outstanding mortgages, encumbrances, or other liens in favor of third parties against the taxpayer that are superior to the lien of the United States. All property is offered for sale "where is" and "as is" and without recourse against the United States. No property or warranty, express or implied, is made as to the validity of the title, quality, quantity, weight, size, or condition of any of the property, or its fitness for any use or purpose. No claim will be considered for allowance or adjustment or for rescission of the sale based on failure of the property to conform with any expressed or implied representation.

Redemption Rights The rights of redemption, as specified in Internal Revenue Code section 6337, are quoted as follows.

Sec. 6337. Redemption of Property

(a) **Before Sale**—Any person whose property has been levied upon shall have the right to pay the amount due, together with the expenses of the proceeding, if any, to the Secretary shall restore such property to him, and all further proceedings in connection with the levy on such property shall cease from the time of such payment.

(b) **Redemption of Real Estate after Sale**

(1) Period—The owners of any real property sold as provided in section 6335, their heirs, executors, or administrators, or any person having any interest therein, or a lien thereon, or any person in their behalf, shall be permitted to redeem the property sold, or any particular tract of such property, at any time within 180 days after the sale thereof.

(2) Price—Such property or tract of property shall be permitted to be redeemed upon payment to the purchaser, or in case he cannot be found in the county in which the property to be redeemed is situated, then to the Secretary, for the use of the purchaser, his heirs or assigns, the amount paid by such purchaser and interest thereon at the rate of 20 percent per month.

Effect of Junior Encumbrances **Sec. 6338(c). Effect of Junior Encumbrances**

A certificate of sale of personal property given or a deed to real property executed pursuant to section 6338 shall discharge such property from all liens, encumbrances, and titles over which the lien of the United States with respect to which the levy was made had priority.

Internal Revenue Service

UNITED STATES POSTAL SERVICE®

Official Business
Penalty for Private Use $300

Form **2434** (Rev. 2-84)

As in the case of a notice of seizure, failure to give the taxpayer a notice of sale, or service of a defective notice, results in noncompliance with one of the conditions precedent to a sale and renders the sale voidable.[527]

---

[527] Although there are some cases to the contrary, strict compliance with the notice provisions has generally been required. Goodwin v. United States, 935 F2d 1061 (9th Cir. 1991) (although notice was sent by certified mail and owner had actual notice, there was not strict compliance with Section 6335(a)); United States v. Powelson, 979 F2d 141 (9th Cir. 1992), cert. denied, 507 US 1029 (1993) (proper notice of sale not given because the Service had not made a reasonable attempt to locate the taxpayer personally before serv-

[c] Time of Sale

A sale must be held not less than ten days nor more than forty days from the date public notice of sale is given.[528] A sale may be adjourned where the interests of either the United States or the taxpayer are best served by the adjournment.[529] Failure to hold the sale of seized property within the statutory thirty-day period designated in Section 6335 affects the validity of the sale.[530] An exception is made to the ten-day waiting period for perishable goods or goods subject to great reduction in value if they are retained, but the taxpayer must be given notice of the appraised value of the property and have the opportunity to pay or post a bond equal to the appraised value of the property.[531]

---

ing him with the notice by mail): Reese v. Scoggins, 506 F2d 967 (5th Cir. 1975) (taxpayer not given notice of adjourned sale); United States v. Conry, 74-1 USTC ¶ 9187 (ND Cal. 1974); Johnson v. Gartlan, 334 F. Supp. 438 (ED Va. 1971), rev'd on other grounds, 470 F2d 1104 (4th Cir.), cert. denied, 414 US 865 (1973); Bartell v. Riddell, 202 F. Supp. 70 (SD Cal. 1962). But see Westaire Properties, Inc. v. Tucker, 89-2 USTC ¶ 9473 (SD Cal. 1989) (lack of compliance with Section 6335(b) excused because notice to corporate taxpayer at corporate address would have been fruitless, and notice was provided to corporation's president and sole shareholder by certified and regular mail); Lawrence v. Beaman, 90-2 USTC ¶ 50,514 (D. Mass. 1990) (actual notice found sufficient; taxpayer also held to have ratified sale by accepting surplus proceeds).

[528] IRC § 6335(d); see also Reg. § 301.6335-1(c).

[529] IRC § 6335(a)(2). Reg. § 301.6335-1(c)(2) specifies that notwithstanding adjournments from time to time, "the sale shall not be later than one month after the date fixed in the original notice of sale." Notice of the adjourned sale should be given to the owner of the property in the same manner as the original notice of sale. Reese v. Scoggins, 506 F2d 967 (5th Cir. 1975); United States v. Conry, 74-1 USTC ¶ 9187 (ND Cal. 1974) (adjournment approved, but failure to give notice of adjourned sale invalidated sale). Cf. Anderson v. United States, 93-1 USTC ¶ 50,249 (ND Cal. 1993) (sale postponed to date more than the seventy days allowed by Sections 6335(d) and 6335(e)(2)(F) permitted because the new date was re-noticed).

[530] If the Service fails to sell the property on the original sale date or on the adjourned date, which may be up to thirty days later, the Service must bid in the property itself or release the property. Anderson v. United States, 44 F3d 795 (9th Cir. 1995) (sale advertised for September 29, 1991, "postponed" until November 14, 1991, as advertised on October 25, but the sale was postponed a second time until March 11, 1992; held, the Service failed to sell the property within forty days after public notice of sale and one month thereafter, and so the property was required to be released). Margiotta v. District Dir., 214 F2d 518 (2d Cir. 1954); Kulawy v. United States, 917 F2d 729 (2d Cir. 1990) (eight days' notice invalidated sale). A sale may be temporarily enjoined by court order, in which case the actual period of suspension should not be included in computing the time for sale under Section 6335(d). See Section 6863(b)(3), providing for a stay of sale of seized property pending a Tax Court decision in the case of a jeopardy assessment.

[531] IRC § 6336; Reg. § 301.6336-1. See Church of Hakeem, Inc. v. United States, 79-2 USTC ¶ 9651 (ND Cal. 1979) (showing a necessity made under Section 6863(b)(3)(B), which is similar to § 6336). A proposed sale before these requirements are complied with may be ignored. Smith v. Flinn, 261 F2d 781 (8th Cir. 1958), modified, 264 F2d 523 (8th Cir. 1959).

[d] Request for Sale

Under Section 6335(f), a taxpayer or owner whose property has been seized by levy has the right to request that the Service sell the property within sixty days, or within any longer period specified by the owner. Within the sixty-day period, the Service must comply or notify the taxpayer of its determination that a sale would not be in the interests of the government. Regulations provide that a request for sale be made in writing to the group manager of the revenue officer whose signature is on the levy[532] and that the request be made within the time specified, and also that the request must include information identifying the owner of the seized property, a description of the property, and a copy of the notice of seizure if available.[533] The group manager must respond in writing within sixty days.[534]

[2] Sale

If any seized property liable to levy is not divisible so as to enable sale of a part of the property to raise the whole amount of the tax and expenses, the whole of the property must be sold.[535] Divisible property may be sold as (1) separate items; (2) in lots or as groups of items; or (3) in the aggregate. All three methods may be employed, in which case the property shall be sold under the method producing the highest total proceeds.[536] Where real and personal property are offered for sale, the real property must be offered first as separate items and the personal property as a group, groups, or separate items before being offered in the aggregate.[537] The Service is given fairly wide discretion under the sale provisions of the Code. Since the objective is to produce

---

[532] Reg. § 301.6335-1(d)(2)(i). The letter should be sent to the attention of the revenue officer's group manager if the manager's name is not known.

[533] Reg. § 301.6335-1(d)(2)(ii).

[534] Reg. § 301.6335-1(d)(3).

[535] IRC § 6335(c); Reg. § 301.6335-1(c)(5)(i) (Offering of property—Sale of indivisible property).

[536] IRC § 6335(c); Reg. § 301.6335-1(c)(5)(ii) (Offering of property—Separately, in groups, or in the aggregate).

[537] If several tracts of realty are to be sold, the costs and expenses of the proceedings should be apportioned to each parcel for purposes of determining the amount to be paid for redemption of any one parcel prior to sale. Failure to prorate costs and expenses incident to preparation of the sale or failure to assign a value to each parcel of real property where sold in the aggregate may be held to prejudice the rights of redemption before sale or after sale. McAndrews v. Belknap, 141 F2d 111 (6th Cir.), cert. denied, 323 US 721 (1944). If the seized property is divisible and a sale of a part thereof would realize an amount sufficient to pay the entire tax and expense, only so much of the divisible property should be sold as is necessary to raise the amount needed. Id. Also, all property need not be sold on the same day.

the highest proceeds from a sale, albeit a forced sale, it would appear that a taxpayer has a basis for relief if the Service fails to exercise this discretion in a commercially reasonable manner. Nevertheless, it has been held that Sections 6335 and 6336 do not require the Service to sell a going business as such to realize the highest price possible for the assets,[538] but the issue is not settled.[539]

The IRS Restructuring and Reform Act of 1998 made several changes to provisions relating to the sale of seized property. The sale of seized property below its minimum bid price is prohibited.[540] Also, the taxpayer is required to be given an accounting of the amount received at the sale which includes the data described in Section 6340, such as the expenses of the sale (but not the name of the purchaser), the amount received from the sale applied to the taxpayer's liability, and the remaining balance of the taxpayer's liability.[541] In addition, within two years after July 22, 1998, the Service adopted a uniform asset disposal mechanism for sales under Section 6335, which eliminates revenue officers from the process, and considers outsourcing.[542]

[a] Minimum Price

Before the sale, the Service's district office must determine a minimum price for which the property will be sold.[543] If no person offers to purchase the property for the minimum price, the property must be declared purchased for the government at the minimum price and the taxpayer's account credited with that amount less the cost of levy and sale.[544] The minimum price is ordinarily computed to be 80 percent or more of the forced sale value of the property

---

[538] Miracle Span Corp. v. United States, 82-1 USTC ¶ 9365 (DSD 1982).

[539] See United States v. Pittman, 449 F2d 623 (7th Cir. 1971) (taxpayer entitled to credit for full value of property seized, not depreciated value resulting from Service inaction).

[540] IRC § 6335(e)(1)(A)(i), as amended by 1998 Act § 3441.

[541] IRC § 6340(c), as amended by 1998 Act § 3442.

[542] 1998 Act § 3443.

[543] IRC § 6335(e)(1); Reg. § 301.6335-1(c)(3) (Determinations relating to minimum price). In general, on and after December 17, 1996, the effective date of revised regulations, the minimum price takes into account the expenses of levy and sale. In determining whether the United States should purchase the property, regulations say the district director should consider, among other factors, the marketability of the property, the cost of maintaining the property, the cost of repairing or restoring the property, and similar factors. See also Reg. § 301.6335-1(c)(4) (Disposition of property at sale). Property will be sold to the highest bidder as long as the bid is at least the amount of the minimum price. If no bidder offers the minimum price, the Service may declare the property sold to the United States for the minimum price; or, if it decides not to bid on the property, the property may be released to the taxpayer, in which case the expenses of the levy and sale would be added to the unpaid tax, and the lien would continue to encumber the property.

[544] IRC § 6343(b); IRM 5.10.4.6 Establishment of Minimum Bid (Jan. 1, 2003).

less encumbrances having priority over the tax lien, but it is not to exceed the lien interest in the property, less costs.[545] This standard gives revenue officers considerable discretion, but as a matter of practice the minimum bid price approximates the forced sale value of the property.[546] The starting point for determining the minimum price for seized property (other than marketable securities) is its "inventory value" (determined at the time of seizure), which is supposed to be based on (1) the wholesale price of the item; (2) its age and condition; (3) an appraisal by others in the business; and (4) any other means a prudent business person would use to establish the value.[547] The minimum price may be the same as or different from the inventory value, depending on facts and circumstances not known at the time of seizure.[548]

[b] Warranties

Only the "property and rights to property" belonging to the taxpayer can be sold at a sale. The government sells nothing more and nothing less than the taxpayer's right, title, and interest in the property or rights to property that have been levied upon and seized subject to any prior mortgages, encumbrances, or liens in favor of third parties.[549] Consequently, the buyer suffers the

---

[545] IRM, Policies of the IRS Handbook, P-5-35. However, there are two exceptions. The minimum price of securities listed on the New York or American stock exchanges, or of unmatured marketable U.S. securities, must be at least 95 percent of the closing price on the day preceding the sale. Matured U.S. securities are not the equivalent of currency and are not offered for sale. See also IRM 5.10.4.6(10) Establishment of the Minimum Bid (Jan. 1, 2003).

[546] Report on Administrative Procedures of the Internal Revenue Service to the Administrative Conference of the United States, S. Doc. No. 94-266, 94th Cong., 2d Sess. 275 (1976).

[547] IRM 5.10.4.6 Establishment of the Minimum Bid (Jan. 1, 2003). The purposes behind establishing the value of seized property is to (1) comply with 31 USC § 66a, which requires a monetary accounting control of seized property by all government agencies, and (2) set a base for establishing the minimum price. See also IRM 5.10.1.3.3.1 Equity Determination–Expenses of Sale (Jan. 1, 2003).

[548] In making the minimum price determination, the Manual advises the revenue officer also to consider (1) other existing liens, encumbrances, and claims against the taxpayer that may affect the bidding at a sale and (2) whether the property is so specialized that the value may be depressed because of the limited market. IRM 5.10.4.6 Establishment of the Minimum Bid, (Jan. 1, 2003).

[549] See IRC § 6339(a)(2) (the sale transfers to the purchaser the taxpayer's "right, title, and interest . . . "); Reg. § 301.6335-1(c)(4)(iii). Commercial Credit Corp. v. Schwartz, 130 F. Supp. 524 (ED Ark. 1955). The property is sold subject to prior mortgages, encumbrances, and liens even if the United States is declared the purchaser of the property. Wells v. Kurtz, 81-2 USTC ¶ 9736 (SD Tex. 1981) (purchasers discovered encumbrances on property after submitting bid; tort action for misrepresentation dismissed under 28 USC § 2680(h), which bars such suits). Reg. § 301.6335-1(c)(5)(iii) (Offering of property— Condition of title and of property).

loss if after the sale, the Service or the buyer discover that the taxpayer did not have right, title, or interest in the property sold. The revenue officer conducting a sale is supposed to emphasize that no warranties are made as to the validity of the title to the property to be sold. The regulations require that the property should be offered for sale "as is" and "where is" and without recourse against the United States.[550]

[c] Method of Sale

The sale of seized property must be conducted by public auction or by public sale under sealed bids.[551] The Service has forms to be used for the making of such bids.[552] If the total bid is $200 or less, the full amount must be remitted with the bid. If the total bid is more than $200, 20 percent of the bid or $200, whichever is greater, must be remitted with the bid.[553] A bid is not considered unless it is received by the revenue officer conducting the sale prior to the opening of the bids.[554] However, the maker of a sealed bid need not be present at the time bids are opened.[555] The revenue officer calls those present to order, announces a bid or bids, and names the unsuccessful bidder(s), to whom he returns their remittances.[556] If the highest bid is greater than the minimum price, the minimum price is not announced. If the highest bid is less than the minimum price, the minimum price is announced and the property is declared purchased for the government at the minimum price.[557]

---

[550] Reg. § 301.6335-1(c)(4)(iii). Reg. § 301.6335-1(c)(5)(iii) (Offering of property— Condition of title and of property).

[551] IRC § 6335(e)(2). If both public auction and sale under sealed bids are used in the same auction, the opening of the sealed bids follows the oral bidding. See Reg. 301.6335-1(c)(6) (Method of sale). See also IRM 5.10.4.7 Determining the Type of Sale (Jan. 1, 2003).

[552] Reg. § 301.6335-1(c)(6) (Method of sale). Reg. § 301.6335-1(c)(5). These forms are available from the Area Territory office.

[553] Reg. § 301.6335-1(c)(5)(iv) (Terms of payment). These and other rules relating to alternative bids, the medium of payment, and the preparation and submission of bids are set forth in Reg. § 301.6335-1(c)(6) (Method of sale). The revenue officer conducting the sale may waive any technical defects in a bid. Reg. § 301.6335-1(c)(6) (Method of sale). However, a defective bid does not give the bidder the right to withdraw the bid after it has been opened. IRM 5.10.5.11 Sealed Bid Sale (Jan. 1, 2003).

[554] Reg. § 301.6335-1(c)(5). Reg. § 301.6335-1(c)(6) (Method of sale).

[555] IRM 5.10.5 Sale Procedures (Jan. 1, 2003).

[556] See Reg. § 301.6335-1(c)(6) (Method of sale). In the event that there are two equal high bids, the successful bidder is determined by drawing lots.

[557] IRM 5.10.5 Sale Procedures (Jan. 1, 2003). The fact that the government is declared the purchaser does not excuse noncompliance with the sale provisions of the Code. McAndrews v. Belknap, 141 F2d 111 (6th Cir.), cert. denied, 323 US 721 (1944); United States v. City of New York, 233 F2d 307 (2d Cir. 1956).

Until full payment is received, the Service retains possession of the sold property, but on acceptance of the bid, the risk of loss and responsibility for preservation of the property shifts to the purchaser. Even if the Service continues to care for the property, it is at the bidder's expense.[558] Regardless of the type of auction, if payment in full is required at the time of acceptance but is not tendered, the property may be immediately resold.[559] If payment of a portion of the price has been deferred but is not paid within the prescribed period, suit may be brought for the unpaid purchase price plus 6 percent interest, or the property may be resold free and clear of any claim of the defaulting purchaser.[560] If there is a dispute about the sale, the aggrieved potential buyer may be required to bring an action against the United States in the Court of Federal Claims. For example when a bidder at a sealed bid sale submitted a bid for $113,000 and a deposit of $22,500, but later learned that the Service could not deliver a deed to the property as the notice of sale represented and would not return the deposit, the bidder could not bring a refund suit under 28 USC § 1346(a)(1). The bidder was not a taxpayer, nor could he sue the government on a claim sounding in tort under the Federal Tort Claims Act because the government did not waive sovereign immunity for such a claim. However, as a contract claim, the case against the government could be brought in the Court of Federal Claims under 28 USC § 1491(a)(1).[561]

---

[558] Reg. § 301.6335-1(c)(8) (Delivery and removal of personal property).

[559] Reg. § 301.6335-1(c)(9) (Default in payment).

[560] Reg. §§ 301.6335-1(c)(6), 301.6335-1(c)(8). In the latter case, the sale is readvertised and the deposit of the defaulting purchaser is forfeited and applied to the account of the taxpayer. The rules for reselling property acquired by the United States for the minimum price in the original sale are generally the same as those applicable to the original sale. See IRC §§ 7505(a), 7506(b); Reg. §§ 301.7505-1(a), 301.7506-1(b); IRM 56(14)3.4, MT 5600-34 (Nov. 15, 1985) (Payment of Bid Price). However, any sale may be adjourned indefinitely, and the district director may enter into agreements with prospective bidders that such persons will bid a specified price at the auction. Resale of realty bid in at an auction by the government may not take place during the 180-day postsale redemption period, but the realty acquired for taxes may be reconveyed by the Service to the taxpayer, his heirs, or other legal representatives within two years of the date it was bid on at auction.

[561] Bonnett Enters., Inc. v. United States, 889 F. Supp. 208 (WD Pa. 1995), citing Cutrubus v. United States, 80-1 USTC ¶ 9174 (D. Utah 1979) (bidder, who made bid and deposit claimed that Service made misrepresentation about car dealership bid on). In *Bonnett Enterprises*, the district court said that the bidder's "problem is not that the United States has not waived sovereign immunity with respect to this suit, or that [the bidder] does not have standing to bring this action because it is not the taxpayer or that [the bidder] has failed to exhaust his administrative remedies. Rather, [the bidder's] suit raises a contractual claim against the United States which is not for the refund of taxes, and therefore exclusive jurisdiction exists in the Court of Federal Claims."

[d] Certificate of Sale or Deed to Property

On payment of the purchase price, a certificate of sale is given to the purchasers of both personal property and real property. After expiration of the period of redemption a deed to real property is given to the purchaser (or his assigns) of unredeemed real property upon surrender of the certificate of sale.[562] The certificate of sale of personal property is prima facie evidence of the right of the revenue officer to make the sale and is conclusive evidence of the regularity of the sale proceedings. It transfers to the purchasers all the delinquent taxpayer's right, title, and interest in the property sold.[563] Because the buyer at a tax sale obtains only a quitclaim deed to the real property, the buyer is responsible for searching the title to the property to determine whether there are any senior liens that might be foreclosed.[564] A deed to real property is prima facie evidence of the facts stated therein and operates as a conveyance of all the taxpayer's right, title, and interest in the premises sold at the time the tax lien attached to the realty, provided the sale has been substantially in compliance with the provisions of law.[565]

---

[562] IRC § 6338; Reg. § 301.6338-1. However, if it is shown that the Service did not adhere to the statutory conditions precedent to sale, the prima facie evidence of the right of the revenue officer to sell seized personal property is rebutted and the sale may be set aside. Margiotta v. District Director, 214 F2d 518 (2d Cir. 1954). But see Silver Bell Indus., Inc. v. United States, 76-1 USTC ¶ 9432 (10th Cir.), cert. denied, 429 US 822 (1976) (sale outside county where property located under general authorization upheld, although special authorization seems to be required by Section 6335(d)). The holder of a certificate of sale has an equitable lien on, but not title to, real property. Only when the property is not redeemed and deed is issued does title pass to the tax sale purchaser. In the meantime, the property is subject to the equitable lien of the tax sale purchaser, and if the property is redeemed, the tax liens revive and may be foreclosed. United States v. Cassel Bros., 82-1 USTC ¶ 9189 (MD Pa. 1981). See Samet v. United States, 242 F. Supp. 214 (MDNC 1965) (1939 Code case).

On the limited rights accorded the purchaser of property at a sale, see United States v. Gaechter Outdoor Adver., Inc., 86 AFTR2d 2000-5456 (10th Cir. 2000) ("We hold that a certificate of sale for real property gives the purchaser only the right to receive either the redemption price, see section 6337(b), or a deed, see section 6338(b), and that only on receipt of the deed does the purchaser obtain the taxpayer's right, title, and interest in the property, see section 6339(c)").

[563] IRC §§ 6339(a)(1), 6339(a)(2); Reg. § 301.6339-1. The certificate also constitutes authority to sell corporate stock or securities (IRC § 6339(a)(3)), a receipt for payment (IRC § 6339(a)(4)), and, where an automobile is involved, authority to sell the automobile (IRC § 6339(a)(5)). Reg. §§ 301.6339-1(a)(3)–301.6339-1(a)(5).

[564] See Horace Martin v. United States, 37 Fed. Cl. 86 (1996) (senior lienor foreclosed with the result that the successful buyer at the tax sale lost the property, as well as his action to obtain a refund of the amount he paid at the sale).

[565] IRC § 6339(b); Reg. § 301.6339-1(b). However, the facts stated on the deed may be rebutted. McAndrews v. Belknap, 141 F2d 111 (6th Cir.), cert. denied, 323 US 721 (1944); cf. Silver Bell Indus., Inc. v. United States, 76-1 USTC ¶ 9432 (10th Cir.), cert. denied, 429 US 822 (1976).

[e] Junior/Senior Lienors

A certificate of sale of personal property or a deed to real property executed by the government after a tax sale discharges the property from all liens, encumbrances, and titles subordinate to the tax lien.[566] For example, a mortgage executed after a notice of lien has been filed is extinguished where the deed is executed and delivered to the purchaser, assuming no redemption within the 180-day period.[567] Of course, the proceeds of the sale must be distributed in accordance with the priority of the liens, encumbrances, or titles. On the other hand, since a purchaser at a sale acquires only the right, title, and interest of the taxpayer, the successful bidder takes the property or rights to property subject to all liens having priority over the tax lien.

[f] Disclosure of Purchasers

A sale is intended to be public, whether conducted by auction or by the solicitation of sealed bids. However, the district director is required to keep records only of the sale of real property situated in his district.[568] These records constitute evidence in any court of the facts stated.

[g] Application of Sale Proceeds

Any moneys realized by seizure and sale[569] are to be applied in the following order: (1) against the expenses of levy and sale;[570] (2) against any unpaid tax specifically imposed against the seized property by any internal revenue law (e.g., alcohol or tobacco tax); (3) against the tax liability for which the levy was made. Any surplus proceeds, including those from the sale

---

[566] IRC § 6339(c). This section codifies the principles of Blacklock v. United States, 208 US 75 (1907), and Commercial Credit Corp. v. Schwartz, 130 F. Supp. 524 (ED Ark. 1955).

[567] Reg. § 301.6339-1(c).

[568] IRC § 6340; Reg. § 301.6340-1.

[569] This provision does not apply to the 50 percent penalty imposed under Section 6332(c)(2) for failure to honor a levy.

[570] IRC § 6342; Reg. § 301.6342-1. Expenses of levy and sale must be determined by the district director (IRC § 6341). These expenses include expenditures or liabilities incurred for protection and preservation of property during the period following service of a levy (e.g., insurance, police or private guards, custodial or maintenance help, rent or storage, utilities, and trucking) as well as actual expenses incurred in connection with the sale of the seized or redeemed property (e.g., advertising). Reg. § 301.6341-1. Expenses of sale may include the amount paid by the United States to redeem the property (IRC § 6342(a)(1)). Where payment is made involuntarily, as in the case of a distraint sale or an execution or judicial sale, the taxpayer does not have the right to direct the application of the sale proceeds to such items as he chooses. O'Dell v. United States, 325 F2d 451 (10th Cir. 1964).

of redeemed property, must be credited or refunded to the person or persons legally entitled to the surplus, which is the taxpayer unless another person establishes a superior claim.[571]

[3] Redemption After Seizure or Sale

Once property has been levied upon and seized, it must be disposed of by sale and the proceeds applied to the taxpayer's liabilities in the manner set forth in the Code. However, before or after the sale, the taxpayer and certain others may redeem the seized property under certain conditions.

The person whose property is seized may redeem from levy both real and personal property at any time before its sale upon payment of the amount of taxes due, along with any expenses or costs in connection with the seizure and contemplated sale.[572] The amount of the tax due must be paid, not merely an amount equal to the value of the property seized or the value of the government's interest in the property. Once payment is made, the property must be restored to the owner and all levy proceedings must cease.[573]

Once the sale occurs, the taxpayer is barred forever from the right to redeem personal property. Where real property has been sold, the taxpayer, his heirs, executors, or administrators, or any person having an interest in or a lien upon the property, or any person in their behalf, may redeem the real property

---

[571] Reg. § 301.6342-1(b). The person legally entitled to the surplus, means "the delinquent taxpayer unless another person establishes a superior claim." Id. Where the purchaser at a tax sale satisfied a mortgage on the property senior to a tax lien, the excess proceeds from the tax sale nevertheless belonged to the taxpayer (actually, the trustee in bankruptcy). Foreclosure of the junior tax lien did not affect the senior mortgage so that any surplus belonged to the mortgagor and was not applicable to the prior mortgage. United States v. Sage, 566 F2d 1114 (9th Cir. 1977). For collection procedures, see IRM 56(15)3, MT 5600-32 (Nov. 15, 1985) (Expenses of Levy and Sale); IRM 56(15)4, MT 5600-32 (Apr. 21, 1987) (Application of Proceeds of Levy).

[572] IRC § 6337(a); Reg. § 301.6337-1.

[573] Reg. § 301.6337-1(a).

within 180 days from the date of sale or payment to the purchaser.[574] This 180-day period is strictly applied.[575]

The redemption price is the purchase price, together with interest at an annual rate of 20 percent.[576] Redemption is made by payment to the purchaser.[577] If the purchaser cannot be found in the county in which the property to be redeemed is situated, payment is to be made "to the Secretary or his delegate for use of the purchaser, his heirs and assigns." Payment contemplates actual delivery of payment within the 180-day period. Consequently, the taxpayer may not rely on such constructive payment rules as the timely mailed, timely paid rule of Section 7502.[578] A check or other draft is not considered payment.[579]

---

[574] IRC § 6337(b)(1), as amended by the Tax Equity and Fiscal Responsibility Act of 1982, § 349A, Pub. L. No. 97-248, 97th Cong., 2d Sess. See Reg. § 301.6337-1(b). The "sale date" is the date of the public-conducted sale. Silver Bell Indus., Inc. v. United States, 76-1 USTC ¶ 9432 (10th Cir.), cert. denied, 429 US 822 (1976). An inchoate right of dower is an "interest" permitting redemption. Samet v. United States, 242 F. Supp. 214 (MDNC 1965). It has been held that the taxpayer's right to redeem is not assignable. United States v. Cassel Bros., 82-1 USTC ¶ 9189 (MD Pa. 1981) (purported redemption ineffective and Service could foreclose tax liens). Where the Service purchases property at a sale and the property can be redeemed after the sale, the effect of the redemption is to restore the property to its owner free only of the tax lien and otherwise fully subject to all prior liens. If the tax lien is senior to a junior lienor, the junior lien is extinguished and the junior lienor may not be entitled to compensation from the Service for extinguishing the junior security interest. See Murray v. United States, 88-1 USTC ¶ 9374 (Cl. Ct. 1988) (junior lienors not entitled to compensation for the "taking" of their lien because the lien was invalid).

[575] Anselmo v. James, 449 F. Supp. 922 (D. Mass. 1978) (the "Great Blizzard" of 1978 did not extend the period); Keely v. Sanders, 99 US 441 (1879) ("courts cannot extend the time, or make any exceptions not made in the statute [providing a right of redemption]"); Howard v. Adle, 538 F. Supp. 504 (ED Mich. 1982) (attempted redemption occurred one day after sale).

[576] IRC § 6337(b)(2). Where the Service lien has been purchased at a lien preclosure sale and the purchase price is paid to the Service in installments, interest at the 20 percent rate, compounded daily, runs from the date of each installment payment. Rosen v. Norton, 970 F2d 1079 (2d Cir. 1992) (taxpayers successful in their attempt to redeem their home only after five years of litigation).

[577] But see Guthrie v. Curnutt, 417 F2d 764 (10th Cir. 1969) (tender of payment held sufficient where purchaser frustrated actual payment).

[578] Silver Bell Indus., Inc. v. United States, 76-1 USTC ¶ 9432 (10th Cir.), cert. denied, 429 US 822 (1976).

[579] Silver Bell Indus., Inc. v. United States, 76-1 USTC ¶ 9432 (10th Cir.), cert. denied, 429 US 822 (1976). See also Fitzhugh v. Ryles, 517 F. Supp. 1361 (ED Ark. 1981) (bank or "envelope" draft not considered cash or equivalent because it did not operate as present assignment of funds).

D   SPECIAL ESTATE AND GIFT TAX LIENS

¶ 14.19   THE SPECIAL ESTATE TAX LIEN—IN GENERAL

The general tax lien attaches to all property belonging to a taxpayer after assessment, demand, and nonpayment of the tax and secures payment of all types of federal taxes, including estate taxes. To secure payment of estate taxes, a second type of lien called the special estate tax lien also exists in favor of the government. Without assessment or notice and demand, the special estate tax lien comes into existence automatically on the date of death. It continues for ten years unless, before the end of the ten-year period, the estate tax is paid in full or becomes unenforceable by expiration of the statute of limitations on collection.[580] Table 14.3 compares the assessment or general tax lien and the special estate tax lien.

TABLE 14.3

Characteristics of General and Special Estate Tax Liens

General Tax Lien	Special Estate Tax Lien
Attaches to all property belonging to the person liable for the tax	Attaches only to property included in and taxed as the gross estate and not used to pay administration expenses
Arises after assessment, notice and demand, and nonpayment	Arises automatically on date of death prior to determination of liability
Notice required to be filed to perfect lien against certain persons dealing with taxpayer	No filing required
Lien continues for ten years	Lien continues for ten years
Lien can be extended by suit, levy, and waiver	Lien cannot be extended

As explained by the Supreme Court in *Detroit Bank v. United States*,[581] provision for the special estate tax lien was based on Congress's belief that there is a greater need of a lien in advance of assessment and demand for payment of estate tax or property passing at and distributed in consequence of death than for other types of taxes. The Court also said that there was less need to protect third persons by way of a recorded notice of the lien because the property passing at death is normally dealt with by probate and estate tax proceedings of public notoriety. However true this observation may have been

---

[580] IRC § 6324(a).

[581] Detroit Bank v. United States 317 US 329, 337 (1943).

at the time *Detroit Bank* was decided, it seems hard to accept today. Purchasers of property from an estate must exercise extreme caution because the special estate tax lien encumbers the property if an estate does not pay estate tax subsequently found to be due. Careful practitioners representing buyers take such precautions as asking the estate representatives for evidence that all estate taxes have been paid, seeking a discharge of the special estate tax lien from the property being purchased, and securing indemnity from the estate should any estate tax liability arise. However, the assurance of obtaining a discharge of property from an estate tax lien or a release of lien from the Service is no longer available in every situation because the estate may not be (at least initially) subject to estate tax. Absent evidence that the Service has been paid, reliance on some form of indemnity from the estate seems to be the method left to protect purchasers of estate property.

The general tax and the special estate tax liens are cumulative security devices to ensure payment of an estate tax. Either or both liens may be available to the government in a particular situation. The different liens operate independently of each other in the sense that each lien comes into existence when the conditions precedent to creation of the lien are met and continue according to the facts and the applicable provisions.[582] To illustrate, the general lien has an unlimited duration as long as collection action is begun within the six-year statutory period of collection, but the life of the special lien is limited to a ten-year period, irrespective of any collection action.[583] Also, even if the statute of limitations on assessment bars assessment of an estate tax against an estate, the government may proceed to enforce the special estate tax lien to collect the estate tax.[584]

Despite their independence, there is some relationship between the two liens. Although the special lien has a duration of no more than ten years, it terminates before the expiration of the ten-year period if the general lien has been extinguished. If the general lien securing an assessed estate tax liability becomes unenforceable because of the expiration of the ten-year statutory period of collection (e.g., without commencement of a collection action), then the special lien also becomes unenforceable "by reason of the lapse of time."[585] Moreover, payments of estate tax reduce the amount of both the general and

---

[582] Detroit Bank v. United States 317 US 329, 337 (1943); Reg. § 301.6324-1(d).

[583] United States v. Cleavenger, 325 F. Supp. 871 (D. Ind. 1971), aff'd, 517 F2d 230 (7th Cir. 1975); United States v. Potemkin, 841 F2d 97 (4th Cir. 1988), aff'g 87-1 USTC ¶ 13,716 (D. Md. 1987) (following *Cleavenger*). Contra United States v. Saleh, 514 F. Supp. 8 (DNJ 1981) (special estate tax lien can be enforced more than ten years after the decedent's death where the foreclosure action is filed within the ten-year period).

[584] Schuster v. Comm'r, 32 TC 998, 1004 (1959), aff'd on this point, 312 F2d 311 (9th Cir. 1962) (transferee assessment was made within four years after estate tax return filed under predecessor of Section 6901).

[585] IRC § 6324(a)(1).

special liens, and so it has been held that deductible expenses incurred in contesting an estate tax deficiency reduce the tax collectible under the special estate tax lien.[586]

Dispute has arisen over whether the ten-year lien is absolute. The Service has contended that it may toll the ten-year period if it commences a collection suit within the ten-year period. Cleavenger rejected the Service's view and held that no action on the part of the Service tolls the ten-year lien. The Service does not follow *Cleavenger*, as shown by the decision in *Saleh*. However, it is unfair to bona fide purchasers of property from an estate to be faced with the secret special estate tax lien solely because shortly before the expiration of the ten-year period the Service decides to act. The lien is a special one, and action within the statutory period does not seem a heavy or unreasonable price for the special benefits the lien gives the Service to collect taxes owed by an estate.

The Eighth Circuit has agreed with the Seventh Circuit in *Cleavenger* and the Fourth Circuit in *Potemkin*, and has held the ten-year period of the special estate tax lien durational, not limitational, so that the government has ten years to enforce its lien before it expires.[587] If the special estate tax lien were limitational, as the government argued successfully in *Saleh*, the government could toll the statute by filing a complaint within the ten-year period. The Eighth Circuit concluded that a durational interpretation created "a bright line for presuming that there will be no title trouble [more than] ten years after the decedent's death due to a tax lien."[588] Conversely, a transfer within the ten-year period will be a red flag of possible title trouble. The circuit court rejected the government's claim that the estate would delay litigation, saying that, in fact, the government had waited nine years after the decedent's death before instituting suit. The court concluded that "the statute places a reasonable burden on the government to prosecute its claim diligently before it expires, and thus that the construction that we propose is not unreasonable."[589]

¶ 14.20 OPERATION OF THE SPECIAL ESTATE TAX LIEN

The special estate tax lien attaches to property includable in the gross estate of a decedent. The term "gross estate" is a creation of the estate tax provisions of the Code, Sections 2031 through 2044. Since the general lien attaches only to property or rights to property owned by the decedent at the time of death and

---

[586] See Harry C. Porter, 52 TC 515 (1969).

[587] United States v. Davis, 52 F3d 781 (8th Cir. 1995).

[588] *Davis*, 52 F3d 781, 782 (8th Cir. 1995).

[589] *Davis*, 52 F3d 781, 783 (8th Cir. 1995).

thus passing through probate, the special lien is far broader than the general lien. Therefore, where probate property is sold by an estate owing estate tax, the purchaser has bought property encumbered by the special lien. Even if the executor of the estate asks for a discharge from personal liability under Section 2204 and has been discharged from personal liability, the special lien is not extinguished. It continues, but shifts from the property transferred to the consideration received by the heirs, legatees, devisees or distributees, provided that the property has been transferred to a "purchaser" or a "holder of a security interest."[590] This shifting lien comes into play under Section 6324(a)(3) only where the executor or other fiduciary has been discharged from personal liability by complying with Section 2204. If there has been no application and discharge, the special lien continues to encumber the transferred property. The special lien attaches to such nonprobate property as dower or curtesy interests, property transferred in contemplation of death, transfers with a retained life estate, transfers taking effect at death, revocable transfers, annuities, joint interests, powers of appointment, and the proceeds of life insurance.[591]

[1] Discharge or Divestment

Property may be discharged or divested from the effects of the special lien, but the circumstances of discharge depend on whether the property is probate or nonprobate. Where probate property is involved, the special estate tax lien is divested automatically from property included in the gross estate that the probate or other court having jurisdiction of the estate allows to be used to pay charges against the estate and administration expenses.[592] Although this approval need not be obtained prior to the payment of an expenditure, the automatic divestiture provision only applies where the expenditures are allowed by a court of competent jurisdiction.[593]

---

[590] Property included in the probate estate is not subject to the shifting lien procedure. Therefore, if probate property is transferred, it remains subject to the special estate tax lien. United States v. Vohland, 675 F2d 1071 (9th Cir. 1982); United States v. Estate of Young, 84-2 USTC ¶ 13,594 (ED Pa. 1984) (special estate tax lien foreclosed against property in hands of bona fide purchaser). Metz v. United States, 933 F2d 802 (10th Cir. 1991) (decedent taxpayer had agreed to transfer house to his grandson's former wife after his death, in exchange for her promise to move in and provide care during his lifetime; held, former wife did not purchase property *transferred* during decedent's lifetime).

[591] See IRC §§ 2034–2042.

[592] IRC § 6324(a)(1). United States v. Security First Nat'l Bank, 30 F. Supp. 113 (SD Cal. 1939). See United States v. McGuire, 42 F. Supp. 337 (DNJ 1941); Rev. Rul. 56-529, 1956-2 CB 948 (types of expenses covered).

[593] United States v. Security First Nat'l Bank, 30 F. Supp. 113 (SD Cal. 1939), appeal dism'd, 113 F2d 491 (9th Cir. 1940) (postpayment approval); Kleine v. United States, 539 F2d 427 (5th Cir. 1976) (allowance of claims by independent executor under

There is another discharge provision peculiar to the special tax lien called the "shifting" lien. Certain third parties are protected against the effect of the general lien by the requirement that the lien be publicly filed in order to be valid against them. The special lien, on the other hand, does not require a notice to be filed for it to be effective. Rather, property sold or transferred to a "purchaser" or "holder of a security interest" is automatically discharged or divested from the effect of the lien, but the lien shifts to the consideration received from the purchaser or the secured lender. This shifting lien attaches to the consideration received, even if a fiduciary obtains a discharge from personal liability after audit of the estate tax return.[594]

The shifting lien procedure is also used when nonprobate property is sold to a purchaser or pledged as security to the holder of a security interest. In this case, the lien shifts from the property sold or secured to all the transferor's property.[595] The shifting estate tax lien attaches not only to property the transferor then owns but to any of his after-acquired property. Thus, property that was not and could not possibly be a part of the decedent's gross estate may become subject to the estate tax lien to the extent of the value of property includable in the gross estate of the decedent who transferred in such a way as to be divested of the estate tax lien.

There are other situations where the special estate tax lien is not effective. For instance, it is not valid against a mechanic's lienor and persons having "superpriority" over filed tax liens.[596] Furthermore, if the lien is not valid as against the lien of the mechanic and person entitled to a superpriority interest, the priority of that person extends to interest and expenses to the extent that under local law the interest or expense has the same priority as the lien or security interest to which it relates.[597] The special estate tax lien attaches to property included in the gross estate even after the property is transferred. In addition, the property is not divested from the effect of the special estate tax lien even if the estate elects to pay the tax in installments, and the special lien provided by Section 6324A is claimed to apply. This is the result at least when only the election has been made, but the executor of the estate has not been discharged, and the Service has not actually filed its lien under Section 6324A.[598]

Texas independent administration system does not constitute an allowance by a court having jurisdiction of the estate for the purposes of Section 6324(a)(1)).

[594] IRC § 6324(a)(3). The discharge of a fiduciary is governed by Section 2204, and the procedure and conditions for discharge are described in Reg. § 20.2204-2.

[595] IRC § 6324(a)(2).

[596] IRC § 6324(c)(1). The persons having superpriority status are set forth in Section 6323(b), discussed at ¶ 16.04[2].

[597] IRC § 6324(c)(2).

[598] Noble v. Soler, 81 AFTR2d 98-395 (SD Ohio 1997).

Perhaps more importantly, the property subject to the special estate tax lien may be discharged from the effect of the lien if the district director finds that the estate tax liability secured by the lien has been fully satisfied or provided for.[599] Since the special lien exists before the amount of the estate tax may have been reported on an estate tax return or before any deficiency assessment may have been made, a determination that the estate tax has been provided for could be speculative. Not surprisingly, therefore, the regulations are far more cautious in describing the circumstances where a discharge is granted. The regulations provide[600] that a discharge is issued only "in case there is actual need therefor," since "the primary purpose" of the discharge is "not to evidence payment or satisfaction of the tax, but to permit the transfer of property free from the lien in case it is necessary to clear title."[601] Application for discharge can be made on Form 4422 (Application for Certificate Discharging Property Subject to Estate Tax Lien). (See Form 14.14.)

[2] Enforcement

Enforcement of the special estate tax lien raises a number of questions. The lien itself may be foreclosed against the specific property encumbered or, after a transfer of the specific property, against all the property of the transferor to which the lien has been shifted. The regulations also state that the property may be seized by levy because it is encumbered by a lien.[602] This position does not seem supported in either the statutory language or policy. The levy statute permits collection of a tax by levy after assessment, notice and demand, and refusal to pay the tax within ten days after notice. The property subject to levy is property either belonging to the person liable to pay the tax or property "on which there is a lien provided in this chapter for payment of such tax."[603] Clearly, the tax referred to in the levy statute is the assessed tax that has been the subject of the notice and demand, and the property subject to the lien referred to is property that the taxpayer has transferred after assessment. Neither circumstances applies to the special estate tax lien. Moreover, except in jeopardy situations, a person said to be liable for a tax has an opportunity to contest the liability, which would not be true if the Service could take enforced collection action by administrative levy before any assessment or opportunity for a preseizure hearing.

---

[599] IRC § 6325(c).

[600] Reg. § 301.6325-1(c)(1).

[601] See Reg. § 301.6325-1(c)(2) for requirements of application for certificate of discharge.

[602] Reg. § 301.6331-1(a).

[603] IRC § 6331.

FORM 14.14
APPLICATION FOR CERTIFICATE DISCHARGING PROPERTY SUBJECT TO ESTATE TAX LIEN

Form **4422** (Rev. October 1986)	Department of the Treasury — Internal Revenue Service **Application for Certificate Discharging Property Subject to Estate Tax Lien**

Name of decedent *(last name, first name, middle initial)* Kraft, Pauline F.	Date of death 12/10/87
Decedent's legal residence at time of death 999 Park Avenue New York, NY 10000	Decedent's SSN 123-45-6789
	Year legal residence was established 1938

To: District Director, Internal Revenue Service, New York, N.Y.

As provided by Internal Revenue Code section 6325(c), I apply for a certificate discharging property subject to an estate tax lien. This property belongs to, or forms a part of, the gross estate of the decedent named above.

Has Form 706 been filed? ☒ Yes ☐ No	If "Yes," give date it was filed. 7/16/88	Amount of tax paid $ 65,000

Give the gross estate values and deductions as reported on Form 706. If Form 706 has not been filed, show approximate amounts.

Gross Estate Values		Gross Estate Values *(Continued)*	
Real estate	$ -0-	All other property	20,047
Stocks and bonds	879,996	**Total Gross Estate**	$ 930,349
Mortgages, notes, and cash	30,306	**Deductions**	
Insurance on decedent's life		Funeral and administrative expenses	$ 85,844
Jointly owned property		Debts of decedent	9,894
Transfers during decedent's life		Marital deduction	
Powers of appointment		Orphans' deduction	
Annuities		Charitable gifts and bequests	
		Total Deductions	$ 95,738

If property is to be sold, transferred, or mortgaged, please complete the following:

(a) Have you made or will you make an election to value certain farm and business real property as provided by Code section 2032A? ☐ Yes ☒ No

(b) Are you going to make a request or was your request already granted to defer payment of estate tax as provided by Code section 6161, 6166, or 6166A? ☐ Yes ☒ No

(c) *(If "Yes," indicate which section.)* ☐ 6161 ☐ 6166 ☐ 6166A

Name and address of the purchaser, transferee, or mortgagee Echab & Co., Inc. 64 Wall Street New York, New York 10000	Relationship to applicant and decedent NONE
	Consideration paid or to be paid $ 38,000

Under penalties of perjury, I declare that I have examined this application, including accompanying schedules and statements, and to the best of my knowledge and belief it is true, correct, and complete.

Applicant Sign Here ▶	Signature /S/ Alan Kraft, Executor	Date signed /S/ Sept. 23, 1988

Applicant's name and address Alan Kraft	Name and address of applicant's attorney Alan Michaels 1 Park Place New York, N.Y. 10000	
Applicant's relationship to estate *(Executor, Administrator, or other title)* Executor	Applicant's phone no. 212/322-0000	Phone no. of applicant's attorney 212/245-0000

For Privacy Act Notice, see back of form.   Form **4422** (Rev. 10-86)

Instructions

1. Attach a statement giving your reasons for applying for this certificate. *(If we have issued any other discharges on this estate, please include the dates and amounts.)*

2. Attach a description of the property for which you want a certificate of discharge. Show the value of the property and the basis of the valuation. If the property consists of real estate, attach a separate legal description, in triplicate, for each parcel.

3. Attach any of the following documents that apply:

Short form of letters testamentary

Copy of will

Copy of sale contract.

Privacy Act Notice

Under the Privacy Act of 1974, we must tell you:

► Our legal right to ask for the information and whether the law says you must give it.

► What major purposes we have in asking for it, and how it will be used.

► What could happen if we do not receive it.

The laws cover:

► Tax returns and any papers filed with them.

► Any questions we need to ask you so we can:

Complete, correct, or process your return.
Figure your tax.
Collect tax, interest, or penalties.

Our legal right to ask for information is Internal Revenue Code sections 6001, 6011, and 6012(a), and their regulations. They say that you must file a return or statement with us for any tax you are liable for. Code section 6109 and its regulations say that you must show your social security number on what you file. This is so we know who you are, and can process your return and papers.

You must fill in all parts of the tax form that apply to you. But you do not have to check boxes for the Presidential Election Campaign Fund.

We ask for tax return information to carry out the Internal Revenue laws of the United States. We need it to figure and collect the right amount of tax.

We may give the information to the Department of Justice and to other Federal agencies, as provided by law. We may also give it to cities, states, the District of Columbia, and U.S. commonwealths or possessions to carry out their tax laws. And we may give it to foreign governments because of tax treaties they have with the United States.

If a return is not filed, or if we don't receive the information we ask for, the law provides that a penalty may be charged. And we may have to disallow the exemptions, exclusions, credits, deductions, or adjustments shown on the tax return. This could make the tax higher or delay any refund. Interest may also be charged.

Please keep this notice with your records. It may help you if we ask you for other information.

If you have questions about the rules for filing and giving information, please call or visit any Internal Revenue Service office.

This is the only notice we must give you to explain the Privacy Act. However, we may give you other notices if we have to examine your return or collect any tax, interest, or penalties.

Form **4422** (Rev. 10-86)

If the special lien may not be enforced by levy, how is it enforced? The lien may be foreclosed against property that it encumbers in a judicial proceeding. Payment of the estate tax secured by the special lien is also ensured by the imposition of personal liability. There are six categories of persons who may have received property subject to the special lien and are personally liable for the amount of the estate tax:[604]

1. The decedent's spouse;
2. The decedent's transferee;
3. A trustee (except the trustee of an employment trust qualified under Section 403(a));
4. A surviving tenant;
5. A person in possession of the property by reason of the exercise or nonexercise or release of a power of appointment; or
6. A beneficiary.

These categories of persons are jointly and severally liable as transferees of property includable in the gross estate.

The categories of persons personally liable for the unpaid estate tax seem broad enough to include nearly any person having or receiving property includable in the gross estate. A trustee is specifically named as a person having personal liability. Thus, it has been held that the trustee of an inter vivos trust, not the beneficiaries, is personally liable under Section 6324(a)(2).[605] The Service has even asserted that an insurer is liable under Section 6324. However, it has been held that an insurance company is not a trustee or beneficiary where it distributes or pays amounts under an insurance policy,[606] although the proceeds of the policy may be reached by enforcement of the lien against the proceeds of the policy in the hands of the beneficiaries. The beneficiaries are the ones who are personally liable as transferees to the extent of the actuarial value of their interest on the date of death.[607]

---

[604] IRC § 6324(a)(2).

[605] Higley v. Comm'r, 69 F2d 160 (8th Cir. 1934). Cf. First W. Bank & Trust Co., 32 TC 1017 (1959), rev'd on other grounds sub nom. Schuster v. Comm'r, 312 F2d 311 (9th Cir. 1962) (trustee had distributed trust corpus to beneficiary before question of liability arose); see also Estate of Irene H. Govern v. Comm'r, TC Memo. 1996-434 (1996) (trustee of marital and family trusts, who was not the executor, held liable for unpaid estate tax and delinquency penalty).

[606] John Hancock Mut. Life Ins. Co. v. Helvering, 128 F2d 745 (DC Cir. 1942); Equitable Life Assurance Soc'y of US, 19 TC 264 (1952).

[607] John Hancock Mutual Life Ins. Co. v. Helvering, 128 F2d 745, 748 (DC Cir. 1942). The beneficiaries are liable in this manner even though they ultimately receive more or less than the actuarial values of their interests. See Brafman v. United States, 384 F2d 863, 864 (5th Cir. 1967). For a case where the beneficiary of an insurance policy was held liable for estate tax under Section 6324(a)(2), see Baptiste v. Comm'r, 63 TCM 2649 (1992); rev'd on other grounds, 29 F3d 433 (8th Cir. 1994).

Personal liability imposed by Section 6324 is transferee liability. The term "transferee" includes with respect to estate taxes "any person who, under (Section) 6324(a)(2) is liable for any part of such (estate) tax."[608] Transferee liability is enforced by two methods: (1) legal action without assessment or (2) assessment under the general transferee provision, Section 6901.[609] Assessment under Section 6901 is not required. The government may assert transferee liability by commencing an action to enforce the statutory liability of Section 6324. On the other hand, the procedures for asserting transferee liability set forth in Section 6901 may be followed. If so, absent jeopardy, a notice of deficiency is sent to the transferee so that he may contest his liability in the Tax Court prior to the payment of the asserted deficiency. In the Tax Court, the burden of proof is on the Commissioner to show that the petitioner transferee is liable for the tax. The substantive liability of a donee for the unpaid estate or gift tax is found in Sections 6901(h) and 6324.[610]

The amount of the liability of the transferee of property under the special estate tax lien is the amount of the estate tax and accrued interest. The transferee's liability is limited, however, to the value of the property transferred. For example, when a beneficiary received life insurance proceeds of $50,000, the beneficiary's liability under the special estate tax lien was limited to that amount even though the total estate tax liability was conceded to be approximately $63,000.[611]

¶ 14.21 THE SPECIAL GIFT TAX LIEN

A special gift tax lien attaches to any and all gifts made during the period for which the donor filed a return and continues for ten years from the date the gifts are made, unless the gift tax is paid in full sooner or becomes unenforce-

---

[608] IRC § 6901(h).

[609] United States v. Russell, 461 F2d 605 (10th Cir. 1972) (holding that a transferee assessment is enforceable by an action in court as well as after assessment under Section 6901).

[610] La Fortune v. Comm'r, 263 F2d 186, 194 (10th Cir. 1958); Estate of Mandels v. Comm'r, 64 TC 61, 66 (1975); Tilton v. Comm'r, 88 TC 590, 595 (1987).

[611] Section 6324(a)(2) provides that a transferee's personal liability is limited "to the extent of the value at the time of the decedent's death" of the property actually transferred. Baptiste v. Comm'r, 29 F3d 433 (8th Cir. July 12, 1994), rev'g 63 TCM 2649 (1992) (rejecting argument that transferee liability becomes a direct obligation of the transferee and should itself be treated as an independent tax bearing interest not subject to the limitation of Section 6324(a)(2)). See also Poinier v. Comm'r, 858 F2d 917 (3d Cir. 1988), cert. denied, 490 US 1019 (1989) (same result as Baptiste where gift tax was involved).

able by reason of lapse of time.[612] If the tax is not paid when due, the donee of any gift becomes personally liable for the tax to the extent of the value of the gift. This personal liability exists as long as there is any gift (including one to another donee) during the year, the tax on which is owing.[613] Because the statute uses the terminology "all gifts" and "any gift," it is clear that irrespective of the $3,000 gift tax exclusion the personal liability and special tax lien apply to the gift.[614] The limit of a donee's liability is the value of the gift received.[615]

The same shifting lien procedure used with respect to the special estate tax lien[616] is found where the special gift tax lien is involved. If any part of the property comprised in the gift is transferred by the donee (or by a transferee of the donee) to a purchaser or a holder of a security interest, the property sold or secured is divested of the lien, but the lien, to the extent of the value of the gift, attaches to all the property (including after-acquired property) of the donee (or the transferee), except the part transferred to the purchaser or a holder of a security interest.[617] As with the special estate tax lien, the gift tax lien is not effective against a mechanic's lienor or the lien or security interest of a person having "superpriority" over a filed tax lien.[618] Also, if the special gift tax lien is not valid against a purchaser, secured party, mechanic lienor, or other superpriority, it also is not valid against interest and expenses attributable to or claimed by these interests.[619]

The provisions dealing with the special gift tax lien are fairly straightforward and the interpretations are consistent with those of the special estate tax

---

[612] IRC § 6324(a). The special gift tax lien also expires after ten years from the date the gifts are made and, in the same manner as the special estate tax lien, the special gift tax lien is durational, not limitational, with the result that the Service must fully enforce its lien within the ten-year period. New England Acceptance Corp. v. United States, 80 AFTR2d 97-6759 (DNH 1997) (reasoning in *Cleavenger* followed; statutory language providing that the special gift tax lien constituted a lien on all gifts for ten years from the date the gifts are made "unambiguously and without qualification invokes durational period"). In *New England Acceptance Corp.*, the Service waited until the final day of the ten-year period to begin its enforcement action against the property in the form of a notice of levy and notice of seizure, and the action was held "insufficient to execute the special gift tax lien within the requisite ten-year period."

[613] Section 6324(b) states: "If the tax is not paid when due, the donee of any gift shall be personally liable for such tax to the extent of the value of such gift." See La Fortune v. Comm'r, 263 F2d 186 (10th Cir. 1958).

[614] Baur v. Comm'r, 145 F2d 338 (3d Cir. 1944).

[615] IRC § 6324(b). It has been held that the donee is not liable for interest on the donor's liability in excess of the value of the gift. Poinier v. Comm'r, 858 F2d 917 (3d Cir. 1988) (a divided court), cert. denied, 109 S. Ct. 1743 (1989).

[616] See supra ¶ 14.19[1].

[617] IRC § 6324(b).

[618] The statutory definition of these superpriority interests is found in Section 6323(b), which is discussed at ¶ 16.04.

[619] See IRC § 6323(e).

lien.[620] However, there has been some litigation involving gifts in trust. Generally, each beneficiary of a trust is considered a separate donee liable to the extent of the actuarial value of the gift, although the interest of that beneficiary may not be capable of valuation and therefore the imposition of personal liability is frustrated.[621] A trustee who fails to recognize potential gift tax liability of a beneficiary may face personal liability, because under Section 6903 the fiduciary who files an appropriate notice with the Service assumes the duties of a beneficiary with respect to the tax liability of the beneficiary.[622]

¶ 14.22 SPECIAL LIEN FOR ESTATE TAX WHERE PAYMENT IS DEFERRED

Section 6324A provides for a special estate tax lien in lieu of the special tax lien of Section 6324 where payment of the estate tax has been deferred under Section 6166. If the executor (1) makes an election under Section 6324A[623] and (2) files a lien agreement signed by each person who has an interest in the property designated in the agreement as collateral for payment of the deferred amount, a lien arises for the deferred amount.[624] The lien agreement is a written agreement signed by each person who has an interest in the property designated in the agreement in which the signing person (1) consents to the creation of a lien against property and (2) designates a responsible person as the agent for the beneficiaries of the estate and the signatories in dealings with the Service on matters arising under Section 6166 or Section 6324A.[625] This consensual lien is against "Section 6166 property," which means interests in property that (1) can be expected to survive the deferral period; (2) are designated in

---

[620] For example, the provisions regarding timeliness of any action asserting personal (transferee) liability for the gift tax are similar to those for the special estate tax liens. La Fortune v. Comm'r, 263 F2d 186, 194 (10th Cir. 1958); Moore v. Comm'r, 1 TC 14 (1943), aff'd, 146 F2d 824 (2d Cir. 1945).

[621] Alma M. Myer, 2 TC 291 (1943), aff'd, 149 F2d 642 (9th Cir. 1945) (even beneficiary of discretionary trust); Charles A.E. Goodhart, 2 TCM 267, 270 (1943) (contingent remainder interest not capable of valuation); cf. Fidelity Trust Co. v. Comm'r, 141 F2d 54, 56 (3d Cir. 1944) (trust estate, not beneficiaries, liable).

[622] Fletcher Trust Co. v. Comm'r, 141 F2d 36 (8th Cir.), cert. denied, 323 US 711 (1944).

[623] IRC § 6324A(a); Reg. § 301.6324A-1(a).

[624] IRC § 6324A(c); Reg. § 301.6324A-1(b).

[625] IRC §§ 6324A(c)(1), 6324A(c)(2). Additional conditions for the agreement may be found in Reg. § 301.6324A-1(b).

the lien agreement; and (3) have a value not greater than the sum of the deferred amount and the required interest amount.[626]

The special estate tax lien of Section 6324A differs from the lien imposed by Section 6324 in two significant ways:

1. The lien created by Section 6324 is nonconsensual, arises automatically, and its existence is not disclosed by filing of a notice. The lien created by Section 6324A is consensual, arises only after a qualifying agreement is filed with the Service, and a notice of the lien is filed in the same manner as a notice of tax lien.[627] In fact, unless a notice of the Section 6324A lien is filed, the lien is not valid against a purchaser, holder of a security interest, or a mechanic's lien or judgment lien creditor in the determination of priority of an assessment lien under Section 6323(a).[628]

2. The special estate tax lien of Section 6324 exists for ten years from the date of death and then ceases. The lien of Section 6324A arises when the executor is discharged under Section 2204 or, if earlier, the date notice of the lien is filed. The lien continues until the liability for the deferred amount is satisfied or becomes unenforceable by reason of lapse of time.[629]

---

[626] IRC § 6324A(b); Reg. § 20.6324A-1(b). See also Reg. § 301.6214A-1(c). A bond can be used to make up any shortfall in the value of property interests suitable for the lien agreement. The terms "deferred amount," "required interest amount," and "deferral period" are defined in Section 6324A(e). Reg. § 20.6324A-1(e).

[627] See IRC § 6324A; Reg. §§ 20.6324A, 301.6324A.

[628] IRC § 6324A(d)(1); Reg. § 20.6324A-1(c)(2).

[629] IRC § 6324A(d)(2); Reg. § 20.6324A-1(c)(1). The statute of limitations on collection is suspended during the period of an extension of time for payment under Section 6166. IRC § 6503(d).

CHAPTER **15**

Avoiding and Minimizing the Effect of Tax Liens and Levies

¶ 15.01 OVERVIEW

It is telling evidence of the Service's tax collection powers that Congress passed two Taxpayer Bills of Rights to limit the scope and circumstances of enforced collection action, as well as to punish its improper use, and in the IRS Restructuring and Reform Act of 1998 (1998 Act) expanded due process procedures for the review of enforced collection action.[1] As the description of liens and levies in Chapter 14 shows, the Service has broad and formidable powers to collect delinquent taxes, and to balance such powers, taxpayers have collection due process rights, which are integrated into the lien and levy procedures.[2] This chapter describes the procedures, both statutory and procedural, available to taxpayers to avoid or minimize the effect of tax liens and levies, apart from the collection due process rights taxpayers have in the lien and levy process. These procedures can be used by taxpayers to survive financially the tax collection process.

---

[1] The first Taxpayer Bill of Rights was part of the Technical and Miscellaneous Revenue Act of 1988, Pub. Law 100-647 (Nov. 10, 1988). The second Taxpayer Bill of Rights was a stand alone measure. Taxpayer Bill of Rights 2, Pub. Law 104-168 (July 30, 1996); IRS Restructuring and Reform Act of 1998, HR 2676, 105th Cong., 2d Sess. § 1002 (hereinafer 1998 Act), Pub. Law 105-206 (July 22, 1998).

[2] The collection due process procedures (Sections 6220 and 6330) are discussed at ¶¶ 14.08 (liens) and 14.13[2] (levies).

Procedures available to taxpayers in the tax collection process include the following:

1. *Taxpayer advocate.* A taxpayer may seek the assistance of a local taxpayer advocate in the National Taxpayer Advocate's organization to resolve problems in dealing with the Service if the Service has not responded to the taxpayer's communications, inquiries, and complaints on a timely basis or at all, or if the taxpayer has or will suffer significant hardship.[3]

2. *Installment payment agreements.* A taxpayer may be able to work out a payment schedule with the Collection personnel using an installment payment agreement or some other collateral agreement.[4]

3. *Offers in compromise.* A taxpayer may be able to settle the amount of tax the Service seeks to collect by using an offer in compromise.[5]

4. *Administrative appeal.* A taxpayer may request an appeal of the lien filing, a release, discharge, or a subordination or certificate of nonattachment of the lien.[6]

5. *Wrongful collection action.* A taxpayer or a third party may bring a civil action against the government regarding the lien[7] or a levy.[8]

6. *Actions by nontaxpayers.* In some instances, a third party may bring a judicial action to minimize the effect of a tax lien or levy to halt collection action.[9]

7. *Collection abuse.* In situations of collection abuse, a taxpayer or a third party may be able to recover damages from the government.[10]

These procedures are not exclusive, and a taxpayer or third party may find that, in practice, the procedures are used in a progression from informal conferences to commencing an action in court.

---

[3] See IRC § 7803(c); see infra ¶ 15.02.

[4] See IRC § 6159; infra ¶ 15.06.

[5] See IRC § 7122; infra ¶ 15.07.

[6] See IRC § 6335; infra ¶¶ 15.08[3]–15.08[6].

[7] See IRC § 7432; infra ¶¶ 15.09[1]–15.09[5].

[8] See IRC § 7426; infra ¶¶ 15.10 and 15.11[3].

[9] See 28 USC 2410; IRC § 7426; infra ¶¶ 15.11[1] and 15.11[2]–15.11[6].

[10] See IRC § 7433; infra ¶ 15.14.

¶ 15.02 MINIMIZING THE EFFECT OF NOTICES: THE TAXPAYER ADVOCATE PROGRAM

[1] The Taxpayer Advocate Service: Section 7803

The IRS Restructuring and Reform Act of 1998 (the 1998 Act) created the Office of the Taxpayer Advocate, headed by the National Taxpayer Advocate.[11] As statutorily mandated, the functions of the Office of the Taxpayer Advocate are (1) to assist taxpayers in resolving problems with the Service; (2) to identify areas in which taxpayers have problems dealing with the Service; (3) to propose changes in the administrative practices of the Service to mitigate the identified taxpayer problems, and (4) to identify potential legislative changes that may be appropriate to mitigate the identified problems.[12]

To give the National Taxpayer Advocate greater prestige and independence, the National Taxpayer Advocate is appointed by the Secretary of the Treasury, after consultation with the Commissioner and the Oversight Board of the Service. The National Taxpayer Advocate reports directly to the Commissioner, and is compensated at the same pay rate as the highest pay rate of any senior Service executive.[13] The National Taxpayer Advocate and the Office of the Taxpayer Advocate supervise and direct the Taxpayer Advocate Service (TAS) Program, formerly the Problems Resolution Program. The National Taxpayer Advocate monitors the allocation of local office taxpayer advocates and develops guidance for Service personnel for referral of taxpayer inquiries to local taxpayer advocates. There are nine area offices (seven field offices and two service center offices), each headed by an Area Taxpayer Advocate who, among other functions, provides program guidance and direction to Local Taxpayer Advocates.[14] There is at least one Local Taxpayer Advocate in each of the fifty states, as well as in each Service center.[15]

---

[11] IRC § 7803(c)(1), as added by the IRS Restructuring and Reform Act of 1998, § 1102(a), effective July 22, 1998. Since 1977, the Service has had a Problems Resolution Program to assist taxpayers in resolving problems with different Service functions, but especially its collection activities. The National Office official administering the Problems Resolution Program was initially the Taxpayer Ombudsman, then changed by the Taxpayer Bill of Rights 2, to the Taxpayer Advocate.

[12] IRC § 7803(c)(2)(A).

[13] IRC §§ 7803(c)(1)(B)(i) and 7803(c)(1)(B)(ii).

[14] IRM 13.1.1.2.1, National Taxpayer Advocate and Deputy National Taxpayer Advocate (Oct. 1, 2001); IRM 13.1.1.2.2, National Office (Oct. 1, 2001).

[15] IRC § 7803(c)(2)(D)(I); IRM 13.1.1.2.3, Area Taxpayer Advocate (ATA) Offices (Oct. 1, 2001).

Local Taxpayer Advocate Service Offices are organized into two functions: casework and systemic analysis and advocacy.[16] Casework units are responsible for resolving all individual and business taxpayer problems that meet the National Taxpayer Advocate's criteria. The systemic analysis and advocacy unit works with operating divisions to identify systemic problems, analyze their causes, propose solutions, and identify potential problems with new systems and procedures. Local Taxpayer Advocates report directly to Area Taxpayer Advocates, and through them to the National Taxpayer Advocate and the Office of the Taxpayer Advocate.[17] Local Taxpayer Advocates do not report to local office management,[18] but they may consult with local supervisory personnel about the operation of a local office.[19] The TAS also has an independent communications system. Each local office of the taxpayer advocate is required to maintain separate phone, facsimile, and other electronic communication access and a separate post office address.[20]

Other measures are intended to give taxpayers confidence in the independence of the Office of the Taxpayer Advocate and its representatives in the field. At the first meeting with a taxpayer, the taxpayer advocate must inform the taxpayer that the TAS operates independent of other Service functional offices, and that it reports directly to Congress through the National Taxpayer Advocate.[21] Taxpayer advocates have the discretion not to disclose the taxpayer's contact information or the information the taxpayer provides to the Service.[22] In addition, taxpayer advocates have greater visibility because each notice of deficiency must include a notice of the taxpayer's right to contact a local taxpayer advocate and the location and telephone number of that advocate's office.[23] If the taxpayer advocate asks an operating division to take action to provide relief to a taxpayer suffering or about to suffer significant hardship, and the operating division refuses, the taxpayer advocate may issue a taxpayer assistance order ordering the function either to cease action or to take action in accordance with the terms of the order.[24]

---

[16] IRM 13.1.1.2.4 Local Taxpayer Advocate (LTA) Offices (Oct. 1, 2001); IRS Program Materials, "The New IRS Stands Up Modernization Conference" (Jan. 13–14, 2000).

[17] IRM 13.1.1.2.4 Local Taxpayer Advocate (LTA) Offices (Oct. 1, 2001); IRS Program Materials, "The New IRS Stands Up Modernization Conference" (Jan. 13–14, 2000).

[18] IRC § 7803(c)(4)(A)(i).

[19] IRC §§ 7803(c)(4)(A)(i) and 7803(c)(4)(A)(ii).

[20] IRC § 7803(c)(4)(B).

[21] IRC § 7803(c)(4)(A)(iii).

[22] IRC § 7803(c)(4)(A)(iv).

[23] IRC § 6212(a), as amended by the IRS Restructuring and Reform Act of 1998, § 1120(b).

[24] IRC § 7811(a).

[2] Assisting Taxpayers

The Office of Taxpayer Advocate's primary role is to assist taxpayers in resolving problems with the Service.[25] The Taxpayer Advocate assists taxpayers in resolving problems in roughly the same way that problems resolution officers did under the IRS Problem Resolution Program (PRP).[26] The key for taxpayer advocate intervention and assistance to a taxpayer is that the taxpayer's problem has not been resolved through "normal channels." Taxpayer advocates will not assist a taxpayer who has not followed or who refuses to follow the Service's normal procedures.

The Taxpayer Advocate has greater authority than the Problem Resolution Program. On January 17, 2001, the Commissioner delegated authority to the National Taxpayer Advocate that includes the same authority granted to the Accounts Management Customer Service Representative.[27] The TAS has the authority to do the following: (1) to report certain accounts as currently not collectible; (2) to release liens not currently open in another Service function if the account has been paid in full and substantiation is provided that no other account is open; (3) to release computer-generated levies; to make trust fund recovery penalty adjustments; (4) to accept installment agreements; and (5) to perform other account management functions.[28]

Because the TAS resolves taxpayer problems with Service functions, it may appear that Appeals and the TAS perform the same functions. Appeals resolves substantive tax disputes between the local office and taxpayers; if the dispute cannot be resolved the taxpayer can challenge the Service's position in court. Taxpayer advocates informally resolve taxpayer problems and Service errors, but they do not interfere with Appeals determinations on substantive issues. On the other hand, the Appeals role in collection due process review proceedings seems to overlap with the role of taxpayer advocates—for example, to the extent that collection personnel have not followed "applicable published administrative guidance (including the Internal Revenue Manual)."[29]

TAS offers taxpayers two general categories of relief: (1) assistance in resolving problems resulting from computer-generated notices from the service center and (2) administrative injunctions, called taxpayer assistance orders, staying various administrative actions.

---

[25] IRC § 7803(c)(2)(A)(i).

[26] IRM 1.2.7.9.2.1, Problem Resolution Program Handbook 2.1, National Office Taxpayer Advocate (Apr. 30, 1998).

[27] Delegation Order No. 267, Authority of the National Taxpayer Advocate to Perform Certain Tax Administration Functions (effective, Jan. 17, 2001).

[28] These functions must be performed in accordance with the adjustments and account-related actions found in IRM 21, Customer Account Services.

[29] See IRC § 7811(a)(3).

[3] Resolving Problems With Service Center Notices

Taxpayer advocates in local offices and service centers are supposed to resolve taxpayer inquiries and responses by ensuring that they are handled by the appropriate function, especially the collection enforcement function in the Small Business and Self-Employed Division. If TAS accepts the case, the first benefit to the taxpayer is that collection is held, pending resolution of the problem.

The TAS has identified the following circumstances or criteria that qualify a taxpayer for additional assistance, including review of the problems the taxpayer has been experiencing:[30]

1. The taxpayer is suffering or about to suffer a significant hardship.
2. The taxpayer is facing an immediate threat of adverse action.
3. The taxpayer will incur significant costs if relief is not granted, including fees for professional representation.
4. The taxpayer will suffer irreparable injury or a long-term adverse "impact" if relief is not granted.
5. The taxpayer has had a delay of more than thirty calendar days to resolve a taxpayer account problem. however, the normal processing period may be more than thirty days, and if so, the taxpayer's inquiry is considered delayed on the day after the prescribed period.
6. The taxpayer has not received a response to an inquiry by the date promised, including a date promised on a Service form.
7. Normal channels, established systems, or procedures have failed to operate as the Service intended, or they have not been successful in resolving the taxpayer's problem.
8. The case is a duplicate congressional/controlled correspondence case.
9. The case does not meet TAS criteria, but it is kept in a local taxpayer advocate office to be worked.

In TAS case processing, the first five criteria are taken from Section 7811(a), which both identifies significant hardship as a basis for the issue of a taxpayer assistance order and defines significant hardship. In turn, Taxpayer Advocate processing divides cases into Criteria 1-4 cases and Criteria 5-7 cases. When an Associate Advocate receives a Criteria 1-4 case, one of the first steps the advocate takes is to suspend collection enforcement action until the claimed hardship can be validated by securing appropriate documentation of an eviction notice, a utility shutoff notice, or a bank notice showing that there are insufficient funds for payroll.[31] The next step in the process is notice to the taxpayer or the taxpayer's representative of TAS involvement in the case. Once hardship has been validated, the Associate Advocate will determine

---

[30] IRM 13.1.7.2, Taxpayer Advocate Case Criteria (Oct. 1, 2001).

[31] IRM 13.1.7.5.2, Initial Case Actions/Contact by the AA/SAA (Criteria 1-4) (Oct. 1, 2001).

whether the hardship should be relieved, and if so, to provide the appropriate relief.[32] All of these actions are supposed to take place within a matter of days.

[4] Taxpayer Assistance Orders: Section 7811

A taxpayer assistance order is an administrative cease and desist order and, when issued in some situations, is similar to a mandatory injunction. Its terms may require the affected Service function within a specified period to accomplish the following: (1) to release property on which collection personnel have levied[33] or (2) "to cease any action, take any action as permitted by law, or refrain from taking any action, with respect to the taxpayer" under the collection provisions of the Code (Chapter 64); under a bankruptcy or receivership subject to the provisions of subchapter B of Chapter 70; under procedures relating to the discovery of liability and enforcement of the tax laws in Chapter 78; or under any other provision of "law" the National Taxpayer Advocate specifically describes in the taxpayer assistance order.[34] A taxpayer assistance order (TAO) is binding on the Service unless the National Taxpayer Advocate, the Commissioner of Internal Revenue, or the Deputy Commissioner of Internal Revenue modifies or rescinds the order, and even then "only if a written explanation of the reason for the modification or rescission is provided to the National Taxpayer Advocate."[35] Any applicable statute of limitations (e.g., the statute of limitations of Section 6501 relating to the assessment or collection of tax) is suspended starting on the date the taxpayer files an application for a TAO with the National Taxpayer Advocate and ending on the date the National Taxpayer Advocate makes a decision on the taxpayer's application (or a later date if the National Taxpayer Advocate's order resulting from a taxpayer's application provides for a continued suspension of the statute of limita-

---

[32] IRM 13.1.7.5.3, Relief Determinations (Step 3) and 7.5.4 Implement Hardship Relief (Step 4) (Oct. 1, 2001).

[33] IRC § 7811(b)(1). Under the terms of a TAO, the Service may be required "within a specified time period" to release property of the taxpayer on which collection personnel has levied, or "to cease any action, take any action as permitted by law, or refrain from taking any action relating to collection, to bankruptcy or receiverships, to the discovery of liability and enforcement of the Code and any other provision of law . . . " The Section 7811 regulations were amended in 1996 to reflect this change. See Reg. § 301.7811-1(d).

[34] IRC § 7811(b)(2).

[35] IRC §§ 7811(c)(1) and 7811(c)(2). Section 7811(c) tracks prior law under which any taxpayer assistance order issued by the Taxpayer Advocate or designee of the Taxpayer Advocate (i.e., the problems resolution function) could be modified or rescinded only by the Taxpayer Advocate (or the Taxpayer Advocate's designee), the Commissioner, or the Deputy Commissioner of Internal Revenue, and then only if a written statement of the reasons for the modification or rescission is provided to the Taxpayer Advocate. IRC § 7811(c), amended by the Taxpayer Bill of Rights 2, § 102(b), effective on the date of enactment, July 30, 1996.

tions).[36] The statute of limitations is not suspended in cases where the Taxpayer Advocate issues an order in the absence of an application for relief by the taxpayer. The National Taxpayer Advocate has the authority to issue a TAO to require a Service function to cease any action, take any action permitted by law, or refrain from taking any action affecting a taxpayer under collection, in a bankruptcy or receivership, in a discovery or enforcement proceeding, or some other provision of law.[37] The form to be used to request a taxpayer assistance order is Form 911.

No TAO may be issued, however, unless the National Taxpayer Advocate (1) "determines the taxpayer is suffering or about to suffer a significant hardship as the result of the manner in which the internal revenue laws are being administered by the [Service]" or (2) the taxpayer meets any other requirements set forth in regulations.[38]

[a] Significant Hardship

Critical to the National Taxpayer Advocate's decision to issue a TAO is the determination that the taxpayer is or is about to suffer "significant hardship." Hardship criteria are statutorily described to include (1) an immediate threat of adverse action; (2) a delay of more than thirty days in resolving a taxpayer account problem; (3) the incurring by the taxpayer of significant costs (including fees for professional representation) if relief is not granted; or (4) irreparable injury to, or a long-term adverse impact on, the taxpayer if relief is not granted.[39] If a Service employee fails to follow "applicable publishable administrative guidance (including the Internal Revenue Manual)," the National Taxpayer Advocate must interpret, "in a manner most favorable to the taxpayer," the hardship criteria considered in determining whether to issue a taxpayer assistance order.[40]

---

[36] IRC § 7811(d).

[37] IRC § 7811(a)(1). The form prescribed for an Application for a Taxpayer Assistance Order (ATAO) is Form 911. See Taxpayer Advocate Service Handbook 7.8, Taxpayer Assistance Order (TAO) Process. As the result of a cross-functional tax force on the authority of the TAS, the Commissioner increased the authority of the TAS to allow it to resolve some taxpayer cases without reference to other parts of the Service. The TAS can generally take the same actions as IRS Customer Service Representatives. The TAS can issue orders directing Service units to take action to prevent a significant hardship or reconsider a determination. See IR-2001-12 (Jan. 24, 2001).

[38] IRC § 7811(a)(1).

[39] IRC § 7811(a)(2). In its 1999 fiscal year, the TAS handled about 93,000 applications for taxpayer assistance orders and granted relief or assistance in 73.5 percent of the cases; of the remaining cases, relief was not considered appropriate in 20 percent of the cases. IRS Annual Report Fiscal Year 1999, at 21.

[40] IRC § 7811(a)(3).

The 1998 amendments regarding "significant hardship" are more under-standable when seen in an historical context. Before 1998, the Taxpayer Advo-cate or the problems resolution officers designated by the Advocate had statutory authority to issue a taxpayer assistance order if the taxpayer was suf-fering or about to suffer "a significant hardship."[41] Regulations restricted tax-payers' opportunity for relief, saying that a significant hardship was "serious privation" caused to the taxpayer by the administrative action, and that it de-pended as much on a consideration of the action the Service had taken or will take as on the financial hardship or inconvenience to the taxpayer.[42] A distinc-tion was drawn between a finding that a taxpayer is suffering or is about to suffer a significant hardship as the result of the manner in which the Service is administering the tax laws and a determination that a TAO would be granted.[43] When problem resolution officers separately examined the taxpayer's behavior and the Service's action and inaction that caused or was about to cause the significant hardship to the taxpayer, in most cases they issued taxpayer assis-tance orders. In a significant number of cases, however, the officers either did not issue orders or believed they were not authorized to do so.[44]

----

[41] The term "significant hardship" first appeared in Section 7811(a) in 1988. IRC § 7811(a), added by the Technical and Miscellaneous Revenue Act of 1988 (TAMRA), § 6230(a), effective January 1, 1989. See also HR Conf. Rep. 1104, Technical and Miscel-laneous Revenue Act of 1988, 100th Cong., 2d Sess. 215, reprinted in 1988-3 CB 705.

[42] Regulations defined "significant hardship" as "a serious privation caused or about to be caused to the taxpayer as the result of the particular manner in which the revenue laws are being administered by the Internal Revenue Service. Mere economic or personal inconvenience to the taxpayer does not constitute significant hardship." Reg. § 301.7811-1(a)(4)(ii).

[43] Reg. § 301.7811-1(a)(5) (1992). At the time, the Problems Resolution Handbook stated that the term "significant hardship" involved a subjective determination made on a case-by-case basis. It cautioned that the determination of the existence of a significant hardship did not guarantee relief for the taxpayer, but only that the taxpayer's case would be reviewed by the problems resolution officer and the Service function involved before the officer made a decision on an appropriate action. IRM 1279, Problems Resolution Handbook, (10)30, Definition of Significant Hardship, MT 1279-75 (Nov. 1, 1994). Later, the same portion of the Manual stated: "No application should be automatically denied. The determination that significant hardship exists does not guarantee relief for the tax-payer." IRM 1.2.7.9, Problem Resolution Program Handbook 3.5.6, Hardship Determina-tion (Apr. 30, 1998).

[44] Despite the apparent limitations on the issuance of a taxpayer assistance order, the Taxpayer Advocate, in his *first annual report* to the House Ways & Means Committee, pointed out that in fiscal year 1996, when 32,150 ATAOs were processed, 76.5 percent of the applications were granted relief or appropriate assistance was otherwise provided. In only five cases did problems resolution officers formally exercise authority to enforce a TAO to create relief for a taxpayer. Taxpayer Advocate's Annual Report to Congress for Fiscal Year 1996, at 4. The Taxpayer Advocate included the following statistics in his Fiscal Year 1996 Annual Report showing how applications for TAOs were processed: 46.2 percent of the TAOs were resolved voluntarily; 6.6 percent Problems Resolution Pro-gram cases were initiated; 12.6 percent of the cases were referred to a particular function

[b] Procedures for Obtaining Taxpayer Assistance Orders

Procedures for obtaining a taxpayer assistance order are fairly straightforward. Taxpayers are required to apply for a taxpayer assistance order.[45] Although no special form is *required*, the Service published Form 911, Application for Taxpayer Assistance Order to Relieve Hardship, for the purpose of seeking this relief.[46] (See Form 15.1.) When Form 911 is filed, the local taxpayer advocate reviews the application to determine if the taxpayer is experiencing substantial hardship (or the hardship is imminent)[47] and, if so, advises the appropriate operating function office. The operating division or function then reviews the account or the relief proposed and reports back to the taxpayer advocate. If the operating division or function refuses to act as requested, the taxpayer advocate issues a TAO, which after review, is sent to the operating division or function involved in enforcement issues.[48]

On receiving a request for a taxpayer assistance order, the taxpayer advocate will first determine whether circumstances listed in the statute are present. Some of these circumstances are readily determinable, such as the threat of adverse action, a delay of more than thirty days in resolving a taxpayer account problem, and the taxpayer's liability for additional costs, including professional fees. Other circumstances are more subjective, such as whether the taxpayer will suffer irreparable injury or long-term adverse effects. The Manual is somewhat more specific in suggesting that officers consider whether the taxpayer will be able to (1) retain housing; (2) obtain food for the taxpayer's family; (3) pay for utilities for the taxpayer's residence; (4) obtain transportation to and from work; (5) remain employed or become unemployed; (6) obtain "essential" medical treatment for the taxpayer's family; (7) make reasonable clothing purchases for the taxpayer's family; (8) continue to provide education for the taxpayer or the taxpayer's family; (9) avoid irreparable damage to the taxpayer's credit rating because the Service acted erroneously or did not reconsider an alternative action; (10) avoid serious financial hardship by, for example, being unable to meet payroll or suffering bankruptcy; or (11) avoid suffering emotional distress because the taxpayer appears "overwhelmed by the enormity of the tax situation she or he is in."[49]

---

for resolution; 3.3 percent were resolved by the problems resolution officer without a TAO; in 7.8 percent of the cases relief was provided before a TAO was issued; and the five TAOs were enforced.

[45] IRC § 7811(a).

[46] Reg. § 301.7811-1T(b)(1). Form 911 may be received by any Service employee.

[47] IRM 13.1.7.2, Taxpayer Advocate Case Criteria; IRM 13.1.7.3, Case Receipt and Assignment; IRM 13.1.7.5.11, Implementing Hardship Relief.

[48] IRM 13.1.7.8.1, Guidelines in Issuing Taxpayer Assistance Orders (Oct. 1, 2001).

[49] IRM 13.1.7.5.3.1, Criteria 1: Considerations for "Hardship" Acceptable Determinations (Oct. 1, 2001).

The issuance of a taxpayer assistance order (Form 9102) occurs when the taxpayer advocate has decided that relief should be granted but the function does not act accordingly.[50] A TAO may require the Service to take remedial actions, such as release of the taxpayer's property from levy.[51]

[5] Identifying Taxpayer Problems and Making Reports

The National Taxpayer Advocate is given the discretion to consult with appropriate supervisory personnel of the Service in carrying out the Advocate's responsibilities. When the National Taxpayer Advocate submits recommendations to the Commissioner, the Commissioner must respond to the Advocate within three months.[52]

The National Taxpayer Advocate is required to submit annual reports to the House Ways and Means Committee and the Senate Finance Committee. One report is due by June 30 of each calendar year, this report includes the objectives of the Office of the Taxpayer Advocate for the next calendar year, together with supporting substantive and statistical analysis.[53] The other report, due not later than December 31 of each calendar year, reports on the activities of the Office of Taxpayer Advocate during the fiscal year that has just ended.[54]

In addition to other information the National Taxpayer Advocate considers appropriate, the Activities Report must include the following:

1. Identify the steps the Office of the Taxpayer Advocate has taken to improve taxpayer services and the Service's responsiveness to those initiatives;
2. Contain recommendations the National Taxpayer Advocate receives from personnel authorized to issue taxpayer assistance orders;
3. Summarize at least twenty of the most serious problems taxpayers encountered;
4. Contain an inventory of the steps taken to improve taxpayer service, recommendations received by the Office of Taxpayer Advocate, and the twenty problems mentioned in item 3, along with the actions the Service has taken and the results of those actions;

---

[50] IRM 13.1.7.8.1, Taxpayer Assistance Order (TAO) Process—Introduction.

[51] IRC § 7811(d).

[52] IRC §§ 7803(c)(2)(D) and 7803(c)(3).

[53] IRC § 7802(d)(2)(B)(i).

[54] IRC § 7803(c)(2)(B). The report on the activities of the Office of the Taxpayer Advocate must cover "full and substantive analysis" of eleven specific subjects ranging from the initiatives that the National Taxpayer Advocate's Office has taken to other information the National Taxpayer Advocate deems advisable to report.

5. Contain an inventory of the steps, recommendations, and serious problems for which actions remain to be completed, and the period during which each item has remained in the inventory;

6. Contain an inventory of the steps, recommendations, and serious problems that have not been taken and addressed, and their period in the inventory;

7. Identify any TAO that the Service did not honor in a timely manner;

8. Contain administrative and legislative recommendations for resolving problems taxpayers encounter in dealing with the Service;

9. Identify areas of the tax law that impose significant compliance burdens on taxpayers and the Service, as well as recommendations for remedying these burdens; and

10. Identify the ten most litigated issues for different taxpayer categories, and provide recommendations for resolving these disputes.[55]

To ensure that Congress receives an unfiltered and candid report on the problems taxpayers are experiencing and what can be done to address them, the National Taxpayer Advocate's two reports are not subject to prior review by the Commissioner, the Secretary of the Treasury, any other officer or employee of the Treasury Department, or the Office of Management and Budget.[56] Treasury nevertheless remains responsible for legislative recommendations; Taxpayer Advocate reports are not legislative recommendations.[57]

---

[55] IRC §§ 7803(c)(2)(B)(ii)(I)−7803(c)(2)(B)(ii)(X).

[56] IRC § 7803(c)(2)(B)(iii).

[57] See IRC § 7803(c)(2)(B)(iv).

FORM 15.1 ————————————————
APPLICATION FOR TAXPAYER ASSISTANCE ORDER TO RELIEVE HARDSHIP

OMB No. 1545-1504

Department of the Treasury — Internal Revenue Service

TAXPAYER ADVOCATE SERVICE

Application for Taxpayer Assistance Order (ATAO)

Form **911**
(Rev. 3-2000)

Section I.   **Taxpayer Information**

1. Name(s) as shown on tax return **ALAN MICHAELS**	4. Your Social Security Number **124-45-6789** 6. Tax Form(s)
	5. Social Security No. of Spouse 7. Tax Period(s)
2. Current mailing address (Number, Street & Apartment Number) **100 MAIN STREET**	8. Employer Identification Number (if applicable)
	9. E-Mail address
3. City, Town or Post Office, State and ZIP Code **ANYTOWN, NJ 07000**	10. Fax number
11. Person to contact **ALAN MICHAELS**	12. Daytime telephone number **201-569-0000** 13. Best time to call **M-F 9-5**

14. Please describe the problem and the significant hardship it is creating. *(If more space is needed, attach additional sheets.)*
    SEE ATTACHED RIDER

15. Please describe the relief you are requesting. *(If more space is needed, attach additional sheets.)*
    SEE ATTACHED RIDER

I understand that Taxpayer Advocate employees may contact third parties in order to respond to this request and I authorize such contacts to be made. Further, by authorizing the Taxpayer Advocate Service to contact third parties, I understand that I will not receive notice, pursuant to section 7602(c) of the Internal Revenue Code, of third parties contacted in connection with this request.

16. Signature of taxpayer or corporate officer	17. Date	18. Signature of spouse	19. Date

Section II.   **Representative Information (if applicable)**

1. Name of Authorized Representative **MICHAEL ALAN**	3. Centralized Authorization File Number (CAF) **2000-00000R**
2. Mailing Address **ONE DAG HAMMARSKJOLD PLAZA** **NEW YORK, NY 10017**	4. Daytime telephone number **212-605-0000**
	5. Fax number **212-605-0001**
6. Signature of Representative	7. Date

Cat. No. 16965S

Form **911** (Rev. 3-2000)

Section III.   (For Internal Revenue Service only)

Taxpayer Name		Taxpayer Identification Number (TIN)	
1. Name of Initiating Employee	2. Employee Telephone Number	3. Operating Division or Function	4. Office
			6. IRS Received Date

5. How Identified & Received (Check the appropriate box)

IRS Function Identified Issue as Meeting TAS Criteria
☐ (r) Functional referral (Functional area identified TP/Rep issue as meeting TAS criteria)
☐ (x) Congressional correspondence/inquiry not addressed to TAS but referred for TAS handling

Taxpayer or Representative Requested TAS Assistance
☐ (c) Taxpayer or representative filed Form 911 or sent other correspondence to TAS
☐ (n) Taxpayer or representative called into a National Taxpayer Advocate (NTA) Toll-Free site
☐ (p) Taxpayer or representative called TAS (other than NTA Toll-Free)
☐ (s) Functional referral (Taxpayer or representative specifically requested TAS assistance)
☐ (w) Taxpayer or representative sought TAS assistance in a TAS walk-in area
☐ (y) Congressional corresp/inquiry addressed to TAS or any Congressional specifically requesting TAS assistance

7. TAS Criteria (Check the appropriate box)
☐ (1) Taxpayer is suffering or about to suffer a significant hardship
☐ (2) Taxpayer is facing an immediate threat of adverse action
☐ (3) Taxpayer will incur significant costs, including fees for professional representation, if relief is not granted
☐ (4) Taxpayer will suffer irreparable injury or long-term adverse impact if relief is not granted
☐ (5) Taxpayer experienced an IRS delay of more than 30 calendar days in resolving an account-related problem or inquiry
☐ (6) Taxpayer did not receive a response or resolution to their problem by the date promised
☐ (7) A system or procedure has either failed to operate as intended or failed to resolve a taxpayer problem or dispute with the IRS
☐ (8) Congressional Duplicate of any criteria or non-criteria case already in TAS or on TAMIS
☐ (9) Any issue/problem not meeting the above TAS criteria but kept in TAS for handling and resolution

8. Initiating Employee. What actions did you take to help resolve the problem?

9. Initiating Employee. State reason(s) why relief was not provided.

Section III Instructions (For Internal Revenue Service only)
1. Enter your name.
2. Enter your telephone number.
3. Enter your function (i.e., ACS, Collection, Examination, Customer Service, etc.). If you are now part of one of the new Business Operating Divisions (Wage & Investment Income, Small Business/Self-Employed, Large/Mid-Size Business, Tax-Exempt/Govt Entity), enter the name of the division.
4. Enter the number/Organization Code for your office. (e.g., 18 for AUSC, 95 for Los Angeles).
5. Check the appropriate box that best reflects how the taxpayer informed us of the problem. For example, did TP call or write an IRS function or TAS? Did TP specifically request TAS assistance/handling or did the function identify the issue as meeting TAS criteria?
6. The IRS Received Date is the date TP/Rep first informed the IRS of the problem. Enter the date the TP/Rep first called, walked in or wrote the IRS to seek assistance with getting the problem resolved.
7. Check the box that best describes the reason/justification for Taxpayer Advocate Service (TAS) assistance and handling.
8. Indicate the actions you took to help resolve taxpayer's problem.
9. State the reason(s) that prevented you from resolving taxpayer's problem and from providing relief. For example, levy proceeds cannot be returned since they were already applied to a valid liability, an overpayment cannot be refunded since the refund statute expired, or current law precludes a specific interest abatement.

Section IV.   (For Taxpayer Advocate Service only)

1. TAMIS CF#	2. BOD/Client	3. How Recd Code	4. Criteria Code	5. IRS Recd Date	6. TAS Recd Date
7. Reopen Ind	8. Func/Unit Assigned	9. Employee Assigned	10. Major Issue Code	11. ATAO Code/Subcode	12. PSD Code
13. Special Case Code	14. Complexity Code	15. Outreach	16. Local Use Code ☐ TP _|_|_|_|_| ☐ Case _|	17. Relief Date	18. TAS Clsd Date
19. Cust Satisfact Cde	20. Root Cause Code				
Hardship ☐ Yes ☐ No	Taxpayer Advocate Signature				Date

Cat. No. 16965S   Form **911** (Rev. 3-2000)

Instructions

When to use this form: Use this form to request relief if any of the following apply to you:

1. You are suffering or about to suffer a significant hardship;
2. You are facing an immediate threat of adverse action;
3. You will incur significant costs, including fees for professional representation, if relief is not granted;
4. You will suffer irreparable injury or long-term adverse impact if relief is not granted;
5. You experienced an IRS delay of more than 30 calendar days in resolving an account-related problem or inquiry;
6. You did not receive a response or resolution to your problem by the date promised;
7. A system or procedure has either failed to operate as intended or failed to resolve your problem or dispute with the IRS.

If an IRS office will not grant the relief requested or will not grant the relief in time to avoid the significant hardship, you may submit this form. No enforcement action will be taken while we are reviewing your application.

Where to Submit This Form: Submit this application to the Taxpayer Advocate office located in the state or city where you reside. For the address of the Taxpayer Advocate in your state or city or for additional information call the National Taxpayer Advocate Toll-Free Number 1-877-777-4778.

Third Party Contact: You should understand that in order to respond to this request you are also authorizing the Taxpayer Advocate Service to contact third parties when necessary and that you will not receive further notice regarding contacted parties. See IRC 7602(c).

Overseas Taxpayers: Taxpayers residing overseas can submit this application by mail to the Taxpayer Advocate, Internal Revenue Service, PO Box 193479, San Juan, Puerto Rico 00919 or in person at 2 Ponce de Leon Avenue, Mercantil Plaza Building, Room GF05A, Hato Rey PR 00918. The application can also be faxed to (787) 759-4535.

Caution: Incomplete applications or applications submitted to an Advocate office outside of your geographical location may result in delays. If you do not hear from us within one week of submitting Form 911, please contact the Taxpayer Advocate office where you originally submitted your application.

Section I Instructions—Taxpayer Information

1. Enter your name(s) as shown on the tax return that relates to this application for relief.
2. Enter your current mailing address, including street number and name and apartment number.
3. Enter your city, town or post office, state and ZIP code.
4. Enter your Social Security Number.
5. Enter the Social Security Number of your spouse if this application relates to a jointly filed return.
6. Enter the number of the Federal tax return or form that relates to this application. For example, an individual taxpayer with an income tax issue would enter Form 1040.
7. Enter the quarterly, annual or other tax period that relates to this application. For example, if this request involves an income tax issue, enter the calendar or fiscal year; if an employment tax issue, enter the calendar quarter.
8. Enter your Employer Identification Number if this relief request involves a business or non-individual entity (e.g., a partnership, corporation, trust, self-employed individual with employees).
9. Enter your E-mail address.
10. Enter your fax number including the area code.
11. Enter the name of the individual we should contact. For partnerships, corporations, trusts, etc., enter the name of the individual authorized to act on the entity's behalf.
12. Enter your daytime telephone number including the area code.
13. Indicate the best time to call you. Please specify a.m. or p.m. hours.
14. Describe the problem and the significant hardship it is creating for you. Specify the actions that the IRS has taken (or not taken) to cause the problem and ensuing hardship. **If the problem involves an IRS delay of more than 30 days in resolving your issue, indicate the date you first contacted the IRS for assistance in resolving your problem.**
15. Describe the relief you are seeking. Specify the actions that you want taken and that you believe necessary to relieve the significant hardship. Furnish if applicable any relevant proof and corroboration as to why relief is warranted or why you cannot or should not meet current IRS demands to satisfy your tax obligations.
16 & 18. If this application is a joint relief request relating to a joint tax liability, both spouses should sign in the appropriate blocks. If only one spouse is requesting relief relating to a joint tax liability, only the requesting spouse has to sign the application. If this application is being submitted for another individual, only a person authorized and empowered to act on that individual's behalf should sign the application.
    NOTE: The signing of this application allows the IRS by law to suspend, for the period of time it takes the Advocate to review and decide upon your request, any applicable statutory periods of limitation relating to the assessment or collection of taxes..
17 & 19. Enter the date the application was signed.

Section II Instructions--Representative Information

Taxpayers: If you wish to have a representative act on your behalf, you must give him/her power of attorney or tax information authorization for the tax return(s) and period(s)involved. For additional information see Form 2848, Power of Attorney and Declaration of Representative or Form 8821, Tax Information Authorization, and the accompanying instructions.

Representatives: If you are an authorized representative submitting this request on behalf of the taxpayer identified in Section I, complete Blocks 1 through 7 of Section II. Attach a copy of Form 2848, Form 8821 or other power of attorney. Enter your Centralized Authorization File (CAF) number in Block 3 of Section II. The CAF number is the unique number that the IRS assigns to a representative after Form 2848 or Form 8821 is filed with an IRS office.

Paperwork Reduction Act Notice: We ask for the information on this form to carry out the Internal Revenue laws of the United States. Your response is voluntary. You are not required to provide the information requested on a form that is subject to the Paperwork Reduction Act unless the form displays a valid OMB control number. Books or records relating to a form or its instructions must be retained as long as their contents may become material in the administration of any Internal Revenue law. Generally, tax returns and return information are confidential, as required by Code section 6103. Although the time needed to complete this form may vary depending on individual circumstances, the estimated average time is 30 minutes. Should you have comments concerning the accuracy of this time estimate or suggestions for making this form simpler, please write to the Internal Revenue Service, Attention: Tax Forms Committee, Western Area Distribution Center, Rancho Cordova, CA 95743-0001.

Cat. No. 16965S   Form **911** (Rev. 3-2000)

¶ 15.03 INFORMAL STEPS IN MINIMIZING THE RISK OF SUMMARY COLLECTION ACTION

[1] Contacts With Collection

Contacts with Collection take place in a different statutory environment since enactment of the IRS Restructuring and Reform Act of 1998. An array of new procedures are available to help taxpayers resolve delinquent tax problems. Taxpayers have due process review rights when Collection files a lien or intends to serve a levy, and these due process rights include the right to administrative review in Appeals and judicial review in the Tax Court. These procedures are part of the lien and levy procedures and are discussed above in connection with those Service collection powers.[58] In voluntary work-out procedures, such as installment payment agreements and offers in compromise, taxpayers also have the right to Appeals review, as described below.[59] Taxpayers are also entitled to be provided with information about the tax liability the Service claims must be paid and information about their rights. Taxpayers should receive explanations or information about a number of different procedures and matters, including the following:

- Joint and several liability and the right of a spouse to limit that liability;
- Taxpayer rights in interviews;
- The criteria for examination selection;
- The Appeals and Collection process;
- Refund disallowance;
- An annual statement to taxpayers with installment payment agreements showing the initial and remaining balance of the unpaid tax;
- The name and address of a new tax matters partner (Section 6231(a)(7)); and
- The conditions under which the taxpayer's return information may be disclosed.[60]

Taxpayers also are protected from certain actions of Collection Enforcement personnel. For example, the statute of limitations on collection may not be extended after December 31, 1999, and before then taxpayers must be given notice of their right to refuse to extend the limitations period.[61]

---

[58] See ¶ 14.08.

[59] See infra ¶¶ 15.06 and 15.07.

[60] 1998 Act §§ 3501–3508.

[61] IRC § 6502, amended by 1998 Act § 3461(a). If the taxpayer agrees to extend the statute before January 1, 2000, the extension on the latest of the ten-year period, December 31, 2002, or, in the case of an installment payment agreement, ninety days after the period of extension provided in the agreement.

Also, no Service official may ask a taxpayer to waive a right to bring a civil action against the government or any government employee for any action involving an internal revenue tax, unless the taxpayer knowingly and voluntarily agrees to waive the right, or if the taxpayer is represented.[62] Although Collection personnel still have wide discretion, it can no longer be said that the exercise of this discretion is subject to no guidelines. Taxpayers and tax practitioners still must be aware of the new procedures and rights, as well as the practical realities of dealing with Collection personnel.

[2] Factors Influencing Collection Action

Taxpayers dealing with Collection Enforcement personnel, especially revenue officers to whom a taxpayer delinquent account (TDA) has been assigned, must take into account both the administrative circumstances in which these officers operate and their attitudes. In any meeting with the revenue officer, the taxpayer has the same rights regarding the time and place of the meeting and possible objections as he would have whenever information is requested from a taxpayer.

[a] What Collection and Taxpayer Want from the Process

Obviously, the objective of Collection Enforcement personnel is to collect delinquent tax quickly and to be able to close the delinquent account as paid in full. Collecting Principles, set out in Service Policy Statement P-5-2, applicable to collection activity and installment agreements, advise revenue officers and other Collection Enforcement personnel as follows:[63]

1. Our first objective when contacting delinquent taxpayers is immediate full payment of disputed liabilities and compliance with all filing and paying requirements.
2. All taxpayers are expected to pay in full. If that is not possible, they should pay the amount that is reasonable; except when business taxpayers cannot pay current taxes, we may need to seize to prevent additional liabilities.
3. We should help taxpayers who try to comply, and take appropriate enforcement actions when taxpayers resist complying. Good judgment is needed in selecting the appropriate collection tool.

---

[62] 1998 Act § 3468(a).

[63] IRM Collecting Contact Handbook, 1.2, Collecting Principles (Sept. 25, 1996). The Collecting Contact Handbook is a new multi-functional handbook that contains procedures for all employees and consolidates existing compliance procedures for, among other actions, conducting an interview of a delinquent taxpayer.

The Collecting Principles are not unreasonable, but suggest the fundamental difference between what Collection Enforcement personnel are looking for and what the delinquent taxpayer is willing or able to do. Some practical realities govern or at least influence the communications and negotiations between the revenue officer and the delinquent taxpayer.

First, the function of Collection Enforcement is to collect the full amount of a delinquent account. The delinquent taxpayer cannot expect sympathy from the personnel involved in this process. It is fair to say that the first impression Collection Enforcement personnel have of the tax delinquent is that the taxpayer has failed to comply with tax obligations when the majority of taxpayers satisfy their obligations on time. This general impression is reinforced by the revenue officer's own experience with his or her tax obligations. As a salaried employee, the revenue officer's tax is withheld. In light of their own experiences, revenue officers find it difficult to understand how a taxpayer can become a tax delinquent, even when the taxpayer is not an employee and may be an independent contractor who has failed to provide for quarterly estimated tax payments. Also, by the time a delinquent account is assigned to a field office, the revenue officer knows that the taxpayer has not responded to notices from the service center and that four or more months have elapsed without the taxpayer's having made a satisfactory effort to work out the delinquency. Appearance is often reality in the tax collection process, and so the transfer of the case to the field suggests to the revenue officer that the taxpayer has failed to take the taxpaying obligations seriously, and it is the revenue officer's job to teach the taxpayer about tax compliance by enforcing return filing and payment obligations. Certain types of tax delinquencies are particularly intolerable to revenue officers. Revenue officers are not sympathetic with delinquent businesses, particularly ones that are habitually delinquent in paying over trust fund taxes withheld from employees.

Second, taxpayers must appreciate the limitations of the collection function. It is not the function of a revenue officer, for example, to determine liability for the tax. Questions of liability are for Examination to decide. Only in unusual cases will the taxpayer be able to establish nonliability for the tax or to compromise the tax in question. Collection Enforcement personnel do not have jurisdiction to determine liability for the ad valorem delinquency, negligence, and fraud penalties, although they may assert a specific penalty, such as the trust fund recovery penalty for failure to pay over employment taxes. Curiously, the revenue officer on the one hand and the taxpayer and the taxpayer's representative on the other have similar objectives. Just as the revenue officer wants to close a case quickly by collecting the delinquent tax, so does the taxpayer. From the taxpayer's point of view, the threat of enforced collection action, the effect of a filed tax lien, and the burden of the Collection intrusion into the taxpayer's affairs makes it imperative for the taxpayer to terminate Collection involvement as soon as the taxpayer's financial situation permits. Surely, any taxpayer not possessed of some self-destructive impulse wants to limit exposure to the tax collection process and does so by paying the delinquent tax due. Consequently, the revenue officer and the taxpayer do not differ over their objectives in the collection process. They differ over ways and means, timing, and each other's perceptions of what is practically possible. On these matters, the taxpayer is the one who must have modest expectations. Often in dealing with Collection, the best a taxpayer can hope to achieve is avoidance of some of the hampering effects of the tax lien and perhaps a portion of the liability attributable to penalties (e.g., the late payment penalty). Ultimately, however, the taxpayer will be required to pay the principal amount of the tax plus accrued interest. Seen in this light, even the most successful encounter with Collection will probably be a limited success from the taxpayer's standpoint. It is the taxpayer's representative's duty to prepare a client for this practical fact.

[b] Discussions with the Revenue Officer

Communications and negotiations between the taxpayer and Collection Enforcement personnel, especially revenue officers, are not easy. In discussions, revenue officers have leverage and the taxpayer, none. The revenue officer is armed with the Code's formidable powers to collect a tax without judicial intervention, which for the most part have been delegated to the revenue officer level. Statutory changes and regulations have limited the revenue officer's discretion to an unprecedented degree. Also, the Manual attempts to prescribe which powers should be exercised and when. Even with these limitations on arbitrary exercise of enforced collection action, revenue officers still have and exercise discretion.[64] Moreover, management of the Service's collection function has not been consistent in its objectives nor in its attitudes towards various collection techniques. These factors have resulted in notable variations in the methods used to dispose of collection matters from local office to local office.[65]

Revenue officers and other collection personnel have wide discretion in the handling of a collection matter. This discretion is not always exercised wisely, even from the government's standpoint. For example, precipitous use of a levy to seize wages of a delinquent taxpayer may serve only to cause the revenue officer's dismissal and the ultimate write-off of the account as uncollectible because the taxpayer cannot obtain employment and has no readily distrainable assets. Revenue officers are also influenced by what they perceive as

---

[64] Many activities (e.g., the seizure of a going business) still depend on the revenue officer's evaluation of the "facts and circumstances" of a particular case. IRM 5.10, Seizure & Sale Handbook 1.2, Pre-Levy Action (Jan. 19, 1999).

[65] Variations among districts in the acceptance of offers in compromise, for example, have long been criticized. See GAO Report, "What the IRS Can Do to Collect More Delinquent Taxes," 51–53 (GGD-82-4 1981).

the wishes of management personnel. Since the National Office evaluates regional accomplishments on the basis of case closings, among other things, a revenue officer may be disinclined to accept a deferred payment agreement because such an agreement delays closings and pushes up inventories.[66]

Collection action taken by the Service must strictly comply with statutory provisions of the Code.[67] Action that is not in accordance with the statutory regime is illegal. The dates when the assessment was made, the notice and demand issued, the notice of lien filed, and the notice of levy served, and the other steps in the collection process should be examined with a view to determining whether any legal defect exists.

In a delinquent account situation, therefore, it is imperative that the taxpayer or the taxpayer's representative build credibility. It is or should be easy to respond immediately to a revenue officer's request to meet with the taxpayer to discuss payment. It is critical that lines of communication between the taxpayer and the Collection Enforcement be kept open if lien filing and enforced collection are to be avoided or delayed. Representatives should establish contact with the collection official as early as possible in the period of delinquency or problem to accomplish the following: (1) persuade the revenue officer to abate the assessment in whole or in part or to negotiate a mutually satisfactory payment agreement; (2) ensure that the revenue officer contacts the representative before any notice of lien is filed or enforced collection action is taken; and (3) learn the revenue officer's temperament and attitude so as to ascertain the likelihood of sudden enforced collection action or of ultimate success in resolving the collection matter.

The more involved the representative is in the matter, the more likely it is that the revenue officer can be persuaded that the taxpayer takes his obligation seriously and that the account will be satisfied in whole or in part. All dealings with collection personnel should be courteous and honest, while at the same

---

[66] It was only in 1998 that the Collection function publicly recognized that its field personnel for years had been focusing on productivity in terms of dollars collected, and that dollars collected was the most important factor in setting program goals and evaluating program accomplishments. IRS, "Use of Enforcement Statistics in the Collection Field Function," January 13, 1998, reproduced by Tax Analysts at Document Number DOC 98-2368. In part, this report concluded,

The Service has created an environment that has placed some taxpayers at risk of abridgment of their rights and some IRS employees at risk of an inappropriate evaluative atmosphere. We can point to no single, overriding factor that led to this environment—an environment that has emphasized increasing productivity without always providing a corresponding emphasis on quality and treatment of taxpayers, and an environment that uses statistical measures in a manner that created a competitive spirit focusing on achievement of goals and results without a corresponding measurement system that focused on appropriateness of case actions and adherence to policy and procedures. Id.

[67] See ¶¶ 14.05, 14.09.

time making clear that all rights, remedies, and procedures to protect the interests of the taxpayer will be used.

Disclosure of some legal defect in the collection process may assist the representative in discussions with a revenue officer, and give the taxpayer's representative greater control over discussions. Although the Service may be able to cure a defect in the collection process, if collection was not made according to law, there are circumstances where seized property must be returned to the taxpayer.[68] In any event, the revenue officer will realize that the officer is dealing with a person who has some knowledge of the collection process. This awareness can translate into some benefit in the negotiations that follow or otherwise help minimize the effect of the lien or levy.

The representative cannot expect the collection official to be of assistance or make suggestions. Consequently, the representative must know what remedies are available and proceed in the direction consistent with the client's interests. The representative's objective should be to funnel information between the revenue officer and the taxpayer. Only in this way can the representative control the course of the matter and determine the extent of disclosure to collection personnel. The representative should also assist in the preparation of any financial statement for the purpose of discussing a deferred payment agreement. This review and monitoring of information is not improper. On the contrary, one of the reasons the revenue officer requests financial statements is to obtain sources for enforced collection action. Although a financial statement may not be falsified, the timing of such information and the manner and circumstances of disclosure may be important to the client.

Dealings with a revenue officer depend on what the representative wants to accomplish for his client. The following are examples of some of the arguments the representative might discuss with the revenue officer:

- Enforced collection action should not be taken because the assessment is invalid (e.g., the assessment is untimely or some procedural requirement has not been complied with).
- Although there is no dispute about liability, the taxpayer is unable to make payment in full at the present time.
- The taxpayer wishes to have a tax lien released because the liability has been paid or security can be provided for the payment of the tax due.
- A filed tax lien is preventing property from being sold or credit from being extended to the taxpayer, thus hampering the realization of income out of which the tax liability may be paid.

---

[68] See, e.g., Kabbaby v. Richardson, 520 F2d 334 (5th Cir. 1975) (cash seized after invalid termination assessment; held, not overpayment for another year and ordered returned). But compare Boyd v. United States, 439 F. Supp. 907 (ED Pa. 1977) (cash seized after invalid assessment because no deficiency notice could be applied to other outstanding assessment).

- The taxpayer cannot or should not be required to make payment of the full amount of the assessment because there is doubt as to liability, or the taxpayer does not now nor is he likely to have the financial resources to pay.

In some instances, it may be necessary to resort to legal action to avoid or discharge the effect of the lien or to halt collection action. Court action tends to be expensive and time-consuming, and the results speculative. The revenue officer may neither appreciate legal technicalities nor be flexible enough to negotiate a mutually satisfactory resolution. One of the few advantages of instituting legal proceedings is that after such action is commenced, the representative's contacts will be with a counsel attorney, Assistant United States Attorney, or Justice Department lawyer, who may be more aware of legal or factual problems in the Service's position and more flexible in negotiations.

While the revenue officer may not be flexible in negotiations, the taxpayer's representative must be flexible and patient, even when sorely pressed to act otherwise.

[c] The First Contact or Interview

Collection personnel are instructed to use the first contact with a taxpayer as a means of collecting the delinquent tax, deciding the appropriate collection procedural alternative, and deciding how to work out an extension to pay or installment payment agreement. The first objective of Collection personnel in contacting the taxpayer is the immediate full payment of the undisputed tax, as well as compliance with all filing and payment obligations. Collection contemplates several outcomes starting with the adjustment of an erroneous account, an extension of time to pay, entering into an installment agreement (streamlined or non-streamlined), determining that the account is currently not collectible, and an offer in compromise.[69]

To determine the appropriate method of full payment, personnel are supposed to use a tiered interview, which has several steps.[70] When a tiered interview is conducted, Collection personnel explain the other options apart from full payment. In order of preference, the options are (1) the taxpayer makes the largest possible payment on the day of the meeting and full payment in ten days; (2) the taxpayer receives a short-term extension to pay; (3) the taxpayer enters into a streamlined installment payment agreement, and (4) the taxpayer enters into a non-streamlined installment agreement.

---

[69] IRM Collecting Contact Handbook, supra 1.1, Introduction. Id., at 2.2.
[70] IRM Collecting Contact Handbook, supra, 105.1.2, Figure 2-1.

The goal of the initial contact is to bring the taxpayer into full compliance with all filing and paying requirements.[71] The revenue officer needs to accomplish the following:

1. Determine the correct status of filing and paying.
2. Demand immediate filing of all delinquent returns.
3. Demand full payment of all delinquent accounts.
4. Verify filing and paying when the taxpayer indicates that the tax was paid, return filed, or both.

The exception to these steps, of course, is when evidence of fraud is found.

The first step is the demand for full payment. If the taxpayer happily agrees, then the tiered interview ends, but the interviewer will ask for information about leviable property if there is to be any deferral, and will also warn of enforcement if payment is not received. The same procedure is followed if the taxpayer agrees to pay the largest possible amount the day of the meeting and to pay the full amount within the next ten days. If the taxpayer wants more time to pay or asks for an installment payment agreement, the next step the Collection interviewer will take is to ask how the taxpayer plans to pay. If the taxpayer proposes to pay the full amount within 60 or 120 days, the taxpayer's proposal will be accepted, and the interview is ended, again with the request for levy sources and a warning of enforcement if payment is not received. If the taxpayer proposes extended payments, the interviewer will ask whether the taxpayer can defer payments on other debts, or borrow or sell assets. The interviewer will point out the disadvantages of a deferred payment arrangement, such as additional interest charges, penalties, and the user fee for an installment payment agreement.[72] If the taxpayer cannot defer other debts, borrow, or sell assets, and the total amount owed is under $10,000, which the taxpayer can pay in full in thirty-six months, Collection will set up a streamlined payment agreement for the minimum amount the taxpayer is able to pay each month, and the interview will be terminated.

If the amount owed is more than $10,000, or the taxpayer cannot pay the amount owed within thirty-six months, the interviewer asks detailed questions about the possibility of deferring payment of other debts, or borrowing or selling assets. The interviewer uses financial information secured from one of the following sources: (1) financial information maintained by the Automated Col-

---

[71] IRM 5.1 General Handbook 10.2(2), Effective First Contact on Taxpayer Cases (Aug. 31, 2000). The Manual also instructs revenue officers to inform taxpayers of their rights, a step that is to be taken at the beginning of the initial contact by providing them with Publication 1, Your Rights As a Taxpayer. IRM 5.1 General Handbook, at 10.4, Rights During Interview (Aug. 31, 2000).

[72] The imposition of a user fee for can be criticized for the obvious reason that the addition of a charge, even a small one, sends the wrong message to a taxpayer who is in sufficiently difficult financial circumstances to require an installment agreement in the first place. The charge is changed periodically and is ($43).

lection System; (2) a Collection Information Statement (CIS) for Wage-earners and Self-employed Individuals, Form 433-A; (3) a Collection Information Statement for Businesses, Form 433-B; or (4) the taxpayer's own financial statement. If the taxpayer cannot pay the liability by deferring other debts, or borrowing or selling assets, then the interviewer conducts a financial analysis using the allowable expense guidelines, described in the financial statement analysis described below. If the taxpayer is a wage earner, and the taxpayer's employer will agree to deduct from payroll, a Payroll Deduction Agreement will be entered into. Similarly, if the taxpayer has a checking account and agrees to a direct debit agreement, the interviewer will set up a Direct Debit Installment Agreement. If the taxpayer is not a wage earner with an employer willing to deduct from payroll and the taxpayer has no checking account, then the interviewer will enter into a General Installment Agreement, Form 433-D.

It obviously will benefit the taxpayer if the taxpayer can propose a practical plan to pay off the liability in the shortest amount of time. Consequently, preparing for the first meeting knowing what the revenue officer will ask and suggest can result in the taxpayer's successfully limiting exposure to the vagaries of collection action.

¶ 15.04 PREPARATION OF FINANCIAL STATEMENTS

In delinquency cases, the revenue officer must determine whether collection action should be enforced or deferred, or whether less than the full liability should be collected because the financial resources of the taxpayer do not permit collection of the full amount. To make this determination, the revenue officer needs to obtain financial information from the taxpayer. Apart from any independent investigation the revenue officer may make, the revenue officer obtains this information by securing a financial statement from the taxpayer. Financial statements in collection cases stand in roughly the same position as tax returns in examinations. The financial statement is a voluntary, albeit required, statement of the matters required to be set forth and is signed under penalties of perjury. Just as the revenue agent examines the correctness of the tax return, the revenue officer investigates the accuracy of the financial statement.

Different financial statement forms are used for different situations, but they all involve, in varying degrees of detail, a statement of the financial condition of the taxpayer (i.e., income and expenses, and assets and liabilities).[73] As described in part above, several basic types of financial statements are used. A comprehensive financial statement, a Statement of Financial Condition

---

[73] See IRM 15.1.1, Expectations (May 1, 2004); IRM 5.15.2, Analyzing Financial Information (May 1, 2004); IRM 5.15.3, Verifying Financial Information (May 1, 2004).

and Other Information (Form 433) is required only for offers in compromise where the offer is based on inability to pay; however, the Form 433 may be called for where complete financial information is considered advisable. Short-form financial statements are also used to determine how individual and business taxpayers can satisfy their tax liabilities; these include the Collection Information Statement for Wage-Earners and Self-Employed, Form 433-A and the Collection Information Statement for Businesses Form 433-B. (See Form 15.2 and Form 15.3, respectively.)[74] A business taxpayer may use its own financial statement (income and balance sheet) as a substitute for the income and expense portion of the Form 433-B. For individuals owing less than $100,000, the Automated Collection System and Client Services Collection Operations at campuses use a Collection Information Statement, Form 433-F.

[1] Balance Sheet

The balance sheet submitted by a taxpayer for collection purposes is only the beginning of the revenue officer's analysis of the taxpayer's ability to pay. A balance sheet prepared by an accountant reflects the assets of a person or business at their original cost, less depreciation. However, the revenue officer is not concerned with historical cost or even fair market value. For tax collection purposes, the forced sale value of property (i.e., the amount it could reasonably bring at a forced sale) is the ultimate question. Thus, certain property, such as jointly owned property, may have a substantial fair market value but a relatively small forced sale value.

[2] The Income and Expense Statement

Another aspect of the financial condition of the delinquent taxpayer becomes apparent under an analysis of his monthly income and expenses. The purpose of this analysis is to provide some objective basis for determining how much a taxpayer can pay the Service over a period of time based on the taxpayer's present income. The taxpayer's potential earning capacity is also a factor. The taxpayer's education, health, profession or trade, age, experience, past and present income, and prospects for the future are all relevant to collection. Finally, not only are the taxpayer's assets and present and future income considered, but also the possibility of collection from transferees and others who may be liable for the amount assessed.

---

[74] Form 433 is discussed further in Saltzman and Saltzman, IRS Practice and Procedure Manual ¶ 9.04 (Warren, Gorham & Lamont, Inc. 2004).

The 1998 Act made use of national and local standards statutorily required.[75] Amended Section 7122(c)(2)(A) requires the Service to develop and publish "national and local allowances designed to provide that taxpayers entering into a compromise have an adequate means to provide for basic living expenses." However, use of these standard allowances is not mandated in all situations. The Service's guidelines providing that revenue officers (1) must determine whether use of the schedules of national and local allowances is "appropriate," considering "the facts and circumstances of the taxpayer," and (2) must not use the schedules "to the extent such use would result in the taxpayer['s] not having adequate means to provide basic living expenses."[76] National and local standards are guidelines the Service has adopted "to provide consistency in certain expense allowances such as groceries and household expenses, housing and transportation."[77] The standard amounts in the national and local guidelines cover basic hiring expenses. If the taxpayer will suffer economic hardship, there may be a deviation from the standards. If standard expenses are exceeded, the taxpayer must provide "reasonable substantiation" (e.g., bank statements or cancelled checks, credit card vouchers, rent/lease receipts and lease agreements, payment coupons, court orders, contracts, and future expenses).

[3] Financial Statement Analysis and Verification

Upon receiving the taxpayer's financial statement, the collection official analyzes and verifies the information, and decides whether to take one or more of the following actions:

- Require payment of the tax liability, in full or in part, from available assets.
- Recommend or initiate collection action if assets are available to pay the liability in full or in part, and the taxpayer refuses to convert assets to cash.
- File a Notice of Federal Tax Lien.
- Allow an extension of time to pay the tax in full.
- Prepare an installment payment agreement explaining the offer in compromise provisions.
- Report the account as currently not collectible.[78]

---

[75] See Act § 3462, amending Section 7122.

[76] IRC § 7122(c)(2)(B). See also ¶ 15.07.

[77] IRM 5.15.1.2.3, Financial Analysis Handbook, Analysis, Substantiation, and Verification of Income and Income and Expenses (May 1, 2004).

[78] IRM 5.15.1.1, Financial Analysis Handbook Expectations (May 1, 2004).

Analysis and verification should take place shortly after receipt. Financial information should be current (no older than twelve months). An in person review/meeting is preferred at the taxpayer's home or place of business. Collection's analysis of the taxpayer's financial information dictates which of the foregoing collection actions to take. Revenue officers are instructed to collect as quickly as possible the full amount of the tax liability, or at least the maximum reasonable amount of that liability, before considering methods other than full and immediate payment.[79] Under this operating principle, the delinquent taxpayer is unlikely to find the revenue officer sympathetic to a delay in the payment of the unpaid tax liability. If the taxpayer has cash equal to the tax liability or assets readily convertible into cash (e.g., stocks, bonds, or the loan value of insurance policies), the revenue officer will demand immediate payment. If the taxpayer can obtain an unsecured loan (e.g., from a credit union), the revenue officer will ask the taxpayer to borrow money to pay the tax liability.

Expense analysis is necessary only if the revenue officer is unable to collect the tax liability from available assets. In general, the amount of income left after the deduction from gross income of allowable expenses and legally required expenses (payments for child support and alimony, as well as federal and state taxes) are considered the taxpayer's disposable income available to apply to the tax liability (that is, gross income less all allowable expenses). The taxpayer is told how much the Service expects the taxpayer to pay, not how the taxpayer should spend money. The revenue officer expects an amount equal to the excess of necessary or not allowable conditional expenses, and will tell the taxpayer that he is responsible for determining what changes in expenses are needed, not what a taxpayer may own. Objective national and local standards and one- and three-year rules are intended to delay or remove entirely the revenue officer from the process of reducing expenses. While in the first instance the taxpayer bears the responsibility of reducing expenses, the revenue officer still reviews the taxpayer's expenses and payment plan.

To establish a consistent framework for evaluating a taxpayer's ability to pay the delinquent tax from disposable income, the National Office has created a standardized list of major expenses as well as questions and answers to assist revenue officers in financial analysis, national standards for total monthly expenses, and national standards for individual expenses.[80] The taxpayer's allowable expenses are divided into two categories: necessary and conditional.[81]

---

[79] IRM 5.15.1.2.3, Financial Analysis Handbook, Analysis, Substantiation, and Verification of Income and Expenses (May 1, 2004).

[80] The Financial Analysis Handbook describes necessary expenses in general, national and local standards for necessary expenses, and "other" necessary expenses. IRM 5.15.1, Financial Expenses Handbook (May 1, 2004); IRM 5.15.1.1, Expectations; IRM 5.15.1.10, Other Expenses (May 1, 2004).

[81] IRM 5.15.1.7, Financial Analysis Handbook, Allowable Expenses (May 1, 2004).

Necessary expenses are expenses that provide for the taxpayer and the tax-payer's family's health and welfare or the production of income. These are minimum amounts that the taxpayer's family needs to live and are divided into three categories: (1) those for which national standards of reasonable amounts have been set (the standards for food, housekeeping supplies, apparel, and ser-vices; standards for personal care products and services come from the Bureau of Labor Statistics Consumer Expenditure Survey for 1992–1993); (2) those for which local standards of reasonable amounts have been established (ex-penses for housing, including utilities and transportation); and (3) other ex-penses, the reasonable amount of which the revenue officer will determine, if the revenue officer decides that the expense is necessary.[82]

Conditional expenses are all other expenses that do not meet the neces-sary expense test; however, these expenses are considered allowable if the tax-payer can pay the full tax liability, including projected interest accruals, within three years. In other words, under the three-year rule, for the taxpayer to be al-lowed what the Service considers to be excessive necessary and conditional expenses, the taxpayer must be able to show that he or she will fully pay the tax liability, including accruals, within three years.[83] On the other hand, if the taxpayer cannot pay the tax liability in full within this three-year period, the taxpayer will be permitted up to one year to modify or eliminate excessive necessary or nonallowable conditional expenses, and during this probationary

---

[82] IRM 5.15.1.8, Financial Analysis Handbook, Necessary Expenses (May 1, 2004); 1.3.2.1, Necessary Expenses: National Standards; 1.3.2.2, Necessary Expenses: Local Standards; 1.3.2.3, Necessary Standards: Other; 1.3.2.4 Necessary Expenses: Other—Un-secured Debts. National Standards are derived from Tables 1, 3, 4 and 5 of the Bureau of Labor Statistics Consumer Expenditure Survey for 1992-93, but these expenses will be up-dated annually as information becomes available from the Bureau. Expenses in the Survey are indicated by income level. As the income level increases, the percentage of income al-located for these expenses decreases. For housing, utilities and transportation, Local Stan-dards have been established by the National Office with the assistance of district offices, and districts may have multiple standards within the district. IRM 5.15.1.9, Financial Analysis Handbook, Local Standards (May 1, 2004). Taxpayers will be allowed the local standard or the amount actually paid, whichever is less. Other expenses in addition to those listed in the National and Local Standards that the Service usually considers to be necessary are taxes, health-care, court-ordered payments, involuntary deductions, account-ing and legal fees for representing the taxpayer before the Service, and minimum pay-ments on secured or legally perfected debts. The taxpayer may be able to prove that other expenses are necessary, but the amounts will have to be reasonable unless the taxpayer will be able to pay the tax liability within three years.

[83] IRM 5.15.1.3.3.1, Financial Analysis Handbook, Allowable Expense Overview (May 1, 2004). If the taxpayer has increased the amount of expenses significantly since the tax liabilities were assessed, the revenue officer may reduce the amount of excessive necessary or conditional expenses incurred after the assessment even if the liability can be fully paid within three years.

period to pay even minimal installments.[84] At the end of this one-year period, if the taxpayer still is unable to reduce nonallowable expenses, the revenue officer will expect to receive payment in the amount of the excessive or non-allowable expenses, and if the taxpayer refuses, will take collection action.

In analyzing the financial statement, the revenue officer does not passively accept the amount of expenses the taxpayer reflects therein; the taxpayer must substantiate the information by providing proof that (1) the expenses are justified and reasonable in amount (according to national and local standards); (2) the expenses are being paid; and (3) the amount of the payments are the amounts the taxpayer reported.[85] To verify the financial statement and the taxpayer's financial condition, the revenue officer will check the information the taxpayer provides from sources both within and outside the Service.

Other information the revenue officer asks for reveals whether the taxpayer is trying to comply and whether he or she would be deserving of the opportunity to pay the tax liability in installments. The revenue officer will determine whether the taxpayer is current in the payment of taxes and the filing of returns, or whether the taxpayer has at least become current since the date of the latest assessment of the current liabilities.[86] The importance of this fact cannot be overstated. Unless the taxpayer can meet current obligations to file returns and pay taxes, the taxpayer does not make a good candidate for deferred collection action by way of an installment payment agreement. If the taxpayer has previously entered into an installment payment agreement and defaulted, the revenue officer will inquire about the reason for the default. Not every default will preclude Collection's entering into an installment agreement. For example, where the taxpayer defaulted because of tax liabilities incurred after the agreement was entered into, the default does not necessarily mean that the taxpayer will not comply with the terms of a new installment agreement. Where the taxpayer defaulted because the taxpayer failed to modify or limit excessive necessary or conditional expenses under either the one-year or three-year rule, this failure to modify suggests that the taxpayer will not comply with the terms of a new installment agreement.[87]

---

[84] IRM 5.15.1.7, Financial Analysis Handbook, Allowable Expense Overview (May 1, 2004).

[85] IRM 5.15.2, Financial Analysis Handbook, Analysis, Substantiation, and Verification of Income and Expenses (May 1, 2004). Proof is requested in the form of check stubs, bank statements, credit card vouchers, rent/lease receipts and leases, payment coupons, court orders, contracts and cancelled checks. Financial statements are submitted under oath, and so a taxpayer who intentionally falsifies the information on the financial statement can be prosecuted for the felony of submitting a false statement to the Service. For cases where this has happened, see ¶ 7A.04[1][a].

[86] IRM 5.14.1.4, Interest-Based Interview (July 1, 2002). See also IRC § 6159(c)(2), describing the circumstances that will preclude an installment payment agreement.

[87] IRM 5.14.1.4, Interest-Based Interview (July 1, 2002).

Also important to the revenue officer is the reason the tax liability was incurred in the first place. If insufficient withholding or estimated tax payments were made, the taxpayer is likely to have known that the tax liability was being incurred and should have taken steps to avoid the creation of the liability or to provide for the payment. On the other hand, if the tax liability arose from an audit, the taxpayer's failure to pay the tax liability may have been because the taxpayer did not expect a liability in the amount assessed, rather than the taxpayer's simply not paying a tax when due.

Collection personnel will demand some payment of the tax out of income available to pay unsecured debt. Even allowable expense items may not be deducted in each month. For example, local property taxes will only be allowed in the month payment must be made unless money for payment is being set aside on a monthly basis. Although some flexibility is provided for "exceptional circumstances," financial statement analysis leads Collection personnel to demand significantly higher monthly payments than were demanded of taxpayers under analyses made under former procedures.

Where an analysis of the taxpayer's financial condition shows that liquidation of assets and payments from present and future income will not result in full payment, the revenue officer is instructed to consider the collection potential of an offer in compromise.

FORM 15.2
COLLECTION INFORMATION STATEMENT FOR INDIVIDUALS

IRS

Department of the Treasury
Internal Revenue Service

www.irs.gov

Form 433-A (Rev. 5-2001)
Catalog Number 20312N

Collection Information Statement for Wage Earners and Self-Employed Individuals

Complete all entry spaces with the most current data available

Important! Write "N/A" (not applicable) in spaces that do not apply. We may require additional information to support "N/A" entries.

Failure to complete all entry spaces may result in rejection or significant delay in the resolution of your account.

Section 1
Personal Information

☑ Check this box when all spaces in Sect. 1 are filled in

1. Full Name(s) MARY SMITH

Street Address 650 WEST ST
City NEW YORK   State NY   Zip 10000
County of Residence NEW YORK
How long at this address? 3 YRS

1a. Home Telephone (212) 555-0000
Best Time To Call: 8 am ___ pm (Enter Hour)

2. Marital Status:
☐ Married   ☐ Separated
☑ Unmarried (single, divorced, widowed)

3. Your Social Security No. (SSN) 123 45 6789
3a. Your Date of Birth (mm/dd/yyyy) 1/1/55
4. Spouse's Social Security No.
4a. Spouse's Date of Birth (mm/dd/yyyy)

5. ☐ Own Home   ☑ Rent   ☐ Other (specify, i.e. share rent, live with relative)

6. List the dependents you can claim on your tax return. (Attach sheet if more space is needed.)

First Name	Relationship	Age	Does this person live with you?	First Name	Relationship	Age	Does this person live with you?
			☐ No ☐ Yes				☐ No ☐ Yes
			☐ No ☐ Yes				☐ No ☐ Yes

Section 2
Your Business Information

☑ Check this box when all spaces in Sect. 2 are filled in and attachments provided.

7. Are you or your spouse self-employed or operate a business? (Check "Yes" if either applies)

☑ No ☐ Yes If yes, provide the following information:
7a. Name of Business
7b. Street Address
City ___ State ___ Zip ___

7c. Employer Identification No., if available
7d. Do you have employees?   ☐ No ☐ Yes
7e. Do you have accounts/notes receivable? ☐ No ☐ Yes
If yes, please complete Section 8 on page 5.

ATTACHMENTS REQUIRED: Please include proof of self-employment income for the **prior 3 months** (e.g., invoices, commissions, sales records, income statement).

Section 3
Employment Information

☑ Check this box when all spaces in Sect. 3 are filled in and attachments provided.

8. Your Employer SALBEC INDUSTRIES INC.
Street Address 100 PARK PLACE
City NEW YORK   State NY   Zip 10000
Work telephone no. (212) 888-0000
May we contact you at work? ☑ No ☐ Yes
8a. How long with this employer? 5 YEARS
8b. Occupation SECRETARY

9. Spouse's Employer
Street Address
City ___ State ___ Zip ___
Work telephone no. (___)
May we contact you at work? ☐ No ☐ Yes
9a. How long with this employer?
9b. Occupation

ATTACHMENTS REQUIRED: Please provide proof of gross earnings and deductions for the past 3 months from each employer (e.g., pay stubs, earnings statements). If year-to-date information is available, send only 1 such statement as long as a **minimum of 3 months** is represented.

Section 4
Other Income Information

☑ Check this box when all spaces in Sect. 4 are filled in and attachments provided.

10. Do you receive income from sources other than your own business or your employer? (Check all that apply.)

☐ Pension   ☐ Social Security   ☐ Other (specify, i.e. child support, alimony, rental)

ATTACHMENTS REQUIRED: Please provide proof of pension/social security/other income for the past 3 months from each payor, including any statements showing deductions. If year-to-date information is available, send only 1 such statement as long as a **minimum of 3 months** is represented.

Page 1 of 6

Section 5 begins on page 2 →
(Rev. 5-2001)

Collection Information Statement for Wage Earners and Self-Employed Individuals   **Form 433-A**

Name MARY SMITH   SSN 123-45-6789

Section 5

Banking, Investment, Cash, Credit, and Life Insurance Information

Complete all entry spaces with the most current data available.

11. CHECKING ACCOUNTS. List all checking accounts. (If you need additional space, attach a separate sheet.)

Type of Account	Full Name of Bank, Savings & Loan, Credit Union or Financial Institution	Bank Routing No.	Bank Account No.	Current Account Balance
11a. Checking	Name UNITED NATIONAL BANK	121000000	7654321	$ 255
	Street Address 25 CEDAR LANE			
	City/State/Zip TEANECK, NJ 07000			
11b. Checking	Name			$
	Street Address			
	City/State/Zip	11c. Total Checking Account Balances		$ 255

12. OTHER ACCOUNTS. List all accounts, including brokerage, savings, and money market, not listed on line 11

Type of Account	Full Name of Bank, Savings & Loan, Credit Union or Financial Institution	Bank Routing No	Bank Account No.	Current Account Balance
12a. SAVINGS	Name UNITED NATIONAL BANK	121000000	3219876	$ 2550
	Street Address 25 CEDAR LANE			
	City/State/Zip TEANECK, NJ 07000			
12b.	Name			$
	Street Address			
	City/State/Zip	12c. Total Other Account Balances		$ 2550

ATTACHMENTS REQUIRED: Please include your current bank statements (checking, savings, money market, and brokerage accounts) for the past three months for all accounts.

13. INVESTMENTS. List all investment assets below. Include stocks, bonds, mutual funds, stock options, certificates of deposits, and retirement assets such as IRAs, Keogh, and 401(k) plans. (If you need additional space, attach a separate sheet.)

✕ Current Value: Indicate the amount you could sell the asset for today.

Name of Company	Number of Shares / Units	✕ Current Value	Loan Amount	Used as collateral on loan?
13a. FIDELITY IRA	N/A	$ 2354	$ 0	☑ No ☐ Yes
13b.				☐ No ☐ Yes
13c.				☐ No ☐ Yes
	13d. Total Investments	$ 2354		

14. CASH ON HAND. Include any money that you have that is not in the bank.

14a. Total Cash on Hand $ 58

15. AVAILABLE CREDIT. List all lines of credit, including credit cards.

Full Name of Credit Institution	Credit Limit	Amount Owed	Available Credit
15a. Name UNITED NATIONAL BANK VISA CARD	5000	4800	$ 200
Street Address 25 CEDAR LAND			
City/State/Zip TEANECK, NJ 07000			
15b. Name			$
Street Address			
City/State/Zip	15c. Total Credit Available		$ 200

Page 2 of 6

Section 5 continued on page 3 →
(Rev. 5-2001)

Collection Information Statement for Wage Earners and Self-Employed Individuals **Form 433-A**

Name MARY SMITH SSN 123-45-6789

Section 5 continued	**16. LIFE INSURANCE.** Do you have life insurance with a cash value? ☑ No ☐ Yes

(Term Life insurance does not have a cash value.)

If yes:

16a. Name of Insurance Company _____

16b. Policy Number(s) _____

16c. Owner of Policy _____

16d. Current Cash Value $ _____ **16e.** Outstanding Loan Balance $ _____

☑ Check this box when all spaces in Sect. 5 are filled in and attachments provided

Subtract "Outstanding Loan Balance" line 16e from "Current Cash Value" line 16d = 16f $ _____

ATTACHMENTS REQUIRED: Please include a statement from the life insurance companies that includes type and cash/loan value amounts. If currently borrowed against, include loan amount and date of loan.

Section 6
Other Information

17. OTHER INFORMATION. Respond to the following questions related to your financial condition: (Attach sheet if you need more space.)

17a. Are there any garnishments against your wages? ☑ No ☐ Yes
If yes, who is the creditor? _____ Date creditor obtained judgement _____ Amount of debt $ _____

17b. Are there any judgments against you? ☑ No ☐ Yes
If yes, who is the creditor? _____ Date creditor obtained judgement _____ Amount of debt $ _____

17c. Are you a party in a lawsuit? ☑ No ☐ Yes
If yes, amount of suit $ _____ Possible completion date _____ Subject matter of suit _____

17d. Did you ever file bankruptcy? ☑ No ☐ Yes
If yes, date filed _____ Date discharged _____

17e. In the past 10 years did you transfer any assets out of your name for less than their actual value? ☑ No ☐ Yes
If yes, what asset? _____ Value of asset at time of transfer $ _____
When was it transferred? _____ To whom was it transferred? _____

17f. Do you anticipate any increase in household income in the next two years? ☐ No ☑ Yes
If yes, why will the income increase? RAISES, BONUSES _____ (Attach sheet if you need more space.)
How much will it increase? $ 3,000-5,000

17g. Are you a beneficiary of a trust or an estate? ☑ No ☐ Yes
If yes, name of the trust or estate _____ Anticipated amount to be received $ _____
When will the amount be received? _____

☑ Check this box when all spaces in Sect. 6 are filled in.

17h. Are you a participant in a profit sharing plan? ☑ No ☐ Yes
If yes, name of plan _____ Value in plan $ _____

Section 7
Assets and Liabilities

18. PURCHASED AUTOMOBILES, TRUCKS AND OTHER LICENSED ASSETS. Include boats, RV's, motorcycles, trailers, etc. (If you need additional space, attach a separate sheet.)

⧗ **Current Value:** Indicate the amount you could sell the asset for today.

	Description (Year, Make, Model, Mileage)	⧗ Current Value	Current Loan Balance	Name of Lender	Purchase Date	Amount of Monthly Payment
18a.	Year _____ Make/Model _____ Mileage	$ ____	$ ____	_____	_____	$ ____
18b.	Year _____ Make/Model _____ Mileage	$ ____	$ ____	_____	_____	$ ____
18c.	Year _____ Make/Model _____ Mileage	$ ____	$ ____	_____	_____	$ ____

Collection Information Statement for Wage Earners and Self-Employed Individuals   Form 433-A

Name **MARY SMITH**   SSN   123-45-6789

Section 7 continued

19. LEASED AUTOMOBILES, TRUCKS AND OTHER LICENSED ASSETS. Include boats, RV's, motorcycles, trailers, etc. (If you need additional space, attach a separate sheet.)

Description (Year, Make, Model)	Lease Balance	Name and Address of Lessor	Lease Date	Amount of Monthly Payment
19a. Year				
Make/Model	$			$
19b. Year				
Make/Model	$			$

ATTACHMENTS REQUIRED: Please include your current statement from lender with monthly car payment amount and current balance of the loan for each vehicle purchased or leased.

20. REAL ESTATE. List all real estate you own. (If you need additional space, attach a separate sheet.)

✕ **Current Value:** Indicate the amount you could sell the asset for today.

✳ **Date of Final Payment:** Enter the date the loan or lease will be fully paid.

Street Address, City, State, Zip, and County	Date Purchased	Purchase Price	✕Current Value	Loan Balance	Name of Lender or Lien Holder	Amount of Monthly Payment	✳Date of Final Payment
20a. LOT 16 BLOCK 1001 ATLANTIC HEIGHTS NJ 02000	5/5/01	$ 10000	$ 10000	$ 0		$	
20b.		$	$	$		$	

ATTACHMENTS REQUIRED: Please include your current statement from lender with monthly payment amount and current balance for each piece of real estate owned.

21. PERSONAL ASSETS. List all Personal assets below. (If you need additional space, attach separate sheet.) *Furniture/Personal Effects* includes the total current market value of your household such as furniture and appliances. *Other Personal Assets* includes all artwork, jewelry, collections (coin/gun, etc.), antiques or other assets.

Description	✕Current Value	Loan Balance	Name of Lender	Amount of Monthly Payment	✳Date of Final Payment
21a. Furniture/Personal Effects	$ 1500	$		$	
Other: (List below)					
21b. Artwork	$	$		$	
21c. Jewelry					
21d.					
21e.					

22. BUSINESS ASSETS. List all business assets and encumbrances below. Include Uniform Commercial Code (UCC) filings (If you need additional space, attach a separate sheet.) *Tools used in Trade or Business* includes the basic tools or books used to conduct your business, excluding automobiles. *Other Business Assets* includes any other machinery, equipment, inventory or other assets.

☑ Check this box when all spaces in Sect. 7 are filled in and attachments provided.

Description	✕Current Value	Loan Balance	Name of Lender	Amount of Monthly Payment	✳Date of Final Payment
22a. Tools used in Trade/Business	$	$		$	
Other: (List below)					
22b. Machinery	$	$		$	
22c. Equipment					
22d.					
22e.					

Page 4 of 6   Section 8 begins on page 5 → (Rev 5-2001)

Collection Information Statement for Wage Earners and Self-Employed Individuals   **Form 433-A**

Name MARY SMITH   SSN   123-45-6789

Section 8 Accounts/ Notes Receivable	**23. ACCOUNTS/NOTES RECEIVABLE** List all accounts separately, including contracts awarded, but not started. (If you need additional space, attach a separate sheet.)			
	Description	Amount Due	Date Due	Age of Account

Use only if needed.

☑ *Check this box if Section 8 not needed.*

23a. Name _____
Street Address _____
City/State/Zip _____
$ _____   _____
☐ 0 - 30 days
☐ 30 - 60 days
☐ 60 - 90 days
☐ 90+ days

23b. Name _____
Street Address _____
City/State/Zip _____
$ _____   _____
☐ 0 - 30 days
☐ 30 - 60 days
☐ 60 - 90 days
☐ 90+ days

23c. Name _____
Street Address _____
City/State/Zip _____
$ _____   _____
☐ 0 - 30 days
☐ 30 - 60 days
☐ 60 - 90 days
☐ 90+ days

23d. Name _____
Street Address _____
City/State/Zip _____
$ _____   _____
☐ 0 - 30 days
☐ 30 - 60 days
☐ 60 - 90 days
☐ 90+ days

23e. Name _____
Street Address _____
City/State/Zip _____
$ _____   _____
☐ 0 - 30 days
☐ 30 - 60 days
☐ 60 - 90 days
☐ 90+ days

23f. Name _____
Street Address _____
City/State/Zip _____
$ _____   _____
☐ 0 - 30 days
☐ 30 - 60 days
☐ 60 - 90 days
☐ 90+ days

23g. Name _____
Street Address _____
City/State/Zip _____
$ _____   _____
☐ 0 - 30 days
☐ 30 - 60 days
☐ 60 - 90 days
☐ 90+ days

23h. Name _____
Street Address _____
City/State/Zip _____
$ _____   _____
☐ 0 - 30 days
☐ 30 - 60 days
☐ 60 - 90 days
☐ 90+ days

23i. Name _____
Street Address _____
City/State/Zip _____
$ _____   _____
☐ 0 - 30 days
☐ 30 - 60 days
☐ 60 - 90 days
☐ 90+ days

23j. Name _____
Street Address _____
City/State/Zip _____
$ _____   _____
☐ 0 - 30 days
☐ 30 - 60 days
☐ 60 - 90 days
☐ 90+ days

23k. Name _____
Street Address _____
City/State/Zip _____
$ _____   _____
☐ 0 - 30 days
☐ 30 - 60 days
☐ 60 - 90 days
☐ 90+ days

23l. Name _____
Street Address _____
City/State/Zip _____
$ _____   _____
☐ 0 - 30 days
☐ 30 - 60 days
☐ 60 - 90 days
☐ 90+ days

☐ Check this box when all spaces in Sect. 8 are filled in.

Add "Amount Due" from lines 23a through 23l = 23m $ _____

Page 5 of 6

Section 9 begins on page 6 →
(Rev. 5-2001)

Collection Information Statement for Wage Earners and Self-Employed Individuals   Form 433-A

Name **MARY SMITH**   SSN **123-45-6789**

Section 9	*Total Income*			*Total Living Expenses*		
Monthly Income and Expense Analysis	Source	Gross Monthly		Expense Items [4]	Actual Monthly	
	24. Wages (Yourself)[1]	$	2042	35. Food, Clothing and Misc.[5]	$	635
	25. Wages (Spouse)[1]			36. Housing and Utilities[6]		490
If only one spouse has a tax liability, but both have income, list the total household income and expenses.	26. Interest - Dividends			37. Transportation[7]		100
	27. Net Income from Business[2]			38. Health Care		75
	28. Net Rental Income[3]			39. Taxes (Income and FICA)		385
	29. Pension/Social Security (Yourself)			40. Court ordered payments		
	30. Pension/Social Security (Spouse)			41. Child/dependent care		
	31. Child Support			42. Life insurance		
	32. Alimony			43. Other secured debt		
	33. Other			44. Other expenses		190
	34. Total Income	$	2042	45. Total Living Expenses	$	1875

[1] **Wages, salaries, pensions, and social security:** Enter your gross monthly wages and/or salaries. Do not deduct withholding or allotments you elect to take out of your pay, such as insurance payments, credit union deductions, car payments etc.
To calculate your gross monthly wages and/or salaries:
    If paid weekly - multiply weekly gross wages by 4.3. Example: $425.89 x 4.3 = $1,831.33
    If paid bi-weekly (every 2 weeks) - multiply bi-weekly gross wages by 2.17. Example: $972.45 x 2.17 = $2,110.22
    If paid semi-monthly (twice each month) - multiply semi-monthly gross wages by 2. Example: $856.23 x 2 = $1,712.46

[2] **Net Income from Business:** Enter your monthly net business income. This is the amount you earn after you pay ordinary and necessary monthly business expenses. This figure should relate to the yearly net profit from your Form 1040 Schedule C. If it is more or less than the previous year, you should attach an explanation. If your net business income is a loss, enter "0". Do not enter a negative number.

[3] **Net Rental Income:** Enter your monthly net rental income. This is the amount you earn after you pay ordinary and necessary monthly rental expenses. If your net rental income is a loss, enter "0". Do not enter a negative number.

[4] **Expenses not generally allowed:** We generally do not allow you to claim tuition for private schools, public or private college expenses, charitable contributions, voluntary retirement contributions, payments on unsecured debts such as credit card bills, cable television and other similar expenses. However, we may allow these expenses, if you can prove that they are necessary for the health and welfare of you or your family or for the production of income.

[5] **Food, Clothing and Misc.:** Total of clothing, food, housekeeping supplies and personal care products for one month.

[6] **Housing and Utilities:** For your principal residence: Total of rent or mortgage payment. Add the average monthly expenses for the following: property taxes, home owner's or renter's insurance, maintenance, dues, fees, and utilities. Utilities include gas, electricity, water, fuel, oil, other fuels, trash collection and telephone.

[7] **Transportation:** Total of lease or purchase payments, vehicle insurance, registration fees, normal maintenance, fuel, public transportation, parking and tolls for one month.

ATTACHMENTS REQUIRED: Please include:

- A copy of your last Form 1040 with all Schedules.

- Proof of all current expenses that you paid for the past 3 months, including utilities, rent, insurance, property taxes, etc.

- Proof of all non-business transportation expenses (e.g., car payments, lease payments, fuel, oil, insurance, parking, registration).

- Proof of payments for health care, including health insurance premiums, co-payments, and other out-of-pocket expenses, for the past 3 months.

- Copies of any court order requiring payment and proof of such payments (e.g., cancelled checks, money orders, earning statements showing such deductions) for the past 3 months.

☑ Check this box when all spaces in Sect. 9 are filled in and attachments provided.

☑ Check this box when all spaces in all sections are filled in and all attachments provided.

⚠ **CAUTION**   *Failure to complete all entry spaces may result in rejection or significant delay in the resolution of your account.*

Certification: Under penalties of perjury, I declare that to the best of my knowledge and belief this statement of assets, liabilities, and other information is true, correct and complete.

Your Signature	Spouse's Signature	Date

Page 6 of 6   (Rev. 5-2001)

How to prepare a
Collection Information Statement (Form 433-A)

Complete all blocks, except shaded areas. Write "N/A" *(Not Applicable)* in those blocks that do not apply to you. **If you don't complete the form, we won't be able to help** determine the best method for you to pay the amount due. The areas explained below are the ones we have found to be the most confusing to people completing the form.

Section 5

Items 11 – Checking Accounts, and 12 – Other Accounts
Enter all accounts, even if there is currently no balance. *Do Not* enter bank loans.

Item 15 – Available Credit
Enter only credit issued by a bank, credit union, or savings and loan *(MasterCard, Visa, overdraft protection, etc.)*.

Section 7

Items 18, 20, 21, and 22 – Automobiles, Trucks, Other Licensed Assets, Real Estate, Personal Assets, and Business Assets

Current Value – Indicate the amount you could sell the asset for today.

Date of Final Payment – Enter the date the loan or lease will be fully paid.

Item 20 – Real Estate
List all property that you own or are purchasing.

Item 21 – Personal Assets
List other assets you own such as artwork, jewelry, antiques, etc.

Section 9

If only one spouse has a tax liability, but both have income, list the total household income and expenses.

TOTAL INCOME

Items 24 and 25 – Wages
Enter your *gross* monthly wages and/or salaries. Do not deduct withholding or allotments you elect to take out of your pay such as insurance payments, credit union deductions, car payments, etc. List these expenses in Items 38 through 44.

Item 27 – Net Business Income
Enter your monthly *net* business income. The net is what you earn after you have paid your ordinary and necessary monthly business expenses.

TOTAL LIVING EXPENSES *(necessary)*

To be necessary, expenses must provide for the health and welfare of you and your family and/or provide for the production of income, and must be reasonable in amount. We may ask you to provide substantiation of certain expenses.

Item 35 – Food, Clothing, and Misc.
This category includes clothing and clothing services, food, housekeeping supplies, personal care products amount from the chart on the back of these instructions, based on your total monthly gross income and the size of your family. If you claim a higher amount, you must substantiate why a higher amount is necessary for each item included in a category.

Item 36 – Housing and Utilities
Enter the monthly rent or mortgage payment for your principal residence. Add the average monthly payment for the following expenses, if they are *not* included in your rent or mortgage payments: property taxes, homeowner's or renter's insurance, parking, necessary maintenance and repair, homeowner dues, condominium fees, and utilities. Utilities includes gas, electricity, water, fuel oil, coal, bottled gas, trash and garbage collection, wood and other fuels, septic cleaning and telephone.

Item 37 – Transportation
Enter your average monthly transportation expenses. Transportation expenses include: lease or purchase payments, insurance, registration fees, normal maintenance, fuel, public transportation, parking and tolls.

Item 43 – Other Secured Debt
Do not enter mortgage payment entered in Item 43, or lease or purchase payments entered in Item 44.

Item 44 – Other Expenses
Enter your average monthly payments for any other *necessary* expenses.

Certification
For joint income tax liabilities, both husband and wife should sign the statement.

IRS
Department of the Treasury
Internal Revenue Service

www.irs.gov

Publication 1854 (Rev. 1-2003)
Catalog Number 21563Q

Total Monthly National Standards
(Except Alaska and Hawaii*)
Effective 01/01/03

TOTAL GROSS MONTHLY INCOME	NUMBER OF PERSONS				
	One	Two	Three	Four	Over Four
Less than $830	344	493	675	838	+125
$831 to $1,249	393	554	679	847	+135
$1,250 to $1,669	458	642	741	877	+145
$1,670 to $2,499	514	716	834	902	+155
$2,500 to $3,329	598	782	895	969	+165
$3,330 to $4,169	670	879	982	1,175	+175
$4,170 to $5,829	701	940	1,020	1,249	+185
$5,830 and over	1,016	1,290	1,414	1,497	+195

Total Monthly Standards for Alaska
Effective 01/01/03

TOTAL GROSS MONTHLY INCOME	NUMBER OF PERSONS				
	One	Two	Three	Four	Over Four
Less than $830	455	651	891	1,106	+165
$831 to $1,249	519	731	895	1,118	+178
$1,250 to $1,669	602	848	978	1,157	+191
$1,670 to $2,499	678	944	1,101	1,190	+205
$2,500 to $3,329	790	1,033	1,181	1,279	+218
$3,330 to $4,169	885	1,161	1,297	1,551	+231
$4,170 to $5,829	925	1,242	1,346	1,649	+244
$5,830 and over	1,342	1,702	1,867	1,976	+257

Total Monthly Standards for Hawaii
Effective 01/01/03

TOTAL GROSS MONTHLY INCOME	NUMBER OF PERSONS				
	One	Two	Three	Four	Over Four
Less than $830	358	512	702	872	+130
$831 to $1,249	409	575	706	881	+140
$1,250 to $1,669	474	667	771	912	+151
$1,670 to $2,499	534	745	867	939	+161
$2,500 to $3,329	622	813	930	1,008	+172
$3,330 to $4,169	697	914	1,021	1,223	+182
$4,170 to $5,829	729	977	1,061	1,299	+192
$5,830 and over	1,056	1,341	1,469	1,557	+203

Expenses include: Housekeeping supplies
Clothing and clothing services
Personal care products and services
Food
Miscellaneous

To find the amount of expenses we can allow you, please read down the Total Gross Monthly Income column until you find your income, then read across to the column that matches the number of persons in your family.

When you have more than four persons in your family, you need to multiply the amount of additional persons over four by the dollar amount in the "Over Four" column; then add the answer to the dollar amount in the "Four" column. For example: when your total monthly income is between $830 and $1,249 and you have six persons in your family, you would multiply $135 by the two members of your family over four to get $270. You then would add this $270 to the $847 allowed to a family of four in your income bracket. As a result, your allowed expenses would equal $1,117 ($270+$847).

* Residents of either Alaska or Hawaii should use the table that outlines the expenses allowed for their state.

FORM 15.3
COLLECTION INFORMATION STATEMENT FOR BUSINESSES

IRS   **Collection Information Statement for Businesses**

Department of the Treasury
Internal Revenue Service

www.irs.gov

Form 433-B (Rev. 5-2001)
Catalog Number 16649P

Complete all entry spaces with the most current data available
Important! Write "N/A" (not applicable) in spaces that do not apply. We may require additional information
to support "N/A" entries.
Failure to complete all entry spaces may result in rejection or significant delay in the resolution of your account.

Section 1		

Business Information	1a. Business Name **BECSAL INDUSTRIES INC.**
	 Business Street Address **1000 LONGVIEW RD.**
	
	 City **NEWARK** State **NJ** Zip **07000**
	 County **ESSEX**
	 1b. Business Telephone (**201**) **555-0000**
	 2a. Employer Identification No. (EIN) **22-7654321**
	 2b. Type of Entity (Check appropriate box below)
	 ☐ Partnership ☑ Corporation ☐ Other ____
	 2c. Type of Business **MFG-GIFTWARE**
		3a. Contact Name **ADAM BLANK**
		 3b. Contact's Business Telephone (**201**) **555-0000**
		    Extension ____ **111**
		    Best Time To Call **9** am **5** pm (Enter Hour)
		 3c. Contact's Home Telephone (**201**) **888-0000**
		    Best Time To Call **7** am ____ pm (Enter Hour)
		 3d. Contact's Other Telephone (____) ____
		    Telephone Type (i.e. fax, cellular, pager)
		 3e. Contact's E-mail Address **ABLANK@BECSAL.COM**

☑ Check this box when all spaces in Sect. 1 are filled in.

Section 2 — Business Personnel and Contacts

4. PERSON RESPONSIBLE FOR DEPOSITING PAYROLL TAXES

4a. Full Name **ADAM BLANK** Title **PRESIDENT**   Social Security Number **123 45 6789**
Home Street Address **18 SEAVIEW TERRACE**   Home Telephone (**201**) **888-0000**
City **RUMSON** State **NJ** Zip **07000**   Ownership Percentage & Shares or Interest **100%**

5. PARTNERS, OFFICERS, MAJOR SHAREHOLDERS, ETC.

5a. Full Name **ADAM BLANK** Title **PRESIDENT**   Social Security Number **123 45 6789**
Home Street Address **18 SEAVIEW TERRACE**   Home Telephone (**201**) **888-0000**
City **RUMSON** State **NJ** Zip **07000**   Ownership Percentage & Shares or Interest **100%**

5b. Full Name ____ Title ____   Social Security Number ____
Home Street Address ____   Home Telephone (____) ____
City ____ State ____ Zip ____   Ownership Percentage & Shares or Interest ____

5c. Full Name ____ Title ____   Social Security Number ____
Home Street Address ____   Home Telephone (____) ____
City ____ State ____ Zip ____   Ownership Percentage & Shares or Interest ____

5d. Full Name ____ Title ____   Social Security Number ____
Home Street Address ____   Home Telephone (____) ____
City ____ State ____ Zip ____   Ownership Percentage & Shares or Interest ____

☑ Check this box when all spaces in Sect. 2 are filled in.

Section 3 — Accounts/Notes Receivable

See page 6 for additional space, if needed.

6. ACCOUNTS/NOTES RECEIVABLE. List all contracts separately, including contracts awarded, but not started.

Description	Amount Due	Date Due	Age of Account
6a. Name **[SEE ATTACHED]** Street Address ____ City/State/Zip ____	$ **38500**	**VARIOUS**	☐ 0 - 30 days ☑ 30 - 60 days ☐ 60 - 90 days ☐ 90+ days
6b. Name **[SEE ATTACHED--UNCOLLECTABLE]** Street Address ____ City/State/Zip ____	$ **23500**	**VARIOUS**	☐ 0 - 30 days ☐ 30 - 60 days ☐ 60 - 90 days ☑ 90+ days

6a + 6b = 6c   6c $ **62000**

Amount from Page 6   6p + ____

6q. Total Accounts/ Notes Receivable   6c + 6p = 6q   = $ **62000**

☑ Check this box when all spaces in Sect. 3 are filled in.

Section 4 begins on page 2 →
(Rev. 5-2001)

Collection Information Statement for Businesses   Form 433-B

Business Name BECSAL INDSUSTRIES INC.   EIN _____ 22-7654321 _____

Section 4

Other Financial Information

7. **OTHER FINANCIAL INFORMATION.** Respond to the following business financial questions.

7a. Does this business have other business relationships (e.g. subsidiary or parent, corporation, partnership, etc.)? .... ☑ No ☐ Yes
If yes, list related EIN _____ Additional EIN _____

7b. Does anyone (e.g. officer, stockholder, partner or employees) have an outstanding loan borrowed from the business? .... ☑ No ☐ Yes
If yes, amount of loan $ _____ Date of loan _____ Current balance $ _____

7c. Are there any judgments or liens against your business? .... ☑ No ☐ Yes
If yes, who is the creditor? _____ Date creditor obtained judgment/lien _____ Amount of debt $ _____

7d. Is your business a party in a lawsuit? .... ☑ No ☐ Yes
If yes, amount of suit $ _____ Possible completion date _____ Subject matter of suit _____

7e. Has your business ever filed bankruptcy? .... ☑ No ☐ Yes
If yes, date filed _____ Date discharged _____ Petition No _____

7f. In the past 10 years have you transferred any assets from your business name for less than their actual value? .... ☑ No ☐ Yes
If yes, what asset? _____ Value of asset at time of transfer $ _____
When was it transferred? _____ To whom or where was it transferred? _____

7g. Do you anticipate any increase in business income (e.g. contracts bid but not yet awarded)? .... ☑ No ☐ Yes
If yes, why will the income increase? _____ (Attach sheet if you need additional space.)
How much will it increase? _____ When will the business income increase? _____

7h. Is your business a beneficiary of a trust, an estate or a life insurance policy? .... ☑ No ☐ Yes
If yes, name of the trust, estate or policy? _____ Anticipated amount to be received? _____
When will the amount be received? _____

☑ Check this box when all spaces in Sect. 4 are filled in

Section 5

Business Assets

☒ **Current Value:** Indicate the amount you could sell the asset for today.

8. **PURCHASED AUTOMOBILES, TRUCKS AND OTHER LICENSED ASSETS.** Include boats, RV's, motorcycles, trailers, etc.
(If you need additional space, attach a separate sheet)

Description (Year, Make, Model, Mileage)	☒ Current Value	Loan Balance	Name of Lender	Purchase Date	Amount of Monthly Payment
8a. Year 1998					
Make/Model FORD EXPLORER					
Mileage 52000	$ 14000	$ 6000	UNITED NAT'L BK	9/98	$ 475
8b. Year					
Make/Model					
Mileage	$	$			$
8c. Year					
Make/Model					
Mileage	$	$			$

9. **LEASED AUTOMOBILES, TRUCKS AND OTHER LICENSED ASSETS.** Include boats, RV's, motorcycles, trailers, etc.
(If you need additional space, attach a separate sheet.)

Description (Year, Make, Model)	Lease Balance	Name of Lessor	Lease Date	Amount of Monthly Payment
9a. Year				
Make/Model	$			$
9b. Year				
Make/Model	$			$

ATTACHMENTS REQUIRED: Please include your current statement from lender with monthly car payment amount and current balance of the loan for each vehicle purchased or leased.

Section 5 continued on page 3 →
(Rev. 5-2001)

Collection Information Statement for Businesses   Form 433-B

Business Name BECSAL INSDUSTRIES INC.   EIN   22-7654321

Section 5 continued	10. REAL ESTATE. List all real estate owned by the business. (If you need additional space, attach a separate sheet.)							
	Street Address, City, State, Zip, and County	Date Purchased	Purchase Price	¤Current Value	Loan Balance	Name of Lender or Lien Holder	Amount of Monthly Payment	*Date of Final Payment
¤ Current Value: Indicate the amount you could sell the asset for today.	10a. _____ _____ _____		$	$	$		$	
*Date of Final Payment: Enter the date the loan or lease will be fully paid.	10b. _____ _____ _____		$	$	$		$	

ATTACHMENTS REQUIRED: Please include your current statement from lender with monthly payment amount and current balance for each piece of real estate owned.

☑ Check this box if you are attaching a depreciation schedule for machinery/ equipment in lieu of completing line 11.	11. BUSINESS ASSETS. List all business assets and encumbrances below. Include Uniform Commercial Code (UCC) filings. (If you need additional space, attach a separate sheet.) Note: If attaching a depreciation schedule, the attachment must include all of the information requested below.						
	Description	¤Current Value	Loan Balance	Name of Lender		Amount of Monthly Payment	*Date of Final Payment
	11a. Machinery	$ 26000	$ 16000	UNITED NAT BANK		$ 650	6/2005
	Equipment						
	Merchandise	45000	0	UNITED NAT BANK		UCC FILING	
	Other Assets: (List below)						
	11b. _____	$	$			$	
	11c. _____						

☑ Check this box when all spaces in Sect. 5 are filled in and attachments provided.

ATTACHMENTS REQUIRED: Please include your current statement from lender with monthly payment amount and current loan balance for assets listed which have an encumbrance.

Section 6	12. INVESTMENTS. List all investment assets below. Include stocks, bonds, mutual funds, stock options and certificates of deposits.				
Investment, Banking and Cash Information	Name of Company	Number of Shares / Units	¤Current Value	Loan Amount	Used as collateral on loan?
	12a. _____		$	$	☐ No ☐ Yes
	12b. _____				☐ No ☐ Yes
	12c. Total Investments	$			

Section 6 continued on page 4 →
(Rev 5-2001)

Collection Information Statement for Businesses   Form 433-B

Business Name BECSAL INSDUSTRIES INC.   EIN   22-7654321

Section 6
continued

Complete all
entry spaces
with the most
current *data*
available.

13. BANK ACCOUNTS. List all checking and savings accounts (If you need additional space, attach a separate sheet.)

	Type of Account	Full Name of Bank, Savings & Loan, Credit Union or Financial Institution	Bank Routing No.	Bank Account No.	Current Account Balance
13a.	Checking	Name UNITED NATIONAL BANK	121000000	123456	$ 4367
		Street Address 25 CEDAR LANE			
		City/State/Zip TEANECK, NJ 07000			
13b.	Checking	Name			$
		Street Address			
		City/State/Zip			
13c.	Savings	Name			$
		Street Address			
		City/State/Zip		**13d. Total Bank Account Balances**	$

ATTACHMENTS REQUIRED: Please include your current bank statements (checking and savings) for the past three months for all accounts.

14. OTHER ACCOUNTS. List all accounts including brokerage accounts, money market, additional checking and savings accounts not listed on line #13 and any other accounts not listed in this section.

	Type of Account	Full Name of Bank, Savings & Loan, Credit Union or Financial Institution	Bank Routing No.	Bank Account No.	Current Account Balance
14a.		Name			$
		Street Address			
		City/State/Zip			
14b.		Name			$
		Street Address			
		City/State/Zip		**14c. Total Other Account Balances**	$

ATTACHMENTS REQUIRED: Please include your current bank statements (checking, savings, money market, and brokerage accounts) for the past three months for all accounts.

15. CASH ON HAND. Include any money that you have that is not in the bank.

      15a. Total Cash on Hand $ 250

16. AVAILABLE CREDIT. List all lines of credit, including credit cards.

	Full Name of Credit Institution	Credit Limit	Amount Owed	Available Credit
16a.	Name			$
	Street Address			
	City/State/Zip			
16b.	Name			$
	Street Address			
	City/State/Zip		**16c. Total Credit Available**	$

☑ Check this box when all spaces in Sect. 6 are filled in and attachments provided.

Page 4 of 6   Section 7 begins on page 5 →
(Rev. 5-2001)

¶ 15.05 INFORMAL METHODS OF SECURING PAYMENT

Collection has authority not only to file notices of lien, but also to forbear in taking such action, including enforced collection action. Indeed, the Service's policy is not to file a notice of lien until after the taxpayer has been contacted and given an opportunity to pay.[88] The Service recognizes that filing a notice of lien may adversely affect the taxpayer's ability to pay,[89] for example, where a taxpayer has assets to secure payment, but insufficient funds to make immediate payment. If the taxpayer can pledge collateral to secure ultimate payment of the tax, he may avoid the filing of liens.[90] The following can be used as collateral: (1) security in the form of a bond from an authorized surety (or one found to be satisfactory); (2) government bonds or notes; and (3) "other security acceptable" in the discretion of the district.[91] (Form 15.4 illustrates a sample bond.) Other acceptable forms of collateral include (1) corporate stocks and bonds; (2) federal, state, and local government securities; and (3) letters of credit.[92] Another type of security that may be acceptable is a mortgage on real or personal property for a term during which payment of the tax is deferred. The Service acknowledges that this form of security may be preferable to the filing of a notice of lien in order to permit the taxpayer to continue in business without the burden of public notice of a lien on the property.[93] However, a mortgage is not satisfactory unless the taxpayer's equity in the property is at least equal to the outstanding tax liability plus additions that would accrue during the deferred payment period. Rather than a bond or mortgage, an escrow arrangement may also serve as a collateral device suitable to protect the government's interest and to allow the taxpayer to continue in business.

These collateral arrangements are governed by so-called collateral agreements. There are no forms for these agreements. (Forms 15.5 and 15.6 illustrate this type of agreement.) They should be prepared in the first instance by

---

[88] IRM 1.2.1, Policies of the IRS P-5-47 (approved October 9, 1996).

[89] IRM 1.2.1, Policies of the IRS P-5-47 (approved October 9, 1996). Courts do not treat an invalid assessment the same way. For a related discussion of the effect on collection of an invalid assessment, see ¶ 10.03[2][c].

[90] This procedure is discretionary with the Service. Collection is not required to accept a collateral agreement and pledge of security even where the security seems satisfactory. Instead, it can demand full payment. See Kadah v. United States, 82-2 USTC ¶ 9473 (NDNY 1982).

[91] Reg. §§ 301.7101-1(b)(1), 301.7101-1(b)(2); IRM 5.6.1.2.1, Bonds (July 15, 1998). In practice, there is no special bond form used by the Collection Division.

[92] IRM 5.6.1.1, Collateral Agreements (July 15, 1998); IRM 5.6.1.2, Types of Acceptable Securities; IRM 5.6.1.2.4, Escrow Arrangements; IRM 5.6.1.2.5, Letter of Credit. See Adolph Coors Co. v. United States, 62 TC 300 (1974) (use of letter of credit). But see Kadah v. United States, 82-2 USTC ¶ 9473 (NDNY 1982) (letter of credit to secure payment of trust fund penalty assessment rejected).

[93] IRM 5.6.1.2.3, Mortgages (July 15, 1998).

the taxpayer's representative and in any event must be approved on behalf of the district director by the Special Procedures Staff and the Counsel. A collateral agreement should contain the following information:

1. Name, identification number, and address of the taxpayer;
2. Name and location of the district director;
3. Taxpayer's business location;
4. Type of tax;
5. Period and balance of the taxpayer's account;
6. Terms of the agreement; and
7. Other pertinent information, such as a recital of the relevant background facts.

FORM 15.4
BOND

Guaranty given by [*indemnity company*], hereinafter called the Guarantor, to the Internal Revenue Service ("the Service"), [*address*], to induce the Service to forbear in the collection of a certain tax liability from [*taxpayer*].

WHEREAS, ... (the "Taxpayer") is indebted to the United States in the amount of $........................... on account of assessed federal employment taxes and interest, together with statutory additions as provided by law and identified as follows:

Dates of assessment	Assessed amounts	Unpaid assessed balances
0/00/00	$...........................	$...........................

WHEREAS, the Taxpayer wishes to defer payment of the said tax pending judicial review of the assessment, and the Service has required the Taxpayer to furnish this bond to forbear in collection of the tax:

In consideration of the foregoing, the Guarantor hereby guarantees the full and prompt payment to the Service of the amount of $..........................., representing the tax liability assessed against [*taxpayer*], on [*date*], on the following terms:

1. If the amount then due or claimed to be due from [*taxpayer*] is less than the amount set forth above, then the Guarantor shall pay such lesser amount, but in no event shall the Guarantor be liable for more than the specific amount set forth above, without the consent of the Guarantor.

2. The term of this Bond shall expire on [*date*], unless it is extended with the consent of the Guarantor.

3. If there is a settlement between the Service and the taxpayer or the guaranty herein provided for is otherwise no longer required, then the Service shall surrender this Guaranty to the Guarantor, along with a letter requesting its cancellation.

[*INDEMNITY COMPANY*]

By: ....

....

Approved and accepted for and on behalf of the United States this ....
day of ...., 20.......

INTERNAL REVENUE SERVICE

FORM 15.5
COLLATERAL AGREEMENT

THIS AGREEMENT made this .... day of ...., 20......., be-tween XYZ Corporation ("XYZ") and John Doe ("Doe"), both of Main Street, New York (hereinafter referred to as "taxpayers"), and the Internal Revenue Service, New York, New York (hereinafter referred to as "the Service").

WHEREAS, XYZ is indebted to the United States of America for the assessed taxes plus statutory additions as provided by law listed in the schedule attached and made part hereof (hereinafter referred to as "the tax liability"). Doe is also claimed by the Service to be liable to the United States of America for the tax liability; however, XYZ has agreed to indemnify Doe in the event he is held liable for all or any portion of the tax liability;

WHEREAS, XYZ has paid the tax due with respect to one employee for each quarter out of which the tax liability of XYZ arises; and has filed claims for refund of the tax payments made with the Service;

WHEREAS, XYZ has represented that it will commence an action for the refund of the taxes it has paid within a reasonable period of time after rejection of the claims for refund or upon the expiration of six months, whichever occurs first, and alleges this action will present to a court for final determination the correct amount, if any, of the tax liability; and

WHEREAS, XYZ and Doe desire to obtain a stay of collection and the forbear-ance of the filing of Notices of Federal Tax Liens, pending a court decision as to the correct amount, if any, of the tax liability.

NOW, THEREFORE, the parties mutually agree as follows:

(1) In consideration for such forbearance by the Service, XYZ will deliver to the Service, before or concurrent with the execution of this Agreement, a letter of credit in the sum of $.............. (amount in words) plus interest at the rate of ....% per annum to .... and at the rate of ....% per annum to .... drawn on the A Bank.

(2) If a final decision of the tax liability, if any, has not been made thirty days prior to the termination of the said letter of credit, then XYZ must obtain an extension of the term of the letter of credit or obtain a new letter of credit having the same terms and conditions as the original letter of credit, except that said terms and conditions shall provide that in addition to the aforesaid interest rates stated in paragraph 1, the rate of interest from .... shall be that as may be established by the Secretary of the Treasury or his delegate under § 6621(b) of the Internal Revenue Code of 1986, and further, the term of the letter of credit shall be extended to a period agreed upon by the Service, provided that the Service may refuse in its discretion, which shall be reasonably exercised, to accept an extension of the letter of credit or a new letter of credit if advised in writing by the United States Attorney for the Southern District of New York that XYZ has failed to prosecute its suit for refund with all deliberate speed.

(3) If XYZ (a) fails to obtain an extended term on the original letter of credit, or (b) fails to obtain a new letter of credit, or (c) if the Service has made a determination that XYZ has failed to prosecute its suit for refund with all deliberate speed, as described in paragraph 2, then the Service may without further notice to

XYZ and Doe make demand for payment of the full amount of the tax liability, plus interest which is due at that time, and present the letter of credit to the A Bank for collection.

(4) This Agreement shall terminate at such time as (a) the District Court of the United States has entered a final judgment; or (b) on the entry of a judgment by a Circuit Court of Appeals, should an appeal to that Court be taken, against either or both XYZ and Doe on the various issues involved; or (c) if a final settlement is entered into between XYZ, Doe and the Service and the United States of America.

(5) If there has been a final judgment either by a United States District Court or a Circuit Court of Appeals in favor of the United States of America against either or both XYZ and Doe on the various issues involved, the Service may present the letter of credit, accompanied by its affidavit attesting to the entry of such a judgment to the A Bank for collection pursuant to the terms of said letter of credit.

(6) If there has been a final judgment either by a United States District Court or a Circuit Court of Appeals in favor of XYZ and Doe on the various issues involved, or if a final settlement is entered into between XYZ, Doe and the Service and the United States of America, and any payments required under such settlement have been made, then the Service shall surrender the letter to the A Bank along with a letter requesting cancellation of the letter of credit and shall mail a copy of this letter of request to XYZ.

The statute of limitations on the collection of the tax liability, plus interest thereon, is suspended during the pendency of this Agreement.

XYZ CORPORATION

By ....

INTERNAL REVENUE SERVICE

By ....

FORM 15.6
COLLATERAL AGREEMENT

THIS AGREEMENT, made this .... day of ...., 20......., between the XYZ CORPORATION of Main Street, Anytown, (hereinafter referred to as "Taxpayer") and the INTERNAL REVENUE SERVICE for the District of .... (hereinafter referred to as "the Service").

WHEREAS, the Taxpayer filed a petition in the United States Tax Court for the purpose of obtaining a redetermination of proposed deficiencies for its taxable years ... ., ..., and .... in the amount of $............., $.......... ... and $............., respectively; and

WHEREAS the United States Tax Court has determined deficiencies to be due from the Taxpayer for the taxable years ...., ..., and .... in the amount of $............., $............., and $..............., respectively, and has determined that the principal amount of tax and interest as of is $.............; and

WHEREAS, the Taxpayer has filed a notice of appeal in the United States Tax Court and intends to prosecute an appeal to the Circuit Court of Appeals with respect to the determination of the Tax Court; and

WHEREAS, on the date the amount of the deficiency as determined by the United States Tax Court is assessed a lien will arise on all property and rights to property of the Taxpayer; and

WHEREAS, the Taxpayer is desirous of satisfying any liability as finally determined by a judgment of a court of competent jurisdiction and of providing the Service with security that the liability, if any, will be paid pending a final judgment in the case; and

WHEREAS, the Service has authority to cause a notice of lien to be filed or to forbear in the filing of a notice of lien; and

WHEREAS, the land and buildings of the Taxpayer have been appraised at a fair market value $.............; and

WHEREAS, the Taxpayer operates a manufacturing facility at Main Street, Anytown, at which are employed approximately 000 employees; and

WHEREAS, the land and buildings owned by the Taxpayer are already encumbered by an Open-End First Mortgage in favor of the A Bank (hereinafter the "Bank");

NOW, THEREFORE, in consideration of the Service's forbearance in the filing of a notice of tax lien as a matter of public record and agreement not to take enforced collection action to secure payment of the liability which is the subject of the Taxpayer's appeal, the Service and the Taxpayer do hereby stipulate and agree as follows:

1. That the Taxpayer agrees to execute a second mortgage (hereinafter the "Second Mortgage") on the real estate and buildings at Main Street, Anytown, as more particularly described in the attached exhibit, in favor of the Service.

2. That Taxpayer will not cause the property to be encumbered in any amount in any way, except that Taxpayer may borrow from the Bank against the Open-End First Mortgage in an amount not to exceed $.............

3. That Taxpayer will make and continue to make payments on any indebtedness secured by the Open-End Mortgage of the Bank.

4. That the Service may in its discretion request proof of payment of any amounts due or to become due on the Open-End First Mortgage Taxpayer has with the Bank.

5. That Taxpayer will prosecute his appeal to the Circuit Court of Appeals with all due diligence.

6. That Taxpayer will pay on notice and demand any deficiency as finally determined by a court of competent jurisdiction.

7. That the Service on satisfaction of the deficiency or liability will issue an appropriate release of the Second Mortgage.

8. That if the deficiency or liability is not satisfied on notice and demand, the Service may foreclose on the Second Mortgage or take such other collection action as the Service in its discretion considers proper.

9. That this Agreement shall terminate two years from the date hereof or, if earlier, the date of a final decision in the Taxpayer's appeal, but if a final decision with respect to the deficiency as determined by the United States Tax Court has not been rendered at the end of the two-year period, then the Agreement may be extended by the parties as they may consent.

XYZ CORPORATION

By ....

INTERNAL REVENUE SERVICE

By ....

¶ 15.06 INSTALLMENT PAYMENT AGREEMENTS

An installment agreement is an agreement between the taxpayer and Collection whereby the taxpayer agrees to pay the taxpayer's tax liability over time in installments, by the end of the term of which the taxpayer will have paid the full amount of the assessed liability, as well as any penalty and interest that has accrued. Installment agreements differ from compromises; they do not reduce the taxpayer's liability. In addition, when a taxpayer enters into an installment agreement, a tax lien may be filed encumbering the taxpayer's property; the taxpayer will be required to extend the statute of limitations on assessment; the statute of limitations will be suspended during any appeal of a rejection or termination of the agreement; and the taxpayer will waive any rights to refunds.[94] An installment agreement nevertheless has the obvious benefit of giving the taxpayer additional time to pay the full liability, rather than requiring the taxpayer to make immediate payment, and the less obvious benefit of a reduced delinquent payment penalty.[95]

[1] Statutory Provisions

The Service "is authorized" to enter into (1) "written agreements with any taxpayer which allows the taxpayer to satisfy liability for payment of any tax in installments" (2) if the Service "determines that such agreement will facilitate collection of such liability."[96] There are two types of installment agreements: mandatory and discretionary. In the case of an individual who has a liability for income tax, Collection is required to ("shall") enter into an installment payment agreement if certain conditions are met.[97] An installment agreement is mandatory (or guaranteed) if, as of the date the individual offers to enter into the agreement:[98] (a) the amount of tax liability, excluding interest, penalties, additions to the tax, and additional amounts, does not exceed $10,000; (b) during any of the prior five years, the taxpayer has not failed to file a return, failed to pay any tax required to be shown on the return, or entered into an installment payment agreement; (c) the Service has decided that the taxpayer is financially unable to pay the delinquent liability in full when due, and the taxpayer submits the information that Collection requires in order to make the determination of inability to pay; (d) the agreement requires full payment of the liability within three years; and (e) the taxpayer agrees to comply with the provisions of the Code for the term of the agreement Similarly, if the taxpayer will pay the delinquent tax within a short period of time (120 days), the taxpayer will be permitted to pay the delinquent tax in installments.[99]

Other installment agreements are discretionary with Collection. According to the general authority for entering into installment agreements, Collection

---

[94] The Manual states: "Installment Agreements are arrangements whereby the Internal Revenue Service allows taxpayers to pay liabilities over time. The only agreements that may be granted are those that provide for full payment of the accounts that are part of the agreements. During the course of agreements, penalty and interest continue to accrue. No levies may be served during installment agreements." IRM 5.14.1.1 Securing Installment Agreements–Overview (Sept. 30, 2004).

[95] See IRC § 6651(h) limiting the failure to pay penalty for individual taxpayers who file returns to 0.25 percent (rather than 0.50 percent) for each month that an installment agreement is in effect for the payment of the tax.

[96] IRC § 6159(a).

[97] IRC § 6159(c).

[98] IRC §§ 6159(c)(1)–6159(c)(5).

[99] See IRM 5.14.1.2 Installment Agreements and Taxpayer Rights (Sept. 30, 2004).

"allows" the taxpayer ("any taxpayer") to satisfy the liability for "any tax" in installments. Individuals who fail the mandatory agreement requirements, taxpayers who are not individuals, and taxpayers who do not have an income tax liability must depend on the Service's administrative judgment and discretion about whether Collection will allow an installment agreement. In the typical situation, a delinquent taxpayer has responded to a contact, a revenue officer has requested full payment of the delinquent tax liability, the taxpayer has responded that full payment cannot be made, and the revenue officer has asked the taxpayer to make some payment.[100] As a matter of administrative practice, the revenue officer must consider an installment payment agreement, and will request that the taxpayer prepare a Collection Information Statement, Form 433-D.[101] On reviewing the taxpayer's financial statement, the revenue officer will reach conclusions about ultimate collection of the liability, and may decide that the taxpayer will be able to pay the amount of the delinquent tax over time or in installments.[102] If a proposed agreement is accepted for processing, but Collection personnel believe that the proposal does not contain sufficient information to evaluate the proposal, Collection can request further information from the taxpayer. However, if the taxpayer does not supply the information within a reasonable period of time, collection can reject the proposed installment payment agreement.[103]

If the revenue officer concludes that an installment agreement is appropriate, and an agreement is entered into with a taxpayer, the agreement remains in effect for its full term subject to certain exceptions. One set of exceptions has to do with the taxpayer's misconduct. The agreement may be terminated for one of the following reasons: (1) the taxpayer provided inaccurate or incomplete information before the date of the agreement or (2) the Service determines that collection is in jeopardy.[104] The second set of exceptions applies because of a change in the taxpayer's financial condition. Collection can also alter, modify, or terminate the installment payment agreement if Collection de-

---

[100] See IRM 5.14.1.2 Installment Agreements and Taxpayer Rights (Sept. 30, 2004).

[101] See IRM 5.14.1.4 Interest-Based Interviews (Sept. 30, 2004). Financial Statements are not required for streamlined, guaranteed, or in certain business agreements where trust fund liabilities have been incurred and the business is still in operation. Id.

[102] To obtain an installment agreement, however, a taxpayer will have to pay a user fee of $43. If the taxpayer fails to meet any of the obligations of the installment agreement, the Service wishes to charge a fee of $24 for processing the restructuring or reinstating of the agreement.

[103] On reviewing the taxpayer's financial statement, the revenue officer may also decide that the taxpayer will be able to pay the amount of the delinquent tax over time or in installments. Treas. Reg. § 301.6331-4(b)(1) (Other actions by Collection while levy action is prohibited).

[104] IRC §§ 6159(b)(2)(A) and 6159(b)(2)(B).

cides that the taxpayer's financial condition has significantly changed[105] (e.g., if the taxpayer's financial condition has deteriorated).[106] The third set of exceptions arises out of the taxpayer's noncompliance with the terms of the installment agreement. Collection may alter, amend, or terminate an installment agreement if the taxpayer has (1) failed to timely pay an installment; (2) failed to remain current in other tax obligations; or (3) failed to supply updated financial information as requested.[107] However, Collection is prohibited from taking any action unless it provides the taxpayer with notice of the intended action at least thirty days before the date of the action, and the notice explains why Collection intends to take the action.[108]

An installment agreement has implications for collection action and the statute of limitations on collection. Section 6331(k) codifies and makes mandatory the Service's previous practice of suspending collection during consideration of a taxpayer's offer to compromise and extends the practice to installment payment agreements.[109] Collection is prohibited from levying on a taxpayer's property and rights to property to collect an unpaid tax during the following periods of time: (1) during the period that the taxpayer's offer for an installment agreement for payment of the unpaid liability is pending with Collection; (2) if the offer is rejected, during the thirty-day period thereafter, and if an appeal is filed within the thirty-period, during the time the appeal is pending; (3) during the period that the installment agreement is in effect; and (4) if the agreement is terminated, for thirty days after the termination of the agreement, and if the taxpayer files an appeal within the thirty-day period, for the period that the appeal is pending.[110]

For purposes of the prohibition of levy action during these periods, "pending" is the key term. A proposed installment payment agreement becomes pending when it is accepted for processing, and remains pending until

---

[105] IRC §§ 6159(b)(3). The Service is aware that the statutory bases for terminating an installment payment agreement are exclusive, and has so advised the field organization. ILM 199922051 (Mar. 26, 1999) (although the Service may impose a condition in an agreement requiring a taxpayer to pay estimated tax and to make federal tax deposits, the taxpayer's failure to comply is not a statutory ground for termination); ILM 199920005 (Feb. 5, 1999) (taxpayers' filing of a Chapter 13 petition in bankruptcy court only suspends, but does not terminate, an installment agreement); ILM 199919008 (Jan. 7, 1999) (failure to extend the statute of limitations on collection is not a statutory ground for terminating an installment agreement; amounts seized were required to be returned).

[106] Reg. § 301.6159-1(c)(3).

[107] IRC § 6159(b)(4).

[108] IRC § 6159(b)(5).

[109] Subject to certain exceptions, Collection did not levy on the taxpayer's property to collect an unpaid tax while offers to enter into installment agreements to pay delinquent taxes were pending.

[110] IRC §§ 6331(k)(2)(A)–6331(k)(2)(D); Reg. §301.6331-4(c) (Statute of limitations).

the Service accepts the proposal, notifies the taxpayer that the proposal has been rejected, or the taxpayer withdraws the proposal.[111] Just when a proposed installment payment agreement is accepted for processing (and therefore is pending, thereby suspending collection action) is left curiously vague. The only clear statement is that Collection is prohibited from accepting a proposed installment agreement for processing if the Service has already sent the case to the Tax Division of the Justice Department for prosecution or defense.[112] A proposed installment agreement, it seems, is accepted for processing when it is received before a Tax Division referral, contains sufficient information to permit the Service to decide whether the proposal is acceptable, and the Service has not returned the offer.

Even if levy is prohibited during the pendency of a proposed or accepted installment agreement, the Service may still take one of the following actions: (1) credit an overpayment against the liability as permitted by the Service's authority to credit an overpayment (Section 6402); (2) file or refile a notice of federal tax lien; and (3) take collection action against a person who is not named in the installment agreement, but who is liable for the tax listed in the installment agreement.[113] When an installment payment agreement is pending, the Service is prohibited from collecting the delinquent tax; consequently, the Service will not refer the case to the Tax Division to institute a collection action.[114] However, the Service may authorize the Tax Division to file a counterclaim or third-party complaint in a refund action where a tax listed in the proposed installment agreement can be disputed, and this counterclaim or third-party complaint can name a person without regard to whether the person is named in the proposal. If the government obtains a judgment against the person, and the case is referred back to the Service for collection, the Service will continue to collect under the terms of the installment payment agreement.

Generally, the term of an installment payment agreement is limited to the ten-year statute of limitations on collection because the projected date of full payment of the tax liability is within the ten-year collection period.[115] Taxpay-

---

[111] Reg. § 301.6331-4(a)(2) (When a proposed installment agreement becomes pending). Note that Section 6331(i)(6) states that a proceeding is pending "beginning on the date [the] proceeding commences and ending on the date that a final order or judgment [in the divisible tax refund suit] from which an appeal may be taken is entered in such proceeding."

[112] Reg. § 301.6331-4(a)(2) (When a proposed installment agreement becomes pending).

[113] Reg. § 301.6331-4(b)(1) (Other actions by Collection while levy action is prohibited).

[114] Reg. § 301.6331-4(b)(2) (Proceedings in court). The regulations suggest that a tax can be disputed in a quiet title action under 28 USC § 2410, but a quiet title action may not be used for this purpose.

[115] IRC § 6502(a). Section 6502(a)(2)(A) extends the statute of limitations on collection in the case of certain installment agreements. See IRM 5.14.2.1 Collection Statute

ers may extend the limitations period to obtain an installment agreement, and Collection will ask for these extensions or waivers of the statutory collection period in connection with granting an installment agreement. In addition, the statute of limitations on collection is suspended during the processing of an installment agreement, for the thirty days after notice that the offer has been rejected, and, if the taxpayer appeals the rejection to Appeals, during the pendency of the appeal.[116] Similarly, if an accepted installment agreement is terminated, the running of the collection statute is suspended for thirty days after termination, and if the taxpayer appeals to the Appeals Office, during the pendency of the appeal. If Collection and the taxpayer agree that the taxpayer's financial condition has changed, Collection may change or terminate the agreement. In any case, absent jeopardy, Collection must give the taxpayer written notice at least thirty days before taking action.[117] The notice will state the reason for the action, and the taxpayer has the opportunity to show that the director's reason for acting is incorrect.

In the case of installment agreements, the normal collection period can be statutorily extended (rather than suspended). Under the terms of an installment agreement, the taxpayer agrees to an extension of the statute of limitations on collection. This agreement or waiver can permit the Service to collect an assessed tax for an extended period that is beyond the normal ten-year statute of limitations on assessment. In this case, the extension is for the period agreed to in the original waiver (which is beyond the otherwise applicable 10-year period), plus ninety days. In other words, collection must be made before the date that is ninety days *after* the extended date for collection agreed to in writing at the time the installment agreement was entered into.[118] This extension

---

Expiration Date (CSED) (Sept. 30, 2004) (no extension beyond the 10-year statutory collection period is requested "except when a reasonable extension . . . will allow an agreement to be accepted. In these cases, waivers of the CSED should be secured.") However, the Service's policy is to limit extensions of the collection statute expiration date to five years beyond the normal expiration for each tax account, plus up to one year. Id.

[116] IRC §§ 6331(k)(3), 6502(a)(2)(A). Note that the statute of limitations is suspended during the period that collection is prohibited. Section 6331(k)(3)(A) states that rules similar to the ones described in Sections 6331(i)(3) and 6331(i)(4) dealing respectively with exceptions to the prohibition on levies during the pendency of a divisible tax refund suit and permitting an injunction restraining a levy in violation of the prohibition, apply to Section 6331(k). Section 6331(k)(3) by reference to Section 6331(i)(5) suspends the statute of limitations on collection for periods when collection is prohibited according to Sections 6331(k)(2)(A)–6331(k)(2)(D), with the exception of the period when the installment agreement is in effect. IRC § 6331(k)(2)(C). See Job Creation and Workers Assistance Act of 2002 (P.L. 107-147) § 416(e)(1), amending Sec. 6331(k)(3), which had previously been amended the Community Renewal Tax Relief Act of 2000 (P.L. 106-554) § 313(b)(3).

[117] Reg. § 301.6159-1(c)(4).

[118] IRC § 6502(a)(2)(A).

permits Collection additional time to collect a tax when it was prohibited from doing so during the term of the installment agreement.

The Service enters into two general categories of installment agreements. One category uses Forms 433-D, 433-G, and 2159, and is entered into in local offices after a face-to-face meeting between the taxpayer and a revenue officer and the taxpayer's submission of financial statements. This category of installment agreement is signed by both the taxpayer and a Collection revenue officer or other Collection employee who has examined and approved the agreement. The other category is the agreement entered into by the Automated Collection System (ACS), the Service Center Collection Branch (SCCB), or Taxpayer Services (TS). This second category of agreement differs from the first category because the agreement is not negotiated in face-to-face meetings or after investigation of a submitted financial statement; it is entered into over the telephone or in response to a letter from the taxpayer. This Service center-generated agreement is then confirmed by letter signed by the Service, but not the taxpayer.[119] The agreement is effective from the date it is signed by the Service until the date provided for in the agreement.

The Service has the discretion to impose other terms and conditions on the taxpayer. Form 433-D not only states that, as a condition of the agreement, the taxpayer must file all returns and pay all taxes owed during the life of the agreement, but also provides space for additional conditions.[120] Revenue officers may add the condition that the taxpayer must meet all estimated tax and federal tax deposit obligations.[121] While the Service may impose conditions, the failure to comply with a condition may not be grounds for termination of the agreement because it is not one of the statutorily provided grounds for termination in Section 6159(b).[122]

During the term of an installment payment agreement, Collection may take action to ensure ultimate payment of the unpaid tax by requesting additional financial information, conducting further investigation that might include the use of a summons, and taking collection action by filing or refiling a notice of lien or taking collection action against a person who, in Collection's view, is liable for the tax but is not a party to the agreement.[123] Termination of

---

[119] See Reg. § 301.6159-1(b)(2).

[120] Reg. § 301.6159-1(b)(1)(B).

[121] In the discussion of the taxpayer's use of an installment agreement, the Manual instructs Service personnel to warn taxpayers of their continuing obligation to make estimated tax payments, and to warn business taxpayers of their obligation to make federal tax deposits. IRM 5.14.1.4 Interest-Based Interview (Sept. 30, 2004).

[122] ILM 199922051 (Mar. 26, 1999) (although the Service may impose the condition that estimated taxes or tax deposits be paid, the taxpayer's failure to do so is not a statutorily permissible ground to terminate the agreement).

[123] Reg. § 301.6159-1(d).

an agreement will result, of course, in collection of the unpaid balance of the assessment.

Appeal of the rejection or termination of an installment agreement is part of the installment agreement process. Before rejecting an installment agreement, Collection must provide for independent administrative review, and permit the taxpayer to appeal the rejection to the Office of Appeals.[124]

Once an installment agreement is entered into, it remains in effect for the term of the agreement.[125] Collection may nevertheless terminate an installment agreement for one of the following reasons: (1) the taxpayer has provided inadequate information; (2) the taxpayer has experienced a significant change in financial condition; or (3) the taxpayer has failed to pay an installment or to provide requested information.[126]

Before an installment agreement is terminated, Section 6159(d) provides for independent administrative review of the proposed termination of installment agreements if the taxpayer so requests. Before taking this action, Collection must provide for independent administrative review to (1) send the taxpayer a notice at least thirty days before taking the action with an explanation of the reason for the intended action, and (2) give the taxpayer the opportunity for administrative appeal of a decision to terminate the installment payment agreement.[127] Regulations provide that if a taxpayer disagrees with a determination to alter, modify, or terminate an installment agreement, the taxpayer may initiate an independent administrative review of the determination by calling the telephone number listed on the notice within thirty days of the notice. If, on calling the number, the dispute still is not resolved to the taxpayer's satisfaction, the taxpayer must speak to the manager and attempt to resolve the dispute. If agreement cannot be reached, the taxpayer then may request Appeals review.[128] Unless Collection gives the taxpayer this notice and permits the taxpayer to file a protest within the next thirty-days, Collection may not terminate an installment agreement because the taxpayer has provided inadequate information, has experienced a significant change in financial condition, or has failed to pay an installment or to provide requested information.

---

[124] IRC § 7122(d).

[125] IRC § 6159(b)(1).

[126] IRC §§ 6159(b)(2)–6159(b)(4).

[127] IRC § 6159(b)(5).

[128] IRC § 7122(d); Reg. § 301.6159-1(c)(4). IRM 5.14.9.3, Independent Administrative Review (Mar. 30, 2002). This review is handled by the Independent Administrative reviewer. IRM 5.14.9.4, Collection Appeals Program (Mar. 30, 2002).

[2] Administrative Procedures

Installment agreements are described as "arrangements whereby the Internal Revenue Service allows taxpayers to pay liabilities over time," but that provide for "full payment."[129] Many of the procedures governing the use of installment agreements are described in regulations.[130] Management personnel are authorized to enter into written installment agreements that allow the taxpayer to satisfy a tax liability by making scheduled periodic payments until the liability is fully satisfied "if the director determines that such an installment agreement will facilitate the collection of the tax liability."[131] Installment agreements are discretionary with the director, and the director has the discretion to require (1) a "reasonable extension of the period of limitations on collection" (although why such a request should be necessary when the statutory period is ten years is unexplained) and (2) terms and conditions that protect the interests of the government, such as requiring the taxpayer to authorize direct debit bank transfers as the method of making the installment payments.[132]

During the term of an installment agreement, penalty and interest continue to accrue, but no levies may be served. When a taxpayer is unable to pay a liability in full, the revenue officer interviews the taxpayer and takes the following steps:

1. Obtains a financial statement from the taxpayer;
2. Determines the date when the taxpayer can make full payment of the liability;
3. Informs the taxpayer of the adverse effects of an installment agreement, including the following:
   a. Interest and penalties will continue to accrue;
   b. A user fee is charged for processing the agreement;
   c. A tax lien may be filed;
   d. A levy may be served if the agreement is terminated;
   e. The taxpayer must pay all current taxes; and
   f. Tax refunds will be offset against the liability;
4. Listens to the taxpayer's reason for not being able to make payment and asks whether the taxpayer can pay the tax liability by deferring payment of other liabilities or by borrowing or selling assets.[133]

---

[129] Administrative procedures for installment agreements are found in the Collection Part of the Manual (Part 5), Chapter 1, or IRM 5.14, Installment Agreements.

[130] Reg. §§ 301.6159-1 et seq., adopted in TD 8583, 59 Fed. Reg. 66,192 (Dec. 23, 1994).

[131] Reg. § 301.6159-1(a).

[132] Reg. § 301.6159-1(b).

[133] IRM 5.14.1.4, Interest-Based Interviews (Sept. 30, 2004).

When an installment agreement is considered to be the best way to collect the liability, the revenue officer researches all outstanding liabilities the taxpayer may have—including the estimated tax liability for the current year—and includes them in the installment agreement.

In addition, despite the pendency of an installment agreement, the revenue officer will also file a notice of lien if it is necessary to protect the Service. The taxpayer's ability to pay governs the amount the taxpayer will be required to pay under the installment agreement, and so the amount of installments can be increased or reduced depending on the taxpayer's current financial condition. Because the Service is better able to monitor monthly payments, the taxpayer is usually required to pay installments on a monthly basis.

Taxpayers are also required to extend the statute of limitations on collection.[134] In most cases, installment agreements must be approved by group managers.[135] If the taxpayer cannot agree with the revenue officer on an installment agreement, the revenue officer is required to notify the taxpayer of the taxpayer's right to independent administrative review[136] and also to Appeals review.[137]

[3] Installment Agreement Forms

Several different forms of installment agreements can be used. When an individual taxpayer is unable to pay a reported tax, the taxpayer may ask the Service for an installment agreement to pay the liability by completing an Installment Agreement Request, Form 9465, and attaching it to the front of the taxpayer's tax return, or to a notice the Service sent to the taxpayer. (See Form 15.6a.) Once it is determined that an installment agreement is appropriate, the Service may use one of the following:

1. *Streamlined installment or guaranteed installment agreement.* A streamlined installment agreement is available to a taxpayer with an unpaid assessment of $25,000 or less, including tax, penalty, and interest, which can be fully paid in sixty months.[138] This type of installment agreement may be processed without financial analysis and management approval. Guaranteed installment agreements are required by Section 6159(c) to be granted if the fol-

---

[134] IRM 5.14.2.1, Collection Statute Expiration Date (CSED): Law, Policy, and Procedures: Group Managers Approve Form 900 Waivers (Sept. 30, 2004).

[135] IRM 5.14.2.1(20), Collection Statute Expiration Date (CSED): Law Policy and Procedures: Group Managers Approve Form 900 Waivers (Sept. 30, 2004).

[136] IRM 5.14.9.3, Independent Administrative Review (Sept. 30, 2004). This review is handled by Collection's Special Procedures staff and the Independent Administrative reviewer.

[137] IRM 5.14.9.4, Collection Appeals Program (Sept. 30, 2004).

[138] IRM 5.14.5.2, Streamlined Installment Agreements (Sept. 30, 2004).

lowing criteria are met: (1) the taxpayer owes income tax of $10,000 or less, excluding penalties and interest; (2) the taxpayer has filed and paid tax for the five prior years; (3) the taxpayer agrees to pay the tax in full within three years; and (4) the taxpayer files all tax returns during the pendency of the agreement.[139]

2. *General installment agreement.* The general installment agreement, Installment Agreement, Form 433-D, contains the terms of the installment agreement, establishing the part payment schedule (i.e., the monthly payment), as well as collection information, such as the taxpayer's employer and bank information for potential levy action if the taxpayer defaults on the agreement. (See Form 15.7.)

3. *Payroll deduction agreement.* A payroll deduction agreement is an agreement where an employer deducts payments from a taxpayer's wages and sends them directly to the Service.[140] A Payroll Deduction Agreement, Form 2159, is used when the taxpayer is a wage earner, and especially when the taxpayer has already defaulted on an installment agreement.

4. *Direct debit installment agreement.* A direct debit installment agreement allows the Service to debit a taxpayer's bank account.[141] This type of agreement is used when a payroll deduction agreement is neither practical nor appropriate. It provides for greater certainty of payment than the general installment agreement; it can be used where the taxpayer has defaulted on a prior installment agreement. There is no separate form for this type of agreement; it is included on the back of the taxpayer's copy of the Installment Agreement, Form 433-D. To put the agreement into force, the taxpayer signs the Form 433-D and initials the portion of the form where the direct debit is provided for. To facilitate the Service's debit arrangement with the taxpayer's bank, the taxpayer attaches a blank, voided check to the Service's copy of Form 433-D.

During the extended payment period, the interests of the government are protected by filing or refiling a notice of lien, if such action is determined to be necessary.

The Service uses Form 433-D (Installment Agreement) to establish a part payment schedule. (See Form 15.7.) Form 433-D also contains collection information, such as data regarding the taxpayer's employer and bank. In addition, Collection uses Form 2159 (Payroll Deduction Agreement), which establishes an arrangement for payroll deductions between the taxpayer, his employer, and the Service, and Form 433-G (Direct Debit Installment Agree-

---

[139] IRM 5.14.5.3, Guaranteed Installment Agreements (Sept. 30, 2004).

[140] IRM 5.14.10.2, Payroll Deduction Agreements (Sept. 30, 2004).

[141] IRM 5.14.10.4, Direct Debit Installment Agreements (Sept. 30, 2004).

ment), which provides for funds to be debited directly from the taxpayer's bank account.[142] (See Forms 15.8 and 15.9.)

A number of differences exist between the installment agreement and payroll deduction and direct debit agreements. To enter into a payroll deduction agreement, Collection must have the cooperation of the employer[143] or the taxpayer's bank. To obtain their cooperation, the Service will disclose to the employer or the bank that the taxpayer has an unpaid tax liability and its amount. This disclosure can have serious consequences to the taxpayer. Installment or direct debit agreements are generally monitored by computer (the IDRS system), while employer remittances under payroll deduction agreements are usually manually processed in the local office. Consequently, from the taxpayer's viewpoint, the installment agreement has the advantage of privacy, but the possible disadvantage of computer monitoring, which requires punctilious compliance by the taxpayer. The payroll deduction or direct debit agreement has the disadvantage of disclosure of the tax delinquency, but the advantage of relative certainty of payment.

The terms of the agreement concerning the amount and frequency of payment depend on the particular facts and circumstances disclosed on the financial statement. The taxpayer is required to pay the maximum amount he is able to pay.[144] If the revenue officer and the taxpayer cannot agree on the amount of installments, the taxpayer may appeal to the immediate manager. Installments are usually made on a monthly basis.[145] Allowable expenses generally cover only those costs necessary for the taxpayer to earn income and basic expenses to provide for the health and welfare of the taxpayer and his family.[146] The taxpayer must also agree to meet current tax obligations and to supply any new financial statements as required. The agreement may be altered, modified, or terminated if the taxpayer fails to perform any of these conditions. If Col-

---

[142] The Direct Debit Installment Agreement permits funds to be automatically debited from the taxpayer's bank account for an agreed-upon installment amount. Since this agreement involves an electronic funds transfer, there is less chance that the taxpayer will forget or miss a payment, and the Service gets immediate access to the funds.

[143] IRM 5.14.10.2, Payroll Deduction Agreements (Sept. 30, 2004).

[144] The taxpayer's financial condition is evaluated on the basis of the taxpayer's financial statement, which the revenue officer analyzes under the guidelines described supra ¶ 15.03[1][b]. See IRM 5.15, Financial Analysis Handbook 1.2, Analyzing and Verifying Financial Information (Nov. 15, 2000), and Financial Analysis Handbook 1.2.3, Analysis, Substantiation, and Verification of Income and Expenses (Nov. 15, 2000).

[145] IRM 5.14.1.4, Interest-Based Interview (Sept. 30, 2004). The Service's integrated data retrieval system (IDRS) is able to monitor monthly payments. If the taxpayer wishes to vary the payments, the payments can be manually monitored. Manual monitoring can be used if the taxpayer wishes to pay amounts greater than the installment amount, or if the taxpayer wishes to make some other payment that would facilitate the payment of the liability before the expiration of the statute of limitations on collection.

[146] See supra ¶ 15.04[3].

lection finds that collection of the tax "is in jeopardy," permission to make installment payments may be terminated.[147] If the installment agreement is terminated for these reasons, the entire amount of any tax liability may be collected by levy on income or salary or by seizure of the taxpayer's property without "further notification."[148]

The Service reserves the right to require new financial statements and to review the agreement periodically.[149] Section 6159 permits the installment agreement to be modified or even terminated if the financial information is not supplied or if it shows that the taxpayer's financial condition has changed significantly. Form 433-D states, "This agreement is based on your current financial circumstances and is subject to revision or cancellation if subsequent financial statements required by IRS reflect a change in your ability to pay." In this situation, the taxpayer is entitled to at least thirty days prior notice and a description from the Service of its reasons for the determination that a significant financial change has taken place.[150]

Even where the taxpayer and the Service enter into an installment agreement, this fact alone is not considered sufficient to withhold filing a notice of lien to protect the interests of the Service during the extended period of collection (in any event, on default, a lien would be filed).[151]

For business taxpayers the process is similar to other taxpayers. The revenue officer examines the business's financial statement, and will take the following possible courses of action:[152]

1. If the taxpayer has the ability to pay delinquent and accrued taxes, immediate payment is requested. Should the business taxpayer refuse to pay, a levy will be served, assets will be seized, or if the levy on the business is not honored, a trust fund penalty against a responsible officer will be assessed.

2. Where the business is unable to pay, Collection action depends on whether the business cannot pay operating expenses and its current taxes. If it can only generate enough funds to stay current in its taxes, the revenue officer will not defer collection, but will levy on and seize property, and make trust fund penalty assessments.

---

[147] IRC §§ 6159(b)(2), 6159(b)(4).

[148] See McGee v. United States, 566 F. Supp. 960 (MD Fla. 1982) (permission to make installment payments withdrawn).

[149] IRM 5.14.4.1, Financial Reviews on Manually Monitored Installment Agreements (Mar. 30, 2002).

[150] IRC § 6159(b)(3).

[151] IRM 5.14.7.2, BMF Installment Agreements—Summary of Interview and Financial Analysis for Business Accounts (Mar. 30, 2002).

[152] IRM 5.14.7.2, BMF Installment Agreements—Summary of Interview and Financial Analysis for Business Accounts (Mar. 30, 2002).

3. If the business can generate sufficient funds to pay expenses and taxes, the revenue officer will enter into an installment agreement providing for payment, in order of priority, of the following liabilities: (a) current taxes; (b) accrued taxes to avoid delinquent accounts; and (c) delinquent taxes.

FORM 15.7
INSTALLMENT AGREEMENT REQUEST

Form **9465** (Rev. December 2003) Department of the Treasury Internal Revenue Service	**Installment Agreement Request** ► If you are filing this form with your tax return, attach it to the front of the return. Otherwise, see instructions.	OMB No. 1545-1350

Caution: *Do not file this form if you are currently making payments on an installment agreement. Instead, call 1-800-829-1040. If you are in bankruptcy or we have accepted your offer-in-compromise, see **Bankruptcy or Offer-in-Compromise** below.*

1	Your first name and initial	Last name		Your social security number
	If a joint return, spouse's first name and initial	Last name		Spouse's social security number
	Your current address (number and street). If you have a P.O. box and no home delivery, enter your box number.			Apt. number
	City, town or post office, state, and ZIP code. If a foreign address, enter city, province or state, and country. Follow the country's practice for entering the postal code.			

2 If this address is new since you filed your last tax return, check here . . . . ► ☐

3	( ) Your home phone number Best time for us to call	4	( ) Your work phone number Ext. Best time for us to call
5	Name of your bank or other financial institution: Address City, state, and ZIP code	6	Your employer's name: Address City, state, and ZIP code

7 Enter the tax return for which you are making this request (for example, Form 1040) . . . . . . ► _____

8 Enter the tax year for which you are making this request (for example, 2003) . . . . ► _____

9	Enter the total amount you owe as shown on your tax return	9	
10	Enter the amount of any payment you are making with your tax return (or notice). See instructions	10	
11	Enter the amount you can pay each month. **Make your payments as large as possible to limit interest and penalty charges.** The charges will continue until you pay in full	11	

12 Enter the date you want to make your payment each month. **Do not** enter a date later than the 28th. . ►

13 If you want to make your payments by electronic funds withdrawal from your checking account, see the instructions and fill in lines 13a and 13b.
► a Routing number ☐☐☐☐☐☐☐☐☐
► b Account number ☐☐☐☐☐☐☐☐☐☐☐☐☐☐☐☐☐

I authorize the U.S. Treasury and its designated Financial Agent to initiate a monthly ACH electronic funds withdrawal entry to the financial institution account indicated for payments of my Federal taxes owed, and the financial institution to debit the entry to this account. This authorization is to remain in full force and effect until I notify the U.S. Treasury Financial Agent to terminate the authorization. To revoke payment, I must contact the U.S. Treasury Financial Agent at **1-800-829-1040** no later than 7 business days prior to the payment (settlement) date. I also authorize the financial institutions involved in the processing of the electronic payments of taxes to receive confidential information necessary to answer inquiries and resolve issues related to the payments.

Your signature	Date	Spouse's signature. If a joint return, **both** must sign.	Date

General Instructions
Section references are to the Internal Revenue Code.

Purpose of Form
Use Form 9465 to request a monthly installment plan if you cannot pay the full amount you owe shown on your tax return (or on a notice we sent you). Generally, you may have up to 60 months to pay. But before requesting an installment agreement, you should consider other less costly alternatives, such as a bank loan. If you have any questions about this request, call 1-800-829-1040.

Guaranteed Installment Agreement. Your request for an installment agreement cannot be turned down if the tax you owe is not more than $10,000 and **all three** of the following apply.

1. During the past 5 tax years, you (and your spouse if you are making a request for a joint tax return) have timely filed all income tax returns and paid any income tax due, and have not entered into an installment agreement for payment of income tax.

2. The IRS determines that you cannot pay the tax owed in full when it is due and you give the IRS any information needed to make that determination.

3. You agree to pay the full amount you owe within 3 years and to comply with the tax laws while the agreement is in effect.

⚠ *A Notice of Federal Tax Lien may be filed to protect the government's interest until you pay in full.*

Bankruptcy or Offer-in-Compromise. If you are in bankruptcy or we have accepted your offer-in-compromise, **do not** file this form. Instead, call 1-800-829-1040 to get the number of your local IRS Insolvency function for bankruptcy or Technical Support function for offer-in-compromise.

For Privacy Act and Paperwork Reduction Act Notice, see back of form.   Cat. No. 14842Y   Form **9465** (Rev. 12-2003)

Form 9465 (Rev. 12-2003)   Page **2**

What Will You Be Charged

You will be charged a $43 fee if your request is approved. **Do not include the fee with this form.** After approving your request, we will bill you for the fee with your first payment.

You will also be charged interest and may be charged a late payment penalty on any tax not paid by its due date, even if your request to pay in installments is granted. To limit interest and penalty charges, file your return on time and pay as much of the tax as possible with your return (or notice).

How Does the Installment Agreement Work

If we approve your request, we will send you a letter. It will tell you how to pay the fee and make your first installment payment. We will usually let you know within 30 days after we receive your request whether it is approved or denied. But if this request is for tax due on a return you filed after March 31, it may take us longer than 30 days to reply.

By approving your request, we agree to let you pay the tax you owe in monthly installments instead of immediately paying the amount in full. In return, you agree to make your monthly payments on time. **You also agree to meet all your future tax liabilities.** This means that you must have enough withholding or estimated tax payments so that your tax liability for future years is paid in full when you timely file your return. Your request for an installment agreement will be denied if all required tax returns have not been filed. Any refund due you in a future year will be applied against the amount you owe.

After we receive each payment, we will send you a letter showing the remaining amount you owe, and the due date and amount of your next payment. But if you choose to have your payments automatically withdrawn from your checking account, you will not receive a letter. Your bank statement is your record of payment. You can also make your payments by credit card. For details on how to pay, see your tax return instructions or visit **www.irs.gov.** We will also give you a statement showing the amount you owe at the beginning of the year, all payments made during the year, and the amount you owe at the end of the year.

If you **do not** make your payments on time or you have an outstanding past-due amount in a future year, you will be in default on your agreement and we may take enforcement actions, such as a Notice of Federal Tax Lien or an IRS levy, to collect the entire amount you owe. To ensure that your payments are made timely, you should consider making them by electronic funds withdrawal (see the instructions for lines 13a and 13b).

Where To File

Attach Form 9465 to the front of your return and send it to the address shown in your tax return booklet. If you have already filed your return or you are filing this form in response to a notice, file Form 9465 by itself with the **Internal Revenue Service Center** at the address below for the place where you live. No street address is needed.

IF you live in . . .	THEN use this address . . .
Alabama, Florida, Georgia, Mississippi, North Carolina, Rhode Island, South Carolina, West Virginia	Atlanta, GA 39901
Maine, Massachusetts, New Hampshire, New York, Vermont	Andover, MA 05501
Delaware, Illinois, Indiana, Iowa, Kansas, Michigan, Minnesota, Missouri, Nebraska, North Dakota, South Dakota, Wisconsin	Kansas City, MO 64999
Connecticut, District of Columbia, Maryland, New Jersey, Pennsylvania	Philadelphia, PA 19255
Arkansas, Colorado, Kentucky, Louisiana, New Mexico, Oklahoma, Tennessee, Texas	Austin, TX 73301
Alaska, Arizona, California, Hawaii, Idaho, Montana, Nevada, Oregon, Utah, Washington, Wyoming	Fresno, CA 93888
Ohio, Virginia	Memphis, TN 37501

If you live in American Samoa or Puerto Rico (or exclude income under section 933); are a nonpermanent resident of Guam or the Virgin Islands *; have an APO, FPO, or foreign address; are a dual-status alien; or file Form 2555, 2555-EZ, or 4563, use this address: *Internal Revenue Service Center, Philadelphia, PA 19255.*

* Permanent residents of Guam and the Virgin Islands cannot use Form 9465.

Specific Instructions

Line 1
If you are making this request for a joint tax return, show the names and social security numbers (SSNs) in the same order as on your tax return.

Line 10
Even if you cannot pay the full amount you owe now, you should pay as much as possible to limit penalty and interest charges. If you are filing this form with your tax return, make the payment with your return. For details on how to pay, see your tax return instructions.

If you are filing this form **by itself**, such as in response to a notice, attach a check or money order payable to the **"United States Treasury."** **Do not send cash.** Be sure to include:

• Your name, address, SSN, and daytime phone number.

• The tax year and tax return (for example, "2003 Form 1040") for which you are making this request.

Line 11
You should try to make your payments large enough so that your balance due will be paid off by the due date of your next tax return.

Line 12
You can choose the date your monthly payment is due. For example, if your rent or mortgage payment is due on the first of the month, you may want to make your installment payments on the 15th. When we approve your request, we will tell you the month and date that your first payment is due.

If we have not replied by the date you chose for your first payment, you may send the first payment to the Internal Revenue Service Center at the address shown on this page that applies to you. See the instructions for line 10 to find out what to write on your payment.

Lines 13a and 13b
To pay by electronic funds withdrawal from your checking account at a bank or other financial institution (such as mutual fund, brokerage firm, or credit union), fill in lines 13a and 13b. Check with your financial institution to make sure that an electronic funds withdrawal is allowed and to get the correct routing and account numbers.

Note: *We will send you a bill for the first payment and the fee. All other payments will be electronically withdrawn.*

Line 13a. The routing number **must be nine** digits. The first two digits of the routing number must be 01 through 12 or 21 through 32. Use a check to verify the routing numbers. But if your check is payable through a financial institution different from the one at which you have your checking account, do not use the routing numbers on that check. Instead, contact your financial institution for the correct routing numbers.

Line 13b. The account number can be up to 17 characters (both numbers and letters). Include hyphens but omit spaces and special symbols. Enter the number from left to right and leave any unused boxes blank. Be sure **not** to include the check number.

Privacy Act and Paperwork Reduction Act Notice. Our legal right to ask for the information on this form is sections 6001, 6011, 6012(a), 6109, and 6159 and their regulations. We will use the information to process your request for an installment agreement. The reason we need your name and social security number is to secure proper identification. We require this information to gain access to the tax information in our files and properly respond to your request. If you do not enter the information, we may not be able to process your request.

You are not required to provide the information requested on a form that is subject to the Paperwork Reduction Act unless the form displays a valid OMB control number. Books or records relating to a form or its instructions must be retained as long as their contents may become material in the administration of any Internal Revenue law. Generally, tax returns and return information are confidential, as required by section 6103. However, we may give this information to the Department of Justice for civil and criminal litigation, and to cities, states, and the District of Columbia to carry out their tax laws. We may also disclose this information to other countries under a tax treaty or to Federal and state agencies to enforce Federal nontax criminal laws and to combat terrorism.

The time needed to complete and file this form will vary depending on individual circumstances. The estimated average time is: **Learning about the law or the form,** 16 min.; **Preparing the form,** 26 min.; and **Copying, assembling, and sending the form to the IRS,** 20 min.

If you have comments concerning the accuracy of this estimate or suggestions for making this form simpler, we would be happy to hear from you. You can write to the Tax Products Coordinating Committee, Western Area Distribution Center, Rancho Cordova, CA 95743-0001. **Do not** send the form to this address. Instead, see **Where To File** on this page.

⊛

FORM 15.8 ————————————————————————————————
INSTALLMENT AGREEMENT INFORMATION

| Form **9433**
 May 1992 | Department of the Treasury—Internal Revenue Service
 Installment Agreement Information |

We use installment agreements to collect the balance you owe in monthly payments. If you can't pay the full amount right now, we will consider a monthly installment agreement for you. We will either approve your request or ask you to fill out a financial statement that will help us understand your financial condition and ability to pay. In certain cases, we may file a Notice of Federal Tax Lien against your property to protect the federal government's interest. However, this is not done routinely. We will notify you of our intent to file a lien before we file it.

Installment agreements are subject to the following conditions: 1) you must make all your payments on time, 2) you must pay all other Federal taxes on time, and 3) you must give current financial information when we ask you for it.

If you pay your taxes right now, you will avoid the additional penalty and interest we will charge you under an installment agreement. You will also be able to keep any future tax refunds.

If you can't pay the full amount, send as much as you can today. Make your check or money order payable to the Internal Revenue Service, and mark the payment with the tax year for which it is intended. Also, complete and detach the bottom of this form (Form 9433) and return it with the bottom of the other notice we enclosed. To help us provide better service, please use the enclosed envelope.

- -

Tax period (from other notice): _____

Your Name:	Social Security Number:
Spouse's Name (joint returns only)	Social Security Number:
Home Telephone Number: ( )	Work Telephone Number: ( )

I am able to pay $ _____ on the _____ day of each month.
(Must be the 1st through the 28th day.)

Your Signature:	Date:	Spouse's Signature (joint returns only):	Date:

Form **9433** (Rev. 5-92)

FORM 15.9
INSTALLMENT AGREEMENT

Form **433-D** (Rev. May 1996)	Department of the Treasury — Internal Revenue Service **Installment Agreement**	check box if installment agreement fee was paid	

Name and address of taxpayer (s)	Social security or employer identification number *(primary)*	*(secondary)*
	Telephone number *(home)*	*(business)*
	Kinds of taxes *(form numbers)*	Tax periods
	Amount owed as of _____ $	Earliest CSED

Employer *(name and address)*	Financial institutions *(names and addresses)*	For assistance: Call 1-800-829-1040 or write: _____ Service Ctr. _____ City, State and Zip Code

I/We agree that the federal taxes shown above, <u>PLUS ALL PENALTIES AND INTEREST PROVIDED BY LAW</u>, will be paid as follows:

$ _____ will be paid on _____ and $ _____ will be paid

no later than the _____ of each month thereafter until the total liability is paid in full. I/we also agree that the above

installment payment will be increased or decreased as follows:

check box if pre-assessed modules included

Date of increase *(or decrease)*		
Amount of increase *(or decrease)*	$	
New installment amount	$	

AGREEMENT LOCATOR NUMBER: _____
(circle)
0.   No future action is required
5   Financial review date: _____
6   Monitor ES compliance:
        Indicator: 1st Qtr ____ 2nd Qtr ____ 3rd Qtr ____
        ES payment: $ _____ $ _____ $ _____

Conditions of this agreement:

- We must receive each payment by the date shown above; if you have a problem, contact us immediately.
- This agreement is based on your current financial condition. We may change or cancel it if our information shows that your ability to pay has changed significantly.
- We may cancel this agreement if you don't give us updated financial information when we ask for it.
- While this agreement is in effect, you must file all federal tax returns and pay any taxes you owe on time.
- We will apply your federal or state tax refunds (if any) to the amount you owe until it is fully paid. (This includes the Alaska Permanent Fund dividend for Alaska residents.)
- You must pay a $43 installment agreement fee, which we have authority to deduct from the first payment.
- If agreement defaults, you must pay a $24 reinstatement fee if agreement is reinstated, which we have authority to deduct from the first payment.

Additional Conditions: (To be completed by IRS)

- If you don't meet the conditions of this agreement, we will cancel it, and may collect the entire amount you owe by levy on your income, bank accounts or other assets, or by seizing your property.
- We will cancel this agreement at any time if we find that collection of the tax is in jeopardy.
- We will apply all payments on this agreement in the best interest of the United States.
- This agreement may require managerial approval. If it is not approved, you will be notified.
- **A NOTICE OF FEDERAL TAX LIEN** *(check one)*
  - ☐ HAS ALREADY BEEN FILED
  - ☐ WILL BE FILED IMMEDIATELY
  - ☐ WILL BE FILED WHEN TAX IS ASSESSED
  - ☐ MAY BE FILED IF THIS AGREEMENT DEFAULTS

Your signature	Title *(if corporate officer or partner)*	Date	Originator's name, title and IDRS assignment number *(or district)*:
Spouse's signature *(if a joint liability)*		Date	
Agreement examined or approved by *(signature, title, function)*		Date	Originator Code:

YOU MAY HAVE YOUR INSTALLMENT AGREEMENT PAYMENT DEDUCTED FROM YOUR CHECKING ACCOUNT EACH MONTH (DIRECT DEBIT); IF YOU CHOOSE THIS OPTION, FOLLOW THE DIRECTIONS ON THE BACK OF YOUR COPY OF THIS FORM.

If you agree to Direct Debit, initial here:

_____

and attach a blank voided check.

- I (we) authorize the IRS and the depository (bank) identified on the attached voided check to deduct payments (debit) from my (our) checking account or correct errors on the account. This authorization remains in effect until I (or either of us) notify IRS in writing to stop or until the liability covered by this agreement is satisfied.
- I (we) understand that if the depository is unable to honor IRS's request for payment due to insufficient funds in my (our) account on the payment due date I (we) will be charged a penalty of $15 or two percent of the payment request, whichever is greater. If the payment request is for less than $15, the penalty is the amount of the request.

Form **433-D** (Rev. 5-96)

INSTRUCTIONS TO TAXPAYER

If not already completed by an IRS employee, in the space provided, enter:

> your name and current address;

> your social security number and/or your employer identification number (whichever applies to your tax liability);

> the complete name and address of your employer(s) and your bank(s);

> your home and work/business telephone number(s);

> the amount you are able to pay now as a partial payment;

> the amount you are able to pay each month (or the amount determined by IRS personnel); and

> the date you prefer to make this payment (this must be the same day for each month, from the 1st to the 28th). We must receive your payment by this date. If you elect the direct debit option, this is the day you want your account debited.

If you choose to have your monthly payment automatically deducted from your checking account (direct debit), put your initials in the space provided in the bottom left corner, give the bank copy to your bank and attach a blank, voided check to the IRS copy of this form.

On the same day each month, your checking account will automatically be debited for the amount of your monthly payment. Be sure to update your checkbook each month. IRS won't send you a reminder notice about this.

When you have finished, sign and date the Installment Agreement and return Part 1 to IRS at the address on the letter which came with the agreement or the address shown on the front page of this form. Retain Part 2 for your records. **Also, make sure you complete the Payment Voucher and include the installment agreement fee with your payment.**

If you have any questions regarding the direct debit process or the completion of this form, please call the toll-free number on the front of this form.

Note: When making an installment, please be sure to:

1. Write your social security or employer identification number on each payment.

2. Make check or money order payable to "Internal Revenue Service."

3. Make each payment in an amount at least equal to that specified in this agreement.

4. Don't double one payment and skip the next without contacting us first.

5. Enclose with each payment a copy of the reminder notice (if you received one), in the envelope provided.

6. Mail your payment on time to the proper IRS office, even if you didn't receive a reminder notice. (Note: we must receive it by the due date.)

7. Contact us immediately if you can't meet the terms of this agreement.

This agreement will not affect your liability (if any) for backup withholding under Public Law 98-67, the Interest and Dividend Tax Compliance Act of 1983.

Instructions for the Payment Voucher

- Enter your Social Security Number in box 1 for individual tax return or Employer Identification Number for business tax return.

- Enter the first four letters of your last name in box 2. See Below for Examples:

Name	Enter	Name	Enter
John Brown	BROW	Juan DeJesus	DEJE
Joan A. Lee	LEE	Jean McCarthy	MCCA
John O'Neil	ONEI	Pedro Torres-Lopez	TORR

If this is a business, enter the first four letters of your business name in box 2. See below for Examples:

Name	Enter
The Meadowlark Co.	MEAD
Smith Flower Shop	SMIT
Burgandy, Olive & Cobalt, Ptrs.	BURG

- Enter the tax year for this request in box 3. If for more than one tax year enter the earliest year.

- If you are filing a joint return enter spouse's SSN in box 4.

- Enter your name and address in box 5.

- Enter the amount of installment agreement fee you are paying on line 6.

- Enter the amount of the first payment you are making on line 7.

- Add lines 6 and 7 and enter the total on line 8.

Form **433-D-V**	**Payment Voucher**	
(May 1996)	▶ Do not staple or attach your payment to this payment voucher.	
Department of the Treasury Internal Revenue Service	▶ See instructions on back of Part 2	

1 Enter your taxpayer identification number	2 Enter the first four letters of your last name or first four letters of business name	3 Enter the tax year for which you are making this request	6 Fee. Enter $43 if this is an initial request. Enter $24 if reinstating a current agreement . . . . $ _____ .00
4 If a joint return, enter your spouses's social security number	5 Enter your name(s) Enter your address Enter your city state, and Zip code		7 Amount of first payment, you are making, if any . . . . $ _____ 8 Total due with this request. Add lines 6 and 7 . . . . $ _____

FORM 15.10 ─────────────────
PAYROLL DEDUCTION AGREEMENT

Form **2159**	Department of the Treasury - Internal Revenue Service
(Rev. April 2003)	**Payroll Deduction Agreement**
	(See Instructions on the back of this page.)

TO: *(Employer - name and address)*
ABC CORPORATION
100 MAIN STREET
FORT LEE, NJ 07000

Regarding: *(Taxpayer - name and address)*
ALAN MICHAELS
279 LINCOLN AVE
FORT LEE, NJ 07000

Contact Person's Name	Telephone *(Include area code)*
JOHN SMITH	201-567-9999

Social security or employer identification number
(Taxpayer)   *(Spouse)*
123-45-6789

EMPLOYER - *See the instructions on the back of Part 2.* The taxpayer identified above on the right named you as an employer. Please read and sign the following statement to agree to withhold amount(s) from the taxpayer's *(employee's)* wages or salary to apply to taxes owed.

I agree to participate in this payroll deduction agreement and will withhold the amount shown below from each wage or salary payment due this employee. I will send the money to the Internal Revenue Service every: *(Check one box.)*
[ ] WEEK [ ] TWO WEEKS [X] MONTH [ ] OTHER *(Specify.)* _____

Signed: _____

Title: VP   Date: _____

Your telephone number *(Include area code)*
(Home)   *(Work or business)*
201-568-0000   201-567-0999

For assistance, call: **1-800-829-0115** *(Business)* or **1-800-829-8374** *(Individual - Self-Employed/Business Owners)*, or **1-800-829-0922** *(Individuals - Wage Earners)*

Or write: HOLTSVILLE, NJ 00501 _____ **Campus**
(City, State, and ZIP Code)

Financial Institution(s) *(Name and address)*
UNITED JERSEY BANK
FORT LEE, NJ 07000

Kinds of taxes *(Form numbers)*	Tax periods	Amount owed as of 8/31/2004
1040	2000, 2001, 2002	$ 4,850, plus all penalties and interest provided by law.

I am paid every: *(Check one)*: [ ] WEEK [X] TWO WEEKS [ ] MONTH [ ] OTHER *(Specify.)*

I agree to have $ _____ 100 deducted from my wage or salary payment beginning _____ 10/1/2004 until the total liability is paid in full. I also agree and authorize this deduction to be increased or decreased as follows:

Date of increase *(or decrease)*	Amount of increase *(or decrease)*	New installment payment amount
4/1/2005	25	125
10/1/2005	25	150

Terms of this agreement - By completing and submitting this agreement, you *(the taxpayer)* agree to the following terms:

- You will make each payment so that we *(IRS)* receive it by the monthly due date stated on the front of this form *If you cannot make a scheduled payment, contact us immediately.*
- This agreement is based on your current financial condition. We may modify or terminate the agreement if our information shows that your ability to pay has significantly changed. You must provide updated financial information when requested.
- While this agreement is in effect, you must file all federal tax returns and pay any *(federal)* taxes you owe on time.
- We will apply your federal tax refunds or overpayments *(if any)* to the amount you owe until it is fully paid.
- You must pay a $43 user fee, which we have authority to deduct from your first payment(s).
- If you default on your installment agreement, you must pay a $24 reinstatement fee if we reinstate the agreement. We have the

authority to deduct this fee from your first payment(s) after the agreement is reinstated.
- We will apply all payments on this agreement in the best interests of the United States.
- **We can terminate your installment agreement if:**
  - You do not make monthly installment payments as agreed.
  - You do not pay any other federal tax debt when due.
  - You do not provide financial information when requested.
- If we terminate your agreement, we may collect the entire amount you owe by levy on your income, bank accounts or other assets, or by seizing your property.
- We may terminate this agreement at any time if we find that collection of the tax is in jeopardy.
- This agreement may require managerial approval. We'll notify you when we approve or don't approve the agreement.

Additional Terms *(To be completed by IRS)*	Note: Internal Revenue Service employees may contact third parties in order to process and maintain this agreement.

Your signature	Title *(If Corporate Officer or Partner)*	Date
Spouse's signature *(If a joint liability)*		Date
Agreement examined or approved by *(Signature, title, function)*		Date

FOR IRS USE ONLY:

AGREEMENT LOCATOR NUMBER: __ __ __ __ __
Input Review Suppress Indicator: "1" *(unless specific balance due IA)*
[ ] Check box if specific balance due IA; input Review Suppress Indicator "6"
Agreement Review Cycle: __ __ __ __ __ __ Earliest CSED _____
[ ] Check box if pre-assessed modules included
Originator's ID: _____ Originator Code: _____
Name: _____ Title: _____

A NOTICE OF FEDERAL TAX LIEN *(Check one box below.)*
[ ] HAS ALREADY BEEN FILED
[ ] WILL BE FILED IMMEDIATELY
[ ] WILL BE FILED WHEN TAX IS ASSESSED
[ ] MAY BE FILED IF THIS AGREEMENT DEFAULTS

Part 1 - Acknowledgement Copy *(Return to IRS)*   www.irs.gov   Form **2159** (Rev. 4-2003)
(HTA)

Agreement Locator Number Designations

XX Position *(the first two numbers)* denotes either the Initiator or Type of Agreement. The XX values are:

00	Form 433-D initiated by AO on an ACS case
01	Service Center and Toll-free initiated agreements
02	AO Field Territory *(revenue officer)* initiated agreements
03	Direct Debit agreements initiated by any function
06	Exam initiated agreements
07	Submission Processing initiated agreements
08	Agreements initiated by other functions
11	Form 2159 agreement initiated by AO or ACS
12	AO or ACS agreement with multiple conditions
20	Status 22/24 accounts -- Call Site/SCCB
90	SCCB initiated agreements – other than status 22 or 26
91	Form 2159 agreement initiated by SCCB
92	SCCB agreement with multiple conditions
99	Up to 120 days extensions

YY Position (the second two numbers) denotes Conditions Affecting the Agreement. The YY values are:

08	Continuous Wage Levy *(from ACS and RO)*
09	All other conditions
12	One year rule *(use for specific BAL DUE module agreements)*
15	In Business Trust Fund *(IBTF)* monitoring required
27	Restricted Interest/Penalty condition present
32	Unassessed modules to be included in agreement
36	Streamlined agreements, less than 60 months, up to $25,000
41	BMF in Business Deferral Level *(SCCB USE ONLY)*
53	Report Currently Not Collectible *(CNC)* if agreement defaults
63	Cross-reference TIN *(Status 63)*
66	File lien in event of default
70	Secondary TP responsible for Joint Liability
80	Review and revise payment amount
99	Up to 120 days extensions

When an agreement has more than one condition, use either 12 or 92 in the "XX" position and assign the primary condition *(YY)* based on the following priorities:

#1-53, #2-08, #3-27, or #4-15

The remaining multiple conditions will be input as a history item on IDRS by SCCB. For example, to construct a history item to record an unassessed module, use the following format:

UM309312 *(Unassessed module, MFT 30, 9312 Tax Period)*; or
UMFILE LIEN *(Unassessed module, file Lien, if appropriate)*

Installment Agreement Originator Codes

20	Collection field function regular agreement
21	Collection field function streamlined agreement
30	Reserved
31	Reserved
50	Field assistance regular agreement
51	Field assistance streamlined agreement
60	Examination regular agreement
61	Examination streamlined agreement
70	Toll-free regular agreement
71	Toll-free streamlined agreement
72	Paper regular agreement
73	Paper streamlined agreement
74	Voice Response Unit (system generated)
75	Automated Collection Branch regular
76	Automated Collection Branch streamlined
77	Automated Collection Branch Voice Response Unit regular *(system generated)*
78	Automated Collection Branch Voice Response Unit streamlined *(system generated)*
80	Other function regular agreement
81	Other function-streamlined agreement
90-91	Reserved for vendors – all streamlined agreements

INSTRUCTIONS TO EMPLOYER

This payroll deduction agreement requires your approval. If you agree to participate, please complete the spaces provided under the employer section on the front of this form.

WHAT YOU SHOULD DO

- Enter the name and telephone number of a contact person. *(This will allow us to contact you if your employee's liability is satisfied ahead of time.)*

- Indicate when you will forward payments to IRS.

- Sign and date the form.

- After you and your employee have completed and signed the form, please return it *(all parts)* to IRS. Use the IRS address on the letter the employee received with the form or the address shown on the front of the form.

HOW TO MAKE PAYMENTS

- ☐ Please deduct the amount your employee agreed with the IRS to have deducted from each wage or salary payment due the employee.

- ☐ Make your check payable to the "United States Treasury." To insure proper credit, please write your employee's name and social security number on each payment.

- ☐ Send the money to the IRS mailing address printed on the letter that came with the agreement. Your employee should give you a copy of this letter. If there is no letter, use the IRS address shown on the front of the form.

Note: The amount of the liability shown on the form may not include all penalties and interest provided by law. Please continue to make payments unless IRS notifies you that the liability has been satisfied. When the amount owed, as shown on the form, is paid in full and IRS hasn't notified you that the liability has been satisfied, please call the appropriate telephone number below to request the final balance due.

If you need assistance, please call the telephone number on the letter that came with the agreement or write to the address shown on the letter. If there's no letter, please call the appropriate telephone number below or write IRS at the address shown on the front of the form.

For assistance, call: 1-800-829-0115 *(Business)*, or
                                 1-800-829-8374 *(Individual – Self-Employed/Business Owners)*, or
                                 1-800-829-0922 *(Individuals – Wage Earners)*

THANK YOU FOR YOUR COOPERATION

INSTRUCTIONS TO TAXPAYER

If not already completed by an IRS employee, please fill in the information in the spaces provided on the front of this form for the following items:

- Your employer's name and address

- Your name*(s) (plus spouse's name if the amount owed is for a joint return)* and current address.

- Your social security number or employer identification number. *(Use the number that appears on the notice(s) you received.)* Also, enter your spouse's social security number if this is a joint liability.

- Your home and work telephone number*(s)*

- The complete name and address of your financial institution*(s)*

- The kind of taxes you owe *(form numbers)* and the tax periods

- The amount you owe as of the date you spoke to IRS

- When you are paid

- The amount you agreed to have deducted from your pay when you spoke to IRS

- The date the deduction is to begin

- The amount of any increase or decrease in the deduction amount, if you agreed to this with IRS; otherwise, leave BLANK

After you complete, sign *(along with your spouse if this is a joint liability)*, and date this agreement form, give it to your participating employer. If you received the form by mail, please give the employer a copy of the letter that came with it.

Your employer should mark the payment frequency on the form and sign it. Then the employer should return all parts of the form to the IRS address on your letter or the address shown in the "For assistance" box on the front of the form.

If you need assistance, please call the appropriate telephone number below or write IRS at the address shown on the form. However, if you received this agreement by mail, please call the telephone number on the letter that came with it or write IRS at the address shown on the letter.

For assistance, call: **1-800-829-0115** *(Business)*, or
                    1-800-829-8374 *(Individual – Self-Employed/Business Owners)*, or
                    1-800-829-0922 *(Individuals – Wage Earners)*

Note: This agreement **will not** affect your liability *(if any)* for backup withholding under Public Law 98-67, the Interest and Dividend Compliance Act of 1983.

Catalog No. 21475H   Form **2159** (Rev. 4-2003)

FORM 15.11
DIRECT DEBIT INSTALLMENT AGREEMENT

Form 433-G (Rev. February 1990)	Department of the Treasury — Internal Revenue Service **Direct Debit Installment Agreement**	Agreement Locator Number

Name and address of taxpayer(s)

Jane James
One Main Street
Anytown, NY 00000

County: _____

Social security or employer identification number
123-45-6789

Kinds of taxes (Form numbers)
1040

Tax periods
1989, 1990

Amount of tax owed
15,000

The undersigned agrees that the Federal taxes shown above, plus any interest and penalties provided by law, will be paid as follows:

$ __3500__ paid with this agreement, $ __500__ to be paid on __October 15, 1993__ and on the same day of each month thereafter until the liability is paid in full and also agrees that the above tax installment payments will be increased or decreased as follows:

Date of increase/decrease		
Amount of increase/decrease		
New installment agreement amount		

Conditions of this agreement

- This agreement is based on your current financial circumstances and is subject to revision or termination if subsequent financial statements required by IRS reflect a change in your ability to pay.
- This agreement may require managerial approval. If it is not approved, you will be so notified.
- All Federal taxes that become due during the term of this agreement must be paid on time.
- All Federal tax returns that become due during the term of this agreement must be filed on time.
- Any Federal or State refunds that might otherwise be due will be applied to this liability until this liability is satisfied.
- This agreement to make installment payments may be terminated and the entire tax liability may be collected by levy on income, bank accounts, or other assets, or by seizure of property if the conditions of this agreement are not met, or if it is determined that collection of these taxes is in jeopardy.
- I (we) authorize the IRS and the Depository (bank) identified on the attached voided check to deduct payments (debit) from my (our) checking account or correct errors on the account. This authorization remains in effect until I (or either of us) notify IRS in writing to stop or until the liability covered by this agreement is satisfied.
- I (we) understand that if the DEPOSITORY is unable to honor IRS's request for payment due to insufficient funds in my (our) account on the payment due date I (we) will be charged a penalty of $15.00 or two percent of the payment request, whichever is greater. If the payment request is for less than $15.00, the penalty is the amount of the request.
- This account is used primarily for personal _____ business _____ transactions (check one)

Additional conditions	Originator's name, IDRS assignment number and function
	13-3-21-16
	John Doe
Attach your blank, voided check here.	For assistance call:
	Or write:

Your signature	Title	Date	
/s/ Jane James		8/19/92	
Spouse's signature (if joint liability)		**Date**	Taxpayer's telephone number:
			(Home):
Agreement examined or approved by (signature)		**Date**	
/s/ Jane James		8/19/92	(Business):

Employer (name & address)
ABC Corporation 1 Elm Street, Anytown, NY 00000

Banks (name & address) and account numbers
United National Bank, 1 Park Place, Anytown, NY 00000

Part 1 - IRS Copy

Form 433-G (Rev. 2-90)

Form 433-G (Rev. February 1990)	Department of the Treasury – Internal Revenue Service **Direct Debit Installment Agreement**

Instructions

Fill out the identifying information on the top part of the form.

Enter your name, address, and social security number or employer identification number in the blanks provided.

Fill in the block for Kinds of Taxes (Form numbers), Tax Periods, and Amount of tax owed if you know the information.

Next, read the section that begins "The undersigned agrees ..." In the first blank space, enter the amount you are paying with this agreement. If you were contacted by an IRS employee regarding this matter, you must pay the amount agreed upon during your interview.

In the second blank space, enter the amount of your monthly installment.

Using your calendar, enter in the last space, the date that is seven weeks from the date you are mailing this form back to us. This is the earliest date IRS will take money from your account electronically. If this date is the 29th, 30th, or 31st of the month, enter the 1st day of the following month as the due date. Remember to record this date and the payment amount in your checkbook.

On the same day of each month, until your liability is satisfied, your bank account will be debited for this agreement amount and forwarded to IRS. For example, if your first payment falls on May 20th, your account will be debited each month on the 20th. You must update your checkbook. You will receive no reminder notices from IRS.

Read the Conditions of Agreement and check the line indicating whether your account is used primarily for business or personal use.

Attach a blank, voided check for the bank account you will use for the agreement. We cannot process your agreement without this check.

Sign and date the agreement. We cannot accept an unsigned agreement.

Finally, fill in the Employer information, Bank information (financial institutions or accounts other than the one on the above check), and your Telephone Numbers.

Be sure to attach the bottom part of your notice or letter (if you received one) to the payment you send along with Parts 1 & 3 of your agreement.

Contact IRS at our toll free number if you have questions regarding the Direct Debit process or the completion of this form.

Form **433-G** (Rev. 2-90)

¶ 15.07 OFFERS IN COMPROMISE

Neither the statute[153] nor the regulations define the term "compromise." The standard dictionary definition of the word—a settlement of difference by consent reached by mutual concessions—has long been the basis for the government's attitude toward the procedure.[154] Unlike an installment agreement, a compromise agreement will settle the taxpayer's liability for less than the full amount and release the taxpayer from a portion of the tax liability assessed. That settlement and release agreement has a cost to the taxpayer in the form of the taxpayer's being required to make full financial disclosure, waive the right to refunds, and perhaps be left with fewer overall tax benefits; in addition, the statute of limitations on collection is suspended. In general, apart from reducing the amount of the outstanding tax liability, the taxpayer has the benefit of unanticipated and disruptive collection action during the pendency of the agreement.

[1] Statutory Requirements

Compromises of tax cases are governed by statute. In general, Section 7122 grants the Service the authority to compromise a case arising under the internal revenue laws, but requires Service personnel to evaluate whether an offer should be accepted or rejected according to guidelines, and establishes procedures for administrative review of rejected offers.[155] When an offer is accepted, the Chief Counsel's opinion of the accepted compromise must be made available in a public file.[156] When the Service accepts an offer, the compromise conclusively settles the liability of the taxpayer specified in the offer, unless the taxpayer has supplied false information, concealed the taxpayer's assets or ability to pay, or the parties discover that there has been a mutual mistake of material fact sufficient to warrant reformation or the setting aside of the compromise.[157]

More specifically, the provisions of Section 7122, while broadly authorizing the compromise of any civil or criminal tax case by the Service, impose the following limitations and requirements:

---

[153] IRC § 7122; Reg. § 301.7122-1.

[154] An offer in compromise is also defined as "an agreement between a taxpayer and the government that settles a tax liability for payment of less than the full amount due." See IRM 5.8.1.1.1, Definition (Nov. 15, 2004).

[155] IRC § 7122(a).

[156] IRC § 7122(b).

[157] Reg. § 301.7122-1(e)(5).

1. The Service's compromise authority is limited to pre-referral cases; that is, the Service may compromise a tax case only if it has not already been referred to the Department of Justice for prosecution or defense. In other words, the Service has authority to compromise a civil (or criminal) tax case during the period it has jurisdiction over the case, and before it refers the case to the Justice Department's Tax Division for prosecution or defense.[158] Once there has been a referral to the Justice Department, the Attorney General or his delegate, not the Service, has final authority to compromise a civil or criminal tax case.[159]

2. Only an official of the Service who has been "duly authorized by the Secretary of the Treasury directly or indirectly by one or more delegations or redelegations of authority" may compromise a tax case.[160]

3. A legal opinion must be obtained from the Chief Counsel[161] setting forth (a) the reasons for the settlement; (b) the amount of the assessed tax, additional amounts, additions to tax, and assessable penalties; and (c) the amount actually paid under the terms of the compromise. This legal opinion must be placed on file. A legal opinion is not necessary where the amount of the assessed tax (plus interest, additional amounts, additions to tax, and assessable penalties)[162] is less than $50,000. When the Service accepts an offer to compromise a tax of $50,000 or more, including penalties and interest, the Chief Counsel is required to file an opinion on the compromise and the reasons for its acceptance.[163] This record of the compromise is kept in the Chief Counsel's office.[164]

---

[158] IRC § 7122(a). There may also be the compromise of a criminal case under Section 7122(a) before the case is referred to the Justice Department.

[159] IRC § 7122(a). Note that 31 USC § 194 has been repealed; instead, see 31 USC § 3711.

[160] IRC §§ 7122(a), 7701(a)(12)(A)(i). Delegations of authority by the Commissioner to accept or reject compromises on behalf of the Service are set forth in Delegation Order (CDO) No. 11 (Nov. 1, 1999). The latest version of CDO No. 11 can be found in the Internal Revenue Bulletin or Cumulative Bulletin and can also be checked through one of the commercial tax services. The officials with authority to execute compromise agreements are listed infra ¶ 15.03[4][e][iii].

[161] IRC § 7122(b). The General Counsel of the Treasury has delegated his functions in compromises to the Chief Counsel, who has redelegated the function to the various Area Counsel. Consequently, each offer in compromise received in an Area/Territory office must be forwarded to the Area Counsel for an opinion if the tax exceeds $50,000.

[162] IRC § 7122(b).

[163] Reg. § 301.7122-1(e)(6). A statement of the amount of assessed tax, the amount of penalties and interest imposed by law, and the amount actually paid under the terms of the compromise will also be put on file. Public access to this information is permitted by Section 6103(k)(1).

[164] IRC § 7122(b).

4. Guidelines for determining whether an offer-in-compromise "is adequate and should be accepted to resolve a dispute" must be prescribed for evaluation of offers.[165] These guidelines are in the form of schedules of national and local allowances "designed to provide that taxpayers entering into a compromise have an adequate means to provide for basic living expenses."[166] In addition, Collection personnel must decide whether the use of the guidelines/schedules is appropriate based on "the facts and circumstances of each taxpayer and must not use the schedules if they would result in the taxpayer's not having adequate means to provide for basic living expenses."[167]

5. Special rules apply to the treatment of offers.[168] Guidelines/schedules provide that Collection personnel must not reject an offer in compromise "solely on the basis of the amount of the offer." Where doubt as to liability is the ground for the offer, the offer cannot be rejected solely because the Service is unable to find the taxpayer's return or return information to verify the liability, and the taxpayer is not required to supply a financial statement.

6. Procedures for administrative review of rejected offers must (a) permit independent administrative review of any rejection of a proposed offer before the taxpayer is formally notified of rejection, and (b) allow the taxpayer to appeal the rejection to the Appeals Office.[169]

Another statute, the levy statute, also applies to compromises. Section 6331(k) prohibits a levy on "any person's property or rights to property" to collect "any" unpaid tax "(A) during the period that an offer-in-compromise by such person under section 7122 of such unpaid tax is pending with the Secretary; and (B) if such offer is rejected by the Secretary, during the thirty days thereafter (and, if an appeal of such rejection is filed within such thirty days, during the period that such appeal is pending)."[170] Should a levy be served in violation of this prohibition, the taxpayer may apply for an injunction enjoining collection.[171] For purposes of the prohibition on collection during the period that an offer is "pending," an offer is pending beginning on the date the offer is accepted for processing.[172] The designation of an offer as pending is critical to the taxpayer. Unless an offer is pending with the Service, the Ser-

---

[165] IRC § 7122(c).

[166] IRC § 7122(c)(2)(A).

[167] IRC § 7122(c)(2)(B).

[168] IRC § 7122(c)(3).

[169] IRC § 7122(d)).

[170] IRC §§ 7122(k)(1)(A), 7122(k)(1)(B). Reg. §§ 301.7122-1(g)(3), 301.7122-1(g)(4).

[171] IRC § 7122(k)(3).

[172] IRC §§ 7122(k)(1)(A), 7122(k)(1)(B) (flush language).

vice is not prohibited from taking levy action.[173] Levy action is also prohibited for thirty days after the rejection of an offer, or while an appeal of a rejection is pending. It is disappointing to describe the Service's procedures in light of these statutory rules. Those procedures show a marked and successful effort to delay every circumstance that might lead to the prohibition of levy action. An offer becomes pending only when the Service accepts it for processing, and this occurs, at least initially, when the offer meets certain minimum requirements.[174]

During the period that the offer is being considered, as well as during any appeal of a rejected offer, the statute of limitations on collection is suspended.[175] Although levy action is prohibited during these periods, Collection may offset an overpayment or other amount against the amount that the taxpayer is attempting to compromise.[176] Suspension of the statute also occurs for the thirty-day period following termination of a compromise agreement and during the appeal of the termination.[177]

Section 7122 was amended by the Taxpayer Bill of Rights 2 and the 1998 Act.[178] To implement these amendments as well as the will of Congress expressed in the legislative history of these changes, Treasury also promulgated regulations that fundamentally change offer in compromise procedures.[179] These regulations are divided into parts covering the following issues: (1) grounds for compromise, Reg. § 301.7122-1(b); (2) special rules for the evaluation of offers, Reg. § 301.7122-1(c); (3) procedures for submission and consideration of offers, Reg..§ 301.7122-1(d); (4) acceptances of offers, rejection of offers, Reg..§ 301.7122-1(e); (5) the effect of offers to compromise on collection activity, Reg. § 301.7122-1(f); (6) deposits, Reg.§ 301.7122-1(g); (7) the statute of limitations, Reg. § 301.7122-1(i); and (8) inspection of accepted offers to compromise, Reg. § 301.7122-1(j). Revenue Procedure 2003-71 sup-

---

[173] IRC §6331(k)(1).

[174] Rev. Proc. 2003-71, 2003-36 IRB 517 (Aug. 21, 2003) at Section 5.01.

[175] IRC § 7122(k)(3).

[176] Reg. § 301.7122-1(g)(5). A deposit a taxpayer has remitted with an offer will not be applied to the tax liability unless the offer is accepted, or unless the taxpayer authorizes the application in writing. If the offer is rejected, the deposit will be refunded to the taxpayer without interest Reg. § 301.7122-1(h).

[177] IRC § 7122(k)(3).

[178] Taxpayer Bill of Rights 2 (Pub. L. No. 104-168).

[179] TD 9007, effective July 18, 2002, contains final regulations reflecting the amendments of Section 7122 made by section 3462 of the 1998 Act and by section 503 of the Taxpayer Bill of Rights 2 (P.L. 104-168). On July 21, 1999, temporary regulations (TD 8829, 64 Fed. Reg. 39020) and a notice of proposed rulemaking (REG-116991-98, 64 Fed. Reg. 39106) adding new Sections 301.7122-0T and 301.7122-1T, effective July 21, 1999, were published in the Federal Register (64 Fed. Reg. 39,020–39,027 (July 21, 1999).

plements and clarifies the regulations.[180] The revenue procedure applies to all offers to compromise a civil or, in rare cases criminal liability, except for offers submitted to the Appeals office or offers submitted after a case has been referred to the Justice Department's Tax Division for defense or prosecution. Consequently, it is necessary to consult not only the relevant statutes, but the regulations, and Revenue Procedure 2003-71 in dealing with offer in compromise issues.

[a] Compromise Policy and Objectives

As the preamble and preliminary portion of the regulations describe, the Service made fundamental changes in its offer in compromise program. First, in policy terms, the Service recognizes that an offer in compromise is a viable collection tool "when it is unlikely that the tax liability can be collected in full and the amount offered reasonably reflects collection potential."[181] The Service's Policy Statement states:[182]

> The Service will accept an offer in compromise when it is unlikely that the tax liability can be collected in full and the amount offered reasonably reflects collection potential. An offer in compromise is a legitimate alternative to declaring the case currently not collectible or to a protracted installment payment agreement. The goal is to achieve collection of what is potentially collectible at the earliest possible time and at the least cost to the Government.

In addition, the Service's objectives are (1) to collect of what can reasonably be collected at the earliest possible time and with the least cost to the government; (2) to achieve a resolution that is in the best interest of both the individual taxpayer and the government; (3) to give taxpayers a fresh start toward future voluntary compliance with all filing and payment requirements; and (4) to collect tax that might not be collected by other means.[183]

---

[180] Rev. Proc. 2003-71, 2003-36 IRB 517 (Aug. 21, 2003), effective November 1, 2003.

[181] The preamble to the regulations refers to the House Conference Report, which states that the Service is expected to consider factors other than doubt as to liability and doubt as to collectibility in deciding whether to compromise the income tax liabilities of individual taxpayers, such as "equity, hardship, and public policy where a compromise of an individual's income tax liability would promote effective tax administration." H. Conf. Rep. 599, 105th Cong., 2d Sess. 289 (1998).

[182] IRM Policies of the IRS P-5-100 (approved Jan. 30, 1992). IRM 5.8.1.1.3, Policy (Nov. 15, 2004).

[183] IRM 5.8.1.1.4, Objectives (Nov. 15, 2004).

[b] Grounds for Compromise

The traditional grounds for compromise have been (1) doubt as to liability and (2) doubt as to collectibility. Doubt as to liability exists when there is a demonstrated genuine dispute about the existence or amount of the correct tax liability.[184] Doubt as to collectibility exists when the taxpayer's assets and income are less than the full amount of the liability.[185] There is now a third ground, promotion of effective tax administration. This third ground permits the Service to compromise a tax liability to "promote effective tax administration when although collection in full could be achieved, collection of the full liability would cause the taxpayer economic hardship," as specially defined.[186]

Also, regardless of the taxpayer's financial circumstances, the Service may compromise to promote effective tax administration where compelling public policy or equity considerations identified by the taxpayer provide sufficient basis for compromising the liability . . . and "due to exceptional circumstances, collection of the full liability would undermine public confidence that the tax laws were being administered in a fair and equitable manner.[187] In addition, the taxpayer must provide some evidence that the circumstances justify compromise, although "a similarly situated taxpayer may have paid his liability in full." Finally, no compromise to promote effective tax administration may be entered into if compromise of the liability would undermine compliance by taxpayers with the tax laws."[188] An offer may be made on one of these three grounds or any combination of the three, in which case, it is called a combination offer.[189]

[i] Doubt as to liability. Offers involving doubt as to liability are relatively infrequent and usually occur where the ninety-day period for filing a

---

[184] Reg. § 301.7122-1(b)(1) (Grounds for compromise—Doubt as to liability).

[185] Reg. § 301.7122-1(b)(2) (Grounds for compromise—Doubt as to collectibility).

[186] Reg. § 301.7122-1(b)(3)(i) (Grounds for compromise—Promote effective tax administration). Taxpayers and practitioners alike often assumed that hardship in paying a delinquent tax assessment alone was a basis for compromise. This was not the case. During the Depression, the Bureau of Internal Revenue solicited the opinion of the Attorney General on whether hardship was a basis for compromise, and the Attorney General opined that if the taxpayer can make payment, hardship should not be considered a basis for compromise, nor should sympathetic or appealing facts, or equity. Opinions of the Attorney General, dated October 24, 1933, and October 2, 1934, known as Op. Att'y Gen. 6, 7, reprinted in XIII-2 CB 442, 445. The Service followed this Opinion for 70 years. By adopting a third ground for compromise for economic hardship, therefore, the Service has modified a long-standing position.

[187] Reg. § 301.7122-1(b)(3)(ii) (Grounds for compromise—Promote effective tax administration).

[188] Reg. § 301.7122-1(b)(3)(iii) (Grounds for compromise—Promote effective tax administration).

[189] IRM 8.13.2.1, Offers in Compromise (June 8, 2000).

Tax Court petition expires without the taxpayer filing a petition.[190] The Service does not consider an offer in compromise a substitute for the normal procedures to determine liability; therefore, the taxpayer must establish that there would be a hardship if the disputed tax had to be paid and a refund suit filed. Where doubt as to liability is supported by evidence, the amount acceptable depends on the hazards of litigation of the particular case. After the taxpayer's liability has been established by a court judgment, there can be no doubt about liability, and no basis exists for a compromise on liability grounds, although the Tax Division of the Justice Department has on occasion settled cases on appeal after a judgment in favor of the government.

[ii] Doubt as to collectibility. Most offers are based on the ground that the taxpayer is unable to pay the full amount of the tax, including additions to the tax, or "the taxpayer's assets and income are less than the full amount of the liability."[191] To determine the taxpayer's ability to pay, Collection will permit the taxpayer to retain "sufficient funds to pay basic living expenses."[192] These basic living expenses are evaluated according to the facts and circumstances of the taxpayer's case and are "guided" by the guidelines the Service has published for national and local living expenses. Notice that the evaluation is to be guided by the national and local living expense guidelines or standards, not that they are controlled by those guidelines.

[iii] Promote effective tax administration. To support a determination that economic hardship exists, the facts must show that (1) the taxpayer is unable to earn a living because the taxpayer has a long-term illness, medical condition, or disability, and it is reasonably foreseeable that the taxpayer's financial resources "will be exhausted providing for care and support during the course of the condition;" (2) the taxpayer has assets, but will be unable to pay for basic living expenses if those assets are sold to pay outstanding tax liabilities; and (3) the taxpayer has assets, but is unable to borrow on the security

---

[190] When an offer is based on doubt as to liability and the case either has been considered by Appeals or is pending in Appeals, the local office will send the case to Appeals for consideration. IRM 5.8.4.9, Identifying Cases Pending in Appeals (Nov. 1, 2000). Appeals may request further investigation from the local office. When the offer is based on doubt as to collectibility and the case is in the Tax Court, the procedures for handling an Appeals case are followed, except that when an offer is to be investigated, Appeals will ordinarily obtain a stipulation agreeing to the proposed liability and will hold the stipulation in escrow. If the local office recommends against the compromise, the taxpayer may appeal. If the offer is accepted, Appeals will see to it that the stipulation is filed with the Tax Court, have the tax assessed, and then send the taxpayer an acceptance letter.

[191] Reg. § 301.7122-1(b)(2) (Grounds for compromise—Doubt as to collectibility).

[192] Reg. § 301.7122-1(b)(2) (Grounds for compromise—Doubt as to collectibility); Reg. § 301.7122-1(c)(2)(i) (Special rules for evaluating offers).

of those assets, and the seizure and sale of the assets "would have sufficient adverse consequences" as to make enforced collection action "unlikely."[193]

Another list illustrates the factors Collection will consider to support a determination that compromise would not undermine other taxpayers' compliance with the tax laws: (1) the taxpayer does not have a history of failing to file and pay taxes; (2) the taxpayer has not deliberately avoided payment of taxes; and (3) the taxpayer has not encouraged other taxpayers to refuse to comply with the tax laws.[194]

[iv] Special rules for the evaluation of offers. Section 7122(c) requires guidelines to be established for revenue officers and other employees to evaluate whether an offer is adequate and should be accepted to resolve the dispute.[195] As part of theses guidelines, Collection developed and published national and local allowances designed to provide taxpayers with basic living expenses for arriving at an acceptable offer. The allowances are to be used by revenue officers to evaluate the taxpayer's particular facts and circumstances.[196] An offer from a low-income taxpayer is not permitted to be rejected solely because of the amount of the offer,[197] and if the offer is based on doubt as to liability, the offer is not to be rejected because of the inability of the Service to locate the taxpayer's return; furthermore, Collection can not require the taxpayer to complete a financial statement.[198]

Doubt as to liability exists where there is a genuine dispute about the existence or amount of the correct tax liability under the law.[199] Assuming a final court decision or judgment has not established the existence of the tax liability, a doubt as to liability offer will be acceptable if it reflects the reasonable equivalent of the amount the Service would expect to collect through litigation; that is, a hazards of litigation settlement.

---

[193] Reg. § 301.7122-1(b)(4)(iv)(B).

[194] Reg. § 301.7121-1(b)(4)(iv)(C).

[195] IRC § 7122(c)(1).

[196] IRC §§ 7122(c)(2)(A) and 7122(c)(2)(B). The Senate Finance Committee stated in its Report that it "believes that the ability of the taxpayer to compromise tax liability and to make payments of tax liability by installment payment agreement enhances taxpayer compliance [and so] the IRS should work with taxpayers who are sincerely trying to meet their obligations and stay in the tax system. Accordingly, the Committee believes that the IRS should make it easier for taxpayers to enter into offer-in-compromise agreements." IRS Restructuring and Reform Bill of 1998, HR 2676, S. Rep. 105-74, 105th Cong. 2d Sess. 88 (Apr. 22, 1998).

[197] IRC § 7122(c)(3)(A).

[198] IRC § 7122(c)(3)(B).

[199] Reg. § 301.7122-1(b)(1). Obviously, that doubt is removed when a judgment establishes the existence of the liability. Id. See Rev. Proc. 2003-71, 2003-36 IRB 517 (Aug. 21, 2003) at section 4, Submitting an offer to compromise).

There is doubt as to collectibility when the taxpayer's assets and income cannot satisfy the full amount of the liability.[200] In evaluating a doubt as to collectibility offer, the revenue officer considers the taxpayer's ability to pay the liability in full, after allowing for the taxpayer's "basic living expenses." Basic living expenses are computed based on the facts and circumstances and the applicable national and local living expenses the Service has published. A doubt as to collectibility offer will be considered acceptable if (1) the Service is unlikely to collect the outstanding tax liability in full and (2) the offer has "reasonable collection potential" (i.e., it is a reasonable reflection of the amount the Service could collect through administrative and judicial remedies).[201] The reasonable collection potential of the taxpayer's case also takes into account the taxpayer's basic living expenses. There is some flexibility where this type of offer is made. An offer to compromise a case based on doubt as to liability may be accepted where the amount offered is less than the total reasonable collection potential of the case when the taxpayer persuades collection personnel that there are special circumstances.

An offer based on the ground that acceptance will promote effective tax administration will be acceptable where the Service could collect the full amount of the tax liability, but full collection would cause the taxpayer economic hardship because the taxpayer will be unable to pay reasonable living expenses.[202]

An effective tax administration offer will also be acceptable where the taxpayer shows that there are "compelling public policy" or "equity considerations." To make this showing, the taxpayer must present information that explains that because of exceptional circumstances, collection of the full liability "would undermine public confidence . . . that the tax laws are being administered in a fair and equitable manner."[203] In addition, the taxpayer has the burden of showing that the circumstances justify compromise, "even though a similarly situated taxpayer may have paid the liability in full."[204]

[c] Acceptance of an Offer

Acceptance of an offer is only made by the Service's sending of a written notice of acceptance to the taxpayer or the taxpayer's representative.[205] As further consideration for accepting the offer, Collection may request that the tax-

---

[200] Rev. Proc. 2003-71, 2003-36 IRB 517 (Aug. 21, 2003) at section 4.02(2).

[201] Rev. Proc. 2003-71, 2003-36 IRB 517 (Aug. 21, 2003) at section 4.02(2).

[202] Rev. Proc. 2003-71, 2003-36 IRB 517 (Aug. 21, 2003) at section 4.02(3). In determining the reasonable collection potential of a case, Collection will take into account current basic living expenses. See Reg. § 301.6343-1(d).

[203] Rev. Proc. 2003-71, 2003-36 IRB 517 (Aug. 21, 2003) at section 4.02(3).

[204] Rev. Proc. 2003-71, 2003-36 IRB 517 (Aug. 21, 2003) at section 4.02(3).

[205] Reg. § 301.7122-1(e)(1).

payer enter into a collateral agreement with the Service or post such security as Collection finds is necessary to ensure collection. A compromise finally concludes the amount of the taxpayer's tax liability as stated in the offer. Neither the taxpayer nor the Service may reopen a case except where (1) false information or documents have been supplied in connection with the offer; (2) the taxpayer has concealed his ability to pay or assets; or (3) it has been discovered that a mutual mistake of material fact has been made, sufficient to cause the offer agreement to be reformed or set aside.[206]

[d] Rejection of an Offer

An offer to compromise has not been rejected until Collection sends the taxpayer a written notice of the rejection and the reasons for the rejection.[207] This notice will not be sent until an independent administrative review of the proposed rejection has been completed. Collection will not take levy action during the period in which it considers the offer and for thirty days after the offer is rejected. The taxpayer may appeal a rejection of the offer to the Office of Appeals if the taxpayer requests an appeal within thirty days after the date on the notice of rejection.[208] The appeal may be made under the collection due process procedures of Section 6330, which permit the taxpayer to appeal the case to the Tax Court or under the Collection Appeals Program, which does not permit Tax Court review. Where Tax Court review is sought, review is for abuse of discretion, a standard that defers to the Service as long as the decision does not represent a "clear error in judgment" on the part of the decisionmaker.[209]

[e] Effect of Offer on Collection Activity

Collection is prohibited during the consideration of an offer, and if the offer is rejected, for an additional thirty days after the rejection to permit the taxpayer to appeal to the Appeals Office, as well as during the consideration of the rejection in Appeals.[210] In addition, during this period, the statute of limitations on collection is suspended.[211] Enforced collection action will be halted

---

[206] Reg. § 301.7122-1(e)(5). Compromise with one taxpayer does not extinguish the liability of any person not named in the offer who is also liable for the tax to which the offer relates, and Collection may take action against that person.

[207] Reg. § 301.7122-1(f)(1).

[208] Reg. § 301.7122-1(f)(5).

[209] See Davis v. Comm'r, 115 TC 35, 39 (2000). See also Fargo v. Comm'r, TC Memo. 2004-12 (where a division of the Court suggested that it might have reached a different decision on the offer in compromise, but nevertheless upheld the Service).

[210] Reg. § 301.7122-1(g)(1).

[211] IRC § 6331(k)(3).

during the processing of an offer; however, if the Service believes collection is in jeopardy, or if the taxpayer submitted the offer solely to delay collection by, for example, failing to file an offer in processable form, the Service may levy to collect the liability.[212]

Even if enforced collection action is not taken during Collection's consideration of the offer, it may offset an overpayment or other amount to the liability that the taxpayer is attempting to compromise to the extent provided by the offset statute, Section 6402.[213]

[f] Deposits

Despite a possible offset, a deposit that a taxpayer makes with the offer in compromise will not be applied to the liability unless the offer is accepted or unless the taxpayer authorizes the application in writing; if the offer is withdrawn or rejected, the deposit will be refunded to the taxpayer without interest.[214]

[g] Statute of Limitations

The statute of limitations on collection is suspended while levy is prohibited.[215] Collection may ask the taxpayer to extend the assessment statute, but must also inform the taxpayer of the right to refuse the extension.[216]

[2] Law of Compromises

The source of the Service's authority to compromise a tax is the statutory language of Section 7122, but the process by which the government and a taxpayer enter a binding compromise agreement is governed by the principles of the law of contracts. The statutory and contractual nature of the compromise are discussed separately.

The statutory requirements for a compromise are not mere directions. They are jurisdictional prerequisites to a valid compromise. The Supreme Court long ago held in *Botany Worsted Mills v. United States*[217] that the Service's authority to enter into a valid compromise agreement exists only where it has strictly complied with the terms of the statute, and in the event of a fail-

---

[212] Reg. § 301.7122-1(g)(3).
[213] Reg. § 301.7122-1(g)(5).
[214] Reg. § 301.7122-1(g).
[215] IRC § 6331(k)(3). See Reg. § 301.7122-1(i)(1)
[216] Reg. § 301.7122-1(i)(2).
[217] Botany Worsted Mills v. United States 278 US 282 (1929).

ure to comply, no agreement binds either the taxpayer or the government. In the case, a deficiency had been asserted against Botany Worsted Mills for additional taxes as a result of disallowed deductions for payments made to members of its board of directors. After protracted negotiations with the chief of the special audit section, a settlement was reached under which Botany Mills accepted a partial disallowance of the deductions, filed an amended return reflecting the settlement, and paid the resulting tax. Later, Botany Mills, wishing to escape the compromise, filed a claim for refund for the tax it paid. When the claim was disallowed, Botany Mills filed a petition in the Court of Claims. The Court of Claims dismissed the petition on the ground that the settlement agreement prevented recovery. In the Supreme Court, the government conceded that the sole statutory authority the Service had to settle a tax case was the predecessor of Sections 7121 and 7122 and that the settlement agreement had not been assented to by the Secretary of the Treasury or his delegate. The Court held that "Congress intended by the statute to prescribe the exclusive method by which tax cases could be compromised, requiring therefor the concurrence by the Commissioner and the Secretary."[218] Because the Service had failed to obtain the statutorily mandated assent, the Supreme Court held that the agreement was binding on neither the taxpayer nor the government.[219]

Even after *Botany Worsted Mills*, the most frequently litigated issue involving the compromise statute arises from the requirement that the compromise must be made by a person with authority to do so. Although authority has been delegated to various officials in the Service, it has not been delegated to revenue officers. A revenue officer (or a revenue agent) has no authority to bind the Service to a compromise, and where a Collection officer or some other employee to whom the delegation authority does not run purports to sign a compromise on behalf of the Service, the compromise is ineffective.[220]

Other rules apply to compromise agreements. According to Section 7122, the civil tax "case" that may be compromised includes not only the principal amount of the tax but interest and penalties as well; in fact, a separate compro-

---

[218] Botany Worsted Mills v. United States 278 US 282, 288 (1929).

[219] Section 3229, the predecessor of Section 7122, authorized the Commissioner of Internal Revenue (not his delegate) to compromise tax claims with the advice and consent of the Secretary of the Treasury and the opinion of the Solicitor of Internal Revenue. In *Botany Worsted Mills*, although the Commissioner may have "ratified" the settlement by making the assessment on the basis of the amended return, neither the consent of the Secretary nor the opinion of the Attorney General had been obtained.

[220] Reimer v. United States, 441 F2d 1129 (5th Cir. 1971) ("under 26 U.S.C. § 7122, the IRS agent named by Reimer had no authority to compromise his tax liability"); Country Gas Serv. Inc. v. United States, 405 F2d 1417 (1st Cir. 1969) (delegation authority to compromise "stops at the district director level"); Brooks v. United States, 833 F2d 1136 (4th Cir. 1987) (letter apparently accepting compromise offer held ineffective, inter alia, because District Director not authorized to accept offers involving liabilities in excess of $100,000).

mise agreement of these parts of the single liability or "case" is impermissible.[221] Also, the amount of any refund agreed to under a compromise may not be used to offset a tax owed for years not involved in the settlement.[222] While the Service literally has the authority to settle a criminal tax case, it views this authority as limited to criminal liability for a violation of a regulatory provision of the Code or a related statute, and then only if the violation was not deliberately committed with an intent to defraud.[223] Regulations[224] provide that acceptance of an offer in compromise of a civil liability does not remit a criminal liability, nor does an acceptance of an offer in compromise of a criminal liability forgive civil liability.

Although Section 7122 gives the Service the authority to compromise a tax case, the compromise agreement itself is a contract, governed by general principles of contract law applicable to other contracts.[225] Among other things, this fact means that a compromise is a legally enforceable promise or set of promises. As such, in order for the compromise to be binding and enforceable, the following elements must be present:

- At least one promisor and one promisee each having legal capacity to act as such in the contract;

---

[221] Reg. § 301.7122-1(c). However, the Service requires specific penalties to be compromised separately and not in connection with taxes, interest, and ad valorem penalties. Based on the proposition that each tax year is a separate cause of action, a taxpayer who entered into a compromise of his 1972 tax year was held barred from a refund for that year arising from a net operating loss carryback from 1974. Hartzog v. United States, 6 Cl. Ct. 835 (1984).

[222] Weisman v. United States, 76-2 USTC ¶ 9731 (DDC 1976).

[223] Reg. § 301.7122-1(b). In a case involving the alleged compromise of a criminal case by a U.S. Attorney, the purpose of the language was said "to facilitate money settlements of tax liability and the settlement of criminal charges are contemplated only when ancillary thereto." United States v. McCue, 178 F. Supp. 426 (D. Conn. 1959), aff'd on other grounds, 301 F2d 451 (2d Cir.), cert. denied, 370 US 939 (1962).

[224] Reg. § 301.7122-1(a)(2).

[225] United States v. Feinberg, 372 F2d 352 (3d Cir. 1967); United States v. Lane, 303 F2d 1 (5th Cir. 1962); Kurio v. United States, 429 F. Supp. 42 (SD Tex. 1970). Sprowles v. United States, 89-2 USTC ¶ 9467 (WD Ky. 1989) (claim that compromise entered into under a mutual mistake over taxpayer's liability rejected; as a matter of law, the compromise agreement established taxpayer's liability). At least where suspension of the limitations period is involved, the Seventh Circuit has properly said that a compromise is a quid pro quo: The proponent agrees to suspend the statute of limitations, and the Service agrees to consider his offer. United States v. McGaughey, 977 F2d 1067 (7th Cir. 1992), reh'g denied, 1993 US App. LEXIS 1099 (7th Cir. 1993) (en banc), cert. denied, 507 US 1019 (1993). On the other hand, it has been said that the waiver of the statute of limitations is not a contract, but the waiver of a defense. Florsheim Bros. Drygoods Co. v. United States, 280 US 453, 466 (1930); Stange v. United States, 282 US 270, 276 (1931). Although a waiver of the limitations period is the voluntary, unilateral waiver of a defense, and therefore is not a contract, contract principles have been applied as a means of determining whether the defense has been waived. See ¶ 5.03[4][a].

- A manifestation of mutual assent (an offer and an acceptance) to the terms by the parties who form the contract and by each promisor to the consideration for his promise;
- Sufficient consideration; and
- An agreement not declared void by statute or common law because, for example, it is not in writing.[226]

When the case is in court, a settlement or compromise is also governed by general contract principles. Tax settlement agreements in the form of letters of offer and acceptance are considered binding even absent a binding stipulation of settlement, filed decision document, or closing agreement or offer in compromise.[227] For example, when the Service sent an offer to settle with investors in a partnership, the taxpayers sent a letter accepting the offer, and the Service sent a closing agreement form to them that they signed and returned, the court held that the taxpayers had accepted the Service's offer; therefore, there was a binding settlement agreement despite the fact that the Service did not execute the closing agreement.[228] A taxpayer makes an offer in compromise on forms prescribed for the purpose.[229] However, a form other than the offer form has been recognized to effect a compromise.[230]

The consideration supporting a compromise agreement is the mutual concessions the parties make. However, as a matter of practice, the Service generally asks that the offer be accompanied by a remittance in the amount offered or a deposit if the offer provides for future installments.[231] As a condition of accepting an offer, the taxpayer may also be required to enter into any collat-

---

[226] Restatement (Second) of Contracts §§ 9 (Parties Required), 18 (Manifestation of Mutual Consent), 71 (Requirement of Exchange), and 110 (The Statute of Frauds—Classes of Contracts Covered). The applicable law would be federal common law of contracts, not state law. Clearfield Trust Co. v. United States, 318 US 363 (1943).

[227] Treaty Pines Inv. Partnership v. Comm'r, 967 F2d 206 (5th Cir. 1992); Spires v. United States, 76 AFTR2d 95-7363 (D. Or. 1995); Robbins Tire & Rubber Co. v. Comm'r, 52 TC 420 (1969); Haiduk v. Comm'r, 60 TCM 864 (1990).

[228] Spires v. United States, 76 AFTR2d 95-7363 (D. Or. 1995) ("General contract law principles govern tax case settlements.").

[229] Reg. § 301.7122-1(d)(1).

[230] See Hamilton v. United States, 324 F2d 960 (Ct. Cl. 1963) (Form 870-AD). See also Stair v. United States, 516 F2d 560 (2d Cir. 1975) (taxpayer was estopped from filing and prosecuting a claim for refund after a Form 870-AD was signed by the taxpayer and the Appellate Division). The effect of the Form 870-AD agreement is discussed at ¶ 9.08[1]. See also Timms v. United States, 678 F2d 831 (9th Cir. 1982) (Form 656 and letters); Finen v. Comm'r, 41 TC 557 (1964) (Form 656 and collateral agreements); Waller v. United States, 767 F. Supp. 1042 (ED Cal. 1991) (original offer on Form 656, later amended by letter was held valid and binding offer in compromise).

[231] IRC § 7809(b); Reg. §§ 301.7122-1(d), 301.7122-1(d)(4). This remittance or deposit is refunded without interest if the offer is withdrawn or rejected unless the taxpayer agrees to the application of the amount to the balance due.

eral agreement or post any security considered necessary to protect the government's interests.[232]

Once the parties enter into the compromise, neither the taxpayer nor the government can reopen the case, except where ground for rescission of a contract exists—that is, where there has been (1) a misrepresentation of the assets of the taxpayer by falsification or concealment or (2) mutual mistake of a material fact.[233] Absent grounds for rescission, a taxpayer who has entered into a valid compromise may not subsequently prosecute a claim for refund.[234] Authorities are divided on the finality of a compromise agreement where it subsequently turns out no tax was due from the taxpayer.[235] In an extreme application of the finality of a compromise, a taxpayer was held bound by a waiver of the statute of limitations in the offer form even where it appeared the limitations period had run prior to the acceptance of the offer.[236] Misrepresentation is ground for rescission.[237] However, the Service says an unintentional mistake in a revenue agent's report does not constitute a misrepresentation.[238]

The ordinary compromise agreement requires performance of the promise of settlement or satisfaction and does not discharge or extinguish the original claim until performance. The Service's remedies on the original claim are

---

[232] Reg. § 301.7122-1(d)(3).

[233] Reg. § 301.7122-1(c). See also Ely & Walker Dry Goods Co. v. United States, 34 F2d 429 (8th Cir. 1929), cert. denied, 281 US 755 (1930); Goodding v. United States, 75-1 USTC ¶ 9401 (SD Iowa 1975); Rosenberg v. United States, 313 F. Supp. 28 (DND 1970). See Timms v. United States, 678 F2d 831 (9th Cir. 1982), cert. denied, 459 US 1068 (1982); Hartzog v. United States, 6 Cl. Ct. 835 (1984) (no mutual mistake of fact found where taxpayer tried to claim a refund for a compromised year on the basis of a net operating loss carryback; the claim had been filed before, but not included in the compromise).

[234] Hamilton v. United States, 324 F2d 960 (Ct. Cl. 1963) (Form 870-AD). See also Morris White Fashions, Inc. v. United States, 176 F. Supp. 760 (SDNY 1959) (claim was allowed but only because a compromise had not been entered into).

[235] Compare Cooper Agency v. United States, 301 F. Supp. (DSC 1969), aff'd per curiam, 422 F2d 1331 (4th Cir.), cert. denied, 400 US 904 (1970) and Seattle-First Nat'l Bank v. United States, 44 F. Supp. 603 (ED Wash. 1942), aff'd, 136 F2d 676 (9th Cir. 1943), aff'd, 321 US 583 (1944) (no refund allowed) with Staten Island Hygeia Ice & Cold Storage Co. v. United States, 85 F2d 68 (2d Cir. 1936) (refund allowed).

[236] United States v. Feinberg 372 F2d 352 (3d Cir. 1967). However, the Service's policy is to advise a taxpayer that the period of limitations has run and to not accept an offer in compromise; however, if the taxpayer wishes to make a voluntary payment, the taxpayer should supply a written statement that the taxpayer has been advised collection of the tax is barred along with the payment. IRM 5.8.1.2.3, Expired liability (Nov. 30, 2001).

[237] United States v. Pittman, 48-2 USTC ¶ 9328 (D. Ga. 1948) (rescission if assets unknown to either party subsequently come to light). See Coy v. United States, 377 F2d 925 (9th Cir. 1967).

[238] Rev. Rul. 73-459, 1973-2 CB 415.

merely suspended. Thus, where a taxpayer defaults on a comproment, the Service may collect the original tax liability, less payment, sue on the compromise agreement.[239]

[3] Decision to File an Offer

An offer in compromise should not be submitted without consideration of both the positive and negative factors in making the offer, both of which are discussed below.

[a] Advantages of Filing an Offer

At least some of the factors in favor of making an offer are as follows:

1. *Payment of less than the full assessed amount.* Obviously, the purpose of making an offer is to liquidate an assessment by paying an amount the taxpayer can pay because he is unable to pay the full amount of the assessed tax. This procedure benefits both the taxpayer and the government. The taxpayer is relieved of the burden of a debt he cannot satisfy and the government obtains some revenue without further proceedings that would only prove unproductive.

2. *Deferred payment.* Unless the offer is a cash offer, the taxpayer's burden in paying the agreed amount may be spread over a term of years and lightened to that extent. Of course, it must be understood that these deferred payments will be made after payment of the taxpayer's current tax liability and will generally be nondeductible payments of the principal amount of the compromised tax liability for an earlier period or periods.

3. *Delay in collection action.* Even in the event an offer is not accepted, collection action against the taxpayer is deferred while the offer is being considered, provided that the offer is not frivolous. Thus, the Service requests a down payment as evidence of the good faith of the offer.

4. *Control over collection action.* Once a taxpayer and the Service enter into a compromise agreement, the taxpayer's dealings with the Service are governed by the terms of the agreement. If the taxpayer performs his end of the bargain, he is assured of no surprise enforced collection.

---

[239] United States v. Lane 303 F2d 1 (5th Cir. 1962). See also United States v. Saladoff, 233 F. Supp. 255 (ED Pa. 1964), aff'd sub nom. United States v. Feinberg, 372 F2d 352 (3d Cir. 1967) (government may also sue for amount of original assessment less payments made under the compromise); Samet v. United States, 242 F. Supp. 214 (MDNC 1965) (Service foreclosed lien against property redeemed after tax sale).

5. *Finality.* Once a compromise agreement is in effect, the taxpayer's liability for the period(s) covered by the agreement is fixed. The Service may not claim that the taxpayer owes any additional liability for the period(s), except in extraordinary circumstances usually arising out of some improper action by the taxpayer.

6. *Release of liens.* Where a collateral agreement is entered into as further consideration for the compromise, the tax liens filed against the taxpayer may be released, thereby increasing possible income (and, of course, revenue to the Service).

[b] Disadvantages of Filing an Offer

The submission of an offer in compromise also has some distinctly negative features, some of which are as follows:

1. *Disclosure of collection sources.* Since no offer is accepted without the preparation and submission of a detailed financial statement, the Service will, in the event it rejects the offer, have a road map to property or rights to property belonging to the taxpayer that are subject to levy or enforcement of the tax lien. The judgment of the taxpayer and his representative that certain property is not readily salable or worthy of collection action is not binding on the Service. Thus, the taxpayer faces the predicament of one of the following situations: (a) not submitting a financial statement and thereby not being able to compromise a liability; (b) submitting a financial statement that opens the possibility of collection action if the offer is rejected; or (c) submitting a financial statement that may be considered false.

2. *Waiver of substantial benefits.* The offer form requires the taxpayer to waive the statute of limitations on collection for a period that may run beyond the normal six-year limitations period. In addition, benefits for periods ending before or during the periods covered by the offer that might have reduced the total liability are waived.

3. *Delay in conclusion of agreement.* The consideration of an offer takes some time, even though the offer states it will be acted upon in "due course." Although this delay benefits the taxpayer because collection action is deferred, the delay may be a source of uncertainty. Mere consideration of an offer, of course, does not constitute acceptance.

4. *Deposit without interest.* The taxpayer is encouraged to make some cash deposit with the offer. This amount does not draw interest during consideration of the offer, and on its return after rejection of the offer represents a likely source of collection. For this reason, a loan by a third party for the purpose of the deposit is advisable.

5. *Immediate collection on default.* Although the Service's procedures on default in a taxpayer's performance of a compromise agreement may seem almost indulgent, they are largely discretionary, and the taxpayer may suffer the effect of immediate Collection action.

6. *Hampering effect of compromise and collateral agreement.* A deferred payment offer does not mean that the tax lien will be released. The taxpayer's property remains encumbered until all payments have been made. The benefit of a future income collateral agreement is that the tax lien may be released, but the taxpayer will be obliged to pay substantial after-tax income to retire the agreed liability. Also, the taxpayer must usually submit a tax form to Special Procedures for a period of ten years; failure to submit a return may result in an unintentional breach of the agreement.

[c] Additional Considerations

When, then, should an offer be submitted? There are obviously no absolute rules applicable in all situations. An offer certainly is indicated if the taxpayer can make a cash offer without being tied down by a collateral agreement under which he may have to pay additional amounts to the Service based on increases in his income. Even a cash offer with a collateral agreement should not be too burdensome if, for example, the taxpayer is over sixty-five and his high-income years are behind him. An analysis of the age, health, and similar circumstances of the taxpayer, as well as analysis of prior liens and other factors relating to the forced sale value of the taxpayer's property in terms of the effect on the likelihood of present and future collection, should help to decide whether to submit an offer.

[4] Preparation of the Offer

A taxpayer must submit an offer to compromise a tax liability on the Service's current version of Form 656, Offer in Compromise, fully completed with no terms stricken or altered, and signed by the taxpayer under penalties of perjury.[240] The Form 656 should include the following: (1) all liabilities covered by the offer; (2) the legal grounds for compromise (doubt as to liability, doubt as to collectibility, promotion of effective tax administration, or a combination

---

[240] Rev. Proc. 2003-71, 2003-36 IRB 517 (Aug. 21, 2003) at section 4. When filed, the offer must be accompanied by a service fee in the amount of $150. Reg. § 300.3 included in TD 9086 (Aug. 4, 2003). The offer should be mailed to the service center indicated in the Offer in Compromise package available from the Service on-line at irs.gov.

of these grounds); (3) the amount the taxpayer proposes to pay; and (4) the payment terms (the amounts and due dates of payments).

These procedures hardly seem onerous. But beneath the offer in compromise terminology and the simple requirement of filing a complete Form 656 lies some hard realities. The taxpayer must not only complete the form, but give the reasons and submit appropriate information to enable Service collection personnel to decide whether the offer should be accepted on the ground that there is doubt about the existence or amount of the legally correct tax liability. The offer is a form of argument. When the taxpayer submits an offer, the taxpayer is presenting a claim to the Service that an outstanding tax liability should be compromised at less than the face amount of the liability. Since the taxpayer is presenting a claim, the taxpayer has the burden of presenting support for the claim and also the burden of persuading Collection personnel that the claim should be approved. When one reflects on the fact that Collection personnel who will act on the offer/claim have reviewed many other offers and have heard many explanations of why the taxpayer is unable to pay the full amount of the liability, one is struck by how formidable a task the taxpayer in straitened financial circumstances faces. It should be remembered, finally, that Service personnel have not only the authority to decide in the first instance (as opposed to final authority) what action should be taken, but also the responsibility for justifying that action.

The Offer in Compromise form contains more than an offer to compromise an assessed liability by paying a lesser amount in cash or in installments. (See Form 15.10.) The form also incorporates (1) a waiver of the statute of limitations on assessment and collection; (2) a waiver of the taxpayer's right to receive refunds or credits from the Service up to the end of the calendar year in which the offer is accepted; and (3) on default, a waiver of the restrictions on assessment and collection, as well as further notice before assessment and collection. Consequently, the offeror/taxpayer promises not only to pay the compromise amount, but to waive substantial rights he otherwise would have had. The offer in compromise may be revoked or withdrawn by the offeror/taxpayer (proponent) or by the death or legally incapacitating insanity of the proponent at any time prior to acceptance.[241] Accordingly, the offer in compromise form should not be executed without careful examination of its terms and consideration of the meaning of the duties imposed and rights waived.

Taxpayers preparing offers in compromise would be wise to consider the following:

1. *Taxpayer's name and address.* The identity of the person submitting the offer is significant because, under the law of some states, the release of one co-obligor releases the other. Consequently, a settlement

---

[241] Reg. § 301.7122-1(d)(4); Restatement (Second) of Contracts §§ 15 (Mental Illness or Defect), 262 (Death or Incapacity of Person Necessary for Performance).

with one taxpayer could operate to release another taxpayer who is jointly liable on the assessment.[242] Therefore, to permit collection of the liability from any other co-obligors, the Service usually requests co-obligors on a joint assessment (other than a husband and wife) to make separate offers.

2. *Total liabilities.* The liabilities included in the offer are important because a compromise agreement conclusively settles the entire liability of the taxpayer (including taxes, ad valorem penalties, and interest) with respect to which the offer in compromise is submitted.[243] However, separate offer forms must be used to compromise each class of tax (e.g., income, gift, estate, employment, or excise) and specific penalties.

3. *Identification of liability.* To avoid any misunderstanding about the liability covered by the compromise, the liability sought to be compromised should be specific and complete; for example, if the liability is transferee liability, it should be described as such.

4. *Basis for compromise.* The legal grounds for compromise must be stated: doubt as to liability, doubt as to collectibility, and to promote effective tax administration.

5. *Amount offered.* The total amount of money offered must be stated. The amount offered does not include money already paid, expected future income, funds attached by levy, or anticipated benefits from capital/net operating losses.

6. *Payment terms.* There are three types of payment terms: (a) cash, payment to be made within ninety days after notice of acceptance; (b) short-term deferred, payment to be made in more than ninety days, but within two years (twenty-four months) or less from the notice of acceptance; or (c) deferred payment, payment to be made within the time remaining on the statute of limitations.[244] Payment of the compromise amount is made with an offer (a cash offer) or, more frequently, payment of all or part of the compromise amount either on notice of the acceptance or in deferred payments (a deferred payment offer). Again, to avoid the Service's taking collection activity because

---

[242] This situation must be distinguished from several liability (e.g. transferees). The Service has ruled that acceptance of an offer in compromise made by one transferee does not compromise the liability of the others, but any payment obtained under the compromise is credited to the transferor's liability, reducing to that extent the liability of the other transferees. Rev. Rul. 72-436, 1972-2 CB 643.

[243] Reg. 301.7122-1(c). For offers accepted after December 31, 1999, interest on the compromised amount is also compromised. IRM 5.8.1.7.1, Taxes, Penalties and Interest Constitute One Liability (Nov. 15, 2004). Moreover, any refund due to the taxpayer under a compromise may not be offset by crediting the amount to other years. Weisman v. United States, 76-2 USTC ¶ 9731 (DDC 1976).

[244] IRM 5.8.1.9.4(3), Payment Terms (Nov. 15, 2004).

it appears that the taxpayer has defaulted on a payment of a deferred payment offer, the offer should reflect the amount, if any, to be deposited at the time the offer is filed, as well as the amounts of any deposits on prior offers and the amount of each deferred payment and the date each is to be made. Consideration should also be given to the allocation of payments. For corporations, interest satisfied by payment is deductible. The Service must follow an allocation made in an agreement,[245] but absent agreement, payments are applied to tax, penalty, and interest beginning with the earliest year.[246]

7. *Standard conditions.* Taxpayers must agree to all the standard conditions as printed on the form. Form 656 provides that the taxpayer not only agrees that the Service may retain all refunds and payments made to the taxpayer's account for the taxable periods covered by the offer, but also waives any amount the taxpayer may be entitled to under the internal revenue laws (by way of refund or credit) for any year ending prior to the end of the calendar year in which the offer is accepted.[247] This waiver should be eliminated in offers based on doubt as to liability or clarified by way of collateral agreement.[248] Form 656 also provides that the offerer/taxpayer must agree both to the waiver of the benefit of any statute of limitations on assessment

---

[245] Robbins Tire & Rubber Co., 52 TC 420 (1969) (acq.). Rev. Rul. 73-304, 1973-2 CB 42.

[246] Rev. Rul. 73-304, 1973-2 CB 42.

[247] Refunds are waived up to "the difference between the liability sought to be compromised and the amount offered," as provided in the Form 656. A taxpayer is permitted to obtain refunds in excess of this amount. However, the Service may require a collateral agreement to be executed as part of the compromise, and the collateral agreement can also contain a waiver of refunds. Whether and to what extent a taxpayer is waiving a right to refunds should be clear from both the offer form and the collateral agreement. See A&A Distribs., Inc. v. United States, 81-1 USTC ¶ 9,136 (conflict between collateral agreement and offer form).

As a contract, the compromise form controls which years' refunds the Service will retain. Therefore, if there is a conflict between the cover letter accompanying the compromise and the compromise agreement, the compromise agreement controls. ILM 199937006 (June 4, 1999), gathering cases.

[248] For an illustrative case construing a provision pertaining to refunds in a compromise agreement prepared by a taxpayer rather than by the Service, see Timms v. United States, 678 F2d 831 (9th Cir. 1982). In *Timms*, the circuit court adopted the rule of contract construction that an ambiguous contract term "should be interpreted against the party drafting the term." However, the court found that the taxpayer was the drafting party and that the taxpayer had failed to provide for the possibility of a refund of taxes paid for certain periods in the event of a change in law.

and collection[249] and to the suspension[250] of the running of the statute of limitations on assessment and collection for the period during which the offer is pending, or for the period an installment under a deferred payment compromise remains unpaid, and for one year thereafter.[251] The purpose of the suspension is to give the Service time to consider the offer and to take action in the event of default.[252]

8. *Explanation of circumstances.* This portion of the offer requires more than an indication. For the reasons described previously, the taxpayer should present the applicable ground and the information (evidence) in support of the ground in a convincing way in a rider to the offer form.

9. *Signatures.* The compromise of the tax liability of a taxpayer jointly liable for an assessed tax may release the joint obligor(s). To avoid a problem on this score, the Service requests that the offer be signed by the proponents or one authorized to bind the proponent (i.e., both a husband and a wife making a joint offer, the president of a corporation, or a partner on behalf of the partnership). The question of whether a compromise will satisfy the liability of both parties and thus prevent collection from the joint obligor depends on state law. Some states say the release of one party does not release the co-obligor. An express reservation may make the liability of the joint obligor certain, but what amount may be collected? Should it be the balance of the liability or only the proportionate share? If a covenant

---

[249] IRC § 6501. Because the compromise form has a waiver provision, the principles applicable to waivers apply. See ¶¶ 5.03[4][a] and 5.04.

[250] IRC § 6331(k)(1). The statute of limitations is suspended for the 30 days following notice of the rejection of the offer to permit the taxpayer to appeal to Appeals, and if the taxpayer does appeal, during the period that the appeal is pending. See United States v. McGee, 993 F2d 184 (9th Cir. 1993) (the Service "does not impliedly reject an offer in compromise by abandoning consideration of the offer").

[251] If the statute of limitations on collection has already run, the Service's policy is to not accept the offer unless the taxpayer is fully aware that collection of the tax is barred. Referral of the taxpayer's case to the Justice Department during the pendency of the consideration of his offer is not an implied rejection of the offer, which would begin the running of the six-year collection period. United States v. Ressler, 576 F2d 650 (5th Cir. 1978); United States v. Holloway, 798 F2d 175 (6th Cir. 1986) (statute of limitations did not begin until the Service formally rejected the offer). For a case where the submission of offers in compromise extended the statute of limitations on collection, see United States v. Spurlin, 90-1 USTC ¶ 50,074 (MD Fla. 1990). See also United States v. Long, 83 AFTR2d 99-1593 (MD Pa. 1999) (computing the suspension period, but refusing to grant a motion for summary judgment to determine whether the taxpayer had crossed out the extension provision, and, if so, the effect of the change on the suspension period).

[252] It is not the Service's practice to request the execution of a formal waiver of the statute of limitations on collection (a Form 900) because the offer form itself contains a waiver. Authority under prior law developed in situations where a separate waiver form was executed.

not to sue releases one obligor, the balance can be collected from the other.[253]

10. *Financial statement.* For offers based on doubt as to collectibility or effective tax administration, a statement of the taxpayer's current financial condition is also required. Individual or self-employed taxpayers must submit Form 433-A, Collection Information Statement for Individuals. Corporations and other business taxpayers must submit Form 433-B, Collection Information Statement for Businesses.[254] The statement is a prerequisite to acceptance of any offer based on doubt as to collectibility and obviously serves as a basis for determining the acceptability of the offer. However, the financial statement also discloses information that will be useful for collection purposes in the event the offer is not accepted. Moreover, because the financial statement is submitted under penalties of perjury, any false information may be a basis for criminal prosecution.[255] Instructions for completing the Form 656 (see Form 15.10) and the supporting financial statement permit assets to reflect their quick sale value, rather than their fair market value. However, both national and local living standards are used to determine the taxpayer's expenses; and unsecured liabilities, including credit card liability, are excluded as taxpayer liabilities in determining the taxpayer's ability to pay.

[5] Submission Procedures

If the taxpayer undertakes to present an offer, the taxpayer must comply with the following procedures: (1) develop information to support an offer on one of the recognized bases (doubt as to liability, doubt as to collectibility, or to promote effective tax administration); (2) complete a Form 656; and (3) complete a financial statement on either Form 433-A, Collection Information Statement for Wage Earners and Self-Employed Individuals, or Form 433-B, Collection Information Statement for Businesses. The offer is sent to the address on Form 656, which will be a Centralized Offer in Compromise site de-

---

[253] See GCM 28417 (Sept. 14, 1954). See also United States v. Wainer, 211 F2d 669 (7th Cir. 1954); United States v. Ross, 176 F. Supp. 932 (D. Neb. 1959).

[254] Taxpayers who submit a Form 433-A for individual tax liabilities who also have an interest in an ongoing business may also be required to submit a Form 433-B for their business. Taxpayer corporations or partnerships must submit Form 433-B, and each shareholder, director, and officer, or each partner must submit a Form 433-A.

[255] IRC § 7206(1). Compare United States v. Cohen, 544 F2d 781 (5th Cir. 1977) (conviction under Section 7206(1) where false Form 433 filed) with United States v. Levy, 533 F2d 969 (5th Cir. 1976) (where Section 7206(1) was held not to apply to an alleged false statement on a Form 433-AB rather than on a Form 433). See ¶ 7A.04[1].

pending on the type of offer and the taxpayer's state of residence. Mailing and receipt of the offer and accompanying information is not the equivalent of the Service's accepting the offer for processing. The Service's reluctance to accept an offer for "processing" is a response to the statutory requirement[256] that the Service halt levy action while an offer in compromise is pending with the Service, including Appeals review, and for thirty days after an offer is rejected.

The minimum requirements for Collection to process an offer are (1) the offer is submitted on the proper version of Form 656 and Form 433-A or Form 433-B; (2) the taxpayer is not in bankruptcy; (3) the taxpayer has complied with all filing and payment listed in the instructions to Form 656; (4) the taxpayer has enclosed the application fee;[257] and (4) the offer meets any other minimum requirements the Service may establish. If these minimum requirements are met, the Service considers the offer processable, but a Service official with delegated authority to accept the offer for processing still must sign the Form 656 to suspend collection action. This is because the date the offer is signed is entered on the Service computers, and it is as of this signing date that the Service considers levy action to be prohibited unless there is a finding that collection is in jeopardy.

Once Collection accepts the offer for processing, the revenue officer begins to gather information to verify the taxpayer's assets and income. If the revenue officer requests additional information necessary to evaluate whether to accept, the taxpayer must supply the additional information or the Service will return the offer.[258] The Service may also return an offer after it has been accepted for processing if (1) the Service decides that the offer was submitted solely to delay collection; (2) the taxpayer fails to file a return or pay a tax liability; (3) the taxpayer files for bankruptcy; (4) the offer is no longer processable; or (5) the offer was accepted for processing in error. Note that when an offer is returned, the Service does not consider the offer ever to have been pending so that it has never been prohibited from levying on the taxpayer's property. Moreover, the return of an offer does not constitute a rejection of the offer.[259] As a result, the taxpayer will not be able to appeal the action to the Appeals office (rejections are appealable).[260] If the Service takes

---

[256] IRC § 6331(k)(1).

[257] The application fee is $150.

[258] Reg. § 301.7122-1(d)(2). The Service may also return an offer if it decides that the taxpayer submitted the offer solely to delay collection, or the taxpayer failed to submit sufficient information to process the offer. If the offer is returned, it is considered pending during the period from the date it was accepted for processing and the date the Service returns the offer to the taxpayer.

[259] Reg. § 301.7122-1(f)(5)(ii); Rev. Proc. 2003-71, 2003-36 IRB 517 (Aug. 21, 2003) at section 5.05. The date an offer is considered returned is the date the Service mails or personally delivers a letter to the taxpayer of the decision to return the offer.

[260] Reg. §§ 301.7122-1(f)(5)(ii), 301.7122-1(g)(4).

collection action after it has returned an offer, the taxpayer may be able to appeal the collection action under the collection due process procedures of Sections 6320 and 6330, or under the Collection Appeals Program.

In addition to the terms on the offer form, the Service may ask the taxpayer to enter into a collateral agreement or to post security if it decides that the additional terms are necessary to protect the Service's interests.[261] Payment under the terms of an offer is acceptable whether the taxpayer agrees to make payment in one or more equal or unequal installments.[262]

Similarly, because the Service has not accepted an offer until it has sent the taxpayer a written acceptance,[263] before the Service has accepted an offer, the taxpayer may withdraw the offer by notifying the Service in writing.[264]

Only when the Service notifies the taxpayer of the acceptance in writing is the offer accepted by the Service.[265] Actions other than a written notice do not constitute acceptance, such as the Service's cashing of a check.[266] Also, the notice of acceptance must be positive, unambiguous, and unequivocal.[267] The requirement of a written notice of acceptance implies that only a notice from a person authorized to enter a compromise on behalf of the Service is effective.[268] On the other hand, if the notice has not been received, the notice is ineffective to create a compromise contract, contrary to the general rule that an acceptance is complete on the mailing of the acceptance. Generally, silence and inaction cannot be construed as an assent to the offer. Although the relations of the parties and circumstances have sometimes justified an offer in assuming that silence indicates assent (e.g., where the offeree takes the benefit of amounts offered to him), the proponent of an offer in compromise is not justified in this assumption.[269]

---

[261] Reg. § 301.7122-1(e)(2).

[262] Reg. § 301.7122-1(e)(3).

[263] Reg. § 301.7122-1(e)(1).

[264] Reg. § 301.7122-1(d)(3). The notice must be sent by certified mail or hand-delivered, or acknowledged by the Service in writing to have been received.

[265] Reg. § 301.7122-1(e)(1).

[266] Moskovitz v. United States, 285 F2d 451 (Ct. Cl. 1961) (deposit); John W. Colbank, 36 TCM 200 (1971) (acceptance of check); Ray Howard, 15 TCM 1152 (1956) (acceptance of check).

[267] See Kurio v. United States, 429 F. Supp. 42 (SD Tex. 1970) (compromise not found where acceptance equivocal).

[268] See Reimer v. United States, 441 F2d 1129 (5th Cir. 1971). But see Tonkonogy v. United States, 417 F. Supp. 78 (SDNY 1976) (taxpayer relied on letter from Service apparently extending time to make payment of a compromise agreement).

[269] See, e.g., United States v. Teti, 75-2 USTC ¶ 9,709 (DC Conn. 1975).

[6] Evaluation of Offers

[a] Offers Based on Doubt as to Collectibility

In evaluating an offer based on doubt as to collectibility, Collection must consider whether, after taking into account the taxpayer's basic living expenses, the taxpayer's assets and income permit the taxpayer to pay the unpaid tax liability. An offer is adequate in the Service's view if it reasonably reflects collection potential by taking into account the following: (1) the amount collectible from the taxpayer's assets; (2) the amount collectible from the taxpayer's present and future income; (3) the amount collectible from third parties (e.g., by use of the trust fund recovery penalty or transferee liability); and (4) the amount the taxpayer should reasonably be expected to raise from assets in which the taxpayer has an interest but which are not available for collection because, for example, they are outside the United States and the Service's normal collection reach, or property held as a tenancy by the entirety.[270] The revenue officer will attempt to identify assets or loan potentials that can be used to effect immediate payment.[271]

There are several steps to processing an offer based on doubt as to collectibility, the promotion of effective tax administration, or both. The collection officer to whom the case is assigned reviews the basic information submitted, requests that the taxpayer supply corrections of incorrect or omitted information, and evaluates the information to determination whether the taxpayer's offer is acceptable.[272] The revenue officer verifies the taxpayer's income and assets to check the taxpayer's representation that the tax liability cannot be paid in full. At least initially, the revenue officer will use information that the Service maintains in various databases including data about the taxpayer or the taxpayer's business, and information returns reporting interest, dividends, and other income. In addition, the revenue officer will have access to other records, such as state motor vehicle records, credit bureau reports, and taxpayer-supplied information.

Investigation of a financial statement usually starts with the taxpayer's current tax return.[273] The return may show, for example, interest or dividends

---

[270] IRM 5.8.4.4, Doubt as to Collectibility (DATC) (Nov. 15, 2004). But see IRS Legal Memorandum 200127009 (concluding that the Service cannot accept an offer in compromise by a general partner to compromise her individual, derivative share of the partnership's employment tax obligations).

[271] IRM 5.8.5.3, Equity in Assets (Nov. 30, 2001). The specific assets identified are cash; securities; life insurance; pension and profit-sharing plans; furniture, fixtures, and personal effects; machinery and equipment; trucks, automobiles, and delivery equipment; receivables; and real estate.

[272] Rev. Proc. 2003-71, 2003-36 IRB 517 (Aug. 21, 2003) at section 6.04(1).

[273] See IRM 5.8.5.2, Financial Analysis—Verification (Nov. 15, 2004).

from assets not reported on the financial statement. The revenue officer can check the accuracy of matters set forth on the financial statement by going to third parties such as a bank or an employer.

Collection's starting point is the value of the taxpayer's assets less encumbrances that have priority over the federal tax lien. "Value" for this analysis is not fair market value, but quick sale or liquidating value; that is, the amount a seller would realize if the seller, under financial pressure, had to sell the property within a short period of time (i.e., under ninety days). In considering a married individual's offer, the nonliable spouse's assets and income generally will not be considered in determining the adequacy of the offer.[274] Also, assets are defined as the taxpayer's net realizable equity in the assets,[275] which is the asset's quick sale value. Future income is defined as an estimate of the taxpayer's ability to pay based on an analysis of gross income, less necessary living expenses, for a specific number of months.[276] In evaluating the taxpayer's income, the Service considers how much of the taxpayer's income is or will be realistically available to pay the delinquent taxes." In evaluating those future prospects, the taxpayer's education, profession or trade, age and experience, health, and past and present income will be considered. In determining future income potential, an evaluation must be made of the likelihood that any increase in real income will be available to pay the delinquent taxes. In general, under these procedures, allowable expenses are divided into two categories: (1) necessary or allowable expenses, which provide for the taxpayer and the taxpayer's family health and welfare, or the production of income, and (2) conditional expenses, which are other expenses of the taxpayer not considered necessary by the Service.[277] Guidelines used by the Service include standardized expenses, national standards for total monthly expenses, and national standards for individual expenses, coupled with local standards for some geographic areas, for such expenses as housing, including utilities and transporta-

---

[274] Reg. § 301.7122-1(c)(2)(ii). An exception to this general rule is that the nonliable spouse's assets and liabilities will be considered if state law permits, unless the taxpayer and the nonliable spouse prove that the collection of the assets would have a "material and adverse" effect on the standard of living of their family.

[275] IRM 5.8.3.1, Net Realizable Equity (Nov. 15, 2004). Quick sale value is the estimate of the price a seller could get for the asset where the seller is under financial pressure to sell the asset in a short period of time. The quick sale value of an asset is considered to be 80 percent of the fair market value of the asset. The quick sale value is an amount less than the fair market value, but greater than the forced sale value which is defined as 75 percent of the fair market value of an asset. The quick sale value of an asset is defined as no less than 80 percent of the property's fair market value. Income and the potential value of assets are also evaluated.

[276] IRM 5.8.5.5, Future Income (Nov. 15, 2004). For cash offers, the projection is made for 48 months; for short-term deferred offers, for 60 months; and for deferred payment offers, for the period of time remaining on the statute of limitations.

[277] IRM 5.8.5.5.1, Allowable Expenses (Nov. 15, 2004); IRM 5.8.5.5.2, Conditional Expenses (Nov. 15, 2004).

tion. The same review of the taxpayer's allowable expenses is conducted in the revenue officer's consideration of an offer in compromise, except that conditional expenses are not considered allowable in an offer in compromise analysis. The amount of these allowable living expenses will be determined on the basis of the facts and circumstances of the taxpayer's particular case, but the national and local living expense standards are intended to be used as a guide in the determination.[278]

Other components of doubt as to collectibility are the amounts collectible from third parties. For example, collectible amounts may come from Collection's asserting the trust fund recovery penalty against other responsible officers, assessing transferee liability, or filing alter ego or nominee liens. In addition, assets or income may be available to the taxpayer, but not to the government. For example, the taxpayer may have net realizable equity in assets outside the country, in property held as a tenancy by the entirety with a nonliable spouse, or in the value of an interest in a business entity.[279]

Any special circumstances of the taxpayer that may warrant consideration in determining reasonable collection potential should be evaluated before determining that the amount offered is inadequate.[280]

[b] Offers Based on Promoting Effective Tax Administration

To compromise a tax liability on effective tax administration grounds, the taxpayer must (1) have filed all required tax returns; (2) not be in a bankruptcy proceeding; (3) submit the offer on the usual form (i.e., Form 656, Offer in Compromise); (4) provide a financial statement; and (5) explain why the Service should consider the offer on these grounds. After these requirements have been met, Collection will determine whether the taxpayer meets the traditional bases for compromise, namely, doubt as to liability or doubt as to collectibility. If no grounds exist to compromise the taxpayer's liability based on

---

[278] Reg. § 301.7122-1(c)(2)(i).

[279] IRM 5.8.4.3, Effective Tax Administration (ETA) and Doubt as to Collectibility With Special Circumstances (DCSC) (Nov. 15, 2004).

[280] The Service generally refuses to consider offers in compromise in bankruptcy cases. However, a bankruptcy court has held that the Service must at least consider a bankruptcy debtor's offer in compromise on the merits, even if a court cannot order it to accept the offer. Duane Alan Mills v. United States (In re Mills, Debtor), 84 AFTR2d 99-5280 (Bankr. SD W. Va. 1999) (Chapter 13 case; court held that the Service's refusal to consider offers from debtors while processing those from other taxpayers was bankruptcy-based discrimination that violated Bankruptcy Code Section 525); Chapman v. United States (In re Chapman), 84 AFTR2d 99-5068 (Bankr. SD W. Va. 1999) (same); see also United States v. Garden State Nat'l Bank, 465 F. Supp. 437 (DNJ 1979) ("While the grant of authority to compromise does not command that a compromise agreement be reached, it does imply a mandate to negotiate, to make the effort, to explore the potential for compromise before deciding unilaterally whether or not to refer.").

these traditional bases, and provided that a compromise based on "effective tax administration considerations" will not undermine compliance with the laws, such a compromise may be entered into when (1) collection of the full liability would create an economic hardship or (2) collection of the full liability would be detrimental to voluntary compliance.[281] Three additional factors must exist before an equity or hardship compromise will be accepted by the Service: (1) the compromised tax liability must first be assessed against the taxpayer; (2) the net equity in the taxpayer's assets, when combined with the taxpayer's anticipated future income, must be greater than the amount owed; and (3) there must exist an exceptional circumstance that warrants consideration of the offer, despite the fact that the assets and future income are sufficient to fully satisfy the tax liability.

[i] Economic hardship. If the foregoing requirements are met, the economic hardship factor is analyzed. Following are examples of economic hardship: (1) the taxpayer has a long-term illness, medical condition, or disability that renders him incapable of earning a living; (2) the taxpayer would be unable to meet basic living expenses if his assets were liquidated to pay the liability; and (3) the taxpayer is unable to borrow against the equity in assets, and the sale of those assets would have sufficient adverse consequences that enforced collection on the part of the Service is unlikely.[282]

A finding of economic hardship will not necessarily mean that a taxpayer makes no payment. Collection will consider the taxpayer's compliance with the Code's filing and payment requirements as well as the taxpayer's deliberate actions to avoid the payment of taxes for the three- to five-year period before the offer. Other factors considered by the Service may be the cause of the delinquency, the length of noncompliance, and the efforts to resolve noncompliance.

[ii] Exceptional circumstances. An offer may also be accepted when exceptional circumstances exist, whatever the taxpayer's financial situation, if collection of the full liability would be detrimental to voluntary compliance of taxpayers in general.[283] One example of an "acceptable exceptional circumstances" compromise offer is where a taxpayer recovers from a serious illness during which he did not file tax returns, only to discover that with tax, penalty, and interest, the liability is more than three times the original tax liability.[284] Another example is the situation where a taxpayer is charged with premature withdrawal penalties based on erroneous advice the taxpayer received from an e-mail inquiry to the Service at its Web site. When this type of

---

[281] IRM 5.8.11.2, Legal Basis for Effective Tax Administration Offer (Nov. 1, 2000).

[282] IRM 5.8. 11.2.1, Economic Hardship (Nov. 30, 2001).

[283] IRM 5.8.11.2.2, Detriment to Voluntary Compliance (Nov. 30, 2001).

[284] IRM 5.8.11.2.2, Detriment to Voluntary Compliance (Nov. 30, 2001).

exceptional circumstance exists, the Service generally expects the taxpayer to offer an amount at least equal to the amount of the assessed tax, exclusive of penalties and interest. Nevertheless, the Manual acknowledges that "equity and fairness" might warrant acceptance of some lesser amount, and, as a result, the Service will consider an offer from a taxpayer who has offered less than the full amount of the tax.

It is possible that a revenue officer may suggest an offer in compromise where a determination is made that the account is not collectible in full and criminal proceedings are not contemplated or pending. For at least two reasons, it is important, from the taxpayer's standpoint, that an offer be one that the revenue officer will recommend for acceptance. First, if the revenue officer considers the offer to be frivolous rather than bona fide, collection action is not stayed, and the offer is immediately rejected.[285] Second, without the approval of the revenue officer, the likelihood of ultimate acceptance is substantially reduced, for the revenue officer's view probably will be representative of the revenue officer's manager's response to the offer, and administrative and psychological inertia tend to confirm a position initially adopted. Consequently, discussions with a revenue officer concerning compromise should be cooperative rather than adversarial. Once some agreement has been reached with the revenue officer, he should be furnished with sufficient information to justify the offer to succeeding levels of review.

[7] The Role of Collateral Agreements

In unusual situations, the Service may ask the taxpayer to agree either to pay additional amounts from future income or to forgo present or future tax benefits, thereby increasing the amount of tax payable and reducing the effective amount of tax abated under the compromise. Although these agreements are the exception and not the rule, they are used as an additional source of collection and to clarify the terms of the offer in compromise.[286] A collateral agreement may be used, for example, where the taxpayer anticipates a substantial increase in future income. A collateral agreement may also be used to make it clear that only one party to the joint assessment is released,[287] and, in delinquency penalty offers involving income tax, to clarify the waiver provisions of the offer and to preclude the allowance of refunds resulting from net operating loss carrybacks to the period covered by the compromise.

Payment under a collateral agreement is limited to the total liability compromised plus additions to the tax (such as interest) accruing during the pen-

---

[285] Reg. § 301.7122-1(d)(4).

[286] See IRM 5.8.6.3, Collateral Agreements—Other Collateral Agreements (May 15, 2004) ("Securing a collateral agreement should be the exception and not the rule.").

[287] See IRM 5.8.6.2, Co-Obligor Agreements (May 15, 2004).

dency of the offer and collateral agreement. If, after payment for the terms of the offer and collateral agreement, there is still a balance due on the liability compromised including accrued interest, the amount is forgiven.

There are four types of collateral agreements in general use: (1) future income agreements; (2) agreements providing for reduction of basis of assets for computing depreciation and gain or loss for tax purposes; (3) agreements involving waivers of net operating losses or unused investment credit carrybacks or carryovers; and (4) agreements involving waivers of bad debt losses or other deductions.[288]

The most frequently used type of agreement is the future income agreement. The Service uses two forms for such agreements: Collateral Agreement—Future Income—Individual (Form 2261) and Collateral Agreement—Future Income—Corporation (Form 2261-A). (See Forms 15.11 and 15.12, respectively.)[289] Future income collateral agreements are considered appropriate when the investigation shows that a substantial increase in future income is likely after release of the lien. The theory is that by releasing the tax lien, the taxpayer's income will increase and the Service can recover amounts in addition to that paid or payable under the compromise agreement. In addition, the Service will participate in windfalls such as bequests.

Under a reduction-of-basis agreement, the taxpayer surrenders present or potential tax benefits from depreciation on certain assets and accelerates the payment of the tax liability. The form used for this purpose is Collateral Agreement—Adjusted Basis of Specific Assets (Form 2261-B). (See Form 15.13.)[290] This type of agreement is used where the basis of assets exceeds the quick-sale value of the assets. For example, if the basis of an asset is $70,000 and its quick-sale value is $60,000, the basis would be reduced to $60,000. This change lowers depreciation deductions, with the result that the taxpayer pays more taxes and might realize higher taxable gain on the sale of the asset, or reduction if not elimination of loss. The term of this type of agreement is generally the life of the asset until the full amount of liability is paid. After the liability is paid, the new basis of the property is the original basis reduced by depreciation that would have been taken in the absence of the compromise.

An agreement waiving losses and investment credits may be entered into with regard to carryovers of net operating losses, capital losses, and unused investment credits. The Service uses a Collateral Agreement—Waiver of Net Operating Losses, Capital Losses, and Unused Investment Credits (Form 2261-C). (See Form 15.14.)[291] This agreement is used where there are carryovers to years ending after the date the offer is accepted, if a corporate taxpayer has al-

---

[288] See IRM 5.8.6.3, Other Collateral Agreements (May 15, 2004).

[289] See IRM 5.8.6.3.1, Future Income (May 15, 2004).

[290] IRM 5.8.6.3.2, Adjusted Basis of Specific Assets (May 15, 2004).

[291] IRM 5.8.6.3.3, Waiver of Losses (May 15, 2004); IRM 5.8.6.3.3.1, Net Operating Loss (May 15, 2004); IRM 5.8.6.3.3.2, Capital Loss (May 15, 2004).

ready entered into a future income agreement on Form 2261-A, which has a waiver of net operating losses. The agreement thus has the effect of increasing the taxpayer's tax liabilities for the affected periods. Similarly, an agreement may be entered into waiving certain disallowed bad debts or other losses.[292]

[8] Acceptance and Followup Procedures

As noted previously, as additional consideration for the acceptance of an offer to compromise, Collection may request that the taxpayer enter into a collateral agreement or post security considered necessary to protect the government's interests.[293] Offers may be accepted when they provide for payment of compromised amounts in one or more equal or unequal payments.[294] Also, if the final payment on an accepted offer is contingent on the immediate and simultaneous release of lien, the payment must be made in accordance with Collection's procedures, which require payment by certified or bank check.[295] An offer is accepted on the date the Service sends the taxpayer a letter of acceptance.[296] The legal effect of the compromise is to settle conclusively the liability of the taxpayer set forth in the offer.[297]

Local Collection offices and the service centers, each with certain fixed responsibilities, are jointly responsible for coordination and follow-up on accepted offers in compromise. Where all the terms of the offer have been met, the local office is responsible for issuing a release of lien.[298] The service center Offer-in-Compromise Technician secures statements of annual income and makes an initial check for compliance with future income agreements and determines what further checks are necessary. The service center also secures sums due and payable under the terms of collateral agreements and prepares the annual reports relating to the collateral agreements. Before the anniversary date, the service center forwards a transmittal letter, along with a statement of annual income to be filled out by the taxpayer. In completing this annual income form, pursuant to the collateral agreement, the taxpayer must attach a copy of his income tax return for the year. After the executed statement and copy of the return are filed by the taxpayer, the Offer-in-Compromise Technician determines whether a payment is due.

---

[292] IRM 5.8.6.3.3., Waiver of Losses (May 15, 2004).

[293] Reg. § 301.7122-1(e)(2).

[294] Reg. § 301.7122-1(e)(3).

[295] Reg. § 301.7122-1(e)(4).

[296] Reg. § 301.7122-1(e)(1); Rev. Proc. 2003-71, 2003-36 IRB 517 (Aug. 21, 2003) at section 8.01.

[297] Rev. Proc. 2003-71, 2003-36 IRB 517 (Aug. 21, 2003) at section 8.02. See IRM 5.8.8.1, Acceptance Processing (Nov. 1, 2000).

[298] Questions about whether there has been compliance are resolved by Area Counsel.

Where the taxpayer submits the required statement of annual income but fails to pay either the installment payment or any payment due under the terms of a collateral agreement, the service center attempts to secure voluntary payment of the amount due. If payment is not received, the file is referred to the local Collection office with a request for follow-up on the delinquent or defaulted taxpayer.

[9] Rejection or Termination of an Offer: Administrative Review

[a] Rejection of the Offer

Before it formally rejects an offer, the Service must complete an independent administrative review of the proposed rejection.[299] During independent administrative review, the offer is still pending and consequently no levy may be made.[300] In Collection, an Independent Administrative Reviewer is responsible for conducting this statutory review. The independent reviewer reviews each case to determine if the proposed rejection or return of the offer is reasonable based on the taxpayer's facts and circumstances and the offer examiner's analysis of the taxpayer's financial information. Also, the review includes an examination of the case file and history to ensure that the investigation was accurate and complete and procedures had been filed with particular attention to the following: (1) financial analysis (including the determination of reasonable collection potential); (2) attempts to communicate with the taxpayer; (3) attempts to negotiate; and (4) special circumstances.[301]

A taxpayer has a statutory right to Appeals review of the rejection of the offer. A taxpayer's offer in compromise is not formally rejected until the Service sends the taxpayer a written notice that it has rejected the offer, with its reasons for doing so.[302] The taxpayer has the right to appeal the action to the Appeals Office.[303] To give the taxpayer time to appeal a rejection of the offer to the Appeals office, no levy is to be made within the thirty-day period after the date of the notice that the offer had been rejected.[304] If the taxpayer administratively appeals the rejection of the offer within thirty days after notice of

---

[299] IRC § 7122(d)(1); Reg. § 301.7122-1(e)(1). See IRM 5.8.12.1, Independent Administrative Review—Overview (May 15, 2004).

[300] IRC § 6331(k)(1)(A).

[301] See IRM 5.8.12.2, Role of the Independent Administrative Reviewer (May 15, 2004).

[302] Rev. Proc. 2003-71, 2003-36 IRB 517 (Aug. 21, 2003) at section 9.02.

[303] Reg. § 301.7122-1(e)(1).

[304] IRC § 6331(k)(1)(A).

the adverse action, Collection may not levy on the taxpayer's property and rights to property during the pendency of the appeal.[305]

Once Appeals receives the case, it has jurisdiction to make decisions on offers in compromise, including offers that the local Collection office or service center determined to be unacceptable.[306] The procedure followed in these appeals is much the same as in a regular appeals, except that with the exception of offers based on doubt as to liability, the subject shifts to the issues of collectibility (with its focus on collection potential from the taxpayer's assets and income) and the requirements for a compromise based on promotion of effective tax administration.[307]

It remains to be said that there are two types of appeals: a collection due process appeal provided by Section 6320 and Section 6330, which contemplates Tax Court review of adverse action, and an equivalent hearing that incorporates the Collection Appeals Program and from which there is no Tax Court appeal.

When a low-income taxpayer has made the offer, the Service may not reject the offer based solely on the amount of the offer; the Service must consider whether the offer complies with one of the three bases for accepting a compromise.[308] Also, the Service is not permitted to reject an offer based on doubt as to liability merely because it is unable to find the taxpayer's return or return information to verify the amount of the liability.[309]

[b] Termination of an Offer

If the taxpayer is delinquent or defaults in making payment under a compromise (or collateral) agreement, the office with jurisdiction over the acceptance of the taxpayer's offer steps back into the picture, either by obtaining payment, modifying the compromise agreement, or by declaring the compromise terminated and instituting collection procedures. Although an effort is made to collect the amount of an offer before declaring it in default, once the offer is actually terminated because of a default, the Service may disregard the amount of the offer and apply all amounts previously deposited or paid against the amount of the liability sought to be compromised; Collection is no longer prohibited from collecting the balance due by levy.[310] The Service may also refer the case to the Justice Department's Tax Division to proceed by suit to col-

---

[305] IRC § 6331(k)(1)(B).

[306] Delegation Order No. 11 (Nov. 1, 1999). The delegation of authority generally runs to Chiefs of Appeals, Assistant Chiefs, and Associate Chiefs, to accept or reject offers.

[307] IRM 8.13.2.4, Consideration of Offers in Compromise (June 8, 2000).

[308] Reg. § 301.7122-1(e)(3).

[309] Reg. § 301.7122-1(e)(4).

[310] See IRC § 6331(k)(1).

lect the entire unpaid balance of the offer. No administrative appeal exists in the case of default.[311] If the taxpayer makes a new offer, he must follow the general compromise procedures—that is, Forms 656 and 433 must be filed, and a thorough investigation will be made of the taxpayer's current financial condition. The fact of the default will weigh heavily against the taxpayer in such a situation.

---

[311] See IRC § 7122(d).

(j)   I/We understand that I/we remain responsible for the full amount of the tax liability, unless and until the IRS accepts the offer in writing and I/we have met all the terms and conditions of the offer. The IRS will not remove the original amount of the tax liability from its records until I/we have met all the terms of the offer.

(k)   I/We understand that the tax I/we offer to compromise is and will remain a tax liability until I/we meet all the terms and conditions of this offer. If I/we file bankruptcy before the terms and conditions of this offer are completed, any claim the IRS files in the bankruptcy proceedings will be a tax claim.

(l)   Once the IRS accepts the offer in writing, I/we have no right to contest, in court or otherwise, the amount of the tax liability.

(m)   The offer is pending starting with the date an authorized IRS official signs this form. The offer remains pending until an authorized IRS official accepts, rejects, returns or acknowledges withdrawal of the offer in writing. If I/we appeal an IRS rejection decision on the offer, the IRS will continue to treat the offer as pending until the Appeals Office accepts or rejects the offer in writing. If I/we don't file a protest within 30 days of the date the IRS notifies me/us of the right to protest the decision, I/we waive the right to a hearing before the Appeals Office about the offer in compromise.

(n)   If I/we fail to meet any of the terms and conditions of the offer and the offer defaults, then the IRS may:

- immediately file suit to collect the entire unpaid balance of the offer

- immediately file suit to collect an amount equal to the original amount of the tax liability as liquidating damages, minus any payment already received under the terms of this offer

- disregard the amount of the offer and apply all amounts already paid under the offer against the original amount of the tax liability

- file suit or levy to collect the original amount of the tax liability, without further notice of any kind.

The IRS will continue to add interest, as Section 6601 of the Internal Revenue Code requires, on the amount the IRS determines is due after default. The IRS will add interest from the date the offer is defaulted until I/we completely satisfy the amount owed.

(o)   The IRS generally files a Notice of Federal Tax Lien to protect the Government's interest on deferred payment offers. Also, the IRS may file a Notice of Federal Tax Lien during the offer investigation. This tax lien will be released when the payment terms of the offer agreement have been satisfied.

(p)   **I/We understand that the IRS employees may contact third parties in order to respond to this request and I/we authorize the IRS to make such contacts. Further, by authorizing the Internal Revenue Service to contact third parties, I/we understand that I will not receive notice, pursuant to section 7602(c) of the Internal Revenue Code, of third parties contacted in connection with this request.**

(q)   If doubt as to collectibility and/or effective tax administration are checked in Item 6 above, I/we are offering to compromise all the tax liabilities assessed against me/us as of the date of this offer and under the taxpayer identification numbers listed in Items 2 and/or 3 above. I/We authorize the IRS to amend Item 5, above, to include any assessed liabilities we failed to list on Form 656.

Item 9 — Explanation of Circumstances

I am requesting an offer in compromise for the reason(s) listed below:

Note: If you are requesting compromise based on doubt as to liability, explain why you don't believe you owe the tax.
If you believe you have special circumstances affecting your ability to fully pay the amount due, explain your situation.
You may attach additional sheets if necessary. Please include your name and SSN or EIN on all additional sheets or
supporting documentation.

_____

_____

_____

_____

_____

Item 10 — Source of Funds

I/We shall obtain the funds to make this offer from the following source(s):

_____

_____

_____

Item 11 — Mandatory Signature(s)

If I/We submit this offer on a substitute form, I/we affirm that this form is a verbatim duplicate of the official Form 656, and I/we agree to be bound by all the terms and conditions set forth in the official Form 656.

Under penalties of perjury, I declare that I have examined this offer, including accompanying schedules and statements, and to the best of my knowledge and belief, it is true, correct and complete.

_____

11(a) Signature of Taxpayer

_____

Date

_____

11(b) Signature of Taxpayer

_____

Date

For Official Use Only

I accept the waiver of the statutory period of limitations on assessment for the Internal Revenue Service, as described in Item 8(e).

_____

Signature of Authorized Internal Revenue Service Official

_____

Title

_____

Date

Item 12 — If this application was prepared by someone other than the taxpayer, please fill in that person's name and address below.

Name: _____

Address: _____
    (if known)

Item 13 **Paid Preparer's Use Only**	Preparer's signature ▶	Date	Check if self-employed ☐	Preparer's CAF no. or PTIN
	Firm's name (or yours if self-employed), address, and ZIP code ▶		EIN	
			Phone no. ( )	

Item 14 **Third Party Designee**	Do you want to allow another person to discuss this offer with the IRS?	☐ Yes. Complete the following.	☐ No
	Designee's name ▶	Phone no. ▶ ( )	

Website Version
Updated October 2004

Department of the Treasury
Internal Revenue Service

www.irs.gov

Form 656 (Rev. 7-2004)
Catalog Number 16728N

Form 656

Offer in Compromise

IMPORTANT! THIS BOOKLET CONTAINS INFORMATION THAT YOU NEED IN ORDER TO PREPARE A COMPLETE AND ACCURATE OFFER IN COMPROMISE. *PLEASE READ THESE INSTRUCTIONS CAREFULLY BEFORE ATTEMPTING TO COMPLETE THE ENCLOSED FORMS.*

CONTENTS

Note: If you have any questions, please call our toll-free number at 1–800–829–1040. You can get forms and publications by calling toll free at 1–800–829–3676 (1–800–TAX–FORM), or by visiting your local Internal Revenue Service (IRS) office or our website at *www.irs.gov.*

Copyright © December 2004

What is an Offer in Compromise?

An Offer in Compromise *(OIC)* is an agreement between the taxpayer and the government that settles a tax liability for payment of less than the full amount owed.

The Service will generally accept an OIC when it is unlikely that the tax liability can be collected in full and the amount offered reasonably reflects collection potential. An OIC is a legitimate alternative to declaring a case currently not collectible or to a "protracted installment agreement." The goal is to achieve collection of what is potentially collectible at the earliest possible time and at the least cost to the government.

Note: *A "protracted installment agreement" is defined as being one that extends **beyond** the period allowed under IRS issued guidelines.*

The success of the Offer in Compromise program will be assured only if taxpayers make adequate compromise proposals consistent with their ability to pay and the Service makes prompt and reasonable decisions. Taxpayers are expected to provide reasonable documentation to verify their ability to pay. The ultimate goal is a compromise which is in the best interest of **both** the taxpayer and the Service. Acceptance of an adequate offer will also result in creating for the taxpayer an expectation of, and a fresh start toward, compliance with all future filing and payment requirements.

- **Doubt as to Collectibility**. Doubt exists that you could **ever** pay the full amount of tax owed. Before the IRS can consider a **doubt as to collectibility** offer *(absent special circumstances)*, the taxpayer **must not** be able to pay the taxes in full either by liquidating assets or through current installment agreement guidelines. You **must** submit the appropriate collection information statement along with all required supporting documents.

- **Doubt as to Liability**. This means that doubt exists that the assessed tax is correct. **Do not use this reason if the sole basis for filing an offer is because you are unable to pay the tax liability.** If you do not think that you owe the tax liability, then you may submit an OIC for **"Doubt as to Liability"** *(see Item 6 on Form 656)*. You **must** submit a detailed written statement explaining why you believe you do not owe the tax that you want to compromise. You are not required to submit a collection information statement if you are submitting an offer on this basis alone.

- **Effective Tax Administration (ETA).** This means that the taxpayer **does not have any doubt** that the tax is correct and there is **no doubt** that the full amount of tax owed could be collected, but an exceptional circumstance exists that would allow us to consider your offer. To be eligible for compromise on this basis, you must demonstrate that the collection of the tax would create an economic hardship or would be unfair and inequitable. If you are requesting an ETA offer, you **must** submit:

  1. A collection information statement with all appropriate attachments, and

  2. A written narrative explaining your special circumstances and why paying the tax liability in full would create an economic hardship or would be unfair and inequitable.

You **must** also attach appropriate documentation that will support your request for an ETA offer such as proof of unusual expenses that would cause you economic hardship if the taxes were collected in full.

The information in this package is designed to assist you in determining if an offer in compromise is the right payment option for you, as well as guide you through the process of completing a complete offer in compromise application package. *Please read and follow the directions carefully!*

1

Step One: Is Your Offer in Compromise (OIC) "Processable?"

(Note: The three questions below do not apply if your offer is based only on doubt as to liability.)

PLEASE DO NOT GO ANY FURTHER WITHOUT FIRST DETERMINING WHETHER OR NOT YOU ARE ELIGIBLE TO HAVE YOUR OFFER IN COMPROMISE PROCESSED AT THIS TIME.

In order to determine whether or not you are eligible to have your offer in compromise processed, please answer the 3 questions below:

	YES	NO
1. Do you currently have an open bankruptcy proceeding? You should contact your Bankruptcy Attorney if you are not certain. If you are involved in an open bankruptcy proceeding, contact your local IRS insolvency office. Any resolution of your outstanding tax liabilities generally must take place within the context of your bankruptcy proceeding.	☐	☐
2. Do you have any unfiled federal tax returns that you are **required** to file? You **must** file all tax returns that you were legally required to file prior to submitting an offer in compromise. This includes but is not limited to:	☐	☐

- All Income Tax, Employment Tax, and Excise Tax returns, along with all required Partnership, Limited Liability Corporations, or closely held Sub-Chapter S Corporation returns.

If you did not file a return for a specific year prior to submitting your OIC because you were not legally required to file the return, then you **must** include a detailed explanation of your circumstances with your OIC.

| 3. If you are a business with employees, have you failed to *timely* make any required federal tax deposits for the current quarter and the two immediate preceding quarters? *(If you have any untimely federal tax deposits for the above quarters or late filing of returns, then you must answer yes to this question.)* | ☐ | ☐ |

If you answered YES to any of the questions above, STOP HERE. You are *not eligible* to have your offer considered or processed at this time. If you answered NO to all of the questions above, then you *may be eligible* to have your offer considered and processed.

Additional Requirements

1. **Offer in Compromise Application Fee** — Your offer must include the $150 application fee or a completed Form 656-A, *Income Certification of Offer in Compromise Application Fee,* if you are requesting an exception of the fee because of your income. Offers received without the $150 fee or a completed Form 656-A will not be accepted for processing. Please see Step 5 on Page 13 of this package for more information on the application fee and to determine if you qualify for the exception.

2. You **must** use the current versions of Form 656, *Offer in Compromise,* and Form 433-A and Form 433-B, Collection Information Statements, which are contained in this package.

- Individual or Self-Employed taxpayers must use Form 433-A, *Collection Information Statement for Wage Earners and Self-Employed Individuals.*

- Corporations and other business taxpayers must use Form 433-B, *Collection Information Statement for Businesses.* We may also require Form 433-A from corporate officers or individual partners.

- **Offers received on outdated forms or without the required information statements will not be considered.**

2

Step Two: What We Need to Fully Evaluate Your Offer

1. COMPLETE AN ACCURATE FORM 656 — Complete all applicable items on Form 656, **which is the official compromise agreement.** You **must** sign Form 656. If someone other than yourself prepared the offer package, then please see the instructions in Step Four, Items 12 and 13, found on Page 11 of this package. If your Form 656 was prepared by an authorized Representative, you **must** include a completed Form 2848, *Power of Attorney and Declaration of Representative*, with your offer. Detailed instructions for the completion of Form 656 are found on Pages 10 and 11 of this package.

Common errors to avoid in completing Form 656:

- The taxpayer's name is missing.

- The street address is missing or incomplete.

- The social security number *(SSN)* or employer identification number *(EIN)* is missing, incomplete, or incorrect.

- The preprinted terms and conditions listed on the Form 656 have been altered or deleted.

- An offer amount or payment term is missing.

- A required signature is missing.

2. COMPLETE AN ACCURATE COLLECTION INFORMATION STATEMENT (Form 433-A and/or Form 433-B) — You **must** provide financial information when you submit offers based on doubt as to collectibility and effective tax administration. **We do not require this information if your offer is based solely on doubt as to liability.** You **must** send us current information that reflects your financial situation for the **three months** immediately prior to the date you submitted your offer in compromise. Collection information statements **must** show all of your assets and income, even those unavailable to us through direct collection action, because you can possibly use them to fund your offer. The offer examiner needs this information to evaluate your offer and may ask you to update it or verify certain financial information. These forms **must** be filled in completely. We may return offer packages that are incomplete. Annotate items that do not apply to you with "N/A." **Provide all the information required to support your financial condition.** Required items of documentation are clearly indicated on the collection information statements with icons.

When only one spouse has a tax liability but both have incomes, only the spouse responsible for the tax debt is required to prepare the necessary collection information statements. The responsible spouse should include **only** his/her assets and liabilities on his/her collection information statements. However, the income and expenses of the entire household is required on their collection information statements. The entire household includes spouse, domestic partner, significant other, children, and others that contribute to the household. This is necessary for the IRS to evaluate the income and expenses allocable to the liable taxpayer.

In States with community property laws, we require collection information statements from both spouses. We may also require financial information on the non-liable spouse, or cohabitant(s), for offer verification purposes, even when community property laws do not apply.

3

3. RESPOND PROMPTLY TO REQUESTS FOR ADDITIONAL INFORMATION — While we are evaluating your offer, we may contact you for any information that is missing, or requires clarification. Respond promptly to any requests for additional information. **If we do not receive this information from you in a timely manner, we will not give your offer any further consideration. It will be returned to you, and *you will forfeit the $150 application fee.***

4. ESTIMATED TAX PAYMENTS MUST BE UP TO DATE FOR THE CURRENT YEAR — We will not process your offer to completion if we determine that your estimated tax payments for the current year's income tax liability are not paid up to date. If we determine this to be the case, you will have one opportunity to make the required payments before we return your offer. If we return your offer because you did not make the estimated tax payments, then your $150 application fee will be forfeited.

4

Step Three: Determining the Amount of Your Offer

Doubt as to Collectibility

Your offer amount must equal or exceed your reasonable collection potential amount. The information provided on the collection information statements *(Form 433-A and Form 433-B)* assists us in determining the reasonable collection potential *(RCP)* of your tax liability. The RCP equals the net equity of your assets plus the amount we could collect from your future income. **If our financial analysis indicates that you have the ability to fully pay the tax liability, either immediately or through an installment agreement, unless special circumstances are involved, your offer will not be accepted. You must offer an amount greater than or equal to the RCP amount. All offer amounts must exceed zero, including doubt as to liability offers.**

If special circumstances cause you to offer an amount less than the RCP, you *must* complete Item 9, "Explanation of Circumstances," on Form 656, explaining your situation. You *must* also attach to Form 656 any supporting documents to help support your special circumstances. Special circumstances may include factors such as advanced age, serious illness from which recovery is unlikely, or any other factors that impact upon your ability to pay the total RCP and continue to provide for the necessary living expenses for you and your family.

If you are a wage earner or self-employed individual, completion of the worksheet on Pages 8 and 9 will give you a good estimate of what an acceptable offer amount may be. You will use the information on your Form 433-A to complete the worksheet.

Doubt as to Liability

Complete Item 9, "Explanation of Circumstances," on Form 656, explaining why, in your judgment, you do not owe the tax liability you want to compromise. Offer the correct tax, penalty, and interest owed based on your judgment in Item 7 on Form 656.

Effective Tax Administration (ETA)

Complete Form 433-A or Form 433-B, as appropriate, and attach to Form 656. You *must* complete Item 9, "Explanation of Circumstances," on Form 656, explaining your exceptional circumstances and why requiring payment of the tax liability in full would either create an economic hardship or would be unfair and inequitable. You *must* also attach to Form 656 any documents to help support your exceptional circumstances.

5

Determine Your Payment Terms

There are three payment plans you and the IRS may agree to:

- **Cash** *(paid in 90 days or less)*;

- **Short-Term Deferred Payment** *(more than 90 days, up to 24 months)*;

- **Deferred Payment** *(offers with payment terms over the remaining statutory period for collecting the tax).*

Cash Offer

You must pay cash offers within 90 days of a written notice of acceptance.

You should offer the realizable value of your assets plus the total amount we could collect over 48 months of payments *(or the remainder of the ten-year statutory period for collection, whichever is less).*

Note: We require full payment of accepted doubt as to liability offers at the time of mutual agreement of the corrected liability. If you're unable to pay the corrected amount, you must also request compromise on the basis of doubt as to collectibility.

Short-Term Deferred Payment Offer

This payment plan requires you to pay the offer within two years of acceptance.

The offer must include the realizable value of your assets plus the amount we could collect over 60 months of payments *(or the remainder of the ten-year statutory period for collection, whichever is less).*

You can pay the short-term deferred payment plan in three ways:

Plan One

- Full payment of the realizable value of your assets within 90 days from the date we accept your offer, and

- Payment within two years of acceptance of the amount we could collect over 60 months *(future income)* or the remaining life of the collection statute, whichever is less.

Plan Two

- Cash payment for a portion of the realizable value of your assets within 90 days from the date we accept your offer, and

- The balance of the realizable value plus the amount we could collect over 60 months *(future income)* or the remaining life of the collection statute, whichever is less, within two years of acceptance.

Plan Three

- The entire offer amount in monthly payments extending over a period not to exceed two years from date of acceptance *(e.g., four payments within 120 days of acceptance).*

For example, on a short-term deferred payment total offer of $16,000, you might propose to pay your realizable value of assets *(e.g., $13,000)* within 90 days of acceptance and the amount of your future income *(e.g., $50 per month for 60 months, or $3,000)* over 6 monthly payments of $500 each, beginning the first month after acceptance.

We may file a Notice of Federal Tax Lien on tax liabilities compromised under short-term payment offers.

6

Deferred Payment Offer

This payment plan requires you to pay the offer amount over the remaining statutory period for collecting the tax.

The offer must include the realizable value of your assets plus the amount we could collect through monthly payments during the remaining life of the collection statute.

- Using the worksheet on Pages 8 and 9, multiply the amount from Item 12, Box O, by the number of months remaining on the collection statute. Add that amount to Item 11, Box N, and use the total as the basis for your offer amount in Item 7 of Form 656.

You can pay the deferred payment plan in three ways:

Plan One

- Full payment of the realizable value of your assets within 90 days from the date we accept your offer, and

- Your "future income" in monthly payments during the remaining life of the collection statute

Plan Two

- Cash payment for a portion of the realizable value of your assets within 90 days from the date we accept your offer, and

- Monthly payments during the remaining life of the collection statute for both the balance of the realizable value and your future income

Plan Three

- The entire offer amount in monthly payments over the life of the collection statute

For example, on a deferred payment offer with 7 years *(84 months)* remaining on the statutory period for collection and a total offer of $25,000, you might propose to pay your realizable value of assets *(e.g., $10,000)* within 90 days and your future income *(e.g., $179 per month for 7 years, or $15,000)* in 84 monthly installments of $179. Alternately, you could also pay the same total $25,000 offer in 84 monthly installments of $298.

Just as with short-term deferred payment offers, we may file a Notice of Federal Tax Lien on tax liabilities compromised under Deferred Payment Offers.

Note: The worksheet on Pages 8 and 9 instructs wage earners and self-employed individuals how to figure the appropriate amount for a Cash, Short-Term Deferred Payment, or Deferred Payment Offer.

Offer in Compromise Worksheet

Please see Pages 8 and 9.

Funding Your Offer

If you do not have the cash to pay your offer amount immediately, you should begin the process of exploring options to finance your offer amount. Options you may want to consider include liquidating assets, obtaining a loan from a lending institution, borrowing on your home equity through a second mortgage or reverse mortgage, or borrowing funds from family members or friends.

7

Worksheet to Calculate an Offer Amount
For use by Wage Earners and Self-Employed Individuals.

Keep this worksheet for your records.
Do not send to IRS.

Use this Worksheet to calculate an offer amount using information from Form 433-A.

1. Enter total checking accounts from Item 11c   **A**

2. Enter total other accounts from Item 12c   **B**

        If less than 0 , enter 0

3. Enter total investments from Item 13d   **C**

4. Enter total cash on hand from Item 14a   **D**

5. Enter life insurance cash value from Item 16f   **E**

6. Enter total accounts/notes receivable from Item 23m   **F**

       Subtotal: Add boxes A through F =   **G**

7. Purchased Automobiles, Trucks, and Other Licensed Assets

	Enter current value for each asset		Enter loan balance for each asset	Individual asset value (if less than 0 , enter 0)
From line 18a	$_____	x .8 = $_____	—$_____	= _____
From line 18b	$_____	x .8 = $_____	—$_____	= _____
From line 18c	$_____	x .8 = $_____	—$_____	= _____
			Subtotal =	**H**

8. Real Estate

	Enter current value for each asset		Enter loan balance for each asset	Individual asset value (if less than 0 , enter 0)
From line 20a	$_____	x .8 = $_____	—$_____	= _____
From line 20b	$_____	x .8 = $_____	—$_____	= _____
			Subtotal =	_____

9. Personal Assets

	Enter current value for each asset		Enter loan balance for each asset	Individual asset value (if less than 0 , enter 0)
From line 21b	$_____	x .8 = $_____	—$_____	= _____
From line 21c	$_____	x .8 = $_____	—$_____	= _____
From line 21d	$_____	x .8 = $_____	—$_____	= _____
From line 21e	$_____	x .8 = $_____	—$_____	= _____
			Subtotal =	**J**
From line 21a	$_____	x .8 = $_____	—$_____	= _____
			Subtract	—$ 7040.00
			Subtotal =	**K**

10. Business Assets

	Enter current value for each asset		Enter loan balance for each asset	Individual asset value (if less than 0 , enter 0)
From line 22b	$_____	x .8 = $_____	—$_____	= _____
From line 22c	$_____	x .8 = $_____	—$_____	= _____
From line 22d	$_____	x .8 = $_____	—$_____	= _____
From line 22e	$_____	x .8 = $_____	—$_____	= _____
			Subtotal =	_____
From line 22a	$_____	x .8 = $_____	—$_____	= _____
			Subtract	—$ 3520.00
			Subtotal =	**M**

8

11. Add amounts in Boxes G through M to obtain your total equity and assets = N [_____]

12. Enter amount from Item 34 $ _____

Enter amount from Item 45 and subtract — $ _____

Net Difference = O [_____]

This amount would be available to pay monthly on your tax liability.

If Box O is 0 or less, STOP. Use the amount from Box N and to base your offer amount in Item 7 of Form 656. **Your offer amount must equal or exceed (*) the amount shown in Box N.**

13a.

If you will pay the offer amount in 90 days or less (i.e., cash offer):

Enter amount from Box O $ _____

Multiply by **x 48**
(or the number of months remaining on the ten-year statutory period for collection, whichever is less)

= P [_____]

Enter amount from Box N + Q [_____]

Add amounts in Box P and Box Q = R [_____]

Use the amount from Box R to base your offer amount in Item 7 of Form 656.

Note: Your offer amount must equal or exceed (*) the amount shown in Box R.

13b.

If you will pay the offer amount in more than 90 days but less than 2 years (i.e., short-term deferred payment offer):

Enter amount from Box O $ _____

Multiply by **x 60**
(or the number of months remaining on the ten-year statutory period for collection, whichever is less)

= S [_____]

Enter amount from Box N + T [_____]

Add amounts in Box S and Box T = U [_____]

Use the amount from Box U to base your offer amount in Item 7 of Form 656.

Note: Your offer amount must equal or exceed (*) the amount shown in Box U.

Note: Do not compute your offer amount using 13a or 13b if your statute expiration date(s) is less than 5 years from the date of your offer. Instead, refer to page 7 under Deferred Payment Offer options 1 through 3.

* Unless you are submitting an offer under effective tax administration or doubt as to collectibility with special circumstances considerations, as described on page 5.

9

Step Four: Completing Form 656, Offer in Compromise

We have included two *Offer in Compromise* forms. Use one form to submit your *Offer in Compromise*. You may use the other form as a worksheet and retain it for your personal records.

Note: If you have any questions about completing this form, you may call toll free at 1–800–829–1040 or visit your local IRS office or our website at www.irs.gov. We may return your offer if you don't follow these instructions.

Item 1:

Enter your name and home or business street address. Show **both names** on a joint offer for joint liabilities. You also should include a mailing address if it is different from your street address.

If you owe a liability —

Jointly with another person and *both of you agree* to submit an offer, send only **one** Form 656, *Offer in Compromise, and* **one** $150 application fee *(or Form 656-A, if applicable)*.

By yourself *(such as employment taxes)*, and other liabilities with another

person *(such as income taxes)*, but **only you** are submitting an offer, then list **all** tax liabilities on **one** Form 656 and submit **one** $150 application fee *(or Form 656-A, if applicable)*.

By yourself and another one jointly, and *both of you* submit an offer, then you must show **all** tax liabilities on your Form 656 and submit **one** $150 application fee *(or Form 656-A, if applicable)*. **The other person** should show **only** the joint tax liability on their Form 656 and submit **one** $150 application fee *(or Form 656-A, if applicable)*.

Item 2:

Enter the social security number(s) for the person(s) submitting the offer. For example, enter the social security number of both spouses when

submitting a joint offer for a joint tax liability. However, when only one spouse submits an offer, enter only that spouse's social security number.

Item 3:

Enter the employer identification number for offers from businesses.

Item 4:

Show the employer identification numbers for all other businesses *(excluding corporate entities)* that you

own or in which you have an ownership interest.

Item 5:

Identify your tax liability and enter the tax year or period. Letters and notices from us and Notices of Federal Tax Lien show

the tax periods for trust fund recovery penalties.

Item 6:

Check the appropriate box(es) describing the basis for your offer.

Doubt as to Liability offers require a statement describing in detail why you think you do not owe the liability. Complete Item 9, "Explanation of Circumstances," explaining your situation.

Doubt as to Collectibility offers require you to complete a Form 433-A, *Collection Information Statement for Wage Earners and Self-Employed Individuals*, if you are an individual taxpayer, or a Form 433-B, *Collection Information Statement for Businesses*, if you are a corporation or other business taxpayer.

Note: Attach to the upper left corner of Form 656 the six (6) pages of the collection information statement(s) and all related documents before you send it to us.

10

Item 6 *(cont'd)*:   **Effective Tax Administration** offers require you to complete a Form 433-A, *Collection Information Statement for Wage Earners and Self-Employed Individuals*, if you are an individual taxpayer, or a Form 433-B, *Collection Information Statement for Businesses*, if you are a corporation or other business taxpayer. Complete Item 9, "Explanation of Circumstances."

Item 7:   Enter the total amount of your offer *(see Page 5, "Determining the Amount of Your Offer")*. Your offer amount cannot include a refund we owe you or amounts you have already paid. Check the appropriate payment box *(cash, short-term deferred payment or deferred payment — see Page 6, "Determine Your Payment Terms")* and describe your payment plan in the spaces provided.

Item 8:   It is important that you understand the requirements listed in this section. Pay particular attention to Items 8(d) and 8(g), as they address the future compliance provision and refunds.

Item 9:   Explain your reason(s) for submitting your offer in the "Explanation of Circumstances." You may attach additional sheets if necessary. Include your name and SSN or EIN on all attachments.

Item 10:   Explain where you will get the funds to pay the amount you are offering.

Item 11:   11(a) and 11(b) **Signature of Taxpayer.** All persons submitting the offer must sign and date Form 656. Include titles of authorized corporate officers, executors, trustees, Powers of Attorney, etc., where applicable.

Item 12:   If someone other than the taxpayer prepared this Offer in Compromise, the taxpayer should insert their name and address *(if known)* in Item 12.

Item 13:   Paid Preparer's Use Only. Self explanatory. Please see the "Privacy Act Notice" on Page 13.

Item 14:   If you want to allow the IRS to discuss your Offer in Compromise with a friend, family member, or any other person, including an individual you paid to prepare this form, check the "Yes" box in Item 14, "Third Party Designee," on your Form 656. Also enter the designee's name and phone number. Checking the "Yes" box allows the IRS to contact another person and discuss with that person any additional information the IRS needs to process your offer. This additional information may include information about tax liabilities you failed to list in Item 5 on your Form 656 or returns you have failed to file. If your contact person is an attorney, CPA, or enrolled agent and you wish to have them represent you regarding this offer, a Form 2848, *Power of Attorney and Declaration of Representative*, should be completed and submitted with your offer.

Note: *Staple in the upper left corner the four (4) pages of Form 656 before you send it to us.*

11

Privacy Act Notice

We ask for the information on this form to carry out the internal revenue laws of the United States. Our authority to request this information is section 7801. Our purpose for requesting the information is to determine if it is in the best interests of the IRS to accept an offer in compromise. You are not required to make an offer in compromise; however, if you choose to do so, you must provide all of the taxpayer information requested. Failure to provide all of the information may prevent us from processing your request. If you are a paid preparer and you prepared the Form 656 for the taxpayer submitting an offer, we request that you complete and sign Item 13 on Form 656, and provide identifying information. Providing this information is voluntary. This information will be used to administer and enforce the internal revenue laws of the United States and may be used to regulate practice before the Internal Revenue Service for those persons subject to Treasury Department Circular No. 230, *Regulations Governing the Practice of Attorneys, Certified Public Accountants, Enrolled Agents, Enrolled Actuaries, and Appraisers before the Internal Revenue Service*. Information on this form may be disclosed to the Department of Justice for civil and criminal litigation. We may also disclose this information to cities, states, and the District of Columbia for use in administering their tax laws, and to Federal and state agencies to enforce nontax criminal laws and to combat terrorism. The authority to disclose information to combat terrorism expired on December 31, 2003. However, legislation is pending that would reinstate this authority. Providing false or fraudulent information on this form may subject you to criminal prosecution and penalties.

Step Five: Offer in Compromise *(OIC)* Application Fee

What is an Offer in Compromise Application Fee?	When you submit an offer in compromise *(OIC)*, the Internal Revenue Service expends resources evaluating your individual financial condition. The OIC	application fee allows the Internal Revenue Service to recover a portion of the cost of processing your OIC.
How much is the fee?	The application fee is $150 for each Form 656 submitted. **Do not send cash**. Please pay either by check or money order and make payable to the	**"United States Treasury."** *(See Offer in Compromise (OIC) Application Fee Worksheet.)*
When is the fee due?	The application fee of $150 is due at the time you submit your OIC for consideration.	
Do all OICs require this fee?	You must remit the application fee along with your Form 656, *Offer in Compromise*, **unless**: (1) Your OIC is based solely on **doubt as to liability** *(see Page 1 of this Offer in Compromise package)*, **or** (2) You certify that your total monthly income is at or below levels based on the poverty guidelines established by the	U.S. Department of Health and Human Services. *(See Offer in Compromise (OIC) Application Fee Worksheet.)* The exception for taxpayers with incomes below these levels only applies to individuals; it does not apply to other entities such as corporations or partnerships.
How do I determine if I qualify for the exception?	To determine if you qualify for the exception, please complete the attached Offer in Compromise *(OIC)* Application Fee Worksheet.	
Is the application fee ever refunded?	If the Internal Revenue Service accepts your OIC based on effective tax administration or special circumstances *(see Pages 1 and 5, respectively, in this Offer in Compromise package)*, the fee will be applied against the amount of the offer, or refunded to you if you	request. In addition, if your offer is determined to be **not** processable as described on Page 2 of this Offer in Compromise package, then your $150 application fee will be returned to you along with your offer.
What happens if I do not submit the application fee with my OIC Form 656?	Except for the two situations described above under "Do all OICs require this fee?" any OIC submitted without the	fee will be returned to you without further consideration.
Where do I call if I have additional questions about OICs and the application fee?	If you have additional questions about an OIC or about the application fee, please call toll free at 1–800–829–1040 or visit our website at *www.irs.gov*.	

Step Six: Where You Need to Send Your Offer

Where to File

IF YOU RESIDE IN

The states of Alaska, Alabama, Arizona, California, Colorado, Hawaii, Idaho, Kentucky, Louisiana, Mississippi, Montana, Nevada, New Mexico, Oregon, Tennessee, Texas, Utah, Washington, Wisconsin or Wyoming,

AND	AND
You are a wage earner, retiree, or a self-employed individual without employees,	You are **OTHER** than a wage earner, retiree, or a self-employed individual without employees,
THEN MAIL	THEN MAIL
Form 656 and attachments to:	Form 656 and attachments to:
Memphis Internal Revenue Service Center COIC Unit **PO Box 30803, AMC** Memphis, TN 38130-0803	Memphis Internal Revenue Service Center COIC Unit **PO Box 30804, AMC** Memphis, TN 38130-0804

IF YOU RESIDE IN

Arkansas, Connecticut, Delaware, District of Columbia, Florida, Georgia, Illinois, Indiana, Iowa, Kansas, Maine, Maryland, Massachusetts, Michigan, Minnesota, Missouri, Nebraska, New Hampshire, New Jersey, New York, North Carolina, North Dakota, Ohio, Oklahoma, Pennsylvania, Puerto Rico, Rhode Island, South Carolina, South Dakota, Vermont, Virginia, West Virginia or have a foreign address,

AND	AND
You are a wage earner, retiree, or a self-employed individual without employees,	You are **OTHER** than a wage earner, retiree, or a self-employed individual without employees,
THEN MAIL	THEN MAIL
Form 656 and attachments to:	Form 656 and attachments to:
Brookhaven Internal Revenue Service Center COIC Unit **PO Box 9007** Holtsville, NY 11742-9007	Brookhaven Internal Revenue Service Center COIC Unit **PO Box 9008** Holtsville, NY 11742-9008

14

Step Seven: What to Expect after the IRS Receives Your Offer

How We Consider Your Offer

An offer examiner will evaluate your offer and may request additional documentation from you to verify financial or other information you provide. The examiner will then make a recommendation to accept or reject the offer. The examiner may also return your offer if you don't provide the requested information.

The examiner may decide that a larger offer amount is necessary to justify acceptance. You will have the opportunity to amend your offer.

Additional Agreements

When you submit certain offers, we may also request that you sign an additional agreement requiring you to:

- Pay a percentage of your future earnings.
- Waive certain present or future tax benefits.

Withholding Collection Activities

There are certain circumstances where we will withhold collection activities while we consider your offer. We will not act to collect the tax liability:

- While we investigate and evaluate your offer.
- For 30 days after we reject an offer.
- While you appeal an offer rejection.
- **However, a Notice of Federal Tax Lien may be filed at any time while your offer is being considered.**

The above do not apply if we find any indication that you submitted your offer to delay collection or cause a delay which will jeopardize our ability to collect the tax.

If you currently have an installment agreement when you submit an offer, you must continue making the agreed upon monthly payments while we consider your offer.

If We Accept Your Offer

If we accept your offer, we will notify you by mail. When you receive your acceptance letter, you must:

- Promptly pay any unpaid amounts that become due under the terms of the offer agreement. You must comply with the payment terms specified in the agreement in a timely manner or your offer and agreement will be in default.

- Comply with all the terms and conditions of the offer, along with those of any additional agreement.

- Promptly notify us of any change of address until you meet the conditions of your offer. Your acceptance letter will indicate the IRS office to contact if your address changes. Your notification allows us to contact you immediately regarding the status of your offer.

We will release all Notices of Federal Tax Lien when you satisfy the payment terms of the offered amount. For an immediate release of a lien, you can submit certified funds with a request letter to the address on the acceptance letter.

Once your offer is accepted, not filing returns or paying taxes when due could result in the default of an accepted offer *(see Item 8(d) of Form 656 for the future compliance provision)*. If you default your agreement, we will reinstate the unpaid amount of the original tax liability, file a Notice of Federal Tax Lien on any tax liability without a filed notice, and resume collection activities. The future compliance provision applies to offers based on **doubt as to collectibility**. In certain cases, the future compliance provision may apply to offers based on **effective tax administration**.

We will not default your offer agreement when you have filed a joint offer with your spouse or ex-spouse as long as you have kept or are keeping all the terms of the agreement, even if your spouse or ex-spouse violates the future compliance provision.

15

Except for offers based on **doubt as to liability**, the offer agreement requires you to forego certain refunds, and to return those refunds to us if they are issued to you by mistake. These conditions are also listed on Form 656, Items 8(g) and 8(h). For example, if your offer was accepted by the IRS in the tax year 2004, the IRS would keep the refund due to you with respect to the tax year 2004, which you would normally receive in calendar year 2005 *(because the due date for filing the tax year 2004 is April 15, 2005).*

If We Reject Your Offer

We'll notify you by mail if we reject your offer. In our letter, we will explain our reason for the rejection. We will also keep your $150 application fee. If your offer is rejected, you have the right to:

- Appeal our decision to the Office of Appeals within thirty days from the date of our letter. The letter will include detailed instructions on how to appeal the rejection.

- Submit another offer with another application fee. You must increase an offer we've rejected as being too low when your financial situation remains unchanged. However, you must provide updated financial information when your financial situation has changed or when the original offer is more than six months old.

16

Step Eight: Offer in Compromise *(OIC)* Summary Checklist

Below is a checklist of items that you should review and complete prior to submitting your Form 656, *Offer in Compromise*. This checklist is solely for your benefit, so do not submit with your offer.

❏ Did you answer YES to any of the three questions on Page 2? If you did, then please do not submit Form 656 because you are not eligible to have your offer considered at this time.

❏ Have you properly completed Form 656, *Offer in Compromise*, by following the instructions on Pages 10 and 11?

❏ The preprinted terms and conditions listed on Form 656 have not changed.

❏ Are you using the most current versions of Form 656, Form 433-A, and Form 433-B as instructed on Page 2.

❏ You included your name *(or names, if joint)*.

❏ You included your social security number *(SSN)* or employer identification number *(EIN)* and it is accurate.

❏ You included an offer amount *(the amount must be greater than zero)* or payment term.

❏ You signed the Form 656. If this is a joint Form 656, both spouses must sign Form 656.

❏ **You either attached the application fee in the designated area on the Form 656 or attached the Form 656-A certification, whichever is applicable.** If you attached Form 656-A, then you *must* complete the Offer in Compromise *(OIC)* Application Fee Worksheet.

❏ If your offer is based on **doubt as to collectibility,** you included complete financial information *(Form 433-A or Form 433-B, or both)* and all attachments.

❏ You signed or initialed in all required places on Form 433-A and/or Form 433-B.

❏ Your offer amount is greater than or equal to the reasonable collection potential *(RCP)* as described on Page 5 and calculated on Page 9.

❏ If applicable, are Items 12 and 14, on Form 656 completed?

❏ If applicable, is Item 13 on Form 656 completed and **signed**?

❏ Have you properly identified where to file your Form 656 from the instructions on Page 14?

If you have any questions, please call our toll-free number at 1–800–829–1040. You can get forms and publications by calling toll free at 1–800–829–3676 (1–800–TAX–FORM), or by visiting your local Internal Revenue Service (IRS) office or our website at *www.irs.gov*.

17

Important Information Regarding the Offer in Compromise *(OIC)*

Statute of Limitations for Collection is Suspended — The statute of limitations for collection of a tax debt is suspended while an OIC is "pending," or being reviewed. The Offer in Compromise is pending starting with the date an authorized IRS employee determines the Form 656, *Offer in Compromise*, can be processed and signs the Form 656. The OIC remains pending until an authorized IRS employee accepts, rejects, returns, or acknowledges withdrawal of the offer in writing. If a taxpayer appeals an OIC that was rejected, the IRS will continue to treat the OIC as pending until the Appeals Office accepts or rejects the OIC in writing.

Taxpayers Must File and Pay Taxes — In order to avoid defaulting an OIC once it is accepted by the IRS, taxpayers must remain in compliance in the filing and payment of all required taxes for a period of five years, or until the offered amount is paid in full, whichever is longer. Failure to comply with these conditions will result in the default of the OIC and the reinstatement of the tax liability.

Federal Tax Liens Are Not Released — If there is a Notice of Federal Tax Lien on record prior to the OIC being submitted, the lien is not released until the terms of the offer in compromise are satisfied, or until the liability is paid, whichever comes first. The IRS generally files a Notice of Federal Tax Lien to protect the Government's interest on deferred payment offers. This tax lien will be released when the payment terms of the offer agreement have been satisfied.

Effect of the Offer on the Taxpayer's Refund — The IRS will keep any refund, including interest due to the taxpayer because of overpayment of any tax or other liability, for tax periods extending through the calendar year that the IRS accepts the offer. The taxpayer may not designate an overpayment ordinarily subject to refund, to which the IRS is entitled, to be applied to estimated tax payments for the following year. This condition does not apply if the offer is based on **doubt as to liability**.

Effect of the Offer on Installment Agreements and Levies — The IRS will keep all payments and credits made, received or applied to the total original tax liability before submission of this offer. The IRS may keep any proceeds from a levy served prior to submission of the offer, but not received at the time the offer is submitted. The taxpayer understands that if they had an installment agreement prior to submitting the offer, he/she must continue to make the payments as agreed while this offer is pending. Installment agreement payments will not be applied against the amount offered.

Public Inspection Files for Accepted Offer in Compromise Files — The law requires IRS to make certain information from accepted Offers in Compromise available for public inspection and review. These public inspection files are located in your local IRS Territory Office. It is important to know that certain information regarding your accepted Offer in Compromise may be publicly known.

Taxpayer Advocate Services — If at anytime you feel that you need help in resolving a tax problem that has not been resolved through normal channels or you are experiencing significant hardship, then you may contact our Taxpayer Advocate Service *(TAS)*. To find more information on TAS or to locate your local TAS office, call the nationwide TAS toll-free number 1–877–777–4778, or visit our website at *www.irs.gov.*

Low Income Taxpayer Clinic *(LITC)* — In addition, each taxpayer has a right to representation but not everyone can afford representation. The Low Income Taxpayer Clinic *(LITC)* was developed to represent low income taxpayers before the IRS for free or for a minimal charge. You can learn about LITC by going to our website at *www.irs.gov* and click on Taxpayer Advocate Services, or you can call the nationwide TAS toll-free number 1–877–777–4778.

18

Terms and Definitions

An understanding of the following terms and conditions will help you to prepare offers based upon **doubt as to collectibility or effective tax administration**.

Current Value — The amount you could reasonably expect from the sale of an asset today. Provide an accurate valuation of each asset. Determine value from realtors, used car dealers, publications, furniture dealers, or other experts on specific types of assets. Please include a copy of any written estimate with your Collection Information Statement.

Expenses Not Generally Allowed — We typically do not allow you to claim tuition for private schools, public or private college expenses, charitable contributions, voluntary retirement contributions, payments on unsecured debts such as credit card bills, cable television charges and other similar expenses as necessary living expenses. However, we can allow these expenses when you can prove that they are necessary for the health and welfare of you or your family or for the production of income.

Future Income — We generally determine the amount we could collect from your future income by subtracting necessary living expenses from your monthly income over a set number of months. For a cash offer, you must offer what you could pay in monthly payments over forty-eight months *(or the remainder of the ten-year statutory period for collection, whichever is less)*. For a short-term deferred offer, you must offer what you could pay in monthly payments over sixty months *(or the remainder of the statutory period for collection, whichever is less)*. For a deferred payment offer, you must offer what you could pay in monthly payments during the remaining time we could legally receive payments.

Necessary Expenses — The allowable payments you make to support you and your family's health and welfare and/or the production of income. This expense allowance does not apply to business entities. Publication 1854, *How to Prepare a Collection Information Statement (Form 433-A)*, explains the National Standard Expenses and gives the allowable amounts. We derive these amounts from the Bureau of Labor Statistics *(BLS)* Consumer Expenditure Survey. We also use information from the Bureau of the Census to determine local expenses for housing, utilities, and transportation.

Note: If the IRS determines that the facts and circumstances of your situation indicate that using the scheduled allowance of necessary expenses is inadequate, we will allow you an adequate means for providing basic living expenses. However, you must provide documentation that supports a determination that using national and local expense standards leaves you an inadequate means of providing for basic living expenses.

Quick Sale Value *(QSV)* — The amount you could reasonably expect from the sale of an asset if you sold it quickly, typically in ninety days or less. This amount generally is less than current value, but may be equal to or higher, based on local circumstances.

Realizable Value — The quick sale value amount minus what you owe to a secured creditor. The creditor must have priority over a filed Notice of Federal Tax Lien before we allow a subtraction from the asset's value.

Reasonable Collection Potential *(RCP)* — The total realizable value of your assets plus your future income. The total is generally your minimum offer amount.

19

IRS

Department of the Treasury
Internal Revenue Service

www.irs.gov

Form 433-A (Rev. 5-2001)
Catalog Number 20312N

Collection Information Statement for Wage Earners and Self-Employed Individuals

Complete all entry spaces with the most current data available.

Important! Write "N/A" (not applicable) in spaces that do not apply. We may require additional information to support "N/A" entries.

Failure to complete all entry spaces may result in rejection or significant delay in the resolution of your account.

Section 1

Personal Information

1. Full Name(s) _____

Street Address _____
City _____ State _____ Zip _____
County of Residence _____
How long at this address? _____

1a. Home Telephone (____) _____ Best Time To Call: ____ am ____ pm (Enter Hour)

2. Marital Status:
☐ Married   ☐ Separated
☐ Unmarried (single, divorced, widowed)

3. Your Social Security No. (SSN) _____
4. Spouse's Social Security No. _____

3a. Your Date of Birth (mm/dd/yyyy) _____
4a. Spouse's Date of Birth (mm/dd/yyyy) _____

5. ☐ Own Home   ☐ Rent   ☐ Other (specify, i.e. share rent, live with relative) _____

6. List the dependents you can claim on your tax return: (Attach sheet if more space is needed.)

First Name	Relationship	Age	Does this person live with you?	First Name	Relationship	Age	Does this person live with you?
			☐ No ☐ Yes				☐ No ☐ Yes
			☐ No ☐ Yes				☐ No ☐ Yes

☐ Check this box when all spaces in Sect. 1 are filled in

Section 2

Your Business Information

7. Are you or your spouse self-employed or operate a business? (Check "Yes" if either applies)

☐ No   ☐ Yes   If yes, provide the following information:

7a. Name of Business _____
7b. Street Address _____
City _____ State _____ Zip _____

7c. Employer Identification No., if available : _____
7d. Do you have employees? ☐ No ☐ Yes
7e. Do you have accounts/notes receivable? ☐ No ☐ Yes
If yes, please complete Section 8 on page 5.

☐ Check this box when all spaces in Sect. 2 are filled in and attachments provided

📎 **ATTACHMENTS REQUIRED:** Please include proof of self-employment income for the **prior 3 months** (e.g., invoices, commissions, sales records, income statement).

Section 3

Employment Information

8. Your Employer _____
Street Address _____
City _____ State _____ Zip _____
Work telephone no. (____) _____
May we contact you at work? ☐ No ☐ Yes
8a. How long with this employer? _____
8b. Occupation _____

9. Spouse's Employer _____
Street Address _____
City _____ State _____ Zip _____
Work telephone no. (____) _____
May we contact you at work? ☐ No ☐ Yes
9a. How long with this employer? _____
9b. Occupation _____

☐ Check this box when all spaces in Sect. 3 are filled in and attachments provided

📎 **ATTACHMENTS REQUIRED:** Please provide proof of gross earnings and deductions for the past 3 months from each employer (e.g., pay stubs, earnings statements). If year-to-date information is available, send only 1 such statement as long as a **minimum of 3 months** is represented.

Section 4

Other Income Information

10. Do you receive income from sources other than your own business or your employer? (Check all that apply.)

☐ Pension   ☐ Social Security   ☐ Other (specify, i.e. child support, alimony, rental) _____

☐ Check this box when all spaces in Sect. 4 are filled in and attachments provided

📎 **ATTACHMENTS REQUIRED:** Please provide proof of pension/social security/other income for the past 3 months from each payor, including any statements showing deductions. If year-to-date information is available, send only 1 such statement as long as a **minimum of 3 months** is represented.

Collection Information Statement for Wage Earners and Self-Employed Individuals **Form 433-A**

Name_____ SSN_____

Section 5	11. CHECKING ACCOUNTS. List all checking accounts. (If you need additional space, attach a separate sheet.)

Section 5

Banking, Investment, Cash, Credit, and Life Insurance Information

Complete all entry spaces with the most current data available.

	Type of Account	Full Name of Bank, Savings & Loan, Credit Union or Financial Institution	Bank Routing No.	Bank Account No.	Current Account Balance
11a. Checking		Name			$
		Street Address			
		City/State/Zip			
11b. Checking		Name			$
		Street Address			
		City/State/Zip		**11c. Total Checking Account Balances**	$

12. OTHER ACCOUNTS. List all acounts, including brokerage, savings, and money market, not listed on line 11.

	Type of Account	Full Name of Bank, Savings & Loan, Credit Union or Financial Institution	Bank Routing No.	Bank Account No.	Current Account Balance
12a.		Name			$
		Street Address			
		City/State/Zip			
12b.		Name			$
		Street Address			
		City/State/Zip		**12c. Total Other Account Balances**	$

ATTACHMENTS REQUIRED: Please include your current bank statements (checking, savings, money market, and brokerage accounts) for the past three months for all accounts.

13. INVESTMENTS. List all investment assets below. Include stocks, bonds, mutual funds, stock options, certificates of deposits, and retirement assets such as IRAs, Keogh, and 401(k) plans. (If you need additional space, attach a separate sheet.)

⊠ **Current Value:** Indicate the amount you could sell the asset for today.

	Name of Company	Number of Shares / Units	⊠ Current Value	Loan Amount	Used as collateral on loan?
13a.			$	$	☐ No ☐ Yes
13b.					☐ No ☐ Yes
13c.					☐ No ☐ Yes
	13d. Total Investments		$		

14. CASH ON HAND. Include any money that you have that is not in the bank.

	14a. Total Cash on Hand	$

15. AVAILABLE CREDIT. List all lines of credit, including credit cards.

	Full Name of Credit Institution	Credit Limit	Amount Owed	Available Credit
15a. Name				$
	Street Address			
	City/State/Zip			
15b. Name				$
	Street Address			
	City/State/Zip	**15c. Total Credit Available**		$

Collection Information Statement for Wage Earners and Self-Employed Individuals   Form 433-A

Name _____   SSN _____

Section 5 continued	**16. LIFE INSURANCE.** Do you have life insurance with a cash value? ☐ No ☐ Yes (Term Life insurance does not have a cash value.) If yes: **16a.** Name of Insurance Company _____ **16b.** Policy Number(s) _____ **16c.** Owner of Policy _____ **16d.** Current Cash Value $ _____ **16e.** Outstanding Loan Balance $ _____ Subtract "Outstanding Loan Balance" line 16e from "Current Cash Value" line 16d = 16f $ _____
☐ Check this box when all spaces in Sect. 5 are filled in and attachments provided.	**ATTACHMENTS REQUIRED:** Please include a statement from the life insurance companies that includes type and cash/loan value amounts. If currently borrowed against, include loan amount and date of loan.

Section 6 Other Information	**17. OTHER INFORMATION.** Respond to the following questions related to your financial condition: (Attach sheet if you need more space.) **17a.** Are there any garnishments against your wages? ☐ No ☐ Yes If yes, who is the creditor?_____ Date creditor obtained judgement_____ Amount of debt $_____ **17b.** Are there any judgments against you? ☐ No ☐ Yes If yes, who is the creditor?_____ Date creditor obtained judgement_____ Amount of debt $_____ **17c.** Are you a party in a lawsuit? ☐ No ☐ Yes If yes, amount of suit $_____ Possible completion date_____ Subject matter of suit_____ **17d.** Did you ever file bankruptcy? ☐ No ☐ Yes If yes, date filed_____ Date discharged_____ **17e.** In the past 10 years did you transfer any assets out of your name for less than their actual value? ☐ No ☐ Yes If yes, what asset?_____ Value of asset at time of transfer $_____ When was it transferred?_____ To whom was it transferred?_____ **17f.** Do you anticipate any increase in household income in the next two years? ☐ No ☐ Yes If yes, why will the income increase? _____ (Attach sheet if you need more space.) How much will it increase? _____ **17g.** Are you a beneficiary of a trust or an estate? ☐ No ☐ Yes If yes, name of the trust or estate_____ Anticipated amount to be received $_____ When will the amount be received?_____ **17h.** Are you a participant in a profit sharing plan? ☐ No ☐ Yes If yes, name of plan _____ Value in plan $_____
☐ Check this box when all spaces in Sect. 6 are filled in.	

Section 7 Assets and Liabilities	**18. PURCHASED AUTOMOBILES, TRUCKS AND OTHER LICENSED ASSETS.** Include boats, RV's, motorcycles, trailers, etc. (If you need additional space, attach a separate sheet.)

Description (Year, Make, Model, Mileage)	⊠ Current Value	Current Loan Balance	Name of Lender	Purchase Date	Amount of Monthly Payment
18a. Year _____ Make/Model _____ Mileage _____	$	$			$
18b. Year _____ Make/Model _____ Mileage _____	$	$			$
18c. Year _____ Make/Model _____ Mileage _____	$	$			$

⊠ Current Value: Indicate the amount you could sell the asset for today.

Section 7 continued on page 4 →
(Rev 5-2001)

Copyright © December 2004

Collection Information Statement for Wage Earners and Self-Employed Individuals   **Form 433-A**

Name _____   SSN _____

Section 7 **continued**	**19.**	**LEASED AUTOMOBILES, TRUCKS AND OTHER LICENSED ASSETS.** Include boats, RV's, motorcycles, trailers, etc. (If you need additional space, attach a separate sheet.)

	Description (Year, Make, Model)	Lease Balance	Name and Address of Lessor	Lease Date	Amount of Monthly Payment
19a.	Year				
	Make/Model	$			$
19b.	Year				
	Make/Model	$			$

ATTACHMENTS REQUIRED: Please include your current statement from lender with monthly car payment amount and current balance of the loan for each vehicle purchased or leased.

20. **REAL ESTATE.** List all real estate you own. (If you need additional space, attach a separate sheet.)

☐ **Current Value:** Indicate the amount you could sell the asset for today.

✳ **Date of Final Payment:** Enter the date the loan or lease will be fully paid.

	Street Address, City, State, Zip, and County	Date Purchased	Purchase Price	☐Current Value	Loan Balance	Name of Lender or Lien Holder	Amount of Monthly Payment	✳Date of Final Payment
20a.			$	$	$		$	
20b.			$	$	$		$	

ATTACHMENTS REQUIRED: Please include your current statement from lender with monthly payment amount and current balance for each piece of real estate owned.

21. PERSONAL ASSETS. List all Personal assets below. (If you need additional space, attach separate sheet.)
Furniture/Personal Effects includes the total current market value of your household such as furniture and appliances.
Other Personal Assets includes all artwork, jewelry, collections (coin/gun, etc.), antiques or other assets.

	Description	☐Current Value	Loan Balance	Name of Lender	Amount of Monthly Payment	✳Date of Final Payment
21a.	Furniture/Personal Effects				$	
	Other: (List below)					
21b.	Artwork	$	$		$	
21c.	Jewelry					
21d.						
21e.						

22. BUSINESS ASSETS. List all business assets and encumbrances below, include Uniform Commercial Code (UCC) filings. (If you need additional space, attach a separate sheet.) *Tools used in Trade or Business* includes the basic tools or books used to conduct your business, excluding automobiles. *Other Business Assets* includes any other machinery, equipment, inventory or other assets.

	Description	☐Current Value	Loan Balance	Name of Lender	Amount of Monthly Payment	✳Date of Final Payment
22a.	Tools used in Trade/Business	$	$		$	
	Other: (List below)					
22b.	Machinery	$	$		$	
22c.	Equipment					
22d.						
22e.						

☐ Check this box when all spaces in Sect. 7 are filled in and attachments provided.

Page 4 of 6   Section 8 begins on page 5 →
                                 (Rev. 5-2001)

Collection Information Statement for Wage Earners and Self-Employed Individuals   Form 433-A

Name _____   SSN _____

Section 8 Accounts/ Notes Receivable *Use only if* *needed.* ☐ Check this box if Section 8 not needed.	**23. ACCOUNTS/NOTES RECEIVABLE.** List all accounts separately, including contracts awarded, but not started. (If you need additional space, attach a separate sheet.)

Description	Amount Due	Date Due	Age of Account
23a. Name _____ Street Address _____ City/State/Zip _____	$ _____	_____	☐ 0 - 30 days ☐ 30 - 60 days ☐ 60 - 90 days ☐ 90+ days
23b. Name _____ Street Address _____ City/State/Zip _____	$ _____		☐ 0 - 30 days ☐ 30 - 60 days ☐ 60 - 90 days ☐ 90+ days
23c. Name _____ Street Address _____ City/State/Zip _____	$ _____		☐ 0 - 30 days ☐ 30 - 60 days ☐ 60 - 90 days ☐ 90+ days
23d. Name _____ Street Address _____ City/State/Zip _____	$ _____		☐ 0 - 30 days ☐ 30 - 60 days ☐ 60 - 90 days ☐ 90+ days
23e. Name _____ Street Address _____ City/State/Zip _____	$ _____		☐ 0 - 30 days ☐ 30 - 60 days ☐ 60 - 90 days ☐ 90+ days
23f. Name _____ Street Address _____ City/State/Zip _____	$ _____		☐ 0 - 30 days ☐ 30 - 60 days ☐ 60 - 90 days ☐ 90+ days
23g. Name _____ Street Address _____ City/State/Zip _____	$ _____		☐ 0 - 30 days ☐ 30 - 60 days ☐ 60 - 90 days ☐ 90+ days
23h. Name _____ Street Address _____ City/State/Zip _____	$ _____		☐ 0 - 30 days ☐ 30 - 60 days ☐ 60 - 90 days ☐ 90+ days
23I. Name _____ Street Address _____ City/State/Zip _____	$ _____		☐ 0 - 30 days ☐ 30 - 60 days ☐ 60 - 90 days ☐ 90+ days
23j. Name _____ Street Address _____ City/State/Zip _____	$ _____		☐ 0 - 30 days ☐ 30 - 60 days ☐ 60 - 90 days ☐ 90+ days
23k. Name _____ Street Address _____ City/State/Zip _____	$ _____		☐ 0 - 30 days ☐ 30 - 60 days ☐ 60 - 90 days ☐ 90+ days
23l. Name _____ Street Address _____ City/State/Zip _____	$ _____		☐ 0 - 30 days ☐ 30 - 60 days ☐ 60 - 90 days ☐ 90+ days

☐ Check this box
when all spaces in
Sect. 8 are filled in

Add "**Amount Due**" from lines 23a through 23l = 23m $ _____

Collection Information Statement for Wage Earners and Self-Employed Individuals   **Form 433-A**

Name_____   SSN_____

Section 9	Total Income		Total Living Expenses	
Monthly Income and Expense Analysis	Source	Gross Monthly	Expense Items [4]	Actual Monthly
	24. Wages (Yourself)[1]	$	35. Food, Clothing and Misc.[5]	$
	25. Wages (Spouse)[1]		36. Housing and Utilities[6]	
If only one spouse has a tax liability, but both have income, list the total household income and expenses.	26. Interest - Dividends		37. Transportation[7]	
	27. Net Income from Business[2]		38. Health Care	
	28. Net Rental Income[3]		39. Taxes (Income and FICA)	
	29. Pension/Social Security (Yourself)		40. Court ordered payments	
	30. Pension/Social Security (Spouse)		41. Child/dependent care	
	31. Child Support		42. Life insurance	
	32. Alimony		43. Other secured debt	
	33. Other		44. Other expenses	
	34. Total Income	$	45. Total Living Expenses	$

[1] **Wages, salaries, pensions, and social security:** Enter your gross monthly wages and/or salaries. Do not deduct withholding or allotments you elect to take out of your pay, such as insurance payments, credit union deductions, car payments etc.
To calculate your gross monthly wages and/or salaries:
>   If paid weekly - multiply weekly gross wages by 4.3. Example: $425.89 x 4.3 = $1,831.33
>   If paid bi-weekly (every 2 weeks) - multiply bi-weekly gross wages by 2.17. Example: $972.45 x 2.17 = $2,110.22
>   If paid semi-monthly (twice each month) - multiply semi-monthly gross wages by 2. Example: $856.23 x 2 = $1,712.46

[2] **Net Income from Business:** Enter your monthly net business income. This is the amount you earn after you pay ordinary and necessary monthly business expenses. This figure should relate to the yearly net profit from your Form 1040 Schedule C. If it is more or less than the previous year, you should attach an explanation. If your net business income is a loss, enter "0". Do not enter a negative number.

[3] **Net Rental Income:** Enter your monthly net rental income. This is the amount you earn after you pay ordinary and necessary monthly rental expenses. If your net rental income is a loss, enter "0". Do not enter a negative number.

[4] **Expenses not generally allowed:** We generally do not allow you to claim tuition for private schools, public or private college expenses, charitable contributions, voluntary retirement contributions, payments on unsecured debts such as credit card bills, cable television and other similar expenses. However, we may allow these expenses, if you can prove that they are necessary for the health and welfare of you or your family or for the production of income.

[5] **Food, Clothing and Misc.:** Total of clothing, food, housekeeping supplies and personal care products for one month.

[6] **Housing and Utilities:** For your principal residence: Total of rent or mortgage payment. Add the average monthly expenses for the following: property taxes, home owner's or renter's insurance, maintenance, dues, fees, and utilities. Utilities include gas, electricity, water, fuel, oil, other fuels, trash collection and telephone.

[7] **Transportation:** Total of lease or purchase payments, vehicle insurance, registration fees, normal maintenance, fuel, public transportation, parking and tolls for one month.

ATTACHMENTS REQUIRED: Please include:

- A copy of your last Form 1040 with all Schedules.

- Proof of all current expenses that you paid for the past 3 months, including utilities, rent, insurance, property taxes, etc.

- Proof of all non-business transportation expenses (e.g., car payments, lease payments, fuel, oil, insurance, parking, registration).

- Proof of payments for health care, including health insurance premiums, co-payments, and other out-of-pocket expenses, for the past 3 months.

- Copies of any court order requiring payment and proof of such payments (e.g., cancelled checks, money orders, earning statements showing such deductions) for the past 3 months.

☐ Check this box when all spaces in Sect. 9 are filled in and attachments provided

☐ Check this box when all spaces in all sections are filled in and all attachments provided

⚠ **CAUTION**   *Failure to complete all entry spaces may result in rejection or significant delay in the resolution of your account.*

Certification: Under penalties of perjury, I declare that to the best of my knowledge and belief this statement of assets, liabilities, and other information is true, correct and complete.

_____   _____   _____
Your Signature   Spouse's Signature   Date

(Rev. 5-2001)

FORM 15.13
COLLATERAL AGREEMENT—FUTURE INCOME—INDIVIDUAL

Form 2261 (Rev. 04-95)	DEPARTMENT OF THE TREASURY – INTERNAL REVENUE SERVICE **Collateral Agreement** Future Income – Individual
Names and Address of Taxpayers John & Mary Jones 1 Park Place New York, NY 10000	**Social Security and Employer Identification Numbers** 123-45-6789 987-65-4321

To: Commissioner of Internal Revenue

The taxpayers identified above have submitted an offer dated 11/1/98 in the amount of $ 25,000. to

compromise unpaid 91,345. tax liability, plus statutory additions, for the taxable periods 1992-1996

The purpose of this collateral agreement (hereinafter referred to as this agreement) is to provide additional consideration for acceptance of the offer in compromise described above. It is understood and agreed:

1. That in addition to the payment of the above amount of $ 25,000 , the taxpayers will pay out of annual income for the years 1998 to 2002 , inclusive

    (a) Nothing on the first $ 42,000 of annual income.

    (b) 10 percent of annual income more than $ 42,000 and not more than $ 50,000 .

    (c) 15 percent of annual income more than $ 50,000 and not more than $ 60,000 .

    (d) 20 percent of annual income more than $ 60,000

2. That the term annual income, as used in this agreement, means adjusted gross income as defined in section 62 of the Internal Revenue Code (except losses from sales or exchanges of property shall not be allowed), plus all nontaxable income and profits or gains from any source whatsoever (including the fair market value of gifts, bequests, devises, and inheritances), minus (a) the federal income tax paid for the year for which annual income is being computed, and (b) any payment made under the terms of the offer in compromise (Form 656), as shown in item 5, for the year in which such payment is made. Annual income shall not be reduced by any overpayments waived in item 7g, Form 656. The annual income shall not be reduced by net operating losses incurred before or after the period covered by this agreement. However, a net operating loss for any year during such period may be deducted from annual income for the following year only. It is also agreed that annual income shall include all income and gains or profits of the taxpayers, regardless of whether these amounts are community income under state law.

3. That in the event close corporations are directly or indirectly controlled or owned by the taxpayers during the existence of this agreement, the computation of annual income shall include their proportionate share of the total corporate annual income in excess of $10,000. The term corporate annual income, as used in this agreement, means the taxable income of the corporation before net operating loss deduction and special deductions (except, in computing such income, the losses from sales or exchanges of property shall not be allowed), plus all nontaxable income, minus (a) dividends paid, and (b) the federal income tax paid for the year for which annual income is being computed. For this purpose, the corporate annual income shall not be reduced by any net operating loss incurred before or after the periods covered by this agreement, but a net operating loss for any year during such period may be deducted from the corporate annual income for the following year only.

4. That the annual payment provided for in this agreement (including interest at the rate established under section 6621 of the Internal Revenue Code (compounded under Code section 6622(a)) on delinquent payments computed from the due date of such payment) shall be paid to the Internal Revenue Service, without notice, on or before the 15th day of the 4th month following the close of the calendar or fiscal year, such payments to be accompanied by a sworn statement and a copy of the taxpayers' federal income tax return. The statement shall refer to this agreement and show the computation of annual income in accordance with items 1, 2, and 3 of this agreement. If the annual income for any year covered by this agreement is insufficient to require a payment under its terms, the taxpayers shall still furnish the Internal Revenue Service a sworn statement of such income and a copy of their federal income tax return. All blocks, records, and accounts shall be open at all reasonable times for inspection by the Internal Revenue Service to verify the annual income shown in the statement. Also, the taxpayers hereby expressly consent to the disclosure to each other of the amount of their respective annual income and of all books, records, and accounts necessary to the computation of their annual income for the purpose of administering this agreement. The payment (if any), the sworn statement, and a copy of the federal income tax return shall be transmitted to:

    Address: Internal Revenu Service, Newark, New Jersey 07000

(Over)   Form **2261** (Rev. 4-95)

5. That the aggregate amount paid under the terms of the offer in compromise and the additional amounts paid under the terms of this agreement shall not exceed an amount equivalent to the liability covered by the offer plus statutory additions that would have become due in the absence of the compromise.

6. That payments made under the terms of this agreement shall be applied first to tax and penalty, in that order, due for the earliest taxable period, then to tax and penalty, in that order, for each succeeding taxable period with no amount to be allocated to interest until the liabilities for taxes and penalties for all taxable periods sought to be compromised have been satisfied.

7. That upon notice to the taxpayers of the acceptance of the offer in compromise of the liability identified in this agreement, the taxpayers shall have no right, in the event of default in payment of any installment of principal or interest due under the terms of the offer and this agreement or in the event any other provision of this agreement is not carried out in accordance with its terms, to contest in court or otherwise the amount of the liability sought to be compromised; and that in the event of such default or noncompliance or in the event the taxpayers become the subject of any proceeding (except a proceeding under the Bankruptcy Act) whereby their affairs are placed under the control and jurisdiction of a court or other party, the United States, at the option of the Commissioner of Internal Revenue or a delegated official, may (a) proceed immediately by suit to collect the entire unpaid balance of the offer and this agreement, or (b) proceed immediately by suit to collect as liquidated damages an amount equal to the tax liability sought to be compromised, minus any payments already received under the terms of the offer and this agreement, with interest at the rate established under section 6621 of the Internal Revenue Code (compounded under Code section 6622(a)) from the date of default, or (c) disregard the amount of such offer and this agreement, apply all amounts previously paid thereunder against the amount of the liability sought to be compromised and, without further notice of any kind, assess and collect by levy or suit (the restrictions against assessment and collection being waived) the balance of such liability. In the event the taxpayers become the subject of any proceeding under the Bankruptcy Act, the offer in compromise and this agreement may be terminated. Upon such termination, the tax liability sought to be compromised, minus any payments already received under the terms of the offer and this agreement, shall become legally enforceable.

8. That the taxpayers waive the benefit of any statute of limitations applicable to the assessment and collection of the liability sought to be compromised and agree to the suspension of the running of the statutory period of limitations on assessment and collection for the period during which the offer in compromise and this agreement are pending, or the period during which any installment under the offer and this agreement remains unpaid, or any provision of this agreement is not carried out in accordance with its terms, and for 1 year thereafter.

9. That when all sums, including interest, due under the terms of the offer in compromise and this agreement, except those sums which may become due and payable under the provisions of item 1 of this agreement, have been paid in full, then and in that event only, all Federal tax liens at that time securing the tax liabilities which are the subject of the offer shall be immediately released. However, if, at the time consideration is being given to the release of the Federal tax liens, there are any sums due and payable under the terms of item 1, they must also be paid before the release of such liens.

This agreement shall be of no force or effect unless the offer in compromise is accepted.

Taxpayer's Signature	Date 11/1/98
Taxpayer's Signature	Date 11/1/98
I accept the waiver of statutory period of limitations for the Internal Revenue Service.	
Signature and Title	Date

Form **2261** (Rev. 4-95)

FORM 15.14
COLLATERAL AGREEMENT—FUTURE INCOME—CORPORATION

Form 2261-A (Rev. 10-94)	Department of the Treasury - Internal Revenue Service
	Collateral Agreement
	Future Income - Individual

Name of Corporation	Employer Identification Number
ABC Corporation	22-7654321

To: Commissioner of Internal Revenue

The taxpayers identified above has submitted an offer dated **September 15, 1995** in the amount of

$ **25,000** to compromise unpaid **94,000** tax liability,

plus statutory additions, for the taxable periods **1988-1990**

The purpose of this collateral agreement (hereinafter referred to as this agreement) is to provide additional consideration for acceptance of the offer in compromise described above. It is understood and agreed:

1. That in addition to the payment of the above amount of $ **25,000**, the taxpayers will pay out of annual income for the years **1996** to **1998**, inclusive

   (a) Nothing on the first $ **30,000** of annual income.

   (b) **20** percent of annual income more than $ **30,000**, and more than $ **50,000**.

   (c) **30** percent of annual income more than $ **50,000**

2. That the term annual income, as used in this agreement, means adjusted gross income before net operating loss deduction and special deductions (except losses from sales or exchanges of property shall not be allowed), plus all nontaxable income, minus (a) the federal income tax paid for the year for which annual income is being computed, and (b) any payment made under the terms of the offer in compromise (Form 656), as shown in item 5, Form 656, for the year in which such payment is made. Annual income shall not be reduced by any overpayments waived in item 7g, Form 656. The annual income shall not be reduced by net operating losses incurred before or after the period covered by this agreement. However, a net operating loss for any year during such period may be deducted from annual income for the following year only.

3. That net operating losses sustained for years ending before the calendar year in which this offer is accepted shall not be claimed as a net operating loss carryover in computing federal income tax.

4. That the annual payment provided for in this agreement (including interest at the annual rate as established under sections 6621(a) and 6622 of the Internal Revenue Code (subject to adjustments as provided by Code section 6621(b)) on delinquent payments computed from the due date of such payments) shall be paid to the Internal Revenue Service on or before the 15th day of the 3rd month following the close of the calendar or fiscal year, such payments to be accompanied by a sworn statement and a copy of the taxpayer's federal income tax return. The statement shall refer to this agreement and show the computation of annual income in accordance with items 1, and 2 of this agreement. If the annual income for any year covered by this agreement is insufficient to require a payment under its terms, the taxpayers shall still furnish the Internal Revenue Service a sworn statement of such income and a copy of their federal income tax return. All blocks, records, and accounts shall be open at all reasonable times for inspection by the Internal Revenue Service to verify the annual income shown in the statement. The payment (if any), the sworn statement, and a copy of the federal income tax return shall be transmitted to:

Address: Internal Revenue Service
15 Warren Street

(Over)   Form 2261-A (Rev. 10-94)

5. That the aggregate amount paid under the terms of the offer in compromise and the additional amounts paid under the terms of this agreement shall not exceed an amount equivalent to the liability covered by the offer plus statutory additions that would become due in the absence of the compromise.

6. That payments made under the terms of this agreement shall be applied first to tax and penalty, in that order, due for the earliest taxable period, then to tax and penalty, in that order, for each succeeding taxable period with no amount to be allocated to interest until the liabilities for taxes and penalties for all taxable periods sought to be compromised have been satisfied.

7. That upon notice to the taxpayers of the acceptance of the offer in compromise of the liability identified in this agreement, the taxpayers shall have no right, in the event of default in payment of any installment of principal or interest due under the terms of the offer and this agreement or in the event any other provision of this agreement is not carried out in accordance with its terms, to contest in court or otherwise the amount of the liability sought to be compromised; and that in the event of such default or noncompliance or in the event the taxpayers become the subject of any proceeding (except a proceeding under the Bankruptcy Act) whereby their affairs are placed under the control and jurisdiction of a court or other party, the United States, at the option of the Commissioner of Internal Revenue or a delegated official, may (a) proceed immediately by suit to collect the entire unpaid balance of the offer and this agreement, or (b) proceed immediately by suit to collect as liquidated damages an amount equal to the tax liability sought to be compromised, minus any payments already received under the terms of the offer and this agreement, with interest at the annual rate established under sections 6621(a) and 6622 of the Internal Revenue Code (subject to adjustments as provided by Code section 6621(b)) from the date of default, or (c) disregard the amount of such offer and this agreement, apply all amounts previously paid thereunder against the amount of the liability sought to be compromised and, without further notice of any kind, assess and collect by levy or suit (the restrictions against assessment and collection being waived) the balance of such liability. In the event the taxpayer becomes the subject of any proceeding under the Bankruptcy Act, the offer in compromise and this agreement may be terminated. Upon such termination, the tax liability sought to be compromised, minus any payments already received under the terms of the offer and this agreement, shall become legally enforceable.

8. That the taxpayer waives the benefit of any statute of limitations applicable to the assessment and collection of the liability sought to be compromised and agrees to the suspension of the running of the statutory period of limitations on assessment and collection for the period during which the offer in compromise and this agreement are pending, or the period during which any installment under the offer and this agreement remains unpaid, or any provision of this agreement is not carried out in accordance with its terms, and for 1 year thereafter.

9. That when all sums, including interest, due under the terms of the offer in compromise and this agreement, except those sums which may become due and payable under the provisions of item 1 of this agreement, have been paid in full, then and in that event only, all federal tax liens at that time securing the tax liabilities which are the subject of the offer shall be immediately released. However, if, at the time consideration is being given to the release of the federal tax liens, there are any sums due and payable under the terms of item 1, they must also be paid before the release of such liens.

This agreement shall be of no force or effect unless the offer in compromise is accepted.

Name of Corporation	Signature and Title of Officer	Date
ABC Corporation	/s/J. Smith	9/16/95

I accept the waiver of statutory period of limitations for the Internal Revenue Service.

Signature and Title		Date

Form 2261-A (Rev. 10-94)

FORM 15.15
COLLATERAL AGREEMENT—ADJUSTED BASIS OF SPECIFIC ASSETS

Form **2261-B** (Rev. May 1988)	DEPARTMENT OF THE TREASURY – INTERNAL REVENUE SERVICE **Collateral Agreement** Adjusted Basis of Specific Assets

Names and Address of Taxpayers	Social Security and Employer Identification Numbers
ABC Transit, Inc. 1000 River Road Teaneck, NJ 07000	22-7654321

To: Commissioner of Internal Revenue

The taxpayers identified above have submitted an offer dated ___9/23/88___ in the amount of $ ___15,000___

to compromise unpaid ___$167,000___ tax liability, plus statutory additions, for the

taxable periods ___1983–1985___ .

The purpose of this collateral agreement (hereinafter referred to as this agreement) is to provide additional consideration for acceptance of the offer in compromise described above. It is understood and agreed:

1. That for the purpose of computing income taxes of the taxpayers for all taxable years beginning after ___1988___ , the basis for certain assets under the existing law for computing depreciation and the gain or loss upon sale, exchange, or other disposition shall be as follows:

Name of asset	Basis
5 MCI Motor Coaches	$ 740,000

   This reduction in basis constitutes a $300,000 reduction from original cost of $1,040,000. For purposes of depreciation, ABC will still be entitled to use MACRS guidelines for similar assets; therefore, depreciation will be based on a 5-year double-declining balance for regular tax and 9-year 150% declining balance for alternative tax calculations.

2. That in no event shall the basis shown in item 1, above, be in excess of the basis that would otherwise be allowable for tax purposes except for this agreement.

3. That the aggregate amount paid under the terms of the offer in compromise and the additional amounts of taxes paid as the result of the reduction of the basis of the assets described above shall not exceed an amount equivalent to the liability covered by the offer plus statutory additions that would have become due in the absence of the compromise.

(Over)   Form 2261-B (Rev. 5-88)

4. That upon notice to the taxpayers of the acceptance of the offer in compromise of the liability identified in this agreement, the taxpayers shall have no right, in the event of default in payment of any installment of principal or interest due under the terms of the offer and this agreement or in the event any other provision of this agreement is not carried out in accordance with its terms, to contest in court or otherwise the amount of the liability sought to be compromised; and that in the event of such default or noncompliance or in the event the taxpayers become the subject of any proceeding (except a proceeding under the Bankruptcy Act) whereby their affairs are placed under the control and jurisdiction of a court or other party, the United States, at the option of the Commissioner of Internal Revenue or a delegated official, may (a) proceed immediately by suit to collect the entire unpaid balance of the offer and this agreement, or (b) proceed immediately by suit to collect as liquidated damages an amount equal to the tax liability sought to be compromised, minus any payments already received under the terms of the offer and this agreement, with interest at the rate established under section 6621 of the Internal Revenue Code from the date of default, or (c) disregard the amount of such offer and this agreement, apply all amounts previously paid thereunder against the amount of the liability sought to be compromised and, without further notice of any kind, assess and collect by levy or suit (the restrictions against assessment and collection being waived) the balance of such liability. In the event the taxpayers become the subject of any proceeding under the Bankruptcy Act, the offer in compromise and this agreement may be terminated. Upon such termination, the tax liability sought to be compromised, minus any payments already received under the terms of the offer and this agreement, shall become legally enforceable.

5. That the taxpayers waive the benefit of any statute of limitations applicable to the assessment and collection of the liability sought to be compromised and agree to the suspension of the running of the statutory period of limitations on assessment and collection for the period during which the offer in compromise and this agreement are pending, or the period during which any installment under the offer and this agreement remains unpaid, or any provision of this agreement is not carried out in accordance with its terms, and for 1 year thereafter.

6. That when all sums, including interest, due under the terms of the offer in compromise and this agreement, except those sums which may become due and payable under the provisions of item 1 of this agreement, have been paid in full, then and in that event only, all Federal tax liens at that time securing the tax liabilities which are the subject of the offer shall be immediately released. However, if, at the time consideration is being given to the release of the Federal tax liens, there are any sums due and payable under the terms of item 1, they must also be paid before the release of such liens.

This agreement shall be of no force or effect unless the offer in compromise is accepted.

Taxpayer's Signature	Date
/S/ Alan Michaels, President	9/23/88
Taxpayer's Signature	Date

I accept the waiver of statutory period of limitations for the Internal Revenue Service.	
Signature and Title	Date

Form 2261-B (Rev. 5-88)

FORM 15.16

COLLATERAL AGREEMENT—WAIVER OF NET OPERATING LOSSES, CAPITAL LOSSES, AND UNUSED INVESTMENT CREDITS

Form 2261-C
(Rev. May 1988)

DEPARTMENT OF THE TREASURY — INTERNAL REVENUE SERVICE
Collateral Agreement
Waiver of Net Operating Losses, Capital Losses, and Unused Investment Credits

Names and Address of Taxpayers	Social Security and Employer Identification Numbers
ABC Transit, Inc. 1000 River Road Teaneck, NJ 07000	22-7654321

To: Commissioner of Internal Revenue

The taxpayers identified above have submitted an offer dated 8/10/88 in the amount of $ 15,000 to compromise unpaid 92,000 tax liability, plus statutory additions, for the taxable periods 1983-1985 .

The purpose of this collateral agreement (hereinafter referred to as this agreement) is to provide additional consideration for acceptance of the offer in compromise described above. It is understood and agreed that for the purpose of computing the taxpayers' Federal income tax for all taxable years beginning after 1987 :

1. That any net operating losses sustained for the years 1988 to 1992 , inclusive, shall not be claimed as net operating loss deductions under the provisions of section 172 of the Internal Revenue Code.

2. That any net capital losses sustained for the years before 1988 shall not be claimed as carryovers or carrybacks under the provisions of section 1212 of the Internal Revenue Code.

3. That any unused investment credits for the years 1983 to 1985 , inclusive, shall not be claimed as investment credit carrybacks or carryovers under the provisions of Internal Revenue Code section 39 or 46, as applicable.

4. That the aggregate amount paid under the terms of the offer in compromise and the additional amounts of taxes paid as the result of the waiver of the losses and credits involved in this agreement shall not exceed an amount equivalent to the liability covered by the offer plus statutory additions that would become due in the absence of the compromise.

5. That upon notice to the taxpayers of the acceptance of the offer in compromise of the liability identified in this agreement, the taxpayers shall have no right, in the event of default in payment of any installment of principal or interest due under the terms of the offer and this agreement or in the event any other provision of this agreement is not carried out in accordance with its terms, to contest in court or otherwise the amount of the liability sought to be compromised; and that in the event of such default or noncompliance or in the event the taxpayers become the subject of any proceeding (except a proceeding under the Bankruptcy Act) whereby their affairs are placed under the control and jurisdiction of a court or other party, the United States, at the option of the Commissioner of Internal Revenue or a delegated official, may (a) proceed immediately by suit to collect the entire unpaid balance of the offer and this agreement, or (b) proceed immediately by suit to collect as liquidated damages an amount equal to the tax liability sought to be compromised, minus any payments already received under the terms of the offer and this agreement, with interest at the rate established under section 6621 of the Internal Revenue Code from the date of default, or (c) disregard the amount of such offer and this agreement, apply all amounts previously paid thereunder against the amount of the liability sought to be compromised and, without further notice of any kind, assess and collect by levy or suit (the restrictions against assessment and collection being waived) the balance of such liability. In the event the taxpayers become the subject of any proceeding under the Bankruptcy Act, the offer in compromise and this agreement may be terminated. Upon such termination, the tax liability sought to be compromised, minus any payments already received under the terms of the offer and this agreement, shall become legally enforceable.

6. That the taxpayers waive the benefit of any statute of limitations applicable to the assessment and collection of the liability sought to be compromised and agree to the suspension of the running of the statutory period of limitations on assessment and collection for the period during which the offer in compromise and this agreement are pending, or the period during which any installment under the offer and this agreement remains unpaid, or any provision of this agreement is not carried out in accordance with its terms, and for 1 year thereafter.

7. That when all sums, including interest, due under the terms of the offer in compromise and this agreement, except those sums which may become due and payable under the provisions of items 1, 2, and 3 of this agreement, have been paid in full, then and in that event only, all Federal tax liens at that time securing the tax liabilities which are the subject of the offer shall be immediately released. However, if, at the time consideration is being given to the release of the Federal tax liens, there are any sums due and payable under the terms of items 1, 2, and 3, they must also be paid before the release of such liens.

This agreement shall be of no force or effect unless the offer in compromise is accepted.

Taxpayers's Signature /S/ Alan Michaels, President	Date 9/23/88
Taxpayer's Signature	Date

I accept the waiver of statutory period of limitations for the Internal Revenue Service.

Signature and Title	Date

Form 2261-C (Rev. 5-88)

TABLE 15.1
Authority to Accept or Reject Offers in Compromise*

Category of Liability and Offer (including any interest, penalty, additional amount or addition to tax)	Regional Commissioners	Regional Counsel	Regional Directors of Appeal; Chiefs and Associate Chiefs; Appeals Offices	District Directors; Assistant District Directors	Service Center Directors; Assistant Service Center Division Chiefs
$250,000 or more based upon doubt as to liability	1	2			
$250,000 or more based upon doubt as to collectibility	1	2			
$250,000 or more based upon doubt as to collectibility and liability	1	2			
Less than $250,000 based upon collectibility and/or liability			2	1	3
Penalties only under $250,000 (including Specific Penalties)			2	1	3

Key: 1—All cases except those under Chief Counsel and Appeals jurisdiction
2—For cases under Appeals jurisdiction
3—When the offer is based on doubt as to liability only; this authority may be redelegated by Service Center Director to Division Chief

¶ 15.08 MINIMIZING THE EFFECT OF TAX LIENS

[1] Administrative Appeal of the Filing of a Notice of Federal Tax Lien

Section 6326 permits the administrative appeal of the filing of federal tax lien and for the release of the lien. After a notice of federal tax lien has been filed, "any person" whose property or rights to property are encumbered by a tax lien is allowed to appeal to the Service for a release of the lien alleging "an error in the filing of the lien."[312] This administrative procedure is intended to be used to correct erroneous filings, not to challenge the underlying assessment of deficiency giving rise to tax lien. Error in the filing of the lien exists only if (1) the tax liability that gave rise to the lien has been satisfied; (2) the liability had been assessed in violation of the Section 6213 restrictions on deficiency assessments; (3) the liability has been assessed in violation of the automatic stay on collection provided in the Bankruptcy Code; or (4) the lien was filed after the expiration of the limitation period on collection.[313]

If there has been an error, a certificate of release of the lien is required to be issued "expeditiously (and to the extent practicable within 14 days)." The certificate of release of lien must include "a statement that such filing of the lien was erroneous."[314] This statement is intended to ensure that the public record shows that the filing of the notice of lien was not the result of the taxpayer's actions and to facilitate the repair of the taxpayer's credit and other financial records. A certificate of release of an erroneous lien must be issued regardless of whether the lien was challenged in an administrative review procedure.

Appeal of the filing of a federal tax lien is made by written application to the Area Collection Enforcement in the small business/self-employed (SB/SE) Division, but should be marked to the attention of the Chief (Special Procedures Function). The appeal must include identifying information (e.g., a copy of the lien), the grounds for the appeal, and substantiating data.[315]

In addition to the statutory right to appeal the filing of a notice of lien, taxpayers have the administrative right to appeal liens, levies, and seizures the

---

[312] IRC § 6326(a).

[313] Reg. §§ 301.6326-1(b)(1)–301.6326-1(b)(4).

[314] IRC § 6326(b).

[315] Reg. §§ 301.6326-1(d)(1) and 301.6326-1(d)(2) (Procedures for Appeal). Although Section 6326 does not say so, the regulations require appeal to be made within one year after the taxpayer becomes aware of the erroneously filed tax lien. Id.

Collection proposes to file or make.[316] The form the taxpayer can use to make this appeal is called Collection Appeal Request (Form 9423). Because notices of federal tax lien may be filed without notice, for example through the Automated Collection System, a taxpayer may be able to appeal only after the collection action has taken place.

[2] Withdrawal of Notice of Lien

Collection has the authority to withdraw a notice of lien after a lien has been filed. Section 6323(j) grants authority for Collection to withdraw a notice of lien in certain circumstances and to apply the other collection provisions of the Code as if the withdrawn notice had not been filed. Collection may withdraw a notice of lien if it determines that (1) the filing of the notice was premature or otherwise not in accordance with the Service's administrative procedures; (2) the taxpayer has entered into an installment payment agreement, unless the agreement provides otherwise; (3) the withdrawal of the notice of lien will facilitate the collection of the tax liability; or (4) with the consent of the taxpayer or Taxpayer Advocate, the withdrawal of the notice will be in the best interests of the taxpayer, as determined by the Taxpayer Advocate and the government.[317] The withdrawal of the notice of lien will be made by filing a notice of withdrawal in the same office the notice of lien was filed; a copy of the notice of withdrawal will be provided to the taxpayer.[318] In addition, if the taxpayer requests it in writing, Collection must "promptly" make reasonable efforts to provide credit reporting agencies and any financial institution or creditor the taxpayer names with notification of the withdrawal of the notice of lien.[319]

Regulations implement the provisions to withdraw a notice of lien. Authorized officials have the authority to withdraw a notice of lien if they decide that specified conditions of withdrawal are present.[320] If one of the conditions is met, Collection will withdraw the notice of lien by filing a notice of withdrawal in the office in which the notice of federal tax lien is filed.[321] Once the notice of withdrawal is filed, collection procedures will apply as if the withdrawn notice had never been filed.

Generally, a taxpayer must file a written request for withdrawal of the lien with the Area/Territory Office in which the lien is filed, marked to the at-

---

[316] The Collection Appeals Program was created in 1996. Ann. 96-5, 1996-4 IRB 1.

[317] IRC §§ 6323(j)(1)(A)–6323(g)(1)(D), added by the Taxpayer Bill of Rights 2, § 501(a), as of the date of enactment, July 30, 1996. See Reg. § 301.6323(j)-1(a).

[318] IRC § 6323(j)(1)(D).

[319] IRC § 6323(j)(2).

[320] Reg. § 301.6323(j)-1(a).

[321] Reg. § 301.6323(j)-1(a).

tention of the Chief, Special Procedures Function.[322] The request must state the taxpayer's name, address, and taxpayer identification number; include a copy of the notice of federal tax lien to be withdrawn; provide an explanation of the grounds on which withdrawal of the notice is requested; list the names and addresses of any credit reporting agency and financial institution or creditor that the taxpayer wishes the director to notify of the withdrawal of the notice of federal tax lien; and request that a notice of the withdrawal of the lien be disclosed to such credit reporting agency, financial institution, or creditor.[323] The taxpayer may supplement the list of parties to which notice of the withdrawal should be sent.[324]

[3] Release of Lien

Section 6325(a) requires a release of lien where (1) there is a finding that the liability for the amount assessed, together with all interest with respect to that assessment, has been fully satisfied; (2) the liability for the amount assessed, together with all interest, has become legally unenforceable; or (3) an acceptable bond is furnished to the Service guaranteeing payment of the amount assessed together with all interest in respect of the assessment within the period of limitations on collection. A release of lien must be granted within thirty days if one of the circumstances in which release may be granted exists.[325] Authority to release a lien has been delegated to district directors who may redelegate to the Chief (Collection Division) and the Chief (Special Procedures Staff). The three circumstances for release of a lien merit further discussion.

[a] Liability Satisfied

Even if the taxpayer has satisfied the liability covered by the lien, the Service itself does not ordinarily take the initiative to clear a taxpayer's title by filing a release of lien. Consequently, the taxpayer must make the application to clear his title. The release procedure is also appropriate even if no lien has been filed if a third person has had actual notice of the assessment, because the procedure is also available for filed and unfiled liens. Some uncertainty exists about the liability that must be satisfied. Section 6325(a) states only that the liability consists of the amount assessed together with any accrued interest. Regulations require that "the entire liability for the tax" be sat-

---

[322] Reg. § 301.6323(j)-1(d).

[323] Reg..§§ 301.6323(j)-1(d)(2)(i)–301.6323(j)-1(d)(2)(iv).

[324] Reg. § 301.6323(j)-1(e).

[325] IRC § 6325(a), as amended by the Tax Equity and Fiscal Responsibility Act of 1982 (TEFRA), § 348, Pub. L. No. 97-248, 97th Cong., 2d Sess. Prior to 1983, releases were discretionary, and no time limit was imposed on IRS action. Reg. § 601.104(c)(3).

isfied.[326] It is the entire liability reflected on a notice of lien that must be satisfied, and this requires payment of the outstanding obligation covered by the lien, including any interest, additional amount, addition to the tax, or assessable penalty, together with any costs such as lien-filing fees, that may have accrued.[327] There is also a distinction between the release of a lien and the determination of the underlying liability. The release of lien conclusively establishes that the tax lien has been extinguished. A release of the tax lien does not itself extinguish the underlying tax liability the taxpayer owes or establish that the underlying tax liability is not owed or has been satisfied.[328]

[b] Liability Unenforceable

A certificate of release of lien may be issued if the tax assessed is unenforceable as a matter of law (e.g., by the expiration of the period of limitations). Unenforceability of the assessment as a matter of fact (e.g., where the tax becomes uncollectible owing to the absence of discoverable property of the taxpayer) is not a basis for the release of a lien,[329] although it may be the basis for a compromise of the assessment. Once the taxpayer's offer in compromise has been accepted and the taxpayer has performed his obligations under the agreement, the tax lien may then be released.[330] There is no direct authority in the Code or regulations for this release, but where a taxpayer has fulfilled his part of a compromise, he has satisfied his liability, even though the original liability itself has been reduced owing to an evaluation of the doubt as to the collectibility of the full amount of the assessment.

The term "legally unenforceable" does not mean "excessive in amount," so that even if an assessment is found to be excessive, the lien arising from the excessive assessment need not be released, but the underlying assessment may be reduced or partially abated under Section 6404(a).[331]

---

[326] Reg. § 301.6325-1(a)(1). Under Reg. § 401.6325-1(c), satisfaction of the tax liability occurs where either (1) authorized Collection management determines as soon as practicable after tender of payment that the entire tax liability has been satisfied in full or (2) the taxpayer provides proof of full payment of the tax liability. The term "proof of full payment" is defined in Reg. § 401.6325-1(d).

[327] Reg. § 401.6325-1(a).

[328] Section 6325(a)(2) supports this view by providing for the filing of a release when a bond securing payment of the liability is accepted. Also, Section 6325(f)(2) permits the Service to revoke the release of lien and reinstate the lien. See ILM 199942036 (Sept. 7, 1999).

[329] Reg. § 301.6325-1(a)(1).

[330] But see Reg. § 301.7122-1(d).

[331] In re Burns, 974 F2d 1064 (9th Cir. 1992) (because some tax was due, assessment was not naked assessment).

[c] Acceptable Bond

The area office has the discretion to issue a certificate of release of any tax lien if it is furnished and accepts a bond guaranteeing the payment of the amount assessed including interest. Payment must be made within the time agreed upon in the bond but not later than six months before the expiration of the statutory period for collection, including extensions. Specific requirements govern the form of bond and the acceptable sureties.[332] The use of an open line of credit or an irrevocable letter of credit, rather than a formal bond, has been approved.[333] One problem with a bond (and with a letter of credit) is that the surety requires collateral to secure its guaranty not to mention some fee for its service. A commercial surety may require security in an amount at least equal to the amount of the bond. If the taxpayer has sufficient property to pledge as collateral, he is only substituting one lien for another. For this reason, it may be better for the taxpayer to explore a collateral agreement with the Service and attempt to obtain some assurances on discharge of the lien when property is sold.

Thus, the Service must issue a certificate of release of lien within thirty days after the day on which the liability is satisfied or unenforceable or a bond is accepted.[334] Once issued, a certificate of release of lien is "conclusive that the lien covered by the certificate is extinguished," provided that the certificate is filed in the appropriate office.[335] However, a filed release of lien is not absolute assurance that the Service does not retain an interest in the taxpayer's property. If the person who acquires the taxpayer's property is a bona fide purchaser or other person entitled to property over an unfiled lien,[336] the person is protected. Where a lien was mistakenly released, the Service successfully contended that a levy it had served before the mistaken release seized the taxpayer's property and the later release of lien did not vitiate the effect of the

---

[332] Reg. § 301.7101-1. See also Treasury Department, Companies Holding Certificate of Authority as Acceptable Sureties on Federal Bonds, Etc., Circ. No. 570.

[333] See Adolph Coors Co. v. Comm'r, 62 TC 300 (1974).

[334] IRC § 6325(a). Reg. § 401.6325-1(a) describes the conditions for release as follows: (a) the liability is legally unenforceable (Reg. § 401.6325-1(b)); (b) the liability secured by any lien is fully satisfied (Reg. § 401.6325-1(c)); (c) a bond is accepted for release of any lien (Reg. § 301.6325-1(a)(2)); or (d) a taxpayer's request for release on the ground that the liability is satisfied or legally unenforceable is received (Reg. § 401.6325-1(f)).

[335] IRC §§ 6325(a), 6325(f). Form 668, Certificate of Release of Federal Tax Lien, is used for this purpose. The release of lien becomes effective as of a date prescribed in the document containing the combined notice of lien and certificate of release. Reg. § 401.6325-1(b).

[336] See IRC § 6323(a).

levy.[337] A request for a release of lien must be submitted to the Chief (Special Procedures Staff) in the district where the notice of lien is filed and must (1) be in writing; (2) provide the taxpayer's name and current address; (3) include a copy of the notice of lien as filed; (4) state the ground on which the request is made (e.g., satisfaction or unenforceability); and (5) if satisfaction is claimed, provide a copy of the canceled check or other evidence of payment.[338]

Proper filing is a prerequisite to the effectiveness of the certificate of release. Proper filing is made if the certificate is filed in the same office that the notice of lien was filed (if notice of lien was filed at all).[339] Some states do not permit a release to be filed in the same office as the notice of lien. In such states, the release is to be filed with the clerk of the appropriate federal district court.[340] It appears that a filing in this place is sufficient to give the release conclusive effect in the same manner as if it were filed "in the same office as the notice of lien."[341]

Although the release of lien is conclusive against third parties, it may nevertheless be revoked if it is erroneously or improvidently granted or if the conditions on which it was issued are breached. If a release is revoked, notice of the revocation is mailed to the taxpayer, who then has an opportunity to appeal the revocation administratively. If a release of lien is revoked and the statute of limitations on collection has not expired, notice of the tax lien may be refiled,[342] because the notice of lien may be refiled in a different office if the taxpayer has relocated since the original filing. Despite refiling of a notice of lien after revocation, a potential problem exists for those who rely on the filed release of lien. A third party is bound by constructive notice of the revocation of a release as long as the notice of revocation has been filed in the

---

[337] American Acceptance Corp. v. Glendora Better Builders, Inc., 550 F2d 1220 (9th Cir. 1977). See also Chevron, USA, Inc. v. United States, 705 F2d 1487 (9th Cir. 1983) (levy served before lien released, and purchaser acquired property at time property was subject to lien). Both *American Acceptance* and *Chevron, USA* rest on the premise that a levy unsatisfied before the lien is released or before it becomes unenforceable by lapse of time effectively transfers property to the Service, thus making the lien unnecessary. This result seems inconsistent with the effect of a levy as interpreted by the Supreme Court in United States v. Whiting Pools, Inc., 462 US 198 (1983), as well as the meaning of Section 6502(a).

[338] Reg. § 401.6325-1(f). If the taxpayer requests that a certificate of release be issued for one of a number of liabilities listed in a notice of lien, the district director will issue a release with respect to the liability that has been paid or has become unenforceable. Reg. § 401.6325-1(e). The Service publishes instructions on requesting a certificate of release of lien. Publication 1450 (Rev. 3-1999), "Instructions on Requesting a Certificate of Release of Lien."

[339] IRC § 6325(f)(1)(A).

[340] IRC § 6325(g).

[341] Reg. § 301.6325-1(f)(2)(iii).

[342] IRC § 6323(g) requires refiling of a notice of lien although IRC § 6323(f)(2) only speaks of filing notice of the revocation.

same office as the original notice of lien. A reinstated and refiled tax lien has no retroactive effect either against those acquiring interests in the interim or against earlier purchasers and junior lienors whose priority position was improved by the release.[343]

[4] Discharge of Lien

A delinquent taxpayer who cannot obtain a bond or pay the tax may nevertheless be able to transfer clear title to particular items of property by obtaining a partial discharge of the property from the tax lien. The Service is authorized to issue a certificate of discharge with respect to specific property where (1) the value of the taxpayer's remaining property is double the amount of the liability; (2) payment is made in an amount equal to the value of the government's interest in the specific property; or (3) the value of the government's interest in the specific property is valueless.[344]

For the fair market value of the taxpayer's property remaining subject to the lien to be at least double the amount of the tax liability, that market value must be twice the sum of two amounts: the amount of the unpaid tax liability secured by the lien and the amount of all other liens on the property that have priority over the lien.[345] Because both the tax lien and a nontax lien having priority are added together, it is possible for a discharge not to be authorized even where the value of the remaining property far exceeds the amount of the tax lien. For example, if the tax lien is $1,000, and the value of the remaining property is $10,000, but the property is subject to a $5,000 mortgage and prior local tax liens of $100, a discharge cannot be issued. The sum of the tax and other prior liens is $6,100. Double this sum is $12,200, but the value of the remaining property is only $10,000.[346]

A discharge is also permitted where the government is paid an amount equal to the value of its interest in the property, which it has by virtue of the lien. In determining the value of the government's interest, the regulations say that the district will take into account (1) the costs and expenses to which the Service has already been put; (2) the value of the property; and (3) the amount

---

[343] IRC § 6325(f)(2). Cf. In re Bowen, 138 F2d 22 (3d Cir. 1943), cert. denied, 320 US 799 (1944).

[344] IRC § 6325(b). A discharge certificate may also be issued without regard to the three statutory situations if one is provided for in a settlement entered into on behalf of the United States by the Justice Department. A certificate of discharge may also be issued if a taxpayer has fully satisfied or provided for estate or gift tax liability. IRC § 6325(c); Reg. § 301.6325-1(c).

[345] Reg. § 301.6325-1(b)(1)(i).

[346] Reg. § 301.6325-1(b)(1)(ii).

of all liens having priority over the tax lien.[347] If, after the value of the lien is determined, the lien is shown to have no value, the district should issue a certificate of discharge as to that item of property.

Issuance of a certificate of discharge is also authorized where property is to be sold and, pursuant to agreement with the district, the proceeds will be held as a fund subject to the tax lien with the same priority the lien had with respect to the discharged property.[348] Under this condition, a mortgagee can first obtain a "Conditional Commitment to Discharge Certain Property from Federal Tax Lien" and avoid the obligation of making the United States a party to a foreclosure proceeding. (See Form 15.17.) The form letter the Service uses for this purpose states that unless the value of the government's interest proves to be greater than a stated amount, the district director will, on payment of the amount and on a proper showing that the taxpayer has been divested of his right, title, and interest in the property exclusive of any redemption right, issue a certificate discharging the property from the effect of the tax lien.

To obtain the discharge, the taxpayer must submit detailed information to the Collection Division's Special Procedures Staff, including an estimate of the fair market value and, where a private sale of the property is contemplated, written appraisals by two disinterested appraisers.[349] These and other points of information to be included are itemized in the Service's instructions, "How to Prepare Application for Certificate of Discharge of Property from Federal Tax Lien." (See Form 15.18. Form 15.19 is a sample application for a certificate of discharge.) Form 669-A (Certificate of Discharge of Property from Federal Tax Lien Under Section 6325(b)(1) of the Internal Revenue Code) is used where discharge is based on the value of the remaining property.[350] (See Form 15.20.) Form 669-B (Certificate of Discharge of Property from Federal Tax Lien Under Section 6325(b)(2)(A) of the Internal Revenue Code) is used where part payment is involved.[351] (See Form 15.21.) Form 669-C (Certificate of Discharge of Property from Federal Tax Lien) is submitted where the government's interest is valueless.[352] (See Form 15.22.) Because the Service must

---

[347] Reg. §§ 301.6325-1(b)(2)(i), 301.6325-1(b)(2)(iii). Although the value of the property usually means its fair market value, in this case, the district may in its discretion consider the forced sale value of the property. Since forced sale value is lower than fair market value, this provision should benefit taxpayers because the value of the property subject to the lien may be less than the amount of the lien.

[348] Reg. § 301.6325-1(b)(3).

[349] Reg. § 301.6325-1(b)(4). See also IRS, How to Prepare Application for Certificate of Discharge of Property from Federal Tax Lien, Doc. No. 5345 (Rev. Nov. 1967).

[350] IRC § 6325(b)(1).

[351] IRS § 6335(b)(2)(A).

[352] IRC § 6325(b)(2)(B).

verify the submitted information, the discharge procedure can be time consuming.

If an agreement cannot be reached with the local office on the amount to be paid for discharge, another procedure is available. To avoid delay of the sale, Collection is permitted to enter into an agreement under which the discharge is granted and the lien is transferred to the proceeds of the property, leaving the dispute to be resolved later.[353] This procedure permits the sale to take place, but the proceeds are frozen pending resolution of the dispute. One condition is applicable to all certificates of discharge. A certificate of discharge issued when the taxpayer disposes of property becomes void if he reacquires the property.[354]

---

[353] IRC § 6325(b)(3).
[354] IRC § 6325(f)(3).

FORM 15.17
CONDITIONAL COMMITMENT TO DISCHARGE CERTAIN PROPERTY FROM FEDERAL TAX LIEN

From: [*Name and address of applicant*]

Re: [*Name and address of taxpayer*]

[*Salutation*]

Your application for a certificate of discharge under the provisions of Section 6325(b)(2)(B) of the Internal Revenue Code has been investigated. Based on the information furnished, I have determined that the interest of the United States under the Federal tax lien(s) outstanding against the taxpayer named above in the following described property is at present valueless.

[*Enter legal description of property*]

I will withhold issuance of a certificate of discharge, however, until the taxpayer through the foreclosure proceeding has been divested of all right, title, and interest (exclusive of any right of redemption) in the property. Unless later circumstances disclose value to the interest of the United States in the property described above, I will on a proper showing that the taxpayer has been divested of all of his right, title, and interest to the property (exclusive of any right of redemption), issue a certificate discharging the property from the Federal tax lien(s) outstanding against the taxpayer named above.

You are allowed to advertise that you have obtained a conditional commitment to discharge the property described above from the Federal tax lien.

Sincerely yours,

....
District Director of Internal Revenue

By: ....
Signature and title

[5] Subordination

A tax lien may be subordinated to another interest where (1) an amount is paid equal to the amount with respect to which the tax lien is subordinated or (2) the district director is persuaded that the amount the government may realize will be increased by issuing the certificate and that issuance will aid in the collection of the tax liability.[355] The issuance of the certificate is left solely to the discretion of the district director, but he is required to act as a prudent businessman would in similar circumstances.[356]

A subordination agreement should be used where the Collection Division's Special Procedures Staff can be satisfied that there is a better chance of ultimate full payment if the taxpayer is allowed to continue in business. The Collection Division may or may not require the taxpayer to make a part payment as consideration for subordination of the tax lien to the lien of the taxpayer's lender.[357] Additional financing by way of commercial loans may be the only alternative open to the small business taxpayer. If new funds are not obtained, the taxpayer and his creditors, including the government, lose. Under these circumstances, the Collection Division should exercise its discretion to issue the certificate subordinating the tax lien to the commercial lender without requiring any part payment. Both situations where subordination of tax liens can be secured are designed to facilitate collection of delinquent tax liabilities by providing more flexible procedures. In the situation where the Service receives payment out of the new funds available to the taxpayer,[358] the government interest cannot be injured because the tax lien is being subordinated only to the extent the Service receives an equivalent amount on a dollar-for-dollar basis. In the situation where the government's lien is subordinated to another creditor's lien,[359] the effect of subordination may increase the value of the government's lien. For example, the value of the property of the taxpayer may be increased if he is able to borrow needed funds to continue operations, or a crop that is subject to the lien and that needs harvesting will have little or no value if funds are not made available to harvest the crop.

Note that the certificate of subordination may be applied for by the creditor who seeks priority to the tax lien, as well as the taxpayer.[360] Applications for subordination are handled by the Special Procedures Staff, which obtains an advisory legal opinion from Area Counsel.[361] If subordination is considered appropriate, a Form 669-D (Certificate of Subordination of Federal Tax Lien Under Section 6325(d)(1) of the Internal Revenue Code) is issued.[362] (See Form 15.23.)

---

[355] IRC §§ 6325(d)(1), 6325(d)(2); Reg. § 301.6325-1(d).

[356] S. Rep. No. 1708, 89th Cong., 2d Sess. (1966), reprinted in 1966-2 CB 876, 887.31 Compare IRC §§ 6325(d)(1) and 6325(d)(2).

[357] Compare IRC §§ 6325(d)(1) and 6325(d)(2).

[358] IRC § 6325(d)(1).

[359] IRC § 6325(d)(2).

[360] The procedure for applying for subordination is set out in Rev. Proc. 68-8, 1968-1 CB 754.

[361] Reg. § 301.6325-1(d)(4).

[362] IRC § 6325(d)(2).

[6] Nonattachment of the Tax Lien

The Code authorizes nonattachment of a tax lien to be certified where, because of confusion of name or otherwise, a person other than the taxpayer is or may be injured by the effect of the lien.[363] The certificate states that a tax lien that was filed against all property and rights to property of one named taxpayer does not, and never did, attach to the property of a person of like or similar name to the actual delinquent taxpayer. An application for a certificate of non-attachment is referred to the Chief (Special Procedures Staff) who reviews and considers the application and determines whether the certificate should be issued.[364]

---

[363] IRC § 6325(e); Reg. § 301.6325-1(e).

[364] See Reg. § 301.6325-1(e). The application, signed under penalty of perjury, should contain the name, address, and TINs of the applicant and spouse; a description of the property for which the certificate is requested; a copy of the notice of lien; a statement of the applicant's address at the time the notice of lien was filed, as well as any later residences; and any other information that might help in the determination. If a representative is involved, a power of attorney must be filed. The information to complete the application is described in IRS Publication 1024, "How to Prepare Application for Certificate of Nonattachment of Federal Tax Lien."

FORM 15.18 ————————————————

HOW TO PREPARE APPLICATION FOR CERTIFICATE OF DISCHARGE OF PROPERTY FROM FEDERAL TAX LIEN

Instructions on How to Apply for a

Certificate of Discharge of Property from Federal Tax Lien

Since there is no standard form available for an application for a Certificate of Discharge of Property from Federal Tax Lien, a computer-generated request will be considered as an application *(please, no handwritten request)*. **Submit your request and all accompanying documents in duplicate to:**

IRS, Attn: Technical Services Group Manager

*(Address to the IRS office in which the lien was filed. Use **Publication 4235**, Technical Services Group Addresses, to determine where to mail your request.)*

Information Required on Application

Give date of the application.

Please **give the name and address of the person applying under section 6325(b)** of the Internal Revenue Code, for a certificate of discharge. See the "*Additional Information*" section of this publication for applicable Internal Revenue Code sections. Give the name and address of the taxpayer, and describe the property as follows:

1. Give a detailed description, including the location of the property for which you are requesting the certificate of discharge. **If real property is involved,** submit a legal copy of the title or deed to the property, and the complete address *(street, city, state, and ZIP code)*. If the certificate is requested under **section 6325(b)(1)**, also give a description of all the taxpayer's remaining property subject to the lien.

2. Show how and when the taxpayer has been or will be divested of all rights, title, and interest in and to the property for which a certificate of discharge is requested.

3. **Attach a copy of each notice of Federal tax lien,** or furnish the following information as it appears on each filed Notice of Federal Tax Lien:

   a. The name of the Internal Revenue Office;

   b. The name and address of the taxpayer against whom the notice was filed;

   c. The serial number shown on the lien;

   d. The taxpayer social security number or employer identification number shown on the lien; and

   e. The date and place the notice was filed.

4. In lieu of the above, a preliminary title report may be substituted listing the required information.

5. List the encumbrances *(or attach a copy of the instrument that created each encumbrance)* on the property which you believe have priority over the Federal tax lien. For each encumbrance show:

   a. The name and address of the holder;

   b. A description of the encumbrance;

   c. The date of the agreement;

   d. The date and place of the recording, if any;

   e. The original principal amount and the interest rate;

   f. The amount due as of the date of the application, if known *(show costs and accrued interest separately)*; and

   g. Your family relationship, if any, to the taxpayer and to the holders of any other encumbrances on the property.

6. In lieu of the above, a preliminary title report may be substituted listing the required information.

7. Itemize all proposed or actual costs, commissions and expenses of any transfer or sale associated with the property.

8. Furnish information to establish the value of the property. If the certificate is requested under **section 6325(b)(1)** furnish an estimate of the fair market value of the property which will remain subject to the lien. In addition:

   a. **If private sale** - Submit written appraisals by two disinterested people qualified to appraise the property, and a brief statement of each appraiser's qualifications.

   b. **If public sale *(auction)* already held** - Give the date and place the sale was held, and the amount for which the property was sold.

   c. **If public sale *(auction)* to be held** - Give the proposed date and place of the sale, and include a statement that the United States will be paid in the proper priority from the proceeds of the sale.

9. Give any other information that might, in your opinion, have bearing upon the application, such as pending judicial actions.

10. The Technical Services Group Manager may request that you furnish additional information.

11. If you are submitting the application under the provisions of **section 6325 (b)(3)**, dealing with the substitution of proceeds of sale, attach a copy of the proposed agreement containing the following:
    a. The name and address of the proposed escrow agent;
    b. The caption, type of account, name and address of depositary for the account.
    c. The condition under which the escrow funds are to be held;
    d. The conditions under which payment will be made from escrow, including the limitation for negotiated settlement of claims against the fund;
    e. The estimated costs of the escrow;
    f. The name and address of any other party you and the Technical Services Group Manager determine to be a party to the escrow agreement;
    g. Your signature, and those of the escrow agent, the Technical Services Group Manager and any other party to the escrow agreement; and
    h. Any other specific information the Technical Services Group Manager requests.

12. Give the name, address and telephone number where you may be reached.

13. Give the name, address and telephone number of your attorney or other representative, if any.

14. **Write the following declaration over your signature and title:** "Under penalties of perjury, I declare that I have examined this application, including any accompanying schedules, exhibits, affidavits, and statements and to the best of my knowledge and belief it is true, correct, and complete."

Additional Information

Please follow the instructions in this publication when applying for a Certificate of Discharge of Property from Federal Tax Lien.

The Technical Services Group Manager has the authority to issue a certificate of discharge of a lien that is filed on any part of a taxpayer's property subject to the lien. The following sections and provisions of the Internal Revenue Code apply:

Section 6325(b)(1) — A specific property may be discharged; if the taxpayer's property remaining subject to the lien has a Fair Market Value *(FMV)* which is double the sum of the balance due: *a)* all Federal Tax Liens, *b)* all other liens. *(FMV=(a+b)x2)*

Section 6325(b)(2)(A) — If there is paid in partial satisfaction of the liability secured by the lien an amount determined to be **not less than the value of the interest** of the United States in the property to be discharged.

Section 6325(b)(2)(B) — It is determined that the interest of the United States in the property to be discharged **has no value.**

Section 6325(b)(3) — If the property subject to the lien is sold, and, under an agreement with the Internal Revenue Service, the proceeds from the sale are to be held as a fund subject to the liens and claims of the United States in the same manner and with the same priority as the liens and claims on the discharged property.

Section 6325(b)(4) — At the request of the non-taxpayer owner, a discharge will be issued on any property subject to a lien. But the owner must deposit an amount equal to the value of the government's interest or furnish an acceptable bond in an amount subject to the government's interest in the property.

1. No payment is required for the issuance of a certificate under **section 6325(b)(1) or 6325(b)(2)(B)** of the Internal Revenue Code. Payment is required for certificates issued under **section 6325(b)(2)(A)**. Do not send the payment with your application. The Technical Services Group Manager will notify you after determining the amount due.

2. The Technical Services Group Manager will have your application investigated to determine whether to issue the certificate and will let you know the outcome.

3. A certificate of discharge under **section 6325(A)** will be issued upon receipt of the amount determined to be the interest of the United States in the subject property under the Federal tax lien. Make payments in cash, or by certified, cashier's, or treasurer's check. It must be drawn on any bank or trust company incorporated under the laws of the United States, or of any state, or possession of the United States. Payment can also be made by United States postal, bank, express, or telegraph money order. *(If you pay by personal check, issuance of the certificate of discharge will be delayed until the bank honors the check.)*

2

4. If application is made under **sections 6325(b)(2)(A) or 6325(b)(2)(B)** and is for the sale of a principal residence, the taxpayer may be eligible for a relocation expense allowance based on an inability to pay, and subject to limitations. This allowance will be taken from sale proceeds and will not reduce the tax liability. To apply for the allowance, complete and submit **Form 12451,** *Request for Relocation Expense Allowance,* **with** the application for discharge.

5. If application is made under provisions of **section 6325(b)(2)(A), or 6325(b)(2)(B)** because a mortgage foreclosure is contemplated, there will be a determination of the amount required for discharge or a determination that the Federal tax lien interest in the property is valueless.

Within 30 days from the date of the application, the applicant will receive a written conditional commitment for a certificate of discharge. When the foreclosure proceeding has been concluded, a certificate of discharge will be issued in accordance with the terms of the commitment letter. Also, see **Publication 487,** *How to Prepare an Application Requesting the United States to Release its Right to Redeem Property by a Federal Tax Lien.*

6. If application is made under the provisions of **section 6325(b)(3),** the Technical Services Group Manager has the authority to approve an escrow agent selected by the applicant. Any reasonable expenses incurred in connection with sale of the property, the holding of the fund, or the distribution of the fund shall be paid by the applicant or from the proceeds of the sale before satisfaction of any claims or liens. Submit a copy of the proposed escrow agreement as part of the application.

7. A certificate of discharge under **section 6325(b)(4)** will be issued when an amount equal to the United States interest in the property is received. The United States interest in the property may be made in the form of cash, other certified funds, or the posting of a bond acceptable to the Secretary.

8. Submit **Form 12180,** *Third Party Contact Form.* Completing this document gives the Internal Revenue Service the authority to contact individuals or companies, if necessary, when determining if the discharge is appropriate.

9. Provide the name, address and telephone number of your attorney or representative as well as the closing attorney or Settlement Company.

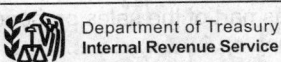

Department of Treasury
Internal Revenue Service

www.irs.gov

Publication 783 (Rev. 1-2004)
Catalog Number 46755I

3

FORM 15.19
APPLICATION FOR PARTIAL DISCHARGE

Internal Revenue Service
290 Broadway
New York, New York 10008

Attention: Chief, Special Procedures Function

Re: Application for Partial Discharge—John Doe

[*Salutation*]

Application is made on behalf of John Doe, c/o XYZ Corp., Anytown, New York, for a certificate of discharge of the following property from the Federal tax lien against John Doe, 1 Main Street, New York, New York. At the present time, the exact amount of the New York State tax liens has not been determined. Accordingly, discharge is sought alternatively under §§ 6325(b)(2)(A), 6325(b)(2)(B) or § 6325(b)(3).

(1) **Description and location of property.** The real property involved is located at 1 Main Street, New York, New York. It is a two-story frame dwelling with a garage under.

(2) **Description of transaction.** The 1 Main Street property is to be sold to an unrelated party on .... The Main Street property is owned jointly by the taxpayer, John Doe, and his estranged wife, Mary Doe.

(3) **Notice of lien** A notice of Federal tax lien was filed in the New York County Clerk's office on ...., under Index No. 00000, Fed. Ser. No. LL00000 against John Doe. The type of tax was employment taxes (100 percent penalty) for the period ended .... The assessment date was ...., and the amount of the lien was $............... (Subsequently, on ...., this lien was refiled under Index No. 00000, Fed. Ser. No. LL00000.)

(4) **Prior liens** There is a $............... mortgage on the property (which the buyer will assume). In addition, a search in the New York County Clerk's Office shows: [*(A), etc.: Describe other filed liens and judgments*].

(5) **Costs of sale** The sales price of the property is $...........................; however, commission of $........................... is payable and as part of the sales proceeds the purchasers will assume a mortgage in the amount of $........................... In addition to prior liens, legal expenses are payable out of the proceeds in the amount of $.............. to (N.) and $.............. to (N). (Describe any other obligations payable out of proceeds.)

(6) **Information regarding value** This is a private sale of property to an unrelated third party and accordingly it is believed that the purchase price reflects the fair market value of the property. (Attach appraisals of the property.)

(7) **Other information.** [*State any other information that might bear on the Service's determination; e.g., "John Doe had been assessed a 100 percent penalty*

and has reduced the balance of this assessment to $............... It is believed that his record of making payments in reduction of the assessment should be taken into account in connection with this application."]

This application is made on the basis of information supplied to me and, to the best of my knowledge and belief, it is true, correct, and complete.

Very truly yours,

FORM 15.20
CERTIFICATE OF DISCHARGE OF PROPERTY FROM FEDERAL TAX LIEN UNDER SECTION 6325(B)(1) OF THE INTERNAL REVENUE CODE

FORM **669-A** (Rev. February 1992)	DEPARTMENT OF THE TREASURY - INTERNAL REVENUE SERVICE **CERTIFICATE OF DISCHARGE OF PROPERTY FROM FEDERAL TAX LIEN** (Sec. 6325(b)(1) of the Internal Revenue Code)

WHEREAS, _____

Of _____ , City of _____

County of _____ , State of _____ .

is indebted to the United States for unpaid internal revenue tax in the sum of _____

_____ Dollars ($ _____)

as evidenced by:

NOTICE OF FEDERAL TAX LIEN SERIAL NUMBER (a)	RECORDING INFORMATION (b)	DATE RECORDED (c)	TAXPAYER IDENTIFICATION NUMBER (d)	AMOUNT SHOWN ON LIEN (e)

WHEREAS, to secure the collection of said tax, notice of the lien of the United States, attaching to all the property and rights to property of the said taxpayer on account of said tax indebtedness, was filed with the

_____ for the

_____ , and also with the _____

_____ , in accordance with the applicable provisions of law.

WHEREAS, the lien of the United States, listed above, for said tax has attached to certain property described as:

Catalog No. 16751C   FORM **669-A** (Rev. 2-92)

(Use this space for continued description of property)

WHEREAS, the District Director of Internal Revenue has determined that if the certificate of discharge is issued with respect to the foregoing property, the other property which will remain subject to the lien of the United States has a fair market value at this time of at least double the sum of: (1) the amount of the liability remaining unsatisfied in respect of such tax and (2) the amount of all prior liens upon such property;

NOW, THEREFORE, THIS INSTRUMENT WITNESSETH, That I, _____ ,

District Director of Internal Revenue at _____ , charged by law with the duty of collecting and enforcing the collection of internal revenue taxes due the United States, and charged with the assessment hereinbefore stated, do, pursuant to the provisions of section 6325(b)(1), of the Internal Revenue Code discharge the property heretofore described from the aforesaid tax lien, saving and reserving, however, the force and effect of said tax lien against and upon all other property or rights to property to which said lien is attached, wheresoever situated.

WITNESS my hand at _____ , on this,

the _____ day of _____ , 19 ___ .

SIGNATURE	TITLE

(NOTE: Certificate of officer authorized by law to take acknowledgments is not essential to the validity of Discharge of Federal Tax Lien. Rev. Rul. 71-466, 1971-2, C.B. 409)

* U.S Government Printing Office 1992-312-711/65015

FORM **669-A** (Rev. 2-92)

FORM 15.21

CERTIFICATE OF DISCHARGE OF PROPERTY FROM FEDERAL TAX LIEN UNDER SECTION 6325(B)(2)(A) OF THE INTERNAL REVENUE CODE

FORM 669-B (Rev. February 1992)	DEPARTMENT OF THE TREASURY - INTERNAL REVENUE SERVICE **Certificate of Discharge of Property from Federal Tax Lien** *(Section 6325(b)(2)(A) of the Internal Revenue Code)*

Whereas, _____

Of _____ , City of _____ ,

County of _____ , State of _____ ,

is indebted to the United States for unpaid internal revenue tax in the sum of _____

_____ Dollars *($ _____)*

as evidenced by:

Notice of Federal Tax Lien Serial Number (a)	Recording Information (b)	Date Recorded (c)	Taxpayer Identification Number (d)	Amount Shown on Lien (e)

Whereas, to secure the collection of said tax, notice of the lien of the United States, attaching to all the property

and rights to property of the said taxpayer on account of said tax indebtedness, was filed with the _____

_____ for the

_____ , and also with the _____

_____ , in accordance with the applicable provisions of law.

Whereas, the lien of the United States, listed above, for said tax has attached to certain property described as:

Form **669-B** (Rev. 2-92)

(Use this space for continued description of property)

    Whereas, the District Director of Internal Revenue has determined that the value of the interest of the United States in the foregoing property, under and by virtue of its aforesaid tax lien, amounts to the sum of _____ _____ dollars *($ _____)* and has authorized the issuance, under the provisions of section 6325(b)(2)(A) of the Internal Revenue Code, of a certificate discharging the above-described property from the tax lien of the United States upon the payment of the sum of _____ dollars *($ _____)* to be applied in part satisfaction of the liability in respect of the tax hereinbefore stated which sum has been paid to be so applied, and the receipt of which sum by me is hereby acknowledged; _____ .

    Now, therefore, this instrument witnesseth, that I, _____ ,

District Director of Internal Revenue at _____ , charged by law with the duty of collecting and enforcing the collection of internal revenue taxes due the United States, and charged with the assessment hereinbefore stated, do, pursuant to the provisions of section 6325(b)(2)(A) of the Internal Revenue Code, discharge the property heretofore described from the aforesaid tax lien, saving and reserving, however, the force and effect of said tax lien against and upon all other property or rights to property to which said lien is attached, wheresoever situated.

    Witness my hand at _____ , on this, the _____ day of _____ , 19 ____ .

Signature	Title

Note: Certificate of officer authorized by law to take acknowledgments is not essential to the validity of Discharge of Federal Tax Lien. Rev. Rul. 71-466, 1971-2, C.B. 409.

Form 669-B (Rev. 2-92)

FORM 15.22
CERTIFICATE OF DISCHARGE OF PROPERTY FROM FEDERAL TAX LIEN

FORM 669-C (Rev. February 1992)	DEPARTMENT OF THE TREASURY - INTERNAL REVENUE SERVICE **CERTIFICATE OF DISCHARGE OF PROPERTY FROM FEDERAL TAX LIEN** *(Sec. 6325(b)(2)(B) of the Internal Revenue Code)*

WHEREAS, _____

Of _____ , City of _____ ,

County of _____ , State of _____ ,

is indebted to the United States for unpaid internal revenue tax in the sum of _____

_____ Dollars ($ _____)

as evidenced by:

NOTICE OF FEDERAL TAX LIEN SERIAL NUMBER (a)	RECORDING INFORMATION (b)	DATE RECORDED (c)	TAXPAYER IDENTIFICATION NUMBER (d)	AMOUNT SHOWN ON LIEN (e)

WHEREAS, to secure the collection of said tax, notice of the lien of the United States, attaching to all the property and rights to property of the said taxpayer on account of said tax indebtedness, was filed with the

_____ for the

_____ , and also with the _____

_____ , in accordance with the applicable provisions of law.

WHEREAS, the lien of the United States, listed above, for said tax has attached to certain property described as:

Form **669-C** (Rev. 2-92)

(Use this space for continued description of property)

WHEREAS, the District Director of Internal Revenue has determined that the interest of the United States in the foregoing property, under and by virtue of its aforesaid tax lien, is now valueless;

NOW, THEREFORE, THIS INSTRUMENT WITNESSETH, That I, _____ , District Director of Internal Revenue at _____ , charged by law with the duty of collecting and enforcing the collection of internal revenue taxes due the United States, and charged with the assessment hereinbefore stated, do, pursuant to the provisions of section 6325(b)(2)(B), of the Internal Revenue Code discharge the property heretofore described from the aforesaid tax lien, saving and reserving, however, the force and effect of said tax lien against and upon all other property or rights to property to which said lien is attached, wheresoever situated.

WITNESS my hand at _____ , on this,

the _____ day of _____ , 19 ___ .

SIGNATURE	TITLE

(NOTE: Certificate of officer authorized by law to take acknowledgments is not essential to the validity of Discharge of Federal Tax Lien. Rev. Rul. 71-466, 1971-2, C.B. 409.)

FORM 669-C (Rev. 2-92)

FORM 15.23 _____

CERTIFICATE OF SUBORDINATION OF FEDERAL TAX LIEN UNDER SECTION 6325(D)(1) OF THE INTERNAL REVENUE CODE

Form 669-D (Rev. February 1992)	DEPARTMENT OF THE TREASURY - INTERNAL REVENUE SERVICE **Certificate of Subordination of Federal Tax Lien** (Section 6325(d)(1) of the Internal Revenue Code)

Whereas, _____

Of _____ , City of _____ ,

County of _____ , State of _____ ,

is indebted to the United States for unpaid internal revenue tax in the sum of _____

_____ Dollars ($ _____)

as evidenced by:

NOTICE OF FEDERAL TAX LIEN SERIAL NUMBER (a)	RECORDING INFORMATION (b)	DATE RECORDED (c)	TAXPAYER IDENTIFICATION NUMBER (d)	AMOUNT SHOWN ON LIEN (e)

Whereas, to secure the collection of said tax, notice of the lien of the United States, attaching to all the property

and rights to property of the said taxpayer on account of said tax indebtedness, was filed with the _____

_____ for the

_____ , and also with the _____ ,

_____ , in accordance with the applicable provisions of law.

Whereas, the lien of the United States, listed above, for said tax has attached to certain property described as:

FORM 669-D (Rev. 2-92)

(Use this space for continued description of property)

Whereas, the District Director of Internal Revenue has determined that upon the payment of the sum of

_____ dollars ($ _____) which amount is

equal to the amount with respect to which the tax lien is subordinated and is to be applied in part satisfaction of the

liability in respect of the tax hereinbefore stated which sum has been paid to be so applied, and the receipt of which

sum by me is hereby acknowledged: _____ , has authorized the

issuance, under the provisions of section 6325(d)(1) of the Internal Revenue Code, of a certificate subordinating the

tax lien of the United States:

     Now, therefore, this instrument witnesseth, that I, _____ ,

District Director of Internal Revenue at _____ , charged by law with the duty

of collecting and enforcing the collection of internal revenue taxes due the United States, and charged with the

assessment hereinbefore stated, do, pursuant to the provisions of section 6325(d)(1) of the Internal Revenue Code,

subordinate the aforesaid tax lien, in the amount heretofore stated to the instrument herein described as _____

_____

saving and reserving, however, the force and effect of said tax lien against and upon all other property or rights to

property to which said lien is attached, wherever situated.

     Witness my hand at _____ , on this,

the _____ day of _____ , 19 ___.

Signature	Title

Note: Certificate of officer authorized by law to take acknowledgments is not essential to the validity of Subordination of Federal Tax Lien.
Rev. Rul. 71-466, 1971-2, C.B. 409

Form 669-D (Rev. 2-92)

¶ 15.09 MINIMIZING THE EFFECT OF LIENS: CIVIL ACTIONS AGAINST THE UNITED STATES BY TAXPAYERS AND THIRD PARTIES PRIOR TO LEVY

When a tax assessment has been made and the Service claims that a lien attaches to property or rights to property, a number of judicial remedies are available to affected taxpayers and third parties before the Service takes enforced collections action by levy. The taxpayer or third person may bring the following five actions:

1. A petition for a declaratory judgment that the tax lien is void or does not attach to the property, or is junior to the third person's lien;
2. An action to quiet title to the property by removing the tax lien as a cloud upon title;
3. An action to foreclose a nontax lien by a third-party lienor;
4. An action by a nontaxpayer to partition the property, where the property involved is jointly owned and only one of the persons is a taxpayer; and
5. An action for damages for failure to release a lien.

Each of these civil actions against the United States will be explored separately in the following sections.

[1] Declaratory Judgments

The Declaratory Judgment Act[365] permits a federal district court to declare the rights and other legal relations of any interested party seeking a declaratory judgment "except with respect to Federal taxes." Consequently, on its face, the statute removes the subject matter jurisdiction of a federal district court to grant a declaratory judgment in a tax case. In this respect the limitation is similar to the provisions of the Anti-Injunction Act,[366] which preclude a court's jurisdiction to enjoin the assessment or collection of an internal revenue tax.[367] However, just as federal courts have issued injunctions in limited types of tax cases, they have also made declaratory judgments in tax cases. Despite the preclusions of the Declaratory Judgment Act, federal courts have declared the

---

[365] 28 USC § 2201.

[366] See the discussion infra at ¶ 15.07.

[367] The statute is literally broader in its preclusion of a declaratory judgment in a case involving the internal revenue laws than the Anti-Injunction Act, but the Supreme Court said in Alexander v. "Americans United" Inc., 416 US 752 (1974), that the federal tax exception to the Declaratory Judgment Act is at least as broad as the prohibition of the Anti-Injunction Act. Consequently, a declaratory judgment may not be obtained in a matter involving federal taxes where an injunction could not also have been obtained.

rights of parties in tax cases where (1) the merits of the tax assessment have not been contested and (2) the attachment of a tax lien to particular property or priority of the tax lien is questioned.[368]

Even where there is a basis for a district court's subject matter jurisdiction to make a declaratory judgment, an independent basis for federal jurisdiction must exist. The Declaratory Judgment Act does not itself confer jurisdiction on federal courts; it merely describes a kind of relief a federal court may grant if jurisdiction otherwise exists. Accordingly, the request for a declaratory judgment must raise a federal question, usually under the internal revenue laws,[369] or there must be diversity jurisdiction. It should be noted that the effect of a court's decision in a quiet title action is not prohibited in tax cases and is very much like a declaratory judgment; therefore, consideration should be given to the commencement of such an action rather than in the form of a declaratory judgment.

[2] Quiet Title Actions: 28 USC Section 2410

A person claiming some interest in property that is either subject to a tax lien or claimed to be subject to a tax lien may institute a proceeding seeking to remove a cloud (the tax lien) from the title. This proceeding is called a quiet title action. Although sovereign immunity at one time prevented the joinder of the United States in this type of proceeding, the United States has now consented to be named a party to a quiet title action where the government claims a mortgage or other lien, including a tax lien, on the property.[370] A quiet title

---

[368] St. Louis Union Trust Co. v. Stone, 570 F2d 833 (8th Cir. 1978) (declaratory judgment action to determine effect of levy and rights of parties); Aqua Bar & Lounge, Inc. v. United States, 539 F2d 935 (3d Cir. 1976) (taxpayer asked the court to determine that a lien did not attach to a liquor license); Bullock v. Latham, 306 F2d 45 (2d Cir. 1962) (third party claimed property did not belong to taxpayer); Tomlinson v. Smith, 128 F2d 808 (7th Cir. 1942) (third party sought a declaration that his lien was superior to the tax lien). When property is subject to a mortgage having priority over a tax lien, the buyer who pays off the mortgage may claim that he is equitably subrogated to the mortgage holder's lien. Han v. United States, 944 F2d 526 (9th Cir. 1991) (applying equitable subrogation under California law); Talbot v. United States, 850 F. Supp. 969 (D. Wyo. 1994) (declaratory judgment action could be brought by third parties who acquired real property formerly owned by taxpayer and his wife as tenants by the entirety because they claimed that the property was being taken to satisfy the taxpayer's liability).

[369] 28 USC § 1340; St. Louis Union Trust Co. v. Stone, 570 F2d 833 (8th Cir. 1978). In Aqua Bar & Lounge, Inc. v. United States, 539 F2d 935 (3d Cir. 1976), the taxpayer apparently raised questions about the procedural regularity of the assessment involved. However, in Bullock v. Latham, 306 F2d 45 (2d Cir. 1962), there had been a seizure so that jurisdiction was found under both 28 USC § 2463 and 28 USC § 1340.

[370] 28 USC § 2410(a)(1). For further description of the use of quiet title actions in collection cases, see infra ¶ 15.12.

action has been used by taxpayers as a means of seeking to determine whether a lien attaches to property,[371] or whether there is a procedural defect in the lien.[372]

The quiet title statute waives sovereign immunity in both quiet title actions (28 USC § 2410(a)(1)) and foreclosure actions (28 USC § 2410(a)(2)). The purpose of the waiver for a quiet title action was to provide "a method . . . to clear real estate titles of questionable or valueless Government liens."[373] Accordingly, the scope of the Section 2410(a)(1) waiver has been held to include a determination of lien priority, as well as of the validity of the tax lien.[374] In the past, where the government had not consented to be joined in these suits, it would move to dismiss the United States as a party and, simultaneously, or shortly thereafter, move to intervene to assert its rights or initiate a new proceeding. The consent statute (Section 2410) avoids these unnecessary procedural steps. However, sovereign immunity is not waived, and a quiet title action is not permitted for a suit analogous to quiet title action, such as for the purpose of requiring the Service to marshal assets by collecting a jeopardy assessment from real property rather than to permit the property to be forfeited.[375]

---

[371] Cole v. Cardoza, 441 F2d 1337 (6th Cir. 1971) (whether tax lien attached to tenancy by the entirety); Benson v. United States, 442 F2d 1221, 1223 n.3 (DC Cir. 1971) (same under District of Columbia law). See Aqua Bar & Lounge, Inc. v. United States, 539 F2d 935 (3d Cir. 1976) (whether tax lien attached to liquor license); Estate of Rao v. United States, 987 F. Supp. 249 (SDNY 1997) (the Service assessed estate tax without sending a notice of deficiency).

[372] United States v. Coson, 286 F2d 453 (9th Cir. 1961); Smith v. Flinn, 261 F2d 781 (8th Cir. 1958), modified, 264 F2d 523 (8th Cir. 1959).

[373] HR Rep. No. 1191, 77th Cong., 1st Sess. 2 (1941); S. Rep. No. 1646, 77th Cong., 2d Sess. 2 (1942).

[374] See Progressive Consumers Federal Credit Union v. United States, 79 F3d 1228 (1st Cir. 1996). The government has argued that a quiet title action under Section 2410(a) is appropriate only where the plaintiff seeks a decree that the government's lien is defective or invalid and seeks to have the cloud removed from his title; that is, in "actual" quiet title actions, not suits analogous to quiet title actions. However, most courts have held that a party may maintain a quiet title action against the United States when the government asserts that a federal lien exists against the property; therefore, under Section 2410(a), lien priority disputes have been considered quiet title actions. Progressive Consumers Fed. Credit Union v. United States, 79 F3d 1228 (1st Cir. 1996) (gathering cases). The quiet title action permitted under Section 2410(a) is in substance a suit for a declaratory judgment, but the Declaratory Judgment Act does not deprive the district court of jurisdiction in this situation as long as the person bringing the action does not challenge the underlying tax assessment. Id.

[375] Raulerson v. United States, 786 F2d 1090 (11th Cir. 1986); Estate of Johnson v. United States, 836 F2d 940 (5th Cir. 1988) (executor who sought a determination that the estate's administrative and funeral expenses took priority over the IRS lien could be viewed as a third party who was able to bring an action to quiet title under 28 USC § 2410(a)).

In a quiet title action brought by a taxpayer, the merits of the tax liability may not be raised.[376] Also, some but not all courts have said that the remedy of a quiet title action is available only to third persons and not to taxpayers.[377] The statutory language of 28 USC Section 2410 does not prohibit an action by taxpayers, and the better view is that, at least where the merits of the tax assessment are not contested, a taxpayer may bring such a proceeding joining the United States.[378]

At any rate, where a third person claims to have an interest in property that the Service believes is subject to its lien, it had long been held that the proper procedure is for the person to institute a quiet title action rather than to pay the tax and sue for refund because that procedure is available only to taxpayers.[379] In *Williams v. United States*,[380] the former wife of the taxpayer could not sell real property because a notice of tax lien had been arising from her former husband's tax liability. Frustrated in her inability to secure a release of lien, the wife paid the husband's tax, filed a claim for refund, and sued for refund. The government objected on grounds that because she was not the taxpayer, the refund court did not have jurisdiction under 28 USC Section 1346, which waives sovereign immunity and grants jurisdiction for taxpayer refund suits. The Supreme Court held that under these circumstances, the divorced wife could properly institute a suit for refund because 28 USC § 1346 was not limited to suits by taxpayers, but to any person whose tax had been erroneously collected.

A number of procedural issues arise in a quiet title action. The government's consent to be named in this type of proceeding does not itself confer jurisdiction on a federal court to hear a quiet title action. Accordingly, a federal court does not have jurisdiction over the action, and the suit should be commenced in an appropriate state court pursuant to the state's procedural

---

[376] Aqua Bar & Lounge, Inc. v. United States, 539 F2d 935 (3d Cir. 1976); Falik v. United States, 343 F2d 38 (2d Cir. 1965); Koff v. United States, 978 F2d 715 (9th Cir. 1992) (taxpayer held to have made attack on merits of assessment, which is impermissible in quiet title action). See PCCE, Inc. v. United States, 82 AFTR2d 98-6914 (9th Cir. 1998) (court construed quiet title action questioning validity of lien that arose because of premature assessment as attack on assessment and thus on merits of tax liability; questionable decision not very convincingly distinguishing Johnson v. United States, 990 F2d 41 (2d Cir. 1993), involving virtually the same facts).

[377] Falik v. United States, 343 F2d 38 (2d Cir. 1965); Globe Prods. Corp. v. United States, 386 F. Supp. 319 (D. Md. 1974. See Mulcahy v. United States, 388 F2d 300, 302 (5th Cir. 1968). Contra Aqua Bar & Lounge, Inc. v. United States, 539 F2d 935 (3d Cir. 1976).

[378] See e.g., Aqua Bar & Lounge, Inc. v. United States, 539 F2d 935 (3d Cir. 1976).

[379] Busse v. United States, 542 F2d 421 (7th Cir. 1976); Phillips v. United States, 346 F2d 999 (2d Cir. 1965). But see United States v. Halton Tractor Co., 258 F2d 612 (9th Cir. 1958); Adams v. United States, 380 F. Supp. 1033 (D. Mont. 1974) (refund action under 28 USC § 1346 proper because payment involuntary).

[380] Williams v. United States, 514 US 527 (1995).

rules unless there are independent grounds for federal jurisdiction, such as diversity of citizenship or a federal matter (i.e., a question arising under the internal revenue laws).[381] The rather stringent requirements for a finding of diversity of citizenship make it unlikely in most cases that such a basis for jurisdiction will be found. On the other hand, original federal jurisdiction may exist if the suit raises a question of federal law rather than merely one of the ownership of property.[382] If the action is commenced in a state court, the government has an absolute right to remove the case to a federal district court.[383] Consequently, there is a lack of symmetry in the jurisdiction of a federal court. Where a quiet title action is brought originally in a federal district court, it may or may not have jurisdiction to hear the case; but if the action is originally brought in a state court and subsequently removed by the United States, the federal district court has jurisdiction to hear the case.

The plaintiff in a quiet title action must satisfy a number of procedural requirements. The complaint or pleading must set forth with particularity the nature of the interest or lien of the United States, including "the name and address of the taxpayer whose liability created the lien and, if the notice of the tax lien was filed, the identity of the Internal Revenue office that filed the notice and the date and place such notice of lien was filed."[384] Where a tax lien has been filed, the plaintiff will not have a problem specifying the government's interest with particularity, but where a lien has not been filed, there is some question as to the effect of a judgment of the court because the plaintiffs may not be able to allege with particularity the nature of the interest or lien of the United States. At any rate, the complaint must be served on the United States, irrespective of any provision of state law, in the same manner as though the action were commenced in a federal district court.[385] The United States then has sixty days after service to appear and answer or otherwise plead. Finally, the person bringing a quiet title action need not request a judicial sale to discharge the government's interest or lien in the property because the statute provides that a judgment or decree in the action has the same effect respecting the discharge of the property from the lien held by the United States as may be provided by applicable local law of the place where the court is sit-

---

[381] Shaw v. United States, 331 F2d 493, 496 (9th Cir. 1964); Remis v. United States, 172 F. Supp. 732 (D. Mass. 1959), aff'd, 273 F2d 293 (1st Cir. 1960).

[382] 28 USC § 1340 is a possible jurisdictional basis for an action in a federal court where the propriety of the lien is at issue. See St. Louis Union Trust Co. v. Stone, 570 F2d 833 (8th Cir. 1978); Aqua Bar & Lounge, Inc. v. United States, 539 F2d 935 (3d Cir. 1976); United States v. Coson, 286 F2d 453 (9th Cir. 1961); Benson v. United States, 442 F2d 1221, 1223 n.3 (DC Cir. 1971). See also Bullock v. Latham, 306 F2d 45 (2d Cir. 1962).

[383] 28 USC § 1441.

[384] 28 USC § 2410(b).

[385] 28 USC § 2410(b); Fed. R. Civ. P. 4.

uated.[386] A person who is successful in a Section 2410 proceeding may also be entitled to attorney fees under Section 7430.[387]

[3] Foreclosure Actions

State laws have different procedures for lienors to foreclose their liens. For example, a lienholder may foreclose a lien in a plenary judicial action or, under the laws of some states, by nonjudicial foreclosure pursuant to a power of sale in the security instrument. Some states permit the lienholder to secure possession of the property by a procedure known as "strict foreclosure" whereby the mortgagee must file an instrument attesting the fact of entry with the proper registrar of deeds within a certain period after the mortgagee enters the property. Under some state procedures, a senior lienholder is permitted to foreclose his lien and sell the property, thereby discharging the tax lien, without any notice to the Service. Obviously, the Service objected strenuously to having its lien cut off by the action of other lienholders. In 1960, the Supreme Court held that a junior tax lien may be discharged on foreclosure of a senior security interest, where state law so provided, although the United States was neither made a party to the proceeding nor had actual notice of the action.[388] Congress responded to this decision by passing the Federal Tax Lien Act of 1966, which added a new Section 7425 and amended 28 USC Section 2410. These statutes provide different rules depending on whether there is a plenary judicial proceeding or a so-called nonjudicial proceeding.

[a] Plenary Judicial Sales

In general, 28 USC Section 2410 permits the joinder of the United States in any civil action to foreclose a mortgage or other lien on real or personal property on which the United States has a tax lien. Section 7425(a) provides rules to determine the effect of the judgment or a judicial sale pursuant to a judgment in a mortgage or other lien foreclosure action in which the United

---

[386] 28 USC § 2410(c).

[387] See Estate of Rao v. United States, 987 F. Supp. 249 (SDNY 1997) (the Service conceded taxpayer's claim that a notice of deficiency had not been sent after taxpayer had brought the matter to the Service's attention, and taxpayer was finally compelled to bring suit to have lien removed; attorney fees allowed).

[388] United States v. Brosnan, 363 US 237 (1960) (tax liens junior to mortgage containing power of sale provision were considered under local law to be cut off by foreclosure of the mortgage through sale at public auction without any judicial proceeding whatsoever); Bank of Am. v. United States, 363 US 237 (1960) (senior mortgage contained confession of judgment provision and, under local law, mortgagee could obtain personal judgment against mortgagor and, without having to join the United States, cut off the junior tax lien by judicial sale pursuant to the judgment).

States has not been joined. If the United States is properly named as a party to a lien or mortgage foreclosure proceeding, a judgment or decree has the same effect on the tax lien of the United States as local law that the place where the court is situated provides with respect to the discharge of junior liens.[389] To join the United States properly, however, the rules of 28 USC Section 2410 must be complied with: (1) the complaint must set forth "with particularity" the nature of the government's interest or lien; (2) the complaint must seek a judicial sale; and (3) the United States must be properly served.[390] If the United States is improperly joined as a party to a judicial proceeding, the effect is the same as if the United States were not joined.[391]

The effect of a failure to join the United States in a lien foreclosure action depends on whether or not a notice of lien was filed when the proceeding was commenced.[392] If the government has properly filed a tax lien before the proceeding commences, but is not joined as a party, a judgment as to the property does not disturb the tax lien with the result that it continues to encumber the property sold.[393] Where the United States is not joined as a party in the court proceeding and either a notice of lien has not been filed at the time the proceeding is commenced, or no provision is made for the filing of a lien (e.g., the special gift or estate tax lien), a judgment or a judicial sale has the same effect with respect to the discharge of the lien as provided by local law.[394] The

---

[389] 28 USC § 2410(c). See Kasdon v. United States, 707 F2d 820 (4th Cir. 1983) (foreclosure sale is not a judicial sale under IRC § 2410(c), because it was not directed by judicial order); United States v. Capobianco, 836 F2d 808 (3d Cir. 1988) (sheriff's sale of real property on foreclosure of purchase-money mortgage qualified as a "judicial sale" under 28 USC § 2410; government received actual timely notice, was made a party to plenary proceeding before judgment was entered, and afterwards had an opportunity to protest distribution of proceeds). In Brightwell v. United States, 805 F. Supp. 1464 (SD Ind. 1992), the district court adopted a view, unprecedented in Indiana, that judicial sale was a proper remedy in actions that begin or are labeled strict foreclosures, and that it had quiet title jurisdiction.

[390] 28 USC §§ 2410(c), 2410(d).

[391] Reg. § 301.7425-1(c)(1).

[392] The rules relating to the proper filing of a notice of lien are set forth in IRC §§ 6323(f) and 6323(g) and are incorporated by reference in the regulations under IRC § 7425. Reg. § 301.7425(c)(2).

[393] Reg. § 301.7425-1(c)(2); United States v. Winterburn, 749 F2d 1283 (9th Cir. 1984) (action under Washington law held to be quiet title action in which United States not named); Hotchkiss v. Starke, 75-2 USTC ¶ 9807 (NDNY 1975) (properly filed tax lien encumbered property sold at judicial sale). Cf. United States v. VonCseh, 354 F. Supp. 315 (SD Tex. 1972) (tax lien was not filed locally, and judicial sale pursuant to judgment was held to discharge the lien). United States v. DelValle & DelValle, Inc., 532 F. Supp. 337 (DPR 1981) (foreclosed property remained subject to lien because no notice given to Service); United States v. Fernandez, 82-1 USTC ¶ 9212 (DPR 1981) (same); United States v. McNeil, 661 F. Supp. 28 (ED Ky. 1987) (foreclosure action in which conditions imposed by 28 USC § 2410(b) were not met did not disturb tax lien).

[394] Reg. § 301.7425-1(c)(3).

result is the same whether the tax lien arose before or after the date the foreclosure action was commenced and regardless of whether notice of the tax lien was filed at any time after the foreclosure action was commenced.[395] However, there is one exception to this rule: Where the government is not joined as a party and the sale discharges the tax lien, the government may still assert its claim against the proceeds of the sale at any time before their distribution is ordered with the same force as though the lien were asserted against the property sold.[396] The effect of provisions dealing with a plenary judicial proceeding is that a junior tax lien is wiped out if the lien is wiped out under the local law of the state where the property is situated. However, the rights of the government are protected by provision for a short redemption period during which the United States may redeem the property.[397] The government has 120 days or the period allowable for redemption under state law, whichever is longer, to redeem real estate sold to satisfy a senior nontax lien. During the redemption period, the Service has time to investigate and determine whether it would be to the government's advantage to redeem the property so that it might be resold for more than the cost of redemption with the resulting benefit to the government.[398]

---

[395] Reg. § 301.7425-1(c)(3)(ii), Ex. (1).

[396] IRC § 7425(a); Reg. § 301.7425(c)(4).

[397] 28 USC § 2410(c); IRC § 7425(d)(1). The objective is to permit the government by the exercise of the right of redemption to purchase property sold at distress prices and to resell the property at a profit. The profit is applied to the taxpayer's liability. Where the purchaser at the sale is the person whose lien is being foreclosed, the amount paid includes the amount underlying the lien to the extent that the lien is satisfied by the sale. However, the amount legally satisfied does not include the amount of the creditor's lien to the extent that the creditor may obtain a deficiency judgment against the debtor taxpayer. Reg. § 301.7425-4(b)(2)(ii). If a creditor purchases property at a below-market price, the government need only tender the below-market price, not the amount of the deficiency claim against the debtor taxpayer. Delta Savings & Loan Ass'n, Inc. v. Internal Revenue Service, 847 F2d 248 (5th Cir. 1988) (creditor could have avoided government's below-market redemption by purchasing property at foreclosure by payment on its debt of an amount equal to the lesser of the property's market value or the value of its debt). Where the Service redeems under IRC § 7425(d), it takes the interest that the redemptionee acquired at the execution sale. Olympic Fed. Sav. & Loan Ass'n v. Regan, 648 F2d 1218 (9th Cir. 1981). Therefore, if the Service decides to redeem, any post-sale purchaser and intervening lienor is divested of title or interest. Also, the Service need not accept payment offered by the redemptionee (i.e., purchaser at the execution sale) of an amount equal to the tax lien. Id. See Black v. United States, 683 F. Supp. 770 (ND Ala. 1987), in which the Service failed to exercise its right of redemption within the 120-day period. The court also found that the correct amount under state law was not tendered—a questionable holding.

[398] IRC § 7180 established a fund for the purchase of redeemed property in the amount of $1 million under the control of the Treasury Department. The fund is reimbursed from proceeds of subsequent sales of real property redeemed in an amount equal to the amount expended out of the fund to make the redemption. The remaining proceeds are applied in satisfaction of the taxpayer's liability. Any surplus is returned to the parties le-

The redemption price is the amount paid by the purchaser at the foreclosure sale, plus interest at the rate of 6 percent from the date of sale.[399] Where the purchaser is a person whose lien is being foreclosed, the amount paid includes the amount of the debt underlying the lien to the extent that the lien is satisfied by the sale. Therefore, the amount the government must tender is the amount paid at the foreclosure sale, even if this amount is less than the amount of the lien.[400] If the lien is fully satisfied, the purchaser cannot receive less than the amount due him at the time of sale. However, where the lien attaches to other property, or where, after sale, the purchaser still has the right to sue for the unpaid balance of the amount due him, the amount does not include this unpaid balance.[401] In addition to the price paid by the purchaser plus interest, the government must pay as part of the redemption price the excess, if any, of expense incurred after the foreclosure in maintaining the property over the income from the property during the period.[402] Where the property is not rented out but is used by the purchaser, the income includes the reasonable rental value of the property.

A sale to satisfy a lien junior to the tax lien is made subject to and does not disturb the tax lien unless the government consents to the sale of the property free of its lien.[403] If at the time the proceeding is commenced, the tax lien is not on file and the United States is not named a party, the tax lien is discharged from the property by the sale, assuming state law so provides.[404] Consequently, if local law provides for the discharge, it is advisable for the junior lienor not to name the United States in the lien foreclosure action.

---

gally entitled to it. The government's right of redemption is triggered by the sale, not the transfer, of property. Southwest Prods. Co. v. United States, 882 F2d 113 (4th Cir. 1989) (when Service tendered bid price plus interest to senior lienor, it became owner of property although property not transferred because of senior lienor's failure to pay closing costs of original public sale).

[399] 28 USC §§ 2410(d)(1), 2410(d)(2). IRC § 7425(d)(2) incorporates 28 USC § 2410(d) by reference.

[400] Equity Mortgage Co. v. Lotus, 504 F2d 1071 (4th Cir. 1974); Bailey v. United States, 78-2 USTC ¶ 9706 (D. Utah 1978); Mikulec v. United States, 705 F2d 599 (2d Cir. 1983).

[401] Reg. § 301.7425-4(b)(2)(ii). Mikulec v. United States, 705 F2d 599 (2d Cir. 1983 (extent to which judgment creditor may obtain a deficiency judgment against judgment debtor is a matter of state law, and under New York law, debtor's property only satisfied judgment to extent of judgment creditor's bid of $50).

[402] 28 USC § 2410(d)(3). Preforeclosure expenses are not considered part of the amount to be paid unless included in the amount of the lien being foreclosed. Reg. § 301.7425-4(b)(2)(ii).

[403] 28 USC § 2410(c).

[404] IRC § 7425(a).

[b] Nonjudicial Sales

In general, where a foreclosure proceeding is a nonjudicial sale, the effect of the proceeding depends on whether or not a notice of lien is on file when the proceeding commences.[405] If a lien is on file, foreclosure made without proper notice to the government does not affect the tax lien, and the lien continues against the property into the hands of a third party.[406] If the notice of lien is not filed (even special gift or estate tax liens, which are not required to be filed) or if the government is notified of the proceeding, the sale has the same effect on the tax lien as local law provides with respect to similar claims. As a result, in a nonjudicial sale, notice of sale must be given to the Service before the tax lien may be discharged. For this reason, classification of a lien enforcement procedure as a nonjudicial sale is quite important. Not surprisingly, therefore, the regulations treat all foreclosure proceedings that are not plenary judicial sales as nonjudicial sales, for which there is some support in

---

[405] IRC § 7425(b). Regulations say that a nonjudicial sale pursuant to a lien that is junior to a tax lien does not divest the tax lien, even if notice of the nonjudicial sale is given to the appropriate district director. Reg. § 301.7425-2(a)(3). This regulation has received judicial approval. Berlin v. United States, 535 F. Supp. 298 (EDNY 1982). The notice of sale must be sent by certified or registered mail to the district director to the attention of the Special Procedures Staff. Reg. § 301.7425-3(a)(1) (Notice of Sale Requirements—In General). Colorado Property Acquisitions, Inc. v. United States, 894 F2d 1173 (10th Cir. 1990) (senior lienholders mailed notice of nonjudicial foreclosure proceedings to the Service by regular mail, not by certified or registered mail; held, because notice did not comply with required type of mailing, sale did not extinguish IRS lien despite its actual notice, but senior lien also not extinguished).

[406] See, e.g., Myers v. United States, 647 F2d 591 (5th Cir. 1981) (tax lien not discharged, and purchaser had no standing to contest underlying tax assessment after Service seized property); Baldwin County Sav. & Loan Ass'n v. United States, 81-2 USTC ¶ 9619 (SD Ala. 1981) (government's junior lien elevated to senior status by foreclosure, and mortgage lien extinguished where senior lienor failed to notify Service in nonjudicial foreclosure); Little v. United States, 704 F2d 1100 (9th Cir. 1983) (government's interest in redeemed property unaffected by foreclosure and sale, because the government did not receive notice of the sale). The result in *Baldwin County* was disapproved in Southern Bank of Lauderdale County v. IRS, 586 F. Supp. 12 (ND Ala. 1984), rev'd, 770 F2d 1001 (11th Cir. 1985). Rather than elevate the junior tax lien to senior status, the district court in *Southern Bank* held that the nonjudicial sale was ineffective as to the Service, but that the IRS lien "could only attach to what the mortgagor had and could not leap ahead of (the senior mortgage lien) simply because (the senior lienor had) purchased at foreclosure." The Court of Appeals reversed the district court in *Southern Bank*, holding that "the sales of the property subject to the tax liens were made subject to and without disturbing the federal tax liens" (footnote omitted).

the legislative history.[407] However, contrary to the regulations, not all nonjudicial proceedings have been held to constitute nonjudicial sales.[408]

A 30–25 day rule applies where the notice requirement is involved. If the tax lien sought to be discharged by the nonjudicial sale is filed more than thirty days before the date of sale, a notice of sale must be given to the district director not less than twenty-five days prior to the date of sale.[409] Obviously, the determination of the "date of sale" is pivotal in determining the operation of the 30-25 day rule. The regulations provide that the date of sale is (1) in the case of a public sale, the date the sale is considered to be held, regardless of the date on which junior liens on the property are divested or the title to the property is transferred under local law; (2) in the case of a private sale, the date title to the property is transferred, regardless of the date junior liens on the property are divested under local law; and (3) in the case of divestment of junior liens on the property, not resulting either from public or private sale, the date on which the junior liens are divested under local law.[410] The regulations also provide some solution to the problem where a notice of judicial sale is not required initially and the date of sale is subsequently postponed. If, because of a postponement of the scheduled sale, more than thirty days elapse between the originally scheduled date of the sale and the actual date of the sale, and a notice of lien is filed more than thirty days before the rescheduled date of the sale, then a notice of the sale is required to be given to the district director.[411] The requirement of a notice of sale is analogous to the particularity require-

---

[407] Reg. § 301.7425-2(a). A forfeiture of a vendee-taxpayer's interest in real property, pursuant to a statutory cancellation of contract for deed, extinguished federal tax liens because the forfeiture was not a nonjudicial sale under Section 7425(b). Johnson v. United States, 799 F2d 374 (8th Cir. 1986) (Reg. § 301.7425-2 held invalid to the extent it treats such forefeitures as nonjudicial sales). Compare Rocky Mountain FSB v. Stanley, 89-2 USTC ¶ 9546 (D. Wyo. 1989) (taxpayers acquired equitable title to real property under Wyoming land sales contract so that the Service, which had filed lien, was entitled to notice before forfeiture).

[408] See, e.g., Runkel v. United States, 527 F2d 914 (9th Cir. 1976) (forfeiture under a Washington real estate sales contract does not constitute a "sale"). CL Galesi v. United States, 406 F. Supp. 623 (D.Vt. 1976), aff'd, 544 F2d 606 (2d Cir. 1976) (strict foreclosure proceeding held to be a judicial sale). Brookbank, Inc. v. Hubbard, 712 F2d 399 (9th Cir. 1983) and Hedlund v. Brellenthin, 520 F. Supp. 81 (WD Wash. 1981) (forfeiture under real estate sales contract is not a "sale" under IRC § 7425(b), and Reg. § 301.7425-2(a) is invalid to the extent it broadens scope of statute). However, Section 7425(c)(4) provides: "For purposes (of the rules in subsection (6)), a sale of property includes any forfeiture of a land sales contract."

[409] IRC § 7425(b); Reg. § 301.7425-2(a). See Baldwin County Sav. & Loan Ass'n v. IRS, 921 F2d 1229 (11th Cir. 1991) (notice to Service was not required, because nonjudicial sale was set for date less than thirty days after Service filed notice of lien, even when sale was rescheduled to date more than thirty days after lien filing).

[410] Reg. § 301.7425-2(b).

[411] Reg. § 301.7425-3(a)(2).

ments of a pleading filed in a plenary judicial proceeding. However, the information required to be included in a proper notice of sale is greater and more detailed than the information that must be included in a complaint in a judicial foreclosure proceeding.[412] Moreover, if the notice of sale is inadequate, the sale is made subject to and does not disturb the lien or title of the United States. Some relief from the notice of sale provisions is provided by the provision for the district director to consent to a sale of the property free of the lien or title of the United States.[413] The consent to sale is within the discretion of the district director where adequate protection is afforded the lien or title of the United States and may involve the partial discharge of the property from the effect of the lien or the release of the lien pursuant to the provisions of Section 6325.

Where nonjudicial sales are involved, the government also has authority to redeem real property sold where the sale is to satisfy a lien prior to the tax lien, even if the government is not entitled to notice because its lien was not filed more than thirty days before the date of sale, if under applicable local law other creditors are afforded a right of redemption.[414] The period of time for redemption in the case of nonjudicial sales is 120 days from the date of sale or the period allowed under local law, whichever is longer.[415] When the

---

[412] Reg. § 301.7425-3(d). The requirements of Reg. § 301.7425-3(d)(2) have been found "ambiguous and overly burdensome," and the regulation's effect "runs contrary to Congress' intent because it places an undue burden on the foreclosing creditor." Edmundson v. United States, 886 F. Supp. 1314 (WD La. 1995) (fifty-four days before the sale, the creditor supplied the Service with notice of sale that complied with nearly all the requirements of the regulation; the Service sent a letter that the notice failed to supply certain information only eight days before the sale, and on the same date that the letter was received, the creditor sent a letter by regular mail supplying the requested information; held, the creditor gave the Service sufficient notice to protect its interests so that its lien was extinguished by the foreclosure and the expiration of the redemption period). The court said that the regulation unreasonably permits the Service to notify the creditor that the notice of sale is inadequate for all purposes because it omits any of the detailed information called for, and requires that "a perfect notice, one that complies with [the] regulation in every way, be received by the I.R.S. not less than 25 days prior to the sale . . . [and this] requirement combined with the latitude the I.R.S. has in responding to inadequate notices [up until five days before the sale], demonstrates why the I.R.S. has too much room to maneuver and delay."

[413] IRC § 7425(c)(2); Reg. § 301.7425-3(d).

[414] Reg. § 301.7425-4(a)(3). Section 7425(b)(1) has been held not to preclude the availability of equitable relief recognized under state law. First Am. Title Ins. Co. v. United States, 848 F2d 969 (9th Cir. 1988) (state law adopted as federal common law; California law applied to determine whether senior lien could survive nonjudicial sale, notice of which was not given to the IRS because of a filing error).

[415] IRC § 7425(d)(1). San Miguel Inv. Co. v. United States, 81-2 USTC ¶ 9589 (D. Colo. 1981) (Service failed to exercise its right of redemption within 120 days after sale; date deed was delivered to purchaser was not applicable date for running of period under Colorado law).

government exercises its right to redeem real property sold at a nonjudicial sale to satisfy a lien prior to the tax lien, the amount to be paid on redemption is the amount prescribed by 28 USC Section 2410(d) in the case of judicial sales.[416] Section 7425(d) permits the Service to redeem "such property" sold to satisfy the tax lien in order to prevent foreclosure purchasers from buying real property at less than its fair market value and then selling it at a profit.[417] When the Service redeems property, therefore, it acquires the entire property purchased by the foreclosure purchaser, not merely the property interest that was subject to the tax lien; if the Service sells the property, any excess profit after all prior liens are satisfied then accrues to the benefit of the taxpayer.[418] However, a party may apply to Collection for a release of the government's right of redemption.[419]

[4] Civil Damages for Failure to Release Lien

Section 7432(a) permits a taxpayer to bring a civil action for damages against the United States in a federal district court if a Service employee "knowingly, or by reason of negligence, fails to release a lien under [S]ection 6325 on property of the taxpayer."[420] If successful, the taxpayer may collect damages equal to the actual, direct economic damages sustained by the taxpayer that,

---

[416] IRC § 7425(d)(2); Reg. 301.7425-4(b)(1). After a redemption by the government, the purchaser at the nonjudicial sale is entitled to expenses incurred in connection with the redemption in excess of income. Regulations have been proposed that require an itemized list to be submitted to the district director within thirty days after the redemption; there will be no reimbursement if this rule is not complied with. Reg. § 301.7425-4(b)(3)(ii).

[417] S. Rep. No. 1708, 1996 USCAN 3722 at 3753.

[418] Vardanega v. IRS, 83 AFTR2d 99-1448 (9th Cir. 1999) (the foreclosure purchaser claimed that the Service could redeem only the portion of the property owned by the taxpayer against which it had a lien, the taxpayer's one-third interest in the property). The circuit court reached this conclusion in part on the basis of the fact that the Service must pay the foreclosure purchaser the amount the purchaser paid at the sale, plus interest and expenses necessary to maintain the property from the time of the sale.

[419] Reg. § 301.7425-4(c)(4). The requirements for the contents of an application for the release of the right of redemption are set forth in Rev. Proc. 68-10, 1968-1 CB 758.

[420] One certificate of release of lien is sufficient to release the original and expired notices of lien. However, if an original notice of lien has been refiled, a separate certificate of release must be issued for the refiled notice. Griswold v. United States, 59 F3d 1571 (11th Cir. 1995) (IRS filed several notices of lien and refiled a notice of lien, and filed certificates of release for all liens but the refiled lien, despite taxpayer's repeated requests). The government contended that it was required to issue only one certificate of release to release multiple notices, and that the Service issues a certificate of release merely by delivering it to the taxpayer. The circuit court rejected these contentions saying that in the case of a refiled lien a separate certificate must be issued, and that to issue the certificate of release when a notice of lien has been filed against the taxpayer, the Service must "either deliver it to the recording office in which the corresponding notice of federal tax

but for the actions of the government, would not have been sustained, plus the costs of the action.[421] In order to recover, the taxpayer is required to show that administrative remedies were exhausted.[422] In order to collect damages under Section 7432, it appears that the taxpayer must show that the employee who failed to release the lien knew or should have known that the requirements of Section 6325, describing the circumstances when the Service is authorized to

---

lien has been filed or deliver it to the taxpayer . . . [who] may then proceed as necessary to file the certificate of release."

One circuit court has held that before a taxpayer may commence a Section 7432(a) action, the taxpayer must make full payment of the liability, one of the circumstances in Section 6325 for the release of lien. PCCE, Inc. v. United States, 82 AFTR2d 98-6914 (9th Cir. 1998). If this view is followed, a taxpayer will be required to suffer greater economic loss in order to be able to bring a suit to recover damages because of the Service's failure to release a lien the taxpayer claims was improperly filed in the first place, a result Congress could not have intended for this remedial statute.

[421] IRC § 7432(a). The cause of action exists for notices of the failure to release the lien provided by the taxpayer to the IRS after December 31, 1988, and damages arising after that date. See also Con. R. 1104, Technical and Miscellaneous Revenue Act of 1988, 100th Cong., 2d Sess. 227, reprinted in 1988-3 CB 717. In an action for wrongful filing of a tax lien, a taxpayer is not entitled to a jury trial. Information Resources, Inc. v. United States, 996 F2d 780 (5th Cir. 1993).

As a district court has said, "in determining whether a taxpayer has a section 7432 cause of action for a knowing or a negligent failure to release a lien when the conditions of section 6325 have been met, the threshold issue is not whether the IRS knew or should have known that the taxes underlying the lien were satisfied or legally unenforceable, but rather, the issue is whether the IRS (or better stated, the proper IRS employee) knew or should have known that the requirements of section 6325 had been met—that there was an actual 'finding' by the district director, or a constructive finding based on the contents of request for release of lien." Bloom v. United States, 84 AFTR2d ¶ 99-5423 (MD Pa. 1999); see also Steffen v. United States, 952 F. Supp. 779, 783 (MD Fla. 1997) (a taxpayer may demonstrate a Section 6325 finding by direct evidence that there had been an actual finding, or circumstantial evidence that a constructive finding had been made because the taxpayer's request for a certificate of release of lien created an obligation to make such a finding).

[422] IRC § 7432(b). Sections 7432 and 7433 have been held applicable only to taxpayers against whom the Service is seeking to collect, not to third parties. Progressive Bank & Trust Co. v. Moore, 91-1 USTC ¶ 50,192 (ED La. 1991). The Service has unsuccessfully argued that in order for a taxpayer to bring an action under Section 7432, the taxpayer must have followed the procedures of Section 6326 for the administrative appeal of liens. Miller v. United States, 763 F. Supp. 1534 (ND Cal. 1991). Proposed regulations under Section 7432 have been published. See Prop. Reg. § 301.7432-1 (June 25, 1991).

An administrative claim for wrongful failure to release a lien under Section 7432 and wrongful collection action under Section 7433 must be mailed to the district director for the district in which the taxpayer resides. Failure to send the administrative claim to the district director as the regulations require has been held to deprive the district court of jurisdiction. Amwest Surety Ins. Co. v. United States, 28 F3d 690 (7th Cir. 1994) (letter to revenue officer violated Treas. Reg. § 301.6343-1(b)(2)); Venen v. United States, 38 F3d 100 (3d Cir. 1994) (letter to revenue agent violated regulations under Sections 7432 and 7433).

release a lien, have been satisfied.[423] Also, the taxpayer must mitigate his damages, and any damage award may be reduced by the amount that could have been reasonably mitigated by the taxpayer.[424] The statute of limitations on bringing the action is two years from the date the cause of action accrues.[425]

[5] Civil Action to Discharge Property From Effect of Lien

The 1998 Act gives third parties new procedures for removing liens from their property. These statutory changes to Section 7426 grow out of the Supreme Court's decision in *United States v. Williams*,[426] which held that a third party who paid another person's tax under protest to remove a lien on the third party's property could bring a refund suit because the third party had no other adequate administrative or judicial remedy. Accordingly, the 1998 Act amended Section 6325, adding a provision for the release or discharge of liens and creating an administrative procedure for the third party, who is the record owner of property against which a tax lien has been filed, to obtain a certificate of discharge of the property from the effect of the lien.[427] The owner of the property is entitled to a certificate of discharge of the lien if the owner (1) deposits an amount of money equal to the value of the Service's interest in the property, as the Service itself determines, or (2) furnishes a bond acceptable to the Service in that amount. The Service is required to refund the amount of a deposit, together with interest at the underpayment rate, and shall release any bond the owner posted if the Service determines that (1) the unsatisfied liability can be satisfied from a source other than the owner's property or (2) the value of the interest of the Service in the property is less than the Service's prior determination of the value of the Service's interest in the property.

---

[423] See Bilzerian v. United States, 86 F3d 1067 (11th Cir. 1996) (circuit court held, contrary to Service's claim, that the lien had been extinguished when taxpayer made a payment satisfying the assessment even when the Service makes what it determines to be an erroneous refund; although the Service conceded that it had intentionally failed to release the lien, the court nevertheless remanded the case on the issue of liability).

[424] IRC §§ 7432(d)(1), 7432(d)(2). Damages an injured taxpayer may recover include lost profits, costs incurred in negotiating the release of lien, loss of goodwill, and attorney fees. Information Resources, Inc. v. United States, 996 F2d 780 (5th Cir. 1993).

[425] IRC § 7432(d)(3). A taxpayer's suit for failure to release a lien was dismissed when he brought the suit more than two years after he learned that the Service had reported the liens to credit services and after he claimed his taxes should have been discharged in his bankruptcy. Richmond v. TRW Info Servs., 80 AFTR2d 97-8160 (SD Cal. 1997) ("the statute of limitations begins to run once plaintiff had a reasonable opportunity to discover all the essential elements of his claims.").

[426] United States v. Williams, 514 US 527 (1995).

[427] IRC § 6325(b)(4), as amended by 1998 Act § 3106(a), effective July 22, 1998.

In addition to the owner's procedural right under Section 6325 to obtain a certificate of discharge of lien by substituting the value of the Service's interest in the owner's property, the owner—and only the owner—may bring a civil action under Section 7426 within 120 days after the date of the certificate of discharge in a district court to release the erroneous lien. In this civil action, the district court will have jurisdiction to determine whether the value of the Service's interest in the property is less than the value that the Service determined.[428] This remedy is the exclusive remedy the owner has to remove the tax lien from the property. If the court determines that the value the Service used for the deposit or bond was excessive, the district court will grant a judgment ordering the refund of the excess portion of the bond or the release of the excess portion of the bond, plus, in the case of a refund, interest from the date of the deposit to the date of the payment of the judgment.

The statute of limitations on collection of the tax from the taxpayer is suspended for the period beginning with the date property or money is wrongfully seized or received by the Service from a third party and ending on the date the Service returns the property pursuant to Section 6343(b) or the date on which the judgment secured pursuant to Section 7426 becomes final, and for thirty days thereafter.[429] However, this period of suspension applies only to the amount wrongfully seized.

A similar suspension statute applies in the case of a wrongfully filed notice of lien.[430] The collection period is suspended for the period beginning on the date the owner is entitled to the certificate of discharge and ending on either the date that is thirty days after the Service refunds the amount of the deposit or releases the bond, or the date the judgment secured under the release of the erroneous lien court proceeding becomes final. Again, the suspension period is limited to the value the Service claimed was the value of its interest in the property.

¶ 15.10 ADMINISTRATIVE REMEDIES TO MINIMIZE THE EFFECT OF LEVIES

Section 6343 provides that the official for a geographical area has authority to release a levy on all or part of the property or rights to property levied upon where (1) it is determined that release of the levy will facilitate collection or (2) the levy was wrongful.[431] The regulations authorize the release of a levy in

---

[428] IRC § 7426(a)(4), as amended by 1998 Act § 3106(b).
[429] IRC § 6503(f)(1), as amended by 1998 Act § 3106(b).
[430] IRC § 6503(f)(2), as amended by 1998 Act § 3106(b).
[431] IRC §§ 6343(a), 6343(b); Reg. § 301.6343-1(a)(1).

still a third situation—that is, where the taxpayer requests the release and complies with one or more of six conditions:

1. The execution of a satisfactory escrow arrangement
2. The delivery of a satisfactory bond
3. The payment of the amount of the government's interest in the property
4. The execution of an assignment of salary and wages in a manner and amount satisfactory to the district director
5. The making of a satisfactory installment payment arrangement
6. The execution of an agreement extending the statute of limitations on collection[432]

Because any one or more of these conditions may be imposed before the levy is released, it is possible for the district to require the taxpayer both to enter into a part-payment agreement and to execute a waiver on the statute of limitations on collection.

Although Section 6343 states that a levy may be released if the local official determines that the release will facilitate collection, regulations mention only one situation where this might happen: where the value of the government's interest in the seized property (or in the part of the seized property to be released) is insufficient to cover the expense of selling the property.[433] However, this situation should not be the sole circumstance where the release of a levy would facilitate collection. Since the levy is used to execute and satisfy a tax lien, a release of the levy should be appropriate in the same situations where it is proper to discharge or subordinate a lien. For example, where a creditor claims a senior lien, it should be possible to obtain a partial discharge of lien from the property and a release of levy, as well as for the purpose of substituting any surplus proceeds. The Service uses Form 668-D (Release of Levy/Release of Property From Levy) for this type of release. (See Form 15.22.)

If a taxpayer obtains release of a levy by meeting one or more of the six conditions or because of the insufficient value of the government's interest, a subsequent levy may still be served, provided of course that the statute of limi-

---

[432] Reg. § 301.6343-1(a)(2).

[433] Reg. § 301.6343-1(a)(3). A notice of levy "must" be released when "(a) the underlying liability has been paid in full, or is no longer enforceable; (b) release of the levy would facilitate collection of the taxes; (c) an installment agreement has been entered into (unless the agreement provides otherwise); (d) the levy is creating an economic hardship; or (e) the fair market value of the property levied upon exceeds the liability so that a partial release does not hinder collection efforts." The taxpayer has the right to request an expedited review of a seizure involving tangible personal assets "essential to the maintenance of a business," but this review is an internal review process within the district Collection Division, not an appeal to the Appeals office, and is limited to tangible personal property, not intangible personal property or real property.

tations on collection has not expired and the property levied upon is otherwise subject to levy.

A levy also may be released where property of a person has been levied upon wrongfully. In this situation, the local official is authorized to remedy the mistake in one of the following ways: (1) by returning the specific property levied upon; (2) by returning an amount of money, equal to the amount of money levied upon (without interest); or (3) by returning an amount of money equal to the amount of money received by the government on the sale of the property, without interest.[434] The Service uses Form 668-E (Release of Levy) for this purpose. (See Form 15.25.) There is a strict statute of limitations imposed for requests to release a wrongful levy. Specific property may be returned at any time.[435] However, where money is to be returned, the amount of money levied upon may be returned at any time, but only if it is returned or a request is made within nine months from the date of the levy.[436]

The making of a request within the nine-month period has critical importance not only for perfecting a claim for wrongful levy of money, but also for a suit for wrongful levy under Section 7426 in the event that the claim is disallowed by the district. A suit for wrongful levy must be brought within nine months from the date of the levy if a request is not filed. If a request is filed, the statutory period for filing is extended another twelve months from the date the request is filed or six months from the date a notice disallowing the request is mailed, whichever is shorter.[437] The administrative request for review of a wrongful levy must be addressed to the local office to the attention of the

---

[434] Reg. § 301.6343-1(b)(1). For the purpose of determining the amount of money received by the government on the sale of property, if property is declared purchased by the government at a sale pursuant to Section 6335(e), the government is treated as having received an amount equal to the minimum price determined by the district director before the sale, or, if larger, the amount received by the government from the resale of the property. A conditional or a "strings-attached" release is not a release of levy within the meaning of Section 6343(a). Baddour, Inc. v. United States, 802 F2d 801 (5th Cir. 1986).

[435] Money that is specifically identifiable (e.g., a coin collection) is treated as specific property. Reg. § 301.6343-1(b)(1).

[436] Reg. § 301.6343-1(b)(1). If the request is made before the expiration of the nine-month period, the money may be returned after a nine-month period if the delay is necessary to investigate and process the request.

[437] IRC §§ 7426, 6532(c). See Dieckmann v. United States, 550 F2d 622 (10th Cir. 1977) (suit brought after nine-month period dismissed for lack of subject matter jurisdiction, despite claim that levy was made by Service without the knowledge of the claimant); Dependable Ins. Co. v. United States, 78-2 USTC ¶ 9721 (D. Md. 1978) (inadequate notice to IRS did not extend nine-month period); DeGregory v. United States, 395 F. Supp. 171 (ED Mich. 1975); American Honda Motor Co. v. United States, 363 F. Supp. 988 (SDNY 1973).

Chief (Special Procedures Staff) as provided in the regulations, or there is no extension of the statutory period for instituting a judicial proceeding.[438]

The Taxpayer Bill of Rights 2 added Section 6343(d), which gives Collection the authority to release a levy and return property in certain situations where the Service already recognized that remedy administratively. Property levied upon will be considered wrongfully levied upon, and subject to the wrongful provisions of Section 6343(b) (except that no interest will be paid), if Collection determines that (1) the levy was premature or otherwise not in accordance with the Service's administrative procedures; (2) the taxpayer has entered into an installment agreement to pay the liability that the Service attempted to collect by the levy, unless the agreement provides otherwise; (3) the return of the property will facilitate collection of the liability; or (4) with the consent of the taxpayer or the Taxpayer Advocate, the return of the property would be in the best interests of the taxpayer, as determined by the Taxpayer Advocate and the government.[439]

A written claim or request is generally necessary to obtain a return of money or property wrongfully levied upon. The request should be sent to the district director of the district making the levy and marked to the attention of the Chief (Special Procedures Staff). The request should contain the following: (1) the name and address of the requester; (2) a description of the property levied upon; (3) the requester's basis for claiming an interest in the property levied upon; (4) the name and address of the taxpayer, and (5) the date of the levy shown on the notice of levy (or the reason why this information cannot be supplied).[440] As a matter of practice, the districts expedite the interest-free refund of money.[441]

---

[438] See Winebrenner v. United States, 924 F2d 851 (9th Cir. 1991); Baddour, Inc. v. United States, 802 F2d 801 (5th Cir. 1986) ("The Regulations under § 6343(b) specifically provide that a written request for the return of property wrongfully levied upon may be submitted to the District Director."); Amwest Sur. Ins. Co. v. United States, 93-2 USTC ¶ 50,439 (SD Ind. 1993) ("A demand that is not addressed to the director marked for the attention of the 'Chief, special procedures staff' is insufficient to comply with the Secretary's explicit regulation.").

[439] Section 6343(d), added by the Taxpayer Bill of Rights 2, § 501(b), effective on the date of enactment, July 30, 1996.

[440] Reg. § 301.6343-1(b)(2). The Service has thirty days after the receipt of the request to notify the requester of any inadequacy in the notice, or it is considered adequate for the purposes of determining the applicable time limit for a wrongful levy action. Reg. § 301.6343-1(b)(3). For a case where the Service failed to notify the claimant of inadequacies within the thirty-day period, see Dependable Ins. Co. v. United States, 78-2 USTC ¶ 9721 (D. Md. 1978).

[441] The Service has said that it will process a claim within seven to ten days and will usually call the Service center for manual processing of a refund. IRS, Report to the Administrative Conference, Administrative Procedures of the Internal Revenue Service, S. Doc. No. 266, 94th Cong., 2d Sess. 263 (1976).

FORM 15.24
RELEASE OF LEVY/RELEASE OF PROPERTY FROM LEVY

Form **668-D**
(Rev. May 1997)

Department of the Treasury — Internal Revenue Service
Release of Levy/Release of Property from Levy

To

Taxpayer(s)

Identifying Number(s)

A notice of levy was served on you and demand was made for the surrender of:

☐ all property, rights to property, money, credits and bank deposits of the taxpayer(s) named above, except as provided in 6332(c) of the Internal Revenue Code—"Special Rule For Banks." See the back of this form regarding this exception.

☐ wages, salary and other income, now owed to or becoming payable to the taxpayer(s) named above.

The box checked below applies to the levy we served on you.

Release of Levy

☐ Under the provisions of Internal Revenue Code section 6343, all property, rights to property, money, credits, and bank deposits of the taxpayer(s) named above are released from the levy.

☐ Under the provisions of Internal Revenue Code section 6343, all wages, salary and other income now owed to or becoming payable to the taxpayer(s) named above are released from the levy.

Release of Property from Levy

☐ Under the provisions of Internal Revenue Code section 6343, all property, rights to property, money, credits, and bank deposits greater than $ _____ are released from the levy. The levy now attaches only to this amount.

☐ The last payment we received from you was $ _____ dated _____ . The amount the taxpayer still owes is $ _____ . When this amount is paid to the Internal Revenue Service, the levy is released. If you sent us a payment after the last payment date shown, subtract that from the amount you send now.

☐ Under the provisions of Internal Revenue code section 6343, all wages, salary and other income ☐ greater than
☐ less than $ _____ each _____ now owed to or becoming payable to the taxpayer(s) named above are released from the levy.

Dated at _____ , 19 ___
(Place) _(Date)_

Signature _____ Telephone Number _____ Title _____

Part 2 — For Taxpayer
Cat. No. 20450C
Form **668-D** (Rev. 05-97)

Excerpts from the Internal Revenue Code

Sec. 6332 Surrender of Property Subject to Levy

(c) Special Rule for Banks.—Any bank (as defined in section 408(n)) shall surrender (subject to an attachment or execution under judicial process) any deposits (including interest thereon) in such bank only after 21 days after service of levy.

* * * * * *

Sec. 6343. Authority to Release Levy and Return Property

(a) Release of Levy and Notice of Release.—

(1) In general.—Under regulations prescribed by the Secretary, the Secretary shall release the levy upon all, or part of, the property or rights to property levied upon and shall promptly notify the person upon whom such levy was made (if any) that such levy has been released if—

(A) the liability for which such levy was made is satisfied or becomes unenforceable by reason of lapse of time,

(B) release of such levy will facilitate the collection of such liability,

(C) the taxpayer has entered into an agreement under section 6159 to satisfy such liability by means of installment payments, unless such agreement provides otherwise,

(D) the Secretary has determined that such levy is creating an economic hardship due to the financial condition of the taxpayer, or

(E) the fair market value of the property exceeds such liability and release of the levy on a part of such property could be made without hindering the collection of such liability.

For purposes of subparagraph (C), the Secretary is not required to release such levy if such release would jeopardize the secured creditor status of the Secretary.

(2) Expedited determination of certain business property.—In the case of any tangible personal property essential in carrying on the trade or business of the taxpayer, the Secretary shall provide for an expedited determination under paragraph (1) if levy on such tangible personal property would prevent the taxpayer from carrying on such trade or business.

(3) Subsequent levy.—The release of levy on any property under paragraph (1) shall not prevent any subsequent levy on such property.

(b) Return of property.—

If the Secretary determines that property has been wrongfully levied upon, it shall be lawful for the Secretary to return . . . an amount equal to the amount of money levied upon . . . any time before the expiration of 9 months from the date of such levy . . . .

(d) Return of Property in Certain Cases.—If—

(1) any property has been levied upon, and

(2) the Secretary determines that—

(A) the levy on such property was premature or otherwise not in accordance with administrative procedures of the Secretary,

(B) the taxpayer has entered into an agreement under section 6159 to satisfy the tax liability for which the levy was imposed by means of installment payments, unless such agreement provides otherwise,

(C) the return of such property will facilitate the collection of the tax liability, or

(D) with the consent of the taxpayer or the Taxpayer Advocate, the return of such property would be in the best interests of the taxpayer (as determined by the Taxpayer Advocate) and the United States,

the provisions of subsection (b) shall apply in the same manner as if such property had been wrongly levied upon, except that no interest shall be allowed

Form **668-D** (Rev. 05-97)

FORM 15.25
RELEASE OF LEVY

Form **668-E** (Rev. July 1989)	Department of the Treasury — Internal Revenue Service **Release of Levy**
Account of	

On the_____day of_____, 19_____, certain property or rights to property belonging

to the above-named taxpayer were levied upon under a levy dated_____, 19_____.

Under the provisions of section 6343, Internal Revenue Code, the following property or rights to property

are released from the levy when the recipient signs the receipt on the back of this form:

Dated at_____this_____day of _____, 19_____.

Signature	Title	Telephone Number

Part 1 — For IRS   Form 668-E (Rev. 7-89)

Receipt for Property returned under Release of Levy

I acknowledge receipt of the property or rights to property listed and described on the front of this form, and I accept the property as being in the same condition as when seized. Further, I waive all claims against the United States for any damages or expenses incurred in connection with this seizure.

Dated at _____ this _____ day of _____ , 19___.

Signature of recipient	

In the presence of:

Name *(Signature)*	Address
Name *(Signature)*	Address

Internal Revenue Code

Sec. 6343. Authority to Release Levy and Return Property.

(a) **Release of Levy and Notice of Release.—**

(1) **In general.—**Under regulations prescribed by the Secretary, the Secretary shall release the levy upon all, or part of, the property or rights to property levied upon and shall promptly notify the person upon whom such levy was made *(if any)* that such levy has been released if—

(A) the liability for which such levy was made is satisfied or becomes unenforceable by reason of lapse of time,

(B) release of such levy will facilitate the collection of such liability,

(C) the taxpayer has entered into an agreement under section 6159 to satisfy such liability by means of installment payments, unless such agreement provides otherwise,

(D) the Secretary has determined that such levy is creating an economic hardship due to the financial condition of the taxpayer, or

(E) the fair market value of the property exceeds such liability and release of the levy on a part of such property could be made without hindering the collection of such liability.

For purposes of subparagraph (C), the Secretary is not required to release such levy if such release would jeopardize the secured creditor status of the Secretary.

(2) **Expedited determination on certain business property.—**In the case of any tangible personal property essential in carrying on the trade or business of the taxpayer, the Secretary shall provide for an expedited determination under paragraph (1) if levy on such tangible personal property would prevent the taxpayer from carrying on such trade or business.

(3) **Subsequent levy.—**The release of levy on any property under paragraph (1) shall not prevent any subsequent levy on such property.

Sec. 6502. Collection after assessment.

(a) **Length of period.—**Where the assessment of any tax imposed by this title has been made within the period of limitation properly applicable thereto, such tax may be collected by levy or by a proceeding in court, but only if the levy is made or the proceeding begun—

(1) within 6 years after the assessment of the tax, or

(2) prior to the expiration of any period for collection agreed upon in writing by the Secretary and the taxpayer before the expiration of such 6-year period *(or, if there is a release of levy under section 6343 after such 6-year period, then before such release).*

(b) **Date when Levy is considered made.—**The date on which a levy on property or rights to property is made shall be the date on which the notice of seizure provided in section 6335(a) is given.

Form 668-E (Rev. 7-89)

¶ 15.11   MINIMIZING THE EFFECT OF LEVIES: JUDICIAL ACTIONS INVOLVING LEVIES

[1] Injunctions

Once enforced collection action has begun, the relief a taxpayer or third person often seeks from the courts is an order restraining the Service from continuing its collection activity. These injunction actions are usually unsuccessful because Congress has specifically prohibited injunctions in tax cases. The Anti-Injunction Act, Section 7421, provides that "no suit for the purpose of restraining the assessment and collection of any tax shall be maintained in any court by any person." The rationale for this statutory prohibition is two-fold. First, an injunction is an equitable remedy that traditionally is unavailable if the person seeking the relief has an adequate legal remedy. Taxpayers may pay the assessed tax and obtain judicial review of the assessment in a refund suit, and, of course, prior to assessment the taxpayer can petition the Tax Court for judicial review. Second, because the tax assessment has been said to have the force of a judgment and, in any event, is supposed to represent a considered finding of the administrator, the requirements of government could not be met if collection of a tax were halted at the option of taxpayers until the conclusion of a time-consuming court action.[442] The statutory language and the force of the rationale behind the statute have made successful injunction actions quite rare.

Despite the absolute prohibition contained in the Anti-Injunction Act, injunctions have nevertheless been granted where (1) the statute itself permits; (2) there is procedural irregularity in the collection process; and (3) the standards of the *Enochs v. Williams Packing & Navigation Co.*[443] and *Commissioner v. Shapiro*[444] have been met.[445] Less clearly, collection may be enjoined (1) where the assessment is based on illegally seized evidence; (2) during a refund suit; and (3) where the taxpayer will suffer irreparable harm.

[a] Statutory Exception

By its own terms, the stated exceptions in Section 7421, the Anti-Injunction Act, do not apply where the Service has failed to send the taxpayer a no-

---

[442] Bull v. United States, 295 US 247 (1935); Phillips v. Comm'r, 283 US 589 (1931).

[443] Enochs v. Williams Packing & Navigation Co., 370 US 1 (1962).

[444] Comm'r. v. Shapiro, 424 US 614 (1976).

[445] Congress had prohibited injunctions to contest the validity of agency actions other than those of the IRS, and courts have also granted limited judicial review. See ¶ 1.03[2][b].

tice of deficiency as required by Section 6212(a) or, after the taxpayer has filed a Tax Court petition in response to an initial notice of deficiency, where the Service has sent a further notice in violation of Section 6212(c). In *Laing v. United States*, the Supreme Court reinstated a taxpayer's injunction action after finding that the Service had failed to send a required notice of deficiency.[446] The Anti-Injunction Act also does not apply where a tax is assessed and collection is made during the ninety-day period granted a taxpayer to file a petition for review in the Tax Court, as well as during the action's pendency in that court.[447] Similarly, in a wrongful levy action brought in a federal district court by a third person, the court has jurisdiction to prohibit the enforcement of the levy or sale of the seized property.[448] This statutory exception incorporates prior case law inferring that an injunction was proper where sought by a third person who claimed that the levy and seizure were wrongful.[449]

That an injunction should be granted where the Service fails to comply with one or more of the statutory provisions excepted from its operation may be implied from the language of Section 7421. Without injunction, these statutory exceptions are reduced to trivial legislative suggestions rather than fundamental procedures governing judicial review of the Service's determination of a taxpayer's liability and the manner in which tax is to be collected by administrative levy. Courts have granted injunctions where one of the statutory exceptions has been violated.[450] However, in some cases, courts have said that in addition to the statutory violation, irreparable harm and an inadequate legal

---

[446] In Laing v. United States, 423 US 161 (1976), the Service had failed to send a notice of deficiency after a termination assessment, a requirement the Supreme Court found to exist, but Congress overruled in the Tax Reform Act of 1976, § 1204, amending Section 6851 of the Code.

[447] Section 7421(a) refers to Section 6213(a). See, e.g., Dierks v. United States, 215 F. Supp 338 (SDNY 1963) (collection attempted before Tax Court decision became final). The Tax Court has been granted jurisdiction to enjoin collection of tax where the restrictions of Section 6213(a) have been violated, provided that a timely petition has been filed in the court. For further discussion of the restrictions on assessment and when a notice of deficiency will be considered to have been sent within the meaning of the statute, see ¶ 10.03[2]. Once the Tax Court has rendered a decision, assessment and collection are prohibited only if the taxpayer posts an appeal bond. IRC § 7485(a)(1). See Akers v. United States, 539 F. Supp. 831 (D. Conn. 1982) (levy after taxpayer apparently failed to post bond).

[448] IRC § 7421(a) refers to IRC §§ 7426(a) and 7426(b)(1). Note that for the purpose of the action, the tax assessment is conclusively presumed to be correct. IRC § 7426(c).

[449] Bullock v. Latham, 306 F2d 45 (2d Cir. 1962); Tomlinson v. Smith, 128 F2d 808 (7th Cir. 1942); Raffaele v. Granger, 196 F2d 620 (3d Cir. 1952) (joint bank account); Pool v. Walsh, 282 F. 620 (9th Cir. 1922) (wrong property seized); Glenn v. American Sur. Co., 160 F2d 977 (6th Cir. 1947) (same).

[450] See the cases cited supra at notes 445, 446, and 448.

remedy must also be shown before the injunction will be granted.[451] This approach shifts the focus of the Anti-Injunction Act from a means of controlling administrative violations of law to an analysis of the taxpayer's actions and ability to pay.[452]

[b] Procedural Irregularities

Where the requirements of law have not been followed, the defects taint the collection process. Thus, where there has been no demand for payment of a tax or a levy within the ten-day grace period provided by Section 6331, collection has been enjoined.[453] For example, in *United States v. Bonaguro*, the court granted the defendant-taxpayer's motion for an order directing the return of allegedly counterfeit currency and suppressing evidence that he possessed the currency at the time of his arrest after finding, inter alia, that the Service had completely failed to take the formal steps under the jeopardy statutes by not even making the internal findings and declaration required under Section 6851(a) nor entertaining the belief required by Section 6861(a).[454]

An injunction has also been granted where it is alleged that the Service has failed to follow the statutory provisions relating to the sale of seized property,[455] provided that the merits of the tax assessment are not contested.

It is possible that an injunction may also be granted where the Service fails to follow its own procedural rules as opposed to statutory requirements, if the failure affects substantial rights of the taxpayer—that is, if the taxpayer is

---

[451] Flynn v. United States, 786 F2d 586 (3d Cir. 1986). See also Philadelphia & Reading Corp. v. Beck, 676 F2d 1159 (7th Cir. 1982). *Flynn* and *Philadelphia Reading Corp.* might be rationalized on the ground that the taxpayers had waived prepayment judicial review. See ¶ 1.05[5][a]. For a critical analysis of the issue, see Andrews, "The Use of the Injunction as a Remedy for an Invalid Federal Tax Assessment," 40 Tax L. Rev. 653 (Summer 1985).

[452] However, if irreparable harm and an inadequate legal remedy can be shown, an injunction has been granted. Jensen v. IRS, 835 F2d 196 (9th Cir. 1987).

[453] See, e.g., Mrizek v. Long, 187 F. Supp. 830 (ND Ill. 1959); LOC Indus., Inc. v. United States, 423 F. Supp. 265 (MD Tenn. 1976); Bauer v. Foley, 404 F2d 1215 (2d Cir. 1968), on rehearing, 408 F2d 1331 (2d Cir. 1969); Steiner v. Nelson, 259 F2d 853 (7th Cir. 1958). See also Shapiro v. Secretary of State, 499 F2d 527 n.12 (DC Cir. 1974), aff'd and remanded sub nom. Comm'r. v. Shapiro, 424 US 614 (1976) ("(i)f proven, this alleged failure by the IRS to adhere to the statute (by failing to send a notice and demand) might well be sufficient basis for an injunction against the levies, assuming the presence of the other essentials of equitable jurisdiction"). See also Stroman v. McCanless, 391 F. Supp. 1344 (ND Tex. 1975) (assessment in violation of agreement).

[454] United States v. Bonaguro, 294 F. Supp. 750 (EDNY 1968), aff'd sub nom. United States v. Dono, 428 F2d 204 (2d Cir.), cert. denied, 400 US 829 (1970). See also Rogan v. Mertens, 153 F2d 937 (9th Cir. 1946).

[455] See Margiotta v. District Director, 214 F2d 518 (2d Cir. 1954), Aqua Bar & Lounge, Inc., v. United States, 539 F2d 935 (3d Cir. 1976).

denied administrative due process. This result is supported by extension of the authority that an injunction is proper where the Service has failed to follow statutory requirements. It is also consistent with the "*Accardi* doctrine", which states that a governmental agency must follow its own self-promulgated rules.[456] However, an injunction is not appropriate in every case where the Service fails to follow its own rules. Some courts have viewed noncompliance with such rules as conference procedures not warranting judicial intervention because the rule (1) did not have the effect of a Treasury Regulation;[457] (2) was for the benefit of the Service, not taxpayers;[458] or (3) gave Service personnel the discretion not to act in accordance with its terms.[459] Still, where the noncompliance is serious enough, an injunction would seem to be an appropriate remedy.[460]

[c] The *Williams Packing/Shapiro* Standard

Despite the seemingly absolute prohibition of the Anti-Injunction Act, the Supreme Court has ruled that an injunction restraining assessment and collection may be granted (1) "if it is clear that under no circumstances could the government ultimately prevail . . . on the basis of information available to it at the time of the suit . . . (taking) the most liberal view of the law and the facts" and (2) "if equity jurisdiction otherwise exists" because the taxpayer has shown extraordinary circumstances causing irreparable harm for which there is no adequate remedy at law.[461] If both these elements are shown, the exaction is merely "in the guise of a tax."[462] The Supreme Court later clarified its position on the required showing that under no circumstances could the government prevail. In *Commissioner v. Shapiro*,[463] it said that the Service may not make

---

[456] Accardi v. Shaughnessy, 347 US 260 (1954), discussed at ¶ 1.06[3]. See United States v. Sourapas, 515 F2d 295 (9th Cir. 1975); United States v. Leahey, 434 F2d 7 (1st Cir. 1970); United States v. Heiner, 420 F2d 809 (4th Cir. 1969) (applying the *Accardi* doctrine to situations where special agents failed to give Miranda-type warnings as required by Service procedure). However, the First Circuit has said in United States v. Irvine, 699 F2d 43 (1st Cir. 1983), that *Leahey* is no longer good law after United States v. Caceres, 440 US 741 (1979).

[457] See, e.g., Luhring v. Glotzbach, 304 F2d 556 (4th Cir. 1962).

[458] United States v. Goldstein, 342 F. Supp. 661 (EDNY 1972).

[459] Einhorn v. DeWitt, 618 F2d 347 (5th Cir. 1980).

[460] Injunction is not prohibited by United States v. Caceres, 440 US 741 (1979), because there the Supreme Court was faced with a request for suppression of clearly relevant evidence obtained after a good faith but unsuccessful effort to comply with a procedural rule. Where the relief sought is not so drastic as suppression, the Supreme Court did not reject the possibility of judicial action.

[461] Enochs v. Williams Packing & Navigation Co., 370 US 1, 7 (1962).

[462] Miller v. Standard Nut Margarine Co., 248 US 498, 509 (1932).

[463] Comm'r v. Shapiro, 424 US 614 (1976).

conclusory allegations as the basis for the assessment (the *Williams Packing* decision indicated that such allegations were sufficient), although the Service may submit affidavits (as opposed to "oral testimony" examination) disclosing the basic facts from which it appears that the government may prevail. If, on the other hand, the facts do not disclose even "probable cause" to support the assessment, a court is entitled to conclude that the government would be unable to prevail at trial.

Prior to *Shapiro*, taxpayers, and to some extent third persons, had a difficult time in successfully petitioning for an injunction because they were unable to show (1) irreparable injury; (2) no likelihood of the government's success; and (3) no adequate remedy at law. Under *Shapiro*, when irreparable injury was alleged, both procedural due process and the *Williams Packing* gloss on the Anti-Injunction Act were found to require the Service to prove that a seizure has at least some basis in fact. The *Shapiro* requirement that the Service make some showing that its assessment has a reasonable basis was not new. It proceeds from due process considerations and is consistent with a number of cases where the Service had no reasonable basis for the amount of tax assessed, and injunctions were granted.[464] This requirement that there be a reasonable basis for the amount of the assessment is also incorporated in the termination and jeopardy assessment provisions. Consequently, where these assessments are made, an injunction proceeding is not necessary because there is a statutorily provided remedy for the prompt judicial review.[465]

[d] Other Situations

It also appears that, at least where the violation is committed by Service officials, a demand for a collection of tax on the basis of illegally seized evidence may be enjoined.[466] However, the Supreme Court will not reach out for a way to avoid the Anti-Injunction Act even if constitutional issues are involved. The constitutional nature of the claim, as distinct from its probability of success under the *Williams Packing* rule, is of no consequence under the

---

[464] See, e.g., United States v. Bonaguro, 294 F. Supp. 750 (EDNY 1968), aff'd sub nom. United States v. Dono, 428 F2d 204 (2d Cir.), cert. denied, 400 US 829 (1970); Pizzarello v. United States, 408 F2d 579 (2d Cir. 1969); Lassoff v. Gray, 266 F2d 745 (6th Cir. 1959); Willits v. Richardson, 497 F2d 240 (5th Cir. 1974). See also Lucia v. United States, 474 F2d 565, 573 (5th Cir. 1973); Rinieri v. Scanlon, 254 F. Supp. 469 (SDNY 1966).

[465] IRC § 7429, added by the Tax Reform Act of 1976, Pub. L. No. 94-455, § 1204, 90 Stat. 1695–1699.

[466] GM Leasing Corp. v. United States, 429 US 338 (1977) (Fourth Amendment rights violated by Service officials). Compare United States v. Janis, 428 US 433 (1976) (exclusionary rule held not to apply to a civil tax case where the violation was committed by state or local police officials).

Anti-Injunction Act.[467] On the other hand, in exceedingly rare cases, an injunction has been obtained where the financial burden imposed by levying against the personal and business property of a taxpayer would result in irreparable injury.[468] Also, where a taxpayer sues for a refund of tax, but has not paid interest on the tax, and where a divisible tax assessment is involved, the Service can attempt to collect an assessment during the pendency of the refund suit. In this situation, the Anti-Injunction Act's collateral purpose of preventing litigation outside the statutory scheme does not apply and an injunction may be granted.[469]

[2] Actions for Wrongful Levy, Surplus Proceeds, and Substituted Sale Proceeds

Once property has actually been levied upon, there is specific statutory authority for suits against the United States in three situations:[470]

1. *Wrongful levy.* Where property of a third person has been wrongfully levied upon to satisfy the tax liability of another;

2. *Surplus proceeds.* After levy, where property of the taxpayer has been sold and a junior lienholder claims all or part of the surplus proceeds of the sale; and

3. *Substituted sale proceeds.* Where the Service has agreed to the sale of property free and clear of the tax lien, has issued a certificate of discharge, and the taxpayer and third persons, including the government, claim an interest in the substituted sale proceeds.

---

[467] Alexander v. "Americans United" Inc., 416 US 752 (1974); Bob Jones Univ. v. Simon, 416 US 725 (1974). These cases practically eliminate prepayment suits to "constitutionalize" the Code. See McGlotten v. Connally, 338 F. Supp. 448 (DC Cir. 1972). See ¶ 1.05[5][a].

[468] Comm'r. v. Shapiro, 424 US 614 (1976); Pizzarello v. United States, 408 F2d 579 (2d Cir. 1969); Midwest Haulers v. Brady, 128 F2d 496 (6th Cir. 1942).

[469] See Bob Jones Univ. v. Simon, 416 US 725, 748 (1974) n.22 ("Petitioner did not bring this case as a refund action. Accordingly, we have no occasion to decide whether the Service is correct in asserting that a district court may not issue an injunction in such a suit, but is restricted in any case to the issuance of a money judgment against the United States. . . . We note, however, that the Service's position with regard to the range of relief available in a refund suit raises several considerations not presented by a preenforcement suit for an injunction"). Nevertheless, one circuit court has ruled that the Service may collect during the pendency of a divisible tax assessment refund suit. Marvel v. United States, 548 F2d 295 (10th Cir. 1977), cert. denied, 431 US 967 (1977) (no collection action had been taken or was threatened, and the Service represented that there was little likelihood of unilateral seizure absent circumstances jeopardizing the availability of funds after judgment).

[470] IRC § 7426(a).

There are separate rules for each of these judicial actions, but they also share certain procedural characteristics.

[3] Wrongful Levy Actions

In general, if a levy has been made on property, or property has been sold pursuant to a levy, any person other than the taxpayer who claims (1) an interest in or lien on the property and (2) that the property was wrongfully levied upon by the Service may bring a civil action directly against the United States in federal district court.[471] Section 7426 creates a remedy against the United

---

[471] IRC § 7426(a)(1). Since the term "levy" includes "the power of distraint by any means," a formal notice of levy need not have been served. IRC § 6331(b). But see Standard Acceptance Co. v. United States, 342 F. Supp. 45 (ND Ill. 1972). Levy does not occur where a setoff has been made. Reg. § 301.7426-1(a)(1). A suit for wrongful levy should be instituted against the United States, not an individual revenue officer. Baddour, Inc. v. United States, 802 F2d 801, 809 (5th Cir. 1986).

Section 7426 also applies when the Service serves a levy on a debt owed to a taxpayer by another federal agency; therefore, another creditor of the taxpayer may use the wrongful levy statute to enforce a priority claim in an amount owed to the taxpayer. Note, however, that Section 7426 does not apply when the payment is requested by a setoff. Reg. § 301.7426-1(a)(1)(ii) (May 20, 1994). Although Section 7426 provides a limited waiver of sovereign immunity allowing third parties to contest an IRS levy when it interferes with their property rights, the person asserting the wrongful levy claim may not be the one against whom the tax is assessed. McGinness v. United States, 90 F3d 143 (6th Cir. 1996). The remedy also applies only to wrongful levies made to seize property, not to the filing of a tax lien. See United States v. Williams, 514 US 527 (1995) ("If the Government has not levied on property—as it has not on [plaintiff's] home—the owner cannot challenge such a levy under 26 U.S.C. section 7426."); Interfirst Bank of Dallas v. United States, 769 F2d 299 (5th Cir. 1985) (when the Service threatened to file a notice of lien, taxpayer turned over account receivable to the Service, and third-party lender instituted action under Section 7426); see also Colonial Baking Co. of Atlanta v. United States, 40 AFTR2d 77-5649 (ND Ga. 1977) (after both lender and the Service perfected liens, the taxpayer turned accounts receivable over to the Service).

When the Service used the Tax Collection Treaty between the United States and the Netherlands to request the assistance of the Netherlands in seizing and selling property of the taxpayer in the Netherlands (the contents of a safe deposit box in a Dutch bank), the district court concluded that the wrongful levy statute waived sovereign immunity for a suit by the taxpayer's daughters who claimed that they owned the property the Dutch authorities seized and sold. In the court's view, the "use of Dutch assistance to obtain payment of an American debt is . . . an exercise of the power granted by section 6331 to seize property belonging to delinquent taxpayers." Miller v. United States, 921 F. Supp. 494 (ND Ohio 1996) (the court also concluded that the term "levy" was broad enough to include any forced taking of property whether or not Code procedures were used).

Persons other than the taxpayer only have standing under Section 7426(a)(1) if they have an interest in the property wrongfully levied on, "such as a fee simple or equivalent interest, a possessory interest, or a security interest in the property levied upon, or a lien on the property at issue; an unsecured interest is not sufficient to confer standing." See Schupert v. United States, 976 F. Supp. 781, 783 (CD Ill. 1997) (citing Security Counsel-

States for the wrongful levy and sale of property.[472] A person claiming an interest in property seized and sold may bring an action against the purchaser at the tax sale, but Section 7426 is inapplicable to such an action.[473] The question of whether the levy was wrongful is not reached unless the party seeking relief under Section 7426 first establishes ownership of or an interest in the seized property.[474]

---

ors, Inc. v. United States, 860 F2d 867, 869 (8th Cir. 1988)); see also McGinness v. United States, 90 F3d 143, 145 (6th Cir. 1996). Courts have held that fiduciaries and escrow agents do not have standing under Section 7426, nor does a disinterested stakeholder. See Lloyd, Kane & Wieder, P.A. v. United States, 757 F. Supp. 683, 684 (D. Md. 1991); Commonwealth of Pa. v. Nationsbank, 83 AFTR2d ¶ 99-2539 (MD Pa. 1999) (bank filed third-party complaint against the Service, but claimed no interest in levied funds and conceded it was a disinterested stakeholder).

[472] Suppose a nontaxpayer's property is seized, and the nontaxpayer institutes a suit for refund in a federal district court pursuant to 28 USC § 1346(a)(1). It has been held that the suit will be dismissed because Section 7426 is the exclusive remedy for nontaxpayers. Snodgrass v. United States, 834 F2d 537, 539 (5th Cir. 1987); Ehlers v. United States, 90-2 USTC ¶ 50,456 (DNJ 1990). But see Martin v. United States, 895 F2d 992 (4th Cir. 1990) (finding that 28 USC § 1346 covers suit by person from whom tax has been collected); WWSM Investors v. United States, 64 F3d 456 (9th Cir. 1995) (finding that under the Supreme Court's decision in Williams, a third party could sue the government under 28 USC § 1346(a)(1) to recover taxes it had paid for another; a divided court).

[473] World Marketing Ltd. v. Hallam, 608 F2d 392 (9th Cir. 1979). See Crow v. Wyoming Timber Prods. Co., 424 F2d 93 (10th Cir. 1970).

[474] See Smith v. United States, 590 F2d 304 (9th Cir. 1979) (claimant failed to establish ownership); Arth v. United States, 735 F2d 1190, 1193 (9th Cir. 1984) ("Property is wrongfully levied if it does not, in whole or in part, belong to the taxpayer against whom the levy originated"). In Arth, the circuit court said that the burden of proof is on the nontaxpayer "to prove that property that appears to be the taxpayer's is actually his." Id. at 1193. Although the third-party nontaxpayer in Arth could trace the funds levied to his separate funds, the district court's factual finding was that the funds, once placed in the taxpayer's account, belonged to the taxpayer. Marotta v. United States, 82-1 USTC ¶ 9115 (NDNY 1981) (where Service has burden of showing some nexus between taxpayer and property seized, claimant must first establish she had an interest in seized property, and she failed to do so). See also Blackburn v. United States, 85-1 USTC ¶ 9166 (MD Tenn. 1984) (wife could not prove purchase of husband's car before lien and levy); Schachle v. United States, 86-2 USTC ¶ 9689 (D. Or. 1986) (plaintiff failed to prove that bonds seized by the Service were her property). In a wrongful levy action, the plaintiff has the initial burden of coming forward with evidence to prove that "he has title or some other ownership of the property and that the government has made a levy on that property because of a tax assessment against another taxpayer, and that after such a showing . . . (is) made by the taxpayer, the burden then shift(s) to the government to prove a nexus." Morris v. United States, 813 F2d 343 (11th Cir. 1987) (Service must justify seizure of a third party's property, but the plaintiff/third party retains "the ultimate burden of proof of persuading the district court that the levy should be overturned" (citations omitted)). Forfeiture of a corporation's articles of incorporation under state law does not operate as a dissolution and conveyance entitling the shareholders to use the wrongful levy statute. Pottorf v. United States, 773 F. Supp. 1491 (D. Kan. 1991) (Kansas law applied); Dubisky

Assuming the claimant establishes ownership of or an interest in the property, a levy is wrongful where (1) the levy is on property exempt from levy;[475] (2) the levy is upon property in which the taxpayer had no interest at the time the lien arose "or thereafter";[476] (3) the levy is on property with respect to which the third person is a purchaser against whom the lien is invalid because notice of lien was not filed at the time of purchase or the purchaser is entitled to "superpriority" status;[477] or (4) the levy or sale pursuant to levy does or will effectively destroy or irreparably injure a senior lienor's interest in the property.[478] A levy may be wrongful as to a senior lien or even if the lienor's rights

v. United States, 62 F3d 182 (7th Cir. 1995) (children of taxpayer donor had the burden of proving that their father had made gifts to them under Illinois law, and failed to show that the district court's adverse finding was clearly erroneous because (1) the father frequently drew funds from the purported trust accounts for his own use; (2) there was virtually no documentary evidence of the existence of the trust; and (3) only small amounts were withdrawn from the accounts for the children).

The analysis can be quite refined when real property is involved. It is established that state law defines the rights of a taxpayer that the Service can sell. When the Service attempted to sell a taxpayer-husband's interest in real property that was the marital abode held as a joint tenancy with right of survivorship, a majority of the circuit court held that the Service could sell only the taxpayer-husband's right of survivorship; the Service could not sell his interest in the homestead without his wife's consent, nor could it sell the right to unilaterally sever the joint tenancy or the right to use and occupy the property. O'Hagan v. United States, 86 F3d 776 (8th Cir. 1996) (applying Minnesota law).

[475] It is difficult to see how a third party (as opposed to the taxpayer) would bring this type of wrongful levy action.

[476] Despite the regulation's reference to the tax lien, it has been held that a levy was wrongful because at the time the levy was served, the taxpayer had no interest in the bank account levied upon because of the bank's setoff. Pittsburgh Nat'l Bank v. United States, 657 F2d 36 (3d Cir. 1981). Compare Texas Commerce Bank-Fort Worth, NA v. United States, 896 F2d 152 (5th Cir. 1990) (bank properly instituted wrongful-levy action because it claimed an interest in the levied funds; bank was not required to surrender the funds to IRS before it instituted a wrongful-levy action). See Morrison v. United States, 83 AFTR2d 99-1507 (WD Pa. 1999) (claimant of a bank account in the name of herself and the taxpayer was held to be the owner of the account because she was the source of the funds in the account). Compare Craig v. United States, 84 AFTR2d 99-6753 (SD Tex. 1999) (beneficiary, who was also executor of his father's estate, opened a checking account in his name as executor of the estate and deposited funds from the estate into the account; held, the evidence showed that the account was the estate's account, not the beneficiary/executor's personal account, and so the Service's levy to collect tax owed by the beneficiary/executor was wrongful because the funds belonged to the estate).

[477] IRC §§ 6323, 6324(a)(2), 6324(b).

[478] Reg. § 301.7426-1(b)(1)(iv)(d). See Trust Co. v. United States, 565 F. Supp. 61 (MD Ga. 1983). The interest of a senior lienor was destroyed when the IRS failed to describe the senior lien in the notice of sale and in the certificate of sale given to the buyer at the tax sale. Bank of Neb. v. United States, 949 F2d 262 (8th Cir. 1991) ("By not registering the Bank's interest on the certificates of sale it issued, the IRS paved the way for (tax sale purchaser) to destroy the bank's interest in the trucks."); compare National Bank

to enforce the lien survive the levy procedure.[479] However, merely because a tax lien is junior to a third person's senior lien does not make the sale of the property subject to the senior nontax lien a "wrongful levy." The regulations were meant to apply to a situation where the senior lienor (A) has a security interest in an obligation that C owes taxpayer B that will be discharged on satisfaction of a levy served on and honored by C, thereby effectively destroying A's security.[480]

Where a wrongful levy action is involved, injunctive relief is available if the court determines that (1) the levy has been wrongful; (2) the levy or sale of property pursuant to the levy would irreparably injure the rights of a third party in the property; and (3) the rights of the third party in the property are superior to the rights of the United States.[481] If the court's determination is in favor of the third party, the injunction is either made permanent where the government does not have possession of the property or, if the government has possession of the property, is continued until the levy is released and the specific property is returned to the person.

If the court determines that the government's levy is wrongful, it may grant one of three alternative types of relief to a third party: (1) the court may order the return of specific property if it is in the government's possession; (2) it may grant a judgment for the amount of money levied upon; or (3) it may grant a judgment for an amount not exceeding the amount received by the United States from the sale of the property or the fair market value of the property immediately before the levy.[482] The return of property wrongfully lev-

---

& Trust Co. v. United States, 589 F2d 1298 (7th Cir. 1978) (bank's interest not destroyed by sale, because property still available as source of collection within state).

[479] Reg. § 301.7426-1(b)(1)(iv).

[480] Reg. § 301.7426.1(b)(2). The regulations also state that the levy is wrongful even if A may sue the taxpayer on the loan or C in tort, and they list some of the factors to be considered in determining whether the property levied upon will remain a realistic source of collection to a senior lienor after levy and sale. See Stratos v. United States, 79-1 USTC ¶ 9,304, (DSC 1979), aff'd mem., 626 F2d 863 (4th Cir. 1980), cert. denied, 449 US 1079 (1981) (senior lienor could not prevent sale after levy under Section 7426). For a case where a levy was held wrongful because it irreparably injured or destroyed a creditor's interest, see CIM Int'l v. United States, 641 F2d 671 (9th Cir. 1981). A creditor of a debtor in bankruptcy claimed proceeds of the sale of property on which the creditor had an attachment lien and the Service had a tax lien. The district court held that the Service had to marshal its claims against the debtor-taxpayer in the bankruptcy. In re Morahan, 85-2 USTC ¶ 9715, 53 Bankr. 489 (D. Me. 1985) (rejecting claims that Service had priority under Section 6323(a) and that sovereign immunity precluded suit).

[481] IRC § 7426(b)(1); Reg. § 301.7426-1(b)(1)(i). In a wrongful levy action, a district court preliminarily enjoined the Service from effecting the levy and the sale of property, claimed to be owned by a trust, to satisfy the liability of its settlor. Palmer v. IRS, 86-2 USTC ¶ 9656 (D. Idaho 1986).

[482] IRC § 7426(b)(2); Reg. §§ 301.7426-1(b)(1)(ii)–301.7426(b)(1)(iv). Where the judgment is under alternatives (2) and (3), the plaintiff is entitled to interest as provided

ied upon can be ordered by the court only where the property is identifiable and still in the government's possession (e.g., a coin collection).[483]

Where the government wrongfully levies upon money, relief in the form of a judgment is in the amount of the money seized.[484] Where the government wrongfully levies upon other property and sells the seized property, the judgment is limited to the amount the government received from its sale or the pre-levy of the property.[485] This limit creates a possible detriment to a senior lienor where the amount received on the sale is deflated. If the property was purchased by the government at the sale, the "amount received" from the sale is the minimum price at which the government would have allowed the property to be sold or, if more, the amount received by the government when it later resold the property. Moreover, a senior lienor is not permitted to recover the damage to the property or loss in value of the property while it is in the custody of the Service.[486]

[4] Surplus Proceeds

The sale of seized property may produce an amount that exceeds the tax claim. If surplus proceeds have been realized from the sale of property, any person (other than the taxpayer) who claims an interest in or lien upon the property junior to the lien or interest of the United States, and that he is legally entitled to all or part of the surplus proceeds, may bring an action against the United

---

by law. IRC § 7426(g). Interest on money wrongfully levied upon is calculated from the date the Service receives the money. Hammond Co. v. United States, 568 F. Supp. 309 (SD Cal. 1983). The Service also reimburses taxpayers for bank charges that arise from wrongful levies on bank accounts, including overdraft charges and bank fees for processing the levy. IR 86-74 (May 20, 1986) (taxpayer should use Form 5646 and send it to address on levy, but a letter with taxpayer's identification number and other information can also be used).

[483] IRC § 7426(b)(2)(A).

[484] Reg. § 301.7426-1(b)(1)(iii).

[485] IRC § 7426(b)(2)(C); Reg. § 301.7426-1(b)(1)(iv). Where a wrongful levy was served before the effective date of the amendment of Section 7426(b)(2)(C), the third party whose property was wrongfully seized was entitled to compensation in the amount of the value of the property on the date of the levy. Baddour, Inc. v. United States, 802 F2d 801 (5th Cir. 1986).

[486] But see United States v. Pittman, 449 F2d 623 (7th Cir. 1971) (taxpayer was entitled to a credit against his tax liability for the amount of deterioration in value of seized property). In general, the policy of Congress announced in the Federal Tort Claims Act, 28 USC § 2680(c), is to deny the right to sue the government for damages for acts relating to tax collection, at least where the claim is for loss of rent and profit as opposed to damage to property. Young v. United States, 75-2 USTC ¶ 9574 (SDNY 1975). However, where a violation of constitutional rights is involved, an action against the revenue officials involved may be maintained. GM Leasing Corp. v. United States, 429 US 338 (1977).

States in a federal district court to recover the surplus proceeds.[487] The term "surplus proceeds" means proceeds in excess of the amount necessary to satisfy the tax liability giving rise to the levy and the expenses of the levy sale.[488] An action for surplus proceeds is based on a kind of wrongful levy, because once a taxpayer's liability is satisfied, the government's retention of the proceeds is wrongful to the person legally entitled to them. Consequently, if a court determines that the interest or lien of any party was transferred to the proceeds of sale of property sold pursuant to a levy, it may grant a judgment against the United States in an amount equal to all or any part of the amount of the surplus proceeds of the sale.

[5] Substituted Sale Proceeds

The Service may issue a certificate of discharge where property subject to a tax lien is sold and, under an agreement with the Service, the proceeds from the sale (substituted sales proceeds) are held as a fund subject to the liens and claims of the United States in the same manner and with the same priority as the liens and claims on the discharged property.[489] The new procedure for the issuance of a certificate of discharge was instituted to aid, for example, in the disposition of property where a dispute exists among competing lienors, including the taxpayer and government, concerning their right to specific property. Where the competing lienors are unable to resolve the matter, the United States may be joined in an action to determine the respective rights of the parties to the substituted sale proceeds.[490] The party bringing the action need not have been a party to the agreement providing for the discharge of the lien if the party claims to be legally entitled to all or any part of the fund from the sale of the property. If the court determines that a party has an interest in or lien on the fund, it has jurisdiction to grant a judgment in an amount equal to all or any part of the fund.

[6] Procedure

It is unnecessary to file a claim for refund before an action under Section 7426 may be commenced.[491] The action must be brought against the United States

---

[487] IRC § 7426(a)(2); Reg. § 301.7426-1(a)(2).

[488] Reg. § 301.7426-1(b)(3).

[489] IRC § 6325(b).

[490] IRC § 7426(a)(3); Reg. § 301.7426-1(a)(3).

[491] IRC § 7426(f). If an administrative claim is filed, however, the claim must be timely filed or else a later suit will be barred. See infra note 250.

and not against any officer or employee of the Service.[492] The action must be brought in a federal, not a state, court. Unlike 28 USC Section 2410, which is a consent statute only (that is, the United States merely consents to its joinder in actions for which jurisdiction otherwise exists under state or federal law), federal district courts are granted specific jurisdiction over actions brought under Section 7426.[493]

Actions under Section 7426 are to be brought only in the judicial district where the property levied on is situated at the time of levy. Where the action does not arise out of a wrongful levy (e.g., in certain cases involving substituted sale agreements), the action is to be brought where the event giving rise to the law suit occurred.[494] In *Gordon v. United States*, the Court of Claims held that it had subject matter jurisdiction under the Tucker Act (28 USC § 1491) to hear an action brought by a person claiming his property had been wrongfully levied upon.[495]

In *The Document Management Group, Inc. v. United States*, the Service improperly levied upon the bank account of the plaintiff corporation, Document Managment Group (DMG), on the erroneous assumption that it was the transferee of a delinquent corporate taxpayer.[496] Immediately following the levy, DMG began negotiations with the Service to release the bank account and its funds. In these discussions, DMG was incorrectly informed that the levy was proper and that it was liable. DMG entered into an installment agreement to pay the uncollected taxes of the delinquent corporate taxpayer. It was subsequently determined that DMG was not the delinquent taxpayer's transferee, and five months later, DMG requested a refund of moneys paid pursuant to the agreement. This claim was denied, and one year and nine months later, DMG brought suit. The Claims Court held that although DMG was a nontaxpayer within the meaning of Section 7701(a)(14), the court could assume jurisdiction and provide judicial relief under the doctrine of implied in-

---

[492] IRC §§ 7426(d), 7426(e). If an officer or employee is named as a party defendant, the United States must be substituted as a party by the court. The summons and complaint must be served on the United States in accordance with Rule 4(m) of the Federal Rules of Civil Procedure. Payne v. United States, 82 AFTR2d 98-6931 (MD Fla. 1998) (wrongful levy suit dismissed because copy of summons and complaint was not timely served on Attorney General; summons and complaint were served within the 120-day period of Rule 4, but not on Attorney General, and good cause for failure was not shown).

[493] 28 USC § 1346(c).

[494] 28 USC § 1402.

[495] Gordon v. United States, 649 F2d 226 (Ct. Cl. 1981). Although finding that its jurisdiction under the Tucker Act was not withdrawn by IRC § 7426, the Court of Claims held that the nine-month limitations period of IRC § 6532(c), rather than the six-year limitations period of 28 USC § 2501, applied to a wrongful levy action in the Court of Claims.

[496] The Document Management Group, Inc. v. United States, 87-1 USTC ¶ 9125, 11 Cl. Ct. 463 (1987)

fact contract jurisdiction. The court further held that the applicable statute of limitations with respect to DMG's claim regarding moneys actually levied from its bank account was the nine-month statute of limitations under Section 7426(a)(1).[497]

The most serious procedural disadvantage in a Section 7426 action is that it must be commenced within an extremely short period of limitations, which has been strictly applied.[498] As a general rule, no suit or proceeding under Sec-

---

[497] However, the six-year statute of limitations under 28 USC § 1491(a)(1) would apply to sums paid by DMG pursuant to its agreement with the Service to remove the levy.

[498] IRC § 6523(c)(2). One court has noted that neither Section 6343(b) nor Reg. § 301.6343-1(b)(1) explicitly requires the claimant to file an administrative claim within nine months of the levy or be time-barred, but that the IRS and the courts have concluded that the requirement exists. Raymond v. United States, 983 F2d 63 (6th Cir. 1993) (claim filed within nine months, but property was returned after nine-month period expired); State Bank of Fraser v. United States, 861 F2d 954, 965–967 (6th Cir. 1988) (bank's written request for return of money was time-barred when filed more than nine months after levy); see the cases cited at ¶ 15.06. See also United Sand & Gravel Contractors, Inc. v. United States, 624 F2d 677 (5th Cir. 1980); Omnibus Fin. Corp. v. United States, 566 F2d 1097 (9th Cir. 1977); Corwin Consultants, Inc. v. Interpublic Group of Cos., Inc., 512 F2d 605 (2d Cir. 1975); Maple Lane Farms v. United States, 82-2 USTC ¶ 9661 (D. Vt. 1982) (suit to recover monies wrongfully levied upon by Service to satisfy tax liability of third person barred because not timely filed within nine-month limitations period). Accord Expoimpe v. United States, 609 F. Supp. 1098 (SD Fla. 1985); Bader v. United States, 86-1 USTC ¶ 9432, 10 Cl. Ct. 78 (Cl. Ct. 1986) (where Service seizes a partner's funds to pay partnership's delinquent taxes, the action is one for wrongful levy subject to nine-month limitations period). The date the nine-month period begins is not the date the affected party learns of the levy, but the date the levy is served. Creditbank v. Milwaukee Elec. Constr., Inc., 707 F. Supp. 513, 515 (SD Fla. 1988); Compagnoni v. United States, 1997 US Dist. LEXIS 7706 (SD Fla. 1997) (levy was served on July 7, 1993, and claimants learned of levies on July 29, 1993, but instituted the wrongful levy action on April 26, 1994, well beyond nine months from the date of the levy; held, the action instituted was untimely). A nontaxpayer has been held to the nine-month statute of limitations of Section 7426, even when the action was commenced as a quiet title action. Winebrenner v. United States, 924 F2d 851 (9th Cir. 1991) (assertion of ownership actions of taxpayer held not to constitute request extending nine-month period); see also Fidelity & Deposit Co. of Md. v. Adelanto, 87 F3d 334 (9th Cir. 1996) (following *Winebrenner* in holding that the exclusive remedy for a third party whose property has been levied upon by the Service is an action under Section 7426, which has a nine-month period to bring the action, not a quiet title action under 28 USC § 2410, which has a six-year statute). Although the person claiming that the levy was wrongful failed to file a claim within the nine-month period, one court has ruled that the claimant is not limited to a wrongful levy action, but can file a suit for refund after the nine-month period and challenge the IRS's seizure, assuming that a claim for refund has been filed. WWSM Investors v. United States, 64 F3d 456 (9th Cir. 1995). The circuit court relied on the Supreme Court's decision that, under 28 USC § 1346(a)(1), a district court had jurisdiction over a third party's suit for the refund of taxes the third party had paid to remove the lien from her property in order to sell it. Williams v. United States, 115 S. Ct. 1611 (1995). One court has held that equitable tolling can apply to a suit under Section 7426 because, unlike Section 6511 (which the Supreme Court held was not subject to equitable

tion 7426 may be begun after nine months from the date of the levy or agreement giving rise to the action.[499] A somewhat longer period of limitations is provided where a claim for administrative refund is filed. Once the nine-month time period has expired, no relief from the statute of limitations is available because most courts have held that the nine-month period is not a statute of limitations, which can be equitably tolled, but a jurisdictional bar, which deprives a district court of jurisdiction and so is unaffected by equitably tolling.[500] Where a request is made for the return of the property, the nine-month period is extended for a period of twelve months from the date of the filing of the request, or for a period of six months from the date of mailing by registered or certified mail by the Service to the person making the request of a no-

---

tolling), Section 6532(c) is "simple in language and construction, like the provision at issue" in Irwin v. Department of Veterans Affairs, 498 US 89 (1990). See Becton Dickinson & Co. v. Wolckenhauer, 82 AFTR2d 98-7184 (DNJ 1998) (court nevertheless held that equitable tolling did not apply because company failed to act actively and diligently; it could have requested extension of nine-month period for filing administrative claim); see also The Gothenburg State Bank & Trust Co. v. United States, 83 AFTR2d ¶ 99-2342 (D. Neb. 1999) (following *Becton Dickenson* and finding that although equitable tolling could apply, there was no evidence that circumstances beyond the control of the bank prevented it from filing a timely claim). On January 20, 1998, the Service served a Notice of Levy on proceeds from the sale of real property held in escrow with All American Land Services, Inc. The taxpayer, La Bonte, claimed a priority interest to the proceeds located in escrow, and negotiations continued with the Service until September 22, 1999, when La Bonte filed a wrongful levy action under Section 7426(a)(1). The taxpayer's suit was untimely because La Bonte did not file suit within nine months of the date of levy. Moreover, the twelve-month exception under Section 6532(c)(2) did not apply because La Bonte failed to address his earlier letter to the district director, as required by Reg. § 301.6343-2(b). Likewise, the court rejected La Bonte's assertion of equitable estoppel because he had failed to establish affirmative misconduct by the government. La Bonte v. United States, 86 AFTR2d 2000-7172 (7th Cir. 2000).

[499] Service of the notice of levy triggers the running of the statute of limitations for purposes of Section 6532(c). Williams v. United States, 947 F2d 37 (2d Cir. 1991) (cases gathered).

[500] Becton Dickinson & Co. v. Wolckenhauer, 85 AFTR2d 2000-1994 (215 F3d 340) (cases on this point gathered). In *Becton Dickinson*, the circuit court rejected an employer's claim that the nine-month period should be equitably tolled, although the employer, which had sued a former employee who had defrauded it for restitution, was unable to secure a judgment giving it an interest in pension and retirement benefits the Service seized until after the nine-month period expired. Similarly, when a levy payment creates an overpayment to a taxpayer's account, money may be returned at any time within nine months after the date of the levy (and a reasonable amount of time after the nine-month period if a timely request has been filed), but the National Office's position is that the overpayment may not be manually refunded if the nine-month period has elapsed. IRS Service Center Advice, SCA 200028036 (June 15, 2000). Once the nine-month period has elapsed, the National Office position is that the normal refund procedures of Section 6511 apply.

tice of disallowance, whichever is shorter.[501] A wrongful levy action also has another procedural disadvantage over which the taxpayer has no control. During the pendency of a wrongful levy action, the statute of limitations on collection is suspended.[502]

¶ 15.12 DECLARATORY JUDGMENT AND QUIET TITLE ACTIONS

Since the prohibition against declaratory judgments is at least as broad as the prohibition against injunctions in tax cases, it seems that a taxpayer may obtain declaratory relief in those situations where an injunction might have been obtained, provided that the merits of the tax assessment are not at issue.[503] Nontaxpayers may obtain a declaration of the rights of the claimants to surplus proceeds after seizure and sale and to substituted sale proceeds under the provisions of Section 7426.[504]

Although declaratory judgment relief is thus available to a limited extent, third persons and taxpayers alike will find courts more receptive to an action to quiet title, especially where the procedural regularity of the seizure and sale is at issue.[505] When a quiet title action is commenced by a taxpayer under 28 USC Section 2410(a), the federal district court does not have jurisdiction to hear a challenge to the underlying tax assessment. (The deficiency and refund procedures must be used for that kind of challenge to be heard by a court.[506]) However, the district court does have jurisdiction to hear a challenge to the

---

[501] The suit must be filed within two nine-month periods in order for the extension to take effect. Williams v. United States, 947 F2d 37 (2d Cir. 1991), supra note 379. If the suit is not filed within one year after the administrative claim is filed, it will be dismissed as untimely, and a creditor, for example, may lose its only procedural remedy. South La. Bank v. United States, 81 AFTR2d 98-492 (ED La. 1997) (creditor filed suit almost two years after its claim was filed).

[502] IRC § 6503(f). United States v. Billings, 79-2 USTC ¶ 9600 (MD Fla. 1979) (period for collecting 1970 assessment suspended during pendency of mortgagee's wrongful levy action, so that 1977 suit to reduce assessment to judgment was timely).

[503] Aqua Bar & Lounge, Inc. v. United States, 539 F2d 935 (3d Cir. 1976).

[504] Where substituted sale proceeds are involved, even a taxpayer may obtain such relief.

[505] Aqua Bar & Lounge, Inc. v. United States, 539 F2d 935 (3d Cir. 1976) (suit by taxpayer); Popp v. Eberlein, 409 F2d 309 (7th Cir.), cert. denied, 396 US 909 (1969); Yanicelli v. Nash, 354 F. Supp. 143 (DNJ 1973).

[506] See Falik v. United States, 343 F2d 38, 42 (2d Cir. 1965); Kulawy v. United States, 917 F2d 729 (2d Cir. 1990) (28 USC § 2410(a) "does not authorize a taxpayer to challenge an IRS assessment of his tax liability"); Aqua Bar & Lounge, Inc. v. United States, 539 F2d 935 (3d Cir. 1976); Elias v. Connett, 908 F2d 521, 527 (9th Cir. 1990).

procedural regularity in the seizure and sale of the taxpayer's property.[507] For example, in *Kulawy v. United States*, an IRS sale of personal property was invalidated in a quiet title action because the Service sold property eight days after the first public notice, rather than ten days as required by Section 6335(d).[508] Where a third person acquires property subject to a lien, he may

---

[507] Aqua Bar & Lounge, Inc. v. United States, 539 F2d 935 (3d Cir. 1976); Robinson v. United States, 920 F2d 1157 (3d Cir. 1990); Kulawy v. United States, 917 F2d 729 (2d Cir. 1990); Pollack v. United States, 819 F2d 144, 145 (6th Cir. 1987); see also Johnson v. United States, 990 F2d 41 (2d Cir. 1993) (validity of lien filed before expiration of time to file appeal held reviewable in a quiet title action). Some courts have erroneously drawn a distinction between irregularities in the assessment of tax and irregularities in its collection with a district court having jurisdiction over the latter type of challenge, but not the former. Schmidt v. King, 913 F2d 837 (10th Cir. 1990) ("The taxpayers . . . do not challenge the procedures used to enforce the tax lien. . . . They attack the procedures of the assessments and notice and demand and, ultimately adjudication of whether they owe taxes."); Olson v. United States, 90-2 USTC ¶ 50,457 (WD Pa. 1990) (misreading "validity of the tax assessment itself" in *Aqua Bar & Lounge*). As long as the taxpayer is not contesting the merits of the tax assessment, a procedural irregularity in the assessment, such as the failure to send a notice and demand, should be subject to challenge in a quiet title action because the irregularity invalidates the lien, and that issue cannot be heard by the Tax Court in a deficiency proceeding. See, e.g., United States v. Coson, 286 F2d 453 (9th Cir. 1961) (quite title action; absence of demand invalidated lien). There is no reason why an untimely assessment should not also be challengeable in a quiet title action. Where the taxpayer claimed no notice of deficiency had been sent, so that the Service assessment was invalid, a quiet title action, rather than an injunction petition, was held proper. Robinson v. United States, supra (adhering to *Aqua Bar & Lounge* and refusing to follow *Schmidt v. King* and *Elias v. Connett*). In an action under Section 2410, a taxpayer is permitted to challenge not only the procedural regularity of the assessment and notice and demand but also the Service's collection activities. Brewer v. United States, 764 F. Supp. 309 (SDNY 1991); Gentry v. United States, 91-2 USTC ¶ 50,374 (ED Tenn. 1991) (following *Brewer*).

When the Service has sold property and no longer claims a lien or mortgage on the property at the time the suit is commenced, the Ninth Circuit has said that a taxpayer may no longer contest the procedural validity of a tax lien under Section 2410. Hughes v. United States, 953 F2d 531 (9th Cir. 1992) (*Kulawy* distinguished on ground that IRS still claimed lien on property at time of suit). Different Ninth Circuit panels have cast doubt about what had been an accepted interpretation of the scope of a taxpayer's action under 28 USC § 2410. As long as a taxpayer does not contest the merits of the assessment, circuit courts, such as the Second Circuit, have held that the taxpayer may raise any procedural defect in the assessment. At least some judges on the Ninth Circuit believe that only certain types of procedural claims may properly be heard under 28 USC § 2410. See Koff v. United States, 3 F3d 1297 (9th Cir. 1993).

[508] Kulawy v. United States, 917 F2d 729 (2d Cir. 1990). The Service contended that the district court did not have jurisdiction under 28 USC § 2410 to quiet title, because the property had been sold and the taxpayer no longer had an "interest" in the property. This argument was rejected because the taxpayer had possession of the property at the time the quiet title action had been commenced. Id. But see McElvain v. United States, 867 F. Supp. 996 (MD Ala. 1994) (once the IRS has sold property or no longer has an interest in or lien on property, a quiet title action to challenge the regularity of the collection action is not permitted). However, where the Service has sold the taxpayer's property, it has

not pay the amount of the tax lien and sue for a refund; rather, an action to quiet title should be commenced.[509] Where a post-levy quiet title action is instituted, the federal district court more clearly has jurisdiction over federal questions.[510]

¶ 15.13 INTERPLEADER

A person may be served with a levy purporting to seize property or rights to property of a taxpayer and also receive notice that others claim an interest in the property. By honoring the levy of one of the claimants, the person may expose himself to double or multiple liability. In this situation, the person is permitted to join the United States and the other claimants in a single action, known as interpleader, which requires the claimants to litigate among themselves to determine which, if any, has a valid claim.

There are four relevant procedural rules for this type of proceeding. First, the United States has consented to be named in an interpleader action by 28 USC Section 2410(a)(5). However, because 28 USC Section 2410 is only a consent statute, some independent basis for federal jurisdiction must be found if the action is brought in a federal district court. Second, if the basis for federal jurisdiction is diversity, 28 USC Section 1335 authorizes commencement of an interpleader action in a federal district court and makes liberal provision as to jurisdiction, venue, and service of process. However, it has been held that

---

been held that the taxpayer may no longer use a quiet title action to challenge the Service's seizure and sale. Kabakjian v. United States, 83 AFTR2d 99-321 (ED Pa. 1999). The distinction seems to be that if the property has been sold at the time the quiet title action has been commenced, the taxpayer cannot bring the action against the United States under 28 USC § 2410 because the United States no longer claims a lien on the property. See Hughes v. United States, 953 F2d 531 (9th Cir. 1992); Brewer v. United States, 764 F. Supp. 309 (SDNY 1991). However, if the quiet title action has been instituted at the time the IRS has a lien, and before it has sold the property, 28 USC § 2410 applies even if the property is later sold. Kulawy v. United States, 917 F2d 729, 733–734 (2d Cir. 1990).

Similarly, where the Service has already collected the taxpayer's property covered by the lien, the Service has successfully contended that there is no longer a ground for a quiet title action. See Urias v. United States, 84 AFTR2d 99-6605 (SD Cal. 1999) ("As to taxpayer's procedural claims, this court does not have jurisdiction because the property at issue belongs to the United States. Therefore no action for quiet title can be brought and the waiver of sovereign immunity under section 2410 does not apply.").

[509] Busse v. United States, 542 F2d 421 (7th Cir. 1976).

[510] 28 USC §§ 1340, 2463. Bullock v. Latham, 306 F2d 45 (2d Cir. 1962); United States v. Coson, 286 F2d 453 (9th Cir. 1961); Seattle Ass'n of Credit Men v. United States, 240 F2d 906 (9th Cir. 1957). See also Aqua Bar & Lounge, Inc. v. United States, 539 F2d 935 (3d Cir. 1976).

the United States is not a citizen of any state for diversity purposes, so that for jurisdiction to exist under 28 USC Section 1335, there must be at least two claimants of different states.[511] Third, if the basis for federal jurisdiction is the existence of a federal question rather than mere title to the property,[512] Rule 22 of the Federal Rules of Civil Procedure provides rules for a nonstatutory interpleader action. Finally, if no basis for federal jurisdiction exists, the procedural rules of the state court in which the action is commenced must be followed (subject to the provisions of 28 USC Section 2410); however, the United States may, and frequently does, remove the action to the appropriate federal district court pursuant to 28 USC Section 1444.

Apart from the jurisdiction problem of where the interpleader action should be brought, the issue of most concern to the interpleading plaintiff is who will pay the attorney fees for such an action.[513] The government's priority includes not only the amount of the tax lien, including the amount of the tax, penalties, and interest reflected in the lien, but also interest that accrues after the lien has been filed.[514] A disinterested stakeholder is not entitled to attorney fees from a fund where the total amount of the fund is insufficient to satisfy prior federal tax liens.[515] However, fees for a stakeholder's counsel have priority over the claims of judgment creditors provided (1) the stakeholder concedes

---

[511] Kent v. Northern Cal. Registered Office of Am. Friends Serv. Comm., 497 F2d 1325 (9th Cir. 1974) (United States is not a citizen of any state so that there must be at least two other claimants of diverse citizenship).

[512] 28 USC §§ 1340 and 2463 would appear to confer jurisdiction over federal questions. See Bullock v. Latham, 306 F2d 45 (2d Cir. 1962); United States v. Coson, 286 F2d 453 (9th Cir. 1961); Seattle Ass'n of Credit Men v. United States, 240 F2d 906 (9th Cir. 1957). See also Aqua Bar & Lounge, Inc. v. United States, 539 F2d 935 (3d Cir. 1976); St. Louis Union Trust Co. v. Stone, 570 F2d 833 (8th Cir. 1978).

[513] For example, in an interpleader action, applying the standards of Federal Rule of Civil Procedure 19, the taxpayer is an indispensable party whose joinder is necessary, even if the taxpayer does not claim an interest in the interpleaded funds, because the taxpayer's interest will be affected by the judgment. Amoco Prod. Co. v. Aspen Group, 83 AFTR2d 99-766 (D. Colo. 1999).

[514] IRC §§ 6321, 6601(a), 6665(a). Interest continues to run on a tax lien when a fund is interpleaded. Paul Revere Life Ins. Co. v. Brock, Jr., 28 F3d 551 (6th Cir. 1994). This rule is contrary to the developed rule in bankruptcy and insolvency proceedings whereby interest is not charged against a debtor for funds that are in a court's custody. See City of New York v. Saper, 336 US 328 (1994). The rationale for the different result in *Paul Revere Life Insurance* seems to be that the statutory provisions of the Code providing for interest do not contain an exception for interpleaded funds.

[515] United States v. Ball Constr. Co., 355 US 587 (1958); Bank of Am. Nat'l Trust & Sav. Ass'n v. Mamokos, 509 F2d 1217 (9th Cir. 1975); United States v. State Nat'l Bank, 421 F2d 519 (2d Cir. 1970) (lien foreclosure action); Spink v. Jones, 499 F2d 339 (5th Cir. 1974). Campagna-Turano Bakery, Inc. v. United States, 632 F2d 39 (7th Cir. 1980).

liability and (2) the fees bear a reasonable relation to the amount of the admitted liability.[516]

¶ 15.14 CIVIL ACTION FOR UNAUTHORIZED COLLECTION ACTION

Section 7433(a) creates a cause of action against the United States "(i)f, in connection with any collection of Federal tax with respect to a taxpayer, any officer or employee of the Internal Revenue Service recklessly or intentionally disregards any provision of (the Code), or any regulation promulgated under (the Code)."[517] The provision, which is part of the Taxpayer Bill of Rights enacted in 1988 (TBOR1), is a limited waiver of the government's sovereign immunity to permit taxpayers to sue the United States where collection personnel—usually revenue officers—engage in collection action in knowing or reckless violation of a Code provision or regulation.[518] Notice that the stat-

---

[516] Fed. R. Civ. P. 22(1); Corwin Consultants, Inc. v. Interpublic Group of Cos., Inc., 375 F. Supp. 186 (SDNY 1974), rev'd and remanded on other issues, 512 F2d 605 (2d Cir. 1975).

[517] Section 7433 was enacted as part of the Technical and Miscellaneous Revenue Act of 1988 (TAMRA). Pub. L. No. 100-647, 102 Stat. 3442 (Nov. 10, 1988). The section applies to actions by IRS personnel after November 10, 1988, the date of enactment. For a case where the claimed illegal action was held not to be actionable because it occurred in October 1988, not after November 10, 1988, see Shaw v. United States, 20 F3d 182 (5th Cir. 1994). For regulations about wrongful collection actions under Section 7433, see Treas. Reg. § 301.7433-1. After enactment of the Taxpayer Bill of Rights 2, which raised the amount the taxpayer may be awarded from $100,000 to $1,000,000, the regulations were modified. In general, under the regulations, the taxpayer must make a claim in writing to the district director, marked to the attention of the Chief, Special Procedures Function, for the district in which the taxpayer resides. The claim must include: (1) the taxpayer's name, current address, current home and work telephone number, convenient time to be reached, and taxpayer identification number; (2) the grounds for the claim, in reasonable detail, including copies of any relevant notices and other documents from the the Service; (3) a description of injury the taxpayer has suffered, including supporting documentation; (4) the dollar amount of the claim, including any damages that have not been incurred but are reasonably foreseeable, again with any substantiating documentation; and (5) the taxpayer's signature or that of his authorized representative.

[518] Taxpayer Bill of Rights, Pub. L. No. 100-647, 102 Stat. 3342 (1988) Sections 7432 and 7433 have been held applicable only to taxpayers against whom the Service is seeking to collect, not to third parties. See Allied/Royal Parking LP v. United States, 83 AFTR2d ¶ 99-415 (9th Cir. 1999) (Section 7433(a) requires that the plaintiff be the direct taxpayer from whom the Service collected the tax, not a third party); Progressive Bank & Trust Co. v. Moore, 91-1 USTC ¶ 50,192 (ED La. 1991); but see Southland Forming, Inc. v. United States, 81 AFTR2d 98-468 (SD Fla. 1997) (finding that the Supreme Court's reasoning in United States v. Williams, 514 US 527 (1995) undermines cases such as *Progressive Bank* (discussed supra) and *Matrix* (discussed infra), and holding that "the term

ute speaks only of illegal collection action. No cause of action is provided for illegal determination of a tax.[519] The distinction is important. For example, when the Service made a wrongful assessment of a trust fund penalty against the wife for her failure to pay over taxes owed by her husband's business, and the Service proceeded to sell her house, the district court was held not to have jurisdiction because it was the determination of the tax that was illegal, not the collection of the illegal assessment.[520] The action must be brought in a federal

---

taxpayer [in Sections 7432 and 7433] includes . . . a party from whom the IRS seeks to collect deficient tax liabilities"). Accordingly, the taxpayer is a corporation, even if the corporation has lost its charter, the corporation is the "taxpayer" for purposes of bringing a wrongful collection action, as long as state law permits the action as part of the winding up of the corporation's affairs. H.W. Reeder, D.O.P.C. v. United States, 84 AFTR2d 99-5119 (9th Cir. 1999) (state law governs, and under Arizona law, a dissolved corporation is winding up its affairs when it institutes an action for wrongful collection; unpublished opinion).

The IRS has unsuccessfully argued that in order for a taxpayer to bring an action under Section 7432, the taxpayer must have followed the procedures of IRC § 6326 for the administrative appeal of liens. Miller v. United States, 763 F. Supp. 1534 (ND Cal. 1991). Unlike other actions authorized by the Code, the action under Section 7433 must name a specific employee, not the United States, Gonsalves v. IRS, 975 F2d 13 (1st Cir. 1992); American Ass'n of Commodity Traders v. Department of Treasury, 598 F2d 1233, 1235 (1st Cir. 1979).

Section 7426 is the sole remedy of a nontaxpayer to contest collection action, and an action under Section 7433 for damages arising out of improper collection action is permitted only to taxpayers. See Matrix Dev. Corp. v. United States, 815 F. Supp. 297 (ED Wis. 1993) (taxpayer's son and daughter and the son's corporation brought wrongful collection action; action dismissed although they were innocent third parties).

[519] Section 7433 applies to violations of the Code collection provisions and applicable regulations. Violations covered by Section 7433 do not include a claim that the taxpayer does not owe the collected tax or that the IRS failed to follow a procedure it stated it would in an IRS publication. See Gonsalves v. IRS, 975 F2d 13 (1st Cir. 1992) (violation of appeal rights in IRS Publication 5); Thomas v. United States, 94-2 USTC ¶ 50,528 (ED Mich. 1994). Many courts have held that Section 7433 does not provide a remedy for lawful collection action to collect an erroneous assessment. Miller v. United States, 66 F3d 220, 222–223 (9th Cir. 1995), cert. denied (taxpayer may recover in a Section 7433 action for a claimed erroneous or illegal assessment); Shaw v. United States, 20 F3d 182, 184 (5th Cir. 1994), cert. denied (based on the plain language of Section 7433, a taxpayer cannot maintain an action for the improper assessment of taxes); Gonsalves v. IRS, supra; see also Bloom v. United States, 84 AFTR2d 99-5423 (MD Pa. 1999) (after gathering cases and reviewing the legislative history, the court held that Section 7433 does not permit recovery on a claim that the IRS engaged in wrongful collection procedures because its actions were based on an erroneous or illegal assessment).

[520] Shaw v. United States, 20 F3d 182, 184 (5th Cir. 1994), cert. denied. Compare Schipper v. United States, 80 AFTR2d 97-8264 (EDNY 1996) (the Service's action to collect an erroneous refund from former spouse held not to be the collection of a tax; therefore, the former spouse was not required to bring her action about the levies served to seize her property as a wrongful collection action under Section 7433, but could make them the subject of a wrongful disclosure action under Section 7431). See Retirement Care Assocs., Inc. v. United States, 3 F. Supp. 2d 1434 (ND Ga. 1998) (based on an affi-

district court within two years after the cause of the action accrues.[521] Recoverable damages are the following: (1) the actual and direct economic damages sustained as a proximate result of the reckless or intentional actions of the Service employee and (2) the costs of the action, or $100,000, whichever is less.[522] The Taxpayer Bill of Rights 2 increased the cap on recovery for damages from $100,000 to $1 million.[523] In establishing his case, the taxpayer must show that all administrative remedies were exhausted and that an effort was made to mitigate damages (a judgment can be reduced by the amount by which damages could reasonably have been mitigated).[524] In a change from prior law, the Taxpayer Bill of Rights 2 gives the court discretion to reduce an award for unauthorized collection action if the court determines that the taxpayer failed to exhaust available administrative remedies.[525]

[1] Negligent Disregard of Code or Regulations

Section 7433 thus permits a taxpayer to bring an action against the United States in federal district court when a collection officer recklessly or intentionally disregards any provision of the Code or regulations. In addition, if the taxpayer establishes 'liability, he or she is permitted to collect up to $1 million

---

davit of a revenue office that was admittedly erroneous in the amount the taxpayer owed, the Service obtained a writ of entry; held, motion for summary judgment denied because taxpayer and related companies presented sufficient evidence to create a genuine issue of material fact as to whether the affidavit in support of the writ of entry was created in reckless or intentional disregard of the Code and whether they had neglected or refused to pay their taxes).

[521] IRC § 7433(a), 7433(d)(3). See, e.g., Miller v. United States, 813 F. Supp. 715 (ND Cal. 1992) (although Service conceded that assessment and lien were illegal because notice of deficiency was not sent, no improper conduct was found, because taxpayer's June 5, 1990, request to release lien was acted upon on July 27, 1990); Johnson v. United States, 83 AFTR2d 99-2158 (ND Ga. 1999) (wrongful acts of collection took place more than two years before the filing of the action).

[522] IRC § 7433(b).

[523] Taxpayer Bill of Rights 2, § 801(a), amending IRC § 7433(b), for actions of IRS employees occurring after the date of enactment, July 30, 1996.

[524] IRC §§ 7433(c)(1), 7433(c)(2). Intentional disregard of a Code provision or regulation had been held not to include alleged constitutional violations, because agents are personally liable for their behavior under *Bivens*, infra; nor does it include a denial of administrative appeal rights. Gonsalves v. IRS, 975 F2d 13 (1st Cir. 1992) (court did not explain why denial of administrative appeal would not violate Statement of Procedural Rules). Failure to send an administrative claim to the district director in accordance with the regulations will deprive the district court of jurisdiction. Amwest Surety Ins. Co. v. United States, 28 F3d 690 (7th Cir. 1994) (letter to revenue officer); Venen v. United States, 38 F3d 100 (3d Cir. 1994) (letter to revenue officer).

[525] Taxpayer Bill of Rights 2, § 802(a), amending IRC § 7433(d)(1), as of the date of enactment, July 30, 1996.

for actual, direct economic damages that are the proximate result of these reckless or intentional acts. The 1998 Act expanded the liability for wrongful collection actions to include liability when a collection officer negligently disregards the Code or regulations, and provides for the recovery of damages of up to $100,000 for actual damages caused by the negligent disregard.[526] To be able to institute a wrongful collection action, the taxpayer must exhaust all available administrative remedies, such as Appeals review.

[2] Civil Damages for Violations of Bankruptcy Procedures

Section 7433 also permits the recovery of damages when a Service official or employee willfully violates an automatic stay in a bankruptcy proceeding (11 USC Section 362) or a discharge provision (11 USC Section 524).[527] These damages are recoverable in the bankruptcy court; however, Section 7433 is the exclusive remedy for the recovery of damages, not the Bankruptcy Code provision for the recovery of sanctions for the violation of the automatic stay (11 USC Section 362). Administrative and litigation costs may be recovered in accordance with Section 7430, but only those costs that are incurred after the filing of the petition in the bankruptcy court.

A taxpayer's cause of action for wrongful collection action is not to be used in negotiations with Collection as part of a quid pro quo. No Service official may ask a taxpayer to waive a right to bring a civil action against the Service or any Service employee for any action involving an internal revenue tax.[528] There are exceptions if the taxpayer agrees to waive the right knowingly and voluntarily, or if the taxpayer is represented.

[3] Recovery of Damages by Persons Other Than Taxpayers

Nontaxpayers may recover damages if collection officials "recklessly or intentionally, or by reason of negligence, disregarded any provision of the [Code]."[529] The amount of the damages is up to $1 million in the case of reckless or intentional conduct, and $100,000 in the case of negligence, but the damages must be actual, direct, economic damages caused by the misconduct. The nontaxpayer must exhaust all administrative remedies before bringing an action.

---

[526] IRC §§ 7433(a) and 7433(b), as amended by 1998 Act § 3102(a), effective as of the date of enactment, July 22, 1998.

[527] IRC § 7433(e), added by 1998 Act § 3102(c).

[528] 1998 Act § 3468(a).

[529] IRC § 7426(h), as amended by 1998 Act § 3102(b), effective July 22, 1998.

¶ 15.15 JUDICIAL ACTION AGAINST COLLECTION OFFICIALS

Where a person's constitutional rights have been violated, a government official may be personally liable for damages unless the official has acted in good faith.[530] Moreover, property may not be forcibly removed from the person of the taxpayer, or the revenue officer may be personally liable for damages arising out of such tortious conduct as trespass, assault and battery, and conversion.[531] The question becomes not whether the revenue officer is entitled to absolute immunity but whether he will be able to establish nonliability on the basis of his honest (subjective) and reasonable (objective) belief that his conduct was lawful.[532] If actions are taken in good faith and on reasonable grounds, revenue officers are qualifiedly immune from liability for civil rights violations.[533] Suits under the Federal Tort Claims Act are barred by the statute

---

[530] Bivens v. Six Unknown Named Agents of Fed. Bureau of Narcotics, 403 US 388 (1971); GM Leasing Corp. v. United States, 429 US 338 (1978). A full discussion of actions against government officials is beyond the scope of this book. But see W. Gelhorn, C. Byse, P. Strauss, T. Rakoff, & R. Schotland, Administrative Law 1165–1208 (1987); C. Koch, Administrative Law & Practice §§ 8.24–8.27 (1985). Since the enactment of Sections 7432 and 7433 awarding damages against the IRS for improper actions by IRS personnel, courts have held that the statutory scheme adequately protects a taxpayer's right to due process, and have dismissed Bivens actions against the IRS for failure to state a claim. Wages v. IRS, 915 F2d 1230 (9th Cir. 1990), cert. denied, 498 US 1096 (1991); Tonn v. United States, 847 F. Supp. 711 (D. Minn. 1993); Cleveland v. United States, 76 AFTR2d 95-7530 (D. Wyo. 1995).

[531] Larson v. Domestic & Foreign Commerce Corp., 337 US 682, reh'g denied, 337 US 682 (1949); Maule Indus. v. Tomlinson, 244 F2d 897 (5th Cir. 1957).

[532] See, e.g., GM Leasing Corp. v. United States, 560 F2d 1011 (10th Cir. 1977) (on remand from the Supreme Court).

[533] Butz v. Economou, 438 US 478, 507 (1978); Harlow v. Fitzgerald, 457 US 800 (1982) ("we have held that qualified immunity would be defeated if an official 'knew or reasonably should have known' that the action he took within his spheres of official responsibility would violate the constitutional rights of the (plaintiff), or, if he took the action with malicious intention to cause a deprivation of constitutional rights or other injury"). For tax cases, see, e.g., Baddour, Inc. v. United States, 802 F2d 801 (5th Cir. 1986) (revenue officer has qualified immunity). See also Todd v. United States, 802 F2d 1152 (9th Cir. 1986); Bothke v. Fluor Eng'rs & Constructors, Inc., 834 F2d 804 (9th Cir. 1987) (IRS agent was entitled to qualified immunity from suit because she acted in an objectively reasonable manner when she construed the taxpayer's protest as a general diatribe directed at the tax system rather than as a request for abatement; her conduct was not so egregious as to violate the taxpayer's constitutional rights). Attorneys are cloaked with absolute immunity when they represent the IRS in a Tax Court case. Fry v. Melaragno, 939 F2d 832 (9th Cir. 1991) (citing Butz v. Economou, supra). However, a revenue agent in the performance of his official duties is entitled only to qualified immunity, except for acts in testifying in the Tax Court, where the agent is entitled to absolute immunity. Id.

itself.[534] Revenue officers are not liable for damages for filing notices of lien and levy even where they have failed to follow procedures described in the Internal Revenue Manual.[535] However, in *Lojeski v. Boandle*, the circuit court stated that it recognized that "a violation by an agency of its own rules can provide a basis for reversal of the agency action."[536] The remedy is the invalidation of agency action, and the basis is federal administrative law rather than constitutional law.[537]

---

[534] 28 USC § 2680(c). See, e.g., Mack v. Kurtz, 575 F2d 488 (5th Cir. 1978) (levy on bank accounts); Joam Co. v. Stiller, 83-1 USTC ¶ 9195 (ND Cal. 1982) (revenue officer levied on wrong property; held, revenue officer is either absolutely immune or entitled to qualified immunity because she acted in good faith, her conduct was objectively reasonable, and she did not violate statutory or constitutional rights she should reasonably have known). See Sato v. Tabor, 579 F. Supp. 1170 (ND Ill. 1983) (collecting cases on immunity of IRS officials charged by taxpayers with constitutional and civil rights violations).

[535] Lojeski v. Boandle, 788 F2d 196 (3d Cir. 1986) (revenue officer filed lien and served levy on individual thought to be taxpayer's nominee without Manual-required approval of regional counsel).

[536] Lojeski v. Boandle, 788 F2d 196,199 (3d Cir. 1986).

[537] Lojeski v. Boandle, 788 F2d 196,199 (3d Cir. 1986), discussing administrative law cases such as Accardi v. Shaughnessy, 347 US 260 (1954). Judicial doctrines controlling IRS discretion are described further at ¶ 1.06.

CHAPTER 16

Priority of Tax Claims

¶ 16.01 DETERMINING THE ISSUE OF PRIORITY: GENERAL PRINCIPLES

This chapter describes how courts determine the relative priority of the Federal tax lien and the liens of other creditors. In cases where there is competition between the Service and a third-party creditor for the taxpayer's property, the focus is on the rules, statutory and decisional, governing disputes between the Internal Revenue Service as a creditor and other creditors of the taxpayer. As Chapter 14 describes, when the Service makes an assessment of tax, gives the taxpayer notice of the assessment, and demands payment, and the taxpayer has neglected or refused to pay the assessment within ten days, a Federal tax lien attaches to all the taxpayer's property and rights to property, both real and personal, tangible and intangible in the amount of the assessment. This tax lien is called a statutory or "silent" lien, because no notice of the lien has been filed. The Service perfects its lien by filing a notice of Federal tax lien. Taxpayers who owe tax also can be expected to owe debts to other creditors. Just as the Internal Revenue Service may state that its claim to the taxpayer's property is prior to the other creditors, nontax creditors may claim that their liens or claims to the taxpayer's property have priority in payment to the tax lien. As lien holders line up to take the taxpayer's property, the stage is set for creditor disputes over which claim or lien has priority. In this priority proceeding, the Service will compete with these other creditors for the right to take the taxpayer's property to satisfy a debt or claim.[1]

As a general rule, where creditors have competing liens, the first lien to arise has priority over the second; that is, the first lien in time is the first lien in right.[2] This general rule is only a starting point in resolving lien priority questions and certainly the relative priority of competing tax and nontax liens. To resolve disputes over the priority of a tax lien and the competing lien or interest, other issues arise about the nature of the claim or lien of the competing creditor, the property secured by the lien, and the form of the transaction between the taxpayer and creditor with an interest in the taxpayer's property competing with the tax lien. Three different statutory regimes have been adopted by Congress to govern the priority of a claim for taxes and other creditors. The Code has long had its own lien priority statute, Section 6323, which is entitled "Priority of Liens" (Sections 6321– 6323). In insolvency situations outside of bankruptcy, other long-standing statutes, 31 USC Sections 3713(a) and 3713(b), grant the government's claim, including any tax claims to have absolute priority.[3] In the event the taxpayer seeks relief under the bankruptcy laws, the Bankruptcy Code has a provision for ordering the payment of creditors, including the claims of the Service, whether those claims are secured or unsecured, and arising before or during the bankruptcy proceeding.[4] Just how each of these sets of statutes works requires some knowledge of creditors rights law, the law of secured transactions, and the bankruptcy laws.

Although there is some overlap and some inconsistency in these statutory provisions, the statutes generally apply in the following different situations:

---

[1] The Service's lien becomes the equivalent of a judgment creditor with a lien. See Bull v. United States, 295 US 247, 260 (1934).

[2] See United States v. City of New Britain, 347 US 81 (1954), applying Rankin v. Scott, 25 US (12 Wheat.) 177, 197 (1827), where Justice Marshall stated: "The principle is believed to be universal, that a prior lien gives a prior claim, which is entitled to prior satisfaction." The Uniform Commercial Code usually adopts this rule as well. See UCC § 9-312(5).

[3] According to the legislative history, the revision and renumbering of Rev. Stat. §§ 3466 and 3467 were not intended to change the substance of the statute. Pub. L. No. 97-258, 96 Stat. 972 (1982), 31 USC § 3713, at 396–397.

[4] 11 USC § 507.

- In cases involving Sections 6321–6323, a tax has been assessed giving rise to the general tax lien, and both the government and a person who is a creditor or other person asserting an interest in or lien upon particular property of the taxpayer claim entitlement to the property.
- In cases involving Sections 3713(a) and 3713(b) of 31 USC, a claim for taxes (which need not have been assessed) is made against the insolvent estate of a deceased taxpayer or against a fiduciary having possession and control of the property of an insolvent living taxpayer in a collective creditor proceeding that has not resulted in bankruptcy.
- In cases involving the Bankruptcy Code, the taxpayer is in bankruptcy, and the government asserts its tax claim or lien.

This Chapter discusses the priority in the context of three types of cases: priority of the general tax lien, priority under 31 USC, and priority under the Bankruptcy Code.[5]

[1] Property Belonging to the Taxpayer

The tax lien attaches to (1) "property and rights to property," and (2) "belonging" to the taxpayer as of the assessment date, not to property belonging to someone else. State law determines whether the interest or right a taxpayer possesses constitutes "property." If under state law the interest of the taxpayer does not constitute "property," then there is nothing to which the tax lien can attach.[6] Suppose a taxpayer/contractor fails to pay laborers and materialmen thereby breaching its construction contract. The Service cannot claim that the taxpayer/contractor has any "property" in retainages due him under a construction contract he has breached, and the claims of those laborers and materialmen risk no competition from the tax lien.[7] Similarly, if property does not or no longer belongs to the taxpayer, then the federal tax lien does not attach. Only the taxpayer's equity in property in his possession under a conditional sales contract, purchase-money mortgage, or Uniform Commercial Code

---

[5] See infra Parts A., B., and C., respectively.

[6] United States v. Durham Lumber Co., 363 US 522 (1960); Aquilino v. United States, 363 US 509 (1960). *Durham Lumber* and *Aquilino* followed and applied United States v. Bess, 357 US 51 (1958) (state law determined whether a taxpayer had "property" in the cash surrender value of an insurance policy). However, not all courts accept the "no property" analysis where there has been an assignment for security purposes. Compare Fine Fashions, Inc. v. United States, 328 F2d 419 (2d Cir. 1964) (argument rejected) with In re Halprin, 280 F2d 407 (3d Cir. 1960) (argument accepted).

[7] United States v. Durham Lumber Co., 363 US 522 (1960); Aquilino v. United States, 363 US 509 (1960).

(UCC) purchase-money security interest "belongs" to the taxpayer.[8] Thus, a purchase-money security interest or mortgage valid under local law does not have to compete with the tax lien on the unpaid balance of the debt despite the fact that the security interest or mortgage arises after notice of the Federal tax lien has been filed.

[2] The Choate Lien Doctrine

In cases involving Sections 3713(a) and 3713(b) of 31 USC, a claim for taxes must be paid first if the estate of a *deceased* taxpayer is insolvent or where a fiduciary has possession and control of the property of an insolvent *living* taxpayer in a collective creditor proceeding that has not resulted in bankruptcy. Under the predecessor of Section 3713(a) of Title 31, in cases where the taxpayer is insolvent, the United States has absolute priority over the claims of other creditors. In these cases, a nontax creditor could collect its lien despite the government's absolute priority where the nontax creditor proved its lien had been perfected so that three matters could be identified: (1) the identity of the lienor; (2) the amount of the lien; and (3) the property to which the lien attached.[9] This requirement came to be known as the "choate lien doctrine". In insolvency cases, no competing lien has been found choate.

Despite the fact that the choate lien doctrine started in insolvency cases, it was later carried over to non-insolvency situations. Where a solvent taxpayer was subject to competing claims from both the government and a private creditor, and the private creditor had obtained, for example, a pre-judgment attachment lien before the tax lien arose, the Supreme Court held that a creditor's attachment lien was incomplete or "inchoate" and therefore ineffective against the later-filed tax lien. Although the creditor's attachment lien seemed to have priority over the tax lien under the general priority principle, *United States v. Security Trust & Savings Bank*[10] held that the pre-judgment attachment lien was contingent upon the creditor's obtaining a favorable final judgment. Since the attachment lien creditor had not obtained that favorable final judgment, its lien was inchoate. In reaching its conclusion, the Court relied on law developed in insolvency cases. In short, despite the general first-in-time, first-in-

---

[8] Rev. Rul. 68-57, 1968-1 CB 553 (quoting the General Explanation of the Federal Tax Lien Act, 1966-2 CB 817, which states that "Although so-called purchase money mortgages are not specifically referred to under [pre-1966] law, it has generally been held that these interests are protected whenever they arise [because] the taxpayer has acquired property or a right to property only to the extent that the value of the whole property or right exceeds the amount of the purchase-money mortgage.").

[9] 31 USC § 3713(a). Spokane County v. United States, 279 US 80 (1929); Illinois ex rel. Gordon v. Campbell, 329 US 362 (1946).

[10] United States v. Security Trust & Sav. Bank, 340 US 47 (1950).

right rule, the government's tax lien prevails over earlier-created liens that are general or inchoate.

After *Security Trust*, even in non-insolvency cases involving a tax lien, the Supreme Court has generally used the choate lien doctrine to find "inchoate" almost every variety with the result that these liens were subordinate to the government's later-arising tax lien.[11] But in the case of solvent taxpayers, from time to time the Supreme Court has found a lien competing with a general tax lien to be choate, usually where it has also recognized the difference between insolvency and solvency situations.[12]

Creditors with liens have lost priority disputes with the Service's later-filed tax lien when they failed to prove the specific property subject to their lien. In *United States v. R.F. Ball Construction Co.*,[13] a surety whose obligation was secured by an assignment of the contractor's receivables due and to become due advanced funds to complete a construction contract. The surety failed to file its assignment as required under Texas law, but both its assignment and its liability under the surety bonds occurred before the tax liens arose, although the amount the surety might have been liable for was not fixed. The balance owed the subcontractor became due after one of the tax assessments was made against him, but before either tax assessment had been perfected by filing. Despite the fact that the tax liens had not been filed at the time the surety became due, the surety's lien nevertheless was held inchoate on the ground that it was indefinite at any given point what the exact amount of the debt protected was or the identity of the property secured. *Ball* failed to explain the basis on which it held the surety's lien inchoate, but the decision was generally believed to rest on the proposition that the lien was inchoate because it was indefinite as to the amount at the time the tax lien was filed.

At this point, it was unclear what facts the Court considered significant, and this uncertainty became even more clouded by the result in a Supreme Court decision some three years after *Ball*. In the case, a creditor's lien arose

---

[11] United States v. Acri, 348 US 211 (1955) (attachment lien); United States v. Liverpool & London Ins. Co., 348 US 215 (1955) (garnishment liens); United States v. Scovil, 348 US 218 (1955) (landlord's lien); United States v. Colotta, 350 US 808 (1955) (mechanic's lien); United States v. White Bear Brewing Co., 350 US 1010 (1956) (mechanic's lien held inchoate, although suit to enforce the lien started but no final judgment yet obtained); United States v. Pioneer Am. Ins. Co., 374 US 84 (1963) (attorney fees added to mortgage debt under terms of mortgage); United States v. Equitable Life Assurance Soc'y of the United States, 384 US 323 (1966) (attorney's lien).

[12] United States v. City of New Britain, 347 US 81 (1954) (real estate and local water rent tax liens on personal property practically indistinguishable from those in *Gilbert Assocs.*, held "choate"); United States v. Vermont, 377 US 351 (1964) (statutory lien on personal property similar to lien in *Gilbert Associates*, held "choate"). See also United States v. Toys of the World Club, Inc., 288 F2d 89 (2d Cir. 1961) (artisan's lien provided by New York law was choate as to property in the possession of the lienor).

[13] United States v. R.F. Ball Constr. Co., 355 US 587 (1958).

from an assignment of accounts that the debtor earned and that were due under an existing contract for a debt. The lien was fixed in amount because the amount of the loans advanced to the contractor had been reflected in notes prior to the tax lien's filing, and under state law such an assignment was perfected when made. The government conceded that the creditor's competing lien was choate,[14] and the Court accepted in *Crest Finance Co. v. United States.*[15]

Thus, a creditor's lien will not be considered inchoate if the amount of the debt is uncertain or "indefinite" (*Ball*), but choate if the debt is in a fixed amount (*Crest Finance*).

Making the choateness of a lien turn on whether the amount of the debt is indefinite or definite hardly provides the certainty of a geometric proof. It has been held that as long as the debt is fixed, payment in the future does not prevent the lien from being choate. Thus, an assignment of a contract right to receive payment in the future (at least where the right to payment is unconditional, as in an installment sale of realty) is choate.[16] In *United States v. Pioneer American Insurance Co.*,[17] moreover, the Supreme Court held that a federal tax lien was entitled to priority over the claim of a mortgagee for a "reasonable attorney's fee" in prosecuting a foreclosure action. The mortgagee had recorded its mortgage before the Service had filed its notice of the federal lien, the mortgagor had defaulted, and the mortgagor had instituted a foreclosure action. The Service had filed the notice of federal tax lien, however, before the entry of the judicial decree that allowed and determined the amount of the attorney's fee. This decision seemed to mean that "reasonable attorney's fees" were not a fixed debt for choateness purposes.

Although there are different views about whether and when the choate lien doctrine applies, some general observations can be made:

- Different standards apply to government claims based on a tax lien arising under Section 6321 and a government claim is based on Section 3713(a) of Title 31 (*New Britain* and *Vermont*). A lien competing with the tax lien of Section 6321 must be choate—that is, the competing lien must be definite in the identity of the lienor, the amount of lien, and the property subject to lien (*Equitable Life*).
- Certain liens are sufficiently choate and specific to defeat a later-filed tax lien. This is the result even if before the notice of the Federal tax lien is filed. These liens were less fixed or identified in character than a

---

[14] The government also conceded that the assignment was a "mortgage" for the purpose of the predecessor of Section 6323, which required a tax lien to be filed in order for it to be valid against a mortgage.

[15] Crest Fin. Co. v. United States, 368 US 347 (1961).

[16] Hammes v. Tucson Newspapers, Inc., 324 F2d 101 (9th Cir. 1963).

[17] United States v. Pioneer Am. Ins. Co., 374 US 84 (1963).

traditional mortgage. At the time the Service files a notice of the Federal tax lien, however, the amount of the debt must be fixed and the property subject to the lien must have been earned and due (*Crest Finance*).[18] If the debt is not fixed when the tax lien is filed, because further advances to or on behalf of the taxpayer/debtor are contemplated and the property assigned as collateral has not been earned and due, the nontax lien is inchoate (*Ball* and *Pioneer American Insurance Co.*).[19]

Federal tax lien versus state tax liens. The choate lien doctrine is applied to resolve the relative priorities of a state tax lien and a filed federal tax lien. In this situation, a close analysis of the state tax law is made. For example, the circuit court examined the New Jersey tax law, which provides that after the Division of Taxation makes a deficiency assessment, gives the taxpayer notice of the assessment and a demand for payment, and the taxpayer fails to pay, the Division has a lien on all of the taxpayer's property and may file a certificate of debt, which has the force and effect of a docketed judgment against the taxpayer for the amount of the debt.[20] The Division then takes all the steps under state law to collect that judgment. The Service conceded that under the New Jersey law, the choate lien doctrine requirements of the identity of the lienor (the Division) and the property subject to the lien (all of the taxpayer's prop-

---

[18] Rice Inv. Co. v. United States, 625 F2d 565 (5th Cir. 1980). See MDC Leasing v. New York Prop. Ins. Underwriting Ass'n, 450 F. Supp. 179 (WDNY 1978), aff'd without opinion, 603 F2d 213 (2d Cir. 1979) (assignee of uncollected insurance proceeds did not have choate lien); Gaeta v. United States, 82-2 USTC 9525 (SDNY 1982) (competing liens of state and assignee became choate only at the time debtor and third party agreed to settlement); Brumfield v. Pana Coals, Inc., 86-2 USTC ¶ 9688 (SD W. Va. 1986) (liens of coal miners were inchoate because property encumbered and amounts of liens were uncertain); American Gen. Life Ins. v. Stein, 87-1 USTC ¶ 9173 (SDNY 1987) (tax lien had priority over doctors' claims to medical insurance proceeds because doctors' claims were inchoate); Lerner v. United States, 87-1 USTC ¶ 9339 (SDNY 1986) (where former wife obtained judgment appointing her receiver of her husband's property with authority to pay herself sums for support "as it becomes due," her lien was held inchoate and did not have priority over a later tax lien, because husband had not actually defaulted at time tax lien arose); United States v. Broady, 89-1 USTC ¶ 9175 (SDNY 1989) (despite terms of proprietary lease providing that tenant shareholder had no right to sales proceeds until after debts to cooperative were paid, the Service had a right to the full sales proceeds, because the lease did not reduce the taxpayer's property rights but only created an inchoate consensual security interest).

[19] See Rev. Rul. 56-41, 1956-1 CB 562 (advance under open-end mortgage does not have priority over intervening tax lien). In a private ruling, the Service held that where the advance was obligatory rather than optional, the nontax lien had priority. Rul. A-619373 (Aug. 24, 1956). Texas Oil & Gas Corp. v. United States, 466 F2d 1040 (5th Cir. 1972), cert. denied, 410 US 929 (1973) (bank's security interest in accounts of a debtor held inchoate at time tax lien filed, because debtor had not yet performed the required services); Peoples Nat'l Bank v. United States, 777 F2d 459 (9th Cir. 1985) (bank's right of setoff held inchoate).

[20] Monica Fuels, Inc. v. United States, 56 F3d 508 (3d Cir. 1995).

erty) had been satisfied, but that the amount of the state liens had not been established because the taxpayer could contest the assessment by filing a protest and requesting a hearing. When the ninety-day period for the taxpayer to file with the state Tax Court lapsed, the circuit court held, the amounts of the assessment "became impervious to challenge and were therefore fixed and specific." A majority of the panel also concluded that the amount of the tax became fixed on the date of the assessment, a view with which one of the panel disagreed. The Service also contended that the New Jersey tax lien was inchoate because it could not be summarily enforced. The court rejected this contention, however, on the ground that the New Jersey statute permitted summary enforcement upon assessment, and the certificate of debt (or, alternatively, a warrant of execution) did not "require the Division to engage in a judicial contest to attain enforcement."

While in *Monica Fuels, Inc.* the Third Circuit closely examined New Jersey tax law, a district court in Alabama analyzed Alabama law to determine whether the amount of the state's liens was established at the time of notice and demand, and whether the state's liens were summarily enforceable. The court concluded that under the state's two-step procedure, the amount of the state tax is not fixed at the time the state issues a notice and demand letter, and its tax lien is not summarily enforceable (a taxpayer has the right to appeal the final assessment within thirty days).[21]

After-acquired property. It also should be noted that the analysis of whether a lien is choate is complicated when the lien priority issue involves after-acquired property. Priority can be determined by looking at when the competing tax and other lien are filed. Some courts, however, have analyzed priority later, when the property at issue comes into existence (e.g., insurance proceeds). If this is done, inevitably the nontax and later tax lien will attach simultaneously. In the case of simultaneous attachment, the federal tax lien has been said to have priority because of the superiority of a government lien.[22] In resolving the issue of the relative priority of a judgment lien and a tax lien in after-acquired property, not a security interest, the Supreme Court stated that the choate lien doctrine continues to be applicable even in the case of a competing security interest in after-acquired property.[23]

---

[21] United States v. Ressler, 81 AFTR2d ¶ 98-1949 (ND Ala. 1998).

[22] See, e.g., MDC Leasing Corp. v. New York Prop. Ins. Underwriting Ass'n, supra; Gaeta v. United States, supra, following United States v. Graham, 96 F. Supp. 318 (SD Cal. 1951), aff'd sub nom. California v. United States, 195 F2d 530 (9th Cir.), cert. denied, 344 US 831 (1952). Contra Southern Rock, Inc. v. B&B Auto Supply, 711 F2d 683 (5th Cir. 1983) (simultaneously perfected security interest and tax lien share in fund in proportion to the claims). See infra ¶ 16.03[2][b], note 63. United States v. J.D. Grainger Co., 945 F2d 259 (9th Cir. 1991) (choate lien doctrine applied to claim of subcontractor under Miller Act, claim held not specific regarding property to which it attached).

[23] See United States v. McDermott, 507 US 447 (1993), discussed infra ¶ 16.03[3]. See KPMG Peat Marwick v. Texas Commerce Bank, 976 F. Supp. 623 (SD Tex. 1997)

[3] The Choate Lien Doctrine and The Federal Tax Lien Act of 1966

In 1966, Congress amended the priority statute in the Code in a comprehensive act called the Federal Tax Lien Act of 1966. Not all courts have concluded that the choate lien doctrine has vitality after the comprehensive amendment of Section 6323 in 1966. Courts that have applied the doctrine have had to navigate their way through Supreme Court cases and Section 6323, and they have usually done so after finding that the competing lienor failed to find protection in Section 6323.[24] Perhaps this is the explanation for the Supreme Court's decision in *McDermott*, which involved the relative priority of a judgment lien and a tax lien in a taxpayer/debtor's after-acquired property.[25] Because Section 6323 does not specifically describe when a judgment lien is perfected for priority purposes, the choate lien doctrine is properly employed to determine whether, at the time the taxpayer/judgment debtor acquired the property, the judgment lien was sufficiently choate to give it priority over the tax lien. Although state law gave the judgment creditor a lien on the after-acquired real property, at the time the judgment lien was perfected under state law, the after-acquired real property had not been identified, and so under the federal choate lien doctrine, the judgment lien was inchoate as to after-acquired property.

Under these circumstances, although the judgment lien was perfected before the tax lien was filed, it was inchoate as to the after-acquired property, while the tax lien was perfected in the property at the time the notice of lien was filed. When the judgment lien creditor perfects its lien on a taxpayer/debtor's existing real property, at a time when the federal tax lien has not been perfected by filing, according to the Supreme Court's decision in *United States v. Estate of Romani*, the judgment lien takes priority, even when the taxpayer/debtor dies, and the Service claims its absolute priority under the Federal Insolvency Statute (31 USC § 3713).[26]

Before 1966, the predecessor of Section 6323 provided that although the tax lien did arise on the date of assessment, purchasers and certain categories

---

(creditor that perfected its security interest under Texas law before the tax lien was filed did not have priority in a partner's partnership distribution and bonus because the security interest was inchoate until the distribution and bonus came into existence at the end of the partnership year, by which time the tax lien had been filed). See also Tri-River Chem. Co., Inc. v. TNT Farms, 83 AFTR2d 99-345 (D. Id. 1998) (lender perfected a security interest before a tax lien was filed, but crop proceeds were "after acquired property," and both the security interest and the tax lien attached at the same time that the crops were planted; held, under *McDermott*, the tax lien had priority over the perfected security interest to the extent of the amount of its lien).

[24] Texas Oil & Gas Corp. v. United States, 466 F2d 1040 (5th Cir. 1972), cert. denied, 410 US 929 (1973); Rice Inv. Co. v. United States, 625 F2d 565 (5th Cir. 1980).

[25] United States v. McDermott, 507 US 447 (1993).

[26] United States v. Estate of Romani, 118 S. Ct. 1478 (1998).

of secured creditors had priority over the tax lien up to the date a notice of tax lien was filed in the appropriate local office designated by state law. Mortgagees, pledgees, purchasers, and judgment lien creditors were given this status. The Federal Tax Lien Act of 1966 (FTLA) was the first comprehensive revision and modernization of the provision of the Code dealing with the relationship of federal tax liens to the interests of other creditors.[27] Briefly, revised Section 6323 has the following key features:

- A list of categories of creditors who are protected against a nonfiled tax lien, expanded to include a mechanic lienor (Section 6323(a));
- The use of the term, "holder of a security interest," used in the Uniform Commercial Code, instead of "mortgagee" and "pledgee" to giving the various types of interests the UCC includes in the term holder of a security interest, priority over an unfiled tax lien whether or not these included interest are definite and complete in all other respects at the time the tax lien is filed;
- Ten categories of interests in properties that have priority even if notice of the lien has been filed (so-called "super-priorities") (Section 6323(c));
- Priority status for creditors' interests arising under three types of financing agreements entered into before tax lien filing even if the creditor continues to advance funds or property comes into existence after tax lien filing; and
- A limited priority for disbursements made within forty-five days after tax lien filing and for interest and expenses attributable to interests having priority over a tax lien (Section 6323(d)).

This comprehensive revision of Section 6323 raises the question of whether the choate lien doctrine is still viable. The answer is yes.[28] Congress intended that Section 6323 replace the choate lien doctrine *only* where the statute specifically applies. For example, the committee reports state that

---

[27] S. Rep. No. 1708, 89th Cong., 2d Sess. (1966), reprinted in 1966-2 CB 876.

[28] Despite the legislative history, the matter is not free from doubt as far as commentators are concerned. Compare Creedon, "Assignments for Security and Federal Tax Liens," 37 Fordham L. Rev. 535, 567 (1969), with Plumb, Federal Tax Liens 100–108 (3d ed. 1972), and Coogan, "The Effect of the Federal Tax Lien Act of 1966 Upon Security Interests Created Under the Uniform Commercial Code," 81 Harv. L. Rev. 1369 (1988).

Court decisions display the same uncertainty. Compare, e.g., Texas Oil & Gas Corp. v. United States, 466 F2d 1040 (5th Cir. 1972), cert. denied, 410 US 929 (1973) (applying the choate lien tests), with Donald v. Madison Indus., Inc., 483 F2d 837 (10th Cir. 1973) (choateness criteria "inappropriate and out-of-date" and "totally obsolete" after FTLA). See Sgro v. United States, 609 F2d 1259 (7th Cir. 1979) (applying choate lien doctrine and Section 6323).

it is intended that, under the bill, the various types of interests defined in Section 6323(a) are to have priority over an unfiled Federal tax lien if they come within the definition of these terms whether or not in all other regards they are definite and complete at the time notice of the tax lien is filed.

The House report specifically states:

Under the decisions of the Supreme Court a mortgagee, pledgee, or judgment creditor is protected at the time the notice of tax lien is filed if the identity of the lienor, the property subject to the lien, and the amount of the lien are all established at such time (citing the *City of New Britain* case). Except as otherwise provided, subsection (2) of new section 6323 retains this basic rule of Federal law.[29]

Consequently, if the interest competing with the tax lien meets the requirements of Section 6323, it need not also meet the requirements of the choate lien doctrine. On the other hand, if the interest fails to find protection under Section 6323, it has priority over a later-filed tax lien only if it meets the standards of choateness.[30]

---

[29] HR Rep. No. 1884, 89th Cong., 2d Sess. (1966), reprinted in 1966-2 CB 815, 839.

[30] See, e.g., Aetna Ins. Co. v. Texas Thermal Indus., 591 F2d 1035, 1038 (5th Cir. 1979) (choateness has been supplanted by the provisions of Section 6323 with respect to tax lien priority questions to which that statute provides unambiguous federal law answers); Sgro v. United States, 609 F2d 1259 (7th Cir. 1979) (applying choate lien doctrine and Section 6323). See also In re Priest, 712 F2d 1326 (9th Cir. 1983) (lien on taxpayer's property created by state statute upon the receipt of delinquent tax return was not sufficiently choate to take priority over a federal tax lien, since the amount of the lien could not be determined until the state taxing authority had computed the actual amount owed to state, including interest, penalties, and fees); Peoples Nat'l Bank v. United States, 777 F2d 459 (9th Cir. 1985) at n. 2 ("the 'choateness' doctrine remains relevant under Section 6323(a), at least as a tool to resolve issues not clearly anticipated by Congress"; cases cited). Transwestern Pipeline Co. v. Allied Bank of Tex., 89-1 USTC 9173 (SD Tex. 1989) ("the choateness rule has been supplanted by the provisions of § 6323 with respect to tax lien priority questions as to which that statute provides an unambiguous federal law answer").

A PRIORITY OF TAX CLAIMS ON INDIVIDUAL CREDITOR PROCEEDINGS

¶ 16.02 PROTECTION OF TRANSACTIONS OCCURRING BEFORE TAX LIEN FILING: SECTION 6323(A)

Section 6323(a) lists four categories of persons whose interests arise before notice of the lien is filed, but after the general tax lien exists and creates an order of priority giving the interests of the four creditors over the unfiled tax lien. The persons listed in Section 6323 are (1) purchasers; (2) holders of security interests; (3) judgment lien creditors; and (4) mechanic lienors. Until a notice of tax lien is filed, transactions of these persons with the taxpayer are protected although a tax lien may already be in existence by way of assessment under Section 6321 on all the taxpayer's "property and rights to property."[31] The definitions of the four interests included in the protected class and the filing rules are discussed in the following sections.[32]

---

[31] The protection of Section 6323 has sometimes been drawn into question where, instead of filing a notice of lien, the Service serves a levy. If a creditor has an unperfected lien at the time of the levy, the government has contended that the levy seizes the taxpayer's property before the creditor can perfect his lien. However, most courts have rejected the contention on the ground that Section 6323 was meant to protect creditors against unrecorded tax liens and that a notice of levy does not constitute notice under Section 6323. Thus, the notice of levy has been held not to be a procedural alternative to filing a notice of lien. City of Vermillion, SD v. Stan Houston Equip. Co., 341 F. Supp. 707 (DSD 1972); Hoover, Inc. v. McCullough Indus., Inc., 351 F. Supp. 1023 (SD Ala. 1972); United States v. Jenison, 484 F. Supp. 747 (DRI 1980). Contra Piontek v. Ceritano, 427 A2d 600 (NJ Super. Ct. App. Div. 1981). See also United States v. Trigg, 465 F2d 1264 (8th Cir. 1972), cert. denied, 410 US 909 (1973) (levy prevented bank from perfecting a security interest in accounts receivable); Southern Rock v. B&B Auto Supply, 711 F2d 683 (5th Cir. 1983) ("serving a notice of levy on accounts receivable does not by itself entitle the government to priority in those accounts over a subsequently perfected security interest").

Circular priority. Where there are multiple lienors, there can be issues of circular priority, and the determination of the priority issue may depend not only on the application of the lien priority regime of Section 6323, but also on the choate lien doctrine. For example, if a holder of the security interest has priority over a tax lien, but a state lien has priority over the holder of the security interest, even if it is prior in time, the state tax lien must be a choate lien in order to have priority over the tax lien. Western Nat'l Bank v. United States, 8 F3d 253 (5th Cir. 1993) (priority of creditors who filed a UCC-1 over tax lien did not invalidate the tax lien, so that even if the state tax lien had priority over the creditors, it did not have priority over the tax lien because it was not choate before the tax lien was filed).

[32] See infra ¶¶ 16.03[1]–16.03[4] (interests), and 16.03[5] (filing rules). Note that when a notice of federal tax lien has not been filed, actual knowledge of the statutory or secret federal tax lien does not affect the lien priority of the purchaser, holder of a security interest, mechanic's lienors, or judgment lien creditor. Rev. Rul. 2003-108, 2003-44

[1] Purchasers

Before 1966, Section 6323 did not define the term "purchaser." Courts held that a purchaser was a person who acquires title to property for a valuable consideration.[33] A valuable consideration, as interpreted by the courts, required more than a nominal amount, but it might be so small an amount as to have little relation to the value of the property acquired.[34] Also, under conditional sales contracts, some courts held that a conditional vendee who took possession but not legal title to property was not a purchaser.[35] In 1966, Section 6321 defined "purchaser entitled to notice of a federal tax lien", as a person who (1) for adequate and full consideration in money or money's worth, (2) acquires an interest (other than a lien or security interest) in property, and (3) whose interest in the property is valid under local law against subsequent purchasers without actual notice.[36]

Adequate or full consideration. By requiring "adequate and full consideration," the definition changes the result reached in *Enochs v. Smith*,[37] which permitted any consideration to qualify as long as it was not nominal in amount. Adequate and full consideration in money or money's worth has a reasonable relationship to the true value of the interest acquired.[38] For purposes of Section 6323(h)(6), "adequate and full consideration in money or money's worth" means that the court must compare the value of the consideration given to the "true value" of the property.[39] True value has been held to be fair mar-

IRB 1. Compare this rule with Section 6323(b) where actual knowledge of the existence of a statutory tax lien is relevant for the effectiveness of certain superpriorities.

[33] See United States v. Scovil, 348 US 218, 221 (1955).

[34] See, e.g., Enochs v. Smith, 359 F2d 924 (5th Cir. 1955).

[35] United States v. Creamer Indus., Inc., 349 F2d 625 (5th Cir. 1965), cert. denied, 382 US 957 (1965); Leipert v. RC Williams & Co., 161 F. Supp. 355 (SDNY 1957).

[36] IRC § 6323(h)(6).

[37] Enochs v. Smith, 359 F2d 924 (5th Cir. 1955).

[38] Reg. § 301.6323(h)-1(f)(3). See, e.g., Jones & Jeffry Constr. Co. v. United States, 77-2 USTC ¶ 9695 (ED Tex. 1977); District Divine Science Church of Allen City v. United States, 80-1 USTC ¶ 9119 (ND Ind. 1979) (property worth $16,000 more than amount of mortgage assumed; also, trustees of alleged purchaser were taxpayers, so church had notice of tax claim).

[39] United States v. McCombs, 928 F. Supp. 261 (WDNY 1995), on remand, United States v. McCombs, 30 F3d 310 (2d Cir. 1994). The district court held that the assumption of a mortgage equals consideration equal to the face amount of the mortgage, especially when the mortgage is paid off. The government's argument that the "purchaser's" inability to pay the mortgage meant assumption was not consideration was rejected because the mortgage was paid off.

ket value, not forced sale value.[40] However, the committee reports[41] and the regulations[42] make it clear that the requirement is not intended to preclude "purchaser" status for a person who is a bona fide purchaser even at a bargain or who is a conditional vendee under a deferred-payment sales contract.[43]

Acquires an interest in property. A purchaser must acquire its interest in the property in a transaction that has the indicia of a vendor-vendee relationship. This term is broader than the normal meaning of "purchase of property." A purchase of property includes (1) a lease of property; (2) a written executory contract to purchase or lease property; (3) an option to purchase or lease property or any interest in property; and (4) an option to renew or extend a lease of property that is not a lien or security in the property.[44] "Purchaser" also includes an assignee of sales proceeds whose interest is perfected before a notice of tax lien is filed.[45]

The interest acquired is good against subsequent purchasers. This element contemplates perfection of the acquired interest under local law. Consequently,

---

[40] United States v. McCombs, 30 F3d 310 (2d Cir. 1994). In *McCombs*, the district court found that consideration that was 67 percent of fair market value was not adequate and full consideration. For fraudulent conveyance purposes, however, the property's value is forced sale value—value in forced foreclosure proceeding. Consideration of $57,800 was held not to be disproportionately small in comparison to forced sale value of $68,526. United States v. McCombs, 30 F3d 310 (2d Cir. 1994).

[41] HR Rep. No. 1884, 89th Cong., 2d Sess. (1966), reprinted in 1966-2 CB 815, 850.

[42] Reg. § 301.6323(a)-1(f)(3).

[43] Thus, the 1966 changes overruled United States v. Creamer Indus., Inc., 349 F2d 625 (5th Cir. 1965), cert. denied, 382 US 957 (1965), and Leipert v. RC Williams & Co., 161 F. Supp. 355 (SDNY 1957). See Engel v. Tinker Nat'l Bank, 269 F. Supp. 199 (EDNY 1967) (applying FTLA).

[44] IRC § 6323(h)(6); Reg. § 301.6323(h)-1(f)(2). The transfer of a marital residence in exchange for the surrender of marital rights in other property pursuant to a divorce decree is not a purchase for "money's worth." Harris v. United States, 588 F. Supp. 835 (ND Tex. 1984), aff'd, 764 F2d 1126 (1985) (applying Reg. § 301.6323(h)-1(f)). See also Newnham v. United States, 813 F2d 1384 (9th Cir. 1987) (seller/taxpayer entered into contract to purchase realty at a time when no tax lien was filed, but later defaulted; held, default did not strip buyer of her status as "purchaser" under Section 6323(h)(6); buyer awarded attorney fees).

[45] See Professional Accounting & Consulting Servs., Inc. v. United States, 80 AFTR2d 97-8350 (MD Fla.) (applying Florida law, an assignee was held not to qualify as a purchaser because before the tax lien was filed, the account debtor had not been given actual notice of assignment, and so the assignment was not perfected under Florida law on the date the tax lien was filed).

a person claiming to be a purchaser may not have that status if the person has not perfected the interest[46] or lost the priority once obtained.[47]

[2] Holders of Security Interests

The "holder of a security interest" as used in Section 6323(a) was meant to include the terms "mortgagee" and "pledgee" under the pre-1966 law and to bring the tax lien statute in line with the UCC, now adopted in all states.[48]

---

[46] See Rodkey v. United States, 87-1 USTC ¶ 9218 (WD Okla. 1987). On May 24, 1985, A purchased real property from B, against whom taxes had been assessed on June 4, 1984, but no tax lien had been filed as of the date of purchase. On June 3, 1985, a tax lien was filed, and on August 9, 1985, A filed his warranty deed. The tax lien had priority over A in the real property because at the time the tax lien was filed, A had not perfected his claim under Oklahoma law against a subsequent purchaser.

[47] A purchaser may have priority over a tax lien at the time that the tax lien is perfected by filing, but lose that priority when the purchase is rescinded. Wasenius v. United States, 1996 US Dist. LEXIS 6113, 96-1 USTC ¶ 50,283 (MD Fla. 1996) (taxpayer made a fraudulent representation about property sold, and the buyers successfully sought rescission of the sale; held, the equitable lien existed on the date the state court granted rescission, and the tax lien was held to have been perfected on that date). In Wasenius, the district court used the choate lien doctrine, as applied by the Supreme Court in McDermott, to disregard the state court's finding that the equitable lien related back to the date the buyers had filed their lis pendens. In McDermott, the judgment lien was held inchoate as to after-acquired property, while in Wasenius, the equitable lien was held inchoate because the relation back finding was not given effect. Compare Progressive Consumers Fed. Credit Union v. United States, 79 F3d 1228 (1st Cir. 1996) (applying the Massachusetts doctrine of unjust enrichment to reinstate the original mortgage that had priority over the tax lien after that mortgage had been discharged and refinanced with a new mortgage). In Progressive Consumers Federal Credit Union, the circuit court said, "the government could not have anticipated its current priority status because from the outset its 1988–1990 liens were clearly junior to MSFCU's 1987 mortgage lien…[and] absent the inadvertent discharge, the government would not have gained serendipitous priority over MSFCU's second mortgage lien in 1992." The same could be said in Wasenius, where the Service could not have anticipated its priority after the rescission of the sales contract.

[48] Actually, under the UCC, the term "security interest" covers such transactions as the chattel mortgage, conditional sales contract, pledge, assignment of accounts, and factoring arrangement. An equitable mortgage has been granted priority over a later-filed tax lien. United States v. Canellis, 490 F. Supp. 1125 (ND Ill. 1980). An equitable lien is not a "security" entitled to super priority under Section 6323(h)(4). Simpson Supply v. American Interiors, 93-2 USTC ¶ 50,405 (D. Neb. 1993).

Suppose a security interest has priority over a tax lien, and a purchaser buys the property from the taxpayer. If the purchaser of property subject to a prior mortgage and a later-filed tax lien pays off the mortgage, the purchaser may be equitably subrogated to the prior lien of the mortgage holder. See Han v. United States, 944 F2d 526 (9th Cir. 1991) (applying California law).

Similarly, when a bank had a choate mortgage lien before the Service filed several tax liens and then refinanced the mortgage, satisfying its first mortgage that was prior in time to the tax liens, the First Circuit applied the Massachusetts law of unjust enrichment

Under the UCC, the term "security interest" covers such transactions as the chattel mortgage, conditional sales contract, pledge, assignment of accounts, and factoring arrangement. Under Section 6323, a security interest is any interest (including a chattel mortgage or pledge) acquired by contract for the purpose of securing payment or performance of an obligation or of indemnifying against loss or liability.[49] A common-law assignment may qualify as a security interest under Section 6323(a) as long as it meets the requirements of Section 6323(h)(1).[50]

---

to reinstate the bank's first mortgage lien without regard to the Service's loss of priority. Progressive Consumers Fed. Credit Union v. United States, 79 F3d 1228 (1st Cir. 1996) (citing *Han* and other cases where liens were found to have priority over the tax lien under various equitable theories to avoid unjust enrichment). The First Circuit reinstated the original mortgage and thus its priority over the tax liens, holding that under Massachusetts law, the doctrine of unjust enrichment applied to set aside the discharge and to reinstate the original mortgage. The fact that tax liens were involved did not preclude the application of state law, the circuit court said, "...because the unjust enrichment doctrine operates only to restore a state created lien to the position it occupied prior to the inadvertent discharge." While federal law determines both the choateness and the priority of competing liens, the unjust enrichment doctrine "equitably determines the effective date of the state created lien independent of other existing liens."

Also, when *B* paid off the note taxpayers gave the holder of a mortgage with priority over a tax lien and then *B* assigned the note and deed of trust to *M*, the circuit court said that *B*'s right of subrogation was assigned to *M*, and so *M* could bring injunction action against the Service. Mort v. United States, 86 F3d 890 (9th Cir. 1996) (*M* was not obligated to first bring action at law against title insurer, which had failed to discover tax lien).

When a grantor trust whose settlor was the guarantor and also the sole shareholder of the obligor corporation satisfied a note secured by a mortgage perfected before the tax lien, the trust was equitably subrogated to the note and mortgage holder's position and priority. Harley J. Robinson Trust v. Ardmore Acres, Inc., 81 AFTR2d ¶ 98-620 (ED Mich. 1998).

[49] IRC § 6323(h)(1); Reg. § 301.6323(h)-1(a).

[50] See Peoples Nat'l Bank v. United States, 608 F. Supp. 672 (WD Wash. 1984), aff'd, 777 F2d 459 (9th Cir. 1985) (note and security agreement covering funds on deposit with bank/lender were not effective assignments because there was no transfer of control of the property assigned). Compare Trust Co. of Columbus v. United States, 735 F2d 447 (11th Cir. 1984) (valid assignment under Georgia law resulted in bank's assignment of a depositor's interest in bank account taking priority over a subsequently filed tax lien). Conzola v. City of Miami, 93-1 USTC ¶ 50,308 (SD Fla. 1993) (assignment was perfected in proceeds of accounts although tax lien was filed before accounts were paid; Nevada's UCC applied). Compare also New Las Vegas Country Club v. Zwerner, 77 AFTR2d ¶ 96-696 (D. Nev. 1996) (restriction on transferability of club membership prevented transfer of a security interest to a nontax creditor, so that the Service was entitled to proceeds of the sale of the membership).

An assignment may be an absolute assignment of property or a collateral assignment. The difference in the type of assignment is important. An absolute or unqualified assignment is a transfer by the debtor of the rights or interest that the debtor has in the property. A collateral assignment is a general intangible, defined in UCC § 9-106 as "personal property, including things in action."

The Section 6323 definition of "security interest" states that a security interest exists (1) where the property is "in existence" (not that the debtor/taxpayer has "rights in the collateral"), (2) where the interest has become protected under local law against a "subsequent judgment lien arising out of an unsecured obligation" (not a person who becomes a "lien creditor before the security interest was perfected"), and (3) to the extent that the holder has parted with money or money's worth.[51] Under the UCC, a security interest is "an interest in personal property or fixtures, which secures payment or per-

---

As a security interest, the collateral assignment is subject to the filing requirements of UCC § 9-401(1)(c), which establishes the filing requirements for the perfection of a security interest in general intangibles. If the assignment is a collateral assignment and the creditor has not perfected its security interest under the state UCC, the creditor will only have an unperfected security interest, and a later-filed tax lien will have priority. See United States v. Talco Contractors, Inc., 83 AFTR2d 99-2897 (WDNY 1999) (bank's debtor made a collateral assignment in condemnation award, but because bank did not perfect its security interest by filing a financing statement, a later-filed tax lien had priority).

Compare the following situation. To secure the payment of fees, an attorney who represented a taxpayer in a tax case that resulted in the assessment of a tax deficiency took back a mortgage in the taxpayer's residence. The Service contended that its later-filed tax lien had priority under Alabama's recording statute because at the time that he filed the mortgage, the attorney had notice of the Service's claim. The district court found for the attorney on the ground that the holder of a security interest who files before the tax lien is filed is entitled to priority under Section 6323(h)(1)(A) as long as the creditor's security interest is perfected under local law against a hypothetical judgment lien creditor, regardless of the filing party's knowledge of the tax claim. United States v. Fletcher, 84 AFTR2d 99-5234 (Bankr. SD Ala. 1999) (following In re Haas, 31 F3d 1081 (11th Cir. 1994)).

The determination that an assignment has effected a transfer of the taxpayer's property rights or interest does not end the analysis. It is important to know what property the taxpayer has actually assigned. For example, a beneficiary's assignment of his interest in a trust has been held not to be an assignment of the trust property, but instead an assignment of the beneficiary's right in the trust—that is, the beneficiary's interest in the trust. David v. Katz, 85 AFTR2d 2000-1458 (ED La. 2000) (beneficiary's interest in trust was choate at the time of assignment, and so assignee creditor's assignment had priority over the tax lien).

[51] IRC § 6323(h)(1). Bank of St. Charles v. Alloy & Steel Fabricators, Inc., 643 F. Supp. 206 (ED La. 1986) (under Louisiana law, a mortgage on real property in favor of a bank gave it a valid lien before a tax lien was filed, although the taxpayer did not have title to the property until after the liens were filed). Compare Crystal Bar, Inc., v. Cosmic, Inc., 758 F. Supp. 543 (DSD 1991) (since purchase of liquor license assigned to taxpayer was security interest, and since no filing was made before tax lien was filed, Service became lien creditor entitled to priority); Citizens State Bank v. United States, 932 F2d 490 (6th Cir. 1991) (Section 6323(h)(1) does not protect security interest once perfected but released before federal tax lien is filed; it protects "present security interests which have been perfected at some point prior to the imposition of the federal tax lien").

formance of an obligation."[52] Thus far, the definitions of a security interest in Section 6323 and UCC are substantially the same.

An unperfected security interest is subordinate to the rights of a "lien creditor" before the security interest is perfected. UCC Section 9-301 provides that "an unperfected security interest is subordinate to the rights of—(b) a person who becomes a lien creditor before the security is perfected...." The section goes on to define a "lien creditor" to mean "a creditor who has acquired a lien on the property involved by attachment, levy, or the like...."[53] Although the Federal Tax Lien Act intended to coordinate the federal tax lien with the UCC, Section 6231(h)(1) uses the term "judgment lien creditor" rather than the UCC term "lien creditor." The result has been that courts have had difficulty in understanding and applying the term "judgment lien creditor" under state law.[54]

An enforceable security interest in collateral under the UCC is created where all of the following have occurred: (1) there is an appropriate agreement that a security interest attach; (2) value is given by the secured party; and (3) the debtor has rights in the collateral.[55] Where these three events (i.e., agreement, value, and acquisition of rights) have occurred, the security interest is said to have "attached" to the collateral. In addition, to achieve maximum possible priority over competing lienors, the secured party must "perfect" his security interest. There are different methods of perfecting a security interest, depending on the type of collateral. A security interest generally is perfected by filing a financing statement.[56] An unperfected security interest is

---

[52] UCC § 1-201(37). The UCC definition of "personal property", which may be the subject of a security interest, is broad enough to include "general intangibles." Because government licenses are generally held to be general intangibles, an FCC license may be the subject of a security interest. If the security interest in the license is perfected by filing under state law before a tax lien is filed, the proceeds from the sale of the license also are subject to the security interest, and the holder of the security interest has priority in the proceeds over the later-filed tax lien. MLQ Investors, LP v. Pacific Quadracasting Inc., 82 AFTR2d ¶ 98-5065 (9th Cir. 1998).

[53] UCC § 9-301(3).

[54] The government has argued and commentators have said that the term "judgment lien creditor" as used in Section 6323 is the equivalent of the interest of a UCC lien creditor, as defined in UCC § 9-301. Litton Indus. Automation Sys., Inc. v. Nationwide Power Corp., 106 F3d 366 (11th Cir. 1997) (agreeing that the "better interpretation" of the term is the one in Reg. § 301.6323(h)-1(g), which defines the term "judgment lien creditor" as "the equivalent to the interest of a UCC lien creditor"). Accordingly, if a security interest is unperfected under state law, it is subordinate to the rights of a tax lien. Litton Indus. Automation Sys., Inc. v. Nationwide Power Corp., 106 F3d 366 (11th Cir. 1997) (analyzing Florida law).

[55] UCC §§ 9-203(1), 9-203(3); UCC § 9-204(1) (1962).

[56] UCC § 9-302. A security interest may also be perfected when it attaches (e.g., a purchase-money security interest in consumer goods other than motor vehicles or fixtures,

subordinate to the rights of "lien creditors" before the security interest is perfected.[57]

[a] Property Must Be in Existence

For purposes of Section 6323(a) unless property subject to the security interest is "in existence," a security interest cannot have attached, and as a result a tax lien has priority over the security interest, even if the tax lien is unfiled. The difference in terminology (i.e., "existence" versus "rights in collateral") between Section 6323 and the UCC probably is not significant. It is likely that Section 6323 does not require physical existence, but only that the taxpayer have some rights in the collateral, as the UCC requires. Collateral is clearly in existence where the debtor owns the goods, inventory, machinery, or equipment. Also, under the UCC, a debtor has rights in collateral where particular goods have been identified as goods to which a sales contract refers and the debtor has special property and insurable interest to the goods.[58] Under these circumstances, property also probably would be "in existence" for the purposes of Section 6323. On the other hand, if no identification has been made, the debtor has no interest in the goods until they are subsequently identified to the contract,[59] and accordingly property would not be "in existence" until that later time. In this connection, the government has argued that a fire insurance payment came into existence only when a judgment was obtained against the insurer, not on the date of the fire when the right to the insurance proceeds accrued. This contention has been rejected.[60] The reasoning is that even if the payment did not come into existence until the judgment, the security interest

---

UCC § 9-302(1)(d)), or by possession of the secured party (e.g., stock certificates, UCC § 9-304(1)).

[57] UCC § 9-301.

[58] UCC § 2-501(1).

[59] UCC § 2-501. See Texas Commerce Bank-Fort Worth, NA v. United States, 896 F2d 152 (5th Cir. 1990) (lender bank had security interest in taxpayer's bank account, but failed to prove funds on deposit existed before tax lien was filed, so that deposited funds were subject to lien when deposited). Compare Jefferson Bank & Trust v. United States, 894 F2d 1241 (10th Cir. 1990) (taxpayer depositor had pledged monies in account as collateral security for bank loan; held, bank's security interest existed before lien filed and was choate). See also Jersey State Bank v. United States, 926 F2d 621 (7th Cir. 1991) (property subject to lien had been fixed when bank exercised right to setoff); In re Siebert Trailers, Inc., 132 Bankr. 37, 91-2 USTC ¶ 50,308 (Bankr. ED Cal. 1991) (refunds claimed on Forms 1139 for tentative refunds did not come into existence before tax liens were filed, because no overpayment exists until the Service offsets overpayment against any taxes owed by taxpayer).

[60] PPG Indus., Inc. v. Hartford Fire Ins. Co., 531 F2d 58 (2d Cir. 1976) (New York law). Accord Paskow v. Calvert Fire Ins. Co., 579 F2d 949 (5th Cir. 1978) (Florida law); Aetna Ins. Co. v. Texas Thermal Indus., Inc., 591 F2d 1035 (5th Cir. 1979) (Texas law); cf. National Fire Ins. Co. v. United States, 77-2 USTC ¶ 9660 (ND Ind. 1977).

was in the debtor's inventory and equipment and continued first in the insurance policy and then in the funds paid out under the policy as "proceeds" of the collateral when "otherwise disposed of."[61]

The major problem with the requirement that property be "in existence" for purposes of protection as a Section 6323 security interest arises where the security is contract rights. Under the UCC, collateral may be purely intangible collateral not evidenced by a writing (e.g., accounts).

Accounts. There may be a conflict between the UCC and Section 6323 definitions where accounts are concerned. Under the 1962 UCC, a "contract right" was described as an account before the right to payment became unconditional by performance by the creditor.[62] However, under the 1972 UCC revision, the term "contract right" was omitted. The term "account" was changed to mean "any right to payment for goods sold or leased or for services rendered...whether or not it has been earned by performance."[63] Regulations appear to take the position that a UCC "account" will not be "in existence" for purposes of the Section 6323 definition until it had been earned by performance, despite the 1972 revision of the UCC.[64] However, the recognition of security interests in contract rights as qualifying for limited superpriority status under Section 6323(c) may indicate that such interests qualify for priority status under Sections 6323(a) and 6323(h)(1).[65] At any rate, in at least two cases

---

[61] UCC § 9-306(1).

[62] UCC § 9-106 (1962). Treasury regulations interpreting "commercial financing security" adopt this definition. See Reg. § 301.6323(c)-1(c)(2)(i).

[63] UCC § 9-106.

[64] See Reg. § 301.6323(c)-1(d), which defines "qualified property" for the purposes of commercial financing security. Regulations distinguish between a "contract right," where right to payment has not been earned by performance, and an "account receivable," which is a right to payment for goods sold or leased or for services rendered not evidenced by an instrument or chattel paper. Regulations state: "An account receivable...is acquired by a taxpayer at the time, and to the extent a right to payment is earned by performance." The protection afforded the holder of a security interest in accounts receivable that arise after the filing of a tax is the forty-five-day protection under the commercial transactions financing agreement rules, discussed infra ¶ 16.05[2]. Because the agreement precedes the lien filing but performance can follow, secured creditors attempt to characterize collateral as a contract right rather than an account receivable to preserve priority over an intervening lien. See St. James, "The Federal Tax Lien in Bankruptcy," 46 Bus. Law. 157, 160 (Nov. 1990).

Section 6323(b)(8) assumes that the notice of tax lien has been filed before the nontax judgment has been perfected under local law. Without specific provision for superpriority of the attorney's lien, the tax lien would have priority. See Capuano v. United States, 955 F2d 1427 (11th Cir. 1992). In *Capuano*, the judgment giving rise to the attorney's lien was choate before the tax lien was filed, so the attorney had priority over the tax lien not because of Section 6323(b)(8), but because his lien was filed first.

[65] Pine Builders, Inc. v. United States, 413 F. Supp. 77, 82 (ED Va. 1976), citing with approval Creedon, "Assignments for Security and Federal Tax Liens," 37 Fordham L. Rev. 535, 563 (1969).

"account" or "contract rights" unearned by complete performance have been held to be in existence for the purposes of an assignment that preceded the filing of a tax lien.[66]

Thus, an assignment of future payments under an existing lease or contract can achieve priority over a later-filed tax lien either when the payments have been earned by performance before tax lien filing (*Pine Builders*); the right to receive payment in the future is unconditional;[67] or the contract or lease was not "property" of the taxpayer at the time the tax lien was filed.[68]

After-acquired property. A security agreement may provide that any or all obligations it covers are to be secured by after-acquired collateral[69] or that the obligation or debt it covers may include future advances.[70] The UCC recognizes that the validity of the security interest in after-acquired property and the security interest for future advances results in a "floating lien" on a shifting collateral in the form of inventory and accounts receivable. If a tax lien arises during the continuation of this type of security agreement, it appears that a security interest does not exist for Section 6323(a) purposes with respect to the property not "in existence" at the time the lien arises, nor would a security interest exist with respect to the amount of future advances. The secured party is provided protection in collateral acquired by the debtor/taxpayer and advances made to him after the tax lien arises even if the lien is filed, although he must follow the rules of Section 6323(c) or Section 6323(d). There is also support for the view that if the security interest is perfected in a class of property and

---

[66] Pine Builders, Inc. v. United States, 413 F. Supp. 77, 82 (ED Va. 1976); Centex Constr. Co. v. Kennedy, 332 F. Supp. 1213 (SD Tex. 1972). See also Atlantic States Constr., Inc. v. Hand et al., 892 F2d 1530 (11th Cir. 1990) (subcontractor's claim constituted an "account" that came into existence before the Service filed the tax lien and bank's previously filed security interest had priority since subcontractor was entitled to lien amount as work under contract was completed); Doan Res. Corp. v. United States, 81-2 USTC ¶ 9523 (ED Mich. 1981). But see Dever v. United States, 81-1 USTC ¶ 9163 (SD Ohio 1980) (assignee held not to have security interest in sales commissions because at time of assignment debtor did not have rights in collateral, a questionable and unexplained partial holding).

[67] Hammes v. Tucson Newspapers, Inc., 324 F2d 101 (9th Cir. 1963).

[68] In re Halprin, 280 F2d 407 (3d Cir. 1960). In *Halprin,* the lender advanced funds to enable the debtor to perform a specific manufacturing contract and took as security an assignment of the debtor's right to payment under the contract. The court concluded that the proceeds of the contract were assigned to the lender as collateral before the tax lien was filed. Compare First Interstate Bank of Utah, N.A. v. IRS, 930 F2d 1521 (10th Cir. 1991) (bank's funds to enable debtor to complete job were for ordinary operation of business, not for asset acquisition, so that contract right was not "collateral or rights in collateral"). The distinction drawn in *First Interstate Bank* is that a purchase-money security interest can qualify only if it is for an asset acquisition; it cannot qualify if it is used to fulfill a preexisting business obligation.

[69] UCC § 9-204(1).

[70] UCC §§ 9-204(3), 9-105(1).

the security agreement provides for a security interest in after-acquired property, the security interest's priority extends to the after-acquired property.[71] The Supreme Court held in *McDermott* that when a judgment under state law attached to after-acquired real property and a tax lien filed after the judgment was perfected, the tax lien had priority.[72] Although the case did not involve a security interest in after-acquired property under the UCC, the Supreme Court, applying the choate lien doctrine, held that the judgment lien did not become choate until the after-acquired real property was purchased (i.e., identified). The Supreme Court, therefore, viewed the judgment lien and the tax lien as attaching to property at the same time, with the tax lien having priority in the case of simultaneous attachment. Reading *McDermott* to apply to the relative priority of a perfected security interest in after-acquired property and a later-filed tax lien ignores the purpose of the Federal Tax Lien Act of 1966 in amending Section 6323. As discussed above, Congress intended to coordinate the UCC and the tax lien priority regime, and to supersede the choate lien doctrine, where Section 6323 provides a rule of priority. However, some courts have applied *McDermott* when a perfected security interest in after-acquired property and a later-filed tax lien compete for priority in after-acquired property.[73]

[b] The Security Must Be Protected Against Judgment Liens

Although the purpose of the FTLA was to coordinate changes in debtor-creditor relationships made by the UCC to the Code, the Section 6323 definitional language of "security interest" differs from the UCC. The Code uses the term "judgment lien" rather than the UCC phrase "lien creditor." Presumably, this language was chosen to be consistent with other parts of Section 6323 (e.g., under Section 6323(a), a "judgment lien creditor" is also entitled to notice of a tax lien). The difference in language has the effect of producing different results under the Code and the UCC. For example, an attachment lien that arises in the gap between attachment and perfection of a security interest has priority over the security interest under the UCC but not under Section 6323, because the attachment lien is not a judgment lien.

Under the UCC, there are different methods of perfection for different types of collateral. Suppose that a secured party's lien attaches to collateral on

---

[71] See J.J. White & R.S. Summers, Uniform Commercial Code 2:321–2:322 (3d ed. 1988); see also McDermott v. Zions First Nat'l Bank, 945 F2d 1475 (10th Cir. 1991), rev'd, rem'd sub nom. United States v. McDermott, 507 US 447 (1993).

[72] United States v. McDermott, 507 US 447 (1993).

[73] See KPMG Peat Marwick v. Texas Commerce Bank, 976 F. Supp. 623 (SD Tex. 1997) (after-acquired property was partnership distribution; tax lien had priority); Tri-River Chem. Co., Inc. v. TNT Farms, 83 AFTR2d 99-345 (D. Id. 1998) (after-acquired property was crop proceeds; tax lien had priority under *McDermott*).

January 1, 1990, but that a tax lien arises on January 15, 1990, and that the security interest is perfected by filing on January 31, 1990. Is the security interest protected against a lien creditor? The answer depends on the type of collateral and security interest involved.[74] For example, temporary automatic perfection is provided for a security interest in instruments or negotiable documents for a period of twenty-one days[75] and for goods in the possession of a bailee[76] or in the proceeds of collateral securing a perfected security interest for a period of ten days.[77] The Treasury regulations recognize that the security interest has priority over a judgment lien (and thus over the tax lien if the security interest is perfected, for example, by filing or possession) during the period of temporary automatic perfection.[78] Also, the tax lien does not have priority over a perfected purchase-money security interest, since at the time the tax lien arises, the taxpayer has no property "belonging" to him, and in any

---

[74] Apart from the automatic perfection of certain security interests on their attachment, a security interest is perfected by taking possession of collateral or filing a financing statement. UCC § 9-302. The method of perfection depends on the type of collateral. Generally, a financing statement is required to be filed to perfect a security interest in most types of property, including general intangibles. UCC § 9-302. However, a security interest in certain types of intangible personal property (letters of credit, instruments, negotiable documents, or chattel paper) may be perfected by taking possession of the property. UCC § 9-305. Consequently, the characterization of property can mean that the security interest was perfected and has priority over a later-filed tax lien, or was unperfected at the time the tax lien was filed and so is not protected against the tax lien. See, e.g., Superior Fin. Corp. v. Haskell, 556 F. Supp. 199 (SDNY 1983) (shares in cooperative apartment type of personal property that could be perfected by possession, so that lender who had possession of stock had perfected security interest at time lien arose).

To secure repayment of loans made to the lessee of leased real property, the lessor granted a lender a security interest in the leased premises and the rental payments due under the lease, and the taxpayer lessee granted the lender a security interest in the lease and the rental payments due under a sublease. The district court held that the property subject to the lender's security interest was the leased property, the leasehold estate, and the rents from the leasehold estate, not rents due on a new sublease entered into after tax liens were filed against the lessee. As a result, the lender had a perfected security interest under West Virginia law prior in time to the perfection of the tax lien. Bank One W. Va., N.A. v. United States, 77 AFTR2d ¶ 96-737 (SD W. Va. 1996).

It also should be noted that a secured party must not only file a financing statement to perfect a security interest, but also refile that financing statement within the time required by state law. See, e.g., Sampson Invs. v. Harold Sampson, 86 AFTR2d 2000-7198 (ED Wis. 2000) (taxpayer's creditor lost priority to other creditors because it failed to refile).

[75] UCC § 9-304(4).

[76] UCC § 9-304(5).

[77] UCC § 9-306(3).

[78] Reg. § 301.6323(h)-1(a)(2)(B)(ii), Ex. (i). However, if the secured party fails to perfect his security interest within the ten-day period, he loses his priority. Security Sav. Bank v. United States, 440 F. Supp. 444 (SD Iowa 1977).

event, under the UCC, a purchase-money security interest is automatically perfected (permanently) as against lien creditors.[79]

The temporary automatic perfection situation and a purchase-money security interest aside, it appears that a tax lien has priority if it exists before a non–purchase-money security interest can be perfected.[80] It has been held that a tax lien executed upon by levy defeats an unperfected non–purchase-money security interest under both Section 9-301(1)(b) of the UCC and the choate lien doctrine.[81] Failure to file a financing statement in all the required places according to local law has also defeated the priority of a security interest over a tax lien.[82] Moreover, it has also been held that solely by virtue of the tax lien a security interest that has not been perfected under local law is subordinate to the tax lien, although a tax levy is not made until after the secured party has repossessed the goods.[83] In view of the developed law, it is imperative that the secured party perfect its security interest without delay in order to avoid an intervening tax lien or loss of priority after the expiration of a period of automatic temporary perfection.

In general, the UCC provides that a security interest is perfected by filing a financing statement and that when a security interest in collateral has been

---

[79] UCC § 9-302(1)(d).

[80] Both Section 6323 and UCC § 9-312(5) are "race" statutes. The first to file or perfect wins the priority race. For a description of the UCC law, see J. White & R. Summers, Uniform Commercial Code § 26-4 (3d ed. 1988). But compare Countryman, Cases and Materials on Debtor and Creditor 409 (2d ed. 1974), with Plumb, Federal Tax Liens 115, 140–141 (3d ed. 1972).

[81] United States v. Trigg, 465 F2d 1264, 1269 (8th Cir. 1972) (bank failed to perfect security interest in contractor's accounts receivable before IRS levy). Without analyzing the state UCC, a taxpayer's promissory notes, executed in favor of a bank and secured by its bank accounts, were held to give the bank a security interest in the bank accounts that had priority over a tax lien filed after the taxpayer defaulted. Trust Co. v. United States, 735 F2d 447 (11th Cir. 1984). The Service has apparently (and erroneously) contended in a priority contest with a secured lender that priority should be determined at the time of assessment rather than lien filing. See Accurate Filter Prod., Inc. v. Dept. of Treasury, 77 AFTR2d ¶ 96-732 (ED Mich. 1996) ("Although the federal tax lien 'arose' prior to the [secured lender's] filing date, it could not defeat a valid prior state law created lien unless it was perfected first through the filing of a 'notice of a Federal Tax Lien'…[which] in this case were not filed until [after the security interest was perfected by filing].").

[82] United States v. Ed Lusk Constr. Co., 504 F2d 328 (10th Cir. 1974). See also George W. Ultch Lumber Co. v. Hall Plastering, Inc., 477 F. Supp. 1060 (WD Mo. 1979). See also Southern Rock, Inc. v. B&B Auto Supply, 711 F2d 683 (5th Cir. 1983).

[83] See Richardson v. United States, 358 F. Supp. 994 (ED Ark. 1973); LB Smith, Inc. v. Foley, 341 F. Supp. 810 (WDNY 1972); cf. United States v. Lebanon Woolen Mills Corp., 241 F. Supp. 393 (DNH 1974); Countryman, Cases and Materials on Debtor and Creditor 409 (2d ed. 1974), at 409. Moreover, if under local law a security interest would be unperfected against a hypothetical judgment creditor who could have obtained a judgment lien against proceeds deposited with a court, the tax lien has priority over the security interest. Dragstrem v. Obermeyer, 549 F2d 20 (7th Cir. 1977).

perfected, the secured party is permitted to realize on the collateral even after the judicial attachment of the collateral by another creditor. The effect of perfection of the security interest is described in UCC Section 9-301, which in substance states that a security interest, unless perfected, is subordinate to, among others, persons who become "lien creditors" before the security interest is perfected. Accordingly, UCC Section 9-301 focuses on the situation where a judicial lien arises in the gap between the creation and perfection of a security interest. For example, if a debtor gives the secured party a security interest on January 1, 1990, and the secured party does not file a financing statement until January 31, 1990, under the UCC, a creditor who obtains a lien by way of attachment on the collateral between January 1 and January 31, 1990, has priority over the secured party.

Although the terminology is different, Congress seems to have intended the same result in requiring that for the purposes of Section 6323(a), a qualifying "security interest" must have been perfected under local law against any hypothetical lien creditor by taking the required steps (usually by filing a financing statement in the appropriate state office) so that the security interest has priority over the lien creditor. Accordingly, a security interest is perfected

by filing before the tax lien arises.[84] If the security interest has not been perfected by filing under local law, the security interest does not have priority

---

[84] See, e.g., Manalis Fin. Co. v. United States, 611 F2d 1270 (9th Cir. 1980); National Equip. Rental, Ltd. v. United States, 78-2 USTC 9780 (CD Cal. 1978); Dragstrem v. Obermeyer, 549 F2d 20 (7th Cir. 1977); United States v. Ed Lusk Constr. Co., 504 F2d 328 (10th Cir. 1974); United States v. Trigg, 465 F2d 1264, 1269 (8th Cir. 1972), cert. denied, 410 US 909 (1973); Nevada Rock & Sand Co. v. United States, 376 F. Supp. 161 (D. Nev. 1974); Fred Kraus & Sons v. United States, 369 F. Supp. 1089 (ND Ind.), aff'd in unpublished opinion, 506 F2d 1404 (7th Cir. 1974); LB Smith, Inc. v. Foley, 341 F. Supp. 810 (WDNY 1972); Coogan, "The Effect of the Federal Tax Lien Act of 1966 Upon Security Interests Created Under the Uniform Commercial Code," 81 Harv. L. Rev. 1369, 1382–1383 (1968).

See also In re Slodov, 436 US 238, 256–257 (1978) (tax liens generally subordinated to "those with a perfected security interest in the property"). Jersey State Bank v. United States, 90-1 USTC ¶ 50,083 (SD Ill. 1990) (lender bank's security interest in depositor's account was protected from judgment creditor under Illinois law; thus, bank's security interest had priority over tax lien), aff'd, 926 F2d 621 (7th Cir. 1991) ("Illinois law would protect the bank's interest in the taxpayer's deposit against a judgment lien creditor of the depositor by allowing the bank to set off the depositor's debt to it with its debt to the depositor (that is, with the deposit) when the creditor appeared on the scene.").

When a county set aside a fund for the payment of construction work, and the contractor was entitled to payment for completion of the construction under the contract it had with the county, a district court held that the contractor was entitled to the fund, and it was subject to the Service's tax lien even though a surety had paid two subcontractors to complete their portion of the contract. Wayne City Bd. of City Comm'rs v. Mendel Inc., 86 AFTR2d 2000-5023 (ND Oh. 2000). In reaching its conclusion, the court found that the contractor's right to the fund was not subject to offset by the county, because the contractor owed no amount to the county, and that accordingly, the tax lien attached to the full amount of the fund. Also, while the surety was subrogated to the contractor's interests in the fund, the surety was not the holder of a perfected security interest because it had failed to file a financing agreement. The court did not consider whether the contractor's contract rights were in existence before the tax lien was filed; instead, it used the choate lien doctrine to determine when the contractor's liens became choate, and these dates were after the tax lien had been filed.

over a tax lien.[85] If the security interest and the tax lien are perfected at the same time, the law is unsettled.[86]

---

[85] However, UCC § 9-301(1)(b) did provide that an unperfected security interest would be subordinate to the right of a person who becomes a lien creditor without knowledge of the security interest and before it is perfected. The Article 9 revisions removed the "notice" element. In a case decided under the previous version, it was said that priority would be granted an unperfected security interest if the secured creditor could establish that all hypothetical judgment lien creditors would have had knowledge of the security interest. Dragstrem v. Obermeyer, 549 F2d 20 (7th Cir. 1977) (the creditor failed).

For other cases where an assignee failed to file under local law, see Dever v. United States, 81-1 USTC ¶ 9163 (SD Ohio 1980) (Ohio law); First Nat'l Bank v. Elgin, 570 F. Supp. 849 (ND Fla. 1983) (bank failed to file financial statement as required by Florida law to protect its interest); American Way Food Serv. Corp. v. IRS, 48 Bankr. 79, 85-1 USTC ¶ 9296 (Bankr. WD Mich. 1985) (buyer of liquor license failed to perfect security interest according to Michigan law). See also Bank of Mount Vernon v. United States, 87-1 USTC ¶ 9245 (ED Ky. 1987) (Kentucky law applied to determine whether bank had a perfected security interest; tax lien had priority over security interest because financing statement was not filed in county required under Kentucky law); United States v. FDIC, 87-2 USTC ¶ 9534 (ND Tex. 1987) (bank had perfected security interest but lost it and priority over tax lien where a mistaken release was filed; Texas law applied). Compare Security Fins. Group, Inc. v. United States, 706 F. Supp. 83 (DDC 1989) (although holder of security interest had not filed in both offices required by Maryland law, under state's "good-faith" exception, holder had priority over tax lien because the Service had reason to have knowledge of holder's security interest).

Where a perfected mortgage lien was erroneously released and subsequently reinstated under state law, the tax lien which was filed after the mortgage lien, was held to have priority. Before the Service had notice of the release, it had the status of a judgment creditor, and under Alabama law, the mortgage was void as to the Service. After the Service had notice of the release, it still had priority over the released mortgage under the "hypothetical judgment lien creditor" test of Section 6323(h)(1), regardless of whether the Service has knowledge of the competing nonfederal interest. Haas v. IRS, 94-2 USTC ¶ 50,496 (11th Cir. 1994) (following Dragstrem v. Obermeyer, 549 F2d 20 (7th Cir. 1977), and distinguishing United States v. Trigg, 465 F2d 1264 (8th Cir. 1972)). See also Cipriano v. Tocco, 757 F. Supp. 1484 (ED Mich. 1991) (assignment of land contract was security interest, perfected under Michigan law when memorandum of land contract was filed).

If a financing statement is filed, the secured creditor's interest may still not have priority over the tax lien under the applicable state UCC where the financing statement does not contain the correct name of the debtor. See Allstate Fin. Corp. v. United States, 109 F3d 1331 (8th Cir. 1997) (Dittrich of Minnesota, Inc. and Zappia Transportation, d/b/a Dittrich of Minnesota, Inc. were sister corporations, and alter egos of one another; held, a financing statement filed in the name of Dittrich of Minnesota, Inc. was perfected as to collateral of Zappia Transportation because it was a filing "under the name of the company that for all practical purposes was the same entity as Zappia.").

[86] Compare MDC Leasing v. New York Prop. Ins. Underwriting, 450 F. Supp. 179, 181 (SDNY 1978), aff'd without opinion, 603 F2d 213, 214 (2d Cir. 1979) ("in the event of simultaneous attachment the federal liens are accorded priority"); and United States v. Graham, 96 F. Supp. 318 (SD Cal. 1951), aff'd sub nom. California v. United States, 195 F2d 530 (9th Cir.), cert. denied, 344 US 831 (1952) (pre-FTLA); with Southern Rock Inc. v. B&B Auto Supply, 711 F2d 683 (5th Cir. 1983) (simultaneously perfected security in-

[c] Value Must Have Been Given in "Money or Money's Worth"

The phrase "money or money's worth" is similar to the requirement under the UCC that value be given by the secured party.[87] In general, "value" is any consideration sufficient to support a simple contract, including the taking of property in satisfaction of or as security for a preexisting claim.[88] Thus, a debtor might owe a creditor a sum of money on an unsecured basis. Subsequently, the debtor and the creditor may enter into a security agreement under which the debtor gives the creditor a security interest in specific goods to secure repayment of the preexisting unsecured claim. Under the UCC, the taking of property as security for a preexisting claim constitutes value. It appears also to constitute "money or money's worth." The tax lien statute requirement that the creditor must have parted with "money or money's worth" is intended to include money previously parted with if, under local law, past consideration is sufficient to support an agreement giving rise to a security interest.[89] There was some authority under prior law that an antecedent obligation that was unliquidated in amount was inchoate and therefore subordinate to a tax lien that did not exist when the security interest was given.[90] However, it appears the provisions of Section 6323 that incorporate local law (i.e., the UCC) no longer require certainty in amount.[91] On the other hand, "money or money's worth" is also a limiting term. It does not include the relinquishment of certain marital rights or consideration in the form of love and affection or a promise of marriage.[92] The effect of the requirement is that the holder of a security interest is protected only to the extent that he has parted with "money or money's worth" prior to the filing of a notice of lien. The lender's security interest does not have priority to the extent of a loan disbursed after the filing of a tax lien, unless the security interest is protected under certain limited conditions from the intervening tax lien by Sections 6323(c) and 6323(d).

---

terest and tax lien "share in fund in proportion to their claims"). See also United States v. Fleming, 474 F. Supp. 904 (SDNY 1979).

The rationale in *B&B Auto Supply* was that giving a filed tax lien priority over a simultaneously recorded security interest would defeat the goal of conforming the tax lien to Article 9 security interests. See United States v. McDermott, 113 S. Ct. 1526 (1993), discussed infra, reversing and remanding McDermott v. Zions First Nat'l Bank, 945 F2d 1475 (10th Cir. 1991) (which had critically distinguished *MDC Leasing, State of California, Southern Rock, Inc.*, and *Fleming*, and held that, once perfected, judgment lien attached to after-acquired property, thereby precluding simultaneous attachments of liens).

[87] UCC § 9-203(1)(b).

[88] UCC § 1-201(44) and Comment 44.

[89] Reg. § 301.6323(h)-1(a)(3).

[90] Empire Standard Life Ins. Co. v. Anderson, 182 F. Supp. 246 (ED Tex. 1960).

[91] See HR Rep. No. 1884, 89th Cong., 2d Sess. (1966), reprinted in 1966-2 CB 815.

[92] Reg. § 301.6323(h)-1(a)(3).

[3] Judgment Lien Creditors

Before the FTLA, the Supreme Court had consistently held that the characterization of a person as a judgment creditor for the purposes of the tax lien was a federal, not a state, question. In *United States v. Gilbert Associates*, a local taxing authority contended that its lien was entitled to priority over the unrecorded tax lien because under state law its lien had the effect of a judgment and therefore it was a judgment creditor. The Supreme Court rejected the state characterization and said that the term as used in the predecessor of Section 6323 was used "in the usual conventional sense of a judgment of a court of record, since all states have such courts."[93] The statute now codifies this interpretation and uses the term "judgment lien creditor."[94] A "judgment lien creditor" under present law is a person who has obtained a valid judgment in a court of record and of competent jurisdiction for the recovery of specific property or a sum of money.[95]

Regulations defining "judgment lien creditor" go further. Where a judgment for a sum of money is involved, a "judgment lien creditor" is a person who has perfected a lien under the judgment on the property involved.[96] Thus, a judgment lien creditor does not include an attachment or garnishment lien or lien lis pendens until that lien has ripened into judgment, even if under local law the lien of the judgment relates back to an earlier date.[97] Therefore, an at-

---

[93] United States v. Gilbert Assocs., 345 US 361, 364 (1953). Both the choate lien doctrine and Section 6323 can be applied in determining whether a state tax lien has priority over a federal tax lien. Under *New Britain*, the state tax lien must be definite with regard to the identity of the lienor, the amount of the lien, and the property subject to the lien. The state tax lien generally is not able to meet these requirements, certainly not at the time a delinquent return is filed. See In re Priest, 712 F2d 1326 (9th Cir. 1983), modified, 725 F2d 477 (1984) (California tax lien); but see Monica Fuels, Inc. v. United States, 56 F3d 508 (3d Cir. 1995) (New Jersey tax lien held choate; see discussion supra ¶ 16.02[2], note 11).

[94] HR Rep. No. 1884, 89th Cong., 2d Sess. (1966), reprinted in 1966-2 CB 815, 840.

[95] Reg. § 301.6323(h)-1(g). A tax lien has been held to have priority over judgment creditor's interest in taxpayer's property, despite the fact that the judgment creditor's interest arose before the tax lien. In this case, the original judgment as to the amount of damages was reversed and remanded, and the tax lien arose before the courts had redetermined the amount of damages. Since the tax lien was filed at a time when the judgment creditor's lien in taxpayer's property was inchoate, the government's interest had priority over the judgment creditor's. Although the final judgment on damages related back to the time when the judgment creditor's rights first arose, the judgment creditor's lien was not choate until the final judgment on damages was entered some two years after the tax lien was filed. Hensley v. Harbin, 196 F3d 613 (6th Cir. 1999).

[96] Reg. § 301.6323(h)-1(g).

[97] Chevron, USA, Inc. v. May Oilfield Serv., Inc., 82-1 USTC ¶ 9408 (D. Wyo. 1982), aff'd, 739 F2d 498 (10th Cir. 1984). But see United States v. Hunt, 513 F2d 129 (10th Cir. 1975) (questionable decision holding a state garnishment lien choate when the proceeds of the lien were paid into court); Warren v. Haggard, 78-2 USTC ¶ 9690 (ED

tachment lien that may give a creditor priority under local law against a competing judgment creditor does not enhance the attaching creditor's position under federal lien law where a tax lien has been filed in the gap between attachment and the docketing of the money judgment.[98]

As they did before FTLA, regulations incorporate the choate lien doctrine and require that the judgment be a "perfected lien" in the subject property. Where real property is involved, the status of a judgment lien creditor is not arrived at until the necessary steps under local law (e.g., recording or docketing) have been taken to perfect the judgment against third parties acquiring liens on the real property.[99] Similarly, if under local law, levy or seizure is

---

Tenn. 1978), aff'd, 627 F2d 1094 (6th Cir. 1980) (lis pendens held inchoate); Middlesex Sav. Bank v. Johnson, 777 F. Supp. 1024 (D. Mass. 1991) (prejudgment attachment did not have priority over tax lien).

When a creditor not only obtains a prejudgment attachment before the filing of a notice of tax lien but also obtains a judgment before the lien is filed, the attachment lien has been found to be choate because the lienor, the property subject to the lien (the attached property), and the amount of the lien (the judgment amount) have been determined. See Floyd v. United States, 77 AFTR2d ¶ 96-1813 (D. Kan. 1996).

[98] This treatment is consistent with the decisions of the Supreme Court holding such liens "inchoate" in United States v. Acri, 348 US 211 (1955); United States v. Liverpool & London Ins. Co., 348 US 215 (1955); and United States v. Security Trust & Sav. Bank, 340 US 47 (1950). See, e.g., United States v. Dishman Indep. Oil Inc., 46 F3d 523 (6th Cir. 1995) (issue was whether a state attachment lien had priority over a federal tax lien if the property subject to the liens was attached prior to the federal tax lien filing, but the final judgment was not entered until after the federal tax lien was filed; Acri followed, and court said that at the time that the federal tax lien was filed, the property subject to the attachment lien and its amount remained uncertain).

[99] Reg. § 301.6323(h)-1(g). In re Vincent Lapiana, et al., 31 Bankr. 738, 83-2 USTC ¶ 9515 (ND Ill. 1983) (reopening of judgment by confession prevents the judgment creditors' lien from being choate under federal law, because the amount of their lien is not fixed until after trial). A judgment creditor perfects his judgment lien on personal property by executing on the property. A writ of garnishment has been held to establish the judgment creditor's right to an amount that is absolutely owed at the time of the writ, but not to future payments, if a tax lien is filed in the interim. Nichols v. Glass, 93-1 USTC ¶ 50,043 (ND Tex. 1992). See KS Fin. Group, Inc. v. Schulman, 73 F. Supp. 2d 1373 (ND Ga. 1999) (unsuccessful postjudgment garnishment held to make judgment lien choate because judgment creditor had done all it could to perfect its interest under Texas law).

The requirement that a judgment be filed in a particular office to be effective can be a requirement of federal law. According to the federal Copyright Act, to be effective as a transfer of a copyright, the judgment must be filed in the Copyright Office, and failure of the judgment creditor to file in that office will give the tax lien priority over the judgment lien in copyright royalties because the judgment lien was not perfected. Broadcast Music, Inc. v. Staenberg, 75 AFTR2d ¶ 95-2754 (CD Cal. 1995) (tax lien was filed properly under Section 6323, and since under Section 6325(f)(5), was not required to be filed in the Copyright Office, it had priority over judgment lien not filed in the Copyright Office). However, the Ninth Circuit reversed the district court and held that (1) the assignments were not subject to the Copyright Act's recording rules; (2) the failure to record them did

necessary before a judgment lien becomes effective against third parties acquiring liens on personal property, then a judgment lien is not perfected under that local law until there has been levy or seizure.[100]

In short, the entry of a judgment by a court probably will not be sufficient to constitute the successful party a judgment lien creditor under Section 6323. The steps that are required under local law to perfect the judgment against third parties in real or personal property, whether it be docketing, recording, or execution, must also be taken if the judgment is to have sufficient status (choateness) to be entitled to notice of a tax lien under Section 6323.[101]

---

not leave the assignments unprotected; and (3) the property was transferred before the tax lien could attach. 104 F3d 1163 (1997).

Even if the judgment is obtained in a foreign jurisdiction and is otherwise entitled to full faith and credit under state law, if the state requires a judgment lien creditor who claims a lien on real property to file a notice of judgment and the foreign judgment creditor fails to do so, the foreign judgment will not be effective against a later tax lien. See Redondo Constr. Corp. v. United States, 82 AFTR2d 98-6675 (6th Cir. 1998) (judgment creditor obtained judgment in Puerto Rico but filed only a lis pendens in Kentucky, rather than notice of judgment Kentucky required to establish lien on realty).

[100] See Durham v. United States, 545 F. Supp. 1093 (DNJ 1982) (government conceded wife with judgment who had caused writ and notice of levy to be served by sheriff on bank was judgment creditor with priority over unfiled tax lien).

Characterization of the property, which is the subject of the judgment, is crucial because different procedures may apply to different types of property. For example, when a creditor obtained a judgment against a judgment debtor that held a limited partnership interest in a partnership, the partnership interest was held to be a chose in action under Georgia law; and under Georgia law, the judgment lien did not attach to a chose until the judgment creditor obtained a charging order, which the judgment creditor had failed to do at the time the tax lien was filed. Prodigy Centers/Atlanta No. 1, L.P. v. T-C Assoc., Ltd., 82 AFTR2d ¶ 98-5145 (11th Cir. 1998).

Suppose a judgment creditor offers to discharge the judgment on the performance of some substituted future performance. The answer is a matter of state law, but the general rule is that the judgment obligation is temporarily suspended pending performance and will be discharged only on performance. In the event of a breach, the creditor may sue on either the original obligation or the new contract, or both, if breach of the accord causes additional damage. United States v. Matthews, 92-2 USTC ¶ 50,566 (ED Wash. 1992) (debtor was still obligated to creditor-taxpayer, and debt was subject to levy). It follows that if an underlying lien has priority over the tax lien, the nontax lien should have priority over the tax lien, even if the judgment obtained by the nontax lien creditor has not been perfected under local law. When a judgment creditor, after obtaining a judgment, garnishes personal property in an effort to execute the judgment, the judgment creditor has perfected the judgment lien on the date of the garnishment. Floyd v. United States, 77 AFTR2d ¶ 96-1813 (D. Kan. 1996) (applying Kansas law).

[101] This action requires some refined analysis of local law. See, e.g., Hartford Provision Co. v. United States, 579 F2d 7 (2d Cir. 1978) (construing Connecticut law where judgment lien was recorded before tax lien but a writ of execution had not been served). Where this analysis is made, the judgment may be upheld. Id.; United States v. Hunt, 513 F2d 129 (10th Cir. 1975). Alternatively, the unfiled tax lien may be given priority because sufficient steps had not been taken. See, e.g., Northwestern State Bank v. United States, 76-2 USTC ¶ 9615 (D. Minn. 1976). Bryan Toyota, Inc. v. Fort Lauderdale Toyota, Inc.,

In effect, this provision is the requirement of perfection adopted by the regulations. Where a judgment creditor does perfect his lien under local law, the lien is entitled to priority over a later-filed tax lien.[102]

Priority issues between a judgment and a tax lien can arise in marital disputes where one spouse obtains a domestic relations order. Treasury Regulation Section 301.6323(h)-1(g) adopts the choate lien doctrine, and so one

---

79-2 USTC ¶ 9517 (SD Fla. 1979), aff'd in unpublished opinion (5th Cir. 1980) (steps under Florida law not taken by state tax department); Mantovani v. Fast Fuel Corp., 494 F. Supp. 72 (SDNY 1980) (execution not delivered to sheriff before lien filed as required by New York law; In re Dulaney, Jr., 29 BR 79, 83-1 USTC ¶ 9201 (WD Va. 1982) (judgment unperfected against third parties under Virginia law); Phillips & Jacobs, Inc. v. Color-Art, Inc., 553 F. Supp. 14 (ND Ga. 1982) (judgment not perfected under Georgia law until after notice of lien filed); New York City Transit Auth. v. Paradise Guard Dogs, 565 F. Supp. 388 (EDNY 1983) (judgment creditor delivered execution to sheriff but no levy was made before the return date of the execution (sixty days after delivery); held, under New York law, judgment creditor did not have judgment lien against taxpayer's personal property because no levy was made before the return date of the execution); Citicorp Sav. v. Agana, 87-1 USTC ¶ 9178 (ND Ind. 1986) (creditor with judgment lien in real property did not have a lien perfected under Indiana law on insurance proceeds before Service filed tax lien). Compare American Express Travel Related Servs. Co. v. Kalish & Rice, Inc., 693 F. Supp. 1436 (SDNY 1988) (judgment lien was perfected under New York law before tax lien filing when judgment execution was delivered to the Marshall). See also Prima Oil & Gas v. Ted's Factoring Serv., 81 Fed. Appx. 290, 92 AFTR2d 2003-7045 (10th Cir. 2003) (judgment creditor who obtained a default judgment failed to serve a writ of garnishment in accordance with Wyoming law with the result that the federal tax lien had priority).

[102] Asher v. United States, 570 F2d 682 (7th Cir. 1978).

A judgment that is apparently perfected may become unperfected under local law. See Gulf Coast Galvanizing, Inc. v. Steel Sales Co., 826 F. Supp. 197 (SD Miss. 1993) (judgment against garnishee held subordinate to federal tax lien because, under Mississippi law, the judgment is a nullity when the garnishee notifies the court of another claim). In an Alabama case, a wife argued that the divorce judgment she obtained against her former husband had priority over a later-filed tax lien against her husband's property. She believed that her judgment was perfected under state law and gave her a general lien on all the husband's property before the federal tax lien was filed. The Service contended that the general lien was not a perfected lien under federal law. Harless v. United States, 86 AFTR2d 2000-5187 (SD Ala. 2000).

It is noteworthy that although the judgment had been perfected under state law, the Service claimed that the judgment was not choate under federal law. The district court held that the Alabama judgment met the choate lien requirements because the judgment established the property encumbered by the lien and the amount of the lien. The property subject to the judgment lien was identified under Alabama law when the wife recorded a certified copy of the judgment. Alabama law created a general lien on all of the husband's property located, subject to levy and sale, in the county of recordation, including the real property the Service claimed under its tax lien. In response to the Service's contention that the judgment did not establish the amount of the wife's lien, the district court held that the state court had awarded the wife $3 million in alimony, and this amount was fixed even if the alimony was payable in installments and the husband had died before paying the second and third installments.

preliminary question is whether the domestic relations order is choate (the answer is likely to be in the affirmative because the spouse's identity and the subject property are identified, and the amount is fixed).[103]

In some states, the determinations of quasi-judicial agencies, such as state or local taxing authorities and workmen's compensation boards, are considered judgments under local law. This characterization is not binding on federal courts interpreting a federal statute, as the Supreme Court held in *Gilbert Associates*, where it concluded that a "judgment creditor" for the purposes of Section 6323 means as used "in the usual, conventional sense of a judgment of a court of record, since all states have such courts."[104] The regulations under FTLA also adopt this position,[105] although the validity of these regulations is drawn into question by the Supreme Court's later opinion in *Vermont*, where a local tax lien arising under a state statute modeled on Section 6321 was held "choate" on assessment, notice, and demand.[106] In *United States v. McDermott*,[107] tax was assessed against the McDermotts on December 9, 1986, but the Service did not file a notice of tax lien until September 9, 1987. In the gap between the assessment and perfection of the tax lien on July 6, 1987, a private creditor docketed a Utah state court judgment. Under Utah law, the judgment created a judgment lien on all of the McDermotts' then-owned and after-acquired real property. After both the judgment lien and the tax lien were filed, the McDermotts acquired title to certain real property. The issue was the relative priority of the tax lien and the judgment lien on the after-acquired real property. The Supreme Court held that the judgment lien did not have priority over the later-filed tax lien. The judgment lien was not perfected with regard

---

[103] United States v. Taylor, 338 F3d 947, 92 AFTR2d 2003-5606 (8th Cir. 2003) (interpleader action involving residue of retirement plan, a stock plan, and a savings plan administered by airline and subject to ERISA, which preempted state law and provided eighteen months for airline to determine whether the domestic relations order qualified as a qualified domestic relations order, which it did, thus giving the wife's domestic-relations-order priority over the tax lien).

[104] United States v. Gilbert Assocs., 345 US 361, 364 (1953).

[105] Reg. § 301.6323(h)-1(g). See In re Thriftway Auto Rental Corp. v. Herzog, 457 F2d 409 (2d Cir. 1972) (city tax warrant had same force as judgment when docketed). Pope v. Birmingham Trust Nat'l Bank, 82-2 USTC 9619 (ND Ala. 1982) (lien of Alabama Department of Industrial Relations held perfected judgment lien). For a case applying Reg. § 301.6323(h)-1(g) and *Gilbert Associates*, and finding a state "court" to qualify as a court of record, see Air Power, Inc. v. United States, 741 F2d 53 (4th Cir. 1984) (Virginia general district court); In re Christina J. Faust v. Wallace G. Faust, 80 AFTR2d ¶ 97-5136 (SD Ind. 1997) (Indiana Department of Revenue tax warrant, which under state law becomes a judgment effective to permit execution by levy, is not a judgment having priority over a tax lien because it was not obtained in a court of record and competent jurisdiction).

[106] United States v. Vermont, 377 US 351 (1964).

[107] United States v. McDermott, 113 S. Ct. 1526 (1993), reversing McDermott v. Zions First Nat'l Bank, NA, 945 F2d 1475 (10th Cir. 1991).

to after-acquired real property because, said the majority, the judgment lien did not attach to the after-acquired realty.

According to the Court's reasoning, perfection requires that a lien attach to the property in question, and a lien cannot attach to property until the debtor acquires rights in the property.[108] Moreover, since the tax lien is valid against a judgment lien as soon as the notice of tax lien has been filed, the federal tax lien was "extant for 'first in time' priority purposes regardless of whether it has yet attached to identifiable property." In other words, at least with regard to the after-acquired property, the tax lien was first in time, although the judgment lien attached to the property at the same time. The majority rejected treatment of the liens as having parity, although they apparently attached simultaneously, while the dissent would have allowed that result.

After *McDermott*, therefore, a judgment lien, even a judgment lien perfected under state law, which state law provides attaches to after-acquired property, does not have priority over a tax lien filed after the perfection of the judgment lien in after-acquired property, because the judgment lien is inchoate in after-acquired property until the taxpayer acquires rights in the property.[109]

[4] Mechanics' Liens

A mechanic's lien is conferred by state statutes and gives those furnishing labor or materials in improving land a lien on the land to secure payment for the work and material furnished.[110] Before 1966, a mechanic's lien that had not actually been reduced to judgment had been held "inchoate" even though it

---

[108] Justice Scalia also said that a security interest is "generally not considered perfected when the financing statement is filed, but only when the security interest has attached to particular property on the debtor's acquisition of that property." This is at best an incomplete statement, because the UCC recognizes perfected security interests in after-acquired property. Congress specifically intended Section 6323 to adopt the same rule as the UCC when tax lien priority was involved. See supra ¶ 16.03[2][a].

[109] See Cotillion Music, Inc. v. Smith, 79 AFTR2d ¶ 97-876 (SDNY 1997) (judgment creditor obtained judgment in April 1994, and tax lien was filed in July 1995, but the tax lien had priority in royalties because until songs composed by the taxpayer/judgment debtor generated royalties, the taxpayer/judgment debtor had "an expectation, but no acquisition," and acquired property only when the royalty payment was made; held, applying *McDermott* the judgment lien was inchoate in the later-paid royalties until paid, and so the tax lien had priority). See Holland v. Penington, In re Buel Penington, Debtor, 82 AFTR2d 98-6309 (ED Ken. 1998) (a judgment lien creditor perfected its lien under state law against debtor's corporation by recording it, and then started an action against the corporation to set aside a fraudulent conveyance the corporation made to debtor; the tax lien against corporation and debtor was held to have priority in proceeds of fraudulent conveyance claim because property had not yet been determined to belong to corporation, so judgment creditor's lien was inchoate under *McDermott*).

[110] See UCC § 9-104(c).

might have arisen before a Federal tax lien.[111] In FTLA, the class of persons entitled to notice of a Federal tax lien, and therefore having priority over an unfiled tax lien, was expanded to include a "mechanic's lienor." Under the statutory definition of this term in Section 6323(h)(2), a mechanic's lienor is a person who under local law has a lien on real property (or on the proceeds of a contract relating to real property) for services, labor, or materials furnished in connection with the construction or improvement of real property. Thus far, the Code definition describes the different types of mechanic's lien statutes.

The definition goes on to say that "a person has a lien on the earliest date such lien becomes valid under local law against subsequent purchasers without actual notice, but not before he begins to furnish the services, labor or materials." Consequently, a mechanic must take appropriate steps under local law to perfect his lien against subsequent purchasers without notice if he is to have priority over a later-filed tax lien.[112] Contrary to the *White Bear* and *Colotta* line of cases, a mechanic need not have perfected his lien by filing or securing a judgment unless state law requires it. Under most state laws and Section 6323, the mechanic's lien arises when the mechanic commences his labor or begins supplying material, even if he does not perfect his lien until long after this time. If the lien arises before the mechanic supplies services or labor (e.g., from the date of the contract), the later date when labor or services are supplied still applies. However, if under local law the mechanic's lien dates from after labor or services have been supplied, it appears that the mechanic's lien arises on this later date for Federal tax lien purposes.[113] In other words, under the Code, the mechanic's lien cannot arise before labor and services are supplied, but it may arise after that date.

Problems with mechanic's liens may arise where the mechanic is a subcontractor and the prime contractor is the delinquent taxpayer. Therefore, to avoid difficulty, the subcontractor may wish to search for a tax lien filed against his prime contractor. If the subcontractor's rights run against the prime contractor, then as a mechanic he is entitled to the notice required by Section

---

[111] United States v. White Bear Brewing Co., 350 US 1010 (1956); United States v. Colotta, 350 US 808 (1955).

[112] Jitney-Jungle Stores of Am., Inc. v. United States, 77-2 USTC ¶ 9751 (SD Miss. 1977). See United States v. Colby Acad., 82-2 USTC ¶ 9450 (EDNY 1981) (claimant required to show it perfected its mechanic's lien under New York law). See also Lawrence v. Albertson's, Inc., 1996 US Dist. LEXIS 19640 (CD Calif. 1996) (although roofers had perfected their liens under California law and their liens were deemed to relate back to the date they began performing services, tax liens had priority because they had been filed and perfected on August 3, 1994, while the services began six days later on August 9, 1994).

[113] For cases applying New York law, see In re Capital Foundry Corp., 64 F. Supp. 885 (EDNY 1946). But cf. In re Chesterfield Developers, Inc., 285 F. Supp. 689 (SDNY 1968). Compare Brumfield v. Pana Coals, Inc., 86-2 USTC ¶ 9688 (SD W. Va. 1986) (mine workers did not have choate lien under West Virginia and federal law).

6323(a). Even a filed tax lien against the prime contractor may not defeat the subcontractor in applying the *Aquilino-Durham Lumber* line of cases,[114] where under state law the prime contractor has "no property" in the proceeds of the prime contract if subcontractors are unpaid because the proceeds constitute a trust fund (as under New York law) or the subcontractors are given a direct right of action against the owner (as under North Carolina law).[115] It has been suggested that the prime contractor can create the "no property" result of the *Aquilino-Durham Lumber* cases by providing in the prime contract for the owner's direct payment to subcontractors on delinquency in payment by the prime contractor.[116]

The priority accorded mechanic's lienors over unfiled tax liens is to be distinguished from the "superpriority" granted repairmen who make small repairs and improvements, even where the notice of the tax lien has been filed.[117] This superpriority is quite limited and applies only (1) with respect to repairs or improvements made on a personal residence containing not more than four dwelling units, and (2) if the contract price on the contract with the owner does not exceed $1,000.

The protection accorded the mechanic's lien should be distinguished from such other statutory liens as the landlord's lien, where no statutory provision has been made. As under pre-1966 law, the likelihood is that a landlord's lien will be inchoate, because the amount of the lien has not been identified or perfected by a final judgment.[118] Similarly, the attorney's lien, which is also a statutory lien, runs the risk of inchoateness except to the extent that it is given superpriority in Section 6323(b)(8). In these situations, it has been suggested that the position of the landlord or attorney might be improved by including such clauses or agreements as would constitute the landlord or attorney the

---

[114] Aquilino v. United States, 363 US 509 (1960); United States v. Durham Lumber Co., 363 US 522 (1960).

[115] See Article 3-A of the New York State Lien Law. Note that under New York law, the federal and state governments are accorded a priority position for the payment of withholding taxes arising out of the job. Flintkote Co. v. United States, 47 FRD 322 (SDNY 1969), aff'd, 435 F2d 556 (2d Cir.), cert. denied, 402 US 944 (1971). See the similar law adopted in Texas. Owens v. Drywall & Acoustical Supply Corp., 325 F. Supp. 397 (SD Tex. 1971).

[116] See Plumb, Federal Tax Liens, 155 (3d ed. 1972).

[117] IRC § 6323(b)(7).

[118] United States v. Scovil, 348 US 218, 221 (1955) (landlord's lien deemed unperfected, even though landlord had initiated enforcement proceedings, where lessee was allowed five days to reacquire property by posting bond). Under the new Section 7425(a), if the landlord filed lis pendens and commenced legal action before the tax liens were filed, the tax lien would be divested from the property, but would be transferred to the proceeds and have priority.

"holder of a security interest."[119] On the other hand, the maritime liens, which are not mentioned in Section 6323 as being entitled to priority over unfiled tax liens, usually have been held by courts to have priority over prior-filed tax liens.[120]

¶ 16.03 THE REQUIREMENT OF A FILED NOTICE OF FEDERAL TAX LIEN

[1] Statutory Rules

A notice of Federal tax lien must be filed if the lien is to be effective (i.e., have priority) over the protected class of creditors and transferees, purchasers, holders of security interests, judgment lien creditors, and mechanic's lienors. As Section 6323(f) states, "[t]he filing of a notice of lien shall be governed solely by this title and shall not be subject to any other Federal law establishing a place or places for the filing of liens or encumbrances under a national filing system." Consequently, a tax lien is properly filed if it is done so according to Section 6323(f) in the single office provided by state law, even if a federal statute, such as the Copyright Act, requires central filing to establish priority.[121] The kind of notice referred to is record notice—that is, the tax lien is not perfected or "valid" against this protected class until notice of the lien

---

[119] For example, the clause in a lease might resemble a chattel mortgage clause securing future advances. However, a financing statement would have to be filed in the same manner as any other security interest, and the landlord without actual notice of the tax lien would be protected from arrears accruing before and forty-five days after the filing of the tax lien. See IRC § 6323(d). See Plumb, Federal Tax Liens, 168, 175–176 (3d ed. 1972).

[120] United States v. Flood, 247 F2d 209, 212 (1st Cir. 1957); United States v. Jane B. Corp., 167 F. Supp. 352 (D. Mass. 1958). Contra The Melissa Trask, 285 F. 781 (D. Mass. 1923).

[121] See Broadcast Music, Inc. v. Staenberg, 75 AFTR2d ¶ 95-2754 (CD Cal. 1995) (requirement that transfers of a copyright, which included the attachment of a tax lien to a copyright, be filed in the Copyright Office, did not apply to the tax lien; tax lien held to have priority).

has been filed[122] in the proper place and form[123] and, to continue its effectiveness against this protected class, is refiled within a specific time.[124]

Proper notice. Substantial compliance in the preparation of a notice of lien has been considered sufficient to establish its validity against a person entitled to notice.[125] Among other things, the proper form means that the lien

---

[122] IRC § 6323(f). In United States v. McCombs, 30 F3d 310 (2d Cir. 1994), the Second Circuit said: "Thus in a priority dispute between the interests of a purchaser or holder of a security interest in property located in New York State (and of the government in a federal tax lien on that same property), section 6324(f)(4) effectively transforms the priority determination in New York from one of 'first in time is first in right' into one in which the first to record is the first in right." In *McCombs*, the finding that a conveyance had been recorded before the government had recorded its tax liens meant the person who had recorded first was protected under Section 6323(a), and that person's interest in the property was superior to the later-filed tax liens, unless the government could prove that there had been a fraudulent conveyance.

[123] IRC § 6323(f).

[124] IRC § 6323(g).

[125] Tony Thornton Auction Serv., Inc. v. United States, 791 F2d 635 (8th Cir. 1986) (lien filed in name of partnership and one partner held valid, although other partner's name was omitted). The National Office has advised that when filing a Notice of Federal Tax Lien concerning a partnership, notice should be given to the persons listed in the Notice. Accordingly, if the Notice lists a partnership and the individual partners, then the Notice should be sent to both the partnership and the partners. See ILM 1999-32-047 (June 16, 1999). See also Weeks v. United States, 87-1 USTC ¶ 9246 (D. Md. 1987) (purchasers of realty from KD Gardner Contracting, Inc. took property subject to tax lien filed under Kenneth Gardner Contracting, Inc., which a "reasonable inspection" (as defined in Section 6323(f)(4)) of clerk's records would have revealed). See also United States v. Sirico, 247 F. Supp. 421, 422 (SDNY 1965) (test is "not absolute perfection in compliance with the statutory requirement for filing the tax lien, but whether there is substantial compliance sufficient to give constructive notice and to alert one to the government's claim"); Hudgins v. IRS, 132 Bankr. 115, 91-2 USTC ¶ 50,397 (ED Va. 1991) ("Where notice of a lien filed against Hudgins Masonry, Inc. was indexed on the same page as the Michael Steven Hudgins, who traded as Hudgins Masonry, this Court finds that there was constructive notice of a lien against the individual Michael Steven Hudgins."); see also Taylor v. IRS, 81 AFTR2d 98-604 (3d Cir. 1998) (tax lien which erroneously identified the taxpayer Selma Taylor as Louis Taylor, a corporation, gave her constructive notice because she had lived with Louis for thirty-two years; the Service was in substantial compliance with the notice requirement). Angello v. United States, 93-2 USTC ¶ 50,391 (MD Pa. 1993) (reasonable search for joint and several liability of Maria and Domenic Angello would have included search of Maria Angello and Domenic Angello individually).

In *Kivel*, the Ninth Circuit stated that "a reasonable inspection of the index" was not to be literally construed, so that "as to documents that are in the actual chain of title the searcher must at least look at such documents as may have a current effect and must then act on the notice imparted." Kivel v. United States, 878 F2d 301, 304 (9th Cir. 1989). See Brightwell v. United States, 805 F. Supp. 1464 (SD Ind. 1992) (gathering cases; purchasers of property had constructive notice of first tax lien fixed for "William S. Van Horn" when correct name on second index card was "William B. Van Horn").

must contain the taxpayer's correct name and have no error of more than a minor nature.[126]

Since 1966, the Code has adopted a "single office" rule for filing tax liens. Thus, if the law of the state in which the real or personal property is situated provides for the filing of liens in a single office, the Federal tax lien must also be filed in that office.[127] However, if state law designates more than

---

[126] United States v. Clark, 81-1 USTC ¶ 9406 (SD Fla. 1981) (Service failed to refile lien containing taxpayer's married name after it had notice of her name change; held, IRS lien of no effect; cases analyzed). Davis v. United States, 728 F Supp 513 (CD Ill. 1989) (where revenue officer had notice that divorced spouse had changed her name, the Service had obligation to refile notice of lien showing new name; incorrect notice extinguished).

Also, when property changes hands from a taxpayer against whose property a lien has properly been filed to a third party and the Service has knowledge of the transfer, a new notice of Federal tax lien must be filed if the Service is to continue to have a perfected tax lien. United States v. LMS Holding Co., 94-1 USTC ¶ 50,045 (ND Okla. 1993) (tax lien filed against the property of bankrupt corporation and property was sold to another corporation, which itself went into bankruptcy; held, the tax lien was avoided in the second bankruptcy because the Service failed to file a notice of lien in the name of the purchaser). The statutory language of Section 6323(f)(4) "plainly required" that the filing of the deed be such that a reasonable inspection will establish that the property is encumbered; therefore, filing under the taxpayer's correct legal name is not dispositive of the sufficiency of the notice. Van Dolen v. IRS, 77 AFTR2d ¶ 96-2040 (MD Tenn. 1996) (after divorce, Genvieve Adkisson's married name was changed to Genvieve Graff; held, nothing in record or index showed that Federal tax liens filed against Genvieve Adkisson or Genvieve Ott Adkisson were notice of lien as to Genvieve Graff).

As the decisions gathered above suggest, no standard has been accepted by all courts. For example, one court rejected as flawed the reasoning of the Eighth Circuit in Tony Thornton Auction Serv., 791 F2d 635 (8th Cir. 1986), and held that a federal tax lien identifying a partnership and only one of the partners, who were husband and wife, did not substantially comply with the statutory requirement and did not give constructive notice of the lien to the husband. Walsh v. United States, 83 AFTR2d 99-930 (WD Pa. 1999).

[127] IRC § 6323(f)(1)(A). In accordance with Section 6323(f), many states have adopted "single office" filing statutes. See, e.g., Rev. Rul. 85-89, 1985-26 IRB 18 (Massachusetts). See also In re Elliott, 67 Bankr. 866, 87-1 USTC ¶ 9118 (Bankr. DRI 1986) (single office for filing liens in Rhode Island in the office of recorder of deeds); In re Aiken, 133 Bankr. 258, 91-2 USTC ¶ 50,502 (D. Me. 1991) (place for filing lien in Maine is same for personal property and realty: Maine county registry of deeds; cases for other states gathered).

Suppose after assessment and the existence of the general assessment lien, Collection, in the course of complying with Section 6323(f), files more than one notice of the assessment lien. Does the filing of duplicate notices of lien violate the requirement of Section 6323(f) because Section 6323(f) refers to "lien" in the singular? A circuit court answered the question in the negative because nothing in the Code prohibits the filing of multiple notices, and in the process the court made some useful distinctions about the general lien and the filing requirement. Bourque v. United States, 80 AFTR2d ¶ 97-6255 (2d Cir. 1997). In rejecting what it termed the taxpayer's clever, but flawed argument, the circuit court said that it "confuses the statutory provisions regarding the placement of a tax lien with those describing what actions the Service must take in order to provide notice of

one office, the Federal tax lien must be filed with the clerk of the district court for the judicial district in which the property subject to the lien is situated.[128] The "single office" rule is met by a state law that designates one office for filing liens on real property and one office for filing liens on personal property, even where the state law designates one office for filing liens on personal property of an individual and one office for filing liens on personal property of a corporation.[129] After a court ruled that Florida had designated two offices for filing liens on personal property because, in addition to its single office rule, it had adopted the federal national filing system for aircraft,[130] Section 6323(f)(1) was amended to make clear that a state's adoption of a federal law establishing a national filing system for personal property does not constitute a second office for filing in that state.[131]

There is an additional requirement in order for the notice of lien to be considered filed for the purposes of Section 6323. In the case of real property, a notice of tax lien must be entered and recorded in a public index at the place of filing maintained by a state.[132] Consequently, a notice of tax lien filed in accordance with the state's single office rule is not "filed" unless it has also been entered and recorded in the public index at the appropriate state office.

Where is property situated? Real property is situated at its physical location.[133] Personal property, whether tangible or intangible, is situated at the resi-

---

such a lien." The general tax lien that arises on assessment of an amount the Service has determined to be due arises automatically, and is enforceable against the taxpayer "regardless of whether the Service chooses to file a notice of it." On the other hand, "[n]otice has its own quite different function. It neither creates the deficiency nor confirms the underlying liability, but is needed instead solely to establish the Service's priority against third-party creditors....It follows that the fact that the word 'lien' is used in the singular to explain its automatic creation tells us nothing about whether multiple notices are not permitted."

[128] IRC § 6323(f)(1)(B). The statute says filing with the clerk of the federal district court is required where a state has "not by law designated one office" for filing notices of liens. If the property subject to the lien is situated in the District of Columbia, the lien must be filed in the office of the Recorder of Deeds of the District of Columbia. IRC § 6323(f)(1)(C).

[129] Reg. § 301.6323(f)-1(d), Ex. (4).

[130] United States v. Air Fla., Inc., 56 BR 732 (SD Fla. 1985).

[131] Technical and Miscellaneous Revenue Act of 1988, §§ 1015(1)(A), 1015(1)(B). Regulations restate the statute by providing that the filing of liens is not subject to federal laws (other than the Code) that establish a federal filing system for liens. Reg. § 301.6323(f)(1), TD 8557, issued July 26, 1994.

[132] IRC § 6323(f)(4). This indexing of the tax lien is required if (1) state law provides that a deed is not valid against a purchaser of the realty without actual notice or knowledge of the existence of the deed, unless the filing of the deed has been entered and recorded in a public index for filing so that a reasonable inspection will reveal the existence of the deed, and (2) an adequate system for the public indexing of federal tax liens is maintained at the office of filing.

[133] IRC § 6323(f)(2)(A).

dence of the taxpayer at the time the notice of lien is filed. Therefore, if state law designates the county clerk's office of the county in which the debtor resides as the office for filing liens on personal property, a tax lien filed in that office is validly filed, even if the taxpayer/debtor subsequently moves to another county within the state or to another state.[134] The place of residence of a corporation or a partnership is the place where its principal executive office is located.[135] The residence of an individual probably means his domicile (roughly speaking, his place of permanent residence, to which he returns or intends to return). The residence of a taxpayer whose residence is not within the United States is considered to be in the District of Columbia.[136] The use of the term "residence," whether of an individual or of an entity, carries with it the problems of determining that status.[137] These rules also apply for the purposes of refiling a notice of lien.[138]

Duration. In general, once a tax lien is filed, it is effective for a period not to exceed ten years, which is the period of limitations for collection. A refiled notice of lien is effective only if it is filed in the office in which the prior notice was filed and, if a change of address notice is received by the Service at least ninety days before the date refiling must be completed, in the appropriate office indicated.[139] If Collection fails to refile a notice of lien, the lien is

---

[134] Reg. §§ 301.6323(f)-1(d), Ex. (1), and 301.6323(f)-1(d), Ex. (2).

[135] Reg. § 301.6323(f)-1(b). See, e.g., In re Dave Thomas Co., 51 Bankr. 66, 85-2 USTC 9630 (Bankr. WD Ky. 1985) ("the situs of the personal property involved is the location of the principal executive office of the debtor" under Kentucky law). "Place of business" has been held to mean the "principal executive office." Dimmitt & Owens Fin., Inc. v. United States, 787 F2d 1186 (7th Cir. 1986) (taxpayer's principal executive office was in Illinois, although its operating plant was in California, so factor lost priority on accounts forty-six days after the lien was filed); Brooks v. United States, 833 F2d 1136 (4th Cir. 1987) ("nerve center" test of *Dimmitt & Owens* followed).

[136] Reg. § 301.6323(f)-1(b).

[137] One court has held that where a taxpayer's residence cannot be determined, filing a notice of lien in the county of the taxpayer's last known address is not sufficient to comply with the provisions of Section 6323(f). Corwin Consultants, Inc. v. Interpublic Group of Cos., Inc., 512 F2d 605 (2d Cir. 1975). The Second Circuit stopped short of holding that for a taxpayer without an ascertainable residence the Service can never properly file its notice of lien, but it called for legislative assistance in resolving this problem. Compare Urban Indus., Inc. v. Thevis, 670 F2d 981 (11th Cir. 1982) (taxpayer residing in Atlanta before incarceration held to have retained Georgia residence during incarceration and found to have continued to be resident of Atlanta during period of escape). See also United States v. Bynum, 81-1 USTC ¶ 9295 (EDNY 1981) (prison not place of residence for purposes of filing requirement; pre-incarceration residence controlled).

[138] Reg. § 301.6323(g)-1(b)(1).

[139] Reg. § 301.6323(g)-1(b)(1). The notice is effective only if it (1) is received in writing from the taxpayer or his representative by the service center for the region in which the former residence was located; (2) relates to any unpaid tax liability of the taxpayer; and (3) states the taxpayer's name and his new address and preferably his identifying number, or the change of address is reflected in a return or amended return of the

not effective after the required refiling expires, against any person without regard to when the interest of the person in the property was acquired. Because of this possibility, a creditor might mistakenly assume that a tax lien that is older than six years is no longer effective and extend credit to a taxpayer. To protect creditors against a lien that is still enforceable after the notice of the Federal tax lien was originally filed, the Service is required to refile its notice of lien within the one-year period after the assessment of the tax.[140] Failure to file within this required refiling period has the effect of nullifying the original tax lien filing as to interests in property arising at any time after the original tax lien filing.[141]

The form the notice of tax lien must take is prescribed by the regulations, which control irrespective of any contrary provision of state law.[142] The Service uses Form 668-Y (Notice of Federal Tax Lien Under Internal Revenue Laws)[143] for this purpose. Form 668-F (Notice of Federal Tax Lien Under Internal Revenue Laws) is used where there is a refiling of notice of lien. (See Form 16.1.)

---

same type of tax. No other communication with the Service is considered an effective notice of change of address. Reg. § 301.6323(g)-1(b)(2).

[140] IRC § 6323(g). For any subsequent refiling, the required refiling period means the one-year period ending with the expiration of six years after the preceding required refiling period for the notice. Reg. § 301.6323(g)-1(c).

[141] Reg. § 301.6323(g)-1(a)(3). The Treasury regulations state two exceptions to this rule: (1) property that is the subject matter of a suit to which the United States is party, commenced prior to the expiration of the six-year period, and (2) property that has been levied upon prior to the end of the six-year period. Id.

Unless the new notice of lien is filed, the Seventh Circuit has said that Form 668-Y operates as a certificate of release of lien, citing Griswold v. United States, 59 F3d 1571, 1579 n.18 (11th Cir. 1995). Municipal Trust & Sav. Co. v. United States, 114 F3d 99 (7th Cir. 1997). Suppose the notice of federal tax lien has the wrong refiling date, thereby erroneously indicating that after that date, when no notice of lien has been refiled, the lien has been released. The circuit court in *Municipal Trust* held that when the Service filed a notice of lien on September 13, 1985, with a clearly erroneous refiling date of March 21, 1985, but refiled liens in 1988 and 1990, a bank, which acquired its interest in 1990, could not claim that it relied to its detriment on the erroneous lien. Municipal Trust & Sav. Co. v. United States, 114 F3d 99 (7th Cir. 1997).

[142] Reg. § 301.6323(f)-1(c). Some states permit liens to be filed electronically or on magnetic media, and the Service can file notices of lien by this method rather than by filing the paper form itself. TD 8174, 1988-16 IRB 24 (Apr. 18, 1988) (adopting temporary regulations to cover the filing of notices of lien by this method).

[143] See Form 14.6 at ¶ 14.03[4].

FORM 16.1
NOTICE OF FEDERAL TAX LIEN UNDER INTERNAL REVENUE LAWS

Form **668-F** (Rev. February 1985)	Department of the Treasury — Internal Revenue Service **Notice of Federal Tax Lien Under Internal Revenue Laws**

District Manhattan	Serial number 987654321	For Optional Use by Recording Office

As provided by sections 6321, 6322, and 6323 of the Internal Revenue Code, notice is given that taxes *(including interest and penalties)* have been assessed against the following-named taxpayer. Demand for payment of this liability has been made, but it remains unpaid. Therefore, there is a lien in favor of the United States on all property and rights to property belonging to this taxpayer for the amount of these taxes, and additional penalties, interest, and costs that may accrue.

Name of taxpayer   Jane Jones

Residence   One Main Street
Anytown, NY

Kind of Tax (a)	MFT (b)	Tax Period Ended (c)	Date of Assessment (d)	Identifying Number (e)	Unpaid Balance of Assessment (f)
1040	30	12/31/97	2/18/00	123–45–7890	117,602
1040	30	12/31/98	2/18/00	123–45–7890	103,514

Place of filing

Total ► $ 221,115

Notice of Federal Tax Lien Refiling

IRS serial number _____ 987654321 _____ Recorder's identification number _____

Notice filed with _____ Clerk's Office, Anytown, NY 11000 _____ Date   2/2/01

Taxpayer's address *(if different than shown above)* _____

Signature _____ /s/ John Doe _____ Title _____ Revenue Officer

This notice was prepared and signed at _____ One Broadway, Anytown, NY _____

on this the _____ 2nd _____ day of _____ February _____ 2000.

Signature _____ /s/ John Doe _____ Title _____ Revenue Officer

Note: Certificate of officer authorized by law to take acknowledgments is not essential to the validity of Notice of Federal Tax Lien. Rev. Rul. 71-466. 1971-2 C.B. 409.

Part 1 – To be kept by recording office   Cat. No. 16742R   Form 668-F (Rev. 2-85)

[2] Federal Tax Lien Filing Procedures

Section 6323 does not require the filing of a notice of Federal tax lien at any particular time. Regulations are also silent on this matter. No definitive set of administrative rules governs lien filing, but collection personnel are given guidelines.[144] Collection personnel should exercise judgment in deciding whether to file a notice of Federal tax lien. In the usual case, the first step is to make a "reasonable effort" to contact the taxpayer.[145] The effort to contact the taxpayer is to afford the taxpayer the opportunity to make payment, explaining the effect lien filing could have on the taxpayer's business and credit. Although computer-generated notices may be sufficient for filing a notice of Federal tax lien without further action, if a notice of Federal tax lien has not been filed previously, a revenue officer will make a determination on whether to file a notice of the tax lien at the same time that the revenue officer attempts to contact the taxpayer to give the taxpayer the opportunity to pay the delinquent amount.[146] If the taxpayer does not make full payment or provide some other security arrangement, the revenue officer will decide whether to file a notice of the lien. Revenue officers are supposed to consider specific criteria in making their decision for or against filing the notice of lien. In general, this criteria would be the taxpayer's compliance history, the taxpayer's actual performance in substantiating claims, and the taxpayer's entering into arrangements to provide for payment, such as collateral agreements.[147]

When the revenue officer makes the decision to file a notice of Federal tax lien, the revenue officer obtains supervisor approval and completes the form notice. In the usual case, the result is that a lien is filed.[148]

---

[144] IRM 5.12.3 Taxpayer Contact (May 20, 2005); IRM 5.12.2.4 Notice of Federal Tax Lien Determination (May 20, 2005); IRM 5.12.2.4.1 Criteria for Filing a NFTL (May 20, 2005); IRM 5.12.2.4.2 Criteria for Not Filing a NFTL (May 20, 2005).

[145] IRM 5.12.3 Taxpayer Contact (May 20, 2005).

[146] IRM 5.12.3 Taxpayer Contact (May 20, 2005). Contact is supposed to be made in person; by telephone; or by a notice sent by certified mail, delivered in person, or left at the taxpayer's last known address. Contact is not necessary if a lien is already on file.

[147] IRM 5.12.2.4 Notice of Federal Tax Lien Determination (May 20, 2005); IRM 5.12.2.4.1 Criteria for Filing a NFTL (May 20, 2005); IRM 5.12.2.4.2 Criteria for Not Filing a NFTL (May 20, 2005).

[148] IRM 5.12.2.6, Preparing the NFTL (May 20, 2005) provides a prototype for preparing the notice of lien; IRM 5.12.2.8 Place for Filing of Notice of Federal Tax Lien (May 20, 2005). A notice is refiled when the collection period is either extended or suspended, IRM 5.12.2.19 Refiling the NFTL (May 20, 2005).

¶ 16.04 PERSONS PROTECTED AGAINST FILED TAX LIENS—SUPERPRIORITIES: SECTION 6323(B)

Prior to 1966, even if a federal tax lien was filed, it was not valid against a mortgagee, pledgee, or purchaser of a security or against certain purchasers of motor vehicles, if the transfer was made for adequate or full consideration in money or money's worth and without notice or knowledge of the existence of the tax lien. These interests were said to be "superpriorites." In 1966, eight other superpriorities were added to the superpriorities for securities and motor vehicles. (See Form 16.1.) Some of these superpriorities are casual or common transactions (e.g., purchases of personal property at retail or in casual sale or those of securities on a motor vehicle) where it could not reasonably be expected that the purchaser check for filed tax liens. Others are transactions that tend to increase the value of the taxpayer's property (e.g., possessory liens attaching to repaired personal property or mechanic's liens for certain repairs and improvements to residential property). Others (e.g., policy and premium loans or passbook loans) do not easily fit into any category, except perhaps transfers of a debtor's funds where checking for liens would be commercially infeasible.

TABLE 16.1
The Ten Superpriorities

Section	Subject	Property Involved	Person Protected	Requires Actual Notice	Has Absolute Priority	Needs Intent to Hinder or Evade
6323(b)(1)	Securities	Security	Purchaser; holder of security interest	Yes	No	No
6323(b)(2)	Motor vehicles	Motor vehicle	Purchaser	Yes	No	No
6323(b)(3)	Retail purchasers	Tangible personal property	Retail purchaser	No	No	No
6323(b)(4)	Casual sales	Tangible personal property	Purchaser	Yes	No	No
6323(b)(5)	Possessory liens	Tangible personal property	Repairman, artisan, mechanic, etc.	No	Yes*	No
6323(b)(6)	Real property and special assessment liens	Real property	Taxing authority	No	Yes*	No
6323(b)(7)	Small repairs and improvements	Residential real property	Mechanic's lienor	No	Yes*	No
6323(b)(8)	Attorney's liens	Judgments and settlements	Attorney	No	Yes*	No
6323(b)(9)	Certain insurance contracts	Cash loan value	Insurer	Yes	No	No
6323(b)(10)	Passbook loans	Savings account	Savings institution	Yes	No*	No

* Qualifications noted in discussion.

Source: IRM, Exhibit 5400-4, MT 5-1 (Aug. 1978).

[1] Actual Notice or Knowledge

Most superpriorities lose their status if at the time that the protected claimant deals with the taxpayer the protected claimant has "actual notice or knowledge" of the existence of the Federal tax lien. According to Section 6323(i), an organization has "actual notice or knowledge," when the organization has actual or constructive knowledge of the existence of the Federal tax lien. Actual notice or knowledge exists from the time the fact is brought to the attention of the individual conducting the transaction for the organization. Constructively, actual notice or knowledge exists from the time the fact would have been brought to the individual's attention, if the organization had exercised due diligence by maintaining routines for communicating information to the person conducting the transaction.[149] Due diligence does not require an individual in the organization to communicate information, unless the communication is part of the individual's regular duties, or unless the individual has reason to know of the transaction and that the transaction would be materially affected by the information.

To appreciate how factual issues complicate Section 6323(i), it is helpful to compare the actual notice or knowledge definition of Section 6323(i) with when a person has notice of a fact for purposes of the UCC. A person has notice of a fact in the UCC definition, when (1) the person has actual knowledge of it; (2) the person has received a notice or notification of it; or (3) from all the facts and circumstances known to the person at the time, the person has reason to know that the fact exists. A person "knows" or has "knowledge" of a fact when he has actual knowledge of it.[150]

---

[149] IRC § 6323(i)(1); Reg. § 301.6323(i)-1(a). For a case where actual notice was found, see United States v. Eads, 82-1 USTC ¶ 9345 (MD Tenn. 1982) (knowledge of bank cashier who signed financing agreement constituted actual knowledge of bank).

[150] UCC § 1-201(25).

[2] The Ten Superpriorities

[a] Securities

Even where a tax lien is filed, Section 6323(b)(1) provides that the lien is not valid with respect to a "security"[151] as against (1) a "purchaser"[152] of the security who at the time of the purchase did not have actual notice or knowledge of the existence of the lien, (2) the "holder of a security interest"[153] who at the time the security interest came into existence did not have actual notice or knowledge of the lien, or (3) a transferee of an interest, who is protected to the same extent that the lien is invalid against his transferor because of exception (1) or (2).[154] The status of the first purchaser can insulate but not taint a later purchaser or creditor. For example, suppose A purchases a security from B, the taxpayer, after a notice of tax lien has been filed, without actual notice or knowledge of the existence of the lien. Not only is A protected, but if A thereafter sells the security to C, who, at the time of the sale, has actual knowledge of the existence of the lien, C is also protected against the federal tax lien.[155] On the other hand, if A had notice of the lien but C did not, C is still protected and is not tainted by A's knowledge.[156]

---

[151] A security is (1) a debt instrument issued by a corporation or a government or political subdivision thereof, with interest coupons or in registered form; (2) a share of stock; (3) a voting trust certificate; (4) a warrant or right to subscribe to or purchase item (1), (2), or (3), or any certificate of interest or participation in, certificate of deposit or receipt for, or temporary or interim certificate for item (1), (2), or (3); (5) a negotiable instrument; or (6) money. IRC § 6323(h)(6) and Reg. § 301.6323(h)-1(a).

Shares in a cooperative apartment do not constitute a security entitling the purchaser to superpriority status.

Malkin v. United States, 645 F. Supp. 229 (SDNY 1986). Negotiability without interference from a tax lien is at the heart of the definition. For example, a bank check endorsed to an individual rendering services had been held to be security, and the endorsee entitled to priority over the tax lien of the endorsee was a holder in due course. Geiselman v. United States, 961 F2d 1 (1st Cir. 1992). The term "money" does not include a generalized right to receive money, because it would bring nonnegotiable instruments as well as accounts receivable within the definition of "security." Christison v. United States, 960 F2d 613 (7th Cir. 1992) (right to payment for goods or services under lease with department store did not constitute money).

[152] The term "purchaser" is defined in IRC § 6323(h)(6) and Reg. § 301.6323(h)-1(f).

[153] The term "security interest" is defined in IRC § 6323(h)(1) and Reg. § 301.6323(h)-1(a).

[154] Reg. § 301.6323(b)-1(a)(1). See also Reg. § 301.6323(b)-1(a)(2), Ex. (5). However, the holder of a security interest in a security does not qualify for the superpriority. Reg. § 301.6323(b)-1(a)(2), Ex. (6).

[155] HR Rep. No. 1884, 89th Cong., 2d Sess. (1966), reprinted in 1966-2 CB 815, 840; Reg. § 301.6323(b)-1(a)(2), Exs. (1), (2) (purchase and sale); HR Rep. No. 1884, 89th Cong., 2d Sess. (1966), reprinted in 1966-2 CB 815, 840, Exs. (3), (4) (security interest).

[156] Reg. § 301.6323(b)-1(a)(2), Ex. (5).

[b] Motor Vehicles

A purchaser of a motor vehicle[157] is protected against a tax lien filed with respect to the property of the seller if (1) the purchaser is without actual notice or knowledge of the existence of the lien at the time of the purchase, and (2) before he obtains such actual notice or knowledge he has acquired possession of the motor vehicle and has not thereafter relinquished possession of the motor vehicle to the seller or his agent.[158]

[c] Personal Property Purchased at Retail

Ordinarily, a retail purchaser of property would be subject to a tax lien against the seller attaching the property before the sale, although the Service prior to 1966 rarely attempted to trace and claim this property after it was in the hands of individual purchasers.[159] To remove this potential liability, Section 6323(b)(3) protects a purchaser at an ordinary retail outlet, even if a notice of tax lien had previously been filed and attached to the article purchased and the purchaser had actual notice or knowledge, unless he intended his purchases to hinder, evade, or defeat the collection of any tax or knew his purchase would achieve the same result.[160] The House report on the FLTA contained the example of a purchaser of a refrigerator who made the purchase at an ordinary retail outlet.[161] This purchaser would be protected under the superpriority for retail sales, even where a tax lien outstanding against the seller had been filed before the purchase had been made. Although this protection is made available to a purchaser with actual notice, the protection is not available if the purchaser (1) intended his purchase to hinder, evade, or defeat the collection of any tax, or (2) knows his purchase will achieve this result.

[d] Personal Property Purchased in Casual Sale

If a person purchases personal property in a casual sale, the purchaser is protected from a tax lien that may have been filed against the seller.[162] The personal property must be household goods, personal effects, or other tangible personal property (described in Section 6334(a), relating to property exempt from levy) purchased other than for resale in a casual sale for less than

---

[157] IRC § 6323(h)(3) defines "motor vehicle."

[158] IRC § 6323(b)(2); Reg. § 301.6323(b)-1(b).

[159] HR Rep. No. 1884, 89th Cong., 2d Sess. (1966), reprinted in 1966-2 CB 815, 817.

[160] Reg. § 301.6323(b)-1(c)(2). A retail sale also includes a going-out-of-business sale that is not a bulk sale or an unusually large (in terms of quantity) sale.

[161] HR Rep. No. 1884, 89th Cong., 2d Sess. (1966), reprinted in 1966-2 CB 815, 840; Reg. § 301.6323(b)-1(c)(3).

[162] IRC § 6323(b)(4).

$1,000.[163] The purchaser is protected only if the purchaser does not have actual notice or knowledge of either (1) the existence of the tax lien,[164] or (2) the fact that the sale is one of a series of sales.[165]

[e] Personal Property Subject to Possessory Loan

A prior-filed tax lien is not valid against tangible personal property subject to a lien under local law securing the reasonable price of the repair of improvement of the property if the holder of the lien is, and has been, continuously in possession of such property from the time his lien arose.[166] For example, if local law gives an automobile mechanic the right to retain possession of an automobile he has repaired as security for payment of the repair bill and the mechanic retains continuous possession of the automobile until his lien is satisfied, a tax lien that has attached to the automobile is not valid to the extent of the repair bill, regardless of when notice of the lien is filed and regardless of whether the mechanic had actual notice at the time he started his work.[167] The protected person under this superpriority is the mechanic who actually repairs and has possession. Unlike most other superpriorities, there is an absolute priority for the mechanic if he meets the criteria of the statute.

[f] Real Property Tax and Special Assessment Liens

A filed notice of federal lien is not valid against a holder of a lien on the real property if under local law, (1) the lien is entitled to priority over security interests in the real property that are prior in time; and (2) the lien either (a) secures a tax of general application based upon the value of property, or (b) secures charges for utilities or public services furnished to the property.[168] The

---

[163] The IRS Restructuring and Reform Act of 1998 (the 1998 Act), HR 2676, 105th Cong. 2d Sess., increases the amount of the superpriority for personal property purchased in a casual sale from $250 to $1,000, subject to cost-of-living increases. IRC § 6321(b)(4), amended by 1998 Act § 3435(a), eff. July 22, 1998.

[164] The House report used the example of a person who purchases a television set from his neighbor and who does not have actual notice or knowledge (1) that a tax lien has attached to the set, or (2) that his purchase is one of a series of sales by his neighbor. HR Rep. No. 1884, 89th Cong., 2d Sess. (1966), reprinted in 1966-2 CB 815, 841. This example is now in the regulations. Reg. § 301.6323(b)-1(d)(3), Ex. (2).

[165] "Series of sales" means separate sales by which a seller plans to dispose of substantially all his household goods, personal effects, and other tangible property exempt from levy. Reg. § 301.6323(b)-1(d)(2).

[166] IRC § 6323(b)(5); Reg. § 301.6323(b)-1(e).

[167] Reg. § 301.6323(b)-1(e); HR Rep. No. 1884, 89th Cong., 2d Sess. (1966), reprinted in 1966-2 CB 815, 841.

[168] IRC § 6323(b)(6); Reg. § 301.6323(b)-1(f). What happens when IRC § 6323(b)(6) gives priority to county and municipal liens, but state law gives the state's lien priority

party protected under all three of the situations is the taxing authority or some-one taking the lien rights of the tax authority. The holder of a lien securing the payment of ad valorem real property taxes to which real property is subject has priority over a federal tax lien that is prior in time. This treatment changes the result in *United States v. Buffalo Savings Bank*,[169] where the Supreme Court held that "the state may not avoid the priority rules of the federal tax lien by the formalistic devise of characterizing subsequently accruing local liens as expenses of sale." Although the result in *Buffalo Savings Bank* has been changed, the statement by the Court is still effective in priority cases. If real estate taxes, whenever they accrue, have priority over mortgages under lo-cal law, they also have priority over federal tax liens. The same result also fol-lows if a lien secures the payment of a special assessment imposed directly on the real property by any taxing authority to defray the cost of a new sewer line, sidewalk, or road paving project arising after the federal tax lien is in ex-istence. The holder of a lien on real property that secures the payment of the cost of electric power or water supplied by a governmental entity (state, local, or federal) to real property also has priority over a federal tax lien. Just as the possessory lien is absolute, the superpriority of local taxes, the special assess-ments lien, or public service lien is absolute.

　　　Some state and local taxes are not covered by the superpriority. These ex-cluded taxes are state and local income, personal property, occupation, and sales taxes. Even if the lien has arisen before the federal tax lien, liens for these taxes must qualify as "choate" by virtue of their being identified as to the taxpayer, amount, and property subject to the lien. The likelihood that the state or local tax lien will satisfy the choate lien has increased since the Su-preme Court's decision in *United States v. Vermont*,[170] where a local tax hav-ing the same generality as the federal assessment lien of Section 6321 was held choate on assessment, notice, and demand.[171] State or local characteriza-tions of the lien as a judgment, so that the taxing authority is said to be a "judgment lien creditor," are not binding on a federal court. The lien, however characterized, still must be a choate lien.[172]

---

over the county and municipal liens? One district court held that the state lien has priority over the federal lien in the amount of the municipal liens, and that the county and munici-pal liens have a position following the lien positions of the Service and the state. United States v. Gleneagles Inv. Co., 584 F. Supp. 671 (MD Pa. 1984).

　[169] United States v. Buffalo Sav. Bank, 371 US 228, 229 (1963). This statutory change was intentional. HR Rep. No. 1884, 89th Cong., 2d Sess. (1966), reprinted in 1966-2 CB 815, 841.

　[170] United States v. Vermont, 377 US 351 (1964).

　[171] The Court acknowledged that this result would not have been reached in applying the choate lien test in an insolvency situation governed by the predecessor of 31 USC § 3713. United States v. City of New Britain, 347 US 81 (1954).

　[172] See, e.g., In re Thriftway Auto Rental Corp. v. Herzog, 457 F2d 409 (2d Cir. 1972) (compare opinion reported at 72-1 USTC ¶ 9311) (under New York law, docketed

[g] Residential Property Subject to a Mechanic's Lien for Small Repairs and Improvements

A superpriority exists for a mechanic who makes small repairs to or improvements on real property. However, since the purpose of the provision is to relieve contractors and others from the burden of searching lien records when they make small repairs and improvements, the property must be a personal residence containing not more than four dwelling units, with the owner occupying one of the units, and the total contract price including labor and material must be $5,000 or less to be eligible for the absolute priority afforded the mechanic's lienor.[173] For example, suppose Jones and his wife own and reside in a house, and also jointly owe Federal income tax for a number of years. The Service has filed a notice of Federal tax lien against Jones and his wife so that lien encumbers the property. After the Federal tax lien has been filed, Jones and his wife sign a contract with a roofer for repairs to the roof of the house at a cost, including labor and materials, of $5,000. The roofer purchases materials from a materialman for $600. If the local law gives the roofer and the materialman mechanic's liens on the property, their liens have priority over the federal tax lien, even if they have actual notice or knowledge of the filed notice of lien.[174] If the contract price were $5,100, the federal tax lien would have priority over the mechanic's liens of both the roofer and the materialman.[175]

[h] Attorney's Liens

An attorney has priority over a tax lien filed before the suit or other proceeding was commenced, even if he has actual notice or knowledge of the filing of the notice of tax lien, if under local law he holds a lien on or a contract enforceable against a judgment or other amount in settlement of a claim, to the extent of his reasonable compensation for obtaining the judgment or procuring

---

city warrant for taxes constituted a statutory lien, enforceable by judgment execution as any other judgment or by administrative action; held, city lien choate when docketed). The Second Circuit appears to say in *Thriftway* that characterization of the lien as a judgment standing alone be ineffective to give it priority. Compare In re Priest, 712 F2d 1326 (9th Cir. 1983) (state statute created lien on receipt of delinquent tax return; held, lien was not sufficiently choate to take priority over federal tax lien because state had not yet computed actual amount owed, including penalties and interest; *Thriftway* distinguished).

[173] IRC § 6323(b)(7); Reg. § 301.6323(b)-1(g). The IRS Restructuring and Reform Act of 1998 increased the amount of a mechanic's lien for certain repairs and improvements from $1,000 to $5,000. IRC § 6323(b)(7), as amended by 1998 Act, § 3435(a), applicable July 22, 1998. This amount is subject to cost-of-living increases.

[174] See Reg. § 301.6323(b)-1(g)(2), Ex. (1).

[175] See Reg. § 301.6323(b)-1(g)(2), Ex. (1).

the settlement.[176] The superpriority granted an attorney's lien is a priority limited to compensation for services the attorney has rendered in obtaining a judgment in favor of the taxpayer or securing a settlement in favor of the taxpayer. Thus, it is supported by the same rationale supporting the superpriorities for certain possessory lienors—the value of the taxpayer's property has been enhanced by the services of the person granted the superpriority.[177]

To the chagrin of attorneys, because their services have not enhanced the value of the taxpayer's property and therefore the value of the Service's lien on the taxpayer's property, the superiority does not apply to a lien for services of the attorney in defending the taxpayer's title to money or property rather than in prosecuting his right to recover money or property.[178] In the former sit-

---

[176] IRC § 6323(b)(8); Reg. § 301.6323(b)-1(h). The Service may seize a taxpayer's chose in action by levy. If it does, is the taxpayer's lawyer who prosecutes the action for the taxpayer entitled to attorney fees, or do the proceeds belong entirely to the Service? Without mentioning the lawyer's superpriority status, a Bankruptcy Court held that the lawyer had priority. In re Birco Mining Co., 10 Bankr. 545, 81-1 USTC ¶ 9401 (Bankr. ND Ala.), aff'd, 14 Bankr. 1017, 81-2 USTC ¶ 9571 (ND Ala. 1981).

[177] The superpriority for attorney's liens is not intended to protect attorneys, but to encourage them to bring suits and obtain judgments that will put their clients in a position to be better able to pay their tax liabilities. United States v. McGaughey, 83 AFTR2d ¶ 99-2023 (SD Ill. 1999) (attorney did not have a superpriority because he did not obtain the judgment or settlement; a receiver of the taxpayer's property obtained an interim compensation order, which was against the Service's interests); see also Montovan v. United States, 864 F. Supp. 519, 523 (ED Va. 1994) ("An attorney is not given a share of the judgment when he merely takes money out of one of the [g]overnment's pockets so that it can be put in another."); United States v. Murray, 963 F. Supp. 52, 56 (D. Mass. 1997). In Reed & Steven v. HIP Health Plan of Fla., Inc. 81 F. Supp. 2d 1335 (SD Fla. 1999), the taxpayer, Reed & Steven, sued HIP for breach of contract. The law firm representing Reed & Steven withdrew as counsel and filed a charging lien for fees of $15,038.40. Reed & Steven was thereafter represented by new counsel who agreed to handle the case based on a 40 percent contingency fee. During the course of the litigation the Service served a Notice of Levy on HIP with respect to plaintiff's outstanding employment tax liability. Thereafter, Reed & Steven agreed to settle the action for $50,000. To resolve the competing claims, HIP filed a Motion to Determine Lien Priorities against the settlement proceeds. Citing Section 6323, the court awarded Reed's current attorney the full amount of the contingency, based on the superiority given to attorney compensation over IRS liens. As to Reed's first attorney's charging lien, the court held that the attorney also had priority over the Service lien because the charging lien satisfied the requirements of Section 6323. However, concerning the amount to be awarded to the first attorney, the court looked to Florida law and the principles of quantum meruit and awarded a "reasonable" amount.

[178] United States v. Kuss, 69-2 USTC ¶ 9492 (ED Pa. 1969); Gilberton Contracting Co. v. Hook, 298 F. Supp. 1367 (ED Pa. 1969). Attorney fees are not entitled to superpriority status where incurred by a person who interpleads funds claimed by the Service and other creditors of the taxpayer. Not only are these fees not covered by Section 6323, they are not choate at the time the tax lien is filed. See Chevron v. May Oilfield Servs., Inc., 739 F2d 498 (10th Cir. 1984). See supra ¶ 16.02[2]. Where city police seized currency from a client in a criminal case, the lawyer who successfully represented the client was

uation, the attorney is assisting in preserving the taxpayer's property, whereas in the latter his services result in the recovery of something of value.[179] It has been suggested that an attorney may improve the position of the nonqualifying attorney's lien by taking a partial assignment of the fund involved during or after the performance of services so as to qualify as a "purchaser"[180] or by taking a security interest in the fund or other property of the client so as to qualify as the holder of a security interest.[181] The House report considered the attorney's lien similar to the repairman's lien in that the attorney's services can be expected to enhance the value of the taxpayer's property.[182]

The superpriority of an attorney's lien is limited where the services involved obtaining a judgment or amount in settlement of a claim or a cause of action against the United States. To the extent that the attorney's services result in a judgment against the United States, and the government is able to offset the judgment or amount owed against any liability the taxpayer owes to the United States, the attorney's lien is likewise reduced.[183] In those cases where the attorney's lien enjoys priority over the federal tax lien, it is limited to rea-

---

held entitled to superpriority for reasonable fees for securing the return of the seized money. State of Nebraska v. Richter, 764 F2d 517 (8th Cir. 1985).

[179] Similarly, where the attorney's services were in connection with a sale of property, the superpriority of the lien has not been recognized. United States v. Fidelity Philadelphia Trust Co., 459 F2d 771 (3d Cir. 1972); United States v. JHW & Gitlitz Deli & Bar, Inc., 499 F. Supp. 1010 (SDNY 1980) (services were not rendered in securing a judgment or settling a claim, but were "of the type that are commonly performed by real estate agents or brokers"). Services rendered that did not result in the actual transfer of funds to the taxpayer-client have been held not covered by the superpriority. Guziak v. Guziak, 609 F. Supp. 65 (WD Wis. 1985) (husband established fund in contemplation of settlement of a divorce action).

[180] See Fritschler, Pellino, Schrank & Rosen, SC v. United States, 716 F. Supp. 1157 (ED Wisc. 1988) (law firm became purchaser of nonrefundable retainer where without notice or knowledge of a tax lien it gave irrevocable promise to represent taxpayer and actually represented him). See Plumb, Federal Tax Liens 173 (3d ed. 1972).

[181] See Plumb, Federal Tax Liens, 173–174 (3d ed. 1972). However, a financing statement must be filed in accordance with the state's UCC.

[182] HR Rep. No. 1884, 89th Cong., 2d Sess. (1966), reprinted in 1966-2 CB 815, 818.

[183] IRC § 6323(b)(8). This provision incorporates the rules of United States v. Munsey Trust Co., 332 US 234 (1974), which held that the United States could set off the amount due for taxes against an amount it owed the taxpayer under a contract. See Hill, Christopher & Phillips v. United States Postal Serv., 535 F. Supp. 804 (DDC 1982) (Postal Service is an entity of U.S. government). For a case applying the set-off exception, see United States v. $319,820.00 in United States Currency, 634 F. Supp. 700 (ND Ga. 1986) (although the government was unsuccessful in a forfeiture proceeding, taxpayer's attorney was not entitled to superpriority status because the attorney's lien was on a judgment against the government and, consequently, the Service was entitled to set off the amount of the tax lien). Thus, an exception to the superpriority of the attorney's lien is a judgment rendered against the United States, where the judgment proceeds may be offset against the tax liability of the attorney's client. See Montavon v. United States, 94-2 USTC ¶ 50,559 (ED Va. 1994) (offset includes levy on proceeds).

sonable compensation for obtaining the judgment or settlement. Generally, reasonable compensation means the amount customarily allowed under local law for an attorney's services for litigating or settling a similar case or administrative claim, or on the basis of the facts and circumstances of each individual case.[184]

[i] Certain Insurance Contracts

An insurer under a life insurance, endowment, or annuity contract with a taxpayer has priority over a notice of tax lien filed against the taxpayer in three situations. First, if an insurer makes a so-called policy loan on a life insurance policy after a notice of tax lien has been filed with respect to the property of the insured, the insurer is protected against the tax lien if the insurer did not have actual notice or knowledge of the existence of the tax lien at the time the policy loan was made.[185]

Second, even after the insurer has actual notice or knowledge of the existence of a federal tax lien, the insurer still has priority, but only with respect to advances, including contractual interest, required to be made automatically to maintain such contract in force where these advances are made under the insurance agreement entered into before the insurer had actual notice or knowledge.[186] Consequently, although an insurer does not have priority for so-called policy loans made after he has actual notice or knowledge that the policy is subject to a tax lien, the insurer may nevertheless continue to make so-called automatic-premium loans to maintain the contract in force and have priority over the federal tax lien with respect to such loans if the agreement to make the automatic-premium loans was entered into before the insurer had actual notice or knowledge.[187]

Third, insurance organizations must, ninety days after service of a notice of levy, pay over to the Service the cash loan value of the contract with cer-

---

[184] Reg. § 301.6323(b)-1(h)(1); HR Rep. No. 1884, 89th Cong., 2d Sess. (1966), reprinted in 1966-2 CB 815, 842. It has been held that "compensation" does not include expenses, unless the attorney was contractually obligated to make the payments and the client was contractually obligated to reimburse the attorney. Miklasz v. United States, 81-1 USTC ¶ 9278 (D. Md. 1980). But see United States v. Collier, 471 F. Supp. 1185 (ED Tenn. 1979) (attorney permitted to retain $500 he incurred as expenses). When the original attorney withdrew during a case for the recovery of a receivable owed to the taxpayer, filed a charging lien under state law, and the successor attorney negotiated the settlement of the claim, the original attorney recovered based on the court's determination of the value of the services performed. Reed & Steven v. HIP Health Plan of Fla., Inc., 81 F. Supp. 2d 1335 (SD Fla. 1999).

[185] IRC § 6323(b)(9); Reg. § 301.6323(b)-1(i).

[186] IRC § 6323(b)(9)(B); Reg. § 301.6323(b)-1(i)(1)(ii).

[187] HR Rep. No. 1884, 89th Cong., 2d Sess. (1966), reprinted in 1966-2 CB 815, 843.

tain adjustments.[188] After the satisfaction of the levy by payment, the insurer has priority over any tax lien with respect to any later policy loans made, unless and until a notification, such as a copy of the notice of lien or notice of levy or a letter or the like, is delivered to the insurer that a tax lien exists against the property or rights to property of the taxpayer.[189]

[j] Passbook Loans

A bank or building and loan association is given superpriority over a filed tax lien with regard to a passbook loan[190] only to the extent that the loan is secured by an account with the bank or association and the institution in fact retains the passbook in its possession until the loan is completely paid off.[191] This protection is available only for passbook loans made before the bank or association obtains actual notice or knowledge of the existence of the tax lien. Where a passbook loan is made before this knowledge and the bank or association subsequently obtains knowledge, the superpriority does not attach to any additional loans made after the knowledge is acquired even if the bank continues to retain the passbook from the preceding protected passbook loan.

¶ 16.05 PROTECTION FOR COMMERCIAL TRANSACTIONS OCCURRING AFTER TAX LIEN FILING: SECTIONS 6323(C) AND 6323(D)

Before 1966, the weight of authority was that, regardless of state law, any lien arising under a security agreement contemplating future advances, such as an open-ended mortgage, was inchoate until the advance was actually made. Consequently, an intervening recorded federal tax lien had priority over advances made after the date of tax lien filing.[192] Any lender who made optional ad-

---

[188] IRC § 6323(b).

[189] IRC § 6323(b)(9)(C); Reg. § 301.6323(b)-1(i)(1)(iii).

[190] A passbook is (1) any tangible evidence of deposit, share, or account that when in the possession of the bank or institution prevents withdrawal of the account balance, or (2) any procedure or system that has this effect. Reg. § 301.6323(b)-1(i)(2).

[191] IRC § 6323(b)(10); Reg. § 301.6323(b)-1(j)(1). The bank or institution must fit the description in either Section 581 (relating to definition of "bank") or Section 591 (relating to deduction for dividends paid on certain deposits by certain savings institutions). The IRS Restructuring and Reform Act of 1998 expanded the superpriority for passbook loans to apply to all deposit-secured loans. IRC § 6324(b)(10), amended by 1998 Act, § 3435(a), eff. July 22, 1998.

[192] Rev. Rul. 56-41, 1956-1 CB 562; United States v. LR Foy Constr. Co., 300 F2d 207 (10th Cir. 1962). See also Hoare v. United States, 294 F2d 823, 826 (9th Cir. 1961);

vances under the security agreement merely increased the value of the tax lien. At the same time, the pre-1966 law was somewhat more favorable to lenders whose loans were secured by after-acquired property.[193]

In FTLA, Congress attempted to ameliorate the condition of persons having dealings with the taxpayer under various types of commercial agreements. In addition to interests that are protected when they arise after the assessment of a tax and before tax lien filing (i.e., purchasers, holders of security interests, mechanic's lienors, and judgment lien creditors) and superpriorities, which are protected even though they arise after tax lien filing, Sections 6323(c) and 6323(d) accord priority to other interests arising under certain types of commercial agreements although those interests arise after tax lien filing. Specifically, Sections 6323(c)(1)–6323(c)(4) provide that security interests arising under three particular types of financing agreements entered into before tax lien filing are protected against the tax lien even where funds are advanced under the agreement and collateral is acquired by the debtor/taxpayer after tax lien filing. These agreements are: transactions financing agreements, real property improvements financing agreements, and obligatory disbursement agreements. Similarly, Section 6323(d) provides that under certain conditions a lender may make additional advances after lien filing secured by collateral that was in existence before tax lien filing. The agreements defined in Section 6323(c) all involve advances made and collateral acquired after tax lien filing, while the agreement defined in Section 6323(d) involves advances made after tax lien filing secured by pre-filing collateral. Each of these agreements is discussed in some detail in the following sections. In addition, the general requirements for these various agreements are summarized in Form 16.2.

United States v. RF Ball Constr. Co., 355 US 587 (1958); United States v. Pioneer Am. Ins. Co., 374 US 84 (1963).

[193] See, e.g., Hoare v. United States, 294 F2d 823, 826 (9th Cir. 1961) (involving a chattel mortgage clause in a lease, permitting substitution of property); United States v. Long Island Drug Co., 115 F2d 983, 986 (2d Cir. 1940) (security assignment of future earnings from personal services); Chrysler Corp. v. Long & Long, Inc., 171 F. Supp. 541 (ED Mich. 1958) (proceeds of goods apparently owned before tax lien filing). But see United States v. Pioneer Am. Ins. Co., 374 US 84 (1963). See Plumb, Federal Tax Liens 103–104 (3d ed. 1972).

TABLE 16.2

Protection for Certain Commercial Transactions Financing Agreements, Etc.

Section	Subject	Who	How	What (Qualified Property)	When
6323(c)(2)	Commercial transactions financing agreements	A person acting in the course of his trade or business (i.e., lender, businessman)	(1) Written agreement before tax lien filed (2) Good against a judgment lien creditor under local law (3) Loan made within forty-five days of tax lien filing	(1) Commercial financing security acquired in ordinary course of trade or business within forth-five days after notice of lien filed (2) Inventory* (3) Intangibles:	Forty–five days after tax lien filing or date of *actual* notice — whichever is earlier (loans only)
6323(c)(2)(D)	"	Purchaser of commercial financing security other than inventory.	"	(a) Accounts receivable (b) Real property mortgage (c) Commercial paper	"
6323(c)(3)(A)(i)	Real property construction or improvement financing agreement	Any person	(1) Written agreement before tax lien filed (2) Good against a judgment lien creditor under local law (3) Loans may be made at any time (4) Must be cash disbursement *Except:* Furnishing of goods or service is same as cash disbursement	(1) Real property with respect to which construction or improvement has been or is to be made (2) Contract proceeds of financed contract	Unlimited
6323(c)(3)(A)(ii) 6323(c)(3)(A)(iii)	" "	" "		(1) Crop (2) Livestock or animals financed (3) Property in existence at time of tax lien filing	
6323(c)(4)	Obligatory disbursement agreement (other than surety)	Person acting in course of trade or business	(1) Written agreement before tax lien filing (2) Good against judgment lien creditor under local law (3) Disbursement required by rights of third parties	(1) Property in existence at tax lien filing (2) Property acquired from disbursements required to be made (3) Property traceable to disbursements (4) Contract proceeds of insured contract† (5) Tangible personal property used in performance of ensured contract†	Unlimited
6323(c)(4)(C)	Obligatory disbursement agreement	"			
6323(d)	General rule	Any person	(1) Written agreement before tax lien filed (2) Valid against judgment creditor under local law (3) Loan made within forty–five days of tax lien filing	Any property in existence and subject to tax lien at time notice of lien is filed	Forty–five days after tax lien filing or date of actual notice, whichever is earlier

* Exclude inventory under Section 6323(c)(2)(D).
† Surety only.

[1] General Requirements to Achieve Protection Under Section 6323(c)(1)

A lender must meet three general requirements to achieve protection under Section 6323(c)(1), as follows:

1. Before tax lien filing, there must be a written agreement under which the security interest arises.
2. The security interest must be in "qualified property."
3. With respect to transactions occurring after the tax lien is filed, the security interest must continue to be perfected under local law against a judgment lien arising at the time the tax lien is filed.

The written agreement. The requirement that the agreement be written differs from the UCC, which states that a security interest is enforceable against the debtor or third party and "attaches" when the three elements (agreement, value, and collateral) exist.[194] The UCC does not require that these events occur in any particular order. In fact, since the UCC is a "notice" type statute, it adopts a "first to file" rule, so that absent a specific rule to the contrary the priority of competing security interests may depend upon the filing of a financing statement, even if the competitor's security interest has attached first.[195] Consequently, the thrust of the UCC is to encourage a lender to file a financing statement before a security agreement between the parties has even been entered into. On the other hand, Section 6323(c) puts a premium on the execution of a security agreement before a tax lien is filed.[196] However, perfection of the security interest before tax lien filing is still important, but in a sense the requirement that there be a written agreement prior to tax lien filing is not unlike other provisions of the Code requiring a "plan," and in any event it has obvious evidentiary and administrative advantages.

Qualified property. The second requirement of Section 6323(c) is that the security interest be in "qualified property," a term specially defined for each of the three types of agreements. These definitions are by no means the same. For example, in a commercial transaction financing agreement the "qualified property" includes only commercial financing security (e.g., accounts and inventory) acquired by the debtor/taxpayer before the forty-sixth day after the date of tax lien filing. No such forty-five-day rule limits the term "qualified property" in a real property construction or improvement financing agreement or

---

[194] UCC §§ 9-203(1), 9-203(2).

[195] UCC § 9-312(5), Comments (4), (5). This is not to suggest that the only way a lender can protect himself under the UCC is to file a financing statement. He must either file or perfect (e.g., by possession, for example).

[196] See Atlantic Nat'l Bank v. United States, 536 F2d 1354 (Ct. Cl. 1976) (secured party lost out to federal tax lien where first assignment of contract proceeds was one day after the tax lien was filed).

obligatory disbursement agreement. The lender's security interest in the real property improved is entitled to priority over an intervening tax lien whenever an advance is made under a construction loan agreement entered into before tax lien filing.

Protection under local law against a judgment lien creditor. The third requirement is that the "security interest which came into existence after tax lien filing...[must be] protected under local law against a judgment lien arising, as of the time of tax lien filing, out of an unsecured obligation."[197] This requirement appears to require that the security interest have attached and been perfected as to amounts advanced and collateral existing at the time the tax lien was filed. If at this point in time, the security interest is perfected, then it continues to be protected against the tax lien on collateral acquired by or advances made to the debtor/taxpayer after tax lien filing, to the extent provided by Sections 6323(c)(2) through 6323(c)(4),

Once again, it is helpful to review the UCC provisions. Under the UCC, "perfection," and thus protection under local law against a judgment lien, cannot occur until the debtor has rights in the collateral.[198] Under the UCC, priority does not depend solely on time of perfection; instead, it may be based on priority in filing before perfection.[199] It must be remembered that under the UCC, filing may occur before a security interest attaches (i.e., before, on agreement, value is given and the debtor has right in the collateral).[200] Under the UCC, if a secured party under a security agreement covering existing and after-acquired collateral files a financing statement and the debtor subsequently acquires property subject to a (non-purchase-money) security interest of a second secured party, who perfects his interest by filing, the first secured party has priority.[201] As to both secured creditors, the last event to occur for perfection is the debtor's acquisition of rights in the collateral. When the debtor acquires rights in the collateral, the competing security interests attach simultaneously. Under the UCC, priority is awarded to the first creditor who has filed a financing statement. In other words, at the time the hypothetical judgment lien is supposed to exist, the priority of a security interest in after-acquired property cannot be protected under local law because the debtor has not yet acquired the property. Consequently, UCC provisions dealing with after-acquired property point to the requirements that the security interest must (1) have attached to existing collateral (by virtue of there being an agreement,

---

[197] IRC § 6323(c)(1).

[198] UCC § 9-303(1). UCC § 9-301(1)(b) states that an unperfected security interest is subordinate to the rights of a person who becomes a "lien creditor" before the security interest is perfected. Thus, the converse must be true: A security interest that is perfected before the rights of the "lien creditor" arise has priority over the lien creditor.

[199] UCC § 9-312, Comment 6.

[200] UCC §§ 9-303(1), 9-203 (UCC § 9-204 (1962)).

[201] UCC § 9-312(5).

value given, and the debtor's having rights in some collateral), and (2) have been perfected by a filed financing statement at the time of tax lien filing.

For the express purpose of conforming the UCC with FTLA, a 1972 amendment of the UCC also provides that if a security interest is perfected at the time the rights of a lien creditor arise, the security interest has priority over the rights of the lien creditor for advances made within 45 days after the date the lien arose.[202] Where the secured party has perfected its security interest by filing a financing statement or taking possession before the rights of the lien creditor have arisen and makes future advances while its interest is perfected, the security interest has the same priority for the future advances as it does with respect to the first advance.[203] These UCC rules apply to competing security interests, not to a security interest competing with an intervening judgment lien creditor. Again, the UCC rules contemplate competing security interests, not a conflict between a secured party making subsequent advances and a judgment lien creditor. To come within the protection of Section 6323(c)(1), the secured creditor must have filed a financing statement before the tax lien has been filed.

[2] Commercial Transactions Financing Agreements

Before the FTLA, a lender or factor was required to search the records before making any additional advance (or purchase of collateral) to be certain that the Service had not recently filed a notice of Federal tax lien. In the FTLA, Congress attempted to strike a balance between the practical requirements of modern commercial finance and protection of the revenue. Section 6323(c) does not dispense with the lender's obligation to search the records for a recently-filed notice of Federal tax lien, but it does reduce the burden of the obligation. Loans made after tax lien filing have priority over the filed tax lien for a 45-day period or sooner if actual notice of the filing is obtained before the 45 days have elapsed. As the committee reports state, Section 6323 gives a financer of inventory, accounts receivable, or the like insurance that his loans or purchases are not inferior to some recently filed tax lien as long as he searches the records at least once every 45 days.[204] Security interests arising under "commercial transactions financing agreements" entered into before tax lien filing in certain cases are protected against the tax lien, even where the funds are advanced under the agreement or the property referred to in the agreement comes into existence after the tax lien filing. A commercial transactions financing agreement qualifies as such for the amount of advances or disburse-

---

[202] UCC § 9-301(4), Comment 7.

[203] UCC § 9-312(7).

[204] S. Rep. No. 1708, 89th Cong., 2d Sess. (1966), reprinted in 1966-2 CB 876, 882; HR Rep. No. 1884, 89th Cong., 2d Sess. (1966), reprinted in 1966-2 CB 815, 821.

ments made before (1) the forty-sixth day after the notice of tax lien is filed, or (2) the date (before the forty-sixth day) on which the lender or purchaser has actual notice or knowledge of the filing of the notice of tax lien.[205]

Qualifying lenders. Not all lenders are protected under the commercial transactions financing agreements. A "commercial transactions financing agreement" is defined to mean a written agreement entered into by (1) a person in the course of its trade or business, (2) either (a) to make loans to the taxpayer, to be secured by "commercial financing security" that the taxpayer acquired in the ordinary course of the taxpayer's trade or business, or (b) to purchase "commercial financing security" (other than inventory) that the taxpayer acquired in the ordinary course of its trade or business.[206] To be protected by Section 6323(c), therefore, the lender (or purchaser of commercial financing security) must be a person in the business of financing commercial transactions or a person who enters into the loan agreement incident to the conduct of a trade or business (e.g., a manufacturer who finances the accounts receivable of one of its customers). This would exclude, for example, a sole shareholder who obtains a lien on the assets of the corporation because the shareholder generally is not in the qualifying trade or business of commercial lending or factoring accounts receivable.[207] Also, the debtor who pledges or sells commercial financing security under a commercial transactions financing agreement must be a person who acquired the security in the ordinary course of its trade or business—that is, the security must not have been on the sale of its machinery and equipment or a bulk sale.[208]

After-acquired property. Not all after-acquired collateral is protected against the filed tax lien. The term "qualified property," for purposes of a commercial transactions financing agreement, includes only commercial financing security acquired by the taxpayer before the forty-sixth day after the day of tax lien filing.[209] A lender or purchaser has priority with respect to any

---

[205] Reg. § 301.6323(c)-1(b). "Actual notice or knowledge" is defined in Reg. § 301.6323(i)-1(a).

[206] IRC § 6323(c)(2); Reg. § 301.6323(c)-1(b). The agreement qualifies whether or not the loans are made at the option of the person agreeing to make the loan. See also Rev. Rul. 72-290, 1972-1 CB 385.

[207] Sgro v. United States, 609 F2d 1259 (7th Cir. 1979).

[208] See Reg. § 301.6323(c)-1(f), Ex. (3) (account receivable, acquired on sale of machinery, held not acquired by the taxpayer in the ordinary course of his business).

[209] IRC § 6323(c)(2)(B). See Texas Oil & Gas Corp. v. United States, 466 F2d 1040 (5th Cir. 1972), cert. denied, 410 US 929 (1973) (tax lien filed in February 1970, and contract entered into in September performed September-November 1970; held, account was acquired by taxpayer more than 45 days after tax lien filing); Rice Inv. Co. v. United States, 625 F2d 565 (5th Cir. 1980) (creditor unable to show that the taxpayer/debtor acquired the inventory before the forty-sixth day after tax lien filing; argument that replacement inventory should be protected was rejected); Shawnee State Bank v. United States, 735 F2d 308 (8th Cir. 1984) (receivables acquired by the debtor/taxpayer more than 45

commercial financing security acquired by the taxpayer during the forty-five-day period, even if he earlier had actual notice or knowledge of the filing of the notice of the tax lien, which precludes him from increasing the amount of his priority by reason of further disbursements.[210] Consequently, although the receipt of actual notice or knowledge of the filing of the notice of lien has the effect of ending the period within which protected disbursements may be made, property acquired by the taxpayer after the lender receives notice or knowledge of the filing and before the forty-sixth day becomes commercial financing security, to which the lender has priority for the loans made before the notice was obtained.

Qualifying security. The term "commercial financing security" means (1) paper of a kind ordinarily arising in commercial transactions; (2) accounts receivable; (3) mortgages on real property; and (4) inventory.[211] In general, "paper of a kind ordinarily arising in commercial transactions" includes any written document customarily used in commercial transactions. For example, this includes paper giving contract rights (as defined in UCC Section 9-106), chattel paper (UCC Section 9-105(b)), documents (UCC Section 9-105(c)), documents to title to personal property, and instruments (UCC Section 9-105(g)), such as negotiable instruments or securities. General intangibles such as patents or copyrights, as they are defined in UCC Section 9-106, are not included. Inventory that is commercial financing security includes raw materials and goods in process, as well as property held by the taxpayer primarily for sale to customers in the ordinary course of his trade or business. Commercial

---

days after first tax lien was filed are not protected by the forty-five-day safe harbor, although the receivables were acquired within 45 days after second tax lien was filed).

Compare In re Tunxis Corp. v. United Bank & Trust Co., 19 Bankr. 256 (D. Conn. 1982) (dates inventory acquired do not have to be proven "as long as it can be shown the property was not acquired when the tax lien could attach"; *Rice* distinguished on facts); Court, Inc. v. United States, 82-2 USTC ¶ 9568 (CD Ill. 1982), aff'd, 712 F2d 258 (7th Cir. 1983) (security interest in accounts that came due because of performance within forty-five days after tax lien filing had priority over tax lien, but tax lien had priority over accounts earned by performance thereafter); In re Downtown Cent. Laboratories, Inc., 82-2 USTC ¶ 9491 (WDNY 1982) (Bankruptcy Court ruled that accounts receivable came into existence after the forty-sixth day after tax liens were filed); Polk County Bank v. United States, 83-1 USTC ¶ 9117 (WD Wis. 1982) (same); United States v. North Side Deposit Bank, 569 F. Supp. 948 (WD Pa. 1983) (creditor-lender's choate lien had priority over a federal tax lien on the debtor's accounts receivable acquired by debtor before the forty-sixth day after the date of tax lien filing; *Texas Oil & Gas* followed); Transwestern Pipeline Co. v. Allied Bk. of Tex., 89-1 USTC ¶ 9173 (SD Tex. 1989) (whether property involved characterized as accounts receivable or inventory, tax lien had priority over bank's security interest because interpleaded fund was from payments for purchases made more than forty-five days after lien filing). Simmons First Nat'l Bank v. United States, 90-1 USTC ¶ 50,069 (ED Ark. 1990) (tax lien had priority over bank that advanced funds under financing agreement more than forty-five days after tax lien filing).

[210] Reg. § 301.6323(c)-1(d).

[211] Reg. § 301.6323(c)-1(c).

financing security includes mortgages on real property, provided the debtor is not the mortgagor.

If "qualified property" consists of commercial financing security acquired by the taxpayer before the forty-sixth day after tax lien filing, when is an account receivable or a "contract right" acquired? According to the regulations, an account receivable is acquired "at the time, and to the extent, a right to payment is earned by performance," and a contract right is acquired by the taxpayer "when a contract is made."[212] Chattel paper, documents of title, negotiable instruments, securities, and mortgages on real estate are acquired by a taxpayer when he obtains rights in the paper or mortgage.[213] Inventory is acquired by the taxpayer when title passes to him.[214]

Proceeds of accounts receivable. If the secured party has priority in collateral acquired by the debtor/taxpayer during the forty-five-day period after tax lien filing, what is the effect of the disposition of the collateral on that priority? In the UCC, "proceeds" includes whatever is received on the sale, exchange, collection, or other disposition of collateral or proceeds.[215] Money,

---

[212] Reg. § 301.6323(c)-1(d). Compare Pine Builders, Inc. v. United States, 413 F. Supp. 77 (ED Va. 1976); Centex Constr. Co. v. Kennedy, 72-1 USTC ¶ 9289 (SD Tex. 1972). As these cases say, a "contract right" can be in existence even if unearned by complete performance for purposes of the definition of a security interest and thus can qualify for protection. See also Breman Bank & Trust Co. v. United States, 131 F3d 1259 (9th Cir. 1997) (rejecting the Service's argument that a service provider does not have a contract right until after performance, and concluding that "a contract need not specifically provide a right to be paid prior to performance in order to generate 'contract rights' pursuant to Treas. Reg. § 301.6323(c)-1(c)"); Doan Res. Corp. v. United States, 81-2 USTC ¶ 9523 (ED Mich. 1981); Court, Inc. v. United States, 82-2 USTC ¶ 9568 (CD Ill. 1982); compare In re May Reporting Servs., Inc., 115 Bankr. 652, 90-2 USTC ¶ 50,464 (Bankr. DSD 1990) (relationship of court reporting service with attorneys held not specific enough to prove that binding enforceable contracts were entered into before forty-sixth day to protect proceeds received after the forty-fifth day).

In a case involving a contract for the performance of services, pledged as collateral for a bank loan, the First Circuit held that as long as the contract was entered into within forty-five days of the tax lien filing, the rights under that contract and all of the proceeds of those rights fall within the protection of Section 6323(c), with the result that the bank had priority over the tax lien. Plymouth Sav. Bank v. United States, 84 AFTR2d 99-5573 (1st Cir. 1999).

[213] Reg. § 301.6323(c)-1(d).

[214] Reg. § 301.6323(c)-1(d). Compare UCC § 2-501(1) (title could pass when goods are identified to sales contract).

[215] UCC § 9-306(1). Insurance payable by reason of loss or damage to the collateral is proceeds, except to the extent that it is payable to a person other than a party to the security agreement. Even under the unamended version of UCC Section 9-306(1), "proceeds" included fire insurance for damaged collateral. PPG Indus., Inc. v. Hartford Fire Ins. Co., 531 F2d 58 (2d Cir. 1976); Paskow v. Calvert Fire Co., 579 F2d 949 (5th Cir. 1978). See Sanchez v. United States, 696 F2d 213 (2d Cir. 1982) (insurance proceeds held not to constitute "proceeds" under New York law before effective date of change to NY

checks, deposit accounts, and the like are "cash proceeds."[216] All other proceeds (e.g., a trade-in car) are "noncash proceeds."[217] At one time, there was a question about the treatment of "proceeds" of collateral resulting from the sale of inventory by the debtor/taxpayer or the collection of accounts. However, the regulations now state that "[t]he term 'proceeds' includes whatever is received when collateral is sold, exchanged, or collected."[218] Consequently, the definition both in the UCC and in the regulations is substantially the same.

Regulations state: "Identifiable proceeds, which arise from the collection or disposition of qualified property by the taxpayer, are considered to be acquired at the time such qualified property is acquired if the secured party has a continuously perfected security interest in the proceeds under local law."[219] UCC Section 9-306(3) provides for such continuous perfection under certain conditions. Consequently, a secured party continues to have priority under Section 6323(c) if, for example, he perfects his security interest in the proceeds within the ten-day grace period. If the secured party has a continuously perfected security interest in accounts acquired by the debtor/taxpayer within the forty-five-day period, he also retains priority in the collection of such accounts after the forty-five-day period.[220] In a case decided while the Treasury regulations under Section 6323 had been issued only in proposed form, the government argued that a security interest in finished products (trucks and trailers) and work in process (inventory-type qualified property)[221] perfected under the state UCC before tax lien filing was inferior to the tax lien with respect to trailers completed after the forty-five-day period. The government contended that the security interest in "finished products" was inchoate and that the debtor did not acquire the collateral until the trailers were completed. The court denied that the choate lien doctrine had continuing viability in the light of Section 6323(c) and held that where property owned by the debtor within the forty-five-day period subsequently undergoes a change from raw materials to finished products and eventually becomes cash proceeds, the secured party does not lose his security in the value of the property that was owned on the

---

UCC § 9-306, following decision of highest New York court; *PPG*, decided before New York court decision, not followed).

[216] UCC § 9-105 defines "deposit account" to mean a demand, time, savings passbook, or similar account maintained with a bank or the like, other than an account evidenced by a certificate of deposit.

[217] UCC § 9-306(1).

[218] Reg. § 301.6323(c)-1(d).

[219] Reg. § 301.6323(c)-1(d).

[220] Reg. § 301.6323(c)-1(d). See Donald v. Madison Indus., Inc., 483 F2d 837 (10th Cir. 1973) (protection held to apply to property received after the forty-five-day period as a trade-in). See Walker v. United States, 636 F. Supp. 61 (ND Okla. 1986) (post-forty-five-day collection of accounts receivable held proceeds entitled to priority over tax lien).

[221] Reg. § 301.6323(c)-1(d).

forty-fifth day, although he would have no right to the "value added" after the forty-fifth day.[222]

Regulations restrict "identifiable proceeds" and provide that the term does not include "money, checks and the like which have been commingled with other cash proceeds."[223] This provision is similar to the UCC rule regarding the perfection of a security interest in proceeds in the event of insolvency proceedings. UCC Sections 9-306(4)(b) and 9-304(4)(c) provide for perfection of a security interest in identifiable cash proceeds in the form of money, checks, and the like that are neither commingled with other money nor deposited in a deposit account prior to the insolvency proceedings. In short, for a secured party to retain priority in cash proceeds, the proceeds must remain identifiable by being deposited in a separate account. However, the priority in proceeds does not continue in property purchased after the forty-fifth day following tax lien filing.[224] This rule is similar under the UCC: Where cash proceeds are deposited into the debtor's business, recipients take free of any claim that the secured party may have in them as proceeds.[225]

Regulations give the following example to illustrate these principles:

EXAMPLE (1):

> (i) On June 1, 1970, a tax is assessed against M, a tool manufacturer, with respect to his delinquent tax liability. On June 15, 1970, M enters into a written financing agreement with X, a bank. The agreement provides that, in consideration of such sums as X may advance to M, X is to have a security interest in all of M's presently owned and subsequently acquired commercial paper, accounts receivable, and inventory (including inventory in the manufacturing stages and raw materials). On July 6, 1970, notice of the tax lien is filed in accordance with § 301.6323(f)-1. On August 3, 1970, without actual notice or knowledge of the tax lien filing, X advances $10,000 to M. On August 5, 1970, M acquires additional inventory through the purchase of raw materials. On August 20, 1970, M has accounts receivable, arising from the sale

---

[222] Donald v. Madison Indus., Inc., 483 F2d 837 (10th Cir. 1973). Under UCC § 9-315, a security interest in raw materials continues in the resulting mass or product in most cases, and where more than one secured party claims an interest in the product, the interests are held to be of equal priority and entitled to share ratably in the product.

[223] Reg. § 301.6323(c)-1(d).

[224] Reg. § 301.6323(c)-1(d). In Donald v. Madison Indus., Inc., 483 F2d 837 (10th Cir. 1973), the court said that the regulation "suggests that once protected collateral is reduced to cash proceeds, it may not be reinvested in similar products and still be considered qualified property. We concur in the conclusion, for while we accept the commercial necessity of allowing continued production of that which is in process, we also recognize the necessity of ending the perpetuity of the taxpayer's liens by payment of his debt and tax obligations with the consequent funds."

[225] UCC § 9-306, Comment 2(c).

of tools, amounting to $5,000. Under local law, X's security interest arising by reason of the $10,000 advance on August 3, 1970, has priority, with respect to the raw materials and accounts receivable, over a judgment lien against M arising July 6, 1970 (the date of tax lien filing) out of an unsecured obligation.

(ii) Because the $10,000 advance was made before the 46th day after the tax lien filing, and the accounts receivable in the amount of $5,000 and the raw materials were acquired by M before such 46th day, X's $10,000 security interest in the accounts receivable and the inventory has priority over the tax lien. The priority of X's security interest also extends to the proceeds, received on or after the 46th day after the tax lien filing, from the liquidation of the accounts receivable and inventory held by M on August 20, 1970, if X has a continuously perfected security interest in identifiable proceeds under local law. However, the priority of X's security interest will not extend to other property acquired with such proceeds.[226]

[3] Real Property Construction or Improvement Financing Agreements

A second type of interest given priority over a filed tax lien is an interest arising under a real property construction or improvement financing agreement. According to the legislative history, the reason priority was given to such security interests is that (as in the case of some superpriority categories) the disbursements generally enhance the value of the property for purposes of the tax lien.[227] The completion of the construction or the improvement of the property or the completion of the raising of the crop or livestock "usually" increases the value of the property underlying the security interest for tax lien purposes by more than the amount of the disbursement granted the priority.[228]

[a] Definition

The term "real property construction or improvement financing agreement" means any written agreement to make cash disbursements, whether or not at the option of the party agreeing to make the disbursements, for the following reasons:

---

[226] Reg. § 301.6323(c)-1(f), Ex. (1).

[227] S. Rep. No. 1708, 89th Cong., 2d Sess. (1966), reprinted in 1966-2 CB 876, 881; HR Rep. No. 1884, 89th Cong., 2d Sess. (1966), reprinted in 1966-2 CB 815, 820.

[228] S. Rep. No. 1708, 89th Cong., 2d Sess. (1966), reprinted in 1966-2 CB 876, 881; HR Rep. No. 1884, 89th Cong., 2d Sess. (1966), reprinted in 1966-2 CB 815, 820.

1. To finance the construction, improvement, or demolition of real property if the agreement provides for a security interest in the real property in which the construction, improvement, or demolition has been or is to be made;
2. To finance a contract to construct, improve, or demolish real property if the agreement provides for a security interest in the proceeds of the contract; and
3. To finance the raising or harvesting of a farm crop or the raising of livestock or other animals if the agreement provides for a security interest in any property subject to the general tax lien at the time of tax lien filing, in the crop raised or harvested, or in the livestock or other animals raised.[229]

For purposes of this type of financing agreement, the holder of the security interest may make disbursements pursuant to the agreement even where he has actual notice or knowledge of the lien at the time the disbursements are made.[230]

[b] Qualified Property

There is no forty-five-day limitation for qualified property under a real property construction or improvement financing agreement,[231] although other limitations are imposed. In the case of cash disbursements made under an agreement to finance the construction or improvement of real property, qualified property includes only the real property with respect to which the construction or improvement has been or is to be made.[232] Thus, with respect to these cash disbursements, a lender has priority over the tax lien only with respect to the real property that is being constructed or improved. Similarly, in the case of disbursements made under an agreement to finance a contract to construct or improve real property, qualified property includes only the proceeds of the construction contract.[233] Consequently, with respect to these cash disbursements made to a construction contractor after a notice of tax lien has been filed, a lender has priority over the tax lien only with respect to the construction contract proceeds, as opposed to the real property. However, even if the agreement also provides for a security interest in the equipment of the contractor, because the qualified property is limited to the contract proceeds, the

---

[229] IRC § 6323(c)(3); Reg. § 301.6323(c)-2(b). For purposes of (1) and (2), construction includes demolition; for purposes of (3), furnishing goods and services is treated as a cash disbursement.

[230] Reg. § 301.6323(c)-2(a).

[231] Reg. § 301.6323(c)-2(d), Exs. (1), (2).

[232] Reg. § 301.6323(c)-2(c)(1). See also Reg. § 301.6323(c)-2(d).

[233] Reg. § 301.6323(c)-2(c)(2). See also Reg. § 301.6323(c)-2(d), Ex. (2).

tax lien has priority over the lender's security interest in the equipment.[234] Finally, in the case of disbursements made under an agreement to finance a farmer or someone who raises livestock or other animals, qualified property includes the crop or the livestock or other animals raised and any property subject to the general tax lien at the time of tax lien filing.[235] Therefore, with respect to disbursements made to a farmer or someone who raises livestock or other animals after a notice of tax lien has been filed, a lender has priority over the tax lien with respect to the crop or the livestock or other animals he has financed, the proceeds of the sale of the crop or livestock, and any other property subject to the lien at the time the notice of tax lien was filed that is subject to the security interest arising under the written agreement.[236] Qualified property for financing agreements involving farmers (and therefore priority over a filed tax lien) is far broader than for contractors and includes literally all property encumbered by the tax lien. The only limitation is with respect to property acquired by the farmer after the date the tax lien was filed. The lender's priority over the tax lien does not extend to property acquired after tax lien filing.[237]

[4] Obligatory Disbursement Agreements

The third category of interest given priority over a filed tax lien is an interest arising from an obligatory disbursement agreement. In general, such an agreement is one entered into by a person, under which he is obliged to make a disbursement because someone other than the taxpayer has relied on his obligation—for example, a surety who agrees to finance a contract entered into by the taxpayer. Priority has been given to the interest arising under this type of agreement as against filed tax liens, because the obligation to make the disbursement arises before the filing of the tax lien, although the disbursements are made after that time.[238] As with real property construction or improvement financing agreements, no limitation is placed on the time during

---

[234] Reg. § 301.6323(c)-2(d).

[235] Reg. § 301.6323(c)-2(c)(3).

[236] Reg. § 301.6323(c)-2(d), Ex. (4).

[237] Reg. § 301.6323(c)-2(d), Ex. (4).

[238] S. Rep. No. 1708, 89th Cong., 2d Sess. (1966), reprinted in 1966-2 CB 876, 882; HR Rep. No. 1884, 89th Cong., 2d Sess. (1966), reprinted in 1966-2 CB 815, 821.
A performance bond given by a surety company is an obligatory disbursement agreement. Despite the legislative history, the Service has argued that the tax lien has priority over payments on a surety bond made after the tax lien was filed. In Amwest Surety Ins. Co. v. United States, 870 F. Supp. 432 (D. Conn. 1994), the court rejected the Service's argument that the surety's payments on the bond were made after tax liens were filed and that any subrogation rights the surety had did not relate back to the time when the insured contractor had earned contract payments. If the surety company makes payments on the

which disbursements may be made after tax lien filing as long as a person is obligated to do so by a written agreement at the time of the tax lien filing. As a result, if an effort is made to foreclose on a federal tax lien before all the potential obligations under an obligatory disbursement agreement are met, these potential obligatory disbursements are given priority over the federal tax lien. In such a case, an amount sufficient to cover the potential obligations usually is set aside and used for these obligations. Only after these obligations have been met is any remainder available to satisfy the liabilities secured by the federal tax lien.[239] Moreover, since the obligor must make disbursements under the terms of the agreement, the fact that he may have actual notice or knowledge of the tax lien filing before the disbursement is made is immaterial.[240]

[a] Definition

"Obligatory disbursement agreement" means a written agreement entered into by a person in the course of his trade or business to make disbursements, but only to the extent of disbursements that are required to be made by reason of the intervention of the rights of a person other than the taxpayer.[241] The obligor must, as in the case of a lender or purchaser under a commercial transactions financing agreement, have assumed his obligation to make disbursements in the course of his trade or business. Accordingly, an issuing bank obligated to honor drafts or other demands for payment on a letter of credit or a bonding company obligated to make payments to indemnify against loss or liability is protected under this provision. This provision does not protect obligors who assume their obligation other than incident to their trade or business (e.g., accommodation indorsers). The requirement that disbursements be made must arise on the happening of an event beyond the obligor's control. Therefore, the required disbursement must be triggered by the intervention of the rights of a third party, such as the good-faith reliance of a supplier of goods or a bank authorized to honor a letter of credit on an issuing bank's obligation under a letter of credit.[242]

---

bond because the contractor has defaulted, the surety company is entitled by equitable subrogation to amounts due under the contract before the tax lien is filed.

[239] S. Rep. No. 1708, 89th Cong., 2d Sess. (1966), reprinted in 1966-2 CB 876, 882; HR Rep. No. 1884, 89th Cong., 2d Sess. (1966), reprinted in 1966-2 CB 815, 821.

[240] Reg. § 301.6323(c)-3(d)(3).

[241] IRC § 6323(c)(4); Reg. § 301.6323(c)-3(b).

[242] Reg. § 301.6323(c)-3(b).

[b] Qualified Property

The property protected from the effect of the tax lien is limited. "Qualified property," where used with respect to an obligatory disbursement agreement, means (1) property subject to the general tax lien belonging to the taxpayer at the time of tax lien filing, and (2) to the extent that the acquisition is directly traceable to the disbursement, property acquired by the taxpayer after tax lien filing.[243]

> **EXAMPLE:** X Bank, pursuant to a written agreement, issues an irrevocable letter of credit to allow A, the taxpayer, to finance the purchase of 100 automobiles. X Bank honors its obligations after the filing of a notice of tax lien. X Bank has priority over the tax lien with respect to the 100 automobiles that were purchased by A with the cash disbursement. In addition, if the written agreement so provides, X Bank's priority extends to any other property whose acquisition is directly traceable to its cash disbursement, such as the proceeds of sale of the automobiles.[244]

However, the regulations appear to limit the tracing to the acquisition of the inventory, not the proceeds of the sale of the inventory.[245]

There are special rules for surety agreements. Where the obligatory disbursement agreement is a surety contract insuring the performance of a contract between the taxpayer and another person, (1) the term "qualified property" is treated as including the proceeds of the insured contract, and (2) if the insured contract is a contract to construct real property, to produce goods, or to furnish services, the term "qualified property" is treated as including any tangible personal property used by the taxpayer in the performance of the insured contract.[246] For example, if a surety company holds a security interest arising from cash disbursements made after tax lien filing under a payment or performance bond on a real estate construction project, the surety has priority over the tax lien not only with respect to the proceeds of the construction contract, but also with respect to any tangible personal property used by the taxpayer-contractor in the construction project. However, priority with respect to tangible personal property used in the performance of an insured contract is available to the surety company only if the security in the property is protected under local law against a judgment lien, arising out of an unsecured obligation, as of the time of tax lien filing.[247]

---

[243] Reg. § 301.6323(c)-3(c).

[244] S. Rep. No. 1708, 89th Cong., 2d Sess. (1966), reprinted in 1966-2 CB 876, 882; HR Rep. No. 1884, 89th Cong., 2d Sess. (1966), reprinted in 1966-2 CB 815, 821.

[245] Reg. § 301.6323(c)-3(d)(3), Ex. (1)(iii).

[246] Reg. § 301.6323(c)-3(d).

[247] See, e.g., International Fidelity Ins. Co. v. United States, 949 F2d 1042 (8th Cir. 1991) (surety's interest in progress payment was not protected under state law against

[5] Disbursements After Tax Lien Filing

Priority over a filed tax lien is granted to security interests in property held by the debtor/taxpayer before tax lien filing in the amount of disbursements made within forty-five days after the date of tax lien filing (unless actual notice or knowledge of the filing is sooner obtained).[248] Section 6323(d) provides that the security interest has priority over a filed tax lien if (1) it comes into existence within forty-five days of federal tax lien filing because of disbursements made after tax lien filing; (2) it is in property in existence at the time of tax lien filing; and (3) as of the time of federal tax lien filing it was perfected against a judgment creditor. The protection provided by Section 6323(d), as in the case of a commercial transactions financing agreement, is designed to make it unnecessary for the holder of the security interest to search the records more often than once every forty-five days for one or more disbursements that are to be made by him.[249]

Section 6323(d) apparently contemplates a situation where a security interest has attached to a taxpayer's existing collateral, and the security interest is perfected at the time the tax lien is filed, because the security agreement provided for future advances, disbursements, or advances. Under the UCC, until the additional value has been given by making the future advance, the security interest has not attached to the extent of the advance.[250] The effect of Section 6323(d) is to permit the lender to increase the amount of his security interest by the amount of post-lien filing advances as long as the advances are made within forty-five days after the date of tax lien filing and he does not otherwise have notice of the lien filing.

There is overlap between this type of agreement and a commercial transactions financing agreement where future advances are involved. However, Section 6323(d) does not require the person making the advance to be a professional lender, as does Section 6323(c), and Section 6323(c) still is necessary to protect a security interest in property acquired by the debtor/taxpayer after tax lien filing.

---

judgment lien, because contractor had not defaulted at time the Service filed its first lien and served its first levy).

[248] IRC § 6323(d).

[249] S. Rep. No. 1708, 89th Cong., 2d Sess. (1966), reprinted in 1966-2 CB 876, 882; HR Rep. No. 1884, 89th Cong., 2d Sess. (1966), reprinted in 1966-2 CB 815, 821.

[250] Reg. § 301.6323(d)-1(b), Ex. (1).

¶ 16.06 PRIORITY OF INTEREST AND EXPENSES

If a lien or security interest has priority over a tax lien, Section 6323(e) also provides priority over a filed tax lien for interest with respect to costs of preserving the collateral related to the lien or security interest. However, for this priority to exist, local law must also give this interest and expense the same priority as the lien or security interest to which it relates. Since the lien or security interest has priority over the tax lien and the interest charges and expenses arise out of the prior lien or security interest, Congress believed that although these charges and expenses might not be fully determinable at the time of tax lien filing, they should also have priority over the tax lien.[251]

The following items of interest and expense are entitled to priority over a filed tax lien, where such priority is permitted by local law:[252]

- Any interest or carrying charges (including finance charges, service charges, and the like) upon the obligation secured.
- The reasonable charges and expenses of an indenture trustee (including, for example, a trustee under a deed of trust) or agent holding the security interest for the benefit of the holder of the security interest.
- The reasonable expenses, including reasonable compensation for attorneys, actually incurred in collection or enforcement of the obligation secured. Thus, a protected holder of a security interest or lien may increase the amount of his encumbrance by the amount of his expenditures incurred to establish the priority of his interest or to collect (by foreclosure or otherwise) the amount due him from the property.[253]
- The reasonable costs of insuring, preserving, or repairing the property subject to the lien or security interest. For example, the amount of a protected security interest may be increased by amounts paid by the security interest holder for fire and casualty insurance on the property and by amounts paid by him to repair the property. In addition, the holder of a security interest in a leasehold may increase the amount of his security interest by the amount of rental payments made to the lessor to preserve the leasehold.[254]
- The reasonable costs of insuring payment of the obligation secured. Thus, the amount of a protected security interest may be increased by

---

[251] S. Rep. No. 1708, 89th Cong., 2d Sess. (1966), reprinted in 1966-2 CB 876, 882; HR Rep. No. 1884, 89th Cong., 2d Sess. (1966), reprinted in 1966-2 CB 815, 821.

[252] IRC §§ 6323(e)(1)–6323(e)(6).

[253] Therefore, IRC § 6323(e)(3) reverses the result reached in United States v. Pioneer Am. Ins. Co., 374 US 84 (1963), and in United States v. Equitable Life Assurance Soc'y of the United States, 384 US 323 (1966).

[254] Reg. § 301.6323(e)-1(c).

amounts paid by the security interest holder for mortgage insurance, such as Federal Housing Administration insurance.

• The amount paid by the holder of the lien or security interest to satisfy any lien on the property to which the lien or security interest relates, but only if the lien so satisfied is entitled to priority over the federal tax lien.[255] For example, if both a security interest and a statutory lien for state sales taxes have priority over a federal tax lien, the holder of the protected security interest may discharge the sales tax lien and increase the amount of his security interest by the amount so expended, even where under local law he is not subrogated to the rights of the holder of the sales tax lien.[256] However, if the holder of the security interest is, within the meaning of Section 6323(i)(2), subrogated to the rights of the holder of the sales tax lien, he is also entitled to any additional protection afforded by that section.

B   PRIORITY OF TAX CLAIMS IN COLLECTIVE INSOLVENCY PROCEEDINGS

¶ 16.07   WHEN PRIORITY EXISTS UNDER 31 USC SECTION 3713(A)

In general, 31 USC Section 3713(a) provides that a debt due the United States must be satisfied (1) wherever the estate of a deceased debtor is insufficient to pay all creditors, and (2) wherever an insolvent living debtor has transferred his property in a collective creditor proceeding that has not resulted in bankruptcy.[257] A fiduciary who makes a distribution in violation of the priority es-

---

[255] In general, Section 6323(i) directs that when local law subrogates a person to the rights of another, that "person shall be subrogated" for purposes of the federal tax lien. This leads to an examination of state subrogation law. See, e.g., First Fed. Sav. Bank of Wabash v. United States, 118 F3d 532 (7th Cir. 1997) (court examined Indiana law and found that when the equities were weighed, the bank, a commercial institution with title insurance, would not be equitably subrogated to defeat an intervening tax lien).

[256] Reg. § 301.6323(e)-1(d).

[257] 31 USC § 3713(a) states:

(1) A claim of the United States Government shall be paid first when—

(A) a person indebted to the Government is insolvent and—

(i) the debtor without enough property to pay all debts make a voluntary assignment of property;

(ii) property of the debtor, if absent, is attached; or

(iii) an act of bankruptcy is committed; or

tablished by 31 USC Section 3713(a) is subjected to personal liability under 31 USC Section 3713(b).[258] The fiduciary (e.g., an executor, administrator, assignee, or receiver) is held personally liable for any diminution in the assets available to pay the government's debt caused by the payment of other debts in violation of the government's priority. Proceedings to enforce fiduciary liability under 31 USC Section 3713(b) are instituted directly by an action in a federal district court or under the transferee liability provisions of Section 6901.[259]

The priority and personal liability provisions have existed in the same or equivalent language since 1797. They apply to every kind of debt due the federal government, but the focus in this section is on only one type of claim: the claim for taxes. Unlike Section 6321, which creates the general tax lien, 31 USC Section 3713(a) creates no lien. The government's priority derives exclusively from the statute. However, both the general tax lien and the government's priority under 31 USC Section 3713(a) may coexist. In fact, the circumstances that give rise to the government's priority under 31 USC Section 3713(a) may have occurred, and the general tax lien may exist as well, because the tax has been assessed. The priority of the government's claim under 31 USC Section 3713(a) does not depend on the secured status of the tax claim. The priority of 31 USC Section 3713(a) applies at the time the property of an insolvent taxpayer has passed to a third person in a non-bankruptcy proceeding. By contrast, the general tax lien attaches to all property and rights to property of the delinquent taxpayer, whether he is insolvent or not, at the time the tax is assessed. Therefore, the general tax lien arising at the time of assessment may already encumber the property of the insolvent taxpayer when his property is transferred to a fiduciary in the non-bankruptcy proceeding. In this situation, the government may assert its priority on the basis of its lien. On the other hand, in insolvency situations where another creditor has claimed to have a lien upon property of the insolvent taxpayer that is prior in time to a later-arising tax lien, the competing nontax lien has been required to meet extremely rigorous tests of perfection because of the government's lien status and its priority under 31 USC Section 3713(a).[260] Consequently, al-

---

(B) the estate of a deceased debtor, in the custody of the executor or administrator, is not enough to pay all debts of the debtor.

(2) This subsection does not apply to a case under title 11.

[258] 31 USC § 3713(b) states:

A representative of a person or an estate (except a trustee acting under title 11) paying any part of a debt of the person or estate before paying a claim of the Government is liable to the extent of the payment for unpaid claims of the Government.

[259] These proceedings are discussed at ¶¶ 17.02 and 17.03.

[260] See United States v. Vermont, 377 US 351 (1964).

though the government's lien status and its priority under Section 3713(a) exist independently, they may be used cumulatively to defeat a competing interest.[261]

Three conditions must exist in a tax case before the government's priority may be established under 31 USC Section 3713(a):

1. There must be a tax debt due the United States;
2. The estate of a deceased taxpayer or a living taxpayer must be insolvent; and
3. Where an insolvent living taxpayer is involved, the taxpayer must have manifested that insolvency by transferring his property voluntarily by making an assignment for the benefit of creditors, having his property attached, or otherwise committing an act of bankruptcy.

The conditions that establish priority under 31 USC Section 3713(a) are different for deceased and living taxpayers. In the case of a deceased taxpayer who

---

[261] It has been contended that where the Service seeks to recover unpaid taxes, Section 6323, rather than former Section 3466, should apply. The contention has been rejected because of its lack of support in the legislative history of FTLA and the distinct purpose of former Section 3466. Nesbitt v. United States, 445 F. Supp. 824 (ND Cal. 1978), aff'd, 622 F2d 433 (9th Cir. 1980), cert. denied, 451 US 984 (1981); Durham v. United States, 545 F. Supp. 1093 (DNJ 1982). Contra, City of Vermillion, SD v. Stan Houston Equip. Co., 341 F. Supp. 707 (DSD 1972).

When a judgment debtor attempted to collect its judgment from the insolvent estate of the deceased taxpayer, a Pennsylvania court held that the judgment lien creditor was entitled to priority under Section 6323, which limits the priority of Section 3713. In re Estate of Francis J. Romani, 688 A2d 703 (Pa. Sup. Ct., 1997), cert. granted, 117 S. Ct. 2506 (1997). Relying on the Supreme Court's decision in United States v. Kimbell Foods, Inc., 440 US 715 (1979), which involved the priority of a federal consensual loan where the debtor was solvent, the Pennsylvania court said that the *Kimbell Foods* case established that the priority of 31 USC § 3713 was not absolute, and that the FTLA expressed Congress's disapproval of "unrestricted federal priority" in tax matters. The Pennsylvania court said its conclusion was supported by the observation in *Kimbell Foods* that the "restrictions on federal tax lien priority are necessary to facilitate commercial stability and to avoid the frustration of expectations of superior lien holders."

In its brief in the Supreme Court, the solicitor general argued that the absolute priority of Section 3713(a)(2), the Bankruptcy Code priority rules, and the tax lien priority rules of Section 6323 are not plainly inconsistent, but rather deal with different situations. Reply Brief for the United States, United States v. Estate of Francis J. Romani, 97 TNT 223–221. In enacting the absolute priority statute, Congress chose to establish greater protection for the government in specified types of insolvencies than in situations where the debtor is not insolvent (and the rights of competing creditors are determined under the tax lien provisions of Section 6323, not under the absolute priority statute) or where the debtor is insolvent but in bankruptcy (and priority is determined under the Bankruptcy Code). According to the solicitor general's argument, the only way for a competing creditor to avoid the absolute priority of Section 3713 is for the debtor to have been divested of title or possession of property by way of seizure or some other equivalent act before the right of priority has accrued to the government.

But the Supreme Court disagreed in United States v. Estate of Francis J. Romani, US 118 S. Ct. 1478 (1989).

owes a tax, mere insolvency of the estate is sufficient to create priority under 31 USC Section 3713(a). On the other hand, an insolvent living taxpayer who owes a tax must also have transferred or been divested of his property in a nonbankruptcy proceeding.[262] The requirement that the living taxpayer must not only be insolvent but have transferred or been divested of possession and control of his property has been interpreted to mean that the priority of Section 3713(a) does not exist in such a case until the date a receiver has been appointed[263] or the date an assignment for the benefit of creditors is executed.[264]

[1] The Tax Debt

"Debt," as used in 31 USC Section 3713(a), includes taxes,[265] although a tax need not have been assessed to constitute a debt within the meaning of 31 USC Section 3713(a). It is sufficient if all the facts giving rise to the tax have occurred and the amount may readily be determined, even if the ultimate liability and the exact amount are not yet known.[266] Thus, income tax liabilities of a decedent that are unassessed at the time of his death constitute a debt due the United States.[267] The tax debt also includes interest[268] and penalties, despite the fact that penalties may not be recoverable in bankruptcy.[269] Typically, the tax debt is owed by the insolvent debtor. However, 31 USC Section 3713(a) may also apply where the delinquent taxpayer has a claim against an insolvent debtor. For example, where the United States acquires the claim a taxpayer-creditor has against an insolvent debtor, the debt of the insolvent debtor becomes a debt due the United States.[270] Thus, the insolvent debtor owes a debt that is due the United States, despite the fact that the debt is not a tax debt and the United States has acquired its claim against the debtor by assignment or levy.

---

[262] United States v. State of Oklahoma, 261 US 253, 259 (1923).

[263] Illinois ex rel. Gordon v. Campbell, 329 US 362 (1946).

[264] Massachusetts v. United States, 333 US 611 (1947).

[265] Price v. United States, 269 US 492 (1926).

[266] Price v. United States, 269 US 492 (1926); Viles v. Comm'r, 233 F2d 376 (6th Cir. 1956).

[267] Rev. Rul. 79-310, 1979-2 CB 404.

[268] United States v. Purdome, 240 F. Supp. 221 (WD Mo. 1965).

[269] United States v. Rome, 414 F. Supp. 517 (D. Mass. 1976).

[270] In re Cherry Valley Homes, Inc., 255 F2d 706 (3d Cir. 1958), cert. denied, 358 US 864 (1958).

[2] Insolvency

Before the priority provided by 31 USC Section 3713(a) applies, the estate of a deceased debtor or the living debtor must be insolvent. The statute does not define in what sense there must be "insolvency." This omission has produced some uncertainty, because insolvency means different things in different situations. Thus, a debtor is insolvent in one sense where the amount of his debts exceeds the book value of his assets (a balance sheet test), while a debtor is insolvent in the equity sense where he is unable to pay his debts as they become due in the ordinary course of business. In applying Section 3713(a) to a situation involving a living debtor (a bank adjudged insolvent under state law), the Supreme Court said: "Mere inability of the debtor to pay all his debts in [the] ordinary course of business is not insolvency within the meaning of 31 USC Section 3713(a)."[271] The statute, the Court observed, requires that there be an insolvent debtor "not having sufficient property to pay all his debts." The "insolvency" referred to in Section 3713(a) is insolvency in the balance sheet sense, not in the equity sense.

The same "asset insufficiency" test, with some qualifications, applies in determining whether a deceased debtor's estate is insolvent. For the purposes of determining the sufficiency of the decedent's assets to pay his debts, only the "estate...in the custody of the executors or administrators" is considered.[272] Consequently, property passing outside probate (e.g., jointly held property or insurance) is not considered in the determination. In other words, the probate estate, not the gross estate for the tax purposes, is the "estate" to be considered for the purpose of Section 3713(a).[273]

Suppose that the assets in the estate of a deceased debtor or the property transferred to a receiver are sufficient to pay all creditors at one point in time but that insolvency develops after some creditors are paid but not the government. Does the priority apply to payments made to creditors before insolvency, because a debt due the United States is entitled to priority "whenever the estate...is insufficient to pay all the debts due from the deceased"? Some early authority supports the view that a series of transfers may result in retroactive priority of the government claim if any one transfer is made at a time when the estate is insolvent.[274] The Tax Court has adopted this rule in Section

---

[271] United States v. State of Oklahoma, 261 US 253, 260 (1923).

[272] 31 USC § 3713(a).

[273] However, it has been suggested that the executor's right to compel contributions toward the estate tax from life insurance beneficiaries (IRC § 2206) and recipients of property subject to a power of appointment included in the gross estate should be added to the "estate" for the purposes of the priority status. Ferguson, "The Fiduciary's Personal Liability for Federal Taxes of the Decedent and His Estate," 25 NYU Inst. on Fed. Tax. 1185, 1196 (1967).

[274] Hatch v. Morosco Holding Co., 50 F2d 138 (2d Cir. 1931).

3713(a) cases, relying on its application in transferee liability cases.[275] However, courts of appeals generally have refused to grant the government "retroactive priority" by relating a later insolvency (and thus priority) back to the initial payment of creditors other than the United States.[276] Consequently, it is only at the time insolvency exists that the priority of the government's debts is established under 31 USC Section 3713(a).

[3] Collective Creditor Proceedings

According to 31 USC Section 3713(a), a debt due the United States must be paid first wherever "any person indebted to the United States is insolvent," and this priority "shall extend as well to (1) cases in which a debtor, not having sufficient property to pay all his debts, makes a voluntary assignment thereof, or (2) in which the estate and effects of an absconding, concealed, or absent debtor are attached by process of law, as to (3) cases in which an act of bankruptcy is committed." A living debtor's insolvency must be manifested in one of these ways before the priority of Section 3713(a) applies.[277] The priority statute thus contemplates collective creditor proceedings, in which possession and control of the insolvent debtor's property are transferred to a fiduciary, as opposed to the recovery of property as the result of an action by an individual creditor against the debtor/taxpayer.[278]

The term "voluntary assignment," as used in Section 3713(a), has been interpreted to include any transfer by a debtor of his property without legal compulsion. Consequently, 31 USC Section 3713(a) has been applied in such proceedings as general assignments for the benefit of creditors, equity receiver-

---

[275] See Burnett Schwartz, 34 TCM 1146 (1975), rev'd, 560 F2d 311 (8th Cir. 1977). In applying the rule, the Tax Court cited such transferee liability cases as Benoit v. Comm'r, 238 F2d 485 (1st Cir. 1956), aff'g on this issue 25 TC 656 (1955) (transferee of corporation); J. Warren Leach, 21 TC 70 (1953); and Burton Ginsberg, 24 TCM 195 (1965). Since transferee liability is based on unjust enrichment, it may be appropriate to disregard the timing of prior transfers when the transferor is rendered insolvent. However, fiduciary liability is based on fault, which is itself tied to an insolvency-causing distribution. In this context, the fiduciary may simply not be at fault at the time of the earlier distribution. Consequently, the series-of-distributions rule should not apply in Rev. Stat. § 3466 cases. See Hochberg & Silbergleit, "Recent Cases Narrow Scope of Executor's Personal Liability for Estate Taxes," 7 Est. Plan. 2 (1980).

[276] Schwartz v. Comm'r, 560 F2d 311 (8th Cir. 1977) (estate); United States v. Lutz, 295 F2d 736 (5th Cir. 1961) (corporation).

[277] United States v. State of Oklahoma, 261 US 253, 259 (1923).

[278] But see United States v. Mr. Hamburg Bronx Corp., 228 F. Supp. 115 (SDNY 1964) (Rev. Stat. § 3466 was applied where creditor recovered in fraudulent conveyance action).

ships,[279] bankruptcy reorganizations,[280] and liquidations of insolvent corporations.[281]

     Section 3713(a) further states that its priority applies as well "to cases in which an act of bankruptcy is committed." This portion of the statute has uncertain application, since the Bankruptcy Reform Act of 1978 amended Section 3713(a) by adding: "(T)he priority established under this section does not apply, however, in a case under title 11 (of the United States Code)."[282] Under the present Bankruptcy Code, an involuntary petition in bankruptcy may be filed by creditors where the debtor (1) is not paying his debts as they come due, or (2) has within 120 days of the petition made assignment or permitted the appointment of a receiver of less than substantially all his property for the benefit of creditors.[283] Although these acts authorize a Bankruptcy Court to grant an involuntary petition in bankruptcy, their occurrence does not necessarily mean that creditors will file such a petition. Consequently, 31 USC Section 3713(a) may still apply in cases where a bankruptcy case is not commenced. As long as the receiver or other person takes charge of the debtor's property in a nonbankruptcy proceeding, 31 USC Sections 3713(a) and 3713(b) apply if the person pays a debt of the debtor in violation of the government's priority.[284] However, once a bankruptcy case is begun, 31 USC Section 3713(a) does not apply. Priorities set forth in the Bankruptcy Code govern distributions, and so the trustee's payment of claims pursuant to the Bankruptcy Code do not render him liable under 31 USC Section 3713(b).

¶ 16.08 THE SCOPE OF THE GOVERNMENT'S PRIORITY UNDER 31 USC SECTION 3713(A)

[1] Exceptions to the Government's Priority

On its face, the priority of 31 USC Section 3713(a) is absolute. A debt due the United States must be paid before the debts of any other creditor. No excep-

---

[279] United States v. Crocker, 313 F2d 946 (9th Cir. 1963).

[280] United States v. Key, 397 US 322 (1970); States v. Anderson, 334 F2d 111 (5th Cir.), cert. denied, 379 US 879 (1964).

[281] Bramwell v. U.S. Fidelity & Guar. Co., 269 US 483 (1926) (state receivership of bank); In re Bonnie Classics, Inc., 116 F. Supp. 646 (SDNY 1953) (winding up under state law with directors or others as trustees).

[282] Bankruptcy Reform Act of 1978, Pub. L. No. 95-598, § 322(a), 92 Stat. 2678.

[283] 11 USC § 303(h).

[284] See Rev. Rul. 77-424, 1977-2 CB 481 (court-appointed receiver was not liable under Rev. Stat. § 3467 where he returned assets to a solvent corporation only because the return did not constitute payment of a "debt" of the corporation).

tions are made in the statute for the payment of administrative expenses (i.e., the costs incurred in collecting, liquidating, and distributing the debtor's property) or for the satisfaction of earlier liens out of the debtor's property or estate. However, this apparently absolute priority is subject to a number of limited exceptions.

First, the costs of administering the estate of the deceased or living debtor may be paid before a tax claim in general because these expenses were not incurred by the debtor but are for the benefit of all creditors, the United States included.[285] These expenses include court costs and reasonable compensation for the fiduciary and attorney.[286] Also, where expenses (including taxes) are incurred in operating the business or liquidating assets, payments or transfers made in the ordinary course of such operations are in the nature of administrative expense and likewise are not subject to the priority of 31 USC Section 3713(a).[287]

Funeral expenses and widow's allowances may also be paid before the government's claim.[288] The basis for allowing these payments is less clear than for administration expenses because, in general, state statutes fixing priority in payments are not binding on the federal government.[289] However, in this case, the rationale seems to be that because these funeral expenses and the widow's allowance are considered charges against the estate, the debtor is, to this ex-

---

[285] Abrams v. United States, 274 F2d 8 (8th Cir. 1960); Kennebec Box Co. v. OS Richards Corp., 5 F2d 951 (2d Cir. 1925); GCM 22499, 1941-1 CB 272. Krulewich v. United States, 94-2 USTC ¶ 50,473 (D. Mass. 1994) (in an assignment for the benefit of creditors, administrative expenses may be paid before the government's claim for taxes).

[286] See Malcolm D. Champlin, 6 TC 280, 285 (1946) (Rev. Stat. § 3467 does not apply to "expenses of administration allowed by any court having jurisdiction thereof").

[287] United States v. State of Okla., 261 US 253 (1923); Southern Ry. Co. v. United States, 306 F2d 119, 125–126 (5th Cir. 1962) (receivership); Colorado Wool Mktg. Ass'n v. Monaghan, 66 F2d 313 (10th Cir. 1933) (receivership). Section 6324(a) permits an executor to make payments free from the special estate tax lien to satisfy administration expenses.

[288] The Service now recognizes this principle. Rev. Rul. 80-112, 1980-1 CB 306 (funeral and administrative expenses, doctor's bills from last illness, wages due household employee, and family allowance). See Schwartz v. Comm'r, 560 F2d 311 (8th Cir. 1977); United States v. Weisburn, 48 F Supp. 393 (ED Pa. 1943) (funeral expenses); GCM 4217, VII-2 CB 162 (1928); IT 2518, IX-1 CB 158 (1930); Grace McKnight, 15 TC 730 (1950) (widow and family allowances); Jessie Smith, 24 BTA 807 (1931). Where the widow's allowance is augmented or superseded by a right in the nature of dower, the government's claim has also been subordinated to this claim. United States v. Broderick, 60-1 USTC ¶ 9438 (SD Ohio 1960).

[289] See United States v. State of Okla., 261 US 253 (1923).

tent, never considered to have had property belonging to him out of which creditors, including the United States, may be paid.[290]

On the other hand, payments of state income taxes, general creditors, and other claims constitute the payment of debts in derogation of the government's priority.[291] Distributions to beneficiaries are clearly not "charges" against the estate of a deceased taxpayer, but are considered payment of a "debt." Distributions to beneficiaries of an insolvent estate may not be made by an executor or administrator before payment of an estate or gift tax due from the estate, because the distribution is considered the payment of a "debt" other than the debt due the United States.[292]

However, it is not always clear when a payment constitutes the payment of a debt. For example, an insurance company that paid out a deceased agent's renewal commissions to his estate before paying estate tax was held to have paid its own debt.[293] Thus, the payment of the fiduciary's own debt does not fall within the statute.[294] Guidelines are not readily available to determine which type of debt is being paid. The estate and gift tax regulations take a hard line in treating distributions as payments of "debts," within the meaning of 31 USC Sections 3713(a) and 3713(b).[295] But where the insolvent taxpayer is a corporation rather than an estate and the tax is an income tax rather than an estate tax, the result may be different.[296] Although there is no apparent basis for a different result simply because there is a difference in the type of tax due

---

[290] Rev. Rul. 80-112, 1980-1 CB 306. See also Igoe v. United States, 717 SW2d 524 (Mo. 1986) (funeral and administration expenses had priority over tax claim under Missouri law).

[291] Rev. Rul. 79-310, 1979-2 CB 404.

[292] Reg. §§ 20.2002-1 (estate tax), 25.2502-2 (gift tax). See United States v. First Huntington Nat'l Bank, 34 F. Supp. 578, 580 (SD W. Va. 1940), aff'd on opinion below per curiam, 117 F2d 376 (4th Cir. 1941); Malcolm D. Champlin, 6 TC 280, 285 (estate tax); Want v. Comm'r, 280 F2d 777 (2d Cir. 1960) (gift tax).

[293] Occidental Life Ins. Co., 50 TC 726 (1968).

[294] Edward G. Leuthesser, 18 TC 1112, 1127–1128 (1952), acq. 1953-2 CB 5; Ethel Posey, 10 TCM 833 (1951). In *Edward G. Leuthesser*, the Tax Court held that a payment by the fiduciaries of their own debts with corporate assets was not a payment of the debts due by the person (corporation) for whom they acted and, therefore, did not come within the terms of the predecessor of Rev. Stat. § 3713. On the basis of this authority the Service has ruled that, to the extent that a receiver returns assets to a corporation, the corporation has the same ability to pay its taxes as before control of the assets was transferred and that, accordingly, the return of assets does not constitute the payment of a debt for the predecessor of Section 3713(b) purposes. Rev. Rul. 77-424, 1977-2 CB 481.

[295] The estate tax regulations state that the executor is personally liable under Section 3713(b) if he "distributes any portion of the estate before all the estate tax is paid." Reg. § 20.2002-1.

[296] Compare the results in Edward G. Leuthesser, 18 TC 1112, 1127–1128 (1952), acq. 1953-2 CB 5, and Rev. Rul. 77-242, 1977-2 CB 489 (no fiduciary liability), with Rev. Rul. 79-310, 1979-2 CB 404 (fiduciary liability).

the United States, it seems that executors have a greater threat of liability than other fiduciaries.

Because of the government's priority under 31 USC Section 3713(a), it seems to make little difference in terms of its priority as against unsecured or secured creditors whether or not the tax claim is secured by a lien. However, if the tax has not been assessed before the collective creditor proceeding, the government relies on its 31 USC Section 3713(a) priority rather than its lien. FTLA, which by amending Section 6323 provided relief to certain classes of creditors and other persons as against unfiled and filed tax liens, did not affect priority in nonbankruptcy insolvency situations to which Section 3713(a) applies.

Where Section 3713(a) is applicable, the government's nonlien tax claims have priority over all unsecured creditors, including wages claims.[297] The relative priority of the claims of secured creditors and the government's priority under Section 3713(a) has been the subject of substantial litigation.[298] In general, Sections 3713(a) and 3713(b) operate only with respect to funds available for payment to creditors. Consequently, it was thought that, to the extent of a secured creditor's lien obtained before the government's priority under Section 3713(a) attached, the fund was reduced. This seems to be true where the debtor has, in an arm's-length transaction, mortgaged property before the circumstances giving rise to the government's priority under Section 3713(a). Although this priority does not apply, the taxpayer has "conveyed" his property prior to the accrual of the government's rights, and no other lien, whatever its nature, comes ahead of the government's priority under Section 3713(a), unless the lien is perfected or "choate."[299] In other words, the government's priority under Section 3713(a) overrides prior inchoate or general liens.

This "choateness" requirement has been interpreted to mean that the prior lien must be definite as to the identity of the lien, the amount of the lien, and the properties to which it attached.[300] Moreover, where a statutory lien on personalty is tested in a collective insolvency proceeding, the lien does not have priority over the tax claim, unless it has been brought judicially or

---

[297] United States v. Emory, 314 US 423, 426 (1941). However, wage claims may constitute an administration expense. See United States v. Wisconsin Valley Trust Co., 233 F. Supp. 73, 79 (WD Wis. 1964); Rev. Rul. 80-112, 1980-1 CB 306 (household employee).

[298] See the discussion of the choate lien doctrine supra ¶ 16.02[2].

[299] Spokane County v. United States, 279 US 80 (1929) (county personal property tax). United States v. Estate of Young, 84-2 USTC ¶ 13,594 (ED Pa. 1984) (Pennsylvania's estate tax lien held inchoate under Section 3713). In *Estate of Young*, the district court rejected Pennsylvania's claim that since its estate tax lien and the federal estate tax lien arose simultaneously, the state and federal liens should share pro rata in the distribution of the proceeds from the estate).

[300] Illinois ex rel. Gordon v. Campbell, 329 US 362, 275 (1946) (after recording lien, state had secured appointment of receiver).

nonjudicially to execution and a seizure of the debtor's property has occurred, fully divesting the debtor of title and placing this title in the hands of the seizing creditor.[301] The Supreme Court has stated that different standards of choateness apply in noninsolvency or individual proceedings and has found in some proceedings some liens existing before the tax lien arose to be choate.[302] But it has not to this point found any lien to be choate in collective proceedings involving insolvent debtors.

The position of the Service regarding mortgages and the hard line the Supreme Court has taken with respect to statutory liens suggest that only where the debtor has been divested of title or possession before the insolvency and other circumstances giving rise to the operation of 31 USC Section 3713(a) have occurred does the government's claim lose its priority to the creditor's statutory lien.[303] Where the secured creditor's lien is consensual it must still withstand the test of choateness, which in insolvency situations has not been affected by FTLA and the limited superpriority granted certain financing agreements. Clearly, where a security agreement contains an after-acquired property and future advances clause, the lien is not choate because the property subject to the lien and the amount of the lien, respectively, are not sufficiently identified or specific.

Finally, in *Estate of Francis J. Romani*, the Supreme Court settled the apparent conflict between the absolute priority accorded to tax claims by 31 USC Section 3713 and the priority granted by Section 6323 to certain creditors who perfected their liens or claims before a tax lien has been perfected by filing.[304] The case involved a competing judgment lien, perfected under Pennsylvania law, and a later-filed tax lien. Under Section 6323, the judgment lien clearly had priority over the tax lien because it had been perfected under Pennsylvania law, and there was no dispute that the judgment lien also was choate. The Court refused to hold that the priority granted to tax claims under the insolvency statute was absolute and rejected the government's claim that 31 USC Section 3713(a) gave the tax claim priority even over antecedent perfected liens of secured creditors. The Court said that the issue was not whether Section 6323 implicitly amended or repealed 31 USC Section 3713(a), but rather

---

[301] United States v. Gilbert Assocs., 345 US 361 (1953); Kentucky v. United States, 383 F2d 13 (6th Cir. 1967). However, even if possession is divested (by levy or distraint), the amount of lien still must be conclusively determined before the collective proceeding is begun. See United States v. Melchiorre 292 F. Supp. 305, 309 (ED Va. 1968). United States v. Estate of Young, 84-2 USTC ¶ 13,594 (ED Pa. 1984).

[302] United States v. Vermont, 377 US 351 (1964). See the discussion in Chapter 14.

[303] See Plumb, Federal Tax Liens 192–193 (3d ed. 1972). The Pennsylvania Supreme Court has held, however, that in enacting the priority provisions of Section 6323, Congress limited unrestricted federal priority in tax matters so that a perfected judgment lien having priority under Section 6323 over a later-filed tax lien did not lose that priority to the tax lien because of the operation of 31 USC § 3713(a).

[304] United States v. Estate of Francis J. Romani, 118 S. Ct. 1478 (1998).

the "proper inquiry is how best to harmonize the impact of two statutes on the Government's power to collect delinquent taxes." Nothing in the long history of the insolvency priority statute, the Court concluded, justifies the view that 31 USC Section 3713(a) authorizes the equivalent of a "secret lien" as a substitute for the expressly authorized tax lien that Section 6323 declares "shall not be valid" against perfected claims of certain creditors. Reasoning that it would be anomalous to conclude that Congress intended the insolvency priority statute to impose greater burdens on creditors than the later-enacted lien priority statute, which was specifically crafted for tax collection purposes, the Court held that the perfected Pennsylvania judgment lien had priority over the tax lien the Service claimed had priority under 31 USC Section 3713(a).[305] It does not appear that *Estate of Romani* will be read broadly and support a general "first in time is first in right" principle (i.e., when a taxpayer is insolvent, a state tax assessment made before a federal tax assessment would have priority because it is "first in time"); instead, *Estate of Romani* requires that the Federal Insolvency Statute controls, unless there is a showing that there is "a specific, inconsistent provision in a later federal statute."[306]

[2] Procedure in Decedents' Estates and Insolvency Proceedings

[a] Notice, Assessment, and Proof of Claim

Where most collective creditor proceedings are involved, the Code provides special notice and, in receivership proceedings, assessment rules. Notice of his qualification must be given to the Service by "every receiver, trustee in a case under title II of the United States Code, assignee for benefit of creditors, or other like fiduciary, and every executor."[307] This notice provision

---

[305] But *Estate of Romani* has been held not to apply to a state lien because no specific statutory regime, such as Section 6323, applies, which needs to be harmonized with 31 USC Section 3713(a); consequently, the absolute priority of the tax claim, applies unless the state claim is a choate lien. Straus, Assignee for the Benefit of Creditors v. United States, 82 AFTR2d 98-7002 (ND Ill. 1998) (insolvent taxpayer had made assignment for benefit of creditors, but state had gained title or possession to taxpayer's property, so that its lien had become choate).

[306] Straus v. United States, 84 AFTR2d 99-5522 (7th Cir. 1999) (competing state and federal tax liens).

[307] IRC § 6036. The regulations require a receiver or other similar fiduciary and an assignee for the benefit of creditors to give notice in writing within ten days of appointment or authorization to the district director of the district in which the debtor is or was required to file returns. Reg. §§ 301.6036-1(a)(2), 301.6036-1(a)(3). The contents of the notice are specified in Reg. § 301.6036-1(a)(4). Failure to supply the notice may subject the fiduciary to criminal penalties (IRC § 7203), as may a false or fraudulent notice (IRC §§ 7206, 7207). "Executor" is defined in Section 2203.

should be distinguished from the notice required under Section 6903, the effect of which is to transfer "the powers, rights, duties, and privileges" of the person for whom the fiduciary is acting with respect to the determination of any tax liability.[308]

The notice under Section 6036 triggers the special rule of Section 6872 for the suspension of the statute of limitations on assessment for the period from the date of the institution of the proceeding to a date thirty days after the date on which the notice from the receiver or other fiduciary is received by the district director, but in no case may the suspension be longer than two years. However, on "the appointment of a receiver for any taxpayer in any receivership proceeding before any federal or state court," Section 6871(a) requires immediate assessment of any income, gift, or estate tax deficiency without the notice and ninety-day waiting period normally required by Section 6213(a).[309]

The Special Procedures Staff in the district Collection Division performs the Service's functions in protecting the government's interests in collecting federal taxes that may properly be claimed in insolvency and decedent estate cases.[310] In insolvency cases, the function of the Special Procedures Staff includes:

- Coordination of efforts to ascertain the commencement of proceedings;
- Preparation of tax claims;
- Control and service functions during the pendency of the proceedings;
- Investigation necessary to determine when any contingency has arisen that requires the services of District Counsel; and
- Closing out the district's file on the case.

The Special Procedures Staff generally learns of a decedent's estate or insolvency proceeding by way of the notice procedure provided by Section 6036. It may learn of such a proceeding from revenue officers and other field personnel, as well as from public notices. Once it is determined that a proceeding has been commenced and what type of proceeding is involved, the processing of the case by the Special Procedures Staff involves:

- A determination whether the case is an "asset" or "no asset" case;
- Notice to the service center to determine all outstanding accounts and to compute penalties and interest to be included in the proof of claim;

---

[308] See, e.g., IRC § 6212(b), which provides for the sending of a notice of deficiency to the last known address of the taxpayer in the absence of a notice under Section 6903 to the district director.

[309] No special provision for immediate assessment of employment or excise taxes is necessary, because the Tax Court has no jurisdiction to review determinations with respect to these taxes.

[310] IRM 57(11)0, MT 5700-8 (Dec. 5, 1986) (Insolvencies, Other Than Bankruptcies, and Decedent's Estates). The organization of the Collection Division and its Special Procedures Staff is described at ¶ 14.02.

- Referral to the Examination Division for a determination of whether any returns of the decedent or debtor are under examination and of any deficiencies, additions to tax, or refunds that may be involved; and
- Notice to the area Collection Division to ensure that all delinquent accounts cases are assigned to a single revenue officer.

Thus, the Special Procedures Staff becomes the focus of information and processing of liabilities for immediate or jeopardy assessment and preparation of a proof of claim.[311]

The Service's claim for taxes is presented as a proof of claim. Form 4490 (Proof of Claim for Internal Revenue Taxes) is used for proceedings other than bankruptcies. For bankruptcies, the Service uses Form 4491 (Proof of Claim for Internal Revenue Taxes—Bankruptcy Proceedings). The proof of claim is prepared by the Special Procedures Staff and filed with the clerk of the court and the fiduciary. If a proof of claim is disputed, the matter is referred to the District Counsel and to the Department of Justice's Tax Division and United States Attorney.[312]

[b] Particular Insolvency Proceedings

[i] Probate proceedings. In a probate proceeding, the decedent's property is in the custody of the state probate court. The filing of a proof of claim is the usual means by which the government asserts a tax claim against a decedent's estate. Although the time and place for filing a proof of claim are prescribed by state law, state statutes of limitations that fix the time for filing proofs of claim are not applicable to the United States.[313] However, once the United States files a proof of claim, it has been held that it has submitted to the jurisdiction of the probate court for all purposes.[314] Thus, if a proof of claim is filed, the court may determine the extent of the government's priority under 31 USC Section 3713(a), and the fiduciary has been held not subject to personal liability as long as he follows the probate court's decree.[315] If the proof of claim is not filed, the fiduciary nevertheless is notified by the Service of the existence of the tax liability, so that he can be held liable if he distributes funds to persons not entitled to priority over the government. Presumably,

---

[311] IRM 57(11)2, MT 5700-8 (Nov. 15, 1985) (Ascertaining Commencement of Proceedings), and IRM 57(11)3, MT 5700-1 (Nov. 15, 1985) (Processing Insolvency and Decedent Cases).

[312] IRM 57(11)4.5, MT 5700-1 (Nov. 15, 1985) (Disputed Tax Claims). See generally IRM 57(11)4– 57(11)4.5, MT 5700-1 (Nov. 15, 1985) (Proof of Claim).

[313] Board of Comm'rs of Jackson County v. United States, 308 US 343 (1939); United States v. Summerlin, 310 US 414 (1940).

[314] United States v. Pate, 47 F. Supp. 965 (WD Ark. 1942).

[315] United States v. Pate, 47 F. Supp. 965 (WD Ark. 1942).

under the rule of *King v. United States*,[316] an executor having notice of the tax claim would be required to press opposition to payments in violation of 31 USC Section 3713(a). Moreover, unless the government's claim has been determined not to be entitled to priority, discharge of the executor of an insolvent estate, approval of his account, or distribution of assets will not relieve him of liability under 31 USC Section 3713(b) for debts due the United States.[317]

The fact that a person dies does not change the restrictions on assessment of income, gift, and estate taxes. Therefore, a notice of deficiency must be issued for these taxes under Section 6212(b).[318] The fiduciary may contest the proposed liability either administratively or by filing a petition in the Tax Court. But where the estate is insufficient to pay all creditors, the tax deficiency determined in the Tax Court must be paid first, as provided in 31 USC Section 3713(a).

[ii] Assignment for the benefit of creditors. A debtor may transfer (or assign) property to a person or persons in trust to apply the property assigned or the proceeds to the payment of his debts. After the transfer, nothing remains in the assignor except the right to claim whatever residue may remain after the debts are paid. As a general rule, the assignee takes the assigned property subject to all encumbrances and to every defect of title to which it was subject in the hands of the assignor, and any defense good against the assignor is good against the assignee. Where taxes are assessed before the assignment, a valid tax lien exists against all the assignor's property whether or not a notice of lien has been filed, since the assignee is not a person protected under Section 6323(a) from a tax lien unless a notice is filed.[319] If a tax lien exists, the assignee takes the property subject to the lien and the government may enforce the lien against the property if necessary. On the other hand, if a general assignment for the benefit of creditors is made prior to the assessment of taxes, the lien cannot attach, because at the time the lien arises, all the taxpayer's property rights have passed to the assignee.[320] In this situation, the government must assert its debt under 31 USC Section 3713(a).

If at the time of assignment the assignor owes taxes and is insolvent, 31 USC Section 3713(a) comes into play to establish the government's priority of

[316] King v. United States, 379 US 329 (1964).

[317] United States v. Weisburn, 48 F. Supp. 393 (ED Pa. 1943).

[318] Section 6212(b) provides that in the absence of notification by a fiduciary, the statutory notice should be sent to the last known address of the decedent.

[319] Dalton v. Peters, 119 F2d 494 (8th Cir. 1941).

[320] Engleman v. Commodity Credit Corp., 107 F. Supp. 930 (SD Cal. 1952); Sisk v. United States, 61-1 USTC ¶ 9476 (ND Okla. 1961).

payments.[321] If the assignor's creditors file a petition to have the assignor adjudicated bankrupt, 31 USC Section 3713(a) specifically provides that the Bankruptcy Code determines the rights of the creditors.

[iii] Receiverships. A general receivership is an independent proceeding to liquidate the debtor's assets and pay liabilities, but it does not always deal with insolvent debtors. A receiver may be appointed, among other reasons, to preserve, protect, and administer property that is involved in a legal action, to take charge of commercial property and receive and disburse rents or profits, or to prevent fraud or loss of property from fraud.[322] The United States itself may apply to the court for the appointment of a receiver in tax cases.[323] On the appointment of a receiver, the assessment of any deficiency for income, estate, and gift tax is required to be made immediately. This assessment is not a jeopardy assessment, and the requirements pertaining to a jeopardy assessment, such as mailing and notices of deficiency, do not apply. However, the receiver is advised by letter in detail how the deficiency was determined.[324]

Once the receiver has taken over the assets of the taxpayer/debtor and the assets are under the control of the court, they are not subject to levy and collection activity.[325] Any assets that are outside the receivership or that are exempt from creditors are as a rule subject to levy.[326] Under Section 6873, any claim allowed in the receivership proceedings and not paid is not discharged but is to be collected from the taxpayer with interest, either by levy or by filing a proceeding in court.[327]

Where the tax liability of the taxpayer has been assessed prior to the receivership, the receiver, like the assignee for the benefit of creditors, takes only the property subject to the tax lien, without the protection afforded certain persons under Section 6323. If taxes are due and owing at the time of the receivership but have not been assessed, the United States has no lien on the assets of the taxpayer, and the priority of payment granted the government under

---

[321] Wing v. United States, 208 F. Supp. 5 (D. Mass. 1962). See also IRM 57(11)5.3, MT 5700-1 (Nov. 15, 1985) (Assignments for the Benefit of Creditors).

[322] 28 USC §§ 754, 959(a). See also IRM 57(11)5.2, MT 5700-1 (Nov. 15, 1985) (Receivership Proceedings).

[323] IRC § 7403(d). See, e.g., United States v. Florida, 178 F. Supp. 627 (ED Ark. 1959), aff'd, 285 F2d 596 (8th Cir. 1960); Goldfine v. United States, 300 F2d 260 (1st Cir. 1962).

[324] Reg. § 301.6871(b)-1(c).

[325] United States v. Allen, 328 F2d 377 (5th Cir. 1964) (notice of levy served after filing of complaint for appointment of receiver but before receiver appointed, held, state court did not acquire jurisdiction over the property levied upon).

[326] Reg. § 301.6871(a)-2.

[327] The normal ten-year period for collection of tax after assessment is suspended under Section 6503(d) while the assets of the taxpayer are in the control or custody of the court and for six months thereafter. IRC § 6503(b).

31 USC Section 3713(a) is its main collection device. Where a taxpayer consents to the appointment of a receiver while he is insolvent, the conditions precedent to the priority of the United States under 31 USC Section 3713(a) are met.[328] On the other hand, a receiver takes a debtor's property subject to the outstanding liens, and his interest is only in any surplus over and above the amount of existing encumbrances. If a tax has been assessed and a levy on the property of the debtor/taxpayer has been made prior to the date of the receivership, the government's right to the property derives from the lien and levy, and it can proceed to sell the property and apply the proceeds to the tax liability.[329]

¶ 16.09 LIABILITY OF FIDUCIARIES UNDER 31 USC SECTION 3713(B)

Section 3713(b) imposes personal liability on every executor, administrator, assignee, or "other person" who distributes the living or deceased debtor's property to other creditors before he satisfies or pays a debt due the United States. Although for convenience, persons subject to personal liability are referred to as fiduciaries, the class of persons subject to personal liability under 31 USC Section 3713(b) is quite broad.[330] Any person who has possession and control of the living or deceased debtor's property is made liable if the person fails to honor the priority set forth in 31 USC Section 3713(a). Thus, it is not the title, but the facts of possession and control, that are determinative.[331]

The personal liability of a fiduciary is subject to three conditions:

1. Liability under 31 USC Section 3713(b) may be imposed only where, by virtue of the insolvency of a deceased debtor's estate or the insolvency and collective creditor proceeding involving a living debtor, the priority of 31 USC Section 3713(a) applies;
2. The fiduciary's liability is limited to debts actually paid before the debt due the United States; and
3. The fiduciary must know or have reason to know of the government's tax claim.

---

[328] New York v. Maclay, 288 US 290 (1932); Illinois ex rel. Gordon v. Campbell, 329 US 362, 375 (1946); United States v. Emory, 314 US 423 (1941); United States v. Butterworth-Judson Corp., 269 US 504 (1926).

[329] United States v. Allen, 328 F2d 377 (5th Cir. 1964); United States v. Eiland, 223 F2d 118 (4th Cir. 1955).

[330] The regulations define "fiduciary" as "a person who holds in trust an estate to which another has the beneficial title or in which another has a beneficial interest, or receives and controls income of another." Reg. § 301.7701-6.

[331] Bramwell v. US Fidelity & Guar. Co., 269 US 483 (1926); King v. United States, 379 US 329 (1964) (debtor-in-possession under Chapter XI of the Old Bankruptcy Act).

The first condition may not be immediately apparent because 31 USC Sections 3713(a) and 3713(b) are separate provisions. However, 31 USC Sections 3713(a) and 3713(b) were at one time part of a single statutory provision, and their division into separate sections did not work any change "in purpose or meaning."[332] Accordingly, the circumstances of personal liability provided in 31 USC Section 3713(b) must be read with the circumstances establishing the government's priority described in 31 USC Section 3713(a).[333]

Since the purpose of 31 USC Section 3713(b) is to protect the government's priority as established in 31 USC Section 3713(a), it follows that personal liability may be imposed on a fiduciary only to the extent that he pays "any debts" of the decedent or his estate or of an insolvent living debtor in violation of the government's priority.[334]

The third condition for the imposition of personal liability cannot be found in either 31 USC Section 3713(a) or 31 USC Section 3713(b) but has been developed from judicial interpretations of the statutes. The courts generally have ruled that a fiduciary is not liable under 31 USC Section 3713(b), unless the fiduciary has notice of the tax claim and elects to satisfy other debts.[335] The required knowledge is either (1) actual knowledge of the liability, or (2) notice of such facts as would put a reasonably prudent person on inquiry of the existence of the unpaid claim.[336] In *Little v. Commissioner*, a recent Tax Court case, a fiduciary of an estate, who did not have actual knowledge of the estate's income tax liabilities, had received Forms W-2 and 1099 and subsequent notices from the Service. The Tax Court held that he had received sufficient information to prompt a reasonably prudent person to inquire about the existence of tax debts owed to the Service, but found that the fiduciary nevertheless did not have sufficient notice of the tax debt to charge him with per-

---

[332] Price v. United States, 269 US 492, 501 (1926); King v. United States, 379 US 329, 336 (1964).

[333] The conditions that must be present before the priority established by 31 USC Section 3713(a) exists are discussed supra ¶ 16.07.

[334] 31 USC Section 3713(b) provides that the fiduciary is liable "to the extent of the payments unpaid claims of the Government." The limited exceptions to the government's priority under 31 USC Section 3713(a) are discussed supra ¶ 16.08.

[335] Want v. Comm'r, 280 F2d 777 (2d Cir. 1960); Viles v. Comm'r, 233 F2d 376 (6th Cir. 1956); Leigh v. Comm'r, 72 TC 1105, 1109 (1979); Fitzgerald v. Comm'r, 4 TC 494, 504 (1944); Irving Trust Co., 36 BTA 146 (1937), acq. 1937-2 CB 15.

[336] Leigh v. Comm'r, 72 TC 1105, 1109 (1979). For a case of actual notice of a tax claim, see United States v. Estate of Lenna A. Kime, 950 F. Supp. 950 (D. Neb. 1996) (personal representative consented to the assessment, the assessment was made, and then he distributed the assests of estate without paying estate tax). See also Allen v. Comm'r, TC Memo. 1999-385 (1999) (son held personally liable for estate tax and penalties due from father's estate: son was fiduciary of father's estate, had knowledge (by virtue of his education and the size of his father's estate) that the estate owed estate tax, but nevertheless ultimately distributed all of estate's assets to himself through various suspicious transfers without paying estate's debts).

sonal liability.[337] In reaching its conclusion in the case, the Tax Court distinguished between reliance on an attorney to perform a required act, such as filing the estate's return, and advising the fiduciary about the existence of a liability or obligation. In the Tax Court's opinion, the fiduciary had acted in a prudent and reasonable manner by promptly forwarding the notices to the estate's attorney, even though the attorney erroneously and repeatedly advised him that because of its modest size, the estate had no income tax liability. Knowing that he had no experience of his own to determine whether the estate had any potential tax liabilities, the fiduciary had consulted an apparently competent attorney about the matter, and so the fiduciary's request for advice was "the reasonable and prudent thing to do." Under the circumstances, the Tax Court found that the fiduciary lacked knowledge of the estate's income tax liabilities at the time he made payments from the estate and did not knowingly disregard debts *because of the Service.* The Service itself has ruled that an executor or administrator of an estate cannot be held personally liable under 31 USC Section 3713(b) for any unpaid income tax liability of a decedent "unless he has either personal knowledge of the debt, or has such knowledge as would put a reasonable prudent man on inquiry."[338] The fiduciary's personal knowledge need not come by way of a formal notice from the Service.[339] Signing an amended return showing additional estate tax, coupled with the administrator's having paid the tax shown on the original return, is evidence of actual or personal knowledge of the debt due under 31 USC Section 3713(b).[340] Further, in general, the fiduciary is not under a duty to inquire of the Service whether any taxes are due, unless there are suspicious circumstances that might have prompted a prudent person to make such an inquiry.[341] Presumably, the executor may rely on a closing letter on conclusion of an estate tax audit, although the Service may reopen the case. An executor may not be chargeable with knowledge of an income or gift tax liability of the decedent.[342] The executor also is not chargeable with knowledge of the existence of assets not included in the estate tax return.[343] However, once a fiduciary has notice of the tax claim, he has been held to be under a duty to make and press objection to paying out deposited funds to nonpriority creditors before provision is made for

---

[337] Little v. Comm'r, 113 TC 474 (1999).

[338] Rev. Rul. 66-43, 1966-1 CB 291. See also Rev. Rul. 79-310, 1979-2 CB 404.

[339] Viles v. Comm'r, 233 F2d 376 (6th Cir. 1956); Paul Haimowitz et al. v. Comm'r, 15 TCM 66 (1956) (executors were informally advised by auditing agents of pending deficiencies before transfers from the estate).

[340] Leigh v. Comm'r, 72 TC 1105, 1109 (1979).

[341] Irving Trust Co., 36 BTA 146 (1937), acq. 1937-2 CB 15, on which Rev. Rul. 66-43, 1966-1 CB 291, was based.

[342] Giovaninni Terranova v. Comm'r, PH TCM ¶ 43,380 (1943).

[343] Occidental Life Ins. Co. v. Comm'r, 50 TC 726 (1968).

the government's claim.[344] In such a case, the fiduciary may not be discharged from liability under 31 USC Section 3713(b) either by his status as agent of the court or by the fact that a court order specifically provides for payment of nonpriority claims, although this absolute liability has not always been imposed.[345]

[1] Proceedings to Enforce Liability Under 31 USC Section 3713(b)

Procedurally, the government may enforce a fiduciary's liability under 31 USC Section 3713(b) in either of two ways: (1) utilize the transferee liability procedures of Section 6901, or (2) institute an action in court under 31 USC Section 3713(b). If the Service elects the first alternative, liability is assessed and collected from the fiduciary in the same manner as an income, gift, or estate tax is collected from a taxpayer and his transferee.[346] Under this summary procedure, a notice of liability similar to the notice of deficiency sent to a taxpayer is sent to the fiduciary. After a notice is sent, the fiduciary may contest the determination in the Tax Court or, after assessment, may pay the tax and sue for a refund in a federal district court or in the Court of Claims. Under the second alternative, the government brings suit against the fiduciary in a district court,[347] thereby cutting off access to the Tax Court.

Where a tax due from a deceased or living taxpayer remains unpaid after normal assessment and collection procedures, the government is not limited to asserting the liability of a fiduciary under 31 USC Section 3713(b). A fiduciary may also be a transferee subject to transferee liability for estate taxes. Section 6324(a)(2) imposes personal liability on a trustee who is a transferee of property includable in the gross estate of a decedent. However, the amount of this personal liability for estate tax is limited to the value of the property received by the trustee at the time of the decedent's death. "Transferee" is defined for purposes of the transferee liability rules to include "any person who, under Section 6324(a)(2), is personally liable" for any part of the unpaid estate tax. In addition to liability under Section 6324, the government may use any creditor's remedy provided by state law to recover from the fiduciary (e.g., under a state fraudulent conveyance act). Transferee liability under Section 6324 or under state law is enforced either by an action against the fiduciary in a federal district court or by way of the transferee liability procedures of Section 6901.

---

[344] King v. United States, 379 US 329 (1964).

[345] United States v. Pate, 47 F. Supp. 965 (WD Ark. 1942) (fiduciary held not liable as long as he followed probate court's decree).

[346] IRC § 6901(a)(1)(B).

[347] See, e.g., United States v. Weisburn, 48 F. Supp. 393 (ED Pa. 1943).

Despite the similarity in procedures for enforcing both 31 USC Section 3713(b) and transferee liability, there are significant differences between the two types of liability. First, the scope of liability differs. The fiduciary is liable for the amount of claims paid before the government's claim—the last opportunity for collection. Transferee liability for estate tax under Section 6324 is limited to the value at the time of the decedent's death of the property received by the trustee. Transferee liability in equity is limited to the value of the assets that the transferee unjustly received when the transferor was insolvent or was rendered insolvent.[348] Second, the nature of the liability differs. Fiduciary liability under 31 USC Section 3713(b) derives from the actions of the fiduciary. If the fiduciary is at fault because he had notice or knowledge of the government's claims, the fiduciary is liable, although he received no personal benefit from the payments. Under Section 6324, transferee liability exists irrespective of fault as the consequence of merely having received property includable in the gross estate. Third, the government may proceed against and collect from the transferees of a decedent under Sections 6324 and 6901 without having to prove the personal liability of the fiduciary or having first proceeded against the estate,[349] as is required under 31 USC Section 3713(b).

[2] Limitations on Liability

The statute of limitations on the assessment of fiduciary liability under Section 6901 is "not later than 1 year after the liability arises or not later than the expiration of the period for collection of the tax in respect of which such liability arises, whichever is later."[350] Income, gift, and estate taxes must be assessed within three years from the date the return is filed, unless (1) there has been a substantial omission; (2) no return has been filed; or (3) the return is false or fraudulent. Thus, assuming no fault on the filing of the return, the earliest time liability may cease is four years after the return is filed. The outside or later limit is expiration of the six-year statute of limitations on collection. It has

---

[348] Kreps v. Comm'r, 42 TC 660, aff'd, 351 F2d 1 (2d Cir. 1965) (applying New York law). An executor is not liable for interest accruing after the Service sends the executor of an estate a notice of liability under 31 USC Section 3713(b). Singleton v. Comm'r, TC Memo. 1996-249 (1996). The Tax Court distinguished an executor's liability under 31 USC Section 3713(b) from the liability of a transferee on the ground that the transferee has the benefit of enjoying the transferred property, while the executor does not. If the executor were liable for funds the executor transferred to a beneficiary, collection of interest from the executor would constitute a penalty ("a punitive act for which there is not legal authority").

[349] Melba Schuster, 32 TC 998 (1959), aff'd in part, 312 F2d 311 (9th Cir. 1962) (transferee liability for estate tax was imposed against a joint tenant, even though the probate estate was solvent, where the taxes had not been timely assessed against the estate).

[350] IRC § 6901(c)(3).

been held that the six-year statute of limitations on collection of the assessment against the fiduciary runs from the date the tax was assessed against the estate, not from the date of the assessment against the fiduciary.[351]

C COLLECTION OF TAX CLAIMS IN BANKRUPTCY [REVISED]

¶ 16.10 BANKRUPTCY LAWS IN GENERAL

In providing for payment of tax claims, the bankruptcy laws differ substantially from the internal revenue laws or the fiduciary liability discussed in Parts A and B of this chapter. The tax lien provisions of the Internal Revenue Code (the Code) reward prompt action by creditors and the Service alike to secure their claims against debtors/taxpayers. Section 6323 is a statute that must be used in a timely manner; for example, to secure priority over the federal tax lien, the holder of a security interest must perfect the interest before the Service files its Notice of Federal Tax Lien. Prompt action by the Service in filing its notice of lien assures priority of the tax claim. On the other hand, bankruptcy law does not always reward a creditor's race of diligence to secure its position, and the bankruptcy law recognizes that payment of tax claims as a priority imposes a burden on other creditors. Under the bankruptcy laws, even if the Service has taken action to improve its position by filing notice of its tax lien, satisfaction of the lien may nevertheless be postponed. Similarly, contrary to the absolute priority accorded federal claims under 31 USC Section 3713(a), the bankruptcy laws recognize that payment of tax claims as a first priority would result in payment by other creditors of the tax claims of the debtor.

The treatment of tax claims in bankruptcy also takes into account the overall objective of the bankruptcy laws to relieve the debtor of his debts and provide him with a fresh start. The "fresh start" for debtors against whom tax claims exist is not as unhampered as other claims; nevertheless, this objective differs from the rather inflexible demands of tax payment incorporated in the internal revenue laws and Revised Statutes.

Before 1978, the law of bankruptcy was composed of (1) the Bankruptcy Act of 1898 and (2) bankruptcy rules.[352] In 1978, Congress made substantial changes in the bankruptcy laws by enacting the Bankruptcy Reform Act (the

---

[351] United States v. Motsinger, 123 F2d 585 (4th Cir. 1941); United States v. Rose, 227 F. Supp. 259 (ED Pa. 1964).

[352] Pursuant to 28 USC Section 2075, the Supreme Court, from 1973 to 1976, promulgated bankruptcy rules, which superseded significant portions of the Bankruptcy Act of 1898.

1978 Act).[353] Among other changes to the bankruptcy system, the 1978 Act gave broad jurisdiction to bankruptcy judges, formerly called referees, to hear cases in which a debtor might be involved. When a bankruptcy judge decided a traditional contract action brought by a debtor against a party which objected to the jurisdiction of the Bankruptcy Court, the jurisdictional provisions of the 1978 Act were drawn into question. In 1982, the Supreme Court, in *Northern Pipeline Construction Co. v. Marathon Pipe Line Co.*,[354] invalidated the 1978 Act because it unconstitutionally granted Article III judicial power to Bankruptcy Court judges who did not have the life tenure and irreducible salaries of district court judges. Congress subsequently passed the Bankruptcy Amendments and Federal Judgeship Act of 1984, which, in general, cured the constitutional problem by providing for the delegation by district courts of their full bankruptcy jurisdiction to bankruptcy judges. Finally, in 1986, Congress passed the Bankruptcy Judges, United States Trustees, and Family Farmer Bankruptcy Act, providing, among other things, for a permanent nationwide United States trustee system under the direction of the Justice Department.

Bankruptcy laws are now found in parts or titles of the United States Code. Title 11, the Bankruptcy Code, incorporates the substantive and procedural provisions for bankruptcy liquidation and rehabilitation cases. Title 28, the Judicial Code, includes the sections that establish bankruptcy jurisdiction, the bankruptcy judges and the Bankruptcy Court, venue and transfer, and the structure of the United States Trustee system.

The Bankruptcy Reform Act of 1994 made significant changes to the Bankruptcy Code, some of which affect tax claims in bankruptcy.[355] Changes to the Bankruptcy Code were made to clarify when the Service may collect taxes from a debtor without violating the automatic stay and when the Service may be sued for damages for violating the automatic stay.

Again in 2003, the Bankruptcy Code and related provisions of the Judicial Code were amended.[356]

The status of a claim for taxes depends on a number of factors, such as (1) whether a notice of lien has been filed before bankruptcy; (2) how long before bankruptcy payment of the taxes was due; (3) whether the claim is for tax, penalty, or interest; and (4) the type of tax (e.g., income, employment, or other excise tax). Bankruptcy affects a tax claim depending on its status as a lien claim (i.e., a claim secured by a lien under Bankruptcy Code Section 506) or a priority claim (i.e., a tax claim entitled to seventh priority under Bankruptcy Code Section 507).

---

[353] For further reading on bankruptcy law for the nonbankruptcy lawyer, see D.G. Epstein, Bankruptcy and Related Law in a Nutshell (West Group 2002).

[354] Northern Pipeline Constr. Co. v. Marathon Pipe Line Co., 458 US 50 (1982).

[355] Pub. L. No. 103-394, eff. Oct. 22, 1994.

[356] Pub. L. No. 108-105, approved Nov. 5, 2003.

Title 11 of the United States Code is divided into seven odd-numbered chapters: Chapters 1 (General Provisions), 3 (Case Administration), and 5 (Creditors, the Debtor and the Estate) apply generally to all cases under Chapters 7 (Liquidation), 9 (Adjustment of Debts of a Municipality) 11 (Reorganization), and 13 (Adjustment of Debts of an Individual with Regular Income).

The operation of the Bankruptcy Code where claims for federal taxes are concerned is more clearly seen by following the course of liquidating bankruptcy under Chapter 7. The following section covers the phases of a liquidating bankruptcy from the commencement of a case to the discharge of the debtor/taxpayer. The balance of the discussion covers a reorganization and rehabilitation under Chapter 11, and wage earners plans under Chapter 13 focusing on (1) the effect of bankruptcy on collection from the taxpayer and (2) the effect of bankruptcy on payment of the tax claim in the bankruptcy proceeding.

¶ 16.11 TAX CLAIM IN A LIQUIDATING BANKRUPTCY UNDER CHAPTER 7

[1] Commencement of a Bankruptcy Case and Its Consequences

A "debtor," whether an individual or an entity, may commence a bankruptcy case by filing with the Bankruptcy Court a petition under the chapter of the Bankruptcy Code under which the debtor seeks protection.[357] Filing a bankruptcy petition is a relatively simple procedure; forms are provided in the Bankruptcy Code itself. Less obvious are the consequences of filing the bankruptcy petition. There are at least two important consequences. First, the filing of a voluntary petition operates as an automatic stay of collection of actions creditors might otherwise take to collect the debts owed to them.[358] Second, commencement of a case under Section 301 "creates an estate" comprised of the debtor's property "wherever located and by whomever held."[359]

From the debtor's standpoint, the stay is necessary to protect the debtor from the collection efforts of creditors. At the same time, the bankruptcy trustee needs time to collect "the property of the estate," and the Bankruptcy

---

[357] 11 USC § 301. Instead of "debtor," Section 301 refers to an "entity." When the debtor files a petition with the Bankruptcy Court, the bankruptcy case is a voluntary case. An involuntary case may be commenced only under Chapters 7 and 11, and against certain persons. 11 USC § 303.

[358] 11 USC §§ 362(a)(1)–362(a)(8).

[359] 11 USC §§ 541(a)(1)–541(a)(7).

Court must have an opportunity to hear and determine the matters that are appropriate before any distribution is made to creditors.

Section 362(a) of the Bankruptcy Code lists specific acts that creditors, including the Service, are prohibited from taking under the automatic stay. The stay is extremely broad and halts nearly all collection action by general creditors. Even the Service may not (1) commence an action in court to enforce a judgment; (2) act to obtain possession of property; (3) create or perfect a lien on property; or (4) set off any debt owing the debtor. However, the automatic stay does not prevent the Service from (1) auditing a debtor's tax returns; (2) issuing a notice of deficiency; (3) making a demand for tax returns; or (4) making an assessment of tax and issuing a notice and demand for payment of the assessment.[360]

The property included in the estate is very broad and includes "all legal or equitable interests of the debtor in property as of *the commencement of the case.*"[361] Thus, the date the bankruptcy petition is filed is a crucial date; property acquired before the petition date becomes property of the estate for distribution to creditors, whereas property acquired after the petition remains the property of the debtor.[362]

[2] Automatic Stay

Bankruptcy Code Section 362(a)(1) "operates as a stay...of...the commencement or continuation...of a judicial proceeding, administrative, or other action or proceeding [i] against the debtor...or [ii] to recover a claim against the debtor."[363] What effect does the automatic stay have on the Service? As amended by the Bankruptcy Reform Act of 1994, the automatic stay no longer prevents the Service from (1) auditing a debtor's tax returns; (2) issuing a notice of deficiency; (3) making a demand for tax returns; or (4) making an assessment of tax and issuing a notice and demand for payment of the assessment.[364] The automatic stay provision does not preclude other Service ac-

---

[360] 11 USC § 362(b)(9).

[361] 11 USC § 541(a)(1).

[362] See 11 USC § 541(a)(2) (postpetition personal-service income belongs to the debtor). However, a creditor whose debt is not discharged in bankruptcy may collect the debt from the debtor's after-acquired property. The same treatment applies for tax claims not discharged in bankruptcy.

[363] 11 USC § 362(a)(8).

[364] 11 USC § 362(b)(9).

tion.[365] However, the automatic stay prohibits the Service from offsetting a postpetition refund against a prepetition tax liability.[366]

Once the automatic stay is in force, the running of the collection period is also suspended. Two Code suspension provisions apply: (1) Section 6503(a)(1) suspends the statute of limitations on assessment during the period in which the Service is prohibited from making an assessment (i.e., the ninety-day or 150-day period after the notice of deficiency during which Section 6213(a) prohibits the Service from assessing income, estate, and gift tax) and for sixty days thereafter, and if a petition is filed in the Tax Court, until the Tax Court's decision becomes final, plus sixty days and (2) Section 6213(f) suspends the running of the ninety-day or 150-day period for filing a Tax Court petition during the bankruptcy stay and for sixty days thereafter.

[a] Scope of the Automatic Stay: Tax Court Cases

The filing of a bankruptcy petition automatically "stays" or enjoins creditors from taking action or continuing to collect their claims or enforce their liens.[367] If the Service has sent the taxpayer a notice of deficiency before filing a bankruptcy petition, Section 6213(f) suspends the time the taxpayer/debtor has to file a petition in the Tax Court "for the period the debtor is prohibited by reason of such [bankruptcy] case from filing a petition in the Tax Court...and for 60 days thereafter."[368] In *McClamma v. Commissioner*, the Tax Court held that the unexpired portion of the ninety-day period provided by Section 6213(a) is added to the sixty days to determine the time during which a discharged debtor could file a petition in the Tax Court.[369] Despite the auto-

---

[365] In re Norton, 717 F2d 767 (3d Cir. 1983). See In re Heritage Village Church & Missionary Fellowship, Inc., 87 BR 401, 88-1 USTC ¶ 9234 (DSC 1988), aff'd, 851 F2d 104 (4th Cir. 1988) (exempt organization status not stayed).

[366] See In re Norton, 717 F2d 767 (3d Cir. 1983) (Service held in contempt for violating automatic stay by offsetting refund in a Chapter 13 case and fined $150). See United States v. Reynolds, 764 F2d 1004 (4th Cir. 1985); United States v. Bulson, 117 BR 537, 91-1 USTC ¶ 50,023 (Bankr. 9th Cir. 1990) (mailing of levy during Chapter 13 proceeding was willful violation of automatic stay). In *Bulson*, the Bankruptcy Appellate Panel held that the debtor was entitled to attorney fees and costs because the Service's violation was willful and because sovereign immunity had been waived by 11 USC Section 106(a). See also Bryant v. IRS, 116 BR 272, 91-1 USTC ¶ 50,124 (Bankr. D. Kan. 1990) (reasonable attorney fees awarded as sanction for stay violation).

[367] 11 USC § 362(a). Once a petition has been filed and the automatic stay is in effect, even a creditor's action already pending in the district court may proceed only if an application is made in the bankruptcy proceeding. NLT Computer Servs. Corp. v. Capital Computer Sys., Inc., 755 F2d 1253 (6th Cir. 1985).

[368] 11 USC § 362(a)(8).

[369] McClamma v. Comm'r, 76 TC 754 (1981) (Tax Court petition filed after bankruptcy petition is subject to automatic stay rule and invalid); Wahlstrum v. Comm'r, 92 TC 703 (1989) (automatic stay precluded filing of petition even though Chapter 13 plan

matic stay, even when the taxpayer/debtor has filed the Tax Court petition, the Tax Court is without jurisdiction, regardless of whether the underlying claim relates to prepetition or postpetition liabilities.[370] The Bankruptcy Court has jurisdiction to determine a debtor/taxpayer's liability even when the taxpayer has filed a Tax Court petition before the bankruptcy, as long as the Tax Court has not adjudicated the claim.[371] Even if the Bankruptcy Court lifts the automatic stay to permit the Tax Court case to proceed, the Bankruptcy Court may also determine the issues itself.[372] The automatic stay prevents the taxpayer/debtor from filing a Tax Court petition during the pendency of the bankruptcy case.

Taking into account these suspension provisions and the Bankruptcy Code's automatic stay, consider the following situations:[373]

1. Suppose the notice of deficiency is issued more than 150 days before the bankruptcy petition is filed. In this situation, the suspension provisions have already run by the date on which the petition is filed. Since the 150-day suspension period (ninety days plus sixty days) has run before the bankruptcy petition date and automatic stay, the Service will be able to make the assessment before the petition and stay.

2. Suppose the notice of deficiency is sent more than ninety days but less than 150 days before the bankruptcy petition. Section 6503(a)(1) suspends the limitation period for the portion of the sixty-day period that has not run. However, if the taxpayer/debtor has not filed a Tax Court petition before the ninety-day period has run, the Service may assess tax. If the taxpayer/debtor has filed a Tax Court petition, the Service may make an assessment only after the Tax Court's decision becomes final.

3. Suppose the notice of deficiency was issued within ninety days before the bankruptcy petition. Section 6213(a) would suspend the running of the balance of the ninety-day period for filing a petition. This unexpired portion would cease to run until the automatic stay suspension period terminates.[374] Thus, the taxpayer/debtor will have the unexpired portion of the ninety-day period plus sixty days to file a petition.

---

had been confirmed). Ever Clean Serv., Inc. v. Comm'r, 45 TCM 349 (1982) (taxpayer's petition dismissed when filed after petition for reorganization).

[370] Halpern v. Comm'r, 96 TC 895 (1991); In re Hunt, 95 BR 442, 89-1 USTC ¶ 9232 (BCND Tex. 1989) (automatic stay of Tax Court proceedings reviewed).

[371] 11 USC §§ 505(a)(1), 505(a)(2).

[372] United States v. Wilson, 974 F2d 514 (4th Cir. 1992) (Bankruptcy Court approved settlement in Tax Court between Service and trustee after Tax Court case had been pending three years, without reinstating automatic stay).

[373] Chief Counsel Notice N(35)(10)-1 (Dec. 1, 1998) Re: Statute of Limitations on Tax Assessment as Affected by Bankruptcy.

[374] IRC § 6213(f).

4. Suppose the notice of deficiency was sent after the bankruptcy petition was filed. Section 6213(f) suspends the running of the period for filing a petition until the automatic stay terminates, plus sixty days. If the automatic stay was violated, Bankruptcy Courts have awarded sanctions against the Service. However, in a decision involving 11 USC Section 106(c), which waives sovereign immunity in general terms, the Supreme Court held that this general waiver did not "unequivocally express" waiver of the government's immunity from actions for monetary relief.[375]

On the other hand, suppose the taxpayer receives a notice of deficiency, files a petition in the Tax Court, and then files a petition in the Bankruptcy Court. Even if the Bankruptcy Court rules on the merits of the tax dispute under 11 USC Section 505, the Tax Court held in *Freytag v. Commissioner*, that the Bankruptcy Court's exercise of jurisdiction does not terminate the Tax Court's jurisdiction over the case, and the Tax Court still retains in personam jurisdiction over the taxpayer/petitioner and subject matter jurisdiction over the taxpayer/petitioner's challenge to the Commissioner's action.[376] Because Congress intended in Section 6871(b) to coordinate the Code's assessment and collection procedures with the jurisdiction of the Bankruptcy Courts, even when the Bankruptcy Court determines the tax liabilities that were at issue in the Tax Court, Section 6503(a) suspends the time when those liabilities may be assessed until the decision of the Tax Court becomes final. As a result, the Tax Court held that the time for making an assessment had not expired, and that a decision of the Tax Court would be entered consistent with the determinations of the Bankruptcy Court.

Different views about the nature of a Tax Court case (i.e., whether it is a suit by the taxpayer because the taxpayer files a petition or a suit against the taxpayer because the notice of deficiency precipitates the petition) have led to different opinions about the effect of the automatic stay on the running of the appeal period. The rationale of the court's conclusion that the stay does not apply was that the taxpayer's petition for redetermination in the Tax Court is (1) not the continuation of an administrative proceeding, but the commencement of an independent judicial proceeding and (2) not a judicial proceeding against the taxpayer because the taxpayer commenced the proceeding.[377] Taking precisely the opposite view of the nature of the Tax Court, another court concluded that the automatic stay suspended the running of the appeal period.[378]

---

[375] United States v. Nordic Village, Inc., 503 US 30 (1992).

[376] Freytag v. Comm'r, 110 TC 35 (1998).

[377] Roberts v. Comm'r, 83 AFTR2d 99-2282 (11th Cir. 1999).

[378] Delpit v. Comm'r, 18 F3d 768 (9th Cir. 1994).

Under the Bankruptcy Code, the Bankruptcy Court has the authority to determine which court will determine the merits of the tax claims, both as to claims against the estate and as to claims against the debtor concerning his personal tax liability for nondischargeable taxes. The Bankruptcy Court may then decide (1) to lift the stay permitting the debtor to litigate in the Tax Court or (2) to determine the debtor's liability for itself. This discretionary jurisdiction created a number of problems, which were addressed by the Bankruptcy Tax Act of 1980 (BTA). To coordinate the Bankruptcy Code and the internal revenue laws in a bankruptcy case, the BTA amended the Code. The ninety-day period within which a debtor/taxpayer must file a petition in the Tax Court to obtain review of a deficiency is "suspended for the period during which the debtor is prohibited by reason of such case from filing a petition in the Tax Court...and for 60 days therafter."[379] Accordingly, if a Bankruptcy Court lifts the stay, a debtor is able to have a deficiency determined in the Tax Court if he files a petition within sixty days after the stay is lifted.

If the debtor files in the Tax Court, the trustee may also intervene as a matter of right in the proceeding,[380] in which case the Tax Court decision is binding on both the debtor and the trustee. If the trustee does not intervene, a Tax Court decision adversely affects the ability of the trustee to litigate the merits of the tax claim in the Bankruptcy Court. The Tax Court decision will not be res judicata or collaterally estop the trustee in the Bankruptcy Court.[381] However, if the debtor's liability is adjudicated in the Bankruptcy Court and his liability for such tax has become res judicata pursuant to the determination, the Service is authorized to make immediate assessment of the tax.[382] After the Bankruptcy Court has made a determination of tax liability under Section 505(a)(1), the Service may assess the tax despite the automatic stay.[383] Again, it is unclear whether a debtor who does not participate in the proceeding is bound by the Bankruptcy Court's determination, because the trustee and the debtor are not in privity. However, because the Service may make immediate assessment, it appears that a debtor ignores a proceeding to determine his tax liability at his peril.

---

[379] IRC § 6213(f). The statute of limitations on assessment is also suspended for the same period. IRC § 6503(i). See McClamma v. Comm'r, 76 TC 754 (1981) (ninety-day period of Section 6213(a) is added to the sixty days to determine the time during which a discharged debtor can file a petition in the Tax Court).

[380] IRC § 7464.

[381] If the trustee is not a party, the judgment of the Tax Court would ordinarily not be binding unless the trustee were in privity with the taxpayer.

[382] IRC § 6871(b).

[383] 11 USC § 505(c). See In re Flaherty, 74 AFTR2d 94-5245 (Bankr. DNH 1994).

[b] Violations of the Stay and Sovereign Immunity

The IRS Restructuring and Reform Act of 1998 (1998 Act) provides that a taxpayer may petition the Bankruptcy Court to recover damages against the Service if any Service personnel willfully violates the automatic stay provision of 11 USC Section 362 by taking any collection action against the taxpayer.[384] The petition under Section 7430 is the exclusive remedy for recovering damages for a Service violation of the automatic stay, except that when the Service violates the automatic stay, the taxpayer may choose to proceed under 11 USC Section 362(h) for recovery of actual damages for the willful violation. If the taxpayer proceeds under 11 USC Section 362(h), then a petition to recover damages in the Bankruptcy Court under Section 7430(e) does not apply. Section 7430 governs the recovery of administrative and litigation costs incurred in the action, and any administrative costs may be awarded only if incurred on or after the date the bankruptcy petition was filed.[385] Consistent with this stay provision, Section 6871 also contemplates that the taxpayer will be sent a notice of deficiency, thereby giving him access to the Tax Court; nevertheless, although a debtor may receive a notice of deficiency, the automatic stay still operates to prevent the taxpayer from commencing a proceeding in the Tax Court. Consequently, a debtor's tax claim is determined by the Bankruptcy Court if it decides against lifting the stay, and only after that determination may the Service make an assessment.[386]

Sovereign immunity will not preclude a Bankruptcy Court from having jurisdiction to impose sanctions on the Service for violating the automatic stay.[387] The Bankruptcy Reform Act of 1994 added a limited waiver of sovereign immunity for the purpose of permitting the Bankruptcy Court to resolve issues about the application of specifically listed provisions of the Bankruptcy Code to governmental units, including the Service.[388] The sovereign immunity

---

[384] IRC § 7430(e)(1), added by 1998 Act, § 3102(c)(1), eff. July 22, 1998.

[385] IRC §§ 7430(c)(2)(A), 7430(c)(2)(B).

[386] 11 USC § 505(c); IRC § 6871(b). See discussion of the determination of tax claims in bankruptcy proceedings, infra ¶ 16.12[1].

[387] See United States v. Nordic Village, Inc., 112 S. Ct. 1011 (1992). The jurisdiction of the Bankruptcy Court to impose sanctions against the Service for violating the automatic stay is analyzed in United States v. Flynn, 73 AFTR2d 94-1028 (Bankr. SD Ga. 1994) (Service liable to debtor when it levied on bank account despite notice of the debtor's bankruptcy, in violation of the automatic stay). If an assessment is made and a notice and demand issued, the tax lien that otherwise would attach to the debtor's property does not take effect except in the following circumstances: (1) the assessed tax is a non-dischargeable debt of the taxpayer and the property or its proceeds are transferred out of the bankruptcy estate to the debtor or (2) the proceeds are otherwise revested in the debtor.

[388] 11 USC § 106(a). The effective date of the Bankruptcy Reform Act of 1994 is October 22, 1994. The waiver applies to such provisions as the automatic stay of 11 USC Section 362 and the discharge injunction of 11 USC Section 524. The waiver of sovereign

waiver of 11 USC Section 106 for the listed sections of the Bankruptcy Code permits the Bankruptcy Court to "issue against a governmental unit an order, process, or judgment" under the Bankruptcy Code or the Federal Rules of Bankruptcy Procedure, "including an order or judgment awarding a money recovery, but not including an award of punitive damages," as well as attorney fees.[389] The Bankruptcy Court's judgment is payable in the same manner as a judgment of a federal district court. Accordingly, if the Service violates the automatic stay, the Bankruptcy Court may award a monetary recovery, including an award under the contempt power of the Bankruptcy Court.[390]

Under this limited waiver of sovereign immunity, if the Service files a proof of claim, it waives sovereign immunity if the trustee brings on a counterclaim against the Service, which is the property of the bankruptcy estate. However, a debtor may recover actual damages only for a willful violation of the stay.[391] In this context, willfulness means "an intentional act with the knowledge of the automatic stay."[392]

After *United States v. Nordic Village*,[393] the government argued that although it had concededly violated the automatic stay by serving a notice of levy, it was not liable to the debtors on sovereign immunity grounds. The Sev-

---

immunity itself creates no cause of action, which is property of the estate. 11 USC § 106(c).

[389] 11 USC § 106(a)(3). While the Bankruptcy Court may order attorney fees, the award must be consistent with the general provision for attorney fees. 28 USC § 2412(d)(2)(A).

[390] 11 USC § 105(a). See Jove Eng'g, Inc. v. IRS, 92 F3d 1539 (11th Cir. 1996) (Service claimed to be liable for contempt of the court's automatic stay); see also Hardy v. United States, 97 F3d 1384 (11th Cir. 1996) (claimed contempt of the discharge injunction).

[391] 11 USC § 362(h). A willful violation for purposes of Bankruptcy Code Section 362(h) does not require a specific intent to violate the automatic stay, only that the defendant knew of the automatic stay and that the defendant's actions that violated the automatic stay were intentional. Herbert v. United States, 1998 Bankr. LEXIS 617 (BAP 9th Cir. 1998) (after the Service received notice, it filed a notice of lien, failed to release the lien, assessed a tax, but only abated part of the assessment; cases gathered; damages of $2,500 approved). Compare A&J Auto Sales, Inc. D/B/A Wise Auto Sales v. United States, 81 AFTR2d 98-2002 (DNH 1998) (Service did not willfully violate the automatic stay when taxpayer/debtor's president told revenue officers that it was about to file a bankruptcy petition that in fact was filed hours later, and then "passively" retained the automobiles seized).

It has been held that a debtor may recover damages for emotional distress caused by a violation of the automatic stay. See Holden v. United States (In re Holden), 83 AFTR2d 99-1049 (BCD Ver. 1998) (cases gathered, which found damages if the distress was not "fleeting" or "inconsequential").

[392] See also Hanna Coal Co. v. IRS, 80 AFTR2d 97-8075 (WD W. Va. 1997) (the Service willfully violated stay by selling property it knew may have belonged to the debtor).

[393] United States v. Nordic Village, 112 S. Ct. 1011 (1992).

enth Circuit rejected the argument.³⁹⁴ The circuit court held that the government had waived its sovereign immunity under Section 106(a) because (1) the Service had filed a proof of claim against the estate; (2) the claim for the attorney fees against the Service was the property of the estate; and (3) there was a logical relationship between the Service's claim and the debtor/taxpayers' claim. The court also held that, under the Bankruptcy Reform Act of 1994, the attorney fees were to be determined in accordance with the provisions of 28 USC Section 2412(d)(2)(A).³⁹⁵ For the Service to be found guilty of contempt for violating the automatic stay pursuant to the power of the Bankruptcy Court described in 11 USC Section 105, the Bankruptcy Court must determine that the Service "(1) knew that the automatic stay was invoked and (2) intended the actions which violated the automatic stay."³⁹⁶

Because the contempt power of the Bankruptcy Court is subject to the limited waiver of sovereign immunity, the Bankruptcy Court is permitted to impose coercive sanctions, not punitive damages. In determining whether a sanction for contempt is coercive, the court must ask "(1) whether the award directly serves the complainant rather than the public interest, and (2) whether the contemnor may control the extent of the award."³⁹⁷ If the Bankruptcy Court finds that the complainant primarily seeks money damages in the form of a fixed noncompensatory fine, then the court is not authorized to order monetary damages because they are punitive and not coercive.

[c] When the Stay Terminates

In general, the stay continues until the case is closed or dismissed or the debtor is discharged.³⁹⁸ Under 11 USC Section 108(c), a period fixed in applicable nonbankruptcy law for commencing an action on a claim against the debtor in a court other than the Bankruptcy Court does not expire until the later of (1) the end of the period, including any suspension of the period beginning with the filing of the commencement of the bankruptcy case or (2) thirty days after the notice of the termination of the stay. Section 6503 pro-

---

³⁹⁴ Price v. United States (In re Price), 42 F3d 1068 (7th Cir. 1994).

³⁹⁵ In re Norton, 717 F2d 767 (3d Cir. 1983) (*Norton* followed; Service violated automatic stay by offsetting refund owed to taxpayer who filed a Chapter 13 plan). However, the Service has been permitted to offset a prepetition refund against a prepetition tax liability. Duguay v. IRS, 85-2 USTC ¶ 9616 (Bankr. WDNY 1985) (Service not stayed from offsetting refund claim in Chapter 7 case; *Norton* distinguished); In re Dominguez, 67 BR 526, 86-2 USTC ¶ 9736 (Bankr. WD Tenn. 1986) (prepetition liability for one year set off against prepetition liability for another year).

³⁹⁶ Jove Eng'g, Inc. v. IRS, 92 F3d 1539 (11th Cir. 1996). This test also applies to the Service's violation of the discharge injunction. Hardy v. United States, 97 F3d 1384 (11th Cir. 1996).

³⁹⁷ Jove Eng'g, Inc. v. IRS, 92 F3d 1539 (11th Cir. 1996).

³⁹⁸ 11 USC § 362(c).

vides for suspension of the statutes of limitation on assessment and collection during the period the Service is prohibited from making an assessment or collection; for sixty days thereafter for assessments; and for six months thereafter for collection.[399] The Tax Court has ruled that when the taxpayer/debtor's bankruptcy petition was dismissed, the automatic stay terminated, and when the case was reinstated, the automatic stay was not reactivated, with the result that the taxpayer/debtor could file a petition in the Tax Court.[400]

Orders of the Bankruptcy Court have required the Tax Court to decide whether the automatic stay prevents its considering the petition of the taxpayer. The Tax Court has ruled that the reopening of a bankruptcy case does not reinstate the automatic stay.[401] Similarly, when the Bankruptcy Court ruled that a creditor's debt and all other debts pursuant to 11 USC Section 727 were nondischargeable, the effect was the denial of discharge, and the order terminated the automatic stay under 11 USC Section 362(a)(8), thereby permitting the continuation of the proceeding in the Tax Court. When the Bankruptcy Court vacated its order, the Tax Court ruled that the automatic stay was not automatically reinstated, but required some further order by the Bankruptcy Court reinstating the stay.[402] In deciding whether the automatic stay prevents its consideration of a case, the Tax Court considers the status of the Bankruptcy Court, and has noted that the Bankruptcy Court, like the Tax Court, has only the jurisdiction and powers that Congress has given it. Accordingly, it has concluded that the automatic stay should be imposed only on the filing of a petition in the Bankruptcy Court because that is all 11 USC Section 362(a) provides.

Although the automatic stay prevents the continuation of a Tax Court case pending on the date the bankruptcy petition is filed, if the Tax Court case is permitted to continue to decision, it has been held that the automatic stay does not stay the ninety-day period for filing a notice of appeal from a Tax Court decision.[403]

---

[399] For further discussion of the suspension under Section 6503(h) and 11 USC Section 108(c), see infra ¶ 16.11[4].

[400] Guerra v. Comm'r, 110 TC 271 (1998); see also Kieu v. Comm'r, 105 TC 387 (1995) (automatic stay terminated when the Bankruptcy Court entered an order granting summary judgment that the taxpayers/debtors were not entitled to discharge of their debts); Allison v. Comm'r, 97 TC 544 (1991) (same, only Bankruptcy Court granted discharge, but subsequently reopened the case); Moody v. Comm'r, 95 TC 655 (1990) (automatic stay terminated when the Bankruptcy Court's confirmation of a Chapter 11 plan and automatic stay was not reinstated despite the Bankruptcy Court's decision to retain jurisdiction over the case).

[401] Allison v. Comm'r, 97 TC 544 (1991).

[402] Kieu v. Comm'r, 105 TC 387 (1995).

[403] Roberts v. Comm'r, 83 AFTR2d 99-2282 (11th Cir. 1999).

[d] Relief From the Stay

Bankruptcy Code Section 362(d) provides for relief from the stay in the following situations: (1) for cause, including the lack of adequate protection of an interest in property of such party in interest or (2) with respect to the stay of an act against property, if—"(A) the debtor does not have an equity in such property; and (B) such property is not necessary to effect an effective reorganization." Among the exceptions to the automatic stay listed in 11 USC Section 362 is an exception for "the commencement or continuation of an action or proceeding by a governmental unit to enforce such governmental unit's police or regulatory power."[404] A creditor may apply for relief from the stay under certain conditions. The conditions do not ordinarily apply in the case of the Service.[405]

The effect of the stay on pending collection action by the Service is unclear. For example, if a deferred-payment agreement had been entered into between the taxpayer and the Service, it seems that further collection under that agreement would be halted outside of bankruptcy. In bankruptcy, collection would depend on whether or not the taxes were entitled to priority under Bankruptcy Code Section 507(a). During the period of the automatic stay, Section 108(c) of the Bankruptcy Code and Section 6503(h) of the Internal Revenue Code suspend the statute of limitations on assessment and collection.[406] Once there is an order of discharge, the automatic stay is lifted, and there is no bar to the Tax Court's hearing the taxpayer's case when the Service does not file a proof of claim in a "no assets" bankruptcy case and the effect of discharge is not determined.[407]

Two tests are used to determine whether an agency's actions fit within this exception—the pecuniary purpose test and the public policy test.[408] Under the pecuniary purpose test, the court determines whether the government's action relates primarily to the protection of the government's pecuniary interest

---

[404] 11 USC § 362(b)(4).

[405] 11 USC § 362(c).

[406] 11 USC § 108(c).

[407] Neilson v. Comm'r, 94 TC 1 (1990) (notice of deficiency mailed after discharge but before the closing of the bankruptcy proceeding); Graham v. Comm'r, 75 TC 389 (1980) (notice of deficiency sent after discharge and after close of bankruptcy proceeding); cf. Wahlstrum v. Comm'r, 92 TC 703 (1989) (confirmation of Chapter 13 plan is not the equivalent of discharge). Moody v. Comm'r, 95 TC 655 (1990) (confirmation of Chapter 11 plan, providing for nondischargeable causes of action against debtor, constituted grant or denial of discharge and termination of automatic stay; *Wahlstrum* distinguished because Chapter 13 does not result in either discharge or denial). Compare Smith v. Comm'r, 96 TC 184 (1991) (waiver of discharge terminated automatic stay before petition was filed). The automatic stay is not reinstated if a bankruptcy case should be reopened; therefore, reopening a bankruptcy case is no bar to any Tax Court action. Roth v. Comm'r, 65 TCM 2778 (1993).

[408] In re Universal Life Church, Debtor, 1997 US App. LEXIS 27266 (9th Cir. 1997).

in the debtor's property or to matters of public safety and welfare. If the action is taken solely for this pecuniary purpose of the governmental unit, the stay is imposed. When the public policy test is applied, the court distinguishes between actions that effectuate public policy and those that adjudicate private rights. When the Service revoked the tax exemption of the Universal Life Church during the pendency of the automatic stay, the circuit court held that while the revocation of the church's exempt status had been a violation of the stay, the Service's action served "a public welfare purpose beyond any pecuniary application in any particular case," because "revocation promotes public welfare by assuring the public and potential donors that contributions will be used for legitimate charitable purposes."[409]

[3] The Bankruptcy Estate

The bankruptcy estate is composed of "all legal or equitable interests of the debtor in property as of the commencement of the case."[410] Thus, the filing of a bankruptcy petition creates an "estate," which includes generally "all legal or equitable interests of the debtor in property as of the commencement of the case."[411] It is "property of the estate" that is distributed to creditors, in the order provided by Bankruptcy Code Section 726.[412] Property in the bankruptcy estate is subject to any liens that encumber the debtor's property when the proceeding begins. However, the Bankruptcy Code gives the trustee certain powers by which he may be able to avoid or set aside the lien.[413] Property includes

---

[409] In re Universal Life Church, Debtor, 1997 US App. LEXIS 27266 (9th Cir. 1997).

[410] 11 USC § 541(a)(1).

[411] 11 USC § 541(a)(1).

[412] 11 USC § 726 provides for distribution in the following order: (1) priority claims; (2) unsecured claims (including creditors who filed late because of absence of knowledge or notice of the case); (3) other tardily filed claims; (4) claims for fines, penalties, and forfeitures; and (5) postpetition interest on claims.

[413] The trustee may do so only if the property is also part of the bankruptcy estate. For example, a tax lien on property exempt in bankruptcy may not be avoided. See, e.g., In re Carlton, 19 BR 73, 82-1 USTC ¶ 9400 (DNM 1982) (lien on proceeds from debtors' homestead). See also In re Halle, 132 BR 186, 91-1 USTC ¶ 50,121 (Bankr. D. Colo. 1991) (prepetition estimated tax remittance was not property of debtor's estate and was not subject to turnover order). Similarly, even if a taxpayer may avoid a transfer of funds under 11 USC Section 522(h) because the property was exempt, the transfer of the funds to the Service pursuant to a levy still may not be set aside, because 11 USC Section 522(c) excepts from the exemption a prebankruptcy tax debt secured by a lien that is properly filed. See also Forrest v. IRS, 226 BR 284, 81 AFTR2d 98-1777 (Bankr. App. Panel, 9th Cir. 1998). (Transfer of estate funds to the Service was potentially voidable because made after commencement of the bankruptcy case and was unauthorized; nevertheless, the transfer was not voided because under 11 USC Section 550(a)(2), the Service received the funds in satisfaction of an antecedent debt, in good faith, and without knowl-

any property turned over under Bankruptcy Code Section 542 or recovered by the trustee under any of his avoiding powers. The property of the estate is comprised of whatever legal or equitable interests the debtor has in the property. This broad definition is intended to advance the Bankruptcy Code's policy of providing equality of distribution among creditors. In some tax cases, it has not been clear whether property was part of the debtor/taxpayer's estate.

The estate also succeeds to all tax attributes of the debtor.[414] This appears to mean that the estate succeeds to net operating loss carryforwards that can be used to offset income of the estate.[415] It has also been held that the estate succeeds to the gain exclusion provided in Section 121 on the sale of a residence.[416] When a debtor is entitled to an earned income tax credit (EITC) for a taxable year, but files a petition in bankruptcy before the end of the year, the EITC is property of the estate because the credit is said to be available at any time during the year.[417] The estate also includes any interest in property that the estate acquires after the commencement of the case,[418] including a tax refund.[419]

---

[414] 11 USC § 346(i)(1).

[415] See In re Luster, 981 F2d 277 (7th Cir. 1992) (loss carryforward is not property of estate under pre-Code law).

[416] See In re Luciano Popa, 218 BR 420, 81 AFTR2d 98-1282 (Bankr. ND Ill. 1998), distinguishing In re Mehr, 153 BR 430 (Bankr. DNJ 1993) and In re Barden, 205 BR 451 (EDNY 1996), aff'd, 105 F3d 821 (2d Cir. 1997) on the ground that Section 121 had been amended and the earlier cases had dealt with the original version of the statute. The estate has been held to succeed to the debtor's earned income tax credit. Johnston v. Hazlett, 222 BR 552, 82 AFTR2d 98-5580 (Bankr. App. Panel, 6th Cir. 1998).

[417] Johnston v. Hazlett (In re Robin L. Johnston, Debtor), 85 AFTR2d 2000-1284 (6th Cir. 2000) (following In re Montgomery, 219 BR 913, 81 AFTR2d 98-1649 (BAP 10th Cir. 1998) and other cases).

[418] 11 USC § 541(a)(7).

[419] See Segal v. Rochelle, 382 US 375 (1966) (claims for refunds of federal income taxes arising from carrybacks of net operating losses sustained before bankruptcy petition constitute property, transferable by debtor and thus passed to trustee); Kokoszka v. Belford, 417 US 642, 648 (1974) (loss carryback property of estate); In re Barowsky, 946 F2d 1516 (10th Cir. 1991) (loss carryback attributable to full year ended before petition). See also In re Linn, 52 BR 63 (Bankr. WD Okla. 1985) (tax refund is property of estate, not earnings from personal services exempt under Oklahoma law). McCullough v. United States, 217 BR 192, 80 AFTR2d 97-8237 (Bankr. ND Tex. 1997) (ordinarily the trustee must file a claim for the refund of the debtor's overpayment within the periods provided by the Code, and the trustee had failed to do so; however, the Bankruptcy Court concluded that the refund of the debtor's overpayment became property of the estate to be distributed to creditors of the estate when, after the petition had been filed, the Service and the debtor had agreed on the amount of the prepetition overpayment). Compare In re Halle, 132 BR 186, 91-1 USTC ¶ 50,121 (Bankr. D. Colo. 1991) (estimated tax remitted before petition was not property of debtor's estate because tax constituted cash bond).

If the Service has already taken action to collect a delinquent tax by levy, ownership of the property seized by the levy is not transferred to the Service. The property is part of the bankruptcy estate, subject to a turnover order of the Bankruptcy Court.[420] In *United States v. Whiting Pools*, the Service served a notice of levy to seize a taxpayer/debtor's tangible personal property, and, on the next day, the taxpayer/debtor filed for reorganization under the Bankruptcy Code. Finding that the levy did not divest the debtor of "legal or equitable ownership," the Supreme Court held that the levy merely brought the seized property into the Service's legal custody, but did not transfer ownership of the property. Consequently, at least where the seized property is subject to sale, property seized by the Service before a petition is filed must be turned over to the Bankruptcy Court.

A debtor does not own an equitable interest in property if it holds the property in trust for another. In the case of trust fund taxes withheld from employees, a debtor employer is a trustee holding the collected taxes for the benefit of the Service. When the debtor employer makes a payment of taxes before bankruptcy, therefore, the payment is not the property of the estate because withheld tax constitutes a trust res and the payment is traceable to the trust res even if the withheld tax was not segregated.[421]

The debtor's claim to a tax refund that the Service owes to the debtor on the date the debtor files a bankruptcy petition is property of the bankruptcy estate, because the "claim" is derived from payments that the debtor otherwise would have owed at the time of bankruptcy. The rationale is that the automatic stay of 11 USC Section 362 prevents the Service from perfecting or enforcing its tax lien, and consequently the lien cannot attach during bankruptcy or afterwards to the extent that the tax claims are dischargeable.[422] If the debtor owes

---

[420] United States v. Whiting Pools, Inc., 462 US 198 (1983) (Bankruptcy Code case where a preorganization levy failed to prevent seized property from being included in the estate and subject to a turnover order). Compare Phelps v. United States, 421 US 330 (1975) (Bankruptcy Act case where a prepetition levy removed the seized property from the debtor's possession and prevented the Bankruptcy Court's exercise of summary jurisdiction). For a description of the legal effect of levies, see ¶ 14.12. Where, prior to the filing of a petition, the Service files a notice of federal tax lien, the tax lien attaches to property that becomes part of the bankruptcy estate. The tax lien also attaches to after-acquired property. In bankruptcy, this does not mean that the Service has a lien on property coming into existence post petition. As one bankruptcy judge rightly said, "[A]t the moment the Debtor filed for bankruptcy relief, his interest in accounts receivable are limited to those acquired through prepetition efforts only...the federal tax liens could not have attached to accounts receivable earned post-petition, because the automatic stay prevents such liens from attaching to post-petition acquisition(s)." In re Larson, 93-2 USTC ¶ 50,508 (ND 1993).

[421] Begier v. IRS, 110 S. Ct. 2258 (1990). Compare In re Sluggo's Chicago Style, Inc., 912 F2d 1073 (9th Cir. 1990) (state requirement of security as condition for doing business, for payment of sales and use tax, did not create trust outside bankruptcy estate).

[422] See In re Braund, 423 F2d 718, 719 (9th Cir. 1970).

both during and after bankruptcy. Collection of tax claims from exempt property involves consideration not only of the Bankruptcy Code, but also of the Internal Revenue Code, which has its own set of exemptions.[433] To analyze the effect of these sometimes inconsistent exemptions, an examination of Bankruptcy Code Section 522 is in order.

Once the bankruptcy petition is filed, the stay on collection prevents enforced collection action during the pendency of the case. If the tax claim is dischargeable, it is not collectible from either bankruptcy-exempt or Section 6334-exempt property.[434] If the prepetition unsecured tax claim is not dischargeable in bankruptcy—and many tax claims are not dischargeable—the claim may be enforced after bankruptcy from property exempt under the Bankruptcy Code but not exempt under Section 6334.[435] Even if the trustee is able to avoid a tax secured by a filed lien by assuming the status of a bona fide purchaser or judgment creditor, the tax lien may still be enforced after bankruptcy from bankruptcy-exempt property.[436] Thus, it appears that the Service may collect Bankruptcy Code-exempt property after, but not during, the bankruptcy case as long as the property is not exempt under Section 6334.

[b] Setoff

Bankruptcy Code Section 362(a)(7) extends the automatic stay to "the setoff of any debt owing to the debtor that arose before the commencement of [the bankruptcy case] against any claim against the debtor." On the other hand, Bankruptcy Code Section 553 effectively preserves ("does not affect") a right of setoff in bankruptcy if the party possesses a right of offset that arose before bankruptcy, so long as certain conditions are met. To satisfy the conditions of Bankruptcy Code Section 553, (1) the creditor must owe a debt that arose before the bankruptcy case; (2) the creditor must also have a claim against the debtor that arose before the bankruptcy case; and (3) the debt and the claim must be mutual or reciprocal obligations. However, because Bankruptcy Code Section 553 is permissive, not mandatory, and a creditor is seeking to set off a mutual debt, the creditor is required to apply to the Bankruptcy Court, so that

---

[433] IRC § 6334. See ¶ 14.14[1] for a description of the property exempt from levy.

[434] 11 USC § 522(c). In re Monteith, 23 BR 601 (ND Ohio 1982) ("property exempted by debtor was not liable to be set off against the tax debt owed by debtor to IRS"). Even if property is exempt from levy under Section 6334, the amount or value of the exempt property may not be stripped from the amount of the Service's secured tax lien. United States v. Barbier, 896 F2d 377 (9th Cir. 1990) (amount of secured tax lien is not affected by exemption from levy); Matter of Voelker, 42 F3d 1050 (7th Cir. 1994).

[435] 11 USC § 522(c)(1).

[436] 11 USC § 522(c)(2)(B). Courts have held that the penalty and statutory additions portion of a federal tax lien are part of the "tax liens" covered by 11 USC Section 522(c)(2)(B). See In re Denarah, 62 F3d 1248, 1251 (9th Cir. 1995); Savage v. United States, 216 BR 919, 80 AFTR2d 97-8247 (Bankr. SD Ga. 1997).

the Bankruptcy Court can exercise its discretion.[437] Reading Section 6402(d) of the Code and Bankruptcy Code Sections 362(a)(7) and 553(a) in conjunction, the filing of a bankruptcy petition operates as an automatic stay of the Service's ability to exercise any right of setoff unless the creditor seeks relief from the stay from the Bankruptcy Court under Bankruptcy Code Section 362(d).[438] When the Service acts unilaterally, therefore, it is subject to sanction for violating the automatic stay.[439]

---

[437] IRS v. Norton (In re Norton), 717 F2d 767 (3d Cir. 1983).

[438] Citizens Bank of Maryland v. Strumpf, 516 US 16, 20 (1995). One Bankruptcy Court has said that 11 USC Section 553 "clearly grants the United States an unqualified right of setoff on overpayment against any federal tax liability of the person who made the overpayment. The automatic stay provisions of 11 USC § 362 prevent the setoff from being made immediately, but no provision of the Bankruptcy Code eliminates the rights granted the United States by [Section 6402 of] the Internal Revenue Code." In re Murry, 15 BR 325 (Bankr. ED Ark. 1981), quoted in Womack v. United States, 188 BR 259, 76 AFTR2d 95-7067 (Bankr. ED Ark. 1995).

[439] When the Service established that it had a right under Bankruptcy Code Section 362 and Section 6402 to set off a taxpayer's overpayment against a tax liability for a prior year, the Bankruptcy Court exercised discretion to lift the stay to allow the Service to offset the prepetition refund against prepetition liability. In re Whitaker, 173 BR 359, 87 AFTR2d 97-8337 (Bankr. SD Ohio 1997) (Chapter 13 case; debtor argued that refund vested in debtor on confirmation of plan).

If the Service withholds a portion of a refund, however, the withholding of the refund may constitute a setoff in violation of the automatic stay, which can be punished by the award of attorney fees to the debtor. See In re Midway Indus. Contractors, Inc., 167 BR 139, 94-1 USTC ¶ 50,268 (Bankr. ND Ill. 1994) (debtor filed a quickie carryback claim for refund in a prepetition year, but the Service delayed in making payment, freezing refund because it had an unpaid penalty assessment also prepetition; held, the Service's delay constituted an unauthorized setoff in violation of the automatic stay); see also In re Rush-Hampton Indus., Inc., 98 F3d 614 (11th Cir. 1996) (Service made unauthorized setoff of 1979 overpayment against prepetition interest; sanction for violation of automatic stay upheld).

When both the refund and the tax claim arose before the bankruptcy case, the Service has been permitted to make the setoff. Breder v. United States (In re Breder), 78 AFTR2d 96-5785 (SD Fla. 1996). Also, when taxes have been overpaid, the debtor's overpayment may be set off against the claim of another government agency's claim against the taxpayer/debtor. HAL Inc. v. United States, 77 AFTR2d 96-2088 (BAP 9th Cir. 1996), aff'd, 122 F3d 851 (9th Cir. 1997).

However, the Service is not permitted to set off a tax refund against the debtor's property that, under 11 USC Section 522, the taxpayer/debtor had claimed was exempt under Kentucky law. Alexander v. IRS, 142 F3d 433, 81 AFTR2d 98-8635 (Bank. WD Ky. 1998). On the other hand, the Service is not required to set off a corporation's income tax against a trust fund recovery penalty and may proceed to collect the penalty separately. Egnatios v. United States, 81 AFTR2d 98-685 (ED Mich. 1998).

¶ 16.12 THE SERVICE AS A CREDITOR: THE CLAIM FOR TAXES

A claim for taxes may be either secured or unsecured. The Service has a secured "claim" under the Bankruptcy Code if it holds a lien on property of the estate.[440] A tax lien is "a statutory lien" under the Bankruptcy Code. A lien means a "charge against or interest in property to secure payment of a debt,"[441] and a statutory lien is defined as a "lien arising solely by force of a statute on specified circumstances or conditions."[442] A secured claimant is entitled to be paid in full out of the security, subject to preservation or disposition charges.[443] Although a tax lien may be valid and entitled to priority outside bankruptcy, the lien may be either invalidated or postponed in bankruptcy.

Prebankruptcy transactions and transfers of property can be set aside and the property brought into the estate under the avoiding powers. The trustee has the power (1) to defeat the lien of a secured creditor (such as the Service) because of the trustee's status as a hypothetical judgement lien creditor or bona fide purchaser of real estate;[444] (2) to set aside a fraudulent conveyance be-

---

[440] 11 USC § 101(33). It follows that a creditor's claim is secured only to the extent that the bankruptcy estate has an interest in the property that serves as collateral. 11 USC Section 506(a) (stating in part that "an allowed claim of a creditor secured by a lien on property in the estate has an interest,…is a secured claim to the extent [] of the value of such creditor's interest in such property…and is an unsecured claim to the extent that the value of such creditor's interest…is less than the amount of such allowed claim"). See Persky v. United States, 82 AFTR2d 98-6664 (ED Pa. 1998) (interest in spendthrift trust was not includable in bankruptcy estate under 11 USC Section 541(c)(2) but was subject to lien under Section 6321; court held that the Service's tax claim did not include debtor's interest in spendthrift trust, a factor in determining debtor's eligibility for Chapter 13 protection). There are few discussions specifically of tax claims in bankruptcy. But see, e.g., St. James, "The Federal Tax Lien in Bankruptcy," 46 Bus. Law. 157 (Nov. 1990).

[441] 11 USC § 101(33).

[442] 11 USC § 101(47). The tax lien arises by reason of the provisions of Section 6321 where a taxpayer neglects or refuses to pay an assessed tax after notice and demand.

[443] The tax lien may not be stripped down to the value of the collateral for the lien (i.e., the property subject to the lien) as of the filing date of the taxpayer's petition. Dewsnup v. Timm, 502 US 410 (1992); In re Cook, 76 AFTR2d 95-5725 (Bankr. MD Fla. 1995) (applying *Dewsnup* to a tax lien when the taxpayer/debtor wanted a determination that his payment of an amount equal to the value of his property on the petition date fully satisfied his tax liability so that the tax lien was unenforceable after his discharge).

[444] 11 USC § 544(a) (the "strong-arm clause").

cause the trustee succeeds to the rights of creditors;[445] and (3) to set aside preferential transfers.[446]

The Service has a general or unsecured claim if (1) it has not obtained a statutory lien or (2) the value of the property subject to its tax lien is less than the amount of its lien. The second type of unsecured claim requires some explanation. A secured claim is secured only to the extent of the value of "such creditor's interest in the estate's interest in such property."[447] For example, if the Service were to have a lien of $10,000 but the value of the property secured by the lien is only $2,000, the Service has a secured claim of $2,000 and an unsecured claim of $8,000. The generality of the tax lien may make this "splitting" of the tax claim less obvious than with creditors with security in specific property, but the distinction nevertheless exists.

[1] The Tax Claim

How is the Service's claim for taxes presented? In a liquidating bankruptcy, the debtor files a list of creditors.[448] The court then sends notice of the proceeding to the listed creditors.[449] To participate in the proceeding and a distribution from the estate, the creditor files a proof of claim.[450] Distribution of the

---

[445] 11 USC § 544(b). A trustee may avoid a debtor's irrevocable election to carry forward net operating losses (NOLs) under the avoiding powers granted to the trustee under 11 USC Section 548. Gibson v. United States (In re Russell), 927 F2d 413 (8th Cir. 1991). On remand, the Bankruptcy Court found that transfer was not made with intent to defraud creditors under 11 USC Section 548(a)(1) because the debtor had relied on an accountant's advice. In re Russell, 154 BR 723, 93-1 USTC ¶ 50,309 (8th Cir. 1993).

[446] 11 USC § 547.

[447] 11 USC § 506(a). For purposes of 11 USC Section 506(a), when collateral subject to a tax lien is retained by the debtor/taxpayer for his use, as in a Chapter 13 plan, the value of the Service's lien is determined by the property's fair market value. Taffi v. United States, 96 F3d 1190 (9th Cir. 1996) (en banc). The purpose of a valuation under 11 USC Section 506(a) in this circumstance, "is not to determine the amount the creditor would receive if it hypothetically had to foreclose and sell the collateral." Taffi v. United States, 96 F3d 1190 (9th Cir. 1996). Accordingly, neither the foreclosure value nor the cost of repossession was considered, because no foreclosure was intended.

[448] 11 USC § 521.

[449] 11 USC § 342.

[450] 11 USC §§ 501, 502, 726. Rules fixing the time for filing a claim do not preclude an increase of the amount of a filed claim. United States v. Kolstad, 928 F2d 171 (5th Cir.), cert. denied, 112 S. Ct. 419 (1991); In re Stavriotis, 977 F2d 1202 (7th Cir. 1992) (the Service was not allowed to amend its claim after bar date, although no plan had been confirmed; delayed amendment prejudiced other creditors). No equitable tolling is allowed to permit the untimely filing of a proof of claim. Gardenhire v. IRS, 85 AFTR2d 2000-1464 (9th Cir. 2000) (180-day period cannot be equitably tolled; claim filed eleven days late was barred).

estate is made to unsecured creditors only if the claim is allowed.[451] However, if a proof of claim is filed, the claim "is deemed allowed, unless a party in interest...objects."[452] In general, if objection is made, the Bankruptcy Court, after notice and hearing, determines the amount of the claim as of the date the petition was filed, although certain claims are not allowable.[453]

Bankruptcy does not alter the burden of proof; therefore, when the substantive law creating the tax obligation puts the burden on the taxpayer, bankruptcy does not reorder the burden.[454] The decision in *Raleigh*[455] settled the law on this issue. Some courts had said that since a properly filed proof of claim is prima facie evidence that the claim is valid, if the trustee objects to the proof of claim, the trustee must come forward with evidence that the claim is invalid; however, the ultimate burden of proving the validity of the claim is on the claimant, even if the claimant is the Service.

---

[451] 11 USC § 726. For a case where the Service filed a proof of claim after the bar date, see United States v. Cardinal Mine Supply, Inc., 916 F2d 1087 (6th Cir. 1990) (tax claim not subordinated to nonpriority unsecured claims, because the Service was not notified and had no knowledge of bankruptcy case).

[452] 11 USC § 502(a).

[453] 11 USC § 502(b).

[454] Raleigh, Chapter 7 Trustee for the Estate of Stoecker v. Ill. Dept. of Rev., 120 S. Ct. 1951 (S. Ct. 2000).

[455] In re Placid Oil Co., 988 F2d 554, 557 (5th Cir. 1993); In re Jules B. LeBlanc, 77 AFTR2d 96-599 (Bankr. MD La. 1996). The Eighth and Tenth Circuits also have concluded that while a properly filed proof of claim is prima facie evidence that the claim is valid and the burden of coming forward with some evidence that the claim is invalid shifts to the trustee who objects to the claim, the ultimate burden of proving the validity of the claim is on the claimant, even if the claimant is a taxing authority. In re Gran, 964 F2d 822, 827–828 (8th Cir. 1992); In re Fullmer, 962 F2d 1463, 1466 (10th Cir. 1992). The Ninth Circuit has held that in a bankruptcy proceeding, a taxing authority, including the Service, has the ultimate burden of proving its claim. California Franchise Tax Bd. v. MacFarlane (In re MacFarlane, (Debtor)), 96 TNT 96-11 (9th Cir. 1996).

The Third and Fourth Circuits reached the opposite conclusion. Resyn Corp. v. United States, 857 F2d 660, 663 (3d Cir. 1988); In re Landbank Equity Corp., 973 F2d 265, 268–272 (4th Cir. 1992) (burden of proof is on the trustee, because nothing in the Bankruptcy Code or in its legislative history that "suggests that [a] dispute between a taxpayer and the Service should be decided in a manner different from that in which the case would be determined outside the bankruptcy context").

Even if the Service has the ultimate burden of proof on a claim, the debtor or trustee who objects to a tax claim still must produce sufficient evidence to rebut the presumption and to shift the burden of producing evidence to the Service. See Brown v. IRS (In re Brown), 82 F2d 801, 805 (8th Cir. 1996) ("We hold the debtors did not provide enough information to meet their burden of producing sufficient evidence to shift the burden of producing evidence to the IRS.").

[2] Claims for Interest

Generally, to avoid unfairness among competing creditors and administrative inconvenience, interest on a tax claim accruing after the date the petition in bankruptcy is filed is not collectible from the bankruptcy estate.[456] This rule was in effect under the Bankruptcy Act, and it is also the result under the Bankruptcy Code. Prepetition interest on a priority tax claim has the same priority as the tax itself; however, even if the principal amount of a claim is allowed, the claim must be disallowed "to the extent that…such claim is for unmatured interest."[457] On distribution of the bankruptcy estate, interest "at the legal rate" is payable on a priority tax claim,[458] but this distribution is provided for only in the unlikely event that a portion of the estate remains after priority claims, unsecured claims, and claims for penalties, fines, and forfeitures are paid in full.[459] Should such a distribution be made, the tax claim and other claims share on a pro rata basis. Also, a priority tax claim is not dischargeable in bankruptcy.[460] Interest continues to run on a nondischargeable tax claim and is a personal liability of the debtor, collectible out of the debtor/taxpayer's after-acquired property.[461]

---

[456] Bruning v. United States, 376 US 358, 362–363 (1964) (Bankruptcy Act); Hanna v. United States, 872 F2d 829 (8th Cir. 1989) (Bankruptcy Code); Jaylaw Drug, Inc. v. United States, 621 F2d 524 (2d Cir. 1980) (same); Woodward v. United States, 113 BR 680, 90-1 USTC ¶ 50,244 (Bankr. D. Or. 1990) (Bankruptcy Code). However, the Service can allocate amounts it receives in such a way as to avoid the issue. See United States v. New York Ins. Dep't, 657 F. Supp. 27 (SDNY 1986) (Service allocated amount to preinsolvency interest).

[457] 11 USC § 502(b)(2). See In re Palmer, 53 BR 545, 85-2 USTC ¶ 9680 (Bankr. ND Tex. 1985) (cases gathered); In re Garcia, 955 F2d 16 (5th Cir. 1992) (approving In re Palmer).

[458] 11 USC § 726(a)(5). The "legal rate" may not be the "annual rate" determined under Section 6621. A number of courts have held that the Service is entitled to postpetition interest on a secured tax claim at the normal statutory rate, even if the claim is nonconsensual. In re Lapiana, 909 F2d 221 (7th Cir. 1990) (reorganization proceeding; "[t]he Treasury bill rate plus three percent is generous but not princely."); Galveston Indep. Sch. Dist. v. Heartland Fed. Sav. & Loan Ass'n, 159 BR 198 (SD Tex. 1993); In the Matter of Greensboro Lumber Co., 183 BR 316, 75 AFTR2d 95-2401 (Bankr. MD Ga. 1995). Daily compounding has also been approved. In the Matter of Greensboro Lumber Co., 183 BR 316, 75 AFTR2d 95-2401 (Bankr. MD Ga. 1995). Interest at the statutory rate is also calculated on the Service's tax claims that are considered administrative expenses. United States v. Cranshaw (In re Allied Mechanical Serv., Inc.), 885 F2d 837 (11th Cir. 1989) (taxes accrued during Chapter 11 period, and were claimed in the converted liquidating bankruptcy).

[459] 11 USC §§ 726(a)(1)–726(a)(4).

[460] 11 USC § 523(a)(1).

[461] Bruning v. United States, 376 US 358, 362–363 (1964). The Bankruptcy Code does not change this rule of law. Moreover, where prepetition tax owed by a bankrupt taxpayer is paid by the trustee in bankruptcy from the estate, postpetition interest on the nondischargeable tax paid in bankruptcy (and the interest accruing on the tax not so paid) can

A tax claim may arise after the Bankruptcy Court acquires jurisdiction over a taxpayer and his estate. If a reorganization proceeding is converted into a liquidating bankruptcy, interest accrued up to the date the petition in bankruptcy is filed on a tax incurred by the trustee or debtor during the reorganization is collectible as an administration expense.[462] A claim for an amount that is less than the value of the property securing it is an oversecured claim. For example, if a $50,000 claim were secured by a lien on property having a value of $75,000, the lien would be oversecured by $25,000 less expenses of selling the property. Bankruptcy Code Section 506(b) allows the holder of an oversecured lien to recover postpetition interest. In *United States v. Ron Pair En-*

---

be collected from the taxpayer after bankruptcy. United States v. River Coal Co., Inc., 748 F2d 1103 (6th Cir. 1984). In re Larson, 862 F2d 112, 119 (7th Cir. 1988). In re Stine, 81 BR 641, 88-2 USTC ¶ 9402 (BCND Fla. 1988) (analyzing authorities).

Relying on *Bruning*, the Second Circuit held that two responsible persons were liable for interest accruing during the corporate bankruptcy and not paid before the confirmation of the corporate employers' plan, although they had entered into a stipulation with the Service providing that unpaid trust fund penalty assessments against them would be abated if the corporation paid the entire trust fund liability, plus accrued interest. Bradley v. United States, 936 F2d 707 (2d Cir. 1991) (if interest were not recoverable from the responsible persons who were separately liable for the trust fund liability and the Service could not collect from the corporation, the liability for interest on nondischargeable tax debts would be avoided, contrary to *Bruning*); In re Chafee, 186 BR 783, 76 AFTR2d 95-5854 (Bankr. NDNY 1995) (*Bradley* followed when the responsible person went into a Chapter 11 proceeding).

[462] 11 USC § 503(b)(1). See Nicholas v. United States, 384 US 678 (1966) (interest on taxes incurred during superseded Chapter XI proceeding payable as administration expense). In re Mark Anthony Constr., Inc., 886 F2d 1101 (9th Cir. 1989) ("interest accruing on taxes due after the filing of the bankruptcy petition is to be treated as an administrative expense of the bankruptcy estate and consequently afforded first priority status"); In re Allied Mechanical Servs., Inc., 885 F2d 837 (11th Cir. 1989) (the Service entitled to administrative expense priority on its claim for interest on post-Chapter 11 petition liability; 11 USC Section 503 construed Bankruptcy Act authority; Nicholas v. United States, 384 US 678, followed).

When a secured creditor agrees to the continued operation of a business as a going concern for the purpose of increasing the ultimate gain in the event of a reorganization or liquidation and the continued operation requires the payment of payroll taxes, then unpaid, postpetition payroll taxes, together with any interest and penalties, are recoverable from the secured collateral under 11 USC Section 506(c) as an expense preserving or disposing of the collateral. United States v. Boatmen's First Nat'l Bank of Kansas City, 5 F3d 1157 (8th Cir. 1993) ("The creditor...in the expectation of an overall benefit, agreed to accept the expenses and risks associated with that anticipated benefit. One of those expenses was payroll taxes, and one of those risks was nonpayment of those taxes and its consequences.").

The claim for taxes incurred in the Chapter 11 proceeding as an administrative expense includes interest that accrued during the proceeding on the taxes, and so interest on the taxes is an administrative expense payable at the same priority as the underlying administrative expense. In re Rocky Mountain Refractories, 205 BR 307, 78 AFTR2d 96-7095 (Bankr. App. Panel, 10th Cir. 1997).

terprises, Inc., the Supreme Court held that postpetition interest on an oversecured tax lien could be recovered even if the lien were nonconsensual rather than consensual, such as a security interest created by agreement between the debtor and the creditor.[463] Suppose that the Service is the oversecured lienor and delays in collecting payment of tax, despite the order of the court to sell the secured property, with the result that interest continues to accrue on the tax lien. Does the delay estop or preclude the Service from collecting the accrued interest eliminating any funds for the payment of junior creditors? In *In re Lapiana*,[464] the Seventh Circuit held that since the competing creditor also had not been diligent, the Service was entitled to collect the additional interest that had accrued. The court also refused to create an equitable defense of estoppel for junior creditors, saying that, after *Ron Pair*, junior lienors are on notice that they must monitor their senior creditors' compliance with payment orders.

[3] Claims for Penalties

Treatment of penalties in bankruptcy depends on whether they are in compensation for actual pecuniary loss or are "true" penalties. An example of a pecuniary loss penalty is the "trust fund recovery penalty" imposed by Section 6672.[465] To call this assessable penalty a "penalty" is misleading. Actually, the trust fund recovery penalty is a collection device intended to recover from responsible officers 100 percent of the withholding tax collected but not paid over to the Service. Nonpecuniary loss penalties do not recover tax, but are in addition to the amount of tax due. Pecuniary loss penalties constitute an allowable tax claim having a seventh priority in payment from the bankruptcy estate regardless of the age of the tax claim.[466] A pecuniary loss penalty is not dis-

---

[463] United States v. Ron Pair Enters., Inc., 489 US 235 (1989). Before the decision in *Ron Pair Enters.*, the Fourth Circuit had held to the contrary. In re Best Repair Co., 789 F2d 1080 (4th Cir. 1986). After the decision in *Best Repair Co.*, the Service ruled that postpetition interest (and pecuniary loss and nonpecuniary penalties) may be claimed against the estate of a bankrupt. Rev. Rul. 87-99, 1987-2 CB 291. This view that postpetition interest on a nondischargeable tax claim is nondischargeable has been accepted by a number of courts. In re Burns, 887 F2d 1541, 1543 (11th Cir. 1989); In re Hanna, 872 F2d 829, 830–831 (8th Cir. 1989).

[464] In re Lapiana, 909 F2d 221 (7th Cir. 1990).

[465] See United States v. Sotelo, 436 US 268 (1978). See the discussion of the trust fund recovery penalty in Chapter 17, Part B. The *Sotelo* decision was codified in Bankruptcy Code Section 507(a)(8)(C). Not only is the trust fund recovery penalty a priority tax and not dischargeable under the Bankruptcy Code, but so, too, is the interest that accrued prior to bankruptcy. Mosbrucker v. United States (In re Mosbrucker), 83 AFTR2d 99-341 (Bankr. App. Panel, 8th Cir. 1998).

[466] 11 USC §§ 507(a)(7)(G), 726(a)(1).

chargeable in bankruptcy.[467] Prepetition nonpecuniary loss or punitive penalties are allowable in bankruptcy, but their payment is deferred. Payment of these penalties is made only after the payment of priority claims and timely and tardily filed unsecured claims.[468]

Section 6658 coordinates the late payment penalties of the Code with the Bankruptcy Code. No late payment penalty is imposed where the unpaid tax was incurred by the debtor before the earlier of the order for relief or, in an involuntary case, the appointment of a trustee where the petition was filed before the return close date or the payment date was on or after the date the petition was filed. Similarly, no late payment penalty is imposed on an estate where the nonpayment occurred pursuant to an order of the Bankruptcy Court finding probable insufficiency of funds to pay administrative expenses. Where trust fund taxes are involved, late payment penalties may be imposed.

Even if a nonpecuniary loss penalty is secured by a tax lien, the lien may be avoided in bankruptcy. Bankruptcy Code Section 726(a) specifically authorizes a trustee to avoid a lien that secures a claim for any penalty that is not compensation for actual pecuniary loss. Nonpecuniary loss penalties attributable to the filing of fraudulent returns, failure to file returns, or the filing of a delinquent return within two years of the date of the petition are nondischargeable.[469] However, a penalty (other than a pecuniary loss penalty) is dischargeable under Bankruptcy Code Section 523(a)(7) as long as the tax is not a priority tax claim that is itself dischargeable, "or the penalty is imposed with respect to a transaction or event that occurred before three years before the

---

[467] 11 USC § 523.

[468] 11 USC §§ 726(a)(1)–726(a)(4). In a reorganization proceeding under Chapter 11, the Bankruptcy Court has been held to have the equitable discretion to subordinate penalties on an individual case basis. Schultz Broadway Inn v. United States, 912 F2d 230, 233 (8th Cir. 1990). Although the Bankruptcy Court has the power not to allow a claim if it is unenforceable against the debtor, it is not empowered under its equitable powers to reduce the amount of an otherwise allowable claim for delinquency penalty. United States v. Sanford, 979 F2d 1511 (11th Cir. 1992).

[469] 11 USC § 523(a)(1). Just what constitutes fraud is determined by the Bankruptcy Court, and for dischargeability purposes, evidence of the taxpayer/debtor's attempt to frustrate collection of tax may not be considered fraud with intent to evade tax. In re Gathwright, 102 BR 211, 89-1 USTC ¶ 9346 (Bankr. D. Or. 1989) (such evidence to be disregarded); see also Peterson v. Comm'r, 132 BR 68, 92-1 USTC ¶ 50,216 (Bankr. D. Wyo. 1991) (taxpayer/debtor claimed excess exemptions on Form W-4, failed to file returns, and made minimal tax payments before filing in bankruptcy; held that government failed to prove willful attempt to evade tax). Although for purposes of the civil fraud penalty, the fraud issue must be decided on preponderance of evidence, for purposes of the exception to discharge, the Service must prove fraud by clear and convincing evidence. The Service has been held to a lesser standard of proof in establishing fraud on a preponderance of the evidence. See Brown v. Felson, 422 US 127 (1979); Graham v. IRS, 973 F2d 1089 (3d Cir. 1992) (Tax Court judgment on civil fraud penalty did not estop taxpayer in bankruptcy proceeding; but fraud issue must be decided on preponderance of evidence, not on clear and convincing evidence standard).

date of the filing of the petition." Based on the plain language of Bankruptcy Code Section 523(a)(7), a penalty for a return required to be filed more than three years before bankruptcy is dischargeable.[470]

Section 507(a)(8) of the Bankruptcy Code, granting priority to taxes, implements a broad general policy against punishing innocent creditors of a bankrupt.[471] It is in light of this policy that courts decide the question of whether an exaction is a tax or a penalty, and, if it is a penalty, whether the penalty is a pecuniary loss penalty or nonpecuniary loss penalty. For example, when a penalty for premature withdrawal of pension plan funds was held to be a nonpecuniary loss penalty, it was subordinate to the claims of general unsecured creditors under a confirmed plan of reorganization.[472] Similarly, excise taxes imposed under ERISA for pension plan underfunding have been held to be penalties imposed to prevent an accumulated funding deficiency under a plan and, consequently, were not expenses of administration or entitled to priority under 11 USC Section 507(a)(8)(E).[473]

Is a penalty under the Internal Revenue Code a penalty for purposes of the Bankruptcy Code? The Supreme Court held that "characterizations in the Internal Revenue Code are not dispositive in the bankruptcy context." Functionally, the Court said, the additional "tax" an employer must pay for an accumulated funding deficiency constitutes punishment for failing to meet the funding standard.[474] Accordingly, the "tax" under Section 4971(a) "was not entitled to a seventh priority as an 'excise tax' under Section 507(a)(7)(E), but instead is, for bankruptcy purposes, a penalty to be dealt with as an ordinary, unsecured claim." The Court also held that the Bankruptcy Court erred in equitably subordinating the claim, because it impermissibly did so categorically

---

[470] In re Burns, 887 F2d 1541 (11th Cir. 1989); Roberts v. United States, 906 F2d 1440 (10th Cir. 1990). But see Cassidy v. Comm'r, 814 F2d 477, 480–481 (7th Cir. 1987). McKay v. United States, 957 F2d 689, 693 (9th Cir. 1992) ("A penalty imposed on unpaid taxes accruing more than three years before the filing of the bankruptcy petition is dischargeable."); In re Roberts, 906 F2d 1440 (10th Cir. 1990); In re Barns, 887 F2d 1541 (11th Cir. 1989); see also Cassidy v. Comm'r, 814 F2d 477, 481 (7th Cir. 1987).

[471] 11 USC § 507(a)(8). One court observed, "In the Chapter 7 context, a uniform rule subordinating penalty claims recognizes that ordinary creditors should receive protection from debtors' punitive obligations." Schultz Broadway Inn v. United States, 912 F2d 230, 233 (8th Cir. 1990).

[472] In re Cassidy, 983 F2d 161 (10th Cir. 1992) (10 percent exaction is a "flat rate penalty bearing no relationship to the direct financial loss of the government").

[473] United States v. Reorganized CF&I Fabricators of Utah, Inc., 518 US 213, 116 S. Ct. 2106 (1996).

[474] United States v. Noland, 48 F3d 210 (6th Cir. 1995)}; rev'd, 517 US 535, 77 AFTR2d 96-2143 (1996) (failure to pay the Federal Unemployment Tax Act (FUTA) tax); United States v. Reorganized CF&I Fabricators of Utah, Inc., 518 US 213, 116 S. Ct. 2106 (1996) (excise tax for failure to pay into a pension fund treated as a penalty).

and generally, as prohibited by *United States v. Noland*,[475] which is discussed later in this subsection. However, the flat tax imposed by Section 4980 on an overfunded pension plan is an excise tax, applying the *Reorganized CF&I* standard to Section 4980, because neither the statute nor the legislative history supports a penalty characterization, and the flat tax merely captures the tax benefit that the employer realized in making the excess contributions.[476]

A tax may be treated as a penalty for purposes of the Bankruptcy Code, even though it is regarded as a "tax" under the Internal Revenue Code.[477] Similarly, it has been held that the 10 percent tax for early withdrawal from a retirement plan under Section 72(t) is a nondischargeable penalty.[478]

While a penalty claim relating to a tax incurred by an estate postpetition is characterized as a postpetition administrative expense, the priority of the tax penalty is subject to the equitable subordination provisions of Section 510(c). Section 510(c) permits the Bankruptcy Court "under principles of equitable subordination, [to] subordinate for purposes of distribution all or part of an allowed claim to all or part of another allowed claim." It is unclear whether under "principles of equitable subordination," a Bankruptcy Court could equitably subordinate a nonpecuniary loss penalty. At stake, of course, is the portion of the estate available to pay nontax creditors, and payment is more likely to the extent that the amount of administrative expenses is reduced. On the other hand, in cases involving the issue, the Service has argued that the equitable subordination of penalties is contrary to the first priority established by Section 726(a)(1), accorded to administrative expenses, including any tax and a penalty relating to the tax and, further, that equitable subordination is limited to instances of creditor misconduct, ordinarily not applicable to the Service.

A number of courts found that prepetition, nonpecuniary loss tax penalties are subject to equitable subordination in the appropriate case without a showing of governmental misconduct.[479] When circuit courts considered whether the

---

[475] United States v. Noland, 48 F3d 210 (6th Cir. 1995); rev'd, 517 US 535, 77 AFTR2d 96-2143 (1996).

[476] In re Juvenile Shoe Corporation of America, 99 F3d 898 (11th Cir. 1996) (accordingly, the assessment constituted an excise tax entitled to a seventh priority); see also In re C-T of Va., Inc., 977 F2d 137 (4th Cir. 1992), cert. denied, 507 US 1004 (1993) (same, but decided before *Reorganized CF&I*).

[477] United States v. Dumler (In re Cassidy), 983 F2d 161 (9th Cir. 1993) (10 percent tax imposed by Section 72(t) for early withdrawal from qualified pension plan is penalty for nonpecuniary loss); *contra*, In re Mansfield Tire & Rubber Co., 942 F2d 1055 (6th Cir. 1991) (declining to recharacterize exaction designated as "tax" by Internal Revenue Code).

[478] Mounier v. United States, 82 AFTR2d 98-6861 (Bankr. SD Cal. 1998).

[479] Burden v. United States, 917 F2d 115 (3d Cir. 1990) (a Chapter 13 case); Schultz Broadway Inn v. United States, 912 F2d 230 (8th Cir. 1990) (liquidating Chapter 11 case); In re Virtual Network Servs. Corp., 902 F2d 1246 (7th Cir. 1990) (liquidating Chapter 11 case).

Bankruptcy Court could equitably subordinate postpetition penalties that were punitive in nature rather than compensatory pecuniary loss penalties, they upheld equitable subordination, because it was consistent with the equitable powers given to Bankruptcy Courts by the Bankruptcy Code and also prevented unfairness to the creditors who supported a business during its attempt to reorganize.[480] In *Noland*, the Supreme Court held that Congress did not intend for the equitable subordination jurisdiction of a Bankruptcy Court order under 11 USC Section 510(c)(1) to be used to modify the normal first priority given to taxes, penalties, and interest as administrative expenses by categorically subordinating all postpetition, noncompensatory penalties in Chapter 7 cases.[481] According to the Court, Congress intended to allow a Bankruptcy Court "to reorder a tax penalty in a given case," applying "principles of equitable subordination" when justified by particular facts.[482]

¶ 16.13 DETERMINATION OF THE TAX CLAIM IN BANKRUPTCY

The Bankruptcy Code gives the Bankruptcy Court jurisdiction to determine the debtor's liability for any unpaid tax, whether or not assessed. Bankruptcy Code Section 505(a)(1) provides that the Bankruptcy Court "may determine the amount or legality of any tax, any fine or penalty relating to a tax, or any addition to tax." If this language appears to give the bankruptcy court declaratory judgment jurisdiction in a tax case, it does. The Declaratory Judgment Act excludes the granting of a declaratory judgment in tax cases, but carves out from the general exception, the granting of a declaratory judgment under Bankruptcy Code Section 505(a)(1). This declaratory judgment jurisdiction is conferred and exists "whether or not (the tax has been) previously assessed, whether or not paid, and whether or not contested before and adjudicated by a judicial or administrative tribunal of competent jurisdiction." There are only two exceptions to this jurisdiction. The Bankruptcy Court is prohibited from determining "the amount of a tax, fine, penalty, or addition to tax if such

---

[480] United States v. Noland, 48 F3d 210 (6th Cir. 1995); rev'd, 517 US 535, 77 AFTR2d 96-21433 (1996) (failure to pay FUTA tax); United States v. Reorganized CF&I Fabricators of Utah, Inc., 518 US 213, 116 S. Ct. 2106 (1996) (excise tax for failure to pay into a pension fund treated as a penalty). The Supreme Court granted certiorari in *Noland* because of the conflict between the Sixth Circuit's opinion in Mansfield Tire & Rubber Co., 942 F2d 1055 (6th Cir. 1991) and the Tenth Circuit's decision in *CF&I* on the characterization of the Section 4971 excise as a penalty. The U.S. Supreme Court reversed the Sixth Circuit's decision in *Noland*. United States v. Noland, 517 US 535, 77 AFTR2d 96-2143 (1996).

[481] United States v. Noland, 517 US 535, 77 AFTR2d 96-2143 (1996).

[482] United States v. Noland, 517 US 535, 77 AFTR2d 96-2143 (1996).

amount or legality was contested before and adjudicated by a judicial or administrative tribunal of competent jurisdiction *before* the commencement of (the bankruptcy) case."[483] The Bankruptcy Court is also prohibited from determining the entitlement of the bankruptcy estate to a tax refund for 120 days after the trustee has filed a claim for refund, unless the Service rules on the claim within the 120-day period.[484]

A trustee is permitted to request an expedited administrative determination of any unpaid liability of the estate incurred during the administration of the estate.[485] If the trustee files a tax return for the tax and makes payment of the tax reported on the return, and submits the return and payment with a request for the determination to "the governmental unit charged with the responsibility for collection or determination of such tax," the trustee, the debtor, and any successor to the debtor are discharged from any liability for the tax unless the governmental unit notifies the trustee within sixty days that the return has been selected for examination. In the case of the Service, the "governmental unit" is the Area Collection Services Office, not the service center/campus where returns are ordinarily required to be filed.[486]

In summary, under the Bankruptcy Code, the Bankruptcy Court has jurisdiction to take the following action:

- The Bankruptcy Court may determine the amount of any claim for taxes, provided liability for the tax has not already been "contested before and adjudicated by" the Tax Court, a district court, or the Court of Federal Claims.
- In the event that the debtor is already contesting a deficiency determination in the Tax Court, the Bankruptcy Court may refuse to lift the automatic stay of Bankruptcy Code Section 362, thereby nullifying the Tax Court proceeding, and determine the tax claim itself.
- In the event that the debtor either has received a notice of deficiency and may file a petition in the Tax Court or is in the course of a Tax Court proceeding, the Bankruptcy Court may lift the stay and permit the Tax Court to decide the issue.

There are limits to the jurisdiction of the Bankruptcy Court in tax cases, and one of them is the government's sovereign immunity. A Bankruptcy Court does not have jurisdiction under 11 USC Section 106(c), which waives sovereign immunity in general terms, to enter a monetary judgment against the Ser-

---

[483] 11 USC § 505(a)(2)(A) (emphasis added).

[484] 11 USC § 505(a)(2)(B).

[485] 11 USC § 505(b)(1).

[486] Rev. Proc. 81-17, 1981-1 CB 688. When the trustee files the return and request in the Service Center, the liability will not be discharged. In re Flaherty, 74 AFTR2d 94-5245 (Bankr. DNH 1994).

vice for the amount of a payment made by the debtor and applied against the trust fund portion of the tax.[487]

¶ 16.14 THE ESTATE

The bankruptcy estate is composed of "all legal or equitable interests of the debtor in property as of the commencement of the case."[488] Thus, property in the bankruptcy estate is subject to any liens that encumber the debtor's property when the proceeding begins. A tax lien is "a statutory lien" under the Bankruptcy Code. A lien means a "charge against or interest in property to secure payment of a debt,"[489] and a statutory lien is defined as a "lien arising solely by force of a statute on specified circumstances or conditions."[490] A secured claimant is entitled to be paid in full out of the security, subject to preservation or disposition charges.[491] As a general matter, claims for taxes secured by valid tax liens must be paid before priority claims are satisfied out of the bankruptcy estate under Bankruptcy Code Section 507. In directing the order or payment before dividends (partial payments) to creditors, Bankruptcy Code Section 726 assumes that secured claims have been paid out of their collateral, because it makes reference to general, not secured, creditors.[492]

Although a tax lien may be valid and entitled to priority outside bankruptcy, the lien may be either invalidated or postponed in bankruptcy. The Bankruptcy Code gives the trustee certain powers by which he may be able to avoid or set aside the lien.[493] Lien avoidance converts a secured tax claim into

---

[487] United States v. Nordic Village, Inc., 112 S. Ct. 1011 (1992) (Section 106(c) does not "unequivocally express" waiver of government's immunity from actions for monetary relief as is required for waiver to be effective).

[488] 11 USC § 541(a)(1).

[489] 11 USC § 101(33).

[490] 11 USC § 101(47). The tax lien arises by reason of the provisions of Section 6321 where a taxpayer neglects or refuses to pay an assessed tax after notice and demand.

[491] The tax lien may not be stripped down to the value of the collateral for the lien (i.e., the property subject to the lien) as of the filing date of the taxpayer's petition. Dewsnup v. Timm, 502 US 410 (1992); In re Cook, 76 AFTR2d 95-5725 (Bankr. MD Fla. 1995) (applying *Dewsnup* to a tax lien when the taxpayer/debtor wanted a determination that his payment of an amount equal to the value of his property on the petition date fully satisfied his tax liability so that the tax lien was unenforceable after his discharge).

[492] See City of Richmond v. Bird, 249 US 174 (1919).

[493] The trustee may do so only if the property is also part of the bankruptcy estate. For example, a tax lien on property exempt in bankruptcy may not be avoided. See, e.g., In re Carlton, 19 BR 73, 82-1 USTC ¶ 9400 (DNM 1982) (lien on proceeds from debtors' homestead). See also In re Halle, 132 BR 186, 91-1 USTC ¶ 50,121 (Bankr. D. Colo. 1991) (prepetition estimated tax remittance was not property of debtor's estate and was not subject to turnover order). Similarly, even if a taxpayer may avoid a transfer of funds

an unsecured one, which nevertheless may be entitled to a seventh-priority position.

There are a number of Bankruptcy Code provisions that the trustee may use to set a tax lien aside. The trustee may assume the status of a lien creditor under Bankruptcy Code Section 544[494] or of a bona fide purchaser under Bankruptcy Code Section 545 to invalidate a tax lien.[495] The trustee also has the power to avoid preferences under Bankruptcy Code Section 547,[496] fraudulent transfers under Bankruptcy Code Section 548,[497] and certain postpetition transactions under Bankruptcy Code Section 549.[498]

[1] Avoidance of Transfers and Obligations

Bankruptcy Code Section 544(a) permits the trustee "to avoid any transfer of property of the debtor or any obligation incurred by the debtor" if the transfer or obligation is avoidable by a hypothetical creditor on a simple contract who holds a judgment lien creditor;[499] by a hypothetical creditor who obtains an execution against the debtor that returned unsatisfied;[500] or by a bona fide purchaser of realty from the debtor who obtains the status of a bona fide purchaser under state law and has perfected the transfer at the time of the

---

under 11 USC Section 522(h) because the property was exempt, the transfer of the funds to the Service pursuant to a levy still may not be set aside, because 11 USC Section 522(c) excepts from the exemption a prebankruptcy tax debt secured by a lien that is properly filed. Forrest v. IRS, 226 BR 284, 81 AFTR2d 98-1777 (Bankr. App. Panel, 9th Cir. 1998).

See also Genova v. Gottlieb (In re Orange County Sanitation Department), 135 F3d 457, 81 AFTR2d 98-545 (Bankr. SDNY 1997). (Transfer of estate funds to the Service was potentially voidable because made after commencement of the bankruptcy case and was unauthorized; nevertheless, the transfer was not avoided because under 11 USC Section 550(a)(2), the Service received the funds in satisfaction of an antecedent debt, in good faith, and without knowledge of the voidability of the transfer.)

[494] 11 USC § 544 (Trustee as lien creditor and as successor to certain creditors or purchasers).

[495] 11 USC § 545 (Statutory liens).

[496] 11 USC § 547 (Preferences). Biddle v. IRS, 31 BR 449, 83-2 USTC ¶ 9471 (Bankr. D. Iowa 1983) (Service transferred debtor's prebankruptcy tax overpayment to Iowa Child Support Recovery Office to be applied to debtor's delinquent child support obligation; held, the payment was not a voidable preferential transfer because (1) the state had a lien against the overpayment under Section 6402(c); (2) the state's lien arose outside the ninety-day period; and (3) the state's lien was a statutory lien and therefore not subject to avoidance).

[497] 11 USC § 548 (Fraudulent transfers and obligations).

[498] 11 USC § 549 (Postpetition transactions).

[499] 11 USC § 544(a)(1).

[500] 11 USC § 544(a)(2).

commencement of the case.[501] A lien is avoidable under Bankruptcy Code Section 544(b) if an actual creditor holding certain unsecured claims could set the transfer or lien aside. It should be noted that Bankruptcy Code Section 545 permits the trustee to avoid a statutory lien if the lien would not be effective against a hypothetical bona fide purchaser of the property.[502] It should also be noted that Bankruptcy Code Section 724(a) allows the trustee to avoid a lien that secures a claim for a nonpecuniary loss penalty.

The trustee's status as a hypothetical judgment lien creditor means that an unfiled tax lien is invalid against a trustee in bankruptcy.[503] This fact is hardly a cause for unsecured creditors to rejoice, because the result may be only to reduce the tax claim to the status of an unsecured claim, sharing a seventh priority with other unsecured tax claims and ranking behind administration expenses and other priority claims, all of which must be paid before any dividend is paid to the unsecured creditors.

However, suppose the Service has filed a notice of tax lien. Can the trustee invalidate a filed tax lien? Even if a tax lien has been filed, it is invalid against a number of claimants granted "superpriority" status by Section 6323, such as the bona fide purchaser of securities, the purchaser of a motor vehicle at retail, or certain commercial lenders. Thus, the trustee under Bankruptcy Code Section 545(2) can assume the status of a bona fide purchaser and comb Section 6323(b) for the opportunity accorded to purchasers of certain property, even if notice of the tax lien has been filed. In such a case, the trustee would have superpriority status over a tax lien. For example, a trustee claiming the status of a bona fide purchaser could defeat federal tax liens on automobiles and securities even though the liens had been perfected by filing prior to the filing of the bankruptcy petition.[504] Also, where the bankrupt was in a retail

---

[501] 11 USC § 544(a)(3).

[502] 11 USC § 545(a).

[503] Section 6323(a) provides that a tax lien is not valid against any "judgment lien creditor" until notice of the lien has been filed.

[504] See Znider v. United States, 167 BR 603, 93-1 USTC ¶ 50,165, (Bankr. D. Calif. 1993), vacated on other grounds, 167 BR 603 (CD Cal. 1993) (debtor-in-possession in Chapter 11 proceeding in status as bona fide purchaser avoided tax liens on corporate stock, money on hand and in the bank, and retirement accounts, as well as a motor vehicle). In *United States v. Hunter (In re Walter)*, the Sixth Circuit held that while Bankruptcy Code Section 545(2) allows the debtor-in-possession or trustee to step into the shoes of a hypothetical bona fide purchaser to avoid a statutory lien, it does not impute possession of property to the debtor-in-possession or trustee. 45 F3d 1023, 75 AFTR2d 95-821 (1995). Therefore, when the court tested the status of the trustee under the purchaser superpriority provisions of Section 6323(b)(2), the trustee was found not to have possession of the tractor (the debtors did). The trustee also failed to meet the requirement that the purchaser not have actual notice. (The debtors/taxpayers had notice of the IRS lien when they filed their petition.) As a result, the tax lien was not invalidated. The Sixth Circuit followed In re Tape City, U.S.A., Inc., 677 F2d 401 (5th Cir. 1982), and In re Trahan, 283 F. Supp. 620, 626 (WD La.), aff'd, 402 F2d 796 (5th Cir. 1968), cert. denied,

business, a tax lien would not seem to be valid against the trustee because it is not valid against a purchaser in the ordinary course, which presumably includes a bona fide purchaser.

[2] Avoidance of Statutory Liens

Section 545 permits the trustee to avoid a statutory lien if the lien would not be effective against a hypothetical bona fide purchaser of the property.[505] A tax lien may not be avoided as a preferential transfer under 11 USC Section 547(b) if it is not avoidable under 11 USC Section 545(2). Once a notice of lien has been filed, it is valid against a bona fide purchaser, unless the purchaser is one of the categories of superpriorities having priority over a filed tax lien, described in Section 6323(b).[506]

Even if a tax lien has been filed, it is invalid against a number of claimants granted "superpriority" status by Section 6323, such as the bona fide purchaser of securities, the purchaser of a motor vehicle at retail, or certain commercial lenders. Thus, the trustee under Bankruptcy Code Section 545(2) can assume the status of a bona fide purchaser and comb Section 6323(b) for the opportunity accorded to purchasers of certain property, even if notice of the tax lien has been filed. In such a case, the trustee would have superpriority status over a tax lien. For example, a trustee claiming the status of a bona fide purchaser could defeat federal tax liens on automobiles and securities even though the liens had been perfected by filing prior to the filing of the bank-

---

394 US 930 (1969), both of which refused to find that hypothetical bona fide purchaser status gave the debtor-in-possession or trustee physical possession of the property in issue, and rejected the reasoning of the *Znider* case.

The Ninth Circuit, followed by the Eighth Circuit, both agree with the result in *Hunter* and say that a bona fide purchaser for purposes of 11 USC Section 545(2) is not necessarily a purchaser for adequate and full consideration, as required by the tax lien priority statute. In re Walter & Battley v. United States (In re Berg), 188 BR 615 (BAP 9th Cir. 1995); Janssen v. United States (In re Janssen), 213 BR 558, 80 AFTR2d 97-7467 (BAP 8th Cir. 1997).

[505] A tax lien may not be avoided as a preferential transfer under 11 USC Section 547(b) if it is not avoidable under 11 USC Section 545(2). Once a notice of lien has been filed, it is valid against a bona fide purchaser, unless the purchaser is one of the categories of superpriorities having priority over a filed tax lien, described in Section 6323(b). See Filipovits v. IRS (In re Filipovits), 76 AFTR2d 95-6934 (Bankr. D Md. 1995) (when the Service levied on taxpayer's bank account within ninety days of taxpayer's filing a Chapter 13 petition, the seizure was held not to be avoidable under 11 USC Section 545 or Section 547).

[506] See Filipovits v. IRS (In re Filipovits), 76 AFTR2d 95-6934 (Bankr. D Md. 1995) (when the Service levied on taxpayer's bank account within ninety days of taxpayer's filing a Chapter 13 petition, the seizure was held not to be avoidable under 11 USC Section 545 or Section 547).

ruptcy petition.[507] Also, where the bankrupt was in a retail business, a tax lien would not seem to be valid against the trustee because it is not valid against a purchaser in the ordinary course, which presumably includes a bona fide purchaser.

In *United States v. Hunter (In re Walter)*, the Sixth Circuit held that while Bankruptcy Code Section 545(2) allows the debtor-in-possession or trustee to step into the shoes of a hypothetical bona fide purchaser to avoid a statutory lien, it does not impute possession of property to the debtor-in-possession or trustee.[508] When the court tested the status of the trustee under the purchaser superpriority provisions of Section 6323(b)(2), the trustee was found not to have possession of the tractor (the debtors did). The trustee also failed to meet the requirement that the purchaser not have actual notice because the debtors/taxpayers had notice of the tax lien when they filed their petition. As a result, the tax lien was not invalidated.[509] A number of courts have held, however, that the status of a "bona fide purchaser" under the Bankruptcy Code is not the equivalent of a "purchaser" under the tax lien priority statute, with the result that debtors have not been allowed to avoid a federal tax lien under 11 USC Section 545(2) by using the superpriority of Section 6323(b)(1)(A).[510]

[3] Fraudulent Transfers and Obligations

The trustee in a bankruptcy proceeding is permitted to avoid any transfer of property that was made on or within one year before the date the petition was

---

[507] See Znider v. United States, 150 BR 239, 93-1 USTC ¶ 50,165 (Bankr. D. Calif. 1993), vacated on other grounds, 167 BR 603 (CD Cal. 1993) (debtor-in-possession in Chapter 11 proceeding in status as bona fide purchaser avoided tax liens on corporate stock, money on hand and in the bank, and retirement accounts, as well as a motor vehicle).

[508] United States v. Hunter (In re Walter), 45 F3d 1023 (6th Cir. 1995).

[509] The Sixth Circuit followed In re Tape City, USA, Inc., 677 F2d 401 (5th Cir. 1982), and In re Trahan, 283 F. Supp. 620, 626 (WD La.), aff'd, 402 F2d 796 (5th Cir. 1968), cert. denied, 394 US 930 (1969), both of which refused to find that hypothetical bona fide purchaser status gave the debtor-in-possession or trustee physical possession of the property in issue, and rejected the reasoning of the *Znider* case. The Ninth Circuit, followed by the Eighth Circuit, both agree with the result in *Hunter* and say that a bona fide purchaser for purposes of 11 USC Section 545(2) is not necessarily a purchaser for adequate and full consideration, as required by the tax lien priority statute. In re Walter & Battley v. United States (In re Berg), 188 BR 615 (BAP 9th Cir. 1995); Janssen v. United States (In re Janssen), 213 BR 558, 80 AFTR2d 97-7467 (BAP 8th Cir. 1997).

[510] Janssen v. United States (In re Janssen), 213 BR 558, 80 AFTR2d 97-7467 (BAP 8th Cir. 1997) (debtor in possession), following In re Walter & Battley v. United States (In re Berg), 188 BR 615 (BAP 9th Cir. 1995) (trustee); United States v. Hunter (In re Walter), 45 F3d 1023, 75 AFTR2d 95-821 (6th Cir. 1995).

filed.[511] One circumstance where the trustee may avoid the transfer is in the case of actual fraud; that is, if the debtor, voluntarily or involuntarily, made the transfer with the intent to defraud a past or future creditor.[512] A debtor's transfer is said to be less than "a reasonably equivalent value" (i.e., fraudulent) if the debtor (1) was insolvent on the date of the transfer (or became insolvent as the result of the transfer);[513] (2) was engaged in business (or was about to engage in business) "for which any property remaining with the debtor was unreasonably small capital";[514] or (3) was intended to incur debts that would be beyond the debtor's ability to pay.[515] For purposes of the first of these constructive fraudulent transfers, "value" means property, or satisfaction or securing of antecedent debt, but does not include an unperformed promise to furnish to the debtor or to a relative of the debtor.[516]

There have been a number of issues peculiar to tax cases arising under the power of the trustee to avoid a fraudulent conveyance. The debtor must have transferred "property," but it may not be obvious that property may include tax attributes. A corporation's Subchapter S election can constitute valuable property of the debtor corporation because its corporate status allowed the corporation to pass on its tax liabilities to its shareholders. When the corporation revokes the election without receiving consideration from the shareholders before the corporation filed for bankruptcy protection, the revocation constitutes a fraudulent transfer.[517] Also, the debtor's right to a net operating loss (NOL) carryback and the resulting tax refunds are interests of the debtor, and the debtor's election to carry the NOL forward rather than back can constitute the transfer of the interest that may be invalidated as a fraudulent transfer under Section 548(a)(2). In this situation, the Service is a transferee of the debtor's right to the loss carryback and the related right to a tax refund.[518] On the other hand, the Service's position is that when the debtor elects to apply an overpayment for a year to estimated taxes for the following year, the election

---

[511] 11 USC § 548(a)(1).

[512] 11 USC § 548(a)(1)(A).

[513] 11 USC § 548(a)(1)(B)(I).

[514] 11 USC § 548(a)(1)(B)(II).

[515] 11 USC § 548(a)(1)(B)(III).

[516] 11 USC § 548(d)(2).

[517] Parker v. Saunders, In re Bakersfield Westar, Inc., Debtor, 82 AFTR2d 98-6877 (BAP 9th Cir. 1998).

[518] United States v. Towers (In re Feiler), 83 AFTR2d 99-2302 (BAP 9th Cir. 1999). See also In re Russell, 927 F2d 413 (8th Cir. 1991) (irrevocable election to carry forward NOLs to offset future income when, without election, NOLs could be used to offset past income held to constitute avoidable fraudulent transfer). In Towers, the Bankruptcy Appellate Panel also held that the trustee's avoidance power is broad enough to avoid a fraudulent transfer of a NOL carryback, even if the debtor has made the election to carry the loss forward before the debtor files a bankruptcy petition.

is irrevocable, and the refund does not constitute a legal or equitable interest of the debtor at the time the bankruptcy petition is filed.[519]

Foreclosure sales can also occur in tax cases, and at least one issue is whether the debtor receives reasonably equivalent value in the exchange. When a home previously owned by a Chapter 11 debtor in possession was sold at a mortgage foreclosure sale shortly before the bankruptcy petition, the debtor sued to avoid the transfer under Section 548, alleging that the fair market value of the property was substantially in excess of the foreclosure price, and the debtor therefore had received less than "reasonably equivalent value" for the property. The Supreme Court held that "a fair and proper price, or a 'reasonably equivalent value,' for foreclosed property, is the price in fact received at the foreclosure sale, so long as all the requirements of the State's foreclosure law have been complied with."[520]

In *United States v. Olsen*,[521] the United States brought an action against the taxpayer to reduce to judgment outstanding assessments and to set aside the transfer of real property to the taxpayer's wife as an alleged fraudulent conveyance or to collect from her property allegedly held as a nominee for the taxpayer. The taxpayer had filed a petition for Chapter 11 reorganization, and the real property became the property of the bankruptcy estate. The taxpayer's wife purchased the real property from the bankruptcy estate and provided notice of the sale to the Service. The sale was conducted and authorized by the Bankruptcy Court. The court, finding that the Service had notice of the sale and failed to object during the bankruptcy, held that the Service waived its right to claim that the transfer was a fraudulent conveyance.

[4] Avoidance of Preferences

Where an insolvent corporation pays a tax deficiency within ninety days before it files a petition in bankruptcy, the Sixth Circuit has held that the payment does not constitute a voidable preference.[522] The circuit court held that, tested as of the date the petition was filed, the Service did not receive more than it would have received in a liquidating bankruptcy under 11 USC Section 548(b)(4). The proceeding in *Tenna Corporation v. United States* had been instituted under Chapter 11, and the competing lienors had been granted superpriority status because they had made loans to the debtor during the

---

[519] ILM 199927037 (Apr. 26, 1999), reprinted in 1999 TNT 132-169 (July 12, 1999).

[520] BFP v. Resolution Trust Corp., 511 US 531 (1994). The same standard has been applied for purposes of a postpetition local tax foreclosure sale that was challenged under Section 549(c) as not being for "present fair equivalent value." T.F. Stone Co., Inc. v. Harper, 72 F3d 466 (5th Cir. 1995).

[521] United States v. Olsen, 87 AFTR2d 2001-863 (D. Ill. DC 2001).

[522] Tenna Corp. v. United States, 801 F2d 819 (6th Cir. 1986).

proceeding. The circuit court said, in part, that potential lenders would not be dissuaded from making loans to a debtor because its balance sheet will not include the prepetition payment as an asset.

In *Begier v. IRS*, the U.S. Supreme Court ruled that a bankruptcy trustee cannot "avoid any voluntary prepetition payment of trust-fund taxes, regardless of the source of the funds."[523] The Court said:

> A payment of withholding constitutes a payment of money held in trust under Internal Revenue Code § 7501(a), and thus will not be a preference because the beneficiary of the trust, the taxing authority, is in a separate class with respect to those taxes, if they have been properly held for payment, as they will have been if the debtor is able to make the payments.

Relying on *Begier*, one court held that the Service's levy on a debtor's bank account to collect employment taxes was an avoidable preference.[524] The court also refused to extend *Begier* to involuntary tax payments. When the Service collects tax within ninety days preceding the filing of a bankruptcy petition, the transfers are void as preferences.[525]

[5] Postponement

The policy of the Bankruptcy Code is to protect certain claims. Property in the estate that is subject to a tax lien that is not avoidable is subordinated under Bankruptcy Code Section 724(b), first to payment of allowable and unavoidable liens senior to the tax lien, and second to all claims having higher priority than tax claims (i.e., Bankruptcy Code Sections 507(a)(1) through 507(a)(6)).[526] Thus, regardless of the age of the tax claim, the tax lien is subordinated to a position between the sixth and seventh priorities; that is, before unsecured priority tax claims are paid. Any excess up to the amount of the tax lien is applied to the lien; that is, the difference between the amount of the first-through sixth-priority payments and the amount of the lien is applied to the tax lien.[527] If there is a holder of an unallowed claim secured by a lien that is not

---

[523] Begier v. IRS, 496 US 53 (1990).

[524] United States v. Borock, 214 BR 481, 80 AFTR2d 97-7926 (ED Mich. 1997).

[525] In re Husher, 131 BR 550 (EDNY 1991) (sovereign immunity rejected, but prejudgment interest not allowed). However, the employer's share of Social Security and Medicare taxes constituted non-trust fund taxes, and so was able to constitute a preferential transfer. Hoffman v. United States, 208 BR 788 (Bankr. D. Conn. 1997).

[526] 11 USC §§ 724(b)(1), 724(b)(2). Irrespective of the tax lien, the property or proceeds from the property are distributed in the following order: (1) administrative expenses; (2) expenses of prior proceedings; (3) certain wage claims; (4) claims for contributions to employee benefit plans; and (5) certain deposits against the purchase or lease of personal property.

[527] 11 USC § 724(b)(3).

avoidable but whose lien is junior to the tax lien, any excess is then applied to the junior nontax lien claim.[528] Finally, any balance is again applied to the tax lien.[529]

The following example illustrates the operation of Bankruptcy Code Section 724(b).

EXAMPLE 16-1: The value of a piece of property subject to a tax lien is $5,000. The amount of the tax lien is $2,500, and the amount of the first-through sixth-priority claims under Bankruptcy Code Section 507 is $2,000. In addition, there is a junior nontax lien of $2,000. In this situation, distribution would be made as follows:

- $2,000 to first- through sixth-priority claims
- $500 to the tax lien
- $2,000 to the junior nontax lien
- $500 to the tax lien

¶ 16.15 DISTRIBUTION OF PROPERTY OF THE ESTATE AND DISCHARGE

There is a purposeful relationship between the priority of tax claims and the exception of these claims from dischargeable debts. Competing interests are at stake where a claim is given priority. The debtor is assured that a greater amount of the priority claim will be satisfied in bankruptcy. Even if the priority claim is not discharged, the debtor simply has less to pay after bankruptcy. On the other hand, unsecured creditors not having priority bear the cost of this preferred payment.

Where tax claims are involved, some priority position is indicated, apart from the debtor's taxpaying obligation, because the Service, unlike other creditors, is prevented by law from obtaining secured status by, for example, the restrictions on assessment and collection when a deficiency is involved. Because the Service does not have as great an opportunity for protection as other creditors before bankruptcy, some priority and preferred status in and after bankruptcy is indicated. These considerations are reflected in the Bankruptcy Code's provision for payment of some but not all tax claims in a seventh-priority position and excepting from discharge those priority claims and certain other tax claims.

---

[528] 11 USC § 724(b)(4).

[529] 11 USC § 724(b)(5).

[1] Priorities

In general, some but not all tax claims are granted a sixth position of priority in payment before the payment of unsecured creditors. Bankruptcy Code Section 724(b) describes and establishes the order of specified expenses and claims. Bankruptcy Code Section 726(a), which governs the order of distribution of the property of the estate, provides that the estate shall be distributed "first, in payment of claims of the kind specified in, and in the order specified in, [Bankruptcy Code] section 507."[530] The expenses and claims granted priority in Bankruptcy Code Section 507(a) over claims for taxes are as follows:

1. Administration expenses.[531] Any tax incurred by the estate is an administration expense,[532] including (a) income and excise taxes incurred by the estate; (b) employees' and employers' shares of employment taxes on wages earned and paid after the petition date; (c) taxes attributable to excess allowances of tentative net operation loss carrybacks (quickie refunds) under Section 6411; (d) any fine, penalty, or reduction in credit attributable to a tax that is incurred in the administration of the estate;[533] and (e) any increase in FUTA tax[534] caused by the trustee's late contribution to a state unemployment fund as to wages earned and paid during administration.[535]

---

[530] 11 USC § 726(a)(1). It has been held that this first priority applies even if the Service fails to file a proof of claim before the bar date because while Congress intended to differentiate between timely and untimely for certain priority distributions described in Section 726, it did not intend Section 507 administration expenses to be included in that scheme. See In re Vecchio, 20 F3d 555 (2d Cir. 1994); In re Pacific Atl. Trading Co., 33 F3d 1064 (9th Cir. 1994); In re Davis, 81 F3d 134 (11th Cir. 1996); Cooper v. IRS (In re Bulldog Trucking, Inc.), 226 BR 174, 80 AFTR2d 97-7564 (WDNC 1997).

[531] These expenses are described in 11 USC Section 503 and 28 USC Section 123.

[532] 11 USC § 503(b)(1)(B)(i). If a tax is an administration expense, interest on that tax is also an administration expense. United States v. Flo-Lizer, Inc., 916 F2d 363 (6th Cir. 1990); compare United States v. Shottenstein, Zox and Dunn, 219 BR 741, 81 AFTR2d 98-1248 (BAP 6th Cir. 1998) (pension underfunding penalty under Section 4971 held not to be an administrative expense because it was not of the type specified in 11 USC Section 503(b)(1)).

[533] Suppose that the debtor files a petition in a bankruptcy proceeding during its fiscal year. Are the taxes due for the full year an administative expense? The answer is *no*, because Bankruptcy Code Section 507(a)(1) grants first priority as an administrative expense to the payment of taxes that are incurred by the bankruptcy estate and are not eighth priority. Even if the entire year's taxes for the prepetition period were considered to be incurred during the administration period, they are entitled to seventh priority; therefore, they do not qualify as administrative expenses. United States v. Hillsborough Holdings Corp. (In re Hillsborough Holdings Corp., Debtor), 116 F3d 1391, 80 AFTR2d 97-1248 (11th Cir. 1997).

[534] IRC § 3302.

[535] If the reduction in FUTA credit is attributable to the debtor's late payment, the claim for additional tax is not allowable. 11 USC § 502(b)(9). Taxes withheld from its

2. Claims in an involuntary case arising during the "gap" period after the filing of the petition but before the order for relief.

3. Wage claims earned within ninety days before the petition date or termination of the debtor's business, whichever occurs first, not to exceed $2,000. Claims for the employees' share of employment taxes are entitled to third priority to the extent that the wages receive third priority.[536]

4. Employee benefit plan claims arising from services within 180 days before the petition or the cessation of the debtor's business, whichever occurs first, but not to exceed the aggregate of $2,000 per claim, less the amount paid under the third priority.[537]

5. Claims up to $2,000 of farmers against grain storage facilities owners or operators, and of fishermen against operators of fish produce or storage facilities.

6. Lay-away-type claims for individuals up to $900 arising from deposits for the purchase, lease, or rental of property for personal or family household use.

Under Bankruptcy Code Section 724(b), a secured tax claim that is not avoidable under the Bankruptcy Code is paid (1) after any allowed secured claim senior to the secured tax claim, and (2) after claims in the first six priority categories up to the amount of the secured tax claim.[538]

Unsecured tax claims meeting the specifications of Bankruptcy Code Section 507(a)(8) are paid in the eighth order of priority. This eighth priority is a compromise reached in the light of a number of factors not otherwise applica-

---

employees' wages but not paid over by a bankrupt employer during an aborted Chapter 11 reorganization are payable as first-priority administrative expenses because the withholding tax liability is one "incurred" by the estate. United States v. Friendship College, Inc., 737 F2d 430 (4th Cir. 1984) (interpreting the exception for sixth-priority taxes in 11 USC Section 503(b)(1)(B)(i) to mean prepetition taxes, and the fact that the postpetition bankruptcy estate was being administered by a debtor-in-possession rather than a trustee to be immaterial); In re Thompson, 67 BR 1, 85-1 USTC ¶ 9243 (Bankr. ND Ohio 1984) (following *Friendship College* and holding that interest and delinquency penalties qualified as first-priority administrative expenses); In re Mansfield Tire & Rubber Co., 80 BR 395, 87-2 USTC ¶ 9542 (Bankr. ND Ohio 1987) (excise tax for underfunding a pension plan held not to be a tax entitled to sixth priority). In re C-T of Va., Inc., 128 BR 628, 91-1 USTC ¶ 50,240 (Bankr. WD Va. 1991) (10 percent tax on reversions of qualified pension plans to employer is not excise tax or pecuniary loss penalty entitled to priority); compare United States v. Shottenstein, Zox and Dunn (In re Unicast), 219 BR 741, 81 AFTR2d 98-1248 (BAP 6th Cir. 1998) (pension underfunding penalty under Section 4971 held not to be an administrative expense because it was not of the type specified in 11 USC Section 503(b)(1)).

[536] See Otte v. United States, 419 US 43 (1974). See also 11 USC § 346(f).

[537] This provision overrules United States v. Embassy Restaurant, 359 US 29 (1958), which held that fringe benefits were not entitled to wage priority status.

[538] See the discussion supra ¶ 16.12[2].

ble in the payment of tax claims. The Bankruptcy Code recognizes that if there are insufficient funds to pay all creditors, payment of taxes in full as a priority claim imposes a burden on the unsecured creditors. On the other hand, the Service, unlike other creditors, is frequently prevented by the internal revenue laws (i.e., restrictions on the assessment and collection of deficiencies) from taking actions available to other creditors to secure or collect their claims. Granting tax claims an eighth priority is a compromise in that taxes are given priority but the priority is limited to recovery of claims arising in a shorter period than would otherwise be available to the Service for collection purposes. Two additional characteristics of the priority accorded tax claims should be observed. First, the priority applies to the tax claims of all taxing authorities — federal, state, and local. Thus, the Service shares the eighth priority with tax claims of these other authorities. Second, should the property of the estate be insufficient, an unsecured tax claim that is not entitled to priority may yet be satisfied as a general unsecured claim along with other unsecured creditors.[539]

Tax claims entitled to payment in an eighth position of priority fall into the following categories:

- Incurred income taxes due for the three years preceding bankruptcy. Bankruptcy Code Section 507(a)(8)(A)(i) specifies income and gross receipts taxes incurred for a year ending on or before the year of the petition if the return due date or extended due date "occurred" within three years before the date of the petition.[540]

- Assessed income and gross receipts taxes if the assessment is made within 240 days before the petition is filed.[541] Because it is the assessment date that controls, the due date of the return may be more than three years before the petition. The 240-day period reflects the period after assessment during which the Service sends multiple notices to the

---

[539] 11 USC § 726(a)(2).

[540] If the tax year ends after the petition is filed, the liability is collectible as a first-priority claim. Hartman v. United States, 110 BR 951, 90-1 USTC ¶ 50,163 (D. Kan. 1990) (assessments did not occur on the sending of a notice of deficiency, but on date of notice and demand that was within 240 days of the filing of bankruptcy petition); see also In re Howell, 120 BR 137 (Bankr. 9th Cir. 1990) (erroneous oral statement of unnamed Service employee regarding assessment date did not preclude finding that actual assessment date was within 240-day period; equitable estoppel rejected); Brickley v. United States, 70 BR 113 (9th Cir. 1987) (taxes incurred more than three years earlier are not discharged if returns for those taxes were filed within three years of Chapter 13 petition but more than three years after the case was converted to liquidating bankruptcy because statute of limitations on collection is suspended by 11 USC Section 108(c) and Section 6503(b). Prepetition interest on taxes that receive priority status have the same priority claim as those taxes. In re Palmer, 53 BR 545, 85-2 USTC 9680 (Bankr. ND Tex. 1985).

[541] 11 USC § 507(a)(8)(A)(ii).

taxpayer requesting payment, after which the Service may take enforced collection action.[542]

- Unassessed income and gross receipts taxes, at the date of the petition but "assessable" as of the petition date;[543] unassessed taxes for tax years still open under the statute of limitations (e.g., by signing a waiver of the statute of limitations); and taxes in litigation in the Tax Court.[544] Thus, taxes in litigation in the Tax Court have sixth priority. Once assessment is made, the priority is determined under the 240-day rule or three-year rule. This subclass of priority tax claims includes transferee liability under Section 6901.

- Withholding taxes, such as wage withholding, employment, excise, and other withholding taxes, in whatever capacity the debtor was required to withhold; that is, employer, responsible person under Section 6672, or lender under Section 3505.[545]

- Employer's share of employment taxes on wages earned and paid before the filing of the petition if the due date of the return or extended due date for these taxes was within three years of the date of the petition (or after the petition was filed).[546]

- Excise taxes the due date for which is within three years of the date of the petition. This category covers not only excise but sales, estate, and gift taxes; gasoline and special fuel taxes; and wagering and truck taxes.

---

[542] If the taxpayer makes an offer in compromise, the running of the 240-day period is stayed pending acceptance, rejection, or withdrawal of the offer. The tax still has priority if the petition is filed within thirty days after the offer is withdrawn. Thus, if an offer is submitted by the debtor after an assessment and is still pending on the petition date, the taxes covered are entitled to sixth priority.

[543] 11 USC § 507(a)(8)(A)(iii).

[544] Taxpayers timely filed their income tax return for 1980, and filed a petition under the Bankruptcy Code more than three years after the return date, but within the statutory period for assessment that had been extended by agreement. The Bankruptcy Court held that additional tax for 1980 was "assessable" after the commencement of the case, and so the taxes were entitled to priority under 11 USC Section 507(a)(8)(A)(iii) and thus were nondischargeable under 11 USC Section 523(a)(1)(A). Longley v. United States, 66 BR 237, 86-2 USTC ¶ 9710 (Bankr. ND Ohio 1986).

[545] The statute thus codifies the result of United States v. Sotelo, 436 US 268 (1978).

[546] 11 USC § 507(a)(8)(D). This priority covers third-priority wage claims paid by the estate. Workers' Compensation premiums have been held to be excise taxes and as such are entitled to priority under 11 USC Section 507(a)(8)(E). See North Dakota Workers Compensation Bureau v. Voightman, 239 BR 380 (Bankr. App. Panel, 8th Cir. 1999) (contains analysis of cases describing the requirements for treatment of an exaction as a tax, as well as an excise tax).

For priority purposes, a claim for erroneous refund or credit of a tax is treated as a claim for the tax to which the refund or credit relates.[547]

These priority tax claims should be compared with the discharge provisions, discussed previously. In general, Bankruptcy Code Sections 523(a)(1) and 523(a)(7) exempt from discharge (1) priority tax claims, including pecuniary loss penalties; (2) taxes that would have been tax claims but for the debtor's failure to file a return, delinquent return, or fraudulent return; and (3) a nonpecuniary loss penalty if it relates to a nondischargeable tax.

When the Bankruptcy Court determines a debtor's tax liability, it renders a declaratory judgment on the issue, which gives the Bankruptcy Court jurisdiction in tax cases that is not shared by any other court.[548] The Bankruptcy Court also has jurisdiction under Bankruptcy Code Section 105 to issue any order necessary or appropriate to carry out the provisions of the Bankruptcy Code. This broad tax jurisdiction has resulted in conflicts with the Service's collection powers, especially in reorganization cases. For example, where a corporate employer is in a Chapter 11 reorganization, some Bankruptcy Courts have enjoined collection of 100 percent penalty assessments against responsible officers. Reviewing courts have generally said the Bankruptcy Court lacks jurisdiction to make these kinds of orders because the responsible officers are not the debtor.[549] However, the "separate taxpayer" analysis cannot be applied

---

[547] 11 USC § 507(c). Bleak v. United States, 817 F2d 1368 (9th Cir. 1987) (claim for erroneous refund of tax is entitled to sixth priority and is nondischargeable under Bankruptcy Act).

[548] The determination made by the Bankruptcy Court is a declaratory judgment because Bankruptcy Code Section 505 is one of the exceptions to the prohibition of declaratory judgments in tax cases. 28 USC § 2201(a). Even when the Service has not determined the amount of the debtor's trust fund liability, or even when it will assess the debtor for unpaid trust fund taxes, and has not filed a proof of claim in a reorganization proceeding, the Bankruptcy Court has jurisdiction under Section 505(a) to enter a declaratory judgment. Kilen v. United States, 129 BR 538, 91-2 USTC ¶ 50,361 (Bankr. ND Ill. 1991). In a Section 505 proceeding, it has been said that the government has the burden of proof (as do other claimants in bankruptcy proceedings), especially where the tax at issue had not been assessed. United States v. Rasbury, 141 BR 752, 92-1 USTC ¶ 50,195 (ND Ala. 1992) (government failed to prove workers were employees).

The Bankruptcy Court's jurisdiction to render a declaratory judgment on the taxpayer/debtor's tax liability does not override the taxpayer/debtor's obligation to file a refund claim and follow other refund procedures required by the Code. United States v. Kearns (In re Kearns), 219 BR 823.81 AFTR2d 98-1425 (BAP 8th Cir. 1998) (under Section 7422(a), the debtor was required to file refund claim for Bankruptcy Court to have jurisdiction); see City of Perth Amboy v. Custom Distrib. Servs., Inc., 224 F3d 235 (3d Cir. 2000) (although a taxpayer was not required to file a claim under county property tax procedures in order to counterclaim for an offset to the county's proof of claim for property taxes, it could not obtain a refund because it had failed to follow the county's refund procedures).

[549] Where a debtor owes employment taxes and an assessment is made against the responsible officers of the debtor under Section 6672, the Bankruptcy Court is said not to

in all situations, partly because the declaratory judgment nature of a Bankruptcy Code Section 505 determination permits the Bankruptcy Court to consider a wide latitude of information[550] that may, under appropriate circumstances, include the liability of a nondebtor for the same tax.[551] Also, in *United States v. Energy Resources Co.*, the Supreme Court upheld a Bankruptcy Court's jurisdiction to order the Service to apply payments to the trust fund portion of employment taxes because the ordered designation was determined by the Bankruptcy Court to be necessary to the success of the reorganization.[552]

By permitting the Bankruptcy Court to designate the payment to the trust fund portion of the liability, the potential liability of nondebtor responsible officers was either reduced or eliminated.[553]

---

have jurisdiction to enjoin collection of the assessment because the liability is separate and distinct from that of the debtor. Huckabee Auto Co., 783 F2d 1546 (11th Cir. 1986), A to Z Welding & Mfg. Co., Inc. v. United States, 803 F2d 932 (8th Cir. 1986) (per curiam); La Salle Rolling Mills, Inc., 832 F2d 390 (7th Cir. 1987). See also Matter of Becker's Motor Transp. Inc., 632 F2d 242 (3d Cir. 1980), cert. denied, 450 US 916 (1981). American Bicycle Ass'n v. United States, 895 F2d 1277 (9th Cir. 1990) (Bankruptcy Court does not have jurisdiction to enjoin the Service from collecting assessment from claimed responsible officer of debtor in Chapter 11).

[550] See generally, 10A Wright, Miller & Kane, Federal Practice and Procedure: Civil 2d § 2751.

[551] But see In re Brandt-Airflex Corp., 843 F2d 90 (2d Cir. 1988), rev'g 69 BR 701 (Bankr. EDNY 1987) (claim that Bankruptcy Court had jurisdiction to determine that a debtor was entitled to credit for tax owed by lender under Section 3505 rejected); cf. Quattrone Accountants, Inc. v. IRS, 895 F2d 921 (3d Cir. 1990) (Bankruptcy Court does have jurisdiction over nondebtor). See also In re Landbank Equity Corp., 973 F2d 265 (4th Cir. 1992) (recognizing that equitable principles apply in bankruptcy proceedings such as equitable subordination in order to protect creditors in manner that is consistent with overall bankruptcy scheme).

[552] United States v. Energy Resources Co., 495 US 545 (1990).

[553] United States v. Energy Resources Co., 495 US 545 (1990). However, the equity jurisdiction of Bankruptcy Court in a reorganization may be greater than that in a Chapter 7 liquidating bankruptcy, especially if no need for the allocation is demonstrated. United States v. Pepperman, 976 F2d 123 (3d Cir. 1992).

When a corporate employer owes employment taxes and its officers file personally for a reorganization, but their corporation does not file for bankruptcy protection, the Bankruptcy Court has jurisdiction over the corporation, but it is not a debtor before the court. Accordingly, *Energy Resources* does not authorize the Bankruptcy Court to use its jurisdiction under 11 USC Sections 1123, 1129, and 105 to order the Service to reallocate the corporate debtor's employment tax payments to the trust fund portion of the taxes in order to improve the chances that the officers' reorganization plan will be successful. Internal Revenue Service v. Kaplan, 104 F3d 589 (3d Cir. 1997) (the officers contended that they had funded the corporation's payments to the Service). Moreover, even if the corporate employer later files under Chapter 11, the Bankruptcy Court cannot order the Service to reallocate employment tax payments the corporation made prepetition under 11 USC Section 105. The Third Circuit approved the inquiry the First Circuit (in In re Energy Resources Co., 871 F2d 223, 234 (1st Cir. 1989)) required the Bankruptcy Court to make

[2] Discharge

As noted previously, the objective of bankruptcy from the debtor's standpoint is, after the distribution of his or her property, to gain a fresh start. A discharge in bankruptcy protects the debtor from any further personal liability on discharged debts. Bankruptcy Code Section 524(a) provides that a discharge voids any judgment with respect to a discharged debt and operates as an injunction against the commencement or continuation of any action to collect the debt.[554] However, despite the fact that the taxpayer/debtor's personal liability for the taxes has been discharged as the result of the Chapter 7 liquidating bankruptcy, and the Service cannot institute an action to collect tax from the taxpayer/debtor personally, federal tax liens continue to attach to the debtor's prepetition property, and the tax lien may be enforced against the property.[555]

The limited waiver of sovereign immunity added to 11 USC Section 106(a) by the Bankruptcy Reform Act of 1994 lists the discharge injunction of Bankruptcy Code Section 524 as one of the provisions to which it applies. Accordingly, the Bankruptcy Court may hold the Service in contempt for violation of the discharge injunction and impose coercive, but not punitive, monetary damages, as well as attorney fees.[556]

A discharge in a bankruptcy case gives real, but limited, relief to a delinquent taxpayer. Whether an individual debtor files under Chapter 7, 11, or 13, the debtor remains subject to tax claims granted priority under Bankruptcy Code Section 507(a)(8) because these claims are one of the exceptions to discharge.[557]

---

before ordering the Service to reallocate payments. Under this inquiry, the Bankruptcy Court must ask "upon consideration of the reorganization plan as a whole, in so far as the particular structure or allocation of payments increases the risk that the IRS may not collect the total tax debt, [whether] that risk [is] nonetheless justified by an offsetting increased likelihood of rehabilitation, i.e., increased likelihood of payments to creditors who might otherwise lose their money."

[554] 11 USC § 727(b). See Conti v. United States, 50 BR 142, 85-2 USTC ¶ 9497 (Bankr. ED Va. 1985) (past due tax notice to debtor after discharge constituted violation of injunction and was subject to civil contempt; attorney fees awarded as compensation). However, a taxpayer's discharge does not prevent collection of the taxpayer's liability from a third party. Kathy B. Enters., Inc. v. United States, 779 F2d 1413 (9th Cir. 1986) (Service collected bankrupt taxpayer's tax from fraudulent transferees of taxpayer).

[555] See Johnson v. Home State Bank, 501 US 78 (1991); In re Isom, 901 F2d 744 (9th Cir. 1990); Avola v. United States, 80 AFTR2d 97-5747 (DNJ 1997) (gathering other cases).

[556] See Hardy v. United States, 97 F3d 1384 (11th Cir. 1996).

[557] 11 USC § 523(a)(1). 11 USC Section 1141 incorporates the provisions of 11 USC Section 523. A corporate debtor is not discharged in a liquidating bankruptcy, 11 USC Section 727(a)(1), or in a reorganization, 11 USC Section 1141(d)(3)(C). See United States v. Isom, 95 BR 148, 89-1 USTC ¶ 9200 (Bank. App. Panel, 9th Cir. 1988), aff'd, 901 F2d 744 (9th Cir. 1990) (the Service filed tax liens before taxpayers filed bankruptcy petition; held, discharge in bankruptcy relieved taxpayers of personal liability for taxes but

Discharge of tax claims in bankruptcy requires consideration of at least three provisions of the Bankruptcy Code: (1) the general discharge provision (Bankruptcy Code Section 727); (2) the exceptions to discharge (Bankruptcy Code Section 523); and (3) the priority accorded to taxes (Bankruptcy Code Section 507(a)(8)). Bankruptcy Code Section 727(b) discharges an individual debtor from all debts that arose before the date of the discharge order "[e]xcept as provided in Section 523" of the Bankruptcy Code. As described earlier, there is a relationship between the exception from discharge of taxes and the priority of taxes in a bankruptcy proceeding. Bankruptcy Code Section 727(a) alone has ten subsections, and the debtor is denied a discharge if he falls afoul of any one of them.

Coordinating the priority for taxes of Bankruptcy Code Section 507(a)(8) with the discharge exceptions of Bankruptcy Code Section 523(a)(1) requires more statutory analysis. In general, Bankruptcy Code Section 523 provides that a discharge under Bankruptcy Code Section 727 does not discharge an individual debtor from

1. Any debt for a tax of the kind and for the periods specified in Bankruptcy Code Section 507(a)(8) for priority tax claims[558] and
2. Tax claims that would have been collected or entitled to priority but for the debtor/taxpayer's own misconduct in filing a false return, failing to file a timely return, or failing to file any return at all.[559]

Coordinating both the priority of the tax claim of Bankruptcy Code Section 507(a)(8) and the exceptions to discharge, in order to be dischargeable, the following criteria must be met:

---

lien on property was still enforceable and so was not required to be released under Section 6325). The Bankruptcy Reform Act of 1994 amended Section 523 to provide that if a debtor pays tax with borrowed funds, the lender, including the issuer of a credit card, has a nondischargeable claim to the extent that the government's claim would be nondischargeable. 11 USC § 523(a)(14) (1994). Even if a taxpayer's personal liability is discharged in bankruptcy, a prebankruptcy tax lien against the debtor taxpayer's property is not discharged. See In re Isom, 95 BR 148, 89-1 USTC ¶ 9200 (Bank. App. Panel, 9th Cir. 1988), aff'd, 901 F2d 744 (9th Cir. 1990); Morris v. United States, 94-1 USTC ¶ 50,035 (Bankr. WD Tenn. 1993) (social security disability benefits of deceased spouse held subject to lien although tax liability of surviving husband discharged).

[558] 11 USC §§ 523(a)(1)(A), 507(a)(8). The exception to discharge also applies to so-called gap tax claims entitled to priority under 11 USC Section 507(a)(2) for tax claims arising in the course of the debtor's business in the gap period between the date of the commencement of the bankruptcy case but before the appointment of the trustee or the order of relief, whichever is earlier.

[559] 11 USC §§ 523(a)(1)(B), 523(a)(1)(C). The Supreme Court has said that Congress intended that the fresh start of a bankruptcy discharge would apply only to the "honest but unfortunate debtor." Grogan v. Garner, 498 US 279, 286–287 (1991).

1. The taxes must be for taxable years, the returns for which were due more than three years (and frequently four years) before the bankruptcy petition was filed;[560]

2. The returns for those taxable years must have been filed at least two years before the bankruptcy petition was filed;[561]

3. The taxes must have been assessed at least 240 days before the bankruptcy petition was filed (taking into account any period of suspension arising out of the submission of an offer in compromise, plus thirty days);[562] and

4. The taxes must not have been taxes the taxpayer/debtor reported on a fraudulent return or willfully in any manner attempted to evade or defeat.[563]

Each of these requirements has been the subject of considerable attention by the courts.

[a] Return Due Within Three Years Before Petition

Taxes for taxable years within three years of the date of the bankruptcy petition are not dischargeable. Bankruptcy Code Section 507(a)(8) provides an eighth priority for a tax for "a taxable year ending on or before the date of the filing of the petition for which a return, if required, is last due, including extensions, after three years before the date of the filing of the petition." The exception from discharge is more complicated than that. If the computation of the three-year rule starts with the date of the bankruptcy petition, the key date for determining whether tax for a taxable year is dischargeable is the date the return for the year is "last due." The date the return for a year may be last due will be affected by such circumstances as whether the taxpayer/debtor had an extension of time to file.[564] For example, suppose an individual taxpayer files a

---

[560] 11 USC §§ 523(a)(1)(A), 507(A)(8)(A)(i).

[561] 11 USC §§ 523(a)(1)(B)(i), 523(a)(1)(B)(ii). See Barber v. United States, 82 AFTR2d 98-7024 (ND Ind. 1998) (failure to file return meant that tax for the year was not nondischargeable, even though the Service prepared substitute return for taxpayer).

[562] 11 USC § 507(a)(8)(A)(ii).

[563] 11 USC § 523(a)(1)(C).

[564] Computation of the three-year period can be complicated when there are serial bankruptcy petitions. During the period that the automatic stay in a prior proceeding is in force, the three-year period does not run. Brickley v. United States, 70 BR 113, 87-1 USTC ¶ 9313 (BAP 9th Cir. 1986); Acosta v. IRS, 184 BR 544, 75 AFTR2d 95-2383 (WD Tenn.) (same). The running of the three-year period is also said to be suspended during the period in which a taxpayer's objection to a tax claim made in a Chapter 11 reorganization is sustained. Montoya v. United States, 965 F2d 554 (7th Cir. 1992) (Chapter 11 proceeding during which tax claim was disallowed, then was allowed one year later, followed successive Chapter 7 proceedings; see also Daniel v. United States, 81 AFTR2d 98-1342 (Bankr. ND Ind. 1998) (*Montoya* followed).

bankruptcy petition on May 1, 2004. Using May 1, 2004, as the measuring

---

But not all courts agree that the suspension provisions of Section 6503(h) apply to suspend the running of the three-year nondischargeability period in 11 USC Section 507(a)(8)(A)(ii), because neither Section 6503(h) nor 11 USC Section 108(c) specifically requires suspension in the case of successive bankruptcy proceedings. Gore v. United States (In re Gore), 182 BR 293, 76 AFTR2d 95-7621 (Bankr. ND Ala. 1995) (taxpayer filed 1990 return without full payment, and his 1991 Chapter 13 petition was dismissed in 1992; the Service assessed the 1990 tax in 1993, and the taxpayer filed a Chapter 7 petition in 1994; held, the three-year nondischargeability period was not suspended during the pendency of the Chapter 13 case; detailed analysis of the law).

Another Bankruptcy Court analyzed the legislative history of Section 108 and disagreed with the conclusions of the Eighth Circuit in *Waugh*, the Third Circuit in *Taylor*, the Seventh Circuit in *Montoya*, and the Ninth Circuit in *Brickley*, holding that the intent of Bankruptcy Code Section 108 is "to preserve the nonbankruptcy limitations periods [of Section 6503(h)(2)] only for nondischargeable taxes, not to employ those periods in determining which taxes are dischargeable." As a result, Section 6503(h)(2) "does not apply to the three-year period in [Bankruptcy Code] section 507(a)(8)(A)(i), and…the three-year period is not tolled for six months after the expiration of the automatic stay." In re Avila, 83 AFTR2d 99-1020 (BC Mass. 1999) (the Service claimed that 1992 taxes were excepted from discharge because, with tolling, the 1992 return was due within three years before the bankruptcy petition was filed; held, although the Service was prevented by the automatic stay from collecting taxes during the debtors' prior bankruptcy proceedings, there was no suspension for an additional six months after the stay in each case, so that the Service had more than three years during which to collect taxes, and the Service's claim was not a secured claim excepted from discharge, but an unsecured claim).

Several circuit courts have held that successive bankruptcy proceedings cannot be used to avoid the three-year requirement. The Third Circuit in *Taylor* said, "it seems clear that Congress intended to provide the government a full and unimpeded three years to collect income taxes; it did not intend to leave a loophole for debtors to engage in tax avoidance, as 'the burden of making up the revenues thus lost must be shifted to other taxpayers'…[so that t]he extension of time provided within section 108(c) of the Bankruptcy Code and section 6503(h) of the Internal Revenue Code would be meaningless if debtors could discharge their tax liability by filing successive bankruptcies." In re Taylor, 81 F3d 20 (3d Cir. 1996); In re Waugh, 109 F3d 489 (8th Cir. 1997) ("Were we to adopt Waugh's limited interpretation of 507(a)(8)(A)(i)'s priority period, future tax debtors could abuse the bankruptcy process by remaining tied up in bankruptcy until the three-year lookback period of section 507(a)(8)(A)(i) expired, then voluntarily dismissing the bankruptcy petition and refiling once the tax liability became dischargeable."). Accord, In re Marcos Occhipinti, 98-1 USTC ¶ 50,112 (Bankr. MD Fla.) (the overwhelming weight of authority is that the three-year lookback periods of 11 USC Section 507(a)(8)(A) are suspended while the debtor's prior bankruptcy case prevented the Service from pursuing full collection activity, with the result that the priority period for tax liabilities that were postpetition in the prior case were also suspended).

Note that the statute of limitations on assessment is suspended under the provisions of Section 6503(h) for the period of the automatic stay and for sixty days thereafter. For a case where the suspension period was computed because the debtor taxpayer claimed that the time for making assessments after his first bankruptcy had expired and, therefore, the assessments were dischargeable in his second bankruptcy, see Richmond v. United States, 80 AFTR2d 97-5701 (SD Cal. 1997), aff'd, 172 F3d 1099, 83 AFTR2d 99-1410 (9th Cir. 1999) (court found that because the Service had not been notified of the Bankruptcy Court's denial of the debtor's discharge, the clock on the running of the assessment period

date, taxes due within the prior three-year period (i.e., after May 1, 2001) would not be eligible for discharge. If the taxpayer obtained an extension to file his 2000 tax return until October 15, 2001, the 2000 tax would also not be dischargeable.[565] However, the nondischargeable taxes due within three years of the petition cannot be converted into older-than-three-year taxes by the simple expedient of filing successive bankruptcy proceedings. In *In re Young*, the Supreme Court held that for purposes of determining whether taxes were due on returns required to be filed within three years of the petition date (dischargeable taxes) or beyond the three-year statute before the petition date (nondischargeable taxes), the three-year period is suspended or tolled during the first bankruptcy proceeding and the second proceeding.[566]

[b] Requirement of Filing Returns More Than Two Years Before Petition

Bankruptcy Code Section 523(a)(1)(B) provides that an individual debtor is not discharged from any tax debt "with respect to which a return, if required (1) was not filed, or (2) was filed after the [due date, including extensions], and after two years before the date of the filing of the petition." This "two-year" rule means that taxpayers/debtors who wish to be discharged from a tax debt for a year must file their return for that year at least two years before filing a petition. If the return is filed within the two-year period before the petition, the tax that was supposed to be reported on the return is excepted from discharge under Bankruptcy Code Section 523(a)(1)(B).[567] A post-assessment

---

did not begin to run until the date it received the notice, and so the assessments were timely).

[565] It has been held that the three-year period for discharge runs from the due date of the return, not the date of actual filing. Reine v. IRS (In re Albert Reine, Sr. et ux.), 92 AFTR2d 2003-5912 (Bank. WD Mo. 2003); Padden v. United States, 80 AFTR2d 97-8246 (Bank. MD Pa. 1997). When debtors filed their 1998 return one week before the April 15, 1999, due date, therefore, they filed their bankruptcy petition one week before the end of the three-year period, and so their tax debt could not be discharged.

[566] In re Young, 535 US 43 (2002) (Chapter 13 followed by a new asset liquidating bankruptcy under Chapter 7, and after the Bankruptcy proceeding was closed, the Service sued for collection of taxes the taxpayer claimed had been discharged).

[567] If the tax was not assessed before the petition date, it at least must be assessable after that date under law or by agreement. 11 USC § 507(a)(8)(A)(iii). If the taxpayer/debtor files a return more than two years before the bankruptcy petition, the tax is dischargeable, even if the taxpayer/debtor filed the return later than the due date under the tax law. However, the taxpayer/debtor must file the return, or at least adopt it, by signing it or some equivalent act. See In re Bergstrom, 949 F2d 341 (10th Cir. 1991); compare In re Hindenlang, 205 BR 874 (Bankr. SD Ohio 1997), rev'd, United States v. Hindenlang, 214 BR 847, 80 AFTR2d 97-6708 (SD Ohio 1997) (Section 6020(b) return is not a return for discharge purposes; taxpayer filed returns after the Service prepared substitute returns and made assessments; the Service's argument that the taxpayer's returns did not consti-

return may still be a return if (1) it purports to be a return; (2) it is executed under penalties of perjury; (3) it contains sufficient data to allow calculation of tax; and (4) it represents an honest and reasonable effort to satisfy the requirements of the tax law.[568]

[c] Requirement That the Tax Has Been Assessed for 240 Days

To be dischargeable, the tax must have been assessed for at least 240 days, which means that the timing of the assessment has real importance for the ultimate discharge of the tax. Clearly, the fact that the Service has approximately eight months to take enforced collection action to collect the tax from the taxpayer will put considerable pressure on the taxpayer to arrange for the payment of the assessed tax or suffer the seizure of property. On the other hand, taxes for old tax years that may not have been assessed before (because the taxpayer has extended the assessment period or assessment has been restricted during the pendency of a Tax Court case) are eligible for discharge as

---

tute "returns" for discharge purposes was rejected), aff'd, 164 F3d 1029, 83 AFTR2d 99-509 (6th Cir. 1999), with Mickens v. United States, 80 AFTR2d 97-6773 (ND Ohio 1997) (concluding that the returns filed after the substitute returns and assessments had no effect for discharge purposes). Note that when the taxpayer files a document that purports to be a return but does not contain sufficient information to constitute a tax return, not only is the tax debt not dischargeable but the conduct may evidence an intent to defraud the Service, and so the tax debt would be nondischargeable under 11 USC Section 523(a)(1)(C). See McGrath v. United States, 217 BR 389, 80 AFTR2d 97-8241 (Bankr. NDNY 1997) (collecting cases).

The Fourth Circuit has held that "income tax forms unjustifiably filed years late, where the IRS has already prepared substitute returns and assessed taxes, do not constitute 'returns' for purposes of 11 U.S.C. § 523(a)(1)(B)(i)." Moroney v. United States, 352 F3d 902 (4th Cir. 2003). The circuit court also held that the Bankruptcy Code did not treat delinquent returns different from other documents purporting to be returns, with the result that the debtor was disqualified from seeking the discharge of his tax debt. On the other hand, the court refused to follow the Service's argument that delinquent returns automatically disqualified the debtor from the discharge of the subject tax, pointing out that another taxpayer/debtor might prove that he had attempted in good faith to comply with the tax laws despite the delinquency.

Some state tax laws require taxpayers to notify the state taxing authority of any IRS tax changes, but a debtor's failure to provide this notice has been held not to constitute the failure to file a "return" for purposes of Bankruptcy Code Section 523(a)(1)(B), because the state tax law referred to the notice of an IRS assessment or tax change as a report, not a return. California Franchise Tax Board v. Marion Dale Jackson (In re Jackson), 1999 TNT 143-27 (9th Cir. 1999); but see In re Blutter, 177 BR 209 (Bankr. SDNY 1995) (Bankruptcy Court rejected debtor's argument that a report was not a return and held that the report of IRS tax changes was a "return" and that the state tax was nondischargeable because "a debtor should not be rewarded with a discharge for failing to comply with his filing obligations").

[568] See Woods v. IRS (In re Woods), 90 AFTR2d 2002-6498 (Bky. SD Ind. 2002) (citing Beard v. Comm'r, 82 TC 766 (1984), aff'd, 793 F2d 139 (6th Cir. 1986)).

long as the tax for those years has been assessed for at least 240 days before the petition is filed. A suspension of the period of assessment or collection will affect the computation of the 240-day period.[569]

[d] Requirement That the Debtor Was Not Delinquent and Did Not Engage in Tax Fraud

Bankruptcy Code Section 523(a)(1)(C) excepts from discharge a tax "with respect to which the debtor made a fraudulent return or willfully attempted in any manner to evade or defeat such tax." This language combines the statutory standards of "fraud" in the civil fraud penalty (Section 6663) and "willful attempt to evade or defeat" in the criminal evasion statute (Section 7201). Because the discharge of a tax claim is at issue, it makes sense to incorporate the civil fraud penalty case law, and since full statutory language of the civil fraud penalty statute is "fraud with intent to evade tax," conduct relevant for the civil fraud penalty and criminal evasion overlap.[570] Consequently, civil fraud penalty cases dealing with proof of fraud should provide the Bankruptcy Courts with adequate guidance and should lead to the results Congress intended; that is, a taxpayer who underpays tax as a result of fraud with an intent to evade tax should not be able to avoid liability by getting a fresh start under the bankruptcy laws. Also, the standard of proof under the discharge

---

[569] The starting point in the 240-day computation is the date of the assessment. A number of courts have concluded that the term "assessed" in Bankruptcy Code Section 507(a)(8)(A)(ii) has the same meaning as it does in the Internal Revenue Code. Hardie v. IRS (In re Hardie), 204 BR 944, 83 AFTR2d 99-2529 (SD Tex. 1996) (gathering cases, and holding that the date of the Tax Court's decision was not the date of assessment because it was not treated as such under the Internal Revenue Code).

The 240-day period can be difficult to compute when there are successive bankruptcy proceedings. When taxes were assessed within the 240-day period before the filing of a petition for a joint Chapter 13 proceeding but the joint petition was dismissed, and individual petitions were filed more than 240 days later, the 240-day period was held suspended until six months after the joint petition had been dismissed. West v. United States (In re West), 5 F3d 423 (9th Cir. 1993). As a result, the 240-day priority period of 11 USC Section 507(a)(8)(A)(ii) was suspended and the IRS tax claim had priority status in the individual Chapter 13 proceedings.

In West, the Ninth Circuit observed that incorporation of Section 6503(h) in Section 108 of the Bankruptcy Code "reflects a policy determination that it would be unfair to allow the statute [of limitations] to run against the government's right to enforce a tax lien when, even if the government did bring suit, it couldn't collect because it couldn't get the taxpayer's assets." West v. United States, 5 F3d 423 at 426. See also In re Richards, 994 F2d 763 (10th Cir. 1993). But see In re Little, 216 BR 769, 80 AFTR2d 97-8148 (Bankr. EDNC 1997) (refusing to toll the 240-day period because of the taxpayers' prior proceeding and rejecting the circuit court decisions cited above on the ground that they were contrary to the plain meaning of the statute, and holding that tax claims were discharged in the taxpayers' subsequent Chapter 13 proceeding under 11 USC Section 1328(a)).

[570] See ¶ 7B.02[3].

provisions is the ordinary preponderance of evidence standard.[571] The lower standard of proof in discharge cases makes it more appropriate to follow the civil fraud penalty cases, where the standard of proof is clear and convincing evidence, rather than the evasion cases, where the elements must be proved beyond a reasonable doubt, because concerns about proof of guilt and elements of the crime tend to merge. Courts nevertheless have adopted different interpretations of the language in 11 USC Section 523(a)(1)(C), although many, if not most, courts apply the civil fraud penalty case law.[572] This approach is consistent with the U.S. Supreme Court's ruling that when the substantive law establishes the burden of proof, in Bankruptcy Court, the burden remains

---

[571] Grogan v. Garner, 498 US 279, 286–287 (1991); Raleigh, Chapter 7 Trustee for the Estate of Stoecker v. Ill. Dept. of Rev., 120 S. Ct. 1951 (S. Ct. 2000).

[572] One court interpreted the language to exclude an attempt to evade collection of the tax, relying on law developed under the criminal evasion statute (IRC § 7201). In re Gathwright, 102 BR 211, 213, 89-1 USTC ¶ 9346 (Bankr. D. Or. 1989).

Several courts have rejected this view but have found affirmative conduct of the type that would support a civil fraud penalty or even an evasion statute. See, e.g., In re Jones, 116 BR 810 (Bankr. D. Kan. 1990) (claim that 11 USC Section 523(a)(1)(C) did not apply to willful attempts to defeat collection); Berzon v. United States, 145 BR 247, 250 (Bankr. ND Ill. 1992) (using badges of fraud found in civil fraud penalty cases); Gilder v. United States, 122 BR 593 (Bankr. D. Fla. 1990) (false withholding statements and failure to file returns were held to be attempt to evade); see also Fernandez v. IRS, 112 BR 888 (Bankr. ND Ohio 1990). See also United States v. Henry Fegeley (In re Henry Fegeley, Annmarie Fegeley, Debtors), 118 F3d 979 (3d Cir. 1997) ("Fegeley had a duty under the tax law, knew he had a duty, and voluntarily and intentionally violated that duty. He also had the financial ability to discharge that duty. The district court correctly found this to be a sufficient basis to prove that Fegeley willfully attempted to defeat his taxes for 1983, 1984, and 1985."). See Graham v. IRS, 108 BR 498, 90-1 USTC ¶ 50,072 (Bankr. ED Pa. 1989) (analyzing whether fraud precluded discharge), aff'd, 131 BR 275, 91-2 USTC ¶ 50,560 (ED Pa. 1991) (Tax Court found that taxpayer/debtor was liable for fraud penalty, but neither res judicata nor collateral estoppel precluded the relitigation of the issue because there had been no trial on the merits in the Tax Court); United States v. Palmer, 85 AFTR2d 2000-1157 (9th Cir. 2000) (same). Similarly, a Tax Court decision entered in accordance with a stipulation of the parties agreeing to negligence penalty does not preclude the Service from taking the position that the returns were fraudulent and therefore the taxes not dischargeable in bankruptcy. Levinson v. United States, 969 F2d 260 (7th Cir. 1992).

One circuit court has held that while the Service has the burden of showing that the debtor's actions were not an honest and reasonable effort to satisfy the tax law, even if a taxpayer has filed a tax return after the Service has made an assessment, the fact that the debtor failed to respond to both the thirty-day and ninety-day letters the Service sent before it assessed tax indicates that the debtor's return serves no tax purpose, and the Service has carried its burden of showing dishonesty. United States v. Hindenlang (In re Hindenlang), 164 F3d 1029, 83 AFTR2d 99-509 (6th Cir. 1998).

Other courts have expressly stated that case law applying the civil fraud penalty are persuasive guidance on the willful evasion element of 11 USC Section 523(a)(1)(C). In re Carapella v. United States, 925 F2d 1474 (11th Cir. 1991) (applying civil fraud penalty standard); Comm'r v. Peterson (In re Peterson), 152 BR 329, 93-1 USTC ¶ 50,095 (D. Wyo. 1993).

where the substantive law put it.[573] Courts have not always agreed about the evidentiary significance of the taxpayer/debtor's failure to pay.[574] Section

---

[573] Raleigh, Chapter 7 Trustee for the Estate of Stoecker v. Ill. Dept. of Rev., 120 S. Ct. 1951 (S. Ct. 2000).

[574] In *In re Haas*, the Eleventh Circuit held that "a debtor's failure to pay his taxes, alone, does not fall within the scope of section 523(a)(1)(C)'s exception to discharge in bankruptcy." 48 F3d 1153 (11th Cir. 1995). The debtor filed accurate returns between 1977 and 1985 but did not pay the taxes due, paying instead personal and business debts. In 1987, he also pled guilty to willfully failing to pay 1980–1982 income taxes and employment taxes for 1984. In 1991, the debtor and his wife filed a joint Chapter 11 bankruptcy petition. The Bankruptcy Court found, however, that the debtor had made no attempt to evade or defeat his tax obligation by concealing assets and the like.

The circuit court concluded that the failure to pay the Service "is not the result of dishonesty but to the defining characteristic of all debtors—insufficient resources to honor all of [their] obligations." The use of limited funds to pay obligations other than taxes did not make the debtor a dishonest debtor, "simply a debtor." The court also thought it was significant for statutory construction purposes that Bankruptcy Code Section 523(a)(1)(C) does not include an attempt to defeat the payment of tax, as does the tax evasion statute, and concluded that "(t)he omission of the words 'or the payment thereof' from section 523(a)(1)(C), in light of Congress's previous inclusion of these words on four previous occasions, indicates that Congress did not intend that a failure to pay taxes, without more, should result in the nondischargeability of a debtor's tax liabilities in bankruptcy." However, another panel in the Eleventh Circuit has said that while the "distinction...between [mere] nonpayment and fraudulent acts of concealment to avoid payment is an attractive reading of section 523(a)(1)(C)," *In re Haas* made clear that discharge was prohibited only "when the actions taken by the debtor affected the assessment of the tax." But the panel "was troubled by [*In re Haas's*] application" to the case before it because the debtor "fraudulently transferred assets to his wife to evade payment of tax debts." Griffith v. United States (In re Griffith), 174 F3d 1222 (11th Cir. 1999). The panel's decision in *Griffith* was vacated and the appeal heard en banc. The full court held that where the debtor has willfully attempted to evade or defeat the payment of tax but has not willfully attempted to evade or defeat assessment, the tax is nevertheless nondischargeable under Bankruptcy Code Section 523(a)(1)(C). Griffith v. United States (In re Leroy Charles Griffith), 85 AFTR2d 2000-1249 (11th Cir. 2000) (the panel distinguished *In re Haas* on the ground that, unlike Haas, Griffith had engaged in fraudulent transfers of assets to prevent the collection of taxes).

On the other hand, it has also been said that failure to pay a known tax is "relevant evidence which a court should consider in the totality of conduct to determine whether...the debtor willfully attempted to evade or defeat taxes." Dalton v. IRS, 77 F3d 1297, 1301 (10th Cir. 1996). Courts have found that nonpayment coupled with a pattern of failing to file tax returns or with other measures to conceal assets or income from the Service suggest that the debtor may have attempted to evade or defeat his tax liabilities. See Toti v. United States, 24 F3d 806 (6th Cir. 1994) (pattern of failing to file returns); In re Bruner, 55 F3d 195 (5th Cir. 1995) (debtors created a shell corporation to which they attempted to attribute their income and conceal assets); In re Birkenstock, 87 F3d 947 (7th Cir. 1996) (debtor failed to file returns and attributed to income to a trust). Without deciding whether it would choose the *Haas* standard that a failure to pay without more was not willful conduct or the *Bruner* test that the exception "encompasses both acts of commission as well as culpable omissions," the Second Circuit has found that under either standard, the tax claim was not dischargeable because the debtor had failed to file returns and

523(c)(1)(C) does not contain the requirement that the debtor engage in affirmative acts of wrongdoing, but it does state that discharge will be denied when the debtor "willfully attempted in any manner to evade or defeat such tax." This omission of the attempt element has led courts to consider whether a discharge will be denied when the taxpayer filed a return but simply failed to pay. The Eleventh Circuit in *In re Haas*[575] held that failure to pay, without more, is insufficient to prevent a discharge because of fraud. On the other hand, the Fifth Circuit has ruled that affirmative misconduct is not required as long as a willful attempt to avoid the liability is done voluntarily, consciously, and intentionally.[576] Also, affirmative acts of wrongdoing may be established by collateral estoppel resulting from the debtor's criminal conviction of tax evasion.[577] One standard clearly does not apply: the case law interpreting willfulness for the 100 percent penalty of Section 6672.[578] This "penalty" is really a collection device and does not require fraud or an intent to evade.

To the extent that these claims are not satisfied in bankruptcy, the debtor remains liable for their payment after bankruptcy.[579] Prepetition interest on

---

had submitted a false affidavit to his employer. Tudisco v. United States (In re Tudisco), 84 AFTR2d 99-5066 (2d Cir. 1999).

Following cases like *In re Bruner*, the Eighth Bankruptcy Appellate Court held that a debtor had willfully attempted to evade or defeat tax because he did not challenge the Service's allegations that he failed to file tax returns and used evasive tactics. (He had entered guilty pleas.) The taxpayer's unsuccessful defense was that his fraud was not material because it did not deceive the Service. May v. Missouri DOR, 86 AFTR2d 2000-5154 (Bankr. App. Panel, 8th Cir. 2000).

[575] In re Haas, 48 F3d 1153 (11th Cir. 1995).

[576] See United States v. Fretz, 244 F3d 1323 (5th Cir. 2001). In the Fifth Circuit, a three-pronged test is used to decide whether a tax liability is dischargeable in the case of a debtor who is financially able to pay his taxes. The three prongs are: (1) did the debtor have a duty to pay the taxes; (2) did the debtor know that he had that duty; and (3) did the debtor voluntarily and intentionally choose not to pay. In re Bruner, 55 F3d 195 (5th Cir. 1995) (Section 523(a)(1)(C) covers a failure to file).

[577] Wilcoxson v. United States (In re Glen Paul Wilcoxson), 89 AFTR2d 2002-576 (Bankr. SD Ala. 2002).

[578] Cases adopting the standard, such as Toti v. United States, 24 F3d 806 (6th Cir. 1994), are misguided, and the Service, which certainly knows better, was quite wrong to make the argument.

[579] The Seventh Circuit has considered the "almost metaphysical" question of whether a liability for trust fund taxes under Section 6672 is "stripped of its underlying character and transformed into a mere contractual obligation once it is incorporated in a confirmed plan of reorganization." In re Official Committee of Unsecured Creditors of White Farm Equipment Co., 943 F2d 752 (7th Cir. 1991). The court considered whether seventh priority should be granted to trust fund taxes in a serial Chapter 11 bankruptcy filing. A serial Chapter 11 filing is a liquidating Chapter 11 case that is commenced to deal with problems that arise in the course of consummation of a prior Chapter 11 plan. Fruehauf Corp. v. Jartran, Inc., 886 F2d 859, 869 n.12 (7th Cir. 1989). The creditors' committee argued that a confirmed plan of reorganization replaces all debts with contractual obligations. Thus, the debt to be discharged in the serial bankruptcy filing would be a mere

these nondischargeable tax claims is also nondischargeable,[580] and even postpetition interest has been found to be nondischargeable.[581] On the other hand, if the tax debt is not entitled to priority, it is dischargeable. If the tax debt is dischargeable, the related penalty is also dischargeable.[582] It also appears from Bankruptcy Code Section 523(a)(7) that even if the tax debt is not dischargeable, a related penalty is dischargeable as long as the transaction or event giving rise to the penalty occurred more than three years before the case was commenced.

For a flow chart summarizing for revenue officers when a tax liability has been discharged in different bankruptcy proceedings, see Figure 16.1.

---

general unsecured claim for breach of the original plan. The court held that the claim for trust fund taxes is not stripped of its underlying character and transformed into a mere contractual obligation, and therefore retains its priority.

[580] See, e.g., In re Larson, 862 F2d 112, 119 (7th Cir. 1988); Cinquegrani v. United States, 93-1 USTC ¶ 50,170 (DCND Ill. 1993).

[581] In re Burns, 887 F2d 1541 (11th Cir. 1989); In re Hanna, 872 F2d 829, 830–831 (8th Cir. 1989). Interest will run on a nondischarged debt after a bankruptcy proceeding. It is well established that an individual Chapter 11 debtor is personally liable for postpetition interest on nondischargeable taxes. In re Turgeon, 158 BR 328 (Bankr. WDNY 1993); In re Hubbard, 161 BR 173 (Bankr. ND Tex. 1993); In re Chaffee, 186 BR 783, 76 AFTR2d 95-5854 (Bankr. NDNY 1995). In re Kirnie, 93-2 USTC ¶ 50,434 (Bankr. ED Pa. 1993) (interest ran on undischarged secured tax claim between first Chapter 13 proceeding and commencement of second Chapter 13 proceeding; In re Bruning followed); IRS v. Cousins, 85 AFTR2d 2000-1379 (1st Cir. 2000) (Chapter 12 debtor liable for postpetition interest).

[582] In re Burns, 887 F2d 1541 (11th Cir. 1989) (where the events occurred more than three years before bankruptcy but taxes were not dischargeable because no return filed, penalty held dischargeable). Roberts v. United States, 906 F2d 1440 (10th Cir. 1990) (accord). In re Hopkins, 131 BR 308, 91-2 USTC ¶ 50,438 (Bankr. ND Tex. 1991); McKay v. United States, 957 F2d 689 (9th Cir. 1992) ("A penalty imposed on unpaid taxes accruing more than three years before the filing of the bankruptcy petition is dischargeable."). But see Cassidy v. Comm'r, 814 F2d 477, 480–481 (7th Cir. 1987); In re Carlton, 19 BR 73, 82-1 USTC ¶ 9400 (DNM 1982); In re Gerulis, 56 BR 283, 85-2 USTC ¶ 9753 (Bankr. D. Minn. 1985).

FIGURE 16.1
DISCHARGEABILITY OF TAXES IN BANKRUPTCY

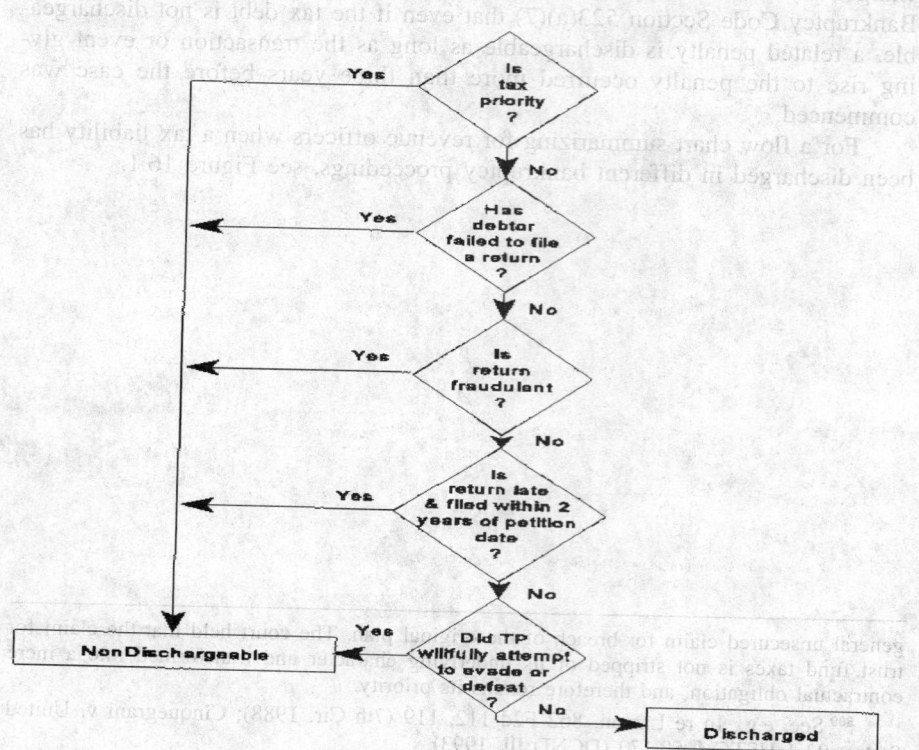

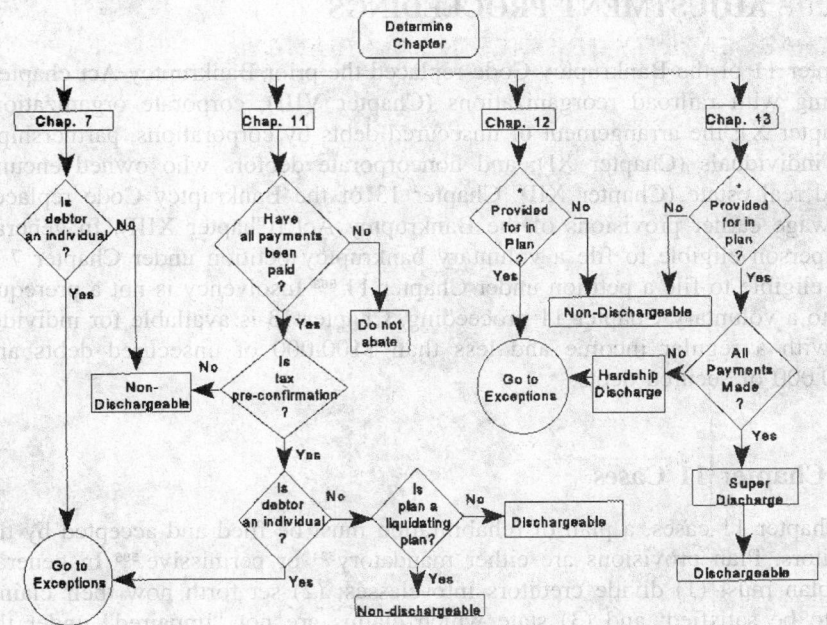

* "Provided for" is interpreted very liberally by the courts. If the IRS is listed as a creditor in the case, consult district counsel prior to denying discharge.

¶ 16.16 TAX CLAIMS IN REORGANIZATIONS AND ADJUSTMENT PROCEEDINGS

Chapter 11 of the Bankruptcy Code replaced the prior Bankruptcy Act chapters dealing with railroad reorganizations (Chapter VIII); corporate organizations (Chapter X); the arrangement of unsecured debts by corporations, partnerships, and individuals (Chapter XI); and noncorporate debtors who owned encumbered real estate (Chapter XII). Chapter 13 of the Bankruptcy Code replaced the wage earner provisions of the Bankruptcy Act (Chapter XIII). In general, any person eligible to file a voluntary bankruptcy petition under Chapter 7 is also eligible to file a petition under Chapter 11.[583] Insolvency is not a prerequisite to a voluntary Chapter 11 proceeding. Chapter 13 is available for individuals with a regular income and less than $100,000 of unsecured debts and $350,000 of secured debts.

[1] Chapter 11 Cases

In Chapter 11 cases, a plan of rehabilitation must be filed and accepted by the creditors. Plan provisions are either mandatory[584] or permissive.[585] In general, the plan must (1) divide creditors into classes; (2) set forth how their claims are to be satisfied; and (3) state which claims are not "impaired" under the plan. Creditors in each class must be treated the same way, unless the creditor consents to less favorable treatment. In addition, the plan must describe adequate means for its execution. A Chapter 11 plan may alter or impair the rights of unsecured creditors, secured creditors, and shareholders, but a plan will not be confirmed unless the Service accepts the plan or the plan makes the following adjustments:

---

[583] An involuntary reorganization proceeding may be commenced by creditors of the debtor. 11 USC § 303. Stockbrokers and commodities dealers are eligible for Chapter 7 but not for Chapter 11. Railroads are eligible for Chapter 11 but not for Chapter 7 liquidating bankruptcy. The Supreme Court has held that the Bankruptcy Code permits individual debtors not engaged in business to file for relief under Chapter 11. Toibb v. Radloff, 111 S. Ct. 2197 (1991).

[584] 11 USC § 1123(a).

[585] 11 USC § 1123(b).

- The plan provides that payment in cash of tax claims may be administrative expenses[586] or "gap" period expenses.[587] This payment must be made on the effective date of the plan.[588]
- The plan provides that payment in cash on the effective date of the plan of tax claims arising out of wages is entitled to third priority under Bankruptcy Code Section 507(a)(3). If the wage class has not accepted the plan (if the plan has been accepted by the wage class, the taxes must be paid in cash but payment may be deferred until the wages are paid).[589]
- The plan provides that payment may be deferred over a six-year period, beginning with the date the taxes were assessed, of unsecured prepetition taxes entitled to priority under Bankruptcy Code Section 507(a)(7).[590]

---

[586] 11 USC § 507(a)(1). In re Lunsford, 134 BR 46, 91-2 USTC ¶ 50,301 (Bankr. MD Fla. 1990) (the Federal Insurance Contributions Act (FICA) and Federal Unemployment Tax Act (FUTA) taxes, including interest, incurred by debtor in possession are administrative expenses). The timing of the liability for employment taxes is important for the debtor-in-possession. The debtor-in-possession is not personally liable for postpetition employment taxes because under 11 USC Section 1107, the debtor-in-possession has all the rights, powers, and duties of the trustee in bankruptcy, operating the estate in a fiduciary capacity. See Bellus v. United States, 125 F3d 821, 80 AFTR2d 97-6674 (9th Cir. 1997). For bankruptcy purposes, however, employment taxes are incurred on the date that the wages are paid, and so the person who may become the debtor-in-possession can be held personally liable for the employment taxes incurred before the Chapter 11 petition. 80 AFTR2d 97-6674 (9th Cir. 1997).

[587] 11 USC § 507(a)(2). The Service is not entitled to postpetition, preconfirmation interest (i.e., "gap period interest") on its secured prepetition tax claims if it fails to include the interest in its claim and to object to the debtor's confirmed plan, which makes no allowance for the payment of gap period interest. United States v. Brumback, 121 F3d 1383 (10th Cir. 1997).

[588] 11 USC § 1129(a)(9)(A).

[589] 11 USC § 1129(a)(9)(B).

[590] 11 USC § 1129(a)(9)(C). The amount of the deferred cash payments must equal the "value" of the allowed claim as of the effective date of the plan. Presumably, this requirement means that the present value of the claim may not be reduced by payment on a deferred or installment basis, so that some interest or other compensation is to be added. However, the terms of deferral and the steps the Service may take if there is a default are not settled by the provision. These matters are the subject of negotiation with the Service. On the payment of interest, see In re Camino Real Landscape Maintenance Contractors, Inc., 818 F2d 1503 (9th Cir. 1987) (Service not entitled to interest at the Section 6621 rate on tax payments deferred under 11 USC Section 1129(a)(9)(C); Bankruptcy Court must make a case-by-case determination of interest debtor would have to pay a creditor on loan of equivalent terms in open market); In re Burgess Wholesale Mfg. Opticians, Inc., 721 F2d 1146 (7th Cir. 1983) (Service is entitled to postpetition interest on an unsecured priority tax claim that was to be paid on an installment basis, where other creditors not paid in full). See also In re Moore, 25 BR 131, 83-1 USTC ¶ 9205 (ND Tx. 1982) (Service is entitled to interest on prepetition priority tax claim where claim is to be paid in in-

The plan of reorganization must be "fair and equitable" with respect to each class of creditors. If the Service does not accept the plan or claims its interest is impaired by the plan and the Service has a secured tax claim, Chapter 11 permits the Service to (1) retain the lien securing the claim, whether the property subject to the lien is retained by the debtor or transferred to another entity; (2) receive on account of the claim deferred cash payments totaling the allowed amount of the claim; or (3) realize the "indubitable equivalent of the claim." With respect to any unsecured nonpriority tax claims, the plan must provide either (1) that the Service receive property with a present value equal to the allowed amount of the claim or (2) that holders of any claims junior to the tax claim will not receive any property under the plan in payment of their junior claims.[591]

Once a plan of reorganization is confirmed, the plan binds the Service whether or not its tax claim is impaired or it has accepted the plan.[592] However, an individual in reorganization is not discharged from taxes that are not

---

stallments; "equivalent value" of Service claim on date of plan did not require use of interest rate of Section 6621, but the rate testified to by experts); In re Milspec, Inc., 82 BR 811, 88-1 USTC ¶ 9263 (BCED Va. 1988) (appropriate rate of interest should be determined by evidence pertaining to the prevailing market rates for a loan of comparable terms). Cf. Architectural Design, Inc. v. IRS, 59 BR 1019, 86-1 USTC ¶ 9409 (WD Va. 1986) (tax claim must be paid with interest at rate provided in Section 6621 for delinquent tax payments; Section 6621 was current market rate applicable to payments on tax liabilities).

The Service must timely file claims for scheduled taxes. Where a claim for corporate income taxes was not presented by the claim bar date, the claims were held untimely (not amendments of timely failed claims), and the claims were not scheduled for payment in the reorganization plan. International Horizons, Inc., 751 F2d 1213 (11th Cir. 1985). However, where 100 percent penalty assessments were made after confirmation of the reorganization plan, it was held that the claim was not discharged but that the plan remained intact with the addition of the subsequently assessed taxes. In re Gurwitch, 54 BR 927 (SD Fla. 1985), aff'd, 794 F2d 584 (11th Cir. 1986).

Plans providing for monthly payments plus a balloon payment have been approved. See, e.g., In re Volli Elec., Inc., 139 BR 451 (CD Ill. 1992); compare In re Mason & Dixon Lines, Inc., 71 BR 300 (Bankr. MDNC 1987) (interest-only plus balloon payment rejected); In re Mahoney, 80 BR 97 (Bankr. SD Cal.) (lump-sum payment in last month of plan rejected). See also IRS v. Taylor, 132 F3d 256 (5th Cir. 1998).

It has been held that even when the Service's tax claim is a secured one, the Bankruptcy Court in a reorganization may order the tax lien claim paid off over six years if the alternative is that the taxpayer will be forced into a liquidating bankruptcy. United States v. TM Bldg. Prods., Ltd., 82 AFTR2d 98-6902 (SD Fla. 1998).

[591] 11 USC § 1129(b)(2)(B). Therefore, if the government receives less than full payment of its claims, the plan may be confirmed if no class junior to the tax claim receives anything at all.

[592] 11 USC §1141(a). The plan is also binding on the Service with respect to collection procedures set forth in the plan. In Martin v. United States, 150 BR 43 (Bankr. SD Cal. 1993), the Service was enjoined from resorting to collection procedures outside the plan, even though the taxes were nondischargeable.

dischargeable in a liquidating bankruptcy under Chapter 7. Thus, an individual debtor remains liable for (1) priority tax claims; (2) taxes attributable to his failure to file, delinquent returns, or fraudulent returns; and (3) nonpecuniary loss penalties attributable to nondischageable taxes.[593] A different result occurs where a partnership or corporation is in reorganization. In reorganizations of these entities, only priority taxes must be provided for before the plan can be confirmed. When the Service's claim is for prepetition taxes that are nondischargeable, the Service is not required to file a claim in the taxpayer/debtor's reorganization bankruptcy proceeding to preserve its right to collect on the debt.[594] The Service may not file a proof of claim in the bankruptcy proceeding and still retain the right to payment of a nondischargeable debt, such as a trust fund recovery penalty. In such a case, the taxpayer/debtor can do one of two things to invoke the Bankruptcy Court's power to determine the amount of

---

[593] 11 USC § 1141(d)(2). Bankruptcy Code Section 1141(d)(2) provides that "(t)he confirmation of a plan does not discharge an individual debtor from any debt excepted from discharge under section 523 of this title." Accordingly, priority tax claims are not discharged when a plan is confirmed. If the Service is owed nondischargeable tax claims, therefore, even after confirmation of the plan, the Service is entitled to enforce the rights it has as they would exist outside bankruptcy. Grynberg v. United States (In re Grynberg), 986 F2d 367, 370 (10th Cir.), cert. denied, 114 S. Ct. 57 (1993). See also United States v. Heisson, 81 AFTR2d 98-306 (D. Mass. 1997) (postpetition-preconfirmation gap interest on a nondischargeable tax claim held subject to collection by the Service outside the reorganization plan; cases gathered and analyzed).

Because Bankruptcy Code Section 523(a)(1)(A) provides that described taxes are not dischargeable "whether or not a claim for such taxes was filed or allowed," it has been said that "Congress has determined that the Service may make a claim for taxes for a particular year in a bankruptcy proceeding, accept the judgment of the Bankruptcy Court, then audit and make additional claims for that same year, even though such conduct may seem inequitable or may impair the debtor's fresh start." DePaolo v. United States (In re DePaolo), 45 F3d 373, 75 AFTR2d 95-662 (10th Cir. 1995) (the Service filed proofs of claim, entered into a stipulation with the taxpayers/debtors regarding payment of the liability, and did not object to the confirmation of the plan; however, after the plan had been confirmed, the taxpayers/debtors had satisfied their obligations under the plan, and the court had closed the proceedings, the Service notified the debtors of its intention to audit one of the years covered by the plan).

However, the Bankruptcy Court has equitable jurisdiction to subordinate penalty claims to actual loss claims of other creditors in certain cases. In re Virtual Network Servs. Corp., 902 F2d 1246 (7th Cir. 1990); Schultz Broadway Inn v. United States, 912 F2d 230 (8th Cir. 1990). When interest accrues on a secured tax claim in the gap period between the date of the debtor's bankruptcy petition and the confirmation date of the debtor's plan of reorganization, it has been held that the interest is dischageable on the consummation of the plan because 11 USC Section 523(a)(7) exempts from discharge only allowed "unsecured claims" for taxes. United States v. Victor (In re Glenn Victor), 211 BR 62, 77 AFTR2d 96-2156 (D. Utah 1996).

[594] See 11 USC § 523(a)(1)(A) (priority taxes excepted from discharge "whether or not a claim for such tax was filed or allowed"). As any holder of a nondischargeable debt may do, the Service is free to pursue the taxpayer outside of bankruptcy. Grynberg v. United States (In re Grynberg), 986 F2d 367, 370 (10th Cir. 1993).

the tax liability: (1) file a motion under Bankruptcy Code Section 505 or (2) file a proof of claim on behalf of the Service and object to it.[595] However, "the confirmation of a plan does not itself invoke the tax determination process."[596]

The Bankruptcy Code grants Bankruptcy Courts residual authority to approve reorganization plans including "any…appropriate provision not inconsistent with the Bankruptcy Code." Bankruptcy Code Section 105 allows Bankruptcy Courts to "issue any order, process or judgment that is necessary or appropriate to carry out the provisions of the Bankruptcy Code." These broad grants of jurisdiction permitted the U.S. Supreme Court, in *United States v. Energy Resources Co.*,[597] to say that even if the payments are considered involuntary and, therefore, not allocable according to the taxpayer's direction, the Bankruptcy Court has the authority to order the Service to apply payments to trust fund liabilities as long as it has determined that this designation is necessary to the success of the reorganization. The possibility that the nontrust fund portion of the taxes might not be paid if the reorganization failed did not limit the Bankruptcy Court's authority even if the trust fund portion of the tax were satisfied, thereby eliminating the use of Section 6672 as a device to collect the trust fund taxes from responsible officers. Before *Energy Resources Co.*, courts had held that Bankruptcy Courts did not have jurisdiction to enjoin the Service from collecting from nondebtors, even when the Bankruptcy Court had determined that the action was necessary for the success of the reorganization.[598] As part of the reorganization plan, assets may be sold and a trustee may be appointed to liquidate and distribute the assets to the creditors of the estate. A trustee appointed to liquidate and distribute property as part of a Chapter 11 bankruptcy plan must file income tax returns and pay income tax.[599] Also, at least where there was no showing that an allocation to the trust

---

[595] See IRS v. Taylor, 132 F3d 256 (5th Cir. 1998) (allowing the Service to collect Section 6672 penalty assessed after Chapter 11 plan was confirmed).

[596] See IRS v. Taylor, 132 F3d 256 (5th Cir. 1998). The court cited with approval United States v. Gurwitch, 794 F2d 584 (11th Cir. 1986).

[597] United States v. Energy Resources Co., 495 US 545 (1990). For further discussion of Bankruptcy Court jurisdiction, see supra ¶ 16.12[1][a]. It has been held that *Energy Resources* applies to Chapter 11 reorganizations but not to Chapter 7 liquidating bankruptcies. United States v. Kare Kemical, Inc., 935 F2d 243 (11th Cir. 1991); see also Jehan-Das, Inc. v. United States, 925 F2d 237 (8th Cir. 1991) (payments of taxes in liquidating bankruptcy were held to be involuntary payments because debtor had "no choice but to pay the funds to the IRS"). *Energy Resources* has been said not to entitle the debtor in a reorganization to decide what portions of a tax liability are secured and unsecured. In re Divine, 127 BR 625, 91-1 USTC ¶ 50,273 (Bankr. D. Minn. 1991).

[598] See cases gathered in United States v. Energy Resources, Inc., 495 US 545 (1990).

[599] Holywell Corp. v. Smith, 112 S. Ct. 1021 (1992). This requirement derives from Section 6012(b)(3), which requires "a receiver, trustee in a case under title 11 of the United States Code, or assignee" to file an income tax return. The trustee was held by the Supreme Court in *Holywell Corp.* to be an "assignee" of the corporate debtors under Sec-

fund portion of the liability was needed for a reorganization or bankruptcy purpose, the Bankruptcy Court's jurisdiction has been held not to be extended by *Energy Resources* to a Chapter 7 bankruptcy.[600]

[2] Chapter 13 Cases

Chapter 13 of the Bankruptcy Code is entitled "Adjustment of Debts of an Individual With Regular Income" and is divided into two subchapters: "Officers, Administration, and the Estate,"[601] and "The Plan."[602] When an individual debtor is insolvent, the debtor has alternative courses of action under Chapters 7 and 13. A proceeding under Chapter 7 is a liquidation proceeding; the debtor's nonexempt assets will be sold, dividends may be distributed to creditors, and a discharge relieves the debtor of further liability. Chapter 13 establishes a reorganization proceeding for individuals with regular income, which permits them to retain their assets and pay creditors out of postpetition income over a three- or five-year period. Not all individual debtors are eligible for a reorganization under Chapter 13. Under 11 USC Section 109(e), "[o]nly an individual with regular income that owes on the date of the filing of the petition, noncontingent, liquidated, unsecured debts of less $250,000 and noncontingent, liquidated, secured debts of less than $750,000" is eligible for a reorganization under Chapter 13. An "individual with regular income" means an "individual whose income is sufficiently stable and regular to enable such individual to make payments under a plan under [Chapter 13], other than a stock or commodity broker."[603] Because Chapter 13 is limited to individuals, a Chapter 13 reorganization is not available to partnerships, corporations, and estates.

An individual debtor's eligibility for Chapter 13 relief turns on the amounts of the individual's debts, unsecured debts of no more than $250,000, and secured debts of no more than $750,000. The Bankruptcy Code defines "debt" as "liability on a claim,"[604] and defines "claim" as a "right to payment,

---

tion 6012(b)(3) because, as provided in the statute, "all" or "substantially all" of the property of the corporate debtors had been transferred to the trustee.

[600] United States v. Pepperman, 976 F2d 123 (3d Cir. 1992) (both corporate employer and responsible officer filed Chapter 7 bankruptcy petitions). Following *Energy Resources*, the Ninth Circuit approved a Bankruptcy Court's order allocating payments in Chapter 11 liquidating plan of reorganization to the trust fund portion of the tax, even when the order would not result in full payment to the Service over the six years provided in Bankruptcy Code Section 1129, and also required the Service to reallocate payments from the secured portion of its claim to the unsecured priority portion. IRS v. Creditor's Committee, 10 F3d 1478 (9th Cir. 1993).

[601] 11 USC §§ 1301–1307.

[602] 11 USC §§ 1321–1330.

[603] 11 USC § 101(30).

[604] 11 USC § 101(12).

whether or not such right is reduced to judgment, liquidated, unliquidated, fixed, contingent, matured, unmatured, disputed, undisputed, legal, equitable, secured, or unsecured."605 When the definitional and eligibility provisions are read together, to be eligible for Chapter 13 relief, only "noncontingent" and "liquidated" rights to payment are considered for purposes of the dollar limitations, terms the Bankruptcy Code does not define. A majority of courts hold that simply because a debt is disputed does not mean that it is contingent and unliquidated, and so disputed debts, which are noncontingent and liquidated, count toward the debt limitation for Chapter 13 eligibility.606 The rationale for this rule is that debtors could circumvent the debt limitation if all they needed to do was "dispute" unsecured claims. Also, a debt is not contingent if it meets the "all events" test; that is, a claim is not contingent if all events giving rise to the liability occurred before the bankruptcy petition. In a tax setting, the tax debt does not become contingent, even when the taxpayer/debtor disputes the amount of the assessment. Assessment is not necessary for a tax debt to be noncontingent because a taxpayer's duty to pay taxes "derives from statute and arises upon his nonpayment of the taxes when due...[, and] is not contingent on any extrinsic event."607 A tax debt has been held to be liquidated when the liability for the tax has been fixed or established by the Service's assessment, as reflected in its Certificate of Assessment.608 Moreover, the amount of the tax liability may be ascertainable from filed tax returns so that the dispute does not make the tax debt either contingent or unliquidated.609 In other words, "where an unsecured claim, though disputed, is both noncontingent and liquidated, the debt that is coextensive with that claim must be included in the calculation that determines the debtor's Chapter 13 eligibility."610

The Chapter 13 debtor begins the case by filing the following:

- A petition;
- A statement listing the debtor's secured and unsecured creditors and their addresses; and

---

605 11 USC § 101(5)(A).

606 Barcal v. Laughlin (In re Barcal), 80 AFTR2d 97-7729 (Bankr. App. Panel, 8th Cir. 1997) (gathering cases).

607 Mazzeo v. United States, 131 F3d 295 (2d Cir. 1997).

608 Barcal v. Laughlin (In re Barcal), 80 AFTR2d 97-7729 (Bankr. App. Panel, 8th Cir. 1997).

609 A debtor's tax debt need not be assessed, however. It has been held that the debtor's debt for unpaid taxes became noncontingent when she filed her tax returns and failed to pay the full amount of the tax reported as due, and the Service sent a notice of deficiency. Geary v. United States, 91 AFTR2d 2003-498 (9th Cir. 2003) ("the mere fact that the government had not secured judgment on its claim for [a] tax deficiency by the time of filing [its claim] does not render such claim contingent").

610 Mazzeo v. United States, 131 F3d 295 (2d Cir. 1997).

> • Any other information that will enable the trustee and the Bankruptcy Court to decide whether to conform the plan the debtor must file.[611]

It is important for a creditor, such as the Service, to be included on the list the debtor is required to file. The clerk of the court will give notice of the meeting of creditors only to those creditors who are on the list. It is necessary for an unsecured creditor to file a proof of claim in order for that claim to be allowed.[612] The creditor is required to file a proof of claim within ninety days after the first date set for the meeting of creditors; therefore, the creditor who does not receive notice of the creditor's meeting may not file a proof of claim.[613] However, it is also important for the debtor to include a creditor, such as the Service, on the list of creditors. If the debtor fails to include a creditor on the list of creditors and the clerk does not give notice to the creditor, the creditor's debt may not be discharged.[614] Where a creditor receives notice, and yet fails to file a proof of claim, the creditor's claim may be discharged.[615]

Because the debtor's statement of financial affairs and schedules are filed at the same time as his or her petition, it may not include postpetition creditors. Bankruptcy Code Section 1305(a) provides that a proof of claim may be filed against the debtor for taxes that become payable while the case is pending. It appears, therefore, that postpetition taxes may be included in a plan and discharged on its completion. A claim for taxes is determined under Bankruptcy Code Section 502, dealing with the allowance of proofs of claim. The amount of the claim is determined as of the date the claim arises, but will be allowed under Bankruptcy Code Section 502, as though it arose before the petition was filed.[616] The Service may file a proof of claim for prepetition taxes where the amount of the tax due is determined after the petition date.[617]

On the filing of a petition, all property of the debtor and all property the debtor acquires, as well as amounts the debtor earns after the commencement of the case, become property of the estate, subject to the order of the Bankruptcy Court and the plan.[618] However, the debtor remains in possession of all property of the estate.[619] Moreover, although a trustee performs certain duties, including advising the debtor and the Bankruptcy Court at the time of the con-

---

[611] Bankruptcy Rules 1002, 1007(a)(1), and 1007(b)(1).

[612] Bankruptcy Rule 3002(a).

[613] Bankruptcy Rule 3002(a); 11 USC § 341(a).

[614] Bankruptcy Rule 2002.

[615] See Reliable Elec. Co. v. Olson Constr. Co., 726 F2d 620 (10th Cir. 1984).

[616] 11 USC § 1305(b).

[617] Where a tax return for a prepetition year is audited after the petition, the tax liability is considered a prepetition liability. In re Easton, 59 BR 714 (Bankr. CD Ill. 1986).

[618] 11 USC § 1306(a).

[619] 11 USC § 1306(b).

firmation hearing[620] and receiving payments prior to the confirmation of the plan,[621] the debtor has the rights and powers of a trustee in dealing with the property of the estate.[622] At any time after a Chapter 13 petition is filed, the debtor may request that it be dismissed.[623] The debtor may also request that the case be converted to a liquidating bankruptcy.[624] If the debtor requests that the Chapter 13 case be dismissed, any payment the debtor may have made to the trustee is subject to levy by the Service.[625] A creditor may also request that the case be converted to a liquidating bankruptcy under Chapter 7 if the debtor fails to promptly act in accordance with the requirements of Chapter 13 (e.g., failing to make payments within thirty days after the plan is filed).[626]

Within fifteen days after the petition is filed, the debtor must file a plan.[627] The plan must contain certain specified provisions (mandatory provisions),[628] such as (1) the submission of sufficient future earnings or future income to the supervision and control of a trustee to ensure that it will be performed; (2) payment in full of priority claims, unless the secured claimant agrees otherwise; and (3) the same treatment for each claim within a particular class. The plan must also provide for payments over three years or, if the court approves, up to five years.[629] The requirement that the debtor's plan provide for "full payment" in deferred cash payments of priority claims applies to tax claims. Tax claims are priority claims and must be paid in full in order for the plan to be confirmed. However, the debtor may wish to pay the tax claim over the period of the plan.[630] If the Service claim is unsecured, under the plan, the tax claim will be paid in full, but without interest.[631] If the tax claim is secured, however, the amount of the claim will be paid in full with interest.[632] Where a plan refers to unsecured tax claims but does not provide for their payment, the Service must file a timely proof of claim and contest the plan treat-

---

[620] 11 USC § 1302(b).

[621] 11 USC § 1326(a).

[622] 11 USC § 1303.

[623] 11 USC § 1307(a).

[624] 11 USC § 1307(b).

[625] See Beam v. IRS (In re Beam), 192 F3d 941 (9th Cir. 1999).

[626] 11 USC § 1307(c).

[627] 11 USC § 1321.

[628] 11 USC § 1322(a).

[629] 11 USC § 1322(c).

[630] Where the debtor provides for the Service claim as a secured or unsecured claim in the plan but the debtor fails to make payments to the Service because it failed to file a timely proof of claim, the debtor was discharged on the completion of the plan. See In re Richards, 50 BR 339 (ED Tenn. 1985); accord In re Goodwin, 58 BR 75 (Bankr. D. Me. 1986).

[631] 11 USC § 1322(a)(2).

[632] 11 USC § 1325(a)(5)(B)(ii).

ment. However, the debtor must give the Service notice, and deceptive information is no notice at all.[633] Where the debtor misrepresents a secured tax lien as an unsecured tax claim, even if the plan is confirmed without objection, the debtor's completion of payments under the plan will not extinguish liens on the debtor/taxpayer's property, because the debtor did not "provide for" the payment of the secured claim.[634] Assuming the nature of the claim is not misrepresented, however, tax claims may be discharged, even if the type of tax involved would not be dischargeable in liquidating bankruptcy.[635] Also, the "full payment" rule does not require that a priority tax claim be paid with interest.[636] Even when interest is provided for in a plan, it may not be the annual rate provided in Section 6621.[637]

In addition, the plan may contain certain other provisions (permissive provisions).[638] Among these permissive provisions, the plan may designate a class or classes of unsecured creditors, provided that the plan does "not discriminate unfairly against any class so designated."[639] The plan may also modify (or leave unaffected) the rights of secured creditors, other than rights involving a claim secured only by a security interest in real property that is the debtor's principal residence. Another permissive provision can provide for the curing or waiver of any default. Also, payments to unsecured creditors may be made at the same time as payments to secured creditors, so that payments under the plan may not be made first to secured creditors. A Chapter 13 plan is permitted to provide for a cure of defaults on any claim, even if the final payment of the claim is due after the date on which the final payment under the plan is due. However, the amount necessary to cure the default will be determined in accordance with the underlying agreement and applicable nonbankruptcy law.

Chapter 13 procedures provide for a creditors' meeting, but creditors do not approve the debtor's plan.[640] After the plan is filed, a creditor may file an objection to the plan.[641] At the confirmation hearing, creditors may file objec-

---

[633] See Deutchman v. Internal Revenue (In re Deutchman), 192 F3d 457 (4th Cir. 1999); Cen-Pen Corp. v. Hanson, 58 F3d 89, 94 (4th Cir. 1995).

[634] Deutchman v. Internal Revenue (In re Deutchman), 192 F3d 457 (4th Cir. 1999).

[635] In re Tomlin, 102 BR 790, 89-2 USTC ¶ 9459 (ED Wash. 1989), aff'd, 907 F2d 114 (9th Cir. 1990); In re Hackney, 20 BR 158, 82-2 USTC ¶ 9421 (D. Id. 1982) (but citing two bankruptcy cases to the contrary).

[636] In re Bruce Martin Smith, 77 AFTR2d 96-1844 (Bankr. MD Fla. 1996).

[637] See, e.g., In re Fisher, 29 BR 542, 83-1 USTC ¶ 9351 (Bankr. D. Kan. 1983) (the appropriate rate in pending unconfirmed and future Chapter 13 proceedings on secured tax claims is the equivalent coupon rate in the sale of fifty-two-week Treasury bills sold every four weeks, plus a 1 percent risk factor; conflicting cases gathered).

[638] 11 USC § 1322(b).

[639] 11 USC § 1322(b)(1).

[640] 11 USC §§ 1324, 1325; Bankruptcy Rule 3015(b).

[641] Bankruptcy Rule 3015(f).

tions, but they do not vote; the Bankruptcy Court will determine whether the plan should be confirmed.[642] The Bankruptcy Court must confirm the plan if the plan meets six requirements.[643] The first two requirements simply stipulate that the plan must comply with the provisions of Chapter 31 and that all required fees are paid. The third requirement is that the debtor must have proposed the plan in good faith and not for any purpose forbidden by law.[644] The fourth requirement includes a "best interests of creditors" test, under which the value of property to be distributed on each unsecured claim on the effective date of the plan must not be less than the amount that would be paid to the claimant in a hypothetical liquidating bankruptcy.[645] In applying this test, it has been held that payment of interest on a tax claim is not required unless all unsecured claims would be paid in full if the estate were liquidated under Chapter 13.[646] A fifth requirement deals with secured claims; in substance it requires that each secured creditor agrees to the plan, the secured creditor is paid the full amount of the secured claim, or the debtor surrenders to the secured claimant the security or collateral for the claim.[647] In determining the value of a secured tax claim in property that will not be sold, the proper measure of the value of the interest is the fair market value of the property, and the debtor is not permitted to deduct hypothetical selling costs of the property.[648] The sixth and final requirement is that the debtor must be able to make all payments under the plan and comply with the plan.[649]

Once a plan is confirmed, the provisions of the plan bind the debtor and each creditor, whether the creditor has objected to the plan, or accepted or rejected it.[650] Unless the plan or court order provides otherwise, confirmation of the plan vests all the property of the estate in the debtor.[651] Moreover, unless the plan or court order provides otherwise, the property vesting in the debtor on confirmation of the plan is free and clear of any claim or interest of any

---

[642] 11 USC § 1324.

[643] 11 USC §§ 1325(a)(1)–1325(a)(6).

[644] 11 USC § 1325(a)(3).

[645] 11 USC § 1325(a)(4).

[646] In re Bruce Martin Smith, 77 AFTR2d 96-1844 (Bankr. MD Fla. 1996).

[647] 11 USC § 1325(a)(5).

[648] See In re Winthrop Old Farms Nurseries, 50 F3d 72, 74 (1st Cir. 1995); In re Rash, 31 F3d 325, 329 (5th Cir. 1994); Lancaster v. United States, 1996 Bankr. LEXIS 554 (Bankr. ND Ala. 1996).

[649] 11 USC § 1325(a)(6).

[650] 11 USC § 1327(a).

[651] 11 USC § 1327(b). Since the plan controls, the failure to deal with the effect of a tax lien in the plan or prepetition taxes can have adverse consequences to the debtor (e.g., a tax lien can attach to property unless the plan provides otherwise). See United States v. Richman, 80 AFTR2d 97-6330 (10th Cir. 1997).

creditor provided for in the plan.[652] In tax cases, some courts hold that the controlling status of the plan means that once the plan is confirmed, the Service may not set off a refund owed to a taxpayer/debtor if it has not objected to the plan.[653] Other courts have upheld the Service's right of setoff because under Bankruptcy Code Section 553(a), its preexisting right of setoff is preserved, despite confirmation or discharge.[654]

The debtor must begin making payments under the plan within thirty days after the plan is filed, even if the plan is not yet confirmed.[655] As soon as the debtor makes all payments due under the plan, the court will grant the debtor's discharge of all debts provided for by the plan or disallowed.[656] Even tax-related debts arising from tax fraud have been held to be dischargeable under Chapter 13.[657] Chapter 13 contains no good faith/fraud requirement, nor any good faith requirement. Nevertheless, a Chapter 13 petition may be dismissed "for cause," and this provision gives jurisdiction to a Bankruptcy Court to dismiss a Chapter 13 petition in an abusive situation.[658] Moreover, a creditor in a Chapter 13 case, such as the Service, may seek the conversion of a Chapter 13 case to Chapter 7 liquidating bankruptcy (where the fraud-related taxes will not be dischargeable), or even the dismissal of the case on the ground that the Chapter 13 debtor has not acted in "good faith," a term that has been said to be determinable on a case-by-case basis because good faith is a term "incapable of precise interpretation."[659] The effect of discharge is the same as if the debtor had been discharged in a liquidating bankruptcy; that is, any creditor is enjoined from collecting its debt after the discharge.[660] If a creditor disregards the discharge injunction, the Bankruptcy Court may hold the creditor, including the Service, in contempt and impose monetary sanctions.[661]

---

[652] 11 USC § 1327(c).

[653] United States v. Norton (In re Norton), 717 F2d 767, 774 (3d Cir. 1983); In re Continental Airlines, 134 F3d 536, 542 (3d Cir. 1998); United States v. Reynolds, 764 F2d 1004 (4th Cir. 1985); In re Johnson, 136 BR 306, 92-1 USTC ¶ 50,001 (Bankr. MD Ga. 1991).

[654] See In re DeLaurentiis Entertainment Group, Inc., 963 F2d 1269, 1276–1277 (9th Cir. 1992); In re Davidovich, 901 F2d 1533, 1539 (10th Cir. 1990); United States v. Munson, 85 AFTR2d 2000-1912 (CD Ill. 2000) (analyzing Seventh Circuit law and finding that if the Service's right of setoff were cut off, the debtor would reap a windfall).

[655] 11 USC § 1326(a)(1).

[656] 11 USC § 1328(a).

[657] In re Ernest Lilley, Jr., 78 AFTR2d 96-5884 (3d Cir. 1996).

[658] See In re Ernest Lilley, Jr., 78 AFTR2d 96-5884 (3d Cir. 1996).

[659] In re Love, 957 F2d 1350, 1355 (7th Cir. 1992) (setting out a list of nonexclusive factors).

[660] 11 USC § 524.

[661] See Hardy v. United States, 97 F3d 1384 (11th Cir. 1996).

CHAPTER 17

Collection From Nontaxpayers—Transferee Liability

B. Collection of Taxes From Withholding Agents

A. COLLECTION OF TAXES FROM TRANSFEREES

¶ 17.01 TRANSFEREE LIABILITY IN GENERAL

Faced with the prospect of having the Internal Revenue Service (the Service) seize their property to collect their unpaid tax obligations, some taxpayers transfer their property to others, for little or no money or money's worth with the understanding that the taxpayers will continue to be able to exercise control over or have the benefit of the transferred property. By transferring their property to others, these taxpayers deplete property that would have been available for tax collection, and hinder the Service's ability to collect a tax debt. Taxpayers who attempt to put their property beyond the reach of the Service, act in the same way as other nontax debtors who attempt to defraud, hinder, or delay the collection efforts of their creditors, and the Service's ability to collect its tax debt is adversely affected in the same way private creditors are when their debtors transfer property to avoid collection. State fraudulent conveyance laws and other statutes, both state and federal, protect creditors from debtors that engage in these tactics. As a creditor, the Service also uses these state and federal debtor/creditor laws to collect tax debts. Although states have adopted such substantive laws as fraudulent conveyance statutes to protect creditors, in tax law, "transferee liability" is primarily a set of procedures, administrative and judicial, governing the manner in which the Service may proceed directly against the transferee of property to collect the tax owed by the transferor, and neither creates nor defines a body of substantive transferee liability law.

What is now Section 6901 was first enacted in 1926 to expedite the Service's collection of the taxpayer's tax from the transferee who was liable for unpaid tax under various state laws.[1] At the time the predecessor of Section 6901 was enacted, law and equity were separate procedures. A creditor could not join in a single action its claim at law against the debtor on the debt and an action in equity to set aside the debtor's transfer of property that hindered collection.[2] When there was a fraudulent conveyance, the common-law procedure was cumbersome and time-consuming. If the transferor was alive or, in the case of a corporation still in existence, the Service was first required to institute an action against the debtor for the unpaid taxes, obtain a judgment for the unpaid taxes that were returned unsatisfied, and then file a bill in equity to

---

[1] Revenue Act of 1926, § 280(a)(1). For legislative history, see S. Rep. No. 52, 69th Cong., 1st Sess. 28–30 (1925); HR Rep. No. 356, 69th Cong., 2d Sess. 42–45 (1926).

[2] The Federal Rules of Civil Procedure "govern the procedure in the United States district courts in all suits of a civil nature whether cognizable as cases at law or in equity" and permit a creditor suing in federal court to join both an action at law and one in equity. Fed. R. Civ. P. 18(a).

set aside the fraudulent conveyance that prevented collection from the taxpayer.[3] The justification for requiring a creditor, such as the Service, to institute an action at law before invoking the procedures of a court of equity to set aside the transfer was that because a jury trial was not available in a court of equity, a proceeding in equity to set aside the transfer would deprive the debtor the right to a trial by jury on the legal claim against the debtor. Until the Service-as-creditor had exhausted its remedy at law by obtaining a judgment for the tax and had taken out an execution on the judgment that was returned unsatisfied, it had not shown a prerequisite to equity jurisdiction: that its remedy at law had been inadequate.[4] Although under state common law the Service had a number of alternatives as a creditor, most states required a judgment against the debtor before the Service-as-creditor could proceed against the transferee under state law.

Under the predecessor of Section 6901, court proceedings could only be brought in a state or federal court, and the Board of Tax Appeals had no jurisdiction to review the Service's determination of transferee liability. In enacting the predecessor of Section 6901, the legislative purpose was not to create substantive rights the Service might enforce or to change the extent of transferee liability under the existing law; rather, it was intended to streamline enforcement of transferee liability, existing under other law, by applying to the transferee the same procedures used to determine and collect the tax deficiency of the transferor.

The original statutory purpose of permitting the enforcement of transferee liability in the Tax Court can be seen in the statutory language of the current Section 6901, which requires that transferee liability must be "assessed, paid, and collected in the same manner and subject to the same provisions and limitations" as the tax liability of the transferor.[5] When the Service wishes to proceed directly against the transferee to assess and collect the taxpayer/transferor's unpaid income, estate tax, or gift tax liability, it must use the same deficiency procedures it is required to use to collect a deficiency in those taxes from the delinquent taxpayer. The Service must send the transferee a notice of transferee liability (the equivalent of a notice of deficiency) asserting the transferee's liability at law or in equity, and give the transferee the option of petitioning for prepayment Tax Court review of the Service's determination or of paying the tax after assessment and filing a suit for refund in an appropriate federal district court of the Court of Federal Claims. The transferee has the

---

[3] According to the Senate Report, the government could proceed in equity by suit against the transferee if the transferor no longer existed (i.e., in the case of a dissolved corporation, or in the case of a deceased individual). S. Rep. No. 52, 69th Cong., 1st Sess. 28–30 (1925). See also Phillips v. Comm'r, 283 US 589, 592 n.2 (1931).

[4] 6A C. Wright, A. Miller & M. Kane, Federal Practice and Procedure; Civil 2d § 1590 (2d ed. 1990).

[5] IRC § 6901(a).

same rights as the taxpayer/transferor to contest liability for the tax, as well as the transferee's liability as a transferee. If the transferee chooses to file a petition for review in the Tax Court, and the Tax Court enters a final adverse decision against the transferee, the Service assesses and collects the tax assessment using the same administrative procedures it would use to collect the tax from the taxpayer transferor. Section 6901 thus "treats the transferee as the taxpayer; [and] so the transferee may contest the transferor's liability either in Tax Court or in a refund suit."[6]

The substantive transferee liability the statute refers to is "the liability at law or in equity" of a transferee of property of a taxpayer in the case of an income tax, a decedent in the case of an estate tax, and a donee in the case of a gift tax.[7] In addition to the transferee's liability at law and equity under state law for payment of the taxpayer/transferor's income, estate, or gift tax debt, transferee liability for purposes of Section 6901 also includes (1) the liability of a fiduciary under 31 USC § 3713 for making transfers from an insolvent estate or debtor before paying a tax debt[8] and (2) the liability of the distributee of an estate or donee under Section 6324 of the Internal Revenue Code (the Code).[9] In addition, when taxes other than income, estate, or gift taxes are involved, transferee liability also includes the liability at law or in equity of a transferee liable for an internal revenue tax if the liability "arises on the liquidation of a partnership or corporation, or on a reorganization within the meaning of Section 368(a)."[10] Whatever the body of law referred to, the purpose is to protect the Service as a creditor from a reduction in the taxpayer's estate caused by a transfer that prevents the collection of tax owed by the taxpayer.

A transferee's liability "at law or in equity" is not determined under Section 6901, but under either state law, the Code, or some other federal law. For state law purposes, the Service is a creditor for the amount of the tax claim and has all the rights a private creditor has under state law when a debtor transfers property in fraud of creditors.[11] The state laws the Service-as-creditor uses to collect a claim for taxes are (1) the state's law of fraudulent conveyances, such as its version of the Uniform Fraudulent Transfer Act (UFTA) or Uniform Fraudulent Conveyance Act (UFCA); (2) state bulk sales acts, that are included in Article 6 (Bulk Transfers) of the state version of the Uniform Commercial Code (UCC); (3) corporation laws dealing with the effect of

---

[6] See United States v. Williams, 514 US 527, 539 (1995).

[7] IRC § 6901(a)(1)(A).

[8] IRC § 6901(a)(1)(B).

[9] IRC § 6901(h).

[10] IRC § 6901(a)(2).

[11] In fact, once tax has been assessed, the Service is the equivalent of a judgment creditor because the assessment "is given the force of a judgment." See Bull v. United States, 295 US 258, 260 (1934). See Chapter 14.

mergers, consolidations, or liquidations on unpaid corporate debts, such as the trust fund doctrine; and (4) the rights of creditors in life insurance benefits.

Transferees and fiduciaries may become personally liable for any unpaid estate and gift tax the taxpayer may owe under other provisions of the Code and other federal laws. Section 6901 expressly provides that the liability of a fiduciary, who becomes personally liable under 31 USC § 3713 for paying a debt of an insolvent estate or person before paying a tax claim, is to be assessed, paid, and collected in the same manner as the taxes for which the liability was incurred.[12] Similarly, 31 USC § 3713. Section 6901 defines a "transferee" to include a donee, heir, devisee, and any other person who is personally liable if an estate tax is not paid when due under Section 6324 of the Code, which makes transferees of an estate personally liable for any unpaid estate tax of the decedent to the extent of the value of the property they receive from the estate or the donor.[13]

The liability of the transferee of a taxpayer's property at equity, which is assessed, paid, and collected under Section 6901, is often the liability of the transferee under state fraudulent conveyance law. It is worth noting, however, that transferee liability procedures are not exclusive. They do not replace the older judicial remedies of instituting proceedings to collect a corporate tax from its shareholders or to set aside a fraudulent conveyance.[14] Similarly, the Service may institute an action to collect a fiduciary's liability under 31 USC § 3713. The transferee may also be held liable for the debts of the debtor under the Bankruptcy Code, which has its own fraudulent conveyance statute,[15] even if the issue of liability is decided in the bankruptcy court, not the Tax Court, under Section 6901.

[1] Statutory Framework

Section 6901 is found in Chapter 71 of the Code, Transferees and Fiduciaries, and simply entitled, "Transferred Assets." Section 6901 and related transferee and fiduciary provisions set out the following definitions and procedures for enforcing transferee liability.

---

[12] Fiduciary liability under 31 USC § 3713 is described at ¶ 16.07.

[13] The special lien for estate and gift taxes of Section 6324 is discussed at ¶ 14.18.

[14] This has long been the case after the enactment of the transferee liability statute. See, e.g., Leighton v. United States, 289 US 506 (1933) (without an assessment against the corporation, the government brought an equity action against corporate shareholders to account for corporate property distributed to them in order that they might be applied to taxes due from their corporation); United States v. Russell, 461 F2d 605 (10th Cir. 1972).

[15] 11 USC § 548.

1. *Definition of "transferee."* For purposes of transferee liability procedures, the term "transferee" is any transferee of property who is liable at law or in equity for the taxpayer's income, estate, or gift tax.[16] A transferee also includes a donee, heir, legatee, devisee, and distributee, and for estate taxes, also includes any person Section 6324(a)(2) makes personally liable for unpaid estate tax.[17] Although a fiduciary's liability under 31 USC § 3713 may be collected under Section 6901, the liability, including the status of the person as a fiduciary, is determined under 31 USC § 3713, and is not defined in Section 6901.[18] When a tax other than an income tax is involved, a "transferee" is any transferee of property who is liable at law or in equity on the liquidation of a partnership or corporation, or a reorganization described in Section 368(a).[19]

2. *Method of collection.* The amounts of liabilities for income, estate, or gift tax of a transferee of property at law or in equity must be assessed, paid, and collected in the same manner and subject to the same provisions and limitations as the tax due from the transferor.[20] The same method of collection applies to the liability of (1) a fiduciary under 31 USC § 3713(b) for an income tax liability of the taxpayer, estate tax of an estate, or gift tax of a donor, or (2) transferee at law or in equity for a tax other than an income, estate, or gift tax, but only if the liability for the other tax arises on the liquidation of a partnership or a corporation, or in a reorganization described in Section 368(a). Thus, a notice of liability must be sent to the transferee offering the transferee the opportunity to file a petition in the Tax Court to obtain prepayment judicial review of the Service's determination of transferee liability, or to pay the amount of the assessment of the transferee liability and sue for refund. For a tax other than an income, estate, or gift tax, the transferee must be given notice of the transferee's right to challenge the transferee by paying a divisible portion of the tax, and suing for refund in a federal district court or the Court of Federal Claims.

3. *Amount of liability.* The liability of a transferee for the tax liability of the transferor of property may be either for the amount of tax shown on the transferor's return or for the amount of any deficiency or underpayment.[21]

4. *Period of limitations—transferees.* The period for making an assessment of transferee liability against an initial transferee's liability is one year longer than the period within which the Service must make an assessment of income, estate, or gift tax against the taxpayer/transferor. This means that, in general, the Service must make an assessment against the initial transferee

---

[16] IRC § 6901(a)(1)(A).

[17] IRC § 6901(h).

[18] IRC § 6901(a)(1)(B).

[19] IRC § 6901(a)(2).

[20] IRC § 6901(a).

[21] IRC § 6901(b).

within one year after the statute of limitations for assessment against the tax-payer/transferor expires.[22] For example, if *A*, an individual, timely files an income tax return for 1997, and the statute of limitations for assessment against *A* under Section 6501 is not extended for any reason, the statute of limitations on assessment against *A* expires April 15, 2001. The Service must make its assessment of transferee liability against an initial transferee (or send a notice of transferee liability) no later than April 15, 2002. Similarly, if the taxpayer's transferee has transferred the taxpayer's property to another person, the Service must assess the transferee liability of the transferee of a transferee within one year after the statute has expired against the preceding transferee. Using the example, this means that the assessment against the transferee of the transferee must be made no later than April 15, 2003. Section 6901 does not extend the period for assessment of transferee liability indefinitely. When the taxpayer's property is successively transferred, no assessment of transferee liability against the transferee of a transferee is permitted to be made more than three years after the statute of limitations for assessment against the initial taxpayer/transferor has expired. If the Service institutes a suit for the collection of the unpaid tax against the taxpayer/transferor or the preceding transferee within the applicable limitations period, however, then the statute of limitations for assessment of transferee liability against the transferee of the taxpayer or the transferee of a transferee does not expire until one year after the return of execution in the collection suit.[23]

5. *Period of limitations—fiduciaries.* A transferee assessment against a fiduciary must be made no later than one year after expiration of the statute of limitations on assessment for the tax giving rise to the fiduciary liability or the statute of limitations on collection of that tax, whichever is later.[24]

6. *Extensions and suspension of the limitations period.* These statutes of limitations can be extended by agreement between the transferee or fiduciary and the Service,[25] or suspended when the Service mails a notice of liability to the transferee or the fiduciary for the period when the Service is prohibited from making an assessment, and for an additional sixty days before it begins to run again.

7. *Burden of proof.* Section 6902(a) allocates the burden of proof in Tax Court transferee proceedings, imposing on the Commissioner the burden of showing that the petitioner "is liable as a transferee of property of a taxpayer,"

---

[22] If the transferor is deceased, or the transferor is a corporation that has terminated its existence, the statute of limitations for assessment against the deceased transferor or dissolved corporation is the same statute of limitations that would apply if the death or termination of corporate existence had not occurred. IRC § 6901(e).

[23] IRC § 6901(c).

[24] IRC § 6901(c)(3).

[25] The form used to extend the statute is a Form 872. See Chapter 5 for discussion of statutes of limitations.

and imposing on the transferee the burden of establishing that the taxpayer/transferor was not liable for the tax. A pretrial discovery rule is provided by statute to assist the transferee in carrying its burden of proof. The discovery rule gives the transferee the right, under the Tax Court's rules,[26] to a preliminary examination of the taxpayer's books, papers, documents, correspondence, and other evidence (or those of the preceding transferee of the taxpayer's property).[27]

8. *Injunctions prohibited.* Sections 6904 and 7421(b) prohibit a transferee from maintaining a suit to restrain enforcement of transferee liability.

9. *Discharge of executor from personal liability.* The executor of an estate may obtain a discharge for personal liability for income and estate tax if, after filing the appropriate return, the executor applies in writing for release from liability for those taxes. After the application is filed, the Service may notify the executor of the amount of the taxes due, and on payment of that amount, the executor will be discharged from liability. If after the application is filed the Service does not notify the executor within nine moths after the date it received the application, the executor is also discharged.[28]

[2] Applicability of State or Federal Law

Generally, the liability of a transferee "at law or in equity" is a question of state, not federal, law.[29] In 1931, the Supreme Court in *Phillips v. Commissioner* rejected the claim that by making the transferee's liability "at law or in equity" depend on state law, the predecessor of Section 6901 violated the constitutional requirement of uniformity because differences in state law might af-

---

[26] See Rule 73, Examination by Transferees, Tax Court Rules of Practice and Procedure.

[27] IRC § 6902(b).

[28] IRC § 6905(a). See Reg. § 301.6905-1. The discharge of an executor from personal liability for income and estate tax due from a decedent or the decedent's estate, liability that will be enforced using the procedures of Section 6901, is related to another provision in this part of the Code—the notice of fiduciary relationship. The filing of a notice of fiduciary relationship, Form 56, is a prerequisite to the fiduciary's assuming, for tax purposes (including tax payment purposes) the powers, rights, duties, and privileges of the party for whom the fiduciary is acting, until the Service is given notice that the relationship is terminated. See Reg. § 301.6903-1.

[29] Certainly that was the intention when the statute was adopted. See Comm'r v. Stern, 357 US 39 (1958) (widow's liability determined under Kentucky law); Kathy B. Enters., Inc. v. United States, 84-2 USTC ¶ 9972 (amended) (D. Ariz. 1984), aff'd on other issues, 779 F2d 1413 (9th Cir. 1986) (Illinois fraudulent conveyance law applied to determine whether corporation owned by taxpayer's wife was liable as transferee); RG Cope, Jr., Inc. v. Comm'r, 781 F2d 852 (11th Cir. 1986).

fect the liability of the transferee.[30] In rejecting this constitutional argument, however, the Court said that "it had no occasion to decide whether the right of the United States to follow transferred assets is limited by any state law." After *Phillips*, the majority of courts applied state law, but both before and after *Phillips*, some courts applied a "general law" that did not distinguish between federal and state decisional law. It was not until the Supreme Court's decision in *Commissioner v. Stern*, decided some twenty-seven years after the *Phillips* case, that the Supreme Court definitively resolved the issue by holding that state, not federal law, applied.[31] In *Stern*, when the deceased taxpayer's estate was insufficient to pay the tax deficiency he owed, the Service claimed that his widow, also the beneficiary of his life insurance policy, was liable as the transferee of the proceeds and the cash surrender value of the policy. Under Kentucky law, however, the widow was not liable to the Service because her husband had paid no premium on the policy in fraud of creditors. Faced with a choice between federal decisional law and Kentucky law, the Supreme Court held that transferee liability is determined under state law because the transferee liability statute merely provided a new procedure, not a definition of a substantive liability, and Congress had not manifested a desire for uniformity of liability. Because Kentucky law did not make the widow a transferee, therefore, neither did the transferee liability statute. In short, *Phillips* held that uniformity was not required under the transferee liability statute as a matter of constitutional law, and *Stern* held that uniformity was not required as a matter of policy, or at least Congress did not express an intention that there be such uniformity as a matter of policy.

Although state law governs whether a person is liable as a transferee, and if so, the extent of a transferee's liability, the principle is subject to important qualifications. First, when state law does not definitively answer a question relating to the transferee's liability in a particular case, federal courts consult judicial principles to protect private creditors as well as the body of federal transferee liability law federal courts developed during the twenty-seven-year period between the Supreme Court's *Phillips* and *Stern* decisions. Second, although state law controls, it is a federal court, not a state court, which independently determines the result under state law.[32] A third qualification is that the supremacy of the federal government prevents the application of state law to certain transferee liability issues. A clear illustration of state law being qualified by federal supremacy is the general principle that even when the Service's claim is made under state law, the Service's claim may not be cut off

---

[30] Phillips v. Comm'r, 283 US 589, 602 (1931).

[31] Comm'r v. Stern, 357 US 39 (1958).

[32] There are many examples of this process cited subsequently. But see, e.g., the Tax Court's decision in Dillman v. Comm'r, 64 TC 797 (1975), in which the court interpreted Wisconsin law.

by a state statute of limitations when the federal period of limitations is still open. Section 6901(c) establishes a statute of limitations for the assessment of transferee liability. In *Summerlin*, the Supreme Court held that "[i]t is well settled that the United States is not bound by state statutes of limitation or subject to the defense of laches in enforcing its rights . . . whether it brings suit in federal or state courts government."[33] Accordingly, the limitations period in Section 6901(c) applies to a claim by the Service, instead of a shorter state statute of limitations, which may apply to other creditors who proceed under the state's law. The rule of *Summerlin* clearly applies under the UFCA, which has an explicit statute of limitations, and courts have permitted the Service to use either the state or federal (usually, the statute of limitations on assessment of Section 6901 or on collection)—whichever statute of limitations is the longer.[34]

The UFTA, which has replaced the UFCA in many states, has a claim or cause of action extinguishment clause, and this clause extinguishes the claim or cause of action unless it is brought generally within four years after the debtor made the transfer with actual intent to defraud or with a constructively fraudulent intent.[35] Even when state law extinguishes the claim or cause of action of the creditor to set aside a fraudulent conveyance unless the action is brought within the statutory period under the state version of the UFTA, most courts hold that under the rule of *Summerlin*, the Service's claim is not extinguished.[36]

---

[33] United States v. Summerlin, 310 US 414, 416 (1940).

[34] See United States v. West Tex. State Bank, 357 F2d 198 (5th Cir. 1966) (applying the statute of limitations of Section 6901); United States v. Fernon, 640 F2d 609 (5th Cir. 1981) (Florida statute of limitations did not apply; Code statute on collection did); United States v. Wurdemann, 663 F2d 50 (8th Cir. 1981); United States v. Wilson, 500 F. Supp. 831 (ND Tex. 1980) (Service not bound by four-year Texas statute of limitations for fraudulent conveyances when action brought within Section 6502, the Code collection statute); United States v. Snyder, 82-2 USTC ¶ 9683 (SD W. Va. 1982) (West Virginia's five-year statute of limitations on fraudulent conveyance actions not applicable, as long as action is timely under statute of limitations on collection); United States v. Freeman, 89-1 USTC ¶ 9127 (ND W. Va. 1988) (West Virginia law applied to set aside fraudulent conveyance, but six-year statute under Section 6502 applied, rather than five-year state statute), aff'd per unpublished opinion (4th Cir. 1990).

In some instances, a longer state statute of limitations has been applied in lieu of Section 6502. United States v. Scott, 167 F2d 301 (8th Cir. 1948) (applying a ten-year statute of limitations provided under state law when the then six-year statute of limitations of Section 6502 had expired). However, it also has been held that, although a state statute of limitations does not apply to the Service, the statute of limitations on collection, Section 6502, governs a Service action to set aside a fraudulent conveyance. United States v. Bushlow, 832 F. Supp. 574 (EDNY 1993).

[35] UFTA § 9.

[36] Compare Stoecklin v. United States, 858 F. Supp. 167, 168 (MD Fla. 1994) (government not bound by extinguishment provision of Florida Transfer Act because of the

Finally, the government need not proceed under state law to assert transferee liability in all situations. If the Service wishes to collect an estate or gift tax liability, it can proceed under Section 6901 to enforce the personal liability of beneficiaries and donees for the unpaid estate and gift taxes under Section 6324. Section 6324 has its own ten-year statute of limitations on transferee liability. Similarly, when a fraudulent conveyance by a bankrupt taxpayer is at issue, the Bankruptcy Code fraudulent transfer provision permits the trustee to set aside any transactions made within one year of the filing of the petition in the bankruptcy court.[37]

¶ 17.02 TRANSFEREE LIABILITY AT LAW OR IN EQUITY— COMMON ELEMENTS

Section 6901 describes transferee liability for purposes of the section as the "liability at law or in equity" of a transferee of property of a taxpayer liable for income taxes, a decedent liable for estate taxes, or a donor liable for gift taxes. The elements of transferee liability at law and in equity are discussed more fully in succeeding sections.

One type of liability at law is the liability of a transferee who assumes the transferor's liability for debts by way of contract. To establish this type of transferee liability at law, the Service must prove the following elements:

* The taxpayer transferred property to another person;
* The taxpayer was liable for the tax at the time of the transfer and at the time transferee liability is asserted;

---

rule of *Summerlin*) and United States v. Bacon, 78 F3d 595 (9th Cir. 1996) (refusing to apply the Washington Transfer Act with a claim extinguishment provision retroactively because of the rule of *Summerlin*, and applying the ten-year statute of limitations on collection of Section 6502(a)(1)) with United States v. Vallelos, 780 F. Supp. 705, 708 (D. Haw. 1992) (finding that the government was bound by the Hawaii Transfer Act claim extinguishment provision), aff'd on other grounds, 990 F2d 1265 (table) (9th Cir. 1993).

The Tax Court, with four judges dissenting, has ruled that California's UFTA, which has a claim extinguishment provision, does not preclude the Service from bringing a fraudulent conveyance claim after the date the claim is extinguished under California law on the ground that even if the extinguishment provision is an element of the cause of action, it is effectively a statute of limitations, which *Summerlin* holds does not bind the Service. Blesson v. Comm'r, 111 TC 172 (1998) (gathering and discussing cases, and distinguishing *Vallelos* on the ground that the transferee liability statute under the Code had not yet expired in the case, unlike *Vallelos*). The dissent argued that a temporal right, which is extinguished under state law, is not a statute of limitations under the Supreme Court's decision in Custer v. McCutcheon, 283 US 514, 519 (1931).

[37] 11 USC § 548(a) (trustee may avoid fraudulent transfers). The trustee may also avoid a fraudulent transfer using state law under 11 USC § 544(b).

- The taxpayer/transferor had a valid contract with the transferee; and
- The transferee, under the terms of that contract, assumed the liabilities of the taxpayer, including the obligation to pay the tax or, specifically, the obligation to pay the taxes of the transferor.

To establish transferee liability in equity, the Service must prove the following elements:

- The taxpayer transferred property to another person;
- The taxpayer was liable for the tax at the time of the transfer and at the time transferee liability is asserted;
- The taxpayer made the transfer after liability for the tax accrued, whether or not the tax was actually assessed at the time of the transfer;
- The taxpayer made the transfer for less than full or adequate consideration or made the transfer with the intention of defrauding creditors;
- The taxpayer/transferor was insolvent at the time of the transfer or the transfer left the taxpayer/transferor insolvent; and
- The government has exhausted all reasonable efforts to collect the tax from the taxpayer/transferor before proceeding against the transferee.

Transferee liability at law and in equity share two common elements: (1) there must have been a transfer of property from the transferor taxpayer to the transferee and (2) the taxpayer/transferor must be liable for the tax both at the time of the transfer and at the time transferee liability is asserted.[38]

[1] Requirement of a Transfer of Property

Section 6901 assumes that a transfer of property has taken place because the same procedure followed to seek payment directly from the taxpayer is used to collect the amount of the liability from "a transferee of property." Without a transfer of property, by its terms, Section 6901 does not apply, therefore, no transferee liability either at law or in equity exists unless there has been a transfer of property by the transferor to the transferee.[39] For example, a person may become liable for the tax of another if the person has agreed to pay the federal tax liability of the other contracting party or has guaranteed the payment of the other party. However, when the United States seeks to recover on a contract between a third party and the taxpayer, the third party's liability is separate and distinct from the payment of taxes and the operation of the trans-

---

[38] The different elements of transferee liability at law and in equity are examined infra ¶¶ 17.03 and 17.04, respectively.

[39] See James M. Denton, 21 TC 295 (1953) (purchase of stock from one officer-shareholder and corporation's purchase from another officer held not to constitute a transfer to still other officer-shareholders).

feree liability statute. The United States sues as a third-party beneficiary under the contract for damages arising from its breach or under the contract of guaranty, not under the theory of transferee liability at law.[40]

A transfer of property does not require a technical transfer of title,[41] but at a minimum beneficial ownership must have been transferred to the transferee.[42] A transfer may be direct or indirect, actual, or constructive. Thus, a direct transfer may occur when a corporation makes direct cash distributions to a shareholder, or it may occur indirectly or constructively when the corporation pays the shareholder's personal liability, or makes payment of moneys for the shareholder's benefit.[43] A constructive transfer may also occur when a corporation pays excessive or unreasonable salaries.[44] The existence and extent of a transferee's liability at law or in equity is determined by applicable state law. Therefore, whether a transaction constitutes a transfer is to be determined under the law of the state in which the transaction occurred.[45]

---

[40] United States v. Scott, 167 F2d 301 (8th Cir. 1948) (six-year limitations period for collection of assessed taxes did not apply; the ten-year Missouri statute of limitations for a claim of money did because the liability was independent of the tax laws).

[41] Hatch v. Morosco Holding Co., 50 F2d 138, 139 (2d Cir. 1931) (a holding company's possession of premises it leased to its subsidiary was found sufficient to render holding company a transferee).

[42] Paulyne E. Tomfohr, 44 BTA 730 (1941) (wife of imprisoned husband held not to be a transferee of real property assigned to her when it was assigned to her for the purpose of disposing of it for husband's benefit); Estate of James A. Fox, 14 TCM 1212, 1216 (1955) (decedent's estate was held not to be a transferee when the property was transferred to the decedent without any intention of passing beneficial ownership to him, and after the transfer, the transferor's partnership continued to use the property).

[43] Fibel v. Comm'r, 44 TC 647, 658 (1965) (corporation's payment of shareholder's tax liabilities and other payments made at the shareholder's directions constituted transfers to the shareholders); Hicks v. Comm'r, 29 TCM 1175, 1184 (1970), aff'd, 73-2 USTC ¶ 9526 (9th Cir. 1973) (although corporation's payments for personal expenses of shareholder were recorded on the corporation's books as receivables, they were found to be transfers).

[44] Charles E. Smith & Sons v. Comm'r, 6 TCM 529 (1947), aff'd, 184 F2d 1011 (6th Cir. 1950), cert. denied, 340 US 953 (1951) (excessive compensation held to have rendered corporation insolvent and president held liable as transferee for excess portion of salary); J. Warren Leach, 21 TC 70 (1953) (same); Bennett E. Meyers, 21 TC 331 (1953); James M. Denton, 21 TC 195 (1953).

For a case in which the court found that a corporation had transferred a promissory note from the buyer of the business to its shareholders because the interest was paid to the shareholders, not the corporation, see Wiltzius v. Comm'r, TC Memo. 1997-117 (1997) (applying Florida fraudulent conveyance law in finding that there was transferee liability).

[45] Comm'r v. Stern, 357 US 39 (1958); Fibel v. Comm'r, 44 TC 647, 658 (1965); Estate of Henry Miller, 42 TC 593, 598 (1964); Rev. Rul. 69-211, 1969-1 CB 305 (applying Virginia law to determine the existence of transferee liability of a church that acquired by gift all of the stock of a Virginia corporation, liquidated the corporation, and disposed of its assets). See Ginsberg v. Comm'r, 305 F2d 664 (2d Cir. 1962) (applying New York law to determine whether a retransfer of property had occurred); Nicholson v. Comm'r, 48

[2] Liability of the Taxpayer/Transferor

For the purposes of assessment and collection of the tax due from a taxpayer/transferor, the transferee is treated in the same manner as the taxpayer. Similarity in the procedure for assessing and collecting the tax from both the transferor and transferee should not mask the fact that it is the unpaid tax of the transferor that the Service is derivative or secondary, not direct or primary.[46] Consequently, unless the taxpayer/transferor is liable for a tax both at the time of the transfer and at the time the transferee liability is asserted, a transferee may not be held liable in equity or at law.[47] A prior judicial determination that the transferor was liable for a tax is binding on the transferee under the doctrine of res judicata.[48] By the same token, a finding that the transferor is not liable for the tax is binding on the government.[49] However, to be binding, the prior determination of liability need not have been made after a hearing on the merits. The doctrine of res judicata applies even when the decision is entered by stipulation of the parties.[50]

TCM 272, 275 (1984) (applying Georgia law to determine whether the delivery of a deed necessary for a valid transfer of real property in that state had occurred); Indiana Nat'l Bank v. United States, 84-2 USTC ¶ 9884 (ND Ill. 1984) (applying Illinois law to determine whether a minister's transfer of his residence to his church was a fraudulent conveyance); United States v. Jones, 86-2 USTC ¶ 9832 (WD Mo. 1986) (although the conveyance had been made twenty years before the Service's suit, a lawyer's conveyance of property to parents was held fraudulent under Missouri law, because the tax assessments had been reduced to judgment).

[46] Phillips-Jones Corp. v. Parmley, 302 US 233, 235–236 (1937). However, Section 6324 imposes primary liability for an unpaid estate tax on transferees. Schuster v. Comm'r, 312 F2d 311, 315 (9th Cir. 1962).

[47] Delia v. Comm'r, 23 TCM 2018, 2020 (1964), aff'd, 362 F2d 400 (6th Cir. 1966) (shareholder held liable as corporation's transferee when, because of a lack of substantiation, salary deductions were denied, giving rise to a corporate tax liability that otherwise would have been eliminated); Cold Metal Process Co. v. Comm'r, 247 F2d 864 (6th Cir. 1957) (a corporation transferred a patent to a shareholder, but the corporate transferor was deemed not to have incurred tax on the income from the royalties on the date of the transfer because the government contested the corporation's right to royalties from the patent); Comm'r v. Henry Hess Co., 210 F2d 553 (9th Cir. 1954) (dissolved corporation held not to be a transferor when, after its dissolution, its shareholders received property that would have been taxable to the corporation if it had remained in existence); John A. Mulligan, 16 TC 1489 (1951); Anne Davis, 23 TCM 1449 (1964).

[48] Egan's Estate v. Comm'r, 260 F2d 779, 785 (8th Cir. 1958); Comm'r v. Henry Hess Co., 210 F2d 553 (9th Cir. 1954); Harrison v. Comm'r, 173 F2d 736, 737 (5th Cir. 1949); First Nat'l Bank v. Comm'r, 112 F2d 260, 262–263 (7th Cir. 1940); Jahncke Serv., Inc., 20 BTA 837, 847 (1930), appeal dismissed, 112 F2d 169 (5th Cir. 1933).

[49] Nora M. Carney, 22 BTA 721 (1931).

[50] David Krueger, 48 TC 824 (1967), overruling Kenner Oil & Gas Co., 32 BTA 186 (1935); Wayne Body Corp., 22 BTA 401 (1931).

Because the transferee's liability derives from the taxpayer's liability, to the extent that the taxpayer-transferor makes unconditional payments of the tax delinquency, the transferee's liability is extinguished.[51] Moreover, because transferees are severally liable, another transferee's payment of the tax extinguishes the remaining transferee's liability, subject to the right of the paying transferee to contribution.[52] However, conditional payments (e.g., payments being made accompanied by claims for refund) do not extinguish the transferee's liability.[53]

¶ 17.03 TRANSFEREE LIABILITY AT LAW

Transferee liability at law is based either on the transferee's express assumption of the transferor's liability (the assumption by contract theory) or on state or federal law imposing liability on the transferee, such as the trust fund doctrine. The difference between liability at law and liability in equity is not that liability at law derives from statute and liability in equity does not. Rather, liability in equity derives from the law of fraudulent conveyances developed by courts of equity that required an application for equitable relief when a conveyance was to be set aside. In fact, much of the law of fraudulent conveyances is now a matter of statute, such as the UFCA and its successor the UFTA.

In the typical situation when transferee liability at law is based on the assumption by contract theory, a purchaser has agreed to buy all the assets of a going business and to assume all its debts. In this type of case, the Commissioner must establish that (1) there was a transfer of property; (2) the transferor was liable for the tax; (3) there was a valid contract between the transferor and the transferee; and (4) the transferee assumed the obligation to pay the tax, by a covenant in the contract. The most frequently asserted statutory bases of transferee liability at law are: (1) Section 6324, for estate and gift tax; (2) state Bulk Sales Acts; and (3) state corporation laws dealing with the treatment of liabilities in consolidations, mergers, and liquidations.

---

[51] JP Quirk, 15 TC 709 (1950), aff'd per curiam, 196 F2d 1022 (5th Cir. 1952); Estate of Samuel Stein, 40 TC 275 (1963).

[52] Phillips-Jones Corp. v. Parmley, 302 US 233 (1937). Similarly, a compromise of the transferee liability of one transferee does not extinguish the liability of other transferees, although the amount of the liability is reduced by the amount paid under the compromise. Rev. Rul. 72-436, 1972-2 CB 643.

[53] Pier v. Comm'r, 96 F2d 642 (9th Cir. 1938) (payment with claim for refund); Stewart C. Holmes, 47 TC 622 (1967).

[1] Assumption of Liability Cases

When liability at law is the theory of liability, it is not necessary for the government to prove (as it must when liability in equity is involved) (1) that the transferor was insolvent[54]; (2) that all remedies of tax collection from the transferor have been exhausted[55]; and (3) the value of the assets transferred. A common issue in assumption by contract cases is whether, under the contract, the transferee actually assumed the tax liability of the transferor.[56] If the transferee purchases all the assets of another, the purchaser is not ordinarily liable for the debts of the transferor.[57] However, when the party who purchases the assets assumes all the liabilities of another, the transferee is liable for any taxes that are outstanding, even if tax liabilities were not specifically assumed.[58] The assumption of "all existing liabilities" of the transferor has been

---

[54] Turnbull, Inc. v. Comm'r, 42 TC 582, 587 (1964), aff'd, 373 F2d 91 (5th Cir.), cert. denied, 389 US 842 (1967); Napsky v. Comm'r, 24 TCM 1578 (1966), aff'd, 371 F2d 189 (7th Cir. 1966).

[55] American Equitable Assurance Co. v. Helvering, 68 F2d 46 (2d Cir. 1933); Napsky v. Comm'r, 24 TCM 1578 (1966), aff'd, 371 F2d 189 (7th Cir. 1966); Georgia, Fla. & Ala. Ry., 31 BTA 1, 6, 7 (1934); Helvering v. Wheeling Mold & Foundry Co., 71 F2d 749, 751 (4th Cir.), cert. denied, 293 US 603 (1934).

[56] The issue is similar to an action based on the government's status as a third-party beneficiary of an agreement. Compare United States v. American Vault Co., 80-1 USTC ¶ 9461 (EDNY 1980) (Service sued individuals as third-party beneficiaries of sales contract rather than as transferees; held, Service failed to prove contract intended to benefit it) with United States v. Jacobs, 304 F. Supp. 613 (SDNY 1969) (escrow agreement bound parties to use reserve to pay taxes).

When an insolvent bank warranted to the acquiring bank that all tax returns had been completely and accurately filed, all taxes had been paid, and there was no pending or threatened litigation or action to materially and adversely affect the assets of the acquired bank, but it turned out that additional taxes were due; the acquiring bank was nevertheless held liable for the taxes. See also United States v. First Dakota Nat'l Bank, 963 F. Supp. 855 (DSD 1997), aff'd, 137 F3d 1077 (8th Cir. 1998) (although the issues were tried to a jury, and the district court had entered a judgment notwithstanding the verdict, the interpretation of the contract was a question of law, and the contract unequivocally established the buyer's intention to assume all liabilities, known or unknown, and the additional liability of $37,000 could not have materially altered negotiations).

[57] There may be exceptions to the rule if the transaction is viewed as a consolidation, de facto merger, or mere continuation of the seller. See the discussion infra ¶ 17.03[6]. See Atlas Tool Co. v. Comm'r, 614 F2d 860, 870–871 (3d Cir. 1980) (dissolution and reincorporation of assets held to be a de facto merger and continuation of the business under New Jersey law); West Tex. Ref. & Dev. Co. v. Comm'r, 68 F2d 77, 81 (10th Cir. 1933).

[58] Kamen Soap Prods. Co. v. Comm'r, 230 F2d 565 (2d Cir. 1956) (agreement that the transferee assumed tax liabilities of shareholders who contributed assets previously held in partnership); Bos Lines, Inc. v. Comm'r, 354 F2d 830 (8th Cir. 1954) (agreement to assume "all liabilities, determined or contingent, known or unknown" of transferee); Helvering v. Wheeling Mold & Foundry Co., 71 F2d 749 (4th Cir.), cert. denied, 293 US

generally held to include any tax liability existing at the time of the transfer, although not determined or assessed until a later time.[59]

Generally, if a corporation sells or transfers its assets to another corporation, the transferee is not liable for the debts, including tax debts, of the transferor corporation, because the transferee has not acquired the liabilities of the transferor corporation.[60] As the circuit court stated in *West Texas Refining & Development Co. v. Commissioner:*

> To this general rule, there are four well-recognized exceptions. . . . (1) Where the purchaser expressly or impliedly agrees to assume (the) debts (of the transferor); (2) where the transaction amounts to a consolidation or merger of the corporations; (3) where the purchasing corporation is merely a continuation of the selling corporation; and (4) where the transaction is entered into fraudulently in order to escape liability for such debts.[61]

Transactions within these exceptions may involve liability at law or in equity or both.

When a purchaser of assets expressly or impliedly agrees to assume the debts of the transferor corporation, the transferee is liable as a transferee at law under the assumption by contract theory.[62] For example, in *Bos Lines, Inc. v. Commissioner*, the liability of a transferee was asserted because the stock of corporation *A* was acquired by corporation *B* in a transaction in which *B* assumed "all liabilities determined or contingent, known or unknown," of *A*. After the purchase of *A*'s stock, *B* liquidated *A*. Subsequently, *C* acquired all of

---

603 (1934) (transferee agreed to pay all "debts" of transferor corporation); Continental Baking Co. v. Helvering, 75 F2d 243 (DC Cir. 1934), cert. denied, 295 US 756 (1935) (transferee held liable for transferor's taxes because it assumed "all existing liabilities," despite the fact that tax liabilities were not included on a list of assumed liabilities, and the tax liability was not determined until after the transfer); American Equitable Assurance Corp. v. Helvering, 68 F2d 46 (2d Cir. 1933); Texsun Supply Corp., 17 TC 433 (1951) (agreement to assume and pay all income tax "heretofore or hereafter owing" by transferor corporation).

[59] California Iron Yards Corp. v. Comm'r, 82 F2d 776 (9th Cir. 1936); Helvering v. Wheeling Mold & Foundry Co., 71 F2d 749 (4th Cir.), cert. denied, 293 US 603 (1934); Shepard v. Comm'r, 101 F2d 595 (7th Cir. 1939); Continental Baking Co. v. Helvering, 75 F2d 243 (DC Cir. 1934), cert. denied, 295 US 756 (1935); Cold Metal Process Co. v. Comm'r, 25 TC 1333 (1956), rev'd on other grounds, 247 F2d 864 (6th Cir. 1957); United States v. Dakota Nat'l Bank, 963 F. Supp. 855 (DSD 1997), aff'd, 137 F3d 1077 (8th Cir. 1998).

[60] West Tex. Ref. & Dev. Co. v. Comm'r, 68 F2d 77 (10th Cir. 1933).

[61] West Tex. Ref. & Dev. Co. v. Comm'r, 68 F2d 77, 81 (10th Cir. 1933).

[62] See Bos Lines, Inc. v. Comm'r, 354 F2d 830 (8th Cir. 1954); Kamen Soap Prods. Co. v. Comm'r, 230 F2d 565 (2d Cir. 1956); Helvering v. Wheeling Mold & Foundry Co., 71 F2d 749 (4th Cir.), cert. denied, 293 US 603 (1934); Continental Baking Co. v. Helvering, 75 F2d 243 (DC Cir. 1934), cert. denied, 295 US 756 (1935).

the capital stock and assets of *B*, including all of the assets *B* had acquired from *A*, and assumed all of *B*'s liabilities, in complete cancellation of the capital stock of *B*. As a result, *C* had assumed *A*'s liabilities, and this assumption subjected *C* to transferee liability at law.

[2] Transferee Liability on the Formation of a Corporation

Transferee liability can be asserted on the formation of the corporation, especially on the incorporation of the assets of a going business.[63] The determination of liability has depended on resolving the issue of whether the stock given in exchange for the assets had any value. The assets of the going business have at least liquidation value, but to the extent that the stock or other property received by the shareholders on the formation of the corporation is less than the value of the assets transferred to the corporation, the corporation is liable as a transferee.

[3] Shareholders as Transferees

It is well established under the trust fund doctrine that distributee-shareholders of a dissolved corporation's assets are liable as transferees for taxes incurred by the corporation before the dissolution.[64] The distribution may be a fraudulent conveyance because the corporation has transferred property at a time

---

[63] Diamondhead Corp. v. Fort Hope Dev., Inc., 78-2 USTC ¶ 9718 (ND Ga. 1978) (sole shareholder formed nominee corporation, and transferred promissory notes to the nominee; held, the nominee gave no value for the notes and the Service therefore was the proper payee). In Tilton v. Comm'r, 88 TC 590 (1987), taxpayer-parents made gifts of property to their children's corporation and to the children individually. The Service contended that as shareholders, the children were liable as indirect transferees under Section 6324(b). The Tax Court assumed without deciding that an indirect donee shareholder may be charged with transferee lliability as a result of a nonshareholder's gratuitous transfer to a corporation. However, it held that the children were not liable as transferees, because the value of their stock had not increased as a result of the transfer (the corporation had assumed debts of the parents as well).

[64] Phillips v. Comm'r, 283 US 589 (1931); Shepard v. Comm'r, 101 F2d 595, 598 (7th Cir. 1939) (applying principles of equity to find that the shareholders held the distributed proceeds of the sale of the corporation's assets as trustees for the benefit of the Service as a creditor of the corporation); Dillman v. Comm'r, 64 TC 797 (1975) (applying Wisconsin law); Lesser v. Comm'r, 47 TC 564 (1967) (applying California law). See also Drew v. United States, 367 F2d 828 (Ct. Cl. 1966). Sebok v. Comm'r, 43 TCM 255 (1982) (applying New York fraudulent conveyance law to the transfer of a corporation's only asset to its sole shareholder for one dollar); Madonia v. United States, 86-1 USTC ¶ 9170 (WDNY 1985) (liquidating distribution held made without fair consideration, because liabilities including accrued taxes exceeded assets and shareholder's percentage interest in compensation and so was constructively fraudulent under New York law).

when it was insolvent. Under the trust fund doctrine, a corporation's creditors are protected from the shareholder's fraudulent action by holding the distributee-shareholders as trustees for the benefit of the corporation's creditors to the extent of the property the shareholders have received. Under the trust fund doctrine, the claims of creditors of a corporation may also be treated as surviving the dissolution of the corporation and may be maintained against the distributee-shareholders.

During the life of a corporation, an employee-shareholder who receives "unreasonable compensation" can be held liable as a transferee if the payment is made at a time when the corporation is insolvent or the payment renders the corporation insolvent.[65] Under the same rationale, payment by an insolvent corporation of a shareholder's personal expenses will constitute a constructive transfer of property of the corporation to the shareholder, or payment under an arrangement that serves no business purpose.[66] The same result is reached when a shareholder personally receives income that properly belongs to the corporation.[67] Generally, a creditor cannot be held liable as a transferee when

---

[65] Charles E. Smith & Sons v. Comm'r, 6 TCM 529 (1947), aff'd, 184 F2d 1011 (6th Cir. 1950), cert. denied, 340 US 953 (1951) (increase in compensation by nearly 1,000 percent and 1,700 percent held unreasonable); J. Warren Leach, 21 TC 70 (1953); Bennett E. Meyers, 21 TC 331 (1953) (sole stockholder withdrew funds from corporation, and officers and corporation reported fictitious salaries; shareholder held liable as transferee for unpaid corporate income taxes); Comm'r v. Renyx, 66 F2d 260 (2d Cir. 1933) (payment to dissolved corporation's treasurer in excess of his salary was a distribution of corporate assets without consideration; treasurer held liable as transferee).

For a case in which a corporation paid compensation to its president and sole shareholder, the Service claimed that the compensation was excessive, and that as a result the president-shareholder was liable as a transferee, but the Tax Court held that the compensation was reasonable based on amounts paid to similarly positioned officers and executives at similar companies, see Solaas v. Comm'r, TC Memo. 1998-25 (1998) (the court rejected the Service's actual and constructive fraud arguments).

A fraudulent transfer may occur where the shareholder attempts to divert compensation to his wife. In Joy Harper Scott v. Comm'r, 70 TC 71 (1978), the taxpayer-shareholder had his wife form a new corporation to perform services actually performed by the husband. The husband received a nominal salary, but the wife was held to be a transferee of distributions made to her.

It has also been held that when a corporation canceled a debt its sole shareholder owed to it while it was insolvent, it paid a dividend to the shareholder sufficient to make him a transferee. Segura v. Comm'r, 77 TC 734 (1981).

[66] United States v. 58th St. Plaza Theatre, Inc., 287 F. Supp. 475 (SDNY 1968) (subleases by corporation of theater property); Estate of Taylor v. Comm'r, 41 TCM 44 (1980); Cockey v. Comm'r, 46 TCM 1564 (1983) (50 percent shareholder was liable as a transferee when, on the sale of the corporation's assets, his share of the proceeds was transferred to his wife in satisfaction of her marital rights).

[67] See Samuel Wilcox, 16 TC 572 (1951), aff'd per curiam sub nom. Bosworth v. Comm'r, 194 F2d 102 (2d Cir. 1952) (lessees paid rents directly to lessor corporation's shareholders so that the corporation was left with insufficient funds to pay tax on the rentals); Estate of Irving Smith, 16 TC 807 (1951) (same); Estate of Robert Harrison, 16 TC

it receives assets in payment of a past due debt. However, a creditor that has been a shareholder of an insolvent corporation, has been held liable as a transferee on the ground that the creditor-shareholder has preferred nontax obligations that do not have priority to the tax claim.[68]

[4] Form of the Acquisition Transaction

Whether a transferee will be determined to be liable for the transferor's tax liability arising from the sale of a target frequently turns on the form of the transaction. As one court summarized decisions in other cases, "[T]he transferee liability of the corporation receiving the assets had been made to turn precisely on . . . whether the vendee corporation's stock was distributed to the vendor corporation, or whether [it] was distributed to the vendor corporation's stockholders."[69] Generally, when the buyer pays fair value for the assets of the target, the buyer is found not to be liable as a transferee because it has left the target's assets at the same value as they were before the sale. Thus, when *B* pays *A* directly in money or stock, *B* is not liable as a transferee because it has left *A* with assets of the same value as those it had prior to the sale.[70] Similarly, when a stockholder sells its stock, it is not liable in equity to a creditor of the corporation or subject to transferee liability for unpaid taxes of the corporation whose stock the transferee sold.[71] But when the vendor corporation receives the consideration and then distributes it to its shareholders, the shareholders are held liable as transferees because the corporation has depleted

---

727 (1951) (same); Comm'r v. Western Union Tel. Co., 141 F2d 774 (2d Cir.), cert. denied, 322 US 751 (1944) (involving payments by Western Union, as lessee of rights of way under 99-year and 999-year leases, directly to shareholders of corporations that were considered to own the property involved). The principle involved also applies where the income of the corporation is fraudulently diverted by shareholders. DiZenzo v. Comm'r, 23 TCM 677 (1964), rev'd in part on other grounds and remanded, 348 F2d 122 (2d Cir. 1965).

[68] Delia v. Comm'r, 362 F2d 400 (6th Cir. 1966) (Ohio law); Weil v. Comm'r, 91 F2d 944 (2d Cir. 1937) (although New York law prohibited a corporation to pay a debt to a shareholder if it refused to pay any notes or obligations when due, no violation of the law was found because the notes or obligations the corporation had failed or refused to pay were not in writing); Powers Photo Engraving Co., 17 TC 393 (1951), aff'd and remanded, 197 F2d 704 (2d Cir. 1952) (transferee shareholder failed to prove that the debt was owed to him as a creditor); see also Estate of LE McKnight, 8 TC 871 (1947) (transferee may be relieved of liability when the transferor's creditors have been paid if the transferee shows that the debts were of a priority character).

[69] Vendig v. Comm'r, 229 F2d 93, 95 (2d Cir. 1956).

[70] Metropolitan Sec. Corp. v. Comm'r, 19 BTA 299 (1930).

[71] Lester L. Robeson, 22 BTA 395, aff'd sub nom. Comm'r v. Bryson, 79 F2d 397 (9th Cir. 1935); Brown's Son Co., 10 TC 840 (1948).

the assets previously available for collection.[72] Even when the vendee or acquiring corporation has paid full value for assets of a corporation with outstanding tax liabilities, the vendee may nevertheless be liable as a transferee when the vendee pays the shareholders of the acquired corporation. For example, when corporation A transfers all of its assets to B for consideration, which B pays to A's shareholders, B is liable for the unpaid income tax of A, which represents the unpaid profits made on the transfer, on the theory that B is a trustee to the extent of the value of the property that it acquired from A. B is liable as a transferee because it has left A without assets.[73]

In other words, transferee liability turns on whether the buyer's consideration for the seller's assets is retained by the seller or whether the consideration for the assets is distributed by the seller.[74] At any rate, if the buyer assumes liabilities of the seller, the assumption includes only those liabilities that were valid and enforceable at the time of the agreement, but not a tax liability that was barred by the statute of limitations.[75] It nevertheless is sometimes difficult to determine whether there is a sale of stock followed by a distribution of the corporate assets of the vendee or acquiring corporation (when the vendee is a transferee) or whether there is a sale of the corporation assets followed by the distribution of the sales proceeds to the shareholders of the vendor or acquired corporation (when the vendor's shareholders are transferees). The critical question is to which party were the assets of the vendee corporation actually dis-

---

[72] Compare Reid Ice Cream Corp. v. Comm'r, 59 F2d 189 (2d Cir. 1932) (purchase price paid to target, which subsequently distributed it to its shareholders; buyer held not liable as transferee for purposes of collecting target's tax on the sale of the target's assets, despite its assumption of the liabilities of the target prior to the sale) with Shepard v. Comm'r, 101 F2d 595, 597 (7th Cir. 1939) (buyer paid target's shareholders directly, leaving target without assets to pay tax on the sale; buyer held liable as transferee for the tax due as the result of the sale of the assets); see also Vendig v. Comm'r, 229 F2d 93 (2d Cir. 1956) (individual shareholder exchanged her stock in corporation for stock of the buyer, which then liquidated the acquired corporation receiving all of its assets). But see Bates Motor Transp. Lines, Inc. v. Comm'r, 200 F2d 20 (7th Cir. 1952) (shareholders dissolved their corporation and sold its stock in exchange for the stock of the buyer, and received the buyer's stock; held, the shareholders were liable as transferees, and it made no difference whether the stock of the buyer had been transferred to the corporation and then to the shareholders in the dissolution of the seller or the shareholders received the stock directly). The Second Circuit said in *Vendig*, 229 F2d 93, 95, "we are convinced that the *Bates* case . . . was wrongly decided."

[73] Shepard v. Comm'r, 101 F2d 595 (7th Cir. 1939) (the purchaser, B, sold A's assets and the tax was incurred as the result of the sale; the Service also claimed A's shareholders were liable as transferees, but the Board of Tax Appeals held that they were not liable); California Iron Yards Corp. v. Comm'r, 82 F2d 776 (9th Cir. 1956).

[74] See Vendig v. Comm'r, 229 F2d 93 (2d Cir. 1956).

[75] Diamond Gardner Corp. v. Comm'r, 38 TC 875 (1962), acq. 1963-1 CB 4.

tributed, not what was the transaction's substance. This applies the judicial doctrine of "substance over form."[76]

[5] Bulk Sales Transactions

Article 6 of the UCC sets forth state Bulk Sales Acts. In general, a bulk transfer of property is any transfer in bulk and not in the ordinary course of the transferor's business, of a major part of the materials, supplies, merchandise, or other inventory of the business. The purpose of Article 6, entitled Bulk Transfers, is to prevent "a merchant, owing debts, from selling out his stock in trade to a friend for any price, pocketing the proceeds, and disappearing leaving his creditors unpaid . . . [by requiring] advance notice to the seller's creditors of the impending sale, since with notice creditors can take steps to impound the proceeds, if they think it necessary."[77] A bulk transfer subject to the Bulk Sales Act is "ineffective against any creditors of the transferor" unless the transferee requires the transferor to furnish a schedule of property and lists of credits, and the transferee gives the creditors notice of the transfer. In 1990, Article 6 of the UCC was modified to reduce the burden of notice and the buyer's strict liability for failure to give notice. As revised, the buyer's liability exists only when the buyer has notice, or, after reasonable inquiry, would have had notice that the seller did not intend to operate the same or a similar business after the sale.[78] Moreover, a buyer is not liable for noncompliance if the buyer makes a good faith effort to comply with Article 6, or believes in good faith that Article 6 does not apply to the sale.[79] If a buyer fails to comply with the notice requirements of a state Bulk Sales Act, however, the buyer is subject to transferee liability at law based on the noncompliance.[80]

---

[76] Compare Vendig v. Comm'r, 229 F2d 93 (2d Cir. 1956) (exchange of preferred stock in vendor for preferred stock in vendee was recognized) with Bates Motor Transp. Lines, Inc. v. Comm'r, 200 F2d 20 (7th Cir. 1952) (sale of stock following a liquidation was held to be, in substance, sale of assets followed by distribution of proceeds to vendor's shareholders).

[77] UCC § 6-101, Purposes at ¶ 2(b) 4 (1991 Official Comment).

[78] UCC § 6-107(3). Furthermore, the buyer's noncompliance does not render the sale ineffective or affect the buyer's title to the goods, but the buyer may be liable to a creditor for damages for the failure to comply. UCC §§ 6-107(1), 6-107(8).

[79] UCC § 6-102(1)(c).

[80] See, e.g., United States v. Goldblatt Bros., 128 F2d 576 (7th Cir.), cert. denied, 317 US 662 (1942) (buyer of assets held liable under Illinois Bulk Sales Act because it had knowledge of the seller's tax liability, but failed to give the Service notice of the sale, as required under by the bulk sales law); Noltze Motor Co. v. Burrows-Moore Pontiac, Inc., 157 F. Supp. 593 (ND Iowa 1958) (applying Iowa law). But see True's Oil Co. v. United States, 64-2 USTC ¶ 9761 (ED Wash. 1964) ("[t]he United States of America (In-

Transferee liability exists if the transaction is entered into fraudulently in order for the transferor corporation to escape liability for its debts. As previously noted, most states have Bulk Sales Acts that require notice to be given to the creditors of the corporation, if the corporation's assets are to be sold in other than the ordinary course. If notice is not given to the Service pursuant to the state Bulk Sales Act, the government may assert that the purchaser is subject to transferee liability at law, although not all courts agree that the Service is a "creditor" for the purposes of Bulk Sales Acts.[81]

[6] Mergers and Consolidations

Many state corporation laws provide that in a merger or consolidation, the surviving corporation is liable for the debts of the constituent corporations.[82] It has been held that the surviving corporation is primarily liable in this situation and, accordingly, is not secondarily liable as a transferee.[83] However, this result is not without its flaws. On a merger or consolidation, there is unquestionably a transfer of property, and furthermore, the surviving corporation's liability derives from the liability of the constituent corporations, which is the nature of transferee liability. The only reason that the surviving corporation is primarily liable is that the constituent corporations no longer exist. In short,

---

ternal Revenue Service) is not one of the taxing agencies accorded first priority under the Bulk Sales Law of the State of Washington").

[81] Compare True's Oil Co. v. United States, 64-2 USTC ¶ 9761 (ED Wash. 1964) (government not a creditor under Washington Bulk Sales Law) with United States v. Goldblatt Bros., 128 F2d 576 (7th Cir.), cert. denied, 317 US 662 (1942) (Illinois law) and Noltze Motor Co. v. Burrows-Moore Pontiac, Inc., 157 F. Supp. 593 (ND Iowa 1958); In re Seminole Motors, Inc., 88-1 USTC ¶ 9252 (ED Okla. 1987) (Service treated as creditor under Oklahoma Bulk Sales Act; failure to give creditors notice of a bulk transfer as required by Oklahoma law tolled the six-month period that the Service had to assert transferee liability).

[82] NY Bus. Corp. Law § 906 (1986); Model Bus. Corp. Act §§ 67–70; Del. Gen. Corp. Law § 259 (1999); Cal. Corp. Code § 1107 (1977).

The transaction need not be in form a merger. When a taxpayer ceases to do business, a second or successor corporation may become liable for the taxes of the taxpayer if the second corporation is the mere continuation of the taxpayer under the de facto merger rule and the interrelated theory of continuation of the business. See Atlas Tool Co. v. Comm'r, 614 F2d 860, 870–871 (3d Cir. 1980); Today's Child Learning Ctr., Inc. v. United States, 81 AFTR2d 98-1362 (ED Pa. 1998). In de facto merger and mere continuation situations, courts consider factors such as continuity of management, personnel, location, assets, and operations.

[83] Comm'r v. Oswego Falls Corp., 71 F2d 673 (2d Cir. 1934) (applying New York law); Missile Sys. Corp. v. Comm'r, 23 TCM 1276 (1964) (applying Delaware law). But cf. Turnbull, Inc. v. Comm'r, 42 TC 582 (1964), aff'd, 373 F2d 91 (5th Cir.), cert. denied, 389 US 842 (1967) (surviving corporation found secondarily liable as transferee based on an agreement between the Service and the surviving corporation).

the statutory provisions merely impose a contract term the parties themselves may have omitted, and the same result should follow as if the term had actually been included in the contract.

On a merger or consolidation, the surviving corporation may be subject to transferee liability, with the theory of liability usually being transferee liability at law. Frequently, on a merger or consolidation, there is an agreement whereby the surviving corporation agrees to assume the liabilities of the constituent or disappearing corporation. For example, in *Texsun Supply Corp.*,[84] *A* and *B* merged under the laws of Louisiana, with *A* as the surviving corporation. In the merger agreement, *A* agreed to assume the payment of all obligations and debts of *B*, including income and other taxes. The Tax Court found *A* to be liable under the assumption by contract theory and because the transaction constituted a merger.[85] The corporation laws of many states contain provisions that the surviving corporation becomes liable for the debts of the constituent corporations disappearing in a merger or consolidation. There is some authority that when such a law exists, the survivor is not liable as a transferee but is primarily liable for the liabilities of the constituent corporations, so that the extended statute of limitations when transferee liability is asserted does not apply.[86] When the agreement governing the merger or consolidation provides for the assumption of liabilities or when a separate agreement admitting transferee liability is executed, the surviving corporation is subject to transferee or secondary liability, not primary liability, under the state law.[87]

If the new corporation is merely a continuation of the transferor, transferee liability applies.[88] For example, transferee liability applies when a

---

[84] Texsun Supply Corp., 17 TC 433 (1951).

[85] See also Turnbull, Inc., 42 TC 582 (1964), aff'd, 373 F2d 91 (5th Cir.), cert. denied, 389 US 842 (1967).

[86] Comm'r v. Oswego Falls Corp., 71 F2d 673 (2d Cir. 1934) (involving the New York Business Corporation Law); Missile Sys. Corp., 23 TCM 1276 (1964). In Southern Pac. Transp. Co. v. Comm'r, 84 TC 367 (1985), the Tax Court held that the Delaware corporation law was like the New York law construed in *Oswego Falls*, so that under Delaware law, the successor corporation in a merger is primarily liable for the debts of the disappearing corporation. However, *Oswego Falls* was distinguished on the ground that the merger agreement in the case expressly provided that the successor constructively obligated itself to pay the liabilities of the disappearing corporation. As a result, the transferee liability statute applied, and the Service's notice of deficiency was timely because there was an additional year to send it to the petitioner-transferee under Section 6901.

[87] In both Texsun Supply Corp., 17 TC 433 (1951), and Turnbull, Inc., 42 TC 582 (1964), aff'd, 373 F2d 91 (5th Cir.), cert. denied, 389 US 842 (1967), the survivor executed a separate agreement admitting transferee liability that was considered by the courts to be at least one of the bases for distinguishing *Oswego Falls*.

[88] Atlas Tool Co. v. Comm'r, 614 F2d 860 (3d Cir. 1980), cert. denied (Type D reorganization); Abegg v. Comm'r, 429 F2d 1209 (2d Cir. 1970) (same). See Estate of Ber-

reincorporation of the corporation constitutes a Type D or Type F reorganization under Section 368, or where a new corporation acquires the assets and business of the old corporation in exchange for the new corporation's stock (a Type C reorganization). If there is merely a recapitalization of an existing corporation (a Type E reorganization), or if the name of the corporation is changed (a variety of Type F reorganization), there is no transferee liability because there is no transfer of assets. Thus, the existing corporation remains primarily liable for the tax. Transferee liability may be imposed in these situations under a number of theories. First, the acquiring corporation may be liable at law under the assumption by contract theory if the governing agreement in the reorganization provides for the assumption of liabilities.[89] Also, liability may be asserted on the theory that the transferee did not give full and adequate consideration for the assets or property acquired.[90] When the shareholders of the old corporation organize the new corporation to take over the assets of the old corporation, the new corporation is in substance a continuation of the old corporation and is considered to have taken the property of the old corporation subject to its liabilities, including those for taxes.[91]

[7] The Special Estate and Gift Tax Lien

Section 6324 imposes on transferees and others, who receive property includable in a decedent's gross estate, personal liability for the unpaid estate tax due from the estate and imposes on donees, who receive gifts during the year, personal liability for the amount of the donor's unpaid gift tax. Transferee liability for estate taxes specifically includes "any person who under Section 6324(a)(2) is personally liable for any part of such tax."[92] When the theory of liability at law is based on Section 6324, therefore, the Service need prove only that (1) the transferee received property subject to estate or gift tax; (2)

---

nard Stauffer, 48 TC 277, 288, 307 (1967), rev'd on another issue, 403 F2d 611 (9th Cir. 1968) (Type F reorganization).

[89] See California Iron Yards Corp. v. Comm'r, 82 F2d 776 (9th Cir. 1956).

[90] See Dardi v. United States, 252 F2d 670 (9th Cir. 1958) (shareholders formed partnership with the assets they received in liquidating distributions from the transferor corporation; adequate consideration held not to have been given); Coffee Pot Holding Corp. v. Comm'r, 113 F2d 415 (5th Cir. 1940); George M. Newcomb, 23 TC 954 (1955).

[91] Atlas Tool Co. v. Comm'r, 614 F2d 860 (3d Cir. 1980), cert. denied (continuity of stockholder interest); Delacroix Corp. v. Comm'r, 84 F2d 442 (5th Cir. 1936); Joy Harper Scott v. Comm'r, 70 TC 71 (1978) (new corporation nominally owned by wife actually continued business of husband's old corporation; held, wife transferee).

[92] IRC § 6901(h). The special gift and estate tax lien of Section 6324 is described in Chapter 14.

the transferor owed the tax in question; and (3) the tax is due and unpaid.[93] Liability under Section 6324 covers transfers of probate and nonprobate assets. However, with respect to probate assets, the Service can also proceed under state laws dealing with distributions of assets of an estate before all claims are fully satisfied.[94]

The beneficiaries who receive property includable in the gross estate of a decedent are personally liable for unpaid estate tax, and donees of property are personally liable for gift tax pursuant to the provisions of Section 6324. One method of enforcing this personal liability is by utilizing the transferee assessment procedures of Section 6901. These procedures are not exclusive. When the tax involved is the decedent's unpaid income tax, transferee liability in equity may be asserted against beneficiaries of an estate if the estate is insolvent or has been completely distributed.[95] The basis of liability is that the beneficiary is a transferee of a transferee; that is, the decedent has transferred property to the estate, which in turn has transferred property to the beneficiary. Under these circumstances, if either the decedent or the estate was insolvent and property was distributed to the beneficiaries, the transfer would be covered under the UFCA, and the executor or administrator will be personally liable under Section 3713(b) for paying a legacy or devise before a debt to the United States.

---

[93] Schuster v. Comm'r, 312 F2d 311 (9th Cir. 1962) (under Section 6324, the transferee's liability is primary, exists if the estate is liable for estate tax, and is limited only by the value of the property received); Want v. Comm'r, 280 F2d 777 (2d Cir. 1960) (trustee liable only to the extent of funds in trust when the notice of deficiency was sent); La Fortune Trust v. Comm'r, 263 F2d 186 (10th Cir. 1958); Baur v. Comm'r 145 F2d 338 (3d Cir. 1944) (donee of nontaxable gift was held personally liable to the extent of its value for the unpaid gift tax the donor owed on another taxable gift to different donor); Groetzinger v. Comm'r, 69 TC 309 (1977); Magill v. Comm'r, 43 TCM 859 (1982) (jointly owned property passing outside probate subject to transferee liability under Section 6324(a)(2).

Consequently, the nature and extent of liability is governed by federal law, not state law. Baptiste v. Comm'r, 29 F3d 1533 (11th Cir. 1994), aff'g 63 TCM 2649 (1992) ("Section 6324(a)(2) imposes a direct and personal liability on petitioner as beneficiary of the proceeds of insurance on decedent's life"). See also Baptiste v. Comm'r, 100 TC 252 (1993) ("[t]he limitation imposed by Section 6324(a)(2) applies to a transferee's liability for unpaid estate tax and for interest accrued thereon owed by a transferor; it does not apply to a transferee's liability for interest accrued on unpaid estate tax owed by the transferee"), aff'd, 29 F3d 433 (8th Cir. 1994), cert. denied, 513 US 1190 (1995).

[94] See, e.g., Magill v. Comm'r, 43 TCM 859 (1982) (Illinois law applied to determine transferee liability, but not the applicable statute of limitations).

[95] See United States v. Floersch, 276 F2d 714 (10th Cir.), cert. denied, 364 US 816 (1960) (transfer of assets to widow from husband's estate rendered the estate insolvent, and under New Mexico law the widow was liable as a transferee for payment of the husband's unpaid taxes); Viles v. Comm'r, 233 F2d 376 (6th Cir. 1956); Sadie D. Leary, 18 TC 139 (1952); Grace McKnight, 15 TC 730 (1950).

A cotenant of jointly owned property who acquires the entire property on the death of a deceased taxpayer has generally been held not to be a transferee for the purposes of Section 6901. Because the surviving joint tenant or tenant by entirety takes the full estate by virtue of the creation of the tenancy and not on the death of the cotenant, the survivor is not a transferee and is not liable for the unpaid income taxes of the deceased tenant.[96] However, when individual partners transferred property to the partnership, although the partnership was a separate entity and the property became partnership property, the individual partners were held transferees.[97]

A beneficiary receiving life insurance proceeds under a policy owned by the deceased taxpayer, is liable as a transferee at law for unpaid estate taxes by virtue of the provisions of Section 6324. The liability of a life insurance beneficiary for the decedent's income taxes depends on whether or not the taxes have been assessed before the death of the decedent. If there has been a tax assessment and a lien has attached to all of the decedent's property and rights to property before the decedent's death, then the beneficiary merely takes the proceeds of the policy subject to the lien. However, only the amount of the proceeds equivalent to the cash surrender value of the policy at the time of the decedent/taxpayer's death is subject to the lien. The balance does not constitute "property or rights to property" of the insured, to which a tax lien could have attached at the time of the insured's death.[98] The Supreme Court held in *Commissioner v. Stern* that if there is no prior federal tax lien, state law determines the existence and extent of the beneficiary's liability. The beneficiary of a life insurance policy is not subject to transferee liability if state law exempts the beneficiary from the claims of the insured's creditors.[99] However, if under state fraudulent conveyance law it can be shown that the deceased taxpayer paid premiums with the intent to defraud creditors, the beneficiary is liable as a transferee in equity for the amount of the premiums paid plus interest, but not for the balance of the proceeds of the policy.[100] In *Stern*, the beneficiary of the insurance policy was the wife of the decedent. When the decedent's estate is the beneficiary of the policy and the proceeds are paid to the estate, which in turn pays them to the widow, the widow is a transferee of the estate and not a beneficiary of the life insurance policy. Ac-

---

[96] Tooley v. Comm'r, 121 F2d 350 (9th Cir. 1941) (California); Irvine v. Helvering, 99 F2d 265 (8th Cir. 1938) (Minnesota); Fecarotta v. United States, 154 F. Supp. 592 (D. Ariz. 1956).

[97] Comm'r v. Kuckenberg, 309 F2d 202 (9th Cir. 1962) (partners of partnership to which assets of liquidated corporation were transferred were held liable as transferees). See also Kamen Soap Prods. Co. v. Comm'r, 230 F2d 565 (2d Cir. 1956) (corporation to which a partnership interest was transferred was held to be a transferee).

[98] United States v. Bess, 357 US 51 (1958).

[99] Comm'r v. Stern, 357 US 39 (1958).

[100] United States v. Truax, 223 F2d 229 (5th Cir. 1955).

cordingly, the widow would be liable as a transferee in equity if the estate were insolvent.[101]

[8] Fiduciary Liability

The liability of a fiduciary for any tax owed to the United States is based on Sections 3713(a) and 3713(b) of Title 31.[102] Fiduciary liability differs from transferee liability. In general, the liability of a fiduciary arises from the priority of a tax claim when a taxpayer is insolvent and when the fiduciary pays, on behalf of the debtor or an estate, debts which do not have the priority over debts due to the United States. This differs from transferee liability, which is asserted when a transferee takes the property of the transferor without full, fair, and adequate consideration to the prejudice of the United States as a creditor. Both an estate and the executor or administrator of the estate, in its representative capacity, can be liable as transferees of the assets of the deceased taxpayer under Section 6901.[103] The estate and its executors are relieved of liability only if a notice of transferee liability has not been received before the assets have been distributed and the executor or administrator dismissed under local law.[104] The executor may apply for release from personal liability by written application and payment of the amount of tax determined under the provisions of Section 6905(a).

¶ 17.04 TRANSFEREE LIABILITY IN EQUITY

The elements of transferee liability in equity derive in substantial part from the requirements of state fraudulent conveyance laws. Therefore, a proper under-

---

[101] Kieferdorf v. Comm'r, 142 F2d 723 (9th Cir.), cert. denied, 323 US 733 (1944).

[102] See supra Chapter 16.

[103] Estate of Henry Miller, 42 TC 593 (1964) (decedent who had withdrawn funds from an insolvent corporation was liable as a transferee to the extent that the funds had been used for his personal benefit, and his estate was held liable for the same amount); Estate of Robert Harrison, 16 TC 727 (1951); Estate of Irving Smith, 16 TC 807 (1951); Estate of LE McKnight, 8 TC 871 (1947); Ewart v. Comm'r, 84 TC 912 (1985), aff'd, 814 F2d 321 (6th Cir. 1987) (co-executor who received property from estate as beneficiary was held liable as transferee under Ohio law because transfer rendered estate insolvent).

When property is distributed to two beneficiaries, they are jointly and severally liable for the primary liability of the estate for estate tax. When the transfer of property from the estate is without consideration and renders the estate insolvent, the transferee beneficiary becomes derivatively liable without the necessity of showing any intent to defraud. Id.

[104] Hulburd v. Comm'r, 296 US 300 (1935).

standing of transferee liability in equity requires some background in the law of fraudulent conveyances. The substantive law of transferee liability varies from state to state, but in most transferee liability cases, the state law involved is its fraudulent conveyance law, which for most states is the state version of the UFCA or its successor, the UFTA.

The modern law of fraudulent conveyances derives from a statute enacted in 1570 during the reign of Queen Elizabeth, which made any transfer made "to delay, hinder or defraud creditors or others" voidable by the persons hindered, delayed, or defrauded. Some states still apply this common-law fraudulent conveyance law. Proof of fraudulent intent was and is difficult, and so circumstantial evidence from which an intent to defraud could be inferred, called badges of fraud, came to be recognized. In the United States, the states recognize various transfers as badges of fraud, however, intrafamily transfers, transfers of property without consideration, transfers of all or a substantial amount of property without consideration, and transfers of all or a substantial amount of property immediately before anticipated litigation are generally considered to be badges of fraud.

In order to conform the many variations in the fraudulent conveyance statutes and common law, in 1918, the UFCA was proposed and remains the fraudulent conveyance law in many states.[105] In 1984, the National Conference of Commissioners on Uniform State Laws approved the UFTA, and this replacement of the UFCA has been adopted in at least thirty-six states, including California, Florida, New Jersey, and Texas, as well as the District of Columbia.

[1] The UFCA and the UFTA

The UFCA and the UFTA have roughly the same structure and basic approach. For example, both have separate provisions for actual fraud and constructive fraud. The UFCA describes as fraudulent, every conveyance made with intent to defraud (Section 7), as well as a conveyance, irrespective of the insolvent's intent, the insolvent makes without a "fair consideration" (Section 4).[106] The UFTA, on the other hand, covers in its Section 4 three provisions of

---

[105] As of January 1, 1997, the UFCA remains in effect in five states, including New York and the Virgin Islands. Uniform Laws Annotated, UFCA General Notes.

[106] UFCA § 4. Section 5 is entitled "Conveyances by Persons in Business"; Section 6, "Conveyances by a Person About to Incur Debts"; and Section 8, "Conveyance of Partnership Property."

Section 548 of the Bankruptcy Code (11 USC § 548) generally incorporates the fraudulent conveyance law as codified in the UFCA, so a law developed under the Bankruptcy Code may be applicable to a fraudulent conveyance outside of a bankruptcy context.

the UFCA: (1) conveyances made with intent to defraud (Section 4); (2) conveyances by persons in business (Section 5); and (3) conveyances by persons about to incur debts (Section 6). Section 4 of the UFTA provides that a transfer is fraudulent as to present and future creditors if the debtor made the transfer (1) with actual intent to defraud or (2) without receiving "reasonably equivalent value" in exchange for the transferred property, and the debtor either (a) was engaged in or about to engage in a business, or a transaction, for which the debtor's remaining assets were "unreasonably small" in relation to the business or transaction, or (b) intended to incur debts beyond the debtor's ability to pay as they became due, or reasonably should have believed that this inability to pay would occur. Section 4 of the UFTA also makes a transfer fraudulent as to creditors whose claims arose before or after the transfer was made if the transfer was actually or constructively fraudulent. A transfer is fraudulent as to a creditor whose claim arose before the transfer under Section 5(a) of the UFTA, if the transfer was made without the debtor's receiving a reasonably equivalent value in exchange for the transfer and the debtor was insolvent at that time or the debtor became insolvent as a result of the transfer. Also, under Section 5(b) of the UFTA, a transfer is fraudulent as to a present creditor if the transfer was made to an insider for an antecedent debt, the debtor was insolvent at the time, and the insider had reasonable cause to believe that the debtor was insolvent.

By judicial interpretation, a "transferee" includes "one who takes property of another without full, fair, and adequate consideration to the prejudice of creditors."[107] By way of illustration, but not by way of limitation, Section 6901 states that the term "transferee" includes "donee, heir, legatee, devisee and distributee."[108] Regulations expand the classes of transferees by adding distributees of a decedent's estate; shareholders of a dissolved corporation; assignees or donees of an insolvent person; successors of a corporation; a party to a reorganization as defined in Section 368 of the Code; and all other classes of distributees.[109] Neither the UFCA nor the UFTA defines a "transferee," but the UFTA does define persons who are "insiders" in their relationship with the debtor when the debtor is an individual, corporation, or a partnership. For individuals, an "insider" includes a relative of the debtor or a general partner of the debtor; a partnership in which the debtor is a general partner; or a relative of a general partner in a partnership which controls the debtor.[110] If the debtor is a corporation, an insider is a director of the debtor; an officer of the debtor;

---

[107] First Nat'l Bank v. Comm'r, 255 F2d 759, 762 (7th Cir. 1958).

[108] IRC § 6901(h).

[109] Reg. § 301.6901-1(b).

[110] UFTA § 1(7)(i). The UFTA also defines a "relative" as "an individual related by consanguinity within the third degree as determined by the common law, a spouse or an individual related to a spouse within the third degree as so determined, and includes an individual in an adoptive relationship within the third degree." UFTA § 1(11).

a person in control of the debtor; a partnership in which the debtor is a general partner; a general partner in a partnership, which is in control of the debtor; or a relative of a general partner, director, officer, or person in control of the debtor.[111] Important classes of transferees are (1) successors of or distributees from corporations and (2) those having dealings with an estate as fiduciary or beneficiary.

[a] Fair Consideration

For the purposes of the UFCA, "fair consideration" uses two comparative value standards: (1) "Fair equivalent" if the transfer is an absolute transfer such as an exchange of property or a gift, and (2) "not disproportionately small" if the transfer is a transfer for security (e.g., under Article 9 of the UCC).[112] Fair consideration also requires good faith, which has been interpreted to exist when there is "(1) an honest belief in the propriety of the activities in question; (2) no attempt to take unconscionable advantage of others; and (3) no attempt to, or knowledge of the fact that the activities in question will, hinder, delay, or defraud others."[113] By contrast, the UFTA uses the term "reasonably equivalent value," which is not completely defined in Section 2, except that value is property, which includes the satisfaction of antecedent debt, the transferee gives temporaneously in exchange for the debtor's property.[114]

[b] Insolvency

The other element of a UFCA fraudulent conveyance is "insolvency," which is defined by Section 2 to exist "when the present 'fair salable value'" of [the debtor's] assets is less than the amount that will be required to pay his probable liability on his existing debts as they become absolute and matured." A transfer by an insolvent debtor is considered to constitute a constructively fraudulent transfer. Under the UFTA, Section 2, "[a] debtor is 'insolvent' if the sum of the debtor's debts is greater than all of the debtor's assets at a fair valuation," and if the debtor is "generally not paying his [or her] debts as they become due."[115] Thus, the UFTA uses both a modified balance sheet test and an equitable insolvency test in determining whether the debtor is insolvent.

---

[111] FTCA § 1(7)(ii).

[112] UFCA § 3.

[113] Tacoma Ass'n of Creditmen v. Lester, 433 P2d 901 (Wash. 1967).

[114] UFTA § 3.

[115] The term "fair valuation" is not defined, but presumably means the valuation of the debtor's assets at their fair market values. Debts, on the other hand, do not include "an

[c] The Transferor's Intent

Under the UFCA and the UFTA, a transfer may be fraudulent if it is made with the actual intent to defraud creditors (actual fraud), thus putting the debtor's subjective intention in issue. A conveyance is fraudulent under Section 7 of the UFCA when it is made "with actual intent, as distinguished from intent presumed in law, to hinder, delay, or defraud either present or future creditors. . . ."[116] For purposes of Section 7 of the UFCA, the focus is on intent, not the adequacy of the consideration or the financial condition of the transferor as it is under Section 2. Usually, this actual intent to defraud is established by the same evidence that constitutes "badges of fraud" under prior law.

On the other hand, Section 4(b) of the UFTA lists objective factors which, among other factors, may be considered by the trier of fact. These objective factors include whether

1. The transfer or obligation was to an insider;
2. The debtor retained possession or control of the property transferred after the transfer;
3. The transfer or obligation was disclosed or concealed;
4. The debtor had been sued or was threatened with suit, before the transfer was made or the obligation incurred;
5. The transfer was of substantially all the debtor's assets;
6. The debtor absconded;
7. The debtor removed or concealed assets;
8. The value of the consideration received by the debtor was reasonably equivalent to the value of the asset transferred or the amount of the obligation incurred;
9. The debtor was insolvent or became insolvent shortly after the transaction was made or the obligation was incurred;
10. The transfer occurred shortly before or shortly after a substantial debt was incurred; and
11. The debtor transferred the essential assets of the business to a lienor who transferred the assets to an insider of the debtor.

---

obligation to the extent that it is secured by a valid lien on property of the debtor not included as an asset." UFTA § 2(e).

[116] For a case applying this distinction, see Carr Enters. v. United States, 539 F. Supp. 528 (DSD 1982), aff'd per curiam, 698 F2d 952 (8th Cir. 1983) (applying South Dakota fraudulent conveyance law, taxpayer's transfer of business and residence to corporation and corporation's stock in a "church" held to have "involved scheme to put their property beyond the reach of government process"); Loving Saviour Church v. United States, 556 F. Supp. 688 (DSD 1983), aff'd, 728 F2d 1085 (8th Cir. 1984) (same).

[d] The Creditor's Remedies

Under the UFCA, the rights of creditors depend on whether their claims have matured. Once a creditor's claim has matured, the creditor may either (1) have the conveyance set aside to the extent necessary to satisfy its claim or (2) disregard the conveyance and levy execution on the property conveyed.[117] In this respect, the UFCA restates the traditional remedies available to a creditor. The remedy of having the conveyance set aside was an equitable remedy usually enforced by a creditor's bill. This remedy was preferable to disregarding the conveyance and attaching or levying execution on the property conveyed. Because the validity of the conveyance was determined in advance of the sale of the property, the amount received on the sale probably would have been higher.

If the rights of the creditor have not matured, under the UFCA a creditor still may proceed in court and may ask the court to (1) restrain the defendant from disposing of the property; (2) appoint a receiver to take charge of the property; (3) set aside the conveyance or annul the obligation; or (4) make any order that the circumstances of the case may require.[118] The UFCA somewhat expands the rights of creditors with unmatured interests in the extent of the remedies available. A prior judgment was generally necessary to maintain an action to set aside a fraudulent conveyance. However, it was not necessary that the creditor's claim be reduced to judgment at the time the conveyance was made, as long as the creditor had a claim at the time of the conveyance, whether that claim was liquidated or contingent.[119]

Under Section 7 of the UFTA, a creditor has such remedies as (1) the avoidance of the transfer to the extent necessary to satisfy the creditor's claim; (2) an attachment or other provisional remedy against the asset transferred or other property of the transferee; or (3) an injunction or the appointment of a receiver.

The transferee does have defenses and protections against these remedies.[120] For example, a present or future creditor may not avoid the constructively fraudulent transfer of an insolvent debtor if the transfer results from (1) a termination of a lease upon default by the debtor when the termination is pursuant to the lease and applicable law or (2) enforcement of a security interest in compliance with Article 9 of the UCC. Similarly, even if the debtor made the transfer with actual fraud, the transfer is not voidable against a person who took the property in good faith and for a reasonably equivalent value. In addition, as long as the transferee took the property in good faith, the trans-

---

[117] UFCA § 9.

[118] UFCA § 10.

[119] See V. Countryman, Cases and Materials on Debtor and Creditor 135 (2d ed. 1974).

[120] UFTA § 8.

feree is entitled to consideration of the value given for the property, even if it was not reasonably equivalent value (e.g., the amount of any judgment).

[2] Elements of Liability in Equity

As the foregoing description of the UFCA and the newer UFTA demonstrates, to hold a transferee liable in equity, it must be established that

- The transferor transferred property to the transferee;
- The transferor was liable for a tax;
- The tax is still unpaid;
- The transfer was made after the tax liability accrued;
- The transfer was made without full and adequate consideration or with the intention to defraud creditors;
- The transfer left the taxpayer/transferor insolvent; and
- The government has exhausted all reasonable procedural remedies against the taxpayer/transferor before proceeding against the transferee.

The taxpayer/transferor's solvency is not an element of proof if the transfer is made with the actual intent to defraud creditors. The requirements of a transfer of assets, the taxpayer/transferor's liability for the tax, and the nonpayment of the tax have already been discussed.[121]

[a] Transfer of Assets Was Made After Accrual of Tax Liability

The rationale of transferee liability is that the transferor, by the transfer of assets, has wrongfully deprived the government of a chance to satisfy the debt out of these assets. Certainly, this chance never existed when the transfer was made before the taxable period involved. However, the government is deprived of a source of collection when property is transferred during or after the period for which the liability has accrued.[122] Notice that the liability need only have accrued; it need not have been assessed.[123]

---

[121] See supra ¶ 17.02. See Gumm v. Comm'r, 93 TC 475, 480 (1989) (factors described).

[122] Blanche S. Sharp, 35 TC 1168, 1175 (1961); Leon Papineau, 28 TC 54, 58 (1957). In *Papineau*, the Tax Court said, "[T]he transferee is retroactively liable for the transferor's taxes in the year of transfer and prior years, and penalty and interest in connection therewith, to the extent of the assets received from the transferor, even though the transferor's liability was unknown at the time of the transfer."

[123] Yagoda v. Comm'r, 39 TC 170 (1962), aff'd, 331 F2d 485 (2d Cir.), cert. denied, 379 US 842 (1964) (when trust was terminated and its assets were distributed, the 1944 and 1945 tax liability had accrued); Scott v. Comm'r, 117 F2d 36 (8th Cir. 1941) (although tax was assessed against a corporation after it had made transfers to its shareholders, the tax was a "potential liability of the corporation, of which the shareholders are

[b] The Transferor Was Insolvent

Insolvency is not required if the debtor transfers property with the actual intent of defrauding any creditor, including the Service. A necessary element of constructive fraud, on the other hand, is the debtor's insolvency. Constructive fraud exists when the debtor, while insolvent, transfers property without receiving fair consideration (the UFCA term) or having received property having a reasonably equivalent value (the UFTA term), or the transfer left the debtor insolvent because the debtor received no property or property not meeting the relevant standard. It is not the transfer of assets alone that establishes liability. The chance to satisfy the tax debt could only be lost if the taxpayer/transferor was already insolvent or was rendered insolvent by the transfer, thereby defeating the possibility of payment of the tax debt.[124]

Insolvency is determined according to state law,[125] although the courts have not always followed this rule.[126] Under Section 2 of the UFCA, insolvency is determined according to a comparative value test and a probable liability test. A person is insolvent when the "present fair salable value" of his or her assets is less than the amount that will be required to pay his or her probable liability on his or her existing debts as they become absolute and matured. The UFCA definition is similar to, although not identical with, the rules in transferee liability cases. In these cases, it is said that insolvency results when the fair market value of the taxpayer's assets at the date of the transfer do not equal or exceed the taxpayer's liabilities on that date.[127] The UFTA also uses a

---

charged with notice"); In re Circle Bar Ranch, Inc., 83-1 USTC ¶ 9246 (MD Fla. 1983) (1978 transfer of assets made after 1973 income tax liability had accrued); RG Cope, Jr., Inc. v. Comm'r, 48 TCM 1053, 1059 (1984) (1976 transfers made after income taxes accrued for 1972–1975).

[124] Ownbey Co. v. Comm'r, 645 F2d 540 (6th Cir. 1981) ("a court must first find that the transferor was insolvent at the time of the transfer or immediately thereafter..." (citations and footnote omitted)). It follows that when there is more than one transfer, the Service is required to prove insolvency on the date of each transfer. Id. Arlington Brown, 24 TC 256 (1955) (no transferee liability found when there was a failure to prove insolvency either before or immediately after the transfers); Charles E. Smith & Sons v. Comm'r, 6 TC Memo. 529 (1947), aff'd, 184 F2d 1011 (6th Cir. 1950), cert. denied, 340 US 953 (1951).

[125] Comm'r v. Stern, 357 US 39 (1958).

[126] See, e.g., Kreps v. Comm'r, 351 F2d 1 (2d Cir. 1965). See also United States v. 58th St. Plaza Theatre, Inc., 287 F. Supp. 475 (SDNY 1968). In these cases, the equity (failure to pay debts as they mature) and bankruptcy (liabilities exceed assets) standards were considered in determining insolvency.

[127] May R. Kierferdorf v. Comm'r, 1 TC 772, 776–777 (1943), aff'd, 142 F2d 723 (9th Cir.), cert. denied, 323 US 733 (1944) (an ordinary definition of "insolvency" is, in effect, a preponderance of liabilities over assets); Mary Stoumen, 27 TC 1014, 1019 (1957). For a case analyzing the assets and liabilities of a transferor for purposes of determining transferor's solvency on the date of the transfer, see Elizalde v. Comm'r, 48 TCM

balance sheet test, which provides that a debtor is insolvent "if the sum of the debtor's debts is greater than all of the debtor's assets at a fair valuation."[128] The UFTA creates a presumption that a debtor is insolvent if the debtor "is generally not paying his [or her] debts as they become due."[129] In some transferee cases, the courts have used the equity test (ability to pay debts as they mature), the balance sheet test, or both. Whichever test the state uses (the common-law test of insolvency, the UFCA, or the UFTA) it should be followed, not a federal standard, because state law controls.[130]

Under the general principles applied in better-decided transferee cases, the UFCA, and the UFTA solvency of the debtor can only be decided after the value of the debtor's assets on the date of the transfer is determined. What assets and liabilities are considered for the purpose of determining solvency? The property of the debtor is usually capable of determination.[131] However, under the UFCA, the term "assets" of a debtor means property not exempt from liability for the debtor's debts.[132] Under general principles of international law, assets of the debtor/taxpayer in a foreign country are excluded because a foreign country will not enforce the tax claims of another; however, assets based in a foreign country having a treaty with the United States providing mutual enforcement of tax obligations, seem to be includable in the term assets.[133]

28, 36–39 (1984) (defective jeopardy assessment not considered a "debt"); Zadorkin v. Comm'r, 49 TCM 1022 (1985) (California law applied, and evidence of insolvency found in Form 433-AB executed eight months after transfer).

[128] UFTA § 2(a).

[129] UFTA § 2(b).

[130] See United States v. Edwards, 572 F. Supp. 1527, 1529 (D. Conn. 1983) (applying Connecticut law, "A person is insolvent for the purpose of determining the existence of a fraudulent conveyance if he is unable to pay his debts existing at the time of the transfer").

[131] The Commissioner may rely on the cash basis books of the debtor and disregard accounts receivable, and if the debtor is insolvent on this basis, the burden of going forward with evidence that the receivables should be considered shifts to the transferee. Kreps v. Comm'r, 351 F2d 1 (2d Cir. 1965).

[132] UFCA § 1. The UFTA provides that an asset means property of the debtor, but does not include property to the extent that it is encumbered by a valid lien, exempt, or held in tenancy by the entireties. UFTA § 1(2). As a result, in determining whether the debtor is insolvent, debts "do not include an obligation to the extent it is secured by a valid lien on property of the debtor not included as an asset." UFTA § 2(e).

[133] United States v. van der Horst, 270 F. Supp. 365 (D. Del. 1967) (tax claims not finally determined as required by the 1948 United States-Netherlands treaty, and so the Netherlands did not have the authority to assist the United States in collecting tax from a U.S. citizen, except in certain circumstances); George M. Newcomb, 23 TC 954 (1955) (at the time, the United States-Canada treaty did not include a collection assistance provision).

The UFTA § 2(d) provides that assets for insolvency purposes do not include "property that has been transferred, concealed, or removed with intent to hinder, delay, or de-

Also, property that is exempt from claims of creditors, such as jointly owned property, has also been excluded from a debtor's assets, at least when a debtor has "no property" for a creditor to attach.[134]

On the other side of the balance sheet, the liabilities of a debtor include "his probable liability on his existing debts as they become absolute and matured."[135] Accrued tax liabilities, even if unknown at the time of the transfer and even if they have not matured by assessment, are included in the liabilities of the debtor/taxpayer for the purpose of determining his or her insolvency on the date of the transfer.[136]

---

fraud creditors or that has been transferred in a manner making the transfer voidable under [the UFTA]."

[134] Louise Noell, 22 TC 1035, 1043 (1954) (tenancy by the entireties exempt under Missouri Law). Cf. May R. Keiferdorf, 1 TC 772 (1943), aff'd, 142 F2d 723 (9th Cir.), cert. denied, 323 US 733 (1944) (insurance proceeds, exempt under California law from execution but held subject to transferee liability in the hands of the widow, were apparently considered an asset of the estate). Therefore, the distinction seems to be whether, under state law, the property "belonged" to the debtor at all. If it did belong to the debtor, it is includable for the purposes of determining solvency, irrespective of any state exemption statute. This rule must be distinguished from state laws declaring the proceeds of life insurance, when paid directly to the beneficiary, to be exempt from the claims of creditors. These proceeds are not property of the estate for the purpose of transferee liability. See Comm'r v. Stern, 357 US 39 (1958). Alonso v. Comm'r, 78 TC 577 (1982) (creation of tenancy by the entirety by husband who failed to retain sufficient property to satisfy existing creditors void under North Carolina law). See also UFTA § 1(2)(iii), stating that an asset does not include property held by the entireties.

[135] UFCA § 2(1).

[136] Kreps v. Comm'r, 351 F2d 1 (2d Cir. 1965); Yagoda v. Comm'r, 331 F2d 485, 492 (2d Cir.), cert. denied, 379 US 842 (1964) ("a transferee is accountable for any accrued liability of the transferor, even though the amount owing may be determined subsequent to the transfer"). See Madonia v. United States, 86-1 USTC ¶ 9170 (WDNY 1985) (1975 liability considered in determining insolvency, despite filing of amended 1975 return in 1978, and trial claim that 1975 taxes were overpaid); United States v. Bushlow, 832 F. Supp. 574 (EDNY 1993) (the Service is deemed to be a creditor as of the date the tax obligation accrues); United States v. Red Stripe, 792 F. Supp. 1338, 1342 (EDNY 1992); United States v. 58th St. Plaza Theatre, Inc., 287 F. Supp. 475, 501 (SDNY 1968). Tax liabilities include interest and penalties. Ownbey Co. v. Comm'r, 645 F2d 540 (6th Cir. 1981).

Compare Cope v. Comm'r, 781 F2d 852 (11th Cir. 1986) (parents failed to file 1974 and 1975 income tax returns, and mother transferred house to son's corporation on January 5, 1976, before the filing of the 1976 return was due and more than a year after the 1974 return was due; held, Service not an existing creditor under Alabama law, although mother admitted joint liability for husband's tax liabilities on December 19, 1976).

[3] The Transfer Was Made Without Full and Adequate Consideration

When a purchaser pays full value in cash for assets conveyed by a transferor, the transferor's creditors are not prejudiced by the transaction.[137] Whether the debtor has received fair consideration under the UFCA or reasonably equivalent value for the assets transferred is a question of valuation of the property received from the transferor and valuation of the property conveyed to the transferor in exchange.[138] It takes no intensive analysis to recognize that a debtor's transfer of property to a family member without consideration is not

---

[137] West Tex. Ref. & Dev. Co. v. Comm'r, 68 F2d 77 (10th Cir. 1933); Stewart Title Guar. Co., 15 TC 556 (1950), acq. 1951-1 CB 3. In *Delpit*, stock in a corporation was sold to a partnership of two unrelated individuals; however, the purchase price for the stock was paid with the corporation's assets, and the price far exceeded the value of the stock. Delpit v. Comm'r, 61 TCM 2303 (1991). The Tax Court held that the taxpayer had received the assets of the transferred corporation, that the stock transferred was not fair consideration for the promissory note and payments made under it, that the transfer was made during and after the accrual of the tax liability, and that the transferred corporation was insolvent at the time of the transfer.

[138] GBG, Inc. v. Comm'r, 43 TCM 169 (1981) (analysis of consideration); Alonso v. Comm'r, 78 TC 577 (1982) (to establish fair consideration, wife had to prove she paid the transferor-husband an amount in excess of the value of the property transferred less the amount of taxes due); Zadorkin v. Comm'r, 49 TCM 1022 (1985) (value of remainder interest in property taxpayer transferred to brother exceeded stipulated consideration); Dardanell Co. Trust v. United States, 88-1 USTC ¶¶ 9260, 9261 (D. Minn. 1986) (trust was subject to transferee liability under the Minnesota UFCA where there was inadequate consideration for the transfers and the transferors were rendered insolvent by the transfer); United States v. Gonzalez, 91-1 USTC ¶ 50,100 (D. Colo. 1991) (quitclaim for nominal cash consideration immediately after assessment; held, fraudulent conveyance under Colorado law, not purchase accorded priority under Section 6323).

When past or future services are involved, and these services are made or promised to be made in the marital setting, the valuation issue can be further complicated. See Galluzzo v. Comm'r, 43 TCM 199, 213 (1981) (executory promise to provide services in future not fair consideration). But see United States v. Pilla, 82-2 USTC ¶ 9500 (D. Minn. 1982), aff'd, 808 F2d 841 (8th Cir. 1983) (transfer made as part of anticipated divorce settlement not fair consideration when divorce never occurs). Compare Mayors v. Comm'r, 48 TCM 680 (1984) (transferee who lived for a period with transferor failed to prove that property transferred was fair consideration for services she rendered to transferor as a homemaker), rev'd, 785 F2d 757 (9th Cir. 1986) (forbearance to exercise a legal right under state law was sufficient consideration for purposes of the California fraudulent conveyance law as long as the transfer in exchange for the forbearance was made in good faith). In a case involving New York law, however, a court noted that a husband's obligation to support his wife and children is an antecedent debt that qualifies as fair consideration. United States v. Laronga, 81 AFTR2d 98-462 (EDNY 1998) (husband's transfer claimed to have been made in recognition of Laronga's obligation to support his wife and minor children, and after the transfer he moved to another state); United States v. Hansel, 81 AFTR2d 98-1382 (NDNY 1998) (claim that children's services on farm gave rise to antecedent debt satisfied by transfer of property rejected because, among other reasons, under New York law father had a right to children's services).

a transfer for valuable consideration.[139] A transfer of property in exchange for the cancellation of an antecedent debt does not ordinarily subject a creditor to transferee liability.[140]

When there are multiple transfers of property, the facts in a case may show both constructive and actual fraud. See United States v. Carlin, 80 AFTR2d 97-7810 (SDNY 1996) (husband transferred property to his wife without consideration when he owed more than $80 million, and indisputably insolvent, proving constructive fraud, and the wife then made several transfers of the property to alter ego corporations without consideration, which were held to constitute actual fraud). See also United States v. Dubey, 82 AFTR2d 98-7050 (ED Cal. 1998) (taxpayers who owed about $1 million transferred several parcels of real estate to trusts without any consideration and also continued to control the property purportedly held in trust held to be a transfer in actual and constructive fraud of the Service as a creditor).

[139] Ethel Hamilton Nau v. Comm'r, 27 TC 999 (1957), aff'd in part and rev'd in part on other grounds, 261 F2d 362 (6th Cir. 1958) (no consideration for transfer from husband to wife); Edelson v. Comm'r, 829 F2d 828 (9th Cir. 1987) (property valued at $149,500 was transferred to wife for $200 two weeks before invalid separate return was filed; New Jersey law applied); Sebok v. Comm'r, 43 TCM 255 (1982) (mortgage expected to generate cash flow of $478.81 until 1982, assigned in 1975 for $1.00, held not transferred for fair consideration, nor for love, affection, and promises of love); Hatcher v. Comm'r, 45 TCM 1244 (1983) (father's transfer of property to son for "love and affection" leaving the father without ample property to pay his debts was not made for valuable consideration under Georgia law); United States v. Thomassen, 610 F. Supp. 386 (D. Neb. 1985) ("one dollar and love and affection" paid to parents held inadequate consideration; Nebraska law analyzed); United States v. Braswell, 85-2 USTC ¶ 9685 (SD Ala. 1985) (property valued at $58,000 was purchased by wife for $500; conveyance found fraudulent under Alabama law).

[140] United States v. Mazzara, 530 F. Supp. 1380 (DNJ 1982) (obligation of support did not constitute antecedent debt, but moneys transferred to wife to pay legitimate debts of husband were for antecedent debts and did not constitute fraudulent conveyances). Compare George M. Newcomb, 23 TC 954 (1955) (past services were not part of consideration where there was no proof of the value of the services).

An alleged concern that if transferor spouse remained part owner of the property with her husband, the value of his mortuary business would be adversely affected (her sole means of support), was held not to constitute reasonably equivalent value because neither the emotional benefit of sparing her husband embarrassment nor his support in the future qualified as "value." VanCampen v. United States, 81 AFTR2d 98-324 (D. Kan. 1997). In a case involving New York law, however, a court noted that a husband's obligation to support his wife and children is an antecedent debt that qualifies as fair consideration. United States v. Laronga, 81 AFTR2d 98-462 (EDNY 1998) (husband's transfer claimed to have been made in recognition of Laronga's obligation to support his wife and minor children, and after the transfer he moved to another state).

When there are multiple transfers of property, the facts in a case may show both constructive and actual fraud. See United States v. Carlin, 80 AFTR2d 97-7810 (SDNY 1996) (husband transferred property to his wife without consideration when he owed more than $80 million, and indisputably insolvent, proving constructive fraud, and the wife then made several transfers of the property to alter ego corporations without consideration, which were held to constitute actual fraud).

In determining the value of the consideration, the amount of a mortgage assumed by the transferee reduces the value of the property transferred (or is part of the consideration given by the transferee).[141] However, when a parent corporation liquidated a subsidiary and claimed that the subsidiary's assets were received to repay advances from the parent to the subsidiary, the Tax Court rejected the argument because the "debt" actually constituted equity and the payment of an obligation of the transferor by the transferee (which does not have priority over the tax claim) is no defense against transferee liability.[142]

[a] Transferor Intended to Defraud

A transfer may be fraudulent because a taxpayer/transferor actually intended to defraud present or future creditors in making the transfer.[143] Intent to defraud is an alternative attack on the validity of a transfer and it is frequently used in conjunction with a claim that the transfer was made by an insolvent. This issue is one of state law and is decided on the basis of the facts involved.[144] The burden of proving "actual intent" is on the party seeking to set

---

[141] United States v. McCombs, 30 F3d 310 (2d Cir. 1994).

[142] Powers Photo Engraving Co., 17 TC 393 (1951), aff'd and remanded, 197 F2d 704 (2d Cir. 1952).

[143] The factors listed in the UFTA set out supra ¶ 17.04[1], should be considered in determining whether there is actual fraud. United States v. Chapman, 84-1 USTC ¶ 9202 (ND Tex. 1984), aff'd, 756 F2d 1237 (5th Cir. 1985) (transfers made before tax lien arose held void under Texas law because they were made with intent to defraud creditors). A finding of fraud can taint not only the first transfer but subsequent transactions as well. Roland v. United States, 838 F2d 1400 (5th Cir. 1988) (Texas law applied; property one was conveyed to son with intent to defraud the Service so that proceeds from sale of property one that were used to purchase property two made property two subject to levy).

[144] A sample of decisions applying state law are United States v. Morgan, 83-2 USTC ¶ 9535 (D. Colo. 1982) (Colorado law applied; fraudulent conveyance found); United States v. Edwards, 572 F. Supp. 1527, 1529 (D. Conn. 1983) (Connecticut law applied; no fraudulent conveyance found); Elizalde v. Comm'r, 48 TCM 28, 36–39 (1984) (actual fraud not found); Cate v. United States, 85-1 USTC ¶ 9114 (ED Tenn. 1984) (Tennessee law applied; no intent to defraud found merely because taxpayer/husband made monthly payments to wife for use of car and house she owned); Midland Ins. Co. v. Friedgood, 86-2 USTC ¶ 9641 (SDNY 1986) (funds sent by a physician to his former nurse in Denmark and used to secure a bail bond for him in New York were held to have been a fraudulent conveyance); United States v. Poio, 87-1 USTC ¶ 9357 (EDNY 1987) (whether conveyance was fraudulent analyzed under New York law); United States v. Bushlow, 832 F. Supp. 574 (EDNY 1993) (transfer of property two months after grand jury testimony admitting tax fraud held evidence of actual fraud under New York law); United States v. Brown, 820 F. Supp. 374 (ND Ill. 1993) (transfer to spouse three months before death of beneficial interest in land trust held to violate Illinois fraudulent conveyance law); United States v. Campbell, 91-1 USTC ¶ 50,106 (ED Mich. 1991) (under Michigan law, intent to defraud must be shown by clear and convincing evidence); United States v. Troyer, 91-2

aside the conveyance, and that actual intent must be proven by clear and convincing evidence.[145]

[b] The Service Has Exhausted All Remedies Against the Transferor

The Service must prove that it has exhausted all possibilities of collection from the primary obligor, the taxpayer/transferor, before proceeding against the transferee.[146] This requirement is not absolute. If a judgment in execution against the taxpayer/transferor would be futile or impossible, the Service need not take these useless steps.[147] Moreover, the requirement that the Service exhaust remedies against the taxpayer/transferor does not require that an assessment be made against the taxpayer/transferor before proceeding against the transferee.[148]

USTC ¶ 50,401 (ND Ind. 1991) (transfers of property to church when taxpayers first became delinquent in tax were held fraudulent under Indiana law); United States v. Parks, 91-1 USTC ¶ 50,263 (D. Utah 1991) (conveyance without consideration made to irrevocable trust within two days after due date for taxpayer's return); Hagaman v. Comm'r, 100 TC 180 (1993) (under either Tennessee or Florida law, actual intent to defraud Service did not require proof that taxpayer was insolvent); United States v. Denlinger, 982 F2d 233 (7th Cir. 1992) (Indiana law applied; fraudulent intent is shown by transfer of property when suit is pending or expected, transfer renders transferor insolvent, transferor retains use of property, and transfer is made for no or little consideration), reh'g denied, No. 91-3183 (7th Cir. 1993).

It is also said that only "an actual intent to hinder and delay" need be proved, "not an actual intent to defraud, and lack of fair consideration gives rise to a rebuttable presumption of fraudulent intent." Atlanta Shipping Corp. v. Chemical Bank, 631 F. Supp. 335, 346–347 (SDNY 1986), aff'd, 818 F2d 240 (2d Cir. 1987), quoted in United States v. Carlin, 80 AFTR2d 97-7810 (SDNY 1996).

[145] The matter is one of state law, but the law in New York is typical. See United States v. McCombs, 94-2 USTC ¶ 50,363 (2d Cir. 1994) (gathering New York cases).

[146] Swan Land & Cattle Co. v. Frank, 148 US 603 (1893) (pretransferee liability case, holding that a claim for damages arising out of fraud in the sale by a corporation must be reduced to judgment against a corporation not yet legally dissolved before the claimant could bring an action against the distributee shareholders); Wire Wheel Corp. v. Comm'r, 16 BTA 737, aff'd, 46 F2d 1013 (2d Cir. 1931).

[147] Coffee Pot Holding Corp. v. Comm'r, 113 F2d 415, 417 (5th Cir. 1940); Ginsberg v. Comm'r, 305 F2d 664, 669 (2d Cir. 1962).

[148] California Iron Yards v. Comm'r, 82 F2d 776, 779 (9th Cir. 1936) (assessment against transferor is not always required before the Service can proceed against the transferee); see also Leighton v. United States, 289 US 506 (1933) (before the transferee liability statute was enacted, the government in an equity proceeding could recover against the distributee shareholders without an assessment against them, and this was not changed when the predecessor of Section 6901 was adopted).

[4] Defenses to Transferee Liability

A person against whom transferee liability is asserted may defend against a finding of liability by proving the negative of one or more of the necessary elements of liability. Thus, liability may be avoided if the transferee can show that

- There has been no transfer[149];
- The tax has been paid by or on behalf of the transferor[150];
- The transfer occurred before the tax liability arose[151];
- The transferor was not liable for the tax[152];
- The transferor was solvent at the time of the transfer[153];
- The transfer was made for full and adequate consideration; or
- The government has not exhausted all reasonable procedural remedies against the taxpayer/transferor.

Liability may also be avoided if the transferee can establish that all or part of the transferred assets were returned before the notice of transferee liability was sent, at least to the extent of the property reconveyed.[154] A transferee may also raise the defense of the statute of limitations if the period of limitations for assessment against the transferee has expired. The transferee bears the burden of proof on this issue.[155]

---

[149] Kizzie Gordon v. Comm'r, 27 BTA 377 (1932).

[150] JP Quirk v. Comm'r, 15 TC 709 (1950). However, a compromise of the liability of one transferee does not extinguish the liability of another transferee, only the amount of the liability is reduced by the amount of the compromise. Rev. Rul. 72-436, 1972-2 CB 643.

[151] See Leon Papineau, 28 TC 54 (1957).

[152] See, e.g., John A. Mulligan, 16 TC 1489 (1951).

[153] CBC Super Mkts., Inc., 54 TC 882, 889 (1970); MH Graham, 26 BTA 301 (1932).

[154] Fada Gobins, 18 TC 1159 (1952), aff'd per curiam, 217 F2d 952 (9th Cir. 1954). Cf. Louise Noell, 22 TC 1035 (1954) (property was returned after the notice, and the transferee was not relieved of liability). See Eyler v. Comm'r, 760 F2d 1129 (11th Cir. 1985) (principle accepted).

[155] Columbia Pictures, Inc., 55 TC 649 (1971).

¶ 17.05 PROCEDURAL ISSUES

[1] The Amount of the Transferee's Liability

The liability at law or in equity referred to in Section 6901 "may be either as to the amount of tax shown on the return or as to any deficiency or underpayment of any tax."[156] A deficiency, in general, is the difference between the actual tax for the taxable period less the amount of tax shown on a return, if a return was filed. A deficiency does not reflect credits for withholding or estimated tax payments. An underpayment incorporates the definition of the deficiencies, at least when a return is timely filed, for the purposes of establishing the base against which negligence and fraud penalties are asserted. However, because the objective of the assertion of transferee liability is the collection of an unpaid tax, it appears that the liability referred to in Section 6901 is the net amount of the unpaid tax, irrespective of the reference to the term "deficiency."

The theory of transferee liability is that collection of taxes has been prejudiced by a transfer of property by the taxpayer to the transferee made without full and adequate consideration. Accordingly, the transferee liability at law or in equity extends to the unpaid taxes of the taxpayer/transferor that have accrued at the time of the transfer, although these taxes need not have been assessed, nor the existence of the tax liability even have been known at the time of the transfer.[157] In general, the liability of the transferee of property that has a value in excess of the tax owed by the transferor includes interest from the date the return was due and such additions to the tax as negligence and fraud penalties.[158]

Two different concepts affect the liability of the transferee for accrued interest, one based on the Code and the other on state law. These different concepts must be kept clearly in mind. Under the Code, the government's rights against the taxpayer/transferor include: (1) interest on deficiencies in tax due from the transferor accruing from the due date for the filing of the return and payment of tax and (2) additions to the tax in the form of delinquency, accuracy-related, and fraud penalties. Accordingly, the Code dictates the amount of

---

[156] IRC § 6901(b).

[157] Elaine Yagoda, 39 TC 170 (1962), aff'd, 331 F2d 485 (2d Cir.), cert. denied, 379 US 842 (1964); Francis L. Hine, 54 TC 1552 (1970), acq. 1971-1 CB 2; Leon Papineau, 28 TC 54 (1957).

[158] Robinette v. Helvering, 139 F2d 285 (6th Cir. 1943), cert. denied, 322 US 745 (1944) (interest); Estate of Stein, 37 TC 945 (1962) (interest); Leo L. Lowy, 35 TC 393 (1960) (interest and fraud penalties); Robert Leslie Bowlin, 31 TC 188 (1958), aff'd per curiam, 273 F2d 610 (6th Cir. 1960) (fraud penalty); Arnold L. Kimmis, 22 TCM 232 (1963) (negligence penalty); Alonso v. Comm'r, 78 TC 577 (1982) (negligence and fraud penalties and interest).

the government's claim. Because the amounts of tax, penalty, and interest constitute the claim of the United States against the taxpayer/transferor, they also measure the claim against the transferred assets followed into the hands of the transferee. State law dictates whether and to what extent the creditor will be entitled to interest and the rate of interest the creditor may recover against the transferee for his or her use of the transferred assets. When the value of the assets transferred is less than the deficiency of the transferor, interest is not allowed on the tax liability itself because the transferee cannot be required to pay any amount in excess of the value of the property transferred; however, interest can be collected if state law so provides for the use of transferred assets.[159] Under state law, the date when interest begins to accrue may depend on whether the fraud was constructive (in which case interest runs from the date of the notice of deficiency) or actual (in which case interest may run from the date of the transfer).[160]

A transferee liable at law because he or she has expressly assumed the transferor's liability is liable for the full amount of the transferor's liability, irrespective of the value of the assets the transferee has received.[161] When transferee liability at law is based on a state statute, it appears that the liability may be limited to the value of the assets received if the state law so provides. However, it is well settled that the liability of the transferee in equity is limited to the value of the assets received from the transferor as of the date of the transfer.[162] It is the value of the assets on the date of the transfer that is con-

---

[159] Estate of Stein, 37 TC 945 (1962). See Patterson v. Sims, 281 F2d 577 (5th Cir. 1960) (under Alabama law, transferee of a constructively fraudulent transfer was not liable for interest until after the filing of a creditor's bill); LeFay v. Comm'r, 44 TCM 582 (1982); Stone v. Comm'r, 50 TCM 683 (1985) (interest due under Florida law from the date of transfer, not the date of Tax Court's decision); Poinier v. Comm'r, 858 F2d 917 (3d Cir. 1988) (under Section 6324, the donee transferee's liability for tax as well as interest is limited to the value of the gift).

[160] Patterson v. Sims, 281 F2d 577 (5th Cir. 1960). See also Pallister v. United States, 182 F. Supp. 720 (SDNY 1960). Cf. Voss v. Wiseman, 234 F2d 237 (10th Cir. 1956) (reaching the same result as *Pallister*, that interest runs from the date of the notice when there is constructive rather than actual fraud, but on the basis of federal rather than state law, which does not control in view of *Stern*). The Tax Court has held that in view of *Stern*'s indication that state law is to be used in determining the "existence and extent" of transferee liability and other authority in the Tenth Circuit, "*Voss* does not preclude us from applying State law to the determination of petitioner's liability for interest in the present case." Stansbury v. Comm'r, 104 TC 486 (1995) (assets of corporation were transferred to its shareholders after the corporation agreed to a tax assessment; held, under Colorado law, the transferee shareholders were liable for interest from the date of the transfers, not only from the date the notices of transferee liability were sent to them).

[161] Bos Lines, Inc. v. Comm'r, 354 F2d 830 (8th Cir. 1973).

[162] Phillips v. Comm'r, 283 US 589 (1931); Kreps v. Comm'r, 351 F2d 1 (2d Cir. 1965); Scott v. Comm'r, 117 F2d 36 (8th Cir. 1941); Benoit v. Comm'r, 238 F2d 485 (1st Cir. 1956); Davis v. Birdsong, 275 F2d 113 (5th Cir. 1960); Drew v. United States, 367

trolling, not the price at which the transferee may have subsequently sold the transferred property.[163] As indicated, the amount of the transferee's liability may be increased by interest provided for by state law for the period the transferred property was held by the transferee. However, the amount of the transferee's liability can be reduced in a number of situations. For example, when property is transferred for less than adequate consideration, the transferee is liable only to the extent of the difference between the consideration paid and the value of the transferred property.[164] When property is transferred subject to a mortgage existing at the time of the transfer, the amount of the mortgage may be deducted from the value of the property transferred.[165] Finally, if a transferee has retransferred property to the transferor before the issuance of a statutory notice of transferee liability, the transferee is generally relieved of liability under state law to the value of the property retransferred.[166]

[2] Several Liability and Contribution

It is settled law that the liability of transferees is several. For example, if a corporation makes liquidating distributions to its shareholders, the entire tax liability up to the value of the property received from the transferor may be collected from one transferee without joining the others.[167] A transferee's individual share of several liability is not limited to his or her pro rata share of the distributions made by the transferor; however, the transferee from whom the entire tax liability of the transferor has been collected does have a right to contribution against other transferees. Thus, even if the Commissioner fails to proceed against all transferees, the transferee who has paid more than his or

---

F2d 828 (Ct. Cl. 1966). When a son took out a mortgage on property owned by his mother, who was liable for unpaid taxes and subject to a Service fraudulent conveyance claim, the mortgagee was not liable, but the son was held liable for the decrease in value of the property attributable to the mortgage. United States v. Bushlow, 832 F. Supp. 574 (EDNY 1993) (mortgage proceeds used to improve son's property).

[163] Bartmer Automatic Self-Serv. Laundry, Inc., 35 TC 317 (1960); Estate of George L. Cury, 23 TC 305 (1954).

[164] Nader v. Comm'r, 323 F2d 139 (7th Cir. 1963).

[165] W. Cleve Stokes, 22 TC 415 (1954); Estate of George L. Cury, 23 TC 305 (1954); Hatcher v. Comm'r, 45 TCM 1244 (1983).

[166] Fada Gobins, 18 TC 1159 (1952), aff'd per curiam, 217 F2d 952 (9th Cir. 1954) (transferee relieved of liability for money and property returned to the transferor, but not for moneys paid in satisfaction of the transferor's debts in the absence of a showing that the debts paid had priority over liability to the Service); cf. Ginsberg v. Comm'r, 305 F2d 664 (2d Cir. 1962) (alleged retransfer found not to have occurred under New York State law).

[167] Phillips v. Comm'r, 283 US 589 (1931); Phillips-Jones Corp. v. Parmley, 302 US 233 (1937).

her proportionate share of the entire tax liability is entitled to obtain contribution from other transferees who have received distributed assets from the transferor.[168]

These rules were established very early in the history of what is now Section 6901. The Supreme Court, in *Phillips v. Commissioner*, not only held that the predecessor of Section 6901 was constitutional, but because each transferee is severally liable to the extent of the assets received, the Commissioner need only pursue one transferee and need not make an assessment against the others. In *Phillips*, the Commissioner elected to proceed only against Phillips and succeeded in obtaining payment of the whole tax from Phillips's estate. In *Phillips-Jones Corp. v. Parmley*, it was held that a transferee, who had paid more than his or her share of a common burden, was entitled to sue for contribution from the other transferees. In such an action, the transferee claiming contribution must prove both that there was a common burden of debt and, as between transferee and the defendants, has paid more than his or her fair share of the common obligations. In the action, each defendant may raise any personal defense.

[3] Statute of Limitations

Section 6901 provides a special statute of limitations that in general permits the Commissioner one year after the running of the statute of limitations for assessment against the taxpayer/transferor to make an assessment against a taxpayer's transferee.[169] If the initial transferee has transferred property, an additional year is added to the period of limitations for assessment.[170] This means that in the case of the initial transferee, the transferee's liability must be assessed within four years after the date the taxpayer/transferor's return is filed.

---

[168] Phillips-Jones Corp. v. Parmley, 302 US 233 (1937). This right to contribution may be asserted by way of joinder of the other transferees in an action brought in a district court or the court of claims, but when the issue of transferee liability is litigated in the Tax Court, unless statutory notices of liability have been issued to the other transferees and they have filed petitions, there will have to be a separate action to obtain contribution.

[169] IRC § 6901(c)(1).

There is a distinction between an action to impose the transferor's tax on the transferee (and collect the transferor's tax from the transferee) and a suit to reach assets the transferor has fraudulently transferred to the transferee. The limitations periods of Section 6501 apply to the first type of transferee proceeding because it involves the determination of the transferor's tax; the other action is ancillary to collecting the judgment against the transferor for those taxes from the transferee who has obtained the transferor's assets fraudulently. See Hall v. United States, 403 F2d 344 (5th Cir. 1968), cert. denied, 394 US 958 (1969); see also United States v. Brickman, 906 F. Supp. 1164 (ND Ill. 1997).

[170] IRC § 6901(c)(2).

Because transferee liability is claimed under state law, the Service can choose either the state statute of limitations on its cause of action or the limitations period determined under Section 6901. The Service will rely on a state statute of limitations when it is more favorable than Section 6901, but if the state provides for a shorter time period, the government is not limited by the state statute, if it is suing in its sovereign capacity to collect taxes.[171] For example, it is not unusual for a transferee to be liable under state law under a contract entered into with the taxpayer/transferor. The statute of limitations on a contract claim is longer than under Section 6901, thus the Service can use that statute of limitations for assessing transferee liability.

This choice of limitation periods is illustrated by *United States v. Scott*,[172] in which Scott agreed to assume tax liabilities and take over X's assets. X died in 1936, but the government sued Scott nine years later, in 1945, as a third-party beneficiary of the contract between Scott and X. The state (Missouri) had a ten-year statute of limitations on contract actions; the circuit court found that the state ten-year statute applied rather than the transferee statute of limitations provided under the Code.[173]

The start date for computing the period of limitations for the assessment of transferee liability is the date the period of limitations against the transferor begins to run. However, the additional one-year period for assessment against an initial transferee runs from the date the period of limitations for assessment against the taxpayer/transferor expires, not from the date of an assessment against the taxpayer/transferor.[174] In fact, the expiration date of the period of limitations against the taxpayer/transferor controls, even if no assessment was ever made or even attempted against the transferor.[175] Because the period of

---

[171] United States v. Summerlin, 310 US 414 (1940); Bruce Dillman v. Comm'r, 64 TC 797 (1975).

[172] United States v. Scott, 167 F2d 301 (8th Cir. 1948).

[173] Also, if the property involved is subject to a tax lien at the time that it is transferred by the taxpayer to the transferee, the government may proceed to foreclose its tax lien at any time when the tax lien is still valid and need not depend on the transferee's liability at law or in equity. United States v. Diamond, 142 F. Supp. 441 (SDNY 1956).

[174] Ann C. Field v. Comm'r, 32 TC 187 (1959), aff'd per curiam, 286 F2d 960 (6th Cir. 1960). The mailing of a statutory notice to the transferor and the transferor's filing of a petition in the Tax Court suspends the running of the statute of limitations on assessment against the transferee as well as the transferor. Elizalde v. Comm'r, 48 TCM 28, 35 (1984) (cases gathered).

Accordingly, the Service has four years to make an assessment against a transferee (the three-year period for assessment against the transferor, plus one additional year), plus the period during which assessment is prohibited (ninety days), plus sixty more days following the prohibition period. If the Service fails to make an assessment within this 4-year-and-150-day period, the assessment is invalid. Dobisch v. United States, 93-2 USTC ¶ 50,522, 156 BR 546 (Bankr. WD Tenn. 1993).

[175] Marce Alexander, 61 TC 278 (1973). See also Bruce Dillman, 64 TC 797 (1975).

limitations for making an assessment against a transferee includes the period of limitations for making an assessment against the transferor, whether or not such an assessment was actually made, the limitations period for a transferee assessment may be extended indefinitely (1) when the transferor has filed a fraudulent return or failed to file a return[176]; (2) for the period provided in a waiver agreement entered into by the transferor[177]; and (3) for a one-year period after the return of execution unsatisfied in a court proceeding against the taxpayer for the collection of the tax begun within the period of limitations on assessment.[178]

The transferee may also extend the period for making a transferee assessment.[179] Further, if a notice of liability under Section 6901 has been mailed to a transferee, the running of the statute of limitations is suspended for the period during which the assessment is prohibited and for the next sixty days.[180]

[4] Burden of Proof and Discovery

In general, the Commissioner has the burden of proof in the Tax Court to show that the transferee/petitioner is liable as a transferee of the taxpayer's property. The burden of proof to show that the taxpayer/transferor was not liable for the tax rests with the transferee/petitioner. Just the opposite allocation

---

[176] Sidney Kreps, 42 TC 660 (1964), aff'd, 351 F2d 1 (2d Cir. 1965); Ann Davis, 23 TCM 1449 (1964) (fraud of transferor); Lenore S. Robinette, 46 BTA 1138, aff'd, 139 F2d 285 (6th Cir. 1943), cert. denied, 322 US 745 (1944); Leo Kubik, 33 TCM 302 (1974) (failure-to-file cases).

[177] IRC § 6901(c). See James M. Denton, 21 TC 295, 300 (1953). See also United States v. Adams Bldg. Co., 531 F2d 342 (6th Cir. 1976), modifying and remanding 74-1 USTC ¶ 9422 (ND Ohio 1975) (waiver of limitations period made in an offer in compromise); United States v. Snyder, 82-2 USTC ¶ 9683 (SD W. Va. 1982) (waiver in offer in compromise form extended statute).

[178] IRC § 6901(c). The same rule applies when a transferee of a transferee is involved. If the Service makes an assessment against the transferor, institutes a collection action against the transferor to collect the assessment, and obtains a judgment, the Service no longer seeks to collect the tax owed by the transferor; the statute of limitations on collection against the transferor stops running and the Service can enforce its judgment at any time. See United States v. Brickman, 906 F. Supp. 1164 (ND Ill. 1997) (involving the transferees of a transferee, against whom the Service had obtained a judgment).

In other words, when the Service takes collection action against a transferor within the applicable period of limitations, the period of limitations for proceeding against the transferor's transferee can be extended indefinitely. Compare United States v. Updike, 281 US 489 (1930), in which the Service made an assessment against the taxpayer/transferor but failed to file a timely collection action against the transferor, so the Court held that the time for the Service to institute a collection action against the transferee had also run.

[179] IRC § 6901(d)(1).

[180] IRC § 6902(b).

of burden of proof seems to make more sense, because, presumably, the transferee has knowledge of the facts surrounding the transfer but none about the tax liability of the transferor. The statutory allocation of the burden of proof is eased somewhat by the statutory rights given the transferee/petitioner to examine the taxpayer/transferor's records.[181] However, it has been held that if the transferee/petitioner is deprived of this statutory right of discovery, the case is not disposed of, especially if the transferee/petitioner can resort to other evidence such as the balance sheet attached to the taxpayer/transferor's tax returns.[182]

Because Section 6901(a) provides that the liability of the transferee is to be assessed and collected in the same manner as that of the taxpayer/transferor, a transferee also has the right to pay the tax and sue for refund after this claim for refund has been denied.[183] In a refund suit, unlike a transferee proceeding in the Tax Court, it has been held that the transferee/plaintiff has the burden of proving the absence of transferee liability.[184] When the United States seeks to establish transferee liability at law or in equity based on a state statute, the burden of proof is on the Service to establish liability and to make out a prima facie case under the relevant state law, as it would if the proceeding took place in the Tax Court.[185] If the transferee claims the defense of a statute of limitations under the Federal Rules of Civil Procedure, the transferee has the burden of affirmatively pleading and proving this defense.

B.　COLLECTION OF TAXES FROM WITHHOLDING AGENTS

¶ 17.06　SCOPE OF SECTION 6672—TRUST FUND RECOVERY PENALTY

The Code requires persons other than taxpayers to function as withholding agents for collecting certain taxes due to the United States. The most common example is the requirement that employers collect and withhold income and Social Security, or more properly, Federal Insurance Contributions Act (FICA), taxes from their employees. Other statutory provisions impose a duty on payors to withhold income tax on certain items of gross income they pay to

---

[181] IRC § 6902(b).

[182] Kreps v. Comm'r, 351 F2d 1 (2d Cir. 1965).

[183] Phillips v. Comm'r, 283 US 589 (1931).

[184] Wehvy v. Patterson, 60-2 USTC ¶ 9611 (ND Ala. 1960); Van Benschoten v. United States, 59-2 USTC ¶ 9782 (SD Cal. 1959).

[185] The elements that the government must establish in a case of liability at law or in equity are set forth in supra ¶¶ 17.03 and 17.04[2], respectively.

nonresident aliens.[186] Similarly, sellers of certain types of property are required to withhold excise taxes on the transactions from the sales prices.[187] Each of these withholding regimes has its own special enforcement procedures, and imposes penalties directly on withholding agents for failure to deposit the amounts they are required to withhold and pay over to the Service. Section 6672 creates a separate and distinct source for collecting withholding taxes the withholding agent has failed to pay over to the Service by imposing personal liability on a person, such as an officer or employee of a corporate withholding agent (or an employee of a partnership, which is a withholding agent), who has a sufficient relationship to the corporate (or partnership) withholding agent as to be under a duty to perform the acts of collecting, accounting for, and paying over the withholding tax.[188] Any responsible person who has a duty "to collect, truthfully account for, and pay over any tax imposed by the [Code], [that] willfully fails to collect such tax, or truthfully account and pay over such tax, or willfully attempts in any manner to evade or defeat any such tax or the payment thereof," is personally liable for a penalty "equal to the total amount of the tax evaded, or not collected, or not collected or not accounted for and paid over."[189] Because the amount of this "penalty" is equal to the amount of the tax that was required to be collected and paid over, the penalty has been called the 100 percent penalty. It also is called the trust fund recovery penalty, because the taxes referred to are taxes the withholding agent is required to hold in trust for the Service.

Although the 100 percent or trust fund recovery penalty applies to all withholding regimes the Code creates, this discussion focuses on withheld income and employment taxes to illustrate how collection may be enforced from persons other than the taxpayers primarily liable for the taxes. Income and employment taxes are by far the most commonly collected and at issue in the case law.

[1] General Observations

Because the trust fund recovery penalty of Section 6672 is used so frequently, some preliminary observations are in order. It should be noted that

---

[186] See IRC §§ 1441 (nonresident aliens), 1442 (foreign corporations), 1443 (foreign tax-exempt organizations). Section 1461 provides that the person required to deduct and withhold the tax is "made liable for the tax. . . ."

[187] See, e.g., IRC §§ 4001–4293, dealing with various retail and manufacturers' excise taxes as well as communications and admissions excise taxes.

[188] IRC § 6671(b).

[189] IRC § 6672(a).

1. The trust fund recovery penalty does not fully compensate the government in the event of a failure to pay over employment taxes. The penalty only compensates the government for the amount of the taxes collected from employers that are not paid over; that is, the trust fund portion of employment taxes and not the portion of the taxes imposed on the employer.

2. The term "penalty" is somewhat misleading. The amount of liability imposed by Section 6672 is equal to the amount of the delinquent trust fund taxes and is not in addition to those taxes. As the Supreme Court has said, "That the funds due are referred to as a penalty when the Government later seeks to recover them does not alter the essential character as taxes. . . . "[190] It follows that the 100 percent or trust fund recovery "penalty" is actually a collection device designed to collect withheld income and the portion of employment taxes the employer collected by paying the employee net wages and should have paid over.[191]

3. Liability for the penalty and the employer's liability for withholding and employment taxes are separate and distinct, but related. There is a distinction between the amount of the liability and the existence of liability for the penalty. The amount of the liability is reduced by the payment of trust fund taxes by the employer and collection from other persons. However, liability for the penalty is a direct and primary obligation of the responsible person for failure to perform the required acts. This liability is separate and distinct from the liability of the employer under the wage-withholding provisions.[192] In this re-

---

[190] United States v. Sotelo, 436 US 268 (1978) ("That the funds due are referred to as a penalty when the Government later seeks to recover them does not alter their essential character as taxes for purposes of the Bankruptcy Act, at least in a case in which, as here, the Section 6672 liability is predicated on a failure to pay over, rather than a failure to collect, the taxes." Id. at 275.). The Service's policy statement is: "The trust fund recovery penalty applicable to withheld income and employment taxes (social security and collected railroad retirement taxes) or collected excise taxes will be used to facilitate collection of and enhance voluntary compliance [with collection and paying over of tax]." IRM, Policies of the IRS Handbook, P-5-60 (approved Feb. 2, 1993).

[191] See, e.g., Emshwiller v. United States, 565 F2d 1336, 1340 (8th Cir. 1976). Nevertheless, the responsible officer who pays the trust fund penalty may not deduct the amount of the payment as a business bad debt, because the conduct punished is willful conduct and deduction would violate public policy. Duncan v. Comm'r, 68 F3d 315 (9th Cir. 1995) (however, the amounts paid to Oregon were held deductible because Oregon imposed liability on employers whether or not their conduct was willful).

[192] United States v. Huckabee Auto Co., 783 F2d 1546 (11th Cir. 1986). Because the liability for the trust fund taxes under Section 6672 is "separate and distinct" from the corporation's liability, the Second Circuit has ruled that interest continues to run on the trust fund liability until it is paid by responsible officers, even if the corporate employer pays the taxes and interest (except for the interest accrued during the corporation's bank-

spect, the trust fund recovery penalty differs from transferee liability, which is derivative (the transferor's liability is being collected from the transferee). In short, there are two bases for liability, but only one amount is collectible when the trust fund recovery penalty is asserted.[193]

4. The penalty is not the only means of collecting withholding and employment taxes when a business is conducted as a proprietorship, or as a partnership. The individual owners or general partners are personally and directly liable for employment taxes. Accordingly, although the penalty applies to "an officer, or employee of a corporation," as to "a member or employee of a partnership, who . . . is under a duty to perform the act in respect of which the violation occurs," the full amount of the tax is collectible in full from a general partner in a partnership.[194]

5. The penalty is not limited to a single "person." The statute says "any person" having the duty to collect and pay over may be liable for the penalty and, accordingly, the penalty may be, and frequently is, asserted against more than one person.[195]

6. No negligence or fraud penalty may be assessed against a person in the event that the trust fund recovery penalty is assessed.[196] The trust

---

ruptcy). Bradley v. United States, 936 F2d 707 (2d Cir. 1991). It is also said that liability for the trust fund recovery penalty arises from the act of collecting trust fund taxes, and so the penalty need not be assessed. Goldston v. United States, 104 F3d 1198 (10th Cir. 1997) (the fact that the penalty assessment was void because it was made in violation of the automatic stay did not prevent the collection of the liability in the Chapter 11 proceeding).

[193] Spivak v. United States, 370 F2d 612 (2d Cir.), cert. denied, 387 US 908 (1967); Datlof v. United States, 370 F2d 655 (3d Cir. 1966); Cash v. Campbell, 346 F2d 670 (5th Cir. 1965); Kelly v. Lethert, 362 F2d 629, 635 (8th Cir. 1966). Cf. McCarty v. United States, 437 F2d 961 (Ct. Cl. 1971) (failure to collect from corporation held to prevent collection of penalty from responsible person); Verdung v. United States, 84-1 USTC ¶ 9324 (ND Ill. 1983) (when a corporate associate had paid most of the 100 percent penalty, the court held that a refund was owed to a responsible officer who had paid over an amount in excess of the remainder of the assessment).

According to the Service's policy statement, "The withheld income and employment or collected excise taxes will be collected only once, whether from the business, from one or more of its responsible persons, or from the business and one or more of its responsible persons." IRM, Policies of the IRS Handbook, P-5-60 (approved Feb. 2, 1993).

[194] IRC § 6671(b).

[195] See Rev. Proc. 69-26, 1969-2 CB 308 (in the event that a refund suit contesting liability for the 100 percent penalty is brought by one responsible person, assessment against other potentially responsible persons without administrative review is authorized in order to bring all potential responsible persons before the court and let it decide which person is responsible within the meaning of Section 6672).

[196] IRC § 6672(a).

fund penalty is the only civil penalty imposed for failure to collect and pay over trust fund taxes.

7. Apart from Section 6672, liability for employment taxes is also imposed on persons who supply financing or funds to an employer. The requirement to collect income and FICA taxes from employees is imposed on employers. However, persons other than employers can directly or indirectly pay the wages of employees. For example, lenders or sureties may pay directly or advance amounts for the payment of employees. Section 3505 imposes liability for trust fund taxes on a commercial lender, surety, or other financing organization that either (1) pays the borrower's employees net wages directly or (2) even if net wages are not paid directly, knows wages are to be paid out of the funds advanced, and has "actual notice or knowledge" that the borrower does not intend to or will not be able to pay over withheld taxes.

[2] Persons Required to Withhold Employment Taxes

Chapter 21, "Federal Insurance Contributions Act," and Chapter 24, "Collection of Income Tax at Source on Wages," of the Code require each "employer" to deduct and withhold FICA and income taxes from each "employee."[197] An employer, for the purposes of the wage-withholding provisions, generally means "the person for whom an individual performs or performed any service of whatever nature, as the employee of that person."[198] Consequently, the status of the payor as the employer of an employee establishes the requirement to withhold.

The apparently straightforward question of whether a payor and payee are employer and employee, however, has confounded both Congress and the courts. For over twenty years, Congress has been attempting to devise a statutory definition of an "employee" from whose wages and salary employers are required to withhold income and FICA taxes, as distinct from an "independent contractor" who is responsible for paying over its own tax. In the meanwhile,

---

[197] IRC §§ 3102(a) (FICA taxes), 3402(a), 3403 (income taxes). The terms "employer" and "employee" are defined in Sections 3401(d) and 3401(c), respectively, for the purpose of income tax withholding. The term "employee" is defined in Section 3121(d) for the purposes of FICA taxes.

[198] IRC § 3401(d). An exception to the general rule is provided where the person for whom the individual performs or performed the service does not have control of the payment of wages for the services. In such cases, the term "employer" means the person having control of the payment of wages. However, for FICA tax purposes, there is only a definition of the term "employee"; the income tax withholding definition of "employer" does not apply.

Congress has provided a temporary rule. If a taxpayer does not treat an individual as a common-law employee for any period, then the worker is not considered to be a common-law employee for employment tax purposes during that period unless the taxpayer has no reasonable basis for not treating the worker as an employee.[199] For any period beginning after December 31, 1978, this relief applies only if the taxpayer files all federal returns required to be filed with respect to the worker on a basis consistent with the taxpayer's treatment of the worker as other than an employee and the taxpayer's treatment is consistent with the treatment after 1977.

The wage withholding provisions of the Code establish the following procedures:

1. *The requirement to file.* The employer is required to file quarterly reports of taxes withheld (Form 941) and to make federal tax deposits with commercial banks designated by regulation as depositories.[200]

2. *Amounts collected are trust funds.* The amount of the tax actually collected or withheld by employers from employees is held to be "a special fund in trust for the United States."[201] Accordingly, any amounts of income and FICA taxes required to be collected from employees are by law trust fund taxes.

3. *The employer's portion of employment taxes.* In addition to collecting and paying over income taxes from employees, employers are required to report and pay their own portion of FICA taxes, as well as federal unemployment tax (FUTA taxes). These employer contributions are referred to as the employer's portion of employment taxes.[202] Consequently, there are two portions of employment taxes: (1) the employee's portion (the withheld tax and the employee's portion of the FICA tax) or trust fund portion, and (2) the employer's portion (the employer's portion of the FICA and the employer's FUTA tax).

---

[199] Revenue Act of 1978, Pub. L. No. 95-600, 95th Cong., 2d Sess. § 530. See Rev. Proc. 81-43, 1981-2 CB 616, for standards applied in determining whether there is a sufficiently reasonable basis for treatment of the worker as other than an employee.

[200] Reg. §§ 31.6071(a)-4 (returns), 31.6071(a)-1 (time for filing), 31.6151-1(a) (time for payment); IRC § 6302 (depositories). To determine an employer's compliance with the employment tax deposit requirements, the Service also has an early warning procedure it calls federal tax deposit alerts. IRM 5611.1, MT 5600-56 (Aug. 10, 1994) (Federal Tax Deposits—Purpose). The federal tax deposit alert process identifies those taxpayers who have fallen behind in their deposit payments before the return (the Form 940) for the year is due. Once they are identified, the Service contacts these taxpayers to resolve the delinquency before the return is due in an attempt to prevent them from pyramiding liabilities. One way this is done is to show taxpayers how a delayed deposit increases penalties.

[201] IRC § 7501(a).

[202] IRC §§ 3101 (FICA), 3301 (FUTA).

4. *Credit even if trust fund taxes are not paid over.* In the event that the employer has no assets, then no taxes, penalties, or interest can be collected from the employer.[203] Employees are nevertheless entitled to credit for the amount of income and FICA taxes withheld whether or not the employer pays over the withheld taxes to the government.[204]

5. *The notice to withhold.* In the event that an employer fails to collect and pay over, it may be required, on notice, to create a special bank account in trust for the withheld taxes.[205] (See Form 17.1.) If the employer fails to comply with these trust provisions, it may be prosecuted under Section 7215 for committing a misdemeanor punishable by a fine of not more than $5,000 or imprisonment for not more than one year, or both.

6. *Criminal penalties.* In aggravated cases of nonpayment, criminal prosecution may be instituted.[206] A felony prosecution might also be brought under one of the criminal statutes described in Section 7206, which deals generally with fraud and false statements. Misdemeanor prosecutions can be based on violations of Section 7204 for fraudulent withholding statements or willful failure to supply such statements given to the Service, or on Section 7203 for willful failure to supply information.

---

[203] Reg. § 301.6672-1.

[204] IRC §§ 1642, 3102(a).

[205] IRC § 7512(a).

[206] See ¶ 7A.05. For example, prosecutions for employment tax violations have been instituted for a willful attempted evasion of the tax under Section 7201 (a felony). Wilson v. United States, 250 F2d 312 (9th Cir. 1957). Prosecutions may also be instituted under Section 7202 (a felony) for willful failure to collect and pay over tax. See, e.g., United States v. Poll, 521 F2d 329 (9th Cir. 1975) (unsuccessful prosecution); United States v. Scharf, 558 F2d 498 (8th Cir. 1977) (successful prosecution).

FORM 17.1 ─────────────────────────────
NOTICE TO MAKE SPECIAL DEPOSITS OF TAXES

Department of Treasury
Internal Revenue Service
Form 2481 (Rev. 3–86)

Notice to Make
Special Deposits
of Taxes

(Section 7512 of the Internal Revenue Code)

Taxpayer's Name and Address

Section 7501 of the Internal Revenue Code provides that whenever any person is required to withhold or collect any internal revenue tax from any other person and to pay over such tax to the United States, the amount of tax so withheld or collected shall be held to be a special fund in trust for the United States. Our records show that you have not paid over to the United States, at the time and in the manner prescribed by the regulations, internal revenue taxes you were required to withhold or collect.

Therefore, under the provisions of section 7912 of the Internal Revenue Code, you are hereby notified that:

Effective immediately, you are required to

(1) Collect, at the time and in the manner prescribed by the law and the regulations, any of the following internal revenue taxes for which you are liable

      Income tax withheld from employees. Employee tax withheld under the Federal Insurance Contributions Act, and Excise taxes on toll telephone service, local telephone service, teletypewriter exchange service and transportation of persons by air.

(2) Establish a bank account in a bank (as defined in section 581 of the Internal Revenue Code) designated as "(Your Name), Trustee, Special Fund in Trust for U.S. under sec. 7512, I.R.C."

(3) Deposit the taxes you withhold or collect in such separate bank account not later than the end of the 2nd banking day after you withhold or collect them.

(4) Keep the taxes so deposited in such separate bank account until you pay them over to the Internal Revenue Service.

In addition to the requirements listed above, and under the provisions of section 6011 of the Internal Revenue Code and regulations, you are further notified that:

Effective for the calendar month in which this notice is delivered, you are required to

File monthly returns on Form 720 for the taxes normally required to be reported quarterly. You must file your monthly returns not later than the 15th day of the 2nd calendar month following the month covered by the return(s).

File monthly returns on Form 941–M for the taxes normally required to be reported quarterly. You must file your monthly returns not later than the 15th day of the month following the month covered by the return(s).

File semimonthly returns on Form 720 for the taxes normally required to be reported quarterly. You must file your semimonthly returns not later than the 2nd day of the 3rd semimonthly period following the semimonthly period for which they are made.

The first monthly or semimonthly return required pursuant to this notice shall cover the month or semimonthly period in which the notice is received and all prior months or semimonthly periods within the calendar quarter that have not yet been reported on a quarterly return.

You should send with each return the full amount of all taxes shown to be due. Payment in this manner makes it unnecessary for you to use Federal tax deposit forms for taxes withheld or collected after receipt of this notice.

Issued under authority of section 7512(a), Internal Revenue Code, this _____ day of _____, 20_____.

_____
District Director of Internal Revenue

The applicable provisions of the Internal Revenue Code referred to in this notice are reproduced on the back of the notice.

Excerpts from the Internal Revenue Code

Sec. 7501

Liability for Taxes Withheld or Collected

(a) General Rule—Whenever any person is required to collect or withhold any internal revenue tax from any other person and to pay over such tax to the United States, the amount of tax so collected or withheld shall be held to be a special fund in trust for the United States * * *

Sec. 7512

Separate Accounting for Certain Collected Taxes, Etc.

(a) General Rule—Whenever any person who is required to collect, account for, and pay over any tax imposed by subtitle C, or chapter 33—

(1) at the time and in the manner prescribed by law or regulations (A) fails to collect, truthfully account for, or pay over such tax, or (B) fails to make deposits, payments, or returns of such tax, and

(2) is notified, by notice delivered in hand to such person, of any such failure,

then all the requirements of subsection (b) shall be complied with. In the case of a corporation, partnership, or trust, notice delivered in hand to an officer, partner, or trustee, shall, for purposes of this section, be deemed to be notice delivered in hand to such corporation, partnership, or trust and to all officers, partners, trustees, and employees thereof.

(b) Requirements.—Any person who is required to collect, account for, and pay over any tax imposed by subtitle C or chapter 33, if notice has been delivered to such person in accordance with subsection (a), shall collect the taxes imposed by subtitle C or chapter 33 which become collectible after delivery of such notice, shall (not later than the end of the second banking day after any amount of such taxes is collected) deposit such amount in a separate account in a bank (as defined in section 581), and shall keep the amount of such taxes in such account until payment over to the United States. Any such account shall be designated as a special fund in trust for the United States, payable to the United States by such person as trustee.

(c) Relief from Further Compliance with Subsection (b)—Whenever the Secretary is satisfied, with respect to any notification made under subsection (a), that all requirements of law and regulations with respect to the taxes imposed by subtitle C or chapter 33, as the case may be, will henceforth be complied with, he may cancel such notification. Such cancellation shall take effect at such time as is specified in the notice of such cancellation.

Sec. 7215

Offenses with Respect to Collected Taxes.

(a) Penalty.—Any person who fails to comply with any provision of section 7512(b) shall, in addition to any other penalties provided by law, be guilty of a misdemeanor, and, upon conviction thereof, shall be fined not more than $5,000, or imprisoned not more than one year, or both, together with the costs of prosecution.

(b) Exceptions—This section shall not apply—

(1) to any person, if such person shows that there was reasonable doubt as to (A) whether the law required collection of tax, or (B) who was required by law to collect tax, and

(2) to any person, if such person shows that the failure to comply with the provisions of section 7512(b) was due to circumstances beyond his control

For purposes of paragraph (2), a lack of funds existing immediately after the payment of wages (whether or not created by the payment of such wages) shall not be considered to be circumstances beyond the control of a person.

Sec. 6331

Levy and Distraint.

(a) Authority of Secretary—If any person liable to pay any tax neglects or refuses to pay the same within 10 days after notice and demand, it shall be lawful for the Secretary to collect such tax (and such further sum as shall be sufficient to cover the expenses of the levy) by levy upon all property and rights to property (except such property as is exempt under section 6334) belonging to such person or on which there is a lien provided in this chapter for the payment of such tax. . . . If the Secretary makes a finding that the collection of such tax is in jeopardy, notice and demand for immediate payment of such tax may be made by the Secretary and, upon failure or refusal to pay such tax, collection thereof by levy shall be lawful without regard to the 10-day period provided in this section.

Sec. 581

Definition of Bank.

For purposes of sections 582 and 584, the term "bank" means a bank or trust company incorporated and doing business under the laws of the United States (including laws relating to the District of Columbia) or of any State, a substantial part of the business of which consists of receiving deposits and making loans and discounts, or of exercising fiduciary powers similar to those permitted to national banks under authority of the Comptroller of the Currency, and which is subject by law to supervision and examination by State, Territorial, or Federal authority having supervision over banking institutions. Such term also means a domestic building and loan association.

Sec. 6011

General Requirement of Return, Statement, or List.

(a) General rule.—When required by regulations prescribed by the Secretary any person made liable for any tax imposed by this title, or with respect to the collection thereof, shall make a return or statement according to the forms and regulations prescribed by the Secretary. * * *

Sec. 6020

Returns Prepared for or Executed by Secretary.

(b) (1) Authority of Secretary to execute return.—If any person fails to make any return required by any internal revenue law or regulation made thereunder at the time prescribed therefor, or makes, willfully or otherwise, a false or fraudulent return, the Secretary shall make such return from his own knowledge and from such information as he can obtain through testimony or otherwise.

Certificate of Delivery
of Form 2481

(Under section 7512, Internal Revenue Code)

I hereby certify that the original of this
Notice was delivered by hand to

Jane Jones, Treasurer, Taxpayer Industries, Inc.

Name and Title

One Main Street, Anytown, NY 00000

on July 15 ___ 20 01 at 10:30 (a.m.) p.m.

Place of Delivery	Revenue Officer (Signature)
Anytown, NY	/s/ Tom Taxes

Internal Revenue Service
Washington, DC 20224

Penalty for Private Use: $300

First Class Mail
Postage and Fees Paid
IRS
Permit No. G–48
Official Business

Although employers are liable for unpaid employment taxes, including penalties and interest, and even potential criminal liability, when they fail to pay over the income and FICA tax they withhold from their employees, employer delinquencies in paying over these employment taxes remain a serious collection problem for the Service. Frequently, corporate or partnership employers unable to obtain outside financing or having insufficient capital to pay all their obligations attempt to continue their business by using the amount of withholding and employment taxes that they were obligated to pay over to the Service to support a failing or cash-strapped business. This ability to borrow the government's tax revenue without its consent is irresistible for some financially troubled businesses because the Service cannot immediately contact all businesses that fail to deposit their withholding and employment taxes on time.

Individuals in control of these businesses are often ignorant of their potential personal liability for the delinquent trust fund deposits. In most cases, persons responsible for deciding how the funds of the employer's business will be spent do not intend to defraud the government. They simply decide to prefer creditors other than the government in a vain hope that the business will "turn the corner" so that sufficient funds will then be available to pay all creditors, including the government. If the business fails, as often is the case, the government bears the cost of the employer's use of the trust fund taxes because it credits employees' income tax and employment tax accounts with the amounts that the employer should have paid over, and that were neither paid over nor otherwise collected out of the assets of the bankrupt business.

To collect burgeoning unpaid trust fund liabilities, the Service routinely asserts liability for the trust fund portion of the liability against responsible officers and employees whenever the employment taxes cannot be immediately collected from the corporation.[207] Section 6672 gives the Service the authority to move more aggressively against those who attempt to use the amount of withholding taxes as a source of current operating capital. To recover the trust fund portion of the taxes for the amounts it has been required to apply, Section 6672 of the Code imposes a penalty equal to the tax required to have been paid over on any person who (1) was required "to collect, truthfully account for and pay over" employment taxes and (2) willfully failed to do so.[208]

---

[207] IRM, Policies of the IRS Handbook, P-5-60 (approved Feb. 2, 1993) ("[i]f a business has failed to collect or pay over income and employment taxes, or has failed to pay over collected excise taxes, the trust fund recovery penalty may be asserted against those determined to have been responsible and willful in failing to pay over the tax").

[208] In 1993, the Service began to refer to the penalty as the trust fund recovery penalty, rather than the 100 percent penalty. IRM, Policies of the IRS Handbook, P-5-60 (approved Feb. 2, 1993).

[3] Persons Required to Withhold From Foreign Taxpayers

Payors of certain types of gross income to nonresident aliens and foreign corporations become withholding agents required to withhold income tax from the payments they make. Section 1441(a) requires payors[209] to withhold 30 percent (or a lower treaty rate) of any payment of U.S.-source fixed or determinable, annual or periodical (FDAP) income[210] to nonresident aliens or foreign partnerships.[211] Section 1442 requires the same withholding tax to be deducted from U.S.-source FDAP income paid to foreign corporations. Section 1445 governs withholding of tax on the disposition by a foreign person of U.S. real property interests,[212] and Section 1446 requires a partnership to withhold tax on a foreign partner's share of the partnership's effectively connected taxable income.[213] These withholding agents must deposit the tax they withhold in a federal reserve bank or authorized financial institution.[214] Deposits of withheld tax must be made quarter-monthly, monthly, or annually, depending on the amount of tax withheld.[215] The higher the amount withheld, the more frequent the required deposits. This determination is made at the withholding agent level, not at the individual foreign payee level.[216]

---

[209] The Code defines a "withholding agent" as "any person required to deduct and withhold any tax under the provisions of [S]ection 1441, 1442, 1443, or 1461." IRC § 7701(a)(16). Although Sections 1445 and 1446 are not mentioned in this definition, persons required to withhold under these sections can safely be called withholding agents because Section 1461 refers to "[e]very person required to deduct and withhold any tax under [Chapter 3] . . . ," which includes Sections 1445 and 1446.

[210] Section 1441(b) provides the following list of income items subject to withholding: interest (other than original issue discount), dividends, rent, salaries, wages, premiums, annuities, compensations, remunerations, emoluments, or other fixed or determinable annual or periodical income, gain on the sale of, or payment on, an original issue discount (OID) obligation to the extent it represents accrual of OID during the foreign person's holding period, and gains from the sale of certain intangible assets.

[211] In October 1997, the Treasury promulgated final regulations under Section 1441, effective for payments made after December 31, 1998. TD 8734, 62 Fed. Reg. 53,465 (Oct. 14, 1997). An analysis of these regulations is beyond the scope of this discussion.

[212] See the regulations under Section 1445 for a complete account of these rules and procedures.

[213] See Rev. Proc. 89-31, 1989-1 CB 895, modified by Rev. Proc. 92-66, 1992-2 CB 428, for rules and procedures for withholding on partnership income allocable to foreign partners.

[214] Reg. § 1.1461-1(a)(1), effective January 1, 1999. See also Reg. § 1.6302-2(a).

[215] Reg. § 1.6302-2(a)(1)(i).

[216] If, at the end of any quarter-monthly period, total undeposited tax is $2,000 or more, quarter-monthly deposits are required within three banking days after the close of the quarter-monthly period. Reg. § 1.6302-2(a)(1)(ii). Monthly deposits are required, within fifteen days after the close of the month, if the withholding agent withholds at least $200, but less than $2,000, during each quarter-monthly period occurring in any calendar month. Reg. § 1.6302-2(a)(1)(i). Annual deposits are required by March 15 of the follow-

By March 15 of the year following the year in which income was paid to a foreign person, every withholding agent must file an income tax return on Form 1042 and an information return on Form 1042-S, regardless of whether withholding was required.[217] If for any reason the total amount of tax required to be withheld was not deposited, the withholding agent must pay the balance when it files the Form 1042.[218] The withholding agent may satisfy the deficiency from either the foreign recipient's property that it controls (if it also underwithheld) or its own funds. If the withholding agent uses its own funds, it may recoup the deficiency by withholding additional tax from future payments made to the foreign recipient.[219]

Although the withholding provisions are mandatory, no penalty is apparently imposed on the withholding agent for merely failing to withhold.[220] Failure to pay tax is another matter, however. Whether or not withholding occurs, the withholding agent is personally liable for the tax required to be withheld.[221] Thus, the tax required to be withheld is an income tax directly imposed on the withholding agent.[222] A withholding agent who fails to withhold (or underwithholds) may end up satisfying the tax liability out of its own funds.[223] Depending on the contractual arrangements between the withholding agent and the recipient of the income, payment of the tax out of the withholding agent's funds may result in either additional FDAP income to the recipient (on which additional withholding could be required), or an advance of funds by the withholding agent to the payee.[224] If the recipient of the income pays the tax, the

---

ing calendar year if the amount of undeposited tax is less than $200 at the close of December. Reg. § 1.6302-2(a)(1)(iv).

[217] Reg. § 1.1461-1(b)(1), effective Jan. 1, 1999.

[218] Reg. § 1.1461-1(a)(1), effective Jan. 1, 1999.

[219] Reg. § 1.1461-2(b), effective Jan. 1, 1999.

[220] Reg. § 1.1461-2(a), effective Jan. 1, 1999.

[221] Section 1461 defines this liability as follows: "Every person required to deduct and withhold any tax under this chapter [Chapter 3] is hereby made liable for such tax and is hereby indemnified against the claims and demands of any person for the amount of any payments made in accordance with the provisions of this chapter."

[222] This is a significant point. Because Section 1461 imposes an income tax liability on the withholding agent, civil penalties applicable to income taxes, such as the substantial understatement penalty in Sections 6662(b)(2) and 6662(d) come into play. See GCM 39,888 (May 1, 1995), revoking GCM 39,686 (concluding that the substantial understatement penalty applies to Form 1042).

[223] This could occur if the withholding agent neither has property of the foreign recipient in its control nor makes future payments to the recipient subject to withholding. In that case, the procedures of Reg. § 1.1461-2(b) are not available. See discussion of adjustments for over withholding and under withholding.

[224] See Reg. §§ 1.1441-2(d)(3), 1.1441-3(f)(1), effective January 1, 1999. If it is characterized as an advance of funds, and the withholding agent fails to collect on the advance, the foreign recipient realizes cancellation of debt income. Although the cancellation

withholding agent is relieved of liability for the tax but remains liable for interest or penalties otherwise applicable to the failure to deduct and withhold, such as the failure-to-deposit penalty.[225]

Section 1461 makes the withholding agent liable for the income tax the agent was required to withhold from the nonresident alien or foreign corporation; thus, persons who are officers or employees of a corporate (or partnership) withholding agent, who willfully fail to collect and pay over the withholding tax, are personally liable under Section 6672 for the trust fund recovery penalty. The Service can collect tax owed by a foreign person on U.S.-source FDAP from three sources: (1) the foreign recipient; (2) the withholding agent; and (3) the withholding agent's responsible officers and employees. Although there have been no reported cases where the Service has used the trust fund recovery penalty to recover unpaid withholding tax from a responsible officer or employee of a withholding agent required to withhold, the regulations plainly contemplate it.[226] It seems unnecessary for the Service to use Section 6672 to recover the unpaid withholding tax from the withholding agent because Section 1461 already makes the withholding agent directly liable for the tax.[227]

[4] Persons Required to Withhold Excise Taxes

There are many excise taxes the Code requires sellers and other persons to collect. Excise taxes are imposed on retail sales of luxury passenger automobiles, special fuels, and heavy trucks and trailers (Chapter 31); manufacturers of automotive and related items, including petroleum products, coal, certain vaccines, and recreational equipment (Chapter 32); facilities and services, such as communications and air transportation (Chapter 33); policies of insurance issued by foreign insurers (Chapter 34); taxes on wagering (Chapter 35); certain other excise taxes (Chapter 36); as well as environmental excise taxes (Chapter

---

of debt (COD) income will be fixed and determinable, annual and periodical (FDAP) income, the withholding agent will not have liability to withhold, provided certain conditions are met. See Reg. § 1.1441-2(d)(3), effective Jan. 1, 1999.

[225] IRC § 1463. Section 6656 imposes a failure-to-deposit penalty on any person who fails to timely deposit any internal revenue tax on the date required under Section 6302, and its accompanying regulations.

[226] Reg. § 1.1461-1(a)(2), effective Jan. 1, 1999.

[227] This does not mean, however, that the Service could not use Section 6672. Section 6671 defines "person" for purposes of Section 6672 to "include" officers, etc. Section 7701(c) says that the term "includes . . . shall not be deemed to exclude other things otherwise within the meaning of the term defined." Arguably, the withholding agent is "otherwise within the meaning" of "person."

38).[228] As many and various as these excise taxes are, they have in common the requirement that the required excise tax paid be timely deposited or the withholding agent is subject to a failure-to-deposit penalty.[229] In addition, the officers and employees of these withholding agents, who have the duty to collect and pay over the excise tax, but who willfully fail to do so, are personally liable under Section 6672 in an amount equal to the amount of the unpaid tax.

¶ 17.07 SECTION 6672—THE RESPONSIBILITY REQUIREMENT

[1] Persons Responsible to Withhold

The statutory definition of the term "person" merely states that it includes, for the purposes of the 100 percent penalty, "an officer or employee of a corporation or a member or employee of a partnership" who is "under a duty" to perform the acts of collecting, accounting for, and paying over income and FICA taxes from employees.[230] The persons listed in the statutory definition are illustrative and not all-inclusive,[231] so that a person other than a corporate employee or officer may be considered to have the duty to perform the required statutory acts. Thus, although officers of the corporation are routinely asserted to be responsible persons for purposes of the 100 percent penalty,[232] persons who are neither corporation officers nor employees may be responsible for col-

---

[228] There are other excise taxes for which withholding may not be apparent or exist, such as various occupational excise taxes (Chapter 40); and various excise taxes on public charities (Chapter 41), private foundations and certain other exempt organizations (Chapter 42), qualified pension plans (Chapter 43), qualified investment entities (Chapter 44), golden parachute payments (Chapter 46), and certain group health plans (Chapter 45).

[229] IRC § 6656(a).

[230] IRC § 6671(b).

[231] See, e.g., Adams v. United States, 504 F2d 73, 75–76 (7th Cir. 1974); Pacific Nat'l Ins. Co. v. United States, 422 F2d 26 (9th Cir.), cert. denied, 398 US 937 (1970). In United States v. Graham, 309 F2d 210, 212 (9th Cir. 1962), the Ninth Circuit said, "The term 'person' does include officer and employee, but certainly does not exclude others. Its scope is illustrated rather than qualified by the specified examples." Section 7701(b) provides that the term "includes" as used in the Code "shall not be deemed to exclude other things otherwise within the meaning of the term defined."

[232] The Service's policy statement was revised in 1993. Before the revision, the IRM's *Policies of the IRS Handbook* stated, "When the person responsible for withholding, collecting and paying over taxes cannot otherwise be determined, the Service will look to the President, Secretary and the Treasurer of the corporation as responsible officers." IRM, Policies of the IRS Handbook, P-5-60 (approved May 30, 1984). The policy statement, as revised in 1993, still makes the status of a person the first of the three fac-

lecting and paying over trust fund taxes. A person may be a director,[233] a prospective purchaser,[234] a surety,[235] a creditor,[236] a lender,[237] a trustee or other fiduciary,[238] or an attorney.[239]

A special rule applies to voluntary board members of tax-exempt organizations to ensure that they are not considered responsible persons. No trust fund recovery penalty is permitted to be imposed against any unpaid volunteer member of any board of trustees or directors of tax-exempt organizations if the member (1) is serving solely in an honorary capacity; (2) does not participate in the day-to-day or financial operations of the organization; and (3) does not have actual knowledge of the failure for which which the penalty is im-

---

tors that establish responsibility, when it states, "Responsibility is a matter of status, duty, and authority."

[233] United States v. Graham, 309 F2d 210 (9th Cir. 1962); In re Summers, 84-1 USTC ¶ 9149 (Bankr. ND Ohio 1983).

[234] Melillo v. United States, 244 F. Supp. 323 (EDNY 1965); Caterino v. United States, 794 F2d 1 (1st Cir. 1986) (prospective purchaser of business who guaranteed loans to it held liable when he became directly involved in its financial and operational problems). See also Fair v. United States, 94-2 USTC ¶ 50,489 (D. Kan. 1994) ("while Fair was not a formal director or officer of Phiron, he had acquired through formal, written agreements with Phiron, effective control over the company").

[235] Pacific Nat'l Ins. Co. v. United States, 504 F2d 73 (7th Cir. 1974).

[236] Walker v. United States, 68-1 USTC ¶ 9370 (D. Okla. 1968). The Service has even asserted that an agent of a debtor of the employer was a responsible person. Haffa v. United States, 516 F2d 931 (7th Cir. 1975); Commonwealth Nat'l Bank v. United States, 665 F2d 743 (5th Cir. 1982) (lender bank and its president held liable as responsible persons); Jones v. United States, 33 F3d 1137 (9th Cir. 1994) (landlord held not a responsible person; although he was "an aggressive landlord who demanded and received cash payments to satisfy rent past due . . . [this] in no way suggests that [he] had the authority to pay payroll taxes").

[237] See infra ¶ 17.11.

[238] Keller v. United States, 46 F3d 851 (8th Cir. 1995) (personal representative "was personally vested under state law with the ultimate responsibility for the estate," and his "authority over the [Inn]: was equivalent to that of an absolute owner, holding it in trust for the benefit of creditors and other interested parties"). National Bank of Commerce v. Phinney, 65-2 USTC ¶ 9512 (SD Tex. 1965). Cf. Kaufman v. Scanlon, 245 F. Supp. 352 (EDNY 1965); Frazier v. United States, 304 F2d 528 (5th Cir. 1962).

Liability of a trustee or fiduciary for employment taxes may be found under provisions other than Section 6672. In United States v. Cole, 733 F2d 651 (9th Cir. 1984), an escrow holder of the proceeds from the sale of assets of an insolvent corporation was held personally laible for the corporation's unpaid federal payroll taxes when he paid the proceeds to other creditors ahead of the United States. Liability was found under 31 USC § 3713, which establishes personal liability for a representative of an insolvent debtor who pays other claimants before paying the claims of the federal government. See infra ¶ 17.11.

[239] Brown v. United States, 464 F2d 590 (5th Cir. 1972), cert. denied, 410 US 908 (1973) (attorney who became "nominal" president of his client's corporation); Wyner v. United States, 82-1 USTC ¶ 9341 (ED Mich. 1982).

posed.[240] This protection from liability is removed, however, if the exception from responsibility results in no person being liable for the penalty.

Responsibility for the purposes of the trust fund recovery penalty is not limited to persons with a formal corporate office. It is generally held that the determination that a person or entity had the statutory duty to collect and pay over withholding taxes is a question of fact. A frequently applied standard in making this determination is whether the person in question had "the final word as to what bills should or should not be paid, and when."[241] This standard is not the only one applied. The key to liability also has been said to be "control of finances within the employer corporation: The power to control the decisionmaking process by which the employer corporation allocates funds to other creditors in preference to its withholding obligations."[242] Another state-

---

[240] IRC § 6672(e), added by Taxpayer Bill of Rights 2, § 904(a), effective on the date of enactment, July 30, 1996. Congress also instructed the Service to develop materials to inform board members of tax-exempt organizations that they may be treated as responsible persons and to instruct Service employees more clearly about the applicability of the penalty to honorary or volunteer members of tax-exempt organizations. At one time, the Service claimed that these board members were liable for the organization's tax. In Rev. Rul. 84-83, 1984-1 CB 264, the Service held that a volunteer member of a board of trustees of a charitable organization may be liable for unpaid employment and withholding taxes in certain circumstances under Section 6672. Carter v. United States, 89-2 USTC ¶ 9446 (SDNY 1989) (officers and directors of not-for-profit organization held liable; summary judgment granted). However, the Service had changed its administrative policy. See IRM, Policies of the IRS Handbook, P-5-60 (approved Feb. 2, 1993).

[241] Wilson v. United States, 250 F2d 312, 316 (9th Cir. 1957) (criminal prosecution involving withholding taxes). This language in Wilson has been applied in 100 percent penalty cases. See also Kiss v. United States, 84-1 USTC ¶ 9169 (D. Alaska 1983) (principal officers were responsible persons where they made the choice not to pay withholding taxes in order to keep their company operating). Bloom v. United States, 272 F2d 215 (9th Cir. 1959), cert. denied, 363 US 803 (1960); United States v. Graham, 309 F2d 210 (9th Cir. 1962); White v. United States, 372 F2d 513 (Ct. Cl. 1967); Hewitt v. United States, 377 F2d 921 (5th Cir. 1967). Hanes v. Longley, 84-2 USTC ¶ 9597 (ND Okla. 1984).

See also Gephart v. United States, 818 F2d 469 (6th Cir. 1987) (accountant/general manager who did not have "final word" but who did have significant control over which creditors were to be paid held to be responsible officer). Cf. Brown v. United States, 464 F2d 590 (5th Cir. 1972), cert. denied, 410 US 908 (1973) (Fifth Circuit stated that in Hewitt, it simply held that a taxpayer who did have the "final word" could not escape liability as a responsible person by asserting that a corporate subordinate was responsible for paying bills and taxes, but not that the officer or employee *must* have the final word to be a responsible person).

[242] Haffa v. United States, 516 F2d 931 (7th Cir. 1975). Latimer v. United States, 593 F. Supp. 881 (ND Ill. 1984). See also Huggins v. United States, 84-1 USTC ¶ 9192 (ND Tex. 1984) ("[a] responsible person is any person who can effectively control the finances or determine which bills should or should not be paid"); Raba v. United States, 977 F2d 941 (5th Cir. 1992) (chief financial officer did not have check-signing authority, but managed financial affairs, including deciding how funds were spent and which creditors were paid); Bradshaw v. United States, 93-2 USTC ¶ 50,532 (D. Utah 1993) (president not a

ment of the standard is that a responsible person is one who exercises full authority over financial affairs and who is therefore ultimately responsible for the decision not to pay the tax.[243]

[2] Standard of Control

Some courts have identified various factors that are considered in determining responsible person status, including: (1) holding an office or owning stock in the corporation; (2) managing the day-to-day operations of the business; (3) making decisions as to disbursement of funds and payment of creditors; (4) check-signing authority.[244] The Fifth Circuit has used these factors to restrict the role of the factfinder in *Barnett v. Internal Revenue Service*.[245] The Fifth Circuit concluded that the issue of responsibility was a matter of law and that even if it were considered a question of fact, "extensive case law . . . narrowly constrains the factfinder's province in Section 6672 cases." Saying that authority over the enterprise's financial or general decision making was indicated by such factors as the ones described, the circuit court found, despite a contrary jury verdict, that Barnett was a responsible person. The court noted that Barnett was a vice president, owned stock in the corporation, managed day-to-day operations, had the authority to hire and fire employees, made decisions about the disbursement of funds and creditors, and had the authority to sign checks.

---

person responsible, because bank retained control over disbursements under overdraft-financing arrangement).

[243] Werner v. United States, 374 F. Supp. 558 (D. Conn. 1974), aff'd per curiam, 512 F2d 1381 (2d Cir. 1975), quoting Melillo v. United States, 244 F. Supp. 323 (EDNY 1965). In United States v. Rem, 38 F3d 634 (2d Cir. 1994), the circuit court said that the determinative question is whether the individual has "significant control over the enterprise's finances," not whether the individual has the final word about which creditors are to be paid. On the other hand, "though § 6672(a) 'is not meant to ensnare those who have merely titular designation,' . . . the section encompasses 'all those connected closely enough with the business to prevent the (tax) default from occurring.'"

[244] Turnbull v. United States, 929 F2d 173, 178 (5th Cir. 1991) (former president was still considered "boss" and retained check-signing authority). Other circuit courts consider these same elements to be controlling on the issue of responsibility. See, e.g., United States v. Rem, 38 F3d 634 (2d Cir. 1994) (factors considered in determining responsible person status are whether the individual (1) is an officer or member of the board of directors; (2) owns shares or possesses an entrepreneurial stake in the company; (3) is active in the management of day-to-day affairs of the company; (4) has the ability to hire and fire employees; (5) makes decisions regarding which, when, and in what order outstanding debts or taxes will be paid; (6) exercises control over daily bank accounts and disbursement records; and (7) has check-signing authority); Jones v. United States, 74 AFTR2d 94-6128 (9th Cir. 1994) (gathering other Ninth Circuit cases). The Service itself says that responsibility is a matter of status, duty, and authority. IRM, Policies of the IRS Handbook, P-5-60 (approved Feb. 2, 1993).

[245] Barnett v. Internal Rev. Serv., 988 F2d 1449 (5th Cir. 1993).

The fact that Barnett was in a satellite office was not sufficient, as a matter of law, to establish lack of effective control. However, other courts, although they recognize that responsibility may be inferred from certain factors, still recognize the role of the trier of fact in making the ultimate finding of liability. The Second Circuit has said that the core question is "significant control," and the power to sign checks and the holding of corporate office "can exist in circumstances where the individual in reality does not possess significant control over corporate finances."[246]

Status alone does not control the issue of responsibility. An extreme application of "the final word" and the "power to control" standards imposes responsibility on shareholders who have nothing to do with the day-to-day operations of the business or on a lender who makes working capital loans to a borrower without any intrusion into its operations. Shareholders as a group might have the final word as a matter of corporate law, or a lender might have the practical ability to control the payment of withholding taxes, but it casts the net of responsibility too far to hold these persons responsible without more. The penalty is imposed on persons who have the duty to collect and pay over, not those having the theoretical authority to do so, and so the concept of responsibility connotes more than a corporate title. It seems fair to say that the statutory duty, and therefore responsibility, arises out of control actually exercised over the financial operations of the business.[247]

As a matter of administrative practice, the Service asserts the trust fund recovery penalty against corporate officers and directors.[248] This administrative practice is elevated to a presumption as a matter of law. Because an assessment is presumptively correct, the burden of coming forward with evidence in any court proceeding must be carried by the person against whom the assessment was made.[249] Consequently, a company's president, vice president, treasurer, and comptroller, as well as an active director, are generally considered responsible persons for purposes of the 100 percent penalty.[250]

---

[246] United States v. Rem, 38 F3d 634 (2d Cir. 1994). See also Jay v. United States, 865 F2d 1175, 1179 (10th Cir. 1989) ("[t]he issues of liability are for the trier of fact to determine, upon all the evidence, taking into account questions of credibility and those reasonable inferences flowing from the evidence which may establish, or fail to establish, that Jay possessed a sufficient degree of authority over corporate decision-making so as to make him a responsible person with Section 6672 of the Code").

[247] See United States v. Rem, 38 F3d 634 (2d Cir. 1994).

[248] IRM, Policies of the IRS Handbook, P-5-60 (Feb. 2, 1993) ("[r]esponsibility is a matter of status, duty and authority"). The Service's policy statment also states that "responsibility and willfulness must both be established" in order for the penalty to be asserted.

[249] United States v. Lease, 346 F2d 696 (2d Cir. 1965).

[250] In Farris, Jr. v. United States, 84-1 USTC ¶ 9263 (Cl. Ct. 1984), the claims court said, "Any high-ranking corporate official, such as a vice president, is considered to be a responsible person, in the absence of evidence to the contrary." Mazo v. United States,

[a] Ministerial Versus Executive Judgment

Courts distinguish between ministerial and executive judgment, however. Employees of a corporation who merely perform the mechanical functions of collection and payment and who do not exercise independent judgment are not responsible when their functions are performed in accordance with the executive judgment of others, whose duty it is to make such decisions.[251] The distinction between a person who performs ministerial acts without exercising independent judgment, and one who performs ministerial acts, but has sufficient authority to pay over trust fund taxes, has led to frequent litigation.[252]

Some courts say that an employee must risk dismissal rather than accede to the nonpayment of taxes.[253] But it is not at all certain whether this view is

---

591 F2d 1151 (5th Cir. 1979) (officers, directors, and general manager); Bloom v. United States, 272 F2d 215 (9th Cir. 1959) (president); Bauer v. United States, 543 F2d 142 (Ct. Cl. 1976) (vice president, secretary, and treasurer); United States v. Graham, 309 F2d 210 (9th Cir. 1962) (directors); Thompson v. United States, 37 Bankr. 211 (Bankr. MD Fla. 1983) (chief executive officer).

[251] The Service itself recognizes that those performing ministerial acts without exercising independent judgment will not be deemed responsible. IRM, Policies of the IRS Handbook, P-5-59 (approved Feb. 2, 1993). The Service's policy statement also says, "In general, nonowner employees of the business entity, who act solely under the dominion and control of others and who are not in a position to make independent decisions on behalf of the business entity, will not be asserted the trust fund recovery penalty."

[252] United States v. Graham, 309 F2d 210 (9th Cir. 1962); Werner v. United States, 374 F. Supp. 558 (D. Conn. 1974). A close question is presented where a board of directors directs the managing executive to continue the business, and there are insufficient funds to pay taxes and other creditors. On the one hand, the executive does have the responsibility of managing the operation, but on the other hand, the executive is legally bound to follow the board's directive. See Cooper v. United States, 539 F. Supp. 117 (ED Va. 1982), aff'd in unpublished opinion (4th Cir. 1983) (foundation director found not to have been instructed not to pay taxes); Carr v. United States, 85-2 USTC ¶ 9542 (ND Ill. 1985) (president who claimed he followed orders of directors held responsible: *Cooper* followed); Schwinger v. United States, 652 F. Supp. 464 (EDNY 1987) (court denied motion for summary judgment that doctor and hospital board member was a responsible person).

Similarly, when an officer retains legal control over a company, including the authority to sign checks, the officer may be liable, even when a lender, under a financing arrangement, refuses to allocate funds to the payment of taxes. See, e.g., Taubman v. United States, 499 F. Supp. 1133 (ED Mich. 1978), aff'd, 635 F2d 1215 (6th Cir. 1980); Totaro v. United States, 533 F. Supp. 71 (WDNY 1981). Compare United States v. Falino, 441 F. Supp. 153 (EDNY 1977) (surety had check-signing authority); First Am. Bank & Trust Co. v. United States, 79-1 USTC ¶ 9205 (WD Okla. 1979) (lender controlled disbursement of checks); Marshall v. United States, 89-1 USTC ¶ 9150 (ND Ill. 1988) (president held responsible despite overdraft financing arrangement with bank). The apparent lesson of the cases finding responsibility is that the officer who has legal authority to act may not acquiesce in the nonpayment of taxes.

[253] Howard v. United States, 711 F2d 729 (5th Cir. 1983) (person is not absolved from liability even if he failed to pay over because of his employer's threats to dismiss

generally accepted.[254] The nature of the officer's duties are also determinative. It is the scope of the officer's authority to act, not the officer's title, that controls the finding. "The central question is whether the individual has significant control over the enterprise's finances."[255] A person may be a director or corporate officer and have nothing to do with payroll, the preparation and signing of checks, and the decision about which creditors to pay. When such facts as these are present, the person is not responsible for the purposes of the trust fund penalty, or at least there is an issue of fact for the trier of fact to hear, taking into account all the evidence and reasonable inferences flowing from

---

him from his job if he paid over the taxes); Hochstein v. United States, 900 F2d 543 (2d Cir. 1990) (a split panel of the Second Circuit ruled that a corporate controller's "good faith belief that he could be prosecuted or fired for not paying the employees or that a bankruptcy court would direct that employees, not the government, be paid, did not excuse his failure to pay"); but see United States v. Rem, 38 F3d 634 (2d Cir. 1994), in which the concurring opinion of Judge Leval says that in *Hochstein*, there was no evidence that a clear instruction not to pay had been given to the controller, and the evidence showed that the financer did not designate how the funds were to be used. Therefore, it was unclear whether Hochstein's payment of taxes would have amounted to noncompliance with the factor's instructions.

[254] In United States v. Rem, 38 F3d 634 (2d Cir. 1994), the Second Circuit clarified its decision in *Hochstein* on the issue of responsibility, and said that the factors used to determine responsibility are not intended to foreclose, for example, probing the substance of an individual's office to determine whether the individual's designation as president was titular and a device to enhance the company to obtain credit.

Other courts have refused to adopt the view in *Howard*. Roth v. United States, 84-1 USTC ¶ 9319 (ND Ala. 1984) (district court refused to follow *Howard* on similar facts when vice president risked termination if he were to pay withholding taxes), rev'd and remanded, 779 F2d 1567 (11th Cir. 1986) (*Howard* followed; dissenting opinion points out absence of finding of willfulness); Freeman v. United States, 603 F. Supp. 272 (D. Ariz. 1985) (following *Howard* and rejecting *Roth*); Kraus v. United States, 85-1 USTC ¶ 9310 (EDNY 1985) (following Howard); cf. Graunke v. United States, 711 F. Supp. 388 (ND Ill. 1989) ("[I]t does not appear that the law has gone so far as to require that a person must disregard checkwriting instructions in order to avoid liability. Rather the focal point in all of the cases is whether the plaintiff possessed a sufficient degree of authority over corporate decisionmaking to make him a responsible person."); Schroeder v. United States, 89-2 USTC ¶ 9474 (ND Ind. 1989) (director of administration and finance not responsible, because he did not have authority to pay creditors on his own and signed checks pursuant to superior's instructions; *Howard* and *Roth* distinguished).

[255] Hochstein v. United States, 900 F2d 543, 547 (2d Cir. 1990); United States v. Rem, 38 F3d 634 (2d Cir. 1994). The core question is "significant control," and the power to sign checks and the holding of corporate office "can exist in circumstances where the individual in reality does not possess significant control over corporate finances." See also Jones v. United States, 74 AFTR2d 94-6128 (9th Cir. 1994) (accord).

the evidence.[256] Similarly, an officer who has been stripped of significant au-

---

[256] There are many federal appellate and Court of Federal Claims cases supporting this point:

1st Circuit: Drummey v. United States, 84-1 USTC ¶ 9105 (D. Mass. 1983) (comptroller of corporation was not liable when approval of chief executive officer was required for all checks drawn on corporation's account). See In re Bourque, 93-1 USTC ¶ 50,327 (Bankr. D. Mass. 1993) (in a questionable decision showing how far some courts will go, a manager of a corporate accounting department was found to be liable under *Hochstein*, 900 F2d 543 (2d Cir. 1990), although she was a single mother with a physically disabled child, and the majority shareholder and president put pressure on her).

2d Circuit: United States v. Rem, 38 F3d 634 (2d Cir. 1994) (nominal president found not to be responsible; distinguishing *Hochstein*, 900 F2d 543 (2d Cir. 1990), when comptroller found responsible, despite claim that he would have been fired if he had paid over trust fund taxes); Abramson v. United States, 85-1 USTC ¶ 9380 (EDNY 1985) (secretary-treasurer who was also board member and principal shareholder was held not liable, because he was not responsible for many payments); United States v. Burger, 717 F. Supp. 245 (SDNY 1989) (director minority shareholder who was not officer and who had no check-signing authority, was held not responsible officer).

3d Circuit: Brounstein v. United States, 979 F2d 952 (3d Cir. 1992) (president who claimed he was only nominal president, and who signed checks under instructions, was held liable because he had exercised authority to sign and issue checks, and signed quarterly withholding tax returns; defense that he acted under instructions rejected). The Third Circuit said, "A corporate officer who fails to pay over to the government withheld taxes when there are funds to do so is not entitled to prefer his own interest in continued employment over that of the government, the beneficiary of a trust created by operation of law when taxes are withheld." Id.

4th Circuit: Turpin v. United States, 91-2 USTC ¶ 50,403 (D. Md. 1991) (categories of facts to be examined are party's status, duties, and authority; secretary-treasurer was held not to be responsible officer, because he had no general authority to sign checks).

5th Circuit: The Fifth Circuit concededly takes a "broad view" of who may be found to be a responsible officer. See Wood v. United States, 808 F2d 411, 415 (5th Cir. 1987).

6th Circuit: Campbell v. Nixon, 207 F. Supp. 826 (ED Mich. 1962); Brennan v. United States, 85-1 USTC ¶ 9113 (ND Ohio 1984) (shareholders were held not responsible persons, because operations were controlled by managers). Because he was not involved in the decision to pay other creditors, an executive vice president primarily responsible for the daily operation of a trucking business was found to be neither a responsible officer nor willful, despite his knowledge of tax delinquencies. Cline v. United States, 997 F2d 191 (6th Cir. 1993) (*Hochstein* and other cases distinguished on ground that responsible persons in those cases paid other corporate obligations while failing to pay withheld taxes that they knew were delinquent). See Corigliano v. United States, 93-2 USTC ¶ 50,418 (ED Pa. 1993) (officer-shareholder and officer-accountant held not to be responsible officers, because they did not have control over corporation's financial affairs).

7th Circuit: Bernardi v. United States, 74-1 USTC ¶ 9170 (ND Ill. 1973), aff'd, 507 F2d 682 (7th Cir. 1974), cert. denied, 422 US 1042 (1975) (vice president of operations and director who cosigned some checks was not responsible, because he was not responsible for payroll, determining credit priorities, or disbursements); Fort v. United States, 85-1 USTC ¶ 9170 (ND Ill. 1981) (corporate officer and director was held not responsible person, because, although he had check-signing authority, this fact "does not mean that he had significant control over the financial decisionmaking").

8th Circuit: United States v. Lumetta, 73-1 USTC ¶ 9386 (ED Mo. 1970) (director and officer was held not to have sufficient control to be responsible); United States v. Strebler, 313 F2d 402 (8th Cir. 1963) (vice president and bookkeeper who prepared checks and tax returns was held not responsible); Keller v. United States, 46 F3d 851 (8th Cir. 1995) (personal representative controlled estate's bank accounts, was authorized to engage in various transactions on behalf of the estate that owned the business, and "in fact exercised that authority by, among other things, employing persons to assist in administering the estate and borrowing money for and making improvements to the Inn").

9th Circuit: Alsheskie v. United States, 31 F3d 837 (9th Cir. 1994) (a divided court found an employee who was president and chairman of the board, but not a shareholder, not to be a responsible officer because he did not have "'significant control' over what bills to pay or not pay since that control remained with the parent corporation . . ."); Jones v. United States, 33 F3d 1137 (9th Cir. 1994) (consultant and general manager who signed checks found not to be responsible person because he signed checks out of the operational account from a list of creditors given to him by the owner, was not authorized to sign checks alone, and was employed for only forty-five days).

10th Circuit: Jay v. United States, 865 F2d 1175 (10th Cir. 1989) (the corporation's comptroller, who possessed checkwriting authority, was not an officer or shareholder, found not liable as a matter of law because his "responsibilities [were] subject to the executive committee's instructions and restrictions on which creditors he should pay").

11th Circuit: Roth v. United States, 84-1 USTC ¶ 9319 (ND Ala. 1984) (vice president not liable when he lacked discretion to decide which creditors should be paid, even though he ran day-to-day affairs of corporation and had limited check-signing authority).

Federal Circuit and U.S. Court of Federal Claims: Godfrey v. United States, 83-2 USTC ¶ 9635 (Cl. Ct. 1983) (two directors, acting jointly with others to keep corporation operating after it was known that substantial withholding taxes remained unpaid, were not liable for the 100 percent penalty, because they had no control over payments of corporate debts and had only limited participation in corporate affairs), rev'd and vacated, 84-2 USTC ¶ 9635 (Fed. Cir. 1984) (finding that third individual, outside director and executive committee chairman, was responsible was reversed absent evidence he exercised control over payment of taxes; his conduct also was not willful, because, although he knew of past delinquencies, he had no actual notice of current delinquencies); Bauer v. United States, 543 F2d 142 (Ct. Cl. 1976); Bolding

thority is not responsible for the purposes of the penalty.[257]

Some courts hold that a person with ultimate authority over the financial affairs of the employer may not avoid responsibility by delegating this authority, although the fact of delegation may be relevant on the issue of willfulness.[258] The distinction between responsibility and willfulness is illustrated by judicial response to a delegation defense. The authority to exercise control

---

v. United States, 565 F2d 663 (Ct. Cl. 1977) (vice president without knowledge); Heimark v. United States, 89-2 USTC ¶ 9499 (Cl. Ct. 1989) (bookkeeper and clerk held title of treasurer, but had little actual authority; cases analyzed); Stewart v. United States, 90-1 USTC ¶ 50,002, 19 Cl. Ct. 1 (1989) (sole shareholder, director, and officer of professional service corporation was held not responsible person when administrator controlled business aspects of practice; *Baur* followed); Schultz v. United States, 19 Cl. Ct. 280, 90-1 USTC ¶ 50,041 (Fed. Cir. 1990) (president was liable not because of office, but because he "actually possessed and exercised ultimate authority and . . . could have ensured taxes were paid").

[257] Maggy v. United States, 560 F2d 1372 (9th Cir. 1977) (president and director who was stripped of "all significant authority" was not responsible after that date). See also Cellura v. United States, 245 F. Supp. 379 (ND Ohio 1965) (manager acting on orders); Werner v. United States, 374 F. Supp. 558 (D. Conn. 1974), aff'd per curiam, 512 F2d 1381 (2d Cir. 1975); Turner v. United States, 83-2 USTC ¶ 9709 (DND 1983) (taxpayer who lost much financial control but who was still actively involved in the business and had authority to sign checks was a responsible person); Pototzky v. United States, 85-1 USTC ¶ 9438 (Cl. Ct. 1985) (officer and director had relinquished day-to-day control at time delinquency occurred).

Lenders exercising control may render themselves liable for trust fund taxes under Section 6672; but the lenders' liability does not necessarily excuse or eliminate liability of the debtor-corporation's officer, because the officer may exercise significant, even if not exclusive, control. See Olsen v. United States, 952 F2d 236 (8th Cir. 1991) (gathering cases); Blankenship v. United States, 93-2 USTC ¶ 50,435 (WD Ky. 1993) (employer's debtor borrowed funds from lender who advanced net payroll to the employer's debtor; held, lender's control did not absolve employer).

[258] Hornsby v. United States, 588 F2d 952 (5th Cir. 1979) ("taxpayer cannot satisfy his burden of proof merely by showing that he delegated his responsibility to someone else"); Lawrence v. United States, 299 F. Supp. 187, 190 (ND Tex. 1959); Koegel v. United States, 437 F. Supp. 176 (SDNY 1977). Thomsen, Jr. v. United States, 887 F2d 12 (1st Cir. 1989) (treasurer who had actual authority to pay was not relieved of responsibility by delegating responsibility for financial matters to another); Keller v. United States, 75 AFTR2d 95-721 (8th Cir. 1995) ("[i]f the responsible person continues to delegate without taking appropriate measures to ensure that future taxes are paid, his failure to take such measures will be considered willful conduct"). Compare United States v. Leuschner, 336 F2d 246 (9th Cir. 1964) (delegator held not to have acted willfully when taxes were not paid over by a bookkeeper). Compare In re Woodson, 15 Bankr. 185 (Bankr. ED Mich. 1981) (majority shareholder and chairman of board who "delegated all the responsibility for payment" of taxes to general manager-president was neither responsible nor willful); Sulger v. United States, 24 Cl. Ct. 535, 91-2 USTC ¶ 50,577 (1991) ("[t]here simply was never the type of complete delegation of authority that could support a conclusion that [chairman of the board and largest stockholder] no longer had the requisite authority to be a 'responsible person'").

over a corporation's financial affairs has been held by a number of circuit courts to be nondelegable. The Ninth Circuit has said that "[t]he authority that permits control carries with it a nondelegable duty to ensure that withholding taxes are duly collected and paid over to the government."[259] Although a person cannot delegate responsibility, the officer who does not exercise control over the corporation's financial affairs, and does not know of the delinquency, ordinarily is not willful.[260]

[b] Factors Evidencing Control

Much case law exists in regard to how much or what kind of control is determinative for holding a person responsible to withhold under Section 6672. The following are various factors the courts have considered:

- The decision to pay creditors is reflected in the checks issued by the employer. Accordingly, a finding of responsibility frequently turns on whether the individual decided which checks should be prepared, for whom, and in what amount, as well as whether the individual had the authority to sign checks.[261]

---

[259] Purcell v. United States, 1 F3d 932 (9th Cir. 1993) (the nondelegability of responsibility has even been said to exist when a president enters into a financing agreement "ceding" his authority to decide which creditors to pay when, on default, the agreement permits the lender to approve payments, including the payment of federal withholding taxes); Bradshaw v. United States, 83 F3d 1175, reh'g denied, 1995 US App. LEXIS 33764 (10th Cir. 1995) (lender refused to authorize payment of taxes, and president held liable as responsible person); compare Alsheshkie v. United States, 31 F3d 837 (9th Cir. 1994) (in nearly the same situation a divided panel of the Ninth Circuit held that the president was not a responsible person, because his authority was limited by the financing arrangement).
See also the discussion of what constitutes "willful conduct" infra ¶ 17.09.

[260] Purcell v. United States, 1 F3d 932 (9th Cir. 1993) (the nondelegability of responsibility has even been said to exist when a president enters into a financing agreement "ceding" his authority to decide which creditors to pay when, on default, the agreement permits the lender to approve payments, including the payment of federal withholding taxes); Bradshaw v. United States, 83 F3d 1175, reh'g denied, 1995 US App. LEXIS 33764 (10th Cir. 1995) (lender refused to authorize payment of taxes, and president held liable as responsible person); compare Alsheshkie v. United States, 31 F3d 837 (9th Cir. 1994) (in nearly the same situation a divided panel of the Ninth Circuit held that the president was not a responsible person, because his authority was limited by the financing arrangement).
See also the discussion of what constitutes "willful conduct" infra ¶ 17.09.

[261] Hornsby v. United States, 588 F2d 952 (5th Cir. 1979); United States v. Graham, 309 F2d 210 (9th Cir. 1962); Cash v. Campbell, 346 F2d 670 (5th Cir. 1965); United States v. Strebler, 313 F2d 402 (8th Cir. 1963). In Bauer v. United States, 543 F2d 142 (Ct. Cl. 1976), the court of claims said, "In each case in this Court, in which a person was found to have possessed a duty under section 6672 of the Code, it has been established by the evidence that he actually signed or cosigned corporate checks." Howard v. United

- That an officer determined the priority of payment and preferred other creditors to the United States may be evidenced by the fact that the officer prepared, signed, or filed payroll tax returns, presumably because it is reasonable to assume that if the officer controlled these acts, he or she could have made any payment that was due.[262]
- To establish officers' duties and authority, the corporation's bylaws are considered.[263]
- The identity of an officer, director, and principal shareholder is evidence of control.[264] The court of claims has said that when a person is a shareholder, officer, and director, there is a rebuttable presumption of responsibility.[265]
- The person who directs the payment of other creditors instead of trust fund taxes is considered responsible for the purposes of the penalty,[266] and this evidence is relevant on the issue of willfulness as well.[267]

[c] Doctrines of Existing Funds and After-Acquired Funds

Section 6672 limits personal liability to a person with the duty to (1) collect; (2) truthfully account for; and (3) pay over the taxes in issue. In Slodov,[268] an orthodontist purchased the stock of three food vending businesses that at the time of the purchase owed about $250,000 in trust fund taxes. Prior management had collected the taxes, but had dissipated the amounts in the operation of the business before Slodov purchased the stock. The sellers of the

---

States, 82-2 USTC ¶ 9567 (ND Tex. 1982), aff'd, 711 F2d 729 (5th Cir. 1983); In re Twomey, 82-2 USTC ¶ 9687 (WDNY 1982).

[262] United States v. Strebler, 313 F2d 402 (8th Cir. 1963); United States v. Graham, 309 F2d 210 (9th Cir. 1962); Horowitz v. United States, 339 F2d 877, 878 (2d Cir. 1965). In Labowitz v. United States, 352 F. Supp. 202, 205 (SDNY 1972), the signing of returns and a partial payment agreement were considered tantamount to an admission of liability.

[263] United States v. Strebler, 313 F2d 402 (8th Cir. 1963); Mussato v. United States, 82-2 USTC ¶ 9498 (D. Colo. 1982) (duties as Treasurer as stated in bylaws analyzed); In re Twomey, 82-2 USTC ¶ 9687 (WDNY 1982).

[264] Frazier v. United States, 304 F2d 528 (5th Cir. 1962); Scherer v. United States, 228 F. Supp. 168, 170 (D. Idaho 1963).

[265] McCarty v. United States, 437 F2d 961 (Ct. Cl. 1971).

[266] United States v. Graham, 309 F2d 210 (9th Cir. 1962); Horowitz v. United States, 339 F2d 877 (2d Cir. 1965); Bloom v. United States, 272 F2d 215 (9th Cir. 1959); Melillo v. United States, 244 F. Supp. 323 (EDNY 1965); Tiffany v. United States, 228 F. Supp. 700, 702 (DNJ 1963). See also Summers v. United States, 89-1 USTC ¶ 9239 (D. Idaho 1989) (sole shareholder and another individual cosigned an operating loan made to corporation; each individual had final authority over payment of creditors).

[267] United States v. Monday, 294 F. Supp. 1384 (D. Wis. 1969), rev'd and remanded, 421 F2d 1210 (7th Cir.), cert. denied, 400 US 821 (1970).

[268] In re Slodov, 436 US 238 (1978).

businesses misrepresented to Slodov that there were sufficient funds in the accounts to pay the taxes, and Slodov in fact sent checks to the Service only to discover that there were insufficient funds to cover the amounts of the checks. Despite this nonpayment in taxes, the Service permitted Slodov to operate the businesses.

After Slodov assumed control of the businesses, the corporations earned sufficient funds for Slodov to have paid the delinquent precontrol taxes, but instead Slodov used these receipts to pay employees' wages, including the current taxes, rent, suppliers, creditors, and other day-to-day expenses of the businesses. Slodov paid no amounts to satisfy the precontrol liability, and eventually the Service assessed the precontrol trust fund taxes against Slodov on the ground that he was a responsible officer of the corporations.

Slodov acknowledged that he was subject to personal liability for the period of time that he had assumed control of the corporations, but argued that because he was not in control of the businesses for the prior periods, he was under no duty to pay the taxes collected by the sellers of the businesses. Slodov's position was that because the obligations of Section 6672 impose personal liability only if the responsible officer was subject to all duties—to collect, to truthfully account for, and to pay over—he was not liable for the penalty. The Supreme Court held that the phrase in Section 6672 apparently limiting the liability of a responsible person to one able to perform all three duties "was meant to limit [Section] 6672 to persons responsible for collection of third party taxes and not to limit it to those persons in a position to perform all three of the enumerated duties with respect to the tax dollars in question."[269] If the duty attaches at the time of collection, responsibility cannot be avoided even if the person is not an officer or the person's duties change by the time taxes are to be paid over and the return filed.[270] Moreover, once the liability exists, it may not be delegated to another. Thus, a controlling officer and seller of stock of a corporation cannot effectively avoid responsibility by entering into a contract whereby the purchaser assumes the liability.[271]

Another troublesome question the Supreme Court faced in *Slodov* was whether Section 6672 imposes personal liability on a responsible person, as Slodov, for precontrol trust fund taxes because sums received after control are

---

[269] In re Slodov, 436 US 238, 247 (1978).

[270] In re Slodov, 436 US 238, 247 (1978); Brown v. United States, 591 F2d 1136 (5th Cir. 1979) (resignation and rescission of authority to sign checks did not prevent finding of responsibility); Kalb v. United States, 505 F2d 506, 509 (2d Cir. 1974), cert. denied, 421 US 979 (1975); Bernardi v. United States, 74-1 USTC ¶ 9170 (ND Ill. 1973), aff'd, 507 F2d 682 (7th Cir. 1974), cert. denied, 422 US 1042 (1975); Seaton v. United States, 254 F. Supp. 161 (WD Mo. 1966); Long v. Bacon, 239 F. Supp. 911 (SD Iowa 1965).

[271] Markel v. United States, 70-2 USTC ¶ 9702 (WD Tex. 1970); Barker v. United States, 72-1 USTC ¶ 9225 (D. Okla. 1972) (indemnity agreement).

impressed with a trust in favor of the Service, and the willful use of those funds to pay other creditors violated the responsible officer's obligation to pay over the trust fund taxes. In addition to noting the Service's admission that it ordinarily allowed persons to take over financially troubled businesses in order to increase the likelihood of repayment of the taxes (and that the argument will defeat that collection opportunity as a practical matter), the Supreme Court rejected the government's argument on the ground that it "would, in effect, make the responsible person assuming control of a business a guarantor for payment of the delinquent taxes simply by undertaking to continue the operation of the business." This construction, the Court held, was precluded by the history and context of Section 6672.[272] The taxpayer must be at fault or "willful" in failing to pay the taxes in question.[273] Such a finding could not be made on the facts of *Slodov* because (1) at the time Slodov assumed control,

---

[272] In re Slodov, 436 US 238, 254 (1978). See Elmore v. United States, 843 F2d 1128 (8th Cir. 1988) (district court decision reversed due to judge's failure to instruct jury on *Slodov* elements of nonliability).

Consequently, it has been said that a person who controls insufficient funds to pay taxes in full does not have effective ability to pay the taxes beyond the funds in the account he or she controls, and such a person is a responsible person only to the extent of the funds entering his or her accounts after the tax liability arises. Morgan v. United States, 937 F2d 281 (5th Cir. 1991) (accountant-officer was liable because he wrote checks to himself and to the state). Following *Slodov*, the Seventh Circuit in *Elmore*, supra, held that the taxpayer is not willful if at the time he assumed control there were no unencumbered funds with which to pay prior tax liabilities and subsequently received funds were not traceable to the taxes collected from employees. In this situation, the taxpayer is not in control or at fault for the prior delinquencies. When the taxpayer is in control and responsible for all the quarters of delinquency, the government is not required to establish that the available funds are traceable to collected taxes. Garsky v. United States, 600 F2d 86 (7th Cir. 1979); Harris v. United States, 92-1 USTC ¶ 50,124 (SD Ind. 1992).

[273] The issue is one of willfulness, therefore, not responsiblity. See, e.g., Howard v. United States, 79-1 USTC ¶ 9130 (6th Cir. 1978); Barrett v. United States, 594 F2d 219 (9th Cir. 1979) (person who paid other creditors before tax deposit was required not liable as a matter of law; evidence of willfulness necessary); Pike v. United States, 563 F. Supp. 428 (SDNY 1983) (president and chairman of the board of corporation was liable for willfully failing to make payments of past due tax liabilities when he was aware of the corporation's liabilities at the time he assumed his new responsibility).

When a responsible officer assumes control over a business with unpaid employment taxes, he pays private creditors at his peril, because the payment of these commercial creditors rather than the Service constitutes "a voluntary, conscious, and intentional act to prefer other creditors over the United States." See Purcell v. United States, 1 F3d 932 (9th Cir. 1993); Davis v. United States, 961 F2d 867 (9th Cir. 1992), cert. denied, 113 S. Ct. 969 (1993); Mazo v. United States, 591 F2d 1151 (5th Cir.), cert. denied, 444 US 842 (1979). However, when a taxpayer was a responsible person during the period of delinquency, but discovered the tax delinquency after the period, courts have generally distinguished *Slodov* and held the responsible officer liable for the trust fund portion of the liability to the extent of unencumbered funds before and after the delinquency was discovered. Kinnie v. United States, 994 F2d 279 (6th Cir. 1993) (gathering cases).

there were no funds with which to satisfy the delinquent taxes and (2) the funds generated after Slodov assumed control were not directly traceable to collected taxes. In the context of the trust created by Section 7501, no trust can exist when, at the time control is assumed, there are no collected funds. Section 7501 does not impress a trust on after-acquired funds.[274]

The Supreme Court's decision in *Slodov* does not answer all the problems that may arise when a person assumes control of a business with preexisting delinquent employment tax liabilities. It appears that if funds are available but are restricted by a perfected security interest having priority over the claim for taxes, then the responsible person may pay the secured creditor without incurring personal liability.[275] However, "the nature and reality of such a security agreement, and not merely its form" will be scrutinized to determine whether the responsible person was acting willfully.[276]

Courts have used the facts and principles of *Slodov* to develop two doctrines. One doctrine, called the existing funds doctrine, is derived from the facts and principles of *Slodov*. The "existing funds" doctrine holds that an individual who does not become a responsible person until after the tax delinquency accrued, is not liable (i.e., does not act willfully) if, at the time the individual assumed control, (1) there are no existing funds traceable to collected but unpaid taxes available to the business; (2) the new responsible person has used after-acquired funds for purposes other than paying down a corporate tax liability prior responsible persons caused to be incurred; and (3) he or she did not otherwise have personal fault in failing to pay the precontrol liability.[277] The other doctrine, called the after-acquired funds doctrine, has been stated in the following terms: "[W]hen a taxpayer has been a 'responsible person' in a corporation throughout the time that tax delinquencies accrued, that person is obligated to apply to the overdue tax all unencumbered funds acquired by the corporation after the individual becomes aware of the delinquency."[278]

---

[274] The taxpayer has the burden of proving that no funds are traceable to collected taxes. Sinder v. United States, 655 F2d 729 (6th Cir. 1981).

[275] See In re Slodov, 436 US 238 (1978); First Nat'l Bank v. United States, 591 F2d 1143 (5th Cir. 1979).

[276] First Nat'l Bank v. United States, 591 F2d 1143 (5th Cir. 1979).

[277] In *Slodov*, the Supreme Court said that "the responsible person . . . does not violate section 6672 by willfully using employer funds for purposes other than satisfaction of the trust-fund tax claims . . . when at the time he assumed control there were no funds with which to satisfy the tax claims and the funds thereafter generated are not directly traceable to collected taxes. . . . " In re Slodov, 436 US 238, 259–260 (1978). See Michaud v. United States, 80 AFTR2d 97-8007 (Fed. Cl. 1997) (applying the doctrine, but finding that there were no existing funds attributable to collected, but unpaid trust fund taxes).

[278] Michaud v. United States, 80 AFTR2d 97-8007 (Fed. Cl. 1997), citing among other cases, *Kinnie*, *Davis*, and *Mazo*.

[3] Lenders and Other Creditors

Lending institutions, sureties, and other creditors who supply funds to a business may exercise controls that render them responsible for collecting and paying over trust fund taxes. In an attempt to safeguard its interests as a creditor, the lender can become a responsible person liable for the payment of employment taxes under Section 6672 or Section 3505.[279]

The measures a lender or other creditor may take to protect an investment without being considered a responsible person present very close questions of fact.[280] At least one court has said that "so long as creditors limit . . . pressure tactics to inducing payments of what is owed . . . and do not seek to take effective control of the debtor in order to improve the debtor's ability to pay . . . the creditor's capacity through threat of collection to make the debtor dance to his tune, ought not to render the creditor a person responsible. . . . "[281]

In resolving this issue, it is reasonable to consider which party had control of the following:

- Business operations in general
- Hiring and firing of employees
- Receipt of funds and the deposit of funds
- Paying bills
- Approving credit given to customers
- Books of the corporation

It is also appropriate to consider who actually operated the business.[282] When employees of the lender or surety supervise the financial operations of the business by receiving and disbursing funds, the lender has effective control and is

---

[279] See the discussion infra ¶ 17.11.

[280] For a further reading on the problem, see Douglas-Hamilton, "When Are Creditors in Control of Debtor Companies?" 26 Bus. Law. 61 (1980). Lawrence, "Lender Control Liability," 62 S. Cal. L. Rev. 1387 (1989); Makel & Chadwick, "Lender Liability for a Borrower's Payroll Taxes," 43 Bus. Law. 507 (1988).

[281] Werner v. United States, 374 F. Supp. 558 (D. Conn. 1974), aff'd per curiam, 512 F2d 1381 (2d Cir. 1975). See also Schink v. United States, 84-1 USTC ¶ 9106 (WD Wash. 1983) (financially, a corporate borrower was completely dependent on a bank, but the bank had no duty to coerce the corporation into paying withholding taxes, as long as it did not intrude into the operations of the borrower's business).

See also Fidelity Bank, NA v. United States, 616 F2d 1181 (10th Cir. 1980) ("we are unwilling to hold that the bank had a duty to (coerce the borrower into paying withholding taxes) when it had not otherwise intruded into the financial or operational aspects of [borrower's] business" because it makes Section 6672 duplicate Section 3505); Mercantile Bank of Kan. City v. United States, 856 F. Supp. 1355 (WD Mo. 1994) (bank did not exercise control over which creditors to pay, although it had the power to do so).

[282] Girard Trust Corn Exch. Bank v. United States, 259 F. Supp. 214 (ED Pa. 1966).

responsible for paying over trust fund taxes.[283] When an attempt to control the disbursements of a debtor by overdraft financing is used, a bank may have effective control over which creditors are paid, especially if checks drawn on the account for taxes are returned for insufficient funds.[284] On the other hand, exercising authority to cosign checks in order to control the proper disbursement of funds does not in itself seem sufficient to establish responsibility.[285]

¶ 17.08 SECTION 6672—THE WILLFULNESS REQUIREMENT

A person may be responsible for collecting, accounting for, and paying over trust fund taxes, but the person is not liable for the trust fund recovery penalty unless the person "willfully" failed to perform the required acts.[286] The term "willfully" is used not only in the trust fund penalty provision, but in criminal statutes of the Code as well. In 1934, the Supreme Court in *United States v. Murdock*, explained that a willful act "often denotes an act which is intentional, or knowing, or voluntary, as distinguished from accidental. But when used in a criminal statute, "willful act" generally means "an act done with a bad purpose . . . without justifiable excuse . . . stubbornly, obstinately, per-

---

[283] Pacific Nat'l Ins. Co. v. United States, 422 F2d 26 (9th Cir. 1970); Anderson v. United States, 561 F2d 162 (8th Cir. 1977); Builders Fin. Co. v. United States, 71-1 USTC ¶ 9150 (ED Mich. 1970), aff'd sub nom. Mueller v. Nixon, 470 F2d 1348 (6th Cir. 1972) (lender and one of its executives held "responsible"). Commonwealth Nat'l Bank v. United States, 665 F2d 743 (5th Cir. 1982) (bank and chairman of board–president); United States v. Security Pac. Bus. Credit, Inc., 956 F2d 703 (7th Cir. 1992) ("Security Pacific took control of Mystic's finances, telling [Mystic] what it could and could not spend money on").

[284] See Dunham v. United States, 70-1 USTC ¶ 9108 (D. Conn. 1970). See also United States v. Park Cities Bank & Trust Co., 481 F2d 738 (5th Cir. 1973) (bank held liable under Section 3505 in an overdraft financing situation even where its employee in charge of the loan falsified bank records). Commonwealth Nat'l Bank v. United States, 665 F2d 743 (5th Cir. 1982) (bank was not liable when it made loans to a corporate employer that was failing to pay over withheld federal employment taxes, because it did not assume control over how the employer's funds were spent); Merchants Nat'l Bank of Mobile v. United States, 878 F2d 1382 (11th Cir. 1989) (bank with control over disbursements refused to honor checks for employment taxes); United States v. Edminston, 84-2 USTC ¶ 9578 (MD Tenn. 1984) (overdraft financing arrangement gave bank control); United States v. Vaccarella, 735 F. Supp. 1421 (SD Ind. 1990) (asset-based lender funded only net payroll).

[285] Haffa v. United States, 516 F2d 931 (7th Cir. 1975).

[286] However, it is also said, "Once it is established that a taxpayer is a responsible person, the burden of proving lack of willfulness is on the taxpayer." Thibodeau v. United States, 828 F2d 1499, 1505 (11th Cir. 1987); Mazo v. United States, 591 F2d 1151 (5th Cir. 1979).

versely. . . . "[287] Over the years, the Supreme Court has changed its definition of the term "willful" in criminal statutes, to mean a voluntary and intentional violation of a known legal duty.[288] Generally, when the same term is used in different provisions of the Code, it is given the same meaning, and so the term "willful," whether it is used in civil or criminal provisions, should have the same meaning, distinguished by the different quantum of evidence necessary to establish willfulness for the different statutes (i.e., more probable than not versus beyond a reasonable doubt). In a criminal tax case, however, courts are also compelled to examine the state of mind of the person accused of willful conduct, in order to determine whether the person charged had the specific intent to defraud. In a criminal failure-to-file tax prosecution, the Supreme Court held that a good faith misunderstanding of the tax law need not be objectively reasonable in order to negate the element of willfulness.[289] In trust fund penalty cases, courts generally have refused to examine the responsible officer's state of mind to determine whether the responsible officer's actions were subjectively reasonable under the circumstances.[290] If the corporation has sufficient unencumbered funds to pay a trust fund liability at the time the responsible person learns of the past liability, the responsible person is under a duty to use those unencumbered funds to pay the past withholding tax liability, and acted willfully as a matter of law if he or she failed to do so.[291]

According to the Service, willfulness exists when "money withheld from employees as taxes, in lieu of being paid over to the government, was know-

---

[287] United States v. Murdock, 290 US 389, 394 (1934).

[288] United States v. Pomponio, 429 US 10 (1976).

[289] United States v. Cheek, 498 US 192 (1991).

[290] Circuit courts have declined to modify the long-standing definition of "willfulness" in Section 6672 as "the voluntary, conscious and intentional" decision not to remit funds properly withheld to the Service. Domanus v. United States, 961 F2d 1323 (7th Cir. 1992). However, a "voluntary, conscious and intentional" act for Section 6672 does not differ materially from a "voluntary, intentional violation" for the criminal tax statutes. But criminal intent also requires the violation of a "known legal duty," and Cheek can be seen as making the determination of a taxpayer's knowledge of the duty a subjective issue of the taxpayer's state of mind. It is unclear whether the court's rejection of a good faith misunderstanding modification of Section 6672's willfulness thereby intended to incorporate an objective standard of willfulness. This does not appear to be the case because the courts, repeating the Cheek modification, simply seemed to have seen no reason to alter the longstanding definition in the Monday case used by the other circuits. Monday v. United States, 421 F2d 1210 (7th Cir. 1970).

[291] United States v. Kim, 111 F3d 1351 (7th Cir. 1997). Funds are unencumbered "only where the taxpayer is legally obligated to use the funds for a purpose other than satisfying the preexisting employment tax liability and if that legal obligation is superior to the interest of the IRS in the funds." Honey v. United States, 963 F2d 1083, 1090 (8th Cir. 1992).

ingly and intentionally used to pay the operating expenses of the business, or for other purposes."[292]

Courts accept the view that willfulness for the purposes of the penalty statute requires deliberate and intentional conduct. It is usually said that willful action under Section 6672 means voluntary, conscious, and intentional, as opposed to accidental, decisions not to pay over trust fund taxes to the United States.[293] At times, courts have attempted to define "willful conduct" in terms of the specific obligations of a responsible officer under the withholding provisions. For example, the Second Circuit has said that "the principal component of willfulness is knowledge: a responsible officer acted willfully within the meaning of [Section] 6672(a) if he (a) knew of the company's obligation to pay withholding taxes and (b) knew that company funds were being used for

---

[292] Rev. Rul. 54-158, 1954-1 CB 247, 249. This revenue ruling was promulgated after some courts had stated or implied that a bad purpose was necessary for the failure to act to be willful under the penalty provisions. See Paddock v. Siemoneit, 218 SW2d 428 (Tex. 1949); Kellems v. United States, 97 F. Supp. 681 (D. Conn. 1951) (the word "willful" in the penalty statute "means 'without reasonable cause,' that is to say 'capricious'"). Id. at 682. In some cases, the courts failed to distinguish between civil and criminal penalties at all. See Cushman v. Wood, 149 F. Supp. 644 (D. Ariz. 1956); Luhrs v. United States, 86-2 USTC ¶ 9709 (ND Ala. 1986) (willfulness found when loans were repaid to president and sole shareholder before company went into Chapter 11).

This position has been adopted by a number of courts. See, e.g., Garsky v. United States, 600 F2d 86, 91 (7th Cir. 1979) ("[a] responsible person's use of funds or his use of funds for payments to other creditors after he is aware of the failure to pay the withholding tax, is willful conduct within the scope of Section 6672"); Harris v. United States, 92-1 USTC ¶ 50,124 (SD Ind. 1992) ("[t]he evidence clearly shows that the taxpayer preferred other creditors over the government, and this is a violation of the law"). The Service's position has been adopted especially by the Fifth Circuit. A responsible officer acts willfully if he or she pays creditors or him or herself after receiving notice that payroll taxes were past due. Morgan v. United States, 937 F2d 281, 285 (5th Cir. 1991); Wood v. United States, 808 F2d 411, 416 (5th Cir. 1987); Raba v. United States, 977 F2d 941 (5th Cir. 1992).

[293] Kalb v. United States, 505 F2d 506, 511 (2d Cir. 1974), cert. denied, 421 US 979 (1975); Bloom v. United States, 272 F2d 215, 223 (9th Cir. 1959), cert. denied, 363 US 803 (1960); Monday v. United States, 421 F2d 1210 (7th Cir. 1970); Spivak v. United States, 370 F2d 612, 615 (2d Cir.), cert. denied, 387 US 908 (1967); Cross v. United States, 311 F2d 90, 94 (4th Cir. 1962); Strebler v. United States, 313 F2d 402 (8th Cir. 1963); Hanes v. Longley, 84-2 USTC ¶ 9597 (ND Okla. 1984); Latimer v. United States, 593 F. Supp. 881 (ND Ill. 1984). For a case in which liability under Section 6672 was found by summary judgment, see Moore v. United States, 87-1 USTC ¶ 9248 (SD W. Va. 1987) (although willfulness "is necessarily a subjective question which, if sufficiently controverted would preclude summary judgment . . . evidence that the responsible person had knowledge of payments to other creditors after he was aware of the failure to pay withholding taxes is sufficient for summary judgment on the question of willfulness"). See also Turner v. United States, 87-1 USTC ¶ 9252 (WD Mich. 1987) (summary judgment for Service).

other purposes instead."[294] Courts have divided, however, about whether the responsible person can negate the willful conduct element by showing that his or her conduct was reasonable under the circumstances. At least at one time, the Third and Fifth Circuits added the words "without reasonable cause" to the definition,[295] but many courts have refused to add this clause to the interpretation of the statutory requirements.[296] The reasons courts give for excluding lack of reasonable cause and justifiable excuse from the standard of willfulness are to avoid a jury's considering either the evil motive associated with criminal liability, but not liability for the trust fund penalty, or irrelevant factors, which might mislead the jury, such as the financial condition of the business or the demands of creditors.[297] Consequently, the exclusion of the qualifying language is for the prophylactic purpose of controlling the jury's deliberations.

Some courts have also taken the issue of willfulness out of the jury's hands altogether. These courts hold that willfulness exists as a matter of law in such situations as where the responsible person fails to investigate an instance of nonpayment or to correct mismanagement after the responsible person receives actual notice of a delinquency, and where the responsible person relies on the representation that withholding taxes will be paid by a person in control of company finances, who has failed to perform those obligations in the

---

[294] United States v. Rem, 38 F3d 634 (2d Cir. 1994).

[295] United States v. Slattery, 333 F2d 844 (3d Cir. 1964); Frazier v. United States, 304 F2d 528 (5th Cir. 1962). See also McCarty v. United States, 437 F2d 961 (Ct. Cl. 1971) (similar language is sometimes considered by the Court of Federal Claims). While the Fifth Circuit has rejected the role of the finder of fact and with it the consideration of reasonable cause, the Tenth Circuit sitting en banc has held that willful conduct for purposes of the trust fund recovery penalty "can be negated by showing the responsible person had reasonable cause for failing to pay withholding taxes held in trust for the government." Finley v. United States, 123 F3d 1342 (10th Cir. 1997) (president and board chairman instructed the secretary-treasurer to pay delinquent taxes, but the secretary-treasurer failed to do so, and bank also refused to turn over collections to the Service). Although it held that willfulness was an issue for the jury, and that reasonable cause could be considered by the jury in determining the issue, the circuit court also concluded that "reasonable cause sufficient to excuse a responsible person's failure to pay withholding taxes should be limited to circumstances in which (1) the taxpayer has made reasonable efforts to protect the trust funds, but (2) those efforts have been frustrated by circumstances outside the taxpayer's control."

[296] See, e.g., Domanus v. United States, 961 F2d 1323 (7th Cir. 1992). The Ninth Circuit has also refused to add this clause. Monday v. United States, 421 F2d 1210 (7th Cir. 1970). Compare Bloom v. United States, 272 F2d 215 (9th Cir. 1959), cert. denied, 363 US 803 (1960), with the language of the Ninth Circuit in Dudley v. United States, 428 F2d 1196 (9th Cir. 1970). The Eighth Circuit has said that "reasonable cause" is "no part of the definition of willfulness," refusing to follow the Fifth Circuit. Olsen v. United States, 952 F2d 236 (8th Cir. 1991).

[297] Monday v. United States, 421 F2d 1210 (7th Cir. 1970).

past.[298] It is precisely because what it called "paradigms of willful conduct" would leave no role for a jury on the issue of willfulness that the Tenth Circuit sitting en banc held that willful conduct for purposes of the trust fund recovery penalty "can be negated by showing the responsible person had reasonable cause for failing to pay withholding taxes held in trust for the government."[299] Consideration of reasonable cause, according to the Tenth Circuit, "sufficient to excuse a responsible person's failure to pay withholding taxes should be limited to circumstances where (1) the taxpayer has made reasonable efforts to protect the trust funds, but (2) those efforts have been frustrated by circumstances outside the taxpayer's control."[300]

Responsible officers have attempted to expand the willfulness inquiry to examination of the reasonableness of the responsible officer's conduct. The Service, however, has sometimes argued that willfulness is virtually the same as negligence, contending that a corporate officer acts willfully within the meaning of Section 6672 when the officer "should have known that taxes owed were not paid."[301] This argument has been rejected, and it is generally accepted that conduct amounting to no more than negligence is not willful for purposes of the penalty.[302] On the other hand, some courts have said that reckless conduct may amount to willfulness, and that gross negligence amounts to reckless conduct. Reckless disregard amounting to willful conduct has been found when the evidence has shown that the responsible person has failed to investigate or to correct mismanagement after having notice that withholding taxes have not been remitted to the government.[303] As one circuit court has

---

[298] See discussion of cases supra note 293. These courts fail to recognize that these instances of willfulness as a matter of law are also situations in which the conduct of the responsible officer has been unreasonable; i.e., the responsible officer's conduct has not met the standard of care a reasonably responsible person would have exercised under the circumstances.

[299] Finley v. United States, 123 F3d 1342 (10th Cir. 1997) (president and board chairman instructed the secretary-treasurer to pay delinquent taxes but the secretary-treasurer failed to do so, and bank also refused to turn over collections to the Service).

[300] Finley v. United States, 123 F3d 1342 (10th Cir. 1997).

[301] Kalb v. United States, 505 F2d 506 (2d Cir. 1974), cert. denied, 421 US 979 (1975).

[302] Kalb v. United States, 505 F2d 506 (2d Cir. 1974), cert. denied, 421 US 979 (1975); Dudley v. United States, 428 F2d 1196, 1200 (9th Cir. 1970). Gustin v. United States 876 F2d 485 (5th Cir. 1989) ("[m]ere negligence, however, does not establish willfulness under the statute"; consultant/president had no notice of unpaid liability); Feist v. United States, 607 F2d 954 (Ct. Cl. 1979) ("mere negligence is not sufficient proof of willfulness"). United States v. McCombs, 30 F3d 310 (2d Cir. 1994) ("mere negligence does not constitute willfulness").

[303] The Second Circuit has said, "At a minimum, the willfulness element denotes 'a reckless disregard for obvious or known risks' and the failure to pay withholding taxes must be 'voluntary, conscious and intentional—as opposed to accidental.'" United States v. McCombs, 30 F3d 310 (2d Cir. 1994); Kalb v. United States, 505 F2d 506 (2d Cir.

said, "Reckless disregard in this context is tantamount to gross negligence and is established if the responsible individual (1) clearly ought to have known that (2) there was a grave risk that withholding taxes were not being paid and if (3) the responsible person was in a position to find out for certain very easily."[304]

1974), cert. denied, 421 US 979 (1975); First Nat'l Bank v. United States, 591 F2d 1143 (5th Cir. 1979); The Third Circuit follows this view. United States v. Vespe, 868 F2d 1328 (3d Cir. 1989) (willfulness includes reckless disregard that exists if the taxpayer clearly ought to have known that there was a grave risk that withholding taxes were not being paid and if he was in a position to find out for certain very easily).

The Ninth Circuit, following the authorities described previously, also says that "'reckless disregard' of whether the taxes are being paid over, as distinguished from actual knowledge of whether they are being paid over, may suffice to establish willfulness." Phillips v. United States, 73 F3d 939 (9th Cir. 1996) (a divided court). See also United States v. Leuschner, 336 F2d 246 (9th Cir. 1964).

See also In re Summers, 84-1 USTC ¶ 9149 (Bankr. ND Ohio 1983); Kielisch v. United States, 86-2 USTC ¶ 9631 (ED Wis. 1986) ("To establish willfulness, it must first be shown that he knew the payroll taxes were not being remitted to the government.... If he did have a lack of knowledge, it stemmed from a 'reckless disregard for obvious and known risks,' and as such, still constitutes willful conduct.").

For a description of fact patterns considered to establish reckless disregard, see Thomsen, Jr. v. United States, 887 F2d 12 (1st Cir. 1989); Dougherty v. United States, 18 Cl. Ct. 335, 887 F2d 12 (Cl. Ct. 1989) (reckless disregard found when tax attorney with authority to pay failed to investigate and correct mismanagement). For other nonmalicious but reckless conduct found to be willful, see Newsome v. United States, 431 F2d 742, 745–746 (5th Cir. 1970) ("[h]owever, he subjects himself to liability under 6672 when he voluntarily and consciously 'risks' the withheld taxes in the operation of the corporation, and subsequently the corporation is unable to remit the withheld taxes"); Hartman v. United States, 538 F2d 1336, 1341 (8th Cir. 1976) (subjective belief that funds will be available from another source); United States v. Hill, 368 F2d 617, 621 (5th Cir. 1966) (desire to continue in business).

[304] United States v. Running, 7 F3d 1293 (7th Cir. 1993). In Wright v. United States, 809 F2d 425 (7th Cir. 1987), the circuit court stated:

> [W]e think gross negligence is enough to establish reckless disregard. Concretely we hold that the "responsible person" is liable if he (1) clearly ought to have known that (2) there was a grave risk that withholding taxes were not being paid and if (3) he was in a position to find out for certain very easily.

The court noted that this was a very small company, that Wright had access to the books, and that Wright had the financial acumen to determine at a "glance" the tax deficiencies. Owing to the company's past history of not paying its withholding and Wright's awareness of its continuing financial deterioration, the circuit court could not say that the lower court clearly erred in finding Wright's failure to inquire reckless. It observed:

> But if a responsible officer knows that the corporation has recently committed such a delinquency and knows that since then its affairs have continued to deteriorate, he runs the risk of being held liable if he fails to take any steps either to ascertain, before signing checks, what the state of the tax withholding account is, or to institute effective financial controls to guard against nonpayment.

However, the Ninth Circuit, in finding that a jury charge, using the language quoted from the Seventh Circuit's opinion in Wright, was proper, the Ninth Circuit in Phillips accepted

[1] Evidence to Negate Willfulness

Whether the standard applied by the court includes the phrase "reasonable cause," facts tending to show that there was no intentional failure to pay over are considered to negate willfulness.[305] These factors have included advice by

---

gross negligence as the equivalent of reckless disregard. Phillips v. United States, 73 F3d 939 (9th Cir. 1996).

[305] A showing that there was no intentional violation of a known legal duty negates willfulness. See, e.g., Howard v. United States, 79-1 USTC ¶ 9130 (6th Cir. 1978) (inexperienced daughter distraught over her father's death preferred creditors over taxes when she took over business). But see White v. United States, 83-1 USTC ¶ 9301 (ND Ga. 1983) (failure of agent to tell acting manager of potential personal liability for unpaid withholding taxes and creditor's attachment of account did not constitute reasonable cause); Smith v. Internal Rev. Serv., 894 F2d 1549 (11th Cir. 1990) ("the fact that SPH had sufficient funds on hand to meet its withholding tax obligations is insufficient to disprove willfulness" of a responsible officer); Hutchinson v. United States, 559 F. Supp. 890 (ND Ohio 1982) (taxpayer who believed that there were sufficient assets to cover tax liability and kept Service apprised of cash flow problems held willful); Howard v. United States, 82-2 USTC ¶ 9567 (ND Tex. 1982), aff'd, 711 F2d 729 (5th Cir. 1983) (chief executive officer's orders not to pay taxes did not constitute reasonable cause). Compare United States v. Davidson, 558 F. Supp. 117 (ED Va. 1982), aff'd in unpublished opinion (4th Cir. 1983) (foundation director found to have acted willfully despite contention that he was following resolution of board of directors). For a careful analysis of whether reckless disregard existed in a case, see Internal Rev. Serv. v. Blais, 85-2 USTC ¶ 9684 (D. Mass. 1985). See also Wright v. United States, 809 F2d 425 (7th Cir. 1987); Rykoff v. United States, 93-1 USTC ¶ 50,104 (CD Cal. 1992) (corporate president's failure to pay over taxes was not willful, because he was prevented from doing so by actions of corporation's bank).

However, an officer's attempt to shift responsibility to a bank for failing to pay over will not always be sufficient to avoid a willfulness finding. Even when a bank exercised control over the corporation's bank account and refused to honor checks to the Service for taxes, it was held that the officer's "voluntary agreement to cede power over the account to the Bank in the event of default, coupled with the knowledge that the other creditors were being paid when the Service was not, is sufficient to make his failure to pay the taxes willful." Bradshaw v. United States, 83 F3d 1175 (10th Cir. 1996). According to the circuit court, the officer's failure to insist on a provision in the loan agreement with the bank altering the bank's power to refuse to honor checks to the Service, in the face of knowledge of the unpaid taxes, also satisfied the willfulness requirement. Finally, the circuit court said that it was convinced that the officer's conduct was willful, because he could have resigned and shut down the business when the bank refused to approve the payment of the taxes. Instead the officer chose to conduct the business and liquidate it later, knowing of the unpaid taxes. This rather strict view of the obligations of the officer of a financially troubled corporation when negotiating with a bank does not mean that the bank might not also be liable as a responsible person, because it "assumes the function of determining whether or not an employer will pay over taxes withheld from its employees." Pacific Nat'l Ins. Co. v. United States, 422 F2d 26, 30 (9th Cir. 1970). The bank may be liable under both Section 6672 and Section 3505. See ¶¶ 17.7[3] and 17.11, respectively.

A reasonable cause defense is said to be "of very limited application." See Kalb v. United States, 505 F2d 506, 509 (2d Cir. 1974), cert. denied, 421 US 979 (1975). A tax-

counsel,[306] assurances of others,[307] and, most frequently, lack of knowledge of the failure to pay over.[308] Courts also have recognized that although reckless disregard may constitute willful conduct, a responsible person may show that his or her conduct was not reckless.[309]

payer's expectation that funds will be available at the end of a quarter does not preclude a willfulness finding. Thibodeau v. United States, 828 F2d 1499, 1506 (11th Cir. 1987). Willfulness also has been found when the officer had hoped that things would have gotten better and that the taxes would have been paid. Wall v. United States, 592 F2d 154, 163 (3d Cir. 1979).

The Second Circuit has held that "voluntary intoxication cannot be a defense to responsible person liability" under the circumstances of the case, which involved a chief executive officer of a multimillion dollar company who was addicted to cocaine, because to permit such a person with ultimate authority over the company's financial affairs to escape liability by claiming some substance addiction "would defeat the purpose of the statute." United States v. Landau, 82 AFTR2d 98-6113 (2d Cir. 1998) (the chief executive officer continued to act as such during the period of delinquency and to draw a salary of over $500,000, while subjecting others earning much less to liability for withheld taxes of over $1 million).

[306] Cash v. Campbell, 346 F2d 670, 672–673 (5th Cir. 1965) (advice by counsel under certain circumstances not to pay the withheld taxes as they became due); Gray Line Co. v. Granquist, 237 F2d 390 (9th Cir. 1956) (by attorney and tax collector); Cross v. United States, 204 F. Supp. 644, 649 (ED Va. 1962) (advice by counsel that there was no tax liability).

[307] Richard v. United States, 72-1 USTC ¶ 9267 (1972). Compare Kadah v. United States, 85-2 USTC ¶ 9449 (NDNY 1985) (assurances of buyer of business did not prevent finding of willfulness). Rykoff v. United States, 94-2 USTC ¶ 50,601 (9th Cir. 1994) (president obtained bank's guarantee that checks paying taxes would be honored; held, when bank withdrew funds to pay taxes, president's failure to pay over was not willful).

[308] Dudley v. United States, 428 F2d 1196 (9th Cir. 1970); United States v. Leuschner, 336 F2d 246 (9th Cir. 1964); United States v. Slattery, 333 F2d 844 (3d Cir. 1964); Markewich v. United States, 61-1 USTC ¶ 9241 (SDNY 1961); Levy v. Tomlinson, 249 F. Supp. 659 (SD Fla. 1965); Belcher v. United States, 6 AFTR2d 5495 (WD Va. 1960); Gordon v. Evans, 62-1 USTC ¶ 9196 (D. Nev. 1961); Schweitzer v. United States, 193 F. Supp. 309 (D. Neb. 1961); Bellah v. Patterson, 197 F. Supp. 522 (ND Ala. 1961); Wiggins v. United States, 188 F. Supp. 374 (ED Tenn. 1960). But see United States v. Charlton, 93-2 USTC ¶ 50,469 (7th Cir. 1993) (attorney who invested in restaurant chain was authorized to borrow money and to sign checks and pay certain employment taxes the restaurants owed; held, the attorney was a responsible officer). Charlton is disturbing because the fact that the attorney/investor had made substantial payments to, and had met with, the Service was used as evidence of his responsibility, a result about which the circuit court also had reservation. The attorney/investor also unsuccessfully argued that he had delegated authority to disburse funds to a management company, but the circuit court said, "The delegation of disbursal authority does not relieve the delegator of liability."

[309] See Feist v. United States, 607 F2d 954 (Ct. Cl. 1979) ("[t]he concomitant of this [reckless disregard] rule must be that absence of willfulness can be proved by an affirmative showing that the responsible person did not disregard his duties, and that he undertook all reasonable efforts to see that such taxes were in fact paid, in circumstances under which the employer had the means of payment and reasonably could be expected to make the payment"). Similarly, a responsible officer who had no actual notice that withholding

Whether lack of knowledge of nonpayment will negate willfulness depends on the facts of the case. For example, in *Markewich v. United States*,[310] an attorney had advanced money to a corporation based on an agreement that he be elected treasurer and that one of his associates be elected secretary. Both were installed as directors. Checks written on behalf of the corporation had to be countersigned by the attorney or his associate. The president prepared the checks, and after discussion, they were signed by the attorney. Signed checks were entrusted to the president for delivery, but the president failed to deliver them. Accordingly, the court held that the attorney may have been responsible, and that because he did not know the checks were not deposited, he may have been negligent, but his acts could not be characterized as willful.

There is a difference between ignorance of the fact of nonpayment and a reckless disregard of the fact of nonpayment, which is illustrated by *United States v. Leuschner*.[311] In this case, an officer-shareholder of two corporations was held not liable for unpaid trust fund taxes owed by one corporation when he relied on an employee of the corporation to pay the taxes. However, the officer-shareholder was liable for the trust fund taxes owed by the successor corporation because he was then aware of the fact that the employee had failed to pay over the taxes due from the predecessor corporation. Once a responsible person knows that his or her agent has failed to pay over trust fund taxes, continued reliance on the agent without any attempt to ensure that trust fund taxes are paid over may, as a matter of law, constitute a "voluntary, conscious and intentional" failure to act.[312]

---

taxes had not been paid, nevertheless had constructive notice of nonpayment on account of his awareness of the employee's mismanagement. Grover v. United States, 691 F. Supp. 1572 (D. Mass. 1988).

[310] Markewich v. United States, 61-1 USTC ¶ 9241 (SDNY 1961).

[311] United States v. Leuschner, 336 F2d 246 (9th Cir. 1964).

[312] See Mazo v. United States, 591 F2d 1151 (5th Cir. 1979), cert. denied, 444 US 842 (1979); Teel v. United States, 529 F2d 903 (9th Cir. 1976); Phillips v. United States, 73 F3d 939 (9th Cir. 1996) (a divided court approved a reckless disregard jury charge in a *Leuschner* situation); see Finley v. United States, 82 F3d 966 (10th Cir. 1996) (president admitted that he received notice of the delinquency and directed the secretary-treasurer to pay taxes, but failed to make further inquiry; held, president's conduct fell short of his obligation under Section 6672 because it amounted to neither an investigation nor a correction of mismanagement); Blake v. United States, 534 F. Supp. 223 (WD La. 1982).

Whether a responsible person's conduct is reasonable, and accordingly not willful, depends on the person's conduct in dealing with the payment or nonpayment of the trust fund taxes at the time they are due, and if a responsible person knows that the trust fund taxes are not being paid, the person acts willfully even if, for example, there is a reasonable expectation that in the future the corporation will have sufficient funds to pay the delinquent taxes. See, e.g., Winter v. United States, 81 AFTR2d 98-1056 (SDNY 1998) (responsible persons claimed that they had a good faith belief that the corporation was entitled to a tax refund).

A responsible person has also been released from liability on grounds closely related to a finding of reasonable cause for nonpayment of the employment taxes. In *McCarty v. United States*,[313] the Service failed to collect from the employer at a time when the employer could have satisfied the liability. The court of claims held that the Service's failure to collect released the responsible person from liability for delinquent taxes to the extent of the collectible but uncollected taxes. This authority in the former court of claims has not been explicitly followed in other courts[314] and seems to be limited to the facts of the case itself.

In *McCarty*, a builder of ships for the navy during the Korean War became delinquent in its taxes. The Service entered a partial payment agreement with the shipbuilder because it did not wish to interfere with the war effort by enforcing its liens. Subsequently, the navy took over the shipbuilder's financial operations and notified the Service that it would only make payments to it out of any excess funds available after completion of the contracts. The Service acquiesced to the navy's position and took no action to foreclose its liens on the shipbuilder's unencumbered property. The Service later assessed the 100 percent penalty against the shipbuilder's president and sole shareholder. The court of claims noted that the Service had a long standing policy of collecting from an employer before proceeding by way of Section 6672 against responsible persons,[315] and had it followed this policy, the responsible person would have been released from liability to the extent of the amount collected. The navy's refusal to pay the Service and the Service's failure to act constituted "acts of commission and failure to act on the part of the government upon which plaintiff could reasonably have relied on grounds for his failure to collect and remit the taxes." Accordingly, the court of claims held that the responsible person was released from liability for the delinquent taxes and the government was barred from collecting them from him.

---

[313] McCarty v. United States, 437 F2d 961 (Ct. Cl. 1971).

[314] But see Glenwal-Schmidt v. United States, 78-2 USTC ¶ 9610 (D. Colo. 1978). In *Mando*, the president and a shareholder of a manufacturer who handled sales and customer service discovered that his brother, who was in charge of finances, had failed to file returns and pay taxes. He informed the Service and worked out installment payment agreements, but the revenue officer treated the brother as the responsible officer. A bankruptcy court found that the Service was estopped from claiming for the first time that the president was liable as a responsible officer when the corporation filed for bankruptcy. Mando v. United States, 93-1 USTC ¶ 50,340, 154 BR 953 (Bankr. ED Ky. 1993).

[315] This was the policy of the Service. IRM, Policies of the IRS Handbook, P-5-60 (approved May 30, 1984). This policy existed before 1977. See United States v. McCarty, 437 F2d 961 (Ct. Cl. 1971). However, the current policy statement only states, "Absent statute considerations, assertion recommendations [for a trust fund penalty assessment] normally will be withheld in cases of approved and adhered to business installment agreements and bankruptcy payment plans." P-5-60 (approved Feb. 2, 1993).

In *Olsen*,[316] a corporate president who met with revenue officers and identified accounts receivable as being available to pay the corporation's withholding taxes was mistakenly informed by the revenue officers that the Service had priority in the accounts. When the Service was unable to collect the accounts, the president was held subject to penalty, despite his claim that if he had known the Service was not going to collect the taxes from the corporation, he would have collected the accounts himself and paid the Service. The president's defense was treated as one of estoppel, but was rejected because the revenue officers acted promptly in notifying the competing lienor of the Service's lien and did nothing to dissipate the assets of the taxpayer as had happened in cases such as *McCarty*.[317]

¶ 17.09 ASSESSMENT AND REVIEW PROCEDURES

In 1993, the Service revised its guidelines for what it had begun to call the trust fund recovery penalty.[318] According to the manual, these guidelines are designed to further the purpose of the trust fund recovery penalty, which is "to facilitate the collection of tax and enhance voluntary compliance."[319] To ensure that all collection sources are considered before a trust fund delinquency investigation of the corporate employer is written off, revenue officers *must* explore the trust fund recovery penalty before reporting outstanding trust fund taxes as uncollectible.[320]

Consistent with prior practice, the guidelines define "responsible person" broadly as "any person or entity that significantly controls the finances of a business or determines which creditors should or should not be paid."[321] Factors to be taken into account are (1) the identity of the person as an officer, director, or shareholder of the corporation; (2) the duties of the officer as set

---

[316] Olsen v. United States, 952 F2d 236 (8th Cir. 1991).

[317] See also Tozier v. United States, 65-2 USTC ¶ 9621 (WD Wash. 1965) (Service permitted corporate assets to be taken by creditors with inferior liens and subordinate to Service lien; held, responsible persons did not act willfully); Mangerie v. United States, 657 F. Supp. 726 (D. Md. 1986) (Service failed to perfect lien after responsible person assigned proceeds of army contract); Anderson v. United States, 77-2 USTC ¶ 9701 (WD La. 1977) (Service was notified of bankruptcy, but failed to file claim in bankruptcy proceeding when there were funds in estate to pay taxes; held, responsible person had reasonable cause).

[318] IRM 5.7, Trust Fund Compliance Handbook (July 31, 1998) (Trust Find Recovery Penalty Assessments).

[319] IRM, Policies of the IRS Handbook, P-5-60 (approved Feb. 2, 1993).

[320] IRM 5.7.3.3, Establishing Responsible Persons (July 31, 1998).

[321] IRM 5.7.3.3, Establishing Responsible Persons (July 31, 1998).

forth in the corporate bylaws; (3) the ability of the person to sign checks, regardless of whether the individual actually did so; (4) the identity of the persons in control of the financial affairs of the business; (5) the identity of persons who hired and fired employees; (6) the identity of persons who had the authority to determine which creditors to pay and those persons who exercised that authority; (7) the identity of persons who signed and filed Form 941, "Employer's Quarterly Federal Tax Return"; (8) the identity of persons who controlled payroll disbursements; (9) the identity of persons who had control of the corporation's voting stock; and (10) the identity of persons who made the federal tax deposit.[322] The guidelines' standard for "willfulness" is "the attitude of a person who, having a free will or choice, either intentionally disregards the law or is plainly indifferent to its requirements."[323]

[1] Revenue Officer Investigation

A revenue officer assigned to the District's Collection Division is the first person to determine which officers or employees were under the duty to collect and pay over trust fund taxes. In making this determination, the revenue officer is instructed to examine all of the following items:[324]

- Articles of incorporation, which show the duties of the officers and directors, along with subsequent resolutions that might change the officers' duties.
- Minutes books and bylaws, which may show who (1) had the responsibility to file returns and pay over withheld taxes; (2) had authority to sign checks, deposit moneys, or make loans on behalf of the corporation; and (3) diverted corporate funds after liability for the taxes accrued.
- Canceled checks and bank statements, because they may show diversions, as well as payments of nontax obligations after the liability had accrued.
- Payroll records and tax returns, which may indicate who had the responsibility for filing.
- Bank records of the business, including signature cards and resolutions, because they indicate both who had authority to sign corporate checks and changes that might have been made. Records of loan and financial statements submitted for the purpose of obtaining loans are also to be reviewed.

---

[322] IRM 5.7.3.3, Establishing Responsible Persons (July 31, 1998).

[323] IRM 5.7.3.4, Establishing Willfulness (July 31, 1998).

[324] IRM 5.7.4, Investigation and Recommendation of Trust Fund Penalty (July 31, 1998).

The revenue officer will interview potential responsible officers and witnesses to determine (1) any business assets available for collection; (2) the business's activities and financial affairs; and (3) the relationship to and business duties of the person interviewed.[325]

The revenue officer may determine that the trust fund recovery penalty is uncollectible. Before making that recommendation, the revenue officer must consider such factors as (1) the current financial condition of the responsible person, including any involvement in a bankruptcy proceeding; (2) the person's income history or potential; (3) the person's asset potential; (4) the compliance value of the assessment; (5) prior trust fund recovery penalty history; and (6) the existence of any prior currently not collectible cases.[326] If it is determined that the penalty is currently not collectible, but that future collection potential exists, the revenue officer will (1) recommend assertion of the penalty; (2) advise the taxpayer that no further action on the taxpayer's part will be necessary, and that a notice of federal tax lien will be filed, if appropriate; and (3) document its action.[327]

Practitioners may wish to explore one option that is provided by the guidelines. When administrative remedies to collect the employer portion of the tax liability and the penalty and interest from the corporation have been exhausted, responsible persons may pay the withheld tax liability on behalf of the corporation, instead of having the liability assessed against them under trust fund recovery penalty procedures.[328] Presumably, taxpayers who take this option will be permitted to treat the payment as a contribution to capital, resulting in reduced capital gain or increased capital loss on the disposition of their shares. The guidelines require that persons taking advantage of this alternative "should" accompany payment with a statement waiving the right to file a claim for a refund.[329]

[2] Administrative Review

After the revenue officer has completed the investigation, the Collection Division is supposed to give the person or persons determined to be responsible, notice of the proposed assessment of the trust fund penalty. (See Form 17.2.) There is no formal district review of the revenue officer's determination.[330]

---

[325] Rev. Proc. 84-78, 1984-2 CB 754. A form questionnaire is frequently used.

[326] IRM 5.7.5, Collectibility Determination (July 31, 1998).

[327] IRM 5.7.5.3, Verification of Inability to Pay (July 31, 1998).

[328] IRM 5.7.5.5, Alternative to Trust Fund Recovery Penalty (July 31, 1998).

[329] IRM 5.7.5.5, Alternative to Trust Fund Recovery Penalty (July 31, 1998).

[330] Procedures for the appeal of 100 percent assessment are found in the Service's Statement of Procedural Rules, 26 CFR §§ 601.106(a)(1)(ii)(c), 601.106(a)(1)(iv)(e).

Next the revenue officer sends the potentially responsible person a letter notifying the person of the opportunity to file a protest and appeal the proposed assessment to the Appeals Division.[331] This letter gives the potentially responsible person sixty days to file the protest. If no such protest is filed the Collection Division will make the trust fund penalty assessment as proposed.

---

[331] IRM 5639.11, MT 5600-45 (May 5, 1993) (Proposed Assessment of Trust Fund Recovery Penalty—Letter 1153 (DO), 60-Day Notification Letter).

FORM 17.2 _____
NOTICE OF PROPOSED ASSESSMENT OF 100 PERCENT PENALTY

Internal Revenue Service
Department of the Treasury
Jane Jones
District Director

Date: June 7, 1990

Employer Identification Number: 00-1234567

Name and Address of Corporation: Taxpayer, Inc.
                                          1776 Main Street
                                          Anytown, NY 00000

Tax Periods Ended: 12-31-86–12-31-87

Kind of Tax: 941

Your Social Security Number: 123-45-6789

Person to Contact:
Contact Telephone Number: (000)222-2222

Dear............................:

   We have reviewed your protest dated May 16, 1990, and determined that you are a responsible person in accordance with Section 6672 of the Internal Revenue Code, relating to liability of the corporation and periods shown above.

   No new facts have been presented to alter that conclusion. The case will be reviewed and will then be forwarded to the Appeals Office for their consideration. You will be contacted for a hearing by an Appeals Officer at that time. If your name, address, or telephone number changes before you are notified of your hearing, please contact us with the changes so that there is no delay in your receipt of the hearing notice.

   If you have any questions, please contact the person whose name and telephone number are shown above.

                                          Sincerely yours,
                                          Group Manager

                                          Letter 1154 (DO) (Rev. 4-89)

In trust fund penalty cases, even an Appeals Office conference often is not a fruitful forum for a disposition of the case. There are at least three reasons why administrative appeal is ineffective in these situations. First, in most cases, there are a number of responsible persons against whom liability has been asserted, thereby reducing doubt as to the group's liability and increasing the likelihood of collection. Second, in light of this situation, there is practically no litigating risk for the government. The government attorney can frequently sit back while the responsible persons joined in a single action inculpate each other.[332] Third, in 100 percent penalty cases, the Service has suffered when administrative accommodations have been made, although there is pressure to increase collections in these cases.

In the past, despite the requirement that the revenue officer send a notice of proposed assessment, thereby permitting the taxpayer to file a protest to appeal the proposed assessment to Appeals, it was not uncommon for assessment to be made without a preassessment notice. The taxpayer against whom there was an outstanding lien and possibly other enforced collection action being taken, was forced to file a claim for abatement of the assessment (or to pay a divisible portion of the tax and claim for refund) and appeal of the denial of the claim to Appeals with the case in postassessment status. Unlike taxpayers who are able to challenge their liability for income, gift, or estate tax in the Tax Court without paying the disputed deficiency in tax, a taxpayer subject to the trust fund recovery penalty had no prepayment judicial forum. If the Collection Division did not send a notice of the proposed assessment to the person believed by the revenue officer to be a responsible person, and the trust fund penalty is assessed, the claimed responsible person was denied prepayment review even at the administrative appeals stage of a challenge to a proposed assessment.

Since 1996, however, the Service is statutorily required to send the taxpayer a preliminary notice of the proposed assessment at least sixty days before any assessment of the penalty, notice of the penalty, and demand for its payment.[333] The notice must be sent to the taxpayer's last known address as determined under Section 6212(b), and also personally delivered to any person

---

[332] Note that the Service cuts short administrative review for other potentially responsible officers and makes assessments once one has instituted a refund suit. Rev. Proc. 84-78, 1984-1 CB 173. This revenue procedure makes clear that the taxpayer is entitled to only one conference with the Appeals Division, instead of having an initial conference with the District Collection Division prior to the Appeals conference.

[333] The Taxpayer Bill of Rights 2, § 901(a), amended Section 6672 by redesignating Section 6672(b) as Section 6672(c) and substituting the preliminary notice requirement as the new Section 6672(b). The provision for proposed assessments made after June 30, 1996. The preliminary notice requirement does not apply if the Service finds that collection is in jeopardy.

against whom the trust fund liability is asserted.[334] When a notice is sent before the expiration of the statute of limitations on assessment of the penalty, the statute of limitations is extended for a ninety-day period beginning on the date the notice was mailed. If the taxpayer files a timely administrative protest of the proposed assessment, the statute of limitations on assessment of the penalty is extended until final action by Appeals, and for thirty days thereafter. Presumably, if the preliminary notice is not sent, the taxpayer's claim for abatement should be granted promptly, and failing that, the taxpayer is entitled to seek an injunction to halt collection in the same manner as the taxpayer may do when a premature assessment of income, gift, or estate tax is made, as provided in Section 6213(b).

Once it has been determined that settlement in the Appeals Office is not possible, the formal notice of assessment is issued. Tax Court review is not available because the Tax Court's jurisdiction does not extend to employment tax cases.[335] Accordingly, no notice of deficiency is sent to the person determined to be a responsible officer. The Service makes an assessment of the trust fund penalty, and then must send the person a notice of the assessment and demand for payment of the amount of the assessment within ten days or enforced collection action will be taken.

Once the Service assesses a trust fund penalty, the Service can take administrative collection action or commence a collection action in court to collect the assessment, unless the person against whom the Service has assessed the penalty takes steps to challenge the assessment in the appropriate district court or the Court of Federal Claims. Under procedures described in Section 6672(c), the person who has received a notice of the trust fund penalty assessment and demand for its payment may statutorily require the Service to withhold administrative and judicial collection of the penalty if, within thirty days after the date of the notice, the responsible person (1) pays a divisible portion of the assessment; (2) files a claim for refund of the amount paid; and (3) furnishes a bond in an amount that is one and one-half times the amount of the assessment.[336] Within thirty days after the claim for refund is denied, the responsible person must commence a refund suit. After December 31, 1999, moreover, if the allegedly responsible person has commenced a suit for refund

---

[334] The IRS Restructuring and Reform Act of 1998 amended Section 6672(b) to make clear that the person against whom the trust fund recovery penalty is asserted receives notice by providing for the personal delivery of the notice, as well as the sending of the notice to the responsible person's last known address in the same manner as a notice of deficiency, as provided for in Section 6212(b). IRC § 6672(b)(1), as amended by Act § 3307(b), effective as of the date of enactment July 22, 1998.

[335] The Tax Court does not have jurisdiction over employment taxes. See IRC §§ 6212(a), 6213(a).

[336] See Rev. Rul. 79-170, 79-1 CB 437 (bonding and surety requirements described in Reg. § 301.7101-1 apply).

of a divisible portion of the assessment, the Service is prohibited from collecting the balance of the assessment.[337]

Because it may be difficult as a practical matter for the person against whom the Service has assessed the penalty to post a bond and avoid collection action, the person must take action to secure the payment of the penalty under a deferred payment or other agreement with the Collection Division. Unless the person assessed the penalty works out an agreement with Collection, the Service can collect the full amount of the assessment by levy and other collection action. The person will be unable to obtain the intervention of a court to enjoin the Service's collection action. The Anti-Injunction Act, Section 7421, prohibits injunctions to restrain the assessment of any tax. For this reason, persons facing collection action often consider bankruptcy protection because when a bankruptcy petition is filed the Service and other creditors are automatically stayed from taking enforced collection action.

When a corporation seeks bankruptcy protection, the automatic stay protects the corporation from enforced collection action, but it does not prevent the Service from collecting trust fund penalty assessments from persons it believes are responsible officers. However, the Supreme Court has held that the bankruptcy court in a Chapter 11 proceeding has jurisdiction to order the Service to apply payments to the trust fund portion of the employment taxes, thereby protecting officers of the employer from trust fund penalty assessments, provided that the bankruptcy court finds that such an order is necessary for the success of the corporate employer's reorganization.[338]

[3] Judicial Review

The general procedures for contesting a trust fund recovery penalty assessment in court are (1) to pay the penalty for one employee for each of the quarters involved; (2) within two years after payment, to file a claim for refund of the tax paid (and abatement of the balance of the assessment); and (3) when the claim is denied (or if no action is taken in six months), to bring a civil action in the appropriate federal district court or the Court of Federal Claims.[339] Thus, unlike the taxpayer who wishes to challenge an income, estate, or gift tax assessment in a refund court, the allegedly responsible person may obtain judicial review and comply with the full payment rule, set out in *Flora v. United States*, without making payment of the full amount of the trust fund penalty

---

[337] IRS Restructuring and Reform Act of 1998, § 3433, amending IRC § 6331(i).

[338] Energy Resources v. United States, Inc., 495 US 545 (1990). See discussion and cases gathered at ¶ 16.12[1][a].

[339] See IRC § 6511(a). For the procedures to be followed in suits for refund in the federal district courts and the Court of Federal Claims, see Section 7422. Refund procedures and such considerations as the choice of forum are described in Chapter 11.

assessment. As the Supreme Court said in *Flora*, "The Government suggests—and we agree—that excise tax deficiencies may be divisible into a tax on each transaction or event and therefore present an entirely different problem with respect to the full-payment rule."[340]

Thus, the trust fund recovery penalty is asserted with respect to a divisible tax or transaction (i.e., the trust fund tax for each employee for each quarter), and so the responsible person who pays a divisible tax, satisfies the full payment requirement of 28 USC § 1346(a)(1), and gives the district court and the Court of Federal Claims jurisdiction over the suit for refund. In the action, the burden of proof is on the taxpayer.[341] Trust fund penalty refund suits are frequently tried before a jury when brought in a district court. At the trial, whether it is a jury or bench trial, the alleged responsible officer has the burden of proving by a preponderance of the evidence, that either or both of the elements of responsibility and willfulness is not present.[342]

Nevertheless, the Service sometimes proceeds to take administrative action to collect the unpaid balance of the penalty assessment. As a result, the advantage the responsible person may gain by the divisible tax exception can be offset as a practical matter by the continuation of the collection action. This result seems contrary to the tax refund procedure contemplated by the Supreme Court because once the person has paid the divisible portion of the trust fund penalty assessment, the Service has rejected the claim for refund, the taxpayer has commenced a refund suit, and the Service has counterclaimed for the balance of the assessment, an injunction will not seek to restrain the assessment

---

[340] Flora v. United States, 362 US 145, 179 n.37 (1960); Steele v. United States, 280 F2d 89 (8th Cir. 1960); Spivak v. United States, 370 F2d 612 (2d Cir.), cert. denied, 387 US 908 (1967).

[341] Horowitz v. United States, 339 F2d 877 (2d Cir. 1965); Datlof v. United States, 370 F2d 655 (3d Cir. 1966). Sinder v. United States, 655 F2d 729 (6th Cir. 1981). But see In re Twomey, 82-2 USTC ¶ 9687 (WDNY 1982) (100 percent penalty was assessed after the taxpayer filed for bankruptcy; held not to have the presumption of "validity" because it violated the automatic-stay provisions under 11 USC § 362(a)(6)).

[342] Hochstein v. United States, 900 F2d 543, 546 (2d Cir. 1990). The same allocation of the burden of proof applies in a collection action the government institutes to collect a trust fund penalty assessment. United States v. McCombs, 30 F3d 310 (2d Cir. 1994). In a bankruptcy proceeding, the Service has the burden of persuasion in establishing trust fund penalty liability, although there are conflicting authorities. See In re Willhelm, 94-2 USTC ¶ 50,485, 173 BR 398 (Bankr. ED Wis. 1994). Because the liability of the responsible person and the corporate employer are separate and distinct, it has been said that the person seeking to disprove liability under Section 6672 cannot carry that burden by showing that the corporate employer was in a position to pay the taxes. Farrington v. United States, 920 F. Supp. 12 (DNH 1996) (government's motion in limine granted precluding evidence that the Service had the obligation to collect tax from the corporate employer in or before its bankruptcy). However, evidence that the corporate employer had sufficient funds to pay the taxes at the time they were due, but failed to do so through no fault of the allegedly responsible person, bears on the issue of willfulness.

and collection of a tax.[343] Nevertheless, when taxpayers have attempted to enjoin collection of the balance of the trust fund penalty assessment before the court, they have not always succeeded because of the stringent requirements of the Anti-Injunction Act.[344]

As of December 31, 1999, the Code makes clear what Supreme Court case law had already suggested. As the result of the IRS Restructuring and Reform Act of 1998 amendment to the levy statute, as of January 1, 2000, no levy may be made to collect the unpaid portion of a divisible tax during the pendency of any refund suit brought by a taxpayer in a proper federal trial court for the recovery of the portion of the divisible tax paid if the decision in the case would be res judicata as to the unpaid tax, or the taxpayer would be collaterally estopped from contesting the unpaid tax by reason of the refund suit.[345] The prohibition does not apply to a levy to carry out an offset under Section 6402, nor a levy served before the refund suit was commenced. The Service also may not institute a separate collection action to collect the balance of the assessment (it may proceed by counterclaim), but the Service is permitted to bring an action related to the taxpayer's refund suit, such as a suit against other responsible persons. If the Service violates the prohibition, the Anti-Injunction Act does not apply, and the taxpayer may ask the refund court to issue an injunction. The statue of limitations on collection is suspended during the pendency of the refund suit.

---

[343] Flora v. United States, 362 US 145 (1960). Also, in Bob Jones Univ. v. Simon, 416 US 725, 748 n.22 (1974), the Supreme Court said:

> [P]etitioner did not bring this case as a refund action. Accordingly, we have no occasion to decide whether the Service is correct in asserting that a district court may not issue an injunction in such a suit, but is restricted in any tax case to the issuance of money judgments against the United States. . . . We note, however, that the Service's position with regard to the range of relief available in a refund suit raises several considerations not presented by a pre-enforcement suit for an injunction. For example, it may be possible to conclude that a suit for a refund is not "for the purpose of restraining the assessment or collection of any tax . . . " and thus that neither the literal terms nor the principal purpose of § 7421(a) are applicable. Moreover, such a suit obviously does not clash with what the Court referred to in Williams Packing . . . as a "collateral objective of the Act—protection of the collector from litigation pending a suit for a refund."

[344] 8 IRC § 7421 (Anti-Injunction Act). See Marvel v. United States, 548 F2d 295 (10th Cir.), cert. denied, 431 US 967 (1977) (taxpayer could not enjoin collection of the balance of divisible tax assessment). However, in *Marvel*, the Service had not actually proceeded to collect and had assured the court that there was "little likelihood of such a unilateral seizure absent circumstances jeopardizing the availability of the revenue after judgment." Id. at 298 n.1. Compare Bullock v. Latham, 306 F2d 45 (2d Cir. 1962); Iraci v. Scanlon, 219 F. Supp. 796 (EDNY 1963).

[345] IRC § 6331(i), as amended by the IRS Restructuring and Reform Act of 1998, § 3433(a), applicable to unpaid tax attributable to taxable periods beginning after December 31, 1999.

[4] Statute of Limitations

Except in cases of a failure to file a return, filing false returns, or willful attempted evasion, the statutory period on assessment is three years after the return is filed.[346] This general rule also applies to the assessment of the 100 percent penalty of Section 6672 against a responsible person.[347] Returns for employment taxes are filed quarterly. If an employment tax return for any period ending with or within a calendar year is filed on or before April 15 of the next year (the return for the fourth quarter), the return is considered filed on April 15 of that calendar year.[348] Consequently, an employment tax return is filed or considered filed on April 15 of the year following the year amounts were required to be collected and paid over. Because the 100 percent penalty is a device for collection of the trust fund portion of these taxes, the penalty should be subject to the same period of limitations as the tax itself, that is, the three-year period following the filing of the employment tax return. The statute of limitations on assessment can remain open more than three years after the

---

[346] IRC § 6501(a).

[347] After about thirty years of acknowledging that a three-year statute of limitations applied to the trust fund penalty, the Service began to take the position that there was no statute of limitations applicable to a trust fund penalty assessment. The argument seems to have derived from the Service's success in tax shelter promoter cases, when courts concluded that no statute of limitations applies to assessment of the Section 6700 penalty. See ¶ 7B.13. The Third Circuit ruled against the Service's unlimited statute of limitations argument, and the Service was unsuccessful in other circuit courts as well. Lauckner v. United States, 68 F3d 69 (3d Cir. 1995), aff'g No. 93-1594 (DNJ 1994); Purcell v. United States, 1 F3d 932 (9th Cir. 1993) (assessment made within time required under Section 7501, and therefore running of time under Section 6502 begun). See also Stallard v. United States, 12 F3d 489 (5th Cir. 1994). The Service made this argument, although its manual recognized a three-year statute of limitations, as did its use of a form requesting the extension of the assessment period for assessing a 100 percent penalty (Form 2750). The Service announced that it no longer will take the position that trust fund recovery penalty assessments are not subject to a statute of limitations. See Action on Decision: Alan R. Lauckner, CC-1996-006, 96 TNT 137-17 (July 15, 1996).

Also, the Service claimed that the trust fund penalty does not apply to particular tax periods. Stallard v. United States, supra (holding that the penalty does apply to specific periods so that when an assessment is made for which no liability exists and the Service fails to show that the assessment was actually made for periods of claimed liability, no proper assessment has been made). But when Service centers issue notices that show the period of the penalty as being the same as the period of the assessment, and the period of the assessment is also one of the periods or quarters of the claimed liability, the taxpayer's liability has been held not to be limited to the last period on the notice. Purcell v. United States, supra. In Stallard, the taxpayer was conceded not to be liable for the period reflected on the notice and the supporting record, the Form 4340 Certificate of Assessments and Payments.

[348] IRC § 6501(b)(2).

date of the failure to act.[349] If the return is filed after April 15, the limitations period is measured from the actual filing date, and if no return is filed, the limitations period remains open indefinitely. Once the tax is assessed, the Service may collect the tax by a levy or proceeding in court within ten years after the assessment.[350] The Section 6672 assessment is collectible within the ten-year period, not the assessment against the employer. Nevertheless, an action against a responsible person has been held timely when brought within ten years of the date of the assessment against the employer.[351] For persons seeking to contest assessments, a refund claim must be filed within two years of the date of payment.[352]

[5] Joint and Several Liability and Contribution

It is well established that a taxpayer who is jointly and severally liable for the payment of an unpaid tax along with the other responsible persons cannot avoid collection on the ground that the government should first collect, or attempt to collect, the tax from the other persons.[353] The obligation to collect and pay over is the individual and primary obligation of the responsible person. For this reason, some courts also have found that the Service need not have first attempted to recover the tax from a corporation,[354] although this may not

---

[349] See, e.g., Lynn v. Scanlon, 234 F. Supp. 140 (EDNY 1964). Periods of limitations on assessment are discussed in Chapter 5.

[350] Reg. § 301.6501(b)-1(b).

[351] Bloom v. United States, 272 F2d 215 (9th Cir. 1959), cert. denied, 363 US 803 (1960); United States v. Allbritten, 218 F. Supp. 701 (D. Kan. 1963).

[352] Kuznitsky v. United States, 93-2 USTC ¶ 50,491 (ND Ill. 1993) (responsible person penalty is a tax for which a return cannot be filed; taxpayer had two years to file for refund under Section 6511).

[353] Phillips v. Comm'r, 283 US 589 (1931) (transferee liability); Kelly v. Lethert, 362 F2d 629 (8th Cir. 1966); Cash v. Campbell, 346 F2d 670 (5th Cir. 1965). Cf. Burack v. United States, 461 F2d 1282 (Ct. Cl. 1972) (Service settled with others and then asserted the penalty for the unrecovered amount); Herzig v. United States, 83-1 USTC ¶ 9232 (ND Ohio 1983) (Service settled with one shareholder and president and obtained judgment against another owner for 100 percent penalty); United States v. DeVito, 82-2 USTC ¶ 9523 (D. Mass. 1982) (Service settled with one responsible person and then assessed 100 percent penalty against treasurer on the basis of the affidavit submitted in the first case).

[354] Spivak v. United States, 370 F2d 612 (2d Cir.), cert. denied, 387 US 908 (1967); Monday v. United States, 421 F2d 1210 (7th Cir. 1970); Datlof v. United States, 370 F2d 655 (3d Cir. 1966); Cash v. Campbell, 346 F2d 670 (5th Cir. 1965); Sage v. United States, 81-2 USTC ¶ 9764 (SD Ill. 1981); Roth v. United States, 83-2 USTC ¶ 9650 (SD Cal. 1983) (Service's failure to timely file a proof of claim in the corporation's bankruptcy proceeding does not prevent it from collecting 100 percent penalty from the responsible corporate officers); Bradley v. United States, 936 F2d 707 (2d Cir. 1991)

be true if the corporation was solvent and had assets available at the time the Service should have collected the liability.[355] Also, because the liability is joint and several, a court will not apportion the liability between or among alleged responsible persons.[356] However, it has been held that despite the existence of joint and several liability, the tax can be collected only once.[357]

Because the penalty is separate and distinct from the employer's liability, it is unclear whether a responsible person who pays the trust fund liability is subrogated to the government's tax claim against the corporate employer.[358]

For many years, despite the joint and several liability of responsible persons, it was doubtful that the responsible person who actually paid the trust fund liability had a right to contribution from other responsible persons. It has long been recognized that the transferee who pays the entire liability has a right of contribution from other transferees; however, jointly and severally liable responsible officers were treated differently from jointly and severally liable transferees.[359] One basis for the different treatment of responsible officers and transferees is that the transferee is liable only to the extent of the value of the assets received from the transferor, while a responsible person is liable for the entire trust fund liability. At any rate, many courts found that a responsible person had no right of contribution from other responsible persons, without discussing the right of the transferee to contribution from other transferees in the analogous but distinguishable situation in which transferee liability has been found.[360] Recognizing that the Service might collect the trust fund recov-

---

(debtor/employer made payment of corporate tax liability that gave rise to assessment during bankruptcy, but interest that accrued during bankruptcy could be collected from responsible officers).

[355] See McCarty v. United States, 437 F2d 961 (Ct. Cl. 1971) (Service's failure to take collection action at a time when the corporation had assets was held to absolve the responsible officer).

[356] Brown v. United States, 591 F2d 1136 (5th Cir. 1979); Hartman v. United States, 538 F2d 1336, 1340 (8th Cir. 1976).

[357] Schink v. United States, 84-1 USTC ¶ 9106 (WD Wash. 1983). See also Verdung v. United States, 84-1 USTC ¶ 9324 (ND Ill. 1983) (partial payment of the 100 percent penalty made by one responsible person must be applied in reduction of the amount owed by another responsible person).

[358] Singer v. District Director, 354 F2d 992 (2d Cir. 1966).

[359] Phillips-Jones Corp. v. Parmley, 302 US 233 (1937).

[360] See, e.g., Rice v. Pearce, 83-2 USTC ¶ 9717 (SD Iowa 1983); DiBenedetto v. United States, 75-1 USTC ¶ 9503 (DRI 1975). Accord Hanhauser v. United States, 45 AFTR2d 80-471, 80-1 USTC ¶ 9139, 85 FRD 89 (MD Pa. 1979); Geiger v. United States, 78-1 USTC ¶ 9395 (D. Md. 1978); Cohen v. United States, 75-1 USTC ¶ 9391 (ED Mich. 1975); Rebelle v. United States, 84-2 USTC ¶ 9717 (MD La. 1984); Rebelle v. United States, 85-2 USTC ¶ 9493 (MD La. 1985) (discussing cases and following *DiBenedetto*); Cook v. United States, 765 F. Supp. 217 (MD Pa. 1991) (clearly defined public policy disfavors allowing claims of contribution or indemnity to interfere with collection under Section 6672; contractual right to indemnity also violates public policy). The

ery penalty from the person from whom it could collect most easily, rather than the person with the greatest culpability, and that the person who had paid the penalty might find it difficult, if not impossible, to force contribution from other responsible persons, Taxpayer Bill of Rights 2 added a new federal right of contribution.[361] Under Section 6672(d), if more than one person is liable for the trust fund recovery penalty, each person who has paid the penalty is "entitled to recover from other persons who are liable for [the] penalty an amount equal to the excess of the amount paid by such person over [that] person's proportionate share of the penalty."[362] However, this right of contribution may not be joined or consolidated as a claim with a collection action the government brings or with a refund suit the responsible officer brings.

¶ 17.10 CONTRIBUTION AND VOLUNTARY PAYMENT OF THE TRUST FUND RECOVERY PENALTY

Financially troubled businesses are faced with a dilemma: If trade creditors and employees are paid, but employment taxes are not, the business may continue for a period, but the responsible persons will be personally liable for trust fund taxes. On the other hand, if trust fund taxes are paid while trade creditors and employees are not, the continuation of the business is also in jeopardy. Sound, albeit unpalatable, advice to such a business starts with the proposition that if any creditor is to be preferred, it is the government rather than a trade creditor. If the corporation is unable to pay nongovernmental creditors, at least its shareholders will not be personally liable unless there is a basis for asserting transferee liability against them.

Corporate officers or other persons who might be considered responsible for paying over trust fund taxes should instruct the Service to apply payments to the trust fund portions of employment taxes accrued during their period of responsibility before making any other application of the payment.[363] However,

---

rationale in part was that the penalty requires intentional conduct, and contribution does not extend in favor of persons engaging in conduct such as that of joint intentional tortfeasors. Sinder v. United States, 655 F2d 729 (6th Cir. 1981).

In *Rebelle*, the court added the further rationale that denial of the right of contribution provides incentive for members of the group of responsible persons to pay over the taxes, because each person is faced with the possibility of bearing the entire penalty.

[361] HR Rep. No. 506, 104th Cong., 2d Sess. 41 (Mar. 28, 1996).

[362] The right of contribution exists for penalties assessed after the date of enactment of the Taxpayer Bill of Rights 2, July 30, 1996.

[363] Rev. Rul. 79-284, 1979-2 CB 83 (voluntary payments are applied as designated, while undesignated payments are applied "in a manner serving the best interest of the Service"). Rev. Rul. 79-284 modified Rev. Rul. 73-305, 1973-2 CB 43, to deal with undesignated payments of taxes other than withheld employment taxes, saying that such payments

the payment only will be applied to the trust fund portion of the liability if the payment is voluntary. This principle derives from debtor-creditor law that permits a debtor who owes money to a creditor on two or more debts and who makes a voluntary payment to the creditor to allocate the payment among the debts.[364] The rule applies in tax cases as well, and is intended to encourage the voluntary payment of debts, "which saves the creditor the costs of collection and delay and thus confers on him a benefit for which the right of allocation is modest compensation."[365] In tax cases, just what constitutes a voluntary payment can be difficult to determine. If payment is made after the withholding tax liability has been assessed, but the Service has not started to take collection action (perhaps only notices and demands for payment have been sent), the payment of the trust fund tax will be considered voluntary.[366] On the other hand, if the payment is made pursuant to a levy, the payment is clearly involuntary.[367] In one case, the Service levied on property and scheduled a public sale, but a private sale of the property was arranged at a higher price before the public sale, the payment of the sale proceeds to the Service was found to be an involuntary payment and the designation to the trust fund portion was disregarded.[368] The elimination of any delinquency in trust fund taxes also eliminates the trust fund penalty. It is necessary to specifically designate a payment as trust fund taxes because the Service's procedure is to consider that any payment on a corporate account represents a payment of the employer portions of the liability (including assessed penalty and interest) unless there is

---

will be applied to tax, penalty, and interest in that order. However, Rev. Rul. 79-284 makes Rev. Rul. 73-305 applicable to employment taxes when *written* instructions are given for the application of a voluntary partial payment. If no instructions are given, the Service will apply payments of withheld employment taxes "in a manner serving its best interests." See Kinnie v. United States, 994 F2d 279 (6th Cir. 1993) (oral instructions alleged to have been given; therefore, Service allocation approved).

[364] Restatement (Second) of Contracts § 258(1) (1981).

[365] Stevens v. United States, 49 F3d 331 (7th Cir. 1995).

[366] Muntwyler v. United States, 703 F2d 1030, 1033 (7th Cir. 1983) (rejecting the suggestion "that a payment is involuntary whenever an agency takes even the slightest action to collect taxes, such as filing a claim or as appears to be a logical extension of the Government's position, telephoning or writing the taxpayer to inform him of taxes due").

[367] Muntwyler v. United States, 703 F2d 1030, 1032–1033 (7th Cir. 1983).

[368] Stevens v. United States, 49 F3d 331 (7th Cir. 1995) (referring to the situation as being an intermediate case, but saying, "Stevens' back was against the wall. The building was going to be sold for the benefit of the IRS whatever he did, and rather than 'volunteering' anything he was trying to minimize his personal liability by maximizing the proceeds of the sale.").

some specific designation to the contrary.[369] Only the balance of the payment, if any, is applied to the trust fund portion of the liability.[370]

The Service does not recognize any right of designation when an enforced collection of the delinquency is made. In Chapter 11 bankruptcy cases, however, the bankruptcy court has authority under the Bankruptcy Code to order the Service to apply payments to trust fund liabilities if the bankruptcy court determines that this designation is necessary to the success of the reorganization.[371] Rather than resolve the issue of whether the payments made were voluntary or involuntary, an issue that had provoked conflicting circuit court opinions, the Supreme Court relied on the broad powers of bankruptcy courts to modify creditor-debtor relationships and to conclude that Section 6672 did not by its terms preclude such a bankruptcy court order. The Service argued that Section 6672 ensured an additional source for collection of trust fund taxes from persons other than the corporate employer if those taxes could not be collected from the corporate employer, and, as a result, the court order frustrated the use of this alternative collection source. The Court rejected this argument saying that the bankruptcy court's order required the Service to collect trust fund taxes, and that Section 6672 still remained an alternative collection

---

[369] IRM, Policies of the IRS Handbook, P-5-60 (approved May 30, 1984). See, e.g., Anderson v. United States, 497 F. Supp. 563 (ED Wis. 1980) (Service properly applied payment to employer's portion, then to trust fund portion, because taxpayer gave no express direction). See also In re Hannan Trucking, Inc. v. United States, 17 Bankr. 475 (ND Tex. 1981) (payment made after due date is not voluntary and cannot be designated—a questionable decision).

When a voluntary payment of employment taxes to the Service is undesignated, the Service has the discretion to apply the payment to the employer's portion, rather than to the trust fund portion, of the taxes. Sotir v. United States, 978 F2d 29 (1st Cir. 1992).

[370] However, it has been held that the Service may not apply a payment to interest and penalties not yet assessed at the time payment is received. First Nat'l Bank v. United States, 591 F2d 1143 (5th Cir. 1979). As a result, a payment may satisfy the trust fund portion of the liability. The rule may be limited to a voluntary payment, and, in effect, the taxpayer has determined that the payment should not be allocated to the unmatured (that is, unassessed) debts for interest and penalties. Stevens v. United States, 95-1 USTC ¶ 50,123 (7th Cir. 1995).

[371] United States v. Energy Resources Co., 495 US 545 (1990). The 100 percent penalty is not avoided by the responsible officers filing a Chapter 7 bankruptcy petition after the corporation also files a Chapter 7 bankruptcy petition. Not only is the 100 percent penalty nondischargeable in the responsible officer's bankruptcy, but the bankruptcy court also does not have jurisdiction to allocate payments from the bankrupt corporation to the trust fund portion of the liability. United States v. Pepperman, 976 F2d 123 (3d Cir. 1992) (in absence of showing that allocation was needed for reorganization or bankruptcy purpose, bankruptcy court's equity jurisdiction was not extended under *Energy Resources* beyond Chapter 11 proceeding).

source for trust fund taxes. It is the Service's position that only taxpayers, not third parties, may designate the application of payments.[372]

The Service's practice is to assert trust fund penalties against all executive officers. However, as noted, a person may be an officer (or a director) of a corporation without having real or effective control over financial affairs, even if he or she has authority to sign checks. Accordingly, the officer's scope of authority in dealing with the payment of taxes should be described.[373] If the person has no authority over tax matters, an employment agreement, resolution, or other official document should clearly state this fact. If the person is to have responsibility, the document should ensure access to information and authority to act. Although contribution among responsible persons is now recognized,[374] an indemnity agreement covering potential liability entered into with principals in the business can provide a contractual basis for contribution. This type of agreement, however, does present a risk of the indemnity agreement being used as evidence of joint and several responsibility for the taxes.[375]

¶ 17.11 SECTION 3505—LIABILITY OF THIRD PARTIES PAYING OR PROVIDING WAGES

In part because it was uncertain whether lenders and sureties could be held liable as responsible persons under Section 6672, Section 3505 was enacted as part of the Federal Tax Lien Act of 1966. Section 3505 imposes personal liability on lenders or other nonemployers who pay wages directly to employees of a common-law employer or, under certain circumstances, to the employer for the purpose of paying these wages.

When a lender is financing the performance of a contract or is providing a business with working capital, enough funds are ordinarily provided to meet

---

[372] See Hewitt v. United States, 377 F2d 921 (5th Cir. 1967), in which a president and majority shareholder sought unsuccessfully to designate the application of funds almost sixteen months after he had severed his connection with the corporation. See also Emshwiller v. United States, 565 F2d 1042 (8th Cir. 1977).

[373] See Hertz, "Personal Liabilities of the Unsuspecting Executive for the Penalties Under Section 6672 and Other Nightmares," 32 NYU Inst. on Fed. Tax'n 1171 (1974).

[374] The right of contribution exists for penalties assessed after the date of the Taxpayer Bill of Rights 2, July 30, 1996. See supra ¶ 17.10.

[375] See Barker v. United States, 72-1 USTC ¶ 9225 (D. Okla. 1972). In re Twomey, 82-2 USTC ¶ 9687 (WDNY 1982) (indemnity of former officer's evidence of responsibility). See United States v. Industrial Crane & Mfg. Corp., 74-1 USTC ¶ 9340 (5th Cir. 1974) (corporation bought an individual's stock and assumed his potential personal liability as responsible officer; held, the Service was able to collect from corporation as a third-party beneficiary, but the corporation was able to offset its liquidated damages for the individual's breach of covenant not to compete).

all obligations, including taxes withheld from wages, as long as the security is sufficient or a stated limit is not exceeded. When the debtor is in financial trouble, the lender's natural inclination is to advance the bare minimum amount of funds necessary to complete the work or to keep the business operating so that the lender's prior loans can be salvaged. A similar situation occurs when a surety attempts to minimize its loss by making only those payments as will enable the contractor to complete its contract.[376] Consequently, the lender or surety knows at the time that it advances funds that no tax will ever be paid, but the worker will get credit for the tax payment even though the tax payment is never remitted to the government. Furthermore, when the debtor fails, claimants, sureties, and lenders entitled to priority under Secton 6323 of the Code could easily come out ahead of the Service, whose lien for withholding taxes arises only after returns become due and assessments are made.

In suits between the Service and the lender or surety, the lender or surety's claim of priority led the Service to advance, and the courts to accept, the argument that the lender's lien, for example, did not have priority over the later-arising federal tax lien because the lender's lien was inchoate under the choate lien doctrine. This argument had potentially unintended consequences in situations outside a contractor's failure to pay withholding tax out of loan proceeds because the choate lien doctrine had not been intended to reach this specific situation. To provide lenders and sureties legislative relief from the choate lien doctrine, it was necessary to strengthen the Service's hand in collecting withholding taxes.[377] Section 3505 statutorily solves the problem by imposing liability on those lenders and sureties who knowingly participate in an arrangement whereby wages are to be paid without setting aside trust fund taxes.

The statutory framework of Section 3505 is straightforward and interesting in its operation. Section 3505(a) imposes liability on third parties, such as lenders and sureties, who make direct payments to employees of the common-law employer on the employer's behalf. Section 3505(b) extends personal liability to the lender, surety, or other person who supplies funds to the common-law employer for the specific purpose of paying wages of the employees of the common-law employer knowing that the employer cannot or will not make timely deposits. Also, as the statute implies, the employer must have failed to pay its withholding and FICA taxes during the times when the lender supplied the funds, and these taxes must have remained unpaid. However, the liability of the lender or surety is limited to 25 percent of the amount supplied to the

---

[376] Except for Miller Act performance bonds on federal contracts (see the 1966 amendment to 40 USC § 279a(d)), bonds obligating sureties to pay "labor" or "wages" are construed not to require sureties to provide for the portion of the wages withheld for taxes. United States v. Crosland Constr. Co., 217 F2d 275, 277 (4th Cir. 1954).

[377] See Plumb, Federal Tax Liens 126 (3d ed. 1972).

employer for this purpose. Section 3505(c) requires that any amounts paid by third persons under Section 3505 are to be credited against the liability of the common-law employer. As this summary description suggests, there are a number of differences between liability under the trust fund recovery penalty of Section 6672 and the liability of sureties and lenders under Section 3505. These differences are summarized in Table 17.1.

TABLE 17.1

Comparison of Sections 6672 and 3505

	Section 6672	Section 3505
Persons liable	Any person required to collect, account for, and pay over, including an officer or employee of a corporation or employee of a partnership under duty to act	Lender, surety, or other person who pays wages directly or supplies funds to employer for payment of wages
Extent of liability	Trust fund portion of tax, i.e., withheld income and employees' share of FICA tax	Direct wage payors—full liability for tax due; suppliers of funds—25 percent of the funds supplied for the wages
Statute of limitations on assessment	Three years from date full-period return is due, i.e., April 15 of year following quarter of delinquency	None
Method of collection	Assessable penalty procedures, including assessment and administrative collection	IRS must institute an action in court
Effect of payment on employer's liability	Section 6672 liability is separate and distinct from employer's liability; administratively, only single liability will be collected	Employer entitled to credit for amount collected from third party under Section 3505

[1] Liability Under Section 3505(a)

If a lender or surety controls the payment of wages by paying them directly to the employees, or through an agent on their behalf, the lender or surety becomes personally liable for the amount of taxes required to be deducted and withheld.[378] Liability under Section 3505(a) flows from the "direct" payment,

---

[378] IRC § 3505(a). The law applies also to payment by an "other person," for example, if the statutory conditions regarding notice and specific purpose are met, a customer or prime contractor seeking to keep a jobber's or subcontractor's labor on the job by making advances against work in progress (as in Abrams v. United States, 72-1 USTC ¶ 9162

not notice to or knowledge of the lender that the tax will not be paid.[379] Accordingly, the surety or lender cannot keep workers on the job in order to perform a bonded obligation or to salvage a loan by paying only the net amount of their wages. The gross payroll must be met, including the tax that the workers are credited with having paid out of these wages. On the other hand, the financing party's obligations under its contract are not enlarged. Once an agreed limit (on a bond or financing arrangement) has been reached, the lender or surety may stop its advances, although this limit will be reached sooner because it involves gross wages. The lender or surety must set aside the amount deducted and withheld and pay it over to the Service.[380] Although it may be the employer in fact of the employees, the lender or surety is not considered the common-law employer,[381] and so may not be subject to taxes imposed on the employer or subject to the employer's obligations to file returns and furnish the employees with W-2 statements.[382]

[2] Liability Under Section 3505(b)

In many cases, the lender or surety does not pay wages directly, but advances to the employer the funds needed for working capital or to meet specific expenses. Section 3505(b) imposes personal liability on a lender or surety that

---

(SD W. Va. 1971)), although not a person, such as a bank's payroll service or a union agent, acting as a mere conduit for the employer's own funds. HR Rep. No. 1884, 89th Cong., 2d Sess. (1966), reprinted in 1966-2 CB 815, 829; Rev. Proc. 67-41, 1967-2 CB 677.

Precedent for such provision is found in Section 3401(d), which treats as an "employer" for purpose of income tax withholding (but not for FICA) tax, "the person having control of the payment of . . . wages." However, the provision failed to meet the situation because it was held not to embrace one who had joint control of the bank account from which payrolls were paid and hence could veto payments of taxes withheld from wages. United States v. Hill, 363 F2d 176 (5th Cir. 1966) (bank and surety); Century Indem. Co. v. Riddell, 317 F2d 681, 686 (9th Cir. 1963) (surety); Venneri Co. v. United States, 340 F2d 337, 340 (Ct. Cl. 1965) (prime contractor).

[379] See United States v. Fred A. Arnold, Inc., 400 F. Supp. 1118 (ND Cal. 1975).

[380] Form 4219 is provided for this purpose. Rev. Proc. 67-41, 1967-2 CB 677.

[381] However, if the surety actually takes over and completes the work, it may incur all the responsibilities of an employer of the workers. National Sur. Co. v. United States, 64-1 USTC ¶ 9197 (D. Kan. 1963); United States v. American Employers Ins. Co., 192 F. Supp. 873, 874 (DND 1961).

[382] The lender or surety making direct payment of wages necessarily has access to the payroll records and knows the gross and net amounts of each wage payment, so the amount to be set aside and paid over can be computed. The contractor or other employer should also know what has been paid in its behalf and can integrate such data with its own payments for reporting purposes. The lender or surety has no responsibility in this regard if the employer fails its reporting obligations. HR Rep. No. 1884, 89th Cong., 2d Sess. (1996), reprinted in 1966-2 CB 815.

advances funds for the specific purpose of paying wages if the lender or surety has "actual notice or knowledge" that the employer "does not intend to or will not be able to make timely payment or deposit of amounts required to be deducted and withheld from these wages."[383] An organization is not chargeable with "actual notice or knowledge" until the particular person conducting the transaction that is affected has notice or knowledge or would have if the organization had exercised "due diligence."[384] "Due diligence" means reasonable routines for communicating significant information and reasonable compliance with these routines. The due diligence requirement of Section 3505(b) incorporates the meaning of that term in the priority provision, Section 6323(i)(1). The government has argued that this requirement imposes a duty on a lender to investigate outside its own organization once it is alerted to "suspicious circumstances." However, this view of due diligence has not been accepted.[385]

[3] Procedures Under Section 3505

The Service bears the burden of proof in establishing that the funds were to be used specifically for the payment of wages and that the lender had actual notice or knowledge. This burden may explain why there are not more Section 3505 cases brought by the Service against sureties and lenders.[386] Actual notice or knowledge no doubt would be found to exist if the employer presented the

---

[383] IRC § 3505(b). This statute has been held constitutional. United States v. Algernon Blair, Inc., 441 F2d 1379 (5th Cir. 1971). For cases finding liability, see Fidelity Bank, NA v. United States, 616 F2d 1181 (10th Cir. 1980); United States v. Park Cities Bank & Trust Co., 481 F2d 738 (5th Cir. 1973); United States v. First Nat'l Bank, 652 F2d 882 (9th Cir. 1981). See also In re Brandt-Airflex Corp., 87-1 USTC ¶ 9194 (Bankr. EDNY), rev'd on other grounds, 87-2 USTC ¶ 9583 (EDNY 1987), aff'd, 843 F2d 90 (2d Cir. 1988).

[384] If the organization is considered to have notice under this standard, the employer's misconduct does not excuse liability. See United States v. Park Cities Bank & Trust Co., 481 F2d 738 (5th Cir. 1973).

[385] United States v. Coconut Grove Bank, 545 F2d 502 (5th Cir. 1977). Cf. United States v. Whilmar Gen. Contractors, Inc., 70-1 USTC ¶ 9428 (ND Tex. 1970); United States v. Estate of Swan, 441 F2d 1082 (5th Cir. 1971) (distinguished by the Fifth Circuit in *Coconut Grove Bank* because it was not a Section 3505(b) case). But see United States v. Metro Constr. Co., 439 F. Supp. 308 (CD Cal. 1977), rev'd on another issue, 602 F2d 879 (9th Cir. 1979) (notice or knowledge was found); United States v. Burchfield & Thomas, Inc., 86-2 USTC ¶ 9652 (ED Ky. 1986) (general contractor held liable for unpaid withholding taxes when it supplied funds for purpose of paying wages of subcontractor).

[386] HR Rep. No. 1884, 89th Cong., 2d Sess. (1996), reprinted in 1966-2 CB 815. See O'Hare v. United States, 878 F2d 953 (6th Cir. 1989) (lender claimed it had no control over disbursements; held, "[c]ontrol, however, is not the test required by [Reg. § 31.3505-1(b)(3)]; the test is actual notice or knowledge").

lender or surety with a list of needs to be met from the funds requested that omitted provision for the withholding taxes, and if there was no evidence of another source of funds from which payment of the taxes was reasonably anticipated. However, this provision has no application to an ordinary working capital loan, even though the lender knows that part of the funds advanced may be used to make wage payments in the ordinary course of business.[387] A lender is not obligated to determine the specific use of a working capital loan or the ability of the borrower to pay the taxes. However, the lender will incur liability if it in fact knows that the loan is to be used to pay net wages, even if the agreement states a different purpose. Thus, a bank having an overdraft financing arrangement with an employer has notice of the employer's inability to make deposits when the loans are credited to a general account out of which creditors are paid while the payroll account out of which taxes are paid is closed.[388]

In some instances, the amount advanced may be less than the total net payroll. In order to avoid imposing liability on the lender or surety for more than the taxes required to be withheld from the wages it actually financed, the lender/surety's liability (if incurred) is limited to 25 percent of the amount advanced. An arbitrary figure had to be used for this provision, because no set percentage of any gross payroll is allocable to taxes due to graduated with-

---

[387] Reg. § 31.3505-1(b)(3); HR Rep. No. 1884, 89th Cong., 2d Sess. (1996), reprinted in 1966-2 CB 815. The regulation states that "[g]enerally, an ordinary working capital loan is a loan which is made to enable the borrower to meet current obligations as they arise . . . [h]owever, section 3505(b) is applicable where the person supplying the funds has actual notice or knowledge (within the meaning of section 6323(i)(1)) at the time of the advance that the funds, or a portion thereof, are to be used specifically to pay net wages, whether or not the written agreement under which the funds are advanced states a different purpose." Reg. § 31.3505-1(b)(3). The "ordinary working capital loan" exception is intended to protect the bank or other lender whose knowledge is only the general knowledge that the expenses of a business include its payroll. For litigation purposes, the Service will treat the term "ordinary working capital loan" as a "loan that would commonly be made by a person or organization in the business of lending money to a person in the taxpayer/employer's business, for the purpose of meeting current obligations." See IRS, Litigation Guideline Memorandum Re: Section 3505 Liability of Lenders and Sureties, LGM GL-14 (May 4, 1994).

[388] Fidelity Bank, NA v. United States, 616 F2d 1181 (10th Cir. 1980); In re Brandt-Airflex Corp., 87-1 USTC ¶ 9194 (Bankr. EDNY), rev'd on other grounds, 87-2 USTC ¶ 9583 (EDNY 1987), aff'd, 843 F2d 90 (2d Cir. 1988). See also United States v. First Nat'l Bank of Circle, 652 F2d 882 (9th Cir. 1981); United States v. Vaccarella, 735 F. Supp. 1421 (SD Ind. 1990) (bank "decided to fund only net payroll, despite its knowledge that this could entail tax liability"). Although the lender must have specific knowledge that all or some portion of the borrowed funds are to be used to meet payroll, it has been held that it is not necessary for the government to prove that lender knew in advance the exact amounts to be used for wages. United States v. Intercontinental Ind., Inc., 635 F2d 1215 (6th Cir. 1980); United States v. Burchfield & Thomas, Inc., 58 AFTR2d 86-5681 (ED Ky. 1979).

holding, differing individual exemptions for income tax purposes, and the wage dollar amount at which old-age insurance tax withholding is terminated. The manner in which the 25 percent limitation is to be determined is unsettled. The Service has argued that the limit embraces only the unpaid employment tax but not the interest for which the third party may become liable.[389] Thus, the limitation does not preclude collection of prejudgment interest. The courts, on the other hand, have held that the liability limitation includes prejudgment interest.[390] Courts have held that the 25 percent limitation is an absolute limitation on the amount of the liability, that the limitation applies to both the collection of tax and prejudgment interest, and, accordingly, that it precludes the collection of tax and prejudgment interest in excess of 25 percent of the amounts supplied for the payment of wages.[391]

It should be noted that, although the liability of lenders under Section 3505 is more specifically defined than under Section 6672, the Service may assert the trust fund recovery penalty instead of liability under Section 3505.[392] If the Service chooses to pursue a lender or surety's liability under Section 3505, it has been held that the Service need not assess the liability against the lender or surety within three years after the return was filed, at least if it makes an assessment against the employer within that period.

In *Jersey Shore State Bank v. United States*,[393] the Supreme Court resolved a split among the circuit courts and held that Section 6303(a) does not

---

[389] Reg. §§ 31.3505-1(b)(1), 31.3505-1(b)(2), Ex. 1. But see Rev. Proc. 67-41, 1967-2 CB 677, § 4.02.

[390] United States v. Metro Constr. Co., 602 F2d 879 (9th Cir. 1979); Taubman v. United States, 449 F. Supp. 520 (ED Mich. 1978); United States v. Terry P. Smith, Inc., 75-2 USTC ¶ 9710 (ND Ohio 1975). See also Rev. Proc. 67-41, 1967-2 CB 677.

[391] United States v. Metro Constr. Co., 602 F2d 879 (9th Cir. 1979); United States v. Intercontinental Ind., Inc., 635 F2d 1215 (6th Cir. 1980); United States v. Hannan Co., 639 F2d 284 (5th Cir. 1981); see also O'Hare v. United States, 878 F2d 953 (6th Cir. 1989); United States v. Security Pac. Credit, Inc., 956 F2d 703 (7th Cir. 1992).

Treasury regulations say that the maximum amount of the lender or surety's liability is 25 percent of the amount of the funds supplied. Reg. § 31.3505-1(d)(2)(iii). Regulations also conform to case law, and make clear that the 25 percent limitation is an absolute cap on the liability of the lender or surety and includes the withholding taxes and prejudgment interest. Reg. § 31.3505-1(b)(1), amended by TD 8604, 60 Fed. Reg. 39,109 (Aug. 1, 1995).

[392] Pacific Nat'l Ins. Co. v. United States, 422 F2d 26 (9th Cir.), cert. denied, 398 US 937 (1970).

[393] Jersey Shore State Bank v. United States, 479 US 442 (1987). It appears that an action against a lender must be commenced within six years after the date of the assessment against the employer. United States v. First Nat'l Bank, 80-1 USTC ¶ 9459 (ND Pa. 1980), approving Reg. § 31.3505-1(d)(1); United States v. Marine Midland Bank, 82-1 USTC ¶ 9362 (WDNY 1962). Although liability under Section 3505 is not assessed and collected by administrative levy, the statute of limitations for collection of withholding taxes from lenders, sureties, and others under Section 3505 is ten years, coextensive with

require the Service to provide notice and demand for payment to a lender before bringing a civil action under Section 3505. The Court pointed out that an employer is subject to summary collection after assessment, but the lender is only subject to collection by way of a civil action. Consequently, the employer has a "far greater need" for a notice and demand than the lender, which could be alerted to its Section 3505 liability when it advances net payroll. The lender could then take steps to protect itself against a lawsuit under Section 3505.

Liability under Section 6672 as a responsible officer and liability as a net payroll financer under Section 3505 are not mutually exclusive. In *Security Pacific Business Credit, Inc.,*[394] the lender was held liable under both statutes because of the terms of the statutes for the trust fund portion of the debtor's taxes as responsible officer, and for preassessment interest as a net payroll lender. The Seventh Circuit rejected the lender's argument that by proceeding under both Sections 6672 and 3505, the Service rendered meaningless the 25 percent cap on the lender's liability. Judge Posner observed:

> There is no reason to believe that by failing to provide for preassessment interest in section 6672 Congress meant to confer a benefit on a lender who should happen to be a responsible person as well—who should, that is, actually compound his wrongdoing. There is no reason to believe that by placing a 25 percent ceiling on a net-payroll lender's liability Congress intended to benefit a responsible person, for it is only by virtue of the money that it has been ordered to pay as a responsible person that Security Pacific can argue that the ceiling has been pierced. The interest assessment under 3505 didn't pierce it, because the government limited that assessment to 25 percent of the loan.[395]

Consequently, the Service may collect the full amount of the unpaid trust fund tax under Section 6672, even if it joins its Section 6672 claim with a claim under Section 3505.

---

the general statute of limitations on collection after assessment provided in Section 6502. Reg. § 31.3505-1(d).

[394] United States v. Security Pac. Bus. Credit, Inc., 956 F2d 703 (7th Cir. 1992).

[395] United States v. Security Pac. Bus. Credit, Inc., 956 F2d 703 (7th Cir. 1992).